Collins

SPANISH DICTIONARY & GRAMMAR

ESSENTIAL EDITION

Published by Collins
An imprint of HarperCollins Publishers
Westerhill Road
Bishopbriggs
Glasgow G64 2QT

Second Edition 2017

10 9 8 7 6 5 4

ISBN 978-0-00-818367-7

www.collins.co.uk/languagesupport

Typeset by Davidson Publishing Solutions, Glasgow

Printed and bound by
CPI Group (UK) Ltd, Croydon, CR0 4YY

200 HarperCollins PUBLISHERS Since 1817

A catalogue record for this book is available from the British Library.

If you would like to comment on any aspect of this book, please contact us at the given address or online.
E-mail: dictionaries@harpercollins.co.uk
facebook.com/collinsdictionary
@collinsdict

Acknowledgements
We would like to thank those authors and publishers who kindly gave permission for copyright material to be used in the Collins Corpus. We would also like to thank Times Newspapers Ltd for providing valuable data.

EDITOR
Susie Beattie

CONTRIBUTORS
Jeremy Butterfield, Mike González, Gerry Breslin, Teresa Álvarez García, Brian Steel, Ana Cristina Llompart, José Miguel Galván Déniz, Val McNulty, José Martín Galera, Lydia Batanaz, José A. Gálvez

FOR THE PUBLISHER
Cordelia Lilly
Janice McNeillie
Sheena Shanks

TECHNICAL SUPPORT
Claire Dimeo
Ross Taggart

Índice de materias

Contents

Introduction

You may be starting Spanish for the first time, or you may wish to extend your knowledge of the language. Perhaps you want to read and study Spanish books, newspapers and magazines, or perhaps simply have a conversation with Spanish speakers. Whatever the reason, whether you're a student, a tourist or want to use Spanish for business, this is the ideal book to help you understand and communicate. This modern, user-friendly dictionary gives priority to everyday vocabulary and the language of current affairs, business, computing and tourism, and, as in all Collins dictionaries, the emphasis is firmly placed on contemporary language and expressions.

How to use the dictionary

Below you will find an outline of how information is presented in your dictionary. Our aim is to give you the maximum amount of detail in the clearest and most helpful way.

Entries

A typical entry in your dictionary will be made up of the following elements:

Phonetic transcription

Phonetics appear in square brackets immediately after the headword. They are shown using the International Phonetic Alphabet (IPA), and a complete list of the symbols used in this system can be found on page x. The pronunciation given is for Castilian Spanish except where a word is solely used in Latin America, when we give the Latin American pronunciation. A further guide to the differences in types of Spanish pronunciation is given on page x.

Grammatical information

All words belong to one of the following parts of speech: noun, verb, adjective, adverb, pronoun, article, conjunction, preposition, abbreviation. Nouns can be singular or plural and, in Spanish, masculine or feminine. Verbs can be transitive, intransitive, reflexive or impersonal. Parts of speech appear in abbreviated form (*n*, *adj*, *adv* etc) and in *italics* immediately after the phonetic spelling of the headword. The gender of noun translations also appears in *italics* immediately following the key element of noun translations, except where this is a regular masculine singular noun ending in "o", or a regular feminine singular noun ending in "a".

Often a word can have more than one part of speech. Just as the English word **chemical** can be an adjective or a noun, the Spanish word **conocido** can be an adjective ("(well-)known") or a noun ("acquaintance"). Similarly, the verb **to walk** is sometimes transitive, ie it takes an object ("to walk the dog") and sometimes intransitive, ie it doesn't take an object ("to walk to school"). To help you find the meaning you are looking for quickly and for clarity of presentation, the different part of speech categories are separated by a triangle ▷.

Meaning divisions

Most words have more than one meaning. Take, for example, **punch**, which can be, amongst other things, a blow with the fist or an object used for making holes. Other words are translated differently depending on the context in which they are used. The transitive verb **to put on**, for example, can be translated by "ponerse", "encender" etc depending on *what* it is you are putting on. To help you select the most appropriate translation in every context, entries are divided according to meaning. Each different meaning is introduced by an "indicator" in *italics* and in brackets. Thus, the examples given above will be shown as follows:

> **punch** [pʌntʃ] *n* (*blow*) golpe *m*, puñetazo; (*tool*) punzón *m*

Likewise, some words can have a different meaning when used to talk about a specific subject area or field. For example **bishop**, which in a religious context means a high-ranking clergyman, is also the name of a chess piece. To show English speakers which translation to use, we have added "subject field labels" in brackets, in this case *(Chess)*:

> **bishop** ['bɪʃəp] *n* obispo; (*Chess*) alfil *m*

Field labels are often shortened to save space. You will find a complete list of abbreviations used in the dictionary on pages viii and ix.

Translations

Most English words have a direct translation in Spanish and vice versa, as shown in the examples given above. Sometimes, however, no exact equivalent exists in the target language. In such cases we have given an approximate equivalent, indicated by the sign ≈. An example is **National Insurance**, the Spanish equivalent of which is "Seguridad Social". There is no exact equivalent since the systems in the two countries are different.

> **National Insurance** *n* (*Brit*) seguro social nacional, ≈ Seguridad *f* Social

On occasion it is impossible to find even an approximate equivalent. This may be the case, for example, with the names of types of food:

> **fabada** [fa'βaða] *nf* *bean and sausage stew*

Here the translation (which doesn't exist) is replaced by an explanation. For increased clarity, the explanation, or "gloss", is shown in *italics*.

It is often the case that a word, or a particular meaning of a word, cannot be translated in isolation. The translation of **Dutch**, for example, is "holandés(-esa)". However, the phrase **to go Dutch** is rendered by "pagar a escote". Even an expression as simple as **washing powder** needs a separate translation since it translates as "detergente (en polvo)", not "polvo para lavar". This is where your dictionary will prove to be particularly informative and useful since it contains an abundance of compounds, phrases and idiomatic expressions.

Levels of formality and familiarity

In English you instinctively know when to say **I'm broke** or **I'm a bit short of cash** and when to say **I don't have any money**. When you are trying to understand someone who is speaking Spanish, however, or when you yourself try to speak Spanish, it is important to know what is polite and what is less so, and what you can say in a relaxed situation but not in a formal context. To help you with this, on the Spanish-English side we have added the label (*fam*) to show that a Spanish meaning or expression is colloquial, while those meanings or expressions which are vulgar are given an exclamation mark (*fam!*), warning you they can cause serious offence. Note also that on the English-Spanish side, colloquial English words are labelled as (*inf*), vulgar or offensive English words as (*inf!*) and vulgar or offensive Spanish translations as (*!*).

Keywords

Words labelled in the text as KEYWORD in English and PALABRA CLAVE in Spanish, such as **have** and **do** or their Spanish equivalents **tener** and **hacer**, have been given special treatment because they form the basic elements of the language. This extra help will ensure that you know how to use these complex words with confidence.

Highlighting

Words that appear with a shaded background, such as **ability** and **abrigo** are words that are specified by or commonly associated with GCSE exams and other exams of a similar level. The highlighting helps you spot your essential exam vocabulary quickly.

Cultural information

Entries which are marked in the main text by a column of dots explain aspects of culture in Spanish- and English-speaking countries. Subject areas covered include politics, education, media and national festivals.

Spanish alphabetical order

In 1994 the **Real Academia Española** and the Spanish American language academies jointly decided to stop treating CH and LL as separate letters in Spanish, thereby bringing it into line with European spelling norms. This means that **chapa** and **lluvia** will appear in letters C and L respectively. Similarly, any words containing **ch** and **ll** in the middle are now included in the same order that they would be in English. Spanish, however still has one more letter than English, with Ñ treated separately, between N and O.

Abreviaturas / Abbreviations

Abreviaturas		Abbreviations
abreviatura	*ab(b)r*	abbreviation
adjetivo, locución adjetiva	*adj*	adjective, adjectival phrase
administración, lenguaje administrativo	*Admin*	administration
adverbio, locución adverbial	*adv*	adverb, adverbial phrase
agricultura	*Agr*	agriculture
alguien	*algn*	
América Latina	*Am*	Latin America
anatomía	*Anat*	anatomy
arquitectura	*Arq, Arch*	architecture
astrología, astronomía	*Astro*	astrology, astronomy
el automóvil	*Aut(o)*	the motor car and motoring
aviación, viajes en avión	*Aviat*	flying, air travel
biología	*Bio(l)*	biology
botánica, flores	*Bot*	botany
inglés británico	*Brit*	British English
química	*Chem*	chemistry
cine	*Cine*	cinema
comercio, finanzas, banca	*Com(m)*	commerce, finance, banking
informática	*Comput*	computing
conjunción	*conj*	conjunction
construcción	*Constr*	building
compuesto	*cpd*	compound element
cocina	*Culin*	cookery
economía	*Econ*	economics
electricidad, electrónica	*Elec*	electricity, electronics
enseñanza, sistema escolar	*Escol*	schooling, schools
España	*Esp*	Spain
especialmente	*esp*	especially
exclamación, interjección	*excl*	exclamation, interjection
femenino	*f*	feminine
lenguaje familiar (! vulgar)	*fam (!)*	informal usage (! particularly offensive)
ferrocarril	*Ferro*	railways
uso figurado	*fig*	figurative use
fotografía	*Foto*	photography
(verbo inglés) del cual la partícula es inseparable	*fus*	(phrasal verb) where the particle is inseparable
generalmente	*gen*	generally
geografía, geología	*Geo*	geography, geology
geometría	*Geom*	geometry
lenguaje familiar (! vulgar)	*inf (!)*	informal usage (! particularly offensive)
informática	*Inform*	computing
invariable	*inv*	invariable
irregular	*irreg*	irregular
lo jurídico	*Jur*	law
América Latina	*LAm*	Latin America
gramática, lingüística	*Ling*	grammar, linguistics

literatura	*Lit*	literature
masculino	*m*	masculine
matemáticas	*Mat(h)*	mathematics
medicina	*Med*	medical term, medicine
masculino/femenino	*m/f*	masculine/feminine
lo militar, el ejército	*Mil*	military matters
música	*Mus*	music
sustantivo	*n*	noun
navegación, náutica	*Naut*	sailing, navigation
sustantivo no empleado en el plural	*no pl*	collective (uncountable) noun, not used in plural
sustantivo numérico	*num*	numeral noun
complemento	*obj*	(grammatical) object
	o.s.	oneself
peyorativo	*pey, pej*	derogatory, pejorative
fotografía	*Phot*	photography
fisiología	*Physiol*	physiology
plural	*pl*	plural
política	*Pol*	politics
participio de pasado	*pp*	past participle
prefijo	*pref*	prefix
preposición	*prep*	preposition
pronombre	*pron*	pronoun
psicología, psiquiatría	*Psico, Psych*	psychology, psychiatry
tiempo pasado	*pt*	past tense
ferrocarril	*Rail*	railways
religión, lo eclesiástico	*Rel*	religion, church service
	sb	somebody
enseñanza, sistema escolar	*Scol*	schooling, schools
singular	*sg*	singular
España	*Sp*	Spain
	sth	something
subjuntivo	*subjun*	subjunctive
sujeto	*su(b)j*	(grammatical) subject
sufijo	*suff*	suffix
tauromaquia	*Taur*	bullfighting
también	*tb*	also
teatro	*Teat*	
técnica, tecnología	*Tec(h)*	technical term, technology
telecomunicaciones	*Telec, Tel*	telecommunications
	Theat	theatre
imprenta, tipografía	*Tip, Typ*	typography, printing
televisión	*TV*	television
sistema universitario	*Univ*	universities
inglés norteamericano	*US*	American English
verbo	*vb*	verb
verbo intransitivo	*vi*	intransitive verb
verbo pronominal	*vr*	reflexive verb
verbo transitivo	*vt*	transitive verb
zoología, animales	*Zool*	zoology
marca registrada	®	registered trademark
indica un equivalente cultural	≈	introduces a cultural equivalent

Spanish Pronunciation

Consonants

b	[b] [β]	See notes on *v* below	*b*om*b*a la*b*or
c	[k]	*c* before *a*, *o* or *u* is pronounced as in *c*at	*c*aja
ce, ci	[θe,θi] [se,si][1]	*c* before *e* or *i* is pronounced as *th* in *th*in in most of Spain, or as *s* in *s*in in Latin America and parts of Spain	*ce*ro, *ci*elo vo*ce*ro, noti*ci*ero
ch	[tʃ]	*ch* is pronounced as *ch* in *ch*air	*ch*iste
d	[d] [ð]	at the beginning of a word or after *l* or *n*, *d* is pronounced as in English. In any other position it is like *th* in *th*e	*d*anés ciu*d*a*d*
g	[g] [ɣ]	*g* before *a*, *o* or *u* is pronounced as in *g*ap if at the beginning of a word or after *n*. In other positions the sound is softened.	*g*afas, *g*uerra pa*g*a
ge, gi	[xe, xi]	*g* before *e* or *i* is pronounced similar to *ch* in Scottish lo*ch*	*g*ente, *g*irar
h		*h* is always silent in Spanish	*h*aber
j	[x]	*j* is pronounced like *ch* in Scottish lo*ch*	*j*ugar
ll	[ʎ]	*ll* is pronounced like the *lli* in mi*lli*on or like the *y* in *y*es	ta*ll*e
ñ	[ɲ]	*ñ* is pronounced like the *ni* in o*ni*on	ni*ñ*o
q	[k]	*q* is pronounced as *k* in *k*ing	*q*ue
r, rr	[r] [rr]	*r* is always pronounced in Spanish, unlike the *r* in dancer. *rr* and *r* at the beginning of a word or syllable are trilled, like a Scottish *r*	quita*r* ga*rr*a
s	[s] [z]	*s* is usually pronounced as in pa*ss*, but before *b*, *d*, *g*, *l*, *m* or *n* it is pronounced as in ro*s*e	quizá*s* i*s*la
v	[b] [β]	*v* is pronounced something like *b*. At the beginning of a word or after *m* or *n* it is pronounced as *b* in *b*oy. In any other position it is pronounced with the lips in position to pronounce *b* of *b*oy, but not meeting	*v*ía di*v*idir
w	[b] [w]	pronounced either like Spanish *b*, or like English *w*	*w*áter *w*hiskey
x	[ks] [s]	*x* is pronounced as in to*x*in except in informal Spanish or at the beginning of a word	tó*x*ico *x*enofobia
z	[θ] [s][1]	*z* is pronounced as *th* in *th*in in most of Spain, or as *s* in *s*in in Latin America and parts of Spain	tena*z* i*z*ada

f, *k*, *l*, *m*, *n*, *p* and *t* are pronounced as in English

[1] Only shown in Latin American entries.

Vowels

a	[a]	Not as long as *a* in f*a*r. When followed by a consonant in the same syllable (ie in a closed syllable), as in am*a*nte, the *a* is short as in b*a*t	p*a*ta
e	[e]	like *e* in th*e*y. In a closed syllable, as in g*e*nte, the *e* is short as in p*e*t	m*e*
i	[i]	as in m*ea*n or mach*i*ne	p*i*no
o	[o]	as in l*o*cal. In a closed syllable, as in contr*o*l, the *o* is short as in c*o*t	l*o*
u	[u]	As in r*u*le. It is silent after *q*, and in *gue*, *gui*, unless marked *güe*, *güi* eg antig*ü*edad, when it is pronounced like *w* in *w*olf	l*u*nes

Semi-vowels

i, y	[j]	pronounced like *y* in *y*es	b*i*en, h*i*elo, *y*unta
u	[w]	unstressed *u* between consonant and vowel is pronounced like *w* in *w*ell. See also notes on *u* above	h*u*evo, f*u*ente, antig*ü*edad

Diphthongs

ai, ay	[ai]	as *i* in r*i*de	b*ai*le
au	[au]	as *ou* in sh*ou*t	*au*to
ei, ey	[ei]	as *ey* in gr*ey*	bu*ey*
eu	[eu]	both elements pronounced independently [e] + [u]	d*eu*da
oi, oy	[oi]	as *oy* in t*oy*	h*oy*

Stress

The rules of stress in Spanish are as follows:

(a) when a word ends in a vowel or in *n* or *s*, the second last syllable is stressed: pa*ta*ta, pa*ta*tas, *co*me, *co*men

(b) when a word ends in a consonant other than *n* or *s*, the stress falls on the last syllable: pa*red*, ha*blar*

(c) when the rules set out in (a) and (b) are not applied, an acute accent appears over the stressed vowel: com*ú*n, geograf*í*a, ingl*é*s

In the phonetic transcription, the symbol ['] precedes the syllable on which the stress falls.

In general, we give the pronunciation of each entry in square brackets after the word in question.

Spanish Verb Forms

1 Gerund **2** Imperative **3** Present **4** Preterite **5** Future **6** Present subjunctive **7** Imperfect subjunctive **8** Past participle **9** Imperfect

acertar **2** acierta **3** acierto, aciertas, acierta, aciertan **6** acierte, aciertes, acierte, acierten

acordar **2** acuerda **3** acuerdo, acuerdas, acuerda, acuerdan **6** acuerde, acuerdes, acuerde, acuerden

advertir **1** advirtiendo **2** advierte **3** advierto, adviertes, advierte, advierten **4** advirtió, advirtieron **6** advierta, adviertas, advierta, advirtamos, advirtáis, adviertan **7** advirtiera *etc*

agradecer **3** agradezco **6** agradezca *etc*

andar **4** anduve, anduviste, anduvo, anduvimos, anduvisteis, anduvieron **7** anduviera *or* anduviese *etc*

aparecer **3** aparezco **6** aparezca *etc*

aprobar **2** aprueba **3** apruebo, apruebas, aprueba, aprueban **6** apruebe, apruebes, apruebe, aprueben

atravesar **2** atraviesa **3** atravieso, atraviesas, atraviesa, atraviesan **6** atraviese, atravieses, atraviese, atraviesen

caber **3** quepo **4** cupe, cupiste, cupo, cupimos, cupisteis, cupieron **5** cabré *etc* **6** quepa *etc* **7** cupiera *etc*

caer **1** cayendo **3** caigo **4** cayó, cayeron **6** caiga *etc* **7** cayera *etc*

calentar **2** calienta **3** caliento, calientas, calienta, calientan **6** caliente, calientes, caliente, calienten

cerrar **2** cierra **3** cierro, cierras, cierra, cierran **6** cierre, cierres, cierre, cierren

COMER **1** comiendo **2** come, comed **3** como, comes, come, comemos, coméis, comen **4** comí, comiste, comió, comimos, comisteis, comieron **5** comeré, comerás, comerá, comeremos, comeréis, comerán **6** coma, comas, coma, comamos, comáis, coman **7** comiera, comieras, comiera, comiéramos, comierais, comieran **8** comido **9** comía, comías, comía, comíamos, comíais, comían

conocer **3** conozco **6** conozca *etc*

contar **2** cuenta **3** cuento, cuentas, cuenta, cuentan **6** cuente, cuentes, cuente, cuenten

costar **2** cuesta **3** cuesto, cuestas, cuesta, cuestan **6** cueste, cuestes, cueste, cuesten

dar **3** doy **4** di, diste, dio, dimos, disteis, dieron **7** diera *etc*

decir **2** di **3** digo **4** dije, dijiste, dijo, dijimos, dijisteis, dijeron **5** diré *etc* **6** diga *etc* **7** dijera *etc* **8** dicho

despertar **2** despierta **3** despierto, despiertas, despierta, despiertan **6** despierte, despiertes, despierte, despierten

divertir **1** divirtiendo **2** divierte **3** divierto, diviertes, divierte, divierten **4** divirtió, divirtieron **6** divierta, diviertas, divierta, divirtamos, divirtáis, diviertan **7** divirtiera *etc*

dormir **1** durmiendo **2** duerme **3** duermo, duermes, duerme, duermen **4** durmió, durmieron **6** duerma, duermas, duerma, durmamos, durmáis, duerman **7** durmiera *etc*

empezar **2** empieza **3** empiezo, empiezas, empieza, empiezan **4** empecé **6** empiece, empieces, empiece, empecemos, empecéis, empiecen

entender **2** entiende **3** entiendo, entiendes, entiende, entienden **6** entienda, entiendas, entienda, entiendan

ESTAR **2** está **3** estoy, estás, está, están **4** estuve, estuviste, estuvo, estuvimos, estuvisteis, estuvieron **6** esté, estés, esté, estén **7** estuviera *etc*

HABER **3** he, has, ha, hemos, habéis, han **4** hube, hubiste, hubo, hubimos, hubisteis, hubieron **5** habré *etc* **6** haya *etc* **7** hubiera *etc*

HABLAR **1** hablando **2** habla, hablad **3** hablo, hablas, habla, hablamos, habláis, hablan **4** hablé, hablaste, habló, hablamos, hablasteis, hablaron **5** hablaré, hablarás, hablará, hablaremos, hablaréis, hablarán **6** hable, hables, hable, hablemos, habléis, hablen **7** hablara *or* hablase, hablaras *or* hablases, habláramos *or* hablásemos, hablarais *or* hablaseis, hablaran *or* hablasen **8** hablado **9** hablaba, hablabas, hablaba, hablábamos, hablabais, hablaban

hacer **2** haz **3** hago **4** hice, hiciste, hizo, hicimos, hicisteis, hicieron **5** haré *etc* **6** haga *etc* **7** hiciera *etc* **8** hecho

instruir **1** instruyendo **2** instruye **3** instruyo, instruyes, instruye, instruyen **4** instruyó, instruyeron **6** instruya *etc* **7** instruyera *etc*

ir **1** yendo **2** ve **3** voy, vas, va, vamos, vais, van **4** fui, fuiste, fue, fuimos, fuisteis, fueron **6** vaya, vayas, vaya, vayamos, vayáis, vayan **7** fuera *etc* **9** iba, ibas, iba, íbamos, ibais, iban

jugar **2** juega **3** juego, juegas, juega, juegan **4** jugué **6** juegue *etc*

leer **1** leyendo **4** leyó, leyeron **7** leyera *etc*

morir **1** muriendo **2** muere **3** muero, mueres, muere, mueren **4** murió, murieron **6** muera, mueras, muera, muramos, muráis, mueran **7** muriera *etc* **8** muerto

mostrar **2** muestra **3** muestro, muestras, muestra, muestran **6** muestre, muestres, muestre, muestren

mover **2** mueve **3** muevo, mueves, mueve, mueven **6** mueva, muevas, mueva, muevan

negar **2** niega **3** niego, niegas, niega, niegan **4** negué **6** niegue, niegues, niegue, neguemos, neguéis, nieguen

ofrecer **3** ofrezco **6** ofrezca *etc*

oír **1** oyendo **2** oye **3** oigo, oyes, oye, oyen **4** oyó, oyeron **6** oiga *etc* **7** oyera *etc*

oler **2** huele **3** huelo, hueles, huele, huelen **6** huela, huelas, huela, huelan

parecer **3** parezco **6** parezca *etc*

pedir **1** pidiendo **2** pide **3** pido, pides, pide, piden **4** pidió, pidieron **6** pida *etc* **7** pidiera *etc*

pensar **2** piensa **3** pienso, piensas, piensa, piensan **6** piense, pienses, piense, piensen

perder **2** pierde **3** pierdo, pierdes, pierde, pierden **6** pierda, pierdas, pierda, pierdan

poder **1** pudiendo **2** puede **3** puedo, puedes, puede, pueden **4** pude, pudiste, pudo, pudimos, pudisteis, pudieron **5** podré *etc* **6** pueda, puedas, pueda, puedan **7** pudiera *etc*

poner **2** pon **3** pongo **4** puse, pusiste, puso, pusimos, pusisteis, pusieron **5** pondré *etc* **6** ponga *etc* **7** pusiera *etc* **8** puesto

preferir **1** prefiriendo **2** prefiere **3** prefiero, prefieres, prefiere, prefieren **4** prefirió, prefirieron **6** prefiera, prefieras, prefiera, prefiramos, prefiráis, prefieran **7** prefiriera *etc*

querer **2** quiere **3** quiero, quieres, quiere, quieren **4** quise, quisiste, quiso, quisimos, quisisteis, quisieron **5** querré *etc* **6** quiera, quieras, quiera, quieran **7** quisiera *etc*

reír **2** ríe **3** río, ríes, ríe, ríen **4** rio, rieron **6** ría, rías, ría, riamos, riais, rían **7** riera *etc*

repetir **1** repitiendo **2** repite **3** repito, repites, repite, repiten **4** repitió, repitieron **6** repita *etc* **7** repitiera *etc*

rogar **2** ruega **3** ruego, ruegas, ruega, ruegan **4** rogué **6** ruegue, ruegues, ruegue, roguemos, roguéis, rueguen

saber **3** sé **4** supe, supiste, supo, supimos, supisteis, supieron **5** sabré *etc* **6** sepa *etc* **7** supiera *etc*

salir **2** sal **3** salgo **5** saldré *etc* **6** salga *etc*

seguir **1** siguiendo **2** sigue **3** sigo, sigues, sigue, siguen **4** siguió, siguieron **6** siga *etc* **7** siguiera *etc*

sentar **2** sienta **3** siento, sientas, sienta, sientan **6** siente, sientes, siente, sienten

sentir **1** sintiendo **2** siente **3** siento, sientes, siente, sienten **4** sintió, sintieron **6** sienta, sientas, sienta, sintamos, sintáis, sientan **7** sintiera *etc*

SER **2** sé **3** soy, eres, es, somos, sois, son **4** fui, fuiste, fue, fuimos, fuisteis, fueron **6** sea *etc* **7** fuera *etc* **9** era, eras, era, éramos, erais, eran

servir **1** sirviendo **2** sirve **3** sirvo, sirves, sirve, sirven **4** sirvió, sirvieron **6** sirva *etc* **7** sirviera *etc*

soñar **2** sueña **3** sueño, sueñas, sueña, sueñan **6** sueñe, sueñes, sueñe, sueñen

tener **2** ten **3** tengo, tienes, tiene, tienen **4** tuve, tuviste, tuvo, tuvimos, tuvisteis, tuvieron **5** tendré *etc* **6** tenga *etc* **7** tuviera *etc*

traer **1** trayendo **3** traigo **4** traje, trajiste, trajo, trajimos, trajisteis, trajeron **6** traiga *etc* **7** trajera *etc*

valer **2** val **3** valgo **5** valdré *etc* **6** valga *etc*

venir **2** ven **3** vengo, vienes, viene, vienen **4** vine, viniste, vino, vinimos, vinisteis, vinieron **5** vendré *etc* **6** venga *etc* **7** viniera *etc*

ver **3** veo **6** vea *etc* **8** visto **9** veía *etc*

vestir **1** vistiendo **2** viste **3** visto, vistes, viste, visten **4** vistió, vistieron **6** vista *etc* **7** vistiera *etc*

VIVIR **1** viviendo **2** vive, vivid **3** vivo, vives, vive, vivimos, vivís, viven **4** viví, viviste, vivió, vivimos, vivisteis, vivieron **5** viviré, vivirás, vivirá, viviremos, viviréis, vivirán **6** viva, vivas, viva, vivamos, viváis, vivan **7** viviera *or* viviese, vivieras *or* vivieses, viviera *or* viviese, viviéramos *or* viviésemos, vivierais *or* vivieseis, vivieran *or* viviesen **8** vivido **9** vivía, vivías, vivía, vivíamos, vivías, vivían

volcar **2** vuelca **3** vuelco, vuelcas, vuelca, vuelcan **4** volqué **6** vuelque, vuelques, vuelque, volquemos, volquéis, vuelquen

volver **2** vuelve **3** vuelvo, vuelves, vuelve, vuelven **6** vuelva, vuelvas, vuelva, vuelvan **8** vuelto

For additional information on Spanish verb formation, see pp 6–75 of the Grammar section.

Números		Numbers
uno (un, una)*	**1**	one
dos	**2**	two
tres	**3**	three
cuatro	**4**	four
cinco	**5**	five
seis	**6**	six
siete	**7**	seven
ocho	**8**	eight
nueve	**9**	nine
diez	**10**	ten
once	**11**	eleven
doce	**12**	twelve
trece	**13**	thirteen
catorce	**14**	fourteen
quince	**15**	fifteen
dieciséis	**16**	sixteen
diecisiete	**17**	seventeen
dieciocho	**18**	eighteen
diecinueve	**19**	nineteen
veinte	**20**	twenty
veintiuno(-ún, -una)*	**21**	twenty-one
veintidós	**22**	twenty-two
treinta	**30**	thirty
treinta y uno(un, una)*	**31**	thirty-one
treinta y dos	**32**	thirty-two
cuarenta	**40**	forty
cincuenta	**50**	fifty
sesenta	**60**	sixty
setenta	**70**	seventy
ochenta	**80**	eighty
noventa	**90**	ninety
cien(ciento)**	**100**	a hundred, one hundred
ciento uno(un, una)*	**101**	a hundred and one
ciento dos	**102**	a hundred and two
ciento cincuenta y seis	**156**	a hundred and fifty-six
doscientos(-as)	**200**	two hundred
trescientos(-as)	**300**	three hundred
quinientos(-as)	**500**	five hundred
mil	**1,000**	a thousand
mil tres	**1,003**	a thousand and three
dos mil	**2,000**	two thousand
un millón	**1,000,000**	a million

*'uno' (+ 'veintiuno' etc) agrees in gender (but not number) with its noun: **treinta y una personas**; the masculine form is shortened to 'un/-ún' unless it stands alone: **veintiún caballos, veintiuno**.

'ciento' is used in compound numbers, except when it multiplies: **ciento diez, but **cien mil**. 'Cien' is used before nouns: **cien hombres, cien casas**.

Números	Numbers
primero (primer, primera) 1°, $1^{er}/1^{a}$, 1^{era}	first, 1st
segundo(-a) $2^{o}/2^{a}$	second, 2nd
tercero (tercer, tercera) 3°, $3^{er}/3^{a}$, 3^{era}	third, 3rd
cuarto(-a) $4^{o}/4^{a}$	fourth, 4th
quinto(-a)	fifth
sexto(-a)	sixth
séptimo(-a)	seventh
octavo(-a)	eighth
noveno(-a); nono(-a)	ninth
décimo(-a)	tenth
undécimo(-a)	eleventh
duodécimo(-a)	twelfth
decimotercero(-a)	thirteenth
decimocuarto(-a)	fourteenth
decimoquinto(-a)	fifteenth
decimosexto(-a)	sixteenth
decimoséptimo(-a)	seventeenth
decimoctavo(-a)	eighteenth
decimonoveno(-a)	nineteenth
vigésimo(-a)	twentieth
vigésimo(-a) primero(-a)	twenty-first
vigésimo(-a) segundo(-a)	twenty-second
trigésimo(-a)	thirtieth
trigésimo(-a) primero(-a)	thirty-first
trigésimo(-a) segundo(-a)	thirty-second
cuadragésimo(-a)	fortieth
quincuagésimo(-a)	fiftieth
sexagésimo(-a)	sixtieth
septuagésimo(-a)	seventieth
octogésimo(-a)	eightieth
nonagésimo(-a)	ninetieth
centésimo(-a)	hundredth
centésimo(-a) primero(-a)	hundred-and-first
milésimo(-a)	thousandth

La hora / The time

¿qué hora es?	*what time is it?*
es la una	it's one o'clock
son las cuatro	it's four o'clock
medianoche, las doce de la noche	midnight
la una (de la madrugada)	one o'clock (in the morning), one (a.m.)
la una y cinco	five past one
la una y diez	ten past one
la una y cuarto *or* quince	a quarter past one, one fifteen
la una y veinticinco	twenty-five past one, one twenty-five
la una y media *or* treinta	half past one, one thirty
las dos menos veinticinco, la una treinta y cinco	twenty-five to two, one thirty-five
las dos menos veinte, la una cuarenta	twenty to two, one forty
las dos menos cuarto, la una cuarenta y cinco	a quarter to two, one forty-five
las dos menos diez, la una cincuenta	ten to two, one fifty
mediodía, las doce (de la mañana)	twelve o'clock, midday, noon
las dos (de la tarde)	two o'clock (in the afternoon), two (p.m.)
las siete (de la tarde)	seven o'clock (in the evening), seven (p.m.)
¿a qué hora?	*at what time?*
a medianoche	at midnight
a las siete	at seven o'clock
a la una	at one o'clock
dentro de veinte minutos	in twenty minutes
hace diez minutos	ten minutes ago

La fecha / The date

hoy	today
mañana	tomorrow
pasado mañana	the day after tomorrow
ayer	yesterday
antes de ayer, anteayer	the day before yesterday
la víspera	the day before, the previous day
el día siguiente	the next *or* following day
la mañana	morning
la tarde	evening

esta mañana	this morning
esta tarde	this evening, this afternoon
ayer por la mañana	yesterday morning
ayer por la tarde	yesterday evening
mañana por la mañana	tomorrow morning
mañana por la tarde	tomorrow evening, tomorrow afternoon
en la noche del sábado al domingo	during Saturday night, during the night of Saturday to Sunday
vendrá el sábado	he's coming on Saturday
los sábados	on Saturdays
todos los sábados	every Saturday
el sábado pasado	last Saturday
el sábado que viene, el próximo sábado	next Saturday
ocho días a partir del sábado	a week on Saturday
quince días a partir del sábado	a fortnight *or* two weeks on Saturday
de lunes a sábado	from Monday to Saturday
todos las días	every day
una vez a la semana	once a week
una vez al mes	once a month
dos veces a la semana	twice a week
hace una semana *u* ocho días	a week ago
hace quince días	a fortnight *or* two weeks ago
el año pasado	last year
dentro de dos días	in two days
dentro de ocho días *o* una semana	in a week
dentro de quince días	in a fortnight *or* two weeks
el mes que viene, el próximo mes	next month
el año que viene, el próximo año	next year
¿a qué o a cuántos estamos?	*what day is it?*
el 1/22 octubre de 2017	the 1st/22nd of October 2017, October 1st/22nd 2017
en 2017	in 2017
mil novicientos noventa y cinco	nineteen ninety-five
44 a. de J.C.	44 BC
14 d. de J.C.	14 AD
en el (siglo) XIX	in the nineteenth century
en los años treinta	in the thirties
érase una vez ...	once upon a time ...

a

PALABRA CLAVE

a [a] *prep* (**a** + **el** = **al**) **1** (*dirección*) to; **fueron a Madrid/Grecia** they went to Madrid/Greece; **me voy a casa** I'm going home
2 (*distancia*): **está a 15 km de aquí** it's 15 km from here
3 (*posición*): **estar a la mesa** to be at table; **al lado de** next to, beside; **a la derecha/izquierda** on the right/left; *ver tb* **puerta**
4 (*tiempo*): **a las 10/a medianoche** at 10/midnight; **¿a qué hora?** (at) what time?; **a la mañana siguiente** the following morning; **a los pocos días** after a few days; **estamos a 9 de julio** it's the 9th of July; **a los 24 años** at the age of 24; **ocho horas al día** eight hours a day; **al año/a la semana** (*Am*) a year/week later
5 (*manera*): **a la francesa** the French way; **a caballo** on horseback; **a oscuras** in the dark; **a rayas** striped; **le echaron a patadas** they kicked him out
6 (*medio, instrumento*): **a lápiz** in pencil; **a mano** by hand; **cocina a gas** gas stove
7 (*razón*): **a dos euros el kilo** at two euros a kilo; **a más de 50 km por hora** at more than 50 km per hour; **poco a poco** little by little
8 (*dativo*): **se lo di a él** I gave it to him; **se lo compré a él** I bought it from him
9 (*complemento directo*): **vi al policía** I saw the policeman
10 (*tras ciertos verbos*): **voy a verle** I'm going to see him; **empezó a trabajar** he started working *o* to work; **sabe a queso** it tastes of cheese
11 (*+infin*): **al verle, le reconocí inmediatamente** when I saw him I recognized him at once; **el camino a recorrer** the distance we *etc* have to travel; **¡a callar!** keep quiet!; **¡a comer!** let's eat!
12: **a que**: **¡a que llueve!** I bet it's going to rain!; **¿a qué viene eso?** what's the meaning of this?; **¿a que sí va a venir?** he IS coming, isn't he?; **¿a que no lo haces? — ¡a que sí!** bet you don't do it! — yes, I WILL!

abad, esa [a'βað, 'ðesa] *nm/f* abbot/abbess
abadía [aβa'ðia] *nf* abbey
abajo [a'βaxo] *adv* (*situación*) (down) below, underneath; (*en edificio*) downstairs; (*dirección*) down, downwards; **~ de** *prep* below, under; **el piso de ~** the downstairs flat; **la parte de ~** the lower part; **¡~ el gobierno!** down with the government!; **cuesta/río ~** downhill/downstream; **de arriba ~** from top to bottom; **el ~ firmante** the undersigned; **más ~** lower *o* further down
abalanzarse [aβalan'θarse] *vr*: **~ sobre** *o* **contra** to throw o.s. at
abalorios [aβa'lorjos] *nmpl* (*chucherías*) trinkets
abanderado, -a [aβande'raðo, a] *nm/f* (*portaestandarte*) standard bearer; (*de un movimiento*) champion, leader; (*Am: linier*) linesman, assistant referee
abandonado, -a [aβando'naðo, a] *adj* derelict; (*desatendido*) abandoned; (*desierto*) deserted; (*descuidado*) neglected
abandonar [aβando'nar] *vt* to leave; (*persona*) to abandon, desert; (*cosa*) to abandon, leave behind; (*descuidar*) to neglect; (*renunciar a*) to give up; (*Inform*) to quit; **abandonarse** *vr*: **~se a** to abandon o.s. to; **~se al alcohol** to take to drink
abandono [aβan'dono] *nm* (*acto*) desertion, abandonment; (*estado*) abandon, neglect; (*renuncia*) withdrawal, retirement; **ganar por ~** to win by default
abanicar [aβani'kar] *vt* to fan
abanico [aβa'niko] *nm* fan; (*Naut*) derrick; **en ~** fan-shaped
abaratar [aβara'tar] *vt* to lower the price of ▷ *vi*, **abaratarse** *vr* to go *o* come down in price
abarcar [aβar'kar] *vt* to include, embrace; (*contener*) to comprise; (*Am*) to monopolize; **quien mucho abarca poco aprieta** don't bite off more than you can chew
abarrotado, -a [aβarro'taðo, a] *adj* packed; **~ de** packed *o* bursting with
abarrotar [aβarro'tar] *vt* (*local, estadio, teatro*) to fill, pack

abarrote [aβa'rrote] *nm* packing; **abarrotes** *nmpl* (*Am*) groceries; **tienda de ~s** (*Am*) grocery store
abarrotero, -a [aβarro'tero, a] *nm/f* (*Am*) grocer
abastecer [aβaste'θer] *vt*: **~ (de)** to supply (with)
abastecimiento [aβasteθi'mjento] *nm* supply
abasto [a'βasto] *nm* supply; (*abundancia*) abundance; **no dar ~ a algo** not to be able to cope with sth
abatible [aβa'tiβle] *adj*: **asiento ~** tip-up seat; (*Auto*) reclining seat
abatido, -a [aβa'tiðo, a] *adj* dejected, downcast; **estar muy ~** to be very depressed
abatimiento [aβati'mjento] *nm* (*depresión*) dejection, depression
abatir [aβa'tir] *vt* (*muro*) to demolish; (*pájaro*) to shoot *o* bring down; (*fig*) to depress; **abatirse** *vr* to get depressed; **~se sobre** to swoop *o* pounce on
abdicación [aβðika'θjon] *nf* abdication
abdicar [aβði'kar] *vi* to abdicate; **~ en algn** to abdicate in favour of sb
abdomen [aβ'ðomen] *nm* abdomen
abdominal [aβðomi'nal] *adj* abdominal ▷ *nm*: **~es** abdominals, stomach muscles; (*Deporte*: *tb*: **ejercicios ~es**) sit-ups
abecedario [aβeθe'ðarjo] *nm* alphabet
abedul [aβe'ðul] *nm* birch
abeja [a'βexa] *nf* bee; (*fig*: *hormiguita*) hard worker
abejorro [aβe'xorro] *nm* bumblebee
aberración [aβerra'θjon] *nf* aberration
abertura [aβer'tura] *nf* = **apertura**
abertzale [aβer'tʃale] *adj*, *nm/f* Basque nationalist
abeto [a'βeto] *nm* fir
abierto, -a [a'βjerto, a] *pp de* **abrir** ▷ *adj* open; (*fig*: *carácter*) frank
abigarrado, -a [aβiɣa'rraðo, a] *adj* multicoloured; (*fig*) motley
abismal [aβis'mal] *adj* (*fig*) vast, enormous
abismo [a'βismo] *nm* abyss; **de sus ideas a las mías hay un ~** our views are worlds apart
abjurar [aβxu'rar] *vt* to abjure, forswear ▷ *vi*: **~ de** to abjure, forswear
ablandar [aβlan'dar] *vt* to soften; (*conmover*) to touch; (*Culin*) to tenderize ▷ *vi*, **ablandarse** *vr* to get softer
abnegación [aβneɣa'θjon] *nf* self-denial
abnegado, -a [aβne'ɣaðo, a] *adj* self-sacrificing
abocado, -a [aβo'kaðo, a] *adj*: **verse ~ al desastre** to be heading for disaster
abochornar [aβotʃor'nar] *vt* to embarrass; **abochornarse** *vr* to get flustered; (*Bot*) to wilt; **~se de** to get embarrassed about
abofetear [aβofete'ar] *vt* to slap (in the face)
abogacía [aβoɣa'θia] *nf* legal profession; (*ejercicio*) practice of the law
abogado, -a [aβo'ɣaðo, a] *nm/f* lawyer; (*notario*) solicitor; (*asesor*) counsel; (*en tribunal*) barrister, advocate, attorney (*US*); **~ defensor** defence lawyer (*Brit*), defense attorney (*US*); **~ del diablo** devil's advocate
abogar [aβo'ɣar] *vi*: **~ por** to plead for; (*fig*) to advocate
abolengo [aβo'lengo] *nm* ancestry, lineage
abolición [aβoli'θjon] *nf* abolition
abolir [aβo'lir] *vt* to abolish; (*cancelar*) to cancel
abolladura [aβoʎa'ðura] *nf* dent
abollar [aβo'ʎar] *vt* to dent
abombarse [aβom'barse] (*Am*) *vr* to go bad
abominable [aβomi'naβle] *adj* abominable
abominación [aβomina'θjon] *nf* abomination
abonado, -a [aβo'naðo, a] *adj* (*deuda*) paid(-up) ▷ *nm/f* subscriber
abonar [aβo'nar] *vt* to pay; (*deuda*) to settle; (*terreno*) to fertilize; (*idea*) to endorse; **abonarse** *vr* to subscribe; **~ dinero en una cuenta** to pay money into an account, credit money to an account
abono [a'βono] *nm* payment; fertilizer; subscription
abordar [aβor'ðar] *vt* (*barco*) to board; (*asunto*) to broach; (*individuo*) to approach
aborigen [aβo'rixen] *nm/f* aborigine
aborrecer [aβorre'θer] *vt* to hate, loathe
abortar [aβor'tar] *vi* (*malparir*) to have a miscarriage; (*deliberadamente*) to have an abortion
aborto [a'βorto] *nm* miscarriage; abortion
abotagado, -a [aβota'ɣaðo, a] *adj* swollen
abotonar [aβoto'nar] *vt* to button (up), do up
abovedado, -a [aβoβe'ðaðo, a] *adj* vaulted, domed
abrasar [aβra'sar] *vt* to burn (up); (*Agr*) to dry up, parch
abrazadera [aβraθa'ðera] *nf* bracket
abrazar [aβra'θar] *vt* to embrace, hug; **abrazarse** *vr* to embrace, hug each other
abrazo [a'βraθo] *nm* embrace, hug; **un ~** (*en carta*) with best wishes
abrebotellas [aβreβo'teʎas] *nm inv* bottle opener
abrecartas [aβre'kartas] *nm inv* letter opener
abrelatas [aβre'latas] *nm inv* tin (*Brit*) *o* can (*US*) opener
abreviar [aβre'βjar] *vt* to abbreviate; (*texto*) to abridge; (*plazo*) to reduce ▷ *vi*: **bueno, para ~** well, to cut a long story short
abreviatura [aβreβja'tura] *nf* abbreviation
abridor [aβri'ðor] *nm* (*de botellas*) bottle opener; (*de latas*) tin (*Brit*) *o* can (*US*) opener
abrigador, a [aβriga'ðor, a] *adj* (*Am*) warm
abrigar [aβri'ɣar] *vt* (*proteger*) to shelter; (*suj*: *ropa*) to keep warm; (*fig*) to cherish; **abrigarse** *vr* (*con ropa*) to cover (o.s.) up; **~se (de)** to take shelter (from), protect o.s. (from); **¡abrígate bien!** wrap up well!

abrigo [a'βriɣo] *nm* (*prenda*) coat, overcoat; (*lugar protegido*) shelter; **al ~ de** in the shelter of

abril [a'βril] *nm* April; *ver tb* **julio**

abrillantador [aβriʎanta'ðor] *nm* polish

abrillantar [aβriʎan'tar] *vt* (*pulir*) to polish; (*fig*) to enhance

abrir [a'βrir] *vt* to open (up); (*camino etc*) to open up; (*apetito*) to whet; (*lista*) to head ▷ *vi* to open; **abrirse** *vr* to open (up); (*extenderse*) to open out; (*cielo*) to clear; **~ un negocio** to start up a business; **en un ~ y cerrar de ojos** in the twinkling of an eye; **~se paso** to find *o* force a way through

abrochar [aβro'tʃar] *vt* (*con botones*) to button (up); (*zapato, con broche*) to do up; **abrocharse** *vr*: **~se los zapatos** to tie one's shoelaces

abrumar [aβru'mar] *vt* to overwhelm; (*sobrecargar*) to weigh down

abrupto, -a [a'βrupto, a] *adj* abrupt; (*empinado*) steep

absceso [aβs'θeso] *nm* abscess

absentismo [aβsen'tismo] *nm* (*de obreros*) absenteeism

absolución [aβsolu'θjon] *nf* (*Rel*) absolution; (*Jur*) acquittal

absoluto, -a [aβso'luto, a] *adj* absolute; (*total*) utter, complete; **en ~** *adv* not at all

absolver [aβsol'βer] *vt* to absolve; (*Jur*) to pardon; (*: acusado*) to acquit

absorbente [aβsor'βente] *adj* absorbent; (*interesante*) absorbing, interesting; (*exigente*) demanding

absorber [aβsor'βer] *vt* to absorb; (*embeber*) to soak up; **absorberse** *vr* to become absorbed

absorción [aβsor'θjon] *nf* absorption; (*Com*) takeover

absorto, -a [aβ'sorto, a] *pp de* **absorber** ▷ *adj* absorbed, engrossed

abstemio, -a [aβs'temjo, a] *adj* teetotal

abstención [aβsten'θjon] *nf* abstention

abstenerse [aβste'nerse] *vr*: **~ (de)** to abstain *o* refrain (from)

abstinencia [aβsti'nenθja] *nf* abstinence; (*ayuno*) fasting

abstracción [aβstrak'θjon] *nf* abstraction

abstracto, -a [aβ'strakto, a] *adj* abstract; **en ~** in the abstract

abstraer [aβstra'er] *vt* to abstract; **abstraerse** *vr* to be *o* become absorbed

abstraído, -a [aβstra'iðo, a] *adj* absent-minded

absuelto [aβ'swelto] *pp de* **absolver**

absurdo, -a [aβ'surðo, a] *adj* absurd ▷ *nm* absurdity; **lo ~ es que ...** the ridiculous thing is that ...

abuchear [aβutʃe'ar] *vt* to boo

abuela [a'βwela] *nf* grandmother; **¡cuéntaselo a tu ~!** (*fam!*) do you think I was born yesterday? (*fam*); **no tener/necesitar ~** (*fam*) to be full of o.s./blow one's own trumpet

abuelo [a'βwelo] *nm* grandfather; (*antepasado*) ancestor; **abuelos** *nmpl* grandparents

abulia [a'βulja] *nf* lethargy

abúlico, -a [a'βuliko, a] *adj* lethargic

abultado, -a [aβul'taðo, a] *adj* bulky

abultar [aβul'tar] *vt* to enlarge; (*aumentar*) to increase; (*fig*) to exaggerate ▷ *vi* to be bulky

abundancia [aβun'danθja] *nf*: **una ~ de** plenty of; **en ~** in abundance

abundante [aβun'dante] *adj* abundant, plentiful

abundar [aβun'dar] *vi* to abound, be plentiful; **~ en una opinión** to share an opinion

aburguesarse [aβurɣe'sarse] *vr* to become middle-class

aburrido, -a [aβu'rriðo, a] *adj* (*hastiado*) bored; (*que aburre*) boring

aburrimiento [aβurri'mjento] *nm* boredom, tedium

aburrir [aβu'rrir] *vt* to bore; **aburrirse** *vr* to be bored, get bored; **~se como una almeja** *u* **ostra** to be bored stiff

abusado, -a [aβu'saðo, a] *adj* (*Am: fam: astuto*) sharp, cunning ▷ *excl*: **¡~!** (*inv*) look out!, careful!

abusar [aβu'sar] *vi* to go too far; **~ de** to abuse

abusivo, -a [aβu'siβo, a] *adj* (*precio*) exorbitant

abuso [a'βuso] *nm* abuse; **~ de confianza** betrayal of trust

abyecto, -a [aβ'jekto, a] *adj* wretched, abject

a/c *abr* (*= al cuidado de*) c/o; (*= a cuenta*) on account

acá [a'ka] *adv* (*lugar*) here; **pasearse de ~ para allá** to walk up and down; **¡vente para ~!** come over here!; **¿de cuándo ~?** since when?

acabado, -a [aka'βaðo, a] *adj* finished, complete; (*perfecto*) perfect; (*agotado*) worn out; (*fig*) masterly ▷ *nm* finish

acabar [aka'βar] *vt* (*llevar a su fin*) to finish, complete; (*consumir*) to use up; (*rematar*) to finish off ▷ *vi* to finish, end; (*morir*) to die; **acabarse** *vr* to finish, stop; (*terminarse*) to be over; (*agotarse*) to run out; **~ con** to put an end to; **~ mal** to come to a sticky end; **esto ~á conmigo** this will be the end of me; **~ de llegar** to have just arrived; **acababa de hacerlo** I had just done it; **~ haciendo** *o* **por hacer algo** to end up (by) doing sth; **¡se acabó!** (*¡basta!*) that's enough!; (*se terminó*) it's all over!; **se me acabó el tabaco** I ran out of cigarettes

acabose [aka'βose] *nm*: **esto es el ~** this is the last straw

acacia [a'kaθja] *nf* acacia

academia [aka'ðemja] *nf* academy; (*Escol*) private school; **~ de idiomas** language school; *ver tb* **colegio**

académico, -a [aka'ðemiko, a] *adj* academic

acaecer [akae'θer] *vi* to happen, occur

acallar [aka'ʎar] *vt* (*silenciar*) to silence; (*calmar*) to pacify
acalorado, -a [akalo'raðo, a] *adj* (*discusión*) heated
acalorarse [akalo'rarse] *vr* (*fig*) to get heated
acampada [akam'paða] *nf*: **ir de ~** to go camping
acampanado, -a [akampa'naðo, a] *adj* flared
acampar [akam'par] *vi* to camp
acanalar [akana'lar] *vt* to groove; (*ondular*) to corrugate
acantilado [akanti'laðo] *nm* cliff
acaparar [akapa'rar] *vt* to monopolize; (*acumular*) to hoard
acariciar [akari'θjar] *vt* to caress; (*esperanza*) to cherish
acarrear [akarre'ar] *vt* to transport; (*fig*) to cause, result in; **le acarreó muchos disgustos** it brought him lots of problems
acaso [a'kaso] *adv* perhaps, maybe ▷ *nm* chance; **¿~ es mi culpa?** (*Am: fam*) what makes you think it's my fault?; **(por) si ~** (just) in case
acatamiento [akata'mjento] *nm* respect; (*de la ley*) observance
acatar [aka'tar] *vt* to respect; (*ley*) to obey, observe
acatarrarse [akata'rrarse] *vr* to catch a cold
acaudalado, -a [akauða'laðo, a] *adj* well-off
acaudillar [akauði'ʎar] *vt* to lead, command
acceder [akθe'ðer] *vi* to accede, agree; **~ a** (*petición etc*) to agree to; (*tener acceso a*) to have access to; (*Inform*) to access
accesible [akθe'siβle] *adj* accessible; **~ a** open to
acceso [ak'θeso] *nm* access, entry; (*camino*) access road; (*Med*) attack, fit; (*de cólera*) fit; (*Pol*) accession; (*Inform*) access; **~ aleatorio/directo/secuencial** *o* **en serie** (*Inform*) random/direct/sequential *o* serial access; **de ~ múltiple** multi-access
accesorio, -a [akθe'sorjo, a] *adj* accessory ▷ *nm* accessory; **accesorios** *nmpl* (*Auto*) accessories, extras; (*Teat*) props
accidentado, -a [akθiðen'taðo, a] *adj* uneven; (*montañoso*) hilly; (*azaroso*) eventful ▷ *nm/f* accident victim
accidental [akθiðen'tal] *adj* accidental; (*empleo*) temporary
accidentarse [akθiðen'tarse] *vr* to have an accident
accidente [akθi'ðente] *nm* accident; **por ~** by chance; **accidentes** *nmpl* (*de terreno*) unevenness *sg*, roughness *sg*; **~ laboral** *o* **de trabajo/de tráfico** industrial/road *o* traffic accident
acción [ak'θjon] *nf* action; (*acto*) action, act; (*Teat*) plot; (*Com*) share; (*Jur*) action, lawsuit; **capital en acciones** share capital; **~ liberada/ordinaria/preferente** fully-paid/ordinary/preference share
accionar [akθjo'nar] *vt* to work, operate; (*ejecutar*) to activate
accionista [akθjo'nista] *nm/f* shareholder
acebo [a'θeβo] *nm* holly; (*árbol*) holly tree
acechanza [aθe'tʃanθa] *nf* = **acecho**
acechar [aθe'tʃar] *vt* to spy on; (*aguardar*) to lie in wait for
acecho [a'θetʃo] *nm*: **estar al ~ (de)** to lie in wait (for)
aceite [a'θeite] *nm* oil; **~ de girasol/oliva** olive/sunflower oil; **~ de hígado de bacalao** cod-liver oil
aceitera [aθei'tera] *nf* oilcan
aceitoso, -a [aθei'toso, a] *adj* oily
aceituna [aθei'tuna] *nf* olive; **~ rellena** stuffed olive
acelerador [aθelera'ðor] *nm* accelerator
acelerar [aθele'rar] *vt* to accelerate; **acelerarse** *vr* to hurry
acelga [a'θelɣa] *nf* chard, beet
acento [a'θento] *nm* accent; (*acentuación*) stress; **~ cerrado** strong *o* thick accent
acentuar [aθen'twar] *vt* to accent; to stress; (*fig*) to accentuate
acepción [aθep'θjon] *nf* meaning
aceptable [aθep'taβle] *adj* acceptable
aceptación [aθepta'θjon] *nf* acceptance; (*aprobación*) approval
aceptar [aθep'tar] *vt* to accept; (*aprobar*) to approve; **~ hacer algo** to agree to do sth
acequia [a'θekja] *nf* irrigation ditch
acera [a'θera] *nf* pavement (*Brit*), sidewalk (*US*)
acerado, -a [aθe'raðo, a] *adj* steel; (*afilado*) sharp; (*fig: duro*) steely; (*: mordaz*) biting
acerbo, -a [a'θerβo, a] *adj* bitter; (*fig*) harsh
acerca [a'θerka]: **~ de** *prep* about, concerning
acercar [aθer'kar] *vt* to bring *o* move nearer; **acercarse** *vr* to approach, come near
acerico [aθe'riko] *nm* pincushion
acero [a'θero] *nm* steel; **~ inoxidable** stainless steel
acérrimo, -a [a'θerrimo, a] *adj* (*partidario*) staunch; (*enemigo*) bitter
acertado, -a [aθer'taðo, a] *adj* correct; (*apropiado*) apt; (*sensato*) sensible
acertar [aθer'tar] *vt* (*blanco*) to hit; (*solución*) to get right; (*adivinar*) to guess ▷ *vi* to get it right, be right; **~ a** to manage to; **~ con** to happen *o* hit on
acertijo [aθer'tixo] *nm* riddle, puzzle
acervo [a'θerβo] *nm* heap; **~ común** undivided estate
achacar [atʃa'kar] *vt* to attribute
achacoso, -a [atʃa'koso, a] *adj* sickly
achaque *etc* [a'tʃake] *vb ver* **achacar** ▷ *nm* ailment
achicar [atʃi'kar] *vt* to reduce; (*humillar*) to humiliate; (*Naut*) to bale out; **achicarse** *vr* (*ropa*) to shrink; (*fig*) to humble o.s.
achicharrar [atʃitʃa'rrar] *vt* to scorch, burn
achichincle [atʃi'tʃinkle] *nm/f* (*Am: fam*) minion

achicoria [atʃi'korja] *nf* chicory
achuras [a'tʃuras] *nf* (*Am: Culin*) offal
aciago, -a [a'θjaɣo, a] *adj* ill-fated, fateful
acicalar [aθika'lar] *vt* to polish; (*adornar*) to bedeck; **acicalarse** *vr* to get dressed up
acicate [aθi'kate] *nm* spur; (*fig*) incentive
acidez [aθi'ðeθ] *nf* acidity
ácido, -a ['aθiðo, a] *adj* sour, acid ▷ *nm* acid; (*fam: droga*) LSD
acierto *etc* [a'θjerto] *vb ver* **acertar** ▷ *nm* success; (*buen paso*) wise move; (*solución*) solution; (*habilidad*) skill, ability; (*al adivinar*) good guess; **fue un ~ suyo** it was a sensible choice on his part
acitronar [aθitro'nar] (*Am*) *vt* (*fam*) to brown
aclamación [aklama'θjon] *nf* acclamation; (*aplausos*) applause
aclamar [akla'mar] *vt* to acclaim; (*aplaudir*) to applaud
aclaración [aklara'θjon] *nf* clarification, explanation
aclarar [akla'rar] *vt* to clarify, explain; (*ropa*) to rinse ▷ *vi* to clear up; **aclararse** *vr* (*suj: persona: explicarse*) to understand; (*fig: asunto*) to become clear; **~se la garganta** to clear one's throat
aclaratorio, -a [aklara'torjo, a] *adj* explanatory
aclimatación [aklimata'θjon] *nf* acclimatization
aclimatar [aklima'tar] *vt* to acclimatize; **aclimatarse** *vr* to become *o* get acclimatized; **~se a algo** to get used to sth
acné [ak'ne] *nm* acne
acobardar [akoβar'ðar] *vt* to daunt, intimidate; **acobardarse** *vr* (*atemorizarse*) to be intimidated; (*echarse atrás*): **~se (ante)** to shrink back (from)
acodarse [ako'ðarse] *vr*: **~ en** to lean on
acogedor, a [akoxe'ðor, a] *adj* welcoming; (*hospitalario*) hospitable
acoger [ako'xer] *vt* to welcome; (*abrigar*) to shelter; **acogerse** *vr* to take refuge; **~se a** (*pretexto*) to take refuge in; (*ley*) to resort to
acogida [ako'xiða] *nf* reception; refuge
acolchar [akol'tʃar] *vt* to pad; (*fig*) to cushion
acomedido, -a [akome'ðiðo, a] (*Am*) *adj* helpful, obliging
acometer [akome'ter] *vt* to attack; (*emprender*) to undertake
acometida [akome'tiða] *nf* attack, assault
acomodado, -a [akomo'ðaðo, a] *adj* (*persona*) well-to-do
acomodador, a [akomoða'ðor, a] *nm/f* usher(ette)
acomodar [akomo'ðar] *vt* to adjust; (*alojar*) to accommodate; **acomodarse** *vr* to conform; (*instalarse*) to install o.s.; (*adaptarse*) to adapt o.s.; **~se (a)** to adapt (to); **¡acomódese a su gusto!** make yourself comfortable!
acomodaticio, -a [akomoða'tiθjo, a] *adj* (*pey*) accommodating, obliging; (*manejable*) pliable
acompañante, -a [akompa'ɲante, a] *nm/f* companion
acompañar [akompa'ɲar] *vt* to accompany, go with; (*documentos*) to enclose; **¿quieres que te acompañe?** do you want me to come with you?; **~ a algn a la puerta** to see sb to the door *o* out; **le acompaño en el sentimiento** please accept my condolences
acomplejar [akomple'xar] *vt* to give a complex to; **acomplejarse** *vr*: **~se (con)** to get a complex (about)
acondicionado, -a [akondiθjo'naðo, a] *adj* (*Tec*) in good condition
acondicionar [akondiθjo'nar] *vt* to get ready, prepare; (*pelo*) to condition
acongojar [akongo'xar] *vt* to distress, grieve
aconsejar [akonse'xar] *vt* to advise, counsel; **~ a algn hacer** *o* **que haga algo** to advise sb to do sth; **aconsejarse** *vr*: **~se con** *o* **de** to consult
acontecer [akonte'θer] *vi* to happen, occur
acontecimiento [akonteθi'mjento] *nm* event
acopio [a'kopjo] *nm* store, stock
acoplamiento [akopla'mjento] *nm* coupling, joint
acoplar [ako'plar] *vt* to fit; (*Elec*) to connect; (*vagones*) to couple
acorazado, -a [akora'θaðo, a] *adj* armour-plated, armoured ▷ *nm* battleship
acordar [akor'ðar] *vt* (*resolver*) to agree, resolve; (*recordar*) to remind; **acordarse** *vr* to agree; **~ hacer algo** to agree to do sth; **~se (de algo)** to remember (sth)
acorde [a'korðe] *adj* (*Mus*) harmonious ▷ *nm* chord; **~ con** (*medidas etc*) in keeping with
acordeón [akorðe'on] *nm* accordion
acordonado, -a [akorðo'naðo, a] *adj* (*calle*) cordoned-off
acorralar [akorra'lar] *vt* to round up, corral; (*fig*) to intimidate
acortar [akor'tar] *vt* to shorten; (*duración*) to cut short; (*cantidad*) to reduce; **acortarse** *vr* to become shorter
acosar [ako'sar] *vt* to pursue relentlessly; (*fig*) to hound, pester; **~ a algn a preguntas** to pester sb with questions
acoso [a'koso] *nm* relentless pursuit; (*fig*) harassment; **~ sexual** sexual harassment
acostar [akos'tar] *vt* (*en cama*) to put to bed; (*en suelo*) to lay down; (*barco*) to bring alongside; **acostarse** *vr* to go to bed; to lie down; **~se con algn** to sleep with sb
acostumbrado, -a [akostum'braðo, a] *adj* (*habitual*) usual; **estar ~ a (hacer) algo** to be used to (doing) sth
acostumbrar [akostum'brar] *vt*: **~ a algn a algo** to get sb used to sth ▷ *vi*: **~ (a hacer algo)** to be in the habit (of doing sth); **acostumbrarse** *vr*: **~se a** to get used to

acotación [akota'θjon] *nf* (*apunte*) marginal note; (*Geo*) elevation mark; (*de límite*) boundary mark; (*Teat*) stage direction
acotamiento [akota'mjento] (*Am*) *nm* hard shoulder (*Brit*), berm (*US*)
ácrata ['akrata] *adj, nm/f* anarchist
acre ['akre] *adj* (*sabor*) sharp, bitter; (*olor*) acrid; (*fig*) biting ▷ *nm* acre
acrecentar [akreθen'tar] *vt* to increase, augment
acreditar [akreði'tar] *vt* (*garantizar*) to vouch for, guarantee; (*autorizar*) to authorize; (*dar prueba de*) to prove; (*Com: abonar*) to credit; (*embajador*) to accredit; **acreditarse** *vr* to become famous; (*demostrar valía*) to prove one's worth; **~se de** to get a reputation for
acreedor, a [akree'ðor, a] *adj*: **~ a** worthy of ▷ *nm/f* creditor; **~ común/diferido/con garantía** (*Com*) unsecured/deferred/secured creditor
acribillar [akriβi'ʎar] *vt*: **~ a balazos** to riddle with bullets
acróbata [a'kroβata] *nm/f* acrobat
acta ['akta] *nf* certificate; (*de comisión*) minutes *pl*, record; **~ de nacimiento/de matrimonio** birth/marriage certificate; **~ notarial** affidavit; **levantar ~** (*Jur*) to make a formal statement *o* deposition
actitud [akti'tuð] *nf* attitude; (*postura*) posture; **adoptar una ~ firme** to take a firm stand
activar [akti'βar] *vt* to activate; (*acelerar*) to speed up
actividad [aktiβi'ðað] *nf* activity; **estar en plena ~** to be in full swing
activo, -a [ak'tiβo, a] *adj* active; (*vivo*) lively ▷ *nm* (*Com*) assets *pl*; **~ y pasivo** assets and liabilities; **~ circulante/fijo/inmaterial/invisible** (*Com*) current/fixed/intangible/invisible assets; **~ realizable** liquid assets; **~s congelados** *o* **bloqueados** frozen assets; **~ tóxico** toxic asset; **estar en ~** (*Mil*) to be on active service
acto ['akto] *nm* act, action; (*ceremonia*) ceremony; (*Teat*) act; **en el ~** immediately; **hacer ~ de presencia** (*asistir*) to attend (formally)
actor [ak'tor] *nm* actor; (*Jur*) plaintiff ▷ *adj*: **parte ~a** prosecution
actriz [ak'triθ] *nf* actress
actuación [aktwa'θjon] *nf* action; (*comportamiento*) conduct, behaviour; (*Jur*) proceedings *pl*; (*desempeño*) performance
actual [ak'twal] *adj* present(-day), current; **el 6 del ~** the 6th of this month
actualidad [aktwali'ðað] *nf* present; **actualidades** *nfpl* (*noticias*) news *sg*; **en la ~** at present; (*hoy día*) nowadays, at present; **ser de gran ~** to be current
actualizar [aktwali'θar] *vt* to update, modernize
actualmente [aktwal'mente] *adv* at present; (*hoy día*) nowadays
actuar [ak'twar] *vi* (*obrar*) to work, operate; (*actor*) to act, perform ▷ *vt* to work, operate; **~ de** to act as
acuarela [akwa'rela] *nf* watercolour
acuario [a'kwarjo] *nm* aquarium; **A~** (*Astro*) Aquarius
acuartelar [akwarte'lar] *vt* (*Mil: alojar*) to quarter
acuático, -a [a'kwatiko, a] *adj* aquatic
acuchillar [akutʃi'ʎar] *vt* (*Tec*) to plane (down), smooth
acuciar [aku'θjar] *vt* to urge on
acuclillarse [akukli'ʎarse] *vr* to crouch down
acudir [aku'ðir] *vi* to attend, turn up; (*ir*) to go; **~ a** to turn to; **~ en ayuda de** to go to the aid of; **~ a una cita** to keep an appointment; **~ a una llamada** to answer a call; **no tener a quién ~** to have nobody to turn to
acuerdo [a'kwerðo] *vb ver* **acordar** ▷ *nm* agreement; (*Pol*) resolution; **~ de pago respectivo** (*Com*) knock-for-knock agreement; **A~ general sobre aranceles aduaneros y comercio** (*Com*) General Agreement on Tariffs and Trade; **tomar un ~** to pass a resolution; **¡de ~!** agreed!; **de ~ con** (*persona*) in agreement with; (*acción, documento*) in accordance with; **de común ~** by common consent; **estar de ~** (*persona*) to agree; **llegar a un ~** to come to an understanding
acumular [akumu'lar] *vt* to accumulate, collect
acuñar [aku'ɲar] *vt* (*moneda*) to mint; (*frase*) to coin
acuoso, -a [a'kwoso, a] *adj* watery
acupuntura [akupun'tura] *nf* acupuncture
acurrucarse [akurru'karse] *vr* to crouch; (*ovillarse*) to curl up
acusación [akusa'θjon] *nf* accusation
acusar [aku'sar] *vt* to accuse; (*revelar*) to reveal; (*denunciar*) to denounce; (*emoción*) to show; **~ recibo** to acknowledge receipt; **su rostro acusó extrañeza** his face registered surprise; **acusarse** *vr*: **~se (de)** to confess (to)
acuse [a'kuse] *nm*: **~ de recibo** acknowledgement of receipt
acústico, -a [a'kustiko, a] *adj* acoustic ▷ *nf* (*de una sala etc*) acoustics *pl*; (*ciencia*) acoustics *sg*
adagio [a'ðaxjo] *nm* adage; (*Mus*) adagio
adaptación [aðapta'θjon] *nf* adaptation
adaptador [aðapta'ðor] *nm* (*Elec*) adapter; **~ universal** universal adapter
adaptar [aðap'tar] *vt* to adapt; (*acomodar*) to fit; (*convertir*): **~ (para)** to convert (to)
adecuado, -a [aðe'kwaðo, a] *adj* (*apto*) suitable; (*oportuno*) appropriate; **el hombre ~ para el puesto** the right man for the job
adecuar [aðe'kwar] *vt* (*adaptar*) to adapt; (*hacer apto*) to make suitable
a. de J.C. *abr* (= *antes de Jesucristo*) B.C.

adelantado, -a [aðelan'taðo, a] *adj* advanced; (*reloj*) fast; **pagar por ~** to pay in advance
adelantamiento [aðelanta'mjento] *nm* advance, advancement; (*Auto*) overtaking
adelantar [aðelan'tar] *vt* to move forward; (*avanzar*) to advance; (*acelerar*) to speed up; (*Auto*) to overtake ▷ *vi* (*ir delante*) to go ahead; (*progresar*) to improve; **adelantarse** *vr* (*tomar la delantera: corredor*) to move forward; **~se a algn** to get ahead of sb; **~se a los deseos de algn** to anticipate sb's wishes
adelante [aðe'lante] *adv* forward(s), onward(s), ahead ▷ *excl* come in!; **de hoy en ~** from now on; **más ~** later on; (*más allá*) further on
adelanto [aðe'lanto] *nm* advance; (*mejora*) improvement; (*progreso*) progress; (*dinero*) advance; **los ~s de la ciencia** the advances of science
adelgazar [aðelɣa'θar] *vt* to thin (down); (*afilar*) to taper ▷ *vi* to get thin; (*con régimen*) to slim down, lose weight
ademán [aðe'man] *nm* gesture; **ademanes** *nmpl* manners; **en ~ de** as if to
además [aðe'mas] *adv* besides; (*por otra parte*) moreover; (*también*) also; **~ de** besides, in addition to
adentrarse [aðen'trarse] *vr*: **~ en** to go into, get inside; (*penetrar*) to penetrate (into)
adentro [a'ðentro] *adv* inside, in; **mar ~** out at sea; **tierra ~** inland ▷ *nm*: **dijo para sus ~s** he said to himself
adepto, -a [a'ðepto, a] *nm/f* supporter
aderezar [aðere'θar] *vt* (*ensalada*) to dress; (*comida*) to season
aderezo [aðe'reθo] *nm* dressing; seasoning
adeudar [aðeu'ðar] *vt* to owe; **adeudarse** *vr* to run into debt; **~ una suma en una cuenta** to debit an account with a sum
adherirse [aðe'rirse] *vr*: **~ a** to adhere to; (*partido*) to join; (*fig*) to follow
adhesión [aðe'sjon] *nf* adhesion; (*fig*) adherence
adicción [aðik'θjon] *nf* addiction
adición [aði'θjon] *nf* addition
adicionar [aðiθjo'nar] *vt* to add
adicto, -a [a'ðikto, a] *adj*: **~ a** (*droga etc*) addicted to; (*dedicado*) devoted to ▷ *nm/f* supporter, follower; (*toxicómano etc*) addict
adiestrar [aðjes'trar] *vt* to train, teach; (*conducir*) to guide, lead; **adiestrarse** *vr* to practise; (*aprender*) to train o.s.
adinerado, -a [aðine'raðo, a] *adj* wealthy
adiós [a'ðjos] *excl* (*para despedirse*) goodbye!, cheerio!; (*al pasar*) hello!
aditivo [aði'tiβo] *nm* additive
adivinanza [aðiβi'nanθa] *nf* riddle
adivinar [aðiβi'nar] *vt* (*profetizar*) to prophesy; (*conjeturar*) to guess
adivino, -a [aði'βino, a] *nm/f* fortune-teller
adj *abr* (= *adjunto*) encl; (= *adjetivo*) adj
adjetivo [aðxe'tiβo] *nm* adjective
adjudicación [aðxuðika'θjon] *nf* award; (*Com*) adjudication
adjudicar [aðxuði'kar] *vt* to award; **adjudicarse** *vr*: **~se algo** to appropriate sth
adjuntar [aðxun'tar] *vt* to attach, enclose
adjunto, -a [að'xunto, a] *adj* attached, enclosed ▷ *nm/f* assistant
administración [aðministra'θjon] *nf* administration; (*dirección*) management; **~ pública** civil service; **A~ de Correos** General Post Office
administrador, a [aðministra'ðor, a] *nm/f* administrator; manager(ess)
administrar [aðminis'trar] *vt* to administer
administrativo, -a [aðministra'tiβo, a] *adj* administrative
admirable [aðmi'raβle] *adj* admirable
admiración [aðmira'θjon] *nf* admiration; (*asombro*) wonder; (*Ling*) exclamation mark
admirar [aðmi'rar] *vt* to admire; (*extrañar*) to surprise; **admirarse** *vr* to be surprised; **se admiró de saberlo** he was amazed to hear it; **no es de ~ que ...** it's not surprising that ...
admisible [aðmi'siβle] *adj* admissible
admisión [aðmi'sjon] *nf* admission; (*reconocimiento*) acceptance
admitir [aðmi'tir] *vt* to admit; (*aceptar*) to accept; (*dudas*) to leave room for; **esto no admite demora** this must be dealt with immediately
admonición [aðmoni'θjon] *nf* warning
ADN *nm abr* (= *ácido desoxirribonucleico*) DNA
adobar [aðo'βar] *vt* (*preparar*) to prepare; (*cocinar*) to season
adobe [a'ðoβe] *nm* adobe, sun-dried brick
adoctrinar [aðoktri'nar] *vt* to indoctrinate
adolecer [aðole'θer] *vi*: **~ de** to suffer from
adolescente [aðoles'θente] *nm/f* adolescent, teenager ▷ *adj* adolescent, teenage
adonde [conj] (to) where
adónde [a'ðonde] *adv* = **dónde**
adopción [aðop'θjon] *nf* adoption
adoptar [aðop'tar] *vt* to adopt
adoptivo, -a [aðop'tiβo, a] *adj* (*padres*) adoptive; (*hijo*) adopted
adoquín [aðo'kin] *nm* paving stone
adorar [aðo'rar] *vt* to adore
adormecer [aðorme'θer] *vt* to put to sleep; **adormecerse** *vr* to become sleepy; (*dormirse*) to fall asleep
adornar [aðor'nar] *vt* to adorn
adorno [a'ðorno] *nm* (*objeto*) ornament; (*decoración*) decoration
adosado, -a [aðo'saðo, a] *adj* (*casa*) semidetached
adosar [aðo'sar] (*Am*) *vt* (*adjuntar*) to attach, enclose (*with a letter*)
adquiera *etc* [að'kjera] *vb ver* **adquirir**
adquirir [aðki'rir] *vt* to acquire, obtain
adquisición [aðkisi'θjon] *nf* acquisition; (*compra*) purchase

adrede [a'ðreðe] *adv* on purpose
adscribir [aðskri'βir] *vt* to appoint; **estuvo adscrito al servicio de ...** he was attached to ...
adscrito [að'skrito] *pp de* **adscribir**
ADSL *nm abbr* ADSL
aduana [a'ðwana] *nf* customs *pl*; (*impuesto*) (customs) duty
aduanero, -a [aðwa'nero, a] *adj* customs *cpd* ▷ *nm/f* customs officer
aducir [aðu'θir] *vt* to adduce; (*dar como prueba*) to offer as proof
adueñarse [aðwe'ɲarse] *vr*: ~ **de** to take possession of
adulación [aðula'θjon] *nf* flattery
adular [aðu'lar] *vt* to flatter
adulterar [aðulte'rar] *vt* to adulterate ▷ *vi* to commit adultery
adulterio [aðul'terjo] *nm* adultery
adúltero, -a [a'ðultero, a] *adj* adulterous ▷ *nm/f* adulterer/adulteress
adulto, -a [a'ðulto, a] *adj, nm/f* adult
adusto, -a [a'ðusto, a] *adj* stern; (*austero*) austere
advenedizo, -a [aðβene'ðiθo, a] *nm/f* upstart
advenimiento [aðβeni'mjento] *nm* arrival; (*al trono*) accession
adverbio [að'βerβjo] *nm* adverb
adversario, -a [aðβer'sarjo, a] *nm/f* adversary
adversidad [aðβersi'ðað] *nf* adversity; (*contratiempo*) setback
adverso, -a [að'βerso, a] *adj* adverse; (*suerte*) bad
advertencia [aðβer'tenθja] *nf* warning; (*prefacio*) preface, foreword
advertir [aðβer'tir] *vt* (*observar*) to notice; (*avisar*): ~ **a algn de** to warn sb about *o* of
Adviento [að'βjento] *nm* Advent
advierta *etc* [að'βjerta], **advirtiendo** *etc* [aðβir'tjendo] *vb ver* **advertir**
adyacente [aðja'θente] *adj* adjacent
aéreo, -a [a'ereo, a] *adj* aerial; (*tráfico*) air *cpd*
aerobic *nm*, **aerobics** (*LAm*) [ae'roβik(s)] *nmpl* aerobics *sg*
aerodeslizador [aeroðesliθa'ðor] *nm* hovercraft
aerodinámico, -a [aeroði'namiko, a] *adj* aerodynamic
aeromodelismo [aeromoðe'lismo] *nm* model aircraft making, aeromodelling
aeromozo, -a [aero'moθo, a] *nm/f* (*Am*) flight attendant, air steward(ess)
aeronáutica [aero'nautika] *nf* aeronautics *sg*
aeronáutico, -a [aero'nautiko, a] *adj* aeronautical
aeronave [aero'naβe] *nm* spaceship
aeroplano [aero'plano] *nm* aeroplane
aeropuerto [aero'pwerto] *nm* airport
aerosol [aero'sol] *nm* aerosol, spray
afabilidad [afaβili'ðað] *nf* affability, pleasantness
afable [a'faβle] *adj* affable, pleasant
afamado, -a [afa'maðo, a] *adj* famous
afán [a'fan] *nm* hard work; (*deseo*) desire; **con** ~ keenly
afanador, a [afana'ðor, a] (*Am*) *nm/f* (*de limpieza*) cleaner
afanar [afa'nar] *vt* to harass; (*fam*) to pinch; **afanarse** *vr*: **~se por** to strive to
afanoso, -a [afa'noso, a] *adj* (*trabajo*) hard; (*trabajador*) industrious
afear [afe'ar] *vt* to disfigure
afección [afek'θjon] *nf* affection; (*Med*) disease
afectación [afekta'θjon] *nf* affectation
afectado, -a [afek'taðo, a] *adj* affected
afectar [afek'tar] *vt* to affect, have an effect on; (*Am: dañar*) to hurt; **por lo que afecta a esto** as far as this is concerned
afectísimo, -a [afek'tisimo, a] *adj* affectionate; **suyo** ~ yours truly
afectivo, -a [afek'tiβo, a] *adj* (*problema etc*) emotional
afecto, -a [a'fekto, a] *adj*: ~ **a** fond of; (*Jur*) subject to ▷ *nm* affection; **tenerle ~ a algn** to be fond of sb
afectuoso, -a [afek'twoso, a] *adj* affectionate
afeitar [afei'tar] *vt* to shave; **afeitarse** *vr* to shave
afeminado, -a [afemi'naðo, a] *adj* effeminate
aferrar [afe'rrar] *vt* to moor; (*fig*) to grasp ▷ *vi* to moor; **aferrarse** *vr* (*agarrarse*) to cling on; **~se a un principio** to stick to a principle; **~se a una esperanza** to cling to a hope
Afganistán [afɣanis'tan] *nm* Afghanistan
afianzamiento [afjanθa'mjento] *nm* strengthening; security
afianzar [afjan'θar] *vt* to strengthen, secure; **afianzarse** *vr* to steady o.s.; (*establecerse*) to become established
afiche [a'fitʃe] *nm* (*Am*) poster
afición [afi'θjon] *nf*: ~ **a** fondness *o* liking for; **la** ~ the fans *pl*; **pinto por** ~ I paint as a hobby
aficionado, -a [afiθjo'naðo, a] *adj* keen, enthusiastic; (*no profesional*) amateur ▷ *nm/f* enthusiast, fan; amateur; **ser ~ a algo** to be very keen on *o* fond of sth
aficionar [afiθjo'nar] *vt*: ~ **a algn a algo** to make sb like sth; **aficionarse** *vr*: **~se a algo** to grow fond of sth
afilado, -a [afi'laðo, a] *adj* sharp
afilar [afi'lar] *vt* to sharpen; **afilarse** *vr* (*cara*) to grow thin
afiliarse [afi'ljarse] *vr* to affiliate
afín [a'fin] *adj* (*parecido*) similar; (*conexo*) related
afinar [afi'nar] *vt* (*Tec*) to refine; (*Mus*) to tune ▷ *vi* (*tocar*) to play in tune; (*cantar*) to sing in tune

afincarse [afin'karse] *vr* to settle
afinidad [afini'ðað] *nf* affinity; (*parentesco*) relationship; **por ~** by marriage
afirmación [afirma'θjon] *nf* affirmation
afirmar [afir'mar] *vt* to affirm, state; (*sostener*) to strengthen; **afirmarse** *vr* (*recuperar el equilibrio*) to steady o.s.; **~se en lo dicho** to stand by what one has said
afirmativo, -a [afirma'tiβo, a] *adj* affirmative
aflicción [aflik'θjon] *nf* affliction; (*dolor*) grief
afligir [afli'xir] *vt* to afflict; (*apenar*) to distress; **afligirse** *vr*: **~se (por** *o* **con** *o* **de)** to grieve (about *o* at); **no te aflijas tanto** you must not let it affect you like this
aflojar [aflo'xar] *vt* to slacken; (*desatar*) to loosen, undo; (*relajar*) to relax ▷ *vi* (*amainar*) to drop; (*bajar*) to go down; **aflojarse** *vr* to relax
aflorar [aflo'rar] *vi* (*Geo, fig*) to come to the surface, emerge
afluente [aflu'ente] *adj* flowing ▷ *nm* (*Geo*) tributary
afluir [aflu'ir] *vi* to flow
afmo., -a. *abr* (= *afectísimo/a suyo/a*) Yours
afónico, -a [a'foniko, a] *adj*: **estar ~** to have a sore throat; to have lost one's voice
aforo [a'foro] *nm* (*Tec*) gauging; (*de teatro etc*) capacity; **el teatro tiene un ~ de 2,000** the theatre can seat 2,000
afortunado, -a [afortu'naðo, a] *adj* fortunate, lucky
afortunadamente [afortunaða'mente] *adv* fortunately, luckily
afrancesado, -a [afranθe'saðo, a] *adj* francophile; (*pey*) Frenchified
afrenta [a'frenta] *nf* affront, insult; (*deshonra*) dishonour (*Brit*), dishonor (*US*), shame
África ['afrika] *nf* Africa; **~ del Sur** South Africa
africano, -a [afri'kano, a] *adj, nm/f* African
afrontar [afron'tar] *vt* to confront; (*poner cara a cara*) to bring face to face
afrutado, -a [afru'taðo, a] *adj* fruity
after ['after] (*pl* **afters** *o* **after**) *nm*, **afterhours** ['afterauars] *nm inv* after-hours club
afuera [a'fwera] *adv* out, outside; **por ~** on the outside; **afueras** *nfpl* outskirts
agachar [aɣa'tʃar] *vt* to bend, bow; **agacharse** *vr* to stoop, bend
agalla [a'ɣaʎa] *nf* (*Zool*) gill; **agallas** *nfpl* (*Med*) tonsillitis *sg*; (*Anat*) tonsils; **tener ~s** (*fam*) to have guts
agarradera [aɣarra'ðera] (*Am*) *nf*, **agarradero** [aɣarra'ðero] *nm* handle; **agarraderas** *nfpl* pull *sg*, influence *sg*
agarrado, -a [aɣa'rraðo, a] *adj* mean, stingy
agarrar [aɣa'rrar] *vt* to grasp, grab; (*Am: tomar*) to take, catch; (*recoger*) to pick up ▷ *vi* (*planta*) to take root; **agarrarse** *vr* to hold on (tightly); (*meterse uno con otro*) to grapple (with each other); **agarrársela con algn** (*Am*) to pick on sb; **agarró y se fue** (*esp Am*: (*fam*)) he upped and went
agarrotar [aɣarro'tar] *vt* (*lío*) to tie tightly; (*persona*) to squeeze tightly; (*reo*) to garrotte; **agarrotarse** *vr* (*motor*) to seize up; (*Med*) to stiffen
agasajar [aɣasa'xar] *vt* to treat well, fête
agencia [a'xenθja] *nf* agency; **~ de créditos/publicidad/viajes** credit/advertising/travel agency; **~ inmobiliaria** estate agent's (office) (*Brit*), real estate office (*US*); **~ matrimonial** marriage bureau
agenciar [axen'θjar] *vt* to bring about; **agenciarse** *vr* to look after o.s.; **~se algo** to get hold of sth
agenda [a'xenda] *nf* diary; **~ electrónica** PDA; **~ telefónica** telephone directory
agente [a'xente] *nm/f* agent; (*tb*: **~ de policía**) policeman/policewoman; **~ de bolsa** stockbroker; **~ de negocios** (*Com*) business agent; **~ de seguros** insurance broker; **~ de tránsito** (*Am*) traffic cop; **~ de viajes** travel agent; **~ inmobiliario** estate agent (*Brit*), realtor (*US*); **~s sociales** social partners
ágil ['axil] *adj* agile, nimble
agilidad [axili'ðað] *nf* agility, nimbleness
agilizar [axili'θar] *vt* (*trámites*) to speed up
agiotista [axjo'tista] (*Am*) *nm/f* (*usurero*) usurer
agitación [axita'θjon] *nf* (*de mano etc*) shaking, waving; (*de líquido etc*) stirring; agitation
agitado, -a [axi'aðo, a] *adj* hectic; (*viaje*) bumpy
agitar [axi'tar] *vt* to wave, shake; (*líquido*) to stir; (*fig*) to stir up, excite; **agitarse** *vr* to get excited; (*inquietarse*) to get worried *o* upset
aglomeración [aɣlomera'θjon] *nf*: **~ de tráfico/gente** traffic jam/mass of people
aglomerar [aɣlome'rar] *vt*, **aglomerarse** *vr* to crowd together
agnóstico, -a [aɣ'nostiko, a] *adj, nm/f* agnostic
agobiar [aɣo'βjar] *vt* to weigh down; (*oprimir*) to oppress; (*cargar*) to burden; **sentirse agobiado por** to be overwhelmed by
agolparse [aɣol'parse] *vr* to crowd together
agonía [aɣo'nia] *nf* death throes *pl*; (*fig*) agony, anguish
agonizante [aɣoni'θante] *adj* dying
agonizar [aɣoni'θar] *vi* to be dying
agosto [a'ɣosto] *nm* August; (*fig*) harvest; **hacer su ~** to make one's pile; *ver tb* **julio**
agotado, -a [aɣo'taðo, a] *adj* (*persona*) exhausted; (*acabado*) finished; (*Com*) sold out; (*: libros*) out of print; (*pila*) flat
agotador, a [aɣota'ðor, a] *adj* exhausting
agotamiento [aɣota'mjento] *nm* exhaustion

agotar [aɣo'tar] *vt* to exhaust; (*consumir*) to drain; (*recursos*) to use up, deplete; **agotarse** *vr* to be exhausted; (*acabarse*) to run out; (*libro*) to go out of print
agraciado, -a [aɣra'θjaðo, a] *adj* (*atractivo*) attractive; (*en sorteo etc*) lucky
agraciar [aɣra'θjar] *vt* (*Jur*) to pardon; (*con premio*) to reward; (*hacer más atractivo*) to make more attractive
agradable [aɣra'ðaβle] *adj* pleasant, nice
agradar [aɣra'ðar] *vt, vi* to please; **él me agrada** I like him; **agradarse** *vr* to like each other
agradecer [aɣraðe'θer] *vt* to thank; (*favor etc*) to be grateful for; **le ~ía me enviara ...** I would be grateful if you would send me ...; **agradecerse** *vr*: **¡se agradece!** much obliged!
agradecido, -a [aɣraðe'θiðo, a] *adj* grateful; **¡muy ~!** thanks a lot!
agradecimiento [aɣraðeθi'mjento] *nm* thanks *pl*; gratitude
agradezca *etc* [aɣra'ðeθka] *vb ver* **agradecer**
agrado [a'ɣraðo] *nm*: **ser de tu** *etc* **~** to be to your *etc* liking
agrandar [aɣran'dar] *vt* to enlarge; (*fig*) to exaggerate; **agrandarse** *vr* to get bigger
agrario, -a [a'ɣrarjo, a] *adj* agrarian, land *cpd*; (*política*) agricultural, farming *cpd*
agravante [aɣra'βante] *adj* aggravating ▷ *nm o f* complication; **con el** *or* **la ~ de que ...** with the further difficulty that ...
agravar [aɣra'βar] *vt* (*pesar sobre*) to make heavier; (*irritar*) to aggravate; **agravarse** *vr* to worsen, get worse
agraviar [aɣra'βjar] *vt* to offend; (*ser injusto con*) to wrong; **agraviarse** *vr* to take offence
agravio [a'ɣraβjo] *nm* offence; wrong; (*Jur*) grievance
agredir [aɣre'ðir] *vt* to attack
agregado [aɣre'ɣaðo] *nm* aggregate; (*persona*) attaché; (*profesor*) assistant professor; **A~** ≈ teacher (*who is not head of department*)
agregar [aɣre'ɣar] *vt* to gather; (*añadir*) to add; (*persona*) to appoint
agresión [aɣre'sjon] *nf* aggression; (*ataque*) attack
agresivo, -a [aɣre'siβo, a] *adj* aggressive
agriar [a'ɣrjar] *vt* (*fig*) to (turn) sour; **agriarse** *vr* to turn sour
agrícola [a'ɣrikola] *adj* farming *cpd*, agricultural
agricultor, a [aɣrikul'tor, a] *nm/f* farmer
agricultura [aɣrikul'tura] *nf* agriculture, farming
agridulce [aɣri'ðulθe] *adj* bittersweet; (*Culin*) sweet and sour
agrietarse [aɣrje'tarse] *vr* to crack; (*la piel*) to chap
agrimensor, a [aɣrimen'sor, a] *nm/f* surveyor
agrio, -a ['aɣrjo, a] *adj* bitter
agronomía [aɣrono'mia] *nf* agronomy, agriculture
agropecuario, -a [aɣrope'kwarjo, a] *adj* farming *cpd*, agricultural
agrupación [aɣrupa'θjon] *nf* group; (*acto*) grouping
agrupar [aɣru'par] *vt* to group; (*Inform*) to block; **agruparse** *vr* (*Pol*) to form a group; (*juntarse*) to gather
agua ['aɣwa] *nf* water; (*Naut*) wake; (*Arq*) slope of a roof; **aguas** *nfpl* (*Med*) water *sg*, urine *sg*; (*Naut*) waters; **~s abajo/arriba** downstream/upstream; **~ bendita/destilada/potable** holy/distilled/drinking water; **~ caliente** hot water; **~ corriente** running water; **~ de colonia** eau de cologne; **~ mineral (con/sin gas)** (fizzy/non-fizzy) mineral water; **~ oxigenada** hydrogen peroxide; **~s jurisdiccionales** territorial waters; **~s mayores** excrement *sg*; **~ pasada no mueve molino** it's no use crying over spilt milk; **estar con el ~ al cuello** to be up to one's neck; **venir como ~ de mayo** to be a godsend
aguacate [aɣwa'kate] *nm* avocado (pear)
aguacero [aɣwa'θero] *nm* (heavy) shower, downpour
aguado, -a [a'ɣwaðo, a] *adj* watery, watered down ▷ *nf* (*Agr*) watering place; (*Naut*) water supply; (*Arte*) watercolour
aguafiestas [aɣwa'fjestas] *nm/f inv* spoilsport
aguafuerte [aɣwa'fwerte] *nf* etching
aguamiel [aɣwa'mjel] (*Am*) *nf* fermented maguey *o* agave juice
aguanieve [aɣwa'njeβe] *nf* sleet
aguantar [aɣwan'tar] *vt* to bear, put up with; (*sostener*) to hold up ▷ *vi* to last; **aguantarse** *vr* to restrain o.s.; **no sé cómo aguanta** I don't know how he can take it
aguante [a'ɣwante] *nm* (*paciencia*) patience; (*resistencia*) endurance; (*Deporte*) stamina
aguar [a'ɣwar] *vt* to water down; (*fig*): **~ la fiesta a algn** to spoil sb's fun
aguardar [aɣwar'ðar] *vt* to wait for
aguardiente [aɣwar'ðjente] *nm* brandy, liquor
aguarrás [aɣwa'rras] *nm* turpentine
aguaviva [aɣwa'biβa] (*RPl*) *nf* jellyfish
agudeza [aɣu'ðeθa] *nf* sharpness; (*ingenio*) wit
agudizar [aɣuði'θar] *vt* to sharpen; (*crisis*) to make worse; **agudizarse** *vr* to worsen, deteriorate
agudo, -a [a'ɣuðo, a] *adj* sharp; (*voz*) high-pitched, piercing; (*dolor, enfermedad*) acute
agüero [a'ɣwero] *nm*: **buen/mal ~** good/bad omen; **ser de buen ~** to augur well; **pájaro de mal ~** bird of ill omen
aguijón [aɣi'xon] *nm* sting; (*fig*) spur
águila ['aɣila] *nf* eagle; (*fig*) genius
aguileño, -a [aɣi'leɲo, a] *adj* (*nariz*) aquiline; (*rostro*) sharp-featured
aguinaldo [aɣi'naldo] *nm* Christmas box

aguja [a'ɣuxa] *nf* needle; (*de reloj*) hand; (*Arq*) spire; (*Tec*) firing-pin; **agujas** *nfpl* (*Zool*) ribs; (*Ferro*) points

agujerear [aɣuxere'ar] *vt* to make holes in; (*penetrar*) to pierce

agujero [aɣu'xero] *nm* hole; (*Com*) deficit

agujetas [aɣu'xetas] *nfpl* stitch *sg*; (*rigidez*) stiffness *sg*

aguzar [aɣu'θar] *vt* to sharpen; (*fig*) to incite; **~ el oído** to prick up one's ears

ahí [a'i] *adv* there; (*allá*) over there; **de ~ que** so that, with the result that; **~ llega** here he comes; **por ~** (*dirección*) that way; **¡hasta ~ hemos llegado!** so it has come to this!; **¡~ va!** (*objeto*) here it comes!; (*individuo*) there he goes!; **~ donde le ve** as sure as he's standing there; **200 o por ~** 200 or so

ahijado, -a [ai'xaðo, a] *nm/f* godson(-daughter)

ahínco [a'inko] *nm* earnestness; **con ~** eagerly

ahogar [ao'ɣar] *vt* (*en agua*) to drown; (*asfixiar*) to suffocate, smother; (*fuego*) to put out; **ahogarse** *vr* (*en agua*) to drown; (*por asfixia*) to suffocate

ahogo [a'oɣo] *nm* (*Med*) breathlessness; (*fig*) distress; (*problema económico*) financial difficulty

ahondar [aon'dar] *vt* to deepen, make deeper; (*fig*) to study thoroughly ▷ *vi*: **~ en** to study thoroughly

ahora [a'ora] *adv* now; (*hace poco*) a moment ago, just now; (*dentro de poco*) in a moment; **~ voy** I'm coming; **~ mismo** right now; **~ bien** now then; **por ~** for the present

ahorcar [aor'kar] *vt* to hang; **ahorcarse** *vr* to hang o.s.

ahorita [ao'rita], **ahoritita** [aori'tita] *adv* (*esp Am*: *fam*: *en este momento*) right now; (*Am*: *hace poco*) just now; (: *dentro de poco*) in a minute

ahorrar [ao'rrar] *vt* (*dinero*) to save; (*esfuerzos*) to save, avoid; **ahorrarse** *vr*: **~se molestias** to save o.s. trouble

ahorro [a'orro] *nm* (*acto*) saving; (*frugalidad*) thrift; **ahorros** *nmpl* (*dinero*) savings

ahuecar [awe'kar] *vt* to hollow (out); (*voz*) to deepen ▷ *vi*: **¡ahueca!** (*fam*) beat it! (*fam*); **ahuecarse** *vr* to give o.s. airs

ahumar [au'mar] *vt* to smoke, cure; (*llenar de humo*) to fill with smoke ▷ *vi* to smoke; **ahumarse** *vr* to fill with smoke

ahuyentar [aujen'tar] *vt* to drive off, frighten off; (*fig*) to dispel

airado, -a [ai'raðo, a] *adj* angry

airar [ai'rar] *vt* to anger; **airarse** *vr* to get angry

aire ['aire] *nm* air; (*viento*) wind; (*corriente*) draught; (*Mus*) tune; **aires** *nmpl*: **darse ~s** to give o.s. airs; **al ~ libre** in the open air; **~ aclimatizado** *o* **acondicionado** air conditioning; **tener ~ de** to look like; **estar de buen/mal ~** to be in a good/bad mood; **estar en el ~** (*Radio*) to be on the air; (*fig*) to be up in the air

airear [aire'ar] *vt* to ventilate; (*fig*: *asunto*) to air; **airearse** *vr* to get some fresh air

airoso, -a [ai'roso, a] *adj* windy; draughty; (*fig*) graceful

aislado, -a [ais'laðo, a] *adj* (*remoto*) isolated; (*incomunicado*) cut off; (*Elec*) insulated

aislar [ais'lar] *vt* to isolate; (*Elec*) to insulate; **aislarse** *vr* to cut o.s. off

ajar [a'xar] *vt* to spoil; (*fig*) to abuse; **ajarse** *vr* to get crumpled; (*fig*: *piel*) to get wrinkled

ajardinado, -a [axarði'naðo, a] *adj* landscaped

ajedrez [axe'ðreθ] *nm* chess

ajeno, -a [a'xeno, a] *adj* (*que pertenece a otro*) somebody else's; **~ a** foreign to; **~ de** free from, devoid of; **por razones ajenas a nuestra voluntad** for reasons beyond our control

ajetreado, -a [axetre'aðo, a] *adj* busy

ajetreo [axe'treo] *nm* bustle

ají [a'xi] *nm* chil(l)i, red pepper; (*salsa*) chil(l)i sauce

ajillo [a'xiʎo] *nm*: **gambas al ~** garlic prawns

ajo ['axo] *nm* garlic; **~ porro** *o* **puerro** leek; **(tieso) como un ~** (*fam*) snobbish; **estar en el ~** to be mixed up in it

ajuar [a'xwar] *nm* household furnishings *pl*; (*de novia*) trousseau; (*de niño*) layette

ajustado, -a [axus'taðo, a] *adj* (*tornillo*) tight; (*cálculo*) right; (*ropa*) tight(-fitting); (*Deporte*: *resultado*) close

ajustar [axus'tar] *vt* (*adaptar*) to adjust; (*encajar*) to fit; (*Tec*) to engage; (*Tip*) to make up; (*apretar*) to tighten; (*concertar*) to agree (on); (*reconciliar*) to reconcile; (*cuenta, deudas*) to settle ▷ *vi* to fit; **ajustarse** *vr*: **~se a** (*precio etc*) to be in keeping with, fit in with; **~ las cuentas a algn** to get even with sb

ajuste [a'xuste] *nm* adjustment; (*Costura*) fitting; (*acuerdo*) compromise; (*de cuenta*) settlement

al [al] = **a+el**; *ver* **a**

ala ['ala] *nf* wing; (*de sombrero*) brim; (*futbolista*) winger; **~ delta** hang-glider; **andar con el ~ caída** to be downcast; **cortar las ~s a algn** to clip sb's wings; **dar ~s a algn** to encourage sb

alabanza [ala'βanθa] *nf* praise

alabar [ala'βar] *vt* to praise

alacena [ala'θena] *nf* cupboard (*Brit*), closet (*US*)

alacrán [ala'kran] *nm* scorpion

alado, -a [a'laðo, a] *adj* winged

alambique *etc* [alam'bike] *vb ver* **alambicar** ▷ *nm* still

alambrada [alam'braða] *nf*, **alambrado** [alam'braðo] *nm* wire fence; (*red*) wire netting

alambre [a'lambre] *nm* wire; **~ de púas** barbed wire

alameda [ala'meða] *nf* (*plantío*) poplar grove; (*lugar de paseo*) avenue, boulevard
álamo ['alamo] *nm* poplar; **~ temblón** aspen
alarde [a'larðe] *nm* show, display; **hacer ~ de** to boast of
alargador [alarɣa'ðor] *nm* extension cable *o* lead
alargar [alar'ɣar] *vt* to lengthen, extend; (*paso*) to hasten; (*brazo*) to stretch out; (*cuerda*) to pay out; (*conversación*) to spin out; **alargarse** *vr* to get longer
alarido [ala'riðo] *nm* shriek
alarma [a'larma] *nf* alarm; **voz de ~** warning note; **dar la ~** to raise the alarm; **~ de incendios** fire alarm
alarmante [alar'mante] *adj* alarming
alarmar [alar'mar] *vt* to alarm; **alarmarse** *vr* to get alarmed
alba ['alβa] *nf* dawn
albacea [alβa'θea] *nm/f* executor/executrix
albahaca [al'βaka] *nf* (*Bot*) basil
Albania [al'βanja] *nf* Albania
albañil [alβa'ɲil] *nm* bricklayer; (*cantero*) mason
albarán [alβa'ran] *nm* (*Com*) delivery note, invoice
albaricoque [alβari'koke] *nm* apricot
albedrío [alβe'ðrio] *nm*: **libre ~** free will
alberca [al'βerka] *nf* reservoir; (*Am*) swimming pool
albergar [alβer'ɣar] *vt* to shelter; (*esperanza*) to cherish; **albergarse** *vr* (*refugiarse*) to shelter; (*alojarse*) to lodge
albergue [al'βerɣe] *vb ver* **albergar** ▷ *nm* shelter, refuge; **~ juvenil** youth hostel
albóndiga [al'βondiɣa] *nf* meatball
albornoz [alβor'noθ] *nm* (*de los árabes*) burnous; (*para el baño*) bathrobe
alborotar [alβoro'tar] *vi* to make a row ▷ *vt* to agitate, stir up; **alborotarse** *vr* to get excited; (*mar*) to get rough
alboroto [alβo'roto] *nm* row, uproar
alborozar [alβoro'θar] *vt* to gladden; **alborozarse** *vr* to rejoice, be overjoyed
alborozo [alβo'roθo] *nm* joy
álbum ['alβum] (*pl* **álbums** *o* **álbumes**) *nm* album; **~ de recortes** scrapbook
albumen [al'βumen] *nm* egg white, albumen
albur [al'βur] (*Am*) *nm* (*juego de palabras*) pun; (*doble sentido*) double entendre
alcachofa [alka'tʃofa] *nf* (globe) artichoke; (*Tip*) golf ball; (*de ducha*) shower head
alcalde, -esa [al'kalde, alkal'desa] *nm/f* mayor(ess)
alcaldía [alkal'dia] *nf* mayoralty; (*lugar*) mayor's office
alcance [al'kanθe] *vb ver* **alcanzar** ▷ *nm* (*Mil, Radio*) range; (*fig*) scope; (*Com*) adverse balance, deficit; **estar al/fuera del ~ de algn** to be within/beyond sb's reach; (*fig*) to be within sb's powers/over sb's head; **de gran ~** (*Mil*) long-range; (*fig*) far-reaching
alcancía [alkan'θia] (*Am*) *nf* (*para ahorrar*) money box; (*para colectas*) collection box
alcantarilla [alkanta'riʎa] *nf* (*de aguas cloacales*) sewer; (*en la calle*) gutter
alcanzar [alkan'θar] *vt* (*algo: con la mano, el pie*) to reach; (*alguien: en el camino etc*) to catch up (with); (*autobús*) to catch; (*suj: bala*) to hit, strike ▷ *vi* (*ser suficiente*) to be enough; **~ algo a algn** to hand sth to sb; **alcánzame la sal, por favor** pass the salt please; **~ a hacer** to manage to do
alcaparra [alka'parra] *nf* (*Bot*) caper
alcatraz [alka'traθ] *nm* gannet
alcayata [alka'jata] *nf* hook
alcázar [al'kaθar] *nm* fortress; (*Naut*) quarter-deck
alcoba [al'koβa] *nf* bedroom
alcohol [al'kol] *nm* alcohol; **no bebe ~** he doesn't drink (alcohol); **~ metílico** methylated spirits *pl* (*Brit*), wood alcohol (*US*)
alcoholemia [alkoo'lemia] *nf* blood alcohol level; **prueba de la ~** breath test
alcohólico, -a [al'koliko, a] *adj, nm/f* alcoholic
alcoholímetro [alko'limetro] *nm* Breathalyser®, drunkometer (*US*)
alcoholismo [alko'lismo] *nm* alcoholism
alcornoque [alkor'noke] *nm* cork tree; (*fam*) idiot
alcurnia [al'kurnja] *nf* lineage
aldaba [al'daβa] *nf* (door) knocker
aldea [al'dea] *nf* village
aldeano, -a [alde'ano, a] *adj* village *cpd* ▷ *nm/f* villager
ale ['ale] *excl* come on!, let's go!
aleación [alea'θjon] *nf* alloy
aleatorio, -a [alea'torjo, a] *adj* random, contingent; **acceso ~** (*Inform*) random access
aleccionar [alekθjo'nar] *vt* to instruct; (*adiestrar*) to train
alegación [aleɣa'θjon] *nf* allegation
alegar [ale'ɣar] *vt* (*dificultad etc*) to plead; (*Jur*) to allege ▷ *vi* (*Am*) to argue; **~ que ...** to give as an excuse that ...
alegato [ale'ɣato] *nm* (*Jur*) allegation; (*escrito*) indictment; (*declaración*) statement; (*Am*) argument
alegoría [aleɣo'ria] *nf* allegory
alegrar [ale'ɣrar] *vt* (*causar alegría*) to cheer (up); (*fuego*) to poke; (*fiesta*) to liven up; **alegrarse** *vr* (*fam*) to get merry *o* tight; **~se de** to be glad about
alegre [a'leɣre] *adj* happy, cheerful; (*fam*) merry, tight; (*chiste*) risqué, blue
alegría [ale'ɣria] *nf* happiness; merriment; **~ vital** joie de vivre
alejamiento [alexa'mjento] *nm* removal; (*distancia*) remoteness
alejar [ale'xar] *vt* to move away, remove; (*fig*) to estrange; **alejarse** *vr* to move away
aleluya [ale'luja] *nm* (*canto*) hallelujah
alemán, -ana [ale'man, ana] *adj, nm/f* German ▷ *nm* (*lengua*) German

Alemania [ale'manja] *nf* Germany
alentador, a [alenta'ðor, a] *adj* encouraging
alentar [alen'tar] *vt* to encourage
alergia [a'lerxja] *nf* allergy
alero [a'lero] *nm* (*de tejado*) eaves *pl*; (*de foca, Deporte*) flipper; (*Auto*) mudguard
alerta [a'lerta] *adj inv, nm* alert
aleta [a'leta] *nf* (*de pez*) fin; (*de ave*) wing; (*de foca, Deporte*) flipper; (*de coche*) mudguard
aletargar [aletar'ɣar] *vt* to make drowsy; (*entumecer*) to make numb; **aletargarse** *vr* to grow drowsy; to become numb
aletear [alete'ar] *vi* to flutter; (*ave*) to flap its wings; (*individuo*) to wave one's arms
alevín [ale'βin] *nm* fry, young fish
alevosía [aleβo'sia] *nf* treachery
alfabeto [alfa'βeto] *nm* alphabet
alfalfa [al'falfa] *nf* alfalfa, lucerne
alfarería [alfare'ria] *nf* pottery; (*tienda*) pottery shop
alfarero, -a [alfa'rero, a] *nm/f* potter
alféizar [al'feiθar] *nm* window-sill
alférez [al'fereθ] *nm* (*Mil*) second lieutenant; (*Naut*) ensign
alfil [al'fil] *nm* (*Ajedrez*) bishop
alfiler [alfi'ler] *nm* pin; (*broche*) clip; (*pinza*) clothes peg (*Brit*) *o* pin (*US*); **~ de gancho** (*Am*) safety pin; **prendido con ~es** shaky
alfiletero [alfile'tero] *nm* needle case
alfombra [al'fombra] *nf* carpet; (*más pequeña*) rug
alfombrar [alfom'brar] *vt* to carpet
alfombrilla [alfom'briʎa] *nf* rug, mat; (*Inform*) mouse mat *o* pad
alforja [al'forxa] *nf* saddlebag
algarabía [alɣara'βia] *nf* (*fam*) gibberish; (*griterío*) hullabaloo
algarroba [alɣa'rroβa] *nf* carob
algarrobo [alɣa'rroβo] *nm* carob tree
algas ['alɣas] *nfpl* seaweed *sg*
algazara [alɣa'θara] *nf* din, uproar
álgebra ['alxeβra] *nf* algebra
álgido, -a ['alxiðo, a] *adj* icy; (*momento etc*) crucial, decisive
algo ['alɣo] *pron* something; (*en frases interrogativas*) anything ▷ *adv* somewhat, rather; **¿~ más?** anything else?; (*en tienda*) is that all?; **por ~ será** there must be some reason for it; **es ~ difícil** it's a bit awkward
algodón [alɣo'ðon] *nm* cotton; (*planta*) cotton plant; **~ de azúcar** candy floss (*Brit*), cotton candy (*US*); **~ hidrófilo** cotton wool (*Brit*), absorbent cotton (*US*)
algodonero, -a [alɣoðo'nero, a] *adj* cotton *cpd* ▷ *nm/f* cotton grower ▷ *nm* cotton plant
alguacil [alɣwa'θil] *nm* bailiff; (*Taur*) mounted official
alguien ['alɣjen] *pron* someone, somebody; (*en frases interrogativas*) anyone, anybody
alguno, -a [al'ɣuno, a] *adj* (*antes de nmsg* **algún**) some; (*después de n*): **no tiene talento ~** he has no talent, he doesn't have any talent ▷ *pron* (*alguien*) someone, somebody; **algún que otro libro** some book or other; **algún día iré** I'll go one *o* some day; **sin interés ~** without the slightest interest; **~ que otro** an occasional one; **~s piensan** some (people) think; **~ de ellos** one of them
alhaja [a'laxa] *nf* jewel; (*tesoro*) precious object, treasure
alhelí [ale'li] *nm* wallflower, stock
aliado, -a [a'ljaðo, a] *adj* allied
alianza [a'ljanθa] *nf* (*Pol etc*) alliance; (*anillo*) wedding ring
aliar [a'ljar] *vt* to ally; **aliarse** *vr* to form an alliance
alias ['aljas] *adv* alias
alicatado [alika'taðo] (*Esp*) *nm* tiling
alicatar [alika'tar] *vt* to tile
alicate [ali'kate] *nm*, **alicates** [ali'kates] *nmpl* pliers *pl*; **~(s) de uñas** nail clippers
aliciente [ali'θjente] *nm* incentive; (*atracción*) attraction
alienación [aljena'θjon] *nf* alienation
aliento [a'ljento] *vb ver* **alentar** ▷ *nm* breath; (*respiración*) breathing; **sin ~** breathless; **de un ~** in one breath; (*fig*) in one go
aligerar [alixe'rar] *vt* to lighten; (*reducir*) to shorten; (*aliviar*) to alleviate; (*mitigar*) to ease; (*paso*) to quicken
alijo [a'lixo] *nm* (*Naut: descarga*) unloading; (*contrabando*) consignment (of smuggled goods)
alimaña [ali'maɲa] *nf* pest
alimentación [alimenta'θjon] *nf* (*comida*) food; (*acción*) feeding; (*tienda*) grocer's (shop); **~ continua** (*en fotocopiadora etc*) stream feed
alimentador [alimenta'ðor] *nm*: **~ de papel** sheet-feeder
alimentar [alimen'tar] *vt* to feed; (*nutrir*) to nourish; **alimentarse** *vr*: **~se (de)** to feed (on)
alimenticio, -a [alimen'tiθjo, a] *adj* food *cpd*; (*nutritivo*) nourishing, nutritious
alimento [ali'mento] *nm* food; (*nutrición*) nourishment; **alimentos** *nmpl* (*Jur*) alimony *sg*
alineación [alinea'θjon] *nf* alignment; (*Deporte*) line-up
alinear [aline'ar] *vt* to align; (*Tip*) to justify; (*Deporte*) to select, pick; **alinearse** *vr* to line up; **~se en** to fall in with
aliñar [ali'ɲar] *vt* (*Culin*) to season; (*ensalada*) to dress
aliño [a'liɲo] *nm* (*Culin*) dressing
alioli [ali'oli] *nm* garlic mayonnaise
alisar [ali'sar] *vt* to smooth
aliso [a'liso] *nm* alder
alistar [ali'star] *vt* to recruit; **alistarse** *vr* to enlist; (*inscribirse*) to enrol; (*Am: prepararse*) to get ready
aliviar [ali'βjar] *vt* (*carga*) to lighten; (*persona*) to relieve; (*dolor*) to relieve, alleviate
alivio [a'liβjo] *nm* alleviation, relief; **~ de luto** half-mourning

aljibe [al'xiβe] *nm* cistern
allá [a'ʎa] *adv* (*lugar*) there; (*por ahí*) over there; (*tiempo*) then; **~ abajo** down there; **más ~** further on; **más ~ de** beyond; **¡~ tú!** that's your problem!
allanamiento [aʎana'mjento] *nm* (*Am Policía*) raid, search; **~ de morada** breaking and entering
allanar [aʎa'nar] *vt* to flatten, level (out); (*igualar*) to smooth (out); (*fig*) to subdue; (*Jur*) to burgle, break into; (*Am Policía*) to raid, search; **allanarse** *vr* to fall down; **~se a** to submit to, accept
allegado, -a [aʎe'ɣaðo, a] *adj* near, close ▷ *nm/f* relation
allí [a'ʎi] *adv* there; **~ mismo** right there; **por ~** over there; (*por ese camino*) that way
alma ['alma] *nf* soul; (*persona*) person; (*Tec*) core; **se le cayó el ~ a los pies** he became very disheartened; **entregar el ~** to pass away; **estar con el ~ en la boca** to be scared to death; **lo siento en el ~** I am truly sorry; **tener el ~ en un hilo** to have one's heart in one's mouth; **estar como ~ en pena** to suffer; **ir como ~ que lleva el diablo** to go at breakneck speed
almacén [alma'θen] *nm* (*depósito*) warehouse, store; (*Mil*) magazine; (*Am*) grocer's shop, food store, grocery store (*US*); **(grandes) almacenes** *nmpl* department store *sg*; **~ depositario** (*Com*) depository
almacenaje [almaθe'naxe] *nm* storage; **~ secundario** backup storage
almacenar [almaθe'nar] *vt* to store, put in storage; (*Inform*) to store; (*proveerse*) to stock up with
almanaque [alma'nake] *nm* almanac
almeja [al'mexa] *nf* clam
almendra [al'mendra] *nf* almond
almendro [al'mendro] *nm* almond tree
almíbar [al'miβar] *nm* syrup
almidón [almi'ðon] *nm* starch
almidonar [almiðo'nar] *vt* to starch
almirantazgo [almiran'taθɣo] *nm* admiralty
almirante [almi'rante] *nm* admiral
almirez [almi'reθ] *nm* mortar
almizcle [al'miθkle] *nm* musk
almohada [almo'aða] *nf* pillow; (*funda*) pillowcase
almohadilla [almoa'ðiʎa] *nf* cushion; (*Tec*) pad; (*Am*) pincushion; (*Inform*) hash key
almohadón [almoa'ðon] *nm* large pillow
almorranas [almo'rranas] *nfpl* piles, haemorrhoids (*Brit*), hemorrhoids (*US*)
almorzar [almor'θar] *vt*: **~ una tortilla** to have an omelette for lunch ▷ *vi* to (have) lunch
almuerzo [al'mwerθo] *vb ver* **almorzar** ▷ *nm* lunch
alocado, -a [alo'kaðo, a] *adj* crazy
alojamiento [aloxa'mjento] *nm* lodging(s) (*pl*); (*viviendas*) housing
alojar [alo'xar] *vt* to lodge; **alojarse** *vr*: **~se en** to stay at; (*bala*) to lodge in
alondra [a'londra] *nf* lark, skylark
alpaca [al'paka] *nf* alpaca
alpargata [alpar'ɣata] *nf* rope-soled shoe, espadrille
Alpes ['alpes] *nmpl*: **los ~** the Alps
alpinismo [alpi'nismo] *nm* mountaineering, climbing
alpinista [alpi'nista] *nm/f* mountaineer, climber
alpino, -a [al'pino, a] *adj* alpine
alpiste [al'piste] *nm* (*semillas*) birdseed; (*Am fam: dinero*) dough; (*fam: alcohol*) booze
alquilar [alki'lar] *vt* (*suj: propietario: inmuebles*) to let, rent (out); (*: coche*) to hire out; (*: TV*) to rent (out); (*suj: alquilador: inmuebles, TV*) to rent; (*: coche*) to hire; **"se alquila casa"** "house to let (*Brit*) *o* for rent (*US*)"
alquiler [alki'ler] *nm* renting; letting; hiring; (*arriendo*) rent; hire charge; **de ~** for hire; **~ de automóviles** car hire
alquimia [al'kimja] *nf* alchemy
alquitrán [alki'tran] *nm* tar
alrededor [alreðe'ðor] *adv* around, about; **alrededores** *nmpl* surroundings; **~ de** *prep* around, about; **mirar a su ~** to look (round) about one
alta ['alta] *nf* (certificate of) discharge; **dar a algn de ~** to discharge sb; **darse de ~** (*Mil*) to join, enrol; (*Deporte*) to declare o.s. fit
altanería [altane'ria] *nf* haughtiness, arrogance
altanero, -a [alta'nero, a] *adj* haughty, arrogant
altar [al'tar] *nm* altar
altavoz [alta'βoθ] *nm* loudspeaker; (*amplificador*) amplifier
alteración [altera'θjon] *nf* alteration; (*alboroto*) disturbance; **~ del orden público** breach of the peace
alterar [alte'rar] *vt* to alter; to disturb; **alterarse** *vr* (*persona*) to get upset
altercado [alter'kaðo] *nm* argument
alternar [alter'nar] *vt* to alternate ▷ *vi* to alternate; (*turnar*) to take turns; **alternarse** *vr* to alternate; (*turnar*) to take turns; **~ con** to mix with
alternativo, -a [alterna'tiβo, a] *adj* alternative; (*alterno*) alternating ▷ *nf* alternative; (*elección*) choice; **alternativas** *nfpl* ups and downs; **tomar la alternativa** (*Taur*) to become a fully-qualified bullfighter
alterno, -a [al'terno, a] *adj* (*Bot, Mat*) alternate; (*Elec*) alternating
Alteza [al'teθa] *nf* (*tratamiento*) Highness
altibajos [alti'βaxos] *nmpl* ups and downs
altiplanicie [altipla'niθje] *nf*, **altiplano** [alti'plano] *nm* high plateau
altisonante [altiso'nante] *adj* high-flown, high-sounding

altitud [alti'tuð] *nf* height; (*Aviat, Geo*) altitude; **a una ~ de** at a height of
altivo, -a [al'tiβo, a] *adj* haughty, arrogant
alto, -a ['alto, a] *adj* high; (*persona*) tall; (*sonido*) high, sharp; (*noble*) high, lofty; (*Geo, clase*) upper ▷ *nm* halt; (*Mus*) alto; (*Geo*) hill; (*Am*) pile ▷ *adv* (*estar*) high; (*hablar*) loud, loudly ▷ *excl* halt!; **la pared tiene dos metros de ~** the wall is two metres high; **en alta mar** on the high seas; **en voz alta** in a loud voice; **las altas horas de la noche** the small (*Brit*) *o* wee (*US*) hours; **en lo ~ de** at the top of; **pasar por ~** to overlook; **~s y bajos** ups and downs; **poner la radio más ~** to turn the radio up; **¡más ~, por favor!** louder, please!
altoparlante [altopar'lante] *nm* (*Am*) loudspeaker
altruismo [al'truismo] *nm* altruism
altura [al'tura] *nf* height; (*Naut*) depth; (*Geo*) latitude; **la pared tiene 1.80 de ~** the wall is 1 metre 80 (cm) high; **a estas ~s** at this stage; **a esta ~ del año** at this time of the year; **estar a la ~ de las circunstancias** to rise to the occasion; **ha sido un partido de gran ~** it has been a terrific match
alubia [a'luβja] *nf* bean; (*judía verde*) French bean; (*judía blanca*) kidney bean
alucinación [aluθina'θjon] *nf* hallucination
alucinante [aluθi'nante] *adj* (*fam: estupendo*) great, super
alucinar [aluθi'nar] *vi* to hallucinate ▷ *vt* to deceive; (*fascinar*) to fascinate
alud [a'luð] *nm* avalanche; (*fig*) flood
aludir [alu'ðir] *vi*: **~ a** to allude to; **darse por aludido** to take the hint; **no te des por aludido** don't take it personally
alumbrado [alum'braðo] *nm* lighting
alumbramiento [alumbra'mjento] *nm* lighting; (*Med*) childbirth, delivery
alumbrar [alum'brar] *vt* to light (up) ▷ *vi* (*iluminar*) to give light; (*Med*) to give birth
aluminio [alu'minjo] *nm* aluminium (*Brit*), aluminum (*US*)
alumno, -a [a'lumno, a] *nm/f* pupil, student
alusión [alu'sjon] *nf* allusion
alusivo, -a [alu'siβo, a] *adj* allusive
aluvión [alu'βjon] *nm* (*Geo*) alluvium; (*fig*) flood; **~ de improperios** torrent of abuse
alverja [al'βerxa] (*Am*) *nf* pea
alza ['alθa] *nf* rise; (*Mil*) sight; **~s fijas/graduables** fixed/adjustable sights; **al** *o* **en ~** (*precio*) rising; **jugar al ~** to speculate on a rising *o* bull market; **cotizarse** *o* **estar en ~** to be rising
alzamiento [alθa'mjento] *nm* (*aumento*) rise, increase; (*acción*) lifting, raising; (*mejor postura*) higher bid; (*rebelión*) rising; (*Com*) fraudulent bankruptcy
alzar [al'θar] *vt* to lift (up); (*precio, muro*) to raise; (*cuello de abrigo*) to turn up; (*Agr*) to gather in; (*Tip*) to gather; **alzarse** *vr* to get up, rise; (*rebelarse*) to revolt; (*Com*) to go fraudulently bankrupt; (*Jur*) to appeal; **~se con el premio** to carry off the prize
ama ['ama] *nf* lady of the house; (*dueña*) owner; (*institutriz*) governess; (*madre adoptiva*) foster mother; **~ de casa** housewife; **~ de cría** *o* **de leche** wet-nurse; **~ de llaves** housekeeper
amabilidad [amaβili'ðað] *nf* kindness; (*simpatía*) niceness
amable [a'maβle] *adj* kind; nice; **es usted muy ~** that's very kind of you
amaestrado, -a [amaes'traðo, a] *adj* (*animal*) trained; (*: en circo etc*) performing
amaestrar [amaes'trar] *vt* to train
amagar [ama'ɣar] *vt, vi* to threaten
amago [a'maɣo] *nm* threat; (*gesto*) threatening gesture; (*Med*) symptom
amainar [amai'nar] *vt* (*Naut*) to lower, take in; (*fig*) to calm ▷ *vi* (*viento*) to die down; **amainarse** *vr* to drop, die down; **el viento amaina** the wind is dropping
amalgama [amal'ɣama] *nf* amalgam
amalgamar [amalɣa'mar] *vt* to amalgamate; (*combinar*) to combine, mix
amamantar [amaman'tar] *vt* to suckle, nurse
amanecer [amane'θer] *vi* to dawn; (*fig*) to appear, begin to show ▷ *nm* dawn; **~ afiebrado** to wake up with a fever
amanerado, -a [amane'raðo, a] *adj* affected
amansar [aman'sar] *vt* to tame; (*persona*) to subdue; **amansarse** *vr* (*persona*) to calm down
amante [a'mante] *adj*: **~ de** fond of ▷ *nm/f* lover
amapola [ama'pola] *nf* poppy
amar [a'mar] *vt* to love
amargado, -a [amar'ɣaðo, a] *adj* bitter; embittered
amargar [amar'ɣar] *vt* to make bitter; (*fig*) to embitter; **amargarse** *vr* to become embittered
amargo, -a [a'marɣo, a] *adj* bitter
amargura [amar'ɣura] *nf* = **amargor**
amarillento, -a [amari'ʎento, a] *adj* yellowish; (*tez*) sallow
amarillo, -a [ama'riʎo, a] *adj, nm* yellow
amarra [a'marra] *nf* (*Naut*) mooring line; **amarras** *nfpl* (*fig*) protection *sg*; **tener buenas ~s** to have good connections; **soltar ~s** (*Naut*) to set sail
amarrado, -a [ama'rraðo, a] (*Am*) *adj* (*fam*) mean, stingy
amarrar [ama'rrar] *vt* to moor; (*sujetar*) to tie up
amartillar [amarti'ʎar] *vt* (*fusil*) to cock
amasar [ama'sar] *vt* (*masa*) to knead; (*mezclar*) to mix, prepare; (*confeccionar*) to concoct
amasijo [ama'sixo] *nm* kneading; mixing; (*fig*) hotchpotch

amateur ['amatur] *nm/f* amateur
amatista [ama'tista] *nf* amethyst
amazona [ama'θona] *nf* horsewoman
Amazonas [ama'θonas] *nm*: **el (Río) ~** the Amazon
ambages [am'baxes] *nmpl*: **sin ~** in plain language
ámbar ['ambar] *nm* amber
ambición [ambi'θjon] *nf* ambition
ambicionar [ambiθjo'nar] *vt* to aspire to
ambicioso, -a [ambi'θjoso, a] *adj* ambitious
ambidextro, -a [ambi'ðekstro, a] *adj* ambidextrous
ambientación [ambjenta'θjon] *nf* (*Cine, Lit etc*) setting; (*Radio etc*) sound effects *pl*
ambientador [ambjenta'ðor] *nm* air freshener
ambiente [am'bjente] *nm* (*tb fig*) atmosphere; (*medio*) environment; (*Am*) room
ambigüedad [ambiɣwe'ðað] *nf* ambiguity
ambiguo, -a [am'biɣwo, a] *adj* ambiguous
ámbito ['ambito] *nm* (*campo*) field; (*fig*) scope
ambos, -as ['ambos, as] *adj pl, pron pl* both
ambulancia [ambu'lanθja] *nf* ambulance
ambulante [ambu'lante] *adj* travelling, itinerant; (*biblioteca*) mobile
ambulatorio [ambula'torio] *nm* state health-service clinic
ameba [a'meβa] *nf* amoeba
amedrentar [ameðren'tar] *vt* to scare
amén [a'men] *excl* amen; **~ de** *prep* besides, in addition to; **en un decir ~** in the twinkling of an eye; **decir ~ a todo** to have no mind of one's own
amenaza [ame'naθa] *nf* threat
amenazar [amena'θar] *vt* to threaten ▷ *vi*: **~ con hacer** to threaten to do
amenidad [ameni'ðað] *nf* pleasantness
ameno, -a [a'meno, a] *adj* pleasant
América [a'merika] *nf* (*continente*) America, the Americas; (EEUU) America; (*Hispanoamérica*) Latin *o* South America; **~ del Norte/del Sur** North/South America; **~ Central/Latina** Central/Latin America
americano, -a [ameri'kano, a] *adj, nm/f* American; Latin *o* South American ▷ *nf* (*abrigo*) coat; (*chaqueta*) jacket
amerindio, -a [ame'rindjo, a] *adj, nm/f* Amerindian, American Indian
amerizar [ameri'θar] *vi* (*Aviat*) to land (on the sea)
ametralladora [ametraʎa'ðora] *nf* machine gun
amianto [a'mjanto] *nm* asbestos
amigable [ami'ɣaβle] *adj* friendly
amígdala [a'miɣðala] *nf* tonsil
amigdalitis [amiɣða'litis] *nf* tonsillitis
amigo, -a [a'miɣo, a] *adj* friendly ▷ *nm/f* friend; (*amante*) lover; **~ de lo ajeno** thief; **~ corresponsal** penfriend; **hacerse ~s** to become friends; **ser ~ de** to like, be fond of; **ser muy ~s** to be close friends
amilanar [amila'nar] *vt* to scare; **amilanarse** *vr* to get scared
aminorar [amino'rar] *vt* to diminish; (*reducir*) to reduce; **~ la marcha** to slow down
amistad [amis'tað] *nf* friendship; **amistades** *nfpl* (*amigos*) friends
amistoso, -a [ami'stoso, a] *adj* friendly
amnesia [am'nesja] *nf* amnesia
amnistía [amnis'tia] *nf* amnesty
amo ['amo] *nm* owner; (*jefe*) boss
amodorrarse [amoðo'rrarse] *vr* to get sleepy
amolar [amo'lar] *vt* to annoy; (*Mex: fam*) to ruin, damage
amoldar [amol'dar] *vt* to mould; (*adaptar*) to adapt
amonestación [amonesta'θjon] *nf* warning; **amonestaciones** *nfpl* marriage banns
amonestar [amone'star] *vt* to warn; (*Rel*) to publish the banns of
amoniaco [amo'njako] *nm* ammonia
amontonar [amonto'nar] *vt* to collect, pile up; **amontonarse** *vr* (*gente*) to crowd together; (*acumularse*) to pile up; (*datos*) to accumulate; (*desastres*) to come one on top of another
amor [a'mor] *nm* love; (*amante*) lover; **hacer el ~** to make love; **~ interesado** cupboard love; **~ propio** self-respect; **por (el) ~ de Dios** for God's sake; **estar al ~ de la lumbre** to be close to the fire
amoratado, -a [amora'taðo, a] *adj* purple, blue with cold; (*con cardenales*) bruised
amordazar [amorða'θar] *vt* to muzzle; (*fig*) to gag
amorfo, -a [a'morfo, a] *adj* amorphous, shapeless
amorío [amo'rio] *nm* (*fam*) love affair
amoroso, -a [amo'roso, a] *adj* affectionate, loving
amortajar [amorta'xar] *vt* (*fig*) to shroud
amortiguador [amortiɣwa'ðor] *nm* shock absorber; (*parachoques*) bumper; (*silenciador*) silencer; **amortiguadores** *nmpl* (*Auto*) suspension *sg*
amortiguar [amorti'ɣwar] *vt* to deaden; (*ruido*) to muffle; (*color*) to soften
amortización [amortiθa'θjon] *nf* redemption; repayment; (*Com*) capital allowance
amotinar [amoti'nar] *vt* to stir up, incite (to riot); **amotinarse** *vr* to mutiny
amparar [ampa'rar] *vt* to protect; **ampararse** *vr* to seek protection; (*de la lluvia etc*) to shelter
amparo [am'paro] *nm* help, protection; **al ~ de** under the protection of
amperio [am'perjo] *nm* ampère, amp
ampliación [amplja'θjon] *nf* enlargement; (*extensión*) extension
ampliar [am'pljar] *vt* to enlarge; to extend
amplificación [amplifika'θjon] *nf* enlargement
amplificador [amplifika'ðor] *nm* amplifier

amplificar [amplifi'kar] *vt* to amplify
amplio, -a ['ampljo, a] *adj* spacious; (*falda etc*) full; (*extenso*) extensive; (*ancho*) wide
amplitud [ampli'tuð] *nf* spaciousness; extent; (*fig*) amplitude; **~ de miras** broadmindedness; **de gran ~** far-reaching
ampolla [am'poʎa] *nf* blister; (*Med*) ampoule
ampuloso, -a [ampu'loso, a] *adj* bombastic, pompous
amputar [ampu'tar] *vt* to cut off, amputate
amueblar [amwe'βlar] *vt* to furnish
amuleto [amu'leto] *nm* (lucky) charm
amurallar [amura'ʎar] *vt* to wall up *o* in
anacronismo [anakro'nismo] *nm* anachronism
ánade ['anaðe] *nm* duck
anagrama [ana'ɣrama] *nm* anagram
anales [a'nales] *nmpl* annals
analfabetismo [analfaβe'tismo] *nm* illiteracy
analfabeto, -a [analfa'βeto, a] *adj, nm/f* illiterate
analgésico [anal'xesiko] *nm* painkiller, analgesic
análisis [a'nalisis] *nm inv* analysis; **~ de costos-beneficios** cost-benefit analysis; **~ de mercados** market research; **~ de sangre** blood test
analista [ana'lista] *nm/f* (*gen*) analyst; (*Pol, Hist*) chronicler; **~ de sistemas** (*Inform*) systems analyst
analizar [anali'θar] *vt* to analyse
analogía [analo'xia] *nf* analogy; **por ~ con** on the analogy of
analógico, -a [ana'loxiko, a] *adj* (*Inform*) analog; (*reloj*) analogue (*Brit*), analog (*US*)
análogo, -a [a'naloɣo, a] *adj* analogous, similar
ananá [ana'na], **ananás** [ana'nas] *nm* pineapple
anaquel [ana'kel] *nm* shelf
anarquía [anar'kia] *nf* anarchy
anarquismo [anar'kismo] *nm* anarchism
anarquista [anar'kista] *nm/f* anarchist
anatomía [anato'mia] *nf* anatomy
anca ['anka] *nf* rump, haunch; **ancas** *nfpl* (*fam*) behind *sg*; **llevar a algn en ~s** to carry sb behind one
ancestral [anθes'tral] *adj* (*costumbre*) age-old
ancho, -a ['antʃo, a] *adj* wide; (*falda*) full; (*fig*) liberal ▷ *nm* width; (*Ferro*) gauge; **le viene muy ~ el cargo** (*fig*) the job is too much for him; **ponerse ~** to get conceited; **quedarse tan ~** to go on as if nothing had happened; **estar a sus anchas** to be at one's ease
anchoa [an'tʃoa] *nf* anchovy
anchura [an'tʃura] *nf* width; (*amplitud*) wideness
anciano, -a [an'θjano, a] *adj* old, aged ▷ *nm/f* old man/woman ▷ *nm* elder
ancla ['ankla] *nf* anchor; **levar ~s** to weigh anchor
ancladero [ankla'ðero] *nm* anchorage
anclar [an'klar] *vi* to (drop) anchor
andadura [anda'ðura] *nf* gait; (*de caballo*) pace
Andalucía [andalu'θia] *nf* Andalusia
andaluz, a [anda'luθ, a] *adj, nm/f* Andalusian
andamiaje [anda'mjaxe], **andamio** [an'damjo] *nm* scaffold(ing)
andar [an'dar] *vt* to go, cover, travel ▷ *vi* to go, walk, travel; (*funcionar*) to go, work; (*estar*) to be ▷ *nm* walk, gait, pace; **andarse** *vr* (*irse*) to go away *o* off; **~ a pie/a caballo/en bicicleta** to go on foot/on horseback/by bicycle; **¡anda!** (*sorpresa*) go on!; **anda en** *o* **por los 40** he's about 40; **¿en qué andas?** what are you up to?; **andamos mal de dinero/tiempo** we're badly off for money/we're short of time; **~se por las ramas** to beat about the bush; **no ~se con rodeos** to call a spade a spade (*fam*); **todo se ~á** all in good time; **anda por aquí** it's round here somewhere; **~ haciendo algo** to be doing sth
andariego, -a [anda'rjeɣo, a] *adj* fond of travelling
andén [an'den] *nm* (*Ferro*) platform; (*Naut*) quayside; (*Am: acera*) pavement (*Brit*), sidewalk (*US*)
Andes ['andes] *nmpl*: **los ~** the Andes
andinismo [andin'ismo] *nm* (*Am*) mountaineering, climbing
Andorra [an'dorra] *nf* Andorra
andrajo [an'draxo] *nm* rag
andrajoso, -a [andra'xoso, a] *adj* ragged
andurriales [andu'rrjales] *nmpl* out-of-the-way place *sg*, the sticks; **en esos ~** in that godforsaken spot
anduve [an'duβe], **anduviera** *etc* [andu'βjera] *vb ver* **andar**
anécdota [a'nekðota] *nf* anecdote, story
anegar [ane'ɣar] *vt* to flood; (*ahogar*) to drown; **anegarse** *vr* to drown; (*hundirse*) to sink
anejo, -a [a'nexo, a] *adj* attached ▷ *nm* (*Arq*) annexe
anemia [a'nemja] *nf* anaemia
anestesia [anes'tesja] *nf* anaesthetic; **~ general/local** general/local anaesthetic
anestesiar [aneste'sjar] *vt* to anaesthetize (*Brit*), anesthetize (*US*)
anexar [anek'sar] *vt* to annex; (*documento*) to attach; (*Inform*) to append
anexión [anek'sjon] *nf*, **anexionamiento** [aneksjona'mjento] *nm* annexation
anexionar [aneksjo'nar] *vt* to annex; **anexionarse** *vr*: **~se un país** to annex a country
anexo, -a [a'nekso, a] *adj* attached ▷ *nm* annexe
anfetamina [anfeta'mina] *nf* amphetamine
anfibio, -a [an'fiβjo, a] *adj* amphibious ▷ *nm* amphibian
anfiteatro [anfite'atro] *nm* amphitheatre; (*Teat*) dress circle

anfitrión, -ona [anfi'trjon, ona] *nm/f* host(ess)
ánfora ['anfora] *nf* (*cántaro*) amphora; (*Am Pol*) ballot box
ángel ['anxel] *nm* angel; **~ de la guarda** guardian angel; **tener ~** to have charm
angélico, -a [an'xeliko, a], **angelical** [anxeli'kal] *adj* angelic(al)
angina [an'xina] *nf* (*Med*) inflammation of the throat; **~ de pecho** angina; **tener ~s** to have tonsillitis, have a sore throat
anglicano, -a [angli'kano, a] *adj, nm/f* Anglican
anglicismo [angli'θismo] *nm* anglicism
anglosajón, -ona [anglosa'xon, 'xona] *adj, nm/f* Anglo-Saxon
angosto, -a [an'gosto, a] *adj* narrow
anguila [an'gila] *nf* eel; **anguilas** *nfpl* slipway *sg*
angula [an'gula] *nf* elver, baby eel
ángulo ['angulo] *nm* angle; (*esquina*) corner; (*curva*) bend
angustia [an'gustja] *nf* anguish
angustiar [angus'tjar] *vt* to distress, grieve; **angustiarse** *vr*: **~se (por)** to be distressed (at, on account of)
anhelante [ane'lante] *adj* eager; (*deseoso*) longing
anhelar [ane'lar] *vt* to be eager for; (*desear*) to long for, desire ▷ *vi* to pant, gasp
anhelo [a'nelo] *nm* eagerness; desire
anhídrido [a'niðriðo] *nm*: **~ carbónico** carbon dioxide
anidar [ani'ðar] *vt* (*acoger*) to take in, shelter ▷ *vi* to nest; (*fig*) to make one's home
anilla [a'niʎa] *nf* ring; **(las) ~s** (*Deporte*) the rings
anillo [a'niʎo] *nm* ring; **~ de boda** wedding ring; **~ de compromiso** engagement ring; **venir como ~ al dedo** to suit to a tee
ánima ['anima] *nf* soul; **las ~s** the Angelus (bell) *sg*
animación [anima'θjon] *nf* liveliness; (*vitalidad*) life; (*actividad*) bustle
animado, -a [ani'maðo, a] *adj* (*vivo*) lively; (*vivaz*) animated; (*concurrido*) bustling; (*alegre*) in high spirits; **dibujos ~s** cartoon *sg*
animador, a [anima'ðor, a] *nm/f* (*TV*) host(ess), compère ▷ *nf* (*Deporte*) cheerleader
animadversión [animaðβer'sjon] *nf* ill-will, antagonism
animal [ani'mal] *adj* animal; (*fig*) stupid ▷ *nm* animal; (*fig*) fool; (*bestia*) brute
animar [ani'mar] *vt* (*Bio*) to animate, give life to; (*fig*) to liven up, brighten up, cheer up; (*estimular*) to stimulate; **animarse** *vr* to cheer up, feel encouraged; (*decidirse*) to make up one's mind
ánimo ['animo] *nm* (*alma*) soul; (*mente*) mind; (*valentía*) courage ▷ *excl* cheer up!; **cobrar ~** to take heart; **dar ~(s) a** to encourage
animoso, -a [ani'moso, a] *adj* brave; (*vivo*) lively
aniquilar [aniki'lar] *vt* to annihilate, destroy
anís [a'nis] *nm* (*grano*) aniseed; (*licor*) anisette
aniversario [aniβer'sarjo] *nm* anniversary
anoche [a'notʃe] *adv* last night; **antes de ~** the night before last
anochecer [anotʃe'θer] *vi* to get dark ▷ *nm* nightfall, dark; **al ~** at nightfall
anodino, -a [ano'ðino, a] *adj* dull, anodyne
anomalía [anoma'lia] *nf* anomaly
anonadado, -a [anona'ðaðo, a] *adj*: **estar ~** to be stunned
anonimato [anoni'mato] *nm* anonymity
anónimo, -a [a'nonimo, a] *adj* anonymous; (*Com*) limited ▷ *nm* (*carta*) anonymous letter; (*: maliciosa*) poison-pen letter
anorak [ano'rak] (*pl* **anoraks**) *nm* anorak
anorexia [ano'reksja] *nf* anorexia
anormal [anor'mal] *adj* abnormal
anotación [anota'θjon] *nf* note; annotation
anotar [ano'tar] *vt* to note down; (*comentar*) to annotate
anquilosamiento [ankilosa'mjento] *nm* (*fig*) paralysis, stagnation
ansia ['ansja] *nf* anxiety; (*añoranza*) yearning
ansiar [an'sjar] *vt* to long for
ansiedad [ansje'ðað] *nf* anxiety
ansioso, -a [an'sjoso, a] *adj* anxious; (*anhelante*) eager; **~ de** *o* **por algo** greedy for sth
antagónico, -a [anta'ɣoniko, a] *adj* antagonistic; (*opuesto*) contrasting
antagonista [antaɣo'nista] *nm/f* antagonist
antaño [an'taɲo] *adv* in years gone by, long ago
Antártico [an'tartiko] *nm*: **el (océano) ~** the Antarctic (Ocean)
ante ['ante] *prep* before, in the presence of; (*encarado con*) faced with ▷ *nm* (*piel*) suede; **~ todo** above all
anteanoche [antea'notʃe] *adv* the night before last
anteayer [antea'jer] *adv* the day before yesterday
antebrazo [ante'βraθo] *nm* forearm
antecedente [anteθe'ðente] *adj* previous ▷ *nm* antecedent; **~s** *nmpl* (*profesionales*) background *sg*; **~s penales** criminal record; **no tener ~s** to have a clean record; **estar en ~s** to be well-informed; **poner a algn en ~s** to put sb in the picture
anteceder [anteθe'ðer] *vt* to precede, go before
antecesor, a [anteθe'sor, a] *nm/f* predecessor
antedicho, -a [ante'ðitʃo, a] *adj* aforementioned
antelación [antela'θjon] *nf*: **con ~** in advance
antemano [ante'mano]: **de ~** *adv* beforehand, in advance
antena [an'tena] *nf* antenna; (*de televisión etc*) aerial; **~ parabólica** satellite dish
antenoche [ante'notʃe] (*Am*) *adv* the night before last

anteojo [ante'oxo] *nm* eyeglass; **anteojos** *nmpl* (*esp Am*) glasses, spectacles
antepasados [antepa'saðos] *nmpl* ancestors
anteponer [antepo'ner] *vt* to place in front; (*fig*) to prefer
anteproyecto [antepro'jekto] *nm* preliminary sketch; (*fig*) blueprint; (*Pol*): **~ de ley** draft bill
anterior [ante'rjor] *adj* preceding, previous
anterioridad [anterjori'ðað] *nf*: **con ~ a** prior to, before
antes ['antes] *adv* sooner; (*primero*) first; (*con anterioridad*) before; (*hace tiempo*) previously, once; (*más bien*) rather ▷ *prep*: **~ de** before ▷ *conj*: **~ (de) que** before; **~ bien** (but) rather; **dos días ~** two days before *o* previously; **mucho/poco ~** long/shortly before; **~ muerto que esclavo** better dead than enslaved; **no quiso venir ~** she didn't want to come any earlier; **tomo el avión ~ que el barco** I take the plane rather than the boat; **~ de** *o* **que nada** (*en el tiempo*) first of all; (*indicando preferencia*) above all; **~ que yo** before me; **cuanto ~, lo ~ posible** as soon as possible; **cuanto ~ mejor** the sooner the better
antesala [ante'sala] *nf* anteroom
antiaéreo, -a [antia'ereo, a] *adj* anti-aircraft
antibalas [anti'βalas] *adj inv*: **chaleco ~** bulletproof jacket
antibiótico [anti'βjotiko] *nm* antibiotic
anticaspa [anti'kaspa] *adj inv* anti-dandruff *cpd*
anticiclón [antiθi'klon] *nm* (*Meteorología*) anti-cyclone
anticipación [antiθipa'θjon] *nf* anticipation; **con 10 minutos de ~** 10 minutes early
anticipado, -a [antiθi'paðo, a] *adj* (in) advance; **por ~** in advance
anticipar [antiθi'par] *vt* to anticipate; (*adelantar*) to bring forward; (*Com*) to advance; **anticiparse** *vr*: **~se a su época** to be ahead of one's time
anticipo [anti'θipo] *nm* (*Com*) advance; *ver tb* **anticipación**
anticonceptivo, -a [antikonθep'tiβo, a] *adj, nm* contraceptive; **métodos ~s** methods of birth control
anticongelante [antikonxe'lante] *nm* antifreeze
anticuado, -a [anti'kwaðo, a] *adj* out-of-date, old-fashioned; (*desusado*) obsolete
anticuario [anti'kwarjo] *nm* antique dealer
anticuerpo [anti'kwerpo] *nm* (*Med*) antibody
antidepresivo [antiðepre'siβo] *nm* antidepressant
antidoping [anti'ðopin] *adj inv* anti-drug; **control ~** drugs test
antídoto [an'tiðoto] *nm* antidote
antiestético, -a [anties'tetiko, a] *adj* unsightly
antifaz [anti'faθ] *nm* mask; (*velo*) veil
antiglobalización [antiglobaliθa'θjon] *nf* anti-globalization; **manifestantes ~** anti-globalization protesters
antiglobalizador, a [antiglobaliθa'ðor, a] *adj* anti-globalization *cpd*
antigualla [anti'ɣwaʎa] *nf* antique; (*reliquia*) relic; **antiguallas** *nfpl* old things
antiguamente [antiɣwa'mente] *adv* formerly; (*hace mucho tiempo*) long ago
antigüedad [antiɣwe'ðað] *nf* antiquity; (*artículo*) antique; (*rango*) seniority
antiguo, -a [an'tiɣwo, a] *adj* old, ancient; (*que fue*) former; **a la antigua** in the old-fashioned way
antillano, -a [anti'ʎano, a] *adj, nm/f* West Indian
Antillas [an'tiʎas] *nfpl*: **las ~** the West Indies, the Antilles; **el mar de las ~** the Caribbean Sea
antílope [an'tilope] *nm* antelope
antinatural [antinatu'ral] *adj* unnatural
antipatía [antipa'tia] *nf* antipathy, dislike
antipático, -a [anti'patiko, a] *adj* disagreeable, unpleasant
antirrobo [anti'rroβo] *nm* (*tb*: **dispositivo ~**: *para casas etc*) burglar alarm; (*: para coches*) car alarm ▷ *adj inv* (*alarma etc*) anti-theft
antisemita [antise'mita] *adj* anti-Semitic ▷ *nm/f* anti-Semite
antiséptico, -a [anti'septiko, a] *adj* antiseptic ▷ *nm* antiseptic
antiterrorismo [antiterro'rismo] *nm* counterterrorism
antiterrorista [antiterro'rista] *adj* antiterrorist, counterterrorist; **la lucha ~** the fight against terrorism
antítesis [an'titesis] *nf inv* antithesis
antivirus [anti'birus] *nm inv* (*Comput*) antivirus program
antojadizo, -a [antoxa'ðiθo, a] *adj* capricious
antojarse [anto'xarse] *vr* (*desear*): **se me antoja comprarlo** I have a mind to buy it; (*pensar*): **se me antoja que ...** I have a feeling that ...
antojo [an'toxo] *nm* caprice, whim; (*rosa*) birthmark; (*lunar*) mole; **hacer a su ~** to do as one pleases
antología [antolo'xia] *nf* anthology
antonomasia [antono'masja] *nf*: **por ~** par excellence
antorcha [an'tortʃa] *nf* torch
antro ['antro] *nm* cavern; **~ de corrupción** (*fig*) den of iniquity
antropófago, -a [antro'pofaɣo, a] *adj, nm/f* cannibal
antropología [antropolo'xia] *nf* anthropology
antropólogo, -a [antro'poloɣo, a] *nm/f* anthropologist
anual [a'nwal] *adj* annual

anualidad [anwali'ðað] *nf* annuity, annual payment; **~ vitalicia** life annuity
anuario [a'nwarjo] *nm* yearbook
anublado, -a [anu'βlaðo, a] *adj* overcast
anudar [anu'ðar] *vt* to knot, tie; (*unir*) to join; **anudarse** *vr* to get tied up; **se me anudó la voz** I got a lump in my throat
anulación [anula'θjon] *nf* (*de un matrimonio*) annulment; (*cancelación*) cancellation; (*de una ley*) repeal
anular [anu'lar] *vt* (*contrato*) to annul, cancel; (*suscripción*) to cancel; (*ley*) to repeal ▷ *nm* ring finger
anunciación [anunθja'θjon] *nf* announcement; **A~** (*Rel*) Annunciation
anunciante [anun'θjante] *nm/f* (*Com*) advertiser
anunciar [anun'θjar] *vt* to announce; (*proclamar*) to proclaim; (*Com*) to advertise
anuncio [a'nunθjo] *nm* announcement; (*señal*) sign; (*Com*) advertisement; (*cartel*) poster; (*Teat*) bill; **~s por palabras** classified ads
anzuelo [an'θwelo] *nm* hook; (*para pescar*) fish hook; **tragar el ~** to swallow the bait
añadido [aɲa'ðiðo] *nm* addition
añadidura [aɲaði'ðura] *nf* addition, extra; **por ~** besides, in addition
añadir [aɲa'ðir] *vt* to add
añejo, -a [a'ɲexo, a] *adj* old; (*vino*) mature; (*jamón*) well-cured
añicos [a'ɲikos] *nmpl*: **hacer ~** to smash, shatter; **hacerse ~** to smash, shatter
añil [a'ɲil] *nm* (*Bot, color*) indigo
año ['aɲo] *nm* year; **¡Feliz A~ Nuevo!** Happy New Year!; **tener 15 ~s** to be 15 (years old); **los ~s 80** the eighties; **~ bisiesto/escolar/fiscal/sabático** leap/school/tax/sabbatical year; **~ fiscal** fiscal *o* tax year; **estar de buen ~** to be in good shape; **en el ~ de la nana** in the year dot; **el ~ que viene** next year
añoranza [aɲo'ranθa] *nf* nostalgia; (*anhelo*) longing
añorar [aɲo'rar] *vt* to long for
apa ['apa] *excl* (*Am*) goodness me!, good gracious!
apabullar [apaβu'ʎar] *vt* (*lit: fig*) to crush
apacentar [apaθen'tar] *vt* to pasture, graze
apacible [apa'θiβle] *adj* gentle, mild
apaciguar [apaθi'ɣwar] *vt* to pacify, calm (down)
apadrinar [apaðri'nar] *vt* to sponsor, support; (*Rel: niño*) to be godfather to
apagado, -a [apa'ɣaðo, a] *adj* (*volcán*) extinct; (*color*) dull; (*voz*) quiet; (*sonido*) muted, muffled; (*persona: apático*) listless; **estar ~** (*fuego, luz*) to be out; (*radio, TV etc*) to be off
apagar [apa'ɣar] *vt* to put out; (*color*) to tone down; (*sonido*) to silence, muffle; (*sed*) to quench; (*Elec, Radio, TV*) to turn off; (*Inform*) to toggle off; **apagarse** *vr* (*luz, fuego*) to go out; (*sonido*) to die away; (*pasión*) to wither; **~ el sistema** (*Inform*) to close *o* shut down
apagón [apa'ɣon] *nm* blackout, power cut
apaisado, -a [apai'saðo, a] *adj* (*papel*) landscape *cpd*
apalabrar [apala'βrar] *vt* to agree to; (*obrero*) to engage
apalear [apale'ar] *vt* to beat, thrash; (*Agr*) to winnow
apañado, -a [apa'ɲaðo, a] *adj* (*mañoso*) resourceful; (*arreglado*) tidy; (*útil*) handy
apañar [apa'ɲar] *vt* to pick up; (*asir*) to take hold of, grasp; (*reparar*) to mend, patch up; **apañarse** *vr* to manage, get along; **apañárselas por su cuenta** to look after number one (*fam*)
apantallar [apanta'ʎar] *vt* (*Am*) to impress
apapachar [apapa'tʃar] *vt* (*Am: fam*) to cuddle, hug
aparador [apara'ðor] *nm* sideboard; (*Am: escaparate*) shop window
aparato [apa'rato] *nm* apparatus; (*máquina*) machine; (*doméstico*) appliance; (*boato*) ostentation; (*Inform*) device; **al ~** (*Telec*) speaking; **~ de facsímil** facsimile (machine), fax; **~ respiratorio** respiratory system; **~ digestivo** digestive system; **~s de mando** (*Aviat etc*) controls
aparatoso, -a [apara'toso, a] *adj* showy, ostentatious
aparcamiento [aparka'mjento] *nm* car park (*Brit*), parking lot (*US*)
aparcar [apar'kar] *vt, vi* to park
aparear [apare'ar] *vt* (*objetos*) to pair, match; (*animales*) to mate; **aparearse** *vr* to form a pair; to mate
aparecer [apare'θer] *vi* to appear; **aparecerse** *vr* to appear; **apareció borracho** he turned up drunk
aparejado, -a [apare'xaðo, a] *adj* fit, suitable; **ir ~ con** to go hand in hand with; **llevar** *o* **traer ~** to involve
aparejador, a [aparexa'ðor, a] *nm/f* (*Arq*) quantity surveyor
aparejo [apa'rexo] *nm* preparation; (*de caballo*) harness; (*Naut*) rigging; (*de poleas*) block and tackle
aparentar [aparen'tar] *vt* (*edad*) to look; (*fingir*): **~ tristeza** to pretend to be sad
aparente [apa'rente] *adj* apparent; (*adecuado*) suitable
aparezca *etc* [apa'reθka] *vb ver* **aparecer**
aparición [apari'θjon] *nf* appearance; (*de libro*) publication; (*de fantasma*) apparition
apariencia [apa'rjenθja] *nf* (outward) appearance; **en ~** outwardly, seemingly
apartado, -a [apar'taðo, a] *adj* separate; (*lejano*) remote ▷ *nm* (*tipográfico*) paragraph; **~ de correos** (*Esp*), **~ postal** (*Am*) post office box
apartamento [aparta'mento] *nm* apartment, flat (*Brit*)
apartamiento [aparta'mjento] *nm* separation; (*aislamiento*) remoteness; (*Am*) apartment, flat (*Brit*)

apartar [apar'tar] *vt* to separate; (*quitar*) to remove; (*Mineralogía*) to extract; **apartarse** *vr* (*separarse*) to separate, part; (*irse*) to move away; (*mantenerse aparte*) to keep away
aparte [a'parte] *adv* (*separadamente*) separately; (*además*) besides ▷ *prep*: **~ de** apart from ▷ *nm* (*Teat*) aside; (*tipográfico*) new paragraph; **"punto y ~"** "new paragraph"
aparthotel [aparto'tel] *nm* serviced apartments
apasionado, -a [apasjo'naðo, a] *adj* passionate; (*pey*) biassed, prejudiced ▷ *nm/f* admirer
apasionante [apasjo'nante] *adj* exciting
apasionar [apasjo'nar] *vt* to excite; **apasionarse** *vr* to get excited; **le apasiona el fútbol** she's crazy about football
apatía [apa'tia] *nf* apathy
apático, -a [a'patiko, a] *adj* apathetic
apátrida [a'patriða] *adj* stateless
Apdo. *nm abr* (= *Apartado (de Correos)*) P.O. Box
apeadero [apea'ðero] *nm* halt, stopping place
apearse [ape'arse] *vr* (*jinete*) to dismount; (*bajarse*) to get down *o* out; (*de coche*) to get out, alight; **no ~ del burro** to refuse to climb down
apechugar [apetʃu'ɣar] *vi*: **~ con algo** to face up to sth
apedrear [apeðre'ar] *vt* to stone
apegarse [ape'ɣarse] *vr*: **~ a** to become attached to
apego [a'peɣo] *nm* attachment, devotion
apelación [apela'θjon] *nf* appeal
apelar [ape'lar] *vi* to appeal; **~ a** (*fig*) to resort to
apellidar [apeʎi'ðar] *vt* to call, name; **apellidarse** *vr*: **se apellida Pérez** her (sur)name's Pérez
apellido [ape'ʎiðo] *nm* surname
apenar [ape'nar] *vt* to grieve, trouble; (*Am*: *avergonzar*) to embarrass; **apenarse** *vr* to grieve; (*Am*: *avergonzarse*) to be embarrassed
apenas [a'penas] *adv* scarcely, hardly ▷ *conj* as soon as, no sooner
apéndice [a'pendiθe] *nm* appendix
apendicitis [apendi'θitis] *nf* appendicitis
aperitivo [aperi'tiβo] *nm* (*bebida*) aperitif; (*comida*) appetizer
apertura [aper'tura] *nf* (*gen*) opening; (*Pol*) openness, liberalization; (*Teat etc*) beginning; **~ de un juicio hipotecario** (*Com*) foreclosure
apesadumbrar [apesaðum'brar] *vt* to grieve, sadden; **apesadumbrarse** *vr* to distress o.s.
apestar [apes'tar] *vt* to infect ▷ *vi*: **~ (a)** to stink (of)
apetecer [apete'θer] *vt*: **¿te apetece una tortilla?** do you fancy an omelette?
apetecible [apete'θiβle] *adj* desirable; (*comida*) appetizing
apetito [ape'tito] *nm* appetite
apetitoso, -a [apeti'toso, a] *adj* (*gustoso*) appetizing; (*fig*) tempting
apiadarse [apja'ðarse] *vr*: **~ de** to take pity on
ápice ['apiθe] *nm* apex; (*fig*) whit, iota; **ni un ~** not a whit; **no ceder un ~** not to budge an inch
apilar [api'lar] *vt* to pile *o* heap up; **apilarse** *vr* to pile up
apiñar [api'ɲar] *vt* to crowd; **apiñarse** *vr* to crowd *o* press together
apio ['apjo] *nm* celery
apisonadora [apisona'ðora] *nf* (*máquina*) steamroller
aplacar [apla'kar] *vt* to placate; **aplacarse** *vr* to calm down
aplanar [apla'nar] *vt* to smooth, level; (*allanar*) to roll flat, flatten; **aplanarse** *vr* (*edificio*) to collapse; (*persona*) to get discouraged
aplastante [aplas'tante] *adj* overwhelming; (*lógica*) compelling
aplastar [aplas'tar] *vt* to squash (flat); (*fig*) to crush
aplatanarse [aplata'narse] *vr* to get lethargic
aplaudir [aplau'ðir] *vt* to applaud
aplauso [a'plauso] *nm* applause; (*fig*) approval, acclaim
aplazamiento [aplaθa'mjento] *nm* postponement
aplazar [apla'θar] *vt* to postpone, defer
aplicación [aplika'θjon] *nf* application; (*esfuerzo*) effort; **aplicaciones de gestión** business applications
aplicado, -a [apli'kaðo, a] *adj* diligent, hard-working
aplicar [apli'kar] *vt* (*ejecutar*) to apply; (*poner en vigor*) to put into effect; (*esfuerzos*) to devote; **aplicarse** *vr* to apply o.s.
aplique *etc* [a'plike] *vb ver* **aplicar** ▷ *nm* wall light *o* lamp
aplomo [a'plomo] *nm* aplomb, self-assurance
apocado, -a [apo'kaðo, a] *adj* timid
apocamiento [apoka'mjento] *nm* timidity; (*depresión*) depression
apocarse [apo'karse] *vr* to feel small *o* humiliated
apócope [a'pokope] *nf* apocopation; **gran es ~ de grande** "gran" is the shortened form of "grande"
apodar [apo'ðar] *vt* to nickname
apoderado [apoðe'raðo] *nm* agent, representative
apoderar [apoðe'rar] *vt* to authorize, empower; (*Jur*) to grant (a) power of attorney to; **apoderarse** *vr*: **~se de** to take possession of
apodo [a'poðo] *nm* nickname
apogeo [apo'xeo] *nm* peak, summit
apolillarse [apoli'ʎarse] *vr* to get moth-eaten
apología [apolo'xia] *nf* eulogy; (*defensa*) defence

apoltronarse [apoltro'narse] *vr* to get lazy
apoplejía [apople'xia] *nf* apoplexy, stroke
apoquinar [apoki'nar] *vt* (*fam*) to cough up, fork out
aporrear [aporre'ar] *vt* to beat (up)
aportar [apor'tar] *vt* to contribute ▷ *vi* to reach port; **aportarse** *vr* (*Am*: *llegar*) to arrive, come
aposentar [aposen'tar] *vt* to lodge, put up
aposento [apo'sento] *nm* lodging; (*habitación*) room
apósito [a'posito] *nm* (*Med*) dressing
aposta [a'posta] *adv* deliberately, on purpose
apostar [apos'tar] *vt* to bet, stake; (*tropas etc*) to station, post ▷ *vi* to bet
a posteriori [aposte'rjori] *adv* at a later date *o* stage; (*Lógica*) a posteriori
apostilla [apos'tiʎa] *nf* note, comment
apóstol [a'postol] *nm* apostle
apóstrofo [a'postrofo] *nm* apostrophe
apoyar [apo'jar] *vt* to lean, rest; (*fig*) to support, back; **apoyarse** *vr*: **~se en** to lean on
apoyo [a'pojo] *nm* support, backing
apreciable [apre'θjaβle] *adj* considerable; (*fig*) esteemed
apreciación [apreθja'θjon] *nf* appreciation; (*Com*) valuation
apreciar [apre'θjar] *vt* to evaluate, assess; (*Com*) to appreciate, value; (*persona*) to respect; (*tamaño*) to gauge, assess; (*detalles*) to notice ▷ *vi* (*Econ*) to appreciate
aprecio [a'preθjo] *nm* valuation, estimate; (*fig*) appreciation
aprehender [apreen'der] *vt* to apprehend, detain; (*ver*) to see, observe
aprehensión [apreen'sjon] *nf* detention, capture
apremiante [apre'mjante] *adj* urgent, pressing
apremiar [apre'mjar] *vt* to compel, force ▷ *vi* to be urgent, press
apremio [a'premjo] *nm* urgency; **~ de pago** demand note
aprender [apren'der] *vt*, *vi* to learn; **~ a conducir** to learn to drive; **aprenderse** *vr*: **~se algo de memoria** to learn sth (off) by heart
aprendiz, a [apren'diθ, a] *nm/f* apprentice; (*principiante*) learner, trainee; **~ de comercio** business trainee
aprendizaje [aprendi'θaxe] *nm* apprenticeship
aprensión [apren'sjon] *nm* apprehension, fear
aprensivo, -a [apren'siβo, a] *adj* apprehensive
apresar [apre'sar] *vt* to seize; (*capturar*) to capture
aprestar [apres'tar] *vt* to prepare, get ready; (*Tec*) to prime, size; **aprestarse** *vr* to get ready
apresurado, -a [apresu'raðo, a] *adj* hurried, hasty
apresuramiento [apresura'mjento] *nm* hurry, haste
apresurar [apresu'rar] *vt* to hurry, accelerate; **apresurarse** *vr* to hurry, make haste; **me apresuré a sugerir que ...** I hastily suggested that ...
apretado, -a [apre'taðo, a] *adj* tight; (*escritura*) cramped
apretar [apre'tar] *vt* to squeeze, press; (*mano*) to clasp; (*dientes*) to grit; (*Tec*) to tighten; (*presionar*) to press together, pack ▷ *vi* to be too tight; **apretarse** *vr* to crowd together; **~ la mano a algn** to shake sb's hand; **~ el paso** to quicken one's step
apretón [apre'ton] *nm* squeeze; **~ de manos** handshake
aprieto [a'prjeto] *vb ver* **apretar** ▷ *nm* squeeze; (*dificultad*) difficulty, predicament; **estar en un ~** to be in a fix; **ayudar a algn a salir de un ~** to help sb out of trouble
a priori [apri'ori] *adv* beforehand; (*Lógica*) a priori
aprisa [a'prisa] *adv* quickly, hurriedly
aprisionar [aprisjo'nar] *vt* to imprison
aprobación [aproβa'θjon] *nf* approval
aprobado [apro'βaðo] *nm* (*nota*) pass mark
aprobar [apro'βar] *vt* to approve (of); (*examen, materia*) to pass ▷ *vi* to pass
apropiación [apropja'θjon] *nf* appropriation
apropiado, -a [apro'pjaðo, a] *adj* appropriate, suitable
apropiarse [apro'pjarse] *vr*: **~ de** to appropriate
aprovechado, -a [aproβe'tʃaðo, a] *adj* industrious, hardworking; (*económico*) thrifty; (*pey*) unscrupulous
aprovechamiento [aproβetʃa'mjento] *nm* use, exploitation
aprovechar [aproβe'tʃar] *vt* to use; (*explotar*) to exploit; (*experiencia*) to profit from; (*oferta, oportunidad*) to take advantage of ▷ *vi* to progress, improve; **aprovecharse** *vr*: **~se de** to make use of; (*pey*) to take advantage of; **¡que aproveche!** enjoy your meal!
aproximación [aproksima'θjon] *nf* approximation; (*de lotería*) consolation prize
aproximadamente [aproksimaða'mente] *adv* approximately
aproximado, -a [aproksi'maðo, a] *adj* approximate
aproximar [aproksi'mar] *vt* to bring nearer; **aproximarse** *vr* to come near, approach
apruebe *etc* [a'prweβe] *vb ver* **aprobar**
aptitud [apti'tuð] *nf* aptitude; (*capacidad*) ability; **~ para los negocios** business sense
apto, -a ['apto, a] *adj* (*hábil*) capable; (*apropiado*): **~ (para)** fit (for), suitable (for); **~/no ~ para menores** (*Cine*) suitable/unsuitable for children
apuesto, -a *etc* [a'pwesto, a] *vb ver* **apostar** ▷ *adj* neat, elegant ▷ *nf* bet, wager

apuntador [apunta'ðor] *nm* prompter
apuntalar [apunta'lar] *vt* to prop up
apuntar [apun'tar] *vt* (*con arma*) to aim at; (*con dedo*) to point at *o* to; (*anotar*) to note (down); (*datos*) to record; (*Teat*) to prompt; **apuntarse** *vr* (*Deporte*: *tanto, victoria*) to score; (*Escol*) to enrol; **~ una cantidad en la cuenta de algn** to charge a sum to sb's account; **~se en un curso** to enrol on a course; **¡yo me apunto!** count me in!
apunte [a'punte] *nm* note; (*Teat*: *voz*) prompt; (: *texto*) prompt book
apuñalar [apuɲa'lar] *vt* to stab
apurado, -a [apu'raðo, a] *adj* needy; (*difícil*) difficult; (*peligroso*) dangerous; (*Am*: *con prisa*) hurried, rushed; **estar en una situación apurada** to be in a tight spot; **estar ~** to be in a hurry
apurar [apu'rar] *vt* (*agotar*) to drain; (*recursos*) to use up; (*molestar*) to annoy; **apurarse** *vr* (*preocuparse*) to worry; (*esp Am*: *darse prisa*) to hurry
apuro [a'puro] *nm* (*aprieto*) fix, jam; (*escasez*) want, hardship; (*vergüenza*) embarrassment; (*Am*: *prisa*) haste, urgency
aquejado, -a [ake'xaðo, a] *adj*: **~ de** (*Med*) afflicted by
aquel, aquella, aquellos, -as [a'kel, a'keʎa, a'keʎos, -as] *adj* that, those *pl* ▷ *pron* that (one), those (ones) *pl*
aquél, aquélla, aquéllos, -as [a'kel, a'keʎa, a'keʎos, -as] *pron* that (one), those (ones) *pl*
aquello [a'keʎo] *pron* that, that business
aquí [a'ki] *adv* (*lugar*) here; (*tiempo*) now; **~ arriba** up here; **~ mismo** right here; **~ yace** here lies; **de ~ a siete días** a week from now
aquietar [akje'tar] *vt* to quieten (down), calm (down)
ara ['ara] *nf* (*altar*) altar; **en ~s de** for the sake of
árabe ['araβe] *adj* Arab, Arabian, Arabic ▷ *nm/f* Arab ▷ *nm* (*Ling*) Arabic
Arabia [a'raβja] *nf* Arabia; **~ Saudí** *o* **Saudita** Saudi Arabia
arado [a'raðo] *nm* plough
Aragón [ara'ɣon] *nm* Aragon
aragonés, -esa [araɣo'nes, esa] *adj, nm/f* Aragonese ▷ *nm* (*Ling*) Aragonese
arancel [aran'θel] *nm* tariff, duty; **~ de aduanas** (customs) duty
arandela [aran'dela] *nf* (*Tec*) washer; (*chorrera*) frill
araña [a'raɲa] *nf* (*Zool*) spider; (*lámpara*) chandelier
arañar [ara'ɲar] *vt* to scratch
arañazo [ara'ɲaθo] *nm* scratch
arar [a'rar] *vt* to plough, till
arbitraje [arβi'traxe] *nm* arbitration
arbitrar [arβi'trar] *vt* to arbitrate in; (*recursos*) to bring together; (*Deporte*) to referee ▷ *vi* to arbitrate
arbitrariedad [arβitrarje'ðað] *nf* arbitrariness; (*acto*) arbitrary act
arbitrario, -a [arβi'trarjo, a] *adj* arbitrary
arbitrio [ar'βitrjo] *nm* free will; (*Jur*) adjudication, decision; **dejar al ~ de algn** to leave to sb's discretion
árbitro ['arβitro] *nm* arbitrator; (*Deporte*) referee; (*Tenis*) umpire
árbol ['arβol] *nm* (*Bot*) tree; (*Naut*) mast; (*Tec*) axle, shaft; **~ de Navidad** Christmas tree
arbolado, -a [arβo'laðo, a] *adj* wooded; (*camino*) tree-lined ▷ *nm* woodland
arboladura [arβola'ðura] *nf* rigging
arbolar [arβo'lar] *vt* to hoist, raise
arboleda [arβo'leða] *nf* grove, plantation
arbusto [ar'βusto] *nm* bush, shrub
arca ['arka] *nf* chest, box; **A~ de la Alianza** Ark of the Covenant; **A~ de Noé** Noah's Ark
arcada [ar'kaða] *nf* arcade; (*de puente*) arch, span; **arcadas** *nfpl* (*náuseas*) retching *sg*
arcaico, -a [ar'kaiko, a] *adj* archaic
arce ['arθe] *nm* maple tree
arcén [ar'θen] *nm* (*de autopista*) hard shoulder; (*de carretera*) verge
archipiélago [artʃi'pjelaɣo] *nm* archipelago
archivador [artʃiβa'ðor] *nm* filing cabinet; **~ colgante** suspension file
archivar [artʃi'βar] *vt* to file (away); (*Inform*) to archive
archivo [ar'tʃiβo] *nm* archive(s) (*pl*); (*Inform*) file; **A~ Nacional** Public Record Office; **~s policíacos** police files; **nombre de ~** (*Inform*) filename; **~ adjunto** (*Inform*) attachment; **~ de seguridad** (*Inform*) backup file
arcilla [ar'θiʎa] *nf* clay
arco ['arko] *nm* arch; (*Mat*) arc; (*Mil, Mus*) bow; (*Am Deporte*) goal; **~ iris** rainbow
arder [ar'ðer] *vti* to burn; **~ sin llama** to smoulder; **estar que arde** (*persona*) to fume
ardid [ar'ðið] *nm* ploy, trick
ardiente [ar'ðjente] *adj* ardent
ardilla [ar'ðiʎa] *nf* squirrel
ardor [ar'ðor] *nm* (*calor*) heat, warmth; (*fig*) ardour; **~ de estómago** heartburn
ardoroso, -a [arðo'roso, a] *adj* passionate
arduo, -a ['arðwo, a] *adj* arduous
área ['area] *nf* area; (*Deporte*) penalty area
arena [a'rena] *nf* sand; (*de una lucha*) arena
arenal [are'nal] *nm* (*terreno arenoso*) sandy area; (*arena movediza*) quicksand
arengar [aren'gar] *vt* to harangue
arenisca [are'niska] *nf* sandstone; (*cascajo*) grit
arenoso, -a [are'noso, a] *adj* sandy
arenque [a'renke] *nm* herring
arete [a'rete] *nm* (*Am*) earring
argamasa [arɣa'masa] *nf* mortar, plaster
Argel [ar'xel] *n* Algiers
Argelia [ar'xelja] *nf* Algeria
argelino, -a [arxe'lino, a] *adj, nm/f* Algerian
Argentina [arxen'tina] *nf*: **(la) ~** Argentina, the Argentine
argentino, -a [arxen'tino, a] *adj* Argentinian; (*de plata*) silvery ▷ *nm/f* Argentinian

argolla [ar'ɣoʎa] *nf* (large) ring; (*Am: de matrimonio*) wedding ring
argot [ar'ɣo] *nm* (*pl* **argots**) [ar'ɣo, ar'ɣos] slang
argucia [ar'ɣuθja] *nf* subtlety, sophistry
argüir [ar'ɣwir] *vt* to deduce; (*discutir*) to argue; (*indicar*) to indicate, imply; (*censurar*) to reproach ▷ *vi* to argue
argumentación [arɣumenta'θjon] *nf* (line of) argument
argumentar [arɣumen'tar] *vt, vi* to argue
argumento [arɣu'mento] *nm* argument; (*razonamiento*) reasoning; (*de novela etc*) plot; (*Cine, TV*) storyline
aria ['arja] *nf* aria
aridez [ari'ðeθ] *nf* aridity, dryness
árido, -a ['ariðo, a] *adj* arid, dry; **áridos** *nmpl* dry goods
Aries ['arjes] *nm* Aries
ariete [a'rjete] *nm* battering ram
ario, -a ['arjo, a] *adj* Aryan
arisco, -a [a'risko, a] *adj* surly; (*insociable*) unsociable
aristocracia [aristo'kraθja] *nf* aristocracy
aristócrata [aris'tokrata] *nm/f* aristocrat
aritmética [arit'metika] *nf* arithmetic
arma ['arma] *nf* arm; **armas** *nfpl* arms; ~ **blanca** blade, knife; (*espada*) sword; ~ **de doble filo** double-edged sword; ~ **de fuego** firearm; **~s cortas** small arms; **~s de destrucción masiva** weapons of mass destruction; **rendir las ~s** to lay down one's arms; **ser de ~s tomar** to be somebody to be reckoned with
armada [ar'maða] *nf* armada; (*flota*) fleet; *ver tb* **armado**
armadillo [arma'ðiʎo] *nm* armadillo
armado, -a [ar'maðo, a] *adj* armed; (*Tec*) reinforced
armador [arma'ðor] *nm* (*Naut*) shipowner
armadura [arma'ðura] *nf* (*Mil*) armour; (*Tec*) framework; (*Zool*) skeleton; (*Física*) armature
armamento [arma'mento] *nm* armament; (*Naut*) fitting-out
armar [ar'mar] *vt* (*soldado*) to arm; (*máquina*) to assemble; (*navío*) to fit out; **~la, ~ un lío** to start a row, kick up a fuss; **armarse** *vr*: **~se de valor** to summon up one's courage
armario [ar'marjo] *nm* wardrobe; (*de cocina, baño*) cupboard; ~ **empotrado** built-in cupboard; **salir del** ~ to come out (of the closet)
armatoste [arma'toste] *nm* (*mueble*) monstrosity; (*máquina*) contraption
armazón [arma'θon] *nf o m* body, chassis; (*de mueble etc*) frame; (*Arq*) skeleton
armiño [ar'miɲo] *nm* stoat; (*piel*) ermine
armisticio [armis'tiθjo] *nm* armistice
armonía [armo'nia] *nf* harmony
armónica [ar'monika] *nf* harmonica
armonioso, -a [armo'njoso, a] *adj* harmonious
armonizar [armoni'θar] *vt* to harmonize; (*diferencias*) to reconcile ▷ *vi* to harmonize; ~ **con** (*fig*) to be in keeping with; (*colores*) to tone in with
arnés [ar'nes] *nm* armour; **arneses** *nmpl* harness *sg*
aro ['aro] *nm* ring; (*tejo*) quoit; (*Am: pendiente*) earring; **entrar por el** ~ to give in
aroma [a'roma] *nm* aroma
aromaterapia [aromate'rapja] *nf* aromatherapy
aromático, -a [aro'matiko, a] *adj* aromatic
arpa ['arpa] *nf* harp
arpía [ar'pia] *nf* (*fig*) shrew
arpillera [arpi'ʎera] *nf* sacking, sackcloth
arpón [ar'pon] *nm* harpoon
arquear [arke'ar] *vt* to arch, bend; **arquearse** *vr* to arch, bend
arqueo [ar'keo] *nm* (*gen*) arching; (*Naut*) tonnage
arqueología [arkeolo'xia] *nf* archaeology
arqueólogo, -a [arke'oloɣo, a] *nm/f* archaeologist
arquero [ar'kero] *nm* archer, bowman; (*Am Deporte*) goalkeeper
arquetipo [arke'tipo] *nm* archetype
arquitecto, -a [arki'tekto, a] *nm/f* architect; ~ **paisajista** *o* **de jardines** landscape gardener
arquitectura [arkitek'tura] *nf* architecture
arrabal [arra'βal] *nm* suburb; (*LAm*) slum; **arrabales** *nmpl* (*afueras*) outskirts
arraigado, -a [arrai'ɣaðo, a] *adj* deep-rooted; (*fig*) established
arraigar [arrai'ɣar] *vt* to establish ▷ *vi*, **arraigarse** *vr* to take root; (*persona*) to settle
arrancar [arran'kar] *vt* (*sacar*) to extract, pull out; (*arrebatar*) to snatch (away); (*pedazo*) to tear off; (*página*) to rip out; (*suspiro*) to heave; (*Auto*) to start; (*Inform*) to boot; (*fig*) to extract ▷ *vi* (*Auto, máquina*) to start; (*ponerse en marcha*) to get going; ~ **información a algn** to extract information from sb; ~ **de** to stem from
arranque *etc* [a'rranke] *vb ver* **arrancar** ▷ *nm* sudden start; (*Auto*) start; (*fig*) fit, outburst
arras ['arras] *nfpl* pledge *sg*, security *sg*
arrasar [arra'sar] *vt* (*aplanar*) to level, flatten; (*destruir*) to demolish
arrastrado, -a [arras'traðo, a] *adj* poor, wretched
arrastrar [arras'trar] *vt* to drag (along); (*fig*) to drag down, degrade; (*suj: agua, viento*) to carry away ▷ *vi* to drag, trail on the ground; **arrastrarse** *vr* to crawl; (*fig*) to grovel; **llevar algo arrastrado** to drag sth along
arrastre [a'rrastre] *nm* drag, dragging; (*Deporte*) crawl; **estar para el** ~ (*fig*) to have had it
arre ['arre] *excl* gee up!
arrear [arre'ar] *vt* to drive on, urge on ▷ *vi* to hurry along

arrebatado, -a [arreβa'taðo, a] *adj* rash, impetuous; (*repentino*) sudden, hasty
arrebatar [arreβa'tar] *vt* to snatch (away), seize; (*fig*) to captivate; **arrebatarse** *vr* to get carried away, get excited
arrebato [arre'βato] *nm* fit of rage, fury; (*éxtasis*) rapture; **en un ~ de cólera** in an outburst of anger
arrecife [arre'θife] *nm* reef
arredrar [arre'ðrar] *vt* (*hacer retirarse*) to drive back; **arredrarse** *vr* (*apartarse*) to draw back; **~se ante algo** to shrink away from sth
arreglado, -a [arre'ɣlaðo, a] *adj* (*ordenado*) neat, orderly; (*moderado*) moderate, reasonable
arreglar [arre'ɣlar] *vt* (*poner orden*) to tidy up; (*algo roto*) to fix, repair; (*problema*) to solve; **arreglarse** *vr* to reach an understanding; **arreglárselas** (*fam*) to get by, manage
arreglo [a'rreɣlo] *nm* settlement; (*orden*) order; (*acuerdo*) agreement; (*Mus*) arrangement, setting; (*Inform*) array; **con ~ a** in accordance with; **llegar a un ~** to reach a compromise
arrellanarse [arreʎa'narse] *vr* to sprawl; **~ en el asiento** to lie back in one's chair
arremangar [arreman'gar] *vt* to roll up, turn up; **arremangarse** *vr* to roll up one's sleeves
arremeter [arreme'ter] *vt* to attack, assault ▷ *vi*: **~ contra algn** to attack sb
arrendador, a [arrenda'ðor, a] *nm/f* landlord/lady
arrendamiento [arrenda'mjento] *nm* letting; (*el alquilar*) hiring; (*contrato*) lease; (*alquiler*) rent
arrendar [arren'dar] *vt* to let; to hire; to lease; to rent
arrendatario, -a [arrenda'tarjo, a] *nm/f* tenant
arreos [a'rreos] *nmpl* (*de caballo*) harness *sg*, trappings
arrepentido, -a [arrepen'tiðo, a] *nm/f* (*Pol*) reformed terrorist
arrepentimiento [arrepenti'mjento] *nm* regret, repentance
arrepentirse [arrepen'tirse] *vr* to repent; **~ de (haber hecho) algo** to regret (doing) sth
arrestar [arres'tar] *vt* to arrest; (*encarcelar*) to imprison
arresto [a'rresto] *nm* arrest; (*Mil*) detention; (*audacia*) boldness, daring; **~ domiciliario** house arrest
arriar [a'rrjar] *vt* (*velas*) to haul down; (*bandera*) to lower, strike; (*un cable*) to pay out

PALABRA CLAVE

arriba [a'rriβa] *adv* **1** (*posición*) above; **desde arriba** from above; **arriba del todo** at the very top, right on top; **Juan está arriba** Juan is upstairs; **lo arriba mencionado** the aforementioned; **aquí/allí arriba** up here/there; **está hasta arriba de trabajo** (*fam*) he's up to his eyes in work (*fam*)
2 (*dirección*) up, upwards; **más arriba** higher *o* further up; **calle arriba** up the street
3: **de arriba abajo** from top to bottom; **mirar a algn de arriba abajo** to look sb up and down
4: **para arriba**: **de 50 euros para arriba** from 50 euros up(wards); **de la cintura (para) arriba** from the waist up
▷ *adj*: **de arriba**: **el piso de arriba** the upstairs flat (*Brit*) *o* apartment; **la parte de arriba** the top *o* upper part
▷ *prep*: **arriba de** (*Am*: *por encima de*) above; **arriba de 200 dólares** more than 200 dollars
▷ *excl*: **¡arriba!** up!; **¡manos arriba!** hands up!; **¡arriba España!** long live Spain!

arribar [arri'βar] *vi* to put into port; (*esp Am*: *llegar*) to arrive
arribista [arri'βista] *nm/f* parvenu(e), upstart
arriendo *etc* [a'rrjendo] *vb ver* **arrendar** ▷ *nm* = **arrendamiento**
arriero [a'rrjero] *nm* muleteer
arriesgado, -a [arrjes'ɣaðo, a] *adj* (*peligroso*) risky; (*audaz*) bold, daring
arriesgar [arrjes'ɣar] *vt* to risk; (*poner en peligro*) to endanger; **arriesgarse** *vr* to take a risk
arrimar [arri'mar] *vt* (*acercar*) to bring close; (*poner de lado*) to set aside; **arrimarse** *vr* to come close *o* closer; **~se a** to lean on; (*fig*) to keep company with; (*buscar ayuda*) to seek the protection of; **arrímate a mí** cuddle up to me
arrinconar [arrinko'nar] *vt* (*colocar*) to put in a corner; (*enemigo*) to corner; (*fig*) to put on one side; (*abandonar*) to push aside
arroba [a'rroβa] *nf* (*peso*) 25 pounds; (*Inform*: *en dirección electrónica*) at sign, @; **tiene talento por ~s** he has loads *o* bags of talent
arrodillarse [arroði'ʎarse] *vr* to kneel (down)
arrogancia [arro'ɣanθja] *nf* arrogance
arrogante [arro'ɣante] *adj* arrogant
arrojar [arro'xar] *vt* to throw, hurl; (*humo*) to emit, give out; (*Com*) to yield, produce; **arrojarse** *vr* to throw *o* hurl o.s.
arrojo [a'rroxo] *nm* daring
arrollador, a [arroʎa'ðor, a] *adj* crushing, overwhelming
arrollar [arro'ʎar] *vt* (*enrollar*) to roll up; (*suj*: *inundación*) to wash away; (*Auto*) to run over; (*Deporte*) to crush
arropar [arro'par] *vt* to cover (up), wrap up; **arroparse** *vr* to wrap o.s. up
arrostrar [arros'trar] *vt* to face (up to); **arrostrarse** *vr*: **~se con algn** to face up to sb
arroyo [a'rrojo] *nm* stream; (*de la calle*) gutter; **poner a algn en el ~** to turn sb onto the streets
arroz [a'rroθ] *nm* rice; **~ con leche** rice pudding

arrozal [arro'θal] *nm* paddy field
arruga [a'rruɣa] *nf* fold; (*de cara*) wrinkle; (*de vestido*) crease
arrugar [arru'ɣar] *vt* to fold; to wrinkle; to crease; **arrugarse** *vr* to get wrinkled; to get creased
arruinar [arrwi'nar] *vt* to ruin, wreck; **arruinarse** *vr* to be ruined
arrullar [arru'ʎar] *vi* to coo ▷ *vt* to lull to sleep
arrumaco [arru'mako] *nm* (*caricia*) caress; (*halago*) piece of flattery
arsenal [arse'nal] *nm* naval dockyard; (*Mil*) arsenal
arsénico [ar'seniko] *nm* arsenic
arte ['arte] *nm* (*gen m en sg, f en pl*) art; (*maña*) skill, guile; **por ~ de magia** (as if) by magic; **no tener ~ ni p~ en algo** to have nothing whatsoever to do with sth; **artes** *nfpl* arts; **Bellas A~s** Fine Art *sg*; **~s y oficios** arts and crafts
artefacto [arte'fakto] *nm* appliance; (*Arqueología*) artefact
arteria [ar'terja] *nf* artery
arterial [arte'rjal] *adj* arterial; (*presión*) blood *cpd*
artesanía [artesa'nia] *nf* craftsmanship; (*artículos*) handicrafts *pl*
artesano, -a [arte'sano, a] *nm/f* artisan, craftsman/woman
ártico, -a ['artiko, a] *adj* Arctic ▷ *nm*: **el (océano) Á~** the Arctic (Ocean)
articulación [artikula'θjon] *nf* articulation; (*Med, Tec*) joint
articulado, -a [artiku'laðo, a] *adj* articulated; jointed
articular [artiku'lar] *vt* to articulate; to join together
artículo [ar'tikulo] *nm* article; (*cosa*) thing, article; (*TV*) feature, report; **~ de fondo** leader, editorial; **artículos** *nmpl* goods; **~s de marca** (*Com*) proprietary goods; **~s de escritorio** stationery
artífice [ar'tifiθe] *nm/f* artist, craftsman; (*fig*) architect
artificial [artifi'θjal] *adj* artificial
artificio [arti'fiθjo] *nm* art, skill; (*artesanía*) craftsmanship; (*astucia*) cunning
artillería [artiʎe'ria] *nf* artillery
artillero [arti'ʎero] *nm* artilleryman, gunner
artilugio [arti'luxjo] *nm* gadget
artimaña [arti'maɲa] *nf* trap, snare; (*astucia*) cunning
artista [ar'tista] *nm/f* (*pintor*) artist, painter; (*Teat*) artist, artiste; **~ de cine** film actor/actress
artístico, -a [ar'tistiko, a] *adj* artistic
artritis [ar'tritis] *nf* arthritis
arveja [ar'βexa] *nf* (*Am*) pea
arzobispo [arθo'βispo] *nm* archbishop
as [as] *nm* ace; **as del fútbol** star player
asa ['asa] *nf* handle; (*fig*) lever
asado [a'saðo] *nm* roast (meat); (*Am: barbacoa*) barbecue

ASADO

Traditional Latin American barbecues, especially in the River Plate area, are celebrated in the open air around a large grill which is used to grill mainly beef and various kinds of spicy pork sausage. They are usually very common during the summer and can go on for several days.

asador [asa'ðor] *nm* (*varilla*) spit; (*aparato*) spit roaster
asadura, asaduras [asa'ðura(s)] *nf(pl)* entrails *pl*, offal *sg*; (*Culin*) chitterlings *pl*
asalariado, -a [asala'rjaðo, a] *adj* paid, wage-earning, salaried ▷ *nm/f* wage earner
asaltador, a [asalta'ðor, a], **asaltante** [asal'tante] *nm/f* assailant
asaltar [asal'tar] *vt* to attack, assault; (*fig*) to assail
asalto [a'salto] *nm* attack, assault; (*Deporte*) round
asamblea [asam'blea] *nf* assembly; (*reunión*) meeting
asar [a'sar] *vt* to roast; **~ al horno/a la parrilla** to bake/grill; **asarse** *vr* (*fig*): **me aso de calor** I'm roasting; **aquí se asa uno vivo** it's boiling hot here
asbesto [as'βesto] *nm* asbestos
ascendencia [asθen'denθja] *nf* ancestry; (*Am: influencia*) ascendancy; **de ~ francesa** of French origin
ascender [asθen'der] *vi* (*subir*) to ascend, rise; (*ser promovido*) to gain promotion ▷ *vt* to promote; **~ a** to amount to
ascendiente [asθen'djente] *nm* influence ▷ *nm/f* ancestor
ascensión [asθen'sjon] *nf* ascent; **la A~** the Ascension
ascenso [as'θenso] *nm* ascent; (*promoción*) promotion
ascensor [asθen'sor] *nm* lift (*Brit*), elevator (*US*)
ascético, -a [as'θetiko, a] *adj* ascetic
asco ['asko] *nm*: **el ajo me da ~** I hate *o* loathe garlic; **hacer ~s de algo** to turn up one's nose at sth; **estar hecho un ~** to be filthy; **poner a algn de ~** to call sb all sorts of names *o* every name under the sun; **¡qué ~!** how revolting *o* disgusting!
ascua ['askwa] *nf* ember; **arrimar el ~ a su sardina** to look after number one; **estar en ~s** to be on tenterhooks
aseado, -a [ase'aðo, a] *adj* clean; (*arreglado*) tidy; (*pulcro*) smart
asear [ase'ar] *vt* (*lavar*) to wash; (*ordenar*) to tidy (up)
asediar [ase'ðjar] *vt* (*Mil*) to besiege, lay siege to; (*fig*) to chase, pester
asedio [a'seðjo] *nm* siege; (*Com*) run

asegurado, a [aseɣu'raðo, a] *adj* insured
asegurador, -a [aseɣura'ðor, a] *nm/f* insurer
asegurar [aseɣu'rar] *vt* (*consolidar*) to secure, fasten; (*dar garantía de*) to guarantee; (*preservar*) to safeguard; (*afirmar: dar por cierto*) to assure, affirm; (*tranquilizar*) to reassure; (*hacer un seguro*) to insure; **asegurarse** *vr* to assure o.s., make sure
asemejarse [aseme'xarse] *vr* to be alike; ~ **a** to be like, resemble
asentado, -a [asen'taðo, a] *adj* established, settled
asentar [asen'tar] *vt* (*sentar*) to seat, sit down; (*poner*) to place, establish; (*alisar*) to level, smooth down *o* out; (*anotar*) to note down ▷ *vi* to be suitable, suit
asentir [asen'tir] *vi* to assent, agree; ~ **con la cabeza** to nod (one's head)
aseo [a'seo] *nm* cleanliness; **aseos** *nmpl* toilet *sg* (*Brit*), cloakroom *sg* (*Brit*), restroom *sg* (*US*)
aséptico, -a [a'septiko, a] *adj* germ-free, free from infection
asequible [ase'kiβle] *adj* (*precio*) reasonable; (*meta*) attainable; (*persona*) approachable
aserradero [aserra'ðero] *nm* sawmill
aserrar [ase'rrar] *vt* to saw
asesinar [asesi'nar] *vt* to murder; (*Pol*) to assassinate
asesinato [asesi'nato] *nm* murder; assassination
asesino, -a [ase'sino, a] *nm/f* murderer, killer; (*Pol*) assassin
asesor, a [ase'sor, a] *nm/f* adviser, consultant; (*Com*) assessor, consultant; ~ **administrativo** management consultant
asesorar [aseso'rar] *vt* (*Jur*) to advise, give legal advice to; (*Com*) to act as consultant to; **asesorarse** *vr*: **~se con** *o* **de** to take advice from, consult
asesoría [aseso'ria] *nf* (*cargo*) consultancy; (*oficina*) consultant's office
asestar [ases'tar] *vt* (*golpe*) to deal; (*arma*) to aim; (*tiro*) to fire
asfalto [as'falto] *nm* asphalt
asfixia [as'fiksja] *nf* asphyxia, suffocation
asfixiar [asfik'sjar] *vt* to asphyxiate, suffocate; **asfixiarse** *vr* to be asphyxiated, suffocate
así [a'si] *adv* (*de esta manera*) in this way, like this, thus; (*aunque*) although; (*tan pronto como*) as soon as; ~ **que** so; ~ **como** as well as; ~ **y todo** even so; **¿no es ~?** isn't it?, didn't you? *etc*; ~ **de grande** this big; **¡~ sea!** so be it!; ~ **es la vida** such is life, that's life
Asia ['asja] *nf* Asia
asiático, -a [a'sjatiko, a] *adj, nm/f* Asian, Asiatic
asidero [asi'ðero] *nm* handle
asiduidad [asiðwi'ðað] *nf* assiduousness
asiduo, -a [a'siðwo, a] *adj* assiduous; (*frecuente*) frequent ▷ *nm/f* regular (customer)
asiento [a'sjento] *vb ver* **asentar, asentir** ▷ *nm* (*mueble*) seat, chair; (*de coche, en tribunal etc*) seat; (*localidad*) seat, place; (*fundamento*) site; ~ **delantero/trasero** front/back seat
asignación [asiɣna'θjon] *nf* (*atribución*) assignment; (*reparto*) allocation; (*sueldo*) salary; (*Com*) allowance; ~ **(semanal)** (weekly) pocket money; ~ **de presupuesto** budget appropriation
asignar [asiɣ'nar] *vt* to assign, allocate
asignatura [asiɣna'tura] *nf* subject; (*curso*) course; ~ **pendiente** (*fig*) matter pending
asilado, -a [asi'laðo, a] *nm/f* refugee
asilo [a'silo] *nm* (*refugio*) asylum, refuge; (*establecimiento*) home, institution; ~ **político** political asylum
asimilación [asimila'θjon] *nf* assimilation
asimilar [asimi'lar] *vt* to assimilate
asimismo [asi'mismo] *adv* in the same way, likewise
asir [a'sir] *vt* to seize, grasp; **asirse** *vr* to take hold; **~se a** *o* **de** to seize
asistencia [asis'tenθja] *nf* presence; (*Teat*) audience; (*Med*) attendance; (*ayuda*) assistance; ~ **social** social *o* welfare work; ~ **en carretera** roadside assistance
asistente, -a [asis'tente, a] *nm/f* assistant ▷ *nm* (*Mil*) orderly ▷ *nf* daily help; **los ~s** those present; ~ **social** social worker
asistido, -a [asis'tiðo, a] *adj* (*Auto: dirección*) power assisted; ~ **por ordenador** computer-assisted
asistir [asis'tir] *vt* to assist, help ▷ *vi*: ~ **a** to attend, be present at
asma ['asma] *nf* asthma
asno ['asno] *nm* donkey; (*fig*) ass
asociación [asoθja'θjon] *nf* association; (*Com*) partnership
asociado, -a [aso'θjaðo, a] *adj* associate ▷ *nm/f* associate; (*Com*) partner
asociar [aso'θjar] *vt* to associate; **asociarse** *vr* to become partners
asolar [aso'lar] *vt* to destroy
asomar [aso'mar] *vt* to show, stick out ▷ *vi* to appear; **asomarse** *vr* to appear, show up; ~ **la cabeza por la ventana** to put one's head out of the window
asombrar [asom'brar] *vt* to amaze, astonish; **asombrarse** *vr*: **~se (de)** (*sorprenderse*) to be amazed (at); (*asustarse*) to be frightened (at)
asombro [a'sombro] *nm* amazement, astonishment; (*susto*) fright
asombroso, -a [asom'broso, a] *adj* amazing, astonishing
asomo [a'somo] *nm* hint, sign; **ni por ~** by no means
aspa ['aspa] *nf* (*cruz*) cross; (*de molino*) sail; **en ~** X-shaped
aspaviento [aspa'βjento] *nm* exaggerated display of feeling; (*fam*) fuss
aspecto [as'pekto] *nm* (*apariencia*) look, appearance; (*fig*) aspect; **bajo ese ~** from that point of view

aspereza [aspe'reθa] *nf* roughness; (*de fruta*) sharpness; (*de carácter*) surliness
áspero, -a ['aspero, a] *adj* (*al tacto*) rough; (*al gusto*) sharp, sour; (*voz*) harsh
aspersión [asper'sjon] *nf* sprinkling; (*Agr*) spraying
aspersor [asper'sor] *nm* sprinkler
aspiración [aspira'θjon] *nf* breath, inhalation; (*Mus*) short pause; **aspiraciones** *nfpl* (*ambiciones*) aspirations
aspirador [aspira'ðor] *nm* = **aspiradora**
aspiradora [aspira'ðora] *nf* vacuum cleaner, Hoover®
aspirante [aspi'rante] *nm/f* (*candidato*) candidate; (*Deporte*) contender
aspirar [aspi'rar] *vt* to breathe in ▷ *vi*: ~ **a** to aspire to
aspirina [aspi'rina] *nf* aspirin
asquear [aske'ar] *vt* to sicken ▷ *vi* to be sickening; **asquearse** *vr* to feel disgusted
asqueroso, -a [aske'roso, a] *adj* disgusting, sickening
asta ['asta] *nf* lance; (*arpón*) spear; (*mango*) shaft, handle; (*Zool*) horn; **a media ~** at half mast
asterisco [aste'risko] *nm* asterisk
asteroide [aste'roiðe] *nm* asteroid
astigmatismo [astiɣma'tismo] *nm* astigmatism
astilla [as'tiʎa] *nf* splinter; (*pedacito*) chip; **astillas** *nfpl* (*leña*) firewood *sg*
astillero [asti'ʎero] *nm* shipyard
astringente [astrin'xente] *adj, nm* astringent
astro ['astro] *nm* star
astrología [astrolo'xia] *nf* astrology
astrólogo, -a [as'troloɣo, a] *nm/f* astrologer
astronauta [astro'nauta] *nm/f* astronaut
astronave [astro'naβe] *nm* spaceship
astronomía [astrono'mia] *nf* astronomy
astronómico, -a [astro'nomiko, a] *adj* (*tb fig*) astronomical
astrónomo, -a [as'tronomo, a] *nm/f* astronomer
astucia [as'tuθja] *nf* astuteness; (*destreza*) clever trick
asturiano, -a [astu'rjano, a] *adj, nm/f* Asturian
astuto, -a [as'tuto, a] *adj* astute; (*taimado*) cunning
asueto [a'sweto] *nm* holiday; (*tiempo libre*) time off; **día de ~** day off; **tarde de ~** (*trabajo*) afternoon off; (*Escol*) half-holiday
asumir [asu'mir] *vt* to assume
asunción [asun'θjon] *nf* assumption; (*Rel*): **A~** Assumption
asunto [a'sunto] *nm* (*tema*) matter, subject; (*negocio*) business; **¡eso es ~ mío!** that's my business!; **~s exteriores** foreign affairs; **~s a tratar** agenda *sg*
asustar [asus'tar] *vt* to frighten; **asustarse** *vr* to be/become frightened
atacar [ata'kar] *vt* to attack
atadura [ata'ðura] *nf* bond, tie
atajar [ata'xar] *vt* (*enfermedad, mal*) to stop; (*ruta de fuga*) to cut off; (*discurso*) to interrupt ▷ *vi* (*persona*) to take a short cut
atajo [a'taxo] *nm* short cut; (*Deporte*) tackle
atañer [ata'ɲer] *vi*: ~ **a** to concern; **en lo que atañe a eso** with regard to that
ataque *etc* [a'take] *vb ver* **atacar** ▷ *nm* attack; **~ cardíaco** heart attack
atar [a'tar] *vt* to tie, tie up; **~ la lengua a algn** (*fig*) to silence sb
atarantado, -a [ataran'taðo, a] *adj* (*Am: aturdido*) dazed
atardecer [atarðe'θer] *vi* to get dark ▷ *nm* evening; (*crepúsculo*) dusk
atareado, -a [atare'aðo, a] *adj* busy
atascar [atas'kar] *vt* to clog up; (*obstruir*) to jam; (*fig*) to hinder; **atascarse** *vr* to stall; (*cañería*) to get blocked up; (*fig*) to get bogged down; (*en discurso*) to dry up
atasco [a'tasko] *nm* obstruction; (*Auto*) traffic jam
ataúd [ata'uð] *nm* coffin
ataviar [ata'βjar] *vt* to deck, array; **ataviarse** *vr* to dress up
atavío [ata'βio] *nm* attire, dress; **atavíos** *nmpl* finery *sg*
atemorizar [atemori'θar] *vt* to frighten, scare; **atemorizarse** *vr* to get frightened *o* scared
Atenas [a'tenas] *nf* Athens
atención [aten'θjon] *nf* attention; (*bondad*) kindness ▷ *excl* (be) careful!, look out!; **en ~ a esto** in view of this
atender [aten'der] *vt* to attend to, look after; (*Tec*) to service; (*enfermo*) to care for; (*ruego*) to comply with; (*Tel*) to answer ▷ *vi* to pay attention; ~ **a** to attend to; (*detalles*) to take care of
atenerse [ate'nerse] *vr*: ~ **a** to abide by, adhere to
atentado [aten'taðo] *nm* crime, illegal act; (*asalto*) assault; (*tb*: **~ terrorista**) terrorist attack; **~ contra la vida de algn** attempt on sb's life; **~ golpista** attempted coup; **~ suicida** suicide bombing, suicide attack
atentamente [atenta'mente] *adv*: **Le saluda ~** Yours faithfully
atentar [aten'tar] *vi*: ~ **a** *o* **contra** to commit an outrage against
atento, -a [a'tento, a] *adj* attentive, observant; (*cortés*) polite, thoughtful; **estar ~ a** (*explicación*) to pay attention to; **su atenta (carta)** (*Com*) your letter
atenuante [ate'nwante] *adj*: **circunstancias ~s** extenuating *o* mitigating circumstances ▷ *nfpl*: **~s** extenuating *o* mitigating circumstances
atenuar [ate'nwar] *vt* to attenuate; (*disminuir*) to lessen, minimize
ateo, -a [a'teo, a] *adj* atheistic ▷ *nm/f* atheist

a

aterciopelado, -a [aterθjope'laðo, a] *adj* velvety
aterido, -a [ate'riðo, a] *adj*: **~ de frío** frozen stiff
aterrador, a [aterra'ðor, a] *adj* frightening
aterrar [ate'rrar] *vt* to frighten; (*aterrorizar*) to terrify; **aterrarse** *vr* to be frightened; to be terrified
aterrizaje [aterri'θaxe] *nm* landing; **~ forzoso** emergency *o* forced landing
aterrizar [aterri'θar] *vi* to land
aterrorizar [aterrori'θar] *vt* to terrify
atesorar [ateso'rar] *vt* to hoard, store up
atestado, -a [ates'taðo, a] *adj* packed ▷ *nm* (*Jur*) affidavit
atestar [ates'tar] *vt* to pack, stuff; (*Jur*) to attest, testify to
atestiguar [atesti'ɣwar] *vt* to testify to, bear witness to
atiborrar [atiβo'rrar] *vt* to fill, stuff; **atiborrarse** *vr* to stuff o.s.
ático ['atiko] *nm* (*desván*) attic; **~ de lujo** penthouse flat
atildar [atil'dar] *vt* to criticize; (*Tip*) to put a tilde over; **atildarse** *vr* to spruce o.s. up
atinado, -a [ati'naðo, a] *adj* correct; (*sensato*) wise, sensible
atinar [ati'nar] *vi* (*acertar*) to be right; **~ con** *o* **en** (*solución*) to hit upon; **~ al blanco** to hit the target; (*fig*) to be right; **~ a hacer** to manage to do
atípico, -a [a'tipiko, a] *adj* atypical
atisbar [atis'βar] *vt* to spy on; (*echar ojeada*) to peep at
atizar [ati'θar] *vt* to poke; (*horno etc*) to stoke; (*fig*) to stir up, rouse
atlántico, -a [at'lantiko, a] *adj* Atlantic ▷ *nm*: **el (océano) A~** the Atlantic (Ocean)
atlas ['atlas] *nm inv* atlas
atleta [at'leta] *nm/f* athlete
atlético, -a [at'letiko, a] *adj* athletic
atletismo [atle'tismo] *nm* athletics *sg*
atmósfera [at'mosfera] *nf* atmosphere
atmosférico, -a [atmos'feriko, a] *adj* atmospheric
atolladero [atoʎa'ðero] *nm*: **estar en un ~** to be in a jam
atollarse [ato'ʎarse] *vr* to get stuck; (*fig*) to get into a jam
atolondrado, -a [atolon'draðo, a] *adj* scatterbrained
atolondramiento [atolondra'mjento] *nm* bewilderment; (*insensatez*) silliness
atómico, -a [a'tomiko, a] *adj* atomic
atomizador [atomiθa'ðor] *nm* atomizer
átomo ['atomo] *nm* atom
atónito, -a [a'tonito, a] *adj* astonished, amazed
atontado, -a [aton'taðo, a] *adj* stunned; (*bobo*) silly, daft
atontar [aton'tar] *vt* to stun; **atontarse** *vr* to become confused
atormentar [atormen'tar] *vt* to torture; (*molestar*) to torment; (*acosar*) to plague, harass
atornillar [atorni'ʎar] *vt* to screw on *o* down
atosigar [atosi'ɣar] *vt* to harass, pester
atracador, a [atraka'ðor, a] *nm/f* robber
atracar [atra'kar] *vt* (*Naut*) to moor; (*robar*) to hold up, rob ▷ *vi* to moor; **atracarse** *vr*: **~se (de)** to stuff o.s. (with)
atracción [atrak'θjon] *nf* attraction
atraco [a'trako] *nm* holdup, robbery
atracón [atra'kon] *nm*: **darse** *o* **pegarse un ~ (de)** (*fam*) to stuff o.s. (with)
atractivo, -a [atrak'tiβo, a] *adj* attractive ▷ *nm* appeal; (*belleza*) attractiveness
atraer [atra'er] *vt* to attract; **dejarse ~ por** to be tempted by
atragantarse [atraɣan'tarse] *vr*: **~ (con algo)** to choke (on sth); **se me ha atragantado el chico ese/el inglés** I can't stand that boy/English
atrancar [atran'kar] *vt* (*con tranca, barra*) to bar, bolt
atrapar [atra'par] *vt* to trap; (*resfriado etc*) to catch
atrás [a'tras] *adv* (*movimiento*) back(wards); (*lugar*) behind; (*tiempo*) previously; **ir hacia ~** to go back(wards); to go to the rear; **estar ~** to be behind *o* at the back
atrasado, -a [atra'saðo, a] *adj* slow; (*pago*) overdue, late; (*país*) backward
atrasar [atra'sar] *vi* to be slow; **atrasarse** *vr* to stay behind; (*tren*) to be *o* run late; (*llegar tarde*) to be late
atraso [a'traso] *nm* slowness; lateness, delay; (*de país*) backwardness; **atrasos** *nmpl* (*Com*) arrears
atravesado, -a [atraβe'saðo, a] *adj*: **un tronco ~ en la carretera** a tree trunk lying across the road
atravesar [atraβe'sar] *vt* (*cruzar*) to cross (over); (*traspasar*) to pierce; (*período*) to go through; (*poner al través*) to lay *o* put across; **atravesarse** *vr* to come in between; (*intervenir*) to interfere
atraviese *etc* [atra'βjese] *vb ver* **atravesar**
atrayente [atra'jente] *adj* attractive
atreverse [atre'βerse] *vr* to dare; (*insolentarse*) to be insolent
atrevido, -a [atre'βiðo, a] *adj* daring; insolent
atrevimiento [atreβi'mjento] *nm* daring; insolence
atribución [atriβu'θjon] *nf* (*Lit*) attribution; **atribuciones** *nfpl* (*Pol*) powers, functions; (*Admin*) responsibilities
atribuir [atriβu'ir] *vt* to attribute; (*funciones*) to confer
atributo [atri'βuto] *nm* attribute
atril [a'tril] *nm* (*para libro*) lectern; (*Mus*) music stand
atrincherarse [atrintʃe'rarse] *vr* (*Mil*) to dig (o.s.) in; **~ en** (*fig*) to hide behind

atrocidad [atroθi'ðað] *nf* atrocity, outrage
atrofiarse [atro'fjarse] *vr* (*tb fig*) to atrophy
atropellar [atrope'ʎar] *vt* (*derribar*) to knock over *o* down; (*empujar*) to push (aside); (*Auto*) to run over *o* down; (*agraviar*) to insult; **atropellarse** *vr* to act hastily
atropello [atro'peʎo] *nm* (*Auto*) accident; (*empujón*) push; (*agravio*) wrong; (*atrocidad*) outrage
atroz [a'troθ] *adj* atrocious, awful
A.T.S. *nm/f abr* (= *Ayudante Técnico Sanitario*) nurse
atuendo [a'twendo] *nm* attire
atún [a'tun] *nm* tuna, tunny
aturdir [atur'ðir] *vt* to stun; (*suj: ruido*) to deafen; (*fig*) to dumbfound, bewilder
atusar [atu'sar] *vt* (*cortar*) to trim; (*alisar*) to smooth (down)
audacia [au'ðaθja] *nf* boldness, audacity
audaz [au'ðaθ] *adj* bold, audacious
audible [au'ðiβle] *adj* audible
audición [auði'θjon] *nf* hearing; (*Teat*) audition; ~ **radiofónica** radio concert
audiencia [au'ðjenθja] *nf* audience; (*Jur*) high court; (*Pol*): ~ **pública** public inquiry
audífono [au'ðifono] *nm* (*para sordos*) hearing aid
audiovisual [auðjoβi'swal] *adj* audio-visual
auditivo, -a [auði'tiβo, a] *adj* hearing *cpd*; (*conducto, nervio*) auditory
auditor [auði'tor] *nm* (*Jur*) judge advocate; (*Com*) auditor
auditoría [auðito'ria] *nf* audit; (*profesión*) auditing
auditorio [auði'torjo] *nm* audience; (*sala*) auditorium
auge ['auxe] *nm* boom; (*clímax*) climax; (*Econ*) expansion; **estar en** ~ to thrive
augurar [auɣu'rar] *vt* to predict; (*presagiar*) to portend
augurio [au'ɣurjo] *nm* omen
aula ['aula] *nf* classroom; (*en universidad etc*) lecture room
aullar [au'ʎar] *vi* to howl, yell
aullido [au'ʎiðo] *nm* howl, yell
aumentar [aumen'tar] *vt* to increase; (*precios*) to put up; (*producción*) to step up; (*con microscopio, anteojos*) to magnify ▷ *vi*, **aumentarse** to increase, be on the increase ▷ *vr* to increase, be on the increase
aumento [au'mento] *nm* increase; rise
aún [a'un] *adv* still, yet; ~ **está aquí** he's still here; ~ **no lo sabemos** we don't know yet; **¿no ha venido ~?** hasn't she come yet?
aun [a'un] *adv* even; ~ **así** even so; ~ **más** even *o* yet more
aunque [a'unke] *conj* though, although, even though
aúpa [a'upa] *excl* up!, come on!; (*fam*): **una función de** ~ a slap-up do; **una paliza de** ~ a good hiding
aureola [aure'ola] *nf* halo
auricular [auriku'lar] *nm* (*Tel*) earpiece, receiver; **auriculares** *nmpl* (*cascos*) headphones
aurora [au'rora] *nf* dawn; ~ **boreal(is)** northern lights *pl*
auscultar [auskul'tar] *vt* (*Med: pecho*) to listen to, sound
ausencia [au'senθja] *nf* absence
ausentarse [ausen'tarse] *vr* to go away; (*por poco tiempo*) to go out
ausente [au'sente] *adj* absent ▷ *nm/f* (*Escol*) absentee; (*Jur*) missing person
auspicios [aus'piθjos] *nmpl* auspices; (*protección*) protection *sg*
austeridad [austeri'ðað] *nf* austerity
austero, -a [aus'tero, a] *adj* austere
austral [aus'tral] *adj* southern ▷ *nm monetary unit of Argentina (1985–1991)*
Australia [aus'tralja] *nf* Australia
australiano, -a [austra'ljano, a] *adj, nm/f* Australian
Austria ['austrja] *nf* Austria
austriaco, -a [aus'trjako, a], **austríaco, -a** [aus'triako, a] *adj* Austrian ▷ *nm/f* Austrian
auténtico, -a [au'tentiko, a] *adj* authentic
autentificar [autentifi'kar] *vt* to authenticate
auto ['auto] *nm* (*coche*) car; (*Jur*) edict, decree; (*: orden*) writ; **autos** *nmpl* (*Jur*) proceedings; (*: acta*) court record *sg*; ~ **de comparecencia** summons, subpoena; ~ **de ejecución** writ of execution
autoadhesivo, -a [autoaðe'siβo, a] *adj* self-adhesive; (*sobre*) self-sealing
autobiografía [autoβjoɣra'fia] *nf* autobiography
autobomba [auto'bomba] *nm* (*RPl*) fire engine
autobronceador, a [autoβronθea'ðor, a] *adj* (self-)tanning
autobús [auto'βus] *nm* bus; ~ **de línea** long-distance coach
autocar [auto'kar] *nm* coach (*Brit*), (passenger) bus (*US*); ~ **de línea** intercity coach *or* bus
autóctono, -a [au'toktono, a] *adj* native, indigenous
autodefensa [autoðe'fensa] *nf* self-defence
autodeterminación [autoðetermina'θjon] *nf* self-determination
autodidacta [autoði'ðakta] *adj* self-taught ▷ *nm/f*: **ser un(a)** ~ to be self-taught
autoescuela [autoes'kwela] *nf* (*Esp*) driving school
autogestión [autoxes'tjon] *nf* self-management
autógrafo [au'toɣrafo] *nm* autograph
autómata [au'tomata] *nm* automaton
automáticamente [auto'matikamente] *adv* automatically
automático, -a [auto'matiko, a] *adj* automatic ▷ *nm* press stud

automatización [automatiθa'θjon] *nf*: ~ **de fábricas** factory automation; ~ **de oficinas** office automation
automotor, -triz [automo'tor, 'triz] *adj* self-propelled ▷ *nm* diesel train
automóvil [auto'moβil] *nm* (motor) car (*Brit*), automobile (*US*)
automovilismo [automoβi'lismo] *nm* (*actividad*) motoring; (*Deporte*) motor racing
automovilista [automoβi'lista] *nm/f* motorist, driver
automovilístico, -a [automoβi'listiko, a] *adj* (*industria*) car *cpd*
autonomía [autono'mia] *nf* autonomy; (*Esp Pol*) autonomy, self-government; (: *comunidad*) autonomous region
autonómico, -a [auto'nomiko, a] *adj* (*Esp Pol*) relating to autonomy, autonomous; **gobierno** ~ autonomous government
autónomo, -a [au'tonomo, a], (*Esp*) **autonómico** *adj* autonomous; (*Inform*) stand-alone, offline
autopista [auto'pista] *nf* motorway (*Brit*), freeway (*US*); ~ **de cuota** (*Am*) *o* **peaje** (*Esp*) toll (*Brit*) *o* turnpike (*US*) road
autopsia [au'topsja] *nf* post-mortem, autopsy
autor, a [au'tor, a] *nm/f* author; **los ~es del atentado** those responsible for the attack
autoridad [autori'ðað] *nf* authority; ~ **local** local authority
autoritario, -a [autori'tarjo, a] *adj* authoritarian
autorización [autoriθa'θjon] *nf* authorization
autorizado, -a [autori'θaðo, a] *adj* authorized; (*aprobado*) approved
autorizar [autori'θar] *vt* to authorize; to approve
autorretrato [autorre'trato] *nm* self-portrait
autoservicio [autoser'βiθjo] *nm* (*tienda*) self-service shop *o* store; (*restaurante*) self-service restaurant
autostop [auto'stop] *nm* hitch-hiking; **hacer** ~ to hitch-hike
autostopista [autosto'pista] *nm/f* hitch-hiker
autosuficiencia [autosufi'θjenθja] *nf* self-sufficiency
autosuficiente [autosufi'θjente] *adj* self-sufficient; (*pey*) smug
autosugestión [autosuxes'tjon] *nf* autosuggestion
autovía [auto'βia] *nf* ≈ dual carriageway (*Brit*), ≈ divided highway (*US*)
auxiliar [auksi'ljar] *vt* to help ▷ *nm/f* assistant
auxilio [auk'siljo] *nm* assistance, help; **primeros ~s** first aid *sg*
Av *abr* (= *Avenida*) Av(e)
aval [a'βal] *nm* guarantee; (*persona*) guarantor
avalancha [aβa'lantʃa] *nf* avalanche > afe
avalar [aβa'lar] *vt* (*Com etc*) to underwrite; (*fig*) to endorse
avance [a'βanθe] *vb ver* **avanzar** ▷ *nm* advance; (*pago*) advance payment; (*Cine*) trailer
avanzado, -a [aβan'θaðo, a] *adj* advanced; **de edad avanzada**, ~ **de edad** elderly
avanzar [aβan'θar] *vt, vi* to advance
avaricia [aβa'riθja] *nf* avarice, greed
avaricioso, -a [aβari'θjoso, a] *adj* avaricious, greedy
avaro, -a [a'βaro, a] *adj* miserly, mean ▷ *nm/f* miser
avasallar [aβasa'ʎar] *vt* to subdue, subjugate
Avda. *abr* (= *Avenida*) Av(e)
AVE ['aβe] *nm abr* (= *Alta Velocidad Española*) ≈ bullet train
ave ['aβe] *nf* bird; ~ **de rapiña** bird of prey
avecinarse [aβeθi'narse] *vr* (*tormenta, fig*) to approach, be on the way
avellana [aβe'ʎana] *nf* hazelnut
avellano [aβe'ʎano] *nm* hazel tree
avemaría [aβema'ria] *nm* Hail Mary, Ave Maria
avena [a'βena] *nf* oats *pl*
avenida [aβe'niða] *nf* (*calle*) avenue
avenir [aβe'nir] *vt* to reconcile; **avenirse** *vr* to come to an agreement, reach a compromise
aventajado, -a [aβenta'xaðo, a] *adj* outstanding
aventajar [aβenta'xar] *vt* (*sobrepasar*) to surpass, outstrip
aventón [aβen'ton] *nm* (*Am*) push; **pedir** ~ to hitch a lift, hitch a ride (*US*)
aventura [aβen'tura] *nf* adventure; ~ **sentimental** love affair
aventurado, -a [aβentu'raðo, a] *adj* risky
aventurero, -a [aβentu'rero, a] *adj* adventurous
avergonzar [aβerɣon'θar] *vt* to shame; (*desconcertar*) to embarrass; **avergonzarse** *vr* to be ashamed; to be embarrassed
avería [aβe'ria] *nf* (*Tec*) breakdown, fault
averiado, -a [aβe'rjaðo, a] *adj* broken-down; **"~"** "out of order"
averiar [aβe'rjar] *vt* to break; **averiarse** *vr* to break down
averiguación [aβeriɣwa'θjon] *nf* investigation
averiguar [aβeri'ɣwar] *vt* to investigate; (*descubrir*) to find out, ascertain
aversión [aβer'sjon] *nf* aversion, dislike; **cobrar ~ a** to take a strong dislike to
avestruz [aβes'truθ] *nm* ostrich
aviación [aβja'θjon] *nf* aviation; (*fuerzas aéreas*) air force
aviador, a [aβja'ðor, a] *nm/f* aviator, airman/woman
aviar [a'βjar] *vt* to prepare, get ready
avícola [a'βikola] *adj* poultry *cpd*

avicultura [aβikul'tura] *nf* poultry farming
avidez [aβi'ðeθ] *nf* avidity, eagerness
ávido, -a ['aβiðo, a] *adj* avid, eager
avinagrado, -a [aβina'ɣraðo, a] *adj* sour, acid
avinagrarse [aβina'ɣrarse] *vr* to go *o* turn sour
avío [a'βio] *nm* preparation; **avíos** *nmpl* gear *sg*, kit *sg*
avión [a'βjon] *nm* aeroplane; (*ave*) martin; **~ de reacción** jet (plane); **por ~** (*Correos*) by air mail
avioneta [aβjo'neta] *nf* light aircraft
avisar [aβi'sar] *vt* (*advertir*) to warn, notify; (*informar*) to tell; (*aconsejar*) to advise, counsel
aviso [a'βiso] *nm* warning; (*noticia*) notice; (*Com*) demand note; (*Inform*) prompt; **~ escrito** notice in writing; **sin previo ~** without warning; **estar sobre ~** to be on the look-out
avispa [a'βispa] *nf* wasp
avispado, -a [aβis'paðo, a] *adj* sharp, clever
avispero [aβis'pero] *nm* wasp's nest
avispón [aβis'pon] *nm* hornet
avistar [aβis'tar] *vt* to sight, spot
avituallar [aβitwa'ʎar] *vt* to supply with food
avivar [aβi'βar] *vt* to strengthen, intensify; **avivarse** *vr* to revive, acquire new life
axila [ak'sila] *nf* armpit
axioma [ak'sjoma] *nm* axiom
ay [ai] *excl* (*dolor*) ow!, ouch!; (*aflicción*) oh!, oh dear!; **¡ay de mi!** poor me!
aya ['aja] *nf* governess; (*niñera*) nanny
ayer [a'jer] *adv, nm* yesterday; **antes de ~** the day before yesterday; **~ por la tarde** yesterday afternoon/evening; **~ mismo** only yesterday
ayo ['ajo] *nm* tutor
ayote [a'jote] *nm* (*Am*) pumpkin
ayuda [a'juða] *nf* help, assistance; (*Med*) enema ▷ *nm* page; **~ humanitaria** humanitarian aid
ayudante, -a [aju'ðante, a] *nm/f* assistant, helper; (*Escol*) assistant; (*Mil*) adjutant
ayudar [aju'ðar] *vt* to help, assist
ayunar [aju'nar] *vi* to fast
ayunas [a'junas] *nfpl*: **estar en ~** (*no haber comido*) to be fasting; (*ignorar*) to be in the dark
ayuno [a'juno] *nm* fast; fasting
ayuntamiento [ajunta'mjento] *nm* (*consejo*) town/city council; (*edificio*) town/city hall; (*cópula*) sexual intercourse
azabache [aθa'βatʃe] *nm* jet
azada [a'θaða] *nf* hoe
azafata [aθa'fata] *nf* air hostess (*Brit*) *o* stewardess
azafrán [aθa'fran] *nm* saffron
azahar [aθa'ar] *nm* orange/lemon blossom
azalea [aθa'lea] *nf* azalea
azar [a'θar] *nm* (*casualidad*) chance, fate; (*desgracia*) misfortune, accident; **por ~** by chance; **al ~** at random
azogue [a'θoɣe] *nm* mercury
azoramiento [aθora'mjento] *nm* alarm; (*confusión*) confusion
azorar [aθo'rar] *vt* to alarm; **azorarse** *vr* to get alarmed
Azores [a'θores] *nfpl*: **las (Islas) ~** the Azores
azotar [aθo'tar] *vt* to whip, beat; (*pegar*) to spank
azote [a'θote] *nm* (*látigo*) whip; (*latigazo*) lash, stroke; (*en las nalgas*) spank; (*calamidad*) calamity
azotea [aθo'tea] *nf* (flat) roof
azteca [aθ'teka] *adj, nm/f* Aztec
azúcar [a'θukar] *nm* sugar
azucarado, -a [aθuka'raðo, a] *adj* sugary, sweet
azucarero, -a [aθuka'rero, a] *adj* sugar *cpd* ▷ *nm* sugar bowl
azucena [aθu'θena] *nf* white lily
azufre [a'θufre] *nm* sulphur
azul [a'θul] *adj, nm* blue; **~ celeste/marino** sky/navy blue
azulejo [aθu'lexo] *nm* tile
azuzar [aθu'θar] *vt* to incite, egg on

b

B.A. *abr* (= *Buenos Aires*) B.A.
baba ['baβa] *nf* spittle, saliva; **se le caía la ~** (*fig*) he was thrilled to bits
babear [baβe'ar] *vi* (*echar saliva*) to slobber; (*niño*) to dribble; (*fig*) to drool, slaver
babel [ba'βel] *nm o f* bedlam
babero [ba'βero] *nm* bib
babor [ba'βor] *nm* port (side); **a ~** to port
babosada [baβo'saða] *nf*: **decir ~s** (*Am*: *fam*) to talk rubbish
baboso, -a [ba'βoso, a] *adj* slobbering; (*Zool*) slimy; (*Am*) silly ▷ *nm/f* (*Am*) fool
babucha [ba'βutʃa] *nf* slipper
baca ['baka] *nf* (*Auto*) luggage *o* roof rack
bacalao [baka'lao] *nm* cod(fish)
bache ['batʃe] *nm* pothole, rut; (*fig*) bad patch
bachillerato [batʃiʎe'rato] *nm two-year advanced secondary school course*; *ver tb* **sistema educativo**
bacinica [baθi'nika], **bacinilla** [baθi'niʎa] *nf* potty
bacteria [bak'terja] *nf* bacterium, germ
bacteriológico, -a [bakterjo'loxico, a] *adj* bacteriological; **guerra bacteriológica** germ warfare
báculo ['bakulo] *nm* stick, staff; (*fig*) support
bádminton ['baðminton] *nm* badminton
bafle ['bafle], **baffle** ['baffle] *nm* (*Elec*) speaker
bagaje [ba'ɣaxe] *nm* baggage; (*fig*) background
bagatela [baɣa'tela] *nf* trinket, trifle
Bahama [ba'ama]: **las (Islas) ~, las ~s** *nfpl* the Bahamas
bahía [ba'ia] *nf* bay
bailar [bai'lar] *vt, vi* to dance
bailarín, -ina [baila'rin, ina] *nm/f* dancer; (*de ballet*) ballet dancer
baile ['baile] *nm* dance; (*formal*) ball
baja ['baxa] *nf* drop, fall; (*Econ*) slump; (*Mil*) casualty; (*paro*) redundancy; **dar de ~** (*soldado*) to discharge; (*empleado*) to dismiss, sack; **darse de ~** (*retirarse*) to drop out; (*Med*) to go sick; (*dimitir*) to resign; **estar de ~** (*enfermo*) to be off sick; (*Bolsa*) to be dropping *o* falling; **jugar a la ~** (*Econ*) to speculate on a fall in prices; *ver tb* **bajo**
bajada [ba'xaða] *nf* descent; (*camino*) slope; (*de aguas*) ebb
bajamar [baxa'mar] *nf* low tide
bajar [ba'xar] *vi* to go *o* come down; (*temperatura, precios*) to drop, fall ▷ *vt* (*cabeza*) to bow; (*escalera*) to go *o* come down; (*radio etc*) to turn down; (*precio, voz*) to lower; (*llevar abajo*) to take down; **bajarse** *vr* (*de vehículo*) to get out; (*de autobús*) to get off; **~ de** (*coche*) to get out of; (*autobús*) to get off; **~le los humos a algn** (*fig*) to cut sb down to size; **~se algo de Internet** to download sth from the internet
bajeza [ba'xeθa] *nf* baseness; (*una bajeza*) vile deed
bajío [ba'xio] *nm* shoal, sandbank; (*Am*) lowlands *pl*
bajo, -a ['baxo, a] *adj* (*terreno*) low(-lying); (*mueble, número, precio*) low; (*piso*) ground *cpd*; (*de estatura*) small, short; (*color*) pale; (*sonido*) faint, soft, low; (*voz, tono*) deep; (*metal*) base; (*humilde*) low, humble ▷ *adv* (*hablar*) softly, quietly; (*volar*) low ▷ *prep* under, below, underneath ▷ *nm* (*Mus*) bass; **hablar en voz baja** to whisper; **~ la lluvia** in the rain
bajón [ba'xon] *nm* fall, drop
bakalao [baka'lao] *nm* (*Mus*) rave music
bala ['bala] *nf* bullet; **~ de goma** plastic bullet
balacear [balaθe'ar] *vt* (*Am, CAm*) to shoot
baladí [bala'ði] *adj* trivial
balance [ba'lanθe] *nm* (*Com*) balance; (*: libro*) balance sheet; (*: cuenta general*) stocktaking; **~ de comprobación** trial balance; **~ consolidado** consolidated balance sheet; **hacer ~** to take stock
balancear [balanθe'ar] *vt* to balance ▷ *vi* to swing (to and fro); (*vacilar*) to hesitate; **balancearse** *vr* to swing (to and fro); (*vacilar*) to hesitate
balanceo [balan'θeo] *nm* swinging
balanza [ba'lanθa] *nf* scales *pl*, balance; **~ comercial** balance of trade; **~ de pagos/de poder(es)** balance of payments/of power; (*Astro*): **B~** Libra
balar [ba'lar] *vi* to bleat
balaustrada [balaus'traða] *nf* balustrade; (*pasamanos*) banister

balazo [ba'laθo] *nm* (*tiro*) shot; (*herida*) bullet wound
balbucear [balβuθe'ar] *vi, vt* to stammer, stutter
balbuceo [balβu'θeo] *nm* stammering, stuttering
balbucir [balβu'θir] *vi, vt* to stammer, stutter
balcánico, -a [bal'kaniko, a] *adj* Balkan
balcón [bal'kon] *nm* balcony
baldar [bal'dar] *vt* to cripple; (*agotar*) to exhaust
balde ['balde] *nm* (*esp Am*) bucket, pail; **de ~** *adv* (for) free, for nothing; **en ~** *adv* in vain
baldío, -a [bal'dio, a] *adj* uncultivated; (*terreno*) waste; (*inútil*) vain ▷ *nm* wasteland
baldosa [bal'dosa] *nf* (*azulejo*) floor tile; (*grande*) flagstone
baldosín [baldo'sin] *nm* tile
Baleares [bale'ares] *nfpl*: **las (Islas) ~** the Balearics, the Balearic Islands
balero [ba'lero] *nm* (*Am: juguete*) cup-and-ball toy
balido [ba'liðo] *nm* bleat, bleating
balín [ba'lin] *nm* pellet; **balines** *nmpl* buckshot *sg*
balística [ba'listika] *nf* ballistics *pl*
baliza [ba'liθa] *nf* (*Aviat*) beacon; (*Naut*) buoy
ballena [ba'ʎena] *nf* whale
ballesta [ba'ʎesta] *nf* crossbow; (*Auto*) spring
ballet (*pl* **ballets**) [ba'le [ba'les] *nm* ballet
balneario, -a [balne'arjo, a] *adj*: **estación balnearia** (bathing) resort ▷ *nm* spa, health resort; (*Am: en la costa*) seaside resort
balón [ba'lon] *nm* ball
baloncesto [balon'θesto] *nm* basketball
balonmano [balon'mano] *nm* handball
balonred [balon'reð] *nm* netball
balonvolea [balombo'lea] *nm* volleyball
balsa ['balsa] *nf* raft; (*Bot*) balsa wood
bálsamo ['balsamo] *nm* balsam, balm
baluarte [ba'lwarte] *nm* bastion, bulwark
bambolearse [bambole'arse] *vr* to swing, sway; (*silla*) to wobble
bamboleo [bambo'leo] *nm* swinging, swaying; wobbling
bambú [bam'bu] *nm* bamboo
banana [ba'nana] *nf* (*Am*) banana
banano [ba'nano] *nm* (*Am*) banana tree; (*fruta*) banana
banca ['banka] *nf* (*asiento*) bench; (*Com*) banking
bancario, -a [ban'karjo, a] *adj* banking *cpd*, bank *cpd*; **giro ~** bank draft
bancarrota [banka'rrota] *nf* bankruptcy; **declararse en** *o* **hacer ~** to go bankrupt
banco ['banko] *nm* bench; (*Escol*) desk; (*Com*) bank; (*Geo*) stratum; **~ comercial** *o* **mercantil** commercial bank; **~ por acciones** joint-stock bank; **~ de crédito/de ahorros** credit/savings bank; **~ de arena** sandbank; **~ de datos** (*Inform*) data bank; **~ de hielo** iceberg
banda ['banda] *nf* band; (*cinta*) ribbon; (*pandilla*) gang; (*Mus*) brass band; (*Naut*) side, edge; **la ~ ancha** broadband; **la B~ Oriental** Uruguay; **~ sonora** soundtrack; **~ transportadora** conveyor belt
bandada [ban'daða] *nf* (*de pájaros*) flock; (*de peces*) shoal
bandazo [ban'daθo] *nm*: **dar ~s** (*coche*) to veer from side to side
bandeja [ban'dexa] *nf* tray; **~ de entrada/salida** in-tray/out-tray
bandera [ban'dera] *nf* (*de tela*) flag; (*estandarte*) banner; **izar la ~** to hoist the flag
banderilla [bande'riʎa] *nf* banderilla; (*tapa*) *savoury appetizer (served on a cocktail stick)*
banderín [bande'rin] *nm* pennant, small flag
banderola [bande'rola] *nf* (*Mil*) pennant
bandido [ban'diðo] *nm* bandit
bando ['bando] *nm* (*edicto*) edict, proclamation; (*facción*) faction; **pasar al otro ~** to change sides; **los ~s** (*Rel*) the banns
bandolera [bando'lera] *nf*: **llevar en ~** to wear across one's chest; **bolsa de ~** shoulder bag
bandolero [bando'lero] *nm* bandit, brigand
banquero [ban'kero] *nm* banker
banqueta [ban'keta] *nf* stool; (*Am: acera*) pavement (*Brit*), sidewalk (*US*)
banquete [ban'kete] *nm* banquet; (*para convidados*) formal dinner; **~ de boda** wedding reception
banquillo [ban'kiʎo] *nm* (*Jur*) dock, prisoner's bench; (*banco*) bench; (*para los pies*) footstool
banquina [ban'kina] *nf* (*RPl*) hard shoulder (*Brit*), berm (*US*)
bañadera [baɲa'ðera] *nf* (*Am*) bath(tub)
bañador [baɲa'ðor] *nm* swimming costume (*Brit*), bathing suit (*US*)
bañar [ba'ɲar] *vt* (*niño*) to bath, bathe; (*objeto*) to dip; (*de barniz*) to coat; **bañarse** *vr* (*en el mar*) to bathe, swim; (*en la bañera*) to have a bath
bañera [ba'ɲera] *nf* (*Esp*) bath(tub)
bañero, -a [ba'ɲero, a] *nm/f* lifeguard ▷ *nf* bath(tub)
bañista [ba'ɲista] *nm/f* bather
baño ['baɲo] *nm* (*en bañera*) bath; (*en río, mar*) dip, swim; (*cuarto*) bathroom; (*bañera*) bath(tub); (*capa*) coating; **darse** *o* **tomar un ~** (*en bañera*) to have *o* take a bath; (*en mar, piscina*) to have a swim; **~ María** bain-marie
baptista [bap'tista] *nm/f* Baptist
baqueta [ba'keta] *nf* (*Mus*) drumstick
bar [bar] *nm* bar
barahúnda [bara'unda] *nf* uproar, hubbub
baraja [ba'raxa] *nf* pack (of cards)
barajar [bara'xar] *vt* (*naipes*) to shuffle; (*fig*) to jumble up
baranda [ba'randa], **barandilla** [baran'diʎa] *nf* rail, railing
barata [ba'rata] *nf* (*Am*) (bargain) sale

baratija [bara'tixa] *nf* trinket; (*fig*) trifle; **baratijas** *nfpl* (*Com*) cheap goods
baratillo [bara'tiʎo] *nm* (*tienda*) junk shop; (*subasta*) bargain sale; (*conjunto de cosas*) second-hand goods *pl*
barato, -a [ba'rato, a] *adj* cheap ▷ *adv* cheap, cheaply
baraúnda [bara'unda] *nf* = **barahúnda**
barba ['barβa] *nf* (*mentón*) chin; (*pelo*) beard; **tener ~** to be unshaven; **hacer algo en las ~s de algn** to do sth under sb's very nose; **reírse en las ~s de algn** to laugh in sb's face
barbacoa [barβa'koa] *nf* (*parrilla*) barbecue; (*carne*) barbecued meat
barbaridad [barβari'ðað] *nf* barbarity; (*acto*) barbarism; (*atrocidad*) outrage; **una ~ de** (*fam*) loads of; **¡qué ~!** (*fam*) how awful!; **cuesta una ~** (*fam*) it costs a fortune
barbarie [bar'βarje] *nf*, **barbarismo** [barβa'rismo] *nm* barbarism; (*crueldad*) barbarity
bárbaro, -a ['barβaro, a] *adj* barbarous, cruel; (*grosero*) rough, uncouth ▷ *nm/f* barbarian ▷ *adv*: **lo pasamos ~** (*fam*) we had a great time; **¡qué ~!** (*fam*) how marvellous!; **un éxito ~** (*fam*) a terrific success; **es un tipo ~** (*fam*) he's a great bloke
barbecho [bar'βetʃo] *nm* fallow land
barbero [bar'βero] *nm* barber, hairdresser
barbilla [bar'βiʎa] *nf* chin, tip of the chin
barbitúrico [barβi'turiko] *nm* barbiturate
barbo ['barβo] *nm*: **~ de mar** red mullet
barbudo, -a [bar'βuðo, a] *adj* bearded
barca ['barka] *nf* (small) boat; **~ pesquera** fishing boat; **~ de pasaje** ferry
barcaza [bar'kaθa] *nf* barge; **~ de desembarco** landing craft
Barcelona [barθe'lona] *nf* Barcelona
barcelonés, -esa [barθelo'nes, esa] *adj* of *o* from Barcelona ▷ *nm/f* native *o* inhabitant of Barcelona
barco ['barko] *nm* boat; (*buque*) ship; (*Com etc*) vessel; **~ de carga** cargo boat; **~ de guerra** warship; **~ de vela** sailing ship; **ir en ~** to go by boat
barda ['barða] *nf* (*Am: de madera*) fence
baremo [ba'remo] *nm* scale; (*tabla de cuentas*) ready reckoner
barítono [ba'ritono] *nm* baritone
barman ['barman] *nm* barman
barniz [bar'niθ] *nm* varnish; (*en la loza*) glaze; (*fig*) veneer
barnizar [barni'θar] *vt* to varnish; (*loza*) to glaze
barómetro [ba'rometro] *nm* barometer
barón [ba'ron] *nm* baron
baronesa [baro'nesa] *nf* baroness
barquero [bar'kero] *nm* boatman
barquillo [bar'kiʎo] *nm* cone, cornet
barra ['barra] *nf* bar, rod; (*Jur*) rail; (*: banquillo*) dock; (*de un bar, café*) bar; (*de pan*) French loaf; (*palanca*) lever; **~ de carmín** *o* **de labios** lipstick; **~ de herramientas** (*Inform*) toolbar; **~ de espaciado** (*Inform*) space bar; **~ inversa** backslash; **~ libre** free bar; **no pararse en ~s** to stick *o* stop at nothing
barraca [ba'rraka] *nf* hut, cabin; (*en Valencia*) thatched farmhouse; (*en feria*) booth
barranca [ba'rranka] *nf* ravine, gully
barranco [ba'rranko] *nm* ravine; (*fig*) difficulty
barrena [ba'rrena] *nf* drill
barrenar [barre'nar] *vt* to drill (through), bore
barrendero, -a [barren'dero, a] *nm/f* street-sweeper
barreno [ba'rreno] *nm* large drill
barrer [ba'rrer] *vt* to sweep; (*quitar*) to sweep away; (*Mil, Naut*) to sweep, rake (with gunfire) ▷ *vi* to sweep up
barrera [ba'rrera] *nf* barrier; (*Mil*) barricade; (*Ferro*) crossing gate; **poner ~s a** to hinder; **~ arancelaria** (*Com*) tariff barrier; **~ comercial** (*Com*) trade barrier
barriada [ba'rrjaða] *nf* quarter, district
barricada [barri'kaða] *nf* barricade
barrida [ba'rriða] *nf*, **barrido** [ba'rriðo] *nm* sweep, sweeping
barriga [ba'rriɣa] *nf* belly; (*panza*) paunch; (*vientre*) guts *pl*; **echar ~** to get middle-age spread
barrigón, -ona [barri'ɣon, ona], **barrigudo, -a** [barri'ɣuðo, a] *adj* potbellied
barril [ba'rril] *nm* barrel, cask; **cerveza de ~** draught beer
barrio ['barrjo] *nm* (*vecindad*) area, neighborhood (*US*); (*en las afueras*) suburb; **~s bajos** poor quarter *sg*; **~ chino** red-light district
barro ['barro] *nm* (*lodo*) mud; (*objetos*) earthenware; (*Med*) pimple
barroco, -a [ba'rroko, a] *adj* Baroque; (*fig*) elaborate ▷ *nm* Baroque
barrote [ba'rrote] *nm* (*de ventana etc*) bar
barruntar [barrun'tar] *vt* (*conjeturar*) to guess; (*presentir*) to suspect
barrunto [ba'rrunto] *nm* guess; suspicion
bartola [bar'tola] *nf*: **a la ~**, **tirarse a la ~** to take it easy, be lazy
bártulos ['bartulos] *nmpl* things, belongings
barullo [ba'ruʎo] *nm* row, uproar
basar [ba'sar] *vt* to base; **basarse** *vr*: **~se en** to be based on
basca ['baska] *nf* nausea
báscula ['baskula] *nf* (platform) scales *pl*
base ['base] *nf* base; **a ~ de** on the basis of, based on; (*mediante*) by means of; **a ~ de bien** in abundance; **~ de conocimiento** knowledge base; **~ de datos** database
básico, -a ['basiko, a] *adj* basic
basílica [ba'silika] *nf* basilica
basket, básquet ['basket] *nm* basketball
básquetbol ['basketbol] *nm* (*Am*) basketball

PALABRA CLAVE

bastante [bas'tante] *adj* **1** (*suficiente*) enough; **bastante dinero** enough *o* sufficient money; **bastantes libros** enough books **2** (*valor intensivo*): **bastante gente** quite a lot of people; **tener bastante calor** to be rather hot; **hace bastante tiempo que ocurrió** it happened quite *o* rather a long time ago ▷ *adv*: **bastante bueno/malo** quite good/ rather bad; **bastante rico** pretty rich; **(lo) bastante inteligente (como) para hacer algo** clever enough *o* sufficiently clever to do sth; **voy a tardar bastante** I'm going to be a while *o* quite some time

bastar [bas'tar] *vi* to be enough *o* sufficient; **bastarse** *vr* to be self-sufficient; **~ para** to be enough to; **¡basta!** (that's) enough!
bastardilla [bastar'ðiʎa] *nf* italics *pl*
bastardo, -a [bas'tarðo, a] *adj, nm/f* bastard
bastidor [basti'ðor] *nm* frame; (*de coche*) chassis; (*Arte*) stretcher; (*Teat*) wing; **entre ~es** behind the scenes
basto, -a ['basto, a] *adj* coarse, rough ▷ *nmpl*: **~s** (*Naipes*) *one of the suits in the Spanish card deck*
bastón [bas'ton] *nm* stick, staff; (*para pasear*) walking stick; **~ de mando** baton
bastoncillo [baston'θiʎo] *nm* (*tb*: **~ de algodón**) cotton bud
basura [ba'sura] *nf* rubbish, refuse (*Brit*), garbage (*US*) ▷ *adj*: **comida/televisión ~** junk food/TV
basurero [basu'rero] *nm* (*hombre*) dustman (*Brit*), garbage collector *o* man (*US*); (*lugar*) rubbish dump; (*cubo*) (rubbish) bin (*Brit*), trash can (*US*)
bata ['bata] *nf* (*gen*) dressing gown; (*cubretodo*) smock, overall; (*Med, Tec etc*) lab(oratory) coat
batalla [ba'taʎa] *nf* battle; **de ~** for everyday use; **~ campal** pitched battle
batallar [bata'ʎar] *vi* to fight
batallón [bata'ʎon] *nm* battalion
batata [ba'tata] *nf* (*Am: Culin*) sweet potato
bate ['bate] *nm* (*Deporte*) bat
bateador [batea'ðor] *nm* (*Deporte*) batter, batsman
batería [bate'ria] *nf* battery; (*Mus*) drums *pl*; (*Teat*) footlights *pl*; **~ de cocina** kitchen utensils *pl*
batido, -a [ba'tiðo, a] *adj* (*camino*) beaten, well-trodden ▷ *nm* (*Culin*) batter; **~ (de leche)** milk shake ▷ *nf* (*Am*) (police) raid
batidora [bati'ðora] *nf* beater, mixer; **~ eléctrica** food mixer, blender
batir [ba'tir] *vt* to beat, strike; (*vencer*) to beat, defeat; (*revolver*) to beat, mix; (*pelo*) to back-comb; **batirse** *vr* to fight; **~ palmas** to clap, applaud
baturro, -a [ba'turro, a] *nm/f* Aragonese peasant
batuta [ba'tuta] *nf* baton; **llevar la ~** (*fig*) to be the boss
baúl [ba'ul] *nm* trunk; (*Am Auto*) boot (*Brit*), trunk (*US*)
bautismo [bau'tismo] *nm* baptism, christening
bautizar [bauti'θar] *vt* to baptize, christen; (*fam: diluir*) to water down; (*dar apodo*) to dub
bautizo [bau'tiθo] *nm* baptism, christening
bayeta [ba'jeta] *nf* (*trapo*) floor cloth; (*Am: pañal*) nappy (*Brit*), diaper (*US*)
bayo, -a ['bajo, a] *adj* bay
bayoneta [bajo'neta] *nf* bayonet
baza ['baθa] *nf* trick; **meter ~** to butt in
bazar [ba'θar] *nm* bazaar
bazo ['baθo] *nm* spleen
bazofia [ba'θofja] *nf* pigswill (*Brit*), hogwash (*US*); (*libro etc*) trash
BCE *nm abr* (= *Banco Central Europeo*) ECB
be [be] *nf name of the letter B*; **be chica/grande** (*Am*) V/B; **be larga** (*Am*) B
beatificar [beatifi'kar] *vt* to beatify
beato, -a [be'ato, a] *adj* blessed; (*piadoso*) pious
bebé (*pl* **bebés**) [be'βe, be'βes], **bebe** (*Am: pl* **bebes**) ['beβe, 'beβes] *nm* baby; **~ de diseño** designer baby
bebedero, -a [beβe'ðero, a] *nm* (*para animales*) drinking trough
bebedor, a [beβe'ðor, a] *adj* hard-drinking
bebé-probeta [be'βe-pro'βeta] (*pl* **bebés-probeta**) *nm/f* test-tube baby
beber [be'βer] *vt, vi* to drink; **~ a sorbos/ tragos** to sip/gulp; **se lo bebió todo** he drank it all up
bebido, -a [be'βiðo, a] *adj* drunk ▷ *nf* drink
beca ['beka] *nf* grant, scholarship
becado, -a [be'kaðo, a] *nm/f* = **becario**
becario, -a [be'karjo, a] *nm/f* scholarship holder, grant holder
bechamel [betʃa'mel] *nf* = **besamel**
bedel [be'ðel] *nm* porter, janitor; (*Univ*) porter
beduino, -a [be'ðwino, a] *adj, nm/f* Bedouin
beige ['beix], **beis** ['beis] *adj, nm* beige
béisbol ['beisβol] *nm* baseball
beldad [bel'dað] *nf* beauty
Belén [be'len] *nm* Bethlehem; **belén** (*de Navidad*) nativity scene, crib
belga ['belɣa] *adj, nm/f* Belgian
Bélgica ['belxika] *nf* Belgium
Belice [be'liθe] *nm* Belize
bélico, -a ['beliko, a] *adj* (*actitud*) warlike
belicoso, -a [beli'koso, a] *adj* (*guerrero*) warlike; (*agresivo*) aggressive, bellicose
beligerante [belixe'rante] *adj* belligerent
bellaco, -a [be'ʎako, a] *adj* sly, cunning ▷ *nm* villain, rogue
bellaquería [beʎake'ria] *nf* (*acción*) dirty trick; (*calidad*) wickedness
belleza [be'ʎeθa] *nf* beauty
bello, -a ['beʎo, a] *adj* beautiful, lovely; **Bellas Artes** Fine Art *sg*

bellota [be'ʎota] *nf* acorn

bemol [be'mol] *nm* (*Mus*) flat; **esto tiene ~es** (*fam*) this is a tough one

bencina [ben'sina] *nf* (*Am*: *gasolina*) petrol (*Brit*), gas (*US*)

bendecir [bende'θir] *vt* to bless; **~ la mesa** to say grace

bendición [bendi'θjon] *nf* blessing

bendito, -a [ben'dito, a] *pp de* **bendecir** ▷ *adj* (*santo*) blessed; (*agua*) holy; (*afortunado*) lucky; (*feliz*) happy; (*sencillo*) simple ▷ *nm/f* simple soul; **¡~ sea Dios!** thank goodness!; **es un ~** he's sweet; **dormir como un ~** to sleep like a log

benedictino, -a [beneðik'tino, a] *adj, nm* Benedictine

beneficencia [benefi'θenθja] *nf* charity

beneficiario, -a [benefi'θjarjo, a] *nm/f* beneficiary; (*de cheque*) payee

beneficio [bene'fiθjo] *nm* (*bien*) benefit, advantage; (*Com*) profit, gain; **a ~ de** for the benefit of; **en ~ propio** to one's own advantage; **~ bruto/neto** gross/net profit; **~ por acción** earnings *pl* per share

beneficioso, -a [benefi'θjoso, a] *adj* beneficial

benéfico, -a [be'nefiko, a] *adj* charitable; **sociedad benéfica** charity (organization)

beneplácito [bene'plaθito] *nm* approval, consent

benevolencia [beneβo'lenθja] *nf* benevolence, kindness

benévolo, -a [be'neβolo, a] *adj* benevolent, kind

benigno, -a [be'niɣno, a] *adj* kind; (*suave*) mild; (*Med*: *tumor*) benign, non-malignant

beodo, -a [be'oðo, a] *adj* drunk ▷ *nm/f* drunkard

berberecho [berβe'retʃo] *nm* cockle

berenjena [beren'xena] *nf* aubergine (*Brit*), eggplant (*US*)

Berlín [ber'lin] *nm* Berlin

berlinés, -esa [berli'nes, esa] *adj* of *o* from Berlin ▷ *nm/f* Berliner

berlinesa [berli'nesa] *nf* (*Am*) doughnut, donut (*US*)

bermejo, -a [ber'mexo, a] *adj* red

bermudas [ber'muðas] *nfpl* Bermuda shorts

berrear [berre'ar] *vi* to bellow, low

berrido [be'rriðo] *nm* bellow(ing)

berrinche [be'rrintʃe] *nm* (*fam*) temper, tantrum

berro ['berro] *nm* watercress

berza ['berθa] *nf* cabbage; **~ lombarda** red cabbage

besamel [besa'mel], **besamela** [besa'mela] *nf* (*Culin*) white sauce, bechamel sauce

besar [be'sar] *vt* to kiss; (*fig*: *tocar*) to graze; **besarse** *vr* to kiss (one another)

beso ['beso] *nm* kiss

bestia ['bestja] *nf* beast, animal; (*fig*) idiot; **~ de carga** beast of burden; **¡~!** you idiot!; **¡no seas ~!** (*bruto*) don't be such a brute!; (*idiota*) don't be such an idiot!

bestial [bes'tjal] *adj* bestial; (*fam*) terrific

bestialidad [bestjali'ðað] *nf* bestiality; (*fam*) stupidity

besugo [be'suɣo] *nm* sea bream; (*fam*) idiot

besuquear [besuke'ar] *vt* to cover with kisses; **besuquearse** *vr* to kiss and cuddle

betabel [beta'bel] *nm* (*Am*) beetroot (*Brit*), beet (*US*)

betún [be'tun] *nm* shoe polish; (*Química*) bitumen, asphalt

biberón [biβe'ron] *nm* feeding bottle

Biblia ['biβlja] *nf* Bible

bibliografía [biβljoɣra'fia] *nf* bibliography

biblioteca [biβljo'teka] *nf* library; (*estantes*) bookcase, bookshelves *pl*; **~ de consulta** reference library

bibliotecario, -a [biβljote'karjo, a] *nm/f* librarian

bicarbonato [bikarβo'nato] *nm* bicarbonate

bíceps ['biθeps] *nm inv* biceps

bicho ['bitʃo] *nm* (*animal*) small animal; (*sabandija*) bug, insect; (*Taur*) bull; **~ raro** (*fam*) queer fish

bici ['biθi] *nf* (*fam*) bike

bicicleta [biθi'kleta] *nf* bicycle, cycle; **ir en ~** to cycle; **~ estática/de montaña** exercise/mountain bike

bidé [bi'ðe] *nm* bidet

bidón [bi'ðon] *nm* (*grande*) drum; (*pequeño*) can

PALABRA CLAVE

bien [bjen] *nm* **1** (*bienestar*) good; **te lo digo por tu bien** I'm telling you for your own good; **el bien y el mal** good and evil

2 (*posesión*): **bienes** goods; **bienes de consumo/equipo** consumer/capital goods; **bienes inmuebles** *o* **raíces/bienes muebles** real estate *sg*/personal property *sg*

▷ *adv* **1** (*de manera satisfactoria, correcta etc*) well; **trabaja/come bien** she works/eats well; **contestó bien** he answered correctly; **oler bien** to smell nice *o* good; **me siento bien** I feel fine; **no me siento bien** I don't feel very well; **se está bien aquí** it's nice here

2 (*frases*): **hiciste bien en llamarme** you were right to call me

3 (*valor intensivo*) very; **un cuarto bien caliente** a nice warm room; **bien de veces** lots of times; **bien se ve que ...** it's quite clear that ...

4: **estar bien**: **estoy muy bien aquí** I feel very happy here; **¿te encuentras bien?** are you all right?; **te está bien la falda** (*ser la talla*) the skirt fits you; (*sentar*) the skirt suits you; **el libro está muy bien** the book is really good; **está bien que vengan** it's all right for them to come; **¡está bien! lo haré** oh all right, I'll do it; **ya está bien de quejas** that's quite enough complaining

5 (*de buena gana*): **yo bien que iría pero ...** I'd gladly go but ...
▷ *excl*: **¡bien!** (*aprobación*) OK!; **¡muy bien!** well done!; **¡qué bien!** great!; **bien, gracias, ¿y usted?** fine thanks, and you?
▷ *adj inv*: **niño bien** rich kid; **gente bien** posh people
▷ *conj* 1: **bien ... bien**: **bien en coche bien en tren** either by car or by train
2: **no bien** (*esp Am*): **no bien llegue te llamaré** as soon as I arrive I'll call you
3: **si bien** even though; *ver tb* **más**

bienal [bje'nal] *adj* biennial
bienaventurado, -a [bjenaβentu'raðo, a] *adj* (*feliz*) happy; (*afortunado*) fortunate; (*Rel*) blessed
bienestar [bjenes'tar] *nm* well-being; **estado de ~** welfare state
bienhechor, a [bjene'tʃor, a] *adj* beneficent ▷ *nm/f* benefactor/benefactress
bienvenido, -a [bjembe'niðo, a] *adj* welcome ▷ *excl* welcome! ▷ *nf* welcome; **dar la bienvenida a algn** to welcome sb
bies ['bjes] *nm*: **falda al ~** bias-cut skirt; **cortar al ~** to cut on the bias
bife ['bife] *nm* (*Am*) steak
bifocal [bifo'kal] *adj* bifocal
bifurcación [bifurka'θjon] *nf* fork; (*Ferro, Inform*) branch
bifurcarse [bifur'karse] *vr* to fork
bigamia [bi'ɣamja] *nf* bigamy
bígamo, -a ['biɣamo, a] *adj* bigamous ▷ *nm/f* bigamist
bigote [bi'ɣote] *nm* (*tb*: **~s**) moustache
bigotudo, -a [biɣo'tuðo, a] *adj* with a big moustache
bikini [bi'kini] *nm* bikini; (*Culin*) toasted cheese and ham sandwich
bilateral [bilate'ral] *adj* bilateral
bilingüe [bi'lingwe] *adj* bilingual
billar [bi'ʎar] *nm* billiards *sg*; **billares** *nmpl* (*lugar*) billiard hall; (*galería de atracciones*) amusement arcade; **~ americano** pool
billete [bi'ʎete] *nm* ticket; (*de banco*) banknote (*Brit*), bill (*US*); (*carta*) note; **~ sencillo, ~ de ida solamente/~ de ida y vuelta** single (*Brit*) *o* one-way (*US*) ticket/return (*Brit*) *o* round-trip (*US*) ticket; **sacar (un) ~** to get a ticket; **un ~ de cinco libras** a five-pound note; **~ electrónico** e-ticket
billetera [biʎe'tera] *nf*, **billetero** [biʎe'tero] *nm* wallet
billón [bi'ʎon] *nm* billion
bimensual [bimen'swal] *adj* twice monthly
bimotor, a [bimo'tor, a] *adj* twin-engined ▷ *nm* twin-engined plane
bingo ['bingo] *nm* (*juego*) bingo; (*sala*) bingo hall
binóculo [bi'nokulo] *nm* pince-nez
binomio [bi'nomjo] *nm* (*Mat*) binomial
biocarburante [biokarβu'rante], **biocombustible** [biokomβus'tiβle] *nm* biofuel
biodegradable [bioðeɣra'ðaβle] *adj* biodegradable
biodiversidad [bioðiβersi'ðað] *nf* biodiversity
biografía [bjoɣra'fia] *nf* biography
biográfico, -a [bio'ɣrafiko, a] *adj* biographical
biógrafo, -a [bi'oɣrafo, a] *nm/f* biographer
biología [biolo'xia] *nf* biology
biológico, -a [bio'loxiko, a] *adj* biological; (*cultivo, producto*) organic; **guerra biológica** biological warfare
biólogo, -a [bi'oloɣo, a] *nm/f* biologist
biométrico, -a [bio'metriko, a] *adj* biometric
biombo ['bjombo] *nm* (folding) screen
biopsia [bi'opsja] *nf* biopsy
biosfera [bios'fera] *nf* biosphere
bioterrorismo [bioterro'rismo] *nm* bioterrorism
bipolar [bipo'lar] *adj* (*Med*) bipolar
biquini [bi'kini] *nm* = **bikini**
birlar [bir'lar] *vt* (*fam*) to pinch
Birmania [bir'manja] *nf* Burma
birome [bi'rome] *nf* (*Am*) ballpoint (pen)
birria ['birrja] *nf* (*fam*): **ser una ~** (*película, libro*) to be rubbish; **ir hecho una ~** to be *o* look a sight
bis [bis] *excl* encore! ▷ *nm* encore ▷ *adv* (*dos veces*) twice; **viven en el 27 ~** they live at 27a
bisabuelo, -a [bisa'βwelo, a] *nm/f* great-grandfather/mother; **bisabuelos** *nmpl* great-grandparents
bisagra [bi'saɣra] *nf* hinge
bisbisar [bisβi'sar], **bisbisear** [bisβise'ar] *vt* to mutter, mumble
bisexual [bisek'swal] *adj, nm/f* bisexual
bisiesto [bi'sjesto] *adj*: **año ~** leap year
bisnieto, -a [bis'njeto, a] *nm/f* great-grandson/daughter; **bisnietos** *nmpl* great-grandchildren
bisonte [bi'sonte] *nm* bison
bistec [bis'tek], **bisté** [bis'te] *nm* steak
bisturí [bistu'ri] *nm* scalpel
bisutería [bisute'ria] *nf* imitation *o* costume jewellery
bit [bit] *nm* (*Inform*) bit; **~ de parada** stop bit; **~ de paridad** parity bit
bitácora [bi'takora] *nf*: **cuaderno de ~** logbook, ship's log
bizco, -a ['biθko, a] *adj* cross-eyed
bizcocho [biθ'kotʃo] *nm* (*Culin*) sponge cake
biznieto, -a [biθ'nieto, a] *nm/f* = **bisnieto**
bizquear [biθke'ar] *vi* to squint
blanco, -a ['blanko, a] *adj* white ▷ *nm/f* white man/woman, white ▷ *nm* (*color*) white; (*en texto*) blank; (*Mil, fig*) target ▷ *nf* (*Mus*) minim; **en ~** blank; **cheque en ~** blank cheque; **votar en ~** to spoil one's vote; **quedarse en ~** to be disappointed; **noche en ~** sleepless night; **ser el ~ de las burlas** to be the butt of jokes; **estar sin blanca** to be broke

blancura [blan'kura] *nf* whiteness
blandir [blan'dir] *vt* to brandish
blando, -a ['blando, a] *adj* soft; (*tierno*) tender, gentle; (*carácter*) mild; (*fam*) cowardly ▷ *nm/f* (*Pol etc*) soft-liner
blandura [blan'dura] *nf* softness; tenderness; mildness
blanqueador [blankea'ðor] *nm* (*Am*) bleach
blanquear [blanke'ar] *vt* to whiten; (*fachada*) to whitewash; (*paño*) to bleach; (*dinero*) to launder ▷ *vi* to turn white
blanquecino, -a [blanke'θino, a] *adj* whitish
blanqueo [blan'keo] *nm* (*de pared*) whitewashing; (*de dinero*) laundering
blanquillo [blan'kiʎo] *nm* (*Am, CAm*) egg
blasfemar [blasfe'mar] *vi* to blaspheme; (*fig*) to curse
blasfemia [blas'femja] *nf* blasphemy
blasón [bla'son] *nm* coat of arms; (*fig*) honour
blasonar [blaso'nar] *vt* to emblazon ▷ *vi* to boast, brag
bledo ['bleðo] *nm*: **(no) me importa un ~** I couldn't care less
blindado, -a [blin'daðo, a] *adj* (*Mil*) armour-plated; (*antibalas*) bulletproof; **coche** *o* (*Am*) **carro ~** armoured car; **puertas blindadas** security doors
blindaje [blin'daxe] *nm* armour, armour-plating
bloc (*pl* **blocs**) [blok, blos] *nm* writing pad; (*Escol*) jotter; **~ de dibujos** sketch pad
blof [blof] *nm* (*Am*) bluff
blofear [blofe'ar] *vi* (*Am*) to bluff
blog [bloɣ] (*pl* **blogs**) *nm* blog
bloguero, -a [blo'ɣero, a] *nm/f* blogger
bloque ['bloke] *nm* (*tb Inform*) block; (*Pol*) bloc; **~ de cilindros** cylinder block
bloquear [bloke'ar] *vt* (*Naut etc*) to blockade; (*aislar*) to cut off; (*Com, Econ*) to freeze; **fondos bloqueados** frozen assets
bloqueo [blo'keo] *nm* blockade; (*Com*) freezing, blocking; **~ mental** mental block
blusa ['blusa] *nf* blouse
boa ['boa] *nf* boa
boato [bo'ato] *nm* show, ostentation
bobada [bo'βaða] *nf* foolish action (*o* statement); **decir ~s** to talk nonsense
bobería [boβe'ria] *nf* = **bobada**
bobina [bo'βina] *nf* (*Tec*) bobbin; (*Foto*) spool; (*Elec*) coil, winding
bobo, -a ['boβo, a] *adj* (*tonto*) daft, silly; (*cándido*) naïve ▷ *nm/f* fool, idiot ▷ *nm* (*Teat*) clown, funny man
boca ['boka] *nf* mouth; (*de crustáceo*) pincer; (*de cañón*) muzzle; (*entrada*) mouth, entrance; **bocas** *nfpl* (*de río*) mouth *sg*; **~ abajo/arriba** face down/up; **a ~ jarro** point-blank; **se me hace la ~ agua** my mouth is watering; **todo salió a pedir de ~** it all turned out perfectly; **en ~ de** (*esp Am*) according to; **la cosa anda de ~ en ~** the story is going the rounds; **¡cállate la ~!** (*fam*) shut up!; **quedarse con la ~ abierta** to be dumbfounded; **no abrir la ~** to keep quiet; **~ de incendios** hydrant; **~ del estómago** pit of the stomach; **~ de metro** tube (*Brit*) *o* subway (*US*) entrance
bocacalle [boka'kaʎe] *nf* side street; **la primera ~** the first turning *o* street
bocadillo [boka'ðiʎo] *nm* sandwich
bocado [bo'kaðo] *nm* mouthful, bite; (*de caballo*) bridle; **~ de Adán** Adam's apple
bocajarro [boka'xarro]: **a ~** *adv* (*Mil*) at point-blank range; **decir algo a ~** to say sth bluntly
bocanada [boka'naða] *nf* (*de vino*) mouthful, swallow; (*de aire*) gust, puff
bocata [bo'kata] *nm* (*fam*) sandwich
bocazas [bo'kaθas] *nm/f inv* (*fam*) bigmouth
boceto [bo'θeto] *nm* sketch, outline
bocha ['botʃa] *nf* bowl; **bochas** *nfpl* bowls *sg*
bochinche [bo'tʃintʃe] *nm* (*fam*) uproar
bochorno [bo'tʃorno] *nm* (*vergüenza*) embarrassment; (*calor*): **hace ~** it's very muggy
bochornoso, -a [botʃor'noso, a] *adj* muggy; embarrassing
bocina [bo'θina] *nf* (*Mus*) trumpet; (*Auto*) horn; (*para hablar*) megaphone; **tocar la ~** (*Auto*) to sound *o* blow one's horn
boda ['boða] *nf* (*tb*: **~s**) wedding, marriage; (*fiesta*) wedding reception; **~s de plata/de oro** silver/golden wedding *sg*
bodega [bo'ðeɣa] *nf* (*de vino*) (wine) cellar; (*bar*) bar; (*restaurante*) restaurant; (*depósito*) storeroom; (*de barco*) hold
bodegón [boðe'ɣon] *nm* (*Arte*) still life
bofe ['bofe] *nm* (*tb*: **~s**: *de res*) lights *pl*; **echar los ~s** to slave (away)
bofetada [bofe'taða] *nf* slap (in the face); **dar de ~s a algn** to punch sb
bofetón [bofe'ton] *nm* = **bofetada**
boga ['boɣa] *nf*: **en ~** in vogue
bogar [bo'ɣar] *vi* (*remar*) to row; (*navegar*) to sail
bogavante [boɣa'βante] *nm* (*Naut*) stroke, first rower; (*Zool*) lobster
Bogotá [boɣo'ta] *n* Bogota
bogotano, -a [boɣo'tano, a] *adj* of *o* from Bogota ▷ *nm/f* native *o* inhabitant of Bogota
bohemio, -a [bo'emjo, a] *adj, nm/f* Bohemian
bohío [bo'io] *nm* (*Am*) shack, hut
boicot [boi'ko(t)] (*pl* **boicots**) *nm* boycott
boicotear [boikote'ar] *vt* to boycott
boicoteo [boiko'teo] *nm* boycott
bóiler ['boiler] *nm* (*Am*) boiler
boina ['boina] *nf* beret
bola ['bola] *nf* ball; (*canica*) marble; (*Naipes*) (grand) slam; (*betún*) shoe polish; (*mentira*) tale, story; **bolas** *nfpl* (*Am*) bolas; **~ de billar** billiard ball; **~ de nieve** snowball
bolchevique [boltʃe'βike] *adj, nm/f* Bolshevik
boleadoras [bolea'ðoras] *nfpl* (*Am*) bolas *sg*
bolear [bole'ar] *vt* (*Am*: *zapatos*) to polish, shine
bolera [bo'lera] *nf* skittle *o* bowling alley

bolero, -a [bo'lero, a] *nm* bolero ▷ *nm/f* (*Am: limpiabotas*) shoeshine boy/girl
boleta [bo'leta] *nf* (*Am: permiso*) pass, permit; (*de rifa*) ticket; (*recibo*) receipt; (*para votar*) ballot; **~ de calificaciones** report card
boletería [bolete'ria] *nf* (*Am*) ticket office
boletín [bole'tin] *nm* bulletin; (*periódico*) journal, review; **~ escolar** (*Esp*) school report; **~ de noticias** news bulletin; **~ de pedido** application form; **~ de precios** price list; **~ de prensa** press release
boleto [bo'leto] *nm* (*esp Am*) ticket; **~ de apuestas** betting slip; **~ de ida y vuelta** (*Am*) round trip ticket; **~ electrónico** (*Am*) e-ticket; **~ redondo** (*Am*) round trip ticket
boli ['boli] *nm* Biro®
boliche [bo'litʃe] *nm* (*bola*) jack; (*juego*) bowls *sg*; (*lugar*) bowling alley; (*Am: tienda*) small grocery store
bólido ['boliðo] *nm* meteorite; (*Auto*) racing car
bolígrafo [bo'liɣrafo] *nm* ball-point pen, Biro®
bolilla [bo'liʎa] *nf* (*Am*) topic
bolillo [bo'liʎo] *nm* (*Costura*) bobbin (for lacemaking); (*Am*) (bread) roll
bolita [bo'lita] *nf* (*Am*) marble
bolívar [bo'liβar] *nm* *monetary unit of Venezuela*
Bolivia [bo'liβja] *nf* Bolivia
boliviano, -a [boli'βjano, a] *adj, nm/f* Bolivian
bollería [boʎe'ria] *nf* cakes *pl* and pastries *pl*
bollo ['boʎo] *nm* (*de pan*) roll; (*dulce*) scone; (*chichón*) bump, lump; (*abolladura*) dent; **bollos** *nmpl* (*Am*) troubles
bolo ['bolo] *nm* skittle; (*píldora*) (large) pill; **(juego de) ~s** skittles *sg*
bolsa ['bolsa] *nf* (*cartera*) purse; (*saco*) bag; (*Am*) pocket; (*de mujer*) handbag; (*Anat*) cavity, sac; (*Com*) stock exchange; (*Minería*) pocket; **~ de agua caliente** hot water bottle; **~ de aire** air pocket; **~ de (la) basura** bin-liner; **~ de dormir** (*Am*) sleeping bag; **~ de papel** paper bag; **~ de plástico** plastic (*o* carrier) bag; **~ de la compra** shopping bag; **"B~ de la propiedad"** "Property Mart"; **~ de trabajo** employment bureau; **jugar a la ~** to play the market
bolsillo [bol'siʎo] *nm* pocket; (*cartera*) purse; **de ~** pocket *cpd*; **meterse a algn en el ~** to get sb eating out of one's hand
bolsista [bol'sista] *nm/f* stockbroker
bolso ['bolso] *nm* (*bolsa*) bag; (*de mujer*) handbag
boludo, -a [bo'luðo, a] (*Am fam!*) *adj* stupid ▷ *nm/f* prat (*!*)
bomba ['bomba] *nf* (*Mil*) bomb; (*Tec*) pump; (*Am: borrachera*) drunkenness ▷ *adj* (*fam*): **noticia ~** bombshell ▷ *adv* (*fam*): **pasarlo ~** to have a great time; **~ atómica/de humo/de retardo** atomic/smoke/time bomb; **~ de gasolina** petrol pump; **~ de incendios** fire engine
bombacha [bom'batʃa] *nf* (*Am*) panties *pl*
bombardear [bombarðe'ar] *vt* to bombard; (*Mil*) to bomb
bombardeo [bombar'ðeo] *nm* bombardment; bombing
bombardero [bombar'ðero] *nm* bomber
bombazo [bom'baθo] *nm* (*Am: explosión*) explosion; (*fam: notición*) bombshell; (*: éxito*) smash hit
bombear [bombe'ar] *vt* (*agua*) to pump (out *o* up); (*Mil*) to bomb; (*Fútbol*) to lob; **bombearse** *vr* to warp
bombero [bom'bero] *nm* fireman; **(cuerpo de) ~s** fire brigade
bombilla [bom'biʎa] (*Esp*) *nf*, **bombillo** [bom'biʎo] (*Am*) *nm* (light) bulb
bombita [bom'bita] *nf* (*Am*) (light) bulb
bombín [bom'bin] *nm* bowler hat
bombo ['bombo] *nm* (*Mus*) bass drum; (*Tec*) drum; (*fam*) exaggerated praise; **hacer algo a ~ y platillo** to make a great song and dance about sth; **tengo la cabeza hecha un ~** I've got a splitting headache
bombón [bom'bon] *nm* chocolate; (*Am: de caramelo*) marshmallow; (*belleza*) gem
bombona [bom'bona] *nf*: **~ de butano** gas cylinder
bonachón, -ona [bona'tʃon, ona] *adj* good-natured
bonaerense [bonae'rense] *adj* of *o* from Buenos Aires ▷ *nm/f* native *o* inhabitant of Buenos Aires
bonanza [bo'nanθa] *nf* (*Naut*) fair weather; (*fig*) bonanza; (*Minería*) rich pocket *o* vein
bondad [bon'dað] *nf* goodness, kindness; **tenga la ~ de** (please) be good enough to
bondadoso, -a [bonda'ðoso, a] *adj* good, kind
bonito, -a [bo'nito, a] *adj* (*lindo*) pretty; (*agradable*) nice ▷ *adv* (*Am fam*) well ▷ *nm* (*atún*) tuna (fish)
bono ['bono] *nm* voucher; (*Finanzas*) bond; **~ de billetes de metro** booklet of metro tickets; **~ del Tesoro** treasury bill
bonobús [bono'βus] *nm* (*Esp*) bus pass
Bono Loto, bonoloto [bono'loto] *nm o f* (*Esp*) *state-run weekly lottery*; *ver tb* **lotería**
boom (*pl* **booms**) [bum, bums] *nm* boom
boquear [boke'ar] *vi* to gasp
boquerón [boke'ron] *nm* (*pez*) (kind of) anchovy; (*agujero*) large hole
boquete [bo'kete] *nm* gap, hole
boquiabierto, -a [bokia'βjerto, a] *adj* open-mouthed (in astonishment); **quedarse ~** to be amazed *o* flabbergasted
boquilla [bo'kiʎa] *nf* (*de riego*) nozzle; (*de cigarro*) cigarette holder; (*Mus*) mouthpiece
borbotón [borβo'ton] *nm*: **salir a borbotones** to gush out
borda ['borða] *nf* (*Naut*) gunwale, rail; **echar *o* tirar algo por la ~** to throw sth overboard
bordado [bor'ðaðo] *nm* embroidery

bordar [bor'ðar] *vt* to embroider
borde ['borðe] *nm* edge, border; (*de camino etc*) side; (*en la costura*) hem; **al ~ de** (*fig*) on the verge *o* brink of ▷ *adj*: **ser ~** (*Esp*: (*fam*)) to be rude
bordear [borðe'ar] *vt* to border
bordillo [bor'ðiʎo] *nm* kerb (*Brit*), curb (*US*)
bordo ['borðo] *nm* (*Naut*) side; **a ~** on board
borla ['borla] *nf* (*gen*) tassel; (*de gorro*) pompon
borlote [bor'lote] *nm* (*Am*) row, uproar
borrachera [borra'tʃera] *nf* (*ebriedad*) drunkenness; (*orgía*) spree, binge
borracho, -a [bo'rratʃo, a] *adj* drunk ▷ *nm/f* (*que bebe mucho*) drunkard, drunk; (*temporalmente*) drunk, drunk man/woman ▷ *nm* (*Culin*) *cake soaked in liqueur or spirit*
borrador [borra'ðor] *nm* (*escritura*) first draft, rough sketch; (*cuaderno*) scribbling pad; (*goma*) rubber (*Brit*), eraser; (*Com*) daybook; (*para pizarra*) duster; **hacer un nuevo ~ de** (*Com*) to redraft
borrar [bo'rrar] *vt* to erase, rub out; (*tachar*) to delete; (*cinta*) to wipe out; (*Inform: archivo*) to delete, erase; (*Pol etc: eliminar*) to deal with
borrasca [bo'rraska] *nf* (*Meteorología*) storm
borrego, -a [bo'rreɣo, a] *nm/f* lamb; (*oveja*) sheep; (*fig*) simpleton ▷ *nm* (*Am: fam*) false rumour
borrico, -a [bo'rriko, a] *nm* donkey; (*fig*) stupid man ▷ *nf* she-donkey; (*fig*) stupid woman
borrón [bo'rron] *nm* (*mancha*) stain; **~ y cuenta nueva** let bygones be bygones
borroso, -a [bo'rroso, a] *adj* vague, unclear; (*escritura*) illegible; (*escrito*) smudgy; (*Foto*) blurred
Bosnia ['bosnja] *nf* Bosnia
bosnio, -a ['bosnjo, a] *adj, nm/f* Bosnian
bosque ['boske] *nm* wood; (*grande*) forest
bosquejar [boske'xar] *vt* to sketch
bosquejo [bos'kexo] *nm* sketch
bostezar [boste'θar] *vi* to yawn
bostezo [bos'teθo] *nm* yawn
bota ['bota] *nf* (*calzado*) boot; (*de vino*) leather wine bottle; **~s de agua** *o* **goma** Wellingtons; **ponerse las ~s** (*fam*) to strike it rich
botánico, -a [bo'taniko, a] *adj* botanical ▷ *nm/f* botanist ▷ *nf* botany
botar [bo'tar] *vt* to throw, hurl; (*Naut*) to launch; (*esp Am fam*) to throw out ▷ *vi* to bounce
bote ['bote] *nm* (*salto*) bounce; (*golpe*) thrust; (*vasija*) tin, can; (*embarcación*) boat; (*Am: pey: cárcel*) jail; **de ~ en ~** packed, jammed full; **~ salvavidas** lifeboat; **dar un ~** to jump; **dar ~s** (*Auto etc*) to bump; **~ de la basura** (*Am*) dustbin (*Brit*), trash can (*US*)
botella [bo'teʎa] *nf* bottle; **~ de vino** (*contenido*) bottle of wine; (*recipiente*) wine bottle
botellín [bote'ʎin] *nm* small bottle
botellón [bote'ʎon] *nm* (*Esp: fam*) outdoor drinking session (*involving groups of young people*)
botica [bo'tika] *nf* chemist's (shop) (*Brit*), pharmacy
boticario, -a [boti'karjo, a] *nm/f* chemist (*Brit*), pharmacist
botijo [bo'tixo] *nm* (earthenware) jug; (*tren*) excursion train
botín [bo'tin] *nm* (*calzado*) half boot; (*polaina*) spat; (*Mil*) booty; (*de ladrón*) loot
botiquín [boti'kin] *nm* (*armario*) medicine chest; (*portátil*) first-aid kit
botón [bo'ton] *nm* button; (*Bot*) bud; (*de florete*) tip; **~ de arranque** (*Auto etc*) starter; **~ de oro** buttercup; **pulsar el ~** to press the button
botones [bo'tones] *nm inv* bellboy, bellhop (*US*)
bóveda ['boβeða] *nf* (*Arq*) vault
boxeador [boksea'ðor] *nm* boxer
boxear [bokse'ar] *vi* to box
boxeo [bok'seo] *nm* boxing
boya ['boja] *nf* (*Naut*) buoy; (*flotador*) float
boyante [bo'jante] *adj* (*Naut*) buoyant; (*feliz*) buoyant; (*próspero*) prosperous
bozal [bo'θal] *nm* (*de caballo*) halter; (*de perro*) muzzle
bracear [braθe'ar] *vi* (*agitar los brazos*) to wave one's arms
bracero [bra'θero] *nm* labourer; (*en el campo*) farmhand
braga ['braɣa] *nf* (*cuerda*) sling, rope; (*de bebé*) nappy, diaper (*US*); **bragas** *nfpl* (*de mujer*) panties
bragueta [bra'ɣeta] *nf* fly (*Brit*), flies *pl* (*Brit*), zipper (*US*)
braille [breil] *nm* braille
bramar [bra'mar] *vi* to bellow, roar
bramido [bra'miðo] *nm* bellow, roar
brasa ['brasa] *nf* live *o* hot coal; **carne a la ~** grilled meat; **dar la ~** (*col: dar la lata, molestar*) to be a pain (*col*); **dar la ~ a algn** to go on at sb (*col*); **¡deja de darme la ~!** stop going on at me! (*col*)
brasero [bra'sero] *nm* brazier; (*Am: chimenea*) fireplace
brasier [bra'sjer] *nm* (*Am*) bra
Brasil [bra'sil] *nm*: **(el) ~** Brazil
brasileño, -a [brasi'leɲo, a] *adj, nm/f* Brazilian
brassier [bra'sjer] *nm* (*Am*) *ver* **brasier**
bravata [bra'βata] *nf* boast
braveza [bra'βeθa] *nf* (*valor*) bravery; (*ferocidad*) ferocity
bravío, -a [bra'βio, a] *adj* wild; (*feroz*) fierce
bravo, -a ['braβo, a] *adj* (*valiente*) brave; (*bueno*) fine, splendid; (*feroz*) ferocious; (*salvaje*) wild; (*mar etc*) rough, stormy; (*Culin*) hot, spicy ▷ *excl* bravo!
bravura [bra'βura] *nf* bravery; ferocity; (*pey*) boast

b

braza ['braθa] *nf* fathom; **nadar a la ~** to swim (the) breast-stroke
brazada [bra'θaða] *nf* stroke
brazalete [braθa'lete] *nm* (*pulsera*) bracelet; (*banda*) armband
brazo ['braθo] *nm* arm; (*Zool*) foreleg; (*Bot*) limb, branch; **brazos** *nmpl* (*braceros*) hands, workers; **~ derecho** (*fig*) right-hand man; **a ~ partido** hand-to-hand; **cogidos** *etc* **del ~** arm in arm; **no dar su ~ a torcer** not to give way easily; **huelga de ~s caídos** sit-down strike
brea ['brea] *nf* pitch, tar
brebaje [bre'βaxe] *nm* potion
brecha ['bretʃa] *nf* (*hoyo, vacío*) gap, opening; (*Mil, fig*) breach
brega ['breɣa] *nf* (*lucha*) struggle; (*trabajo*) hard work
breva ['breβa] *nf* (*Bot*) early fig; (*puro*) flat cigar; **¡no caerá esa ~!** no such luck!
breve ['breβe] *adj* short, brief; **en ~** (*pronto*) shortly; (*en pocas palabras*) in short ▷ *nf* (*Mus*) breve
brevedad [breβe'ðað] *nf* brevity, shortness; **con** *o* **a la mayor ~** as soon as possible
brezal [bre'θal] *nm* moor(land), heath
brezo ['breθo] *nm* heather
bribón, -ona [bri'βon, ona] *adj* idle, lazy ▷ *nm/f* (*vagabundo*) vagabond; (*pícaro*) rascal, rogue
bricolaje [briko'laxe] *nm* do-it-yourself, DIY
brida ['briða] *nf* bridle, rein; (*Tec*) clamp; **a toda ~** at top speed
bridge [britʃ] *nm* (*Naipes*) bridge
brigada [bri'ɣaða] *nf* (*unidad*) brigade; (*trabajadores*) squad, gang ▷ *nm* ≈ sergeant major
brillante [bri'ʎante] *adj* brilliant; (*color*) bright; (*joya*) sparkling ▷ *nm* diamond
brillar [bri'ʎar] *vi* (*tb fig*) to shine; (*joyas*) to sparkle; **~ por su ausencia** to be conspicuous by one's absence
brillo ['briʎo] *nm* shine; (*brillantez*) brilliance; (*fig*) splendour; **sacar ~ a** to polish
brincar [brin'kar] *vi* to skip about, hop about, jump about; **está que brinca** he's hopping mad
brinco ['brinko] *nm* jump, leap; **a ~s** by fits and starts; **de un ~** at one bound
brindar [brin'dar] *vi*: **~ a** *o* **por** to drink (a toast) to ▷ *vt* to offer, present; **le brinda la ocasión de** it offers *o* affords him the opportunity to; **brindarse** *vr*: **~se a hacer algo** to offer to do sth
brindis ['brindis] *nm inv* toast; (*Taur*) (ceremony of) dedication
brío ['brio] *nm* spirit, dash
brioso, -a [bri'oso, a] *adj* spirited, dashing
brisa ['brisa] *nf* breeze
británico, -a [bri'taniko, a] *adj* British ▷ *nm/f* Briton, British person; **los ~s** the British
brizna ['briθna] *nf* (*hebra*) strand, thread; (*de hierba*) blade; (*de tabaco*) leaf; (*trozo*) piece
broca ['broka] *nf* (*Costura*) bobbin; (*Tec*) drill bit; (*clavo*) tack
brocal [bro'kal] *nm* rim
brocha ['brotʃa] *nf* (large) paintbrush; **~ de afeitar** shaving brush; **pintor de ~ gorda** painter and decorator; (*fig*) poor painter
broche ['brotʃe] *nm* brooch
broma ['broma] *nf* joke; (*inocentada*) practical joke; **en ~** in fun, as a joke; **gastar una ~ a algn** to play a joke on sb; **tomar algo a ~** to take sth as a joke; **~ pesada** practical joke
bromear [brome'ar] *vi* to joke
bromista [bro'mista] *adj* fond of joking ▷ *nm/f* joker, wag
bronca ['bronka] *nf* row; (*regañada*) ticking-off; **armar una ~** to kick up a fuss; **echar una ~ a algn** to tell sb off
bronce ['bronθe] *nm* bronze; (*latón*) brass
bronceado, -a [bronθe'aðo, a] *adj* bronze *cpd*; (*por el sol*) tanned ▷ *nm* (sun)tan; (*Tec*) bronzing
bronceador [bronθea'ðor] *nm* suntan lotion
broncearse [bronθe'arse] *vr* to get a suntan
bronco, -a ['bronko, a] *adj* (*manera*) rude, surly; (*voz*) harsh
bronquios ['bronkjos] *nmpl* bronchial tubes
bronquitis [bron'kitis] *nf inv* bronchitis
brotar [bro'tar] *vt* (*tierra*) to produce ▷ *vi* (*Bot*) to sprout; (*aguas*) to gush (forth); (*lágrimas*) to well up; (*Med*) to break out
brote ['brote] *nm* (*Bot*) shoot; (*Med, fig*) outbreak
bruces ['bruθes]: **de ~** *adv*: **caer** *o* **dar de ~** to fall headlong, fall flat
bruja ['bruxa] *nf* witch
brujería [bruxe'ria] *nf* witchcraft
brujo ['bruxo] *nm* wizard, magician
brújula ['bruxula] *nf* compass
bruma ['bruma] *nf* mist
brumoso, -a [bru'moso, a] *adj* misty
bruñido [bru'ɲiðo] *nm* polish
bruñir [bru'ɲir] *vt* to polish
brusco, -a ['brusko, a] *adj* (*súbito*) sudden; (*áspero*) brusque
Bruselas [bru'selas] *nf* Brussels
brutal [bru'tal] *adj* brutal
brutalidad [brutali'ðað] *nf* brutality
bruto, -a ['bruto, a] *adj* (*idiota*) stupid; (*bestial*) brutish; (*peso*) gross ▷ *nm* brute; **a la bruta, a lo ~** roughly; **en ~** raw, unworked
Bs.As. *abr* = **Buenos Aires**
bucal [bu'kal] *adj* oral; **por vía ~** orally
bucear [buθe'ar] *vi* to dive ▷ *vt* to explore
buceo [bu'θeo] *nm* diving; (*fig*) investigation
bucle ['bukle] *nm* curl; (*Inform*) loop
budismo [bu'ðismo] *nm* Buddhism
budista [bu'ðista] *adj, nm/f* Buddhist
buen [bwen] *adj ver* **bueno**
buenamente [bwena'mente] *adv* (*fácilmente*) easily; (*voluntariamente*) willingly
buenaventura [bwenaβen'tura] *nf* (*suerte*) good luck; (*adivinación*) fortune; **decir** *o* **echar la ~ a algn** to tell sb's fortune

buenmozo [bwen'moθo] *adj* (*Am*) handsome

PALABRA CLAVE

bueno, -a ['bweno, a] (*antes de nmsg* **buen**) *adj*
1 (*excelente etc*) good; (*Med*) well; **es un libro bueno, es un buen libro** it's a good book; **hace bueno, hace buen tiempo** the weather is fine, it is fine; **es buena persona** he's a good sort; **el bueno de Paco** good old Paco; **fue muy bueno conmigo** he was very nice *o* kind to me; **ya está bueno** he's fine now
2 (*apropiado*): **ser bueno para** to be good for; **creo que vamos por buen camino** I think we're on the right track
3 (*irónico*): **le di un buen rapapolvo** I gave him a good *o* real ticking off; **¡buen conductor estás hecho!** some driver *o* a fine driver you are!; **¡estaría bueno que ...!** a fine thing it would be if ...!
4 (*atractivo, sabroso*): **está bueno este bizcocho** this sponge is delicious; **Julio está muy bueno** (*fam*) Julio's gorgeous
5 (*saludos*): **¡buen día!** (*Am*), **¡buenos días!** (good) morning!; **¡buenas (tardes)!** good afternoon!; (*más tarde*) good evening!; **¡buenas noches!** good night!
6 (*otras locuciones*): **estar de buenas** to be in a good mood; **por las buenas o por las malas** by hook or by crook; **de buenas a primeras** all of a sudden
7 (*grande*) good, big; **un buen número de ...** a good number of ...; **un buen trozo de ...** a nice big piece of ...
▷ *excl*: **¡bueno!** all right!; **bueno, ¿y qué?** well, so what?; **bueno, lo que pasa es que ...** well, the thing is ...; **pero ¡bueno!** well, I like that!; **bueno, pues ...** right, (then) ...

Buenos Aires [bweno'saires] *nm* Buenos Aires
buey [bwei] *nm* ox
búfalo ['bufalo] *nm* buffalo
bufanda [bu'fanda] *nf* scarf
bufar [bu'far] *vi* to snort
bufete [bu'fete] *nm* (*despacho de abogado*) lawyer's office; **establecer su ~** to set up in legal practice
buffer ['bufer] *nm* (*Inform*) buffer
bufón [bu'fon] *nm* clown
buhardilla [buar'ðiʎa] *nf* attic
búho ['buo] *nm* owl; (*fig*) hermit, recluse
buhonero [buo'nero] *nm* pedlar
buitre ['bwitre] *nm* vulture
bujía [bu'xia] *nf* (*vela*) candle; (*Elec*) candle (power); (*Auto*) spark plug
bula ['bula] *nf* (papal) bull
bulbo ['bulβo] *nm* (*Bot*) bulb
bulevar [bule'βar] *nm* boulevard
Bulgaria [bul'ɣarja] *nf* Bulgaria
búlgaro, -a ['bulɣaro, a] *adj, nm/f* Bulgarian
bulimia [bu'limja] *nf* bulimia
bulla ['buʎa] *nf* (*ruido*) uproar; (*de gente*) crowd; **armar** *o* **meter ~** to kick up a row
bullicio [bu'ʎiθjo] *nm* (*ruido*) uproar; (*movimiento*) bustle
bullir [bu'ʎir] *vi* (*hervir*) to boil; (*burbujear*) to bubble; (*moverse*) to move, stir; (*insectos*) to swarm; **~ de** (*fig*) to teem *o* seethe with
bulto ['bulto] *nm* (*paquete*) package; (*fardo*) bundle; (*tamaño*) size, bulkiness; (*Med*) swelling, lump; (*silueta*) vague shape; (*estatua*) bust, statue; **hacer ~** to take up space; **escurrir el ~** to make o.s. scarce; (*fig*) to dodge the issue
buñuelo [bu'ɲwelo] *nm* ≈ doughnut, ≈ donut (*US*); (*fruta de sartén*) fritter
buque ['buke] *nm* ship, vessel; **~ de guerra** warship; **~ mercante** merchant ship; **~ de vela** sailing ship
burbuja [bur'βuxa] *nf* bubble; **~ inmobiliaria** housing bubble; **hacer ~s** to bubble; (*gaseosa*) to fizz
burbujear [burβuxe'ar] *vi* to bubble
burdel [bur'ðel] *nm* brothel
burdo, -a ['burðo, a] *adj* coarse, rough
burgués, -esa [bur'ɣes, esa] *adj* middle-class, bourgeois; **pequeño ~** lower middle-class; (*Pol, pey*) petty bourgeois
burguesía [burɣe'sia] *nf* middle class, bourgeoisie
burla ['burla] *nf* (*mofa*) gibe; (*broma*) joke; (*engaño*) trick; **hacer ~ de** to make fun of
burladero [burla'ðero] *nm* (bullfighter's) refuge
burlador, a [burla'ðor, a] *adj* mocking ▷ *nm/f* mocker; (*bromista*) joker ▷ *nm* (*libertino*) seducer
burlar [bur'lar] *vt* (*engañar*) to deceive; (*seducir*) to seduce ▷ *vi* to joke; **burlarse** *vr* to joke; **~se de** to make fun of
burlesco, -a [bur'lesko, a] *adj* burlesque
burlón, -ona [bur'lon, ona] *adj* mocking
buró [bu'ro] *nm* bureau
burocracia [buro'kraθja] *nf* bureaucracy
burócrata [bu'rokrata] *nm/f* bureaucrat
buromática [buro'matika] *nf* office automation
burrada [bu'rraða] *nf* stupid act; **decir ~s** to talk nonsense; **hacer ~s** to act stupid; **una ~** (*Esp*: *mucho*) a (hell of a) lot
burro, -a ['burro, a] *nm/f* (*Zool*) donkey; (*fig*) ass, idiot ▷ *adj* stupid; **caerse del ~** to realise one's mistake; **no ver tres en un ~** to be as blind as a bat
bursátil [bur'satil] *adj* stock-exchange *cpd*
bus [bus] *nm* bus
busca ['buska] *nf* search, hunt ▷ *nm* bleeper, pager; **en ~ de** in search of
buscador, a [buska'ðor, a] *nm/f* searcher ▷ *nm* (*Internet*) search engine
buscar [bus'kar] *vt* to look for; (*objeto perdido*) to have a look for; (*beneficio*) to seek; (*enemigo*)

to seek out; (*traer*) to bring, fetch; (*provocar*) to provoke; (*Inform*) to search ▷ *vi* to look, search, seek; **ven a ~me a la oficina** come and pick me up at the office; **~le 3 *o* 4 pies al gato** to split hairs; **"~ y reemplazar"** (*Inform*) "search and replace"; **se busca secretaria** secretary wanted; **se la buscó** he asked for it

buscona [bus'kona] *nf* whore

busque *etc* ['buske] *vb ver* **buscar**

búsqueda ['buskeða] *nf* = **busca**

busto ['busto] *nm* (*Anat, Arte*) bust

butaca [bu'taka] *nf* armchair; (*de cine, teatro*) stall, seat

butano [bu'tano] *nm* butane (gas); **bombona de ~** gas cylinder

buzo ['buθo] *nm* diver; (*Am: chandal*) tracksuit

buzón [bu'θon] *nm* (*gen*) letter box; (*en la calle*) pillar box (*Brit*); (*Telec*) mailbox; **echar al ~** to post

buzonear [buθone'ar] *vt* to leaflet

C

C. *abr* (= *centígrado*) C.; (= *compañía*) Co

c. *abr* (= *capítulo*) ch

C/ *abr* (= *calle*) St, Rd

c.a. *abr* (= *corriente alterna*) A.C.

cabal [ka'βal] *adj* (*exacto*) exact; (*correcto*) right, proper; (*acabado*) finished, complete; **cabales** *nmpl*: **estar en sus ~es** to be in one's right mind

cábala ['kaβala] *nf* (*Rel*) cab(b)ala; (*fig*) cabal, intrigue; **cábalas** *nfpl* guess *sg*, supposition *sg*; **hacer ~s** to guess

cabalgadura [kaβalɣa'ðura] *nf* mount, horse

cabalgar [kaβal'ɣar] *vt, vi* to ride

cabalgata [kaβal'ɣata] *nf* procession; *ver tb* **Reyes Magos**

caballa [ka'βaʎa] *nf* mackerel

caballeresco, -a [kaβaʎe'resko, a] *adj* noble, chivalrous

caballería [kaβaʎe'ria] *nf* mount; (*Mil*) cavalry

caballeriza [kaβaʎe'riθa] *nf* stable

caballerizo [kaβaʎe'riθo] *nm* groom, stableman

caballero [kaβa'ʎero] *nm* gentleman; (*de la orden de caballería*) knight; (*trato directo*) sir; **"C~s"** "Gents"

caballerosidad [kaβaʎerosi'ðað] *nf* chivalry

caballete [kaβa'ʎete] *nm* (*Agr*) ridge; (*Arte*) easel; (*Tec*) trestle

caballito [kaβa'ʎito] *nm* (*caballo pequeño*) small horse, pony; (*juguete*) rocking horse;

caballitos *nmpl* merry-go-round *sg*; **~ de mar** seahorse; **~ del diablo** dragonfly
caballo [ka'βaʎo] *nm* horse; (*Ajedrez*) knight; (*Naipes*) ≈ queen; **ir en ~** to ride; **~ de carreras** racehorse; **~ de vapor** *o* **de fuerza** horsepower; **es su ~ de batalla** it's his hobby-horse; **~ blanco** (*Com*) backer; *ver tb* **Baraja Española**
cabaña [ka'βaɲa] *nf* (*casita*) hut, cabin
cabaré, cabaret (*pl* **cabarets**) [kaβa're, kaβa'res] *nm* cabaret
cabecear [kaβeθe'ar] *vt, vi* to nod
cabecera [kaβe'θera] *nf* (*gen*) head; (*de distrito*) chief town; (*de cama*) headboard; (*Imprenta*) headline
cabecilla [kaβe'θiʎa] *nm* ringleader
cabellera [kaβe'ʎera] *nf* (head of) hair; (*de cometa*) tail
cabello [ka'βeʎo] *nm* (*tb*: **~s**) hair *sg*; **~ de ángel** *confectionery and pastry filling made of pumpkin and syrup*
cabelludo [kaβe'ʎuðo] *adj ver* **cuero**
caber [ka'βer] *vi* (*entrar*) to fit, go; **caben tres más** there's room for three more; **cabe preguntar si...** one might ask whether...; **cabe que venga más tarde** he may come later
cabestrillo [kaβes'triʎo] *nm* sling
cabestro [ka'βestro] *nm* halter
cabeza [ka'βeθa] *nf* head; (*Pol*) chief, leader; **~ de ajo** bulb of garlic; **~ de familia** head of the household; **~ rapada** skinhead; **caer de ~** to fall head first; **sentar la ~** to settle down; **~ de lectura/escritura** read/write head; **~ impresora** *o* **de impresión** printhead
cabezada [kaβe'θaða] *nf* (*golpe*) butt; **dar una ~** to nod off
cabezazo [kaβe'θaθo] *nm* (*golpe*) headbutt; (*Fútbol*) header
cabezón, -ona [kaβe'θon, ona] *adj* with a big head; (*vino*) heady; (*obstinado*) pig-headed
cabezota [kaβe'θota] *adj inv* obstinate, stubborn
cabida [ka'βiða] *nf* space; **dar ~ a** to make room for; **tener ~ para** to have room for
cabildo [ka'βildo] *nm* (*de iglesia*) chapter; (*Pol*) town council
cabina [ka'βina] *nf* cabin; (*de avión*) cockpit; (*de camión*) cab; **~ telefónica** (tele)phone box (*Brit*) *o* booth
cabizbajo, -a [kaβiθ'βaxo, a] *adj* crestfallen, dejected
cable ['kaβle] *nm* cable; (*de aparato*) lead; **~ aéreo** (*Elec*) overhead cable; **conectar con ~** (*Inform*) to hardwire
cabo ['kaβo] *nm* (*de objeto*) end, extremity; (*Mil*) corporal; (*Naut*) rope, cable; (*Geo*) cape; (*Tec*) thread; **al ~ de tres días** after three days; **de ~ a rabo** *o* **~** from beginning to end; (*libro: leer*) from cover to cover; **llevar a ~** to carry out; **atar ~s** to tie up the loose ends; **C~ de Buena Esperanza** Cape of Good Hope; **C~ de Hornos** Cape Horn; **las Islas de C~ Verde** the Cape Verde Islands
cabra ['kaβra] *nf* goat; **estar como una ~** (*fam*) to be nuts
cabré *etc* [ka'βre] *vb ver* **caber**
cabrear [kaβre'ar] *vt* to annoy; **cabrearse** *vr* (*enfadarse*) to fly off the handle
cabrío, -a [ka'βrio, a] *adj* goatish; **macho ~** (he-)goat, billy goat
cabriola [ka'βrjola] *nf* caper
cabritilla [kaβri'tiʎa] *nf* kid, kidskin
cabrito [ka'βrito] *nm* kid
cabrón [ka'βron] *nm* cuckold; (*fam!*) bastard (*!*)
cabronada [kaβro'naða] *nf* (*fam!*): **hacer una ~ a algn** to be a bastard to sb
caca ['kaka] *nf* (*palabra de niños*) pooh ▷ *excl*: **no toques, ¡~!** don't touch, it's dirty!
cacahuete [kaka'wete] *nm* (*Esp*) peanut
cacao [ka'kao] *nm* cocoa; (*Bot*) cacao
cacarear [kakare'ar] *vi* (*persona*) to boast; (*gallina*) to cluck; (*gallo*) to crow
cacarizo, -a [kaka'riθo, a] *adj* (*Am*) pockmarked
cacería [kaθe'ria] *nf* hunt
cacerola [kaθe'rola] *nf* pan, saucepan
cachalote [katʃa'lote] *nm* sperm whale
cacharro [ka'tʃarro] *nm* (*cazo*) pot; (*cerámica*) piece of pottery; (*fam*) useless object; **cacharros** *nmpl* pots and pans
cachear [katʃe'ar] *vt* to search, frisk
cachemir [katʃe'mir] *nm* cashmere
cacheo [ka'tʃeo] *nm* searching, frisking
cachetada [katʃe'taða] *nf* (*Am*: *fam*: *bofetada*) slap
cachete [ka'tʃete] *nm* (*Anat*) cheek; (*bofetada*) slap (in the face)
cachimba [ka'tʃimba] *nf*, **cachimbo** [ka'tʃimbo] *nm* (*Am*) pipe
cachiporra [katʃi'porra] *nf* truncheon
cachivache [katʃi'βatʃe] *nm* piece of junk; **cachivaches** *nmpl* trash *sg*, junk *sg*
cacho ['katʃo] *nm* (small) bit; (*Am*: *cuerno*) horn
cachondearse [katʃonde'arse] *vr*: **~ de algn** to tease sb
cachondeo [katʃon'deo] *nm* (*fam*) farce, joke; (*guasa*) laugh
cachondo, -a [ka'tʃondo, a] *adj* (*Zool*) on heat; (*caliente*) randy, sexy; (*gracioso*) funny
cachorro, -a [ka'tʃorro, a] *nm/f* (*de perro*) pup, puppy; (*de león*) cub
cachucha [ka'tʃutʃa] (*Méx*: *fam*) *nf* cap
cacique [ka'θike] *nm* chief, local ruler; (*Pol*) local party boss; (*fig*) despot
caco ['kako] *nm* pickpocket
cacto ['kakto] *nm*, **cactus** ['kaktus] *nm inv* cactus
cada ['kaða] *adj inv* each; (*antes de número*) every; **~ día** each day, every day; **~ dos días** every other day; **~ uno/a** each one, every one; **~ vez más/menos** more and more/less and

less; ~ **vez que ...** whenever, every time (that) ...; **uno de ~ diez** one out of every ten; **¿~ cuánto?** how often?
cadalso [ka'ðalso] *nm* scaffold
cadáver [ka'ðaβer] *nm* (dead) body, corpse
cadena [ka'ðena] *nf* chain; (*TV*) channel; **reacción en ~** chain reaction; **trabajo en ~** assembly line work; **~ midi/mini** (*Mus*) midi/mini system; **~ montañosa** mountain range; **~ perpetua** (*Jur*) life imprisonment; **~ de caracteres** (*Inform*) character string
cadencia [ka'ðenθja] *nf* cadence, rhythm
cadera [ka'ðera] *nf* hip
cadete [ka'ðete] *nm* cadet
caducar [kaðu'kar] *vi* to expire
caducidad [kaðuθi'ðað] *nf*: **fecha de ~** expiry date; (*de comida*) sell-by date
caduco, -a [ka'ðuko, a] *adj* (*idea etc*) outdated, outmoded; **de hoja caduca** deciduous
caer [ka'er] *vi* to fall; (*premio*) to go; (*sitio*) to be, lie; (*pago*) to fall due; **caerse** *vr* to fall (down); **dejar ~** to drop; **estar al ~** to be due to happen; (*persona*) to be about to arrive; **me cae bien/mal** I like/don't like him; **~ en la cuenta** to catch on; **su cumpleaños cae en viernes** her birthday falls on a Friday; **se me ha caído el guante** I've dropped my glove
café (*pl* **cafés**) [ka'fe, ka'fes] *nm* (*bebida, planta*) coffee; (*lugar*) café ▷ *adj* (*color*) brown; **~ con leche** white coffee; **~ solo**, **~ negro** (*Am*) (small) black coffee
cafeína [kafe'ina] *nf* caffein(e)
cafetal [kafe'tal] *nm* coffee plantation
cafetera [kafe'tera] *nf ver* **cafetero**
cafetería [kafete'ria] *nf* cafe
cafetero, -a [kafe'tero, a] *adj* coffee *cpd* ▷ *nf* coffee pot; **ser muy ~** to be a coffee addict
cagalera [kaɣa'lera] *nf* (*fam!*): **tener ~** to have the runs
cagar [ka'ɣar] (*fam!*) *vt* to shit (*!*); (*fig*) to bungle, mess up ▷ *vi* to have a shit (*!*); **cagarse** *vr*: **¡me cago en diez** *etc*! Christ! (*!*)
caído, -a [ka'iðo, a] *adj* fallen; (*Inform*) down ▷ *nf* fall; (*declive*) slope; (*disminución*) fall, drop; **~ del cielo** out of the blue; **a la caída del sol** at sunset; **sufrir una caída** to have a fall
caiga *etc* ['kaiɣa] *vb ver* **caer**
caimán [kai'man] *nm* alligator
caja ['kaxa] *nf* box; (*ataúd*) coffin, casket (*US*); (*para reloj*) case; (*de ascensor*) shaft; (*Com*) cash box; (*Econ*) fund; (*donde se hacen los pagos*) cashdesk; (*en supermercado*) checkout, till; (*Tip*) case; (*de parking*) pay station; **~ de ahorros** savings bank; **~ de cambios** gearbox; **~ de fusibles** fuse box; **~ fuerte** *o* **de caudales** safe, strongbox; **ingresar en ~** to be paid in
cajero, -a [ka'xero, a] *nm/f* cashier; (*en banco*) (bank) teller ▷ *nm*: **~ automático** cash dispenser, automatic telling machine, ATM
cajetilla [kaxe'tiʎa] *nf* (*de cigarrillos*) packet
cajón [ka'xon] *nm* big box; (*de mueble*) drawer
cajuela [kax'wela] (*Méx*) *nf* (*Auto*) boot (*Brit*), trunk (*US*)
cal [kal] *nf* lime; **cerrar algo a ~ y canto** to shut sth firmly
cala ['kala] *nf* (*Geo*) cove, inlet; (*de barco*) hold
calabacín [kalaβa'θin] *nm* (*Bot*) baby marrow; (*: más pequeño*) courgette (*Brit*), zucchini (*US*)
calabacita (*Am*) [kalaβa'θita] *nf* courgette (*Brit*), zucchini (*US*)
calabaza [kala'βaθa] *nf* (*Bot*) pumpkin; **dar ~s a** (*candidato*) to fail
calabozo [kala'βoθo] *nm* (*cárcel*) prison; (*celda*) cell
calado, -a [ka'laðo, a] *adj* (*prenda*) lace *cpd* ▷ *nm* (*Tec*) fretwork; (*Naut*) draught ▷ *nf* (*de cigarrillo*) puff; **estar ~ (hasta los huesos)** to be soaked (to the skin)
calamar [kala'mar] *nm* squid
calambre [ka'lambre] *nm* (*Elec*) shock; (*tb*: **~s**) cramp
calamidad [kalami'ðað] *nf* calamity, disaster; (*persona*): **es una ~** he's a dead loss
calamina [kala'mina] *nf* calamine
calaña [ka'laɲa] *nf* model, pattern; (*fig*) nature, stamp
calar [ka'lar] *vt* to soak, drench; (*penetrar*) to pierce, penetrate; (*comprender*) to see through; (*vela, red*) to lower; **calarse** *vr* (*Auto*) to stall; **~se las gafas** to stick one's glasses on
calavera [kala'βera] *nf* skull
calcañal [kalka'ɲal], **calcañar** [kalka'ɲar] *nm* heel
calcar [kal'kar] *vt* (*reproducir*) to trace; (*imitar*) to copy
calceta [kal'θeta] *nf* (knee-length) stocking; **hacer ~** to knit
calcetín [kalθe'tin] *nm* sock
calcinar [kalθi'nar] *vt* to burn, blacken
calcio ['kalθjo] *nm* calcium
calco ['kalko] *nm* tracing
calcomanía [kalkoma'nia] *nf* transfer
calculador, a [kalkula'ðor, a] *adj* calculating ▷ *nf* calculator
calcular [kalku'lar] *vt* (*Mat*) to calculate, compute; **~ que ...** to reckon that ...
cálculo ['kalkulo] *nm* calculation; (*Med*) (gall) stone; (*Mat*) calculus; **~ de costo** costing; **~ diferencial** differential calculus; **obrar con mucho ~** to act cautiously
caldear [kalde'ar] *vt* to warm (up), heat (up); (*metales*) to weld
caldera [kal'dera] *nf* boiler
calderilla [kalde'riʎa] *nf* (*moneda*) small change
caldero [kal'dero] *nm* small boiler
caldo ['kaldo] *nm* stock; (*consomé*) consommé; **~ de cultivo** (*Bio*) culture medium; **poner a ~ a algn** to tear sb off a strip; **los ~s jerezanos** sherries
caldoso, -a [kal'doso, a] *adj* (*guisado*) juicy; (*sopa*) thin

calefacción [kalefak'θjon] *nf* heating; **~ central** central heating
calefón [kale'fon] *nm* (*RPl*) boiler
caleidoscopio [kaleiðos'kopjo] *nm* kaleidoscope
calendario [kalen'darjo] *nm* calendar
calentador [kalenta'ðor] *nm* heater
calentamiento [kalenta'mjento] *nm* (*Deporte*) warm-up; **~ global** global warming
calentar [kalen'tar] *vt* to heat (up); (*fam: excitar*) to turn on; (*Am: enfurecer*) to anger; **calentarse** *vr* to heat up, warm up; (*fig: discusión etc*) to get heated
calentón, -ona [kalen'ton, ona] (*RPl: fam*) *adj* (*sexualmente*) horny, randy (*Brit*)
calentura [kalen'tura] *nf* (*Med*) fever, (high) temperature; (*de boca*) mouth sore
calenturiento, -a [kalentu'rjento, a] *adj* (*mente*) overactive
calesita [kale'sita] *nf* (*Am*) merry-go-round, carousel
calibrar [kali'βrar] *vt* to gauge, measure
calibre [ka'liβre] *nm* (*de cañón*) calibre, bore; (*diámetro*) diameter; (*fig*) calibre
calidad [kali'ðað] *nf* quality; **de ~** quality *cpd*; **~ de borrador** (*Inform*) draft quality; **~ de carta** *o* **de correspondencia** (*Inform*) letter quality; **~ texto** (*Inform*) text quality; **~ de vida** quality of life; **en ~ de** in the capacity of
cálido, -a ['kaliðo, a] *adj* hot; (*fig*) warm
caliente [ka'ljente] *vb ver* **calentar** ▷ *adj* hot; (*fig*) fiery; (*disputa*) heated; (*fam: cachondo*) randy
califa [ka'lifa] *nm* caliph
calificación [kalifika'θjon] *nf* qualification; (*de alumno*) grade, mark; **~ de sobresaliente** first-class mark
calificado, -a [kalifi'kado, a] *adj* (*Am: competente*) qualified; (*obrero*) skilled
calificar [kalifi'kar] *vt* to qualify; (*alumno*) to grade, mark; **~ de** to describe as
caligrafía [kaliɣra'fia] *nf* calligraphy
calima [ka'lima] *nf* (*cerca del mar*) mist
cáliz ['kaliθ] *nm* (*Bot*) calyx; (*Rel*) chalice
caliza [ka'liθa] *nf* limestone
callado, -a [ka'ʎaðo, a] *adj* quiet, silent
callar [ka'ʎar] *vt* (*asunto delicado*) to keep quiet about, say nothing about; (*omitir*) to pass over in silence; (*persona, oposición*) to silence ▷ *vi*, **callarse** *vr* to keep quiet, be silent; (*dejar de hablar*) to stop talking; **¡calla!** be quiet!; **¡cállate!, ¡cállese!** shut up!; **¡cállate la boca!** shut your mouth!
calle ['kaʎe] *nf* street; (*Deporte*) lane; **~ arriba/abajo** up/down the street; **~ de sentido único** one-way street; **~ mayor** (*Esp*) high (*Brit*) *o* main (*US*) street; **~ peatonal** pedestrianized *o* pedestrian street; **~ principal** (*Am*) high (*Brit*) *o* main (*US*) street; **poner a algn (de patitas) en la ~** to kick sb out
calleja [ka'ʎexa] *nf* alley, narrow street
callejear [kaʎexe'ar] *vi* to wander (about) the streets
callejero, -a [kaʎe'xero, a] *adj* street *cpd* ▷ *nm* street map
callejón [kaʎe'xon] *nm* alley, passage; (*Geo*) narrow pass; **~ sin salida** cul-de-sac; (*fig*) blind alley
callejuela [kaʎe'xwela] *nf* side-street, alley
callista [ka'ʎista] *nm/f* chiropodist
callo ['kaʎo] *nm* callus; (*en el pie*) corn; **callos** *nmpl* (*Culin*) tripe *sg*
callosidad [kaʎosi'ðað] *nf* (*de pie*) corn; (*de mano*) callus
calloso, -a [ka'ʎoso, a] *adj* horny, rough
calma ['kalma] *nf* calm; (*pachorra*) slowness; (*Com, Econ*) calm, lull; **~ chicha** dead calm; **¡~!, ¡con ~!** take it easy!
calmante [kal'mante] *adj* soothing ▷ *nm* sedative, tranquillizer
calmar [kal'mar] *vt* to calm, calm down; (*dolor*) to relieve ▷ *vi*, **calmarse** *vr* (*tempestad*) to abate; (*mente etc*) to become calm
calmoso, -a [kal'moso, a] *adj* calm, quiet
calor [ka'lor] *nm* heat; (*calor agradable*) warmth; **entrar en ~** to get warm; **tener ~** to be *o* feel hot
caloría [kalo'ria] *nf* calorie
calorífero, -a [kalo'rifero, a] *adj* heat-producing, heat-giving ▷ *nm* heating system
calumnia [ka'lumnja] *nf* slander; (*por escrito*) libel
calumnioso, -a [kalum'njoso, a] *adj* slanderous; libellous
caluroso, -a [kalu'roso, a] *adj* hot; (*sin exceso*) warm; (*fig*) enthusiastic
calva ['kalβa] *nf* bald patch; (*en bosque*) clearing
calvario [kal'βarjo] *nm* stations *pl* of the cross; (*fig*) cross, heavy burden
calvicie [kal'βiθje] *nf* baldness
calvo, -a ['kalβo, a] *adj* bald; (*terreno*) bare, barren; (*tejido*) threadbare ▷ *nm* bald man
calza ['kalθa] *nf* wedge, chock
calzado, -a [kal'θaðo, a] *adj* shod ▷ *nm* footwear ▷ *nf* roadway, highway
calzador [kalθa'ðor] *nm* shoehorn
calzar [kal'θar] *vt* (*zapatos etc*) to wear; (*un mueble*) to put a wedge under; (*Tec: rueda etc*) to scotch; **calzarse** *vr*: **~se los zapatos** to put on one's shoes; **¿qué (número) calza?** what size do you take?
calzón [kal'θon] *nm* (*tb*: **calzones**) shorts *pl*; (*Am: de hombre*) pants *pl*; (*: de mujer*) panties *pl*
calzoncillos [kalθon'θiʎos] *nmpl* underpants
cama ['kama] *nf* bed; (*Geo*) stratum; **~ individual/de matrimonio** single/double bed; **hacer la ~** to make the bed; **guardar ~** to be ill in bed
camada [ka'maða] *nf* litter; (*de personas*) gang, band
camafeo [kama'feo] *nm* cameo

camaleón [kamale'on] *nm* chameleon
cámara ['kamara] *nf* (*Pol etc*) chamber; (*habitación*) room; (*sala*) hall; (*Cine*) cine camera; (*fotográfica*) camera; **~ de aire** inner tube; **~ alta/baja** upper/lower house; **~ de comercio** chamber of commerce; **~ digital** digital camera; **~ de gas** gas chamber; **~ de vídeo** video camera; **a ~ lenta** in slow motion; **~ frigorífica** cold-storage room
camarada [kama'raða] *nm* comrade, companion
camarero, -a [kama'rero, a] *nm* waiter ▷ *nf* (*en restaurante*) waitress; (*en casa, hotel*) maid
camarilla [kama'riʎa] *nf* (*clan*) clique; (*Pol*) lobby
camarín [kama'rin] *nm* (*Teat*) dressing room
camarógrafo, -a [kama'rografo, a] *nm/f* (*Am*) cameraman/camerawoman
camarón [kama'ron] *nm* shrimp
camarote [kama'rote] *nm* (*Naut*) cabin
cambiable [kam'bjaβle] *adj* (*variable*) changeable, variable; (*intercambiable*) interchangeable
cambiante [kam'bjante] *adj* variable
cambiar [kam'bjar] *vt* to change; (*trocar*) to exchange ▷ *vi* to change; **cambiarse** *vr* (*mudarse*) to move; (*de ropa*) to change; **~ de idea** *u* **opinión** to change one's mind; **~se de ropa** to change (one's clothes)
cambiazo [kam'bjaθo] *nm*: **dar el ~ a algn** to swindle sb
cambio ['kambjo] *nm* change; (*trueque*) exchange; (*Com*) rate of exchange; (*oficina*) bureau de change; (*dinero menudo*) small change; **a ~ de** in return *o* exchange for; **en ~** on the other hand; (*en lugar de eso*) instead; **~ climático** climate change; **~ de divisas** (*Com*) foreign exchange; **~ de línea** (*Inform*) line feed; **~ de página** (*Inform*) form feed; **~ a término** (*Com*) forward exchange; **~ de velocidades** gear lever; **~ de vía** points *pl*
cambista [kam'bista] *nm* (*Com*) exchange broker
camelar [kame'lar] *vt* (*con mujer*) to flirt with; (*persuadir*) to sweet-talk
camelia [ka'melia] *nf* camellia
camello [ka'meʎo] *nm* camel; (*fam*: *traficante*) pusher
camelo [ka'melo] *nm*: **me huele a ~** it smells fishy
camerino [kame'rino] *nm* (*Teat*) dressing room
camilla [ka'miʎa] *nf* (*Med*) stretcher
caminante [kami'nante] *nm/f* traveller
caminar [kami'nar] *vi* (*marchar*) to walk, go; (*viajar*) to travel, journey ▷ *vt* (*recorrer*) to cover, travel
caminata [kami'nata] *nf* long walk; (*por el campo*) hike
camino [ka'mino] *nm* way, road; (*sendero*) track; **a medio ~** halfway (there); **en el ~** on the way, en route; **~ de** on the way to; **~ particular** private road; **~ vecinal** country road; **C~s, Canales y Puertos** (*Univ*) Civil Engineering; **ir por buen ~** (*fig*) to be on the right track; **C~ de Santiago** Way of St James; *see note*

CAMINO DE SANTIAGO

The *Camino de Santiago* is a medieval pilgrim route stretching from the Pyrenees to Santiago de Compostela in north-west Spain, where tradition has it the body of the Apostle James is buried. Nowadays it is a popular tourist route as well as a religious one. The *concha* (cockleshell) is a symbol of the *Camino de Santiago*, because it is said that when St James' body was found it was covered in shells.

camión [ka'mjon] *nm* lorry, truck (*US*); (*Am*: *autobús*) bus; **~ cisterna** tanker; **~ de la basura** dustcart, refuse lorry; **~ de mudanzas** removal (*Brit*) *o* moving (*US*) van; **~ de bomberos** fire engine
camionero [kamjo'nero] *nm* lorry *o* truck (*US*) driver, trucker (*esp US*)
camioneta [kamjo'neta] *nf* van, small truck
camionista [kamjo'nista] *nm/f* (*Am*) lorry *o* truck driver
camisa [ka'misa] *nf* shirt; (*Bot*) skin; **~ de dormir** nightdress; **~ de fuerza** straitjacket
camiseta [kami'seta] *nf* tee-shirt; (*ropa interior*) vest; (*de deportista*) top
camisón [kami'son] *nm* nightdress, nightgown
camorra [ka'morra] *nf*: **armar ~** to kick up a row; **buscar ~** to look for trouble
camorrista [kamo'rrista] *nm/f* thug
camote [ka'mote] *nm* (*Am*) sweet potato; (*bulbo*) tuber, bulb; (*fam*: *enamoramiento*) crush
campal [kam'pal] *adj*: **batalla ~** pitched battle
campamento [kampa'mento] *nm* camp
campana [kam'pana] *nf* bell
campanada [kampa'naða] *nf* peal
campanario [kampa'narjo] *nm* belfry
campanilla [kampa'niʎa] *nf* (*campana*) small bell
campaña [kam'paɲa] *nf* (*Mil, Pol*) campaign; **hacer ~ (en pro de/contra)** to campaign (for/against); **~ de venta** sales campaign; **~ electoral** election campaign
campechano, -a [kampe'tʃano, a] *adj* (*franco*) open
campeón, -ona [kampe'on, ona] *nm/f* champion
campeonato [kampeo'nato] *nm* championship
cámper ['kamper] *nm o f* (*Am*) caravan (*Brit*), trailer (*US*)
campera [kam'pera] *nf* (*RPl*) anorak

campesino, -a [kampe'sino, a] *adj* country *cpd*, rural; (*gente*) peasant *cpd* ▷ *nm/f* countryman/woman; (*agricultor*) farmer
campestre [kam'pestre] *adj* country *cpd*, rural
camping ['kampin] *nm* camping; (*lugar*) campsite; **ir de** *o* **hacer ~** to go camping
campiña [kam'piɲa] *nf* countryside
campista [kam'pista] *nm/f* camper
campo ['kampo] *nm* (*fuera de la ciudad*) country, countryside; (*Agr, Elec, Inform*) field; (*de fútbol*) pitch; (*de golf*) course; (*Mil*) camp; **~ de batalla** battlefield; **~ de minas** minefield; **~ petrolífero** oilfield; **~ visual** field of vision; **~ de concentración/de internación/de trabajo** concentration/internment/labour camp; **~ de deportes** sports ground, playing field
camposanto [kampo'santo] *nm* cemetery
campus ['kampus] *nm inv* (*Univ*) campus
camuflaje [kamu'flaxe] *nm* camouflage
camuflar [kamu'flar] *vt* to camouflage
cana ['kana] *nf ver* **cano**
Canadá [kana'ða] *nm* Canada
canadiense [kana'ðjense] *adj, nm/f* Canadian ▷ *nf* fur-lined jacket
canal [ka'nal] *nm* canal; (*Geo*) channel, strait; (*de televisión*) channel; (*de tejado*) gutter; **C~ de la Mancha** English Channel; **C~ de Panamá** Panama Canal
canaleta [kana'leta] *nf* (*Am: de tejado*) gutter
canalizar [kanali'θar] *vt* to channel
canalla [ka'naʎa] *nf* rabble, mob ▷ *nm* swine
canalón [kana'lon] *nm* (*conducto vertical*) drainpipe; (*del tejado*) gutter; **canalones** *nmpl* (*Culin*) cannelloni
canapé (*pl* **canapés**) [kana'pe, kana'pes] *nm* sofa, settee; (*Culin*) canapé
Canarias [ka'narjas] *nfpl*: **las (Islas) ~** the Canaries, the Canary Isles
canario, -a [ka'narjo, a] *adj* of *o* from the Canary Isles ▷ *nm/f* native *o* inhabitant of the Canary Isles ▷ *nm* (*Zool*) canary
canasta [ka'nasta] *nf* (round) basket
canastilla [kanas'tiʎa] *nf* small basket; (*de niño*) layette
canasto [ka'nasto] *nm* large basket
cancela [kan'θela] *nf* (wrought-iron) gate
cancelación [kanθela'θjon] *nf* cancellation
cancelar [kanθe'lar] *vt* to cancel; (*una deuda*) to write off
cáncer ['kanθer] *nm* (*Med*) cancer; **C~** (*Astro*) Cancer
cancerígeno, -a [kanθe'rixeno, a] *adj* carcinogenic
cancha ['kantʃa] *nf* (*de baloncesto, tenis etc*) court; (*Am: de fútbol etc*) pitch; **~ de tenis** (*Am*) tennis court
canciller [kanθi'ʎer] *nm* chancellor; **C~** (*Am*) Foreign Minister, ≈ Foreign Secretary (*Brit*)
canción [kan'θjon] *nf* song; **~ de cuna** lullaby
cancionero [kanθjo'nero] *nm* song book
candado [kan'daðo] *nm* padlock
candela [kan'dela] *nf* candle
candelero [kande'lero] *nm* (*para vela*) candlestick; (*de aceite*) oil lamp
candente [kan'dente] *adj* red-hot; (*tema*) burning
candidato, -a [kandi'ðato, a] *nm/f* candidate; (*para puesto*) applicant
candidez [kandi'ðeθ] *nf* (*sencillez*) simplicity; (*simpleza*) naiveté
cándido, -a ['kandiðo, a] *adj* simple; naive
candil [kan'dil] *nm* oil lamp
candilejas [kandi'lexas] *nfpl* (*Teat*) footlights
candor [kan'dor] *nm* (*sinceridad*) frankness; (*inocencia*) innocence
canela [ka'nela] *nf* cinnamon
canelones [kane'lones] *nmpl* cannelloni
cangrejo [kan'grexo] *nm* crab
canguro [kan'guro] *nm* (*Zool*) kangaroo; (*de niños*) baby-sitter; **hacer de ~** to baby-sit
caníbal [ka'niβal] *adj, nm/f* cannibal
canica [ka'nika] *nf* marble
canijo, -a [ka'nixo, a] *adj* frail, sickly
canilla [ka'niʎa] *nf* (*Tec*) bobbin; (*Am*) tap (*Brit*), faucet (*US*)
canino, -a [ka'nino, a] *adj* canine ▷ *nm* canine (tooth)
canjear [kanxe'ar] *vt* to exchange; (*trocar*) to swap
cano, -a ['kano, a] *adj* grey-haired, white-haired ▷ *nf* (*tb*: **canas**) white *o* grey hair; **tener canas** to be going grey
canoa [ka'noa] *nf* canoe
canon ['kanon] *nm* canon; (*pensión*) rent; (*Com*) tax
canónico, -a [ka'noniko, a] *adj*: **derecho ~** canon law
canónigo [ka'noniɣo] *nm* canon
canonizar [kanoni'θar] *vt* to canonize
canoso, -a [ka'noso, a] *adj* (*pelo*) grey (*Brit*), gray (*US*); (*persona*) grey-haired
cansado, -a [kan'saðo, a] *adj* tired, weary; (*tedioso*) tedious, boring; **estoy ~ de hacerlo** I'm sick of doing it
cansancio [kan'sanθjo] *nm* tiredness, fatigue
cansar [kan'sar] *vt* (*fatigar*) to tire, tire out; (*aburrir*) to bore; (*fastidiar*) to bother; **cansarse** *vr* to tire, get tired; (*aburrirse*) to get bored
cantábrico, -a [kan'taβriko, a] *adj* Cantabrian; **Mar C~** Bay of Biscay; **(Montes) C~s, Cordillera Cantábrica** Cantabrian Mountains
cantante [kan'tante] *adj* singing ▷ *nm/f* singer
cantar [kan'tar] *vt* to sing ▷ *vi* to sing; (*insecto*) to chirp; (*rechinar*) to squeak; (*fam: criminal*) to squeal ▷ *nm* (*acción*) singing; (*canción*) song; (*poema*) poem; **~ a algn las cuarenta** to tell sb a few home truths; **~ a dos voces** to sing a duet

cántara ['kantara] *nf* large pitcher
cántaro ['kantaro] *nm* pitcher, jug; **llover a ~s** to rain cats and dogs
cantautor, a [kantau'tor, a] *nm/f* singer-songwriter
cante ['kante] *nm Andalusian folk song*; **~ jondo** flamenco singing
cantera [kan'tera] *nf* quarry
cantero [kan'tero] *nm* (*Am*: *arriate*) border
cantidad [kanti'ðað] *nf* quantity, amount; (*Econ*) sum ▷ *adv* (*fam*) a lot; **~ alzada** lump sum; **~ de** lots of
cantilena [kanti'lena] *nf* = **cantinela**
cantimplora [kantim'plora] *nf* water bottle, canteen
cantina [kan'tina] *nf* canteen; (*de estación*) buffet; (*esp Am*) bar
cantinela [kanti'nela] *nf* ballad, song
cantinero, -a [kanti'nero, a] *nm/f* (*Am*) barman/barmaid, bartender (*US*)
canto ['kanto] *nm* singing; (*canción*) song; (*borde*) edge, rim; (*de un cuchillo*) back; **~ rodado** boulder
cantor, a [kan'tor, a] *nm/f* singer
canturrear [kanturre'ar] *vi* to sing softly
canutas [ka'nutas] *nfpl*: **pasarlas ~** (*fam*) to have a rough time (of it)
canuto [ka'nuto] *nm* (*tubo*) small tube; (*fam*: *porro*) joint
caña ['kaɲa] *nf* (*Bot*: *tallo*) stem, stalk; (*carrizo*) reed; (*vaso*) tumbler; (*de cerveza*) glass of beer; (*Anat*) shinbone; (*Am*: *aguardiente*) cane liquor; **~ de azúcar** sugar cane; **~ de pescar** fishing rod
cañada [ka'ɲaða] *nf* (*entre dos montañas*) gully, ravine; (*camino*) cattle track
cáñamo ['kaɲamo] *nm* (*Bot*) hemp
cañería [kaɲe'ria] *nf* piping; (*tubo*) pipe
caño ['kaɲo] *nm* (*tubo*) tube, pipe; (*de aguas servidas*) sewer; (*Mus*) pipe; (*Naut*) navigation channel; (*de fuente*) jet
cañón [ka'ɲon] *nm* (*Mil*) cannon; (*de fusil*) barrel; (*Geo*) canyon, gorge
cañonera [kaɲo'nera] *nf* (*tb*: **lancha ~**) gunboat
caoba [ka'oβa] *nf* mahogany
caos ['kaos] *nm* chaos
caótico, -a [ka'otiko, a] *adj* chaotic
cap. *abr* (= *capítulo*) ch.
capa ['kapa] *nf* cloak, cape; (*Culin*) coating; (*Geo*) layer, stratum; (*de pintura*) coat; **de ~ y espada** cloak-and-dagger; **so ~ de** under the pretext of; **~ de ozono** ozone layer; **~s sociales** social groups
capacidad [kapaθi'ðað] *nf* (*medida*) capacity; (*aptitud*) capacity, ability; **una sala con ~ para 900** a hall seating 900; **~ adquisitiva** purchasing power
capacitación [kapaθita'θjon] *nf* training
capacitar [kapaθi'tar] *vt*: **~ a algn para algo** to qualify sb for sth; (*Tec*) to train sb for sth; **capacitarse** *vr*: **~se para algo** to qualify for sth
capar [ka'par] *vt* to castrate, geld
caparazón [kapara'θon] *nm* (*Zool*) shell
capataz [kapa'taθ] *nm* foreman, charge hand
capaz [ka'paθ] *adj* able, capable; (*amplio*) capacious, roomy; **es ~ que venga mañana** (*Am*) he'll probably come tomorrow
capcioso, -a [kap'θjoso, a] *adj* wily, deceitful; **pregunta capciosa** trick question
capea [ka'pea] *nf* (*Taur*) bullfight with young bulls
capear [kape'ar] *vt* (*dificultades*) to dodge; **~ el temporal** to weather the storm
capellán [kape'ʎan] *nm* chaplain; (*sacerdote*) priest
caperuza [kape'ruθa] *nf* hood; (*de bolígrafo*) cap
capicúa [kapi'kua] *adj inv* (*número, fecha*) reversible ▷ *nf reversible number, e.g. 1441*
capilar [kapi'lar] *adj* hair *cpd*
capilla [ka'piʎa] *nf* chapel
capital [kapi'tal] *adj* capital ▷ *nm* (*Com*) capital ▷ *nf* (*de nación*) capital (city); (*tb*: **~ de provincia**) provincial capital, ≈ county town; **~ activo/en acciones** working/share *o* equity capital; **~ arriesgado** venture capital; **~ autorizado** *o* **social** authorised capital; **~ emitido** issued capital; **~ improductivo** idle money; **~ invertido** *o* **utilizado** capital employed; **~ pagado** paid-up capital; **~ de riesgo** risk capital; **~ social** equity *o* share capital; **inversión de ~es** capital investment; *ver tb* **provincia**
capitalismo [kapita'lismo] *nm* capitalism
capitalista [kapita'lista] *adj, nm/f* capitalist
capitalizar [kapitali'θar] *vt* to capitalize
capitán [kapi'tan] *nm* captain; (*fig*) leader
capitanear [kapitane'ar] *vt* to captain
capitolio [kapi'toljo] *nm* capitol
capitulación [kapitula'θjon] *nf* (*rendición*) capitulation, surrender; (*acuerdo*) agreement, pact; **capitulaciones matrimoniales** marriage contract *sg*
capitular [kapitu'lar] *vi* to come to terms, make an agreement; (*Mil*) to surrender
capítulo [ka'pitulo] *nm* chapter
capo [ka'po] *nm* drugs baron
capó [ka'po] *nm* (*Auto*) bonnet (*Brit*), hood (*US*)
capón [ka'pon] *nm* (*gallo*) capon
caporal [kapo'ral] *nm* chief, leader
capota [ka'pota] *nf* (*de mujer*) bonnet; (*Auto*) hood (*Brit*), top (*US*)
capote [ka'pote] *nm* (*abrigo*: *de militar*) greatcoat; (*de torero*) cloak
capricho [ka'pritʃo] *nm* whim, caprice
caprichoso, -a [kapri'tʃoso, a] *adj* capricious
Capricornio [kapri'kornjo] *nm* Capricorn
cápsula ['kapsula] *nf* capsule; **~ espacial** space capsule
captar [kap'tar] *vt* (*comprender*) to understand; (*Radio*) to pick up; (*atención, apoyo*) to attract
captura [kap'tura] *nf* capture; (*Jur*) arrest; **~ de pantalla** screenshot

capturar [kaptu'rar] *vt* to capture; (*Jur*) to arrest; (*datos*) to input
capucha [ka'putʃa] *nf* hood, cowl
capuchón [kapu'tʃon] *nm* (*Esp*: *de bolígrafo*) cap
capullo [ka'puʎo] *nm* (*Zool*) cocoon; (*Bot*) bud; (*fam!*) idiot
caqui ['kaki] *nm* khaki
cara ['kara] *nf* (*Anat, de moneda*) face; (*aspecto*) appearance; (*de disco*) side; (*fig*) boldness; (*descaro*) cheek, nerve ▷ *prep*: **~ a** facing; **de ~ a** opposite, facing; **dar la ~** to face the consequences; **echar algo en ~ a algn** to reproach sb for sth; **¿~ o cruz?** heads or tails?; **¡qué ~ más dura!** what a nerve!; **de una ~** (*disquete*) single-sided
carabina [kara'βina] *nf* carbine, rifle; (*persona*) chaperone
Caracas [ka'rakas] *nm* Caracas
caracol [kara'kol] *nm* (*Zool*) snail; (*concha*) (sea)shell; **escalera de ~** spiral staircase
caracolear [karakole'ar] *vi* (*caballo*) to prance about
carácter (*pl* **caracteres**) [ka'rakter, karak'teres] *nm* character; **caracteres de imprenta** (*Tip*) type(face) *sg*; **~ libre** (*Inform*) wildcard character; **tener buen/mal ~** to be good-natured/bad tempered
característico, -a [karakte'ristiko, a] *adj* characteristic ▷ *nf* characteristic
caracterizar [karakteri'θar] *vt* (*distinguir*) to characterize, typify; (*honrar*) to confer a distinction on
caradura [kara'ðura] *nm/f* cheeky person; **es un ~** he's got a nerve
carajillo [kara'xiʎo] *nm* *black coffee with brandy*
carajo [ka'raxo] *nm* (*esp Am fam!*): **¡~!** shit! (!); **¡qué ~!** what the hell!; **me importa un ~** I don't give a damn
caramba [ka'ramba] *excl* well!, good gracious!
carámbano [ka'rambano] *nm* icicle
caramelo [kara'melo] *nm* (*dulce*) sweet; (*azúcar fundido*) caramel
carantoñas [karan'toɲas] *nfpl*: **hacer ~ a algn** to (try to) butter sb up
caraqueño, -a [kara'keɲo, a] *adj* of *o* from Caracas ▷ *nm/f* native *o* inhabitant of Caracas
carátula [ka'ratula] *nf* (*máscara*) mask; (*Teat*): **la ~** the stage
caravana [kara'βana] *nf* caravan; (*fig*) group; (*de autos*) tailback
carbo ['carβo] *nm* (*inf*: = *carbohidrato*) carb
carbón [kar'βon] *nm* coal; **~ de leña** charcoal; **papel ~** carbon paper
carboncillo [karβon'θiʎo] *nm* (*Arte*) charcoal
carbonilla [karβo'niʎa] *nf* coal dust
carbonizar [karβoni'θar] *vt* to carbonize; (*quemar*) to char; **quedar carbonizado** (*Elec*) to be electrocuted
carbono [kar'βono] *nm* carbon; **~ neutral** carbon-neutral
carburador [karβura'ðor] *nm* carburettor
carburante [karβu'rante] *nm* fuel
carca ['karka] *adj, nm/f inv* reactionary
carcajada [karka'xaða] *nf* (loud) laugh, guffaw
carcajearse [karkaxe'arse] *vr* to roar with laughter
cárcel ['karθel] *nf* prison, jail; (*Tec*) clamp
carcelero, -a [karθe'lero, a] *adj* prison *cpd* ▷ *nm/f* warder
carcoma [kar'koma] *nf* woodworm
carcomer [karko'mer] *vt* to bore into, eat into; (*fig*) to undermine; **carcomerse** *vr* to become worm-eaten; (*fig*) to decay
carcomido, -a [karko'miðo, a] *adj* worm-eaten; (*fig*) rotten
cardar [kar'ðar] *vt* (*Tec*) to card, comb; (*pelo*) to backcomb
cardenal [karðe'nal] *nm* (*Rel*) cardinal; (*Med*) bruise
cárdeno, -a ['karðeno, a] *adj* purple; (*lívido*) livid
cardiaco, -a [kar'ðiako, a], **cardíaco, a** [kar'ðiako, a] *adj* cardiac; (*ataque*) heart *cpd*
cardinal [karði'nal] *adj* cardinal
cardo ['karðo] *nm* thistle
carear [kare'ar] *vt* to bring face to face; (*comparar*) to compare; **carearse** *vr* to come face to face, meet
carecer [kare'θer] *vi*: **~ de** to lack, be in need of
carencia [ka'renθja] *nf* lack; (*escasez*) shortage; (*Med*) deficiency
carente [ka'rente] *adj*: **~ de** lacking in, devoid of
carestía [kares'tia] *nf* (*escasez*) scarcity, shortage; (*Com*) high cost; **época de ~** period of shortage
careta [ka'reta] *nf* mask
carga ['karɣa] *nf* (*peso, Elec*) load; (*de barco*) cargo, freight; (*Finanzas*) tax, duty; (*Mil*) charge; (*Inform*) loading; (*obligación, responsabilidad*) duty, obligation; **~ aérea** (*Com*) air cargo; **~ útil** (*Com*) payload; **la ~ fiscal** the tax burden
cargado, -a [kar'ɣaðo, a] *adj* loaded; (*Elec*) live; (*café, té*) strong; (*cielo*) overcast
cargamento [karɣa'mento] *nm* (*acción*) loading; (*mercancías*) load, cargo
cargar [kar'ɣar] *vt* (*barco, arma*) to load; (*Elec*) to charge; (*impuesto*) to impose; (*Com*: *algo en cuenta*) to charge, debit; (*Mil*: *enemigo*) to charge; (*Inform*) to load ▷ *vi* (*Auto*) to load (up); (*inclinarse*) to lean; **~ con** to pick up, carry away; (*peso*: *fig*) to shoulder, bear; **cargarse** *vr* (*fam*: *estropear*) to break; (: *matar*) to bump off; (*Elec*) to become charged
cargo ['karɣo] *nm* (*Com etc*) charge, debit; (*puesto*) post, office; (*responsabilidad*) duty, obligation; (*fig*) weight, burden; (*Jur*) charge; **altos ~s** high-ranking officials; **una cantidad en ~ a algn** a sum chargeable to sb;

hacerse ~ de to take charge of *o* responsibility for

carguero [kar'ɣero] *nm* freighter, cargo boat; (*avión*) freight plane

Caribe [ka'riβe] *nm*: **el ~** the Caribbean; **del ~** Caribbean

caribeño, -a [kari'βeɲo, a] *adj* Caribbean

caricatura [karika'tura] *nf* caricature

caricia [ka'riθja] *nf* caress; (*a animal*) pat, stroke

caridad [kari'ðað] *nf* charity

caries ['karjes] *nf inv* (*Med*) tooth decay

cariño [ka'riɲo] *nm* affection, love; (*caricia*) caress; (*en carta*) love ...; **tener ~ a** to be fond of

cariñoso, -a [kari'ɲoso, a] *adj* affectionate

carisma [ka'risma] *nm* charisma

carismático, -a [karis'matiko, a] *adj* charismatic

caritativo, -a [karita'tiβo, a] *adj* charitable

cariz [ka'riθ] *nm*: **tener** *o* **tomar buen/mal ~** to look good/bad

carmesí [karme'si] *adj, nm* crimson

carmín [kar'min] *nm* (*color*) carmine; (*tb*: **~ de labios**) lipstick

carnal [kar'nal] *adj* carnal; **primo ~** first cousin

carnaval [karna'βal] *nm* carnival; *see note*

CARNAVAL

The 3 days before *miércoles de ceniza* (Ash Wednesday), when fasting traditionally starts, are the time for *carnaval*, an exuberant celebration which dates back to pre-Christian times. Although in decline during the Franco years, the *carnaval* has grown in popularity recently in Spain, Cádiz and Tenerife being particularly well-known for their celebrations. *El martes de carnaval* (Shrove Tuesday) is the biggest day, with colourful street parades, fancy dress, fireworks and a general party atmosphere.

carne ['karne] *nf* flesh; (*Culin*) meat; **se me pone la ~ de gallina sólo verlo** I get the creeps just seeing it; **~ de cerdo/de cordero/de ternera/de vaca** pork/lamb/veal/beef; **~ molida** (*LAm*) Brit, ground meat (*US*); **~ picada** (*Esp*) mince (*Brit*), ground meat (*US*); **~ de gallina** (*fig*) gooseflesh

carné [kar'ne] (*pl* **carnés**) (*Esp*) *nm*: **~ de conducir** driving licence (*Brit*), driver's license (*US*); **~ de identidad** identity card; **~ de socio** membership card

carnero [kar'nero] *nm* sheep, ram; (*carne*) mutton

carnet (*pl* **carnets**) [kar'ne, kar'nes] *nm* (*Esp*) = **carné**

carnicería [karniθe'ria] *nf* butcher's (shop); (*fig*: *matanza*) carnage, slaughter

carnicero, -a [karni'θero, a] *adj* carnivorous ▷ *nm/f* (*tb fig*) butcher ▷ *nm* carnivore

carnívoro, -a [kar'niβoro, a] *adj* carnivorous ▷ *nm* carnivore

carnoso, -a [kar'noso, a] *adj* beefy, fat

caro, -a ['karo, a] *adj* dear; (*Com*) dear, expensive ▷ *adv* dear, dearly; **vender ~** to sell at a high price

carpa ['karpa] *nf* (*pez*) carp; (*de circo*) big top; (*Am*: *de camping*) tent

carpeta [kar'peta] *nf* folder, file

carpintería [karpinte'ria] *nf* carpentry, joinery

carpintero [karpin'tero] *nm* carpenter; **pájaro ~** woodpecker

carraspear [karraspe'ar] *vi* (*aclararse la garganta*) to clear one's throat

carraspera [karras'pera] *nf* hoarseness

carrera [ka'rrera] *nf* (*acción*) run(ning); (*espacio recorrido*) run; (*certamen*) race; (*trayecto*) course; (*profesión*) career; (*Escol, Univ*) course; (*de taxi*) ride; (*en medias*) ladder; **a la ~** at (full) speed; **caballo de ~(s)** racehorse; **~ de obstáculos** (*Deporte*) steeplechase; **~ de armamentos** arms race

carreta [ka'rreta] *nf* wagon, cart

carrete [ka'rrete] *nm* reel, spool; (*Tec*) coil

carretera [karre'tera] *nf* (main) road, highway; **~ nacional** ≈ A road (*Brit*), ≈ state highway (*US*); **~ de circunvalación** ring road

carretilla [karre'tiʎa] *nf* trolley; (*Agr*) (wheel) barrow

carril [ka'rril] *nm* furrow; (*de autopista*) lane; (*Ferro*) rail

carril bici (*pl* **carriles bici**) [karil'βiθi, kariles'βiθi] *nm* cycle lane, bikeway (*US*)

carrillo [ka'rriʎo] *nm* (*Anat*) cheek; (*Tec*) pulley

carrito [ka'rrito] *nm* trolley

carro ['karro] *nm* cart, wagon; (*Mil*) tank; (*Am*: *coche*) car; (*Tip*) carriage; **~ blindado** armoured car; **~ patrulla** (*Am*) patrol *o* panda (*Brit*) car

carrocería [karroθe'ria] *nf* body, bodywork *no pl* (*Brit*)

carroña [ka'rroɲa] *nf* carrion *no pl*

carroza [ka'rroθa] *nf* (*vehículo*) coach ▷ *nm/f* (*fam*) old fogey

carruaje [ka'rrwaxe] *nm* carriage

carrusel [karru'sel] *nm* merry-go-round, roundabout (*Brit*)

carta ['karta] *nf* letter; (*Culin*) menu; (*naipe*) card; (*mapa*) map; (*Jur*) document; **~ de crédito** credit card; **~ de crédito documentaria** (*Com*) documentary letter of credit; **~ de crédito irrevocable** (*Com*) irrevocable letter of credit; **~ certificada/urgente** registered/special delivery letter; **~ marítima** chart; **~ de pedido** (*Com*) order; **~ verde** (*Auto*) green card; **~ de vinos** wine list; **echar una ~ al correo** to post a letter; **echar las ~s a algn** to tell sb's fortune

cartabón [karta'βon] *nm* set square
cartearse [karte'arse] *vr* to correspond
cartel [kar'tel] *nm* (*anuncio*) poster, placard; (*Escol*) wall chart; (*Com*) cartel
cartelera [karte'lera] *nf* hoarding, billboard; (*en periódico etc*) listings *pl*, entertainments guide; **"en ~"** "showing"
cartera [kar'tera] *nf* (*de bolsillo*) wallet; (*de colegial, cobrador*) satchel; (*Am: de señora*) handbag (*Brit*), purse (*US*); (*para documentos*) briefcase; (*Com*) portfolio; **ministro sin ~** (*Pol*) minister without portfolio; **ocupa la ~ de Agricultura** he is Minister of Agriculture; **~ de pedidos** (*Com*) order book; **efectos en ~** (*Econ*) holdings
carterista [karte'rista] *nm/f* pickpocket
cartero [kar'tero] *nm* postman
cartilla [kar'tiʎa] *nf* (*Escol*) primer, first reading book; **~ de ahorros** savings book
cartografía [kartoɣgra'fia] *nf* cartography
cartón [kar'ton] *nm* cardboard; **~ piedra** papier-mâché
cartucho [kar'tutʃo] *nm* (*Mil*) cartridge; (*bolsita*) paper cone; **~ de datos** (*Inform*) data cartridge; **~ de tinta** ink cartridge
cartulina [kartu'lina] *nf* fine cardboard, card
casa ['kasa] *nf* house; (*hogar*) home; (*edificio*) building; (*Com*) firm, company; **~ consistorial** town hall; **~ de huéspedes** boarding house; **~ de socorro** first aid post; **~ de citas** (*fam*) brothel; **~ independiente** detached house; **~ rural** (*de alquiler*) holiday cottage; (*pensión*) rural B&B; **~ rodante** (*CS*) caravan (*Brit*), trailer (*US*); **en ~** at home; **ir a ~** to go home; **salir de ~** to go out; (*para siempre*) to leave home; **echar la ~ por la ventana** (*gastar*) to spare no expense; *ver tb* **hotel**
casadero, -a [kasa'ðero, a] *adj* marriageable
casado, -a [ka'saðo, a] *adj* married ▷ *nm/f* married man/woman
casamiento [kasa'mjento] *nm* marriage, wedding
casar [ka'sar] *vt* to marry; (*Jur*) to quash, annul; **casarse** *vr* to marry, get married; **~se por lo civil** to have a civil wedding, get married in a registry office (*Brit*)
cascabel [kaska'βel] *nm* (small) bell; (*Zool*) rattlesnake
cascada [kas'kaða] *nf* waterfall
cascanueces [kaska'nweθes] *nm inv* (a pair of) nutcrackers, nutcracker *sg*
cascar [kas'kar] *vt* to split; (*nuez*) to crack ▷ *vi* to chatter; **cascarse** *vr* to crack, split, break (open)
cáscara ['kaskara] *nf* (*de huevo, fruta seca*) shell; (*de fruta*) skin; (*de limón*) peel
casco ['kasko] *nm* (*de bombero, soldado*) helmet; (*cráneo*) skull; (*Naut: de barco*) hull; (*Zool: de caballo*) hoof; (*botella*) empty bottle; (*de ciudad*): **el ~ antiguo** the old part; **el ~ urbano** the town centre; **los ~s azules** the UN peace-keeping force, the blue helmets
cascote [kas'kote] *nm* piece of rubble; **cascotes** *nmpl* rubble *sg*
caserío [kase'rio] *nm* hamlet, group of houses; (*casa*) farmhouse
casero, -a [ka'sero, a] *adj* (*pan etc*) home-made; **ser muy ~** (*persona*) to be home-loving; **"comida casera"** "home cooking" ▷ *nm/f* (*propietario*) landlord/lady; (*Com*) house agent
caseta [ka'seta] *nf* hut; (*para bañista*) cubicle; (*de feria*) stall
casete [ka'sete] *nm o f* cassette; **~ digital** digital audio tape, DAT
casi ['kasi] *adv* almost; **~ nunca** hardly ever, almost never; **~ nada** next to nothing; **~ te caes** you almost *o* nearly fell
casilla [ka'siʎa] *nf* (*casita*) hut, cabin; (*Teat*) box office; (*para cartas*) pigeonhole; (*Ajedrez*) square; **C~ postal** *o* **de Correo(s)** (*Am*) P.O. Box; **sacar a algn de sus ~s** to drive sb round the bend (*fam*), make sb lose his temper
casillero [kasi'ʎero] *nm* (*para cartas*) pigeonholes
casino [ka'sino] *nm* club; (*de juego*) casino
caso ['kaso] *nm* case; (*suceso*) event; **en ~ de ...** in case of ...; **el ~ es que** the fact is that; **en el mejor de los ~s** at best; **en ese ~** in that case; **en todo ~** in any case; **en último ~** as a last resort; **hacer ~ a** to pay attention to; **hacer ~ omiso de** to fail to mention, pass over; **hacer** *o* **venir al ~** to be relevant
caspa ['kaspa] *nf* dandruff
casquillo [kas'kiʎo] *nm* (*de bombilla*) fitting; (*de bala*) cartridge case
cassette [ka'set] *nf o m* = **casete**
casta ['kasta] *nf* caste; (*raza*) breed
castaña [kas'taɲa] *nf ver* **castaño**
castañetear [kastaɲete'ar] *vi* (*dientes*) to chatter
castaño, -a [kas'taɲo, a] *adj* chestnut(-coloured), brown ▷ *nm* chestnut tree ▷ *nf* chestnut; (*fam: golpe*) punch; **~ de Indias** horse chestnut tree
castañuelas [kasta'ɲwelas] *nfpl* castanets
castellano, -a [kaste'ʎano, a] *adj* Castilian; (*fam*) Spanish ▷ *nm/f* Castilian; (*fam*) Spaniard ▷ *nm* (*Ling*) Castilian, Spanish; *see note*

CASTELLANO

The term *castellano* is now the most widely used term in Spain and Spanish America to refer to the Spanish language, since español is too closely associated with Spain as a nation. Of course some people maintain that *castellano* should only refer to the type of Spanish spoken in Castilla.

castidad [kasti'ðað] *nf* chastity, purity
castigar [kasti'ɣar] *vt* to punish; (*Deporte*) to penalize; (*afligir*) to afflict

castigo [kas'tiɣo] *nm* punishment; (*Deporte*) penalty
Castilla [kas'tiʎa] *nf* Castile
castillo [kas'tiʎo] *nm* castle
castizo, -a [kas'tiθo, a] *adj* (*Ling*) pure; (*de buena casta*) purebred, pedigree; (*auténtico*) genuine
casto, -a ['kasto, a] *adj* chaste, pure
castor [kas'tor] *nm* beaver
castrar [kas'trar] *vt* to castrate; (*gato*) to doctor; (*Bot*) to prune
castrense [kas'trense] *adj* army *cpd*, military
casual [ka'swal] *adj* chance, accidental
casualidad [kaswali'ðað] *nf* chance, accident; (*combinación de circunstancias*) coincidence; **da la ~ de que ...** it (just) so happens that ...; **¡qué ~!** what a coincidence!
cataclismo [kata'klismo] *nm* cataclysm
catador [kata'ðor] *nm* taster
catalán, -ana [kata'lan, ana] *adj, nm/f* Catalan ▷ *nm* (*Ling*) Catalan
catalejo [kata'lexo] *nm* telescope
catalizador [kataliθa'ðor] *nm* catalyst; (*Auto*) catalytic converter
catalogar [katalo'ɣar] *vt* to catalogue; **~ (de)** (*fig*) to classify as
catálogo [ka'taloɣo] *nm* catalogue
Cataluña [kata'luɲa] *nf* Catalonia
cataplasma [kata'plasma] *nf* (*Med*) poultice
catapulta [kata'pulta] *nf* catapult
catar [ka'tar] *vt* to taste, sample
catarata [kata'rata] *nf* (*Geo*) (water)fall; (*Med*) cataract
catarro [ka'tarro] *nm* catarrh; (*constipado*) cold
catarsis [ka'tarsis] *nf* catharsis
catastro [ka'tastro] *nm* property register
catástrofe [ka'tastrofe] *nf* catastrophe
catear [kate'ar] *vt* (*fam: examen, alumno*) to fail
catecismo [kate'θismo] *nm* catechism
cátedra ['kateðra] *nf* (*Univ*) chair, professorship; (*Escol*) principal teacher's post; **sentar ~ sobre un argumento** to take one's stand on an argument
catedral [kate'ðral] *nf* cathedral
catedrático, -a [kate'ðratiko, a] *nm/f* professor; (*Escol*) principal teacher
categoría [kateɣo'ria] *nf* category; (*rango*) rank, standing; (*calidad*) quality; **de ~** (*hotel*) top-class; **de baja ~** (*oficial*) low-ranking; **de segunda ~** second-rate; **no tiene ~** he has no standing
categórico, -a [kate'ɣoriko, a] *adj* categorical
catequesis [kate'kesis] *nf* catechism lessons
cateto, -a [ka'teto, a] *nm/f* yokel
catolicismo [katoli'θismo] *nm* Catholicism
católico, -a [ka'toliko, a] *adj, nm/f* Catholic
catorce [ka'torθe] *num* fourteen
catre ['katre] *nm* camp bed (*Brit*), cot (*US*); (*fam*) pit
cauce ['kauθe] *nm* (*de río*) riverbed; (*fig*) channel
caucho ['kautʃo] *nm* rubber; (*Am: llanta*) tyre
caución [kau'θjon] *nf* bail
caudal [kau'ðal] *nm* (*de río*) volume, flow; (*fortuna*) wealth; (*abundancia*) abundance
caudaloso, -a [kauða'loso, a] *adj* (*río*) large; (*persona*) wealthy, rich
caudillo [kau'ðiʎo] *nm* leader, chief
causa ['kausa] *nf* cause; (*razón*) reason; (*Jur*) lawsuit, case; **a** *o* **por ~ de** because of, on account of
causar [kau'sar] *vt* to cause
cautela [kau'tela] *nf* caution, cautiousness
cauteloso, -a [kaute'loso, a] *adj* cautious, wary
cautivar [kauti'βar] *vt* to capture; (*fig*) to captivate
cautiverio [kauti'βerjo] *nm*, **cautividad** [kautiβi'ðað] *nf* captivity
cautivo, -a [kau'tiβo, a] *adj, nm/f* captive
cauto, -a ['kauto, a] *adj* cautious, careful
cava ['kaβa] *nf* (*bodega*) (wine) cellar ▷ *nm* (*vino*) *champagne-type wine*
cavar [ka'βar] *vt* to dig; (*Agr*) to dig over
caverna [ka'βerna] *nf* cave, cavern
caviar [ka'βjar] *nm* caviar(e)
cavidad [kaβi'ðað] *nf* cavity
cavilar [kaβi'lar] *vt* to ponder
cayado [ka'jaðo] *nm* (*de pastor*) crook; (*de obispo*) crozier
cayendo *etc* [ka'jendo] *vb ver* **caer**
caza ['kaθa] *nf* (*acción: gen*) hunting; (*: con fusil*) shooting; (*una caza*) hunt, chase; (*animales*) game; **coto de ~** hunting estate ▷ *nm* (*Aviat*) fighter; **ir de ~** to go hunting; **~ mayor** game hunting
cazador, a [kaθa'ðor, a] *nm/f* hunter/ huntress ▷ *nf* jacket
cazar [ka'θar] *vt* to hunt; (*perseguir*) to chase; (*prender*) to catch; **~las al vuelo** to be pretty sharp
cazo ['kaθo] *nm* saucepan
cazuela [ka'θwela] *nf* (*vasija*) pan; (*guisado*) casserole
CC *abr* (*= compensación de carbono*) carbon offsetting
CC.OO. *nfpl abr* = **Comisiones Obreras**
CD *nm abr* (*= compact disc*) CD; (Pol: *= Cuerpo Diplomático*) CD (*= Diplomatic Corps*)
CD-ROM [θeðe'rom] *nm abr* CD-ROM
CE *nm abr* (*= Consejo de Europa*) Council of Europe
cebada [θe'βaða] *nf* barley
cebar [θe'βar] *vt* (*animal*) to fatten (up); (*anzuelo*) to bait; (*Mil, Tec*) to prime; **cebarse** *vr*: **~se en** to vent one's fury on, take it out on
cebo ['θeβo] *nm* (*gen: para animales*) feed, food; (*para peces, fig*) bait; (*de arma*) charge
cebolla [θe'βoʎa] *nf* onion
cebolleta [θebo'ʎeta] *nf* spring onion
cebra ['θeβra] *nf* zebra; **paso de ~** zebra crossing
cecear [θeθe'ar] *vi* to lisp
ceceo [θe'θeo] *nm* lisp

cedazo [θe'ðaθo] *nm* sieve
ceder [θe'ðer] *vt* (*entregar*) to hand over; (*renunciar a*) to give up, part with ▷ *vi* (*renunciar*) to give in, yield; (*disminuir*) to diminish, decline; (*romperse*) to give way; (*viento*) to drop; (*fiebre etc*) to abate; **"ceda el paso"** (*Auto*) "give way"
cederom [θeðe'rom] *nm* CD-ROM
cedro ['θeðro] *nm* cedar
cédula ['θeðula] *nf* certificate, document; ~ **de identidad** (*Am*) identity card; ~ **electoral** (*Am*) ballot; ~ **en blanco** blank cheque; *ver tb* **Documento Nacional de Identidad**
cegar [θe'ɣar] *vt* to blind; (*tubería etc*) to block up, stop up ▷ *vi* to go blind; **cegarse** *vr*: **~se (de)** to be blinded (by)
ceguera [θe'ɣera] *nf* blindness
ceja ['θexa] *nf* eyebrow; **~s pobladas** bushy eyebrows; **arquear las ~s** to raise one's eyebrows; **fruncir las ~s** to frown
cejar [θe'xar] *vi* (*fig*) to back down; **no** ~ to keep it up, stick at it
celada [θe'laða] *nf* ambush, trap
celador, a [θela'ðor, a] *nm/f* (*de edificio*) watchman; (*de museo etc*) attendant; (*de cárcel*) warder
celda ['θelda] *nf* cell
celebración [θeleβra'θjon] *nf* celebration
celebrar [θele'βrar] *vt* to celebrate; (*alabar*) to praise ▷ *vi* to be glad; **celebrarse** *vr* to occur, take place
célebre ['θeleβre] *adj* famous
celebridad [θeleβri'ðað] *nf* fame; (*persona*) celebrity
celeste [θe'leste] *adj* sky-blue; (*cuerpo etc*) heavenly ▷ *nm* sky blue
celestial [θeles'tjal] *adj* celestial, heavenly
celibato [θeli'βato] *nm* celibacy
célibe ['θeliβe] *adj, nm/f* celibate
celo¹ ['θelo] *nm* zeal; (*Rel*) fervour; (*pey*) envy; **celos** *nmpl* jealousy *sg*; **dar ~s a algn** to make sb jealous; **tener ~s de algn** to be jealous of sb; **en** ~ (*animales*) on heat
celo²® ['θelo] *nm* Sellotape®
celofán [θelo'fan] *nm* Cellophane®
celoso, -a [θe'loso, a] *adj* (*envidioso*) jealous; (*trabajador*) zealous; (*desconfiado*) suspicious
celta ['θelta] *adj* Celtic ▷ *nm/f* Celt
célula ['θelula] *nf* cell
celular [θelu'lar] *nm* (*LAm*) mobile (phone) (*Brit*), cellphone (*US*)
celulitis [θelu'litis] *nf* (*enfermedad*) cellulitis; (*grasa*) cellulite
celuloide [θelu'loiðe] *nm* celluloid
celulosa [θelu'losa] *nf* cellulose
cementerio [θemen'terjo] *nm* cemetery, graveyard; ~ **de coches** scrap yard
cemento [θe'mento] *nm* cement; (*hormigón*) concrete; (*Am: cola*) glue
cena ['θena] *nf* evening meal, dinner
cenagal [θena'ɣal] *nm* bog, quagmire
cenar [θe'nar] *vt* to have for dinner, dine on ▷ *vi* to have dinner, dine
cenicero [θeni'θero] *nm* ashtray
cenit [θe'nit] *nm* zenith
ceniza [θe'niθa] *nf* ash, ashes *pl*
censar [θen'sar] *vt* to take a census of
censo ['θenso] *nm* census; ~ **electoral** electoral roll
censura [θen'sura] *nf* (*Pol*) censorship; (*moral*) censure, criticism
censurar [θensu'rar] *vt* (*idea*) to censure; (*cortar: película*) to censor
centella [θen'teʎa] *nf* spark
centellear [θenteʎe'ar] *vi* (*metal*) to gleam; (*estrella*) to twinkle; (*fig*) to sparkle
centelleo [θente'ʎeo] *nm* gleam(ing); twinkling; sparkling
centena [θen'tena] *nf* hundred
centenar [θente'nar] *nm* hundred
centenario, -a [θente'narjo, a] *adj* hundred year-old ▷ *nm* centenary; **ser** ~ to be one hundred years old
centeno [θen'teno] *nm* rye
centésimo, -a [θen'tesimo, a] *adj, nm* hundredth
centígrado [θen'tiɣraðo] *adj* centigrade
centímetro [θen'timetro] *nm* centimetre (*Brit*), centimeter (*US*)
céntimo, -a ['θentimo, a] *adj* hundredth ▷ *nm* cent
centinela [θenti'nela] *nm* sentry, guard
centollo, -a [θen'toʎo, a] *nm/f* large (*o* spider) crab
central [θen'tral] *adj* central ▷ *nf* head office; (*Tec*) plant; (*Telec*) exchange; ~ **eléctrica** power station; ~ **nuclear** nuclear power station; ~ **telefónica** telephone exchange
centralita [θentra'lita] *nf* switchboard
centralización [θentraliθa'θjon] *nf* centralization
centralizar [θentrali'θar] *vt* to centralize
centrar [θen'trar] *vt* to centre
céntrico, -a ['θentriko, a] *adj* central
centrifugar [θentrifu'ɣar] *vt* (*ropa*) to spin-dry
centrífugo, -a [θent'rifuɣo, a] *adj* centrifugal
centrista [θen'trista] *adj* centre *cpd*
centro ['θentro] *nm* centre; **ser de** ~ (*Pol*) to be a moderate; ~ **de acogida (para niños)** children's home; ~ **de beneficios** (*Com*) profit centre; ~ **cívico** community centre; ~ **comercial** shopping centre; ~ **de informática** computer centre; ~ **(de determinación) de costos** (*Com*) cost centre; ~ **delantero** (*Deporte*) centre forward; ~ **de atención al cliente** call centre; ~ **de salud** health centre; ~ **docente** teaching institution; ~ **escolar** school; ~ **juvenil** youth club; ~ **social** community centre; ~ **turístico** (*lugar muy visitado*) tourist centre; ~ **urbano** urban area, city

centroamericano, -a [θentroameri'kano, a] *adj, nm/f* Central American
ceñido, -a [θe'ɲiðo, a] *adj* tight
ceñir [θe'ɲir] *vt* (*rodear*) to encircle, surround; (*ajustar*) to fit (tightly); (*apretar*) to tighten; **ceñirse** *vr*: **~se algo** to put sth on; **~se al asunto** to stick to the matter in hand
ceño ['θeɲo] *nm* frown, scowl; **fruncir el ~** to frown, knit one's brow
CEOE *nf abr* (= *Confederación Española de Organizaciones Empresariales*) ≈ CBI (*Brit*)
cepillar [θepi'ʎar] *vt* to brush; (*madera*) to plane (down)
cepillo [θe'piʎo] *nm* brush; (*para madera*) plane; (*Rel*) poor box, alms box; **~ de dientes** toothbrush
cepo ['θepo] *nm* (*de caza*) trap
cera ['θera] *nf* wax; **~ de abejas** beeswax
cerámica [θe'ramika] *nf* pottery; (*arte*) ceramics *sg*
cerca ['θerka] *nf* fence ▷ *adv* near, nearby, close; **por aquí ~** nearby ▷ *prep*: **~ de** (*cantidad*) nearly, about; (*distancia*) near, close to ▷ *nmpl*: **~s** foreground *sg*
cercanía [θerka'nia] *nf* nearness, closeness; **cercanías** *nfpl* outskirts, suburbs; **tren de ~s** commuter *o* local train
cercano, -a [θer'kano, a] *adj* close, near; (*pueblo etc*) nearby; **C~ Oriente** Near East
cercar [θer'kar] *vt* to fence in; (*rodear*) to surround
cerciorar [θerθjo'rar] *vt* (*asegurar*) to assure; **cerciorarse** *vr*: **~se (de)** (*descubrir*) to find out (about); (*asegurarse*) to make sure (of)
cerco ['θerko] *nm* (*Agr*) enclosure; (*Am*) fence; (*Mil*) siege
cerda ['θerða] *nf* (*de cepillo*) bristle; (*Zool*) sow
cerdada [θer'ðaða] *nf* (*fam*): **hacer una ~ a algn** to play a dirty trick on sb
cerdo ['θerðo] *nm* pig; **carne de ~** pork
cereal [θere'al] *nm* cereal; **cereales** *nmpl* cereals, grain *sg*
cerebral [θere'βral] *adj* (*tb fig*) cerebral; (*tumor*) brain *cpd*
cerebro [θe'reβro] *nm* brain; (*fig*) brains *pl*; **ser un ~** (*fig*) to be brilliant
ceremonia [θere'monja] *nf* ceremony; **reunión de ~** formal meeting; **hablar sin ~** to speak plainly
ceremonial [θeremo'njal] *adj, nm* ceremonial
ceremonioso, -a [θeremo'njoso, a] *adj* ceremonious; (*cumplido*) formal
cereza [θe'reθa] *nf* cherry
cerilla [θe'riʎa] *nf*, **cerillo** [se'riʎo] *nm* (*Am*) match
cerner [θer'ner] *vt* to sift, sieve; **cernerse** *vr* to hover
cero ['θero] *nm* nothing, zero; (*Deporte*) nil; **8 grados bajo ~** 8 degrees below zero; **a partir de ~** from scratch
cerquillo [θer'kiʎo] *nm* (*Am*) fringe (*Brit*), bangs *pl* (*US*)
cerrado, -a [θe'rraðo, a] *adj* closed, shut; (*con llave*) locked; (*tiempo*) cloudy, overcast; (*curva*) sharp; (*acento*) thick, broad; **a puerta cerrada** (*Jur*) in camera
cerradura [θerra'ðura] *nf* (*acción*) closing; (*mecanismo*) lock
cerrajero, -a [θerra'xero, a] *nm/f* locksmith
cerrar [θe'rrar] *vt* to close, shut; (*paso, carretera*) to close; (*grifo*) to turn off; (*trato, cuenta, negocio*) to close ▷ *vi* to close, shut; (*la noche*) to come down; **~ con llave** to lock; **~ el sistema** (*Inform*) to close *o* shut down the system; **~ un trato** to strike a bargain; **cerrarse** *vr* to close, shut; (*herida*) to heal
cerro ['θerro] *nm* hill; **andar por las ~s de Úbeda** to wander from the point, digress
cerrojo [θe'rroxo] *nm* (*herramienta*) bolt; (*de puerta*) latch
certamen [θer'tamen] *nm* competition, contest
certero, -a [θer'tero, a] *adj* accurate
certeza [θer'teθa], **certidumbre** [θerti'ðumbre] *nf* certainty
certidumbre [θerti'ðumβre] *nf* = **certeza**
certificado, -a [θertifi'kaðo, a] *adj* certified; (*Correos*) registered ▷ *nm* certificate; **~ médico** medical certificate
certificar [θertifi'kar] *vt* (*asegurar, atestar*) to certify
cervatillo [θerβa'tiʎo] *nm* fawn
cervecería [θerβeθe'ria] *nf* (*fábrica*) brewery; (*taberna*) public house, pub
cerveza [θer'βeθa] *nf* beer; **~ de barril** draught beer
cervical [θerβi'kal] *adj* cervical
cesación [θesa'θjon] *nf* cessation, suspension
cesante [θe'sante] *adj* redundant; (*Am*) unemployed; (*ministro*) outgoing; (*diplomático*) recalled ▷ *nm/f* redundant worker
cesar [θe'sar] *vi* to cease, stop; (*de un trabajo*) to leave ▷ *vt* (*en el trabajo*) to dismiss; (*alto cargo*) to remove from office
cesárea [θe'sarea] *nf* Caesarean (section)
cese ['θese] *nm* (*de trabajo*) dismissal; (*de pago*) suspension
césped ['θespeð] *nm* grass, lawn
cesta ['θesta] *nf* basket
cesto ['θesto] *nm* (large) basket, hamper
cetro ['θetro] *nm* sceptre
CFC *nm abr* (= *clorofluorocarbono*) CFC
cfr. *abr* (= *confróntese, compárese*) cf
Ch, ch [tʃe] *nf former letter in the Spanish alphabet*
chabacano, -a [tʃaβa'kano, a] *adj* vulgar, coarse
chabola [tʃa'βola] *nf* shack; **barriada** *or* **barrio de ~s** shanty town
chacal [tʃa'kal] *nm* jackal
chacha ['tʃatʃa] *nf* (*fam*) maid
cháchara ['tʃatʃara] *nf* chatter; **estar de ~** to chatter away

chacra ['tʃakra] *nf* (*Am*) smallholding
chafa ['tʃafa] *adj* (*Am: fam*) useless, dud
chafar [tʃa'far] *vt* (*aplastar*) to crush, flatten; (*arruinar*) to ruin
chal [tʃal] *nm* shawl
chalado, -a [tʃa'laðo, a] *adj* (*fam*) crazy
chalé (*pl* **chalés**) [tʃa'le, tʃa'les] *nm* = **chalet**
chaleco [tʃa'leko] *nm* waistcoat, vest (*US*); **~ antibala** bulletproof vest; **~ salvavidas** life jacket; **~ de seguridad**, **~ reflectante** (*Aut*) high-visibility vest
chalet (*pl* **chalets**) [tʃa'le, tʃa'les] *nm* villa, ≈ detached house; **~ adosado** semi-detached house
chalupa [tʃa'lupa] *nf* launch, boat
chamaco, -a [tʃa'mako, a] *nm/f* (*Am*) kid
champán [tʃam'pan], **champaña** [tʃam'paɲa] *nm* champagne
champiñón [tʃampi'ɲon] *nm* mushroom
champú [tʃam'pu] (*pl* **champúes** *o* **champús**) *nm* shampoo
chamuscar [tʃamus'kar] *vt* to scorch, singe
chance ['tʃanθe] *nm* (*a veces nf*) (*Am*) chance, opportunity
chancho, -a ['tʃantʃo, a] *nm/f* (*Am*) pig
chanchullo [tʃan'tʃuʎo] *nm* (*fam*) fiddle, wangle
chandal [tʃan'dal] *nm* tracksuit; **~ (de tactel)** shellsuit
chantaje [tʃan'taxe] *nm* blackmail; **hacer ~ a uno** to blackmail sb
chapa ['tʃapa] *nf* (*de metal*) plate, sheet; (*de madera*) board, panel; (*de botella*) bottle top; (*insignia*) (lapel) badge; (*Am: Auto: tb:* **~ de matrícula**) number (*Brit*) *o* license (*US*) plate; (*Am: cerradura*) lock; **de 3 ~s** (*madera*) 3-ply
chapado, -a [tʃa'paðo, a] *adj* (*metal*) plated; (*muebles etc*) finished; **~ en oro** gold-plated
chaparrón [tʃapa'rron] *nm* downpour, cloudburst
chaperón [tʃape'ron] *nm* (*Am*): **hacer de ~** to play gooseberry
chaperona [tʃape'rona] *nf* (*Am*): **hacer de ~** to play gooseberry
chapotear [tʃapote'ar] *vt* to sponge down ▷ *vi* (*fam*) to splash about
chapucero, -a [tʃapu'θero, a] *adj* rough, crude ▷ *nm/f* bungler
chapulín [tʃapu'lin] *nm* (*Am*) grasshopper
chapurrar [tʃapurr'ar], **chapurrear** [tʃapurre'ar] *vt* (*idioma*) to speak badly
chapuza [tʃa'puθa] *nf* botched job
chapuzón [tʃapu'θon] *nm*: **darse un ~** to go for a dip
chaqué [tʃa'ke] *nm* morning coat
chaqueta [tʃa'keta] *nf* jacket; **cambiar la ~** (*fig*) to change sides
chaquetón [tʃake'ton] *nm* (three-quarter-length) coat
charca ['tʃarka] *nf* pond, pool
charco ['tʃarko] *nm* pool, puddle
charcutería [tʃarkute'ria] *nf* (*tienda*) *shop selling chiefly pork meat products*; (*productos*) cooked pork meats *pl*
charla ['tʃarla] *nf* talk, chat; (*conferencia*) lecture
charlar [tʃar'lar] *vi* to talk, chat
charlatán, -ana [tʃarla'tan, ana] *nm/f* chatterbox; (*estafador*) trickster
charol¹ [tʃa'rol] *nm* varnish; (*cuero*) patent leather
charol² [tʃa'rol] *nm*, **charola** [tʃa'rola] *nf* (*Am*) tray
charro, -a ['tʃarro [a] *adj* Salamancan; (*Am*) Mexican; (*ropa*) loud, gaudy; (*costumbres*) traditional ▷ *nm/f* Salamancan ▷ *nm* (*vaquero*) typical Mexican
chárter ['tʃarter] *adj inv*: **vuelo ~** charter flight
chascarrillo [tʃaska'rriʎo] *nm* (*fam*) funny story
chasco ['tʃasko] *nm* (*broma*) trick, joke; (*desengaño*) disappointment
chasis ['tʃasis] *nm inv* (*Auto*) chassis; (*Foto*) plate holder
chasquear [tʃaske'ar] *vt* (*látigo*) to crack; (*lengua*) to click
chasquido [tʃas'kiðo] *nm* (*de lengua*) click; (*de látigo*) crack
chat [tʃat] *nm* (*Internet*) chat room
chatarra [tʃa'tarra] *nf* scrap (metal)
chatear [tʃate'ar] *vi* (*Internet*) to chat
chato, -a ['tʃato, a] *adj* flat; (*nariz*) snub ▷ *nm* wine tumbler; **beber unos ~s** to have a few drinks
chaucha (*Am*) ['tʃautʃa] *nf* runner (*Brit*) *o* pole (*US*) bean
chaval, a [tʃa'βal, a] *nm/f* kid (*fam*), lad/lass
chavo, -a ['tʃaβo, a] *nm/f* (*Am: fam*) guy/girl
checar [tʃe'kar] *vt* (*Am*): **~ tarjeta** (*al entrar*) to clock in *o* on; (*al salir*) to clock off *o* out
checo, -a ['tʃeko, a] *adj, nm/f* Czech ▷ *nm* (*Ling*) Czech
checoeslovaco, -a [tʃekoeslo'βako, a], **checoslovaco, -a** [tʃekoslo'βako, a] *adj, nm/f* Czech, Czechoslovak
Checoeslovaquia [tʃekoeslo'βakja], **Checoslovaquia** [tʃekoslo'βakja] *nf* Czechoslovakia
cheque ['tʃeke] *nm* cheque (*Brit*), check (*US*); **cobrar un ~** to cash a cheque; **~ abierto/en blanco/cruzado** open/blank/crossed cheque; **~ al portador** cheque payable to bearer; **~ de viajero** traveller's cheque
chequeo [tʃe'keo] *nm* (*Med*) check-up; (*Auto*) service
chequera [tʃe'kera] *nf* (*Am*) chequebook (*Brit*), checkbook (*US*)
chévere ['tʃeβere] *adj* (*Am*) great, fabulous (*fam*)
chicano, -a [tʃi'kano, a] *adj, nm/f* chicano, Mexican-American
chícharo ['tʃitʃaro] *nm* (*Am*) pea
chicharrón [tʃitʃa'rron] *nm* (pork) crackling

chichón [tʃi'tʃon] *nm* bump, lump
chicle ['tʃikle] *nm* chewing gum
chico, -a ['tʃiko, a] *adj* small, little ▷ *nm/f* child; (*muchacho*) boy; (*muchacha*) girl
chiflado, -a [tʃi'flaðo, a] *adj* (*fam*) crazy, round the bend ▷ *nm/f* nutcase
chiflar [tʃi'flar] *vt* to hiss, boo ▷ *vi* (*esp Am*) to whistle
chilango, -a [tʃi'lango, a] *adj* (*Am*) of *o* from Mexico City
Chile ['tʃile] *nm* Chile
chile ['tʃile] *nm* chilli pepper
chileno, -a [tʃi'leno, a] *adj, nm/f* Chilean
chillar [tʃi'ʎar] *vi* (*persona*) to yell, scream; (*animal salvaje*) to howl; (*cerdo*) to squeal; (*puerta*) to creak
chillido [tʃi'ʎiðo] *nm* (*de persona*) yell, scream; (*de animal*) howl; (*de frenos*) screech(ing)
chillón, -ona [tʃi'ʎon, ona] *adj* (*niño*) noisy; (*color*) loud, gaudy
chimenea [tʃime'nea] *nf* chimney; (*hogar*) fireplace
China ['tʃina] *nf*: **(la)** ~ China
china ['tʃina] *nf* pebble
chinche ['tʃintʃe] *nf* bug; (*Tec*) drawing pin (*Brit*), thumbtack (*US*) ▷ *nm/f* nuisance, pest
chincheta [tʃin'tʃeta] *nf* drawing pin (*Brit*), thumbtack (*US*)
chingado, -a [tʃin'gaðo, a] *adj* (*esp Am fam!*) lousy, bloody (*!*); **hijo de la chingada** bastard (*!*), son of a bitch (*US*) (*!*)
chingar [tʃin'gar] *vt* (*Am: fam!*) to fuck (up) (*!*), screw (up) (*!*); **chingarse** *vr* (*Am: emborracharse*) to get pissed (*Brit*), get plastered; (*: fracasar*) to fail
chino, -a ['tʃino, a] *adj, nm/f* Chinese ▷ *nm* (*Ling*) Chinese
chipirón [tʃipi'ron] *nm* squid
Chipre ['tʃipre] *nf* Cyprus
chipriota [tʃi'prjota], **chipriote** [tʃi'prjote] *adj* Cypriot, Cyprian ▷ *nm/f* Cypriot
chiquillo, -a [tʃi'kiʎo, a] *nm/f* kid (*fam*), youngster, child
chiquito, -a [tʃi'kito, a] *adj* very small, tiny ▷ *nm/f* kid (*fam*)
chirimoya [tʃiri'moja] *nf* custard apple
chiringuito [tʃirin'gito] *nm* small open-air bar
chiripa [tʃi'ripa] *nf* fluke; **por** ~ by chance
chirriar [tʃi'rrjar] *vi* (*goznes*) to creak, squeak; (*pájaros*) to chirp, sing
chirrido [tʃi'rriðo] *nm* creak(ing), squeak(ing); (*de pájaro*) chirp(ing)
chis [tʃis] *excl* sh!
chisme ['tʃisme] *nm* (*habladurías*) piece of gossip; (*fam: objeto*) thingummyjig
chismoso, -a [tʃis'moso, a] *adj* gossiping ▷ *nm/f* gossip
chispa ['tʃispa] *nf* spark; (*fig*) sparkle; (*ingenio*) wit; (*fam*) drunkenness
chispeante [tʃispe'ante] *adj* (*tb fig*) sparkling
chispear [tʃispe'ar] *vi* to spark; (*lloviznar*) to drizzle
chisporrotear [tʃisporrote'ar] *vi* (*fuego*) to throw out sparks; (*leña*) to crackle; (*aceite*) to hiss, splutter
chiste ['tʃiste] *nm* joke, funny story; ~ **verde** blue joke
chistera [tʃis'tera] *nf* top hat
chistoso, -a [tʃis'toso, a] *adj* (*gracioso*) funny, amusing; (*bromista*) witty
chivatazo [tʃiβa'taθo] *nm* (*fam*) tip-off; **dar ~** to inform
chivo, -a ['tʃiβo, a] *nm/f* (billy/nanny-)goat; ~ **expiatorio** scapegoat
chocante [tʃo'kante] *adj* startling; (*extraño*) odd; (*ofensivo*) shocking
chocar [tʃo'kar] *vi* (*coches etc*) to collide, crash; (*Mil, fig*) to clash ▷ *vt* to shock; (*sorprender*) to startle; ~ **con** to collide with; (*fig*) to run into, run up against; **¡chócala!** (*fam*) put it there!
chochear [tʃotʃe'ar] *vi* to dodder, be senile
chocho, -a ['tʃotʃo, a] *adj* doddering, senile; (*fig*) soft, doting
choclo (*Am*) ['tʃoklo] *nm* (*grano*) sweetcorn; (*mazorca*) corn on the cob
chocolate [tʃoko'late] *adj* chocolate ▷ *nm* chocolate; (*fam*) dope, marijuana
chocolatina [tʃokola'tina] *nf* chocolate
chófer ['tʃofer], **chofer** [tʃo'fer] (*esp Am*) *nm* driver
chollo ['tʃoʎo] *nm* (*fam*) bargain, snip
choque ['tʃoke] *vb ver* **chocar** ▷ *nm* (*impacto*) impact; (*golpe*) jolt; (*Auto*) crash; (*fig*) conflict; ~ **frontal** head-on collision
chorizo [tʃo'riθo] *nm hard pork sausage (type of salami)*; (*ladrón*) crook
chorrada [tʃo'rraða] *nf* (*fam*): **¡es una ~!** that's crap! (*!*); **decir ~s** to talk crap (*!*)
chorrear [tʃorre'ar] *vt* to pour ▷ *vi* to gush (out), spout (out); (*gotear*) to drip, trickle
chorro ['tʃorro] *nm* jet; (*caudalito*) dribble, trickle; (*fig*) stream; **salir a ~s** to gush forth; **con propulsión a ~** jet-propelled
choza ['tʃoθa] *nf* hut, shack
chubasco [tʃu'βasko] *nm* squall
chubasquero [tʃuβas'kero] *nm* cagoule, raincoat
chuchería [tʃutʃe'ria] *nf* trinket
chuleta [tʃu'leta] *nf* chop, cutlet; (*Escol etc: fam*) crib
chulo, -a ['tʃulo, a] *adj* (*encantador*) charming; (*aire*) proud; (*pey*) fresh; (*fam: estupendo*) great, fantastic ▷ *nm* (*pícaro*) rascal; (*madrileño*) working-class person from Madrid; (*rufián: tb:* **~ de putas**) pimp
chungo, -a ['tʃungo, a] (*fam*) *adj* lousy ▷ *nf*: **estar de chunga** to be in a merry mood
chupa ['tʃupa] *nf* (*fam*) jacket
chupado, -a [tʃu'paðo, a] *adj* (*delgado*) skinny, gaunt; **está ~** (*fam*) it's simple, it's dead easy
chupaleta [tʃupa'leta] *nf* (*Am*) lollipop
chupar [tʃu'par] *vt* to suck; (*absorber*) to absorb; **chuparse** *vr* to grow thin; **para ~se los dedos** mouthwatering

chupete [tʃu'pete] *nm* dummy (*Brit*), pacifier (*US*)
chupetín [tʃupe'tin] *nf* (*Am*) lollipop
chupetón [tʃupe'ton] *nm* suck
chupito [tʃu'pito] *nm* (*fam*) shot
chupón [tʃu'pon] *nm* (*piruleta*) lollipop; (*Am: chupete*) dummy (*Brit*), pacifier (*US*)
churrasco [tʃu'rrasko] *nm* (*Am*) barbecue, barbecued meat
churrería [tʃurre'ria] *nf stall or shop which sells "churros"*
churretón [tʃurre'ton] *nm* stain
churro, -a ['tʃurro, a] *adj* coarse ▷ *nm* (*Culin*) (type of) fritter; *see note*; (*chapuza*) botch, mess

CHURRO

Churros, long fritters made with flour and water, are very popular in much of Spain and are often eaten with thick hot chocolate, either for breakfast or as a snack. In Madrid, they eat a thicker variety of churro called *porra*.

chusco, -a ['tʃusko, a] *adj* funny
chusma ['tʃusma] *nf* rabble, mob
chutar [tʃu'tar] *vi* (*Deporte*) to shoot (at goal); **esto va que chuta** it's going fine
Cía. *abr* (= *compañía*) Co.
cianuro [θja'nuro] *nm* cyanide
cibercafé [θiβerka'fe] *nm* cybercafé
cibernauta [θiβer'nauta] *nm/f* cybernaut
cibernética [θiβer'netika] *nf* cybernetics *sg*
ciberterrorista [θiβerterro'rista] *nm/f* cyberterrorist
cicatriz [θika'triθ] *nf* scar
cicatrizar [θikatri'θar] *vt* to heal; **cicatrizarse** *vr* to heal (up), form a scar
ciclismo [θi'klismo] *nm* cycling
ciclista [θi'klista] *adj* cycle *cpd* ▷ *nm/f* cyclist
ciclo ['θiklo] *nm* cycle
ciclomotor [θiklomo'tor] *nm* moped
ciclón [θi'klon] *nm* cyclone
cicloturismo [θiklotu'rismo] *nm* touring by bicycle
ciego, -a *etc* ['θjeɣo, a] *vb ver* **cegar** ▷ *adj* blind ▷ *nm/f* blind man/woman; **a ciegas** blindly; **me puse ciega mariscos** (*fam*) I stuffed myself with seafood
cielo ['θjelo] *nm* sky; (*Rel*) heaven; (*Arq*: *tb*: **~ raso**) ceiling; **¡~s!** good heavens!; **ver el ~ abierto** to see one's chance
ciempiés [θjem'pjes] *nm inv* centipede
cien [θjen] *num ver* **ciento**
ciénaga ['θjenaɣa] *nf* marsh, swamp
ciencia ['θjenθja] *nf* science; **ciencias** *nfpl* science *sg*; **saber algo a ~ cierta** to know sth for certain
ciencia-ficción ['θjenθjafik'θjon] *nf* science fiction
científico, -a [θjen'tifiko, a] *adj* scientific ▷ *nm/f* scientist
ciento ['θjento], **cien** *num* hundred; **pagar al 10 por ~** to pay at 10 per cent
cierne *etc* ['θjerne] *vb ver* **cerner** ▷ *nm*: **en ~** in blossom; **en ~(s)** (*fig*) in its infancy
cierre ['θjerre] *vb ver* **cerrar** ▷ *nm* closing, shutting; (*con llave*) locking; (*Radio, TV*) close-down; **~ de cremallera** zip (fastener); **precios de ~** (*Bolsa*) closing prices; **~ del sistema** (*Inform*) system shutdown
cierro *etc vb ver* **cerrar**
cierto, -a ['θjerto, a] *adj* sure, certain; (*un tal*) a certain; (*correcto*) right, correct; **~ hombre** a certain man; **ciertas personas** certain *o* some people; **sí, es ~** yes, that's correct; **por ~** by the way; **lo ~ es que ...** the fact is that ...; **estar en lo ~** to be right
ciervo ['θjerβo] *nm* (*Zool*) deer; (*: macho*) stag
cierzo ['θjerθo] *nm* north wind
cifra ['θifra] *nf* number, figure; (*cantidad*) number, quantity; (*secreta*) code; **~ global** lump sum; **~ de negocios** (*Com*) turnover; **en ~s redondas** in round figures; **~ de referencia** (*Com*) benchmark; **~ de ventas** (*Com*) sales figures
cifrar [θi'frar] *vt* to code, write in code; (*resumir*) to abridge; (*calcular*) to reckon
cigala [θi'ɣala] *nf* Norway lobster
cigarra [θi'ɣarra] *nf* cicada
cigarrillo [θiɣa'rriʎo] *nm* cigarette; **~ electrónico** e-cigarette
cigarro [θi'ɣarro] *nm* cigarette; (*puro*) cigar
cigüeña [θi'ɣweɲa] *nf* stork
cilíndrico, -a [θi'lindriko, a] *adj* cylindrical
cilindro [θi'lindro] *nm* cylinder
cima ['θima] *nf* (*de montaña*) top, peak; (*de árbol*) top; (*fig*) height
címbalo ['θimbalo] *nm* cymbal
cimbrear [θimbre'ar] *vt* to brandish; **cimbrearse** *vr* to sway
cimentar [θimen'tar] *vt* to lay the foundations of; (*fig: reforzar*) to strengthen; (*: fundar*) to found
cimiento *etc* [θi'mjento] *vb ver* **cimentar** ▷ *nm* foundation
cinc [θink] *nm* zinc
cincel [θin'θel] *nm* chisel
cincelar [θinθe'lar] *vt* to chisel
cinco ['θinko] *num* five; (*fecha*) fifth; **las ~** five o'clock; **no estar en sus ~** (*fam*) to be off one's rocker
cincuenta [θin'kwenta] *num* fifty
cine ['θine] *nm* cinema; **el ~ mudo** silent films *pl*; **hacer ~** to make films
cineasta [θine'asta] *nm/f* (*director de cine*) film-maker *o* director
cinematográfico, -a [θinemato'ɣrafiko, a] *adj* cine-, film *cpd*
cínico, -a ['θiniko, a] *adj* cynical; (*descarado*) shameless ▷ *nm/f* cynic
cinismo [θi'nismo] *nm* cynicism
cinta ['θinta] *nf* band, strip; (*de tela*) ribbon; (*película*) reel; (*de máquina de escribir*) ribbon; (*métrica*) tape measure; (*magnetofónica*) tape;

~ **adhesiva** sticky tape; ~ **aislante** insulating tape; ~ **de vídeo** videotape; ~ **de carbón** carbon ribbon; ~ **magnética** (*Inform*) magnetic tape; ~ **métrica** tape measure; ~ **de múltiples impactos** (*en impresora*) multistrike ribbon; ~ **de tela** (*para máquina de escribir*) fabric ribbon; ~ **transportadora** conveyor belt

cinto ['θinto] *nm* belt, girdle

cintura [θin'tura] *nf* waist; (*medida*) waistline

cinturón [θintu'ron] *nm* belt; (*fig*) belt, zone; ~ **salvavidas** lifebelt; ~ **de seguridad** safety belt

ciprés [θi'pres] *nm* cypress (tree)

circo ['θirko] *nm* circus

circuito [θir'kwito] *nm* circuit; (*Deporte*) lap; **TV por ~ cerrado** closed-circuit TV; ~ **experimental** (*Inform*) breadboard; ~ **impreso** printed circuit; ~ **lógico** (*Inform*) logical circuit

circulación [θirkula'θjon] *nf* circulation; (*Auto*) traffic; **"cerrado a la ~ rodada"** "closed to vehicles"

circular [θirku'lar] *adj, nf* circular ▷ *vt* to circulate ▷ *vi* to circulate; (*dinero*) to be in circulation; (*Auto*) to drive; (*autobús*) to run; **"circule por la derecha"** "keep (to the) right"

círculo ['θirkulo] *nm* circle; (*centro*) clubhouse; (*Pol*) political group; ~ **vicioso** vicious circle

circuncidar [θirkunθi'dar] *vt* to circumcise

circundar [θirkun'dar] *vt* to surround

circunferencia [θirkunfe'renθja] *nf* circumference

circunscribir [θirkunskri'βir] *vt* to circumscribe; **circunscribirse** *vr* to be limited

circunscripción [θirkunskrip'θjon] *nf* division; (*Pol*) constituency

circunspecto, -a [θirkuns'pekto, a] *adj* circumspect, cautious

circunstancia [θirkuns'tanθja] *nf* circumstance; **~s agravantes/extenuantes** aggravating/extenuating circumstances; **estar a la altura de las ~s** to rise to the occasion

circunvalación [θirkumbala'θjon] *nf*: **carretera de** ~ ring road

cirio ['θirjo] *nm* (wax) candle

cirrosis [θi'rrosis] *nf* cirrhosis (of the liver)

ciruela [θi'rwela] *nf* plum; ~ **pasa** prune

cirugía [θiru'xia] *nf* surgery; ~ **estética** *o* **plástica** plastic surgery

cirujano [θiru'xano] *nm* surgeon

cisne ['θisne] *nm* swan; **canto de** ~ swan song

cisterna [θis'terna] *nf* cistern, tank

cita ['θita] *nf* appointment, meeting; (*de novios*) date; (*referencia*) quotation; **acudir/faltar a una ~** to turn up for/miss an appointment

citación [θita'θjon] *nf* (*Jur*) summons *sg*

citar [θi'tar] *vt* to make an appointment with, arrange to meet; (*Jur*) to summons; (*un autor, texto*) to quote; **citarse** *vr*: **~se con algn** to arrange to meet sb; **se ~on en el cine** they arranged to meet at the cinema

citología [θitolo'xia] *nf* smear test

cítrico, -a ['θitriko, a] *adj* citric ▷ *nm*: **~s** citrus fruits

ciudad [θju'ðað] *nf* town; (*capital de país etc*) city; ~ **universitaria** university campus; **C~ del Cabo** Cape Town; **la C~ Condal** Barcelona

ciudadanía [θjuðaða'nia] *nf* citizenship

ciudadano, -a [θjuða'ðano, a] *adj* civic ▷ *nm/f* citizen

cívico, -a ['θiβiko, a] *adj* civic; (*fig*) public-spirited

civil [θi'βil] *adj* civil ▷ *nm* (*guardia*) policeman

civilización [θiβiliθa'θjon] *nf* civilization

civilizar [θiβili'θar] *vt* to civilize

civismo [θi'βismo] *nm* public spirit

cizaña [θi'θaɲa] *nf* (*fig*) discord; **sembrar ~** to sow discord

cl *abr* (= *centilitro*) cl

clamar [kla'mar] *vt* to clamour for, cry out for ▷ *vi* to cry out, clamour

clamor [kla'mor] *nm* (*grito*) cry, shout; (*fig*) clamour, protest

clan [klan] *nm* clan; (*de gángsters*) gang

clandestino, -a [klandes'tino, a] *adj* clandestine; (*Pol*) underground

clara ['klara] *nf* (*de huevo*) egg white

claraboya [klara'βoja] *nf* skylight

clarear [klare'ar] *vi* (*el día*) to dawn; (*el cielo*) to clear up, brighten up; **clarearse** *vr* to be transparent

clarete [kla'rete] *nm* rosé (wine)

claridad [klari'ðað] *nf* (*del día*) brightness; (*de estilo*) clarity

clarificar [klarifi'kar] *vt* to clarify

clarín [kla'rin] *nm* bugle

clarinete [klari'nete] *nm* clarinet

clarividencia [klariβi'ðenθja] *nf* clairvoyance; (*fig*) far-sightedness

claro, -a ['klaro, a] *adj* clear; (*luminoso*) bright; (*color*) light; (*evidente*) clear, evident; (*poco espeso*) thin ▷ *nm* (*en bosque*) clearing ▷ *adv* clearly ▷ *excl*: **¡~ que sí!** of course!; **¡~ que no!** of course not!; **hablar ~** (*fig*) to speak plainly; **a las claras** openly; **no sacamos nada en ~** we couldn't get anything definite

clase ['klase] *nf* class; (*tipo*) kind, sort; (*Escol etc*) class; (*: aula*) classroom; ~ **alta/media/obrera** upper/middle/working class; **dar ~s** to teach; **~s particulares** private lessons *o* tuition *sg*

clásico, -a ['klasiko, a] *adj* classical; (*fig*) classic

clasificación [klasifika'θjon] *nf* classification; (*Deporte*) league (table); (*Com*) ratings *pl*

clasificar [klasifi'kar] *vt* to classify; (*Inform*) to sort; **clasificarse** *vr* (*Deporte*: *en torneo*) to qualify
claudicar [klauði'kar] *vi* (*fig*) to back down
claustro ['klaustro] *nm* cloister; (*Univ*) staff; (*junta*) senate
claustrofobia [klaustro'foβja] *nf* claustrophobia
cláusula ['klausula] *nf* clause; ~ **de exclusión** (*Com*) exclusion clause
clausura [klau'sura] *nf* closing, closure
clausurar [klausu'rar] *vt* (*congreso etc*) to close, bring to a close; (*Pol etc*) to adjourn; (*cerrar*) to close (down)
clavar [kla'βar] *vt* (*tablas etc*) to nail (together); (*con alfiler*) to pin; (*clavo*) to hammer in; (*cuchillo*) to stick, thrust; (*mirada*) to fix; (*fam*: *estafar*) to cheat
clave ['klaβe] *nf* key; (*Mus*) clef ▷ *adj inv* key *cpd*; ~ **de acceso** password; ~ **lada** (*Am*) dialling (*Brit*) *o* area (*US*) code
clavel [kla'βel] *nm* carnation
clavícula [kla'βikula] *nf* collar bone
clavija [kla'βixa] *nf* peg, pin; (*Mus*) peg; (*Elec*) plug
clavo ['klaβo] *nm* (*de metal*) nail; (*Bot*) clove; **dar en el** ~ (*fig*) to hit the nail on the head
claxon ['klakson] (*pl* **claxons**) *nm* horn; **tocar el** ~ to sound one's horn
clemencia [kle'menθja] *nf* mercy, clemency
cleptómano, -a [klep'tomano, a] *nm/f* kleptomaniac
clerical [kleri'kal] *adj* clerical
clérigo ['kleriɣo] *nm* priest, clergyman
clero ['klero] *nm* clergy
clicar [kli'kar] *vi* (*Inform*) to click; **clica en el icono** click on the icon; ~ **dos veces** to double-click
cliché [kli'tʃe] *nm* cliché; (*Tip*) stencil; (*Foto*) negative
cliente, -a ['kljente, a] *nm/f* client, customer
clientela [kljen'tela] *nf* clientele, customers *pl*; (*Com*) goodwill; (*Med*) patients *pl*
clima ['klima] *nm* climate
climatizado, -a [klimati'θaðo, a] *adj* air-conditioned
clímax ['klimaks] *nm inv* climax
clínico, -a ['kliniko, a] *adj* clinical ▷ *nf* clinic; (*particular*) private hospital
clip (*pl* **clips**) [klip, klis] *nm* paper clip
clítoris ['klitoris] *nm inv* clitoris
cloaca [klo'aka] *nf* sewer, drain
clonación [klona'θjon] *nf* cloning
clonar [klo'nar] *vt* to clone
clorhídrico, -a [klo'ridriko, a] *adj* hydrochloric
cloro ['kloro] *nm* chlorine
clorofila [kloro'fila] *nf* chlorophyl(l)
club (*pl* **clubs** *o* **clubes**) [klub, klus, 'kluβes] *nm* club; ~ **de jóvenes** youth club; ~ **nocturno** night club
cm *abr* (= *centímetro*) cm
C.N.T. *nf abr* (*Esp*: = *Confederación Nacional de Trabajo*) *Anarchist Union Confederation*; (*Am*) = **Confederación Nacional de Trabajadores**
coacción [koak'θjon] *nf* coercion, compulsion
coaccionar [koakθjo'nar] *vt* to coerce, compel
coagular [koaɣu'lar] *vt*, **coagularse** *vr* (*sangre*) to clot; (*leche*) to curdle
coágulo [ko'aɣulo] *nm* clot
coalición [koali'θjon] *nf* coalition
coartada [koar'taða] *nf* alibi
coartar [koar'tar] *vt* to limit, restrict
coba ['koβa] *nf*: **dar ~ a algn** (*adular*) to suck up to sb
cobarde [ko'βarðe] *adj* cowardly ▷ *nm/f* coward
cobardía [koβar'ðia] *nf* cowardice
cobaya [ko'βaja] *nf* guinea pig
cobertizo [koβer'tiθo] *nm* shelter
cobertor [koβer'tor] *nm* bedspread
cobertura [koβer'tura] *nf* cover; (*Com*) coverage; ~ **de dividendo** (*Com*) dividend cover; **no tengo** ~ (*Telec*) I can't get a signal
cobija [ko'βixa] *nf* (*Am*) blanket
cobijar [koβi'xar] *vt* (*cubrir*) to cover; (*abrigar*) to shelter; **cobijarse** *vr* to take shelter
cobijo [ko'βixo] *nm* shelter
cobra ['koβra] *nf* cobra
cobrador, a [koβra'ðor, a] *nm/f* (*de autobús*) conductor/conductress; (*de impuestos, gas*) collector
cobrar [ko'βrar] *vt* (*cheque*) to cash; (*sueldo*) to collect, draw; (*objeto*) to recover; (*precio*) to charge; (*deuda*) to collect ▷ *vi* to be paid; **cobrarse** *vr* to recover, get on well; **cóbrese al entregar** cash on delivery (COD) (*Brit*), collect on delivery (COD) (*US*); **a** ~ (*Com*) receivable; **cantidades por** ~ sums due; **¿me cobra, por favor?** (*en tienda*) how much do I owe you?; (*en restaurante*) can I have the bill, please?
cobre ['koβre] *nm* copper; (*Am fam*) cent; **cobres** *nmpl* (*Mús*) brass instruments
cobro ['koβro] *nm* (*de cheque*) cashing; (*pago*) payment; **presentar al** ~ to cash; *ver tb* **llamada**
cocaína [koka'ina] *nf* cocaine
cocción [kok'θjon] *nf* (*Culin*) cooking; (*el hervir*) boiling
cocear [koθe'ar] *vi* to kick
cocer [ko'θer] *vt, vi* to cook; (*en agua*) to boil; (*en horno*) to bake
coche ['kotʃe] *nm* (*Auto*) car, automobile (*US*); (*de tren, de caballos*) coach, carriage; (*para niños*) pram (*Brit*), baby carriage (*US*); **ir en** ~ to drive; ~ **de bomberos** fire engine; ~ **celular** police van, patrol wagon (*US*); ~ **(comedor)** (*Ferro*) (dining) car; ~ **de carreras** racing car; ~**-escuela** learner car; ~ **fúnebre** hearse
coche-bomba ['kotʃe'βomba] (*pl* **coches-bomba**) *nm* car bomb

coche-cama ['kotʃe'kama] (*pl* **coches-cama**) *nm* (*Ferro*) sleeping car, sleeper
cochera [ko'tʃera] *nf* garage; (*de autobuses, trenes*) depot
coche-restaurante ['kotʃerestau'rante] (*pl* **coches-restaurante**) *nm* (*Ferro*) dining-car, diner
cochinillo [kotʃi'niʎo] *nm* piglet, suckling pig
cochino, -a [ko'tʃino, a] *adj* filthy, dirty ▷ *nm/f* pig
cocido, -a [ko'θiðo, a] *adj* boiled; (*fam*) plastered ▷ *nm* stew
cociente [ko'θjente] *nm* quotient
cocina [ko'θina] *nf* kitchen; (*aparato*) cooker, stove; (*actividad*) cookery; **~ casera** home cooking; **~ eléctrica** electric cooker; **~ francesa** French cuisine; **~ de gas** gas cooker
cocinar [koθi'nar] *vt, vi* to cook
cocinero, -a [koθi'nero, a] *nm/f* cook
coco ['koko] *nm* coconut; (*fantasma*) bogeyman; (*fam*: *cabeza*) nut; **comer el ~ a algn** (*fam*) to brainwash sb
cocodrilo [koko'ðrilo] *nm* crocodile
cocotero [koko'tero] *nm* coconut palm
cóctel ['koktel] *nm* (*bebida*) cocktail; (*reunión*) cocktail party; **~ Molotov** Molotov cocktail, petrol bomb
codazo [ko'ðaθo] *nm*: **dar un ~ a algn** to nudge sb
codear [koðe'ar] *vi* to elbow, jostle; **codearse** *vr*: **~se con** to rub shoulders with
codicia [ko'ðiθja] *nf* greed; (*fig*) lust
codiciar [koði'θjar] *vt* to covet
codicioso, -a [koði'θjoso, a] *adj* covetous
codificar [koðifi'kar] *vt* (*mensaje*) to (en)code; (*leyes*) to codify
código ['koðiɣo] *nm* code; **~ de barras** (*Com*) bar code; **~ binario** binary code; **~ de caracteres** (*Inform*) character code; **~ de (la) circulación** highway code; **~ de la zona** (*Am*) dialling (*Brit*) *o* area (*US*) code; **~ postal** postcode; **~ civil** common law; **~ de control** (*Inform*) control code; **~ máquina** (*Inform*) machine code; **~ militar** military law; **~ de operación** (*Inform*) operational *o* machine code; **~ penal** penal code; **~ de práctica** code of practice
codillo [ko'ðiʎo] *nm* (*Zool*) knee; (*Tec*) elbow (joint)
codo ['koðo] *nm* (*Anat, de tubo*) elbow; (*Zool*) knee; **hablar por los ~s** to talk nineteen to the dozen
codorniz [koðor'niθ] *nf* quail
coerción [koer'θjon] *nf* coercion
coetáneo, -a [koe'taneo, a] *nm/f*: **~s** contemporaries
coexistir [koeksis'tir] *vi* to coexist
cofradía [kofra'ðia] *nf* brotherhood, fraternity; *ver tb* **Semana Santa**
cofre ['kofre] *nm* (*baúl*) trunk; (*de joyas*) box; (*de dinero*) chest; (*Am Auto*) bonnet (*Brit*), hood (*US*)
coger [ko'xer] *vt* (*Esp*) to take (hold of); (*objeto caído*) to pick up; (*frutas*) to pick, harvest; (*resfriado, ladrón, pelota*) to catch; (*Am fam!*) to lay (*!*) ▷ *vi*: **~ por el buen camino** to take the right road; **cogerse** *vr* (*el dedo*) to catch; **~ a algn desprevenido** to take sb unawares; **~se a algo** to get hold of sth
cogollo [ko'ɣoʎo] *nm* (*de lechuga*) heart; (*fig*) core, nucleus
cogorza [ko'ɣorθa] *nf* (*fam*): **agarrar una ~** to get smashed
cogote [ko'ɣote] *nm* back *o* nape of the neck
cohabitar [koaβi'tar] *vi* to live together, cohabit
cohecho [ko'etʃo] *nm* (*acción*) bribery; (*soborno*) bribe
coherencia [koe'renθja] *nf* coherence
coherente [koe'rente] *adj* coherent
cohesión [koe'sjon] *nm* cohesion
cohete [ko'ete] *nm* rocket
cohibido, -a [koi'βiðo, a] *adj* (*Psico*) inhibited; (*tímido*) shy; **sentirse ~** to feel embarrassed
cohibir [koi'βir] *vt* to restrain, restrict; **cohibirse** *vr* to feel inhibited
coima ['koima] *nf* (*Am fam*) bribe
coincidencia [koinθi'ðenθja] *nf* coincidence
coincidir [koinθi'ðir] *vi* (*en idea*) to coincide, agree; (*en lugar*) to coincide
coito ['koito] *nm* intercourse, coitus
coja *etc vb ver* **coger**
cojear [koxe'ar] *vi* (*persona*) to limp, hobble; (*mueble*) to wobble, rock
cojera [ko'xera] *nf* lameness; (*andar cojo*) limp
cojín [ko'xin] *nm* cushion
cojinete [koxi'nete] *nm* small cushion, pad; (*Tec*) (ball) bearing
cojo, -a *etc* ['koxo, a] *vb ver* **coger** ▷ *adj* (*que no puede andar*) lame, crippled; (*mueble*) wobbly ▷ *nm/f* lame person
cojón [ko'xon] *nm* (*fam!*) ball (*!*), testicle; **¡cojones!** shit! (*!*)
cojonudo, -a [koxo'nuðo, a] *adj* (*Esp fam*) great, fantastic
col [kol] *nf* cabbage; **~es de Bruselas** Brussels sprouts
cola ['kola] *nf* tail; (*de gente*) queue; (*lugar*) end, last place; (*para pegar*) glue, gum; (*de vestido*) train; **hacer ~** to queue (up)
colaboración [kolaβora'θjon] *nf* (*gen*) collaboration; (*en periódico*) contribution
colaborador, a [kolaβora'ðor, a] *nm/f* collaborator; contributor
colaborar [kolaβo'rar] *vi* to collaborate
colado, -a [ko'laðo, a] *adj* (*metal*) cast ▷ *nf*: **hacer la colada** to do the washing
colador [kola'ðor] *nm* (*de té*) strainer; (*para verduras etc*) colander

colapsar [kolap'sar] *vt* (*tráfico etc*) to bring to a standstill
colapso [ko'lapso] *nm* collapse; ~ **nervioso** nervous breakdown
colar [ko'lar] *vt* (*líquido*) to strain off; (*metal*) to cast ▷ *vi* to ooze, seep (through); **colarse** *vr* to jump the queue; (*en mitin*) to sneak in; (*equivocarse*) to slip up; ~**se en** to get into without paying; (*en una fiesta*) to gatecrash
colateral [kolate'ral] *nm* collateral
colcha ['koltʃa] *nf* bedspread
colchón [kol'tʃon] *nm* mattress; ~ **inflable** air bed, inflatable mattress
colchoneta [koltʃo'neta] *nf* (*en gimnasio*) mat; ~ **hinchable** air bed, inflatable mattress
colear [kole'ar] *vi* (*perro*) to wag its tail
colección [kolek'θjon] *nf* collection
coleccionar [kolekθjo'nar] *vt* to collect
coleccionista [kolekθjo'nista] *nm/f* collector
colecta [ko'lekta] *nf* collection
colectivo, -a [kolek'tiβo, a] *adj* collective, joint ▷ *nm* (*Am*: *autobús*) (small) bus; (*taxi*) collective taxi
colector [kolek'tor] *nm* collector; (*sumidero*) sewer
colega [ko'leɣa] *nm/f* colleague; (*Esp*: *amigo*) mate
colegiado, -a [kole'xjaðo, a] *adj* (*profesional*) registered ▷ *nm/f* referee
colegial, a [kole'xjal, a] *adj* (*Escol etc*) school *cpd*, college *cpd* ▷ *nm/f* schoolboy/girl
colegio [ko'lexjo] *nm* college; (*escuela*) school; (*de abogados etc*) association; ~ **de internos** boarding school; **ir al** ~ to go to school; ~ **electoral** polling station; ~ **mayor** (*Esp*) hall of residence; *see note*

COLEGIO

A *colegio* is normally a private primary or secondary school. In the state system it means a primary school although these are also called *escuela*. State secondary schools are called *institutos*. Extracurricular subjects, such as computing or foreign languages, are offered in private schools called *academias*.

colegir [kole'xir] *vt* (*juntar*) to collect, gather; (*deducir*) to infer, conclude
cólera ['kolera] *nf* (*ira*) anger; **montar en** ~ to get angry ▷ *nm* (*Med*) cholera
colérico, -a [ko'leriko, a] *adj* angry, furious
colesterol [koleste'rol] *nm* cholesterol
coleta [ko'leta] *nf* pigtail
coletilla [kole'tiʎa] *nf* (*en carta*) postscript; (*en conversación*) filler phrase
colgante [kol'ɣante] *adj* hanging; *ver* **puente** ▷ *nm* (*joya*) pendant
colgar [kol'ɣar] *vt* to hang (up); (*tender*: *ropa*) to hang out ▷ *vi* to hang; (*teléfono*) to hang up; **no cuelgue** please hold
cólico ['koliko] *nm* colic
coliflor [koli'flor] *nf* cauliflower
colilla [ko'liʎa] *nf* cigarette end, butt
colina [ko'lina] *nf* hill
colindante [kolin'dante] *adj* adjacent, neighbouring
colindar [kolin'dar] *vi* to adjoin, be adjacent
colisión [koli'sjon] *nf* collision; ~ **frontal** head-on crash
collar [ko'ʎar] *nm* necklace; (*de perro*) collar
colmado, -a [kol'maðo, a] *adj* full ▷ *nm* grocer's (shop) (*Brit*), grocery store (*US*)
colmar [kol'mar] *vt* to fill to the brim; (*fig*) to fulfil, realize
colmena [kol'mena] *nf* beehive
colmillo [kol'miʎo] *nm* (*diente*) eye tooth; (*de elefante*) tusk; (*de perro*) fang
colmo ['kolmo] *nm* height, summit; **para** ~ **de desgracias** to cap it all; **¡eso es ya el** ~**!** that's beyond a joke!
colocación [koloka'θjon] *nf* (*acto*) placing; (*empleo*) job, position; (*situación*) place, position; (*Com*) placement
colocar [kolo'kar] *vt* to place, put, position; (*poner en empleo*) to find a job for; ~ **dinero** to invest money; **colocarse** *vr* to place o.s.; (*conseguir trabajo*) to find a job
Colombia [ko'lombja] *nf* Colombia
colombiano, -a [kolom'bjano, a] *adj, nm/f* Colombian
colonia [ko'lonja] *nf* colony; (*de casas*) housing estate; (*agua de colonia*) cologne; ~ **escolar** summer camp (for schoolchildren); ~ **proletaria** (*Am*) shantytown
colonización [koloniθa'θjon] *nf* colonization
colonizador, a [koloniθa'ðor, a] *adj* colonizing ▷ *nm/f* colonist, settler
colonizar [koloni'θar] *vt* to colonize
colono [ko'lono] *nm* (*Pol*) colonist, settler; (*Agr*) tenant farmer
coloquial [kolo'kjal] *adj* colloquial
coloquio [ko'lokjo] *nm* conversation; (*congreso*) conference
color [ko'lor] *nm* colour; **a todo** ~ in full colour; **verlo todo** ~ **de rosa** to see everything through rose-coloured spectacles; **le salieron los** ~**es** she blushed
colorado, -a [kolo'raðo, a] *adj* (*rojo*) red; (*Am*: *chiste*) rude, blue; **ponerse** ~ to blush
colorante [kolo'rante] *nm* colouring (matter)
colorar [kolo'rar] *vt* to colour; (*teñir*) to dye
colorear [kolore'ar] *vt* to colour
colorete [kolo'rete] *nm* blusher
colorido [kolo'riðo] *nm* colour(ing)
coloso [ko'loso] *nm* colossus
columna [ko'lumna] *nf* column; (*pilar*) pillar; (*apoyo*) support; ~ **blindada** (*Mil*) armoured column; ~ **vertebral** spine, spinal column; (*fig*) backbone

columpiar [kolum'pjar] *vt* to swing; **columpiarse** *vr* to swing
columpio [ko'lumpjo] *nm* swing
colza ['kolθa] *nf* rape; **aceite de ~** rapeseed oil
coma ['koma] *nf* comma ▷ *nm* (*Med*) coma
comadre [ko'maðre] *nf* (*madrina*) godmother; (*vecina*) neighbour; (*chismosa*) gossip
comadrear [komaðre'ar] *vi* (*esp Am*) to gossip
comadrona [koma'ðrona] *nf* midwife
comal [ko'mal] *nm* (*Am*) griddle
comandancia [koman'danθja] *nf* command
comandante [koman'dante] *nm* commandant; (*grado*) major
comandar [koman'dar] *vt* to command
comarca [ko'marka] *nf* region; *ver tb* **provincia**
comba ['komba] *nf* (*curva*) curve; (*en viga*) warp; (*cuerda*) skipping rope; **saltar a la ~** to skip
combar [kom'bar] *vt* to bend, curve
combate [kom'bate] *nm* fight; (*fig*) battle; **fuera de ~** out of action
combatiente [komba'tjente] *nm* combatant
combatir [komba'tir] *vt* to fight, combat
combi ['kombi] *nm* fridge-freezer
combinación [kombina'θjon] *nf* combination; (*Química*) compound; (*bebida*) cocktail; (*plan*) scheme, setup; (*prenda*) slip
combinar [kombi'nar] *vt* to combine; (*colores*) to match
combustible [kombus'tiβle] *nm* fuel
combustión [kombus'tjon] *nf* combustion
comedia [ko'meðja] *nf* comedy; (*Teat*) play, drama; (*fig*) farce
comediante [kome'ðjante] *nm/f* (comic) actor/actress
comedido, -a [kome'ðiðo, a] *adj* moderate
comedor, a [kome'ðor, a] *nm/f* (*persona*) glutton ▷ *nm* (*habitación*) dining room; (*restaurante*) restaurant; (*cantina*) canteen
comensal [komen'sal] *nm/f* fellow guest/diner
comentar [komen'tar] *vt* to comment on; (*fam*) to discuss; **comentó que...** he made the comment that...
comentario [komen'tarjo] *nm* comment, remark; (*Lit*) commentary; **comentarios** *nmpl* gossip *sg*; **dar lugar a ~s** to cause gossip
comentarista [komenta'rista] *nm/f* commentator
comenzar [komen'θar] *vt, vi* to begin, start, commence; **~ a hacer algo** to begin *o* start doing *o* to do sth
comer [ko'mer] *vt* to eat; (*Damas, Ajedrez*) to take, capture ▷ *vi* to eat; (*almorzar*) to have lunch; **comerse** *vr* to eat up; (*párrafo etc*) to skip; **~ el coco a** (*fam*) to brainwash; **¡a ~!** food's ready!
comercial [komer'θjal] *adj* commercial; (*relativo al negocio*) business *cpd*
comercializar [komerθjali'θar] *vt* (*producto*) to market; (*pey*) to commercialize
comerciante [komer'θjante] *nm/f* trader, merchant; (*tendero*) shopkeeper; **~ exclusivo** (*Com*) sole trader
comerciar [komer'θjar] *vi* to trade, do business
comercio [ko'merθjo] *nm* commerce, trade; (*tienda*) shop, store; (*negocio*) business; (*grandes empresas*) big business; (*fig*) dealings *pl*; **~ autorizado** (*Com*) licensed trade; **~ electrónico** e-commerce; **~ exterior** foreign trade
comestible [komes'tiβle] *adj* eatable, edible ▷ *nm*: **~s** food *sg*, foodstuffs; (*Com*) groceries
cometa [ko'meta] *nm* comet ▷ *nf* kite
cometer [kome'ter] *vt* to commit
cometido [kome'tiðo] *nm* (*misión*) task, assignment; (*deber*) commitment
comezón [kome'θon] *nf* itch, itching
cómic (*pl* **cómics**) ['komik, 'komiks] *nm* comic
comicios [ko'miθjos] *nmpl* elections; (*voto*) voting *sg*
cómico, -a ['komiko, a] *adj* comic(al) ▷ *nm/f* comedian; (*de teatro*) (comic) actor/actress
comida [ko'miða] *nf* (*alimento*) food; (*almuerzo, cena*) meal; (*de mediodía*) lunch; (*Am*) dinner; **~ basura** junk food; **~ chatarra** (*Am*) junk food
comidilla [komi'ðiʎa] *nf*: **ser la ~ del barrio** *o* **pueblo** to be the talk of the town
comienzo [ko'mjenθo] *vb ver* **comenzar** ▷ *nm* beginning, start; **dar ~ a un acto** to begin a ceremony; **~ del archivo** (*Inform*) top-of-file
comillas [ko'miʎas] *nfpl* quotation marks
comilón, -ona [komi'lon, ona] *adj* greedy ▷ *nf* (*fam*) blow-out
comino [ko'mino] *nm* cumin (seed); **no me importa un ~** I don't give a damn!
comisaría [komisa'ria] *nf* police station, precinct (*US*); (*Mil*) commissariat
comisario [komi'sarjo] *nm* (*Mil etc*) commissary; (*Pol*) commissar
comisión [komi'sjon] *nf* (*Com: pago*) commission, rake-off (*fam*); (*: junta*) board; (*encargo*) assignment; **~ mixta/permanente** joint/standing committee; **Comisiones Obreras** (*Esp: formerly*) *Communist Union Confederation*
comité (*pl* **comités**) [komi'te, komi'tes] *nm* committee; **~ de empresa** works council
comitiva [komi'tiβa] *nf* suite, retinue
como ['komo] *adv* as; (*tal como*) like; (*aproximadamente*) about, approximately ▷ *conj* (*ya que, puesto que*) as, since; (*en seguida que*) as soon as; (*si: +subjun*) if; **¡~ no!** of course!; **~ no lo haga hoy** unless he does it today; **~ si** as if; **es tan alto ~ ancho** it is as high as it is wide
cómo ['komo] *adv* how?, why? ▷ *excl* what?, I beg your pardon? ▷ *nm*: **el ~ y el porqué**

the whys and wherefores; **¿~ está Ud?** how are you?; **¿~ no?** why not?; **¡~ no!** (*esp Am*) of course!; **¿~ son?** what are they like?
cómoda ['komoða] *nf* chest of drawers
comodidad [komoði'ðað] *nf* comfort; **venga a su ~** come at your convenience
comodín [komo'ðin] *nm* joker; (*Inform*) wild card; **símbolo ~** wild-card character
cómodo, -a ['komoðo, a] *adj* comfortable; (*práctico, de fácil uso*) convenient
comodón, -ona [komo'ðon, ona] *adj* comfort-loving ▷ *nm/f*: **ser un(a) ~/-ona** to like one's home comforts
compact [kom'pakt] (*pl* **compacts**) *nm* (*tb*: **~ disc**) compact disk player
compacto, -a [kom'pakto, a] *adj* compact
compadecer [kompaðe'θer] *vt* to pity, be sorry for; **compadecerse** *vr*: **~se de** to pity, be sorry for
compadre [kom'paðre] *nm* (*padrino*) godfather; (*esp Am: amigo*) friend, pal
compaginar [kompaxi'nar] *vt*: **~ A con B** to bring A into line with B; **compaginarse** *vr*: **~se con** to tally with, square with
compañerismo [kompaɲe'rismo] *nm* comradeship
compañero, -a [kompa'ɲero, a] *nm/f* companion; (*novio*) boyfriend/girlfriend; **~ de clase** classmate
compañía [kompa'ɲia] *nf* company; **~ afiliada** associated company; **~ concesionaria** franchiser; **~ (no) cotizable** (un)listed company; **~ inversionista** investment trust; **hacer ~ a algn** to keep sb company
comparación [kompara'θjon] *nf* comparison; **en ~ con** in comparison with
comparar [kompa'rar] *vt* to compare
comparativo, -a [kompara'tiβo, a] *adj* comparative
comparecer [kompare'θer] *vi* to appear (in court)
comparsa [kom'parsa] *nm/f* extra
compartimento [komparti'mento], **compartimiento** [komparti'mjento] *nm* (*Ferro*) compartment; (*de mueble, cajón*) section; **~ estanco** (*fig*) watertight compartment
compartir [kompar'tir] *vt* to share; (*dinero, comida etc*) to divide (up), share (out)
compás [kom'pas] *nm* (*Mus*) beat, rhythm; (*Mat*) compasses *pl*; (*Naut etc*) compass; **al ~** in time
compasión [kompa'sjon] *nf* compassion, pity
compasivo, -a [kompa'siβo, a] *adj* compassionate
compatibilidad [kompatiβili'ðað] *nf* (*tb Inform*) compatibility
compatible [kompa'tiβle] *adj* compatible
compatriota [kompa'trjota] *nm/f* compatriot, fellow countryman/woman
compendiar [kompen'djar] *vt* to summarize; (*libro*) to abridge
compendio [kom'pendjo] *nm* summary; abridgement
compenetrarse [kompene'trarse] *vr* to be in tune; (*fig*): **~ (muy) bien** to get on (very) well together
compensación [kompensa'θjon] *nf* compensation; (*Jur*) damages *pl*; (*Com*) clearing; **~ de carbono** carbon offsetting
compensar [kompen'sar] *vt* to compensate; (*pérdida*) to make up for
competencia [kompe'tenθja] *nf* (*incumbencia*) domain, field; (*Com*) receipt; (*Jur, habilidad*) competence; (*rivalidad*) competition
competente [kompe'tente] *adj* (*Jur, persona*) competent; (*conveniente*) suitable
competición [kompeti'θjon] *nf* competition
competir [kompe'tir] *vi* to compete
competitivo, -a [kompeti'tiβo, a] *adj* competitive
compilar [kompi'lar] *vt* to compile
compinche [kom'pintʃe] *nm/f* (*LAm: fam*) mate, buddy (*US*)
complacencia [kompla'θenθja] *nf* (*placer*) pleasure; (*satisfacción*) satisfaction; (*buena voluntad*) willingness
complacer [kompla'θer] *vt* to please; **complacerse** *vr* to be pleased
complaciente [kompla'θjente] *adj* kind, obliging, helpful
complejo, -a [kom'plexo, a] *adj, nm* complex
complementario, -a [komplemen'tarjo, a] *adj* complementary
complemento [komple'mento] *nm* (*de moda, diseño*) accessory; (*Ling*) complement
completar [komple'tar] *vt* to complete
completo, -a [kom'pleto, a] *adj* complete; (*perfecto*) perfect; (*lleno*) full ▷ *nm* full complement
complexión [komple'ksjon] *nf* constitution
complicación [komplika'θjon] *nf* complication
complicado, -a [kompli'kaðo, a] *adj* complicated; **estar ~ en** to be mixed up in
complicar [kompli'kar] *vt* to complicate
cómplice ['kompliθe] *nm/f* accomplice
complot (*pl* **complots**) [kom'plo(t), kom'plos] *nm* plot; (*conspiración*) conspiracy
componente [kompo'nente] *adj, nm* component
componer [kompo'ner] *vt* to make up, put together; (*Mus, Lit, Imprenta*) to compose; (*algo roto*) to mend, repair; (*adornar*) to adorn; (*arreglar*) to arrange; (*reconciliar*) to reconcile; **componerse** *vr*: **~se de** to consist of; **componérselas para hacer algo** to manage to do sth

comportamiento [komporta'mjento] *nm* behaviour, conduct
comportarse [kompor'tarse] *vr* to behave
composición [komposi'θjon] *nf* composition
compositor, a [komposi'tor, a] *nm/f* composer
compostura [kompos'tura] *nf* (*reparación*) mending, repair; (*composición*) composition; (*acuerdo*) agreement; (*actitud*) composure
compra ['kompra] *nf* purchase; **compras** *nfpl* purchases, shopping *sg*; **hacer la ~/ir de ~s** to do the/go shopping; **~ a granel** (*Com*) bulk buying; **~ proteccionista** (*Com*) support buying
comprador, a [kompra'ðor, a] *nm/f* buyer, purchaser
comprar [kom'prar] *vt* to buy, purchase; **~ deudas** (*Com*) to factor
comprender [kompren'der] *vt* to understand; (*incluir*) to comprise, include
comprensible [kompren'siβle] *adj* understandable
comprensión [kompren'sjon] *nf* understanding; (*totalidad*) comprehensiveness
comprensivo, -a [kompren'siβo, a] *adj* comprehensive; (*actitud*) understanding
compresa [kom'presa] *nf* compress; **~ higiénica** sanitary towel (*Brit*) *o* napkin (*US*)
comprimido, -a [kompri'miðo, a] *adj* compressed ▷ *nm* (*Med*) pill, tablet; **en caracteres ~s** (*Tip*) condensed
comprimir [kompri'mir] *vt* to compress; (*fig*) to control; (*Inform*) to compress, zip
comprobante [kompro'βante] *nm* proof; (*Com*) voucher; **~ (de pago)** receipt; **~ de compra** proof of purchase
comprobar [kompro'βar] *vt* to check; (*probar*) to prove; (*Tec*) to check, test
comprometer [komprome'ter] *vt* to compromise; (*exponer*) to endanger; **comprometerse** *vr* to compromise o.s.; (*involucrarse*) to get involved
compromiso [kompro'miso] *nm* (*obligación*) obligation; (*cita*) engagement, date; (*cometido*) commitment; (*convenio*) agreement; (*dificultad*) awkward situation; **libre de ~** (*Com*) without obligation
compuesto, -a [kom'pwesto, a] *pp de* **componer** ▷ *adj*: **~ de** composed of, made up of ▷ *nm* compound; (*Med*) preparation
compungido, -a [kompun'xiðo, a] *adj* remorseful
computador [komputa'ðor] *nm*, **computadora** [komputa'ðora] *nf* computer; **~ central** mainframe computer; **~ especializado** dedicated computer; **~ personal** personal computer
cómputo ['komputo] *nm* calculation

comulgar [komul'ɣar] *vi* to receive communion
común [ko'mun] *adj* (*gen*) common; (*corriente*) ordinary; **por lo ~** generally ▷ *nm*: **el ~** the community
comunicación [komunika'θjon] *nf* communication; (*informe*) report
comunicado [komuni'kaðo] *nm* announcement; **~ de prensa** press release
comunicar [komuni'kar] *vt* to communicate; (*Arq*) to connect ▷ *vi* to communicate; to send a report; **comunicarse** *vr* to communicate; **está comunicando** (*Telec*) the line's engaged (*Brit*) *o* busy (*US*)
comunicativo, -a [komunika'tiβo, a] *adj* communicative
comunidad [komuni'ðað] *nf* community; **~ autónoma** (*Esp*) autonomous region; **~ de vecinos** residents' association; **C~ Económica Europea (CEE)** European Economic Community (EEC)
comunión [komu'njon] *nf* communion
comunismo [komu'nismo] *nm* communism
comunista [komu'nista] *adj, nm/f* communist
comunitario, -a [komuni'tarjo, a] *adj* (*de la CE*) Community *cpd*, EC *cpd*

PALABRA CLAVE

con [kon] *prep* **1** (*medio, compañía, modo*) with; **comer con cuchara** to eat with a spoon; **café con leche** white coffee; **estoy con un catarro** I've got a cold; **pasear con algn** to go for a walk with sb; **con habilidad** skilfully
2 (*a pesar de*): **con todo, merece nuestros respetos** all the same *o* even so, he deserves our respect
3 (*para con*): **es muy bueno para con los niños** he's very good with (the) children
4 (*+infin*): **con llegar tan tarde se quedó sin comer** by arriving *o* because he arrived so late he missed out on eating; **con estudiar un poco apruebas** with a bit of studying you should pass
5 (*queja*): **¡con las ganas que tenía de ir!** and I really wanted to go (too)!
▷ *conj*: **con que**: **será suficiente con que le escribas** it will be enough if you write to her

conato [ko'nato] *nm* attempt; **~ de robo** attempted robbery
concebir [konθe'βir] *vt* to conceive; (*imaginar*) to imagine ▷ *vi* to conceive
conceder [konθe'ðer] *vt* to concede
concejal, a [konθe'xal, a] *nm/f* town councillor
concejo [kon'θexo] *nm* council
concentración [konθentra'θjon] *nf* concentration

concentrar [konθen'trar] *vt* to concentrate; **concentrarse** *vr* to concentrate

concéntrico, -a [kon'θentriko, a] *adj* concentric

concepción [konθep'θjon] *nf* conception

concepto [kon'θepto] *nm* concept; **por ~ de** as, by way of; **tener buen ~ de algn** to think highly of sb; **bajo ningún ~** under no circumstances

concernir [konθer'nir] *vi* to concern; **en lo que concierne a ...** with regard to ...; **en lo que a mí concierne** as far as I'm concerned

concertar [konθer'tar] *vt* (*Mus*) to harmonize; (*acordar: precio*) to agree; (*: tratado*) to conclude; (*trato*) to arrange, fix up; (*combinar: esfuerzos*) to coordinate; (*reconciliar: personas*) to reconcile ▷ *vi* to harmonize, be in tune

concesión [konθe'sjon] *nf* concession; (*Com: fabricación*) licence

concesionario, -a [konθesjo'narjo, a] *nm/f* (*Com*) (licensed) dealer, agent, concessionaire; (*: de venta*) franchisee; (*: de transportes etc*) contractor

concha ['kontʃa] *nf* shell; (*Am fam!*) cunt (*!*)

conchabarse [kontʃa'βarse] *vr*: **~ contra** to gang up on

conciencia [kon'θjenθja] *nf* (*moral*) conscience; (*conocimiento*) awareness; **libertad de ~** freedom of worship; **tener/tomar ~ de** to be/become aware of; **tener la ~ limpia** *o* **tranquila** to have a clear conscience; **tener plena ~ de** to be fully aware of

concienciar [konθjen'θjar] *vt* to make aware; **concienciarse** *vr* to become aware

concienzudo, -a [konθjen'θuðo, a] *adj* conscientious

concierto [kon'θjerto] *vb ver* **concertar** ▷ *nm* concert; (*obra*) concerto

conciliar [konθi'ljar] *vt* to reconcile ▷ *adj* (*Rel*) council *cpd*; **~ el sueño** to get to sleep

concilio [kon'θiljo] *nm* council

conciso, -a [kon'θiso, a] *adj* concise

conciudadano, -a [konθjuða'ðano, a] *nm/f* fellow citizen

concluir [konklu'ir] *vt* (*acabar*) to conclude; (*inferir*) to infer, deduce ▷ *vi*, **concluirse** *vr* to conclude; **todo ha concluido** it's all over

conclusión [konklu'sjon] *nf* conclusion; **llegar a la ~ de que ...** to come to the conclusion that ...

concluyente [konklu'jente] *adj* (*prueba, información*) conclusive

concordar [konkor'ðar] *vt* to reconcile ▷ *vi* to agree, tally

concordia [kon'korðja] *nf* harmony

concretar [konkre'tar] *vt* to make concrete, make more specific; (*problema*) to pinpoint; **concretarse** *vr* to become more definite

concreto, -a [kon'kreto, a] *adj, nm* (*Am*) concrete; **en ~** (*en resumen*) to sum up; (*específicamente*) specifically; **no hay nada en ~** there's nothing definite

concurrencia [konku'rrenθja] *nf* turnout

concurrido, -a [konku'rriðo, a] *adj* (*calle*) busy; (*local: reunión*) crowded

concurrir [konku'rrir] *vi* (*juntarse: ríos*) to meet, come together; (*: personas*) to gather, meet

concursante [konkur'sante] *nm* competitor

concursar [konkur'sar] *vi* to compete

concurso [kon'kurso] *nm* (*de público*) crowd; (*Escol, Deporte, competición*) competition; (*Com*) invitation to tender; (*examen*) open competition; (*TV etc*) quiz; (*ayuda*) help, cooperation

condal [kon'dal] *adj*: **la ciudad ~** Barcelona

conde ['konde] *nm* count

condecoración [kondekora'θjon] *nf* (*Mil*) medal, decoration

condecorar [kondeko'rar] *vt* to decorate

condena [kon'dena] *nf* sentence; **cumplir una ~** to serve a sentence

condenación [kondena'θjon] *nf* condemnation; (*Rel*) damnation

condenar [konde'nar] *vt* to condemn; (*Jur*) to convict; **condenarse** *vr* (*Jur*) to confess (one's guilt); (*Rel*) to be damned

condensar [konden'sar] *vt* to condense

condesa [kon'desa] *nf* countess

condescender [kondesθen'der] *vi* to acquiesce, comply

condición [kondi'θjon] *nf* (*gen*) condition; (*rango*) social class; **condiciones** *nfpl* (*cualidades*) qualities; (*estado*) condition; **a ~ de que ...** on condition that ...; **las condiciones del contrato** the terms of the contract; **condiciones de trabajo** working conditions; **condiciones de venta** conditions of sale

condicional [kondiθjo'nal] *adj* conditional

condicionar [kondiθjo'nar] *vt* (*acondicionar*) to condition; **~ algo a algo** to make sth conditional *o* dependent on sth

condimento [kondi'mento] *nm* seasoning

condolerse [kondo'lerse] *vr* to sympathize

condominio [kondo'minjo] *nm* (*Com*) joint ownership; (*Am*) condominium, apartment

condón [kon'don] *nm* condom

conducir [kondu'θir] *vt* to take, convey; (*Elec etc*) to carry; (*Auto*) to drive; (*negocio*) to manage ▷ *vi* to drive; (*fig*) to lead; **conducirse** *vr* to behave

conducta [kon'dukta] *nf* conduct, behaviour

conducto [kon'dukto] *nm* pipe, tube; (*fig*) channel; (*Elec*) lead; **por ~ de** through

conductor, a [konduk'tor, a] *adj* leading, guiding ▷ *nm* (*Física*) conductor; (*de vehículo*) driver

conduje *etc* [kon'duxe] *vb ver* **conducir**

conduzco *etc* [kon'duθko] *vb ver* **conducir**

conectado, -a [konek'taðo, a] *adj* (*Elec*) connected, plugged in; (*Inform*) on-line

conectar [konek'tar] *vt* to connect (up); (*enchufar*) plug in; (*Inform*) to toggle on; **conectarse** *vr* (*Inform*) to log in *or* on
conejillo [kone'xiʎo] *nm*: **~ de Indias** guinea pig
conejo [ko'nexo] *nm* rabbit
conexión [konek'sjon] *nf* connection; (*Inform*) logging in *or* on
confección [konfek'θjon] *nf* (*preparación*) preparation, making-up; (*industria*) clothing industry; (*producto*) article; **de ~** (*ropa*) off-the-peg
confeccionar [konfekθjo'nar] *vt* to make (up)
confederación [konfeðera'θjon] *nf* confederation
conferencia [konfe'renθja] *nf* conference; (*lección*) lecture; (*Telec*) call; **~ de cobro revertido** (*Telec*) reversed-charge (*Brit*) *o* collect (*US*) call; **~ cumbre** summit (conference); **~ de prensa** press conference
conferir [konfe'rir] *vt* to award
confesar [konfe'sar] *vt* (*admitir*) to confess, admit; (*error*) to acknowledge; (*crimen*) to own up to
confesión [konfe'sjon] *nf* confession
confesionario [konfesjo'narjo] *nm* confessional
confeti [kon'feti] *nm* confetti
confiado, -a [kon'fjaðo, a] *adj* (*crédulo*) trusting; (*seguro*) confident; (*presumido*) conceited, vain
confianza [kon'fjanθa] *nf* trust; (*aliento, confidencia*) confidence; (*familiaridad*) intimacy, familiarity; (*pey*) vanity, conceit; **margen de ~** credibility gap; **tener ~ con algn** to be on close terms with sb
confiar [kon'fjar] *vt* to entrust ▷ *vi* (*fiarse*) to trust; (*contar con*) to rely; **confiarse** *vr* to put one's trust in; **~ en algn** to trust sb; **~ en que ...** to hope that ...
confidencia [konfi'ðenθja] *nf* confidence
confidencial [konfiðen'θjal] *adj* confidential
confidente [konfi'ðente] *nm/f* confidant/confidante; (*policial*) informer
configurar [konfiɣu'rar] *vt* to shape, form
confín [kon'fin] *nm* limit; **confines** *nmpl* confines, limits
confinar [konfi'nar] *vi* to confine; (*desterrar*) to banish
confirmación [konfirma'θjon] *nf* confirmation; (*Rel*) Confirmation
confirmar [konfir'mar] *vt* to confirm; (*Jur etc*) to corroborate; **la excepción confirma la regla** the exception proves the rule
confiscar [konfis'kar] *vt* to confiscate
confite [kon'fite] *nm* sweet (*Brit*), candy (*US*)
confitería [konfite'ria] *nf* confectionery; (*tienda*) confectioner's (shop)
confitura [konfi'tura] *nf* jam
conflictivo, -a [konflik'tiβo, a] *adj* (*asunto, propuesta*) controversial; (*país, situación*) troubled
conflicto [kon'flikto] *nm* conflict; (*fig*) clash; (*: dificultad*): **estar en un ~** to be in a jam; **~ laboral** labour dispute
confluir [konflu'ir] *vi* (*ríos etc*) to meet; (*gente*) to gather
conformar [konfor'mar] *vt* to shape, fashion ▷ *vi* to agree; **conformarse** *vr* to conform; (*resignarse*) to resign o.s.; **~se con algo** to be happy with sth
conforme [kon'forme] *adj* alike, similar; (*correspondiente*): **~ con** in line with; (*de acuerdo*) agreed, in agreement; (*satisfecho*) satisfied ▷ *adv* as ▷ *excl* agreed! ▷ *nm* agreement ▷ *prep*: **~ a** in accordance with; **estar ~s (con algo)** to be in agreement (with sth); **quedarse ~ (con algo)** to be satisfied (with sth)
conformidad [konformi'ðað] *nf* (*semejanza*) similarity; (*acuerdo*) agreement; (*resignación*) resignation; **de/en ~ con** in accordance with; **dar su ~** to consent
conformista [konfor'mista] *nm/f* conformist
confort (*pl* **conforts**) [kon'for, kon'for(t)s] *nm* comfort
confortable [konfor'taβle] *adj* comfortable
confortar [konfor'tar] *vt* to comfort
confraternizar [konfraterni'θar] *vi* to fraternize
confrontar [konfron'tar] *vt* to confront; (*dos personas*) to bring face to face; (*cotejar*) to compare ▷ *vi* to border
confundir [konfun'dir] *vt* (*borrar*) to blur; (*equivocar*) to mistake, confuse; (*mezclar*) to mix; (*turbar*) to confuse; **confundirse** *vr* (*hacerse borroso*) to become blurred; (*turbarse*) to get confused; (*equivocarse*) to make a mistake; (*mezclarse*) to mix
confusión [konfu'sjon] *nf* confusion
confuso, -a [kon'fuso, a] *adj* (*gen*) confused; (*recuerdo*) hazy; (*estilo*) obscure
congelado, -a [konxe'laðo, a] *adj* frozen ▷ *nmpl*: **~s** frozen food *sg o* foods
congelador [konxela'ðor] *nm* freezer, deep freeze
congelar [konxe'lar] *vt* to freeze; **congelarse** *vr* (*sangre, grasa*) to congeal
congénere [kon'xenere] *nm/f*: **sus ~s** his peers
congeniar [konxe'njar] *vi* to get on (*Brit*) *o* along (*US*) (well)
congestión [konxes'tjon] *nf* congestion
congestionar [konxestjo'nar] *vt* to congest; **congestionarse** *vr* to become congested; **se le congestionó la cara** his face became flushed
congoja [kon'goxa] *nf* distress, grief
congraciarse [kongra'θjarse] *vr* to ingratiate o.s.

congratular [kongratu'lar] *vt* to congratulate
congregación [kongreɣa'θjon] *nf* congregation
congregar [kongre'ɣar] *vt* to gather together; **congregarse** *vr* to gather together
congresista [kongre'sista] *nm/f* delegate, congressman/woman
congreso [kon'greso] *nm* congress; **C~ de los Diputados** (*Esp Pol*) ≈ House of Commons (*Brit*), House of Representatives (*US*); *ver tb* **Cortes**
conífera [ko'nifera] *nf* conifer
conjetura [konxe'tura] *nf* guess; (*Com*) guesstimate
conjeturar [konxetu'rar] *vt* to guess
conjugación [konxuɣa'θjon] *nf* conjugation
conjugar [konxu'ɣar] *vt* to combine, fit together; (*Ling*) to conjugate
conjunción [konxun'θjon] *nf* conjunction
conjunto, -a [kon'xunto, a] *adj* joint, united ▷ *nm* whole; (*Mus*) band; (*de ropa*) ensemble; (*Inform*) set; **en ~** as a whole; **~ integrado de programas** (*Inform*) integrated software suite
conjurar [konxu'rar] *vt* (*Rel*) to exorcise; (*peligro*) to ward off ▷ *vi* to plot
conmemoración [konmemora'θjon] *nf* commemoration
conmemorar [konmemo'rar] *vt* to commemorate
conmigo [kon'miɣo] *pron* with me
conminar [konmi'nar] *vt* to threaten
conmoción [konmo'θjon] *nf* shock; (*Pol*) disturbance; (*fig*) upheaval; **~ cerebral** (*Med*) concussion
conmovedor, a [konmoβe'ðor, a] *adj* touching, moving; (*emocionante*) exciting
conmover [konmo'βer] *vt* to shake, disturb; (*fig*) to move; **conmoverse** *vr* (*fig*) to be moved
conmutador [konmuta'ðor] *nm* switch; (*Am Telec*) switchboard; (*: central*) telephone exchange
connotación [konnota'θjon] *nf* connotation
cono ['kono] *nm* cone; **C~ Sur** Southern Cone
conocedor, a [konoθe'ðor, a] *adj* expert, knowledgeable ▷ *nm/f* expert, connoisseur
conocer [kono'θer] *vt* to know; (*por primera vez*) to meet, get to know; (*entender*) to know about; (*reconocer*) to recognize; **conocerse** *vr* (*una persona*) to know o.s.; (*dos personas*) to (get to) know each other; **~ a algn de vista** to know sb by sight; **darse a ~** (*presentarse*) to make o.s. known; **se conoce que ...** (*parece*) apparently ...
conocido, -a [kono'θiðo, a] *adj* (well-)known ▷ *nm/f* acquaintance
conocimiento [konoθi'mjento] *nm* knowledge; (*Med*) consciousness; (*Naut*: *tb*: **~ de embarque**) bill of lading; **conocimientos** *nmpl* (*personas*) acquaintances; (*saber*) knowledge *sg*; **hablar con ~ de causa** to speak from experience; **~ (de embarque) aéreo** (*Com*) air waybill
conozco *etc* [ko'noθko] *vb ver* **conocer**
conque ['konke] *conj* and so, so then
conquista [kon'kista] *nf* conquest
conquistador, a [konkista'ðor, a] *adj* conquering ▷ *nm* conqueror
conquistar [konkis'tar] *vt* (*Mil*) to conquer; (*puesto, simpatía*) to win; (*enamorar*) to win the heart of
consagrar [konsa'ɣrar] *vt* (*Rel*) to consecrate; (*fig*) to devote
consciente [kons'θjente] *adj* conscious; **ser** *o* **estar ~ de** to be aware of
consecución [konseku'θjon] *nf* acquisition; (*de fin*) attainment
consecuencia [konse'kwenθja] *nf* consequence, outcome; (*firmeza*) consistency; **de ~** of importance
consecuente [konse'kwente] *adj* consistent
consecutivo, -a [konseku'tiβo, a] *adj* consecutive
conseguir [konse'ɣir] *vt* to get, obtain; (*sus fines*) to attain
consejería [konsexe'ria] *nf* (*Pol*) ministry (*in a regional government*)
consejero, -a [konse'xero, a] *nm/f* adviser, consultant; (*Pol*) minister (*in a regional government*); (*Com*) director; (*en comisión*) member
consejo [kon'sexo] *nm* advice; (*Pol*) council; (*Com*) board; **un ~** a piece of advice; **~ de administración** board of directors; **~ de guerra** court-martial; **~ de ministros** cabinet meeting; **C~ de Europa** Council of Europe
consenso [kon'senso] *nm* consensus
consentimiento [konsenti'mjento] *nm* consent
consentir [konsen'tir] *vt* (*permitir, tolerar*) to consent to; (*mimar*) to pamper, spoil; (*aguantar*) to put up with ▷ *vi* to agree, consent; **~ que algn haga algo** to allow sb to do sth
conserje [kon'serxe] *nm* caretaker; (*portero*) porter
conserva [kon'serβa] *nf*: **en ~** (*alimentos*) tinned (*Brit*), canned; **conservas** (*tb*: **~s alimenticias**) tinned (*Brit*) *o* canned foods
conservación [konserβa'θjon] *nf* conservation; (*de alimentos, vida*) preservation
conservador, a [konserβa'ðor, a] *adj* (*Pol*) conservative ▷ *nm/f* conservative
conservante [konser'βante] *nm* preservative
conservar [konser'βar] *vt* (*gen*) to preserve; (*recursos*) to conserve, keep; (*alimentos, vida*) to preserve; **conservarse** *vr* to survive
conservatorio [konserβa'torjo] *nm* (*Mus*) conservatoire, conservatory; (*Am*) greenhouse

considerable [konsiðe'raβle] *adj* considerable
consideración [konsiðera'θjon] *nf* consideration; (*estimación*) respect; **de ~** important; **De mi** *o* **nuestra (mayor) ~** (*Am*) Dear Sir(s) *o* Madam; **tomar en ~** to take into account
considerado, -a [konsiðe'raðo, a] *adj* (*atento*) considerate; (*respetado*) respected
considerar [konsiðe'rar] *vt* (*gen*) to consider; (*meditar*) to think about; (*tener en cuenta*) to take into account
consigna [kon'siɣna] *nf* (*orden*) order, instruction; (*para equipajes*) left-luggage office (*Brit*), checkroom (*US*)
consigo [kon'siɣo] *vb ver* **conseguir** ▷ *pron* (*m*) with him; (*f*) with her; (*usted*) with you; (*reflexivo*) with o.s.
consiguiendo *etc* [konsi'ɣjendo] *vb ver* **conseguir**
consiguiente [konsi'ɣjente] *adj* consequent; **por ~** and so, therefore, consequently
consistente [konsis'tente] *adj* consistent; (*sólido*) solid, firm; (*válido*) sound; **~ en** consisting of
consistir [konsis'tir] *vi*: **~ en** (*componerse de*) to consist of; (*ser resultado de*) to be due to
consola [kon'sola] *nf* console, control panel; (*mueble*) console table; **~ de juegos** games console; **~ de mandos** (*Inform*) control console; **~ de visualización** visual display console
consolación [konsola'θjon] *nf* consolation
consolar [konso'lar] *vt* to console
consolidar [konsoli'ðar] *vt* to consolidate
consomé (*pl* **consomés**) [konso'me, konso'mes] *nm* consommé, clear soup
consonante [konso'nante] *adj* consonant, harmonious ▷ *nf* consonant
consorcio [kon'sorθjo] *nm* (*Com*) consortium, syndicate
conspiración [konspira'θjon] *nf* conspiracy
conspirador, a [konspira'ðor, a] *nm/f* conspirator
conspirar [konspi'rar] *vi* to conspire
constancia [kons'tanθja] *nf* (*gen*) constancy; (*certeza*) certainly; **dejar ~ de algo** to put sth on record
constante [kons'tante] *adj, nf* constant
constar [kons'tar] *vi* (*evidenciarse*) to be clear *o* evident; **~ (en)** to appear (in); **~ de** to consist of; **hacer ~** to put on record; **me consta que ...** I have evidence that ...; **que conste que lo hice por ti** believe me, I did it for your own good
constatar [konsta'tar] *vt* (*controlar*) to check; (*observar*) to note
constelación [konstela'θjon] *nf* constellation
consternación [konsterna'θjon] *nf* consternation
constipado, -a [konsti'paðo, a] *adj*: **estar ~** to have a cold ▷ *nm* cold
constiparse [konsti'parse] *vr* to catch a cold
constitución [konstitu'θjon] *nf* constitution; **Día de la C~** (*Esp*) Constitution Day (*6th December*)
constitucional [konstituθjo'nal] *adj* constitutional
constituir [konstitu'ir] *vt* (*formar, componer*) to constitute, make up; (*fundar, erigir, ordenar*) to constitute, establish; (*ser*) to be; **constituirse** *vr* (*Pol etc: cuerpo*) to be composed; (*: fundarse*) to be established
constitutivo, -a [konstitu'tiβo, a] *adj* constitutive, constituent
constituyente [konstitu'jente] *adj* constituent
constreñir [konstre'ɲir] *vt* (*obligar*) to compel, oblige; (*restringir*) to restrict
construcción [konstruk'θjon] *nf* construction, building
constructivo, -a [konstruk'tiβo, a] *adj* constructive
constructor, a [konstruk'tor, a] *nm/f* builder
construir [konstru'ir] *vt* to build, construct
construyendo *etc* [konstru'jendo] *vb ver* **construir**
consuelo *etc* [kon'swelo] *vb ver* **consolar** ▷ *nm* consolation, solace
cónsul ['konsul] *nm* consul
consulado [konsu'laðo] *nm* (*sede*) consulate; (*cargo*) consulship
consulta [kon'sulta] *nf* consultation; (*Med: consultorio*) consulting room; (*Inform*) enquiry; **horas de ~** surgery hours; **obra de ~** reference book
consultar [konsul'tar] *vt* to consult; **~ un archivo** (*Inform*) to interrogate a file; **~ algo con algn** to discuss sth with sb
consultorio [konsul'torjo] *nm* (*Med*) surgery
consumar [konsu'mar] *vt* to complete, carry out; (*crimen*) to commit; (*sentencia*) to carry out
consumición [konsumi'θjon] *nf* consumption; (*bebida*) drink; (*comida*) food; **~ mínima** cover charge
consumidor, a [konsumi'ðor, a] *nm/f* consumer
consumir [konsu'mir] *vt* to consume; **consumirse** *vr* to be consumed; (*persona*) to waste away
consumismo [konsu'mismo] *nm* (*Com*) consumerism
consumo [kon'sumo] *nm* consumption; **bienes de ~** consumer goods
contabilidad [kontaβili'ðað] *nf* accounting, book-keeping; (*profesión*) accountancy; (*Com*): **~ analítica** variable costing; **~ de costos** cost accounting; **~ de doble partida** double-entry book-keeping; **~ de gestión**

management accounting; **~ por partida simple** single-entry book-keeping

contabilizar [kontaβi'liθar] *vt* to enter in the accounts

contable [kon'taβle] *nm/f* bookkeeper; (*licenciado*) accountant; **~ de costos** (*Com*) cost accountant

contactar [kontak'tar] *vi*: **~ con algn** to contact sb

contacto [kon'takto] *nm* contact; (*Auto*) ignition; **lentes de ~** contact lenses; **estar en ~ con** to be in touch with

contado, -a [kon'taðo, a] *adj*: **~s** (*escasos*) numbered, scarce, few ▷ *nm*: **al ~** for cash; **pagar al ~** to pay (in) cash; **precio al ~** cash price

contador [konta'ðor] *nm* (*aparato*) meter; (*Am: contable*) accountant

contagiar [konta'xjar] *vt* (*enfermedad*) to pass on, transmit; (*persona*) to infect; **contagiarse** *vr* to become infected

contagio [kon'taxjo] *nm* infection

contagioso, -a [konta'xjoso, a] *adj* infeccioso; (*fig*) catching

contaminación [kontamina'θjon] *nf* (*gen*) contamination; (*del ambiente etc*) pollution

contaminar [kontami'nar] *vt* (*gen*) to contaminate; (*aire, agua*) to pollute; (*fig*) to taint

contante [kon'tante] *adj*: **dinero ~ (y sonante)** hard cash

contar [kon'tar] *vt* (*páginas, dinero*) to count; (*anécdota etc*) to tell ▷ *vi* to count; **contarse** *vr* to be counted, figure; **~ con** to rely on, count on; **sin ~** not to mention; **le cuento entre mis amigos** I reckon him among my friends

contemplación [kontempla'θjon] *nf* contemplation; **no andarse con contemplaciones** not to stand on ceremony

contemplar [kontem'plar] *vt* to contemplate; (*mirar*) to look at

contemporáneo, -a [kontempo'raneo, a] *adj, nm/f* contemporary

contendiente [konten'djente] *nm/f* contestant

contenedor [kontene'ðor] *nm* container; (*de escombros*) skip; **~ de (la) basura** wheelie-bin (*Brit*); **~ de vidrio** bottle bank

contener [konte'ner] *vt* to contain, hold; (*risa etc*) to hold back, contain; **contenerse** *vr* to control *o* restrain o.s.

contenido, -a [konte'niðo, a] *adj* (*moderado*) restrained; (*risa etc*) suppressed ▷ *nm* contents *pl*, content

contentar [konten'tar] *vt* (*satisfacer*) to satisfy; (*complacer*) to please; (*Com*) to endorse; **contentarse** *vr* to be satisfied

contento, -a [kon'tento, a] *adj* contented, content; (*alegre*) pleased; (*feliz*) happy

contestación [kontesta'θjon] *nf* answer, reply; **~ a la demanda** (*Jur*) defence plea

contestador [kontesta'ðor] *nm*: **~ automático** answering machine

contestar [kontes'tar] *vt* to answer (back), reply; (*Jur*) to corroborate, confirm

contestatario, -a [kontesta'tarjo, a] *adj* anti-establishment, nonconformist

contexto [kon'teksto] *nm* context

contienda [kon'tjenda] *nf* contest, struggle

contigo [kon'tiɣo] *pron* with you

contiguo, -a [kon'tiɣwo, a] *adj* (*de al lado*) next; (*vecino*) adjacent, adjoining

continental [kontinen'tal] *adj* continental

continente [konti'nente] *adj, nm* continent

contingencia [kontin'xenθja] *nf* contingency; (*riesgo*) risk; (*posibilidad*) eventuality

contingente [kontin'xente] *adj* contingent ▷ *nm* contingent; (*Com*) quota

continuación [kontinwa'θjon] *nf* continuation; **a ~** then, next

continuamente [kon'tinwamente] *adv* (*sin interrupción*) continuously; (*a todas horas*) constantly

continuar [konti'nwar] *vt* to continue, go on with; (*reanudar*) to resume ▷ *vi* to continue, go on; **~ hablando** to continue talking *o* to talk

continuidad [kontinwi'ðað] *nf* continuity

continuo, -a [kon'tinwo, a] *adj* (*sin interrupción*) continuous; (*acción perseverante*) continual

contorno [kon'torno] *nm* outline; (*Geo*) contour; **contornos** *nmpl* neighbourhood *sg*, surrounding area *sg*

contorsión [kontor'sjon] *nf* contortion

contra ['kontra] *prep* against; (*Com: giro*) on ▷ *adv* against ▷ *adj, nm/f* (*Pol fam*) counter-revolutionary ▷ *nm* con ▷ *nf*: **la C~ (nicaragüense)** the Contras *pl*

contraataque [kontraa'take] *nm* counterattack

contrabajo [kontra'βaxo] *nm* double bass

contrabandista [kontraβan'dista] *nm/f* smuggler

contrabando [kontra'βando] *nm* (*acción*) smuggling; (*mercancías*) contraband; **~ de armas** gun-running

contracción [kontrak'θjon] *nf* contraction

contrachapado [kontratʃa'paðo] *nm* plywood

contracorriente [kontrako'rrjente] *nf* cross-current

contradecir [kontraðe'θir] *vt* to contradict

contradicción [kontraðik'θjon] *nf* contradiction; **espíritu de ~** contrariness

contradictorio, -a [kontraðik'torjo, a] *adj* contradictory

contraer [kontra'er] *vt* to contract; (*hábito*) to acquire; (*limitar*) to restrict; **contraerse** *vr* to contract; (*limitarse*) to limit o.s.

contraespionage [kontraespjo'naxe] *nm* counter-espionage

contrafuerte [kontra'fwerte] *nm* (*Arq*) buttress
contragolpe [kontra'ɣolpe] *nm* backlash
contraluz [kontra'luθ] *nm o f* view against the light; (*Foto etc*) back lighting; **a ~** against the light
contramaestre [kontrama'estre] *nm* foreman
contraofensiva [kontraofen'siβa] *nf* counteroffensive
contrapartida [kontrapar'tiða] *nf* (*Com*) balancing entry; **como ~ (de)** in return (for), as *o* in compensation (for)
contrapelo [kontra'pelo]: **a ~** *adv* the wrong way
contrapesar [kontrape'sar] *vt* to counterbalance; (*fig*) to offset
contrapeso [kontra'peso] *nm* counterweight; (*fig*) counterbalance; (*Com*) makeweight
contraportada [kontrapor'taða] *nf* (*de revista*) back cover
contraproducente [kontraproðu'θente] *adj* counterproductive
contrariar [kontra'rjar] *vt* (*oponerse*) to oppose; (*poner obstáculo*) to impede; (*enfadar*) to vex
contrariedad [kontrarje'ðað] *nf* (*oposición*) opposition; (*obstáculo*) obstacle, setback; (*disgusto*) vexation, annoyance
contrario, -a [kon'trarjo, a] *adj* contrary; (*persona*) opposed; (*sentido, lado*) opposite ▷ *nm/f* enemy, adversary; (*Deporte*) opponent; **al ~**, **por el ~** on the contrary; **de lo ~** otherwise
contrarreloj [kontrarre'lo(x)] *nf* (*tb*: **prueba ~**) time trial
contrarrestar [kontrarres'tar] *vt* to counteract
contrasentido [kontrasen'tiðo] *nm* contradiction; **es un ~ que él ...** it doesn't make sense for him to ...
contraseña [kontra'seɲa] *nf* countersign; (*frase*) password
contrastar [kontras'tar] *vt* to verify ▷ *vi* to contrast
contraste [kon'traste] *nm* contrast
contrata [kon'trata] *nf* (*Jur*) written contract; (*empleo*) hiring
contratar [kontra'tar] *vt* (*firmar un acuerdo para*) to contract for; (*empleados, obreros*) to hire, engage; (*Deporte*) to sign up; **contratarse** *vr* to sign on
contratiempo [kontra'tjempo] *nm* (*revés*) setback; (*accidente*) mishap; **a ~** (*Mus*) off-beat
contratista [kontra'tista] *nm/f* contractor
contrato [kon'trato] *nm* contract; **~ de compraventa** contract of sale; **~ a precio fijo** fixed-price contract; **~ a término** forward contract; **~ de trabajo** contract of employment *o* service
contravenir [kontraβe'nir] *vi*: **~ a** to contravene, violate
contraventana [kontraβen'tana] *nf* shutter
contribución [kontriβu'θjon] *nf* (*municipal etc*) tax; (*ayuda*) contribution; **exento de contribuciones** tax-free
contribuir [kontriβu'ir] *vt, vi* to contribute; (*Com*) to pay (in taxes)
contribuyente [kontriβu'jente] *nm/f* (*Com*) taxpayer; (*que ayuda*) contributor
contrincante [kontrin'kante] *nm* opponent, rival
control [kon'trol] *nm* control; (*inspección*) inspection, check; (*Com*): **~ de calidad** quality control; **~ de cambios** exchange control; **~ de costos** cost control; **~ de créditos** credit control; **~ de existencias** stock control; **~ de precios** price control; **~ de pasaportes** passport inspection
controlador, a [kontrola'ðor, a] *nm/f* controller; **~ aéreo** air-traffic controller
controlar [kontro'lar] *vt* to control; to inspect, check; (*Com*) to audit
controversia [kontro'βersja] *nf* controversy
contundente [kontun'dente] *adj* (*prueba*) conclusive; (*fig: argumento*) convincing; **instrumento ~** blunt instrument
contusión [kontu'sjon] *nf* bruise
convalecencia [kombale'θenθja] *nf* convalescence
convalecer [kombale'θer] *vi* to convalesce, get better
convaleciente [kombale'θjente] *adj, nm/f* convalescent
convalidar [kombali'ðar] *vt* (*título*) to recognize
convencer [komben'θer] *vt* to convince; (*persuadir*) to persuade
convencimiento [kombenθi'mjento] *nm* (*acción*) convincing; (*persuasión*) persuasion; (*certidumbre*) conviction; **tener el ~ de que ...** to be convinced that ...
convención [komben'θjon] *nf* convention
convencional [kombenθjo'nal] *adj* conventional
conveniencia [kombe'njenθja] *nf* suitability; (*conformidad*) agreement; (*utilidad, provecho*) usefulness; **conveniencias** *nfpl* conventions; (*Com*) property *sg*; **ser de la ~ de algn** to suit sb
conveniente [kombe'njente] *adj* suitable; (*útil*) useful; (*correcto*) fit, proper; (*aconsejable*) advisable
convenio [kom'benjo] *nm* agreement, treaty; **~ de nivel crítico** threshold agreement
convenir [kombe'nir] *vi* (*estar de acuerdo*) to agree; (*ser conveniente*) to suit, be suitable; **"sueldo a ~"** "salary to be agreed"; **conviene recordar que ...** it should be remembered that ...

convento [kom'bento] *nm* monastery; (*de monjas*) convent
convenza *etc* [kom'benθa] *vb ver* **convencer**
convergencia [komber'xenθja] *nf* convergence
converger [komber'xer], **convergir** [komber'xir] *vi* to converge; **sus esfuerzos convergen a un fin común** their efforts are directed towards the same objective
conversación [kombersa'θjon] *nf* conversation
conversar [komber'sar] *vi* to talk, converse
conversión [komber'sjon] *nf* conversion
convertir [komber'tir] *vt* to convert; (*transformar*) to transform, turn; (*Com*) to (ex) change; **convertirse** *vr* (*Rel*) to convert
convexo, -a [kom'bekso, a] *adj* convex
convicción [kombik'θjon] *nf* conviction
convicto, -a [kom'bikto, a] *adj* convicted; (*condenado*) condemned
convidado, -a [kombi'ðaðo, a] *nm/f* guest
convidar [kombi'ðar] *vt* to invite; **~ a algn a una cerveza** to buy sb a beer
convincente [kombin'θente] *adj* convincing
convite [kom'bite] *nm* invitation; (*banquete*) banquet
convivencia [kombi'βenθja] *nf* coexistence, living together
convivir [kombi'βir] *vi* to live together; (*Pol*) to coexist
convocar [kombo'kar] *vt* to summon, call (together)
convocatoria [komboka'torja] *nf* summons *sg*; (*anuncio*) notice of meeting; (*Escol*) examination session
convulsión [kombul'sjon] *nf* convulsion; (*Pol etc*) upheaval
conyugal [konju'ɣal] *adj* conjugal; **vida ~** married life
cónyuge ['konyuxe] *nm/f* spouse, partner
coñac (*pl* **coñacs**) ['koɲa(k), 'koɲas] *nm* cognac, brandy
coñazo [ko'ɲaθo] *nm* (*fam*) pain; **dar el ~** to be a real pain
coño ['koɲo] (*fam!*) *nm* cunt (*!*); (*Am pey*) Spaniard ▷ *excl* (*enfado*) shit (*!*); (*sorpresa*) bloody hell (*!*); **¡qué ~!** what a pain in the arse! (*!*)
cool [kul] *adj* (*fam*) cool
cooperación [koopera'θjon] *nf* cooperation
cooperar [koope'rar] *vi* to cooperate
cooperativo, -a [koopera'tiβo, a] *adj* cooperative ▷ *nf* cooperative
coordinador, a [koorðina'ðor, a] *nm/f* coordinator ▷ *nf* coordinating committee
coordinar [koorði'nar] *vt* to coordinate
copa ['kopa] *nf* (*tb Deporte*) cup; (*vaso*) glass; (*de árbol*) top; (*de sombrero*) crown; **copas** *nfpl* (*Naipes*) *one of the suits in the Spanish card deck*; **(tomar una) ~** (to have a) drink; **ir de ~s** to go out for a drink; *ver tb* **Baraja Española**
copar [ko'par] *vt* (*puestos*) to monopolize
copia ['kopja] *nf* copy; (*Arte*) replica; (*Com etc*) duplicate; (*Inform*): **~ impresa** hard copy; **~ de respaldo** *o* **de seguridad** backup copy; **hacer ~ de seguridad** to back up; **~ de trabajo** working copy
copiar [ko'pjar] *vt* to copy; **~ al pie de la letra** to copy word for word
copiloto [kopi'loto] *nm* (*Aviat*) co-pilot; (*Auto*) co-driver
copioso, -a [ko'pjoso, a] *adj* copious, plentiful
copipegar [kopipe'ɣar] *vt* (*Inform*) to copy and paste
copla ['kopla] *nf* verse; (*canción*) (popular) song
copo ['kopo] *nm*: **~s de maíz** cornflakes; **~ de nieve** snowflake
coqueta [ko'keta] *adj* flirtatious, coquettish ▷ *nf* (*mujer*) flirt
coquetear [kokete'ar] *vi* to flirt
coraje [ko'raxe] *nm* courage; (*ánimo*) spirit; (*ira*) anger
coral [ko'ral] *adj* choral ▷ *nf* choir ▷ *nm* (*Zool*) coral
coraza [ko'raθa] *nf* (*armadura*) armour; (*blindaje*) armour-plating
corazón [kora'θon] *nm* heart; (*Bot*) core; **corazones** *nmpl* (*Naipes*) hearts; **de buen ~** kind-hearted; **de todo ~** wholeheartedly; **estar mal del ~** to have heart trouble
corazonada [koraθo'naða] *nf* impulse; (*presentimiento*) presentiment, hunch
corbata [kor'βata] *nf* tie
corchea [kor'tʃea] *nf* quaver
corchete [kor'tʃete] *nm* catch, clasp; **corchetes** *nmpl* (*Tip*) square brackets
corcho ['kortʃo] *nm* cork; (*Pesca*) float
cordel [kor'ðel] *nm* cord, line
cordero [kor'ðero] *nm* lamb; (*piel*) lambskin
cordial [kor'ðjal] *adj* cordial ▷ *nm* cordial, tonic
cordialidad [korðjali'ðað] *nf* warmth, cordiality
cordillera [korði'ʎera] *nf* range (of mountains)
Córdoba ['korðoβa] *nf* Cordova
cordón [kor'ðon] *nm* (*cuerda*) cord, string; (*de zapatos*) lace; (*Elec*) flex, wire (*US*); (*Mil etc*) cordon; **~ umbilical** umbilical cord
cordura [kor'ðura] *nf* (*Med*) sanity; (*fig*) good sense; **con ~** (*obrar, hablar*) sensibly
coreografía [koreoɣra'fia] *nf* choreography
córner (*pl* **córners**) ['korner, 'korners] *nm* corner (kick)
corneta [kor'neta] *nf* bugle
cornisa [kor'nisa] *nf* cornice
coro ['koro] *nm* chorus; (*conjunto de cantores*) choir
corona [ko'rona] *nf* crown; (*de flores*) garland
coronación [korona'θjon] *nf* coronation
coronar [koro'nar] *vt* to crown
coronel [koro'nel] *nm* colonel
coronilla [koro'niʎa] *nf* (*Anat*) crown (of the head); **estar hasta la ~ (de)** to be utterly fed up (with)

corporación [korpora'θjon] *nf* corporation
corporal [korpo'ral] *adj* corporal, bodily
corporativo, -a [korpora'tiβo, a] *adj* corporate
corpulento, -a [korpu'lento, a] *adj* (*persona*) heavily-built
corral [ko'rral] *nm* (*patio*) farmyard; (*Agr*: *de aves*) poultry yard; (*redil*) pen
correa [ko'rrea] *nf* strap; (*cinturón*) belt; (*de perro*) lead, leash; **~ transportadora** conveyor belt; **~ del ventilador** (*Auto*) fan belt
corrección [korrek'θjon] *nf* correction; (*reprensión*) rebuke; (*cortesía*) good manners; (*Inform*): **~ por líneas** line editing; **~ en pantalla** screen editing; **~ (de pruebas)** (*Tip*) proofreading
correccional [korrekθjo'nal] *nm* reformatory
correcto, -a [ko'rrekto, a] *adj* correct; (*persona*) well-mannered
corrector, a [korrek'tor, a] *nm/f*: **~ de pruebas** proofreader
corredizo, -a [korre'ðiθo, a] *adj* (*puerta etc*) sliding; (*nudo*) running
corredor, a [korre'ðor, a] *adj* running; (*rápido*) fast ▷ *nm/f* (*Deporte*) runner ▷ *nm* (*pasillo*) corridor; (*balcón corrido*) gallery; (*Com*) agent, broker; **~ de bienes raíces** real-estate broker; **~ de bolsa** stockbroker; **~ de seguros** insurance broker
corregir [korre'xir] *vt* (*error*) to correct; (*amonestar, reprender*) to rebuke, reprimand; **corregirse** *vr* to reform
correo [ko'rreo] *nm* post, mail; (*persona*) courier; **Correos** *nmpl* Post Office *sg*; **~ aéreo** airmail; **~ basura** (*por carta*) junk mail; (*por Internet*) spam; **~ certificado** registered mail; **~ electrónico** email, electronic mail; **~ urgente** special delivery; **~ web** webmail; **a vuelta de ~** by return (of post)
correr [ko'rrer] *vt* to run; (*viajar*) to cover, travel; (*riesgo*) to run; (*aventura*) to have; (*cortinas*) to draw; (*cerrojo*) to shoot ▷ *vi* to run; (*líquido*) to run, flow; (*rumor*) to go round; **correrse** *vr* to slide, move; (*colores*) to run; (*fam*: *tener orgasmo*) to come; **echar a ~** to break into a run; **~ con los gastos** to pay the expenses; **eso corre de mi cuenta** I'll take care of that
correspondencia [korrespon'denθja] *nf* correspondence; (*Ferro*) connection; (*reciprocidad*) return; **~ directa** (*Com*) direct mail
corresponder [korrespon'der] *vi* to correspond; (*convenir*) to be suitable; (*pertenecer*) to belong; (*tocar*) to concern; (*favor*) to repay; **corresponderse** *vr* (*por escrito*) to correspond; (*amarse*) to love one another; **"a quien corresponda"** "to whom it may concern"
correspondiente [korrespon'djente] *adj* corresponding; (*respectivo*) respective
corresponsal [korrespon'sal] *nm/f* (newspaper) correspondent; (*Com*) agent
corrido, -a [ko'rriðo, a] *adj* (*avergonzado*) abashed; (*fluido*) fluent ▷ *nf* run, dash; (*de toros*) bullfight; **de ~** fluently; **tres noches corridas** three nights running; **un kilo ~** a good kilo
corriente [ko'rrjente] *adj* (*agua*) running; (*fig*) flowing; (*dinero, cuenta etc*) current; (*común*) ordinary, normal ▷ *nf* current; (*fig*: *tendencia*) course ▷ *nm* current month; **~ de aire** draught; **~ eléctrica** electric current; **las ~s modernas del arte** modern trends in art; **estar al ~ de** to be informed about
corrija *etc* [ko'rrixa] *vb ver* **corregir**
corrillo [ko'rriʎo] *nm* ring, circle (of people); (*fig*) clique
corro ['korro] *nm* ring, circle (of people); (*baile*) ring-a-ring-a-roses; **la gente hizo ~** the people formed a ring
corroborar [korroβo'rar] *vt* to corroborate
corroer [korro'er] *vt* (*tb fig*) to corrode, eat away; (*Geo*) to erode
corromper [korrom'per] *vt* (*madera*) to rot; (*fig*) to corrupt
corrosivo, -a [korro'siβo, a] *adj* corrosive
corrupción [korrup'θjon] *nf* rot, decay; (*fig*) corruption
corrupto, -a [ko'rrupto, a] *adj* corrupt
corsé [kor'se] *nm* corset
cortacésped [korta'θespeð] *nm* lawn mower
cortado, -a [kor'taðo, a] *adj* (*con cuchillo*) cut; (*leche*) sour; (*confuso*) confused; (*desconcertado*) embarrassed; (*tímido*) shy ▷ *nm* white coffee (with a little milk)
cortafuegos [korta'fweɣos] *nm inv* (*en el bosque*) firebreak, fire lane (*US*); (*Internet*) firewall
cortalápices [korta'lapiθes], **cortalápiz** [korta'lapiθ] *nm inv* (pencil) sharpener
cortapegar [kortape'ɣar] *vt* (*Inform*) to cut and paste
cortar [kor'tar] *vt* to cut; (*suministro*) to cut off; (*un pasaje*) to cut out; (*comunicación, teléfono*) to cut off ▷ *vi* to cut; (*Am Telec*) to hang up; **cortarse** *vr* (*turbarse*) to become embarrassed; (*leche*) to turn, curdle; **~ por lo sano** to settle things once and for all; **~se el pelo** to have one's hair cut; **se cortó la línea** *o* **el teléfono** I got cut off
cortauñas [korta'uɲas] *nm inv* nail clippers *pl*
corte ['korte] *nm* cut, cutting; (*filo*) edge; (*de tela*) piece, length; (*Costura*) tailoring ▷ *nf* (*real*) (royal) court; **~ y confección** dressmaking; **~ de corriente** *o* **luz** power cut; **~ de pelo** haircut; **me da ~ pedírselo** I'm embarrassed to ask him for it; **¡qué ~ le di!** I left him with no comeback!; **C~ Internacional de Justicia** International Court of Justice; **las C~s** the Spanish Parliament *sg*; **hacer la ~ a** to woo, court; *see note*

CORTES

The Spanish Parliament, *Las Cortes (Españolas)*, has a Lower and an Upper Chamber, the *Congreso de los Diputados* and the *Senado* respectively. Members of Parliament are called *diputados* and are elected in national elections by proportional representation. Some Senate members, *senadores*, are chosen by being voted in during national elections and others are appointed by the regional parliaments.

cortejar [korte'xar] *vt* to court
cortejo [kor'texo] *nm* entourage; **~ fúnebre** funeral procession, cortège
cortés [kor'tes] *adj* courteous, polite
cortesía [korte'sia] *nf* courtesy
corteza [kor'teθa] *nf* (*de árbol*) bark; (*de pan*) crust; (*de fruta*) peel, skin; (*de queso*) rind
cortijo [kor'tixo] *nm* (*Esp*) farm, farmhouse
cortina [kor'tina] *nf* curtain; **~ de humo** smoke screen
corto, -a ['korto, a] *adj* (*breve*) short; (*tímido*) bashful; **~ de luces** not very bright; **~ de oído** hard of hearing; **~ de vista** short-sighted; **estar ~ de fondos** to be short of funds
cortocircuito [kortoθir'kwito] *nm* short-circuit
cortometraje [kortome'traxe] *nm* (*Cine*) short
corvo, -a ['korβo, a] *adj* curved; (*nariz*) hooked ▷ *nf* back of knee
cosa ['kosa] *nf* thing; (*asunto*) affair; **~ de** about; **eso es ~ mía** that's my business; **es poca ~** it's not important; **¡qué ~ más rara!** how strange!
coscorrón [kosko'rron] *nm* bump on the head
cosecha [ko'setʃa] *nf* (*Agr*) harvest; (*acto*) harvesting; (*de vino*) vintage; (*producción*) yield
cosechar [kose'tʃar] *vt* to harvest, gather (in)
coser [ko'ser] *vt* to sew; (*Med*) to stitch (up)
cosmético, -a [kos'metiko, a] *adj, nm* cosmetic ▷ *nf* cosmetics *pl*
cosmos ['kosmos] *nm* cosmos
cosquillas [kos'kiʎas] *nfpl*: **hacer ~** to tickle; **tener ~** to be ticklish
costa ['kosta] *nf* (*Geo*) coast; **C~ Brava** Costa Brava; **C~ Cantábrica** Cantabrian Coast; **C~ de Marfil** Ivory Coast; **C~ del Sol** Costa del Sol; **a ~** (*Com*) at cost; **a ~ de** at the expense of; **a toda ~** at any price
costado [kos'taðo] *nm* side; **de ~** (*dormir*) on one's side; **español por los 4 ~s** Spanish through and through
costal [kos'tal] *nm* sack
costanera [kosta'nera] *nf* (*Am*) promenade, sea front
costar [kos'tar] *vt* (*valer*) to cost; **me cuesta hablarle** I find it hard to talk to him; **¿cuánto cuesta?** how much does it cost?
Costa Rica [kosta'rika] *nf* Costa Rica
costarricense [kostarri'θense], **costarriqueño, -a** [kostarri'keɲo, a] *adj, nm/f* Costa Rican
coste ['koste] *nm* (*Com*): **~ promedio** average cost; **~s fijos** fixed costs; *ver* **costo**
costear [koste'ar] *vt* to pay for; (*Com etc*) to finance; (*Naut*) to sail along the coast of; **costearse** *vr* (*negocio*) to pay for itself, cover its costs
costero, -a [kos'tero, a] *adj* coastal, coast *cpd*
costilla [kos'tiʎa] *nf* rib; (*Culin*) cutlet
costo ['kosto] *nm* cost, price; **~ directo** direct cost; **~ de expedición** shipping charges; **~ de sustitución** replacement cost; **~ unitario** unit cost; **~ de la vida** cost of living
costoso, -a [kos'toso, a] *adj* costly, expensive
costra ['kostra] *nf* (*corteza*) crust; (*Med*) scab
costumbre [kos'tumbre] *nf* custom, habit; **como de ~** as usual
costura [kos'tura] *nf* sewing, needlework; (*confección*) dressmaking; (*zurcido*) seam
costurera [kostu'rera] *nf* dressmaker
costurero [kostu'rero] *nm* sewing box *o* case
cota ['kota] *nf* (*Geo*) height above sea level; (*fig*) height
cotarro [ko'tarro] *nm*: **dirigir el ~** (*fam*) to rule the roost
cotejar [kote'xar] *vt* to compare
cotidiano, -a [koti'ðjano, a] *adj* daily, day to day
cotilla [ko'tiʎa] *nf* busybody, gossip
cotillear [kotiʎe'ar] *vi* to gossip
cotilleo [koti'ʎeo] *nm* gossip(ing)
cotización [kotiθa'θjon] *nf* (*Com*) quotation, price; (*de club*) dues *pl*
cotizar [koti'θar] *vt* (*Com*) to quote, price; **cotizarse** *vr* (*fig*) to be highly prized; **~se a** to sell at, fetch; (*Bolsa*) to stand at, be quoted at
coto ['koto] *nm* (*terreno cercado*) enclosure; (*de caza*) reserve; (*Com*) price-fixing agreement; **poner ~ a** to put a stop to
cotorra [ko'torra] *nf* (*Zool: loro*) parrot; (*fam: persona*) windbag
coyote [ko'jote] *nm* coyote, prairie wolf
coyuntura [kojun'tura] *nf* (*Anat*) joint; (*fig*) juncture, occasion; **esperar una ~ favorable** to await a favourable moment
coz [koθ] *nf* kick
crack [krak] *nm* (*droga*) crack
cráneo ['kraneo] *nm* skull, cranium
cráter ['krater] *nm* crater
crayón [kra'jon] *nm* (*Am: lápiz*) (coloured) pencil; (*cera*) crayon
creación [krea'θjon] *nf* creation
creador, a [krea'ðor, a] *adj* creative ▷ *nm/f* creator

crear [kre'ar] *vt* to create, make; (*originar*) to originate; (*Inform: archivo*) to create; **crearse** *vr* (*comité etc*) to be set up
creativo, -a [krea'tiβo, a] *adj* creative
crecer [kre'θer] *vi* to grow; (*precio*) to rise; **crecerse** *vr* (*engreírse*) to get cocky
creces ['kreθes]: **con ~** *adv* amply, fully
crecido, -a [kre'θiðo, a] *adj* (*persona, planta*) full-grown; (*cantidad*) large ▷ *nf* (*de río*) spate, flood
creciente [kre'θjente] *adj* growing; (*cantidad*) increasing; (*luna*) crescent ▷ *nm* crescent
crecimiento [kreθi'mjento] *nm* growth; (*aumento*) increase; (*Com*) rise
credencial [kreðen'θjal] *nf* (*Am: tarjeta*) card; **credenciales** *nfpl* credentials; **~ de socio** (*Am*) membership card
crédito ['kreðito] *nm* credit; **a ~** on credit; **dar ~ a** to believe (in); **~ al consumidor** consumer credit; **~ rotativo** *o* **renovable** revolving credit
credo ['kreðo] *nm* creed
crédulo, -a ['kreðulo, a] *adj* credulous
creencia [kre'enθja] *nf* belief
creer [kre'er] *vt, vi* to think, believe; (*considerar*) to think, consider; **creerse** *vr* to believe o.s. (to be); **~ en** to believe in; **creo que sí/no** I think/don't think so; **¡ya lo creo!** I should think so!
creíble [kre'iβle] *adj* credible, believable
creído, -a [kre'iðo, a] *adj* (*engreído*) conceited
crema ['krema] *adj inv* cream (coloured) ▷ *nf* cream; (*natillas*) custard; **~ batida** (*Am*) whipped cream; **~ pastelera** (confectioner's) custard; **la ~ de la sociedad** the cream of society
cremallera [krema'ʎera] *nf* zip (fastener) (*Brit*), zipper (*US*)
crematorio [krema'torjo] *nm* crematorium (*Brit*), crematory (*US*)
crepe ['krepe] *nf* (*Esp*) pancake
crepitar [krepi'tar] *vi* (*fuego*) to crackle
crepúsculo [kre'puskulo] *nm* twilight, dusk
crespo, -a ['krespo, a] *adj* (*pelo*) curly
crespón [kres'pon] *nm* crêpe
cresta ['kresta] *nf* (*Geo, Zool*) crest
cretino, -a [kre'tino, a] *adj* cretinous ▷ *nm/f* cretin
creyendo *etc* [kre'jendo] *vb ver* **creer**
creyente [kre'jente] *nm/f* believer
creyó *etc* [kre'jo] *vb ver* **creer**
crezco *etc vb ver* **crecer**
cría ['kria] *vb ver* **criar** ▷ *nf* (*de animales*) rearing, breeding; (*animal*) young; *ver tb* **crío**
criada [kri'aða] *nf ver* **criado, a**
criadero [kria'ðero] *nm* nursery; (*Zool*) breeding place
criado, -a [kri'aðo, a] *nm* servant ▷ *nf* servant, maid
criador [kria'ðor] *nm* breeder
crianza [kri'anθa] *nf* rearing, breeding; (*fig*) breeding; (*Med*) lactation
criar [kri'ar] *vt* (*amamantar*) to suckle, feed; (*educar*) to bring up; (*producir*) to grow, produce; (*animales*) to breed; **criarse** *vr* to grow (up); **~ cuervos** to nourish a viper in one's bosom; **Dios los cría y ellos se juntan** birds of a feather flock together
criatura [kria'tura] *nf* creature; (*niño*) baby, (small) child
criba ['kriβa] *nf* sieve
cribar [kri'βar] *vt* to sieve
crimen ['krimen] *nm* crime; **~ pasional** crime of passion
criminal [krimi'nal] *adj, nm/f* criminal
crin [krin] *nf* (*tb*: **~es**) mane
crío, -a ['krio, a] *nm/f* (*fam: chico*) kid ▷ *nf* (*de animales*) rearing, breeding; (*animal*) young
cripta ['kripta] *nf* crypt
crisis ['krisis] *nf inv* crisis; **~ nerviosa** nervous breakdown
crisma ['krisma] *nf*: **romperle la ~ a algn** (*fam*) to knock sb's block off
crismas ['krismas] *nm inv* (*Esp*) Christmas card
crispación [krispa'θjon] *nf* tension
crispar [kris'par] *vt* (*músculo*) to cause to contract; (*nervios*) to set on edge
cristal [kris'tal] *nm* crystal; (*de ventana*) glass, pane; (*lente*) lens; **de ~** glass *cpd*; **~ ahumado/tallado** smoked/cut glass
cristalino, -a [krista'lino, a] *adj* crystalline; (*fig*) clear ▷ *nm* lens of the eye
cristalizar [kristali'θar] *vt, vi* to crystallize
cristiandad [kristjan'dað] *nf*, **cristianismo** [kristja'nismo] *nm* Christianity
cristianismo [kristja'nismo] *nm* Christianity
cristiano, -a [kris'tjano, a] *adj, nm/f* Christian; **hablar en ~** to speak proper Spanish; (*fig*) to speak clearly
Cristo ['kristo] *nm* (*dios*) Christ; (*crucifijo*) crucifix
criterio [kri'terjo] *nm* criterion; (*juicio*) judgement; (*enfoque*) attitude, approach; (*punto de vista*) view, opinion; **~ de clasificación** (*Inform*) sort criterion
criticar [kriti'kar] *vt* to criticize
crítico, -a ['kritiko, a] *adj* critical ▷ *nm* critic ▷ *nf* criticism; (*Teat etc*) review, notice; **la crítica** the critics *pl*
Croacia [kro'aθja] *nf* Croatia
croar [kro'ar] *vi* to croak
croata [kro'ata] *adj, nm/f* Croat(ian) ▷ *nm* (*Ling*) Croat(ian)
croissan, croissant [krwa'san] *nm* croissant
crol ['krol] *nm* crawl
cromo ['kromo] *nm* chrome; (*Tip*) coloured print
cromosoma [kromo'soma] *nm* chromosome
crónico, -a ['kroniko, a] *adj* chronic ▷ *nf* chronicle, account; (*de periódico*) feature, article

cronología [kronolo'xia] *nf* chronology
cronológico, -a [krono'loxiko, a] *adj* chronological
cronometrar [kronome'trar] *vt* to time
cronómetro [kro'nometro] *nm* (*Deporte*) stopwatch; (*Tec etc*) chronometer
croqueta [kro'keta] *nf* croquette, rissole
cruce ['kruθe] *vb ver* **cruzar** ▷ *nm* (*para peatones*) crossing; (*de carreteras*) crossroads; (*Auto etc*) junction, intersection; (*Bio*: *proceso*) crossbreeding; **luces de ~** dipped headlights
crucero [kru'θero] *nm* (*Naut*: *barco*) cruise ship; (: *viaje*) cruise
crucial [kru'θjal] *adj* crucial
crucificar [kruθifi'kar] *vt* to crucify; (*fig*) to torment
crucifijo [kruθi'fixo] *nm* crucifix
crucigrama [kruθi'ɣrama] *nm* crossword (puzzle)
cruda ['kruða] *nf* (*Am*: *fam*) hangover
crudo, -a ['kruðo, a] *adj* raw; (*no maduro*) unripe; (*petróleo*) crude; (*rudo, cruel*) cruel; (*agua*) hard; (*clima etc*) harsh ▷ *nm* crude (oil)
cruel [krwel] *adj* cruel
crueldad [krwel'ðað] *nf* cruelty
crujido [kru'xiðo] *nm* (*de madera etc*) creak
crujiente [kru'xjente] *adj* (*galleta etc*) crunchy
crujir [kru'xir] *vi* (*madera etc*) to creak; (*dedos*) to crack; (*dientes*) to grind; (*nieve, arena*) to crunch
cruz [kruθ] *nf* cross; (*de moneda*) tails *sg*; (*fig*) burden; **~ gamada** swastika; **C~ Roja** Red Cross
cruzado, -a [kru'θaðo, a] *adj* crossed ▷ *nm* crusader ▷ *nf* crusade
cruzar [kru'θar] *vt* to cross; (*palabras*) to exchange; **cruzarse** *vr* (*líneas etc*) to cross, intersect; (*personas*) to pass each other; **~se de brazos** to fold one's arms; (*fig*) not to lift a finger to help; **~se con algn en la calle** to pass sb in the street
cuaderno [kwa'ðerno] *nm* notebook; (*de escuela*) exercise book; (*Naut*) logbook
cuadra ['kwaðra] *nf* (*caballeriza*) stable; (*Am*) (city) block
cuadrado, -a [kwa'ðraðo, a] *adj* square ▷ *nm* (*Mat*) square
cuadrar [kwa'ðrar] *vt* to square; (*Tip*) to justify ▷ *vi*: **~ con** (*cuenta*) to square with, tally with; **cuadrarse** *vr* (*soldado*) to stand to attention; **~ por la derecha/izquierda** to right-/left-justify
cuadriculado, -a [kwaðriku'laðo, a] *adj*: **papel ~** squared *o* graph paper
cuadrilátero [kwaðri'latero] *nm* (*Deporte*) boxing ring; (*Geom*) quadrilateral
cuadrilla [kwa'ðriʎa] *nf* (*de amigos*) party, group; (*de delincuentes*) gang; (*de obreros*) team
cuadro ['kwaðro] *nm* square; (*Pintura*) painting; (*Teat*) scene; (*diagrama*: *tb*: **~ sinóptico**) chart, table, diagram; (*Deporte, Med*) team; (*Pol*) executive; **~ de mandos** control panel; **a ~s** check *cpd*; **tela a ~s** checked (*Brit*) *o* chequered (*US*) material
cuádruplo, -a ['kwaðruplo, a], **cuádruple** ['kwaðruple] *adj* quadruple
cuajar [kwa'xar] *vt* to thicken; (*leche*) to curdle; (*sangre*) to congeal; (*adornar*) to adorn; (*Culin*) to set ▷ *vi* (*nieve*) to lie; (*fig*) to become set, become established; (*idea*) to be received, be acceptable; **cuajarse** *vr* to curdle; to congeal; (*llenarse*) to fill up
cuajo ['kwaxo] *nm*: **de ~** (*arrancar*) by the roots; (*cortar*) completely; **arrancar algo de ~** to tear sth out by its roots
cual [kwal] *adv* like, as ▷ *pron*: **el ~** *etc* which; (*persona*: *sujeto*) who; (: *objeto*) whom; **lo ~** (*relativo*) which; **allá cada ~** every man to his own taste; **son a ~ más gandul** each is as idle as the other; **cada ~** each one ▷ *adj* such as; **tal ~** just as it is
cuál [kwal] *pron interrogativo* which (one), what
cualesquier [kwales'kjer], **cualesquiera** [kwales'kjera] *adj pl, pron pl de* **cualquier, cualquiera**
cualidad [kwali'ðað] *nf* quality
cualquier [kwal'kjer], **cualquiera** [kwal'kjera] (*pl* **cualesquier(a)**) *adj* any ▷ *pron* anybody, anyone; (*quienquiera*) whoever; **en ~ momento** any time; **~ día/libro** any day/book; **en ~ parte** anywhere; **~a que sea** whichever it is; (*persona*) whoever it is; **un coche ~a servirá** any car will do; **no es un hombre ~a** he isn't just anybody; **eso ~a lo sabe hacer** anybody can do that; **es un ~a** he's a nobody
cuando ['kwando] *adv* when; (*aún si*) if, even if ▷ *conj* (*puesto que*) since ▷ *prep*: **yo, ~ niño ...** when I was a child *o* as a child I ...; **~ no sea así** even if it is not so; **~ más** at (the) most; **~ menos** at least; **~ no** if not, otherwise; **de ~ en ~** from time to time; **ven ~ quieras** come when(ever) you like
cuándo ['kwando] *adv* when; **¿desde ~?**, **¿de ~ acá?** since when?
cuantía [kwan'tia] *nf* (*importe*: *de pérdidas, deuda, daños*) extent; (*importancia*) importance
cuantioso, -a [kwan'tjoso, a] *adj* substantial

PALABRA CLAVE

cuanto, -a ['kwanto, a] *adj* **1** (*todo*): **tiene todo cuanto desea** he's got everything he wants; **le daremos cuantos ejemplares necesite** we'll give him as many copies as *o* all the copies he needs; **cuantos hombres la ven** all the men who see her
2: **unos cuantos**: **había unos cuantos periodistas** there were (quite) a few journalists
3 (*+más*): **cuanto más vino bebas peor te sentirás** the more wine you drink the worse

you'll feel; **cuantos más, mejor** the more the merrier
▷ *pron*: **tiene cuanto desea** he has everything he wants; **tome cuanto/ cuantos quiera** take as much/many as you want
▷ *adv*: **en cuanto**: **en cuanto profesor** as a teacher; **en cuanto a mí** as for me; *ver tb* **antes**
▷ *conj* **1**: **cuanto más gana menos gasta** the more he earns the less he spends; **cuanto más joven se es más se es confiado** the younger you are the more trusting you are
2: **en cuanto**: **en cuanto llegue/llegué** as soon as I arrive/arrived

cuánto, -a ['kwanto, a] *adj* (*exclamación*) what a lot of; (*interrogativo*: *sg*) how much?; (: *pl*) how many? ▷ *pron, adv* how; (*interrogativo*: *sg*) how much?; (: *pl*) how many? ▷ *excl*: **¡~ me alegro!** I'm so glad!; **¡cuánta gente!** what a lot of people!; **¿~ tiempo?** how long?; **¿~ cuesta?** how much does it cost?; **¿a ~s estamos?** what's the date?; **¿~ hay de aquí a Bilbao?** how far is it from here to Bilbao?; **Señor no sé ~s** Mr. So-and-So
cuarenta [kwa'renta] *num* forty
cuarentena [kwaren'tena] *nf* (*Med etc*) quarantine; (*conjunto*) forty(-odd)
cuaresma [kwa'resma] *nf* Lent
cuarta ['kwarta] *nf ver* **cuarto**
cuartear [kwarte'ar] *vt* to quarter; (*dividir*) to divide up; **cuartearse** *vr* to crack, split
cuartel [kwar'tel] *nm* (*de ciudad*) quarter, district; (*Mil*) barracks *pl*; **~ de bomberos** (*Am*) fire station; **~ general** headquarters *pl*
cuarteto [kwar'teto] *nm* quartet
cuartilla [kwar'tiʎa] *nf* (*hoja*) sheet (of paper); **cuartillas** *nfpl* (*Tip*) copy *sg*
cuarto, -a ['kwarto, a] *adj* fourth ▷ *nm* (*Mat*) quarter, fourth; (*habitación*) room ▷ *nf* (*Mat*) quarter, fourth; (*palmo*) span; **~ de baño** bathroom; **~ de estar** living room; **~ de hora** quarter (of an) hour; **~ de kilo** quarter kilo; **~s de final** quarter finals; **no tener un ~** to be broke (*fam*)
cuarzo ['kwarθo] *nm* quartz
cuatrimestre [kwatri'mestre] *nm* four-month period
cuatro ['kwatro] *num* four; **las ~** four o'clock; **el ~ de octubre** (on) the fourth of October; *ver tb* **seis**
cuatrocientos, -as [kwatro'θjentos, as] *num* four hundred; *ver tb* **seiscientos**
Cuba ['kuβa] *nf* Cuba
cuba ['kuβa] *nf* cask, barrel; **estar como una ~** (*fam*) to be sloshed
cubalibre [kuβa'liβre] *nm* (white) rum and coke®
cubano, -a [ku'βano, a] *adj, nm/f* Cuban
cubata [ku'βata] *nm* = **cubalibre**
cubeta [ku'βeta] *nf* (*balde*) bucket, tub
cúbico, -a ['kuβiko, a] *adj* cubic
cubierto, -a [ku'βjerto, a] *pp de* **cubrir** ▷ *adj* covered; (*cielo*) overcast ▷ *nm* cover; (*en la mesa*) place ▷ *nf* cover, covering; (*neumático*) tyre; (*Naut*) deck; **cubiertos** *nmpl* cutlery *sg*; **a ~** under cover; **a ~ de** covered with *o* in; **precio del ~** cover charge
cubil [ku'βil] *nm* den
cubilete [kuβi'lete] *nm* (*en juegos*) cup
cubito [ku'βito] *nm*: **~ de hielo** ice cube
cubo ['kuβo] *nm* cube; (*balde*) bucket, tub; (*Tec*) drum; **~ de (la) basura** dustbin (*Brit*), trash can (*US*)
cubrecama [kuβre'kama] *nm* bedspread
cubrir [ku'βrir] *vt* to cover; (*vacante*) to fill; (*Bio*) to mate with; (*gastos*) to meet; **cubrirse** *vr* (*cielo*) to become overcast; (*Com*: *gastos*) to be met *o* paid; (: *deuda*) to be covered; **~ las formas** to keep up appearances; **lo cubrieron las aguas** the waters closed over it; **el agua casi me cubría** I was almost out of my depth
cucaracha [kuka'ratʃa] *nf* cockroach
cuchara [ku'tʃara] *nf* spoon; (*Tec*) scoop
cucharada [kutʃa'raða] *nf* spoonful; **~ colmada** heaped spoonful
cucharadita [kutʃara'ðita] *nf* teaspoonful
cucharilla [kutʃa'riʎa] *nf* teaspoon
cucharón [kutʃa'ron] *nm* ladle
cuchichear [kutʃitʃe'ar] *vi* to whisper
cuchilla [ku'tʃiʎa] *nf* (large) knife; (*de arma blanca*) blade; **~ de afeitar** razor blade; **pasar a ~** to put to the sword
cuchillada [kutʃi'ʎaða] *nf* (*golpe*) stab; (*herida*) knife *o* stab wound
cuchillo [ku'tʃiʎo] *nm* knife
cuchitril [kutʃi'tril] *nm* hovel; (*habitación etc*) pigsty
cuclillas [ku'kliʎas] *nfpl*: **en ~** squatting
cuco, -a ['kuko, a] *adj* pretty; (*astuto*) sharp ▷ *nm* cuckoo
cucurucho [kuku'rutʃo] *nm* paper cone, cornet
cueca ['kweka] *nf Chilean national dance*
cuello ['kweʎo] *nm* (*Anat*) neck; (*de vestido, camisa*) collar
cuenca ['kwenka] *nf* (*Anat*) eye socket; (*Geo*: *valle*) bowl, deep valley; (: *fluvial*) basin
cuenco ['kwenko] *nm* (earthenware) bowl
cuenta ['kwenta] *vb ver* **contar** ▷ *nf* (*cálculo*) count, counting; (*en café, restaurante*) bill (*Brit*), check (*US*); (*Com*) account; (*de collar*) bead; (*fig*) account; **a fin de ~s** in the end; **en resumidas ~s** in short; **caer en la ~** to catch on; **dar ~ a algn de sus actos** to account to sb for one's actions; **darse ~ de** to realize; **tener en ~** to bear in mind; **echar ~s** to take stock; **~ atrás** countdown; **~ corriente/de ahorros/a plazo (fijo)** current/savings/ deposit account; **~ de caja** cash account; **~ de capital** capital account; **~ por cobrar** account receivable; **~ de correo** (*Internet*)

email account; ~ **de crédito** credit *o* loan account; ~ **de gastos e ingresos** income and expenditure account; ~ **por pagar** account payable; **abonar una cantidad en ~ a algn** to credit a sum to sb's account; **ajustar** *o* **liquidar una ~** to settle an account; **pasar la ~** to send the bill

cuentakilómetros [kwentaki'lometros] *nm inv* (*de distancias*) ≈ milometer, clock; (*velocímetro*) speedometer

cuento ['kwento] *vb ver* **contar** ▷ *nm* story; (*Lit*) short story; ~ **chino** tall story; ~ **de hadas** fairy tale *o* story; **es el ~ de nunca acabar** it's an endless business; **eso no viene a ~** that's irrelevant

cuerda ['kwerða] *nf* rope; (*hilo*) string; (*de reloj*) spring; (*Mus: de violín etc*) string; (*Mat*) chord; (*Anat*) cord; ~ **floja** tightrope; **~s vocales** vocal cords; **dar ~ a un reloj** to wind up a clock

cuerdo, -a ['kwerðo, a] *adj* sane; (*prudente*) wise, sensible

cuerno ['kwerno] *nm* (*Zool: gen*) horn; (*: de ciervo*) antler; **poner los ~s a** (*fam*) to cuckold; **saber a ~ quemado** to leave a nasty taste

cuero ['kwero] *nm* (*Zool*) skin, hide; (*Tec*) leather; **en ~s** stark naked; ~ **cabelludo** scalp

cuerpo ['kwerpo] *nm* body; (*cadáver*) corpse; (*fig*) main part; ~ **de bomberos** fire brigade; ~ **diplomático** diplomatic corps; **luchar ~ a ~** to fight hand-to-hand; **tomar ~** (*plan etc*) to take shape

cuervo ['kwerβo] *nm* (*Zool*) raven, crow; *ver* **criar**

cuesta ['kwesta] *vb ver* **costar** ▷ *nf* slope; (*en camino etc*) hill; ~ **arriba/abajo** uphill/downhill; **a ~s** on one's back

cueste *etc vb ver* **costar**

cuestión [kwes'tjon] *nf* matter, question, issue; (*riña*) quarrel, dispute; **eso es otra ~** that's another matter

cuestionario [kwestjo'narjo] *nm* questionnaire

cuete ['kwete] *adj* (*Am: fam*) drunk ▷ *nm* (*cohete*) rocket; (*fam: embriaguez*) drunkenness; (*Culin*) steak

cueva ['kweβa] *nf* cave

cuidado [kwi'ðaðo] *nm* care, carefulness; (*preocupación*) care, worry ▷ *excl* careful!, look out!; **eso me tiene sin ~** I'm not worried about that

cuidadoso, -a [kwiða'ðoso, a] *adj* careful; (*preocupado*) anxious

cuidar [kwi'ðar] *vt* (*Med*) to care for; (*ocuparse de*) to take care of, look after; (*detalles*) to pay attention to ▷ *vi*: ~ **de** to take care of, look after; **cuidarse** *vr* to look after o.s.; **~se de hacer algo** to take care to do sth

culata [ku'lata] *nf* (*de fusil*) butt

culebra [ku'leβra] *nf* snake; ~ **de cascabel** rattlesnake

culebrón [kule'βron] *nm* (*fam*) soap (opera)

culinario, -a [kuli'narjo, a] *adj* culinary, cooking *cpd*

culminación [kulmina'θjon] *nf* culmination

culminar [kulmi'nar] *vi* to culminate

culo ['kulo] *nm* (*fam: asentaderas*) bottom, backside, bum (*Brit*); (*: ano*) arse(hole) (*Brit!*), ass(hole) (*US!*); (*de vaso*) bottom

culpa ['kulpa] *nf* fault; (*Jur*) guilt; **culpas** *nfpl* sins; **por ~ de** through, because of; **echar la ~ a algn** to blame sb for sth; **tener la ~ (de)** to be to blame (for)

culpabilidad [kulpaβili'ðað] *nf* guilt

culpable [kul'paβle] *adj* guilty ▷ *nm/f* culprit; **confesarse ~** to plead guilty; **declarar ~ a algn** to find sb guilty

culpar [kul'par] *vt* to blame; (*acusar*) to accuse

cultivar [kulti'βar] *vt* to cultivate; (*cosecha*) to raise; (*talento*) to develop

cultivo [kul'tiβo] *nm* (*acto*) cultivation; (*plantas*) crop; (*Bio*) culture

culto, -a ['kulto, a] *adj* (*cultivado*) cultivated; (*que tiene cultura*) cultured, educated ▷ *nm* (*homenaje*) worship; (*religión*) cult; (*Pol etc*) cult

cultura [kul'tura] *nf* culture

cultural [kultu'ral] *adj* cultural

culturismo [kultu'rismo] *nm* body-building

cumbia ['kumbja] *nf popular Colombian dance*

cumbre ['kumbre] *nf* summit, top; (*fig*) top, height; **conferencia (en la) ~** summit (conference)

cumpleaños [kumple'aɲos] *nm inv* birthday

cumplido, -a [kum'pliðo, a] *adj* complete, perfect; (*abundante*) plentiful; (*cortés*) courteous ▷ *nm* compliment; **visita de ~** courtesy call

cumplidor, a [kumpli'ðor, a] *adj* reliable

cumplimentar [kumplimen'tar] *vt* to congratulate; (*órdenes*) to carry out

cumplimiento [kumpli'mjento] *nm* (*de un deber*) fulfilment, execution, performance; (*acabamiento*) completion; (*Com*) expiry, end

cumplir [kum'plir] *vt* (*orden*) to carry out, obey; (*promesa*) to carry out, fulfil; (*condena*) to serve; (*años*) to reach, attain ▷ *vi* (*pago*) to fall due; (*plazo*) to expire; **cumplirse** *vr* (*plazo*) to expire; (*plan etc*) to be fulfilled; (*vaticinio*) to come true; **hoy cumple dieciocho años** he is eighteen today; ~ **con** (*deber*) to carry out, fulfil

cúmulo ['kumulo] *nm* (*montón*) heap; (*nube*) cumulus

cuna ['kuna] *nf* cradle, cot; **canción de ~** lullaby

cundir [kun'dir] *vi* (*noticia, rumor, pánico*) to spread; (*rendir*) to go a long way

cuneta [ku'neta] *nf* ditch

cuña ['kuɲa] *nf* (*Tec*) wedge; (*Com*) advertising spot; (*Med*) bedpan; **tener ~s** to have influence

cuñado, -a [ku'ɲaðo, a] *nm/f* brother/sister-in-law

C

cuota ['kwota] *nf* (*parte proporcional*) share; (*cotización*) fee, dues *pl*; ~ **inicial** (*Com*) down payment
cupe *etc* ['kupe] *vb ver* **caber**
cupiera *etc* [ku'pjera] *vb ver* **caber**
cupo *etc* ['kupo] *vb ver* **caber** ▷ *nm* quota, share; (*Com*): ~ **de importación** import quota; ~ **de ventas** sales quota
cupón [ku'pon] *nm* coupon; ~ **de la ONCE** *o* **de los ciegos** ONCE lottery ticket; *ver tb* **lotería**
cúpula ['kupula] *nf* (*Arq*) dome
cura ['kura] *nf* (*curación*) cure; (*método curativo*) treatment ▷ *nm* priest; ~ **de emergencia** emergency treatment
curación [kura'θjon] *nf* cure; (*acción*) curing
curandero, -a [kuran'dero, a] *nm/f* healer; (*pej*) quack
curar [ku'rar] *vt* (*Med*: *herida*) to treat, dress; (: *enfermo*) to cure; (*Culin*) to cure, salt; (*cuero*) to tan ▷ *vi*, **curarse** *vr* to get well, recover
curiosear [kurjose'ar] *vt* to glance at, look over ▷ *vi* to look round, wander round; (*explorar*) to poke about
curiosidad [kurjosi'ðað] *nf* curiosity
curioso, -a [ku'rjoso, a] *adj* curious; (*aseado*) neat ▷ *nm/f* bystander, onlooker; **¡qué ~!** how odd!
curita [ku'rita] *nf* (*Am*) sticking plaster
currante [ku'rrante] *nm/f* (*fam*) worker
currar [ku'rrar] *vi* (*fam*), **currelar** [kurre'lar] *vi* (*fam*) to work
currículo [ku'rrikulo], **currículum** [ku'rrikulum] *nm* curriculum vitae
curro ['kurro] *nm* (*fam*) work, job
cursar [kur'sar] *vt* (*Escol*) to study
cursi ['kursi] *adj* (*fam*) pretentious; (: *amanerado*) affected
cursilada [kursi'laða] *nf*: **¡qué ~!** how tacky!
cursillo [kur'siʎo] *nm* short course
cursiva [kur'siβa] *nf* italics *pl*
curso ['kurso] *nm* (*dirección*) course; (*fig*) progress; (*Escol*) school year; (*Univ*) academic year; **en** ~ (*año*) current; (*proceso*) going on, under way; **moneda de ~ legal** legal tender
cursor [kur'sor] *nm* (*Inform*) cursor; (*Tec*) slide
curtido, -a [kur'tiðo, a] *adj* (*cara etc*) weather-beaten; (*fig*: *persona*) experienced
curtir [kur'tir] *vt* (*piel*) to tan; (*fig*) to harden
curul [ku'rul] *nm* (*Am*: *escaño*) seat
curvo, -a ['kurβo, a] *adj* (*gen*) curved; (*torcido*) bent ▷ *nf* (*gen*) curve, bend; **curva de rentabilidad** (*Com*) break-even chart
cúspide ['kuspiðe] *nf* (*Geo*) summit, peak; (*fig*) top, pinnacle
custodia [kus'toðja] *nf* (*cuidado*) safekeeping; (*Jur*) custody
custodiar [kusto'ðjar] *vt* (*conservar*) to keep, take care of; (*vigilar*) to guard
custodio [kus'toðjo] *nm* guardian, keeper
cutáneo, -a [ku'taneo, a] *adj* skin *cpd*
cutícula [ku'tikula] *nf* cuticle
cutis ['kutis] *nm inv* skin, complexion
cutre ['kutre] *adj* (*fam*: *lugar*) grotty; (: *persona*) naff
cuyo, -a ['kujo, a] *pron* (*de quien*) whose; (*de que*) whose, of which; **la señora en cuya casa me hospedé** the lady in whose house I stayed; **el asunto ~s detalles conoces** the affair the details of which you know; **por ~ motivo** for which reason; **en ~ caso** in which case
C.V. *abr* (= *Curriculum Vitae*) CV; (= *caballos de vapor*) H.P.

d

D. *abr* (= *Don*) Esq
dádiva ['daðiβa] *nf* (*donación*) donation; (*regalo*) gift
dadivoso, -a [daði'βoso, a] *adj* generous
dado, -a ['daðo, a] *pp de* **dar** ▷ *nm* die; **dados** *nmpl* dice ▷ *adj*: **en un momento ~** at a certain point; **ser ~ a (hacer algo)** to be very fond of (doing sth); **~ que** *conj* given that
daltónico, -a [dal'toniko, a] *adj* colour-blind
dama ['dama] *nf* (*gen*) lady; (*Ajedrez*) queen; **damas** *nfpl* draughts; **primera ~** (*Teat*) leading lady; (*Pol*) president's wife, first lady (*US*); **~ de honor** (*de reina*) lady-in-waiting; (*de novia*) bridesmaid
damasco [da'masko] *nm* (*tela*) damask; (*Am*: *árbol*) apricot tree; (: *fruta*) apricot
damnificar [damnifi'kar] *vt* to harm; (*persona*) to injure
danés, -esa [da'nes, esa] *adj* Danish ▷ *nm/f* Dane ▷ *nm* (*Ling*) Danish
danza ['danθa] *nf* (*gen*) dancing; (*una danza*) dance
danzar [dan'θar] *vt, vi* to dance
dañar [da'ɲar] *vt* (*objeto*) to damage; (*persona*) to hurt; (*estropear*) to spoil; **dañarse** *vr* (*objeto*) to get damaged
dañino, -a [da'ɲino, a] *adj* harmful
daño ['daɲo] *nm* (*a un objeto*) damage; (*a una persona*) harm, injury; **~s y perjuicios** (*Jur*) damages; **hacer ~ a** to damage; (*persona*) to hurt, injure; **hacerse ~** to hurt o.s.
dañoso, -a [da'ɲoso, a] *adj* harmful

PALABRA CLAVE

dar [dar] *vt* **1** (*gen*) to give; (*obra de teatro*) to put on; (*film*) to show; (*fiesta*) to have; **dar algo a algn** to give sb sth *o* sth to sb; **dar una patada a algn/algo** to kick sb/sth, give sb/sth a kick; **dar un susto a algn** to give sb a fright; **dar de beber a algn** to give sb a drink; **dar de comer** to feed
2 (*producir*: *intereses*) to yield; (: *fruta*) to produce
3 (*locuciones +n*): **da gusto escucharle** it's a pleasure to listen to him; **me da pena/asco** it frightens/sickens me; *ver tb* **paseo** *y otros sustantivos*
4 (*+ n*: *= perífrasis de verbo*): **me da asco** it sickens me
5 (*considerar*): **dar algo por descontado/entendido** to take sth for granted/as read; **dar algo por concluido** to consider sth finished; **le dieron por desaparecido** they gave him up as lost
6 (*hora*): **el reloj dio las seis** the clock struck six (o'clock)
7: **me da lo mismo** it's all the same to me; *ver tb* **igual**; **más**
8: **¡y dale!** (*¡otra vez!*) not again!; **estar/seguir dale que dale** *o* **dale que te pego** *o* (*Am*) **dale y dale** to go/keep on and on
▷ *vi* **1**: **dar a** (*habitación*) to overlook, look on to; (*accionar*: *botón etc*) to press, hit
2: **dar con**: **dimos con él dos horas más tarde** we came across him two hours later; **al final di con la solución** I eventually came up with the answer
3: **dar en** (*blanco, suelo*) to hit; **el sol me da en la cara** the sun is shining (right) in my face
4: **dar de sí** (*zapatos etc*) to stretch, give
5: **dar para** to be enough for; **nuestro presupuesto no da para más** our budget's really tight
6: **dar por**: **le ha dado por estudiar música** now he's into studying music
7: **dar que hablar** to set people talking; **una película que da que pensar** a thought-provoking film
darse *vr* **1**: **darse un baño** to have a bath; **darse un golpe** to hit o.s.
2: **darse por vencido** to give up; **con eso me doy por satisfecho** I'd settle for that
3 (*ocurrir*): **se han dado muchos casos** there have been a lot of cases
4: **darse a**: **se ha dado a la bebida** he's taken to drinking
5: **se me dan bien/mal las ciencias** I'm good/bad at science
6: **dárselas de**: **se las da de experto** he fancies himself *o* poses as an expert

dardo ['darðo] *nm* dart
dársena ['darsena] *nf* (*Naut*) dock
datar [da'tar] *vi*: **~ de** to date from

dátil ['datil] *nm* date
dato ['dato] *nm* fact, piece of information; (*Mat*) datum; **datos** *nmpl* (*Inform*) data; **~s de entrada/salida** input/output data; **~s personales** personal details
dcha. *abr* (= *derecha*) r (= *right*)
d. de C. *abr* (= *después de Cristo*) A.D. (= *Anno Domini*)

PALABRA CLAVE

de [de] *prep* (**de** + **el** = **del**) **1** (*posesión, pertenencia*) of; **la casa de Isabel/mis padres** Isabel's/ my parents' house; **es de ellos/ella** it's theirs/hers; **un libro de Unamuno** a book by Unamuno
2 (*origen, distancia, con números*) from; **soy de Gijón** I'm from Gijón; **de 8 a 20** from 8 to 20; **5 metros de largo** 5 metres long; **salir del cine** to go out of *o* leave the cinema; **de ... en ...** from ... to ...; **de 2 en 2** 2 by 2, 2 at a time; **9 de cada 10** 9 out of every 10
3 (*valor descriptivo*): **una copa de vino** a glass of wine; **una silla de madera** a wooden chair; **la mesa de la cocina** the kitchen table; **un viaje de dos días** a two-day journey; **un billete de 50 euros** a 50-euro note; **un niño de tres años** a three-year-old (child); **una máquina de coser** a sewing machine; **la ciudad de Madrid** the city of Madrid; **el tonto de Juan** that idiot Juan; **ir vestido de gris** to be dressed in grey; **la niña del vestido azul** the girl in the blue dress; **la chica del pelo largo** the girl with long hair; **trabaja de profesora** she works as a teacher; **de lado** sideways; **de atrás/ delante** rear/front
4 (*hora, tiempo*): **a las 8 de la mañana** at 8 o'clock in the morning; **de día/noche** by day/night; **de hoy en ocho días** a week from now; **de niño era gordo** as a child he was fat
5 (*comparaciones*): **más/menos de cien personas** more/less than a hundred people; **el más caro de la tienda** the most expensive in the shop; **menos/más de lo pensado** less/more than expected
6 (*causa*): **del calor** from the heat; **de puro tonto** out of sheer stupidity
7 (*tema*) about; **clases de inglés** English classes; **¿sabes algo de él?** do you know anything about him?; **un libro de física** a physics book
8 (*adj+de+infin*): **fácil de entender** easy to understand
9 (*oraciones pasivas*): **fue respetado de todos** he was loved by all
10 (*condicional+infin*) if; **de ser posible** if possible; **de no terminarlo hoy** if I *etc* don't finish it today

dé [de] *vb ver* **dar**
deambular [deambu'lar] *vi* to stroll, wander
debajo [de'βaxo] *adv* underneath; **~ de** below, under; **por ~ de** beneath
debate [de'βate] *nm* debate
debatir [deβa'tir] *vt* to debate; **debatirse** *vr* to struggle
deber [de'βer] *nm* duty ▷ *vt* to owe ▷ *vi*: **debe (de)** it must, it should; **deberse** *vr*: **~se a** to be owing *o* due to; **deberes** *nmpl* (*Escol*) homework *sg*; **debo hacerlo** I must do it; **debe de ir** he should go; **¿qué** *o* **cuánto le debo?** how much is it?
debido, -a [de'βiðo, a] *adj* proper, due; **~ a** due to, because of; **en debida forma** duly
débil ['deβil] *adj* weak; (*persona: físicamente*) feeble; (*salud*) poor; (*voz, ruido*) faint; (*luz*) dim
debilidad [deβili'ðað] *nf* weakness; feebleness; dimness; **tener ~ por algn** to have a soft spot for sb
debilitar [deβili'tar] *vt* to weaken; **debilitarse** *vr* to grow weak
débito ['deβito] *nm* debit; (*deuda*) debt; **~ bancario** (*Am*) direct debit (*Brit*) *o* billing (*US*)
debutar [deβu'tar] *vi* to make one's debut
década ['dekaða] *nf* decade
decadencia [deka'ðenθja] *nf* (*estado*) decadence; (*proceso*) decline, decay
decaer [deka'er] *vi* (*declinar*) to decline; (*debilitarse*) to weaken; (*salud*) to fail; (*negocio*) to fall off
decaído, -a [deka'iðo, a] *adj*: **estar ~** (*persona*) to be down
decaimiento [dekai'mjento] *nm* (*declinación*) decline; (*desaliento*) discouragement; (*Med: depresión*) depression
decano, -a [de'kano, a] *nm/f* (*Univ etc*) dean; (*de grupo*) senior member
decapitar [dekapi'tar] *vt* to behead
decena [de'θena] *nf*: **una ~** ten (or so)
decencia [de'θenθja] *nf* (*modestia*) modesty; (*honestidad*) respectability
decente [de'θente] *adj* decent
decepción [deθep'θjon] *nf* disappointment
decepcionar [deθepθjo'nar] *vt* to disappoint
decidir [deθi'ðir] *vt* (*persuadir*) to convince, persuade; (*resolver*) to decide ▷ *vi* to decide; **decidirse** *vr*: **~se a** to make up one's mind to; **~se por** to decide *o* settle on, choose
decimal [deθi'mal] *adj, nm* decimal
décimo, -a ['deθimo, a] *num* tenth ▷ *nf* (*Mat*) tenth; **tiene unas décimas de fiebre** he has a slight temperature
decimoctavo, -a [deθimok'taβo, a] *num* eighteenth; *ver tb* **sexto**
decimocuarto, -a [deθimo'kwarto, a] *num* fourteenth; *ver tb* **sexto**
decimonoveno, -a [deθimono'βeno, a] *num* nineteenth; *ver tb* **sexto**
decimoquinto, -a [deθimo'kinto, a] *num* fifteenth; *ver tb* **sexto**
decimoséptimo, -a [deθimo'septimo, a] *num* seventeenth; *ver tb* **sexto**

decimosexto, -a [deθimo'seksto, a] *num* sixteenth; *ver tb* **sexto**
decimotercero, -a [deθimoter'θero, a] *num* thirteenth; *ver tb* **sexto**
decir [de'θir] *vt* (*expresar*) to say; (*contar*) to tell; (*hablar*) to speak; (*indicar*) to show; (*revelar*) to reveal; (*fam: nombrar*) to call ▷ *nm* saying; **decirse** *vr*: **se dice** it is said, they say; (*se cuenta*) the story goes; **¿cómo se dice en inglés "cursi"?** what's the English for "cursi"?; **~ para** *o* **entre sí** to say to o.s.; **~ por ~** to talk for talking's sake; **dar que ~ (a la gente)** to make people talk; **querer ~** to mean; **es ~** that is to say, namely; **ni que ~ tiene que ...** it goes without saying that ...; **como quien dice** so to speak; **¡quién lo diría!** would you believe it!; **el qué dirán** gossip; **¡diga!**, **¡dígame!** (*en tienda etc*) can I help you?; (*Telec*) hello?; **le dije que fuera más tarde** I told her to go later; **es un ~** it's just a phrase
decisión [deθi'sjon] *nf* decision; (*firmeza*) decisiveness; (*voluntad*) determination
decisivo, -a [deθi'siβo, a] *adj* decisive
declamar [dekla'mar] *vt, vi* to declaim; (*versos etc*) to recite
declaración [deklara'θjon] *nf* (*manifestación*) statement; (*de amor*) declaration; (*explicación*) explanation; (*Jur: testimonio*) evidence; **~ de derechos** (*Pol*) bill of rights; **~ de impuestos** (*Com*) tax return; **~ de ingresos** *o* **de la renta** income tax return; **~ jurada** affidavit; **falsa ~** (*Jur*) misrepresentation
declarar [dekla'rar] *vt* to declare ▷ *vi* to declare; (*Jur*) to testify; **declararse** *vr* (*a una chica*) to propose; (*guerra, incendio*) to break out; **~ culpable/inocente a algn** to find sb guilty/not guilty; **~se culpable/inocente** to plead guilty/not guilty
declinar [dekli'nar] *vt* (*gen, Ling*) to decline; (*Jur*) to reject ▷ *vi* (*el día*) to draw to a close
declive [de'kliβe] *nm* (*cuesta*) slope; (*inclinación*) incline; (*fig*) decline; (*Com: tb:* **~ económico**) slump
decolorarse [dekolo'rarse] *vr* to become discoloured
decomiso [deko'miso] *nm* seizure
decoración [dekora'θjon] *nf* decoration; (*Teat*) scenery, set; **~ de escaparates** window dressing
decorado [deko'raðo] *nm* (*Cine, Teat*) scenery, set
decorador, a [dekora'ðor, a] *nm/f* (*de interiores*) (interior) decorator; (*Teat*) stage *o* set designer
decorar [deko'rar] *vt* to decorate
decorativo, -a [dekora'tiβo, a] *adj* ornamental, decorative
decoro [de'koro] *nm* (*respeto*) respect; (*dignidad*) decency; (*recato*) propriety
decoroso, -a [deko'roso, a] *adj* (*decente*) decent; (*modesto*) modest; (*digno*) proper
decrecer [dekre'θer] *vi* to decrease, diminish; (*nivel de agua*) to go down; (*días*) to draw in
decrépito, -a [de'krepito, a] *adj* decrepit
decretar [dekre'tar] *vt* to decree
decreto [de'kreto] *nm* decree; (*Pol*) act
decreto-ley [dekreto'lei] (*pl* **decretos-leyes**) *nm* decree
dedal [de'ðal] *nm* thimble
dedicación [deðika'θjon] *nf* dedication; **con ~ exclusiva** *o* **plena** full-time
dedicar [deði'kar] *vt* (*libro*) to dedicate; (*tiempo, dinero*) to devote; (*palabras: decir, consagrar*) to dedicate, devote; **dedicarse** *vr*: **~se a (hacer algo)** to devote o.s. to (doing sth); (*carrera, estudio*) to go in for (doing sth), take up (doing sth); **¿a qué se dedica usted?** what do you do (for a living)?
dedicatoria [deðika'torja] *nf* (*de libro*) dedication
dedo ['deðo] *nm* finger; (*de vino etc*) drop; **~ (del pie)** toe; **~ pulgar** thumb; **~ índice** index finger; **~ mayor** *o* **cordial** middle finger; **~ anular** ring finger; **~ meñique** little finger; **contar con los ~s** to count on one's fingers; **comerse los ~s** to get very impatient; **entrar a ~** to get a job by pulling strings; **hacer ~** (*fam*) to hitch (a lift); **poner el ~ en la llaga** to put one's finger on it; **no tiene dos ~s de frente** he's pretty dim
deducción [deðuk'θjon] *nf* deduction
deducir [deðu'θir] *vt* (*concluir*) to deduce, infer; (*Com*) to deduct
defecto [de'fekto] *nm* defect, flaw; (*de cara*) imperfection; **~ de pronunciación** speech defect; **por ~** (*Inform*) default; **~ latente** (*Com*) latent defect
defectuoso, -a [defek'twoso, a] *adj* defective, faulty
defender [defen'der] *vt* to defend; (*ideas*) to uphold; (*causa*) to champion; (*amigos*) to stand up for; **defenderse** *vr* to defend o.s.; **~se bien** to give a good account of o.s.; **me defiendo en inglés** (*fig*) I can get by in English
defensa [de'fensa] *nf* defence; (*Naut*) fender ▷ *nm* (*Deporte*) defender, back; **en ~ propia** in self-defence
defensivo, -a [defen'siβo, a] *adj* defensive ▷ *nf*: **a la defensiva** on the defensive
defensor, -a [defen'sor, a] *adj* defending ▷ *nm/f* (*abogado defensor*) defending counsel; (*protector*) protector; **~ del pueblo** (*Esp*) ≈ ombudsman
deferente [defe'rente] *adj* deferential
deficiencia [defi'θjenθja] *nf* deficiency
deficiente [defi'θjente] *adj* (*defectuoso*) defective; **~ en** lacking *o* deficient in ▷ *nm/f*: **ser un ~ mental** to have learning difficulties
déficit (*pl* **déficits**) ['defiθit] *nm* (*Com*) deficit; (*fig*) lack, shortage; **~ presupuestario** budget deficit

deficitario, -a [defiθi'tarjo, a] *adj* (*Com*) in deficit; (: *empresa*) loss-making
definición [defini'θjon] *nf* definition; (*Inform*: *de pantalla*) resolution
definir [defi'nir] *vt* (*determinar*) to determine, establish; (*decidir, Inform*) to define; (*aclarar*) to clarify
definitivo, -a [defini'tiβo, a] *adj* (*edición, texto*) definitive; (*fecha*) definite; **en definitiva** definitively; (*en conclusión*) finally; (*en resumen*) in short
deforestación [deforesta'θjon] *nf* deforestation
deformación [deforma'θjon] *nf* (*alteración*) deformation; (*Radio etc*) distortion
deformar [defor'mar] *vt* (*gen*) to deform; **deformarse** *vr* to become deformed
deforme [de'forme] *adj* (*informe*) deformed; (*feo*) ugly; (*mal hecho*) misshapen
defraudar [defrau'ðar] *vt* (*decepcionar*) to disappoint; (*estafar*) to cheat; to defraud; **~ impuestos** to evade tax
defunción [defun'θjon] *nf* death, demise
degeneración [dexenera'θjon] *nf* (*de las células*) degeneration; (*moral*) degeneracy
degenerar [dexene'rar] *vi* to degenerate; (*empeorar*) to get worse
degollar [deɣo'ʎar] *vt* to slaughter
degradar [deɣra'ðar] *vt* to debase, degrade; (*Inform*: *datos*) to corrupt; **degradarse** *vr* to demean o.s.
degustación [deɣusta'θjon] *nf* sampling, tasting
deificar [deifi'kar] *vt* (*persona*) to deify
dejadez [dexa'ðeθ] *nf* (*negligencia*) neglect; (*descuido*) untidiness, carelessness
dejado, -a [de'xaðo, a] *adj* (*desaliñado*) slovenly; (*negligente*) careless; (*indolente*) lazy
dejar [de'xar] *vt* (*gen*) to leave; (*permitir*) to allow, let; (*abandonar*) to abandon, forsake; (*actividad, empleo*) to give up; (*beneficios*) to produce, yield ▷ *vi*: **~ de** (*parar*) to stop; (*no hacer*) to fail to; **dejarse** *vr* (*abandonarse*) to let o.s. go; **no puedo ~ de fumar** I can't give up smoking; **no dejes de visitarles** don't fail to visit them; **no dejes de comprar un billete** make sure you buy a ticket; **~ a un lado** to leave *o* set aside; **~ caer** to drop; **~ entrar/ salir** to let in/out; **~ pasar** to let through; **¡déjalo!** (*no te preocupes*) don't worry about it; **te dejo en tu casa** I'll drop you off at your place; **deja mucho que desear** it leaves a lot to be desired; **~se persuadir** to allow o.s. to *o* let o.s. be persuaded; **¡déjate de tonterías!** stop messing about!
dejo ['dexo] *nm* (*Ling*) accent
del [del] = **de + el**; *ver* **de**
delantal [delan'tal] *nm* apron
delante [de'lante] *adv* in front; (*enfrente*) opposite; (*adelante*) ahead ▷ *prep*: **~ de** in front of, before; **la parte de ~** the front part; **estando otros ~** with others present
delantero, -a [delan'tero, a] *adj* front; (*patas de animal*) fore ▷ *nm* (*Deporte*) forward, striker ▷ *nf* (*de vestido, casa etc*) front part; (*Teat*) front row; (*Deporte*) forward line; **llevar la delantera (a algn)** to be ahead (of sb)
delatar [dela'tar] *vt* to inform on *o* against, betray; **los delató a la policía** he reported them to the police
delator, -a [dela'tor, a] *nm/f* informer
delegación [deleɣa'θjon] *nf* (*acción, delegados*) delegation; (*Com*: *oficina*) district office, branch; **~ de poderes** (*Pol*) devolution; **~ de policía** (*Am*) police station
delegado, -a [dele'ɣaðo, a] *nm/f* delegate; (*Com*) agent
delegar [dele'ɣar] *vt* to delegate
deletrear [deletre'ar] *vt* (*tb fig*) to spell (out)
deleznable [deleθ'naβle] *adj* (*frágil*) fragile; (*fig*: *malo*) poor; (: *excusa*) feeble
delfín [del'fin] *nm* dolphin
delgadez [delɣa'ðeθ] *nf* thinness, slimness
delgado, -a [del'ɣaðo, a] *adj* thin; (*persona*) slim, thin; (*tierra*) poor; (*tela etc*) light, delicate ▷ *adv*: **hilar (muy) ~** (*fig*) to split hairs
deliberación [deliβera'θjon] *nf* deliberation
deliberar [deliβe'rar] *vt* to debate, discuss ▷ *vi* to deliberate
delicadeza [delika'ðeθa] *nf* delicacy; (*refinamiento, sutileza*) refinement
delicado, -a [deli'kaðo, a] *adj* delicate; (*sensible*) sensitive; (*rasgos*) dainty; (*gusto*) refined; (*situación*: *difícil*) tricky; (: *violento*) embarrassing; (*punto, tema*) sore; (*persona*: *difícil de contentar*) hard to please; (: *sensible*) touchy, hypersensitive; (: *atento*) considerate
delicia [de'liθja] *nf* delight
delicioso, -a [deli'θjoso, a] *adj* (*gracioso*) delightful; (*exquisito*) delicious
delimitar [delimi'tar] *vt* to delimit; (*función, responsabilidades*) to define
delincuencia [delin'kwenθja] *nf*: **~ juvenil** juvenile delinquency; **cifras de la ~** crime rate
delincuente [delin'kwente] *nm/f* delinquent; (*criminal*) criminal; **~ sin antecedentes** first offender; **~ habitual** hardened criminal
delineante [deline'ante] *nm/f* draughtsman/ draughtswoman; (*US*) draftsman/ draftswoman
delinear [deline'ar] *vt* to delineate; (*dibujo*) to draw; (*contornos, fig*) to outline; **~ un proyecto** to outline a project
delinquir [delin'kir] *vi* to commit an offence
delirante [deli'rante] *adj* delirious
delirar [deli'rar] *vi* to be delirious, rave; (*fig*: *desatinar*) to talk nonsense
delirio [de'lirjo] *nm* (*Med*) delirium; (*palabras insensatas*) ravings *pl*; **~ de grandeza** megalomania; **~ de persecución** persecution mania; **con ~** (*fam*) madly; **¡fue el ~!** (*fam*) it was great!

delito [de'lito] *nm (gen)* crime; *(infracción)* offence
delta ['delta] *nm* delta
demacrado, -a [dema'kraðo, a] *adj* emaciated; **estar ~** to look pale and drawn, be wasted away
demagogia [dema'ɣoxja] *nf* demagogy, demagoguery
demagogo [dema'ɣoɣo] *nm* demagogue
demanda [de'manda] *nf (pedido, Com)* demand; *(petición)* request; *(pregunta)* inquiry; *(reivindicación)* claim; *(Jur)* action, lawsuit; *(Teat)* call; *(Elec)* load; **~ de pago** demand for payment; **escribir en ~ de ayuda** to write asking for help; **entablar ~** *(Jur)* to sue; **presentar ~ de divorcio** to sue for divorce; **~ final** final demand; **~ indirecta** derived demand; **~ de mercado** market demand
demandante [deman'dante] *nm/f* claimant; *(Jur)* plaintiff
demandar [deman'dar] *vt (gen)* to demand; *(Jur)* to sue, file a lawsuit against, start proceedings against; **~ a algn por calumnia/daños y perjuicios** to sue sb for libel/damages
demarcación [demarka'θjon] *nf (de terreno)* demarcation
demás [de'mas] *adj*: **los ~ niños** the other children, the remaining children ▷ *pron*: **los/las ~** the others, the rest (of them); **lo ~** the rest (of it); **por ~** moreover; *(en vano)* in vain; **y ~** etcetera
demasía [dema'sia] *nf (exceso)* excess, surplus; **comer en ~** to eat to excess
demasiado, -a [dema'sjaðo, a] *adj*: **~ vino** too much wine ▷ *adv (antes de adj, adv)* too; **~s libros** too many books; **¡es ~!** it's too much!; **es ~ pesado para levantar** it is too heavy to lift; **~ lo sé** I know it only too well; **hace ~ calor** it's too hot; **~ despacio** too slowly; **~s** too many
demencia [de'menθja] *nf (locura)* madness
demente [de'mente] *adj* mad, insane ▷ *nm/f* lunatic
democracia [demo'kraθja] *nf* democracy
demócrata [de'mokrata] *nm/f* democrat
democrático, -a [demo'kratiko, a] *adj* democratic
demoler [demo'ler] *vt* to demolish; *(edificio)* to pull down
demolición [demoli'θjon] *nf* demolition
demonio [de'monjo] *nm* devil, demon; **¡~s!** hell!, damn!; **¿cómo ~s?** how the hell?; **¿qué ~s será?** what the devil can it be?; **¿dónde ~ lo habré dejado?** where the devil can I have left it?; **tener el ~ en el cuerpo** *(no parar)* to be always on the go
demora [de'mora] *nf* delay
demorar [demo'rar] *vt (retardar)* to delay, hold back; *(dilatar)* to hold up ▷ *vi* to linger, stay on; **demorarse** *vr* to linger, stay on; *(retrasarse)* to take a long time; **~se en hacer algo** *(esp Am)* to take time doing sth
demos ['demos] *vb ver* **dar**
demostración [demostra'θjon] *nf (gen)* demonstration; *(de cariño, fuerza)* show; *(de teorema)* proof; *(de amistad)* gesture; *(de cólera, gimnasia)* display; **~ comercial** commercial exhibition
demostrar [demos'trar] *vt (probar)* to prove; *(mostrar)* to show; *(manifestar)* to demonstrate
demostrativo, -a [demostra'tiβo, a] *adj* demonstrative
demudado, -a [demu'ðaðo, a] *adj (rostro)* pale; *(fig)* upset; **tener el rostro ~** to look pale
den [den] *vb ver* **dar**
denegar [dene'ɣar] *vt (rechazar)* to refuse; *(negar)* to deny; *(Jur)* to reject
denigrar [deni'ɣrar] *vt (desacreditar)* to denigrate; *(injuriar)* to insult
denominación [denomina'θjon] *nf (acto)* naming; *(clase)* denomination; *see note*

DENOMINACIÓN

The *denominación de origen*, often abbreviated to D.O., is a prestigious product classification given to designated regions by the awarding body, the *Consejo Regulador de la Denominación de Origen*, when their produce meets the required quality and production standards. It is often associated with *manchego* cheeses and many of the wines from the Rioja and Ribera de Duero regions.

denominador [denomina'ðor] *nm*: **~ común** common denominator
denotar [deno'tar] *vt (indicar)* to indicate, denote
densidad [densi'ðað] *nf (Física)* density; *(fig)* thickness
denso, -a ['denso, a] *adj (apretado)* solid; *(espeso, pastoso)* thick, dense; *(fig)* heavy
dentadura [denta'ðura] *nf* (set of) teeth *pl*; **~ postiza** false teeth *pl*
dental [den'tal] *adj* dental
dentera [den'tera] *nf (sensación desagradable)* the shivers *pl*; *(grima)*: **dar ~ a algn** to set sb's teeth on edge
dentífrico, -a [den'tifriko, a] *adj* dental, tooth *cpd* ▷ *nm* toothpaste; **pasta dentífrica** toothpaste
dentista [den'tista] *nm/f* dentist
dentro ['dentro] *adv* inside ▷ *prep*: **~ de** in, inside, within; **por ~** (on the) inside; **allí ~** in there; **mirar por ~** to look inside; **~ de lo posible** as far as possible; **~ de todo** all in all; **~ de tres meses** within three months
denuncia [de'nunθja] *nf (delación)* denunciation; *(acusación)* accusation; *(de accidente)* report; **hacer** *o* **poner una ~** to report an incident to the police

denunciar [denun'θjar] *vt* to report; (*delatar*) to inform on *o* against
departamento [departa'mento] *nm* (*sección*) department, section; (*Am*: *piso*) flat (*Brit*), apartment (*US*); (*distrito*) department, province; **~ de envíos** (*Com*) dispatch department; **~ de máquinas** (*Naut*) engine room
departir [depar'tir] *vi* to talk, converse
dependencia [depen'denθja] *nf* dependence; (*Pol*) dependency; (*Com*) office, section; (*sucursal*) branch office; (*Arq*: *cuarto*) room; **dependencias** *nfpl* outbuildings
depender [depen'der] *vi*: **~ de** to depend on; (*contar con*) to rely on; (*autoridad*) to be under, be answerable to; **depende** it (all) depends; **no depende de mí** it's not up to me
dependienta [depen'djenta] *nf* saleswoman, shop assistant
dependiente [depen'djente] *adj* dependent ▷ *nm* salesman, shop assistant
depilar [depi'lar] *vt* (*con cera*: *piernas*) to wax; (*cejas*) to pluck
depilatorio, -a [depila'torjo, a] *adj* depilatory ▷ *nm* hair remover
deplorable [deplo'raβle] *adj* deplorable
deplorar [deplo'rar] *vt* to deplore
deponer [depo'ner] *vt* (*armas*) to lay down; (*rey*) to depose; (*gobernante*) to oust; (*ministro*) to remove from office ▷ *vi* (*Jur*) to give evidence; (*declarar*) to make a statement
deportar [depor'tar] *vt* to deport
deporte [de'porte] *nm* sport; **hacer ~** to play sports
deportista [depor'tista] *adj* sports *cpd* ▷ *nm/f* sportsman(-woman)
deportivo, -a [depor'tiβo, a] *adj* (*club, periódico*) sports *cpd* ▷ *nm* sports car
depositante [deposi'tante] *nm/f* depositor
depositar [deposi'tar] *vt* (*dinero*) to deposit; (*mercaderías*) to put away, store; **depositarse** *vr* to settle; **~ la confianza en algn** to place one's trust in sb
depositario, -a [deposi'tarjo, a] *nm/f* trustee; **~ judicial** official receiver
depósito [de'posito] *nm* (*gen*) deposit; (*de mercaderías*) warehouse, store; (*de animales, coches*) pound; (*de agua, gasolina etc*) tank; (*en retrete*) cistern; **~ afianzado** bonded warehouse; **~ bancario** bank deposit; **~ de cadáveres** mortuary; **~ de maderas** timber yard; **~ de suministro** feeder bin
depravar [depra'βar] *vt* to deprave, corrupt; **depravarse** *vr* to become depraved
depreciar [depre'θjar] *vt* to depreciate, reduce the value of; **depreciarse** *vr* to depreciate, lose value
depredador, a [depreða'ðor, a] (*Zool*) *adj* predatory ▷ *nm* predator
depresión [depre'sjon] *nf* (*gen, Med*) depression; (*hueco*) hollow; (*en horizonte, camino*) dip; (*merma*) drop; (*Econ*) slump, recession; **~ nerviosa** nervous breakdown
deprimido, -a [depri'miðo, a] *adj* depressed
deprimir [depri'mir] *vt* to depress; **deprimirse** *vr* (*persona*) to become depressed
deprisa [de'prisa] *adv* quickly, hurriedly
depuración [depura'θjon] *nf* purification; (*Pol*) purge
depuradora [depura'ðora] *nf* (*de agua*) water-treatment plant; (*tb*: **~ de aguas residuales**) sewage farm
depurar [depu'rar] *vt* to purify; (*purgar*) to purge
derecha [de'retʃa] *nf ver* **derecho**
derecho, -a [de'retʃo, a] *adj* right, right-hand ▷ *nm* (*privilegio*) right; (*título*) claim, title; (*lado*) right(-hand) side; (*leyes*) law ▷ *nf* right(-hand) side; (*Pol*) right ▷ *adv* straight, directly; **derechos** *nmpl* dues; (*profesionales*) fees; (*impuestos*) taxes; (*de autor*) royalties; **la(s) derecha(s)** (*Pol*) the Right; **~s civiles** civil rights; **~s de patente** patent rights; **~s portuarios** (*Com*) harbour dues; **~ de propiedad literaria** copyright; **~ de timbre** (*Com*) stamp duty; **~ de votar** right to vote; **~ a voto** voting right; **Facultad de D~** Faculty of Law; **a derechas** rightly, correctly; **de derechas** (*Pol*) right-wing; **"reservados todos los ~s"** "all rights reserved"; **¡no hay ~!** it's not fair!; **tener ~ a** to have a right to; **a la derecha** on the right; (*dirección*) to the right; **siga todo ~** carry *o* (*Brit*) go straight on
deriva [de'riβa] *nf*: **ir** *o* **estar a la ~** to drift, be adrift
derivado, -a [deri'βaðo, a] *adj* derived ▷ *nm* (*Ling*) derivative; (*Industria, Química*) by-product
derivar [deri'βar] *vt* to derive; (*desviar*) to direct ▷ *vi* to derive, be derived; (*Naut*) to drift; **derivarse** *vr* to derive, be derived; **~(se) de** (*consecuencia*) to spring from
dermoprotector, a [dermoprotek'tor, a] *adj* protective
derramamiento [derrama'mjento] *nm* (*dispersión*) spilling; (*fig*) squandering; **~ de sangre** bloodshed
derramar [derra'mar] *vt* to spill; (*verter*) to pour out; (*esparcir*) to scatter; **derramarse** *vr* to pour out; **~ lágrimas** to weep
derrame [de'rrame] *nm* (*de líquido*) spilling; (*de sangre*) shedding; (*de tubo etc*) overflow; (*pérdida*) leakage; (*Med*) discharge; (*declive*) slope; **~ cerebral** brain haemorrhage; **~ sinovial** water on the knee
derrapar [derra'par] *vi* to skid
derredor [derre'ðor] *adv*: **al** *o* **en ~ de** around, about
derretido, -a [derre'tiðo, a] *adj* melted; (*metal*) molten; **estar ~ por algn** (*fig*) to be crazy about sb
derretir [derre'tir] *vt* (*gen*) to melt; (*nieve*) to thaw; (*fig*) to squander; **derretirse** *vr* to melt
derribar [derri'βar] *vt* to knock down; (*construcción*) to demolish; (*persona, gobierno, político*) to bring down

derrocar [derro'kar] *vt* (*gobierno*) to bring down, overthrow; (*ministro*) to oust
derrochar [derro'tʃar] *vt* (*dinero, recursos*) to squander; (*energía, salud*) to be bursting with *o* full of
derroche [de'rrotʃe] *nm* (*despilfarro*) waste, squandering; (*exceso*) extravagance; **con un ~ de buen gusto** with a fine display of good taste
derrota [de'rrota] *nf* (*Naut*) course; (*Mil*) defeat, rout; **sufrir una grave ~** (*fig*) to suffer a grave setback
derrotar [derro'tar] *vt* (*gen*) to defeat
derrotero [derro'tero] *nm* (*rumbo*) course; **tomar otro ~** (*fig*) to adopt a different course
derruir [derru'ir] *vt* to demolish, tear down
derrumbar [derrum'bar] *vt* to throw down; (*despeñar*) to fling *o* hurl down; (*edificio*) to knock down; (*volcar*) to upset; **derrumbarse** *vr* (*hundirse*) to collapse; (*: techo*) to fall in, cave in; (*fig: esperanzas*) to collapse
des [des] *vb ver* **dar**
desabotonar [desaβoto'nar] *vt* to unbutton, undo ▷ *vi* (*flores*) to blossom; **desabotonarse** *vr* to come undone
desabrido, -a [desa'βriðo, a] *adj* (*comida*) insipid, tasteless; (*persona: soso*) dull; (*: antipático*) rude, surly; (*respuesta*) sharp; (*tiempo*) unpleasant
desabrochar [desaβro'tʃar] *vt* (*botones, broches*) to undo, unfasten; **desabrocharse** *vr* (*ropa etc*) to come undone
desacato [desa'kato] *nm* (*falta de respeto*) disrespect; (*Jur*) contempt
desacertado, -a [desaθer'taðo, a] *adj* (*equivocado*) mistaken; (*inoportuno*) unwise
desacierto [desa'θjerto] *nm* (*error*) mistake, error; (*dicho*) unfortunate remark
desaconsejado, -a [desakonse'xaðo, a] *adj* ill-advised
desaconsejar [desakonse'xar] *vt*: **~ algo a algn** to advise sb against sth
desacorde [desa'korðe] *adj* (*Mus*) discordant; (*fig: opiniones*) conflicting; **estar ~ con algo** to disagree with sth
desacreditar [desakreði'tar] *vt* (*desprestigiar*) to discredit, bring into disrepute; (*denigrar*) to run down
desacuerdo [desa'kwerðo] *nm* (*conflicto*) disagreement, discord; (*error*) error, blunder; **en ~** out of keeping
desafiar [desa'fjar] *vt* (*retar*) to challenge; (*enfrentarse a*) to defy
desafilado, -a [desafi'laðo, a] *adj* blunt
desafinado, -a [desafi'naðo, a] *adj*: **estar ~** to be out of tune
desafinar [desafi'nar] *vi* to be out of tune; **desafinarse** *vr* to go out of tune
desafío [desa'fio] *nm* (*reto*) challenge; (*combate*) duel; (*resistencia*) defiance
desaforado, -a [desafo'raðo, a] *adj* (*grito*) ear-splitting; (*comportamiento*) outrageous
desafortunadamente [desafortunaða'mente] *adv* unfortunately
desafortunado, -a [desafortu'naðo, a] *adj* (*desgraciado*) unfortunate, unlucky
desagradable [desaɣra'ðaβle] *adj* (*fastidioso, enojoso*) unpleasant; (*irritante*) disagreeable; **ser ~ con algn** to be rude to sb
desagradar [desaɣra'ðar] *vi* (*disgustar*) to displease; (*molestar*) to bother
desagradecido, -a [desaɣraðe'θiðo, a] *adj* ungrateful
desagrado [desa'ɣraðo] *nm* (*disgusto*) displeasure; (*contrariedad*) dissatisfaction; **con ~** unwillingly
desagraviar [desaɣra'βjar] *vt* to make amends to
desagravio [desa'ɣraβjo] *nm* (*satisfacción*) amends; (*compensación*) compensation
desagüe [de'saɣwe] *nm* (*de un líquido*) drainage; (*cañería: tb:* **tubo de ~**) drainpipe; (*salida*) outlet, drain
desaguisado, -a [desaɣi'saðo, a] *adj* illegal ▷ *nm* outrage
desahogado, -a [desao'ɣaðo, a] *adj* (*holgado*) comfortable; (*espacioso*) roomy
desahogar [desao'ɣar] *vt* (*aliviar*) to ease, relieve; (*ira*) to vent; **desahogarse** *vr* (*distenderse*) to relax; (*desfogarse*) to let off steam (*fam*); (*confesarse*) to confess, get sth off one's chest (*fam*)
desahogo [desa'oɣo] *nm* (*alivio*) relief; (*comodidad*) comfort, ease; **vivir con ~** to be comfortably off
desahuciar [desau'θjar] *vt* (*enfermo*) to give up hope for; (*inquilino*) to evict
desahucio [de'sauθjo] *nm* eviction
desairar [desai'rar] *vt* (*menospreciar*) to slight, snub; (*cosa*) to disregard; (*Com*) to default on
desaire [des'aire] *nm* (*menosprecio*) slight; (*falta de garbo*) unattractiveness; **dar** *o* **hacer un ~ a algn** to offend sb; **¿me va usted a hacer ese ~?** I won't take no for an answer!
desajustar [desaxus'tar] *vt* (*desarreglar*) to disarrange; (*desconcertar*) to throw off balance; (*fig: planes*) to upset; **desajustarse** *vr* to get out of order; (*aflojarse*) to loosen
desajuste [desa'xuste] *nm* (*de máquina*) disorder; (*avería*) breakdown; (*situación*) imbalance; (*desacuerdo*) disagreement
desalentador, -a [desalenta'ðor, a] *adj* discouraging
desalentar [desalen'tar] *vt* (*desanimar*) to discourage; **desalentarse** *vr* to get discouraged
desaliento *etc* [desa'ljento] *vb ver* **desalentar** ▷ *nm* discouragement; (*abatimiento*) depression
desaliño [desa'liɲo] *nm* (*descuido*) slovenliness; (*negligencia*) carelessness
desalmado, -a [desal'maðo, a] *adj* (*cruel*) cruel, heartless
desalojar [desalo'xar] *vt* (*gen*) to remove, expel; (*expulsar, echar*) to eject; (*abandonar*) to move out of ▷ *vi* to move out; **la policía**

desalojó el local the police cleared people out of the place
desamarrar [desama'rrar] *vt* to untie; (*Naut*) to cast off
desamor [desa'mor] *nm* (*frialdad*) indifference; (*odio*) dislike
desamparado, -a [desampa'raðo, a] *adj* (*persona*) helpless; (*lugar*: *expuesto*) exposed; (: *desierto*) deserted
desamparar [desampa'rar] *vt* (*abandonar*) to desert, abandon; (*Jur*) to leave defenceless; (*barco*) to abandon
desandar [desan'dar] *vt*: **~ lo andado** *o* **el camino** to retrace one's steps
desangrar [desan'grar] *vt* to bleed; (*fig*: *persona*) to bleed dry; (*lago*) to drain; **desangrarse** *vr* to lose a lot of blood; (*morir*) to bleed to death
desanimado, -a [desani'maðo, a] *adj* (*persona*) downhearted; (*espectáculo, fiesta*) dull
desanimar [desani'mar] *vt* (*desalentar*) to discourage; (*deprimir*) to depress; **desanimarse** *vr* to lose heart
desapacible [desapa'θiβle] *adj* unpleasant
desaparecer [desapare'θer] *vi* to disappear; (*el sol, la luz*) to vanish; (*desaparecer de vista*) to drop out of sight; (*efectos, señales*) to wear off ▷ *vt* (*esp Am Pol*) to cause to disappear; (: *eufemismo*) to murder
desaparecido, -a [desapare'θiðo, a] *adj* missing; (*especie*) extinct ▷ *nm/f* (*Am Pol*) kidnapped *o* missing person
desaparición [desapari'θjon] *nf* disappearance; (*de especie etc*) extinction
desapasionado, -a [desapasjo'naðo, a] *adj* dispassionate, impartial
desapego [desa'peɣo] *nm* (*frialdad*) coolness; (*distancia*) detachment
desapercibido, -a [desaperθi'βiðo, a] *adj* unnoticed; (*desprevenido*) unprepared; **pasar ~** to go unnoticed
desaprensivo, -a [desapren'siβo, a] *adj* unscrupulous
desaprobar [desapro'βar] *vt* (*reprobar*) to disapprove of; (*condenar*) to condemn; (*no consentir*) to reject
desaprovechado, -a [desaproβe'tʃaðo, a] *adj* (*oportunidad, tiempo*) wasted; (*estudiante*) slack
desaprovechar [desaproβe'tʃar] *vt* to waste; (*talento*) not to use to the full ▷ *vi* (*perder terreno*) to lose ground
desarmador [desarma'ðor] *nm* (*Am*) screwdriver
desarmar [desar'mar] *vt* (*Mil, fig*) to disarm; (*Tec*) to take apart, dismantle
desarme [de'sarme] *nm* disarmament
desarraigar [desarrai'ɣar] *vt* to uproot; (*fig*: *costumbre*) to root out; (: *persona*) to banish
desarraigo [desa'rraiɣo] *nm* uprooting
desarreglado, -a [desarre'ɣlaðo, a] *adj* (*desordenado*) disorderly, untidy; (*hábitos*) irregular
desarreglar [desarre'ɣlar] *vt* to mess up; (*desordenar*) to disarrange; (*trastocar*) to upset, disturb
desarreglo [desa'rreɣlo] *nm* (*de casa, persona*) untidiness; (*desorden*) disorder; (*Tec*) trouble; (*Med*) upset; **viven en el mayor ~** they live in complete chaos
desarrollar [desarro'ʎar] *vt* (*gen*) to develop; (*extender*) to unfold; (*teoría*) to explain; **desarrollarse** *vr* to develop; (*ocurrir*) to take place; (*extenderse*) to open (out); (*film*) to develop; (*fig*) to grow; (*tener lugar*) to take place; **aquí desarrollan un trabajo muy importante** they carry on *o* out very important work here; **la acción se desarrolla en Roma** (*Cine etc*) the scene is set in Rome
desarrollo [desa'rroʎo] *nm* development; (*de acontecimientos*) unfolding; (*de industria, mercado*) expansion, growth; **país en vías de ~** developing country; **la industria está en pleno ~** industry is expanding steadily; **~ sostenible** sustainable development
desarticular [desartiku'lar] *vt* (*huesos*) to dislocate, put out of joint; (*objeto*) to take apart; (*grupo terrorista etc*) to break up
desaseo [desa'seo] *nm* (*suciedad*) dirtiness; (*desarreglo*) untidiness
desasir [desa'sir] *vt* to loosen; **desasirse** *vr* to extricate o.s.; **~se de** to let go, give up
desasosegar [desasose'ɣar] *vt* (*inquietar*) to disturb, make uneasy; **desasosegarse** *vr* to become uneasy
desasosiego *etc* [desaso'sjeɣo] *vb ver* **desasosegar** ▷ *nm* (*intranquilidad*) uneasiness, restlessness; (*ansiedad*) anxiety; (*Pol etc*) unrest
desastrado, -a [desas'traðo, a] *adj* (*desaliñado*) shabby; (*sucio*) dirty
desastre [de'sastre] *nm* disaster; **¡un ~!** how awful!; **la función fue un ~** the show was a shambles
desastroso, -a [desas'troso, a] *adj* disastrous
desatado, -a [desa'taðo, a] *adj* (*desligado*) untied; (*violento*) violent, wild
desatar [desa'tar] *vt* (*nudo*) to untie; (*paquete*) to undo; (*perro, odio*) to unleash; (*misterio*) to solve; (*separar*) to detach; **desatarse** *vr* (*zapatos*) to come untied; (*tormenta*) to break; (*perder control de sí mismo*) to lose self-control; **~se en injurias** to pour out a stream of insults
desatascar [desatas'kar] *vt* (*cañería*) to unblock, clear
desatender [desaten'der] *vt* (*no prestar atención a*) to disregard; (*abandonar*) to neglect
desatento, -a [desa'tento, a] *adj* (*distraído*) inattentive; (*descortés*) discourteous
desatinado, -a [desati'naðo, a] *adj* foolish, silly
desatino [desa'tino] *nm* (*idiotez*) foolishness, folly; (*error*) blunder; **desatinos** *nmpl*

nonsense *sg*; **¡qué ~!** how silly!, what rubbish!

desatornillar [desatorni'ʎar] *vt* to unscrew

desatrancar [desatran'kar] *vt* (*puerta*) to unbolt; (*cañería*) to unblock

desautorizado, -a [desautori'θaðo, a] *adj* unauthorized

desautorizar [desautori'θar] *vt* (*oficial*) to deprive of authority; (*informe*) to deny

desavenencia [desaβe'nenθja] *nf* (*desacuerdo*) disagreement; (*discrepancia*) quarrel

desaventajado, -a [desaβenta'xaðo, a] *adj* (*inferior*) inferior; (*poco ventajoso*) disadvantageous

desayunar [desaju'nar] *vi*, **desayunarse** *vr* to have breakfast ▷ *vt* to have for breakfast; **~ con café** to have coffee for breakfast; **~ con algo** (*fig*) to get the first news of sth

desayuno [desa'juno] *nm* breakfast

desazón [desa'θon] *nf* (*angustia*) anxiety; (*Med*) discomfort; (*fig*) annoyance

desazonar [desaθo'nar] *vt* (*fig*) to annoy, upset; **desazonarse** *vr* (*enojarse*) to be annoyed; (*preocuparse*) to worry, be anxious

desbandarse [desβan'darse] *vr* (*Mil*) to disband; (*fig*) to flee in disorder

desbarajuste [desβara'xuste] *nm* confusion, disorder; **¡qué ~!** what a mess!

desbaratar [desβara'tar] *vt* (*gen*) to mess up; (*plan*) to spoil; (*deshacer, destruir*) to ruin ▷ *vi* to talk nonsense; **desbaratarse** *vr* (*máquina*) to break down; (*persona: irritarse*) to fly off the handle (*fam*)

desbloquear [desβloke'ar] *vt* (*negociaciones, tráfico*) to get going again; (*Com: cuenta*) to unfreeze

desbocado, -a [desβo'kaðo, a] *adj* (*caballo*) runaway; (*herramienta*) worn

desbordar [desβor'ðar] *vt* (*sobrepasar*) to go beyond; (*exceder*) to exceed ▷ *vi*, **desbordarse** *vr* (*líquido, río*) to overflow; (*entusiasmo*) to erupt; (*persona: exaltarse*) to get carried away

descabalgar [deskaβal'ɣar] *vi* to dismount

descabellado, -a [deskaβe'ʎaðo, a] *adj* (*disparatado*) wild, crazy; (*insensato*) preposterous

descabellar [deskaβe'ʎar] *vt* to ruffle; (*Taur: toro*) to give the coup de grace to

descafeinado, -a [deskafei'naðo, a] *adj* decaffeinated ▷ *nm* decaffeinated coffee, de-caff

descalabro [deska'laβro] *nm* blow; (*desgracia*) misfortune

descalificación [deskalifika'θjon] *nf* disqualification; **descalificaciones** *nfpl* discrediting *sg*

descalificar [deskalifi'kar] *vt* to disqualify; (*desacreditar*) to discredit

descalzar [deskal'θar] *vt* (*zapato*) to take off; (*persona*) to take the shoes off

descalzo, -a [des'kalθo, a] *adj* barefoot(ed); (*fig*) destitute; **estar (con los pies) ~(s)** to be barefooted

descambiar [deskam'bjar] *vt* to exchange

descaminado, -a [deskami'naðo, a] *adj* (*equivocado*) on the wrong road; (*fig*) misguided; **en eso no anda usted muy ~** you're not far wrong there

descampado [deskam'paðo] *nm* open space, piece of empty ground; **comer al ~** to eat in the open air

descansado, -a [deskan'saðo, a] *adj* (*gen*) rested; (*que tranquiliza*) restful

descansar [deskan'sar] *vt* (*gen*) to rest; (*apoyar*): **~ (sobre)** to lean (on) ▷ *vi* to rest, have a rest; (*echarse*) to lie down; (*cadáver, restos*) to lie; **¡que usted descanse!** sleep well!; **~ en** (*argumento*) to be based on

descansillo [deskan'siʎo] *nm* (*de escalera*) landing

descanso [des'kanso] *nm* (*reposo*) rest; (*alivio*) relief; (*pausa*) break; (*Deporte*) interval, half time; **día de ~** day off; **~ de enfermedad/maternidad** sick/maternity leave; **tomarse unos días de ~** to take a few days' leave *o* rest

descapotable [deskapo'taβle] *nm* (*tb*: **coche ~**) convertible

descarado, -a [deska'raðo, a] *adj* (*sin vergüenza*) shameless; (*insolente*) cheeky

descarga [des'karɣa] *nf* (*Arq, Elec, Mil*) discharge; (*Naut*) unloading; (*Inform*) download

descargable [deskar'ɣaβle] *adj* downloadable

descargar [deskar'ɣar] *vt* to unload; (*golpe*) to let fly; (*arma*) to fire; (*Elec*) to discharge; (*pila*) to run down; (*conciencia*) to relieve; (*Com*) to take up; (*persona: de una obligación*) to release; (*: de una deuda*) to free; (*Jur*) to clear ▷ *vi* (*río*): **~ (en)** to flow (into); **descargarse** *vr* to unburden o.s.; **~se de algo** to get rid of sth; **~se algo de Internet** to download sth from the internet

descargo [des'karɣo] *nm* (*de obligación*) release; (*Com: recibo*) receipt; (*: de deuda*) discharge; (*Jur*) evidence; **~ de una acusación** acquittal on a charge

descarnado, -a [deskar'naðo, a] *adj* scrawny; (*fig*) bare; (*estilo*) straightforward

descaro [des'karo] *nm* nerve

descarriar [deska'rrjar] *vt* (*descaminar*) to misdirect; (*fig*) to lead astray; **descarriarse** *vr* (*perderse*) to lose one's way; (*separarse*) to stray; (*pervertirse*) to err, go astray

descarrilamiento [deskarrila'mjento] *nm* (*de tren*) derailment

descarrilar [deskarri'lar] *vi* to be derailed

descartar [deskar'tar] *vt* (*rechazar*) to reject; (*eliminar*) to rule out; **descartarse** *vr* (*Naipes*) to discard; **~se de** to shirk

descascarillado, -a [deskaskari'ʎaðo, a] *adj* (*paredes*) peeling

descendencia [desθen'denθja] *nf* (*origen*) origin, descent; (*hijos*) offspring; **morir sin dejar ~** to die without issue

descender [desθen'der] *vt* (*bajar*: *escalera*) to go down ▷ *vi* to descend; (*temperatura, nivel*) to fall, drop; (*líquido*) to run; (*cortina etc*) to hang; (*fuerzas, persona*) to fail, get weak; **~ de** to be descended from

descendiente [desθen'djente] *nm/f* descendant

descenso [des'θenso] *nm* descent; (*de temperatura*) drop; (*de producción*) downturn; (*de calidad*) decline; (*Minería*) collapse; (*bajada*) slope; (*fig*: *decadencia*) decline; (*de empleado etc*) demotion

descifrar [desθi'frar] *vt* (*escritura*) to decipher; (*mensaje*) to decode; (*problema*) to puzzle out; (*misterio*) to solve

descodificador [deskoðifika'ðor] *nm* decoder

descodificar [deskoðifi'kar] *vt* to decode

descolgar [deskol'ɣar] *vt* (*bajar*) to take down; (*desde una posición alta*) to lower; (*de una pared etc*) to unhook; (*teléfono*) to pick up; **descolgarse** *vr* to let o.s. down; **~se por** (*bajar escurriéndose*) to slip down; (*pared*) to climb down; **dejó el teléfono descolgado** he left the phone off the hook

descollar [desko'ʎar] *vi* (*sobresalir*) to stand out; (*montaña etc*) to rise; **la obra que más descuella de las suyas** his most outstanding work

descolorido, -a [deskolo'riðo, a] *adj* (*color, tela*) faded; (*pálido*) pale; (*fig*: *estilo*) colourless

descompaginar [deskompaxi'nar] *vt* (*desordenar*) to disarrange, mess up

descompasado, -a [deskompa'saðo, a] *adj* (*sin proporción*) out of all proportion; (*excesivo*) excessive; (*hora*) unearthly

descomponer [deskompo'ner] *vt* (*gen, Ling, Mat*) to break down; (*desordenar*) to disarrange, disturb; (*materia orgánica*) to rot, decompose; (*Tec*) to put out of order; (*facciones*) to distort; (*estómago etc*) to upset; (*: planes*) to mess up; (*persona*: *molestar*) to upset; (*irritar*) to annoy; **descomponerse** *vr* (*corromperse*) to rot, decompose; (*estómago*) to get upset; (*el tiempo*) to change (for the worse); (*Tec*) to break down

descomposición [deskomposi'θjon] *nf* (*de un objeto*) breakdown; (*de fruta etc*) decomposition; (*putrefacción*) rotting; (*de cara*) distortion; **~ de vientre** (*Med*) stomach upset, diarrhoea, diarrhea (US)

descompostura [deskompos'tura] *nf* (*Tec*) breakdown, fault; (*desorganización*) disorganization; (*desorden*) untidiness; (*Am*: *diarrea*) diarrhoea, diarrhea (US)

descompuesto, -a [deskom'pwesto, a] *pp de* **descomponer** ▷ *adj* (*corrompido*) decomposed; (*roto*) broken (down)

descomunal [deskomu'nal] *adj* (*enorme*) huge; (*fam*: *excelente*) fantastic

desconcertado, -a [deskonθer'taðo, a] *adj* disconcerted, bewildered

desconcertar [deskonθer'tar] *vt* (*confundir*) to baffle; (*incomodar*) to upset, put out; (*orden*) to disturb; **desconcertarse** *vr* (*turbarse*) to be upset; (*confundirse*) to be bewildered

desconchado, -a [deskon'tʃaðo, a] *adj* (*pintura*) peeling

desconcierto *etc* [deskon'θjerto] *vb ver* **desconcertar** ▷ *nm* (*gen*) disorder; (*desorientación*) uncertainty; (*inquietud*) uneasiness; (*confusión*) bewilderment

desconectar [deskonek'tar] *vt* to disconnect; (*desenchufar*) to unplug; (*radio, televisión*) to switch off; (*Inform*) to toggle off

desconfianza [deskon'fjanθa] *nf* distrust

desconfiar [deskon'fjar] *vi* to be distrustful; **~ de** (*sospechar*) to mistrust, suspect; (*no tener confianza en*) to have no faith *o* confidence in; **desconfío de ello** I doubt it; **desconfíe de las imitaciones** (*Com*) beware of imitations

descongelar [deskonxe'lar] *vt* (*nevera*) to defrost; (*comida*) to thaw; (*Auto*) to de-ice; (*Com, Pol*) to unfreeze

descongestionar [desconxestjo'nar] *vt* (*cabeza, tráfico*) to clear; (*calle, ciudad*) to relieve congestion in; (*fig*: *despejar*) to clear

desconocer [deskono'θer] *vt* (*ignorar*) not to know, be ignorant of; (*no aceptar*) to deny; (*repudiar*) to disown

desconocido, -a [deskono'θiðo, a] *adj* unknown; (*que no se conoce*) unfamiliar; (*no reconocido*) unrecognized ▷ *nm/f* stranger; (*recién llegado*) newcomer; **está ~** he is hardly recognizable

desconocimiento [deskonoθi'mjento] *nm* (*falta de conocimientos*) ignorance; (*repudio*) disregard

desconsiderado, -a [deskonsiðe'raðo, a] *adj* inconsiderate; (*insensible*) thoughtless

desconsolar [deskonso'lar] *vt* to distress; **desconsolarse** *vr* to despair

desconsuelo [deskon'swelo] *vb ver* **desconsolar** ▷ *nm* (*tristeza*) distress; (*desesperación*) despair

descontado, -a [deskon'taðo, a] *adj*: **por ~** of course; **dar por ~ (que)** to take it for granted (that)

descontar [deskon'tar] *vt* (*deducir*) to take away, deduct; (*rebajar*) to discount

descontento, -a [deskon'tento, a] *adj* dissatisfied ▷ *nm* dissatisfaction, discontent

descontrol [deskon'trol] *nm* (*fam*) lack of control

descontrolarse [deskontro'larse] *vr* (*persona*) to lose control

desconvocar [deskombo'kar] *vt* to call off

descorazonar [deskoraθo'nar] *vt* to discourage, dishearten; **descorazonarse** *vr* to get discouraged, lose heart

descorchar [deskor'tʃar] *vt* to uncork, open

descorrer [desko'rrer] *vt* (*cortina, cerrojo*) to draw back; (*velo*) to remove

descortés [deskor'tes] *adj* (*mal educado*)

discourteous; (*grosero*) rude
descoser [desko'ser] *vt* to unstitch; **descoserse** *vr* to come apart (at the seams); (*fam: descubrir un secreto*) to blurt out a secret; **~se de risa** to split one's sides laughing
descosido, -a [desko'siðo, a] *adj* (*costura*) unstitched; (*desordenado*) disjointed ▷ *nm*: **como un ~** (*obrar*) wildly; (*beber, comer*) to excess; (*estudiar*) like mad
descrédito [des'kreðito] *nm* discredit; **caer en ~** to fall into disrepute; **ir en ~ de** to be to the discredit of
descreído, -a [deskre'iðo, a] *adj* (*incrédulo*) incredulous; (*falto de fe*) unbelieving
descremado, -a [deskre'maðo, a] *adj* skimmed
describir [deskri'βir] *vt* to describe
descripción [deskrip'θjon] *nf* description
descrito [des'krito] *pp de* **describir**
descuartizar [deskwarti'θar] *vt* (*animal*) to carve up, cut up; (*fig: hacer pedazos*) to tear apart
descubierto, -a [desku'βjerto, a] *pp de* **descubrir** ▷ *adj* uncovered, bare; (*persona*) bare-headed; (*cielo*) clear; (*coche*) open; (*campo*) treeless ▷ *nm* (*lugar*) open space; (*Com: en el presupuesto*) shortage; (*: bancario*) overdraft; **al ~** in the open; **poner al ~** to lay bare; **quedar al ~** to be exposed; **estar en ~** to be overdrawn
descubrimiento [deskuβri'mjento] *nm* (*hallazgo*) discovery; (*de criminal, fraude*) detection; (*revelación*) revelation; (*de secreto etc*) disclosure; (*de estatua etc*) unveiling
descubrir [desku'βrir] *vt* to discover, find; (*petróleo*) to strike; (*inaugurar*) to unveil; (*vislumbrar*) to detect; (*sacar a luz: crimen*) to bring to light; (*revelar*) to reveal, show; (*poner al descubierto*) to expose to view; (*naipes*) to lay down; (*quitar la tapa de*) to uncover; (*cacerola*) to take the lid off; (*enterarse de: causa, solución*) to find out; (*divisar*) to see, make out; (*delatar*) to give away, betray; **descubrirse** *vr* to reveal o.s.; (*quitarse sombrero*) to take off one's hat; (*confesar*) to confess; (*fig: salir a luz*) to come out *o* to light
descuento [des'kwento] *vb ver* **descontar** ▷ *nm* discount; **~ del 3%** 3% off; **con ~** at a discount; **~ por pago al contado** (*Com*) cash discount; **~ por volumen de compras** (*Com*) volume discount
descuidado, -a [deskwi'ðaðo, a] *adj* (*sin cuidado*) careless; (*desordenado*) untidy; (*olvidadizo*) forgetful; (*dejado*) neglected; (*desprevenido*) unprepared
descuidar [deskwi'ðar] *vt* (*dejar*) to neglect; (*olvidar*) to overlook ▷ *vi*, **descuidarse** *vr* (*distraerse*) to be careless; (*estar desaliñado*) to let o.s. go; (*desprevenirse*) to drop one's guard; **¡descuida!** don't worry!
descuido [des'kwiðo] *nm* (*dejadez*) carelessness; (*olvido*) negligence; (*un descuido*) oversight; **al ~** casually; (*sin cuidado*) carelessly; **al menor ~** if my *etc* attention wanders for a minute; **con ~** thoughtlessly; **por ~** by an oversight

PALABRA CLAVE

desde ['desðe] *prep* **1** (*lugar*) from; **desde Burgos hasta mi casa hay 30 km** it's 30 km from Burgos to my house; **desde lejos** from a distance
2 (*posición*): **hablaba desde el balcón** she was speaking from the balcony
3 (*tiempo: +adv, n*): **desde ahora** from now on; **desde entonces/la boda** since then/the wedding; **desde niño** since I *etc* was a child; **desde tres años atrás** since three years ago
4 (*tiempo: +vb*) since; for; **nos conocemos desde 1978/desde hace 20 años** we've known each other since 1978/for 20 years; **no le veo desde 1983/desde hace 5 años** I haven't seen him since 1983/for 5 years; **¿desde cuándo vives aquí?** how long have you lived here?
5 (*gama*): **desde los más lujosos hasta los más económicos** from the most luxurious to the most reasonably priced
6: **desde luego (que no)** of course (not)
▷ *conj*: **desde que**: **desde que recuerdo** for as long as I can remember; **desde que llegó no ha salido** he hasn't been out since he arrived

desdecir [desðe'θir] *vi*: **~ de** (*no merecer*) to be unworthy of; (*no corresponder*) to clash with; **desdecirse** *vr*: **~se de** to go back on
desdén [des'ðen] *nm* scorn
desdeñar [desðe'ɲar] *vt* (*despreciar*) to scorn
desdicha [des'ðitʃa] *nf* (*desgracia*) misfortune; (*infelicidad*) unhappiness
desdichado, -a [desði'tʃaðo, a] *adj* (*sin suerte*) unlucky; (*infeliz*) unhappy; (*día*) ill-fated ▷ *nm/f* (*pobre desgraciado*) poor devil
desdoblar [desðo'βlar] *vt* (*extender*) to spread out; (*desplegar*) to unfold
desear [dese'ar] *vt* to want, desire, wish for; **¿qué desea la señora?** (*tienda etc*) what can I do for you, madam?; **estoy deseando que esto termine** I'm longing for this to finish
desecar [dese'kar] *vt*, **desecarse** *vr* to dry up
desechar [dese'tʃar] *vt* (*basura*) to throw out *o* away; (*ideas*) to reject, discard; (*miedo*) to cast aside; (*plan*) to drop
desecho [de'setʃo] *nm* (*desprecio*) contempt; (*lo peor*) dregs *pl*; **desechos** *nmpl* rubbish *sg*, waste *sg*; **de ~** (*hierro*) scrap; (*producto*) waste; (*ropa*) cast-off
desembalar [desemba'lar] *vt* to unpack
desembarazado, -a [desembara'θaðo, a] *adj* (*libre*) clear, free; (*desenvuelto*) free and easy
desembarazar [desembara'θar] *vt* (*desocupar*) to clear; (*desenredar*) to free;

desembarazarse *vr*: **~se de** to free o.s. of, get rid of
desembarcar [desembar'kar] *vt* (*personas*) to land; (*mercancías etc*) to unload ▷ *vi*, **desembarcarse** *vr* (*de barco, avión*) to disembark
desembocadura [desemboka'ðura] *nf* (*de río*) mouth; (*de calle*) opening
desembocar [desembo'kar] *vi*: **~ en** to flow into; (*fig*) to result in
desembolso [desem'bolso] *nm* payment
desembragar [desembra'ɣar] *vt* (*Tec*) to disengage, release ▷ *vi* (*Auto*) to declutch
desembrollar [desembro'ʎar] *vt* (*madeja*) to unravel; (*asunto, malentendido*) to sort out
desemejanza [deseme'xanθa] *nf* dissimilarity
desempaquetar [desempake'tar] *vt* (*regalo*) to unwrap; (*mercancía*) to unpack
desempatar [desempa'tar] *vi* to break a tie; **volvieron a jugar para ~** they held a play-off
desempate [desem'pate] *nm* (*Fútbol*) replay, play-off; (*Tenis*) tie-break(er)
desempeñar [desempe'ɲar] *vt* (*cargo*) to hold; (*papel*) to play; (*deber, función*) to perform, carry out; (*lo empeñado*) to redeem; **desempeñarse** *vr* to get out of debt; **~ un papel** (*fig*) to play (a role)
desempeño [desem'peɲo] *nm* occupation; (*de lo empeñado*) redeeming; **de mucho ~** very capable
desempleado, -a [desemple'aðo, a] *adj* unemployed, out of work ▷ *nm/f* unemployed person
desempleo [desem'pleo] *nm* unemployment
desempolvar [desempol'βar] *vt* (*muebles etc*) to dust; (*lo olvidado*) to revive
desencadenar [desenkaðe'nar] *vt* to unchain; (*ira*) to unleash; (*provocar*) to cause, set off; **desencadenarse** *vr* to break loose; (*tormenta*) to burst; (*guerra*) to break out; **se desencadenó una lucha violenta** a violent struggle ensued
desencajar [desenka'xar] *vt* (*hueso*) to put out of joint; (*mandíbula*) to dislocate; (*mecanismo, pieza*) to disconnect, disengage
desencanto [desen'kanto] *nm* disillusionment, disenchantment
desenchufar [desentʃu'far] *vt* to unplug, disconnect
desenfadado, -a [desenfa'ðaðo, a] *adj* (*desenvuelto*) uninhibited; (*descarado*) forward; (*en el vestir*) casual
desenfado [desen'faðo] *nm* (*libertad*) freedom; (*comportamiento*) free and easy manner; (*descaro*) forwardness; (*desenvoltura*) self-confidence
desenfocado, -a [desenfo'kaðo, a] *adj* (*Foto*) out of focus
desenfrenado, -a [desenfre'naðo, a] *adj* (*descontrolado*) uncontrolled; (*inmoderado*) unbridled
desenfreno [desen'freno] *nm* (*vicio*) wildness; (*falta de control*) lack of self-control; (*de pasiones*) unleashing
desenganchar [desengan'tʃar] *vt* (*gen*) to unhook; (*Ferro*) to uncouple; (*Tec*) to disengage
desengañar [desenga'ɲar] *vt* to disillusion; (*abrir los ojos a*) to open the eyes of; **desengañarse** *vr* to become disillusioned; **¡desengáñate!** don't you believe it!
desengaño [desen'gaɲo] *nm* disillusionment; (*decepción*) disappointment; **sufrir un ~ amoroso** to be disappointed in love
desenlace *etc* [desen'laθe] *nm* outcome; (*Lit*) ending
desenmarañar [desenmara'ɲar] *vt* (*fig*) to unravel
desenmascarar [desenmaska'rar] *vt* to unmask, expose
desenredar [desenre'ðar] *vt* (*pelo*) to untangle; (*problema*) to sort out
desenroscar [desenros'kar] *vt* (*tornillo etc*) to unscrew
desentenderse [desenten'derse] *vr*: **~ de** to pretend not to know about; (*apartarse*) to have nothing to do with
desenterrar [desente'rrar] *vt* to exhume; (*tesoro, fig*) to unearth, dig up
desentonar [desento'nar] *vi* (*Mus*) to sing (*o* play) out of tune; (*no encajar*) to be out of place; (*color*) to clash
desentrañar [desentra'ɲar] *vt* (*misterio*) to unravel
desentumecer [desentume'θer] *vt* (*pierna etc*) to stretch; (*Deporte*) to loosen up
desenvoltura [desembol'tura] *nf* (*libertad, gracia*) ease; (*descaro*) free and easy manner; (*al hablar*) fluency
desenvolver [desembol'βer] *vt* (*paquete*) to unwrap; (*fig*) to develop; **desenvolverse** *vr* (*desarrollarse*) to unfold, develop; (*suceder*) to go off; (*prosperar*) to prosper; (*arreglárselas*) to cope
deseo [de'seo] *nm* desire, wish; **~ de saber** thirst for knowledge; **buen ~** good intentions *pl*; **arder en ~s de algo** to yearn for sth
deseoso, -a [dese'oso, a] *adj*: **estar ~ de hacer** to be anxious to do
desequilibrado, -a [desekili'βraðo, a] *adj* unbalanced ▷ *nm/f* unbalanced person; **~ mental** mentally disturbed person
desertar [deser'tar] *vt* (*Jur: derecho de apelación*) to forfeit ▷ *vi* to desert; **~ de sus deberes** to neglect one's duties
desértico, -a [de'sertiko, a] *adj* desert *cpd*; (*vacío*) deserted
desertor, a [deser'tor, a] *nm/f* deserter
desesperación [desespera'θjon] *nf* desperation, despair; (*irritación*) fury; **es una ~** it's maddening; **es una ~ tener que ...** it's infuriating to have to ...

desesperado, -a [desespe'raðo, a] *adj* (*persona*: *sin esperanza*) desperate; (*caso, situación*) hopeless; (*esfuerzo*) furious ▷ *nm*: **como un ~** like mad ▷ *nf*: **hacer algo a la desesperada** to do sth as a last resort *o* in desperation

desesperar [desespe'rar] *vt* to drive to despair; (*exasperar*) to drive to distraction ▷ *vi*: **~ de** to despair of; **desesperarse** *vr* to despair, lose hope

desestabilizar [desestaβili'θar] *vt* to destabilize

desestimar [desesti'mar] *vt* (*menospreciar*) to have a low opinion of; (*rechazar*) to reject

desfachatez [desfatʃa'teθ] *nf* (*insolencia*) impudence; (*descaro*) rudeness

desfalco [des'falko] *nm* embezzlement

desfallecer [desfaʎe'θer] *vi* (*perder las fuerzas*) to become weak; (*desvanecerse*) to faint

desfasado, -a [desfa'saðo, a] *adj* (*anticuado*) old-fashioned; (*Tec*) out of phase

desfase [des'fase] *nm* (*diferencia*) gap

desfavorable [desfaβo'raβle] *adj* unfavourable

desfigurar [desfiɣu'rar] *vt* (*cara*) to disfigure; (*cuerpo*) to deform; (*cuadro, monumento*) to deface; (*Foto*) to blur; (*sentido*) to twist; (*suceso*) to misrepresent

desfiladero [desfila'ðero] *nm* gorge, defile

desfilar [desfi'lar] *vi* to parade; **~on ante el general** they marched past the general

desfile [des'file] *nm* procession; (*Mil*) parade; **~ de modelos** fashion show

desfogar [desfo'ɣar] *vt* (*fig*) to vent ▷ *vi* (*Naut*: *tormenta*) to burst; **desfogarse** *vr* (*fig*) to let off steam

desgajar [desɣa'xar] *vt* (*arrancar*) to tear off; (*romper*) to break off; (*naranja*) to split into segments; **desgajarse** *vr* to come off

desgana [des'ɣana] *nf* (*falta de apetito*) loss of appetite; (*renuencia*) unwillingness; **hacer algo a ~** to do sth unwillingly

desganado, -a [desɣa'naðo, a] *adj*: **estar ~** (*sin apetito*) to have no appetite; (*sin entusiasmo*) to have lost interest

desgarrador, a [desɣarra'ðor, a] *adj* heartrending

desgarrar [desɣa'rrar] *vt* to tear (up); (*fig*) to shatter

desgarro [des'ɣarro] *nm* (*en tela*) tear; (*aflicción*) grief; (*descaro*) impudence

desgastar [desɣas'tar] *vt* (*deteriorar*) to wear away *o* down; (*estropear*) to spoil; **desgastarse** *vr* to get worn out

desgaste [des'ɣaste] *nm* wear (and tear); (*de roca*) erosion; (*de cuerda*) fraying; (*de metal*) corrosion; **~ económico** drain on one's resources

desglosar [desɣlo'sar] *vt* to detach; (*factura*) to break down

desgracia [des'ɣraθja] *nf* misfortune; (*accidente*) accident; (*vergüenza*) disgrace; (*contratiempo*) setback; **por ~** unfortunately; **en el accidente no hay que lamentar ~s personales** there were no casualties in the accident; **caer en ~** to fall from grace; **tener la ~ de** to be unlucky enough to

desgraciado, -a [desɣra'θjaðo, a] *adj* (*sin suerte*) unlucky, unfortunate; (*miserable*) wretched; (*infeliz*) miserable ▷ *nm/f* (*malvado*) swine; (*infeliz*) poor creature; **¡esa radio desgraciada!** (*esp Am*) that lousy radio!

desgravación [desɣraβa'θjon] *nf* (*Com*): **~ de impuestos** tax relief; **~ personal** personal allowance

desgravar [desɣra'βar] *vt* (*producto*) to reduce the tax *o* duty on

desgreñado, -a [desɣre'ɲaðo, a] *adj* dishevelled

desguace [des'ɣwaθe] *nm* (*de coches*) scrapping; (*lugar*) scrapyard

desguazar [desɣwa'θar] *vt* (*coche*) to scrap

deshabitado, -a [desaβi'taðo, a] *adj* uninhabited

deshacer [desa'θer] *vt* (*lo hecho*) to undo, unmake; (*proyectos*: *arruinar*) to spoil; (*casa*) to break up; (*Tec*) to take apart; (*enemigo*) to defeat; (*diluir*) to melt; (*contrato*) to break; (*intriga*) to solve; (*cama*) to strip; (*maleta*) to unpack; (*paquete*) to unwrap; (*nudo*) to untie; (*costura*) to unpick; **deshacerse** *vr* (*desatarse*) to come undone; (*estropearse*) to be spoiled; (*descomponerse*) to fall to pieces; (*disolverse*) to melt; (*despedazarse*) to come apart *o* undone; **~se de** to get rid of; (*Com*) to dump, unload; **~se en** (*cumplidos, elogios*) to be lavish with; **~se en lágrimas** to burst into tears; **~se por algo** to be crazy about sth

deshecho, -a [de'setʃo, a] *pp de* **deshacer** ▷ *adj* (*lazo, nudo*) undone; (*roto*) smashed; (*despedazado*) in pieces; (*cama*) unmade; (*Med*: *persona*) weak, emaciated; (*: salud*) broken; **estoy ~** I'm shattered

deshelar [dese'lar] *vt* (*cañería*) to thaw; (*heladera*) to defrost

desheredar [desere'ðar] *vt* to disinherit

deshidratar [desiðra'tar] *vt* to dehydrate

deshielo *etc* [des'jelo] *vb ver* **deshelar** ▷ *nm* thaw

deshinchar [desin'tʃar] *vt* (*neumático*) to let down; (*herida etc*) to reduce (the swelling of); **deshincharse** *vr* (*neumático*) to go flat; (*hinchazón*) to go down

deshonesto, -a [deso'nesto, a] *adj* (*no honrado*) dishonest; (*indecente*) indecent

deshonra [de'sonra] *nf* (*deshonor*) dishonour; (*vergüenza*) shame

deshonrar [deson'rar] *vt* to dishonour

deshora [de'sora]: **a ~** *adv* at the wrong time; (*llegar*) unexpectedly; (*acostarse*) at some unearthly hour

deshuesadero [deswesa'ðero] *nm* (*Am*) junkyard

deshuesar [deswe'sar] *vt* (*carne*) to bone; (*fruta*) to stone

desierto, -a [de'sjerto, a] *adj* (*casa, calle, negocio*) deserted; (*paisaje*) bleak ▷ *nm* desert
designar [desiɣ'nar] *vt* (*nombrar*) to designate; (*indicar*) to fix
designio [de'siɣnjo] *nm* plan; **con el ~ de** with the intention of
desigual [desi'ɣwal] *adj* (*lucha*) unequal; (*diferente*) different; (*terreno*) uneven; (*tratamiento*) unfair; (*cambiadizo: tiempo*) changeable; (*: carácter*) unpredictable
desigualdad [desiɣwal'ðað] *nf* (*Econ, Pol*) inequality; (*de carácter, tiempo*) unpredictability; (*de escritura*) unevenness; (*de terreno*) roughness
desilusión [desilu'sjon] *nf* disillusionment; (*decepción*) disappointment
desilusionar [desilusjo'nar] *vt* to disillusion; (*decepcionar*) to disappoint; **desilusionarse** *vr* to become disillusioned
desinfectar [desinfek'tar] *vt* to disinfect
desinflar [desin'flar] *vt* to deflate; **desinflarse** *vr* (*neumático*) to go down *o* flat
desintegración [desinteɣra'θjon] *nf* disintegration; **~ nuclear** nuclear fission
desinterés [desinte'res] *nm* (*desgana*) lack of interest; (*altruismo*) unselfishness
desintoxicación [desintoksika'θjon] *nf* detox
desintoxicar [desintoksi'kar] *vt* to detoxify; **desintoxicarse** *vr* (*drogadicto*) to undergo detoxification; **~se de** (*rutina, trabajo*) to get away from
desistir [desis'tir] *vi* (*renunciar*) to stop, desist; **~ de** (*empresa*) to give up; (*derecho*) to waive
desleal [desle'al] *adj* (*infiel*) disloyal; (*Com: competencia*) unfair
deslealtad [desleal'tað] *nf* disloyalty
desleír [desle'ir] *vt* (*líquido*) to dilute; (*sólido*) to dissolve
deslenguado, -a [deslen'gwaðo, a] *adj* (*grosero*) foul-mouthed
desligar [desli'ɣar] *vt* (*desatar*) to untie, undo; (*separar*) to separate; **desligarse** *vr* (*de un compromiso*) to extricate o.s.
desliz [des'liθ] *nm* (*fig*) lapse; **~ de lengua** slip of the tongue; **cometer un ~** to slip up
deslizar [desli'θar] *vt* to slip, slide; **deslizarse** *vr* (*escurrirse: persona*) to slip, slide; (*: coche*) to skid; (*aguas mansas*) to flow gently; (*error*) to creep in; (*tiempo*) to pass; (*persona: irse*) to slip away; **~se en un cuarto** to slip into a room
deslucido, -a [deslu'θiðo, a] *adj* dull; (*torpe*) awkward, graceless; (*deslustrado*) tarnished; (*fracasado*) unsuccessful; **quedar ~** to make a poor impression
deslucir [deslu'θir] *vt* (*deslustrar*) to tarnish; (*estropear*) to spoil, ruin; (*persona*) to discredit; **la lluvia deslució el acto** the rain ruined the ceremony
deslumbrar [deslum'brar] *vt* (*con la luz*) to dazzle; (*cegar*) to blind; (*impresionar*) to dazzle; (*dejar perplejo a*) to puzzle, confuse
desmadrarse [desma'ðrarse] *vr* (*fam: descontrolarse*) to run wild; (*divertirse*) to let one's hair down
desmadre [des'maðre] *nm* (*fam: desorganización*) chaos; (*: jaleo*) commotion
desmán [des'man] *nm* (*exceso*) outrage; (*abuso de poder*) abuse
desmandarse [desman'darse] *vr* (*portarse mal*) to behave badly; (*excederse*) to get out of hand; (*caballo*) to bolt
desmano [des'mano]: **a ~** *adv*: **me coge** *o* **pilla a ~** it's out of my way
desmantelar [desmante'lar] *vt* (*deshacer*) to dismantle; (*casa*) to strip; (*organización*) to disband; (*Mil*) to raze; (*andamio*) to take down; (*Naut*) to unrig
desmaquillador [desmakiʎa'ðor] *nm* make-up remover
desmaquillarse [desmaki'ʎarse] *vr* to take off one's make-up
desmarcarse [desmar'karse] *vr*: **~ de** (*Deporte*) to get clear of; (*fig*) to distance o.s. from
desmayado, -a [desma'jaðo, a] *adj* (*sin sentido*) unconscious; (*carácter*) dull; (*débil*) faint, weak; (*color*) pale
desmayar [desma'jar] *vi* to lose heart; **desmayarse** *vr* (*Med*) to faint
desmayo [des'majo] *nm* (*Med: acto*) faint; (*estado*) unconsciousness; (*depresión*) dejection; (*de voz*) faltering; **sufrir un ~** to have a fainting fit
desmedido, -a [desme'ðiðo, a] *adj* excessive; (*ambición*) boundless
desmejorar [desmexo'rar] *vt* (*dañar*) to impair, spoil; (*Med*) to weaken
desmembrar [desmem'brar] *vt* (*Med*) to dismember; (*fig*) to separate
desmemoriado, -a [desmemo'rjaðo, a] *adj* forgetful, absent-minded
desmentir [desmen'tir] *vt* (*contradecir*) to contradict; (*refutar*) to deny; (*rumor*) to scotch ▷ *vi*: **~ de** to refute; **desmentirse** *vr* to contradict o.s.
desmenuzar [desmenu'θar] *vt* (*deshacer*) to crumble; (*carne*) to chop; (*examinar*) to examine closely
desmerecer [desmere'θer] *vt* to be unworthy of ▷ *vi* (*deteriorarse*) to deteriorate
desmesurado, -a [desmesu'raðo, a] *adj* (*desmedido*) disproportionate; (*enorme*) enormous; (*ambición*) boundless; (*descarado*) insolent
desmontable [desmon'taβle] *adj* (*que se quita*) detachable; (*en compartimientos*) sectional; (*que se puede plegar etc*) collapsible, folding
desmontar [desmon'tar] *vt* (*deshacer*) to dismantle; (*motor*) to strip down; (*máquina*) to take apart; (*escopeta*) to uncock; (*tienda de campaña*) to take down; (*tierra*) to level; (*quitar los árboles a*) to clear; (*jinete*) to throw ▷ *vi* to dismount
desmoralizar [desmorali'θar] *vt* to demoralize

desmoronar [desmoro'nar] *vt* to wear away, erode; **desmoronarse** *vr* (*edificio, dique*) to collapse; (*economía*) to decline

desnatado, -a [desna'taðo, a] *adj* skimmed; (*yogur*) low-fat

desnivel [desni'βel] *nm* (*de terreno*) unevenness; (*Pol*) inequality; (*diferencia*) difference

desnudar [desnu'ðar] *vt* (*desvestir*) to undress; (*despojar*) to strip; **desnudarse** *vr* (*desvestirse*) to get undressed

desnudez [desnu'ðeθ] *nf* (*de persona*) nudity; (*fig*) bareness

desnudo, -a [des'nuðo, a] *adj* (*cuerpo*) naked; (*árbol, brazo*) bare; (*paisaje*) flat; (*estilo*) unadorned; (*verdad*) plain ▷ *nm/f* nude; **~ de** devoid *o* bereft of; **la retrató al ~** he painted her in the nude; **poner al ~** to lay bare

desnutrición [desnutri'θjon] *nf* malnutrition

desnutrido, -a [desnu'triðo, a] *adj* undernourished

desobedecer [desoβeðe'θer] *vt, vi* to disobey

desobediencia [desoβe'ðjenθja] *nf* disobedience

desobediente [desoβe'ðjente] *adj* disobedient

desocupado, -a [desoku'paðo, a] *adj* at leisure; (*desempleado*) unemployed; (*deshabitado*) empty, vacant

desocupar [desoku'par] *vt* to vacate; **desocuparse** *vr* (*quedar libre*) to be free; **se ha desocupado aquella mesa** that table's free now

desodorante [desoðo'rante] *nm* deodorant

desolación [desola'θjon] *nf* (*de lugar*) desolation; (*fig*) grief

desolar [deso'lar] *vt* to ruin, lay waste

desorbitado, -a [desorβi'taðo, a] *adj* (*excesivo: ambición*) boundless; (*deseos*) excessive; (*precio*) exorbitant; **con los ojos ~s** pop-eyed

desorden [de'sorðen] *nm* confusion; (*de casa, cuarto*) mess; (*político*) disorder; **desórdenes** *nmpl* (*alborotos*) disturbances; (*excesos*) excesses; **en ~** (*gente*) in confusion

desordenado, -a [desorðe'naðo, a] *adj* (*habitación, persona*) untidy; (*objetos revueltos*) in a mess, jumbled; (*conducta*) disorderly

desorganización [desorɣaniθa'θjon] *nf* (*de persona*) disorganization; (*en empresa, oficina*) disorder, chaos

desorganizar [desorɣani'θar] *vt* to disorganize

desorientar [desorjen'tar] *vt* (*extraviar*) to mislead; (*confundir, desconcertar*) to confuse; **desorientarse** *vr* (*perderse*) to lose one's way

desovar [deso'βar] *vi* (*peces*) to spawn; (*insectos*) to lay eggs

despabilado, -a [despaβi'laðo, a] *adj* (*despierto*) wide-awake; (*fig*) alert, sharp

despabilar [despaβi'lar] *vt* (*despertar*) to wake up; (*fig: persona*) to liven up; (*trabajo*) to get through quickly ▷ *vi*, **despabilarse** *vr* to wake up; (*fig*) to get a move on

despachar [despa'tʃar] *vt* (*negocio*) to do, complete; (*resolver: problema*) to settle; (*correspondencia*) to deal with; (*fam: comida*) to polish off; (*: bebida*) to knock back; (*enviar*) to send, dispatch; (*vender*) to sell, deal in; (*Com: cliente*) to attend to; (*billete*) to issue; (*mandar ir*) to send away ▷ *vi* (*decidirse*) to get things settled; (*apresurarse*) to hurry up; **despacharse** *vr* to finish off; (*apresurarse*) to hurry up; **~se de algo** to get rid of sth; **~se a su gusto con algn** to give sb a piece of one's mind; **¿quién despacha?** is anybody serving?

despacho [des'patʃo] *nm* (*oficina*) office; (*: en una casa*) study; (*de paquetes*) dispatch; (*Com: venta*) sale (of goods); (*comunicación*) message; **~ de billetes** *o* **boletos** (*Am*) booking office; **~ de localidades** box office; **géneros sin ~** unsaleable goods; **tener buen ~** to find a ready sale

despacio [des'paθjo] *adv* (*lentamente*) slowly; (*esp Am: en voz baja*) softly; **¡~!** take it easy!

desparpajo [despar'paxo] *nm* (*desenvoltura*) self-confidence; (*pey*) nerve

desparramar [desparra'mar] *vt* (*esparcir*) to scatter; (*líquido*) to spill

despavorido, -a [despaβo'riðo, a] *adj* terrified

despecho [des'petʃo] *nm* spite; **a ~ de** in spite of; **por ~** out of (sheer) spite

despectivo, -a [despek'tiβo, a] *adj* (*despreciativo*) derogatory; (*Ling*) pejorative

despedazar [despeða'θar] *vt* to tear to pieces

despedida [despe'ðiða] *nf* (*adiós*) goodbye, farewell; (*antes de viaje*) send-off; (*en carta*) closing formula; (*de obrero*) sacking; (*Inform*) logout; **cena/función de ~** farewell dinner/performance; **regalo de ~** parting gift; **~ de soltero/soltera** stag/hen party

despedir [despe'ðir] *vt* (*visita*) to see off, show out; (*empleado*) to dismiss; (*inquilino*) to evict; (*objeto*) to hurl; (*olor etc*) to give out *o* off; **despedirse** *vr* (*dejar un empleo*) to give up one's job; (*Inform*) to log out *o* off; **~se de** to say goodbye to; **se despidieron** they said goodbye to each other

despegar [despe'ɣar] *vt* to unstick; (*sobre*) to open ▷ *vi* (*avión*) to take off; (*cohete*) to blast off; **despegarse** *vr* to come loose, come unstuck; **sin ~ los labios** without uttering a word

despego [des'peɣo] *nm* detachment

despegue *etc* [des'peɣe] *vb ver* **despegar** ▷ *nm* takeoff; (*de cohete*) blast-off

despeinado, -a [despei'naðo, a] *adj* dishevelled, unkempt

despeinar [despei'nar] *vt* (*pelo*) to ruffle; **¡me has despeinado todo!** you've completely ruined my hairdo!

d

despejado, -a [despe'xaðo, a] *adj* (*lugar*) clear, free; (*cielo*) clear; (*persona*) wide-awake, bright
despejar [despe'xar] *vt* (*gen*) to clear; (*misterio*) to clarify, clear up; (*Mat*: *incógnita*) to find ▷ *vi* (*el tiempo*) to clear; **despejarse** *vr* (*tiempo, cielo*) to clear (up); (*misterio*) to become clearer; (*cabeza*) to clear; **¡despejen!** (*moverse*) move along!; (*salirse*) everybody out!
despellejar [despeʎe'xar] *vt* (*animal*) to skin; (*criticar*) to criticize unmercifully; (*fam*: *arruinar*) to fleece
despenalizar [despenali'θar] *vt* to decriminalize
despensa [des'pensa] *nf* (*armario*) larder; (*Naut*) storeroom; (*provisión de comestibles*) stock of food
despeñadero [despeɲa'ðero] *nm* (*Geo*) cliff, precipice
despeñar [despe'ɲar] *vt* (*arrojar*) to fling down; **despeñarse** *vr* to fling o.s. down; (*caer*) to fall headlong; (*coche*) to tumble over
desperdicio [desper'ðiθjo] *nm* (*despilfarro*) squandering; (*residuo*) waste; **desperdicios** *nmpl* (*basura*) rubbish *sg*, refuse *sg*, garbage *sg* (*US*); (*residuos*) waste *sg*; **~s de cocina** kitchen scraps; **el libro no tiene ~** the book is excellent from beginning to end
desperezarse [despere'θarse] *vr* to stretch
desperfecto [desper'fekto] *nm* (*deterioro*) slight damage; (*defecto*) flaw, imperfection
despertador [desperta'ðor] *nm* alarm clock; **~ de viaje** travelling clock
despertar [desper'tar] *vt* (*persona*) to wake up; (*recuerdos*) to revive; (*esperanzas*) to raise; (*sentimiento*) to arouse ▷ *vi* to awaken, wake up; **despertarse** *vr* to awaken, wake up ▷ *nm* awakening; **~se a la realidad** to wake up to reality
despido *etc* [des'piðo] *vb ver* **despedir** ▷ *nm* dismissal, sacking; **~ improcedente** *o* **injustificado** wrongful dismissal; **~ injusto** unfair dismissal; **~ libre** right to hire and fire; **~ voluntario** voluntary redundancy
despierto, -a [des'pjerto, a] *pp de* **despertar** ▷ *adj* awake; (*fig*) sharp, alert
despilfarrar [despilfa'rrar] *vt* (*gen*) to waste; (*dinero*) to squander
despilfarro [despil'farro] *nm* (*derroche*) squandering; (*lujo desmedido*) extravagance
despistado, -a [despis'taðo, a] *adj* (*distraído*) vague, absent-minded; (*poco práctico*) unpractical; (*confuso*) confused; (*desorientado*) off the track ▷ *nm/f* (*persona distraída*) scatterbrain, absent-minded person
despistar [despis'tar] *vt* to throw off the track *o* scent; (*fig*) to mislead, confuse; **despistarse** *vr* to take the wrong road; (*fig*) to become confused
despiste [des'piste] *nm* (*Auto etc*) swerve; (*error*) slip; (*distracción*) absent-mindedness; **un ~** a mistake *o* slip; **tiene un terrible ~** he's terribly absent-minded
desplazamiento [desplaθa'mjento] *nm* displacement; (*viaje*) journey; (*de opinión, votos*) shift, swing; (*Inform*) scrolling; **~ hacia arriba/abajo** (*Inform*) scroll up/down
desplazar [despla'θar] *vt* (*gen*) to move; (*Física, Naut, Tec*) to displace; (*tropas*) to transfer; (*suplantar*) to take the place of; (*fig*) to oust; (*Inform*) to scroll; **desplazarse** *vr* (*persona, vehículo*) to travel, go; (*objeto*) to move, shift; (*votos, opinión*) to shift, swing
desplegable [desple'ɣable] *adj* (*libro, tb Inform*) pop-up
desplegar [desple'ɣar] *vt* (*tela, papel*) to unfold, open out; (*bandera*) to unfurl; (*alas*) to spread; (*Mil*) to deploy; (*manifestar*) to display
despliegue *etc* [des'pljeɣe] *vb ver* **desplegar** ▷ *nm* unfolding, opening; deployment, display
desplomarse [desplo'marse] *vr* (*edificio, gobierno, persona*) to collapse; (*derrumbarse*) to topple over; (*precios*) to slump; **se ha desplomado el techo** the ceiling has fallen in
desplumar [desplu'mar] *vt* (*ave*) to pluck; (*fam*: *estafar*) to fleece
despoblado, -a [despo'βlaðo, a] *adj* (*sin habitantes*) uninhabited; (*con pocos habitantes*) depopulated; (*con insuficientes habitantes*) underpopulated ▷ *nm* deserted spot
despojar [despo'xar] *vt* (*a alguien*: *de sus bienes*) to divest of, deprive of; (*casa*) to strip, leave bare; (*de su cargo*) to strip of; **despojarse** *vr* (*desnudarse*) to undress; **~se de** (*ropa, hojas*) to shed; (*poderes*) to relinquish
despojo [des'poxo] *nm* (*acto*) plundering; (*objetos*) plunder, loot; **despojos** *nmpl* (*de ave, res*) offal *sg*
desposado, -a [despo'saðo, a] *adj, nm/f* newly-wed
desposar [despo'sar] *vt* (*sacerdote*: *pareja*) to marry; **desposarse** *vr* (*casarse*) to marry, get married
desposeer [despose'er] *vt* (*despojar*) to dispossess; **~ a algn de su autoridad** to strip sb of his authority
déspota ['despota] *nm/f* despot
despotismo [despo'tismo] *nm* despotism
despotricar [despotri'kar] *vi*: **~ contra** to moan *o* complain about
despreciar [despre'θjar] *vt* (*desdeñar*) to despise, scorn; (*afrentar*) to slight
desprecio [des'preθjo] *nm* scorn, contempt; slight
desprender [despren'der] *vt* (*soltar*) to loosen; (*separar*) to separate; (*desatar*) to unfasten; (*olor*) to give off; **desprenderse** *vr* (*botón*: *caerse*) to fall off; (*broche*) to come unfastened; (*olor, perfume*) to be given off; **~se de** to follow from; **~se de algo** (*ceder*) to give sth up; (*desembarazarse*) to get rid of sth; **~se de algo que ...** to draw from sth that ...; **se desprende que ...** it transpires that ...

desprendimiento [desprendi'mjento] *nm* (*gen*) loosening; (*generosidad*) disinterestedness; (*indiferencia*) detachment; (*de gas*) leak; (*de tierra, rocas*) landslide; **~ de retina** detachment of the retina
despreocupado, -a [despreoku'paðo, a] *adj* (*sin preocupación*) unworried, unconcerned; (*tranquilo*) nonchalant; (*en el vestir*) casual; (*negligente*) careless
despreocuparse [despreoku'parse] *vr* to be carefree, not to worry; (*dejar de inquietarse*) to stop worrying; (*ser indiferente*) to be unconcerned; **~ de** to have no interest in
desprestigiar [despresti'xjar] *vt* (*criticar*) to run down, disparage; (*desacreditar*) to discredit
desprevenido, -a [despreβe'niðo, a] *adj* (*no preparado*) unprepared, unready; **coger** (*Esp*) *o* **agarrar a algn ~** (*Am*) to catch sb unawares
desproporcionado, -a [desproporθjo'naðo, a] *adj* disproportionate, out of proportion
desprovisto, -a [despro'βisto, a] *adj*: **~ de** devoid of; **estar ~ de** to lack
después [des'pwes] *adv* afterwards, later; (*desde entonces*) since (then); (*próximo paso*) next; **poco ~** soon after; **un año ~** a year later; **~ se debatió el tema** next the matter was discussed ▷ *prep*: **~ de** (*tiempo*) after, since; (*orden*) next (to); **~ de comer** after lunch; **~ de corregido el texto** after the text had been corrected; **~ de esa fecha** (*pasado*) since that date; (*futuro*) from *o* after that date; **~ de todo** after all; **~ de verlo** after seeing it, after I *etc* saw it; **mi nombre está ~ del tuyo** my name comes next to yours ▷ *conj*: **~ (de) que** after; **~ (de) que lo escribí** after *o* since I wrote it, after writing it
desquiciado, -a [deski'θjaðo, a] *adj* deranged
desquite [des'kite] *nm* (*satisfacción*) satisfaction; (*venganza*) revenge
destacado, -a [desta'kaðo, a] *adj* outstanding
destacar [desta'kar] *vt* (*Arte: hacer resaltar*) to make stand out; (*subrayar*) to emphasize, point up; (*Mil*) to detach, detail; (*Inform*) to highlight ▷ *vi* (*resaltarse*) to stand out; (*persona*) to be outstanding *o* exceptional; **destacarse** *vr* (*resaltarse*) to stand out; (*persona*) to be outstanding *o* exceptional; **quiero ~ que...** I wish to emphasize that...; **~(se) contra** *o* **en** *o* **sobre** to stand out *o* be outlined against
destajo [des'taxo] *nm*: **a ~** (*por pieza*) by the job; (*con afán*) eagerly; **trabajar a ~** to do piecework; (*fig*) to work one's fingers to the bone
destapar [desta'par] *vt* (*botella*) to open; (*cacerola*) to take the lid off; (*descubrir*) to uncover; **destaparse** *vr* (*descubrirse*) to get uncovered; (*revelarse*) to reveal one's true character
destartalado, -a [destarta'laðo, a] *adj* (*desordenado*) untidy; (*casa etc: grande*) rambling; (*: ruinoso*) tumbledown
destello [des'teʎo] *nm* (*de diamante*) sparkle; (*de metal*) glint; (*de estrella*) twinkle; (*de faro*) signal light; **no tiene un ~ de verdad** there's not a grain of truth in it
destemplado, -a [destem'plaðo, a] *adj* (*Mus*) out of tune; (*voz*) harsh; (*Med*) out of sorts; (*Meteorología*) unpleasant, nasty
desteñir [deste'ɲir] *vt* to fade ▷ *vi*, **desteñirse** *vr* to fade; **esta tela no destiñe** this fabric will not run
desternillarse [desterni'ʎarse] *vr*: **~ de risa** to split one's sides laughing
desterrar [deste'rrar] *vt* (*exilar*) to exile; (*fig*) to banish, dismiss
destetar [deste'tar] *vt* to wean
destiempo [des'tjempo]: **a ~** *adv* at the wrong time
destierro *etc* [des'tjerro] *vb ver* **desterrar** ▷ *nm* exile; **vivir en el ~** to live in exile
destilar [desti'lar] *vt* to distil; (*pus, sangre*) to ooze; (*fig: rebosar*) to exude; (*: revelar*) to reveal ▷ *vi* (*gotear*) to drip
destilería [destile'ria] *nf* distillery; **~ de petróleo** oil refinery
destinar [desti'nar] *vt* (*funcionario*) to appoint, assign; (*fondos*) to set aside; **es un libro destinado a los niños** it is a book (intended *o* meant) for children; **una carta que viene destinada a usted** a letter for you, a letter addressed to you
destinatario, -a [destina'tarjo, a] *nm/f* addressee; (*Com*) payee
destino [des'tino] *nm* (*suerte*) destiny; (*de viajero*) destination; (*función*) use; (*puesto*) post, placement; **~ público** public appointment; **salir con ~ a** to leave for; **con ~ a Londres** (*avión, barco*) (bound) for London; (*carta*) to London
destituir [destitu'ir] *vt* (*despedir*) to dismiss; (*: ministro, funcionario*) to remove from office
destornillador [destorniʎa'ðor] *nm* screwdriver
destornillar [destorni'ʎar] *vt* (*tornillo*) to unscrew; **destornillarse** *vr* to unscrew
destreza [des'treθa] *nf* (*habilidad*) skill; (*maña*) dexterity
destrozar [destro'θar] *vt* (*romper*) to smash, break (up); (*estropear*) to ruin; (*nervios*) to shatter; **~ a algn en una discusión** to crush sb in an argument
destrozo [des'troθo] *nm* (*acción*) destruction; (*desastre*) smashing; **destrozos** *nmpl* (*pedazos*) pieces; (*daños*) havoc *sg*
destrucción [destruk'θjon] *nf* destruction
destruir [destru'ir] *vt* to destroy; (*casa*) to demolish; (*equilibrio*) to upset; (*proyecto*) to spoil; (*esperanzas*) to dash; (*argumento*) to demolish
desuso [de'suso] *nm* disuse; **caer en ~** to fall into disuse, become obsolete; **una expresión caída en ~** an obsolete expression
desvalido, -a [desβa'liðo, a] *adj* (*desprotegido*) destitute; (*sin fuerzas*) helpless; **niños ~s** waifs and strays

d

desvalijar [desβali'xar] *vt* (*persona*) to rob; (*casa, tienda*) to burgle; (*coche*) to break into
desván [des'βan] *nm* attic
desvanecer [desβane'θer] *vt* (*disipar*) to dispel; (*recuerdo, temor*) to banish; (*borrar*) to blur; **desvanecerse** *vr* (*humo etc*) to vanish, disappear; (*duda*) to be dispelled; (*color*) to fade; (*recuerdo, sonido*) to fade away; (*Med*) to pass out
desvanecimiento [desβaneθi'mjento] *nm* (*desaparición*) disappearance; (*de dudas*) dispelling; (*de colores*) fading; (*evaporación*) evaporation; (*Med*) fainting fit
desvariar [desβa'rjar] *vi* (*enfermo*) to be delirious; (*delirar*) to talk nonsense
desvarío [desβa'rio] *nm* delirium; (*desatino*) absurdity; **desvaríos** *nmpl* ravings
desvelar [desβe'lar] *vt* to keep awake; **desvelarse** *vr* (*no poder dormir*) to stay awake; (*vigilar*) to be vigilant *o* watchful; **~se por algo** (*inquietarse*) to be anxious about sth; (*poner gran cuidado*) to take great care over sth
desvencijado, -a [desβenθi'xaðo, a] *adj* (*silla*) rickety; (*máquina*) broken-down
desventaja [desβen'taxa] *nf* disadvantage; (*inconveniente*) drawback
desventura [desβen'tura] *nf* misfortune
desvergonzado, -a [desβerɣon'θaðo, a] *adj* (*sin vergüenza*) shameless; (*descarado*) insolent ▷ *nm/f* shameless person
desvergüenza [desβer'ɣwenθa] *nf* (*descaro*) shamelessness; (*insolencia*) impudence; (*mala conducta*) effrontery; **esto es una ~** this is disgraceful; **¡qué ~!** what a nerve!
desvestir [desβes'tir] *vt* to undress; **desvestirse** *vr* to undress
desviación [desβja'θjon] *nf* deviation; (*Auto: rodeo*) diversion, detour; (*: carretera de circunvalación*) ring road (Brit), circular route (US); **~ de la circulación** traffic diversion; **es una ~ de sus principios** it is a departure from his usual principles
desviar [des'βjar] *vt* to turn aside; (*balón, flecha, golpe*) to deflect; (*pregunta*) to parry; (*ojos*) to avert, turn away; (*río*) to alter the course of; (*navío*) to divert, re-route; (*conversación*) to sidetrack; **desviarse** *vr* (*apartarse del camino*) to turn aside; (*: barco*) to go off course; (*Auto: dar un rodeo*) to make a detour; **~se de un tema** to get away from the point
desvío [des'βio] *vb ver* **desviar** ▷ *nm* (*desviación*) detour, diversion; (*fig*) indifference
desvirgar [desβir'ɣar] *vt* to deflower
desvirtuar [desβir'twar] *vt* (*estropear*) to spoil; (*argumento, razonamiento*) to detract from; (*efecto*) to counteract; (*sentido*) to distort; **desvirtuarse** *vr* to spoil
desvitalizar [desβitali'θar] *vt* (*nervio*) to numb
desvivirse [desβi'βirse] *vr*: **~ por** to long for, crave for; **~ por los amigos** to do anything for one's friends
detallar [deta'ʎar] *vt* to detail; (*asunto por asunto*) to itemize
detalle [de'taʎe] *nm* detail; (*fig*) gesture, token; **al ~** in detail; (*Com*) retail *cpd*; **comercio al ~** retail trade; **vender al ~** to sell retail; **no pierde ~** he doesn't miss a trick; **me observaba sin perder ~** he watched my every move; **tiene muchos ~s** she is very considerate
detallista [deta'ʎista] *nm/f* retailer ▷ *adj* (*meticuloso*) meticulous; **comercio ~** retail trade
detectar [detek'tar] *vt* to detect
detective [detek'tiβe] *nm/f* detective; **~ privado** private detective
detector [detek'tor] *nm* (*Naut, Tec etc*) detector; **~ de mentiras/de minas** lie/mine detector
detención [deten'θjon] *nf* (*acción*) stopping; (*estancamiento*) stoppage; (*retraso*) holdup, delay; (*Jur: arresto*) arrest; (*prisión*) detention; (*cuidado*) care; **~ de juego** (*Deporte*) stoppage of play; **~ ilegal** unlawful detention
detener [dete'ner] *vt* (*gen*) to stop; (*Jur: arrestar*) to arrest; (*: encarcelar*) to detain; (*objeto*) to keep; (*retrasar*) to hold up, delay; (*aliento*) to hold; **detenerse** *vr* to stop; **~se en** (*demorarse*) to delay over, linger over
detenidamente [deteniða'mente] *adv* (*minuciosamente*) carefully; (*extensamente*) at great length
detenido, -a [dete'niðo, a] *adj* (*arrestado*) under arrest; (*minucioso*) detailed; (*examen*) thorough; (*tímido*) timid ▷ *nm/f* person under arrest, prisoner
detenimiento [deteni'mjento] *nm* care; **con ~** thoroughly; (*observar, considerar*) carefully
detergente [deter'xente] *adj, nm* detergent
deteriorar [deterjo'rar] *vt* to spoil, damage; **deteriorarse** *vr* to deteriorate
deterioro [dete'rjoro] *nm* deterioration
determinación [determina'θjon] *nf* (*empeño*) determination; (*decisión*) decision; (*de fecha, precio*) settling, fixing
determinado, -a [determi'naðo, a] *adj* (*preciso*) certain; (*Ling: artículo*) definite; (*persona: resuelto*) determined; **un día ~** on a certain day; **no hay ningún tema ~** there is no particular theme
determinar [determi'nar] *vt* (*plazo*) to fix; (*precio*) to settle; (*daños, impuestos*) to assess; (*pleito*) to decide; (*causar*) to cause; **determinarse** *vr* to decide; **el reglamento determina que ...** the rules lay it down *or* state that ...; **aquello determinó la caída del gobierno** that brought about the fall of the government; **esto le determinó** this decided him
detestar [detes'tar] *vt* to detest
detonación [detona'θjon] *nf* detonation; (*sonido*) explosion
detonante [deto'nante] *nm* (*fig*) trigger

detonar [deto'nar] *vi* to detonate

detractor, a [detrak'tor, a] *adj* disparaging ▷ *nm/f* detractor

detrás [de'tras] *adv* (*tb*: **por ~**) behind; (*atrás*) at the back ▷ *prep*: **~ de** behind; **por ~ de algn** (*fig*) behind sb's back; **salir de ~** to come out from behind; **por ~** behind

detrimento [detri'mento] *nm*: **en ~ de** to the detriment of

deuda [de'uða] *nf* (*condición*) indebtedness, debt; (*cantidad*) debt; **~ a largo plazo** long-term debt; **~ exterior/pública** foreign/national debt; **~ incobrable** *o* **morosa** bad debt; **~s activas/pasivas** assets/liabilities; **contraer ~s** to get into debt

deudor, a [deu'ðor, a] *nm/f* debtor; **~ hipotecario** mortgager; **~ moroso** slow payer

devaluación [deβalwa'θjon] *nf* devaluation

devaluar [deβalu'ar] *vt* to devalue

devastar [deβas'tar] *vt* (*destruir*) to devastate

devengar [deβen'gar] *vt* (*salario*: *ganar*) to earn; (*: tener que cobrar*) to be due; (*intereses*) to bring in, accrue, earn

deveras [de'βeras] *nf inv* (*Am*): **un amigo de (a) ~** a true *o* real friend

devoción [deβo'θjon] *nf* devotion; (*afición*) strong attachment

devolución [deβolu'θjon] *nf* (*reenvío*) return, sending back; (*reembolso*) repayment; (*Jur*) devolution

devolver [deβol'βer] *vt* to return; (*lo extraviado, prestado*) to give back; (*a su sitio*) to put back; (*carta al correo*) to send back; (*Com*) to repay, refund; (*visita, la palabra*) to return; (*salud, vista*) to restore; (*fam*: *vomitar*) to throw up ▷ *vi* (*fam*) to be sick; **devolverse** *vr* (*Am*) to return; **~ mal por bien** to return ill for good; **~ la pelota a algn** to give sb tit for tat

devorar [deβo'rar] *vt* to devour; (*comer ávidamente*) to gobble up; (*fig*: *fortuna*) to run through; **todo lo devoró el fuego** the fire consumed everything; **le devoran los celos** he is consumed with jealousy

devoto, -a [de'βoto, a] *adj* (*Rel*: *persona*) devout; (*: obra*) devotional; (*amigo*): **~ (de algn)** devoted (to sb) ▷ *nm/f* admirer; **los devotos** *nmpl* (*Rel*) the faithful; **su muy ~** your devoted servant

devuelto [de'βwelto], **devuelva** *etc* [de'βwelβa] *vb ver* **devolver**

di [di] *vb ver* **dar, decir**

día ['dia] *nm* day; **~ de asueto** day off; **~ feriado** (*Am*) *o* **festivo** (public) holiday; **~ hábil/inhábil** working/non-working day; **~ lunes** (*Am*) Monday; **~ lectivo** teaching day; **~ libre** day off; **D~ de Reyes** Epiphany (*6 January*); **D~ de la Independencia** Independence Day; **¿qué ~ es?** what's the date?; **estar/poner al ~** to be/keep up to date; **el ~ de hoy/de mañana** today/tomorrow; **el ~ menos pensado** when you least expect it; **al ~ siguiente** on the following day; **todos los ~s** every day; **un ~ sí y otro no** every other day; **vivir al ~** to live from hand to mouth; **de ~** during the day, by day; **es de ~** it's daylight; **del ~** (*estilos*) fashionable; (*menú*) today's; **de un ~ para otro** any day now; **en pleno ~** in full daylight; **en su ~** in due time; **¡hasta otro ~!** so long!

diabetes [dja'betes] *nf* diabetes *sg*

diabético, -a [dja'betiko, a] *adj, nm/f* diabetic

diablo ['djaβlo] *nm* (*tb fig*) devil; **pobre ~** poor devil; **hace un frío de todos los ~s** it's hellishly cold

diablura [dja'βlura] *nf* prank; (*travesura*) mischief

diadema [dja'ðema] *nf* (*para el pelo*) Alice band, headband; (*joya*) tiara

diafragma [dja'fraɣma] *nm* diaphragm

diagnosis [djaɣ'nosis] *nf inv*, **diagnóstico** [diaɣ'nostiko] *nm* diagnosis

diagnosticar [djaɣnosti'kar] *vt* to diagnose

diagnóstico [diaɣ'nostiko] *nm* = **diagnosis**

diagonal [djaɣo'nal] *adj* diagonal ▷ *nf* (*Geom*) diagonal; **en ~** diagonally

diagrama [dja'ɣrama] *nm* diagram; **~ de barras** (*Com*) bar chart; **~ de dispersión** (*Com*) scatter diagram; **~ de flujo** (*Inform*) flowchart

dial [di'al] *nm* dial

dialecto [dja'lekto] *nm* dialect

dialogar [djalo'ɣar] *vt* to write in dialogue form ▷ *vi* (*conversar*) to have a conversation; **~ con** (*Pol*) to hold talks with

diálogo ['djaloɣo] *nm* dialogue

diamante [dja'mante] *nm* diamond

diámetro [di'ametro] *nm* diameter; **~ de giro** (*Auto*) turning circle; **faros de gran ~** wide-angle headlights

diana ['djana] *nf* (*Mil*) reveille; (*de blanco*) centre, bull's-eye

diapositiva [djaposi'tiβa] *nf* (*Foto*) slide, transparency

diario, -a ['djarjo, a] *adj* daily ▷ *nm* newspaper; (*libro diario*) diary; (*: Com*) daybook; (*Com*: *gastos*) daily expenses; **~ de navegación** (*Naut*) logbook; **~ hablado** (*Radio*) news (bulletin); **~ de sesiones** parliamentary report; **a ~** daily; **de** *o* **para ~** everyday

diarrea [dja'rrea] *nf* diarrhoea

dibujante [diβu'xante] *nm/f* (*de bosquejos*) sketcher; (*de dibujos animados*) cartoonist; (*de moda*) designer; **~ de publicidad** commercial artist

dibujar [diβu'xar] *vt* to draw, sketch; **dibujarse** *vr* (*emoción*) to show; **~se contra** to be outlined against

dibujo [di'βuxo] *nm* drawing; (*Tec*) design; (*en papel, tela*) pattern; (*en periódico*) cartoon; (*fig*) description; **~s animados** cartoons; **~ del natural** drawing from life

diccionario [dikθjo'narjo] *nm* dictionary

dice *etc vb ver* **decir**

dicho, -a ['ditʃo, a] *pp de* **decir** ▷ *adj* (*susodicho*) aforementioned ▷ *nm* saying; (*proverbio*) proverb; (*ocurrencia*) bright remark ▷ *nf* (*buena suerte*) good luck; **mejor ~** rather; **~ y hecho** no sooner said than done
dichoso, -a [di'tʃoso, a] *adj* (*feliz*) happy; (*afortunado*) lucky; **¡aquel ~ coche!** (*fam*) that blessed car!
diciembre [di'θjembre] *nm* December; *ver tb* **julio**
dictado [dik'taðo] *nm* dictation; **escribir al ~** to take dictation; **los ~s de la conciencia** (*fig*) the dictates of conscience
dictador [dikta'ðor] *nm* dictator
dictadura [dikta'ðura] *nf* dictatorship
dictamen [dik'tamen] *nm* (*opinión*) opinion; (*informe*) report; **~ contable** auditor's report; **~ facultativo** (*Med*) medical report
dictar [dik'tar] *vt* (*carta*) to dictate; (*Jur: sentencia*) to pass; (*decreto*) to issue; (*Am: clase*) to give; (*: conferencia*) to deliver
didáctico, -a [di'ðaktiko, a] *adj* didactic; (*material*) teaching *cpd*; (*juguete*) educational
diecinueve [djeθinu'eβe] *num* nineteen; (*fecha*) nineteenth; *ver tb* **seis**
dieciocho [djeθi'otʃo] *num* eighteen; (*fecha*) eighteenth; *ver tb* **seis**
dieciséis [djeθi'seis] *num* sixteen; (*fecha*) sixteenth; *ver tb* **seis**
diecisiete [djeθi'sjete] *num* seventeen; (*fecha*) seventeenth; *ver tb* **seis**
diente ['djente] *nm* (*Anat, Tec*) tooth; (*Zool*) fang; (*: de elefante*) tusk; (*de ajo*) clove; **~ de león** dandelion; **~s postizos** false teeth; **enseñar los ~s** (*fig*) to show one's claws; **hablar entre ~s** to mutter, mumble; **hincar el ~ en** (*comida*) to bite into
diera *etc* ['djera] *vb ver* **dar**
diesel ['disel] *adj*: **motor ~** diesel engine
diestro, -a ['djestro, a] *adj* (*derecho*) right; (*hábil*) skilful; (*: con las manos*) handy ▷ *nm* (*Taur*) matador ▷ *nf* right hand; **a ~ y siniestro** (*sin método*) wildly
dieta ['djeta] *nf* diet; **dietas** *nfpl* expenses; **estar a ~** to be on a diet
dietético, -a [dje'tetiko, a] *adj* dietetic ▷ *nm/f* dietician ▷ *nf* dietetics *sg*
diez [djeθ] *num* ten; (*fecha*) tenth; **hacer las ~ de últimas** (*Naipes*) to sweep the board; *ver tb* **seis**
diezmar [djeθ'mar] *vt* to decimate
difamación [difama'θjon] *nf* slander; libel
difamar [difa'mar] *vt* (*Jur: hablando*) to slander; (*: por escrito*) to libel
diferencia [dife'renθja] *nf* difference; **a ~ de** unlike; **hacer ~ entre** to make a distinction between; **~ salarial** (*Com*) wage differential
diferenciar [diferen'θjar] *vt* to differentiate between ▷ *vi* to differ; **diferenciarse** *vr* to differ, be different; (*distinguirse*) to distinguish o.s.
diferente [dife'rente] *adj* different
diferido [dife'riðo] *nm*: **en ~** (*TV etc*) recorded
diferir [dife'rir] *vt* to defer
difícil [di'fiθil] *adj* difficult; (*tiempos, vida*) hard; (*situación*) delicate; **es un hombre ~** he's a difficult man to get on with
dificultad [difikul'tað] *nf* difficulty; (*problema*) trouble; (*objeción*) objection
dificultar [difikul'tar] *vt* (*complicar*) to complicate, make difficult; (*estorbar*) to obstruct; **las restricciones dificultan el comercio** the restrictions hinder trade
difundir [difun'dir] *vt* (*calor, luz*) to diffuse; (*Radio*) to broadcast; **difundirse** *vr* to spread (out); **~ una noticia** to spread a piece of news
difunto, a [di'funto, a] *adj* dead, deceased ▷ *nm/f* deceased (person); **el ~** the deceased
difusión [difu'sjon] *nf* (*de calor, luz*) diffusion; (*de noticia, teoría*) dissemination; (*de programa*) broadcasting; (*programa*) broadcast
difuso, -a [di'fuso, a] *adj* (*luz*) diffused; (*conocimientos*) widespread; (*estilo, explicación*) wordy
diga *etc* ['diɣa] *vb ver* **decir**
digerir [dixe'rir] *vt* to digest; (*fig*) to absorb; (*reflexionar sobre*) to think over
digestión [dixes'tjon] *nf* digestion; **corte de ~** indigestion
digestivo, -a [dixes'tiβo, a] *adj* digestive ▷ *nm* (*bebida*) liqueur, digestif
digital [dixi'tal] *adj* (*Inform*) digital; (*dactilar*) finger *cpd* ▷ *nf* (*Bot*) foxglove; (*droga*) digitalis
dignarse [diɣ'narse] *vr* to deign to
dignidad [diɣni'ðað] *nf* dignity; (*honra*) honour; (*rango*) rank; (*persona*) dignitary; **herir la ~ de algn** to hurt sb's pride
digno, -a ['diɣno, a] *adj* worthy; (*persona: honesto*) honourable; **~ de elogio** praiseworthy; **~ de mención** worth mentioning; **es ~ de verse** it is worth seeing; **poco ~** unworthy
digo *etc vb ver* **decir**
dije *etc* ['dixe], **dijera** *etc* [di'xera] *vb ver* **decir**
dilapidar [dilapi'ðar] *vt* to squander, waste
dilatado, -a [dila'taðo, a] *adj* dilated; (*período*) long drawn-out; (*extenso*) extensive
dilatar [dila'tar] *vt* (*gen*) to dilate; (*prolongar*) to prolong; (*aplazar*) to delay; **dilatarse** *vr* (*pupila etc*) to dilate; (*agua*) to expand
dilema [di'lema] *nm* dilemma
diligencia [dili'xenθja] *nf* diligence; (*rapidez*) speed; (*ocupación*) errand, job; (*carruaje*) stagecoach; **diligencias** *nfpl* (*Jur*) formalities; **~s judiciales** judicial proceedings; **~s previas** inquest *sg*
diligente [dili'xente] *adj* diligent; **poco ~** slack
diluir [dilu'ir] *vt* to dilute; (*aguar, fig*) to water down
diluvio [di'luβjo] *nm* deluge, flood; **un ~ de cartas** (*fig*) a flood of letters
dimensión [dimen'sjon] *nf* dimension; **dimensiones** *nfpl* size *sg*; **tomar las**

dimensiones de to take the measurements of

diminutivo [diminu'tiβo] *nm* diminutive

diminuto, -a [dimi'nuto, a] *adj* tiny, diminutive

dimisión [dimi'sjon] *nf* resignation

dimitir [dimi'tir] *vt* (*cargo*) to give up; (*despedir*) to sack ▷ *vi* to resign

dimos ['dimos] *vb ver* **dar**

Dinamarca [dina'marka] *nf* Denmark

dinámico, -a [di'namiko, a] *adj* dynamic ▷ *nf* dynamics *sg*

dinamita [dina'mita] *nf* dynamite

dinamo [di'namo], **dínamo** ['dinamo] *nf, nm en Am* dynamo

dinastía [dinas'tia] *nf* dynasty

dineral [dine'ral] *nm* fortune

dinero [di'nero] *nm* money; (*dinero en circulación*) currency; **~ caro** (*Com*) dear money; **~ contante (y sonante)** hard cash; **~ de curso legal** legal tender; **~ efectivo** *o* **metálico** cash, ready cash; **~ suelto** (loose) change; **es hombre de** he is a man of means; **andar mal de ~** to be short of money; **ganar ~ a espuertas** to make money hand over fist

dinosaurio [dino'saurjo] *nm* dinosaur

dio [djo] *vb ver* **dar**

diócesis ['djoθesis] *nf inv* diocese

dios [djos] *nm* god; **D~** God; **D~ mediante** God willing; **a D~ gracias** thank heaven; **a la buena de D~** any old how; **una de D~ es Cristo** an almighty row; **D~ los cría y ellos se juntan** birds of a feather flock together; **como D~ manda** as is proper; **¡D~ mío!** (oh) my God!; **¡por D~!** for God's sake!

diosa ['djosa] *nf* goddess

diploma [di'ploma] *nm* diploma

diplomacia [diplo'maθja] *nf* diplomacy; (*fig*) tact

diplomado, -a [diplo'maðo, a] *adj* qualified ▷ *nm/f* holder of a diploma; (*Univ*) graduate; *ver tb* **licenciado**

diplomático, -a [diplo'matiko, a] *adj* (*cuerpo*) diplomatic; (*que tiene tacto*) tactful ▷ *nm/f* diplomat

diptongo [dip'tongo] *nm* diphthong

diputación [diputa'θjon] *nf* deputation; (*tb*: **~ provincial**) ≈ county council; **~ permanente** (*Pol*) standing committee

diputado, -a [dipu'taðo, a] *nm/f* delegate; (*Pol*) ≈ member of parliament (*Brit*), ≈ representative (*US*); *ver tb* **Corte**

dique ['dike] *nm* dyke; (*rompeolas*) breakwater; **~ de contención** dam

diré *etc* [di're] *vb ver* **decir**

dirección [direk'θjon] *nf* direction; (*fig: tendencia*) trend; (*señas, tb Inform*) address; (*Auto*) steering; (*gerencia*) management; (*de periódico*) editorship; (*en escuela*) headship; (*Pol*) leadership; (*junta*) board of directors; (*despacho*) director's/manager's/headmaster's/editor's office; **~ administrativa** office management; **~ asistida** power-assisted steering; **D~ General de Seguridad/Turismo** State Security/Tourist Office; **"~ única"** "one-way street"; **"~ prohibida"** "no entry"; **tomar la ~ de una empresa** to take over the running of a company

direccional [direkθjo'nal] *nf* (*Am: Auto*) indicator

directa [di'rekta] *nf* (*Auto*) top gear

directivo, -a [direk'tiβo, a] *adj* (*junta*) managing; (*función*) administrative ▷ *nm/f* (*Com*) manager ▷ *nf* (*norma*) directive; (*tb*: **junta directiva**) board of directors

directo, -a [di'rekto, a] *adj* direct; (*línea*) straight; (*inmediato*) immediate; (*tren*) through; (*TV*) live; **programa en ~** live programme; **transmitir en ~** to broadcast live

director, a [direk'tor, a] *adj* leading ▷ *nm/f* director; (*Escol*) head (teacher) (*Brit*), principal (*US*), (*gerente*) manager/manageress; (*de compañía*) president; (*jefe*) head; (*Prensa*) editor; (*de prisión*) governor; (*Mus*) conductor; **~ adjunto** assistant manager; **~ de cine** film director; **~ comercial** marketing manager; **~ ejecutivo** executive director; **~ de empresa** company director; **~ general** general manager; **~ gerente** managing director; **~ de sucursal** branch manager

directorio [direk'torjo] *nm* (*Inform*) directory; (*Am: telefónico*) phone book

dirigente [diri'xente] *adj* leading ▷ *nm/f* (*Pol*) leader; **los ~s del partido** the party leaders

dirigir [diri'xir] *vt* to direct; (*acusación*) to level; (*carta*) to address; (*obra de teatro, film*) to direct; (*Mus*) to conduct; (*comercio*) to manage; (*expedición*) to lead; (*sublevación*) to head; (*periódico*) to edit; (*guiar*) to guide; **dirigirse** *vr*: **~se a** to go towards, make one's way towards; (*hablar con*) to speak to; **~se a algn solicitando algo** to apply to sb for sth; **"diríjase a ..."** "apply to ..."

dirija *etc* [di'rixa] *vb ver* **dirigir**

discernir [disθer'nir] *vt* to discern ▷ *vi* to distinguish

disciplina [disθi'plina] *nf* discipline

discípulo, -a [dis'θipulo, a] *nm/f* disciple; (*seguidor*) follower; (*Escol*) pupil

Discman® ['diskman] *nm* Discman®, personal CD player

disco ['disko] *nm* disc (*Brit*), disk (*US*); (*Deporte*) discus; (*Telec*) dial; (*Auto: semáforo*) light; (*Mus*) record; (*Inform*) disk; **~ de arranque** boot disk; **~ compacto** compact disc; **~ de densidad sencilla/doble** single/double density disk; **~ de larga duración** long-playing record (LP); **~ flexible** *o* **floppy** floppy disk; **~ de freno** brake disc; **~ maestro** master disk; **~ de reserva** backup

disk; ~ **rígido** hard disk; ~ **de una cara/dos caras** single-/double-sided disk; ~ **virtual** RAMdisk
discográfico, -a [disko'ɣrafiko, a] *adj* record *cpd*; **casa discográfica** record company; **sello** ~ label
disconforme [diskon'forme] *adj* differing; **estar ~ (con)** to be in disagreement (with)
discontinuo, -a [diskon'tinwo, a] *adj* discontinuous; (*Auto*: *línea*) broken
discordia [dis'korðja] *nf* discord
discoteca [disko'teka] *nf* disco(theque)
discreción [diskre'θjon] *nf* discretion; (*reserva*) prudence; **¡a ~!** (*Mil*) stand easy!; **añadir azúcar a** ~ (*Culin*) add sugar to taste; **comer a** ~ to eat as much as one wishes
discrecional [diskreθjo'nal] *adj* (*facultativo*) discretionary; **parada** ~ request stop
discrepancia [diskre'panθja] *nf* (*diferencia*) discrepancy; (*desacuerdo*) disagreement
discrepar [diskre'par] *vi* to disagree
discreto, -a [dis'kreto, a] *adj* (*diplomático*) discreet; (*sensato*) sensible; (*reservado*) quiet; (*sobrio*) sober; (*mediano*) fair, fairly good; **le daremos un plazo** ~ we'll allow him a reasonable time
discriminación [diskrimina'θjon] *nf* discrimination
discriminar [diskrimi'nar] *vt* to discriminate against; (*diferenciar*) to discriminate between
disculpa [dis'kulpa] *nf* excuse; (*pedir perdón*) apology; **pedir ~s a/por** to apologize to/for
disculpar [diskul'par] *vt* to excuse, pardon; **disculparse** *vr* to excuse o.s.; to apologize
discurrir [disku'rrir] *vt* to contrive, think up ▷ *vi* (*pensar, reflexionar*) to think, meditate; (*recorrer*) to roam, wander; (*río*) to flow; (*el tiempo*) to pass, flow by
discurso [dis'kurso] *nm* speech; ~ **de clausura** closing speech; **pronunciar un** ~ to make a speech; **en el ~ del tiempo** with the passage of time
discusión [disku'sjon] *nf* (*diálogo*) discussion; (*riña*) argument; **tener una** ~ to have an argument
discutible [disku'tiβle] *adj* debatable; **de mérito** ~ of dubious worth
discutir [disku'tir] *vt* (*debatir*) to discuss; (*pelear*) to argue about; (*contradecir*) to argue against ▷ *vi* to discuss; (*disputar*) to argue; ~ **de política** to argue about politics; **¡no discutas!** don't argue!
disecar [dise'kar] *vt* (*para conservar*: *animal*) to stuff; (: *planta*) to dry
diseminar [disemi'nar] *vt* to disseminate, spread
disentir [disen'tir] *vi* to dissent, disagree
diseñador, a [diseɲa'dor, a] *nm/f* designer
diseñar [dise'ɲar] *vt, vi* to design
diseño [di'seɲo] *nm* (*Tec*) design; (*Arte*) drawing; (*Costura*) pattern; **de ~ italiano** Italian-designed; ~ **asistido por ordenador** computer-assisted design, CAD
disfraz [dis'fraθ] *nm* (*máscara*) disguise; (*traje*) fancy dress; (*excusa*) pretext; **bajo el ~ de** under the cloak of
disfrazar [disfra'θar] *vt* to disguise; **disfrazarse** *vr* to dress (o.s.) up; **~se de** to disguise o.s. as
disfrutar [disfru'tar] *vt* to enjoy ▷ *vi* to enjoy o.s.; **¡que disfrutes!** have a good time!; ~ **de** to enjoy, possess; ~ **de buena salud** to enjoy good health
disgregar [disɣre'ɣar] *vt* (*desintegrar*) to disintegrate; (*manifestantes*) to disperse; **disgregarse** *vr* to disintegrate, break up
disgustar [disɣus'tar] *vt* (*no gustar*) to displease; (*contrariar, enojar*) to annoy; to upset; **disgustarse** *vr* to get upset; (*dos personas*) to fall out; **estaba muy disgustado con el asunto** he was very upset about the affair
disgusto [dis'ɣusto] *nm* (*repugnancia*) disgust; (*contrariedad*) annoyance; (*desagrado*) displeasure; (*tristeza*) grief; (*riña*) quarrel; (*desgracia*) misfortune; **hacer algo a** ~ to do sth unwillingly; **matar a algn a ~s** to drive sb to distraction
disidente [disi'ðente] *nm* dissident
disimular [disimu'lar] *vt* (*ocultar*) to hide, conceal ▷ *vi* to dissemble
disipar [disi'par] *vt* (*duda, temor*) to dispel; (*esperanza*) to destroy; (*fortuna*) to squander; **disiparse** *vr* (*nubes*) to vanish; (*dudas*) to be dispelled; (*indisciplinarse*) to dissipate
diskette [dis'ket] *nm* (*Inform*) diskette, floppy disk
dislexia [dis'leksja] *nf* dyslexia
dislocar [dislo'kar] *vt* (*gen*) to dislocate; (*tobillo*) to sprain; **dislocarse** *vr* (*articulación*) to sprain, dislocate
disminución [disminu'θjon] *nf* decrease, reduction
disminuido, -a [disminu'iðo, a] *nm/f*: ~ **mental/físico** person with learning difficulties/a physical disability
disminuir [disminu'ir] *vt* to decrease, diminish; (*estrechar*) to lessen; (*temperatura*) to lower; (*gastos, raciones*) to cut down; (*dolor*) to relieve; (*autoridad, prestigio*) to weaken; (*entusiasmo*) to damp ▷ *vi* (*días*) to grow shorter; (*precios, temperatura*) to drop, fall; (*velocidad*) to slacken; (*población*) to decrease; (*beneficios, número*) to fall off; (*memoria, vista*) to fail
disolución [disolu'θjon] *nf* (*acto*) dissolution; (*Química*) solution; (*Com*) liquidation; (*moral*) dissoluteness
disolvente [disol'βente] *nm* solvent, thinner
disolver [disol'βer] *vt* (*gen*) to dissolve; (*manifestación*) to break up; **disolverse** *vr* to dissolve; (*Com*) to go into liquidation
dispar [dis'par] *adj* (*distinto*) different; (*irregular*) uneven

disparar [dispa'rar] *vt, vi* to shoot, fire; **dispararse** *vr* (*arma de fuego*) to go off; (*persona: marcharse*) to rush off; (*: enojarse*) to lose control; (*caballo*) to bolt
disparatado, -a [dispara'taðo, a] *adj* crazy
disparate [dispa'rate] *nm* (*tontería*) foolish remark; (*error*) blunder; **decir ~s** to talk nonsense; **¡qué ~!** how absurd!; **costar un ~** to cost a hell of a lot
disparo [dis'paro] *nm* shot; (*acto*) firing; **disparos** *nmpl* shooting *sg*, exchange *sg* of shots, shots; **~ inicial** (*de cohete*) blast-off
dispensar [dispen'sar] *vt* to dispense; (*ayuda*) to give; (*honores*) to grant; (*disculpar*) to excuse; **¡usted dispense!** I beg your pardon!; **~ a algn de hacer algo** to excuse sb from doing sth
dispersar [disper'sar] *vt* to disperse; (*manifestación*) to break up; **dispersarse** *vr* to scatter
disperso, -a [dis'perso, a] *adj* scattered
disponer [dispo'ner] *vt* (*arreglar*) to arrange; (*ordenar*) to put in order; (*preparar*) to prepare, get ready ▷ *vi*: **~ de** to have, own; **disponerse** *vr*: **~se para** to prepare to, prepare for; **la ley dispone que ...** the law provides that ...; **no puede ~ de esos bienes** she cannot dispose of those properties
disponible [dispo'niβle] *adj* available; (*tiempo*) spare; (*dinero*) on hand
disposición [disposi'θjon] *nf* arrangement, disposition; (*voluntad*) willingness; (*de casa, Inform*) layout; (*ley*) order; (*cláusula*) provision; (*aptitud*) aptitude; **~ de ánimo** attitude of mind; **última ~** last will and testament; **a la ~ de** at the disposal of; **a su ~** at your service
dispositivo [disposi'tiβo] *nm* device, mechanism; **~ de alimentación** hopper; **~ de almacenaje** storage device; **~ periférico** peripheral (device); **~ de seguridad** safety catch; (*fig*) security measure
dispuesto, -a [dis'pwesto, a] *pp de* **disponer** ▷ *adj* (*arreglado*) arranged; (*preparado*) disposed; (*persona: dinámico*) bright; **estar ~/poco ~ a hacer algo** to be inclined/reluctant to do sth
disputa [dis'puta] *nf* (*discusión*) dispute, argument; (*controversia*) controversy
disputar [dispu'tar] *vt* (*discutir*) to dispute, question; (*contender*) to contend for; (*carrera*) to compete in ▷ *vi* to argue
disquete [dis'kete] *nm* (*Inform*) diskette, floppy disk
disquetera [diske'tera] *nf* disk drive
distancia [dis'tanθja] *nf* distance; (*de tiempo*) interval; **~ de parada** braking distance; **~ del suelo** (*Auto etc*) height off the ground; **a gran** *o* **a larga ~** long-distance; **mantenerse a ~** to keep one's distance; (*fig*) to remain aloof; **guardar las ~s** to keep one's distance
distanciar [distan'θjar] *vt* to space out; **distanciarse** *vr* to become estranged
distante [dis'tante] *adj* distant
distar [dis'tar] *vi*: **dista 5 km de aquí** it is 5 km from here; **¿dista mucho?** is it far?; **dista mucho de la verdad** it's very far from the truth
diste ['diste], **disteis** ['disteis] *vb ver* **dar**
distensión [disten'sjon] *nf* distension; (*Pol*) détente; **~ muscular** (*Med*) muscular strain
distinción [distin'θjon] *nf* distinction; (*elegancia*) elegance; (*honor*) honour; **a ~ de** unlike; **sin ~** indiscriminately; **sin ~ de edades** irrespective of age
distinguido, -a [distin'giðo, a] *adj* distinguished; (*famoso*) prominent, well-known; (*elegante*) elegant
distinguir [distin'gir] *vt* to distinguish; (*divisar*) to make out; (*escoger*) to single out; (*caracterizar*) to mark out; **distinguirse** *vr* to be distinguished; (*destacarse*) to distinguish o.s.; **a lo lejos no se distingue** it's not visible from a distance
distintivo, -a [distin'tiβo, a] *adj* distinctive; (*signo*) distinguishing ▷ *nm* (*de policía etc*) badge; (*fig*) characteristic
distinto, -a [dis'tinto, a] *adj* different; (*claro*) clear; **~s** several, various
distorsión [distor'sjon] *nf* (*Anat*) twisting; (*Radio etc*) distortion
distorsionar [distorsjo'nar] *vt, vi* to distort
distracción [distrak'θjon] *nf* distraction; (*pasatiempo*) hobby, pastime; (*olvido*) absent-mindedness, distraction
distraer [distra'er] *vt* (*atención*) to distract; (*divertir*) to amuse; (*fondos*) to embezzle ▷ *vi* to be relaxing; **distraerse** *vr* (*entretenerse*) to amuse o.s.; (*perder la concentración*) to allow one's attention to wander; **~ a algn de su pensamiento** to divert sb from his train of thought; **el pescar distrae** fishing is a relaxation
distraído, -a [distra'iðo, a] *adj* (*gen*) absent-minded; (*desatento*) inattentive; (*entretenido*) amusing ▷ *nm*: **hacerse el ~** to pretend not to notice; **con aire ~** idly; **me miró distraída** she gave me a casual glance
distribuidor, a [distriβui'ðor, a] *nm/f* (*persona: gen*) distributor; (*: Correos*) sorter; (*: Com*) dealer, agent; **su ~ habitual** your regular dealer
distribuir [distriβu'ir] *vt* to distribute; (*prospectos*) to hand out; (*cartas*) to deliver; (*trabajo*) to allocate; (*premios*) to award; (*dividendos*) to pay; (*peso*) to distribute; (*Arq*) to plan
distrito [dis'trito] *nm* (*sector, territorio*) region; (*barrio*) district; **~ electoral** constituency; **~ postal** postal district; **D~ Federal** (*Am*) Federal District
disturbio [dis'turβjo] *nm* disturbance; (*desorden*) riot; **los disturbios** *nmpl* the troubles

disuadir [diswa'ðir] *vt* to dissuade
disuelto [di'swelto] *pp de* **disolver**
disyuntiva [disjun'tiβa] *nf* (*dilema*) dilemma
DIU ['diu] *nm abr* (= *dispositivo intrauterino*) IUD
diurno, -a ['djurno, a] *adj* day *cpd*, diurnal
divagar [diβa'ɣar] *vi* (*desviarse*) to digress
diván [di'βan] *nm* divan
divergencia [diβer'xenθja] *nf* divergence
diversidad [diβersi'ðað] *nf* diversity, variety
diversificar [diβersifi'kar] *vt* to diversify
diversión [diβer'sjon] *nf* (*gen*) entertainment; (*actividad*) hobby, pastime
diverso, -a [di'βerso, a] *adj* diverse; (*diferente*) different ▷ *nm*: **~s** (*Com*) sundries; **~s libros** several books
divertido, -a [diβer'tiðo, a] *adj* (*chiste*) amusing, funny; (*fiesta etc*) enjoyable; (*película, libro*) entertaining; **está ~** (*irónico*) this is going to be fun
divertir [diβer'tir] *vt* (*entretener, recrear*) to amuse, entertain; **divertirse** *vr* (*pasarlo bien*) to have a good time; (*distraerse*) to amuse o.s.
dividendo [diβi'ðendo] *nm* (*Com*) *usu pl* dividend, dividends; **~ definitivo** final dividend; **~s por acción** earnings per share
dividir [diβi'ðir] *vt* (*gen*) to divide; (*separar*) to separate; (*distribuir*) to distribute, share out
divierta *etc* [di'βjerta] *vb ver* **divertir**
divino, -a [di'βino, a] *adj* divine; (*fig*) lovely
divirtiendo *etc* [diβir'tjendo] *vb ver* **divertir**
divisa [di'βisa] *nf* (*emblema*) emblem, badge; **divisas** *nfpl* currency *sg*; (*Com*) foreign exchange *sg*; **control de ~s** exchange control; **~ de reserva** reserve currency
divisar [diβi'sar] *vt* to make out, distinguish
división [diβi'sjon] *nf* division; (*de partido*) split; (*de país*) partition
divorciado, -a [diβor'θjaðo, a] *adj* divorced; (*opinión*) split ▷ *nm/f* divorcé(e)
divorciar [diβor'θjar] *vt* to divorce; **divorciarse** *vr* to get divorced
divorcio [di'βorθjo] *nm* divorce; (*fig*) split
divulgar [diβul'ɣar] *vt* (*desparramar*) to spread; (*popularizar*) to popularize; (*hacer circular*) to divulge, circulate; **divulgarse** *vr* (*secreto*) to leak out; (*rumor*) to get about
DNI *nm abr* (*Esp*) = **Documento Nacional de Identidad**

DNI

The *Documento Nacional de Identidad* is a Spanish ID card which must be carried at all times and produced on request for the police. It contains the holder's photo, fingerprints and personal details. It is also known as the *DNI* or *carnet de identidad*.

Dña. *abr* (= *Doña*) Mrs
do [do] *nm* (*Mus*) C
dobladillo [doβla'ðiʎo] *nm* (*de vestido*) hem; (*de pantalón: vuelta*) turn-up (*Brit*), cuff (*US*)
doblaje [do'βlaxe] *nm* (*Cine*) dubbing
doblar [do'βlar] *vt* to double; (*papel*) to fold; (*caño*) to bend; (*la esquina*) to turn, go round; (*film*) to dub ▷ *vi* to turn; (*campana*) to toll; **doblarse** *vr* (*plegarse*) to fold (up), crease; (*encorvarse*) to bend; **~ a la derecha/izquierda** to turn right/left
doble ['doβle] *adj* (*gen*) double; (*de dos aspectos*) dual; (*cuerda*) thick; (*fig*) two-faced ▷ *nm* double ▷ *nm/f* (*Teat*) double, stand-in; **dobles** *nmpl* (*Deporte*) doubles *sg*; **~ o nada** double or quits; **~ página** double-page spread; **con ~ sentido** with a double meaning; **el ~** twice the quantity *o* as much; **su sueldo es el ~ del mío** his salary is twice (as much as) mine; (*Inform*): **~ cara** double-sided; **~ densidad** double density; **~ espacio** double spacing
doblegar [doβle'ɣar] *vt* to fold, crease; **doblegarse** *vr* to yield
doblez [do'βleθ] *nm* (*pliegue*) fold, hem ▷ *nf* (*falsedad*) duplicity
doce ['doθe] *num* twelve; (*fecha*) twelfth; **las ~** twelve o'clock; *ver tb* **seis**
docena [do'θena] *nf* dozen; **por ~s** by the dozen
docente [do'θente] *adj*: **personal ~** teaching staff; **centro ~** educational institution
dócil ['doθil] *adj* (*pasivo*) docile; (*manso*) gentle; (*obediente*) obedient
doctor, a [dok'tor, a] *nm/f* doctor; **~ en filosofía** Doctor of Philosophy
doctorado [dokto'raðo] *nm* doctorate
doctrina [dok'trina] *nf* doctrine, teaching
documentación [dokumenta'θjon] *nf* documentation; (*de identidad etc*) papers *pl*
documental [dokumen'tal] *adj, nm* documentary
documentar [dokumen'tar] *vt* to document; **documentarse** *vr* to gather information
documento [doku'mento] *nm* (*certificado*) document; (*Jur*) exhibit; **documentos** *nmpl* papers; **~ adjunto** (*Inform*) attachment; **~ justificativo** voucher; **D~ Nacional de Identidad** national identity card; *ver* **DNI**
dogma ['doɣma] *nm* dogma
dogmático, -a [doɣ'matiko, a] *adj* dogmatic
dólar ['dolar] *nm* dollar
doler [do'ler] *vt, vi* to hurt; (*fig*) to grieve; **dolerse** *vr* (*de su situación*) to grieve, feel sorry; (*de las desgracias ajenas*) to sympathize; (*quejarse*) to complain; **me duele el brazo** my arm hurts; **no me duele el dinero** I don't mind about the money; **¡ahí le duele!** you've put your finger on it!
dolor [do'lor] *nm* pain; (*fig*) grief, sorrow; **~ de cabeza** headache; **~ de estómago** stomach ache; **~ de oídos** earache; **~ sordo** dull ache
dolorido, -a [dolo'riðo, a] *adj* (*Med*) sore; **la parte dolorida** the part which hurts
doloroso, -a [dolo'roso, a] *adj* (*Med*) painful; (*fig*) distressing

domar [do'mar] *vt* to tame
domesticar [domesti'kar] *vt* to tame
doméstico, -a [do'mestiko, a] *adj* domestic; (*vida, servicio*) home; (*tareas*) household; (*animal*) tame, pet ▷ *nm/f* servant; **economía doméstica** home economy; **gastos ~s** household expenses
domiciliación [domiθilja'θjon] *nf*: **~ de pagos** (*Com*) direct debit
domiciliar [domiθi'ljar] *vt* to domicile; **domiciliarse** *vr* to take up (one's) residence
domicilio [domi'θiljo] *nm* home; **~ particular** private residence; **~ social** (*Com*) head office, registered office; **servicio a ~** delivery service; **sin ~ fijo** of no fixed abode
dominante [domi'nante] *adj* dominant; (*persona*) domineering
dominar [domi'nar] *vt* (*gen*) to dominate; (*países*) to rule over; (*adversario*) to overpower; (*caballo, nervios, emoción*) to control; (*incendio, epidemia*) to bring under control; (*idiomas*) to be fluent in ▷ *vi* to dominate, prevail; **dominarse** *vr* to control o.s.
domingo [do'mingo] *nm* Sunday; **D~ de Ramos** Palm Sunday; **D~ de Resurrección** Easter Sunday; *ver tb* **sábado**; **Semana Santa**
dominguero, -a [domin'gero, a] *adj* Sunday *cpd*
dominical [domini'kal] *adj* Sunday *cpd*; **periódico ~** Sunday newspaper
dominicano, -a [domini'kano, a] *adj, nm/f* Dominican
dominio [do'minjo] *nm* (*tierras*) domain; (*Pol*) dominion; (*autoridad*) power, authority; (*supremacía*) supremacy; (*de las pasiones*) grip, hold; (*de idioma*) command; **ser del ~ público** to be widely known
don [don] *nm* (*talento*) gift; **D~ Juan Gómez** Mr Juan Gómez, Juan Gómez Esq. (*Brit*); **tener ~ de gentes** to know how to handle people; **~ de lenguas** gift for languages; **~ de mando** (qualities of) leadership; **~ de palabra** gift of the gab; *see note*

DON

Don or *doña* is a term used before someone's first name – eg Don Diego, Doña Inés – when showing respect or being polite to someone of a superior social standing or to an older person. It is becoming somewhat rare, but it does however continue to be used with names and surnames in official documents and in correspondence: eg Sr. D. Pedro Rodríguez Hernández, Sra. Dña Inés Rodríguez Hernández.

dona ['dona] *nf* (*Am*) doughnut, donut (*US*)
donación [dona'θjon] *nf* donation
donaire [do'naire] *nm* charm
donante [do'nante] *nm/f* donor; **~ de sangre** blood donor
donar [do'nar] *vt* to donate
donativo [dona'tiβo] *nm* donation
doncella [don'θeʎa] *nf* (*criada*) maid
donde ['donde] *adv* where ▷ *prep*: **el coche está allí ~ el farol** the car is over there by the lamppost *o* where the lamppost is; **por ~** through which; **a ~** to where, to which; **en ~** where, in which; **es a ~ vamos nosotros** that's where we're going
dónde ['donde] *adv interrogativo* where?; **¿a ~ vas?** where are you going (to)?; **¿de ~ vienes?** where have you been?; **¿en ~?** where?; **¿por ~?** where?, whereabouts?; **¿por ~ se va al estadio?** how do you get to the stadium?
dondequiera [donde'kjera] *adv* anywhere ▷ *conj*: **~ que** wherever; **por ~** everywhere, all over the place
donut® [do'nut] *nm* (*Esp*) doughnut, donut (*US*)
doña ['doɲa] *nf*: **~ Alicia** Alicia; **D~ Carmen Gómez** Mrs Carmen Gómez; *ver tb* **don**
dopar [do'par] *vt* to dope, drug
doping ['dopin] *nm* doping, drugging
dorado, -a [do'raðo, a] *adj* (*color*) golden; (*Tec*) gilt
dorar [do'rar] *vt* (*Tec*) to gild; (*Culin*) to brown, cook lightly; **~ la píldora** to sweeten the pill
dormir [dor'mir] *vt*: **~ la siesta** to have an afternoon nap ▷ *vi* to sleep; **dormirse** *vr* (*persona, brazo, pierna*) to fall asleep; **~la** (*fam*) to sleep it off; **~ la mona** (*fam*) to sleep off a hangover; **~ como un lirón** *o* **tronco** to sleep like a log; **~ a pierna suelta** to sleep soundly
dormitar [dormi'tar] *vi* to doze
dormitorio [dormi'torjo] *nm* bedroom; **~ común** dormitory
dorsal [dor'sal] *adj* dorsal ▷ *nm* (*Deporte*) number
dorso ['dorso] *nm* (*de mano*) back; (*de hoja*) other side; **escribir algo al ~** to write sth on the back; **"véase al ~"** "see other side", "please turn over"
dos [dos] *num* two; (*fecha*) second; **los ~** the two of them, both of them; **cada ~ por tres** every five minutes; **de ~ en ~** in twos; **estamos a ~** (*Tenis*) the score is deuce; *ver tb* **seis**
doscientos, -as [dos'θjentos, as] *num* two hundred
dosis ['dosis] *nf inv* dose, dosage
dossier [do'sjer] *nm* dossier, file
dotado, -a [do'taðo, a] *adj* gifted; **~ de** (*persona*) endowed with; (*máquina*) equipped with
dotar [do'tar] *vt* to endow; (*Tec*) to fit; (*barco*) to man; (*oficina*) to staff
dote ['dote] *nf* (*de novia*) dowry; **dotes** *nfpl* (*talentos*) gifts
doy [doj] *vb ver* **dar**
dragón [dra'ɣon] *nm* dragon

d

drama ['drama] *nm* drama; (*obra*) play
dramático, -a [dra'matiko, a] *adj* dramatic ▷ *nm/f* dramatist; (*actor*) actor; **obra dramática** play
dramaturgo, -a [drama'turɣo, a] *nm/f* dramatist, playwright
drástico, -a ['drastiko, a] *adj* drastic
drenaje [dre'naxe] *nm* drainage
droga ['droɣa] *nf* drug; (*Deporte*) dope; **el problema de la ~** the drug problem
drogadicto, -a [droɣa'ðikto, a] *nm/f* drug addict
drogar [dro'ɣar] *vt* to drug; (*Deporte*) to dope; **drogarse** *vr* to take drugs
drogodependencia [droɣoðepen'denθja] *nf* drug addiction
droguería [droɣe'ria] *nf* ≈ hardware shop (*Brit*) *o* store (*US*)
dromedario [drome'ðarjo] *nm* dromedary
ducha ['dutʃa] *nf* (*baño*) shower; (*Med*) douche
ducharse [du'tʃarse] *vr* to take a shower
duda ['duða] *nf* doubt; **sin ~** no doubt, doubtless; **¡sin ~!** of course!; **no cabe ~** there is no doubt about it; **no le quepa ~** make no mistake about it; **no quiero poner en ~ su conducta** I don't want to call his behaviour into question; **sacar a algn de la ~** to settle sb's doubts; **tengo una ~** I have a query
dudar [du'ðar] *vt* to doubt ▷ *vi* to doubt, have doubts; **~ acerca de algo** to be uncertain about sth; **dudó en comprarlo** he hesitated to buy it; **dudan que sea verdad** they doubt whether *o* if it's true
dudoso, -a [du'ðoso, a] *adj* (*incierto*) hesitant; (*sospechoso*) doubtful; (*conducta*) dubious
duela *etc vb ver* **doler**
duelo ['dwelo] *vb ver* **doler** ▷ *nm* (*combate*) duel; (*luto*) mourning; **batirse en ~** to fight a duel
duende ['dwende] *nm* imp, goblin; **tiene ~** he's got real soul
dueño, -a ['dweɲo, a] *nm/f* (*propietario*) owner; (*de pensión, taberna*) landlord(-lady); (*de casa, perro*) master/mistress; (*empresario*) employer; **ser ~ de sí mismo** to have self-control; (*libre*) to be one's own boss; **eres ~ de hacer como te parezca** you're free to do as you think fit; **hacerse ~ de una situación** to take command of a situation
duerma *etc* ['dwerma] *vb ver* **dormir**
dulce ['dulθe] *adj* sweet; (*carácter, clima*) gentle, mild ▷ *adv* gently, softly ▷ *nm* sweet
dulcería [dulθe'ria] *nf* (*Am*) confectioner's (shop)
dulzón, -ona [dul'θon, ona] *adj* (*alimento*) sickly-sweet, too sweet; (*canción etc*) gooey
dulzura [dul'θura] *nf* sweetness; (*ternura*) gentleness
duna ['duna] *nf* dune
dúo ['duo] *nm* duet, duo
duodécimo, -a [duo'deθimo, a] *adj* twelfth; *ver tb* **sexto, a**
dúplex ['dupleks] *nm inv* (*piso*) duplex (apartment); (*Telec*) link-up; (*Inform*): **~ integral** full duplex
duplicar [dupli'kar] *vt* (*hacer el doble de*) to duplicate; (*cantidad*) to double; **duplicarse** *vr* to double
duque ['duke] *nm* duke
duquesa [du'kesa] *nf* duchess
durable [du'raβle] *adj* durable
duración [dura'θjon] *nf* (*de película, disco etc*) length; (*de pila etc*) life; (*curso: de acontecimientos etc*) duration; **~ media de la vida** average life expectancy; **de larga ~** (*enfermedad*) lengthy; (*pila*) long-life; (*disco*) long-playing; **de poca ~** short
duradero, -a [dura'ðero, a] *adj* (*tela*) hard-wearing; (*fe, paz*) lasting
durante [du'rante] *adv* during; **~ toda la noche** all night long; **habló ~ una hora** he spoke for an hour
durar [du'rar] *vi* (*permanecer*) to last; (*recuerdo*) to remain; (*ropa*) to wear (well)
durazno [du'rasno] *nm* (*Am: fruta*) peach; (*: árbol*) peach tree
durex ['dureks] *nm* (*Am: tira adhesiva*) Sellotape® (*Brit*), Scotch tape® (*US*)
dureza [du'reθa] *nf* (*cualidad*) hardness; (*de carácter*) toughness
durmiente [dur'mjente] *adj* sleeping ▷ *nm/f* sleeper
duro, -a ['duro, a] *adj* hard; (*carácter*) tough; (*pan*) stale; (*cuello, puerta*) stiff; (*clima, luz*) harsh ▷ *adv* hard ▷ *nm* (*moneda*) five peseta coin; **el sector ~ del partido** the hardliners *pl* in the party; **ser ~ con algn** to be tough with *o* hard on sb; **~ de mollera** (*torpe*) dense; **~ de oído** hard of hearing; **trabajar ~** to work hard; **estar sin un ~** to be broke
DVD *nm abr* (*= disco de vídeo digital*) DVD

e

E *abr* (= *este*) E
e [e] *conj* (*delante de* **i-** *e* **hi-** *pero no* **hie-**) and; *ver tb* **y**
ebanista [eβa'nista] *nm/f* cabinetmaker
ébano ['eβano] *nm* ebony
e-book ['ibuk] *nm* e-book
ebrio, -a ['eβrjo, a] *adj* drunk
ebullición [eβuʎi'θjon] *nf* boiling; **punto de ~** boiling point
e-card ['ikard] *nf* e-card
eccema [ek'θema] *nm* (*Med*) eczema
echar [e'tʃar] *vt* to throw; (*agua, vino*) to pour (out); (*Culin*) to put in, add; (*dientes*) to cut; (*discurso*) to give; (*empleado: despedir*) to fire, sack; (*hojas*) to sprout; (*cartas*) to post; (*humo*) to emit, give out; (*reprimenda*) to deal out; (*cuenta*) to make up; (*freno*) to put on ▷ *vi*: **~ a correr** to start running *o* to run, break into a run; **~ a llorar** to burst into tears; **~ a reír** to burst out laughing; **echarse** *vr* to lie down; **~ llave a** to lock (up); **~ abajo** (*gobierno*) to overthrow; (*edificio*) to demolish; **~ mano a** to lay hands on; **~ una mano a algn** (*ayudar*) to give sb a hand; **~ la buenaventura a algn** to tell sb's fortune; **~ la culpa a** to lay the blame on; **~ de menos** to miss; **~ una mirada** to give a look; **~ sangre** to bleed; **~se atrás** to throw o.s. back(wards); (*fig*) to back out; **~se una novia** to get o.s. a girlfriend; **~se una siestecita** to have a nap
eclesiástico, -a [ekle'sjastiko, a] *adj* ecclesiastical; (*autoridades etc*) church *cpd* ▷ *nm* clergyman
eclipsar [eklip'sar] *vt* to eclipse; (*fig*) to outshine, overshadow
eclipse [e'klipse] *nm* eclipse
eco ['eko] *nm* echo; **encontrar un ~ en** to produce a response from; **hacerse ~ de una opinión** to echo an opinion; **tener ~** to catch on
ecografía [ekoɣra'fia] *nf* ultrasound
ecología [ekolo'xia] *nf* ecology
ecológico, -a [eko'loxiko, a] *adj* ecological; (*producto, método*) environmentally-friendly; (*agricultura*) organic
ecologista [ekolo'xista] *adj* environmental, conservation *cpd* ▷ *nm/f* environmentalist
economato [ekono'mato] *nm* cooperative store
economía [ekono'mia] *nf* (*sistema*) economy; (*carrera*) economics; (*cualidad*) thrift; **~ dirigida** planned economy; **~ doméstica** housekeeping; **~ de mercado** market economy; **~ mixta** mixed economy; **~ sumergida** black economy; **hacer ~s** to economize; **~s de escala** economies of scale
económico, -a [eko'nomiko, a] *adj* (*barato*) cheap, economical; (*persona*) thrifty; (*Com: año etc*) financial; (*: situación*) economic
economista [ekono'mista] *nm/f* economist
ecosistema [ekosis'tema] *nm* ecosystem
ecu ['eku] *nm* ecu
ecuación [ekwa'θjon] *nf* equation
Ecuador [ekwa'ðor] *nm* Ecuador
ecuador [ekwa'ðor] *nm* equator
ecuánime [e'kwanime] *adj* (*carácter*) level-headed; (*estado*) calm
ecuatoriano, -a [ekwato'rjano, a] *adj, nm/f* Ecuador(i)an
ecuestre [e'kwestre] *adj* equestrian
eczema [ek'θema] *nm* = **eccema**
edad [e'ðað] *nf* age; **¿qué ~ tienes?** how old are you?; **tiene ocho años de ~** he is eight (years old); **de ~ corta** young; **ser de ~ mediana/avanzada** to be middle-aged/getting on; **ser mayor de ~** to be of age; **llegar a mayor ~** to come of age; **ser menor de ~** to be under age; **la E~ Media** the Middle Ages; **la E~ de Oro** the Golden Age
edición [eði'θjon] *nf* (*acto*) publication; (*ejemplar*) edition; **"al cerrar la ~"** (*Tip*) "stop press"
edicto [e'ðikto] *nm* edict, proclamation
edificar [edifi'kar] *vt, vi* (*Arq*) to build
edificio [eði'fiθjo] *nm* building; (*fig*) edifice, structure
Edimburgo [eðim'burɣo] *nm* Edinburgh
editar [eði'tar] *vt* (*publicar*) to publish; (*preparar textos, tb Inform*) to edit
editor, a [eði'tor, a] *nm/f* (*que publica*) publisher; (*redactor*) editor ▷ *adj*: **casa ~a** publishing company

editorial [eðito'rjal] *adj* editorial ▷ *nm* leading article, editorial; (*tb*: **casa ~**) publisher

edredón [eðre'ðon] *nm* eiderdown, quilt; **~ nórdico** continental quilt, duvet

educación [eðuka'θjon] *nf* education; (*crianza*) upbringing; (*modales*) (good) manners *pl*; (*formación*) training; **sin ~** ill-mannered; **¡qué falta de ~!** how rude!

educado, -a [eðu'kaðo, a] *adj* well-mannered; **mal ~** ill-mannered

educar [eðu'kar] *vt* to educate; (*criar*) to bring up; (*voz*) to train

educativo, -a [eðuka'tiβo, a] *adj* educational; (*política*) education *cpd*

EE.UU. *nmpl abr* (= *Estados Unidos*) USA

efectista [efek'tista] *adj* sensationalist

efectivamente [efektiβa'mente] *adv* (*como respuesta*) exactly, precisely; (*verdaderamente*) really; (*de hecho*) in fact

efectivo, -a [efek'tiβo, a] *adj* effective; (*real*) actual, real ▷ *nm*: **pagar en ~** to pay (in) cash; **hacer ~ un cheque** to cash a cheque

efecto [e'fekto] *nm* effect, result; (*objetivo*) purpose, end; **efectos** *nmpl* (*personales*) effects; (*bienes*) goods; (*Com*) assets; (*Econ*) bills, securities; **~ 2000** millennium bug; **~ invernadero** greenhouse effect; **~s de consumo** consumer goods; **~s a cobrar** bills receivable; **~s especiales** special effects; **~s personales** personal effects; **~s secundarios** side effects; **~s sonoros** sound effects; **hacer** *o* **surtir ~** to have the desired effect; **hacer ~** (*impresionar*) to make an impression; **llevar algo a ~** to carry sth out; **en ~** in fact; (*respuesta*) exactly, indeed

efectuar [efek'twar] *vt* to carry out; (*viaje*) to make

eficacia [efi'kaθja] *nf* (*de persona*) efficiency; (*de medicamento etc*) effectiveness

eficaz [efi'kaθ] *adj* (*persona*) efficient; (*acción*) effective

eficiente [efi'θjente] *adj* efficient

efusivo, -a [efu'siβo, a] *adj* effusive; **mis más efusivas gracias** my warmest thanks

EGB *nf abr* (*Esp Escol*: = *Educación General Básica*) *primary education for six- to fourteen-year olds*; *ver tb* **sistema educativo**

egipcio, -a [e'xipθjo, a] *adj, nm/f* Egyptian

Egipto [e'xipto] *nm* Egypt

egoísmo [eɣo'ismo] *nm* egoism

egoísta [eɣo'ista] *adj* egoistical, selfish ▷ *nm/f* egoist

egregio, -a [e'ɣrexjo, a] *adj* eminent, distinguished

Eire ['eire] *nm* Eire

ej. *abr* (= *ejemplo*) eg

eje ['exe] *nm* (*Geo, Mat*) axis; (*Pol, fig*) axis, main line; (*de rueda*) axle; (*de máquina*) shaft, spindle

ejecución [exeku'θjon] *nf* execution; (*cumplimiento*) fulfilment; (*actuación*) performance; (*Jur*: *embargo de deudor*) attachment

ejecutar [exeku'tar] *vt* to execute, carry out; (*matar*) to execute; (*cumplir*) to fulfil; (*Mus*) to perform; (*Jur*: *embargar*) to attach, distrain; (*deseos*) to fulfil; (*Inform*) to run

ejecutivo, -a [exeku'tiβo, a] *adj, nm/f* executive; **el (poder) ~** the executive (power)

ejemplar [exem'plar] *adj* exemplary ▷ *nm* example; (*Zool*) specimen; (*de libro*) copy; (*de periódico*) number, issue; **~ de regalo** complimentary copy; **sin ~** unprecedented

ejemplo [e'xemplo] *nm* example; (*caso*) instance; **por ~** for example; **dar ~** to set an example

ejercer [exer'θer] *vt* to exercise; (*funciones*) to perform; (*negocio*) to manage; (*influencia*) to exert; (*un oficio*) to practise; (*poder*) to wield ▷ *vi*: **~ de** to practise as

ejercicio [exer'θiθjo] *nm* exercise; (*Mil*) drill; (*Com*) fiscal *o* financial year; (*período*) tenure; **~ acrobático** (*Aviat*) stunt; **~ comercial** business year; **~s espirituales** (*Rel*) retreat *sg*; **hacer ~** to take exercise

ejercitar [exerθi'tar] *vt* to exercise; (*Mil*) to drill

ejército [e'xerθito] *nm* army; **E~ del Aire/de Tierra** Air Force/Army; **~ de ocupación** army of occupation; **~ permanente** standing army; **entrar en el ~** to join the army, join up

ejote [e'xote] *nm* (*Am*) green bean

PALABRA CLAVE

el [el] (*fem* **la**, *neutro* **lo**, *pl* **los, las**) *artículo definido* **1** the; **el libro/la mesa/los estudiantes/las flores** the book/table/students/flowers; **me gusta el fútbol** I like football; **está en la cama** she's in bed

2 (*con n abstracto o propio*: *no se traduce*): **el amor/la juventud** love/youth; **el Conde Drácula** Count Dracula

3 (*posesión*: *se traduce a menudo por adj posesivo*): **romperse el brazo** to break one's arm; **levantó la mano** he put his hand up; **se puso el sombrero** she put her hat on

4 (*valor descriptivo*): **tener la boca grande/los ojos azules** to have a big mouth/blue eyes

5 (*con días*) on; **me iré el viernes** I'll leave on Friday; **los domingos suelo ir a nadar** on Sundays I generally go swimming

6 (*lo + adj*): **lo difícil/caro** what is difficult/expensive; (*cuán*): **no se da cuenta de lo pesado que es** he doesn't realize how boring he is

▷ *pron demostrativo* **1**: **mi libro y el de usted** my book and yours; **las de Pepe son mejores** Pepe's are better; **no la(s) blanca(s) sino la(s) gris(es)** not the white one(s) but the grey one(s)

2: **lo de**: **lo de ayer** what happened

yesterday; **lo de las facturas** that business about the invoices
▷ *pron relativo*: **el que** *etc* **1** (*indef*): **el (los) que quiera(n) que se vaya(n)** anyone who wants to can leave; **llévese el/la que más le guste** take the one you like best
2 (*def*): **el que compré ayer** the one I bought yesterday; **los que se van** those who leave
3: **lo que**: **lo que pienso yo/más me gusta** what I think/like most
▷ *conj*: **el que**: **el que lo diga** the fact that he says so; **el que sea tan vago me molesta** his being so lazy bothers me
▷ *excl*: **¡el susto que me diste!** what a fright you gave me!
▷ *pron personal* **1** (*persona*: *m*) him; (: *f*) her; (: *pl*) them; **lo/las veo** I can see him/them
2 (*animal, cosa*: *sg*) it; (: *pl*) them; **lo** (*o* **la**) **veo** I can see it; **los** (*o* **las**) **veo** I can see them
3: **lo** (*como sustituto de frase*): **no lo sabía** I didn't know; **ya lo entiendo** I understand now

él [el] *pron* (*persona*) he; (*cosa*) it; (*después de prep*: *persona*) him; (: *cosa*) it; **mis libros y los de él** my books and his
elaboración [elaβora'θjon] *nf* (*producción*) manufacture; **~ de presupuestos** (*Com*) budgeting
elaborar [elaβo'rar] *vt* (*producto*) to make, manufacture; (*preparar*) to prepare; (*madera, metal etc*) to work; (*proyecto etc*) to work on *o* out
elasticidad [elastiθi'ðað] *nf* elasticity
elástico, -a [e'lastiko, a] *adj* elastic; (*flexible*) flexible ▷ *nm* elastic; (*gomita*) elastic band
elección [elek'θjon] *nf* election; (*selección*) choice, selection; **elecciones parciales** by-election *sg*; **elecciones generales** general election *sg*
electorado [elekto'raðo] *nm* electorate, voters *pl*
electoral [elekto'ral] *adj* electoral
electricidad [elektriθi'ðað] *nf* electricity
electricista [elektri'θista] *nm/f* electrician
eléctrico, -a [e'lektriko, a] *adj* electric
electrificar [elektrifi'kar] *vt* to electrify
electrizar [elektri'θar] *vt* (*Ferro, fig*) to electrify
electro... [elektro] *pref* electro...
electrocardiograma [elektrokarðjo'ɣrama] *nm* electrocardiogram
electrocución [elektroku'θjon] *nf* electrocution
electrocutar [elektroku'tar] *vt* to electrocute
electrodo [elek'troðo] *nm* electrode
electrodomésticos [elektroðo'mestikos] *nmpl* (electrical) household appliances; (*Com*) white goods
electroimán [electroi'man] *nm* electromagnet
electromagnético, -a [elektromaɣ'netiko, a] *adj* electromagnetic
electrón [elek'tron] *nm* electron
electrónico, -a [elek'troniko, a] *adj* electronic ▷ *nf* electronics *sg*
electrotecnia [elektro'teknja] *nf* electrical engineering
electrotécnico, -a [elektro'tekniko, a] *nm/f* electrical engineer
electrotren [elektro'tren] *nm* express electric train
elefante [ele'fante] *nm* elephant
elegancia [ele'ɣanθja] *nf* elegance, grace; (*estilo*) stylishness
elegante [ele'ɣante] *adj* elegant, graceful; (*estiloso*) stylish, fashionable; (*traje etc*) smart; (*decoración*) tasteful
elegía [ele'xia] *nf* elegy
elegir [ele'xir] *vt* (*escoger*) to choose, select; (*optar*) to opt for; (*presidente*) to elect
elemental [elemen'tal] *adj* (*claro, obvio*) elementary; (*fundamental*) elemental, fundamental
elemento [ele'mento] *nm* element; (*fig*) ingredient; (*Am*) person, individual; (*tipo raro*) odd person; (*de pila*) cell; **elementos** *nmpl* elements, rudiments; **estar en su ~** to be in one's element; **vino a verle un ~** someone came to see you
elepé [ele'pe] *nm* LP
elevación [eleβa'θjon] *nf* elevation; (*acto*) raising, lifting; (*de precios*) rise; (*Geo etc*) height, altitude
elevado, -a [ele'βaðo, a] *pp de* **elevar** ▷ *adj* high
elevador [eleβa'ðor] *nm* (*Am*) lift (*Brit*), elevator (*US*)
elevar [ele'βar] *vt* to raise, lift (up); (*precio*) to put up; (*producción*) to step up; (*informe etc*) to present; **elevarse** *vr* (*edificio*) to rise; (*precios*) to go up; (*transportarse, enajenarse*) to get carried away; **la cantidad se eleva a ...** the total amounts to ...
eligiendo *etc* [eli'xjenðo], **elija** *etc* [e'lixa] *vb ver* **elegir**
eliminar [elimi'nar] *vt* to eliminate, remove; (*olor, persona*) to get rid of; (*Deporte*) to eliminate, knock out
eliminatoria [elimina'torja] *nf* heat, preliminary (round)
elite [e'lite], **élite** ['elite] *nf* elite, élite
elitista [eli'tista] *adj* elitist
elixir [elik'sir] *nm* elixir; (*tb*: **~ bucal**) mouthwash
ella ['eʎa] *pron* (*persona*) she; (*cosa*) it; (*después de prep*: *persona*) her; (*cosa*) it; **de ~** hers
ellas ['eʎas] *pron ver* **ellos**
ello ['eʎo] *pron neutro* it; **es por ~ que ...** that's why ...
ellos, -as ['eʎos, as] *pron personal pl* they; (*después de prep*) them; **de ~** theirs
elocuencia [elo'kwenθja] *nf* eloquence

e

elocuente [elo'kwente] *adj* eloquent; (*fig*) significant; **un dato ~** a fact which speaks for itself
elogiar [elo'xjar] *vt* to praise, eulogize
elogio [e'loxjo] *nm* praise; **queda por encima de todo ~** it's beyond praise; **hacer ~ de** to sing the praises of
elote [e'lote] *nm* (*Am*) corn on the cob
eludir [elu'ðir] *vt* (*evitar*) to avoid, evade; (*escapar*) to escape, elude
email ['imeil] *nm* (*gen*) e-mail *m*; (*dirección*) e-mail address; **mandar un ~ a algn** to e-mail sb, send sb an e-mail
emanar [ema'nar] *vi*: **~ de** to emanate from, come from; (*derivar de*) to originate in
emancipar [emanθi'par] *vt* to emancipate; **emanciparse** *vr* to become emancipated, free o.s.
embadurnar [embaður'nar] *vt* to smear
embajada [emba'xaða] *nf* embassy
embajador, a [embaxa'ðor, a] *nm/f* ambassador/ambassadress
embalar [emba'lar] *vt* (*envolver*) to parcel, wrap (up); (*envasar*) to package ▹ *vi* to sprint; **embalarse** *vr* to go fast
embalsamar [embalsa'mar] *vt* to embalm
embalse [em'balse] *nm* (*presa*) dam; (*lago*) reservoir
embarazada [embara'θaða] *adj f* pregnant ▹ *nf* pregnant woman
embarazar [embara'θar] *vt* to obstruct, hamper; **embarazarse** *vr* (*aturdirse*) to become embarrassed; (*confundirse*) to get into a mess
embarazo [emba'raθo] *nm* (*de mujer*) pregnancy; (*impedimento*) obstacle, obstruction; (*timidez*) embarrassment
embarazoso, -a [embara'θoso, a] *adj* (*molesto*) awkward; (*violento*) embarrassing
embarcación [embarka'θjon] *nf* (*barco*) boat, craft; (*acto*) embarkation; **~ de arrastre** trawler; **~ de cabotaje** coasting vessel
embarcadero [embarka'ðero] *nm* pier, landing stage
embarcar [embar'kar] *vt* (*cargamento*) to ship, stow; (*persona*) to embark, put on board; (*fig*): **~ a algn en una empresa** to involve sb in an undertaking; **embarcarse** *vr* to embark, go on board; (*marinero*) to sign on; (*Am*: *en tren etc*) to get on, get in
embargar [embar'ɣar] *vt* (*frenar*) to restrain; (*sentidos*) to overpower; (*Jur*) to seize, impound
embargo [em'barɣo] *nm* (*Jur*) seizure; (*Com etc*) embargo; **sin ~** still, however, nonetheless
embargue *etc* [em'barɣe] *vb ver* **embargar**
embarque *etc* [em'barke] *vb ver* **embarcar** ▹ *nm* shipment, loading
embaucar [embau'kar] *vt* to trick, fool
embeber [embe'βer] *vt* (*absorber*) to absorb, soak up; (*empapar*) to saturate ▹ *vi* to shrink; **embeberse** *vr*: **~se en un libro** to be engrossed *o* absorbed in a book
embellecer [embeʎe'θer] *vt* to embellish, beautify
embestida [embes'tiða] *nf* attack, onslaught; (*carga*) charge
embestir [embes'tir] *vt* to attack, assault; to charge, attack ▹ *vi* to attack
emblema [em'blema] *nm* emblem
embobado, -a [embo'βaðo, a] *adj* (*atontado*) stunned, bewildered
embolia [em'bolja] *nf* (*Med*) clot, embolism; **~ cerebral** clot on the brain
émbolo ['embolo] *nm* (*Auto*) piston
embolsar [embol'sar] *vt* to pocket
emborrachar [emborra'tʃar] *vt* to make drunk, intoxicate; **emborracharse** *vr* to get drunk
emboscada [embos'kaða] *nf* (*celada*) ambush
embotar [embo'tar] *vt* to blunt, dull; **embotarse** *vr* (*adormecerse*) to go numb
embotellamiento [emboteʎa'mjento] *nm* (*Auto*) traffic jam
embotellar [embote'ʎar] *vt* to bottle; **embotellarse** *vr* (*circulación*) to get into a jam
embragar [embra'ɣar] *vt* (*Auto, Tec*) to engage; (*partes*) to connect ▹ *vi* to let in the clutch
embrague *etc* [em'braɣe] *vb ver* **embragar** ▹ *nm* (*tb*: **pedal de ~**) clutch
embriagar [embrja'ɣar] *vt* (*emborrachar*) to make drunk; (*alegrar*) to delight; **embriagarse** *vr* (*emborracharse*) to get drunk
embriaguez [embrja'ɣeθ] *nf* (*borrachera*) drunkenness
embrión [em'brjon] *nm* embryo
embrollar [embro'ʎar] *vt* (*asunto*) to confuse, complicate; (*persona*) to involve, embroil; **embrollarse** *vr* (*confundirse*) to get into a muddle *o* mess
embrollo [em'broʎo] *nm* (*enredo*) muddle, confusion; (*aprieto*) fix, jam
embromar [embro'mar] *vt* (*burlarse de*) to tease, make fun of; (*Am fam*: *molestar*) to annoy
embrujado, -a [embru'xaðo, a] *adj* (*persona*) bewitched; **casa embrujada** haunted house
embrujo [em'bruxo] *nm* (*de mirada etc*) charm, magic
embrutecer [embrute'θer] *vt* (*atontar*) to stupefy; **embrutecerse** *vr* to be stupefied
embudo [em'buðo] *nm* funnel
embuste [em'buste] *nm* trick; (*mentira*) lie; (*humorístico*) fib
embustero, -a [embus'tero, a] *adj* lying, deceitful ▹ *nm/f* (*tramposo*) cheat; (*mentiroso*) liar; (*humorístico*) fibber
embutido [embu'tiðo] *nm* (*Culin*) sausage; (*Tec*) inlay
embutir [embu'tir] *vt* to insert; (*Tec*) to inlay; (*llenar*) to pack tight, cram
emergencia [emer'xenθja] *nf* emergency; (*surgimiento*) emergence
emerger [emer'xer] *vi* to emerge, appear

emigración [emiɣra'θjon] *nf* emigration; (*de pájaros*) migration
emigrante [emi'ɣrante] *adj, nm/f* emigrant
emigrar [emi'ɣrar] *vi* (*personas*) to emigrate; (*pájaros*) to migrate
eminencia [emi'nenθja] *nf* eminence; (*en títulos*): **Su E~** His Eminence; **Vuestra E~** Your Eminence
eminente [emi'nente] *adj* eminent, distinguished; (*elevado*) high
emisario [emi'sarjo] *nm* emissary
emisión [emi'sjon] *nf* (*acto*) emission; (*Com etc*) issue; (*Radio, TV: acto*) broadcasting; (*: programa*) broadcast, programme, program (*US*); **~ de acciones** (*Com*) share issue; **~ gratuita de acciones** (*Com*) rights issue; **~ de valores** (*Com*) flotation
emisor, a [emi'sor, a] *nm* transmitter ▷ *nf* radio *o* broadcasting station
emitir [emi'tir] *vt* (*olor etc*) to emit, give off; (*moneda etc*) to issue; (*opinión*) to express; (*voto*) to cast; (*señal*) to send out; (*Radio*) to broadcast; **~ una señal sonora** to beep
emoción [emo'θjon] *nf* emotion; (*excitación*) excitement; (*sentimiento*) feeling; **¡qué ~!** how exciting!; (*irónico*) what a thrill!
emocionado, -a [emoθjo'naðo, a] *adj* deeply moved, stirred
emocionante [emoθjo'nante] *adj* (*excitante*) exciting, thrilling
emocionar [emoθjo'nar] *vt* (*excitar*) to excite, thrill; (*conmover*) to move, touch; (*impresionar*) to impress; **emocionarse** *vr* to get excited
emoticón [emoti'kon], **emoticono** [emoti'kono] *nm* smiley, emoticon
emotivo, -a [emo'tiβo, a] *adj* emotional
empacar [empa'kar] *vt* (*gen*) to pack; (*en caja*) to bale, crate
empacho [em'patʃo] *nm* (*Med*) indigestion; (*fig*) embarrassment
empadronarse [empaðro'narse] *vr* (*Pol: como elector*) to register
empalagoso, -a [empala'ɣoso, a] *adj* cloying; (*fig*) tiresome
empalmar [empal'mar] *vt* to join, connect ▷ *vi* (*dos caminos*) to meet, join
empalme [em'palme] *nm* joint, connection; (*de vías*) junction; (*de trenes*) connection
empanada [empa'naða] *nf* pie, pasty
empantanarse [empanta'narse] *vr* to get swamped; (*fig*) to get bogged down
empañarse [empa'ɲarse] *vr* (*nublarse*) to get misty, steam up
empapar [empa'par] *vt* (*mojar*) to soak, saturate; (*absorber*) to soak up, absorb; **empaparse** *vr*: **~se de** to soak up
empapelar [empape'lar] *vt* (*paredes*) to paper
empaquetar [empake'tar] *vt* to pack, parcel up; (*Com*) to package
emparedado [empare'ðaðo] *nm* sandwich
emparejar [empare'xar] *vt* to pair ▷ *vi* to catch up
empastar [empas'tar] *vt* (*embadurnar*) to paste; (*diente*) to fill
empaste [em'paste] *nm* (*de diente*) filling
empatar [empa'tar] *vi* to draw, tie; **~on a dos** they drew two-all
empate [em'pate] *nm* draw, tie; **un ~ a cero** a no-score draw
empecé [empe'θe], **empecemos** *etc* [empe'θemos] *vb ver* **empezar**
empedernido, -a [empeðer'niðo, a] *adj* hard, heartless; (*fijado*) hardened, inveterate; **un fumador ~** a heavy smoker
empedrado, -a [empe'ðraðo, a] *adj* paved ▷ *nm* paving
empedrar [empe'ðrar] *vt* to pave
empeine [em'peine] *nm* (*de pie, zapato*) instep
empellón [empe'ʎon] *nm* push, shove; **abrirse paso a empellones** to push *o* shove one's way past *o* through
empeñado, -a [empe'ɲaðo, a] *adj* (*persona*) determined; (*objeto*) pawned
empeñar [empe'ɲar] *vt* (*objeto*) to pawn, pledge; (*persona*) to compel; **empeñarse** *vr* (*obligarse*) to bind o.s., pledge o.s.; (*endeudarse*) to get into debt; **~se en hacer** to be set on doing, be determined to do
empeño [em'peɲo] *nm* (*determinación*) determination; (*cosa prendada*) pledge; **casa de ~s** pawnshop; **con ~** insistently; (*con celo*) eagerly; **tener ~ en hacer algo** to be bent on doing sth
empeorar [empeo'rar] *vt* to make worse, worsen ▷ *vi* to get worse, deteriorate
empequeñecer [empekeɲe'θer] *vt* to dwarf; (*fig*) to belittle
emperador [empera'ðor] *nm* emperor
emperatriz [empera'triθ] *nf* empress
empezar [empe'θar] *vt, vi* to begin, start; **empezó a llover** it started to rain; **bueno, para ~** well, to start with
empiece *etc* [em'pjeθe] *vb ver* **empezar**
empiezo *etc* [em'pjeθo] *vb ver* **empezar**
empinar [empi'nar] *vt* to raise; (*botella*) to tip up; **empinarse** *vr* (*persona*) to stand on tiptoe; (*animal*) to rear up; (*camino*) to climb steeply; **~ el codo** to booze (*fam*)
empírico, -a [em'piriko, a] *adj* empirical
emplaste [em'plaste], **emplasto** [em'plasto] *nm* (*Med*) plaster
emplasto [em'plasto] *nm* (*Med*) plaster
emplazamiento [emplaθa'mjento] *nm* site, location; (*Jur*) summons *sg*
emplazar [empla'θar] *vt* (*ubicar*) to site, place, locate; (*Jur*) to summons; (*convocar*) to summon
empleado, -a [emple'aðo, a] *nm/f* (*gen*) employee; (*de banco etc*) clerk; **~ público** civil servant
emplear [emple'ar] *vt* (*usar*) to use, employ; (*dar trabajo a*) to employ; **emplearse** *vr* (*conseguir trabajo*) to be employed; (*ocuparse*) to occupy o.s.; **~ mal el tiempo** to waste time; **¡te está bien empleado!** it serves you right!

e

empleo [em'pleo] *nm* (*puesto*) job; (*puestos: colectivamente*) employment; (*uso*) use, employment; **"modo de ~"** "instructions for use"
empobrecer [empoβre'θer] *vt* to impoverish; **empobrecerse** *vr* to become poor *o* impoverished
empollar [empo'ʎar] *vt* to incubate; (*Escol fam*) to swot (up) ▷ *vi* (*gallina*) to brood; (*Escol fam*) to swot
empollón, -ona [empo'ʎon, ona] *nm/f* (*Escol fam*) swot
emporio [em'porjo] *nm* emporium, trading centre; (*Am: gran almacén*) department store
empotrado, -a [empo'traðo, a] *adj* (*armario etc*) built-in
emprendedor, a [emprende'ðor, a] *adj* enterprising
emprender [empren'der] *vt* to undertake; (*empezar*) to begin, embark on; (*acometer*) to tackle, take on; **~ marcha a** to set out for
empresa [em'presa] *nf* enterprise; (*Com: sociedad*) firm, company; (*: negocio*) business; (*esp Teat*) management; **~ filial** (*Com*) affiliated company; **~ matriz** (*Com*) parent company
empresariales [empresa'rjales] *nfpl* business studies
empresario, -a [empre'sarjo, a] *nm/f* (*Com*) businessman(-woman), entrepreneur; (*Tec*) manager; (*Mus: de ópera etc*) impresario; **~ de pompas fúnebres** undertaker (*Brit*), mortician (*US*)
empréstito [em'prestito] *nm* (public) loan; (*Com*) loan capital
empujar [empu'xar] *vt* to push, shove
empuje [em'puxe] *nm* thrust; (*presión*) pressure; (*fig*) vigour, drive
empujón [empu'xon] *nm* push, shove; **abrirse paso a empujones** to shove one's way through
empuñar [empu'ɲar] *vt* (*asir*) to grasp, take (firm) hold of; **~ las armas** (*fig*) to take up arms
emular [emu'lar] *vt* to emulate; (*rivalizar*) to rival
emulsión [emul'sjon] *nf* emulsion

PALABRA CLAVE

en [en] *prep* **1** (*posición*) in; (*: sobre*) on; **está en el cajón** it's in the drawer; **en Argentina/La Paz** in Argentina/La Paz; **en el colegio/la oficina** at school/the office; **en casa** at home; **está en el suelo/quinto piso** it's on the floor/the fifth floor; **en el periódico** in the paper
2 (*dirección*) into; **entró en el aula** she went into the classroom; **meter algo en el bolso** to put sth into one's bag; **ir de puerta en puerta** to go from door to door
3 (*tiempo*) in; on; **en 1605/3 semanas/invierno** in 1605/3 weeks/winter; **en (el mes de) enero** in (the month of) January; **en aquella ocasión/época** on that occasion/at that time
4 (*precio*) for; **lo vendió en 20 dólares** he sold it for 20 dollars
5 (*diferencia*) by; **reducir/aumentar en una tercera parte/un 20 por ciento** to reduce/increase by a third/20 per cent
6 (*manera, forma*): **en avión/autobús** by plane/bus; **escrito en inglés** written in English; **en serio** seriously; **en espiral/círculo** in a spiral/circle
7 (*después de vb que indica gastar etc*) on; **han cobrado demasiado en dietas** they've charged too much to expenses; **se le va la mitad del sueldo en comida** half his salary goes on food
8 (*tema, ocupación*): **experto en la materia** expert on the subject; **trabaja en la construcción** he works in the building industry
9 (*adj + en + infin*): **lento en reaccionar** slow to react

enagua, enaguas [enaɣwa(s)] *nf(pl)* (*esp Am*) petticoat *sg*, underskirt *eg*
enajenación [enaxena'θjon] *nf*, **enajenamiento** [enaxena'mjento] *nm* alienation; (*fig: distracción*) absent-mindedness; (*: embelesamiento*) rapture, trance; **~ mental** mental derangement
enajenar [enaxe'nar] *vt* to alienate; (*fig*) to carry away
enamorado, -a [enamo'raðo, a] *adj* in love ▷ *nm/f* lover; **estar ~ (de)** to be in love (with)
enamorar [enamo'rar] *vt* to win the love of; **enamorarse** *vr*: **~se (de)** to fall in love (with)
enano, -a [e'nano, a] *adj* tiny, dwarf ▷ *nm/f* person of small stature; (*pey*) runt
enardecer [enarðe'θer] *vt* (*pasiones*) to fire, inflame; (*persona*) to fill with enthusiasm; **enardecerse** *vr* to get excited; **~se por** to get enthusiastic about
encabezamiento [enkaβeθa'mjento] *nm* (*de carta*) heading; (*Com*) billhead, letterhead; (*de periódico*) headline; (*preámbulo*) foreword, preface; **~ normal** (*Tip etc*) running head
encabezar [enkaβe'θar] *vt* (*movimiento, revolución*) to lead, head; (*lista*) to head; (*carta*) to put a heading to; (*libro*) to entitle
encadenar [enkaðe'nar] *vt* to chain (together); (*poner grilletes a*) to shackle
encajar [enka'xar] *vt* (*ajustar*): **~ en** to fit (into); (*meter a la fuerza*) to push in; (*máquina etc*) to house; (*partes*) to join; (*fam: golpe*) to give, deal; (*entremeter*) to insert ▷ *vi* to fit (well); (*fig: corresponder a*) to match; **encajarse** *vr*: **~se en un sillón** to squeeze into a chair
encaje [en'kaxe] *nm* (*labor*) lace
encalar [enka'lar] *vt* (*pared*) to whitewash
encallar [enka'ʎar] *vi* (*Naut*) to run aground

encaminar [enkami'nar] *vt* to direct, send; **encaminarse** *vr*: **~se a** to set out for; **~ por** (*expedición etc*) to route via
encandilar [enkandi'lar] *vt* to dazzle; (*persona*) to daze, bewilder
encantado, -a [enkan'taðo, a] *adj* (*hechizado*) bewitched; (*muy contento*) delighted; **¡~!** how do you do!, pleased to meet you
encantador, a [enkanta'ðor, a] *adj* charming, lovely ▷ *nm/f* magician, enchanter/enchantress
encantar [enkan'tar] *vt* to charm, delight; (*cautivar*) to fascinate; (*hechizar*) to bewitch, cast a spell on; **me encanta eso** I love that
encanto [en'kanto] *nm* (*magia*) spell, charm; (*fig*) charm, delight; (*expresión de ternura*) sweetheart; **como por ~** as if by magic
encarcelar [enkarθe'lar] *vt* to imprison, jail
encarecer [enkare'θer] *vt* to put up the price of ▷ *vi*, **encarecerse** *vr* to get dearer
encarecimiento [enkareθi'mjento] *nm* price increase
encargado, -a [enkar'ɣaðo, a] *adj* in charge ▷ *nm/f* agent, representative; (*responsable*) person in charge
encargar [enkar'ɣar] *vt* to entrust; (*Com*) to order; (*recomendar*) to urge, recommend; **encargarse** *vr*: **~se de** to look after, take charge of; **~ algo a algn** to put sb in charge of sth
encargo [en'karɣo] *nm* (*pedido*) assignment, job; (*responsabilidad*) responsibility; (*recomendación*) recommendation; (*Com*) order
encariñarse [enkari'ɲarse] *vr*: **~ con** to grow fond of, get attached to
encarnación [enkarna'θjon] *nf* incarnation, embodiment
encarnizado, -a [enkarni'θaðo, a] *adj* (*lucha*) bloody, fierce
encarrilar [enkarri'lar] *vt* (*tren*) to put back on the rails; (*fig*) to correct, put on the right track
encasillar [enkasi'ʎar] *vt* (*Teat*) to typecast; (*clasificar: pey*) to pigeonhole
encasquetar [enkaske'tar] *vt* (*sombrero*) to pull down *o* on; **encasquetarse** *vr*: **~se el sombrero** to pull one's hat down *o* on; **~ algo a algn** to offload sth onto sb
encauzar [enkau'θar] *vt* to channel; (*fig*) to direct
encendedor [enθende'ðor] *nm* lighter
encender [enθen'der] *vt* (*con fuego*) to light; (*incendiar*) to set fire to; (*luz, radio*) to put on, switch on; (*Inform*) to toggle on, switch on; (*avivar: pasiones etc*) to inflame; (*despertar: entusiasmo*) to arouse; (*odio*) to awaken; **encenderse** *vr* to catch fire; (*excitarse*) to get excited; (*de cólera*) to flare up; (*el rostro*) to blush
encendido, -a [enθen'diðo, a] *adj* alight; (*aparato*) (switched) on; (*mejillas*) glowing; (*cara: por el vino etc*) flushed; (*mirada*) passionate ▷ *nm* (*Auto*) ignition; (*de faroles*) lighting
encerado, -a [enθe'raðo, a] *adj* (*suelo*) waxed, polished ▷ *nm* (*Escol*) blackboard; (*hule*) oilcloth
encerar [enθe'rar] *vt* (*suelo*) to wax, polish
encerrar [enθe'rrar] *vt* (*confinar*) to shut in *o* up; (*con llave*) to lock in *o* up; (*comprender, incluir*) to include, contain; **encerrarse** *vr* to shut *o* lock o.s. up *o* in
encestar [enθes'tar] *vi* to score a basket
encharcado, -a [entʃar'kaðo, a] *adj* (*terreno*) flooded
encharcar [entʃar'kar] *vt* to swamp, flood; **encharcarse** *vr* to become flooded
enchufado, -a [entʃu'faðo, a] *nm/f* (*fam*) well-connected person
enchufar [entʃu'far] *vt* (*Elec*) to plug in; (*Tec*) to connect, fit together; (*Com*) to merge
enchufe [en'tʃufe] *nm* (*Elec: clavija*) plug; (*: toma*) socket; (*de dos tubos*) joint, connection; (*fam: influencia*) contact, connection; (*puesto*) cushy job; **~ de clavija** jack plug; **tiene un ~ en el ministerio** he can pull strings at the ministry
encía [en'θia] *nf* (*Anat*) gum
enciclopedia [enθiklo'peðja] *nf* encyclopaedia
encienda *etc* [en'θjenda] *vb ver* **encender**
encierro *etc* [en'θjerro] *vb ver* **encerrar** ▷ *nm* shutting in *o* up; (*calabozo*) prison; (*Agr*) pen; (*Taur*) penning
encima [en'θima] *adv* (*sobre*) above, over; (*además*) besides; **~ de** (*en*) on, on top of; (*sobre*) above, over; (*además de*) besides, on top of; **por ~ de** over; **¿llevas dinero ~?** have you (got) any money on you?; **se me vino ~** it took me by surprise
encina [en'θina] *nf* (holm) oak
encinta [en'θinta] *adj f* pregnant
enclave [en'klaβe] *nm* enclave
enclenque [en'klenke] *adj* weak, sickly
encoger [enko'xer] *vt* (*gen*) to shrink, contract; (*fig: asustar*) to scare; (*: desanimar*) to discourage; **encogerse** *vr* to shrink, contract; (*fig*) to cringe; **~se de hombros** to shrug one's shoulders
encolar [enko'lar] *vt* (*engomar*) to glue, paste; (*pegar*) to stick down
encolerizar [enkoleri'θar] *vt* to anger, provoke; **encolerizarse** *vr* to get angry
encomendar [enkomen'dar] *vt* to entrust, commend; **encomendarse** *vr*: **~se a** to put one's trust in
encomiar [enko'mjar] *vt* to praise, pay tribute to
encomienda *etc* [enko'mjenda] *vb ver* **encomendar** ▷ *nf* (*encargo*) charge, commission; (*elogio*) tribute; (*Am*) parcel, package; **~ postal** (*Am: servicio*) parcel post
encono [en'kono] *nm* (*rencor*) rancour, spite

encontrado, -a [enkon'traðo, a] *adj* (*contrario*) contrary, conflicting; (*hostil*) hostile
encontrar [enkon'trar] *vt* (*hallar*) to find; (*inesperadamente*) to meet, run into; **encontrarse** *vr* to meet (each other); (*situarse*) to be (situated); (*persona*) to find o.s., be; (*entrar en conflicto*) to crash, collide; **~se con** to meet; **~se bien (de salud)** to feel well; **no se encuentra aquí en este momento** he's not in at the moment
encorvar [enkor'βar] *vt* to curve; (*inclinar*) to bend (down); **encorvarse** *vr* to bend down, bend over
encrespar [enkres'par] *vt* (*cabellos*) to curl; (*fig*) to anger, irritate; **encresparse** *vr* (*el mar*) to get rough; (*fig*) to get cross *o* irritated
encrucijada [enkruθi'xaða] *nf* crossroads *sg*; (*empalme*) junction
encuadernación [enkwaðerna'θjon] *nf* binding; (*taller*) binder's
encuadernador, a [enkwaðerna'ðor, a] *nm/f* bookbinder
encuadrar [enkwa'ðrar] *vt* (*retrato*) to frame; (*ajustar*) to fit, insert; (*encerrar*) to contain
encubrir [enku'βrir] *vt* (*ocultar*) to hide, conceal; (*criminal*) to harbour, shelter; (*ayudar*) to be an accomplice in
encuentro [en'kwentro] *vb ver* **encontrar** ▷ *nm* (*de personas*) meeting; (*Auto etc*) collision, crash; (*Deporte*) match, game; (*Mil*) encounter
encuerado, -a [enkwe'raðo, a] *adj* (*Am*) nude, naked
encuesta [en'kwesta] *nf* inquiry, investigation; (*sondeo*) public opinion poll; **~ judicial** post-mortem
encumbrado, -a [enkum'braðo, a] *adj* eminent, distinguished
encumbrar [enkum'brar] *vt* (*persona*) to exalt; **encumbrarse** *vr* (*fig*) to become conceited
endeble [en'deβle] *adj* (*argumento, excusa, persona*) weak
endémico, -a [en'demiko, a] *adj* endemic
endemoniado, -a [endemo'njaðo, a] *adj* possessed (of the devil); (*travieso*) devilish
enderezar [endere'θar] *vt* (*poner derecho*) to straighten (out); (*: verticalmente*) to set upright; (*fig*) to straighten *o* sort out; (*dirigir*) to direct; **enderezarse** *vr* (*persona sentada*) to sit up straight
endeudarse [endeu'ðarse] *vr* to get into debt
endiablado, -a [endja'βlaðo, a] *adj* devilish, diabolical; (*humorístico*) mischievous
endibia [en'diβja] *nf* endive
endilgar [endil'ɣar] *vt* (*fam*): **~ algo a algn** to lumber sb with sth; **~ un sermón a algn** to give sb a lecture
endiñar [endi'ɲar] *vt*: **~ algo a algn** to land sth on sb
endomingarse [endomin'garse] *vr* to dress up, put on one's best clothes
endosar [endo'sar] *vt* (*cheque etc*) to endorse
endulzar [endul'θar] *vt* to sweeten; (*suavizar*) to soften
endurecer [endure'θer] *vt* to harden; **endurecerse** *vr* to harden, grow hard
endurecido, -a [endure'θiðo, a] *adj* (*duro*) hard; (*fig*) hardy, tough; **estar ~ a algo** to be hardened *o* used to sth
enema [e'nema] *nm* (*Med*) enema
enemigo, -a [ene'miɣo, a] *adj* enemy, hostile ▷ *nm/f* enemy ▷ *nf* enmity, hostility; **ser ~ de** (*persona*) to dislike; (*tendencia*) to be inimical to
enemistad [enemis'tað] *nf* enmity
enemistar [enemis'tar] *vt* to make enemies of, cause a rift between; **enemistarse** *vr* to become enemies; (*amigos*) to fall out
energía [ener'xia] *nf* (*vigor*) energy, drive; (*empuje*) push; (*Tec, Elec*) energy, power; **~ atómica/eléctrica/eólica** atomic/electric/wind power; **~ solar** solar energy *o* power; **~s renovables** renewable energy sources
enérgico, -a [e'nerxiko, a] *adj* (*gen*) energetic; (*ataque*) vigorous; (*ejercicio*) strenuous; (*medida*) bold; (*voz, modales*) forceful
energúmeno, -a [ener'ɣumeno, a] *nm/f* madman(-woman); **ponerse como un ~ con algn** to get furious with sb
enero [e'nero] *nm* January; *ver tb* **julio**
enésimo, -a [e'nesimo, a] *adj* (*Mat*) nth; **por enésima vez** (*fig*) for the umpteenth time
enfadado, -a [enfa'ðaðo, a] *adj* angry, annoyed
enfadar [enfa'ðar] *vt* to anger, annoy; **enfadarse** *vr* to get angry *o* annoyed
enfado [en'faðo] *nm* (*enojo*) anger, annoyance; (*disgusto*) trouble, bother
énfasis ['enfasis] *nm* emphasis, stress; **poner ~ en** to stress
enfático, -a [en'fatiko, a] *adj* emphatic
enfermar [enfer'mar] *vt* to make ill ▷ *vi* to fall ill, be taken ill; **su actitud me enferma** his attitude makes me sick; **~ del corazón** to develop heart trouble
enfermedad [enferme'ðað] *nf* illness; **~ venérea** venereal disease
enfermera [enfer'mera] *nf ver* **enfermero**
enfermería [enferme'ria] *nf* infirmary; (*de colegio etc*) sick bay
enfermero, -a [enfer'mero, a] *nm* (male) nurse ▷ *nf* nurse; **enfermera jefa** matron
enfermizo, -a [enfer'miθo, a] *adj* (*persona*) sickly, unhealthy; (*fig*) unhealthy
enfermo, -a [en'fermo, a] *adj* ill, sick ▷ *nm/f* invalid, sick person; (*en hospital*) patient; **caer** *o* **ponerse ~** to fall ill
enflaquecer [enflake'θer] *vt* (*adelgazar*) to make thin; (*debilitar*) to weaken

enfocar [enfo'kar] *vt* (*foto etc*) to focus; (*problema etc*) to consider, look at
enfoque *etc* [en'foke] *vb ver* **enfocar** ▷ *nm* focus; (*acto*) focusing; (*óptica*) approach
enfrascarse [enfras'karse] *vr*: **~ en un libro** to bury o.s. in a book
enfrentamiento [enfrenta'mjento] *nm* confrontation
enfrentar [enfren'tar] *vt* (*peligro*) to face (up to), confront; (*oponer*) to bring face to face; **enfrentarse** *vr* (*dos personas*) to face *o* confront each other; (*Deporte: dos equipos*) to meet; **~se a** *o* **con** to face up to, confront
enfrente [en'frente] *adv* opposite; **~ de** *prep* opposite, facing; **la casa de ~** the house opposite, the house across the street
enfriamiento [enfria'mjento] *nm* chilling, refrigeration; (*Med*) cold, chill
enfriar [enfri'ar] *vt* (*alimentos*) to cool, chill; (*algo caliente*) to cool down; (*habitación*) to air, freshen; (*entusiasmo*) to dampen; **enfriarse** *vr* to cool down; (*Med*) to catch a chill; (*amistad*) to cool
enfurecer [enfure'θer] *vt* to enrage, madden; **enfurecerse** *vr* to become furious, fly into a rage; (*mar*) to get rough
engalanar [engala'nar] *vt* (*adornar*) to adorn; (*ciudad*) to decorate; **engalanarse** *vr* to get dressed up
enganchar [engan'tʃar] *vt* to hook; (*ropa*) to hang up; (*dos vagones*) to hitch up; (*Tec*) to couple, connect; (*Mil*) to recruit; (*fam: atraer: persona*) to rope into; **engancharse** *vr* (*Mil*) to enlist, join up; **~se (a)** (*drogas*) to get hooked (on)
enganche [en'gantʃe] *nm* hook; (*Tec*) coupling, connection; (*acto*) hooking (up); (*Mil*) recruitment, enlistment; (*Am: depósito*) deposit
engañar [enga'ɲar] *vt* to deceive; (*estafar*) to cheat, swindle ▷ *vi*: **las apariencias engañan** appearances are deceptive; **engañarse** *vr* (*equivocarse*) to be wrong; (*asimismo*) to deceive *o* kid o.s.; **engaña a su mujer** he's unfaithful to *o* cheats on his wife
engaño [en'gaɲo] *nm* deceit; (*estafa*) trick, swindle; (*error*) mistake, misunderstanding; (*ilusión*) delusion
engañoso, -a [enga'ɲoso, a] *adj* (*tramposo*) crooked; (*mentiroso*) dishonest, deceitful; (*aspecto*) deceptive; (*consejo*) misleading
engarzar [engar'θar] *vt* (*joya*) to set, mount; (*fig*) to link, connect
engatusar [engatu'sar] *vt* (*fam*) to coax
engendrar [enxen'drar] *vt* to breed; (*procrear*) to beget; (*fig*) to cause, produce
engendro [en'xendro] *nm* (*Bio*) foetus; (*fig*) monstrosity; (*: idea*) brainchild
englobar [englo'βar] *vt* (*comprender*) to include, comprise; (*incluir*) to lump together
engomar [engo'mar] *vt* to glue, stick
engordar [engor'ðar] *vt* to fatten ▷ *vi* to get fat, put on weight
engorroso, -a [engo'rroso, a] *adj* bothersome, trying
engranaje [engra'naxe] *nm* (*Auto*) gear; (*juego*) gears *pl*
engrandecer [engrande'θer] *vt* to enlarge, magnify; (*alabar*) to praise, speak highly of; (*exagerar*) to exaggerate
engrasar [engra'sar] *vt* (*Tec: poner grasa*) to grease; (*: lubricar*) to lubricate, oil; (*manchar*) to make greasy
engreído, -a [engre'iðo, a] *adj* vain, conceited
engrosar [engro'sar] *vt* (*ensanchar*) to enlarge; (*aumentar*) to increase; (*hinchar*) to swell
enhebrar [ene'βrar] *vt* to thread
enhorabuena [enora'βwena] *excl*: **¡~!** congratulations! ▷ *nf*: **dar la ~ a** to congratulate
enigma [e'niɣma] *nm* enigma; (*problema*) puzzle; (*misterio*) mystery
enjabonar [enxaβo'nar] *vt* to soap; (*barba*) to lather; (*fam: adular*) to soft-soap; (*: reganar*) to tick off
enjambre [en'xamβre] *nm* swarm
enjaular [enxau'lar] *vt* to (put in a) cage; (*fam*) to jail, lock up
enjuagar [enxwa'ɣar] *vt* (*ropa*) to rinse (out)
enjuague *etc* [en'xwaɣe] *vb ver* **enjuagar** ▷ *nm* (*Med*) mouthwash; (*de ropa*) rinse, rinsing
enjugar [enxu'ɣar] *vt* to wipe (off); (*lágrimas*) to dry; (*déficit*) to wipe out
enjuiciar [enxwi'θjar] *vt* (*Jur: procesar*) to prosecute, try; (*fig*) to judge
enjuto, -a [en'xuto, a] *adj* dry, dried up; (*fig*) lean, skinny
enlace *etc* [en'laθe] *vb ver* **enlazar** ▷ *nm* link, connection; (*relación*) relationship; (*tb*: **~ matrimonial**) marriage; (*de trenes*) connection; **~ de datos** data link; **~ sindical** shop steward; **~ telefónico** telephone link-up
enlatado, -a [enla'taðo, a] *adj* (*alimentos, productos*) tinned, canned
enlazar [enla'θar] *vt* (*unir con lazos*) to bind together; (*atar*) to tie; (*conectar*) to link, connect; (*Am*) to lasso
enlodar [enlo'ðar] *vt* to cover in mud; (*fig: manchar*) to stain; (*: rebajar*) to debase
enloquecer [enloke'θer] *vt* to drive mad ▷ *vi*, **enloquecerse** *vr* to go mad
enlutado, -a [enlu'taðo, a] *adj* (*persona*) in mourning
enmarañar [enmara'ɲar] *vt* (*enredar*) to tangle up, entangle; (*complicar*) to complicate; (*confundir*) to confuse; **enmarañarse** *vr* (*enredarse*) to become entangled; (*confundirse*) to get confused
enmarcar [enmar'kar] *vt* (*cuadro*) to frame; (*fig*) to provide a setting for
enmascarar [enmaska'rar] *vt* to mask; (*intenciones*) to disguise; **enmascararse** *vr* to put on a mask

enmendar [enmen'dar] *vt* to emend, correct; (*constitución etc*) to amend; (*comportamiento*) to reform; **enmendarse** *vr* to reform, mend one's ways
enmienda *etc* [en'mjenda] *vb ver* **enmendar** ▷ *nf* correction; amendment; reform
enmohecerse [enmoe'θerse] *vr* (*metal*) to rust, go rusty; (*muro, plantas*) to go mouldy
enmudecer [enmuðe'θer] *vt* to silence ▷ *vi*, **enmudecerse** *vr* (*perder el habla*) to fall silent; (*guardar silencio*) to remain silent; (*por miedo*) to be struck dumb
ennegrecer [enneɣre'θer] *vt* (*poner negro*) to blacken; (*oscurecer*) to darken; **ennegrecerse** *vr* to turn black; (*oscurecerse*) to get dark, darken
ennoblecer [ennoβle'θer] *vt* to ennoble
enojadizo, -a [enoxa'ðiθo, a] *adj* irritable, short-tempered
enojado, -a [eno'xaðo, a] *adj* (*Am*) angry
enojar [eno'xar] (*esp Am*) *vt* (*encolerizar*) to anger; (*disgustar*) to annoy, upset; **enojarse** *vr* to get angry; to get annoyed
enojo [e'noxo] *nm* (*esp Am: cólera*) anger; (*irritación*) annoyance; **enojos** *nmpl* trials, problems
enojoso, -a [eno'xoso, a] *adj* annoying
enorgullecerse [enorɣuʎe'θerse] *vr* to be proud; ~ **de** to pride o.s. on, be proud of
enorme [e'norme] *adj* enormous, huge; (*fig*) monstrous
enormidad [enormi'ðað] *nf* hugeness, immensity
enoturismo [enotu'rismo] *nm* wine tourism
enraizar [enrai'θar] *vi* to take root
enrarecido, -a [enrare'θiðo, a] *adj* rarefied
enredadera [enreða'ðera] *nf* (*Bot*) creeper, climbing plant
enredar [enre'ðar] *vt* (*cables, hilos etc*) to tangle (up), entangle; (*situación*) to complicate, confuse; (*meter cizaña*) to sow discord among *o* between; (*implicar*) to embroil, implicate; **enredarse** *vr* to get entangled, get tangled (up); (*situación*) to get complicated; (*persona*) to get embroiled; (*Am: fam*) to meddle
enredo [en'reðo] *nm* (*maraña*) tangle; (*confusión*) mix-up, confusion; (*intriga*) intrigue; (*apuro*) jam; (*amorío*) love affair
enrevesado, -a [enreβe'saðo, a] *adj* (*asunto*) complicated, involved
enriquecer [enrike'θer] *vt* to make rich; (*fig*) to enrich; **enriquecerse** *vr* to get rich
enrojecer [enroxe'θer] *vt* to redden ▷ *vi* (*persona*) to blush; **enrojecerse** *vr* to blush
enrolar [enro'lar] *vt* (*Mil*) to enlist; (*reclutar*) to recruit; **enrolarse** *vr* (*Mil*) to join up; (*afiliarse*) to enrol, sign on
enrollar [enro'ʎar] *vt* to roll (up), wind (up); **enrollarse** *vr*: **~se con algn** to get involved with sb
enroscar [enros'kar] *vt* (*torcer, doblar*) to twist; (*arrollar*) to coil (round), wind; (*tornillo, rosca*) to screw in; **enroscarse** *vr* to coil, wind
ensalada [ensa'laða] *nf* salad; (*lío*) mix-up
ensaladilla [ensala'ðiʎa] *nf* (*tb:* **~ rusa**) ≈ Russian salad
ensalzar [ensal'θar] *vt* (*alabar*) to praise, extol; (*exaltar*) to exalt
ensambladura [ensambla'ðura] *nf*, **ensamblaje** [ensam'blaxe] *nm* assembly; (*Tec*) joint
ensamblar [ensam'blar] *vt* (*montar*) to assemble; (*madera etc*) to join
ensanchar [ensan'tʃar] *vt* (*hacer más ancho*) to widen; (*agrandar*) to enlarge, expand; (*Costura*) to let out; **ensancharse** *vr* to get wider, expand; (*pey*) to give o.s. airs
ensanche [en'santʃe] *nm* (*de calle*) widening; (*de negocio*) expansion
ensangrentar [ensangren'tar] *vt* to stain with blood
ensañarse [ensa'ɲarse] *vr*: **~ con** to treat brutally
ensartar [ensar'tar] *vt* (*gen*) to string (together); (*carne*) to spit, skewer
ensayar [ensa'jar] *vt* to test, try (out); (*Teat*) to rehearse
ensayista [ensa'jista] *nm/f* essayist
ensayo [en'sajo] *nm* test, trial; (*Química*) experiment; (*Teat*) rehearsal; (*Deporte*) try; (*Escol, Lit*) essay; **pedido de ~** (*Com*) trial order; **~ general** (*Teat*) dress rehearsal; (*Mus*) full rehearsal
enseguida [ense'ɣuiða] *adv* at once, right away; **~ termino** I've nearly finished, I shan't be long now
ensenada [ense'naða] *nf* inlet, cove
enseñanza [ense'ɲanθa] *nf* (*educación*) education; (*acción*) teaching; (*doctrina*) teaching, doctrine; **~ primaria/secundaria/superior** primary/secondary/higher education
enseñar [ense'ɲar] *vt* (*educar*) to teach; (*instruir*) to teach, instruct; (*mostrar, señalar*) to show
enseres [en'seres] *nmpl* belongings
ensillar [ensi'ʎar] *vt* to saddle (up)
ensimismarse [ensimis'marse] *vr* (*abstraerse*) to become lost in thought; (*estar absorto*) to be lost in thought; (*Am*) to become conceited
ensordecer [ensorðe'θer] *vt* to deafen ▷ *vi* to go deaf
ensortijado, -a [ensorti'xaðo, a] *adj* (*pelo*) curly
ensuciar [ensu'θjar] *vt* (*manchar*) to dirty, soil; (*fig*) to defile; **ensuciarse** *vr* (*mancharse*) to get dirty; (*niño*) to dirty one's nappy
ensueño [en'sweɲo] *nm* (*sueño*) dream, fantasy; (*ilusión*) illusion; (*soñando despierto*) daydream; **de ~** dream-like
entablado [enta'βlaðo] *nm* (*piso*) floorboards *pl*; (*armazón*) boarding
entablar [enta'βlar] *vt* (*recubrir*) to board (up); (*Ajedrez, Damas*) to set up; (*conversación*) to strike up; (*Jur*) to file ▷ *vi* to draw

entablillar [entaβli'ʎar] *vt* (*Med*) to (put in a) splint
entallado, -a [enta'ʎaðo, a] *adj* waisted
entallar [enta'ʎar] *vt* (*traje*) to tailor ▷ *vi*: **el traje entalla bien** the suit fits well
ente ['ente] *nm* (*organización*) body, organization; (*compañía*) company; (*fam*: *persona*) odd character; (*ser*) being; **~ público** (*Esp*) state(-owned) body
entender [enten'der] *vt* (*comprender*) to understand; (*darse cuenta*) to realize; (*querer decir*) to mean ▷ *vi* to understand; (*creer*) to think, believe ▷ *nm*: **a mi ~** in my opinion; **~ de** to know all about; **~ algo de** to know a little about; **~ en** to deal with, have to do with; **entenderse** *vr* (*comprenderse*) to be understood; (*2 personas*) to get on together; (*ponerse de acuerdo*) to agree, reach an agreement; **dar a ~ que ...** to lead to believe that ...; **~se mal** to get on badly; **¿entiendes?** (do you) understand?
entendido, -a [enten'diðo, a] *adj* (*comprendido*) understood; (*hábil*) skilled; (*inteligente*) knowledgeable ▷ *nm/f* (*experto*) expert ▷ *excl* agreed!
entendimiento [entendi'mjento] *nm* (*comprensión*) understanding; (*inteligencia*) mind, intellect; (*juicio*) judgement
enterado, -a [ente'raðo, a] *adj* well-informed; **estar ~ de** to know about, be aware of; **no darse por ~** to pretend not to understand
enteramente [entera'mente] *adv* entirely, completely
enterar [ente'rar] *vt* (*informar*) to inform, tell; **enterarse** *vr* to find out, get to know; **para que te enteres ...** (*fam*) for your information ...
entereza [ente'reθa] *nf* (*totalidad*) entirety; (*fig*: *de carácter*) strength of mind; (*honradez*) integrity
enterito [ente'rito] *nm* (*Am*) boiler suit (*Brit*), overalls (*US*)
enternecer [enterne'θer] *vt* (*ablandar*) to soften; (*apiadar*) to touch, move; **enternecerse** *vr* to be touched, be moved
entero, -a [en'tero, a] *adj* (*total*) whole, entire; (*fig*: *recto*) honest; (: *firme*) firm, resolute ▷ *nm* (*Mat*) integer; (*Com*: *punto*) point; (*Am*: *pago*) payment; **las acciones han subido dos ~s** the shares have gone up two points
enterrador [enterra'ðor] *nm* gravedigger
enterrar [ente'rrar] *vt* to bury; (*fig*) to forget
entibiar [enti'βjar] *vt* (*enfriar*) to cool; (*calentar*) to warm; **entibiarse** *vr* (*fig*) to cool
entidad [enti'ðað] *nf* (*empresa*) firm, company; (*organismo*) body; (*sociedad*) society; (*Filosofía*) entity
entienda *etc* [en'tjenda] *vb ver* **entender**
entierro [en'tjerro] *vb ver* **enterrar** ▷ *nm* (*acción*) burial; (*funeral*) funeral
entomología [entomolo'xia] *nf* entomology
entonación [entona'θjon] *nf* (*Ling*) intonation; (*fig*) conceit
entonar [ento'nar] *vt* (*canción*) to intone; (*colores*) to tone; (*Med*) to tone up ▷ *vi* to be in tune; **entonarse** *vr* (*engreírse*) to give o.s. airs
entonces [en'tonθes] *adv* then, at that time; **desde ~** since then; **en aquel ~** at that time; **(pues) ~** and so; **el ~ embajador de España** the then Spanish ambassador
entornar [entor'nar] *vt* (*puerta, ventana*) to half close, leave ajar; (*los ojos*) to screw up
entorno [en'torno] *nm* setting, environment; **~ de redes** (*Inform*) network environment
entorpecer [entorpe'θer] *vt* (*entendimiento*) to dull; (*impedir*) to obstruct, hinder; (: *tránsito*) to slow down, delay
entrado, -a [en'traðo, a] *adj*: **~ en años** elderly; **(una vez) ~ el verano** in the summer(time), when summer comes ▷ *nf* (*acción*) entry, access; (*sitio*) entrance, way in; (*principio*) beginning; (*Com*) receipts *pl*, takings *pl*; (*Culin*) entrée; (*Deporte*) innings *sg*; (*Teat*) house, audience; (*para el cine etc*) ticket; (*Inform*) input; (*Econ*): **entradas** *nfpl* income *sg*; **entradas brutas** gross receipts; **entradas y salidas** (*Com*) income and expenditure; **entrada de aire** (*Tec*) air intake *o* inlet; **de entrada** from the outset; **"entrada gratis"** "admission free"; **tiene entradas** he's losing his hair
entramparse [entram'parse] *vr* to get into debt
entrante [en'trante] *adj* next, coming; (*Pol*) incoming ▷ *nm* inlet; (*Culin*) starter; **entrantes** *nmpl* starters; **mes/año ~** next month/year
entraña [en'traɲa] *nf* (*fig*: *centro*) heart, core; (*raíz*) root; **entrañas** *nfpl* (*Anat*) entrails; (*fig*) heart *sg*
entrañable [entra'ɲaβle] *adj* (*persona, lugar*) dear; (*relación*) close; (*acto*) intimate
entrañar [entra'ɲar] *vt* to entail
entrar [en'trar] *vt* (*introducir*) to bring in; (*persona*) to show in; (*Inform*) to input ▷ *vi* (*meterse*) to go *o* come in, enter; (*comenzar*): **~ diciendo** to begin by saying; **entré en** *o* **a** (*Am*) **la casa** I went into the house; **le ~on ganas de reír** he felt a sudden urge to laugh; **me entró sed/sueño** I started to feel thirsty/sleepy; **no me entra** I can't get the hang of it
entre ['entre] *prep* (*dos*) between; (*en medio de*) among(st); (*por*): **se abrieron paso ~ la multitud** they forced their way through the crowd; **~ una cosa y otra** what with one thing and another; **~ más estudia más aprende** (*Am*) the more he studies the more he learns
entreabrir [entrea'βrir] *vt* to half-open, open halfway
entrecejo [entre'θexo] *nm*: **fruncir el ~** to frown

entrecortado, -a [entrekor'taðo, a] *adj* (*respiración*) laboured, difficult; (*habla*) faltering

entredicho [entre'ðitʃo] *nm* (*Jur*) injunction; **poner en ~** to cast doubt on; **estar en ~** to be in doubt

entrega [en'treɣa] *nf* (*de mercancías*) delivery; (*de premios*) presentation; (*de novela etc*) instalment; **"~ a domicilio"** "door-to-door delivery service"

entregar [entre'ɣar] *vt* (*dar*) to hand (over), deliver; (*ejercicios*) to hand in; **entregarse** *vr* (*rendirse*) to surrender, give in, submit; **~se a** (*dedicarse*) to devote o.s. to; **a ~** (*Com*) to be supplied

entrelazar [entrela'θar] *vt* to entwine

entremeses [entre'meses] *nmpl* hors d'œuvres

entremeter [entreme'ter] *vt* to insert, put in; **entremeterse** *vr* to meddle, interfere

entremetido, -a [entreme'tiðo, a] *adj* meddling, interfering

entremezclar [entremeθ'klar] *vt* to intermingle; **entremezclarse** *vr* to intermingle

entrenador, a [entrena'ðor, a] *nm/f* trainer, coach

entrenamiento [entrena'mjento] *nm* training

entrenar [entre'nar] *vt* (*Deporte*) to train; (*caballo*) to exercise ▷ *vi*, **entrenarse** *vr* to train

entrepierna [entre'pjerna] *nf* (*tb*: **~s**) crotch, crutch

entresacar [entresa'kar] *vt* to pick out, select

entresuelo [entre'swelo] *nm* mezzanine, entresol; (*Teat*) dress *o* first circle

entretanto [entre'tanto] *adv* meanwhile, meantime

entretecho [entre'tetʃo] *nm* (*Am*) attic

entretejer [entrete'xer] *vt* to interweave

entretener [entrete'ner] *vt* (*divertir*) to entertain, amuse; (*detener*) to hold up, delay; (*mantener*) to maintain; **entretenerse** *vr* (*divertirse*) to amuse o.s.; (*retrasarse*) to delay, linger; **no le entretengo más** I won't keep you any longer

entretenido, -a [entrete'niðo, a] *adj* entertaining, amusing

entretenimiento [entreteni'mjento] *nm* entertainment, amusement; (*mantenimiento*) upkeep, maintenance

entretiempo [entre'tjempo] *nm*: **ropa de ~** *clothes for spring and autumn*

entrever [entre'βer] *vt* to glimpse, catch a glimpse of

entrevista [entre'βista] *nf* interview

entrevistador, a [entreβista'ðor, a] *nm/f* interviewer

entrevistar [entreβis'tar] *vt* to interview; **entrevistarse** *vr*: **~se con** to have an interview with, see; **el ministro se entrevistó con el Rey ayer** the minister had an audience with the King yesterday

entristecer [entriste'θer] *vt* to sadden, grieve; **entristecerse** *vr* to grow sad

entrometerse [entrome'terse] *vr*: **~ (en)** to interfere (in *o* with)

entroncar [entron'kar] *vi* to be connected *o* related

entumecer [entume'θer] *vt* to numb, benumb; **entumecerse** *vr* (*por el frío*) to go *o* become numb

entumecido, -a [entume'θiðo, a] *adj* numb, stiff

enturbiar [entur'βjar] *vt* (*el agua*) to make cloudy; (*fig*) to confuse; **enturbiarse** *vr* (*oscurecerse*) to become cloudy; (*fig*) to get confused, become obscure

entusiasmar [entusjas'mar] *vt* to excite, fill with enthusiasm; (*gustar mucho*) to delight; **entusiasmarse** *vr*: **~se con** *o* **por** to get enthusiastic *o* excited about

entusiasmo [entu'sjasmo] *nm* enthusiasm; (*excitación*) excitement

entusiasta [entu'sjasta] *adj* enthusiastic ▷ *nm/f* enthusiast

enumerar [enume'rar] *vt* to enumerate

enunciación [enunθja'θjon] *nf*, **enunciado** [enun'θjaðo] *nm* enunciation; (*declaración*) declaration, statement

envainar [embai'nar] *vt* to sheathe

envalentonar [embalento'nar] *vt* to give courage to; **envalentonarse** *vr* (*pey: jactarse*) to boast, brag

envanecer [embane'θer] *vt* to make conceited; **envanecerse** *vr* to grow conceited

envasar [emba'sar] *vt* (*empaquetar*) to pack, wrap; (*enfrascar*) to bottle; (*enlatar*) to can; (*embolsar*) to pocket

envase [em'base] *nm* packing, wrapping; bottling; canning; pocketing; (*recipiente*) container; (*paquete*) package; (*botella*) bottle; (*lata*) tin (*Brit*), can

envejecer [embexe'θer] *vt* to make old, age ▷ *vi*, **envejecerse** *vr* (*volverse viejo*) to grow old; (*parecer viejo*) to age

envenenar [embene'nar] *vt* to poison; (*fig*) to embitter

envergadura [emberɣa'ðura] *nf* (*expansión*) expanse; (*Naut*) breadth; (*fig*) scope; **un programa de gran ~** a wide-ranging programme

envés [em'bes] *nm* (*de tela*) back, wrong side

enviar [em'bjar] *vt* to send; **~ un mensaje a algn** (*por móvil*) to text sb, send sb a text message

enviciar [embi'θjar] *vt* to corrupt ▷ *vi* (*trabajo etc*) to be addictive; **enviciarse** *vr*: **~se (con** *o* **en)** to get addicted (to)

envidia [em'biðja] *nf* envy; **tener ~ a** to envy, be jealous of

envidiar [embi'ðjar] *vt* (*desear*) to envy; (*tener celos de*) to be jealous of
envío [em'bio] *nm* (*acción*) sending; (*de mercancías*) consignment; (*de dinero*) remittance; (*en barco*) shipment; **gastos de ~** postage and packing; **~ contra reembolso** COD shipment
enviudar [embju'ðar] *vi* to be widowed
envoltorio [embol'torjo] *nm* package
envoltura [embol'tura] *nf* (*cobertura*) cover; (*embalaje*) wrapper, wrapping
envolver [embol'βer] *vt* to wrap (up); (*cubrir*) to cover; (*enemigo*) to surround; (*implicar*) to involve, implicate
envuelto [em'bwelto], **envuelva** *etc* [em'bwelβa] *vb ver* **envolver**
enyesar [enje'sar] *vt* (*pared*) to plaster; (*Med*) to put in plaster
enzarzarse [enθar'θarse] *vr*: **~ en algo** to get mixed up in sth; (*disputa*) to get involved in sth
epicentro [epi'θentro] *nm* epicentre
épico, -a ['epiko, a] *adj* epic ▷ *nf* epic (poetry)
epidemia [epi'ðemja] *nf* epidemic
epidermis [epi'ðermis] *nf* epidermis
epilepsia [epi'lepsja] *nf* epilepsy
epiléptico, -a [epi'leptiko, a] *adj, nm/f* epileptic
epílogo [e'piloɣo] *nm* epilogue
episodio [epi'soðjo] *nm* episode; (*suceso*) incident
epístola [e'pistola] *nf* epistle
epíteto [e'piteto] *nm* epithet
época ['epoka] *nf* period, time; (*temporada*) season; (*Historia*) age, epoch; **hacer ~** to be epoch-making
equidad [eki'ðað] *nf* equity, fairness
equilibrar [ekili'βrar] *vt* to balance
equilibrio [eki'liβrjo] *nm* balance, equilibrium; **mantener/perder el ~** to keep/lose one's balance; **~ político** balance of power
equilibrista [ekili'βrista] *nm/f* (*funámbulo*) tightrope walker; (*acróbata*) acrobat
equipaje [eki'paxe] *nm* luggage (*Brit*), baggage (*US*); (*avíos*) equipment, kit; **~ de mano** hand luggage; **hacer el ~** to pack
equipar [eki'par] *vt* (*proveer*) to equip
equiparar [ekipa'rar] *vt* (*igualar*) to put on the same level; (*comparar*): **~ con** to compare with; **equipararse** *vr*: **~se con** to be on a level with
equipo [e'kipo] *nm* (*conjunto de cosas*) equipment; (*Deporte, grupo*) team; (*de obreros*) shift; (*de máquinas*) plant; (*turbinas etc*) set; **~ de caza** hunting gear; **~ de música** music centre; **~ físico** (*Inform*) hardware; **~ manos libres** hands-free kit; **~ médico** medical team
equis ['ekis] *nf* (the letter) X
equitación [ekita'θjon] *nf* (*acto*) riding; (*arte*) horsemanship
equitativo, -a [ekita'tiβo, a] *adj* equitable, fair
equivalente [ekiβa'lente] *adj, nm* equivalent
equivaler [ekiβa'ler] *vi*: **~ a** to be equivalent *o* equal to; (*en rango*) to rank as
equivocación [ekiβoka'θjon] *nf* mistake, error; (*malentendido*) misunderstanding
equivocado, -a [ekiβo'kaðo, a] *adj* wrong, mistaken
equivocarse [ekiβo'karse] *vr* to be wrong, make a mistake; **~ de camino** to take the wrong road
equívoco, -a [e'kiβoko, a] *adj* (*dudoso*) suspect; (*ambiguo*) ambiguous ▷ *nm* ambiguity; (*malentendido*) misunderstanding
era ['era] *vb ver* **ser** ▷ *nf* era, age; (*Agr*) threshing floor
erais ['erais], **éramos** ['eramos], **eran** ['eran] *vb ver* **ser**
erario [e'rarjo] *nm* exchequer, treasury
eras ['eras], **eres** ['eres] *vb ver* **ser**
e-reader ['irider] *nm* e-reader
erección [erek'θjon] *nf* erection
erguir [er'ɣir] *vt* to raise, lift; (*poner derecho*) to straighten; **erguirse** *vr* to straighten up
erigir [eri'xir] *vt* to erect, build; **erigirse** *vr*: **~se en** to set o.s. up as
erizado, -a [eri'θaðo, a] *adj* bristly
erizarse [eri'θarse] *vr* (*pelo: de perro*) to bristle; (*: de persona*) to stand on end
erizo [e'riθo] *nm* hedgehog; **~ de mar** sea urchin
ermita [er'mita] *nf* hermitage
ermitaño, -a [ermi'taɲo, a] *nm/f* hermit
erosión [ero'sjon] *nf* erosion
erosionar [erosjo'nar] *vt* to erode
erótico, -a [e'rotiko, a] *adj* erotic
erotismo [ero'tismo] *nm* eroticism
erradicar [erraði'kar] *vt* to eradicate
errante [e'rrante] *adj* wandering, errant
errar [e'rrar] *vi* (*vagar*) to wander, roam; (*equivocarse*) to be mistaken ▷ *vt*: **~ el camino** to take the wrong road; **~ el tiro** to miss
errata [e'rrata] *nf* misprint
erróneo, -a [e'rroneo, a] *adj* (*equivocado*) wrong, mistaken; (*falso*) false, untrue
error [e'rror] *nm* error, mistake; (*Inform*) bug; **~ de imprenta** misprint; **~ de lectura/escritura** (*Inform*) read/write error; **~ sintáctico** syntax error; **~ judicial** miscarriage of justice
eructar [eruk'tar] *vt* to belch, burp
eructo [e'rukto] *nm* belch
erudito, -a [eru'ðito, a] *adj* erudite, learned ▷ *nm/f* scholar; **los ~s en esta materia** the experts in this field
erupción [erup'θjon] *nf* eruption; (*Med*) rash; (*de violencia*) outbreak; (*de ira*) outburst
es [es] *vb ver* **ser**
esa ['esa], **esas** ['esas] *adj demostrativo, pron ver* **ese**
ésa ['esa], **ésas** ['esas] *pron ver* **ése**

esbelto, -a [es'βelto, a] *adj* slim, slender
esbozo [es'βoθo] *nm* sketch, outline
escabeche [eska'βetʃe] *nm* brine; (*de aceitunas etc*) pickle; **en ~** pickled
escabroso, -a [eska'βroso, a] *adj* (*accidentado*) rough, uneven; (*fig*) tough, difficult; (*: atrevido*) risqué
escabullirse [eskaβu'ʎirse] *vr* to slip away; (*largarse*) to clear out
escacharrar [eskatʃa'rrar] *vt* (*fam*) to break; **escacharrarse** *vr* to get broken
escafandra [eska'fandra] *nf* (*buzo*) diving suit; (*escafandra espacial*) spacesuit
escala [es'kala] *nf* (*proporción, Mus*) scale; (*de mano*) ladder; (*Aviat*) stopover; (*de colores etc*) range; **~ de tiempo** time scale; **~ de sueldos** salary scale; **una investigación a ~ nacional** a nationwide inquiry; **reproducir a ~** to reproduce to scale; **hacer ~ en** (*gen*) to stop off at *o* call in at; (*Aviat*) to stop over in
escalafón [eskala'fon] *nm* (*escala de salarios*) salary scale, wage scale
escalar [eska'lar] *vt* to climb, scale ▷ *vi* (*Mil, Pol*) to escalate
escalera [eska'lera] *nf* stairs *pl*, staircase; (*escala*) ladder; (*Naipes*) run; (*de camión*) tailboard; **~ mecánica** escalator; **~ de caracol** spiral staircase; **~ de incendios** fire escape
escalerilla [eskale'riʎa] *nf* (*de avión*) steps *pl*
escalfar [eskal'far] *vt* (*huevos*) to poach
escalinata [eskali'nata] *nf* staircase
escalofriante [eskalo'frjante] *adj* chilling
escalofrío [eskalo'frio] *nm* (*Med*) chill; **escalofríos** *nmpl* (*fig*) shivers
escalón [eska'lon] *nm* step, stair; (*de escalera*) rung; (*fig: paso*) step; (*al éxito*) ladder
escalope [eska'lope] *nm* (*Culin*) escalope
escama [es'kama] *nf* (*de pez, serpiente*) scale; (*de jabón*) flake; (*fig*) resentment
escamar [eska'mar] *vt* (*pez*) to scale; (*producir recelo*) to make wary
escamotear [eskamote'ar] *vt* (*fam: robar*) to lift, swipe; (*hacer desaparecer*) to make disappear
escampar [eskam'par] *vb impersonal* to stop raining
escanciar [eskan'θjar] *vt* (*vino*) to pour (out)
escandalizar [eskandali'θar] *vt* to scandalize, shock; **escandalizarse** *vr* to be shocked; (*ofenderse*) to be offended
escándalo [es'kandalo] *nm* scandal; (*alboroto, tumulto*) row, uproar; **armar un ~** to make a scene; **¡es un ~!** it's outrageous!
escandaloso, -a [eskanda'loso, a] *adj* scandalous, shocking; (*risa*) hearty; (*niño*) noisy
escandinavo, -a [eskandi'naβo, a] *adj, nm/f* Scandinavian
escanear [eskane'ar] *vt* to scan
escaneo [es'kaneo] *nm* scanning
escáner [es'kaner] *nm* scanner
escaño [es'kaɲo] *nm* bench; (*Pol*) seat
escapar [eska'par] *vi* (*gen*) to escape, run away; (*Deporte*) to break away; **escaparse** *vr* to escape, get away; (*agua, gas, noticias*) to leak (out); **se me escapa su nombre** his name escapes me
escaparate [eskapa'rate] *nm* shop window; (*Com*) showcase; **ir de ~s** to go window shopping
escape [es'kape] *nm* (*huida*) escape; (*de agua, gas*) leak; (*de motor*) exhaust; **salir a ~** to rush out
escaquearse [eskake'arse] *vr* (*fam*) to duck out
escarabajo [eskara'βaxo] *nm* beetle
escaramuza [eskara'muθa] *nf* skirmish; (*fig*) brush
escarbar [eskar'βar] *vt* (*gallina*) to scratch; (*fig*) to inquire into, investigate
escarceos [eskar'θeos] *nmpl*: **en sus ~ con la política** in his occasional forays into politics; **~ amorosos** love affairs
escarcha [es'kartʃa] *nf* frost
escarchado, -a [eskar'tʃaðo, a] *adj* (*Culin: fruta*) crystallized
escarlata [eskar'lata] *adj inv* scarlet
escarlatina [eskarla'tina] *nf* scarlet fever
escarmentar [eskarmen'tar] *vt* to punish severely ▷ *vi* to learn one's lesson; **¡para que escarmientes!** that'll teach you!
escarmiento *etc* [eskar'mjento] *vb ver* **escarmentar** ▷ *nm* (*ejemplo*) lesson; (*castigo*) punishment
escarnio [es'karnjo] *nm* mockery; (*injuria*) insult
escarola [eska'rola] *nf* (*Bot*) endive
escarpado, -a [eskar'paðo, a] *adj* (*pendiente*) sheer, steep; (*rocas*) craggy
escasear [eskase'ar] *vi* to be scarce
escasez [eska'seθ] *nf* (*falta*) shortage, scarcity; (*pobreza*) poverty; **vivir con ~** to live on the breadline
escaso, -a [es'kaso, a] *adj* (*poco*) scarce; (*raro*) rare; (*ralo*) thin, sparse; (*limitado*) limited; (*recursos*) scanty; (*público*) sparse; (*posibilidad*) slim; (*visibilidad*) poor
escatimar [eskati'mar] *vt* (*limitar*) to skimp (on), be sparing with; **no ~ esfuerzos (para)** to spare no effort (to)
escayola [eska'jola] *nf* plaster
escayolar [eskajo'lar] *vt* to put in plaster
escena [es'θena] *nf* scene; (*decorado*) scenery; (*escenario*) stage; **poner en ~** to put on
escenario [esθe'narjo] *nm* (*Teat*) stage; (*Cine*) set; (*fig*) scene; **el ~ del crimen** the scene of the crime; **el ~ político** the political scene
escenografía [esθenoɣra'fia] *nf* set *o* stage design
escepticismo [esθepti'θismo] *nm* scepticism
escéptico, -a [es'θeptiko, a] *adj* sceptical ▷ *nm/f* sceptic
escisión [esθi'sjon] *nf* (*Med*) excision; (*fig, Pol*) split; **~ nuclear** nuclear fission

esclarecer [esklare'θer] *vt* (*iluminar*) to light up, illuminate; (*misterio, problema*) to shed light on
esclavitud [esklaβi'tuð] *nf* slavery
esclavizar [esklaβi'θar] *vt* to enslave
esclavo, -a [es'klaβo, a] *nm/f* slave
esclusa [es'klusa] *nf* (*de canal*) lock; (*compuerta*) floodgate
escoba [es'koβa] *nf* broom; **pasar la ~** to sweep up
escobilla [esko'βiʎa] *nf* brush
escocer [esko'θer] *vi* to burn, sting; **escocerse** *vr* to chafe, get chafed
escocés, -esa [esko'θes, esa] *adj* Scottish; (*whisky*) Scotch ▷ *nm/f* Scotsman(-woman), Scot ▷ *nm* (*Ling*) Scots *sg*; **tela escocesa** tartan
Escocia [es'koθja] *nf* Scotland
escoger [esko'xer] *vt* to choose, pick, select
escogido, -a [esko'xiðo, a] *adj* chosen, selected; (*calidad*) choice, select; (*persona*): **ser muy ~** to be very fussy
escolar [esko'lar] *adj* school *cpd* ▷ *nm/f* schoolboy(-girl), pupil
escollo [es'koʎo] *nm* (*arrecife*) reef, rock; (*fig*) pitfall
escolta [es'kolta] *nf* escort
escoltar [eskol'tar] *vt* to escort; (*proteger*) to guard
escombros [es'kombros] *nmpl* (*basura*) rubbish *sg*; (*restos*) debris *sg*
esconder [eskon'der] *vt* to hide, conceal; **esconderse** *vr* to hide
escondidas [eskon'diðas] *nfpl* (*Am*) hide-and-seek *sg*; **a ~** secretly; **hacer algo a ~ de algn** to do sth behind sb's back
escondite [eskon'dite] *nm* hiding place; (*juego*) hide-and-seek
escondrijo [eskon'drixo] *nm* hiding place, hideout
escopeta [esko'peta] *nf* shotgun; **~ de aire comprimido** air gun
escoria [es'korja] *nf* (*desecho mineral*) slag; (*fig*) scum, dregs *pl*
Escorpio [es'korpjo] *nm* (*Astro*) Scorpio
escorpión [eskor'pjon] *nm* scorpion
escotado, -a [esko'taðo, a] *adj* low-cut
escote [es'kote] *nm* (*de vestido*) low neck; **pagar a ~** to share the expenses
escotilla [esko'tiʎa] *nf* (*Naut*) hatchway
escozor [esko'θor] *nm* (*dolor*) sting(ing)
escribano, -a [eskri'βano, a], **escribiente** [eskri'βjente] *nm/f* clerk; (*secretario judicial*) court *o* lawyer's clerk
escribible [eskri'βiβle] *adj* writable
escribir [eskri'βir] *vt, vi* to write; **~ a máquina** to type; **¿cómo se escribe?** how do you spell it?
escrito, -a [es'krito, a] *pp de* **escribir** ▷ *adj* written, in writing; (*examen*) written ▷ *nm* (*documento*) document; (*manuscrito*) text, manuscript; **por ~** in writing
escritor, a [eskri'tor, a] *nm/f* writer
escritorio [eskri'torjo] *nm* desk; (*oficina*) office; (*Inform*) desktop
escritura [eskri'tura] *nf* (*acción*) writing; (*caligrafía*) (hand)writing; (*Jur: documento*) deed; (*Com*) indenture; **~ de propiedad** title deed; **Sagrada E~** (Holy) Scripture; **~ social** articles *pl* of association
escrúpulo [es'krupulo] *nm* scruple; (*minuciosidad*) scrupulousness
escrupuloso, -a [eskrupu'loso, a] *adj* scrupulous
escrutar [eskru'tar] *vt* to scrutinize, examine; (*votos*) to count
escrutinio [eskru'tinjo] *nm* (*examen atento*) scrutiny; (*Pol: recuento de votos*) count(ing)
escuadra [es'kwaðra] *nf* (*Tec*) square; (*Mil etc*) squad; (*Naut*) squadron; (*de coches etc*) fleet
escuadrilla [eskwa'ðriʎa] *nf* (*de aviones*) squadron; (*Am: de obreros*) gang
escuadrón [eskwa'ðron] *nm* squadron
escuálido, -a [es'kwaliðo, a] *adj* skinny, scraggy; (*sucio*) squalid
escucha [es'kutʃa] *nf* (*acción*) listening ▷ *nm* (*Telec: sistema*) monitor; (*oyente*) listener; **estar a la ~** to listen in; **estar de ~** to spy; **~s telefónicas** (phone)tapping *sg*
escuchar [esku'tʃar] *vt* to listen to; (*consejo*) to heed; (*esp Am: oír*) to hear ▷ *vi* to listen; **escucharse** *vr*: **se escucha muy mal** (*Telec*) it's a very bad line
escudarse [esku'ðarse] *vr*: **~ en** (*fig*) to hide behind
escudilla [esku'ðiʎa] *nf* bowl, basin
escudo [es'kuðo] *nm* shield; **~ de armas** coat of arms
escudriñar [eskuðri'ɲar] *vt* (*examinar*) to investigate, scrutinize; (*mirar de lejos*) to scan
escuela [es'kwela] *nf* (*tb fig*) school; **~ normal** teacher training college; **~ técnica superior** *university offering five-year courses in engineering and technical subjects*; **~ universitaria** *university offering three-year diploma courses*; **~ de párvulos** kindergarten; **~ de artes y oficios** (*Esp*) ≈ technical college; **~ de choferes** (*Am*) driving school; **~ de manejo** (*Am*) driving school; *ver tb* **colegio**
escueto, -a [es'kweto, a] *adj* plain; (*estilo*) simple; (*explicación*) concise
escuincle [es'kwinkle] *nm* (*Am fam*) kid
esculpir [eskul'pir] *vt* to sculpt; (*grabar*) to engrave; (*tallar*) to carve
escultor, a [eskul'tor, a] *nm/f* sculptor
escultura [eskul'tura] *nf* sculpture
escupidera [eskupi'ðera] *nf* spittoon
escupir [esku'pir] *vt* to spit (out) ▷ *vi* to spit
escupitajo [eskupi'taxo] *nm* (*fam*) gob of spit
escurreplatos [eskurre'platos] *nm inv* plate rack
escurridero [eskurri'ðero] *nm* (*Am*) draining board (*Brit*), drainboard (*US*)
escurridizo, -a [eskurri'ðiθo, a] *adj* slippery

e

escurridor [eskurri'ðor] *nm* colander
escurrir [esku'rrir] *vt* (*ropa*) to wring out; (*verduras, platos*) to drain ▷ *vi* (*los líquidos*) to drip; **escurrirse** *vr* (*secarse*) to drain; (*resbalarse*) to slip, slide; (*escaparse*) to slip away
ese¹ ['ese] *nf* (the letter) S; **hacer ~s** (*carretera*) to zigzag; (*borracho*) to reel about
ese² ['ese], **esa** ['esa], **esos** ['esos], **esas** ['esas] *adj demostrativo* that *sg*, those *pl* ▷ *pron* that (one) *sg*, those (ones) *pl*; **~ ... este ...** the former ... the latter ...; **¡no me vengas con esas!** don't give me any more of that nonsense!
ése ['ese], **ésa** ['esa], **ésos** ['esos], **ésas** ['esas] *pron* that (one) *sg*, those (ones) *pl*
esencia [e'senθja] *nf* essence
esencial [esen'θjal] *adj* essential; (*principal*) chief; **lo ~** the main thing
esfera [es'fera] *nf* sphere; (*de reloj*) face; **~ de acción** scope; **~ terrestre** globe
esférico, -a [es'feriko, a] *adj* spherical
esforzado, -a [esfor'θaðo, a] *adj* (*enérgico*) energetic, vigorous
esforzarse [esfor'θarse] *vr* to exert o.s., make an effort
esfuerzo [es'fwerθo] *vb ver* **esforzarse** ▷ *nm* effort; **sin ~** effortlessly
esfumarse [esfu'marse] *vr* (*apoyo, esperanzas*) to fade away; (*persona*) to vanish
esgrima [es'ɣrima] *nf* fencing
esgrimir [esɣri'mir] *vt* (*arma*) to brandish; (*argumento*) to use ▷ *vi* to fence
esguince [es'ɣinθe] *nm* (*Med*) sprain
eslabón [esla'βon] *nm* link; **~ perdido** (*Bio, fig*) missing link
eslálom [es'lalom] *nm* slalom
eslavo, -a [es'laβo, a] *adj* Slav, Slavonic ▷ *nm/f* Slav ▷ *nm* (*Ling*) Slavonic
eslip [ez'lip] *nm* pants *pl* (*Brit*), briefs *pl*
eslogan [es'loɣan] *nm* (*pl* **eslogans**) slogan
eslovaco, -a [eslo'βako, a] *adj, nm/f* Slovak, Slovakian ▷ *nm* (*Ling*) Slovak, Slovakian
Eslovaquia [eslo'βakja] *nf* Slovakia
esmaltar [esmal'tar] *vt* to enamel
esmalte [es'malte] *nm* enamel; **~ de uñas** nail varnish *o* polish
esmerado, -a [esme'raðo, a] *adj* careful, neat
esmeralda [esme'ralda] *nf* emerald
esmerarse [esme'rarse] *vr* (*aplicarse*) to take great pains, exercise great care; (*afanarse*) to work hard; (*hacer lo mejor*) to do one's best
esmero [es'mero] *nm* (great) care
esnob [es'nob] *adj inv* (*persona*) snobbish; (*coche etc*) posh ▷ *nm/f* snob
esnobismo [esno'βismo] *nm* snobbery
eso ['eso] *pron* that, that thing *o* matter; **~ de su coche** that business about his car; **~ de ir al cine** all that about going to the cinema; **a ~ de las cinco** at about five o'clock; **en ~** thereupon, at that point; **por ~** therefore; **~ es** that's it; **nada de ~** far from it; **¡~ sí que es vida!** now this is really living!; **por ~ te lo dije** that's why I told you; **y ~ que llovía** in spite of the fact it was raining
esófago [e'sofaɣo] *nm* (*Anat*) oesophagus
esos ['esos] *adj demostrativo ver* **ese**
ésos ['esos] *pron ver* **ése**
esotérico, -a [eso'teriko, a] *adj* esoteric
espabilado, -a [espaβi'laðo, a] *adj* quick-witted
espabilar [espaβi'lar] *vt*, **espabilarse** *vr* = **despabilar(se)**
espachurrar [espatʃu'rrar] *vt* to squash; **espachurrarse** *vr* to get squashed
espacial [espa'θjal] *adj* (*del espacio*) space *cpd*
espaciar [espa'θjar] *vt* to space (out)
espacio [es'paθjo] *nm* space; (*Mus*) interval; (*Radio, TV*) programme, program (*US*); **el ~** space; **ocupar mucho ~** to take up a lot of room; **a dos ~s, a doble ~** (*Tip*) double-spaced; **por ~ de** during, for; **~ aéreo/exterior** air/outer space
espacioso, -a [espa'θjoso, a] *adj* spacious, roomy
espada [es'paða] *nf* sword ▷ *nm* swordsman; (*Taur*) matador; **espadas** *nfpl* (*Naipes*) *one of the suits in the Spanish card deck*; **estar entre la ~ y la pared** to be between the devil and the deep blue sea
espaguetis [espa'ɣetis] *nmpl* spaghetti *sg*
espalda [es'palda] *nf* (*gen*) back; (*Natación*) backstroke; **~s** *nfpl* (*hombros*) shoulders; **a ~s de algn** behind sb's back; **estar de ~s** to have one's back turned; **tenderse de ~s** to lie (down) on one's back; **volver la ~ a algn** to cold-shoulder sb
espaldilla [espal'ðiʎa] *nf* shoulder blade
espantadizo, -a [espanta'ðiθo, a] *adj* timid, easily frightened
espantajo [espan'taxo] *nm*, **espantapájaros** [espanta'paxaros] *nm inv* scarecrow
espantar [espan'tar] *vt* (*asustar*) to frighten, scare; (*ahuyentar*) to frighten off; (*asombrar*) to horrify, appal; **espantarse** *vr* to get frightened *o* scared; to be appalled
espanto [es'panto] *nm* (*susto*) fright; (*terror*) terror; (*asombro*) astonishment; **¡qué ~!** how awful!
espantoso, -a [espan'toso, a] *adj* frightening, terrifying; (*ruido*) dreadful
España [es'paɲa] *nf* Spain; **la ~ de pandereta** touristy Spain
español, a [espa'ɲol, a] *adj* Spanish ▷ *nm/f* Spaniard ▷ *nm* (*Ling*) Spanish; *ver tb* **castellano**
esparadrapo [espara'ðrapo] *nm* surgical tape
esparcimiento [esparθi'mjento] *nm* (*dispersión*) spreading; (*derramamiento*) scattering; (*fig*) cheerfulness

esparcir [espar'θir] *vt* to spread; (*derramar*) to scatter; **esparcirse** *vr* to spread (out); to scatter; (*divertirse*) to enjoy o.s.
espárrago [es'parraɣo] *nm* (*tb*: **~s**) asparagus; **estar hecho un ~** to be as thin as a rake; **¡vete a freír ~s!** (*fam*) go to hell!
esparto [es'parto] *nm* esparto (grass)
espasmo [es'pasmo] *nm* spasm
espátula [es'patula] *nf* (*Med*) spatula; (*Arte*) palette knife; (*Culin*) fish slice
especia [es'peθja] *nf* spice
especial [espe'θjal] *adj* special
especialidad [espeθjali'ðað] *nf* speciality, specialty (*US*); (*Escol*: *ramo*) specialism
especialista [espeθja'lista] *nm/f* specialist; (*Cine*) stuntman(-woman)
especializado, -a [espeθjali'θaðo, a] *adj* specialized; (*obrero*) skilled
especialmente [espeθjal'mente] *adv* particularly, especially
especie [es'peθje] *nf* (*Bio*) species; (*clase*) kind, sort; **pagar en ~** to pay in kind
especificar [espeθifi'kar] *vt* to specify
específico, -a [espe'θifiko, a] *adj* specific
espécimen [es'peθimen] (*pl* **especímenes**) *nm* specimen
espectáculo [espek'takulo] *nm* (*gen*) spectacle; (*Teat etc*) show; (*función*) performance; **dar un ~** to make a scene
espectador, a [espekta'ðor, a] *nm/f* spectator; (*de incidente*) onlooker; **los espectadores** *nmpl* (*Teat*) the audience *sg*
espectro [es'pektro] *nm* ghost; (*fig*) spectre
especulación [espekula'θjon] *nf* speculation; **~ bursátil** speculation on the Stock Market
especular [espeku'lar] *vt, vi* to speculate
espejismo [espe'xismo] *nm* mirage
espejo [es'pexo] *nm* mirror; (*fig*) model; **~ retrovisor** rear-view mirror; **mirarse al ~** to look (at o.s.) in the mirror
espeleología [espeleolo'xia] *nf* potholing
espeluznante [espeluθ'nante] *adj* horrifying, hair-raising
espera [es'pera] *nf* (*pausa, intervalo*) wait; (*Jur*: *plazo*) respite; **en ~ de** waiting for; (*con expectativa*) expecting; **en ~ de su contestación** awaiting your reply
esperanza [espe'ranθa] *nf* (*confianza*) hope; (*expectativa*) expectation; **hay pocas ~s de que venga** there is little prospect of his coming; **~ de vida** life expectancy
esperanzar [esperan'θar] *vt* to give hope to
esperar [espe'rar] *vt* (*aguardar*) to wait for; (*tener expectativa de*) to expect; (*desear*) to hope for ▷ *vi* to wait; to expect; to hope; **esperarse** *vr*: **como podía ~se** as was to be expected; **hacer ~ a algn** to keep sb waiting; **ir a ~ a algn** to go and meet sb; **~ un bebé** to be expecting (a baby)
esperma [es'perma] *nf* sperm
espermatozoide [espermato'θoiðe] *nm* spermatozoid
espesar [espe'sar] *vt* to thicken; **espesarse** *vr* to thicken, get thicker
espeso, -a [es'peso, a] *adj* thick; (*bosque*) dense; (*nieve*) deep; (*sucio*) dirty
espesor [espe'sor] *nm* thickness; (*de nieve*) depth
espía [es'pia] *nm/f* spy
espiar [espi'ar] *vt* (*observar*) to spy on ▷ *vi*: **~ para** to spy for
espiga [es'piɣa] *nf* (*Bot*: *de trigo etc*) ear; (: *de flores*) spike
espigón [espi'ɣon] *nm* (*Bot*) ear; (*Naut*) breakwater
espina [es'pina] *nf* thorn; (*de pez*) bone; **~ dorsal** (*Anat*) spine; **me da mala ~** I don't like the look of it
espinaca [espi'naka] *nf* (*tb*: **~s**) spinach
espinazo [espi'naθo] *nm* spine, backbone
espinilla [espi'niʎa] *nf* (*Anat*: *tibia*) shin(bone); (: *en la piel*) blackhead
espino [es'pino] *nm* hawthorn
espinoso, -a [espi'noso, a] *adj* (*planta*) thorny, prickly; (*fig*) bony; (*asunto*) difficult; (*problema*) knotty
espionaje [espjo'naxe] *nm* spying, espionage
espiral [espi'ral] *adj, nf* spiral; **la ~ inflacionista** the inflationary spiral
espirar [espi'rar] *vt, vi* to breathe out, exhale
espiritista [espiri'tista] *adj, nm/f* spiritualist
espíritu [es'piritu] *nm* spirit; (*mente*) mind; (*inteligencia*) intelligence; (*Rel*) spirit, soul; **E~ Santo** Holy Ghost; **con ~ amplio** with an open mind
espiritual [espiri'twal] *adj* spiritual
espita [es'pita] *nf* tap (*Brit*), faucet (*US*)
espléndido, -a [es'plendiðo, a] *adj* (*magnífico*) magnificent, splendid; (*generoso*) generous, lavish
esplendor [esplen'dor] *nm* splendour
espolear [espole'ar] *vt* to spur on
espoleta [espo'leta] *nf* (*de bomba*) fuse
espolvorear [espolβore'ar] *vt* to dust, sprinkle
esponja [es'ponxa] *nf* sponge; (*fig*) sponger
esponjoso, -a [espon'xoso, a] *adj* spongy
espontaneidad [espontanei'ðað] *nf* spontaneity
espontáneo, -a [espon'taneo, a] *adj* spontaneous; (*improvisado*) impromptu; (*persona*) natural
esporádico, -a [espo'raðiko, a] *adj* sporadic
esposa [es'posa] *nf ver* **esposo**
esposar [espo'sar] *vt* to handcuff
esposo, -a [es'poso, a] *nm* husband ▷ *nf* wife; **esposas** *nfpl* handcuffs
espray [es'prai] *nm* spray
espuela [es'pwela] *nf* spur; (*fam*: *trago*) one for the road
espuma [es'puma] *nf* foam; (*de cerveza*) froth, head; (*de jabón*) lather; (*de olas*) surf; **~ de afeitar** shaving foam

espumadera [espuma'ðera] *nf* skimmer
espumoso, -a [espu'moso, a] *adj* frothy, foamy; (*vino*) sparkling
esqueje [es'kexe] *nm* (*Bot*) cutting
esquela [es'kela] *nf*: **~ mortuoria** announcement of death
esquelético, -a [eske'letiko, a] *adj* (*fam*) skinny
esqueleto [eske'leto] *nm* skeleton; (*lo esencial*) bare bones (of a matter); **en ~** unfinished
esquema [es'kema] *nm* (*diagrama*) diagram; (*dibujo*) plan; (*plan*) scheme; (*Filosofía*) schema
esquemático, -a [eske'matiko, a] *adj* schematic; **un resumen ~** a brief outline
esquí [es'ki] (*pl* **esquís**) *nm* (*objeto*) ski; (*deporte*) skiing; **~ acuático** water-skiing; **hacer ~** to go skiing
esquiar [es'kjar] *vi* to ski
esquilar [eski'lar] *vt* to shear
esquimal [eski'mal] *adj, nm/f* Eskimo
esquina [es'kina] *nf* corner; **doblar la ~** to turn the corner
esquinazo [eski'naθo] *nm*: **dar ~ a algn** to give sb the slip
esquirol [eski'rol] *nm* (*Esp*) strikebreaker, blackleg
esquivar [eski'βar] *vt* to avoid; (*evadir*) to dodge, elude
esquivo, -a [es'kiβo, a] *adj* (*altanero*) aloof; (*desdeñoso*) scornful, disdainful
esta ['esta] *adj demostrativo, pron ver* **este**
ésta ['esta] *pron ver* **éste**
está [es'ta] *vb ver* **estar**
estabilidad [estaβili'ðað] *nf* stability
estabilizador, a [estabiliθa'ðor, a] *adj* (*Foto*) antishake
estabilizar [estaβili'θar] *vt* to stabilize; (*fijar*) to make steady; (*precios*) to peg; **estabilizarse** *vr* to become stable
estable [es'taβle] *adj* stable
establecer [estaβle'θer] *vt* to establish; (*fundar*) to set up; (*colonos*) to settle; (*récord*) to set (up); **establecerse** *vr* to establish o.s.; (*echar raíces*) to settle (down); (*Com*) to start up
establecimiento [estaβleθi'mjento] *nm* establishment; (*fundación*) institution; (*de negocio*) start-up; (*de colonias*) settlement; (*local*) establishment; **~ comercial** business house
establo [es'taβlo] *nm* (*Agr*) stall; (*para vacas*) cowshed; (*para caballos*) stable; (*: esp Am*) barn
estaca [es'taka] *nf* stake, post; (*de tienda de campaña*) peg
estacada [esta'kaða] *nf* (*cerca*) fence, fencing; (*palenque*) stockade; **dejar a algn en la ~** to leave sb in the lurch
estación [esta'θjon] *nf* station; (*del año*) season; **~ de autobuses/ferrocarril** bus/railway station; **~ balnearia (de turistas)** seaside resort; **~ de servicio** service station; **~ terminal** terminus; **~ de trabajo** (*Com*) work station; **~ transmisora** transmitter; **~ de visualización** display unit
estacionamiento [estaθjona'mjento] *nm* (*Auto*) parking; (*Mil*) stationing
estacionar [estaθjo'nar] *vt* (*Auto*) to park; (*Mil*) to station
estacionario, -a [estaθjo'narjo, a] *adj* stationary; (*Com: mercado*) slack
estada [es'taða], **estadía** [esta'ðia] *nf* (*Am*) stay
estadio [es'taðjo] *nm* (*fase*) stage, phase; (*Deporte*) stadium
estadista [esta'ðista] *nm* (*Pol*) statesman; (*Estadística*) statistician
estadística [esta'ðistika] *nf* (*una estadística*) figure, statistic; (*ciencia*) statistics *sg*
estado [es'taðo] *nm* (*Pol: condición*) state; **~ civil** marital status; **~ de ánimo** state of mind; **~ de cuenta(s)** bank statement, statement of accounts; **~ de excepción** (*Pol*) state of emergency; **~ financiero** (*Com*) financial statement; **~ mayor** (*Mil*) staff; **~ de pérdidas y ganancias** (*Com*) profit and loss statement, operating statement; **E~s Unidos (EE.UU.)** United States (of America) (USA); **estar en ~ (de buena esperanza)** to be pregnant
estadounidense [estaðouni'ðense] *adj* United States *cpd*, American ▷ *nm/f* United States citizen, American
estafa [es'tafa] *nf* swindle, trick; (*Com etc*) racket
estafar [esta'far] *vt* to swindle, defraud
estafeta [esta'feta] *nf* (*oficina de correos*) post office; **~ diplomática** diplomatic bag
estáis *vb ver* **estar**
estallar [esta'ʎar] *vi* to burst; (*bomba*) to explode, go off; (*volcán*) to erupt; (*vidrio*) to shatter; (*látigo*) to crack; (*epidemia, guerra, rebelión*) to break out; **~ en llanto** to burst into tears
estallido [esta'ʎiðo] *nm* explosion; (*de látigo, trueno*) crack; (*fig*) outbreak
Estambul [estam'bul] *nm* Istanbul
estampa [es'tampa] *nf* (*impresión, imprenta*) print, engraving; (*imagen, figura: de persona*) appearance
estampado, -a [estam'paðo, a] *adj* printed ▷ *nm* (*impresión: acción*) printing; (*: efecto*) print; (*marca*) stamping
estampar [estam'par] *vt* (*imprimir*) to print; (*marcar*) to stamp; (*metal*) to engrave; (*poner sello en*) to stamp; (*fig*) to stamp, imprint
estampida [estam'piða] *nf* stampede
estampido [estam'piðo] *nm* bang, report
estampilla [estam'piʎa] *nf* (*sello de goma*) (rubber) stamp; (*Am*) (postage) stamp
están [es'tan] *vb ver* **estar**
estancado, -a [estan'kaðo, a] *adj* (*agua*) stagnant
estancar [estan'kar] *vt* (*aguas*) to hold up, hold back; (*Com*) to monopolize; (*fig*) to

block, hold up; **estancarse** *vr* to stagnate
estancia [es'tanθja] *nf* (*permanencia*) stay; (*sala*) room; (*Am*) farm, ranch
estanciero [estan'sjero] *nm* (*Am*) farmer, rancher
estanco, -a [es'tanko, a] *adj* watertight ▷ *nm* tobacconist's (shop); *see note*

ESTANCO

Cigarettes, tobacco, postage stamps and official forms are all sold under state monopoly and usually through a shop called an *estanco*. Tobacco products are also sold in *quioscos* and bars but are generally more expensive. The number of *estanco* licences is regulated by the state.

estándar [es'tandar] *adj, nm* standard
estandarizar [estandari'θar] *vt* to standardize
estandarte [estan'darte] *nm* banner, standard
estanque *etc* [es'tanke] *vb ver* **estancar** ▷ *nm* (*lago*) pool, pond; (*Agr*) reservoir
estanquero, -a [estan'kero, a] *nm/f* tobacconist
estante [es'tante] *nm* (*armario*) rack, stand; (*biblioteca*) bookcase; (*anaquel*) shelf; (*Am*) prop
estantería [estante'ria] *nf* shelving, shelves *pl*
estaño [es'taɲo] *nm* tin

PALABRA CLAVE

estar [es'tar] *vi* **1** (*posición*) to be; **está en la plaza** it's in the square; **¿está Juan?** is Juan in?; **estamos a 30 km de Junín** we're 30 km from Junín
2 (*+ adj o adv*: *estado*) to be; **estar enfermo** to be ill; **está muy elegante** he's looking very smart; **estar lejos** to be far (away); **¿cómo estás?** how are you keeping?
3 (*+ gerundio*) to be; **estoy leyendo** I'm reading
4 (*uso pasivo*): **está condenado a muerte** he's been condemned to death; **está envasado en ...** it's packed in ...
5: **estar a**: **¿a cuántos estamos?** what's the date today?; **estamos a 9 de mayo** it's the 9th of May; **las manzanas están a 1,50 euros** apples are (selling at) 1.5 euros; **estamos a 25 grados** it's 25 degrees today
6 (*locuciones*): **¿estamos?** (*¿de acuerdo?*) okay?; (*¿listo?*) ready?; **¡ya está bien!** that's enough!; **¿está la comida?** is dinner ready?; **¡ya está!**, **¡ya estuvo!** (*Am*) that's it!
7: **estar con**: **está con gripe** he's got (the) flu
8: **estar de**: **estar de vacaciones/viaje** to be on holiday/away *o* on a trip; **está de camarero** he's working as a waiter
9: **estar para**: **está para salir** he's about to leave; **no estoy para bromas** I'm not in the mood for jokes
10: **estar por** (*propuesta etc*) to be in favour of; (*persona etc*) to support, side with; **está por limpiar** it still has to be cleaned; **¡estoy por dejarlo!** I think I'm going to leave this!
11: **estar sin**: **estar sin dinero** to have no money; **está sin terminar** it isn't finished yet
estarse *vr*: **se estuvo en la cama toda la tarde** he stayed in bed all afternoon; **¡estáte quieto!** stop fidgeting!
12 (*+ que*): **está que rabia** (*fam*) he's hopping mad (*fam*); **estoy que me caigo de sueño** I'm terribly sleepy, I can't keep my eyes open

estárter [es'tarter] *nm* (*Auto*) choke
estas ['estas] *adj demostrativo, pron ver* **este**
éstas ['estas] *pron ver* **éste**
estatal [esta'tal] *adj* state *cpd*
estático, -a [es'tatiko, a] *adj* static
estatua [es'tatwa] *nf* statue
estatura [esta'tura] *nf* stature, height
estatus [es'tatus] *nm inv* status
estatuto [esta'tuto] *nm* (*Jur*) statute; (*de ciudad*) bye law; (*de comité*) rule; **~s sociales** (*Com*) articles of association
este¹ ['este] *adj* (*lado*) east; (*dirección*) easterly ▷ *nm* east; **en la parte del ~** in the eastern part
este² ['este], **esta** ['esta], **estos** ['estos], **estas** ['estas] *adj demostrativo* this *sg*, these *pl*; (*Am: como muletilla*) er, um ▷ *pron* this (one) *sg*, these (ones) *pl*; **ese ... ~ ...** the former ... the latter ...
éste ['este], **ésta** ['esta], **éstos** ['estos], **éstas** ['estas] *pron* this (one) *sg*, these (ones) *pl*
esté [es'te] *vb ver* **estar**
estela [es'tela] *nf* wake, wash; (*fig*) trail
estelar [este'lar] *adj* (*Astro*) stellar; (*Teat*) star *cpd*
estén [es'ten] *vb ver* **estar**
estenografía [estenoɣra'fia] *nf* shorthand
estepa [es'tepa] *nf* (*Geo*) steppe
estera [es'tera] *nf* (*alfombra*) mat; (*tejido*) matting
estéreo [es'tereo] *adj inv, nm* stereo
estereotipo [estereo'tipo] *nm* stereotype
estéril [es'teril] *adj* sterile, barren; (*fig*) vain, futile
esterilizar [esterili'θar] *vt* to sterilize
esterlina [ester'lina] *adj*: **libra ~** pound sterling
estés [es'tes] *vb ver* **estar**
estético, -a [es'tetiko, a] *adj* aesthetic ▷ *nf* aesthetics *sg*
estiércol [es'tjerkol] *nm* dung, manure
estigma [es'tiɣma] *nm* stigma
estilarse [esti'larse] *vr* (*estar de moda*) to be in fashion; (*usarse*) to be used
estilo [es'tilo] *nm* style; (*Tec*) stylus; (*Natación*) stroke; **~ de vida** lifestyle; **al ~ de** in the style

of; **algo por el ~** something along those lines

estima [es'tima] *nf* esteem, respect

estimación [estima'θjon] *nf* (*evaluación*) estimation; (*aprecio, afecto*) esteem, regard

estimado, -a [esti'maðo, a] *adj* esteemed; **"E~ Señor"** "Dear Sir"

estimar [esti'mar] *vt* (*evaluar*) to estimate; (*valorar*) to value; (*apreciar*) to esteem, respect; (*pensar, considerar*) to think, reckon

estimulante [estimu'lante] *adj* stimulating ▷ *nm* stimulant

estimular [estimu'lar] *vt* to stimulate; (*excitar*) to excite; (*animar*) to encourage

estímulo [es'timulo] *nm* stimulus; (*ánimo*) encouragement

estío [es'tio] *nm* summer

estipulación [estipula'θjon] *nf* stipulation, condition

estipular [estipu'lar] *vt* to stipulate

estirado, -a [esti'raðo, a] *adj* (*tenso*) (stretched *o* drawn) tight; (*fig: persona*) stiff, pompous; (*engreído*) stuck-up

estirar [esti'rar] *vt* to stretch; (*dinero, suma etc*) to stretch out; (*cuello*) to crane; (*discurso*) to spin out; **~ la pata** (*fam*) to kick the bucket; **estirarse** *vr* to stretch

estirón [esti'ron] *nm* pull, tug; (*crecimiento*) spurt, sudden growth; **dar un ~** (*niño*) to shoot up

estirpe [es'tirpe] *nf* stock, lineage

estival [esti'βal] *adj* summer *cpd*

esto ['esto] *pron* this, this thing *o* matter; (*como muletilla*) er, um; **~ de la boda** this business about the wedding; **en ~** at this *o* that point; **por ~** for this reason

Estocolmo [esto'kolmo] *nm* Stockholm

estofa [es'tofa] *nf*: **de baja ~** poor-quality

estofado [esto'faðo] *nm* stew

estofar [esto'far] *vt* (*bordar*) to quilt; (*Culin*) to stew

estómago [es'tomaɣo] *nm* stomach; **tener ~** to be thick-skinned

estorbar [estor'βar] *vt* to hinder, obstruct; (*fig*) to bother, disturb ▷ *vi* to be in the way

estorbo [es'torβo] *nm* (*molestia*) bother, nuisance; (*obstáculo*) hindrance, obstacle

estornudar [estornu'ðar] *vi* to sneeze

estornudo [estor'nuðo] *nm* sneeze

estos ['estos] *adj demostrativo ver* **este**

éstos ['estos] *pron ver* **éste**

estoy [es'toi] *vb ver* **estar**

estrado [es'traðo] *nm* (*tarima*) platform; (*Mus*) bandstand; **estrados** *nmpl* law courts

estrafalario, -a [estrafa'larjo, a] *adj* odd, eccentric; (*desarreglado*) slovenly, sloppy

estrago [es'traɣo] *nm* ruin, destruction; **hacer ~s en** to wreak havoc among

estragón [estra'ɣon] *nm* (*Culin*) tarragon

estrambótico, -a [estram'botiko, a] *adj* odd, eccentric; (*peinado, ropa*) outlandish

estrangulador, -a [estrangula'ðor, a] *nm/f* strangler ▷ *nm* (*Tec*) throttle; (*Auto*) choke

estrangulamiento [estrangula'mjento] *nm* (*Auto*) bottleneck

estrangular [estrangu'lar] *vt* (*persona*) to strangle; (*Med*) to strangulate

estraperlo [estra'perlo] *nm* black market

estratagema [estrata'xema] *nf* (*Mil*) stratagem; (*astucia*) cunning

estrategia [estra'texja] *nf* strategy

estratégico, -a [estra'texiko, a] *adj* strategic

estratificar [estratifi'kar] *vt* to stratify

estrato [es'trato] *nm* stratum, layer

estrechar [estre'tʃar] *vt* (*reducir*) to narrow; (*vestido*) to take in; (*persona*) to hug, embrace; **estrecharse** *vr* (*reducirse*) to narrow, grow narrow; (*2 personas*) to embrace; **~ la mano** to shake hands

estrechez [estre'tʃeθ] *nf* narrowness; (*de ropa*) tightness; (*intimidad*) intimacy; (*Com*) want *o* shortage of money; **estrecheces** *nfpl* financial difficulties

estrecho, -a [es'tretʃo, a] *adj* narrow; (*apretado*) tight; (*íntimo*) close, intimate; (*miserable*) mean ▷ *nm* strait; **~ de miras** narrow-minded; **E~ de Gibraltar** Straits of Gibraltar

estrella [es'treʎa] *nf* star; **~ fugaz** shooting star; **~ de mar** starfish; **tener (buena)/mala ~** to be lucky/unlucky

estrellado, -a [estre'ʎaðo, a] *adj* (*forma*) star-shaped; (*cielo*) starry; (*huevos*) fried

estrellar [estre'ʎar] *vt* (*hacer añicos*) to smash (to pieces); (*huevos*) to fry; **estrellarse** *vr* to smash; (*chocarse*) to crash; (*fracasar*) to fail

estremecer [estreme'θer] *vt* to shake; **estremecerse** *vr* to shake, tremble; **~ de** (*horror*) to shudder with; (*frío*) to shiver with

estremecimiento [estremeθi'mjento] *nm* (*temblor*) trembling, shaking

estrenar [estre'nar] *vt* (*vestido*) to wear for the first time; (*casa*) to move into; (*película, obra de teatro*) to première; **estrenarse** *vr* (*persona*) to make one's début; (*película*) to have its première; (*Teat*) to open

estreno [es'treno] *nm* (*primer uso*) first use; (*Cine etc*) première

estreñido, -a [estre'ɲiðo, a] *adj* constipated

estreñimiento [estreɲi'mjento] *nm* constipation

estreñir [estre'ɲir] *vt* to constipate

estrépito [es'trepito] *nm* noise, racket; (*fig*) fuss

estrepitoso, -a [estrepi'toso, a] *adj* noisy; (*fiesta*) rowdy

estrés [es'tres] *nm* stress

estría [es'tria] *nf* groove; **~s (en el cutis)** stretchmarks

estribación [estriβa'θjon] *nf* (*Geo*) spur; **estribaciones** *nfpl* foothills

estribar [estri'βar] *vi* (*Archit*): **~ en** to rest on, be supported by; **la dificultad estriba en el texto** the difficulty lies in the text

estribillo [estri'βiʎo] *nm* (*Lit*) refrain; (*Mus*) chorus
estribo [es'triβo] *nm* (*de jinete*) stirrup; (*de coche, tren*) step; (*de puente*) support; (*Geo*) spur; **perder los ~s** to fly off the handle
estribor [estri'βor] *nm* (*Naut*) starboard
estricnina [estrik'nina] *nf* strychnine
estricto, -a [es'trikto, a] *adj* (*riguroso*) strict; (*severo*) severe
estridente [estri'ðente] *adj* (*color*) loud; (*voz*) raucous
estrofa [es'trofa] *nf* verse
estropajo [estro'paxo] *nm* scourer
estropeado, -a [estrope'aðo, a] *adj*: **está ~** it's not working
estropear [estrope'ar] *vt* (*arruinar*) to spoil; (*dañar*) to damage; (*: máquina*) to break; **estropearse** *vr* (*objeto*) to get damaged; (*coche*) to break down; (*la piel etc*) to be ruined
estructura [estruk'tura] *nf* structure
estruendo [es'trwendo] *nm* (*ruido*) racket, din; (*fig: alboroto*) uproar, turmoil
estrujar [estru'xar] *vt* (*apretar*) to squeeze; (*aplastar*) to crush; (*fig*) to drain, bleed
estuario [es'twarjo] *nm* estuary
estuche [es'tutʃe] *nm* box, case
estudiante [estu'ðjante] *nm/f* student
estudiantil [estuðjan'til] *adj inv* student *cpd*
estudiar [estu'ðjar] *vt* to study; (*propuesta*) to think about *o* over; **~ para abogado** to study to become a lawyer
estudio [es'tuðjo] *nm* study; (*encuesta*) research; (*proyecto*) plan; (*piso*) studio flat; (*Cine, Arte, Radio*) studio; **estudios** *nmpl* studies; (*erudición*) learning *sg*; **cursar** *o* **hacer ~s** to study; **~ de casos prácticos** case study; **~ de desplazamientos y tiempos** (*Com*) time and motion study; **~s de motivación** motivational research *sg*; **~ del trabajo** (*Com*) work study; **~ de viabilidad** (*Com*) feasibility study
estudioso, -a [estu'ðjoso, a] *adj* studious
estufa [es'tufa] *nf* heater, fire
estupefaciente [estupefa'θjente] *adj, nm* narcotic
estupefacto, -a [estupe'fakto, a] *adj* speechless, thunderstruck
estupendamente [estupenda'mente] *adv* (*fam*): **estoy ~** I feel great; **le salió ~** he did it very well
estupendo, -a [estu'pendo, a] *adj* wonderful, terrific; (*fam*) great; **¡~!** that's great!, fantastic!
estupidez [estupi'ðeθ] *nf* (*torpeza*) stupidity; (*acto*) stupid thing (to do); **fue una ~ mía** that was a silly thing for me to do *o* say
estúpido, -a [es'tupiðo, a] *adj* stupid, silly
estupor [estu'por] *nm* stupor; (*fig*) astonishment, amazement
estupro [es'tupro] *nm* rape
estuve *etc* [es'tuβe], **estuviera** *etc* [estu'βjera] *vb ver* **estar**
esvástica [es'βastika] *nf* swastika
ETA ['eta] *nf abr* (*Pol: = Euskadi Ta Askatasuna*) ETA
etapa [e'tapa] *nf* (*de viaje*) stage; (*Deporte*) leg; (*parada*) stopping place; (*fig*) stage, phase; **por ~s** gradually, in stages
etarra [e'tarra] *adj* ETA *cpd* ▷ *nm/f* member of ETA
etc. *abr* (= *etcétera*) etc
etcétera [et'θetera] *adv* etcetera
eternidad [eterni'ðað] *nf* eternity
eternizarse [eterni'θarse] *vr*: **~ en hacer algo** to take ages to do sth
eterno, -a [e'terno, a] *adj* eternal, everlasting; (*despectivo*) never-ending
ético, -a ['etiko, a] *adj* ethical ▷ *nf* ethics
etiqueta [eti'keta] *nf* (*modales*) etiquette; (*rótulo*) label, tag; (*en Twitter*) hashtag; **de ~** formal
etnia ['etnja] *nf* ethnic group
étnico, -a ['etniko, a] *adj* ethnic
Eucaristía [eukaris'tia] *nf* Eucharist
eufemismo [eufe'mismo] *nm* euphemism
euforia [eu'forja] *nf* euphoria
eunuco [eu'nuko] *nm* eunuch
euro ['euro] *nm* (*moneda*) euro
eurodiputado, -a [euroðipu'taðo, a] *nm/f* Euro MP, MEP
Europa [eu'ropa] *nf* Europe
europeo, -a [euro'peo, a] *adj, nm/f* European
Euskadi [eus'kaði] *nm* the Basque Provinces *pl*
euskera, eusquera [eus'kera] *nm* (*Ling*) Basque; *ver tb* **Lengua**
eutanasia [euta'nasja] *nf* euthanasia
evacuación [eβakwa'θjon] *nf* evacuation
evacuar [eβa'kwar] *vt* to evacuate
evadir [eβa'ðir] *vt* to evade, avoid; **evadirse** *vr* to escape
evaluación [eβalwa'θjon] *nf* evaluation, assessment
evaluar [eβa'lwar] *vt* to evaluate, assess
evangélico, -a [eβan'xeliko, a] *adj* evangelical
evangelio [eβan'xeljo] *nm* gospel
evaporar [eβapo'rar] *vt* to evaporate; **evaporarse** *vr* to vanish
evasión [eβa'sjon] *nf* escape, flight; (*fig*) evasion; **~ fiscal** *o* **tributaria** tax evasion; **~ de capitales** flight of capital
evasivo, -a [eβa'siβo, a] *adj* evasive, non-committal ▷ *nf* (*pretexto*) excuse; **contestar con evasivas** to avoid giving a straight answer
evento [e'βento] *nm* event; (*eventualidad*) eventuality
eventual [eβen'twal] *adj* possible, conditional (upon circumstances); (*trabajador*) casual, temporary
evidencia [eβi'ðenθja] *nf* evidence, proof; **poner en ~** to make clear; **ponerse en ~** (*persona*) to show o.s. up
evidenciar [eβiðen'θjar] *vt* (*hacer patente*) to make evident; (*probar*) to prove, show; **evidenciarse** *vr* to be evident

e

evidente [eβi'ðente] *adj* obvious, clear, evident
evitar [eβi'tar] *vt* (*evadir*) to avoid; (*impedir*) to prevent; (*peligro*) to escape; (*molestia*) to save; (*tentación*) to shun; **~ hacer algo** to avoid doing sth; **si puedo ~lo** if I can help it
evocar [eβo'kar] *vt* to evoke, call forth
evolución [eβolu'θjon] *nf* (*desarrollo*) evolution, development; (*cambio*) change; (*Mil*) manoeuvre
evolucionar [eβoluθjo'nar] *vi* to evolve; (*Mil, Aviat*) to manoeuvre
ex [eks] *adj* ex-; **el ex ministro** the former minister, the ex-minister
exacerbar [eksaθer'βar] *vt* to irritate, annoy
exactamente [eksakta'mente] *adv* exactly
exactitud [eksakti'tuð] *nf* exactness; (*precisión*) accuracy; (*puntualidad*) punctuality
exacto, -a [ek'sakto, a] *adj* exact; accurate; punctual; **¡~!** exactly!; **eso no es del todo ~** that's not quite right; **para ser ~** to be precise
exageración [eksaxera'θjon] *nf* exaggeration
exagerar [eksaxe'rar] *vt* to exaggerate; (*exceder*) to overdo
exaltado, -a [eksal'taðo, a] *adj* (*apasionado*) over-excited, worked up; (*exagerado*) extreme; (*fanático*) hot-headed; (*discurso*) impassioned ▷ *nm/f* (*fanático*) hothead; (*Pol*) extremist
exaltar [eksal'tar] *vt* to exalt, glorify; **exaltarse** *vr* (*excitarse*) to get excited *o* worked up
examen [ek'samen] *nm* examination; (*de problema*) consideration; **~ de** (*encuesta*) inquiry into; **~ de ingreso** entrance examination; **~ de conducir** driving test; **~ de ingreso** entrance examination; **~ eliminatorio** qualifying examination
examinar [eksami'nar] *vt* to examine; (*poner a prueba*) to test; (*inspeccionar*) to inspect; **examinarse** *vr* to be examined, take an examination
exasperar [eksaspe'rar] *vt* to exasperate; **exasperarse** *vr* to get exasperated, lose patience
excavador, a [ekskaβa'ðor, a] *nm/f* (*persona*) excavator ▷ *nf* (*Tec*) digger
excavar [ekska'βar] *vt* to excavate, dig (out)
excedencia [eksθe'ðenθja] *nf* (*Mil*) leave; (*Escol*) sabbatical; **estar en ~** to be on leave; **pedir** *o* **solicitar la ~** to ask for leave
excedente [eksθe'ðente] *adj, nm* excess, surplus
exceder [eksθe'ðer] *vt* to exceed, surpass; **excederse** *vr* (*extralimitarse*) to go too far; (*sobrepasarse*) to excel o.s.
excelencia [eksθe'lenθja] *nf* excellence; **E~** Excellency; **por ~** par excellence
excelente [eksθe'lente] *adj* excellent
excelso, -a [eks'θelso, a] *adj* lofty, sublime
excentricidad [eksθentriθi'ðað] *nf* eccentricity
excéntrico, -a [eks'θentriko, a] *adj, nm/f* eccentric
excepción [eksθep'θjon] *nf* exception; **a ~ de** with the exception of, except for; **la ~ confirma la regla** the exception proves the rule
excepcional [eksθepθjo'nal] *adj* exceptional
excepto [eks'θepto] *adv* excepting, except (for)
exceptuar [eksθep'twar] *vt* to except, exclude
excesivo, -a [eksθe'siβo, a] *adj* excessive
exceso [eks'θeso] *nm* excess; (*Com*) surplus; **~ de equipaje/peso** excess luggage/weight; **~ de velocidad** speeding; **en** *o* **por ~** excessively
excitación [eksθita'θjon] *nf* (*sensación*) excitement; (*acción*) excitation
excitado, -a [eksθi'taðo, a] *adj* excited; (*emociones*) aroused
excitar [eksθi'tar] *vt* to excite; (*incitar*) to urge; (*emoción*) to stir up; (*esperanzas*) to raise; (*pasión*) to arouse; **excitarse** *vr* to get excited
exclamación [eksklama'θjon] *nf* exclamation
exclamar [ekskla'mar] *vi* to exclaim; **exclamarse** *vr*: **~se (contra)** to complain (about)
excluir [eksklu'ir] *vt* to exclude; (*dejar fuera*) to shut out; (*solución*) to reject; (*posibilidad*) to rule out
exclusión [eksklu'sjon] *nf* exclusion
exclusiva [eksklu'siβa] *nf ver* **exclusivo**
exclusivo, -a [eksklu'siβo, a] *adj* exclusive ▷ *nf* (*Prensa*) exclusive, scoop; (*Com*) sole right *o* agency; **derecho ~** sole *o* exclusive right
Excma., Excmo. *abr* (= *Excelentísima, Excelentísimo*) *courtesy title*
excomulgar [ekskomul'ɣar] *vt* (*Rel*) to excommunicate
excomunión [ekskomu'njon] *nf* excommunication
excremento [ekskre'mento] *nm* excrement
excursión [ekskur'sjon] *nf* excursion, outing; **ir de ~** to go (off) on a trip
excursionista [ekskursjo'nista] *nm/f* (*turista*) sightseer
excusa [eks'kusa] *nf* excuse; (*disculpa*) apology; **presentar sus ~s** to excuse o.s.
excusar [eksku'sar] *vt* to excuse; (*evitar*) to avoid, prevent; **excusarse** *vr* (*disculparse*) to apologize
exento, -a [ek'sento, a] *pp de* **eximir** ▷ *adj* exempt
exequias [ek'sekjas] *nfpl* funeral rites
exfoliar [eksfo'ljar] *vt* to exfoliate
exhalar [eksa'lar] *vt* to exhale, breathe out; (*olor etc*) to give off; (*suspiro*) to breathe, heave
exhaustivo, -a [eksaus'tiβo, a] *adj* (*análisis*) thorough; (*estudio*) exhaustive
exhausto, -a [ek'sausto, a] *adj* exhausted, worn-out

exhibición [eksiβi'θjon] *nf* exhibition; (*demostración*) display, show; (*de película*) showing; (*de equipo*) performance
exhibir [eksi'βir] *vt* to exhibit; to display, show; (*cuadros*) to exhibit; (*artículos*) to display; (*pasaporte*) to show; (*película*) to screen; (*mostrar con orgullo*) to show off; **exhibirse** *vr* (*mostrarse en público*) to show o.s. off; (*fam: indecentemente*) to expose o.s.
exhortación [eksorta'θjon] *nf* exhortation
exhortar [eksor'tar] *vt*: **~ a** to exhort to
exigencia [eksi'xenθja] *nf* demand, requirement
exigente [eksi'xente] *adj* demanding; (*profesor*) strict; **ser ~ con algn** to be hard on sb
exigir [eksi'xir] *vt* (*gen*) to demand, require; (*impuestos*) to exact, levy; **~ el pago** to demand payment
exiliado, -a [eksi'ljaðo, a] *adj* exiled, in exile ▷ *nm/f* exile
exilio [ek'siljo] *nm* exile
eximio, -a [ek'simjo, a] *adj* (*eminente*) distinguished, eminent
eximir [eksi'mir] *vt* to exempt
existencia [eksis'tenθja] *nf* existence; **existencias** *nfpl* stock *sg*; **~ de mercancías** (*Com*) stock-in-trade; **tener en ~** to have in stock; **amargar la ~ a algn** to make sb's life a misery
existir [eksis'tir] *vi* to exist, be
éxito ['eksito] *nm* (*resultado*) result, outcome; (*triunfo*) success; (*Mus, Teat*) hit; **~ editorial** bestseller; **~ rotundo** smash hit; **tener ~** to be successful
éxodo ['eksoðo] *nm* exodus; **el ~ rural** the drift from the land
exonerar [eksone'rar] *vt* to exonerate; **~ de una obligación** to free from an obligation
exorbitante [eksorβi'tante] *adj* (*precio*) exorbitant; (*cantidad*) excessive
exorcizar [eksorθi'θar] *vt* to exorcize
exótico, -a [ek'sotiko, a] *adj* exotic
expandir [ekspan'dir] *vt* to expand; (*Com*) to expand, enlarge; **expandirse** *vr* to expand, spread
expansión [ekspan'sjon] *nf* expansion; (*recreo*) relaxation; **la ~ económica** economic growth; **economía en ~** expanding economy
expansionarse [ekspansjo'narse] *vr* (*dilatarse*) to expand; (*recrearse*) to relax
expansivo, -a [ekspan'siβo, a] *adj* expansive; (*efusivo*) communicative; **onda expansiva** shock wave
expatriarse [ekspa'trjarse] *vr* to emigrate; (*Pol*) to go into exile
expectativa [ekspekta'tiβa] *nf* (*espera*) expectation; (*perspectiva*) prospect; **~ de vida** life expectancy; **estar a la ~** to wait and see (what will happen)
expedición [ekspeði'θjon] *nf* (*excursión*) expedition; **gastos de ~** shipping charges
expediente [ekspe'ðjente] *nm* expedient; (*Jur: procedimiento*) action, proceedings *pl*; (*: papeles*) dossier, file, record; **~ judicial** court proceedings *pl*; **~ académico** (student's) record
expedir [ekspe'ðir] *vt* (*despachar*) to send, forward; (*pasaporte*) to issue; (*cheque*) to make out
expedito, -a [ekspe'ðito, a] *adj* (*libre*) clear, free
expendedor, a [ekspende'ðor, a] *nm/f* (*vendedor*) dealer; (*Teat*) ticket agent ▷ *nm* (*aparato*) (vending) machine; **~ de cigarrillos** cigarette machine
expendeduría [ekspendedu'ria] *nf* (*estanco*) tobacconist's (shop) (*Brit*), cigar store (*US*)
expensas [eks'pensas] *nfpl* (*Jur*) costs; **a ~ de** at the expense of
experiencia [ekspe'rjenθja] *nf* experience
experimentado, -a [eksperimen'taðo, a] *adj* experienced
experimentar [eksperimen'tar] *vt* (*en laboratorio*) to experiment with; (*probar*) to test, try out; (*notar, observar*) to experience; (*deterioro, pérdida*) to suffer; (*aumento*) to show; (*sensación*) to feel
experimento [eksperi'mento] *nm* experiment
experto, -a [eks'perto, a] *adj* expert ▷ *nm/f* expert
expiar [ekspi'ar] *vt* to atone for
expirar [ekspi'rar] *vi* to expire
explanada [ekspla'naða] *nf* (*paseo*) esplanade; (*a orillas del mar*) promenade
explayarse [ekspla'jarse] *vr* (*en discurso*) to speak at length; **~ con algn** to confide in sb
explicación [eksplika'θjon] *nf* explanation
explicar [ekspli'kar] *vt* to explain; (*teoría*) to expound; (*Univ*) to lecture in; **explicarse** *vr* to explain (o.s.); **no me lo explico** I can't understand it
explícito, -a [eks'pliθito, a] *adj* explicit
explique *etc* [eks'plike] *vb ver* **explicar**
explorador, a [eksplora'ðor, a] *nm/f* (*pionero*) explorer; (*Mil*) scout ▷ *nm* (*Med*) probe; (*radar*) (radar) scanner
explorar [eksplo'rar] *vt* to explore; (*Med*) to probe; (*radar*) to scan
explosión [eksplo'sjon] *nf* explosion
explosivo, -a [eksplo'siβo, a] *adj* explosive
explotación [eksplota'θjon] *nf* exploitation; (*de planta etc*) running; (*de mina*) working; (*de recurso*) development; **~ minera** mine; **gastos de ~** operating costs
explotar [eksplo'tar] *vt* to exploit; (*planta*) to run, operate; (*mina*) to work ▷ *vi* (*bomba etc*) to explode, go off
exponer [ekspo'ner] *vt* to expose; (*cuadro*) to display; (*vida*) to risk; (*idea*) to explain; (*teoría*) to expound; (*hechos*) to set out; **exponerse** *vr*: **~se a (hacer) algo** to run the risk of (doing) sth

exportación [eksporta'θjon] *nf* (*acción*) export; (*mercancías*) exports *pl*
exportar [ekspor'tar] *vt* to export
exposición [eksposi'θjon] *nf* (*gen*) exposure; (*de arte*) show, exhibition; (*Com*) display; (*feria*) show, fair; (*explicación*) explanation; (*de teoría*) exposition; (*narración*) account, statement
exprés [eks'pres] *adj inv* (*café*) espresso ▷ *nm* (*Ferro*) express (train)
expresamente [ekspresa'mente] *adv* (*decir*) clearly; (*concretamente*) expressly; (*a propósito*) on purpose
expresar [ekspre'sar] *vt* to express; (*redactar*) to phrase, put; (*emoción*) to show; **expresarse** *vr* to express o.s.; (*dato*) to be stated; **como abajo se expresa** as stated below
expresión [expre'sjon] *nf* expression; **~ familiar** colloquialism
expresivo, -a [ekspre'siβo, a] *adj* expressive; (*cariñoso*) affectionate
expreso, -a [eks'preso, a] *adj* (*explícito*) express; (*claro*) specific, clear; (*tren*) fast ▷ *nm* (*Ferro*) fast train
express [eks'pres] *adv* (*Am*): **enviar algo ~** to send sth special delivery
exprimidor [eksprimi'ðor] *nm* (lemon) squeezer
exprimir [ekspri'mir] *vt* (*fruta*) to squeeze; (*zumo*) to squeeze out
ex profeso [ekspro'feso] *adv* expressly
expropiar [ekspro'pjar] *vt* to expropriate
expuesto, -a [eks'pwesto, a] *pp de* **exponer** ▷ *adj* exposed; (*cuadro etc*) on show, on display; **según lo ~ arriba** according to what has been stated above
expulsar [ekspul'sar] *vt* (*echar*) to eject, throw out; (*alumno*) to expel; (*despedir*) to sack, fire; (*Deporte*) to send off
expulsión [ekspul'sjon] *nf* expulsion; sending-off
exquisito, -a [ekski'sito, a] *adj* exquisite; (*comida*) delicious; (*afectado*) affected
éxtasis ['ekstasis] *nm* (*tb droga*) ecstasy
extender [eksten'der] *vt* to extend; (*los brazos*) to stretch out, hold out; (*mapa, tela*) to spread (out), open (out); (*mantequilla*) to spread; (*certificado*) to issue; (*cheque, recibo*) to make out; (*documento*) to draw up; **extenderse** *vr* to extend; (*terreno*) to stretch *o* spread (out); (*persona: en el suelo*) to stretch out; (*en el tiempo*) to extend, last; (*costumbre, epidemia*) to spread; (*guerra*) to escalate; **~se sobre un tema** to enlarge on a subject
extendido, -a [eksten'diðo, a] *adj* (*abierto*) spread out, open; (*brazos*) outstretched; (*costumbre etc*) widespread
extensión [eksten'sjon] *nf* (*de terreno, mar*) expanse, stretch; (*Mus*) range; (*de conocimientos*) extent; (*de programa*) scope; (*de tiempo*) length, duration; (*Telec*) extension; **~ de plazo** (*Com*) extension; **en toda la ~ de la palabra** in every sense of the word; **de ~** (*Inform*) add-on
extenso, -a [eks'tenso, a] *adj* extensive
extenuar [ekste'nwar] *vt* (*debilitar*) to weaken
exterior [ekste'rjor] *adj* (*de fuera*) external; (*afuera*) outside, exterior; (*apariencia*) outward; (*deuda, relaciones*) foreign ▷ *nm* exterior, outside; (*aspecto*) outward appearance; (*Deporte*) wing(er); (*países extranjeros*) abroad; **asuntos ~es** foreign affairs; **al ~** outwardly, on the outside; **en el ~** abroad; **noticias del ~** foreign *o* overseas news
exteriorizar [eksterjori'θar] *vt* (*emociones*) to show, reveal
exterminar [ekstermi'nar] *vt* to exterminate
exterminio [ekster'minjo] *nm* extermination
externo, -a [eks'terno, a] *adj* (*exterior*) external, outside; (*superficial*) outward ▷ *nm/f* day pupil
extinguir [ekstin'gir] *vt* (*fuego*) to extinguish, put out; (*raza, población*) to wipe out; **extinguirse** *vr* (*fuego*) to go out; (*Bio*) to die out, become extinct
extinto, -a [eks'tinto, a] *adj* extinct
extintor [ekstin'tor] *nm* (fire) extinguisher
extirpar [ekstir'par] *vt* (*vicios*) to eradicate, stamp out; (*Med*) to remove (surgically)
extra ['ekstra] *adj inv* (*tiempo*) extra; (*vino*) vintage; (*chocolate*) good-quality; (*gasolina*) high-octane ▷ *nm/f* extra ▷ *nm* extra; (*bono*) bonus; (*periódico*) special edition
extracción [ekstrak'θjon] *nf* extraction; (*en lotería*) draw; (*de carbón*) mining
extracto [eks'trakto] *nm* extract
extractor [ekstrak'tor] *nm* (*tb*: **~ de humos**) extractor fan
extradición [ekstraði'θjon] *nf* extradition
extraer [ekstra'er] *vt* to extract, take out
extraescolar [ekstraesko'lar] *adj*: **actividad ~** extracurricular activity
extralimitarse [ekstralimi'tarse] *vr* to go too far
extranjero, -a [ekstran'xero, a] *adj* foreign ▷ *nm/f* foreigner ▷ *nm* foreign countries *pl*; **en el ~** abroad
extrañar [ekstra'ɲar] *vt* (*sorprender*) to find strange *o* odd; (*echar de menos*) to miss; **extrañarse** *vr* (*sorprenderse*) to be amazed, be surprised; (*distanciarse*) to become estranged, grow apart; **me extraña** I'm surprised
extrañeza [ekstra'ɲeθa] *nf* (*rareza*) strangeness, oddness; (*asombro*) amazement, surprise
extraño, -a [eks'traɲo, a] *adj* (*extranjero*) foreign; (*raro, sorprendente*) strange, odd
extraordinario, -a [ekstraorði'narjo, a] *adj* extraordinary; (*edición, número*) special ▷ *nm* (*de periódico*) special edition; **horas extraordinarias** overtime *sg*
extrarradio [ekstra'rraðjo] *nm* suburbs *pl*

extravagancia [ekstraβa'ɣanθja] *nf* oddness; outlandishness; (*rareza*) peculiarity; **extravagancias** *nfpl* (*tonterías*) nonsense *sg*
extravagante [ekstraβa'ɣante] *adj* (*excéntrico*) eccentric; (*estrafalario*) outlandish
extraviado, -a [ekstra'βjaðo, a] *adj* lost, missing
extraviar [ekstra'βjar] *vt* to mislead, misdirect; (*perder*) to lose, misplace; **extraviarse** *vr* to lose one's way, get lost; (*objeto*) to go missing, be mislaid
extravío [ekstra'βio] *nm* loss; (*fig*) misconduct
extremar [ekstre'mar] *vt* to carry to extremes; **extremarse** *vr* to do one's utmost, make every effort
extremaunción [ekstremaun'θjon] *nf* extreme unction, last rites *pl*
extremidad [ekstremi'ðað] *nf* (*punta*) extremity; (*fila*) edge; **extremidades** *nfpl* (*Anat*) extremities
extremista [ekstre'mista] *adj, nm/f* extremist
extremo, -a [eks'tremo, a] *adj* extreme; (*más alejado*) furthest; (*último*) last ▷ *nm* end; (*situación*) extreme; **E~ Oriente** Far East; **en último ~** as a last resort; **pasar de un ~ a otro** (*fig*) to go from one extreme to the other; **con ~** in the extreme; **la extrema derecha** (*Pol*) the far right; **~ derecho/izquierdo** (*Deporte*) outside right/left
extrovertido, -a [ekstroβer'tiðo, a] *adj* extrovert, outgoing ▷ *nm/f* extrovert
exuberancia [eksuβe'ranθja] *nf* exuberance
exuberante [eksuβe'rante] *adj* exuberant; (*fig*) luxuriant, lush
eyaculación [ejakula'θjon] *nf* ejaculation
eyacular [ejaku'lar] *vt, vi* to ejaculate

f

fa [fa] *nm* (*Mus*) F
fabada [fa'βaða] *nf bean and sausage stew*
fábrica ['faβrika] *nf* factory; **~ de moneda** mint; **marca de ~** trademark; **precio de ~** factory price
fabricación [faβrika'θjon] *nf* (*manufactura*) manufacture; (*producción*) production; **de ~ casera** home-made; **de ~ nacional** home produced; **~ en serie** mass production
fabricante [faβri'kante] *nm/f* manufacturer
fabricar [faβri'kar] *vt* (*manufacturar*) to manufacture, make; (*construir*) to build; (*cuento*) to fabricate, devise; **~ en serie** to mass-produce
fábula ['faβula] *nf* (*cuento*) fable; (*chisme*) rumour; (*mentira*) fib
fabuloso, -a [faβu'loso, a] *adj* fabulous, fantastic
facción [fak'θjon] *nf* (*Pol*) faction; **facciones** *nfpl* (*del rostro*) features
faceta [fa'θeta] *nf* facet
facha ['fatʃa] (*fam*) *nm/f* fascist, right-wing extremist ▷ *nf* (*aspecto*) look; (*cara*) face; **¡qué ~ tienes!** you look a sight!
fachada [fa'tʃaða] *nf* (*Arq*) façade, front; (*Tip*) title page; (*fig*) façade, outward show
facial [fa'θjal] *adj* facial
fácil ['faθil] *adj* (*simple*) easy; (*sencillo*) simple, straightforward; (*probable*) likely; (*respuesta*) facile; **~ de usar** (*Inform*) user-friendly
facilidad [faθili'ðað] *nf* (*capacidad*) ease; (*sencillez*) simplicity; (*de palabra*) fluency;

facilidades *nfpl* facilities; **"~es de pago"** (*Com*) "credit facilities", "payment terms"
facilitar [faθili'tar] *vt* (*hacer fácil*) to make easy; (*proporcionar*) to provide; (*documento*) to issue; **le agradecería me ~a ...** I would be grateful if you could let me have ...
fácilmente ['faθilmente] *adv* easily
facsímil [fak'simil] *nm* (*documento*) facsimile; **enviar por ~** to fax
factible [fak'tiβle] *adj* feasible
factor [fak'tor] *nm* factor; (*Com*) agent; (*Ferro*) freight clerk
factura [fak'tura] *nf* (*cuenta*) bill; (*nota de pago*) invoice; (*hechura*) manufacture; **presentar ~ a** to invoice
facturación [faktura'θjon] *nf* (*Com*) invoicing; (*: ventas*) turnover; **~ de equipajes** luggage check-in; **~ online** online check-in
facturar [faktu'rar] *vt* (*Com*) to invoice, charge for; (*Aviat*) to check in; (*equipaje*) to register, check (US)
facultad [fakul'tað] *nf* (*aptitud, Escol etc*) faculty; (*poder*) power
facultativo, -a [fakulta'tiβo, a] *adj* optional; (*de un oficio*) professional; **prescripción facultativa** medical prescription
faena [fa'ena] *nf* (*trabajo*) work; (*quehacer*) task, job; **~s domésticas** housework *sg*
fagot [fa'ɣot] *nm* (*Mus*) bassoon
faisán [fai'san] *nm* pheasant
faja ['faxa] *nf* (*para la cintura*) sash; (*de mujer*) corset; (*de tierra*) strip
fajo ['faxo] *nm* (*de papeles*) bundle; (*de billetes*) role, wad
falange [fa'lanxe] *nf*: **la F~** (*Pol*) the Falange
falda ['falda] *nf* (*prenda de vestir*) skirt; (*Geo*) foothill; **~ pantalón** culottes *pl*, split skirt; **~ escocesa** kilt
falla ['faʎa] *nf* (*defecto*) fault, flaw; **~ humana** (*Am*) human error
fallar [fa'ʎar] *vt* (*Jur*) to pronounce sentence on; (*Naipes*) to trump ▷ *vi* (*memoria*) to fail; (*plan*) to go wrong; (*motor*) to miss; **~ a algn** to let sb down
Fallas ['faʎas] *nfpl see note*

FALLAS

In the week of the 19th of March (the feast of St Joseph, San José), Valencia honours its patron saint with a spectacular *fiesta* called *las Fallas*. The *Fallas* are huge sculptures, made of wood, cardboard, paper and cloth, depicting famous politicians and other targets for ridicule, which are set alight and burned by the *falleros*, members of the competing local groups who have just spent months preparing them.

fallecer [faʎe'θer] *vi* to pass away, die
fallecimiento [faʎeθi'mjento] *nm* decease, demise
fallido, -a [fa'ʎiðo, a] *adj* vain; (*intento*) frustrated, unsuccessful
fallo ['faʎo] *nm* (*Jur*) verdict, ruling; (*decisión*) decision; (*de jurado*) findings; (*fracaso*) failure; (*Deporte*) miss; (*Inform*) bug; **~ cardíaco** heart failure; **~ humano** (*Esp*) human error
falo ['falo] *nm* phallus
falsear [false'ar] *vt* to falsify; (*firma etc*) to forge ▷ *vi* (*Mus*) to be out of tune
falsedad [false'ðað] *nf* falseness; (*hipocresía*) hypocrisy; (*mentira*) falsehood
falsificar [falsifi'kar] *vt* (*firma etc*) to forge; (*voto etc*) to rig; (*moneda*) to counterfeit
falso, -a ['falso, a] *adj* false; (*erróneo*) wrong, mistaken; (*firma, documento*) forged; (*moneda etc*) fake; **en ~** falsely; **dar un paso en ~** to trip; (*fig*) to take a false step
falta ['falta] *nf* (*defecto*) fault, flaw; (*privación*) lack, want; (*ausencia*) absence; (*carencia*) shortage; (*equivocación*) mistake; (*Jur*) default; (*Deporte*) foul; (*Tenis*) fault; **~ de ortografía** spelling mistake; **~ de respeto** disrespect; **echar en ~** to miss; **hacer ~ hacer algo** to be necessary to do sth; **me hace ~ una pluma** I need a pen; **~ de educación** bad manners *pl*; **~ de ortografía** spelling mistake; **sin ~** without fail; **por ~ de** through *o* for lack of
faltar [fal'tar] *vi* (*escasear*) to be lacking, be wanting; (*ausentarse*) to be absent, be missing; **¿falta algo?** is anything missing?; **falta mucho todavía** there's plenty of time yet; **¿falta mucho?** is there long to go?; **faltan dos horas para llegar** there are two hours to go till arrival; **~ (al respeto) a algn** to be disrespectful to sb; **~ a una cita** to miss an appointment; **~ a la verdad** to lie; **¡no faltaba más!** (*no hay de qué*) don't mention it!
falto, -a ['falto, a] *adj* (*desposeído*) deficient, lacking; (*necesitado*) poor, wretched; **estar ~ de** to be short of
fama ['fama] *nf* (*renombre*) fame; (*reputación*) reputation
famélico, -a [fa'meliko, a] *adj* starving
familia [fa'milja] *nf* family; **~ numerosa** large family; **~ política** in-laws *pl*
familiar [fami'ljar] *adj* (*relativo a la familia*) family *cpd*; (*conocido, informal*) familiar; (*estilo*) informal; (*Ling*) colloquial ▷ *nm/f* relative, relation
familiaridad [familjari'ðað] *nf* familiarity; (*informalidad*) homeliness
familiarizarse [familjari'θarse] *vr*: **~ con** to familiarize o.s. with
famoso, -a [fa'moso, a] *adj* (*renombrado*) famous
fan (*pl* **fans**) [fan, fans] *nm* fan
fanático, -a [fa'natiko, a] *adj* fanatical ▷ *nm/f* fanatic; (*Cine, Deporte etc*) fan
fanatismo [fana'tismo] *nm* fanaticism

fanfarrón, -ona [fanfa'rron, ona] *adj* boastful; (*pey*) showy
fanfarronear [fanfarrone'ar] *vi* to boast
fango ['fango] *nm* mud
fangoso, -a [fan'goso, a] *adj* muddy
fantasía [fanta'sia] *nf* fantasy, imagination; (*Mus*) fantasia; (*capricho*) whim; **joyas de ~** imitation jewellery *sg*
fantasma [fan'tasma] *nm* (*espectro*) ghost, apparition; (*presumido*) show-off
fantástico, -a [fan'tastiko, a] *adj* (*irreal, fam*) fantastic
fanzine [fan'θine] *nm* fanzine
faquir [fa'kir] *nm* fakir
faraón [fara'on] *nm* Pharaoh
faraónico, -a [fara'oniko, a] *adj* Pharaonic; (*fig*) grandiose
faringe [fa'rinxe] *nf* pharynx
faringitis [farin'xitis] *nf* pharyngitis
farmacéutico, -a [farma'θeutiko, a] *adj* pharmaceutical ▷ *nm/f* chemist (*Brit*), pharmacist
farmacia [far'maθja] *nf* (*ciencia*) pharmacy; (*tienda*) chemist's (shop) (*Brit*), pharmacy, drugstore (*US*); **~ de turno** duty chemist; **~ de guardia** all-night chemist
fármaco ['farmako] *nm* medicine, drug
faro ['faro] *nm* (*Naut: torre*) lighthouse; (*señal*) beacon; (*Auto*) headlamp; **~s antiniebla** fog lamps; **~s delanteros/traseros** headlights/ rear lights
farol [fa'rol] *nm* (*luz*) lantern, lamp; (*Ferro*) headlamp; (*poste*) lamppost; **echarse un ~** (*fam*) to show off
farola [fa'rola] *nf* street lamp (*Brit*) *o* light (*US*), lamppost
farra ['farra] *nf* (*Am: fam*) party; **ir de ~** to go on a binge
farsa ['farsa] *nf* farce
farsante [far'sante] *nm/f* fraud, fake
fascículo [fas'θikulo] *nm* part, instalment (*Brit*), installment (*US*)
fascinante (fasθi'nante) *adj* fascinating
fascinar [fasθi'nar] *vt* to fascinate; (*encantar*) to captivate
fascismo [fas'θismo] *nm* fascism
fascista [fas'θista] *adj, nm/f* fascist
fase ['fase] *nf* phase
fashion ['faʃon] *adj* (*fam*) trendy
fastidiar [fasti'ðjar] *vt* (*disgustar*) to annoy, bother; (*estropear*) to spoil; **fastidiarse** *vr* (*disgustarse*) to get annoyed *o* cross; **¡no fastidies!** you're joking!; **¡que se fastidie!** (*fam*) he'll just have to put up with it!
fastidio [fas'tiðjo] *nm* (*disgusto*) annoyance
fastidioso, -a [fasti'ðjoso, a] *adj* (*molesto*) annoying
fastuoso, -a [fas'twoso, a] *adj* (*espléndido*) magnificent; (*banquete etc*) lavish
fatal [fa'tal] *adj* (*gen*) fatal; (*desgraciado*) ill-fated; (*fam: malo, pésimo*) awful ▷ *adv* terribly; **lo pasó ~** he had a terrible time (of it)
fatalidad [fatali'ðað] *nf* (*destino*) fate; (*mala suerte*) misfortune
fatiga [fa'tiɣa] *nf* (*cansancio*) fatigue, weariness; **fatigas** *nfpl* hardships
fatigar [fati'ɣar] *vt* to tire, weary; **fatigarse** *vr* to get tired
fatigoso, -a [fati'ɣoso, a] *adj* (*que cansa*) tiring
fatuo, -a ['fatwo, a] *adj* (*vano*) fatuous; (*presuntuoso*) conceited
fauces ['fauθes] *nfpl* (*Anat*) gullet *sg*; (*fam*) jaws
fauna ['fauna] *nf* fauna
favor [fa'βor] *nm* favour (*Brit*), favor (*US*); **haga el ~ de ...** would you be so good as to ..., kindly ...; **por ~** please; **a ~** in favo(u)r; **a ~ de** in favo(u)r of; (*Com*) to the order of
favorable [faβo'raβle] *adj* favourable (*Brit*), favorable (*US*); (*condiciones etc*) advantageous
favorecer [faβore'θer] *vt* to favour (*Brit*), favor (*US*); (*amparar*) to help; (*vestido etc*) to become, flatter; **este peinado le favorece** this hairstyle suits him
favorito, -a [faβo'rito, a] *adj, nm/f* favourite (*Brit*), favorite (*US*)
fax [faks] *nm inv* fax; **mandar por ~** to fax
faz [faθ] *nf* face; **la ~ de la tierra** the face of the earth
fe [fe] *nf* (*Rel*) faith; (*confianza*) belief; (*documento*) certificate; **de buena fe** (*Jur*) bona fide; **prestar fe a** to believe, credit; **actuar con buena/mala fe** to act in good/bad faith; **dar fe de** to bear witness to; **fe de erratas** errata
fealdad [feal'dað] *nf* ugliness
febrero [fe'βrero] *nm* February; *ver tb* **julio**
febril [fe'βril] *adj* feverish; (*movido*) hectic
fecha ['fetʃa] *nf* date; **~ límite** *o* **tope** closing *o* last date; **~ límite de venta** (*de alimentos*) sell-by date; **~ de caducidad** (*de alimentos*) sell-by date; (*de contrato*) expiry date; **con ~ adelantada** postdated; **en ~ próxima** soon; **hasta la ~** to date, so far; **~ de vencimiento** (*Com*) due date; **~ de vigencia** (*Com*) effective date
fechar [fe'tʃar] *vt* to date
fechoría [fetʃo'ria] *nf* misdeed
fecundar [fekun'dar] *vt* (*generar*) to fertilize, make fertile
fecundo, -a [fe'kundo, a] *adj* (*fértil*) fertile; (*fig*) prolific; (*productivo*) productive
federación [feðera'θjon] *nf* federation
federal [feðe'ral] *adj* federal
felicidad [feliθi'ðað] *nf* (*satisfacción, contento*) happiness; **felicidades** *nfpl* best wishes, congratulations; (*en cumpleaños*) happy birthday
felicitación [feliθita'θjon] *nf* (*tarjeta*) greetings card; **felicitaciones** *nfpl* (*enhorabuena*) congratulations; **~ navideña** *o* **de Navidad** Christmas Greetings
felicitar [feliθi'tar] *vt* to congratulate

feligrés, -esa [feli'ɣres, esa] *nm/f* parishioner
felino, -a [fe'lino, a] *adj* cat-like; (*Zool*) feline ▷ *nm* feline
feliz [fe'liθ] *adj* (*contento*) happy; (*afortunado*) lucky
felpudo [fel'puðo] *nm* doormat
femenino, -a [feme'nino, a] *adj* feminine; (*Zool etc*) female ▷ *nm* (*Ling*) feminine
feminista [femi'nista] *adj, nm/f* feminist
fenomenal [fenome'nal] *adj* phenomenal; (*fam*) great, terrific
fenómeno [fe'nomeno] *nm* phenomenon; (*fig*) freak, accident ▷ *adv*: **lo pasamos ~** we had a great time ▷ *excl* great!, marvellous!
feo, -a ['feo, a] *adj* (*gen*) ugly; (*desagradable*) bad, nasty ▷ *nm* insult; **hacer un ~ a algn** to offend sb; **más ~ que Picio** as ugly as sin
féretro ['feretro] *nm* (*ataúd*) coffin; (*sarcófago*) bier
feria ['ferja] *nf* (*gen*) fair; (*Am: mercado*) market; (*descanso*) holiday, rest day; (*Am: cambio*) small change; (*Am: mercado*) village market; **~ comercial** trade fair; **~ de muestras** trade show
feriado, -a [fe'rjaðo, a] (*Am*) *adj*: **día ~** (public) holiday ▷ *nm* (public) holiday
fermentar [fermen'tar] *vi* to ferment
ferocidad [feroθi'ðað] *nf* fierceness, ferocity
feroz [fe'roθ] *adj* (*cruel*) cruel; (*salvaje*) fierce
férreo, -a ['ferreo, a] *adj* iron *cpd*; (*Tec*) ferrous; (*fig*) (of) iron
ferretería [ferrete'ria] *nf* (*tienda*) ironmonger's (shop) (*Brit*), hardware store
ferretero [ferre'tero] *nm* ironmonger
ferrocarril [ferroka'rril] *nm* railway, railroad (*US*); **~ de vía estrecha/única** narrow-gauge/single-track railway *o* line
ferroviario, -a [ferrovja'rjo, a] *adj* rail *cpd*, railway *cpd* (*Brit*), railroad *cpd* (*US*) ▷ *nm*: **~s** railway (*Brit*) *o* railroad (*US*) workers
ferry ['ferri] (*pl* **ferrys** *o* **ferries**) *nm* ferry
fértil ['fertil] *adj* (*productivo*) fertile; (*rico*) rich
fertilidad [fertili'ðað] *nf* (*gen*) fertility; (*productividad*) fruitfulness
fertilizante [fertili'θante] *nm* fertilizer
fertilizar [fertili'θar] *vt* to fertilize
ferviente [fer'βjente] *adj* fervent
fervor [fer'βor] *nm* fervour (*Brit*), fervor (*US*)
fervoroso, -a [ferβo'roso, a] *adj* fervent
festejar [feste'xar] *vt* (*agasajar*) to wine and dine, fête; (*galantear*) to court; (*celebrar*) to celebrate
festejo [fes'texo] *nm* (*diversión*) entertainment; (*galanteo*) courtship; (*fiesta*) celebration; **festejos** *nmpl* (*fiestas*) festivals
festín [fes'tin] *nm* feast, banquet
festival [festi'βal] *nm* festival
festividad [festiβi'ðað] *nf* festivity
festivo, -a [fes'tiβo, a] *adj* (*de fiesta*) festive; (*fig*) witty; (*Cine, Lit*) humorous; **día ~** holiday
fétido, -a ['fetiðo, a] *adj* (*hediondo*) foul-smelling
feto ['feto] *nm* foetus; (*fam*) monster
fiable [fi'aβle] *adj* (*persona*) trustworthy; (*máquina*) reliable
fiador, a [fia'ðor, a] *nm/f* (*Jur*) surety, guarantor; (*Com*) backer; **salir ~ por algn** to stand bail for sb
fiambre ['fjambre] *adj* (*Culin*) served cold ▷ *nm* (*Culin*) cold meat (*Brit*), cold cut (*US*); (*fam*) corpse, stiff
fiambrera [fjam'brera] *nf* ≈ lunch box, ≈ dinner pail (*US*)
fianza ['fjanθa] *nf* surety; (*Jur*): **libertad bajo ~** release on bail
fiar [fi'ar] *vt* (*salir garante de*) to guarantee; (*Jur*) to stand bail *o* bond (*US*) for; (*vender a crédito*) to sell on credit; (*secreto*) to confide ▷ *vi*: **~ (de)** to trust (in); **ser de ~** to be trustworthy; **fiarse** *vr*: **~se de** to trust (in), rely on; **~se de algn** to rely on sb
fibra ['fiβra] *nf* fibre (*Brit*), fiber (*US*); (*fig*) vigour (*Brit*), vigor (*US*); **~ óptica** (*Inform*) optical fibre (*Brit*) *o* fiber (*US*)
ficción [fik'θjon] *nf* fiction
ficha ['fitʃa] *nf* (*Telec*) token; (*en juegos*) counter, marker; (*en casino*) chip; (*Com, Econ*) tally, check (*US*); (*Inform*) file; (*tarjeta*) (index) card; (*Elec*) plug; (*en hotel*) registration form; **~ policíaca** police dossier
fichaje [fi'tʃaxe] *nm* signing(-up)
fichar [fi'tʃar] *vt* (*archivar*) to file, index; (*Deporte*) to sign (up) ▷ *vi* (*deportista*) to sign (up); (*obrero*) to clock in *o* on; **estar fichado** to have a record
fichero [fi'tʃero] *nm* card index; (*archivo*) filing cabinet; (*Com*) box file; (*Inform*) file, archive; (*de policía*) criminal records; **~ activo** (*Inform*) active file; **~ archivado** (*Inform*) archived file; **~ indexado** (*Inform*) index file; **~ de reserva** (*Inform*) backup file; **~ de tarjetas** card index; **nombre de ~** filename
ficticio, -a [fik'tiθjo, a] *adj* (*imaginario*) fictitious; (*falso*) fabricated
fidelidad [fiðeli'ðað] *nf* (*lealtad*) fidelity, loyalty; (*exactitud: de dato etc*) accuracy; **alta ~** high fidelity, hi-fi
fideos [fi'ðeos] *nmpl* noodles
fiebre ['fjeβre] *nf* (*Med*) fever; (*fig*) fever, excitement; **~ amarilla/del heno** yellow/hay fever; **~ palúdica** malaria; **tener ~** to have a temperature; **~ aftosa** foot-and-mouth disease
fiel [fjel] *adj* (*leal*) faithful, loyal; (*fiable*) reliable; (*exacto*) accurate ▷ *nm* (*aguja*) needle, pointer; **los fieles** *nmpl* the faithful
fieltro ['fjeltro] *nm* felt
fiera ['fjera] *nf* *ver* **fiero**
fiero, -a ['fjero, a] *adj* (*cruel*) cruel; (*feroz*) fierce; (*duro*) harsh ▷ *nm/f* (*fig*) fiend ▷ *nf* (*animal feroz*) wild animal *o* beast; (*fig*) dragon
fierro ['fjerro] *nm* (*Am*) iron
fiesta ['fjesta] *nf* party; (*de pueblo*) festival; **la ~ nacional** bullfighting; **(día de) ~**

(public) holiday; **mañana es ~** it's a holiday tomorrow; **~ mayor** annual festival; **~ patria** (*Am*) independence day; **~ de guardar** (*Rel*) day of obligation; *see note*

FIESTA

Fiestas can be official public holidays (such as the *Día de la Constitución*), or special holidays for each *comunidad autónoma*, many of which are religious feast days. All over Spain there are also special local *fiestas* for a patron saint or the Virgin Mary. These often last several days and can include religious processions, carnival parades, bullfights, dancing and feasts of typical local produce.

figura [fi'ɣura] *nf* (*gen*) figure; (*forma, imagen*) shape, form; (*Naipes*) face card
figurado, -a [fiɣu'raðo, a] *adj* figurative
figurante [fiɣu'rante] *nm/f* (*Teat*) walk-on part; (*Cine*) extra
figurar [fiɣu'rar] *vt* (*representar*) to represent; (*fingir*) to feign ▷ *vi* to figure; **figurarse** *vr* (*imaginarse*) to imagine; (*suponer*) to suppose; **ya me lo figuraba** I thought as much
fijador [fixa'ðor] *nm* (*Foto etc*) fixative; (*de pelo*) gel
fijar [fi'xar] *vt* (*gen*) to fix; (*cartel*) to post, put up; (*estampilla*) to affix, stick (on); (*pelo*) to set; (*fig*) to settle (on), decide; **fijarse** *vr*: **~se en** to notice; **¡fíjate!** just imagine!; **¿te fijas?** see what I mean?
fijo, -a ['fixo, a] *adj* (*gen*) fixed; (*firme*) firm; (*permanente*) permanent; (*trabajo*) steady; (*colorfast*) fast ▷ *adv*: **mirar ~** to stare
fila ['fila] *nf* row; (*Mil*) rank; (*cadena*) line; (*en marcha*) file; **~ india** single file; **ponerse en ~** to line up, get into line; **primera ~** front row
filántropo, -a [fi'lantropo, a] *nm/f* philanthropist
filatelia [fila'telja] *nf* philately, stamp collecting
filete [fi'lete] *nm* (*de carne*) fillet steak; (*de cerdo*) tenderloin; (*pescado*) fillet; (*Mecánica: rosca*) thread
filiación [filja'θjon] *nf* (*Pol etc*) affiliation; (*señas*) particulars *pl*; (*Mil, Policía*) records *pl*
filial [fi'ljal] *adj* filial ▷ *nf* subsidiary; (*sucursal*) branch
Filipinas [fili'pinas] *nfpl*: **las (Islas) ~** the Philippines
filipino, -a [fili'pino, a] *adj, nm/f* Philippine
film [film] (*pl* **films**) *nm* = **filme**
filmar [fil'mar] *vt* to film, shoot
filme ['filme] *nm* film, movie (*US*)
filo ['filo] *nm* (*gen*) edge; **sacar ~ a** to sharpen; **al ~ del medio día** at about midday; **de doble ~** double-edged
filología [filolo'xia] *nf* philology; **~ inglesa** (*Univ*) English Studies
filón [fi'lon] *nm* (*Minería*) vein, lode; (*fig*) gold mine
filosofía [filoso'fia] *nf* philosophy
filósofo, -a [fi'losofo, a] *nm/f* philosopher
filtrar [fil'trar] *vt, vi* to filter, strain; (*información*) to leak; **filtrarse** *vr* to filter; (*fig: dinero*) to dwindle
filtro ['filtro] *nm* (*Tec, utensilio*) filter
fin [fin] *nm* end; (*objetivo*) aim, purpose; **a ~ de cuentas** at the end of the day; **al ~ y al cabo** when all's said and done; **a ~ de** in order to; **por ~** finally; **en ~** (*resumiendo*) in short; **¡en ~!** (*resignación*) oh, well!; **~ de archivo** (*Inform*) end-of-file; **~ de semana** weekend; **sin ~** endless(ly)
final [fi'nal] *adj* final ▷ *nm* end, conclusion ▷ *nf* (*Deporte*) final; **al ~** in the end; **a ~es de** at the end of
finalidad [finali'ðað] *nf* finality; (*propósito*) purpose, aim
finalista [fina'lista] *nm/f* finalist
finalizar [finali'θar] *vt* to end, finish ▷ *vi* to end, come to an end; **~ la sesión** (*Inform*) to log out *o* off
financiar [finan'θjar] *vt* to finance
financiero, -a [finan'θjero, a] *adj* financial ▷ *nm/f* financier
finanzas [fi'nanθas] *nfpl* finances
finca ['finka] *nf* (*casa de recreo*) house in the country; (*Esp: bien inmueble*) property, land; (*Am: granja*) farm
finde ['finde] *nm abbr* (*fam:* = *fin de semana*) weekend
fingir [fin'xir] *vt* (*simular*) to simulate, feign; (*pretextar*) to sham, fake ▷ *vi* (*aparentar*) to pretend; **fingirse** *vr*: **~se dormido** to pretend to be asleep
finlandés, -esa [finlan'des, esa] *adj* Finnish ▷ *nm/f* Finn ▷ *nm* (*Ling*) Finnish
Finlandia [fin'landja] *nf* Finland
fino, -a ['fino, a] *adj* fine; (*delgado*) slender; (*de buenas maneras*) polite, refined; (*inteligente*) shrewd; (*punta*) sharp; (*gusto*) discriminating; (*oído*) sharp; (*jerez*) fino, dry ▷ *nm* (*jerez*) dry sherry
firma ['firma] *nf* signature; (*Com*) firm, company
firmamento [firma'mento] *nm* firmament
firmante [fir'mante] *adj, nm/f* signatory; **los abajo ~s** the undersigned
firmar [fir'mar] *vt* to sign; **~ un contrato** (*Com: colocarse*) to sign on; **firmado y sellado** signed and sealed
firme ['firme] *adj* firm; (*estable*) stable; (*sólido*) solid; (*constante*) steady; (*decidido*) resolute; (*duro*) hard; **¡~s!** (*Mil*) attention!; **oferta en ~** (*Com*) firm offer ▷ *nm* road (surface)
firmemente [firme'mente] *adv* firmly
firmeza [fir'meθa] *nf* firmness; (*constancia*) steadiness; (*solidez*) solidity

f

fiscal [fis'kal] *adj* fiscal ▷ *nm* (*Jur*) public prosecutor, ≈ district attorney (*US*); **año ~** tax *o* fiscal year
fisco ['fisko] *nm* (*hacienda*) treasury, exchequer; **declarar algo al ~** to declare sth for tax purposes
fisgar [fis'ɣar] *vt* to pry into
fisgón, -ona [fis'ɣon, ona] *adj* nosey
fisgonear [fisɣone'ar] *vt* to poke one's nose into ▷ *vi* to pry, spy
físico, -a ['fisiko, a] *adj* physical ▷ *nm* physique; (*aspecto*) appearance, looks *pl* ▷ *nm/f* physicist ▷ *nf* physics *sg*
fisioterapia [fisjote'rapja] *nf* physiotherapy
fisura [fi'sura] *nf* crack; (*Med*) fracture
fláccido, -a ['flakθiðo, a], **flácido, -a** ['flaθiðo, a] *adj* flabby
flaco, -a ['flako, a] *adj* (*muy delgado*) skinny, thin; (*débil*) weak, feeble
flagrante [fla'ɣrante] *adj* flagrant
flama ['flama] *nf* (*Am*) flame
flamable [fla'maβle] *adj* (*Am*) flammable
flamante [fla'mante] *adj* (*fam*) brilliant; (*: nuevo*) brand-new
flamenco, -a [fla'menko, a] *adj* (*de Flandes*) Flemish; (*baile, música*) flamenco ▷ *nm/f* Fleming; **los ~s** the Flemish ▷ *nm* (*Ling*) Flemish; (*baile, música*) flamenco; (*Zool*) flamingo
flamingo [fla'mingo] *nm* (*Am*) flamingo
flan [flan] *nm* creme caramel
flaquear [flake'ar] *vi* (*debilitarse*) to weaken; (*persona*) to slack
flaqueza [fla'keθa] *nf* (*delgadez*) thinness, leanness; (*fig*) weakness
flash [flaʃ] (*pl* **flashes**) [flas] *nm* (*Foto*) flash; (*Inform*): **~ drive** flash drive
flauta ['flauta] (*Mus*) *nf* flute ▷ *nm/f* flautist, flute player; **¡la gran ~!** (*Am*) my God!; **hijo de la gran ~** (*Am*: (*fam!*)) bastard (*!*), son of a bitch (*US!*)
flecha ['fletʃa] *nf* arrow
flechazo [fle'tʃaθo] *nm* (*acción*) bowshot; (*fam*): **fue un ~** it was love at first sight
fleco ['fleko] *nm* fringe
flema ['flema] *nm* phlegm
flemón [fle'mon] *nm* (*Med*) gumboil
flequillo [fle'kiʎo] *nm* (*de pelo*) fringe, bangs (*US*)
flete ['flete] *nm* (*carga*) freight; (*alquiler*) charter; (*precio*) freightage; **~ debido** (*Com*) freight forward; **~ sobre compras** (*Com*) freight inward
flexible [flek'siβle] *adj* flexible; (*individuo*) compliant
flexión [flek'sjon] *nf* (*Deporte*) bend; (*: en el suelo*) press-up
flexo ['flekso] *nm* adjustable table lamp
flipper ['fliper] *nm* pinball machine
flirtear [flirte'ar] *vi* to flirt
flojear [floxe'ar] *vi* (*piernas: al andar*) to give way; (*alumno*) to do badly; (*cosecha, mercado*) to be poor
flojera [flo'xera] *nf* (*Am*) laziness; **me da ~** I can't be bothered
flojo, -a ['floxo, a] *adj* (*gen*) loose; (*sin fuerzas*) limp; (*débil*) weak; (*viento*) light; (*bebida*) weak; (*trabajo*) poor; (*actitud*) slack; (*precio*) low; (*Com: mercado*) dull, slack; (*Am*) lazy
flor [flor] *nf* flower; (*piropo*) compliment; **la ~ y nata de la sociedad** (*fig*) the cream of society; **en la ~ de la vida** in the prime of life; **a ~ de** on the surface of
flora ['flora] *nf* flora
florecer [flore'θer] *vi* (*Bot*) to flower, bloom; (*fig*) to flourish
floreciente [flore'θjente] *adj* (*Bot*) in flower, flowering; (*fig*) thriving
florería [flore'ria] *nf* (*Am*) florist's (shop)
florero [flo'rero] *nm* vase
florista [flo'rista] *nm/f* florist
floristería [floriste'ria] *nf* florist's (shop)
flota ['flota] *nf* fleet
flotador [flota'ðor] *nm* (*gen*) float; (*para nadar*) rubber ring; (*de cisterna*) ballcock
flotar [flo'tar] *vi* to float
flote ['flote] *nm*: **a ~** afloat; **salir a ~** (*fig*) to get back on one's feet
fluctuar [fluk'twar] *vi* (*oscilar*) to fluctuate
fluidez [flui'ðeθ] *nf* fluidity; (*fig*) fluency
fluido, -a ['flwiðo, a] *adj* fluid; (*lenguaje*) fluent; (*estilo*) smooth ▷ *nm* (*líquido*) fluid
fluir [flu'ir] *vi* to flow
flujo ['fluxo] *nm* flow; (*Pol*) swing; (*Naut*) rising tide; **~ y reflujo** ebb and flow; **~ de sangre** (*Med*) haemorrhage (*Brit*), hemorrhage (*US*); **~ positivo/negativo de efectivo** (*Com*) positive/negative cash flow
flúor ['fluor] *nm* fluorine; (*en dentífrico*) fluoride
fluorescente [flwores'θente] *adj* fluorescent ▷ *nm* (*tb*: **tubo ~**) fluorescent tube
fluvial [fluβi'al] *adj* (*navegación, cuenca*) fluvial, river *cpd*
FMI *nm abr* (= *Fondo Monetario Internacional*) IMF
fobia ['fobja] *nf* phobia; **~ a las alturas** fear of heights
foca ['foka] *nf* seal
foco ['foko] *nm* focus; (*centro*) focal point; (*fuente*) source; (*de incendio*) seat; (*Elec*) floodlight; (*Teat*) spotlight; (*Am*) (light) bulb, light
fofo, -a ['fofo, a] *adj* (*esponjoso*) soft, spongy; (*músculo*) flabby
fogata [fo'ɣata] *nf* (*hoguera*) bonfire
fogón [fo'ɣon] *nm* (*de cocina*) ring, burner
fogoso, -a [fo'ɣoso, a] *adj* spirited
folio ['foljo] *nm* (*hoja*) sheet (of paper), page
folklore [fol'klore] *nm* folklore
folklórico, -a [fol'kloriko, a] *adj* traditional
follaje [fo'ʎaxe] *nm* foliage
follar [fo'ʎar] *vt, vi* (*fam!*) to fuck (*!*)

folleto [fo'ʎeto] *nm* pamphlet; (*Com*) brochure; (*prospecto*) leaflet; (*Escol etc*) handout

follón [fo'ʎon] *nm* (*fam*: *lío*) mess; (: *conmoción*) fuss, rumpus, shindy; **armar un ~** to kick up a fuss; **se armó un ~** there was a hell of a row

fomentar [fomen'tar] *vt* (*Med*) to foment; (*fig*: *promover*) to promote, foster; (*odio etc*) to stir up

fomento [fo'mento] *nm* (*fig*: *ayuda*) fostering; (*promoción*) promotion

fonda ['fonda] *nf* ≈ boarding house; *ver tb* **hotel**

fondo ['fondo] *nm* (*de caja etc*) bottom; (*medida*) depth; (*de coche, sala*) back; (*Arte etc*) background; (*reserva*) fund; (*fig*: *carácter*) nature; **fondos** *nmpl* (*Com*) funds, resources; **~ de escritorio** (*Inform*) wallpaper; **F~ Monetario Internacional** International Monetary Fund; **~ del mar** sea bed *o* floor; **una investigación a ~** a thorough investigation; **en el ~** at bottom, deep down; **tener buen ~** to be good-natured

fonética [fo'netika] *nf* phonetics *sg*

fono ['fono] *nm* (*Am*) telephone (number)

fonobuzón [fonoβu'θon] *nm* voice mail

fontanería [fontane'ria] *nf* plumbing

fontanero [fonta'nero] *nm* plumber

footing ['futin] *nm* jogging; **hacer ~** to jog

forastero, -a [foras'tero, a] *nm/f* stranger

forcejear [forθexe'ar] *vi* (*luchar*) to struggle

fórceps ['forθeps] *nm inv* forceps *pl*

forense [fo'rense] *adj* forensic ▷ *nm/f* pathologist

forestal [fores'tal] *adj* forest *cpd*

forjar [for'xar] *vt* to forge; (*formar*) to form

forma ['forma] *nf* (*figura*) form, shape; (*molde*) mould, pattern; (*Med*) fitness; (*método*) way, means; **estar en ~** to be fit; **~ de pago** (*Com*) method of payment; **las ~s** the conventions; **de ~ que ...** so that ...; **de todas ~s** in any case

formación [forma'θjon] *nf* (*gen*) formation; (*enseñanza*) training; **~ profesional** vocational training; **~ fuera del trabajo** off-the-job training; **~ en el trabajo** *o* **sobre la práctica** on-the-job training

formal [for'mal] *adj* (*gen*) formal; (*fig*: *persona*) serious; (: *ooo*: *de fiar*) reliable; (*conducta*) steady

formalidad [formali'ðað] *nf* formality; seriousness; reliability; steadiness

formalizar [formali'θar] *vt* (*Jur*) to formalize; (*plan*) to draw up; (*situación*) to put in order, regularize; **formalizarse** *vr* (*situación*) to be put in order, be regularized

formar [for'mar] *vt* (*componer*) to form, shape; (*constituir*) to make up, constitute; (*Escol*) to train, educate ▷ *vi* (*Mil*) to fall in; (*Deporte*) to line up; **formarse** *vr* (*Escol*) to be trained (*o* educated); (*cobrar forma*) to form, take form; (*desarrollarse*) to develop

formatear [formate'ar] *vt* (*Inform*) to format

formato [for'mato] *nm* (*Inform*) format; **sin ~** (*disco, texto*) unformatted; **~ de registro** record format

formidable [formi'ðaβle] *adj* (*temible*) formidable; (*asombroso*) tremendous

fórmula ['formula] *nf* formula

formular [formu'lar] *vt* (*queja*) to lodge; (*petición*) to draw up; (*pregunta*) to pose, formulate; (*idea*) to formulate

formulario [formu'larjo] *nm* form; **~ de solicitud/de pedido** (*Com*) application/order form; **llenar un ~** to fill in a form; **~ continuo desplegable** (*Inform*) fanfold paper

fornido, -a [for'niðo, a] *adj* well-built

foro ['foro] *nm* (*gen*) forum; (*Jur*) court; **~ de debate/discusión** (*Internet*) discussion forum, message board

forrar [fo'rrar] *vt* (*abrigo*) to line; (*libro*) to cover; (*coche*) to upholster; **forrarse** *vr* (*fam*) to line one's pockets

forro ['forro] *nm* (*de cuaderno*) cover; (*costura*) lining; (*de sillón*) upholstery; **~ polar** fleece

fortalecer [fortale'θer] *vt* to strengthen; **fortalecerse** *vr* to fortify o.s.; (*opinión etc*) to become stronger

fortaleza [forta'leθa] *nf* (*Mil*) fortress, stronghold; (*fuerza*) strength; (*determinación*) resolution

fortuito, -a [for'twito, a] *adj* accidental, chance *cpd*

fortuna [for'tuna] *nf* (*suerte*) fortune, (good) luck; (*riqueza*) fortune, wealth

forzar [for'θar] *vt* (*puerta*) to force (open); (*compeler*) to compel; (*violar*) to rape; (*ojos etc*) to strain

forzoso, -a [for'θoso, a] *adj* necessary; (*inevitable*) inescapable; (*obligatorio*) compulsory

fosa ['fosa] *nf* (*sepultura*) grave; (*en tierra*) pit; (*Med*) cavity; **~s nasales** nostrils

fosforescente [fosfores'θente] *adj* phosphorescent

fósforo ['fosforo] *nm* (*Química*) phosphorus; (*esp Am*: *cerilla*) match

fósil ['fosil] *adj* fossil, fossilized ▷ *nm* fossil

foso ['foso] *nm* ditch; (*Teat*) pit; (*Auto*): **~ de reconocimiento** inspection pit

foto ['foto] *nf* photo, snap(shot); **sacar una ~** to take a photo *o* picture; **~ (de) carné** passport(-size) photo

fotocopia [foto'kopja] *nf* photocopy

fotocopiadora [fotokopja'ðora] *nf* photocopier

fotocopiar [fotoko'pjar] *vt* to photocopy

fotogénico, -a [foto'xeniko, a] *adj* photogenic

fotografía [fotoɣra'fia] *nf* (*arte*) photography; (*una fotografía*) photograph

fotografiar [fotoɣra'fjar] *vt* to photograph

f

fotógrafo, -a [fo'toɣrafo, a] *nm/f* photographer
fotomatón [fotoma'ton] *nm* (*cabina*) photo booth
fotonovela [fotono'βela] *nf* photo-story
FP *nf abr* (*Esp*: *Escol, Com*) = **Formación Profesional** ▷ *nm abr* (*Pol*) = **Frente Popular**
frac (*pl* **fracs** *o* **fraques**) [frak, 'frakes] *nm* dress coat, tails
fracasar [fraka'sar] *vi* (*gen*) to fail; (*plan etc*) to fall through
fracaso [fra'kaso] *nm* (*desgracia, revés*) failure; (*de negociaciones etc*) collapse, breakdown
fracción [frak'θjon] *nf* fraction; (*Pol*) faction, splinter group
fraccionamiento [fraksjona'mjento] *nm* (*Am*) housing estate
fractura [frak'tura] *nf* fracture, break
fragancia [fra'ɣanθja] *nf* (*olor*) fragrance, perfume
fraganti [fra'ɣanti]: **in ~** *adv*: **coger a algn in fraganti** to catch sb red-handed
fragata [fra'ɣata] *nf* frigate
frágil ['fraxil] *adj* (*débil*) fragile; (*Com*) breakable; (*fig*) frail, delicate
fragmento [fraɣ'mento] *nm* fragment; (*pedazo*) piece; (*de discurso*) excerpt; (*de canción*) snatch
fragua ['fraɣwa] *nf* forge
fraguar [fra'ɣwar] *vt* to forge; (*fig*) to concoct ▷ *vi* to harden
fraile ['fraile] *nm* (*Rel*) friar; (: *monje*) monk
frambuesa [fram'bwesa] *nf* raspberry
francés, -esa [fran'θes, esa] *adj* French ▷ *nm/f* Frenchman(-woman) ▷ *nm* (*Ling*) French
Francia ['franθja] *nf* France
franco, -a ['franko, a] *adj* (*cándido*) frank, open; (*Com*: *exento*) free ▷ *nm* (*moneda*) franc; **~ de derechos** duty-free; **~ al costado del buque** (*Com*) free alongside ship; **~ puesto sobre vagón** (*Com*) free on rail; **~ a bordo** free on board
francotirador, a [frankotira'ðor, a] *nm/f* sniper
franela [fra'nela] *nf* flannel
franja ['franxa] *nf* fringe; (*de uniforme*) stripe; (*de tierra etc*) strip
franquear [franke'ar] *vt* (*camino*) to clear; (*carta, paquete*) to frank, stamp; (*obstáculo*) to overcome; (*Com etc*) to free, exempt
franqueo [fran'keo] *nm* postage
franqueza [fran'keθa] *nf* frankness
franquismo [fran'kismo] *nm*: **el ~** (*sistema*) the Franco system; (*período*) the Franco years; *see note*
franquista [fran'kista] *adj* pro-Franco ▷ *nm/f* supporter of Franco
frasco ['frasko] *nm* bottle, flask; **~ al vacío** (vacuum) flask
frase ['frase] *nf* sentence; (*locución*) phrase, expression; **~ hecha** set phrase; (*pey*) stock phrase
fraternal [frater'nal] *adj* brotherly, fraternal
fraterno, -a [fra'terno, a] *adj* brotherly, fraternal
fraude ['frauðe] *nm* (*cualidad*) dishonesty; (*acto*) fraud, swindle
fraudulento, -a [frauðu'lento, a] *adj* fraudulent
frazada [fra'saða] *nf* (*Am*) blanket
frecuencia [fre'kwenθja] *nf* frequency; **con ~** frequently, often; **~ de red** (*Inform*) mains frequency; **~ del reloj** (*Inform*) clock speed; **~ telefónica** voice frequency
frecuentar [frekwen'tar] *vt* (*lugar*) to frequent; (*persona*) to see frequently *o* often; **~ la buena sociedad** to mix in high society
frecuente [fre'kwente] *adj* frequent; (*costumbre*) common; (*vicio*) rife
fregadero [freɣa'ðero] *nm* (kitchen) sink
fregar [fre'ɣar] *vt* (*frotar*) to scrub; (*platos*) to wash (up); (*Am*: *fam*: *fastidiar*) to annoy; (: *malograr*) to screw up
freidora [frei'ðora] *nf* deep-fat fryer
freír [fre'ir] *vt* to fry
frenar [fre'nar] *vt* to brake; (*fig*) to check
frenazo [fre'naθo] *nm*: **dar un ~** to brake sharply
frenesí [frene'si] *nm* frenzy
frenético, -a [fre'netiko, a] *adj* frantic; **ponerse ~** to lose one's head
freno ['freno] *nm* (*Tec, Auto*) brake; (*de cabalgadura*) bit; (*fig*) check; **~ de mano** handbrake
frente ['frente] *nm* (*Arq, Mil, Pol*) front; (*de objeto*) front part ▷ *nf* forehead, brow; **~ de batalla** battle front; **hacer ~ común con algn** to make common cause with sb; **~ a** in front of; (*en situación opuesta a*) opposite; **chocar de ~** to crash head-on; **hacer ~ a** to face up to
fresa ['fresa] *nf* (*Esp*: *fruta*) strawberry; (*de dentista*) drill
fresco, -a ['fresko, a] *adj* (*nuevo*) fresh; (*huevo*) newly-laid; (*frío*) cool; (*descarado*) cheeky, bad-mannered ▷ *nm* (*aire*) fresh air; (*Arte*) fresco; (*Am*: *bebida*) fruit juice *o* drink ▷ *nm/f* (*fam*) shameless person; (*persona insolente*) impudent person; **tomar el ~** to get some fresh air; **ser un ~** to have a nerve; **¡qué ~!** what a cheek!
frescura [fres'kura] *nf* freshness; (*descaro*) cheek, nerve; (*calma*) calmness
frialdad [frjal'dað] *nf* (*gen*) coldness; (*indiferencia*) indifference
fricción [frik'θjon] *nf* (*gen*) friction; (*acto*) rub(bing); (*Med*) massage; (*Pol, fig etc*) friction, trouble
frigidez [frixi'ðeθ] *nf* frigidity
frigo ['friɣo] *nm* fridge
frigorífico, -a [friɣo'rifiko, a] *adj* refrigerating ▷ *nm* refrigerator; (*camión*) freezer lorry *o* truck (US); **instalación frigorífica** cold-storage plant

frijol [fri'xol], **fríjol** ['frixol] *nm* kidney bean
frío, -a *etc* ['frio, a] *vb ver* **freír** ▷ *adj* cold; (*fig: indiferente*) unmoved, indifferent; (*poco entusiasta*) chilly ▷ *nm* cold(ness); indifference; **hace ~** it's cold; **tener ~** to be cold; **¡qué ~!** how cold it is!
frito, -a ['frito, a] *pp de* **freír** ▷ *adj* fried ▷ *nm* fry; **me trae ~ ese hombre** I'm sick and tired of that man; **fritos** *nmpl* fried food; **~s variados** mixed grill
frívolo, -a ['friβolo, a] *adj* frivolous
frontal [fron'tal] *adj* frontal ▷ *nm*: **choque ~** head-on collision
frontera [fron'tera] *nf* frontier; (*línea divisoria*) border; (*zona*) frontier area
fronterizo, -a [fronte'riθo, a] *adj* frontier *cpd*; (*contiguo*) bordering
frontón [fron'ton] *nm* (*Deporte: cancha*) pelota court; (*: juego*) pelota
frotar [fro'tar] *vt* to rub; (*fósforo*) to strike; **frotarse** *vr*: **~se las manos** to rub one's hands
fructífero, -a [fruk'tifero, a] *adj* productive, fruitful
frugal [fru'ɣal] *adj* frugal
fruncir [frun'θir] *vt* to pucker; (*Costura*) to gather; (*ceño*) to frown; (*labios*) to purse; **~ el ceño** to knit one's brow
frustración [frustra'θjon] *nf* frustration
frustrar [frus'trar] *vt* to frustrate; **frustrarse** *vr* to be frustrated; (*plan etc*) to fail
fruta ['fruta] *nf* fruit
frutería [frute'ria] *nf* fruit shop
frutero, -a [fru'tero, a] *adj* fruit *cpd* ▷ *nm/f* fruiterer ▷ *nm* fruit dish *o* bowl
frutilla [fru'tiʎa] *nf* (*Am*) strawberry
fruto ['fruto] *nm* (*Bot*) fruit; (*fig: resultado*) result, outcome; (*: beneficio*) benefit; **~s secos** nuts and dried fruit
fucsia ['fuksja] *nf* fuchsia
fue [fwe] *vb ver* **ser, ir**
fuego ['fweɣo] *nm* (*gen*) fire; (*Culin: gas*) burner, ring; (*Mil*) fire; (*fig: pasión*) fire, passion; **~ amigo** friendly fire; **~s artificiales** *o* **de artificio** fireworks; **prender ~ a** to set fire to; **a ~ lento** on a low flame *o* gas; **¡alto el ~!** cease fire!; **estar entre dos ~s** to be in the crossfire; **¿tienes ~?** have you (got) a light?
fuente ['fwente] *nf* fountain; (*manantial, fig*) spring; (*origen*) source; (*plato*) large dish; **~ de alimentación** (*Inform*) power supply; **de ~ desconocida/fidedigna** from an unknown/reliable source
fuera ['fwera] *vb ver* **ser, ir** ▷ *adv* out(side); (*en otra parte*) away; (*excepto, salvo*) except, save ▷ *prep*: **~ de** outside; (*fig*) besides; **~ de alcance** out of reach; **~ de combate** out of action; (*boxeo*) knocked out; **~ de sí** beside o.s.; **por ~** (on the) outside; **los de ~** strangers, newcomers; **estar ~** (*en el extranjero*) to be abroad
fuera-borda [fwera'βorða] *nm inv* (*barco*) speedboat; (*motor*) outboard engine *o* motor
fuero ['fwero] *nm* (*carta municipal*) municipal charter; (*leyes locales*) local *o* regional law code; (*privilegio*) privilege; (*autoridad*) jurisdiction; (*fig*): **en mi** *etc* **~ interno ...** in my *etc* heart of hearts ..., deep down ...
fuerte ['fwerte] *adj* strong; (*golpe*) hard; (*ruido*) loud; (*comida*) rich; (*lluvia*) heavy; (*dolor*) intense ▷ *adv* strongly; hard; loud(ly) ▷ *nm* (*Mil*) fort, strongpoint; (*fig*): **ser ~ en** to be good at; **el canto no es mi ~** singing is not my strong point
fuerza ['fwerθa] *vb ver* **forzar** ▷ *nf* (*fortaleza*) strength; (*Tec, Elec*) power; (*coacción*) force; (*violencia*) violence; (*Mil: tb:* **~s**) forces *pl*; **~ de arrastre** (*Tec*) pulling power; **~ de brazos** manpower; **~ mayor** force majeure; **~ bruta** brute force; **~s armadas (FF.AA.)** armed forces; **~ del orden público (F.O.P.)** police (forces); **~s aéreas** air force *sg*; **~ vital** vitality; **a ~ de** by (dint of); **cobrar ~s** to recover one's strength; **tener ~s para** to have the strength to; **hacer algo a la ~** to be forced to do sth; **con ~ legal** (*Com*) legally binding; **a la ~** forcibly, by force; **por ~** of necessity; **~ de voluntad** willpower
fuga ['fuɣa] *nf* (*huida*) flight, escape; (*de enamorados*) elopement; (*de gas etc*) leak; **~ de cerebros** (*fig*) brain drain
fugarse [fu'ɣarse] *vr* to flee, escape
fugaz [fu'ɣaθ] *adj* fleeting
fugitivo, -a [fuxi'tiβo, a] *adj* fugitive, fleeing ▷ *nm/f* fugitive
fui *etc* [fwi] *vb ver* **ser, ir**
fulano, -a [fu'lano, a] *nm/f* so-and-so, what's-his-name
fulgor [ful'ɣor] *nm* brilliance
fulminante [fulmi'nante] *adj* (*pólvora*) fulminating; (*fig: mirada*) withering; (*Med*) sudden, serious; (*fam*) terrific, tremendous; (*éxito, golpe*) sudden; **ataque ~** stroke
fulminar [fulmi'nar] *vt*: **caer fulminado por un rayo** to be struck down by lightning; **~ a algn con la mirada** to look daggers at sb
fumador, a [fuma'ðor, a] *nm/f* smoker; **no ~** non-smoker
fumar [fu'mar] *vt, vi* to smoke; **fumarse** *vr* (*disipar*) to squander; **~ en pipa** to smoke a pipe
fumigar [fumi'ɣar] *vt* to fumigate
funámbulo, -a [fu'nambulo, a], **funambulista** [funambu'lista] *nm/f* tightrope walker
función [fun'θjon] *nf* function; (*de puesto*) duties *pl*; (*Teat etc*) show; **entrar en funciones** to take up one's duties; **~ de tarde/de noche** matinée/evening performance
funcional [funθjo'nal] *adj* functional
funcionamiento [funθjona'mjento] *nm* functioning; (*Tec*) working; **en ~** (*Com*) on stream; **entrar en ~** to come into operation

f

funcionar [funθjo'nar] *vi* (*gen*) to function; (*máquina*) to work; **"no funciona"** "out of order"
funcionario, -a [funθjo'narjo, a] *nm/f* official; (*público*) civil servant
funda ['funda] *nf* (*gen*) cover; (*de almohada*) pillowcase; ~ **protectora del disco** (*Inform*) disk-jacket
fundación [funda'θjon] *nf* foundation
fundamental [fundamen'tal] *adj* fundamental, basic
fundamentalismo [fundamenta'lismo] *nm* fundamentalism
fundamentalista [fundamenta'lista] *adj, nm/f* fundamentalist
fundamentar [fundamen'tar] *vt* (*poner base*) to lay the foundations of; (*establecer*) to found; (*fig*) to base
fundamento [funda'mento] *nm* (*base*) foundation; (*razón*) grounds *pl*; **eso carece de ~** that is groundless
fundar [fun'dar] *vt* to found; (*crear*) to set up; (*fig: basar*): ~ **(en)** to base *o* found (on); **fundarse** *vr*: **~se en** to be founded on
fundición [fundi'θjon] *nf* (*acción*) smelting; (*fábrica*) foundry; (*Tip*) font
fundir [fun'dir] *vt* (*gen*) to fuse; (*metal*) to smelt, melt down; (*nieve etc*) to melt; (*Com*) to merge; (*estatua*) to cast; **fundirse** *vr* (*colores etc*) to merge, blend; (*unirse*) to fuse together; (*Elec: fusible, lámpara etc*) to blow; (*nieve etc*) to melt
fúnebre ['funeβre] *adj* funeral *cpd*, funereal
funeral [fune'ral] *nm* funeral
funeraria [fune'rarja] *nf* undertaker's (*Brit*), mortician's (*US*)
funesto, -a [fu'nesto, a] *adj* ill-fated; (*desastroso*) fatal
funicular [funiku'lar] *nm* (*tren*) funicular; (*teleférico*) cable car
furgón [fur'ɣon] *nm* wagon
furgoneta [furɣo'neta] *nf* (*Auto, Com*) (transit) van (*Brit*), pickup (truck) (*US*)
furia ['furja] *nf* (*ira*) fury; (*violencia*) violence
furibundo, -a [furi'βundo, a] *adj* furious
furioso, -a [fu'rjoso, a] *adj* (*iracundo*) furious; (*violento*) violent
furor [fu'ror] *nm* (*cólera*) rage; (*pasión*) frenzy, passion; **hacer ~** to be a sensation
furtivo, -a [fur'tiβo, a] *adj* furtive ▷ *nm* poacher
furúnculo [fu'runkulo] *nm* (*Med*) boil
fusible [fu'siβle] *nm* fuse
fusil [fu'sil] *nm* rifle
fusilar [fusi'lar] *vt* to shoot
fusión [fu'sjon] *nf* (*gen*) melting; (*unión*) fusion; (*Com*) merger, amalgamation
fusta ['fusta] *nf* (*látigo*) riding crop
fútbol ['futβol] *nm* football (*Brit*), soccer (*US*); ~ **americano** American football (*Brit*), football (*US*); ~ **sala** indoor football (*Brit*) *o* soccer (*US*)
futbolín [futβo'lin] *nm* table football
futbolista [futβo'lista] *nm/f* footballer
fútil ['futil] *adj* trifling
futilidad [futili'ðað], **futileza** [futi'leθa] *nf* triviality
futón [fu'ton] *nm* futon
futuro, -a [fu'turo, a] *adj* future ▷ *nm* future; (*Ling*) future tense; **futuros** *nmpl* (*Com*) futures

g

gabacho, -a [ga'βatʃo, a] *adj* Pyrenean; (*fam*) Frenchified ▷ *nm/f* Pyrenean villager; (*fam*) Frenchy

gabán [ga'βan] *nm* overcoat

gabardina [gaβar'ðina] *nf* (*tela*) gabardine; (*prenda*) raincoat

gabinete [gaβi'nete] *nm* (*Pol*) cabinet; (*estudio*) study; (*de abogados etc*) office; **~ de consulta/de lectura** consulting/reading room

gaceta [ga'θeta] *nf* gazette

gachas ['gatʃas] *nfpl* porridge *sg*

gafar [ga'far] *vt* (*fam*: *traer mala suerte*) to put a jinx on

gafas ['gafas] *nfpl* glasses; **~ oscuras** dark glasses; **~ de sol** sunglasses

gafe ['gafe] *adj*: **ser ~** to be jinxed ▷ *nm* (*fam*) jinx

gaita ['gaita] *nf* flute; (*tb*: **~ gallega**) bagpipes *pl*; (*dificultad*) bother; (*cosa engorrosa*) tough job

gajes ['gaxes] *nmpl* (*salario*) pay *sg*; **los ~ del oficio** occupational hazards; **~ y emolumentos** perquisites

gajo ['gaxo] *nm* (*gen*) bunch; (*de árbol*) bough; (*de naranja*) segment

gala ['gala] *nf* full dress; (*fig*: *lo mejor*) cream, flower; **galas** *nfpl* finery *sg*; **estar de ~** to be in one's best clothes; **hacer ~ de** to display, show off; **tener algo a ~** to be proud of sth

galán [ga'lan] *nm* lover, gallant; (*hombre atractivo*) ladies' man; (*Teat*): **primer ~** leading man

galante [ga'lante] *adj* gallant; (*atento*) charming; (*cortés*) polite

galantear [galante'ar] *vt* (*hacer la corte a*) to court, woo

galantería [galante'ria] *nf* (*caballerosidad*) gallantry; (*cumplido*) politeness; (*piropo*) compliment

galápago [ga'lapaɣo] *nm* (*Zool*) turtle, sea/freshwater turtle (*US*)

galardón [galar'ðon] *nm* award, prize

galardonar [galarðo'nar] *vt* (*premiar*) to reward; (*una obra*) to award a prize for

galaxia [ga'laksja] *nf* galaxy

galera [ga'lera] *nf* (*nave*) galley; (*carro*) wagon; (*Med*) hospital ward; (*Tip*) galley

galería [gale'ria] *nf* (*gen*) gallery; (*balcón*) veranda(h); (*de casa*) corridor; (*fam*: *público*) audience; **~ secreta** secret passage; **~ comercial** shopping mall

Gales ['gales] *nm*: **(el País de) ~** Wales

galés, -esa [ga'les, esa] *adj* Welsh ▷ *nm/f* Welshman(-woman) ▷ *nm* (*Ling*) Welsh

galgo, -a ['galɣo, a] *nm/f* greyhound

Galicia [ga'liθja] *nf* Galicia

galimatías [galima'tias] *nm inv* (*asunto*) rigmarole; (*lenguaje*) gibberish, nonsense

gallardía [gaʎar'ðia] *nf* (*galantería*) dash; (*gracia*) gracefulness; (*valor*) bravery; (*elegancia*) elegance; (*nobleza*) nobleness

gallego, -a [ga'ʎeɣo, a] *adj* Galician; (*Am pey*) Spanish ▷ *nm/f* Galician; (*Am pey*) Spaniard ▷ *nm* (*Ling*) Galician

galleta [ga'ʎeta] *nf* biscuit (*Brit*), cookie (*US*); (*fam*: *bofetada*) whack, slap

gallina [ga'ʎina] *nf* hen ▷ *nm* (*fam*) chicken; **~ ciega** blind man's buff; **~ llueca** broody hen

gallinero [gaʎi'nero] *nm* (*criadero*) henhouse; (*Teat*) gods *sg*, top gallery; (*voces*) hubbub

gallo ['gaʎo] *nm* cock, rooster; (*Mus*) false *o* wrong note; (*cambio de voz*) break in the voice; **en menos que canta un ~** in an instant

galón [ga'lon] *nm* (*Costura*) braid; (*Mil*) stripe; (*medida*) gallon

galopante [galo'pante] *adj* galloping

galopar [galo'par] *vi* to gallop

gama ['gama] *nf* (*Mus*) scale; (*fig*) range; (*Zool*) doe

gamba ['gamba] *nf* prawn (*Brit*), shrimp (*US*)

gamberrada [gambe'rraða] *nf* act of hooliganism

gamberro, -a [gam'berro, a] *nm/f* hooligan, lout

gamuza [ga'muθa] *nf* chamois; (*bayeta*) duster; (*Am*: *piel*) suede

gana ['gana] *nf* (*deseo*) desire, wish; (*apetito*) appetite; (*voluntad*) will; (*añoranza*) longing; **de buena ~** willingly; **de mala ~** reluctantly; **me da ~s de** I feel like, I want to; **tener ~s de** to feel like; **no me da la (real) ~** I (really) don't feel like it; **son ~s de molestar** they're just trying to be awkward

ganadería [ganaðe'ria] *nf* (*ganado*) livestock; (*ganado vacuno*) cattle *pl*; (*cría, comercio*) cattle raising

ganadero, -a [gana'ðero, a] *adj* stock *cpd* ▷ *nm/f* (*hacendado*) rancher

ganado [ga'naðo] *nm* livestock; **~ caballar/cabrío** horses *pl*/goats *pl*; **~ lanar** *u* **ovejuno** sheep *pl*; **~ porcino/vacuno** pigs *pl*/cattle *pl*

ganador, -a [gana'ðor, a] *adj* winning ▷ *nm/f* winner; (*Econ*) earner

ganancia [ga'nanθja] *nf* (*lo ganado*) gain; (*aumento*) increase; (*beneficio*) profit; **ganancias** *nfpl* (*ingresos*) earnings; (*beneficios*) profit *sg*, winnings; **~s y pérdidas** profit and loss; **~ bruta/líquida** gross/net profit; **~s de capital** capital gains; **sacar ~ de** to draw profit from

ganar [ga'nar] *vt* (*obtener*) to get, obtain; (*sacar ventaja*) to gain; (*Com*) to earn; (*Deporte, premio*) to win; (*derrotar*) to beat; (*alcanzar*) to reach; (*Mil: objetivo*) to take; (*apoyo*) to gain, win ▷ *vi* (*Deporte*) to win; **ganarse** *vr*: **~se la vida** to earn one's living; **se lo ha ganado** he deserves it; **~ tiempo** to gain time

ganchillo [gan'tʃiʎo] *nm* (*para croché*) crochet hook; (*arte*) crochet

gancho ['gantʃo] *nm* (*gen*) hook; (*colgador*) hanger; (*pey: revendedor*) tout; (*fam: atractivo*) sex appeal; (*Boxeo: golpe*) hook

gandul, -a [gan'dul, a] *adj, nm/f* good-for-nothing, layabout

ganga ['ganga] *nf* (*cosa*) bargain; (*chollo*) cushy job

gangrena [gan'grena] *nf* gangrene

gansada [gan'saða] *nf* (*fam*) stupid thing (to do)

ganso, -a ['ganso, a] *nm/f* (*Zool*) gander/goose; (*fam*) idiot

ganzúa [gan'θua] *nf* skeleton key ▷ *nm/f* burglar

garabatear [garaβate'ar] *vt* to scribble, scrawl

garabato [gara'βato] *nm* (*gancho*) hook; (*garfio*) grappling iron; (*escritura*) scrawl, scribble; (*fam*) sex appeal

garaje [ga'raxe] *nm* garage

garajista [gara'xista] *nm/f* mechanic

garante [ga'rante] *adj* responsible ▷ *nm/f* guarantor

garantía [garan'tia] *nf* guarantee; (*seguridad*) pledge; (*compromiso*) undertaking; (*Jur: caución*) warranty; **de máxima ~** absolutely guaranteed; **~ de trabajo** job security

garantizar [garanti'θar] *vt* (*hacerse responsable de*) to vouch for; (*asegurar*) to guarantee

garbanzo [gar'βanθo] *nm* chickpea

garbo ['garβo] *nm* grace, elegance; (*desenvoltura*) jauntiness; (*de mujer*) glamour; **andar con ~** to walk gracefully

garete [ga'rete] *nm*: **irse al ~** to go to the dogs

garfio ['garfjo] *nm* grappling iron; (*gancho*) hook; (*Alpinismo*) climbing iron

garganta [gar'ɣanta] *nf* (*interna*) throat; (*externa, de botella*) neck; (*Geo: barranco*) ravine; (*desfiladero*) narrow pass

gargantilla [garɣan'tiʎa] *nf* necklace

gárgara ['garɣara] *nf* gargle, gargling; **hacer ~s** to gargle; **¡vete a hacer ~s!** (*fam*) go to blazes!

gargarear [garɣare'ar] *vi* (*Am*) to gargle

garita [ga'rita] *nf* cabin, hut; (*Mil*) sentry box; (*puesto de vigilancia*) lookout post

garito [ga'rito] *nm* (*lugar*) gaming house *o* den

garra ['garra] *nf* (*de gato, Tec*) claw; (*de ave*) talon; (*fam*) hand, paw; (*fig: de canción etc*) bite; **caer en las ~s de algn** to fall into sb's clutches

garrafa [ga'rrafa] *nf* carafe, decanter

garrapata [garra'pata] *nf* (*Zool*) tick

garrote [ga'rrote] *nm* (*palo*) stick; (*porra*) club, cudgel; (*suplicio*) garrotte

garza ['garθa] *nf* heron

gas [gas] *nm* gas; (*vapores*) fumes *pl*; **~es de escape** exhaust (fumes); **~es lacrimógenos** tear gas *sg*

gasa ['gasa] *nf* gauze; (*de pañal*) nappy liner

gaseoso, -a [gase'oso, a] *adj* gassy, fizzy ▷ *nf* lemonade, pop (*fam*)

gasoil [ga'soil], **gasóleo** [ga'soleo] *nm* diesel (oil)

gasolina [gaso'lina] *nf* petrol, gas(oline) (*US*); **~ sin plomo** unleaded petrol

gasolinera [gasoli'nera] *nf* petrol (*Brit*) *o* gas (*US*) station

gastado, -a [gas'taðo, a] *adj* (*dinero*) spent; (*ropa*) worn out; (*usado: frase etc*) trite

gastar [gas'tar] *vt* (*dinero, tiempo*) to spend; (*consumir*) to use (up), consume; (*desperdiciar*) to waste; (*llevar*) to wear; **gastarse** *vr* to wear out; (*terminarse*) to run out; (*estropearse*) to waste; **~ en** to spend on; **~ bromas** to crack jokes; **¿qué número gastas?** what size (shoe) do you take?

gasto ['gasto] *nm* (*desembolso*) expenditure, spending; (*cantidad gastada*) outlay, expense; (*consumo, uso*) use; (*desgaste*) waste; **gastos** *nmpl* (*desembolsos*) expenses; (*cargos*) charges, costs; **~ corriente** (*Com*) revenue expenditure; **~ fijo** (*Com*) fixed charge; **~s bancarios** bank charges; **~s corrientes** running expenses; **~s de distribución** (*Com*) distribution costs; **~s generales** overheads; **~s de mantenimiento** maintenance expenses; **~s operacionales** operating costs; **~s de tramitación** (*Com*) handling charge *sg*; **~s vencidos** (*Com*) accrued charges; **cubrir ~s** to cover expenses; **meterse en ~s** to incur expense

gastronomía [gastrono'mia] *nf* gastronomy

gata ['gata] *nf* (*Zool*) she-cat; **andar a ~s** to go on all fours

gatear [gate'ar] *vi* (*andar a gatas*) to go on all fours

gatillo [ga'tiʎo] *nm* (*de arma de fuego*) trigger; (*de dentista*) forceps
gato ['gato] *nm* (*Zool*) cat; (*Tec*) jack; **~ de Angora** Angora cat; **~ montés** wildcat; **dar a algn ~ por liebre** to take sb in; **aquí hay ~ encerrado** there's something fishy here; **andar a gatas** to go on all fours
gaucho, -a ['gautʃo, a] *adj, nm/f* gaucho

GAUCHO

Gauchos are the herdsmen or riders of the Southern Cone plains. Although popularly associated with Argentine folklore, *gauchos* belong equally to the cattle-raising areas of Southern Brazil and Uruguay. *Gauchos'* traditions and clothing reflect their mixed ancestry and cultural roots. Their baggy trousers are Arabic in origin, while the horse and guitar are inherited from the Spanish conquistadors; the poncho, maté and *boleadoras* (strips of leather weighted at either end with stones) form part of the Indian tradition.

gaveta [ga'βeta] *nf* drawer
gaviota [ga'βjota] *nf* seagull
gay [ge] *adj, nm* gay, homosexual
gazapo [ga'θapo] *nm* young rabbit
gazpacho [gaθ'patʃo] *nm* gazpacho
gel [xel] *nm* gel; **~ de baño/ducha** bath/shower gel
gelatina [xela'tina] *nf* jelly; (*polvos etc*) gelatine
gema ['xema] *nf* gem
gemelo, -a [xe'melo, a] *adj, nm/f* twin; **gemelos** *nmpl* (*de camisa*) cufflinks; **~s de campo** field glasses, binoculars; **~s de teatro** opera glasses
gemido [xe'miðo] *nm* (*quejido*) moan, groan; (*lamento*) wail, howl
Géminis ['xeminis] *nm* (*Astro*) Gemini
gemir [xe'mir] *vi* (*quejarse*) to moan, groan; (*animal*) to whine; (*viento*) to howl
gen [xen] *nm* gene
generación [xenera'θjon] *nf* generation; **primera/segunda/tercera/cuarta ~** (*Inform*) first/second/third/fourth generation
general [xene'ral] *adj* general; (*común*) common; (*pey: corriente*) rife; (*frecuente*) usual ▷ *nm* general; **~ de brigada/de división** brigadier-/major-general; **por lo** *o* **en ~** in general
Generalitat [jenerali'tat] *nf regional government of Catalonia*; **~ Valenciana** *regional government of Valencia*
generalizar [xenerali'θar] *vt* to generalize; **generalizarse** *vr* to become generalized, spread; (*difundirse*) to become widely known
generalmente [xeneral'mente] *adv* generally
generar [xene'rar] *vt* to generate
género ['xenero] *nm* (*clase*) kind, sort; (*tipo*) type; (*Bio*) genus; (*Ling*) gender; (*Com*) material; **géneros** *nmpl* (*productos*) goods; **~ humano** human race; **~ chico** (*zarzuela*) Spanish operetta; **~s de punto** knitwear *sg*
generosidad [xenerosi'ðað] *nf* generosity
generoso, -a [xene'roso, a] *adj* generous
genético, -a [xe'netiko, a] *adj* genetic ▷ *nf* genetics *sg*
genial [xe'njal] *adj* inspired; (*idea*) brilliant; (*estupendo*) wonderful; (*afable*) genial
genio ['xenjo] *nm* (*carácter*) nature, disposition; (*humor*) temper; (*facultad creadora*) genius; **mal ~** bad temper; **~ vivo** quick *o* hot temper; **de mal ~** bad-tempered
genital [xeni'tal] *adj* genital ▷ *nm*: **~es** genitals, genital organs
gente ['xente] *nf* (*personas*) people *pl*; (*raza*) race; (*nación*) nation; (*parientes*) relatives *pl*; **~ bien/baja** posh/lower-class people *pl*; **~ menuda** (*niños*) children *pl*; **es buena ~** (*fam: esp Am*) he's a good sort; **una ~ como Vd** (*Am*) a person like you
gentil [xen'til] *adj* (*elegante*) graceful; (*encantador*) charming; (*Rel*) gentile
gentileza [xenti'leθa] *nf* grace; charm; (*cortesía*) courtesy; **por ~ de** by courtesy of
gentío [xen'tio] *nm* crowd, throng
genuino, -a [xe'nwino, a] *adj* genuine
geoetiquetar [xeoetike'tar] *vt* to geotag
geografía [xeoɣra'fia] *nf* geography
geográfico, -a [xeo'ɣrafiko, a] *adj* geographic(al)
geología [xeolo'xia] *nf* geology
geometría [xeome'tria] *nf* geometry
geranio [xe'ranjo] *nm* (*Bot*) geranium
gerencia [xe'renθja] *nf* management; (*cargo*) post of manager; (*oficina*) manager's office
gerente [xe'rente] *nm/f* (*supervisor*) manager; (*jefe*) director
geriatría [xerja'tria] *nf* (*Med*) geriatrics *sg*
geriátrico, -a [xer'jatriko, a] *adj* geriatric
germen ['xermen] *nm* germ
germinar [xermi'nar] *vi* to germinate; (*brotar*) to sprout
gerundio [xe'rundjo] *nm* (*Ling*) gerund
gestación [xesta'θjon] *nf* gestation
gesticulación [xestikula'θjon] *nf* (*ademán*) gesticulation; (*mueca*) grimace
gesticular [xestiku'lar] *vi* (*con ademanes*) to gesticulate; (*con muecas*) to make faces
gestión [xes'tjon] *nf* management; (*diligencia, acción*) negotiation; **hacer las gestiones preliminares** to do the groundwork; **~ de cartera** (*Com*) portfolio management; **~ financiera** (*Com*) financial management; **~ interna** (*Inform*) housekeeping; **~ de personal** personnel management; **~ de riesgos** (*Com*) risk management
gestionar [xestjo'nar] *vt* (*tratar de arreglar*) to try to arrange; (*llevar*) to manage

gesto ['xesto] *nm* (*mueca*) grimace; (*ademán*) gesture; **hacer ~s** to make faces
gestoría [xesto'ria] *nf agency undertaking business with government departments, insurance companies etc*
Gibraltar [xiβral'tar] *nm* Gibraltar
gibraltareño, -a [xiβralta'reɲo, a] *adj* of *o* from Gibraltar, Gibraltarian ▷ *nm/f* Gibraltarian
giga ['giɣa] *nm abr* gig (= *gigabyte*)
gigabyte ['giɣaβait] *nm* gigabyte
gigante [xi'ɣante] *adj, nm/f* giant
gigantesco, -a [xiɣan'tesko, a] *adj* gigantic
gilipollas [xili'poʎas] (*fam*) *adj inv* daft ▷ *nm/f* berk (*Brit*), jerk (*esp US*)
gilipollez [xilipo'ʎez] *nf* (*fam*): **es una ~** that's a load of crap (*!*); **decir gilipolleces** to talk crap (*!*)
gimnasia [xim'nasja] *nf* gymnastics *pl*; **confundir la ~ con la magnesia** to get things mixed up
gimnasio [xim'nasjo] *nm* gym(nasium)
gimnasta [xim'nasta] *nm/f* gymnast
gimnástica [xim'nastika] *nf* gymnastics *sg*
gimotear [ximote'ar] *vi* to whine, whimper; (*lloriquear*) to snivel
ginebra [xi'neβra] *nf* gin
ginecología [xinekolo'xia] *nf* gyn(a)ecology
ginecólogo, -a [xine'koloɣo, a] *nm/f* gyn(a)ecologist
gira ['xira] *nf* tour, trip
girar [xi'rar] *vt* (*dar la vuelta*) to turn (around); (*: rápidamente*) to spin; (*Com: giro postal*) to draw; (*comerciar: letra de cambio*) to issue ▷ *vi* to turn (round); (*dar vueltas*) to rotate; (*rápido*) to spin; **la conversación giraba en torno a las elecciones** the conversation centred on the election; **~ en descubierto** to overdraw
girasol [xira'sol] *nm* sunflower
giratorio, -a [xira'torjo, a] *adj* (*gen*) revolving; (*puente*) swing *cpd*; (*silla*) swivel *cpd*
giro ['xiro] *nm* (*movimiento*) turn, revolution; (*Ling*) expression; (*Com*) draft; (*de sucesos*) trend, course; **~ bancario** bank draft, bank giro; **~ de existencias** (*Com*) stock turnover; **~ postal** money order
gis [xis] *nm* (*Am*) chalk
gitano, -a [xi'tano, a] *adj, nm/f* gypsy
glacial [gla'θjal] *adj* icy, freezing
glaciar [gla'θjar] *nm* glacier
glándula ['glandula] *nf* (*Anat, Bot*) gland
global [glo'βal] *adj* (*en conjunto*) global; (*completo*) total; (*investigación*) full; (*suma*) lump *cpd*
globalización [gloβaliθa'θjon] *nf* globalization
globo ['gloβo] *nm* (*esfera*) globe, sphere; (*aeróstato, juguete*) balloon
glóbulo ['gloβulo] *nm* globule; (*Anat*) corpuscle; **~ blanco/rojo** white/red corpuscle
gloria ['glorja] *nf* glory; (*fig*) delight; (*delicia*) bliss
glorieta [glo'rjeta] *nf* (*de jardín*) bower, arbour, arbor (*US*); (*Auto*) roundabout (*Brit*), traffic circle (*US*); (*plaza redonda*) circus; (*cruce*) junction
glorificar [glorifi'kar] *vt* (*enaltecer*) to glorify, praise
glorioso, -a [glo'rjoso, a] *adj* glorious
glosa ['glosa] *nf* comment; (*explicación*) gloss
glosar [glo'sar] *vt* (*comentar*) to comment on
glosario [glo'sarjo] *nm* glossary
glotón, -ona [glo'ton, ona] *adj* gluttonous, greedy ▷ *nm/f* glutton
glucosa [glu'kosa] *nf* glucose
gobernación [goβerna'θjon] *nf* government, governing; (*Pol*) Provincial Governor's office; **Ministro de la G~** Minister of the Interior, Home Secretary (*Brit*)
gobernador, -a [goβerna'ðor, a] *adj* governing ▷ *nm/f* governor
gobernante [goβer'nante] *adj* governing ▷ *nm* ruler, governor ▷ *nf* (*en hotel etc*) housekeeper
gobernar [goβer'nar] *vt* (*dirigir*) to guide, direct; (*Pol*) to rule, govern ▷ *vi* to govern; (*Naut*) to steer; **~ mal** to misgovern
gobierno [go'βjerno] *vb ver* **gobernar** ▷ *nm* (*Pol*) government; (*gestión*) management; (*dirección*) guidance, direction; (*Naut*) steering; (*puesto*) governorship
goce *etc* ['goθe] *vb ver* **gozar** ▷ *nm* enjoyment
gol [gol] *nm* goal
golf [golf] *nm* golf
golfo, -a ['golfo, a] *nm/f* (*pilluelo*) street urchin; (*vagabundo*) tramp; (*gorrón*) loafer; (*gamberro*) lout ▷ *nm* (*Geo*) gulf ▷ *nf* (*fam: prostituta*) slut, whore, hooker (*US*)
golondrina [golon'drina] *nf* swallow
golosina [golo'sina] *nf* titbit; (*dulce*) sweet
goloso, -a [go'loso, a] *adj* sweet-toothed; (*fam: glotón*) greedy
golpe ['golpe] *nm* blow; (*de puño*) punch; (*de mano*) smack; (*de remo*) stroke; (*Fútbol*) kick; (*Tenis etc*) hit, shot; (*mala suerte*) misfortune; (*fam: atraco*) job, heist (*US*); (*fig: choque*) clash; **no dar ~** to be bone idle; **de un ~** with one blow; **de ~** suddenly; **~ (de estado)** coup (d'état); **~ de gracia** coup de grâce (*tb fig*); **~ de fortuna/maestro** stroke of luck/genius; **cerrar una puerta de ~** to slam a door
golpear [golpe'ar] *vt, vi* to strike, knock; (*asestar*) to beat; (*de puño*) to punch; (*golpetear*) to tap; (*mesa*) to bang
golpista [gol'pista] *adj*: **intentona ~** coup attempt ▷ *nm/f* participant in a coup (d'état)
goma ['goma] *nf* (*caucho*) rubber; (*elástico*) elastic; (*tira*) rubber *o* elastic (*Brit*) band; (*fam: preservativo*) condom; (*droga*) hashish; (*explosivo*) plastic explosive; **~ (de borrar)** eraser, rubber (*Brit*); **~ de mascar** chewing

gum; ~ **de pegar** gum, glue; ~ **espuma** foam rubber

gomina [go'mina] *nf* hair gel

gomita [go'mita] *nf* rubber *o* elastic (*Brit*) band

gordo, -a ['gorðo, a] *adj* (*gen*) fat; (*persona*) plump; (*agua*) hard; (*fam*) enormous ▷ *nm/f* fat man *o* woman; **el (premio)** ~ (*en lotería*) first prize; **¡~!** (*fam*) fatty!

gordura [gor'ðura] *nf* fat; (*corpulencia*) fatness, stoutness

gorila [go'rila] *nm* gorilla; (*fam*) tough, thug; (*guardaespaldas*) bodyguard

gorjear [gorxe'ar] *vi* to twitter, chirp

gorra ['gorra] *nf* (*gen*) cap; (*de niño*) bonnet; (*militar*) bearskin; ~ **de montar/de paño/de punto/de visera** riding/cloth/knitted/peaked cap; **andar** *o* **ir** *o* **vivir de** ~ to sponge, scrounge; **entrar de** ~ (*fam*) to gatecrash

gorrión [go'rrjon] *nm* sparrow

gorro ['gorro] *nm* cap; (*de niño, mujer*) bonnet; **estoy hasta el** ~ I am fed up

gorrón, -ona [go'rron, ona] *nm* pebble; (*Tec*) pivot ▷ *nm/f* scrounger

gorronear [gorrone'ar] *vi* (*fam*) to sponge, scrounge

gota ['gota] *nf* (*gen*) drop; (*de pintura*) blob; (*de sudor*) bead; (*Med*) gout; ~ **a** ~ drop by drop; **caer a ~s** to drip

gotear [gote'ar] *vi* to drip; (*escurrir*) to trickle; (*salirse*) to leak; (*cirio*) to gutter; (*lloviznar*) to drizzle

gotera [go'tera] *nf* leak

gótico, -a ['gotiko, a] *adj* Gothic

gozar [go'θar] *vi* to enjoy o.s.; ~ **de** (*disfrutar*) to enjoy; (*poseer*) to possess; ~ **de buena salud** to enjoy good health

gozne ['goθne] *nm* hinge

gozo ['goθo] *nm* (*alegría*) joy; (*placer*) pleasure; **¡mi ~ en el pozo!** that's torn it!, just my luck!

gr *abr* (= *gramo(s)*) g

grabación [graβa'θjon] *nf* recording

grabado, -a [gra'βaðo, a] *adj* (*Mus*) recorded; (*en cinta*) taped, on tape ▷ *nm* print, engraving; ~ **al agua fuerte** etching; ~ **al aguatinta** aquatint; ~ **en cobre** copperplate; ~ **en madera** woodcut; ~ **rupestre** rock carving

grabador, -a [graβa'ðor, a] *nm/f* engraver ▷ *nf* tape-recorder; **~a de cassettes** cassette recorder; **~a de CD/DVD** CD/DVD writer

grabar [gra'βar] *vt* to engrave; (*discos, cintas*) to record; (*impresionar*) to impress

gracia ['graθja] *nf* (*encanto*) grace, gracefulness; (*Rel*) grace; (*chiste*) joke; (*humor*) humour, wit; **¡muchas ~s!** thanks very much!; **~s a** thanks to; **tener** ~ (*chiste etc*) to be funny; **¡qué ~!** how funny!; (*irónico*) what a nerve!; **no me hace** ~ (*broma*) it's not funny; (*plan*) I am not too keen; **con ~s anticipadas/repetidas** thanking you in advance/again; **dar las ~s a algn por algo** to thank sb for sth

gracioso, -a [gra'θjoso, a] *adj* (*garboso*) graceful; (*chistoso*) funny; (*cómico*) comical; (*agudo*) witty; (*título*) gracious ▷ *nm/f* (*Teat*) comic character, fool; **su graciosa Majestad** His/Her Gracious Majesty

grada ['graða] *nf* (*de escalera*) step; (*de anfiteatro*) tier, row; **gradas** *nfpl* (*de estadio*) terraces

gradación [graða'θjon] *nf* gradation; (*serie*) graded series

gradería [graðe'ria] *nf* (*gradas*) (flight of) steps *pl*; (*de anfiteatro*) tiers *pl*, rows *pl*; ~ **cubierta** covered stand

grado ['graðo] *nm* degree; (*etapa*) stage, step; (*nivel*) rate; (*de parentesco*) order of lineage; (*de aceite, vino*) grade; (*grada*) step; (*Escol*) class, year, grade (*US*); (*Univ*) degree; (*Ling*) degree of comparison; (*Mil*) rank; **de buen** ~ willingly; **en sumo ~, en ~ superlativo** in the highest degree; ~ **centígrado/Fahrenheit** degree centigrade/Fahrenheit

graduación [graðwa'θjon] *nf* (*acto*) gradation; (*clasificación*) rating; (*del alcohol*) proof, strength; (*Escol*) graduation; (*Mil*) rank; **de alta** ~ high-ranking

gradual [gra'ðwal] *adj* gradual

graduar [gra'ðwar] *vt* (*gen*) to graduate; (*medir*) to gauge; (*Tec*) to calibrate; (*Univ*) to confer a degree on; (*Mil*) to commission; **graduarse** *vr* to graduate; **~se la vista** to have one's eyes tested

gráfico, -a ['grafiko, a] *adj* graphic; (*fig: vívido*) vivid, lively ▷ *nm* diagram ▷ *nf* graph; ~ **de barras** (*Com*) bar chart; ~ **de sectores** *o* **de tarta** (*Com*) pie chart; **gráficos** *nmpl* (*tb Inform*) graphics; **~s empresariales** (*Com*) business graphics

grajo ['graxo] *nm* rook

Gral. *abr* (*Mil*: = *General*) Gen.

gramático, -a [gra'matiko, a] *nm/f* (*persona*) grammarian ▷ *nf* grammar

gramo ['gramo] *nm* gramme (*Brit*), gram (*US*)

gran [gran] *adj ver* **grande**

grana ['grana] *nf* (*Bot*) seedling; (*color*) scarlet; **ponerse como la** ~ to go as red as a beetroot

granada [gra'naða] *nf* pomegranate; (*Mil*) grenade; ~ **de mano** hand grenade; ~ **de metralla** shrapnel shell

granate [gra'nate] *adj inv* maroon ▷ *nm* garnet; (*color*) maroon

Gran Bretaña [grambre'taɲa] *nf* Great Britain

grande ['grande], **gran** *adj* (*de tamaño*) big, large; (*alto*) tall; (*distinguido*) great; (*impresionante*) grand ▷ *nm* grandee; **¿cómo es de ~?** how big is it?, what size is it?; **pasarlo en** ~ to have a tremendous time

grandeza [gran'deθa] *nf* greatness; (*tamaño*) bigness; (*esplendor*) grandness; (*nobleza*) nobility

g

grandioso, -a [gran'djoso, a] *adj* magnificent, grand

granel [gra'nel] *nm* (*montón*) heap; **a ~** (*Com*) in bulk

granero [gra'nero] *nm* granary, barn

granito [gra'nito] *nm* (*Agr*) small grain; (*roca*) granite

granizado [grani'θaðo] *nm* iced drink; **~ de café** iced coffee

granizar [grani'θar] *vi* to hail

granizo [gra'niθo] *nm* hail

granja ['granxa] *nf* (*gen*) farm; **~ avícola** chicken *o* poultry farm

granjear [granxe'ar] *vt* (*cobrar*) to earn; (*ganar*) to win; (*avanzar*) to gain; **granjearse** *vr* (*amistad etc*) to gain for o.s.

granjero, -a [gran'xero, a] *nm/f* farmer

grano ['grano] *nm* grain; (*semilla*) seed; (*baya*) berry; (*Med*) pimple, spot; (*partícula*) particle; (*punto*) speck; **granos** *nmpl* cereals; **~ de café** coffee bean; **ir al ~** to get to the point

granuja [gra'nuxa] *nm* rogue; (*golfillo*) urchin

grapa ['grapa] *nf* staple; (*Tec*) clamp; (*sujetador*) clip, fastener; (*Arq*) cramp

grapadora [grapa'ðora] *nf* stapler

grasa ['grasa] *nf ver* **graso**

grasiento, -a [gra'sjento, a] *adj* greasy; (*de aceite*) oily; (*mugriento*) filthy

graso, -a ['graso, a] *adj* fatty; (*aceitoso*) greasy, oily ▷ *nf* (*gen*) grease; (*de cocina*) fat, lard; (*sebo*) suet; (*mugre*) filth; (*Auto*) oil; (*lubricante*) grease; **grasa de ballena** blubber; **grasa de pescado** fish oil

gratificación [gratifika'θjon] *nf* (*propina*) tip; (*aguinaldo*) gratuity; (*bono*) bonus; (*recompensa*) reward

gratificar [gratifi'kar] *vt* (*dar propina*) to tip; (*premiar*) to reward; **"se ~á"** "a reward is offered"

gratinar [grati'nar] *vt* to cook au gratin

gratis ['gratis] *adv* free, for nothing

gratitud [grati'tuð] *nf* gratitude

grato, -a ['grato, a] *adj* (*agradable*) pleasant, agreeable; (*bienvenido*) welcome; **nos es ~ informarle que ...** we are pleased to inform you that ...

gratuito, -a [gra'twito, a] *adj* (*gratis*) free; (*sin razón*) gratuitous; (*acusación*) unfounded

grava ['graβa] *nf* (*guijos*) gravel; (*piedra molida*) crushed stone; (*en carreteras*) road metal

gravamen [gra'βamen] *nm* (*carga*) burden; (*impuesto*) tax; **libre de ~** (*Econ*) free from encumbrances

gravar [gra'βar] *vt* to burden; (*Com*) to tax; (*Econ*) to assess for tax; **~ con impuestos** to burden with taxes

grave ['graβe] *adj* heavy; (*fig, Med*) grave, serious; (*importante*) important; (*herida*) severe; (*Mus*) low, deep; (*Ling*: *acento*) grave; **estar ~** to be seriously ill

gravedad [graβe'ðað] *nf* gravity; (*fig*) seriousness; (*grandeza*) importance; (*dignidad*) dignity; (*Mus*) depth

gravilla [gra'βiʎa] *nf* gravel

gravitar [graβi'tar] *vi* to gravitate; **~ sobre** to rest on

gravoso, -a [gra'βoso, a] *adj* (*pesado*) burdensome; (*costoso*) costly

graznar [graθ'nar] *vi* (*cuervo*) to squawk; (*pato*) to quack; (*hablar ronco*) to croak

Grecia ['greθja] *nf* Greece

gremio ['gremjo] *nm* trade, industry; (*asociación*) professional association, guild

greña ['greɲa] *nf* (*cabellos*) shock of hair; (*maraña*) tangle; **andar a la ~** to bicker, squabble

gresca ['greska] *nf* uproar; (*trifulca*) row

griego, -a ['grjeɣo, a] *adj* Greek, Grecian ▷ *nm/f* Greek ▷ *nm* (*Ling*) Greek

grieta ['grjeta] *nf* crack; (*hendidura*) chink; (*quiebra*) crevice; (*Med*) chap; (*Pol*) rift

grifo ['grifo] *nm* tap (*Brit*), faucet (*US*); (*Am*) petrol (*Brit*) *o* gas (*US*) station

grilletes [gri'ʎetes] *nmpl* fetters, shackles

grillo ['griʎo] *nm* (*Zool*) cricket; (*Bot*) shoot; **grillos** *nmpl* shackles, irons

gripa ['gripa] *nf* (*Am*) flu, influenza

gripe ['gripe] *nf* flu, influenza; **~ porcina** swine flu; **~ aviar** bird flu

gris [gris] *adj* grey

gritar [gri'tar] *vt, vi* to shout, yell; **¡no grites!** stop shouting!

grito ['grito] *nm* shout, yell; (*de horror*) scream; **a ~ pelado** at the top of one's voice; **poner el ~ en el cielo** to scream blue murder; **es el último ~** (*de moda*) it's all the rage

grosella [gro'seʎa] *nf* (red)currant; **~ negra** blackcurrant

grosería [grose'ria] *nf* (*actitud*) rudeness; (*comentario*) vulgar comment; (*palabrota*) swearword

grosero, -a [gro'sero, a] *adj* (*poco cortés*) rude, bad-mannered; (*ordinario*) vulgar, crude

grosor [gro'sor] *nm* thickness

grotesco, -a [gro'tesko, a] *adj* grotesque; (*absurdo*) bizarre

grúa ['grua] *nf* (*Tec*) crane; (*de petróleo*) derrick; **~ corrediza** *o* **móvil/de pescante/puente/de torre** travelling/jib/overhead/tower crane

grueso, -a ['grweso, a] *adj* thick; (*persona*) stout; (*calidad*) coarse ▷ *nm* bulk; (*espesor*) thickness; (*densidad*) density; (*de gente*) main body, mass; **el ~ de** the bulk of

grulla ['gruʎa] *nf* (*Zool*) crane

grumo ['grumo] *nm* (*coágulo*) clot, lump; (*masa*) dollop

gruñido [gru'ɲiðo] *nm* grunt, growl; (*fig*) grumble

gruñir [gru'ɲir] *vi* (*animal*) to grunt, growl; (*fam*) to grumble

grupa ['grupa] *nf* (*Zool*) rump

grupo ['grupo] *nm* group; (*Tec*) unit, set; (*de árboles*) cluster; ~ **sanguíneo** blood group; ~ **de presión** pressure group

gruta ['gruta] *nf* grotto

guacamole [gwaka'mole] *nm* (*Am*) avocado salad

guacho, -a ['gwatʃo, a] *nm/f* (*Am*) homeless child

guadaña [gwa'ðaɲa] *nf* scythe

guagua ['gwaɣwa] *nf* (*Am, Canarias*) bus; (*Am: criatura*) baby

guajolote [gwajo'lote] *nm* (*Am*) turkey

guante ['gwante] *nm* glove; **~s de goma** rubber gloves; **se ajusta como un ~** it fits like a glove; **echar el ~ a algn** to catch hold of sb; (*fig: policía*) to catch sb

guantera [gwan'tera] *nf* glove compartment

guapo, -a ['gwapo, a] *adj* good-looking; (*mujer*) pretty, attractive; (*hombre*) handsome; (*elegante*) smart ▷ *nm* lover, gallant; (*Am fam*) tough guy, bully

guarda ['gwarða] *nm/f* (*persona*) warden, keeper ▷ *nf* (*acto*) guarding; (*custodia*) custody; (*Tip*) flyleaf, endpaper; **~ forestal** game warden; **~ jurado** (armed) security guard

guardabarros [gwarða'βarros] *nm inv* mudguard (*Brit*), fender (*US*)

guardabosques [gwarda'βoskes] *nm inv* gamekeeper

guardacostas [gwarda'kostas] *nm inv* coastguard vessel ▷ *nm/f* guardian, protector

guardador, a [gwarða'ðor, a] *adj* protective; (*tacaño*) mean, stingy ▷ *nm/f* guardian, protector

guardaespaldas [gwardaes'paldas] *nm/f inv* bodyguard

guardameta [gwarða'meta] *nm* goalkeeper

guardapolvo [gwarda'polβo] *nm* dust cover; (*prenda de vestir*) overalls *pl*

guardar [gwar'ðar] *vt* (*gen*) to keep; (*vigilar*) to guard, watch over; (*conservar*) to put away; (*dinero: ahorrar*) to save; (*promesa etc*) to keep; (*ley*) to observe; (*rencor*) to bear, harbour; (*Inform: archivo*) to save; **guardarse** *vr* (*preservarse*) to protect o.s.; **~se de algo** (*evitar*) to avoid sth; **~ cama** to stay in bed

guardarropa [gwarða'rropa] *nm* (*armario*) wardrobe; (*en establecimiento público*) cloakroom

guardería [gwarðe'ria] *nf* nursery

guardia ['gwarðja] *nf* (*Mil*) guard; (*cuidado*) care, custody ▷ *nm/f* guard; (*policía*) policeman(-woman); **estar de ~** to be on guard; **montar ~** to mount guard; **la G~ Civil** the Civil Guard; **~ municipal** *o* **urbana** municipal police; **un ~ civil** a Civil Guard(sman); **un(a) ~ nacional** a policeman(-woman); **~ urbano** traffic policeman

guardián, -ana [gwar'ðjan, ana] *nm/f* (*gen*) guardian, keeper

guarecer [gware'θer] *vt* (*proteger*) to protect; (*abrigar*) to shelter; **guarecerse** *vr* to take refuge

guarida [gwa'riða] *nf* (*de animal*) den, lair; (*de persona*) haunt, hideout; (*refugio*) refuge

guarnecer [gwarne'θer] *vt* (*equipar*) to provide; (*adornar*) to adorn; (*Tec*) to reinforce

guarnición [gwarni'θjon] *nf* (*de vestimenta*) trimming; (*de piedra*) mount; (*Culin*) garnish; (*arneses*) harness; (*Mil*) garrison

guarrada [gwa'rraða] (*fam*) *nf* (*cosa sucia*) dirty mess; (*acto o dicho obsceno*) obscenity; **hacer una ~ a algn** to do the dirty on sb

guarrería [gwarre'ria] *nf* = **guarrada**

guarro, -a ['gwarro, a] *nm/f* (*fam*) pig; (*fig*) dirty *o* slovenly person

guasa ['gwasa] *nf* joke; **con** *o* **de ~** jokingly, in fun

guasón, -ona [gwa'son, ona] *adj* witty; (*bromista*) joking ▷ *nm/f* wit; joker

Guatemala [gwate'mala] *nf* Guatemala

guay [gwai] *adj* (*fam*) super, great

gubernamental [guβernamen'tal], **gubernativo, -a** [guβerna'tiβo, a] *adj* governmental

güero, -a ['gwero, a] *adj* (*Am*) blond(e)

guerra ['gerra] *nf* war; (*arte*) warfare; (*pelea*) struggle; **~ atómica/bacteriológica/nuclear/de guerrillas** atomic/germ/nuclear/guerrilla warfare; **Primera/Segunda G~ Mundial** First/Second World War; **~ de precios** (*Com*) price war; **~ civil/fría** civil/cold war; **~ a muerte** fight to the death; **de ~** military, war *cpd*; **estar en ~** to be at war; **dar ~** to be a nuisance; **dar ~ a algn** to give s.o. a lot of bother

guerrear [gerre'ar] *vi* to wage war

guerrero, -a [ge'rrero, a] *adj* fighting; (*carácter*) warlike ▷ *nm/f* warrior

guerrilla [ge'rriʎa] *nf* guerrilla warfare; (*tropas*) guerrilla band *o* group

guerrillero, -a [gerri'ʎero, a] *nm/f* guerrilla (fighter); (*contra invasor*) partisan

gueto ['geto] *nm* ghetto

guía ['gia] *vb ver* **guiar** ▷ *nm/f* (*persona*) guide ▷ *nf* (*libro*) guidebook; (*manual*) handbook; **~ de ferrocarriles** railway timetable; **~ telefónica** telephone directory; **~ del turista/del viajero** tourist/traveller's guide

guiar [gi'ar] *vt* to guide, direct; (*dirigir*) to lead; (*orientar*) to advise; (*Auto*) to steer; **guiarse** *vr*: **~se por** to be guided by

guijarro [gi'xarro] *nm* pebble

guillotina [giʎo'tina] *nf* guillotine

guinda ['ginda] *nf* morello cherry; (*licor*) cherry liqueur

guindilla [gin'diʎa] *nf* chil(l)i pepper

guiñapo [gi'ɲapo] *nm* (*harapo*) rag; (*persona*) rogue

guiñar [gi'ɲar] *vi* to wink

guiño ['giɲo] *nm* (*parpadeo*) wink; (*muecas*) grimace; **hacer ~s a** (*enamorados*) to make eyes at

guión [gi'on] *nm* (*Ling*) hyphen, dash; (*esquema*) summary, outline; (*Cine*) script
guionista [gjo'nista] *nm/f* scriptwriter
guiri ['giri] *nm/f* (*fam, pey*) foreigner
guirnalda [gir'nalda] *nf* garland
guisa ['gisa] *nf*: **a ~ de** as, like
guisado [gi'saðo] *nm* stew
guisante [gi'sante] *nm* pea
guisar [gi'sar] *vt, vi* to cook; (*fig*) to arrange
guiso ['giso] *nm* cooked dish
guitarra [gi'tarra] *nf* guitar
guitarrista [gita'rrista] *nm/f* guitarist
gula ['gula] *nf* gluttony, greed
gusano [gu'sano] *nm* maggot, worm; (*de mariposa, polilla*) caterpillar; (*lombriz*) earthworm; (*fig*) worm; (*ser despreciable*) creep; **~ de seda** silk-worm
gustar [gus'tar] *vt* to taste, sample ▷ *vi* to please, be pleasing; **~ de algo** to like *o* enjoy sth; **me gustan las uvas** I like grapes; **le gusta nadar** she likes *o* enjoys swimming; **¿gusta Ud?** would you like some?; **como Ud guste** as you wish
gusto ['gusto] *nm* (*sentido, sabor*) taste; (*agrado*) liking; (*placer*) pleasure; **tiene un ~ amargo** it has a bitter taste; **tener buen ~** to have good taste; **sobre ~s no hay nada escrito** there's no accounting for tastes; **de buen/mal ~** in good/bad taste; **sentirse a ~** to feel at ease; **¡mucho** *o* **tanto ~ (en conocerle)!** how do you do?, pleased to meet you; **el ~ es mío** the pleasure is mine; **tomar ~ a** to take a liking to; **con ~** willingly, gladly
gustoso, -a [gus'toso, a] *adj* (*sabroso*) tasty; (*agradable*) pleasant; (*con voluntad*) willing, glad; **lo hizo ~** he did it gladly
gutural [gutu'ral] *adj* guttural

h

ha[1] [a] *vb ver* **haber**
ha[2] *abr* (= *Hectárea(s)*) ha
haba ['aβa] *nf* bean; **son ~s contadas** it goes without saying; **en todas partes cuecen ~s** it's the same (story) the whole world over
Habana [a'βana] *nf*: **la ~** Havana
habano [a'βano] *nm* Havana cigar
habéis *vb ver* **haber**

PALABRA CLAVE

haber [a'βer] *vb auxiliar* **1** (*tiempos compuestos*) to have; **había comido** I have/had eaten; **antes/después de haberlo visto** before seeing/after seeing *o* having seen it; **si lo hubiera sabido habría ido** if I had known I would have gone
2: **¡haberlo dicho antes!** you should have said so before!; **¿habrase visto (cosa igual)?** have you ever seen anything like it?
3: **haber de**: **he de hacerlo** I must do it; **ha de llegar mañana** it should arrive tomorrow
▷ *vb impersonal* **1** (*existencia*: *sg*) there is; (: *pl*) there are; **hay un hermano/dos hermanos** there is one brother/there are two brothers; **¿cuánto hay de aquí a Sucre?** how far is it from here to Sucre?; **habrá unos 4 grados** it must be about 4 degrees; **no hay quien te entienda** there's no understanding you
2 (*obligación*): **hay que hacer algo** something must be done; **hay que apuntarlo para**

acordarse you have to write it down to remember
3: **¡hay que ver!** well I never!
4: **¡no hay de** *o* **por** (*Am*) **qué!** don't mention it!, not at all!
5: **¿qué hay?** (*¿qué pasa?*) what's up?, what's the matter?; (*¿qué tal?*) how's it going?
haberse *vr*: **habérselas con algn** to have it out with sb
▷ *vt*: **he aquí unas sugerencias** here are some suggestions; **todos los inventos habidos y por haber** all inventions present and future; **en el encuentro habido ayer** in yesterday's game
▷ *nm* (*en cuenta*) credit side
haberes *nmpl* assets; **¿cuánto tengo en el haber?** how much do I have in my account?; **tiene varias novelas en su haber** he has several novels to his credit

habichuela [aβi'tʃwela] *nf* kidney bean
hábil ['aβil] *adj* (*listo*) clever, smart; (*capaz*) fit, capable; (*experto*) expert; **día ~** working day
habilidad [aβili'ðað] *nf* (*gen*) skill, ability; (*inteligencia*) cleverness; (*destreza*) expertness, expertise; (*Jur*) competence; **~ (para)** fitness (for); **tener ~ manual** to be clever with one's hands
habilitar [aβili'tar] *vt* to qualify; (*autorizar*) to authorize; (*capacitar*) to enable; (*dar instrumentos*) to equip; (*financiar*) to finance
hábilmente [aβil'mente] *adv* skilfully, expertly
habitación [aβita'θjon] *nf* (*cuarto*) room; (*casa*) dwelling, abode; (*Bio: morada*) habitat; **~ sencilla** *o* **individual** single room; **~ doble** *o* **de matrimonio** double room
habitante [aβi'tante] *nm/f* inhabitant
habitar [aβi'tar] *vt* (*residir en*) to inhabit; (*ocupar*) to occupy ▷ *vi* to live
hábitat (*pl* **hábitats**) ['aβitat, 'aβitats] *nm* habitat
hábito ['aβito] *nm* habit; **tener el ~ de hacer algo** to be in the habit of doing sth
habitual [aβi'twal] *adj* habitual
habituar [aβi'twar] *vt* to accustom;
habituarse *vr*: **~se a** to get used to
habla ['aβla] *nf* (*capacidad de hablar*) speech; (*idioma*) language; (*dialecto*) dialect; **perder el ~** to become speechless; **de ~ francesa** French-speaking; **estar al ~** to be in contact; (*Telec*) to be on the line; **¡González al ~!** (*Telec*) Gonzalez speaking!
hablador, a [aβla'ðor, a] *adj* talkative ▷ *nm/f* chatterbox
habladuría [aβlaðu'ria] *nf* rumour;
habladurías *nfpl* gossip *sg*
hablante [a'βlante] *adj* speaking ▷ *nm/f* speaker
hablar [a'βlar] *vt* to speak, talk ▷ *vi* to speak;
hablarse *vr* to speak to each other; **~ con** to speak to; **¡hable!, ¡puede ~!** (*Telec*) you're through!; **de eso ni ~** no way, that's out of the question; **~ alto/bajo/claro** to speak loudly/quietly/plainly *o* bluntly; **~ de** to speak of *o* about; **"se habla inglés"** "English spoken here"; **no se hablan** they are not on speaking terms
habré *etc* [a'βre] *vb ver* **haber**
hacedor, a [aθe'ðor, a] *nm/f* maker
hacendado, -a [aθen'daðo, a] *adj* property-owning ▷ *nm* (*Am*) rancher, farmer; (*terrateniente*) large landowner
hacendoso, -a [aθen'doso, a] *adj* industrious, hard-working

PALABRA CLAVE

hacer [a'θer] *vt* 1 (*fabricar, producir, conseguir*) to make; (*construir*) to build; **hacer una película/un ruido** to make a film/noise; **el guisado lo hice yo** I made *o* cooked the stew; **hacer amigos** to make friends
2 (*ejecutar: trabajo etc*) to do: **hacer la colada** to do the washing; **hacer la comida** to do the cooking; **¿qué haces?** what are you doing?; **¡eso está hecho!** you've got it!; **hacer el tonto/indio** to act the fool/clown; **hacer el malo** *o* **el papel del malo** (*Teat*) to play the villain
3 (*estudios, algunos deportes*) to do; **hacer español/económicas** to do *o* study Spanish/economics; **hacer yoga/gimnasia** to do yoga/go to the gym
4 (*transformar, incidir en*): **esto lo hará más difícil** this will make it more difficult; **salir te hará sentir mejor** going out will make you feel better; **te hace más joven** it makes you look younger
5 (*cálculo*): **2 y 2 hacen 4** 2 and 2 make 4; **éste hace 100** this one makes 100
6 (*+ sub*): **esto hará que ganemos** this will make us win; **harás que no quiera venir** you'll stop him wanting to come
7 (*como sustituto de vb*) to do; **él bebió y yo hice lo mismo** he drank and I did likewise
8: **no hace más que criticar** all he does is criticize
▷ *vb semi-auxiliar* (*+ infin*) 1 (*directo*): **les hice venir** I made *o* had them come; **hacer trabajar a los demás** to get others to work
2 (*por intermedio de otros*): **hacer reparar algo** to get sth repaired
▷ *vi* 1: **haz como que no lo sabes** act as if you don't know; **hiciste bien en decírmelo** you were right to tell me
2 (*ser apropiado*): **si os hace** if it's alright with you
3: **hacer de**: **hacer de madre para uno** to be like a mother to sb; (*Teat*): **hacer de Otelo** to play Othello; **la tabla hace de mesa** the board does as a table
▷ *vb impersonal* 1: **hace calor/frío** it's hot/cold; *ver tb* **bueno**; **sol**; **tiempo**

2 (*tiempo*): **hace tres años** three years ago; **hace un mes que voy/no voy** I've been going/I haven't been for a month; **no le veo desde hace mucho** I haven't seen him for a long time
3: **¿cómo has hecho para llegar tan rápido?** how did you manage to get here so quickly?
hacerse *vr* **1** (*volverse*) to become; **se hicieron amigos** they became friends; **hacerse viejo** to get *o* grow old; **se hace tarde** it's getting late
2: **hacerse algo**: **me hice un traje** I got a suit made
3 (*acostumbrarse*): **hacerse a** to get used to; **hacerse a la idea** to get used to the idea
4: **se hace con huevos y leche** it's made out of eggs and milk; **eso no se hace** that's not done
5 (*obtener*): **hacerse de** *o* **con algo** to get hold of sth
6 (*fingirse*): **hacerse el sordo/sueco** to turn a deaf ear/pretend not to notice

hacha ['atʃa] *nf* axe; (*antorcha*) torch
hachazo [a'tʃaθo] *nm* axe blow
hachís [a'tʃis] *nm* hashish
hacia ['aθja] *prep* (*en dirección de, actitud*) towards; (*cerca de*) near; (*actitud*) towards; **~ adelante/atrás** forwards/backwards; **~ arriba/abajo** up(wards)/down(wards); **~ mediodía** about noon
hacienda [a'θjenda] *nf* (*propiedad*) property; (*finca*) farm; (*Am*) ranch; **~ pública** public finance; **(Ministerio de) H~** Exchequer (*Brit*), Treasury Department (*US*)
hada ['aða] *nf* fairy; **~ madrina** fairy godmother
haga *etc* ['aɣa] *vb ver* **hacer**
Haití [ai'ti] *nm* Haiti
halagar [ala'ɣar] *vt* (*lisonjear*) to flatter
halago [a'laɣo] *nm* (*adulación*) flattery
halagüeño, -a [ala'ɣweɲo, a] *adj* flattering
halcón [al'kon] *nm* falcon, hawk
hálito ['alito] *nm* breath
hallar [a'ʎar] *vt* (*gen*) to find; (*descubrir*) to discover; (*toparse con*) to run into; **hallarse** *vr* to be (situated); (*encontrarse*) to find o.s.; **se halla fuera** he is away; **no se halla** he feels out of place
hallazgo [a'ʎaθɣo] *nm* discovery; (*cosa*) find
halógeno, a [a'loxeno, a] *adj*: **faro ~** halogen lamp
halterofilia [altero'filja] *nf* weightlifting
hamaca [a'maka] *nf* hammock
hambre ['ambre] *nf* hunger; (*carencia*) famine; (*inanición*) starvation; (*fig*) longing; **tener ~** to be hungry; **¡me muero de ~!** I'm starving!
hambriento, -a [am'brjento, a] *adj* hungry, starving ▷ *nm/f* starving person; **los ~s** the hungry; **~ de** hungry *o* longing for
hambruna [am'bruna] *nf* famine
hamburguesa [ambur'ɣesa] *nf* hamburger, burger
hamburguesería [amburɣese'ria] *nf* burger bar
hampón [am'pon] *nm* thug
hámster ['xamster] *nm* hamster
han [an] *vb ver* **haber**
haragán, -ana [ara'ɣan, ana] *adj, nm/f* good-for-nothing
harapiento, -a [ara'pjento, a] *adj* tattered, in rags
harapo [a'rapo] *nm* rag
haré *etc* [a're] *vb ver* **hacer**
harina [a'rina] *nf* flour; **~ de maíz** cornflour (*Brit*), cornstarch (*US*); **~ de trigo** wheat flour; **eso es ~ de otro costal** that's another kettle of fish
hartar [ar'tar] *vt* to satiate, glut; (*fig*) to tire, sicken; **hartarse** *vr* (*de comida*) to fill o.s., gorge o.s.; (*cansarse*): **~se de** to get fed up with
hartazgo [ar'taθɣo] *nm* surfeit, glut
harto, -a ['arto, a] *adj* (*lleno*) full; (*cansado*) fed up ▷ *adv* (*bastante*) enough; (*muy*) very; **estar ~ de** to be fed up with; **¡estoy ~ de decírtelo!** I'm sick and tired of telling you (so)!
hartura [ar'tura] *nf* (*exceso*) surfeit; (*abundancia*) abundance; (*satisfacción*) satisfaction
has[1] [as] *vb ver* **haber**
has[2] *abr* (= *Hectáreas*) ha
hasta ['asta] *adv* even ▷ *prep* (*alcanzando a*) as far as, up/down to; (*de tiempo: a tal hora*) till, until; (*: antes de*) before ▷ *conj*: **~ que** until; **~ luego** *o* **ahora/el sábado** (*fam*) see you soon/on Saturday; **~ pronto** see you soon; **~ la fecha** (up) to date; **~ nueva orden** until further notice; **~ en Valencia hiela a veces** even in Valencia it freezes sometimes
hastiar [as'tjar] *vt* (*gen*) to weary; (*aburrir*) to bore; **hastiarse** *vr*: **~se de** to get fed up with
hastío [as'tio] *nm* weariness; boredom
hatillo [a'tiʎo] *nm* belongings *pl*, kit; (*montón*) bundle, heap
hay [ai] *vb ver* **haber**
Haya ['aja] *nf*: **la ~** The Hague
haya *etc* ['aja] *vb ver* **haber** ▷ *nf* beech tree
haz [aθ] *vb ver* **hacer** ▷ *nm* bundle, bunch; (*rayo: de luz*) beam ▷ *nf*: **~ de la tierra** face of the earth
hazaña [a'θaɲa] *nf* feat, exploit; **sería una ~** it would be a great achievement
hazmerreír [aθmerre'ir] *nm inv* laughing stock
he [e] *vb ver* **haber** ▷ *adv*: **he aquí** here is, here are; **he aquí por qué ...** that is why ...
hebilla [e'βiʎa] *nf* buckle, clasp
hebra ['eβra] *nf* thread; (*Bot: fibra*) fibre, grain
hebreo, -a [e'βreo, a] *adj, nm/f* Hebrew ▷ *nm* (*Ling*) Hebrew

hechicero, -a [etʃi'θero, a] *nm/f* sorcerer/sorceress
hechizar [etʃi'θar] *vt* to cast a spell on, bewitch
hechizo [e'tʃiθo] *nm* witchcraft, magic; (*acto de magia*) spell, charm
hecho, -a ['etʃo, a] *pp de* **hacer** ▷ *adj* complete; (*maduro*) mature; (*carne*) done; (*Costura*) ready-to-wear ▷ *nm* deed, act; (*dato*) fact; (*cuestión*) matter; (*suceso*) event ▷ *excl* agreed!, done!; **¡bien ~!** well done!; **de ~** in fact, as a matter of fact; (*Pol etc: adj, adv*) de facto; **de ~ y de derecho** de facto and de jure; **~ a la medida** made-to-measure; **a lo ~, pecho** it's no use crying over spilt milk; **el ~ es que ...** the fact is that ...
hechura [e'tʃura] *nf* making, creation; (*producto*) product; (*forma*) form, shape; (*de persona*) build; (*Tec*) craftsmanship
hectárea [ek'tarea] *nf* hectare
heder [e'ðer] *vi* to stink, smell; (*fig*) to be unbearable
hediondo, -a [e'ðjondo, a] *adj* stinking
hedor [e'ðor] *nm* stench
hegemonía [exemo'nia] *nf* hegemony
helada [e'laða] *nf* frost
heladera [ela'ðera] *nf* (*Am: refrigerador*) refrigerator
heladería [elaðe'ria] *nf* ice-cream stall (*o* parlour)
helado, -a [e'laðo, a] *adj* frozen; (*glacial*) icy; (*fig*) chilly, cold ▷ *nm* ice-cream; **dejar ~ a algn** to dumbfound sb
helar [e'lar] *vt* to freeze, ice (up); (*dejar atónito*) to amaze; (*desalentar*) to discourage ▷ *vi*, **helarse** *vr* to freeze; (*Aviat, Ferro etc*) to ice (up), freeze up; (*líquido*) to set
helecho [e'letʃo] *nm* bracken, fern
hélice ['eliθe] *nf* spiral; (*Tec*) propeller; (*Mat*) helix
helicóptero [eli'koptero] *nm* helicopter
helio ['eljo] *nm* helium
hematoma [ema'toma] *nm* bruise
hembra ['embra] *nf* (*Bot, Zool*) female; (*mujer*) woman; (*Tec*) nut; **un elefante ~** a she-elephant
hemiciclo [emi'θiklo] *nm*: **el ~** (*Pol*) the floor
hemisferio [emis'ferjo] *nm* hemisphere
hemorragia [emo'rraxja] *nf* haemorrhage (*Brit*), hemorrhage (*US*)
hemorroides [emo'rroiðes] *nfpl* haemorrhoids (*Brit*), hemorrhoids (*US*)
hemos ['emos] *vb ver* **haber**
hendidura [endi'ðura] *nf* crack, split; (*Geo*) fissure
heno ['eno] *nm* hay
hepatitis [epa'titis] *nf inv* hepatitis
herbicida [erβi'θiða] *nm* weedkiller
herbívoro, -a [er'βiβoro, a] *adj* herbivorous
herboristería [erβoriste'ria] *nf* herbalist's shop
heredad [ere'ðað] *nf* landed property; (*granja*) farm
heredar [ere'ðar] *vt* to inherit
heredero, -a [ere'ðero, a] *nm/f* heir(ess); **~ del trono** heir to the throne
hereditario, -a [ereði'tarjo, a] *adj* hereditary
hereje [e'rexe] *nm/f* heretic
herencia [e'renθja] *nf* inheritance; (*fig*) heritage; (*Bio*) heredity
herido, -a [e'riðo, a] *adj* injured, wounded; (*fig*) offended ▷ *nm/f* casualty ▷ *nf* wound, injury
herir [e'rir] *vt* to wound, injure; (*fig*) to offend; (*conmover*) to touch, move
hermana [er'mana] *nf ver* **hermano**
hermanación [ermana'θjon] *nf* (*de ciudades*) twinning
hermanado, -a [erma'naðo, a] *adj* (*ciudad*) twinned
hermanastro, -a [erma'nastro, a] *nm/f* stepbrother(-sister)
hermandad [erman'dað] *nf* brotherhood; (*de mujeres*) sisterhood; (*sindicato etc*) association
hermano, -a [er'mano, a] *adj* similar ▷ *nm* brother ▷ *nf* sister; **~ gemelo** twin brother; **~ político** brother-in-law; **~ primo** first cousin; **mis ~s** my brothers, my brothers and sisters; **hermana política** sister-in-law
hermético, -a [er'metiko, a] *adj* hermetic; (*fig*) watertight
hermoso, -a [er'moso, a] *adj* beautiful, lovely; (*estupendo*) splendid; (*guapo*) handsome
hermosura [ermo'sura] *nf* beauty; (*de hombre*) handsomeness
hernia ['ernja] *nf* hernia, rupture; **~ discal** slipped disc
herniarse [er'njarse] *vr* to rupture o.s.; (*fig*) to break one's back
héroe ['eroe] *nm* hero
heroína [ero'ina] *nf* (*mujer*) heroine; (*droga*) heroin
heroinómano, -a [eroi'nomano, a] *nm/f* heroin addict
heroísmo [ero'ismo] *nm* heroism
herradura [erra'ðura] *nf* horseshoe
herramienta [erra'mjenta] *nf* tool
herrería [erre'ria] *nf* smithy; (*Tec*) forge
herrero [e'rrero] *nm* blacksmith
herrumbre [e'rrumbre] *nf* rust
hervidero [erβi'ðero] *nm* (*fig*) swarm; (*Pol etc*) hotbed
hervir [er'βir] *vi* to boil; (*burbujear*) to bubble; (*fig*): **~ de** to teem with; **~ a fuego lento** to simmer
hervor [er'βor] *nm* boiling; (*fig*) ardour, fervour
heterosexual [eterosek'swal] *adj, nm/f* heterosexual
híbrido, -a ['iβriðo, a] *adj* hybrid
hice *etc* ['iθe] *vb ver* **hacer**

hidratante [iðra'tante] *adj*: **crema ~** moisturizing cream, moisturizer
hidratar [iðra'tar] *vt* to moisturize
hidrato [i'ðrato] *nm* hydrate; **~ de carbono** carbohydrate
hidráulico, -a [i'ðrauliko, a] *adj* hydraulic ▷ *nf* hydraulics *sg*
hidro... [iðro] *pref* hydro..., water-...
hidrodeslizador [iðrodesliθa'ðor] *nm* hovercraft
hidroeléctrico, -a [iðroe'lektriko, a] *adj* hydroelectric
hidrofobia [iðro'foβja] *nf* hydrophobia, rabies
hidrógeno [i'ðroxeno] *nm* hydrogen
hiedra ['jeðra] *nf* ivy
hiel [jel] *nf* gall, bile; (*fig*) bitterness
hielo ['jelo] *vb ver* **helar** ▷ *nm* (*gen*) ice; (*escarcha*) frost; (*fig*) coldness, reserve; **romper el ~** (*fig*) to break the ice
hiena ['jena] *nf* (*Zool*) hyena
hierba ['jerβa] *nf* (*pasto*) grass; (*Culin, Med: planta*) herb; **mala ~** weed; (*fig*) evil influence
hierbabuena [jerβa'βwena] *nf* mint
hierro ['jerro] *nm* (*metal*) iron; (*objeto*) iron object; **~ acanalado** corrugated iron; **~ colado** *o* **fundido** cast iron; **de ~** iron *cpd*
hígado ['iɣaðo] *nm* liver; **hígados** *nmpl* (*fig*) guts; **echar los ~s** to wear o.s. out
higiene [i'xjene] *nf* hygiene
higiénico, -a [i'xjeniko, a] *adj* hygienic
higo ['iɣo] *nm* fig; **~ seco** dried fig; **~ chumbo** prickly pear; **de ~s a brevas** once in a blue moon
higuera [i'gera] *nf* fig tree
hijastro, -a [i'xastro, a] *nm/f* stepson(-daughter)
hijo, -a ['ixo, a] *nm/f* son/daughter, child; (*uso vocativo*) dear; **hijos** *nmpl* children, sons and daughters; **sin ~s** childless; **~/hija político/a** son-/daughter-in-law; **~ pródigo** prodigal son; **~ adoptivo** adopted child; **~ de papá/mamá** daddy's/mummy's boy; **~ de puta** (*fam!*) bastard (*!*), son of a bitch (*!*); **~ único** only child; **cada ~ de vecino** any Tom, Dick or Harry
hilar [i'lar] *vt* to spin; (*fig*) to reason, infer; **~ delgado** to split hairs
hilera [i'lera] *nf* row, file
hilo ['ilo] *nm* thread; (*Bot*) fibre; (*tela*) linen; (*de metal*) wire; (*de agua*) trickle, thin stream; (*de luz*) beam, ray; (*de conversación*) thread, theme; (*de pensamientos*) train; **~ dental** dental floss; **colgar de un ~** (*fig*) to hang by a thread; **traje de ~** linen suit
hilvanar [ilβa'nar] *vt* (*Costura*) to tack (*Brit*), baste (*US*); (*fig*) to do hurriedly
himno ['imno] *nm* hymn; **~ nacional** national anthem
hincapié [inka'pje] *nm*: **hacer ~ en** to emphasize, stress
hincar [in'kar] *vt* to drive (in), thrust (in); (*diente*) to sink; **hincarse** *vr*: **~se de rodillas** (*esp Am*) to kneel down
hincha ['intʃa] *nm/f* (*fam: Deporte*) fan
hinchado, -a [in'tʃaðo, a] *adj* (*gen*) swollen; (*persona*) pompous ▷ *nf* (group of) supporters *o* fans
hinchar [in'tʃar] *vt* (*gen*) to swell; (*inflar*) to blow up, inflate; (*fig*) to exaggerate; **hincharse** *vr* (*inflarse*) to swell up; (*fam: llenarse*) to stuff o.s.; (*fig*) to get conceited; **~se de reír** to have a good laugh
hinchazón [intʃa'θon] *nf* (*Med*) swelling; (*protuberancia*) bump, lump; (*altivez*) arrogance
hindú [in'du] *adj, nm/f* Hindu
hinojo [i'noxo] *nm* fennel
hipermercado [ipermer'kaðo] *nm* hypermarket, superstore
hipertensión [iperten'sjon] *nf* high blood pressure, hypertension
hípico, -a ['ipiko, a] *adj* horse *cpd*, equine; **club ~** riding club
hipnosis [ip'nosis] *nf inv* hypnosis
hipnotismo [ipno'tismo] *nm* hypnotism
hipnotizar [ipnoti'θar] *vt* to hypnotize
hipo ['ipo] *nm* hiccups *pl*; **quitar el ~ a algn** to cure sb's hiccups
hipocresía [ipokre'sia] *nf* hypocrisy
hipócrita [i'pokrita] *adj* hypocritical ▷ *nm/f* hypocrite
hipódromo [i'poðromo] *nm* racetrack
hipopótamo [ipo'potamo] *nm* hippopotamus
hipoteca [ipo'teka] *nf* mortgage; **redimir una ~** to pay off a mortgage
hipotecar [ipote'kar] *vt* to mortgage; (*fig*) to jeopardize
hipótesis [i'potesis] *nf inv* hypothesis; **es una ~ (nada más)** that's just a theory
hiriente [i'rjente] *adj* offensive, wounding
hispánico, -a [is'paniko, a] *adj* Hispanic, Spanish
hispano, -a [is'pano, a] *adj* Hispanic, Spanish, Hispano- ▷ *nm/f* Spaniard
Hispanoamérica [ispanoa'merika] *nf* Spanish *o* Latin America
hispanoamericano, -a [ispanoameri'kano, a] *adj, nm/f* Spanish *o* Latin American
histeria [is'terja] *nf* hysteria
histérico, -a [is'teriko, a] *adj* hysterical
historia [is'torja] *nf* history; (*cuento*) story, tale; **historias** *nfpl* (*chismes*) gossip *sg*; **dejarse de ~s** to come to the point; **pasar a la ~** to go down in history
historiador, a [istorja'ðor, a] *nm/f* historian
historial [isto'rjal] *nm* record; (*profesional*) curriculum vitae, c.v., résumé (*US*); (*Med*) case history
histórico, -a [is'toriko, a] *adj* historical; (*fig*) historic
historieta [isto'rjeta] *nf* tale, anecdote; (*de dibujos*) comic strip

hito ['ito] *nm* (*fig*) landmark; (*objetivo*) goal, target; (*fig*) milestone
hizo ['iθo] *vb ver* **hacer**
hocico [o'θiko] *nm* snout; (*fig*) grimace
hockey ['xoki] *nm* hockey; **~ sobre hielo** ice hockey
hogar [o'ɣar] *nm* fireplace, hearth; (*casa*) home; (*vida familiar*) home life
hogareño, -a [oɣa'reɲo, a] *adj* home *cpd*; (*persona*) home-loving
hoguera [o'ɣera] *nf* (*gen*) bonfire; (*para herejes*) stake
hoja ['oxa] *nf* (*gen*) leaf; (*de flor*) petal; (*de hierba*) blade; (*de papel*) sheet; (*página*) page; (*formulario*) form; (*de puerta*) leaf; **~ de afeitar** razor blade; **~ de cálculo electrónica** spreadsheet; **~ informativa** leaflet, handout; **~ de ruta** road map; **~ de solicitud** application form; **~ de trabajo** (*Inform*) worksheet; **de ~ ancha** broad-leaved; **de ~ caduca/perenne** deciduous/evergreen
hojalata [oxa'lata] *nf* tin(plate)
hojaldre [o'xaldre] *nm* (*Culin*) puff pastry
hojear [oxe'ar] *vt* to leaf through, turn the pages of
hojuela [o'xwela] *nf* (*Am*) flake
hola ['ola] *excl* hello!
Holanda [o'landa] *nf* Holland
holandés, -esa [olan'des, esa] *adj* Dutch ▷ *nm/f* Dutchman(-woman); **los holandeses** the Dutch ▷ *nm* (*Ling*) Dutch
holgado, -a [ol'ɣaðo, a] *adj* loose, baggy; (*rico*) well-to-do
holgar [ol'ɣar] *vi* (*descansar*) to rest; (*sobrar*) to be superfluous; **huelga decir que** it goes without saying that
holgazán, -ana [olɣa'θan, ana] *adj* idle, lazy ▷ *nm/f* loafer
holgura [ol'ɣura] *nf* looseness, bagginess; (*Tec*) play, free movement; (*vida*) comfortable living, luxury
hollín [o'ʎin] *nm* soot
hombre ['ombre] *nm* man; (*raza humana*): **el ~** man(kind) ▷ *excl*: **¡sí ~!** (*claro*) of course!; (*para énfasis*) man, old chap; **~ de negocios** businessman; **~-rana** frogman; **~ de bien** *o* **pro** honest man; **~ de confianza** right-hand man; **~ de estado** statesman; **el ~ medio** the average man
hombrera [om'brera] *nf* shoulder strap
hombro ['ombro] *nm* shoulder; **arrimar el ~** to lend a hand; **encogerse de ~s** to shrug one's shoulders
hombruno, -a [om'bruno, a] *adj* mannish
homenaje [ome'naxe] *nm* (*gen*) homage; (*tributo*) tribute; **un partido ~** a benefit match
homeopatía [omeopa'tia] *nf* hom(o)eopathy
homeopático, -a [omeo'patiko, a] *adj* hom(o)eopathic
homicida [omi'θiða] *adj* homicidal ▷ *nm/f* murderer
homicidio [omi'θiðjo] *nm* murder, homicide; (*involuntario*) manslaughter
homologar [omolo'ɣar] *vt* (*Com*) to standardize; (*Escol*) to officially approve; (*Deporte*) to officially recognize; (*sueldos*) to equalize
homólogo, -a [o'moloɣo, a] *nm/f* counterpart, opposite number
homosexual [omosek'swal] *adj, nm/f* homosexual
honda ['onda] *nf* (*CS*) catapult
hondo, -a ['ondo, a] *adj* deep; **lo ~** the depth(s) (*pl*), the bottom; **con ~ pesar** with deep regret
hondonada [ondo'naða] *nf* hollow, depression; (*cañón*) ravine; (*Geo*) lowland
hondura [on'dura] *nf* depth, profundity
Honduras [on'duras] *nf* Honduras
hondureño, -a [ondu'reɲo, a] *adj, nm/f* Honduran
honestidad [onesti'ðað] *nf* purity, chastity; (*decencia*) decency
honesto, -a [o'nesto, a] *adj* chaste; decent, honest; (*justo*) just
hongo ['ongo] *nm* (*Bot: gen*) fungus; (*: comestible*) mushroom; (*: venenoso*) toadstool; (*sombrero*) bowler (hat) (*Brit*), derby (*US*); **~s del pie** foot rot *sg*, athlete's foot *sg*
honor [o'nor] *nm* (*gen*) honour (*Brit*), honor (*US*); (*gloria*) glory; **~ profesional** professional etiquette; **en ~ a la verdad** to be fair
honorable [ono'raβle] *adj* honourable (*Brit*), honorable (*US*)
honorario, -a [ono'rarjo, a] *adj* honorary ▷ *nm*: **~s** fees
honra ['onra] *nf* (*gen*) honour (*Brit*), honor (*US*); (*renombre*) good name; **~s fúnebres** funeral rites; **tener algo a mucha ~** to be proud of sth
honradez [onra'ðeθ] *nf* honesty; (*de persona*) integrity
honrado, -a [on'raðo, a] *adj* honest, upright
honrar [on'rar] *vt* to honour (*Brit*) *o* honor (*US*); **honrarse** *vr*: **~se con algo/de hacer algo** to be honoured by sth/to do sth
honroso, -a [on'roso, a] *adj* (*honrado*) honourable (*Brit*) *o* honorable (*US*); (*respetado*) respectable
hora ['ora] *nf* hour; (*tiempo*) time; **¿qué ~ es?** what time is it?; **¿a qué ~?** at what time?; **media ~** half an hour; **a la ~ de comer/de recreo** at lunchtime/at playtime; **a primera ~** first thing (in the morning); **a última ~** at the last moment; **"última ~"** "stop press"; **noticias de última ~** last-minute news; **a altas ~s** in the small hours; **a la ~ en punto** on the dot; **¡a buena ~!** about time, too!; **en mala ~** unluckily; **pedir ~** to make an appointment; **dar la ~** to strike the hour; **poner el reloj en ~** to set one's watch; **~s de oficina/de trabajo** office/working hours;

~s de visita visiting times; **~s extras** *o* **extraordinarias** overtime *sg*; **~s pico** (*Am*) rush *o* peak hours; **~s punta** rush hours; **no ver la ~ de** to look forward to; **¡ya era ~!** and about time too!
horadar [ora'ðar] *vt* to drill, bore
horario, -a [o'rarjo, a] *adj* hourly, hour *cpd* ▷ *nm* timetable; **~ comercial** business hours
horca ['orka] *nf* gallows *sg*; (*Agr*) pitchfork
horcajadas [orka'xaðas]: **a ~** *adv* astride
horchata [or'tʃata] *nf* *cold drink made from tiger nuts and water*, tiger nut milk
horda ['orða] *nf* horde
horizontal [oriθon'tal] *adj* horizontal
horizonte [ori'θonte] *nm* horizon
horma ['orma] *nf* mould; **~ (de calzado)** last; **~ de sombrero** hat block
hormiga [or'miɣa] *nf* ant; **hormigas** *nfpl* (*Med*) pins and needles
hormigón [ormi'ɣon] *nm* concrete; **~ armado/pretensado** reinforced/ prestressed concrete
hormigonera [ormiɣon'era] *nf* cement mixer
hormigueo [ormi'ɣeo] *nm* (*comezón*) itch; (*fig*) uneasiness
hormiguero [ormi'ɣero] *nm* (*Zool*) ants' nest; **era un ~** it was swarming with people
hormona [or'mona] *nf* hormone
hornada [or'naða] *nf* batch of loaves (*etc*)
hornillo [or'niʎo] *nm* (*cocina*) portable stove; **~ de gas** gas ring
horno ['orno] *nm* (*Culin*) oven; (*Tec*) furnace; (*para cerámica*) kiln; **~ microondas** microwave (oven); **alto ~** blast furnace; **~ crematorio** crematorium
horóscopo [o'roskopo] *nm* horoscope
horquilla [or'kiʎa] *nf* hairpin; (*Agr*) pitchfork
horrendo, -a [o'rrendo, a] *adj* horrendous, frightful
horrible [o'rriβle] *adj* horrible, dreadful
horripilante [orripi'lante] *adj* hair-raising, horrifying
horror [o'rror] *nm* horror, dread; (*atrocidad*) atrocity; **¡qué ~!** (*fam*) how awful!; **estudia ~es** he studies a hell of a lot
horrorizar [orrori'θar] *vt* to horrify, frighten; **horrorizarse** *vr* to be horrified
horroroso, -a [orro'roso, a] *adj* horrifying, ghastly
hortaliza [orta'liθa] *nf* vegetable
hortelano, -a [orte'lano, a] *nm/f* (market) gardener
hortera [or'tera] *adj* (*fam*) tacky
horterada [orte'raða] *nf* (*fam*): **es una ~** it's really naff
hortofrutícola [ortofru'tikola] *adj* fruit and vegetable *cpd*
hosco, -a ['osko, a] *adj* dark; (*persona*) sullen, gloomy
hospedar [ospe'ðar] *vt* to put up; **hospedarse** *vr*: **~se (con/en)** to stay *o* lodge (with/at)
hospital [ospi'tal] *nm* hospital
hospitalario, -a [ospita'larjo, a] *adj* (*acogedor*) hospitable
hospitalidad [ospitali'ðað] *nf* hospitality
hospitalizar [ospitali'θar] *vt* to send *o* take to hospital, hospitalize
hostal [os'tal] *nm* small hotel; *ver tb* **hotel**
hostelería [ostele'ria] *nf* hotel business *o* trade
hostia ['ostja] *nf* (*Rel*) host, consecrated wafer; (*fam: golpe*) whack, punch ▷ *excl*: **¡~(s)!** (*fam!*) damn!
hostigar [osti'ɣar] *vt* to whip; (*fig*) to harass, pester
hostil [os'til] *adj* hostile
hostilidad [ostili'ðað] *nf* hostility
hotdog [ot'dog] *nm* (*Am*) hot dog
hotel [o'tel] *nm* hotel; *see note*

HOTEL

In Spain you can choose from the following categories of accommodation, in descending order of quality and price: hotel (from 5 stars to 1), *hostal, pensión, casa de huéspedes, fonda*. Quality can vary widely even within these categories. The State also runs luxury hotels called *paradores*, which are usually sited in places of particular historical interest and are often historic buildings themselves.

hotelero, -a [ote'lero, a] *adj* hotel *cpd* ▷ *nm/f* hotelier
hoy [oi] *adv* (*este día*) today; (*en la actualidad*) now(adays) ▷ *nm* present time; **~ (en) día** now(adays); **el día de ~, ~ día** (*Am*) this very day; **~ por ~** right now; **de ~ en ocho días** a week today; **de ~ en adelante** from now on
hoyo ['ojo] *nm* hole, pit; (*tumba*) grave; (*Golf*) hole; (*Med*) pockmark
hoyuelo [oj'welo] *nm* dimple
hoz [oθ] *nf* sickle
hube *etc* ['uβe] *vb ver* **haber**
hucha ['utʃa] *nf* money box
hueco, -a ['weko, a] *adj* (*vacío*) hollow, empty; (*resonante*) booming; (*sonido*) resonant; (*persona*) conceited; (*estilo*) pompous ▷ *nm* hollow, cavity; (*agujero*) hole; (*de escalera*) well; (*de ascensor*) shaft; (*vacante*) vacancy; **~ de la mano** hollow of the hand
huelga ['welɣa] *vb ver* **holgar** ▷ *nf* strike; **declararse en ~** to go on strike, come out on strike; **~ general** general strike; **~ de hambre** hunger strike; **~ oficial** official strike
huelguista [wel'ɣista] *nm/f* striker
huella ['weʎa] *nf* (*acto de pisar, pisada*) tread(ing); (*marca del paso*) footprint, footstep;

(*: de animal, máquina*) track; **~ dactilar** *o* **digital** fingerprint; **sin dejar ~** without leaving a trace

huelo *etc vb ver* **oler**

huérfano, -a ['werfano, a] *adj* orphan(ed); (*fig*) unprotected ▷ *nm/f* orphan

huerta ['werta] *nf* market garden (*Brit*), truck farm (*US*); (*de Murcia, Valencia*) irrigated region

huerto ['werto] *nm* kitchen garden; (*de árboles frutales*) orchard

hueso ['weso] *nm* (*Anat*) bone; (*de fruta*) stone, pit (*US*); **sin ~** (*carne*) boned; **estar en los ~s** to be nothing but skin and bone; **ser un ~** (*profesor*) to be terribly strict; **un ~ duro de roer** a hard nut to crack

huésped, a ['wespeð, a] *nm/f* (*invitado*) guest; (*habitante*) resident; (*anfitrión*) host(ess)

huesudo, -a [we'suðo, a] *adj* bony, big-boned

huevas ['weβas] *nfpl* eggs, roe *sg*; (*Am: fam!*) balls (!)

huevera [we'βera] *nf* eggcup

huevo ['weβo] *nm* egg; (*fam!*) ball (!), testicle; **~ duro/escalfado/estrellado** *o* **frito/pasado por agua** hard-boiled/poached/fried/soft-boiled egg; **~s revueltos** scrambled eggs; **~ tibio** (*Am*) soft-boiled egg; **me costó un** (*fam!*) it was hard work; **tener ~s** (*fam!*) to have guts

huida [u'iða] *nf* escape, flight; **~ de capitales** (*Com*) flight of capital

huidizo, -a [ui'ðiθo, a] *adj* (*tímido*) shy; (*pasajero*) fleeting

huir [u'ir] *vt* (*escapar*) to flee, escape; (*evadir*) to avoid ▷ *vi* to flee, run away

hule ['ule] *nm* (*encerado*) oilskin; (*esp Am*) rubber

hulera [u'lera] *nf* (*Am*) catapult

humanidad [umani'ðað] *nf* (*género humano*) man(kind); (*cualidad*) humanity; (*fam: gordura*) corpulence

humanitario, -a [umani'tarjo, a] *adj* humanitarian; (*benévolo*) humane

humano, -a [u'mano, a] *adj* (*gen*) human; (*humanitario*) humane ▷ *nm* human; **ser ~** human being

humareda [uma'reða] *nf* cloud of smoke

humedad [ume'ðað] *nf* (*del clima*) humidity; (*de pared etc*) dampness; **a prueba de ~** damp-proof

humedecer [umeðe'θer] *vt* to moisten, wet; **humedecerse** *vr* to get wet

húmedo, -a ['umeðo, a] *adj* (*mojado*) damp, wet; (*tiempo etc*) humid

humildad [umil'dað] *nf* humility, humbleness

humilde [u'milde] *adj* humble, modest; (*clase etc*) low, modest

humillación [umiʎa'θjon] *nf* humiliation

humillante [umi'ʎante] *adj* humiliating

humillar [umi'ʎar] *vt* to humiliate; **humillarse** *vr* to humble o.s., grovel

humo ['umo] *nm* (*de fuego*) smoke; (*gas nocivo*) fumes *pl*; (*vapor*) steam, vapour; **humos** *nmpl* (*fig*) conceit *sg*; **irse todo en ~** (*fig*) to vanish without trace; **bajar los ~s a algn** to take sb down a peg or two

humor [u'mor] *nm* (*disposición*) mood, temper; (*lo que divierte*) humour; **de buen/mal ~** in a good/bad mood

humorismo [umo'rismo] *nm* humour

humorista [umo'rista] *nm/f* comic

humorístico, -a [umo'ristiko, a] *adj* funny, humorous

hundimiento [undi'mjento] *nm* (*gen*) sinking; (*colapso*) collapse

hundir [un'dir] *vt* to sink; (*edificio, plan*) to ruin, destroy; **hundirse** *vr* to sink, collapse; (*fig: arruinarse*) to be ruined; (*desaparecer*) to disappear; **se hundió la economía** the economy collapsed; **se hundieron los precios** prices slumped

húngaro, -a ['ungaro, a] *adj, nm/f* Hungarian ▷ *nm* (*Ling*) Hungarian, Magyar

Hungría [un'gria] *nf* Hungary

huracán [ura'kan] *nm* hurricane

huraño, -a [u'raɲo, a] *adj* shy; (*antisocial*) unsociable

hurgar [ur'ɣar] *vt* to poke, jab; (*remover*) to stir (up); **hurgarse** *vr*: **~se (las narices)** to pick one's nose

hurón [u'ron] *nm* (*Zool*) ferret

hurtadillas [urta'ðiʎas]: **a ~** *adv* stealthily, on the sly

hurtar [ur'tar] *vt* to steal; **hurtarse** *vr* to hide, keep out of the way

hurto ['urto] *nm* theft, stealing; (*lo robado*) (piece of) stolen property, loot

husmear [usme'ar] *vt* (*oler*) to sniff out, scent; (*fam*) to pry into ▷ *vi* to smell bad

huso ['uso] *nm* (*Tec*) spindle; (*de torno*) drum

huy ['ui] *excl* (*dolor*) ow!, ouch!; (*sorpresa*) well!; (*alivio*) phew!; **¡~, perdona!** oops, sorry!

huyo *etc vb ver* **huir**

i

iba *etc* ['iβa] *vb ver* **ir**
ibérico, -a [i'βeriko, a] *adj* Iberian; **la Península ibérica** the Iberian Peninsula
iberoamericano, -a [iβeroameri'kano, a] *adj, nm/f* Latin American
íbice ['iβiθe] *nm* ibex
Ibiza [i'βiθa] *nf* Ibiza
iceberg [iθe'ber] *nm* iceberg
icono [i'kono] *nm* (*tb Inform*) icon
iconoclasta [ikono'klasta] *adj* iconoclastic ▹ *nm/f* iconoclast
ictericia [ikte'riθja] *nf* jaundice
I+D *nf abr* (= *Investigación y Desarrollo*) R&D
ida ['iða] *nf* going, departure; **~ y vuelta** round trip, return; **~s y ven~s** comings and goings
idea [i'ðea] *nf* idea; (*impresión*) opinion; (*propósito*) intention; **~ genial** brilliant idea; **a mala ~** out of spite; **no tengo la menor ~** I haven't a clue
ideal [iðe'al] *adj, nm* ideal
idealista [iðea'lista] *adj* idealistic ▹ *nm/f* idealist
idealizar [iðeali'θar] *vt* to idealize
idear [iðe'ar] *vt* to think up; (*aparato*) to invent; (*viaje*) to plan
ídem ['iðem] *pron* ditto
idéntico, -a [i'ðentiko, a] *adj* identical
identidad [iðenti'ðað] *nf* identity; **~ corporativa** corporate identity *o* image
identificación [iðentifika'θjon] *nf* identification
identificar [iðentifi'kar] *vt* to identify; **identificarse** *vr*: **~se con** to identify with
ideología [iðeolo'xia] *nf* ideology
idilio [i'ðiljo] *nm* love affair
idioma [i'ðjoma] *nm* language
idiota [i'ðjota] *adj* idiotic ▹ *nm/f* idiot
idiotez [iðjo'teθ] *nf* idiocy
idolatrar [iðola'trar] *vt* (*fig*) to idolize
ídolo ['iðolo] *nm* (*tb fig*) idol
idóneo, -a [i'ðoneo, a] *adj* suitable
iglesia [i'ɣlesja] *nf* church; **~ parroquial** parish church; **¡con la ~ hemos topado!** now we're really up against it!
iglú [i'ɣlu] *nm* igloo; (*contenedor*) bottle bank
ignominia [iɣno'minja] *nf* ignominy
ignorancia [iɣno'ranθja] *nf* ignorance; **por ~** through ignorance
ignorante [iɣno'rante] *adj* ignorant, uninformed ▹ *nm/f* ignoramus
ignorar [iɣno'rar] *vt* not to know, be ignorant of; (*no hacer caso a*) to ignore; **ignoramos su paradero** we don't know his whereabouts
igual [i'ɣwal] *adj* equal; (*similar*) like, similar; (*mismo*) (the) same; (*constante*) constant; (*temperatura*) even ▹ *nm/f* equal; **al ~ que** *prep, conj* like, just like; **~ que** the same as; **sin ~** peerless; **me da** *o* **es ~** I don't care, it makes no difference; **no tener ~** to be unrivalled; **son ~es** they're the same
igualada [iɣwa'laða] *nf* equalizer
igualar [iɣwa'lar] *vt* (*gen*) to equalize, make equal; (*terreno*) to make even; (*allanar, nivelar*) to level (off); (*Com*) to agree upon; **igualarse** *vr* (*platos de balanza*) to balance out; **~se (a)** (*equivaler*) to be equal (to)
igualdad [iɣwal'dað] *nf* equality; (*similaridad*) sameness; (*uniformidad*) uniformity; **en ~ de condiciones** on an equal basis
igualmente [iɣwal'mente] *adv* equally; (*también*) also, likewise ▹ *excl* the same to you!
ikurriña [iku'rriɲa] *nf* Basque flag
ilegal [ile'ɣal] *adj* illegal
ilegítimo, -a [ile'xitimo, a] *adj* illegitimate
ileso, -a [i'leso, a] *adj* unhurt, unharmed
ilícito, -a [i'liθito, a] *adj* illicit
ilimitado, -a [ilimi'taðo, a] *adj* unlimited
ilógico, -a [i'loxiko, a] *adj* illogical
iluminación [ilumina'θjon] *nf* illumination; (*alumbrado*) lighting; (*fig*) enlightenment
iluminar [ilumi'nar] *vt* to illuminate, light (up); (*fig*) to enlighten
ilusión [ilu'sjon] *nf* illusion; (*quimera*) delusion; (*esperanza*) hope; (*emoción*) excitement, thrill; **hacerse ilusiones** to build up one's hopes; **no te hagas ilusiones** don't build up your hopes *o* get too excited
ilusionado, -a [ilusjo'naðo, a] *adj* excited
ilusionar [ilusjo'nar] *vt*: **~ a algn** (*falsamente*) to build up sb's hopes ▹ *vi*: **le ilusiona ir de vacaciones** he's looking forward to going on holiday; **ilusionarse** *vr* (*falsamente*) to build up one's hopes; (*entusiasmarse*) to get excited;

me ilusiona mucho el viaje I'm really excited about the trip
ilusionista [ilusjo'nista] *nm/f* conjurer
iluso, -a [i'luso, a] *adj* gullible, easily deceived ▷ *nm/f* dreamer, visionary
ilusorio, -a [ilu'sorjo, a] *adj* (*de ilusión*) illusory, deceptive; (*esperanza*) vain
ilustración [ilustra'θjon] *nf* illustration; (*saber*) learning, erudition; **la I~** the Enlightenment
ilustrado, -a [ilus'traðo, a] *adj* illustrated; learned
ilustrar [ilus'trar] *vt* to illustrate; (*instruir*) to instruct; (*explicar*) to explain, make clear; **ilustrarse** *vr* to acquire knowledge
ilustre [i'lustre] *adj* famous, illustrious
imagen [i'maxen] *nf* (*gen*) image; (*dibujo, TV*) picture; (*Rel*) statue; **ser la viva ~ de** to be the spitting *o* living image of; **a su ~** in one's own image
imaginación [imaxina'θjon] *nf* imagination; (*fig*) fancy; **ni por ~** on no account; **no se me pasó por la ~ que ...** it never even occurred to me that ...
imaginar [imaxi'nar] *vt* (*gen*) to imagine; (*idear*) to think up; (*suponer*) to suppose; **imaginarse** *vr* to imagine; **¡imagínate!** just imagine!, just fancy!; **imagínese que ...** suppose that ...; **me imagino que sí** I should think so
imaginario, -a [imaxi'narjo, a] *adj* imaginary
imaginativo, -a [imaxina'tiβo, a] *adj* imaginative ▷ *nf* imagination
imán [i'man] *nm* magnet
imbécil [im'beθil] *nm/f* imbecile, idiot
imbuir [imbu'ir] *vi* to imbue
imitación [imita'θjon] *nf* imitation; (*parodia*) mimicry; **a ~ de** in imitation of; **desconfíe de las imitaciones** (*Com*) beware of copies *o* imitations
imitar [imi'tar] *vt* to imitate; (*parodiar, remedar*) to mimic, ape; (*copiar*) to follow
impaciencia [impa'θjenθja] *nf* impatience
impaciente [impa'θjente] *adj* impatient; (*nervioso*) anxious
impacto [im'pakto] *nm* impact; (*esp Am: fig*) shock
impar [im'par] *adj* odd ▷ *nm* odd number
imparcial [impar'θjal] *adj* impartial, fair
imparcialidad [imparθjali'ðað] *nf* impartiality, fairness
impartir [impar'tir] *vt* to impart, give
impasible [impa'siβle] *adj* impassive
impávido, -a [im'paβiðo, a] *adj* fearless, intrepid
impecable [impe'kaβle] *adj* impeccable
impedimento [impeði'mento] *nm* impediment, obstacle
impedir [impe'ðir] *vt* (*obstruir*) to impede, obstruct; (*estorbar*) to prevent; **~ a algn hacer** *o* **que algn haga algo** to prevent sb (from) doing sth; **~ el tráfico** to block the traffic
impeler [impe'ler] *vt* to drive, propel; (*fig*) to impel
impenetrable [impene'traβle] *adj* impenetrable; (*fig*) incomprehensible
imperar [impe'rar] *vi* (*reinar*) to rule, reign; (*fig*) to prevail, reign; (*precio*) to be current
imperativo, -a [impera'tiβo, a] *adj* (*persona*) imperious; (*urgente, Ling*) imperative
imperceptible [imperθep'tiβle] *adj* imperceptible
imperdible [imper'ðiβle] *nm* safety pin
imperdonable [imperðo'naβle] *adj* unforgivable, inexcusable
imperfección [imperfek'θjon] *nf* imperfection; (*falla*) flaw, fault
imperfecto, -a [imper'fekto, a] *adj* faulty, imperfect ▷ *nm* (*Ling*) imperfect tense
imperial [impe'rjal] *adj* imperial
imperialismo [imperja'lismo] *nm* imperialism
imperio [im'perjo] *nm* empire; (*autoridad*) rule, authority; (*fig*) pride, haughtiness; **vale un ~** (*fig*) it's worth a fortune
imperioso, -a [impe'rjoso, a] *adj* imperious; (*urgente*) urgent; (*imperativo*) imperative
impermeable [imperme'aβle] *adj* (*a prueba de agua*) waterproof ▷ *nm* raincoat, mac (*Brit*)
impersonal [imperso'nal] *adj* impersonal
impertérrito, -a [imper'territo, a] *adj* undaunted
impertinencia [imperti'nenθja] *nf* impertinence
impertinente [imperti'nente] *adj* impertinent
imperturbable [impertur'βaβle] *adj* imperturbable; (*sereno*) unruffled; (*impasible*) impassive
ímpetu ['impetu] *nm* (*impulso*) impetus, impulse; (*impetuosidad*) impetuosity; (*violencia*) violence
impetuoso, -a [impe'twoso, a] *adj* impetuous; (*río*) rushing; (*acto*) hasty
impío, -a [im'pio, a] *adj* impious, ungodly; (*cruel*) cruel, pitiless
implacable [impla'kaβle] *adj* implacable, relentless
implantar [implan'tar] *vt* (*costumbre*) to introduce; (*Bio*) to implant; **implantarse** *vr* to be introduced
implemento [imple'mento] *nm* (*Am*) tool, implement
implicar [impli'kar] *vt* to involve; (*entrañar*) to imply; **esto no implica que ...** this does not mean that ...
implícito, -a [im'pliθito, a] *adj* (*tácito*) implicit; (*sobreentendido*) implied
implorar [implo'rar] *vt* to beg, implore
imponente [impo'nente] *adj* (*impresionante*) impressive, imposing; (*solemne*) grand ▷ *nm/f* (*Com*) depositor
imponer [impo'ner] *vt* (*gen*) to impose; (*tarea*) to set; (*exigir*) to exact; (*miedo*) to inspire;

(*Com*) to deposit; **imponerse** *vr* to assert o.s.; (*prevalecer*) to prevail; (*costumbre*) to grow up; **~se un deber** to assume a duty
imponible [impo'niβle] *adj* (*Com*) taxable, subject to tax; (*importación*) dutiable, subject to duty; **no ~** tax-free, tax-exempt (*US*)
impopular [impopu'lar] *adj* unpopular
importación [importa'θjon] *nf* (*acto*) importing; (*mercancías*) imports *pl*
importancia [impor'tanθja] *nf* importance; (*valor*) value, significance; (*extensión*) size, magnitude; **no dar ~ a** to consider unimportant; (*fig*) to make light of; **no tiene ~** it's nothing
importante [impor'tante] *adj* important; valuable, significant
importar [impor'tar] *vt* (*del extranjero*) to import; (*costar*) to amount to; (*implicar*) to involve ▷ *vi* to be important, matter; **me importa un rábano** *or* **un bledo** I couldn't care less, I don't give a damn; **¿le importa que fume?** do you mind if I smoke?; **¿te importa prestármelo?** would you mind lending it to me?; **¿qué importa?** what difference does it make?; **no importa** it doesn't matter; **no le importa** he doesn't care, it doesn't bother him; **"no importa precio"** "cost no object"
importe [im'porte] *nm* (*cantidad*) amount; (*valor*) value
importunar [importu'nar] *vt* to bother, pester
imposibilidad [imposiβili'ðað] *nf* impossibility; **mi ~ para hacerlo** my inability to do it
imposibilitar [imposiβili'tar] *vt* to make impossible, prevent
imposible [impo'siβle] *adj* impossible; (*insoportable*) unbearable, intolerable; **es ~** it's out of the question; **es ~ de predecir** it's impossible to forecast *o* predict
imposición [imposi'θjon] *nf* imposition; (*Com*) tax; (*inversión*) deposit; **efectuar una ~** to make a deposit
impostor, a [impos'tor, a] *nm/f* impostor
impotencia [impo'tenθja] *nf* impotence
impotente [impo'tente] *adj* impotent
impracticable [imprakti'kaβle] *adj* (*irrealizable*) impracticable; (*intransitable*) impassable
imprecar [impre'kar] *vi* to curse
impreciso, -a [impre'θiso, a] *adj* imprecise, vague
impregnar [impreɣ'nar] *vt* to impregnate; (*fig*) to pervade; **impregnarse** *vr* to become impregnated
imprenta [im'prenta] *nf* (*acto*) printing; (*aparato*) press; (*casa*) printer's; (*letra*) print
imprescindible [impresθin'diβle] *adj* essential, vital
impresión [impre'sjon] *nf* impression; (*Imprenta*) printing; (*edición*) edition; (*Foto*) print; (*marca*) imprint; **~ digital** fingerprint
impresionable [impresjo'naβle] *adj* (*sensible*) impressionable
impresionante [impresjo'nante] *adj* impressive; (*tremendo*) tremendous; (*maravilloso*) great, marvellous
impresionar [impresjo'nar] *vt* (*conmover*) to move; (*afectar*) to impress, strike; (*película fotográfica*) to expose; **impresionarse** *vr* to be impressed; (*conmoverse*) to be moved
impreso, -a [im'preso, a] *pp de* **imprimir** ▷ *adj* printed ▷ *nm* printed paper/book *etc*; **impresos** *nmpl* printed matter *sg*; **~ de solicitud** application form
impresora [impre'sora] *nf* (*Inform*) printer; **~ de chorro de tinta** ink-jet printer; **~ (por) láser** laser printer; **~ de línea** line printer
imprevisto, -a [impre'βisto, a] *adj* unforeseen; (*inesperado*) unexpected ▷ *nm*: **~s** (*dinero*) incidentals, unforeseen expenses
imprimir [impri'mir] *vt* to stamp; (*textos*) to print; (*Inform*) to output, print out
improbable [impro'βaβle] *adj* improbable; (*inverosímil*) unlikely
improcedente [improθe'ðente] *adj* inappropriate; (*Jur*) inadmissible
improductivo, -a [improðuk'tiβo, a] *adj* unproductive
improperio [impro'perjo] *nm* insult; **improperios** *nmpl* abuse *sg*
impropiedad [impropje'ðað] *nf* impropriety (of language)
impropio, -a [im'propjo, a] *adj* improper; (*inadecuado*) inappropriate
improvisación [improβisa'θjon] *nf* improvization
improvisado, -a [improβi'saðo, a] *adj* improvised, impromptu
improvisar [improβi'sar] *vt* to improvise; (*comida*) to rustle up ▷ *vi* to improvise; (*Mus*) to extemporize; (*Teat etc*) to ad-lib
improviso [impro'βiso] *adv*: **de ~** unexpectedly, suddenly; (*Mus etc*) impromptu
imprudencia [impru'ðenθja] *nf* imprudence; (*indiscreción*) indiscretion; (*descuido*) carelessness
imprudente [impru'ðente] *adj* unwise, imprudent; (*indiscreto*) indiscreet
impúdico, -a [im'puðiko, a] *adj* shameless; (*lujurioso*) lecherous
impudor [impu'ðor] *nm* shamelessness; (*lujuria*) lechery
impuesto, -a [im'pwesto, a] *pp de* **imponer** ▷ *adj* imposed ▷ *nm* tax; **anterior al ~** pre-tax; **sujeto a ~** taxable; **~ ambiental** green tax, environmental tax; **~ de lujo** luxury tax; **~ de plusvalía** capital gains tax; **~ sobre la propiedad** property tax; **~ sobre la renta** income tax; **~ sobre la renta de las personas físicas (IRPF)** personal income tax; **~ sobre la riqueza** wealth tax; **~ de transferencia de capital** capital transfer

tax; **~ de venta** sales tax; **~ sobre el valor añadido (IVA)** value added tax (VAT)
impugnar [impuɣ'nar] *vt* to oppose, contest; (*refutar*) to refute, impugn
impulsar [impul'sar] *vt* to drive; (*promover*) to promote, stimulate
impulsivo, -a [impul'siβo, a] *adj* impulsive
impulso [im'pulso] *nm* impulse; (*fuerza, empuje*) thrust, drive; (*fig: sentimiento*) urge, impulse; **a ~s del miedo** driven on by fear
impune [im'pune] *adj* unpunished
impureza [impu'reθa] *nf* impurity; (*fig*) lewdness
impuro, -a [im'puro, a] *adj* impure; lewd
imputar [impu'tar] *vt*: **~ a** to attribute to, to impute to
inacabable [inaka'βaβle] *adj* (*infinito*) endless; (*interminable*) interminable
inaccesible [inakθe'siβle] *adj* inaccessible; (*fig: precio*) beyond one's reach, prohibitive; (*individuo*) aloof
inacción [inak'θjon] *nf* inactivity
inaceptable [inaθep'taβle] *adj* unacceptable
inactividad [inaktiβi'ðað] *nf* inactivity; (*Com*) dullness
inactivo, -a [inak'tiβo, a] *adj* inactive; (*Com*) dull; (*población*) non-working
inadaptación [inaðapta'θjon] *nf* maladjustment
inadecuado, -a [inaðe'kwaðo, a] *adj* (*insuficiente*) inadequate; (*inapto*) unsuitable
inadmisible [inaðmi'siβle] *adj* inadmissible
inadvertido, -a [inaðβer'tiðo, a] *adj* (*no visto*) unnoticed
inagotable [inaɣo'taβle] *adj* inexhaustible
inaguantable [inaɣwan'taβle] *adj* unbearable
inalámbrico, -a [ina'lambriko, a] *adj* cordless, wireless
inalterable [inalte'raβle] *adj* immutable, unchangeable
inanición [inani'θjon] *nf* starvation
inanimado, -a [inani'maðo, a] *adj* inanimate
inapreciable [inapre'θjaβle] *adj* invaluable
inaudito, -a [inau'ðito, a] *adj* unheard-of
inauguración [inauɣura'θjon] *nf* inauguration; (*de exposición*) opening
inaugurar [inauɣu'rar] *vt* to inaugurate; (*exposición*) to open
inca ['inka] *nm/f* Inca
incaico, -a [in'kaiko, a] *adj* Inca
incalculable [inkalku'laβle] *adj* incalculable
incandescente [inkandes'θente] *adj* incandescent
incansable [inkan'saβle] *adj* tireless, untiring
incapacidad [inkapaθi'ðað] *nf* incapacity; (*incompetencia*) incompetence; **~ física/mental** physical/mental disability
incapacitar [inkapaθi'tar] *vt* (*inhabilitar*) to incapacitate, handicap; (*descalificar*) to disqualify
incapaz [inka'paθ] *adj* incapable; **~ de hacer algo** unable to do sth
incautación [inkauta'θjon] *nf* seizure, confiscation
incautarse [inkau'tarse] *vr*: **~ de** to seize, confiscate
incauto, -a [in'kauto, a] *adj* (*imprudente*) incautious, unwary
incendiar [inθen'djar] *vt* to set fire to; (*fig*) to inflame; **incendiarse** *vr* to catch fire
incendiario, -a [inθen'djarjo, a] *adj* incendiary ▷ *nm/f* fire-raiser, arsonist
incendio [in'θendjo] *nm* fire; **~ intencionado** arson
incentivo [inθen'tiβo] *nm* incentive
incertidumbre [inθerti'ðumbre] *nf* (*inseguridad*) uncertainty; (*duda*) doubt
incesante [inθe'sante] *adj* incessant
incesto [in'θesto] *nm* incest
incidencia [inθi'ðenθja] *nf* (*Mat*) incidence; (*fig*) effect
incidente [inθi'ðente] *nm* incident
incidir [inθi'ðir] *vi*: **~ en** (*influir*) to influence; (*afectar*) to affect; **~ en un error** to be mistaken
incienso [in'θjenso] *nm* incense
incierto, -a [in'θjerto, a] *adj* uncertain
incineración [inθinera'θjon] *nf* incineration; (*de cadáveres*) cremation
incinerar [inθine'rar] *vt* to burn; (*cadáveres*) to cremate
incipiente [inθi'pjente] *adj* incipient
incisión [inθi'sjon] *nf* incision
incisivo, -a [inθi'siβo, a] *adj* sharp, cutting; (*fig*) incisive
incitar [inθi'tar] *vt* to incite, rouse
incivil [inθi'βil] *adj* rude, uncivil
inclemencia [inkle'menθja] *nf* (*severidad*) harshness, severity; (*del tiempo*) inclemency
inclinación [inklina'θjon] *nf* (*gen*) inclination; (*de tierras*) slope, incline; (*de cabeza*) nod, bow; (*fig*) leaning, bent
inclinado, -a [inkli'naðo, a] *adj* (*objeto*) leaning; (*superficie*) sloping
inclinar [inkli'nar] *vt* to incline; (*cabeza*) to nod, bow; **inclinarse** *vi* to lean, slope ▷ *vr* to lean, slope; (*en reverencia*) to bow; (*encorvarse*) to stoop; **~se a** (*parecerse*) to take after, resemble; **~se ante** to bow down to; **me inclino a pensar que ...** I'm inclined to think that ...
incluir [inklu'ir] *vt* to include; (*incorporar*) to incorporate; (*meter*) to enclose; **todo incluido** (*Com*) inclusive, all-in
inclusive [inklu'siβe] *adv* inclusive ▷ *prep* including
incluso, -a [in'kluso, a] *adj* included ▷ *adv* inclusively; (*hasta*) even
incógnita [in'koɣnita] *nf* (*Mat*) unknown quantity; (*fig*) mystery
incógnito [in'koɣnito] *nm*: **de ~** incognito
incoherente [inkoe'rente] *adj* incoherent

incoloro, -a [inko'loro, a] *adj* colourless
incólume [in'kolume] *adj* safe; (*indemne*) unhurt, unharmed
incomodar [inkomo'ðar] *vt* to inconvenience; (*molestar*) to bother, trouble; (*fastidiar*) to annoy; **incomodarse** *vr* to put o.s. out; (*fastidiarse*) to get annoyed; **no se incomode** don't bother
incomodidad [inkomoði'ðað] *nf* inconvenience; (*fastidio, enojo*) annoyance; (*de vivienda*) discomfort
incómodo, -a [in'komoðo, a] *adj* (*inconfortable*) uncomfortable; (*molesto*) annoying; (*inconveniente*) inconvenient; **sentirse ~** to feel ill at ease
incomparable [inkompa'raβle] *adj* incomparable
incompatible [inkompa'tiβle] *adj* incompatible
incompetencia [inkompe'tenθja] *nf* incompetence
incompetente [inkompe'tente] *adj* incompetent
incompleto, -a [inkom'pleto, a] *adj* incomplete, unfinished
incomprendido, -a [inkompren'diðo, a] *adj* misunderstood
incomprensible [inkompren'siβle] *adj* incomprehensible
incomunicado, -a [inkomuni'kaðo, a] *adj* (*aislado*) cut off, isolated; (*confinado*) in solitary confinement
inconcebible [inkonθe'βiβle] *adj* inconceivable
inconcluso, -a [inkon'kluso, a] *adj* (*inacabado*) unfinished
incondicional [inkondiθjo'nal] *adj* unconditional; (*apoyo*) wholehearted; (*partidario*) staunch
inconexo, -a [inko'nekso, a] *adj* unconnected; (*desunido*) disconnected; (*incoherente*) incoherent
inconformista [inkonfor'mista] *adj, nm/f* nonconformist
inconfundible [inkonfun'diβle] *adj* unmistakable
incongruente [inkon'grwente] *adj* incongruous
inconmensurable [inkonmensu'raβle] *adj* immeasurable, vast
inconsciencia [inkons'θjenθja] *nf* unconsciousness; (*fig*) thoughtlessness
inconsciente [inkons'θjente] *adj* unconscious; thoughtless; (*ignorante*) unaware; (*involuntario*) unwitting
inconsecuente [inkonse'kwente] *adj* inconsistent
inconsiderado, -a [inkonsiðe'raðo, a] *adj* inconsiderate
inconsistente [inkonsis'tente] *adj* inconsistent; (*Culin*) lumpy; (*endeble*) weak; (*tela*) flimsy
inconstancia [inkons'tanθja] *nf* inconstancy; (*de tiempo*) changeability; (*capricho*) fickleness
inconstante [inkons'tante] *adj* inconstant; changeable; fickle
incontable [inkon'taβle] *adj* countless, innumerable
incontestable [inkontes'taβle] *adj* unanswerable; (*innegable*) undeniable
incontinencia [inkonti'nenθja] *nf* incontinence
inconveniencia [inkombe'njenθja] *nf* unsuitability, inappropriateness; (*falta de cortesía*) impoliteness
inconveniente [inkombe'njente] *adj* unsuitable; impolite ▷ *nm* obstacle; (*desventaja*) disadvantage; **el ~ es que ...** the trouble is that ...; **no hay ~ en** *o* **para hacer eso** there is no objection to doing that; **no tengo ~** I don't mind
incordiar [inkor'ðjar] *vt* (*fam*) to hassle
incorporación [inkorpora'θjon] *nf* incorporation; (*fig*) inclusion
incorporar [inkorpo'rar] *vt* to incorporate; (*abarcar*) to embody; (*Culin*) to mix; **incorporarse** *vr* to sit up; **~se a** to join
incorrección [inkorrek'θjon] *nf* incorrectness, inaccuracy; (*descortesía*) bad-mannered behaviour
incorrecto, -a [inko'rrekto, a] *adj* incorrect, wrong; (*comportamiento*) bad-mannered
incorregible [inkorre'xiβle] *adj* incorrigible
incredulidad [inkreðuli'ðað] *nf* incredulity; (*escepticismo*) scepticism
incrédulo, -a [in'kreðulo, a] *adj* incredulous, unbelieving; sceptical
increíble [inkre'iβle] *adj* incredible
incremento [inkre'mento] *nm* increment; (*aumento*) rise, increase; **~ de precio** rise in price
increpar [inkre'par] *vt* to reprimand
incruento, -a [in'krwento, a] *adj* bloodless
incrustar [inkrus'tar] *vt* to incrust; (*piedras: en joya*) to inlay; (*fig*) to graft; (*Tec*) to set
incubar [inku'βar] *vt* to incubate; (*fig*) to hatch
inculcar [inkul'kar] *vt* to inculcate
inculpar [inkul'par] *vt*: **~ de** (*acusar*) to accuse of; (*achacar, atribuir*) to charge with, blame for
inculto, -a [in'kulto, a] *adj* (*persona*) uneducated, uncultured; (*fig: grosero*) uncouth ▷ *nm/f* ignoramus
incumplimiento [inkumpli'mjento] *nm* non-fulfilment; (*Com*) repudiation; **~ de contrato** breach of contract; **por ~** by default
incurable [inku'raβle] *adj* (*enfermedad*) incurable; (*paciente*) incurably ill
incurrir [inku'rrir] *vi*: **~ en** to incur; (*crimen*) to commit; **~ en un error** to make a mistake
indagación [indaɣa'θjon] *nf* investigation; (*búsqueda*) search; (*Jur*) inquest

indagar [inda'ɣar] *vt* to investigate; to search; (*averiguar*) to ascertain
indecencia [inde'θenθja] *nf* indecency; (*dicho*) obscenity
indecente [inde'θente] *adj* indecent, improper; (*lascivo*) obscene
indecible [inde'θiβle] *adj* unspeakable; (*indescriptible*) indescribable
indeciso, -a [inde'θiso, a] *adj* (*por decidir*) undecided; (*vacilante*) hesitant
indefenso, -a [inde'fenso, a] *adj* defenceless
indefinido, -a [indefi'niðo, a] *adj* indefinite; (*vago*) vague, undefined
indeleble [inde'leβle] *adj* indelible
indemne [in'demne] *adj* (*objeto*) undamaged; (*persona*) unharmed, unhurt
indemnizar [indemni'θar] *vt* to indemnify; (*compensar*) to compensate
independencia [indepen'denθja] *nf* independence
independiente [indepen'djente] *adj* (*libre*) independent; (*autónomo*) self-sufficient; (*Inform*) stand alone
indeseable [indese'aβle] *adj, nm/f* undesirable
indeterminado, -a [indetermi'naðo, a] *adj* (*tb Ling*) indefinite; (*desconocido*) indeterminate
India ['india] *nf*: **la ~** India
indicación [indika'θjon] *nf* indication; (*dato*) piece of information; (*señal*) sign; (*sugerencia*) suggestion, hint; **indicaciones** *nfpl* (*Com*) instructions
indicado, -a [indi'kaðo, a] *adj* (*momento, método*) right; (*tratamiento*) appropriate; (*solución*) likely
indicador [indika'ðor] *nm* indicator; (*Tec*) gauge, meter; (*aguja*) hand, pointer; (*de carretera*) road sign; **~ de encendido** (*Inform*) power-on indicator
indicar [indi'kar] *vt* (*mostrar*) to indicate, show; (*suj*: *termómetro etc*) to read, register; (*señalar*) to point to
indicativo, -a [indika'tiβo, a] *adj* indicative ▷ *nm* (*Radio*) call sign; **~ de nacionalidad** (*Auto*) national identification plate
índice ['indiθe] *nm* index; (*catálogo*) catalogue; (*Anat*) index finger, forefinger; **~ del coste de (la) vida** cost-of-living index; **~ de crédito** credit rating; **~ de materias** table of contents; **~ de natalidad** birth rate; **~ de precios al por menor (IPM)** (*Com*) retail price index (RPI)
indicio [in'diθjo] *nm* indication, sign; (*en pesquisa etc*) clue
indiferencia [indife'renθja] *nf* indifference; (*apatía*) apathy
indiferente [indife'rente] *adj* indifferent; **me es ~** it makes no difference to me
indígena [in'dixena] *adj* indigenous, native ▷ *nm/f* native
indigencia [indi'xenθja] *nf* poverty, need
indigestión [indixes'tjon] *nf* indigestion
indigesto, -a [indi'xesto, a] *adj* undigested; (*indigerible*) indigestible; (*fig*) turgid
indignación [indiɣna'θjon] *nf* indignation
indignar [indiɣ'nar] *vt* to anger, make indignant; **indignarse** *vr*: **~se por** to get indignant about
indigno, -a [in'diɣno, a] *adj* (*despreciable*) low, contemptible; (*inmerecido*) unworthy
indio, -a ['indjo, a] *adj, nm/f* Indian
indirecto, -a [indi'rekto, a] *adj* indirect ▷ *nf* insinuation, innuendo; (*sugerencia*) hint
indiscreción [indiskre'θjon] *nf* (*imprudencia*) indiscretion; (*irreflexión*) tactlessness; (*acto*) gaffe, faux pas; **..., si no es ~ ...**, if I may say so
indiscreto, -a [indis'kreto, a] *adj* indiscreet
indiscriminado, -a [indiskrimi'naðo, a] *adj* indiscriminate
indiscutible [indisku'tiβle] *adj* indisputable, unquestionable
indispensable [indispen'saβle] *adj* indispensable, essential
indisponer [indispo'ner] *vt* to spoil, upset; (*salud*) to make ill; **indisponerse** *vr* to fall ill; **~se con algn** to fall out with sb
indisposición [indisposi'θjon] *nf* indisposition; (*desgana*) unwillingness
indispuesto, -a [indis'pwesto, a] *pp de* **indisponer** ▷ *adj* (*enfermo*) unwell, indisposed; **sentirse ~** to feel unwell *o* indisposed
indistinto, -a [indis'tinto, a] *adj* indistinct; (*vago*) vague
individual [indiβi'ðwal] *adj* individual; (*habitación*) single ▷ *nm* (*Deporte*) singles *sg*
individuo, -a [indi'βiðwo, a] *adj* individual ▷ *nm* individual
índole ['indole] *nf* (*naturaleza*) nature; (*clase*) sort, kind
indolencia [indo'lenθja] *nf* indolence, laziness
indomable [indo'maβle] *adj* (*animal*) untameable; (*espíritu*) indomitable
indómito, -a [in'domito, a] *adj* indomitable
inducir [indu'θir] *vt* to induce; (*inferir*) to infer; (*persuadir*) to persuade; **~ a algn en el error** to mislead sb
indudable [indu'ðaβle] *adj* undoubted; (*incuestionable*) unquestionable; **es ~ que ...** there is no doubt that ...
indulgencia [indul'xenθja] *nf* indulgence; (*Jur etc*) leniency; **proceder sin ~ contra** to proceed ruthlessly against
indultar [indul'tar] *vt* (*perdonar*) to pardon, reprieve; (*librar de pago*) to exempt
indulto [in'dulto] *nm* pardon; exemption
industria [in'dustrja] *nf* industry; (*habilidad*) skill; **~ agropecuaria** farming and fishing; **~ pesada** heavy industry; **~ petrolífera** oil industry
industrial [indus'trjal] *adj* industrial ▷ *nm* industrialist

industrializar [industrjali'θar] *vt* to industrialize; **industrializarse** *vr* to become industrialized
inédito, -a [i'neðito, a] *adj* (*libro*) unpublished; (*nuevo*) new
inefable [ine'faβle] *adj* ineffable, indescribable
ineficaz [inefi'kaθ] *adj* (*inútil*) ineffective; (*ineficiente*) inefficient
ineludible [inelu'ðiβle] *adj* inescapable, unavoidable
ineptitud [inepti'tuð] *nf* ineptitude, incompetence
inepto, -a [i'nepto, a] *adj* inept, incompetent
inequívoco, -a [ine'kiβoko, a] *adj* unequivocal; (*inconfundible*) unmistakable
inercia [i'nerθja] *nf* inertia; (*pasividad*) passivity
inerme [i'nerme] *adj* (*sin armas*) unarmed; (*indefenso*) defenceless
inerte [i'nerte] *adj* inert; (*inmóvil*) motionless
inescrutable [ineskru'taβle] *adj* inscrutable
inesperado, -a [inespe'raðo, a] *adj* unexpected, unforeseen
inestable [ines'taβle] *adj* unstable
inestimable [inesti'maβle] *adj* inestimable; **de valor ~** invaluable
inevitable [ineβi'taβle] *adj* inevitable
inexactitud [ineksakti'tuð] *nf* inaccuracy
inexacto, -a [inek'sakto, a] *adj* inaccurate; (*falso*) untrue
inexorable [inekso'raβle] *adj* inexorable
inexperto, -a [ineks'perto, a] *adj* (*novato*) inexperienced
infalible [infa'liβle] *adj* infallible; (*indefectible*) certain, sure; (*plan*) foolproof
infame [in'fame] *adj* infamous
infamia [in'famja] *nf* infamy; (*deshonra*) disgrace
infancia [in'fanθja] *nf* infancy, childhood; **jardín de la ~** nursery school
infante [in'fante] *nm* (*hijo del rey*) infante, prince
infantería [infante'ria] *nf* infantry
infantil [infan'til] *adj* child's, children's; (*pueril, aniñado*) infantile; (*cándido*) childlike
infarto [in'farto] *nm* (*tb*: **~ de miocardio**) heart attack
infatigable [infati'ɣaβle] *adj* tireless, untiring
infección [infek'θjon] *nf* infection
infeccioso, -a [infek'θjoso, a] *adj* infectious
infectar [infek'tar] *vt* to infect; **infectarse** *vr*: **~se (de)** (*tb fig*) to become infected (with)
infeliz [infe'liθ] *adj* (*desgraciado*) unhappy, wretched; (*inocente*) gullible ▷ *nm/f* (*desgraciado*) wretch; (*inocentón*) simpleton
inferior [infe'rjor] *adj* inferior; (*situación, Mat*) lower ▷ *nm/f* inferior, subordinate; **cualquier número ~ a nueve** any number less than *o* under *o* below nine; **una cantidad ~** a lesser quantity
inferioridad [inferjori'ðað] *nf* inferiority; **estar en ~ de condiciones** to be at a disadvantage
inferir [infe'rir] *vt* (*deducir*) to infer, deduce; (*causar*) to cause
infernal [infer'nal] *adj* infernal
infestar [infes'tar] *vt* to infest
infidelidad [infiðeli'ðað] *nf* infidelity, unfaithfulness
infiel [in'fjel] *adj* unfaithful, disloyal; (*falso*) inaccurate ▷ *nm/f* infidel, unbeliever
infierno [in'fjerno] *nm* hell; **¡vete al ~!** go to hell; **está en el quinto ~** it's at the back of beyond
infiltrar [infil'trar] *vt* to infiltrate; **infiltrarse** *vr* to infiltrate; **~se en** to infiltrate in(to); (*persona*) to work one's way in(to)
ínfimo, -a ['infimo, a] *adj* (*vil*) vile, mean; (*más bajo*) lowest; (*peor*) worst; (*miserable*) wretched
infinidad [infini'ðað] *nf* infinity; (*abundancia*) great quantity; **~ de** vast numbers of; **~ de veces** countless times
infinitivo [infini'tiβo] *nm* infinitive
infinito, -a [infi'nito, a] *adj* infinite; (*fig*) boundless ▷ *adv* infinitely ▷ *nm* infinite; (*Mat*) infinity; **hasta lo ~** ad infinitum
inflación [infla'θjon] *nf* (*hinchazón*) swelling; (*monetaria*) inflation; (*fig*) conceit
inflacionario, -a [inflaθjo'narjo, a] *adj* inflationary
inflamable [infla'maβle] *adj* flammable
inflamar [infla'mar] *vt* to set on fire; (*Med, fig*) to inflame; **inflamarse** *vr* to catch fire; to become inflamed
inflar [in'flar] *vt* (*hinchar*) to inflate, blow up; (*fig*) to exaggerate; **inflarse** *vr* to swell (up); (*fig*) to get conceited
inflexible [inflek'siβle] *adj* inflexible; (*fig*) unbending
infligir [infli'xir] *vt* to inflict
influencia [in'flwenθja] *nf* influence
influenciar [inflwen'θjar] *vt* to influence
influir [influ'ir] *vt* to influence ▷ *vi* to have influence, carry weight; **~ en** *o* **sobre** to influence, affect; (*contribuir a*) to have a hand in
influjo [in'fluxo] *nm* influence; **~ de capitales** (*Econ etc*) capital influx
influya *etc vb ver* **influir**
influyente [influ'jente] *adj* influential
información [informa'θjon] *nf* information; (*noticias*) news *sg*; (*informe*) report; (*Inform: datos*) data; (*Jur*) inquiry; **I~** (*oficina*) information desk; (*Telec*) Directory Enquiries (*Brit*), Directory Assistance (*US*); (*mostrador*) Information Desk; **una ~** a piece of information; **abrir una ~** (*Jur*) to begin proceedings; **~ deportiva** (*en periódico*) sports section
informal [infor'mal] *adj* informal
informante [infor'mante] *nm/f* informant

informar [infor'mar] *vt* (*gen*) to inform; (*revelar*) to reveal, make known ▷ *vi* (*Jur*) to plead; (*denunciar*) to inform; (*dar cuenta de*) to report on; **informarse** *vr* to find out; **~se de** to inquire into

informática [infor'matika] *nf ver* **informático**

informático, -a [infor'matiko, a] *adj* computer *cpd* ▷ *nf* (*Tec*) information technology; computing; (*Escol*) computer science *o* studies; **~ de gestión** commercial computing

informativo, -a [informa'tiβo, a] *adj* (*libro*) informative; (*folleto*) information *cpd*; (*Radio, TV*) news *cpd* ▷ *nm* (*Radio, TV*) news programme

informe [in'forme] *adj* shapeless ▷ *nm* report; (*dictamen*) statement; (*Mil*) briefing; (*Jur*) plea; **informes** *nmpl* information *sg*; (*datos*) data; **~ anual** annual report; **~ del juez** summing-up

infortunio [infor'tunjo] *nm* misfortune

infracción [infrak'θjon] *nf* infraction, infringement; (*Auto*) offence

in fraganti [infra'ɣanti] *adv*: **pillar a algn ~** to catch sb red-handed

infranqueable [infranke'aβle] *adj* impassable; (*fig*) insurmountable

infravalorar [infraβalo'rar] *vt* to undervalue; (*Finanzas*) to underestimate

infringir [infrin'xir] *vt* to infringe, contravene

infructuoso, -a [infruk'twoso, a] *adj* fruitless, unsuccessful

infundado, -a [infun'daðo, a] *adj* groundless, unfounded

infundir [infun'dir] *vt* to infuse, instil; **~ ánimo a algn** to encourage sb; **~ miedo a algn** to intimidate sb

infusión [infu'sjon] *nf* infusion; **~ de manzanilla** camomile tea

ingeniar [inxe'njar] *vt* to think up, devise; **ingeniarse** *vr* to manage; **~se para** to manage to

ingeniería [inxenje'ria] *nf* engineering; **~ genética** genetic engineering; **~ de sistemas** (*Inform*) systems engineering

ingeniero, -a [inxe'njero, a] *nm/f* engineer; (*Am*) courtesy title; **~ de sonido** sound engineer; **~ de caminos** civil engineer

ingenio [in'xenjo] *nm* (*talento*) talent; (*agudeza*) wit; (*habilidad*) ingenuity, inventiveness; (*Tec*): **~ azucarero** sugar refinery

ingenioso, -a [inxe'njoso, a] *adj* ingenious, clever; (*divertido*) witty

ingenuidad [inxenwi'ðað] *nf* ingenuousness; (*sencillez*) simplicity

ingenuo, -a [in'xenwo, a] *adj* ingenuous

ingerir [inxe'rir] *vt* to ingest; (*tragar*) to swallow; (*consumir*) to consume

Inglaterra [ingla'terra] *nf* England

ingle ['ingle] *nf* groin

inglés, -esa [in'gles, esa] *adj* English ▷ *nm/f* Englishman(-woman) ▷ *nm* (*Ling*) English; **los ingleses** the English

ingratitud [ingrati'tuð] *nf* ingratitude

ingrato, -a [in'grato, a] *adj* ungrateful; (*tarea*) thankless

ingrediente [ingre'ðjente] *nm* ingredient; **ingredientes** *nmpl* (*Am: tapas*) titbits

ingresar [ingre'sar] *vt* (*dinero*) to deposit ▷ *vi* to come *o* go in; **~ a** (*esp Am*) to enter; **~ en** (*club*) to join; (*Mil, Escol*) to enrol in; **~ en el hospital** to go into hospital

ingreso [in'greso] *nm* (*entrada*) entry; (*: en hospital etc*) admission; (*Mil, Escol*) enrolment; **ingresos** *nmpl* (*dinero*) income *sg*; (*: Com*) takings *pl*; **~ gravable** taxable income *sg*; **~s accesorios** fringe benefits; **~s brutos** gross receipts; **~s devengados** earned income *sg*; **~s exentos de impuestos** non-taxable income *sg*; **~s personales disponibles** disposable personal income *sg*

inhabilitar [inaβili'tar] *vt* (*Pol, Med*): **~ a algn (para hacer algo)** to disqualify sb (from doing sth)

inhabitable [inaβi'taβle] *adj* uninhabitable

inhalar [ina'lar] *vt* to inhale

inherente [ine'rente] *adj* inherent

inhibir [ini'βir] *vt* to inhibit; (*Rel*) to restrain; **inhibirse** *vr* to keep out

inhóspito, -a [i'nospito, a] *adj* (*región, paisaje*) inhospitable

inhumano, -a [inu'mano, a] *adj* inhuman

inicial [ini'θjal] *adj, nf* initial

iniciar [ini'θjar] *vt* (*persona*) to initiate; (*empezar*) to begin, commence; (*conversación*) to start up; **~ a algn en un secreto** to let sb into a secret; **~ la sesión** (*Inform*) to log in *o* on

iniciativa [iniθja'tiβa] *nf* initiative; (*liderazgo*) leadership; **~ privada** private enterprise

inicio [i'niθjo] *nm* start, beginning

inicuo, -a [i'nikwo, a] *adj* iniquitous

ininterrumpido, -a [ininterrum'piðo, a] *adj* uninterrupted; (*proceso*) continuous; (*progreso*) steady

injerencia [inxe'renθja] *nf* interference

injertar [inxer'tar] *vt* to graft

injerto [in'xerto] *nm* graft; **~ de piel** skin graft

injuria [in'xurja] *nf* (*agravio, ofensa*) offence; (*insulto*) insult; **injurias** *nfpl* abuse *sg*

injuriar [inxu'rjar] *vt* to insult

injurioso, -a [inxu'rjoso, a] *adj* offensive; insulting

injusticia [inxus'tiθja] *nf* injustice, unfairness; **con ~** unjustly

injusto, -a [in'xusto, a] *adj* unjust, unfair

inmadurez [inmaðu'reθ] *nf* immaturity

inmaduro, -a [inma'ðuro, a] *adj* immature; (*fruta*) unripe

i

inmediaciones [inmeðja'θjones] *nfpl* neighbourhood *sg*, environs
inmediatamente [in meðjata'mente] *adv* immediately
inmediato, -a [inme'ðjato, a] *adj* immediate; (*contiguo*) adjoining; (*rápido*) prompt; (*próximo*) neighbouring, next; **de ~** (*esp Am*) immediately
inmejorable [inmexo'raβle] *adj* unsurpassable; (*precio*) unbeatable
inmenso, -a [in'menso, a] *adj* immense, huge
inmerecido, -a [inmere'θiðo, a] *adj* undeserved
inmigración [inmiɣra'θjon] *nf* immigration
inmigrante [inmi'ɣrante] *adj, nm/f* immigrant
inminente [inmi'nente] *adj* imminent, impending
inmiscuirse [inmisku'irse] *vr* to interfere, meddle
inmobiliario, -a [inmoβi'ljarjo, a] *adj* real-estate *cpd*, property *cpd* ▷ *nf* estate agency
inmolar [inmo'lar] *vt* to immolate, sacrifice
inmoral [inmo'ral] *adj* immoral
inmortal [inmor'tal] *adj* immortal
inmortalizar [inmortali'θar] *vt* to immortalize
inmóvil [in'moβil] *adj* immobile
inmovilizar [inmoβili'θar] *vt* to immobilize; (*paralizar*) to paralyse; **inmovilizarse** *vr*: **se le ha inmovilizado la pierna** her leg was paralysed
inmueble [in'mweβle] *adj*: **bienes ~s** real estate *sg*, landed property *sg* ▷ *nm* property
inmundicia [inmun'diθja] *nf* filth
inmundo, -a [in'mundo, a] *adj* filthy
inmune [in'mune] *adj*: **~ (a)** (*Med*) immune (to)
inmunidad [inmuni'ðað] *nf* immunity; (*fisco*) exemption; **~ diplomática/parlamentaria** diplomatic/parliamentary immunity
inmunitario, -a [inmuni'tarjo, a] *adj*: **sistema ~** immune system
inmunización [inmuniθa'θjon] *nf* immunization
inmunizar [inmuni'θar] *vt* to immunize
inmutable [inmu'taβle] *adj* immutable; **permaneció ~** he didn't flinch
inmutarse [inmu'tarse] *vr* to turn pale; **no se inmutó** he didn't turn a hair; **siguió sin ~** he carried on unperturbed
innato, -a [in'nato, a] *adj* innate
innecesario, -a [inneθe'sarjo, a] *adj* unnecessary
innoble [in'noβle] *adj* ignoble
innovación [innoβa'θjon] *nf* innovation
innovar [inno'βar] *vt* to introduce
inocencia [ino'θenθja] *nf* innocence
inocentada [inoθen'taða] *nf* practical joke
inocente [ino'θente] *adj* (*ingenuo*) naive, innocent; (*no culpable*) innocent; (*sin malicia*) harmless ▷ *nm/f* simpleton; **día de los (Santos) I~s** ≈ April Fools' Day; *see note*

DÍA DE LOS INOCENTES

The 28th December, *el día de los (Santos) Inocentes*, is when the Church commemorates the story of Herod's slaughter of the innocent children of Judea in the time of Christ. On this day Spaniards play *inocentadas* (practical jokes) on each other, much like our April Fools' Day pranks, eg typically sticking a *monigote* (cut-out paper figure) on someone's back, or broadcasting unlikely news stories.

inodoro, -a [ino'ðoro, a] *adj* odourless ▷ *nm* toilet (*Brit*), lavatory (*Brit*), washroom (*US*)
inofensivo, -a [inofen'siβo, a] *adj* inoffensive
inolvidable [inolβi'ðaβle] *adj* unforgettable
inoperante [inope'rante] *adj* ineffective
inopinado, -a [inopi'naðo, a] *adj* unexpected
inoportuno, -a [inopor'tuno, a] *adj* untimely; (*molesto*) inconvenient; (*inapropiado*) inappropriate
inoxidable [inoksi'ðaβle] *adj* stainless; **acero ~** stainless steel
inquebrantable [inkeβran'taβle] *adj* unbreakable; (*fig*) unshakeable
inquietar [inkje'tar] *vt* to worry, trouble; **inquietarse** *vr* to worry, get upset
inquieto, -a [in'kjeto, a] *adj* anxious, worried; **estar ~ por** to be worried about
inquietud [inkje'tuð] *nf* anxiety, worry
inquilino, -a [inki'lino, a] *nm/f* tenant; (*Com*) lessee
inquirir [inki'rir] *vt* to enquire into, investigate
insaciable [insa'θjaβle] *adj* insatiable
insalubre [insa'luβre] *adj* unhealthy; (*condiciones*) insanitary
inscribir [inskri'βir] *vt* to inscribe; (*en lista*) to put; (*en censo*) to register; **inscribirse** *vr* to register; (*Escol etc*) to enrol
inscripción [inskrip'θjon] *nf* inscription; (*Escol etc*) enrolment; (*en censo*) registration
insecticida [insekti'θiða] *nm* insecticide
insecto [in'sekto] *nm* insect
inseguridad [inseɣuri'ðað] *nf* insecurity; **~ ciudadana** lack of safety in the streets
inseguro, -a [inse'ɣuro, a] *adj* insecure; (*inconstante*) unsteady; (*incierto*) uncertain
inseminación [insemina'θjon] *nf*: **~ artificial** artificial insemination (A.I.)
insensato, -a [insen'sato, a] *adj* foolish, stupid
insensibilidad [insensiβili'ðað] *nf* (*gen*) insensitivity; (*dureza de corazón*) callousness

insensible [insen'siβle] *adj* (*gen*) insensitive; (*movimiento*) imperceptible; (*sin sensación*) numb
inseparable [insepa'raβle] *adj* inseparable
insertar [inser'tar] *vt* to insert
inservible [inser'βiβle] *adj* useless
insidioso, -a [insi'ðjoso, a] *adj* insidious
insignia [in'siɣnja] *nf* (*señal distintiva*) badge; (*estandarte*) flag
insignificante [insiɣnifi'kante] *adj* insignificant
insinuar [insi'nwar] *vt* to insinuate, imply; **insinuarse** *vr*: **~se con algn** to ingratiate o.s. with sb
insípido, -a [in'sipiðo, a] *adj* insipid
insistencia [insis'tenθja] *nf* insistence
insistir [insis'tir] *vi* to insist; **~ en algo** to insist on sth; (*enfatizar*) to stress sth
in situ [in'situ] *adv* on the spot, in situ
insociable [inso'θjaβle] *adj* unsociable
insolación [insola'θjon] *nf* (*Med*) sunstroke
insolencia [inso'lenθja] *nf* insolence
insolente [inso'lente] *adj* insolent
insólito, -a [in'solito, a] *adj* unusual
insoluble [inso'luβle] *adj* insoluble
insolvencia [insol'βenθja] *nf* insolvency
insomnio [in'somnjo] *nm* insomnia
insondable [inson'daβle] *adj* bottomless
insonorizado, -a [insonori'θaðo, a] *adj* (*cuarto etc*) soundproof
insoportable [insopor'taβle] *adj* unbearable
insospechado, -a [insospe'tʃaðo, a] *adj* (*inesperado*) unexpected
inspección [inspek'θjon] *nf* inspection, check; **I~** inspectorate; **~ técnica (de vehículos)** ≈ MOT (test) (*Brit*)
inspeccionar [inspekθjo'nar] *vt* (*examinar*) to inspect, examine; (*controlar*) to check
inspector, a [inspek'tor, a] *nm/f* inspector
inspiración [inspira'θjon] *nf* inspiration
inspirar [inspi'rar] *vt* to inspire; (*Med*) to inhale; **inspirarse** *vr*: **~se en** to be inspired by
instalación [instala'θjon] *nf* (*equipo*) fittings *pl*, equipment; **~ eléctrica** wiring
instalar [insta'lar] *vt* (*establecer*) to instal; (*erguir*) to set up, erect; **instalarse** *vr* to establish o.s.; (*en una vivienda*) to move into
instancia [ins'tanθja] *nf* (*solicitud*) application; (*ruego*) request; (*Jur*) petition; **a ~ de** at the request of; **en última ~** as a last resort
instantáneo, -a [instan'taneo, a] *adj* instantaneous ▷ *nf* snap(shot); **café ~** instant coffee
instante [ins'tante] *nm* instant, moment; **al ~** right now; **en un ~** in a flash
instar [ins'tar] *vt* to press, urge
instaurar [instau'rar] *vt* (*costumbre*) to establish; (*normas, sistema*) to bring in, introduce; (*gobierno*) to install
instigar [insti'ɣar] *vt* to instigate
instinto [ins'tinto] *nm* instinct; **por ~** instinctively
institución [institu'θjon] *nf* institution, establishment; **~ benéfica** charitable foundation
instituir [institu'ir] *vt* to establish; (*fundar*) to found
instituto [insti'tuto] *nm* (*gen*) institute; **I~ Nacional de Enseñanza** (*Esp*) ≈ comprehensive (*Brit*) *o* high (*US*) school; **I~ Nacional de Industria (INI)** (*Esp Com*) ≈ National Enterprise Board (*Brit*)
institutriz [institu'triθ] *nf* governess
instrucción [instruk'θjon] *nf* instruction; (*enseñanza*) education, teaching; (*Jur*) proceedings *pl*; (*Mil*) training; (*Deporte*) coaching; (*conocimientos*) knowledge; (*Inform*) statement; **instrucciones para el uso** directions for use; **instrucciones de funcionamiento** operating instructions
instructivo, -a [instruk'tiβo, a] *adj* instructive
instructor [instruk'tor] *nm* instructor
instruir [instru'ir] *vt* (*gen*) to instruct; (*enseñar*) to teach, educate; (*Jur*: *proceso*) to prepare, draw up; **instruirse** *vr* to learn, teach o.s.
instrumento [instru'mento] *nm* (*gen, Mus*) instrument; (*herramienta*) tool, implement; (*Com*) indenture; (*Jur*) legal document; **~ de percusión/cuerda/viento** percussion/string(ed)/wind instrument
insubordinarse [insuβorði'narse] *vr* to rebel
insuficiencia [insufi'θjenθja] *nf* (*carencia*) lack; (*inadecuación*) inadequacy; **~ cardíaca/renal** heart/kidney failure
insuficiente [insufi'θjente] *adj* (*gen*) insufficient; (*Escol*: *nota*) unsatisfactory
insufrible [insu'friβle] *adj* insufferable
insular [insu'lar] *adj* insular
insulina [insu'lina] *nf* insulin
insultar [insul'tar] *vt* to insult
insulto [in'sulto] *nm* insult
insumisión [insumi'sjon] *nf* *refusal to do military service or community service*
insumiso, -a [insu'miso, a] *adj* (*rebelde*) rebellious ▷ *nm/f* (*Pol*) *person who refuses to do military service or community service*; *ver tb* **mili**
insuperable [insupe'raβle] *adj* (*excelente*) unsurpassable; (*problema etc*) insurmountable
insurgente [insur'xente] *adj, nm/f* insurgent
insurrección [insurrek'θjon] *nf* insurrection, rebellion
intachable [inta'tʃaβle] *adj* irreproachable
intacto, -a [in'takto, a] *adj* (*sin tocar*) untouched; (*entero*) intact
integral [inte'ɣral] *adj* integral; (*completo*) complete; (*Tec*) built-in; **pan ~** wholemeal bread
integrar [inte'ɣrar] *vt* to make up, compose; (*Mat, fig*) to integrate

integridad [inteɣri'ðað] *nf* wholeness; (*carácter, tb Inform*) integrity; **en su ~** completely
integrismo [inte'ɣrismo] *nm* fundamentalism
integrista [inte'ɣrista] *adj, nm/f* fundamentalist
íntegro, -a ['inteɣro, a] *adj* whole, entire; (*texto*) uncut, unabridged; (*honrado*) honest
intelectual [intelek'twal] *adj, nm/f* intellectual
inteligencia [inteli'xenθja] *nf* intelligence; (*ingenio*) ability; **~ artificial** artificial intelligence
inteligente [inteli'xente] *adj* intelligent
inteligible [inteli'xiβle] *adj* intelligible
intemperie [intem'perje] *nf*: **a la ~** outdoors, out in the open, exposed to the elements
intempestivo, -a [intempes'tiβo, a] *adj* untimely
intención [inten'θjon] *nf* intention, purpose; **con segundas intenciones** maliciously; **con ~** deliberately
intencionado, -a [intenθjo'naðo, a] *adj* deliberate; **bien ~** well-meaning; **mal ~** ill-disposed, hostile
intensidad [intensi'ðað] *nf* (*gen*) intensity; (*Elec, Tec*) strength; (*de recuerdo*) vividness; **llover con ~** to rain hard
intensivo, -a [inten'siβo, a] *adj* intensive; **curso ~** crash course
intenso, -a [in'tenso, a] *adj* intense; (*impresión*) vivid; (*sentimiento*) profound, deep
intentar [inten'tar] *vt* (*tratar*) to try, attempt
intento [in'tento] *nm* (*intención*) intention, purpose; (*tentativa*) attempt
interactivo, -a [interak'tiβo, a] *adj* interactive; (*Inform*): **computación interactiva** interactive computing
intercalar [interka'lar] *vt* to insert; (*Inform: archivos, texto*) to merge
intercambio [inter'kambjo] *nm* (*canje*) exchange; (*trueque*) swap
interceder [interθe'ðer] *vi* to intercede
interceptar [interθep'tar] *vt* to intercept, cut off; (*Auto*) to hold up
intercesión [interθe'sjon] *nf* intercession
interés [inte'res] *nm* (*gen, Com*) interest; (*importancia*) concern; (*parte*) share, part; (*pey*) self-interest; **~ compuesto** compound interest; **~ simple** simple interest; **con un ~ de 9 por ciento** at an interest of 9%; **dar a ~** to lend at interest; **tener ~ en** (*Com*) to hold a share in; **intereses acumulados** accrued interest *sg*; **intereses por cobrar** interest receivable *sg*; **intereses creados** vested interests; **intereses por pagar** interest payable *sg*
interesado, -a [intere'saðo, a] *adj* interested; (*prejuiciado*) prejudiced; (*pey*) mercenary, self-seeking ▷ *nm/f* person concerned; (*firmante*) the undersigned
interesante [intere'sante] *adj* interesting
interesar [intere'sar] *vt* to interest, be of interest to ▷ *vi* to interest, be of interest; (*importar*) to be important; **interesarse** *vr*: **~se en** *o* **por** to take an interest in; **no me interesan los toros** bullfighting does not appeal to me
interferencia [interfe'renθja] *nf* interference
interferir [interfe'rir] *vt* to interfere with; (*Telec*) to jam ▷ *vi* to interfere
interfón [inter'fon] *nm* (*Am*) = **interfono**
interfono [inter'fono] *nm* intercom, entry phone
interino, -a [inte'rino, a] *adj* temporary; (*empleado etc*) provisional ▷ *nm/f* temporary holder of a post; (*Med*) locum; (*Escol*) supply teacher; (*Teat*) stand-in
interior [inte'rjor] *adj* inner, inside; (*Com*) domestic, internal ▷ *nm* interior, inside; (*fig*) soul, mind; (*Deporte*) inside forward; **Ministerio del I~** ≈ Home Office (*Brit*), ≈ Department of the Interior (*US*); **dije para mí ~** I said to myself
interjección [interxek'θjon] *nf* interjection
interlocutor, a [interloku'tor, a] *nm/f* speaker; (*al teléfono*) person at the other end (of the line); **mi ~** the person I was speaking to
intermediario, -a [interme'ðjarjo, a] *adj* (*mediador*) mediating ▷ *nm/f* intermediary, go-between; (*mediador*) mediator
intermedio, -a [inter'meðjo, a] *adj* intermediate; (*tiempo*) intervening ▷ *nm* interval; (*Pol*) recess
interminable [intermi'naβle] *adj* endless, interminable
intermitente [intermi'tente] *adj* intermittent ▷ *nm* (*Auto*) indicator
internacional [internaθjo'nal] *adj* international
internado [inter'naðo] *nm* boarding school
internar [inter'nar] *vt* to intern; (*en un manicomio*) to commit; **internarse** *vr* (*penetrar*) to penetrate; **~se en** to go into *o* right inside; **~se en un estudio** to study a subject in depth
internauta [inter'nauta] *nm/f* web surfer, internet user
Internet [inter'net] *nm o nf* internet, Internet
interno, -a [in'terno, a] *adj* internal, interior; (*Pol etc*) domestic ▷ *nm/f* (*alumno*) boarder
interponer [interpo'ner] *vt* to interpose, put in; **interponerse** *vr* to intervene
interpretación [interpreta'θjon] *nf* interpretation; (*Mus, Teat*) performance; **mala ~** misinterpretation
interpretar [interpre'tar] *vt* to interpret; (*Teat, Mus*) to perform, play
intérprete [in'terprete] *nm/f* (*Ling*) interpreter, translator; (*Mus, Teat*) performer, artist(e)

interrogación [interroɣa'θjon] *nf* interrogation; (*Ling*: *tb*: **signo de ~**) question mark; (*Telec*) polling
interrogante [interro'ɣante] *adj* questioning ▷ *nm* question mark; (*fig*) question mark, query
interrogar [interro'ɣar] *vt* to interrogate, question
interrumpir [interrum'pir] *vt* to interrupt; (*vacaciones*) to cut short; (*servicio*) to cut off; (*tráfico*) to block
interrupción [interrup'θjon] *nf* interruption
interruptor [interrup'tor] *nm* (*Elec*) switch
intersección [intersek'θjon] *nf* intersection; (*Auto*) junction
interurbano, -a [interur'βano, a] *adj* inter city; (*Telec*) long-distance
intervalo [inter'βalo] *nm* interval; (*descanso*) break; **a ~s** at intervals, every now and then
intervención [interβen'θjon] *nf* supervision; (*Com*) audit(ing); (*Med*) operation; (*Telec*) tapping; (*participación*) intervention; **~ quirúrgica** surgical operation; **la política de no ~** the policy of non-intervention
intervenir [interβe'nir] *vt* (*controlar*) to control, supervise; (*Com*) to audit; (*Med*) to operate on; (*Telec*) to tap ▷ *vi* (*participar*) to take part, participate; (*mediar*) to intervene
interventor, a [interβen'tor, a] *nm/f* inspector; (*Com*) auditor
interviú [inter'βju] *nf* interview
intestino [intes'tino] *nm* intestine
intimar [inti'mar] *vt* to intimate, announce; (*mandar*) to order ▷ *vi*, **intimarse** *vr* to become friendly
intimidad [intimi'ðað] *nf* intimacy; (*familiaridad*) familiarity; (*vida privada*) private life; (*Jur*) privacy
íntimo, -a ['intimo, a] *adj* intimate; (*pensamientos*) innermost; (*vida*) personal, private; **una boda íntima** a quiet wedding
intolerable [intole'raβle] *adj* intolerable, unbearable
intolerancia [intole'ranθja] *nf* intolerance
intoxicación [intoksika'θjon] *nf* poisoning; **~ alimenticia** food poisoning
intranet [intra'net] *nf* intranet
intranquilizarse [intrankili'θarse] *vr* to get worried *o* anxious
intranquilo, -a [intran'kilo, a] *adj* worried
intransigente [intransi'xente] *adj* intransigent
intransitable [intransi'taβle] *adj* impassable
intransitivo, -a [intransi'tiβo, a] *adj* intransitive
intrepidez [intrepi'ðeθ] *nf* courage, bravery
intrépido, -a [in'trepiðo, a] *adj* intrepid, fearless
intriga [in'triɣa] *nf* intrigue; (*plan*) plot
intrigar [intri'ɣar] *vt*, *vi* to intrigue
intrincado, -a [intrin'kaðo, a] *adj* intricate
intrínseco, -a [in'trinseko, a] *adj* intrinsic
introducción [introðuk'θjon] *nf* introduction; (*de libro*) foreword; (*Inform*) input
introducir [introðu'θir] *vt* (*gen*) to introduce; (*moneda*) to insert; (*Inform*) to input, enter
intromisión [intromi'sjon] *nf* interference, meddling
introvertido, -a [introβer'tiðo, a] *adj*, *nm/f* introvert
intruso, -a [in'truso, a] *adj* intrusive ▷ *nm/f* intruder
intuición [intwi'θjon] *nf* intuition
intuir [intu'ir] *vt* to know by intuition, intuit
inundación [inunda'θjon] *nf* flood(ing)
inundar [inun'dar] *vt* to flood; (*fig*) to swamp, inundate
inusitado, -a [inusi'taðo, a] *adj* unusual
inútil [i'nutil] *adj* useless; (*esfuerzo*) vain, fruitless
inutilidad [inutili'ðað] *nf* uselessness
inutilizar [inutili'θar] *vt* to make unusable, put out of action; (*incapacitar*) to disable; **inutilizarse** *vr* to become useless
invadir [imba'ðir] *vt* to invade
invalidar [imbali'ðar] *vt* to invalidate
inválido, -a [im'baliðo, a] *adj* invalid; (*Jur*) null and void ▷ *nm/f* invalid
invariable [imba'rjable] *adj* invariable
invasión [imba'sjon] *nf* invasion
invasor, a [imba'sor, a] *adj* invading ▷ *nm/f* invader
invencible [imben'θiβle] *adj* invincible; (*timidez, miedo*) unsurmountable
invención [imben'θjon] *nf* invention
inventar [imben'tar] *vt* to invent
inventario [imben'tarjo] *nm* inventory; (*Com*) stocktaking
inventiva [imben'tiβa] *nf* inventiveness
invento [im'bento] *nm* invention; (*fig*) brainchild; (*pey*) silly idea
inventor, a [imben'tor, a] *nm/f* inventor
invernadero [imberna'ðero] *nm* greenhouse
invernar [imber'nar] *vi* (*Zool*) to hibernate
inverosímil [imbero'simil] *adj* implausible
inversión [imber'sjon] *nf* (*Com*) investment; **~ de capitales** capital investment; **inversiones extranjeras** foreign investment *sg*
inverso, a [im'berso, a] *adj* inverse, opposite; **en el orden ~** in reverse order; **a la inversa** inversely, the other way round
inversor, -a [imber'sor, a] *nm/f* (*Com*) investor
invertebrado, -a [imberte'βraðo, a] *adj*, *nm* invertebrate
invertir [imber'tir] *vt* (*Com*) to invest; (*volcar*) to turn upside down; (*tiempo etc*) to spend
investigación [imbestiɣa'θjon] *nf* investigation; (*indagación*) inquiry; (*Univ*) research; **~ y desarrollo** (*Com*) research and development (R & D); **~ de los medios de**

publicidad media research; **~ del mercado** market research
investigar [imbesti'ɣar] *vt* to investigate; (*estudiar*) to do research into
investir [imbes'tir] *vt*: **~ a algn con algo** to confer sth on sb; **fue investido Doctor Honoris Causa** he was awarded an honorary doctorate
invicto, -a [im'bikto, a] *adj* unconquered
invidente [imbi'ðente] *adj* sightless ▷ *nm/f* blind person; **los ~s** the sightless
invierno [im'bjerno] *nm* winter
invisible [imbi'siβle] *adj* invisible; **exportaciones/importaciones ~s** invisible exports/imports
invitación [imbita'θjon] *nf* invitation
invitado, -a [imbi'taðo, a] *nm/f* guest
invitar [imbi'tar] *vt* to invite; (*incitar*) to entice; **~ a algn a hacer algo** to invite sb to do sth; **~ a algo** to pay for sth; **nos invitó a cenar fuera** she took us out for dinner; **invito yo** it's on me
in vitro [im'bitro] *adv* in vitro
invocar [imbo'kar] *vt* to invoke, call on
involucrar [imbolu'krar] *vt*: **~ algo en un discurso** to bring something irrelevant into a discussion; **~ a algn en algo** to involve sb in sth; **involucrarse** *vr* (*interesarse*) to get involved
involuntario, -a [imbolun'tarjo, a] *adj* involuntary; (*ofensa etc*) unintentional
inyección [injek'θjon] *nf* injection
inyectar [injek'tar] *vt* to inject
ión [i'on] *nm* ion
IPC *nm abr* (*Esp*: = *índice de precios al consumo*) CPI
iPod® ['ipoð] (*pl* **iPods**) *nm* iPod®

PALABRA CLAVE

ir [ir] *vi* **1** to go; (*a pie*) to walk; (*viajar*) to travel; **ir caminando** to walk; **fui en tren** I went *o* travelled by train; **voy a la calle** I'm going out; **ir en coche/en bicicleta** to drive/cycle; **ir a pie** to walk, go on foot; **ir de pesca** to go fishing; **¡(ahora) voy!** (I'm just) coming!
2: **ir (a) por**: **ir (a) por el médico** to fetch the doctor
3 (*progresar*: *persona, cosa*) to go; **el trabajo va muy bien** work is going very well; **¿cómo te va?** how are things going?; **me va muy bien** I'm getting on very well; **le fue fatal** it went awfully badly for him
4 (*funcionar*): **el coche no va muy bien** the car isn't running very well
5 (*sentar*): **me va estupendamente** (*ropa, color*) it suits me really well; (*medicamento*) it works really well for me; **ir bien con algo** to go well with sth; **te va estupendamente ese color** that colour suits you fantastically well
6 (*aspecto*): **iba muy bien vestido** he was very well dressed; **ir con zapatos negros** to wear black shoes
7 (*locuciones*): **¿vino? — ¡que va!** did he come? — of course not!; **vamos, no llores** come on, don't cry; **¡vaya coche!** (*admiración*) what a car!, that's some car!; (*desprecio*) that's a terrible car!; **¡vaya!** (*regular*) so so; (*desagrado*) come on!; **¡vamos!** come on!; **¡que le vaya bien!** (*adiós*) take care!
8: **no vaya a ser**: **tienes que correr, no vaya a ser que pierdas el tren** you'll have to run so as not to miss the train
9: **no me** *etc* **va ni me viene** I *etc* don't care
▷ *vb auxiliar* **1**: **ir a**: **voy/iba a hacerlo hoy** I am/was going to do it today
2 (*+gerundio*): **iba anocheciendo** it was getting dark; **todo se me iba aclarando** everything was gradually becoming clearer to me
3 (*+pp = pasivo*): **van vendidos 300 ejemplares** 300 copies have been sold so far
irse *vr* **1**: **¿por dónde se va al zoológico?** which is the way to the zoo?
2 (*marcharse*) to leave; **ya se habrán ido** they must already have left *o* gone; **¡vámonos!**, **¡nos fuimos!** (*Am*) let's go!; **¡vete!** go away!; **¡vete a saber!** your guess is as good as mine!, who knows!

ira ['ira] *nf* anger, rage
iracundo, -a [ira'kundo, a] *adj* irascible
Irak [i'rak] *nm* = **Iraq**
Irán [i'ran] *nm* Iran
iraní [ira'ni] *adj, nm/f* Iranian
Iraq [i'rak] *nm* Iraq
iraquí [ira'ki] *adj, nm/f* Iraqi
irascible [iras'θiβle] *adj* irascible
iris ['iris] *nm inv* (*arco iris*) rainbow; (*Anat*) iris
Irlanda [ir'landa] *nf* Ireland; **~ del Norte** Northern Ireland, Ulster
irlandés, -esa [irlan'des, esa] *adj* Irish ▷ *nm/f* Irishman(-woman) ▷ *nm* (*Ling*) Gaelic, Irish; **los irlandeses** *nmpl* the Irish
ironía [iro'nia] *nf* irony
irónico, -a [i'roniko, a] *adj* ironic(al)
IRPF *nm abr* (*Esp*) = **impuesto sobre la renta de las personas físicas**
irracional [irraθjo'nal] *adj* irrational
irreal [irre'al] *adj* unreal
irrecuperable [irrekupe'raβle] *adj* irrecoverable, irretrievable
irreflexión [irreflek'sjon] *nf* thoughtlessness; (*ímpetu*) rashness
irregular [irreɣu'lar] *adj* irregular; (*situación*) abnormal, anomalous; **margen izquierdo/derecho ~** (*texto*) ragged left/right (margin)
irregularidad [irreɣulari'ðað] *nf* irregularity
irremediable [irreme'ðjaβle] *adj* irremediable; (*vicio*) incurable
irreparable [irrepa'raβle] *adj* (*daños*) irreparable; (*pérdida*) irrecoverable
irreprochable [irrepro'tʃaβle] *adj* irreproachable
irresistible [irresis'tiβle] *adj* irresistible

irresoluto, -a [irreso'luto, a] *adj* irresolute, hesitant; (*sin resolver*) unresolved
irrespetuoso, -a [irrespe'twoso, a] *adj* disrespectful
irresponsable [irrespon'saβle] *adj* irresponsible
irreversible [irreβer'siβle] *adj* irreversible
irrevocable [irreβo'kaβle] *adj* irrevocable
irrigar [irri'ɣar] *vt* to irrigate
irrisorio, -a [irri'sorjo, a] *adj* derisory, ridiculous; (*precio*) bargain *cpd*
irritación [irrita'θjon] *nf* irritation
irritar [irri'tar] *vt* to irritate, annoy; **irritarse** *vr* to get angry, lose one's temper
irrupción [irrup'θjon] *nf* irruption; (*invasión*) invasion
IRTP *nm abr* (*Esp: = impuesto sobre el rendimiento del trabajo personal*) ≈ PAYE
isla ['isla] *nf* (*Geo*) island; **I~s Británicas** British Isles; **I~s Filipinas/Malvinas/Canarias** Philippines/Falklands/Canaries
Islam [is'lam] *nm* Islam
islámico, -a [is'lamiko, a] *adj* Islamic
islandés, -esa [islan'des, esa] *adj* Icelandic ▷ *nm/f* Icelander ▷ *nm* (*Ling*) Icelandic
Islandia [is'landja] *nf* Iceland
isleño, -a [is'leɲo, a] *adj* island *cpd* ▷ *nm/f* islander
isotónico, -a [iso'toniko, a] *adj* isotonic
Israel [isra'el] *nm* Israel
israelí [israe'li] *adj, nm/f* Israeli
istmo ['istmo] *nm* isthmus; **el I~ de Panamá** the Isthmus of Panama
Italia [i'talja] *nf* Italy
italiano, -a [ita'ljano, a] *adj, nm/f* Italian ▷ *nm* (*Ling*) Italian
itinerario [itine'rarjo] *nm* itinerary, route
ITV *nf abr* (= *Inspección Técnica de Vehículos*) ≈ MOT (test) (*Brit*)
IVA ['iβa] *nm abr* (*Esp Com: = Impuesto sobre el Valor Añadido*) VAT
izar [i'θar] *vt* to hoist
izdo., izq.° *abr* (= *izquierdo*) L, l
izquierda [iθ'kjerða] *nf ver* **izquierdo**
izquierdista [iθkjer'ðista] *adj* leftist, left-wing ▷ *nm/f* left-winger, leftist
izquierdo, -a [iθ'kjerðo, a] *adj* left ▷ *nf* left; (*Pol*) left (wing); **a la izquierda** on the left; (*torcer etc*) (to the) left; **es un cero a la izquierda** (*fam*) he is a nonentity; **conducción por la izquierda** left-hand drive

J

jabalí [xaβa'li] *nm* wild boar
jabalina [xaβa'lina] *nf* javelin
jabón [xa'βon] *nm* soap; (*fam: adulación*) flattery; **~ de afeitar** shaving soap; **~ de tocador** toilet soap; **dar ~ a algn** to soft-soap sb
jabonar [xaβo'nar] *vt* to soap
jaca ['xaka] *nf* pony
jacal [xa'kal] *nm* (*Am*) shack
jacinto [xa'θinto] *nm* hyacinth
jactarse [xak'tarse] *vr*: **~ (de)** to boast *o* brag (about *o* of)
jadear [xaðe'ar] *vi* to pant, gasp for breath
jadeo [xa'ðeo] *nm* panting, gasping
jaguar [xa'ɣwar] *nm* jaguar
jaiba ['xaiβa] *nf* (*Am*) crab
jalar [xa'lar] *vt* (*Am*) to pull
jalbegue [xal'βeɣe] *nm* whitewash
jalea [xa'lea] *nf* jelly
jaleo [xa'leo] *nm* racket, uproar; **armar un ~** to kick up a racket
jalón [xa'lon] *nm* (*Am*) tug
Jamaica [xa'maika] *nf* Jamaica
jamás [xa'mas] *adv* never, not ... ever; (*interrogativo*) ever; **¿~ se vio tal cosa?** did you ever see such a thing?
jamón [xa'mon] *nm* ham; **~ (de) York** boiled ham; **~ dulce/serrano** boiled/cured ham
Japón [xa'pon] *nm*: **el ~** Japan
japonés, -esa [xapo'nes, esa] *adj, nm/f* Japanese ▷ *nm* (*Ling*) Japanese
jaque ['xake] *nm*: **~ mate** checkmate

jaqueca [xa'keka] *nf* (very bad) headache, migraine
jarabe [xa'raβe] *nm* syrup; **~ para la tos** cough syrup *o* mixture
jarcia ['xarθja] *nf* (*Naut*) ropes *pl*, rigging
jardín [xar'ðin] *nm* garden; **~ botánico** botanical garden; **~ de (la) infancia** (*Esp*) *o* **de niños** (*Am*) *o* **infantil** kindergarten, nursery school
jardinaje [xarði'naxe] *nm* gardening
jardinería [xarðine'ria] *nf* gardening
jardinero, -a [xarði'nero, a] *nm/f* gardener
jarra ['xarra] *nf* jar; (*jarro*) jug; (*de leche*) churn; (*de cerveza*) mug; **de** *o* **en ~s** with arms akimbo
jarro ['xarro] *nm* jug
jarrón [xa'rron] *nm* vase; (*Arqueología*) urn
jaula ['xaula] *nf* cage; (*embalaje*) crate
jauría [xau'ria] *nf* pack of hounds
jazmín [xaθ'min] *nm* jasmine
J. C. *abr* = **Jesucristo**
jeans [jins, dʒins] *nmpl* (*Am*) jeans, denims; **unos ~** a pair of jeans
jeep® (*pl* **jeeps**) [jip, jips] *nm* jeep®
jefa ['xefa] *nf ver* **jefe**
jefatura [xefa'tura] *nf* (*liderazgo*) leadership; (*sede*) central office; **J~ de la aviación civil** ≈ Civil Aviation Authority; **~ de policía** police headquarters *sg*
jefe, -a ['xefe, a] *nm/f* (*gen*) chief, head; (*patrón*) boss; (*Pol*) leader; (*Com*) manager(ess); **~ de camareros** head waiter; **~ de cocina** chef; **~ ejecutivo** (*Com*) chief executive; **~ de estación** stationmaster; **~ de estado** head of state; **~ de oficina** (*Com*) office manager; **~ de producción** (*Com*) production manager; **~ supremo** commander-in-chief; **~ de estudios** (*Escol*) director of studies; **~ de gobierno** head of government; **ser el ~** (*fig*) to be the boss
jengibre [xen'xiβre] *nm* ginger
jeque ['xeke] *nm* sheik(h)
jerarquía [xerar'kia] *nf* (*orden*) hierarchy; (*rango*) rank
jerárquico, -a [xe'rarkiko, a] *adj* hierarchic(al)
jerez [xe'reθ] *nm* sherry; **J~ de la Frontera** Jerez
jerga ['xerɣa] *nf* (*tela*) coarse cloth; (*lenguaje*) jargon; **~ informática** computer jargon
jerigonza [xeri'ɣonθa] *nf* (*jerga*) jargon, slang; (*galimatías*) nonsense, gibberish
jeringa [xe'ringa] *nf* syringe; (*Am*) annoyance, bother; **~ de engrase** grease gun
jeringar [xerin'gar] *vt* to annoy, bother
jeringuilla [xerin'guiʎa] *nf* syringe
jeroglífico [xero'ɣlifiko] *nm* hieroglyphic
jersey [xer'sei] (*pl* **jerseys**) *nm* jersey, pullover, jumper
Jerusalén [xerusa'len] *n* Jerusalem
Jesucristo [xesu'kristo] *nm* Jesus Christ
jesuita [xe'swita] *adj, nm* Jesuit
Jesús [xe'sus] *nm* Jesus; **¡~!** good heavens!; (*al estornudar*) bless you!
jet (*pl* **jets**) [jet, jet] *nm* jet (plane) ▷ *nf*: **la ~** the jet set
jeta ['xeta] *nf* (*Zool*) snout; (*fam: cara*) mug; **¡que ~ tienes!** (*fam: insolencia*) you've got a nerve!
jilguero [xil'ɣero] *nm* goldfinch
jinete, -a [xi'nete, a] *nm/f* horseman(-woman)
jipijapa [xipi'xapa] *nm* (*Am*) straw hat
jirafa [xi'rafa] *nf* giraffe
jirón [xi'ron] *nm* rag, shred
jitomate [xito'mate] *nm* (*Am*) tomato
jocoso, -a [xo'koso, a] *adj* humorous, jocular
joder [xo'ðer] (*fam!*) *vt* to fuck (*!*), screw (*!*); (*fig: fastidiar*) to piss off (*!*), bug; **joderse** *vr* (*fracasar*) to fail; **¡~!** damn it!; **se jodió todo** everything was ruined
jogging ['joɣin] *nm* (*Am*) tracksuit (*Brit*), sweat suit (*US*)
jornada [xor'naða] *nf* (*viaje de un día*) day's journey; (*camino o viaje entero*) journey; (*día de trabajo*) working day; **~ de 8 horas** 8-hour day; **(trabajar a) ~ partida** (to work a) split shift
jornal [xor'nal] *nm* (day's) wage
jornalero, -a [xorna'lero, a] *nm/f* (day) labourer
joroba [xo'roβa] *nf* hump
jorobado, -a [xoro'βaðo, a] *adj* hunchbacked ▷ *nm/f* hunchback
jota ['xota] *nf* letter J; (*danza*) *Aragonese dance*; (*fam*) jot, iota; **no saber ni ~** to have no idea
joven ['xoβen] *adj* young ▷ *nm* young man, youth ▷ *nf* young woman, girl
jovial [xo'βjal] *adj* cheerful, jolly
jovialidad [xoβjali'ðað] *nf* cheerfulness
joya ['xoja] *nf* jewel, gem; (*fig: persona*) gem; **~s de fantasía** imitation jewellery *sg*
joyería [xoje'ria] *nf* (*joyas*) jewellery; (*tienda*) jeweller's (shop)
joyero [xo'jero] *nm* (*persona*) jeweller; (*caja*) jewel case
Juan [xwan] *nm*: **Noche de San ~** *ver* **noche**
juanete [xwa'nete] *nm* (*del pie*) bunion
jubilación [xuβila'θjon] *nf* (*retiro*) retirement
jubilado, -a [xuβi'lado, a] *adj* retired ▷ *nm/f* retired person, pensioner (*Brit*), senior citizen
jubilar [xuβi'lar] *vt* to pension off, retire; (*fam*) to discard; **jubilarse** *vr* to retire
júbilo ['xuβilo] *nm* joy, rejoicing
jubiloso, -a [xuβi'loso, a] *adj* jubilant
judía [xu'ðia] *nf ver* **judío**
judicial [xuði'θjal] *adj* judicial
judío, -a [xu'ðio, a] *adj* Jewish ▷ *nm* Jew ▷ *nf* Jewish woman; (*Culin*) bean; **judía blanca** haricot bean; **judía verde** French *o* string bean
judo ['juðo] *nm* judo

juego ['xweɣo] *vb ver* **jugar** ▷ *nm* (*gen*) play; (*pasatiempo, partido*) game; (*en casino*) gambling; (*deporte*) sport; (*conjunto*) set; (*herramientas*) kit; **~ de azar** game of chance; **~ de café** coffee set; **~ de caracteres** (*Inform*) font; **~ limpio/sucio** fair/foul *o* dirty play; **~ de mesa** board game; **~ de palabras** pun, play on words; **J~s Olímpicos** Olympic Games; **~ de programas** (*Inform*) suite of programs; **fuera de ~** (*Deporte*: *persona*) offside; (*: pelota*) out of play; **por ~** in fun, for fun

juerga ['xwerɣa] *nf* binge; (*fiesta*) party; **ir de ~** to go out on a binge

jueves ['xweβes] *nm inv* Thursday; *ver tb* **sábado**

juez [xweθ] *nm/f* judge; (*Tenis*) umpire; **~ de instrucción** examining magistrate; **~ de línea** linesman; **~ de paz** justice of the peace; **~ de salida** starter

jugada [xu'ɣaða] *nf* play; **buena ~** good move (*o* shot *o* stroke) *etc*

jugador, a [xuɣa'ðor, a] *nm/f* player; (*en casino*) gambler

jugar [xu'ɣar] *vt* to play; (*en casino*) to gamble; (*apostar*) to bet ▷ *vi* to play; to gamble; (*Com*) to speculate; **jugarse** *vr* to gamble (away); **~se el todo por el todo, ~ al fútbol** to play football, to stake one's all, go for bust; **¿quién juega?** whose move is it?; **¡me la han jugado!** (*fam*) I've been had!

juglar [xu'ɣlar] *nm* minstrel

jugo ['xuɣo] *nm* (*Bot, de fruta*) juice; (*fig*) essence, substance; **~ de naranja** (*esp Am*) orange juice

jugoso, -a [xu'ɣoso, a] *adj* juicy; (*fig*) substantial, important

juguete [xu'ɣete] *nm* toy

juguetear [xuɣete'ar] *vi* to play

juguetería [xuɣete'ria] *nf* toyshop

juguetón, -ona [xuɣe'ton, ona] *adj* playful

juicio ['xwiθjo] *nm* judgement; (*sana razón*) sanity, reason; (*opinión*) opinion; (*Jur*: *proceso*) trial; **estar fuera de ~** to be out of one's mind; **a mi ~** in my opinion

juicioso, -a [xwi'θjoso, a] *adj* wise, sensible

julio ['xuljo] *nm* July; **el uno** *o* **el primero de ~** the first of July; **en el mes de ~** during July; **en ~ del año que viene** in July of next year

jumper ['dʒumper] *nm* (*Am*) pinafore dress (*Brit*), jumper (*US*)

junco ['xunko] *nm* rush, reed

jungla ['xungla] *nf* jungle

junio ['xunjo] *nm* June; *ver tb* **julio**

junta ['xunta] *nf ver* **junto**

juntar [xun'tar] *vt* to join, unite; (*maquinaria*) to assemble, put together; (*dinero*) to collect; **juntarse** *vr* to join, meet; (*reunirse*: *personas*) to meet, assemble; (*arrimarse*) to approach, draw closer; **~se con algn** to join sb

junto, -a ['xunto, a] *adj* joined; (*unido*) united; (*anexo*) near, close; (*contiguo, próximo*) next, adjacent ▷ *nf* (*asamblea*) meeting, assembly; (*comité, consejo*) board, council, committee; (*Mil, Pol*) junta; (*articulación*) joint ▷ *adv*: **todo ~** all at once ▷ *prep*: **~ a** near (to), next to; **~s** together; **~ con** (together) with; **junta constitutiva** (*Com*) statutory meeting; **junta directiva** (*Com*) board of management; **junta general extraordinaria** (*Com*) extraordinary general meeting

jurado [xu'raðo] *nm* (*Jur*: *individuo*) juror; (*: grupo*) jury; (*de concurso*: *grupo*) panel (of judges); (*: individuo*) member of a panel

juramento [xura'mento] *nm* oath; (*maldición*) oath, curse; **bajo ~** on oath; **prestar ~** to take the oath; **tomar ~ a** to swear in, administer the oath to

jurar [xu'rar] *vt, vi* to swear; **~ en falso** to commit perjury; **jurárselas a algn** to have it in for sb

jurídico, -a [xu'riðiko, a] *adj* legal, juridical

jurisdicción [xurisðik'θjon] *nf* (*poder, autoridad*) jurisdiction; (*territorio*) district

jurisprudencia [xurispru'ðenθja] *nf* jurisprudence

jurista [xu'rista] *nm/f* jurist

justamente [xusta'mente] *adv* justly, fairly; (*precisamente*) just, exactly

justicia [xus'tiθja] *nf* justice; (*equidad*) fairness, justice; **de ~** deservedly

justiciero, -a [xusti'θjero, a] *adj* just, righteous

justificación [xustifika'θjon] *nf* justification; **~ automática** (*Inform*) automatic justification

justificante [xustifi'kante] *nm* voucher; **~ médico** sick note

justificar [xustifi'kar] *vt* (*tb Tip*) to justify; (*probar*) to verify

justo, -a ['xusto, a] *adj* (*equitativo*) just, fair, right; (*preciso*) exact, correct; (*ajustado*) tight ▷ *adv* (*precisamente*) exactly, precisely; (*apenas a tiempo*) just in time; **¡~!** that's it!, correct!; **llegaste muy ~** you just made it; **vivir muy ~** to be hard up

juvenil [xuβe'nil] *adj* youthful

juventud [xuβen'tuð] *nf* (*adolescencia*) youth; (*jóvenes*) young people *pl*

juzgado [xuθ'ɣaðo] *nm* tribunal; (*Jur*) court

juzgar [xuθ'ɣar] *vt* to judge; **a ~ por ...** to judge by ..., judging by ...; **~ mal** to misjudge; **júzguelo usted mismo** see for yourself

K

L

karaoke [kara'oke] *nm* karaoke
kárate ['karate], **karate** [ka'rate] *nm* karate
Kg, kg *abr* (= *kilogramo(s)*) K, kg
kilo ['kilo] *nm* kilo
kilogramo [kilo'ɣramo] *nm* kilogramme (*Brit*), kilogram (*US*)
kilometraje [kilome'traxe] *nm* distance in kilometres, ≈ mileage
kilómetro [ki'lometro] *nm* kilometre (*Brit*), kilometer (*US*)
kilovatio [kilo'βatjo] *nm* kilowatt
kiosco ['kjosko] *nm* = **quiosco**
kiwi ['kiwi] *nm* kiwi (fruit)
kleenex® [kli'neks] *nm* paper handkerchief, tissue
km *abr* (= *kilómetro(s)*) km
Kosovo [koso'βo] *nm* Kosovo
kv *abr* (= *kilovatio*) kw

l *abr* (= *litro(s)*) l; (= *libro*) bk
la [la] *artículo definido fsg* the ▷ *pron* her; (*en relación a usted*) you; (*en relación a una cosa*) it ▷ *nm* (*Mus*) A; **está en la cárcel** he's in jail; **la del sombrero rojo** the woman/girl/one in the red hat
laberinto [laβe'rinto] *nm* labyrinth
labia ['laβja] *nf* fluency; (*pey*) glibness; **tener mucha ~** to have the gift of the gab
labial [la'βjal] *adj* labial
labio ['laβjo] *nm* lip; (*de vasija etc*) edge, rim; **~ inferior/superior** lower/upper lip
labor [la'βor] *nf* labour; (*Agr*) farm work; (*tarea*) job, task; (*Costura*) needlework, sewing; (*punto*) knitting; **~ de equipo** teamwork; **~ de ganchillo** crochet; **~es domésticas** *o* **del hogar** household chores
laborable [laβo'raβle] *adj* (*Agr*) workable; **día ~** working day
laboral [laβo'ral] *adj* (*accidente, conflictividad*) industrial; (*jornada*) working; (*derecho, relaciones*) labour *cpd*
laboralista [laβora'lista] *adj*: **abogado ~** labour lawyer
laborar [laβo'rar] *vi* to work
laboratorio [laβora'torjo] *nm* laboratory
laborioso, -a [laβo'rjoso, a] *adj* (*persona*) hard-working; (*trabajo*) tough
laborista [laβo'rista] (*Pol*) *adj*: **Partido L~** Labour Party ▷ *nm/f* Labour Party member *o* supporter

labrado, -a [la'βraðo, a] *adj* worked; (*madera*) carved; (*metal*) wrought ▷ *nm* (*Agr*) cultivated field

labrador, a [laβra'ðor, a] *adj* farming *cpd* ▷ *nm/f* farmer

labranza [la'βranθa] *nf* (*Agr*) cultivation

labrar [la'βrar] *vt* (*gen*) to work; (*madera etc*) to carve; (*fig*) to cause, bring about

labriego, -a [la'βrjeɣo, a] *nm/f* peasant

laca ['laka] *nf* lacquer; (*de pelo*) hairspray; **~ de uñas** nail varnish

lacayo [la'kajo] *nm* lackey

lacerar [laθe'rar] *vt* to lacerate

lacio, -a ['laθjo, a] *adj* (*pelo*) lank, straight

lacón [la'kon] *nm* shoulder of pork

lacónico, -a [la'koniko, a] *adj* laconic

lacra ['lakra] *nf* (*defecto*) blemish; **~ social** social disgrace

lacrar [la'krar] *vt* (*cerrar*) to seal (with sealing wax)

lacre ['lakre] *nm* sealing wax

lacrimoso, -a [lakri'moso, a] *adj* tearful

lactancia [lak'tanθja] *nf* lactation, breast-feeding

lactar [lak'tar] *vt, vi* to suckle, breast-feed

lácteo, -a ['lakteo, a] *adj*: **productos ~s** dairy products

ladear [laðe'ar] *vt* to tip, tilt ▷ *vi* to tilt; **ladearse** *vr* to lean; (*Deporte*) to swerve; (*Aviat*) to bank, turn

ladera [la'ðera] *nf* slope

ladino, -a [la'ðino, a] *adj* cunning

lado ['laðo] *nm* (*gen*) side; (*fig*) protection; (*Mil*) flank; **~ izquierdo** left(-hand) side; **~ a ~** side by side; **al ~ de** next to, beside; **hacerse a un ~** to stand aside; **poner de ~** to put on its side; **poner a un ~** to put aside; **me da de ~** I don't care; **por un ~ ..., por otro ~ ...** on the one hand ..., on the other (hand) ...; **por todos ~s** on all sides, all round (*Brit*)

ladrar [la'ðrar] *vi* to bark

ladrido [la'ðriðo] *nm* bark, barking

ladrillo [la'ðriʎo] *nm* (*gen*) brick; (*azulejo*) tile

ladrón, -ona [la'ðron, ona] *nm/f* thief

lagar [la'ɣar] *nm* (wine/oil) press

lagartija [laɣar'tixa] *nf* (small) lizard, wall lizard

lagarto [la'ɣarto] *nm* (*Zool*) lizard; (*Am*) alligator

lago ['laɣo] *nm* lake

lágrima ['laɣrima] *nf* tear

lagrimal [laɣri'mal] *nm* (inner) corner of the eye

laguna [la'ɣuna] *nf* (*lago*) lagoon; (*en escrito, conocimientos*) gap

laico, -a ['laiko, a] *adj* lay ▷ *nm/f* layman(-woman)

lamentable [lamen'taβle] *adj* lamentable, regrettable; (*miserable*) pitiful

lamentar [lamen'tar] *vt* (*sentir*) to regret; (*deplorar*) to lament; **lamentarse** *vr* to lament; **lo lamento mucho** I'm very sorry

lamento [la'mento] *nm* lament

lamer [la'mer] *vt* to lick

lámina ['lamina] *nf* (*plancha delgada*) sheet; (*para estampar, estampa*) plate; (*grabado*) engraving

laminar [lami'nar] *vt* (*en libro*) to laminate; (*Tec*) to roll

lámpara ['lampara] *nf* lamp; **~ de alcohol/gas** spirit/gas lamp; **~ de pie** standard lamp

lamparón [lampa'ron] *nm* (*Med*) scrofula; (*mancha*) (large) grease spot

lampiño, -a [lam'piɲo, a] *adj* (*sin pelo*) hairless

lana ['lana] *nf* wool; (*tela*) woollen (*Brit*) *o* woolen (*US*) cloth; (*Am fam: dinero*) dough; **(hecho) de ~** wool *cpd*

lance *etc* ['lanθe] *vb ver* **lanzar** ▷ *nm* (*golpe*) stroke; (*suceso*) event, incident

lancha ['lantʃa] *nf* launch; **~ motora** motorboat; **~ de pesca** fishing boat; **~ salvavidas/torpedera** lifeboat/torpedo boat; **~ neumática** rubber dinghy

lanero, -a [la'nero, a] *adj* wool *cpd*

langosta [lan'gosta] *nf* (*insecto*) locust; (*crustáceo*) lobster; (*: de río*) crayfish

langostino [langos'tino] *nm* prawn; (*de agua dulce*) crayfish

languidecer [langiðe'θer] *vi* to languish

languidez [langi'ðeθ] *nf* languor

lánguido, -a ['langiðo, a] *adj* (*gen*) languid; (*sin energía*) listless

lanilla [la'niʎa] *nf* nap; (*tela*) thin flannel cloth

lanudo, -a [la'nuðo, a] *adj* woolly, fleecy

lanza ['lanθa] *nf* (*arma*) lance, spear; **medir ~s** to cross swords

lanzadera [lanθa'ðera] *nf* shuttle

lanzado, -a [lan'θaðo, a] *adj* (*atrevido*) forward; (*decidido*) determined; **ir ~** (*rápido*) to fly along

lanzamiento [lanθa'mjento] *nm* (*gen*) throwing; (*Naut, Com*) launch, launching; **~ de pesos** putting the shot

lanzar [lan'θar] *vt* (*gen*) to throw; (*con violencia*) to fling; (*Deporte: pelota*) to bowl, to pitch (*US*); (*Naut, Com*) to launch; (*Jur*) to evict; (*grito*) to give, utter; **lanzarse** *vr* to throw o.s.; (*fig*) to take the plunge; **~se a** (*fig*) to embark upon

lapa ['lapa] *nf* limpet

La Paz *nf* La Paz

lapicero [lapi'θero] *nm* pencil; (*Am*) propelling (*Brit*) *o* mechanical (*US*) pencil; (*: bolígrafo*) ballpoint pen, Biro®

lápida ['lapiða] *nf* stone; **~ conmemorativa** memorial stone; **~ mortuoria** headstone

lapidar [lapi'ðar] *vt* to stone; (*Tec*) to polish, lap

lapidario, -a [lapi'ðarjo, a] *adj, nm* lapidary

lápiz ['lapiθ] *nm* pencil; **~ de color** coloured pencil; **~ de labios** lipstick; **~ de ojos** eyebrow pencil; **~ óptico** *o* **luminoso** light pen

lapón, -ona [la'pon, ona] *adj* Lapp ▷ *nm/f* Laplander, Lapp ▷ *nm* (*Ling*) Lapp
Laponia [la'ponja] *nf* Lapland
lapso ['lapso] *nm* lapse; (*error*) error; ~ **de tiempo** interval of time
lapsus ['lapsus] *nm inv* error, mistake
largar [lar'ɣar] *vt* (*soltar*) to release; (*aflojar*) to loosen; (*lanzar*) to launch; (*fam*) to let fly; (*velas*) to unfurl; (*Am*) to throw; **largarse** *vr* (*fam*) to beat it; **~se a** (*Am*) to start to
largo, -a ['larɣo, a] *adj* (*longitud*) long; (*tiempo*) lengthy; (*persona: alta*) tall; (*: fig*) generous ▷ *nm* length; (*Mus*) largo; **dos años ~s** two long years; **a ~ plazo** in the long term; **tiene nueve metros de ~** it is nine metres long; **a lo ~** (*posición*) lengthways; **a lo ~ de** along; (*tiempo*) all through, throughout; **a la larga** in the long run; **me dio largas con una promesa** she put me off with a promise; **¡~ de aquí!** (*fam*) clear off!
largometraje [larɣome'traxe] *nm* full-length *o* feature film
largura [lar'ɣura] *nf* length
laringe [la'rinxe] *nf* larynx
laringitis [larin'xitis] *nf* laryngitis
larva ['larβa] *nf* larva
las [las] *artículo definido fpl* the ▷ *pron* them; **~ que cantan** the ones/women/girls who sing
lasaña [la'saɲa] *nf* lasagne, lasagna
lascivo, -a [las'θiβo, a] *adj* lewd
láser ['laser] *nm* laser
lástima ['lastima] *nf* (*pena*) pity; **dar ~** to be pitiful; **es una ~ que** it's a pity that; **¡qué ~!** what a pity!; **estar hecho una ~** to be a sorry sight
lastimar [lasti'mar] *vt* (*herir*) to wound; (*ofender*) to offend; **lastimarse** *vr* to hurt o.s.
lastimero, -a [lasti'mero, a] *adj* pitiful, pathetic
lastre ['lastre] *nm* (*Tec, Naut*) ballast; (*fig*) dead weight
lata ['lata] *nf* (*metal*) tin; (*envase*) tin, can; (*fam*) nuisance; **en ~** tinned; **dar (la) ~** to be a nuisance
latente [la'tente] *adj* latent
lateral [late'ral] *adj* side, lateral ▷ *nm* (*Teat*) wings *pl*
latido [la'tiðo] *nm* (*del corazón*) beat; (*de herida*) throb(bing)
latifundio [lati'fundjo] *nm* large estate
latifundista [latifun'dista] *nm/f* owner of a large estate
latigazo [lati'ɣaθo] *nm* (*golpe*) lash; (*sonido*) crack; (*fig: regaño*) dressing-down
látigo ['latiɣo] *nm* whip
latín [la'tin] *nm* Latin; **saber (mucho) ~** (*fam*) to be pretty sharp
latino, -a [la'tino, a] *adj* Latin
Latinoamérica [latinoa'merika] *nf* Latin America
latinoamericano, -a [latinoameri'kano, a] *adj, nm/f* Latin American
latir [la'tir] *vi* (*corazón, pulso*) to beat
latitud [lati'tuð] *nf* (*Geo*) latitude; (*fig*) breadth, extent
latón [la'ton] *nm* brass
latoso, -a [la'toso, a] *adj* (*molesto*) annoying; (*aburrido*) boring
laúd [la'uð] *nm* lute
laurel [lau'rel] *nm* (*Bot*) laurel; (*Culin*) bay
lava ['laβa] *nf* lava
lavabo [la'βaβo] *nm* (*jofaina*) washbasin; (*retrete*) lavatory (*Brit*), toilet (*Brit*), washroom (*US*)
lavadero [laβa'ðero] *nm* laundry
lavado [la'βaðo] *nm* washing; (*de ropa*) wash, laundry; (*Arte*) wash; **~ de cerebro** brainwashing; **~ en seco** dry-cleaning
lavadora [laβa'ðora] *nf* washing machine
lavanda [la'βanda] *nf* lavender
lavandería [laβande'ria] *nf* laundry; **~ automática** launderette
lavaplatos [laβa'platos] *nm inv* dishwasher
lavar [la'βar] *vt* to wash; (*borrar*) to wipe away; **lavarse** *vr* to wash o.s.; **~se las manos** to wash one's hands; (*fig*) to wash one's hands of it; **~se los dientes** to brush one's teeth; **~ y marcar** (*pelo*) to shampoo and set; **~ en seco** to dry-clean; **~ los platos** to wash the dishes
lavarropas [laβa'rropas] *nm inv* (*RPl*) washing machine
lavavajillas [laβaβa'xiʎas] *nm inv* dishwasher
laxante [lak'sante] *nm* laxative
lazada [la'θaða] *nf* bow
lazarillo [laθa'riʎo] *nm*: **perro de ~** guide dog
lazo ['laθo] *nm* knot; (*lazada*) bow; (*para animales*) lasso; (*trampa*) snare; (*vínculo*) tie; **~ corredizo** slipknot
le [le] *pron* (*directo*) him (*o* her); (*: en relación a usted*) you; (*indirecto*) to him (*o* her *o* it); (*: a usted*) to you
leal [le'al] *adj* loyal
lealtad [leal'tað] *nf* loyalty
lebrel [le'βrel] *nm* greyhound
lección [lek'θjon] *nf* lesson; **~ práctica** object lesson; **dar lecciones** to teach, give lessons; **dar una ~ a algn** (*fig*) to teach sb a lesson
leche ['letʃe] *nf* milk; (*fam!*) semen, spunk (*!*); **dar una ~ a algn** (*fam*) to belt sb; **estar de mala ~** (*fam*) to be in a foul mood; **tener mala ~** (*fam*) to be a nasty piece of work; **~ condensada/en polvo** condensed/powdered milk; **~ desnatada** skimmed milk; **~ de magnesia** milk of magnesia; **¡~!** hell!
lechera [le'tʃera] *nf ver* **lechero**
lechería [letʃe'ria] *nf* dairy
lechero, -a [le'tʃero, a] *adj* milk *cpd* ▷ *nm* milkman ▷ *nf* (*vendedora*) milkwoman; (*recipiente*) milk pan; (*para servir*) milk churn
lecho ['letʃo] *nm* (*cama, de río*) bed; (*Geo*) layer; **~ mortuorio** deathbed

lechón [le'tʃon] *nm* sucking (*Brit*) *o* suckling (*US*) pig
lechoso, -a [le'tʃoso, a] *adj* milky
lechuga [le'tʃuɣa] *nf* lettuce
lechuza [le'tʃuθa] *nf* (barn) owl
lectivo, -a [lek'tiβo, a] *adj* (*horas*) teaching *cpd*; **año** *o* **curso ~** (*Escol*) school year; (*Univ*) academic year
lector, a [lek'tor, a] *nm/f* reader; (*Escol, Univ*) (conversation) assistant ▷ *nm*: **~ de discos compactos** CD player; **~ óptico de caracteres** (*Inform*) optical character reader; **~ de libros electrónicos** e-reader ▷ *nf*: **~a de fichas** (*Inform*) card reader
lectura [lek'tura] *nf* reading; **~ de marcas sensibles** (*Inform*) mark sensing
leer [le'er] *vt* to read; **~ entre líneas** to read between the lines
legado [le'ɣaðo] *nm* (*don*) bequest; (*herencia*) legacy; (*enviado*) legate
legajo [le'ɣaxo] *nm* file, bundle (of papers)
legal [le'ɣal] *adj* legal, lawful; (*persona*) trustworthy
legalidad [leɣali'ðað] *nf* legality
legalizar [leɣali'θar] *vt* to legalize; (*documento*) to authenticate
legaña [le'ɣaɲa] *nf* sleep (*in eyes*)
legar [le'ɣar] *vt* to bequeath, leave
legendario, -a [lexen'darjo, a] *adj* legendary
legión [le'xjon] *nf* legion
legionario, -a [lexjo'narjo, a] *adj* legionary ▷ *nm* legionnaire
legislación [lexisla'θjon] *nf* legislation; (*leyes*) laws *pl*; **~ antimonopolio** (*Com*) anti-trust legislation
legislar [lexis'lar] *vt* to legislate
legislativo, -a [lexisla'tiβo, a] *adj*: **(elecciones) legislativas** ≈ general election
legislatura [lexisla'tura] *nf* (*Pol*) period of office
legitimar [lexiti'mar] *vt* to legitimize
legítimo, -a [le'xitimo, a] *adj* (*genuino*) authentic; (*legal*) legitimate, rightful
lego, -a ['leɣo, a] *adj* (*Rel*) secular; (*ignorante*) ignorant ▷ *nm* layman
legua ['leɣwa] *nf* league; **se ve (*o* nota) a la ~** you can tell (it) a mile off
legumbres [le'ɣumbres] *nfpl* pulses
leído, -a [le'iðo, a] *adj* well-read
lejanía [lexa'nia] *nf* distance
lejano, -a [le'xano, a] *adj* far-off; (*en el tiempo*) distant; (*fig*) remote; **L~ Oriente** Far East
lejía [le'xia] *nf* bleach
lejos ['lexos] *adv* far, far away; **a lo ~** in the distance; **de** *o* **desde ~** from a distance; **está muy ~** it's a long way (away); **¿está ~?** is it far?; **~ de** *prep* far from
lelo, -a ['lelo, a] *adj* silly ▷ *nm/f* idiot
lema ['lema] *nm* motto; (*Pol*) slogan
lencería [lenθe'ria] *nf* (*telas*) linen, drapery; (*ropa interior*) lingerie
lengua ['lengwa] *nf* tongue; (*Ling*) language; **~ materna** mother tongue; **~ de tierra** (*Geo*) spit *o* tongue of land; **dar a la ~** to chatter; **morderse la ~** to hold one's tongue; **sacar la ~ a algn** (*fig*) to cock a snook at sb
lenguado [len'gwaðo] *nm* sole
lenguaje [len'gwaxe] *nm* language; (*forma de hablar*) (mode of) speech; **~ comercial** business language; **~ ensamblador** *o* **de alto nivel** (*Inform*) high-level language; **~ máquina** (*Inform*) machine language; **~ original** source language; **~ periodístico** journalese; **~ de programación** (*Inform*) programming language; **en ~ llano** ≈ in plain English
lengüeta [len'gweta] *nf* (*Anat*) epiglottis; (*de zapatos*) tongue; (*Mus*) reed
lente ['lente] *nm o nf* lens; (*lupa*) magnifying glass; **lentes** *nmpl* glasses; **~s bifocales/de sol** (*Am*) bifocals/sunglasses; **~s de contacto** contact lenses; **~s progresivas** varifocal lenses
lenteja [len'texa] *nf* lentil
lentejuela [lente'xwela] *nf* sequin
lentilla [len'tiʎa] *nf* contact lens
lentitud [lenti'tuð] *nf* slowness; **con ~** slowly
lento, -a ['lento, a] *adj* slow
leña ['leɲa] *nf* firewood; **dar ~ a** to thrash; **echar ~ al fuego** to add fuel to the flames
leñador, a [leɲa'ðor, a] *nm/f* woodcutter
leño ['leɲo] *nm* (*trozo de árbol*) log; (*madera*) timber; (*fig*) blockhead
Leo ['leo] *nm* (*Astro*) Leo
león [le'on] *nm* lion; **~ marino** sea lion
leona [le'ona] *nf* lioness
leonino, -a [leo'nino, a] *adj* leonine
leopardo [leo'parðo] *nm* leopard
leotardos [leo'tarðos] *nmpl* tights
lepra ['lepra] *nf* leprosy
leproso, -a [le'proso, a] *nm/f* leper
lerdo, -a ['lerðo, a] *adj* (*lento*) slow; (*patoso*) clumsy
les [les] *pron* (*directo*) them; (*: en relación a ustedes*) you; (*indirecto*) to them; (*: a ustedes*) to you
lesbiana [les'βjana] *adj, nf* lesbian
lesión [le'sjon] *nf* wound, lesion; (*Deporte*) injury
lesionado, -a [lesjo'naðo, a] *adj* injured ▷ *nm/f* injured person
lesionar [lesjo'nar] *vt* (*dañar*) to hurt; (*herir*) to wound; **lesionarse** *vr* to get hurt
letal [le'tal] *adj* lethal
letanía [leta'nia] *nf* litany; (*retahíla*) long list
letargo [le'tarɣo] *nm* lethargy
letra ['letra] *nf* letter; (*escritura*) handwriting; (*Com*) letter, bill, draft; (*Mus*) lyrics *pl*; **letras** *nfpl* (*Univ*) arts; **~ bastardilla/negrilla** italics *pl*/bold type; **~ de cambio** bill of exchange; **~ de imprenta** print; **~ inicial/mayúscula/minúscula** initial/capital/small letter; **lo tomó al pie de la ~** he took it literally; **~ bancaria** (*Com*) bank draft; **~ de patente** (*Com*) letters patent *pl*; **escribir cuarto ~s a algn** to drop a line to sb

l

letrado, -a [le'traðo, a] *adj* learned; (*fam*) pedantic ▷ *nm/f* lawyer
letrero [le'trero] *nm* (*cartel*) sign; (*etiqueta*) label
letrina [le'trina] *nf* latrine
leucemia [leu'θemja] *nf* leukaemia
leucocito [leuko'θito] *nm* white blood cell, leucocyte
levadizo, -a [leβa'ðiθo, a] *adj*: **puente ~** drawbridge
levadura [leβa'ðura] *nf* yeast, leaven; **~ de cerveza** brewer's yeast
levantamiento [leβanta'mjento] *nm* raising, lifting; (*rebelión*) revolt, rising; (*Geo*) survey; **~ de pesos** weightlifting
levantar [leβan'tar] *vt* (*gen*) to raise; (*del suelo*) to pick up; (*hacia arriba*) to lift (up); (*plan*) to make, draw up; (*mesa*) to clear; (*campamento*) to strike; (*fig*) to cheer up, hearten; **levantarse** *vr* to get up; (*enderezarse*) to straighten up; (*rebelarse*) to rebel; (*sesión*) to be adjourned; (*niebla*) to lift; (*viento*) to rise; **~se (de la cama)** to get up, get out of bed; **~ el ánimo** to cheer up
levante [le'βante] *nm* east; (*viento*) east wind; **el L~** *region of Spain extending from Castellón to Murcia*
levar [le'βar] *vti*: **~ (anclas)** to weigh anchor
leve ['leβe] *adj* light; (*fig*) trivial; (*mínimo*) slight
levedad [leβe'ðað] *nf* lightness; (*fig*) levity
levita [le'βita] *nf* frock coat
léxico, -a ['leksiko, a] *adj* lexical ▷ *nm* (*vocabulario*) vocabulary; (*Ling*) lexicon
ley [lei] *nf* (*gen*) law; (*metal*) standard; **decreto-~** decree law; **de buena ~** (*fig*) genuine; **según la ~** in accordance with the law, by law, in law
leyenda [le'jenda] *nf* legend; (*Tip*) inscription
leyó *etc vb ver* **leer**
liar [li'ar] *vt* to tie (up); (*unir*) to bind; (*envolver*) to wrap (up); (*enredar*) to confuse; (*cigarrillo*) to roll; **liarse** *vr* (*fam*) to get involved; (*confundirse*) to get mixed up; **~se a palos** to get involved in a fight
Líbano ['liβano] *nm*: **el ~** the Lebanon
libar [li'βar] *vt* to suck
libelo [li'βelo] *nm* satire, lampoon; (*Jur*) petition
libélula [li'βelula] *nf* dragonfly
liberación [liβera'θjon] *nf* liberation; (*de la cárcel*) release
liberal [liβe'ral] *adj, nm/f* liberal
liberar [liβe'rar] *vt* to liberate
libertad [liβer'tað] *nf* liberty, freedom; **~ de asociación/de culto/de prensa/de comercio/de palabra** freedom of association/of worship/of the press/of trade/of speech; **~ condicional** probation; **~ bajo palabra** parole; **~ bajo fianza** bail; **estar en ~** to be free; **poner a algn en ~** to set sb free
libertar [liβer'tar] *vt* (*preso*) to set free; (*de una obligación*) to release; (*eximir*) to exempt
libertinaje [liβerti'naxe] *nm* licentiousness
libertino, -a [liβer'tino, a] *adj* permissive ▷ *nm/f* permissive person
libidinoso, -a [liβiði'noso, a] *adj* lustful; (*viejo*) lecherous
libra ['liβra] *nf* pound; **L~** (*Astro*) Libra; **~ esterlina** pound sterling
librador, a [liβra'ðor, a] *nm/f* drawer
libramiento [liβra'mjento] (*Am*) *nm* ring road (*Brit*), beltway (*US*)
librar [li'βrar] *vt* (*de peligro*) to save; (*batalla*) to wage, fight; (*de impuestos*) to exempt; (*cheque*) to make out; (*Jur*) to exempt; **librarse** *vr*: **~se de** to escape from, free o.s. from; **de buena nos hemos librado** we're well out of that
libre ['liβre] *adj* (*gen*) free; (*lugar*) unoccupied; (*tiempo*) spare; (*asiento*) vacant; (*de deudas*) free of debts; (*Com*): **~ a bordo** free on board; **~ de franqueo** post-free; **~ de impuestos** free of tax; **tiro ~** free kick; **los 100 metros ~** the 100 metres freestyle (race); **al aire ~** in the open air; **¿estás ~?** are you free?
librería [liβre'ria] *nf* (*tienda*) bookshop; (*estante*) bookcase; **~ de ocasión** secondhand bookshop
librero, -a [li'βrero, a] *nm/f* bookseller
libreta [li'βreta] *nf* notebook; (*pan*) one-pound loaf; **~ de ahorros** savings book
libro ['liβro] *nm* book; **~ de actas** minute book; **~ de bolsillo** paperback; **~ de cabecera** bedside book; **~ de caja** (*Com*) cashbook; **~ de caja auxiliar** (*Com*) petty cash book; **~ de cocina** cookery book (*Brit*), cookbook (*US*); **~ de consulta** reference book; **~ de cuentas** account book; **~ de cuentos** storybook; **~ de cheques** cheque (*Brit*) *o* check (*US*) book; **~ de entradas y salidas** (*Com*) daybook; **~ de honor** visitors' book; **~ diario** journal; **~ electrónico** e-book; **~ mayor** (*Com*) general ledger; **~ de reclamaciones** complaints book; **~ de texto** textbook
Lic. *abr* = **Licenciado, a**
licencia [li'θenθja] *nf* (*gen*) licence; (*permiso*) permission; **~ por enfermedad/con goce de sueldo** sick/paid leave; **~ de armas/de caza** gun/game licence; **~ de exportación** (*Com*) export licence; **~ poética** poetic licence
licenciado, -a [liθen'θjaðo, a] *adj* licensed ▷ *nm/f* graduate; **L~ en Filosofía y Letras** ≈ Bachelor of Arts; *see note*

LICENCIADO

When students finish University after an average of five years they receive the degree of *licenciado*. If the course is only three years such as Nursing, or if they choose not to do the optional two-year specialization, they are awarded the degree of *diplomado*. *Cursos de posgrado*, postgraduate courses, are becoming increasingly popular, especially one-year specialist courses called *masters*.

licenciar [liθen'θjar] *vt* (*empleado*) to dismiss; (*permitir*) to permit, allow; (*soldado*) to discharge; (*estudiante*) to confer a degree upon; **licenciarse** *vr*: **~se en derecho** to graduate in law; **~se en letras** to get an arts degree
licenciatura [liθenθja'tura] *nf* (*título*) degree; (*estudios*) degree course
licencioso, -a [liθen'θjoso, a] *adj* licentious
liceo [li'θeo] *nm* (*esp Am*) (high) school
licitar [liθi'tar] *vt* to bid for ▷ *vi* to bid
lícito, -a ['liθito, a] *adj* (*legal*) lawful; (*justo*) fair, just; (*permisible*) permissible
licor [li'kor] *nm* spirits *pl* (*Brit*), liquor (*US*); (*con hierbas etc*) liqueur
licra® ['likra] *nf* Lycra®
licuadora [likwa'ðora] *nf* blender
licuar [li'kwar] *vt* to liquidize
lid [lið] *nf* combat; (*fig*) controversy
líder ['liðer] *nm/f* leader
liderato [liðe'rato] *nm* = **liderazgo**
liderazgo [liðe'raθɣo] *nm* leadership
lidia ['liðja] *nf* bullfighting; (*una lidia*) bullfight; **toros de ~** fighting bulls
lidiar [li'ðjar] *vt, vi* to fight
liebre ['ljeβre] *nf* hare; **dar gato por ~** to con
lienzo ['ljenθo] *nm* linen; (*Arte*) canvas; (*Arq*) wall
liga ['liɣa] *nf* (*de medias*) garter, suspender; (*confederación*) league; (*Am: gomita*) rubber band
ligadura [liɣa'ðura] *nf* bond, tie; (*Med, Mus*) ligature
ligamento [liɣa'mento] *nm* (*Anat*) ligament; (*atadura*) tie; (*unión*) bond
ligar [li'ɣar] *vt* (*atar*) to tie; (*unir*) to join; (*Med*) to bind up; (*Mus*) to slur; (*fam*) to get off with, pick up ▷ *vi* to mix, blend; (*fam*) to get off with sb; (*2 personas*) to get off with one another; (*fam*): **(él) liga mucho** he pulls a lot of women; **ligarse** *vr* (*fig*) to commit o.s.; **~ con** (*fam*) to get off with, pick up; **~se a algn** to get off with *o* pick up sb
ligereza [lixe'reθa] *nf* lightness; (*rapidez*) swiftness; (*agilidad*) agility; (*superficialidad*) flippancy
ligero, -a [li'xero, a] *adj* (*de peso*) light; (*tela*) thin; (*rápido*) swift, quick; (*ágil*) agile, nimble; (*de importancia*) slight; (*de carácter*) flippant, superficial ▷ *adv* quickly, swiftly; **a la ligera** superficially; **juzgar a la ligera** to jump to conclusions
light ['lait] *adj inv* (*cigarrillo*) low-tar; (*comida*) diet *cpd*
ligue *etc* ['liɣe] *vb ver* **ligar** ▷ *nm/f* boyfriend/girlfriend ▷ *nm* (*persona*) pick-up
liguero [li'ɣero] *nm* suspender (*Brit*) *o* garter (*US*) belt
lija ['lixa] *nf* (*Zool*) dogfish; **(papel de) ~** sandpaper
lijar [li'xar] *vt* to sand
lila ['lila] *adj inv, nf* lilac ▷ *nm* (*fam*) twit
lima ['lima] *nf* file; (*Bot*) lime; **~ de uñas** nail file; **comer como una ~** to eat like a horse
limar [li'mar] *vt* to file; (*alisar*) to smooth over; (*fig*) to polish up
limbo ['limbo] *nm* (*Rel*) limbo; **estar en el ~** to be on another planet
limitación [limita'θjon] *nf* limitation, limit; **~ de velocidad** speed limit
limitar [limi'tar] *vt* to limit; (*reducir*) to reduce, cut down ▷ *vi*: **~ con** to border on; **limitarse** *vr*: **~se a** to limit *o* confine o.s. to
límite ['limite] *nm* (*gen*) limit; (*fin*) end; (*frontera*) border; **como ~** at (the) most; (*fecha*) at the latest; **no tener ~s** to know no bounds; **~ de crédito** (*Com*) credit limit; **~ de página** (*Inform*) page break; **~ de velocidad** speed limit
limítrofe [li'mitrofe] *adj* bordering, neighbouring
limón [li'mon] *nm* lemon ▷ *adj*: **amarillo ~** lemon-yellow
limonada [limo'naða] *nf* lemonade
limonero [limo'nero] *nm* lemon tree
limosna [li'mosna] *nf* alms *pl*; **pedir ~** to beg; **vivir de ~** to live on charity
limpiabotas [limpja'βotas] *nm/f inv* bootblack (*Brit*), shoeshine boy/girl
limpiador, a [limpja'ðor, a] *adj* cleaning, cleansing ▷ *nm/f* cleaner; = **limpiaparabrisas**
limpiaparabrisas [limpjapara'βrisas] *nm inv* windscreen (*Brit*) *o* windshield (*US*) wiper
limpiar [lim'pjar] *vt* to clean; (*con trapo*) to wipe; (*quitar*) to wipe away; (*zapatos*) to shine, polish; (*casa*) to tidy up; (*Inform*) to debug; (*fig*) to clean up; (*: purificar*) to cleanse, purify; (*Mil*) to mop up; **~ en seco** to dry-clean
limpieza [lim'pjeθa] *nf* (*estado*) cleanliness; (*acto*) cleaning; (*: de las calles*) cleansing; (*: de zapatos*) polishing; (*habilidad*) skill; (*fig: Policía*) clean-up; (*pureza*) purity; (*Mil*): **operación de ~** mopping-up operation; **~ étnica** ethnic cleansing; **~ en seco** dry cleaning
limpio, -a ['limpjo, a] *adj* clean; (*moralmente*) pure; (*ordenado*) tidy; (*despejado*) clear; (*Com*) clear, net; (*fam*) honest ▷ *adv*: **jugar ~** to play fair; **pasar a ~** to make a fair copy; **sacar algo en ~** to get benefit from sth; **~ de** free from
linaje [li'naxe] *nm* lineage, family
linaza [li'naθa] *nf* linseed; **aceite de ~** linseed oil
lince ['linθe] *nm* lynx; **ser un ~** (*fig: observador*) to be very observant; (*: astuto*) to be shrewd
linchar [lin'tʃar] *vt* to lynch
lindar [lin'dar] *vi* to adjoin; **~ con** to border on; (*Arq*) to abut on

linde ['linde] *nm o nf* boundary
lindero, -a [lin'dero, a] *adj* adjoining ▷ *nm* boundary
lindo, -a ['lindo, a] *adj* pretty, lovely ▷ *adv* (*esp Am*: *fam*) nicely, very well; **canta muy ~** (*Am*) he sings beautifully; **se divertían de lo ~** they enjoyed themselves enormously
línea ['linea] *nf* (*gen, moral, Pol etc*) line; (*talle*) figure; (*Inform*): **en ~** on line; **fuera de ~** off line; **~ de estado** status line; **~ de formato** format line; **~ aérea** airline; **~ de alto el fuego** ceasefire line; **~ de fuego** firing line; **~ de meta** goal line; (*de carrera*) finishing line; **~ de montaje** assembly line; **~ discontinua** (*Auto*) broken line; **~ dura** (*Pol*) hard line; **~ recta** straight line; **la ~ de 2008** (*moda*) the 2008 look
lingote [lin'gote] *nm* ingot
lingüista [lin'gwista] *nm/f* linguist
lingüística [lin'gwistika] *nf* linguistics *sg*
linimento [lini'mento] *nm* liniment
lino ['lino] *nm* linen; (*Bot*) flax
linóleo [li'noleo] *nm* lino, linoleum
linterna [lin'terna] *nf* lantern, lamp; **~ eléctrica** *o* **a pilas** torch (*Brit*), flashlight (*US*)
lío ['lio] *nm* bundle; (*desorden*) muddle, mess; (*fam*: *follón*) fuss; (: *relación amorosa*) affair; **armar un ~** to make a fuss; **meterse en un ~** to get into a jam; **tener un ~ con algn** to be having an affair with sb
lipotimia [lipo'timja] *nf* blackout
liquen ['liken] *nm* lichen
liquidación [likiða'θjon] *nf* liquidation; (*de cuenta*) settlement; **venta de ~** clearance sale
liquidar [liki'ðar] *vt* (*Química*) to liquefy; (*Com*) to liquidate; (*deudas*) to pay off; (*empresa*) to wind up; **~ a algn** to bump sb off, rub sb out (*fam*)
liquidez [liki'ðeθ] *nf* liquidity
líquido, -a ['likiðo, a] *adj* liquid; (*ganancia*) net ▷ *nm* liquid; (*Com*: *efectivo*) ready cash *o* money; (: *ganancia*) net amount *o* profit; **~ imponible** net taxable income
lira ['lira] *nf* (*Mus*) lyre; (*moneda*) lira
lírico, -a ['liriko, a] *adj* lyrical
lirio ['lirjo] *nm* (*Bot*) iris
lirón [li'ron] *nm* (*Zool*) dormouse; (*fig*) sleepyhead
Lisboa [lis'βoa] *nf* Lisbon
lisiado, -a [li'sjaðo, a] *adj* injured ▷ *nm/f* cripple
lisiar [li'sjar] *vt* to maim; **lisiarse** *vr* to injure o.s.
liso, -a ['liso, a] *adj* (*terreno*) flat; (*cabello*) straight; (*superficie*) even; (*tela*) plain; **lisa y llanamente** in plain language, plainly
lisonja [li'sonxa] *nf* flattery
lisonjear [lisonxe'ar] *vt* to flatter; (*fig*) to please
lisonjero, -a [lison'xero, a] *adj* flattering; (*agradable*) gratifying, pleasing ▷ *nm/f* flatterer
lista ['lista] *nf* list; (*en escuela*) school register; (*de libros*) catalogue; (*tb*: **~ de correos**) poste restante, general delivery (*US*); (*tb*: **~ de platos**) menu; (*tb*: **~ de precios**) price list; **pasar ~** to call the roll; (*Escol*) to call the register; **~ de direcciones** mailing list; **~ electoral** electoral roll; **~ de espera** waiting list; **tela a ~s** striped material
listado, -a [lis'taðo, a] *adj* striped ▷ *nm* (*Com, Inform*) listing; **~ paginado** (*Inform*) paged listing
listo, -a ['listo, a] *adj* (*perspicaz*) smart, clever; (*preparado*) ready; **~ para usar** ready-to-use; **¿estás ~?** are you ready?; **pasarse de ~** to be too clever by half
listón [lis'ton] *nm* (*de tela*) ribbon; (*de madera, metal*) strip
litera [li'tera] *nf* (*en barco, tren*) berth; (*en dormitorio*) bunk, bunk bed
literal [lite'ral] *adj* literal
literario, -a [lite'rarjo, a] *adj* literary
literato, -a [lite'rato, a] *adj* literary ▷ *nm/f* writer
literatura [litera'tura] *nf* literature
litigar [liti'ɣar] *vt* to fight ▷ *vi* (*Jur*) to go to law; (*fig*) to dispute, argue
litigio [li'tixjo] *nm* (*Jur*) lawsuit; (*fig*): **en ~ con** in dispute with
litografía [litoɣra'fia] *nf* lithography; (*una litografía*) lithograph
litoral [lito'ral] *adj* coastal ▷ *nm* coast, seaboard
litro ['litro] *nm* litre, liter (*US*)
liviano, -a [li'βjano, a] *adj* (*persona*) fickle; (*cosa, objeto*) trivial; (*Am*) light
lívido, -a ['liβiðo, a] *adj* livid
llaga ['ʎaɣa] *nf* wound
llama ['ʎama] *nf* flame; (*fig*) passion; (*Zool*) llama; **en ~s** burning, ablaze
llamada [ʎa'maða] *nf* call; (*a la puerta*) knock; (: *al timbre*) ring; **~ a cobro revertido** reverse-charge call; **~ al orden** call to order; **~ de atención** warning; **~ a pie de página** reference note; **~ a procedimiento** (*Inform*) procedure call; **~ interurbana** trunk call; **~ metropolitana** (*Esp*), **~ local** (*Am*) local call; **~ por cobrar** (*Am*) reverse-charge call
llamamiento [ʎama'mjento] *nm* call; **hacer un ~ a algn para que haga algo** to appeal to sb to do sth
llamar [ʎa'mar] *vt* to call; (*convocar*) to summon; (*invocar*) to invoke; (*atraer con gesto*) to beckon; (*atención*) to attract; (*Telec*: *tb*: **~ por teléfono**) to call, ring up, telephone; (*Mil*) to call up ▷ *vi* (*por teléfono*) to phone; (*a la puerta*) to knock (*o* ring); (*por señas*) to beckon; **llamarse** *vr* to be called, be named; **¿cómo se llama usted?** what's your name?; **¿quién llama?** (*Telec*) who's calling?, who's that?; **no me llama la atención** (*fam*) I don't fancy it
llamarada [ʎama'raða] *nf* (*llamas*) blaze; (*rubor*) flush; (*fig*) flare-up

llamativo, -a [ʎama'tiβo, a] *adj* showy; (*color*) loud
llamear [ʎame'ar] *vi* to blaze
llano, -a ['ʎano, a] *adj* (*superficie*) flat; (*persona*) straightforward; (*estilo*) clear ▷ *nm* plain, flat ground
llanta ['ʎanta] *nf* (wheel) rim; (*Am*: *neumático*) tyre; (: *cámara*) (inner) tube; **~ de repuesto** (*Am*) spare tyre
llanto ['ʎanto] *nm* weeping; (*fig*) lamentation; (*canción*) dirge, lament
llanura [ʎa'nura] *nf* (*lisura*) flatness, smoothness; (*Geo*) plain
llave ['ʎaβe] *nf* key; (*de gas, agua*) tap (*Brit*), faucet (*US*); (*Mecánica*) spanner; (*de la luz*) switch; (*Mus*) key; **~ inglesa** monkey wrench; **~ maestra** master key; **~ de contacto**, **~ de encendido** (*Am*: *Auto*) ignition key; **~ de paso** stopcock; **echar ~ a** to lock up
llavero [ʎa'βero] *nm* keyring
llavín [ʎa'βin] *nm* latchkey
llegada [ʎe'ɣaða] *nf* arrival
llegar [ʎe'ɣar] *vt* to bring up, bring over ▷ *vi* to arrive; (*bastar*) to be enough; **llegarse** *vr*: **~se a** to approach; **~ a** (*alcanzar*) to reach; to manage to, succeed in; **~ a saber** to find out; **~ a ser famoso/el jefe** to become famous/the boss; **~ a las manos** to come to blows; **~ a las manos de** to come into the hands of; **no llegues tarde** don't be late; **esta cuerda no llega** this rope isn't long enough
llenar [ʎe'nar] *vt* to fill; (*superficie*) to cover; (*espacio, tiempo*) to fill, take up; (*formulario*) to fill in *o* out; (*fig*) to heap; **llenarse** *vr* to fill (up); **~se de** (*fam*) to stuff o.s. with
lleno, -a ['ʎeno, a] *adj* full, filled; (*repleto*) full up ▷ *nm* (*abundancia*) abundance; (*Teat*) full house; **dar de ~ contra un muro** to hit a wall head-on
llevadero, -a [ʎeβa'ðero, a] *adj* bearable, tolerable
llevar [ʎe'βar] *vt* to take; (*ropa*) to wear; (*cargar*) to carry; (*quitar*) to take away; (*en coche*) to drive; (*transportar*) to transport; (*ruta*) to follow, keep to; (*traer*: *dinero*) to carry; (*conducir*) to lead; (*Mat*) to carry; (*aguantar*) to bear; (*negocio*) to conduct, direct; to manage ▷ *vi* (*suj*: *camino etc*): **~ a** to lead to; **llevarse** *vr* to carry off, take away; **llevamos dos días aquí** we have been here for two days; **él me lleva dos años** he's two years older than me; **~ adelante** (*fig*) to carry forward; **~ por delante a uno** (*en coche etc*) to run sb over; (*fig*) to ride roughshod over sb; **~ la ventaja** to be winning *o* in the lead; **~ los libros** (*Com*) to keep the books; **llevo las de perder** I'm likely to lose; **no las lleva todas consigo** he's not all there; **nos llevó a cenar fuera** she took us out for a meal; **~se a uno por delante** (*atropellar*) to run sb over; **~se bien** to get on well (together)
llorar [ʎo'rar] *vt* to cry, weep ▷ *vi* to cry, weep; (*ojos*) to water; **~ a moco tendido** to sob one's heart out; **~ de risa** to cry with laughter
lloriquear [ʎorike'ar] *vi* to snivel, whimper
lloro ['ʎoro] *nm* crying, weeping
llorón, -ona [ʎo'ron, ona] *adj* tearful ▷ *nm/f* cry-baby
lloroso, -a [ʎo'roso, a] *adj* (*gen*) weeping, tearful; (*triste*) sad, sorrowful
llover [ʎo'βer] *vi* to rain; **~ a cántaros** *o* **a cubos** *o* **a mares** to rain cats and dogs, pour (down); **ser una cosa llovida del cielo** to be a godsend; **llueve sobre mojado** it never rains but it pours
llovizna [ʎo'βiθna] *nf* drizzle
lloviznar [ʎoβiθ'nar] *vi* to drizzle
llueve *etc* ['ʎweβe] *vb ver* **llover**
lluvia ['ʎuβja] *nf* rain; (*cantidad*) rainfall; (*fig*: *de balas etc*) hail, shower; **~ radioactiva** radioactive fallout; **día de ~** rainy day; **una ~ de regalos** a shower of gifts
lluvioso, -a [ʎu'βjoso, a] *adj* rainy
lo [lo] *artículo definido neutro*: **lo bueno** the good ▷ *pron* (*en relación a una persona*) him; (*en relación a una cosa*) it; **lo mío** what is mine; **lo difícil es que …** the difficult thing about it is that …; **no saben lo aburrido que es** they don't know how boring it is; **viste a lo americano** he dresses in the American style; **lo de** that matter of; **lo que** what, that which; **toma lo que quieras** take what(ever) you want; **lo que sea** whatever; **¡toma lo que he dicho!** I stand by what I said!; *ver tb* **el**
loa ['loa] *nf* praise
loable [lo'aβle] *adj* praiseworthy
loar [lo'ar] *vt* to praise
lobato [lo'βato] *nm* (*Zool*) wolf cub
lobo ['loβo] *nm* wolf; **~ de mar** (*fig*) sea dog; **~ marino** seal
lóbrego, -a ['loβreɣo, a] *adj* dark; (*fig*) gloomy
lóbulo ['loβulo] *nm* lobe
local [lo'kal] *adj* local ▷ *nm* place, site; (*oficinas*) premises *pl*
localidad [lokali'ðað] *nf* (*barrio*) locality; (*lugar*) location; (*Teat*) seat, ticket
localizar [lokali'θar] *vt* (*ubicar*) to locate, find; (*encontrar*) to find, track down; (*restringir*) to localize; (*situar*) to place
loción [lo'θjon] *nf* lotion, wash
loco, -a ['loko, a] *adj* mad; (*fig*) wild, mad ▷ *nm/f* madman(-woman); **~ de atar**, **~ de remate**, **~ rematado** raving mad; **a lo ~** without rhyme or reason; **ando ~ con el examen** the exam is driving me crazy; **estar ~ con** *o* **por algo/por algn** to be mad about sth/sb; **estar ~ de alegría** to be overjoyed *o* over the moon
locomoción [lokomo'θjon] *nf* locomotion
locomotora [lokomo'tora] *nf* engine, locomotive
locuaz [lo'kwaθ] *adj* loquacious, talkative
locución [loku'θjon] *nf* expression
locura [lo'kura] *nf* madness; (*acto*) crazy act

locutor, a [loku'tor, a] *nm/f* (*Radio*) announcer; (*comentarista*) commentator; (*TV*) newscaster, newsreader
locutorio [loku'torjo] *nm* (*Telec*) telephone box *o* booth; (*negocio*) *shop or internet café providing telephone services*
lodo ['lodo] *nm* mud
lógico, -a ['loxiko, a] *adj* logical; (*correcto*) natural; (*razonable*) reasonable ▷ *nm* logician ▷ *nf* logic; **es ~ que ...** it stands to reason that ...; **ser de una lógica aplastante** to be as clear as day
login ['loxin] *nm* login
logístico, -a [lo'xistiko, a] *adj* logistical ▷ *nf* logistics *pl*
logotipo [loɣo'tipo] *nm* logo
logrado, -a [lo'ɣraðo, a] *pp de* **lograr** ▷ *adj* (*interpretación, reproducción*) polished, excellent
lograr [lo'ɣrar] *vt* (*obtener*) to get, obtain; (*conseguir*) to achieve, attain; **~ hacer** to manage to do; **~ que algn venga** to manage to get sb to come; **~ acceso a** (*Inform*) to access
logro ['loɣro] *nm* achievement, success; (*Com*) profit
lóker ['loker] *nm* (*Am*) locker
loma ['loma] *nf* hillock, low ridge
lombriz [lom'briθ] *nf* (earth)worm
lomo ['lomo] *nm* (*de animal*) back; (*Culin: de cerdo*) pork loin; (*: de vaca*) rib steak; (*de libro*) spine
lona ['lona] *nf* canvas
loncha ['lontʃa] *nf* = **lonja**
lonche ['lontʃe] *nm* (*Am*) lunch
lonchería [lontʃe'ria] *nf* (*Am*) snack bar, diner (*US*)
Londres ['londres] *nm* London
longaniza [longa'niθa] *nf* pork sausage
longevidad [lonxeβi'ðað] *nf* longevity
longitud [lonxi'tuð] *nf* length; (*Geo*) longitude; **tener tres metros de ~** to be three metres long; **~ de onda** wavelength; **salto de ~** long jump
longitudinal [lonxituði'nal] *adj* longitudinal
lonja ['lonxa] *nf* slice; (*de tocino*) rasher; (*Com*) market, exchange; **~ de pescado** fish market
loro ['loro] *nm* parrot
los [los] *artículo definido mpl* the ▷ *pron* them; (*en relación a ustedes*) you; **mis libros y ~ tuyos** my books and yours
losa ['losa] *nf* stone; **~ sepulcral** gravestone
lote ['lote] *nm* portion, share; (*Com*) lot; (*Inform*) batch
lotería [lote'ria] *nf* lottery; (*juego*) lotto; **le tocó la ~** he won a big prize in the lottery; (*fig*) he struck lucky; **~ nacional** national lottery; **~ primitiva** (*Esp*) *type of state-run lottery*; *see note*

LOTERÍA

Millions of euros are spent every year on *loterías*, lotteries. There is the weekly *Lotería Nacional* which is very popular especially at Christmas. Other weekly lotteries are the *Bono Loto* and the *(Lotería) Primitiva*. One of the most famous lotteries is run by the wealthy and influential society for the blind, *la ONCE*, and the form is called *el cupón de la ONCE* or *el cupón de los ciegos*.

loza ['loθa] *nf* crockery; **~ fina** china
lozanía [loθa'nia] *nf* (*lujo*) luxuriance
lozano, -a [lo'θano, a] *adj* luxuriant; (*animado*) lively
lubina [lu'βina] *nf* (*Zool*) sea bass
lubricante [luβri'kante] *adj, nm* lubricant
lubricar [luβri'kar], **lubrificar** [luβrifi'kar] *vt* to lubricate
lucero [lu'θero] *nm* (*Astro*) bright star; (*fig*) brilliance; **~ del alba/de la tarde** morning/evening star
luces ['luθes] *nfpl de* **luz**
lucha ['lutʃa] *nf* fight, struggle; **~ de clases** class struggle; **~ libre** wrestling
luchar [lu'tʃar] *vi* to fight
lucidez [luθi'ðeθ] *nf* lucidity
lúcido, -a ['luθiðo, a] *adj* (*persona*) lucid; (*mente*) logical; (*idea*) crystal-clear
luciérnaga [lu'θjernaɣa] *nf* glow-worm
lucimiento [luθi'mjento] *nm* (*brillo*) brilliance; (*éxito*) success
lucir [lu'θir] *vt* to illuminate, light (up); (*ostentar*) to show off ▷ *vi* (*brillar*) to shine; (*Am: parecer*) to look, seem; **lucirse** *vr* (*irónico*) to make a fool of o.s.; (*presumir*) to show off; **la casa luce limpia** the house looks clean
lucro ['lukro] *nm* profit, gain; **~s y daños** (*Com*) profit and loss *sg*
lúdico, -a ['luðiko, a] *adj* playful; (*actividad*) recreational
ludopatía [luðopa'tia] *nf* addiction to gambling (*o* videogames)
luego ['lweɣo] *adv* (*después*) next; (*más tarde*) later, afterwards; (*Am fam: en seguida*) at once, immediately; **desde ~** of course; **¡hasta ~!** see you later!, so long!; **¿y ~?** what next?
lugar [lu'ɣar] *nm* place; (*sitio*) spot; (*pueblo*) village, town; **en ~ de** instead of; **en primer ~** in the first place, firstly; **dar ~ a** to give rise to; **hacer ~** to make room; **fuera de ~** out of place; **sin ~ a dudas** without doubt, undoubtedly; **tener ~** to take place; **~ común** commonplace; **yo en su ~** if I were him; **no hay ~ para preocupaciones** there is no cause for concern
lugareño, -a [luɣa'reɲo, a] *adj* village *cpd* ▷ *nm/f* villager
lugarteniente [luɣarte'njente] *nm* deputy
lúgubre ['luɣuβre] *adj* mournful
lujo ['luxo] *nm* luxury; (*fig*) profusion, abundance; **de ~** luxury *cpd*, de luxe
lujoso, -a [lu'xoso, a] *adj* luxurious
lujuria [lu'xurja] *nf* lust
lumbago [lum'baɣo] *nm* lumbago

lumbre ['lumbre] *nf* (*luz*) light; (*fuego*) fire; **cerca de la ~** near the fire, at the fireside; **¿tienes ~?** (*para cigarro*) have you got a light?

lumbrera [lum'brera] *nf* luminary; (*fig*) leading light

luminoso, -a [lumi'noso, a] *adj* luminous, shining; (*idea*) bright, brilliant

luna ['luna] *nf* moon; (*vidrio: escaparate*) plate glass; (*: de un espejo*) glass; (*: de gafas*) lens; (*fig*) crescent; **~ creciente/llena/menguante/nueva** crescent/full/waning/new moon; **~ de miel** honeymoon; **estar en la ~** to have one's head in the clouds

lunar [lu'nar] *adj* lunar ▷ *nm* (*Anat*) mole; **tela a ~es** spotted material

lunes ['lunes] *nm inv* Monday; *ver tb* **sábado**

lupa ['lupa] *nf* magnifying glass

lustrar [lus'trar] *vt* (*esp Am: mueble*) to polish; (*zapatos*) to shine

lustre ['lustre] *nm* polish; (*fig*) lustre; **dar ~ a** to polish

lustroso, -a [lus'troso, a] *adj* shining

luterano, -a [lute'rano, a] *adj* Lutheran

luto ['luto] *nm* mourning; (*congoja*) grief, sorrow; **llevar el** *o* **vestirse de ~** to be in mourning

Luxemburgo [luksem'burɣo] *nm* Luxembourg

luz [luθ] (*pl* **luces**) *nf* (*tb fig*) light; (*fam*) electricity; **dar a ~ un niño** to give birth to a child; **sacar a la ~** to bring to light; **dar la ~** to switch on the light; **encender** (*Esp*) *o* **prender** (*Am*)/**apagar la ~** to switch the light on/off; **les cortaron la ~** their (electricity) supply was cut off; **a la ~ de** in the light of; **a todas luces** by any reckoning; **hacer la ~ sobre** to shed light on; **tener pocas luces** to be dim *o* stupid; **~ de la luna/del sol** *o* **solar** moonlight/sunlight; **~ eléctrica** electric light; **~ roja/verde** red/green light; **~ de cruce** (*Auto*) dipped headlight; **~ de freno** brake light; **~ intermitente/trasera** flashing/rear light; **luces de tráfico** traffic lights; **el Siglo de las Luces** the Age of Enlightenment; **traje de luces** bullfighter's costume

m

m *abr* (= *metro(s)*) m; (= *minuto(s)*) min., m; (= *masculino*) m., masc

macana [ma'kana] *nf* (*Am: porra*) club; (*: mentira*) lie, fib; (*: tontería*) piece of nonsense

macarra [ma'karra] *nm* (*fam*) thug

macarrones [maka'rrones] *nmpl* macaroni *sg*

macedonia [maθe'ðonja] *nf*: **~ de frutas** fruit salad

macerar [maθe'rar] *vt* (*Culin*) to soak, macerate; **macerarse** *vr* to soak, soften

maceta [ma'θeta] *nf* (*de flores*) pot of flowers; (*para plantas*) flowerpot

machacar [matʃa'kar] *vt* to crush, pound; (*moler*) to grind (up); (*aplastar*) to mash ▷ *vi* (*insistir*) to go on, keep on

machete [ma'tʃete] *nm* machete, (large) knife

machetear [matʃete'ar] *vt* (*Am*) to swot (*Brit*), grind away (*US*)

machismo [ma'tʃismo] *nm* sexism; male chauvinism

machista [ma'tʃista] *adj, nm* sexist; male chauvinist

macho ['matʃo] *adj* male; (*fig*) virile ▷ *nm* male; (*fig*) he-man, tough guy (*US*); (*Tec: perno*) pin, peg; (*Elec*) pin, plug; (*Costura*) hook

macizo, -a [ma'θiθo, a] *adj* (*grande*) massive; (*fuerte, sólido*) solid ▷ *nm* mass, chunk; (*Geo*) massif

macramé [makra'me] *nm* macramé

mácula ['makula] *nf* stain, blemish

madeja [ma'ðexa] *nf* (*de lana*) skein, hank; (*de pelo*) mass, mop

madera [ma'ðera] *nf* wood; (*fig*) nature, character; (*: aptitud*) aptitude; **una ~** a piece of wood; **~ contrachapada** *o* **laminada** plywood; **tiene buena ~** he's made of solid stuff; **tiene ~ de futbolista** he's got the makings of a footballer
madero [ma'ðero] *nm* beam; (*fig*) ship
madrastra [ma'ðrastra] *nf* stepmother
madre ['maðre] *adj* mother *cpd*; (*Am*) tremendous ▷ *nf* mother; (*de vino etc*) dregs *pl*; **~ adoptiva/política/soltera** foster mother/mother-in-law/unmarried mother; **la M~ Patria** the Mother Country; **sin ~** motherless; **¡~ mía!** oh dear!; **¡tu ~!** (*fam!*) fuck off! (*!*); **salirse de ~** (*río*) to burst its banks; (*persona*) to lose all self-control
madreperla [maðre'perla] *nf* mother-of-pearl
madreselva [maðre'selβa] *nf* honeysuckle
Madrid [ma'ðrið] *n* Madrid
madriguera [maðri'ɣera] *nf* burrow
madrileño, -a [maðri'leɲo, a] *adj* of *o* from Madrid ▷ *nm/f* native *o* inhabitant of Madrid
madrina [ma'ðrina] *nf* godmother; (*Arq*) prop, shore; (*Tec*) brace; **~ de boda** bridesmaid
madrugada [maðru'ɣaða] *nf* early morning, small hours; (*alba*) dawn, daybreak; **a las cuarto de la ~** at four o'clock in the morning
madrugador, a [maðruɣa'ðor, a] *adj* early-rising
madrugar [maðru'ɣar] *vi* to get up early; (*fig*) to get ahead
madurar [maðu'rar] *vt, vi* (*fruta*) to ripen; (*fig*) to mature
madurez [maðu'reθ] *nf* ripeness; (*fig*) maturity
maduro, -a [ma'ðuro, a] *adj* ripe; (*fig*) mature; **poco ~** unripe
maestra [ma'estra] *nf ver* **maestro**
maestría [maes'tria] *nf* mastery; (*habilidad*) skill, expertise; (*Am*) Master's Degree
maestro, -a [ma'estro, a] *adj* masterly; (*perito*) skilled, expert; (*principal*) main; (*educado*) trained ▷ *nm/f* master/mistress; (*profesor*) teacher ▷ *nm* (*autoridad*) authority; (*Mus*) maestro; (*experto*) master; (*obrero*) skilled workman; **~ albañil** master mason; **~ de obras** foreman
mafia ['mafja] *nf* mafia; **la M~** the Mafia
magdalena [maɣða'lena] *nf* fairy cake
magia ['maxja] *nf* magic
mágico, -a ['maxiko, a] *adj* magic(al) ▷ *nm/f* magician
magisterio [maxis'terjo] *nm* (*enseñanza*) teaching; (*profesión*) teaching profession; (*maestros*) teachers *pl*
magistrado [maxis'traðo] *nm* magistrate; **Primer M~** (*Am*) President, Prime Minister
magistral [maxis'tral] *adj* magisterial; (*fig*) masterly
magnánimo, -a [maɣ'nanimo, a] *adj* magnanimous
magnate [maɣ'nate] *nm* magnate, tycoon; **~ de la prensa** press baron
magnético, -a [maɣ'netiko, a] *adj* magnetic
magnetismo [maɣne'tismo] *nm* magnetism
magnetizar [maɣneti'θar] *vt* to magnetize
magnetofón [maɣneto'fon], **magnetófono** [maɣne'tofono] *nm* tape recorder
magnetofónico, -a [maɣneto'foniko, a] *adj*: **cinta magnetofónica** recording tape
magnífico, -a [maɣ'nifiko, a] *adj* splendid, magnificent
magnitud [maɣni'tuð] *nf* magnitude
mago, -a ['maɣo, a] *nm/f* magician, wizard; **los Reyes M~s** the Magi, the Three Wise Men; *ver tb* **Reyes Magos**
magro, -a ['maɣro, a] *adj* (*persona*) thin, lean; (*carne*) lean
magullar [maɣu'ʎar] *vt* (*amoratar*) to bruise; (*dañar*) to damage; (*fam: golpear*) to bash, beat
mahometano, -a [maome'tano, a] *adj* Mohammedan
mahonesa [mao'nesa] *nf* mayonnaise
maître ['metre] *nm* head waiter
maíz [ma'iθ] *nm* maize (*Brit*), corn (*US*); sweet corn
majadero, -a [maxa'ðero, a] *adj* silly, stupid
majestad [maxes'tað] *nf* majesty; **Su M~** His/Her Majesty; **(Vuestra) M~** Your Majesty
majestuoso, -a [maxes'twoso, a] *adj* majestic
majo, -a ['maxo, a] *adj* nice; (*guapo*) attractive, good-looking; (*elegante*) smart
mal [mal] *adv* badly; (*equivocadamente*) wrongly; (*con dificultad*) with difficulty ▷ *adj* = **malo** ▷ *nm* evil; (*desgracia*) misfortune; (*daño*) harm, damage; (*Med*) illness ▷ *conj*: **~ que le pese** whether he likes it or not; **me entendió ~** he misunderstood me; **hablar ~ de algn** to speak ill of sb; **huele ~** it smells bad; **ir de ~ en peor** to go from bad to worse; **oigo/veo ~** I can't hear/see very well; **si ~ no recuerdo** if my memory serves me right; **¡menos ~!** just as well!; **~ que bien** rightly or wrongly; **no hay ~ que por bien no venga** every cloud has a silver lining; **~ de ojo** evil eye
malabarismo [malaβa'rismo] *nm* juggling
malabarista [malaβa'rista] *nm/f* juggler
malaconsejado, -a [malakonse'xaðo, a] *adj* ill-advised
malaria [ma'larja] *nf* malaria
malcriado, -a [mal'krjaðo, a] *adj* (*consentido*) spoiled
maldad [mal'dað] *nf* evil, wickedness
maldecir [malde'θir] *vt* to curse ▷ *vi*: **~ de** to speak ill of
maldición [maldi'θjon] *nf* curse; **¡~!** curse it!, damn!
maldito, -a [mal'dito, a] *adj* (*condenado*) damned; (*perverso*) wicked ▷ *nm*: **el ~** the

devil; **¡~ sea!** damn it!; **no le hace ~ (el) caso** he doesn't take a blind bit of notice

maleante [male'ante] *adj* wicked ▷ *nm/f* criminal, crook

malecón [male'kon] *nm* pier, jetty; (*rompeolas*) breakwater; (*LAm: paseo*) sea front, promenade

maledicencia [maleðiˈθenθja] *nf* slander, scandal

maleducado, -a [maleðu'kaðo, a] *adj* bad-mannered, rude

maleficio [male'fiθjo] *nm* curse, spell

malentendido [malenten'diðo] *nm* misunderstanding

malestar [males'tar] *nm* (*gen*) discomfort; (*enfermedad*) indisposition; (*fig: inquietud*) uneasiness; (*Pol*) unrest; **siento un ~ en el estómago** my stomach is upset

maleta [ma'leta] *nf* case, suitcase; (*Auto*) boot (*Brit*), trunk (*US*); **hacer la ~** to pack

maletera [male'tera] *nf* (*Am Auto*) boot (*Brit*), trunk (*US*)

maletero [male'tero] *nm* (*Auto*) boot (*Brit*), trunk (*US*); (*persona*) porter

maletín [male'tin] *nm* small case, bag; (*portafolio*) briefcase

malévolo, -a [ma'leβolo, a] *adj* malicious, spiteful

maleza [ma'leθa] *nf* (*malas hierbas*) weeds *pl*; (*arbustos*) thicket

malgastar [malɣas'tar] *vt* (*tiempo, dinero*) to waste; (*recursos*) to squander; (*salud*) to ruin

malhechor, a [male'tʃor, a] *nm/f* delinquent; (*criminal*) criminal

malherido, -a [male'riðo, a] *adj* badly injured

malhumorado, -a [malumo'raðo, a] *adj* bad-tempered

malicia [ma'liθja] *nf* (*maldad*) wickedness; (*astucia*) slyness, guile; (*mala intención*) malice, spite; (*carácter travieso*) mischievousness

malicioso, -a [mali'θjoso, a] *adj* wicked, evil; sly, crafty; malicious, spiteful; mischievous

maligno, -a [ma'liɣno, a] *adj* evil; (*dañino*) pernicious, harmful; (*malévolo*) malicious; (*Med*) malignant ▷ *nm*: **el ~** the devil

malla ['maʎa] *nf* (*de una red*) mesh; (*red*) network; (*Am: de baño*) swimsuit; (*de ballet, gimnasia*) leotard; **mallas** *nfpl* tights; **~ de alambre** wire mesh

Mallorca [ma'ʎorka] *nf* Majorca

malo, -a ['malo, a] *adj* (**mal** *antes de nmsg*) bad; (*calidad*) poor; (*falso*) false; (*espantoso*) dreadful; (*niño*) naughty ▷ *nm/f* villain ▷ *nm* (*Cine fam*) bad guy ▷ *nf* spell of bad luck; **estar ~** to be ill; **andar a malas con algn** to be on bad terms with sb; **estar de malas** (*mal humor*) to be in a bad mood; **lo ~ es que ...** the trouble is that ...

malograr [malo'ɣrar] *vt* to spoil; (*plan*) to upset; (*ocasión*) to waste; **malograrse** *vr* (*plan etc*) to fail, come to grief; (*persona*) to die before one's time

malparado, -a [malpa'raðo, a] *adj*: **salir ~** to come off badly

malpensado, -a [malpen'saðo, a] *adj* nasty

malsano, -a [mal'sano, a] *adj* unhealthy

Malta ['malta] *nf* Malta

malta ['malta] *nf* malt

malteada [malte'aða] *nf* (*Am*) milk shake

maltratar [maltra'tar] *vt* to ill-treat, mistreat

maltrecho, -a [mal'tretʃo, a] *adj* battered, damaged

malva ['malβa] *nf* mallow; **~ loca** hollyhock; **(de color de) ~** mauve

malvado, -a [mal'βaðo, a] *adj* evil, villainous

malvavisco [malβa'βisko] *nm* marshmallow

malversar [malβer'sar] *vt* to embezzle, misappropriate

Malvinas [mal'βinas] *nfpl*: **islas ~** Falkland Islands

malware ['malwer] *nm* malware

mama ['mama] (*pl* **mamas**) *nf* (*de animal*) teat, (*de mujer*) breast

mamá [ma'ma] *nf* (*fam*) mum, mummy

mamar [ma'mar] *vt* (*pecho*) to suck; (*fig*) to absorb, assimilate ▷ *vi* to suck; **dar de ~** to (breast-)feed; (*animal*) to suckle

mamarracho [mama'rratʃo] *nm* sight, mess

mambo ['mambo] *nf* (*Mus*) mambo

mameluco [mameluko] (*Am*) *nm* dungarees *pl* (*Brit*), overalls *pl* (*US*)

mamífero, -a [ma'mifero, a] *adj* mammalian, mammal *cpd* ▷ *nm* mammal

mamón, -ona [ma'mon, ona] *adj* small, baby *cpd* ▷ *nm/f* small baby; (*fam!*) wanker (*!*)

mampara [mam'para] *nf* (*entre habitaciones*) partition; (*biombo*) screen

mampostería [mamposte'ria] *nf* masonry

mamut [ma'mut] *nm* mammoth

manada [ma'naða] *nf* (*Zool*) herd; (*: de leones*) pride; (*: de lobos*) pack; **llegaron en ~s** (*fam*) they came in droves

Managua [ma'naɣwa] *n* Managua

manantial [manan'tjal] *nm* spring; (*fuente*) fountain; (*fig*) source

manar [ma'nar] *vt* to run with, flow with ▷ *vi* to run, flow; (*abundar*) to abound

mancha ['mantʃa] *nf* stain, mark; (*de tinta*) blot; (*de vegetación*) patch; (*imperfección*) stain, blemish, blot; (*boceto*) sketch, outline; **la M~** La Mancha

manchar [man'tjar] *vt* to stain, mark; (*Zool*) to patch; (*ensuciar*) to soil, dirty; **mancharse** *vr* to get dirty; (*fig*) to dirty one's hands

manchego, -a [man'tʃeɣo, a] *adj* of *o* from La Mancha ▷ *nm/f* native *o* inhabitant of La Mancha

mancilla [man'θiʎa] *nf* stain, blemish

manco, -a ['manko, a] *adj* (*de un brazo*) one-armed; (*de una mano*) one-handed; (*fig*) defective, faulty; **no ser ~** to be useful *o* active

m

mancomunar [mankomu'nar] *vt* to unite, bring together; (*recursos*) to pool; (*Jur*) to make jointly responsible
mancomunidad [mankomuni'ðað] *nf* union, association; (*comunidad*) community; (*Jur*) joint responsibility
mandado [man'daðo] *nm* (*orden*) order; (*recado*) commission, errand
mandamiento [manda'mjento] *nm* (*orden*) order, command; (*Rel*) commandment; **~ judicial** warrant
mandar [man'dar] *vt* (*ordenar*) to order; (*dirigir*) to lead, command; (*país*) to rule over; (*enviar*) to send; (*pedir*) to order, ask for ▷ *vi* to be in charge; (*pey*) to be bossy; **mandarse** *vr*: **~se mudar** (*Am*: (*fam*)) to go away, clear off; **¿mande?** pardon?, excuse me? (*US*); **¿manda usted algo más?** is there anything else?; **~ a algn a paseo** *o* **a la porra** to tell sb to go to hell; **se lo ~emos por correo** we'll post it to you; **~ hacer un traje** to have a suit made
mandarín [manda'rin] *nm* petty bureaucrat
mandarina [manda'rina] *nf* (*fruta*) tangerine, mandarin (orange)
mandatario, -a [manda'tarjo, a] *nm/f* (*representante*) agent; **primer ~** (*esp Am*) head of state
mandato [man'dato] *nm* (*orden*) order; (*Pol*: *período*) term of office; (: *territorio*) mandate; **~ judicial** (search) warrant
mandíbula [man'diβula] *nf* jaw
mandil [man'dil] *nm* (*delantal*) apron
mando ['mando] *nm* (*Mil*) command; (*de país*) rule; (*el primer lugar*) lead; (*Pol*) term of office; (*Tec*) control; **~ a la izquierda** left-hand drive; **los altos ~s** the high command *sg*; **~ por botón** push-button control; **~ a distancia** remote control; **al ~ de** in charge of; **tomar el ~** to take the lead
mandolina [mando'lina] *nf* mandolin(e)
mandón, -ona [man'don, ona] *adj* bossy, domineering
manejable [mane'xaβle] *adj* manageable; (*fácil de usar*) handy
manejar [mane'xar] *vt* to manage; (*máquina*) to work, operate; (*caballo etc*) to handle; (*casa*) to run, manage; (*Am Auto*) to drive ▷ *vi* (*Am Auto*) to drive; **manejarse** *vr* (*comportarse*) to act, behave; (*arreglárselas*) to manage; **"~ con cuidado"** "handle with care"
manejo [ma'nexo] *nm* (*de bicicleta*) handling; (*de negocio*) management, running; (*Auto*) driving; (*facilidad de trato*) ease, confidence; (*de idioma*) command; **manejos** *nmpl* intrigues; **tengo ~ del francés** I have a good command of French
manera [ma'nera] *nf* way, manner, fashion; (*Arte, Lit etc*: *estilo*) manner, style; **maneras** *nfpl* (*modales*) manners; **su ~ de ser** the way he is; (*aire*) his manner; **de mala ~** (*fam*) badly, unwillingly; **de ninguna ~** no way, by no means; **de otra ~** otherwise; **de todas ~s** at any rate; **en gran ~** to a large extent; **sobre ~** exceedingly; **a mi ~ de ver** in my view; **no hay ~ de persuadirle** there's no way of convincing him
manga ['manga] *nf* (*de camisa*) sleeve; (*de riego*) hose; **de ~ corta/larga** short-/long-sleeved; **andar ~ por hombro** (*desorden*) to be topsy-turvy; **tener ~ ancha** to be easy-going
mangar [man'gar] *vt* (*unir*) to plug in; (*fam*: *birlar*) to pinch, nick, swipe; (*mendigar*) to beg
mango ['mango] *nm* handle; (*Bot*) mango; **~ de escoba** broomstick
mangonear [mangone'ar] *vt* to boss about ▷ *vi* to be bossy
manguera [man'gera] *nf* (*de riego*) hose; (*tubo*) pipe; **~ de incendios** fire hose
maní [ma'ni] (*pl* **maníes** *o* **manises**) *nm* (*Am*: *cacahuete*) peanut; (: *planta*) groundnut plant
manía [ma'nia] *nf* (*Med*) mania; (*fig*: *moda*) rage, craze; (*disgusto*) dislike; (*malicia*) spite; **tiene ~s** she's a bit fussy; **coger ~ a algn** to take a dislike to sb; **tener ~ a algn** to dislike sb
maníaco, -a [ma'niako, a] *adj* maniac(al) ▷ *nm/f* maniac
maniatar [manja'tar] *vt* to tie the hands of
maniático, -a [ma'njatiko, a] *adj* maniac(al); (*loco*) crazy; (*tiquismiquis*) fussy ▷ *nm/f* maniac
manicomio [mani'komjo] *nm* psychiatric hospital (*Brit*), insane asylum (*US*)
manicuro, -a [mani'kuro, a] *nm/f* manicurist ▷ *nf* manicure
manifestación [manifesta'θjon] *nf* (*declaración*) statement, declaration; (*demostración*) show, display; (*Pol*) demonstration; (*concentración*) mass meeting
manifestante [manifes'tante] *nm/f* demonstrator
manifestar [manifes'tar] *vt* to show, manifest; (*declarar*) to state, declare; **manifestarse** *vr* to show, become apparent; (*Pol*: *desfilar*) to demonstrate; (: *reunirse*) to hold a mass meeting
manifiesto, -a [mani'fjesto, a] *vb ver* **manifestar** ▷ *adj* clear, manifest ▷ *nm* manifesto; (*Anat, Naut*) manifest; **poner algo de ~** (*aclarar*) to make sth clear; (*revelar*) to reveal sth; **quedar ~** to be plain *o* clear
manija [ma'nixa] *nf* handle
manillar [mani'ʎar] *nm* handlebars *pl*
maniobra [ma'njoβra] *nf* manœuvring; (*manejo*) handling; (*fig*: *movimiento*) manœuvre, move; (: *estratagema*) trick, stratagem; **maniobras** *nfpl* manœuvres
maniobrar [manio'βrar] *vt* to manœuvre; (*manejar*) to handle ▷ *vi* to manœuvre
manipulación [manipula'θjon] *nf* manipulation; (*Com*) handling
manipular [manipu'lar] *vt* to manipulate; (*manejar*) to handle
maniquí [mani'ki] *nm/f* model ▷ *nm* dummy

manirroto, -a [mani'rroto, a] *adj* lavish, extravagant ▷ *nm/f* spendthrift
manitas [ma'nitas] *adj inv* good with one's hands ▷ *nm/f inv*: **ser un ~** to be very good with one's hands
manivela [mani'βela] *nf* crank
manjar [man'xar] *nm* (tasty) dish
mano[1] ['mano] *nf* hand; (*Zool*) foot, paw; (*de pintura*) coat; (*serie*) lot, series; **a ~** by hand; **a ~ derecha/izquierda** on (*o* to) the right(-hand side)/left(-hand side); **a ~s llenas** lavishly, generously; **hecho a ~** handmade; **robo a ~ armada** armed robbery; **darse la(s) ~(s)** to shake hands; **de primera ~** (at) first hand; **de segunda ~** (at) second hand; **echar ~ de** to make use of; **echar una ~** to lend a hand; **echar una ~ a** to lay hands on; **está en tus ~s** it's up to you; **estrechar la ~ a algn** to shake sb's hand; **~ de obra** labour, manpower; **~ de santo** sure remedy; **¡~s a la obra!** to work!; **~s libres** hands-free; **Pedro es mi ~ derecha** Pedro is my right-hand man; **se le fue la ~** his hand slipped; (*fig*) he went too far; **traer** *o* **llevar algo entre ~s** to deal *o* be busy with sth
mano[2] ['mano] *nm* (*Am fam*) friend, mate
manojo [ma'noxo] *nm* handful, bunch; **~ de llaves** bunch of keys
manopla [ma'nopla] *nf* (*paño*) flannel; **manoplas** *nfpl* mittens
manoseado, -a [manose'aðo, a] *adj* well-worn
manosear [manose'ar] *vt* (*tocar*) to handle, touch; (*desordenar*) to mess up, rumple; (*insistir en*) to overwork; (*acariciar*) to caress, fondle; (*pey: persona*) to feel *o* touch up
manos libres *adj inv* (*teléfono, dispositivo*) hands-free ▷ *nm inv* hands-free kit
manotazo [mano'taθo] *nm* slap, smack
mansalva [man'salβa]: **a ~** *adv* indiscriminately
mansedumbre [manse'ðumbre] *nf* gentleness, meekness; (*de animal*) tameness
mansión [man'sjon] *nf* mansion
manso, -a ['manso, a] *adj* gentle, mild; (*animal*) tame
manta ['manta] *nf* blanket; (*Am*) poncho
manteca [man'teka] *nf* fat; (*Am*) butter; **~ de cacahuete/cacao** peanut/cocoa butter; **~ de cerdo** lard
mantecado [mante'kaðo] *nm* (*Esp: dulce navideño*) *Christmas sweet made from flour, almonds and lard*; (*helado*) ice cream
mantel [man'tel] *nm* tablecloth
mantendré *etc* [manten'dre] *vb ver* **mantener**
mantener [mante'ner] *vt* to support, maintain; (*alimentar*) to sustain; (*conservar*) to keep; (*Tec*) to maintain, service; **mantenerse** *vr* (*seguir de pie*) to be still standing; (*no ceder*) to hold one's ground; (*subsistir*) to sustain o.s., keep going; **~ algo en equilibrio** to keep sth balanced; **~se a distancia** to keep one's distance; **~se firme** to hold one's ground
mantenimiento [manteni'mjento] *nm* maintenance; sustenance; (*sustento*) support
mantequilla [mante'kiʎa] *nf* butter
mantilla [man'tiʎa] *nf* mantilla; **mantillas** *nfpl* baby clothes; **estar en ~s** (*persona*) to be terribly innocent; (*proyecto*) to be in its infancy
manto ['manto] *nm* (*capa*) cloak; (*de ceremonia*) robe, gown
mantón [man'ton] *nm* shawl
mantuve *etc* [man'tuβe] *vb ver* **mantener**
manual [ma'nwal] *adj* manual ▷ *nm* manual, handbook; **habilidad ~** manual skill
manubrio [ma'nuβrio] *nm* (*Am Auto*) steering wheel
manufactura [manufak'tura] *nf* manufacture; (*fábrica*) factory
manufacturado, -a [manufaktu'raðo, a] *adj* manufactured
manuscrito, -a [manus'krito, a] *adj* handwritten ▷ *nm* manuscript
manutención [manuten'θjon] *nf* maintenance; (*sustento*) support
manzana [man'θana] *nf* apple; (*Arq*) block; **~ de la discordia** (*fig*) bone of contention
manzanilla [manθa'niʎa] *nf* (*planta*) camomile; (*infusión*) camomile tea; (*vino*) manzanilla
manzano [man'θano] *nm* apple tree
maña ['maɲa] *nf* (*gen*) skill, dexterity; (*pey*) guile; (*costumbre*) habit; (*una maña*) trick, knack; **con ~** craftily
mañana [ma'ɲana] *adv* tomorrow ▷ *nm* future ▷ *nf* morning; **de** *o* **por la ~** in the morning; **¡hasta ~!** see you tomorrow!; **pasado ~** the day after tomorrow; **~ por la ~** tomorrow morning
mañanero, -a [maɲa'nero, a] *adj* early-rising
maño, -a ['maɲo, a] *adj* Aragonese ▷ *nm/f* native *o* inhabitant of Aragon
mañoso, -a [ma'ɲoso, a] *adj* (*hábil*) skilful; (*astuto*) smart, clever
mapa ['mapa] *nm* map
maple ['maple] *nm* (*Am*) maple
maqueta [ma'keta] *nf* (scale) model
maquillador, a [makiʎa'ðor, a] *nm/f* (*Teat etc*) make-up artist ▷ *nf* (*Am: Com*) bonded assembly plant
maquillaje [maki'ʎaxe] *nm* make-up; (*acto*) making up
maquillar [maki'ʎar] *vt* to make up; **maquillarse** *vr* to put on (some) make-up
máquina ['makina] *nf* machine; (*de tren*) locomotive, engine; (*Foto*) camera; (*Am: coche*) car; (*fig*) machinery; (*: proyecto*) plan, project; **a toda ~** at full speed; **escrito a ~** typewritten; **~ de afeitar** electric razor; **~ de coser** sewing machine; **~ de escribir**

typewriter; **~ fotográfica** camera; **~ de coser/lavar** sewing/washing machine; **~ de facsímil** facsimile (machine), fax; **~ de franqueo** franking machine; **~ tragaperras** fruit machine; (*Com*) slot machine
maquinación [makina'θjon] *nf* machination, plot
maquinal [maki'nal] *adj* (*fig*) mechanical, automatic
maquinaria [maki'narja] *nf* (*máquinas*) machinery; (*mecanismo*) mechanism, works *pl*
maquinilla [maki'niʎa] *nf* small machine; (*torno*) winch; **~ de afeitar** razor; **~ eléctrica** electric razor
maquinista [maki'nista] *nm/f* (*Ferro*) engine driver (*Brit*), engineer (*US*); (*Tec*) operator; (*Naut*) engineer
mar [mar] *nm* sea; **~ de fondo** groundswell; **~ llena** high tide; **~ adentro** *o* **afuera** out at sea; **en alta ~** on the high seas; **por ~** by sea *o* boat; **hacerse a la ~** to put to sea; **a ~es** in abundance; **un ~ de** lots of; **es la ~ de guapa** she is ever so pretty; **el M~ Negro/Báltico** the Black/Baltic Sea; **el M~ Muerto/Rojo** the Dead/Red Sea; **el M~ del Norte** the North Sea
maraca [ma'raka] *nf* maraca
maraña [ma'raɲa] *nf* (*maleza*) thicket; (*confusión*) tangle
maravilla [mara'βiʎa] *nf* marvel, wonder; (*Bot*) marigold; **hacer ~s** to work wonders; **a (las mil) ~s** wonderfully well
maravillar [maraβi'ʎar] *vt* to astonish, amaze; **maravillarse** *vr* to be astonished, be amazed
maravilloso, -a [maraβi'ʎoso, a] *adj* wonderful, marvellous
marca ['marka] *nf* mark; (*sello*) stamp; (*Com*) make, brand; (*de ganado*) brand; (*: acto*) branding; (*Naut*) seamark; (*: boya*) marker; (*Deporte*) record; **de ~** excellent, outstanding; **~ de fábrica** trademark; **~ propia** own brand; **~ registrada** registered trademark
marcado, -a [mar'kaðo, a] *adj* marked, strong
marcador [marka'ðor] *nm* marker; (*rotulador*) marker (pen); (*de libro*) bookmark; (*Deporte*) scoreboard; (*: persona*) scorer
marcapasos [marka'pasos] *nm inv* pacemaker
marcar [mar'kar] *vt* to mark; (*número de teléfono*) to dial; (*gol*) to score; (*números*) to record, keep a tally of; (*el pelo*) to set; (*ganado*) to brand; (*suj: termómetro*) to read, register; (*: reloj*) to show; (*tarea*) to assign; (*Com*) to put a price on ▷ *vi* (*Deporte*) to score; (*Telec*) to dial; **mi reloj marca las dos** it's two o'clock by my watch; **~ el compás** (*Mus*) to keep time; **~ el paso** (*Mil*) to mark time
marcha ['martʃa] *nf* march; (*Deporte*) walk; (*Tec*) running, working; (*Auto*) gear; (*velocidad*) speed; (*fig*) progress; (*curso*) course; **dar ~ atrás** to reverse, put into reverse; **estar en ~** to be under way, be in motion; **hacer algo sobre la ~** to do sth as you *etc* go along; **poner en ~** to put into gear; **ponerse en ~** to start, get going; **a ~s forzadas** (*fig*) with all speed; **¡en ~!** (*Mil*) forward march!; (*fig*) let's go!; **"~ moderada"** (*Auto*) "drive slowly"; **que tiene** *o* **de mucha ~** (*fam*) very lively
marchar [mar'tʃar] *vi* (*ir*) to go; (*funcionar*) to work, go; (*fig*) to go, proceed; **marcharse** *vr* to go (away), leave; **todo marcha bien** everything is going well
marchitar [martʃi'tar] *vt* to wither, dry up; **marchitarse** *vr* (*Bot*) to wither; (*fig*) to fade away
marchito, -a [mar'tʃito, a] *adj* withered, faded; (*fig*) in decline
marchoso, -a [mar'tʃoso, a] *adj* (*fam: animado*) lively; (*: moderno*) modern
marcial [mar'θjal] *adj* martial, military
marciano, -a [mar'θjano, a] *adj* Martian, of *o* from Mars
marco ['marko] *nm* frame; (*Deporte*) goalposts *pl*; (*moneda*) mark; (*fig*) setting; (*contexto*) framework; **~ de chimenea** mantelpiece
marea [ma'rea] *nf* tide; (*llovizna*) drizzle; **~ alta/baja** high/low tide; **~ negra** oil slick
mareado, -a [mare'aðo, a] *adj*: **estar ~** (*con náuseas*) to feel sick; (*aturdido*) to feel dizzy
marear [mare'ar] *vt* (*fig: irritar*) to annoy, upset; (*Med*): **~ a algn** to make sb feel sick; **marearse** *vr* (*tener náuseas*) to feel sick; (*desvanecerse*) to feel faint; (*aturdirse*) to feel dizzy; (*fam: emborracharse*) to get tipsy
maremoto [mare'moto] *nm* tidal wave
mareo [ma'reo] *nm* (*náusea*) sick feeling; (*en viaje*) travel sickness; (*aturdimiento*) dizziness; (*fam: lata*) nuisance
marfil [mar'fil] *nm* ivory
margarina [marɣa'rina] *nf* margarine
margarita [marɣa'rita] *nf* (*Bot*) daisy; **(rueda) ~** (*en máquina impresora*) daisy wheel
margen ['marxen] *nm* (*borde*) edge, border; (*fig*) margin, space ▷ *nf* (*de río etc*) bank; **~ de beneficio** *o* **de ganancia** profit margin; **~ comercial** mark-up; **~ de confianza** credibility gap; **dar ~ para** to give an opportunity for; **dejar a algn al ~** to leave sb out (in the cold); **mantenerse al ~** to keep out (of things); **al ~ de lo que digas** despite what you say
marginal [marxi'nal] *adj* (*tema, error*) minor; (*grupo*) fringe *cpd*; (*anotación*) marginal
marginar [marxi'nar] *vt* to exclude; (*socialmente*) to marginalize, ostracize
maría [ma'ria] *nf* (*fam: mujer*) housewife
mariachi [ma'rjatʃi] *nm* (*música*) mariachi music; (*grupo*) mariachi band; (*persona*) mariachi musician

MARIACHI

Mariachi music is the musical style most characteristic of Mexico. From the state of Jalisco in the 19th century, this music spread rapidly throughout the country, until each region had its own particular style of the mariachi "sound". A mariachi band can be made up of several singers, up to eight violins, two trumpets, guitars, a *vihuela* (an old form of guitar), and a harp. The dance associated with this music is called the *zapateado*.

marica [ma'rika] *nm* (*fam!*) sissy; (*homosexual*) queer (*!*)
maricón [mari'kon] *nm* (*fam!*) queer (*!*)
marido [ma'riðo] *nm* husband
marihuana [mari'wana] *nf* marijuana, cannabis
marimacho [mari'matʃo] *nf* (*fam*) mannish woman
marina [ma'rina] *nf* navy; **~ mercante** merchant navy
marinero, -a [mari'nero, a] *adj* sea *cpd*; (*barco*) seaworthy ▷ *nm* sailor, seaman
marino, -a [ma'rino, a] *adj* sea *cpd*, marine ▷ *nm* sailor; **~ de agua dulce/de cubierta/de primera** landlubber/deckhand/able seaman
marioneta [marjo'neta] *nf* puppet
mariposa [mari'posa] *nf* butterfly
mariquita [mari'kita] *nm* (*fam*) sissy; (*homosexual*) queer (*!*) ▷ *nf* (*Zool*) ladybird (Brit), ladybug (US)
marisco [ma'risko] *nm* (*tb*: **~s**) shellfish, seafood
marisma [ma'risma] *nf* marsh, swamp
marítimo, -a [ma'ritimo, a] *adj* sea *cpd*, maritime
marmita [mar'mita] *nf* pot
mármol ['marmol] *nm* marble
marqués, -esa [mar'kes, esa] *nm/f* marquis/marchioness
marranada [marra'naða] *nf* (*fam*): **es una ~** that's disgusting; **hacer una ~ a algn** to do the dirty on sb
marrano, -a [ma'rrano, a] *adj* filthy, dirty ▷ *nm* (*Zool*) pig; (*malo*) swine; (*sucio*) dirty pig
marrón [ma'rron] *adj* brown
marroquí [marro'ki] *adj, nm/f* Moroccan ▷ *nm* Morocco (leather)
Marruecos [ma'rrwekos] *nm* Morocco
martes ['martes] *nm inv* Tuesday; **~ de carnaval** Shrove Tuesday; *ver tb* **Carnaval**; **sábado**; **~ y trece** ≈ Friday 13th

MARTES Y TRECE

According to Spanish superstition Tuesday is an unlucky day, even more so if it falls on the 13th of the month.

martillar [marti'ʎar], **martillear** [martiʎe'ar] *vt* to hammer
martillo [mar'tiʎo] *nm* hammer; (*de presidente de asamblea, comité*) gavel; **~ neumático** pneumatic drill (Brit), jackhammer (US)
mártir ['martir] *nm/f* martyr
martirio [mar'tirjo] *nm* martyrdom; (*fig*) torture, torment
maruja [ma'ruxa] *nf* (*fam*) = **maría**
marxismo [mark'sismo] *nm* Marxism
marxista [mark'sista] *adj, nm/f* Marxist
marzo ['marθo] *nm* March; *ver tb* **julio**
mas [mas] *conj* but

PALABRA CLAVE

más [mas] *adj, adv* **1**: **más (que, de)** (*compar*) more (than), ...+ er (than); **más grande/inteligente** bigger/more intelligent; **trabaja más (que yo)** he works more (than me); **más de seis** more than six; **es más de medianoche** it's after midnight; **durar más** to last longer; *ver tb* **cada**
2 (*superl*): **el más** the most, ...+ est; **el más grande/inteligente (de)** the biggest/most intelligent (in)
3 (*negativo*): **no tengo más dinero** I haven't got any more money; **no viene más por aquí** he doesn't come round here any more; **no sé más** I don't know any more, that's all I know
4 (*adicional*): **un kilómetro más** one more kilometre; **no le veo más solución que ...** I see no other solution than to ...; **¿algo más?** anything else?; (*en tienda*) will that be all?; **¿quién más?** anybody else?
5 (*+ adj: valor intensivo*): **¡qué perro más sucio!** what a filthy dog!; **¡es más tonto!** he's so stupid!
6 (*locuciones*): **más o menos** more or less; **los más** most people; **es más** in fact, furthermore; **más bien** rather; **¡qué más da!** what does it matter!; *ver tb* **no**
7: **por más**: **por más que lo intento** no matter how much *o* hard I try; **por más que quisiera ayudar** much as I should like to help
8: **de más**: **veo que aquí estoy de más** I can see I'm not needed here; **tenemos uno de más** we've got one extra
9 (*Am*): **no más** only, just; **ayer no más** just yesterday
▷ *prep*: **2 más 2 son 4** 2 and *o* plus 2 are 4
▷ *nm inv*: **este trabajo tiene sus más y sus menos** this job's got its good points and its bad points

masa ['masa] *nf* (*mezcla*) dough; (*volumen*) volume, mass; (*Física*) mass; **en ~** en masse; **las ~s** (*Pol*) the masses
masacre [ma'sakre] *nf* massacre
masaje [ma'saxe] *nm* massage; **dar ~ a** to massage

m

mascar [mas'kar] *vt, vi* to chew; (*fig*) to mumble, mutter
máscara ['maskara] *nf* (*tb Inform*) mask ▷ *nm/f* masked person; **~ antigás** gas mask
mascarada [maska'raða] *nf* masquerade
mascarilla [maska'riʎa] *nf* mask; (*vaciado*) deathmask; (*de maquillaje*) face pack
mascota [mas'kota] *nf* mascot
masculino, -a [masku'lino, a] *adj* masculine; (*Bio*) male ▷ *nm* (*Ling*) masculine
mascullar [masku'ʎar] *vt* to mumble, mutter
masía [ma'sia] *nf* farmhouse
masificación [masifika'θjon] *nf* overcrowding
masilla [ma'siʎa] *nf* putty
masivo, -a [ma'siβo, a] *adj* (*en masa*) mass
masón [ma'son] *nm* (free)mason
masoquista [maso'kista] *adj* masochistic ▷ *nm/f* masochist
mastectomía [mastekto'mia] *nf* mastectomy
máster (*pl* **masters**) ['master, 'masters] *nm* master's degree; *ver tb* **licenciado**
masticar [masti'kar] *vt* to chew; (*fig*) to ponder over
mástil ['mastil] *nm* (*de navío*) mast; (*de guitarra*) neck
mastín [mas'tin] *nm* mastiff
masturbación [masturβa'θjon] *nf* masturbation
masturbarse [mastur'βarse] *vr* to masturbate
mata ['mata] *nf* (*arbusto*) bush, shrub; (*de hierbas*) tuft; (*campo*) field; (*manojo*) tuft, blade; **matas** *nfpl* scrub *sg*; **~ de pelo** mop of hair; **a salto de ~** (*día a día*) from day to day; (*al azar*) haphazardly
matadero [mata'ðero] *nm* slaughterhouse, abattoir
matador, a [mata'ðor, a] *adj* killing ▷ *nm/f* killer ▷ *nm* (*Taur*) matador, bullfighter
matamoscas [mata'moskas] *nm inv* (*palo*) fly swat
matanza [ma'tanθa] *nf* slaughter
matar [ma'tar] *vt* to kill; (*tiempo, pelota*) to kill ▷ *vi* to kill; **matarse** *vr* (*suicidarse*) to kill o.s., commit suicide; (*morir*) to be *o* get killed; (*gastarse*) to wear o.s. out; **~ el hambre** to stave off hunger; **~ a algn a disgustos** to make sb's life a misery; **~las callando** to go about things slyly; **~se trabajando** to kill o.s. with work; **~se por hacer algo** to struggle to do sth
matasellos [mata'seʎos] *nm inv* postmark
mate ['mate] *adj* (*sin brillo: color*) dull, matt ▷ *nm* (*en ajedrez*) (check)mate; (*Am: hierba*) maté; (*: vasija*) gourd
matemáticas [mate'matikas] *nfpl* mathematics
matemático, -a [mate'matiko, a] *adj* mathematical ▷ *nm/f* mathematician
materia [ma'terja] *nf* (*gen*) matter; (*Tec*) material; (*Escol*) subject; **en ~ de** on the subject of; (*en cuanto a*) as regards; **~ prima** raw material; **entrar en ~** to get down to business
material [mate'rjal] *adj* material; (*dolor*) physical; (*real*) real; (*literal*) literal ▷ *nm* material; (*Tec*) equipment; **~ de construcción** building material; **~es de derribo** rubble *sg*
materialismo [materja'lismo] *nm* materialism
materialista [materja'lista] *adj* materialist(ic)
materialmente [materjal'mente] *adv* materially; (*fig*) absolutely
maternal [mater'nal] *adj* motherly, maternal
maternidad [materni'ðað] *nf* motherhood, maternity
materno, -a [ma'terno, a] *adj* maternal; (*lengua*) mother *cpd*
matinal [mati'nal] *adj* morning *cpd*
matiz [ma'tiθ] *nm* shade; (*de sentido*) shade, nuance; (*de ironía etc*) touch
matizar [mati'θar] *vt* (*variar*) to vary; (*Arte*) to blend; **~ de** to tinge with
matón [ma'ton] *nm* bully
matorral [mato'rral] *nm* thicket
matraca [ma'traka] *nf* rattle; (*fam*) nuisance
matrícula [ma'trikula] *nf* (*registro*) register; (*Escol: inscripción*) registration; (*Auto*) registration number; (*: placa*) number plate; **~ de honor** (*Univ*) *top marks in a subject at university with the right to free registration the following year*
matricular [matriku'lar] *vt* to register, enrol
matrimonial [matrimo'njal] *adj* matrimonial
matrimonio [matri'monjo] *nm* (*pareja*) (married) couple; (*acto*) marriage; **~ civil/ clandestino** civil/secret marriage; **contraer ~ (con)** to marry
matriz [ma'triθ] *nf* (*Anat*) womb; (*Tec*) mould; (*Mat*) matrix; **casa ~** (*Com*) head office
matrona [ma'trona] *nf* (*mujer de edad*) matron; (*comadrona*) midwife
matufia [ma'tufja] *nf* (*Am: fam*) put-up job
maullar [mau'ʎar] *vi* to mew, miaow
mausoleo [mauso'leo] *nm* mausoleum
maxilar [maksi'lar] *nm* jaw(bone)
máxima ['maksima] *nf ver* **máximo**
máxime ['maksime] *adv* especially
máximo, -a ['maksimo, a] *adj* maximum; (*más alto*) highest; (*más grande*) greatest ▷ *nm* maximum ▷ *nf* maxim; **~ jefe** *o* **líder** (*Am*) President, leader; **como ~** at most; **al ~** to the utmost
maxisingle [maksi'singel] *nm* twelve-inch (single)
maya ['maja] *adj* Mayan ▷ *nm/f* Maya(n)
mayo ['majo] *nm* May; *ver tb* **julio**

mayonesa [majo'nesa] *nf* mayonnaise
mayor [ma'jor] *adj* main, chief; (*adulto*) grown-up, adult; (*Jur*) of age; (*de edad avanzada*) elderly; (*Mus*) major; (*comparativo: de tamaño*) bigger; (*: de edad*) older; (*superlativo: de tamaño*) biggest; (*tb fig*) greatest; (*: de edad*) oldest ▷ *nm* chief, boss; (*adulto*) adult; **mayores** *nmpl* (*antepasados*) ancestors; **al por ~** wholesale; **~ de edad** adult; *ver tb* **mayores**
mayoral [majo'ral] *nm* foreman
mayordomo [major'ðomo] *nm* butler
mayores [ma'jores] *nmpl* grown-ups; **llegar a ~** to get out of hand
mayoría [majo'ria] *nf* majority, greater part; **en la ~ de los casos** in most cases; **en su ~** on the whole
mayorista [majo'rista] *nm/f* wholesaler
mayoritario, -a [majori'tarjo, a] *adj* majority *cpd*; **gobierno ~** majority government
mayúsculo, -a [ma'juskulo, a] *adj* (*fig*) big, tremendous ▷ *nf* capital (letter); **mayúsculas** *nfpl* capitals; (*Tip*) upper case *sg*
mazapán [maθa'pan] *nm* marzipan
mazo ['maθo] *nm* (*martillo*) mallet; (*de mortero*) pestle; (*de flores*) bunch; (*Deporte*) bat
me [me] *pron* (*directo*) me; (*indirecto*) (to) me; (*reflexivo*) (to) myself; **¡dámelo!** give it to me!; **me lo compró** (*de mí*) he bought it from me; (*para mí*) he bought it for me
meandro [me'andro] *nm* meander
mear [me'ar] (*fam*) *vt* to piss on (*!*) ▷ *vi* to pee, piss (*!*), have a piss (*!*); **mearse** *vr* to wet o.s.
mecánica [me'kanika] *nf ver* **mecánico**
mecánico, -a [me'kaniko, a] *adj* mechanical; (*repetitivo*) repetitive ▷ *nm/f* mechanic ▷ *nf* (*estudio*) mechanics *sg*; (*mecanismo*) mechanism
mecanismo [meka'nismo] *nm* mechanism; (*engranaje*) gear
mecanografía [mekanoɣra'fia] *nf* typewriting
mecanógrafo, -a [meka'noɣrafo, a] *nm/f* (copy) typist
mecate [me'kate] *nm* (*Am*) rope
mecedor (*Am*) [mese'ðor] *nm*, **mecedora** [meθe'ðora] *nf* rocking chair
mecer [me'θer] *vt* (*cuna*) to rock; **mecerse** *vr* to rock; (*rama*) to sway
mecha ['metʃa] *nf* (*de vela*) wick; (*de bomba*) fuse; **a toda ~** at full speed; **ponerse ~s** to streak one's hair
mechero [me'tʃero] *nm* (cigarette) lighter
mechón [me'tʃon] *nm* (*gen*) tuft; (*manojo*) bundle; (*de pelo*) lock
medalla [me'ðaʎa] *nf* medal
media ['meðja] *nf ver* **medio**
mediación [meða'θjon] *nf* mediation; **por ~ de** through
mediado, -a [me'ðjaðo, a] *adj* half-full; (*trabajo*) half-completed; **a ~s de** in the middle of, halfway through
mediano, -a [me'ðjano, a] *adj* (*regular*) medium, average; (*mediocre*) mediocre ▷ *nf* (*Aut*) central reservation, median (*US*); **(de tamaño) ~** medium-sized
medianoche [meðja'notʃe] *nf* midnight
mediante [me'ðjante] *adv* by (means of), through
mediar [me'ðjar] *vi* (*tiempo*) to elapse; (*interceder*) to mediate, intervene; (*existir*) to exist; **media el hecho de que ...** there is the fact that ...
medicación [meðika'θjon] *nf* medication, treatment
medicamento [meðika'mento] *nm* medicine, drug
medicina [meði'θina] *nf* medicine
medicinal [meðici'nal] *adj* medicinal
medición [meði'θjon] *nf* measurement
médico, -a ['meðiko, a] *adj* medical ▷ *nm/f* doctor; **~ de cabecera** family doctor; **~ pediatra** paediatrician; **~ residente** house physician, intern (*US*)
medida [me'ðiða] *nf* measure; (*medición*) measurement; (*de camisa, zapato etc*) size, fitting; (*moderación*) moderation, prudence; **en cierta/gran ~** up to a point/to a great extent; **un traje a la ~** a made to measure suit; **~ de cuello** collar size; **a ~ de** in proportion to; (*de acuerdo con*) in keeping with; **con ~** with restraint; **sin ~** immoderately; **a ~ que ...** (at the same time) as ...; **tomar ~s** to take steps
medidor [meði'ðor] *nm* (*Am*) meter
medieval [meðje'βal] *adj* medieval
medio, -a ['meðjo, a] *adj* half (a); (*punto*) mid, middle; (*promedio*) average ▷ *adv* half-; (*esp Am: un tanto*) rather, quite ▷ *nm* (*centro*) middle, centre; (*método*) means, way; (*ambiente*) environment ▷ *nf* (*prenda de vestir*) stocking; (*Am*) sock; (*promedio*) average; **medias** *nfpl* tights; **media hora** half an hour; **~ litro** half a litre; **las tres y media** half past three; **M~ Oriente** Middle East; **a ~ camino** halfway (there); **~ dormido** half asleep; **~ enojado** (*esp Am*) rather annoyed; **lo dejó a ~s** he left it half-done; **ir a ~s** to go fifty-fifty; **~ de transporte** means of transport; **a ~ terminar** half finished; **en ~** in the middle; (*entre*) in between; **por ~ de** by (means of), through; **en los ~s financieros** in financial circles; **encontrarse en su ~** to be in one's element; **~ ambiente** environment; **~ circulante** (*Com*) money supply; *ver tb* **medios**
medioambiental [meðjoambjen'tal] *adj* environmental
mediocre [me'ðjokre] *adj* middling, average; (*pey*) mediocre
mediodía [meðjo'ðia] *nm* midday, noon
medios ['meðjos] *nmpl* means, resources; **los ~ de comunicación** the media
medir [me'ðir] *vt* (*gen*) to measure ▷ *vi* to measure; **medirse** *vr* (*moderarse*) to be

m

moderate, act with restraint; **¿cuánto mides? — mido 1.50 m** how tall are you? — I am 1.50 m tall
meditabundo, -a [meðita'βundo, a] *adj* pensive
meditar [meði'tar] *vt* to ponder, think over, meditate on; (*planear*) to think out ▷ *vi* to ponder, think, meditate
mediterráneo, -a [meðite'rraneo, a] *adj* Mediterranean ▷ *nm*: **el (mar) M~** the Mediterranean (Sea)
médula ['meðula] *nf* (*Anat*) marrow; (*Bot*) pith; **~ espinal** spinal cord; **hasta la ~** (*fig*) to the core
medusa [me'ðusa] *nf* (*Esp*) jellyfish
megafonía [meɣgafo'nia] *nf* PA *o* public address system
megáfono [me'ɣafono] *nm* megaphone
megalómano, -a [meɣa'lomano, a] *nm/f* megalomaniac
megapíxel [meɣa'piksel] (*pl* **megapixels** *or* **megapíxeles**) *nm* megapixel
mejicano, -a [mexi'kano, a] *adj, nm/f* Mexican
Méjico ['mexiko] *nm* Mexico
mejilla [me'xiʎa] *nf* cheek
mejillón [mexi'ʎon] *nm* mussel
mejor [me'xor] *adj, adv* (*comparativo*) better; (*superlativo*) best; **lo ~** the best thing; **lo ~ de la vida** the prime of life; **a lo ~** probably; (*quizá*) maybe; **~ dicho** rather; **tanto ~** so much the better; **es el ~ de todos** he's the best of all
mejora [me'xora] *nf*, **mejoramiento** [mexora'mjento] *nm* improvement
mejorar [mexo'rar] *vt* to improve, make better ▷ *vi*, **mejorarse** *vr* to improve, get better; (*Com*) to do well, prosper; **~ a** to be better than; **los negocios mejoran** business is picking up
mejunje [me'xunxe] *nm* (*pey*) concoction
melancolía [melanko'lia] *nf* melancholy
melancólico, -a [melan'koliko, a] *adj* (*triste*) sad, melancholy; (*soñador*) dreamy
melena [me'lena] *nf* (*de persona*) long hair; (*Zool*) mane
mellizo, -a [me'ʎiθo, a] *adj, nm/f* twin
melocotón [meloko'ton] *nm* (*Esp*) peach
melodía [melo'ðia] *nf* melody; (*tonada*) tune; (*de móvil*) ringtone
melodrama [melo'ðrama] *nm* melodrama
melodramático, -a [meloðra'matiko, a] *adj* melodramatic
melón [me'lon] *nm* melon
meloso, -a [me'loso, a] *adj* honeyed, sweet; (*empalagoso*) sickly, cloying; (*voz*) sweet; (*zalamero*) smooth
membrana [mem'brana] *nf* membrane
membrete [mem'brete] *nm* letterhead; **papel con ~** headed notepaper
membrillo [mem'briʎo] *nm* quince; **carne de ~** quince jelly
memorable [memo'raβle] *adj* memorable
memorándum [memo'randum] *nm* (*libro*) notebook; (*comunicación*) memorandum
memoria [me'morja] *nf* (*gen*) memory; (*artículo*) (learned) paper; **memorias** *nfpl* (*de autor*) memoirs; **~ anual** annual report; **aprender algo de ~** to learn sth by heart; **si tengo buena ~** if my memory serves me right; **venir a la ~** to come to mind; (*Inform*): **~ auxiliar** backing storage; **~ de acceso aleatorio** random access memory, RAM; **~ del teclado** keyboard memory; **~ fija** read-only memory, ROM; **~ flash** flash drive; **~ USB** USB stick
memorizar [memori'θar] *vt* to memorize
menaje [me'naxe] *nm* (*muebles*) furniture; (*tb*: **artículos de ~**) household items *pl*; **~ de cocina** kitchenware
mención [men'θjon] *nf* mention; **digno de ~** noteworthy; **hacer ~ de** to mention
mencionar [menθjo'nar] *vt* to mention; (*nombrar*) to name; **sin ~ ...** let alone ...
mendigar [mendi'ɣar] *vt* to beg (for)
mendigo, -a [men'diɣo, a] *nm/f* beggar
mendrugo [men'druɣo] *nm* crust
menear [mene'ar] *vt* to move; (*cola*) to wag; (*cadera*) to swing; (*fig*) to handle; **menearse** *vr* to shake; (*balancearse*) to sway; (*moverse*) to move; (*fig*) to get a move on
menester [menes'ter] *nm* (*necesidad*) necessity; **menesteres** *nmpl* (*deberes*) duties; **es ~ hacer algo** it is necessary to do sth, sth must be done
menestra [me'nestra] *nf*: **~ de verduras** vegetable stew
menguante [men'gwante] *adj* decreasing, diminishing; (*luna*) waning; (*marea*) ebb *cpd*
menguar [men'gwar] *vt* to lessen, diminish; (*fig*) to discredit ▷ *vi* to diminish, decrease; (*fig*) to decline
menopausia [meno'pausja] *nf* menopause
menor [me'nor] *adj* (*más pequeño: comparativo*) smaller; (*número*) less, lesser; (*: superlativo*) smallest; (*número*) least; (*más joven: comparativo*) younger; (*: superlativo*) youngest; (*Mus*) minor ▷ *nmf* (*joven*) young person, juvenile; **Juanito es ~ que Pepe** Juanito is younger than Pepe; **ella es la ~ de todas** she is the youngest of all; **no tengo la ~ idea** I haven't the faintest idea; **al por ~** retail; **~ de edad** minor
Menorca [me'norka] *nf* Minorca

PALABRA CLAVE

menos [menos] *adj* **1**: **menos (que, de)** (*compar: cantidad*) less (than); (*: número*) fewer (than); **con menos entusiasmo** with less enthusiasm; **menos gente** fewer people; *ver tb* **cada**

2 (*superl*): **es el que menos culpa tiene** he is the least to blame; **donde menos problemas hay** where there are fewest problems

▷ *adv* **1** (*compar*): **menos (que, de)** less (than); **me gusta menos que el otro** I like it less than the other one; **menos de cinco** less than five; **menos de lo que piensas** less than you think
2 (*superl*): **es el menos listo (de su clase)** he's the least bright (in his class); **de todas ellas es la que menos me agrada** out of all of them she's the one I like least; **(por) lo menos** at (the very) least; **es lo menos que puedo hacer** it's the least I can do; **lo menos posible** as little as possible
3 (*locuciones*): **no quiero verle y menos visitarle** I don't want to see him let alone visit him; **tenemos siete (de) menos** we're seven short; **eso es lo de menos** that's the least of it; **¡todo menos eso!** anything but that!; **al/por lo menos** at (the very) least; **si al menos** if only; **¡menos mal!** thank goodness!
▷ *prep* except; (*cifras*) minus; **todos menos él** everyone except (for) him; **5 menos 2** 5 minus 2; **las 7 menos 20** (*hora*) 20 to 7
▷ *conj*: **a menos que**: **a menos que venga mañana** unless he comes tomorrow

menoscabar [menoska'βar] *vt* (*estropear*) to damage, harm; (*fig*) to discredit
menospreciar [menospre'θjar] *vt* to underrate, undervalue; (*despreciar*) to scorn, despise
mensaje [men'saxe] *nm* message; **enviar un ~ a algn** (*por móvil*) to text sb, send sb a text message; **~ de error** (*Inform*) error message; **~ de texto** text message; **~ electrónico** email
mensajear [mensaxe'ar] *vt* to send text messages
mensajero, -a [mensa'xero, a] *nm/f* messenger
menso, -a ['menso, a] *adj* (*Am: fam*) stupid
menstruación [menstrwa'θjon] *nf* menstruation
menstruar [mens'trwar] *vi* to menstruate
mensual [men'swal] *adj* monthly; **10 euros ~es** 10 euros a month
mensualidad [menswali'ðað] *nf* (*salario*) monthly salary; (*Com*) monthly payment *o* instalment
menta ['menta] *nf* mint
mental [men'tal] *adj* mental
mentalidad [mentali'ðað] *nf* mentality
mentalizar [mentali'θar] *vt* (*sensibilizar*) to make aware; (*convencer*) to convince; (*preparar mentalmente*) to prepare mentally; **mentalizarse** *vr* (*concienciarse*) to become aware; (*prepararse mentalmente*) to prepare o.s. mentally; **~se (de)** to get used to the idea (of); **~se de que ...** (*convencerse*) to get it into one's head that ...
mentar [men'tar] *vt* to mention, name; **~ la madre a algn** to swear at sb
mente ['mente] *nf* mind; (*inteligencia*) intelligence; **no tengo en ~ hacer eso** it is not my intention to do that
mentecato, -a [mente'kato, a] *adj* silly, stupid ▷ *nm/f* fool, idiot
mentir [men'tir] *vi* to lie; **¡miento!** sorry, I'm wrong!
mentira [men'tira] *nf* (*una mentira*) lie; (*acto*) lying; (*invención*) fiction; **~ piadosa** white lie; **una ~ como una casa** a whopping great lie (*fam*); **parece ~ que ...** it seems incredible that ..., I can't believe that ...
mentiroso, -a [menti'roso, a] *adj* lying; (*falso*) deceptive ▷ *nm/f* liar
menú [me'nu] *nm* (*tb Inform*) menu; (*tb*: **~ del día**) set meal; **~ turístico** tourist menu; **guiado por ~** (*Inform*) menu-driven
menudo, -a [me'nuðo, a] *adj* (*pequeño*) small, tiny; (*sin importancia*) petty, insignificant; **¡~ negocio!** (*fam*) some deal!; **a ~** often, frequently
meñique [me'ɲike] *nm* little finger
meollo [me'oʎo] *nm* (*fig*) essence, core
mercadillo [merka'ðiʎo] *nm* (*Esp*) flea market
mercado [mer'kaðo] *nm* market; **~ en baja** falling market; **M~ Común** Common Market; **~ de demanda/de oferta** seller's/buyer's market; **~ laboral** labour market; **~ objetivo** target market; **~ de productos básicos** commodity market; **~ de pulgas** (*Am*) flea market; **~ de valores** stock market; **~ exterior/interior** *o* **nacional/libre** overseas/home/free market
mercancía [merkan'θia] *nf* commodity; **mercancías** *nfpl* goods, merchandise *sg*; **~s en depósito** bonded goods; **~s perecederas** perishable goods
mercantil [merkan'til] *adj* mercantile, commercial
mercenario, -a [merθe'narjo, a] *adj, nm* mercenary
mercería [merθe'ria] *nf* (*artículos*) haberdashery (*Brit*), notions *pl* (*US*); (*tienda*) haberdasher's shop (*Brit*), drapery (*Brit*), notions store (*US*)
mercurio [mer'kurjo] *nm* mercury
merecer [mere'θer] *vt* to deserve, merit ▷ *vi* to be deserving, be worthy; **merece la pena** it's worthwhile
merecido, -a [mere'θiðo, a] *adj* (well) deserved; **llevarse su ~** to get one's deserts
merendar [meren'dar] *vt* to have for tea ▷ *vi* to have tea; (*en el campo*) to have a picnic
merendero [meren'dero] *nm* ((*open-air*) *café*: *en el campo*) picnic spot
merengue [me'renge] *nm* meringue
meridiano [meri'ðjano] *nm* (*Astro, Geo*) meridian; **la explicación es de una claridad meridiana** the explanation is as clear as day
merienda [me'rjenda] *vb ver* **merendar** ▷ *nf* (light) tea, afternoon snack; (*de campo*) picnic; **~ de negros** free-for-all

m

mérito ['merito] *nm* merit; (*valor*) worth, value; **hacer ~s** to make a good impression; **restar ~ a** to detract from
merluza [mer'luθa] *nf* hake; **coger una ~** (*fam*) to get sozzled
merma ['merma] *nf* decrease; (*pérdida*) wastage
mermar [mer'mar] *vt* to reduce, lessen ▷ *vi* to decrease, dwindle
mermelada [merme'laða] *nf* jam; **~ de naranja** marmalade
mero, -a ['mero, a] *adj* mere, simple; (*Am fam*) very ▷ *adv* (*Am*) just, right ▷ *nm* (*Zool*) grouper; **el ~ ~** (*Am*: (*fam*)) the boss
merodear [meroðe'ar] *vi* (*Mil*) to maraud; (*de noche*) to prowl (about); (*curiosear*) to snoop around
mes [mes] *nm* month; (*salario*) month's pay; **el ~ corriente** this *o* the current month
mesa ['mesa] *nf* table; (*de trabajo*) desk; (*Com*) counter; (*en mitin*) platform; (*Geo*) plateau; (*Arq*) landing; **~ de noche/de tijera/de operaciones** *u* **operatoria** bedside/folding/ operating table; **~ electoral** *officials in charge of a polling station*; **~ redonda** (*reunión*) round table; **~ digitalizadora** (*Inform*) graph pad; **~ directiva** board; **~ y cama** bed and board; **poner/quitar la ~** to lay/clear the table
mesero, -a [me'sero, a] *nm/f* (*Am*) waiter/ waitress
meseta [me'seta] *nf* (*Geo*) tableland; (*Arq*) landing
mesilla [me'siʎa], **mesita** [me'sita] *nf*: **~ de noche** bedside table
mesón [me'son] *nm* inn
mestizo, -a [mes'tiθo, a] *adj* mixed-race; (*Zool*) crossbred ▷ *nm/f* person of mixed race
mesura [me'sura] *nf* (*calma*) calm; (*moderación*) moderation, restraint; (*cortesía*) courtesy
meta ['meta] *nf* goal; (*de carrera*) finish; (*fig*) goal, aim, objective
metabolismo [metaβo'lismo] *nm* metabolism
metáfora [me'tafora] *nf* metaphor
metal [me'tal] *nm* (*materia*) metal; (*Mus*) brass
metálico, -a [me'taliko, a] *adj* metallic; (*de metal*) metal ▷ *nm* (*dinero contante*) cash
metalurgia [meta'lurxja] *nf* metallurgy
metedura [mete'ðura] *nf*: **~ de pata** (*fam*) blunder
meteorito [meteo'rito] *nm* meteorite
meteoro [mete'oro] *nm* meteor
meteorología [meteorolo'xia] *nf* meteorology
meter [me'ter] *vt* (*colocar*) to put, place; (*introducir*) to put in, insert; (*involucrar*) to involve; (*causar*) to make, cause; **meterse** *vr*: **~se en** to go into, enter; (*fig*) to interfere in, meddle in; **~se a** to start; **~se a escritor** to become a writer; **~se con algn** to provoke sb, pick a quarrel with sb; **~ prisa a algn** to hurry sb up
meticuloso, -a [metiku'loso, a] *adj* meticulous, thorough
metódico, -a [me'toðiko, a] *adj* methodical
metodismo [meto'ðismo] *nm* Methodism
método ['metoðo] *nm* method
metodología [metoðolo'xia] *nf* methodology
metralla [me'traʎa] *nf* shrapnel
metralleta [metra'ʎeta] *nf* sub-machine-gun
métrico, -a ['metriko, a] *adj* metric ▷ *nf* metrics *pl*; **cinta métrica** tape measure
metro ['metro] *nm* metre; (*tren*: *tb*: **metropolitano**) underground (*Brit*), subway (*US*); (*instrumento*) rule; **~ cuadrado/cúbico** square/cubic metre
metrópoli [me'tropoli], **metrópolis** [me'tropolis] *nf* (*ciudad*) metropolis; (*colonial*) mother country
metrosexual [metrosexu'al] *adj, nm* metrosexual
mexicano, -a [mexi'kano, a] *adj, nm/f* (*Am*) Mexican
México ['mexiko] *nm* (*Am*) Mexico; **Ciudad de ~** Mexico City
mezcla ['meθkla] *nf* mixture; (*fig*) blend
mezclar [meθ'klar] *vt* to mix (up); (*armonizar*) to blend; (*combinar*) to merge; **mezclarse** *vr* to mix, mingle; **~ en** to get mixed up in, get involved in
mezquino, -a [meθ'kino, a] *adj* (*cicatero*) mean ▷ *nm/f* (*avaro*) mean person; (*miserable*) petty individual
mezquita [meθ'kita] *nf* mosque
mg *abr* (= *miligramo(s)*) mg
mi [mi] *adj posesivo* my ▷ *nm* (*Mus*) E
mí [mi] *pron* me, myself; **¿y a mí qué?** so what?
mía ['mia] *pron ver* **mío**
miaja ['mjaxa] *nf* crumb; **ni una ~** (*fig*) not the least little bit
miau [mjau] *nm* miaow
michelín [mitʃe'lin] *nm* (*fam*) spare tyre
micro ['mikro] *nm* (*Radio*) mike, microphone; (*Am*: *pequeño*) minibus; (*: grande*) coach, bus
microbio [mi'kroβjo] *nm* microbe
microbús [mikro'βus] *nm* minibus
microfilm (*pl* **microfilms**) [mikro'film, mikro'films] *nm* microfilm
micrófono [mi'krofono] *nm* microphone
microonda [mikro'onda] *nf*, **microondas** [mikro'ondas] *nm inv* microwave; **(horno) ~s** microwave (oven)
micropago [mikro'paɣo] *nm* micropayment
microscópico, -a [mikros'kopiko, a] *adj* microscopic
microscopio [mikros'kopjo] *nm* microscope
miedo ['mjeðo] *nm* fear; (*nerviosismo*) apprehension, nervousness; **meter ~ a** to scare, frighten; **tener ~** to be afraid; **de ~** wonderful, marvellous; **¡qué ~!** (*fam*) how awful!; **me da ~** it scares me; **hace un frío de ~** (*fam*) it's terribly cold

miedoso, -a [mje'ðoso, a] *adj* fearful, timid
miel [mjel] *nf* honey; **no hay ~ sin hiel** there's no rose without a thorn
miembro ['mjembro] *nm* limb; (*socio*) member; (*de institución*) fellow; **~ viril** penis
mientes *etc* ['mjentes] *vb ver* **mentar, mentir** ▷ *nfpl*: **no parar ~ en** to pay no attention to; **traer a las ~** to recall
mientras ['mjentras] *conj* while; (*duración*) as long as ▷ *adv* meanwhile; **~ (que)** whereas; **~ tanto** meanwhile; **~ más tiene, más quiere** the more he has, the more he wants
miércoles ['mjerkoles] *nm inv* Wednesday; **~ de ceniza** Ash Wednesday; *ver tb* **Carnaval**; **sábado**
mierda ['mjerða] *nf* (*fam!*) shit (!), crap (!); (*fig*) filth, dirt; **¡vete a la ~!** go to hell!
miga ['miɣa] *nf* crumb; (*fig*: *meollo*) essence; **hacer buenas ~s** (*fam*) to get on well; **esto tiene su ~** there's more to this than meets the eye
migaja [mi'ɣaxa] *nf*: **una ~ de** (*un poquito*) a little; **migajas** *nfpl* crumbs; (*pey*) left overs
migración [miɣra'θjon] *nf* migration
migratorio, -a [miɣra'torjo, a] *adj* migratory
mil [mil] *num* thousand; **dos ~ libras** two thousand pounds
milagro [mi'laɣro] *nm* miracle; **hacer ~s** (*fig*) to work wonders
milagroso, -a [mila'ɣroso, a] *adj* miraculous
milésima [mi'lesima] *nf* (*de segundo*) thousandth
milésimo, -a [mi'lesimo, a] *num* thousandth
mili ['mili] *nf*: **hacer la ~** (*fam*) to do one's military service; *see note*

MILI

La mili, military service, is compulsory in Spain although the number of months' service has been reduced and recruits are now posted close to their home town. There continues to be strong opposition from *objetores de conciencia*, conscientious objectors, who are obliged to do *Prestación Social Sustitutoria* in place of military service; this usually involves doing community service and lasts longer. Those who refuse to do either of these, *los insumisos*, can be sent to prison.

milicia [mi'liθja] *nf* (*Mil*) militia; (*servicio militar*) military service
miligramo [mili'ɣramo] *nm* milligram
milímetro [mi'limetro] *nm* millimetre (*Brit*), millimeter (*US*)
militante [mili'tante] *adj* militant
militar [mili'tar] *adj* military ▷ *nm/f* soldier ▷ *vi* to serve in the army; (*fig*) to militate, fight
militarismo [milita'rismo] *nm* militarism
milla ['miʎa] *nf* mile; **~ marina** nautical mile
millar [mi'ʎar] *num* thousand; **a ~es** in thousands
millón [mi'ʎon] *num* million
millonario, -a [miʎo'narjo, a] *nm/f* millionaire
milusos [mi'lusos] *nm inv* (*Am*) odd-job man
mimar [mi'mar] *vt* to spoil, pamper
mimbre ['mimbre] *nm* wicker; **de ~** wicker *cpd*, wickerwork
mímica ['mimika] *nf* (*para comunicarse*) sign language; (*imitación*) mimicry
mimo ['mimo] *nm* (*caricia*) caress; (*de niño*) spoiling; (*Teat*) mime; (*: actor*) mime artist
mina ['mina] *nf* mine; (*pozo*) shaft; (*de lápiz*) lead refill; **hullera** *o* **~ de carbón** coal mine
minar [mi'nar] *vt* to mine; (*fig*) to undermine
mineral [mine'ral] *adj* mineral ▷ *nm* (*Geo*) mineral; (*mena*) ore
minero, -a [mi'nero, a] *adj* mining *cpd* ▷ *nm/f* miner
miniatura [minja'tura] *adj inv, nf* miniature
minicadena [minika'ðena] *nf* (*Mus*) mini hi-fi
MiniDisc® [mini'disk] *nm* MiniDisc®
minidisco [mini'ðisko] *nm* diskette
minifalda [mini'falda] *nf* miniskirt
minifundio [mini'fundjo] *nm* smallholding, small farm
minimizar [minimi'θar] *vt* to minimize
mínimo, -a ['minimo, a] *adj* minimum; (*insignificante*) minimal ▷ *nm* minimum; **precio/salario ~** minimum price/wage; **lo ~ que pueden hacer** the least they can do
minino, -a [mi'nino, a] *nm/f* (*fam*) puss, pussy
ministerio [minis'terjo] *nm* ministry (*Brit*), department (*US*); **M~ de Asuntos Exteriores** Foreign Office (*Brit*), State Department (*US*); **M~ del Comercio e Industria** Department of Trade and Industry; **M~ de (la) Gobernación** *o* **del Interior** ≈ Home Office (*Brit*), Ministry of the Interior; **M~ de Hacienda** Treasury (*Brit*), Treasury Department (*US*)
ministro, -a [mi'nistro, a] *nm/f* minister, secretary (*esp US*); **M~ de Hacienda** Chancellor of the Exchequer, Secretary of the Treasury (*US*); **M~ de (la) Gobernación** *o* **del Interior** ≈ Home Secretary (*Brit*), Secretary of the Interior (*US*)
minoría [mino'ria] *nf* minority
minorista [mino'rista] *nm* retailer
minucioso, -a [minu'θjoso, a] *adj* thorough, meticulous; (*prolijo*) very detailed
minúsculo, -a [mi'nuskulo, a] *adj* tiny, minute ▷ *nf* small letter; **minúsculas** *nfpl* (*Tip*) lower case *sg*
minusválido, -a [minus'βaliðo, a] *adj* (physically) disabled ▷ *nm/f* disabled person
minuta [mi'nuta] *nf* (*de comida*) menu; (*de abogado etc*) fee

minutero [minu'tero] *nm* minute hand
minuto [mi'nuto] *nm* minute
mío, -a ['mio, a] *adj, pron*: **el ~** mine; **un amigo ~** a friend of mine; **lo ~** what is mine; **los ~s** my people, my relations
miope ['mjope] *adj* short-sighted
miopía [mjo'pia] *nf* near- *o* short-sightedness
mira ['mira] *nf* (*de arma*) sight(s) *pl*; (*fig*) aim, intention; **de amplias/estrechas ~s** broad-/narrow-minded
mirada [mi'raða] *nf* look, glance; (*expresión*) look, expression; **~ de soslayo** sidelong glance; **~ fija** stare, gaze; **~ perdida** distant look; **clavar la ~ en** to stare at; **echar una ~ a** to glance at; **levantar/bajar la ~** to look up/down; **resistir la ~ de algn** to stare sb out
mirado, -a [mi'raðo, a] *adj* (*sensato*) sensible; (*considerado*) considerate; **bien/mal ~** well/not well thought of; **bien ~ ...** all things considered ...
mirador [mira'ðor] *nm* viewpoint, vantage point
mirar [mi'rar] *vt* to look at; (*observar*) to watch; (*considerar*) to consider, think over; (*vigilar, cuidar*) to watch, look after ▷ *vi* to look; (*Arq*) to face; **mirarse** *vr* (*dos personas*) to look at each other; **~ algo/a algn de reojo** *o* **de través** to look askance at sth/sb; **~ algo/a algn por encima del hombro** to look down on sth/sb; **~ bien/mal** to think highly of/have a poor opinion of; **~ fijamente** to stare *o* gaze at; **~ por** (*fig*) to look after; **~ por la ventana** to look out of the window; **~se al espejo** to look at o.s. in the mirror; **~se a los ojos** to look into each other's eyes
mirilla [mi'riʎa] *nf* (*agujero*) spyhole, peephole
mirlo ['mirlo] *nm* blackbird
misa ['misa] *nf* mass; **~ del gallo** midnight mass (*on Christmas Eve*); **~ de difuntos** requiem mass; **como en ~** in dead silence; **estos datos van a ~** (*fig*) these facts are utterly trustworthy
miserable [mise'raβle] *adj* (*avaro*) mean, stingy; (*nimio*) miserable, paltry; (*lugar*) squalid; (*fam*) vile, despicable ▷ *nm/f* (*malvado*) rogue
miseria [mi'serja] *nf* misery; (*pobreza*) poverty; (*tacañería*) meanness, stinginess; (*condiciones*) squalor; **una ~** a pittance
misericordia [miseri'korðja] *nf* (*compasión*) compassion, pity; (*perdón*) forgiveness, mercy
misil [mi'sil] *nm* missile
misión [mi'sjon] *nf* mission; (*tarea*) job, duty; (*Pol*) assignment; **misiones** *nfpl* (*Rel*) overseas missions
misionero, -a [misjo'nero, a] *nm/f* missionary
mismo, -a ['mismo, a] *adj* (*semejante*) same; (*después de pronombre*) -self; (*para énfasis*) very ▷ *adv*: **aquí/ayer/hoy ~** right here/only yesterday/this very day; **ahora ~** right now ▷ *conj*: **lo ~ que** just like, just as; **por lo ~** for the same reason; **el ~ traje** the same suit; **en ese ~ momento** at that very moment; **vino el ~ Ministro** the Minister himself came; **yo ~ lo vi** I saw it myself; **lo hizo por sí ~** he did it by himself; **lo ~** the same (thing); **da lo ~** it's all the same; **quedamos en las mismas** we're no further forward
misterio [mis'terjo] *nm* mystery; (*lo secreto*) secrecy
misterioso, -a [miste'rjoso, a] *adj* mysterious; (*inexplicable*) puzzling
mitad [mi'tað] *nf* (*medio*) half; (*centro*) middle; **~ (y) ~** half-and-half; (*fig*) yes and no; **a ~ de precio** (at) half-price; **en** *o* **a ~ del camino** halfway along the road; **cortar por la ~** to cut through the middle
mitigar [miti'ɣar] *vt* to mitigate; (*dolor*) to relieve; (*sed*) to quench; (*ira*) to appease; (*preocupación*) to allay; (*soledad*) to alleviate
mitin ['mitin] *nm* (*esp Pol*) meeting
mito ['mito] *nm* myth
mitología [mitolo'xia] *nf* mythology
mixto, -a ['miksto, a] *adj* mixed; (*comité*) joint
ml *abr* (= *mililitro(s)*) ml
mm *abr* (= *milímetro(s)*) mm
mobiliario [moβi'ljarjo] *nm* furniture
mocasín [moka'sin] *nm* moccasin
mochila [mo'tʃila] *nf* rucksack (*Brit*), backpack
moción [mo'θjon] *nf* motion; **~ compuesta** (*Pol*) composite motion
moco ['moko] *nm* mucus; **mocos** *nmpl* (*fam*) snot; **limpiarse los ~s** to blow one's nose; **no es ~ de pavo** it's no trifle
moda ['moða] *nf* fashion; (*estilo*) style; **de** *o* **a la ~** in fashion, fashionable; **pasado de ~** out of fashion; **vestido a la última ~** trendily dressed
modal [mo'ðal] *adj* modal ▷ *nm*: **modales** *nmpl* manners
modalidad [moðali'ðað] *nf* (*clase*) kind, variety; (*manera*) way; (*Inform*) mode; **~ de texto** (*Inform*) text mode
modelar [moðe'lar] *vt* to model
modelo [mo'ðelo] *adj inv* model ▷ *nm/f* model ▷ *nm* (*patrón*) pattern; (*norma*) standard
módem ['moðem] *nm* (*Inform*) modem
moderado, -a [moðe'raðo, a] *adj* moderate
moderar [moðe'rar] *vt* to moderate; (*violencia*) to restrain, control; (*velocidad*) to reduce; **moderarse** *vr* to restrain o.s., control o.s.
modernizar [moðerni'θar] *vt* to modernize; (*Inform*) to upgrade
moderno, -a [mo'ðerno, a] *adj* modern; (*actual*) present-day; (*equipo etc*) up-to-date
modestia [mo'ðestja] *nf* modesty
modesto, -a [mo'ðesto, a] *adj* modest
módico, -a ['moðiko, a] *adj* moderate, reasonable

modificar [moðifi'kar] *vt* to modify
modismo [mo'ðismo] *nm* idiom
modisto, -a [mo'ðisto, a] *nm/f* (*diseñador*) couturier, designer; (*que confecciona*) dressmaker
modo ['moðo] *nm* (*manera, forma*) way, manner; (*Inform, Mus*) mode; (*Ling*) mood; **modos** *nmpl* manners; **"~ de empleo"** "instructions for use"; **~ de gobierno** form of government; **a ~ de** like; **de este ~** in this way; **de ningún ~** in no way; **de todos ~s** at any rate; **de un ~ u otro** (in) one way or another
modorra [mo'ðorra] *nf* drowsiness
módulo ['moðulo] *nm* module; (*de mueble*) unit
mofarse [mo'farse] *vr*: **~ de** to mock, scoff at
mofle ['mofle] *nm* (*Am*) silencer (*Brit*), muffler (*US*)
mogollón [moɣo'ʎon] (*fam*) *nm*: **~ de discos** *etc* loads of records *etc* ▷ *adv*: **un ~** a hell of a lot
moho ['moo] *nm* (*Bot*) mould, mildew; (*en metal*) rust
mohoso, -a [mo'oso, a] *adj* mouldy; rusty
mojado, -a [mo'xaðo, a] *adj* wet; (*húmedo*) damp; (*empapado*) drenched
mojar [mo'xar] *vt* to wet; (*humedecer*) to damp(en), moisten; (*calar*) to soak; **mojarse** *vr* to get wet; **~ el pan en el café** to dip *o* dunk one's bread in one's coffee
mojón [mo'xon] *nm* (*hito*) landmark; (*en un camino*) signpost; (*tb*: **~ kilométrico**) milestone
molcajete (*Am*) [molka'xete] *nm* mortar
moldavo, -a [mol'ðaβo, a] *adj, nm/f* Moldavian, Moldovan
molde ['molde] *nm* mould; (*vaciado*) cast; (*de costura*) pattern; (*fig*) model
moldeado [molde'aðo] *nm* soft perm
moldear [molde'ar] *vt* to mould; (*en yeso etc*) to cast
mole ['mole] *nf* mass, bulk; (*edificio*) pile
molécula [mo'lekula] *nf* molecule
moler [mo'ler] *vt* to grind, crush; (*pulverizar*) to pound; (*trigo etc*) to mill; (*cansar*) to tire out, exhaust; **~ a algn a palos** to give sb a beating
molestar [moles'tar] *vt* to bother; (*fastidiar*) to annoy; (*incomodar*) to inconvenience, put out; (*perturbar*) to trouble, upset ▷ *vi* to be a nuisance; **molestarse** *vr* to bother; (*incomodarse*) to go to a lot of trouble; (*ofenderse*) to take offence; **¿le molesta el ruido?** do you mind the noise?; **siento ~le** I'm sorry to trouble you
molestia [mo'lestja] *nf* bother, trouble; (*incomodidad*) inconvenience; (*Med*) discomfort; **es una ~** it's a nuisance; **no es ninguna ~** it's no trouble at all
molesto, -a [mo'lesto, a] *adj* (*que fastidia*) annoying; (*incómodo*) inconvenient; (*inquieto*) uncomfortable, ill at ease; (*enfadado*) annoyed; **estar ~** (*Med*) to be in some discomfort; **estar ~ con algn** (*fig*) to be cross with sb; **me sentí ~** I felt embarrassed
molido, -a [mo'liðo, a] *adj* (*machacado*) ground; (*pulverizado*) powdered; **estar ~** (*fig*) to be exhausted *o* dead beat
molinillo [moli'niʎo] *nm* hand mill; **~ de carne/café** mincer/coffee grinder
molino [mo'lino] *nm* (*edificio*) mill; (*máquina*) grinder
molusco [mo'lusko] *nm* mollusc
momentáneo, -a [momen'taneo, a] *adj* momentary
momento [mo'mento] *nm* (*gen*) moment; (*Tec*) momentum; **de ~** at the moment, for the moment; **en ese ~** at that moment, just then; **por el ~** for the time being
momia ['momja] *nf* mummy
mona ['mona] *nf ver* **mono**
monaguillo [mona'ɣiʎo] *nm* altar boy
monarca [mo'narka] *nm/f* monarch, ruler
monarquía [monar'kia] *nf* monarchy
monárquico, -a [mo'narkiko, a] *nm/f* royalist, monarchist
monasterio [monas'terjo] *nm* monastery
mondadientes [monda'ðjentes] *nm inv* toothpick
mondar [mon'dar] *vt* (*limpiar*) to clean; (*pelar*) to peel; **mondarse** *vr*: **~se de risa** (*fam*) to split one's sides laughing
mondongo [mon'dongo] *nm* (*Am*) tripe
moneda [mo'neða] *nf* (*tipo de dinero*) currency, money; (*pieza*) coin; **una ~ de 50 céntimos** a 50-cent coin; **~ de curso** legal tender; **~ extranjera** foreign exchange; **~ única** single currency; **es ~ corriente** (*fig*) it's common knowledge
monedero [mone'ðero] *nm* purse
monetario, -a [mone'tarjo, a] *adj* monetary, financial
mongólico, -a [mon'goliko, a] *adj, nm/f* Mongol
monigote [moni'ɣote] *nm* (*dibujo*) doodle; (*de papel*) cut-out figure; (*pey*) wimp; *ver tb* **inocente**
monitor, a [moni'tor, a] *nm/f* instructor, coach ▷ *nm* (*TV*) set; (*Inform*) monitor; **~ en color** colour monitor
monja ['monxa] *nf* nun
monje ['monxe] *nm* monk
mono, -a ['mono, a] *adj* (*bonito*) lovely, pretty; (*gracioso*) nice, charming ▷ *nm/f* monkey, ape ▷ *nm* dungarees *pl*; (*traje de faena*) overalls *pl*; (*fam: de drogadicto*) cold turkey; **una chica muy mona** a very pretty girl; **dormir la ~** to sleep it off
monóculo [mo'nokulo] *nm* monocle
monografía [monoɣra'fia] *nf* monograph
monologuista [monolo'ɣista] *nmf* stand-up (comedian)
monomando [mono'mando] *nm* (*tb*: **grifo ~**) mixer tap
monoparental [monoparen'tal] *adj*: **familia ~** single-parent family

monopatín [monopa'tin] *nm* skateboard
monopolio [mono'poljo] *nm* monopoly; **~ total** absolute monopoly
monopolizar [monopoli'θar] *vt* to monopolize
monotonía [monoto'nia] *nf* (*sonido*) monotone; (*fig*) monotony
monótono, -a [mo'notono, a] *adj* monotonous
monstruo ['monstrwo] *nm* monster ▷ *adj inv* fantastic
monstruoso, -a [mons'trwoso, a] *adj* monstrous
monta ['monta] *nf* total, sum; **de poca ~** unimportant, of little account
montacargas [monta'karɣas] *nm inv* service lift (*Brit*), freight elevator (*US*)
montaje [mon'taxe] *nm* assembly; (*organización*) fitting up; (*Teat*) décor; (*Cine*) montage
montaña [mon'taɲa] *nf* (*monte*) mountain; (*sierra*) mountains *pl*, mountainous area; (*Am*: *selva*) forest; **~ rusa** roller coaster
montañero, -a [monta'ɲero, a] *adj* mountain *cpd* ▷ *nm/f* mountaineer, climber
montañés, -esa [monta'ɲes, esa] *adj* mountain *cpd*; (*de Santander*) of *o* from the Santander region ▷ *nm/f* highlander; native *o* inhabitant of the Santander region
montañismo [monta'ɲismo] *nm* mountaineering, climbing
montañoso, -a [monta'ɲoso, a] *adj* mountainous
montar [mon'tar] *vt* (*subir a*) to mount, get on; (*caballo etc*) to ride; (*Tec*) to assemble, put together; (*negocio*) to set up; (*colocar*) to lift on to; (*Cine*: *película*) to edit; (*Teat*: *obra*) to stage, put on; (*Culin*: *batir*) to whip, beat ▷ *vi* to mount, get on; (*sobresalir*) to overlap; **~ en bicicleta** to ride a bicycle; **~ en cólera** to get angry; **~ a caballo** to ride, go horseriding; **~ un número** *o* **numerito** to make a scene; **tanto monta** it makes no odds
montaraz [monta'raθ] *adj* mountain *cpd*, highland *cpd*; (*pey*) uncivilized
monte ['monte] *nm* (*montaña*) mountain; (*bosque*) woodland; (*área sin cultivar*) wild area, wild country; **~ de piedad** pawnshop; **~ alto** forest; **~ bajo** scrub(land)
monto ['monto] *nm* total, amount
montón [mon'ton] *nm* heap, pile; **un ~ de** (*fig*) heaps of, lots of; **a montones** by the score, galore
monumental [monumen'tal] *adj* (*tb fig*) monumental; **zona ~** area of historical interest
monumento [monu'mento] *nm* monument; (*de conmemoración*) memorial
monzón [mon'θon] *nm* monsoon
moño ['moɲo] *nm* (*de pelo*) bun; **estar hasta el ~** (*fam*) to be fed up to the back teeth
moqueta [mo'keta] *nf* fitted carpet
mora ['mora] *nf* (*Bot*) mulberry; (: *zarzamora*) blackberry; (*Com*): **en ~** in arrears
morado, -a [mo'raðo, a] *adj* purple, violet ▷ *nm* bruise ▷ *nf* (*casa*) dwelling, abode; **pasarlas moradas** to have a tough time of it
moral [mo'ral] *adj* moral ▷ *nf* (*ética*) ethics *pl*; (*moralidad*) morals *pl*, morality; (*ánimo*) morale; **tener baja la ~** to be in low spirits
moraleja [mora'lexa] *nf* moral
moralidad [morali'ðað] *nf* morals *pl*, morality
moralizar [morali'θar] *vt* to moralize
moratón [mora'ton] *nm* bruise
morbo ['morβo] *nm* (*fam*) morbid pleasure
morboso, -a [mor'βoso, a] *adj* morbid
morcilla [mor'θiʎa] *nf* blood sausage, ≈ black pudding (*Brit*)
mordaz [mor'ðaθ] *adj* (*crítica*) biting, scathing
mordaza [mor'ðaθa] *nf* (*para la boca*) gag; (*Tec*) clamp
morder [mor'ðer] *vt* to bite; (*mordisquear*) to nibble; (*fig*: *consumir*) to eat away, eat into ▷ *vi*, **morderse** *vr* to bite; **está que muerde** he's hopping mad; **~se la lengua** to hold one's tongue
mordisco [mor'ðisko] *nm* bite
moreno, -a [mo'reno, a] *adj* (*color*) (dark) brown; (*de tez*) dark; (*de pelo moreno*) dark-haired; (*negro*) black ▷ *nm/f* (*de tez*) dark-skinned man/woman; (*de pelo*) dark-haired man/woman
morfina [mor'fina] *nf* morphine
moribundo, -a [mori'βundo, a] *adj* dying ▷ *nm/f* dying person
morir [mo'rir] *vi* to die; (*fuego*) to die down; (*luz*) to go out; **morirse** *vr* to die; (*fig*) to be dying; (*Ferro etc*: *vías*) to end; (*calle*) to come out; **fue muerto a tiros/en un accidente** he was shot (dead)/was killed in an accident; **~ de frío/hambre** to die of cold/starve to death; **¡me muero de hambre!** (*fig*) I'm starving!; **~se por algo** to be dying for sth; **~se por algn** to be crazy about sb
mormón, -ona [mor'mon, ona] *nm/f* Mormon
moro, -a ['moro, a] *adj* Moorish ▷ *nm/f* Moor; **¡hay ~s en la costa!** watch out!
moroso, -a [mo'roso, a] *adj* (*lento*) slow ▷ *nm* (*Com*) bad debtor, defaulter; **deudor ~** (*Com*) slow payer
morral [mo'rral] *nm* haversack
morriña [mo'rriɲa] *nf* homesickness; **tener ~** to be homesick
morro ['morro] *nm* (*Zool*) snout, nose; (*Auto, Aviat*) nose; (*fam*: *labio*) (thick) lip; **beber a ~** to drink from the bottle; **caer de ~** to nosedive; **estar de ~s (con algn)** to be in a bad mood (with sb); **tener ~** to have a nerve
morsa ['morsa] *nf* walrus
morse ['morse] *nm* Morse (code)
mortadela [morta'ðela] *nf* mortadella, bologna sausage

mortaja [mor'taxa] *nf* shroud; (*Tec*) mortise; (*Am*) cigarette paper
mortal [mor'tal] *adj* mortal; (*golpe*) deadly
mortalidad [mortali'ðað], **mortandad** [mortan'dað] *nf* mortality
mortero [mor'tero] *nm* mortar
mortífero, -a [mor'tifero, a] *adj* deadly, lethal
mortificar [mortifi'kar] *vt* to mortify; (*atormentar*) to torment
mosaico [mo'saiko] *nm* mosaic
mosca ['moska] *nf* fly; **por si las ~s** just in case; **estar ~** (*desconfiar*) to smell a rat; **tener la ~ en** *o* **detrás de la oreja** to be wary
Moscú [mos'ku] *nm* Moscow
mosquear [moske'ar] (*fam*) *vt* (*hacer sospechar*) to make suspicious; (*fastidiar*) to annoy; **mosquearse** *vr* (*enfadarse*) to get annoyed; (*ofenderse*) to take offence
mosquita [mos'kita] *nf*: **parece una ~ muerta** he looks as though butter wouldn't melt in his mouth
mosquitero [moski'tero] *nm* mosquito net
mosquito [mos'kito] *nm* mosquito
mostaza [mos'taθa] *nf* mustard
mosto ['mosto] *nm* unfermented grape juice
mostrador [mostra'ðor] *nm* (*de tienda*) counter; (*de café*) bar
mostrar [mos'trar] *vt* to show; (*exhibir*) to display, exhibit; (*explicar*) to explain; **mostrarse** *vr*: **~se amable** to be kind; to prove to be kind; **no se muestra muy inteligente** he doesn't seem (to be) very intelligent; **~ en pantalla** (*Inform*) to display
mota ['mota] *nf* speck, tiny piece; (*en diseño*) dot
mote ['mote] *nm* (*apodo*) nickname
motín [mo'tin] *nm* (*del pueblo*) revolt, rising; (*del ejército*) mutiny
motivación [motiβa'θjon] *nf* motivation
motivar [moti'βar] *vt* (*causar*) to cause, motivate; (*explicar*) to explain, justify
motivo [mo'tiβo] *nm* motive, reason; (*Arte, Mus*) motif; **con ~ de** (*debido a*) because of; (*en ocasión de*) on the occasion of; (*con el fin de*) in order to; **sin ~** for no reason at all
moto ['moto] *nf*, **motocicleta** [motoθi'kleta] *nf* motorbike (*Brit*), motorcycle
motociclista [motoθi'klista] *nm/f* motorcyclist, biker
motoneta [moto'neta] *nf* (*Am*) (motor) scooter
motor, a [mo'tor, a] *adj* (*Tec*) motive; (*Anat*) motor ▷ *nm* motor, engine; **~ a chorro** *o* **de reacción/de explosión** jet engine/internal combustion engine; **~ de búsqueda** (*Internet*) search engine ▷ *nf* motorboat
motorista [moto'rista] *nm/f* (*esp Am: automovilista*) motorist; (*: motociclista*) motorcyclist
motosierra [moto'sjerra] *nf* mechanical saw
motriz [mo'triz] *adj*: **fuerza ~** motive power; (*fig*) driving force
movedizo, -a [moβe'ðiθo, a] *adj* (*inseguro*) unsteady; (*fig*) unsettled, changeable; (*persona*) fickle
mover [mo'βer] *vt* to move; (*cambiar de lugar*) to shift; (*cabeza: para negar*) to shake; (*: para asentir*) to nod; (*accionar*) to drive; (*fig*) to cause, provoke; **moverse** *vr* to move; (*mar*) to get rough; (*viento*) to rise; (*fig: apurarse*) to get a move on; (*: transformarse*) to be on the move
movido, -a [mo'βiðo, a] *adj* (*Foto*) blurred; (*persona: activo*) active; (*mar*) rough; (*día*) hectic ▷ *nf* move; **la movida madrileña** the Madrid scene
móvil ['moβil] *adj* mobile; (*pieza de máquina*) moving; (*mueble*) movable ▷ *nm* (*motivo*) motive; (*teléfono*) mobile, cellphone (*US*)
movilidad [moβili'ðað] *nf* mobility
movilizar [moβili'θar] *vt* to mobilize
movimiento [moβi'mjento] *nm* (*gen, Lit, Pol*) movement; (*Tec*) motion; (*actividad*) activity; (*Mus*) tempo; **el M~** the Falangist Movement; **~ de bloques** (*Inform*) block move; **~ de mercancías** (*Com*) turnover, volume of business; **~ obrero/sindical** workers'/trade union movement; **~ sísmico** earth tremor
mozo, -a ['moθo, a] *adj* (*joven*) young; (*soltero*) single, unmarried ▷ *nm/f* (*joven*) youth, young man/girl; (*camarero*) waiter; (*camarera*) waitress; **~ de estación** porter
MP3 *nm* MP3; **reproductor (de) ~** MP3 player
mucama [mu'kama] *nf* (*Am*) maid
muchacho, -a [mu'tʃatʃo, a] *nm/f* (*niño*) boy/girl; (*criado*) servant/servant *o* maid
muchedumbre [mutʃe'ðumbre] *nf* crowd

PALABRA CLAVE

mucho, -a ['mutʃo, a] *adj* **1** (*cantidad*) a lot of, much; (*número*) lots of, a lot of, many; **mucho dinero** a lot of money; **hace mucho calor** it's very hot; **muchas amigas** lots *o* a lot of *o* many friends
2 (*sg: fam*): **ésta es mucha casa para él** this house is much too big for him; **había mucho borracho** there were a lot *o* lots of drunks
▷ *pron*: **tengo mucho que hacer** I've got a lot to do; **muchos dicen que ...** a lot of people say that ...; *ver tb* **tener**
▷ *adv* **1**: **me gusta mucho** I like it a lot *o* very much; **lo siento mucho** I'm very sorry; **come mucho** he eats a lot; **trabaja mucho** he works hard; **¿te vas a quedar mucho?** are you going to be staying long?; **mucho más/menos** much *o* a lot more/less
2 (*respuesta*) very; **¿estás cansado? — ¡mucho!** are you tired? — very!
3 (*locuciones*): **como mucho** at (the) most; **el mejor con mucho** by far the best; **¡ni mucho menos!** far from it!; **no es rico ni**

m

mucho menos he's far from being rich **4**: **por mucho que**: **por mucho que le creas** however much *o* no matter how much you believe him

muda ['muða] *nf* (*de ropa*) change of clothing; (*Zool*) moult; (*de serpiente*) slough
mudanza [mu'ðanθa] *nf* (*cambio*) change; (*de casa*) move; **estar de ~** to be moving
mudar [mu'ðar] *vt* to change; (*Zool*) to shed ▷ *vi* to change; **mudarse** *vr* (*la ropa*) to change; **~se de casa** to move house
mudo, -a ['muðo, a] *adj* with a speech impairment; (*callado*: *película*) silent; (*Ling*: *letra*) mute; (*: consonante*) voiceless; **quedarse ~ (de)** (*fig*) to be dumb with; **quedarse ~ de asombro** to be speechless
mueble ['mweβle] *nm* piece of furniture; **muebles** *nmpl* furniture *sg*
mueca ['mweka] *nf* face, grimace; **hacer ~s a** to make faces at
muela ['mwela] *vb ver* **moler** ▷ *nf* (*diente*) tooth; (*: de atrás*) back tooth; (*de molino*) millstone; (*de afilar*) grindstone; **~ del juicio** wisdom tooth
muelle ['mweʎe] *adj* (*blando*) soft; (*fig*) soft, easy ▷ *nm* spring; (*Naut*) wharf; (*malecón*) pier
muermo ['mwermo] *nm* (*fam*) wimp
muerte ['mwerte] *nf* death; (*homicidio*) murder; **dar ~ a** to kill; **de mala ~** (*fam*) lousy, rotten; **es la ~** (*fam*) it's deadly boring
muerto, -a ['mwerto, a] *pp de* **morir** ▷ *adj* dead; (*color*) dull ▷ *nm/f* dead man(-woman); (*difunto*) deceased; (*cadáver*) corpse; **cargar con el ~** (*fam*) to carry the can; **echar el ~ a algn** to pass the buck; **hacer el ~** (*nadando*) to float; **estar ~ de cansancio** to be dead tired; **Día de los M~s** (*Am*) All Souls' Day

DÍA DE LOS MUERTOS

All Souls' Day (or "Day of the Dead") in Mexico coincides with All Saints' Day, which is celebrated in the Catholic countries of Latin America on November 1st and 2nd. All Souls' Day is actually a celebration which begins in the evening of October 31st and continues until November 2nd. It is a combination of the Catholic tradition of honouring the Christian saints and martyrs, and the ancient Mexican or Aztec traditions, in which death was not something sinister. For this reason all the dead are honoured by bringing offerings of food, flowers and candles to the cemetery.

muesca ['mweska] *nf* nick
muestra *etc* ['mwestra] *vb ver* **mostrar** ▷ *nf* (*señal*) indication, sign; (*demostración*) demonstration; (*prueba*) proof; (*estadística*) sample; (*modelo*) model, pattern; (*testimonio*) token; **dar ~s de** to show signs of; **~ al azar** (*Com*) random sample
muestreo [mwes'treo] *nm* sample, sampling
muestro *etc vb ver* **mostrar**
muevo *etc* [mweβa] *vb ver* **mover**
mugir [mu'xir] *vi* (*vaca*) to moo
mugre ['muɣre] *nf* dirt, filth, muck
mugriento, -a [mu'ɣrjento, a] *adj* dirty, filthy, mucky
mujer [mu'xer] *nf* woman; (*esposa*) wife
mujeriego [muxe'rjeɣo] *nm* womaniser
mula ['mula] *nf* mule
mulato, -a [mu'lato, a] *adj, nm/f* mulatto (*pey*)
muleta [mu'leta] *nf* (*para andar*) crutch; (*Taur*) *stick with red cape attached*
mullido, -a [mu'ʎiðo, a] *adj* (*cama*) soft; (*hierba*) soft, springy
multa ['multa] *nf* fine; **echar** *o* **poner una ~ a** to fine
multar [mul'tar] *vt* to fine; (*Deporte*) to penalize
multicines [multi'θine] *nmpl* multiscreen cinema
multicolor [multiko'lor] *adj* multicoloured
multimillonario, -a [multimiʎo'narjo, a] *adj* (*contrato*) multimillion pound *o* dollar *cpd* ▷ *nm/f* multimillionaire/-millionairess
multinacional [multinaθjo'nal] *adj, nf* multinational
múltiple ['multiple] *adj* multiple, many *pl*, numerous; **de tarea ~** (*Inform*) multi-tasking; **de usuario ~** (*Inform*) multi-user
multiplicar [multipli'kar] *vt* (*Mat*) to multiply; (*fig*) to increase; **multiplicarse** *vr* (*Bio*) to multiply; (*fig*) to be everywhere at once
múltiplo ['multiplo] *adj, nm* multiple
multitud [multi'tuð] *nf* (*muchedumbre*) crowd; **~ de** lots of
mundano, -a [mun'dano, a] *adj* worldly; (*de moda*) fashionable
mundial [mun'djal] *adj* world-wide, universal; (*guerra, récord*) world *cpd*
mundo ['mundo] *nm* world; (*ámbito*) world, circle; **el otro ~** the next world; **el ~ del espectáculo** show business; **todo el ~** everybody; **tener ~** to be experienced, know one's way around; **el ~ es un pañuelo** it's a small world; **no es nada del otro ~** it's nothing special; **se le cayó el ~ (encima)** his world fell apart
munición [muni'θjon] *nf* (*Mil*: *provisiones*) stores *pl*, supplies *pl*; (*: de armas*) ammunition
municipal [muniθi'pal] *adj* (*elección*) municipal; (*concejo*) town *cpd*, local; (*piscina etc*) public ▷ *nm* (*guardia*) policeman
municipio [muni'θipjo] *nm* (*ayuntamiento*) town council, corporation; (*territorio administrativo*) town, municipality
muñeca [mu'ɲeka] *nf* (*Anat*) wrist; (*juguete*) doll

muñeco [mu'ɲeko] *nm* (*figura*) figure; (*marioneta*) puppet; (*fig*) puppet, pawn; (*niño*) pretty little boy; ~ **de nieve** snowman
muñequera [muɲe'kera] *nf* wristband
mural [mu'ral] *adj* mural, wall *cpd* ▷ *nm* mural
muralla [mu'raʎa] *nf* (city) wall(s) *pl*
murciélago [mur'θjelaɣo] *nm* bat
murmullo [mur'muʎo] *nm* murmur(ing); (*cuchicheo*) whispering; (*de arroyo*) murmur, rippling; (*de hojas, viento*) rustle, rustling; (*ruido confuso*) hum(ming)
murmuración [murmura'θjon] *nf* gossip; (*críticas*) backbiting
murmurar [murmu'rar] *vi* to murmur, whisper; (*criticar*) to criticize; (*cotillear*) to gossip
muro ['muro] *nm* wall; ~ **de contención** retaining wall
mus [mus] *nm card game*
muscular [musku'lar] *adj* muscular
músculo ['muskulo] *nm* muscle
musculoso, -a [musku'loso, a] *adj* muscular
museo [mu'seo] *nm* museum; ~ **de arte** *o* **de pintura** art gallery; ~ **de cera** waxworks
musgo ['musɣo] *nm* moss
musical [musi'kal] *adj, nm* musical
músico, -a ['musiko, a] *adj* musical ▷ *nm/f* musician ▷ *nf* music; **irse con la música a otra parte** to clear off
musitar [musi'tar] *vt, vi* to mutter, mumble
muslo ['muslo] *nm* thigh; (*de pollo*) leg, drumstick
mustio, -a ['mustjo, a] *adj* (*persona*) depressed, gloomy; (*planta*) faded, withered
musulmán, -ana [musul'man, ana] *nm/f* Moslem, Muslim
mutación [muta'θjon] *nf* (*Bio*) mutation; (*: cambio*) (sudden) change
mutilar [muti'lar] *vt* to mutilate; (*a una persona*) to maim
mutismo [mu'tismo] *nm* silence
mutuamente [mutwa'mente] *adv* mutually
mutuo, -a ['mutwo, a] *adj* mutual
muy [mwi] *adv* very; (*demasiado*) too; **M~ Señor mío** Dear Sir; ~ **bien** (*de acuerdo*) all right; ~ **de noche** very late at night; **eso es ~ de él** that's just like him; **eso es ~ español** that's typically Spanish

n

N *abr* (= *norte*) N
n/ *abr* = **nuestro, a**
nabo ['naβo] *nm* turnip
nácar ['nakar] *nm* mother-of-pearl
nacer [na'θer] *vi* to be born; (*huevo*) to hatch; (*vegetal*) to sprout; (*río*) to rise; (*fig*) to begin, originate, have its origins; **nací en Barcelona** I was born in Barcelona; **nació para poeta** he was born to be a poet; **nadie nace enseñado** we all have to learn; **nació una sospecha en su mente** a suspicion formed in her mind
nacido, -a [na'θiðo, a] *adj* born; **recién ~** newborn
naciente [na'θjente] *adj* new, emerging; (*sol*) rising
nacimiento [naθi'mjento] *nm* birth; (*fig*) birth, origin; (*de Navidad*) Nativity; (*linaje*) descent, family; (*de río*) source; **ciego de ~** blind from birth
nación [na'θjon] *nf* nation; (*pueblo*) people; **Naciones Unidas** United Nations
nacional [naθjo'nal] *adj* national; (*Com, Econ*) domestic, home *cpd*
nacionalidad [naθjonali'ðað] *nf* nationality; (*Esp, Pol*) autonomous region
nacionalismo [naθjona'lismo] *nm* nationalism
nacionalista [naθjona'lista] *adj, nm/f* nationalist
nacionalizar [naθjonali'θar] *vt* to nationalize; **nacionalizarse** *vr* (*persona*) to become naturalized

nada ['naðaa] *pron* nothing ▷ *adv* not at all, in no way ▷ *nf* nothingness; **no decir ~ (más)** to say nothing (else), not to say anything (else); **¡~ más!** that's all; **de ~** don't mention it; **~ de eso** nothing of the kind; **antes de ~** right away; **como si ~** as if it didn't matter; **no ha sido ~** it's nothing; **la ~** the void
nadador, a [naða'ðor, a] *nm/f* swimmer
nadar [na'ðar] *vi* to swim; **~ en la abundancia** (*fig*) to be rolling in money
nadie ['naðje] *pron* nobody, no-one; **~ habló** nobody spoke; **no había ~** there was nobody there, there wasn't anybody there; **es un don ~** he's a nobody *o* nonentity
nado ['naðo]: **a ~** *adv*: **pasar a ~** to swim across
nafta ['nafta] *nf* (*Am*) petrol (*Brit*), gas(oline) (*US*)
náhuatl ['nawatl] *adj, nm* Nahuatl
naipe ['naipe] *nm* (playing) card; **naipes** *nmpl* cards
nalgas ['nalɣas] *nfpl* buttocks
nalguear [nalɣe'ar] *vt* (*Am, CAm*) to spank
nana ['nana] *nf* lullaby
napias ['napjas] *nfpl* (*fam*) conk *sg*
naranja [na'ranxa] *adj inv, nf* orange; **media ~** (*fam*) better half; **¡~s de la China!** nonsense!
naranjada [naran'xaða] *nf* orangeade
naranjo [na'ranxo] *nm* orange tree
narcisista [narθi'sista] *adj* narcissistic
narciso [nar'θiso] *nm* narcissus
narcótico, -a [nar'kotiko, a] *adj, nm* narcotic
narcotizar [narkoti'θar] *vt* to drug
narcotráfico [narko'trafiko] *nm* narcotics *o* drug trafficking
nardo ['narðo] *nm* lily
narigón, -ona [nari'ɣon, ona], **narigudo, -a** [nari'ɣuðo, a] *adj* big-nosed
nariz [na'riθ] *nf* nose; **narices** *nfpl* nostrils; **¡narices!** (*fam*) rubbish!; **delante de las narices de algn** under one's (very) nose; **estar hasta las narices** to be completely fed up; **meter las narices en algo** to poke one's nose into sth; **~ chata/respingona** snub/turned-up nose
narración [narra'θjon] *nf* narration
narrador, a [narra'ðor, a] *nm/f* narrator
narrar [na'rrar] *vt* to narrate, recount
narrativo, -a [narra'tiβo, a] *adj* narrative ▷ *nf* narrative, story
nata ['nata] *nf* cream (*tb fig*); (*en leche cocida etc*) skin; **~ batida** whipped cream
natación [nata'θjon] *nf* swimming
natal [na'tal] *adj* natal; (*país*) native; **ciudad ~** home town
natalidad [natali'ðað] *nf* birth rate
natillas [na'tiʎas] *nfpl* (egg) custard *sg*
natividad [natiβi'ðað] *nf* nativity
nativo, -a [na'tiβo, a] *adj, nm/f* native
nato, -a ['nato, a] *adj* born; **un músico ~** a born musician
natural [natu'ral] *adj* natural; (*fruta etc*) fresh ▷ *nm/f* native ▷ *nm* disposition, temperament; **buen ~** good nature; **fruta al ~** fruit in its own juice
naturaleza [natura'leθa] *nf* nature; (*género*) nature, kind; **~ muerta** still life
naturalidad [naturali'ðað] *nf* naturalness
naturalización [naturaliθa'θjon] *nf* naturalization
naturalizarse [naturali'θarse] *vr* to become naturalized; (*aclimatarse*) to become acclimatized
naturalmente [natural'mente] *adv* naturally; (*de modo natural*) in a natural way; **¡~!** of course!
naturista [natu'rista] *adj* (*Med*) naturopathic ▷ *nm/f* naturopath
naufragar [naufra'ɣar] *vi* (*barco*) to sink; (*gente*) to be shipwrecked; (*fig*) to fail
naufragio [nau'fraxjo] *nm* shipwreck
náufrago, -a ['naufraɣo, a] *nm/f* castaway, shipwrecked person
náusea ['nausea] *nf* nausea; **me da ~s** it makes me feel sick
nauseabundo, -a [nausea'βundo, a] *adj* nauseating, sickening
náutico, -a ['nautiko, a] *adj* nautical; **club ~** sailing *o* yacht club ▷ *nf* navigation, seamanship
navaja [na'βaxa] *nf* (*cortaplumas*) clasp knife (*Brit*), penknife; **~ (de afeitar)** razor
navajazo [naβa'xaθo] *nm* (*herida*) gash; (*acto*) slash
naval [na'βal] *adj* (*Mil*) naval; **construcción ~** shipbuilding; **sector ~** shipbuilding industry
Navarra [na'βarra] *nf* Navarre
nave ['naβe] *nf* (*barco*) ship, vessel; (*Arq*) nave; **~ espacial** spaceship; **quemar las ~s** to burn one's boats; **~ industrial** factory premises *pl*
navegación [naβeɣa'θjon] *nf* navigation; (*viaje*) sea journey; **~ aérea** air traffic; **~ costera** coastal shipping; **~ fluvial** river navigation
navegador [naβeɣa'ðor] *nm* (*Inform*) browser; (*de coche*) sat nav
navegante [naβe'ɣante] *nm/f* navigator
navegar [naβe'ɣar] *vi* (*barco*) to sail; (*avión*) to fly ▷ *vt* to sail; to fly; (*dirigir el rumbo de*) to navigate; **~ por Internet** to surf the Net
Navidad [naβi'ðað] *nf* Christmas; **Navidades** *nfpl* Christmas time *sg*; **día de ~** Christmas Day; **por ~es** at Christmas (time); **¡Feliz ~!** Merry Christmas!
navideño, -a [naβi'ðeɲo, a] *adj* Christmas *cpd*
navío [na'βio] *nm* ship
nazca *etc vb ver* **nacer**
nazi ['naθi] *adj, nm/f* Nazi
nazismo [na'θismo] *nm* Nazism
NE *abr* (= *nor(d)este*) NE
neblina [ne'βlina] *nf* mist
nebuloso, -a [neβu'loso, a] *adj* foggy; (*calinoso*) misty; (*indefinido*) nebulous, vague ▷ *nf* nebula

necedad [neθe'ðað] *nf* foolishness; (*una necedad*) foolish act
necesario, -a [neθe'sarjo, a] *adj* necessary; **si fuera** *o* **fuese ~** if need(s) be
neceser [neθe'ser] *nm* toilet bag; (*bolsa grande*) holdall
necesidad [neθesi'ðað] *nf* need; (*lo inevitable*) necessity; (*miseria*) poverty, need; **en caso de ~** in case of need *o* emergency; **hacer sus ~es** to relieve o.s.
necesitado, -a [neθesi'taðo, a] *adj* needy, poor; **~ de** in need of
necesitar [neθesi'tar] *vt* to need, require ▷ *vi*: **~ de** to have need of; **necesitarse** *vr* to be needed; (*en anuncios*): **"necesitase coche"** "car wanted"
necio, -a ['neθjo, a] *adj* foolish ▷ *nm/f* fool
necrología [nekrolo'xia] *nf* obituary
necrópolis [ne'kropolis] *nf inv* cemetery
néctar ['nektar] *nm* nectar
nectarina [nekta'rina] *nf* nectarine
nefasto, -a [ne'fasto, a] *adj* ill-fated, unlucky
negación [neɣa'θjon] *nf* negation; (*Ling*) negative; (*rechazo*) refusal, denial
negado, -a [ne'ɣaðo, a] *adj*: **~ para** inept at, unfitted for
negar [ne'ɣar] *vt* (*renegar, rechazar*) to refuse; (*prohibir*) to refuse, deny; (*desmentir*) to deny; **negarse** *vr*: **~se a hacer algo** to refuse to do sth
negativo, -a [neɣa'tiβo, a] *adj* negative ▷ *nm* (*Foto*) negative; (*Mat*) minus ▷ *nf* (*gen*) negative; (*rechazo*) refusal, denial; **negativa rotunda** flat refusal
negligencia [neɣli'xenθja] *nf* negligence
negligente [neɣli'xente] *adj* negligent
negociable [neɣo'θjaβle] *adj* negotiable
negociación [neɣoθja'θjon] *nf* negotiation
negociado [neɣo'θjaðo] *nm* department, section
negociante [neɣo'θjante] *nm/f* businessman(-woman)
negociar [neɣo'θjar] *vt, vi* to negotiate; **~ en** to deal in, trade in
negocio [ne'ɣoθjo] *nm* (*Com*) business; (*asunto*) affair, business; (*operación comercial*) deal, transaction; (*Am*) shop, store; (*lugar*) place of business; **los ~s** business *sg*; **hacer ~** to do business; **el ~ del libro** the book trade; **~ autorizado** licensed trade; **hombre de ~s** businessman; **~ sucio** shady deal; **hacer un buen ~** to pull off a profitable deal; **¡mal ~!** it looks bad!
negra ['neɣra] *nf* (*Mus*) crotchet; *ver* **negro**
negro, -a ['neɣro, a] *adj* black; (*suerte*) awful, atrocious; (*humor etc*) sad; (*lúgubre*) gloomy ▷ *nm* (*color*) black ▷ *nm/f* black person ▷ *nf* (*Mus*) crotchet; **~ como la boca del lobo** pitch-black; **estoy ~ con esto** I'm getting desperate about it; **ponerse ~** (*fam*) to get cross
negrura [ne'ɣrura] *nf* blackness
nene, -a ['nene, a] *nm/f* baby, small child
nenúfar [ne'nufar] *nm* water lily
neologismo [neolo'xismo] *nm* neologism
neón [ne'on] *nm* neon; **luces/lámpara de ~** neon lights/lamp
neoyorquino, -a [neojor'kino, a] *adj* New York *cpd* ▷ *nm/f* New Yorker
nepotismo [nepo'tismo] *nm* nepotism
nervio ['nerβjo] *nm* (*Anat*) nerve; (*: tendón*) tendon; (*fig*) vigour; (*Tec*) rib; **crispar los ~s a algn**, **poner los ~s de punta a algn** to get on sb's nerves
nerviosismo [nerβjo'sismo] *nm* nervousness, nerves *pl*
nervioso, -a [ner'βjoso, a] *adj* nervous; (*sensible*) nervy, highly-strung; (*impaciente*) restless; **¡no te pongas ~!** take it easy!
neto, -a ['neto, a] *adj* clear; (*limpio*) clean; (*Com*) net
neumático, -a [neu'matiko, a] *adj* pneumatic ▷ *nm* (*Esp*) tyre (*Brit*), tire (*US*); **~ de recambio** spare tyre
neumonía [neumo'nia] *nf* pneumonia; **~ asiática** SARS
neura ['neura] (*fam*) *nm/f* (*persona*) neurotic ▷ *nf* (*obsesión*) obsession
neurálgico, -a [neu'ralxiko, a] *adj* neuralgic; (*fig: centro*) nerve *cpd*
neurastenia [neuras'tenja] *nf* neurasthenia; (*fig*) excitability
neurólogo, -a [neu'roloɣo, a] *nm/f* neurologist
neurona [neu'rona] *nf* neuron
neutral [neu'tral] *adj* neutral
neutralizar [neutrali'θar] *vt* to neutralize; (*contrarrestar*) to counteract
neutro, -a ['neutro, a] *adj* (*Bio, Ling*) neuter
neutrón [neu'tron] *nm* neutron
nevado, -a [ne'βaðo, a] *adj* snow-covered; (*montaña*) snow-capped; (*fig*) snowy, snow-white ▷ *nf* snowstorm; (*caída de nieve*) snowfall
nevar [ne'βar] *vi* to snow ▷ *vt* (*fig*) to whiten
nevera [ne'βera] *nf* (*Esp*) refrigerator (*Brit*), icebox (*US*)
nevería [neβe'ria] *nf* (*Am*) ice-cream parlour
nevisca [ne'βiska] *nf* flurry of snow
nexo ['nekso] *nm* link, connection
ni [ni] *conj* nor, neither; (*tb*: **ni siquiera**) not even; **ni que** not even if; **ni blanco ni negro** neither white nor black; **ni el uno ni el otro** neither one nor the other
Nicaragua [nika'raɣwa] *nf* Nicaragua
nicaragüense [nikara'ɣwense] *adj, nm/f* Nicaraguan
nicho ['nitʃo] *nm* niche
nicotina [niko'tina] *nf* nicotine
nido ['niðo] *nm* nest; (*fig*) hiding place; **~ de ladrones** den of thieves
niebla ['njeβla] *nf* fog; (*neblina*) mist; **hay ~** it is foggy

n

niego *etc* ['njeɣo], **niegue** *etc* ['njeɣe] *vb ver* **negar**
nieto, -a ['njeto, a] *nm/f* grandson/ granddaughter; **nietos** *nmpl* grandchildren
nieve ['njeβe] *vb ver* **nevar** ▷ *nf* snow; (*Am*) ice cream; **copo de ~** snowflake
Nilo ['nilo] *nm*: **el (Río) ~** the Nile
nimiedad [nimje'ðað] *nf* small-mindedness; (*trivialidad*) triviality; (*una nimiedad*) trifle, tiny detail
nimio, -a ['nimjo, a] *adj* trivial, insignificant
ninfa ['ninfa] *nf* nymph
ninfómana [nin'fomana] *nf* nymphomaniac
ningún [nin'gun] *adj ver* **ninguno**
ninguno, -a [nin'guno, a] *adj* (*antes de nmsg* **ningún**) no ▷ *pron* (*nadie*) nobody; (*ni uno*) none, not one; (*ni uno ni otro*) neither; **de ninguna manera** by no means, not at all; **no voy a ninguna parte** I'm not going anywhere
niña ['niɲa] *nf ver* **niño**
niñera [ni'ɲera] *nf* nursemaid, nanny
niñería [niɲe'ria] *nf* childish act
niñez [ni'ɲeθ] *nf* childhood; (*infancia*) infancy
niño, -a ['niɲo, a] *adj* (*joven*) young; (*inmaduro*) immature ▷ *nm* (*chico*) boy, child ▷ *nf* girl, child; (*Anat*) pupil; **los ~s** the children; **~ bien** rich kid; **~ expósito** foundling; **~ de pecho** babe-in-arms; **~ prodigio** child prodigy; **de ~** as a child; **ser el ~ mimado de algn** to be sb's pet; **ser la niña de los ojos de algn** to be the apple of sb's eye
nipón, -ona [ni'pon, ona] *adj, nm/f* Japanese; **los nipones** the Japanese
níquel ['nikel] *nm* nickel
niquelar [nike'lar] *vt* (*Tec*) to nickel-plate
níspero ['nispero] *nm* medlar
nitidez [niti'ðeθ] *nf* (*claridad*) clarity; (*: de atmósfera*) brightness; (*: de imagen*) sharpness
nítido, -a ['nitiðo, a] *adj* bright; (*fig*) pure; (*imagen*) clear, sharp
nitrato [ni'trato] *nm* nitrate
nitrógeno [ni'troxeno] *nm* nitrogen
nitroglicerina [nitroɣliθe'rina] *nf* nitroglycerine
nivel [ni'βel] *nm* (*Geo*) level; (*norma*) level, standard; (*altura*) height; **~ de aceite** oil level; **~ de aire** spirit level; **~ de vida** standard of living; **al ~ de** on a level with, at the same height as; (*fig*) on a par with; **a 900m sobre el ~ del mar** at 900m above sea level
nivelar [niβe'lar] *vt* to level out; (*fig*) to even up; (*Com*) to balance
NN. UU. *nfpl abr* (= *Naciones Unidas*) UN *sg*
NO *abr* (= *noroeste*) NW
no [no] *adv* no; (*con verbo*) not ▷ *excl* no!; **no tengo nada** I don't have anything, I have nothing; **no es el mío** it's not mine; **ahora no** not now; **¿no lo sabes?** don't you know?; **no mucho** not much; **no bien termine, lo entregaré** as soon as I finish I'll hand it over; **ayer no más** just yesterday; **¡pase no más!** come in!; **¡a que no lo sabes!** I bet you don't know!; **¡cómo no!** of course!; **pacto de no agresión** non-aggression pact; **los países no alineados** the non-aligned countries; **el no va más** the ultimate; **la no intervención** non-intervention
noble ['noβle] *adj, nm/f* noble; **los ~s** the nobility *sg*
nobleza [noβ'leθa] *nf* nobility
noche ['notʃe] *nf* night, night-time; (*la tarde*) evening; (*fig*) darkness; **de ~, por la ~** at night; **ayer por la ~** last night; **esta ~** tonight; **(en) toda la ~** all night; **hacer ~ en un sitio** to spend the night in a place; **se hace de ~** it's getting dark; **es de ~** it's dark; **N~ de San Juan** *see note*

NOCHE DE SAN JUAN

The *Noche de San Juan* on the 24th June is a *fiesta* coinciding with the summer solstice and which has taken the place of other ancient pagan festivals. Traditionally fire plays a major part in these festivities with celebrations and dancing taking place around bonfires in towns and villages across the country.

Nochebuena [notʃe'βwena] *nf* Christmas Eve; *see note*

NOCHEBUENA

On *Nochebuena* in Spanish homes there is normally a large supper when family members come from all over to be together. The more religiously inclined attend *la misa del gallo* at midnight. The tradition of receiving Christmas presents from Santa Claus that night is becoming more and more widespread and gradually replacing the tradition of *los Reyes Magos* (the Three Wise Men) on the 6th of January.

Nochevieja [notʃe'βjexa] *nf* New Year's Eve; *ver tb* **uvas**
noción [no'θjon] *nf* notion; **nociones** *nfpl* elements, rudiments
nocivo, -a [no'θiβo, a] *adj* harmful
noctámbulo, -a [nok'tambulo, a] *nm/f* sleepwalker
nocturno, -a [nok'turno, a] *adj* (*de la noche*) nocturnal, night *cpd*; (*de la tarde*) evening *cpd* ▷ *nm* nocturne
nogal [no'ɣal] *nm* walnut tree; (*madera*) walnut
nómada ['nomaða] *adj* nomadic ▷ *nm/f* nomad
nombramiento [nombra'mjento] *nm* naming; (*para un empleo*) appointment; (*Pol etc*) nomination; (*Mil*) commission

nombrar [nom'brar] *vt* (*gen*) to name; (*mencionar*) to mention; (*designar*) to appoint, nominate; (*Mil*) to commission

nombre ['nombre] *nm* name; (*sustantivo*) noun; (*fama*) renown; **~ y apellidos** name in full; **poner ~ a** to call, name; **~ común/propio** common/proper noun; **~ de pila/de soltera** Christian/maiden name; **~ de fichero** (*Inform*) file name; **en ~ de** in the name of, on behalf of; **sin ~** nameless; **su conducta no tiene ~** his behaviour is utterly despicable

nomenclatura [nomenkla'tura] *nf* nomenclature

nomeolvides [nomeol'βiðes] *nm inv* forget-me-not

nómina ['nomina] *nf* (*lista*) list; (*Com*: *tb*: **~s**) payroll; (*hoja*) payslip

nominal [nomi'nal] *adj* nominal; (*valor*) face *cpd*; (*Ling*) noun *cpd*, substantival

nominar [nomi'nar] *vt* to nominate

nominativo, -a [nomina'tiβo, a] *adj* (*Ling*) nominative; (*Com*): **un cheque ~ a X** a cheque made out to X

non [non] *adj* odd, uneven ▷ *nm* odd number; **pares y ~es** odds and evens

nono, -a ['nono, a] *num* ninth

nordeste [nor'ðeste] *adj* north-east, north-eastern, north-easterly ▷ *nm* north-east; (*viento*) north-east wind, north easterly

nórdico, -a ['norðiko, a] *adj* (*del norte*) northern, northerly; (*escandinavo*) Nordic, Norse ▷ *nm/f* northerner; (*escandinavo*) Norseman/-woman ▷ *nm* (*Ling*) Norse

noreste [no'reste] *adj, nm* = **nordeste**

noria ['norja] *nf* (*Agr*) waterwheel; (*de carnaval*) big (*Brit*) *o* Ferris (*US*) wheel

norma ['norma] *nf* standard, norm, rule; (*patrón*) pattern; (*método*) method

normal [nor'mal] *adj* (*corriente*) normal; (*habitual*) usual, natural; (*Tec*) standard; **Escuela N~** teacher training college; **(gasolina) ~** two-star petrol

normalidad [normali'ðað] *nf* normality

normalizar [normali'θar] *vt* (*reglamentar*) to normalize; (*Com, Tec*) to standardize; **normalizarse** *vr* to return to normal

normalmente [normal'mente] *adv* (*con normalidad*) normally; (*habitualmente*) usually

normando, -a [nor'mando, a] *adj, nm/f* Norman

normativo, -a [norma'tiβo, a] *adj*: **es ~ en todos los coches nuevos** it is standard in all new cars ▷ *nf* rules *pl*, regulations *pl*

noroeste [noro'este] *adj* north-west, north-western, north-westerly ▷ *nm* north-west; (*viento*) north-west wind, north-westerly

norte ['norte] *adj* north, northern, northerly ▷ *nm* north; (*fig*) guide

norteamericano, -a [norteameri'kano, a] *adj, nm/f* (North) American

Noruega [no'rweɣa] *nf* Norway

noruego, -a [no'rweɣo, a] *adj, nm/f* Norwegian ▷ *nm* (*Ling*) Norwegian

nos [nos] *pron* (*directo*) us; (*indirecto*) (to) us; (*reflexivo*) (to) ourselves; (*recíproco*) (to) each other; **~ levantamos a las siete** we get up at seven

nosotros, -as [no'sotros, as] *pron* (*sujeto*) we; (*después de prep*) us; **~ (mismos)** ourselves

nostalgia [nos'talxja] *nf* nostalgia, homesickness

nota ['nota] *nf* note; (*Escol*) mark; (*de fin de año*) report; (*Univ etc*) footnote; (*Com*) account; **~ de aviso** advice note; **~ de crédito/débito** credit/debit note; **~ de gastos** expenses claim; **~ de sociedad** gossip column; **tomar ~s** to take notes

notable [no'taβle] *adj* noteworthy, notable; (*Escol etc*) outstanding ▷ *nm/f* notable

notar [no'tar] *vt* to notice, note; (*percibir*) to feel; (*ver*) to see; **notarse** *vr* to be obvious; **se nota que ...** one observes that ...

notarial [nota'rjal] *adj* (*estilo*) legal; **acta ~** affidavit

notario [no'tarjo] *nm* notary; (*abogado*) solicitor

noticia [no'tiθja] *nf* (*información*) piece of news; (*TV etc*) news item; **las ~s** the news *sg*; **según nuestras ~s** according to our information; **tener ~s de algn** to hear from sb

noticiario [noti'θjarjo] *nm* (*Cine*) newsreel; (*TV*) news bulletin

noticiero [noti'θjero] *nm* newspaper, gazette; (*Am*: *tb*: **~ telediario**) news bulletin

notificación [notifika'θjon] *nf* notification

notificar [notifi'kar] *vt* to notify, inform

notoriedad [notorje'ðað] *nf* fame, renown

notorio, -a [no'torjo, a] *adj* (*público*) well-known; (*evidente*) obvious

novato, -a [no'βato, a] *adj* inexperienced ▷ *nm/f* beginner, novice

novecientos, -as [noβe'θjentos, as] *num* nine hundred

novedad [noβe'ðað] *nf* (*calidad de nuevo*) newness, novelty; (*noticia*) piece of news; (*cambio*) change, (new) development; (*sorpresa*) surprise; **novedades** *nfpl* (*noticia*) latest (news) *sg*

novedoso, -a [noβe'ðoso, a] *adj* novel

novel [no'βel] *adj* new; (*inexperto*) inexperienced ▷ *nm/f* beginner

novela [no'βela] *nf* novel; **~ policíaca** detective story

novelero, -a [noβe'lero, a] *adj* highly imaginative

novelesco, -a [noβe'lesko, a] *adj* fictional; (*romántico*) romantic; (*fantástico*) fantastic

novelista [noβe'lista] *nm/f* novelist

noveno, -a [no'βeno, a] *num* ninth

noventa [no'βenta] *num* ninety

novia ['noβja] *nf ver* **novio**

noviazgo [no'βjaθɣo] *nm* engagement

novicio, -a [no'βiθjo, a] *nm/f* novice
noviembre [no'βjembre] *nm* November; *ver tb* **julio**
novillada [noβi'ʎaða] *nf* (*Taur*) *bullfight with young bulls*
novillero [noβi'ʎero] *nm* novice bullfighter
novillo [no'βiʎo] *nm* young bull, bullock; **hacer ~s** (*fam*) to play truant (*Brit*) *o* hooky (*US*)
novio, -a ['noβjo, a] *nm/f* boyfriend/girlfriend; (*prometido*) fiancé/fiancée; (*recién casado*) bridegroom/bride; **los ~s** the newly-weds
N. S. *abr* = **Nuestro Señor**
nubarrón [nuβa'rron] *nm* storm cloud
nube ['nuβe] *nf* cloud; (*Med: ocular*) cloud, film; (*fig*) mass; **una ~ de críticas** a storm of criticism; **los precios están por las ~s** prices are sky-high; **estar en las ~s** to be away with the fairies
nublado, -a [nu'βlaðo, a] *adj* cloudy ▷ *nm* storm cloud
nublar [nu'βlar] *vt* (*oscurecer*) to darken; (*confundir*) to cloud; **nublarse** *vr* to cloud over
nuboso, -a [nu'βoso, a] *adj* cloudy
nuca ['nuka] *nf* nape of the neck
nuclear [nukle'ar] *adj* nuclear
núcleo ['nukleo] *nm* (*centro*) core; (*Física*) nucleus; **~ urbano** city centre
nudillo [nu'ðiʎo] *nm* knuckle
nudista [nu'dista] *adj, nm/f* nudist
nudo ['nuðo] *nm* knot; (*unión*) bond; (*de problema*) crux; (*Ferro*) junction; (*fig*) lump; **~ corredizo** slipknot; **con un ~ en la garganta** with a lump in one's throat
nudoso, -a [nu'ðoso, a] *adj* knotty; (*tronco*) gnarled; (*bastón*) knobbly
nuera ['nwera] *nf* daughter-in-law
nuestro, -a ['nwestro, a] *adj posesivo* our ▷ *pron* ours; **~ padre** our father; **un amigo ~** a friend of ours; **es el ~** it's ours; **los ~s** our people; (*Deporte*) our *o* the local team *o* side
nueva ['nweβa] *nf ver* **nuevo**
nuevamente [nweβa'mente] *adv* (*otra vez*) again; (*de nuevo*) anew
Nueva York [-'jork] *nf* New York
Nueva Zelanda [-θe'landa], **Nueva Zelandia** [-θe'landja] *nf* New Zealand
nueve ['nweβe] *num* nine
nuevo, -a ['nweβo, a] *adj* (*gen*) new ▷ *nf* piece of news; **¿qué hay de ~?** (*fam*) what's new?; **de ~** again
nuez [nweθ] (*pl* **nueces**) *nf* nut; (*del nogal*) walnut; **~ de Adán** Adam's apple; **~ moscada** nutmeg
nulidad [nuli'ðað] *nf* (*incapacidad*) incompetence; (*abolición*) nullity; (*individuo*) nonentity; **es una ~** he's a dead loss
nulo, -a ['nulo, a] *adj* (*inepto, torpe*) useless; (*inválido*) (null and) void; (*Deporte*) drawn, tied
núm. *abr* (= *número*) no.
numeración [numera'θjon] *nf* (*cifras*) numbers *pl*; (*arábiga, romana etc*) numerals *pl*; **~ de línea** (*Inform*) line numbering
numerador [numera'ðor] *nm* (*Mat*) numerator
numeral [nume'ral] *nm* numeral
numerar [nume'rar] *vt* to number; **numerarse** *vr* (*Mil etc*) to number off
numérico, -a [nu'meriko, a] *adj* numerical
número ['numero] *nm* (*gen*) number; (*tamaño: de zapato*) size; (*ejemplar: de diario*) number, issue; (*Teat etc*) turn, act, number; **sin ~** numberless, unnumbered; **~ binario** (*Inform*) binary number; **~ de matrícula/de teléfono** registration/telephone number; **~ personal de identificación** (*Inform etc*) personal identification number; **~ impar/par** odd/even number; **~ romano** Roman numeral; **~ de serie** (*Com*) serial number; **~ atrasado** back number
numeroso, -a [nume'roso, a] *adj* numerous; **familia numerosa** large family
numerus ['numerus] *nm*: **~ clausus** (*Univ*) restricted *o* selective entry
nunca ['nunka] *adv* (*jamás*) never; (*con verbo negativo*) ever; **~ lo pensé** I never thought it; **no viene ~** he never comes; **~ más** never again; **más que ~** more than ever
nuncio ['nunθjo] *nm* (*Rel*) nuncio
nupcial [nup'θjal] *adj* wedding *cpd*
nupcias ['nupθjas] *nfpl* wedding *sg*, nuptials
nutria ['nutrja] *nf* otter
nutrición [nutri'θjon] *nf* nutrition
nutrido, -a [nu'triðo, a] *adj* (*alimentado*) nourished; (*fig: grande*) large; (*abundante*) abundant; **mal ~** undernourished; **~ de** full of
nutrir [nu'trir] *vt* (*alimentar*) to nourish; (*dar de comer*) to feed; (*fig*) to strengthen
nutritivo, -a [nutri'tiβo, a] *adj* nourishing, nutritious
nylon [ni'lon] *nm* nylon

ñ o

ñango, -a ['ɲango, a] *adj* (*Am*) puny
ñapa ['ɲapa] *nf* (*Am*) extra
ñata ['ɲata] *nf* (*Am*: *fam*) nose; *ver tb* **ñato**
ñato, -a ['ɲato, a] *adj* (*Am*) snub-nosed
ñoñería [ɲoɲe'ria], **ñoñez** [ɲo'ɲeθ] *nf* insipidness
ñoño, -a ['ɲoɲo, a] *adj* (*fam*: *tonto*) silly, stupid; (*soso*) insipid; (*persona*) spineless; (*Esp*: *película, novela*) sentimental
ñoquis ['ɲokis] *nmpl* (*Culin*) gnocchi

O *abr* (= *oeste*) W
o [o] *conj* or; **o ... o** either ... or; **o sea** that is
o/ *nm* (*Com*: = *orden*) o
oasis [o'asis] *nm inv* oasis
obcecarse [oβθe'karse] *vr* to become obsessed; **~ en hacer** to insist on doing
obedecer [oβeðe'θer] *vt* to obey; **~ a** (*Med etc*) to yield to; (*fig*): **~ a ..., ~ al hecho de que ...** to be due to ..., arise from ...
obediencia [oβe'ðjenθja] *nf* obedience
obediente [oβe'ðjente] *adj* obedient
obertura [oβer'tura] *nf* overture
obesidad [oβesi'ðað] *nf* obesity
obeso, -a [o'βeso, a] *adj* obese
obispo [o'βispo] *nm* bishop
obituario [oβi'twarjo] *nm* (*Am*) obituary
objeción [oβxe'θjon] *nf* objection; **hacer una ~, poner objeciones** to raise objections, object
objetar [oβxe'tar] *vt, vi* to object
objetivo, -a [oβxe'tiβo, a] *adj* objective ▷ *nm* objective; (*fig*) aim; (*Foto*) lens
objeto [oβ'xeto] *nm* (*cosa*) object; (*fin*) aim
objetor, a [oβxe'tor, a] *nm/f* objector; **~ de conciencia** conscientious objector; *ver tb* **mili**
oblicuo, -a [o'βlikwo, a] *adj* oblique; (*mirada*) sidelong
obligación [oβliɣa'θjon] *nf* obligation; (*Com*) bond, debenture
obligar [oβli'ɣar] *vt* to force; **obligarse** *vr*: **~se a** to commit o.s. to

obligatorio, -a [oβliɣa'torjo, a] *adj* compulsory, obligatory
oboe [o'βoe] *nm* oboe; (*músico*) oboist
obra ['oβra] *nf* work; (*producción*) piece of work; (*Arq*) construction, building; (*libro*) book; (*Mus*) opus; (*Teat*) play; ~ **de arte** work of art; ~ **maestra** masterpiece; ~ **de consulta** reference book; **~s completas** complete works; ~ **benéfica** charity; **"~s"** (*en carretera*) "men at work"; **~s públicas** public works; **por ~ de** thanks to (the efforts of); **~s son amores y no buenas razones** actions speak louder than words
obrar [o'βrar] *vt* to work; (*tener efecto*) to have an effect on ▷ *vi* to act, behave; (*tener efecto*) to have an effect; **la carta obra en su poder** the letter is in his/her possession
obrero, -a [o'βrero, a] *adj* working; (*movimiento*) labour *cpd*; **clase obrera** working class ▷ *nm/f* (*gen*) worker; (*sin oficio*) labourer
obscenidad [oβsθeni'ðað] *nf* obscenity
obsceno, -a [oβs'θeno, a] *adj* obscene
obscu... *pref* = **oscu...**
obsequiar [oβse'kjar] *vt* (*ofrecer*) to present; (*agasajar*) to make a fuss of, lavish attention on
obsequio [oβ'sekjo] *nm* (*regalo*) gift; (*cortesía*) courtesy, attention
obsequioso, -a [oβse'kjoso, a] *adj* attentive
observación [oβserβa'θjon] *nf* observation; (*reflexión*) remark; (*objeción*) objection
observador, a [oβserβa'ðor, a] *adj* observant ▷ *nm/f* observer
observancia [oβser'βanθja] *nf* observance
observar [oβser'βar] *vt* to observe; (*notar*) to notice; (*leyes*) to observe, respect; (*reglas*) to abide by; **observarse** *vr* to keep to, observe
observatorio [oβserβa'torjo] *nm* observatory; ~ **del tiempo** weather station
obsesión [oβse'sjon] *nf* obsession
obsesionar [oβsesjo'nar] *vt* to obsess
obsesivo, -a [obse'siβo, a] *adj* obsessive
obseso, -a [oβ'seso, a] *nm/f* (*sexual*) sex maniac
obsoleto, -a [oβso'leto, a] *adj* obsolete
obstaculizar [oβstakuli'θar] *vt* (*dificultar*) to hinder, hamper
obstáculo [oβs'takulo] *nm* (*gen*) obstacle; (*impedimento*) hindrance, drawback
obstante [oβs'tante]: **no** ~ *adv* nevertheless; (*de todos modos*) all the same ▷ *prep* in spite of
obstetra [oβs'tetra] *nm/f* obstetrician
obstetricia [oβste'triθja] *nf* obstetrics *sg*
obstinado, -a [oβsti'naðo, a] *adj* (*gen*) obstinate; (*terco*) stubborn
obstinarse [oβsti'narse] *vr* to be obstinate; ~ **en** to persist in
obstrucción [oβstruk'θjon] *nf* obstruction
obstruir [oβstru'ir] *vt* to obstruct; (*bloquear*) to block; (*estorbar*) to hinder
obtener [oβte'ner] *vt* (*conseguir*) to obtain; (*ganar*) to gain; (*premio*) to win
obturador [oβtura'ðor] *nm* (*Foto*) shutter
obtuso, -a [oβ'tuso, a] *adj* (*filo*) blunt; (*Mat, fig*) obtuse
obviar [oβ'βjar] *vt* to obviate, remove
obvio, -a ['oββjo, a] *adj* obvious
oca ['oka] *nf* goose; (*tb*: **juego de la ~**) ≈ snakes and ladders
ocasión [oka'sjon] *nf* (*oportunidad*) opportunity, chance; (*momento*) occasion, time; (*causa*) cause; **de ~** secondhand; **con ~ de** on the occasion of; **en algunas ocasiones** sometimes; **aprovechar la ~** to seize one's opportunity
ocasionar [okasjo'nar] *vt* to cause
ocaso [o'kaso] *nm* sunset; (*fig*) decline
occidental [okθiðen'tal] *adj* western ▷ *nm/f* westerner ▷ *nm* west
occidente [okθi'ðente] *nm* west; **el O~** the West
O.C.D.E. *nf abr* (= *Organización de Cooperación y Desarrollo Económicos*) OECD
océano [o'θeano] *nm* ocean; **el ~ Índico** the Indian Ocean
ochenta [o'tʃenta] *num* eighty
ocho ['otʃo] *num* eight; (*fecha*) eighth; ~ **días** a week; **dentro de ~ días** within a week
ochocientos, -as [otʃo'θjentos, as] *num* eight hundred
ocio ['oθjo] *nm* (*tiempo*) leisure; (*pey*) idleness; **"guía del ~"** "what's on"
ociosidad [oθjosi'ðað] *nf* idleness
ocioso, -a [o'θjoso, a] *adj* (*inactivo*) idle; (*inútil*) useless
octanaje [okta'naxe] *nm*: **de alto ~** high octane
octano [ok'tano] *nm* octane
octavilla [okta'βiʎa] *nm* leaflet, pamphlet
octavo, -a [ok'taβo, a] *num* eighth
octogenario, -a [oktoxe'narjo, a] *adj, nm/f* octogenarian
octubre [ok'tuβre] *nm* October; *ver tb* **julio**
ocular [oku'lar] *adj* ocular, eye *cpd*; **testigo ~** eyewitness
oculista [oku'lista] *nm/f* oculist
ocultar [okul'tar] *vt* (*esconder*) to hide; (*callar*) to conceal; (*disfrazar*) to screen; **ocultarse** *vr* to hide (o.s.); **~se a la vista** to keep out of sight
oculto, -a [o'kulto, a] *adj* hidden; (*fig*) secret
ocupación [okupa'θjon] *nf* occupation; (*tenencia*) occupancy
ocupado, -a [oku'paðo, a] *adj* (*persona*) busy; (*plaza*) occupied, taken; (*teléfono*) engaged; **¿está ocupada la silla?** is that seat taken?
ocupar [oku'par] *vt* (*gen*) to occupy; (*puesto*) to hold, fill; (*individuo*) to engage; (*obreros*) to employ; (*confiscar*) to seize; **ocuparse** *vr*: **~se de** *o* **en** to concern o.s. with; (*cuidar*) to look after; **~se de lo suyo** to mind one's own business
ocurrencia [oku'rrenθja] *nf* (*ocasión*) occurrence; (*agudeza*) witticism; (*idea*) bright idea

ocurrir [oku'rrir] *vi* to happen; **ocurrirse** *vr*: **se me ocurrió que ...** it occurred to me that ...; **¿se te ocurre algo?** can you think of *o* come up with anything?; **¿qué ocurre?** what's going on?
odiar [o'ðjar] *vt* to hate
odio ['oðjo] *nm* (*gen*) hate, hatred; (*disgusto*) dislike
odioso, -a [o'ðjoso, a] *adj* (*gen*) hateful; (*malo*) nasty
odisea [oði'sea] *nf* odyssey
odontólogo, -a [oðon'toloɣo, a] *nm/f* dentist, dental surgeon
oeste [o'este] *nm* west; **una película del ~** a western
ofender [ofen'der] *vt* (*agraviar*) to offend; (*insultar*) to insult; **ofenderse** *vr* to take offence
ofensa [o'fensa] *nf* offence; (*insulto*) slight
ofensivo, -a [ofen'siβo, a] *adj* (*insultante*) insulting; (*Mil*) offensive ▷ *nf* offensive
oferta [o'ferta] *nf* offer; (*propuesta*) proposal; (*para contrato*) bid, tender; **la ~ y la demanda** supply and demand; **artículos en ~** goods on offer; **~ excedentaria** (*Com*) excess supply; **~ monetaria** money supply; **~ pública de adquisición (OPA)** (*Com*) takeover bid; **~s de trabajo** (*en periódicos*) situations vacant column
offset ['ofset] *nm* offset
oficial [ofi'θjal] *adj* official ▷ *nm* official; (*Mil*) officer
oficina [ofi'θina] *nf* office; **~ de correos** post office; **~ de empleo** employment agency; **~ de información** information bureau; **~ de objetos perdidos** lost property office (*Brit*), lost-and-found department (*US*); **~ de turismo** tourist office; **~ principal** (*Com*) head office, main branch
oficinista [ofiθi'nista] *nm/f* clerk; **los ~s** white-collar workers
oficio [o'fiθjo] *nm* (*profesión*) profession; (*puesto*) post; (*Rel*) service; (*función*) function; (*comunicado*) official letter; **ser del ~** to be an old hand; **tener mucho ~** to have a lot of experience; **~ de difuntos** funeral service; **de ~** officially
oficioso, -a [ofi'θjoso, a] *adj* (*pey*) officious; (*no oficial*) unofficial, informal
ofimática [ofi'matika] *nf* office automation
ofrecer [ofre'θer] *vt* (*dar*) to offer; (*proponer*) to propose; **ofrecerse** *vr* (*persona*) to offer o.s., volunteer; (*situación*) to present itself; **¿qué se le ofrece?, ¿se le ofrece algo?** what can I do for you?, can I get you anything?
ofrecimiento [ofreθi'mjento] *nm* offer, offering
ofrendar [ofren'dar] *vt* to offer, contribute
oftalmólogo, -a [oftal'moloɣo, a] *nm/f* ophthalmologist
ofuscación [ofuska'θjon] *nf*, **ofuscamiento** [ofuska'mjento] *nm* (*fig*) bewilderment
ofuscar [ofus'kar] *vt* (*confundir*) to bewilder; (*enceguecer*) to dazzle, blind
oída [o'iða] *nf*: **de ~s** by hearsay
oído [o'iðo] *nm* (*Anat, Mus*) ear; (*sentido*) hearing; **~ interno** inner ear; **de ~** by ear; **apenas pude dar crédito a mis ~s** I could scarcely believe my ears; **hacer ~s sordos a** to turn a deaf ear to
oigo *etc vb ver* **oír**
oír [o'ir] *vt* (*gen*) to hear; (*esp Am: escuchar*) to listen to; **¡oye!** (*sorpresa*) I say!, say! (*US*); **¡oiga!** excuse me!; (*Telec*) hullo?; **~ misa** to attend mass; **como quien oye llover** without paying (the slightest) attention
ojal [o'xal] *nm* buttonhole
ojalá [oxa'la] *excl* if only (it were so)!, some hope! ▷ *conj* if only...!, would that...!; **~ que venga hoy** I hope he comes today; **¡~ pudiera!** I wish I could!
ojeada [oxe'aða] *nf* glance; **echar una ~ a** to take a quick look at
ojera [o'xera] *nf*: **tener ~s** to have bags under one's eyes
ojeriza [oxe'riθa] *nf* ill-will; **tener ~ a** to have a grudge against, have it in for
ojeroso, -a [oxe'roso, a] *adj* haggard
ojo ['oxo] *nm* eye; (*de puente*) span; (*de cerradura*) keyhole ▷ *excl* careful!; **tener ~ para** to have an eye for; **~s saltones** bulging *o* goggle eyes; **~ de buey** porthole; **~ por ~** an eye for an eye; **en un abrir y cerrar de ~s** in the twinkling of an eye; **a ~s vistas** openly; (*crecer etc*) before one's (very) eyes; **a ~ (de buen cubero)** roughly; **~s que no ven, corazón que no siente** out of sight, out of mind; **ser el ~ derecho de algn** (*fig*) to be the apple of sb's eye
okey ['okei] *excl* (*Am*) O.K.
okupa [o'kupa] *nm/f* (*fam*) squatter
ola ['ola] *nf* wave; **~ de calor/frío** heatwave/cold spell; **la nueva ~** the latest fashion; (*Cine, Mus*) (the) new wave
olé [o'le] *excl* bravo!, olé!
oleada [ole'aða] *nf* big wave, swell; (*fig*) wave
oleaje [ole'axe] *nm* swell
óleo ['oleo] *nm* oil
oleoducto [oleo'ðukto] *nm* (oil) pipeline
oler [o'ler] *vt* (*gen*) to smell; (*inquirir*) to pry into; (*fig: sospechar*) to sniff out ▷ *vi* to smell; **~ a** to smell of; **huele mal** it smells bad, it stinks
olfatear [olfate'ar] *vt* to smell; (*fig: sospechar*) to sniff out; (*inquirir*) to pry into
olfato [ol'fato] *nm* sense of smell
oligarquía [oliɣar'kia] *nf* oligarchy
olimpiada [olim'piaða] *nf*: **la ~** *o* **las ~s** the Olympics
olímpicamente [o'limpikamente] *adv*: **pasar ~ de algo** to totally ignore sth
olímpico, -a [o'limpiko, a] *adj* Olympian; (*deportes*) Olympic
oliva [o'liβa] *nf* (*aceituna*) olive; **aceite de ~** olive oil

O

olivo [o'liβo] *nm* olive tree
olla ['oʎa] *nf* pan; (*para hervir agua*) kettle; (*comida*) stew; **~ a presión** pressure cooker; **~ podrida** *type of Spanish stew*
olmo ['olmo] *nm* elm (tree)
olor [o'lor] *nm* smell
oloroso, -a [olo'roso, a] *adj* scented
olvidadizo, -a [olβiða'ðiθo, a] *adj* (*desmemoriado*) forgetful; (*distraído*) absent-minded
olvidar [olβi'ðar] *vt* to forget; (*omitir*) to omit; (*abandonar*) to leave behind; **olvidarse** *vr* (*fig*) to forget o.s.; **se me olvidó** I forgot
olvido [ol'βiðo] *nm* oblivion; (*acto*) oversight; (*descuido*) slip; (*despiste*) forgetfulness; **caer en el ~** to fall into oblivion
ombligo [om'bliɣo] *nm* navel
omelette [ome'lete] *nf* (*Am*) omelet(te)
ominoso, -a [omi'noso, a] *adj* ominous
omisión [omi'sjon] *nf* (*abstención*) omission; (*descuido*) neglect
omiso, -a [o'miso, a] *adj*: **hacer caso ~ de** to ignore, pass over
omitir [omi'tir] *vt* to leave *o* miss out, omit
omnipotente [omnipo'tente] *adj* omnipotent
omnívoro, -a [om'niβoro, a] *adj* omnivorous
omoplato [omo'plato], **omóplato** [o'moplato] *nm* shoulder-blade
OMS *nf abr* (= *Organización Mundial de la Salud*) WHO
once ['onθe] *num* eleven; **onces** *nfpl* tea break *sg*
onda ['onda] *nf* wave; **~ corta/larga/media** short/long/medium wave; **~s acústicas/hertzianas** acoustic/Hertzian waves; **~ sonora** sound wave
ondear [onde'ar] *vi* to wave; (*tener ondas*) to be wavy; (*agua*) to ripple; **ondearse** *vr* to swing, sway
ondulación [ondula'θjon] *nf* undulation
ondulado, -a [ondu'laðo, a] *adj* wavy ▷ *nm* wave
ondulante [ondu'lante] *adj* undulating
ondular [ondu'lar] *vt* (*el pelo*) to wave ▷ *vi*, **ondularse** *vr* to undulate
oneroso, -a [one'roso, a] *adj* onerous
ONG *nf abr* (= *organización no gubernamental*) NGO
ONU ['onu] *nf abr ver* **Organización de las Naciones Unidas**
OPA ['opa] *nf abr* (= *Oferta Pública de Adquisición*) takeover bid
opaco, -a [o'pako, a] *adj* opaque; (*fig*) dull
ópalo ['opalo] *nm* opal
opción [op'θjon] *nf* (*gen*) option; (*derecho*) right, option; **no hay ~** there is no alternative
opcional [opθjo'nal] *adj* optional
O.P.E.P. [o'pep] *nf abr* (= *Organización de Países Exportadores de Petróleo*) OPEC
ópera ['opera] *nf* opera; **~ bufa** *o* **cómica** comic opera
operación [opera'θjon] *nf* (*gen*) operation; (*Com*) transaction, deal; **~ a plazo** (*Com*) forward transaction; **operaciones accesorias** (*Inform*) housekeeping; **operaciones a término** (*Com*) futures
operador, a [opera'ðor, a] *nm/f* operator; (*Cine*: *proyección*) projectionist; (: *rodaje*) cameraman
operar [ope'rar] *vt* (*producir*) to produce, bring about; (*Med*) to operate on ▷ *vi* (*Com*) to operate, deal; **operarse** *vr* to occur; (*Med*) to have an operation; **se han operado grandes cambios** great changes have been made *o* have taken place
opereta [ope'reta] *nf* operetta
opinar [opi'nar] *vt* (*estimar*) to think ▷ *vi* (*enjuiciar*) to give one's opinion; **~ bien de** to think well of
opinión [opi'njon] *nf* (*creencia*) belief; (*criterio*) opinion; **la ~ pública** public opinion
opio ['opjo] *nm* opium
oponente [opo'nente] *nm/f* opponent
oponer [opo'ner] *vt* (*resistencia*) to put up, offer; (*negativa*) to raise; **oponerse** *vr* (*objetar*) to object; (*estar frente a frente*) to be opposed; (*dos personas*) to oppose each other; **~ A a B** to set A against B; **me opongo a pensar que ...** I refuse to believe *o* think that ...
oporto [o'porto] *nm* port
oportunidad [oportuni'ðað] *nf* (*ocasión*) opportunity; (*posibilidad*) chance
oportunismo [oportu'nismo] *nm* opportunism
oportunista [oportu'nista] *nm/f* opportunist; (*infección*) opportunistic
oportuno, -a [opor'tuno, a] *adj* (*en su tiempo*) opportune, timely; (*respuesta*) suitable; **en el momento ~** at the right moment
oposición [oposi'θjon] *nf* opposition; **oposiciones** *nfpl* (*Escol*) public examinations; **ganar un puesto por oposiciones** to win a post by public competitive examination; **hacer oposiciones a, presentarse a unas oposiciones a** to sit a competitive examination for; *see note*
opositar [oposi'tar] *vi* to sit a public entrance examination
opositor, -a [oposi'tor, a] *nm/f* (*Admin*) candidate to a public examination; (*adversario*) opponent; **~ (a)** candidate (for)
opresión [opre'sjon] *nf* oppression
opresivo, -a [opre'siβo, a] *adj* oppressive
opresor, a [opre'sor, a] *nm/f* oppressor
oprimir [opri'mir] *vt* to squeeze; (*asir*) to grasp; (*pulsar*) to press; (*fig*) to oppress
optar [op'tar] *vi* (*elegir*) to choose; **~ a** *o* **por** to opt for
optativo, -a [opta'tiβo, a] *adj* optional
óptico, -a ['optiko, a] *adj* optic(al) ▷ *nm/f* optician ▷ *nf* (*ciencia*) optics *sg*; (*tienda*) optician's; (*fig*) viewpoint; **desde esta óptica** from this point of view

optimismo [opti'mismo] *nm* optimism

optimista [opti'mista] *nm/f* optimist

óptimo, -a ['optimo, a] *adj* (*el mejor*) very best

opuesto, -a [o'pwesto, a] *pp de* **oponer** ▷ *adj* (*contrario*) opposite; (*antagónico*) opposing

opulencia [opu'lenθja] *nf* opulence

opulento, -a [opu'lento, a] *adj* opulent

oración [ora'θjon] *nf* (*Rel*) prayer; (*Ling*) sentence

oráculo [o'rakulo] *nm* oracle

orador, a [ora'ðor, a] *nm/f* orator; (*conferenciante*) speaker

oral [o'ral] *adj* oral; **por vía ~** (*Med*) orally

orangután [orangu'tan] *nm* orang-utan

orar [o'rar] *vi* (*Rel*) to pray

oratoria [ora'torja] *nf* oratory

órbita ['orβita] *nf* orbit; (*Anat*: *ocular*) (eye-) socket

orden ['orðen] *nm* (*gen*) order; (*Inform*) command; **~ público** public order, law and order; (*números*): **del ~ de** about; **de primer ~** first-rate; **en ~ de prioridad** in order of priority ▷ *nf* (*gen*) order; **~ bancaria** banker's order; **~ de compra** (*Com*) purchase order; **~ del día** agenda; **eso ahora está a la ~ del día** that is now the order of the day; **a la ~ de usted** at your service; **dar la ~ de hacer algo** to give the order to do sth

ordenado, -a [orðe'naðo, a] *adj* (*metódico*) methodical; (*arreglado*) orderly

ordenador [orðena'ðor] *nm* computer; **~ central** mainframe computer; **~ de gestión** business computer; **~ portátil** laptop (computer); **~ de sobremesa** desktop computer

ordenamiento [orðena'mjento] *nm* legislation

ordenanza [orðe'nanθa] *nf* ordinance; **~s municipales** by-laws ▷ *nm* (*Com etc*) messenger; (*Mil*) orderly; (*bedel*) porter

ordenar [orðe'nar] *vt* (*mandar*) to order; (*poner orden*) to put in order, arrange; **ordenarse** *vr* (*Rel*) to be ordained

ordeñar [orðe'ɲar] *vt* to milk

ordinario, -a [orði'narjo, a] *adj* (*común*) ordinary, usual; (*vulgar*) vulgar, common

orégano [o'reɣano] *nm* oregano

oreja [o'rexa] *nf* ear; (*Mecánica*) lug, flange

orfanato [orfa'nato], **orfanatorio** [orfana'torjo] *nm* orphanage

orfandad [orfan'dað] *nf* orphanhood

orfebrería [orfeβre'ria] *nf* gold/silver work

orgánico, -a [or'ɣaniko, a] *adj* organic

organigrama [orɣani'ɣrama] *nm* flow chart; (*de organización*) organization chart

organismo [orɣa'nismo] *nm* (*Bio*) organism; (*Pol*) organization; **O~ Internacional de Energía Atómica** International Atomic Energy Agency

organista [orɣa'nista] *nm/f* organist

organización [orɣaniθa'θjon] *nf* organization; **O~ de las Naciones Unidas (ONU)** United Nations Organization; **O~ del Tratado del Atlántico Norte (OTAN)** North Atlantic Treaty Organization (NATO)

organizar [orɣani'θar] *vt* to organize

órgano ['orɣano] *nm* organ

orgasmo [or'ɣasmo] *nm* orgasm

orgía [or'xia] *nf* orgy

orgullo [or'ɣuʎo] *nm* (*altanería*) pride; (*autorrespeto*) self-respect

orgulloso, -a [orɣu'ʎoso, a] *adj* (*gen*) proud; (*altanero*) haughty

orientación [orjenta'θjon] *nf* (*posición*) position; (*dirección*) direction; **~ profesional** occupational guidance

oriental [orjen'tal] *adj* oriental; (*región etc*) eastern ▷ *nm/f* oriental

orientar [orjen'tar] *vt* (*situar*) to orientate; (*señalar*) to point; (*dirigir*) to direct; (*guiar*) to guide; **orientarse** *vr* to get one's bearings; (*decidirse*) to decide on a course of action

oriente [o'rjente] *nm* east; **el O~** the East, the Orient; **Cercano/Medio/Lejano O~** Near/Middle/Far East

origen [o'rixen] *nm* origin; (*nacimiento*) lineage, birth; **dar ~ a** to cause, give rise to

original [orixi'nal] *adj* (*nuevo*) original; (*extraño*) odd, strange ▷ *nm* original; (*Tip*) manuscript; (*Tec*) master (copy)

originalidad [orixinali'ðað] *nf* originality

originar [orixi'nar] *vt* to start, cause; **originarse** *vr* to originate

originario, -a [orixi'narjo, a] *adj* (*nativo*) native; (*primordial*) original; **ser ~ de** to originate from; **país ~** country of origin

orilla [o'riʎa] *nf* (*borde*) border; (*de río*) bank; (*de bosque, tela*) edge; (*de mar*) shore; **a ~s de** on the banks of

orín [o'rin] *nm* rust

orina [o'rina] *nf* urine

orinal [ori'nal] *nm* (chamber) pot

orinar [ori'nar] *vi* to urinate; **orinarse** *vr* to wet o.s.

orines [o'rines] *nmpl* urine *sg*

oriundo, -a [o'rjundo, a] *adj*: **~ de** native of

ornar [or'nar] *vt* to adorn

ornitología [ornitolo'xia] *nf* ornithology, bird watching

oro ['oro] *nm* gold; **~ en barras** gold ingots; **de ~** gold, golden; **no es ~ todo lo que reluce** all that glitters is not gold; **hacerse de ~** to make a fortune; *ver tb* **oros**

oropel [oro'pel] *nm* tinsel

oros ['oros] *nmpl* (*Naipes*) *one of the suits in the Spanish card deck*

orquesta [or'kesta] *nf* orchestra; **~ de cámara/sinfónica** chamber/symphony orchestra; **~ de jazz** jazz band

orquestar [orkes'tar] *vt* to orchestrate

orquídea [or'kiðea] *nf* orchid

ortiga [or'tiɣa] *nf* nettle
ortodoncia [orto'ðonθja] *nf* orthodontics *sg*
ortodoxo, -a [orto'ðokso, a] *adj* orthodox
ortografía [ortoɣra'fia] *nf* spelling
ortopedia [orto'peðja] *nf* orthop(a)edics *sg*
ortopédico, -a [orto'peðiko, a] *adj* orthop(a)edic
oruga [o'ruɣa] *nf* caterpillar
orzuelo [or'θwelo] *nm* (*Med*) stye
os [os] *pron* (*gen*) you; (*a vosotros*) (to) you; (*reflexivo*) (to) yourselves; (*mutuo*) (to) each other; **vosotros os laváis** you wash yourselves; **¡callaros!** (*fam*) shut up!
osa ['osa] *nf* (she-)bear; **O~ Mayor/Menor** Great/Little Bear, Ursa Major/Minor
osadía [osa'ðia] *nf* daring; (*descaro*) impudence
osar [o'sar] *vi* to dare
oscilación [osθila'θjon] *nf* (*movimiento*) oscillation; (*fluctuación*) fluctuation; (*vacilación*) hesitation; (*de columpio*) swinging, movement to and fro
oscilar [osθi'lar] *vi* to oscillate; to fluctuate; to hesitate
oscurecer [oskure'θer] *vt* to darken ▷ *vi* to grow dark; **oscurecerse** *vr* to grow *o* get dark
oscuridad [oskuri'ðað] *nf* obscurity; (*tinieblas*) darkness
oscuro, -a [os'kuro, a] *adj* dark; (*fig*) obscure; (*indefinido*) confused; (*cielo*) overcast, cloudy; (*futuro etc*) uncertain; **a oscuras** in the dark
óseo, -a ['oseo, a] *adj* bony; (*Med etc*) bone *cpd*
oso ['oso] *nm* bear; **~ blanco/gris/pardo** polar/grizzly/brown bear; **~ de peluche** teddy bear; **~ hormiguero** anteater; **hacer el ~** to play the fool
ostensible [osten'siβle] *adj* obvious
ostentación [ostenta'θjon] *nf* (*gen*) ostentation; (*acto*) display
ostentar [osten'tar] *vt* (*gen*) to show; (*pey*) to flaunt, show off; (*poseer*) to have, possess
ostentoso, -a [osten'toso, a] *adj* ostentatious, showy
ostión [os'tjon] *nm* (*Am*) = **ostra**
ostra ['ostra] *nf* oyster ▷ *excl*: **¡~s!** (*fam*) sugar!
OTAN ['otan] *nf abr ver* **Organización del Tratado del Atlántico Norte**
otear [ote'ar] *vt* to observe; (*fig*) to look into
otitis [o'titis] *nf* earache
otoñal [oto'ɲal] *adj* autumnal
otoño [o'toɲo] *nm* autumn, fall (*US*)
otorgamiento [otorɣa'mjento] *nm* conferring, granting; (*Jur*) execution
otorgar [otor'ɣar] *vt* (*conceder*) to concede; (*dar*) to grant; (*poderes*) to confer; (*premio*) to award
otorrinolaringólogo, -a [otorrinolarin'goloɣo, a] *nm/f* (*Med*: *tb*: **otorrino**) ear, nose and throat specialist

PALABRA CLAVE

otro, -a ['otro, a] *adj* **1** (*distinto*: *sg*) another; (: *pl*) other; **otra cosa/persona** something/someone else; **con otros amigos** with other *o* different friends; **a/en otra parte** elsewhere, somewhere else
2 (*adicional*): **tráigame otro café (más), por favor** can I have another coffee please; **otros 10 días más** another 10 days
▷ *pron* **1** (*sg*) another one; **el otro** the other one; **(los) otros** (the) others; **¡otra!** (*Mus*) more!; **de otro** somebody *o* someone else's; **que lo haga otro** let somebody *o* someone else do it; **ni uno ni otro** neither one nor the other
2 (*recíproco*): **se odian (la) una a (la) otra** they hate one another *o* each other
3: **otro tanto**: **comer otro tanto** to eat the same *o* as much again; **recibió una decena de telegramas y otras tantas llamadas** he got about ten telegrams and as many calls

outlet ['autlet] *nm* outlet store
ovación [oβa'θjon] *nf* ovation
oval [o'βal], **ovalado, a** [oβa'laðo, a] *adj* oval
óvalo ['oβalo] *nm* oval
ovario [o'βarjo] *nm* ovary
oveja [o'βexa] *nf* sheep; **~ negra** (*fig*) black sheep (of the family)
overol [oβe'rol] *nm* (*Am*) overalls *pl*
ovillo [o'βiʎo] *nm* (*de lana*) ball; (*fig*) tangle; **hacerse un ~** to curl up (into a ball)
OVNI ['oβni] *nm abr* (= *objeto volante (o volador) no identificado*) UFO
ovulación [oβula'θjon] *nf* ovulation
óvulo ['oβulo] *nm* ovum
oxidación [oksiða'θjon] *nf* rusting
oxidar [oksi'ðar] *vt* to rust; **oxidarse** *vr* to go rusty; (*Tec*) to oxidize
óxido ['oksiðo] *nm* oxide
oxigenado, -a [oksixe'naðo, a] *adj* (*Química*) oxygenated; (*pelo*) bleached
oxígeno [ok'sixeno] *nm* oxygen
oyente [o'jente] *nm/f* listener, hearer; (*Escol*) unregistered *o* occasional student
oyes *etc vb ver* **oír**
ozono [o'θono] *nm* ozone

p

P *abr* (*Rel*: = *padre*) Fr.; (= *pregunta*) Q; = **papa**

pabellón [paβe'ʎon] *nm* bell tent; (*Arq*) pavilion; (*de hospital etc*) block, section; (*bandera*) flag; **~ de conveniencia** (*Com*) flag of convenience; **~ de la oreja** outer ear

pábilo ['paβilo] *nm* wick

pacer [pa'θer] *vi* to graze ▷ *vt* to graze on

pachanguero, -a [patʃan'gero, a] *adj* (*pey: música*) *noisy and catchy*

paciencia [pa'θjenθja] *nf* patience; **¡~!** be patient!; **¡~ y barajar!** don't give up!; **perder la ~** to lose one's temper

paciente [pa'θjente] *adj, nm/f* patient

pacificación [paθifika'θjon] *nf* pacification

pacificar [paθifi'kar] *vt* to pacify; (*tranquilizar*) to calm

pacífico, -a [pa'θifiko, a] *adj* peaceful; (*persona*) peaceable; (*existencia*) peaceful; **el (Océano) P~** the Pacific (Ocean)

pacifismo [paθi'fismo] *nm* pacifism

pacifista [paθi'fista] *nm/f* pacifist

pack [pak] *nm* (*de yogures, latas*) pack; (*de vacaciones*) package

pacotilla [pako'tiʎa] *nf* trash; **de ~** shoddy

pactar [pak'tar] *vt* to agree to, agree on ▷ *vi* to come to an agreement

pacto ['pakto] *nm* (*tratado*) pact; (*acuerdo*) agreement

padecer [paðe'θer] *vt* (*sufrir*) to suffer; (*soportar*) to endure, put up with; (*ser víctima de*) to be a victim of ▷ *vi*: **~ de** to suffer from

padecimiento [paðeθi'mjento] *nm* suffering

pádel ['paðel] *nm* paddle tennis

padrastro [pa'ðrastro] *nm* stepfather

padre ['paðre] *nm* father ▷ *adj* (*fam*): **un éxito ~** a tremendous success; **padres** *nmpl* parents; **~ espiritual** confessor; **P~ Nuestro** Lord's Prayer; **~ político** father-in-law; **García ~** García senior; **¡tu ~!** (*fam!*) up yours! (*!*)

padrino [pa'ðrino] *nm* godfather; (*fig*) sponsor, patron; **padrinos** *nmpl* godparents; **~ de boda** best man

padrón [pa'ðron] *nm* (*censo*) census, roll; (*de socios*) register

padrote [pa'ðrote] (*Am: fam*) *nm* pimp

paella [pa'eʎa] *nf* paella, *dish of rice with meat, shellfish etc*

paga ['paγa] *nf* (*dinero pagado*) payment; (*sueldo*) pay, wages *pl*

pagadero, -a [paγa'ðero, a] *adj* payable; **~ a la entrega/a plazos** payable on delivery/in instalments

pagano, -a [pa'γano, a] *adj, nm/f* pagan, heathen

pagar [pa'γar] *vt* (*gen*) to pay; (*las compras, crimen*) to pay for; (*deuda*) to pay (off); (*fig: favor*) to repay ▷ *vi* to pay; **pagarse** *vr*: **~se con algo** to be content with sth; **~ al contado/a plazos** to pay (in) cash/in instalments; **¡me las ~ás!** I'll get you for this!

pagaré [paγa're] *nm* I.O.U

página ['paxina] *nf* page; **~ de inicio** (*Inform*) home page; **~ personal** (*Internet*) personal web page; **~ web** (*Internet*) web page

pago ['paγo] *nm* (*dinero*) payment; (*fig*) return; **~ anticipado/a cuenta/a la entrega/en especie/inicial** advance payment/payment on account/cash on delivery/payment in kind/down payment; **~ a título gracioso** ex gratia payment; **en ~ de** in return for

pág(s). *abr* (= *página(s)*) p(p)

pague *etc* ['paγe] *vb ver* **pagar**

país [pa'is] *nm* (*gen*) country; (*región*) land; **los P~es Bajos** the Low Countries; **el P~ Vasco** the Basque Country

paisaje [pai'saxe] *nm* countryside, landscape; (*vista*) scenery

paisano, -a [pai'sano, a] *adj* of the same country ▷ *nm/f* (*compatriota*) fellow countryman(-woman); **vestir de ~** (*soldado*) to be in civilian clothes; (*guardia*) to be in plain clothes

paja ['paxa] *nf* straw; (*fig*) trash, rubbish; (*en libro, ensayo*) padding, waffle; **riñeron por un quítame allá esas ~s** they quarrelled over a trifle

pajar [pa'xar] *nm* hay loft

pajarita [paxa'rita] *nf* bow tie

pájaro ['paxaro] *nm* bird; (*fam: astuto*) clever fellow; **tener la cabeza a ~s** to be featherbrained; **~ carpintero** woodpecker

pajita [pa'xita] *nf* (drinking) straw

pala ['pala] *nf* (*de mango largo*) spade; (*de mango corto*) shovel; (*raqueta etc*) bat; (*: de tenis*) racquet; (*Culin*) slice; **~ matamoscas** fly swat; **~ mecánica** power shovel
palabra [pa'laβra] *nf* (*gen, promesa*) word; (*facultad*) (power of) speech; (*derecho de hablar*) right to speak; **faltar a su ~** to go back on one's word; **quedarse con la ~ en la boca** to stop short; (*en reunión, comité etc*): **tomar la ~** to speak, take the floor; **pedir la ~** to ask to be allowed to speak; **tener la ~** to have the floor; **no encuentro ~s para expresarme** words fail me
palabrería [palaβre'ria] *nf* hot air
palabrota [pala'βrota] *nf* swearword
palacio [pa'laθjo] *nm* palace; (*mansión*) mansion, large house; **~ de justicia** courthouse; **~ municipal** town/city hall
paladar [pala'ðar] *nm* palate
paladear [palaðe'ar] *vt* to taste
palanca [pa'lanka] *nf* lever; (*fig*) pull, influence; **~ de cambio** (*Auto*) gear lever, gearshift (*US*); **~ de freno** (*Auto*) brake lever; **~ de gobierno** *o* **de control** (*Inform*) joystick
palangana [palan'gana] *nf* washbasin
palco ['palko] *nm* box
Palestina [pales'tina] *nf* Palestine
palestino, -a [pales'tino, a] *adj, nm/f* Palestinian
palestra [pa'lestra] *nf*: **salir** *o* **saltar a la ~** to come into the spotlight
paleto, -a [pa'leto, a] *nm/f* yokel, hick (*US*) ▷ *nf* (*pala*) small shovel; (*Arte*) palette; (*Anat*) shoulder blade; (*Deporte: de ping-pong*) bat; (*Am: helado*) ice lolly (*Brit*), Popsicle® (*US*)
paliar [pa'ljar] *vt* (*mitigar*) to mitigate; (*disfrazar*) to conceal
paliativo [palja'tiβo] *nm* palliative
palidecer [paliðe'θer] *vi* to turn pale
palidez [pali'ðeθ] *nf* paleness
pálido, -a ['paliðo, a] *adj* pale
palillo [pa'liʎo] *nm* small stick; (*para dientes*) toothpick; **~s (chinos)** chopsticks; **estar hecho un ~** to be as thin as a rake
palio ['paljo] *nm* canopy
paliza [pa'liθa] *nf* beating, thrashing; **dar** *o* **propinar** (*fam*) **una ~ a algn** to give sb a thrashing
palma ['palma] *nf* (*Anat*) palm; (*árbol*) palm tree; **batir** *o* **dar ~s** to clap, applaud; **llevarse la ~** to triumph, win
palmada [pal'maða] *nf* slap; **palmadas** *nfpl* clapping *sg*, applause *sg*
palmar [pal'mar] *vi* (*tb*: **~la**) to die, kick the bucket
palmarés [palma'res] *nm* (*lista*) list of winners; (*historial*) track record
palmear [palme'ar] *vi* to clap
palmera [pal'mera] *nf* (*Bot*) palm tree
palmo ['palmo] *nm* (*medida*) span; (*fig*) small amount; **~ a ~** inch by inch
palmotear [palmote'ar] *vi* to clap, applaud
palmoteo [palmo'teo] *nm* clapping, applause
palo ['palo] *nm* stick; (*poste*) post, pole; (*mango*) handle, shaft; (*golpe*) blow, hit; (*de golf*) club; (*de béisbol*) bat; (*Naut*) mast; (*Naipes*) suit; **vermut a ~ seco** straight vermouth; **de tal ~ tal astilla** like father like son
paloma [pa'loma] *nf* dove, pigeon; **~ mensajera** carrier *o* homing pigeon
palomilla [palo'miʎa] *nf* moth; (*Tec: tuerca*) wing nut; (*soporte*) bracket
palomitas [palo'mitas] *nfpl* popcorn *sg*
palpar [pal'par] *vt* to touch, feel
palpitación [palpita'θjon] *nf* palpitation
palpitante [palpi'tante] *adj* palpitating; (*fig*) burning
palpitar [palpi'tar] *vi* to palpitate; (*latir*) to beat
palta ['palta] *nf* (*Am*) avocado
palúdico, -a [pa'luðiko, a] *adj* marshy
paludismo [palu'ðismo] *nm* malaria
pamela [pa'mela] *nf* sun hat
pampa ['pampa] *nf* (*Am*) pampa(s), prairie
pan [pan] *nm* bread; (*una barra*) loaf; **~ de molde** sliced loaf; **~ integral** wholemeal bread; **~ rallado** breadcrumbs *pl*; **~ tostado** (*Am: tostada*) toast; **eso es ~ comido** it's a cinch; **llamar al ~ ~ y al vino vino** to call a spade a spade
pana ['pana] *nf* corduroy
panadería [panaðe'ria] *nf* baker's (shop)
panadero, -a [pana'ðero, a] *nm/f* baker
Panamá [pana'ma] *nm* Panama
panameño, -a [pana'meɲo, a] *adj* Panamanian
pancarta [pan'karta] *nf* placard, banner
panceta [pan'θeta] *nf* bacon
pancho, -a ['pantʃo, a] *adj*: **estar tan ~** to remain perfectly calm ▷ *nm* (*Am*) hot dog
pancito [pan'sito] *nm* (*Am*) (bread) roll
páncreas ['pankreas] *nm* pancreas
panda ['panda] *nm* panda ▷ *nf* gang
pandereta [pande'reta] *nf* tambourine
pandilla [pan'diʎa] *nf* set, group; (*de criminales*) gang; (*pey*) clique
panecillo [pane'θiʎo] *nm* (bread) roll
panel [pa'nel] *nm* panel; **~ acústico** acoustic screen; **~ solar** solar panel
panfleto [pan'fleto] *nm* (*Pol etc*) pamphlet; lampoon
pánico ['paniko] *nm* panic
panificadora [panifika'ðora] *nf* bakery
panorama [pano'rama] *nm* panorama; (*vista*) view
panqué [pan'ke], **panqueque** [pan'keke] *nm* (*Am*) pancake
pantalla [pan'taʎa] *nf* (*de cine*) screen; (*cubreluz*) lampshade; (*Inform*) screen, display; **servir de ~ a** to be a blind for; **~ de ayuda** help screen; **~ de cristal líquido** liquid crystal display; **~ de plasma** plasma screen; **~ plana** flatscreen; **~ táctil** touch screen

pantalón, pantalones [panta'lon(es)] *nm(pl)* trousers *pl*, pants *pl* (*US*); **pantalones cortos** shorts *pl*; **pantalones vaqueros** jeans *pl*
pantano [pan'tano] *nm* (*ciénaga*) marsh, swamp; (*depósito: de agua*) reservoir; (*fig*) jam, fix, difficulty
panteón [pante'on] *nm* (*monumento*) pantheon
pantera [pan'tera] *nf* panther
pantimedias [panti'meðjas] *nfpl* (*Am*) = **pantis**
pantis ['pantis] *nmpl* tights (*Brit*), pantyhose (*US*)
pantomima [panto'mima] *nf* pantomime
pantorrilla [panto'rriʎa] *nf* calf (of the leg)
pants [pants] *nmpl* (*Am*) tracksuit (*Brit*), sweat suit (*US*)
pantufla [pan'tufla] *nf* slipper
panty(s) ['panti(s)] *nm(pl)* tights (*Brit*), pantyhose (*US*)
panza ['panθa] *nf* belly, paunch
panzón, -ona [pan'θon, ona], **panzudo, -a** [pan'θuðo, a] *adj* fat, potbellied
pañal [pa'ɲal] *nm* nappy, diaper (*US*); (*fig*) early stages, infancy *sg*; **estar todavía en ~es** to be still wet behind the ears
pañería [paɲe'ria] *nf* (*artículos*) drapery; (*tienda*) draper's (shop), dry-goods store (*US*)
paño ['paɲo] *nm* (*tela*) cloth; (*pedazo de tela*) (piece of) cloth; (*trapo*) duster, rag; **~ de cocina** dishcloth; **~ higiénico** sanitary towel; **~s menores** underclothes; **~s calientes** (*fig*) half-measures; **no andarse con ~s calientes** to pull no punches
pañuelo [pa'ɲwelo] *nm* handkerchief, hanky (*fam*); (*para la cabeza*) (head)scarf
papa ['papa] *nf* (*Am: patata*) potato; **~s fritas** (*Am*) French fries, chips (*Brit*); (*de bolsa*) crisps (*Brit*), potato chips (*US*), potato ▷ *nm*: **el P~** the Pope
papá [pa'pa] *nm* (*pl* **papás**) (*fam*) dad, daddy, pop (*US*); **papás** *nmpl* parents; **hijo de ~** Hooray Henry (*fam*)
papada [pa'paða] *nf* double chin
papagayo [papa'ɣajo] *nm* parrot
papalote [papa'lote] *nm* (*Am*) kite
papanatas [papa'natas] *nm inv* (*fam*) sucker, simpleton
paparrucha [papa'rrutʃa] *nf* (*tontería*) piece of nonsense
papaya [pa'paja] *nf* papaya
papear [pape'ar] *vt, vi* (*fam*) to eat
papel [pa'pel] *nm* (*gen*) paper; (*hoja de papel*) sheet of paper; (*Teat*) part, role; **papeles** *nmpl* identification papers; **~ de calco/carbón/de cartas** tracing paper/carbon paper/stationery; **~ continuo** (*Inform*) continuous stationery; **~ de arroz/envolver/fumar** rice/wrapping/cigarette paper; **~ de aluminio/higiénico** tinfoil/toilet paper; **~ del** *o* **de pagos al Estado** government bonds *pl*; **~ de lija** sandpaper; **~ moneda** paper money; **~ plegado (en abanico** *o* **en acordeón)** fanfold paper; **~ pintado** wallpaper; **~ secante** blotting paper; **~ térmico** thermal paper
papeleo [pape'leo] *nm* red tape
papelera [pape'lera] *nf* (*cesto*) wastepaper basket; (*escritorio*) desk; **~ de reciclaje** (*Inform*) wastebasket
papelería [papele'ria] *nf* (*tienda*) stationer's (shop)
papeleta [pape'leta] *nf* (*pedazo de papel*) slip *o* bit of paper; (*Pol*) ballot paper; (*Escol*) report; **¡vaya ~!** this is a tough one!
paperas [pa'peras] *nfpl* mumps *sg*
papilla [pa'piʎa] *nf* (*de bebé*) baby food; (*pey*) mush; **estar hecho ~** to be dog-tired
paquete [pa'kete] *nm* (*caja*) packet; (*bulto*) parcel; (*Am fam*) nuisance, bore; (*Inform*) package (*of software*); (*de vacaciones*) package tour; **~ de aplicaciones** (*Inform*) applications package; **~ integrado** (*Inform*) integrated package; **~ de gestión integrado** combined management suite; **~s postales** parcel post *sg*
par [par] *adj* (*igual*) like, equal; (*Mat*) even ▷ *nm* equal; (*de guantes*) pair; (*de veces*) couple; (*título*) peer; (*Golf, Com*) par ▷ *nf* par; **~es o nones** odds or evens; **abrir de ~ en ~** to open wide; **a la ~** par; **sobre/bajo la ~** above/below par
para ['para] *prep* for; **no es ~ comer** it's not for eating; **decir ~ sí** to say to o.s.; **¿~ qué lo quieres?** what do you want it for?; **se casaron ~ separarse otra vez** they married only to separate again; **~ entonces** by then *o* that time; **lo tendré ~ mañana** I'll have it for tomorrow; **ir ~ casa** to go home, head for home; **~ profesor es muy estúpido** he's very stupid for a teacher; **¿quién es usted ~ gritar así?** who are you to shout like that?; **tengo bastante ~ vivir** I have enough to live on
parabién [para'βjen] *nm* congratulations *pl*
parábola [pa'raβola] *nf* parable; (*Mat*) parabola
parabólica [para'βolika] *nf* (*tb:* **antena ~**) satellite dish
parabrisas [para'βrisas] *nm inv* windscreen, windshield (*US*)
paracaídas [paraka'iðas] *nm inv* parachute
paracaidista [parakai'ðista] *nm/f* parachutist; (*Mil*) paratrooper
parachoques [para'tʃokes] *nm inv* bumper, fender (*US*); shock absorber
parada [pa'raða] *nf ver* **parado**
paradero [para'ðero] *nm* stopping-place; (*situación*) whereabouts
parado, -a [pa'raðo, a] *adj* (*persona*) motionless, standing still; (*fábrica*) closed, at a standstill; (*coche*) stopped; (*Am: de pie*) standing (up); (*sin empleo*) unemployed, idle;

P

(*confuso*) confused ▷ *nf* (*gen*) stop; (*acto*) stopping; (*de industria*) shutdown, stoppage; (*lugar*) stopping-place; **salir bien ~** to come off well; **parada de autobús** bus stop; **parada discrecional** request stop; **parada en seco** sudden stop; **parada de taxis** taxi rank
paradoja [para'ðoxa] *nf* paradox
parador [para'ðor] *nm* (*Esp*) (luxury) hotel (*owned by the state*)
paráfrasis [pa'rafrasis] *nf inv* paraphrase
paragolpes [para'golpes] *nm inv* (*Am: Auto*) bumper, fender (*US*)
paraguas [pa'raɣwas] *nm inv* umbrella
Paraguay [para'ɣwai] *nm*: **el ~** Paraguay
paraguayo, -a [para'ɣwajo, a] *adj, nm/f* Paraguayan
paraíso [para'iso] *nm* paradise, heaven; **~ fiscal** (*Com*) tax haven
paraje [pa'raxe] *nm* place, spot
paralelo, -a [para'lelo, a] *adj, nm* parallel; **en ~** (*Elec, Inform*) (in) parallel
parálisis [pa'ralisis] *nf inv* paralysis; **~ cerebral** cerebral palsy; **~ progresiva** creeping paralysis
paralítico, -a [para'litiko, a] *adj, nm/f* paralytic
paralizar [parali'θar] *vt* to paralyse; **paralizarse** *vr* to become paralysed; (*fig*) to come to a standstill
paramilitar [paramili'tar] *adj* paramilitary
páramo ['paramo] *nm* bleak plateau
parangón [paran'gon] *nm*: **sin ~** incomparable
paranoia [para'noia] *nf* paranoia
paranoico, -a [para'noiko, a] *adj, nm/f* paranoid
paranormal [paranor'mal] *adj* paranormal
parapente [para'pente] *nm* (*deporte*) paragliding; (*aparato*) paraglider
parapléjico, -a [para'plexiko, a] *adj, nm/f* paraplegic
parar [pa'rar] *vt* to stop; (*progreso etc*) to check, halt; (*golpe*) to ward off ▷ *vi* to stop; (*hospedarse*) to stay, put up; **pararse** *vr* to stop; (*Am*) to stand up; **no ~ de hacer algo** to keep on doing sth; **ha parado de llover** it has stopped raining; **van a ~ en la comisaría** they're going to end up in the police station; **no sabemos en qué va a ~ todo esto** we don't know where all this is going to end; **~se a hacer algo** to stop to do sth; **~se en** to pay attention to
pararrayos [para'rrajos] *nm inv* lightning conductor
parásito, -a [pa'rasito, a] *nm/f* parasite
parasol [para'sol] *nm* parasol, sunshade
parcela [par'θela] *nf* plot, piece of ground, smallholding
parche ['partʃe] *nm* patch
parchís [par'tʃis] *nm* ludo
parcial [par'θjal] *adj* (*pago*) part-; (*eclipse*) partial; (*juez*) prejudiced, biased; (*Pol*) partisan
parcialidad [parθjali'ðað] *nf* (*prejuicio*) prejudice, bias
parco, -a ['parko, a] *adj* (*frugal*) sparing; (*moderado*) moderate
pardillo, -a [par'ðiʎo, a] *adj* (*pey*) provincial ▷ *nm/f* (*pey*) country bumpkin ▷ *nm* (*Zool*) linnet
pardo, -a ['parðo, a] *adj* (*color*) brown; (*cielo*) overcast; (*voz*) flat, dull
parear [pare'ar] *vt* (*juntar, hacer par*) to match, put together; (*calcetines*) to put into pairs; (*Bio*) to mate, pair
parecer [pare'θer] *nm* (*opinión*) opinion, view; (*aspecto*) looks *pl* ▷ *vi* (*tener apariencia*) to seem, look; (*asemejarse*) to look like, seem like; (*aparecer, llegar*) to appear; **parecerse** *vr* to look alike, resemble each other; **según parece** evidently, apparently; **~se a** to look like, resemble; **al ~** apparently; **me parece que** I think (that), it seems to me that
parecido, -a [pare'θiðo, a] *adj* similar ▷ *nm* similarity, likeness, resemblance; **~ a** like, similar to; **bien ~** good-looking, nice-looking
pared [pa'reð] *nf* wall; **~ divisoria/medianera** dividing/party wall; **subirse por las ~es** (*fam*) to go up the wall
parejo, -a [pa'rexo, a] *adj* (*igual*) equal; (*liso*) smooth, even ▷ *nf* (*dos*) pair; (*: de personas*) couple; (*el otro: de un par*) other one (of a pair); (*: persona*) partner; (*de Guardias*) Civil Guard patrol
parentela [paren'tela] *nf* relations *pl*
parentesco [paren'tesko] *nm* relationship
paréntesis [pa'rentesis] *nm inv* parenthesis; (*digresión*) digression; (*en escrito*) bracket
parezco *etc vb ver* **parecer**
parida [pa'riða] *nf*: **~ mental** (*fam*) dumb idea
paridad [pari'ðað] *nf* (*Econ*) parity
pariente, -a [pa'rjente, a] *nm/f* relative, relation
parir [pa'rir] *vt* to give birth to ▷ *vi* (*mujer*) to give birth, have a baby; (*yegua*) to foal; (*vaca*) to calve
París [pa'ris] *nm* Paris
paritario, -a [pari'tarjo, a] *adj* equal
parka ['parka] *nf* (*Am*) anorak
parking ['parkin] *nm* car park, parking lot (*US*)
parlamentar [parlamen'tar] *vi* (*negociar*) to parley
parlamentario, -a [parlamen'tarjo, a] *adj* parliamentary ▷ *nm/f* member of parliament
parlamento [parla'mento] *nm* (*Pol*) parliament; (*Jur*) speech
parlanchín, -ina [parlan'tʃin, ina] *adj* loose-tongued, indiscreet ▷ *nm/f* chatterbox
parlar [par'lar] *vi* to chatter (away)
parlotear [parlote'ar] *vi* to chatter, prattle

paro ['paro] *nm* (*huelga*) stoppage (of work), strike; (*desempleo*) unemployment; **~ cardiaco** cardiac arrest; **estar en ~** (*Esp*) to be unemployed; **subsidio de ~** unemployment benefit; **hay ~ en la industria** work in the industry is at a standstill; **~ del sistema** (*Inform*) system shutdown
parodia [pa'roðja] *nf* parody
parodiar [paro'ðjar] *vt* to parody
parpadear [parpaðe'ar] *vi* (*los ojos*) to blink; (*luz*) to flicker
párpado ['parpaðo] *nm* eyelid
parque ['parke] *nm* (*lugar verde*) park; (*Am: munición*) ammunition; **~ de atracciones/de bomberos/zoológico** fairground/fire station/zoo; **~ infantil/temático/zoológico** playground/theme park/zoo
parqué, parquet [par'ke] *nm* parquet
parquímetro [par'kimetro] *nm* parking meter
parra ['parra] *nf* grapevine
párrafo ['parrafo] *nm* paragraph; **echar un ~** (*fam*) to have a chat
parranda [pa'rranda] *nf* (*fam*) spree, binge
parrilla [pa'rriʎa] *nf* (*Culin*) grill; (*Am Auto*) roof rack; **~ (de salida)** (*Auto*) starting grid; **(carne a la) ~** grilled meat, barbecue
parrillada [parri'ʎaða] *nf* barbecue
párroco ['parroko] *nm* parish priest
parroquia [pa'rrokja] *nf* parish; (*iglesia*) parish church; (*Com*) clientele, customers *pl*
parroquiano, -a [parro'kjano, a] *nm/f* parishioner; client, customer
parte ['parte] *nm* message; (*informe*) report ▷ *nf* part; (*lado, cara*) side; (*de reparto*) share; (*Jur*) party; **en alguna ~ de Europa** somewhere in Europe; **en cualquier ~** anywhere; **por ahí no se va a ninguna ~** that leads nowhere; (*fig*) this is getting us nowhere; **en** *o* **por todas ~s** everywhere; **en gran ~** to a large extent; **la mayor ~ de los españoles** most Spaniards; **de algún tiempo a esta ~** for some time past; **de ~ de algn** on sb's behalf; **¿de ~ de quién?** (*Telec*) who is speaking?; **por ~ de** on the part of; **yo por mi ~** I for my part; **por una ~ ... por otra ~** on the one hand, ... on the other (hand); **dar ~ a algn** to report to sb; **tomar ~** to take part; **~ meteorológico** weather forecast *o* report
partera [par'tera] *nf* midwife
partición [parti'θjon] *nf* division, sharing-out; (*Pol*) partition
participación [partiθipa'θjon] *nf* (*acto*) participation, taking part; (*parte*) share; (*Com*) share, stock (*US*); (*de lotería*) shared prize; (*aviso*) notice, notification; **~ en los beneficios** profit-sharing; **~ minoritaria** minority interest
participante [partiθi'pante] *nm/f* participant
participar [partiθi'par] *vt* to notify, inform ▷ *vi* to take part, participate; **~ en una empresa** (*Com*) to invest in an enterprise; **le participo que ...** I have to tell you that ...
partícipe [par'tiθipe] *nm/f* participant; **hacer ~ a algn de algo** to inform sb of sth
particular [partiku'lar] *adj* (*especial*) particular, special; (*individual, personal*) private, personal ▷ *nm* (*punto, asunto*) particular, point; (*individuo*) individual; **tiene coche ~** he has a car of his own; **no dijo mucho sobre el ~** he didn't say much about the matter
particularizar [partikulari'θar] *vt* to distinguish; (*especificar*) to specify; (*detallar*) to give details about
partida [par'tiða] *nf* (*salida*) departure; (*Com*) entry, item; (*juego*) game; (*grupo, bando*) band, group; **mala ~** dirty trick; **~ de nacimiento/matrimonio/defunción** birth/marriage/death certificate; **echar una ~** to have a game
partidario, -a [parti'ðarjo, a] *adj* partisan ▷ *nm/f* (*Deporte*) supporter; (*Pol*) partisan
partido [par'tiðo] *nm* (*Pol*) party; (*encuentro*) game, match; (*apoyo*) support; (*equipo*) team; **~ amistoso** (*Deporte*) friendly (game); **~ de fútbol** football match; **sacar ~ de** to profit from, benefit from; **tomar ~** to take sides
partir [par'tir] *vt* (*dividir*) to split, divide; (*compartir, distribuir*) to share (out), distribute; (*romper*) to break open, split open; (*rebanada*) to cut (off); (*vi: ponerse en camino*) to set off, set out; (*comenzar*) to start (off *o* out); **partirse** *vr* to crack *o* split *o* break (in two *etc*); **a ~ de** (starting) from; **~se de risa** to split one's sides (laughing)
partitura [parti'tura] *nf* score
parto ['parto] *nm* birth, delivery; (*fig*) product, creation; **estar de ~** to be in labour
parvulario [parβu'larjo] *nm* nursery school, kindergarten
pasa ['pasa] *nf ver* **paso**
pasable [pa'saβle] *adj* passable
pasacintas [pasa'θintas] *nm* (*Am*) cassette player
pasada [pa'saða] *nf ver* **pasado**
pasadizo [pasa'ðiθo] *nm* (*pasillo*) passage, corridor; (*callejuela*) alley
pasado, -a [pa'saðo, a] *adj* past; (*malo: comida, fruta*) bad; (*muy cocido*) overdone; (*anticuado*) out of date ▷ *nm* past; (*Ling*) past (tense) ▷ *nf* passing, passage; (*acción de pulir*) rub, polish; **~ mañana** the day after tomorrow; **el mes ~** last month; **~s dos días** after two days; **lo ~, ~** let bygones be bygones; **~ de moda** old-fashioned; **~ por agua** (*huevo*) boiled; **estar ~ de vueltas** *o* **de rosca** (*grifo, tuerca*) to be worn; **de pasada** in passing, incidentally; **una mala pasada** a dirty trick

P

pasador [pasa'ðor] *nm* (*gen*) bolt; (*de pelo*) slide; (*horquilla*) grip; **pasadores** *nmpl* (*Am: cordones*) shoelaces
pasaje [pa'saxe] *nm* (*gen*) passage; (*pago de viaje*) fare; (*los pasajeros*) passengers *pl*; (*pasillo*) passageway
pasajero, -a [pasa'xero, a] *adj* passing; (*situación, estado*) temporary; (*amor, enfermedad*) brief; (*ave*) migratory ▷ *nm/f* passenger; (*viajero*) traveller
pasamanos [pasa'manos] *nm inv* rail, handrail; (*de escalera*) banister
pasamontañas [pasamon'taɲas] *nm inv* balaclava (helmet)
pasaporte [pasa'porte] *nm* passport
pasar [pa'sar] *vt* (*gen*) to pass; (*tiempo*) to spend; (*durezas*) to suffer, endure; (*noticia*) to give, pass on; (*película*) to show; (*persona*) to take, conduct; (*río*) to cross; (*barrera*) to pass through; (*falta*) to overlook, tolerate; (*contrincante*) to surpass, do better than; (*coche*) to overtake; (*contrabando*) to smuggle (in/out); (*enfermedad*) to give, infect with ▷ *vi* (*gen*) to pass, go; (*terminarse*) to be over; (*ocurrir*) to happen; **pasarse** *vr* (*efectos*) to pass, be over; (*flores*) to fade; (*comida*) to go bad, go off; (*fig*) to overdo it, go too far *o* over the top; **~ la aspiradora** to do the vacuuming *or* hoovering, to hoover; **~ de** to go beyond, exceed; **¡pase!** come in!; **nos hicieron ~** they showed us in; **~ por** to fetch; **~ por alto** to skip; **~ por una crisis** to go through a crisis; **se hace ~ por médico** he passes himself off as a doctor; **~lo bien/ bomba** *o* **de maravilla** to have a good/great time; **¡que lo pases bien!** have a good time!; **~se al enemigo** to go over to the enemy; **~se de la raya** to go too far; **¡no te pases!** don't try me!; **se me pasó** I forgot; **se me pasó el turno** I missed my turn; **no se le pasa nada** nothing escapes him, he misses nothing; **ya se te ~á** you'll get over it; **¿qué pasa?** what's happening?, what's going on?, what's up?; **¿qué te pasa?** what's wrong?; **¡cómo pasa el tiempo!** time just flies!; **pase lo que pase** come what may; **el autobús pasa por nuestra casa** the bus goes past our house
pasarela [pasa'rela] *nf* footbridge; (*en barco*) gangway
pasatiempo [pasa'tjempo] *nm* pastime, hobby; (*distracción*) amusement
Pascua, pascua ['paskwa] *nf*: **~ (de Resurrección)** Easter; **~ de Navidad** Christmas; **Pascuas** *nfpl* Christmas time *sg*; **¡felices ~s!** Merry Christmas!; **de ~s a Ramos** once in a blue moon; **hacer la ~ a** (*fam*) to annoy, bug
pase ['pase] *nm* pass; (*Cine*) performance, showing; (*Com*) permit; (*Jur*) licence
pasear [pase'ar] *vt* to take for a walk; (*exhibir*) to parade, show off ▷ *vi* to walk, go for a walk; **pasearse** *vr* to walk, go for a walk; **~ en coche** to go for a drive
paseo [pa'seo] *nm* (*distancia corta*) (short) walk, stroll; (*avenida*) avenue; **~ marítimo** promenade; **dar un ~** to go for a walk; **~ en bicicleta** (bike) ride; **~ en barco** boat trip; **mandar a algn a ~** to tell sb to go to blazes; **¡vete a ~!** get lost!
pasillo [pa'siʎo] *nm* passage, corridor
pasión [pa'sjon] *nf* passion
pasional [pasjo'nal] *adj* passionate; **crimen ~** crime of passion
pasivo, -a [pa'siβo, a] *adj* passive; (*inactivo*) inactive ▷ *nm* (*Com*) liabilities *pl*, debts *pl*; (*de cuenta*) debit side; **~ circulante** current liabilities
pasma ['pasma] *nm* (*fam*) cop
pasmar [pas'mar] *vt* (*asombrar*) to amaze, astonish; **pasmarse** *vr* to be amazed *o* astonished
pasmo ['pasmo] *nm* amazement, astonishment; (*fig*) wonder, marvel
pasmoso, -a [pas'moso, a] *adj* amazing, astonishing
paso, -a ['paso, a] *adj* dried ▷ *nm* (*gen, de baile*) step; (*modo de andar*) walk; (*huella*) footprint; (*rapidez*) speed, pace, rate; (*camino accesible*) way through, passage; (*cruce*) crossing; (*pasaje*) passing, passage; (*Rel*) *religious float or sculpture*; (*Geo*) pass; (*estrecho*) strait; (*fig*) step, measure; (*apuro*) difficulty ▷ *nf* raisin; **pasa de Corinto /de Esmirna** currant/sultana; **~ a ~** step by step; **a ese ~** (*fig*) at that rate; **salir al ~ de** *o* **a** to waylay; **salir del ~** to get out of trouble; **dar un ~ en falso** to trip; (*fig*) to take a false step; **estar de ~** to be passing through; **~ atrás** step backwards; (*fig*) backward step; **~ elevado/subterráneo** flyover/subway, underpass (*US*); **prohibido el ~** no entry; **ceda el ~** give way; **~ a nivel** (*Ferro*) level-crossing; **~ (de) cebra** (*Esp*) zebra crossing; **~ de peatones** pedestrian crossing; **~ elevado** flyover
pasota [pa'sota] *adj, nm/f* (*fam*) ≈ dropout; **ser un (tipo) ~** to be a bit of a dropout; (*ser indiferente*) not to care about anything
pasta ['pasta] *nf* (*gen*) paste; (*Culin: masa*) dough; (*: de bizcochos etc*) pastry; (*fam*) money, dough; (*encuadernación*) hardback; **pastas** *nfpl* (*bizcochos*) pastries, small cakes; (*espaguetis etc*) pasta *sg*; **~ de dientes** *o* **dentífrica** toothpaste; **~ de madera** wood pulp
pastar [pas'tar] *vt, vi* to graze
pastel [pas'tel] *nm* (*dulce*) cake; (*Arte*) pastel; (*fig*) plot; **pasteles** *nmpl* pastry *sg*, confectionery *sg*; **~ de carne** meat pie
pastelería [pastele'ria] *nf* cake shop, pastry shop
pasteurizado, -a [pasteuri'θaðo, a] *adj* pasteurized
pastilla [pas'tiʎa] *nf* (*de jabón, chocolate*) cake, bar; (*píldora*) tablet, pill

pasto ['pasto] *nm* (*hierba*) grass; (*lugar*) pasture, field; (*fig*) food, nourishment
pastor, a [pas'tor, a] *nm/f* shepherd(ess) ▷ *nm* clergyman, pastor; (*Zool*) sheepdog; **~ alemán** Alsatian
pata ['pata] *nf* (*pierna*) leg; (*pie*) foot; (*de muebles*) leg; **~s arriba** upside down; **a cuatro ~s** on all fours; **meter la ~** to put one's foot in it; **~ de cabra** (*Tec*) crowbar; **~s de gallo** crow's feet; **metedura de ~** (*fam*) gaffe; **tener buena/mala ~** to be lucky/unlucky
patada [pa'taða] *nf* stamp; (*puntapié*) kick; **a ~s** in abundance; (*trato*) roughly; **echar a algn a ~s** to kick sb out
patalear [patale'ar] *vi* to stamp one's feet
patata [pa'tata] *nf* potato; **~s fritas** *o* **a la española** chips, French fries; (*de bolsa*) crisps; **ni ~** (*fam*) nothing at all; **no entendió ni ~** he didn't understand a single word
paté [pa'te] *nm* pâté
patear [pate'ar] *vt* (*pisar*) to stamp on, trample (on); (*pegar con el pie*) to kick ▷ *vi* to stamp (with rage), stamp one's foot
patentar [paten'tar] *vt* to patent
patente [pa'tente] *adj* obvious, evident; (*Com*) patent ▷ *nf* patent
patera [pa'tera] *nf* boat
paternal [pater'nal] *adj* fatherly, paternal
paterno, -a [pa'terno, a] *adj* paternal
patético, -a [pa'tetiko, a] *adj* pathetic, moving
patilla [pa'tiʎa] *nf* (*de gafas*) sidepiece; **patillas** *nfpl* sideburns
patín [pa'tin] *nm* skate; (*de tobogán*) runner; **~ de hielo** ice skate; **~ de ruedas** roller skate
patinaje [pati'naxe] *nm* skating
patinar [pati'nar] *vi* to skate; (*resbalarse*) to skid, slip; (*fam*) to slip up, blunder
patines de ruedas *nmpl* rollerskates
patineta [pati'neta] *nf* (*Am: patinete*) scooter; (*monopatín*) skateboard
patinete [pati'nete] *nm* scooter
patio ['patjo] *nm* (*de casa*) patio, courtyard; **~ de recreo** playground
pato ['pato] *nm* duck; **pagar el ~** (*fam*) to take the blame, carry the can
patológico, -a [pato'loxiko, a] *adj* pathological
patoso, -a [pa'toso, a] *adj* awkward, clumsy
patotero [pato'tero] *nm* (*Am*) hooligan, lout
patraña [pa'traɲa] *nf* story, fib
patria ['patrja] *nf* native land, mother country; **~ chica** home town
patrimonio [patri'monjo] *nm* inheritance; (*fig*) heritage; (*Com*) net worth
patriota [pa'trjota] *nm/f* patriot
patriótico, -a [pa'trjotiko, a] *adj* patriotic
patriotismo [patrjo'tismo] *nm* patriotism
patrocinador, a [patroθina'ðor, a] *nm/f* sponsor
patrocinar [patroθi'nar] *vt* to sponsor; (*apoyar*) to back, support
patrocinio [patro'θinjo] *nm* sponsorship; backing, support
patrón, -ona [pa'tron, ona] *nm/f* (*jefe*) boss, chief, master/mistress; (*propietario*) landlord(-lady); (*Rel*) patron saint ▷ *nm* (*Costura*) pattern; (*Tec*) standard; **~ oro** gold standard
patronal [patro'nal] *adj*: **la clase ~** management; **cierre ~** lockout
patronato [patro'nato] *nm* sponsorship; (*acto*) patronage; (*Com*) employers' association; (*fundación*) trust; **el ~ de turismo** the tourist board
patrulla [pa'truʎa] *nf* patrol
pausa ['pausa] *nf* pause; (*intervalo*) break; (*interrupción*) interruption; (*Tec: en videograbadora*) hold; **con ~** slowly
pausado, -a [pau'saðo, a] *adj* slow, deliberate
pauta ['pauta] *nf* line, guide line
pava ['paβa] *nf* (*Am*) kettle
pavimento [paβi'mento] *nm* (*Arq*) flooring; (*de losa*) pavement, paving
pavo ['paβo] *nm* turkey; (*necio*) silly thing, idiot; **~ real** peacock; **¡no seas ~!** don't be silly!
pavor [pa'βor] *nm* dread, terror
payaso, -a [pa'ʝaso, a] *nm/f* clown
payo, -a ['pajo, a] *adj, nm/f* non-gipsy
paz [paθ] *nf* peace; (*tranquilidad*) peacefulness, tranquillity; **dejar a algn en ~** to leave sb alone *o* in peace; **hacer las paces** to make peace; (*fig*) to make up; **¡déjame en ~!** leave me alone!, **¡haya ~!** stop it!
PC *nm abr* (*Pol: = Partido Comunista*) CP ▷ *nm* PC, personal computer
P.D. *abr* (*= posdata*) P.S.
peaje [pe'axe] *nm* toll; **autopista de ~** toll motorway, turnpike (*US*)
peatón [pea'ton] *nm* pedestrian; **paso de peatones** pedestrian crossing, crosswalk (*US*)
peatonal [peato'nal] *adj* pedestrian
peca ['peka] *nf* freckle
pecado [pe'kaðo] *nm* sin
pecador, a [peka'ðor, a] *adj* sinful ▷ *nm/f* sinner
pecaminoso, -a [pekami'noso, a] *adj* sinful
pecar [pe'kar] *vi* (*Rel*) to sin; (*fig*): **~ de generoso** to be too generous
pecera [pe'θera] *nf* fish tank; (*redonda*) goldfish bowl
pecho ['petʃo] *nm* (*Anat*) chest; (*de mujer*) breast(s *pl*), bosom; (*corazón*) heart, breast; (*valor*) courage, spirit; **dar el ~ a** to breast-feed; **tomar algo a ~** to take sth to heart; **no le cabía en el ~** he was bursting with happiness
pechuga [pe'tʃuɣa] *nf* breast
pecoso, -a [pe'koso, a] *adj* freckled

P

peculiar [peku'ljar] *adj* special, peculiar; (*característico*) typical, characteristic
peculiaridad [pekuljari'ðað] *nf* peculiarity; special feature, characteristic
pedagogía [peðaɣo'ɣia] *nf* education
pedal [pe'ðal] *nm* pedal; **~ de embrague** clutch (pedal); **~ de freno** footbrake
pedalear [peðale'ar] *vi* to pedal
pédalo ['peðalo] *nm* pedalo, pedal boat
pedante [pe'ðante] *adj* pedantic ▷ *nm/f* pedant
pedantería [peðante'ria] *nf* pedantry
pedazo [pe'ðaθo] *nm* piece, bit; **hacerse ~s** to fall to pieces; (*romperse*) to smash, shatter; **un ~ de pan** a scrap of bread; (*fig*) a terribly nice person
pedernal [peðer'nal] *nm* flint
pedestal [peðes'tal] *nm* base; **tener/poner a algn en un ~** to put sb on a pedestal
pediatra [pe'ðjatra] *nm/f* paediatrician (*Brit*), pediatrician (*US*)
pedicuro, -a [peði'kuro, a] *nm/f* chiropodist (*Brit*), podiatrist (*US*)
pedido [pe'ðiðo] *nm* (*Com: mandado*) order; (*petición*) request; **~s en cartera** (*Com*) backlog *sg*
pedigrí [peði'ɣri] *nm* pedigree
pedir [pe'ðir] *vt* to ask for, request; (*comida, Com: mandar*) to order; (*exigir: precio*) to ask; (*necesitar*) to need, demand, require ▷ *vi* to ask; **~ prestado** to borrow; **~ disculpas** to apologize; **me pidió que cerrara la puerta** he asked me to shut the door; **¿cuánto piden por el coche?** how much are they asking for the car?
pedo ['peðo] (*fam*) *adj inv*: **estar ~** to be pissed (*!*) ▷ *nm* fart (*!*)
pedrada [pe'ðraða] *nf* throw of a stone; (*golpe*) blow from a stone; **herir a algn de una ~** to hit sb with a stone
pega ['peɣa] *nf* (*dificultad*) snag; **de ~** false, dud; **poner ~s** to raise objections
pegadizo, -a [peɣa'ðiθo, a] *adj* (*canción etc*) catchy
pegajoso, -a [peɣa'xoso, a] *adj* sticky, adhesive
pegamento [peɣa'mento] *nm* gum, glue
pegar [pe'ɣar] *vt* (*papel, sellos*) to stick (on); (*con cola*) to glue; (*cartel*) to post, stick up; (*coser*) to sew (on); (*unir: partes*) to join, fix together; (*Inform*) to paste; (*Med*) to give, infect with; (*dar: golpe*) to give, deal ▷ *vi* (*adherirse*) to stick, adhere; (*Inform*) to paste; (*ir juntos: colores*) to match, go together; (*golpear*) to hit; (*quemar: el sol*) to strike hot, burn; **pegarse** *vr* (*gen*) to stick; (*dos personas*) to hit each other, fight; **~le a algo** to be a great one for sth; **~ un grito** to let out a yell; **~ un salto** to jump (with fright); **~ fuego** to catch fire; **~ en** to touch; **~se un tiro** to shoot o.s.; **no pega** that doesn't seem right; **ese sombrero no pega con el abrigo** that hat doesn't go with the coat
pegatina [peɣa'tina] *nf* (*Pol etc*) sticker
pego ['peɣo] *nm*: **dar el ~** (*pasar por verdadero*) to look like the real thing
pegote [pe'ɣote] *nm* (*fam*) eyesore, sight; (*fig*) patch, ugly mend; **tirarse ~s** (*fam*) to come on strong
peinado [pei'naðo] *nm* (*en peluquería*) hairdo; (*estilo*) hair style
peinar [pei'nar] *vt* to comb sb's hair; (*con un cierto estilo*) to style; **peinarse** *vr* to comb one's hair
peine ['peine] *nm* comb
peineta [pei'neta] *nf* ornamental comb
p.ej. *abr* (= *por ejemplo*) e.g.
Pekín [pe'kin] *n* Peking
pelado, -a [pe'laðo, a] *adj* (*cabeza*) shorn; (*fruta*) peeled; (*campo, tb fig*) bare; (*fam: sin dinero*) broke
pelaje [pe'laxe] *nm* (*Zool*) fur, coat; (*fig*) appearance
pelambre [pe'lambre] *nm* long hair, mop
pelar [pe'lar] *vt* (*fruta, patatas*) to peel; (*cortar el pelo a*) to cut the hair of; (*quitar la piel: animal*) to skin; (*ave*) to pluck; (*habas etc*) to shell; **pelarse** *vr* (*la piel*) to peel off; **voy a ~me** I'm going to get my hair cut; **corre que se las pela** (*fam*) he runs like nobody's business
peldaño [pel'daɲo] *nm* step; (*de escalera portátil*) rung
pelea [pe'lea] *nf* (*lucha*) fight; (*discusión*) quarrel, row
peleado, -a [pele'aðo, a] *adj*: **estar ~ (con algn)** to have fallen out (with sb)
pelear [pele'ar] *vi* to fight; **pelearse** *vr* to fight; (*reñir*) to fall out, quarrel
pelela [pe'lela] *nf* (*Am*) potty
peletería [pelete'ria] *nf* furrier's, fur shop
peliagudo, -a [pelja'ɣuðo, a] *adj* tricky
pelícano [pe'likano] *nm* pelican
película [pe'likula] *nf* (*Cine*) film, movie (*US*); (*cobertura ligera*) film, thin covering; (*Foto: rollo*) roll *o* reel of film; **~ de dibujos (animados)** cartoon film; **~ muda** silent film; **de ~** (*fam*) astonishing, out of this world
peligrar [peli'ɣrar] *vi* to be in danger
peligro [pe'liɣro] *nm* danger; (*riesgo*) risk; **"~ de muerte"** "danger"; **correr ~ de** to be in danger of, run the risk of; **con ~ de la vida** at the risk of one's life
peligroso, -a [peli'ɣroso, a] *adj* dangerous; risky
pelirrojo, -a [peli'rroxo, a] *adj* red-haired, red-headed ▷ *nm/f* redhead
pellejo [pe'ʎexo] *nm* (*de animal*) skin, hide; **salvar el ~** to save one's skin
pellizcar [peʎiθ'kar] *vt* to pinch, nip
pellizco [pe'ʎiθko] *nm* pinch
pelma ['pelma] *nm/f*, **pelmazo** [pel'maθo] *nm* (*fam*) pain (in the neck)

pelo ['pelo] *nm* (*cabellos*) hair; (*de barba, bigote*) whisker; (*de animal: piel*) fur, coat; (*de perro etc*) hair, coat; (*de ave*) down; (*de tejido*) nap; (*Tec*) fibre; **a ~** bareheaded; (*desnudo*) naked; **al ~** just right; **venir al ~** to be exactly what one needs; **un hombre de ~ en pecho** a brave man; **por los ~s** by the skin of one's teeth; **escaparse por un ~** to have a close shave; **se me pusieron los ~s de punta** my hair stood on end; **no tener ~s en la lengua** to be outspoken, not mince words; **con ~s y señales** in minute detail; **tomar el ~ a algn** to pull sb's leg
pelón, -ona [pe'lon, ona] *adj* hairless, bald
pelota [pe'lota] *nf* ball; (*fam: cabeza*) nut (*fam*); **en ~(s)** stark naked; **~ vasca** pelota; **devolver la ~ a algn** (*fig*) to turn the tables on sb; **hacer la ~ (a algn)** to creep (to sb)
pelotera [pelo'tera] *nf* (*fam*) barney
pelotón [pelo'ton] *nm* (*Mil*) squad, detachment
peluca [pe'luka] *nf* wig
peluche [pe'lutʃe] *nm*: **muñeco de ~** soft toy
peludo, -a [pe'luðo, a] *adj* hairy, shaggy
peluquería [peluke'ria] *nf* hairdresser's; (*para hombres*) barber's (shop)
peluquero, -a [pelu'kero, a] *nm/f* hairdresser; barber
pelusa [pe'lusa] *nf* (*Bot*) down; (*Costura*) fluff
pelvis ['pelβis] *nf* pelvis
pena ['pena] *nf* (*congoja*) grief, sadness; (*remordimiento*) regret; (*dificultad*) trouble; (*dolor*) pain; (*Am: vergüenza*) shame; (*Jur*) sentence; (*Deporte*) penalty; **~ capital** capital punishment; **~ de muerte** death penalty; **~ pecuniaria** fine; **merecer** *o* **valer la ~** to be worthwhile; **a duras ~s** with great difficulty; **so ~ de** on pain of; **me dan ~** I feel sorry for them; **¿no te da ~ hacerlo?** (*Am*) aren't you embarrassed doing that?; **¡qué ~!** what a shame *o* pity!
penal [pe'nal] *adj* penal ▷ *nm* (*cárcel*) prison
penalidad [penali'ðað] *nf* (*problema, dificultad*) trouble, hardship; (*Jur*) penalty, punishment; **penalidades** *nfpl* trouble *sg*, hardship *sg*
penalizar [penali'θar] *vt* to penalize
penalti, penalty [pe'nalti] *nm* (*Deporte*) penalty
penalty [pe'nalti] (*pl* **penaltys** *o* **penalties**) *nm* penalty (kick)
penar [pe'nar] *vt* to penalize; (*castigar*) to punish ▷ *vi* to suffer
pendiente [pen'djente] *adj* pending, unsettled ▷ *nm* earring ▷ *nf* hill, slope; **tener una asignatura ~** to have to resit a subject
péndulo ['pendulo] *nm* pendulum
pene ['pene] *nm* penis
penetración [penetra'θjon] *nf* (*acto*) penetration; (*agudeza*) sharpness, insight
penetrante [pene'trante] *adj* (*herida*) deep; (*persona, arma*) sharp; (*sonido*) penetrating, piercing; (*mirada*) searching; (*viento, ironía*) biting
penetrar [pene'trar] *vt* to penetrate, pierce; (*entender*) to grasp ▷ *vi* to penetrate, go in; (*entrar*) to enter; (*líquido*) to soak in; (*emoción*) to pierce
penicilina [peniθi'lina] *nf* penicillin
península [pe'ninsula] *nf* peninsula; **P~ Ibérica** Iberian Peninsula
peninsular [peninsu'lar] *adj* peninsular
penique [pe'nike] *nm* penny; **peniques** *nmpl* pence
penitencia [peni'tenθja] *nf* (*remordimiento*) penitence; (*castigo*) penance; **en ~** as a penance
penitenciaría [penitenθja'ria] *nf* prison, penitentiary
penitenciario, -a [peniten'θjarjo, a] *adj* prison *cpd*
penoso, -a [pe'noso, a] *adj* laborious, difficult; (*lamentable*) distressing
pensador, a [pensa'ðor, a] *nm/f* thinker
pensamiento [pensa'mjento] *nm* (*gen*) thought; (*mente*) mind; (*idea*) idea; (*Bot*) pansy; **no se le pasó por el ~** it never occurred to him
pensar [pen'sar] *vt* to think; (*considerar*) to think over, think out; (*proponerse*) to intend, plan, propose; (*imaginarse*) to think up, invent ▷ *vi* to think; **~ en** to think of *o* about; (*anhelar*) to aim at, aspire to; **dar que ~ a algn** to give sb food for thought
pensativo, -a [pensa'tiβo, a] *adj* thoughtful, pensive
pensión [pen'sjon] *nf* (*casa*) ≈ guest house; (*dinero*) pension; (*cama y comida*) board and lodging; **~ de jubilación** retirement pension; **~ escalada** graduated pension; **~ completa** full board; **media ~** half board
pensionista [pensjo'nista] *nm/f* (*jubilado*) (old-age) pensioner; (*el que vive en una pensión*) lodger; (*Escol*) boarder
penúltimo, -a [pe'nultimo, a] *adj* penultimate, second last
penumbra [pe'numbra] *nf* half-light, semi-darkness
penuria [pe'nurja] *nf* shortage, want
peña ['peɲa] *nf* (*roca*) rock; (*acantilado*) cliff, crag; (*grupo*) group, circle; (*Am: club*) folk club; (*Deporte*) supporters' club
peñasco [pe'ɲasko] *nm* large rock, boulder
peñón [pe'ɲon] *nm* crag; **el P~** the Rock (of Gibraltar)
peón [pe'on] *nm* labourer; (*Am*) farm labourer, farmhand; (*Tec*) spindle, shaft; (*Ajedrez*) pawn
peonza [pe'onθa] *nf* spinning top
peor [pe'or] *adj* (*comparativo*) worse; (*superlativo*) worst ▷ *adv* worse; worst; **de mal en ~** from bad to worse; **tanto ~** so much the worse; **A es ~ que B** A is worse than B; **Z es el ~ de todos** Z is the worst of all

P

pepinillo [pepi'niʎo] *nm* gherkin
pepino [pe'pino] *nm* cucumber; **(no) me importa un ~** I don't care one bit
pepita [pe'pita] *nf* (*Bot*) pip; (*Minería*) nugget
pepito [pe'pito] *nm* (*Esp*: *tb*: **~ de ternera**) steak sandwich
pequeñez [peke'ɲeθ] *nf* smallness, littleness; (*trivialidad*) trifle, triviality
pequeño, -a [pe'keɲo, a] *adj* small, little; (*cifra*) small, low; (*bajo*) short; **~ burgués** lower middle-class
pera ['pera] *adj inv* classy; **niño ~** spoiled upper-class brat ▷ *nf* pear; **eso es pedir ~s al olmo** that's asking the impossible
peral [pe'ral] *nm* pear tree
percance [per'kanθe] *nm* setback, misfortune
per cápita [per'kapita] *adj*: **renta ~** per capita income
percatarse [perka'tarse] *vr*: **~ de** to notice, take note of
percebe [per'θeβe] *nm* (*Zool*) barnacle; (*fam*) idiot
percepción [perθep'θjon] *nf* (*vista*) perception; (*idea*) notion, idea; (*Com*) collection
perceptible [perθep'tiβle] *adj* perceptible, noticeable; (*Com*) payable, receivable
percha ['pertʃa] *nf* (*poste*) pole, support; (*gancho*) peg; (*de abrigos*) coat stand; (*colgador*) coat hanger; (*ganchos*) coat hooks *pl*; (*de ave*) perch
percibir [perθi'βir] *vt* to perceive, notice; (*ver*) to see; (*peligro etc*) to sense; (*Com*) to earn, receive, get
percusión [perku'sjon] *nf* percussion
perdedor, a [perðe'ðor, a] *adj* losing ▷ *nm/f* loser
perder [per'ðer] *vt* to lose; (*tiempo, palabras*) to waste; (*oportunidad*) to lose, miss; (*tren*) to miss ▷ *vi* to lose; **perderse** *vr* (*extraviarse*) to get lost; (*desaparecer*) to disappear, be lost to view; (*arruinarse*) to be ruined; **echar a ~** (*comida*) to spoil, ruin; (*oportunidad*) to waste; **tener buen ~** to be a good loser; **¡no te lo pierdas!** don't miss it!; **he perdido la costumbre** I have got out of the habit
perdición [perði'θjon] *nf* perdition; (*fig*) ruin
pérdida ['perðiða] *nf* loss; (*de tiempo*) waste; (*Com*) net loss; **pérdidas** *nfpl* (*Com*) losses; **¡no tiene ~!** you can't go wrong!; **~ contable** (*Com*) book loss
perdido, -a [per'ðiðo, a] *adj* lost; **estar ~ por** to be crazy about; **es un caso ~** he is a hopeless case
perdigón [perði'ɣon] *nm* pellet
perdiz [per'ðiθ] *nf* partridge
perdón [per'ðon] *nm* (*disculpa*) pardon, forgiveness; (*clemencia*) mercy; **¡~!** sorry!, I beg your pardon!; **con ~** if I may, if you don't mind
perdonar [perðo'nar] *vt* to pardon, forgive; (*la vida*) to spare; (*excusar*) to exempt, excuse ▷ *vi* to pardon, forgive; **¡perdone (usted)!** sorry!, I beg your pardon!; **perdone, pero me parece que ...** excuse me, but I think ...
perdurable [perðu'raβle] *adj* lasting; (*eterno*) everlasting
perdurar [perðu'rar] *vi* (*resistir*) to last, endure; (*seguir existiendo*) to stand, still exist
perecedero, -a [pereθe'ðero, a] *adj* perishable
perecer [pere'θer] *vi* to perish, die
peregrinación [pereɣrina'θjon] *nf* (*Rel*) pilgrimage
peregrino, -a [pere'ɣrino, a] *adj* (*extraño*) strange; (*singular*) rare ▷ *nm/f* pilgrim
perejil [pere'xil] *nm* parsley
perenne [pe'renne] *adj* perennial
perentorio, -a [peren'torjo, a] *adj* (*urgente*) urgent; (*terminante*) peremptory; (*fijo*) set, fixed
pereza [pe'reθa] *nf* (*flojera*) laziness; (*lentitud*) sloth, slowness
perezoso, -a [pere'θoso, a] *adj* lazy; slow, sluggish
perfección [perfek'θjon] *nf* perfection; **a la ~** to perfection
perfeccionar [perfekθjo'nar] *vt* to perfect; (*mejorar*) to improve; (*acabar*) to complete, finish
perfectamente [perfekta'mente] *adv* perfectly
perfecto, -a [per'fekto, a] *adj* perfect ▷ *nm* (*Ling*) perfect (tense)
perfidia [per'fiðja] *nf* perfidy, treachery
perfil [per'fil] *nm* (*parte lateral*) profile; (*silueta*) silhouette, outline; (*Tec*) (cross) section; **perfiles** *nmpl* features; (*fig*) social graces; **~ del cliente** (*Com*) customer profile; **en ~** from the side, in profile
perfilado, -a [perfi'laðo, a] *adj* (*bien formado*) well-shaped; (*largo*: *cara*) long
perfilar [perfi'lar] *vt* (*trazar*) to outline; (*dar carácter a*) to shape, give character to; **perfilarse** *vr* to be silhouetted (*en* against); **el proyecto se va perfilando** the project is taking shape
perforación [perfora'θjon] *nf* perforation; (*con taladro*) drilling
perforadora [perfora'ðora] *nf* drill; (*tb*: **~ de fichas**) card-punch
perforar [perfo'rar] *vt* to perforate; (*agujero*) to drill, bore; (*papel*) to punch a hole in ▷ *vi* to drill, bore
perfume [per'fume] *nm* perfume, scent
perfumería [perfume'ria] *nf* perfume shop
pericia [pe'riθja] *nf* skill, expertise
periferia [peri'ferja] *nf* periphery; (*de ciudad*) outskirts *pl*
periférico, -a [peri'feriko, a] *adj* peripheral ▷ *nm* (*Inform*) peripheral; (*Am*: *Auto*) ring road (*Brit*), beltway (*US*); **barrio ~** outlying district

ión) to pilot; (*barco*) to
t; (*de aparato*) (pilot)
, tail light; (*conductor*)
a ~ pilot plant; **luz ~**
ico automatic pilot
] *nm* (*polvo*) paprika
nf pepper
nm pepper, pimiento
, *nm* badge
eka] *nf* art gallery
wood
intbrush
'diskos] *nm/f inv* disc
perforar) to prick, pierce;
e; (*incitar*) to prod;
lus fam) to be DJ;
a) to inject o.s.;
uncture; **no ~ ni cortar**
ner un neumático
uncture *o* a flat tyre
nm (*perforación*) prick; (*de*
US); (*fig*) prod
oint; (*aguijón*) spike;
); **~ moruno** shish
mall slice of omelette
nm table tennis
nm penguin
l: **hacer sus primeros**
teps
tree); **vivir en el**
back of beyond
, (*gota*) spot, drop;
look(s) *pl*; (*medida*) pint;
k good, look well; **por la**
, a] *adj* spotted; (*de*
ful ▷ *nf* piece of political
pl political graffiti *sg*;
me viene que ni ~ it
βjos] *nm inv* (*Esp*)
paint ▷ *vi* to paint; (*fam*)
nt; **pintarse** *vr* to put on
as solo para hacer algo
by o.s.; **no pinta nada**
nm/f painter; **~ de**
painter; (*fig*) bad
o'resko, a] *adj*
painting; **~ a la**
ur; **~ al óleo** oil painting;
nting
l) claw; (*para colgar ropa*)
pin (US); (*Tec*) pincers *pl*;
lar) tweezers
el pino) pine cone; (*fruta*)
p

piñata [pi'ɲata] *nf* piñata (*figurine hung up*
parties to be beaten with sticks until sweets or presents fall out)
piñón [pi'ɲon] *nm* (*Bot*) pine nut; (*Tec*) pir
pío, -a ['pio, a] *adj* (*devoto*) pious, devout; (*misericordioso*) merciful ▷ *nm*: **no decir ni** not to breathe a word
piojo ['pjoxo] *nm* louse
pionero, -a [pjo'nero, a] *adj* pioneering ▷ *nm/f* pioneer
pipa ['pipa] *nf* pipe; (*Bot*) seed, pip; (*de gira* sunflower seed
pipí [pi'pi] *nm* (*fam*): **hacer ~** to have a wee wee)
pique *etc* ['pike] *vb ver* **picar** ▷ *nm* (*resentimiento*) pique, resentment; (*rivalida* rivalry, competition; **irse a ~** to sink; (*fi* to be ruined; **tener un ~ con algn** to hav grudge against sb
piqueta [pi'keta] *nf* pick(axe)
piquete [pi'kete] *nm* (*agujerito*) small hole (*Mil*) squad, party; (*de obreros*) picket; (*Am insecto*) bite; **~ secundario** secondary pic
pirado, -a [pi'raðo, a] *adj* (*fam*) round the bend ▷ *nm/f* nutter
piragua [pi'raɣwa] *nf* canoe
piragüismo [pira'ɣwismo] *nm* (*Deporte*) canoeing
pirámide [pi'ramiðe] *nf* pyramid
piraña [pi'raɲa] *nf* piranha
pirarse [pi'rarse] *vr*: **~(las)** (*largarse*) to bea (*fam*); (*Escol*) to cut class
pirata [pi'rata] *adj*: **edición/disco ~** pira edition/bootleg record ▷ *nm* pirate; (*tb*: **~ informático**) hacker
Pirineo, Pirineos [piri'neo(s)] *nm(pl)* Pyrenees *pl*
pirómano, -a [pi'romano, a] *nm/f* (*Psico*) pyromaniac; (*Jur*) arsonist
piropo [pi'ropo] *nm* compliment, (piece o flattery; **echar ~s a** to make flirtatious remarks to
pirueta [pi'rweta] *nf* pirouette
piruleta [piru'leta] *nf* lollipop
pis [pis] *nm* (*fam*) pee; **hacer ~** to have a p (*para niños*) to wee-wee
pisada [pi'saða] *nf* (*paso*) footstep; (*huella* footprint
pisar [pi'sar] *vt* (*caminar sobre*) to walk on, tread on; (*apretar con el pie*) to press; (*fig*) t trample on, walk all over ▷ *vi* to tread, st walk; **~ el acelerador** to step on the accelerator; **~ fuerte** (*fig*) to act determi
piscifactoría [pisθifakto'ria] *nf* fish far
piscina [pis'θina] *nf* swimming pool
Piscis ['pisθis] *nm* (*Astro*) Pisces
piso ['piso] *nm* (*suelo*: *de edificio*) floor; (*Am* ground; (*apartamento*) flat, apartment; **primer ~** (*Esp*) first *o* second (US) floor; (ground *o* first (US) floor
pisotear [pisote'ar] *vt* to trample (on *o* underfoot); (*fig*: *humillar*) to trample on

perilla [pe'riʎa] *nf* (*barba*) goatee; (*Am*: *de puerta*) doorknob, door handle
perímetro [pe'rimetro] *nm* perimeter
periódico, -a [pe'rjoðiko, a] *adj* periodic(al) ▷ *nm* (news)paper; **~ dominical** Sunday (news)paper
periodismo [perjo'ðismo] *nm* journalism
periodista [perjo'ðista] *nm/f* journalist
periodo [pe'rjoðo], **período** [pe'rioðo] *nm* period; **~ contable** (*Com*) accounting period
peripecias [peri'peθjas] *nfpl* adventures
periquito [peri'kito] *nm* budgerigar, budgie (*fam*)
perito, -a [pe'rito, a] *adj* (*experto*) expert; (*diestro*) skilled, skilful ▷ *nm/f* expert; skilled worker; (*técnico*) technician
perjudicar [perxuði'kar] *vt* (*gen*) to damage, harm; (*fig*) to prejudice
perjudicial [perxuði'θjal] *adj* damaging, harmful; (*en detrimento*) detrimental
perjuicio [per'xwiθjo] *nm* damage, harm; **en/sin ~ de** to the detriment of/without prejudice to
perjurar [perxu'rar] *vi* to commit perjury
perla ['perla] *nf* pearl; **me viene de ~s** it suits me fine
permanecer [permane'θer] *vi* (*quedarse*) to stay, remain; (*seguir*) to continue to be
permanencia [perma'nenθja] *nf* (*duración*) permanence; (*estancia*) stay
permanente [perma'nente] *adj* (*que queda*) permanent; (*constante*) constant; (*comisión etc*) standing ▷ *nf* perm; **hacerse una ~** to have one's hair permed
permisible [permi'siβle] *adj* permissible, allowable
permiso [per'miso] *nm* permission; (*licencia*) permit, licence (*Brit*), license (*US*); **con ~** excuse me; **estar de ~** (*Mil*) to be on leave; **~ de conducir** *o* **conductor** driving licence (*Brit*), driver's license (*US*); **~ de exportación/importación** export/import licence; **~ por asuntos familiares** compassionate leave; **~ por enfermedad** (*Am*) sick leave
permitir [permi'tir] *vt* to permit, allow; **permitirse** *vr*: **~se algo** to allow o.s. sth; **no me puedo ~ ese lujo** I can't afford that; **¿me permite?** may I?; **si lo permite el tiempo** weather permitting
pernera [per'nera] *nf* trouser leg
pernicioso, -a [perni'θjoso, a] *adj* (*maligno*, *Med*) pernicious; (*persona*) wicked
perno ['perno] *nm* bolt
pero ['pero] *conj* but; (*aún*) yet ▷ *nm* (*defecto*) flaw, defect; (*reparo*) objection; **¡no hay ~ que valga!** there are no buts about it
perol [pe'rol] *nm*, **perola** [pe'rola] *nf* pan
perpendicular [perpendiku'lar] *adj* perpendicular; **el camino es ~ al río** the road is at right angles to the river
perpetrar [perpe'trar] *vt* to perpetrate
perpetuar [perpe'twar] *vt* to perpetuate

perpetuo, -a [per'petwo, a] *adj* perpetual; (*Jur etc*: *condena*) life *cpd*
perplejo, -a [per'plexo, a] *adj* perplexed, bewildered
perra ['perra] *nf* (*Zool*) bitch; (*fam*: *dinero*) money; (: *manía*) mania, crazy idea; (: *rabieta*) tantrum; **estar sin una ~** to be flat broke
perrera [pe'rrera] *nf* kennel
perrito [pe'rrito] *nm* (*tb*: **~ caliente**) hot dog
perro ['perro] *nm* dog; **~ caliente** hot dog; **"~ peligroso"** "beware of the dog"; **ser ~ viejo** to be an old hand; **tiempo de ~s** filthy weather; **~ que ladra no muerde** his bark is worse than his bite
persa ['persa] *adj*, *nm/f* Persian ▷ *nm* (*Ling*) Persian
persecución [perseku'θjon] *nf* pursuit, hunt, chase; (*Rel*, *Pol*) persecution
perseguir [perse'ɣir] *vt* to pursue, hunt; (*cortejar*) to chase after; (*molestar*) to pester, annoy; (*Rel*, *Pol*) to persecute; (*Jur*) to prosecute
perseverante [perseβe'rante] *adj* persevering, persistent
perseverar [perseve'rar] *vi* to persevere, persist; **~ en** to persevere in, persist with
persiana [per'sjana] *nf* (Venetian) blind
persignarse [persiɣ'narse] *vr* to cross o.s.
persistente [persis'tente] *adj* persistent
persistir [persis'tir] *vi* to persist
persona [per'sona] *nf* person; **10 ~s** 10 people; **~ mayor** elderly person; **tercera ~** third party; (*Ling*) third person; **en ~** in person *o* the flesh; **por ~** a head; **es buena ~** he's a good sort
personaje [perso'naxe] *nm* important person, celebrity; (*Teat*) character
personal [perso'nal] *adj* (*particular*) personal; (*para una persona*) single, for one person ▷ *nm* (*plantilla*) personnel, staff; (*Naut*) crew; (*fam*: *gente*) people
personalidad [personali'ðað] *nf* personality; (*Jur*) status
personalizar [personali'θar] *vt* to personalize ▷ *vi* (*al hablar*) to name names
personarse [perso'narse] *vr* to appear in person; **~ en** to present o.s. at, report to
personificar [personifi'kar] *vt* to personify
perspectiva [perspek'tiβa] *nf* perspective; (*vista*, *panorama*) view, panorama; (*posibilidad futura*) outlook, prospect; **tener algo en ~** to have sth in view
perspicacia [perspi'kaθja] *nf* discernment, perspicacity
perspicaz [perspi'kaθ] *adj* shrewd
persuadir [perswa'ðir] *vt* (*gen*) to persuade; (*convencer*) to convince; **persuadirse** *vr* to become convinced
persuasión [perswa'sjon] *nf* (*acto*) persuasion; (*convicción*) conviction
persuasivo, -a [perwa'siβo, a] *adj* persuasive; convincing

P

pertenecer [pertene'θer] *vi*: **~ a** to belong to; (*fig*) to concern
perteneciente [pertene'θjente] *adj*: **~ a** belonging to
pertenencia [perte'nenθja] *nf* ownership; **pertenencias** *nfpl* possessions, property *sg*
pertenezca *etc* [perte'neθka] *vb ver* **pertenecer**
pértiga ['pertiɣa] *nf* pole; **salto de ~** pole vault
pertinaz [perti'naθ] *adj* (*persistente*) persistent; (*terco*) obstinate
pertinente [perti'nente] *adj* relevant, pertinent; (*apropiado*) appropriate; **~ a** concerning, relevant to
perturbación [perturβa'θjon] *nf* (*Pol*) disturbance; (*Med*) upset, disturbance; **~ del orden público** breach of the peace
perturbador, a [perturβa'ðor, a] *adj* (*que perturba*) perturbing, disturbing; (*subversivo*) subversive
perturbar [pertur'βar] *vt* (*el orden*) to disturb; (*Med*) to upset, disturb; (*mentalmente*) to perturb
Perú [pe'ru] *nm*: **el ~** Peru
peruano, -a [pe'rwano, a] *adj, nm/f* Peruvian
perversión [perβer'sjon] *nf* perversion
perverso, -a [perβerso, a] *adj* perverse; (*depravado*) depraved
pervertido, -a [perβer'tiðo, a] *adj* perverted ▷ *nm/f* pervert
pervertir [perβer'tir] *vt* to pervert, corrupt
pesa ['pesa] *nf* weight; (*Deporte*) shot
pesadez [pesa'ðeθ] *nf* (*calidad de pesado*) heaviness; (*lentitud*) slowness; (*aburrimiento*) tediousness; **es una ~ tener que ...** it's a bind having to ...
pesadilla [pesa'ðiʎa] *nf* nightmare, bad dream; (*fig*) worry, obsession
pesado, -a [pe'saðo, a] *adj* (*gen*) heavy; (*lento*) slow; (*difícil, duro*) tough, hard; (*aburrido*) tedious, boring; (*bochornoso*) sultry ▷ *nm/f* bore; **tener el estómago ~** to feel bloated; **¡no seas ~!** come off it!
pesadumbre [pesa'ðumbre] *nf* grief, sorrow
pésame ['pesame] *nm* expression of condolence, message of sympathy; **dar el ~** to express one's condolences
pesar [pe'sar] *vt* to weigh; (*fig*) to weigh heavily on; (*afligir*) to grieve ▷ *vi* to weigh; (*ser pesado*) to weigh a lot, be heavy; (*fig: opinión*) to carry weight ▷ *nm* (*sentimiento*) regret; (*pena*) grief, sorrow; **no pesa mucho** it's not very heavy; **a ~ de (que)** in spite of, despite; **no me pesa haberlo hecho** I'm not sorry I did it
pesca ['peska] *nf* (*acto*) fishing; (*cantidad de pescado*) catch; **~ de altura/en bajura** deep sea/coastal fishing; **ir de ~** to go fishing
pescadería [peskaðe'ria] *nf* fish shop, fishmonger's
pescadilla [peska'ðiʎa] *nf* whiting
pescado [pes'kaðo] *nm* fish
pescador, a [peska'ðor, a] *nm/f* fisherman(-woman)
pescar [pes'kar] *vt* (*coger*) to catch; (*tratar de coger*) to fish for; (*fam: lograr*) to get hold of, land; (*conseguir: trabajo*) to manage to get; (*sorprender*) to catch unawares ▷ *vi* to fish, go fishing
pescuezo [pes'kweθo] *nm* neck
pesebre [pe'seβre] *nm* manger
peseta [pe'seta] *nf* peseta
pesimismo [pesi'mismo] *nm* pessimism
pesimista [pesi'mista] *adj* pessimistic ▷ *nm/f* pessimist
pésimo, -a ['pesimo, a] *adj* awful, dreadful
peso ['peso] *nm* weight; (*balanza*) scales *pl*; (*Am Com*) *monetary unit*; (*moneda*) peso; (*Deporte*) shot; **~ bruto/neto** gross/net weight; **~ mosca/pesado** fly-/heavyweight; **de poco ~** light(weight); **levantamiento de ~s** weightlifting; **vender a ~** to sell by weight; **argumento de ~** weighty argument; **eso cae de su ~** that goes without saying
pesquero, -a [pes'kero, a] *adj* fishing *cpd*
pesquisa [pes'kisa] *nf* inquiry, investigation
pestaña [pes'taɲa] *nf* (*Anat*) eyelash; (*borde*) rim
pestañear [pestaɲe'ar] *vi* to blink
peste ['peste] *nf* plague; (*fig*) nuisance; (*mal olor*) stink, stench; **~ negra** Black Death; **echar ~s** to swear, fume
pesticida [pesti'θiða] *nm* pesticide
pestilencia [pesti'lenθja] *nf* (*mal olor*) stink, stench
pestillo [pes'tiʎo] *nm* bolt, latch; (*cerrojo*) catch; (*picaporte*) (door) handle
petaca [pe'taka] *nf* (*de cigarrillos*) cigarette case; (*de pipa*) tobacco pouch; (*Am: maleta*) suitcase
pétalo ['petalo] *nm* petal
petanca [pe'tanka] *nf* *a game in which metal bowls are thrown at a target bowl*
petardo [pe'tarðo] *nm* firework, firecracker
petición [peti'θjon] *nf* (*pedido*) request, plea; (*memorial*) petition; (*Jur*) plea; **a ~ de** at the request of; **~ de aumento de salarios** wage demand *o* claim
peto ['peto] *nm* dungarees *pl*, overalls *pl* (*US*); (*corpiño*) bodice; (*Taur*) horse's padding
petrificar [petrifi'kar] *vt* to petrify
petróleo [pe'troleo] *nm* oil, petroleum
petrolero, -a [petro'lero, a] *adj* petroleum *cpd* ▷ *nm* (*Com*) oil man; (*buque*) (oil) tanker
peyorativo, -a [pejora'tiβo, a] *adj* pejorative
pez [peθ] *nm* fish; **~ de colores** goldfish; **~ espada** swordfish; **estar como el ~ en el agua** to feel completely at home
pezón [pe'θon] *nm* teat, nipple
pezuña [pe'θuɲa] *nf* hoof
piadoso, -a [pja'ðoso, a] *adj* (*devoto*) pious, devout; (*misericordioso*) kind, merciful
pianista [pja'nista] *nm/f* pianist
piano ['pjano] *nm* piano; **~ de cola** grand piano
piar [pjar] *vi* to cheep
PIB *nm abr* (*Esp Com: = Producto Interno Bruto*
pibe, -a ['piβe, a] *nm/f* (*Am*) boy/girl, kid, child
picadero [pika'ðero] *nm* riding school
picadillo [pika'ðiʎo] *nm* mince, minced
picado, -a [pi'kaðo, a] *adj* pricked, punct
(*Culin*) minced, chopped; (*mar*) choppy; (*diente*) bad; (*tabaco*) cut; (*enfadado*) cross
picador [pika'ðor] *nm* (*Taur*) picador; (*mi*
faceworker
picadora [pika'ðora] *nf* mincer
picadura [pika'ðura] *nf* (*pinchazo*) punctu
(*de abeja*) sting; (*de mosquito*) bite; (*tabaco picado*) cut tobacco
picana [pi'kana] (*Am*) *nf* (*Agr*) cattle prod; *para tortura*) electric prod
picante [pi'kante] *adj* (*comida, sabor*) hot; (*comentario*) racy, spicy
picaporte [pika'porte] *nm* (*tirador*) handl
(*pestillo*) latch
picar [pi'kar] *vt* (*agujerear, perforar*) to prick, puncture; (*billete*) to punch, clip; (*abeja*) to
sting; (*mosquito, serpiente*) to bite; (*Culin*) to
mince, chop; (*persona*) to nibble (at); (*incit*
to incite, goad; (*dañar, irritar*) to annoy, bother; (*quemar: lengua*) to burn, sting ▷ *vi*
(*pez*) to bite, take the bait; (*el sol*) to burn, scorch; (*abeja, Med*) to sting; (*mosquito*) to b
picarse *vr* (*agriarse*) to turn sour, go off; (*m*
to get choppy; (*ofenderse*) to take offence;
pican los ojos my eyes sting; **me pica el**
brazo my arm itches
picardía [pikar'ðia] *nf* villainy; (*astucia*) slyness, craftiness; (*una picardía*) dirty trick
(*palabra*) rude/bad word *o* expression
pícaro, -a ['pikaro, a] *adj* (*malicioso*) villainous; (*travieso*) mischievous ▷ *nm* (*astuto*) sly sort; (*sinvergüenza*) rascal, scoundrel
pichi ['pitʃi] *nm* (*Esp*) pinafore dress (*Brit*), jumper (*US*)
pichón, -ona [pi'tʃon, ona] *nm/f* (*de paloma*) young pigeon; (*apelativo*) darling, dearest
pico ['piko] *nm* (*de ave*) beak; (*punta agudo*) peak, sharp point; (*Tec*) pick, pickaxe; (*Geo*) peak, summit; (*labia*) talkativeness; **no abrir el ~** to keep quiet; **~ parásito** (*Elec*) spike; **y ~** and a bit; **las seis y ~** six and a bi
son las tres y ~ it's just after three; **tiene 5**
libros y ~ he has 50-odd books; **me costó u**
~ it cost me quite a bit
picor [pi'kor] *nm* itch; (*ardor*) sting(ing feeling)
picoso, -a (*Am*) [pi'koso, a] *adj* (*comida*) hot
picotear [pikote'ar] *vt* to peck ▷ *vi* to nibble, pick
picudo, -a [pi'kuðo, a] *adj* pointed, with a point

pilotar [pilo'tar] *vt* (*a*
steer
piloto [pi'loto] *nm* pi
light; (*Auto*) rear lig
driver ▷ *adj inv*: **plan**
side light; **~ automá**
pimentón [pimen'to
pimienta [pi'mjenta
pimiento [pi'mjento
pin (*pl* **pins**) [pin, pin
pinacoteca [pinako
pinar [pi'nar] *nm* pin
pincel [pin'θel] *nm* p
pinchadiscos [pintʃ
jockey, DJ
pinchar [pin'tʃar] *vt*
(*neumático*) to punctu
(*Inform*) to click ▷ *vi*
pincharse *vr* (*con drc*
(*neumático*) to burst,
(*fam*) to cut no ice; **t**
pinchado to have a
pinchazo [pin'tʃaθo
llanta) puncture, fla
pincho ['pintʃo] *nm*
(*Culin*) savoury (snac
kebab; **~ de tortilla**
ping-pong ['pimpor
pingüino [pin'gwin
pinitos [pi'nitos] *nm*
~ to take one's first
pino ['pino] *nm* pine
quinto ~ to live at t
pinta ['pinta] *nf* spo
(*aspecto*) appearance
tener buena ~ to lo
~ by the look of it
pintado, -a [pin'tad
muchos colores) colou
graffiti; **pintados**
me sienta que ni ~
suits me a treat
pintalabios [pinta
lipstick
pintar [pin'tar] *vt* t
to count, be impor
make-up; **pintárs**
to manage to do st
(*fam*) he has no say
pintor, a [pin'tor, a
brocha gorda hou
painter
pintoresco, -a [pi
picturesque
pintura [pin'tura]
acuarela waterco
~ rupestre cave pa
pinza ['pinθa] *nf* (*Z*
clothes peg, cloth
pinzas *nfpl* (*para d*
piña ['piɲa] *nf* (*frut*
pineapple; (*fig*) gr

pisotón [piso'ton] *nm* (*con el pie*) stamp
pista ['pista] *nf* track, trail; (*indicio*) clue; (*Inform*) track; ~ **de auditoría** (*Com*) audit trail; ~ **de aterrizaje** runway; ~ **de baile** dance floor; ~ **de tenis** tennis court; ~ **de hielo** ice rink; **estar sobre la ~ de algn** to be on sb's trail
pisto ['pisto] *nm* (*Culin*) ratatouille; **darse ~** (*fam*) to show off
pistola [pis'tola] *nf* pistol; (*Tec*) spray-gun
pistolero, -a [pisto'lero, a] *nm/f* gunman, gangster ▷ *nf* holster
pistón [pis'ton] *nm* (*Tec*) piston; (*Mus*) key
pitar [pi'tar] *vt* (*hacer sonar*) to blow; (*partido*) to referee; (*rechiflar*) to whistle at, boo; (*actor, obra*) to hiss ▷ *vi* to whistle; (*Auto*) to sound *o* toot one's horn; (*Am*) to smoke; **salir pitando** to beat it
pitido [pi'tiðo] *nm* whistle; (*sonido agudo*) beep; (*sonido corto*) pip
pitillera [piti'ʎera] *nf* cigarette case
pitillo [pi'tiʎo] *nm* cigarette
pito ['pito] *nm* whistle; (*de coche*) horn; (*cigarrillo*) cigarette; (*fam: de marihuana*) joint; (*fam!*) prick (*!*); **me importa un ~** I don't care two hoots
pitón [pi'ton] *nm* (*Zool*) python
pitonisa [pito'nisa] *nf* fortune-teller
pitorreo [pito'rreo] *nm* joke, laugh; **estar de ~** to be in a joking mood
píxel ['piksel] *nm* (*Inform*) pixel
piyama [pi'jama] *nm* (*Am*) pyjamas *pl*, pajamas (*US*) *pl*
pizarra [pi'θarra] *nf* (*piedra*) slate; (*encerado*) blackboard; ~ **blanca** whiteboard; ~ **interactiva** interactive whiteboard
pizarrón [piθa'rron] *nm* (*Am*) blackboard
pizca ['piθka] *nf* pinch, spot; (*fig*) spot, speck, trace; **ni ~** not a bit
pizza ['pitsa] *nf* pizza
placa ['plaka] *nf* plate; (*Med*) dental plate; (*distintivo*) badge; ~ **de matrícula** number plate; ~ **madre** (*Inform*) mother board; ~ **fotovoltaica** solar panel
placaje [pla'kaxe] *nm* tackle
placard [pla'kar] *nm* (*Am*) built-in cupboard, (clothes) closet (*US*)
placenta [pla'θenta] *nf* placenta; (*tras el parto*) afterbirth
placentero, -a [plaθen'tero, a] *adj* pleasant, agreeable
placer [pla'θer] *nm* pleasure ▷ *vt* to please; **a ~** at one's pleasure
plácido, -a ['plaθiðo, a] *adj* placid
plaga ['plaɣa] *nf* (*Zool*) pest; (*Med*) plague; (*fig*) swarm; abundance
plagar [pla'ɣar] *vt* to infest, plague; (*llenar*) to fill; **plagado de** riddled with; **han plagado la ciudad de carteles** they have plastered the town with posters
plagiar [pla'gjar] *vt* to plagiarize; (*Am*) to kidnap
plagio ['plaxjo] *nm* plagiarism; (*Am*) kidnap
plan [plan] *nm* (*esquema, proyecto*) plan; (*idea, intento*) idea, intention; (*de curso*) programme; ~ **cotizable de jubilación** contributory pension scheme; ~ **de estudios** curriculum, syllabus; ~ **de incentivos** (*Com*) incentive scheme; **tener ~** (*fam*) to have a date; **tener un ~** (*fam*) to have an affair; **en ~ de cachondeo** for a laugh; **en ~ económico** (*fam*) on the cheap; **vamos en ~ de turismo** we're going as tourists; **si te pones en ese ~ ...** if that's your attitude ...
plana ['plana] *nf ver* **plano**
plancha ['plantʃa] *nf* (*para planchar*) iron; (*rótulo*) plate, sheet; (*Naut*) gangway; (*Culin*) grill; **pescado a la ~** grilled fish; ~ **de pelo** straighteners; **a la ~** (*Culin*) grilled
planchado, -a [plan'tʃaðo, a] *adj* (*ropa*) ironed; (*traje*) pressed ▷ *nm* ironing
planchar [plan'tʃar] *vt* to iron ▷ *vi* to do the ironing
planeador [planea'ðor] *nm* glider
planear [plane'ar] *vt* to plan ▷ *vi* to glide
planeta [pla'neta] *nm* planet
planicie [pla'niθje] *nf* plain
planificación [planifika'θjon] *nf* planning; ~ **corporativa** (*Com*) corporate planning; ~ **familiar** family planning; **diagrama de ~** (*Com*) planner
plano, -a ['plano, a] *adj* flat, level, even; (*liso*) smooth ▷ *nm* (*Mat, Tec, Aviat*) plane; (*Foto*) shot; (*Arq*) plan; (*Geo*) map; (*de ciudad*) map, street plan ▷ *nf* sheet of paper, page; (*Tec*) trowel; **primer ~** close-up; **caer de ~** to fall flat; **rechazar algo de ~** to turn sth down flat; **le daba el sol de ~** (*fig*) the sun shone directly on it; **en primera plana** on the front page; **plana mayor** staff
planta ['planta] *nf* (*Bot, Tec*) plant; (*Anat*) sole of the foot, foot; (*piso*) floor; (*Am: personal*) staff; ~ **baja** ground floor
plantación [planta'θjon] *nf* (*Agr*) plantation; (*acto*) planting
plantar [plan'tar] *vt* (*Bot*) to plant; (*puesto*) to put in; (*levantar*) to erect, set up; **plantarse** *vr* to stand firm; ~ **a algn en la calle** to chuck sb out; **dejar plantado a algn** (*fam*) to stand sb up; **~se en** to reach, get to
plantear [plante'ar] *vt* (*problema*) to pose; (*dificultad*) to raise; **se lo ~é** I'll put it to him
plantilla [plan'tiʎa] *nf* (*de zapato*) insole; (*personal*) personnel; **ser de ~** to be on the staff
plantón [plan'ton] *nm* (*Mil*) guard, sentry; (*fam*) long wait; **dar (un) ~ a algn** to stand sb up
plañir [pla'ɲir] *vi* to mourn
plasma ['plasma] *nm* plasma
plasta ['plasta] *nm/f* (*Esp: fam*) bore ▷ *nf* soft mass, lump; (*desastre*) botch, mess ▷ *adj* (*Esp: fam*) boring
plástico, -a ['plastiko, a] *adj* plastic ▷ *nf* (art of) sculpture, modelling ▷ *nm* plastic

P

Plastilina® [plasti'lina] *nf* Plasticine®
plata ['plata] *nf* (*metal*) silver; (*cosas hechas de plata*) silverware; (*Am*) cash, dough (*fam*); **hablar en ~** to speak bluntly *o* frankly
plataforma [plata'forma] *nf* platform; **~ de lanzamiento/perforación** launch(ing) pad/ drilling rig
plátano ['platano] *nm* (*fruta*) banana; (*árbol*) plane tree; banana tree
platea [pla'tea] *nf* (*Teat*) pit
plateado, -a [plate'aðo, a] *adj* silver; (*Tec*) silver-plated
plática ['platika] *nf* (*Am*) talk, chat; (*Rel*) sermon
platicar [plati'kar] *vi* (*Am*) to talk, chat
platillo [pla'tiʎo] *nm* saucer; (*de limosnas*) collecting bowl; **platillos** *nmpl* cymbals; **~ volador** *o* **volante** flying saucer; **pasar el ~** to pass the hat round
platina [pla'tina] *nf* (*Mus*) tape deck
platino [pla'tino] *nm* platinum; **platinos** *nmpl* (*Auto*) (contact) points
plato ['plato] *nm* plate, dish; (*parte de comida*) course; (*guiso*) dish; **~ frutero/sopero** fruit/ soup dish; **primer ~** first course; **~ combinado** set main course (*served on one plate*); **~ fuerte** main course; **pagar los ~s rotos** (*fam*) to carry the can (*fam*)
plató [pla'to] *nm* set
platónico, -a [pla'toniko, a] *adj* platonic
playa ['plaja] *nf* beach; (*costa*) seaside; **~ de estacionamiento** (*Am*) car park
playero, -a [pla'jero, a] *adj* beach *cpd* ▷ *nf* (*Am: camiseta*) T-shirt; **playeras** *nfpl* canvas shoes; (*Tenis*) tennis shoes
plaza ['plaθa] *nf* square; (*mercado*) market(place); (*sitio*) room, space; (*en vehículo*) seat, place; (*colocación*) post, job; **~ de abastos** food market; **~ mayor** main square; **~ de toros** bullring; **hacer la ~** to do the daily shopping; **reservar una ~** to reserve a seat; **el hotel tiene 100 ~s** the hotel has 100 beds
plazo ['plaθo] *nm* (*lapso de tiempo*) time, period, term; (*fecha de vencimiento*) expiry date; (*pago parcial*) instalment; **a corto/largo ~** short-/ long-term; **comprar a ~s** to buy on hire purchase, pay for in instalments; **nos dan un ~ de ocho días** they allow us a week
plazoleta [plaθo'leta], **plazuela** [pla'θwela] *nf* small square
pleamar [plea'mar] *nf* high tide
plebe ['pleβe] *nf*: **la ~** the common people *pl*, the masses *pl*; (*pey*) the plebs *pl*
plebeyo, -a [ple'βejo, a] *adj* plebeian; (*pey*) coarse, common
plebiscito [pleβis'θito] *nm* plebiscite
plegable [ple'ɣaβle] *adj* pliable; (*silla*) folding
plegar [ple'ɣar] *vt* (*doblar*) to fold, bend; (*Costura*) to pleat; **plegarse** *vr* to yield, submit
pleito ['pleito] *nm* (*Jur*) lawsuit, case; (*fig*) dispute, feud; **pleitos** *nmpl* litigation *sg*; **entablar ~** to bring an action *o* a lawsuit; **poner ~** to sue
plenilunio [pleni'lunjo] *nm* full moon
plenitud [pleni'tuð] *nf* plenitude, fullness; (*abundancia*) abundance
pleno, -a ['pleno, a] *adj* full; (*completo*) complete ▷ *nm* plenum; **en ~** as a whole; (*por unanimidad*) unanimously; **en ~ día** in broad daylight; **en ~ verano** at the height of summer; **en plena cara** full in the face
pletina *nf* (*Mus*) tape deck
pliego ['pljeɣo] *vb ver* **plegar** ▷ *nm* (*hoja*) sheet (of paper); (*carta*) sealed letter/document; **~ de condiciones** details *pl*, specifications *pl*
pliegue ['pljeɣe] *vb ver* **plegar** ▷ *nm* fold, crease; (*de vestido*) pleat
plisado [pli'saðo] *nm* pleating
plomería [plome'ria] *nf* (*Am*) plumbing
plomero [plo'mero] *nm* (*Am*) plumber
plomo ['plomo] *nm* (*metal*) lead; (*Elec*) fuse; **sin ~** unleaded; **caer a ~** to fall heavily *o* flat
pluma ['pluma] *nf* (*Zool*) feather; (*para escribir*): **~ (estilográfica)** ink pen; **~ fuente** (*Am*) fountain pen
plumero [plu'mero] *nm* (*quitapolvos*) feather duster; **ya te veo el ~** I know what you're up to
plumón [plu'mon] *nm* (*de ave*) down; (*Am*) felt-tip pen
plural [plu'ral] *adj* plural ▷ *nm*: **en ~** in the plural
pluralidad [plurali'ðað] *nf* plurality; **una ~ de votos** a majority of votes
pluriempleo [pluriem'pleo] *nm* having more than one job
plus [plus] *nm* bonus
plusvalía [plusβa'lia] *nf* (*mayor valor*) appreciation, added value; (*Com*) goodwill
plutocracia [pluto'kraθja] *nf* plutocracy
PNB *nm abr* (*Esp Com: = Producto Nacional Bruto*) GNP
población [poβla'θjon] *nf* population; (*pueblo, ciudad*) town, city; **~ activa** working population
poblado, -a [po'βlaðo, a] *adj* inhabited; (*barba*) thick; (*cejas*) bushy ▷ *nm* (*aldea*) village; (*pueblo*) (small) town; **~ de** (*lleno de*) filled with; **densamente ~** densely populated
poblador, a [poβla'ðor, a] *nm/f* settler, colonist
poblar [po'βlar] *vt* (*colonizar*) to colonize; (*fundar*) to found; (*habitar*) to inhabit; **poblarse** *vr*: **~se de** to fill up with; (*irse cubriendo*) to become covered with
pobre ['poβre] *adj* poor ▷ *nm/f* poor person; (*mendigo*) beggar; **los ~s** the poor; **¡~!** poor thing!; **~ diablo** (*fig*) poor wretch *o* devil
pobreza [po'βreθa] *nf* poverty; **~ energética** fuel poverty
pocilga [po'θilɣa] *nf* pigsty
pocillo [po'siʎo] *nm* (*Am*) coffee cup

perilla [pe'riʎa] *nf* (*barba*) goatee; (*Am: de puerta*) doorknob, door handle
perímetro [pe'rimetro] *nm* perimeter
periódico, -a [pe'rjoðiko, a] *adj* periodic(al) ▷ *nm* (news)paper; **~ dominical** Sunday (news)paper
periodismo [perjo'ðismo] *nm* journalism
periodista [perjo'ðista] *nm/f* journalist
periodo [pe'rjoðo], **período** [pe'rioðo] *nm* period; **~ contable** (*Com*) accounting period
peripecias [peri'peθjas] *nfpl* adventures
periquito [peri'kito] *nm* budgerigar, budgie (*fam*)
perito, -a [pe'rito, a] *adj* (*experto*) expert; (*diestro*) skilled, skilful ▷ *nm/f* expert; skilled worker; (*técnico*) technician
perjudicar [perxuði'kar] *vt* (*gen*) to damage, harm; (*fig*) to prejudice
perjudicial [perxuði'θjal] *adj* damaging, harmful; (*en detrimento*) detrimental
perjuicio [per'xwiθjo] *nm* damage, harm; **en/sin ~ de** to the detriment of/without prejudice to
perjurar [perxu'rar] *vi* to commit perjury
perla ['perla] *nf* pearl; **me viene de ~s** it suits me fine
permanecer [permane'θer] *vi* (*quedarse*) to stay, remain; (*seguir*) to continue to be
permanencia [perma'nenθja] *nf* (*duración*) permanence; (*estancia*) stay
permanente [perma'nente] *adj* (*que queda*) permanent; (*constante*) constant; (*comisión etc*) standing ▷ *nf* perm; **hacerse una ~** to have one's hair permed
permisible [permi'siβle] *adj* permissible, allowable
permiso [per'miso] *nm* permission; (*licencia*) permit, licence (*Brit*), license (*US*); **con ~** excuse me; **estar de ~** (*Mil*) to be on leave; **~ de conducir** *o* **conductor** driving licence (*Brit*), driver's license (*US*); **~ de exportación/importación** export/import licence; **~ por asuntos familiares** compassionate leave; **~ por enfermedad** (*Am*) sick leave
permitir [permi'tir] *vt* to permit, allow; **permitirse** *vr*: **~se algo** to allow o.s. sth; **no me puedo ~ ese lujo** I can't afford that; **¿me permite?** may I?; **si lo permite el tiempo** weather permitting
pernera [per'nera] *nf* trouser leg
pernicioso, -a [perni'θjoso, a] *adj* (*maligno, Med*) pernicious; (*persona*) wicked
perno ['perno] *nm* bolt
pero ['pero] *conj* but; (*aún*) yet ▷ *nm* (*defecto*) flaw, defect; (*reparo*) objection; **¡no hay ~ que valga!** there are no buts about it
perol [pe'rol] *nm*, **perola** [pe'rola] *nf* pan
perpendicular [perpendiku'lar] *adj* perpendicular; **el camino es ~ al río** the road is at right angles to the river
perpetrar [perpe'trar] *vt* to perpetrate
perpetuar [perpe'twar] *vt* to perpetuate
perpetuo, -a [per'petwo, a] *adj* perpetual; (*Jur etc: condena*) life *cpd*
perplejo, -a [per'plexo, a] *adj* perplexed, bewildered
perra ['perra] *nf* (*Zool*) bitch; (*fam: dinero*) money; (*: manía*) mania, crazy idea; (*: rabieta*) tantrum; **estar sin una ~** to be flat broke
perrera [pe'rrera] *nf* kennel
perrito [pe'rrito] *nm* (*tb*: **~ caliente**) hot dog
perro ['perro] *nm* dog; **~ caliente** hot dog; **"~ peligroso"** "beware of the dog"; **ser ~ viejo** to be an old hand; **tiempo de ~s** filthy weather; **~ que ladra no muerde** his bark is worse than his bite
persa ['persa] *adj, nm/f* Persian ▷ *nm* (*Ling*) Persian
persecución [perseku'θjon] *nf* pursuit, hunt, chase; (*Rel, Pol*) persecution
perseguir [perse'ɣir] *vt* to pursue, hunt; (*cortejar*) to chase after; (*molestar*) to pester, annoy; (*Rel, Pol*) to persecute; (*Jur*) to prosecute
perseverante [perseβe'rante] *adj* persevering, persistent
perseverar [perseve'rar] *vi* to persevere, persist; **~ en** to persevere in, persist with
persiana [per'sjana] *nf* (Venetian) blind
persignarse [persiɣ'narse] *vr* to cross o.s.
persistente [persis'tente] *adj* persistent
persistir [persis'tir] *vi* to persist
persona [per'sona] *nf* person; **10 ~s** 10 people; **~ mayor** elderly person; **tercera ~** third party; (*Ling*) third person; **en ~** in person *o* the flesh; **por ~** a head; **es buena ~** he's a good sort
personaje [perso'naxe] *nm* important person, celebrity; (*Teat*) character
personal [perso'nal] *adj* (*particular*) personal; (*para una persona*) single, for one person ▷ *nm* (*plantilla*) personnel, staff; (*Naut*) crew; (*fam: gente*) people
personalidad [personali'ðað] *nf* personality; (*Jur*) status
personalizar [personali'θar] *vt* to personalize ▷ *vi* (*al hablar*) to name names
personarse [perso'narse] *vr* to appear in person; **~ en** to present o.s. at, report to
personificar [personifi'kar] *vt* to personify
perspectiva [perspek'tiβa] *nf* perspective; (*vista, panorama*) view, panorama; (*posibilidad futura*) outlook, prospect; **tener algo en ~** to have sth in view
perspicacia [perspi'kaθja] *nf* discernment, perspicacity
perspicaz [perspi'kaθ] *adj* shrewd
persuadir [perswa'ðir] *vt* (*gen*) to persuade; (*convencer*) to convince; **persuadirse** *vr* to become convinced
persuasión [perswa'sjon] *nf* (*acto*) persuasion; (*convicción*) conviction
persuasivo, -a [perwa'siβo, a] *adj* persuasive; convincing

P

pertenecer [pertene'θer] *vi*: ~ **a** to belong to; (*fig*) to concern
perteneciente [pertene'θjente] *adj*: ~ **a** belonging to
pertenencia [perte'nenθja] *nf* ownership; **pertenencias** *nfpl* possessions, property *sg*
pertenezca *etc* [perte'neθka] *vb ver* **pertenecer**
pértiga ['pertiɣa] *nf* pole; **salto de** ~ pole vault
pertinaz [perti'naθ] *adj* (*persistente*) persistent; (*terco*) obstinate
pertinente [perti'nente] *adj* relevant, pertinent; (*apropiado*) appropriate; ~ **a** concerning, relevant to
perturbación [perturβa'θjon] *nf* (*Pol*) disturbance; (*Med*) upset, disturbance; ~ **del orden público** breach of the peace
perturbador, a [perturβa'ðor, a] *adj* (*que perturba*) perturbing, disturbing; (*subversivo*) subversive
perturbar [pertur'βar] *vt* (*el orden*) to disturb; (*Med*) to upset, disturb; (*mentalmente*) to perturb
Perú [pe'ru] *nm*: **el** ~ Peru
peruano, -a [pe'rwano, a] *adj, nm/f* Peruvian
perversión [perβer'sjon] *nf* perversion
perverso, -a [perβerso, a] *adj* perverse; (*depravado*) depraved
pervertido, -a [perβer'tiðo, a] *adj* perverted ▷ *nm/f* pervert
pervertir [perβer'tir] *vt* to pervert, corrupt
pesa ['pesa] *nf* weight; (*Deporte*) shot
pesadez [pesa'ðeθ] *nf* (*calidad de pesado*) heaviness; (*lentitud*) slowness; (*aburrimiento*) tediousness; **es una ~ tener que ...** it's a bind having to ...
pesadilla [pesa'ðiʎa] *nf* nightmare, bad dream; (*fig*) worry, obsession
pesado, -a [pe'saðo, a] *adj* (*gen*) heavy; (*lento*) slow; (*difícil, duro*) tough, hard; (*aburrido*) tedious, boring; (*bochornoso*) sultry ▷ *nm/f* bore; **tener el estómago** ~ to feel bloated; **¡no seas ~!** come off it!
pesadumbre [pesa'ðumbre] *nf* grief, sorrow
pésame ['pesame] *nm* expression of condolence, message of sympathy; **dar el** ~ to express one's condolences
pesar [pe'sar] *vt* to weigh; (*fig*) to weigh heavily on; (*afligir*) to grieve ▷ *vi* to weigh; (*ser pesado*) to weigh a lot, be heavy; (*fig: opinión*) to carry weight ▷ *nm* (*sentimiento*) regret; (*pena*) grief, sorrow; **no pesa mucho** it's not very heavy; **a ~ de (que)** in spite of, despite; **no me pesa haberlo hecho** I'm not sorry I did it
pesca ['peska] *nf* (*acto*) fishing; (*cantidad de pescado*) catch; ~ **de altura/en bajura** deep sea/coastal fishing; **ir de** ~ to go fishing
pescadería [peskaðe'ria] *nf* fish shop, fishmonger's
pescadilla [peska'ðiʎa] *nf* whiting
pescado [pes'kaðo] *nm* fish
pescador, a [peska'ðor, a] *nm/f* fisherman(-woman)
pescar [pes'kar] *vt* (*coger*) to catch; (*tratar de coger*) to fish for; (*fam: lograr*) to get hold of, land; (*conseguir: trabajo*) to manage to get; (*sorprender*) to catch unawares ▷ *vi* to fish, go fishing
pescuezo [pes'kweθo] *nm* neck
pesebre [pe'seβre] *nm* manger
peseta [pe'seta] *nf* peseta
pesimismo [pesi'mismo] *nm* pessimism
pesimista [pesi'mista] *adj* pessimistic ▷ *nm/f* pessimist
pésimo, -a ['pesimo, a] *adj* awful, dreadful
peso ['peso] *nm* weight; (*balanza*) scales *pl*; (*Am Com*) *monetary unit*; (*moneda*) peso; (*Deporte*) shot; ~ **bruto/neto** gross/net weight; ~ **mosca/pesado** fly-/heavyweight; **de poco** ~ light(weight); **levantamiento de ~s** weightlifting; **vender a** ~ to sell by weight; **argumento de** ~ weighty argument; **eso cae de su** ~ that goes without saying
pesquero, -a [pes'kero, a] *adj* fishing *cpd*
pesquisa [pes'kisa] *nf* inquiry, investigation
pestaña [pes'taɲa] *nf* (*Anat*) eyelash; (*borde*) rim
pestañear [pestaɲe'ar] *vi* to blink
peste ['peste] *nf* plague; (*fig*) nuisance; (*mal olor*) stink, stench; ~ **negra** Black Death; **echar ~s** to swear, fume
pesticida [pesti'θiða] *nm* pesticide
pestilencia [pesti'lenθja] *nf* (*mal olor*) stink, stench
pestillo [pes'tiʎo] *nm* bolt, latch; (*cerrojo*) catch; (*picaporte*) (door) handle
petaca [pe'taka] *nf* (*de cigarrillos*) cigarette case; (*de pipa*) tobacco pouch; (*Am: maleta*) suitcase
pétalo ['petalo] *nm* petal
petanca [pe'tanka] *nf a game in which metal bowls are thrown at a target bowl*
petardo [pe'tarðo] *nm* firework, firecracker
petición [peti'θjon] *nf* (*pedido*) request, plea; (*memorial*) petition; (*Jur*) plea; **a ~ de** at the request of; ~ **de aumento de salarios** wage demand *o* claim
peto ['peto] *nm* dungarees *pl*, overalls *pl* (*US*); (*corpiño*) bodice; (*Taur*) horse's padding
petrificar [petrifi'kar] *vt* to petrify
petróleo [pe'troleo] *nm* oil, petroleum
petrolero, -a [petro'lero, a] *adj* petroleum *cpd* ▷ *nm* (*Com*) oil man; (*buque*) (oil) tanker
peyorativo, -a [pejora'tiβo, a] *adj* pejorative
pez [peθ] *nm* fish; ~ **de colores** goldfish; ~ **espada** swordfish; **estar como el ~ en el agua** to feel completely at home
pezón [pe'θon] *nm* teat, nipple
pezuña [pe'θuɲa] *nf* hoof
piadoso, -a [pja'ðoso, a] *adj* (*devoto*) pious, devout; (*misericordioso*) kind, merciful

pianista [pja'nista] *nm/f* pianist
piano ['pjano] *nm* piano; **~ de cola** grand piano
piar [pjar] *vi* to cheep
PIB *nm abr* (*Esp Com:* = *Producto Interno Bruto*) GDP
pibe, -a ['piβe, a] *nm/f* (*Am*) boy/girl, kid, child
picadero [pika'ðero] *nm* riding school
picadillo [pika'ðiʎo] *nm* mince, minced meat
picado, -a [pi'kaðo, a] *adj* pricked, punctured; (*Culin*) minced, chopped; (*mar*) choppy; (*diente*) bad; (*tabaco*) cut; (*enfadado*) cross
picador [pika'ðor] *nm* (*Taur*) picador; (*minero*) faceworker
picadora [pika'ðora] *nf* mincer
picadura [pika'ðura] *nf* (*pinchazo*) puncture; (*de abeja*) sting; (*de mosquito*) bite; (*tabaco picado*) cut tobacco
picana [pi'kana] (*Am*) *nf* (*Agr*) cattle prod; (*Pol: para tortura*) electric prod
picante [pi'kante] *adj* (*comida, sabor*) hot; (*comentario*) racy, spicy
picaporte [pika'porte] *nm* (*tirador*) handle; (*pestillo*) latch
picar [pi'kar] *vt* (*agujerear, perforar*) to prick, puncture; (*billete*) to punch, clip; (*abeja*) to sting; (*mosquito, serpiente*) to bite; (*Culin*) to mince, chop; (*persona*) to nibble (at); (*incitar*) to incite, goad; (*dañar, irritar*) to annoy, bother; (*quemar: lengua*) to burn, sting ▷ *vi* (*pez*) to bite, take the bait; (*el sol*) to burn, scorch; (*abeja, Med*) to sting; (*mosquito*) to bite; **picarse** *vr* (*agriarse*) to turn sour, go off; (*mar*) to get choppy; (*ofenderse*) to take offence; **me pican los ojos** my eyes sting; **me pica el brazo** my arm itches
picardía [pikar'ðia] *nf* villainy; (*astucia*) slyness, craftiness; (*una picardía*) dirty trick; (*palabra*) rude/bad word *o* expression
pícaro, -a ['pikaro, a] *adj* (*malicioso*) villainous; (*travieso*) mischievous ▷ *nm* (*astuto*) sly sort; (*sinvergüenza*) rascal, scoundrel
pichi ['pitʃi] *nm* (*Esp*) pinafore dress (*Brit*), jumper (*US*)
pichón, -ona [pi'tʃon, ona] *nm/f* (*de paloma*) young pigeon; (*apelativo*) darling, dearest
pico ['piko] *nm* (*de ave*) beak; (*punta agudo*) peak, sharp point; (*Tec*) pick, pickaxe; (*Geo*) peak, summit; (*labia*) talkativeness; **no abrir el ~** to keep quiet; **~ parásito** (*Elec*) spike; **y ~** and a bit; **las seis y ~** six and a bit; **son las tres y ~** it's just after three; **tiene 50 libros y ~** he has 50-odd books; **me costó un ~** it cost me quite a bit
picor [pi'kor] *nm* itch; (*ardor*) sting(ing feeling)
picoso, -a (*Am*) [pi'koso, a] *adj* (*comida*) hot
picotear [pikote'ar] *vt* to peck ▷ *vi* to nibble, pick
picudo, -a [pi'kuðo, a] *adj* pointed, with a point
pidió *etc vb ver* **pedir**
pido *etc vb ver* **pedir**
pie [pje] (*pl* **pies**) *nm* (*gen, Mat*) foot; (*de cama, página, escalera*) foot, bottom; (*Teat*) cue; (*fig: motivo*) motive, basis; (*: fundamento*) foothold; **~s planos** flat feet; **ir a ~** to go on foot, walk; **estar de ~** to be standing (up); **ponerse de ~** to stand up; **al ~ de la letra** (*citar*) literally, verbatim; (*copiar*) exactly, word for word; **de ~s a cabeza** from head to foot; **en ~ de guerra** on a war footing; **sin ~s ni cabeza** pointless, absurd; **dar ~ a** to give cause for; **hacer ~** (*en el agua*) to touch (the) bottom; **no dar ~ con bola** to be no good at anything; **saber de qué ~ cojea algn** to know sb's weak spots
piedad [pje'ðað] *nf* (*lástima*) pity, compassion; (*clemencia*) mercy; (*devoción*) piety, devotion; **tener ~ de** to take pity on
piedra ['pjeðra] *nf* stone; (*roca*) rock; (*de mechero*) flint; (*Meteorología*) hailstone; **primera ~** foundation stone; **~ de afilar** grindstone; **~ arenisca/caliza** sand / limestone; **~ preciosa** precious stone
piel [pjel] *nf* (*Anat*) skin; (*Zool*) skin, hide; (*de oso*) fur; (*cuero*) leather; (*Bot*) skin, peel ▷ *nm/f*: **~ roja** redskin
pienso *etc* ['pjenso] *vb ver* **pensar** ▷ *nm* (*Agr*) feed
piercing ['pjersiŋ] *nm* piercing
pierdo *etc* ['pjerðo] *vb ver* **perder**
pierna ['pjerna] *nf* leg; **en ~s** bare-legged
pieza ['pjeθa] *nf* piece; (*esp Am: habitación*) room; (*Mus*) piece, composition; (*Teat*) work, play; **~ de recambio** *o* **repuesto** spare (part), extra (*US*); **~ de ropa** article of clothing; **quedarse de una ~** to be dumbfounded
pigmento [piɣ'mento] *nm* pigment
pigmeo, -a [piɣ'meo, a] *adj, nm/f* pigmy
pijama [pi'xama] *nm* pyjamas *pl*
pijo, -a ['pixo, a] *nm/f* (*fam*) upper-class twit
pila ['pila] *nf* (*Elec*) battery; (*montón*) heap, pile; (*de fuente*) sink; (*Rel: tb:* **~ bautismal**) font; **nombre de ~** Christian *o* first name; **tengo una ~ de cosas que hacer** (*fam*) I have heaps *o* stacks of things to do
pilar [pi'lar] *nm* pillar; (*de puente*) pier; (*fig*) prop, mainstay
Pilates [pi lates] *nm* Pilates
píldora ['pildora] *nf* pill; **la ~ (anticonceptiva)** the pill; **tragarse la ~** to be taken in
pileta [pi'leta] *nf* basin, bowl; (*Am: de cocina*) sink; (*: piscina*) swimming pool
pillaje [pi'ʎaxe] *nm* pillage, plunder
pillar [pi'ʎar] *vt* (*saquear*) to pillage, plunder; (*fam: coger*) to catch; (*: agarrar*) to grasp, seize; (*: entender*) to grasp, catch on to; (*suj: coche etc*) to run over; **pillarse** *vr*: **~se un dedo con la puerta** to catch one's finger in the door; **~ un resfriado** (*fam*) to catch a cold
pillo, -a ['piʎo, a] *adj* villainous; (*astuto*) sly, crafty ▷ *nm/f* rascal, rogue, scoundrel

P

pilotar [pilo'tar] *vt* (*avión*) to pilot; (*barco*) to steer
piloto [pi'loto] *nm* pilot; (*de aparato*) (pilot) light; (*Auto*) rear light, tail light; (*conductor*) driver ▷ *adj inv*: **planta ~** pilot plant; **luz ~** side light; **~ automático** automatic pilot
pimentón [pimen'ton] *nm* (*polvo*) paprika
pimienta [pi'mjenta] *nf* pepper
pimiento [pi'mjento] *nm* pepper, pimiento
pin (*pl* **pins**) [pin, pins] *nm* badge
pinacoteca [pinako'teka] *nf* art gallery
pinar [pi'nar] *nm* pinewood
pincel [pin'θel] *nm* paintbrush
pinchadiscos [pintʃa'diskos] *nm/f inv* disc jockey, DJ
pinchar [pin'tʃar] *vt* (*perforar*) to prick, pierce; (*neumático*) to puncture; (*incitar*) to prod; (*Inform*) to click ▷ *vi* (*Mus fam*) to be DJ; **pincharse** *vr* (*con droga*) to inject o.s.; (*neumático*) to burst, puncture; **no ~ ni cortar** (*fam*) to cut no ice; **tener un neumático pinchado** to have a puncture *o* a flat tyre
pinchazo [pin'tʃaθo] *nm* (*perforación*) prick; (*de llanta*) puncture, flat (*US*); (*fig*) prod
pincho ['pintʃo] *nm* point; (*aguijón*) spike; (*Culin*) savoury (snack); **~ moruno** shish kebab; **~ de tortilla** small slice of omelette
ping-pong ['pimpon] *nm* table tennis
pingüino [pin'gwino] *nm* penguin
pinitos [pi'nitos] *nmpl*: **hacer sus primeros ~** to take one's first steps
pino ['pino] *nm* pine (tree); **vivir en el quinto ~** to live at the back of beyond
pinta ['pinta] *nf* spot; (*gota*) spot, drop; (*aspecto*) appearance, look(s) *pl*; (*medida*) pint; **tener buena ~** to look good, look well; **por la ~** by the look of it
pintado, -a [pin'taðo, a] *adj* spotted; (*de muchos colores*) colourful ▷ *nf* piece of political graffiti; **pintados** *nfpl* political graffiti *sg*; **me sienta que ni ~, me viene que ni ~** it suits me a treat
pintalabios [pinta'laβjos] *nm inv* (*Esp*) lipstick
pintar [pin'tar] *vt* to paint ▷ *vi* to paint; (*fam*) to count, be important; **pintarse** *vr* to put on make-up; **pintárselas solo para hacer algo** to manage to do sth by o.s.; **no pinta nada** (*fam*) he has no say
pintor, a [pin'tor, a] *nm/f* painter; **~ de brocha gorda** house painter; (*fig*) bad painter
pintoresco, -a [pinto'resko, a] *adj* picturesque
pintura [pin'tura] *nf* painting; **~ a la acuarela** watercolour; **~ al óleo** oil painting; **~ rupestre** cave painting
pinza ['pinθa] *nf* (*Zool*) claw; (*para colgar ropa*) clothes peg, clothespin (*US*); (*Tec*) pincers *pl*; **pinzas** *nfpl* (*para depilar*) tweezers
piña ['piɲa] *nf* (*fruto del pino*) pine cone; (*fruta*) pineapple; (*fig*) group
piñata [pi'ɲata] *nf* piñata (*figurine hung up at parties to be beaten with sticks until sweets or presents fall out*)
piñón [pi'ɲon] *nm* (*Bot*) pine nut; (*Tec*) pinion
pío, -a ['pio, a] *adj* (*devoto*) pious, devout; (*misericordioso*) merciful ▷ *nm*: **no decir ni ~** not to breathe a word
piojo ['pjoxo] *nm* louse
pionero, -a [pjo'nero, a] *adj* pioneering ▷ *nm/f* pioneer
pipa ['pipa] *nf* pipe; (*Bot*) seed, pip; (*de girasol*) sunflower seed
pipí [pi'pi] *nm* (*fam*): **hacer ~** to have a wee(-wee)
pique *etc* ['pike] *vb ver* **picar** ▷ *nm* (*resentimiento*) pique, resentment; (*rivalidad*) rivalry, competition; **irse a ~** to sink; (*familia*) to be ruined; **tener un ~ con algn** to have a grudge against sb
piqueta [pi'keta] *nf* pick(axe)
piquete [pi'kete] *nm* (*agujerito*) small hole; (*Mil*) squad, party; (*de obreros*) picket; (*Am*: *de insecto*) bite; **~ secundario** secondary picket
pirado, -a [pi'raðo, a] *adj* (*fam*) round the bend ▷ *nm/f* nutter
piragua [pi'raɣwa] *nf* canoe
piragüismo [pira'ɣwismo] *nm* (*Deporte*) canoeing
pirámide [pi'ramiðe] *nf* pyramid
piraña [pi'raɲa] *nf* piranha
pirarse [pi'rarse] *vr*: **~(las)** (*largarse*) to beat it (*fam*); (*Escol*) to cut class
pirata [pi'rata] *adj*: **edición/disco ~** pirate edition/bootleg record ▷ *nm* pirate; (*tb*: **~ informático**) hacker
Pirineo, Pirineos [piri'neo(s)] *nm(pl)* Pyrenees *pl*
pirómano, -a [pi'romano, a] *nm/f* (*Psico*) pyromaniac; (*Jur*) arsonist
piropo [pi'ropo] *nm* compliment, (piece of) flattery; **echar ~s a** to make flirtatious remarks to
pirueta [pi'rweta] *nf* pirouette
piruleta [piru'leta] *nf* lollipop
pis [pis] *nm* (*fam*) pee; **hacer ~** to have a pee; (*para niños*) to wee-wee
pisada [pi'saða] *nf* (*paso*) footstep; (*huella*) footprint
pisar [pi'sar] *vt* (*caminar sobre*) to walk on, tread on; (*apretar con el pie*) to press; (*fig*) to trample on, walk all over ▷ *vi* to tread, step, walk; **~ el acelerador** to step on the accelerator; **~ fuerte** (*fig*) to act determinedly
piscifactoría [pisθifakto'ria] *nf* fish farm
piscina [pis'θina] *nf* swimming pool
Piscis ['pisθis] *nm* (*Astro*) Pisces
piso ['piso] *nm* (*suelo*: *de edificio*) floor; (*Am*) ground; (*apartamento*) flat, apartment; **primer ~** (*Esp*) first *o* second (*US*) floor; (*Am*) ground *o* first (*US*) floor
pisotear [pisote'ar] *vt* to trample (on *o* underfoot); (*fig*: *humillar*) to trample on

pisotón ['piso'ton] *nm (con el pie)* stamp
pista ['pista] *nf* track, trail; *(indicio)* clue; *(Inform)* track; **~ de auditoría** *(Com)* audit trail; **~ de aterrizaje** runway; **~ de baile** dance floor; **~ de tenis** tennis court; **~ de hielo** ice rink; **estar sobre la ~ de algn** to be on sb's trail
pisto ['pisto] *nm (Culin)* ratatouille; **darse ~** *(fam)* to show off
pistola [pis'tola] *nf* pistol; *(Tec)* spray-gun
pistolero, -a [pisto'lero, a] *nm/f* gunman, gangster ▷ *nf* holster
pistón [pis'ton] *nm (Tec)* piston; *(Mus)* key
pitar [pi'tar] *vt (hacer sonar)* to blow; *(partido)* to referee; *(rechiflar)* to whistle at, boo; *(actor, obra)* to hiss ▷ *vi* to whistle; *(Auto)* to sound *o* toot one's horn; *(Am)* to smoke; **salir pitando** to beat it
pitido [pi'tiðo] *nm* whistle; *(sonido agudo)* beep; *(sonido corto)* pip
pitillera [piti'ʎera] *nf* cigarette case
pitillo [pi'tiʎo] *nm* cigarette
pito ['pito] *nm* whistle; *(de coche)* horn; *(cigarrillo)* cigarette; *(fam: de marihuana)* joint; *(fam!)* prick *(!)*; **me importa un ~** I don't care two hoots
pitón [pi'ton] *nm (Zool)* python
pitonisa [pito'nisa] *nf* fortune-teller
pitorreo [pito'rreo] *nm* joke, laugh; **estar de ~** to be in a joking mood
píxel ['piksel] *nm (Inform)* pixel
piyama [pi'jama] *nm (Am)* pyjamas *pl*, pajamas *(US) pl*
pizarra [pi'θarra] *nf (piedra)* slate; *(encerado)* blackboard; **~ blanca** whiteboard; **~ interactiva** interactive whiteboard
pizarrón [piθa'rron] *nm (Am)* blackboard
pizca ['piθka] *nf* pinch, spot; *(fig)* spot, speck, trace; **ni ~** not a bit
pizza ['pitsa] *nf* pizza
placa ['plaka] *nf* plate; *(Med)* dental plate; *(distintivo)* badge; **~ de matrícula** number plate; **~ madre** *(Inform)* mother board; **~ fotovoltaica** solar panel
placaje [pla'kaxe] *nm* tackle
placard [pla'kar] *nm (Am)* built-in cupboard, (clothes) closet *(US)*
placenta [pla'θenta] *nf* placenta; *(tras el parto)* afterbirth
placentero, -a [plaθen'tero, a] *adj* pleasant, agreeable
placer [pla'θer] *nm* pleasure ▷ *vt* to please; **a ~** at one's pleasure
plácido, -a ['plaθiðo, a] *adj* placid
plaga ['plaɣa] *nf (Zool)* pest; *(Med)* plague; *(fig)* swarm; abundance
plagar [pla'ɣar] *vt* to infest, plague; *(llenar)* to fill; **plagado de** riddled with; **han plagado la ciudad de carteles** they have plastered the town with posters
plagiar [pla'gjar] *vt* to plagiarize; *(Am)* to kidnap
plagio ['plaxjo] *nm* plagiarism; *(Am)* kidnap
plan [plan] *nm (esquema, proyecto)* plan; *(idea, intento)* idea, intention; *(de curso)* programme; **~ cotizable de jubilación** contributory pension scheme; **~ de estudios** curriculum, syllabus; **~ de incentivos** *(Com)* incentive scheme; **tener ~** *(fam)* to have a date; **tener un ~** *(fam)* to have an affair; **en ~ de cachondeo** for a laugh; **en ~ económico** *(fam)* on the cheap; **vamos en ~ de turismo** we're going as tourists; **si te pones en ese ~ ...** if that's your attitude ...
plana ['plana] *nf ver* **plano**
plancha ['plantʃa] *nf (para planchar)* iron; *(rótulo)* plate, sheet; *(Naut)* gangway; *(Culin)* grill; **pescado a la ~** grilled fish; **~ de pelo** straighteners; **a la ~** *(Culin)* grilled
planchado, -a [plan'tʃaðo, a] *adj (ropa)* ironed; *(traje)* pressed ▷ *nm* ironing
planchar [plan'tʃar] *vt* to iron ▷ *vi* to do the ironing
planeador [planea'ðor] *nm* glider
planear [plane'ar] *vt* to plan ▷ *vi* to glide
planeta [pla'neta] *nm* planet
planicie [pla'niθje] *nf* plain
planificación [planifika'θjon] *nf* planning; **~ corporativa** *(Com)* corporate planning; **~ familiar** family planning; **diagrama de ~** *(Com)* planner
plano, -a ['plano, a] *adj* flat, level, even; *(liso)* smooth ▷ *nm (Mat, Tec, Aviat)* plane; *(Foto)* shot; *(Arq)* plan; *(Geo)* map; *(de ciudad)* map, street plan ▷ *nf* sheet of paper, page; *(Tec)* trowel; **primer ~** close-up; **caer de ~** to fall flat; **rechazar algo de ~** to turn sth down flat; **le daba el sol de ~** *(fig)* the sun shone directly on it; **en primera plana** on the front page; **plana mayor** staff
planta ['planta] *nf (Bot, Tec)* plant; *(Anat)* sole of the foot, foot; *(piso)* floor; *(Am: personal)* staff; **~ baja** ground floor
plantación [planta'θjon] *nf (Agr)* plantation; *(acto)* planting
plantar [plan'tar] *vt (Bot)* to plant; *(puesto)* to put in; *(levantar)* to erect, set up; **plantarse** *vr* to stand firm; **~ a algn en la calle** to chuck sb out; **dejar plantado a algn** *(fam)* to stand sb up; **~se en** to reach, get to
plantear [plante'ar] *vt (problema)* to pose; *(dificultad)* to raise; **se lo ~é** I'll put it to him
plantilla [plan'tiʎa] *nf (de zapato)* insole; *(personal)* personnel; **ser de ~** to be on the staff
plantón [plan'ton] *nm (Mil)* guard, sentry; *(fam)* long wait; **dar (un) ~ a algn** to stand sb up
plañir [pla'ɲir] *vi* to mourn
plasma ['plasma] *nm* plasma
plasta ['plasta] *nm/f (Esp: fam)* bore ▷ *nf* soft mass, lump; *(desastre)* botch, mess ▷ *adj (Esp: fam)* boring
plástico, -a ['plastiko, a] *adj* plastic ▷ *nf* (art of) sculpture, modelling ▷ *nm* plastic

P

Plastilina® [plasti'lina] *nf* Plasticine®
plata ['plata] *nf* (*metal*) silver; (*cosas hechas de plata*) silverware; (*Am*) cash, dough (*fam*); **hablar en ~** to speak bluntly *o* frankly
plataforma [plata'forma] *nf* platform; **~ de lanzamiento/perforación** launch(ing) pad/ drilling rig
plátano ['platano] *nm* (*fruta*) banana; (*árbol*) plane tree; banana tree
platea [pla'tea] *nf* (*Teat*) pit
plateado, -a [plate'aðo, a] *adj* silver; (*Tec*) silver-plated
plática ['platika] *nf* (*Am*) talk, chat; (*Rel*) sermon
platicar [plati'kar] *vi* (*Am*) to talk, chat
platillo [pla'tiʎo] *nm* saucer; (*de limosnas*) collecting bowl; **platillos** *nmpl* cymbals; **~ volador** *o* **volante** flying saucer; **pasar el ~** to pass the hat round
platina [pla'tina] *nf* (*Mus*) tape deck
platino [pla'tino] *nm* platinum; **platinos** *nmpl* (*Auto*) (contact) points
plato ['plato] *nm* plate, dish; (*parte de comida*) course; (*guiso*) dish; **~ frutero/sopero** fruit/ soup dish; **primer ~** first course; **~ combinado** set main course (*served on one plate*); **~ fuerte** main course; **pagar los ~s rotos** (*fam*) to carry the can (*fam*)
plató [pla'to] *nm* set
platónico, -a [pla'toniko, a] *adj* platonic
playa ['plaja] *nf* beach; (*costa*) seaside; **~ de estacionamiento** (*Am*) car park
playero, -a [pla'jero, a] *adj* beach *cpd* ▷ *nf* (*Am: camiseta*) T-shirt; **playeras** *nfpl* canvas shoes; (*Tenis*) tennis shoes
plaza ['plaθa] *nf* square; (*mercado*) market(place); (*sitio*) room, space; (*en vehículo*) seat, place; (*colocación*) post, job; **~ de abastos** food market; **~ mayor** main square; **~ de toros** bullring; **hacer la ~** to do the daily shopping; **reservar una ~** to reserve a seat; **el hotel tiene 100 ~s** the hotel has 100 beds
plazo ['plaθo] *nm* (*lapso de tiempo*) time, period, term; (*fecha de vencimiento*) expiry date; (*pago parcial*) instalment; **a corto/largo ~** short-/ long-term; **comprar a ~s** to buy on hire purchase, pay for in instalments; **nos dan un ~ de ocho días** they allow us a week
plazoleta [plaθo'leta], **plazuela** [pla'θwela] *nf* small square
pleamar [plea'mar] *nf* high tide
plebe ['pleβe] *nf*: **la ~** the common people *pl*, the masses *pl*; (*pey*) the plebs *pl*
plebeyo, -a [ple'βejo, a] *adj* plebeian; (*pey*) coarse, common
plebiscito [pleβis'θito] *nm* plebiscite
plegable [ple'ɣaβle] *adj* pliable; (*silla*) folding
plegar [ple'ɣar] *vt* (*doblar*) to fold, bend; (*Costura*) to pleat; **plegarse** *vr* to yield, submit
pleito ['pleito] *nm* (*Jur*) lawsuit, case; (*fig*) dispute, feud; **pleitos** *nmpl* litigation *sg*; **entablar ~** to bring an action *o* a lawsuit; **poner ~** to sue
plenilunio [pleni'lunjo] *nm* full moon
plenitud [pleni'tuð] *nf* plenitude, fullness; (*abundancia*) abundance
pleno, -a ['pleno, a] *adj* full; (*completo*) complete ▷ *nm* plenum; **en ~** as a whole; (*por unanimidad*) unanimously; **en ~ día** in broad daylight; **en ~ verano** at the height of summer; **en plena cara** full in the face
pletina *nf* (*Mus*) tape deck
pliego ['pljeɣo] *vb ver* **plegar** ▷ *nm* (*hoja*) sheet (of paper); (*carta*) sealed letter/document; **~ de condiciones** details *pl*, specifications *pl*
pliegue ['pljeɣe] *vb ver* **plegar** ▷ *nm* fold, crease; (*de vestido*) pleat
plisado [pli'saðo] *nm* pleating
plomería [plome'ria] *nf* (*Am*) plumbing
plomero [plo'mero] *nm* (*Am*) plumber
plomo ['plomo] *nm* (*metal*) lead; (*Elec*) fuse; **sin ~** unleaded; **caer a ~** to fall heavily *o* flat
pluma ['pluma] *nf* (*Zool*) feather; (*para escribir*): **~ (estilográfica)** ink pen; **~ fuente** (*Am*) fountain pen
plumero [plu'mero] *nm* (*quitapolvos*) feather duster; **ya te veo el ~** I know what you're up to
plumón [plu'mon] *nm* (*de ave*) down; (*Am*) felt-tip pen
plural [plu'ral] *adj* plural ▷ *nm*: **en ~** in the plural
pluralidad [plurali'ðað] *nf* plurality; **una ~ de votos** a majority of votes
pluriempleo [pluriem'pleo] *nm* having more than one job
plus [plus] *nm* bonus
plusvalía [plusβa'lia] *nf* (*mayor valor*) appreciation, added value; (*Com*) goodwill
plutocracia [pluto'kraθja] *nf* plutocracy
PNB *nm abr* (*Esp Com*: = *Producto Nacional Bruto*) GNP
población [poβla'θjon] *nf* population; (*pueblo, ciudad*) town, city; **~ activa** working population
poblado, -a [po'βlaðo, a] *adj* inhabited; (*barba*) thick; (*cejas*) bushy ▷ *nm* (*aldea*) village; (*pueblo*) (small) town; **~ de** (*lleno de*) filled with; **densamente ~** densely populated
poblador, a [poβla'ðor, a] *nm/f* settler, colonist
poblar [po'βlar] *vt* (*colonizar*) to colonize; (*fundar*) to found; (*habitar*) to inhabit; **poblarse** *vr*: **~se de** to fill up with; (*irse cubriendo*) to become covered with
pobre ['poβre] *adj* poor ▷ *nm/f* poor person; (*mendigo*) beggar; **los ~s** the poor; **¡~!** poor thing!; **~ diablo** (*fig*) poor wretch *o* devil
pobreza [po'βreθa] *nf* poverty; **~ energética** fuel poverty
pocilga [po'θilɣa] *nf* pigsty
pocillo [po'siʎo] *nm* (*Am*) coffee cup

pócima ['poθima], **poción** [po'θjon] *nf* potion; (*brebaje*) concoction, nasty drink

PALABRA CLAVE

poco, -a ['poko, a] *adj* **1** (*sg*) little, not much; **poco tiempo** little *o* not much time; **de poco interés** of little interest, not very interesting; **poca cosa** not much
2 (*pl*) few, not many; **unos pocos** a few, some; **pocos niños comen lo que les conviene** few children eat what they should
▷ *adv* **1** little, not much; **cuesta poco** it doesn't cost much; **poco más o menos** more or less
2 (+ *adj*: *negativo, antónimo*): **poco amable/inteligente** not very nice/intelligent
3: **por poco me caigo** I almost fell
4 (*tiempo*): **poco después** soon after that; **dentro de poco** shortly; **hace poco** a short time ago, not long ago; **a poco de haberse casado** shortly after getting married
5: **poco a poco** little by little
6 (*Am*): **¿a poco no está divino?** isn't it just divine?; **de a poco** gradually
▷ *nm* a little, a bit; **un poco triste/de dinero** a little sad/money

podar [po'ðar] *vt* to prune
podcast ['poðkast] *nm* podcast
podcastear [poðkaste'ar] *vi* to podcast
poder [po'ðer] *vi* **1** (*capacidad*) can, be able to; **no puedo hacerlo** I can't do it, I'm unable to do it
2 (*permiso*) can, may, be allowed to; **¿se puede?** may I (*o* we)?; **puedes irte ahora** you may go now; **no se puede fumar en este hospital** smoking is not allowed in this hospital
3 (*posibilidad*) may, might, could; **puede llegar mañana** he may *o* might arrive tomorrow; **pudiste haberte hecho daño** you might *o* could have hurt yourself; **¡podías habérmelo dicho antes!** you might have told me before!
4: **puede (ser)** perhaps; **puede que lo sepa Tomás** Tomás may *o* might know
5: **¡no puedo más!** I've had enough!; **no pude menos que dejarlo** I couldn't help but leave it; **es tonto a más no** ~ he's as stupid as they come
6: ~ **con**: **no puedo con este crío** this kid's too much for me; **¿puedes con eso?** can you manage that?
7: **él me puede** (*fam*) he's stronger than me
▷ *nm* power; **el** ~ the Government; ~ **adquisitivo** purchasing power; **detentar** *u* **ocupar** *o* **estar en el** ~ to be in power *o* office; **estar** *u* **obrar en** ~ **de** to be in the hands *o* possession of; **por** ~**(es)** by proxy; ~ **judicial** judiciary

poderoso, -a [poðe'roso, a] *adj* powerful
podio ['poðjo] *nm* podium
podium ['poðjum] = **podio**
podólogo, -a [po'ðoloɣo, a] *nm/f* chiropodist (*Brit*), podiatrist (*US*)
podrido, -a [po'ðriðo, a] *adj* rotten, bad; (*fig*) rotten, corrupt
podrir [po'ðrir] = **pudrir**
poema [po'ema] *nm* poem
poesía [poe'sia] *nf* poetry
poeta [po'eta] *nm* poet
poético, -a [po'etiko, a] *adj* poetic(al)
poetisa [poe'tisa] *nf* (woman) poet
póker ['poker] *nm* poker
polaco, -a [po'lako, a] *adj* Polish ▷ *nm/f* Pole ▷ *nm* (*Ling*) Polish
polar [po'lar] *adj* polar
polaridad [polari'ðað] *nf* polarity
polea [po'lea] *nf* pulley
polémica [po'lemika] *nf* polemics *sg*; (*una polémica*) controversy
polémico, -a [po'lemiko, a] *adj* polemic(al)
polen ['polen] *nm* pollen
poleo [po'leo] *nm* pennyroyal
policía [poli'θia] *nm/f* policeman(-woman) ▷ *nf* police; *see note*

POLICÍA

There are two branches of the police, both armed: the *policía nacional*, in charge of national security and public order in general, and the *policía municipal*, with duties of regulating traffic and policing the local community. Catalonia and the Basque Country have their own police forces, the *Mossos d'Esquadra* and the *Ertzaintza* respectively.

policíaco, -a [poli'θiako, a] *adj* police *cpd*; **novela policíaca** detective story
policial [poli'θjal] *adj* police *cpd*
polideportivo [poliðepor'tiβo] *nm* sports centre
poliéster [poli'ester] *nm* polyester
polietileno [polieti'leno] *nm* polythene (*Brit*), polyethylene (*US*)
poligamia [poli'ɣamja] *nf* polygamy
polígono [po'liɣono] *nm* (*Mat*) polygon; (*solar*) building lot; (*zona*) area; (*unidad vecina*) housing estate; ~ **industrial** industrial estate
polígrafo [po'liɣrafo] *nm* polygraph
polilla [po'liʎa] *nf* moth
polio ['poljo] *nf* polio
politécnico [poli'tekniko] *nm* polytechnic
político, -a [po'litiko, a] *adj* political; (*discreto*) tactful; (*pariente*) in-law ▷ *nm/f* politician ▷ *nf* politics *sg*; (*económica, agraria*) policy; **padre** ~ father-in-law; **política exterior/de ingresos y precios** foreign/prices and incomes policy

póliza ['poliθa] *nf* certificate, voucher; (*impuesto*) tax *o* fiscal stamp; **~ de seguro(s)** insurance policy
polizón [poli'θon] *nm* (*Aviat, Naut*) stowaway
pollera [po'ʎera] *nf* (*criadero*) hencoop; (*Am*) skirt, overskirt
pollería [poʎe'ria] *nf* poulterer's (shop)
pollo ['poʎo] *nm* chicken; (*joven*) young man; (*señorito*) playboy; **~ asado** roast chicken
polo ['polo] *nm* (*Geo, Elec*) pole; (*helado*) ice lolly (*Brit*), Popsicle® (*US*); (*Deporte*) polo; (*suéter*) polo-neck; **P~ Norte/Sur** North/South Pole; **esto es el ~ opuesto de lo que dijo antes** this is the exact opposite of what he said before
Polonia [po'lonja] *nf* Poland
poltrona [pol'trona] *nf* reclining chair, easy chair
polución [polu'θjon] *nf* pollution; **~ ambiental** environmental pollution
polvera [pol'βera] *nf* powder compact
polvo ['polβo] *nm* dust; (*Química, Culin, Med*) powder; (*fam!*) screw (*!*); **polvos** *nmpl* (*maquillaje*) powder *sg*; **en ~** powdered; **~ de talco** talcum powder; **estar hecho ~** to be worn out *o* exhausted; **hacer algo ~** to smash sth; **hacer ~ a algn** to shatter sb; *ver tb* **polvos**
pólvora ['polβora] *nf* gunpowder; (*fuegos artificiales*) fireworks *pl*; **propagarse como la ~** (*noticia*) to spread like wildfire
polvoriento, -a [polβo'rjento, a] *adj* (*superficie*) dusty; (*sustancia*) powdery
pomada [po'maða] *nf* cream
pomelo [po'melo] *nm* grapefruit
pómez ['pomeθ] *nf*: **piedra ~** pumice stone
pomo ['pomo] *nm* knob, handle
pompa ['pompa] *nf* (*burbuja*) bubble; (*bomba*) pump; (*esplendor*) pomp, splendour; **~s fúnebres** funeral *sg*
pomposo, -a [pom'poso, a] *adj* splendid, magnificent; (*pey*) pompous
pómulo ['pomulo] *nm* cheekbone
pon [pon] *vb ver* **poner**
ponchadura [pontʃa'dura] *nf* (*Am*) puncture (*Brit*), flat (*US*)
ponchar [pon'tʃar] *vt* (*Am: llanta*) to puncture
ponche ['pontʃe] *nm* punch
poncho ['pontʃo] *nm* (*Am*) poncho, cape
ponderar [ponde'rar] *vt* (*considerar*) to weigh up, consider; (*elogiar*) to praise highly, speak in praise of
pondré *etc* [pon'dre] *vb ver* **poner**

PALABRA CLAVE

poner [po'ner] *vt* **1** to put; (*colocar*) to place, set; (*ropa*) to put on; (*problema, la mesa*) to set; (*interés*) to show; (*telegrama*) to send; (*obra de teatro*) to put on; (*película*) to show; **ponlo más alto** turn it up; **¿qué ponen en el Excelsior?** what's on at the Excelsior?; **poner algo a secar** to put sth (out) to dry; **¡no pongas esa cara!** don't look at me like that!
2 (*tienda*) to open; (*instalar: gas etc*) to put in; (*radio, TV*) to switch *o* turn on
3 (*suponer*): **pongamos que ...** let's suppose that ...
4 (*contribuir*): **el gobierno ha puesto otro millón** the government has contributed another million
5 (*Telec*): **póngame con el Sr. López** can you put me through to Mr. López?
6: **poner de**: **le han puesto de director general** they've appointed him general manager
7 (*+ adj*) to make; **me estás poniendo nerviosa** you're making me nervous
8 (*dar nombre*): **al hijo le pusieron Diego** they called their son Diego
9 (*estar escrito*) to say; **¿qué pone aquí?** what does it say here?
▷ *vi* (*gallina*) to lay
ponerse *vr* **1** (*colocarse*): **se puso a mi lado** he came and stood beside me; **tú ponte en esa silla** you go and sit on that chair; **ponerse en camino** to set off
2 (*vestido, cosméticos*) to put on; **¿por qué no te pones el vestido nuevo?** why don't you put on *o* wear your new dress?
3 (*sol*) to set
4 (*+ adj*) to get, become; to turn; **ponerse enfermo/gordo/triste** to get ill/fat/sad; **se puso muy serio** he got very serious; **después de lavarla la tela se puso azul** after washing it the material turned blue; **¡no te pongas así!** don't be like that!; **ponerse cómodo** to make o.s. comfortable
5: **ponerse a**, **se puso a llorar** he started to cry; **tienes que ponerte a estudiar** you must get down to studying; **ponerse a bien con algn** to make it up with sb; **ponerse a mal con algn** to get on the wrong side of sb
6 (*Am*): **se me pone que ...** it seems to me that ..., I think that ...

pongo *etc* ['pongo] *vb ver* **poner**
poniente [po'njente] *nm* west; (*viento*) west wind
pontificado [pontifi'kaðo] *nm* papacy, pontificate
pontífice [pon'tifiθe] *nm* pope, pontiff; **el Sumo P~** His Holiness the Pope
pontón [pon'ton] *nm* pontoon
ponzoña [pon'θoɲa] *nf* poison, venom
pop [pop] *adj inv, nm* (*Mus*) pop
popa ['popa] *nf* stern; **a ~** astern, abaft; **de ~ a proa** fore and aft
popote [po'pote] *nm* (*Am*) straw
popular [popu'lar] *adj* popular; (*del pueblo*) of the people
popularidad [populari'ðað] *nf* popularity

PALABRA CLAVE

por [por] *prep* **1** (*objetivo*) for; **luchar por la patria** to fight for one's country; **hazlo por mí** do it for my sake
2 (+ *infin*): **por no llegar tarde** so as not to arrive late; **por citar unos ejemplos** to give a few examples
3 (*causa*) out of, because of; **no es por eso** that's not the reason; **por escasez de fondos** through *o* for lack of funds
4 (*tiempo*): **por la mañana/noche** in the morning/at night; **se queda por una semana** she's staying (for) a week
5 (*lugar*): **pasar por Madrid** to pass through Madrid; **ir a Guayaquil por Quito** to go to Guayaquil via Quito; **caminar por la calle** to walk along the street; **por allí** over there; **se va por ahí** we have to go that way; **¿hay un banco por aquí?** is there a bank near here?; **¿por dónde?** which way?; **está por el norte** it's somewhere in the north; **por todo el país** throughout the country
6 (*cambio, precio*): **te doy uno nuevo por el que tienes** I'll give you a new one (in return) for the one you've got; **lo vendí por 15 dólares** I sold it for 15 dollars
7 (*valor distributivo*): **30 euros por hora/cabeza** 30 euros an *o* per hour/a *o* per head; **10 por ciento** 10 per cent; **80 (kms) por hora** 80 (km) an *o* per hour
8 (*modo, medio*) by; **por correo/avión** by post/air; **día por día** day by day; **por orden** in order; **entrar por la entrada principal** to go in through the main entrance
9 (*agente*) by; **hecho por él** done by him; **"dirigido por"** "directed by"
10: **10 por 10 son 100** 10 by 10 is 100
11 (*en lugar de*): **vino él por su jefe** he came instead of his boss
12: **por mí que revienten** as far as I'm concerned they can drop dead
13 (*evidencia*): **por lo que dicen** judging by *o* from what they say
14: **estar/quedar por hacer** to be still *o* remain to be done
15: **por (muy) difícil que sea** however hard it is *o* may be; **por más que lo intente** no matter how *o* however hard I try
16: **por qué** why; **¿por qué?** why?; **¿por qué no?** why not?; **¿por?** (*fam*) why (do you ask)?

porcelana [porθe'lana] *nf* porcelain; (*china*) china
porcentaje [porθen'taxe] *nm* percentage; **~ de actividad** (*Inform*) hit rate
porción [por'θjon] *nf* (*parte*) portion, share; (*cantidad*) quantity, amount
pordiosero, -a [porðjo'sero, a] *nm/f* beggar
porfía [por'fia] *nf* persistence; (*terquedad*) obstinacy
porfiado, -a [por'fjaðo, a] *adj* persistent; obstinate
porfiar [por'fjar] *vi* to persist, insist; (*disputar*) to argue stubbornly
pormenor [porme'nor] *nm* detail, particular
porno ['porno] *adj inv* porno ▷ *nm* porn
pornografía [pornoɣra'fia] *nf* pornography
poro ['poro] *nm* pore
pororó [poro'ro] *nm* (*Am*) popcorn
poroso, -a [po'roso, a] *adj* porous
poroto [po'roto] *nm* (*Am*) kidney bean
porque ['porke] *conj* (*a causa de*) because; (*ya que*) since; (*con el fin de*) so that, in order that; **~ sí** because I feel like it
porqué [por'ke] *nm* reason, cause
porquería [porke'ria] *nf* (*suciedad*) filth, muck, dirt; (*acción*) dirty trick; (*objeto*) small thing, trifle; (*fig*) rubbish
porra ['porra] *nf* (*arma*) stick, club; (*cachiporra*) truncheon; **¡~s!** oh heck!; **¡vete a la ~!** go to heck!
porrazo [po'rraθo] *nm* (*golpe*) blow; (*caída*) bump; **de un ~** in one go
porro ['porro] *nm* (*fam: droga*) joint
porrón [po'rron] *nm glass wine jar with a long spout*
portaaviones [port(a)a'βjones] *nm inv* aircraft carrier
portada [por'taða] *nf* (*Tip*) title page; (*: de revista*) cover
portador, a [porta'ðor, a] *nm/f* carrier, bearer; (*Com*) bearer, payee; (*Med*) carrier; **ser ~ del virus del sida** to be HIV-positive
portaequipajes [portaeki'paxes] *nm inv* boot (*Brit*), trunk (*US*); (*baca*) luggage rack
portafolio [porta'foljo], **portafolios** [porta'foljos] *nm* (*Am*) briefcase; **~(s) de inversiones** (*Com*) investment portfolio
portal [por'tal] *nm* (*entrada*) vestibule, hall; (*pórtico*) porch, doorway; (*puerta de entrada*) main door; (*Deporte*) goal; (*Internet*) portal; **portales** *nmpl* arcade *sg*
portamaletas [portama'letas] *nm inv* (*Auto: maletero*) boot; (*: baca*) roof rack
portamonedas [portamo'neðas] *nm inv* (*LAm*) purse
portar [por'tar] *vt* to carry, bear; **portarse** *vr* to behave, conduct o.s.; **~se mal** to misbehave; **se portó muy bien conmigo** he treated me very well
portátil [por'tatil] *adj* portable; **(ordenador) ~** laptop (computer)
portaviones [porta'βjones] *nm inv* aircraft carrier
portavoz [porta'βoθ] *nm/f* spokesman(-woman)
portazo [por'taθo] *nm*: **dar un ~** to slam the door
porte ['porte] *nm* (*Com*) transport; (*precio*) transport charges *pl*; (*Correos*) postage; **~ debido** (*Com*) carriage forward; **~ pagado** (*Com*) carriage paid, post-paid

P

portento [por'tento] *nm* marvel, wonder
portentoso, -a [porten'toso, a] *adj* marvellous, extraordinary
porteño, -a [por'teɲo, a] *adj* of *o* from Buenos Aires ▷ *nm/f* native *o* inhabitant of Buenos Aires
portería [porte'ria] *nf* (*oficina*) porter's office; (*gol*) goal
portero, -a [por'tero, a] *nm/f* porter; (*conserje*) caretaker; (*ujier*) doorman; (*Deporte*) goalkeeper; ~ **automático** (*Esp*) entry phone
pórtico ['portiko] *nm* (*porche*) portico, porch; (*fig*) gateway; (*arcada*) arcade
portilla [por'tiʎa] *nf*, **portillo** [por'tiʎo] *nm* gate
portorriqueño, -a [portorri'keɲo, a] *adj, nm/f* Puerto Rican
Portugal [portu'ɣal] *nm* Portugal
portugués, -esa [portu'ɣes, esa] *adj, nm/f* Portuguese ▷ *nm* (*Ling*) Portuguese
porvenir [porβe'nir] *nm* future
pos [pos]: **en ~ de** *prep* after, in pursuit of
posada [po'saða] *nf* (*refugio*) shelter, lodging; (*mesón*) guest house; **dar ~ a** to give shelter to, take in
posaderas [posa'ðeras] *nfpl* backside *sg*, buttocks
posar [po'sar] *vt* (*en el suelo*) to lay down, put down; (*la mano*) to place, put gently ▷ *vi* to sit, pose; **posarse** *vr* to settle; (*pájaro*) to perch; (*avión*) to land, come down
posavasos [posa'basos] *nm inv* coaster; (*para cerveza*) beermat
posdata [pos'ðata] *nf* postscript
pose ['pose] *nf* (*Arte, afectación*) pose
poseedor, a [posee'ðor, a] *nm/f* owner, possessor; (*de récord, puesto*) holder
poseer [pose'er] *vt* to have, possess, own; (*ventaja*) to enjoy; (*récord, puesto*) to hold
poseído, -a [pose'iðo, a] *adj* possessed; **estar muy ~ de** to be very vain about
posesión [pose'sjon] *nf* possession; **tomar ~ (de)** to take over
posesivo, -a [pose'siβo, a] *adj* possessive
posgrado [pos'ɣraðo] *nm* = **postgrado**
posibilidad [posiβili'ðað] *nf* possibility; (*oportunidad*) chance
posibilitar [posiβili'tar] *vt* to make possible, permit; (*hacer factible*) to make feasible
posible [po'siβle] *adj* possible; (*factible*) feasible ▷ *nm*: **~s** means; (*bienes*) funds, assets; **de ser ~** if possible; **en** *o* **dentro de lo ~** as far as possible; **lo antes ~** as quickly as possible
posición [posi'θjon] *nf* (*gen*) position; (*rango social*) status
positivo, -a [posi'tiβo, a] *adj* positive ▷ *nf* (*Foto*) print
poso ['poso] *nm* sediment; (*heces*) dregs *pl*
posoperatorio, -a [posopera'torjo, a] *adj, nm* = **postoperatorio**
posponer [pospo'ner] *vt* (*relegar*) to put behind *o* below; (*aplazar*) to postpone
posta ['posta] *nf* (*de caballos*) relay, team; **a ~** on purpose, deliberately
postal [pos'tal] *adj* postal ▷ *nf* postcard
poste ['poste] *nm* (*de telégrafos*) post, pole; (*columna*) pillar
póster (*pl* **posters**) ['poster, 'posters] *nm* poster
postergar [poster'ɣar] *vt* (*esp Am*) to put off, postpone, delay
posteridad [posteri'ðað] *nf* posterity
posterior [poste'rjor] *adj* back, rear; (*siguiente*) following, subsequent; (*más tarde*) later; **ser ~ a** to be later than
posterioridad [posterjori'ðað] *nf*: **con ~** later, subsequently
postgrado [post'ɣraðo] *nm*: **curso de ~** postgraduate course
postizo, -a [pos'tiθo, a] *adj* false, artificial; (*sonrisa*) false, phoney ▷ *nm* hairpiece
postoperatorio, -a [postopera'torjo, a] *adj* postoperative ▷ *nm* postoperative period
postor, a [pos'tor, a] *nm/f* bidder; **mejor ~** highest bidder
postrado, -a [pos'traðo, a] *adj* prostrate
postre ['postre] *nm* sweet, dessert ▷ *nf*: **a la ~** in the end, when all is said and done; **para ~** (*fam*) to crown it all; **llegar a los ~s** (*fig*) to come too late
postrero, -a [pos'trero, a] *adj* (*antes de nmsg* **postrer**) (*último*) last; (*: que viene detrás*) rear
postulado [postu'laðo] *nm* postulate
póstumo, -a ['postumo, a] *adj* posthumous
postura [pos'tura] *nf* (*del cuerpo*) posture, position; (*fig*) attitude, position
potable [po'taβle] *adj* drinkable; **agua ~** drinking water
potaje [po'taxe] *nm* thick vegetable soup
pote ['pote] *nm* pot, jar
potencia [po'tenθja] *nf* power; (*capacidad*) capacity; **~ (en caballos)** horsepower; **en ~** potential, in the making; **las grandes ~s** the great powers
potencial [poten'θjal] *adj, nm* potential
potenciar [poten'θjar] *vt* (*promover*) to promote; (*fortalecer*) to boost
potente [po'tente] *adj* powerful
potro ['potro] *nm* (*Zool*) colt; (*Deporte*) vaulting horse
pozo ['poθo] *nm* well; (*de río*) deep pool; (*de mina*) shaft; **~ negro** cesspool; **ser un ~ de ciencia** (*fig*) to be deeply learned
PP *abr* (= *por poderes*) pp; (= *porte pagado*) carriage paid ▷ *nm abr* = **Partido Popular**
práctica ['praktika] *nf ver* **práctico**
practicable [prakti'kaβle] *adj* practicable; (*camino*) passable, usable
prácticamente ['praktikamente] *adv* practically
practicante [prakti'kante] *nm/f* (*Med: ayudante de doctor*) medical assistant;

(: *enfermero*) nurse; (*el que practica algo*) practitioner ▷ *adj* practising
practicar [prakti'kar] *vt* to practise; (*deporte*) to go in for, play; (*ejecutar*) to carry out, perform
práctico, -a ['praktiko, a] *adj* (*gen*) practical; (*conveniente*) handy; (*instruido: persona*) skilled, expert ▷ *nf* practice; (*método*) method; (*arte, capacidad*) skill; **en la práctica** in practice
practique *etc* [prak'tike] *vb ver* **practicar**
pradera [pra'ðera] *nf* meadow; (*de Canadá*) prairie
prado ['praðo] *nm* (*campo*) meadow, field; (*pastizal*) pasture; (*Am*) lawn
Praga ['praɣa] *nf* Prague
pragmático, -a [praɣ'matiko, a] *adj* pragmatic
preámbulo [pre'ambulo] *nm* preamble, introduction; **decir algo sin ~s** to say sth without beating about the bush
precalentamiento [prekalenta'mjento] *nm* (*Deporte*) warm-up
precario, -a [pre'karjo, a] *adj* precarious
precaución [prekau'θjon] *nf* (*medida preventiva*) preventive measure, precaution; (*prudencia*) caution, wariness
precaver [preka'βer] *vt* to guard against; (*impedir*) to forestall; **precaverse** *vr*: **~se de** *o* **contra algo** to (be on one's) guard against sth
precavido, -a [preka'βiðo, a] *adj* cautious, wary
precedencia [preθe'ðenθja] *nf* precedence; (*prioridad*) priority; (*superioridad*) greater importance, superiority
precedente [preθe'ðente] *adj* preceding; (*anterior*) former ▷ *nm* precedent; **sin ~(s)** unprecedented; **establecer** *o* **sentar un ~** to establish *o* set a precedent
preceder [preθe'ðer] *vt, vi* to precede, go/come before
precepto [pre'θepto] *nm* precept
preciado, -a [pre'θjaðo, a] *adj* (*estimado*) esteemed, valuable
preciar [pre'θjar] *vt* to esteem, value; **preciarse** *vr* to boast; **~se de** to pride o.s. on
precintar [preθin'tar] *vt* (*local*) to seal off; (*producto*) to seal
precinto [pre'θinto] *nm* (*Com*: *tb*: **~ de garantía**) seal
precio ['preθjo] *nm* (*de mercado*) price; (*costo*) cost; (*valor*) value, worth; (*de viaje*) fare; **~ de coste** *o* **de cobertura** cost price; **~ al contado** cash price; **~ al detalle** *o* **al por menor** retail price; **~ al detallista** trade price; **~ de entrega inmediata** spot price; **~ de oferta** offer price, bargain price; **~ de salida** upset price; **~ tope** top price; **~ unitario** unit price; **no tener ~** (*fig*) to be priceless; **"no importa ~"** "cost no object"
preciosidad [preθjosi'ðað] *nf* (*valor*) (high) value, (great) worth; (*encanto*) charm; (*cosa bonita*) beautiful thing; **es una ~** it's lovely, it's really beautiful
precioso, -a [pre'θjoso, a] *adj* precious; (*de mucho valor*) valuable; (*fam*) lovely, beautiful
precipicio [preθi'piθjo] *nm* cliff, precipice; (*fig*) abyss
precipitación [preθipita'θjon] *nf* (*prisa*) haste; (*lluvia*) rainfall; (*Química*) precipitation
precipitado, -a [preθipi'taðo, a] *adj* hasty, rash; (*salida*) hasty, sudden ▷ *nm* (*Química*) precipitate
precipitar [preθipi'tar] *vt* (*arrojar*) to hurl, throw; (*apresurar*) to hasten; (*acelerar*) to speed up, accelerate; (*Química*) to precipitate; **precipitarse** *vr* to throw o.s.; (*apresurarse*) to rush; (*actuar sin pensar*) to act rashly; **~se hacia** to rush towards
precisamente [preθisa'mente] *adv* precisely; (*justo*) precisely, exactly, just; **~ por eso** for that very reason; **~ fue él quien lo dijo** as a matter of fact he said it; **no es eso ~** it's not really that
precisar [preθi'sar] *vt* (*necesitar*) to need, require; (*fijar*) to determine exactly, fix; (*especificar*) to specify; (*señalar*) to pinpoint
precisión [preθi'sjon] *nf* (*exactitud*) precision
preciso, -a [pre'θiso, a] *adj* (*exacto*) precise; (*necesario*) necessary, essential; (*estilo, lenguaje*) concise; **es ~ que lo hagas** you must do it
preconcebido, -a [prekonθe'βiðo, a] *adj* preconceived
precoz [pre'koθ] *adj* (*persona*) precocious; (*calvicie*) premature
precursor, a [prekur'sor, a] *nm/f* precursor
predecesor, a [preðeθe'sor, a] *nm/f* predecessor
predecir [preðe'θir] *vt* to predict, foretell, forecast
predestinado, -a [preðesti'naðo, a] *adj* predestined
predeterminar [preðetermi'nar] *vt* to predetermine
predicado [preði'kaðo] *nm* predicate
predicador, a [preðika'ðor, a] *nm/f* preacher
predicar [preði'kar] *vt, vi* to preach
predicción [preðik'θjon] *nf* prediction; (*pronóstico*) forecast; **~ del tiempo** weather forecast(ing)
predilecto, -a [preði'lekto, a] *adj* favourite
predisponer [preðispo'ner] *vt* to predispose; (*pey*) to prejudice
predisposición [preðisposi'θjon] *nf* predisposition, inclination; prejudice, bias; (*Med*) tendency
predominante [preðomi'nante] *adj* predominant; (*preponderante*) prevailing; (*interés*) controlling
predominar [preðomi'nar] *vt* to dominate ▷ *vi* to predominate; (*prevalecer*) to prevail
predominio [preðo'minjo] *nm* predominance; prevalence
preescolar [preesko'lar] *adj* preschool

P

prefabricado, -a [prefaβri'kaðo, a] *adj* prefabricated
prefacio [pre'faθjo] *nm* preface
preferencia [prefe'renθja] *nf* preference; **de ~** preferably, for preference; **localidad de ~** reserved seat
preferible [prefe'riβle] *adj* preferable
preferido, -a [prefe'riðo, a] *adj, nm/f* favourite, favorite (*US*)
preferir [prefe'rir] *vt* to prefer
prefiero *etc* [pre'fjero] *vb ver* **preferir**
prefijo [pre'fixo] *nm* prefix; (*Tel*) (dialling) code
pregonar [preɣo'nar] *vt* to proclaim, announce; (*mercancía*) to hawk
pregunta [pre'ɣunta] *nf* question; **~ capciosa** catch question; **hacer una ~** to ask a question; **~s frecuentes** FAQs, frequently asked questions
preguntar [preɣun'tar] *vt* to ask; (*cuestionar*) to question ▷ *vi* to ask; **preguntarse** *vr* to wonder; **~ por algn** to ask for sb; **~ por la salud de algn** to ask after sb's health
preguntón, -ona [preɣun'ton, ona] *adj* inquisitive
prehistórico, -a [preis'toriko, a] *adj* prehistoric
prejuicio [pre'xwiθjo] *nm* prejudgement; (*preconcepción*) preconception; (*pey*) prejudice, bias
preliminar [prelimi'nar] *adj, nm* preliminary
preludio [pre'luðjo] *nm* (*Mus, fig*) prelude
premamá [prema'ma] *adj*: **vestido ~** maternity dress
prematrimonial [prematrimo'njal] *adj*: **relaciones ~es** premarital sex
prematuro, -a [prema'turo, a] *adj* premature
premeditación [premeðita'θjon] *nf* premeditation
premeditar [premeði'tar] *vt* to premeditate
premiar [pre'mjar] *vt* to reward; (*en un concurso*) to give a prize to
premio ['premjo] *nm* reward; prize; (*Com*) premium; **~ gordo** first prize
premisa [pre'misa] *nf* premise
premonición [premoni'θjon] *nf* premonition
premura [pre'mura] *nf* (*prisa*) haste, urgency
prenatal [prena'tal] *adj* antenatal, prenatal
prenda ['prenda] *nf* (*de ropa*) garment, article of clothing; (*garantía*) pledge; (*fam*) darling!; **prendas** *nfpl* talents, gifts; **dejar algo en ~** to pawn sth; **no soltar ~** to give nothing away; (*fig*) not to say a word
prendar [pren'dar] *vt* to captivate, enchant; **~se de algo** to fall in love with sth
prendedor [prende'ðor] *nm* brooch
prender [pren'der] *vt* (*captar*) to catch, capture; (*detener*) to arrest; (*coser*) to pin, attach; (*sujetar*) to fasten; (*Am*) to switch on ▷ *vi* to catch; (*arraigar*) to take root; **prenderse** *vr* (*encenderse*) to catch fire
prendido, -a [pren'diðo, a] *adj* (*Am: luz*) on
prensa ['prensa] *nf* press; **la P~** the press; **tener mala ~** to have *o* get a bad press; **la ~ nacional** the national press
prensar [pren'sar] *vt* to press
preñado, -a [pre'ɲaðo, a] *adj* (*mujer*) pregnant; **~ de** pregnant with, full of
preocupación [preokupa'θjon] *nf* worry, concern; (*ansiedad*) anxiety
preocupado, -a [preoku'paðo, a] *adj* worried, concerned; anxious
preocupar [preoku'par] *vt* to worry; **preocuparse** *vr* to worry; **~se de algo** (*hacerse cargo de algo*) to take care of sth; **~se por algo** to worry about sth
preparación [prepara'θjon] *nf* (*acto*) preparation; (*estado*) preparedness, readiness; (*entrenamiento*) training
preparado, -a [prepa'raðo, a] *adj* (*dispuesto*) prepared; (*Culin*) ready (to serve) ▷ *nm* (*Med*) preparation; **¡~s, listos, ya!** ready, steady, go!
preparar [prepa'rar] *vt* (*disponer*) to prepare, get ready; (*Tec: tratar*) to prepare, process, treat; (*entrenar*) to teach, train; **prepararse** *vr*: **~se a** *o* **para hacer algo** to prepare *o* get ready to do sth
preparativo, -a [prepara'tiβo, a] *adj* preparatory, preliminary ▷ *nm*: **~s** *nmpl* preparations
preparatoria [prepara'torja] *nf* (*Am*) sixth form college (*Brit*), senior high school (*US*)
preposición [preposi'θjon] *nf* preposition
prepotencia [prepo'tenθja] *nf* abuse of power; (*Pol*) high-handedness; (*soberbia*) arrogance
prepotente [prepo'tente] *adj* (*Pol*) high-handed; (*soberbio*) arrogant
prerrogativa [prerroɣa'tiβa] *nf* prerogative, privilege
presa ['presa] *nf* (*cosa apresada*) catch; (*víctima*) victim; (*de animal*) prey; (*de agua*) dam; **hacer ~ en** to clutch (on to), seize; **ser ~ de** (*fig*) to be a prey to
presagiar [presa'xjar] *vt* to presage
presagio [pre'saxjo] *nm* omen
prescindir [presθin'dir] *vi*: **~ de** (*privarse de*) to do without, go without; (*descartar*) to dispense with; **no podemos ~ de él** we can't manage without him
prescribir [preskri'βir] *vt* to prescribe
prescripción [preskrip'θjon] *nf* prescription; **~ facultativa** medical prescription
presencia [pre'senθja] *nf* presence; **en ~ de** in the presence of
presencial [presen'θjal] *adj*: **testigo ~** eyewitness
presenciar [presen'θjar] *vt* to be present at; (*asistir a*) to attend; (*ver*) to see, witness
presentación [presenta'θjon] *nf* presentation; (*introducción*) introduction

presentador, a [presenta'ðor, a] *nm/f* compère
presentar [presen'tar] *vt* to present; (*ofrecer*) to offer; (*mostrar*) to show, display; (*renuncia*) to tender; (*moción*) to propose; (*a una persona*) to introduce; **presentarse** *vr* (*llegar inesperadamente*) to appear, turn up; (*ofrecerse: como candidato*) to run, stand; (*aparecer*) to show, appear; (*solicitar empleo*) to apply; **~ al cobro** (*Com*) to present for payment; **~se a la policía** to report to the police
presente [pre'sente] *adj* present ▷ *nm* present; (*Ling*) present (tense); (*regalo*) gift; **los ~s** those present; **hacer ~** to state, declare; **tener ~** to remember, bear in mind; **la carta ~, la ~** this letter
presentimiento [presenti'mjento] *nm* premonition, presentiment
presentir [presen'tir] *vt* to have a premonition of
preservación [preserβa'θjon] *nf* protection, preservation
preservar [preser'βar] *vt* to protect, preserve
preservativo [preserβa'tiβo] *nm* sheath, condom
presidencia [presi'ðenθja] *nf* presidency; (*de comité*) chairmanship; **ocupar la ~** to preside, be in *o* take the chair
presidente [presi'ðente] *nm/f* president; (*de comité*) chairman(-woman); (*en parlamento*) speaker; (*Jur*) presiding magistrate
presidiario [presi'ðjarjo] *nm* convict
presidio [pre'siðjo] *nm* prison, penitentiary
presidir [presi'ðir] *vt* (*dirigir*) to preside at, preside over; (*: comité*) to take the chair at; (*dominar*) to dominate, rule ▷ *vi* to preside; to take the chair
presión [pre'sjon] *nf* pressure; **~ atmosférica** atmospheric *o* air pressure; **~ arterial** *o* **sanguínea** blood pressure; **a ~** under pressure
presionar [presjo'nar] *vt* to press; (*botón*) to push, press; (*fig*) to press, put pressure on ▷ *vi*: **~ para** *o* **por** to press for
preso, -a ['preso, a] *adj*: **estar ~ de terror** *o* **pánico** to be panic-stricken ▷ *nm/f* prisoner; **tomar** *o* **llevar ~ a algn** to arrest sb, take sb prisoner
prestación [presta'θjon] *nf* (*aportación*) lending; (*Inform*) capability; (*servicio*) service; (*subsidio*) benefit; **prestaciones** *nfpl* (*Auto*) performance features; **~ de juramento** oath-taking; **~ personal** obligatory service; **P~ Social Sustitutoria** community service for conscientious objectors; *ver tb* **mili**
prestado, -a [pres'taðo, a] *adj* on loan; **dar algo ~** to lend sth; **pedir ~** to borrow
prestamista [presta'mista] *nm/f* moneylender
préstamo ['prestamo] *nm* loan; **~ con garantía** loan against collateral; **~ hipotecario** mortgage
prestar [pres'tar] *vt* to lend, loan; (*atención*) to pay; (*ayuda*) to give; (*servicio*) to do, render; (*juramento*) to take, swear; **prestarse** *vr* (*ofrecerse*) to offer *o* volunteer
presteza [pres'teθa] *nf* speed, promptness
prestigio [pres'tixjo] *nm* prestige; (*reputación*) face; (*renombre*) good name
prestigioso, -a [presti'xjoso, a] *adj* (*honorable*) prestigious; (*famoso, renombrado*) renowned, famous
presto, -a ['presto, a] *adj* (*rápido*) quick, prompt; (*dispuesto*) ready ▷ *adv* at once, right away
presumido, -a [presu'miðo, a] *adj* conceited
presumir [presu'mir] *vt* to presume ▷ *vi* (*darse aires*) to be conceited; **según cabe ~** as may be presumed, presumably; **~ de listo** to think o.s. very smart
presunción [presun'θjon] *nf* presumption; (*sospecha*) suspicion; (*vanidad*) conceit
presunto, -a [pre'sunto, a] *adj* (*supuesto*) supposed, presumed; (*así llamado*) so-called
presuntuoso, -a [presun'twoso, a] *adj* conceited, presumptuous
presuponer [presupo'ner] *vt* to presuppose
presupuesto [presu'pwesto] *pp de* **presuponer** ▷ *nm* (*Finanzas*) budget; (*estimación: de costo*) estimate; **asignación de ~** (*Com*) budget appropriation
presuroso, -a [presu'roso, a] *adj* (*rápido*) quick, speedy; (*que tiene prisa*) hasty
pretencioso, -a [preten'θjoso, a] *adj* pretentious
pretender [preten'der] *vt* (*intentar*) to try to, seek to; (*reivindicar*) to claim; (*buscar*) to seek, try for; (*cortejar*) to woo, court; **~ que** to expect that; **¿qué pretende usted?** what are you after?
pretendiente [preten'djente] *nm/f* (*candidato*) candidate, applicant; (*amante*) suitor; (*al trono*) pretender
pretensión [preten'sjon] *nf* (*aspiración*) aspiration; (*reivindicación*) claim; (*orgullo*) pretension
pretexto [pre'teksto] *nm* pretext; (*excusa*) excuse; **so ~ de** under pretext of
prevalecer [preβale'θer] *vi* to prevail
prevención [preβen'θjon] *nf* (*preparación*) preparation; (*estado*) preparedness, readiness; (*medida*) prevention; (*previsión*) foresight, forethought; (*precaución*) precaution
prevenido, -a [preβe'niðo, a] *adj* prepared, ready; (*cauteloso*) cautious; **estar ~** (*preparado*) to be ready; **ser ~** (*cuidadoso*) to be cautious; **hombre ~ vale por dos** forewarned is forearmed
prevenir [preβe'nir] *vt* (*impedir*) to prevent; (*prever*) to foresee, anticipate; (*predisponer*) to prejudice, bias; (*avisar*) to warn; (*preparar*) to prepare, get ready; **prevenirse** *vr* to get ready, prepare; **~se contra** to take precautions against

P

preventivo, -a [preβen'tiβo, a] *adj* preventive, precautionary

prever [pre'βer] *vt* to foresee; (*anticipar*) to anticipate

previo, -a ['preβjo, a] *adj* (*anterior*) previous, prior; (*preliminar*) preliminary ▷ *prep*: **~ acuerdo de los otros** subject to the agreement of the others; **~ pago de los derechos** on payment of the fees

previsión [preβi'sjon] *nf* (*perspicacia*) foresight; (*predicción*) forecast; (*prudencia*) caution; **~ de ventas** (*Com*) sales forecast

previsor, a [preβi'sor, a] *adj* (*precavido*) far-sighted; (*prudente*) thoughtful

previsto, -a [pre'βisto, a] *pp de* **prever** ▷ *adj* anticipated, forecast

prima ['prima] *nf ver* **primo**

primacía [prima'θia] *nf* primacy

primario, -a [pri'marjo, a] *adj* primary ▷ *nf* primary education; *ver tb* **sistema educativo**

primavera [prima'βera] *nf* (*temporada*) spring; (*período*) springtime

Primer Ministro [pri'mer-] *nm* Prime Minister

primero, -a [pri'mero, a] *adj* (*antes de nmsg* **primer**) first; (*fig*) prime; (*anterior*) former; (*básico*) fundamental ▷ *adv* first; (*más bien*) sooner, rather ▷ *nf* (*Auto*) first gear; (*Ferro*) first class; **de primera** (*fam*) first-class, first-rate; **de buenas a primeras** suddenly; **primera dama** (*Teat*) leading lady; **primera plana** front page

primicia [pri'miθja] *nf* (*Prensa*) scoop; **primicias** *nfpl* (*tb fig*) first fruits

primitivo, -a [primi'tiβo, a] *adj* primitive; (*original*) original; (*Com: acción*) ordinary ▷ *nf*: **(Lotería) Primitiva** *weekly state-run lottery*; *ver tb* **lotería**

primo, -a ['primo, a] *adj* (*Mat*) prime ▷ *nm/f* cousin; (*fam*) fool, idiot ▷ *nf* (*Com*) bonus; (*de seguro*) premium; (*a la exportación*) subsidy; **~ hermano** first cousin; **materias primas** raw materials; **hacer el ~** to be taken for a ride

primogénito, -a [primo'xenito, a] *adj* first-born

primor [pri'mor] *nm* (*cuidado*) care; **es un ~** it's lovely

primordial [primor'ðjal] *adj* basic, fundamental

primoroso, -a [primo'roso, a] *adj* exquisite, fine

princesa [prin'θesa] *nf* princess

principal [prinθi'pal] *adj* principal, main; (*más destacado*) foremost; (*piso*) first, second (*US*); (*Inform*) foreground ▷ *nm* (*jefe*) chief, principal

príncipe ['prinθipe] *nm* prince; **~ heredero** crown prince; **P~ de Asturias** *King's son and heir to the Spanish throne*; **~ de Gales** (*tela*) check

principiante [prinθi'pjante] *nm/f* beginner; (*novato*) novice

principio [prin'θipjo] *nm* (*comienzo*) beginning, start; (*origen*) origin; (*base*) rudiment, basic idea; (*moral*) principle; **a ~s de** at the beginning of; **desde el ~** from the first; **en un ~** at first

pringar [prin'gar] *vt* (*Culin: pan*) to dip; (*ensuciar*) to dirty; **pringarse** *vr* to get splashed *o* soiled; **~ a algn en un asunto** (*fam*) to involve sb in a matter

pringoso, -a [prin'goso, a] *adj* greasy; (*pegajoso*) sticky

pringue *etc* ['pringe] *vb ver* **pringar** ▷ *nm* (*grasa*) grease, fat, dripping

prioridad [priori'ðað] *nf* priority; (*Auto*) right of way

prisa ['prisa] *nf* (*apresuramiento*) hurry, haste; (*rapidez*) speed; (*urgencia*) (sense of) urgency; **a** *o* **de ~** quickly; **correr ~** to be urgent; **darse ~** to hurry up; **estar de** *o* **tener ~** to be in a hurry

prisión [pri'sjon] *nf* (*cárcel*) prison; (*período de cárcel*) imprisonment

prisionero, -a [prisjo'nero, a] *nm/f* prisoner

prismáticos [pris'matikos] *nmpl* binoculars

privación [priβa'θjon] *nf* deprivation; (*falta*) want, privation; **privaciones** *nfpl* hardships, privations

privado, -a [pri'βaðo, a] *adj* (*particular*) private; (*Pol: favorito*) favourite (*Brit*), favorite (*US*); **en ~** privately, in private; **"~ y confidencial"** "private and confidential"

privar [pri'βar] *vt* to deprive; **privarse** *vr*: **~se de** (*abstenerse de*) to deprive o.s. of; (*renunciar a*) to give up

privativo, -a [priβa'tiβo, a] *adj* exclusive

privatizar [priβati'θar] *vt* to privatize

privilegiado, -a [priβile'xjaðo, a] *adj* privileged; (*memoria*) very good ▷ *nm/f* (*afortunado*) privileged person

privilegiar [priβile'xjar] *vt* to grant a privilege to; (*favorecer*) to favour

privilegio [priβi'lexjo] *nm* privilege; (*concesión*) concession

pro [pro] *nm o nf* profit, advantage ▷ *prep*: **asociación ~ ciegos** association for the blind ▷ *pref*: **~ soviético/americano** pro-Soviet/-American; **en ~ de** on behalf of, for; **los ~s y los contras** the pros and cons

proa ['proa] *nf* (*Naut*) bow, prow; **de ~** bow *cpd*, fore; *ver tb* **popa**

probabilidad [proβaβili'ðað] *nf* probability, likelihood; (*oportunidad, posibilidad*) chance, prospect

probable [pro'βaβle] *adj* probable, likely; **es ~ que** (*+ subjun*) it is probable *o* likely that; **es ~ que no venga** he probably won't come

probador [proβa'ðor] *nm* (*persona*) taster (*of wine etc*); (*en una tienda*) fitting room

probar [pro'βar] *vt* (*demostrar*) to prove; (*someter a prueba*) to test, try out; (*ropa*) to try on; (*comida*) to taste ▷ *vi* to try; **probarse** *vr*: **~se un traje** to try on a suit

probeta [pro'βeta] *nf* test tube
problema [pro'βlema] *nm* problem
procedencia [proθe'ðenθja] *nf* (*principio*) source, origin; (*lugar de salida*) point of departure
procedente [proθe'ðente] *adj* (*razonable*) reasonable; (*conforme a derecho*) proper, fitting; ~ **de** coming from, originating in
proceder [proθe'ðer] *vi* (*avanzar*) to proceed; (*actuar*) to act; (*ser correcto*) to be right (and proper), be fitting ▷ *nm* (*comportamiento*) behaviour, conduct; **no procede obrar así** it is not right to act like that; ~ **de** to come from, originate in
procedimiento [proθeði'mjento] *nm* procedure; (*proceso*) process; (*método*) means, method; (*trámite*) proceedings *pl*
procesado, -a [proθe'saðo, a] *nm/f* accused (person)
procesador [proθesa'ðor] *nm*: ~ **de textos** (*Inform*) word processor
procesar [proθe'sar] *vt* to try, put on trial; (*Inform*) to process
procesión [proθe'sjon] *nf* procession; **la ~ va por dentro** he keeps his troubles to himself
proceso [pro'θeso] *nm* process; (*Jur*) trial; (*lapso*) course (of time); (*Inform*): ~ **(automático) de datos** (automatic) data processing; ~ **no prioritario** background process; ~ **por pasadas** batch processing; ~ **en tiempo real** real-time programming
proclamar [prokla'mar] *vt* to proclaim
procreación [prokrea'θjon] *nf* procreation
procrear [prokre'ar] *vt, vi* to procreate
procurador, a [prokura'ðor, a] *nm/f* attorney, solicitor
procurar [proku'rar] *vt* (*intentar*) to try, endeavour; (*conseguir*) to get, obtain; (*asegurar*) to secure; (*producir*) to produce
prodigar [proði'ɣar] *vt* to lavish; **prodigarse** *vr*: **~se en** to be lavish with
prodigio [pro'ðixjo] *nm* prodigy; (*milagro*) wonder, marvel; **niño ~** child prodigy
prodigioso, -a [proði'xjoso, a] *adj* prodigious, marvellous
pródigo, -a ['proðiɣo, a] *adj* (*rico*) rich, productive; **hijo ~** prodigal son
producción [proðuk'θjon] *nf* production; (*suma de productos*) output; (*producto*) product; ~ **en serie** mass production
producir [proðu'θir] *vt* to produce; (*generar*) to cause, bring about; (*impresión*) to give; (*Com: interés*) to bear; **producirse** *vr* (*cambio*) to come about, happen; (*hacerse*) to be produced, be made; (*estallar*) to break out; (*accidente*) to take place; (*problema etc*) to arise
productividad [proðuktiβi'ðað] *nf* productivity
productivo, -a [proðuk'tiβo, a] *adj* productive; (*provechoso*) profitable
producto [pro'ðukto] *nm* (*resultado*) product; (*producción*) production; ~ **alimenticio** foodstuff; ~ **(nacional) bruto** gross (national) product; ~ **interno bruto** gross domestic product
productor, a [proðuk'tor, a] *adj* productive, producing ▷ *nm/f* producer
proeza [pro'eθa] *nf* exploit, feat
profanar [profa'nar] *vt* to desecrate, profane
profano, -a [pro'fano, a] *adj* profane ▷ *nm/f* (*inexperto*) layman(-woman); **soy ~ en música** I don't know anything about music
profecía [profe'θia] *nf* prophecy
proferir [profe'rir] *vt* (*palabra, sonido*) to utter; (*injuria*) to hurl, let fly
profesar [profe'sar] *vt* (*declarar*) to profess; (*practicar*) to practise
profesión [profe'sjon] *nf* profession; (*en formulario*) occupation; (*confesión*) avowal; **abogado de ~, de ~ abogado** a lawyer by profession
profesional [profesjo'nal] *adj* professional
profesor, a [profe'sor, a] *nm/f* teacher; (*instructor*) instructor; ~ **de universidad** lecturer; ~ **adjunto** assistant lecturer, associate professor (*US*)
profesorado [profeso'raðo] *nm* (*profesión*) teaching profession; (*cuerpo*) teaching staff, faculty (*US*); (*cargo*) professorship
profeta [pro'feta] *nm/f* prophet
profetizar [profeti'θar] *vt, vi* to prophesy
prófugo, -a ['profuɣo, a] *nm/f* fugitive; (*desertor*) deserter
profundidad [profundi'ðað] *nf* depth; **tener una ~ de 30 cm** to be 30 cm deep
profundizar [profundi'θar] (*fig*) *vt* to go into deeply, study in depth ▷ *vi*: ~ **en** to go into deeply
profundo, -a [pro'fundo, a] *adj* deep; (*misterio, pensador*) profound; **poco ~** shallow
profusión [profu'sjon] *nf* (*abundancia*) profusion; (*prodigalidad*) wealth
progenitor [proxeni'tor] *nm* ancestor; **progenitores** *nmpl* (*fam*) parents
programa [pro'ɣrama] *nm* programme; (*Inform*) program; ~ **de estudios** curriculum, syllabus; ~ **verificador de ortografía** (*Inform*) spelling checker
programación [proɣrama'θjon] *nf* (*Inform*) programming; ~ **estructurada** structured programming
programador, a [proɣrama'ðor, a] *nm/f* (computer) programmer; ~ **de aplicaciones** applications programmer
programar [proɣra'mar] *vt* (*Inform*) to program
progre ['proɣre] *adj* (*fam*) liberal
progresar [proɣre'sar] *vi* to progress, make progress
progresión [proɣres'jon] *nf*: ~ **geométrica/aritmética** geometric/arithmetic progression
progresista [proɣre'sista] *adj, nm/f* progressive

P

progresivo, -a [proɣre'siβo, a] *adj* progressive; (*gradual*) gradual; (*continuo*) continuous
progreso [pro'ɣreso] *nm* (*tb*: **~s**) progress; **hacer ~s** to progress, advance
prohibición [proiβi'θjon] *nf* prohibition, ban; **levantar la ~ de** to remove the ban on
prohibir [proi'βir] *vt* to prohibit, ban, forbid; **se prohíbe fumar** no smoking; **"prohibido el paso"** "no entry"
prójimo, -a ['proximo, a] *nm* fellow man ▷ *nm/f* (*vecino*) neighbour
proletariado [proleta'rjaðo] *nm* proletariat
proletario, -a [prole'tarjo, a] *adj, nm/f* proletarian
proliferación [prolifera'θjon] *nf* proliferation; **~ de armas nucleares** spread of nuclear arms
proliferar [prolife'rar] *vi* to proliferate
prolífico, -a [pro'lifiko, a] *adj* prolific
prolijo, -a [pro'lixo, a] *adj* long-winded, tedious; (*Am*) neat
prólogo ['proloɣo] *nm* prologue; (*preámbulo*) preface, introduction
prolongación [prolonga'θjon] *nf* extension
prolongado, -a [prolon'gaðo, a] *adj* (*largo*) long; (*alargado*) lengthy
prolongar [prolon'gar] *vt* (*gen*) to extend; (*en el tiempo*) to prolong; (*calle, tubo*) to make longer, extend; **prolongarse** *vr* (*alargarse*) to extend, go on
promedio [pro'meðjo] *nm* average; (*de distancia*) middle, mid-point
promesa [pro'mesa] *nf* promise ▷ *adj*: **jugador ~** promising player; **faltar a una ~** to break a promise
prometer [prome'ter] *vt* to promise ▷ *vi* to show promise; **prometerse** *vr* (*dos personas*) to get engaged
prometido, -a [prome'tiðo, a] *adj* promised; engaged ▷ *nm/f* fiancé/fiancée
prominente [promi'nente] *adj* prominent
promiscuo, -a [pro'miskwo, a] *adj* promiscuous
promoción [promo'θjon] *nf* promotion; (*año*) class, year; **~ por correspondencia directa** (*Com*) direct mailshot; **~ de ventas** sales promotion *o* drive
promocionar [promoθjo'nar] *vt* (*Com*: *dar publicidad*) to promote
promontorio [promon'torjo] *nm* promontory
promotor [promo'tor] *nm* promoter; (*instigador*) instigator
promover [promo'βer] *vt* to promote; (*causar*) to cause; (*juicio*) to bring; (*motín*) to instigate, stir up
promulgar [promul'ɣar] *vt* to promulgate; (*fig*) to proclaim
pronombre [pro'nombre] *nm* pronoun
pronosticar [pronosti'kar] *vt* to predict, foretell, forecast
pronóstico [pro'nostiko] *nm* prediction, forecast; (*profecía*) omen; (*Med*: *diagnóstico*) prognosis; **de ~ leve** slight, not serious; **~ del tiempo** weather forecast
pronto, -a ['pronto, a] *adj* (*rápido*) prompt, quick; (*preparado*) ready ▷ *adv* quickly, promptly; (*en seguida*) at once, right away; (*dentro de poco*) soon; (*temprano*) early ▷ *nm* urge, sudden feeling; **tener ~s de enojo** to be quick-tempered; **al ~** at first; **de ~** suddenly; **tiene unos ~s muy malos** he gets ratty all of a sudden (*inf*); **¡hasta ~!** see you soon!; **lo más ~ posible** as soon as possible; **por lo ~** meanwhile, for the present; **tan ~ como** as soon as
pronunciación [pronunθja'θjon] *nf* pronunciation
pronunciar [pronun'θjar] *vt* to pronounce; (*discurso*) to make, deliver; (*Jur*: *sentencia*) to pass, pronounce; **pronunciarse** *vr* to revolt, rise, rebel; (*declararse*) to declare o.s.; **~se sobre** to pronounce on
propagación [propaɣa'θjon] *nf* propagation; (*difusión*) spread(ing)
propaganda [propa'ɣanda] *nf* (*política*) propaganda; (*comercial*) advertising; **hacer ~ de** (*Com*) to advertise
propagar [propa'ɣar] *vt* to propagate; (*difundir*) to spread, disseminate; **propagarse** *vr* (*Bio*) to propagate; (*fig*) to spread
propano [pro'pano] *nm* propane
propasarse [propa'sarse] *vr* (*excederse*) to go too far; (*sexualmente*) to take liberties
propensión [propen'sjon] *nf* inclination, propensity
propenso, -a [pro'penso, a] *adj*: **~ a** prone *o* inclined to; **ser ~ a hacer algo** to be inclined *o* have a tendency to do sth
propiamente [propja'mente] *adv* properly; (*realmente*) really, exactly; **~ dicho** real, true
propicio, -a [pro'piθjo, a] *adj* favourable, propitious
propiedad [propje'ðað] *nf* property; (*posesión*) possession, ownership; (*conveniencia*) suitability; (*exactitud*) accuracy; **~ particular** private property; **~ pública** (*Com*) public ownership; **ceder algo a algn en ~** to transfer to sb the full rights over sth
propietario, -a [propje'tarjo, a] *nm/f* owner, proprietor
propina [pro'pina] *nf* tip; **dar algo de ~** to give something extra
propio, -a ['propjo, a] *adj* own, of one's own; (*característico*) characteristic, typical; (*conveniente*) proper; (*mismo*) selfsame, very; **el ~ ministro** the minister himself; **¿tienes casa propia?** have you a house of your own?; **eso es muy ~ de él** that's just like him; **tiene un olor muy ~** it has a smell of its own
proponer [propo'ner] *vt* to propose, put forward; (*candidato*) to propose, nominate; (*problema*) to pose; **proponerse** *vr* to propose, plan, intend

proporción [propor'θjon] *nf* proportion; (*Mat*) ratio; (*razón, porcentaje*) rate; **proporciones** *nfpl* dimensions; (*fig*) size *sg*; **en ~ con** in proportion to
proporcionado, -a [proporθjo'naðo, a] *adj* proportionate; (*regular*) medium, middling; (*justo*) just right; **bien ~** well-proportioned
proporcional [proporθjo'nal] *adj* proportional; **~ a** proportional to
proporcionar [proporθjo'nar] *vt* (*dar*) to give, supply, provide; **esto le proporciona una renta anual de ...** this brings him in a yearly income of ...
proposición [proposi'θjon] *nf* proposition; (*propuesta*) proposal
propósito [pro'posito] *nm* (*intención*) purpose; (*intento*) aim, intention ▷ *adv*: **a ~** by the way, incidentally; (*a posta*) on purpose, deliberately; **a ~ de** about, with regard to
propuesto, -a [pro'pwesto, a] *pp de* **proponer** ▷ *nf* proposal
propugnar [propuɣ'nar] *vt* to uphold
propulsar [propul'sar] *vt* to drive, propel; (*fig*) to promote, encourage
propulsión [propul'sjon] *nf* propulsion; **~ a chorro** *o* **por reacción** jet propulsion
prórroga ['prorroɣa] *nf* (*gen*) extension; (*Jur*) stay; (*Com*) deferment; (*Deporte*) extra time
prorrogar [prorro'ɣar] *vt* (*período*) to extend; (*decisión*) to defer, postpone
prorrumpir [prorrum'pir] *vi* to burst forth, break out; **~ en gritos** to start shouting; **~ en lágrimas** to burst into tears
prosa ['prosa] *nf* prose
prosaico, -a [pro'saiko, a] *adj* prosaic, dull
proscripción [proskrip'θjon] *nf* prohibition, ban; banishment; proscription
proscrito, -a [pros'krito, a] *adj* (*prohibido*) banned; (*desterrado*) outlawed ▷ *nm/f* (*exilado*) exile; (*bandido*) outlaw
prosecución [proseku'θjon] *nf* continuation; (*persecución*) pursuit
proseguir [prose'ɣir] *vt* to continue, carry on, proceed with; (*investigación, estudio*) to pursue ▷ *vi* to continue, go on
prospección [prospek'θjon] *nf* exploration; (*del petróleo, del oro*) prospecting
prospecto [pros'pekto] *nm* prospectus; (*folleto*) leaflet, sheet of instructions
prosperar [prospe'rar] *vi* to prosper, thrive, flourish
prosperidad [prosperi'ðað] *nf* prosperity; (*éxito*) success
próspero, -a ['prospero, a] *adj* prosperous, thriving; (*que tiene éxito*) successful
prostíbulo [pros'tiβulo] *nm* brothel
prostitución [prostitu'θjon] *nf* prostitution
prostituir [prosti'twir] *vt* to prostitute; **prostituirse** *vr* to prostitute o.s., become a prostitute
prostituta [prosti'tuta] *nf* prostitute
protagonista [protaɣo'nista] *nm/f* protagonist; (*Lit: personaje*) main character, hero/heroine
protagonizar [protaɣoni'θar] *vt* to head, take the chief role in
protección [protek'θjon] *nf* protection
protector, a [protek'tor, a] *adj* protective, protecting; (*tono*) patronizing ▷ *nm/f* protector; (*bienhechor*) patron; (*de la tradición*) guardian
proteger [prote'xer] *vt* to protect; **~ contra grabación** *o* **contra escritura** (*Inform*) to write-protect
protegido, -a [prote'xiðo, a] *nm/f* protégé/protégée
proteína [prote'ina] *nf* protein
prótesis ['protesis] *nf* (*Med*) prosthesis
protesta [pro'testa] *nf* protest; (*declaración*) protestation
protestante [protes'tante] *adj* Protestant
protestar [protes'tar] *vt* to protest, declare; (*fe*) to protest ▷ *vi* to protest; (*objetar*) to object; **cheque protestado por falta de fondos** cheque referred to drawer
protocolo [proto'kolo] *nm* protocol; **sin ~s** (*formalismo*) informal(ly)
protón [pro'ton] *nm* proton
prototipo [proto'tipo] *nm* prototype; (*ideal*) model
protuberancia [protuβe'ranθja] *nf* protuberance
prov. *abr* (= *provincia*) prov.
provecho [pro'βetʃo] *nm* advantage, benefit; (*Finanzas*) profit; **¡buen ~!** bon appétit!; **en ~ de** to the benefit of; **sacar ~ de** to benefit from, profit by
proveer [proβe'er] *vt* to provide, supply; (*preparar*) to provide, get ready; (*vacante*) to fill; (*negocio*) to transact, dispatch ▷ *vi*: **~ a** to provide for; **proveerse** *vr*: **~se de** to provide o.s. with
provenir [proβe'nir] *vi*: **~ de** to come from
proverbio [pro'βerβjo] *nm* proverb
providencia [proβi'ðenθja] *nf* providence; (*previsión*) foresight; **providencias** *nfpl* measures, steps
provincia [pro'βinθja] *nf* province; (*Esp: Admin*) ≈ county, ≈ region (*Scot*); **un pueblo de ~(s)** a country town; *see note*

PROVINCIA

Spain is divided up into 55 administrative *provincias*, including the islands, and territories in North Africa. Each one has a *capital de provincia*, which generally bears the same name. *Provincias* are grouped by geography, history and culture into *comunidades autónomas*. It should be noted that the term *comarca* normally has a purely geographical function in Spanish, but in Catalonia it designates administrative boundaries.

provinciano, -a [proβin'θjano, a] *adj* provincial; (*del campo*) country *cpd*
provisión [proβi'sjon] *nf* provision; (*abastecimiento*) provision, supply; (*medida*) measure, step
provisional [proβisjo'nal] *adj* provisional
provocación [proβoka'θjon] *nf* provocation
provocar [proβo'kar] *vt* to provoke; (*alentar*) to tempt, invite; (*causar*) to bring about, lead to; (*promover*) to promote; (*estimular*) to rouse, stir, stimulate; (*protesta, explosión*) to cause, spark off; (*Am*): **¿te provoca un café?** would you like a coffee?
provocativo, -a [proβoka'tiβo, a] *adj* provocative
proxeneta [prokse'neta] *nm/f* go-between; (*de prostitutas*) pimp/procuress
próximamente [proksima'mente] *adv* shortly, soon
proximidad [proksimi'ðað] *nf* closeness, proximity
próximo, -a ['proksimo, a] *adj* near, close; (*vecino*) neighbouring; (*el que viene*) next; **en fecha próxima** at an early date; **el mes ~** next month
proyectar [projek'tar] *vt* (*objeto*) to hurl, throw; (*luz*) to cast, shed; (*Cine*) to screen, show; (*planear*) to plan
proyectil [projek'til] *nm* projectile, missile; **~ (tele)dirigido** guided missile
proyecto [pro'jekto] *nm* plan; (*idea*) project; (*estimación de costo*) detailed estimate; **tener algo en ~** to be planning sth; **~ de ley** (*Pol*) bill
proyector [projek'tor] *nm* (*Cine*) projector
prudencia [pru'ðenθja] *nf* (*sabiduría*) wisdom, prudence; (*cautela*) care
prudente [pru'ðente] *adj* sensible, wise, prudent; (*cauteloso*) careful
prueba ['prweβa] *vb ver* **probar** ▷ *nf* proof; (*ensayo*) test, trial; (*cantidad*) taste, sample; (*saboreo*) testing, sampling; (*de ropa*) fitting; (*Deporte*) event; **a ~** on trial; (*Com*) on approval; **a ~ de** proof against; **a ~ de agua/fuego** waterproof/fireproof; **~ de capacitación** (*Com*) proficiency test; **~ de fuego** (*fig*) acid test; **~ de vallas** hurdles; **someter a ~** to put to the test; **¿tiene usted ~ de ello?** can you prove it?, do you have proof?
prurito [pru'rito] *nm* itch; (*de bebé*) nappy rash; (*anhelo*) urge
psico... [siko] *pref* psycho...
psicoanálisis [sikoa'nalisis] *nm* psychoanalysis
psicología [sikolo'xia] *nf* psychology
psicológico, -a [siko'loxiko, a] *adj* psychological
psicólogo, -a [si'koloɣo, a] *nm/f* psychologist
psicópata [si'kopata] *nm/f* psychopath
psicosis [si'kosis] *nf inv* psychosis
psicosomático, -a [sikoso'matiko, a] *adj* psychosomatic
psiquiatra [si'kjatra] *nm/f* psychiatrist
psiquiátrico, -a [si'kjatriko, a] *adj* psychiatric ▷ *nm* psychiatric hospital
psíquico, -a ['sikiko, a] *adj* psychic(al)
PSOE [pe'soe] *nm abr* = **Partido Socialista Obrero Español**
PSS *nf abr* (*Hist*: = *Prestación Social Sustitutoria*) *community service for conscientious objectors*
púa ['pua] *nf* sharp point; (*Bot, Zool*) prickle, spine; (*para guitarra*) plectrum; **alambre de ~s** barbed wire
pub [puβ/paβ/paf] *nm* bar
pubertad [puβer'tað] *nf* puberty
publicación [puβlika'θjon] *nf* publication
publicar [puβli'kar] *vt* (*editar*) to publish; (*hacer público*) to publicize; (*divulgar*) to make public, divulge
publicidad [puβliθi'ðað] *nf* publicity; (*Com*) advertising; **dar ~ a** to publicize, give publicity to; **~ gráfica** display advertising; **~ en el punto de venta** point-of-sale advertising
publicitario, -a [puβliθi'tarjo, a] *adj* publicity *cpd*; advertising *cpd*
público, -a ['puβliko, a] *adj* public ▷ *nm* public; (*Teat etc*) audience; (*Deporte*) spectators *pl*, crowd; (*en restaurantes etc*) clients *pl*; **el gran ~** the general public; **hacer ~** to publish; (*difundir*) to disclose; **~ objetivo** (*Com*) target audience
puchero [pu'tʃero] *nm* (*Culin*: *olla*) cooking pot; (*: guiso*) stew; **hacer ~s** to pout
pucho ['putʃo] (*Am*: *fam*) *nm* cigarette, fag (*Brit*)
pude *etc vb ver* **poder**
púdico, -a ['puðiko, a] *adj* modest; (*pudibundo*) bashful
pudiera *etc vb ver* **poder**
pudiente [pu'ðjente] *adj* (*opulento*) wealthy; (*poderoso*) powerful
pudor [pu'ðor] *nm* modesty; (*vergüenza*) (sense of) shame
pudrir [pu'ðrir] *vt* to rot; (*fam*) to upset, annoy; **pudrirse** *vr* to rot, decay; (*fig*) to rot, languish
pueblo ['pweβlo] *vb ver* **poblar** ▷ *nm* people; (*nación*) nation; (*aldea*) village; (*plebe*) common people; (*población pequeña*) small town, country town
puedo *etc* ['pweðo] *vb ver* **poder**
puente ['pwente] *nm* (*gen*) bridge; (*Naut*: *tb*: **~ de mando**) bridge; (*: cubierta*) deck; **~ aéreo** shuttle service; **~ colgante** suspension bridge; **~ levadizo** drawbridge; **hacer (el) ~** (*fam*) to take a long weekend

HACER PUENTE

When a public holiday in Spain falls on a Tuesday or Thursday it is common practice for employers to make the Monday or Friday a holiday as well and to give everyone a four-day weekend. This is known as *hacer puente*. When a named public holiday such as the *Día de la Constitución* falls on a Tuesday or Thursday, people refer to the whole holiday period as e.g. the *puente de la Constitución*.

puenting ['pwentin] *nm* bungee jumping
puerco, -a ['pwerko, a] *adj* (*sucio*) dirty, filthy; (*obsceno*) disgusting ▷ *nm/f* pig/sow; **~ espín** porcupine
pueril [pwe'ril] *adj* childish
puerro ['pwerro] *nm* leek
puerta ['pwerta] *nf* door; (*de jardín*) gate; (*portal*) doorway; (*fig*) gateway; (*gol*) goal; (*Inform*) port; **a la ~** at the door; **a ~ cerrada** behind closed doors; **~ corredera/giratoria** sliding/swing *o* revolving door; **~ principal/trasera** *o* **de servicio** front/back door; **~ (de transmisión en) paralelo/serie** (*Inform*) parallel/serial port; **tomar la ~** (*fam*) to leave
puerto ['pwerto] *nm* (*tb Inform*) port; (*de mar*) seaport; (*paso*) pass; (*fig*) haven, refuge; **llegar a ~** (*fig*) to get over a difficulty
Puerto Rico [pwerto'riko] *nm* Puerto Rico
puertorriqueño, -a [pwertorri'keɲo, a] *adj, nm/f* Puerto Rican
pues [pwes] *adv* (*entonces*) then; (*¡entonces!*) well, well then; (*así que*) so ▷ *conj* (*porque*) since; **¡~ sí!** yes!, certainly!; **~ ... no sé** well ... I don't know
puesto, -a ['pwesto, a] *pp de* **poner** ▷ *adj* dressed ▷ *nm* (*lugar, posición*) place; (*trabajo*) post, job; (*Mil*) post; (*Com*) stall; (*quiosco*) kiosk ▷ *conj*: **~ que** since, as ▷ *nf* (*apuesta*) bet, stake; **tener algo ~** to have sth on, be wearing sth; **~ de mercado** market stall; **~ de policía** police station; **~ de socorro** first aid post; **puesta en escena** staging; **puesta al día** updating; **puesta en marcha** starting; **puesta a punto** fine tuning; **puesta del sol** sunset; **puesta a cero** (*Inform*) reset
púgil ['puxil] *nm* boxer
pugna ['puɣna] *nf* battle, conflict
pugnar [puɣ'nar] *vi* (*luchar*) to struggle, fight; (*pelear*) to fight
pujar [pu'xar] *vt* (*precio*) to raise, push up ▷ *vi* (*en licitación*) to bid, bid up; (*fig: esforzarse*) to struggle, strain
pulcro, -a ['pulkro, a] *adj* neat, tidy
pulga ['pulɣa] *nf* flea; **tener malas ~s** to be short-tempered
pulgada [pul'ɣaða] *nf* inch
pulgar [pul'ɣar] *nm* thumb
pulir [pu'lir] *vt* to polish; (*alisar*) to smooth; (*fig*) to polish up, touch up
pulla ['puʎa] *nf* cutting remark
pulmón [pul'mon] *nm* lung; **a pleno ~** (*respirar*) deeply; (*gritar*) at the top of one's voice; **~ de acero** iron lung
pulmonía [pulmo'nia] *nf* pneumonia
pulpa ['pulpa] *nf* pulp; (*de fruta*) flesh, soft part
pulpería [pulpe'ria] *nf* (*Am*) small grocery store
púlpito ['pulpito] *nm* pulpit
pulpo ['pulpo] *nm* octopus
pulque ['pulke] *nm* pulque

PULQUE

Pulque is a thick, white, alcoholic drink which is very popular in Mexico. In ancient times it was considered sacred by the Aztecs. It is produced by fermenting the juice of the *maguey*, a Mexican cactus similar to the agave. It can be drunk by itself or mixed with fruit or vegetable juice.

pulsación [pulsa'θjon] *nf* beat, pulsation; (*Anat*) throb(bing); (*en máquina de escribir*) tap; (*de pianista, mecanógrafo*) touch; **~ (de una tecla)** (*Inform*) keystroke; **~ doble** (*Inform*) strikeover; **pulsaciones** pulse rate
pulsador [pulsa'ðor] *nm* button, push button
pulsar [pul'sar] *vt* (*tecla*) to touch, tap; (*Mus*) to play; (*botón*) to press, push ▷ *vi* to pulsate; (*latir*) to beat, throb
pulsera [pul'sera] *nf* bracelet; **reloj de ~** wristwatch
pulso ['pulso] *nm* (*Med*) pulse; (*fuerza*) strength; (*firmeza*) steadiness, steady hand; **hacer algo a ~** to do sth unaided *o* by one's own efforts
pulverizador [pulβeriθa'ðor] *nm* spray, spray gun
pulverizar [pulβeri'θar] *vt* to pulverize; (*líquido*) to spray
puna ['puna] *nf* (*Am Med*) mountain sickness
punición [puni'θjon] *nf* punishment
punitivo, -a [puni'tiβo, a] *adj* punitive
punki ['punki] *adj, nm/f* punk
punta ['punta] *nf* point, tip; (*extremidad*) end; (*promontorio*) headland; (*Costura*) corner; (*Tec*) small nail; (*fig*) touch, trace; **horas ~s** peak hours, rush hours; **sacar ~ a** to sharpen; **de ~** on end; **de ~ a ~** from one end to the other; **estar de ~** to be edgy; **ir de ~ en blanco** to be all dressed up to the nines; **tener algo en la ~ de la lengua** to have sth on the tip of one's tongue; **se le pusieron los pelos de ~** her hair stood on end
puntada [pun'taða] *nf* (*Costura*) stitch
puntal [pun'tal] *nm* prop, support
puntapié [punta'pje ʃ] (*pl* **puntapiés**) *nm* kick; **echar a algn a ~s** to kick sb out
puntear [punte'ar] *vt* to tick, mark; (*Mus*) to pluck
puntería [punte'ria] *nf* (*de arma*) aim, aiming; (*destreza*) marksmanship
puntero, -a [pun'tero, a] *adj* leading ▷ *nm* (*señal, Inform*) pointer; (*dirigente*) leader

P

puntiagudo, -a [puntja'ɣuðo, a] *adj* sharp, pointed
puntilla [pun'tiʎa] *nf* (*Tec*) tack, braid; (*Costura*) lace edging; **(andar) de ~s** (to walk) on tiptoe
punto ['punto] *nm* (*gen*) point; (*señal diminuta*) spot, dot; (*lugar*) spot, place; (*momento*) point, moment; (*en un examen*) mark; (*tema*) item; (*Costura*) stitch; (*Inform*: *impresora*) pitch; (: *pantalla*) pixel; **a ~** ready; **estar a ~ de** to be on the point of *o* about to; **llegar a ~** to come just at the right moment; **al ~** at once; **en ~** on the dot; **estar en su ~** (*Culin*) to be done to a turn; **hasta cierto ~** to some extent; **hacer ~** to knit; **poner un motor en ~** to tune an engine; **~ de partida/de congelación/de fusión** starting/freezing/melting point; **~ de vista** point of view, viewpoint; **~ muerto** dead centre; (*Auto*) neutral (gear); **~s a tratar** matters to be discussed, agenda *sg*; **~ final** full stop; **dos ~s** colon; **~ y coma** semicolon; **~ acápite** (*Am*) full stop, new paragraph; **~ de interrogación** question mark; **~s suspensivos** suspension points; **~ de equilibrio/de pedido** (*Com*) breakeven/reorder point; **~ inicial** *o* **de partida** (*Inform*) home; **~ de referencia/de venta** (*Com*) benchmark point/point-of-sale
puntocom [punto'kom] *nf inv, adj inv* dotcom, dot.com
puntuación [puntwa'θjon] *nf* punctuation; (*puntos*: *en examen*) mark(s) *pl*; (: *Deporte*) score
puntual [pun'twal] *adj* (*a tiempo*) punctual; (*cálculo*) exact, accurate; (*informe*) reliable
puntualidad [puntwali'ðað] *nf* punctuality; exactness, accuracy; reliability
puntualizar [puntwali'θar] *vt* to fix, specify
puntuar [pun'twar] *vt* (*Ling, Tip*) to punctuate; (*examen*) to mark ▷ *vi* (*Deporte*) to score, count
punzada [pun'θaða] *nf* (*puntura*) prick; (*Med*) stitch; (*dolor*) twinge (of pain)
punzante [pun'θante] *adj* (*dolor*) shooting, sharp; (*herramienta*) sharp; (*comentario*) biting
punzar [pun'θar] *vt* to prick, pierce ▷ *vi* to shoot, stab
puñado [pu'ɲaðo] *nm* handful (*tb fig*); **a ~s** by handfuls
puñal [pu'ɲal] *nm* dagger
puñalada [puɲa'laða] *nf* stab
puñetazo [puɲe'taθo] *nm* punch
puño ['puɲo] *nm* (*Anat*) fist; (*cantidad*) fistful, handful; (*Costura*) cuff; (*de herramienta*) handle; **como un ~** (*verdad*) obvious; (*palpable*) tangible, visible; **de ~ y letra del poeta** in the poet's own handwriting
pupila [pu'pila] *nf* (*Anat*) pupil
pupitre [pu'pitre] *nm* desk
puré [pu're] (*pl* **purés**) *nm* puree; (*sopa*) (thick) soup; **~ de patatas** (*Esp*), **~ de papas** (*Am*) mashed potatoes; **estar hecho ~** (*fig*) to be knackered
pureza [pu'reθa] *nf* purity
purga ['purɣa] *nf* purge
purgante [pur'ɣante] *adj, nm* purgative
purgar [pur'ɣar] *vt* to purge; (*Pol*: *depurar*) to purge, liquidate; **purgarse** *vr* (*Med*) to take a purge
purgatorio [purɣa'torjo] *nm* purgatory
purificar [purifi'kar] *vt* to purify; (*refinar*) to refine
puritano, -a [puri'tano, a] *adj* (*actitud*) puritanical; (*iglesia, tradición*) puritan ▷ *nm/f* puritan
puro, -a ['puro, a] *adj* pure; (*depurado*) unadulterated; (*oro*) solid; (*cielo*) clear; (*verdad*) simple, plain ▷ *adv*: **de ~ cansado** out of sheer tiredness ▷ *nm* cigar; **por pura casualidad** by sheer chance
púrpura ['purpura] *nf* purple
purpúreo, -a [pur'pureo, a] *adj* purple
pus [pus] *nm* pus
puse *etc* ['puse] *vb ver* **poner**
pusiera *etc vb ver* **poder**
pústula ['pustula] *nf* pimple, sore
puta ['puta] *nf* whore, prostitute
putada [pu'taða] *nf* (*fam!*): **hacer una ~ a algn** to play a dirty trick on sb; **¡qué ~!** what a pain in the arse! (*!*)
putrefacción [putrefak'θjon] *nf* rotting, putrefaction
pútrido, -a ['putriðo, a] *adj* rotten
puzzle ['puθle] *nm* puzzle
PVP *abr* (*Esp*: = *Precio Venta al Público*) ≈ RRP
PYME ['pime] *nf abr* (= *Pequeña y Mediana Empresa*) SME

q

que [ke] *conj* **1** (*con oración subordinada: muchas veces no se traduce*) that; **dijo que vendría** he said (that) he would come; **espero que lo encuentres** I hope (that) you find it; **dile que me llame** ask him to call me; *ver tb* **el**
2 (*en oración independiente*): **¡que entre!** send him in; **¡que aproveche!** enjoy your meal!; **¡que se mejore tu padre!** I hope your father gets better; **¡que lo haga él!** he can do it!; (*orden*) get him to do it!
3 (*enfático*): **¿me quieres? — ¡que sí!** do you love me? — of course!; **te digo que sí** I'm telling you
4 (*consecutivo: muchas veces no se traduce*) that; **es tan grande que no lo puedo levantar** it's so big (that) I can't lift it
5 (*comparaciones*) than; **yo que tú/él** if I were you/him; *ver tb* **más**; **menos**
6 (*valor disyuntivo*): **que le guste o no** whether he likes it or not; **que venga o que no venga** whether he comes or not
7 (*porque*): **no puedo, que tengo que quedarme en casa** I can't, I've got to stay in
8: **siguió toca que toca** he kept on playing
▷ *pron* **1** (*cosa*) that, which; (*+ prep*) which; **el sombrero que te compraste** the hat (that *o* which) you bought; **la cama en que dormí** the bed (that *o* which) I slept in; **el día (en) que ella nació** the day (when) she was born
2 (*persona: suj*) that, who; (*: objeto*) that, whom; **el amigo que me acompañó al museo** the friend that *o* who went to the museum with me; **la chica que invité** the girl (that *o* whom) I invited

qué [ke] *adj* what?, which? ▷ *pron* what?; **¡~ divertido/asco!** how funny/revolting!; **¡~ día más espléndido!** what a glorious day!; **¿~ edad tienes?** how old are you?; **¿de ~ me hablas?** what are you saying to me?; **¿~ tal?** how are you?, how are things?; **¿~ hay (de nuevo)?** what's new?; **¿~ más?** anything else?

quebrada [ke'βraða] *nf ver* **quebrado**

quebradero [keβra'ðero] *nm*: **~ de cabeza** headache, worry

quebradizo, -a [keβra'ðiθo, a] *adj* fragile; (*persona*) frail

quebrado, -a [ke'βraðo, a] *adj* (*roto*) broken; (*terreno*) rough, uneven ▷ *nm/f* bankrupt ▷ *nm* (*Mat*) fraction ▷ *nf* ravine; **~ rehabilitado** discharged bankrupt

quebrantar [keβran'tar] *vt* (*infringir*) to violate, transgress; **quebrantarse** *vi* (*persona*) to fail in health

quebranto [ke'βranto] *nm* damage, harm; (*decaimiento*) exhaustion; (*dolor*) grief, pain

quebrar [ke'βrar] *vt* to break, smash ▷ *vi* to go bankrupt; **quebrarse** *vr* to break, get broken; (*Med*) to be ruptured

quedada [ke'ðaða] *nf* meet-up

quedar [ke'ðar] *vi* to stay, remain; (*encontrarse*) to be; (*restar*) to remain, be left; **quedarse** *vr* to remain, stay (behind); **~ en** (*acordar*) to agree on/to; (*acabar siendo*) to end up as; **~ por hacer** to be still to be done; **~ ciego/mudo** to be left blind/with a speech impairment; **no te queda bien ese vestido** that dress doesn't suit you; **quedamos a las seis** we agreed to meet at six; **eso queda muy lejos** that's a long way (away); **nos quedan 12 kms para llegar al pueblo** there are still 12 km before we get to the village; **no queda otra** there's no alternative; **~se (con) algo** to keep sth; **~se con algn** (*fam*) to swindle sb; **~se en nada** to come to nothing *o* nought; **~se frito** (*inf*) to fall asleep, to crash out; **~se sin** to run out of

quedo, -a ['keðo, a] *adj* still ▷ *adv* softly, gently

quehacer [kea'θer] *nm* task, job; **~es (domésticos)** household chores

queja ['kexa] *nf* complaint

quejarse [ke'xarse] *vr* (*enfermo*) to moan, groan; (*protestar*) to complain; **~ de que ...** to complain (about the fact) that ...

quejido [ke'xiðo] *nm* moan

quejoso, -a [ke'xoso, a] *adj* complaining

quemado, -a [ke'maðo, a] *adj* burnt; (*irritado*) annoyed

quemadura [kema'ðura] *nf* burn, scald; (*de sol*) sunburn; (*de fusible*) blow-out

quemar [ke'mar] *vt* to burn; (*fig: malgastar*) to burn up, squander; (*Com: precios*) to slash, cut; (*fastidiar*) to annoy, bug ▷ *vi* to be burning hot; **quemarse** *vr* (*consumirse*) to burn (up); (*del sol*) to get sunburnt
quemarropa [kema'rropa]: **a ~** *adv* point-blank
quemazón [kema'θon] *nf* burn; (*calor*) intense heat; (*sensación*) itch
quepo *etc* ['kepo] *vb ver* **caber**
querella [ke'reʎa] *nf* (*Jur*) charge; (*disputa*) dispute
querellarse [kere'ʎarse] *vr* to file a complaint

PALABRA CLAVE

querer [ke'rer] *vt* **1** (*desear*) to want; **quiero más dinero** I want more money; **quisiera** *o* **querría un té** I'd like a tea; **sin querer** unintentionally; **quiero ayudar/que vayas** I want to help/you to go; **como Vd quiera** as you wish, as you please; **ven cuando quieras** come when you like; **lo hizo sin querer** he didn't mean to do it; **no quiero** I don't want to; **le pedí que me dejara ir pero no quiso** I asked him to let me go but he refused
2 (*preguntas: para pedir u ofrecer algo*): **¿quiere abrir la ventana?** could you open the window?; **¿quieres echarme una mano?** can you give me a hand?; **¿quiere un café?** would you like some coffee?
3 (*amar*) to love; (*tener cariño a*) to be fond of; **te quiero** I love you; **quiere mucho a sus hijos** he's very fond of his children
4 (*requerir*): **esta planta quiere más luz** this plant needs more light
5: **querer decir** to mean; **¿qué quieres decir?** what do you mean?

querido, -a [ke'riðo, a] *adj* dear ▷ *nm/f* darling; (*amante*) lover; **nuestra querida patria** our beloved country
quesería [kese'ria] *nf* dairy; (*fábrica*) cheese factory
queso ['keso] *nm* cheese; **~ rallado** grated cheese; **~ crema** (*Am*), **~ de untar** (*Esp*) cream cheese; **~ manchego** *sheep's milk cheese made in La Mancha*; **dárselas con ~ a algn** (*fam*) to take sb in
quicio ['kiθjo] *nm* hinge; **estar fuera de ~** to be beside o.s.; **sacar a algn de ~** to drive sb up the wall
quiebra ['kjeβra] *nf* break, split; (*Com*) bankruptcy; (*Econ*) slump
quiebro *etc* ['kjeβro] *vb ver* **quebrar** ▷ *nm* (*del cuerpo*) swerve
quien [kjen] *pron relativo* (*suj*) who; (*complemento*) whom; (*indefinido*): **~ dice eso es tonto** whoever says that is a fool; **hay ~ piensa que** there are those who think that; **no hay ~ lo haga** no-one will do it; **~ más, ~ menos tiene sus problemas** everybody has problems
quién [kjen] *pron interrogativo* who; (*complemento*) whom; **¿~ es?** who is it?, who's there?; (*Telec*) who's calling?
quienquiera [kjen'kjera] (*pl* **quienesquiera**) *pron* whoever
quiero *etc* ['kjero] *vb ver* **querer**
quieto, -a ['kjeto, a] *adj* still; (*carácter*) placid; **¡estáte ~!** keep still!
quietud [kje'tuð] *nf* stillness
quijada [ki'xaða] *nf* jaw, jawbone
quilate [ki'late] *nm* carat
quilla ['kiʎa] *nf* keel
quimera [ki'mera] *nf* (*sueño*) pipe dream
quimérico, -a [ki'meriko, a] *adj* fantastic
químico, -a ['kimiko, a] *adj* chemical ▷ *nm/f* chemist ▷ *nf* chemistry
quimioterapia [kimiote'rapia] *nf* chemotherapy
quincalla [kin'kaʎa] *nf* hardware, ironmongery (*Brit*)
quince ['kinθe] *num* fifteen; **~ días** a fortnight
quinceañero, -a [kinθea'ɲero, a] *adj* fifteen-year-old; (*adolescente*) teenage ▷ *nm/f* fifteen-year-old; (*adolescente*) teenager
quincena [kin'θena] *nf* fortnight; (*pago*) fortnightly pay
quincenal [kinθe'nal] *adj* fortnightly
quiniela [ki'njela] *nf* football pools *pl*; **quinielas** *nfpl* pools coupon *sg*
quinientos, -as [ki'njentos, as] *num* five hundred
quinina [ki'nina] *nf* quinine
quinqui ['kinki] *nm* delinquent
quinta ['kinta] *nf ver* **quinto**
quinteto [kin'teto] *nm* quintet
quinto, -a ['kinto, a] *adj* fifth ▷ *nm* (*Mil*) conscript, draftee ▷ *nf* country house; (*Mil*) call-up, draft
quiosco ['kjosko] *nm* (*de música*) bandstand; (*de periódicos*) news stand (*also selling sweets, cigarettes etc*)
quirófano [ki'rofano] *nm* operating theatre
quirúrgico, -a [ki'rurxiko, a] *adj* surgical
quise *etc* ['kise] *vb ver* **querer**
quisiera *etc vb ver* **querer**
quisquilloso [kiski'ʎoso, a] *adj* (*susceptible*) touchy; (*meticuloso*) pernickety
quiste ['kiste] *nm* cyst
quitaesmalte [kitaes'malte] *nm* nail polish remover
quitamanchas [kita'mantʃas] *nm inv* stain remover
quitanieves [kita'njeβes] *nm inv* snowplough (*Brit*), snowplow (*US*)
quitar [ki'tar] *vt* to remove, take away; (*ropa*) to take off; (*dolor*) to relieve; (*vida*) to take; (*valor*) to reduce; (*hurtar*) to remove, steal ▷ *vi*: **¡quita de ahí!** get away!; **quitarse** *vr* to

withdraw; (*mancha*) to come off *o* out; (*ropa*) to take off; **me quita mucho tiempo** it takes up a lot of my time; **el café me quita el sueño** coffee stops me sleeping; **~ de en medio a algn** to get rid of sb; **~se algo de encima** to get rid of sth; **~se del tabaco** to give up smoking; **se quitó el sombrero** he took off his hat
quite ['kite] *nm* (*en esgrima*) parry; (*evasión*) dodge; **estar al ~** to be ready to go to sb's aid
Quito ['kito] *n* Quito
quizá [ki'θa]
quizás [ki'θas] *adv* perhaps, maybe

r

rabadilla [raβa'ðiʎa] *nf* base of the spine
rábano ['raβano] *nm* radish; **me importa un ~** I don't give a damn
rabia ['raβja] *nf* (*Med*) rabies *sg*; (*fig: ira*) fury, rage; **¡qué ~!** isn't it infuriating!; **me da ~** it maddens me; **tener ~ a algn** to have a grudge against sb
rabiar [ra'βjar] *vi* to have rabies; to rage, be furious; **~ por algo** to long for sth
rabieta [ra'βjeta] *nf* tantrum, fit of temper
rabino [ra'βino] *nm* rabbi
rabioso, -a [ra'βjoso, a] *adj* rabid; (*fig*) furious
rabo ['raβo] *nm* tail
racha ['ratʃa] *nf* gust of wind; (*serie*) string, series; **buena/mala ~** spell of good/bad luck
racial [ra'θjal] *adj* racial, race *cpd*
racimo [ra'θimo] *nm* bunch
raciocinio [raθjo'θinjo] *nm* reason; (*razonamiento*) reasoning
ración [ra'θjon] *nf* portion; **raciones** *nfpl* rations
racional [raθjo'nal] *adj* (*razonable*) reasonable; (*lógico*) rational
racionalizar [raθjonali'θar] *vt* to rationalize; (*Com*) to streamline
racionar [raθjo'nar] *vt* to ration (out)
racismo [ra'θismo] *nm* racialism, racism
racista [ra'θista] *adj, nm/f* racist
radar [ra'ðar] *nm* radar
radiactividad [raðjaktiβi'ðað] *nf* radioactivity

radiactivo, -a [raðjak'tiβo, a] *adj* radioactive
radiador [raðja'ðor] *nm* radiator
radiante [ra'ðjante] *adj* radiant
radical [raði'kal] *adj, nm/f* radical ▷ *nm* (*Ling*) root; (*Mat*) square-root sign
radicar [raði'kar] *vi* to take root; **~ en** (*dificultad, problema*) to lie in; (*solución*) to consist in; **radicarse** *vr* to establish o.s., put down (one's) roots
radio ['raðjo] *nf* radio; (*aparato*) radio (set) ▷ *nm* (*Mat*) radius; (*Am*) radio; (*Química*) radium; **~ de acción** extent of one's authority, sphere of influence
radioactividad [raðjoaktiβi'ðað] *nf* radioactivity
radioactivo, -a [raðjoak'tiβo, a] *adj* radioactive
radioaficionado, -a [raðjoafiθjo'naðo, a] *nm/f* radio ham
radiocasete [raðjoka'sete] *nm* radiocassette (player)
radiodifusión [raðjodifu'sjon] *nf* broadcasting
radioemisora [raðjoemi'sora] *nf* transmitter, radio station
radiografía [raðjoɣra'fia] *nf* X-ray
radionovela [raðjono'βela] *nf* radio series
radiotaxi [raðjo'taksi] *nm* radio taxi
radioterapia [raðjote'rapja] *nf* radiotherapy
radioyente [raðjo'jente] *nm/f* listener
ráfaga ['rafaɣa] *nf* gust; (*de luz*) flash; (*de tiros*) burst
raído, -a [ra'iðo, a] *adj* (*ropa*) threadbare; (*persona*) shabby
raigambre [rai'ɣambre] *nf* (*Bot*) roots *pl*; (*fig*) tradition
raíz [ra'iθ] (*pl* **raíces**) *nf* root; **~ cuadrada** square root; **a ~ de** as a result of; (*después de*) immediately after
raja ['raxa] *nf* (*de melón etc*) slice; (*hendidura*) slit, split; (*grieta*) crack
rajar [ra'xar] *vt* to split; (*fam*) to slash; **rajarse** *vr* to split, crack; **~se de** to back out of
rajatabla [raxa'taβla]: **a ~** *adv* (*estrictamente*) strictly, to the letter
rallador [raʎa'ðor] *nm* grater
rallar [ra'ʎar] *vt* to grate
ralo, -a ['ralo, a] *adj* thin, sparse
rama ['rama] *nf* bough, branch; **andarse por las ~s** (*fig: fam*) to beat about the bush
ramaje [ra'maje] *nm* branches *pl*, foliage
ramal [ra'mal] *nm* (*de cuerda*) strand; (*Ferro*) branch line; (*Auto*) branch (road)
rambla ['rambla] *nf* (*avenida*) avenue
ramera [ra'mera] *nf* whore, hooker (*US*)
ramificación [ramifika'θjon] *nf* ramification
ramificarse [ramifi'karse] *vr* to branch out
ramillete [rami'ʎete] *nm* bouquet; (*fig*) select group
ramo ['ramo] *nm* branch, twig; (*sección*) department, section; (*sector*) field, sector
rampa ['rampa] *nf* ramp; **~ de acceso** entrance ramp
ramplón, -ona [ram'plon, ona] *adj* uncouth, coarse
rana ['rana] *nf* frog; **salto de ~** leapfrog; **cuando las ~s críen pelos** when pigs fly
ranchero [ran'tʃero] *nm* (*Am*) rancher; (*pequeño propietario*) smallholder
rancho ['rantʃo] *nm* (*Mil*) food; (*Am: grande*) ranch; (*: pequeño*) small farm
rancio, -a ['ranθjo, a] *adj* (*comestibles*) stale, rancid; (*vino*) aged, mellow; (*fig*) ancient
rango ['rango] *nm* rank; (*prestigio*) standing
ranura [ra'nura] *nf* groove; (*de teléfono etc*) slot; **~ de expansión** (*Inform*) expansion slot
rap [rap] *nm* (*Mus*) rap
rapar [ra'par] *vt* to shave; (*los cabellos*) to crop
rapaz [ra'paθ] (*nf* **rapaza**) *nm/f* young boy/girl ▷ *adj* (*Zool*) predatory
rapaza [ra'paθa] *nf* young girl
rape ['rape] *nm* quick shave; (*pez*) monkfish; **al ~** cropped
rapé [ra'pe] *nm* snuff
rápidamente ['rapiðarmente] *adv* quickly
rapidez [rapi'ðeθ] *nf* speed, rapidity
rápido, -a ['rapiðo, a] *adj* fast, quick ▷ *adv* quickly ▷ *nm* (*Ferro*) express; **rápidos** *nmpl* rapids
rapiña [ra'piɲa] *nm* robbery; **ave de ~** bird of prey
raptar [rap'tar] *vt* to kidnap
rapto ['rapto] *nm* kidnapping; (*impulso*) sudden impulse; (*éxtasis*) ecstasy, rapture
raqueta [ra'keta] *nf* racquet
raquítico, -a [ra'kitiko, a] *adj* stunted; (*fig*) poor, inadequate
raquitismo [raki'tismo] *nm* rickets *sg*
raramente [rara'mente] *adv* rarely
rareza [ra'reθa] *nf* rarity; (*fig*) eccentricity
raro, -a ['raro, a] *adj* (*poco común*) rare; (*extraño*) odd, strange; (*excepcional*) remarkable; **¡qué ~!** how (very) odd!; **¡(qué) cosa más rara!** how strange!
ras [ras] *nm*: **a ~ de** level with; **a ~ de tierra** at ground level
rasar [ra'sar] *vt* to level
rascacielos [raska'θjelos] *nm inv* skyscraper
rascar [ras'kar] *vt* (*con las uñas etc*) to scratch; (*raspar*) to scrape; **rascarse** *vr* to scratch (o.s.)
rasgar [ras'ɣar] *vt* to tear, rip (up)
rasgo ['rasɣo] *nm* (*con pluma*) stroke; **rasgos** *nmpl* features, characteristics; **a grandes ~s** in outline, broadly
rasguñar [rasɣu'ɲar] *vt* to scratch; (*bosquejar*) to sketch
rasguño [ras'ɣuɲo] *nm* scratch
raso, -a ['raso, a] *adj* (*liso*) flat, level; (*a baja altura*) very low ▷ *nm* satin; (*campo llano*) flat country; **cielo ~** clear sky; **al ~** in the open
raspado [ras'paðo] *nm* (*Med*) scrape
raspadura [raspa'ðura] *nf* (*acto*) scrape,

scraping; (*marca*) scratch; **raspaduras** *nfpl* (*de papel etc*) scrapings
raspar [ras'par] *vt* to scrape; (*arañar*) to scratch; (*limar*) to file ▷ *vi* (*manos*) to be rough; (*vino*) to be sharp, have a rough taste
rastra ['rastra] *nf* (*Agr*) rake; **a ~s** by dragging; (*fig*) unwillingly
rastreador [rastrea'ðor] *nm* tracker; **~ de minas** minesweeper
rastrear [rastre'ar] *vt* (*seguir*) to track; (*minas*) to sweep
rastrero, -a [ras'trero, a] *adj* (*Bot, Zool*) creeping; (*fig*) despicable, mean
rastrillar [rastri'ʎar] *vt* to rake
rastrillo [ras'triʎo] *nm* rake; (*Am*) safety razor
rastro ['rastro] *nm* (*Agr*) rake; (*pista*) track, trail; (*vestigio*) trace; (*mercado*) flea market; **el R~** *the Madrid flea market*; **perder el ~** to lose the scent; **desaparecer sin ~** to vanish without trace
rastrojo [ras'troxo] *nm* stubble
rasurado [rasu'raðo] *nm* (*Am*) shaving
rasurador [rasura'ðor] *nm*, **rasuradora** (*Am*) [rasura'ðora] *nf* electric shaver *o* razor
rasurar [rasu'rar] *vt* (*Am*) to shave; **rasurarse** *vr* to shave
rata ['rata] *nf* rat
ratear [rate'ar] *vt* (*robar*) to steal
ratero, -a [ra'tero, a] *adj* light-fingered ▷ *nm/f* (*carterista*) pickpocket; (*ladrón*) petty thief; (*Am: de casas*) burglar
ratificar [ratifi'kar] *vt* to ratify
rato ['rato] *nm* while, short time; **a ~s** from time to time; **al poco ~** shortly after, soon afterwards; **~s libres** *o* **de ocio** leisure *sg*, spare *o* free time *sg*; **hay para ~** there's still a long way to go; **pasar el ~** to kill time; **pasar un buen/mal ~** to have a good/rough time
ratón [ra'ton] *nm* (*tb Inform*) mouse
ratonera [rato'nera] *nf* mousetrap
raudal [rau'ðal] *nm* torrent; **a ~es** in abundance; **entrar a ~es** to pour in
raya ['raja] *nf* line; (*marca*) scratch; (*en tela*) stripe; (*puntuación*) dash; (*de pelo*) parting; (*límite*) boundary; (*pez*) ray; **a ~s** striped; **pasarse de la ~** to overstep the mark; **tener a ~** to keep in check
rayar [ra'jar] *vt* to line; to scratch; (*subrayar*) to underline ▷ *vi*: **~ en** *o* **con** to border on; **al ~ el alba** at first light; **~ a algn** (*col*) to do sb's head in (*col*); **está siempre rayándome con esa historia** he's doing my head in with that business (*col*)
rayo ['rajo] *nm* (*del sol*) ray, beam; (*de luz*) shaft; (*en una tormenta*) (flash of) lightning; **~ solar** *o* **de sol** sunbeam; **~s infrarrojos** infrared rays; **~s X** X-rays; **como un ~** like a shot; **la noticia cayó como un ~** the news was a bombshell; **pasar como un ~** to flash past
raza ['raθa] *nf* race; (*de animal*) breed; **~ humana** human race; **de pura ~** (*caballo*) thoroughbred; (*perro etc*) pedigree
razón [ra'θon] *nf* reason; (*justicia*) right, justice; (*razonamiento*) reasoning; (*motivo*) reason, motive; (*proporción*) rate; (*Mat*) ratio; **a ~ de 10 cada día** at the rate of 10 a day; **"~: ..."** "inquiries to ..."; **en ~ de** with regard to; **perder la ~** to go out of one's mind; **dar ~ a algn** to agree that sb is right; **dar ~ de** to give an account of, report on; **tener/no tener ~** to be right/wrong; **~ directa/inversa** direct/inverse proportion; **~ de ser** raison d'être
razonable [raθo'naβle] *adj* reasonable; (*justo, moderado*) fair
razonamiento [raθona'mjento] *nm* (*juicio*) judgement; (*argumento*) reasoning
razonar [raθo'nar] *vt, vi* to reason, argue
RDSI *nf abr* (= *Red Digital de Servicios Integrados*) ISDN
re [re] *nm* (*Mus*) D
reacción [reak'θjon] *nf* reaction; **avión a ~** jet plane; **~ en cadena** chain reaction
reaccionar [reakθjo'nar] *vi* to react
reaccionario, -a [reakθjo'narjo, a] *adj* reactionary
reacio, -a [re'aθjo, a] *adj* stubborn; **ser** *o* **estar ~ a** to be opposed to
reactivar [reakti'βar] *vt* to reactivate; (*economía*) revitalize; **reactivarse** *vr* (*economía*) to be on the upturn
reactor [reak'tor] *nm* reactor; (*avión*) jet plane; **~ nuclear** nuclear reactor
readaptación [reaðapta'θjon] *nf*: **~ profesional** industrial retraining
readmitir [reaðmi'tir] *vt* to readmit
reajuste [rea'xuste] *nm* readjustment; **~ salarial** wage increase; **~ de plantilla** rationalization
real [re'al] *adj* real; (*del rey, fig*) royal; (*espléndido*) grand ▷ *nm* (*de feria*) fairground
realce *etc* [re'alθe] *vb ver* **realzar** ▷ *nm* (*Tec*) embossing; **poner de ~** to emphasize
real-decreto [re'alde'kreto] (*pl* **reales-decretos**) *nm* royal decree
realidad [reali'ðað] *nf* reality; (*verdad*) truth; **~ virtual** virtual reality; **en ~** in fact
realismo [rea'lismo] *nm* realism
realista [rea'lista] *nm/f* realist
realización [realiθa'θjon] *nf* fulfilment, realization; (*Com*) selling up (*Brit*), conversion into money (*US*); **~ de plusvalías** profit-taking
realizador, a [realiθa'ðor, a] *nm/f* film-maker; (*TV etc*) producer
realizar [reali'θar] *vt* (*objetivo*) to achieve; (*plan*) to carry out; (*viaje*) to make, undertake; (*Com*) to realize; **realizarse** *vr* to come about, come true; **~se como persona** to fulfil one's aims in life
realmente [real'mente] *adv* really, actually
realojar [realo'xar] *vt* to rehouse
realquilar [realki'lar] *vt* (*subarrendar*) to sublet; (*alquilar de nuevo*) to relet

r

realzar [real'θar] *vt* (*Tec*) to raise; (*embellecer*) to enhance; (*acentuar*) to highlight
reanimar [reani'mar] *vt* to revive; (*alentar*) to encourage; **reanimarse** *vr* to revive
reanudar [reanu'ðar] *vt* (*renovar*) to renew; (*historia, viaje*) to resume
reaparición [reapari'θjon] *nf* reappearance; (*vuelta*) return
rearme [re'arme] *nm* rearmament
reavivar [reaβi'βar] *vt* (*persona*) to revive; (*fig*) to rekindle
rebaja [re'βaxa] *nf* reduction, lowering; (*Com*) discount; **rebajas** *nfpl* (*Com*) sale; **"grandes ~s"** "big reductions", "sale"
rebajar [reβa'xar] *vt* (*bajar*) to lower; (*reducir*) to reduce; (*precio*) to cut; (*disminuir*) to lessen; (*humillar*) to humble; **rebajarse** *vr*: **~se a hacer algo** to stoop to doing sth
rebanada [reβa'naða] *nf* slice
rebañar [reβa'ɲar] *vt* (*comida*) to scrape up; (*plato*) to scrape clean
rebaño [re'βaɲo] *nm* herd; (*de ovejas*) flock
rebasar [reβa'sar] *vt* (*tb*: **~ de**) to exceed; (*Auto*) to overtake
rebatir [reβa'tir] *vt* to refute; (*rebajar*) to reduce; (*ataque*) to repel
rebeca [re'βeka] *nf* cardigan
rebelarse [reβe'larse] *vr* to rebel, revolt
rebelde [re'βelde] *adj* rebellious; (*niño*) unruly ▷ *nm/f* rebel; **ser ~ a** to be in revolt against, rebel against
rebeldía [reβel'dia] *nf* rebelliousness; (*desobediencia*) disobedience; (*Jur*) default
rebelión [reβe'ljon] *nf* rebellion
reblandecer [reβlande'θer] *vt* to soften
rebobinar [reβoβi'nar] *vt* to rewind
rebosante [reβo'sante] *adj*: **~ de** (*fig*) brimming *o* overflowing with
rebosar [reβo'sar] *vi* to overflow; (*abundar*) to abound, be plentiful; **~ de salud** to be bursting *o* brimming with health
rebotar [reβo'tar] *vt* to bounce; (*rechazar*) to repel ▷ *vi* (*pelota*) to bounce; (*bala*) to ricochet
rebote [re'βote] *nm* rebound; **de ~** on the rebound
rebozado, -a [reβo'θaðo, a] *adj* (*Culin*) fried in batter *o* breadcrumbs *o* flour
rebozar [reβo'θar] *vt* to wrap up; (*Culin*) to fry in batter *etc*
rebuscado, -a [reβus'kaðo, a] *adj* (*amanerado*) affected; (*palabra*) recherché; (*idea*) far-fetched
rebuscar [reβus'kar] *vi* (*en bolsillo, cajón*) to fish; (*en habitación*) to search high and low
rebuznar [reβuθ'nar] *vi* to bray
recabar [reka'βar] *vt* (*obtener*) to manage to get; **~ fondos** to collect money
recado [re'kaðo] *nm* message; (*encargo*) errand; **dejar/tomar un ~** (*Telec*) to leave/take a message
recaer [reka'er] *vi* to relapse; **~ en** to fall to *o* on; (*criminal etc*) to fall back into, relapse into; (*premio*) to go to
recaída [reka'iða] *nf* relapse
recalcar [rekal'kar] *vt* (*fig*) to stress, emphasize
recalcitrante [rekalθi'trante] *adj* recalcitrant
recalentamiento [rekalenta'mjento] *nm*: **~ global** global warming
recalentar [rekalen'tar] *vt* (*comida*) to warm up, reheat; (*demasiado*) to overheat; **recalentarse** *vr* to overheat, get too hot
recámara [re'kamara] *nf* side room; (*Am*) bedroom
recambio [re'kambjo] *nm* spare; (*de pluma*) refill; **piezas de ~** spares
recapacitar [rekapaθi'tar] *vi* to reflect
recapitular [rekapitu'lar] *vt* to recap
recargable [rekar'ɣaβle] *adj* (*batería, pila*) rechargeable; (*mechero, pluma*) refillable
recargado, -a [rekar'ɣaðo, a] *adj* overloaded; (*exagerado*) over-elaborate
recargar [rekar'ɣar] *vt* to overload; (*batería*) to recharge; (*mechero, pluma*) to refill; (*tarjeta de móvil*) to top up
recargo [re'karɣo] *nm* surcharge; (*aumento*) increase
recatado, -a [reka'taðo, a] *adj* (*modesto*) modest, demure; (*prudente*) cautious
recato [re'kato] *nm* (*modestia*) modesty, demureness; (*cautela*) caution
recauchutado, -a [rekautʃu'taðo, a] *adj* remould *cpd*
recaudación [rekauða'θjon] *nf* (*acción*) collection; (*cantidad*) takings *pl*; (*en deporte*) gate; (*oficina*) tax office
recaudador, a [rekauða'ðor, a] *nm/f* tax collector
recaudar [rekau'ðar] *vt* to collect
recelar [reθe'lar] *vt*: **~ que** (*sospechar*) to suspect that; (*temer*) to fear that ▷ *vi*: **~(se) de** to distrust
recelo [re'θelo] *nm* distrust, suspicion
receloso, -a [reθe'loso, a] *adj* distrustful, suspicious
recepción [reθep'θjon] *nf* reception; (*acto de recibir*) receipt
recepcionista [reθepθjo'nista] *nm/f* receptionist
receptáculo [reθep'takulo] *nm* receptacle
receptivo, -a [reθep'tiβo, a] *adj* receptive
receptor, a [reθep'tor, a] *nm/f* recipient ▷ *nm* (*Telec*) receiver; **descolgar el ~** to pick up the receiver
recesión [reθe'sjon] *nf* (*Com*) recession
receta [re'θeta] *nf* (*Culin*) recipe; (*Med*) prescription
recetar [reθe'tar] *vt* to prescribe
rechazar [retʃa'θar] *vt* to repel, drive back; (*idea*) to reject; (*oferta*) to turn down
rechazo [re'tʃaθo] *nm* (*de fusil*) recoil; (*rebote*) rebound; (*negación*) rebuff; rejection
rechifla [re'tʃifla] *nf* hissing, booing; (*fig*) derision

rechinar [retʃi'nar] *vi* to creak; (*dientes*) to grind; (*máquina*) to clank, clatter; (*metal seco*) to grate; (*motor*) to hum
rechistar [retʃis'tar] *vi*: **sin ~** without complaint
rechoncho, -a [re'tʃontʃo, a] *adj* (*fam*) stocky, thickset (*Brit*), heavy-set (*US*)
rechupete [retʃu'pete]: **de ~** *adj* (*comida*) delicious
recibidor [reθiβi'ðor] *nm* entrance hall
recibimiento [reθiβi'mjento] *nm* reception, welcome
recibir [reθi'βir] *vt* to receive; (*dar la bienvenida*) to welcome; (*salir al encuentro de*) to go and meet ▷ *vi* to entertain; **recibirse** *vr*: **~se de** to qualify as
recibo [re'θiβo] *nm* receipt; **acusar ~ de** to acknowledge receipt of
reciclable [reθi'klaβle] *adj* recyclable
reciclaje [reθi'klaxe] *nm* recycling; (*de trabajadores*) retraining; **cursos de ~** refresher courses
reciclar [reθi'klar] *vt* to recycle; (*trabajador*) to retrain
recién [re'θjen] *adv* recently, newly; (*Am*) just, recently; **~ casado** newly-wed; **el ~ llegado** the newcomer; **el ~ nacido** the newborn child; **~ a las seis** only at six o'clock
reciente [re'θjente] *adj* recent; (*fresco*) fresh
recientemente [reθjente'mente] *adv* recently
recinto [re'θinto] *nm* enclosure; (*área*) area, place
recio, -a ['reθjo, a] *adj* strong, tough; (*voz*) loud ▷ *adv* hard; loud(ly)
recipiente [reθi'pjente] *nm* (*objeto*) container, receptacle; (*persona*) recipient
reciprocidad [reθiproθi'ðað] *nf* reciprocity
recíproco, -a [re'θiproco, a] *adj* reciprocal
recital [reθi'tal] *nm* (*Mus*) recital; (*Lit*) reading
recitar [reθi'tar] *vt* to recite
reclamación [reklama'θjon] *nf* claim, demand; (*queja*) complaint; **libro de reclamaciones** complaints book; **~ salarial** pay claim
reclamar [rekla'mar] *vt* to claim, demand ▷ *vi*: **~ contra** to complain about; **~ a algn en justicia** to take sb to court
reclamo [re'klamo] *nm* (*anuncio*) advertisement; (*tentación*) attraction
reclinar [rekli'nar] *vt* to recline, lean; **reclinarse** *vr* to lean back
recluir [reklu'ir] *vt* to intern, confine
reclusión [reklu'sjon] *nf* (*prisión*) prison; (*refugio*) seclusion; **~ perpetua** life imprisonment
recluta [re'kluta] *nm/f* recruit ▷ *nf* recruitment
reclutamiento [rekluta'mjento] *nm* recruitment
reclutar [reklu'tar] *vt* (*datos*) to collect; (*dinero*) to collect up
recobrar [reko'βrar] *vt* (*recuperar*) to recover; (*rescatar*) to get back; (*ciudad*) to recapture; (*tiempo*) to make up (for); **recobrarse** *vr* to recover
recochineo [rekotʃi'neo] *nm* (*fam*) mickey-taking
recodo [re'koðo] *nm* (*de río, camino*) bend
recogedor, a [rekoxe'ðor, a] *nm* dustpan ▷ *nm(f)* picker, harvester
recoger [reko'xer] *vt* to collect; (*Agr*) to harvest; (*fruta*) to pick; (*levantar*) to pick up; (*juntar*) to gather; (*pasar a buscar*) to come for, get; (*dar asilo*) to give shelter to; (*faldas*) to gather up; (*mangas*) to roll up; (*pelo*) to put up; **recogerse** *vr* (*retirarse*) to retire; **me recogieron en la estación** they picked me up at the station
recogido, -a [reko'xiðo, a] *adj* (*lugar*) quiet, secluded; (*pequeño*) small ▷ *nf* (*Correos*) collection; (*Agr*) harvest; **recogida de datos** (*Inform*) data capture
recolección [rekolek'θjon] *nf* (*Agr*) harvesting; (*colecta*) collection
recomendación [rekomenda'θjon] *nf* (*sugerencia*) suggestion, recommendation; (*referencia*) reference; **carta de ~ para** letter of introduction to
recomendar [rekomen'dar] *vt* to suggest, recommend; (*confiar*) to entrust
recompensa [rekom'pensa] *nf* reward, recompense; (*compensación*): **~ (de una pérdida)** compensation (for a loss); **como** *o* **en ~ por** in return for
recompensar [rekompen'sar] *vt* to reward, recompense
recomponer [rekompo'ner] *vt* to mend; (*Inform*: *texto*) to reformat
reconciliación [rekonθilja'θjon] *nf* reconciliation
reconciliar [rekonθi'ljar] *vt* to reconcile; **reconciliarse** *vr* to become reconciled
recóndito, -a [re'kondito, a] *adj* (*lugar*) hidden, secret
reconfortar [rekonfor'tar] *vt* to comfort
reconocer [rekono'θer] *vt* to recognize; (*registrar*) to search; (*Med*) to examine; **~ los hechos** to face the facts
reconocido, -a [rekono'θiðo, a] *adj* recognized; (*agradecido*) grateful
reconocimiento [rekonoθi'mjento] *nm* recognition; (*registro*) search; (*inspección*) examination; (*gratitud*) gratitude; (*confesión*) admission; **~ óptico de caracteres** (*Inform*) optical character recognition; **~ de la voz** (*Inform*) speech recognition
reconquista [rekon'kista] *nf* reconquest; **la R~** the Reconquest (of Spain)
reconstituyente [rekonstitu'jente] *nm* tonic
reconstruir [rekonstru'ir] *vt* to reconstruct
reconversión [recomber'sjon] *nf* restructuring, reorganization; (*tb*: **~ industrial**) rationalization

r

recopilación [rekopila'θjon] *nf* (*resumen*) summary; (*compilación*) compilation
recopilar [rekopi'lar] *vt* to compile
récord ['rekorð] *adj inv* record; **cifras ~** record figures ▷ *nm* (*pl* **records** *o* **récords** ['rekorð]) record; **batir el ~** to break the record
recordar [rekor'ðar] *vt* (*acordarse de*) to remember; (*traer a la memoria*) to recall; (*recordar a otro*) to remind ▷ *vi* to remember; **recuérdale que me debe cinco dólares** remind him that he owes me five dollars; **que yo recuerde** as far as I can remember; **creo ~, si mal no recuerdo** if my memory serves me right
recordatorio [rekorða'torjo] *nm* (*de fallecimiento*) in memoriam card; (*de bautizo, comunión*) *commemorative card*
recorrer [reko'rrer] *vt* (*país*) to cross, travel through; (*distancia*) to cover; (*registrar*) to search; (*repasar*) to look over
recorrido [reko'rriðo] *nm* run, journey; **tren de largo ~** main-line *o* inter-city (*Brit*) train
recortado, -a [rekor'taðo, a] *adj* uneven, irregular
recortar [rekor'tar] *vt* (*papel*) to cut out; (*el pelo*) to trim; (*dibujar*) to draw in outline; **recortarse** *vr* to stand out, be silhouetted
recorte [re'korte] *nm* (*acción, de prensa*) cutting; (*de telas, chapas*) trimming; **~ presupuestario** budget cut; **~ salarial** wage cut
recostado, -a [rekos'taðo, a] *adj* leaning; **estar ~** to be lying down
recostar [rekos'tar] *vt* to lean; **recostarse** *vr* to lie down
recoveco [reko'βeko] *nm* (*de camino, río etc*) bend; (*en casa*) cubbyhole
recreación [rekrea'θjon] *nf* recreation
recrear [rekre'ar] *vt* (*entretener*) to entertain; (*volver a crear*) to recreate
recreativo, -a [rekrea'tiβo, a] *adj* recreational
recreo [re'kreo] *nm* recreation; (*Escol*) break, playtime
recriminar [rekrimi'nar] *vt* to reproach ▷ *vi* to recriminate; **recriminarse** *vr* to reproach each other
recrudecer [rekruðe'θer] *vt, vi* to worsen; **recrudecerse** *vr* to worsen
recta ['rekta] *nf ver* **recto**
rectangular [rektangu'lar] *adj* rectangular
rectángulo, -a [rek'tangulo, a] *adj* rectangular ▷ *nm* rectangle
rectificar [rektifi'kar] *vt* to rectify; (*volverse recto*) to straighten ▷ *vi* to correct o.s.
rectitud [rekti'tuð] *nf* straightness; (*fig*) rectitude
recto, -a ['rekto, a] *adj* straight; (*persona*) honest, upright; (*estricto*) strict; (*juez*) fair; (*juicio*) sound ▷ *nm* rectum; (*Atletismo*) straight ▷ *nf* straight line; **siga todo ~** go straight on; **en el sentido ~ de la palabra** in the proper sense of the word; **recta final** *o* **de llegada** home straight
rector, a [rek'tor, a] *adj* governing ▷ *nm/f* head, chief; (*Escol*) rector, president (*US*)
recuadro [re'kwaðro] *nm* box; (*Tip*) inset
recubrir [reku'βir] *vt*: **~ (con)** (*pintura, crema*) to cover (with)
recuento [re'kwento] *nm* inventory; **hacer el ~ de** to count *o* reckon up
recuerdo [re'kwerðo] *vb ver* **recordar** ▷ *nm* souvenir; **recuerdos** *nmpl* memories; **¡~s a tu madre!** give my regards to your mother!; **"R~ de Mallorca"** "a present from Majorca"; **contar los ~s** to reminisce
recular [reku'lar] *vi* to back down
recuperable [rekupe'raβle] *adj* recoverable
recuperación [rekupera'θjon] *nf* recovery; **~ de datos** (*Inform*) data retrieval
recuperar [rekupe'rar] *vt* to recover; (*tiempo*) to make up; (*Inform*) to retrieve; **recuperarse** *vr* to recuperate
recurrir [reku'rrir] *vi* (*Jur*) to appeal; **~ a** to resort to; (*persona*) to turn to
recurso [re'kurso] *nm* resort; (*medio*) means *pl*, resource; (*Jur*) appeal; **como último ~** as a last resort; **~s económicos** economic resources; **~s naturales** natural resources
recusar [reku'sar] *vt* to reject, refuse
red [reð] *nf* net, mesh; (*Ferro, Inform*) network; (*Elec, de agua*) mains, supply system; (*de tiendas*) chain; (*trampa*) trap; **la R~** (*Internet*) the Net; **estar conectado con la ~** to be connected to the mains; **~ local** (*Inform*) local area network; **~ de transmisión** (*Inform*) data network
redacción [reðak'θjon] *nf* (*acción*) writing; (*Escol*) essay, composition; (*limpieza de texto*) editing; (*personal*) editorial staff
redactar [reðak'tar] *vt* to draw up, draft; (*periódico, Inform*) to edit
redactor, a [reðak'tor, a] *nm/f* writer; (*en periódico*) editor
redada [re'ðaða] *nf* (*Pesca*) cast, throw; (*fig*) catch; **~ policial** police raid, round-up
rededor [reðe'ðor] *nm*: **al** *o* **en ~** around, round about
redención [reðen'θjon] *nf* redemption
redentor, a [reðen'tor, a] *adj* redeeming ▷ *nm/f* (*Com*) redeemer
redescubrir [reðesku'βrir] *vt* to rediscover
redicho, -a [re'ðitʃo, a] *adj* affected
redil [re'ðil] *nm* sheepfold
redimir [reði'mir] *vt* to redeem; (*rehén*) to ransom
rédito ['reðito] *nm* interest, yield
redoblar [reðo'βlar] *vt* to redouble ▷ *vi* (*tambor*) to roll
redomado, -a [reðo'maðo, a] *adj* (*astuto*) sly, crafty; (*perfecto*) utter
redonda [re'ðonda] *nf ver* **redondo**
redondear [reðonde'ar] *vt* to round, round off; (*cifra*) to round up

redondel [reðon'del] *nm (círculo)* circle; *(Taur)* bullring, arena; *(Auto)* roundabout
redondo, -a [re'ðondo, a] *adj (circular)* round; *(completo)* complete ▷ *nf*: **a la redonda** around, round about; **en muchas millas a la redonda** for many miles around; **rehusar en ~** to give a flat refusal
reducción [reðuk'θjon] *nf* reduction; **~ del activo** *(Com)* divestment; **~ de precios** *(Com)* price-cutting
reducido, -a [reðu'θiðo, a] *adj* reduced; *(limitado)* limited; *(pequeño)* small; **quedar ~ a** to be reduced to
reducir [reðu'θir] *vt* to reduce, limit; *(someter)* to bring under control; **reducirse** *vr* to diminish; *(Mat)*: **~ (a)** to reduce (to), convert (into); **~ las millas a kilómetros** to convert miles into kilometres; **~se a** *(fig)* to come *o* boil down to
reducto [re'ðukto] *nm* redoubt
redundancia [reðun'danθja] *nf* redundancy
reedición [re(e)ði'θjon] *nf* reissue
reeditar [re(e)ði'tar] *vt* to reissue
reelección [re(e)lek'θjon] *nf* re-election
reelegir [re(e)le'xir] *vt* to re-elect
reembolsar [re(e)mbol'sar] *vt (persona)* to reimburse; *(dinero)* to repay, pay back; *(depósito)* to refund
reembolso [re(e)m'bolso] *nm* reimbursement; refund; **enviar algo contra ~** to send sth cash on delivery; **contra ~ del flete** freight forward; **~ fiscal** tax rebate
reemplazar [re(e)mpla'θar] *vt* to replace
reemplazo [re(e)m'plaθo] *nm* replacement; **de ~** *(Mil)* reserve
reencuentro [re(e)n'kwentro] *nm* reunion
reengancharse [re(e)ngan'tʃarse] *vr (Mil)* to re-enlist
reescribible [reeskri'βiβle] *adj* rewritable
reestreno [re(e)s'treno] *nm* rerun
reestructurar [re(e)struktu'rar] *vt* to restructure
refacción [refak'θjon] *nf (Am)* repair(s); **refacciones** *nfpl (piezas de repuesto)* spare parts
referencia [refe'renθja] *nf* reference; **con ~ a** with reference to; **hacer ~ a** to refer *o* allude to; **~ comercial** *(Com)* trade reference
referéndum [refe'rendum] *(pl* **referéndums***) nm* referendum
referente [refe'rente] *adj*: **~ a** concerning, relating to
réferi ['referi] *nm/f (Am)* referee
referir [refe'rir] *vt (contar)* to tell, recount; *(relacionar)* to refer, relate; **referirse** *vr*: **~se a** to refer to; **~ al lector a un apéndice** to refer the reader to an appendix; **~ a** *(Com)* to convert into; **por lo que se refiere a eso** as for that, as regards that
refilón [refi'lon]: **de ~** *adv* obliquely; **mirar a algn de ~** to look out of the corner of one's eye at sb
refinado, -a [refi'naðo, a] *adj* refined
refinamiento [refina'mjento] *nm* refinement; **~ por pasos** *(Inform)* stepwise refinement
refinar [refi'nar] *vt* to refine
refinería [refine'ria] *nf* refinery
reflejar [refle'xar] *vt* to reflect; **reflejarse** *vr* to be reflected
reflejo, -a [re'flexo, a] *adj* reflected; *(movimiento)* reflex ▷ *nm* reflection; *(Anat)* reflex; *(en el pelo)*: **~s** *nmpl* highlights; **tiene el pelo castaño con ~s rubios** she has chestnut hair with blond streaks
reflexión [reflek'sjon] *nf* reflection
reflexionar [refleksjo'nar] *vt* to reflect on ▷ *vi* to reflect; *(detenerse)* to pause (to think); **¡reflexione!** you think it over!
reflexivo, -a [reflek'siβo, a] *adj* thoughtful; *(Ling)* reflexive
reflujo [re'fluxo] *nm* ebb
reforma [re'forma] *nf* reform; *(Arq etc)* repair; **~ agraria** agrarian reform
reformar [refor'mar] *vt* to reform; *(modificar)* to change, alter; *(texto)* to revise; *(Arq)* to repair; **reformarse** *vr* to mend one's ways
reformatorio [reforma'torjo] *nm* reformatory; **~ de menores** remand home
reformista [refor'mista] *adj, nm/f* reformist
reforzar [refor'θar] *vt* to strengthen; *(Arq)* to reinforce; *(fig)* to encourage
refractario, -a [refrak'tarjo, a] *adj (Tec)* heat-resistant; **ser ~ a una reforma** to resist *o* be opposed to a reform
refrán [re'fran] *nm* proverb, saying
refregar [refre'ɣar] *vt* to scrub
refrenar [refre'nar] *vt* to check, restrain
refrendar [refren'dar] *vt (firma)* to endorse, countersign; *(ley)* to approve
refrescante [refres'kante] *adj* refreshing, cooling
refrescar [refres'kar] *vt* to refresh ▷ *vi* to cool down; **refrescarse** *vr* to get cooler; *(tomar aire fresco)* to go out for a breath of fresh air; *(beber)* to have a drink
refresco [re'fresko] *nm* soft drink, cool drink; **"~s"** "refreshments"
refriega *etc* [re'frjeɣa] *vb ver* **refregar** ▷ *nf* scuffle, brawl
refrigeración [refrixera'θjon] *nf* refrigeration; *(de casa)* air-conditioning
refrigerador [refrixera'ðor] *nm,* **refrigeradora** *(Am)* [refrixera'ðora] *nf* refrigerator, icebox *(US)*
refrigerar [refrixe'rar] *vt* to refrigerate; *(sala)* to air-condition
refrito [re'frito] *nm (Culin)*: **un ~ de cebolla y tomate** sautéed onions and tomatoes; **un ~** *(fig)* a rehash
refuerzo *etc* [re'fwerθo] *vb ver* **reforzar** ▷ *nm* reinforcement; *(Tec)* support
refugiado, -a [refu'xjaðo, a] *nm/f* refugee
refugiarse [refu'xjarse] *vr* to take refuge, shelter

refugio [re'fuxjo] *nm* refuge; (*protección*) shelter; (*Auto*) street *o* traffic island; **~ alpino** *o* **de montaña** mountain hut; **~ subterráneo** (*Mil*) underground shelter
refulgir [reful'xir] *vi* to shine, be dazzling
refunfuñar [refunfu'ɲar] *vi* to grunt, growl; (*quejarse*) to grumble
refutar [refu'tar] *vt* to refute
regadera [reɣa'ðera] *nf* watering can; (*Am*) shower; **estar como una ~** (*fam*) to be as mad as a hatter
regadío [rega'ðio] *nm* irrigated land
regalado, -a [reɣa'laðo, a] *adj* comfortable, luxurious; (*gratis*) free, for nothing; **lo tuvo ~** it was handed to him on a plate
regalar [reɣa'lar] *vt* (*dar*) to give (as a present); (*entregar*) to give away; (*mimar*) to pamper, make a fuss of; **regalarse** *vr* to treat o.s. to
regalía [reɣa'lia] *nf* privilege, prerogative; (*Com*) bonus; (*de autor*) royalty
regaliz [reɣa'liθ] *nm* liquorice
regalo [re'ɣalo] *nm* (*obsequio*) gift, present; (*gusto*) pleasure; (*comodidad*) comfort
regañadientes [reɣaɲa'ðjentes]: **a ~** *adv* reluctantly
regañar [reɣa'ɲar] *vt* to scold ▷ *vi* to grumble; (*dos personas*) to fall out, quarrel
regañón, -ona [reɣa'ɲon, ona] *adj* nagging
regar [re'ɣar] *vt* to water, irrigate; (*fig*) to scatter, sprinkle
regatear [reɣate'ar] *vt* (*Com*) to bargain over; (*escatimar*) to be mean with ▷ *vi* to bargain, haggle; (*Deporte*) to dribble; **no ~ esfuerzo** to spare no effort
regateo [reɣa'teo] *nm* bargaining; (*Deporte*) dribbling; (*con el cuerpo*) swerve, dodge
regazo [re'ɣaθo] *nm* lap
regencia [re'xenθja] *nf* regency
regeneración [rexenera'θjon] *nf* regeneration
regenerar [rexene'rar] *vt* to regenerate
regentar [rexen'tar] *vt* to direct, manage; (*puesto*) to hold in an acting capacity; (*negocio*) to be in charge of
regente, -a [re'xente, a] *adj* (*príncipe*) regent; (*director*) managing ▷ *nm* (*Com*) manager; (*Pol*) regent
régimen ['reximen] (*pl* **regímenes** [re'ximenes]) *nm* regime; (*reinado*) rule; (*Med*) diet; (*reglas*) (set of) rules *pl*; (*manera de vivir*) lifestyle; **estar a ~** to be on a diet
regimiento [rexi'mjento] *nm* regiment
regio, -a ['rexjo, a] *adj* royal, regal; (*fig: suntuoso*) splendid; (*Am fam*) great, terrific
región [re'xjon] *nf* region; (*área*) area
regional [rexjo'nal] *adj* regional
regir [re'xir] *vt* to govern, rule; (*dirigir*) to manage, run; (*Econ, Jur, Ling*) to govern ▷ *vi* to apply, be in force
registrador [rexistra'ðor] *nm* registrar, recorder
registrar [rexis'trar] *vt* (*buscar*) to search; (*en cajón*) to look through; (*inspeccionar*) to inspect; (*anotar*) to register, record; (*Inform*) to log; (*Mus*) to record; **registrarse** *vr* to register; (*ocurrir*) to happen
registro [re'xistro] *nm* (*acto*) registration; (*Mus, libro*) register; (*lista*) list, record; (*Inform*) record; (*inspección*) inspection, search; **~ civil** registry office; **~ electoral** voting register; **~ de la propiedad** land registry (office)
regla ['reɣla] *nf* (*ley*) rule, regulation; (*de medir*) ruler, rule; (*Med: período*) period; **en ~** in order; (*regla científica*) law, principle; **no hay ~ sin excepción** every rule has its exception
reglamentación [reɣlamenta'θjon] *nf* (*acto*) regulation; (*lista*) rules *pl*
reglamentar [reɣlamen'tar] *vt* to regulate
reglamentario, -a [reɣlamen'tarjo, a] *adj* statutory; **en la forma reglamentaria** in the properly established way
reglamento [reɣla'mento] *nm* rules *pl*, regulations *pl*; **~ del tráfico** highway code
reglar [re'ɣlar] *vt* (*acciones*) to regulate; **reglarse** *vr*: **~se por** to be guided by
regocijarse [reɣoθi'xarse] *vr*: **~ de** *o* **por** to rejoice at, be glad about
regocijo [reɣo'θixo] *nm* joy, happiness
regodearse [reɣoðe'arse] *vr* to be glad, be delighted; (*pey*): **~ con** *o* **en** to gloat over
regodeo [reɣo'ðeo] *nm* delight; (*pey*) perverse pleasure
regrabadora [regraβa'ðora] *nf* rewriter; **~ de DVD** DVD rewriter
regresar [reɣre'sar] *vi* to come/go back, return; **regresarse** *vr* (*Am*) to return
regresivo, -a [reɣre'siβo, a] *adj* backward; (*fig*) regressive
regreso [re'ɣreso] *nm* return; **estar de ~** to be back, be home
reguero [re'ɣero] *nm* (*de sangre*) trickle; (*de humo*) trail
regulación [reɣula'θjon] *nf* regulation; (*Tec*) adjustment; (*control*) control; **~ de empleo** redundancies *pl*; **~ del tráfico** traffic control
regulador [reɣula'ðor] *nm* (*Tec*) regulator; (*de radio etc*) knob, control
regular [reɣu'lar] *adj* regular; (*normal*) normal, usual; (*común*) ordinary; (*organizado*) regular, orderly; (*mediano*) average; (*fam*) not bad, so-so ▷ *adv*: **estar ~** to be so-so *o* alright ▷ *vt* (*controlar*) to control, regulate; (*Tec*) to adjust; **por lo ~** as a rule
regularidad [reɣulari'ðað] *nf* regularity; **con ~** regularly
regularizar [reɣulari'θar] *vt* to regularize
regusto [re'ɣusto] *nm* aftertaste
rehabilitación [reaβilita'θjon] *nf* rehabilitation; (*Arq*) restoration
rehabilitar [reaβili'tar] *vt* to rehabilitate; (*Arq*) to restore; (*reintegrar*) to reinstate

rehacer [rea'θer] *vt* (*reparar*) to mend, repair; (*volver a hacer*) to redo, repeat; **rehacerse** *vr* (*Med*) to recover
rehén [re'en] *nm/f* hostage
rehogar [reo'ɣar] *vt* to sauté, toss in oil
rehuir [reu'ir] *vt* to avoid, shun
rehusar [reu'sar] *vt, vi* to refuse
reina ['reina] *nf* queen
reinado [rei'naðo] *nm* reign
reinante [rei'nante] *adj* (*fig*) prevailing
reinar [rei'nar] *vi* to reign; (*fig: prevalecer*) to prevail, be general
reincidir [reinθi'ðir] *vi* to relapse; (*criminal*) to repeat an offence
reincorporarse [reinkorpo'rarse] *vr*: **~ a** to rejoin
reino ['reino] *nm* kingdom; **~ animal/vegetal** animal/plant kingdom; **el R~ Unido** the United Kingdom
reinserción [reinser'θjon] *nf* rehabilitation
reinsertar [reinser'tar] *vt* to rehabilitate
reintegrar [reinte'ɣrar] *vt* (*reconstituir*) to reconstruct; (*persona*) to reinstate; (*dinero*) to refund, pay back; **reintegrarse** *vr*: **~se a** to return to
reír [re'ir] *vi* to laugh; **reírse** *vr* to laugh; **~se de** to laugh at
reiterado, -a [reite'raðo, a] *adj* repeated
reiterar [reite'rar] *vt* to reiterate; (*repetir*) to repeat
reivindicación [reiβindika'θjon] *nf* (*demanda*) claim, demand; (*justificación*) vindication
reivindicar [reiβindi'kar] *vt* to claim
reja ['rexa] *nf* (*de ventana*) grille, bars *pl*; (*en la calle*) grating
rejilla [re'xiʎa] *nf* grating, grille; (*muebles*) wickerwork; (*de ventilación*) vent; (*de coche etc*) luggage rack
rejoneador [rexonea'ðor] *nm* mounted bullfighter
rejuvenecer [rexuβene'θer] *vt, vi* to rejuvenate
relación [rela'θjon] *nf* relation, relationship; (*Mat*) ratio; (*lista*) list; (*narración*) report; **~ costo-efectivo** *o* **costo-rendimiento** (*Com*) cost-effectiveness; **relaciones** *nfpl* (*enchufes*) influential friends, connections; **relaciones carnales** sexual relations; **relaciones comerciales** business connections; **relaciones empresariales/humanas** industrial/human relations; **relaciones laborales/públicas** labour/public relations; **con ~ a, en ~ con** in relation to; **estar en** *o* **tener buenas relaciones con** to be on good terms with
relacionar [relaθjo'nar] *vt* to relate, connect; **relacionarse** *vr* to be connected *o* linked
relajación [relaxa'θjon] *nf* relaxation
relajado, -a [rela'xaðo, a] *adj* (*disoluto*) loose; (*cómodo*) relaxed; (*Med*) ruptured
relajar [rela'xar] *vt* to relax; **relajarse** *vr* to relax
relamerse [rela'merse] *vr* to lick one's lips
relamido, -a [rela'miðo, a] *adj* (*pulcro*) overdressed; (*afectado*) affected
relámpago [re'lampaɣo] *nm* flash of lightning ▷ *adj* lightning *cpd*; **como un ~** as quick as lightning, in a flash; **visita/huelga ~** lightning visit/strike
relampaguear [relampaɣe'ar] *vi* to flash
relanzar [relan'θar] *vt* to relaunch
relatar [rela'tar] *vt* to tell, relate
relatividad [relatiβi'ðað] *nf* relativity
relativo, -a [rela'tiβo, a] *adj* relative; **en lo ~ a** concerning
relato [re'lato] *nm* (*narración*) story, tale
relax [re'las] *nm* rest; **"R~"** (*en anuncio*) "Personal services"
relegar [rele'ɣar] *vt* to relegate; **~ algo al olvido** to banish sth from one's mind
relevante [rele'βante] *adj* eminent, outstanding
relevar [rele'βar] *vt* (*sustituir*) to relieve; **relevarse** *vr* to relay; **~ a algn de un cargo** to relieve sb of his post
relevo [re'leβo] *nm* relief; **carrera de ~s** relay race; **coger** *o* **tomar el ~** to take over, stand in
relieve [re'ljeβe] *nm* (*Arte, Tec*) relief; (*fig*) prominence, importance; **bajo ~** bas-relief; **un personaje de ~** an important man; **dar ~ a** to highlight
religión [reli'xjon] *nf* religion
religioso, -a [reli'xjoso, a] *adj* religious ▷ *nm/f* monk/nun
relinchar [relin'tʃar] *vi* to neigh
relincho [re'lintʃo] *nm* neigh; (*acto*) neighing
reliquia [re'likja] *nf* relic; **~ de familia** heirloom
rellano [re'ʎano] *nm* (*Arq*) landing
rellenar [reʎe'nar] *vt* (*llenar*) to fill up; (*Culin*) to stuff; (*Costura*) to pad; (*formulario etc*) to fill in *o* out
relleno, -a [re'ʎeno, a] *adj* full up; (*Culin*) stuffed ▷ *nm* stuffing; (*de tapicería*) padding
reloj [re'lo(x)] *nm* clock; **poner el ~ (en hora)** to set one's watch (*o* the clock); **~ de pie** grandfather clock; **~ (de pulsera)** wristwatch; **~ de sol** sundial; **~ despertador** alarm (clock); **~ digital** digital watch; **como un ~** like clockwork; **contra (el) ~** against the clock
relojería [reloxe'ria] (*tienda*) watchmaker's (shop); **aparato de ~** clockwork; **bomba de ~** time bomb
relojero, -a [relo'xero, a] *nm/f* clockmaker; watchmaker
reluciente [relu'θjente] *adj* brilliant, shining
relucir [relu'θir] *vi* to shine; (*fig*) to excel; **sacar algo a ~** to show sth off
relumbrar [relum'brar] *vi* to dazzle, shine brilliantly

remachar [rema'tʃar] *vt* to rivet; (*fig*) to hammer home, drive home
remache [re'matʃe] *nm* rivet
remanente [rema'nente] *nm* remainder; (*Com*) balance; (*de producto*) surplus
remangar [reman'gar] *vt* to roll up; **remangarse** *vr* to roll one's sleeves up
remanso [re'manso] *nm* pool
remar [re'mar] *vi* to row
rematado, -a [rema'taðo, a] *adj* complete, utter; **es un loco ~** he's a raving lunatic
rematar [rema'tar] *vt* to finish off; (*animal*) to put out of its misery; (*Com*) to sell off cheap ▷ *vi* to end, finish off; (*Deporte*) to shoot
remate [re'mate] *nm* end, finish; (*punta*) tip; (*Deporte*) shot; (*Arq*) top; (*Com*) auction sale; **de** *o* **para ~** to crown it all (*Brit*), to top it off
remedar [reme'ðar] *vt* to imitate
remediar [reme'ðjar] *vt* (*gen*) to remedy; (*subsanar*) to make good, repair; (*evitar*) to avoid; **sin poder ~lo** without being able to prevent it
remedio [re'meðjo] *nm* remedy; (*alivio*) relief, help; (*Jur*) recourse, remedy; **poner ~ a** to correct, stop; **no tener más ~** to have no alternative; **¡qué ~!** there's no choice!; **como último ~** as a last resort; **sin ~** inevitable; (*Med*) hopeless
remedo [re'meðo] *nm* imitation; (*pey*) parody
remendar [remen'dar] *vt* to repair; (*con parche*) to patch; (*fig*) to correct
remesa [re'mesa] *nf* remittance; (*Com*) shipment
remiendo *etc* [re'mjendo] *vb ver* **remendar** ▷ *nm* mend; (*con parche*) patch; (*cosido*) darn; (*fig*) correction
remilgado, -a [remil'ɣaðo, a] *adj* prim; (*afectado*) affected
remilgo [re'milɣo] *nm* primness; (*afectación*) affectation
reminiscencia [reminis'θenθja] *nf* reminiscence
remiso, -a [re'miso, a] *adj* slack, slow
remite [re'mite] *nm* (*en sobre*) name and address of sender
remitente [remi'tente] *nm/f* (*Correos*) sender
remitir [remi'tir] *vt* to remit, send ▷ *vi* to slacken; (*en carta*): **remite: X** sender: X
remo ['remo] *nm* (*de barco*) oar; (*Deporte*) rowing; **cruzar un río a ~** to row across a river
remojar [remo'xar] *vt* to steep, soak; (*galleta etc*) to dip, dunk; (*fam*) to celebrate with a drink
remojo [re'moxo] *nm* steeping, soaking; (*por la lluvia*) drenching, soaking; **dejar la ropa en ~** to leave clothes to soak
remolacha [remo'latʃa] *nf* beet, beetroot (*Brit*)
remolcador [remolka'ðor] *nm* (*Naut*) tug; (*Auto*) breakdown lorry
remolcar [remol'kar] *vt* to tow
remolino [remo'lino] *nm* eddy; (*de agua*) whirlpool; (*de viento*) whirlwind; (*de gente*) crowd
remolque *etc* [re'molke] *vb ver* **remolcar** ▷ *nm* tow, towing; (*cuerda*) towrope; **llevar a ~** to tow
remontar [remon'tar] *vt* to mend; (*obstáculo*) to negotiate, get over; **remontarse** *vr* to soar; **~se a** (*Com*) to amount to; (*en tiempo*) to go back to, date from; **~ el vuelo** to soar
remorder [remor'ðer] *vt* to distress, disturb; **~le la conciencia a algn** to have a guilty conscience
remordimiento [remorði'mjento] *nm* remorse
remoto, -a [re'moto, a] *adj* remote
remover [remo'βer] *vt* to stir; (*tierra*) to turn over; (*objetos*) to move round
remozar [remo'θar] *vt* (*Arq*) to refurbish; (*fig*) to brighten *o* polish up
remuneración [remunera'θjon] *nf* remuneration
remunerar [remune'rar] *vt* to remunerate; (*premiar*) to reward
renacer [rena'θer] *vi* to be reborn; (*fig*) to revive
renacimiento [renaθi'mjento] *nm* rebirth; **el R~** the Renaissance
renacuajo [rena'kwaxo] *nm* (*Zool*) tadpole
renal [re'nal] *adj* renal, kidney *cpd*
rencilla [ren'θiʎa] *nf* quarrel; **rencillas** *nfpl* bickering *sg*
rencor [ren'kor] *nm* rancour, bitterness; (*resentimiento*) ill feeling, resentment; **guardar ~ a** to have a grudge against
rencoroso, -a [renko'roso, a] *adj* spiteful
rendición [rendi'θjon] *nf* surrender
rendido, -a [ren'diðo, a] *adj* (*sumiso*) submissive; (*agotado*) worn-out, exhausted; (*enamorado*) devoted
rendija [ren'dixa] *nf* (*hendidura*) crack; (*abertura*) aperture; (*fig*) rift, split; (*Jur*) loophole
rendimiento [rendi'mjento] *nm* (*producción*) output; (*Com*) yield, profit(s) (*pl*); (*Tec, Com*) efficiency; **~ de capital** (*Com*) return on capital
rendir [ren'dir] *vt* (*vencer*) to defeat; (*producir*) to produce; (*dar beneficio*) to yield; (*agotar*) to exhaust ▷ *vi* to pay; (*Com*) to yield, produce; **rendirse** *vr* (*someterse*) to surrender; (*ceder*) to yield; (*cansarse*) to wear o.s. out; **~ homenaje** *o* **culto a** to pay homage to; **el negocio no rinde** the business doesn't pay
renegado, -a [rene'ɣaðo, a] *adj, nm/f* renegade
renegar [rene'ɣar] *vt* (*negar*) to deny vigorously ▷ *vi* (*blasfemar*) to blaspheme; **~ de** (*renunciar*) to renounce; (*quejarse*) to complain about
RENFE ['renfe] *nf abr* (*Esp: Ferro*) = **Red Nacional de Ferrocarriles Españoles**

renglón [ren'glon] *nm* (*línea*) line; (*Com*) item, article; **a ~ seguido** immediately after
renombrado, -a [renom'braðo, a] *adj* renowned
renombre [re'nombre] *nm* renown
renovable [reno'βaβle] *adj* renewable
renovación [renoβa'θjon] *nf* (*de contrato*) renewal; (*Arq*) renovation
renovar [reno'βar] *vt* to renew; (*Arq*) to renovate; (*sala*) to redecorate
renta ['renta] *nf* (*ingresos*) income; (*beneficio*) profit; (*alquiler*) rent; **~ gravable** *o* **imponible** taxable income; **~ nacional (bruta)** (gross) national income; **~ no salarial** unearned income; **~ sobre el terreno** (*Com*) ground rent; **~ vitalicia** annuity; **política de ~s** incomes policy; **vivir de sus ~s** to live on one's private income
rentabilizar [rentaβili'θar] *vt* to make profitable
rentable [ren'taβle] *adj* profitable; **no ~** unprofitable
rentar [ren'tar] *vt* to produce, yield; (*Am*) to rent
renuencia [re'nwenθja] *nf* reluctance
renuncia [re'nunθja] *nf* resignation
renunciar [renun'θjar] *vt* to renounce, give up ▷ *vi* to resign; **~ a** (*tabaco, alcohol etc*) to give up; (*oferta, oportunidad*) to turn down; (*puesto*) to resign; **~ a hacer algo** to give up doing sth
reñido, -a [re'ɲiðo, a] *adj* (*batalla*) bitter, hard-fought; **estar ~ con algn** to be on bad terms with sb; **está ~ con su familia** he has fallen out with his family
reñir [re'ɲir] *vt* (*regañar*) to scold ▷ *vi* (*estar peleado*) to quarrel, fall out; (*combatir*) to fight
reo ['reo] *nm/f* culprit, offender; (*Jur*) accused
reojo [re'oxo]: **de ~** *adv* out of the corner of one's eye
reparación [repara'θjon] *nf* (*acto*) mending, repairing; (*Tec*) repair; (*fig*) amends, reparation; **"reparaciones en el acto"** "repairs while you wait"
reparador, -a [repara'ðor, a] *adj* refreshing; (*comida*) fortifying ▷ *nm* repairer
reparar [repa'rar] *vt* to repair; (*fig*) to make amends for; (*suerte*) to retrieve; (*observar*) to observe ▷ *vi*: **~ en** (*darse cuenta de*) to notice; (*poner atención en*) to pay attention to; **sin ~ en los gastos** regardless of the cost
reparo [re'paro] *nm* (*advertencia*) observation; (*duda*) doubt; (*dificultad*) difficulty; (*escrúpulo*) scruple, qualm; **poner ~s (a)** to raise objections (to); (*criticar*) to criticize; **no tuvo ~ en hacerlo** he did not hesitate to do it
repartición [reparti'θjon] *nf* distribution; (*división*) division
repartidor, a [reparti'ðor, a] *nm/f* distributor; **~ de leche** milkman
repartir [repar'tir] *vt* to distribute, share out; (*Com, Correos*) to deliver; (*Mil*) to partition; (*libros*) to give out; (*comida*) to serve out; (*Naipes*) to deal
reparto [re'parto] *nm* distribution; (*Com, Correos*) delivery; (*Teat, Cine*) cast; (*Am: urbanización*) housing estate (*Brit*), real estate development (*US*); **"~ a domicilio"** "home delivery service"
repasar [repa'sar] *vt* (*Escol*) to revise; (*Mecánica*) to check, overhaul; (*Costura*) to mend
repaso [re'paso] *nm* revision; (*Mecánica*) overhaul, checkup; (*Costura*) mending; **~ general** servicing, general overhaul; **curso de ~** refresher course
repatriar [repa'trjar] *vt* to repatriate; **repatriarse** *vr* to return home
repecho [re'petʃo] *nm* steep incline
repelente [repe'lente] *adj* repellent, repulsive
repeler [repe'ler] *vt* to repel; (*idea, oferta*) to reject
repente [re'pente] *nm* sudden movement; (*fig*) impulse; **de ~** suddenly; **~ de ira** fit of anger
repentino, -a [repen'tino, a] *adj* sudden; (*imprevisto*) unexpected
repercusión [reperku'sjon] *nf* repercussion; **de amplia** *o* **ancha ~** far-reaching
repercutir [reperku'tir] *vi* (*objeto*) to rebound; (*sonido*) to echo; **~ en** (*fig*) to have repercussions *o* effects on
repertorio [reper'torjo] *nm* list; (*Teat*) repertoire
repesca [re'peska] *nf* (*Escol fam*) resit
repetición [repeti'θjon] *nf* repetition
repetir [repe'tir] *vt* to repeat; (*plato*) to have a second helping of; (*Teat*) to give as an encore, sing *etc* again ▷ *vi* to repeat; (*sabor*) to come back; **repetirse** *vr* to repeat o.s.; (*suceso*) to recur
repetitivo, -a [repeti'tiβo, a] *adj* repetitive, repetitious
repicar [repi'kar] *vi* (*campanas*) to ring (out)
repipi [re'pipi] *adj* la-di-da ▷ *nf*: **es una ~** she's a little madam
repique *etc* [re'pike] *vb ver* **repicar** ▷ *nm* pealing, ringing
repiqueteo [repike'teo] *nm* pealing; (*de tambor*) drumming
repisa [re'pisa] *nf* ledge, shelf; **~ de chimenea** mantelpiece; **~ de ventana** windowsill
repito *etc vb ver* **repetir**
replantear [replante'ar] *vt* (*cuestión pública*) to readdress; (*problema personal*) to reconsider; (*en reunión*) to raise again; **replantearse** *vr*: **~se algo** to reconsider sth
replegarse [reple'ɣarse] *vr* to fall back, retreat
repleto, -a [re'pleto, a] *adj* replete, full up; **~ de** filled *o* crammed with
réplica ['replika] *nf* answer; (*Arte*) replica; **derecho de ~** right of *o* to reply

r

replicar [repli'kar] *vi* to answer; (*objetar*) to argue, answer back
repliegue *etc* [re'pljeɣe] *vb ver* **replegarse** ▷ *nm* (*Mil*) withdrawal
repoblación [repoβla'θjon] *nf* repopulation; (*de río*) restocking; **~ forestal** reafforestation
repoblar [repo'βlar] *vt* to repopulate; to restock; (*con árboles*) to reafforest
repollito [repo'ʎito] *nm* (*Am*): **~s de Bruselas** (Brussels) sprouts
repollo [re'poʎo] *nm* cabbage
reponer [repo'ner] *vt* to replace, put back; (*máquina*) to re-set; (*Teat*) to revive; **reponerse** *vr* to recover; **~ que** to reply that
reportaje [repor'taxe] *nm* report, article; **~ gráfico** illustrated report
reportero, -a [repor'tero, a] *nm/f* reporter; **~ gráfico/a** news photographer
reposacabezas [reposaka'βeθas] *nm inv* headrest
reposado, -a [repo'saðo, a] *adj* (*descansado*) restful; (*tranquilo*) calm
reposar [repo'sar] *vi* to rest, repose; (*muerto*) to lie, rest
reposición [reposi'θjon] *nf* replacement; (*Cine*) second showing; (*Teat*) revival
reposo [re'poso] *nm* rest
repostar [repos'tar] *vt* to replenish; (*Auto*) to fill up (with petrol *o* gasoline)
repostería [reposte'ria] *nf* (*arte*) confectionery, pastry-making; (*tienda*) confectioner's (shop)
repostero, -a [repos'tero, a] *nm/f* confectioner
reprender [repren'der] *vt* to reprimand; (*niño*) to scold
represa [re'presa] *nf* dam; (*lago artificial*) lake, pool
represalia [repre'salja] *nf* reprisal; **tomar ~s** to take reprisals, retaliate
representación [representa'θjon] *nf* representation; (*Teat*) performance; **en ~ de** representing; **por ~** by proxy
representante [represen'tante] *nm/f* (*Pol, Com*) representative; (*Teat*) performer
representar [represen'tar] *vt* to represent; (*significar*) to mean; (*Teat*) to perform; (*edad*) to look; **representarse** *vr* to imagine; **tal acto ~ía la guerra** such an act would mean war
representativo, -a [representa'tiβo, a] *adj* representative
represión [repre'sjon] *nf* repression
represivo, -a [repre'siβo, a] *adj* repressive
reprimenda [repri'menda] *nf* reprimand, rebuke
reprimir [repri'mir] *vt* to repress; **reprimirse** *vr*: **~se de hacer algo** to stop o.s. from doing sth
reprobar [repro'βar] *vt* to censure, reprove
réprobo, -a ['reproβo, a] *nm/f* reprobate
reprochar [repro'tʃar] *vt* to reproach; (*censurar*) to condemn, censure
reproche [re'protʃe] *nm* reproach
reproducción [reproðuk'θjon] *nf* reproduction
reproducir [reproðu'θir] *vt* to reproduce; **reproducirse** *vr* to breed; (*situación*) to recur
reproductor, a [reproðuk'tor, a] *adj* reproductive ▷ *nm*: **~ de CD** CD player; **~ MP3/MP4** MP3/MP4 player
reptil [rep'til] *nm* reptile
república [re'puβlika] *nf* republic; **R~ Dominicana** Dominican Republic; **R~ Federal Alemana (RFA)** Federal Republic of Germany
republicano, -a [repuβli'kano, a] *adj, nm/f* republican
repudiar [repu'ðjar] *vt* to repudiate; (*fe*) to renounce
repudio [re'puðjo] *nm* repudiation
repuesto [re'pwesto] *pp de* **reponer** ▷ *nm* (*pieza de recambio*) spare (part); (*abastecimiento*) supply; **rueda de ~** spare wheel; **y llevamos otro de ~** and we have another as a spare *o* in reserve
repugnancia [repuɣ'nanθja] *nf* repugnance
repugnante [repuɣ'nante] *adj* repugnant, repulsive
repugnar [repuɣ'nar] *vt* to disgust ▷ *vi*, **repugnarse** *vr* (*contradecirse*) to contradict each other
repujar [repu'xar] *vt* to emboss
repulsa [re'pulsa] *nf* rebuff
repulsión [repul'sjon] *nf* repulsion, aversion
repulsivo, -a [repul'siβo, a] *adj* repulsive
reputación [reputa'θjon] *nf* reputation
reputar [repu'tar] *vt* to consider, deem
requemado, -a [reke'maðo, a] *adj* (*quemado*) scorched; (*bronceado*) tanned
requerimiento [rekeri'mjento] *nm* request; (*demanda*) demand; (*Jur*) summons
requerir [reke'rir] *vt* (*pedir*) to ask, request; (*exigir*) to require; (*ordenar*) to call for; (*llamar*) to send for, summon
requesón [reke'son] *nm* cottage cheese
requete... [rekete] *pref* extremely
réquiem ['rekjem] *nm* requiem
requisa [re'kisa] *nf* (*inspección*) survey, inspection; (*Mil*) requisition
requisar [reki'sar] *vt* (*Mil*) to requisition; (*confiscar*) to seize, confiscate
requisito [reki'sito] *nm* requirement, requisite; **~ previo** prerequisite; **tener los ~s para un cargo** to have the essential qualifications for a post
res [res] *nf* beast, animal
resabio [re'saβjo] *nm* (*maña*) vice, bad habit; (*dejo*) (unpleasant) aftertaste
resaca [re'saka] *nf* (*en el mar*) undertow, undercurrent; (*fig*) backlash; (*fam*) hangover
resaltar [resal'tar] *vi* to project, stick out; (*fig*) to stand out
resarcir [resar'θir] *vt* to compensate; (*pagar*) to repay; **resarcirse** *vr* to make up for;

~ **a algn de una pérdida** to compensate sb for a loss; ~ **a algn de una cantidad** to repay sb a sum

resbaladero [resβala'ðero] *nm* (*Am*) slide

resbaladizo, -a [resβala'ðiθo, a] *adj* slippery

resbalar [resβa'lar] *vi* to slip, slide; (*fig*) to slip (up); **resbalarse** *vr* to slip, slide; (*fig*) to slip (up); **le resbalaban las lágrimas por las mejillas** tears were trickling down his cheeks

resbalón [resβa'lon] *nm* (*acción*) slip; (*deslizamiento*) slide; (*fig*) slip

rescatar [reska'tar] *vt* (*salvar*) to save, rescue; (*objeto*) to get back, recover; (*cautivos*) to ransom

rescate [res'kate] *nm* rescue; (*de objeto*) recovery; **pagar un** ~ to pay a ransom

rescindir [resθin'dir] *vt* (*contrato*) to annul, rescind

rescisión [resθi'sjon] *nf* cancellation

rescoldo [res'koldo] *nm* embers *pl*

resecar [rese'kar] *vt* to dry off, dry thoroughly; (*Med*) to cut out, remove; **resecarse** *vi* to dry up

reseco, -a [re'seko, a] *adj* very dry; (*fig*) skinny

resentido, -a [resen'tiðo, a] *adj* resentful; **es un** ~ he's bitter

resentimiento [resenti'mjento] *nm* resentment, bitterness

resentirse [resen'tirse] *vr* (*debilitarse*: *persona*) to suffer; ~ **con** to resent; ~ **de** (*sufrir las consecuencias de*) to feel the effects of; ~ **de** (*o* **por**) **algo** to resent sth, be bitter about sth

reseña [re'seɲa] *nf* (*cuenta*) account; (*informe*) report; (*Lit*) review

reseñar [rese'ɲar] *vt* to describe; (*Lit*) to review

reserva [re'serβa] *nf* reserve; (*reservación*) reservation; **a ~ de que ...** unless ...; **con toda** ~ in strictest confidence; **de** ~ spare; **tener algo de** ~ to have sth in reserve; ~ **de indios** Indian reservation; (*Com*): ~ **para amortización** depreciation allowance; ~ **de caja** *o* **en efectivo** cash reserves; **~s del Estado** government stock; **~s en oro** gold reserves

reservación [reserβa'θjon] *nf* (*LAm*) reservation

reservado, -a [reser'βaðo, a] *adj* reserved; (*retraído*) cold, distant ▷ *nm* private room; (*Ferro*) reserved compartment

reservar [reser'βar] *vt* (*guardar*) to keep; (*Ferro, Teat etc*) to reserve, book; **reservarse** *vr* to save o.s.; (*callar*) to keep to o.s.; ~ **con exceso** to overbook

resfriado [res'friaðo] *nm* cold

resfriarse [res'friarse] *vr* to cool off; (*Med*) to catch (a) cold

resguardar [resɣwar'ðar] *vt* to protect, shield; **resguardarse** *vr*: **~se de** to guard against

resguardo [res'ɣwarðo] *nm* defence; (*vale*) voucher; (*recibo*) receipt, slip

residencia [resi'ðenθja] *nf* residence; (*Univ*) hall of residence; ~ **para ancianos** *o* **jubilados** residential home, old people's home

residencial [resiðen'θjal] *adj* residential ▷ *nf* (*urbanización*) housing estate (*Brit*), real estate development (*US*)

residente [resi'ðente] *adj, nm/f* resident

residir [resi'ðir] *vi* to reside, live; ~ **en** to reside *o* lie in; (*consistir en*) to consist of

residuo [re'siðwo] *nm* residue; **~s atmosféricos** *o* **radiactivos** fallout *sg*

resignación [resiɣna'θjon] *nf* resignation

resignarse [resiɣ'narse] *vr*: ~ **a** *o* **con** to resign o.s. to, be resigned to

resina [re'sina] *nf* resin

resistencia [resis'tenθja] *nf* (*dureza*) endurance, strength; (*oposición, Elec*) resistance; **la R~** (*Mil*) the Resistance

resistente [resis'tente] *adj* strong, hardy; (*Tec*) resistant; ~ **al calor** heat-resistant

resistir [resis'tir] *vt* (*soportar*) to bear; (*oponerse a*) to resist, oppose; (*aguantar*) to put up with ▷ *vi* to resist; (*aguantar*) to last, endure; **resistirse** *vr*: **~se a** to refuse to, resist; **no puedo ~ este frío** I can't bear *o* stand this cold; **me resisto a creerlo** I refuse to believe it; **se le resiste la química** chemistry escapes her

resollar [reso'ʎar] *vi* to breathe noisily, wheeze

resolución [resolu'θjon] *nf* resolution; (*decisión*) decision; (*moción*) motion; ~ **judicial** legal ruling; **tomar una** ~ to take a decision

resoluto, -a [reso'luto, a] *adj* resolute

resolver [resol'βer] *vt* to resolve; (*solucionar*) to solve, resolve; (*decidir*) to decide, settle; **resolverse** *vr* to make up one's mind

resonancia [reso'nanθja] *nf* (*del sonido*) resonance; (*repercusión*) repercussion; (*fig*) wide effect, impact

resonante [reso'nante] *adj* resonant, resounding; (*fig*) tremendous

resonar [reso'nar] *vi* to ring, echo

resoplar [reso'plar] *vi* to snort; (*por cansancio*) to puff

resoplido [reso'pliðo] *nm* heavy breathing

resorte [re'sorte] *nm* spring; (*fig*) lever

resortera [resor'tera] *nf* (*Am*) catapult

respaldar [respal'dar] *vt* to back (up), support; (*Inform*) to back up; **respaldarse** *vr* to lean back; **~se con** *o* **en** (*fig*) to take one's stand on

respaldo [res'paldo] *nm* (*de sillón*) back; (*fig*) support, backing

respectivo, -a [respek'tiβo, a] *adj* respective; **en lo ~ a** with regard to

respecto [res'pekto] *nm*: **al** ~ on this matter; **con ~ a, ~ de** with regard to, in relation to

respetable [respe'taβle] *adj* respectable
respetar [respe'tar] *vt* to respect
respeto [res'peto] *nm* respect; (*acatamiento*) deference; **respetos** *nmpl* respects; **por ~ a** out of consideration for; **presentar sus ~s a** to pay one's respects to
respetuoso, -a [respe'twoso, a] *adj* respectful
respingo [res'pingo] *nm* start, jump
respiración [respira'θjon] *nf* breathing; (*Med*) respiration; (*ventilación*) ventilation; **~ asistida** artificial respiration (*by machine*)
respirar [respi'rar] *vt, vi* to breathe; **no dejar ~ a algn** to keep on at sb; **estuvo escuchándole sin ~** he listened to him in complete silence
respiratorio, -a [respira'torjo, a] *adj* respiratory
respiro [res'piro] *nm* breathing; (*fig: descanso*) respite, rest; (*Com*) period of grace
resplandecer [resplande'θer] *vi* to shine
resplandeciente [resplande'θjente] *adj* resplendent, shining
resplandor [resplan'dor] *nm* brilliance, brightness; (*del fuego*) blaze
responder [respon'der] *vt* to answer ▷ *vi* to answer; (*fig*) to respond; (*pey*) to answer back; (*corresponder*) to correspond; **~ a** (*situación etc*) to respond to; **~ a una pregunta** to answer a question; **~ a una descripción** to fit a description; **~ de** *o* **por** to answer for
respondón, -ona [respon'don, ona] *adj* cheeky
responsabilidad [responsaβili'ðað] *nf* responsibility; **bajo mi ~** on my authority; **~ ilimitada** (*Com*) unlimited liability
responsabilizarse [responsaβili'θarse] *vr* to make o.s. responsible, take charge
responsable [respon'sable] *adj* responsible; **la persona ~** the person in charge; **hacerse ~ de algo** to assume responsibility for sth
respuesta [res'pwesta] *nf* answer, reply; (*reacción*) response
resquebrajar [reskeβra'xar] *vt* to crack, split; **resquebrajarse** *vr* to crack, split
resquemor [reske'mor] *nm* resentment
resquicio [res'kiθjo] *nm* chink; (*hendidura*) crack
resta ['resta] *nf* (*Mat*) remainder
restablecer [restaβle'θer] *vt* to re-establish, restore; **restablecerse** *vr* to recover
restallar [resta'ʎar] *vi* to crack
restante [res'tante] *adj* remaining; **lo ~** the remainder; **los ~s** the rest, those left (over)
restar [res'tar] *vt* (*Mat*) to subtract; (*descontar*) to deduct; (*fig*) to take away ▷ *vi* to remain, be left
restauración [restaura'θjon] *nf* restoration
restaurante [restau'rante] *nm* restaurant
restaurar [restau'rar] *vt* to restore
restitución [restitu'θjon] *nf* return, restitution
restituir [restitu'ir] *vt* (*devolver*) to return, give back; (*rehabilitar*) to restore
resto ['resto] *nm* (*residuo*) rest, remainder; (*apuesta*) stake; **restos** *nmpl* remains; (*Culin*) leftovers, scraps; **~s mortales** mortal remains
restorán [resto'ran] *nm* (*Am*) restaurant
restregar [restre'ɣar] *vt* to scrub, rub
restricción [restrik'θjon] *nf* restriction; **sin ~ de** without restrictions on *o* as to; **hablar sin restricciones** to talk freely
restrictivo, -a [restrik'tiβo, a] *adj* restrictive
restringir [restrin'xir] *vt* to restrict, limit
resucitar [resuθi'tar] *vt, vi* to resuscitate, revive
resuello *etc* [re'sweʎo] *vb ver* **resollar** ▷ *nm* (*aliento*) breath
resuelto, -a [re'swelto, a] *pp de* **resolver** ▷ *adj* resolute, determined; **estar ~ a algo** to be set on sth; **estar ~ a hacer algo** to be determined to do sth
resultado [resul'taðo] *nm* result; (*conclusión*) outcome; **resultados** *nmpl* (*Inform*) output *sg*; **dar ~** to produce results
resultante [resul'tante] *adj* resulting, resultant
resultar [resul'tar] *vi* (*ser*) to be; (*llegar a ser*) to turn out to be; (*salir bien*) to turn out well; (*seguir*) to ensue; **~ a** (*Com*) to amount to; **~ de** to stem from; **~ en** to result in, produce; **resulta que ...** (*en consecuencia*) it follows that ...; (*parece que*) it seems that ...; **el conductor resultó muerto** the driver was killed; **no resultó** it didn't work *o* come off; **me resulta difícil hacerlo** it's difficult for me to do it
resumen [re'sumen] *nm* summary, résumé; **en ~** in short
resumir [resu'mir] *vt* to sum up; (*condensar*) to summarize; (*cortar*) to abridge, cut down; **resumirse** *vr*: **la situación se resume en pocas palabras** the situation can be summed up in a few words
resurgir [resur'xir] *vi* (*reaparecer*) to reappear
resurrección [resurrek'θjon] *nf* resurrection
retablo [re'taβlo] *nm* altarpiece
retaguardia [reta'ɣwarðja] *nf* rearguard
retahíla [reta'ila] *nf* series, string; (*de injurias*) volley, stream
retal [re'tal] *nm* remnant
retar [re'tar] *vt* (*gen*) to challenge; (*desafiar*) to defy, dare
retardar [retar'ðar] *vt* (*demorar*) to delay; (*hacer más lento*) to slow down; (*retener*) to hold back
retardo [re'tarðo] *nm* delay
retazo [re'taθo] *nm* snippet (*Brit*), fragment
retención [reten'θjon] *nf* retention; (*de pago*) deduction; (*tráfico*) hold-up; **~ fiscal** deduction for tax purposes; **~ de llamadas** (*Telec*) hold facility
retener [rete'ner] *vt* (*guardar*) to retain, keep; (*intereses*) to withhold

reticente [reti'θente] *adj* (*insinuador*) insinuating; (*engañoso*) deceptive; (*postura*) reluctant; **ser ~ a hacer algo** to be reluctant *o* unwilling to do sth
retina [re'tina] *nf* retina
retintín [retin'tin] *nm* jangle, jingle; **decir algo con ~** to say sth sarcastically
retirado, -a [reti'raðo, a] *adj* (*lugar*) remote; (*vida*) quiet; (*jubilado*) retired ▷ *nf* (*Mil*) retreat; (*de dinero*) withdrawal; (*de embajador*) recall; **batirse en retirada** to retreat
retirar [reti'rar] *vt* to withdraw; (*la mano*) to draw back; (*quitar*) to remove; (*dinero*) to take out, withdraw; (*jubilar*) to retire, pension off; **retirarse** *vr* to retreat, withdraw; (*jubilarse*) to retire; (*acostarse*) to retire, go to bed
retiro [re'tiro] *nm* retreat; (*jubilación, tb Deporte*) retirement; (*pago*) pension; (*lugar*) quiet place
reto ['reto] *nm* dare, challenge
retocar [reto'kar] *vt* (*fotografía*) to touch up, retouch
retoño [re'toɲo] *nm* sprout, shoot; (*fig*) offspring, child
retoque *etc* [re'toke] *vb ver* **retocar** ▷ *nm* retouching
retorcer [retor'θer] *vt* to twist; (*argumento*) to turn, twist; (*manos, lavado*) to wring; **retorcerse** *vr* to become twisted; (*persona*) to writhe; **~se de dolor** to writhe in *o* squirm with pain
retorcido, -a [retor'θiðo, a] *adj* (*tb fig*) twisted
retorcijón [retorθi'xon] *nm* (*Am*: *tb*: **~ de tripas**) stomach cramp
retorcimiento [retorθi'mjento] *nm* twist, twisting; (*fig*) deviousness
retórico, -a [re'toriko, a] *adj* rhetorical; (*pey*) affected, windy ▷ *nf* rhetoric; (*pey*) affectedness
retornable [retor'naβle] *adj* returnable
retornar [retor'nar] *vt* to return, give back ▷ *vi* to return, go/come back
retorno [re'torno] *nm* return; **~ del carro** (*Inform, Tip*) carriage return
retortijón [retorti'xon] *nm* twist, twisting; **~ de tripas** stomach cramp
retozar [reto'θar] *vi* (*juguetear*) to frolic, romp; (*saltar*) to gambol
retozón, -ona [reto'θon, ona] *adj* playful
retracción [retrak'θjon] *nf* retraction
retractarse [retrak'tarse] *vr* to retract; **me retracto** I take that back
retraerse [retra'erse] *vr* to retreat, withdraw
retraído, -a [retra'iðo, a] *adj* shy, retiring
retraimiento [retrai'mjento] *nm* retirement; (*timidez*) shyness
retransmisión [retransmi'sjon] *nf* repeat (broadcast)
retransmitir [retransmi'tir] *vt* (*mensaje*) to relay; (*TV etc*) to repeat, retransmit; (*: en vivo*) to broadcast live
retrasado, -a [retra'saðo, a] *adj* late; (*fam!*: *mentalmente*) backward (!), with a learning disability; (*país etc*) underdeveloped; **estar ~** (*reloj*) to be slow; (*persona, industria*) to be *o* lag behind
retrasar [retra'sar] *vt* (*demorar*) to postpone, put off; (*retardar*) to slow down ▷ *vi* (*atrasarse*) to be late; (*reloj*) to be slow; (*producción*) to fall (off); (*quedarse atrás*) to lag behind; **retrasarse** *vr* to be late; to be slow; to fall (off); to lag behind
retraso [re'traso] *nm* (*demora*) delay; (*lentitud*) slowness; (*tardanza*) lateness; (*atraso*) backwardness; **retrasos** *nmpl* (*Com*) arrears; (*deudas*) deficit *sg*, debts; **llegar con ~** to arrive late; **llegar con 25 minutos de ~** to be 25 minutes late; **llevo un ~ de seis semanas** I'm six weeks behind (with my work *etc*); **~ mental** learning disability
retratar [retra'tar] *vt* (*Arte*) to paint the portrait of; (*fotografiar*) to photograph; (*fig*) to depict, describe; **retratarse** *vr* to have one's portrait painted; to have one's photograph taken
retrato [re'trato] *nm* portrait; (*Foto*) photograph; (*descripción*) portrayal, depiction; (*fig*) likeness; **ser el vivo ~ de** to be the spitting image of
retrato-robot [re'tratoro'βo(t)] (*pl* **retratos-robot**) *nm* Identikit® picture
retreta [re'treta] *nf* retreat
retrete [re'trete] *nm* toilet
retribución [retriβu'θjon] *nf* (*recompensa*) reward; (*pago*) pay, payment
retribuir [retriβu'ir] *vt* (*recompensar*) to reward; (*pagar*) to pay
retro... [retro] *pref* retro...
retroactivo, -a [retroak'tiβo, a] *adj* retroactive, retrospective; **dar efecto ~ a un pago** to backdate a payment
retroceder [retroθe'ðer] *vi* (*echarse atrás*) to move back(wards); (*fig*) to back down; **no ~** to stand firm; **la policía hizo ~ a la multitud** the police forced the crowd back
retroceso [retro'θeso] *nm* backward movement; (*Med*) relapse; (*Com*) recession, depression; (*fig*) backing down
retrógrado, -a [re'troɣraðo, a] *adj* retrograde, retrogressive; (*Pol*) reactionary
retropropulsión [retropropul'sjon] *nf* jet propulsion
retrospectivo, -a [retrospek'tiβo, a] *adj* retrospective; **mirada retrospectiva** backward glance
retrovisor [retroβi'sor] *nm* rear-view mirror
retuit [re'twit] *nm* (*en Twitter*) retweet
retuitear [retwite'ar] *vt* (*en Twitter*) to retweet
retumbar [retum'bar] *vi* to echo, resound; (*continuamente*) to reverberate
reuma ['reuma] *nm* rheumatism
reumatismo [reuma'tismo] *nm* rheumatism
reunificar [reunifi'kar] *vt* to reunify
reunión [reu'njon] *nf* (*asamblea*) meeting; (*fiesta*) party; **~ en la cumbre** summit meeting; **~ de ventas** (*Com*) sales meeting

r

reunir [reu'nir] *vt* (*juntar*) to reunite, join (together); (*recoger*) to gather (together); (*personas*) to bring *o* get together; (*cualidades*) to combine; **reunirse** *vr* (*personas: en asamblea*) to meet, gather; **reunió a sus amigos para discutirlo** he got his friends together to talk it over
revalidar [reβali'ðar] *vt* (*ratificar*) to confirm, ratify
revalorar [reβalo'rar] *vt* to revalue, reassess
revalorizar [reβalori'θar] *vt* to revalue, reassess
revancha [re'βantʃa] *nf* revenge; (*Deporte*) return match; (*Boxeo*) return fight
revelación [reβela'θjon] *nf* revelation
revelado [reβe'laðo] *nm* developing
revelar [reβe'lar] *vt* to reveal; (*secreto*) to disclose; (*mostrar*) to show; (*Foto*) to develop
reventa [re'βenta] *nf* resale; (*especulación*) speculation; (*de entradas*) touting
reventar [reβen'tar] *vt* to burst, explode; (*molestar*) to annoy, rile ▷ *vi*, **reventarse** *vr* (*estallar*) to burst, explode; **me revienta tener que ponérmelo** I hate having to wear it; **~ de** (*fig*) to be bursting with; **~ por** to be bursting to
reventón [reβen'ton] *nm* (*Auto*) blow-out (*Brit*), flat (*US*)
reverberación [reβerβera'θjon] *nf* reverberation
reverberar [reβerβe'rar] *vi* (*luz*) to play, be reflected; (*superficie*) to shimmer; (*nieve*) to glare; (*sonido*) to reverberate
reverencia [reβe'renθja] *nf* reverence; (*inclinación*) bow
reverenciar [reβeren'θjar] *vt* to revere
reverendo, -a [reβe'rendo, a] *adj* reverend; (*fam*) big, awful; **un ~ imbécil** an awful idiot
reverente [reβe'rente] *adj* reverent
reversa [re'βersa] *nf* (*Am*) (reverse) gear
reversible [reβer'siβle] *adj* reversible
reverso [re'βerso] *nm* back, other side; (*de moneda*) reverse
revertir [reβer'tir] *vi* to revert; **~ en beneficio de** to be to the advantage of; **~ en perjuicio de** to be to the detriment of
revés [re'βes] *nm* back, wrong side; (*fig*) reverse, setback; (*Deporte*) backhand; **al ~** the wrong way round; (*de arriba abajo*) upside down; (*ropa*) inside out; **y al ~** and vice versa; **volver algo del ~** to turn sth round; (*ropa*) to turn sth inside out; **los reveses de la fortuna** the blows of fate
revestir [reβes'tir] *vt* (*poner*) to put on; (*cubrir*) to cover, coat; (*cualidad*) to have, possess; **revestirse** *vr* (*Rel*) to put on one's vestments; (*ponerse*) to put on; **~ con** *o* **de** to arm o.s. with; **el acto revestía gran solemnidad** the ceremony had great dignity
revisar [reβi'sar] *vt* (*examinar*) to check; (*texto etc*) to revise; (*Jur*) to review
revisión [reβi'sjon] *nf* revision; **~ aduanera** customs inspection; **~ de cuentas** audit; **~ salarial** wage review
revisor, a [reβi'sor, a] *nm/f* inspector; (*Ferro*) ticket collector; **~ de cuentas** auditor
revista [re'βista] *vb ver* **revestir** ▷ *nf* magazine, review; (*Teat*) revue; (*inspección*) inspection; **~ literaria** literary review; **~ de libros** book reviews (page); **~ del corazón** *magazine featuring celebrity gossip and real-life romance stories*; **pasar ~ a** to review, inspect
revivir [reβi'βir] *vt* (*recordar*) to revive memories of ▷ *vi* to revive
revocación [reβoka'θjon] *nf* repeal
revocar [reβo'kar] *vt* (*decisión*) to revoke; (*Arq*) to plaster
revolcar [reβol'kar] *vt* to knock down, send flying; **revolcarse** *vr* to roll about
revolotear [reβolote'ar] *vi* to flutter
revoltijo [reβol'tixo] *nm* mess, jumble
revoltoso, -a [reβol'toso, a] *adj* (*travieso*) naughty, unruly
revolución [reβolu'θjon] *nf* revolution
revolucionar [reβoluθjo'nar] *vt* to revolutionize
revolucionario, -a [reβoluθjo'narjo, a] *adj, nm/f* revolutionary
revolver [reβol'βer] *vt* (*desordenar*) to disturb, mess up; (*agitar*) to shake; (*líquido*) to stir; (*mover*) to move about; (*Pol*) to stir up ▷ *vi*: **~ en** to go through, rummage (about) in; **revolverse** *vr* (*en cama*) to toss and turn; (*Meteorología*) to break, turn stormy; **~se contra** to turn on *o* against; **han revuelto toda la casa** they've turned the whole house upside down
revólver [re'βolβer] *nm* revolver
revuelo [re'βwelo] *nm* fluttering; (*fig*) commotion; **armar** *o* **levantar un gran ~** to cause a great stir
revuelto, -a [re'βwelto, a] *pp de* **revolver** ▷ *adj* (*mezclado*) mixed-up, in disorder; (*mar*) rough; (*tiempo*) unsettled ▷ *nf* (*motín*) revolt; (*agitación*) commotion; **todo estaba ~** everything was in disorder *o* was topsy-turvy
revulsivo [reβul'siβo] *nm*: **servir de ~** to have a salutary effect
rey [rei] *nm* king; **Día de R~es** Twelfth Night; **los R~es Magos** the Three Wise Men, the Magi; **los R~es** the King and Queen; *see note*

REYES MAGOS

The night before the 6th of January (the Epiphany), which is a holiday in Spain, children go to bed expecting *los Reyes Magos*, the Three Wise Men who visited the baby Jesus, to bring them presents. Twelfth night processions, known as *cabalgatas*, take place that evening, when 3 people dressed as *los Reyes Magos* arrive in the town by land or sea to the delight of the children.

reyerta [re'jerta] *nf* quarrel, brawl
rezagado, -a [reθa'ɣaðo, a] *adj*: **quedar ~** to be left behind; (*estar retrasado*) to be late, be behind ▷ *nm/f* straggler
rezagar [reθa'ɣar] *vt* (*dejar atrás*) to leave behind; (*retrasar*) to delay, postpone; **rezagarse** *vr* (*atrasarse*) to fall behind
rezar [re'θar] *vi* to pray; **~ con** (*fam*) to concern, have to do with
rezo ['reθo] *nm* prayer
rezongar [reθon'gar] *vi* to grumble; (*murmurar*) to mutter; (*refunfuñar*) to growl
rezumar [reθu'mar] *vt* to ooze ▷ *vi* to leak; **rezumarse** *vr* to leak out
ría ['ria] *nf* estuary
riachuelo [rja'tʃwelo] *nm* stream
riada [ri'aða] *nf* flood
ribera [ri'βera] *nf* (*de río*) bank; (*: área*) riverside
ribete [ri'βete] *nm* (*de vestido*) border; (*fig*) addition
ribetear [riβete'ar] *vt* to edge, border
ricino [ri'θino] *nm*: **aceite de ~** castor oil
rico, -a ['riko, a] *adj* (*adinerado*) rich, wealthy; (*lujoso*) luxurious; (*comida*) delicious; (*niño*) lovely, cute ▷ *nm/f* rich person; **nuevo ~** nouveau riche
rictus ['riktus] *nm* (*mueca*) sneer, grin; **~ de amargura** bitter smile
ridiculez [riðiku'leθ] *nf* absurdity
ridiculizar [riðikuli'θar] *vt* to ridicule
ridículo, -a [ri'ðikulo, a] *adj* ridiculous; **hacer el ~** to make a fool of o.s.; **poner a algn en ~** to make a fool of sb; **ponerse en ~** to make a fool of o.s.
riego *etc* ['rjeɣo] *vb ver* **regar** ▷ *nm* (*aspersión*) watering; (*irrigación*) irrigation; **~ sanguíneo** blood flow *o* circulation
riel [rjel] *nm* rail
rienda ['rjenda] *nf* rein; (*fig*) restraint, moderating influence; **dar ~ suelta a** to give free rein to; **llevar las ~s** to be in charge
riesgo ['rjesɣo] *nm* risk; **seguro a** *o* **contra todo ~** comprehensive insurance; **~ para la salud** health hazard; **correr el ~ de** to run the risk of
rifa ['rifa] *nf* (*lotería*) raffle
rifar [ri'far] *vt* to raffle
rifle ['rifle] *nm* rifle
rigidez [rixi'ðeθ] *nf* rigidity, stiffness; (*fig*) strictness
rígido, -a ['rixiðo, a] *adj* rigid, stiff; (*moralmente*) strict, inflexible; (*cara*) wooden, expressionless
rigor [ri'ɣor] *nm* strictness, rigour; (*dureza*) toughness; (*inclemencia*) harshness; (*meticulosidad*) accuracy; **el ~ del verano** the hottest part of the summer; **con todo ~ científico** with scientific precision; **de ~** de rigueur, essential; **después de los saludos de ~** after the inevitable greetings
riguroso, -a [riɣu'roso, a] *adj* rigorous; (*Meteorología*) harsh; (*severo*) severe
rimar [ri'mar] *vi* to rhyme
rimbombante [rimbom'bante] *adj* (*fig*) pompous
rímel, rímmel ['rimel] *nm* mascara
rímmel ['rimel] *nm* = **rímel**
rin [rin] *nm* (*Am*) (wheel) rim
rincón [rin'kon] *nm* corner (*inside*)
ring [riŋ] *nm* (*Boxeo*) ring
rinoceronte [rinoθe'ronte] *nm* rhinoceros
riña ['riɲa] *nf* (*disputa*) argument; (*pelea*) brawl
riñón [ri'ɲon] *nm* kidney; **me costó un ~** (*fam*) it cost me an arm and a leg; **tener riñones** to have guts
río ['rio] *vb ver* **reír** ▷ *nm* river; (*fig*) torrent, stream; **~ abajo/arriba** downstream/upstream; **cuando el ~ suena, agua lleva** there's no smoke without fire; **R~ de la Plata** River Plate
rioja [ri'oxa] *nm*: **~** rioja wine ▷ *nf*: **La R~** La Rioja
rioplatense [riopla'tense] *adj* of *o* from the River Plate region ▷ *nm/f* native *o* inhabitant of the River Plate region
riqueza [ri'keθa] *nf* wealth, riches *pl*; (*cualidad*) richness
risa ['risa] *nf* laughter; (*una risa*) laugh; **¡qué ~!** what a laugh!; **caerse** *o* **morirse de ~** to split one's sides laughing, die laughing; **tomar algo a ~** to laugh sth off
risco ['risko] *nm* crag, cliff
risible [ri'siβle] *adj* ludicrous, laughable
risotada [riso'taða] *nf* guffaw, loud laugh
ristra ['ristra] *nf* string
risueño, -a [ri'sweɲo, a] *adj* (*sonriente*) smiling; (*contento*) cheerful
ritmo ['ritmo] *nm* rhythm; **a ~ lento** slowly; **trabajar a ~ lento** to go slow; **~ cardíaco** heart rate
rito ['rito] *nm* rite
ritual [ri'twal] *adj, nm* ritual
rival [ri'βal] *adj, nm/f* rival
rivalidad [riβali'ðað] *nf* rivalry, competition
rivalizar [riβali'θar] *vi*: **~ con** to rival, vie with
rizado, -a [ri'θaðo, a] *adj* (*pelo*) curly; (*superficie*) ridged; (*terreno*) undulating; (*mar*) choppy ▷ *nm* curls *pl*
rizar [ri'θar] *vt* to curl; **rizarse** *vr* (*el pelo*) to curl; (*agua*) to ripple; (*el mar*) to become choppy
rizo ['riθo] *nm* curl; (*en agua*) ripple
RNE *nf abr* = **Radio Nacional de España**
robar [ro'βar] *vt* to rob; (*objeto*) to steal; (*casa etc*) to break into; (*Naipes*) to draw; (*atención*) to steal, capture; (*paciencia*) to exhaust
roble ['roβle] *nm* oak
robledal [roβle'ðal], **robledo** [ro'βleðo] *nm* oakwood
robo ['roβo] *nm* robbery, theft; (*objeto robado*) stolen article *o* goods *pl*; **¡esto es un ~!** this is daylight robbery!

r

robot [ro'βo(t)] (*pl* **robots**) *adj, nm* robot ▷ *nm* (*tb:* **~ de cocina**) food processor
robustecer [roβuste'θer] *vt* to strengthen
robusto, -a [ro'βusto, a] *adj* robust, strong
roca ['roka] *nf* rock; **la R~** the Rock (of Gibraltar)
roce *etc* ['roθe] *vb ver* **rozar** ▷ *nm* rub, rubbing; (*caricia*) brush; (*Tec*) friction; (*en la piel*) graze; **tener ~ con** to have a brush with
rociar [ro'θjar] *vt* to sprinkle, spray
rocín [ro'θin] *nm* nag, hack
rocío [ro'θio] *nm* dew
rock [rok] *adj inv, nm* (*Mus*) rock (*cpd*)
rockero, -a [ro'kero, a] *adj* rock *cpd* ▷ *nm/f* rocker
rocola [ro'kola] *nf* (*Am*) jukebox
rocoso, -a [ro'koso, a] *adj* rocky
rodaballo [roða'baʎo] *nm* turbot
rodado, -a [ro'ðaðo, a] *adj* (*con ruedas*) wheeled ▷ *nf* rut
rodaja [ro'ðaxa] *nf* (*raja*) slice
rodaje [ro'ðaxe] *nm* (*Cine*) shooting, filming; (*Auto*): **en ~** running in
rodamiento [roða'mjento] *nm* (*Auto*) tread
rodar [ro'ðar] *vt* (*vehículo*) to wheel (along); (*escalera*) to roll down; (*viajar por*) to travel (over) ▷ *vi* to roll; (*coche*) to go, run; (*Cine*) to shoot, film; (*persona*) to move about (from place to place), drift; **echarlo todo a ~** (*fig*) to mess it all up
rodear [roðe'ar] *vt* to surround ▷ *vi* to go round; **rodearse** *vr*: **~se de amigos** to surround o.s. with friends
rodeo [ro'ðeo] *nm* (*ruta indirecta*) long way round, roundabout way; (*desvío*) detour; (*evasión*) evasion; (*Am*) rodeo; **dejarse de ~s** to talk straight; **hablar sin ~s** to come to the point, speak plainly
rodilla [ro'ðiʎa] *nf* knee; **de ~s** kneeling; **ponerse de ~s** to kneel (down)
rodillo [ro'ðiʎo] *nm* roller; (*Culin*) rolling-pin; (*en máquina de escribir, impresora*) platen
rododendro [roðo'ðendro] *nm* rhododendron
roedor, a [roe'ðor, a] *adj* gnawing ▷ *nm* rodent
roer [ro'er] *vt* (*masticar*) to gnaw; (*corroer, fig*) to corrode
rogar [ro'ɣar] *vt* (*pedir*) to beg, ask for ▷ *vi* (*suplicar*) to beg, plead; **rogarse** *vr*: **se ruega no fumar** please do not smoke; **~ que** (+ *subjun*) to ask to ...; **ruegue a este señor que nos deje en paz** please ask this gentleman to leave us alone; **no se hace de ~** he doesn't have to be asked twice
rojizo, -a [ro'xiθo, a] *adj* reddish
rojo, -a ['roxo, a] *adj* red ▷ *nm* red (colour); (*Pol*) red; **ponerse ~** to turn red, blush; **al ~ vivo** red-hot
rol [rol] *nm* list, roll; (*esp Am: papel*) role
rollito [ro'ʎito] *nm* (*tb:* **~ de primavera**) spring roll
rollizo, -a [ro'ʎiθo, a] *adj* (*objeto*) cylindrical; (*persona*) plump
rollo, -a ['roʎo, a] *adj* (*fam*) boring, tedious ▷ *nm* roll; (*de cuerda*) coil; (*de madera*) log; (*fam*) bore; (*discurso*) boring speech; **¡qué ~!** what a carry-on!; **la conferencia fue un ~** the lecture was a big drag
Roma ['roma] *nf* Rome; **por todas partes se va a ~** all roads lead to Rome
romance [ro'manθe] *nm* (*amoroso*) romance; (*Ling*) Romance language; (*Lit*) ballad; **hablar en ~** to speak plainly
románico, -a [ro'maniko, a] *adj, nm* Romanesque
romano, -a [ro'mano, a] *adj* Roman, of Rome ▷ *nm/f* Roman; **a la romana** in batter
romanticismo [romanti'θismo] *nm* romanticism
romántico, -a [ro'mantiko, a] *adj* romantic
rombo ['rombo] *nm* (*Geom*) rhombus; (*diseño*) diamond; (*Tip*) lozenge
romería [rome'ria] *nf* (*Rel*) pilgrimage; (*excursión*) trip, outing; *see note*

ROMERÍA

Originally a pilgrimage to a shrine or church to express devotion to Our Lady or a local Saint, the *romería* has also become a rural *fiesta* which accompanies the pilgrimage. People come from all over to attend, bringing their own food and drink, and spend the day in celebration.

romero, -a [ro'mero, a] *nm/f* pilgrim ▷ *nm* rosemary
romo, -a ['romo, a] *adj* blunt; (*fig*) dull
rompecabezas [rompeka'βeθas] *nm inv* riddle, puzzle; (*juego*) jigsaw (puzzle)
rompehielos [rompe'jelos] *nm inv* icebreaker
rompehuelgas (*Am*) [rompe'welɣas] *nm inv* strikebreaker, scab
rompeolas [rompe'olas] *nm inv* breakwater
romper [rom'per] *vt* to break; (*hacer pedazos*) to smash; (*papel, tela etc*) to tear, rip; (*relaciones*) to break off ▷ *vi* (*olas*) to break; (*sol, diente*) to break through; **~ un contrato** to break a contract; **~ a** to start (suddenly) to; **~ a llorar** to burst into tears; **~ con algn** to fall out with sb; **ha roto con su novio** she has broken up with her fiancé
rompimiento [rompi'mjento] *nm* (*acto*) breaking; (*fig*) break; (*quiebra*) crack; **~ de relaciones** breaking off of relations
ron [ron] *nm* rum
roncar [ron'kar] *vi* (*al dormir*) to snore; (*animal*) to roar
roncha ['rontʃa] *nf* (*cardenal*) bruise; (*hinchazón*) swelling
ronco, -a ['ronko, a] *adj* (*afónico*) hoarse; (*áspero*) raucous
ronda ['ronda] *nf* (*de bebidas etc*) round;

(*patrulla*) patrol; (*de naipes*) hand, game; **ir de ~** to do one's round
rondar [ron'dar] *vt* to patrol; (*a una persona*) to hang round; (*molestar*) to harass; (*a una chica*) to court ▷ *vi* to patrol; (*fig*) to prowl round; (*Mus*) to go serenading
ronquido [ron'kiðo] *nm* snore, snoring
ronronear [ronrone'ar] *vi* to purr
ronroneo [ronro'neo] *nm* purr
roña ['roɲa] *nf* (*en veterinaria*) mange; (*mugre*) dirt, grime; (*óxido*) rust
roñica [ro'ɲika] *nm/f* (*fam*) skinflint
roñoso, -a [ro'ɲoso, a] *adj* (*mugriento*) filthy; (*tacaño*) mean
ropa ['ropa] *nf* clothes *pl*, clothing; **~ blanca** linen; **~ de cama** bed linen; **~ de color** coloureds *pl*; **~ interior** underwear; **~ lavada** *o* **para lavar** washing; **~ planchada** ironing; **~ sucia** dirty clothes *pl*, dirty washing; **~ usada** secondhand clothes
ropaje [ro'paxe] *nm* gown, robes *pl*
ropero [ro'pero] *nm* linen cupboard; (*guardarropa*) wardrobe
rosa ['rosa] *adj inv* pink ▷ *nf* rose; (*Anat*) red birthmark; **~ de los vientos** the compass; **estar como una ~** to feel as fresh as a daisy; **(color) de ~** pink
rosado, -a [ro'saðo, a] *adj* pink ▷ *nm* rosé
rosal [ro'sal] *nm* rosebush
rosario [ro'sarjo] *nm* (*Rel*) rosary; (*fig: serie*) string; **rezar el ~** to say the rosary
rosca ['roska] *nf* (*de tornillo*) thread; (*de humo*) coil, spiral; (*pan, postre*) ring-shaped roll/pastry; **hacer la ~ a algn** (*fam*) to suck up to sb; **pasarse de ~** (*fig*) to go too far
rosetón [rose'ton] *nm* rosette; (*Arq*) rose window
rosquilla [ros'kiʎa] *nf* ring-shaped cake; (*de humo*) ring
rostro ['rostro] *nm* (*cara*) face; (*fig*) cheek
rotación [rota'θjon] *nf* rotation; **~ de cultivos** crop rotation
rotativo, -a [rota'tiβo, a] *adj* rotary ▷ *nm* newspaper
roto, -a ['roto, a] *pp de* **romper** ▷ *adj* broken; (*en pedazos*) smashed; (*tela, papel*) torn; (*vida*) shattered ▷ *nm* (*en vestido*) hole, tear
rotonda [ro'tonda] *nf* roundabout
rótula ['rotula] *nf* kneecap; (*Tec*) ball-and-socket joint
rotulador [rotula'ðor] *nm* felt-tip pen
rotular [rotu'lar] *vt* (*carta, documento*) to head, entitle; (*objeto*) to label
rótulo ['rotulo] *nm* (*título*) heading, title; (*etiqueta*) label; (*letrero*) sign
rotundamente [rotunda'mente] *adv* (*negar*) flatly; (*responder, afirmar*) emphatically
rotundo, -a [ro'tundo, a] *adj* round; (*enfático*) emphatic
rotura [ro'tura] *nf* (*rompimiento*) breaking; (*Med*) fracture
roturar [rotu'rar] *vt* to plough
roulote [ru'lote] *nf* caravan (*Brit*), trailer (*US*)
rozadura [roθa'ðura] *nf* abrasion, graze
rozar [ro'θar] *vt* (*frotar*) to rub; (*arañar*) to scratch; (*ensuciar*) to dirty; (*Med*) to graze; (*tocar ligeramente*) to shave, skim; (*fig*) to touch *o* border on; **rozarse** *vr* to rub (together); **~ con** (*fam*) to rub shoulders with
Rte. *abr* = **remite; remitente**
RTVE *nf abr* (*TV*) = **Radiotelevisión Española**
rubí [ru'βi] *nm* ruby; (*de reloj*) jewel
rubio, -a ['ruβjo, a] *adj* fair-haired, blond(e) ▷ *nm/f* blond/blonde; **tabaco ~** Virginia tobacco; **(cerveza) rubia** lager
rubor [ru'βor] *nm* (*sonrojo*) blush; (*timidez*) bashfulness
ruborizarse [ruβori'θarse] *vr* to blush
ruboroso, -a [ruβo'roso, a] *adj* blushing
rúbrica ['ruβrika] *nf* (*título*) title, heading; (*de la firma*) flourish; **bajo la ~ de** under the heading of
rubricar [ruβri'kar] *vt* (*firmar*) to sign with a flourish; (*concluir*) to sign and seal
rudeza [ru'ðeθa] *nf* (*tosquedad*) coarseness; (*sencillez*) simplicity
rudimentario, -a [ruðimen'tarjo, a] *adj* rudimentary, basic
rudo, -a ['ruðo, a] *adj* (*sin pulir*) unpolished; (*grosero*) coarse; (*violento*) violent; (*sencillo*) simple
rueda ['rweða] *nf* wheel; (*círculo*) ring, circle; (*rodaja*) slice, round; (*en impresora etc*) sprocket; **~ de auxilio** (*Am*) spare tyre; **~ delantera/trasera/de repuesto** front/back/spare wheel; **~ impresora** (*Inform*) print wheel; **~ de prensa** press conference; **~ gigante** (*Am*) big (*Brit*) *o* Ferris (*US*) wheel
ruedo *etc* ['rweðo] *vb ver* **rodar** ▷ *nm* (*contorno*) edge, border; (*de vestido*) hem; (*círculo*) circle; (*Taur*) arena, bullring; (*esterilla*) (round) mat
ruego *etc* ['rweɣo] *vb ver* **rogar** ▷ *nm* request; **a ~ de** at the request of; **"~s y preguntas"** "question and answer session"
rufián [ru'fjan] *nm* scoundrel
rugby ['ruɣβi] *nm* rugby
rugido [ru'xiðo] *nm* roar
rugir [ru'xir] *vi* to roar; (*toro*) to bellow; (*estómago*) to rumble
rugoso, -a [ru'ɣoso, a] *adj* (*arrugado*) wrinkled; (*áspero*) rough; (*desigual*) ridged
ruido ['rwiðo] *nm* noise; (*sonido*) sound; (*alboroto*) racket, row; (*escándalo*) commotion, rumpus; **~ de fondo** background noise; **hacer** *o* **meter ~** to cause a stir
ruidoso, -a [rwi'ðoso, a] *adj* noisy, loud; (*fig*) sensational
ruin [rwin] *adj* contemptible, mean
ruina ['rwina] *nf* ruin; (*hundimiento*) collapse; (*de persona*) ruin, downfall; **estar hecho una ~** to be a wreck; **la empresa le llevó a la ~** the venture ruined him (financially)
ruindad [rwin'dað] *nf* lowness, meanness; (*acto*) low *o* mean act

r

ruinoso, -a [rwi'noso, a] *adj* ruinous; (*destartalado*) dilapidated, tumbledown; (*Com*) disastrous
ruiseñor [rwise'ɲor] *nm* nightingale
rulero [ru'lero] *nm* (*Am*) roller
ruleta [ru'leta] *nf* roulette
rulo ['rulo] *nm* (*para el pelo*) curler
Rumania [ru'manja] *nf* Rumania
rumano, -a [ru'mano, a] *adj, nm/f* Rumanian
rumba ['rumba] *nf* rumba
rumbo ['rumbo] *nm* (*ruta*) route, direction; (*ángulo de dirección*) course, bearing; (*fig*) course of events; **con ~ a** in the direction of; **ir con ~ a** to be heading for; (*Naut*) to be bound for
rumboso, -a [rum'boso, a] *adj* (*generoso*) generous
rumiante [ru'mjante] *nm* ruminant
rumiar [ru'mjar] *vt* to chew; (*fig*) to chew over ▷ *vi* to chew the cud
rumor [ru'mor] *nm* (*ruido sordo*) low sound; (*murmuración*) murmur, buzz
rumorearse [rumore'arse] *vr*: **se rumorea que** it is rumoured that
runrún [run'run] *nm* (*de voces*) murmur, sound of voices; (*fig*) rumour; (*de una máquina*) whirr
rupestre [ru'pestre] *adj* rock *cpd*; **pintura ~** cave painting
ruptura [rup'tura] *nf* (*gen*) rupture; (*disputa*) split; (*de contrato*) breach; (*de relaciones*) breaking-off
rural [ru'ral] *adj* rural
Rusia ['rusja] *nf* Russia
ruso, -a ['ruso, a] *adj, nm/f* Russian ▷ *nm* (*Ling*) Russian
rústico, -a ['rustiko, a] *adj* rustic; (*ordinario*) coarse, uncouth ▷ *nm/f* yokel ▷ *nf*: **libro en rústica** paperback (book)
ruta ['ruta] *nf* route
rutina [ru'tina] *nf* routine; **~ diaria** daily routine; **por ~** as a matter of course
rutinario, -a [ruti'narjo, a] *adj* routine

S

S *abr* (= *san, santo, a*) St.; (= *sur*) S
s. *abr* (*tb*: **S.**: = *siglo*) c.; (= *siguiente*) foll.
S.ª *abr* (= *Sierra*) Mts
S.A. *abr* (= *Sociedad Anónima*) Ltd., Inc. (US); (= *Su Alteza*) H.H.
sábado ['saβaðo] *nm* Saturday; (*de los judíos*) Sabbath; **del ~ en ocho días** a week on Saturday; **un ~ sí y otro no, cada dos ~s** every other Saturday; **S~ Santo** Holy Saturday; *ver tb* **Semana Santa**
sábana ['saβana] *nf* sheet; **se le pegan las ~s** he can't get up in the morning
sabandija [saβan'dixa] *nf* (*bicho*) bug; (*fig*) louse
sabañón [saβa'ɲon] *nm* chilblain
sabelotodo [saβelo'toðo] *nm/f inv* know-all
saber [sa'βer] *vt* to know; (*llegar a conocer*) to find out, learn; (*tener capacidad de*) to know how to ▷ *vi*: **~ a** to taste of, taste like ▷ *nm* knowledge, learning; **saberse** *vr*: **se sabe que ...** it is known that ...; **no se sabe** nobody knows; **a ~** namely; **¿sabes conducir/nadar?** can you drive/swim?; **¿sabes francés?** do you *o* can you speak French?; **~ de memoria** to know by heart; **lo sé** I know; **hacer ~** to inform, let know; **que yo sepa** as far as I know; **vete** *o* **anda a ~** your guess is as good as mine, who knows!; **¿sabe?** (*fam*) you know (what I mean)?; **le sabe mal que otro la saque a bailar** it upsets him that anybody else should ask her to dance

sabiduría [saβiðu'ria] *nf* (*conocimientos*) wisdom; (*instrucción*) learning; ~ **popular** folklore
sabiendas [sa'βjendas]: **a ~** *adv* knowingly; **a ~ de que ...** knowing full well that ...
sabio, -a ['saβjo, a] *adj* (*docto*) learned; (*prudente*) wise, sensible
sable [sa'βle] *nm* sabre
sabor [sa'βor] *nm* taste, flavour; (*fig*) flavour; **sin ~** flavourless
saborear [saβore'ar] *vt* to taste, savour; (*fig*) to relish
sabotaje [saβo'taxe] *nm* sabotage
saboteador, a [saβotea'ðor, a] *nm/f* saboteur
sabotear [saβote'ar] *vt* to sabotage
sabré *etc* [sa'βre] *vb ver* **saber**
sabroso, -a [sa'βroso, a] *adj* tasty; (*fig fam*) racy, salty
sacacorchos [saka'kortʃos] *nm inv* corkscrew
sacapuntas [saka'puntas] *nm inv* pencil sharpener
sacar [sa'kar] *vt* to take out; (*fig: extraer*) to get (out); (*quitar*) to remove, get out; (*hacer salir*) to bring out; (*fondos: de cuenta*) to draw out, withdraw; (*obtener: legado etc*) to get; (*demostrar*) to show; (*conclusión*) to draw; (*novela etc*) to publish, bring out; (*ropa*) to take off; (*obra*) to make; (*premio*) to receive; (*entradas*) to get; (*Tenis*) to serve; (*Fútbol*) to put into play; **~ adelante** (*niño*) to bring up; (*negocio*) to carry on, go on with; **~ a algn a bailar** to get sb up to dance; **~ a algn de sí** to infuriate sb; **~ una foto** to take a photo; **~ la lengua** to stick out one's tongue; **~ buenas/malas notas** to get good/bad marks
sacarina [saka'rina] *nf* saccharin(e)
sacerdote [saθer'ðote] *nm* priest
saciar [sa'θjar] *vt* (*hartar*) to satiate; (*fig*) to satisfy; **saciarse** *vr* (*de comida*) to get full up; (*fig*) to be satisfied
saco ['sako] *nm* bag; (*grande*) sack; (*contenido*) bagful; (*Am: chaqueta*) jacket; **~ de dormir** sleeping bag
sacramento [sakra'mento] *nm* sacrament
sacrificar [sakrifi'kar] *vt* to sacrifice; (*animal*) to slaughter; (*perro etc*) to put to sleep; **sacrificarse** *vr* to sacrifice o.s.
sacrificio [sakri'fiθjo] *nm* sacrifice
sacrilegio [sakri'lexjo] *nm* sacrilege
sacrílego, -a [sa'krileɣo, a] *adj* sacrilegious
sacristán [sakris'tan] *nm* verger
sacristía [sakris'tia] *nf* sacristy
sacro, -a ['sakro, a] *adj* sacred
sacudida [saku'ðiða] *nf* (*agitación*) shake, shaking; (*sacudimiento*) jolt, bump; (*fig*) violent change; (*Pol etc*) upheaval; **~ eléctrica** electric shock
sacudir [saku'ðir] *vt* to shake; (*golpear*) to hit; (*ala*) to flap; (*alfombra*) to beat; **~ a algn** (*fam*) to belt sb
sádico, -a ['saðiko, a] *adj* sadistic ▷ *nm/f* sadist
sadismo [sa'ðismo] *nm* sadism
sadomasoquismo [saðomaso'kismo] *nm* sadomasochism, S & M
sadomasoquista [saðomaso'kista] *adj* sadomasochistic ▷ *nm/f* sadomasochist
saeta [sa'eta] *nf* (*flecha*) arrow; (*Mus*) *sacred song in flamenco style*
safari [sa'fari] *nm* safari
sagacidad [saɣaθi'ðað] *nf* shrewdness, cleverness
sagaz [sa'ɣaθ] *adj* shrewd, clever
Sagitario [saxi'tarjo] *nm* (*Astro*) Sagittarius
sagrado, -a [sa'ɣraðo, a] *adj* sacred, holy
Sáhara ['saara] *nm*: **el ~** the Sahara (desert)
sal [sal] *vb ver* **salir** ▷ *nf* salt; (*gracia*) wit; (*encanto*) charm; **~es de baño** bath salts; **~ gorda** *o* **de cocina** kitchen *o* cooking salt
sala ['sala] *nf* (*cuarto grande*) large room; (*tb*: **~ de estar**) living room; (*Teat*) house, auditorium; (*de hospital*) ward; **~ de apelación** court; **~ de conferencias** lecture hall; **~ de espera** waiting room; **~ de embarque** departure lounge; **~ de estar** living room; **~ de juntas** (*Com*) boardroom; **~ VIP** (*en aeropuerto, discoteca*) VIP lounge
salado, -a [sa'laðo, a] *adj* salty; (*fig*) witty, amusing; **agua salada** salt water
salar [sa'lar] *vt* to salt, add salt to
salariado, -a [sala'rjaðo, a] *adj* (*empleado*) salaried
salarial [sala'rjal] *adj* (*aumento, revisión*) wage *cpd*, salary *cpd*, pay *cpd*
salario [sa'larjo] *nm* wage, pay
salchicha [sal'tʃitʃa] *nf* (pork) sausage
salchichón [saltʃi'tʃon] *nm* (salami-type) sausage
saldar [sal'dar] *vt* to pay; (*vender*) to sell off; (*fig*) to settle, resolve
saldo ['saldo] *nm* (*pago*) settlement; (*de una cuenta*) balance; (*lo restante*) remnant(s) (*pl*), remainder; (*de móvil*) credit; **saldos** *nmpl* (*en tienda*) sale; (*Com*): **~ anterior** balance brought forward; **~ acreedor/deudor** *o* **pasivo** credit/debit balance; **~ final** final balance
saldré *etc* [sal'dre] *vb ver* **salir**
salero [sa'lero] *nm* salt cellar; (*ingenio*) wit; (*encanto*) charm
salgo *etc* ['salɣa] *vb ver* **salir**
salida [sa'liða] *nf* (*puerta etc*) exit, way out; (*acto*) leaving, going out; (*de tren, Aviat*) departure; (*Com, Tec*) output, production; (*fig*) way out; (*resultado*) outcome; (*Com: oportunidad*) opening; (*Geo, válvula*) outlet; (*de gas*) leak; (*ocurrencia*) joke; **calle sin ~** cul-de-sac; **~ de baño** (*Am*) bathrobe; **a la ~ del teatro** after the theatre; **dar la ~** (*Deporte*) to give the starting signal; **~ de incendios** fire escape; **~ impresa** (*Inform*) hard copy; **no hay ~** there's no way out of it; **no tenemos otra ~** we have no option; **tener ~s** to be witty
salido, -a [sa'liðo, a] *adj* (*fam*) randy

S

saliente [sa'ljente] *adj* (*Arq*) projecting; (*sol*) rising; (*fig*) outstanding

PALABRA CLAVE

salir [sa'lir] *vi* **1** (*persona*) to come *o* go out; (*tren, avión*) to leave; **Juan ha salido** Juan has gone out; **salió de la cocina** he came out of the kitchen; **salimos de Madrid a las ocho** we left Madrid at eight (o'clock); **salió corriendo (del cuarto)** he ran out (of the room); **salir de un apuro** to get out of a jam
2 (*pelo*) to grow; (*diente*) to come through; (*disco, libro*) to come out; (*planta, número de lotería*) to come up; **salir a la superficie** to come to the surface; **anoche salió en la tele** she appeared *o* was on TV last night; **salió en todos los periódicos** it was in all the papers; **le salió un trabajo** he got a job
3 (*resultar*): **la muchacha nos salió muy trabajadora** the girl turned out to be a very hard worker; **la comida te ha salido exquisita** the food was delicious; **sale muy caro** it's very expensive; **la entrevista que hice me salió bien/mal** the interview I did turned out *o* went well/badly; **nos salió a 50 euros cada uno** it worked out at 50 euros each; **no salen las cuentas** it doesn't work out *o* add up; **salir ganando** to come out on top; **salir perdiendo** to lose out
4 (*Deporte*) to start; (*Naipes*) to lead
5: **salir con algn** to go out with sb
6: **salir adelante**: **no sé como haré para salir adelante** I don't know how I'll get by
salirse *vr* **1** (*líquido*) to spill; (*animal*) to escape
2 (*desviarse*): **salirse de la carretera** to leave *o* go off the road; **salirse de lo normal** to be unusual; **salirse del tema** to get off the point
3: **salirse con la suya** to get one's own way

saliva [sa'liβa] *nf* saliva
salmo ['salmo] *nm* psalm
salmón [sal'mon] *nm* salmon
salmonete [salmo'nete] *nm* red mullet
salmuera [sal'mwera] *nf* pickle, brine
salón [sa'lon] *nm* (*de casa*) living-room, lounge; (*muebles*) lounge suite; **~ de belleza** beauty parlour; **~ de baile** dance hall; **~ de actos/sesiones** assembly hall
salpicadera [salpika'ðera] *nf* (*Am*) mudguard (*Brit*), fender (*US*)
salpicadero [salpika'ðero] *nm* (*Auto*) dashboard
salpicar [salpi'kar] *vt* (*de barro, pintura*) to splash; (*rociar*) to sprinkle, spatter; (*esparcir*) to scatter
salpicón [salpi'kon] *nm* (*acto*) splashing; (*Culin*) meat *o* fish salad; (*tb*: **~ de marisco**) seafood salad
salsa ['salsa] *nf* sauce; (*con carne asada*) gravy; (*fig*) spice; **~ mayonesa** mayonnaise; **estar en su ~** (*fam*) to be in one's element
saltamontes [salta'montes] *nm inv* grasshopper
saltar [sal'tar] *vt* to jump (over), leap (over); (*dejar de lado*) to skip, miss out ▷ *vi* to jump, leap; (*pelota*) to bounce; (*al aire*) to fly up; (*quebrarse*) to break; (*al agua*) to dive; (*fig*) to explode, blow up; (*botón*) to come off; (*corcho*) to pop out; **saltarse** *vr* (*omitir*) to skip, miss; **salta a la vista** it's obvious; **~se todas las reglas** to break all the rules
saltear [salte'ar] *vt* (*robar*) to rob (in a holdup); (*asaltar*) to assault, attack; (*Culin*) to sauté
saltimbanqui [saltim'banki] *nm/f* acrobat
salto ['salto] *nm* jump, leap; (*al agua*) dive; **a ~s** by jumping; **~ de agua** waterfall; **~ de altura** high jump; **~ de cama** negligee; **~ mortal** somersault; (*Inform*): **~ de línea** line feed; **~ de línea automático** wordwrap; **~ de página** formfeed
saltón, -ona [sal'ton, ona] *adj* (*ojos*) bulging, popping; (*dientes*) protruding
salubre [sa'luβre] *adj* healthy, salubrious
salud [sa'luð] *nf* health; **estar bien/mal de ~** to be in good/poor health; **¡(a su) ~!** cheers!, good health!; **beber a la ~ de** to drink (to) the health of
saludable [salu'ðaβle] *adj* (*de buena salud*) healthy; (*provechoso*) good, beneficial
saludar [salu'ðar] *vt* to greet; (*Mil*) to salute; **ir a ~ a algn** to drop in to see sb; **salude de mi parte a X** give my regards to X; **le saluda atentamente** (*en carta*) yours faithfully
saludo [sa'luðo] *nm* greeting; **~s** (*en carta*) best wishes, regards; **un ~ afectuoso** *o* **cordial** yours sincerely
salva ['salβa] *nf* (*Mil*) salvo; **una ~ de aplausos** thunderous applause
salvación [salβa'θjon] *nf* salvation; (*rescate*) rescue
salvado [sal'βaðo] *nm* bran
salvador [salβa'ðor] *nm* rescuer, saviour; **el S~** the Saviour; **El S~** El Salvador; **San S~** San Salvador
salvadoreño, -a [salβaðo'reɲo, a] *adj, nm/f* Salvadoran, Salvadorian
salvaguardar [salβaɣwar'ðar] *vt* to safeguard; (*Inform*) to back up, make a backup copy of
salvajada [salβa'xaða] *nf* savage deed, atrocity
salvaje [sal'βaxe] *adj* wild; (*tribu*) savage
salvajismo [salβa'xismo] *nm* savagery
salvamanteles [salβaman'teles] *nm inv* table mat
salvamento [salβa'mento] *nm* (*acción*) rescue; (*de naufragio*) salvage; **~ y socorrismo** life-saving
salvapantallas [salβapan'taʎas] *nm inv* screensaver

salvar [sal'βar] *vt* (*rescatar*) to save, rescue; (*resolver*) to overcome, resolve; (*cubrir distancias*) to cover, travel; (*hacer excepción*) to except, exclude; (*un barco*) to salvage; **salvarse** *vr* to save o.s., escape; **¡sálvese el que pueda!** every man for himself!
salvavidas [salβa'βiðas] *adj inv*: **bote/chaleco/cinturón ~** lifeboat/lifejacket/lifebelt
salvia ['salβja] *nf* sage
salvo, -a ['salβo, a] *adj* safe ▷ *prep* except (for), save; **~ error u omisión** (*Com*) errors and omissions excepted; **a ~** out of danger; **~ que** unless
salvoconducto [salβokon'dukto] *nm* safe-conduct
samba ['samba] *nf* samba
san [san] *n* (*apócope de* **santo**) saint; **~ Juan** St. John; *ver tb* **noche**
sanar [sa'nar] *vt* (*herida*) to heal; (*persona*) to cure ▷ *vi* (*persona*) to get well, recover; (*herida*) to heal
sanatorio [sana'torjo] *nm* sanatorium
sanción [san'θjon] *nf* sanction
sancionar [sanθjo'nar] *vt* to sanction
sancochado, -a [sanko'tʃaðo, a] *adj* (*Am: Culin*) underdone, rare
sandalia [san'dalja] *nf* sandal
sandez [san'deθ] *nf* (*cualidad*) foolishness; (*acción*) stupid thing; **decir sandeces** to talk nonsense
sandía [san'dia] *nf* watermelon
sandinista [sanði'nista] *adj, nm/f* Sandinist(a)
sandwich ['sandwitʃ] (*pl* **sandwichs** *o* **sandwiches**) *nm* sandwich
saneamiento [sanea'mjento] *nm* sanitation
sanear [sane'ar] *vt* to drain; (*indemnizar*) to compensate; (*Econ*) to reorganize
Sanfermines [sanfer'mines] *nmpl see note*

SANFERMINES

The *Sanfermines* are a week of *fiestas* in Pamplona, the capital of Navarre, made famous by Ernest Hemingway. From the 7th of July, the feast of San Fermín, crowds of mainly young people take to the streets drinking, singing and dancing. Early in the morning bulls are released along the narrow streets leading to the bullring, and people risk serious injury by running out in front of them, a custom which is also typical of many Spanish villages.

sangrar [san'grar] *vt, vi* to bleed; (*texto*) to indent
sangre ['sangre] *nf* blood; **~ fría** sangfroid; **a ~ fría** in cold blood
sangría [san'gria] *nf* (*Med*) bleeding; (*Culin*) sangria (*sweetened drink of red wine with fruit*), ≈ fruit cup
sangriento, -a [san'grjento, a] *adj* bloody
sanguijuela [sangi'xwela] *nf* (*Zool, fig*) leech
sanguinario, -a [sangi'narjo, a] *adj* bloodthirsty
sanguíneo, -a [san'gineo, a] *adj* blood *cpd*
sanidad [sani'ðað] *nf* sanitation; (*calidad de sano*) health, healthiness; **~ pública** public health (department)
San Isidro [sani'sidro] *nm patron saint of Madrid*

SAN ISIDRO

San Isidro is the patron saint of Madrid, and gives his name to the week-long festivities which take place around the 15th May. Originally an 18th-century trade fair, the *San Isidro* celebrations now include music, dance, a famous *romería*, theatre and bullfighting.

sanitario, -a [sani'tarjo, a] *adj* sanitary; (*de la salud*) health *cpd* ▷ *nm*: **~s** *nmpl* toilets (*Brit*), restroom *sg* (*US*)
sano, -a ['sano, a] *adj* healthy; (*sin daños*) sound; (*comida*) wholesome; (*entero*) whole, intact; **~ y salvo** safe and sound
Santiago [san'tjaɣo] *nm*: **~ (de Chile)** Santiago
santiamén [santja'men] *nm*: **en un ~** in no time at all
santidad [santi'ðað] *nf* holiness, sanctity
santificar [santifi'kar] *vt* to sanctify
santiguarse [santi'ɣwarse] *vr* to make the sign of the cross
santo, -a ['santo, a] *adj* holy; (*fig*) wonderful, miraculous ▷ *nm/f* saint ▷ *nm* saint's day; **hacer su santa voluntad** to do as one jolly well pleases; **¿a ~ de qué ...?** why on earth ...?; **se le fue el ~ al cielo** he forgot what he was about to say; **~ y seña** password; *see note*

SANTO

As well as celebrating their birthday Spaniards have traditionally celebrated *el santo*, their Saint's day, when the Saint they were called after at birth, eg San Pedro or la Virgen de los Dolores, is honoured in the Christian calendar. This is a custom which is gradually dying out.

santuario [san'twarjo] *nm* sanctuary, shrine
saña ['saɲa] *nf* rage, fury
sapo ['sapo] *nm* toad
saque *etc* ['sake] *vb ver* **sacar** ▷ *nm* (*Tenis*) service, serve; (*Fútbol*) throw-in; **~ inicial** kick-off; **~ de esquina** corner (kick); **tener buen ~** to eat heartily
saquear [sake'ar] *vt* (*Mil*) to sack; (*robar*) to loot, plunder; (*fig*) to ransack

saqueo [sa'keo] *nm* sacking; looting, plundering; ransacking
sarampión [saram'pjon] *nm* measles *sg*
sarcasmo [sar'kasmo] *nm* sarcasm
sarcástico, -a [sar'kastiko, a] *adj* sarcastic
sarcófago [sar'kofaɣo] *nm* sarcophagus
sardina [sar'ðina] *nf* sardine
sardónico, -a [sar'ðoniko, a] *adj* sardonic; (*irónico*) ironical, sarcastic
sargento [sar'xento] *nm* sergeant
sarmiento [sar'mjento] *nm* vine shoot
sarna ['sarna] *nf* itch; (*Med*) scabies
sarpullido [sarpu'ʎiðo] *nm* (*Med*) rash
sarro ['sarro] *nm* deposit; (*en dientes*) tartar, plaque
sartén [sar'ten] *nf* frying pan; **tener la ~ por el mango** to rule the roost
sastre ['sastre] *nm* tailor
sastrería [sastre'ria] *nf* (*arte*) tailoring; (*tienda*) tailor's (shop)
Satanás [sata'nas] *nm* Satan
satélite [sa'telite] *nm* satellite
sátira ['satira] *nf* satire
satisfacción [satisfak'θjon] *nf* satisfaction
satisfacer [satisfa'θer] *vt* to satisfy; (*gastos*) to meet; (*deuda*) to pay; (*Com: letra de cambio*) to honour (*Brit*), honor (*US*); (*pérdida*) to make good; **satisfacerse** *vr* to satisfy o.s., be satisfied; (*vengarse*) to take revenge
satisfecho, -a [satis'fetʃo, a] *pp de* **satisfacer** ▷ *adj* satisfied; (*contento*) content(ed), happy; (*tb*: **~ de sí mismo**) self-satisfied, smug
saturación [satura'θjon] *nf* saturation; **llegar a la ~** to reach saturation point
saturar [satu'rar] *vt* to saturate; **saturarse** *vr* (*mercado, aeropuerto*) to reach saturation point; **¡estoy saturado de tanta televisión!** I can't take any more television!
sauce ['sauθe] *nm* willow; **~ llorón** weeping willow
saudí [sau'ði] *adj, nm/f* Saudi
sauna ['sauna] *nf* sauna
savia ['saβja] *nf* sap
saxo ['sakso] *nm* sax
saxofón [sakso'fon] *nm* saxophone
sazonado, -a [saθo'naðo, a] *adj* (*fruta*) ripe; (*Culin*) flavoured, seasoned
sazonar [saθo'nar] *vt* to ripen; (*Culin*) to flavour, season
scooter [e'skuter] *nf* (*Esp*) scooter
Scotch® [skotʃ] *nm* (*Am*) Sellotape® (*Brit*), Scotch tape® (*US*)
screenshot [es'krinʃot] *nm* screenshot
SE *abr* (*= sudeste*) SE

PALABRA CLAVE

se [se] *pron* **1** (*reflexivo: sg: m*) himself; (*: f*) herself; (*: pl*) themselves; (*: cosa*) itself; (*: de Vd*) yourself; (*: de Vds*) yourselves; (*indefinido*) oneself; **se mira en el espejo** he looks at himself in the mirror; **¡siéntese!** sit down!; **se durmió** he fell asleep; **se está preparando** she's getting (herself) ready; *para usos léxicos del pron ver el vb en cuestión, p. ej.* **arrepentirse**
2 (*como complemento indirecto*) to him; to her; to them; to it; to you; **se lo dije ayer** (*a Vd*) I told you yesterday; **se compró un sombrero** he bought himself a hat; **se rompió la pierna** he broke his leg; **cortarse el pelo** to get one's hair cut; (*uno mismo*) to cut one's hair; **se comió un pastel** he ate a cake
3 (*uso recíproco*) each other, one another; **se miraron (el uno al otro)** they looked at each other *o* one another
4 (*en oraciones pasivas*): **se han vendido muchos libros** a lot of books have been sold; **"se vende coche"** "car for sale"
5 (*impers*): **se dice que** people say that, it is said that; **allí se come muy bien** the food there is very good, you can eat very well there

sé [se] *vb ver* **saber, ser**
sea *etc* ['sea] *vb ver* **ser**
sebo ['seβo] *nm* fat, grease
seca ['seka] *nf ver* **seco**
secador [seka'ðor] *nm*: **~ para el pelo** hairdryer
secadora [seka'ðora] *nf* tumble dryer; **~ centrífuga** spin-dryer
secano [se'kano] *nm* (*Agr: tb*: **tierra de ~**) dry land *o* region; **cultivo de ~** dry farming
secar [se'kar] *vt* to dry; (*superficie*) to wipe dry; (*frente, suelo*) to mop; (*líquido*) to mop up; (*tinta*) to blot; **secarse** *vr* to dry (off); (*río, planta*) to dry up
sección [sek'θjon] *nf* section; (*Com*) department; **~ deportiva** (*en periódico*) sports page(s)
seco, -a ['seko, a] *adj* dry; (*fruta*) dried; (*persona: magro*) thin, skinny; (*carácter*) cold; (*antipático*) disagreeable; (*respuesta*) sharp, curt ▷ *nf* dry season; **habrá pan a secas** there will be just bread; **decir algo a secas** to say sth curtly; **parar en ~** to stop dead
secretaría [sekreta'ria] *nf* secretariat; (*oficina*) secretary's office
secretario, -a [sekre'tarjo, a] *nm/f* secretary; **~ adjunto** (*Com*) assistant secretary
secreto, -a [se'kreto, a] *adj* secret; (*información*) confidential; (*persona*) secretive ▷ *nm* secret; (*calidad*) secrecy
secta ['sekta] *nf* sect
sectario, -a [sek'tarjo, a] *adj* sectarian
sector [sek'tor] *nm* sector (*tb Inform*); (*de opinión*) section; (*fig: campo*) area, field; **~ privado/público** (*Com: Econ*) private/public sector
secuela [se'kwela] *nf* consequence
secuencia [se'kwenθja] *nf* sequence
secuestrar [sekwes'trar] *vt* to kidnap; (*avión*) to hijack; (*bienes*) to seize, confiscate

secuestro [se'kwestro] *nm* kidnapping; hijack; seizure, confiscation
secular [seku'lar] *adj* secular
secundar [sekun'dar] *vt* to second, support
secundario, -a [sekun'darjo, a] *adj* secondary; (*carretera*) side *cpd*; (*Inform*) background *cpd* ▷ *nf* secondary education; *ver tb* **sistema educativo**
sed [seð] *nf* thirst; (*fig*) thirst, craving; **tener ~** to be thirsty
seda ['seða] *nf* silk; **~ dental** dental floss
sedal [se'ðal] *nm* fishing line
sedán [se'ðan] *nm* (*Am*) saloon (*Brit*), sedan (*US*)
sedante [se'ðante] *nm* sedative
sede ['seðe] *nf* (*de gobierno*) seat; (*de compañía*) headquarters *pl*, head office; **Santa S~** Holy See
sedentario, -a [seðen'tarjo, a] *adj* sedentary
sediento, -a [se'ðjento, a] *adj* thirsty
sedimentar [seðimen'tar] *vt* to deposit; **sedimentarse** *vr* to settle
sedimento [seði'mento] *nm* sediment
sedoso, -a [se'ðoso, a] *adj* silky, silken
seducción [seðuk'θjon] *nf* seduction
seducir [seðu'θir] *vt* to seduce; (*sobornar*) to bribe; (*cautivar*) to charm, fascinate; (*atraer*) to attract
seductor, a [seðuk'tor, a] *adj* seductive; charming, fascinating; attractive; (*engañoso*) deceptive, misleading ▷ *nm/f* seducer
segadora-trilladora [seɣa'ðoratriʎa'ðora] *nf* combine harvester
segar [se'ɣar] *vt* (*mies*) to reap, cut; (*hierba*) to mow, cut; (*esperanzas*) to ruin
seglar [se'ɣlar] *adj* secular, lay
segregación [seɣreɣa'θjon] *nf* segregation; **~ racial** racial segregation
segregar [seɣre'ɣar] *vt* to segregate, separate
seguido, -a [se'ɣiðo, a] *adj* (*continuo*) continuous, unbroken; (*recto*) straight ▷ *adv* (*directo*) straight (on); (*después*) after; (*Am: a menudo*) often ▷ *nf*: **en seguida** at once, right away; **cinco días ~s** five days running, five days in a row; **en seguida termino** I've nearly finished, I shan't be long now
seguimiento [seɣi'mjento] *nm* chase, pursuit; (*continuación*) continuation
seguir [se'ɣir] *vt* to follow; (*venir después*) to follow on, come after; (*proseguir*) to continue; (*perseguir*) to chase, pursue; (*indicio*) to follow up; (*mujer*) to court ▷ *vi* (*gen*) to follow; (*continuar*) to continue, carry *o* go on; **seguirse** *vr* to follow; **a ~** to be continued; **sigo sin comprender** I still don't understand; **sigue lloviendo** it's still raining; **sigue** (*en carta*) P.T.O.; (*en libro, TV*) continued; **"hágase ~"** "please forward"; **¡siga!** (*Am: pase*) come in!
según [se'ɣun] *prep* according to ▷ *adv*: **~ (y conforme)** it all depends ▷ *conj* as; **~ esté el tiempo** depending on the weather; **~ me consta** as far as I know; **está ~ lo dejaste** it is just as you left it
segundo, -a [se'ɣundo, a] *adj* second; (*en discurso*) secondly ▷ *nm* (*gen, medida de tiempo*) second; (*piso*) second floor ▷ *nf* (*sentido*) second meaning; **~ (de a bordo)** (*Naut*) first mate; **segunda (clase)** (*Ferro*) second class; **segunda (marcha)** (*Auto*) second (gear); **de segunda mano** second hand
seguramente [seɣura'mente] *adv* surely; (*con certeza*) for sure, with certainty; (*probablemente*) probably; **¿lo va a comprar?** — **~** is he going to buy it? — I should think so
seguridad [seɣuri'ðað] *nf* safety; (*del estado, de casa etc*) security; (*certidumbre*) certainty; (*confianza*) confidence; (*estabilidad*) stability; **~ social** social security; **~ contra incendios** fire precautions *pl*; **~ en sí mismo** (self-) confidence
seguro, -a [se'ɣuro, a] *adj* (*cierto*) sure, certain; (*fiel*) trustworthy; (*libre de peligro*) safe; (*bien defendido, firme*) secure; (*datos etc*) reliable; (*fecha*) firm ▷ *adv* for sure, certainly ▷ *nm* (*dispositivo*) safety device; (*de cerradura*) tumbler; (*de arma*) safety catch; (*Com*) insurance; **~ contra accidentes/incendios** fire/accident insurance; **~ contra terceros/a todo riesgo** third party/ comprehensive insurance; **~ dotal con beneficios** with-profits endowment assurance; **S~ de Enfermedad** ≈ National Insurance; **~ marítimo** marine insurance; **~ mixto** endowment assurance; **~ temporal** term insurance; **~ de vida** life insurance; **~s sociales** social security *sg*
seis [seis] *num* six; **~ mil** six thousand; **tiene ~ años** she is six (years old); **unos ~** about six; **hoy es el ~** today is the sixth
seiscientos, -as [seis'θjentos, as] *num* six hundred
seísmo [se'ismo] *nm* tremor, earthquake
selección [selek'θjon] *nf* selection; **~ múltiple** multiple choice; **~ nacional** (*Deporte*) national team
seleccionar [selekθjo'nar] *vt* to pick, choose, select
selectividad [selektiβi'ðað] *nf* (*Univ*) entrance examination; *see note*

SELECTIVIDAD

School leavers wishing to go on to University sit the dreaded *selectividad* in June, with resits in September. When student numbers are too high for a particular course only the best students get their choice. Some of the others then wait a year to sit the exam again rather than do a course they don't want.

selecto, -a [se'lekto, a] *adj* select, choice; (*escogido*) selected

S

sellar [se'ʎar] *vt* (*documento oficial*) to seal; (*pasaporte, visado*) to stamp; (*marcar*) to brand; (*pacto, labios*) to seal
sello ['seʎo] *nm* stamp; (*precinto*) seal; (*fig*: *tb*: **~ distintivo**) hallmark; **~ fiscal** revenue stamp; **~s de prima** (*Com*) trading stamps
selva ['selβa] *nf* (*bosque*) forest, woods *pl*; (*jungla*) jungle; **la S~ Negra** the Black Forest
semáforo [se'maforo] *nm* (*Auto*) traffic lights *pl*; (*Ferro*) signal
semana [se'mana] *nf* week; **~ inglesa** five-day (working) week; **~ laboral** working week; **S~ Santa** Holy Week; **entre ~** during the week; *see note*

SEMANA SANTA

Semana Santa is a holiday in Spain all regions take *Viernes Santo*, Good Friday, *Sábado Santo*, Holy Saturday, and *Domingo de Resurrección*, Easter Sunday. Other holidays at this time vary according to each region. There are spectacular procesiones all over the country, with members of *cofradías* (brotherhoods) dressing in hooded robes and parading their *pasos* (religious floats or sculptures) through the streets. Seville has the most renowned celebrations, on account of the religious fervour shown by the locals.

semanal [sema'nal] *adj* weekly
semanario [sema'narjo] *nm* weekly (magazine)
semblante [sem'blante] *nm* face; (*fig*) look
sembrar [sem'brar] *vt* to sow; (*objetos*) to sprinkle, scatter about; (*noticias etc*) to spread
semejante [seme'xante] *adj* (*parecido*) similar; (*tal*) such; **~s** alike, similar ▷ *nm* fellow man, fellow creature; **son muy ~s** they are very much alike; **nunca hizo cosa ~** he never did such a thing
semejanza [seme'xanθa] *nf* similarity, resemblance; **a ~ de** like, as
semejar [seme'xar] *vi* to seem like, resemble; **semejarse** *vr* to look alike, be similar
semen ['semen] *nm* semen
semental [semen'tal] *nm* (*macho*) stud
semestral [semes'tral] *adj* half-yearly, bi-annual
semicírculo [semi'θirkulo] *nm* semicircle
semiconsciente [semikons'θjente] *adj* semiconscious
semidesnatado, -a [semiðesna'taðo, a] *adj* semi-skimmed
semifinal [semifi'nal] *nf* semifinal
semiinconsciente [semi(i)nkons'θjente] *adj* semiconscious
semilla [se'miʎa] *nf* seed
seminario [semi'narjo] *nm* (*Rel*) seminary; (*Escol*) seminar
sémola ['semola] *nf* semolina
sempiterno, -a [sempi'terno, a] *adj* everlasting
Sena ['sena] *nm*: **el ~** the (river) Seine
senado [se'naðo] *nm* senate; *ver tb* **Las Cortes (españolas)**
senador, a [sena'ðor, a] *nm/f* senator
sencillez [senθi'ʎeθ] *nf* simplicity; (*de persona*) naturalness
sencillo, -a [sen'θiʎo, a] *adj* simple; (*carácter*) natural, unaffected; (*billete*) single ▷ *nm* (*disco*) single; (*Am*) small change
senda ['senda] *nf*, **sendero** [sen'dero] *nm* path, track; **Sendero Luminoso** the Shining Path (guerrilla movement)
senderismo [sende'rismo] *nm* hiking
sendero [sen'dero] *nm* path, track
sendos, -as ['sendos, as] *adj pl*: **les dio ~ golpes** he hit both of them
senil [se'nil] *adj* senile
seno ['seno] *nm* (*Anat*) bosom, bust; (*fig*) bosom; **senos** *nmpl* breasts; **~ materno** womb
sensación [sensa'θjon] *nf* sensation; (*sentido*) sense; (*sentimiento*) feeling; **causar** *o* **hacer ~** to cause a sensation
sensacional [sensaθjo'nal] *adj* sensational
sensatez [sensa'teθ] *nf* common sense
sensato, -a [sen'sato, a] *adj* sensible
sensibilidad [sensiβili'ðað] *nf* sensitivity; (*para el arte*) feel
sensibilizar [sensiβili'θar] *vt*: **~ a la población/opinión pública** to raise public awareness
sensible [sen'sible] *adj* sensitive; (*apreciable*) perceptible, appreciable; (*pérdida*) considerable
sensiblero, -a [sensi'βlero, a] *adj* sentimental, slushy
sensitivo, -a [sensi'tiβo, a] *adj* sense *cpd*
sensorial [senso'rjal] *adj* sensory
sensual [sen'swal] *adj* sensual
sentado, -a [sen'taðo, a] *adj* (*establecido*) settled; (*carácter*) sensible ▷ *nf* sitting; (*Pol*) sit-in, sit-down protest; **dar por ~** to take for granted, assume; **dejar algo ~** to establish sth firmly; **estar ~** to sit, be sitting (down); **de una sentada** at one sitting
sentar [sen'tar] *vt* to sit, seat; (*fig*) to establish ▷ *vi* (*vestido*) to suit; (*alimento*): **~ bien/mal a** to agree/disagree with; **sentarse** *vr* (*persona*) to sit, sit down; (*el tiempo*) to settle (down); (*los depósitos*) to settle; **¡siéntese!** (do) sit down, take a seat
sentencia [sen'tenθja] *nf* (*máxima*) maxim, saying; (*Jur*) sentence; **~ de muerte** death sentence
sentenciar [senten'θjar] *vt* to sentence
sentido, -a [sen'tiðo, a] *adj* (*pérdida*) regrettable; (*carácter*) sensitive ▷ *nm* sense; (*sentimiento*) feeling; (*significado*) sense, meaning; (*dirección*) direction; **mi más ~ pésame** my deepest sympathy; **~ del humor**

sense of humour; ~ **común** common sense; **en el buen ~ de la palabra** in the best sense of the word; **sin ~** meaningless; **tener ~** to make sense; **~ único** one-way (street)

sentimental [sentimen'tal] *adj* sentimental; **vida ~** love life

sentimiento [senti'mjento] *nm* (*emoción*) feeling, emotion; (*sentido*) sense; (*pesar*) regret, sorrow

sentir [sen'tir] *vt* to feel; (*percibir*) to perceive, sense; (*esp Am: oír*) to hear; (*lamentar*) to regret, be sorry for; (*música etc*) to have a feeling for ▷ *vi* to feel; (*lamentarse*) to feel sorry ▷ *nm* opinion, judgement; **sentirse** *vr* to feel; **lo siento** I'm sorry; **~se mejor/mal** to feel better/ill; **~se como en su casa** to feel at home

seña ['seɲa] *nf* sign; (*Mil*) password; **señas** *nfpl* address *sg*; **~s personales** personal description *sg*; **por más ~s** moreover; **dar ~s de** to show signs of

señal [se'ɲal] *nf* sign; (*síntoma*) symptom; (*indicio*) indication; (*Ferro: Telec*) signal; (*marca*) mark; (*Com*) deposit; (*Inform*) marker, mark; **en ~ de** as a token of, as a sign of; **dar ~es de** to show signs of; **~ de auxilio/de peligro** distress/danger signal; **~ de llamada** ringing tone; **~ para marcar** dialling tone

señalar [seɲa'lar] *vt* to mark; (*indicar*) to point out, indicate; (*significar*) to denote; (*referirse a*) to allude to; (*fijar*) to fix, settle; (*pey*) to criticize

señalizar [seɲali'θar] *vt* (*Auto*) to put up road signs on; (*Ferro*) to put signals on; (*Auto: ruta*): **está bien señalizada** it's well signposted

señor, a [se'ɲor, a] *adj* (*fam*) lordly ▷ *nm* (*hombre*) man; (*caballero*) gentleman; (*dueño*) owner, master; (*trato: antes de nombre propio*) Mr; (*: hablando directamente*) sir ▷ *nf* (*dama*) lady; (*trato: antes de nombre propio*) Mrs; (*: hablando directamente*) madam; (*esposa*) wife; **los ~es González** Mr and Mrs González; **S~ Don Jacinto Benavente** (*en sobre*) Mr J. Benavente, J. Benavente Esq.; **S~ Director ...** (*de periódico*) Dear Sir ...; **~ juez** my lord, your worship (US); **~ Presidente** Mr Chairman *o* President; **Muy ~ mío** Dear Sir; **Muy ~es nuestros** Dear Sirs; **Nuestro S~** (*Rel*) Our Lord; **¿está la ~a?** is the lady of the house in?; **la ~a de Smith** Mrs Smith; **Nuestra S~a** (*Rel*) Our Lady

señorita [seɲo'rita] *nf* (*gen*) Miss; (*mujer joven*) young lady; (*maestra*) schoolteacher

señorito [seɲo'rito] *nm* young gentleman; (*lenguaje de criados*) master; (*pey*) toff

señuelo [se'ɲwelo] *nm* decoy

sepa *etc* ['sepa] *vb ver* **saber**

separación [separa'θjon] *nf* separation; (*división*) division; (*distancia*) gap, distance; **~ de bienes** division of property

separado, -a [sepa'raðo, a] *adj* separate; (*Tec*) detached; **vive ~ de su mujer** he is separated from his wife; **por ~** separately

separar [sepa'rar] *vt* to separate; (*silla (de la mesa)*) to move away; (*Tec: pieza*) to detach; (*persona: de un cargo*) to remove, dismiss; (*dividir*) to divide; **separarse** *vr* (*parte*) to come away; (*partes*) to come apart; (*persona*) to leave, go away; (*matrimonio*) to separate

separatismo [separa'tismo] *nm* (*Pol*) separatism

sepia ['sepja] *nf* cuttlefish

septentrional [septentrjo'nal] *adj* north *cpd*, northern

septiembre [sep'tjembre] *nm* September; *ver tb* **julio**

séptimo, -a ['septimo, a] *adj, nm* seventh

sepulcral [sepul'kral] *adj* sepulchral; (*fig*) gloomy, dismal; (*silencio, atmósfera*) deadly

sepulcro [se'pulkro] *nm* tomb, grave, sepulchre

sepultar [sepul'tar] *vt* to bury; (*en accidente*) to trap; **quedaban sepultados en la caverna** they were trapped in the cave

sepultura [sepul'tura] *nf* (*acto*) burial; (*tumba*) grave, tomb; **dar ~ a** to bury; **recibir ~** to be buried

sepulturero, -a [sepultu'rero, a] *nm/f* gravedigger

sequedad [seke'ðað] *nf* dryness; (*fig*) brusqueness, curtness

sequía [se'kia] *nf* drought

séquito ['sekito] *nm* (*de rey etc*) retinue; (*Pol*) followers *pl*

PALABRA CLAVE

ser [ser] *vi* **1** (*descripción, identidad*) to be; **es médica/muy alta** she's a doctor/very tall; **la familia es de Cuzco** his (*o* her *etc*) family is from Cuzco; **ser de madera** to be made of wood; **soy Ana** I'm Ana

2 (*propiedad*): **es de Joaquín** it's Joaquín's, it belongs to Joaquín

3 (*horas, fechas, números*): **es la una** it's one o'clock; **son las seis y media** it's half-past six; **es el 1 de junio** it's the first of June; **somos/son seis** there are six of us/them; **2 y 2 son 4** 2 and 2 are *o* make 4

4 (*suceso*): **¿qué ha sido eso?** what was that?; **la fiesta es en mi casa** the party's at my house; **¿qué será de mí?** what will become of me?; **"érase una vez ..."** "once upon a time ..."

5 (*en oraciones pasivas*): **ha sido descubierto ya** it's already been discovered

6: **es de esperar que ...** it is to be hoped *o* I *etc* hope that ...

7 (*locuciones con sub*): **o sea** that is to say; **sea él sea su hermana** either him or his sister; **tengo que irme, no sea que mis hijos estén esperándome** I have to go in case my

S

children are waiting for me
8: **a** *o* **de no ser por él ...** but for him ...
9: **a no ser que**: **a no ser que tenga uno ya** unless he's got one already
▷ *nm* being; **ser humano** human being; **ser vivo** living creature

Serbia ['serβja] *nf* Serbia
serbio, -a ['serβjo, a] *adj* Serbian ▷ *nm/f* Serb
serenarse [sere'narse] *vr* to calm down; (*mar*) to grow calm; (*tiempo*) to clear up
serenidad [sereni'ðað] *nf* calmness
sereno, -a [se'reno, a] *adj* (*persona*) calm, unruffled; (*tiempo*) fine, settled; (*ambiente*) calm, peaceful ▷ *nm* night watchman
serial [se'rjal] *nm* serial
serie ['serje] *nf* series; (*cadena*) sequence, succession; (*TV etc*) serial; (*de inyecciones*) course; **fuera de ~** out of order; (*fig*) special, out of the ordinary; **fabricación en ~** mass production; (*Inform*): **interface/impresora en ~** serial interface/printer
seriedad [serje'ðað] *nf* seriousness; (*formalidad*) reliability; (*de crisis*) gravity, seriousness
serigrafía [seriɣra'fia] *nf* silk screen printing
serio, -a ['serjo, a] *adj* serious; reliable, dependable; grave, serious; **poco ~** (*actitud*) undignified; (*carácter*) unreliable; **en ~** seriously
sermón [ser'mon] *nm* (*Rel*) sermon
seropositivo, -a [seroposi'tiβo, a] *adj* HIV-positive
serpentear [serpente'ar] *vi* to wriggle; (*camino, río*) to wind, snake
serpentina [serpen'tina] *nf* streamer
serpiente [ser'pjente] *nf* snake; **~ boa** boa constrictor; **~ de cascabel** rattlesnake
serranía [serra'nia] *nf* mountainous area
serrano, -a [se'rrano, a] *adj* highland *cpd*, hill *cpd* ▷ *nm/f* highlander
serrar [se'rrar] *vt* to saw
serrín [se'rrin] *nm* sawdust
serrucho [se'rrutʃo] *nm* handsaw
service ['serβis] *nm* (*Am*: *Auto*) service
servicio [ser'βiθjo] *nm* service; (*Am Auto*) service; (*Culin etc*) set; **servicios** *nmpl* toilet(s) (*pl*); **estar de ~** to be on duty; **~ aduanero** *o* **de aduana** customs service; **~ a domicilio** home delivery service; **~ incluido** (*en hotel etc*) service charge included; **~ militar** military service; **~ público** (*Com*) public utility
servidor, a [serβi'ðor, a] *nm/f* servant ▷ *nm* (*Inform*) server; **su seguro ~ (s.s.s.)** yours faithfully; **un ~** (*el que habla o escribe*) your humble servant
servidumbre [serβi'ðumbre] *nf* (*sujeción*) servitude; (*criados*) servants *pl*, staff
servil [ser'βil] *adj* servile
servilleta [serβi'ʎeta] *nf* serviette, napkin
servir [ser'βir] *vt* to serve; (*comida*) to serve out *o* up; (*Tenis etc*) to serve ▷ *vi* to serve; (*camarero*) to serve, wait; (*tener utilidad*) to be of use, be useful; **servirse** *vr* to serve *o* help o.s.; **¿en qué puedo ~le?** how can I help you?; **~ vino a algn** to pour out wine for sb; **~ de guía** to act *o* serve as a guide; **no sirve para nada** it's no use at all; **~se de algo** to make use of sth, use sth; **sírvase pasar** please come in
sesenta [se'senta] *num* sixty
sesgo ['sesɣo] *nm* slant; (*fig*) slant, twist
sesión [se'sjon] *nf* (*Pol*) session, sitting; (*Cine*) showing; (*Teat*) performance; **abrir/levantar la ~** to open/close *o* adjourn the meeting; **la segunda ~** the second house
seso ['seso] *nm* brain; (*fig*) intelligence; **sesos** *nmpl* (*Culin*) brains; **devanarse los ~s** to rack one's brains
sesudo, -a [se'suðo, a] *adj* sensible, wise
set (*pl* **sets**) [set, sets] *nm* (*Tenis*) set
seta ['seta] *nf* mushroom; **~ venenosa** toadstool
setecientos, -as [sete'θjentos, as] *num* seven hundred
setenta [se'tenta] *num* seventy
seto ['seto] *nm* fence; **~ vivo** hedge
seudo... [seuðo] *pref* pseudo...
seudónimo [seu'ðonimo] *nm* pseudonym
severidad [seβeri'ðað] *nf* severity
severo, -a [se'βero, a] *adj* severe; (*disciplina*) strict; (*frío*) bitter
Sevilla [se'βiʎa] *nf* Seville
sevillano, -a [seβi'ʎano, a] *adj* of *o* from Seville ▷ *nm/f* native *o* inhabitant of Seville
sexo ['sekso] *nm* sex; **el ~ femenino/masculino** the female/male sex
sexto, -a ['seksto, a] *num* sixth; **Juan S~** John the Sixth
sexual [sek'swal] *adj* sexual; **vida ~** sex life
sexualidad [sekswali'ðað] *nf* sexuality
si [si] *conj* if; (*en pregunta indirecta*) if, whether ▷ *nm* (*Mus*) B; **si ... si ...** whether ... or ...; **me pregunto si ...** I wonder if *o* whether ...; **si no** if not, otherwise; **¡si fuera verdad!** if only it were true!; **por si viene** in case he comes
sí [si] *adv* yes ▷ *nm* consent ▷ *pron* (*uso impersonal*) oneself; (*sg*: *m*) himself; (: *f*) herself; (: *de cosa*) itself; (: *de usted*) yourself; (*pl*) themselves; (: *de ustedes*) yourselves; (: *recíproco*) each other; **él no quiere pero yo sí** he doesn't want to but I do; **ella sí vendrá** she will certainly come, she is sure to come; **claro que sí** of course; **creo que sí** I think so; **porque sí** because that's the way it is; (*porque lo digo yo*) because I say so; **¡sí que lo es!** I'll say it is!; **¡eso sí que no!** never!; **se ríe de sí misma** she laughs at herself; **cambiaron una mirada entre sí** they gave each other a look; **de por sí** in itself
siamés, -esa [sja'mes, esa] *adj*, *nm/f* Siamese

sibarita [siβa'rita] *adj* sybaritic ▷ *nm/f* sybarite
sicario [si'karjo] *nm* hired killer
SIDA ['siða] *nm abr* (= *síndrome de inmunodeficiencia adquirida*) AIDS
siderúrgico, -a [siðe'rurxico, a] *adj* iron and steel *cpd*
sidra ['siðra] *nf* cider
siembra *etc* ['sjembra] *vb ver* **sembrar** ▷ *nf* sowing
siempre ['sjempre] *adv* always; (*todo el tiempo*) all the time; (*Am*: *así y todo*) still ▷ *conj*: **~ que ...** (+ *indic*) whenever ...; (+ *subjun*) provided that ...; **es lo de ~** it's the same old story; **como ~** as usual; **para ~** forever; **~ me voy mañana** (*Am*) I'm still leaving tomorrow
sien [sjen] *nf* (*Anat*) temple
siento *etc* ['sjento] *vb ver* **sentar, sentir**
sierra ['sjerra] *vb ver* **serrar** ▷ *nf* (*Tec*) saw; (*Geo*) mountain range; **S~ Leona** Sierra Leone
siervo, -a ['sjerβo, a] *nm/f* slave
siesta ['sjesta] *nf* siesta, nap; **dormir la** *o* **echarse una** *o* **tomar una ~** to have an afternoon nap *o* a doze
siete ['sjete] *num* seven ▷ *excl* (*Am fam*): **¡la gran ~!** wow!, hell!; **hijo de la gran ~** (*fam!*) bastard (*!*), son of a bitch (*US*) (*!*)
sífilis ['sifilis] *nf* syphilis
sifón [si'fon] *nm* syphon; **whisky con ~** whisky and soda
sigilo [si'xilo] *nm* secrecy; (*discreción*) discretion
sigla ['siɣla] *nf* initial, abbreviation
siglo ['siɣlo] *nm* century; (*fig*) age; **S~ de las Luces** Age of Enlightenment; **S~ de Oro** Golden Age
significación [siɣnifika'θjon] *nf* significance
significado [siɣnifi'kaðo] *nm* significance; (*de palabra etc*) meaning
significar [siɣnifi'kar] *vt* to mean, signify; (*notificar*) to make known, express
significativo, -a [siɣnifika'tiβo, a] *adj* significant
signo ['siɣno] *nm* sign; **~ de admiración** *o* **exclamación** exclamation mark; **~ igual** equals sign; **~ de interrogación** question mark; **~ de más/de menos** plus/minus sign; **~s de puntuación** punctuation marks
sigo *etc vb ver* **seguir**
siguiente [si'ɣjente] *adj* following; (*próximo*) next
siguió *etc vb ver* **seguir**
sílaba ['silaβa] *nf* syllable
silbar [sil'βar] *vt, vi* to whistle; (*silbato*) to blow; (*Teat etc*) to hiss
silbato [sil'βato] *nm* (*instrumento*) whistle
silbido [sil'βiðo] *nm* whistle, whistling; (*abucheo*) hiss
silenciador [silenθja'ðor] *nm* silencer
silenciar [silen'θjar] *vt* (*persona*) to silence; (*escándalo*) to hush up
silencio [si'lenθjo] *nm* silence, quiet; **en el ~ más absoluto** in dead silence; **guardar ~** to keep silent
silencioso, -a [silen'θjoso, a] *adj* silent, quiet
silicio [si'liθjo] *nm* silicon
silla ['siʎa] *nf* (*asiento*) chair; (*tb*: **~ de montar**) saddle; **~ de ruedas** wheelchair
sillín [si'ʎin] *nm* saddle, seat
sillón [si'ʎon] *nm* armchair, easy chair
silueta [si'lweta] *nf* silhouette; (*de edificio*) outline; (*figura*) figure
silvestre [sil'βestre] *adj* (*Bot*) wild; (*fig*) rustic, rural
simbólico, -a [sim'boliko, a] *adj* symbolic(al)
simbolizar [simboli'θar] *vt* to symbolize
símbolo ['simbolo] *nm* symbol; **~ gráfico** (*Inform*) icon
simetría [sime'tria] *nf* symmetry
simétrico, -a [si'metriko, a] *adj* symmetrical
simiente [si'mjente] *nf* seed
similar [simi'lar] *adj* similar
simio ['simjo] *nm* ape
simpatía [simpa'tia] *nf* liking; (*afecto*) affection; (*amabilidad*) kindness; (*de ambiente*) friendliness; (*de persona, lugar*) charm, attractiveness; (*solidaridad*) mutual support, solidarity; **tener ~ a** to like; **la famosa ~ andaluza** that well-known Andalusian charm
simpático, -a [sim'patiko, a] *adj* nice, pleasant; (*bondadoso*) kind; **no le hemos caído muy ~s** she didn't much take to us
simpatizante [simpati'θante] *nm/f* sympathizer
simpatizar [simpati'θar] *vi*: **~ con** to get on well with
simple ['simple] *adj* simple; (*elemental*) simple, easy; (*mero*) mere; (*puro*) pure, sheer ▷ *nm/f* simpleton; **un ~ soldado** an ordinary soldier
simpleza [sim'pleθa] *nf* simpleness; (*necedad*) silly thing
simplicidad [simpliθi'ðað] *nf* simplicity
simplificar [simplifi'kar] *vt* to simplify
simposio [sim'posjo] *nm* symposium
simulacro [simu'lakro] *nm* (*apariencia*) semblance; (*fingimiento*) sham
simular [simu'lar] *vt* to simulate; (*fingir*) to feign, sham
simultáneo, -a [simul'taneo, a] *adj* simultaneous
sin [sin] *prep* without; (*a no ser por*) but for ▷ *conj*: **~ que** (+ *subjun*) without; **~ decir nada** without a word; **~ verlo yo** without my seeing it; **platos ~ lavar** unwashed *o* dirty dishes; **la ropa está ~ lavar** the clothes are unwashed; **~ que lo sepa él** without his knowing; **~ embargo** however

sinagoga [sina'ɣoɣa] *nf* synagogue
sinceridad [sinθeri'ðað] *nf* sincerity
sincero, -a [sin'θero, a] *adj* sincere; (*persona*) genuine; (*opinión*) frank; (*felicitaciones*) heartfelt
sincronizar [sinkroni'θar] *vt* to synchronize
sindical [sindi'kal] *adj* union *cpd*, trade-union *cpd*
sindicalista [sindika'lista] *adj* trade-union *cpd* ▷ *nm/f* trade unionist
sindicato [sindi'kato] *nm* (*de trabajadores*) trade(s) *o* labor (*US*) union; (*de negociantes*) syndicate
síndrome ['sindrome] *nm* syndrome; **~ de abstinencia** withdrawal symptoms; **~ de la clase turista** economy-class syndrome
sine qua non [sine'kwanon] *adj*: **condición ~** sine qua non
sinfín [sin'fin] *nm*: **un ~ de** a great many, no end of
sinfonía [sinfo'nia] *nf* symphony
sinfónico, -a [sin'foniko, a] *adj* (*música*) symphonic; **orquesta sinfónica** symphony orchestra
singular [singu'lar] *adj* singular; (*fig*) outstanding, exceptional; (*pey*) peculiar, odd ▷ *nm* (*Ling*) singular; **en ~** in the singular
singularidad [singulari'ðað] *nf* singularity, peculiarity
singularizar [singulari'θar] *vt* to single out; **singularizarse** *vr* to distinguish o.s., stand out
siniestro, -a [si'njestro, a] *adj* left; (*fig*) sinister ▷ *nm* (*accidente*) accident; (*desastre*) natural disaster
sinnúmero [sin'numero] *nm* = **sinfín**
sino ['sino] *nm* fate, destiny ▷ *conj* (*pero*) but; (*salvo*) except, save; **no son 8 ~ 9** there are not 8 but 9; **todos ~ él** all except him
sinónimo, -a [si'nonimo, a] *adj* synonymous ▷ *nm* synonym
sintaxis [sin'taksis] *nf* syntax
síntesis ['sintesis] *nf inv* synthesis
sintético, -a [sin'tetiko, a] *adj* synthetic
sintetizar [sinteti'θar] *vt* to synthesize
sintió *vb ver* **sentir**
síntoma ['sintoma] *nm* symptom
sintomático, -a [sinto'matiko, a] *adj* symptomatic
sintonía [sinto'nia] *nf* (*Radio*) tuning; (*melodía*) signature tune
sintonizar [sintoni'θar] *vt* (*Radio*) to tune (in) to, pick up
sinvergüenza [simber'ɣwenθa] *nm/f* rogue, scoundrel; **¡es un ~!** he's got a nerve!
sionismo [sjo'nismo] *nm* Zionism
siquiera [si'kjera] *conj* even if, even though ▷ *adv* (*esp Am*) at least; **ni ~** not even; **~ bebe algo** at least drink something
sirena [si'rena] *nf* siren, mermaid; (*bocina*) siren, hooter
Siria ['sirja] *nf* Syria
sirio, -a ['sirjo, a] *adj*, *nm/f* Syrian
sirviente, -a [sir'βjente, a] *nm/f* servant
sirvo *etc vb ver* **servir**
sisear [sise'ar] *vt*, *vi* to hiss
sísmico, -a ['sismiko, a] *adj*: **movimiento ~** earthquake
sismógrafo [sis'moɣrafo] *nm* seismograph
sistema [sis'tema] *nm* system; (*método*) method; **~ binario** (*Inform*) binary system; **~ de alerta inmediata** early-warning system; **~ de facturación** (*Com*) invoicing system; **~ educativo** educational system; **~ impositivo** *o* **tributario** taxation, tax system; **~ métrico** metric system; **~ operativo (en disco)** (*Inform*) (disk-based) operating system; *see note*

SISTEMA EDUCATIVO

The reform of the Spanish *sistema educativo* (education system) begun in the early 90s has replaced the courses EGB, BUP and COU with the following: *Primaria* a compulsory 6 years; *Secundaria* a compulsory 4 years; *Bachillerato* an optional 2 year secondary school course, essential for those wishing to go on to higher education.

sistemático, -a [siste'matiko, a] *adj* systematic
sitiar [si'tjar] *vt* to besiege, lay siege to
sitio ['sitjo] *nm* (*lugar*) place; (*espacio*) room, space; (*Mil*) siege; **~ de taxis** (*Am*: *parada*) taxi stand *o* rank (*Brit*); **~ web** website; **¿hay ~?** is there any room?; **hay ~ de sobra** there's plenty of room
situación [sitwa'θjon] *nf* situation, position; (*estatus*) position, standing
situado, -a [si'twaðo, a] *adj* situated, placed; **estar ~** (*Com*) to be financially secure
situar [si'twar] *vt* to place, put; (*edificio*) to locate, situate
slip [es'lip] (*pl* **slips**) *nm* pants *pl*, briefs *pl*
SME *nm abr* (= *Sistema Monetario Europeo*) EMS; **(mecanismo de cambios del) ~** ERM
smoking [(e)'smokin] (*pl* **smokings**) *nm* dinner jacket (*Brit*), tuxedo (*US*)
SMS *nm* (*mensaje*) text (message), SMS (message)
snob [es'nob] = **esnob**
SO *abr* (= *suroeste*) SW
so [so] *excl* whoa!; **¡so burro!** you idiot! ▷ *prep* under
sobaco [so'βako] *nm* armpit
sobar [so'βar] *vt* (*tela*) to finger; (*ropa*) to rumple, mess up; (*músculos*) to rub, massage; (*comida*) to play around with
soberanía [soβera'nia] *nf* sovereignty
soberano, -a [soβe'rano, a] *adj* sovereign; (*fig*) supreme ▷ *nm/f* sovereign; **los ~s** the king and queen

soberbio, -a [so'βerβjo, a] *adj* (*orgulloso*) proud; (*altivo*) haughty, arrogant; (*fig*) magnificent, superb ▷ *nf* pride; haughtiness, arrogance; magnificence
sobornar [soβor'nar] *vt* to bribe
soborno [so'βorno] *nm* (*un soborno*) bribe; (*el soborno*) bribery
sobra ['soβra] *nf* excess, surplus; **sobras** *nfpl* left-overs, scraps; **de ~** surplus, extra; **lo sé de ~** I'm only too aware of it; **tengo de ~** I've more than enough
sobrado, -a [so'βraðo, a] *adj* (*más que suficiente*) more than enough; (*superfluo*) excessive ▷ *adv* too, exceedingly; **sobradas veces** repeatedly
sobrante [so'βrante] *adj* remaining, extra ▷ *nm* surplus, remainder
sobrar [so'βrar] *vt* to exceed, surpass ▷ *vi* (*tener de más*) to be more than enough; (*quedar*) to remain, be left (over)
sobrasada [soβra'saða] *nf* ≈ sausage spread
sobre ['soβre] *prep* (*gen*) on; (*encima*) on (top of); (*por encima de, arriba de*) over, above; (*más que*) more than; (*además*) in addition to, besides; (*alrededor de*) about; (*porcentaje*) in, out of; (*tema*) about, on ▷ *nm* envelope; **~ todo** above all; **3 ~ 100** 3 in a 100, 3 out of every 100; **un libro ~ Tirso** a book about Tirso; **~ de ventanilla** window envelope
sobrecama [soβre'kama] *nf* bedspread
sobrecargar [soβrekar'ɣar] *vt* (*camión*) to overload; (*Com*) to surcharge
sobrecoger [soβreko'xer] *vt* (*sobresaltar*) to startle; (*asustar*) to scare; **sobrecogerse** *vr* (*sobresaltarse*) to be startled; (*asustarse*) to get scared; (*quedar impresionado*): **~se (de)** to be overawed (by)
sobredosis [soβre'ðosis] *nf inv* overdose
sobreentender [soβreenten'der] *vt* to understand; (*adivinar*) to deduce, infer; **sobreentenderse** *vr*: **se sobreentiende que ...** it is implied that ...
sobreescribir [soβreeskri'βir] *vt* (*Inform*) to overwrite
sobrehumano, -a [soβreu'mano, a] *adj* superhuman
sobrellevar [soβreʎe'βar] *vt* (*fig*) to bear, endure
sobremesa [soβre'mesa] *nf* (*después de comer*) sitting on after a meal; (*Inform*) desktop; **durante la ~** after dinner; **conversación de ~** table talk
sobrenatural [soβrenatu'ral] *adj* supernatural
sobrenombre [soβre'nombre] *nm* nickname
sobrepasar [soβrepa'sar] *vt* to exceed, surpass
sobreponer [soβrepo'ner] *vt* (*poner encima*) to put on top; (*añadir*) to add; **sobreponerse** *vr*: **~se a** to overcome
sobresaliente [soβresa'ljente] *adj* projecting; (*fig*) outstanding, excellent; (*Univ etc*) first class ▷ *nm* (*Univ etc*) first class (mark), distinction
sobresalir [soβresa'lir] *vi* to project, jut out; (*fig*) to stand out, excel
sobresaltar [soβresal'tar] *vt* (*asustar*) to scare, frighten; (*sobrecoger*) to startle
sobresalto [soβre'salto] *nm* (*movimiento*) start; (*susto*) scare; (*turbación*) sudden shock
sobrescribir [soβreskri'βir] *vt* = **sobreescribir**
sobretodo [soβre'toðo] *nm* overcoat
sobrevenir [soβreβe'nir] *vi* (*ocurrir*) to happen (unexpectedly); (*resultar*) to follow, ensue
sobreviviente [soβreβi'βjente] *adj* surviving ▷ *nm/f* survivor
sobrevivir [soβreβi'βir] *vi* to survive; (*persona*) to outlive; (*objeto etc*) to outlast
sobrevolar [soβreβo'lar] *vt* to fly over
sobriedad [soβrje'ðað] *nf* sobriety, soberness; (*moderación*) moderation, restraint
sobrino, -a [so'βrino, a] *nm/f* nephew/niece
sobrio, -a ['soβrjo, a] *adj* sober; (*moderado*) moderate, restrained
socarrón, -ona [soka'rron, ona] *adj* (*sarcástico*) sarcastic, ironic(al)
socavar [soka'βar] *vt* to undermine; (*excavar*) to dig underneath *o* below
socavón [soka'βon] *nm* (*en mina*) gallery; (*hueco*) hollow; (*en la calle*) hole
sociable [so'θjaβle] *adj* (*persona*) sociable, friendly; (*animal*) social
social [so'θjal] *adj* social; (*Com*) company *cpd*
socialdemócrata [soθjalde'mokrata] *adj* social-democratic ▷ *nm/f* social democrat
socialista [soθja'lista] *adj, nm/f* socialist
socializar [soθjali'θar] *vt* to socialize
sociedad [soθje'ðað] *nf* society; (*Com*) company; **~ de ahorro y préstamo** savings and loan society; **~ anónima (S.A.)** limited company (Ltd) (*Brit*), incorporated company (Inc) (*US*); **~ de beneficiencia** friendly society (*Brit*), benefit association (*US*); **~ de cartera** investment trust; **~ comanditaria** (*Com*) co-ownership; **~ conjunta** (*Com*) joint venture; **~ de consumo** consumer society; **~ inmobiliaria** building society (*Brit*), savings and loan (society) (*US*); **~ de responsabilidad limitada** (*Com*) private limited company
socio, -a ['soθjo, a] *nm/f* (*miembro*) member; (*Com*) partner; **~ activo** active partner; **~ capitalista** *o* **comanditario** sleeping *o* silent (*US*) partner
sociología [soθjolo'xia] *nf* sociology
sociólogo, -a [so'θjoloɣo, a] *nm/f* sociologist
socorrer [soko'rrer] *vt* to help
socorrismo [soko'rrismo] *nm* life-saving
socorrista [soko'rrista] *nm/f* first aider; (*en piscina, playa*) lifeguard
socorro [so'korro] *nm* (*ayuda*) help, aid; (*Mil*) relief; **¡~!** help!
soda ['soða] *nf* (*sosa*) soda; (*bebida*) soda (water)

sódico, -a ['soðiko, a] *adj* sodium *cpd*
sofá [so'fa] *nm* sofa, settee
sofá-cama [so'fakama] *nm* studio couch, sofa bed
sofisticación [sofistika'θjon] *nf* sophistication
sofisticado, -a [sofisti'kaðo, a] *adj* sophisticated
sofocar [sofo'kar] *vt* to suffocate; (*apagar*) to smother, put out; **sofocarse** *vr* to suffocate; (*fig*) to blush, feel embarrassed
sofoco [so'foko] *nm* suffocation; (*azoro*) embarrassment
sofreír [sofre'ir] *vt* to fry lightly
soft ['sof], **software** ['sofwer] *nm* (*Inform*) software
soga ['soɣa] *nf* rope
sois [sois] *vb ver* **ser**
soja ['soxa] *nf* soya
sojuzgar [soxuθ'ɣar] *vt* to subdue, rule despotically
sol [sol] *nm* sun; (*luz*) sunshine, sunlight; (*Mus*) G; ~ **naciente/poniente** rising/setting sun; **tomar el** ~ to sunbathe; **hace** ~ it is sunny
solamente [sola'mente] *adv* only, just
solapa [so'lapa] *nf* (*de chaqueta*) lapel; (*de libro*) jacket
solapado, -a [sola'paðo, a] *adj* (*intenciones*) underhand; (*gestos, movimiento*) sly
solar [so'lar] *adj* solar, sun *cpd* ▷ *nm* (*terreno*) plot (of ground); (*local*) undeveloped site
solaz [so'laθ] *nm* recreation, relaxation
solazar [sola'θar] *vt* (*divertir*) to amuse; **solazarse** *vr* to enjoy o.s., relax
soldado [sol'daðo] *nm* soldier; ~ **raso** private
soldador [solda'ðor] *nm* soldering iron; (*persona*) welder
soldar [sol'dar] *vt* to solder, weld; (*unir*) to join, unite
soleado, -a [sole'aðo, a] *adj* sunny
soledad [sole'ðað] *nf* solitude; (*estado infeliz*) loneliness
solemne [so'lemne] *adj* solemn; (*tontería*) utter; (*error*) complete
solemnidad [solemni'ðað] *nf* solemnity
soler [so'ler] *vi* to be in the habit of, be accustomed to; **suele salir a las ocho** she usually goes out at 8 o'clock; **solíamos ir todos los años** we used to go every year
solfeo [sol'feo] *nm* sol-fa, singing of scales; **ir a clases de** ~ to take singing lessons
solicitar [soliθi'tar] *vt* (*permiso*) to ask for, seek; (*puesto*) to apply for; (*votos*) to canvass for; (*atención*) to attract; (*persona*) to pursue, chase after
solícito, -a [so'liθito, a] *adj* (*diligente*) diligent; (*cuidadoso*) careful
solicitud [soliθi'tuð] *nf* (*calidad*) great care; (*petición*) request; (*a un puesto*) application
solidaridad [soliðari'ðað] *nf* solidarity; **por** ~ **con** (*Pol etc*) out of *o* in solidarity with
solidario, -a [soli'ðarjo, a] *adj* (*participación*) joint, common; (*compromiso*) mutually binding; **hacerse** ~ **de** to declare one's solidarity with
solidarizarse [soliðari'θarse] *vr*: ~ **con algn** to support sb, sympathize with sb
solidez [soli'ðeθ] *nf* solidity
sólido, -a ['soliðo, a] *adj* solid; (*Tec*) solidly made; (*bien construido*) well built
soliloquio [soli'lokjo] *nm* soliloquy
solista [so'lista] *nm/f* soloist
solitario, -a [soli'tarjo, a] *adj* (*persona*) lonely, solitary; (*lugar*) lonely, desolate ▷ *nm/f* (*reclusa*) recluse; (*en la sociedad*) loner ▷ *nm* solitaire ▷ *nf* tapeworm
sollozar [soʎo'θar] *vi* to sob
sollozo [so'ʎoθo] *nm* sob
solo[1], -a ['solo, a] *adj* (*único*) single, sole; (*sin compañía*) alone; (*Mus*) solo; (*solitario*) lonely; **hay una sola dificultad** there is just one difficulty; **a solas** alone, by o.s.
solo[2], sólo ['solo] *adv* only, just; (*exclusivamente*) solely; **tan** ~ only just
solomillo [solo'miʎo] *nm* sirloin
solsticio [sols'tiθjo] *nm* solstice
soltar [sol'tar] *vt* (*dejar ir*) to let go of; (*desprender*) to unfasten, loosen; (*librar*) to release, set free; (*amarras*) to cast off; (*Auto: freno etc*) to release; (*suspiro*) to heave; (*risa etc*) to let out; **soltarse** *vr* (*desanudarse*) to come undone; (*desprenderse*) to come off; (*adquirir destreza*) to become expert; (*en idioma*) to become fluent
soltero, -a [sol'tero, a] *adj* single, unmarried ▷ *nm* bachelor ▷ *nf* single woman, spinster
solterón [solte'ron] *nm* confirmed bachelor
solterona [solte'rona] *nf* spinster, maiden lady; (*pey*) old maid
soltura [sol'tura] *nf* looseness, slackness; (*de los miembros*) agility, ease of movement; (*en el hablar*) fluency, ease
soluble [so'luβle] *adj* (*Química*) soluble; (*problema*) solvable; ~ **en agua** soluble in water
solución [solu'θjon] *nf* solution; ~ **de continuidad** break in continuity
solucionar [soluθjo'nar] *vt* (*problema*) to solve; (*asunto*) to settle, resolve
solventar [solβen'tar] *vt* (*pagar*) to settle, pay; (*resolver*) to resolve
solvente [sol'βente] *adj* solvent, free of debt
sombra ['sombra] *nf* shadow; (*como protección*) shade; **sombras** *nfpl* darkness *sg*, shadows; **sin** ~ **de duda** without a shadow of doubt; **tener buena/mala** ~ (*suerte*) to be lucky/unlucky; (*carácter*) to be likeable/disagreeable
sombrero [som'brero] *nm* hat; ~ **hongo** bowler (hat), derby (*US*); ~ **de copa** *o* **de pelo** (*Am*) top hat
sombrilla [som'briʎa] *nf* parasol, sunshade

sombrío, -a [som'brio, a] *adj* (*oscuro*) dark; (*fig*) sombre, sad; (*persona*) gloomy
somero, -a [so'mero, a] *adj* superficial
someter [some'ter] *vt* (*país*) to conquer; (*persona*) to subject to one's will; (*informe*) to present, submit; **someterse** *vr* to give in, yield, submit; **~ a** to subject to; **~se a** to submit to; **~se a una operación** to undergo an operation
somier [so'mjer] (*pl* **somiers**) *nm* spring mattress
somnífero [som'nifero] *nm* sleeping pill *o* tablet
somnolencia [somno'lenθja] *nf* sleepiness, drowsiness
somos ['somos] *vb ver* **ser**
son [son] *vb ver* **ser** ▷ *nm* sound; **en ~ de broma** as a joke
sonaja [so'naxa] *nf* (*Am*) = **sonajero**
sonajero [sona'xero] *nm* (baby's) rattle
sonambulismo [sonambu'lismo] *nm* sleepwalking
sonámbulo, -a [so'nambulo, a] *nm/f* sleepwalker
sonar [so'nar] *vt* (*campana*) to ring; (*trompeta, sirena*) to blow ▷ *vi* to sound; (*hacer ruido*) to make a noise; (*Ling*) to be sounded, be pronounced; (*ser conocido*) to sound familiar; (*campana*) to ring; (*reloj*) to strike, chime; **sonarse** *vr*: **~se (la nariz)** to blow one's nose; **es un nombre que suena** it's a name that's in the news; **me suena ese nombre** that name rings a bell
sonda ['sonda] *nf* (*Naut*) sounding; (*Tec*) bore, drill; (*Med*) probe
sondear [sonde'ar] *vt* to sound; to bore (into), drill; to probe, sound; (*fig*) to sound out
sondeo [son'deo] *nm* sounding; boring, drilling; (*encuesta*) poll, enquiry; **~ de la opinión pública** public opinion poll
sónico, -a ['soniko, a] *adj* sonic, sound *cpd*
sonido [so'niðo] *nm* sound
sonoro, -a [so'noro, a] *adj* sonorous; (*resonante*) loud, resonant; (*Ling*) voiced; **efectos ~s** sound effects
sonreír [sonre'ir] *vi*, **sonreírse** *vr* to smile
sonriente [son'rjente] *adj* smiling
sonrisa [son'risa] *nf* smile
sonrojar [sonro'xar] *vt*: **~ a algn** to make sb blush; **sonrojarse** *vr*: **~se (de)** to blush (at)
sonrojo [son'roxo] *nm* blush
sonsacar [sonsa'kar] *vt* to wheedle, coax; **~ a algn** to pump sb for information
soñador, a [soɲa'ðor, a] *nm/f* dreamer
soñar [so'ɲar] *vt, vi* to dream; **~ con** to dream about *o* of; **soñé contigo anoche** I dreamed about you last night
soñoliento, -a [soɲo'ljento, a] *adj* sleepy, drowsy
sopa ['sopa] *nf* soup; **~ de fideos** noodle soup
sopero, -a [so'pero, a] *adj* (*plato, cuchara*) soup *cpd* ▷ *nm* soup plate ▷ *nf* soup tureen
sopesar [sope'sar] *vt* to try the weight of; (*fig*) to weigh up
soplar [so'plar] *vt* (*polvo*) to blow away, blow off; (*inflar*) to blow up; (*vela*) to blow out; (*ayudar a recordar*) to prompt; (*birlar*) to nick; (*delatar*) to split on ▷ *vi* to blow; (*delatar*) to squeal; (*beber*) to booze, bend the elbow
soplo ['soplo] *nm* blow, puff; (*de viento*) puff, gust
soplón, -ona [so'plon, ona] *nm/f* (*fam: chismoso*) telltale; (*: de policía*) informer, grass
sopor [so'por] *nm* drowsiness
soporífero, -a [sopo'rifero, a] *adj* sleep-inducing; (*fig*) soporific ▷ *nm* sleeping pill
soportable [sopor'taβle] *adj* bearable
soportal [sopor'tal] *nm* porch; **soportales** *nmpl* arcade *sg*
soportar [sopor'tar] *vt* to bear, carry; (*fig*) to bear, put up with
soporte [so'porte] *nm* support; (*fig*) pillar, support; (*Inform*) medium; **~ de entrada/salida** input/output medium
soprano [so'prano] *nf* soprano
sor [sor] *nf*: **S~ María** Sister Mary
sorber [sor'βer] *vt* (*chupar*) to sip; (*inhalar*) to sniff, inhale; (*absorber*) to soak up, absorb
sorbete [sor'βete] *nm* iced fruit drink
sorbo ['sorβo] *nm* (*trago*) gulp, swallow; (*chupada*) sip; **beber a ~s** to sip
sordera [sor'ðera] *nf* deafness
sórdido, -a ['sorðiðo, a] *adj* dirty, squalid
sordo, -a ['sorðo, a] *adj* (*persona*) deaf; (*ruido*) dull; (*Ling*) voiceless ▷ *nm/f* deaf person; **quedarse ~** to go deaf
sordomudo, -a [sorðo'muðo, a] *adj* speech-and-hearing impaired ▷ *nm/f* person with a speech and hearing impairment
sorna ['sorna] *nf* (*malicia*) slyness; (*tono burlón*) sarcastic tone
soroche [so'rotʃe] *nm* (*Am Med*) mountain sickness
sorprendente [sorpren'dente] *adj* surprising
sorprender [sorpren'der] *vt* to surprise; (*asombrar*) to amaze; (*sobresaltar*) to startle; (*coger desprevenido*) to catch unawares; **sorprenderse** *vr*: **~se (de)** to be surprised *o* amazed (at)
sorpresa [sor'presa] *nf* surprise
sortear [sorte'ar] *vt* to draw lots for; (*rifar*) to raffle; (*dificultad*) to dodge, avoid
sorteo [sor'teo] *nm* (*en lotería*) draw; (*rifa*) raffle
sortija [sor'tixa] *nf* ring; (*rizo*) ringlet, curl
sosegado, -a [sose'ɣaðo, a] *adj* quiet, calm
sosegar [sose'ɣar] *vt* to quieten, calm; (*el ánimo*) to reassure ▷ *vi* to rest
sosiego *etc* [so'sjeɣo] *vb ver* **sosegar** ▷ *nm* quiet(ness), calm(ness)
soslayar [sosla'jar] *vt* (*preguntas*) to get round
soslayo [sos'lajo]: **de ~** *adv* obliquely, sideways; **mirar de ~** to look out of the corner of one's eye (at)

S

soso, -a ['soso, a] *adj* (*Culin*) tasteless; (*fig*) dull, uninteresting
sospecha [sos'petʃa] *nf* suspicion
sospechar [sospe'tʃar] *vt* to suspect ▷ *vi*: **~ de** to be suspicious of
sospechoso, -a [sospe'tʃoso, a] *adj* suspicious; (*testimonio, opinión*) suspect ▷ *nm/f* suspect
sostén [sos'ten] *nm* (*apoyo*) support; (*sujetador*) bra; (*alimentación*) sustenance, food
sostener [soste'ner] *vt* to support; (*mantener*) to keep up, maintain; (*alimentar*) to sustain, keep going; **sostenerse** *vr* to support o.s.; (*seguir*) to continue, remain
sostenido, -a [soste'niðo, a] *adj* continuous, sustained; (*prolongado*) prolonged; (*Mus*) sharp ▷ *nm* (*Mus*) sharp
sota ['sota] *nf* (*Naipes*) ≈ jack
sotana [so'tana] *nf* (*Rel*) cassock
sótano ['sotano] *nm* basement
soviético, -a [so'βjetiko, a] *adj, nm/f* Soviet; **los ~s** the Soviets, the Russians
soy [soi] *vb ver* **ser**
soya ['soja] *nf* (*Am*) soya (bean)
spot [es'pot] (*pl* **spot**) *nm* (*publicitario*) ad
spyware [es'paiwer] *nm* spyware
squash [es'kwas] *nm* (*Deporte*) squash
Sr. *abr* (= *Señor*) Mr
Sra. *abr* (= *Señora*) Mrs
Sras. *abr* (= *Señoras*) Mrs
S.R.C. *abr* (= *se ruega contestación*) R.S.V.P.
Sres., Srs. *abr* (= *Señores*) Messrs
Srta. *abr* = **Señorita**
Sta. *abr* (= *Santa*) St; (= *Señorita*) Miss
stand (*pl* **stands**) [es'tan, es'tan(s)] *nm* (*Com*) stand
status ['status, es'tatus] *nm inv* status
Sto. *abr* (= *Santo*) St
stop (*pl* **stops**) [es'top, es'top(s)] *nm* (*Auto*) stop sign
su [su] *pron* (*de él*) his; (*de ella*) her; (*de una cosa*) its; (*de ellos, ellas*) their; (*de usted, ustedes*) your
suave ['swaβe] *adj* gentle; (*superficie*) smooth; (*trabajo*) easy; (*música, voz*) soft, sweet; (*clima, sabor*) mild
suavidad [swaβi'ðað] *nf* gentleness; (*de superficie*) smoothness; (*de música*) softness, sweetness
suavizante [swaβi'θante] *nm* (*de ropa*) softener; (*del pelo*) conditioner
suavizar [swaβi'θar] *vt* to soften; (*quitar la aspereza*) to smooth (out); (*pendiente*) to ease; (*colores*) to tone down; (*carácter*) to mellow; (*dureza*) to temper
subalimentado, -a [suβalimen'taðo, a] *adj* undernourished
subasta [su'βasta] *nf* auction; **poner en** *o* **sacar a pública ~** to put up for public auction; **~ a la rebaja** Dutch auction
subastar [suβas'tar] *vt* to auction (off)
subcampeón, -ona [suβkampe'on, ona] *nm/f* runner-up
subconsciente [suβkons'θjente] *adj* subconscious
subdesarrollado, -a [suβðesarro'ʎaðo, a] *adj* underdeveloped
subdesarrollo [suβðesa'rroʎo] *nm* underdevelopment
subdirector, a [suβðirek'tor, a] *nm/f* assistant *o* deputy manager
súbdito, -a ['suβðito, a] *nm/f* subject
subdividir [suβðiβi'ðir] *vt* to subdivide
subestimar [suβesti'mar] *vt* to underestimate, underrate
subido, -a [su'βiðo, a] *adj* (*color*) bright, strong; (*precio*) high ▷ *nf* (*de montaña etc*) ascent, climb; (*de precio*) rise, increase; (*pendiente*) slope, hill
subir [su'βir] *vt* (*objeto*) to raise, lift up; (*cuesta, calle*) to go up; (*colina, montaña*) to climb; (*precio*) to raise, put up; (*empleado etc*) to promote ▷ *vi* to go/come up; (*a un coche*) to get in; (*a un autobús, tren*) to get on; (*precio*) to rise, go up; (*en el empleo*) to be promoted; (*río, marea*) to rise; **subirse** *vr* to get up, climb; **~se a un coche** to get in(to) a car
súbito, -a ['suβito, a] *adj* (*repentino*) sudden; (*imprevisto*) unexpected
subjetivo, -a [suβxe'tiβo, a] *adj* subjective
subjuntivo [suβxun'tiβo] *nm* subjunctive (mood)
sublevación [suβleβa'θjon] *nf* revolt, rising
sublevar [suβle'βar] *vt* to rouse to revolt; **sublevarse** *vr* to revolt, rise
sublime [su'βlime] *adj* sublime
subliminal [suβlimi'nal] *adj* subliminal
submarinismo [suβmari'nismo] *nm* scuba diving
submarinista [suβmari'nista] *nm/f* underwater explorer
submarino, -a [suβma'rino, a] *adj* underwater ▷ *nm* submarine
subnormal [suβnor'mal] *adj* subnormal ▷ *nm/f* subnormal person
subordinado, -a [suβorði'naðo, a] *adj, nm/f* subordinate
subrayar [suβra'jar] *vt* to underline; (*recalcar*) to underline, emphasize
subrepticio, -a [suβrep'tiθjo, a] *adj* surreptitious
subsanar [suβsa'nar] *vt* (*reparar*) to rectify; (*perdonar*) to excuse; (*sobreponerse a*) to overcome
subscribir [suβskri'βir] *vt* = **suscribir**
subsidiariedad [suβsiðjarie'ðað] *nf* (*Pol*) subsidiarity
subsidiario, -a [suβsi'ðjarjo, a] *adj* subsidiary
subsidio [suβ'siðjo] *nm* (*ayuda*) aid, financial help; (*subvención*) subsidy, grant; (*de enfermedad, paro etc*) benefit, allowance
subsistencia [suβsis'tenθja] *nf* subsistence
subsistir [suβsis'tir] *vi* to subsist; (*vivir*) to

live; (*sobrevivir*) to survive, endure
subte ['suβte] *nm* (*RPl*) underground (*Brit*), subway (*US*)
subterráneo, -a [suβte'rraneo, a] *adj* underground, subterranean ▷ *nm* underpass, underground passage; (*Am*) underground railway, subway (*US*)
subtitulado, -a [suβtitu'laðo, a] *adj* subtitled
subtítulo [suβ'titulo] *nm* subtitle, subheading
suburbano, -a [suβur'βano, a] *adj* suburban
suburbio [su'βurβjo] *nm* (*barrio*) slum quarter; (*afueras*) suburbs *pl*
subvención [suββen'θjon] *nf* subsidy, subvention, grant; ~ **estatal** state subsidy *o* support; ~ **para la inversión** (*Com*) investment grant
subvencionar [suββenθjo'nar] *vt* to subsidize
subversión [suββer'sjon] *nf* subversion
subversivo, -a [suββer'siβo, a] *adj* subversive
subyugar [suβju'ɣar] *vt* (*país*) to subjugate, subdue; (*enemigo*) to overpower; (*voluntad*) to dominate
succión [suk'θjon] *nf* suction
sucedáneo, -a [suθe'ðaneo, a] *adj* substitute ▷ *nm* substitute (food)
suceder [suθe'ðer] *vi* to happen; ~ **a** (*seguir*) to succeed, follow; **lo que sucede es que ...** the fact is that ...; ~ **al trono** to succeed to the throne
sucesión [suθe'sjon] *nf* succession; (*serie*) sequence, series; (*hijos*) issue, offspring
sucesivamente [suθesiβa'mente] *adv*: **y así** ~ and so on
sucesivo, -a [suθe'siβo, a] *adj* successive, following; **en lo** ~ in future, from now on
suceso [su'θeso] *nm* (*hecho*) event, happening; (*incidente*) incident
suciedad [suθje'ðað] *nf* (*estado*) dirtiness; (*mugre*) dirt, filth
sucinto, -a [su'θinto, a] *adj* (*conciso*) succinct, concise
sucio, -a ['suθjo, a] *adj* dirty; (*mugriento*) grimy; (*manchado*) grubby; (*borroso*) smudged; (*conciencia*) bad; (*conducta*) vile; (*táctica*) dirty, unfair
Sucre ['sukre] *n* Sucre
suculento, -a [suku'lento, a] *adj* (*sabroso*) tasty; (*jugoso*) succulent
sucumbir [sukum'bir] *vi* to succumb
sucursal [sukur'sal] *nf* branch (office); (*filial*) subsidiary
sudadera [suða'ðera] *nf* sweatshirt
Sudáfrica [su'ðafrika] *nf* South Africa
Sudamérica [suða'merika] *nf* South America
sudamericano, -a [suðameri'kano, a] *adj, nm/f* South American
sudar [su'ðar] *vt, vi* to sweat; (*Bot*) to ooze, give out *o* off
sudeste [su'ðeste] *adj* south-east(ern); (*rumbo, viento*) south-easterly ▷ *nm* south-east; (*viento*) south-east wind
sudoeste [suðo'este] *adj* south-west(ern); (*rumbo, viento*) south-westerly ▷ *nm* south-west; (*viento*) south-west wind
sudoku [su'doku] *nm* sudoku
sudor [su'ðor] *nm* sweat
sudoroso, -a [suðo'roso, a] *adj* sweaty, sweating
Suecia ['sweθja] *nf* Sweden
sueco, -a ['sweko, a] *adj* Swedish ▷ *nm/f* Swede ▷ *nm* (*Ling*) Swedish; **hacerse el** ~ to pretend not to hear *o* understand
suegro, -a ['sweɣro, a] *nm/f* father-/mother-in-law; **los ~s** one's in-laws
suela ['swela] *nf* (*de zapato, tb pescado*) sole
sueldo ['sweldo] *vb ver* **soldar** ▷ *nm* pay, wage(s) (*pl*)
suelo ['swelo] *vb ver* **soler** ▷ *nm* (*tierra*) ground; (*de casa*) floor
suelto, -a *etc* ['swelto, a] *vb ver* **soltar** ▷ *adj* loose; (*libre*) free; (*separado*) detached; (*ágil*) quick, agile; (*fue corre*) fluent, flowing ▷ *nm* (loose) change, small change; **está muy ~ en inglés** he is very good at *o* fluent in English
sueñito [swe'ɲito] *nm* (*Am*) nap
sueño ['sweɲo] *vb ver* **soñar** ▷ *nm* sleep; (*somnolencia*) sleepiness, drowsiness; (*lo soñado, fig*) dream; ~ **pesado** *o* **profundo** deep *o* heavy sleep; **tener** ~ to be sleepy
suero ['swero] *nm* (*Med*) serum; (*de leche*) whey
suerte ['swerte] *nf* (*fortuna*) luck; (*azar*) chance; (*destino*) fate, destiny; (*condición*) lot; (*género*) sort, kind; **lo echaron a ~s** they drew lots *o* tossed up for it; **tener** ~ to be lucky; **de otra** ~ otherwise, if not; **de ~ que** so that, in such a way that
suéter ['sweter] (*pl* **suéters**) *nm* sweater
suficiente [sufi'θjente] *adj* enough, sufficient ▷ *nm* (*Escol*) pass
sufragar [sufra'ɣar] *vt* (*ayudar*) to help; (*gastos*) to meet; (*proyecto*) to pay for
sufragio [su'fraxjo] *nm* (*voto*) vote; (*derecho de voto*) suffrage
sufrido, -a [su'friðo, a] *adj* (*de carácter fuerte*) tough; (*paciente*) long-suffering, patient; (*tela*) hard-wearing; (*color*) that does not show the dirt; (*marido*) complaisant
sufrimiento [sufri'mjento] *nm* suffering
sufrir [su'frir] *vt* (*padecer*) to suffer; (*soportar*) to bear, stand, put up with; (*apoyar*) to hold up, support ▷ *vi* to suffer
sugerencia [suxe'renθja] *nf* suggestion
sugerir [suxe'rir] *vt* to suggest; (*sutilmente*) to hint; (*idea: incitar*) to prompt
sugestión [suxes'tjon] *nf* suggestion; (*sutil*) hint; (*poder*) hypnotic power
sugestionar [suxestjo'nar] *vt* to influence

sugestivo, -a [suxes'tiβo, a] *adj* stimulating; (*atractivo*) attractive; (*fascinante*) fascinating
suicida [sui'θiða] *adj* suicidal ▷ *nm/f* suicidal person; (*muerto*) suicide, person who has committed suicide
suicidarse [suiθi'ðarse] *vr* to commit suicide, kill o.s.
suicidio [sui'θiðjo] *nm* suicide
Suiza ['swiθa] *nf* Switzerland
suizo, -a ['swiθo, a] *adj, nm/f* Swiss ▷ *nm* sugared bun
sujeción [suxe'θjon] *nf* subjection
sujetador [suxeta'ðor] *nm* fastener, clip; (*prenda femenina*) bra, brassiere
sujetar [suxe'tar] *vt* (*fijar*) to fasten; (*detener*) to hold down; (*fig*) to subject, subjugate; (*pelo etc*) to keep *o* hold in place; (*papeles*) to fasten together; **sujetarse** *vr* to subject o.s.
sujeto, -a [su'xeto, a] *adj* fastened, secure ▷ *nm* subject; (*individuo*) individual; (*fam: tipo*) fellow, character, type, guy (*US*); **~ a** subject to
suma ['suma] *nf* (*cantidad*) total, sum; (*de dinero*) sum; (*acto*) adding (up), addition; **en ~** in short; **~ y sigue** (*Com*) carry forward
sumamente [suma'mente] *adv* extremely, exceedingly
sumar [su'mar] *vt* to add (up); (*reunir*) to collect, gather ▷ *vi* to add up
sumario, -a [su'marjo, a] *adj* brief, concise ▷ *nm* summary
sumergir [sumer'xir] *vt* to submerge; (*hundir*) to sink; (*bañar*) to immerse, dip; **sumergirse** *vr* (*hundirse*) to sink beneath the surface
sumidero [sumi'ðero] *nm* drain, sewer; (*Tec*) sump
suministrar [suminis'trar] *vt* to supply, provide
suministro [sumi'nistro] *nm* supply; (*acto*) supplying, providing
sumir [su'mir] *vt* to sink, submerge; (*fig*) to plunge; **sumirse** *vr* (*objeto*) to sink; **~se en el estudio** to become absorbed in one's studies
sumisión [sumi'sjon] *nf* (*acto*) submission; (*calidad*) submissiveness, docility
sumiso, -a [su'miso, a] *adj* submissive, docile
sumo, -a ['sumo, a] *adj* great, extreme; (*mayor*) highest, supreme ▷ *nm* sumo (wrestling); **a lo ~** at most
suntuoso, -a [sun'twoso, a] *adj* sumptuous, magnificent; (*lujoso*) lavish
supe *etc* ['supe] *vb ver* **saber**
supeditar [supeði'tar] *vt* to subordinate; (*sojuzgar*) to subdue; (*oprimir*) to oppress; **supeditarse** *vr*: **~se a** to subject o.s. to
super... [super] *pref* super..., over...
súper ['super] *adj* (*fam*) super, great ▷ *nf* (*gasolina*) four-star (petrol)
superación [supera'θjon] *nf* (*tb*: **~ personal**) self-improvement
superar [supe'rar] *vt* (*sobreponerse a*) to overcome; (*rebasar*) to surpass, do better than; (*pasar*) to go beyond; (*marca, récord*) to break; (*etapa: dejar atrás*) to get past; **superarse** *vr* to excel o.s.
superávit [supe'raβit] (*pl* **superávits**) *nm* surplus
superbueno, a [super'bweno, a] *adj* great, fantastic
superficial [superfi'θjal] *adj* superficial; (*medida*) surface *cpd*
superficie [super'fiθje] *nf* surface; (*área*) area; **grandes ~s** (*Com*) superstores
superfluo, -a [su'perflwo, a] *adj* superfluous
superintendente [superinten'dente] *nm/f* supervisor, superintendent
superior [supe'rjor] *adj* (*piso, clase*) upper; (*temperatura, número, nivel*) higher; (*mejor: calidad, producto*) superior, better ▷ *nm/f* superior
superioridad [superjori'ðað] *nf* superiority
superlativo, -a [superla'tiβo, a] *adj, nm* superlative
supermercado [supermer'kaðo] *nm* supermarket
superponer [superpo'ner] *vt* to superimpose; (*Inform*) to overstrike
supersónico, -a [super'soniko, a] *adj* supersonic
superstición [supersti'θjon] *nf* superstition
supersticioso, -a [supersti'θjoso, a] *adj* superstitious
supervisar [superβi'sar] *vt* to supervise; (*Com*) to superintend
supervisor, a [superβi'sor, a] *nm/f* supervisor
supervivencia [superβi'βenθja] *nf* survival
superviviente [superβi'βjente] *adj* surviving ▷ *nm/f* survivor
supiera *etc vb ver* **saber**
suplantar [suplan'tar] *vt* (*persona*) to supplant; (*hacerse pasar por otro*) to take the place of
suplementario, -a [suplemen'tarjo, a] *adj* supplementary
suplemento [suple'mento] *nm* supplement
suplente [su'plente] *adj* substitute; (*disponible*) reserve ▷ *nm/f* substitute
supletorio, -a [suple'torjo, a] *adj* supplementary; (*adicional*) extra ▷ *nm* supplement; **mesa supletoria** spare table; **teléfono ~** extension
súplica ['suplika] *nf* request; (*Rel*) supplication; (*Jur: instancia*) petition; **súplicas** *nfpl* entreaties
suplicar [supli'kar] *vt* (*cosa*) to beg (for), plead for; (*persona*) to beg, plead with; (*Jur*) to appeal to, petition
suplicio [su'pliθjo] *nm* torture; (*tormento*) torment; (*emoción*) anguish; (*experiencia penosa*) ordeal

suplir [su'plir] *vt* (*compensar*) to make good, make up for; (*reemplazar*) to replace, substitute ▷ *vi*: ~ **a** to take the place of, substitute for

supo *etc* ['supo] *vb ver* **saber**

suponer [supo'ner] *vt* to suppose; (*significar*) to mean; (*acarrear*) to involve ▷ *vi* to count, have authority; **era de ~ que ...** it was to be expected that ...

suposición [suposi'θjon] *nf* supposition

supositorio [suposi'torjo] *nm* suppository

supremacía [suprema'θia] *nf* supremacy

supremo, -a [su'premo, a] *adj* supreme

supresión [supre'sjon] *nf* suppression; (*de derecho*) abolition; (*de dificultad*) removal; (*de palabra etc*) deletion; (*de restricción*) cancellation, lifting

suprimir [supri'mir] *vt* to suppress; (*derecho, costumbre*) to abolish; (*dificultad*) to remove; (*palabra etc, Inform*) to delete; (*restricción*) to cancel, lift

supuesto, -a [su'pwesto, a] *pp de* **suponer** ▷ *adj* (*hipotético*) supposed; (*falso*) false ▷ *nm* assumption, hypothesis ▷ *conj*: ~ **que** since; **dar por ~ algo** to take sth for granted; **por ~** of course

supurar [supu'rar] *vi* to fester, suppurate

sur [sur] *adj* southern; (*rumbo*) southerly ▷ *nm* south; (*viento*) south wind

suramericano, -a [surameri'kano, a] *adj* South American ▷ *nm/f* South American

surcar [sur'kar] *vt* to plough; (*superficie*) to cut, score

surco ['surko] *nm* (*en metal, disco*) groove; (*Agr*) furrow

sureste [su'reste] = **sudeste**

surf [surf] *nm* surfing

surfear [surfe'ar] *vt*: ~ **el Internet** to surf the internet

surgir [sur'xir] *vi* to arise, emerge; (*dificultad*) to come up, crop up

suroeste [suro'este] *nm* south-west

surtido, -a [sur'tiðo, a] *adj* mixed, assorted ▷ *nm* (*selección*) selection, assortment; (*abastecimiento*) supply, stock

surtidor [surti'ðor] *nm* (*chorro*) jet, spout; (*fuente*) fountain; ~ **de gasolina** petrol (*Brit*) *o* gas (*US*) pump

surtir [sur'tir] *vt* to supply, provide; (*efecto*) to have, produce ▷ *vi* to spout, spurt; **surtirse** *vr*: **~se de** to provide o.s. with

susceptible [susθep'tiβle] *adj* susceptible; (*sensible*) sensitive; ~ **de** capable of

suscitar [susθi'tar] *vt* to cause, provoke; (*discusión*) to start; (*duda, problema*) to raise; (*interés, sospechas*) to arouse

suscribir [suskri'βir] *vt* (*firmar*) to sign; (*respaldar*) to subscribe to, endorse; (*Com: acciones*) to take out an option on; **suscribirse** *vr* to subscribe; **~ a algn a una revista** to take out a subscription to a journal for sb

suscripción [suskrip'θjon] *nf* subscription

susodicho, -a [suso'ditʃo, a] *adj* above-mentioned

suspender [suspen'der] *vt* (*objeto*) to hang (up), suspend; (*trabajo*) to stop, suspend; (*Escol*) to fail; (*interrumpir*) to adjourn; (*atrasar*) to postpone

suspense [sus'pense] *nm* suspense; **película/novela de ~** thriller

suspensión [suspen'sjon] *nf* suspension; (*fig*) stoppage, suspension; (*Jur*) stay; **~ de fuego** *o* **de hostilidades** ceasefire, cessation of hostilities; **~ de pagos** suspension of payments

suspenso, -a [sus'penso, a] *adj* hanging, suspended; (*Escol*) failed ▷ *nm* (*Escol*) fail(ure); **quedar** *o* **estar en ~** to be pending; **película** *o* **novela de ~** (*Am*) thriller

suspicacia [suspi'kaθja] *nf* suspicion, mistrust

suspicaz [suspi'kaθ] *adj* suspicious, distrustful

suspirar [suspi'rar] *vi* to sigh

suspiro [sus'piro] *nm* sigh

sustancia [sus'tanθja] *nf* substance; **~ gris** (*Anat*) grey matter; **sin ~** lacking in substance, shallow

sustancial [sustan'θjal] *adj* substantial

sustancioso, -a [sustan'θjoso, a] *adj* substantial; (*discurso*) solid

sustantivo, -a [sustan'tiβo, a] *adj* substantive; (*Ling*) substantival, noun *cpd* ▷ *nm* noun, substantive

sustentar [susten'tar] *vt* (*alimentar*) to sustain, nourish; (*objeto*) to hold up, support; (*idea, teoría*) to maintain, uphold; (*fig*) to sustain, keep going

sustento [sus'tento] *nm* support; (*alimento*) sustenance, food

sustituir [sustitu'ir] *vt* to substitute, replace

sustituto, -a [susti'tuto, a] *nm/f* substitute, replacement

susto ['susto] *nm* fright, scare; **dar un ~ a algn** to give sb a fright; **darse** *o* **pegarse un ~** (*fam*) to get a fright

sustraer [sustra'er] *vt* to remove, take away; (*Mat*) to subtract

sustrato [sus'trato] *nm* substratum

susurrar [susu'rrar] *vi* to whisper

susurro [su'surro] *nm* whisper

sutil [su'til] *adj* (*aroma*) subtle; (*tenue*) thin; (*hilo, hebra*) fine; (*olor*) delicate; (*brisa*) gentle; (*diferencia*) fine, subtle; (*inteligencia*) sharp, keen

sutileza [suti'leθa] *nf* subtlety; (*delgadez*) thinness; (*delicadeza*) delicacy; (*agudeza*) keenness

suturar [sutu'rar] *vt* to suture; (*juntar con puntos*) to stitch

suyo, -a ['sujo, a] *adj* (*con artículo o después del verbo* **ser**: *de él*) his; (*: de ella*) hers; (*: de ellos, ellas*) theirs; (*: de usted, ustedes*) yours; (*después de un nombre*: *de él*) of his; (*: de ella*) of hers;

(*: de ellos, ellas*) of theirs; (*: de usted, ustedes*) of yours; **lo ~** (what is) his; (*su parte*) his share, what he deserves; **los ~s** (*su familia*) one's family *o* relations; (*sus partidarios*) one's own people *o* supporters; **~ afectísimo** (*en carta*) yours faithfully *o* sincerely; **de ~** in itself; **eso es muy ~** that's just like him; **hacer de las suyas** to get up to one's old tricks; **ir a la suya, ir a lo ~** to go one's own way; **salirse con la suya** to get one's way; **un amigo ~** a friend of his (*o* hers *o* theirs *o* yours)

t

Tabacalera [taβaka'lera] *nf Spanish state tobacco monopoly*
tabaco [ta'βako] *nm* tobacco; (*fam*) cigarettes *pl*
tábano ['taβano] *nm* horsefly
tabaquería [tabake'ria] *nf* tobacconist's (*Brit*), cigar store (*US*)
taberna [ta'βerna] *nf* bar
tabernero, -a [taβer'nero, a] *nm/f* (*encargado*) publican; (*camarero*) barman/barmaid
tabique [ta'βike] *nm* (*pared*) thin wall; (*para dividir*) partition
tabla ['taβla] *nf* (*de madera*) plank; (*estante*) shelf; (*de anuncios*) board; (*lista, catálogo*) list; (*de vestido*) pleat; (*Arte*) panel; **tablas** *nfpl* (*Taur, Teat*) boards; **estar** *o* **quedar en ~s** to draw; **~ de consulta** (*Inform*) lookup table
tablado [ta'βlaðo] *nm* (*plataforma*) platform; (*suelo*) plank floor; (*Teat*) stage
tablao [ta'βlao] *nm* (*tb*: **~ flamenco**) flamenco show
tablero [ta'βlero] *nm* (*de madera*) plank, board; (*pizarra*) blackboard; (*de ajedrez, damas*) board; (*Auto*) dashboard; **~ de gráficos** (*Inform*) graph pad; **~ de mandos** (*Am: Auto*) dashboard
tablet ['tablet] *nf* (*Inform*) tablet
tableta [ta'βleta] *nf* (*Med, Inform*) tablet; (*de chocolate*) bar
tablón [ta'βlon] *nm* (*de suelo*) plank; (*de techo*) beam; (*de anuncios*) notice board
tabú [ta'βu] *nm* taboo
tabular [taβu'lar] *vt* to tabulate; (*Inform*) to tab

taburete [taβu'rete] *nm* stool
tacaño, -a [ta'kaɲo, a] *adj* (*avaro*) mean; (*astuto*) crafty
tacha ['tatʃa] *nf* (*defecto*) flaw, defect; (*Tec*) stud; **poner ~ a** to find fault with; **sin ~** flawless
tachar [ta'tʃar] *vt* (*borrar*) to cross out; (*corregir*) to correct; (*criticar*) to criticize; **~ de** to accuse of
tacho ['tatʃo] *nm* (*Am*) bucket, pail; **~ de la basura** rubbish bin (*Brit*), trash can (*US*)
tácito, -a ['taθito, a] *adj* tacit; (*acuerdo*) unspoken; (*Ling*) understood; (*ley*) unwritten
taciturno, -a [taθi'turno, a] *adj* (*callado*) silent; (*malhumorado*) sullen
taco ['tako] *nm* (*Billar*) cue; (*libro de billetes*) book; (*manojo de billetes*) wad; (*Am*) heel; (*tarugo*) peg; (*fam: bocado*) snack; (*: palabrota*) swear word; (*: trago de vino*) swig; (*México*) filled tortilla; **armarse** *o* **hacerse un ~** to get into a mess
tacón [ta'kon] *nm* heel; **de ~ alto** high-heeled
taconear [takone'ar] *vi* (*dar golpecitos*) to tap with one's heels; (*Mil etc*) to click one's heels
taconeo [tako'neo] *nm* (heel) tapping *o* clicking
táctico, -a ['taktiko, a] *adj* tactical ▷ *nf* tactics *pl*
tacto ['takto] *nm* touch; (*acción*) touching; (*fig*) tact
tafetán [tafe'tan] *nm* taffeta; **tafetanes** *nmpl* (*fam*) frills; **~ adhesivo** *o* **inglés** sticking plaster
tafilete [tafi'lete] *nm* morocco leather
tahona [ta'ona] *nf* (*panadería*) bakery; (*molino*) flour mill
taimado, -a [tai'maðo, a] *adj* (*astuto*) sly; (*resentido*) sullen
taita ['taita] *nm* dad, daddy
tajada [ta'xaða] *nf* slice; (*fam*) rake-off; **sacar ~** to get one's share
tajante [ta'xante] *adj* sharp; (*negativa*) emphatic; **es una persona ~** he's an emphatic person
tajar [ta'xar] *vt* to cut, slice
tajo ['taxo] *nm* (*corte*) cut; (*filo*) cutting edge; (*Geo*) cleft
tal [tal] *adj* such; **un ~ García** a man called García; **~ vez** perhaps ▷ *pron* (*persona*) someone, such a one; (*cosa*) something, such a thing; **~ como** such as; **~ para cual** tit for tat; (*dos iguales*) two of a kind; **hablábamos de que si ~ si cual** we were talking about this, that and the other ▷ *adv*: **~ como** (*igual*) just as; **~ cual** (*como es*) just as it is; **~ el padre, cual el hijo** like father, like son; **¿qué ~?** how are things?; **¿qué ~ te gusta?** how do you like it? ▷ *conj*: **con ~ (de) que** provided that
taladradora [talaðra'ðora] *nf* drill; **~ neumática** pneumatic drill
taladrar [tala'ðrar] *vt* to drill; (*fig: ruido*) to pierce
taladro [ta'laðro] *nm* (*gen*) drill; (*hoyo*) drill hole; **~ neumático** pneumatic drill
talante [ta'lante] *nm* (*humor*) mood; (*voluntad*) will, willingness
talar [ta'lar] *vt* to fell, cut down; (*fig*) to devastate
talco ['talko] *nm* (*polvos*) talcum powder; (*Mineralogía*) talc
talega [ta'leɣa] *nf* sack
talego [ta'leɣo] *nm* sack; **tener ~** (*fam*) to have money
talento [ta'lento] *nm* talent; (*capacidad*) ability; (*don*) gift
Talgo ['talgo] *nm abr* (*Ferro: = tren articulado ligero Goicoechea Oriol*) *high-speed train*
talismán [talis'man] *nm* talisman
talla ['taʎa] *nf* (*estatura, fig, Med*) height, stature; (*de ropa*) size, fitting; (*palo*) measuring rod; (*Arte: de madera*) carving; (*de piedra*) sculpture
tallado, -a [ta'ʎaðo, a] *adj* carved ▷ *nm* (*de madera*) carving; (*de piedra*) sculpture
tallar [ta'ʎar] *vt* (*trabajar*) to work, carve; (*grabar*) to engrave; (*medir*) to measure; (*repartir*) to deal ▷ *vi* to deal
tallarín [taʎa'rin] *nm* noodle
talle ['taʎe] *nm* (*Anat*) waist; (*medida*) size; (*física*) build; (*: de mujer*) figure; (*fig*) appearance; **de ~ esbelto** with a slim figure
taller [ta'ʎer] *nm* (*Tec*) workshop; (*fábrica*) factory; (*Auto*) garage; (*de artista*) studio
tallo ['taʎo] *nm* (*de planta*) stem; (*de hierba*) blade; (*brote*) shoot; (*col*) cabbage; (*Culin*) candied peel
talón [ta'lon] *nm* (*gen*) heel; (*Com*) counterfoil; (*cheque*) cheque (*Brit*), check (*US*); (*Tec*) rim; **~ de Aquiles** Achilles heel
talonario [talo'narjo] *nm* (*de cheques*) chequebook (*Brit*), checkbook (*US*); (*de billetes*) book of tickets; (*de recibos*) receipt book
tamaño, -a [ta'maɲo, a] *adj* (*tan grande*) such a big; (*tan pequeño*) such a small ▷ *nm* size; **de ~ natural** full-size; **¿de qué ~ es?** what size is it?
tamarindo [tama'rindo] *nm* tamarind
tambalearse [tambale'arse] *vr* (*persona*) to stagger; (*mueble*) to wobble; (*vehículo*) to sway
también [tam'bjen] *adv* (*igualmente*) also, too, as well; (*además*) besides; **estoy cansado — yo ~** I'm tired — so am I *o* me too
tambor [tam'bor] *nm* drum; (*Anat*) eardrum; **~ del freno** brake drum; **~ magnético** (*Inform*) magnetic drum
Támesis ['tamesis] *nm* Thames
tamiz [ta'miθ] *nm* sieve
tamizar [tami'θar] *vt* to sieve
tampoco [tam'poko] *adv* nor, neither; **yo ~ lo compré** I didn't buy it either
tampón [tam'pon] *nm* plug; (*Med*) tampon

t

tan [tan] *adv* so; ~ **es así que** so much so that; **¡qué cosa ~ rara!** how strange!; **no es una idea ~ buena** it is not such a good idea
tanatorio [tana'torjo] *nm* (*privado*) funeral home *o* parlour; (*público*) mortuary
tanda ['tanda] *nf* (*gen*) series; (*de inyecciones*) course; (*juego*) set; (*turno*) shift; (*grupo*) gang
tanga ['tanga] *nm* (*bikini*) tanga; (*ropa interior*) tanga briefs
tangente [tan'xente] *nf* tangent; **salirse por la ~** to go off at a tangent
Tánger ['tanxer] *n* Tangier
tangerina [tanxe'rina] *nf* (*Am*) tangerine
tangible [tan'xiβle] *adj* tangible
tango ['tango] *nm* tango
tanque ['tanke] *nm* (*gen*) tank; (*Auto, Naut*) tanker
tanqueta [tan'keta] *nf* (*Mil*) small tank, armoured vehicle
tantear [tante'ar] *vt* (*calcular*) to reckon (up); (*medir*) to take the measure of; (*probar*) to test, try out; (*tomar la medida*: *persona*) to take the measurements of; (*considerar*) to weigh up; (*persona*: *opinión*) to sound out ▷ *vi* (*Deporte*) to score
tanteo [tan'teo] *nm* (*cálculo aproximado*) (rough) calculation; (*prueba*) test, trial; (*Deporte*) scoring; (*adivinanzas*) guesswork; **al ~** by trial and error

PALABRA CLAVE

tanto, -a ['tanto, a] *adj* (*cantidad*) so much, as much; **tantos** so many, as many; **20 y tantos** 20-odd
▷ *adv* (*cantidad*) so much, as much; (*tiempo*) so long, as long; **tanto tú como yo** both you and I; **tanto como eso** as much as that; **tanto más ... cuanto que** it's all the more ... because; **tanto mejor/peor** so much the better/the worse; **tanto si viene como si va** whether he comes or whether he goes; **tanto es así que** so much so that; **por tanto, por lo tanto** therefore; **me he vuelto ronco de** *o* **con tanto hablar** I have become hoarse with so much talking
▷ *conj*: **con tanto que** provided (that); **en tanto que** while; **hasta tanto (que)** until such time as
▷ *nm* **1** (*suma*) certain amount; (*proporción*) so much; **un tanto perezoso** somewhat lazy
2 (*punto*) point; (*gol*) goal
3 (*locuciones*): **tanto alzado** agreed price; **tanto por ciento** percentage; **al tanto** up to date; **estar al tanto de los acontecimientos** to be fully abreast of events; **al tanto de que** because of the fact that
▷ *pron*: **cado uno paga tanto** each one pays so much; **uno de tantos** one of many; **a tantos de agosto** on such and such a day in August; **entre tanto** meanwhile

tapa ['tapa] *nf* (*de caja, olla*) lid; (*de botella*) top; (*de libro*) cover; (*de comida*) snack
tapadera [tapa'ðera] *nf* lid, cover
tapar [ta'par] *vt* (*cubrir*) to cover; (*envolver*) to wrap *o* cover up; (*la vista*) to obstruct; (*persona, falta*) to conceal; (*Am*) to fill; **taparse** *vr* to wrap o.s. up
taparrabo [tapa'rraβo] *nm* loincloth
tapete [ta'pete] *nm* table cover; **estar sobre el ~** (*fig*) to be under discussion
tapia ['tapja] *nf* (garden) wall
tapiar [ta'pjar] *vt* to wall in
tapicería [tapiθe'ria] *nf* tapestry; (*para muebles*) upholstery; (*tienda*) upholsterer's (shop)
tapiz [ta'piθ] *nm* (*alfombra*) carpet; (*tela tejida*) tapestry
tapizar [tapi'θar] *vt* (*pared*) to wallpaper; (*suelo*) to carpet; (*muebles*) to upholster
tapón [ta'pon] *nm* (*de botella*) top; (*corcho*) stopper; (*Tec*) plug; (*Med*) tampon; **~ de rosca** *o* **de tuerca** screw-top
taquigrafía [takiɣra'fia] *nf* shorthand
taquígrafo, -a [ta'kiɣrafo, a] *nm/f* shorthand writer, stenographer (US)
taquilla [ta'kiʎa] *nf* (*de estación etc*) booking office; (*de teatro*) box office; (*suma recogida*) takings *pl*; (*archivador*) filing cabinet
taquillero, -a [taki'ʎero, a] *adj*: **función taquillera** box office success ▷ *nm/f* ticket clerk
taquimecanografía [takimekanoɣra'fia] *nf* shorthand and typing
tara ['tara] *nf* (*defecto*) defect; (*Com*) tare
tarántula [ta'rantula] *nf* tarantula
tararear [tarare'ar] *vi* to hum
tardanza [tar'ðanθa] *nf* (*demora*) delay; (*lentitud*) slowness
tardar [tar'ðar] *vi* (*tomar tiempo*) to take a long time; (*llegar tarde*) to be late; (*demorar*) to delay; **¿tarda mucho el tren?** does the train take long?; **a más ~** at the (very) latest; **~ en hacer algo** to be slow *o* take a long time to do sth; **no tardes en venir** come soon, come before long
tarde ['tarðe] *adv* (*hora*) late; (*fuera de tiempo*) too late ▷ *nf* (*de día*) afternoon; (*de noche*) evening; **~ o temprano** sooner or later; **de ~ en ~** from time to time; **¡buenas ~s!** (*de día*) good afternoon!; (*de noche*) good evening!; **a** *o* **por la ~** in the afternoon; in the evening
tardío, -a [tar'ðio, a] *adj* (*retrasado*) late; (*lento*) slow (to arrive)
tardo, -a ['tarðo, a] *adj* (*lento*) slow; (*torpe*) dull; **~ de oído** hard of hearing
tarea [ta'rea] *nf* task; **tareas** *nfpl* (*Escol*) homework *sg*; **~ de ocasión** chore
tarifa [ta'rifa] *nf* (*lista de precios*) price list; (*Com*) tariff; **~ básica** basic rate; **~ completa** all-in cost; **~ a destajo** piece rate; **~ doble** double time
tarima [ta'rima] *nf* (*plataforma*) platform

tarjeta [tar'xeta] *nf* card; **~ postal/de crédito/de Navidad** postcard/credit card/Christmas card; **~ de circuitos** (*Inform*) circuit board; **~ cliente** loyalty card; **~ comercial** (*Com*) calling card; **~ dinero** cash card; **~ gráficos** (*Inform*) graphics card; **~ monedero** electronic purse *o* wallet; **~ de embarque** boarding pass; **~ de memoria** memory card; **~ prepago** top-up card; **~ SIM** SIM card
tarot [ta'rot] *nm* tarot
tarro ['tarro] *nm* jar, pot
tarta ['tarta] *nf* (*pastel*) cake; (*torta*) tart
tartamudear [tartamuðe'ar] *vi* to stutter, stammer
tartamudo, -a [tarta'muðo, a] *adj* stuttering, stammering ▷ *nm/f* stutterer, stammerer
tártaro, -a ['tartaro, a] *adj*: **salsa tártara** tartar(e) sauce ▷ *nm* Tartar ▷ *nm* (*Química*) tartar
tasa ['tasa] *nf* (*precio*) (fixed) price, rate; (*valoración*) valuation; (*medida, norma*) measure, standard; **~ básica** (*Com*) basic rate; **~ de cambio** exchange rate; **de ~ cero** (*Com*) zero-rated; **~s de aeropuerto** airport tax; **~ de crecimiento** growth rate; **~ de interés/de nacimiento** rate of interest/birth rate; **~ de rendimiento** (*Com*) rate of return; **~s universitarias** university fees
tasación [tasa'θjon] *nf* assessment, valuation; (*fig*) appraisal
tasador, a [tasa'ðor, a] *nm/f* valuer; (*Com: de impuestos*) assessor
tasar [ta'sar] *vt* (*arreglar el precio*) to fix a price for; (*valorar*) to value, assess; (*limitar*) to limit
tasca ['taska] *nf* (*fam*) pub
tata ['tata] *nm* (*fam*) dad(dy) ▷ *nf* (*niñera*) nanny, maid
tatarabuelo, -a [tatara'βwelo, a] *nm/f* great-great-grandfather/mother; **los ~s** one's great-great-grandparents
tatuaje [ta'twaxe] *nm* (*dibujo*) tattoo; (*acto*) tattooing
tatuar [ta'twar] *vt* to tattoo
taurino, -a [tau'rino, a] *adj* bullfighting *cpd*
Tauro ['tauro] *nm* Taurus
tauromaquia [tauro'makja] *nf* (art of) bullfighting
taxi ['taksi] *nm* taxi
taxista [tak'sista] *nm/f* taxi driver
taza ['taθa] *nf* cup; (*de retrete*) bowl; **~ para café** coffee cup; **~ de café** cup of coffee
tazón [ta'θon] *nm* mug, large cup; (*escudilla*) basin
te [te] *pron* (*complemento de objeto*) you; (*complemento indirecto*) (to) you; (*reflexivo*) (to) yourself; **¿te duele mucho el brazo?** does your arm hurt a lot?; **te equivocas** you're wrong; **¡cálmate!** calm yourself!
té [te] (*pl* **tés**) *nm* tea; (*reunión*) tea party
tea ['tea] *nf* (*antorcha*) torch
teatral [tea'tral] *adj* theatre *cpd*; (*fig*) theatrical
teatro [te'atro] *nm* theatre; (*Lit*) plays *pl*, drama; **el ~** (*carrera*) the theatre, acting; **~ de aficionados/de variedades** amateur/variety theatre, vaudeville theater (*US*); **hacer ~** (*fig*) to make a fuss
tebeo [te'βeo] *nm* children's comic
techo ['tetʃo] *nm* (*externo*) roof; (*interno*) ceiling
tecla ['tekla] *nf* (*Inform, Mus, Tip*) key; (*Inform*): **~ de anulación/de borrar** cancel/delete key; **~ de control/de edición** control/edit key; **~ con flecha** arrow key; **~ programable** user-defined key; **~ de retorno/de tabulación** return/tab key; **~ del cursor** cursor key; **~s de control direccional del cursor** cursor control keys
teclado [te'klaðo] *nm* keyboard (*tb Inform*); **~ numérico** (*Inform*) numeric keypad
teclear [tekle'ar] *vi* to strum; (*fam*) to drum ▷ *vt* (*Inform*) to key (in), type in, keyboard
tecleo [te'kleo] *nm* (*Mus: sonido*) strumming; (*: forma de tocar*) fingering; (*fam*) drumming
técnico, -a ['tekniko, a] *adj* technical ▷ *nm* technician; (*experto*) expert ▷ *nf* (*procedimientos*) technique; (*tecnología*) technology; (*arte, oficio*) craft
tecnicolor [tekniko'lor] *nm* Technicolor®
tecnócrata [tek'nokrata] *nm/f* technocrat
tecnología [teknolo'xia] *nf* technology; **~ de estado sólido** (*Inform*) solid-state technology; **~ de la información** information technology
tecnológico, -a [tekno'loxiko, a] *adj* technological
tecolote [teko'lote] *nm* (*Am*) owl
tedio ['teðjo] *nm* (*aburrimiento*) boredom; (*apatía*) apathy; (*fastidio*) depression
tedioso, -a [te'ðjoso, a] *adj* boring; (*cansado*) wearisome, tedious
teja ['texa] *nf* (*azulejo*) tile; (*Bot*) lime (tree)
tejado [te'xaðo] *nm* (tiled) roof
tejano, -a [te'xano, a] *adj, nm/f* Texan ▷ *nmpl*: **~s** (*vaqueros*) jeans
tejemaneje [texema'nexe] *nm* (*actividad*) bustle; (*lío*) fuss, to-do; (*intriga*) intrigue
tejer [te'xer] *vt* to weave; (*tela de araña*) to spin; (*Am*) to knit; (*fig*) to fabricate ▷ *vi*: **~ y des~** to chop and change
tejido [te'xiðo] *nm* fabric; (*estofa, tela*) (knitted) material; (*telaraña*) web; (*Anat*) tissue; (*textura*) texture
tel. *abr* (= *teléfono*) tel.
tela ['tela] *nf* (*material*) material; (*de fruta, en líquido*) skin; (*del ojo*) film; **hay ~ para rato** there's lots to talk about; **poner en ~ de juicio** to (call in) question; **~ de araña** cobweb, spider's web
telar [te'lar] *nm* (*máquina*) loom; (*de teatro*) gridiron; **telares** *nmpl* textile mill *sg*
telaraña [tela'raɲa] *nf* cobweb, spider's web
tele ['tele] *nf* (*fam*) TV

tele... [tele] *pref* tele...
telebasura [teleβa'sura] *nf* trash TV
telecomunicación [telekomunika'θjon] *nf* telecommunication
teleconferencia [telekonfe'renθja] *nf* (*reunión*) teleconference; (*sistema*) teleconferencing
telecontrol [telekon'trol] *nm* remote control
telediario [tele'ðjarjo] *nm* television news
teledifusión [teleðifu'sjon] *nf* (television) broadcast
teledirigido, -a [teleðiri'xiðo, a] *adj* remote-controlled
teléf. *abr* (= *teléfono*) tel.
teleférico [tele'feriko] *nm* (*tren*) cable-railway; (*de esquí*) ski-lift
telefonear [telefone'ar] *vi* to telephone
telefónico, -a [tele'foniko, a] *adj* telephone *cpd* ▷ *nf*: **Telefónica** (*Esp*) *Spanish national telephone company*, ≈ British Telecom
telefonillo [telefo'niʎo] *nm* (*de puerta*) intercom
telefonista [telefo'nista] *nm/f* telephonist
teléfono [te'lefono] *nm* (tele)phone; ~ **móvil** mobile phone; **está hablando por** ~ he's on the phone; **llamar a algn por** ~ to ring sb (up) *o* phone sb (up); ~ **celular** (*Am*) mobile phone; ~ **con cámara** camera phone; ~ **inalámbrico** cordless phone
telegrafía [teleɣra'fia] *nf* telegraphy
telégrafo [te'leɣrafo] *nm* telegraph; (*fam: persona*) telegraph boy
telegrama [tele'ɣrama] *nm* telegram
teleimpresor [teleimpre'sor] *nm* teleprinter
telenovela [teleno'βela] *nf* soap (opera)
teleobjetivo [teleobxe'tiβo] *nm* telephoto lens
telepatía [telepa'tia] *nf* telepathy
telepático, -a [tele'patiko, a] *adj* telepathic
telerrealidad [telerreali'ðað] *nf* reality TV
telescópico, -a [tele'skopiko, a] *adj* telescopic
telescopio [tele'skopjo] *nm* telescope
telesilla [tele'siʎa] *nm* chairlift
telespectador, a [telespekta'ðor, a] *nm/f* viewer
telesquí [teles'ki] *nm* ski-lift
teletarjeta [teletar'xeta] *nf* phonecard
teletex [tele'teks], **teletexto** [tele'teksto] *nm* teletext
teletipo [tele'tipo] *nm* teletype(writer)
teletrabajador, a [teletraβaxa'ðor, a] *nm/f* teleworker
teletrabajo [teletra'βaxo] *nm* teleworking
televentas [tele'βentas] *nfpl* telesales
televidente [teleβi'ðente] *nm/f* viewer
televisar [teleβi'sar] *vt* to televise
televisión [teleβi'sjon] *nf* television; ~ **en color/por satélite** colour/satellite television; ~ **digital** digital television
televisor [teleβi'sor] *nm* television set
télex ['teleks] *nm* telex; **máquina** ~ telex (machine); **enviar por** ~ to telex
telón [te'lon] *nm* curtain; ~ **de boca/seguridad** front/safety curtain; ~ **de acero** (*Pol*) iron curtain; ~ **de fondo** backcloth, background
telonero, -a [telo'nero, a] *nm/f* support act; **los ~s** (*Mus*) the support band
tema ['tema] *nm* (*asunto*) subject, topic; (*Mus*) theme; **~s de actualidad** current affairs ▷ *nf* (*obsesión*) obsession; (*manía*) ill-will; **tener ~ a algn** to have a grudge against sb
temario [te'marjo] *nm* (*Escol*) set of topics; (*de una conferencia*) agenda
temático, -a [te'matiko, a] *adj* thematic ▷ *nf* subject matter
temblar [tem'blar] *vi* to shake, tremble; (*de frío*) to shiver
tembleque [tem'bleke] *adj* shaking ▷ *nm* shaking
temblón, -ona [tem'blon, ona] *adj* shaking
temblor [tem'blor] *nm* trembling; (*de tierra*) earthquake
tembloroso, -a [temblo'roso, a] *adj* trembling
temer [te'mer] *vt* to fear ▷ *vi* to be afraid; **temo que Juan llegue tarde** I am afraid Juan may be late
temerario, -a [teme'rarjo, a] *adj* (*imprudente*) rash; (*descuidado*) reckless; (*arbitrario*) hasty
temeridad [temeri'ðað] *nf* (*imprudencia*) rashness; (*audacia*) boldness
temeroso, -a [teme'roso, a] *adj* (*miedoso*) fearful; (*que inspira temor*) frightful
temible [te'miβle] *adj* fearsome
temor [te'mor] *nm* (*miedo*) fear; (*duda*) suspicion
témpano ['tempano] *nm* (*Mus*) kettledrum; ~ **de hielo** ice floe
temperamento [tempera'mento] *nm* temperament; **tener** ~ to be temperamental
temperatura [tempera'tura] *nf* temperature
tempestad [tempes'tað] *nf* storm; ~ **en un vaso de agua** (*fig*) storm in a teacup
tempestuoso, -a [tempes'twoso, a] *adj* stormy
templado, -a [tem'plaðo, a] *adj* (*moderado*) moderate; (*: en el comer*) frugal; (*: en el beber*) abstemious; (*agua*) lukewarm; (*clima*) mild; (*Mus*) in tune, well-tuned
templanza [tem'planθa] *nf* moderation; (*en el beber*) abstemiousness; (*del clima*) mildness
templar [tem'plar] *vt* (*moderar*) to moderate; (*furia*) to restrain; (*calor*) to reduce; (*solución*) to dilute; (*afinar*) to tune (up); (*acero*) to temper; (*tuerca*) to tighten up ▷ *vi* to moderate; **templarse** *vr* to be restrained
temple ['temple] *nm* (*humor*) mood; (*coraje*) courage; (*ajuste*) tempering; (*afinación*) tuning; (*pintura*) tempera
templo ['templo] *nm* (*iglesia*) church; (*pagano etc*) temple; ~ **metodista** Methodist chapel

temporada [tempo'raða] *nf* time, period; (*estación, social, Deporte*) season; **en plena ~** at the height of the season
temporal [tempo'ral] *adj* (*no permanente*) temporary; (*Rel*) temporal ▷ *nm* storm
tempranero, -a [tempra'nero, a] *adj* (*Bot*) early; (*persona*) early-rising
temprano, -a [tem'prano, a] *adj* early ▷ *adv* early; (*demasiado pronto*) too soon, too early; **lo más ~ posible** as soon as possible
ten [ten] *vb ver* **tener**
tenaces [te'naθes] *adj pl ver* **tenaz**
tenacidad [tenaθi'ðað] *nf* (*gen*) tenacity; (*dureza*) toughness; (*terquedad*) stubbornness
tenacillas [tena'θiʎas] *nfpl* (*gen*) tongs; (*para el pelo*) curling tongs; (*Med*) forceps
tenaz [te'naθ] *adj* (*material*) tough; (*persona*) tenacious; (*pegajoso*) sticky; (*terco*) stubborn
tenaza, tenazas [te'naθ(as)] *nf(pl)* (*Med*) forceps; (*Tec*) pliers; (*Zool*) pincers
tendedero [tende'ðero] *nm* (*para ropa*) drying-place; (*cuerda*) clothes line
tendencia [ten'denθja] *nf* tendency; (*proceso*) trend; **~ imperante** prevailing tendency; **~ del mercado** run of the market; **tener ~ a** to tend *o* have a tendency to
tendencioso, -a [tenden'θjoso, a] *adj* tendentious
tender [ten'der] *vt* (*extender*) to spread out; (*ropa*) to hang out; (*vía férrea, cable*) to lay; (*cuerda*) to stretch; (*trampa*) to set ▷ *vi* to tend; **tenderse** *vr* to lie down; (*fig: dejarse llevar*) to let o.s. go; (*: dejar ir*) to let things go; **~ la cama/la mesa** (*Am*) to make the bed/lay the table
tenderete [tende'rete] *nm* (*puesto*) stall; (*carretilla*) barrow; (*exposición*) display of goods
tendero, -a [ten'dero, a] *nm/f* shopkeeper
tendido, -a [ten'diðo, a] *adj* (*acostado*) lying down, flat; (*colgado*) hanging ▷ *nm* (*ropa*) washing; (*Taur*) front rows *pl* of seats; (*colocación*) laying; (*Arq: enyesado*) coat of plaster; **a galope ~** flat out
tendón [ten'don] *nm* tendon
tendré *etc* [ten'dre] *vb ver* **tener**
tenebroso, -a [tene'βroso, a] *adj* (*oscuro*) dark; (*fig*) gloomy; (*siniestro*) sinister
tenedor [tene'ðor] *nm* (*Culin*) fork; (*poseedor*) holder; **~ de libros** book-keeper; **~ de acciones** shareholder; **~ de póliza** policyholder
teneduría [teneðu'ria] *nf* keeping; **~ de libros** book-keeping
tenencia [te'nenθja] *nf* (*de casa*) tenancy; (*de oficio*) tenure; (*de propiedad*) possession; **~ asegurada** security of tenure; **~ ilícita de armas** illegal possession of weapons

PALABRA CLAVE

tener [te'ner] *vt* **1** (*poseer, gen*) to have; (*en la mano*) to hold; **¿tienes un boli?** have you got a pen?; **va a tener un niño** she's going to have a baby; **tiene los ojos azules** he's got blue eyes; **¡ten (o tenga)!, ¡aquí tienes (o tiene)!** here you are!
2 (*edad, medidas*) to be; **tiene siete años** she's seven (years old); **tiene 15 cm de largo** it's 15 cm long
3 (*sentimientos, sensaciones*): **tener sed/hambre/frío/calor** to be thirsty/hungry/cold/hot; **tener celos** to be jealous; **tener cuidado** to be careful; **tener razón** to be right; **tener suerte** to be lucky
4 (*considerar*): **lo tengo por brillante** I consider him to be brilliant; **tener en mucho a algn** to think very highly of sb
5 (*+ pp, + adj, + gerundio*): **tengo terminada ya la mitad del trabajo** I've done half the work already; **tenía el sombrero puesto** he had his hat on; **tenía pensado llamarte** I had been thinking of phoning you; **nos tiene hartos** we're fed up with him; **me ha tenido tres horas esperando** he kept me waiting three hours
6: **tener que hacer algo** to have to do sth; **tengo que acabar este trabajo hoy** I have to finish this job today
7: **¿qué tienes, estás enfermo?** what's the matter with you, are you ill?
8 (*locuciones*): **¿conque ésas tenemos?** so it's like that, then?; **no las tengo todas conmigo** I'm a bit unsure (about it); **lo tiene difícil** he'll have a hard job
tenerse *vr* **1**: **tenerse en pie** to stand up
2: **tenerse por** to think o.s.; **se tiene por un gran cantante** he thinks himself a great singer

tengo *etc* ['tengo] *vb ver* **tener**
tenia ['tenja] *nf* tapeworm
teniente [te'njente] *nm* lieutenant; (*ayudante*) deputy; **~ coronel** lieutenant colonel
tenis ['tenis] *nm* tennis; **~ de mesa** table tennis
tenista [te'nista] *nm/f* tennis player
tenor [te'nor] *nm* (*tono*) tone; (*sentido*) meaning; (*Mus*) tenor; **a ~ de** on the lines of
tensar [ten'sar] *vt* to tauten; (*arco*) to draw
tensión [ten'sjon] *nf* tension; (*Tec*) stress; (*Med*): **~ arterial** blood pressure; **~ nerviosa** nervous strain; **tener la ~ alta** to have high blood pressure
tenso, -a ['tenso, a] *adj* tense; (*relaciones*) strained
tentación [tenta'θjon] *nf* temptation
tentáculo [ten'takulo] *nm* tentacle
tentador, a [tenta'ðor, a] *adj* tempting ▷ *nm/f* tempter/temptress
tentar [ten'tar] *vt* (*tocar*) to touch, feel; (*seducir*) to tempt; (*atraer*) to attract; (*probar*) to try (out); (*Med*) to probe; **~ hacer algo** to try to do sth

t

tentativa [tenta'tiβa] *nf* attempt; **~ de asesinato** attempted murder
tentempié [tentem'pje] *nm* (*fam*) snack
tenue ['tenwe] *adj* (*delgado*) thin, slender; (*alambre*) fine; (*insustancial*) tenuous; (*sonido*) faint; (*neblina*) light; (*lazo, vínculo*) slight
teñir [te'ɲir] *vt* to dye; (*fig*) to tinge; **teñirse** *vr* to dye; **~se el pelo** to dye one's hair
teología [teolo'xia] *nf* theology
teorema [teo'rema] *nm* theorem
teoría [teo'ria] *nf* theory; **en ~** in theory
teóricamente [te'orikamente] *adv* theoretically
teórico, -a [te'oriko, a] *adj* theoretic(al) ▷ *nm/f* theoretician, theorist
teorizar [teori'θar] *vi* to theorize
tequila [te'kila] *nm o f* tequila
terapéutico, -a [tera'peutiko, a] *adj* therapeutic(al) ▷ *nf* therapeutics *sg*
terapia [te'rapja] *nf* therapy; **~ laboral** occupational therapy
tercer [ter'θer] *adj ver* **tercero**
tercermundista [terθermun'dista] *adj* Third World *cpd*
tercero, -a [ter'θero, a] *adj* third (*antes de nmsg* **tercer**) ▷ *nm* (*árbitro*) mediator; (*Jur*) third party
terceto [ter'θeto] *nm* trio
terciado, -a [ter'θjaðo, a] *adj* slanting; **azúcar ~** brown sugar
terciar [ter'θjar] *vt* (*Mat*) to divide into three; (*inclinarse*) to slope; (*llevar*) to wear across one's chest ▷ *vi* (*participar*) to take part; (*hacer de árbitro*) to mediate; **terciarse** *vr* to arise
terciario, -a [ter'θjarjo, a] *adj* tertiary
tercio ['terθjo] *nm* third
terciopelo [terθjo'pelo] *nm* velvet
terco, -a ['terko, a] *adj* obstinate, stubborn; (*material*) tough
tergal® [ter'ɣal] *nm* Terylene®, Dacron® (*US*)
tergiversar [terxiβer'sar] *vt* to distort ▷ *vi* to prevaricate
termal [ter'mal] *adj* thermal
termas ['termas] *nfpl* hot springs
térmico, -a ['termiko, a] *adj* thermic, thermal, heat *cpd*
terminación [termina'θjon] *nf* (*final*) end; (*conclusión*) conclusion, ending
terminal [termi'nal] *adj* terminal ▷ *nm* (*Elec, Inform*) terminal; **~ conversacional** interactive terminal; **~ de pantalla** visual display unit ▷ *nf* (*Aviat, Ferro*) terminal
terminante [termi'nante] *adj* (*final*) final, definitive; (*tajante*) categorical
terminantemente [terminante'mente] *adv*: **~ prohibido** strictly forbidden
terminar [termi'nar] *vt* (*completar*) to complete, finish; (*concluir*) to end ▷ *vi* (*llegar a su fin*) to end; (*parar*) to stop; (*acabar*) to finish; **terminarse** *vr* to come to an end; **~ por hacer algo** to end up (by) doing sth
término ['termino] *nm* end, conclusion; (*parada*) terminus; (*límite*) boundary; (*en discusión*) point; (*Ling, Com*) term; **~ medio** average; (*fig*) middle way; **en otros ~s** in other words; **en último ~** (*a fin de cuentas*) in the last analysis; (*como último recurso*) as a last resort; **~ medio** average; (*fig*) middle way; **en ~s de** in terms of; **según los ~s del contrato** according to the terms of the contract
terminología [terminolo'xia] *nf* terminology
termita [ter'mita] *nf* termite
termo(s)® ['termo(s)] *nm* Thermos® (flask)
termodinámico, -a [termoði'namiko, a] *adj* thermodynamic ▷ *nf* thermodynamics *sg*
termómetro [ter'mometro] *nm* thermometer
termonuclear [termonukle'ar] *adj* thermonuclear
termostato [termos'tato] *nm* thermostat
ternero, -a [ter'nero, a] *nm/f* (*animal*) calf ▷ *nf* (*carne*) veal, beef
terno ['terno] *nm* (*traje*) three-piece suit; (*conjunto*) set of three
ternura [ter'nura] *nf* (*trato*) tenderness; (*palabra*) endearment; (*cariño*) fondness
terquedad [terke'ðað] *nf* obstinacy; (*dureza*) harshness
terrado [te'rraðo] *nm* terrace
terraplén [terra'plen] *nm* (*Agr*) terrace; (*Ferro*) embankment; (*Mil*) rampart; (*cuesta*) slope
terráqueo, -a [te'rrakeo, a] *adj*: **globo ~** globe
terrateniente [terrate'njente] *nm* landowner
terraza [te'rraθa] *nf* (*balcón*) balcony; (*techo*) flat roof; (*Agr*) terrace
terremoto [terre'moto] *nm* earthquake
terrenal [terre'nal] *adj* earthly
terreno, -a [te'rreno, a] *adj* (*de la tierra*) earthly, worldly ▷ *nm* (*tierra*) land; (*parcela*) plot; (*suelo*) soil; (*fig*) field; **un ~** a piece of land; **sobre el ~** on the spot; **ceder/perder ~** to give/lose ground; **preparar el ~ (a)** (*fig*) to pave the way (for)
terrestre [te'rrestre] *adj* terrestrial; (*ruta*) land *cpd*
terrible [te'rriβle] *adj* (*espantoso*) terrible; (*aterrador*) dreadful; (*tremendo*) awful
territorial [territo'rjal] *adj* territorial
territorio [terri'torjo] *nm* territory; **~ bajo mandato** mandated territory
terrón [te'rron] *nm* (*de azúcar*) lump; (*de tierra*) clod, lump; **terrones** *nmpl* land *sg*
terror [te'rror] *nm* terror
terrorífico, -a [terro'rifiko, a] *adj* terrifying
terrorismo [terro'rismo] *nm* terrorism
terrorista [terro'rista] *adj, nm/f* terrorist; **~ suicida** suicide bomber
terroso, -a [te'rroso, a] *adj* earthy

terruño [te'rruɲo] *nm* (*pedazo*) clod; (*parcela*) plot; (*fig*) native soil; **apego al ~** attachment to one's native soil
terso, -a ['terso, a] *adj* (*liso*) smooth; (*pulido*) polished; (*fig: estilo*) flowing
tersura [ter'sura] *nf* smoothness; (*brillo*) shine
tertulia [ter'tulja] *nf* (*reunión informal*) social gathering; (*grupo*) group, circle; (*sala*) clubroom; **~ literaria** literary circle
tesina [te'sina] *nf* dissertation
tesis ['tesis] *nf inv* thesis
tesón [te'son] *nm* (*firmeza*) firmness; (*tenacidad*) tenacity
tesorero, -a [teso'rero, a] *nm/f* treasurer
tesoro [te'soro] *nm* treasure; (*Com, Pol*) treasury; **T~ público** (*Pol*) Exchequer
test (*pl* **tests**) [tes(t), tes(t)] *nm* test
testaferro [testa'ferro] *nm* figurehead
testamentaría [testamenta'ria] *nf* execution of a will
testamentario, -a [testamen'tarjo, a] *adj* testamentary ▷ *nm/f* executor/executrix
testamento [testa'mento] *nm* will
testar [tes'tar] *vi* to make a will
testarudo, -a [testa'ruðo, a] *adj* stubborn
testículo [tes'tikulo] *nm* testicle
testificar [testifi'kar] *vt* to testify; (*fig*) to attest ▷ *vi* to give evidence
testigo [tes'tiɣo] *nm/f* witness; **~ de cargo/descargo** witness for the prosecution/defence; **~ ocular** eye witness; **poner a algn por ~** to cite sb as a witness
testimonial [testimo'njal] *adj* (*prueba*) testimonial; (*gesto*) token
testimoniar [testimo'njar] *vt* to testify to; (*fig*) to show
testimonio [testi'monjo] *nm* testimony; **en ~ de** as a token *o* mark of; **falso ~** perjured evidence, false witness
teta ['teta] *nf* (*de biberón*) teat; (*Anat*) nipple; (*fam*) breast; (*fam!*) tit (*!*)
tétanos ['tetanos] *nm* tetanus
tetera [te'tera] *nf* teapot; **~ eléctrica** (electric) kettle
tetilla [te'tiʎa] *nf* (*Anat*) nipple; (*de biberón*) teat
tétrico, -a ['tetriko, a] *adj* gloomy, dismal
textear [tekste'ar] *vt* (*LAm*) to text
textil [teks'til] *adj* textile
texto ['teksto] *nm* text
textual [teks'twal] *adj* textual; **palabras ~es** exact words
textura [teks'tura] *nf* (*de tejido*) texture; (*de mineral*) structure
tez [teθ] *nf* (*cutis*) complexion; (*color*) colouring
ti [ti] *pron* you; (*reflexivo*) yourself
tía ['tia] *nf* (*pariente*) aunt; (*fam: mujer*) girl
tibieza [ti'βjeθa] *nf* (*temperatura*) tepidness; (*fig*) coolness
tibio, -a ['tiβjo, a] *adj* lukewarm, tepid
tiburón [tiβu'ron] *nm* shark
tic [tik] *nm* (*ruido*) click; (*de reloj*) tick; **~ nervioso** (*Med*) nervous tic
tictac [tik'tak] *nm* (*de reloj*) tick tock
tiempo ['tjempo] *nm* (*gen*) time; (*época, período*) age, period; (*Meteorología*) weather; (*Ling*) tense; (*edad*) age; (*de juego*) half; **a ~** in time; **a un** *o* **al mismo ~** at the same time; **al poco ~** very soon (after); **andando el ~** in due course; **cada cierto ~** every so often; **con ~** in time; **con el ~** eventually; **se quedó poco ~** he didn't stay very long; **hace poco ~** not long ago; **mucho ~** a long time; **de ~ en ~** from time to time; **en mis ~s** in my time; **en los buenos ~s** in the good old days; **hace buen/mal ~** the weather is fine/bad; **estar a ~** to be in time; **hace ~** some time ago; **hacer ~** to while away the time; **¿qué ~ tiene?** how old is he?; **motor de 2 ~s** two-stroke engine; **~ compartido** (*Inform*) time sharing; **~ de ejecución** (*Inform*) run time; **~ inactivo** (*Com*) downtime; **~ libre** spare time; **~ de paro** (*Com*) idle time; **a ~ partido** (*trabajar*) part-time; **~ preferencial** (*Com*) prime time; **en ~ real** (*Inform*) real time; **primer ~** first half
tienda ['tjenda] *vb ver* **tender** ▷ *nf* shop; (*más grande*) store; (*Naut*) awning; **~ de campaña** tent; **~ de comestibles** grocer's (shop) (*Brit*), grocery (store) (*US*)
tiene *etc* ['tjene] *vb ver* **tener**
tienta ['tjenta] *vb ver* **tentar** ▷ *nf* (*Med*) probe; (*fig*) tact; **andar a ~s** to grope one's way along
tiento *etc* ['tjento] *vb ver* **tentar** ▷ *nm* (*tacto*) touch; (*precaución*) wariness; (*pulso*) steady hand; (*Zool*) feeler, tentacle
tierno, -a ['tjerno, a] *adj* (*blando, dulce*) tender; (*fresco*) fresh
tierra ['tjerra] *nf* earth; (*suelo*) soil; (*mundo*) world; (*país*) country, land; (*Elec*) earth, ground (*US*); **~ adentro** inland; **~ natal** native land; **echar ~ a un asunto** to hush an affair up; **no es de estas ~s** he's not from these parts; **la T~ Santa** the Holy Land
tieso, -a ['tjeso, a] *adj* (*rígido*) rigid; (*duro*) stiff; (*fig: testarudo*) stubborn; (*fam: orgulloso*) conceited ▷ *adv* strongly
tiesto ['tjesto] *nm* flowerpot; (*pedazo*) piece of pottery
tifoidea [tifoi'ðea] *nf* typhoid
tifón [ti'fon] *nm* (*huracán*) typhoon; (*de mar*) tidal wave
tifus ['tifus] *nm* typhus; **~ icteroides** yellow fever
tigre ['tiɣre] *nm* tiger; (*Am*) jaguar
tijera [ti'xera] *nf* (*una tijera*) (pair of) scissors *pl*; (*Zool*) claw; (*persona*) gossip; **de ~** folding; **tijeras** *nfpl* scissors; (*para plantas*) shears; **unas ~s** a pair of scissors
tijeretear [tixerete'ar] *vt* to snip ▷ *vi* (*fig*) to meddle
tila ['tila] *nf* (*Bot*) lime tree; (*Culin*) lime flower tea

tildar [til'dar] *vt*: ~ **de** to brand as
tilde ['tilde] *nf* (*defecto*) defect; (*trivialidad*) triviality; (*Tip*) tilde
tilín [ti'lin] *nm* tinkle
tilo ['tilo] *nm* lime tree
timar [ti'mar] *vt* (*robar*) to steal; (*estafar*) to swindle; (*persona*) to con; **timarse** *vr* (*fam*): **~se con algn** to make eyes at sb
timbal [tim'bal] *nm* small drum
timbrar [tim'brar] *vt* to stamp; (*sellar*) to seal; (*carta*) to postmark
timbre ['timbre] *nm* (*sello*) stamp; (*campanilla*) bell; (*tono*) timbre; (*Com*) stamp duty
timidez [timi'ðeθ] *nf* shyness
tímido, -a ['timiðo, a] *adj* shy, timid
timo ['timo] *nm* swindle; **dar un ~ a algn** to swindle sb
timón [ti'mon] *nm* helm, rudder; (*Am*) steering wheel; **coger el ~** (*fig*) to take charge
timonel [timo'nel] *nm* helmsman
tímpano ['timpano] *nm* (*Anat*) eardrum; (*Mus*) small drum
tina ['tina] *nf* tub; (*Am*: *baño*) bath(tub)
tinaja [ti'naxa] *nf* large earthen jar
tinglado [tin'glaðo] *nm* (*cobertizo*) shed; (*fig*: *truco*) trick; (*intriga*) intrigue; **armar un ~** to lay a plot
tinieblas [ti'njeβlas] *nfpl* darkness *sg*; (*sombras*) shadows; **estamos en ~ sobre sus proyectos** (*fig*) we are in the dark about his plans
tino ['tino] *nm* (*habilidad*) skill; (*Mil*) marksmanship; (*juicio*) insight; (*moderación*) moderation; **sin ~** immoderately; **coger el ~** to get the feel *o* hang of it
tinta ['tinta] *nf* ink; (*Tec*) dye; (*Arte*) colour; **~ china** Indian ink; **tintas** *nfpl* (*fig*) shades; **medias ~s** (*fig*) half measures; **saber algo de buena ~** to have sth on good authority
tinte ['tinte] *nm* dye; (*acto*) dyeing; (*fig*) tinge; (*barniz*) veneer
tintero [tin'tero] *nm* inkwell; **se le quedó en el ~** he clean forgot about it
tintinear [tintine'ar] *vt* to tinkle
tinto, -a ['tinto, a] *nm* red wine
tintorería [tintore'ria] *nf* dry cleaner's
tintura [tin'tura] *nf* (*acto*) dyeing; (*Química*) dye; (*farmacéutico*) tincture
tío ['tio] *nm* (*pariente*) uncle; (*fam*: *hombre*) bloke, guy (US)
tiovivo [tio'βiβo] *nm* merry-go-round
típico, -a ['tipiko, a] *adj* typical; (*pintoresco*) picturesque
tiple ['tiple] *nm* soprano (voice) ▷ *nf* soprano
tipo ['tipo] *nm* (*clase*) type, kind; (*norma*) norm; (*patrón*) pattern; (*fam*: *hombre*) fellow, bloke, guy (US); (*Anat*) build; (: *de mujer*) figure; (*Imprenta*) type; **~ bancario/de descuento** bank/discount rate; **~ de interés** interest rate; **~ de interés vigente** (*Com*) standard rate; **~ de cambio** exchange rate; **~ base** (*Com*) base rate; **~ a término** (*Com*) forward rate; **dos ~s sospechosos** two suspicious characters; **~ de letra** (*Inform, Tip*) typeface; **~ de datos** (*Inform*) data type
tipografía [tipoɣra'fia] *nf* (*tipo*) printing; (*lugar*) printing press
tipográfico, -a [tipo'ɣrafiko, a] *adj* printing
tipógrafo, -a [ti'poɣrafo, a] *nm/f* printer
tíquet ['tiket] (*pl* **tíquets**) *nm* ticket; (*en tienda*) cash slip
tiquismiquis [tikis'mikis] *nm* fussy person ▷ *nmpl* (*querellas*) squabbling *sg*; (*escrúpulos*) silly scruples
tira ['tira] *nf* strip; (*fig*) abundance ▷ *nm*: **~ y afloja** give and take; (*cautela*) caution; **la ~ de ...** (*fam*) lots of ...
tirabuzón [tiraβu'θon] *nm* corkscrew; (*rizo*) curl
tirachinas [tira'tʃinas] *nm inv* catapult
tiradero [tira'ðero] *nm* (*Am*) rubbish dump
tirado, -a [ti'raðo, a] *adj* (*barato*) dirt-cheap; (*fam*: *fácil*) very easy ▷ *nf* (*acto*) cast, throw; (*distancia*) distance; (*serie*) series; (*Tip*) printing, edition; **de una tirada** at one go; **está ~** (*fam*) it's a cinch
tirador, a [tira'ðor, a] *nm/f* (*persona*) shooter ▷ *nm* (*mango*) handle; (*Elec*) flex; **~ certero** sniper
tiralíneas [tira'lineas] *nm inv* ruling-pen
tiranía [tira'nia] *nf* tyranny
tiránico, -a [ti'raniko, a] *adj* tyrannical
tiranizar [tirani'θar] *vt* (*pueblo, empleado*) to tyrannize
tirano, -a [ti'rano, a] *adj* tyrannical ▷ *nm/f* tyrant
tirante [ti'rante] *adj* (*cuerda*) tight, taut; (*relaciones*) strained ▷ *nm* (*Arq*) brace; (*Tec*) stay; (*correa*) shoulder strap; **tirantes** *nmpl* braces, suspenders (US)
tirantez [tiran'teθ] *nf* tightness; (*fig*) tension
tirar [ti'rar] *vt* to throw; (*volcar*) to upset; (*derribar*) to knock down *o* over; (*tiro*) to fire; (*cohete*) to launch; (*bomba*) to drop; (*edificio*) to pull down; (*desechar*) to throw out *o* away; (*disipar*) to squander; (*imprimir*) to print; (*dar*: *golpe*) to deal ▷ *vi* (*disparar*) to shoot; (*dar un tirón*) to pull; (*fig*) to draw; (*interesar*) to appeal; (*fam*: *andar*) to go; (*tender a*) to tend to; (*Deporte*) to shoot; **tirarse** *vr* to throw o.s.; (*fig*) to demean o.s.; (*fam!*) to screw (!); **~ abajo** to bring down, destroy; **tira más a su padre** he takes more after his father; **~ de algo** to pull *o* tug (on) sth; **ir tirando** to manage; **~ a la derecha** to turn *o* go right; **a todo ~** at the most
tirita [ti'rita] *nf* (sticking) plaster, Band-Aid® (US)
tiritar [tiri'tar] *vi* to shiver
tiro ['tiro] *nm* (*lanzamiento*) throw; (*disparo*) shot; (*tiroteo*) shooting; (*Deporte*) shot; (*Tenis, Golf*) drive; (*alcance*) range; (*de escalera*) flight (of stairs); (*golpe*) blow; (*engaño*) hoax; **~ al blanco** target practice; **caballo de ~** cart-

horse; **andar de ~s largos** to be all dressed up; **al ~** (*Am*) at once; **de a ~** (*Am*: *fam*) completely; **se pegó un ~** he shot himself; **le salió el ~ por la culata** it backfired on him
tiroides [ti'roiðes] *nm inv* thyroid
tirón [ti'ron] *nm* (*sacudida*) pull, tug; **de un ~** in one go; **dar un ~ a** to pull at, tug at
tiroteo [tiro'teo] *nm* exchange of shots, shooting; (*escaramuza*) skirmish
tísico, -a ['tisiko, a] *adj, nm/f* consumptive
tisis ['tisis] *nf* consumption, tuberculosis
titánico, -a [ti'taniko, a] *adj* titanic
títere ['titere] *nm* puppet; **no dejar ~ con cabeza** to turn everything upside-down
titilar [titi'lar] *vi* (*luz, estrella*) to twinkle; (*párpado*) to flutter
titiritero, -a [titiri'tero, a] *nm/f* (*acróbata*) acrobat; (*malabarista*) juggler
titubeante [tituβe'ante] *adj* (*inestable*) shaky, tottering; (*farfullante*) stammering; (*dudoso*) hesitant
titubear [tituβe'ar] *vi* to stagger; (*tartamudear*) to stammer; (*vacilar*) to hesitate
titubeo [titu'βeo] *nm* staggering; stammering; hesitation
titulado, -a [titu'laðo, a] *adj* (*libro*) entitled; (*persona*) titled
titular [titu'lar] *adj* titular ▷ *nm/f* (*de oficina*) occupant; (*de pasaporte*) holder ▷ *nm* headline ▷ *vt* to title; **titularse** *vr* to be entitled
título ['titulo] *nm* (*gen*) title; (*de diario*) headline; (*certificado*) professional qualification; (*universitario*) university degree; (*Com*) bond; (*fig*) right; **títulos** *nmpl* qualifications; **a ~ de** by way of; (*en calidad de*) in the capacity of; **a ~ de curiosidad** as a matter of interest; **~ de propiedad** title deed; **~s convertibles de interés fijo** (*Com*) convertible loan stock *sg*
tiza ['tiθa] *nf* chalk; **una ~** a piece of chalk
tiznar [tiθ'nar] *vt* to blacken; (*manchar*) to smudge, stain; (*fig*) to tarnish
tizón [ti'θon], **tizo** ['tiθo] *nm* brand; (*fig*) stain
TLC *nm abr* (= *Tratado de Libre Comercio*) NAFTA
toalla [to'aʎa] *nf* towel
tobillo [to'βiʎo] *nm* ankle
tobogán [toβo'ɣan] *nm* toboggan; (*montaña rusa*) roller-coaster; (*resbaladilla*) chute, slide
toca ['toka] *nf* headdress
tocadiscos [toka'ðiskos] *nm inv* record player
tocado, -a [to'kaðo, a] *adj* (*fruta etc*) rotten; (*fam*) touched ▷ *nm* headdress; **estar ~ de la cabeza** (*fam*) to be weak in the head
tocador [toka'ðor] *nm* (*mueble*) dressing table; (*cuarto*) boudoir; (*neceser*) toilet case; (*fam*) ladies' room
tocante [to'kante]: **~ a** *prep* with regard to; **en lo ~ a** as for, so far as concerns
tocar [to'kar] *vt* to touch; (*sentir*) to feel; (*con la mano*) to handle; (*Mus*) to play; (*campana*) to ring; (*tambor*) to beat; (*trompeta*) to blow; (*topar con*) to run into, strike; (*referirse a*) to allude to; (*estar emparentado con*) to be related to ▷ *vi* (*a la puerta*) to knock (on *o* at the door); (*ser el turno*) to fall to, be the turn of; (*ser hora*) to be due; (*atañer*) to concern; **tocarse** *vr* (*cubrirse la cabeza*) to cover one's head; (*tener contacto*) to touch (each other); **~le a algn** to fall to sb's lot; **~ en** (*Naut*) to call at; **por lo que a mí me toca** as far as I am concerned; **te toca a ti** it's your turn; **esto toca en la locura** this verges on madness
tocateja [toka'texa] (*fam*): **a ~** *adv* in readies
tocayo, -a [to'kajo, a] *nm/f* namesake
tocino [to'θino] *nm* (bacon) fat; **~ de panceta** bacon
todavía [toða'βia] *adv* (*aun*) even; (*aún*) still, yet; **~ más** yet *o* still more; **~ no** not yet; **~ en 1970** as late as 1970; **está lloviendo ~** it's still raining

PALABRA CLAVE

todo, -a ['toðo, a] *adj* **1** (*sg*) all; **toda la carne** all the meat; **toda la noche** all night, the whole night; **todo el libro** the whole book; **toda una botella** a whole bottle; **todo lo contrario** quite the opposite; **está toda sucia** she's all dirty; **a toda velocidad** at full speed; **por todo el país** throughout the whole country; **es todo un hombre** he's every inch a man; **soy todo oídos** I'm all ears
2 (*pl*) all; every; **todos los libros** all the books; **todas las noches** every night; **todos los que quieran salir** all those who want to leave; **todos vosotros** all of you
▷ *pron* **1** everything, all; **todos** everyone, everybody; **lo sabemos todo** we know everything; **todos querían más tiempo** everybody *o* everyone wanted more time; **nos marchamos todos** all of us left; **corriendo y todo, no llegaron a tiempo** even though they ran, they still didn't arrive in time
2 (*con preposición*): **a pesar de todo** even so, in spite of everything; **con todo él me sigue gustando** even so I still like him; **le llamaron de todo** they called him all the names under the sun; **no me agrada del todo** I don't entirely like it
▷ *adv* all; **vaya todo seguido** keep straight on *o* ahead
▷ *nm*: **como un todo** as a whole; **arriba del todo** at the very top; **todo a cien** ≈ pound store (*Brit*), ≈ dollar store (*US*)

todocamino [toðoka'mino] *nm* four-wheel drive, SUV (*esp US*)
todopoderoso, -a [toðopoðe'roso, a] *adj* all powerful; (*Rel*) almighty
todoterreno [toðote'rreno] *nm* (*tb*: **vehículo ~**) four-wheel drive, SUV (*esp US*)
toga ['toɣa] *nf* toga; (*Escol*) gown

Tokio ['tokjo] *n* Tokyo
toldo ['toldo] *nm* (*para el sol*) sunshade; (*en tienda*) marquee; (*fig*) pride
tole ['tole] *nm* (*fam*) commotion
tolerancia [tole'ranθja] *nf* tolerance
tolerante [tole'rante] *adj* tolerant; (*sociedad*) liberal; (*fig*) open-minded
tolerar [tole'rar] *vt* to tolerate; (*resistir*) to endure
toma ['toma] *nf* (*gen*) taking; (*Med*) dose; (*Elec*: *tb*: **~ de corriente**) socket; (*Mec*) inlet; **~ de posesión** (*por presidente*) taking up office; **~ de tierra** (*Aviat*) landing
tomacorriente [tomako'rrjente] *nm* (*Am*) socket
tomar [to'mar] *vt* (*gen, Cine, Foto, TV*) to take; (*actitud*) to adopt; (*aspecto*) to take on; (*notas*) to take down; (*beber*) to drink ▷ *vi* to take; (*Am*) to drink; **tomarse** *vr* to take; **~se por** to consider o.s. to be; **¡toma!** here you are!; **~ asiento** to sit down; **~ a algn por loco** to think sb mad; **~ a bien/a mal** to take well/ badly; **~ en serio** to take seriously; **~ el pelo a algn** to pull sb's leg; **~la con algn** to pick a quarrel with sb; **~ el sol** to sunbathe; **~ por escrito** to write down; **toma y daca** give and take
tomate [to'mate] *nm* tomato
tomatera [toma'tera] *nf* tomato plant
tomavistas [toma'βistas] *nm inv* movie camera
tomillo [to'miʎo] *nm* thyme
tomo ['tomo] *nm* (*libro*) volume; (*fig*) importance
ton [ton] *abr* = **tonelada** ▷ *nm*: **sin ~ ni son** without rhyme or reason
tonada [to'naða] *nf* tune
tonalidad [tonali'ðað] *nf* tone
tonel [to'nel] *nm* barrel
tonelada [tone'laða] *nf* ton; **~(s) métrica(s)** metric ton(s)
tonelaje [tone'laxe] *nm* tonnage
tonelero [tone'lero] *nm* cooper
tongo ['tongo] *nm* (*Deporte*) fix
tónico, -a ['toniko, a] *adj* tonic ▷ *nm* (*Med*) tonic ▷ *nf* (*Mus*) tonic; (*fig*) keynote
tonificar [tonifi'kar] *vt* to tone up
tono ['tono] *nm* (*Mus*) tone; (*altura*) pitch; (*color*) shade; **fuera de ~** inappropriate; **~ de llamada** ringtone; **~ de marcar** (*Telec*) dialling tone; **darse ~** to put on airs
tontería [tonte'ria] *nf* (*estupidez*) foolishness; (*una tontería*) silly thing; **tonterías** *nfpl* rubbish *sg*, nonsense *sg*
tonto, -a ['tonto, a] *adj* stupid; (*ridículo*) silly ▷ *nm/f* fool; (*payaso*) clown; **a tontas y a locas** anyhow; **hacer(se) el ~** to act the fool
topacio [to'paθjo] *nm* topaz
topar [to'par] *vt* (*tropezar*) to bump into; (*encontrar*) to find, come across; (*cabra etc*) to butt ▷ *vi*: **~ contra** *o* **en** to run into; **~ con** to run up against; **el problema topa en eso** that's where the problem lies
tope ['tope] *adj* maximum ▷ *nm* (*fin*) end; (*límite*) limit; (*Ferro*) buffer; (*Auto*) bumper; **al ~** end to end; **fecha ~** closing date; **precio ~** top price; **sueldo ~** maximum salary; **~ de tabulación** tab stop
tópico, -a ['topiko, a] *adj* topical; (*Med*) local ▷ *nm* platitude, cliché; **de uso ~** for external application
topo ['topo] *nm* (*Zool*) mole; (*fig*) blunderer
topografía [topoɣra'fia] *nf* topography
topógrafo, -a [to'poɣrafo, a] *nm/f* topographer; (*agrimensor*) surveyor
toque *etc* ['toke] *vb ver* **tocar** ▷ *nm* touch; (*Mus*) beat; (*de campana*) chime, ring; (*Mil*) bugle call; (*fig*) crux; **dar un ~ a** to test; **dar el último ~ a** to put the final touch to; **~ de queda** curfew
toqué *etc vb ver* **tocar**
toquetear [tokete'ar] *vt* to finger; (*fam!*) to touch up
toquilla [to'kiʎa] *nf* (*pañuelo*) headscarf; (*chal*) shawl
tórax ['toraks] *nm inv* thorax
torbellino [torbe'ʎino] *nm* whirlwind; (*fig*) whirl
torcedura [torθe'ðura] *nf* twist; (*Med*) sprain
torcer [tor'θer] *vt* to twist; (*la esquina*) to turn; (*Med*) to sprain; (*cuerda*) to plait; (*ropa, manos*) to wring; (*persona*) to corrupt; (*sentido*) to distort ▷ *vi* (*cambiar de dirección*) to turn; (*desviar*) to turn off; **torcerse** *vr* to twist; (*doblar*) to bend; (*desviarse*) to go astray; (*fracasar*) to go wrong; **~ el gesto** to scowl; **~se un pie** to twist one's foot; **el coche torció a la derecha** the car turned right
torcido, -a [tor'θiðo, a] *adj* twisted; (*fig*) crooked ▷ *nm* curl
tordo, -a ['torðo, a] *adj* dappled ▷ *nm* thrush
torear [tore'ar] *vt* (*fig: evadir*) to dodge; (*jugar con*) to tease; (*toro*) to fight ▷ *vi* to fight bulls
toreo [to'reo] *nm* bullfighting
torero, -a [to'rero, a] *nm/f* bullfighter
tormenta [tor'menta] *nf* storm; (*fig: confusión*) turmoil
tormento [tor'mento] *nm* torture; (*fig*) anguish
tornar [tor'nar] *vt* (*devolver*) to return, give back; (*transformar*) to transform ▷ *vi* to go back; **tornarse** *vr* (*ponerse*) to become; (*volver*) to return
tornasolado, -a [tornaso'laðo, a] *adj* (*brillante*) iridescent; (*reluciente*) shimmering
torneo [tor'neo] *nm* tournament
tornillo [tor'niʎo] *nm* screw; **apretar los ~s a algn** to apply pressure on sb; **le falta un ~** (*fam*) he's got a screw loose
torniquete [torni'kete] *nm* (*puerta*) turnstile; (*Med*) tourniquet
torno ['torno] *nm* (*Tec: grúa*) winch; (*: de carpintero*) lathe; (*tambor*) drum; **~ de banco** vice, vise (*US*); **en ~ (a)** round, about

toro ['toro] *nm* bull; (*fam*) he-man; **los ~s** bullfighting *sg*
toronja [to'ronxa] *nf* grapefruit
torpe ['torpe] *adj* (*poco hábil*) clumsy, awkward; (*movimiento*) sluggish; (*necio*) dim; (*lento*) slow; (*indecente*) crude; (*no honrado*) dishonest
torpedo [tor'peðo] *nm* torpedo
torpeza [tor'peθa] *nf* (*falta de agilidad*) clumsiness; (*lentitud*) slowness; (*rigidez*) stiffness; (*error*) mistake; (*crudeza*) obscenity
torre ['torre] *nf* tower; (*de petróleo*) derrick; (*de electricidad*) pylon; (*Ajedrez*) rook; (*Aviat, Mil, Naut*) turret
torrefacto, -a [torre'fakto, a] *adj* roasted; **café ~** high roast coffee
torrente [to'rrente] *nm* torrent
tórrido, -a ['torriðo, a] *adj* torrid
torrija [to'rrixa] *nf* fried bread; **~s** French toast *sg*
torsión [tor'sjon] *nf* twisting
torso ['torso] *nm* torso
torta ['torta] *nf* cake; (*fam*) slap; **~ de huevos** (*Am*) omelette; **no entendió ni ~** he didn't understand a word of it
tortazo [tor'taθo] *nm* (*bofetada*) slap; (*de coche*) crash
tortícolis [tor'tikolis] *nm inv* stiff neck
tortilla [tor'tiʎa] *nf* omelette; (*Am*) maize pancake; **~ francesa/española** plain/potato omelette; **cambiar** *o* **volver la ~ a algn** to turn the tables on sb
tórtola ['tortola] *nf* turtledove
tortuga [tor'tuɣa] *nf* tortoise; **~ marina** turtle
tortuoso, -a [tor'twoso, a] *adj* winding
tortura [tor'tura] *nf* torture
torturar [tortu'rar] *vt* to torture
tos [tos] *nf inv* cough; **~ ferina** whooping cough
tosco, -a ['tosko, a] *adj* coarse
toser [to'ser] *vi* to cough; **no hay quien le tosa** he's in a class by himself
tostado, -a [tos'taðo, a] *adj* toasted; (*por el sol*) dark brown; (*piel*) tanned ▷ *nf* tan; (*pan*) piece of toast; **tostadas** *nfpl* toast *sg*
tostador [tosta'ðor] *nm*, **tostadora** [tosta'ðora] (*Am*) *nf* toaster
tostar [tos'tar] *vt* to toast; (*café*) to roast; (*al sol*) to tan; **tostarse** *vr* to get brown
tostón [tos'ton] *nm*: **ser un ~** to be a drag
total [to'tal] *adj* total ▷ *adv* in short; (*al fin y al cabo*) when all is said and done ▷ *nm* total; **en ~** in all; **~ que** to cut a long story short; **~ de comprobación** (*Inform*) hash total; **~ debe/haber** (*Com*) debit/assets total
totalidad [totali'ðað] *nf* whole
totalitario, -a [totali'tarjo, a] *adj* totalitarian
totalmente [to'talmente] *adv* totally
tóxico, -a ['toksiko, a] *adj* toxic ▷ *nm* poison
toxicómano, -a [toksi'komano, a] *adj* addicted to drugs ▷ *nm/f* drug addict
toxina [to'ksina] *nf* toxin
tozudo, -a [to'θuðo, a] *adj* obstinate
traba ['traβa] *nf* bond, tie; (*cadena*) fetter; **poner ~s a** to restrain
trabajador, a [traβaxa'ðor, a] *nm/f* worker ▷ *adj* hard-working; **~ autónomo** *o* **por cuenta propia** self-employed person
trabajar [traβa'xar] *vt* to work; (*arar*) to till; (*empeñarse en*) to work at; (*empujar: persona*) to push; (*convencer*) to persuade ▷ *vi* to work; (*esforzarse*) to strive; **¡a ~!** let's get to work!; **~ por hacer algo** to strive to do sth
trabajo [tra'βaxo] *nm* work; (*tarea*) task; (*Pol*) labour; (*fig*) effort; **tomarse el ~ de** to take the trouble to; **~ por turno/a destajo** shift work/piecework; **~ en equipo** teamwork; **~ en proceso** (*Com*) work-in-progress; **~s forzados** hard labour *sg*
trabajoso, -a [traβa'xoso, a] *adj* hard; (*Med*) pale
trabalenguas [traβa'lengwas] *nm inv* tongue twister
trabar [tra'βar] *vt* (*juntar*) to join, unite; (*atar*) to tie down, fetter; (*agarrar*) to seize; (*amistad*) to strike up; **trabarse** *vr* to become entangled; (*reñir*) to squabble; **se le traba la lengua** he gets tongue-tied
tracción [trak'θjon] *nf* traction; **~ delantera/trasera** front-wheel/rear-wheel drive
tractor [trak'tor] *nm* tractor
tradición [traði'θjon] *nf* tradition
tradicional [traðiθjo'nal] *adj* traditional
traducción [traðuk'θjon] *nf* translation; **~ asistida por ordenador** computer-assisted translation
traducir [traðu'θir] *vt* to translate; **traducirse** *vr*: **~se en** (*fig*) to entail, result in
traductor, a [traðuk'tor, a] *nm/f* translator
traer [tra'er] *vt* to bring; (*llevar*) to carry; (*ropa*) to wear; (*incluir*) to carry; (*fig*) to cause; **traerse** *vr*: **~se algo** to be up to sth; **~se bien/mal** to dress well/badly; **traérselas** to be annoying; **~ consigo** to involve, entail; **es un problema que se las trae** it's a difficult problem
traficar [trafi'kar] *vi* to trade; **~ con** (*pey*) to deal illegally in
tráfico ['trafiko] *nm* (*Com*) trade; (*Auto*) traffic
tragaluz [traɣa'luθ] *nm* skylight
tragamonedas [traɣamo'neðas] *nm inv*, **tragaperras** [traɣa'perras] *nm inv* slot machine
tragar [tra'ɣar] *vt* to swallow; (*devorar*) to devour, bolt down; **tragarse** *vr* to swallow; (*tierra*) to absorb, soak up; **no le puedo ~** (*persona*) I can't stand him
tragedia [tra'xeðja] *nf* tragedy
trágico, -a ['traxiko, a] *adj* tragic
trago ['traɣo] *nm* (*de líquido*) drink; (*comido de golpe*) gulp; (*fam: de bebida*) swig; (*desgracia*)

blow; **echar un ~** to have a drink; **~ amargo** (*fig*) hard time

traición [trai'θjon] *nf* treachery; (*Jur*) treason; (*una traición*) act of treachery

traicionar [traiθjo'nar] *vt* to betray

traicionero, -a [traiθjo'nero, a] = **traidor, a**

traidor, a [trai'ðor, a] *adj* treacherous ▷ *nm/f* traitor

traigo *etc* ['traiɣo] *vb ver* **traer**

trailer (*pl* **trailers**) ['trailer, 'trailer(s)] *nm* trailer

traje ['traxe] *vb ver* **traer** ▷ *nm* (*gen*) dress; (*de hombre*) suit; (*traje típico*) costume; (*fig*) garb; **~ de baño** swimsuit; **~ de luces** bullfighter's costume; **~ hecho a la medida** made-to-measure suit

trajera *etc* [tra'xera] *vb ver* **traer**

trajín [tra'xin] *nm* haulage; (*fam: movimiento*) bustle; **trajines** *nmpl* goings-on

trajinar [traxi'nar] *vt* (*llevar*) to carry, transport ▷ *vi* (*moverse*) to bustle about; (*viajar*) to travel around

trama ['trama] *nf* (*fig*) link; (*: intriga*) plot; (*de tejido*) weft

tramar [tra'mar] *vt* to plot; (*Tec*) to weave; **tramarse** *vr* (*fig*): **algo se está tramando** there's something going on

tramitar [trami'tar] *vt* (*asunto*) to transact; (*negociar*) to negotiate; (*manejar*) to handle

trámite ['tramite] *nm* (*paso*) step; (*Jur*) transaction; **trámites** *nmpl* (*burocracia*) paperwork *sg*, procedures; (*Jur*) proceedings

tramo ['tramo] *nm* (*de tierra*) plot; (*de escalera*) flight; (*de vía*) section

tramoya [tra'moja] *nf* (*Teat*) piece of stage machinery; (*fig*) trick

tramoyista [tramo'jista] *nm/f* scene shifter; (*fig*) trickster

trampa ['trampa] *nf* trap; (*en el suelo*) trapdoor; (*prestidigitación*) conjuring trick; (*engaño*) trick; (*fam*) fiddle; **caer en la ~** to fall into the trap; **hacer ~s** (*trampear*) to cheat

trampear [trampe'ar] *vt, vi* to cheat

trampolín [trampo'lin] *nm* trampoline; (*de piscina etc*) diving board

tramposo, -a [tram'poso, a] *adj* crooked, cheating ▷ *nm/f* crook, cheat

tranca ['tranka] *nf* (*palo*) stick; (*viga*) beam; (*de puerta, ventana*) bar; (*borrachera*) binge; **a ~s y barrancas** with great difficulty

trancar [tran'kar] *vt* to bar ▷ *vi* to stride along

trance ['tranθe] *nm* (*momento difícil*) difficult moment; (*situación crítica*) critical situation; (*estado de hipnosis*) trance; **estar en ~ de muerte** to be at death's door

tranco ['tranko] *nm* stride

tranquilamente [tran'kilamente] *adv* (*sin preocupaciones: leer, trabajar*) peacefully; (*sin enfadarse: hablar, discutir*) calmly

tranquilidad [trankili'ðað] *nf* (*calma*) calmness, stillness; (*paz*) peacefulness

tranquilizante [trankili'θante] *nm* tranquillizer

tranquilizar [trankili'θar] *vt* (*calmar*) to calm (down); (*asegurar*) to reassure; **tranquilizarse** *vr* to calm down

tranquilo, -a [tran'kilo, a] *adj* (*calmado*) calm; (*apacible*) peaceful; (*mar*) calm; (*mente*) untroubled

transacción [transak'θjon] *nf* transaction

transatlántico, -a [transat'lantiko, a] *adj* transatlantic ▷ *nm* (ocean) liner

transbordador [transβorða'ðor] *nm* ferry

transbordar [transβor'ðar] *vt* to transfer; **transbordarse** *vr* to change

transbordo [trans'βorðo] *nm* transfer; **hacer ~** to change (trains)

transcender [transθen'der] *vt* = **trascender**

transcribir [transkri'βir] *vt* to transcribe

transcurrir [transku'rrir] *vi* (*tiempo*) to pass; (*hecho*) to turn out

transcurso [trans'kurso] *nm* passing, lapse; **~ del tiempo** lapse (of time); **en el ~ de ocho días** in the course of a week

transeúnte [transe'unte] *adj* transient ▷ *nm/f* passer-by

transexual [transe'kswal] *adj, nm/f* transsexual

transferencia [transfe'renθja] *nf* transference; (*Com*) transfer; **~ bancaria** banker's order; **~ de crédito** (*Com*) credit transfer; **~ electrónica de fondos** (*Com*) electronic funds transfer

transferir [transfe'rir] *vt* to transfer; (*aplazar*) to postpone

transformación [transforma'θjon] *nf* transformation

transformador [transforma'ðor] *nm* transformer

transformar [transfor'mar] *vt* to transform; (*convertir*) to convert

tránsfuga ['transfuɣa] *nm/f* (*Mil*) deserter; (*Pol*) turncoat

transfusión [transfu'sjon] *nf* (*tb*: **~ de sangre**) (blood) transfusion

transgénico, -a [trans'xeniko, a] *adj* genetically modified

transgredir [transɣre'dir] *vt* to transgress

transición [transi'θjon] *nf* transition; **período de ~** transitional period

transido, -a [tran'siðo, a] *adj* overcome; **~ de angustia** beset with anxiety; **~ de dolor** racked with pain

transigir [transi'xir] *vi* to compromise; (*ceder*) to make concessions

transistor [transis'tor] *nm* transistor

transitar [transi'tar] *vi* to go (from place to place)

transitivo, -a [transi'tiβo, a] *adj* transitive

tránsito ['transito] *nm* transit; (*Auto*) traffic; (*parada*) stop; **horas de máximo ~** rush hours; **"se prohíbe el ~"** "no thoroughfare"

transitorio, -a [transi'torjo, a] *adj* transitory

transmisión [transmi'sjon] *nf* (*Radio, TV*) transmission, broadcast(ing); (*transferencia*) transfer; **~ en circuito** hookup; **~ en directo/exterior** live/outside broadcast; **~ de datos (en paralelo/en serie)** (*Inform*) (parallel/serial) data transfer *o* transmission; **plena/media ~ bidireccional** (*Inform*) full/half duplex

transmitir [transmi'tir] *vt* to transmit; (*Radio, TV*) to broadcast; (*enfermedad*) to give, pass on

transparencia [transpa'renθja] *nf* transparency; (*claridad*) clearness, clarity; (*foto*) slide

transparentar [transparen'tar] *vt* to reveal ▷ *vi* to be transparent

transparente [transpa'rente] *adj* transparent; (*aire*) clear; (*ligero*) diaphanous ▷ *nm* curtain

transpirar [transpi'rar] *vi* to perspire; (*fig*) to transpire

transponer [transpo'ner] *vt* to transpose; (*cambiar de sitio*) to move about ▷ *vi* (*desaparecer*) to disappear; (*ir más allá*) to go beyond; **transponerse** *vr* to change places; (*ocultarse*) to hide; (*sol*) to go down

transportar [transpor'tar] *vt* to transport; (*llevar*) to carry

transporte [trans'porte] *nm* transport; (*Com*) haulage; **Ministerio de T~s** Ministry of Transport

transversal [transβer'sal] *adj* transverse, cross ▷ *nf* (*tb*: **calle ~**) cross street

tranvía [tram'bia] *nm* tram, streetcar (US)

trapeador [trapea'ðor] *nm* (*Am*) mop

trapear [trape'ar] *vt* (*Am*) to mop

trapecio [tra'peθjo] *nm* trapeze

trapecista [trape'θista] *nm/f* trapeze artist

trapero, -a [tra'pero, a] *nm/f* ragman

trapicheos [trapi'tʃeos] *nmpl* (*fam*) schemes, fiddles

trapo ['trapo] *nm* (*tela*) rag; (*de cocina*) cloth; **trapos** *nmpl* (*fam*: *de mujer*) clothes, dresses; **a todo ~** under full sail; **soltar el ~** (*llorar*) to burst into tears

tráquea ['trakea] *nf* trachea, windpipe

traqueteo [trake'teo] *nm* (*crujido*) crack; (*golpeteo*) rattling

tras [tras] *prep* (*detrás*) behind; (*después*) after; **~ de** besides; **día ~ día** day after day; **uno ~ otro** one after the other

trasatlántico [trasat'lantiko] *nm* (*barco*) (cabin) cruiser

trascendencia [trasθen'denθja] *nf* (*importancia*) importance; (*en filosofía*) transcendence

trascendental [trasθenden'tal] *adj* important; transcendental

trascender [trasθen'der] *vi* (*oler*) to smell; (*noticias*) to come out, leak out; (*sucesos, sentimientos*) to spread, have a wide effect; **~ a** (*afectar*) to reach, have an effect on; (*oler a*) to smack of; **en su novela todo trasciende a romanticismo** everything in his novel smacks of romanticism

trasegar [trase'ɣar] *vt* (*mover*) to move about; (*vino*) to decant

trasero, -a [tra'sero, a] *adj* back, rear ▷ *nm* (*Anat*) bottom; **traseros** *nmpl* ancestors

trasfondo [tras'fondo] *nm* background

trasgredir [trasɣre'ðir] *vt* to contravene

trashumante [trasu'mante] *adj* migrating

trasladar [trasla'ðar] *vt* to move; (*persona*) to transfer; (*postergar*) to postpone; (*copiar*) to copy; (*interpretar*) to interpret; **trasladarse** *vr* (*irse*) to go; (*mudarse*) to move; **~se a otro puesto** to move to a new job

traslado [tras'laðo] *nm* move; (*mudanza*) move, removal; (*de persona*) transfer; (*copia*) copy; **~ de bloque** (*Inform*) block move, cut-and-paste

traslucir [traslu'θir] *vt* to show; **traslucirse** *vr* to be translucent; (*fig*) to be revealed

trasluz [tras'luθ] *nm* reflected light; **al ~** against *o* up to the light

trasnochado, -a [trasno'tʃaðo, a] *adj* dated

trasnochador, a [trasnotʃa'ðor, a] *adj* given to staying up late ▷ *nm/f* (*fig*) night owl

trasnochar [trasno'tʃar] *vi* (*acostarse tarde*) to stay up late; (*no dormir*) to have a sleepless night; (*pasar la noche*) to stay the night

traspapelar [traspape'lar] *vt* (*documento, carta*) to mislay, misplace

traspasar [traspa'sar] *vt* (*bala*) to pierce, go through; (*propiedad*) to sell, transfer; (*calle*) to cross over; (*límites*) to go beyond; (*ley*) to break; **"traspaso negocio"** "business for sale"

traspaso [tras'paso] *nm* (*venta*) transfer, sale; (*fig*) anguish

traspié [tras'pje] (*pl* **traspiés**) *nm* (*caída*) stumble; (*tropezón*) trip; (*fig*) blunder

trasplantar [trasplan'tar] *vt* to transplant

trasplante [tras'plante] *nm* transplant

traspuesto, -a [tras'pwesto, a] *adj*: **quedarse ~** to doze off

trastada [tras'taða] *nf* (*fam*) prank

trastazo [tras'taθo] *nm* (*fam*) bump; **darse un ~** (*persona*) to bump o.s.; (*en coche*) to have a bump

traste ['traste] *nm* (*Mus*) fret; **dar al ~ con algo** to ruin sth; **ir al ~** to fall through

trastero [tras'tero] *nm* lumber room

trastienda [tras'tjenda] *nf* back room (*of shop*); **obtener algo por la ~** to get sth by underhand means

trasto ['trasto] *nm* (*mueble*) piece of furniture; (*tarro viejo*) old pot; (*pey*: *cosa*) piece of junk; (: *persona*) dead loss; **trastos** *nmpl* (*Teat*) scenery *sg*; **tirar los ~s a la cabeza** to have a blazing row

trastocar [trasto'kar] *vt* (*papeles*) to mix up

trastornado, -a [trastor'naðo, a] *adj* (*loco*) mad; (*agitado*) crazy

t

trastornar [trastor'nar] *vt* to overturn, upset; (*fig*: *ideas*) to confuse; (: *nervios*) to shatter; (: *persona*) to drive crazy; **trastornarse** *vr* (*plan*) to fall through; (*volverse loco*) to go mad *o* crazy
trastorno [tras'torno] *nm* (*acto*) overturning; (*confusión*) confusion; (*Pol*) disturbance, upheaval; (*Med*) upset; **~ estomacal** stomach upset; **~ mental** mental disorder, breakdown
trasvase [tras'βase] *nm* (*de río*) diversion
tratable [tra'taβle] *adj* friendly
tratado [tra'taðo] *nm* (*Pol*) treaty; (*Com*) agreement; (*Lit*) treatise
tratamiento [trata'mjento] *nm* treatment; (*Tec*) processing; (*de problema*) handling; **~ de datos** (*Inform*) data processing; **~ de gráficos** (*Inform*) graphics; **~ de márgenes** margin settings; **~ de textos** (*Inform*) word processing; **~ por lotes** (*Inform*) batch processing; **~ de tú** familiar address
tratar [tra'tar] *vt* (*ocuparse de*) to treat; (*manejar*, *Tec*) to handle; (*Inform*) to process; (*Med*) to treat; (*dirigirse a*: *persona*) to address ▷ *vi*: **~ de** (*hablar sobre*) to deal with, be about; (*intentar*) to try to; **tratarse** *vr* to treat each other; **~ con** (*Com*) to trade in; (*negociar con*) to negotiate with; (*tener tratos con*) to have dealings with; **se trata de la nueva piscina** it's about the new pool; **¿de qué se trata?** what's it about?
trato ['trato] *nm* dealings *pl*; (*relaciones*) relationship; (*comportamiento*) manner; (*Com*, *Jur*) agreement, contract; (*título*) (form of) address; **de ~ agradable** pleasant; **de fácil ~** easy to get on with; **~ equitativo** fair deal; **¡~ hecho!** it's a deal!; **malos ~s** ill-treatment *sg*
trauma ['trauma] *nm* trauma
través [tra'βes] *nm* (*contratiempo*) reverse; **al ~** across, crossways; **a ~ de** across; (*sobre*) over; (*por*) through; **de ~** across; (*de lado*) sideways
travesaño [traβe'saɲo] *nm* (*Arq*) crossbeam; (*Deporte*) crossbar
travesía [traβe'sia] *nf* (*calle*) cross-street; (*Naut*) crossing
travesti [tra'βesti] *nm/f* transvestite
travesura [traβe'sura] *nf* (*broma*) prank; (*ingenio*) wit
travieso, -a [tra'βjeso, a] *adj* (*niño*) naughty; (*adulto*) restless; (*ingenioso*) witty ▷ *nf* crossing; (*Arq*) crossbeam; (*Ferro*) sleeper
trayecto [tra'jekto] *nm* (*ruta*) road, way; (*viaje*) journey; (*tramo*) stretch; (*curso*) course; **final del ~** end of the line
trayectoria [trajek'torja] *nf* trajectory; (*desarrollo*) development; (*fig*) path; **la ~ actual del partido** the party's present line
traza ['traθa] *nf* (*Arq*) plan, design; (*aspecto*) looks *pl*; (*señal*) sign; (*engaño*) trick; (*habilidad*) skill; (*Inform*) trace
trazado, -a [tra'θaðo, a] *adj*: **bien ~** shapely, well-formed ▷ *nm* (*Arq*) plan, design; (*fig*) outline; (*de carretera etc*) line, route
trazar [tra'θar] *vt* (*Arq*) to plan; (*Arte*) to sketch; (*fig*) to trace; (*itinerario*: *hacer*) to plot; (*plan*) to draw up
trazo ['traθo] *nm* (*línea*) line; (*bosquejo*) sketch; **trazos** *nmpl* (*de cara*) lines, features
trébol ['treβol] *nm* (*Bot*) clover; **tréboles** *nmpl* (*Naipes*) clubs
trece ['treθe] *num* thirteen; **estar en sus ~** to stand firm
trecho ['tretʃo] *nm* (*distancia*) distance; (*de tiempo*) while; (*fam*) piece; **de ~ en ~** at intervals
tregua ['treɣwa] *nf* (*Mil*) truce; (*fig*) lull, respite; **sin ~** without respite
treinta ['treinta] *num* thirty
tremendo, -a [tre'mendo, a] *adj* (*terrible*) terrible; (*imponente*: *cosa*) imposing; (*fam*: *fabuloso*) tremendous; (*divertido*) entertaining
trémulo, -a ['tremulo, a] *adj* quivering; (*luz*) flickering
tren [tren] *nm* (*Ferro*) train; **~ de aterrizaje** undercarriage; **~ directo/expreso/(de) mercancías/de pasajeros/suplementario** through/fast/goods *o* freight/passenger/ relief train; **~ de cercanías** suburban train; **~ de vida** way of life
trenca ['trenka] *nf* duffel coat
trenza ['trenθa] *nf* (*de pelo*) plait
trenzar [tren'θar] *vt* (*el pelo*) to plait ▷ *vi* (*en baile*) to weave in and out; **trenzarse** *vr* (*Am*) to become involved
trepar [tre'par] *vt*, *vi* to climb; (*Tec*) to drill
trepidar [trepi'ðar] *vi* to shake, vibrate
tres [tres] *num* three; (*fecha*) third; **las ~** three o'clock
trescientos, -as [tres'θjentos, as] *num* three hundred
tresillo [tre'siʎo] *nm* three-piece suite; (*Mus*) triplet
treta ['treta] *nf* (*Com etc*) gimmick; (*fig*) trick
triangular [trjangu'lar] *adj* triangular
triángulo [tri'angulo] *nm* triangle
tribal [tri'βal] *adj* tribal
tribu ['triβu] *nf* tribe
tribuna [tri'βuna] *nf* (*plataforma*) platform; (*Deporte*) stand; (*fig*) public speaking; **~ de la prensa** press box; **~ del acusado** (*Jur*) dock; **~ del jurado** jury box
tribunal [triβu'nal] *nm* (*en juicio*) court; (*comisión*, *fig*) tribunal; (*Escol*: *examinadores*) board of examiners; **T~ Supremo** High Court, Supreme Court (US); **T~ de Justicia de las Comunidades Europeas** European Court of Justice; **~ popular** jury
tributar [triβu'tar] *vt* to pay; (*las gracias*) to give; (*cariño*) to show
tributo [tri'βuto] *nm* (*Com*) tax
triciclo [tri'θiklo] *nm* tricycle
tricotar [triko'tar] *vi* to knit

trifulca [tri'fulka] *nf* (*fam*) row, shindy
trigal [tri'ɣal] *nm* wheat field
trigo ['triɣo] *nm* wheat; **trigos** *nmpl* wheat field(s) (*pl*)
trigueño, -a [tri'ɣeɲo, a] *adj* (*pelo*) corn-coloured; (*piel*) olive-skinned
trillado, -a [tri'ʎaðo, a] *adj* threshed; (*fig*) trite, hackneyed
trilladora [triʎa'ðora] *nf* threshing machine
trillar [tri'ʎar] *vt* (*Agr*) to thresh; (*fig*) to frequent
trimestral [trimes'tral] *adj* quarterly; (*Escol*) termly
trimestre [tri'mestre] *nm* (*Escol*) term; (*Com*) quarter, financial period; (*: pago*) quarterly payment
trinar [tri'nar] *vi* (*Mus*) to trill; (*ave*) to sing, warble; (*rabiar*) to fume, be angry; **está que trina** he's hopping mad
trincar [trin'kar] *vt* (*atar*) to tie up; (*Naut*) to lash; (*agarrar*) to pinion
trinchar [trin'tʃar] *vt* to carve
trinchera [trin'tʃera] *nf* (*fosa*) trench; (*para vía*) cutting; (*impermeable*) trench-coat
trineo [tri'neo] *nm* sledge
trinidad [trini'ðað] *nf* trio; (*Rel*): **la T~** the Trinity
trino ['trino] *nm* trill
trío ['trio] *nm* trio
tripa ['tripa] *nf* (*Anat*) intestine; (*fig: fam*) belly; **tripas** *nfpl* (*Anat*) insides; (*Culin*) tripe *sg*; **tener mucha ~** to be fat; **me duelen las ~s** I have a stomach ache
triple ['triple] *adj* triple; (*tres veces*) threefold
triplicado, -a [tripli'kaðo, a] *adj*: **por ~** in triplicate
triplicar [tripli'kar] *vt* to treble
triplo, -a ['triplo, a] *adj* = **triple**
trípode ['tripoðe] *nm* tripod
tripulación [tripula'θjon] *nf* crew
tripulante [tripu'lante] *nm/f* crewman/woman
tripular [tripu'lar] *vt* (*barco*) to man; (*Auto*) to drive
triquiñuela [triki'ɲwela] *nf* trick
tris [tris] *nm* crack; **en un ~** in an instant; **estar en un ~ de hacer algo** to be within an inch of doing sth
triste ['triste] *adj* (*afligido*) sad; (*sombrío*) melancholy, gloomy; (*desolado*) desolate; (*lamentable*) sorry, miserable; (*viejo*) old; (*único*) single; **no queda sino un ~ penique** there's just one miserable penny left
tristeza [tris'teθa] *nf* (*aflicción*) sadness; (*melancolía*) melancholy; (*de lugar*) desolation; (*pena*) misery
triturar [tritu'rar] *vt* (*moler*) to grind; (*mascar*) to chew; (*documentos*) to shred
triunfal [triun'fal] *adj* triumphant; (*arco*) triumphal
triunfar [triun'far] *vi* (*tener éxito*) to triumph; (*ganar*) to win; (*Naipes*) to be trumps; **triunfan corazones** hearts are trumps; **~ en la vida** to succeed in life
triunfo [tri'unfo] *nm* triumph; (*Naipes*) trump
trivial [tri'βjal] *adj* trivial
trivializar [triβjali'θar] *vt* to minimize, play down
triza ['triθa] *nf* bit, piece; **hacer algo ~s** to smash sth to bits; (*papel*) to tear sth to shreds
trocar [tro'kar] *vt* (*Com*) to exchange; (*dinero, de lugar*) to change; (*palabras*) to exchange; (*confundir*) to confuse; **trocarse** *vr* (*confundirse*) to get mixed up; (*transformarse*): **~se (en)** to change (into)
trocear [troθe'ar] *vt* to cut up
trocha ['trotʃa] *nf* (*sendero*) by-path; (*atajo*) short cut
troche ['trotʃe]: **a ~ y moche** *adv* helter-skelter, pell-mell
trofeo [tro'feo] *nm* (*premio*) trophy
trola ['trola] *nf* (*fam*) fib
tromba ['tromba] *nf* whirlwind; **~ de agua** downpour
trombón [trom'bon] *nm* trombone
trombosis [trom'bosis] *nf inv* thrombosis
trompa ['trompa] *nf* (*Mus*) horn; (*de elefante*) trunk; (*trompo*) humming top; (*hocico*) snout; (*Anat*) tube, duct ▷ *nm* (*Mus*) horn player; **~ de Falopio** Fallopian tube; **cogerse una ~** (*fam*) to get tight
trompada [trom'paða] *nf* = **trompazo**
trompazo [trom'paθo] *nm* (*choque*) bump, bang; (*puñetazo*) punch
trompeta [trom'peta] *nf* trumpet; (*clarín*) bugle ▷ *nm* trumpeter
trompetilla [trompe'tiʎa] *nf* ear trumpet
trompicón [trompi'kon]: **a trompicones** *adv* in fits and starts
trompo ['trompo] *nm* spinning top
trompón [trom'pon] *nm* bump
tronar [tro'nar] *vt* (*Am*) to shoot, execute; (*examen*) to flunk ▷ *vi* to thunder; (*fig*) to rage; (*fam*) to go broke
tronchar [tron'tʃar] *vt* (*árbol*) to chop down; (*fig: vida*) to cut short; (*esperanza*) to shatter; (*persona*) to tire out; **troncharse** *vr* to fall down; **~se de risa** to split one's sides with laughter
tronco ['tronko] *nm* (*de árbol, Anat*) trunk; (*de planta*) stem; **estar hecho un ~** to be sound asleep
trono ['trono] *nm* throne
tropa ['tropa] *nf* (*Mil*) troop; (*soldados*) soldiers *pl*; (*soldados rasos*) ranks *pl*; (*gentío*) mob
tropel [tro'pel] *nm* (*muchedumbre*) crowd; (*prisa*) rush; (*montón*) throng; **acudir** (*etc*) **en ~** to come (*etc*) in a mad rush
tropelía [trope'lia] *nm* outrage
tropezar [trope'θar] *vi* to trip, stumble; (*fig*) to slip up; **tropezarse** *vr* (*dos personas*) to run into each other; **~ con** (*encontrar*) to run into; (*topar con*) to bump into

t

tropezón [trope'θon] *nm* trip; (*fig*) blunder; (*traspié*): **dar un ~** to trip
tropical [tropi'kal] *adj* tropical
trópico ['tropiko] *nm* tropic
tropiezo *etc* [tro'pjeθo] *vb ver* **tropezar** ▷ *nm* (*error*) slip, blunder; (*desgracia*) misfortune; (*revés*) setback; (*obstáculo*) snag; (*discusión*) quarrel
trotamundos [trota'mundos] *nm inv* globetrotter
trotar [tro'tar] *vi* to trot; (*viajar*) to travel about
trote ['trote] *nm* trot; (*fam*) travelling; **de mucho ~** hard-wearing
trozar [tro'θar] *vt* (*Am*) to cut up, cut into pieces
trozo ['troθo] *nm* bit, piece; (*Lit, Mus*) passage; **a ~s** in bits
trucha ['trutʃa] *nf* (*pez*) trout; (*Tec*) crane
truco ['truko] *nm* (*habilidad*) knack; (*engaño*) trick; (*Cine*) trick effect *o* photography; **trucos** *nmpl* billiards *sg*; **~ publicitario** advertising gimmick
trueno ['trweno] *vb ver* **tronar** ▷ *nm* (*gen*) thunder; (*estampido*) boom; (*de arma*) bang
trueque ['trweke] *vb ver* **trocar** ▷ *nm* exchange; (*Com*) barter
trufa ['trufa] *nf* (*Bot*) truffle; (*fig*: *fam*) fib
truhán, -ana [tru'an, ana] *nm/f* rogue
truncar [trun'kar] *vt* (*cortar*) to truncate; (*la vida etc*) to cut short; (*el desarrollo*) to stunt
tu [tu] *adj* your
tú [tu] *pron* you
tubérculo [tu'βerkulo] *nm* (*Bot*) tuber
tuberculosis [tuβerku'losis] *nf inv* tuberculosis
tubería [tuβe'ria] *nf* pipes *pl*, piping; (*conducto*) pipeline
tubo ['tuβo] *nm* tube, pipe; **~ de desagüe** drainpipe; **~ de ensayo** test-tube; **~ de escape** exhaust (pipe); **~ digestivo** alimentary canal
tuerca ['twerka] *nf* (*Tec*) nut
tuerto, -a ['twerto, a] *adj* (*torcido*) twisted; (*ciego*) blind in one eye ▷ *nm/f* one-eyed person ▷ *nm* (*ofensa*) wrong; **a tuertas** upside-down
tuerza *etc* ['twerθa] *vb ver* **torcer**
tuétano ['twetano] *nm* (*Anat*: *médula*) marrow; (*Bot*) pith; **hasta los ~s** through and through, utterly
tufo ['tufo] *nm* vapour; (*fig*: *pey*) stench
tugurio [tu'ɣurjo] *nm* slum
tuit [twit] *nm* (*en Twitter*) tweet
tuitear [twite'ar] *vt* (*en Twitter*) to tweet
tul [tul] *nm* tulle
tulipán [tuli'pan] *nm* tulip
tullido, -a [tu'ʎiðo, a] *adj* crippled; (*cansado*) exhausted
tumba ['tumba] *nf* (*sepultura*) tomb; (*sacudida*) shake; (*voltereta*) somersault; **ser (como) una ~** to keep one's mouth shut
tumbar [tum'bar] *vt* to knock down; (*doblar*) to knock over; (*fam*: *suj*: *olor*) to overpower ▷ *vi* to fall down; **tumbarse** *vr* (*echarse*) to lie down; (*extenderse*) to stretch out
tumbo ['tumbo] *nm* (*caída*) fall; (*de vehículo*) jolt; (*momento crítico*) critical moment; **dar ~s** to stagger
tumbona [tum'bona] *nf* (*butaca*) easy chair; (*de playa*: *para acostarse*) lounger; (*para sentarse*) deckchair (*Brit*), beach chair (*US*)
tumor [tu'mor] *nm* tumour
tumulto [tu'multo] *nm* turmoil; (*Pol*: *motín*) riot
tuna ['tuna] *nf* (*Mus*) student music group; *ver tb* **tuno**; *see note*

TUNA

A *tuna* is made up of university students, or quite often former students, who dress up in costumes from the *Edad de Oro*, the Spanish Golden Age. These musical troupes go through the town playing their guitars, lutes and tambourines and serenade the young ladies in the halls of residence, or make impromptu appearances at weddings or parties singing traditional Spanish songs for a few pesetas.

tunante [tu'nante] *adj* rascally ▷ *nm* rogue, villain; **¡~!** you villain!
tunda ['tunda] *nf* (*de tela*) shearing; (*de golpes*) beating
túnel ['tunel] *nm* tunnel
Túnez ['tuneθ] *nm* Tunis
tuning ['tunin] *nm* (*Auto*) car styling, modding (*inf*)
tuno, -a ['tuno, a] *nm/f* (*fam*) rogue ▷ *nm* (*Mus*) *member of a "tuna"*; *ver* **tuna**
tuntún [tun'tun]: **al ~** *adv* thoughtlessly
tupé [tu'pe] *nm* quiff
tupido, -a [tu'piðo, a] *adj* (*denso*) dense; (*fig*: *torpe*) dim; (*tela*) close-woven
turba ['turβa] *nf* (*combustible*) turf; (*muchedumbre*) crowd
turbación [turβa'θjon] *nf* (*molestia*) disturbance; (*preocupación*) worry
turbado, -a [tur'βaðo, a] *adj* (*molesto*) disturbed; (*preocupado*) worried
turbante [tur'βante] *nm* turban
turbar [tur'βar] *vt* (*molestar*) to disturb; (*incomodar*) to upset; **turbarse** *vr* to be disturbed
turbina [tur'βina] *nf* turbine
turbio, -a ['turβjo, a] *adj* (*agua etc*) cloudy; (*vista*) dim, blurred; (*tema*) unclear, confused; (*negocio*) shady ▷ *adv* indistinctly
turbo ['turβo] *adj inv* turbo(-charged) ▷ *nm* (*tb coche*) turbo
turbulencia [turβu'lenθja] *nf* turbulence; (*fig*) restlessness

turbulento, -a [turβu'lento, a] *adj* turbulent; (*fig*: *intranquilo*) restless; (: *ruidoso*) noisy
turco, -a ['turko, a] *adj* Turkish ▷ *nm/f* Turk ▷ *nm* (*Ling*) Turkish
turismo [tu'rismo] *nm* tourism; (*coche*) saloon car; **hacer ~** to go travelling (abroad)
turista [tu'rista] *nm/f* tourist; (*vacacionista*) holidaymaker (*Brit*), vacationer (*US*)
turístico, -a [tu'ristiko, a] *adj* tourist *cpd*
turnar [tur'nar] *vi*, **turnarse** *vr* to take (it in) turns
turno ['turno] *nm* (*de trabajo*) shift; (*oportunidad, orden de prioridad*) opportunity; (*Deporte etc*) turn; **es su ~** it's his turn (next); **~ de día/de noche** day/night shift
turquesa [tur'kesa] *nf* turquoise
Turquía [tur'kia] *nf* Turkey
turrón [tu'rron] *nm* (*dulce*) nougat; (*fam*) sinecure, cushy job *o* number
tute ['tute] *nm* (*Naipes*) *card game*; **darse un ~** to break one's back
tutear [tute'ar] *vt* to address as familiar "tú"; **tutearse** *vr* to be on familiar terms
tutela [tu'tela] *nf* (*legal*) guardianship; (*instrucción*) guidance; **estar bajo la ~ de** (*fig*) to be under the protection of
tutelar [tute'lar] *adj* tutelary ▷ *vt* to protect
tutor, a [tu'tor, a] *nm/f* (*legal*) guardian; (*Escol*) tutor; **~ de curso** form master/ mistress
tuve *etc* ['tuβe] *vb ver* **tener**
tuviera *etc vb ver* **tener**
tuyo, -a ['tujo, a] *adj* yours, of yours ▷ *pron* yours; **un amigo ~** a friend of yours; **los ~s** (*fam*) your relations, your family
TV *nf abr* (= *televisión*) TV
TVE *nf abr* = **Televisión Española**

U

u [u] *conj* or
ubicado, -a [uβi'kaðo, a] *adj* (*esp Am*) situated
ubicar [uβi'kar] *vt* (*esp Am*) to place, situate; (: *fig*) to install in a post; (: *encontrar*) to find; **ubicarse** *vr* to be situated, be located
ubre ['uβre] *nf* udder
UCI ['uθi] *sigla f* (= *Unidad de Cuidados Intensivos*) ICU
Ud(s). *abr* = **usted(es)**
UE *nf abr* (= *Unión Europea*) EU
UEFA [w'efa] *nf abr* (= *Unión de Asociaciones de Fútbol Europeo*) UEFA
UEO *nf abr* (= *Unión Europea Occidental*) WEU
ufanarse [ufa'narse] *vr* to boast; **~ de** to pride o.s. on
ufano, -a [u'fano, a] *adj* (*arrogante*) arrogant; (*presumido*) conceited
UGT *nf abr ver* **Unión General de Trabajadores**
ujier [u'xjer] *nm* usher; (*portero*) doorkeeper
úlcera ['ulθera] *nf* ulcer
ulcerar [ulθe'rar] *vt* to make sore; **ulcerarse** *vr* to ulcerate
ulterior [ulte'rjor] *adj* (*más allá*) farther, further; (*subsecuente, siguiente*) subsequent
últimamente ['ultimamente] *adv* (*recientemente*) lately, recently; (*finalmente*) finally; (*como último recurso*) as a last resort
ultimar [ulti'mar] *vt* to finish; (*finalizar*) to finalize; (*Am*: *matar*) to kill
ultimátum [ulti'matum] *nm* (*pl* **ultimátums**) ultimatum

último, -a ['ultimo, a] *adj* last; (*más reciente*) latest, most recent; (*más bajo*) bottom; (*más alto*) top; (*fig*) final, extreme; **en las últimas** on one's last legs; **por ~** finally
ultra ['ultra] *adj* ultra ▷ *nm/f* extreme right-winger
ultracongelar [ultrakonxe'lar] *vt* to deep-freeze
ultraderecha [ultraðe'retʃa] *nf* extreme right (wing)
ultrajar [ultra'xar] *vt* (*escandalizar*) to outrage; (*insultar*) to insult, abuse
ultraje [ul'traxe] *nm* outrage; insult
ultraligero [ultrali'xero] *nm* microlight (*Brit*), microlite (*US*)
ultramar [ultra'mar] *nm*: **de** *o* **en ~** abroad, overseas; **los países de ~** the overseas countries
ultramarino, -a [ultrama'rino, a] *adj* overseas, foreign ▷ *nmpl*: **~s** groceries; **tienda de ~s** grocer's (shop)
ultranza [ul'tranθa]: **a ~** *adv* to the death; (*a toda costa*) at all costs; (*completo*) outright; (*Pol etc*) out-and-out, extreme; **un nacionalista a ~** a rabid nationalist
ultrasónico, -a [ultra'soniko, a] *adj* ultrasonic
ultratumba [ultra'tumba] *nf*: **la vida de ~** the next life; **una voz de ~** a ghostly voice
ultravioleta [ultraβjo'leta] *adj inv* ultraviolet
ulular [ulu'lar] *vi* to howl; (*búho*) to hoot
umbilical [umbili'kal] *adj*: **cordón ~** umbilical cord
umbral [um'bral] *nm* (*gen*) threshold; **~ de rentabilidad** (*Com*) break-even point
UME *nf abr* (= *Unión Monetaria y Económica*) EMU

PALABRA CLAVE

un, una [un, 'una] **1** *artículo indefinido* a; (*antes de vocal*) an; **una mujer/naranja** a woman/ an orange
2: **unos** (*o* **unas**): **hay unos regalos para ti** there are some presents for you; **hay unas cervezas en la nevera** there are some beers in the fridge; *ver tb* **uno**
3 (*enfático*): **¡hace un frío!** it's so cold!; **¡tiene una casa!** he's got some house!

unánime [u'nanime] *adj* unanimous
unanimidad [unanimi'ðað] *nf* unanimity; **por ~** unanimously
unción [un'θjon] *nf* anointing
undécimo, -a [un'deθimo, a] *adj, nm/f* eleventh
UNED [u'ned] *nf abr* (*Esp Univ*: = *Universidad Nacional de Enseñanza a Distancia*) ≈ Open University (*Brit*)
ungir [un'xir] *vt* to rub with ointment; (*Rel*) to anoint
ungüento [un'gwento] *nm* ointment; (*fig*) salve, balm
únicamente ['unikamente] *adv* solely; (*solamente*) only
único, -a ['uniko, a] *adj* only; (*solo*) sole, single; (*sin par*) unique; **hijo ~** only child
unidad [uni'ðað] *nf* unity; (*Tec*) unit; **~ móvil** (*TV*) mobile unit; (*Inform*): **~ central** system unit, central processing unit; **~ de control** control unit; **~ de disco** disk drive; **~ de entrada/salida** input/output device; **~ de información** data item; **~ periférica** peripheral device; **~ de presentación visual** *o* **de visualización** visual display unit; **~ procesadora central** central processing unit
unido, -a [u'niðo, a] *adj* joined, linked; (*fig*) united
unifamiliar [unifamil'jar] *adj*: **vivienda ~** single-family home
unificar [unifi'kar] *vt* to unite, unify
uniformar [unifor'mar] *vt* to make uniform; (*persona*) to put into uniform; (*Tec*) to standardize
uniforme [uni'forme] *adj* uniform, equal; (*superficie*) even ▷ *nm* uniform
uniformidad [uniformi'ðað] *nf* uniformity; (*llaneza*) levelness, evenness
unilateral [unilate'ral] *adj* unilateral
unión [u'njon] *nf* (*gen*) union; (*acto*) uniting, joining; (*calidad*) unity; (*Tec*) joint; (*fig*) closeness, togetherness; **en ~ con** (together) with, accompanied by; **~ aduanera** customs union; **U~ General de Trabajadores (UGT)** (*Esp*) *Socialist Union Confederation*; **U~ Europea** European Union; **la U~ Soviética** the Soviet Union; **punto de ~** (*Tec*) junction
unir [u'nir] *vt* (*juntar*) to join, unite; (*atar*) to tie, fasten; (*combinar*) to combine ▷ *vi* (*ingredientes*) to mix well; **unirse** *vr* to join together, unite; (*empresas*) to merge; **les une una fuerte simpatía** they are bound by (a) strong affection; **~se en matrimonio** to marry
unisex [uni'seks] *adj inv* unisex
unísono [u'nisono] *nm*: **al ~** in unison
universal [uniβer'sal] *adj* universal; (*mundial*) world *cpd*; **historia ~** world history
universidad [uniβersi'ðað] *nf* university; **~ laboral** polytechnic, poly
universitario, -a [uniβersi'tarjo, a] *adj* university *cpd* ▷ *nm/f* (*profesor*) lecturer; (*estudiante*) (university) student; (*graduado*) graduate
universo [uni'βerso] *nm* universe

PALABRA CLAVE

uno, -a ['uno, a] *adj* one; **es todo uno** it's all one and the same; **unos pocos** a few; **unos cien** about a hundred
▷ *pron* **1** one; **quiero uno solo** I only want one; **uno de ellos** one of them; **una de dos** either one or the other; **no doy una hoy**

I can't do anything right today
2 (*alguien*) somebody, someone; **conozco a uno que se te parece** I know somebody *o* someone who looks like you; **unos querían quedarse** some (people) wanted to stay
3 (*impersonal*) one; **uno mismo** oneself; **uno nunca sabe qué hacer** one never knows what to do
4: **unos ... otros ...** some ... others; **una y otra son muy agradables** they're both very nice; **(los) uno(s) a (los) otro(s)** each other, one another
▷ *nf* one; **es la una** it's one o'clock
▷ *num* (number) one; **el día uno** the first; *ver tb* **un**

untar [un'tar] *vt* (*gen*) to rub; (*mantequilla*) to spread; (*engrasar*) to grease, oil; (*Med*) to rub (with ointment); (*fig*) to bribe; **untarse** *vr* (*fig*) to be crooked; **~ el pan con mantequilla** to spread butter on one's bread

uña ['uɲa] *nf* (*Anat*) nail; (*del pie*) toenail; (*garra*) claw; (*casco*) hoof; (*arrancaclavos*) claw; **ser ~ y carne** to be as thick as thieves; **enseñar** *o* **mostrar** *o* **sacar las ~s** to show one's claws

uperizado, -a [uperi'θaðo, a] *adj*: **leche uperizada** UHT milk

uralita® [ura'lita] *nf* corrugated asbestos cement

uranio [u'ranjo] *nm* uranium

urbanidad [urβani'ðað] *nf* courtesy, politeness

urbanismo [urβa'nismo] *nm* town planning

urbanización [urβaniθa'θjon] *nf* (*colonia, barrio*) estate, housing scheme

urbanizar [urβani'θar] *vt* (*zona*) to develop, urbanize

urbano, -a [ur'βano, a] *adj* (*de ciudad*) urban, town *cpd*; (*cortés*) courteous, polite

urbe ['urβe] *nf* large city, metropolis

urdimbre [ur'ðimbre] *nf* (*de tejido*) warp; (*intriga*) intrigue

urdir [ur'ðir] *vt* to warp; (*fig*) to plot, contrive

urgencia [ur'xenθja] *nf* urgency; (*prisa*) haste, rush; (*emergencia*) emergency; **salida de ~** emergency exit; **servicios de ~** emergency services; **"U~s"** "Casualty"

urgente [ur'xente] *adj* urgent; (*insistente*) insistent; **carta ~** registered (*Brit*) *o* special delivery (*US*) letter

urgir [ur'xir] *vi* to be urgent; **me urge** I'm in a hurry for it; **me urge terminarlo** I must finish it as soon as I can

urinario, -a [uri'narjo, a] *adj* urinary ▷ *nm* urinal, public lavatory, comfort station (*US*)

urna ['urna] *nf* urn; (*Pol*) ballot box; **acudir a las ~s** (*fig: persona*) to (go and) vote; (*: gobierno*) to go to the country

urología [urolo'xia] *nf* urology

urraca [u'rraka] *nf* magpie

URSS *nf abr* (*Historia: = Unión de Repúblicas Socialistas Soviéticas*) USSR

Uruguay [uru'ɣwai] *nm*: **El ~** Uruguay

uruguayo, -a [uru'ɣwajo, a] *adj, nm/f* Uruguayan

usado, -a [u'saðo, a] *adj* (*gen*) used; (*ropa etc*) worn; **muy ~** worn out; (*de segunda mano*) secondhand

usanza [u'sanθa] *nf* custom, usage

usar [u'sar] *vt* to use; (*ropa*) to wear; (*tener costumbre*) to be in the habit of ▷ *vi*: **~ de** to make use of; **usarse** *vr* to be used; (*ropa*) to be worn *o* in fashion

uso ['uso] *nm* use; (*Mecánica etc*) wear; (*costumbre*) usage, custom; (*moda*) fashion; **al ~** in keeping with custom; **al ~ de** in the style of; **de ~ externo** (*Med*) for external use; **estar en el ~ de la palabra** to be speaking, have the floor; **~ y desgaste** (*Com*) wear and tear

usted [us'teð] *pron* (*sg formal: abr* **Ud.** *o* **Vd.**) you *sg*; **~es** (*pl formal: abr* **Uds.** *o* **Vds.**) you *pl*; (*Am: formal y fam*) you *pl*

usual [u'swal] *adj* usual

usuario, -a [usw'arjo, a] *nm/f* user; **~ final** (*Com*) end user

usufructo [usu'frukto] *nm* use; **~ vitalicio (de)** life interest (in)

usura [u'sura] *nf* usury

usurero, -a [usu'rero, a] *nm/f* usurer

usurpar [usur'par] *vt* to usurp

utensilio [uten'siljo] *nm* tool; (*Culin*) utensil

útero ['utero] *nm* uterus, womb

útil ['util] *adj* useful; (*servible*) usable, serviceable ▷ *nm* tool; **día ~** working day, weekday; **es muy ~ tenerlo aquí cerca** it's very handy having it here close by

utilidad [utili'ðað] *nf* usefulness, utility; (*Com*) profit; **~es líquidas** net profit *sg*

utilizar [utili'θar] *vt* to use, utilize; (*explotar*) to harness

utopía [uto'pia] *nf* Utopia

utópico, -a [u'topiko, a] *adj* Utopian

uva ['uβa] *nf* grape; **~ pasa** raisin; **~ de Corinto** currant; **estar de mala ~** to be in a bad mood; *see note*

UVA

In Spain *las uvas* play a big part on New Years' Eve (*Nochevieja*), when on the stroke of midnight people from every part of Spain, at home, in restaurants or in the *plaza mayor* eat a grape for each stroke of the clock of the Puerta del Sol in Madrid. It is said to bring luck for the following year.

UVI ['uβi] *nf abr* (*Esp Med: = unidad de vigilancia intensiva*) ICU

V

v. *abr* (*= voltio*) v; (*= ver, véase*) v.; (*Lit: = verso*) v
va [ba] *vb ver* **ir**
vaca ['baka] *nf* (*animal*) cow; (*carne*) beef; (*cuero*) cowhide; **~s flacas/gordas** (*fig*) bad/good times
vacaciones [baka'θjones] *nfpl* holiday(s); **estar/irse** *o* **marcharse de ~** to be/go (away) on holiday
vacante [ba'kante] *adj* vacant, empty ▷ *nf* vacancy
vaciar [ba'θjar] *vt* to empty (out); (*ahuecar*) to hollow out; (*moldear*) to cast; (*Inform*) to dump ▷ *vi* (*río*): **~ en** to flow into; **vaciarse** *vr* to empty; (*fig*) to blab, spill the beans
vaciedad [baθje'ðað] *nf* emptiness
vacilación [baθila'θjon] *nf* hesitation
vacilante [baθi'lante] *adj* unsteady; (*habla*) faltering; (*luz*) flickering; (*fig*) hesitant
vacilar [baθi'lar] *vi* to be unsteady; to falter; to flicker; to hesitate, waver; (*persona*) to stagger, stumble; (*memoria*) to fail; (*esp Am: divertirse*) to have a great time
vacilón [baθi'lon] *nm* (*esp Am*): **estar** *o* **ir de ~** to have a great time
vacío, -a [ba'θio, a] *adj* empty; (*puesto*) vacant; (*desocupado*) idle; (*vano*) vain; (*charla etc*) light, superficial ▷ *nm* emptiness; (*Física*) vacuum; (*un vacío*) (empty) space; **hacer el ~ a algn** to send sb to Coventry
vacuna [ba'kuna] *nf* vaccine
vacunar [baku'nar] *vt* to vaccinate; **vacunarse** *vr* to get vaccinated
vacuno, -a [ba'kuno, a] *adj* bovine; **ganado ~** cattle
vacuo, -a ['bakwo, a] *adj* empty
vadear [baðe'ar] *vt* (*río*) to ford; (*problema*) to overcome; (*persona*) to sound out
vado ['baðo] *nm* ford; (*solución*) solution; (*descanso*) respite; **"~ permanente"** "keep clear"
vagabundo, -a [baɣa'βundo, a] *adj* wandering; (*pey*) vagrant ▷ *nm/f* (*errante*) wanderer; (*vago*) tramp, bum (*US*)
vagamente [baɣa'mente] *adv* vaguely
vagancia [ba'ɣanθja] *nf* (*pereza*) idleness, laziness; (*vagabundeo*) vagrancy
vagar [ba'ɣar] *vi* to wander; (*pasear*) to saunter up and down; (*no hacer nada*) to idle ▷ *nm* leisure
vagina [ba'xina] *nf* vagina
vago, -a ['baɣo, a] *adj* vague; (*perezoso*) lazy; (*ambulante*) wandering ▷ *nm/f* (*vagabundo*) tramp, bum (*US*); (*perezoso*) lazybones *sg*, idler
vagón [ba'ɣon] *nm* (*de pasajeros*) carriage; (*de mercancías*) wagon; **~ cama/restaurante** sleeping/dining car
vaguear [baɣe'ar] *vi* to laze around
vaguedad [baɣe'ðað] *nf* vagueness
vaho ['bao] *nm* (*vapor*) vapour, steam; (*olor*) smell; (*respiración*) breath; **vahos** *nmpl* (*Med*) inhalation *sg*
vaina ['baina] *nf* sheath ▷ *nm* (*Am*) nuisance
vainilla [bai'niʎa] *nf* vanilla
vainita [bai'nita] *nf* (*Am*) green *o* French bean
vais [bais] *vb ver* **ir**
vaivén [bai'βen] *nm* to-and-fro movement; (*de tránsito*) coming and going; **vaivenes** *nmpl* (*fig*) ups and downs
vajilla [ba'xiʎa] *nf* crockery, dishes *pl*; (*una vajilla*) service; **~ de porcelana** chinaware
valdré *etc vb ver* **valer**
vale ['bale] *nm* voucher; (*recibo*) receipt; (*pagaré*) I.O.U.; **~ de regalo** gift voucher *o* token
valedero, -a [bale'ðero, a] *adj* valid
valenciano, -a [balen'θjano, a] *adj, nm/f* Valencian ▷ *nm* (*Ling*) Valencian
valentía [balen'tia] *nf* courage, bravery; (*pey*) boastfulness; (*acción*) heroic deed
valentón, -ona [balen'ton, ona] *adj* blustering
valer [ba'ler] *vt* to be worth; (*Mat*) to equal; (*costar*) to cost; (*amparar*) to aid, protect ▷ *vi* (*ser útil*) to be useful; (*ser válido*) to be valid; **valerse** *vr* to take care of o.s. ▷ *nm* worth, value; **~ la pena** to be worthwhile; **¿vale?** O.K.?; **¡vale!** (*¡basta!*) that'll do!; **¡eso no vale!** that doesn't count!; **no vale nada** it's no good; (*mercancía*) it's worthless; (*argumento*) it's no use; **no vale para nada** he's no good at all; **más vale tarde que nunca** better late than never; **más vale que nos vayamos** we'd better go; **~se de** to make use of, take advantage of; **~se por sí mismo** to help *o*

manage by o.s.; **¡eso a mí no me vale!** (*Am*: *fam*: *no importar*) I couldn't care less about that
valeroso, -a [bale'roso, a] *adj* brave, valiant
valgo *etc* ['balɣo] *vb ver* **valer**
valía [ba'lia] *nf* worth; **de gran ~** (*objeto*) very valuable
validar [bali'ðar] *vt* to validate; (*Pol*) to ratify
validez [bali'ðeθ] *nf* validity; **dar ~ a** to validate
válido, -a ['baliðo, a] *adj* valid
valiente [ba'ljente] *adj* brave, valiant; (*audaz*) bold; (*pey*) boastful; (*con ironía*) fine, wonderful ▷ *nm/f* brave man/woman
valija [ba'lixa] *nf* case; (*Am*) suitcase; (*mochila*) satchel; (*Correos*) mailbag; **~ diplomática** diplomatic bag
valioso, -a [ba'ljoso, a] *adj* valuable; (*rico*) wealthy
valla ['baʎa] *nf* fence; (*Deporte*) hurdle; (*fig*) barrier; **~ publicitaria** hoarding (*esp Brit*), billboard (*esp US*)
vallar [ba'ʎar] *vt* to fence in
valle ['baʎe] *nm* valley, vale
valor [ba'lor] *nm* value, worth; (*precio*) price; (*valentía*) valour, courage; (*importancia*) importance; (*cara*) nerve, cheek (*fam*); **sin ~** worthless; **~ adquisitivo** *o* **de compra** purchasing power; **dar ~ a** to attach importance to; **quitar ~ a** to minimize the importance of; (*Com*): **~ según balance** book value; **~ comercial** *o* **de mercado** market value; **~ contable/desglosado** asset/break-up value; **~ de escasez** scarcity value; **~ intrínseco** intrinsic value; **~ a la par** par value; **~ neto** net worth; **~ de rescate/de sustitución** surrender/replacement value; *ver tb* **valores**
valoración [balora'θjon] *nf* valuation
valorar [balo'rar] *vt* to value; (*tasar*) to price; (*fig*) to assess
valores [ba'lores] *nmpl* (*Com*) securities; **~ en cartera** *o* **habidos** investments
vals [bals] *nm* waltz
válvula ['balβula] *nf* valve
vamos ['bamos] *vb ver* **ir**
vampiro, -iresa [bam'piro, i'resa] *nm/f* vampire ▷ *nf* (*Cine*) vamp, femme fatale
van [ban] *vb ver* **ir**
vanagloriarse [banaɣlo'rjarse] *vr* to boast
vandalismo [banda'lismo] *nm* vandalism
vándalo, -a ['bandalo, a] *nm/f* vandal
vanguardia [ban'gwardja] *nf* vanguard; **de ~** (*Arte*) avant-garde; **estar en** *o* **ir a la ~ de** (*fig*) to be in the forefront of
vanguardista [bangwar'ðista] *adj* avant-garde
vanidad [bani'ðað] *nf* vanity; (*inutilidad*) futility; (*irrealidad*) unreality
vanidoso, -a [bani'ðoso, a] *adj* vain, conceited
vano, -a ['bano, a] *adj* (*irreal*) unreal; (*irracional*) unreasonable; (*inútil*) vain, useless; (*persona*) vain, conceited; (*frívolo*) frivolous
vapor [ba'por] *nm* vapour; (*vaho*) steam; (*de gas*) fumes *pl*; (*neblina*) mist; **vapores** *nmpl* (*Med*) hysterics; **al ~** (*Culin*) steamed; **~ de agua** water vapour
vaporizador [baporiθa'ðor] *nm* (*de perfume etc*) spray
vaporizar [bapori'θar] *vt* to vaporize; (*perfume*) to spray
vaporoso, -a [bapo'roso, a] *adj* vaporous; (*vahoso*) steamy; (*tela*) light, airy
vapulear [bapule'ar] *vt* to thrash; (*fig*) to slate
vaquero, -a [ba'kero, a] *adj* cattle *cpd* ▷ *nm* cowboy; **vaqueros** *nmpl* jeans
vaquilla [ba'kiʎa] *nf* heifer
vara ['bara] *nf* stick, pole; (*Tec*) rod; **~ mágica** magic wand
variable [ba'rjaβle] *adj, nf* variable (*tb Inform*)
variación [barja'θjon] *nf* variation; **sin ~** unchanged
variado, -a [ba'rjaðo, a] *adj* varied; (*dulces, galletas*) assorted; **entremeses ~s** a selection of starters
variante [ba'rjante] *adj* variant ▷ *nf* (*alternativa*) alternative; (*Auto*) bypass
variar [ba'rjar] *vt* (*cambiar*) to change; (*poner variedad*) to vary; (*modificar*) to modify; (*cambiar de posición*) to switch around ▷ *vi* to vary; **~ de** to differ from; **~ de opinión** to change one's mind; **para ~** just for a change
varicela [bari'θela] *nf* chicken pox
varices [ba'riθes] *nfpl* varicose veins
variedad [barje'ðað] *nf* variety
varilla [ba'riʎa] *nf* stick; (*Bot*) twig; (*Tec*) rod; (*de rueda*) spoke; **~ mágica** magic wand
vario, -a ['barjo, a] *adj* (*variado*) varied; (*multicolor*) motley; (*cambiable*) changeable; **~s** various, several
variopinto, -a [barjo'pinto, a] *adj* diverse; **un público ~** a mixed audience
varita [ba'rita] *nf*: **~ mágica** magic wand
varón [ba'ron] *nm* male, man
varonil [baro'nil] *adj* manly
Varsovia [bar'soβja] *nf* Warsaw
vas [bas] *vb ver* **ir**
vasco, -a ['basko, a], **vascongado a** [baskon'gaðo, a] *adj, nm/f* Basque ▷ *nm* (*Ling*) Basque ▷ *nfpl*: **las V~ngadas** the Basque Country *sg o* Provinces
vascuence [bas'kwenθe] *nm* (*Ling*) Basque
vasectomía [basekto'mia] *nf* vasectomy
vaselina [base'lina] *nf* Vaseline®
vasija [ba'sixa] *nf* (earthenware) vessel
vaso ['baso] *nm* glass, tumbler; (*Anat*) vessel; (*cantidad*) glass(ful); **~ de vino** glass of wine; **~ para vino** wineglass
vástago ['bastaɣo] *nm* (*Bot*) shoot; (*Tec*) rod; (*fig*) offspring
vasto, -a ['basto, a] *adj* vast, huge
Vaticano [bati'kano] *nm*: **el ~** the Vatican; **la Ciudad del ~** the Vatican City

vaticinio [bati'θinjo] *nm* prophecy
vatio ['batjo] *nm* (*Elec*) watt
vaya *etc* ['baja] *vb ver* **ir**
Vd. *abr* = **usted**
Vds. *abr* = **ustedes**
ve [be] *vb ver* **ir, ver**
vecindad [beθin'dað] *nf*, **vecindario** [beθin'darjo] *nm* neighbourhood; (*habitantes*) residents *pl*
vecino, -a [be'θino, a] *adj* neighbouring ▷ *nm/f* neighbour; (*residente*) resident; **somos ~s** we live next door to one another
vector [bek'tor] *nm* vector
veda ['beða] *nf* prohibition; (*temporada*) close season
vedado [be'ðaðo] *nm* preserve
vedar [be'ðar] *vt* (*prohibir*) to ban, prohibit; (*idea, plan*) to veto; (*impedir*) to stop, prevent
vega ['beɣa] *nf* fertile plain *o* valley
vegetación [bexeta'θjon] *nf* vegetation
vegetal [bexe'tal] *adj, nm* vegetable
vegetar [bexe'tar] *vi* to vegetate
vegetariano, -a [bexeta'rjano, a] *adj, nm/f* vegetarian
vegetativo, -a [bexeta'tiβo, a] *adj* vegetative
vehemencia [bee'menθja] *nf* (*insistencia*) vehemence; (*pasión*) passion; (*fervor*) fervour; (*violencia*) violence
vehemente [bee'mente] *adj* vehement; passionate; fervent; violent
vehículo [be'ikulo] *nm* vehicle; (*Med*) carrier; **~ de servicio público** public service vehicle; **~ espacial** spacecraft
veía *etc vb ver* **ver**
veinte ['beinte] *num* twenty; (*orden, fecha*) twentieth; **el siglo ~** the twentieth century
vejación [bexa'θjon] *nf* vexation; (*humillación*) humiliation
vejar [be'xar] *vt* (*irritar*) to annoy, vex; (*humillar*) to humiliate
vejatorio, -a [bexa'torjo, a] *adj* humiliating, degrading
vejez [be'xeθ] *nf* old age
vejiga [be'xiɣa] *nf* (*Anat*) bladder
vela ['bela] *nf* (*de cera*) candle; (*Naut*) sail; (*insomnio*) sleeplessness; (*vigilia*) vigil; (*Mil*) sentry duty; (*fam*) snot; **a toda ~** (*Naut*) under full sail; **estar a dos ~s** (*fam*) to be skint; **pasar la noche en ~** to have a sleepless night
velado, -a [be'laðo, a] *adj* veiled; (*sonido*) muffled; (*Foto*) blurred ▷ *nf* soirée
velador [bela'ðor] *nm* watchman; (*candelero*) candlestick; (*Am*) bedside table
velar [be'lar] *vt* (*vigilar*) to keep watch over; (*cubrir*) to veil ▷ *vi* to stay awake; **~ por** to watch over, look after
velatorio [bela'torjo] *nm* (funeral) wake
veleidad [belei'ðað] *nf* (*ligereza*) fickleness; (*capricho*) whim
velero [be'lero] *nm* (*Naut*) sailing ship; (*Aviat*) glider
veleta [be'leta] *nm/f* fickle person ▷ *nf* weather vane
veliz [be'lis] *nm* (*Am*) suitcase
vello ['beʎo] *nm* down, fuzz
velo ['belo] *nm* veil; **~ de paladar** (*Anat*) soft palate
velocidad [beloθi'ðað] *nf* speed; (*Tec*) rate, pace, velocity; (*Mecánica, Auto*) gear; **¿a qué ~?** how fast?; **de alta ~** high-speed; **cobrar ~** to pick up *o* gather speed; **meter la segunda ~** to change into second gear; **~ máxima de impresión** (*Inform*) maximum print speed
velocímetro [belo'θimetro] *nm* speedometer
velorio [be'lorjo] *nm* (*Am*) (funeral) wake
veloz [be'loθ] *adj* fast, swift
ven [ben] *vb ver* **venir**
vena ['bena] *nf* vein; (*fig*) vein, disposition; (*Geo*) seam, vein
venado [be'naðo] *nm* deer; (*Culin*) venison
vencedor, a [benθe'ðor, a] *adj* victorious ▷ *nm/f* victor, winner
vencer [ben'θer] *vt* (*dominar*) to defeat, beat; (*derrotar*) to vanquish; (*superar, controlar*) to overcome, master ▷ *vi* (*triunfar*) to win (through), triumph; (*pago*) to fall due; (*plazo*) to expire; **dejarse ~** to yield, give in
vencido, -a [ben'θiðo, a] *adj* (*derrotado*) defeated, beaten; (*Com*) payable, due ▷ *adv*: **pagar ~** to pay in arrears; **le pagan por meses ~s** he is paid at the end of the month; **darse por ~** to give up
vencimiento [benθi'mjento] *nm* collapse; (*Com: de plazo*) expiration; **a su ~** when it falls due
venda ['benda] *nf* bandage
vendaje [ben'daxe] *nm* bandage, dressing
vendar [ben'dar] *vt* to bandage; **~ los ojos** to blindfold
vendaval [benda'βal] *nm* (*viento*) gale; (*huracán*) hurricane
vendedor, a [bende'ðor, a] *nm/f* seller; **~ ambulante** hawker, pedlar (*Brit*), peddler (*US*)
vender [ben'der] *vt* to sell; (*comerciar*) to market; (*traicionar*) to sell out, betray; **venderse** *vr* (*estar a la venta*) to be on sale; **~ al contado/al por mayor/al por menor/a plazos** to sell for cash/wholesale/retail/on credit; **"se vende"** "for sale"; **"véndese coche"** "car for sale"; **~ al descubierto** to sell short
vendimia [ben'dimja] *nf* grape harvest; **la ~ de 1973** the 1973 vintage
vendimiar [bendi'mjar] *vi* to pick grapes
vendré *etc* [ben'dre] *vb ver* **venir**
veneno [be'neno] *nm* poison; (*de serpiente*) venom
venenoso, -a [bene'noso, a] *adj* poisonous; venomous
venerable [bene'raβle] *adj* venerable
venerar [bene'rar] *vt* (*respetar*) to revere; (*reconocer*) to venerate; (*adorar*) to worship

venéreo, -a [be'nereo, a] *adj* venereal; **enfermedad venérea** venereal disease
venezolano, -a [beneθo'lano, a] *adj, nm/f* Venezuelan
Venezuela [bene'θwela] *nf* Venezuela
venganza [ben'ganθa] *nf* vengeance, revenge
vengar [ben'gar] *vt* to avenge; **vengarse** *vr* to take revenge
vengativo, -a [benga'tiβo, a] *adj* (*persona*) vindictive
vengo *etc vb ver* **venir**
venia ['benja] *nf* (*perdón*) pardon; (*permiso*) consent; **con su ~** by your leave
venial [be'njal] *adj* venial
venida [be'niða] *nf* (*llegada*) arrival; (*regreso*) return; (*fig*) rashness
venidero, -a [beni'ðero, a] *adj* coming, future; **en lo ~** in (the) future
venir [be'nir] *vi* to come; (*llegar*) to arrive; (*ocurrir*) to happen; **venirse** *vr*: **~se abajo** to collapse; **~ a menos** (*persona*) to lose status; (*empresa*) to go downhill; **~ bien** to be suitable, come just right; (*ropa, gusto*) to suit; **~ mal** to be unsuitable *o* inconvenient, come awkwardly; **el año que viene** next year; **¡ven acá!** come (over) here!; **¡venga!** (*fam*) come on!
venta ['benta] *nf* (*Com*) sale; (*posada*) inn; **~ a plazos** hire purchase; **"en ~"** "for sale"; **~ al contado/al por mayor/al por menor** *o* **al detalle** cash sale/wholesale/retail; **~ a domicilio** door-to-door selling; **~ y arrendamiento al vendedor** sale and lease back; **~ de liquidación** clearance sale; **estar de** *o* **en ~** to be (up) for sale *o* on the market; **~s brutas** gross sales; **~s a término** forward sales
ventaja [ben'taxa] *nf* advantage; **llevar la ~** (*en carrera*) to be leading *o* ahead
ventajoso, -a [benta'xoso, a] *adj* advantageous
ventana [ben'tana] *nf* window; **~ de guillotina/galería** sash/bay window; **~ de la nariz** nostril
ventanilla [venta'niʎa] *nf* (*de taquilla, tb Inform*) window
ventilación [bentila'θjon] *nf* ventilation; (*corriente*) draught; (*fig*) airing
ventilador [bentila'ðor] *nm* ventilator; (*eléctrico*) fan
ventilar [benti'lar] *vt* to ventilate; (*poner a secar*) to put out to dry; (*fig*) to air, discuss
ventisca [ben'tiska] *nf* blizzard
ventisquero [bentis'kero] *nm* snowdrift
ventosidad [bentosi'ðað] *nf* flatulence
ventoso, -a [ben'toso, a] *adj* windy ▷ *nf* (*Zool*) sucker; (*instrumento*) suction pad
ventrílocuo, -a [ben'trilokwo, a] *nm/f* ventriloquist
ventura [ben'tura] *nf* (*felicidad*) happiness; (*buena suerte*) luck; (*destino*) fortune; **a la (buena) ~** at random
venturoso, -a [bentu'roso, a] *adj* happy; (*afortunado*) lucky, fortunate
veo *etc vb ver* **ver**
ver [ber] *vt, vi* to see; (*mirar*) to look at, watch; (*investigar*) to look into; (*entender*) to see, understand; **verse** *vr* (*encontrarse*) to meet; (*dejarse ver*) to be seen; (*hallarse: en un apuro*) to find o.s., be ▷ *nm* looks *pl*, appearance; **a ~** let's see; **a ~ si ...** I wonder if ...; **por lo que veo** apparently; **dejarse ~** to become apparent; **no tener nada que ~ con** to have nothing to do with; **a mi modo de ~** as I see it; **merece ~se** it's worth seeing; **no lo veo** I can't see it; **¡nos vemos!** see you (later)!; **¡habrase visto!** did you ever! (*fam*); **¡viera(n)** *o* **hubiera(n) visto qué casa!** (*Am: fam*) if only you'd seen the house!, what a house!; **ya se ve que ...** it is obvious that ...; **si te vi no me acuerdo** they *etc* just don't want to know; **ya ~emos** we'll see
vera ['bera] *nf* edge, verge; (*de río*) bank; **a la ~ de** near, next to
veracidad [beraθi'ðað] *nf* truthfulness
veraneante [berane'ante] *nm/f* holidaymaker, (summer) vacationer (*US*)
veranear [berane'ar] *vi* to spend the summer
veraneo [bera'neo] *nm* summer holiday; **estar de ~** to be away on (one's summer) holiday; **lugar de ~** holiday resort
veraniego, -a [bera'njeɣo, a] *adj* summer *cpd*
verano [be'rano] *nm* summer
veras ['beras] *nfpl* truth *sg*; **de ~** really, truly; **esto va de ~** this is serious
veraz [be'raθ] *adj* truthful
verbal [ber'βal] *adj* verbal; (*mensaje etc*) oral
verbena [ber'βena] *nf* street party; (*baile*) open-air dance
verbo ['berβo] *nm* verb
verboso, -a [ber'βoso, a] *adj* verbose
verdad [ber'ðað] *nf* (*lo verídico*) truth; (*fiabilidad*) reliability ▷ *adv* really; **¿~?, ¿no es ~?** isn't it?, aren't you?, don't you? *etc*; **de ~** *adj* real, proper; **a decir ~, no quiero** to tell (you) the truth, I don't want to; **la pura ~** the plain truth
verdadero, -a [berða'ðero, a] *adj* (*veraz*) true, truthful; (*fiable*) reliable; (*fig*) real
verde ['berðe] *adj* green; (*fruta etc*) green, unripe; (*chiste etc*) blue, smutty, dirty ▷ *nm* green; **viejo ~** dirty old man; **poner ~ a algn** to give sb a dressing-down
verdear [berðe'ar], **verdecer** [berðe'θer] *vi* to turn green
verdor [ber'ðor] *nm* (*lo verde*) greenness; (*Bot*) verdure; (*fig*) youthful vigour
verdugo [ber'ðuɣo] *nm* executioner; (*Bot*) shoot; (*cardenal*) weal
verdulería [berðule'ria] *nf* greengrocer's (shop)
verdulero, -a [berðu'lero, a] *nm/f* greengrocer

verdura [ber'ðura] *nf* greenness; **verduras** *nfpl* (*Culin*) greens
vereda [be'reða] *nf* path; (*Am*) pavement, sidewalk (*US*); **meter a algn en ~** to bring sb into line
veredicto [bere'ðikto] *nm* verdict
vergel [ber'xel] *nm* lush garden
vergonzoso, -a [berɣon'θoso, a] *adj* shameful; (*tímido*) timid, bashful
vergüenza [ber'ɣwenθa] *nf* shame, sense of shame; (*timidez*) bashfulness; (*pudor*) modesty; **tener ~** to be ashamed; **me da ~ decírselo** I feel too shy *o* it embarrasses me to tell him; **¡qué ~!** (*de situación*) what a disgrace!; (*a persona*) shame on you!
verídico, -a [be'riðiko, a] *adj* true, truthful
verificar [berifi'kar] *vt* to check; (*corroborar*) to verify (*tb Inform*); (*testamento*) to prove; (*llevar a cabo*) to carry out; **verificarse** *vr* to occur, happen; (*mitin etc*) to be held; (*profecía etc*) to come *o* prove true
verja ['berxa] *nf* (*cancela*) iron gate; (*cerca*) railing(s) (*pl*); (*rejado*) grating
vermut [ber'mu] (*pl* **vermuts**) *nm* vermouth ▷ *nf* (*esp Am*) matinée
verosímil [bero'simil] *adj* likely, probable; (*relato*) credible
verruga [be'rruɣa] *nf* wart
versado, -a [ber'saðo, a] *adj*: **~ en** versed in
versátil [ber'satil] *adj* versatile
versión [ber'sjon] *nf* version; (*traducción*) translation
verso ['berso] *nm* verse; **un ~** a line of poetry; **~ libre/suelto** free/blank verse
vértebra ['berteβra] *nf* vertebra
vertebrado, -a [berte'βraðo, a] *adj, nm/f* vertebrate
vertebral [berte'βral] *adj* vertebral; **columna ~** spine
verter [ber'ter] *vt* (*vaciar*) to empty, pour (out); (*sin querer*) to spill; (*basura*) to dump ▷ *vi* to flow
vertical [berti'kal] *adj* vertical; (*postura, piano etc*) upright ▷ *nf* vertical
vértice ['bertiθe] *nm* vertex, apex
vertidos [ber'tiðos] *nmpl* waste *sg*
vertiente [ber'tjente] *nf* slope; (*fig*) aspect
vertiginoso, -a [bertixi'noso, a] *adj* giddy, dizzy
vértigo ['bertiɣo] *nm* vertigo; (*mareo*) dizziness; (*actividad*) intense activity; **de ~** (*fam: velocidad*) giddy; (*: ruido*) tremendous; (*: talento*) fantastic
vesícula [be'sikula] *nf* blister; **~ biliar** gall bladder
vespa® ['bespa] *nf* (motor) scooter
vespertino, -a [besper'tino, a] *adj* evening *cpd*
vespino® [bes'pino] *nm o f* ≈ moped
vestíbulo [bes'tiβulo] *nm* hall; (*de teatro*) foyer
vestido [bes'tiðo] *nm* (*ropa*) clothes *pl*, clothing; (*de mujer*) dress, frock
vestidor [besti'ðor] *nm* (*Am: Deporte*) changing (*Brit*) *o* locker (*US*) room
vestigio [bes'tixjo] *nm* (*trazo*) trace; (*señal*) sign; **vestigios** *nmpl* remains
vestimenta [besti'menta] *nf* clothing
vestir [bes'tir] *vt* (*poner: ropa*) to put on; (*llevar: ropa*) to wear; (*cubrir*) to clothe, cover; (*pagar: la ropa*) to clothe, pay for the clothing of; (*sastre*) to make clothes for ▷ *vi* (*ponerse: ropa*) to dress; (*verse bien*) to look good; **vestirse** *vr* to get dressed, dress o.s.; **traje de ~** (*formal*) formal suit; **estar vestido de** to be dressed *o* clad in; (*como disfraz*) to be dressed as
vestuario [bes'twarjo] *nm* clothes *pl*, wardrobe; (*Teat: para actores*) dressing room; (*: para público*) cloakroom; (*Deporte*) changing room
veta ['beta] *nf* (*vena*) vein, seam; (*raya*) streak; (*de madera*) grain
vetar [be'tar] *vt* to veto
veterano, -a [bete'rano, a] *adj, nm/f* veteran
veterinario, -a [beteri'narjo, a] *nm/f* vet(erinary surgeon) ▷ *nf* veterinary science
veto ['beto] *nm* veto
vetusto, -a [be'tusto, a] *adj* ancient
vez [beθ] *nf* time; (*turno*) turn; **a la ~ que** at the same time as; **a su ~** in its turn; **cada ~ más/menos** more and more/less and less; **una ~** once; **dos veces** twice; **de una ~** in one go; **de una ~ para siempre** once and for all; **en ~ de** instead of; **a veces** sometimes; **otra ~** again; **una y otra ~** repeatedly; **muchas veces** (*con frecuencia*) often; **pocas veces** seldom; **de ~ en cuando** from time to time; **7 veces 9** 7 times 9; **hacer las veces de** to stand in for; **tal ~** perhaps; **¿lo viste alguna ~?** did you ever see it?; **¿cuántas veces?** how often?; **érase una ~** once upon a time (there was)
vía ['bia] *nf* (*calle*) road; (*ruta*) track, route; (*Ferro*) line; (*fig*) way; (*Anat*) passage, tube ▷ *prep* via, by way of; **por ~ bucal** orally; **por ~ judicial** by legal means; **por ~ oficial** through official channels; **por ~ de** by way of; **en ~s de** in the process of; **un país en ~s de desarrollo** a developing country; **~ aérea** airway; **V~ Láctea** Milky Way; **~ pública** public highway *o* thoroughfare; **~ única** one-way street; **el tren está en la ~ 8** the train is (standing) at platform 8
viable ['bjaβle] *adj* (*Com*) viable; (*plan etc*) feasible
viaducto [bja'ðukto] *nm* viaduct
viajante [bja'xante] *nm* commercial traveller, traveling salesman (*US*)
viajar [bja'xar] *vi* to travel, journey
viaje ['bjaxe] *nm* journey; (*gira*) tour; (*Naut*) voyage; (*Com: carga*) load; **los ~s** travel *sg*; **estar de ~** to be on a journey; **~ de ida y vuelta** round trip; **~ de novios** honeymoon

viajero, -a [bja'xero, a] *adj* travelling (*Brit*), traveling (*US*); (*Zool*) migratory ▷ *nm/f* (*quien viaja*) traveller; (*pasajero*) passenger
vial [bjal] *adj* road *cpd*, traffic *cpd*
víbora ['biβora] *nf* viper; (*Am: venenoso*) poisonous snake
vibración [biβra'θjon] *nf* vibration
vibrador [biβra'ðor] *nm* vibrator
vibrante [bi'βrante] *adj* vibrant, vibrating
vibrar [bi'βrar] *vt* to vibrate ▷ *vi* to vibrate; (*pulsar*) to throb, beat, pulsate
vicario [bi'karjo] *nm* curate
vicegerente [biθexe'rente] *nm/f* assistant manager
vicepresidente [biθepresi'ðente] *nm/f* vice president; (*de comité etc*) vice-chairman
viceversa [biθe'βersa] *adv* vice versa
viciado, -a [bi'θjaðo, a] *adj* (*corrompido*) corrupt; (*contaminado*) foul, contaminated
viciar [bi'θjar] *vt* (*pervertir*) to pervert; (*adulterar*) to adulterate; (*falsificar*) to falsify; (*Jur*) to nullify; (*estropear*) to spoil; (*sentido*) to twist; **viciarse** *vr* to become corrupted; (*aire, agua*) to be(come) polluted
vicio ['biθjo] *nm* (*libertinaje*) vice; (*mala costumbre*) bad habit; (*mimo*) spoiling; (*alabeo*) warp, warping; **de** *o* **por ~** out of sheer habit
vicioso, -a [bi'θjoso, a] *adj* (*muy malo*) vicious; (*corrompido*) depraved; (*mimado*) spoiled ▷ *nm/f* depraved person; (*adicto*) addict
vicisitud [biθisi'tuð] *nf* vicissitude
víctima ['biktima] *nf* victim; (*de accidente etc*) casualty
victoria [bik'torja] *nf* victory
victorioso, -a [bikto'rjoso, a] *adj* victorious
vicuña [bi'kuɲa] *nf* vicuna
vid [bið] *nf* vine
vida ['biða] *nf* life; (*duración*) lifetime; (*modo de vivir*) way of life; **¡~!, ¡~ mía!** (*saludo cariñoso*) my love!; **de por ~** for life; **de ~ airada** *o* **libre** loose-living; **en la/mi ~** never; **estar con ~** to be still alive; **ganarse la ~** to earn one's living; **¡esto es ~!** this is the life!; **le va la ~ en esto** his life depends on it
vidente [bi'ðente] *nm/f* (*adivino*) clairvoyant; (*no ciego*) sighted person
vídeo ['biðeo] *nm* video; (*aparato*) video (recorder); **cinta de ~** videotape; **película de ~** videofilm; **grabar en ~** to record, (video) tape; **~ compuesto/inverso** (*Inform*) composite/reverse video
videoblog [biðeo'bloɣ] *nm* videoblog
videocámara [biðeo'kamara] *nf* video camera; (*pequeña*) camcorder
videocasete, videocassette [biðeoka'set] *nm* video cassette
videoclip [biðeo'klip] *nm* (music) video
videoclub [biðeo'klub] *nm* video club; (*tienda*) video shop
videojuego [biðeo'xweɣo] *nm* video game
videollamada [biðeoʎa'mada] *nf* video call
videoteléfono [biðeote'lefono] *nf* videophone
vidriero, -a [bi'ðrjero, a] *nm/f* glazier ▷ *nf* (*ventana*) stained-glass window; (*Am: de tienda*) shop window; (*puerta*) glass door
vidrio ['biðrjo] *nm* glass; (*Am*) window; **~ cilindrado/inastillable** plate/splinter-proof glass
vidrioso, -a [bi'ðrjoso, a] *adj* glassy; (*frágil*) fragile, brittle; (*resbaladizo*) slippery
vieira ['bjeira] *nf* scallop
viejo, -a ['bjexo, a] *adj* old ▷ *nm/f* old man/woman; **mi ~/vieja** (*fam*) my old man/woman; **hacerse** *o* **ponerse ~** to grow *o* get old
Viena ['bjena] *nf* Vienna
viene *etc* ['bjene] *vb ver* **venir**
vienés, -esa [bje'nes, esa] *adj, nm/f* Viennese
viento ['bjento] *nm* wind; **hacer ~** to be windy; **contra ~ y marea** at all costs; **ir ~ en popa** to go splendidly; (*negocio*) to prosper
vientre ['bjentre] *nm* belly; (*matriz*) womb; **vientres** *nmpl* bowels; **hacer de ~** to have a movement of the bowels
viernes ['bjernes] *nm inv* Friday; **V~ Santo** Good Friday; *ver tb* **Semana Santa**; **sábado**
Vietnam [bjet'nam] *nm*: **el ~** Vietnam
vietnamita [bjetna'mita] *adj, nm/f* Vietnamese
viga ['biɣa] *nf* beam, rafter; (*de metal*) girder
vigencia [bi'xenθja] *nf* validity; (*de contrato etc*) term, life; **estar/entrar en ~** to be in/come into effect *o* force
vigente [bi'xente] *adj* valid, in force; (*imperante*) prevailing
vigésimo, -a [bi'xesimo, a] *num* twentieth
vigía [bi'xia] *nm* look-out ▷ *nf* (*atalaya*) watchtower; (*acción*) watching
vigilancia [bixi'lanθja] *nf* vigilance; **tener a algn bajo ~** to keep watch on sb
vigilante [bixi'lante] *adj* vigilant ▷ *nm* caretaker; (*en cárcel*) warder; (*en almacén*) shopwalker (*Brit*), floor-walker (*US*); **~ jurado** security guard (*licensed to carry a gun*); **~ nocturno** night watchman
vigilar [bixi'lar] *vt* to watch over; (*cuidar*) to look after, keep an eye on ▷ *vi* to be vigilant; (*hacer guardia*) to keep watch; **~ por** to take care of
vigilia [vi'xilja] *nf* wakefulness; (*Rel*) vigil; fast; **comer de ~** to fast
vigor [bi'ɣor] *nm* vigour, vitality; **en ~** in force; **entrar/poner en ~** to come/put into effect
vigoroso, -a [biɣo'roso, a] *adj* vigorous
VIH *nm abr* (= *virus de inmunodeficiencia humana*) HIV; **~ negativo/positivo** HIV-negative/-positive
vil [bil] *adj* vile, low
vileza [bi'leθa] *nf* vileness; (*acto*) base deed
vilipendiar [bilipen'djar] *vt* to vilify, revile
villa ['biʎa] *nf* (*casa*) villa; (*pueblo*) small town; (*municipalidad*) municipality; **la V~** (*Esp*) Madrid; **~ miseria** shanty town

villancico [biʎan'θiko] *nm* (Christmas) carol
villorrio [bi'ʎorrjo] *nm* one-horse town, dump; (*Am*: *barrio pobre*) shanty town
vilo ['bilo]: **en ~** *adv* in the air, suspended; (*fig*) on tenterhooks, in suspense; **estar** *o* **quedar en ~** to be left in suspense
vinagre [bi'naɣre] *nm* vinegar
vinagrera [bina'ɣrera] *nf* vinegar bottle; **vinagreras** *nfpl* cruet stand *sg*
vinagreta [bina'ɣreta] *nf* vinaigrette, French dressing
vinculación [binkula'θjon] *nf* (*lazo*) link, bond; (*acción*) linking
vincular [binku'lar] *vt* to link, bind
vínculo ['binkulo] *nm* link, bond
vine *etc vb ver* **venir**
vinicultor, -a [binikul'tor, a] *nm/f* wine grower
vinicultura [binikul'tura] *nf* wine growing
viniera *etc vb ver* **venir**
vino ['bino] *vb ver* **venir** ▷ *nm* wine; **~ de solera/seco/tinto** vintage/dry/red wine; **~ de Jerez** sherry; **~ de Oporto** port (wine)
viña ['biɲa] *nf*, **viñedo** [bi'ɲeðo] *nm* vineyard
viñeta [bi'ɲeta] *nf* (*en historieta*) cartoon
viola ['bjola] *nf* viola
violación [bjola'θjon] *nf* violation; (*Jur*) offence, infringement; (*estupro*): **~ (sexual)** rape; **~ de contrato** (*Com*) breach of contract
violar [bjo'lar] *vt* to violate; (*Jur*) to infringe; (*cometer estupro*) to rape
violencia [bjo'lenθja] *nf* (*fuerza*) violence, force; (*embarazo*) embarrassment; (*acto injusto*) unjust act
violentar [bjolen'tar] *vt* to force; (*casa*) to break into; (*agredir*) to assault; (*violar*) to violate
violento, -a [bjo'lento, a] *adj* violent; (*furioso*) furious; (*situación*) embarrassing; (*acto*) forced, unnatural; (*difícil*) awkward; **me es muy ~** it goes against the grain with me
violeta [bjo'leta] *nf* violet
violín [bjo'lin] *nm* violin
violón [bjo'lon] *nm* double bass
viraje [bi'raxe] *nm* turn; (*de vehículo*) swerve; (*de carretera*) bend; (*fig*) change of direction
virar [bi'rar] *vi* to turn; to swerve; to change direction
virgen ['birxen] *adj* virgin; (*cinta*) blank ▷ *nm/f* virgin; **la Santísima V~** (*Rel*) the Blessed Virgin
virginidad [birxini'ðað] *nf* virginity
Virgo ['birɣo] *nm* Virgo
viril [bi'ril] *adj* virile
virilidad [birili'ðað] *nf* virility
virtual [bir'twal] *adj* (*real*) virtual; (*en potencia*) potential
virtud [bir'tuð] *nf* virtue; **en ~ de** by virtue of
virtuoso, -a [bir'twoso, a] *adj* virtuous ▷ *nm/f* virtuoso
viruela [bi'rwela] *nf* smallpox; **viruelas** *nfpl* pockmarks; **~s locas** chickenpox *sg*
virulento, -a [biru'lento, a] *adj* virulent
virus ['birus] *nm inv* virus
visa ['bisa] *nf*, (*Am*) **visado** [bi'saðo] *nm* visa; **~ de permanencia** residence permit
víscera ['bisθera] *nf* internal organ; **vísceras** *nfpl* entrails
visceral [bisθe'ral] *adj* (*odio*) deep-rooted; **reacción ~** gut reaction
viscoso, -a [bis'koso, a] *adj* viscous
visera [bi'sera] *nf* visor
visibilidad [bisiβili'ðað] *nf* visibility
visible [bi'siβle] *adj* visible; (*fig*) obvious; **exportaciones/importaciones ~s** (*Com*) visible exports/imports
visillo [bi'siʎo] *nm* lace curtain
visión [bi'sjon] *nf* (*Anat*) vision, (eye)sight; (*fantasía*) vision, fantasy; (*panorama*) view; **ver visiones** to see *o* be seeing things
visionario, -a [bisjo'narjo, a] *adj* (*que prevé*) visionary; (*alucinado*) deluded ▷ *nm/f* visionary; (*chalado*) lunatic
visita [bi'sita] *nf* call, visit; (*persona*) visitor; **horas/tarjeta de ~** visiting hours/card; **~ de cortesía/de cumplido/de despedida** courtesy/formal/farewell visit; **hacer una ~** to pay a visit; **ir de ~** to go visiting
visitante [bisi'tante] *adj* visiting ▷ *nm/f* visitor
visitar [bisi'tar] *vt* to visit, call on; (*inspeccionar*) to inspect
vislumbrar [bislum'brar] *vt* to glimpse, catch a glimpse of
vislumbre [bis'lumbre] *nf* glimpse; (*centelleo*) gleam; (*idea vaga*) glimmer
viso ['biso] *nm* (*de metal*) glint, gleam; (*de tela*) sheen; (*aspecto*) appearance; **hay un ~ de verdad en esto** there is an element of truth in this
visón [bi'son] *nm* mink
visor [bi'sor] *nm* (*Foto*) viewfinder
víspera ['bispera] *nf* day before; **la ~** *o* **en ~s de** on the eve of
vista ['bista] *nf* sight, vision; (*capacidad de ver*) (eye)sight; (*mirada*) look(s) (*pl*); (*Foto etc*) view; (*Jur*) hearing ▷ *nm* customs officer; **a primera ~** at first glance; **~ general** overview; **fijar** *o* **clavar la ~ en** to stare at; **hacer la ~ gorda** to turn a blind eye; **volver la ~** to look back; **está a la ~ que** it's obvious that; **a la ~** (*Com*) at sight; **en ~ de** in view of; **en ~ de que** in view of the fact that; **¡hasta la ~!** so long!, see you!; **con ~s a** with a view to; *ver tb* **visto, a**
vistazo [bis'taθo] *nm* glance; **dar** *o* **echar un ~ a** to glance at
visto, -a *etc* ['bisto, a] *vb ver* **vestir** ▷ *pp de* **ver** ▷ *adj* seen; (*considerado*) considered ▷ *nm*: **~ bueno** approval; **"~ bueno"** "approved"; **por lo ~** apparently; **dar el ~ bueno a algo** to give sth the go-ahead; **está ~ que** it's clear

that; **está bien/mal** ~ it's acceptable/ unacceptable; **está muy** ~ it is very common; **estaba** ~ it had to be; ~ **que** *conj* since, considering that
vistoso, -a [bis'toso, a] *adj* colourful; (*alegre*) gay; (*pey*) gaudy
visual [bi'swal] *adj* visual
vital [bi'tal] *adj* life *cpd*, living *cpd*; (*fig*) vital; (*persona*) lively, vivacious
vitalicio, -a [bita'liθjo, a] *adj* for life
vitalidad [bitali'ðað] *nf* vitality; (*de persona, negocio*) energy; (*de ciudad*) liveliness
vitamina [bita'mina] *nf* vitamin
viticultor, a [bitikul'tor, a] *nm/f* vine grower
viticultura [bitikul'tura] *nf* vine growing
vitorear [bitore'ar] *vt* to cheer, acclaim
vítores ['bitores] *nmpl* cheers
vítreo, -a ['bitreo, a] *adj* vitreous
vitrina [bi'trina] *nf* glass case; (*en casa*) display cabinet; (*Am*) shop window
vituperio [bitu'perjo] *nm* (*condena*) condemnation; (*censura*) censure; (*insulto*) insult
viudo, -a ['bjuðo, a] *adj* widowed ▷ *nm* widower ▷ *nf* widow
viva ['biβa] *excl* hurrah! ▷ *nm* cheer; **¡~ el rey!** long live the King!
vivacidad [biβaθi'ðað] *nf* (*vigor*) vigour; (*vida*) vivacity
vivaracho, -a [biβa'ratʃo, a] *adj* jaunty, lively; (*ojos*) bright, twinkling
vivaz [bi'βaθ] *adj* (*que dura*) enduring; (*vigoroso*) vigorous; (*vivo*) lively
vivencia [bi'βenθja] *nf* experience
víveres ['biβeres] *nmpl* provisions
vivero [bi'βero] *nm* (*Horticultura*) nursery; (*para peces*) fishpond; (: *Com*) fish farm; (*fig*) hotbed
viveza [bi'βeθa] *nf* liveliness; (*agudeza*: *mental*) sharpness
vivienda [bi'βjenda] *nf* (*alojamiento*) housing; (*morada*) dwelling; **~s protegidas** *o* **sociales** council housing *sg* (*Brit*), public housing *sg* (*US*); (*una vivienda*) house; (*piso*) flat (*Brit*), apartment (*US*)
viviente [bi'βjente] *adj* living
vivir [bi'βir] *vt* (*experimentar*) to live *o* go through ▷ *vi* (*gen, Com*): ~ **(de)** to live (by, off, on) ▷ *nm* life, living; **¡viva!** hurray!; **¡viva el rey!** long live the king!
vivo, -a ['biβo, a] *adj* living, live, alive; (*fig*) vivid; (*movimiento*) quick; (*color*) bright; (*protesta*) strong; (*persona*: *astuto*) smart, clever; **en** ~ (*TV etc*) live; **llegar a lo** ~ to cut to the quick
V.O. *abr* = **versión original**
vocablo [bo'kaβlo] *nm* (*palabra*) word; (*término*) term
vocabulario [bokaβu'larjo] *nm* vocabulary, word list
vocación [boka'θjon] *nf* vocation
vocacional [bokasjo'nal] *nf* (*Am*) ≈ technical college
vocal [bo'kal] *adj* vocal ▷ *nm/f* member (of a committee *etc*) ▷ *nm* non-executive director ▷ *nf* vowel
vocalizar [bokali'θar] *vt* to vocalize
vocear [boθe'ar] *vt* (*para vender*) to cry; (*aclamar*) to acclaim; (*fig*) to proclaim ▷ *vi* to yell
vocerío [boθe'rio] *nm* shouting; (*escándalo*) hullabaloo
vocero, -a [bo'θero, a] *nm/f* (*Am*) spokesman/ woman
voces ['boθes] *pl de* **voz**
vociferar [boθife'rar] *vt* to shout; (*jactarse*) to proclaim boastfully ▷ *vi* to yell
vodka ['boðka] *nm* vodka
vol *abr* = **volumen**
volado, -a [bo'laðo, a] *adj*: **estar** ~ (*fam*: *inquieto*) to be worried; (: *loco*) to be crazy ▷ *adv* (*Am*) in a rush, hastily
volador, a [bola'ðor, a] *adj* flying
volandas [bo'landas]: **en** ~ *adv* in o through the air; (*fig*) swiftly
volante [bo'lante] *adj* flying ▷ *nm* (*de máquina, coche*) steering wheel; (*de reloj*) balance; (*nota*) note; **ir al** ~ to be at the wheel, be driving
volar [bo'lar] *vt* (*demoler*) to blow up, demolish ▷ *vi* to fly; (*fig*: *correr*) to rush, hurry; (*fam*: *desaparecer*) to disappear; **voy volando** I must dash; **¡cómo vuela el tiempo!** how time flies!
volátil [bo'latil] *adj* volatile; (*fig*) changeable
volcán [bol'kan] *nm* volcano
volcánico, -a [bol'kaniko, a] *adj* volcanic
volcar [bol'kar] *vt* to upset, overturn; (*tumbar, derribar*) to knock over; (*vaciar*) to empty out ▷ *vi* to overturn; **volcarse** *vr* to tip over; (*barco*) to capsize
voleibol [bolei'βol] *nm* volleyball
volqué [bol'ke], **volquemos** *etc* [bol'kemos] *vb ver* **volcar**
volquete [bol'kete] *nm* dumper, dump truck (*US*)
voltaje [bol'taxe] *nm* voltage
voltear [bolte'ar] *vt* to turn over; (*volcar*) to knock over; (*doblar*) to peal ▷ *vi* to roll over; **voltearse** *vr* (*Am*) to turn round; ~ **a hacer algo** (*Am*) to do sth again
voltereta [bolte'reta] *nf* somersault; ~ **sobre las manos** handspring; ~ **lateral** cartwheel
voltio ['boltjo] *nm* volt
voluble [bo'luβle] *adj* fickle
volumen [bo'lumen] *nm* volume; ~ **monetario** money supply; ~ **de negocios** turnover; **bajar el** ~ to turn down the volume; **poner la radio a todo** ~ to turn the radio up full
voluminoso, -a [bolumi'noso, a] *adj* voluminous; (*enorme*) massive
voluntad [bolun'tað] *nf* will, willpower; (*deseo*) desire, wish; (*afecto*) fondness; **a** ~

at will; (*cantidad*) as much as one likes; **buena ~** goodwill; **mala ~** ill will, malice; **por causas ajenas a mi ~** for reasons beyond my control

voluntario, -a [bolun'tarjo, a] *adj* voluntary ▷ *nm/f* volunteer

voluntarioso, -a [bolunta'rjoso, a] *adj* headstrong

voluptuoso, -a [bolup'twoso, a] *adj* voluptuous

volver [bol'βer] *vt* to turn; (*boca abajo*) to turn (over); (*voltear*) to turn round, turn upside down; (*poner del revés*) to turn inside out; (*devolver*) to return; (*transformar*) to change, transform; (*manga*) to roll up ▷ *vi* to return, go/come back; **volverse** *vr* to turn round; (*llegar a ser*) to become; **~ la espalda** to turn one's back; **~ bien por mal** to return good for evil; **~ a hacer** to do again; **~ en sí** to come to *o* round, regain consciousness; **~ la vista atrás** to look back; **~ triste** *etc* **a algn** to make sb sad *etc*; **~ loco a algn** to drive sb mad; **~se loco** to go mad

vomitar [bomi'tar] *vt, vi* to vomit

vómito ['bomito] *nm* (*acto*) vomiting; (*resultado*) vomit

voracidad [boraθi'ðað] *nf* voracity

voraz [bo'raθ] *adj* voracious; (*fig*) fierce

vórtice ['bortiθe] *nm* whirlpool; (*de aire*) whirlwind

vos [bos] *pron* (*Am*) you

vosotros, -as [bo'sotros, as] *pron* you *pl*; (*reflexivo*) yourselves; **entre ~** among yourselves

votación [bota'θjon] *nf* (*acto*) voting; (*voto*) vote; **~ a mano alzada** show of hands; **someter algo a ~** to put sth to the vote

votar [bo'tar] *vt* (*Pol*: *partido etc*) to vote for; (*proyecto*: *aprobar*) to pass; (*Rel*) to vow ▷ *vi* to vote

voto ['boto] *nm* vote; (*promesa*) vow; (*maldición*) oath, curse; **votos** *nmpl* (good) wishes; **~ de bloque/de grupo** block/card vote; **~ de censura/de (des)confianza/de gracias** vote of censure/(no) confidence/thanks; **dar su ~** to cast one's vote

voy [boi] *vb ver* **ir**

voz [boθ] *nf* voice; (*grito*) shout; (*chisme*) rumour; (*Ling*: *palabra*) word; (*: forma*) voice; **dar voces** to shout, yell; **llamar a algn a voces** to shout to sb; **llevar la ~ cantante** (*fig*) to be the boss; **tener la ~ tomada** to be hoarse; **tener ~ y voto** to have the right to speak; **en ~ baja** in a low voice; **a ~ en cuello** *o* **en grito** at the top of one's voice; **de viva ~** verbally; **en ~ alta** aloud; **~ de mando** command

vuelco *etc* ['bwelko] *vb ver* **volcar** ▷ *nm* spill, overturning; (*fig*) collapse; **mi corazón dio un ~** my heart missed a beat

vuelo ['bwelo] *vb ver* **volar** ▷ *nm* flight; (*encaje*) lace, frill; (*de falda etc*) loose part; (*fig*) importance; **de altos ~s** (*fig*: *plan*) grandiose; (*: persona*) ambitious; **alzar el ~** to take flight; (*fig*) to dash off; **coger al ~** to catch in flight; **~ de bajo coste** low-cost flight; **~ en picado** dive; **~ libre** hang-gliding; **~ regular** scheduled flight; **falda de mucho ~** full *o* wide skirt

vuelque *etc* ['bwelke] *vb ver* **volcar**

vuelta ['bwelta] *nf* turn; (*curva*) bend, curve; (*regreso*) return; (*revolución*) revolution; (*paseo*) stroll; (*circuito*) lap; (*de papel, tela*) reverse; (*de pantalón*) turn-up (*Brit*), cuff (*US*); (*cambio*) change; **~ a empezar** back to square one; **~ al mundo** world trip; **~ ciclista** (*Deporte*) (cycle) tour; **V~ de Francia** Tour de France; **~ cerrada** hairpin bend; **a la ~** (*Esp*) on one's return; **a la ~ de la esquina, a la ~** (*Am*) round the corner; **a ~ de correo** by return of post; **dar ~s** to turn, revolve; (*cabeza*) to spin; **dar(se) la ~** (*volverse*) to turn round; **dar ~s a una idea** to turn over an idea (in one's mind); **dar una ~** to go for a walk; (*en coche*) to go for a drive; **dar media ~** (*Auto*) to do a U-turn; (*fam*) to beat it; **estar de ~** (*fam*) to be back; **poner a algn de ~ y media** to heap abuse on sb; **no tiene ~ de hoja** there's no alternative

vuelto ['bwelto] *pp de* **volver** ▷ *nm* (*Am*: *moneda*) change

vuelvo *etc* ['bwelβo] *vb ver* **volver**

vuestro, -a ['bwestro, a] *adj* your; (*después de n*) of yours ▷ *pron*: **el ~/la vuestra/los ~s/las vuestras** yours; **lo ~** (what is) yours; **un amigo ~** a friend of yours; **una idea vuestra** an idea of yours

vulgar [bul'ɣar] *adj* (*ordinario*) vulgar; (*común*) common

vulgaridad [bulɣari'ðað] *nf* commonness; (*acto*) vulgarity; (*expresión*) coarse expression; **vulgaridades** *nfpl* banalities

vulgarizar [bulɣari'θar] *vt* to popularize

vulgo ['bulɣo] *nm* common people

vulnerable [bulne'raβle] *adj* vulnerable

vulnerar [bulne'rar] *vt* (*Jur, Com*) to violate; (*derechos*) to violate, to interfere with; (*reputación*) to harm, damage

vulva ['bulβa] *nf* vulva

W X

walkie-talkie [walki'talki] *nm* walkie-talkie
walkman® ['wal(k)man] *nm* Walkman®
wáter ['bater] *nm* (*taza*) toilet; (*Am: lugar*) toilet (*Brit*), rest room (*US*)
waterpolo [water'polo] *nm* waterpolo
web [web] *nm o nf* (*página*) website; (*red*) (World Wide) Web
webserie [web'serje] *nf* webseries
web site ['websait] *nm* website
webcam ['webkam] *nf* webcam
webmaster ['webmaster] *nm/f* webmaster
website ['websait] *nm* website
western ['western] (*pl* **westerns**) *nm* western
whisky ['wiski] *nm* whisky
wifi ['waifai] *nm* Wi-Fi
wiki ['wiki] *nf* wiki
windsurf ['winsurf] *nm* windsurfing; **hacer ~** to go windsurfing

xenofobia [seno'foβja] *nf* xenophobia
xenófobo, -a [se'nofoβo, a] *adj* xenophobic ▷ *nm/f* xenophobe
xerografía [seroɣra'fia] *nf* xerography
xilófono [si'lofono] *nm* xylophone
xocoyote, -a [ksoko'jote, a] *nm/f* (*Am*) baby of the family, youngest child

Y

y [i] *conj* and; (*Am fam*: *pues*) well; (*hora*): **la una y cinco** five past one; **¿y eso?** why?, how so?; **¿y los demás?** what about the others?; **y bueno ...** (*Am*) well ...
ya [ja] *adv* (*gen*) already; (*ahora*) now; (*en seguida*) at once; (*pronto*) soon ▷ *excl* all right!; (*por supuesto*) of course! ▷ *conj* (*ahora que*) now that; **ya no** not any more, no longer; **ya lo sé** I know; **ya dice que sí, ya dice que no** first he says yes, then he says no; **¡ya, ya!** yes, yes!; (*con impaciencia*) all right!, O.K.!; **¡ya está bien!** that's (quite) enough!; **¡ya voy!** (*enfático*: *no se suele traducir*) coming!; **ya que** since
yacer [ja'θer] *vi* to lie
yacimiento [jaθi'mjento] *nm* bed, deposit; (*arqueológico*) site; **~ petrolífero** oilfield
yanqui ['janki] *adj* Yankee ▷ *nm/f* Yank, Yankee
yate ['jate] *nm* yacht
yazco *etc* ['jaθko] *vb ver* **yacer**
yedra ['jeðra] *nf* ivy
yegua ['jeɣwa] *nf* mare
yema ['jema] *nf* (*del huevo*) yolk; (*Bot*) leaf bud; (*fig*) best part; **~ del dedo** fingertip
yermo, -a ['jermo, a] *adj* barren; (*de gente*) uninhabited ▷ *nm* waste land
yerno ['jerno] *nm* son-in-law
yerto, -a ['jerto, a] *adj* stiff
yesca ['jeska] *nf* tinder
yeso ['jeso] *nm* (*Geo*) gypsum; (*Arq*) plaster
yo [jo] *pron personal* I; **soy yo** it's me, it is I; **yo que tú/usted** if I were you
yodo ['joðo] *nm* iodine
yoga ['joɣa] *nm* yoga
yogur [jo'ɣur], **yogurt** [jo'ɣurt] *nm* yogurt
yuca ['juka] *nf* (*Bot*) yucca; (*alimento*) cassava, manioc root
yudo ['juðo] *nm* judo
yugo ['juɣo] *nm* yoke
Yugoslavia [juɣos'laβja] *nf* Yugoslavia
yugular [juɣu'lar] *adj* jugular
yunque ['junke] *nm* anvil
yunta ['junta] *nf* yoke
yuntero [jun'tero] *nm* ploughman
yute ['jute] *nm* jute
yuxtaponer [jukstapo'ner] *vt* to juxtapose
yuxtaposición [jukstaposi'θjon] *nf* juxtaposition
yuyo ['jujo] *nm* (*Am*: *mala hierba*) weed

Z

zafar [θa'far] *vt* (*soltar*) to untie; (*superficie*) to clear; **zafarse** *vr* (*escaparse*) to escape; (*ocultarse*) to hide o.s. away; (*Tec*) to slip off; **~se de** (*persona*) to get away from
zafio, -a ['θafjo, a] *adj* coarse
zafiro [θa'firo] *nm* sapphire
zaga ['θaɣa] *nf* rear; **a la ~** behind, in the rear
zagal [θa'ɣal] *nm* boy, lad
zaguán [θa'ɣwan] *nm* hallway
zaherir [θae'rir] *vt* (*criticar*) to criticize; (*fig: herir*) to wound
zaino, -a ['θaino, a] *adj* (*color de caballo*) chestnut; (*pérfido*) treacherous; (*animal*) vicious
zalamería [θalame'ria] *nf* flattery
zalamero, -a [θala'mero, a] *adj* flattering; (*relamido*) suave
zamarra [θa'marra] *nf* (*piel*) sheepskin; (*chaqueta*) sheepskin jacket
zambullirse [θambu'ʎirse] *vr* to dive; (*ocultarse*) to hide o.s.
zampar [θam'par] *vt* (*esconder*) to hide *o* put away (hurriedly); (*comer*) to gobble; (*arrojar*) to hurl ▷ *vi* to eat voraciously; **zamparse** *vr* (*chocar*) to bump; (*fig*) to gatecrash
zanahoria [θana'orja] *nf* carrot
zancada [θan'kaða] *nf* stride
zancadilla [θanka'ðiʎa] *nf* trip; (*fig*) stratagem; **echar la ~ a algn** to trip sb up
zanco ['θanko] *nm* stilt
zancudo, -a [θan'kuðo, a] *adj* long-legged ▷ *nm* (*Am*) mosquito
zángano ['θangano] *nm* drone; (*holgazán*) idler, slacker
zanja ['θanxa] *nf* (*fosa*) ditch; (*tumba*) grave
zanjar [θan'xar] *vt* (*fosa*) to ditch, trench; (*problema*) to surmount; (*conflicto*) to resolve
zapata [θa'pata] *nf* half-boot; (*Mecánica*) shoe
zapatear [θapate'ar] *vt* (*tocar*) to tap with one's foot; (*patear*) to kick; (*fam*) to ill-treat ▷ *vi* to tap with one's feet
zapatería [θapate'ria] *nf* (*oficio*) shoemaking; (*tienda*) shoe-shop; (*fábrica*) shoe factory
zapatero, -a [θapa'tero, a] *nm/f* shoemaker; **~ remendón** cobbler
zapatilla [θapa'tiʎa] *nf* slipper; (*Tec*) washer; (*de deporte*) training shoe
zapato [θa'pato] *nm* shoe
zapping ['θapin] *nm* channel-hopping; **hacer ~** to channel-hop, flick through the channels
zar [θar] *nm* tsar, czar
zarandear [θarande'ar] *vt* to sieve; (*fam*) to shake vigorously
zarpa ['θarpa] *nf* (*garra*) claw, paw; **echar la ~ a** to claw at; (*fam*) to grab
zarpar [θar'par] *vi* to weigh anchor
zarpazo [θar'paθo] *nm*: **dar un ~** to claw
zarza ['θarθa] *nf* (*Bot*) bramble
zarzal [θar'θal] *nm* (*matorral*) bramble patch
zarzamora [θarθa'mora] *nf* blackberry
zarzuela [θar'θwela] *nf* Spanish light opera; **la Z~** *home of the Spanish Royal Family*
zigzag [θiɣ'θaɣ] *adj* zigzag
zigzaguear [θiɣθaɣe'ar] *vi* to zigzag
zinc [θink] *nm* zinc
zíper ['siper] *nm* (*Am*) zip, zipper (*US*)
zócalo ['θokalo] *nm* (*Arq*) plinth, base; (*de pared*) skirting board
zoclo ['θoklo] *nm* (*Am*) skirting board (*Brit*), baseboard (*US*)
zoco ['θoko] *nm* (Arab) market, souk
zodíaco [θo'ðiako] *nm* zodiac; **signo del ~** star sign
zona ['θona] *nf* zone; **~ cero** Ground Zero; **~ euro** Eurozone; **los países de la ~ euro** the Eurozone countries; **~ fronteriza** border area; **~ del dólar** (*Com*) dollar area; **~ de fomento** *o* **de desarrollo** development area; **~ roja** (*Am*) red-light district
zonzo, -a ['θonθo, a] (*Am*) *adj* silly ▷ *nm/f* fool
zoo ['θoo] *nm* zoo
zoología [θoolo'xia] *nf* zoology
zoológico, -a [θoo'loxiko, a] *adj* zoological ▷ *nm* (*tb*: **parque ~**) zoo
zoólogo, -a [θo'oloɣo, a] *nm/f* zoologist
zoom [θum] *nm* zoom lens
zopenco, -a [θo'penko, a] (*fam*) *adj* dull, stupid ▷ *nm/f* clot, nitwit
zopilote [θopi'lote] *nm* (*Am*) buzzard
zoquete [θo'kete] *nm* (*de madera*) block; (*de pan*) crust; (*fam*) blockhead
zorro, -a ['θorro, a] *adj* crafty ▷ *nm/f* fox/vixen ▷ *nf* (*fam*) whore, tart, hooker (*US*)

zozobra [θo'θoβra] *nf* (*fig*) anxiety
zozobrar [θoθo'βrar] *vi* (*hundirse*) to capsize; (*fig*) to fail
zueco ['θweko] *nm* clog
zumbar [θum'bar] *vt* (*burlar*) to tease; (*golpear*) to hit ▷ *vi* to buzz; (*fam*) to be very close; **zumbarse** *vr*: **~se de** to tease; **me zumban los oídos** I have a buzzing *o* ringing in my ears
zumbido [θum'biðo] *nm* buzzing; (*fam*) punch; **~ de oídos** buzzing *o* ringing in the ears
zumo ['θumo] *nm* juice; (*ganancia*) profit; **~ de naranja** (fresh) orange juice
zurcir [θur'θir] *vt* (*coser*) to darn; (*fig*) to put together; **¡que las zurzan!** to blazes with them!
zurdo, -a ['θurðo, a] *adj* (*mano*) left; (*persona*) left-handed
zurrar [θu'rrar] *vt* (*Tec*) to dress; (*fam: pegar duro*) to wallop; (*: aplastar*) to flatten; (*: criticar*) to criticize harshly
zurrón [θu'rron] *nm* pouch
zutano, -a [θu'tano, a] *nm/f* so-and-so

a

A, a [eɪ] *n* (*letter*) A, a; (*Scol*: *mark*) ≈ sobresaliente; (*Mus*): **A** la *m*; **A for Andrew**, (*US*) **A for Able** A de Antonio; **A road** *n* (*Brit Aut*) ≈ carretera nacional

KEYWORD

a [ə] *indef art* (*before vowel and silent h* **an**) **1** un(a); **a book** un libro; **an apple** una manzana; **she's a nurse** (ella) es enfermera; **I haven't got a car** no tengo coche
2 (*instead of the number "one"*) un(a); **a year ago** hace un año; **a hundred/thousand pounds** cien/mil libras
3 (*in expressing ratios, prices etc*): **three a day/week** tres al día/a la semana; **10 km an hour** 10 km por hora; **£5 a person** £5 por persona; **30p a kilo** 30p el kilo; **three times a month** tres veces al mes

A2 *n* (*Brit Scol*) *segunda parte de los "A levels" (módulos 4–6)*
AA *n abbr* (*Brit*: *= Automobile Association*) ≈ RACE *m* (*Sp*); (*= Alcoholics Anonymous*) A.A.; (*US*: *= Associate in/of Arts*) *título universitario*; = **anti-aircraft**
AAA *n abbr* (*= American Automobile Association*) ≈ RACE *m* (*Sp*); ['θriː'eɪz] (*Brit*: *= Amateur Athletics Association*) *asociación de atletismo amateur*
aback [ə'bæk] *adv*: **to be taken ~** quedar(se) desconcertado
abandon [ə'bændən] *vt* abandonar; (*renounce*) renunciar a ▷ *n* abandono; (*wild behaviour*): **with ~** con desenfreno; **to ~ ship** abandonar el barco
abate [ə'beɪt] *vi* moderarse; (*lessen*) disminuir; (*calm down*) calmarse
abattoir ['æbətwɑːʳ] *n* (*Brit*) matadero
abbey ['æbɪ] *n* abadía
abbot ['æbət] *n* abad *m*
abbreviate [ə'briːvɪeɪt] *vt* abreviar
abbreviation [əbriːvɪ'eɪʃən] *n* (*short form*) abreviatura; (*act*) abreviación *f*
ABC *n abbr* (*= American Broadcasting Company*) *cadena de televisión*
abdicate ['æbdɪkeɪt] *vt, vi* abdicar
abdication [æbdɪ'keɪʃən] *n* abdicación *f*
abdomen ['æbdəmən] *n* abdomen *m*
abduct [æb'dʌkt] *vt* raptar, secuestrar
abduction [æb'dʌkʃən] *n* rapto, secuestro
abductor [æb'dʌktəʳ] *n* raptor(a) *m(f)*, secuestrador(a) *m(f)*
aberration [æbə'reɪʃən] *n* aberración *f*; **in a moment of mental ~** en un momento de enajenación mental
abet [ə'bɛt] *vt see* **aid**
abeyance [ə'beɪəns] *n*: **in ~** (*law*) en desuso; (*matter*) en suspenso
abide [ə'baɪd] *vt*: **I can't ~ it/him** no lo/le puedo ver *or* aguantar; **to ~ by** *vt fus* atenerse a
abiding [ə'baɪdɪŋ] *adj* (*memory etc*) perdurable
ability [ə'bɪlɪtɪ] *n* habilidad *f*, capacidad *f*; (*talent*) talento; **to the best of my ~** lo mejor que pueda *etc*
abject ['æbdʒɛkt] *adj* (*poverty*) sórdido; (*apology*) rastrero; (*coward*) vil
ablaze [ə'bleɪz] *adj* en llamas, ardiendo
able ['eɪbl] *adj* capaz; (*skilled*) hábil; **to be ~ to do sth** poder hacer algo
able-bodied ['eɪbl'bɔdɪd] *adj* sano; **~ seaman** marinero de primera
ably ['eɪblɪ] *adv* hábilmente
abnormal [æb'nɔːməl] *adj* anormal
aboard [ə'bɔːd] *adv* a bordo ▷ *prep* a bordo de; **~ the train** en el tren
abode [ə'bəud] *n* (*old*) morada; (*Law*) domicilio; **of no fixed ~** sin domicilio fijo
abolish [ə'bɔlɪʃ] *vt* suprimir, abolir
abolition [æbəu'lɪʃən] *n* supresión *f*, abolición *f*
aborigine [æbə'rɪdʒɪnɪ] *n* aborigen *m/f*
abort [ə'bɔːt] *vt* abortar; (*Comput*) interrumpir ▷ *vi* (*Comput*) interrumpir el programa
abortion [ə'bɔːʃən] *n* aborto; **to have an ~** abortar
abortive [ə'bɔːtɪv] *adj* fracasado
abound [ə'baund] *vi*: **to ~ (in** *or* **with)** abundar (de *or* en)

KEYWORD

about [ə'baut] *adv* **1** (*approximately*) más o menos, aproximadamente; **about a**

hundred/thousand *etc* unos(-as) *or* como cien/mil *etc*; **it takes about 10 hours** se tarda unas *or* más o menos 10 horas; **at about two o'clock** sobre las dos; **I've just about finished** casi he terminado
2 (*referring to place*) por todas partes; **to leave things lying about** dejar las cosas (tiradas) por ahí; **to run about** correr por todas partes; **to walk about** pasearse, ir y venir; **is Paul about?** ¿está por aquí Paul?; **it's the other way about** es al revés
3: **to be about to do sth** estar a punto de hacer algo; **I'm not about to do all that for nothing** no pienso hacer todo eso para nada
▷ *prep* **1** (*relating to*) de, sobre, acerca de; **a book about London** un libro sobre *or* acerca de Londres; **what is it about?** (*book, film*) ¿de qué se trata?; **we talked about it** hablamos de eso *or* ello; **what** *or* **how about doing this?** ¿qué tal si hacemos esto?
2 (*referring to place*) por; **to walk about the town** caminar por la ciudad

about face, about turn *n* (*Mil*) media vuelta; (*fig*) cambio radical
above [ə'bʌv] *adv* encima, por encima, arriba ▷ *prep* encima de; (*greater than*: *in number*) más de; (: *in rank*) superior a; **mentioned ~** susodicho; **~ all** sobre todo; **he's not ~ a bit of blackmail** es capaz hasta de hacer chantaje
above board *adj* legítimo
abrasive [ə'breɪzɪv] *adj* abrasivo
abreast [ə'brɛst] *adv* uno al lado de otro; **to keep ~ of** mantenerse al corriente de
abridge [ə'brɪdʒ] *vt* abreviar
abroad [ə'brɔːd] *adv* (*be*) en el extranjero; (*go*) al extranjero; **there is a rumour ~ that ...** corre el rumor de que ...
abrupt [ə'brʌpt] *adj* (*sudden*: *departure*) repentino; (*manner*) brusco
abruptly [ə'brʌptlɪ] *adv* (*leave*) repentinamente; (*speak*) bruscamente
abscess ['æbsɪs] *n* absceso
abscond [əb'skɔnd] *vi* fugarse
absence ['æbsəns] *n* ausencia; **in the ~ of** (*person*) en ausencia de; (*thing*) a falta de
absent ['æbsənt] *adj* ausente; **~ without leave (AWOL)** ausente sin permiso
absentee [æbsən'tiː] *n* ausente *m/f*
absent-minded [æbsənt'maɪndɪd] *adj* distraído
absolute ['æbsəluːt] *adj* absoluto; **~ monopoly** monopolio total
absolutely [æbsə'luːtlɪ] *adv* totalmente; **oh yes, ~!** ¡claro *or* por supuesto que sí!
absolution [æbsə'luːʃən] *n* (*Rel*) absolución *f*
absolve [əb'zɔlv] *vt*: **to ~ sb (from)** absolver a algn (de)
absorb [əb'zɔːb] *vt* absorber; **to be ~ed in a book** estar absorto en un libro
absorbent [əb'zɔːbənt] *adj* absorbente
absorbent cotton *n* (*US*) algodón *m* hidrófilo
absorbing [əb'zɔːbɪŋ] *adj* absorbente; (*book etc*) interesantísimo
absorption [əb'zɔːpʃən] *n* absorción *f*
abstain [əb'steɪn] *vi*: **to ~ (from)** abstenerse (de)
abstention [əb'stɛnʃən] *n* abstención *f*
abstract ['æbstrækt] *adj* abstracto
absurd [əb'səːd] *adj* absurdo
ABTA ['æbtə] *n abbr* = **Association of British Travel Agents**
abundance [ə'bʌndəns] *n* abundancia
abundant [ə'bʌndənt] *adj* abundante
abuse [ə'bjuːs] *n* (*insults*) insultos *mpl*, improperios *mpl*; (*misuse*) abuso ▷ *vt* [ə'bjuːz] (*ill-treat*) maltratar; (*take advantage of*) abusar de; **open to ~** sujeto al abuso
abusive [ə'bjuːsɪv] *adj* ofensivo
abysmal [ə'bɪzməl] *adj* pésimo; (*failure*) garrafal; (*ignorance*) supino
abyss [ə'bɪs] *n* abismo
AC *abbr* (= *alternating current*) corriente *f* alterna ▷ *n abbr* (*US*) = **athletic club**
academic [ækə'dɛmɪk] *adj* académico, universitario; (*pej*: *issue*) puramente teórico ▷ *n* estudioso(-a); (*lecturer*) profesor(a) *m(f)* universitario(-a)
academic year *n* (*Univ*) año académico
academy [ə'kædəmɪ] *n* (*learned body*) academia; (*school*) instituto, colegio
accelerate [æk'sɛləreɪt] *vi* acelerar
acceleration [æksɛlə'reɪʃən] *n* aceleración *f*
accelerator [æk'sɛləreɪtə[r]] *n* (*Brit*) acelerador *m*
accent ['æksɛnt] *n* acento; (*fig*) énfasis *m*
accentuate [æk'sɛntjueɪt] *vt* (*syllable*) acentuar; (*need, difference etc*) recalcar, subrayar
accept [ək'sɛpt] *vt* aceptar; (*approve*) aprobar; (*concede*) admitir
acceptable [ək'sɛptəbl] *adj* aceptable, admisible
acceptance [ək'sɛptəns] *n* aceptación *f*; aprobación *f*; **to meet with general ~** recibir la aprobación general
access ['æksɛs] *n* acceso ▷ *vt* (*Comput*) acceder a; **the burglars gained ~ through a window** los ladrones lograron entrar por una ventana; **to have ~ to** tener acceso a
accessible [æk'sɛsəbl] *adj* (*place, person*) accesible; (*knowledge etc*) asequible
accessory [æk'sɛsərɪ] *n* accesorio; (*Law*): **~ to** cómplice de; **toilet accessories** artículos *mpl* de tocador
accident ['æksɪdənt] *n* accidente *m*; (*chance*) casualidad *f*; **by ~** (*unintentionally*) sin querer; (*by coincidence*) por casualidad; **~s at work** accidentes *mpl* de trabajo; **to meet with** *or* **to have an ~** tener *or* sufrir un accidente
accidental [æksɪ'dɛntl] *adj* accidental, fortuito

accidentally [æksɪ'dɛntəlɪ] *adv* sin querer; por casualidad
Accident and Emergency Department *n* (*Brit*) Urgencias *fpl*
accident insurance *n* seguro contra accidentes
accident-prone ['æksɪdənt'prəun] *adj* propenso a los accidentes
acclaim [ə'kleɪm] *vt* aclamar, aplaudir ▷ *n* aclamación *f*, aplausos *mpl*
acclimatize [ə'klaɪmətaɪz], **acclimate** (*US*) [ə'klaɪmət] *vt*: **to become ~d** aclimatarse
accommodate [ə'kɔmədeɪt] *vt* alojar, hospedar; (: *car, hotel etc*) tener cabida para; (*oblige, help*) complacer; **this car ~s four people comfortably** en este coche caben cuatro personas cómodamente
accommodating [ə'kɔmədeɪtɪŋ] *adj* servicial, complaciente
accommodation *n*, **accommodations** (*US*) *npl* [əkɔmə'deɪʃən(z)] alojamiento; **"~ to let"** "se alquilan habitaciones"; **seating ~** asientos *mpl*
accompaniment [ə'kʌmpənɪmənt] *n* acompañamiento
accompany [ə'kʌmpənɪ] *vt* acompañar
accomplice [ə'kʌmplɪs] *n* cómplice *m/f*
accomplish [ə'kʌmplɪʃ] *vt* (*finish*) concluir; (*aim*) realizar; (*task*) llevar a cabo
accomplished [ə'kʌmplɪʃt] *adj* experto, hábil
accomplishment [ə'kʌmplɪʃmənt] *n* (*ending*) conclusión *f*; (*bringing about*) realización *f*; (*skill*) talento
accord [ə'kɔ:d] *n* acuerdo ▷ *vt* conceder; **of his own ~** espontáneamente; **with one ~** de *or* por común acuerdo
accordance [ə'kɔ:dəns] *n*: **in ~ with** de acuerdo con
according [ə'kɔ:dɪŋ]: **~ to** *prep* según; (*in accordance with*) conforme a; **it went ~ to plan** salió según lo previsto
accordingly [ə'kɔ:dɪŋlɪ] *adv* (*thus*) por consiguiente, en consecuencia; (*appropriately*) de acuerdo con esto
accordion [ə'kɔ:dɪən] *n* acordeón *m*
accost [ə'kɔst] *vt* abordar, dirigirse a
account [ə'kaunt] *n* (*Comm*) cuenta, factura; (*report*) informe *m*; **accounts** *npl* (*Comm*) cuentas *fpl*; **"~ payee only"** "únicamente en cuenta del beneficiario"; **your ~ is still outstanding** su cuenta está todavía pendiente; **of little ~** de poca importancia; **on ~** a crédito; **to buy sth on ~** comprar algo a crédito; **on no ~** bajo ningún concepto; **on ~ of** a causa de, por motivo de; **to take into ~, take ~ of** tener en cuenta; **to keep an ~ of** llevar la cuenta de; **to bring sb to ~ for sth/for having done sth** pedirle cuentas a algn por algo/por haber hecho algo; **account for** *vt fus* (*explain*) explicar; **all the children were ~ed for** no faltaba ningún niño
accountability [əkauntə'bɪlɪtɪ] *n* responsabilidad *f*
accountable [ə'kauntəbl] *adj*: **~ (for)** responsable (de)
accountancy [ə'kauntənsɪ] *n* contabilidad *f*
accountant [ə'kauntənt] *n* contable *m/f*, contador(a) *m(f)* (*LAm*)
account number *n* (*at bank etc*) número de cuenta
accumulate [ə'kju:mjuleɪt] *vt* acumular ▷ *vi* acumularse
accumulation [əkju:mju'leɪʃən] *n* acumulación *f*
accuracy ['ækjurəsɪ] *n* (*of total*) exactitud *f*; (*of description etc*) precisión *f*
accurate ['ækjurɪt] *adj* (*number*) exacto; (*answer*) acertado; (*shot*) certero
accurately ['ækjurɪtlɪ] *adv* (*count, shoot, answer*) con precisión
accusation [ækju'zeɪʃən] *n* acusación *f*
accuse [ə'kju:z] *vt* acusar; (*blame*) echar la culpa a; **to ~ sb (of sth)** acusar a algn (de algo)
accused [ə'kju:zd] *n* acusado(-a)
accuser [ə'kju:zə^r] *n* acusador(a) *m(f)*
accustom [ə'kʌstəm] *vt* acostumbrar; **to ~ o.s. to sth** acostumbrarse a algo
accustomed [ə'kʌstəmd] *adj*: **~ to** acostumbrado a
AC/DC *abbr* (= *alternating current/direct current*) CA/CC
ace [eɪs] *n* as *m*
ache [eɪk] *n* dolor *m* ▷ *vi* doler; (*yearn*): **to ~ to do sth** ansiar hacer algo; **I've got stomach ~** *or* (*US*) **a stomach ~** tengo dolor de estómago, me duele el estómago; **my head ~s** me duele la cabeza
achieve [ə'tʃi:v] *vt* (*reach*) alcanzar; (*realize*) realizar; (*victory, success*) lograr, conseguir
achievement [ə'tʃi:vmənt] *n* (*completion*) realización *f*; (*success*) éxito
Achilles heel [ə'kɪli:z-] *n* talón *m* de Aquiles
acid ['æsɪd] *adj* ácido; (*bitter*) agrio ▷ *n* (*Chem, inf*: *LSD*) ácido
acid rain *n* lluvia ácida
acid test *n* (*fig*) prueba de fuego
acknowledge [ək'nɔlɪdʒ] *vt* (*letter*: *also*: **~ receipt of**) acusar recibo de; (*fact*) reconocer
acknowledgement [ək'nɔlɪdʒmənt] *n* acuse *m* de recibo; reconocimiento; **~s** (*in book*) agradecimientos *mpl*
acne ['æknɪ] *n* acné *m*
acorn ['eɪkɔ:n] *n* bellota
acoustic [ə'ku:stɪk] *adj* acústico
acoustics [ə'ku:stɪks] *n, npl* acústica *sg*
acquaint [ə'kweɪnt] *vt*: **to ~ sb with sth** (*inform*) poner a algn al corriente de algo; **to be ~ed with** (*person*) conocer; (*fact*) estar al corriente de
acquaintance [ə'kweɪntəns] *n* conocimiento; (*person*) conocido(-a); **to make sb's ~** conocer a algn

acquiesce [ækwɪ'ɛs] *vi* (*agree*): **to ~ (in)** consentir (en), conformarse (con)
acquire [ə'kwaɪəʳ] *vt* adquirir
acquisition [ækwɪ'zɪʃən] *n* adquisición *f*
acquit [ə'kwɪt] *vt* absolver, exculpar; **to ~ o.s. well** salir con éxito
acquittal [ə'kwɪtl] *n* absolución *f*, exculpación *f*
acre ['eɪkəʳ] *n* acre *m*
acrid ['ækrɪd] *adj* (*smell*) acre; (*fig*) mordaz, sarcástico
acrobat ['ækrəbæt] *n* acróbata *m/f*
acrobatic [ækrə'bætɪk] *adj* acrobático
acrobatics [ækrə'bætɪks] *npl* acrobacia *sg*
acronym ['ækrənɪm] *n* siglas *fpl*
across [ə'krɔs] *prep* (*on the other side of*) al otro lado de; (*crosswise*) a través de ▷ *adv* de un lado a otro, de una parte a otra a través, al través; **to run/swim ~** atravesar corriendo/nadando; **~ from** enfrente de; **the lake is 12 km ~** el lago tiene 12 km de ancho; **to get sth ~ to sb** (*fig*) hacer comprender algo a algn
acrylic [ə'krɪlɪk] *adj* acrílico
act [ækt] *n* acto, acción *f*; (*Theat*) acto; (*in music-hall etc*) número; (*Law*) decreto, ley *f* ▷ *vi* (*behave*) comportarse; (*Theat*) actuar; (*pretend*) fingir; (*take action*) tomar medidas ▷ *vt* (*part*) hacer, representar; **~ of God** fuerza mayor; **it's only an ~** es cuento; **to catch sb in the ~** coger a algn in fraganti *or* con las manos en la masa; **to ~ Hamlet** hacer el papel de Hamlet; **to ~ as** actuar *or* hacer de; **~ing in my capacity as chairman, I ...** en mi calidad de presidente, yo ...; **it ~s as a deterrent** sirve para disuadir; **he's only ~ing** está fingiendo nada más; **act on** *vt*: **to ~ on sth** actuar *or* obrar sobre algo; **act out** *vt* (*event*) representar; (*fantasies*) realizar; **act up** *vi* (*inf: person*) portarse mal
acting ['æktɪŋ] *adj* suplente ▷ *n*: **to do some ~** hacer algo de teatro; **he is the ~ manager** es el gerente en funciones
action ['ækʃən] *n* acción *f*, acto; (*Mil*) acción *f*; (*Law*) proceso, demanda ▷ *vt* (*Comm*) llevar a cabo; **to put a plan into ~** poner un plan en acción *or* en marcha; **killed in ~** (*Mil*) muerto en acto de servicio *or* en combate; **out of ~** (*person*) fuera de combate; (*thing*) averiado, estropeado; **to take ~** tomar medidas; **to bring an ~ against sb** entablar *or* presentar demanda contra algn
action replay *n* (*TV*) repetición *f*
activate ['æktɪveɪt] *vt* activar
active ['æktɪv] *adj* activo, enérgico; (*volcano*) en actividad; **to play an ~ part in** colaborar activamente en
actively ['æktɪvlɪ] *adv* (*participate*) activamente; (*discourage, dislike*) enérgicamente
activist ['æktɪvɪst] *n* activista *m/f*
activity [æk'tɪvɪtɪ] *n* actividad *f*
activity holiday *n* *vacaciones con actividades organizadas*
actor ['æktəʳ] *n* actor *m*
actress ['aektrɪs] *n* actriz *f*
actual ['æktjuəl] *adj* verdadero, real
actually ['æktjuəlɪ] *adv* realmente, en realidad
acumen ['ækjumən] *n* perspicacia; **business ~** talento para los negocios
acupuncture ['ækjupʌŋktʃəʳ] *n* acupuntura
acute [ə'kju:t] *adj* agudo
acutely [ə'kju:tlɪ] *adv* profundamente, extremadamente
AD *adv abbr* (= *Anno Domini*) d.C. ▷ *n abbr* (*US Mil*) = **active duty**
ad [æd] *n abbr* = **advertisement**
Adam ['ædəm] *n* Adán; **~'s apple** *n* nuez *f* (de la garganta)
adamant ['ædəmənt] *adj* firme, inflexible
adapt [ə'dæpt] *vt* adaptar; (*reconcile*) acomodar ▷ *vi*: **to ~ (to)** adaptarse (a), ajustarse (a)
adaptability [ədæptə'bɪlɪtɪ] *n* (*of person, device etc*) adaptabilidad *f*
adaptable [ə'dæptəbl] *adj* (*device*) adaptable; (*person*) acomodadizo, que se adapta
adaptation [ædæp'teɪʃən] *n* adaptación *f*
adapter, adaptor [ə'dæptəʳ] *n* (*Elec*) adaptador *m*; (*for several plugs*) ladrón *m*
add [æd] *vt* añadir, agregar (*esp LAm*); (*figures: also*: **~ up**) sumar ▷ *vi*: **to ~ to** (*increase*) aumentar, acrecentar ▷ *n* (*Internet*): **thanks for the ~** gracias por agregarme; **add on** *vt* añadir; **add up** *vt* (*figures*) sumar ▷ *vi* (*fig*): **it doesn't ~ up** no tiene sentido; **it doesn't ~ up to much** es poca cosa, no tiene gran *or* mucha importancia
addendum [ə'dɛndəm] *n* ad(d)enda *m or f*
adder ['ædəʳ] *n* víbora
addict ['ædɪkt] *n* (*to drugs etc*) adicto(-a); (*enthusiast*) aficionado(-a), entusiasta *m/f*; **heroin ~** heroinómano(-a)
addicted [ə'dɪktɪd] *adj*: **to be ~ to** ser adicto a; ser aficionado a
addiction [ə'dɪkʃən] *n* (*to drugs etc*) adicción *f*; (*enthusiasm*) afición *f*
addictive [ə'dɪktɪv] *adj* que causa adicción
addition [ə'dɪʃən] *n* (*adding up*) adición *f*; (*thing added*) añadidura, añadido; **in ~** además, por añadidura; **in ~ to** además de
additional [ə'dɪʃənl] *adj* adicional
additive ['ædɪtɪv] *n* aditivo
address [ə'drɛs] *n* dirección *f*, señas *fpl*; (*speech*) discurso; (*Comput*) dirección *f* ▷ *vt* (*letter*) dirigir; (*speak to*) dirigirse a, dirigir la palabra a; **form of ~** tratamiento; **absolute/relative ~** (*Comput*) dirección *f* absoluta/relativa; **to ~ o.s. to sth** (*issue, problem*) abordar
address book *n* agenda (de direcciones)
addressee [ædrɛ'si:] *n* destinatario(-a)
adenoids ['ædɪnɔɪdz] *npl* vegetaciones *fpl* (adenoideas)
adept ['ædɛpt] *adj*: **~ at** experto *or* ducho en

adequate ['ædɪkwɪt] *adj* (*satisfactory*) adecuado; (*enough*) suficiente; **to feel ~ to a task** sentirse con fuerzas para una tarea
adequately ['ædɪkwɪtlɪ] *adv* adecuadamente
adhere [əd'hɪə^r] *vi*: **to ~ to** adherirse a; (*fig*: *abide by*) observar
adhesive [əd'hi:zɪv] *adj, n* adhesivo
adhesive tape *n* (*Brit*) cinta adhesiva; (*US Med*) esparadrapo
ad hoc [æd'hɔk] *adj* (*decision*) ad hoc; (*committee*) formado con fines específicos ▷ *adv* ad hoc
adjacent [ə'dʒeɪsənt] *adj*: **~ to** contiguo a, inmediato a
adjective ['ædʒɛktɪv] *n* adjetivo
adjoining [ə'dʒɔɪnɪŋ] *adj* contiguo, vecino
adjourn [ə'dʒə:n] *vt* aplazar; (*session*) suspender, levantar; (*US*: *end*) terminar ▷ *vi* suspenderse; **the meeting has been ~ed till next week** se ha levantado la sesión hasta la semana que viene; **they ~ed to the pub** (*inf*) se trasladaron al bar
adjournment [ə'dʒə:nmənt] *n* (*period*) suspensión *f*; (*postponement*) aplazamiento
adjudicate [ə'dʒu:dɪkeɪt] *vi* sentenciar ▷ *vt* (*contest*) hacer de árbitro en, juzgar; (*claim*) decidir
adjust [ə'dʒʌst] *vt* (*change*) modificar; (*arrange*) arreglar; (*machine*) ajustar ▷ *vi*: **to ~ (to)** adaptarse (a)
adjustable [ə'dʒʌstəbl] *adj* ajustable
adjustment [ə'dʒʌstmənt] *n* adaptación *f*; arreglo; (*of prices, wages*) ajuste *m*
ad-lib [æd'lɪb] *vt, vi* improvisar ▷ *adv*: **ad lib** a voluntad, a discreción
admin ['ædmin] *n abbr* (*inf*) = **administration**
administer [əd'mɪnɪstə^r] *vt* proporcionar; (*justice*) administrar
administration [ædmɪnɪ'streɪʃən] *n* administración *f*; (*government*) gobierno; **the A~** (*US*) la Administración
administrative [əd'mɪnɪstrətɪv] *adj* administrativo
administrator [əd'mɪnɪstreɪtə^r] *n* administrador(a) *m(f)*
admirable ['ædmərəbl] *adj* admirable
admiral ['ædmərəl] *n* almirante *m*
Admiralty ['ædmərəltɪ] *n* (*Brit*) Ministerio de Marina, Almirantazgo
admiration [ædmə'reɪʃən] *n* admiración *f*
admire [əd'maɪə^r] *vt* admirar
admirer [əd'maɪərə^r] *n* admirador(a) *m(f)*; (*suitor*) pretendiente *m*
admiring [əd'maɪərɪŋ] *adj* (*expression*) de admiración
admissible [əd'mɪsəbl] *adj* admisible
admission [əd'mɪʃən] *n* (*to exhibition, nightclub*) entrada; (*enrolment*) ingreso; (*confession*) confesión *f*; **"~ free"** "entrada gratis *or* libre"; **by his own ~** él mismo reconoce que
admit [əd'mɪt] *vt* dejar entrar, dar entrada a; (*permit*) admitir; (*acknowledge*) reconocer; **"this ticket ~s two"** "entrada para dos personas"; **children not ~ted** se prohíbe la entrada a (los) menores de edad; **to be ~ted to hospital** ingresar en el hospital; **I must ~ that ...** debo reconocer que ...; **admit of** *vt fus* admitir, permitir; **admit to** *vt fus* confesarse culpable de
admittance [əd'mɪtəns] *n* entrada; **"no ~"** "se prohíbe la entrada", "prohibida la entrada"
admittedly [əd'mɪtədlɪ] *adv* es cierto que
admonish [əd'mɔnɪʃ] *vt* amonestar; (*advise*) aconsejar
ad nauseam [æd'nɔ:sɪæm] *adv* hasta la saciedad
ado [ə'du:] *n*: **without (any) more ~** sin más (ni más)
adolescence [ædəu'lɛsns] *n* adolescencia
adolescent [ædəu'lɛsnt] *adj, n* adolescente *m/f*
adopt [ə'dɔpt] *vt* adoptar
adopted [ə'dɔptɪd] *adj* adoptivo
adoption [ə'dɔpʃən] *n* adopción *f*
adorable [ə'dɔ:rəbl] *adj* adorable
adore [ə'dɔ:^r] *vt* adorar
adoring [ə'dɔ:rɪŋ] *adj*: **to his ~ public** a un público que le adora *or* le adoraba *etc*
adorn [ə'dɔ:n] *vt* adornar
adrenalin [ə'drɛnəlɪn] *n* adrenalina
Adriatic [eɪdrɪ'ætɪk] *n*: **the ~ (Sea)** el (Mar) Adriático
adrift [ə'drɪft] *adv* a la deriva; **to come ~** (*boat*) ir a la deriva, soltarse; (*wire, rope etc*) soltarse
ADSL *n abbr* (= *asymmetrical digital subscriber line*) ADSL *m*
adult ['ædʌlt] *n* adulto(-a) ▷ *adj*: **~ education** educación *f* para adultos
adultery [ə'dʌltərɪ] *n* adulterio
advance [əd'vɑ:ns] *n* adelanto, progreso; (*money*) anticipo; (*Mil*) avance *m* ▷ *vt* avanzar, adelantar; (*money*) anticipar ▷ *vi* avanzar, adelantarse; **in ~** por adelantado; (*book*) con antelación; **to make ~s to sb** (*gen*) hacer una proposición a algn; (*amorously*) insinuarse a algn
advanced *adj* avanzado; (*Scol*: *studies*) adelantado; **~ in years** entrado en años
advantage [əd'vɑ:ntɪdʒ] *n* (*also Tennis*) ventaja; **to take ~ of** aprovecharse de; **it's to our ~** es ventajoso para nosotros
advantageous [ædvən'teɪdʒəs] *adj* ventajoso, provechoso
advent ['ædvənt] *n* advenimiento; **A~** Adviento
adventure [əd'vɛntʃə^r] *n* aventura
adventure playground *n* parque *m* infantil
adventurous [əd'vɛntʃərəs] *adj* aventurero; (*bold*) arriesgado
adverb ['ædvə:b] *n* adverbio
adversary ['ædvəsərɪ] *n* adversario, contrario

a

adverse ['ædvə:s] *adj* adverso, contrario; **~ to** adverso a
adversity [əd'və:sɪtɪ] *n* infortunio
advert ['ædvə:t] *n abbr* (*Brit*) = **advertisement**
advertise ['ædvətaɪz] *vi* hacer propaganda; (*in newspaper etc*) poner un anuncio, anunciarse; **to ~ for** (*staff*) buscar por medio de anuncios ▷ *vt* anunciar
advertisement [əd'və:tɪsmənt] *n* anuncio
advertiser ['ædvətaɪzəʳ] *n* anunciante *m/f*
advertising ['ædvətaɪzɪŋ] *n* publicidad *f*, propaganda; anuncios *mpl*; (*industry*) industria publicitaria
advertising agency *n* agencia de publicidad
advice [əd'vaɪs] *n* consejo, consejos *mpl*; (*notification*) aviso; **a piece of ~** un consejo; **to take legal ~** consultar a un abogado; **to ask (sb) for ~** pedir consejo (a algn)
advisable [əd'vaɪzəbl] *adj* aconsejable, conveniente
advise [əd'vaɪz] *vt* aconsejar; **to ~ sb of sth** (*inform*) informar a algn de algo; **to ~ sb against sth/doing sth** desaconsejar algo a algn/aconsejar a algn que no haga algo; **you will be well/ill ~d to go** deberías/no deberías ir
advisedly [əd'vaɪzɪdlɪ] *adv* deliberadamente
adviser [əd'vaɪzəʳ] *n* consejero(-a); (*business adviser*) asesor(a) *m(f)*
advisory [ad'vaɪzərɪ] *adj* consultivo; **in an ~ capacity** como asesor
advocate ['ædvəkeɪt] *vt* (*argue for*) abogar por; (*give support to*) ser partidario de ▷ *n* ['ædvəkɪt] abogado(-a); (*supporter*): **~ of** defensor(a) *m(f)* de
Aegean [i:'dʒi:ən] *n*: **the ~ (Sea)** el (Mar) Egeo
aerial ['ɛərɪəl] *n* antena ▷ *adj* aéreo
aerobatics [ɛərəu'bætɪks] *npl* acrobacia aérea
aerobics [ɛə'rəubɪks] *nsg* aerobic *m*, aerobismo (*LAm*)
aeroplane ['ɛərəpleɪn] *n* (*Brit*) avión *m*
aerosol ['ɛərəsɔl] *n* aerosol *m*
aesthetic [i:s'θɛtɪk] *adj* estético
afar [ə'fɑ:ʳ] *adv* lejos; **from ~** desde lejos
affair [ə'fɛəʳ] *n* asunto; (*also*: **love ~**) aventura *f* amorosa; **~s** (*business*) asuntos *mpl*; **the Watergate ~** el asunto (de) Watergate
affect [ə'fɛkt] *vt* afectar, influir en; (*move*) conmover
affected [ə'fɛktɪd] *adj* afectado
affection [ə'fɛkʃən] *n* afecto, cariño
affectionate [ə'fɛkʃənɪt] *adj* afectuoso, cariñoso
affinity [ə'fɪnɪtɪ] *n* afinidad *f*
affirm [ə'fə:m] *vt* afirmar
affirmative [ə'fə:mətɪv] *adj* afirmativo
afflict [ə'flɪkt] *vt* afligir
affluence ['æfluəns] *n* opulencia, riqueza
affluent ['aefluənt] *adj* acomodado; **the ~ society** la sociedad opulenta
afford [ə'fɔ:d] *vt* poder permitirse; (*provide*) proporcionar; **can we ~ a car?** ¿podemos permitirnos el gasto de comprar un coche?
affordable [ə'fɔ:dəbl] *adj* asequible
Afghanistan [æf'gænɪstæn] *n* Afganistán *m*
afield [ə'fi:ld] *adv*: **far ~** muy lejos
afloat [ə'fləut] *adv* (*floating*) a flote; (*at sea*) en el mar
afoot [ə'fut] *adv*: **there is something ~** algo se está tramando
afraid [ə'freɪd] *adj*: **to be ~ of** (*person*) tener miedo a; (*thing*) tener miedo de; **to be ~ to** tener miedo de, temer; **I am ~ that** me temo que; **I'm ~ so** lo siento, pero es así, me temo que sí; **I'm ~ not** lo siento, pero no
afresh [ə'frɛʃ] *adv* de nuevo, otra vez
Africa ['æfrɪkə] *n* África
African ['æfrɪkən] *adj, n* africano(-a) *m(f)*
African-American *adj, n* afroamericano(-a)
Afro-American ['æfrəuə'mɛrɪkən] *adj, n* afroamericano(-a) *m(f)*
aft [ɑ:ft] *adv* (*be*) en popa; (*go*) a popa
after ['ɑ:ftəʳ] *prep* (*time*) después de; (*place, order*) detrás de, tras ▷ *adv* después ▷ *conj* después (de) que; **what/who are you ~?** ¿qué/a quién buscas?; **the police are ~ him** la policía le está buscando; **~ having done/ he left** después de haber hecho/después de que se marchó; **~ dinner** después de cenar *or* comer; **the day ~ tomorrow** pasado mañana; **to ask ~ sb** preguntar por algn; **~ all** después de todo, al fin y al cabo; **~ you!** ¡pase usted!; **quarter ~ two** (*US*) las dos y cuarto
afterbirth ['ɑ:ftəbə:θ] *n* placenta
after-effects ['ɑ:ftərɪfɛkts] *npl* secuelas *fpl*, efectos *mpl*
afterlife ['ɑ:ftəlaɪf] *n* vida después de la muerte
aftermath ['ɑ:ftəmɑ:θ] *n* consecuencias *fpl*, resultados *mpl*
afternoon [ɑ:ftə'nu:n] *n* tarde *f*; **good ~!** ¡buenas tardes!
afters ['ɑ:ftəz] *n* (*inf*: *dessert*) postre *m*
after-sales service [ɑ:ftə'seɪlz-] *n* (*Brit Comm*: *for car, washing machine etc*) servicio de asistencia pos-venta
after-shave ['ɑ:ftəʃeɪv], **after-shave lotion** *n* loción *f* para después del afeitado, aftershave *m*
aftersun ['ɑ:ftəsʌn], **aftersun lotion** *n* aftersun *m inv*
aftertaste ['ɑ:ftəteɪst] *n* regusto
afterthought ['ɑ:ftəθɔ:t] *n* ocurrencia (tardía)
afterwards ['ɑ:ftəwədz] *adv* después, más tarde
again [ə'gɛn] *adv* otra vez, de nuevo; **to do sth ~** volver a hacer algo; **~ and ~** una y otra vez; **now and ~** de vez en cuando
against [ə'gɛnst] *prep* (*opposed*) en contra de; (*close to*) contra, junto a; **I was leaning ~ the**

desk estaba apoyado en el escritorio; **(as) ~** frente a
age [eɪdʒ] *n* edad *f*; (*old age*) vejez *f*; (*period*) época ▷ *vi* envejecer(se) ▷ *vt* envejecer; **what ~ is he?** ¿qué edad *or* cuántos años tiene?; **he is 20 years of ~** tiene 20 años; **under ~** menor de edad; **to come of ~** llegar a la mayoría de edad; **it's been ~s since I saw you** hace siglos que no te veo
aged [eɪdʒd] *adj*: **~ 10** de 10 años de edad ▷ *npl* ['eɪdʒɪd]: **the ~** los ancianos
age group *n*: **to be in the same ~** tener la misma edad; **the 40 to 50 ~** las personas de 40 a 50 años
ageing ['eɪdʒɪŋ] *adj* que envejece; (*pej*) en declive ▷ *n* envejecimiento
age limit *n* límite *m* de edad, edad *f* tope
agency ['eɪdʒənsɪ] *n* agencia; **through** *or* **by the ~ of** por medio de
agenda [ə'dʒɛndə] *n* orden *m* del día; **on the ~** (*Comm*) en el orden del día
agent ['eɪdʒənt] *n* (*gen*) agente *m/f*; (*representative*) representante *m/f* delegado(-a)
aggravate ['ægrəveɪt] *vt* agravar; (*annoy*) irritar, exasperar
aggravating ['ægrəveɪtɪŋ] *adj* irritante, molesto
aggravation [ægrə'veɪʃən] *n* agravamiento
aggregate ['ægrɪgeɪt] *n* conjunto
aggression [ə'grɛʃən] *n* agresión *f*
aggressive [ə'grɛsɪv] *adj* agresivo; (*vigorous*) enérgico
aggressor [ə'grɛsə^r] *n* agresor(a) *m(f)*
aggrieved [ə'gri:vd] *adj* ofendido, agraviado
aggro ['ægrəu] *n* (*inf*: *physical violence*) bronca; (*bad feeling*) mal rollo; (*hassle*) rollo, movida
aghast [ə'gɑ:st] *adj* horrorizado
agile ['ædʒaɪl] *adj* ágil
agility [ə'dʒɪlɪtɪ] *n* agilidad *f*
agitate ['ædʒɪteɪt] *vt* (*shake*) agitar; (*trouble*) inquietar; **to ~ for** hacer campaña en pro de *or* en favor de
agitated ['ædʒɪteɪtɪd] *adj* agitado
AGM *n abbr* = **annual general meeting**
agnostic [æg'nɔstɪk] *adj, n* agnóstico(-a) *m(f)*
ago [ə'gəu] *adv*: **two days ~** hace dos días; **not long ~** hace poco; **how long ~?** ¿hace cuánto tiempo?; **as long ~ as 1980** ya en 1980
agog [ə'gɔg] *adj* (*anxious*) ansioso; (*excited*): **(all) ~ (for)** (todo) emocionado (por)
agonize ['ægənaɪz] *vi*: **to ~ (over)** atormentarse (por)
agonized ['ægənaɪzd] *adj* angustioso
agonizing ['ægənaɪzɪŋ] *adj* (*pain*) atroz; (*suspense*) angustioso
agony ['ægənɪ] *n* (*pain*) dolor *m* atroz; (*distress*) angustia; **to be in ~** retorcerse de dolor
agony aunt *n* (*Brit inf*) consejera sentimental
agree [ə'gri:] *vt* (*price*) acordar, quedar en ▷ *vi* (*statements etc*) coincidir, concordar; **to ~ (with)** (*person*) estar de acuerdo (con), ponerse de acuerdo (con); **to ~ to do** aceptar hacer; **to ~ to sth** consentir en algo; **to ~ that** (*admit*) estar de acuerdo en que; **it was ~d that ...** se acordó que ...; **garlic doesn't ~ with me** el ajo no me sienta bien
agreeable [ə'gri:əbl] *adj* agradable; (*person*) simpático; (*willing*) de acuerdo, conforme
agreed [ə'gri:d] *adj* (*time, place*) convenido
agreement [ə'gri:mənt] *n* acuerdo; (*Comm*) contrato; **in ~** de acuerdo, conforme; **by mutual ~** de común acuerdo
agricultural [ægrɪ'kʌltʃərəl] *adj* agrícola
agriculture ['ægrɪkʌltʃə^r] *n* agricultura
aground [ə'graund] *adv*: **to run ~** encallar, embarrancar
ahead [ə'hɛd] *adv* delante; **~ of** delante de; (*fig*: *schedule etc*) antes de; **~ of time** antes de la hora; **to be ~ of sb** (*fig*) llevar ventaja *or* la delantera a algn; **go right** *or* **straight ~** siga adelante; **they were (right) ~ of us** iban (justo) delante de nosotros
aid [eɪd] *n* ayuda, auxilio ▷ *vt* ayudar, auxiliar; **in ~ of** a beneficio de; **with the ~ of** con la ayuda de; **to ~ and abet** (*Law*) ser cómplice
aide [eɪd] *n* (*Pol*) ayudante *m/f*
AIDS [eɪdz] *n abbr* (= *acquired immune (or immuno-)deficiency syndrome*) SIDA *m*, sida *m*
ailing ['eɪlɪŋ] *adj* (*person, economy*) enfermizo
ailment ['eɪlmənt] *n* enfermedad *f*, achaque *m*
aim [eɪm] *vt* (*gun*) apuntar; (*missile, remark*) dirigir; (*blow*) asestar ▷ *vi* (*also*: **take ~**) apuntar ▷ *n* puntería; (*objective*) propósito, meta; **to ~ at** (*objective*) aspirar a, pretender; **to ~ to do** tener la intención de hacer, aspirar a hacer
aimless ['eɪmlɪs] *adj* sin propósito, sin objeto
ain't [eɪnt] (*inf*) = **am not**; **aren't**; **isn't**
air [ɛə^r] *n* aire *m*; (*appearance*) aspecto ▷ *vt* (*room*) ventilar; (*clothes, bed, grievances, ideas*) airear; (*views*) hacer público ▷ *cpd* aéreo; **to throw sth into the ~** (*ball etc*) lanzar algo al aire; **by ~** (*travel*) en avión; **to be on the ~** (*Radio, TV*: *programme*) estarse emitiendo; (: *station*) estar en antena
airbag ['ɛəbæg] *n* airbag *m inv*
air bed *n* (*Brit*) colchoneta inflable *or* neumática
airborne ['ɛəbɔ:n] *adj* (*in the air*) en el aire; (*Mil*) aerotransportado; **as soon as the plane was ~** tan pronto como el avión estuvo en el aire
air-conditioned ['ɛəkən'dɪʃənd] *adj* climatizado
air conditioning [-kən'dɪʃənɪŋ] *n* aire *m* acondicionado
aircraft ['ɛəkrɑ:ft] *n pl inv* avión *m*
aircraft carrier *n* porta(a)viones *m inv*
airfield ['ɛəfi:ld] *n* campo de aviación
Air Force *n* fuerzas aéreas *fpl*, aviación *f*
air freshener *n* ambientador *m*
air gun *n* escopeta de aire comprimido

air hostess (*Brit*) *n* azafata, aeromoza (*LAm*)
airing ['ɛərɪŋ] *n*: **to give an ~ to** (*linen*) airear; (*room*) ventilar; (*fig: ideas etc*) airear, someter a discusión
airing cupboard *n* (*Brit*) armario *m* para oreo
air letter *n* (*Brit*) carta aérea
airlift ['ɛəlɪft] *n* puente *m* aéreo
airline ['ɛəlaɪn] *n* línea aérea
airliner ['ɛəlaɪnəʳ] *n* avión *m* de pasajeros
airmail ['ɛəmeɪl] *n*: **by ~** por avión
airplane ['ɛəpleɪn] *n* (*US*) avión *m*
air pocket *n* bolsa de aire
airport ['ɛəpɔːt] *n* aeropuerto
air rage *n conducta agresiva de pasajeros a bordo de un avión*
air raid *n* ataque *m* aéreo
air rifle *n* escopeta de aire comprimido
airsick ['ɛəsɪk] *adj*: **to be ~** marearse (en avión)
airspace *n* espacio aéreo
airspeed ['ɛəspiːd] *n* velocidad *f* de vuelo
airstrip ['ɛəstrɪp] *n* pista de aterrizaje
air terminal *n* terminal *f*
airtight ['ɛətaɪt] *adj* hermético
air time *n* (*Radio, TV*) tiempo en antena
air traffic control *n* control *m* de tráfico aéreo
air traffic controller *n* controlador(a) *m(f)* aéreo(-a)
airway ['ɛəweɪ] *n* (*Aviat*) vía aérea; (*Anat*) vía respiratoria
airy ['ɛərɪ] *adj* (*room*) bien ventilado; (*manners*) desenfadado
aisle [aɪl] *n* (*of church*) nave *f* lateral; (*of theatre, plane*) pasillo
aisle seat *n* (*on plane*) asiento de pasillo
ajar [ə'dʒɑːʳ] *adj* entreabierto
akin [ə'kɪn] *adj*: **~ to** semejante a
à la carte [ælæ'kɑːt] *adv* a la carta
alarm [ə'lɑːm] *n* alarma; (*anxiety*) inquietud *f* ▷ *vt* asustar, alarmar
alarm call *n* (*in hotel etc*) alarma
alarm clock *n* despertador *m*
alarmed [ə'lɑːmd] *adj* (*person*) alarmado, asustado; (*house, car etc*) con alarma
alarming [ə'lɑːmɪŋ] *adj* alarmante
alas [ə'læs] *adv* desgraciadamente ▷ *excl* ¡ay!
Albania [æl'beɪnɪə] *n* Albania
albatross ['ælbətrɔs] *n* albatros *m*
albeit [ɔːl'biːɪt] *conj* (*although*) aunque
album ['ælbəm] *n* álbum *m*; (*L.P.*) elepé *m*
alcohol ['ælkəhɔl] *n* alcohol *m*
alcohol-free ['ælkəhɔlfriː] *adj* sin alcohol
alcoholic [ælkə'hɔlɪk] *adj, n* alcohólico(-a) *m(f)*
alcoholism ['ælkəhɔlɪzəm] *n* alcoholismo
alcove ['ælkəuv] *n* nicho, hueco
ale [eɪl] *n* cerveza
alert [ə'ləːt] *adj* alerta *inv*; (*sharp*) despierto, atento ▷ *n* alerta *m*, alarma ▷ *vt* poner sobre aviso; **to ~ sb (to sth)** poner sobre aviso *or* alertar a algn (de algo); **to ~ sb to the dangers of sth** poner sobre aviso *or* alertar a algn de los peligros de algo; **to be on the ~** estar alerta *or* sobre aviso
A level *n abbr* (*Brit Scol: = Advanced level*) ≈ Bachillerato
algebra ['ældʒɪbrə] *n* álgebra
Algeria [æl'dʒɪərɪə] *n* Argelia
Algerian [æl'dʒɪərɪən] *adj, n* argelino(-a) *m(f)*
alias ['eɪlɪəs] *adv* alias, conocido por ▷ *n* alias *m*; (*of criminal*) apodo; (*of writer*) seudónimo
alibi ['ælɪbaɪ] *n* coartada
alien ['eɪlɪən] *n* (*foreigner*) extranjero(-a); (*extraterrestrial*) extraterrestre *m/f* ▷ *adj*: **~ to** ajeno a
alienate ['eɪlɪəneɪt] *vt* enajenar, alejar
alight [ə'laɪt] *adj* ardiendo ▷ *vi* apearse, bajar
align [ə'laɪn] *vt* alinear
alignment [ə'laɪnmənt] *n* alineación *f*; **the desks are out of ~** los pupitres no están bien alineados
alike [ə'laɪk] *adj* semejantes, iguales ▷ *adv* igualmente, del mismo modo; **to look ~** parecerse
alimony ['ælɪmənɪ] *n* (*Law*) pensión *f* alimenticia
alive [ə'laɪv] *adj* (*gen*) vivo; (*lively*) alegre
alkali ['ælkəlaɪ] *n* álcali *m*

KEYWORD

all [ɔːl] *adj* todo(-a) *sg*, todos(-as) *pl*; **all day** todo el día; **all night** toda la noche; **all men** todos los hombres; **all five came** vinieron los cinco; **all the books** todos los libros; **all the time/his life** todo el tiempo/toda su vida; **for all their efforts** a pesar de todos sus esfuerzos

▷ *pron* **1** todo; **I ate it all, I ate all of it** me lo comí todo; **all of them** todos (ellos); **all of us went** fuimos todos; **all the boys went** fueron todos los chicos; **is that all?** ¿eso es todo?, ¿algo más?; (*in shop*) ¿algo más?, ¿alguna cosa más?

2 (*in phrases*): **above all** sobre todo; por encima de todo; **after all** después de todo; **at all**: **anything at all** lo que sea; **not at all** (*in answer to question*) en absoluto; (*in answer to thanks*) ¡de nada!, ¡no hay de qué!; **I'm not at all tired** no estoy nada cansado(-a); **anything at all will do** cualquier cosa viene bien; **all in all** a fin de cuentas

▷ *adv*: **all alone** completamente solo(-a); **to be/feel all in** estar rendido; **it's not as hard as all that** no es tan difícil como lo pintas; **all the more/the better** tanto más/mejor; **all but** casi; **the score is two all** están empatados a dos

Allah ['ælə] *n* Alá *m*
all-around ['ɔːlə'raund] *adj* (*US*) = **all-round**
allay [ə'leɪ] *vt* (*fears*) aquietar; (*pain*) aliviar
allegation [ælɪ'geɪʃən] *n* alegato

allege [ə'lɛdʒ] *vt* pretender; **he is ~d to have said ...** se afirma que él dijo ...
alleged [ə'lɛdʒd] *adj* supuesto, presunto
allegedly [ə'lɛdʒɪdlɪ] *adv* supuestamente, según se afirma
allegiance [ə'li:dʒəns] *n* lealtad *f*
allegory ['ælɪgərɪ] *n* alegoría
allergic [ə'lə:dʒɪk] *adj*: **~ to** alérgico a
allergy ['ælədʒɪ] *n* alergia
alleviate [ə'li:vɪeɪt] *vt* aliviar
alley ['ælɪ] *n* (*street*) callejuela; (*in garden*) paseo
alleyway ['ælɪweɪ] *n* callejón *m*
alliance [ə'laɪəns] *n* alianza
allied ['ælaɪd] *adj* aliado; (*related*) relacionado
alligator ['ælɪgeɪtə^r] *n* caimán *m*
all-in ['ɔ:lɪn] *adj, adv* (*Brit*: *charge*) todo incluido
all-in wrestling *n* lucha libre
alliteration [əlɪtə'reɪʃən] *n* aliteración *f*
all-night ['ɔ:l'naɪt] *adj* (*café*) abierto toda la noche; (*party*) que dura toda la noche
allocate ['æləkeɪt] *vt* (*share out*) repartir; (*devote*) asignar
allocation [ælə'keɪʃən] *n* (*of money*) ración *f*, cuota; (*distribution*) reparto
allot [ə'lɔt] *vt* asignar; **in the ~ted time** en el tiempo asignado
allotment [ə'lɔtmənt] *n* porción *f*; (*garden*) parcela
all-out ['ɔ:laut] *adj* (*effort etc*) supremo ▷ *adv*: **all out** con todas las fuerzas, a fondo
allow [ə'lau] *vt* (*permit*) permitir, dejar; (*a claim*) admitir; (*sum to spend, time estimated*) dar, conceder; (*concede*): **to ~ that** reconocer que; **to ~ sb to do** permitir a algn hacer; **smoking is not ~ed** prohibido *or* se prohíbe fumar; **he is ~ed to ...** se le permite ...; **we must ~ three days for the journey** debemos dejar tres días para el viaje; **allow for** *vt fus* tener en cuenta
allowance [ə'lauəns] *n* concesión *f*; (*payment*) subvención *f*, pensión *f*; (*discount*) descuento, rebaja; (*tax allowance*) desgravación *f*; **to make ~s for** (*person*) disculpar a; (*thing*: *take into account*) tener en cuenta
alloy ['ælɔɪ] *n* aleación *f*
all right *adv* (*feel, work*) bien; (*as answer*) ¡de acuerdo!, ¡está bien!
all-round [ɔ:l'raund] *adj* completo; (*view*) amplio
all-rounder [ɔ:l'raundə^r] *n*: **to be a good ~** ser una persona que hace de todo
all-time ['ɔ:l'taɪm] *adj* (*record*) de todos los tiempos
allude [ə'lu:d] *vi*: **to ~ to** aludir a
alluring [ə'ljuərɪŋ] *adj* seductor(a), atractivo
allusion [ə'lu:ʒən] *n* referencia, alusión *f*
ally *n* ['ælaɪ] aliado(-a) ▷ *vt* [ə'laɪ]: **to ~ o.s. with** aliarse con
almighty [ɔ:l'maɪtɪ] *adj* todopoderoso; (*row etc*) imponente
almond ['ɑ:mənd] *n* (*fruit*) almendra; (*tree*) almendro
almost ['ɔ:lməust] *adv* casi; **he ~ fell** casi *or* por poco se cae
alms [ɑ:mz] *npl* limosna *sg*
aloft [ə'lɔft] *adv* arriba
alone [ə'ləun] *adj* solo ▷ *adv* solo, solamente; **to leave sb ~** dejar a algn en paz; **to leave sth ~** no tocar algo; **let ~ ...** y mucho menos ..., y no digamos ...
along [ə'lɔŋ] *prep* a lo largo de, por ▷ *adv*: **is he coming ~ with us?** ¿viene con nosotros?; **he was limping ~** iba cojeando; **~ with** junto con; **all ~** (*all the time*) desde el principio
alongside [ə'lɔŋ'saɪd] *prep* al lado de ▷ *adv* (*Naut*) de costado; **we brought our boat ~** atracamos nuestro barco
aloof [ə'lu:f] *adj* distante ▷ *adv*: **to stand ~** mantenerse a distancia
aloud [ə'laud] *adv* en voz alta
alphabet ['ælfəbɛt] *n* alfabeto
alphabetical [ælfə'bɛtɪkəl] *adj* alfabético; **in ~ order** por orden alfabético
alpine ['ælpaɪn] *adj* alpino, alpestre
Alps [ælps] *npl*: **the ~** los Alpes
already [ɔ:l'rɛdɪ] *adv* ya
alright ['ɔ:l'raɪt] *adv* (*Brit*) = **all right**
Alsatian [æl'seɪʃən] *n* (*dog*) pastor *m* alemán
also ['ɔ:lsəu] *adv* también, además
altar ['ɔltə^r] *n* altar *m*
alter ['ɔltə^r] *vt* cambiar, modificar ▷ *vi* cambiar, modificarse
alteration [ɔltə'reɪʃən] *n* cambio, modificación *f*; **alterations** *npl* (*Arch*) reformas *fpl*; (*Sewing*) arreglos *mpl*; **timetable subject to ~** el horario puede cambiar
altercation [ɔltə'keɪʃən] *n* altercado
alternate [ɔl'tə:nɪt] *adj* alterno ▷ *vi* ['ɔltəneɪt]: **to ~ (with)** alternar (con); **on ~ days** en días alternos
alternately [ɔl'tə:nɪtlɪ] *adv* alternativamente, por turno
alternating ['ɔltəneɪtɪŋ] *adj* (*current*) alterno
alternative [ɔl'tə:nətɪv] *adj* alternativo ▷ *n* alternativa; **~ medicine** medicina alternativa
alternatively [ɔl'tə:nətɪvlɪ] *adv*: **~ one could ...** por otra parte se podría ...
alternative medicine *n* medicina alternativa
alternator ['ɔltəneɪtə^r] *n* (*Aut*) alternador *m*
although [ɔ:l'ðəu] *conj* aunque, si bien
altitude ['æltɪtju:d] *n* altitud *f*, altura
alto ['æltəu] *n* (*female*) contralto *f*; (*male*) alto
altogether [ɔ:ltə'gɛðə^r] *adv* completamente, del todo; (*on the whole, in all*) en total, en conjunto; **how much is that ~?** ¿cuánto es todo *or* en total?
altruism ['æltruɪzəm] *n* altruismo
aluminium [ælju'mɪnɪəm], **aluminum** (*US*) [ə'lu:mɪnəm] *n* aluminio
always ['ɔ:lweɪz] *adv* siempre
Alzheimer's ['æltshaɪməz] *n* (*also*: **~ disease**) enfermedad *f* de Alzheimer

AM *abbr* (= *amplitude modulation*) A.M. *f* ▷ *n abbr* (*Pol*: *in Wales*) = **Assembly Member**
am [æm] *vb see* **be**
a.m. *adv abbr* (= *ante meridiem*) de la mañana
amalgamate [ə'mælgəmeɪt] *vi* amalgamarse ▷ *vt* amalgamar
amass [ə'mæs] *vt* amontonar, acumular
amateur ['æmətəʳ] *n* aficionado(-a), amateur *m/f*; **~ dramatics** dramas *mpl* presentados por aficionados, representación *f* de aficionados
amateurish ['æmətərɪʃ] *adj* (*pej*) torpe, inexperto
amaze [ə'meɪz] *vt* asombrar, pasmar; **to be ~d (at)** asombrarse (de)
amazed *adj* [ə'meɪzd] asombrado
amazement [ə'meɪzmənt] *n* asombro, sorpresa; **to my ~** para mi sorpresa
amazing [ə'meɪzɪŋ] *adj* extraordinario, asombroso; (*bargain, offer*) increíble
Amazon ['æməzən] *n* (*Geo*) Amazonas *m*; (*Mythology*) amazona ▷ *cpd*: **the ~ basin/jungle** la cuenca/selva del Amazonas
ambassador [æm'bæsədəʳ] *n* embajador(a) *m(f)*
amber ['æmbəʳ] *n* ámbar *m*; **at ~** (*Brit Aut*) en amarillo
ambiguity [æmbɪ'gjuɪtɪ] *n* ambigüedad *f*; (*of meaning*) doble sentido
ambiguous [æm'bɪgjuəs] *adj* ambiguo
ambition [æm'bɪʃən] *n* ambición *f*; **to achieve one's ~** realizar su ambición
ambitious [æm'bɪʃəs] *adj* ambicioso; (*plan*) grandioso
amble ['æmbl] *vi* (*gen*: *also*: **~ along**) deambular, andar sin prisa
ambulance ['æmbjuləns] *n* ambulancia
ambush ['æmbuʃ] *n* emboscada ▷ *vt* tender una emboscada a; (*fig*) coger (*Sp*) *or* agarrar (*LAm*) por sorpresa
amen [ɑː'mɛn] *excl* amén
amenable [ə'miːnəbl] *adj*: **~ to** (*advice etc*) sensible a
amend [ə'mɛnd] *vt* (*law, text*) enmendar; **to make ~s** (*apologize*) enmendarlo, dar cumplida satisfacción
amendment [ə'mɛndmənt] *n* enmienda
amenities [ə'miːnɪtɪz] *npl* comodidades *fpl*
America [ə'mɛrɪkə] *n* América (del Norte); (*USA*) Estados *mpl* Unidos
American [ə'mɛrɪkən] *adj, n* (norte) americano(-a) *m(f)*, estadounidense *m/f*
American football *n* (*Brit*) fútbol *m* americano
amiable ['eɪmɪəbl] *adj* (*kind*) amable, simpático
amicable ['æmɪkəbl] *adj* amistoso, amigable
amid [ə'mɪd], **amidst** [ə'mɪdst] *prep* entre, en medio de
amiss [ə'mɪs] *adv*: **to take sth ~** tomar algo a mal; **there's something ~** pasa algo
ammonia [ə'məunɪə] *n* amoníaco
ammunition [æmju'nɪʃən] *n* municiones *fpl*; (*fig*) argumentos *mpl*
amnesia [æm'niːzɪə] *n* amnesia
amnesty ['æmnɪstɪ] *n* amnistía; **to grant an ~ to** amnistiar (a); **A~ International** Amnistía Internacional
amok [ə'mɔk] *adv*: **to run ~** enloquecerse, desbocarse
among [ə'mʌŋ], **amongst** [ə'mʌŋst] *prep* entre, en medio de
amorous ['æmərəs] *adj* cariñoso
amount [ə'maunt] *n* (*gen*) cantidad *f*; (*of bill etc*) suma, importe *m* ▷ *vi*: **to ~ to** (*total*) sumar; (*be same as*) equivaler a, significar; **this ~s to a refusal** esto equivale a una negativa; **the total ~** (*of money*) la suma total
amp [æmp], **ampère** ['æmpɛəʳ] *n* amperio; **a 13 ~ plug** un enchufe de 13 amperios
amphetamine [æm'fɛtəmiːn] *n* anfetamina
amphibian [æm'fɪbɪən] *n* anfibio
ample ['æmpl] *adj* (*spacious*) amplio; (*abundant*) abundante; **to have ~ time** tener tiempo de sobra
amplifier ['æmplɪfaɪəʳ] *n* amplificador *m*
amplify ['æmplɪfaɪ] *vt* amplificar, aumentar; (*explain*) explicar
amply ['æmplɪ] *adv* ampliamente
amputate ['æmpjuteɪt] *vt* amputar
Amtrak ['æmtræk] *n* (*US*) *empresa nacional de ferrocarriles de los EEUU*
amuse [ə'mjuːz] *vt* divertir; (*distract*) distraer, entretener; **to ~ o.s. with sth/by doing sth** distraerse con algo/haciendo algo; **he was ~d at the joke** le divirtió el chiste
amusement [ə'mjuːzmənt] *n* diversión *f*; (*pastime*) pasatiempo; (*laughter*) risa; **much to my ~** con gran regocijo mío
amusement arcade *n* salón *m* de juegos
amusement park *n* parque *m* de atracciones
amusing [ə'mjuːzɪŋ] *adj* divertido
an [æn, ən, n] *indef art see* **a**
anaemia [ə'niːmɪə] *n* anemia
anaemic [ə'niːmɪk] *adj* anémico; (*fig*) flojo
anaesthetic [ænɪs'θɛtɪk] *n* anestesia; **local/general ~** anestesia local/general
anaesthetist [æ'niːsθɪtɪst] *n* anestesista *m/f*
anagram ['ænəgræm] *n* anagrama *m*
anal ['eɪnl] *adj* anal
analogous [ə'næləgəs] *adj*: **~ to** *or* **with** análogo a
analogue, analog ['ænəlɔg] *adj* analógico
analogy [ə'nælədʒɪ] *n* analogía; **to draw an ~ between** señalar la analogía entre
analyse ['ænəlaɪz] *vt* (*Brit*) analizar
analysis (*pl* **analyses**) [ə'næləsɪs, -siːz] *n* análisis *m inv*
analyst ['ænəlɪst] *n* (*political analyst, psychoanalyst*) analista *m/f*
analyze ['ænəlaɪz] *vt* (*US*) = **analyse**
anarchic [æ'nɑːkɪk] *adj* anárquico
anarchist ['ænəkɪst] *adj, n* anarquista *m/f*
anarchy ['ænəkɪ] *n* anarquía, desorden *m*

anathema [ə'næθɪmə] *n*: **that is ~ to him** eso es pecado para él
anatomy [ə'nætəmɪ] *n* anatomía
ancestor ['ænsɪstəʳ] *n* antepasado
ancestry ['ænsɪstrɪ] *n* ascendencia, abolengo
anchor ['æŋkəʳ] *n* ancla, áncora ▷ *vi* (*also*: **to drop ~**) anclar, echar el ancla ▷ *vt* (*fig*) sujetar, afianzar; **to weigh ~** levar anclas
anchor man, anchor woman *n* (*Radio, TV*) presentador(a) *m(f)*
anchovy ['æntʃəvɪ] *n* anchoa
ancient ['eɪnʃənt] *adj* antiguo; **~ monument** monumento histórico
ancillary [æn'sɪlərɪ] *adj* (*worker, staff*) auxiliar
and [ænd] *conj* y; (*before i, hi*) e; **~ so on** etcétera; **try ~ come** procura venir; **better ~ better** cada vez mejor
Andalusia [ændə'lu:zɪə] *n* Andalucía
Andean ['ændɪən] *adj* andino(-a); **~ high plateau** altiplanicie *f*, altiplano (*LAm*)
Andes ['ændi:z] *npl*: **the ~** los Andes
Andorra [æn'dɔ:rə] *n* Andorra
anecdote ['ænɪkdəut] *n* anécdota
anemia [ə'ni:mɪə] *n* (*US*) = **anaemia**
anemic [ə'ni:mɪk] *adj* (*US*) = **anaemic**
anesthetic [ænɪs'θɛtɪk] *adj, n* (*US*) = **anaesthetic**
anesthetist [æ'ni:sθɪtɪst] *n* (*US*) = **anaesthetist**
anew [ə'nju:] *adv* de nuevo, otra vez
angel ['eɪndʒəl] *n* ángel *m*
angel dust *n* polvo de ángel
anger ['æŋgəʳ] *n* ira, cólera, enojo (*LAm*) ▷ *vt* enojar, enfurecer
angina [æn'dʒaɪnə] *n* angina (del pecho)
angle ['æŋgl] *n* ángulo; **from their ~** desde su punto de vista
angler ['æŋgləʳ] *n* pescador(a) *m(f)* (de caña)
Anglican ['æŋglɪkən] *adj, n* anglicano(-a)
angling ['æŋglɪŋ] *n* pesca con caña
Anglo- [æŋgləu] *pref* anglo...
angrily ['æŋgrɪlɪ] *adv* enojado, enfadado
angry ['æŋgrɪ] *adj* enfadado, enojado (*esp LAm*); **to be ~ with sb/at sth** estar enfadado con algn/por algo; **to get ~** enfadarse, enojarse (*esp LAm*)
anguish ['æŋgwɪʃ] *n* (*physical*) tormentos *mpl*; (*mental*) angustia
anguished ['æŋgwɪʃt] *adj* angustioso
angular ['æŋgjuləʳ] *adj* (*shape*) angular; (*features*) anguloso
animal ['ænɪməl] *adj, n* animal *m*; (*pej*: *person*) bestia
animal rights [-raɪts] *npl* derechos *mpl* de los animales
animate *vt* ['ænɪmeɪt] (*enliven*) animar; (*encourage*) estimular, alentar ▷ *adj* ['ænɪmɪt] vivo, animado
animated ['ænɪmeɪtɪd] *adj* vivo, animado
animation [ænɪ'meɪʃən] *n* animación *f*
animosity [ænɪ'mɔsɪtɪ] *n* animosidad *f*, rencor *m*
aniseed ['ænɪsi:d] *n* anís *m*
ankle ['æŋkl] *n* tobillo *m*
ankle sock *n* calcetín *m*
annex *n* ['ænɛks] (*Brit*: *also*: **annexe**: *building*) edificio anexo ▷ *vt* [æ'nɛks] (*territory*) anexionar
annihilate [ə'naɪəleɪt] *vt* aniquilar
annihilation [ənaɪə'leɪʃən] *n* aniquilación *f*
anniversary [ænɪ'və:sərɪ] *n* aniversario
announce [ə'nauns] *vt* (*gen*) anunciar; (*inform*) comunicar; **he ~d that he wasn't going** declaró que no iba
announcement [ə'naunsmənt] *n* (*gen*) anuncio; (*declaration*) declaración *f*; **I'd like to make an ~** quisiera anunciar algo
announcer [ə'naunsəʳ] *n* (*Radio*) locutor(a) *m(f)*; (*TV*) presentador(a) *m(f)*
annoy [ə'nɔɪ] *vt* molestar, fastidiar, fregar (*LAm*), embromar (*LAm*); **to be ~ed (at sth/ with sb)** estar enfadado *or* molesto (por algo/ con algn); **don't get ~ed!** ¡no se enfade!
annoyance [ə'nɔɪəns] *n* enojo; (*thing*) molestia
annoying [ə'nɔɪɪŋ] *adj* molesto, fastidioso, fregado (*LAm*), embromado (*LAm*); (*person*) pesado
annual ['ænjuəl] *adj* anual ▷ *n* (*Bot*) anual *m*; (*book*) anuario
annual general meeting *n* junta general anual
annually ['ænjuəlɪ] *adv* anualmente, cada año
annual report *n* informe *m or* memoria anual
annul [ə'nʌl] *vt* anular; (*law*) revocar
annum ['ænəm] *n see* **per annum**
anomaly [ə'nɔməlɪ] *n* anomalía
anon. [ə'nɔn] *abbr* = **anonymous**
anonymity [ænə'nɪmɪtɪ] *n* anonimato
anonymous [ə'nɔnɪməs] *adj* anónimo; **to remain ~** quedar en el anonimato
anorak ['ænəræk] *n* anorak *m*
anorexia [ænə'rɛksɪə] *n* (*Med*) anorexia
anorexic [ænə'rɛksɪk] *adj, n* anoréxico(-a) *m(f)*
another [ə'nʌðəʳ] *adj*: **~ book** otro libro; **~ beer?** ¿(quieres) otra cerveza?; **in ~ five years** en cinco años más ▷ *pron* otro; *see also* **one**
answer ['ɑ:nsəʳ] *n* respuesta, contestación *f*; (*to problem*) solución *f* ▷ *vi* contestar, responder ▷ *vt* (*reply to*) contestar a, responder a; (*problem*) resolver; **to ~ the phone** contestar el teléfono; **in ~ to your letter** contestando *or* en contestación a su carta; **to ~ the bell** *or* **the door** abrir la puerta; **answer back** *vi* replicar, ser respondón(-ona); **answer for** *vt fus* responder de *or* por; **answer to** *vt fus* (*description*) corresponder a
answerable ['ɑ:nsərəbl] *adj*: **~ to sb for sth** responsable ante algn de algo

answering machine ['ɑːnsərɪŋ-] *n* contestador *m* automático
answerphone ['ɑːnsəfəun] *n* (*esp Brit*) contestador *m* (automático)
ant [ænt] *n* hormiga
antagonism [æn'tægənɪzəm] *n* antagonismo *m*
antagonistic [æntægə'nɪstɪk] *adj* antagónico; (*opposed*) contrario, opuesto
antagonize [æn'tægənaɪz] *vt* provocar la enemistad de
Antarctic [ænt'ɑːktɪk] *adj* antártico ▷ *n*: **the ~** el Antártico
Antarctica [æn'tɑːktɪkə] *n* Antártida
Antarctic Circle *n* Círculo Polar Antártico
Antarctic Ocean *n* Océano Antártico
antelope ['æntɪləup] *n* antílope *m*
antenatal [æntɪ'neɪtl] *adj* prenatal
antenna [æn'tɛnə] (*pl* **antennae** [-niː]) *n* antena
anthem ['ænθəm] *n*: **national ~** himno nacional
anthology [æn'θɔlədʒɪ] *n* antología
anthrax ['ænθræks] *n* ántrax *m*
anthropologist [ænθrə'pɔlədʒɪst] *n* antropólogo(-a)
anthropology [ænθrə'pɔlədʒɪ] *n* antropología
anti... [æntɪ] *pref* anti...
anti-aircraft ['æntɪ'ɛəkrɑːft] *adj* antiaéreo
antibiotic [æntɪbaɪ'ɔtɪk] *adj, n* antibiótico
antibody ['æntɪbɔdɪ] *n* anticuerpo
anticipate [æn'tɪsɪpeɪt] *vt* (*foresee*) prever; (*expect*) esperar, contar con; (*forestall*) anticiparse a, adelantarse a; **this is worse than I ~d** esto es peor de lo que esperaba; **as ~d** según se esperaba
anticipation [æntɪsɪ'peɪʃən] *n* previsión *f*; esperanza; anticipación *f*
anticlimax [æntɪ'klaɪmæks] *n* decepción *f*
anticlockwise [æntɪ'klɔkwaɪz] *adv* en dirección contraria a la de las agujas del reloj
antics ['æntɪks] *npl* gracias *fpl*
antidepressant [ˌæntɪdɪ'presnt] *n* antidepresivo
antidote ['æntɪdəut] *n* antídoto
antifreeze ['æntɪfriːz] *n* anticongelante *m*
anti-globalization ['æntɪgləubəlaɪ'zeɪʃən] *n* antiglobalización *f*; **~ protesters** manifestantes *m/fpl* antiglobalización
antihistamine [æntɪ'hɪstəmiːn] *n* antihistamínico
antiperspirant ['æntɪpəːspɪrənt] *n* antitranspirante *m*
antiquated ['æntɪkweɪtɪd] *adj* anticuado
antique [æn'tiːk] *n* antigüedad *f* ▷ *adj* antiguo
antique dealer *n* anticuario(-a)
antique shop *n* tienda de antigüedades
anti-Semitism [æntɪ'sɛmɪtɪzəm] *n* antisemitismo
antiseptic [æntɪ'sɛptɪk] *adj, n* antiséptico
antishake ['æntɪʃeɪk] *adj* estabilizador
antisocial [æntɪ'səuʃəl] *adj* antisocial
antivirus [æntɪ'vaɪərəs] *adj* antivirus; **~ software** antivirus *m*
antlers ['æntləz] *npl* cornamenta
anvil ['ænvɪl] *n* yunque *m*
anxiety [æŋ'zaɪətɪ] *n* (*worry*) inquietud *f*; (*eagerness*) ansia, anhelo
anxious ['æŋkʃəs] *adj* (*worried*) inquieto; (*keen*) deseoso; **to be ~ to do** tener muchas ganas de hacer; **I'm very ~ about you** me tienes muy preocupado

KEYWORD

any ['ɛnɪ] *adj* **1** (*in questions etc*) algún/alguna; **have you any butter/children?** ¿tienes mantequilla/hijos?; **if there are any tickets left** si quedan billetes, si queda algún billete
2 (*with negative*): **I haven't any money/books** no tengo dinero/libros
3 (*no matter which*) cualquier; **any excuse will do** valdrá *or* servirá cualquier excusa; **choose any book you like** escoge el libro que quieras; **any teacher you ask will tell you** cualquier profesor al que preguntes te lo dirá
4 (*in phrases*): **in any case** de todas formas, en cualquier caso; **any day now** cualquier día (de estos); **at any moment** en cualquier momento, de un momento a otro; **at any rate** en todo caso; **any time: come (at) any time** ven cuando quieras; **he might come (at) any time** podría llegar de un momento a otro
▷ *pron* **1** (*in questions etc*): **have you got any?** ¿tienes alguno/a?; **can any of you sing?** ¿sabe cantar alguno de vosotros/ustedes?
2 (*with negative*): **I haven't any (of them)** no tengo ninguno
3 (*no matter which one(s)*): **take any of those books (you like)** toma el libro que quieras de ésos
▷ *adv* **1** (*in questions etc*): **do you want any more soup/sandwiches?** ¿quieres más sopa/bocadillos?; **are you feeling any better?** ¿te sientes algo mejor?
2 (*with negative*): **I can't hear him any more** ya no le oigo; **don't wait any longer** no esperes más

anybody ['ɛnɪbɔdɪ] *pron* cualquiera, cualquier persona; (*in interrogative sentences*) alguien; (*in negative sentences*): **I don't see ~** no veo a nadie
anyhow ['ɛnɪhau] *adv* de todos modos, de todas maneras; (*carelessly*) de cualquier manera; (*haphazardly*) de cualquier modo; **I shall go ~** iré de todas maneras
anyone ['ɛnɪwʌn] *pron* = **anybody**
anyplace ['ɛnɪpleɪs] *adv* (*US*) = **anywhere**
anything ['ɛnɪθɪŋ] *pron* cualquier cosa;

(in interrogative sentences) algo; *(in negative sentences)* nada; *(everything)* todo; **~ else?** ¿algo más?; **can you see ~?** ¿ves algo?; **he'll eat ~** come de todo *or* lo que sea; **it can cost ~ between £15 and £20** puede costar entre 15 y 20 libras
anytime ['ɛnɪtaɪm] *adv (at any moment)* en cualquier momento, de un momento a otro; *(whenever)* no importa cuándo, cuando quiera
anyway ['ɛnɪweɪ] *adv (at any rate)* de todos modos, de todas formas; **I shall go ~** iré de todos modos; *(besides)*: **~, I couldn't come even if I wanted to** además, no podría venir aunque quisiera; **why are you phoning, ~?** ¿entonces, por qué llamas?, ¿por qué llamas, pues?
anywhere ['ɛnɪwɛəʳ] *adv* dondequiera; *(interrogative)* en algún sitio; *(negative sense)* en ningún sitio; *(everywhere)* en *or* por todas partes; **I don't see him ~** no le veo en ningún sitio; **are you going ~?** ¿vas a algún sitio?; **~ in the world** en cualquier parte del mundo
apart [ə'pɑ:t] *adv* aparte, separadamente; **10 miles ~** separados por 10 millas; **to take ~** desmontar; **~ from** *prep* aparte de
apartheid [ə'pɑ:teɪt] *n* apartheid *m*
apartment [ə'pɑ:tmənt] *n (US)* piso, departamento *(LAm)*, apartamento; *(room)* cuarto
apartment block *or* **building** *n (US)* bloque *m* de apartamentos
apathetic [æpə'θɛtɪk] *adj* apático, indiferente
apathy ['æpəθɪ] *n* apatía, indiferencia
ape [eɪp] *n* mono ▷ *vt* imitar, remedar
aperitif [ə'pɛrɪti:f] *n* aperitivo
aperture ['æpətʃjuəʳ] *n* rendija, resquicio; *(Phot)* abertura
APEX ['eɪpɛks] *n abbr (Aviat: = advance purchase excursion)* tarifa *f* APEX
apex ['eɪpɛks] *n* ápice *m*; *(fig)* cumbre *f*
aphorism ['æfərɪzəm] *n* aforismo
aphrodisiac [æfrəu'dɪzɪæk] *adj, n* afrodisíaco
apiece [ə'pi:s] *adv* cada uno
apologetic [əpɔlə'dʒɛtɪk] *adj (look, remark)* de disculpa
apologize [ə'pɔlədʒaɪz] *vi*: **to ~ (for sth to sb)** disculparse (con algn por algo)
apology [ə'pɔlədʒɪ] *n* disculpa, excusa; **please accept my apologies** le ruego me disculpe
apostle [ə'pɔsl] *n* apóstol *m/f*
apostrophe [ə'pɔstrəfɪ] *n* apóstrofo *m*
app *n abbr (Comput)* = **application**
appal [ə'pɔ:l] *vt* horrorizar, espantar
appalling [ə'pɔ:lɪŋ] *adj* espantoso; *(awful)* pésimo; **she's an ~ cook** es una cocinera malísima
apparatus [æpə'reɪtəs] *n (equipment)* equipo; *(organization)* aparato; *(in gymnasium)* aparatos *mpl*
apparel [ə'pærl] *n (US)* indumentaria
apparent [ə'pærənt] *adj* aparente; *(obvious)* manifiesto, evidente; **it is ~ that** está claro que
apparently [ə'pærəntlɪ] *adv* por lo visto, al parecer, dizque *(LAm)*
appeal [ə'pi:l] *vi (Law)* apelar ▷ *n (Law)* apelación *f*; *(request)* llamamiento, llamado *(LAm)*; *(plea)* petición *f*; *(charm)* atractivo, encanto; **to ~ for** solicitar; **to ~ to** *(person)* rogar a, suplicar a; *(thing)* atraer, interesar; **to ~ to sb for mercy** rogarle misericordia a algn; **it doesn't ~ to me** no me atrae, no me llama la atención; **right of ~** derecho de apelación
appealing [ə'pi:lɪŋ] *adj (nice)* atractivo; *(touching)* conmovedor(a), emocionante
appear [ə'pɪəʳ] *vi* aparecer, presentarse; *(Law)* comparecer; *(publication)* salir (a luz), publicarse; *(seem)* parecer; **to ~ on TV/in "Hamlet"** salir por la tele/hacer un papel en "Hamlet"; **it would ~ that** parecería que
appearance [ə'pɪərəns] *n* aparición *f*; *(look, aspect)* apariencia, aspecto; **to keep up ~s** salvar las apariencias; **to all ~s** al parecer
appease [ə'pi:z] *vt (pacify)* apaciguar; *(satisfy)* satisfacer
appendices [ə'pɛndɪsi:z] *npl of* **appendix**
appendicitis [əpɛndɪ'saɪtɪs] *n* apendicitis *f*
appendix *(pl* **appendices***)* [ə'pɛndɪks, -dɪsi:z] *n* apéndice *m*; **to have one's ~ out** operarse de apendicitis
appetite ['æpɪtaɪt] *n* apetito; *(fig)* deseo, anhelo; **that walk has given me an ~** ese paseo me ha abierto el apetito
appetizer ['æpɪtaɪzəʳ] *n (drink)* aperitivo; *(food)* tapas *fpl (Sp)*
applaud [ə'plɔ:d] *vt, vi* aplaudir
applause [ə'plɔ:z] *n* aplausos *mpl*
apple ['æpl] *n* manzana
apple pie *n* pastel *m* de manzana, pay *m* de manzana *(LAm)*
apple tree *n* manzano
appliance [ə'plaɪəns] *n* aparato; **electrical ~s** electrodomésticos *mpl*
applicable [ə'plɪkəbl] *adj* aplicable, pertinente; **the law is ~ from January** la ley es aplicable *or* se pone en vigor a partir de enero; **to be ~ to** referirse a
applicant ['æplɪkənt] *n* candidato(-a); solicitante *m/f*
application [æplɪ'keɪʃən] *n (also Comput)* aplicación *f*; *(for a job, a grant etc)* solicitud *f*
application form *n* solicitud *f*
applied [ə'plaɪd] *adj (science, art)* aplicado
apply [ə'plaɪ] *vt*: **to ~ (to)** aplicar (a); *(fig)* emplear (para) ▷ *vi*: **to ~ to** *(ask)* dirigirse a; *(be suitable for)* ser aplicable a; *(be relevant to)* tener que ver con; **to ~ for** *(permit, grant, job)* solicitar; **to ~ the brakes** echar el freno; **to ~ o.s. to** aplicarse a, dedicarse a
appoint [ə'pɔɪnt] *vt (to post)* nombrar; *(date, place)* fijar, señalar

appointment [ə'pɔɪntmənt] *n* (*engagement*) cita; (*date*) compromiso; (*act*) nombramiento; (*post*) puesto; **to make an ~ (with)** (*doctor*) pedir hora (con); (*friend*) citarse (con); **"~s"** "ofertas de trabajo"; **by ~** mediante cita
apportion [ə'pɔːʃən] *vt* repartir
appraisal [ə'preɪzl] *n* evaluación *f*
appreciably [ə'priːʃəblɪ] *adv* sensiblemente, de manera apreciable
appreciate [ə'priːʃɪeɪt] *vt* (*like*) apreciar, tener en mucho; (*be grateful for*) agradecer; (*be aware of*) comprender ▷ *vi* (*Comm*) aumentar en valor; **I ~d your help** agradecí tu ayuda
appreciation [əpriːʃɪ'eɪʃən] *n* apreciación *f*; (*gratitude*) reconocimiento, agradecimiento; (*Comm*) aumento en valor
appreciative [ə'priːʃɪətɪv] *adj* agradecido
apprehend [æprɪ'hɛnd] *vt* percibir; (*arrest*) detener
apprehension [æprɪ'hɛnʃən] *n* (*fear*) aprensión *f*
apprehensive [æprɪ'hɛnsɪv] *adj* aprensivo
apprentice [ə'prɛntɪs] *n* aprendiz(a) *m(f)* ▷ *vt*: **to be ~d to** estar de aprendiz con
apprenticeship [ə'prɛntɪsʃɪp] *n* aprendizaje *m*; **to serve one's ~** hacer el aprendizaje
approach [ə'prəutʃ] *vi* acercarse ▷ *vt* acercarse a; (*be approximate*) aproximarse a; (*ask, apply to*) dirigirse a; (*problem*) abordar ▷ *n* acercamiento; aproximación *f*; (*access*) acceso; (*proposal*) proposición *f*; (*to problem etc*) enfoque *m*; **to ~ sb about sth** hablar con algn sobre algo
approachable [ə'prəutʃəbl] *adj* (*person*) abordable; (*place*) accesible
appropriate [ə'prəuprɪɪt] *adj* apropiado, conveniente ▷ *vt* [-rɪeɪt] (*take*) apropiarse de; (*allot*): **to ~ sth for** destinar algo a; **~ for** *or* **to** apropiado para; **it would not be ~ for me to comment** no estaría bien *or* sería pertinente que yo diera mi opinión
approval [ə'pruːvəl] *n* aprobación *f*, visto bueno; **on ~** (*Comm*) a prueba; **to meet with sb's ~** obtener la aprobación de algn
approve [ə'pruːv] *vt* aprobar; **approve of** *vt fus* aprobar; **they don't ~ of her** (ella) no les parece bien
approved school [ə'pruːvd-] *n* (*Brit*) correccional *m*
approx. *abbr* (= *approximately*) aprox
approximate [ə'prɔksɪmɪt] *adj* aproximado
approximately [ə'prɔksɪmɪtlɪ] *adv* aproximadamente, más o menos
approximation [əprɔksɪ'meɪʃən] *n* aproximación *f*
Apr. *abbr* (= *April*) abr
apr *n abbr* (= *annual percentage rate*) tasa de interés anual
apricot ['eɪprɪkɔt] *n* albaricoque *m* (*Sp*), damasco (*LAm*)
April ['eɪprəl] *n* abril *m*; *see also* **July**
April Fools' Day *n* ≈ día *m* de los (Santos) Inocentes
apron ['eɪprən] *n* delantal *m*; (*Aviat*) pista
apt [æpt] *adj* (*to the point*) acertado, oportuno; (*appropriate*) apropiado; **~ to do** (*likely*) propenso a hacer
aptitude ['æptɪtjuːd] *n* aptitud *f*, capacidad *f*
aquarium [ə'kwɛərɪəm] *n* acuario
Aquarius [ə'kwɛərɪəs] *n* Acuario
Arab ['ærəb] *adj, n* árabe *m/f*
Arabia [ə'reɪbɪə] *n* Arabia
Arabian [ə'reɪbɪən] *adj* árabe, arábigo
Arabian Desert *n* Desierto de Arabia
Arabian Sea *n* Mar *m* de Omán
Arabic ['ærəbɪk] *adj* (*language, manuscripts*) árabe, arábigo ▷ *n* árabe *m*; **~ numerals** numeración *f* arábiga
arable ['ærəbl] *adj* cultivable
Aragon ['ærəgən] *n* Aragón *m*
arbitrary ['ɑːbɪtrərɪ] *adj* arbitrario
arbitration [ɑːbɪ'treɪʃən] *n* arbitraje *m*; **the dispute went to ~** el conflicto laboral fue sometido al arbitraje
arbitrator ['ɑːbɪtreɪtə^r] *n* árbitro
arc [ɑːk] *n* arco
arcade [ɑː'keɪd] *n* (*Arch*) arcada; (*round a square*) soportales *mpl*; (*shopping arcade*) galería comercial
arch [ɑːtʃ] *n* arco; (*vault*) bóveda; (*of foot*) puente *m* ▷ *vt* arquear
archaeological [ɑːkɪə'lɔdʒɪkl] *adj* arqueológico
archaeologist [ɑːkɪ'ɔlədʒɪst] *n* arqueólogo(-a)
archaeology [ɑːkɪ'ɔlədʒɪ] *n* arqueología
archaic [ɑː'keɪɪk] *adj* arcaico
archbishop [ɑːtʃ'bɪʃəp] *n* arzobispo
archenemy ['ɑːtʃ'ɛnəmɪ] *n* enemigo jurado
archeology *etc* [ɑːkɪ'ɔlədʒɪ] (US) *see* **archaeology** *etc*
archery ['ɑːtʃərɪ] *n* tiro al arco
architect ['ɑːkɪtɛkt] *n* arquitecto(-a)
architectural [ɑːkɪ'tɛktʃərəl] *adj* arquitectónico
architecture ['ɑːkɪtɛktʃə^r] *n* arquitectura
archive ['ɑːkaɪv] *n often pl* (*also Comput*) archivo; **archives** *npl* archivo *sg*
Arctic ['ɑːktɪk] *adj* ártico ▷ *n*: **the ~** el Ártico
Arctic Circle *n* Círculo Polar Ártico
Arctic Ocean *n* Océano (Glacial) Ártico
ardent ['ɑːdənt] *adj* (*desire*) ardiente; (*supporter, lover*) apasionado
are [ɑː^r] *vb see* **be**
area ['ɛərɪə] *n* área; (*Math etc*) superficie *f*, extensión *f*; (*zone*) región *f*, zona; (*of knowledge, experience*) campo; **the London ~** la zona de Londres
area code *n* (*US Tel*) prefijo
arena [ə'riːnə] *n* arena; (*of circus*) pista; (*for bullfight*) plaza, ruedo
aren't [ɑːnt] = **are not**
Argentina [ɑːdʒən'tiːnə] *n* Argentina

Argentinian [ɑːdʒən'tɪnɪən] *adj, n* argentino(-a) *m(f)*
arguable ['ɑːgjuəbl] *adj*: **it is ~ whether ...** es dudoso que + *subjun*
arguably ['ɑːgjuəblɪ] *adv*: **it is ~ ...** es discutiblemente ...
argue ['ɑːgjuː] *vt* (*debate*: *case, matter*) mantener, argüir ▷ *vi* (*quarrel*) discutir; (*reason*) razonar, argumentar; **to ~ that** sostener que; **to ~ about sth (with sb)** pelearse (con algn) por algo
argument ['ɑːgjumənt] *n* (*reasons*) argumento; (*quarrel*) discusión *f*; (*debate*) debate *m*; **~ for/against** argumento en pro/contra de
argumentative [ɑːgju'mɛntətɪv] *adj* discutidor(a)
Aries ['ɛərɪz] *n* Aries *m*
arise [ə'raɪz] (*pt* **arose**, *pp* **arisen** [ə'rɪzn]) *vi* (*rise up*) levantarse, alzarse; (*emerge*) surgir, presentarse; **to ~ from** derivar de; **should the need ~** si fuera necesario
aristocracy [ærɪs'tɔkrəsɪ] *n* aristocracia
aristocrat ['ærɪstəkræt] *n* aristócrata *m/f*
aristocratic [ərɪstə'krætɪk] *adj* aristocrático
arithmetic [ə'rɪθmətɪk] *n* aritmética
Ark [ɑːk] *n*: **Noah's ~** el Arca *f* de Noé
arm [ɑːm] *n* (*Anat*) brazo ▷ *vt* armar; **~ in ~** cogidos del brazo; *see also* **arms**
armaments ['ɑːməmənts] *npl* (*weapons*) armamentos *mpl*
armchair ['ɑːmtʃɛə^r] *n* sillón *m*, butaca
armed [ɑːmd] *adj* armado; **the ~ forces** las fuerzas armadas
armed robbery *n* robo a mano armada
Armenia [ɑː'miːnɪə] *n* Armenia
armour, armor (*US*) ['ɑːmə^r] *n* armadura
armoured car, armored car (*US*) *n* coche *m* or carro (*LAm*) blindado
armpit ['ɑːmpɪt] *n* sobaco, axila
armrest ['ɑːmrɛst] *n* reposabrazos *m inv*, brazo
arms [ɑːmz] *npl* (*weapons*) armas *fpl*; (*Heraldry*) escudo *sg*
army ['ɑːmɪ] *n* ejército; (*fig*) multitud *f*
A road *n* (*Brit*) ≈ carretera *f* nacional
aroma [ə'rəumə] *n* aroma *m*, fragancia
aromatherapy [ərəumə'θɛrəpɪ] *n* aromaterapia
arose [ə'rəuz] *pt of* **arise**
around [ə'raund] *adv* alrededor; (*in the area*) a la redonda ▷ *prep* alrededor de
arousal [ə'rauzəl] *n* (*sexual*) excitación *f*; (*of feelings, interest*) despertar *m*
arouse [ə'rauz] *vt* despertar; (*anger*) provocar
arrange [ə'reɪndʒ] *vt* arreglar, ordenar; (*programme*) organizar; (*appointment*) concertar ▷ *vi*: **we have ~d for a taxi to pick you up** hemos organizado todo para que le recoja un taxi; **to ~ to do sth** quedar en hacer algo; **it was ~d that ...** se quedó en que ...
arrangement [ə'reɪndʒmənt] *n* arreglo; (*agreement*) acuerdo; **arrangements** *npl* (*plans*) planes *mpl*, medidas *fpl*; (*preparations*) preparativos *mpl*; **to come to an ~ (with sb)** llegar a un acuerdo (con algn); **by ~** a convenir; **I'll make ~s for you to be met** haré los preparativos para que le estén esperando
arrant ['ærənt] *adj*: **~ nonsense** una verdadera tontería
array [ə'reɪ] *n* (*Comput*) matriz *f*; **~ of** (*things*) serie *f* or colección *f* de; (*people*) conjunto de
arrears [ə'rɪəz] *npl* atrasos *mpl*; **in ~** (*Comm*) en mora; **to be in ~ with one's rent** estar retrasado en el pago del alquiler
arrest [ə'rɛst] *vt* detener; (*sb's attention*) llamar ▷ *n* detención *f*; **under ~** detenido
arrival [ə'raɪvəl] *n* llegada, arribo (*LAm*); **new ~** recién llegado(-a)
arrive [ə'raɪv] *vi* llegar, arribar (*LAm*); **arrive at** *vt fus* (*decision, solution*) llegar a
arrogance ['ærəgəns] *n* arrogancia, prepotencia (*LAm*)
arrogant ['ærəgənt] *adj* arrogante, prepotente (*LAm*)
arrow ['ærəu] *n* flecha
arse [ɑːs] *n* (*Brit inf!*) culo, trasero
arsenal ['ɑːsɪnl] *n* arsenal *m*
arsenic ['ɑːsnɪk] *n* arsénico
arson ['ɑːsn] *n* incendio provocado
art [ɑːt] *n* arte *m*; (*skill*) destreza; (*technique*) técnica; **Arts** *npl* (*Scol*) Letras *fpl*; **work of ~** obra de arte
art college *n* escuela *f* de Bellas Artes
artefact ['ɑːtɪfækt] *n* artefacto
artery ['ɑːtərɪ] *n* (*Med: road etc*) arteria
artful ['ɑːtful] *adj* (*cunning*: *person, trick*) mañoso
art gallery *n* pinacoteca, museo de pintura; (*Comm*) galería de arte
arthritis [ɑː'θraɪtɪs] *n* artritis *f*
artichoke ['ɑːtɪtʃəuk] *n* alcachofa; **Jerusalem ~** aguaturma
article ['ɑːtɪkl] *n* artículo, objeto, cosa; (*in newspaper*) artículo; (*Brit Law: training*); **articles** *npl* contrato *sg* de aprendizaje; **~s of clothing** prendas *fpl* de vestir
articulate *adj* [ɑː'tɪkjulɪt] (*speech*) claro; (*person*) que se expresa bien ▷ *vi* [ɑː'tɪkjuleɪt] articular ▷ *vt* [ɑː'tɪkjuleɪt] expresar
articulated lorry *n* (*Brit*) trailer *m*
artificial [ɑːtɪ'fɪʃəl] *adj* artificial; (*teeth etc*) postizo
artificial insemination *n* inseminación *f* artificial
artificial respiration *n* respiración *f* artificial
artillery [ɑː'tɪlərɪ] *n* artillería
artisan ['ɑːtɪzæn] *n* artesano(-a)
artist ['ɑːtɪst] *n* artista *m/f*; (*Mus*) intérprete *m/f*
artistic [ɑː'tɪstɪk] *adj* artístico
artistry ['ɑːtɪstrɪ] *n* arte *m*, habilidad *f* (artística)

art school *n* escuela de bellas artes
artwork ['ɑːtwəːk] *n* material *m* gráfico

KEYWORD

as [æz] *conj* **1** (*referring to time: while*) mientras; (*: when*) cuando; **she wept as she told her story** lloraba mientras contaba lo que le ocurrió; **as the years go by** con el paso de los años, a medida que pasan los años; **he came in as I was leaving** entró cuando me marchaba; **as from tomorrow** a partir de *or* desde mañana
2 (*in comparisons*): **as big as** tan grande como; **twice as big as** el doble de grande que; **as much money/many books as** tanto dinero/tantos libros como; **as soon as** en cuanto, no bien (*LAm*)
3 (*since, because*) como, ya que; **as I don't speak German I can't understand him** como no hablo alemán no le entiendo, no le entiendo ya que no hablo alemán
4 (*although*): **much as I like them, ...** aunque me gustan, ...
5 (*referring to manner, way*): **do as you wish** haz lo que quieras; **as she said** como dijo; **he gave it to me as a present** me lo dio de regalo; **it's on the left as you go in** según se entra, a la izquierda
6 (*concerning*): **as for** *or* **to that** por *or* en lo que respecta a eso
7: **as if** *or* **though** como si; **he looked as if he was ill** parecía como si estuviera enfermo, tenía aspecto de enfermo; *see also* **long**; **such**; **well**
▷ *prep* (*in the capacity of*): **he works as a barman** trabaja de barman; **as chairman of the company, he ...** como presidente de la compañía, ...

a.s.a.p. *abbr* (= *as soon as possible*) cuanto antes, lo más pronto posible
asbestos [æz'bɛstəs] *n* asbesto, amianto
ascend [ə'sɛnd] *vt* subir, ascender
ascendancy [ə'sɛndənsɪ] *n* ascendiente *m*, dominio
ascent [ə'sɛnt] *n* subida; (*slope*) cuesta, pendiente *f*; (*of plane*) ascenso
ascertain [æsə'teɪn] *vt* averiguar
ascetic [ə'sɛtɪk] *adj* ascético
ASCII ['æskiː] *n abbr* (= *American Standard Code for Information Interchange*) ASCII
ascribe [ə'skraɪb] *vt*: **to ~ sth to** atribuir algo a
ash [æʃ] *n* ceniza; (*tree*) fresno
ashamed [ə'ʃeɪmd] *adj* avergonzado; **to be ~ of** avergonzarse de
ashen ['æʃn] *adj* pálido
ashore [ə'ʃɔːʳ] *adv* en tierra; (*swim etc*) a tierra
ashtray ['æʃtreɪ] *n* cenicero
Ash Wednesday *n* miércoles *m* de Ceniza
Asia ['eɪʃə] *n* Asia
Asian ['eɪʃən], **Asiatic** [eɪsɪ'ætɪk] *adj, n* asiático(-a) *m(f)*
aside [ə'saɪd] *adv* a un lado ▷ *n* aparte *m*; **~ from** *prep* (*as well as*) aparte *or* además de
ask [ɑːsk] *vt* (*question*) preguntar; (*demand*) pedir; (*invite*) invitar ▷ *vi*: **to ~ about sth** preguntar acerca de algo; **to ~ sb sth/to do sth** preguntar algo a algn/pedir a algn que haga algo; **to ~ sb about sth** preguntar algo a algn; **to ~ (sb) a question** hacer una pregunta (a algn); **to ~ sb the time** preguntar la hora a algn; **to ~ sb out to dinner** invitar a cenar a algn; **ask after** *vt fus* preguntar por; **ask for** *vt fus* pedir; **it's just ~ing for trouble** *or* **for it** es buscarse problemas
askance [ə'skɑːns] *adv*: **to look ~ at sb** mirar con recelo a algn
asking price *n* (*Comm*) precio inicial
asleep [ə'sliːp] *adj* dormido; **to fall ~** dormirse, quedarse dormido
asparagus [əs'pærəgəs] *n* espárragos *mpl*
aspect ['æspɛkt] *n* aspecto, apariencia; (*direction in which a building etc faces*) orientación *f*
aspersions [əs'pəːʃənz] *npl*: **to cast ~ on** difamar a, calumniar a
asphyxiate [æs'fɪksɪeɪt] *vt* asfixiar
asphyxiation [aesfɪksɪ'eɪʃən] *n* asfixia
aspirate ['æspəreɪt] *vt* aspirar ▷ *adj* ['æspərɪt] aspirado
aspirations [æspə'reɪʃənz] *npl* aspiraciones *fpl*; (*ambition*) ambición *f*
aspire [əs'paɪəʳ] *vi*: **to ~ to** aspirar a, ambicionar
aspirin ['æsprɪn] *n* aspirina
aspiring [əs'paɪərɪŋ] *adj*: **an ~ actor** un aspirante a actor
ass [æs] *n* asno, burro; (*inf*) imbécil *m/f*; (*US inf!*) culo, trasero
assailant [ə'seɪlənt] *n* agresor(a) *m(f)*
assassin [ə'sæsɪn] *n* asesino(-a)
assassinate [ə'sæsɪneɪt] *vt* asesinar
assassination [əsæsɪ'neɪʃən] *n* asesinato
assault [ə'sɔːlt] *n* (*gen: attack*) asalto; (*Law*) agresión *f* ▷ *vt* asaltar, agredir; (*sexually*) violar
assemble [ə'sɛmbl] *vt* reunir, juntar; (*Tech*) montar ▷ *vi* reunirse, juntarse
assembly [ə'sɛmblɪ] *n* (*meeting*) reunión *f*, asamblea; (*parliament*) parlamento; (*construction*) montaje *m*
assembly line *n* cadena de montaje
assent [ə'sɛnt] *n* asentimiento, aprobación *f* ▷ *vi* consentir, asentir; **to ~ (to sth)** consentir (en algo)
assert [ə'səːt] *vt* afirmar; (*insist on*) hacer valer; **to ~ o.s.** imponerse
assertion [ə'səːʃən] *n* afirmación *f*
assertive [ə'səːtɪv] *adj* enérgico, agresivo, perentorio
assess [ə'sɛs] *vt* valorar, calcular; (*tax, damages*) fijar; (*property etc: for tax*) gravar

assessment [əˈsɛsmənt] *n* valoración *f*; gravamen *m*; (*judgment*): **~ (of)** juicio (sobre)
assessor [əˈsɛsəʳ] *n* asesor(a) *m(f)*; (*of tax*) tasador(a) *m(f)*
asset [ˈæsɛt] *n* posesión *f*; (*quality*) ventaja; **assets** *npl* (*funds*) activo *sg*, fondos *mpl*
assiduous [əˈsɪdjuəs] *adj* asiduo
assign [əˈsaɪn] *vt* (*date*) fijar; (*task*) asignar; (*resources*) destinar; (*property*) traspasar
assignment [əˈsaɪnmənt] *n* asignación *f*; (*task*) tarea
assimilate [əˈsɪmɪleɪt] *vt* asimilar
assimilation [əsɪmɪˈleɪʃən] *n* asimilación *f*
assist [əˈsɪst] *vt* ayudar
assistance [əˈsɪstəns] *n* ayuda, auxilio
assistant [əˈsɪstənt] *n* ayudante *m/f*; (*Brit*: *also*: **shop ~**) dependiente(-a) *m(f)*
associate [*adj, n* əˈsəuʃɪɪt, *vt, vi* əˈsəuʃɪeɪt] *adj* asociado ▷ *n* socio(-a), colega *m/f*; (*in crime*) cómplice *m/f*; (*member*) miembro(-a) ▷ *vt* asociar; (*ideas*) relacionar ▷ *vi*: **to ~ with sb** tratar con algn; **~ director** subdirector(a) *m(f)*; **~d company** compañía afiliada
association [əsəusɪˈeɪʃən] *n* asociación *f*; (*Comm*) sociedad *f*; **in ~ with** en asociación con
assorted [əˈsɔːtɪd] *adj* surtido, variado; **in ~ sizes** en distintos tamaños
assortment [əˈsɔːtmənt] *n* (*of shapes, colours*) surtido; (*of books*) colección *f*; (*of people*) mezcla
Asst. *abbr* = **Assistant**
assume [əˈsjuːm] *vt* (*suppose*) suponer; (*responsibilities etc*) asumir; (*attitude, name*) adoptar, tomar
assumed name [əˈsjuːmd-] *n* nombre *m* falso
assumption [əˈsʌmpʃən] *n* (*supposition*) suposición *f*, presunción *f*; (*act*) asunción *f*; **on the ~ that** suponiendo que
assurance [əˈʃuərəns] *n* garantía, promesa; (*confidence*) confianza, aplomo; (*Brit*: *insurance*) seguro; **I can give you no ~s** no puedo hacerle ninguna promesa
assure [əˈʃuəʳ] *vt* asegurar
assured [əˈʃuəd] *adj* seguro
asterisk [ˈæstərɪsk] *n* asterisco
asteroid [ˈæstərɔɪd] *n* asteroide *m*
asthma [ˈæsmə] *n* asma
astonish [əˈstɔnɪʃ] *vt* asombrar, pasmar
astonished [əˈstɔnɪʃt] *adj* estupefacto, pasmado; **to be ~ (at)** asombrarse (de)
astonishing [əˈstɔnɪʃɪŋ] *adj* asombroso, pasmoso; **I find it ~ that ...** me asombra *or* pasma que ...
astonishment [əˈstɔnɪʃmənt] *n* asombro, sorpresa; **to my ~** con gran sorpresa mía
astound [əˈstaund] *vt* asombrar, pasmar
astounding [əˈstaundɪŋ] *adj* asombroso
astray [əˈstreɪ] *adv*: **to go ~** extraviarse; **to lead ~** llevar por mal camino; **to go ~ in one's calculations** equivocarse en sus cálculos
astride [əˈstraɪd] *prep* a caballo *or* horcajadas sobre
astrologer [əsˈtrɔlədʒəʳ] *n* astrólogo(-a)
astrology [əsˈtrɔlədʒɪ] *n* astrología
astronaut [ˈæstrənɔːt] *n* astronauta *m/f*
astronomer [əsˈtrɔnəməʳ] *n* astrónomo(-a)
astronomical [æstrəˈnɔmɪkəl] *adj* astronómico
astronomy [aesˈtrɔnəmɪ] *n* astronomía
astute [əsˈtjuːt] *adj* astuto
asylum [əˈsaɪləm] *n* (*refuge*) asilo; (*hospital*) manicomio; **to seek political ~** pedir asilo político

KEYWORD

at [æt] *prep* **1** (*referring to position*) en; (*direction*) a; **at the top** en lo alto; **at home/school** en casa/la escuela; **to look at sth/sb** mirar algo/a algn
2 (*referring to time*): **at four o'clock** a las cuatro; **at night** por la noche; **at Christmas** en Navidad; **at times** a veces
3 (*referring to rates, speed etc*): **at £1 a kilo** a una libra el kilo; **two at a time** de dos en dos; **at 50 km/h** a 50 km/h
4 (*referring to manner*): **at a stroke** de un golpe; **at peace** en paz
5 (*referring to activity*): **to be at work** estar trabajando; (*in office*) estar en el trabajo; **to play at cowboys** jugar a los vaqueros; **to be good at sth** ser bueno en algo
6 (*referring to cause*): **shocked/surprised/annoyed at sth** asombrado/sorprendido/fastidiado por algo; **I went at his suggestion** fui a instancias suyas
▷ *n* (*symbol @*) arroba

ate [ɛt, eɪt] *pt of* **eat**
atheism [ˈeɪθɪɪzəm] *n* ateísmo
atheist [ˈeɪθɪɪst] *n* ateo(-a)
Athens [ˈæθɪnz] *n* Atenas *f*
athlete [ˈæθliːt] *n* atleta *m/f*
athletic [æθˈlɛtɪk] *adj* atlético
athletics [æθˈlɛtɪks] *n* atletismo
Atlantic [ətˈlæntɪk] *adj* atlántico ▷ *n*: **the ~ (Ocean)** el (Océano) Atlántico
atlas [ˈætləs] *n* atlas *m inv*
A.T.M. *n abbr* (= *Automated Telling Machine*) *cajero automático*
atmosphere [ˈætməsfɪəʳ] *n* (*air*) atmósfera; (*fig*) ambiente *m*
atom [ˈætəm] *n* átomo
atom bomb *n* bomba atómica
atomic [əˈtɔmɪk] *adj* atómico
atomic bomb *n* bomba atómica
atomizer [ˈætəmaɪzəʳ] *n* atomizador *m*
atone [əˈtəun] *vi*: **to ~ for** expiar
A to Z® *n* guía alfabética; (*map*) callejero
atrocious [əˈtrəuʃəs] *adj* atroz; (*fig*) horrible, infame
atrocity [əˈtrɔsɪtɪ] *n* atrocidad *f*

attach [ə'tætʃ] *vt* sujetar; (*stick*) pegar; (*document, email, letter*) adjuntar; **to be ~ed to sb/sth** (*like*) tener cariño a algn/algo; **the ~ed letter** la carta adjunta
attaché [ə'tæʃeɪ] *n* agregado(-a)
attaché case *n* (*Brit*) maletín *m*
attachment [ə'tætʃmənt] *n* (*tool*) accesorio; (*Comput*) archivo *o* documento adjunto; (*love*): **~ (to)** apego (a), cariño (a)
attack [ə'tæk] *vt* (*Mil*) atacar; (*criminal*) agredir, asaltar; (*criticize*) criticar; (*task etc*) emprender ▷ *n* ataque *m*, asalto; (*on sb's life*) atentado; (*fig*: *criticism*) crítica; **heart ~** infarto (de miocardio)
attacker [ə'tækəʳ] *n* agresor(a) *m(f)*, asaltante *m/f*
attain [ə'teɪn] *vt* (*also*: **~ to**) alcanzar; (*achieve*) lograr, conseguir
attainments [ə'teɪnmənts] *npl* (*skill*) talento *sg*
attempt [ə'tɛmpt] *n* tentativa, intento; (*attack*) atentado ▷ *vt* intentar, tratar de; **he made no ~ to help** ni siquiera intentó ayudar
attempted [ə'tɛmptɪd] *adj*: **~ murder/burglary/suicide** tentativa *or* intento de asesinato/robo/suicidio
attend [ə'tɛnd] *vt* asistir a; (*patient*) atender; **attend to** *vt fus* (*needs, affairs etc*) ocuparse de; (*speech etc*) prestar atención a; (*customer*) atender a
attendance [ə'tɛndəns] *n* asistencia, presencia; (*people present*) concurrencia
attendant [ə'tɛndənt] *n* sirviente(-a) *m(f)*, ayudante *m/f*; (*Theat*) acomodador(a) *m(f)* ▷ *adj* concomitante
attention [ə'tɛnʃən] *n* atención *f* ▷ *excl* (*Mil*) ¡firme(s)!; **for the ~ of ...** (*Admin*) a la atención de ...; **it has come to my ~ that ...** me he enterado de que ...
attentive [ə'tɛntɪv] *adj* atento; (*polite*) cortés
attest [ə'tɛst] *vi*: **to ~ to** dar fe de
attic ['ætɪk] *n* desván *m*, altillo (*LAm*), entretecho (*LAm*)
attitude ['ætɪtjuːd] *n* (*gen*) actitud *f*; (*disposition*) disposición *f*
attorney [ə'təːnɪ] *n* (*US*: *lawyer*) abogado(-a); (*having proxy*) apoderado
Attorney General *n* (*Brit*) ≈ Presidente *m* del Consejo del Poder Judicial (*Sp*); (*US*) ≈ ministro de Justicia
attract [ə'trækt] *vt* atraer; (*attention*) llamar
attraction [ə'trækʃən] *n* (*gen*) encanto, atractivo; (*Physics*) atracción *f*; (*towards sth*) atracción *f*
attractive [ə'træktɪv] *adj* atractivo
attribute ['ætrɪbjuːt] *n* atributo ▷ *vt* [ə'trɪbjuːt]: **to ~ sth to** atribuir algo a; (*accuse*) achacar algo a
attrition [ə'trɪʃən] *n*: **war of ~** guerra de agotamiento *or* desgaste
atypical [eɪ'tɪpɪkl] *adj* atípico
aubergine ['əubəʒiːn] *n* (*Brit*) berenjena; (*colour*) morado
auburn ['ɔːbən] *adj* color castaño rojizo
auction ['ɔːkʃən] *n* (*also*: **sale by ~**) subasta ▷ *vt* subastar
auctioneer [ɔːkʃə'nɪəʳ] *n* subastador(a) *m(f)*
audacious [ɔː'deɪʃəs] *adj* (*bold*) audaz, osado; (*impudent*) atrevido, descarado
audacity [ɔː'dæsɪtɪ] *n* audacia, atrevimiento; (*pej*) descaro
audible ['ɔːdɪbl] *adj* audible, que se puede oír
audience ['ɔːdɪəns] *n* auditorio; (*gathering*) público; (*Radio*) radioescuchas *mpl*; (*TV*) telespectadores *mpl*; (*interview*) audiencia
audio-typist ['ɔːdɪəu'taɪpɪst] *n* mecanógrafo(-a) de dictáfono
audiovisual [ɔːdɪəu'vɪzjuəl] *adj* audiovisual
audit ['ɔːdɪt] *vt* revisar, intervenir
audition [ɔː'dɪʃən] *n* audición *f* ▷ *vi*: **to ~ for the part of** hacer una audición para el papel de
auditor ['ɔːdɪtəʳ] *n* interventor(a) *m(f)*, censor(a) *m(f)* de cuentas
auditorium [ɔːdɪ'tɔːrɪəm] *n* auditorio
Aug. *abbr* (= *August*) ag
augur ['ɔːgəʳ] *vi*: **it ~s well** es de buen agüero
August ['ɔːgəst] *n* agosto; *see also* **July**
aunt [ɑːnt] *n* tía
auntie, aunty ['ɑːntɪ] *n diminutive of* **aunt**
au pair ['əu'pɛəʳ] *n* (*also*: **~ girl**) chica *f* au pair
aura ['ɔːrə] *n* aura; (*atmosphere*) ambiente *m*
auspicious [ɔːs'pɪʃəs] *adj* propicio, de buen augurio
austere [ɔs'tɪəʳ] *adj* austero; (*manner*) adusto
austerity [ɔ'stɛrɪtɪ] *n* austeridad *f*
Australasia [ɔːstrə'leɪzɪə] *n* Australasia
Australia [ɔs'treɪlɪə] *n* Australia
Australian [ɔs'treɪlɪən] *adj, n* australiano(-a) *m(f)*
Austria ['ɔstrɪə] *n* Austria
Austrian ['ɔstrɪən] *adj, n* austríaco(-a) *m(f)*
authentic [ɔː'θɛntɪk] *adj* auténtico
authenticity [ɔːθɛn'tɪsɪtɪ] *n* autenticidad *f*
author ['ɔːθəʳ] *n* autor(a) *m(f)*
authoritarian [ɔːθɔrɪ'tɛərɪən] *adj* autoritario
authoritative [ɔː'θɔrɪtətɪv] *adj* autorizado; (*manner*) autoritario
authority [ɔː'θɔrɪtɪ] *n* autoridad *f*; **the authorities** *npl* las autoridades; **to have ~ to do sth** tener autoridad para hacer algo
authorization [ɔːθəraɪ'zeɪʃən] *n* autorización *f*
authorize ['ɔːθəraɪz] *vt* autorizar
auto ['ɔːtəu] *n* (*US*) coche *m*, carro (*LAm*), auto (*LAm*), automóvil *m*
autobiography [ɔːtəbaɪ'ɔgrəfɪ] *n* autobiografía
autograph ['ɔːtəgrɑːf] *n* autógrafo ▷ *vt* firmar; (*photo etc*) dedicar
automated ['ɔːtəmeɪtɪd] *adj* automatizado
automatic [ɔːtə'mætɪk] *adj* automático ▷ *n* (*gun*) pistola automática; (*washing machine*) lavadora

a

automatically [ɔːtəˈmætɪklɪ] *adv* automáticamente
automation [ɔːtəˈmeɪʃən] *n* automatización *f*
automobile [ˈɔːtəməbiːl] *n* (*US*) coche *m*, carro (*LAm*), auto (*LAm*), automóvil *m*
autonomous [ɔːˈtɔnəməs] *adj* autónomo
autonomy [ɔːˈtɔnəmɪ] *n* autonomía
autopsy [ˈɔːtɔpsɪ] *n* autopsia
autumn [ˈɔːtəm] *n* otoño
auxiliary [ɔːgˈzɪlɪərɪ] *adj* auxiliar
Av. *abbr* (*= avenue*) Av., Avda
avail [əˈveɪl] *vt*: **to ~ o.s. of** aprovechar(se) de, valerse de ▷ *n*: **to no ~** en vano, sin resultado
availability [əveɪləˈbɪlɪtɪ] *n* disponibilidad *f*
available [əˈveɪləbl] *adj* disponible; (*obtainable*) asequible; **to make sth ~ to sb** poner algo a la disposición de algn; **is the manager ~?** ¿está libre el gerente?
avalanche [ˈævəlɑːnʃ] *n* alud *m*, avalancha
Ave. *abbr* (*= avenue*) Av., Avda
avenge [əˈvɛndʒ] *vt* vengar
avenue [ˈævənjuː] *n* avenida; (*fig*) camino, vía
average [ˈævərɪdʒ] *n* promedio, media ▷ *adj* (*mean*) medio; (*ordinary*) regular, corriente ▷ *vt* alcanzar un promedio de; **on ~** por término medio; **average out** *vi*: **to ~ out at** salir a un promedio de
averse [əˈvəːs] *adj*: **to be ~ to sth/doing** sentir aversión *or* antipatía por algo/por hacer
aversion [əˈvəːʃən] *n* aversión *f*, repugnancia
avert [əˈvəːt] *vt* prevenir; (*blow*) desviar; (*one's eyes*) apartar
aviary [ˈeɪvɪərɪ] *n* pajarera
aviation [eɪvɪˈeɪʃən] *n* aviación *f*
avid [ˈævɪd] *adj* ávido, ansioso
avocado [ævəˈkɑːdəu] *n* (*Brit: also:* **~ pear**) aguacate *m*, palta (*LAm*)
avoid [əˈvɔɪd] *vt* evitar, eludir
avoidable [əˈvɔɪdəbl] *adj* evitable, eludible
await [əˈweɪt] *vt* esperar, aguardar; **long ~ed** largamente esperado
awake [əˈweɪk] (*pt* **awoke**, *pp* **awoken** *or* **awaked**) *adj* despierto ▷ *vt* despertar ▷ *vi* despertarse; **to be ~** estar despierto
awakening [əˈweɪknɪŋ] *n* despertar *m*
award [əˈwɔːd] *n* (*prize*) premio; (*medal*) condecoración *f*; (*Law*) fallo, sentencia; (*act*) concesión *f* ▷ *vt* (*prize*) otorgar, conceder; (*Law: damages*) adjudicar
aware [əˈwɛəʳ] *adj* consciente; (*awake*) despierto; (*informed*) enterado; **to become ~ of** darse cuenta de, enterarse de; **I am fully ~ that** sé muy bien que
awareness [əˈwɛənɪs] *n* conciencia, conocimiento
awash [əˈwɔʃ] *adj* inundado
away [əˈweɪ] *adv* (*gen*) fuera; (*far away*) lejos; **two kilometres ~** a dos kilómetros (de distancia); **two hours ~ by car** a dos horas en coche; **the holiday was two weeks ~** faltaban dos semanas para las vacaciones; **~ from** lejos de, fuera de; **he's ~ for a week** estará ausente una semana; **he's ~ in Barcelona** está en Barcelona; **to take ~** llevar(se); **to work/pedal ~** seguir trabajando/pedaleando; **to fade ~** desvanecerse; (*sound*) apagarse
away game *n* (*Sport*) partido de fuera
awe [ɔː] *n* respeto, admiración *f* respetuosa
awe-inspiring [ˈɔːɪnspaɪərɪŋ] *adj* imponente, pasmoso
awesome [ˈɔːsəm] (*esp US*) *adj* (*excellent*) formidable; = **awe-inspiring**
awful [ˈɔːfəl] *adj* terrible; **an ~ lot of** (*people, cars, dogs*) la mar de, muchísimos
awfully [ˈɔːfəlɪ] *adv* (*very*) terriblemente
awhile [əˈwaɪl] *adv* (durante) un rato, algún tiempo
awkward [ˈɔːkwəd] *adj* (*clumsy*) desmañado, torpe; (*shape, situation*) incómodo; (*difficult: question*) difícil; (*problem*) complicado
awning [ˈɔːnɪŋ] *n* (*of shop*) toldo; (*of window etc*) marquesina
awoke [əˈwəuk], **awoken** [əˈwəukən] *pt, pp of* **awake**
AWOL [ˈeɪwɔl] *abbr* (*Mil etc*) = **absent without leave**
awry [əˈraɪ] *adv*: **to be ~** estar descolocado *or* atravesado; **to go ~** salir mal, fracasar
axe, ax (*US*) [æks] *n* hacha ▷ *vt* (*employee*) despedir; (*project etc*) cortar; (*jobs*) reducir; **to have an ~ to grind** (*fig*) tener un interés creado *or* algún fin interesado
axes [ˈæksiːz] *npl of* **axis**
axis (*pl* **axes**) [ˈæksɪs, -siːz] *n* eje *m*
axle [ˈæksl] *n* eje *m*, árbol *m*
ay, aye [aɪ] *excl* (*yes*) sí; **the ayes** los que votan a favor
azalea [əˈzeɪlɪə] *n* azalea
Azerbaijan [æzəbaɪˈdʒɑːn] *n* Azerbaiyán *m*
Aztec [ˈæztɛk] *adj, n* azteca *m/f*

b

B, b [biː] *n* (*letter*) B, b *f*; (*Scol*: *mark*) N; (*Mus*): **B** si *m*; **B for Benjamin**, (*US*) **B for Baker** B de Barcelona; **B road** (*Brit Aut*) ≈ carretera secundaria

BA *n abbr* = **British Academy**; (*Scol*) = **Bachelor of Arts**

babble [ˈbæbl] *vi* farfullar

baboon [bəˈbuːn] *n* mandril *m*

baby [ˈbeɪbɪ] *n* bebé *m/f*; (*US*: *inf*: *darling*) mi amor

baby carriage *n* (*US*) cochecito

baby-sit [ˈbeɪbɪsɪt] *vi* hacer de canguro

baby-sitter [ˈbeɪbɪsɪtəʳ] *n* canguro *m/f*

baby wipe *n* toallita húmeda (*para bebés*)

bachelor [ˈbætʃələʳ] *n* soltero; **B~ of Arts/Science (BA/BSc)** licenciado(-a) en Filosofía y Letras/Ciencias

back [bæk] *n* (*of person*) espalda; (*of animal*) lomo; (*of hand, page*) dorso; (*as opposed to front*) parte *f* de atrás; (*of room*) fondo; (*of chair*) respaldo; (*of page*) reverso; (*Football*) defensa *m*; **to have one's ~ to the wall** (*fig*) estar entre la espada y la pared; **to break the ~ of a job** hacer lo más difícil de un trabajo; **~ to front** al revés; **at the ~ of my mind was the thought that ...** en el fondo tenía la idea de que ... ▷ *vt* (*candidate*: *also*: **~ up**) respaldar, apoyar; (*horse*: *at races*) apostar a; (*car*) dar marcha atrás a *or* con ▷ *vi* (*car etc*) dar marcha atrás ▷ *adj* de atrás; **~ seats/wheels** (*Aut*) asientos *mpl* traseros, ruedas *fpl* traseras; **~ garden/room** jardín *m*/habitación *f* de atrás; **~ payments** pagos *mpl* con efecto retroactivo; **~ rent** renta atrasada; **to take a ~ seat** (*fig*) pasar a segundo plano ▷ *adv* (*not forward*) (hacia) atrás; **he's ~** (*returned*) ha vuelto; **he ran ~** volvió corriendo; **throw the ball ~** (*restitution*) devuelve la pelota; **can I have it ~?** ¿me lo devuelve?; **he called ~** (*again*) volvió a llamar; **~ and forth** de acá para allá; **as far ~ as the 13th century** ya en el siglo XIII; **when will you be ~?** ¿cuándo volverá?; **back down** *vi* echarse atrás; **back on to** *vt fus*: **the house ~s on to the golf course** por atrás la casa da al campo de golf; **back out** *vi* (*of promise*) volverse atrás; **back up** *vt* (*support*: *person*) apoyar, respaldar; (*theory*) defender; (*car*) dar marcha atrás a; (*Comput*) hacer una copia de reserva de

backache [ˈbækeɪk] *n* dolor *m* de espalda

backbencher [ˈbækˈbɛntʃəʳ] *n* (*Brit*) *diputado sin cargo oficial en el gobierno o la oposición*

back benches *npl* (*Brit*) *ver nota*

backbone [ˈbækbəun] *n* columna vertebral; **the ~ of the organization** el pilar de la organización

backcloth [ˈbækklɔθ] *n* telón *m* de fondo

backdate [bækˈdeɪt] *vt* (*letter*) poner fecha atrasada a; **~d pay rise** aumento de sueldo con efecto retroactivo

back door *n* puerta *f* trasera

backdrop [ˈbækdrɔp] *n* = **backcloth**

backer [ˈbækəʳ] *n* partidario(-a); (*Comm*) promotor(a) *m(f)*

backfire [bækˈfaɪəʳ] *vi* (*Aut*) petardear; (*plans*) fallar, salir mal

backgammon [ˈbækgæmən] *n* backgammon *m*

background [ˈbækgraund] *n* fondo; (*of events*) antecedentes *mpl*; (*basic knowledge*) bases *fpl*; (*experience*) conocimientos *mpl*, educación *f* ▷ *cpd* (*noise, music*) de fondo; (*Comput*) secundario; **~ reading** lectura de preparación; **family ~** origen *m*, antecedentes *mpl* familiares

backhand [ˈbækhænd] *n* (*Tennis*: *also*: **~ stroke**) revés *m*

backhanded [ˈbækˈhændɪd] *adj* (*fig*) ambiguo, equívoco

backhander [ˈbækˈhændəʳ] *n* (*Brit*: *bribe*) soborno

backing [ˈbækɪŋ] *n* (*fig*) apoyo, respaldo; (*Comm*) respaldo financiero; (*Mus*) acompañamiento

backlash [ˈbæklæʃ] *n* reacción *f* (en contra)

backlog [ˈbæklɔg] *n*: **~ of work** trabajo atrasado

back number *n* (*of magazine etc*) número atrasado

backpack [ˈbækpæk] *n* mochila

backpacker [ˈbækpækəʳ] *n* mochilero(-a)

back pay *n* atrasos *mpl*

backpedal [ˈbækpɛdl] *vi* (*fig*) volverse/echarse atrás

b

backseat driver ['bæksi:t-] *n pasajero que se empeña en aconsejar al conductor*
backside ['bæksaɪd] *n* (*inf*) trasero
backslash ['bækslæʃ] *n* pleca, barra inversa
backstage [bæk'steɪdʒ] *adv* entre bastidores
backstroke ['bækstrəuk] *n* espalda
backtrack ['bæktræk] *vi* (*fig*) = **backpedal**
backup ['bækʌp] *adj* (*train, plane*) suplementario; (*Comput: disk, file*) de reserva ▷ *n* (*support*) apoyo; (*also*: **~ file**) copia de reserva; (*US: congestion*) embotellamiento, retención *f*
backward ['bækwəd] *adj* (*movement*) hacia atrás; (*person, country*) atrasado; (*shy*) tímido
backwards ['bækwədz] *adv* (*move, go*) hacia atrás; (*read a list*) al revés; (*fall*) de espaldas; **to know sth ~** *or* (*US*) **~ and forwards** (*inf*) saberse algo al dedillo
backwater ['bækwɔ:tə^r] *n* (*fig*) lugar *m* atrasado *or* apartado
backyard [bæk'jɑ:d] *n* patio trasero
bacon ['beɪkən] *n* tocino, bacon *m*, beicon *m*
bacteria [bæk'tɪərɪə] *npl* bacterias *fpl*
bad [bæd] *adj* malo; (*serious*) grave; (*meat, food*) podrido, pasado; **to go ~** pasarse; **to have a ~ time of it** pasarlo mal; **I feel ~ about it** (*guilty*) me siento culpable; **~ debt** (*Comm*) cuenta incobrable; **in ~ faith** de mala fe
baddie, baddy ['bædɪ] *n* (*inf: Cine etc*) malo(-a)
bade [bæd [beɪd] *pt of* **bid**
badge [bædʒ] *n* insignia; (*metal badge*) chapa; (*of policeman*) placa; (*stick-on*) pegatina
badger ['bædʒə^r] *n* tejón *m*
badly ['bædlɪ] *adv* (*work, dress etc*) mal; **to reflect ~ on sb** influir negativamente en la reputación de algn; **~ wounded** gravemente herido; **he needs it ~** le hace mucha falta; **to be ~ off (for money)** andar mal de dinero; **things are going ~** las cosas van muy mal
bad-mannered ['bæd'mænəd] *adj* mal educado
badminton ['bædmɪntən] *n* bádminton *m*
bad-tempered ['bæd'tɛmpəd] *adj* de mal genio *or* carácter; (*temporary*) de mal humor
baffle ['bæfl] *vt* desconcertar, confundir
baffling ['bæflɪŋ] *adj* incomprensible
bag [bæg] *n* bolsa; (*handbag*) bolso; (*satchel*) mochila; (*case*) maleta; (*of hunter*) caza ▷ *vt* (*inf: take*) coger (*Sp*), agarrar (*LAm*), pescar; **~s of** (*inf: lots of*) un montón de; **to pack one's ~s** hacer las maletas
baggage ['bægɪdʒ] *n* equipaje *m*
baggage allowance *n* límite *m* de equipaje
baggage (re)claim *n* recogida de equipajes
baggy ['bægɪ] *adj* (*trousers*) ancho, holgado
bag lady *n* (*inf*) *mujer sin hogar cargada de bolsas*
bagpipes ['bægpaɪps] *npl* gaita *sg*
Bahamas [bə'hɑ:məz] *npl*: **the ~** las (Islas) Bahama
bail [beɪl] *n* fianza ▷ *vt* (*prisoner: also*: **grant ~ to**) poner en libertad bajo fianza; (*boat: also*: **~ out**) achicar; **on ~** (*prisoner*) bajo fianza; **to be released on ~** ser puesto en libertad bajo fianza; **to ~ sb out** pagar la fianza de algn; *see also* **bale**
bailiff ['beɪlɪf] *n* alguacil *m*
bait [beɪt] *n* cebo ▷ *vt* poner el cebo en
bake [beɪk] *vt* cocer (al horno) ▷ *vi* (*cook*) cocerse; (*be hot*) hacer un calor terrible
baked beans *npl* judías *fpl* en salsa de tomate
baked potato *n* patata al horno
baker ['beɪkə^r] *n* panadero(-a)
baker's dozen *n* docena del fraile
bakery ['beɪkərɪ] *n* (*for bread*) panadería; (*for cakes*) pastelería
baking ['beɪkɪŋ] *n* (*act*) cocción *f*; (*batch*) hornada
baking powder *n* levadura (en polvo)
balaclava [bælə'klɑ:və] *n* (*also*: **~ helmet**) pasamontañas *m inv*
balance ['bæləns] *n* equilibrio; (*Comm: sum*) balance *m*; (*remainder*) resto; (*scales*) balanza ▷ *vt* equilibrar; (*budget*) nivelar; (*account*) saldar; (*compensate*) compensar; **~ of trade/payments** balanza de comercio/pagos; **~ carried forward** balance *m* pasado a cuenta nueva; **~ brought forward** saldo de hoja anterior; **to ~ the books** hacer el balance
balanced ['bælənst] *adj* (*personality, diet*) equilibrado; (*report*) objetivo
balance sheet *n* balance *m*
balcony ['bælkənɪ] *n* (*open*) balcón *m*; (*closed*) galería; (*in theatre*) anfiteatro
bald [bɔ:ld] *adj* calvo; (*tyre*) liso
baldness ['bɔ:ldnɪs] *n* calvicie *f*
bale [beɪl] *n* (*Agr*) paca, fardo; **bale out** *vi* (*of a plane*) lanzarse en paracaídas ▷ *vt* (*Naut*) achicar; **to ~ sb out of a difficulty** sacar a algn de un apuro
Balearic Islands [bælɪ'ærɪk-] *npl*: **the ~** las (Islas) Baleares
balk [bɔ:k] *vi*: **to ~ (at)** resistirse (a); (*horse*) plantarse (ante)
ball [bɔ:l] *n* (*sphere*) bola; (*football*) balón *m*; (*for tennis, golf etc*) pelota; (*of wool, string*) ovillo; (*dance*) baile *m*; **to be on the ~** (*fig: competent*) ser un enterado; (*: alert*) estar al tanto; **to play ~ (with sb)** jugar a la pelota (con algn); (*fig*) cooperar; **to start the ~ rolling** (*fig*) empezar; **the ~ is in your court** (*fig*) le toca a usted
ballad ['bæləd] *n* balada, romance *m*
ballast ['bæləst] *n* lastre *m*
ball bearing *n* cojinete *m* de bolas
ballerina [bælə'ri:nə] *n* bailarina
ballet ['bæleɪ] *n* ballet *m*
ballet dancer *n* bailarín(-ina) *m(f)* (de ballet)
balloon [bə'lu:n] *n* globo; (*in comic strip*) bocadillo ▷ *vi* dispararse
ballot ['bælət] *n* votación *f*
ballot box *n* urna (electoral)

ballot paper *n* papeleta
ballpark ['bɔːlpɑːk] *n* (*US*) estadio de béisbol
ball-point pen ['bɔːlpɔɪnt-] *n* bolígrafo
ballroom ['bɔːlrum] *n* salón *m* de baile
balm [bɑːm] *n* (*also fig*) bálsamo
balmy ['bɑːmɪ] *adj* (*breeze, air*) suave; (*inf*) = **barmy**
Baltic ['bɔːltɪk] *adj* báltico ▷ *n*: **the ~ (Sea)** el (Mar) Báltico
bamboo [bæm'buː] *n* bambú *m*
ban [bæn] *n* prohibición *f* ▷ *vt* prohibir; (*exclude*) excluir; **he was ~ned from driving** le retiraron el carnet de conducir
banal [bə'nɑːl] *adj* banal, vulgar
banana [bə'nɑːnə] *n* plátano, banana (*LAm*)
band [bænd] *n* (*group*) banda; (*gang*) pandilla; (*strip*) faja, tira; (*at a dance*) orquesta; (*Mil*) banda; (*rock band*) grupo; **band together** *vi* juntarse, asociarse
bandage ['bændɪdʒ] *n* venda, vendaje *m* ▷ *vt* vendar
Band-Aid® ['bændeɪd] *n* (*US*) tirita, curita (*LAm*)
B & B *n abbr* = **bed and breakfast**
bandit ['bændɪt] *n* bandido; **one-armed ~** máquina tragaperras
bandwagon ['bændwægən] *n*: **to jump on the ~** (*fig*) subirse al carro
bandy ['bændɪ] *vt* (*jokes, insults*) intercambiar
bandy-legged ['bændɪ'lɛgd] *adj* patizambo
bang [bæŋ] *n* (*of gun, exhaust*) estallido; (*of door*) portazo; (*blow*) golpe *m* ▷ *vt* (*door*) cerrar de golpe; (*one's head*) golpear ▷ *vi* estallar ▷ *adv*: **to be ~ on time** (*inf*) llegar en punto; **to ~ the door** dar un portazo; **to ~ into sth** chocar con algo, golpearse contra algo; *see also* **bangs**
banger ['bæŋəʳ] *n* (*Brit*: *car*: *also*: **old ~**) armatoste *m*, cacharro; (*Brit inf*: *sausage*) salchicha; (*firework*) petardo
Bangladesh [bæŋglə'dɛʃ] *n* Bangladesh *f*
bangle ['bæŋgl] *n* brazalete *m*, ajorca
bangs [bæŋz] *npl* (*US*) flequillo *sg*
banish ['bænɪʃ] *vt* desterrar
banister ['bænɪstəʳ] *n*, **banisters** ['bænɪstəz] *npl* barandilla *f*, pasamanos *m inv*
banjo (*pl* **banjoes** *or* **banjos**) ['bændʒəu] *n* banjo
bank [bæŋk] *n* (*Comm*) banco; (*of river, lake*) ribera, orilla; (*of earth*) terraplén *m* ▷ *vi* (*Aviat*) ladearse; (*Comm*): **to ~ with** tener la cuenta en; **bank on** *vt fus* contar con
bank account *n* cuenta bancaria
bank balance *n* saldo
bank card *n* = **banker's card**
bank charges *npl* comisión *fsg*
bank draft *n* letra de cambio
banker ['bæŋkəʳ] *n* banquero; **~'s card** (*Brit*) tarjeta bancaria; **~'s order** orden *f* bancaria
bank giro *n* giro bancario
bank holiday *n* (*Brit*) día *m* festivo *or* de fiesta; *ver nota*

BANK HOLIDAY

El término *bank holiday* se aplica en el Reino Unido a todo día festivo oficial en el que cierran bancos y comercios. Los más destacados coinciden con Navidad, Semana Santa, finales de mayo y finales de agosto. Al contrario que en los países de tradición católica, no se celebran las festividades dedicadas a los santos.

banking ['bæŋkɪŋ] *n* banca
bank loan *n* préstamo bancario
bank manager *n* director(a) *m(f)* (de sucursal) de banco
banknote ['bæŋknəut] *n* billete *m* de banco
bank rate *n* tipo de interés bancario
bankrupt ['bæŋkrʌpt] *n* quebrado(-a) ▷ *adj* quebrado, insolvente; **to go ~** quebrar, hacer bancarrota; **to be ~** estar en quiebra
bankruptcy ['bæŋkrʌptsɪ] *n* quiebra, bancarrota
bank statement *n* extracto de cuenta
banner ['bænəʳ] *n* bandera; (*in demonstration*) pancarta
bannister(s) ['bænɪstə(z)] *n(pl)* = **banister(s)**
banns [bænz] *npl* amonestaciones *fpl*
banquet ['bæŋkwɪt] *n* banquete *m*
banter ['bæntəʳ] *n* guasa, bromas *fpl*
baptism ['bæptɪzəm] *n* bautismo; (*act*) bautizo
baptize [bæp'taɪz] *vt* bautizar
bar [bɑːʳ] *n* barra; (*on door*) tranca; (*of window, cage*) reja; (*of soap*) pastilla; (*of chocolate*) tableta; (*fig*: *hindrance*) obstáculo; (*prohibition*) prohibición *f*; (*pub*) bar *m*, cantina (*esp LAm*); (*counter*: *in pub*) barra, mostrador *m*; (*Mus*) barra ▷ *vt* (*road*) obstruir; (*window, door*) atrancar; (*person*) excluir; (*activity*) prohibir; **behind ~s** entre rejas; **the B~** (*Law*: *profession*) la abogacía; (: *people*) el cuerpo de abogados; **~ none** sin excepción
barbarian [bɑː'bɛərɪən] *n* bárbaro(-a)
barbaric [bɑː'bærɪk] *adj* bárbaro
barbarity [bɑː'bærɪtɪ] *n* barbaridad *f*
barbecue ['bɑːbɪkjuː] *n* barbacoa, asado (*LAm*)
barbed wire ['bɑːbd-] *n* alambre *m* de espino
barber ['bɑːbəʳ] *n* peluquero, barbero
barber's (shop), (*US*) **barber (shop)** *n* peluquería
Barcelona [bɑːsɪ'ləunə] *n* Barcelona
bar chart *n* gráfico de barras
bar code *n* código de barras
bare [bɛəʳ] *adj* desnudo; (*trees*) sin hojas; (*head*) descubierto ▷ *vt* desnudar; **to ~ one's teeth** enseñar los dientes
bareback ['bɛəbæk] *adv* a pelo
barefaced ['bɛəfeɪst] *adj* descarado
barefoot ['bɛəfut] *adj, adv* descalzo
barely ['bɛəlɪ] *adv* apenas
bargain ['bɑːgɪn] *n* pacto; (*transaction*)

negocio; (*good buy*) ganga ▷ *vi* negociar; (*haggle*) regatear; **into the ~** además, por añadidura; **bargain for** *vt fus* (*inf*): **he got more than he ~ed for** le resultó peor de lo que esperaba
bargaining ['bɑːgənɪŋ] *n* negociación *f*, regateo; **~ table** mesa de negociaciones
barge [bɑːdʒ] *n* barcaza; **barge in** *vi* irrumpir; (*in conversation*) entrometerse; **barge into** *vt fus* dar contra
baritone ['bærɪtəun] *n* barítono
barium meal ['bɛərɪəm-] *n* (*Med*) sulfato de bario
bark [bɑːk] *n* (*of tree*) corteza; (*of dog*) ladrido ▷ *vi* ladrar
barley ['bɑːlɪ] *n* cebada
barley sugar *n* azúcar *m* cande
barmaid ['bɑːmeɪd] *n* camarera
barman ['bɑːmən] *n* camarero, barman *m*
barmy ['bɑːmɪ] *adj* (*inf*) chiflado, chalado
barn [bɑːn] *n* granero; (*for animals*) cuadra
barnacle ['bɑːnəkl] *n* percebe *m*
barometer [bə'rɔmɪtə^r] *n* barómetro
baron ['bærən] *n* barón *m*; (*fig*) magnate *m*; **the press ~s** los magnates de la prensa
baroness ['bærənɪs] *n* baronesa
baroque [bə'rɔk] *adj* barroco
barrack ['bærək] *vt* (*Brit*) abuchear
barracks ['bærəks] *npl* cuartel *msg*
barrage ['bærɑːʒ] *n* (*Mil*) cortina de fuego; (*dam*) presa; (*fig*: *of criticism etc*) lluvia, aluvión *m*; **a ~ of questions** una lluvia de preguntas
barrel ['bærəl] *n* barril *m*; (*of wine*) tonel *m*, cuba; (*of gun*) cañón *m*
barren ['bærən] *adj* estéril
barrette [bə'rɛt] *n* (*US*) pasador *m* (*LAm, Sp*), broche *m* (*Mex*)
barricade [bærɪ'keɪd] *n* barricada ▷ *vt* cerrar con barricadas
barrier ['bærɪə^r] *n* barrera; (*crash barrier*) barrera
barrier cream *n* crema protectora
barring ['bɑːrɪŋ] *prep* excepto, salvo
barrister ['bærɪstə^r] *n* (*Brit*) abogado(-a)
barrow ['bærəu] *n* (*cart*) carretilla
bartender ['bɑːtɛndə^r] *n* (*US*) camarero, barman *m*
barter ['bɑːtə^r] *vt*: **to ~ sth for sth** trocar algo por algo
base [beɪs] *n* base *f* ▷ *vt*: **to ~ sth on** basar *or* fundar algo en ▷ *adj* bajo, infame; **to ~ at** (*troops*) estacionar en; **I'm ~d in London** (*work*) trabajo en Londres
baseball ['beɪsbɔːl] *n* béisbol *m*
baseball cap *n* gorra *f* de béisbol
baseline ['beɪslaɪn] *n* (*Tennis*) línea de fondo
basement ['beɪsmənt] *n* sótano
bases ['beɪsiːz] *npl of* **basis**; ['beɪsɪz] *npl of* **base**
bash [bæʃ] *n*: **I'll have a ~ (at it)** lo intentaré ▷ *vt* (*inf*) golpear; **bash up** *vt* (*inf*: *car*) destrozar; (*: person*) aporrear, vapulear
bashful ['bæʃful] *adj* tímido, vergonzoso
basic ['beɪsɪk] *adj* (*salary etc*) básico; (*elementary*: *principles*) fundamental
basically ['beɪsɪklɪ] *adv* fundamentalmente, en el fondo
basics *npl*: **the ~** los fundamentos
basil ['bæzl] *n* albahaca
basin ['beɪsn] *n* (*vessel*) cuenco, tazón *m*; (*Geo*) cuenca; (*also*: **wash~**) palangana, jofaina; (*in bathroom*) lavabo
basis ['beɪsɪs] (*pl* **bases** [-siːz]) *n* base *f*; **on a part-time/trial ~** a tiempo parcial/a prueba; **on the ~ of what you've said** en base a lo que has dicho
bask [bɑːsk] *vi*: **to ~ in the sun** tomar el sol
basket ['bɑːskɪt] *n* cesta, cesto
basketball ['bɑːskɪtbɔːl] *n* baloncesto
Basque [bæsk] *adj, n* vasco(-a) *m(f)*
Basque Country *n* Euskadi *m*, País *m* Vasco
bass [beɪs] *n* (*Mus*) bajo
bassoon [bə'suːn] *n* fagot *m*
bastard ['bɑːstəd] *n* bastardo(-a); (*inf!*) cabrón *m*, hijo de puta (*!*)
bat [bæt] *n* (*Zool*) murciélago; (*for ball games*) palo; (*for cricket, baseball*) bate *m*; (*Brit*: *for table tennis*) pala ▷ *vt*: **he didn't ~ an eyelid** ni pestañeó, ni se inmutó
batch [bætʃ] *n* lote *m*, remesa; (*of bread*) hornada
bated ['beɪtɪd] *adj*: **with ~ breath** sin respirar
bath [bɑːθ, *pl* bɑːðz] *n* (*act*) baño; (*bathtub*) bañera, tina (*esp LAm*) ▷ *vt* bañar; **to have a ~** bañarse, darse un baño; *see also* **baths**
bathe [beɪð] *vi* bañarse; (*US*) darse un baño, bañarse ▷ *vt* (*wound etc*) lavar; (*US*) bañar, dar un baño a
bather ['beɪðə^r] *n* bañista *m/f*
bathing ['beɪðɪŋ] *n* baño
bathing cap *n* gorro de baño
bathing costume, bathing suit (*US*) *n* bañador *m*, traje *m* de baño
bathing trunks *npl* bañador *msg*
bathrobe ['bɑːθrəub] *n* albornoz *m*
bathroom ['bɑːθrum] *n* (cuarto de) baño
baths [bɑːðz] *npl* piscina *sg*
bath towel *n* toalla de baño
bathtub ['bɑːθtʌb] *n* bañera
baton ['bætən] *n* (*Mus*) batuta; (*weapon*) porra
battalion [bə'tælɪən] *n* batallón *m*
batter ['bætə^r] *vt* maltratar; (*wind, rain*) azotar ▷ *n* batido
battered ['bætəd] *adj* (*hat, pan*) estropeado
battery ['bætərɪ] *n* batería; (*of torch*) pila
battery charger *n* cargador *m* de baterías
battery farming *n* cría intensiva
battle ['bætl] *n* batalla; (*fig*) lucha ▷ *vi* luchar; **that's half the ~** (*inf*) ya hay medio camino andado; **to fight a losing ~** (*fig*) luchar por una causa perdida
battlefield ['bætlfiːld] *n* campo *m* de batalla
battleship ['bætlʃɪp] *n* acorazado

b

batty ['bætɪ] *adj* (*inf: person*) chiflado; (*: idea*) de chiflado
bauble ['bɔ:bl] *n* chuchería
bawdy ['bɔ:dɪ] *adj* indecente; (*joke*) verde
bawl [bɔ:l] *vi* chillar, gritar
bay [beɪ] *n* (*Geo*) bahía; (*for parking*) parking *m*, estacionamiento; (*loading bay*) patio de carga; (*Bot*) laurel *m* ▷ *vi* aullar; **to hold sb at ~** mantener a alguien a raya
bay leaf *n* (hoja de) laurel *m*
bayonet ['beɪənɪt] *n* bayoneta
bay window *n* ventana salediza
bazaar [bə'zɑ:ʳ] *n* bazar *m*
bazooka [bə'zu:kə] *n* bazuca
BB *n abbr* (*Brit: = Boys' Brigade*) *organización juvenil para chicos*
BBC *n abbr* (*= British Broadcasting Corporation*) BBC *f*; *ver nota*

BBC

La *BBC* es el organismo público británico de radio y televisión, autónomo en cuanto a su política de programas pero regulado por un estatuto ("BBC charter") que ha de aprobar el Parlamento. Además de cadenas nacionales de televisión y de radio, transmite también un servicio informativo mundial ("BBC World Service"). A no tener publicidad, se financia a través de operaciones comerciales paralelas y del cobro de una licencia anual obligatoria ("TV licence") para los que tienen aparato de televisión.

BC *adv abbr* (*= before Christ*) a. de J.C.

KEYWORD

be [bi:] (*pt* **was, were**, *pp* **been**) *aux vb* **1** (*with present participle: forming continuous tenses*): **what are you doing?** ¿qué estás haciendo?, ¿qué haces?; **they're coming tomorrow** vienen mañana; **I've been waiting for you for hours** llevo horas esperándote
2 (*with pp: forming passives*) ser (*but often replaced by active or reflexive constructions*); **to be murdered** ser asesinado; **the box had been opened** habían abierto la caja; **the thief was nowhere to be seen** no se veía al ladrón por ninguna parte
3 (*in tag questions*): **it was fun, wasn't it?** fue divertido, ¿no? *or* ¿verdad?; **he's good-looking, isn't he?** es guapo, ¿no te parece?; **she's back again, is she?** entonces, ¿ha vuelto?
4 (*+to +infin*): **the house is to be sold** (*necessity*) hay que vender la casa; (*future*) van a vender la casa; **he's not to open it** no tiene que abrirlo; **he was to have come yesterday** debía de haber venido ayer; **am I to understand that ...?** ¿debo entender que ...?
▷ *vb +complement* **1** (*with n or num complement*) ser; **he's a doctor** es médico; **2 and 2 are 4** 2 y 2 son 4
2 (*with adj complement: expressing permanent or inherent quality*) ser; (*: expressing state seen as temporary or reversible*) estar; **I'm English** soy inglés(-esa); **she's tall/pretty** es alta/bonita; **he's young** es joven; **be careful/good/quiet** ten cuidado/pórtate bien/cállate; **I'm tired** estoy cansado(-a); **I'm warm** tengo calor; **it's dirty** está sucio(-a)
3 (*of health*) estar; **how are you?** ¿cómo estás?; **he's very ill** está muy enfermo; **I'm better now** ya estoy mejor
4 (*of age*) tener; **how old are you?** ¿cuántos años tienes?; **I'm sixteen (years old)** tengo dieciséis años
5 (*cost*) costar; ser; **how much was the meal?** ¿cuánto fue *or* costó la comida?; **that'll be £5.75, please** son £5.75, por favor; **this shirt is £17** esta camisa cuesta £17
▷ *vi* **1** (*exist, occur etc*) existir, haber; **the best singer that ever was** el mejor cantante que existió jamás; **is there a God?** ¿hay un Dios?, ¿existe Dios?; **be that as it may** sea como sea; **so be it** así sea
2 (*referring to place*) estar; **I won't be here tomorrow** no estaré aquí mañana
3 (*referring to movement*): **where have you been?** ¿dónde has estado?
▷ *impers vb* **1** (*referring to time*): **it's 5 o'clock** son las 5; **it's the 28th of April** estamos a 28 de abril
2 (*referring to distance*): **it's 10 km to the village** el pueblo está a 10 km
3 (*referring to the weather*): **it's too hot/cold** hace demasiado calor/frío; **it's windy today** hace viento hoy
4 (*emphatic*): **it's me** soy yo; **it was Maria who paid the bill** fue María la que pagó la cuenta

beach [bi:tʃ] *n* playa ▷ *vt* varar
beacon ['bi:kən] *n* (*lighthouse*) faro; (*marker*) guía; (*radio beacon*) radiofaro
bead [bi:d] *n* cuenta, abalorio; (*of dew, sweat*) gota; **beads** *npl* (*necklace*) collar *m*
beak [bi:k] *n* pico
beaker ['bi:kəʳ] *n* vaso
beam [bi:m] *n* (*Arch*) viga; (*of light*) rayo, haz *m* de luz; (*Radio*) rayo ▷ *vi* brillar; (*smile*) sonreír; **to drive on full** *or* **main ~** conducir con las luces largas
bean [bi:n] *n* judía, fríjol/frijol *m* (*esp LAm*); **runner/broad ~** habichuela/haba; **coffee ~** grano de café
beanpole ['bi:npəul] *n* (*inf*) espárrago
bean sprouts ['bi:nsprauts] *npl* brotes *mpl* de soja
bear [bɛəʳ] (*pt* **bore**, *pp* **borne**) *n* oso; (*Stock Exchange*) bajista *m* ▷ *vt* (*weight etc*) llevar; (*cost*) pagar; (*responsibility*) tener; (*traces, signs*)

mostrar; (*produce: fruit*) dar; (*Comm: interest*) devengar; (*endure*) soportar, aguantar; (*stand up to*) resistir a; (*children*) tener, dar a luz; (*fruit*) dar ▷ *vi*: **to ~ right/left** torcer a la derecha/izquierda; **I can't ~ him** no le puedo ver, no lo soporto; **to bring pressure to ~ on sb** ejercer presión sobre algn; **bear on** *vt fus* tener que ver con, referirse a; **bear out** *vt fus* (*suspicions*) corroborar, confirmar; (*person*) confirmar lo dicho por; **bear up** *vi* (*cheer up*) animarse; **he bore up well under the strain** resistió bien la presión; **bear with** *vt fus* (*sb's moods, temper*) tener paciencia con

beard [bɪəd] *n* barba

bearded ['bɪədɪd] *adj* con barba

bearer ['bɛərəʳ] *n* (*of news, cheque*) portador(a) *m(f)*; (*of passport*) titular *m/f*

bearing ['bɛərɪŋ] *n* porte *m*; (*connection*) relación *f*; **(ball) bearings** *npl* cojinetes *mpl* a bolas; **to take a ~** marcarse; **to find one's ~s** orientarse

beast [bi:st] *n* bestia; (*inf*) bruto, salvaje *m*

beastly ['bi:stlɪ] *adj* bestial; (*awful*) horrible

beat [bi:t] (*pt* **beat**, *pp* **beaten**) *n* (*of heart*) latido; (*Mus*) ritmo, compás *m*; (*of policeman*) ronda ▷ *vt* (*hit*) golpear, pegar; (*eggs*) batir; (*defeat*) vencer, derrotar; (*better*) sobrepasar; (*drum*) redoblar; (*rhythm*) marcar ▷ *vi* (*heart*) latir; **off the ~en track** aislado; **to ~ about the bush** andarse con rodeos; **to ~ it** largarse; **that ~s everything!** (*inf*) ¡eso es el colmo!; **to ~ on a door** dar golpes en una puerta; **beat down** ▷ *vt* (*door*) derribar a golpes; (*price*) conseguir rebajar, regatear; (*seller*) hacer rebajar el precio *vi* (*rain*) llover a cántaros; (*sun*) caer de plomo; **beat off** *vt* rechazar; **beat up** *vt* (*inf: person*) dar una paliza a

beating ['bi:tɪŋ] *n* paliza, golpiza (*LAm*); **to take a ~** recibir una paliza

beautiful ['bju:tɪful] *adj* hermoso, bello, lindo (*esp LAm*)

beautifully ['bju:tɪfəlɪ] *adv* de maravilla

beauty ['bju:tɪ] *n* belleza, hermosura; (*concept, person*) belleza; **the ~ of it is that ...** lo mejor de esto es que ...

beauty parlour, (*US*) **beauty parlor** *n* salón *m* de belleza

beauty salon *n* salón *m* de belleza

beauty sleep *n*: **to get one's ~** *no perder horas de sueño*

beauty spot *n* lunar *m* postizo; (*Brit: Tourism*) lugar *m* pintoresco

beaver ['bi:vəʳ] *n* castor *m*

became [bɪ'keɪm] *pt of* **become**

because [bɪ'kɔz] *conj* porque; **~ of** *prep* debido a, a causa de

beck [bɛk] *n*: **to be at the ~ and call of** estar a disposición de

beckon ['bɛkən] *vt* (*also*: **~ to**) llamar con señas

become [bɪ'kʌm] (*irreg: like* **come**) *vi + noun* hacerse, llegar a ser *+ adj* ponerse, volverse ▷ *vt* (*suit*) favorecer, sentar bien a; **to ~ fat** engordar; **to ~ angry** enfadarse; **it became known that ...** se descubrió que ...

becoming [bɪ'kʌmɪŋ] *adj* (*behaviour*) decoroso; (*clothes*) favorecedor(a)

bed [bɛd] *n* cama; (*of flowers*) macizo; (*of sea, lake*) fondo; (*of river*) lecho; (*of coal, clay*) capa; **to go to ~** acostarse; **bed down** *vi* acostarse

bed and breakfast *n* ≈ pensión *f*; *ver nota*

BED AND BREAKFAST

Se llama *Bed and Breakfast* a la casa de hospedaje particular, o granja si es en el campo, que ofrece cama y desayuno a tarifas inferiores a las de un hotel. El servicio se suele anunciar con carteles colocados en las ventanas del establecimiento, en el jardín o en la carretera y en ellos aparece a menudo únicamente el símbolo "B & B".

bedclothes ['bɛdkləuðz] *npl* ropa de cama

bedding ['bɛdɪŋ] *n* ropa de cama

bed linen *n* (*Brit*) ropa *f* de cama

bedraggled [bɪ'drægld] *adj* desastrado

bedridden ['bɛdrɪdn] *adj* postrado (en cama)

bedroom ['bɛdrum] *n* dormitorio, alcoba

bed settee *n* sofá cama *m*

bedside ['bɛdsaɪd] *n*: **at sb's ~** a la cabecera de alguien

bedside lamp *n* lámpara de noche

bedside table *n* mesilla de noche

bedsit ['bɛdsɪt], **bedsitter** ['bɛdsɪtəʳ] *n* (*Brit*) estudio

bedspread ['bɛdsprɛd] *n* cubrecama *m*, colcha

bedtime ['bɛdtaɪm] *n* hora de acostarse; **it's ~** es hora de acostarse *or* de irse a la cama

bee [bi:] *n* abeja; **to have a ~ in one's bonnet (about sth)** tener una idea fija (de algo)

beech [bi:tʃ] *n* haya

beef [bi:f] *n* carne *f* de vaca; **roast ~** rosbif *m*; **beef up** *vt* (*inf*) reforzar

beefburger ['bi:fbə:gəʳ] *n* hamburguesa

beefeater ['bi:fi:təʳ] *n* *alabardero de la Torre de Londres*

beehive ['bi:haɪv] *n* colmena

beeline ['bi:laɪn] *n*: **to make a ~ for** ir derecho a

been [bi:n] *pp of* **be**

beeper ['bi:pəʳ] *n* (*of doctor etc*) busca *m inv*

beer [bɪəʳ] *n* cerveza

beer belly *n* (*inf*) barriga (*de bebedor de cerveza*)

beer garden *n* (*Brit*) terraza *f* de verano, jardín *m* (de un bar)

beet [bi:t] *n* (*US*) remolacha

beetle ['bi:tl] *n* escarabajo

beetroot ['bi:tru:t] *n* (*Brit*) remolacha

before [bɪ'fɔːʳ] *prep* (*of time*) antes de; (*of space*) delante de ▷ *conj* antes (de) que ▷ *adv* (*time*) antes; (*space*) delante, adelante; **~ going** antes de marcharse; **~ she goes** antes de que se vaya; **the week ~** la semana anterior; **I've never seen it ~** no lo he visto nunca
beforehand [bɪ'fɔːhænd] *adv* de antemano, con anticipación
befriend [bɪ'frɛnd] *vt* ofrecer amistad a
beg [bɛg] *vi* pedir limosna, mendigar ▷ *vt* pedir, rogar; (*entreat*) suplicar; **to ~ sb to do sth** rogar a algn que haga algo; *see also* **pardon**
began [bɪ'gæn] *pt of* **begin**
beggar ['bɛgəʳ] *n* mendigo(-a)
begin (*pt* **began**, *pp* **begun**) [bɪ'gɪn, -gæn, -gʌn] *vt, vi* empezar, comenzar; **to ~ doing** *or* **to do sth** empezar a hacer algo; **I can't ~ to thank you** no encuentro palabras para agradecerle; **to ~ with, I'd like to know ...** en primer lugar, quisiera saber ...; **~ning from Monday** a partir del lunes
beginner [bɪ'gɪnəʳ] *n* principiante *m/f*
beginning [bɪ'gɪnɪŋ] *n* principio, comienzo; **right from the ~** desde el principio
begun [bɪ'gʌn] *pp of* **begin**
behalf [bɪ'hɑːf] *n*: **on ~ of** (*US*), **in ~ of** en nombre de, por; (*for benefit of*) en beneficio de; **on my/his ~** por mí/él
behave [bɪ'heɪv] *vi* (*person*) portarse, comportarse; (*thing*) funcionar; (*well*: *also*: **~ o.s.**) portarse bien
behaviour, behavior (*US*) [bɪ'heɪvjəʳ] *n* comportamiento, conducta
behead [bɪ'hɛd] *vt* decapitar
beheld [bɪ'hɛld] *pt, pp of* **behold**
behind [bɪ'haɪnd] *prep* detrás de ▷ *adv* detrás, por detrás, atrás ▷ *n* trasero; **to be ~ (schedule)** ir retrasado; **~ the scenes** (*fig*) entre bastidores; **we're ~ them in technology** (*fig*) nos dejan atrás en tecnología; **to leave sth ~** olvidar *or* dejarse algo; **to be ~ with sth** estar atrasado en algo; **to be ~ with payments (on sth)** estar atrasado en el pago (de algo)
behold [bɪ'həuld] (*irreg*: *like* **hold**) *vt* contemplar
beige [beɪʒ] *adj* (color) beige
Beijing ['beɪ'dʒɪŋ] *n* Pekín *m*
being ['biːɪŋ] *n* ser *m*; **to come into ~** nacer, aparecer
Beirut [beɪ'ruːt] *n* Beirut *m*
Belarus [bɛlə'rus] *n* Bielorrusia
belated [bɪ'leɪtɪd] *adj* atrasado, tardío
belch [bɛltʃ] *vi* eructar ▷ *vt* (*also*: **~ out**: *smoke etc*) vomitar, arrojar
belfry ['bɛlfrɪ] *n* campanario
Belgian ['bɛldʒən] *adj, n* belga *m/f*
Belgium ['bɛldʒəm] *n* Bélgica
belie [bɪ'laɪ] *vt* (*give false impression of*) desmentir, contradecir
belief [bɪ'liːf] *n* (*opinion*) opinión *f*; (*trust, faith*) fe *f*; (*acceptance as true*) creencia; **it's beyond ~** es increíble; **in the ~ that** creyendo que
believable [bɪ'liːvəbl] *adj* creíble
believe [bɪ'liːv] *vt, vi* creer; **to ~ (that)** creer (que); **to ~ in** (*God, ghosts*) creer en; (*method*) ser partidario de; **he is ~d to be abroad** se cree que está en el extranjero; **I don't ~ in corporal punishment** no soy partidario del castigo corporal
believer [bɪ'liːvəʳ] *n* (*in idea, activity*) partidario(-a); (*Rel*) creyente *m/f*, fiel *m/f*
belittle [bɪ'lɪtl] *vt* despreciar
Belize [bɛ'liːz] *n* Belice *f*
bell [bɛl] *n* campana; (*small*) campanilla; (*on door*) timbre *m*; (*animal's*) cencerro; (*on toy etc*) cascabel *m*; **that rings a ~** (*fig*) eso me suena
bellboy ['bɛlbɔɪ], **bellhop** (*US*) ['bɛlhɔp] *n* botones *m inv*
belligerent [bɪ'lɪdʒərənt] *adj* (*at war*) beligerante; (*fig*) agresivo
bellow ['bɛləu] *vi* bramar; (*person*) rugir ▷ *vt* (*orders*) gritar
bell pepper *n* (*esp US*) pimiento, pimentón *m* (*LAm*)
belly ['bɛlɪ] *n* barriga, panza
belly button (*inf*) *n* ombligo
bellyful ['bɛlɪful] *n*: **to have had a ~ of ...** (*inf*) estar más que harto de ...
belong [bɪ'lɔŋ] *vi*: **to ~ to** pertenecer a; (*club etc*) ser socio de; **this book ~s here** este libro va aquí
belongings [bɪ'lɔŋɪŋz] *npl* (*also*: **personal ~**) pertenencias *fpl*
Belorussia [bɛləu'rʌʃə] *n* Bielorrusia
beloved [bɪ'lʌvɪd] *adj, n* querido(-a) *m(f)*, amado(-a) *m(f)*
below [bɪ'ləu] *prep* bajo, debajo de; (*less than*) inferior a ▷ *adv* abajo, (por) debajo; **see ~** véase más abajo
belt [bɛlt] *n* cinturón *m*; (*Tech*) correa, cinta ▷ *vt* (*thrash*) pegar con correa; **industrial ~** cinturón industrial; **belt out** *vt* (*song*) cantar a voz en grito *or* a grito pelado; **belt up** *vi* (*Aut*) ponerse el cinturón de seguridad; (*fig, inf*) cerrar el pico
beltway ['bɛltweɪ] *n* (*US Aut*) carretera de circunvalación
bemused [bɪ'mjuːzd] *adj* perplejo
bench [bɛntʃ] *n* banco; (*Brit Pol*): **the Government/Opposition ~es** (los asientos de) los miembros del Gobierno/de la Oposición; **the B~** (*Law*) el tribunal; (*people*) la magistratura
bend [bɛnd] (*pt, pp* **bent**) *vt* doblar; (*body, head*) inclinar ▷ *vi* inclinarse; (*road*) curvarse ▷ *n* (*Brit*: *in road, river*) recodo; (*in pipe*) codo; *see also* **bends**; **bend down** *vi* inclinarse, doblarse; **bend over** *vi* inclinarse
bends [bɛndz] *npl* (*Med*) *apoplejía por cambios bruscos de presión*

b

beneath [bɪ'niːθ] *prep* bajo, debajo de; (*unworthy of*) indigno de ▷ *adv* abajo, (por) debajo
benefactor ['bɛnɪfæktəʳ] *n* bienhechor *m*
beneficial [bɛnɪ'fɪʃəl] *adj*: **~ to** beneficioso para
beneficiary [bɛnɪ'fɪʃərɪ] *n* (*Law*) beneficiario(-a)
benefit ['bɛnɪfɪt] *n* beneficio, provecho; (*allowance of money*) subsidio ▷ *vt* beneficiar ▷ *vi*: **he'll ~ from it** le sacará provecho; **unemployment ~** subsidio de desempleo
Benelux ['bɛnɪlʌks] *n* Benelux *m*
benevolent [bɪ'nɛvələnt] *adj* benévolo
benign [bɪ'naɪn] *adj* (*person*) benigno; (*Med*) benigno; (*smile*) afable
bent [bɛnt] *pt, pp of* **bend** ▷ *n* inclinación *f* ▷ *adj* (*wire, pipe*) doblado, torcido; **to be ~ on** estar empeñado en
bequest [bɪ'kwɛst] *n* legado
bereaved [bɪ'riːvd] *adj* afligido ▷ *n*: **the ~** los allegados *mpl* del difunto
bereavement [bɪ'riːvmənt] *n* aflicción *f*
beret ['bɛreɪ] *n* boina
berk [bəːk] *n* (*Brit inf*) capullo(-a) (*!*)
Berlin [bəː'lɪn] *n* Berlín *m*
berm [bəːm] *n* (*US Aut*) arcén *m*
Bermuda [bəː'mjuːdə] *n* las (Islas) Bermudas
berry ['bɛrɪ] *n* baya
berserk [bə'səːk] *adj*: **to go ~** perder los estribos
berth [bəːθ] *n* (*bed*) litera; (*cabin*) camarote *m*; (*for ship*) amarradero ▷ *vi* atracar, amarrar; **to give sb a wide ~** (*fig*) evitar encontrarse con algn
beseech (*pt, pp* **besought**) [bɪ'siːtʃ, -'sɔːt] *vt* suplicar
beset (*pt, pp* **beset**) [bɪ'sɛt] *vt* (*person*) acosar ▷ *adj*: **a policy ~ with dangers** una política rodeada de peligros
beside [bɪ'saɪd] *prep* junto a, al lado de; (*compared with*) comparado con; **to be ~ o.s. with anger** estar fuera de sí; **that's ~ the point** eso no tiene nada que ver
besides [bɪ'saɪdz] *adv* además ▷ *prep* (*as well as*) además de; (*except*) excepto
besiege [bɪ'siːdʒ] *vt* (*town*) sitiar; (*fig*) asediar
best [bɛst] *adj* (el/la) mejor ▷ *adv* (lo) mejor; **the ~ part of** (*most*) la mayor parte de; **at ~** en el mejor de los casos; **to make the ~ of sth** sacar el mejor partido de algo; **to do one's ~** hacer todo lo posible; **to the ~ of my knowledge** que yo sepa; **to the ~ of my ability** como mejor puedo; **the ~ thing to do is ...** lo mejor (que se puede hacer) es ...; **he's not exactly patient at the ~ of times** no es que tenga mucha paciencia precisamente
best-before date *n* fecha de consumo preferente
best man *n* padrino de boda
bestow [bɪ'stəu] *vt* otorgar; (*honour, praise*) dispensar; **to ~ sth on sb** conceder *or* dar algo a algn
bestseller ['bɛst'sɛləʳ] *n* éxito de ventas, bestseller *m*
bet [bɛt] *n* apuesta ▷ *vt, vi* (*pt, pp* **bet** *or* **betted**): **to ~ (on)** apostar (a); **it's a safe ~** (*fig*) es cosa segura
betray [bɪ'treɪ] *vt* traicionar; (*trust*) faltar a; (*inform on*) delatar
betrayal [bɪ'treɪəl] *n* traición *f*
better ['bɛtəʳ] *adj* mejor ▷ *adv* mejor ▷ *vt* mejorar; (*record etc*) superar ▷ *n*: **to get the ~ of sb** quedar por encima de algn; **you had ~ do it** más vale que lo hagas; **he thought ~ of it** cambió de parecer; **to get ~** mejorar(se); **that's ~!** ¡eso es!; **I had ~ go** tengo que irme; **a change for the ~** una mejora; **~ off** *adj* más acomodado
betting ['bɛtɪŋ] *n* juego, apuestas *fpl*
betting shop *n* (*Brit*) casa de apuestas
between [bɪ'twiːn] *prep* entre ▷ *adv* (*also*: **in ~**: *time*) mientras tanto; (*: place*) en medio; **the road ~ here and London** la carretera de aquí a Londres; **we only had 5 ~ us** teníamos sólo 5 entre todos
beverage ['bɛvərɪdʒ] *n* bebida
beware [bɪ'wɛəʳ] *vi*: **to ~ (of)** tener cuidado (con) ▷ *excl* ¡cuidado!; **"~ of the dog"** "perro peligroso"
bewildered [bɪ'wɪldəd] *adj* aturdido, perplejo
bewildering [bɪ'wɪldərɪŋ] *adj* desconcertante
beyond [bɪ'jɔnd] *prep* más allá de; (*past: understanding*) fuera de; (*after: date*) después de, más allá de; (*above*) superior a ▷ *adv* (*in space*) más allá; (*in time*) posteriormente; **~ doubt** fuera de toda duda; **~ repair** irreparable
bias ['baɪəs] *n* (*prejudice*) prejuicio; (*preference*) predisposición *f*
biased, biassed ['baɪəst] *adj* parcial; **to be ~ against** tener perjuicios contra
biathlon [baɪ'æθlən] *n* biatlón *m*
bib [bɪb] *n* babero
Bible ['baɪbl] *n* Biblia
bibliography [bɪblɪ'ɔgrəfɪ] *n* bibliografía
bicarbonate of soda [baɪ'kɑːbənɪt-] *n* bicarbonato sódico
biceps ['baɪsɛps] *n* bíceps *m*
bicker ['bɪkəʳ] *vi* reñir
bicycle ['baɪsɪkl] *n* bicicleta
bicycle pump *n* bomba de bicicleta
bid [bɪd] *n* (*at auction*) oferta, puja, postura; (*attempt*) tentativa, conato ▷ *vi* (*pt, pp* **bid**) hacer una oferta ▷ *vt* (*pt* **bade** [bæd], *pp* **bidden** ['bɪdn]) (*offer*) ofrecer; **to ~ sb good day** dar a algn los buenos días
bidder ['bɪdəʳ] *n*: **the highest ~** el mejor postor
bidding ['bɪdɪŋ] *n* (*at auction*) ofertas *fpl*, puja; (*order*) orden *f*, mandato
bide [baɪd] *vt*: **to ~ one's time** esperar el momento adecuado
bidet ['biːdeɪ] *n* bidet *m*

bifocals [baɪ'fəuklz] *npl* gafas *fpl or* anteojos *mpl* (*LAm*) bifocales
big [bɪg] *adj* grande; (*brother, sister*) mayor; ~ **business** gran negocio; **to do things in a ~ way** hacer las cosas en grande
bigamy ['bɪgəmɪ] *n* bigamia
biggish ['bɪgɪʃ] *adj* más bien grande; (*man*) más bien alto
bigheaded ['bɪg'hɛdɪd] *adj* engreído
bigot ['bɪgət] *n* fanático(-a), intolerante *m/f*
bigoted ['bɪgətɪd] *adj* fanático, intolerante
bigotry ['bɪgətrɪ] *n* fanatismo, intolerancia
big toe *n* dedo gordo (del pie)
big top *n* (*circus*) circo; (*main tent*) carpa principal
big wheel *n* (*at fair*) noria
bike [baɪk] *n* bici *f*
bike lane *n* carril *m* de bicicleta, carril *m* bici
bikini [bɪ'ki:nɪ] *n* bikini *m*
bilateral [baɪ'lætərl] *adj* (*agreement*) bilateral
bilingual [baɪ'lɪŋgwəl] *adj* bilingüe
bill [bɪl] *n* (*gen*) cuenta; (*invoice*) factura; (*Pol*) proyecto de ley; (*US: banknote*) billete *m*; (*of bird*) pico; (*notice*) cartel *m*; (*Theat*) programa *m* ▷ *vt* extender *or* pasar la factura a; **may I have the ~ please?** ¿puede traerme la cuenta, por favor?; **~ of exchange** letra de cambio; **~ of lading** conocimiento de embarque; **~ of sale** escritura de venta; **"post no ~s"** "prohibido fijar carteles"; **to fit** *or* **fill the ~** (*fig*) cumplir con los requisitos
billboard ['bɪlbɔ:d] *n* valla publicitaria
billet ['bɪlɪt] *n* alojamiento ▷ *vt*: **to ~ sb (on sb)** alojar a algn (con algn)
billfold ['bɪlfəuld] *n* (*US*) cartera
billiards ['bɪljədz] *n* billar *m*
billion ['bɪljən] *n* (*Brit*) billón *m*; (*US*) mil millones *mpl*
bimbo ['bɪmbəu] *n* (*inf*) tía buena sin seso
bin [bɪn] *n* (*gen*) cubo *or* bote *m* (*LAm*) de la basura; **litter~** *n* (*Brit*) papelera
binary ['baɪnərɪ] *adj* (*Math*) binario; ~ **code** código binario
bind (*pt, pp* **bound**) [baɪnd, baund] *vt* atar, liar; (*wound*) vendar; (*book*) encuadernar; (*oblige*) obligar; **bind over** *vt* (*Law*) obligar por vía legal; **bind up** *vt* (*wound*) vendar; **to be bound up in** (*work, research etc*) estar absorto en; **to be bound up with** (*person*) estar estrechamente ligado a ▷ *n* (*inf: nuisance*) lata
binder ['baɪndə^r] *n* (*file*) archivador *m*
binding ['baɪndɪŋ] *adj* (*contract*) vinculante
binge [bɪndʒ] *n* borrachera, juerga; **to go on a ~** ir de juerga
bingo ['bɪŋgəu] *n* bingo *m*
bin-liner ['bɪnlaɪnə^r] *n* bolsa de la basura
binoculars [bɪ'nɔkjuləz] *npl* prismáticos *mpl*, gemelos *mpl*
biochemistry [baɪə'kɛmɪstrɪ] *n* bioquímica
biodegradable ['baɪəudɪ'greɪdəbl] *adj* biodegradable
biodiversity ['baɪəudaɪ'və:sɪtɪ] *n* biodiversidad *f*
biofuel ['baɪəufjuəl] *n* biocombustible *m*, biocarburante *m*
biographer [baɪ'ɔgrəfə^r] *n* biógrafo(-a)
biographical [baɪə'græfɪkəl] *adj* biográfico
biography [baɪ'ɔgrəfɪ] *n* biografía
biological [baɪə'lɔdʒɪkəl] *adj* biológico; (*products, foodstuffs etc*) orgánico(-a)
biological clock *n* reloj *m* biológico
biologist [baɪ'ɔlədʒɪst] *n* biólogo(-a)
biology [baɪ'ɔlədʒɪ] *n* biología
biometric [baɪə'mɛtrɪk] *adj* biométrico
biopic ['baɪəupɪk] *n* filme *m* biográfico
biopsy ['baɪɔpsɪ] *n* biopsia
biosphere ['baɪəsfɪə^r] *n* biosfera
bioterrorism ['baɪəu'tɛrərɪzəm] *n* bioterrorismo
bipolar [baɪ'pəulə^r] *adj* bipolar
birch [bə:tʃ] *n* abedul *m*; (*cane*) vara
bird [bə:d] *n* ave *f*, pájaro; (*Brit inf: girl*) chica
birdcage ['bə:dkeɪdʒ] *n* jaula
bird flu *n* gripe aviar
bird of prey *n* ave *f* de presa
bird's-eye view ['bə:dzaɪ-] *n* vista de pájaro
bird-watcher *n* ornitólogo(-a)
bird-watching *n*: **he likes to go ~ on Sundays** los domingos le gusta ir a ver pájaros
Biro® ['baɪrəu] *n* bolígrafo
birth [bə:θ] *n* nacimiento; (*Med*) parto; **to give ~ to** parir, dar a luz a; (*fig*) dar origen a
birth certificate *n* partida de nacimiento
birth control *n* control *m* de natalidad; (*methods*) métodos *mpl* anticonceptivos
birthday ['bə:θdeɪ] *n* cumpleaños *m inv*
birthmark *n* antojo, marca de nacimiento
birthplace ['bə:θpleɪs] *n* lugar *m* de nacimiento
birth rate *n* (tasa de) natalidad *f*
Biscay ['bɪskeɪ] *n*: **the Bay of ~** el Mar Cantábrico, el golfo de Vizcaya
biscuit ['bɪskɪt] *n* (*Brit*) galleta
bisect [baɪ'sɛkt] *vt* (*also Math*) bisecar
bisexual ['baɪ'sɛksjuəl] *adj, n* bisexual *m/f*
bishop ['bɪʃəp] *n* obispo; (*Chess*) alfil *m*
bistro ['bi:strəu] *n* café-bar *m*
bit [bɪt] *pt of* **bite** ▷ *n* trozo, pedazo, pedacito; (*Comput*) bit *m*; (*for horse*) freno, bocado; **a ~ of** un poco de; **a ~ mad** un poco loco; **~ by ~** poco a poco; **to come to ~s** (*break*) hacerse pedazos; **to do one's ~** aportar su granito de arena; **bring all your ~s and pieces** trae todas tus cosas
bitch [bɪtʃ] *n* (*dog*) perra; (*inf!: woman*) zorra (*!*)
bite [baɪt] *vt, vi* (*pt* **bit** [bɪt], *pp* **bitten** ['bɪtn]) morder; (*insect etc*) picar ▷ *n* (*wound: of dog, snake etc*) mordedura; (*of insect*) picadura; (*mouthful*) bocado; **to ~ one's nails** morderse las uñas; **let's have a ~ (to eat)** vamos a comer algo
bitten ['bɪtn] *pp of* **bite**
bitter ['bɪtə^r] *adj* amargo; (*wind, criticism*) cortante, penetrante; (*icy: weather*) glacial;

(*battle*) encarnizado ▷ *n* (*Brit: beer*) *cerveza típica británica a base de lúpulos*
bitterness ['bɪtənɪs] *n* amargura; (*anger*) rencor *m*
bizarre [bɪ'zɑːʳ] *adj* raro, extraño
blab [blæb] *vi* cantar ▷ *vt* (*also*: **~ out**) soltar, contar
black [blæk] *adj* (*colour*) negro; (*dark*) oscuro ▷ *n* (*colour*) color *m* negro; (*person*): **B~** negro(-a) ▷ *vt* (*shoes*) lustrar; (*Brit Industry*) boicotear; **to give sb a ~ eye** ponerle a algn el ojo morado; **~ coffee** café *m* solo; **there it is in ~ and white** (*fig*) ahí está bien claro; **to be in the ~** (*in credit*) tener saldo positivo; **~ and blue** *adj* amoratado; **black out** *vi* (*faint*) desmayarse
blackberry ['blækbərɪ] *n* zarzamora
blackbird ['blækbəːd] *n* mirlo
blackboard ['blækbɔːd] *n* pizarra
black box *n* (*Aviat*) caja negra
blackcurrant ['blæk'kʌrənt] *n* grosella negra
black economy *n* economía sumergida
blacken ['blækən] *vt* ennegrecer; (*fig*) denigrar
black hole *n* (*Astro*) agujero negro
black ice *n* hielo invisible en la carretera
blackleg ['blæklɛg] *n* (*Brit*) esquirol *m/f*
blacklist ['blæklɪst] *n* lista negra ▷ *vt* poner en la lista negra
blackmail ['blækmeɪl] *n* chantaje *m* ▷ *vt* chantajear
black market *n* mercado negro, estraperlo
blackout ['blækaut] *n* (*Elec*) apagón *m*; (*TV*) bloqueo informativo; (*fainting*) desmayo, pérdida de conocimiento
black pepper *n* pimienta *f* negra
black pudding *n* morcilla
Black Sea *n*: **the ~** el Mar Negro
black sheep *n* oveja negra
blacksmith ['blæksmɪθ] *n* herrero
black spot *n* (*Aut*) punto negro
bladder ['blædəʳ] *n* vejiga
blade [bleɪd] *n* hoja; (*cutting edge*) filo; **a ~ of grass** una brizna de hierba
blame [bleɪm] *n* culpa ▷ *vt*: **to ~ sb for sth** echar a algn la culpa de algo; **to be to ~ (for)** tener la culpa (de); **I'm not to ~** yo no tengo la culpa; **and I don't ~ him** y lo comprendo perfectamente
blameless ['bleɪmlɪs] *adj* (*person*) inocente
bland [blænd] *adj* suave; (*taste*) soso
blank [blæŋk] *adj* en blanco; (*shot*) de fogueo; (*look*) sin expresión ▷ *n* blanco, espacio en blanco; (*cartridge*) cartucho sin bala *or* de fogueo; **to draw a ~** (*fig*) no conseguir nada; **my mind is a ~** no puedo recordar nada
blank cheque, blank check (*US*) *n* cheque *m* en blanco
blanket ['blæŋkɪt] *n* manta, frazada (*LAm*), cobija (*LAm*); (*of snow*) capa; (*of fog*) manto ▷ *adj* (*statement, agreement*) comprensivo, general; **to give ~ cover** (*insurance policy*) dar póliza a todo riesgo
blare [blɛəʳ] *vi* (*brass band, horns, radio*) resonar
blasphemous ['blæsfɪməs] *adj* blasfemo
blasphemy ['blæsfɪmɪ] *n* blasfemia
blast [blɑːst] *n* (*of wind*) ráfaga, soplo; (*of whistle*) toque *m*; (*of explosive*) explosión *f*; (*force*) choque *m* ▷ *vt* (*blow up*) volar; (*blow open*) abrir con carga explosiva ▷ *excl* (*Brit inf*) ¡maldito sea!; **(at) full ~** (*also fig*) a toda marcha; **blast off** *vi* (*spacecraft etc*) despegar
blast-off ['blɑːstɔf] *n* (*Space*) lanzamiento
blatant ['bleɪtənt] *adj* descarado
blaze [bleɪz] *n* (*fire*) fuego; (*flames*) llamarada; (*glow: of fire, sun etc*) resplandor *m*; (*fig*) arranque *m* ▷ *vi* (*fire*) arder en llamas; (*fig*) brillar ▷ *vt*: **to ~ a trail** (*fig*) abrir (un) camino; **in a ~ of publicity** bajo los focos de la publicidad
blazer ['bleɪzəʳ] *n* *chaqueta de uniforme de colegial o de socio de club*
bleach [bliːtʃ] *n* (*also*: **household ~**) lejía ▷ *vt* (*linen*) blanquear
bleached [bliːtʃt] *adj* (*hair*) decolorado; (*clothes*) blanqueado
bleachers ['bliːtʃəz] *npl* (*US Sport*) gradas *fpl*
bleak [bliːk] *adj* (*countryside*) desierto; (*landscape*) desolado, desierto; (*weather*) desapacible; (*smile*) triste; (*prospect, future*) poco prometedor(a)
bleary-eyed ['blɪərɪ'aɪd] *adj*: **to be ~** tener ojos de cansado
bleat [bliːt] *vi* balar
bled [blɛd] *pt, pp of* **bleed**
bleed (*pt, pp* **bled**) [bliːd, blɛd] *vt* sangrar; (*brakes, radiator*) desaguar ▷ *vi* sangrar; **my nose is ~ing** me está sangrando la nariz
bleep [bliːp] *n* pitido ▷ *vi* pitar ▷ *vt* llamar por el busca
bleeper ['bliːpəʳ] *n* (*of doctor etc*) busca *m*
blemish ['blɛmɪʃ] *n* marca, mancha; (*on reputation*) tacha
blend [blɛnd] *n* mezcla ▷ *vt* mezclar ▷ *vi* (*colours etc*) combinarse, mezclarse
blender ['blɛndəʳ] *n* (*Culin*) batidora
bless (*pt, pp* **blessed** *or* **blest**) [blɛs, blɛst] *vt* bendecir; **~ you!** (*after sneeze*) ¡Jesús!
blessed ['blɛsɪd] *adj* (*Rel: holy*) santo, bendito; (*: happy*) dichoso; **every ~ day** cada santo día
blessing ['blɛsɪŋ] *n* bendición *f*; (*advantage*) beneficio, ventaja; **to count one's ~s** agradecer lo que se tiene; **it was a ~ in disguise** no hay mal que por bien no venga
blew [bluː] *pt of* **blow**
blight [blaɪt] *vt* (*hopes etc*) frustrar, arruinar
blimey ['blaɪmɪ] *excl* (*Brit inf*) ¡caray!
blind [blaɪnd] *adj* ciego ▷ *n* (*for window*) persiana ▷ *vt* cegar; (*dazzle*) deslumbrar; **to ~ sb to ...** (*deceive*) cegar a algn a ...; **the blind** *npl* los ciegos
blind alley *n* callejón *m* sin salida
blind corner *n* (*Brit*) esquina *or* curva sin visibilidad
blind date *n* cita a ciegas

blindfold ['blaɪndfəuld] *n* venda ▷ *adj, adv* con los ojos vendados ▷ *vt* vendar los ojos a
blinding ['blaɪndɪŋ] *adj* (*flash, light*) cegador; (*pain*) intenso
blindingly ['blaɪndɪŋlɪ] *adv*: **it's ~ obvious** salta a la vista
blindly ['blaɪndlɪ] *adv* a ciegas, ciegamente
blindness ['blaɪndnɪs] *n* ceguera
blind spot *n* (*Aut*) ángulo muerto; **to have a ~ about sth** estar ciego para algo
blink [blɪŋk] *vi* parpadear, pestañear; (*light*) oscilar; **to be on the ~** (*inf*) estar estropeado
blinkers ['blɪŋkəz] *npl* (*esp Brit*) anteojeras *fpl*
blip [blɪp] *n* señal *f* luminosa; (*on graph*) pequeña desviación *f*; (*fig*) pequeña anomalía
bliss [blɪs] *n* felicidad *f*
blissful ['blɪsful] *adj* dichoso; **in ~ ignorance** feliz en la ignorancia
blister ['blɪstəʳ] *n* (*on skin, paint*) ampolla ▷ *vi* ampollarse
blistering ['blɪstərɪŋ] *adj* (*heat*) abrasador(a)
blithely ['blaɪðlɪ] *adv* alegremente, despreocupadamente
blizzard ['blɪzəd] *n* ventisca
bloated ['bləutɪd] *adj* hinchado
blob [blɔb] *n* (*drop*) gota; (*stain, spot*) mancha
block [blɔk] *n* (*also Comput*) bloque *m*; (*in pipes*) obstáculo; (*of buildings*) manzana, cuadra (*LAm*) ▷ *vt* (*gen*) obstruir, cerrar; (*progress*) estorbar; (*Comput*) agrupar; **~ of flats** (*Brit*) bloque *m* de pisos; **mental ~** bloqueo mental; **~ and tackle** (*Tech*) aparejo de polea; **3 ~s from here** a 3 manzanas *or* cuadras (*LAm*) de aquí; **block up** *vt* tapar, obstruir; (*pipe*) atascar
blockade [blɔ'keɪd] *n* bloqueo ▷ *vt* bloquear
blockage ['blɔkɪdʒ] *n* estorbo, obstrucción *f*
block booking *n* reserva en grupo
blockbuster ['blɔkbʌstəʳ] *n* (*book*) best-seller *m*; (*film*) éxito de público
block capitals *npl* mayúsculas *fpl*
block letters *npl* mayúsculas *fpl*
blog [blɔg] *n* (*Comput*) blog *m* ▷ *vi* bloguear
blogger ['blɔgəʳ] *n* (*inf: person*) bloguero(-a)
bloke [bləuk] *n* (*Brit inf*) tipo, tío
blond, blonde [blɔnd] *adj, n* rubio(-a) *m(f)*
blood [blʌd] *n* sangre *f*; **new ~** (*fig*) gente *f* nueva
blood bank *n* banco de sangre
blood count *n* recuento de glóbulos rojos y blancos
blood donor *n* donante *m/f* de sangre
blood group *n* grupo sanguíneo
bloodhound ['blʌdhaund] *n* sabueso
blood poisoning *n* septicemia, envenenamiento de la sangre
blood pressure *n* tensión *f*, presión *f* sanguínea; **to have high/low ~** tener la tensión alta/baja
bloodshed ['blʌdʃɛd] *n* baño de sangre
bloodshot ['blʌdʃɔt] *adj* inyectado en sangre
bloodstream ['blʌdstri:m] *n* corriente *f* sanguínea
blood test *n* análisis *m* de sangre
bloodthirsty ['blʌdθə:stɪ] *adj* sanguinario
blood transfusion *n* transfusión *f* de sangre
blood type *n* grupo sanguíneo
blood vessel *n* vaso sanguíneo
bloody ['blʌdɪ] *adj* sangriento; (*Brit inf!*): **this ~ ...** este condenado *or* puñetero *or* fregado (*LAm*) ... (*!*) ▷ *adv* (*Brit inf!*): **~ strong/good** terriblemente fuerte/bueno
bloody-minded ['blʌdɪ'maɪndɪd] *adj* (*Brit inf*) con malas pulgas
bloom [blu:m] *n* floración *f*; **in ~** en flor ▷ *vi* florecer
blossom ['blɔsəm] *n* flor *f* ▷ *vi* florecer; (*fig*) desarrollarse; **to ~ into** (*fig*) convertirse en
blot [blɔt] *n* borrón *m* ▷ *vt* (*dry*) secar; (*stain*) manchar; **to ~ out** *vt* (*view*) tapar; (*memories*) borrar; **to be a ~ on the landscape** estropear el paisaje; **to ~ one's copy book** (*fig*) manchar su reputación
blotchy ['blɔtʃɪ] *adj* (*complexion*) lleno de manchas
blotting paper ['blɔtɪŋ-] *n* papel *m* secante
blouse [blauz] *n* blusa
blow [bləu] (*pt* **blew**, *pp* **blown**) *n* golpe *m* ▷ *vi* soplar; (*fuse*) fundirse ▷ *vt* (*glass*) soplar; (*fuse*) quemar; (*instrument*) tocar; **to come to ~s** llegar a golpes; **to ~ one's nose** sonarse; **blow away** *vt* llevarse, arrancar; **blow down** *vt* derribar; **blow off** *vt* arrebatar; **blow out** *vt* apagar ▷ *vi* apagarse; (*tyre*) reventar; **blow over** *vi* amainar; **blow up** *vi* estallar ▷ *vt* volar; (*tyre*) inflar; (*Phot*) ampliar
blow-dry ['bləudraɪ] *n* secado con secador de mano ▷ *vt* secar con secador de mano
blowlamp ['bləulæmp] *n* (*Brit*) soplete *m*, lámpara de soldar
blown [bləun] *pp of* **blow**
blow-out ['bləuaut] *n* (*of tyre*) pinchazo; (*inf: big meal*) banquete *m*, festín *m*
blowtorch ['bləutɔ:tʃ] *n* = **blowlamp**
blue [blu:] *adj* azul; **~ film** película porno; **~ joke** chiste verde; **once in a ~ moon** de higos a brevas; **to come out of the ~** (*fig*) ser completamente inesperado; *see also* **blues**
bluebell ['blu:bɛl] *n* campanilla, campánula azul
blueberry *n* arándano
bluebottle ['blu:bɔtl] *n* moscarda, mosca azul
blue cheese *n* queso azul
blueprint ['blu:prɪnt] *n* proyecto; **~ (for)** (*fig*) anteproyecto (de)
blues [blu:z] *npl*: **the ~** (*Mus*) el blues; **to have the ~** estar triste
bluetit [blu:tɪt] *n* herrerillo *m* (común)
bluff [blʌf] *vi* tirarse un farol, farolear ▷ *n* bluff *m*, farol *m*; (*Geo*) precipicio, despeñadero; **to call sb's ~** coger a algn en un renuncio

blunder ['blʌndə^{r}] *n* patinazo, metedura de pata ▷ *vi* cometer un error, meter la pata; **to ~ into sb/sth** tropezar con algn/algo
blunt [blʌnt] *adj* (*knife*) desafilado; (*person*) franco, directo ▷ *vt* embotar, desafilar; **this pencil is ~** este lápiz está despuntado; **~ instrument** (*Law*) instrumento contundente
blur [bləː^{r}] *n* aspecto borroso; **to become a ~** hacerse borroso ▷ *vt* (*vision*) enturbiar; (*memory*) empañar
blurb [bləːb] *n* propaganda
blurred [bləːd] *adj* borroso
blurt [bləːt]: **to ~ out** *vt* (*say*) descolgarse con, dejar escapar
blush [blʌʃ] *vi* ruborizarse, ponerse colorado ▷ *n* rubor *m*
blusher ['blʌʃə^{r}] *n* colorete *m*
blustery ['blʌstərɪ] *adj* (*weather*) tempestuoso, tormentoso
BMA *n abbr* = **British Medical Association**
BO *n abbr* (*inf*: = *body odour*) olor *m* a sudor; (*US*) = **box office**
boar [bɔː^{r}] *n* verraco, cerdo
board [bɔːd] *n* tabla, tablero; (*on wall*) tablón *m*; (*for chess etc*) tablero; (*committee*) junta, consejo; (*in firm*) mesa *or* junta directiva; (*Naut, Aviat*): **on ~** a bordo ▷ *vt* (*ship*) embarcarse en; (*train*) subir a; **full ~** (*Brit*) pensión *f* completa; **half ~** (*Brit*) media pensión; **~ and lodging** alojamiento y comida; **to go by the ~** (*fig*) irse por la borda; **above ~** (*fig*) sin tapujos; **across the ~** (*fig*: *adv*) en todos los niveles; (: *adj*) general; **board up** *vt* (*door*) tapar, cegar
boarder ['bɔːdə^{r}] *n* huésped(a) *m(f)*; (*Scol*) interno(-a)
board game *n* juego de tablero
boarding card ['bɔːdɪŋ-] *n* (*Brit*: *Aviat, Naut*) tarjeta de embarque
boarding house ['bɔːdɪŋ-] *n* casa de huéspedes
boarding party ['bɔːdɪŋ-] *n* brigada de inspección
boarding pass ['bɔːdɪŋ-] *n* (*US*) = **boarding card**
boarding school ['bɔːdɪŋ-] *n* internado
board meeting *n* reunión *f* de la junta directiva
board room *n* sala de juntas
boast [bəust] *vi*: **to ~ (about** *or* **of)** alardear (de) ▷ *vt* ostentar ▷ *n* alarde *m*, baladronada
boat [bəut] *n* barco, buque *m*; (*small*) barca, bote *m*; **to go by ~** ir en barco
boater ['bəutə^{r}] *n* (*hat*) canotié *m*
boat people *npl refugiados que huyen en barca*
bob [bɔb] *vi* (*boat, cork on water*: *also*: **~ up and down**) menearse, balancearse ▷ *n* (*Brit inf*) = **shilling**; **bob up** *vi* (re)aparecer de repente
bobby ['bɔbɪ] *n* (*Brit inf*) poli *m/f*
bobby pin *n* (*US*) horquilla
bobsleigh ['bɔbsleɪ] *n* bob *m*, trineo de competición *f*
bode [bəud] *vi*: **to ~ well/ill (for)** ser de buen/mal agüero (para)
bodily ['bɔdɪlɪ] *adj* (*comfort, needs*) corporal; (*pain*) corpóreo ▷ *adv* (*in person*) en persona; (*carry*) corporalmente; (*lift*) en peso
body ['bɔdɪ] *n* cuerpo; (*corpse*) cadáver *m*; (*of car*) caja, carrocería; (*also*: **~ stocking**) body *m*; (*fig*: *organization*) organización *f*; (: *public body*) organismo; (: *quantity*) masa; (: *of speech, document*) parte *f* principal; **ruling ~** directiva; **in a ~** todos juntos, en masa
body blow *n* (*fig*) palo
body-building ['bɔdɪ'bɪldɪŋ] *n* culturismo
bodyguard ['bɔdɪgɑːd] *n* guardaespaldas *m inv*
body language *n* lenguaje *m* gestual
body search *n* cacheo; **to carry out a ~ on sb** registrar a algn; **to submit to** *or* **undergo a ~** ser registrado
bodywork ['bɔdɪwəːk] *n* carrocería
bog [bɔg] *n* pantano, ciénaga ▷ *vt*: **to get ~ged down** (*fig*) empantanarse, atascarse
boggle ['bɔgl] *vi*: **the mind ~s!** ¡no puedo creerlo!
bogus ['bəugəs] *adj* falso, fraudulento; (*person*) fingido
boil [bɔɪl] *vt* hervir; (*eggs*) pasar por agua ▷ *vi* hervir; (*fig*: *with anger*) estar furioso ▷ *n* (*Med*) furúnculo, divieso; **to bring to the ~** calentar hasta que hierva; **to come to the** (*Brit*) *or* **a** (*US*) **~** comenzar a hervir; **~ed egg** huevo pasado por agua; **~ed potatoes** patatas *fpl or* papas *fpl* (*LAm*) cocidas; **boil down** *vi* (*fig*): **to ~ down to** reducirse a; **boil over** *vi* (*liquid*) salirse; (*anger, resentment*) llegar al colmo
boiler ['bɔɪlə^{r}] *n* caldera
boiler suit *n* (*Brit*) mono, overol *m* (*LAm*)
boiling ['bɔɪlɪŋ] *adj*: **I'm ~ (hot)** (*inf*) estoy asado
boiling point *n* punto de ebullición *f*
boil-in-the-bag [bɔɪlɪnðə'bæg] *adj*: **~ meals** platos que se cuecen en su misma bolsa
boisterous ['bɔɪstərəs] *adj* (*noisy*) bullicioso; (*excitable*) exuberante; (*crowd*) tumultuoso
bold [bəuld] *adj* (*brave*) valiente, audaz; (*pej*) descarado; (*outline*) grueso; (*colour*) llamativo; **~ type** (*Typ*) negrita
Bolivia [bə'lɪvɪə] *n* Bolivia
Bolivian [bə'lɪvɪən] *adj, n* boliviano(-a) *m(f)*
bollard ['bɔləd] *n* (*Brit Aut*) poste *m*
bolshy ['bɔlʃɪ] *adj* (*Brit inf*) protestón(-ona); **to be in a ~ mood** tener el día protestón
bolster ['bəulstə^{r}] *n* travesero, cabezal *m*; **bolster up** *vt* reforzar; (*fig*) alentar
bolt [bəult] *n* (*lock*) cerrojo; (*with nut*) perno, tornillo ▷ *adv*: **~ upright** rígido, erguido ▷ *vt* (*door*) echar el cerrojo a; (*food*) engullir ▷ *vi* fugarse; (*horse*) desbocarse
bomb [bɔm] *n* bomba ▷ *vt* bombardear

b

bombard [bɔm'bɑːd] *vt* bombardear; (*fig*) asediar
bombardment [bɔm'bɑːdmənt] *n* bombardeo
bombastic [bɔm'bæstɪk] *adj* rimbombante; (*person*) pomposo
bomb disposal *n* desactivación *f* de explosivos
bomb disposal expert *n* artificiero(-a)
bomber ['bɔməʳ] *n* (*Aviat*) bombardero; (*terrorist*) persona que pone bombas
bombing ['bɔmɪŋ] *n* bombardeo
bomb scare *n* amenaza de bomba
bombshell ['bɔmʃɛl] *n* obús *m*, granada; (*fig*) bomba
bomb site *n* lugar *m* donde estalló una bomba
bona fide ['bəunə'faɪdɪ] *adj* genuino, auténtico
bonanza [bə'nænzə] *n* bonanza
bond [bɔnd] *n* (*binding promise*) fianza; (*Finance*) bono; (*link*) vínculo, lazo; **in ~** (*Comm*) en depósito bajo fianza
bondage ['bɔndɪdʒ] *n* esclavitud *f*
bone [bəun] *n* hueso; (*of fish*) espina ▷ *vt* deshuesar; quitar las espinas a; **~ of contention** manzana de la discordia
bone idle *adj* gandul
bone marrow *n* médula; **~ transplant** transplante *m* de médula
bonfire ['bɔnfaɪəʳ] *n* hoguera, fogata
bonkers ['bɔŋkəz] *adj* (*Brit inf*) majareta
bonnet ['bɔnɪt] *n* gorra; (*Brit*: *of car*) capó *m*
bonus ['bəunəs] *n* (*payment*) paga extraordinaria, plus *m*; (*fig*) bendición *f*
bony ['bəunɪ] *adj* (*arm, face*) huesudo; (*Med*: *tissue*) huesudo; (*meat*) lleno de huesos; (*fish*) lleno de espinas; (*thin*: *person*) flaco, delgado
boo [buː] *excl* ¡uh! ▷ *vt* abuchear
booby trap ['buːbɪ-] *n* (*Mil etc*) trampa explosiva
book [buk] *n* libro; (*notebook*) libreta; (*of stamps etc*) librillo; **~s** (*Comm*) cuentas *fpl*, contabilidad *f* ▷ *vt* (*ticket, seat, room*) reservar; (*driver*) fichar; (*Football*) amonestar; **to keep the ~s** llevar las cuentas *or* los libros; **by the ~** según las reglas; **to throw the ~ at sb** echar un rapapolvo a algn; **book in** *vi* (*at hotel*) registrarse; **book up** *vt*: **all seats are ~ed up** todas las plazas están reservadas; **the hotel is ~ed up** el hotel está completo
bookcase ['bukkeɪs] *n* librería, estante *m* para libros
booking ['bukɪŋ] *n* reserva
booking office *n* (*Brit*: *Rail*) despacho de billetes *or* boletos (*LAm*); (*: Theat*) taquilla, boletería (*LAm*)
book-keeping ['buk'kiːpɪŋ] *n* contabilidad *f*
booklet ['buklɪt] *n* folleto
bookmaker ['bukmeɪkəʳ] *n* corredor *m* de apuestas
bookmark ['bukmɑːk] *n* (*Comput*) favorito, marcador *m*
bookseller ['buksɛləʳ] *n* librero(-a)
bookshelf ['bukʃɛlf] *n* estante *m*
bookshop ['bukʃɔp] *n* librería
bookstall ['bukstɔːl] *n* quiosco de libros
book store *n* = **bookshop**
book token *n* vale *m* para libros
boom [buːm] *n* (*noise*) trueno, estampido; (*in prices etc*) alza rápida; (*Econ*) boom *m*, auge *m* ▷ *vi* (*cannon*) hacer gran estruendo, retumbar; (*Econ*) estar en alza
boomerang ['buːməræŋ] *n* bumerang *m* (*also fig*) ▷ *vi*: **to ~ on sb** (*fig*) ser contraproducente para algn
boon [buːn] *n* favor *m*, beneficio
boost [buːst] *n* estímulo, empuje *m* ▷ *vt* estimular, empujar; (*increase*: *sales, production*) aumentar; **to give a ~ to** (*morale*) levantar; **it gave a ~ to his confidence** le dio confianza en sí mismo
booster ['buːstəʳ] *n* (*Med*) reinyección *f*; (*TV*) repetidor *m*; (*Elec*) elevador *m* de tensión; (*also*: **~ rocket**) cohete *m*
boot [buːt] *n* bota; (*ankle boot*) botín *m*, borceguí *m*; (*Brit*: *of car*) maleta, maletero, baúl *m* (*LAm*) ▷ *vt* dar un puntapié a; (*Comput*) arrancar; **to ~** (*in addition*) además, por añadidura; **to give sb the ~** (*inf*) despedir a algn, poner a algn en la calle
booth [buːð] *n* (*at fair*) barraca; (*telephone booth, voting booth*) cabina
booty ['buːtɪ] *n* botín *m*
booze [buːz] (*inf*) *n* bebida ▷ *vi* emborracharse
border ['bɔːdəʳ] *n* borde *m*, margen *m*; (*of a country*) frontera; (*for flowers*) arriate *m* ▷ *adj* fronterizo; **the B~s** *región fronteriza entre Escocia e Inglaterra*; **border on** *vt fus* lindar con; (*fig*) rayar en
borderline ['bɔːdəlaɪn] *n* (*fig*) frontera; **on the ~** en el límite
bore [bɔːʳ] *pt of* **bear** ▷ *vt* (*hole*) hacer; (*person*) aburrir ▷ *n* (*person*) pelmazo, pesado; (*of gun*) calibre *m*
bored [bɔːd] *adj* aburrido; **he's ~ to tears** *or* **to death** *or* **stiff** está aburrido como una ostra, está muerto de aburrimiento
boredom ['bɔːdəm] *n* aburrimiento
boring ['bɔːrɪŋ] *adj* aburrido, pesado
born [bɔːn] *adj*: **to be ~** nacer; **I was ~ in 1960** nací en 1960
born-again [bɔːnə'gɛn] *adj*: **~ Christian** evangelista *m/f*
borne [bɔːn] *pp of* **bear**
borough ['bʌrə] *n* municipio
borrow ['bɔrəu] *vt*: **to ~ sth (from sb)** tomar algo prestado (a alguien); **may I ~ your car?** ¿me prestas tu coche?
borrower ['bɔrəuəʳ] *n* prestatario(-a)
borstal ['bɔːstl] *n* (*Brit*) reformatorio (de menores)

Bosnia ['bɔznɪə] *n* Bosnia
Bosnia-Herzegovina, Bosnia-Hercegovina ['bɔːsnɪəhɛrzə'gəuviːnə] *n* Bosnia-Herzegovina
Bosnian ['bɔznɪən] *adj, n* bosnio(-a)
bosom ['buzəm] *n* pecho; (*fig*) seno
boss [bɔs] *n* jefe(-a) *m(f)*; (*employer*) patrón(-ona) *m(f)*; (*political etc*) cacique *m* ▷ *vt* (*also*: **~ about** *or* **around**) mangonear; **stop ~ing everyone about!** ¡deja de dar órdenes *or* de mangonear a todos!
bossy ['bɔsɪ] *adj* mandón(-ona)
bosun ['bəusn] *n* contramaestre *m*
botanist ['bɔtənɪst] *n* botanista *m/f*
botany ['bɔtənɪ] *n* botánica
botch [bɔtʃ] *vt* (*also*: **~ up**) arruinar, estropear
both [bəuθ] *adj, pron* ambos(-as), los/las dos; **~ of us went, we ~ went** fuimos los dos, ambos fuimos ▷ *adv*: **~ A and B** tanto A como B
bother ['bɔðə^r] *vt* (*worry*) preocupar; (*disturb*) molestar, fastidiar, fregar (*LAm*), embromar (*LAm*) ▷ *vi* (*gen*): **to ~ o.s.** molestarse ▷ *n* (*trouble*) dificultad *f*; (*nuisance*) molestia, lata; **what a ~!** ¡qué lata! ▷ *excl* ¡maldita sea!, ¡caramba!; **I'm sorry to ~ you** perdona que te moleste; **to ~ doing** tomarse la molestia de hacer; **please don't ~** no te molestes
bottle ['bɔtl] *n* botella; (*small*) frasco; (*baby's*) biberón *m* ▷ *vt* embotellar; **~ of wine/milk** botella de vino/de leche; **wine/milk ~** botella de vino/de leche; **bottle up** *vt* (*fig*) contener, reprimir
bottle bank *n* contenedor *m* de vidrio, iglú *m*
bottleneck ['bɔtlnɛk] *n* embotellamiento
bottle-opener ['bɔtləupnə^r] *n* abrebotellas *m inv*
bottom ['bɔtəm] *n* (*of box, sea*) fondo; (*buttocks*) trasero, culo; (*of page, mountain, tree*) pie *m*; (*of list*) final *m* ▷ *adj* (*lowest*) más bajo; (*last*) último; **to get to the ~ of sth** (*fig*) llegar al fondo de algo
bottomless ['bɔtəmlɪs] *adj* sin fondo, insondable
bottom line *n*: **the ~** lo fundamental; **the ~ is he has to go** el caso es que tenemos que despedirle
botulism ['bɔtjulɪzəm] *n* botulismo
bough [bau] *n* rama
bought [bɔːt] *pt, pp of* **buy**
boulder ['bəuldə^r] *n* canto rodado
bounce [bauns] *vi* (*ball*) (re)botar; (*cheque*) ser rechazado ▷ *vt* hacer (re)botar ▷ *n* (*rebound*) (re)bote *m*; **he's got plenty of ~** (*fig*) tiene mucha energía
bouncer ['baunsə^r] *n* (*inf*) forzudo, gorila *m*
bouncy castle® ['baunsɪ-] *n* castillo inflable
bound [baund] *pt, pp of* **bind** ▷ *n* (*leap*) salto *gen pl* (*limit*) límite *m* ▷ *vi* (*leap*) saltar ▷ *adj*: **~ by** rodeado de; **to be ~ to do sth** (*obliged*) tener el deber de hacer algo; **he's ~ to come** es seguro que vendrá; **"out of ~s to the public"** "prohibido el paso"; **~ for** con destino a
boundary ['baundrɪ] *n* límite *m*, lindero
boundless ['baundlɪs] *adj* ilimitado
bouquet ['bukeɪ] *n* (*of flowers*) ramo, ramillete *m*; (*of wine*) aroma *m*
bourbon ['buəbən] *n* (*US*: *also*: **~ whiskey**) whisky *m* americano, bourbon *m*
bourgeois ['bueʒwɑː] *adj, n* burgués(-esa) *m(f)*
bout [baut] *n* (*of malaria etc*) ataque *m*; (*Boxing etc*) combate *m*, encuentro
boutique [buː'tiːk] *n* boutique *f*, tienda de ropa
bow [bəu] *n* (*knot*) lazo; (*weapon*) arco; (*Mus*) arco [bau] (*of the head*) reverencia; (*Naut*: *also*: **~s**) proa ▷ *vi* [bau] inclinarse, hacer una reverencia; (*yield*): **to ~ to** *or* **before** ceder ante, someterse a; **to ~ to the inevitable** resignarse a lo inevitable
bowels ['bauəlz] *npl* intestinos *mpl*, vientre *m*; (*fig*) entrañas *fpl*
bowl [bəul] *n* tazón *m*, cuenco; (*for washing*) palangana, jofaina; (*ball*) bola; (*US*: *stadium*) estadio ▷ *vi* (*Cricket*) arrojar la pelota; *see also* **bowls**
bow-legged ['bəu'lɛgɪd] *adj* estevado
bowler ['bəulə^r] *n* (*Cricket*) lanzador *m* (de la pelota); (*Brit*: *also*: **~ hat**) hongo, bombín *m*
bowling ['bəulɪŋ] *n* (*game*) bolos *mpl*, bochas *fpl*
bowling alley *n* bolera
bowling green *n* pista para bochas
bowls [bəulz] *n* juego de los bolos, bochas *fpl*
bow tie ['bəu-] *n* corbata de lazo, pajarita
box [bɔks] *n* (*also*: **cardboard ~**) caja, cajón *m*; (*for jewels*) estuche *m*; (*for money*) cofre *m*; (*crate*) cofre *m*, arca; (*Theat*) palco ▷ *vt* encajonar ▷ *vi* (*Sport*) boxear
boxer ['bɔksə^r] *n* (*person*) boxeador *m*; (*dog*) bóxer *m*
boxer shorts ['bɔksəʃɔːts] *npl* bóxers; **a pair of ~** unos bóxers
boxing ['bɔksɪŋ] *n* (*Sport*) boxeo, box *m* (*LAm*)
Boxing Day *n* (*Brit*) día *m* de San Esteban
boxing gloves *npl* guantes *mpl* de boxeo
boxing ring *n* ring *m*, cuadrilátero
box number *n* (*for advertisements*) apartado
box office *n* taquilla, boletería (*LAm*)
boxroom ['bɔksrum] *n* trastero
boy [bɔɪ] *n* (*young*) niño; (*older*) muchacho, chico; (*son*) hijo
boy band *n* boy band *m* (*grupo musical de chicos*)
boycott ['bɔɪkɔt] *n* boicot *m* ▷ *vt* boicotear
boyfriend ['bɔɪfrɛnd] *n* novio
boyish ['bɔɪɪʃ] *adj* de muchacho, inmaduro
boy scout *n* boy scout *m*
bra [brɑː] *n* sostén *m*, sujetador *m*, corpiño (*LAm*)
brace [breɪs] *n* refuerzo, abrazadera; (*Brit*: *on teeth*) corrector *m*, aparato; (*tool*) berbiquí *m*

▷ *vt* asegurar, reforzar; **to ~ o.s. (for)** (*fig*) prepararse (para); *see also* **braces**
bracelet [ˈbreɪslɪt] *n* pulsera, brazalete *m*, pulso (*LAm*)
braces [ˈbreɪsɪz] *npl* (*on teeth*) corrector *m*; (*Brit*: *for trousers*) tirantes *mpl*, suspensores *mpl* (*LAm*)
bracing [ˈbreɪsɪŋ] *adj* vigorizante, tónico
bracket [ˈbrækɪt] *n* (*Tech*) soporte *m*, puntal *m*; (*group*) clase *f*, categoría; (*also*: **brace ~**) soporte *m*, abrazadera; (*also*: **round ~**) paréntesis *m inv*; (*gen*): **square ~** corchete *m* ▷ *vt* (*fig*: *also*: **~ together**) agrupar; **income ~** nivel *m* económico; **in ~s** entre paréntesis
brag [bræg] *vi* jactarse
braid [breɪd] *n* (*trimming*) galón *m*; (*of hair*) trenza
Braille [breɪl] *n* Braille *m*
brain [breɪn] *n* cerebro; **brains** *npl* sesos *mpl*; **she's got ~s** es muy lista
brainchild [ˈbreɪntʃaɪld] *n* invención *f*
braindead [ˈbreɪndɛd] *adj* (*Med*) clínicamente muerto; (*inf*) subnormal, tarado
brainfood [ˈbreɪnfu:d] *n* alimentos *pl* para el cerebro
brainwash [ˈbreɪnwɔʃ] *vt* lavar el cerebro a
brainwave [ˈbreɪnweɪv] *n* idea luminosa *or* genial, inspiración *f*
brainy [ˈbreɪnɪ] *adj* muy listo *or* inteligente
braise [breɪz] *vt* cocer a fuego lento
brake [breɪk] *n* (*on vehicle*) freno ▷ *vt, vi* frenar
brake fluid *n* líquido de frenos
brake light *n* luz *f* de frenado
bran [bræn] *n* salvado
branch [brɑ:ntʃ] *n* rama; (*fig*) ramo; (*Comm*) sucursal *f* ▷ *vi* ramificarse; (*fig*) extenderse; **branch off** *vi*: **a small road ~es off to the right** hay una carretera pequeña que sale hacia la derecha; **branch out** *vi* (*fig*) extenderse
brand [brænd] *n* marca; (*fig*: *type*) tipo; (*iron*) hierro de marcar ▷ *vt* (*cattle*) marcar con hierro candente
brand name *n* marca
brand-new [ˈbrændˈnju:] *adj* flamante, completamente nuevo
brandy [ˈbrændɪ] *n* coñac *m*, brandy *m*
brash [bræʃ] *adj* (*rough*) tosco; (*cheeky*) descarado
brass [brɑ:s] *n* latón *m*; **the ~** (*Mus*) los cobres
brass band *n* banda de metal
brassière [ˈbræsɪəʳ] *n* sostén *m*, sujetador *m*, corpiño (*LAm*)
brass tacks *npl*: **to get down to ~** ir al grano
brat [bræt] *n* (*pej*) mocoso(-a)
bravado [brəˈvɑ:dəu] *n* fanfarronería
brave [breɪv] *adj* valiente, valeroso ▷ *n* guerrero indio ▷ *vt* (*challenge*) desafiar; (*resist*) aguantar
bravery [ˈbreɪvərɪ] *n* valor *m*, valentía
bravo [brɑ:ˈvəu] *excl* ¡bravo!, ¡olé!
brawl [brɔ:l] *n* pelea, reyerta ▷ *vi* pelearse
bray [breɪ] *n* rebuzno ▷ *vi* rebuznar
brazen [ˈbreɪzn] *adj* descarado, cínico ▷ *vt*: **to ~ it out** echarle cara al asunto
brazier [ˈbreɪzɪəʳ] *n* brasero
Brazil [brəˈzɪl] *n* (el) Brasil
Brazilian [brəˈzɪlɪən] *adj, n* brasileño(-a) *m(f)*
breach [bri:tʃ] *vt* abrir brecha en ▷ *n* (*gap*) brecha; (*estrangement*) ruptura; (*breaking*): **~ of confidence** abuso de confianza; **~ of contract** infracción *f* de contrato; **~ of the peace** perturbación *f* del orden público; **in ~ of** por incumplimiento *or* infracción de
bread [brɛd] *n* pan *m*; (*inf*: *money*) pasta, lana (*LAm*); **~ and butter** *n* pan con mantequilla; (*fig*) pan (de cada día) ▷ *adj* común y corriente; **to earn one's daily ~** ganarse el pan; **to know which side one's ~ is buttered (on)** saber dónde aprieta el zapato
breadbin [ˈbrɛdbɪn] *n* panera
breadbox [ˈbrɛdbɔks] *n* (*US*) panera
breadcrumbs [ˈbrɛdkrʌmz] *npl* migajas *fpl*; (*Culin*) pan *msg* rallado
breadline [ˈbrɛdlaɪn] *n*: **on the ~** en la miseria
breadth [brɛtθ] *n* anchura; (*fig*) amplitud *f*
breadwinner [ˈbrɛdwɪnəʳ] *n* sostén *m* de la familia
break [breɪk] *vb* (*pt* **broke**, *pp* **broken**) ▷ *vt* (*gen*) romper; (*promise*) faltar a; (*fall*) amortiguar; (*journey*) interrumpir; (*law*) violar, infringir; (*record*) batir; (*news*) comunicar ▷ *vi* romperse, quebrarse; (*storm*) estallar; (*weather*) cambiar; (*news etc*) darse a conocer ▷ *n* (*gap*) abertura; (*crack*) grieta; (*fracture*) fractura; (*in relations*) ruptura; (*rest*) descanso; (*time*) intervalo; (*: at school*) (período de) recreo; (*holiday*) vacaciones *fpl*; (*chance*) oportunidad *f*; (*escape*) evasión *f*, fuga; **to ~ with sb** (*fig*) romper con algn; **to ~ even** *vi* cubrir los gastos; **to ~ free** *or* **loose** *vi* escaparse; **lucky ~** (*inf*) chiripa, racha de buena suerte; **to have** *or* **take a ~** (*few minutes*) descansar; **without a ~** sin descanso *or* descansar; **break down** *vt* (*door etc*) echar abajo, derribar; (*resistance*) vencer, acabar con; (*figures, data*) analizar, descomponer; (*undermine*) acabar con ▷ *vi* estropearse; (*Med*) sufrir un colapso; (*Aut*) averiarse, descomponerse (*LAm*); (*person*) romper a llorar; (*talks*) fracasar; **break in** *vt* (*horse etc*) domar ▷ *vi* (*burglar*) forzar una entrada; **break into** *vt fus* (*house*) forzar; **break off** *vi* (*speaker*) pararse, detenerse; (*branch*) partir ▷ *vt* (*talks*) suspender; (*engagement*) romper; **break open** *vt* (*door etc*) abrir por la fuerza, forzar; **break out** *vi* estallar; (*prisoner*) escaparse; **to ~ out in spots** salir a algn granos; **break through** *vi*: **the sun broke through** asomó el sol ▷ *vt fus* (*defences, barrier, crowd*) abrirse paso por; **break up** *vi* (*marriage*) deshacerse; (*ship*) hacerse

pedazos; (*crowd, meeting*) disolverse; (*Scol*) terminar (el curso); (*line*) cortarse ▷ *vt* (*rocks etc*) partir; (*journey*) partir; (*fight etc*) acabar con; **the line's** *or* **you're ~ing up** se corta
breakable ['breɪkəbl] *adj* quebradizo ▷ *n*: **~s** cosas *fpl* frágiles
breakage ['breɪkɪdʒ] *n* rotura; **to pay for ~s** pagar por los objetos rotos
breakdown ['breɪkdaun] *n* (*Aut*) avería; (*in communications*) interrupción *f*; (*Med*: *also*: **nervous ~**) colapso, crisis *f* nerviosa; (*of marriage, talks*) fracaso; (*of figures*) desglose *m*
breakdown truck, breakdown van *n* (camión *m*) grúa
breaker ['breɪkəʳ] *n* rompiente *m*, ola grande
breakfast ['brɛkfəst] *n* desayuno
break-in ['breɪkɪn] *n* robo con allanamiento de morada
breaking and entering ['breɪkɪŋənd'ɛntərɪŋ] *n* (*Law*) violación *f* de domicilio, allanamiento de morada
breaking point ['breɪkɪŋ-] *n* punto de ruptura
breakthrough ['breɪkθru:] *n* ruptura; (*fig*) avance *m*, adelanto
break-up ['breɪkʌp] *n* (*of partnership, marriage*) disolución *f*
breakwater ['breɪkwɔ:təʳ] *n* rompeolas *m inv*
breast [brɛst] *n* (*of woman*) pecho, seno; (*chest*) pecho; (*of bird*) pechuga
breast-feed ['brɛstfi:d] *vt, vi* (*irreg*: *like* **feed**) amamantar, dar el pecho
breaststroke ['brɛststrəuk] *n* braza de pecho
breath [brɛθ] *n* aliento, respiración *f*; **to take a deep ~** respirar hondo; **out of ~** sin aliento, sofocado; **to go out for a ~ of air** salir a tomar el fresco
Breathalyser® ['brɛθəlaɪzəʳ] *n* (*Brit*) alcoholímetro *m*; **~ test** *n* prueba de alcoholemia
breathe [bri:ð] *vt, vi* respirar; (*noisily*) resollar; **I won't ~ a word about it** no diré ni una palabra de ello; **breathe in** *vt*, ▷ *vi* aspirar; **breathe out** *vt*, ▷ *vi* espirar
breather ['bri:ðəʳ] *n* respiro, descanso
breathing ['bri:ðɪŋ] *n* respiración *f*
breathing space *n* (*fig*) respiro, pausa
breathless ['brɛθlɪs] *adj* sin aliento, jadeante; (*with excitement*) pasmado
breathtaking ['brɛθteɪkɪŋ] *adj* imponente, pasmoso
breath test *n* prueba de la alcoholemia
bred [brɛd] *pt, pp of* **breed**
breed [bri:d] (*pt, pp* **bred**) *vt* criar; (*fig*: *hate, suspicion*) crear, engendrar ▷ *vi* reproducirse, procrear ▷ *n* raza, casta
breeding ['bri:dɪŋ] *n* (*of person*) educación *f*
breeze [bri:z] *n* brisa
breezy ['bri:zɪ] *adj* de mucho viento, ventoso; (*person*) despreocupado
brevity ['brɛvɪtɪ] *n* brevedad *f*
brew [bru:] *vt* (*tea*) hacer; (*beer*) elaborar; (*plot*) tramar ▷ *vi* hacerse; elaborarse; tramarse; (*fig*: *trouble*) prepararse; (*storm*) amenazar
brewer ['bru:əʳ] *n* cervecero, fabricante *m* de cerveza
brewery ['bru:ərɪ] *n* fábrica de cerveza
briar ['braɪəʳ] *n* (*thorny bush*) zarza; (*wild rose*) escaramujo, rosa silvestre
bribe [braɪb] *n* soborno ▷ *vt* sobornar, cohechar; **to ~ sb to do sth** sobornar a algn para que haga algo
bribery ['braɪbərɪ] *n* soborno, cohecho
bric-a-brac ['brɪkəbræk] *n inv* baratijas *fpl*
brick [brɪk] *n* ladrillo
bricklayer ['brɪkleɪəʳ] *n* albañil *m*
bridal ['braɪdl] *adj* nupcial
bride [braɪd] *n* novia
bridegroom ['braɪdgru:m] *n* novio
bridesmaid ['braɪdzmeɪd] *n* dama de honor
bridge [brɪdʒ] *n* puente *m*; (*Naut*) puente *m* de mando; (*of nose*) caballete *m*; (*Cards*) bridge *m* ▷ *vt* (*river*) tender un puente sobre; (*fig*): **to ~ a gap** llenar un vacío
bridle ['braɪdl] *n* brida, freno ▷ *vt* poner la brida a; (*fig*) reprimir, refrenar ▷ *vi* (*in anger etc*) picarse
bridle path *n* camino de herradura
brief [bri:f] *adj* breve, corto ▷ *n* (*Law*) escrito ▷ *vt* (*inform*) informar; (*instruct*) dar instrucciones a; **in ~ ...** en resumen ...; **to ~ sb (about sth)** informar a algn (sobre algo)
briefcase ['bri:fkeɪs] *n* cartera, portafolio(s) *m inv* (*LAm*)
briefing ['bri:fɪŋ] *n* (*Press*) informe *m*
briefly ['bri:flɪ] *adv* (*smile, glance*) brevemente; (*explain, say*) brevemente, en pocas palabras
briefs [bri:fs] *npl* (*for men*) calzoncillos *mpl*; (*for women*) bragas *fpl*
brigade [brɪ'geɪd] *n* (*Mil*) brigada
brigadier [brɪgə'dɪəʳ] *n* general *m* de brigada
bright [braɪt] *adj* brillante; (*room*) luminoso; (*day*) de sol; (*person*: *clever*) listo, inteligente; (: *lively*) alegre, animado; (*colour*) vivo; (*future*) prometedor(a); **to look on the ~ side** mirar el lado bueno
brighten ['braɪtn] (*also*: **~ up**) *vt* (*room*) hacer más alegre ▷ *vi* (*weather*) despejarse; (*person*) animarse, alegrarse
brill [brɪl] *adj* (*Brit inf*) guay
brilliance ['brɪljəns] *n* brillo, brillantez *f*; (*fig*: *of person*) inteligencia
brilliant ['brɪljənt] *adj* (*light, idea, person, success*) brillante; (*clever*) genial
brim [brɪm] *n* borde *m*; (*of hat*) ala
brine [braɪn] *n* (*Culin*) salmuera
bring (*pt, pp* **brought**) [brɪŋ, brɔ:t] *vt* (*thing*) traer; (*person*) conducir; **to ~ sth to an end** terminar con algo; **I can't ~ myself to sack him** no soy capaz de echarle; **bring about** *vt* ocasionar, producir; **bring back** *vt* volver a traer; (*return*) devolver; **bring down** *vt*

(*government, plane*) derribar; (*price*) rebajar; **bring forward** *vt* adelantar; (*Bookkeeping*) sumar y seguir; **bring in** *vt* (*harvest*) recoger; (*person*) hacer entrar *or* pasar; (*object*) traer; (*Pol: bill, law*) presentar; (*Law: verdict*) pronunciar; (*produce: income*) producir, rendir; **bring off** *vt* (*task, plan*) lograr, conseguir; (*deal*) cerrar; **bring on** *vt* (*illness, attack*) producir, causar; (*player, substitute*) sacar (de la reserva), hacer salir; **bring out** *vt* (*object*) sacar; (*new product*) sacar; (*book*) publicar; **bring round** *vt* (*unconscious person*) hacer volver en sí; (*convince*) convencer; **bring up** *vt* (*person*) educar, criar; (*carry up*) subir; (*question*) sacar a colación; (*food: vomit*) devolver, vomitar

brink [brɪŋk] *n* borde *m*; **on the ~ of doing sth** a punto de hacer algo; **she was on the ~ of tears** estaba al borde de las lágrimas

brisk [brɪsk] *adj* (*walk*) enérgico, vigoroso; (*speedy*) rápido; (*wind*) fresco; (*trade*) activo, animado; (*abrupt*) brusco; **business is ~** el negocio va bien *or* a paso activo

bristle ['brɪsl] *n* cerda ▷ *vi* (*fur*) erizarse; **to ~ in anger** temblar de rabia

Brit [brɪt] *n abbr* (*inf: = British person*) británico(-a)

Britain ['brɪtən] *n* (*also:* **Great ~**) Gran Bretaña

British ['brɪtɪʃ] *adj* británico; **the British** *npl* los británicos; **the British Isles** *npl* las Islas Británicas

British Summer Time *n hora de verano británica*

Briton ['brɪtən] *n* británico(-a)

brittle ['brɪtl] *adj* quebradizo, frágil

broach [brəutʃ] *vt* (*subject*) abordar

broad [brɔːd] *adj* ancho; (*range*) amplio; (*accent*) cerrado ▷ *n* (*US inf*) tía; **in ~ daylight** en pleno día; **the ~ outlines** las líneas generales

broadband ['brɔːdbænd] *n* banda ancha

broad bean *n* haba

broadcast ['brɔːdkɑːst] (*pt, pp* **broadcast**) *n* emisión *f* ▷ *vt* (*Radio*) emitir; (*TV*) transmitir ▷ *vi* emitir; transmitir

broadcaster ['brɔːdkɑːstəʳ] *n* locutor(a) *m(f)*

broadcasting ['brɔːdkɑːstɪŋ] *n* radiodifusión *f*, difusión *f*

broaden ['brɔːdn] *vt* ampliar ▷ *vi* ensancharse; **to ~ one's mind** hacer más tolerante a algn

broadly ['brɔːdlɪ] *adv* en general

broad-minded ['brɔːd'maɪndɪd] *adj* tolerante, liberal

broadsheet ['brɔːdʃiːt] *n* (*Brit*) periódico de gran formato (*no sensacionalista*); *see also* **quality press**

broccoli ['brɔkəlɪ] *n* brécol *m*, bróculi *m*

brochure ['brəuʃjuəʳ] *n* folleto

brogue [brəug] *n* (*accent*) acento regional; (*shoe*) (*tipo de*) *zapato de cuero grueso*

broil [brɔɪl] *vt* (*US*) asar a la parrilla

broiler ['brɔɪləʳ] *n* (*grill*) parilla; (*fowl*) pollo (para asar)

broke [brəuk] *pt of* **break** ▷ *adj* (*inf*) pelado, sin blanca; **to go ~** quebrar

broken ['brəukən] *pp of* **break** ▷ *adj* (*stick*) roto; (*fig: marriage*) deshecho; (*: promise, vow*) violado; **~ leg** pierna rota; **in ~ English** en un inglés chapurreado

broken-down ['brəukn'daun] *adj* (*car*) averiado; (*machine*) estropeado; (*house*) destartalado

broken-hearted ['brəukn'hɑːtɪd] *adj* con el corazón destrozado

broker ['brəukəʳ] *n* corredor(a) *m(f)* de bolsa

brolly ['brɔlɪ] *n* (*Brit inf*) paraguas *m inv*

bronchitis [brɔŋ'kaɪtɪs] *n* bronquitis *f*

bronze [brɔnz] *n* bronce *m*

brooch [brəutʃ] *n* broche *m*

brood [bruːd] *n* camada, cría; (*children*) progenie *f* ▷ *vi* (*hen*) empollar; **to ~ over** dar vueltas a

broom [brum] *n* escoba; (*Bot*) retama

broomstick ['brumstɪk] *n* palo de escoba

Bros. *abbr* (*Comm: = Brothers*) Hnos

broth [brɔθ] *n* caldo

brothel ['brɔθl] *n* burdel *m*

brother ['brʌðəʳ] *n* hermano

brotherhood ['brʌðəhud] *n* hermandad *f*

brother-in-law ['brʌðərɪn'lɔː] *n* cuñado

brought [brɔːt] *pt, pp of* **bring**

brow [brau] *n* (*forehead*) frente *f*; (*eyebrow*) ceja; (*of hill*) cumbre *f*

brown [braun] *adj* marrón; (*hair*) castaño; (*tanned*) moreno ▷ *n* (*colour*) marrón *m* ▷ *vt* (*tan*) poner moreno; (*Culin*) dorar; **to go ~** (*person*) ponerse moreno; (*leaves*) dorarse

brown bread *n* pan *m* integral

Brownie ['braunɪ] *n* niña exploradora

brown paper *n* papel *m* de estraza

brown rice *n* arroz *m* integral

brown sugar *n* azúcar *m* moreno

browse [brauz] *vi* (*animal*) pacer; (*among books*) hojear libros; **to ~ through a book** hojear un libro

browser ['brauzəʳ] *n* (*Comput*) navegador *m*

bruise [bruːz] *n* (*on person*) cardenal *m*, moretón *m* ▷ *vt* (*leg etc*) magullar; (*fig: feelings*) herir

brunch [brʌntʃ] *n desayuno-almuerzo*

brunette [bruː'nɛt] *n* morena, morocha (*LAm*)

brunt [brʌnt] *n*: **to bear the ~ of** llevar el peso de

brush [brʌʃ] *n* cepillo, escobilla (*LAm*); (*large*) escoba; (*for painting, shaving etc*) brocha; (*artist's*) pincel *m*; (*Bot*) maleza ▷ *vt* (*sweep*) barrer; (*groom*) cepillar; (*gen*): **to ~ past, ~ against** rozar al pasar; **to have a ~ with the police** tener un roce con la policía; **brush aside** *vt* rechazar, no hacer caso a; **brush up** *vt* (*knowledge*) repasar, refrescar

brushwood ['brʌʃwud] *n* (*bushes*) maleza; (*sticks*) leña
Brussels ['brʌslz] *n* Bruselas
Brussels sprout *n* col *f* de Bruselas
brutal ['bru:tl] *adj* brutal
brutality [bru:'tælɪtɪ] *n* brutalidad *f*
brute [bru:t] *n* bruto; (*person*) bestia ▷ *adj*: **by ~ force** por la fuerza bruta
BSc *abbr* (= *Bachelor of Science*) *licenciado en Ciencias*
BSE *n abbr* (= *bovine spongiform encephalopathy*) encefalopatía espongiforme bovina
bubble ['bʌbl] *n* burbuja; (*in paint*) ampolla ▷ *vi* burbujear, borbotar
bubble bath *n* espuma para el baño
bubble gum *n* chicle *m* (de globo)
bubblejet printer ['bʌbldʒɛt-] *n* impresora de inyección por burbujas
bubbly ['bʌblɪ] *adj* (*person*) vivaracho; (*liquid*) con burbujas ▷ *n* (*inf*) champán *m*
buck [bʌk] *n* (*rabbit*) macho; (*deer*) gamo; (*US inf*) dólar *m* ▷ *vi* corcovear; **to pass the ~ (to sb)** echar (a algn) el muerto; **buck up** *vi* (*cheer up*) animarse, cobrar ánimo ▷ *vt*: **to ~ one's ideas up** poner más empeño
bucket ['bʌkɪt] *n* cubo, balde *m* (*esp LAm*) ▷ *vi*: **the rain is ~ing (down)** (*inf*) está lloviendo a cántaros
Buckingham Palace ['bʌkɪŋəm-] *n* el Palacio de Buckingham
buckle ['bʌkl] *n* hebilla ▷ *vt* abrochar con hebilla ▷ *vi* torcerse, combarse; **buckle down** *vi* poner empeño
bud [bʌd] *n* (*of plant*) brote *m*, yema; (*of flower*) capullo ▷ *vi* brotar, echar brotes
Buddhism ['budɪzm] *n* Budismo
Buddhist ['budɪst] *adj*, *n* budista *m/f*
budding ['bʌdɪŋ] *adj* en ciernes, en embrión
buddy ['bʌdɪ] *n* (*US*) compañero, compinche *m*
budge [bʌdʒ] *vt* mover; (*fig*) hacer ceder ▷ *vi* moverse
budgerigar ['bʌdʒərɪɡɑ:ʳ] *n* periquito
budget ['bʌdʒɪt] *n* presupuesto ▷ *vi*: **to ~ for sth** presupuestar algo; **I'm on a tight ~** no puedo gastar mucho; **she works out her ~ every month** planea su presupuesto todos los meses
budgie ['bʌdʒɪ] *n* = **budgerigar**
buff [bʌf] *adj* (*colour*) color de ante; (*inf*: *person*: *well-muscled*) escultural ▷ *n* (*enthusiast*) entusiasta *m/f*
buffalo ['bʌfələu] (*pl* **buffalo** *or* **buffaloes**) *n* (*Brit*) búfalo; (*US*: *bison*) bisonte *m*
buffer ['bʌfəʳ] *n* amortiguador *m*; (*Rail*) tope *m*; (*Comput*) memoria intermedia, buffer *m*
buffer zone *n* zona (que sirve de) colchón
buffet ['bufeɪ] *n* (*Brit*: *bar*) bar *m*, cafetería; (*food*) buffet *m* ▷ *vt* ['bʌfɪt] (*strike*) abofetear; (*wind etc*) golpear
buffet car *n* (*Brit Rail*) coche-restaurante *m*
bug [bʌɡ] *n* (*insect*) chinche *m*; (*: gen*) bicho, sabandija; (*germ*) microbio, bacilo; (*spy device*) micrófono oculto; (*Comput*) fallo, error *m* ▷ *vt* (*annoy*) fastidiar; (*room*) poner un micrófono oculto en; (*phone*) pinchar; **I've got the travel ~** (*fig*) me encanta viajar; **it really ~s me** me fastidia *or* molesta mucho
bugle ['bju:ɡl] *n* corneta, clarín *m*
build [bɪld] *n* (*of person*) talle *m*, tipo ▷ *vt* (*pt, pp* **built** [bɪlt]) construir, edificar; **build on** *vt fus* (*fig*) basar en; **build up** *vt* (*morale, forces, production*) acrecentar; (*Med*) fortalecer; (*stocks*) acumular; (*establish*: *business*) fomentar, desarrollar; (*: reputation*) crear(se); (*increase*: *production*) aumentar; **don't ~ your hopes up too soon** no te hagas demasiadas ilusiones
builder ['bɪldəʳ] *n* constructor(a) *m(f)*; (*contractor*) contratista *m/f*
building ['bɪldɪŋ] *n* (*act*) construcción *f*; (*habitation, offices*) edificio
building site *n* obra, solar *m* (*Sp*)
building society *n* (*Brit*) sociedad *f* de préstamo inmobiliario
build-up ['bɪldʌp] *n* (*publicity*): **to give sb/sth a good ~** hacer mucha propaganda de algn/algo
built [bɪlt] *pt, pp of* **build**
built-in ['bɪlt'ɪn] *adj* (*cupboard*) empotrado; (*device*) interior, incorporado; **~ obsolescence** caducidad *f* programada
built-up ['bɪltʌp] *adj* (*area*) urbanizado
bulb [bʌlb] *n* (*Bot*) bulbo; (*Elec*) bombilla, bombillo (*LAm*), foco (*LAm*)
Bulgaria [bʌl'ɡɛərɪə] *n* Bulgaria
Bulgarian [bʌl'ɡɛərɪən] *adj* búlgaro ▷ *n* búlgaro(-a); (*Ling*) búlgaro
bulge [bʌldʒ] *n* bulto; (*in birth rate, sales*) alza, aumento ▷ *vi* bombearse, pandearse; (*pocket etc*) hacer bulto; **to ~ (with)** rebosar (de)
bulimia [bə'lɪmɪə] *n* bulimia
bulimic [bju:'lɪmɪk] *adj*, *n* bulímico(-a) *m/f*
bulk [bʌlk] *n* (*mass*) bulto, volumen *m*; (*major part*) grueso; **in ~** (*Comm*) a granel; **the ~ of** la mayor parte de; **to buy in ~** comprar en grandes cantidades
bulky ['bʌlkɪ] *adj* voluminoso, abultado
bull [bul] *n* toro; (*Stock Exchange*) alcista *m/f* de bolsa; (*Rel*) bula
bulldog ['buldɔɡ] *n* dogo
bulldoze ['buldəuz] *vt* mover con excavadora; **I was ~d into doing it** (*fig, inf*) me obligaron a hacerlo
bulldozer ['buldəuzəʳ] *n* buldozer *m*, excavadora
bullet ['bulɪt] *n* bala; **~ wound** balazo
bulletin ['bulɪtɪn] *n* comunicado, parte *m*; (*journal*) boletín *m*
bulletin board *n* (*US*) tablón *m* de anuncios; (*Comput*) tablero de noticias
bulletproof ['bulɪtpru:f] *adj* a prueba de balas; **~ vest** chaleco antibalas

bullfight ['bulfaɪt] *n* corrida de toros
bullfighter ['bulfaɪtəʳ] *n* torero
bullfighting ['bulfaɪtɪŋ] *n* los toros *mpl*, el toreo; (*art of bullfighting*) tauromaquia
bullion ['buljən] *n* oro *or* plata en barras
bullock ['bulək] *n* novillo
bullring ['bulrɪŋ] *n* plaza de toros
bull's-eye ['bulzaɪ] *n* blanco, diana
bullshit ['bulʃɪt] (*inf!*) *excl* chorradas ▷ *n* chorradas *fpl* ▷ *vi* decir chorradas ▷ *vt*: **to ~ sb** quedarse con algn
bully ['bulɪ] *n* valentón *m*, matón *m* ▷ *vt* intimidar, tiranizar
bum [bʌm] *n* (*Brit*: *inf*: *backside*) culo; (: *tramp*) vagabundo; (*inf*: *esp US*: *idler*) holgazán(-ana) *m(f)*, flojo(-a)
bumblebee ['bʌmblbi:] *n* abejorro
bump [bʌmp] *n* (*blow*) tope *m*, choque *m*; (*jolt*) sacudida; (*noise*) choque *m*, topetón *m*; (*on road etc*) bache *m*; (*on head*) chichón *m* ▷ *vt* (*strike*) chocar contra, topetar ▷ *vi* dar sacudidas; **bump into** *vt fus* chocar contra, tropezar con; (*person*) topar con; (*inf*: *meet*) tropezar con, toparse con
bumper ['bʌmpəʳ] *n* (*Brit*) parachoques *m inv* ▷ *adj*: **~ crop/harvest** cosecha abundante
bumper cars *npl* (*US*) autos *or* coches *mpl* de choque
bumpy ['bʌmpɪ] *adj* (*road*) lleno de baches; (*journey, flight*) agitado
bun [bʌn] *n* (*Brit*: *cake*) pastel *m*; (*US*: *bread*) bollo; (*of hair*) moño
bunch [bʌntʃ] *n* (*of flowers*) ramo; (*of keys*) manojo; (*of bananas*) piña; (*of people*) grupo; (*pej*) pandilla; **bunches** *npl* (*in hair*) coletas *fpl*
bundle ['bʌndl] *n* (*gen*) bulto, fardo; (*of sticks*) haz *m*; (*of papers*) legajo ▷ *vt* (*also*: **~ up**) atar, envolver; **to ~ sth/sb into** meter algo/a algn precipitadamente en
bung [bʌŋ] *n* tapón *m*, bitoque *m* ▷ *vt* (*throw*: *also*: **~ into**) arrojar; (*also*: **~ up**: *pipe, hole*) tapar; **my nose is ~ed up** (*inf*) tengo la nariz atascada *or* taponada
bungalow ['bʌŋgələu] *n* bungalow *m*, chalé *m*
bungee jumping ['bʌndʒi:'dʒʌmpɪŋ] *n* puenting *m*, banyi *m*
bungle ['bʌŋgl] *vt* chapucear
bunion ['bʌnjən] *n* juanete *m*
bunk [bʌŋk] *n* litera; **~ beds** *npl* literas *fpl*
bunker ['bʌŋkəʳ] *n* (*coal store*) carbonera; (*Mil*) refugio; (*Golf*) bunker *m*
bunk off *vi*: **to ~ school** (*Brit*: *inf*) pirarse las clases; **I'll ~ at 3 this afternoon** me voy a pirar a las 3 esta tarde
bunny ['bʌnɪ] *n* (*also*: **~ rabbit**) conejito
bunting ['bʌntɪŋ] *n* empavesada, banderas *fpl*
buoy [bɔɪ] *n* boya; **buoy up** *vt* mantener a flote; (*fig*) animar
buoyant ['bɔɪənt] *adj* (*ship*) capaz de flotar; (*carefree*) boyante, optimista; (*Comm*: *market, prices etc*) sostenido; (: *economy*) boyante
BUPA ['bu:pə] *n abbr* (= *British United Provident Association*) *seguro médico privado*
burden ['bə:dn] *n* carga ▷ *vt* cargar; **to be a ~ to sb** ser una carga para algn
bureau (*pl* **bureaux**) ['bjuərəu, -z] *n* (*Brit*: *writing desk*) escritorio, buró *m*; (*US*: *chest of drawers*) cómoda; (*office*) oficina, agencia
bureaucracy [bjuə'rɔkrəsɪ] *n* burocracia
bureaucrat ['bjuərəkræt] *n* burócrata *m/f*
bureaucratic [bjuərə'krætɪk] *adj* burocrático
bureau de change [-də'ʃɑ̃ʒ] (*pl* **bureaux de change**) *n* caja *f* de cambio
bureaux ['bjuərəuz] *npl of* **bureau**
burger ['bə:gəʳ] *n* hamburguesa
burglar ['bə:gləʳ] *n* ladrón(-ona) *m(f)*
burglar alarm *n* alarma *f* contra robo
burglarize ['bə:gləraɪz] *vt* (*US*) robar (con allanamiento)
burglary ['bə:glərɪ] *n* robo con allanamiento *or* fractura, robo de una casa
burgle ['bə:gl] *vt* robar (con allanamiento)
Burgundy ['bə:gəndɪ] *n* Borgoña
burial ['bɛrɪəl] *n* entierro
burly ['bə:lɪ] *adj* fornido, membrudo
Burma ['bə:mə] *n* Birmania
burn [bə:n] *vb* (*pt, pp* **burned** *or* **burnt**) ▷ *vt* quemar; (*house*) incendiar ▷ *vi* quemarse, arder; incendiarse; (*sting*) escocer ▷ *n* (*Med*) quemadura; **the cigarette ~t a hole in her dress** se ha quemado el vestido con el cigarrillo; **I've ~t myself!** ¡me he quemado!; **burn down** *vt* incendiar; **burn out** *vt* (*writer etc*): **to ~ o.s. out** agotarse
burner ['bə:nəʳ] *n* (*gas*) quemador *m*
burning ['bə:nɪŋ] *adj* (*building, forest*) en llamas; (*hot*: *sand etc*) abrasador(a); (*ambition*) ardiente
Burns' Night [bə:nz-] *n ver nota*

BURNS' NIGHT

Cada veinticinco de enero los escoceses celebran la llamada *Burns' Night* (noche de Burns), en honor al poeta escocés Robert Burns (1759-1796). Es tradición hacer una cena en la que, al son de la música de la gaita escocesa, se sirve "haggis", plato tradicional de asadura de cordero cocida en el estómago del animal, acompañado de nabos y puré de patatas. Durante la misma se recitan poemas del autor y varios discursos conmemorativos de carácter festivo.

burnt [bə:nt] *pt, pp of* **burn**
burp [bə:p] (*inf*) *n* eructo ▷ *vi* eructar
burrow ['bʌrəu] *n* madriguera ▷ *vt* hacer una madriguera
bursary ['bə:sərɪ] *n* (*Brit*) beca
burst [bə:st] *vb* (*pt, pp* **burst**) ▷ *vt* (*balloon, pipe*) reventar; (*banks etc*) romper ▷ *vi* reventarse; romperse; (*tyre*) pincharse ▷ *n* (*explosion*)

estallido; (*also*: **~ pipe**) reventón *m*; **the river has ~ its banks** el río se ha desbordado; **to ~ into flames** estallar en llamas; **to ~ out laughing** soltar la carcajada; **to ~ into tears** deshacerse en lágrimas; **to be ~ing with** reventar de; **a ~ of energy** una explosión de energía; **a ~ of applause** una salva de aplausos; **a ~ of speed** un acelerón; **to ~ open** abrirse de golpe; **burst into** *vt fus* (*room etc*) irrumpir en

bury ['bɛrɪ] *vt* enterrar; (*body*) enterrar, sepultar; **to ~ the hatchet** enterrar el hacha (de guerra), echar pelillos a la mar

bus [bʌs] *n* autobús *m*, camión *m* (*LAm*)

bus boy *n* (*US*) ayudante *m/f* de camarero

bus conductor *n* cobrador(a) *m(f)*

bush [buʃ] *n* arbusto; (*scrub land*) monte *m* bajo; **to beat about the ~** andar(se) con rodeos

bushed [buʃt] *adj* (*inf*) molido

bush fire *n* incendio en el monte

bushy ['buʃɪ] *adj* (*beard, eyebrows*) poblado; (*hair*) espeso; (*fur*) tupido

busily ['bɪzɪlɪ] *adv* afanosamente

business ['bɪznɪs] *n* (*matter, affair*) asunto; (*trading*) comercio, negocios *mpl*; (*firm*) empresa, casa; (*occupation*) oficio; **to be away on ~** estar en viaje de negocios; **it's my ~ to ...** me toca *or* corresponde ...; **it's none of my ~** no es asunto mío; **he means ~** habla en serio; **he's in the insurance ~** se dedica a los seguros; **I'm here on ~** estoy aquí por mi trabajo; **to do ~ with sb** hacer negocios con algn

business card *n* tarjeta de visita

business class *n* (*Aviat*) clase *f* preferente

businesslike ['bɪznɪslaɪk] *adj* (*company*) serio; (*person*) eficiente

businessman ['bɪznɪsmən] *n* hombre *m* de negocios

business trip *n* viaje *m* de negocios

businesswoman ['bɪznɪswumən] *n* mujer *f* de negocios

busker ['bʌskəʳ] *n* (*Brit*) músico(-a) ambulante

bus pass *n* bonobús

bus route *n* recorrido del autobús

bus shelter *n* parada cubierta

bus station *n* estación *f or* terminal *f* de autobuses

bus-stop ['bʌsstɔp] *n* parada de autobús, paradero (*LAm*)

bust [bʌst] *n* (*Anat*) pecho; (*sculpture*) busto ▷ *adj* (*inf*: *broken*) roto, estropeado ▷ *vt* (*inf*: *Police*: *arrest*) detener; **to go ~** quebrar

bustle ['bʌsl] *n* bullicio, movimiento ▷ *vi* menearse, apresurarse

bustling ['bʌslɪŋ] *adj* (*town*) animado, bullicioso

bust-up ['bʌstʌp] *n* (*inf*) riña

busy ['bɪzɪ] *adj* ocupado, atareado; (*shop, street*) concurrido, animado ▷ *vt*: **to ~ o.s. with** ocuparse en; **he's a ~ man** (*normally*) es un hombre muy ocupado; (*temporarily*) está muy ocupado; **the line's ~** (*esp US*) está comunicando

busybody ['bɪzɪbɔdɪ] *n* entrometido(-a)

busy signal *n* (*US Tel*) señal *f* de comunicando

KEYWORD

but [bʌt] *conj* **1** pero; **he's not very bright, but he's hard-working** no es muy inteligente, pero es trabajador

2 (*in direct contradiction*) sino; **he's not English but French** no es inglés sino francés; **he didn't sing but he shouted** no cantó sino que gritó

3 (*showing disagreement, surprise etc*): **but that's far too expensive!** ¡pero eso es carísimo!; **but it does work!** ¡(pero) sí que funciona!

▷ *prep* (*apart from, except*) menos, salvo; **we've had nothing but trouble** no hemos tenido más que problemas; **no one but him can do it** nadie más que él puede hacerlo; **the last but one** el penúltimo; **who but a lunatic would do such a thing?** ¡sólo un loco haría una cosa así!; **but for you/your help** si no fuera por ti/tu ayuda; **anything but that** cualquier cosa menos eso

▷ *adv* (*just, only*): **she's but a child** no es más que una niña; **had I but known** si lo hubiera sabido; **I can but try** al menos lo puedo intentar; **it's all but finished** está casi acabado

butch [butʃ] *adj* (*pej*: *woman*) machirula, marimacho; (*inf*: *man*) muy macho

butcher ['butʃəʳ] *n* carnicero(-a) ▷ *vt* hacer una carnicería con; (*cattle etc for meat*) matar; **~'s (shop)** carnicería

butler ['bʌtləʳ] *n* mayordomo

butt [bʌt] *n* (*cask*) tonel *m*; (*for rain*) tina; (*thick end*) cabo, extremo; (*of gun*) culata; (*of cigarette*) colilla; (*Brit fig*: *target*) blanco ▷ *vt* dar cabezadas contra, topetar; **butt in** *vi* (*interrupt*) interrumpir

butter ['bʌtəʳ] *n* mantequilla, manteca (*LAm*) ▷ *vt* untar con mantequilla

buttercup ['bʌtəkʌp] *n* ranúnculo

butterfly ['bʌtəflaɪ] *n* mariposa; (*Swimming*: *also*: **~ stroke**) (braza de) mariposa

buttocks ['bʌtəks] *npl* nalgas *fpl*

button ['bʌtn] *n* botón *m* ▷ *vt* (*also*: **~ up**) abotonar, abrochar ▷ *vi* abrocharse

buttress ['bʌtrɪs] *n* contrafuerte *m*; (*fig*) apoyo, sostén *m*

buxom ['bʌksəm] *adj* (*woman*) frescachona, rolliza

buy [baɪ] *vb* (*pt, pp* **bought**) ▷ *vt* comprar ▷ *n* compra; **to ~ sb sth/sth from sb** comprarle algo a algn; **to ~ sb a drink** invitar a algn a tomar algo; **a good/bad ~** una buena/mala compra; **buy back** *vt* volver a comprar;

buy in *vt* proveerse *or* abastecerse de; **buy into** *vt fus* comprar acciones en; **buy off** *vt* (*inf: bribe*) sobornar; **buy out** *vt* (*partner*) comprar la parte de; **buy up** *vt* (*property*) acaparar; (*stock*) comprar todas las existencias de

buyer ['baɪə^r] *n* comprador(a) *m(f)*; **~'s market** mercado favorable al comprador

buy-out ['baɪaut] *n* (*Comm*) adquisición *f* de (la totalidad de) las acciones

buzz [bʌz] *n* zumbido; (*inf: phone call*) llamada (telefónica) ▷ *vt* (*call on intercom*) llamar; (*with buzzer*) hacer sonar; (*Aviat: plane, building*) pasar rozando ▷ *vi* zumbar; **my head is ~ing** me zumba la cabeza; **buzz off** *vi* (*Brit: inf*) largarse

buzzer ['bʌzə^r] *n* timbre *m*

buzz word *n* palabra que está de moda

KEYWORD

by [baɪ] *prep* **1** (*referring to cause, agent*) por; de; **abandoned by his mother** abandonado por su madre; **surrounded by enemies** rodeado de enemigos; **a painting by Picasso** un cuadro de Picasso

2 (*referring to method, manner, means*): **by bus/car/train** en autobús/coche/tren; **to pay by cheque** pagar con cheque; **by moonlight/candlelight** a la luz de la luna/una vela; **by saving hard, he ...** ahorrando, ...

3 (*via, through*) por; **we came by Dover** vinimos por Dover

4 (*close to, past*): **the house by the river** la casa junto al río; **she rushed by me** pasó a mi lado como una exhalación; **I go by the post office every day** paso por delante de Correos todos los días

5 (*time: not later than*) para; (*: during*): **by daylight** de día; **by 4 o'clock** para las cuatro; **by this time tomorrow** mañana a estas horas; **by the time I got here it was too late** cuando llegué ya era demasiado tarde

6 (*amount*): **by the metre/kilo** por metro/kilo; **paid by the hour** pagado por hora

7 (*in measurements, sums*): **to divide/multiply by 3** dividir/multiplicar por 3; **a room 3 metres by 4** una habitación de 3 metros por 4; **it's broader by a metre** es un metro más ancho; **the bus missed me by inches** no me pilló el autobús por un pelo

8 (*according to*) según, de acuerdo con; **it's 3 o'clock by my watch** según mi reloj, son las tres; **it's all right by me** por mí, está bien

9: **(all) by oneself** *etc* todo solo; **he did it (all) by himself** lo hizo él solo; **he was standing (all) by himself in a corner** estaba de pie solo en un rincón

10: **by the way** a propósito, por cierto; **this wasn't my idea, by the way** pues, no fue idea mía

▷ *adv* **1** *see* **go, pass** *etc*

2: **by and by** finalmente; **they'll come back by and by** acabarán volviendo; **by and large** en líneas generales, en general

bye ['baɪ], **bye-bye** ['baɪ'baɪ] *excl* adiós, hasta luego, chao (*esp LAm*)

by-election ['baɪɪlɛkʃən] *n* (*Brit*) elección *f* parcial; *ver nota*

Byelorussia [bjɛləu'rʌʃə] *n* Bielorrusia

bygone ['baɪgɔn] *adj* pasado, del pasado ▷ *n*: **let ~s be ~s** lo pasado, pasado está

bypass ['baɪpɑːs] *n* carretera de circunvalación; (*Med*) (operación *f* de) bypass *m* ▷ *vt* evitar

by-product ['baɪprɔdʌkt] *n* subproducto, derivado

bystander ['baɪstændə^r] *n* espectador(a) *m(f)*

byte [baɪt] *n* (*Comput*) byte *m*, octeto

byword ['baɪwəːd] *n*: **to be a ~ for** ser sinónimo de

by-your-leave ['baɪjɔː'liːv] *n*: **without so much as a ~** sin decir nada, sin dar ningún tipo de explicación

C

C, c [siː] *n* (*letter*) C, c *f*; (*Mus*): **C** do *m*; **C for Charlie** C de Carmen
C *abbr* (= *Celsius*, *centigrade*) C
c *abbr* (= *century*) S.; (= *circa*) hacia; (*US etc*) = **cent(s)**
CA *n abbr* = **Central America**; (*Brit*) = **chartered accountant**
CAA *n abbr* (*Brit*: = *Civil Aviation Authority*) *organismo de control y desarrollo de la aviación civil*
cab [kæb] *n* taxi *m*; (*of truck*) cabina
cabaret ['kæbəreɪ] *n* cabaret *m*
cabbage ['kæbɪdʒ] *n* col *f*, berza
cabbie, cabby ['kæbɪ] *n* (*inf*) taxista *m/f*
cabin ['kæbɪn] *n* cabaña; (*on ship*) camarote *m*
cabin crew *n* tripulación *f* de cabina
cabin cruiser *n* yate *m* de motor
cabinet ['kæbɪnɪt] *n* (*Pol*) consejo de ministros; (*furniture*) armario; (*also*: **display ~**) vitrina
cabinet minister *n* ministro(-a) (del gabinete)
cable ['keɪbl] *n* cable *m* ▷ *vt* cablegrafiar
cable car *n* teleférico
cable television *n* televisión *f* por cable
cache [kæʃ] *n* (*of drugs*) alijo; (*of arms*) zulo
cackle ['kækl] *vi* cacarear
cactus (*pl* **cacti**) ['kæktəs, -taɪ] *n* cacto
caddie, caddy ['kædɪ] *n* (*Golf*) cadi *m*
cadet [kə'dɛt] *n* (*Mil*) cadete *m*; **police ~** cadete *m* de policía
cadge [kædʒ] *vt* gorronear
Caesarean, Cesarean (*US*) [siː'zɛərɪən] *adj*: **~ (section)** cesárea
café ['kæfeɪ] *n* café *m*
cafeteria [kæfɪ'tɪərɪə] *n* cafetería (*con autoservicio para comer*)
caffeine ['kæfiːn] *n* cafeína
cage [keɪdʒ] *n* jaula ▷ *vt* enjaular
cagey ['keɪdʒɪ] *adj* (*inf*) cauteloso, reservado
cagoule [kə'guːl] *n* chubasquero
cahoots [kə'huːts] *n*: **to be in ~ (with sb)** estar conchabado (con algn)
cajole [kə'dʒəul] *vt* engatusar
cake [keɪk] *n* (*large*) tarta; (*small*) pastel *m*; (*of soap*) pastilla; **he wants to have his ~ and eat it** (*fig*) quiere estar en misa y repicando; **it's a piece of ~** (*inf*) es pan comido
caked [keɪkt] *adj*: **~ with** cubierto de
calamity [kə'læmɪtɪ] *n* calamidad *f*
calcium ['kælsɪəm] *n* calcio
calculate ['kælkjuleɪt] *vt* (*estimate*: *chances*, *effect*) calcular; **calculate on** *vt fus*: **to ~ on sth/on doing sth** contar con algo/con hacer algo
calculation [kælkju'leɪʃən] *n* cálculo, cómputo
calculator ['kælkjuleɪtə^r] *n* calculadora
calculus ['kælkjuləs] *n* cálculo
calendar ['kæləndə^r] *n* calendario; **~ month/year** *n* mes *m*/año civil
calf (*pl* **calves**) [kɑːf, kɑːvz] *n* (*of cow*) ternero, becerro; (*of other animals*) cría; (*also*: **~skin**) piel *f* de becerro; (*Anat*) pantorrilla, canilla (*LAm*)
calibre, caliber (*US*) ['kælɪbə^r] *n* calibre *m*
call [kɔːl] *vt* (*gen*) llamar; (*Tel*) llamar; (*announce*: *flight*) anunciar; (*meeting*, *strike*) convocar ▷ *vi* (*shout*) llamar; (*telephone*) llamar (por teléfono), telefonear; (*visit*: *also*: **~ in**, **~ round**) hacer una visita ▷ *n* (*shout*) llamada, llamado (*LAm*); (*Tel*) llamada, llamado (*LAm*); (*of bird*) canto; (*appeal*) llamamiento, llamado (*LAm*); (*summons*: *for flight etc*) llamada; (*fig*: *lure*) llamada; **to be ~ed** (*person*, *object*) llamarse; **to ~ sb names** poner verde a algn; **let's ~ it a day** (*inf*) ¡dejémoslo!, ¡ya está bien!; **who is ~ing?** ¿de parte de quién?; **London ~ing** (*Radio*) aquí Londres; **on ~** (*nurse*, *doctor etc*) de guardia; **please give me a ~ at seven** despiérteme *or* llámeme a las siete, por favor; **long-distance ~** conferencia (interurbana); **to make a ~** llamar por teléfono; **port of ~** puerto de escala; **to pay a ~ on sb** pasarse a ver a algn; **there's not much ~ for these items** estos artículos no tienen mucha demanda; **call at** *vt fus* (*ship*) hacer escala en, tocar en; (*train*) parar en; **call back** *vi* (*return*) volver; (*Tel*) volver a llamar; **call for** *vt fus* (*demand*) pedir, exigir; (*fetch*) pasar a recoger; **call in** *vt* (*doctor*, *expert*, *police*) llamar; **call off** *vt* (*cancel*: *meeting*, *race*) cancelar; (*: deal*) anular; (*: strike*) desconvocar; **call on** *vt fus*

(*visit*) ir a ver; (*turn to*) acudir a; **call out** *vi* gritar, dar voces ▷ *vt* (*doctor*) llamar; (*police, troops*) hacer intervenir; **call up** *vt* (*Mil*) llamar a filas
callbox ['kɔ:lbɔks] *n* (*Brit*) cabina telefónica
call centre *n* (*Brit*) centro de atención al cliente
caller ['kɔ:ləʳ] *n* visita *f*; (*Tel*) usuario(-a); **hold the line, ~!** ¡no cuelgue!
call girl *n* prostituta
call-in ['kɔ:lɪn] *n* (*US*) *programa de línea abierta al público*
calling ['kɔ:lɪŋ] *n* vocación *f*; (*profession*) profesión *f*
calling card *n* tarjeta de visita
callous ['kæləs] *adj* insensible, cruel
calm [kɑ:m] *adj* tranquilo; (*sea*) tranquilo, en calma ▷ *n* calma, tranquilidad *f* ▷ *vt* calmar, tranquilizar; **calm down** *vi* calmarse, tranquilizarse ▷ *vt* calmar, tranquilizar
calmly ['kɑ:mlɪ] *adv* tranquilamente, con calma
calmness ['kɑ:mnɪs] *n* calma
Calor gas® ['kæləʳ-] *n* butano, camping gas® *m inv*
calorie ['kælərɪ] *n* caloría; **low-~ product** producto bajo en calorías
calves [kɑ:vz] *npl of* **calf**
camber ['kæmbəʳ] *n* (*of road*) combadura
Cambodia [kæm'bəudjə] *n* Camboya
camcorder ['kæmkɔ:dəʳ] *n* videocámara
came [keɪm] *pt of* **come**
camel ['kæməl] *n* camello
camera ['kæmərə] *n* cámara *or* máquina fotográfica; (*Cine, TV*) cámara; (*movie camera*) cámara, tomavistas *m inv*; **in ~** (*Law*) a puerta cerrada
cameraman ['kæmərəmən] *n* cámara *m*
camera phone *n* teléfono *m* con cámara
camouflage ['kæməflɑ:ʒ] *n* camuflaje *m* ▷ *vt* camuflar
camp [kæmp] *n* campamento, camping *m*; (*Mil*) campamento; (*for prisoners*) campo; (*fig: faction*) bando ▷ *vi* acampar ▷ *adj* afectado, afeminado; **to go ~ing** ir de *or* hacer camping
campaign [kæm'peɪn] *n* (*Mil, Pol etc*) campaña ▷ *vi*: **to ~ (for/against)** hacer campaña (a favor de/en contra de)
campaigner [kæm'peɪnəʳ] *n*: **~ for** defensor(a) *m(f)* de; **~ against** persona que hace campaña contra
campbed ['kæmpbɛd] *n* (*Brit*) cama plegable
camper ['kæmpəʳ] *n* campista *m/f*; (*vehicle*) caravana
campground ['kæmpgraund] *n* (*US*) camping *m*, campamento
camping ['kæmpɪŋ] *n* camping *m*
campsite ['kæmpsaɪt] *n* camping *m*
campus ['kæmpəs] *n* campus *m*
can¹ [kæn] *n* (*of oil, water*) bidón *m*; (*tin*) lata, bote *m* ▷ *vt* enlatar; (*preserve*) conservar en lata; **a ~ of beer** una lata *or* un bote de cerveza; **to carry the ~** (*inf*) pagar el pato

KEYWORD

can² (*negative* **cannot, can't**, *conditional and pt* **could**) *aux vb* **1** (*be able to*) poder; **you can do it if you try** puedes hacerlo si lo intentas; **I can't see you** no te veo; **can you hear me?** (*not translated*) ¿me oyes?
2 (*know how to*) saber; **I can swim/play tennis/drive** sé nadar/jugar al tenis/ conducir; **can you speak French?** ¿hablas *or* sabes hablar francés?
3 (*may*) poder; **can I use your phone?** ¿me dejas *or* puedo usar tu teléfono?; **could I have a word with you?** ¿podría hablar contigo un momento?
4 (*expressing disbelief, puzzlement etc*): **it can't be true!** ¡no puede ser (verdad)!; **what CAN he want?** ¿qué querrá?
5 (*expressing possibility, suggestion etc*): **he could be in the library** podría estar en la biblioteca; **she could have been delayed** puede que se haya retrasado

Canada ['kænədə] *n* Canadá *m*
Canadian [kə'neɪdɪən] *adj, n* canadiense *m/f*
canal [kə'næl] *n* canal *m*
canary [kə'nɛərɪ] *n* canario
Canary Islands, Canaries [kə'nɛərɪz] *npl* las (Islas) Canarias
cancel ['kænsəl] *vt* cancelar; (*train*) suprimir; (*appointment, cheque*) anular; (*cross out*) tachar; **cancel out** *vt* (*Math*) anular; (*fig*) contrarrestar; **they ~ each other out** se anulan mutuamente
cancellation [kænsə'leɪʃən] *n* cancelación *f*; supresión *f*
cancer ['kænsəʳ] *n* cáncer *m*; **C~** (*Astro*) Cáncer *m*
candid ['kændɪd] *adj* franco, abierto
candidate ['kændɪdeɪt] *n* candidato(-a)
candle ['kændl] *n* vela; (*in church*) cirio
candlelight ['kændllaɪt] *n*: **by ~** a la luz de una vela
candlestick ['kændlstɪk] *n* (*single*) candelero; (: *low*) palmatoria; (*bigger, ornate*) candelabro
candour, candor (*US*) ['kændəʳ] *n* franqueza
candy ['kændɪ] *n* azúcar *m* cande; (*US*) caramelo ▷ *vt* (*fruit*) escarchar
candy bar (*US*) *n* barrita (*dulce*)
candyfloss ['kændɪflɔs] *n* (*Brit*) algodón *m* (azucarado)
cane [keɪn] *n* (*Bot*) caña; (*for baskets, chairs etc*) mimbre *m*; (*stick*) vara, palmeta; (*for walking*) bastón *m* ▷ *vt* (*Brit Scol*) castigar (con palmeta); **~ liquor** caña
canister ['kænɪstəʳ] *n* bote *m*, lata
cannabis ['kænəbɪs] *n* canabis *m*
canned [kænd] *adj* en lata, de lata; (*inf: music*) grabado; (: *drunk*) mamado

cannibal ['kænɪbəl] *n* caníbal *m/f*, antropófago(-a)
cannon (*pl* **cannon** *or* **cannons**) ['kænən] *n* cañón *m*
cannot ['kænɔt] = **can not**
canoe [kə'nuː] *n* canoa; (*Sport*) piragua
canoeing [kə'nuːɪŋ] *n* (*Sport*) piragüismo
canon ['kænən] *n* (*clergyman*) canónigo; (*standard*) canon *m*
canonize ['kænənaɪz] *vt* canonizar
can opener *n* abrelatas *m inv*
canopy ['kænəpɪ] *n* dosel *m*, toldo
can't [kænt] = **can not**
cantankerous [kæn'tæŋkərəs] *adj* arisco, malhumorado
canteen [kæn'tiːn] *n* (*eating place*) comedor *m*; (*Brit*: *of cutlery*) juego
canter ['kæntəʳ] *n* medio galope ▷ *vi* ir a medio galope
canvas ['kænvəs] *n* (*material*) lona; (*painting*) lienzo; (*Naut*) velamen *m*; **under ~** (*camping*) en tienda de campaña
canvass ['kænvəs] (*Pol*) *vi*: **to ~ for** solicitar votos por ▷ *vt* (*district*) hacer campaña (puerta a puerta) en; (: *person*) hacer campaña (puerta a puerta) a favor de; (*Comm*: *district*) sondear el mercado en; (: *citizens*, *opinions*) sondear
canyon ['kænjən] *n* cañón *m*
cap [kæp] *n* (*hat*) gorra; (*for swimming*) gorro; (*of pen*) capuchón *m*; (*of bottle*) tapón *m*, tapa; (: *metal*) chapa; (*contraceptive*) diafragma *m* ▷ *vt* (*outdo*) superar; (*limit*) recortar; (*Brit Sport*) seleccionar (para el equipo nacional); **and to ~ it all, he ...** y para colmo, él ...
capability [keɪpə'bɪlɪtɪ] *n* capacidad *f*
capable ['keɪpəbl] *adj* capaz
capacity [kə'pæsɪtɪ] *n* capacidad *f*; (*position*) calidad *f*; **filled to ~** lleno a reventar; **this work is beyond my ~** este trabajo es superior a mí; **in an advisory ~** como asesor
cape [keɪp] *n* capa; (*Geo*) cabo
caper ['keɪpəʳ] *n* (*Culin*: *also*: **~s**) alcaparra; (*prank*) travesura
capital ['kæpɪtl] *n* (*also*: **~ city**) capital *f*; (*money*) capital *m*; (*also*: **~ letter**) mayúscula
capital gains tax *n* impuesto sobre la plusvalía
capitalism ['kæpɪtəlɪzəm] *n* capitalismo
capitalist ['kæpɪtəlɪst] *adj*, *n* capitalista *m/f*
capitalize ['kæpɪtəlaɪz] *vt* (*Comm*: *provide with capital*) capitalizar; **capitalize on** *vt fus* (*fig*) sacar provecho de, aprovechar
capital punishment *n* pena de muerte
Capitol ['kæpɪtl] *n*: **the ~** el Capitolio

CAPITOL

El Capitolio (*Capitol*) es el edificio en el que se reúne el Congreso de los Estados Unidos ("Congress"), situado en la ciudad de Washington. Por extensión, también se suele llamar así al edificio en el que tienen lugar las sesiones parlamentarias de la cámara de representantes de muchos de los estados.

capitulate [kə'pɪtjuleɪt] *vi* capitular, rendirse
Capricorn ['kæprɪkɔːn] *n* Capricornio
caps [kæps] *abbr* (= *capital letters*) may
capsize [kæp'saɪz] *vt* volcar, hacer zozobrar ▷ *vi* volcarse, zozobrar
capsule ['kæpsjuːl] *n* cápsula
Capt. *abbr* = **Captain**
captain ['kæptɪn] *n* capitán *m* ▷ *vt* capitanear, ser el capitán de
caption ['kæpʃən] *n* (*heading*) título; (*to picture*) leyenda, pie *m*
captivate ['kæptɪveɪt] *vt* cautivar, encantar
captive ['kæptɪv] *adj*, *n* cautivo(-a) *m(f)*
captivity [kæp'tɪvɪtɪ] *n* cautiverio
captor ['kæptəʳ] *n* captor(a) *m(f)*
capture ['kæptʃəʳ] *vt* capturar; (*place*) tomar; (*attention*) captar, llamar ▷ *n* captura; toma; (*Comput*: *also*: **data ~**) formulación *f* de datos
car [kɑːʳ] *n* coche *m*, carro (*LAm*), automóvil *m*, auto (*LAm*); (*US Rail*) vagón *m*; **by ~** en coche
carafe [kə'ræf] *n* jarra
caramel ['kærəməl] *n* caramelo
carat ['kærət] *n* quilate *m*; **18-~ gold** oro de 18 quilates
caravan ['kærəvæn] *n* (*Brit*) caravana, rulot *m*; (*of camels*) caravana
caravan site *n* (*Brit*) camping *m* para caravanas
carb [kɑːb] *n abbr* (*inf*: = *carbohydrate*) carbohidrato
carbohydrates [kɑːbəu'haɪdreɪts] *npl* (*foods*) hidratos *mpl* de carbono
car bomb *n* coche-bomba *m*
carbon ['kɑːbən] *n* carbono
carbon copy *n* copia al carbón
carbon dioxide *n* dióxido de carbono, anhídrido carbónico
carbon footprint *n* huella de carbono
carbon monoxide *n* monóxido de carbono
carbon-neutral [kɑːbn'njuːtrəl] *adj* carbono neutral
carbon offsetting [-'ɔfsɛtɪŋ] *n* compensación *f* de carbono
carbon paper *n* papel *m* carbón
car boot sale *n* mercadillo (*de objetos usados expuestos en el maletero del coche*)
carburettor, carburetor (*US*) [kɑːbju'rɛtəʳ] *n* carburador *m*
card [kɑːd] *n* (*thin cardboard*) cartulina; (*playing card*) carta, naipe *m*; (*visiting card*, *greetings card etc*) tarjeta; (*index card*) ficha; **membership ~** carnet *m*; **to play ~s** jugar a las cartas *or* los naipes
cardboard ['kɑːdbɔːd] *n* cartón *m*, cartulina

cardboard city *n* zona de marginados sin hogar (*que se refugian entre cartones*)
card game *n* juego de naipes *or* cartas
cardiac ['kɑ:dıæk] *adj* cardíaco
cardigan ['kɑ:dıgən] *n* chaqueta (de punto), rebeca
cardinal ['kɑ:dınl] *adj* cardinal; (*importance, principal*) esencial ▷ *n* cardenal *m*
cardinal number *n* número cardinal
card index *n* fichero
cardphone ['kɑ:dfəun] *n* *cabina que funciona con tarjetas telefónicas*
care [kɛə^r] *n* cuidado; (*worry*) preocupación *f*; (*charge*) cargo, custodia ▷ *vi*: **to ~ about** preocuparse por; **~ of (c/o)** en casa de, al cuidado de; (*on letter*) para (entregar a); **in sb's ~** a cargo de algn; **the child has been taken into ~** pusieron al niño bajo custodia del gobierno; **"with ~"** "¡frágil!"; **to take ~ to** cuidarse de, tener cuidado de; **to take ~ of** *vt* cuidar; (*details, arrangements*) encargarse de; **I don't ~** no me importa; **I couldn't ~ less** me trae sin cuidado; **care for** *vt fus* cuidar; (*like*) querer
career [kə'rıə^r] *n* carrera (profesional); (*occupation*) profesión *f* ▷ *vi* (*also*: **~ along**) correr a toda velocidad
carefree ['kɛəfri:] *adj* despreocupado
careful ['kɛəful] *adj* cuidadoso; (*cautious*) cauteloso; **(be) ~!** ¡(ten) cuidado!; **he's very ~ with his money** mira mucho el dinero; (*pej*) es muy tacaño
carefully ['kɛəfəlı] *adv* con cuidado, cuidadosamente
caregiver ['kɛəgıvə^r] *n* (*US*: *professional*) enfermero(-a) *m/f*; (*unpaid*) *persona que cuida a un pariente o vecino*
careless ['kɛəlıs] *adj* descuidado; (*heedless*) poco atento
carelessness ['kɛəlısnıs] *n* descuido, falta de atención
carer ['kɛərə^r] *n* (*professional*) enfermero(-a) *m/f*; (*unpaid*) *persona que cuida a un pariente o vecino*
caress [kə'rɛs] *n* caricia ▷ *vt* acariciar
caretaker ['kɛəteıkə^r] *n* portero(-a), conserje *m/f*
car-ferry ['kɑ:fɛrı] *n* transbordador *m* para coches
cargo (*pl* **cargoes**) ['kɑ:gəu] *n* cargamento, carga
car hire *n* alquiler *m* de coches
Caribbean [kærı'bi:ən] *adj* caribe, caribeño; **the ~ (Sea)** el (Mar) Caribe
caricature ['kærıkətjuə^r] *n* caricatura
caring ['kɛərıŋ] *adj* humanitario
carnal ['kɑ:nl] *adj* carnal
carnation [kɑ:'neıʃən] *n* clavel *m*
carnival ['kɑ:nıvəl] *n* carnaval *m*; (*US*) parque *m* de atracciones
carnivore ['kɑ:nıvɔ:^r] *n* carnívoro(-a)
carnivorous [kɑ:'nıvrəs] *adj* carnívoro
carol ['kærəl] *n*: **(Christmas) ~** villancico
carousel [kærə'sɛl] *n* (*US*) tiovivo, caballitos *mpl*
carp [kɑ:p] *n* (*fish*) carpa; **carp at** *or* **about** *vt fus* sacar faltas de
car park *n* (*Brit*) aparcamiento, parking *m*, playa de estacionamiento (*LAm*)
carpenter ['kɑ:pıntə^r] *n* carpintero(-a)
carpentry ['kɑ:pıntrı] *n* carpintería
carpet ['kɑ:pıt] *n* alfombra ▷ *vt* alfombrar; **fitted ~** moqueta
carpet bombing *n* bombardeo de arrasamiento
carpet slippers *npl* zapatillas *fpl*
carpet sweeper [-'swi:pə^r] *n* cepillo mecánico
car phone *n* teléfono de coche
car rental *n* (*US*) alquiler *m* de coches
carriage ['kærıdʒ] *n* (*Brit Rail*) vagón *m*; (*horse-drawn*) coche *m*; (*for goods*) transporte *m*; (*of typewriter*) carro; (*bearing*) porte *m*; **~ forward** porte *m* debido; **~ free** franco de porte; **~ paid** porte pagado; **~ inwards/outwards** gastos *mpl* de transporte a cargo del comprador/vendedor
carriageway ['kærıdʒweı] *n* (*Brit*: *part of road*) calzada; **dual ~** autovía
carrier ['kærıə^r] *n* transportista *m/f*; (*company*) empresa de transportes; (*Med*) portador(a) *m(f)*
carrier bag *n* (*Brit*) bolsa de papel *or* plástico
carrot ['kærət] *n* zanahoria
carry ['kærı] *vt* (*person*) llevar; (*transport*) transportar; (*a motion, bill*) aprobar; (*involve*: *responsibilities etc*) entrañar, conllevar; (*Comm*: *stock*) tener en existencia; (*interest*) llevar; (*Math*: *figure*) llevarse ▷ *vi* (*sound*) oírse; **to get carried away** (*fig*) entusiasmarse; **this loan carries 10% interest** este empréstito devenga un interés del 10 por ciento; **carry forward** *vt* (*Math, Comm*) pasar a la página/columna siguiente; **carry on** *vi* (*continue*) seguir (adelante), continuar; (*inf*: *complain*) montar el número ▷ *vt* seguir, continuar; **carry out** *vt* (*orders*) cumplir; (*investigation*) llevar a cabo, realizar
carrycot ['kærıkɔt] *n* (*Brit*) cuna portátil, capazo
carry-on ['kærı'ɔn] *n* (*inf*) follón *m*
cart [kɑ:t] *n* carro, carreta ▷ *vt* (*inf*: *transport*) cargar con
carton ['kɑ:tən] *n* caja (de cartón); (*of milk etc*) bote *m*; (*of cigarettes*) cartón *m*
cartoon [kɑ:'tu:n] *n* (*Press*) chiste *m*; (*comic strip*) historieta, tira cómica; (*film*) dibujos *mpl* animados
cartoonist [kɑ:'tu:nıst] *n* humorista *m/f* gráfico
cartridge ['kɑ:trıdʒ] *n* cartucho
cartwheel ['kɑ:twi:l] *n*: **to turn a ~** dar una voltereta lateral

carve [kɑ:v] *vt* (*meat*) trinchar; (*wood*) tallar; (*stone*) cincelar, esculpir; (*on tree*) grabar; **carve up** *vt* dividir, repartir; (*meat*) trinchar
carving ['kɑ:vɪŋ] *n* (*in wood etc*) escultura; (*design*) talla
carving knife *n* trinchante *m*
car wash *n* túnel *m* de lavado
case [keɪs] *n* (*container*) caja; (*Med*) caso; (*for jewels etc*) estuche *m*; (*Law*) causa, proceso; (*Brit*: *also*: **suit~**) maleta; **lower/upper ~** (*Typ*) caja baja/alta; **in ~ of** en caso de; **in any ~** en todo caso; **just in ~** por si acaso; **to have a good ~** tener buenas razones; **there's a strong ~ for reform** hay razones sólidas para exigir una reforma
cash [kæʃ] *n* (dinero en) efectivo; (*inf*: *money*) dinero ▷ *vt* cobrar, hacer efectivo; **to pay (in) ~** pagar al contado; **~ on delivery (COD)** entrega contra reembolso; **~ with order** paga al hacer el pedido; **to be short of ~** estar pelado, estar sin blanca; **cash in** *vt* (*insurance policy etc*) cobrar ▷ *vi*: **to ~ in on sth** sacar partido *or* aprovecharse de algo
cash and carry *n* cash and carry *m*, autoservicio mayorista
cashback ['kæʃ'bæk] *n* (*discount*) devolución *f*; (*at supermarket etc*) *retirada de dinero en efectivo de un establecimiento donde se ha pagado con tarjeta; también dinero retirado*
cashbook ['kæʃbuk] *n* libro de caja
cash card *n* tarjeta *f* de(l) cajero (automático)
cash desk *n* (*Brit*) caja
cash dispenser *n* cajero automático
cashew [kæ'ʃu:] *n* (*also*: **~ nut**) anacardo
cash flow *n* flujo de fondos, cash-flow *m*, movimiento de efectivo
cashier [kæ'ʃɪəʳ] *n* cajero(-a) ▷ *vt* (*Mil*) destituir, expulsar
cashmere ['kæʃmɪəʳ] *n* cachemir *m*, cachemira
cash point *n* cajero automático
cash register *n* caja
casing ['keɪsɪŋ] *n* revestimiento
casino [kə'si:nəu] *n* casino
casket ['kɑ:skɪt] *n* cofre *m*, estuche *m*; (*US*: *coffin*) ataúd *m*
casserole ['kæsərəul] *n* (*food, pot*) cazuela
cassette [kæ'sɛt] *n* cas(s)et(t)e *m or f*
cassette player, cassette recorder *n* cas(s)et(t)e *m*
cast [kɑ:st] (*pt, pp* **cast**) *vt* (*throw*) echar, arrojar, lanzar; (*skin*) mudar, perder; (*metal*) fundir; (*Theat*): **to ~ sb as Othello** dar a algn el papel de Otelo ▷ *n* (*Theat*) reparto; (*mould*) forma, molde *m*; (*also*: **plaster ~**) vaciado; **to ~ loose** soltar; **to ~ one's vote** votar; **cast aside** *vt* (*reject*) descartar, desechar; **cast away** *vt* desechar; **cast down** *vt* derribar; **cast off** *vi* (*Naut*) soltar amarras; (*Knitting*) cerrar los puntos ▷ *vt* (*Knitting*) cerrar; **to ~ sb off** abandonar a algn, desentenderse de algn; **cast on** *vt* (*Knitting*) montar
castanets [kæstə'nɛts] *npl* castañuelas *fpl*
castaway ['kɑ:stəwəɪ] *n* náufrago(-a)
caster sugar ['kɑ:stəʳ-] *n* (*Brit*) azúcar *m* extrafino
Castile [kæs'ti:l] *n* Castilla
Castilian [kæs'tɪlɪən] *adj, n* castellano(-a) ▷ *n* (*Ling*) castellano
casting vote ['kɑ:stɪŋ-] *n* (*Brit*) voto decisivo
cast iron *n* hierro fundido *or* colado
cast-iron ['kɑ:staɪən] *adj* (*lit*) (hecho) de hierro fundido *or* colado; (*fig*: *alibi*) irrebatible; (*will*) férreo
castle ['kɑ:sl] *n* castillo; (*Chess*) torre *f*
castor ['kɑ:stəʳ] *n* (*wheel*) ruedecilla
castor oil *n* aceite *m* de ricino
castrate [kæs'treɪt] *vt* castrar
casual ['kæʒjul] *adj* (*by chance*) fortuito; (*irregular*: *work etc*) eventual, temporero; (*unconcerned*) despreocupado; (*informal*: *clothes*) de sport
casually ['kæzjulɪ] *adv* por casualidad; de manera despreocupada
casualty ['kæʒjultɪ] *n* víctima, herido; (*dead*) muerto; (*Mil*) baja; **heavy casualties** numerosas bajas *fpl*
casualty ward *n* urgencias *fpl*
cat [kæt] *n* gato
Catalan ['kætəlæn] *adj, n* catalán(-ana) *m(f)*
catalogue, catalog (*US*) ['kætəlɔg] *n* catálogo ▷ *vt* catalogar
Catalonia [kætə'ləunɪə] *n* Cataluña
catalyst ['kætəlɪst] *n* catalizador *m*
catalytic converter [kætə'lɪtɪkkən'və:təʳ] *n* catalizador *m*
catapult ['kætəpʌlt] *n* tirachinas *m inv*
cataract ['kætərækt] *n* (*Med*) cataratas *fpl*
catarrh [kə'tɑ:ʳ] *n* catarro
catastrophe [kə'tæstrəfɪ] *n* catástrofe *f*
catch [kætʃ] (*pt, pp* **caught**) *vt* coger (*Sp*), agarrar (*LAm*); (*arrest*) atrapar, coger (*Sp*); (*grasp*) asir; (*breath*) recobrar; (*person*: *by surprise*) pillar; (*attract*: *attention*) captar; (*Med*) pillar, coger; (*also*: **~ up**) alcanzar ▷ *vi* (*fire*) encenderse; (*in branches etc*) engancharse ▷ *n* (*fish etc*) captura; (*act of catching*) cogida; (*trick*) trampa; (*of lock*) pestillo, cerradura; **to ~ fire** prenderse; (*house*) incendiarse; **to ~ sight of** divisar; **catch on** *vi* (*understand*) caer en la cuenta; (*grow popular*) tener éxito, cuajar; **catch out** *vt* (*fig*: *with trick question*) hundir; **catch up** *vi* (*fig*) ponerse al día
catching ['kætʃɪŋ] *adj* (*Med*) contagioso
catchment area ['kætʃmənt-] *n* (*Brit*) zona de captación
catch phrase *n* frase *f* de moda
catchy ['kætʃɪ] *adj* (*tune*) pegadizo
category ['kætɪgərɪ] *n* categoría
cater ['keɪtəʳ] *vi*: **to ~ for** (*Brit*) abastecer a; (*needs*) atender a; (*consumers*) proveer a
caterer ['keɪtərəʳ] *n* abastecedor(a) *m(f)*, proveedor(a) *m(f)*
catering ['keɪtərɪŋ] *n* (*trade*) hostelería

C

caterpillar ['kætəpɪlə^r] *n* oruga
caterpillar track *n* rodado de oruga
cat flap *n* gatera
cathedral [kə'θi:drəl] *n* catedral *f*
catholic ['kæθəlɪk] *adj* católico; **C~** *adj, n* (*Rel*) católico(-a) *m(f)*
Catseye® ['kætsaɪ] *n* (*Brit Aut*) catadióptrico
cattle ['kætl] *npl* ganado *sg*
catty ['kætɪ] *adj* malicioso
catwalk ['kætwɔ:k] *n* pasarela
caucus ['kɔ:kəs] *n* (*Pol: local committee*) comité *m* local; (*: US: to elect candidates*) comité *m* electoral; (*: group*) camarilla política
caught [kɔ:t] *pt, pp of* **catch**
cauliflower ['kɔlɪflauə^r] *n* coliflor *f*
cause [kɔ:z] *n* causa; (*reason*) motivo, razón *f* ▷ *vt* causar; (*provoke*) provocar; **to ~ sb to do sth** hacer que algn haga algo
caution ['kɔ:ʃən] *n* cautela, prudencia; (*warning*) advertencia, amonestación *f* ▷ *vt* amonestar
cautious ['kɔ:ʃəs] *adj* cauteloso, prudente, precavido
cavalry ['kævəlrɪ] *n* caballería
cave [keɪv] *n* cueva, caverna ▷ *vi*: **to go caving** ir en una expedición espeleológica; **cave in** *vi* (*roof etc*) derrumbarse, hundirse
caveman ['keɪvmæn] *n* cavernícola *m*
caviar, caviare ['kævɪɑ:^r] *n* caviar *m*
cavity ['kævɪtɪ] *n* hueco, cavidad *f*
cavort [kə'vɔ:t] *vi* hacer cabrioladas
CB *n abbr* (*= Citizens' Band (Radio)*) *frecuencias de radio usadas para la comunicación privada*; (*Brit: = Companion of (the Order of) the Bath*) *título de nobleza*
CBE *n abbr* (*Brit: = Companion of (the Order of) the British Empire*) *título de nobleza*
CBI *n abbr* (*= Confederation of British Industry*) ≈ C.E.O.E. *f* (*Sp*)
CBS *n abbr* (*US: = Columbia Broadcasting System*) *cadena de radio y televisión*
cc *abbr* (*= cubic centimetres*) cc, cm³; (*on letter etc*) = **carbon copy**
CCTV *n abbr* = **closed-circuit television**
CD *n abbr* (*= compact disc*) CD *m*; (*Mil: Brit: = Civil Defence (Corps); US: = Civil Defense*) defensa civil ▷ *abbr* (*Brit: = Corps Diplomatique*) CD
CD player *n* reproductor *m* de CD
CD-ROM ['si:'di:'rɔm] *n abbr* (*= compact disc read-only memory*) CD-ROM *m*
CD writer *n* grabadora *f* de CDs
cease [si:s] *vt* cesar
ceasefire ['si:sfaɪə^r] *n* alto *m* el fuego
ceaseless ['si:slɪs] *adj* incesante
cedar ['si:də^r] *n* cedro
ceilidh ['keɪlɪ] *n* *baile con música y danzas tradicionales escocesas o irlandesas*
ceiling ['si:lɪŋ] *n* techo; (*fig: upper limit*) límite *m*, tope *m*
celebrate ['sɛlɪbreɪt] *vt* celebrar; (*have a party*) festejar ▷ *vi*: **let's ~!** ¡vamos a celebrarlo!
celebrated ['sɛlɪbreɪtɪd] *adj* célebre
celebration [sɛlɪ'breɪʃən] *n* celebración *f*, festejo
celebrity [sɪ'lɛbrɪtɪ] *n* celebridad *f*
celery ['sɛlərɪ] *n* apio
celibacy ['sɛlɪbəsɪ] *n* celibato
cell [sɛl] *n* celda; (*Biol*) célula; (*Elec*) elemento
cellar ['sɛlə^r] *n* sótano; (*for wine*) bodega
cello ['tʃɛləu] *n* violoncelo
Cellophane® ['sɛləfeɪn] *n* celofán *m*
cellphone ['sɛlfəun] *n* móvil
cellular ['sɛljulə^r] *adj* celular
Celsius ['sɛlsɪəs] *adj* centígrado
Celt [kɛlt, sɛlt] *n* celta *m/f*
Celtic ['kɛltɪk, 'sɛltɪk] *adj* celta, céltico ▷ *n* (*Ling*) celta *m*
cement [sə'mɛnt] *n* cemento ▷ *vt* cementar; (*fig*) cimentar
cement mixer *n* hormigonera
cemetery ['sɛmɪtrɪ] *n* cementerio
cenotaph ['sɛnətɑ:f] *n* cenotafio
censor ['sɛnsə^r] *n* censor(a) *m(f)* ▷ *vt* (*cut*) censurar
censorship ['sɛnsəʃɪp] *n* censura
censure ['sɛnʃə^r] *vt* censurar
census ['sɛnsəs] *n* censo
cent [sɛnt] *n* (*US: unit of dollar*) centavo; (*unit of euro*) céntimo; *see also* **per**
centenary [sɛn'ti:nərɪ], **centennial** [sɛn'tɛnɪəl] (*US*) *n* centenario
center ['sɛntə^r] *n* (*US*) = **centre**
centigrade ['sɛntɪgreɪd] *adj* centígrado
centimetre, centimeter (*US*) ['sɛntɪmi:tə^r] *n* centímetro
centipede ['sɛntɪpi:d] *n* ciempiés *m inv*
central ['sɛntrəl] *adj* central; (*house etc*) céntrico
Central America *n* Centroamérica
Central American *adj, n* centroamericano(-a) *m(f)*
central heating *n* calefacción *f* central
central reservation *n* (*Brit Aut*) mediana
centre, center (*US*) ['sɛntə^r] *n* centro ▷ *vt* centrar; **to ~ (on)** (*concentrate*) concentrar (en)
centre-forward ['sɛntə'fɔ:wəd] *n* (*Sport*) delantero centro
centre-half ['sɛntə'hɑ:f] *n* (*Sport*) medio centro
centre-stage ['sɛntəsteɪdʒ] *n*: **to take ~** pasar a primer plano
century ['sɛntjurɪ] *n* siglo; **20th ~** siglo veinte; **in the twentieth ~** en el siglo veinte
CEO *n abbr* = **chief executive officer**
ceramic [sɪ'ræmɪk] *adj* de cerámica
cereal ['si:rɪəl] *n* cereal *m*
ceremony ['sɛrɪmənɪ] *n* ceremonia; **to stand on ~** hacer ceremonias, andarse con cumplidos
cert [sə:t] *n* (*Brit inf*): **it's a dead ~** ¡es cosa segura!
certain ['sə:tən] *adj* seguro; (*correct*) cierto; (*particular*) cierto; **for ~** a ciencia cierta; **a ~ Mr Smith** un tal Sr. Smith

certainly ['sə:tənlɪ] *adv* desde luego, por supuesto
certainty ['sə:təntɪ] *n* certeza, certidumbre *f*, seguridad *f*
certificate [sə'tɪfɪkɪt] *n* certificado
certified ['sə:tɪfaɪd] *adj*: **~ mail** (*US*) correo certificado
certified public accountant *n* (*US*) contable *m/f* diplomado(-a)
certify ['sə:tɪfaɪ] *vt* certificar; (*declare insane*) declarar loco
cervical ['sə:vɪkl] *adj*: **~ cancer** cáncer *m* cervical; **~ smear** citología
cervix ['sə:vɪks] *n* cerviz *f*, cuello del útero
Cesarean [sɪ'zεərɪən] *adj*, *n* (*US*) = **Caesarean**
cessation [sə'seɪʃən] *n* cese *m*, suspensión *f*
CET *n abbr* (= *Central European Time*) *hora de Europa central*
cf. *abbr* (= *compare*) cfr
CFC *n abbr* (= *chlorofluorocarbon*) CFC *m*
ch. *abbr* (= *chapter*) cap
chafe [tʃeɪf] *vt* (*rub*) rozar; (*irritate*) irritar; **to ~ (against)** (*fig*) irritarse *or* enojarse (con)
chain [tʃeɪn] *n* cadena; (*of mountains*) cordillera; (*of events*) sucesión *f* ▷ *vt* (*also*: **~ up**) encadenar
chain reaction *n* reacción *f* en cadena
chain-smoke ['tʃeɪnsməuk] *vi* fumar un cigarrillo tras otro
chain store *n* tienda de una cadena, ≈ grandes almacenes *mpl*
chair [tʃεə^r] *n* silla; (*armchair*) sillón *m*; (*of university*) cátedra ▷ *vt* (*meeting*) presidir; **the ~** (*US*: *electric chair*) la silla eléctrica; **please take a ~** siéntese *or* tome asiento, por favor
chairlift ['tʃεəlɪft] *n* telesilla *m*
chairman ['tʃεəmən] *n* presidente *m*
chairperson ['tʃεəpə:sn] *n* presidente(-a) *m(f)*
chairwoman ['tʃεəwumən] *n* presidenta
chalet ['ʃæleɪ] *n* chalet *m* (de madera)
chalice ['tʃælɪs] *n* cáliz *m*
chalk [tʃɔ:k] *n* (*Geo*) creta; (*for writing*) tiza, gis *m* (*LAm*); **chalk up** *vt* apuntar; (*fig*: *success, victory*) apuntarse
chalkboard ['tʃɔ:kbɔ:d] (*US*) *n* pizarrón (*LAm*), pizarra (*Sp*)
challenge ['tʃælɪndʒ] *n* desafío, reto ▷ *vt* desafiar, retar; (*statement, right*) poner en duda; **to ~ sb to do sth** retar a algn a que haga algo
challenger ['tʃælɪndʒə^r] *n* (*Sport*) contrincante *m/f*
challenging ['tʃælɪndʒɪŋ] *adj* que supone un reto; (*tone*) de desafío
chamber ['tʃeɪmbə^r] *n* cámara, sala
chambermaid ['tʃeɪmbəmeɪd] *n* camarera
chamber music *n* música de cámara
champagne [ʃæm'peɪn] *n* champaña *m*, champán *m*
champers ['ʃæmpəz] *nsg* (*inf*) champán *m*
champion ['tʃæmpɪən] *n* campeón(-ona) *m(f)*; (*of cause*) defensor(a) *m(f)*, paladín *m/f* ▷ *vt* defender, apoyar
championship ['tʃæmpɪənʃɪp] *n* campeonato
chance [tʃɑ:ns] *n* (*coincidence*) casualidad *f*; (*luck*) suerte *f*; (*fate*) azar *m*; (*opportunity*) ocasión *f*, oportunidad *f*, chance *m or f* (*LAm*); (*likelihood*) posibilidad *f*; (*risk*) riesgo ▷ *vt* arriesgar, probar ▷ *adj* fortuito, casual; **to ~ it** arriesgarse, intentarlo; **to take a ~** arriesgarse; **by ~** por casualidad; **it's the ~ of a lifetime** es la oportunidad de su vida; **the ~s are that ...** lo más probable es que ...; **to ~ to do sth** (*happen*) hacer algo por casualidad; **chance (up)on** *vt fus* tropezar(se) con
chancellor ['tʃɑ:nsələ^r] *n* canciller *m*; **C~ of the Exchequer** (*Brit*) Ministro de Economía y Hacienda; *see also* **Downing Street**
chancy ['tʃɑ:nsɪ] *adj* (*inf*) arriesgado
chandelier [ʃændə'lɪə^r] *n* araña (de luces)
change [tʃeɪndʒ] *vt* cambiar; (*clothes, house*) cambiarse de, mudarse de; (*transform*) transformar ▷ *vi* cambiar(se); (*change trains*) hacer transbordo; (*be transformed*): **to ~ into** transformarse en ▷ *n* cambio; (*alteration*) modificación *f*, transformación *f*; (*coins*) suelto; (*money returned*) vuelta, vuelto (*LAm*); **to ~ one's mind** cambiar de opinión *or* idea; **to ~ gear** (*Aut*) cambiar de marcha; **she ~d into an old skirt** se puso una falda vieja; **for a ~** para variar; **can you give me ~ for £1?** ¿tiene cambio de una libra?; **keep the ~** quédese con la vuelta; **change over** *vi* (*from sth to sth*) cambiar; (*players etc*) cambiar(se) ▷ *vt* cambiar
changeable ['tʃeɪndʒəbl] *adj* (*weather*) cambiable; (*person*) variable
change machine *n* máquina de cambio
changeover ['tʃeɪndʒəuvə^r] *n* (*to new system*) cambio
changing ['tʃeɪndʒɪŋ] *adj* cambiante
changing room *n* (*Brit*) vestuario
channel ['tʃænl] *n* (*TV*) canal *m*; (*of river*) cauce *m*; (*of sea*) estrecho; (*groove, fig*: *medium*) conducto, medio ▷ *vt* (*river etc*) encauzar; **to ~ into** (*fig*: *interest, energies*) encauzar a, dirigir a; **the (English) C~** el Canal (de la Mancha); **the C~ Islands** las Islas Anglonormandas; **~s of communication** canales *mpl* de comunicación; **green/red ~** (*Customs*) pasillo verde/rojo
Channel Tunnel *n*: **the ~** el túnel del Canal de la Mancha, el Eurotúnel
chant [tʃɑ:nt] *n* (*also Rel*) canto; (*of crowd*) gritos *mpl* ▷ *vt* cantar; (*slogan, word*) repetir a gritos; **the demonstrators ~ed their disapproval** los manifestantes corearon su desaprobación
chaos ['keɪɔs] *n* caos *m*
chaotic [keɪ'ɔtɪk] *adj* caótico

C

chap [tʃæp] *n* (*Brit inf*: *man*) tío, tipo; **old ~** amigo (mío)
chapel ['tʃæpəl] *n* capilla
chaplain ['tʃæplɪn] *n* capellán *m*
chapped [tʃæpt] *adj* agrietado
chapter ['tʃæptə^r] *n* capítulo
char [tʃɑː^r] *vt* (*burn*) carbonizar, chamuscar
character ['kærɪktə^r] *n* carácter *m*, naturaleza, índole *f*; (*in novel, film*) personaje *m*; (*role*) papel *m*; (*individuality*) carácter *m*; (*Comput*) carácter *m*; **a person of good ~** una persona de buena reputación
characteristic [kærɪktə'rɪstɪk] *adj* característico ▷ *n* característica
characterize ['kærɪktəraɪz] *vt* caracterizar
charcoal ['tʃɑːkəul] *n* carbón *m* vegetal; (*Art*) carboncillo
charge [tʃɑːdʒ] *n* carga; (*Law*) cargo, acusación *f*; (*cost*) precio, coste *m*; (*responsibility*) cargo; (*task*) encargo ▷ *vt* (*Law*): **to ~ (with)** acusar (de); (*gun, battery*) cargar; (*Mil*: *enemy*) cargar; (*price*) pedir; (*customer*) cobrar; (*person*: *with task*) encargar ▷ *vi* precipitarse; (*make pay*) cobrar; **charges** *npl*: **bank ~s** comisiones *fpl* bancarias; **extra ~** recargo, suplemento; **free of ~** gratis; **to reverse the ~s** (*Brit Tel*) llamar a cobro revertido; **to take ~ of** hacerse cargo de, encargarse de; **to be in ~ of** estar encargado de; **how much do you ~?** ¿cuánto cobra usted?; **to ~ an expense (up) to sb's account** cargar algo a cuenta de algn; **~ it to my account** póngalo *or* cárguelo a mi cuenta
charge card *n* tarjeta de cuenta
charge hand ['tʃɑːdʒhænd] *n* capataz *m*
charger ['tʃɑːdʒə^r] *n* (*also*: **battery ~**) cargador *m* (de baterías)
chariot ['tʃærɪət] *n* carro
charisma [kæ'rɪzmə] *n* carisma *m*
charismatic [kærɪz'mætɪk] *adj* carismático
charitable ['tʃærɪtəbl] *adj* caritativo
charity ['tʃærɪtɪ] *n* (*gen*) caridad *f*; (*organization*) organización *f* benéfica; (*money, gifts*) limosnas *fpl*
charity shop *n* (*Brit*) *tienda de artículos de segunda mano que dedica su recaudación a causas benéficas*
charm [tʃɑːm] *n* encanto, atractivo; (*spell*) hechizo; (*object*) amuleto; (*on bracelet*) dije *m* ▷ *vt* encantar; hechizar
charming ['tʃɑːmɪŋ] *adj* encantador(a); (*person*) simpático
chart [tʃɑːt] *n* (*table*) cuadro; (*graph*) gráfica; (*map*) carta de navegación; (*weather chart*) mapa *m* meteorológico ▷ *vt* (*course*) trazar; (*progress*) seguir; (*sales*) hacer una gráfica de; **to be in the ~s** (*record, pop group*) estar en la lista de éxitos
charter ['tʃɑːtə^r] *vt* (*bus*) alquilar; (*plane, ship*) fletar ▷ *n* (*document*) estatuto, carta; **on ~** en alquiler, alquilado
chartered accountant *n* (*Brit*) contable *m/f* diplomado(-a)
charter flight *n* vuelo chárter
chase [tʃeɪs] *vt* (*pursue*) perseguir; (*hunt*) cazar ▷ *n* persecución *f*; caza; **to ~ after** correr tras; **chase up** *vt* (*information*) tratar de conseguir; **to ~ sb up about sth** recordar algo a algn
chasm ['kæzəm] *n* abismo
chassis ['ʃæsɪ] *n* chasis *m*
chaste [tʃeɪst] *adj* casto
chastity ['tʃæstɪtɪ] *n* castidad *f*
chat [tʃæt] *vi* (*also*: **have a ~**) charlar; (*Internet*) chatear ▷ *n* charla; (*Internet*) chat *m*; **chat up** *vt* (*inf*: *girl*) ligar con, enrollarse con
chatline ['tʃætlaɪn] *n* línea (telefónica) múltiple, party line *f*
chat room *n* (*Internet*) chat *m*, canal *m* de charla
chat show *n* (*Brit*) programa *m* de entrevistas
chatter ['tʃætə^r] *vi* (*person*) charlar; (*teeth*) castañetear ▷ *n* (*of birds*) parloteo; (*of people*) charla, cháchara
chatterbox ['tʃætəbɔks] *n* parlanchín(-ina) *m(f)*
chattering classes ['tʃætərɪŋ'klɑːsɪz] *npl*: **the ~** (*inf, pej*) los intelectualillos
chatty ['tʃætɪ] *adj* (*style*) informal; (*person*) hablador(a)
chauffeur ['ʃəufə^r] *n* chófer *m*
chauvinist ['ʃəuvɪnɪst] *n* (*also*: **male ~**) machista *m*; (*nationalist*) chovinista *m/f*, patriotero(-a) *m(f)*
cheap [tʃiːp] *adj* barato; (*joke*) de mal gusto, chabacano; (*poor quality*) de mala calidad; (*reduced*: *ticket*) económico; (*: fare*) barato ▷ *adv* barato
cheap day return *n billete de ida y vuelta el mismo día*
cheaply ['tʃiːplɪ] *adv* barato, a bajo precio
cheat [tʃiːt] *vi* hacer trampa; (*in exam*) copiar ▷ *vt* estafar, timar ▷ *n* trampa; estafa; (*person*) tramposo(-a); **to ~ sb (out of sth)** estafar (algo) a algn; **cheat on** *vt fus* engañar; **he's been ~ing on his wife** ha estado engañando a su esposa
check [tʃɛk] *vt* (*examine*) controlar; (*facts*) comprobar; (*count*) contar; (*halt*) frenar; (*restrain*) refrenar, restringir ▷ *vi*: **to ~ with sb** consultar con algn; (*official etc*) informarse por ▷ *n* (*inspection*) control *m*, inspección *f*; (*curb*) freno; (*bill*) nota, cuenta; (*US*) = **cheque**; (*pattern*) *gen pl* cuadro ▷ *adj* (*also*: **~ed**: *pattern, cloth*) a cuadros; **to keep a ~ on sth/sb** controlar algo/a algn; **check in** *vi* (*in hotel*) registrarse; (*at airport*) facturar ▷ *vt* (*luggage*) facturar; **check off** *vt* (*esp US*: *check*) comprobar; (*cross off*) tachar; **check out** *vi* (*of hotel*) desocupar la habitación ▷ *vt* (*investigate*: *story*) comprobar; (*: person*) informarse sobre; **check up** *vi*: **to ~ up on sth** comprobar algo; **to ~ up on sb** investigar a algn

checkbook ['tʃɛkbuk] *n* (*US*) = **chequebook**
checked [tʃɛkt] *adj* a cuadros *inv*
checkered ['tʃɛkəd] *adj* (*US*) = **chequered**
checkers ['tʃɛkəz] *n* (*US*) damas *fpl*
check-in ['tʃɛkɪn] *n* (*also*: **~ desk**: *at airport*) mostrador *m* de facturación
checking account ['tʃɛkɪŋ-] *n* (*US*) cuenta corriente
checklist ['tʃɛklɪst] *n* lista
checkmate ['tʃɛkmeɪt] *n* jaque *m* mate
checkout ['tʃɛkaut] *n* (*in supermarket*) caja
checkpoint ['tʃɛkpɔɪnt] *n* (punto de) control *m*, retén *m* (*LAm*)
checkroom ['tʃɛkrum] *n* (*US*) consigna
checkup ['tʃɛkʌp] *n* (*Med*) reconocimiento general; (*of machine*) revisión *f*
cheddar ['tʃedə^r] *n* (*also*: **~ cheese**) queso *m* cheddar
cheek [tʃi:k] *n* mejilla; (*impudence*) descaro; **what a ~!** ¡qué cara!
cheekbone ['tʃi:kbəun] *n* pómulo
cheeky ['tʃi:kɪ] *adj* fresco, descarado
cheep [tʃi:p] *n* (*of bird*) pío ▷ *vi* piar
cheer [tʃɪə^r] *vt* vitorear, ovacionar; (*gladden*) alegrar, animar ▷ *vi* dar vivas ▷ *n* viva *m*; **cheers** *npl* vítores *mpl*; **~s!** ¡salud!; **cheer on** *vt* (*person etc*) animar con aplausos *or* gritos; **cheer up** *vi* animarse ▷ *vt* alegrar, animar
cheerful ['tʃɪəful] *adj* alegre
cheerio [tʃɪərɪ'əu] *excl* (*Brit*) ¡hasta luego!
cheerleader ['tʃɪəli:də^r] *n* animador(a) *m(f)*
cheese [tʃi:z] *n* queso
cheeseboard ['tʃi:zbɔ:d] *n* tabla de quesos
cheeseburger ['tʃi:zbə:gə^r] *n* hamburguesa con queso
cheesecake ['tʃi:zkeɪk] *n* pastel *m* de queso
cheetah ['tʃi:tə] *n* guepardo
chef [ʃɛf] *n* jefe(-a) *m(f)* de cocina
chemical ['kɛmɪkəl] *adj* químico ▷ *n* producto químico
chemist ['kɛmɪst] *n* (*Brit*: *pharmacist*) farmacéutico(-a); (*scientist*) químico(-a); **~'s (shop)** *n* (*Brit*) farmacia
chemistry ['kɛmɪstrɪ] *n* química
chemotherapy [ki:məu'θɛrəpɪ] *n* quimioterapia
cheque, check (*US*) [tʃɛk] *n* cheque *m*; **to pay by ~** pagar con cheque
chequebook, checkbook (*US*) ['tʃɛkbuk] *n* talonario (de cheques), chequera (*LAm*)
cheque card *n* (*Brit*) tarjeta de identificación bancaria
chequered, checkered (*US*) ['tʃɛkəd] *adj* (*fig*) accidentado; (*pattern*) de cuadros
cherish ['tʃɛrɪʃ] *vt* (*love*) querer, apreciar; (*protect*) cuidar; (*hope etc*) abrigar
cherry ['tʃɛrɪ] *n* cereza; (*also*: **~ tree**) cerezo
chess [tʃɛs] *n* ajedrez *m*
chessboard ['tʃɛsbɔ:d] *n* tablero (de ajedrez)
chest [tʃɛst] *n* (*Anat*) pecho; (*box*) cofre *m*; **to get sth off one's ~** (*inf*) desahogarse; **~ of drawers** *n* cómoda
chestnut ['tʃɛsnʌt] *n* castaña; (*also*: **~ tree**) castaño; (*colour*) castaño ▷ *adj* (color) castaño *inv*
chesty ['tʃɛstɪ] *adj* (*cough*) de bronquios, de pecho
chew [tʃu:] *vt* mascar, masticar
chewing gum ['tʃu:ɪŋ-] *n* chicle *m*
chic [ʃi:k] *adj* elegante
Chicano [tʃɪ'kɑ:nəu] *adj, n* chicano(-a)
chick [tʃɪk] *n* pollito, polluelo; (*US inf*) chica
chicken ['tʃɪkɪn] *n* gallina, pollo; (*food*) pollo; (*inf*: *coward*) gallina *m/f*; **chicken out** *vi* (*inf*) rajarse; **to ~ out of doing sth** rajarse y no hacer algo
chickenpox ['tʃɪkɪnpɔks] *n* varicela
chickpea ['tʃɪkpi:] *n* garbanzo
chicory ['tʃɪkərɪ] *n* (*for coffee*) achicoria; (*salad*) escarola
chief [tʃi:f] *n* jefe(-a) *m(f)* ▷ *adj* principal, máximo (*esp LAm*); **C~ of Staff** (*esp Mil*) Jefe *m* del Estado mayor
chief executive, chief executive officer (*US*) *n* director *m* general
chiefly ['tʃi:flɪ] *adv* principalmente
chiffon ['ʃɪfɔn] *n* gasa
chilblain ['tʃɪlbleɪn] *n* sabañón *m*
child (*pl* **children**) [tʃaɪld, 'tʃɪldrən] *n* niño(-a); (*offspring*) hijo(-a)
child abuse *n* (*with violence*) malos tratos *mpl* a niños; (*sexual*) abuso *m* sexual de niños
child benefit *n* (*Brit*) subsidio por cada hijo pequeño
childbirth ['tʃaɪldbə:θ] *n* parto
childcare ['tʃaɪldkɛə^r] *n* cuidado de los niños
childhood ['tʃaɪldhud] *n* niñez *f*, infancia
childish ['tʃaɪldɪʃ] *adj* pueril, infantil
childlike ['tʃaɪldlaɪk] *adj* de niño, infantil
child minder *n* (*Brit*) niñera, madre *f* de día
child prodigy *n* niño(-a) prodigio *inv*
children ['tʃɪldrən] *npl of* **child**
children's home *n* centro de acogida para niños
Chile ['tʃɪlɪ] *n* Chile *m*
Chilean ['tʃɪlɪən] *adj, n* chileno(-a) *m(f)*
chill [tʃɪl] *n* frío; (*Med*) resfriado ▷ *adj* frío ▷ *vt* enfriar; (*Culin*) refrigerar; **chill out** *vi* (*esp US inf*) tranquilizarse
chilling ['tʃɪlɪŋ] *adj* escalofriante
chilly ['tʃɪlɪ] *adj* frío
chime [tʃaɪm] *n* repique *m*, campanada ▷ *vi* repicar, sonar
chimney ['tʃɪmnɪ] *n* chimenea
chimney sweep *n* deshollinador *m*
chimpanzee [tʃɪmpæn'zi:] *n* chimpancé *m*
chin [tʃɪn] *n* mentón *m*, barbilla
China ['tʃaɪnə] *n* China
china ['tʃaɪnə] *n* porcelana; (*crockery*) loza
Chinese [tʃaɪ'ni:z] *adj* chino ▷ *n pl inv* chino(-a); (*Ling*) chino
chink [tʃɪŋk] *n* (*opening*) rendija, hendedura; (*noise*) tintineo

chinwag ['tʃɪnwæg] *n (Brit inf)*: **to have a ~** echar una parrafada

chip [tʃɪp] *n gen pl (Culin: Brit)* patata *or (LAm)* papa frita; *(: US: also:* **potato ~**) patata *or (LAm)* papa frita; *(of wood)* astilla; *(stone)* lasca; *(in gambling)* ficha; *(Comput)* chip *m* ▷ *vt (cup, plate)* desconchar; **when the ~s are down** *(fig)* a la hora de la verdad; **chip in** *vi (inf: interrupt)* interrumpir, meterse; *(: contribute)* contribuir

chip shop *n ver nota*

CHIP SHOP

Se denomina *chip shop* o *fish-and-chip shop* a un tipo de tienda popular de comida rápida en la que se despachan platos tradicionales británicos, principalmente filetes de pescado rebozado frito y patatas fritas.

chiropodist [kɪ'rɔpədɪst] *n (Brit)* podólogo(-a)

chirp [tʃə:p] *vi* gorjear; *(cricket)* cantar ▷ *n (of cricket)* canto

chisel ['tʃɪzl] *n (for wood)* escoplo; *(for stone)* cincel *m*

chit [tʃɪt] *n* nota

chitchat ['tʃɪttʃæt] *n* chismes *mpl*, habladurías *fpl*

chivalry ['ʃɪvəlrɪ] *n* caballerosidad *f*

chives [tʃaɪvz] *npl* cebollinos *mpl*

chlorine ['klɔ:ri:n] *n* cloro

choc-ice ['tʃɔkaɪs] *n (Brit)* helado *m* cubierto de chocolate

chock-a-block ['tʃɔkə'blɔk], **chock-full** [tʃɔk'ful] *adj* atestado

chocolate ['tʃɔklɪt] *n* chocolate *m*; *(sweet)* bombón *m*

choice [tʃɔɪs] *n* elección *f*; *(preference)* preferencia ▷ *adj* escogido; **I did it by** *or* **from ~** lo hice de buena gana; **a wide ~** un gran surtido, una gran variedad

choir ['kwaɪə^r] *n* coro

choirboy ['kwaɪəbɔɪ] *n* niño de coro

choke [tʃəuk] *vi* ahogarse; *(on food)* atragantarse ▷ *vt* ahogar; *(block)* atascar ▷ *n (Aut)* estárter *m*

cholera ['kɔlərə] *n* cólera *m*

cholesterol [kɔ'lɛstərəl] *n* colesterol *m*

choose [tʃu:z] *(pt* **chose** [tʃəuz], *pp* **chosen** [tʃəuzn]) *vt* escoger, elegir; *(team)* seleccionar; **to ~ between** elegir *or* escoger entre; **to ~ from** escoger entre; **to ~ to do sth** optar por hacer algo

choosy ['tʃu:zɪ] *adj* remilgado

chop [tʃɔp] *vt (wood)* cortar, talar; *(Culin: also:* **~ up**) picar ▷ *n* tajo, golpe *m* cortante; *(Culin)* chuleta; **chops** *npl (jaws)* boca *sg*; **to get the ~** *(inf: project)* ser suprimido; *(: person: be sacked)* ser despedido; **chop down** *vt (tree)* talar; **chop off** *vt* cortar (de un tajo)

chopper ['tʃɔpə^r] *n (helicopter)* helicóptero

choppy ['tʃɔpɪ] *adj (sea)* picado, agitado

chopsticks ['tʃɔpstɪks] *npl* palillos *mpl*

chord [kɔ:d] *n (Mus)* acorde *m*

chore [tʃɔ:^r] *n* faena, tarea; *(routine task)* trabajo rutinario

choreographer [kɔrɪ'ɔgrəfə^r] *n* coreógrafo(-a)

choreography [kɔrɪ'ɔgrəfɪ] *n* coreografía

chortle ['tʃɔ:tl] *vi* reírse satisfecho

chorus ['kɔ:rəs] *n* coro; *(repeated part of song)* estribillo

chose [tʃəuz] *pt of* **choose**

chosen ['tʃəuzn] *pp of* **choose**

Christ [kraɪst] *n* Cristo

christen ['krɪsn] *vt* bautizar

christening ['krɪsnɪŋ] *n* bautizo

Christian ['krɪstɪən] *adj, n* cristiano(-a) *m(f)*

Christianity [krɪstɪ'ænɪtɪ] *n* cristianismo

Christian name *n* nombre *m* de pila

Christmas ['krɪsməs] *n* Navidad *f*; **Merry ~!** ¡Felices Navidades!

Christmas card *n* crismas *m inv*, tarjeta de Navidad

Christmas carol *n* villancico *m*

Christmas Day *n* día *m* de Navidad

Christmas Eve *n* Nochebuena

Christmas pudding *n (esp Brit)* pudín *m* de Navidad

Christmas tree *n* árbol *m* de Navidad

chrome [krəum] *n* = **chromium plating**

chromium ['krəumɪəm] *n* cromo; *(also:* **~ plating**) cromado

chromosome ['krəuməsəum] *n* cromosoma *m*

chronic ['krɔnɪk] *adj* crónico; *(fig: liar, smoker)* empedernido

chronicle ['krɔnɪkl] *n* crónica

chronological [krɔnə'lɔdʒɪkəl] *adj* cronológico

chrysanthemum [krɪ'sænθəməm] *n* crisantemo

chubby ['tʃʌbɪ] *adj* rechoncho

chuck [tʃʌk] *(inf) vt* lanzar, arrojar; *(Brit: also:* **~ in, ~ up**) abandonar; **chuck out** *vt (person)* echar (fuera); *(rubbish etc)* tirar

chuckle ['tʃʌkl] *vi* reírse entre dientes

chuffed [tʃʌft] *adj (inf)*: **to be ~ (about sth)** estar encantado (con algo)

chug [tʃʌg] *vi (also:* **~ along**: *train)* ir despacio; *(: fig)* ir tirando

chum [tʃʌm] *n* amiguete(-a) *m(f)*, coleguilla *m/f*

chunk [tʃʌŋk] *n* pedazo, trozo

Chunnel [tʃʌnl] *n* = **Channel Tunnel**

church [tʃə:tʃ] *n* iglesia; **the C~ of England** la Iglesia Anglicana

churchyard ['tʃə:tʃjɑ:d] *n* cementerio, camposanto

churn [tʃə:n] *n (for butter)* mantequera; *(for milk)* lechera; **churn out** *vt* producir en serie

chute [ʃu:t] *n (also:* **rubbish ~**) vertedero; *(Brit: children's slide)* tobogán *m*

chutney ['tʃʌtnɪ] *n salsa picante de frutas y especias*
CIA *n abbr* (*US*: = *Central Intelligence Agency*) CIA *f*, Agencia Central de Inteligencia
CID *n abbr* (*Brit*: = *Criminal Investigation Department*) ≈ B.I.C. *f* (*Sp*)
cider ['saɪdə^r] *n* sidra
cigar [sɪ'gɑː^r] *n* puro
cigarette [sɪgə'rɛt] *n* cigarrillo, pitillo
cigarette case *n* pitillera
cigarette end *n* colilla
cigarette lighter *n* mechero
Cinderella [sɪndə'rɛlə] *n* Cenicienta
cinders ['sɪndəz] *npl* cenizas *fpl*
cine-camera ['sɪnɪ'kæmərə] *n* (*Brit*) cámara cinematográfica
cinema ['sɪnəmə] *n* cine *m*
cinnamon ['sɪnəmən] *n* canela
circle ['səːkl] *n* círculo; (*in theatre*) anfiteatro ▷ *vi* dar vueltas ▷ *vt* (*surround*) rodear, cercar; (*move round*) dar la vuelta a
circuit ['səːkɪt] *n* circuito; (*track*) pista; (*lap*) vuelta
circuitous [səː'kjuɪtəs] *adj* indirecto
circular ['səːkjulə^r] *adj* circular ▷ *n* circular *f*; (*as advertisement*) panfleto
circulate ['səːkjuleɪt] *vi* circular; (*person: socially*) alternar, circular ▷ *vt* poner en circulación
circulation [səːkju'leɪʃən] *n* circulación *f*; (*of newspaper etc*) tirada
circumcise ['səːkəmsaɪz] *vt* circuncidar
circumference [sə'kʌmfərəns] *n* circunferencia
circumstances ['səːkəmstənsɪz] *npl* circunstancias *fpl*; (*financial condition*) situación *f* económica; **in the ~** en or dadas las circunstancias; **under no ~** de ninguna manera, bajo ningún concepto
circumvent ['səːkəmvɛnt] *vt* (*rule etc*) burlar
circus ['səːkəs] *n* circo; (*also*: **C~**: *in place names*) Plaza
cirrhosis [sɪ'rəusɪs] *n* (*also*: **~ of the liver**) cirrosis *f inv*
CIS *n abbr* (= *Commonwealth of Independent States*) CEI *f*
cissy ['sɪsɪ] *n* = **sissy**
cistern ['sɪstən] *n* tanque *m*, depósito; (*in toilet*) cisterna
citation [saɪ'teɪʃən] *n* cita; (*Law*) citación *f*; (*Mil*) mención *f*
cite [saɪt] *vt* citar
citizen ['sɪtɪzn] *n* (*Pol*) ciudadano(-a); (*of city*) habitante *m/f*, vecino(-a)
Citizens' Advice Bureau *n* (*Brit*) *organización voluntaria británica que aconseja especialmente en temas legales o financieros*
citizenship ['sɪtɪznʃɪp] *n* ciudadanía; (*Brit Scol*) civismo
citric ['sɪtrɪk] *adj*: **~ acid** ácido cítrico
citrus fruits ['sɪtrəs-] *npl* cítricos *mpl*
city ['sɪtɪ] *n* ciudad *f*; **the C~** *centro financiero de Londres*
city centre *n* centro de la ciudad
City Hall *n* (*US*) ayuntamiento
City Technology College *n* (*Brit*) ≈ Centro de formación profesional
civic ['sɪvɪk] *adj* cívico; (*authorities*) municipal
civic centre *n* (*Brit*) centro de administración municipal
civil ['sɪvɪl] *adj* civil; (*polite*) atento, cortés; (*well-bred*) educado
civil defence *n* protección *f* civil
civil engineer *n* ingeniero(-a) de caminos
civil engineering *n* ingeniería de caminos
civilian [sɪ'vɪlɪən] *adj* civil; (*clothes*) de paisano ▷ *n* civil *m/f*
civilization [sɪvɪlaɪ'zeɪʃən] *n* civilización *f*
civilized ['sɪvɪlaɪzd] *adj* civilizado
civil law *n* derecho civil
civil liberties *npl* libertades *fpl* civiles
civil rights *npl* derechos *mpl* civiles
civil servant *n* funcionario(-a) (del Estado)
Civil Service *n* administración *f* pública
civil war *n* guerra civil
civvies ['sɪvɪz] *npl*: **in ~** (*inf*) de paisano
CJD *n abbr* (= *Creutzfeldt-Jakob disease*) *enfermedad de Creutzfeldt-Jakob*
clad [klæd] *adj*: **~ (in)** vestido (de)
claim [kleɪm] *vt* exigir, reclamar; (*rights etc*) reivindicar; (*assert*) pretender ▷ *vi* (*for insurance*) reclamar ▷ *n* (*for expenses*) reclamación *f*; (*Law*) demanda; (*pretension*) pretensión *f*; **to put in a ~ for sth** presentar una demanda por algo
claimant ['kleɪmənt] *n* (*Admin, Law*) demandante *m/f*
claim form *n* solicitud *f*
clairvoyant [klɛə'vɔɪənt] *n* clarividente *m/f*
clam [klæm] *n* almeja; **clam up** *vi* (*inf*) cerrar el pico
clamber ['klæmbə^r] *vi* trepar
clammy ['klæmɪ] *adj* (*cold*) frío y húmedo; (*sticky*) pegajoso
clamour, clamor (*US*) ['klæmə^r] *n* (*noise*) clamor *m*; (*protest*) protesta ▷ *vi*: **to ~ for sth** clamar por algo, pedir algo a voces
clamp [klæmp] *n* abrazadera; (*laboratory clamp*) grapa; (*wheel clamp*) cepo ▷ *vt* afianzar (con abrazadera); **clamp down on** *vt fus* (*government, police*) poner coto a
clampdown ['klæmpdaun] *n* restricción *f*; **there has been a ~ on terrorism** se ha puesto coto al terrorismo
clan [klæn] *n* clan *m*
clang [klæŋ] *n* estruendo ▷ *vi* sonar con estruendo
clanger [klæŋə^r] *n*: **to drop a ~** (*Brit*: (*inf*)) meter la pata
clap [klæp] *vi* aplaudir ▷ *vt* (*hands*) batir ▷ *n* (*of hands*) palmada; **to ~ one's hands** dar palmadas, batir las palmas; **a ~ of thunder** un trueno

clapping ['klæpɪŋ] *n* aplausos *mpl*
claptrap ['klæptræp] *n* (*inf*) gilipolleces *fpl*
claret ['klærət] *n* burdeos *m inv*
clarification [klærɪfɪ'keɪʃən] *n* aclaración *f*
clarify ['klærɪfaɪ] *vt* aclarar
clarinet [klærɪ'nɛt] *n* clarinete *m*
clarity ['klærɪtɪ] *n* claridad *f*
clash [klæʃ] *n* estruendo; (*fig*) choque *m* ▷ *vi* enfrentarse; (*beliefs*) chocar; (*disagree*) estar en desacuerdo; (*colours*) desentonar; (*two events*) coincidir
clasp [klɑːsp] *n* (*hold*) apretón *m*; (*of necklace, bag*) cierre *m* ▷ *vt* abrochar; (*hand*) apretar; (*embrace*) abrazar
class [klɑːs] *n* (*gen*) clase *f*; (*group, category*) clase *f*, categoría ▷ *cpd* de clase ▷ *vt* clasificar
classic ['klæsɪk] *adj* clásico ▷ *n* (*work*) obra clásica, clásico; **classics** *npl* (*Univ*) clásicas *fpl*
classical ['klæsɪkəl] *adj* clásico; ~ **music** música clásica
classification [klæsɪfɪ'keɪʃən] *n* clasificación *f*
classified ['klæsɪfaɪd] *adj* (*information*) reservado
classified advertisement *n* anuncio por palabras
classify ['klæsɪfaɪ] *vt* clasificar
classmate ['klɑːsmeɪt] *n* compañero(-a) de clase
classroom ['klɑːsrum] *n* aula
classroom assistant *n* profesor(a) *m(f)* de apoyo
classy ['klɑːsɪ] *adj* (*inf*) elegante, con estilo
clatter ['klætəʳ] *n* ruido, estruendo; (*of hooves*) trápala ▷ *vi* hacer ruido *or* estruendo
clause [klɔːz] *n* cláusula; (*Ling*) oración *f*
claustrophobia [klɔːstrə'fəubɪə] *n* claustrofobia
claustrophobic [klɔːstrə'fəubɪk] *adj* claustrofóbico; **I feel** ~ me entra claustrofobia
claw [klɔː] *n* (*of cat*) uña; (*of bird of prey*) garra; (*of lobster*) pinza; (*Tech*) garfio ▷ *vi*: **to ~ at** arañar; (*tear*) desgarrar
clay [kleɪ] *n* arcilla
clean [kliːn] *adj* limpio; (*record, reputation*) bueno, intachable; (*joke*) decente; (*copy*) en limpio; (*lines*) bien definido ▷ *vt* limpiar; (*hands etc*) lavar ▷ *adv*: **he ~ forgot** lo olvidó por completo; **to come ~** (*inf: admit guilt*) confesarlo todo; **to have a ~ driving licence** tener el carnet de conducir sin sanciones; **to ~ one's teeth** lavarse los dientes; **clean off** *vt* limpiar; **clean out** *vt* limpiar (a fondo); **clean up** *vt* limpiar, asear ▷ *vi* (*fig: make profit*): **to ~ up on** sacar provecho de
clean-cut ['kliːn'kʌt] *adj* bien definido; (*outline*) nítido; (*person*) de buen parecer
cleaner ['kliːnəʳ] *n* encargado(-a) *m(f)* de la limpieza; (*also*: **dry ~**) tintorero(-a); (*substance*) producto para la limpieza
cleaning ['kliːnɪŋ] *n* limpieza
cleanliness ['klɛnlɪnɪs] *n* limpieza
cleanse [klɛnz] *vt* limpiar
cleanser ['klɛnzəʳ] *n* detergente *m*; (*cosmetic*) loción *f or* crema limpiadora
clean-shaven ['kliːn'ʃeɪvn] *adj* bien afeitado
cleansing department ['klɛnzɪŋ-] *n* (*Brit*) servicio municipal de limpieza
clean sweep *n*: **to make a ~** (*Sport*) arrasar, barrer
clear [klɪəʳ] *adj* claro; (*road, way*) libre; (*profit*) neto; (*majority*) absoluto ▷ *vt* (*space*) despejar, limpiar; (*Law: suspect*) absolver; (*obstacle*) salvar, saltar por encima de; (*debt*) liquidar; (*cheque*) aceptar; (*site, woodland*) desmontar ▷ *vi* (*fog etc*) despejarse ▷ *n*: **to be in the ~** (*out of debt*) estar libre de deudas; (*out of suspicion*) estar fuera de toda sospecha; (*out of danger*) estar fuera de peligro ▷ *adv*: **~ of** a distancia de; **to make o.s. ~** explicarse claramente; **to make it ~ to sb that ...** hacer entender a algn que ...; **I have a ~ day tomorrow** mañana tengo el día libre; **to keep ~ of sth/sb** evitar algo/a algn; **to ~ a profit of ...** sacar una ganancia de ...; **to ~ the table** recoger *or* quitar la mesa; **clear away** *vt* (*things, clothes etc*) quitar (de en medio); (*dishes*) retirar; **clear off** *vi* (*inf: leave*) marcharse, mandarse mudar (*LAm*); **clear up** *vt* limpiar; (*mystery*) aclarar, resolver
clearance ['klɪərəns] *n* (*removal*) despeje *m*; (*permission*) acreditación *f*
clear-cut ['klɪə'kʌt] *adj* bien definido, claro
clearing ['klɪərɪŋ] *n* (*in wood*) claro
clearing bank *n* (*Brit*) banco central
clearly ['klɪəlɪ] *adv* claramente; (*evidently*) sin duda
clearway ['klɪəweɪ] *n* (*Brit*) *carretera en la que no se puede estacionar*
clef [klɛf] *n* (*Mus*) clave *f*
cleft [klɛft] *n* (*in rock*) grieta, hendedura
clemency ['klɛmənsɪ] *n* clemencia
clench [klɛntʃ] *vt* apretar, cerrar
clergy ['kləːdʒɪ] *n* clero
clergyman ['kləːdʒɪmən] *n* clérigo
clerical ['klɛrɪkəl] *adj* de oficina; (*Rel*) clerical; (*error*) de copia
clerk [klɑːk, (*US*) kləːk] *n* oficinista *m/f*; (*US*) dependiente(-a) *m(f)*, vendedor(a) *m(f)*; **C~ of the Court** secretario(-a) de juzgado
clever ['klɛvəʳ] *adj* (*mentally*) inteligente, listo; (*skilful*) hábil; (*device, arrangement*) ingenioso
clew [kluː] *n* (*US*) = **clue**
cliché ['kliːʃeɪ] *n* cliché *m*, frase *f* hecha
click [klɪk] *vt* (*tongue*) chasquear ▷ *vi* (*Comput*) hacer clic; **to ~ one's heels** taconear; **to ~ on an icon** hacer clic en un icono
client ['klaɪənt] *n* cliente *m/f*
clientele [kliːɑ̃ːn'tɛl] *n* clientela
cliff [klɪf] *n* acantilado
climate ['klaɪmɪt] *n* clima *m*; (*fig*) clima *m*, ambiente *m*
climate change *n* cambio climático

climax ['klaımæks] *n* (*of battle, career*) apogeo; (*of film, book*) punto culminante, clímax; (*sexual*) orgasmo

climb [klaım] *vi* subir, trepar; (*plane*) elevarse, remontar el vuelo ▷ *vt* (*stairs*) subir; (*tree*) trepar a; (*mountain*) escalar ▷ *n* subida, ascenso; **to ~ over a wall** saltar una tapia; **climb down** *vi* (*fig*) volverse atrás

climbdown ['klaımdaun] *n* vuelta atrás

climber ['klaımə^r] *n* escalador(a) *m(f)*

climbing ['klaımıŋ] *n* escalada

clinch [klıntʃ] *vt* (*deal*) cerrar; (*argument*) remachar

cling [klıŋ] (*pt, pp* **clung** [klʌŋ]) *vi*: **to ~ (to)** agarrarse (a); (*clothes*) pegarse (a)

clingfilm ['klıŋfılm] *n* plástico adherente

clinic ['klınık] *n* clínica

clinical ['klınıkl] *adj* clínico; (*fig*) frío, impasible

clink [klıŋk] *vi* tintinear

clip [klıp] *n* (*for hair*) horquilla; (*also*: **paper ~**) sujetapapeles *m inv*, clip *m*; (*clamp*) grapa ▷ *vt* (*cut*) cortar; (*hedge*) podar; (*also*: **~ together**) unir

clippers ['klıpəz] *npl* (*for gardening*) tijeras *fpl* de podar; (*for hair*) maquinilla *sg*; (*for nails*) cortauñas *m inv*

clipping ['klıpıŋ] *n* (*from newspaper*) recorte *m*

clique [kli:k] *n* camarilla

cloak [kləuk] *n* capa, manto ▷ *vt* (*fig*) encubrir, disimular

cloakroom ['kləukrum] *n* guardarropa *m*; (*Brit*: *WC*) lavabo, aseos *mpl*, baño (*esp LAm*)

clock [klɔk] *n* reloj *m*; (*in taxi*) taxímetro; **to work against the ~** trabajar contra reloj; **around the ~** las veinticuatro horas; **to sleep round the ~** dormir un día entero; **30,000 on the ~** (*Aut*) treinta mil millas en el cuentakilómetros; **clock in, clock on** *vi* fichar, picar; **clock off, clock out** *vi* fichar *or* picar la salida; **clock up** *vt* hacer

clockwise ['klɔkwaız] *adv* en el sentido de las agujas del reloj

clockwork ['klɔkwə:k] *n* aparato de relojería ▷ *adj* (*toy, train*) de cuerda

clog [klɔg] *n* zueco, chanclo ▷ *vt* atascar ▷ *vi* (*also*: **~ up**) atascarse

cloister ['klɔıstə^r] *n* claustro

clone [kləun] *n* clon *m* ▷ *vt* clonar

close [*adj, adv* kləus, *vb, n* kləuz] *adj* cercano, próximo; (*near*): **~ (to)** cerca (de); (*print, weave*) tupido, compacto; (*friend*) íntimo; (*connection*) estrecho; (*examination*) detallado, minucioso; (*weather*) bochornoso; (*atmosphere*) sofocante; (*room*) mal ventilado ▷ *adv* cerca; **~ by, ~ at hand** muy cerca; **~ to** *prep* cerca de; **to have a ~ shave** (*fig*) escaparse por un pelo; **how ~ is Edinburgh to Glasgow?** ¿qué distancia hay de Edimburgo a Glasgow?; **at ~ quarters** de cerca ▷ *vt* cerrar; (*end*) concluir, terminar ▷ *vi* (*shop etc*) cerrar; (*end*) concluir(se), terminar(se) ▷ *n* (*end*) fin *m*, final *m*, conclusión *f*; **to bring sth to a ~** terminar algo; **close down** *vi* cerrar definitivamente; **close in** *vi* (*hunters*) acercarse rodeando, rodear; (*evening, night*) caer; (*fog*) cerrarse; **to ~ in on sb** rodear *or* cercar a algn; **the days are closing in** los días son cada vez más cortos; **close off** *vt* (*area*) cerrar al tráfico *or* al público

closed [kləuzd] *adj* (*shop etc*) cerrado

closed-circuit ['kləuzd'sə:kıt] *adj*: **~ television** televisión *f* por circuito cerrado

closed shop *n* *empresa en la que todo el personal está afiliado a un sindicato*

close-knit ['kləus'nıt] *adj* (*fig*) muy unido

closely ['kləuslı] *adv* (*study*) con detalle; (*listen*) con atención; (*watch*) de cerca; **we are ~ related** somos parientes cercanos; **a ~ guarded secret** un secreto rigurosamente guardado

close season [kləuz-] *n* (*Football*) temporada de descanso; (*Hunting*) veda

closet ['klɔzıt] *n* (*cupboard*) armario, placar(d) *m* (*LAm*)

close-up ['kləusʌp] *n* primer plano

closing time *n* hora de cierre

closure ['kləuʒə^r] *n* cierre *m*

clot [klɔt] *n* (*gen*: *also*: **blood ~**) coágulo; (*inf*: *idiot*) imbécil *m/f* ▷ *vi* (*blood*) coagularse

cloth [klɔθ] *n* (*material*) tela, paño; (*table cloth*) mantel *m*; (*rag*) trapo

clothe [kləuð] *vt* vestir; (*fig*) revestir

clothes [kləuðz] *npl* ropa *sg*; **to put one's ~ on** vestirse, ponerse la ropa; **to take one's ~ off** desvestirse, desnudarse

clothes brush *n* cepillo (para la ropa)

clothes line *n* cuerda (para tender la ropa)

clothes peg, clothes pin (*US*) *n* pinza

clothing ['kləuðıŋ] *n* = **clothes**

cloud [klaud] *n* nube *f*; (*storm cloud*) nubarrón *m* ▷ *vt* (*liquid*) enturbiar; **every ~ has a silver lining** no hay mal que por bien no venga; **to ~ the issue** empañar el problema; **cloud over** *vi* (*also fig*) nublarse

cloudburst ['klaudbə:st] *n* chaparrón *m*

cloudy ['klaudı] *adj* nublado; (*liquid*) turbio

clout [klaut] *n* (*fig*) influencia, peso ▷ *vt* dar un tortazo a

clove [kləuv] *n* clavo; **~ of garlic** diente *m* de ajo

clover ['kləuvə^r] *n* trébol *m*

clown [klaun] *n* payaso ▷ *vi* (*also*: **~ about, ~ around**) hacer el payaso

cloying ['klɔııŋ] *adj* (*taste*) empalagoso

club [klʌb] *n* (*society*) club *m*; (*weapon*) porra, cachiporra; (*also*: **golf ~**) palo ▷ *vt* aporrear ▷ *vi*: **to ~ together** (*join forces*) unir fuerzas; **clubs** *npl* (*Cards*) tréboles *mpl*

club car *n* (*US Rail*) coche *m* salón

club class *n* (*Aviat*) clase *f* preferente

clubhouse ['klʌbhaus] *n* *local social, sobre todo en clubs deportivos*

club soda *n* (*US*) soda

cluck [klʌk] *vi* cloquear
clue [klu:] *n* pista; (*in crosswords*) indicación *f*; **I haven't a ~** no tengo ni idea
clump [klʌmp] *n* (*of trees*) grupo
clumsy ['klʌmzɪ] *adj* (*person*) torpe; (*tool*) difícil de manejar
clung [klʌŋ] *pt, pp of* **cling**
cluster ['klʌstəʳ] *n* grupo; (*Bot*) racimo ▷ *vi* agruparse, apiñarse
clutch [klʌtʃ] *n* (*Aut*) embrague *m*; (*pedal*) (pedal *m* de) embrague *m*; **to fall into sb's ~es** caer en las garras de algn ▷ *vt* agarrar
clutter ['klʌtəʳ] *vt* (*also*: **~ up**) atestar, llenar desordenadamente ▷ *n* desorden *m*, confusión *f*
cm *abbr* (= *centimetre*) cm
CND *n abbr* (*Brit*: = *Campaign for Nuclear Disarmament*) *plataforma pro desarme nuclear*
Co. *abbr* = **county**; **company**
c/o *abbr* (= *care of*) c/a, a/c
coach [kəutʃ] *n* (*bus*) autocar *m* (*Sp*), autobús *m*; (*horse-drawn*) coche *m*; (*ceremonial*) carroza; (*of train*) vagón *m*, coche *m*; (*Sport*) entrenador(a) *m(f)*, instructor(a) *m(f)* ▷ *vt* (*Sport*) entrenar; (*student*) preparar, enseñar
coach station *n* (*Brit*) estación *f* de autobuses *etc*
coach trip *n* excursión *f* en autocar
coal [kəul] *n* carbón *m*
coalfield ['kəulfi:ld] *n* yacimiento de carbón
coalition [kəuə'lɪʃən] *n* coalición *f*
coal man *n* carbonero
coalmine ['kəulmaɪn] *n* mina de carbón
coarse [kɔ:s] *adj* basto, burdo; (*vulgar*) grosero, ordinario
coast [kəust] *n* costa, litoral *m* ▷ *vi* (*Aut*) ir en punto muerto
coastal ['kəustl] *adj* costero
coastguard ['kəustgɑ:d] *n* guardacostas *m inv*
coastline ['kəustlaɪn] *n* litoral *m*
coat [kəut] *n* (*jacket*) chaqueta, saco (*LAm*); (*overcoat*) abrigo; (*of animal*) pelo, pelaje, lana; (*of paint*) mano *f*, capa ▷ *vt* cubrir, revestir
coat hanger *n* percha, gancho (*LAm*)
coating ['kəutɪŋ] *n* capa, baño
coat of arms *n* escudo de armas
coax [kəuks] *vt* engatusar
cob [kɔb] *n see* **corn**
cobbled ['kɔbld] *adj*: **~ street** calle *f* empedrada, calle *f* adoquinada
cobbler ['kɔbləʳ] *n* zapatero (remendón)
cobbles ['kɔblz], **cobblestones** ['kɔblstəunz] *npl* adoquines *mpl*
cobweb ['kɔbwɛb] *n* telaraña
cocaine [kə'keɪn] *n* cocaína
cock [kɔk] *n* (*rooster*) gallo; (*male bird*) macho ▷ *vt* (*gun*) amartillar
cockerel ['kɔkərl] *n* gallito, gallo joven
cock-eyed ['kɔkaɪd] *adj* bizco; (*fig*: *crooked*) torcido; (*: idea*) disparatado
cockle ['kɔkl] *n* berberecho
cockney ['kɔknɪ] *n habitante de ciertos barrios de Londres*
cockpit ['kɔkpɪt] *n* (*in aircraft*) cabina
cockroach ['kɔkrəutʃ] *n* cucaracha
cocktail ['kɔkteɪl] *n* combinado, cóctel *m*; **prawn ~** cóctel *m* de gambas
cocktail cabinet *n* mueble-bar *m*
cocktail party *n* cóctel *m*
cocky ['kɔkɪ] *adj* farruco, flamenco
cocoa ['kəukəu] *n* cacao; (*drink*) chocolate *m*
coconut ['kəukənʌt] *n* coco
cod [kɔd] *n* bacalao
COD *abbr* (= *cash on delivery*, *US*: = *collect on delivery*) C.A.E.
code [kəud] *n* código; (*cipher*) clave *f*; (*Tel*) prefijo; **~ of behaviour** código de conducta; **~ of practice** código profesional
codger [kɔdʒəʳ] *n* (*Brit inf*): **an old ~** un abuelo
cod-liver oil ['kɔdlɪvəʳ-] *n* aceite *m* de hígado de bacalao
coeducational [kəuɛdju'keɪʃənl] *adj* mixto
coercion [kəu'ə:ʃən] *n* coacción *f*
coffee ['kɔfɪ] *n* café *m*; **white ~** (*US*), **~ with cream** café con leche
coffee bar *n* (*Brit*) cafetería
coffee bean *n* grano de café
coffee break *n* descanso (para tomar café)
coffee maker *n* máquina de hacer café, cafetera
coffeepot ['kɔfɪpɔt] *n* cafetera
coffee shop *n* café *m*
coffee table *n* mesita baja
coffin ['kɔfɪn] *n* ataúd *m*
cog [kɔg] *n* diente *m*
cogent ['kəudʒənt] *adj* lógico, convincente
cognac ['kɔnjæk] *n* coñac *m*
coherent [kəu'hɪərənt] *adj* coherente
coil [kɔɪl] *n* rollo; (*of rope*) vuelta; (*of smoke*) espiral *f*; (*Aut, Elec*) bobina, carrete *m*; (*contraceptive*) DIU *m* ▷ *vt* enrollar
coin [kɔɪn] *n* moneda ▷ *vt* acuñar; (*word*) inventar, acuñar
coinage ['kɔɪnɪdʒ] *n* moneda
coin-box ['kɔɪnbɔks] *n* (*Brit*) caja recaudadora
coincide [kəuɪn'saɪd] *vi* coincidir
coincidence [kəu'ɪnsɪdəns] *n* casualidad *f*, coincidencia
Coke® [kəuk] *n* Coca Cola® *f*
coke [kəuk] *n* (*coal*) coque *m*
colander ['kɔləndəʳ] *n* escurridor *m*
cold [kəuld] *adj* frío ▷ *n* frío; (*Med*) resfriado; **it's ~** hace frío; **to be ~** tener frío; **to catch a ~** resfriarse, acatarrarse, coger un catarro; **in ~ blood** a sangre fría; **the room's getting ~** está empezando a hacer frío en la habitación; **to give sb the ~ shoulder** tratar a algn con frialdad
cold sore *n* calentura, herpes *m* labial
cold sweat *n*: **to be in a ~ (about sth)** tener sudores fríos (por algo)
cold turkey *n* (*inf*) mono

Cold War *n*: **the ~** la guerra fría
coleslaw ['kəulslɔ:] *n* ensalada de col con zanahoria
colic ['kɔlɪk] *n* cólico
colicky ['kɔlɪkɪ] *adj*: **to be ~** tener un cólico
collaborate [kə'læbəreɪt] *vi* colaborar
collaboration [kəlæbə'reɪʃən] *n* colaboración *f*; (*Pol*) colaboracionismo
collapse [kə'læps] *vi* (*gen*) hundirse, derrumbarse; (*Med*) sufrir un colapso ▷ *n* (*gen*) hundimiento, derrumbamiento; (*Med*) colapso; (*of government*) caída; (*of plans, scheme*) fracaso; (*of business*) ruina
collapsible [kə'læpsəbl] *adj* plegable
collar ['kɔlə^r] *n* (*of coat, shirt*) cuello; (*for dog*) collar *m*; (*Tech*) collar *m* ▷ *vt* (*inf*: *person*) agarrar; (: *object*) birlar
collarbone ['kɔləbəun] *n* clavícula
collateral [kɔ'lætərəl] *n* (*Comm*) garantía subsidiaria
colleague ['kɔli:g] *n* colega *m/f*; (*at work*) compañero(-a) *m(f)*
collect [kə'lɛkt] *vt* reunir; (*as a hobby*) coleccionar; (*Brit*: *call and pick up*) recoger; (*wages*) cobrar; (*debts*) recaudar; (*donations, subscriptions*) colectar ▷ *vi* (*crowd*) reunirse ▷ *adv*: **to call ~** (*US Tel*) llamar a cobro revertido; **to ~ one's thoughts** reponerse, recobrar el dominio de sí mismo; **~ on delivery (COD)** (*US*) entrega contra reembolso
collection [kə'lɛkʃən] *n* colección *f*; (*of fares, wages*) cobro; (*of post*) recogida
collective [kə'lɛktɪv] *adj* colectivo
collector [kə'lɛktə^r] *n* coleccionista *m/f*; (*of taxes etc*) recaudador(a) *m(f)*; **~'s item** *or* **piece** pieza de coleccionista
college ['kɔlɪdʒ] *n* colegio; (*of technology, agriculture etc*) escuela
collide [kə'laɪd] *vi* chocar
collie ['kɔlɪ] *n* (*dog*) collie *m*, perro pastor escocés
colliery ['kɔlɪərɪ] *n* (*Brit*) mina de carbón
collision [kə'lɪʒən] *n* choque *m*, colisión *f*; **to be on a ~ course** (*also fig*) ir rumbo al desastre
colloquial [kə'ləukwɪəl] *adj* coloquial
cologne [kə'ləun] *n* (*also*: **eau de ~**) (agua de) colonia
Colombia [kə'lɔmbɪə] *n* Colombia
Colombian [kə'lɔmbɪən] *adj, n* colombiano(-a) *m(f)*
colon ['kəulən] *n* (*sign*) dos puntos; (*Med*) colon *m*
colonel ['kə:nl] *n* coronel *m*
colonial [kə'ləunɪəl] *adj* colonial
colonize ['kɔlənaɪz] *vt* colonizar
colony ['kɔlənɪ] *n* colonia
color ['kʌlə^r] *n* (*US*) = **colour**
colossal [kə'lɔsl] *adj* colosal
colour, color (*US*) ['kʌlə^r] *n* color *m* ▷ *vt* colorear, pintar; (*dye*) teñir; (*fig*: *account*) adornar; (: *judgement*) distorsionar ▷ *vi* (*blush*) sonrojarse; **colours** *npl* (*of party, club*) colores *mpl*; **colour in** *vt* colorear
colour-blind, color-blind (*US*) ['kʌləblaɪnd] *adj* daltónico
coloured, colored (*US*) ['kʌləd] *adj* de color; (*photo*) en color; (*inf!*: *of race*) de color
colour film, color film (*US*) *n* película en color
colourful, colorful (*US*) ['kʌləful] *adj* lleno de color; (*person*) pintoresco
colouring, coloring (*US*) ['kʌlərɪŋ] *n* colorido, color; (*substance*) colorante *m*
colour television, color television (*US*) *n* televisión *f* en color
colt [kəult] *n* potro
column ['kɔləm] *n* columna; (*fashion column, sports column etc*) sección *f*, columna; **the editorial ~** el editorial
columnist ['kɔləmnɪst] *n* columnista *m/f*
coma ['kəumə] *n* coma *m*
comb [kəum] *n* peine *m*; (*ornamental*) peineta ▷ *vt* (*hair*) peinar; (*area*) registrar a fondo, peinar
combat ['kɔmbæt] *n* combate *m* ▷ *vt* combatir
combination [kɔmbɪ'neɪʃən] *n* (*gen*) combinación *f*
combine [kəm'baɪn] *vt* combinar; (*qualities*) reunir ▷ *vi* combinarse ▷ *n* ['kɔmbaɪn] (*Econ*) cartel *m*; (*also*: **~ harvester**) cosechadora; **a ~d effort** un esfuerzo conjunto

KEYWORD

come [kʌm] (*pt* **came**, *pp* **come**) *vi* **1** (*movement towards*) venir; **to come running** venir corriendo; **come with me** ven conmigo
2 (*arrive*) llegar; **he's come here to work** ha venido aquí para trabajar; **to come home** volver a casa; **we've just come from Seville** acabamos de llegar de Sevilla; **coming!** ¡voy!
3 (*reach*): **to come to** llegar a; **the bill came to £40** la cuenta ascendía a cuarenta libras
4 (*occur*): **an idea came to me** se me ocurrió una idea; **if it comes to it** llegado el caso
5 (*be, become*): **to come loose/undone** *etc* aflojarse/desabrocharse, desatarse *etc*; **I've come to like him** por fin ha llegado a gustarme
come about *vi* suceder, ocurrir
come across *vt fus* (*person*) encontrarse con; (*thing*) encontrar ▷ *vi*: **to come across well/badly** causar buena/mala impresión
come along *vi* (*Brit*: *progress*) ir
come away *vi* (*leave*) marcharse; (*become detached*) desprenderse
come back *vi* (*return*) volver; (*reply*): **can I come back to you on that one?** volvamos sobre ese punto
come by *vt fus* (*acquire*) conseguir
come down *vi* (*price*) bajar; (*building*) derrumbarse; (*be demolished*) ser derribado

come forward *vi* presentarse
come from *vt fus* (*place, source*) ser de
come in *vi* (*visitor*) entrar; (*train, report*) llegar; (*fashion*) ponerse de moda; (*on deal etc*) entrar
come in for *vt fus* (*criticism etc*) recibir
come into *vt fus* (*money*) heredar; (*be involved*) tener que ver con; **to come into fashion** ponerse de moda
come off *vi* (*button*) soltarse, desprenderse; (*attempt*) salir bien
come on *vi* (*pupil, work, project*) marchar; (*lights*) encenderse; (*electricity*) volver; **come on!** ¡vamos!
come out *vi* (*fact*) salir a la luz; (*book, sun*) salir; (*stain*) quitarse; **to come out (on strike)** declararse en huelga; **to come out for/against** declararse a favor/en contra de
come over *vt fus*: **I don't know what's come over him!** ¡no sé lo que le pasa!
come round *vi* (*after faint, operation*) volver en sí
come through *vi* (*survive*) sobrevivir; (*telephone call*): **the call came through** recibimos la llamada
come to *vi* (*wake*) volver en sí; (*total*) sumar; **how much does it come to?** ¿cuánto es en total?, ¿a cuánto asciende?
come under *vt fus* (*heading*) entrar dentro de; (*influence*) estar bajo
come up *vi* (*sun*) salir; (*problem*) surgir; (*event*) aproximarse; (*in conversation*) mencionarse
come up against *vt fus* (*resistance etc*) tropezar con
come upon *vt fus* (*find*) dar con
come up to *vt fus* llegar hasta; **the film didn't come up to our expectations** la película no fue tan buena como esperábamos
come up with *vt fus* (*idea*) sugerir; (*money*) conseguir

comeback ['kʌmbæk] *n* (*reaction*) reacción *f*; (*response*) réplica; **to make a ~** (*Theat*) volver a las tablas
comedian [kə'mi:dɪən] *n* humorista *m/f*
comedienne [kəmi:dɪ'ɛn] *n* humorista
comedy ['kɔmɪdɪ] *n* comedia
comet ['kɔmɪt] *n* cometa *m*
comeuppance [kʌm'ʌpəns] *n*: **to get one's ~** llevar su merecido
comfort ['kʌmfət] *n* comodidad *f*, confort *m*; (*well-being*) bienestar *m*; (*solace*) consuelo; (*relief*) alivio ▷ *vt* consolar
comfortable ['kʌmfətəbl] *adj* cómodo; (*income*) adecuado; (*majority*) suficiente; **I don't feel very ~ about it** la cosa me tiene algo preocupado
comfortably ['kʌmfətəblɪ] *adv* (*sit*) cómodamente; (*live*) holgadamente
comfort station *n* (*US*) servicios *mpl*
comic ['kɔmɪk] *adj* (*also*: **~al**) cómico, gracioso ▷ *n* (*comedian*) cómico; (*magazine*) tebeo; (*for adults*) cómic *m*
comic book (*US*) *n* libro *m* de cómics
comic strip *n* tira cómica
coming ['kʌmɪŋ] *n* venida, llegada ▷ *adj* que viene; (*next*) próximo; (*future*) venidero; **~(s) and going(s)** *n(pl)* ir y venir *m*, ajetreo; **in the ~ weeks** en las próximas semanas
comma ['kɔmə] *n* coma
command [kə'mɑ:nd] *n* orden *f*, mandato; (*Mil: authority*) mando; (*mastery*) dominio; (*Comput*) orden *f*, comando ▷ *vt* (*troops*) mandar; (*give orders to*) mandar, ordenar; (*be able to get*) disponer de; (*deserve*) merecer; **to have at one's ~** (*money, resources etc*) disponer de; **to have/take ~ of** estar al/asumir el mando de
commandeer [kɔmən'dɪə[r]] *vt* requisar
commander [kə'mɑ:ndə[r]] *n* (*Mil*) comandante *m/f*, jefe(-a) *m(f)*
commandment [kə'mɑ:ndmənt] *n* (*Rel*) mandamiento
commando [kə'mɑ:ndəu] *n* comando
commemorate [kə'mɛməreɪt] *vt* conmemorar
commemoration [kəmɛmə'reɪʃən] *n* conmemoración *f*
commemorative [kə'mɛmərətɪv] *adj* conmemorativo
commence [kə'mɛns] *vt, vi* comenzar
commencement (*US*) [kə'mɛnsmənt] *n* (*Univ*) (ceremonia de) graduación *f*
commend [kə'mɛnd] *vt* (*praise*) elogiar, alabar; (*recommend*) recomendar; (*entrust*) encomendar
commensurate [kə'mɛnʃərɪt] *adj*: **~ with** en proporción a
comment ['kɔmɛnt] *n* comentario ▷ *vt*: **to ~ that** comentar *or* observar que ▷ *vi*: **to ~ (on)** comentar, hacer comentarios (sobre); **"no ~"** (*written*) "sin comentarios"; (*spoken*) "no tengo nada que decir"
commentary ['kɔməntərɪ] *n* comentario
commentator ['kɔmənteɪtə[r]] *n* comentarista *m/f*
commerce ['kɔmə:s] *n* comercio
commercial [kə'mə:ʃəl] *adj* comercial ▷ *n* (*TV*) anuncio
commercial break *n* intermedio para publicidad
commercialism [kə'mə:ʃəlɪzəm] *n* comercialismo
commercial television *n* televisión *f* comercial
commiserate [kə'mɪzəreɪt] *vi*: **to ~ with** compadecerse de, condolerse de
commission [kə'mɪʃən] *n* (*committee, fee, order for work of art etc*) comisión *f*; (*act*) perpetración *f* ▷ *vt* (*Mil*) nombrar; (*work of art*) encargar; **out of ~** (*machine*) fuera de servicio; **~ of inquiry** comisión *f* investigadora; **I get 10% ~** me dan el diez por ciento de comisión; **to ~ sb to do sth** encargar a algn que haga algo; **to ~ sth from sb** (*painting etc*) encargar algo a algn

commissionaire [kəmɪʃəˈnɛəʳ] *n* (*Brit*) portero, conserje *m*
commissioner [kəˈmɪʃənəʳ] *n* comisario; (*Police*) comisario *m* de policía
commit [kəˈmɪt] *vt* (*act*) cometer; (*resources*) dedicar; (*to sb's care*) entregar; **to ~ o.s. (to do)** comprometerse (a hacer); **to ~ suicide** suicidarse; **to ~ sb for trial** remitir a algn al tribunal
commitment [kəˈmɪtmənt] *n* compromiso
committed [kəˈmɪtɪd] *adj* (*writer, politician etc*) comprometido
committee [kəˈmɪtɪ] *n* comité *m*; **to be on a ~** ser miembro(-a) de un comité
commodity [kəˈmɔdɪtɪ] *n* mercancía
common [ˈkɔmən] *adj* (*gen*) común; (*pej*) ordinario ▷ *n* campo común; **in ~** en común; **in ~ use** de uso corriente
common cold *n*: **the ~** el resfriado
common denominator *n* común denominador *m*
commoner [ˈkɔmənəʳ] *n* plebeyo(-a)
common land *n* campo comunal, ejido
common law *n* ley *f* consuetudinaria
common-law [ˈkɔmənlɔː] *adj*: **~ wife** esposa de hecho
commonly [ˈkɔmənlɪ] *adv* comúnmente
Common Market *n* Mercado Común
commonplace [ˈkɔmənpleɪs] *adj* corriente
common room [ˈkɔmənrum] *n* sala de reunión
Commons [ˈkɔmənz] *npl* (*Brit Pol*): **the ~** (la Cámara de) los Comunes
common sense *n* sentido común
Commonwealth [ˈkɔmənwɛlθ] *n*: **the ~** la Comunidad (Británica) de Naciones, la Commonwealth; *ver nota*

COMMONWEALTH

La *Commonwealth* es la asociación de estados soberanos independientes y territorios asociados que formaban parte del antiguo Imperio Británico. Éste pasó a llamarse así después de la Segunda Guerra Mundial, aunque ya desde 1931 se le conocía como "British Commonwealth of Nations". Todos los estados miembros reconocen al monarca británico como "Head of the Commonwealth".

commotion [kəˈməuʃən] *n* tumulto, confusión *f*
communal [ˈkɔmjuːnl] *adj* comunal; (*kitchen*) común
commune [ˈkɔmjuːn] *n* (*group*) comuna ▷ *vi* [kəˈmjuːn]: **to ~ with** comunicarse con
communicate [kəˈmjuːnɪkeɪt] *vt* comunicar ▷ *vi*: **to ~ (with)** comunicarse (con); (*in writing*) estar en contacto (con)
communication [kəmjuːnɪˈkeɪʃən] *n* comunicación *f*
communication cord *n* (*Brit*) timbre *m* de alarma
communion [kəˈmjuːnɪən] *n* (*also*: **Holy C~**) comunión *f*
communiqué [kəˈmjuːnɪkeɪ] *n* comunicado, parte *m*
communism [ˈkɔmjunɪzəm] *n* comunismo
communist [ˈkɔmjunɪst] *adj, n* comunista *m/f*
community [kəˈmjuːnɪtɪ] *n* comunidad *f*; (*large group*) colectividad *f*; (*local*) vecindario
community centre *n* centro social
community chest *n* (*US*) fondo social
community service *n* trabajo *m* comunitario (*prestado en lugar de cumplir una pena de prisión*)
commutation ticket [kɔmjuˈteɪʃən-] *n* (*US*) billete *m* de abono
commute [kəˈmjuːt] *vi viajar a diario de casa al trabajo* ▷ *vt* conmutar
commuter [kəˈmjuːtəʳ] *n persona que viaja a diario de casa al trabajo*
compact [kəmˈpækt] *adj* compacto; (*style*) conciso; (*dense*) apretado ▷ *n* [ˈkɔmpækt] (*pact*) pacto; (*also*: **powder ~**) polvera
compact disc *n* compact disc *m*, disco compacto
compact disc player *n* lector *m or* reproductor *m* de discos compactos
companion [kəmˈpænɪən] *n* compañero(-a)
companionship [kəmˈpænjənʃɪp] *n* compañerismo
company [ˈkʌmpənɪ] *n* (*gen*) compañía; (*Comm*) empresa, compañía; **to keep sb ~** acompañar a algn; **Smith and C~** Smith y Compañía
company car *n* coche *m* de la empresa
company director *n* director(a) *m(f)* de empresa
company secretary *n* (*Brit*) administrador(a) *m(f)* de empresa
comparable [ˈkɔmpərəbl] *adj* comparable
comparative [kəmˈpærətɪv] *adj* (*freedom, luxury, cost*) relativo; (*study, linguistics*) comparado
comparatively [kəmˈpærətɪvlɪ] *adv* (*relatively*) relativamente
compare [kəmˈpɛəʳ] *vt* comparar ▷ *vi*: **to ~ (with)** poder compararse (con); **~d with** *or* **to** comparado con *or* a; **how do the prices ~?** ¿cómo son los precios en comparación?
comparison [kəmˈpærɪsn] *n* comparación *f*; **in ~ (with)** en comparación (con)
compartment [kəmˈpɑːtmənt] *n* compartim(i)ento; (*Rail*) departamento, compartimento
compass [ˈkʌmpəs] *n* brújula; **compasses** *npl* compás *m*; **within the ~ of** al alcance de
compassion [kəmˈpæʃən] *n* compasión *f*
compassionate [kəmˈpæʃənɪt] *adj* compasivo; **on ~ grounds** por compasión

compassionate leave *n* permiso por asuntos familiares
compatible [kəm'pætɪbl] *adj* compatible
compel [kəm'pɛl] *vt* obligar
compelling [kəm'pɛlɪŋ] *adj* (*fig*: *argument*) convincente
compensate ['kɔmpənseɪt] *vt* compensar ▷ *vi*: **to ~ for** compensar
compensation [kɔmpən'seɪʃən] *n* (*for loss*) indemnización *f*
compère ['kɔmpɛəʳ] *n* presentador(a) *m(f)*
compete [kəm'pi:t] *vi* (*take part*) competir; (*vie with*) competir, hacer la competencia
competent ['kɔmpɪtənt] *adj* competente, capaz
competition [kɔmpɪ'tɪʃən] *n* (*contest*) concurso; (*Sport*) competición *f*; (*Econ*: *rivalry*) competencia; **in ~ with** en competencia con
competitive [kəm'pɛtɪtɪv] *adj* (*Econ, Sport*) competitivo; (*spirit*) competidor(a), de competencia; (*selection*) por concurso
competitor [kəm'pɛtɪtəʳ] *n* (*rival*) competidor(a) *m(f)*; (*participant*) concursante *m/f*
compile [kəm'paɪl] *vt* recopilar
complacency [kəm'pleɪsnsɪ] *n* autosatisfacción *f*
complacent [kəm'pleɪsənt] *adj* autocomplaciente
complain [kəm'pleɪn] *vi* (*gen*) quejarse; (*Comm*) reclamar
complaint [kəm'pleɪnt] *n* (*gen*) queja; (*Comm*) reclamación *f*; (*Law*) demanda, querella; (*Med*) enfermedad *f*
complement ['kɔmplɪmənt] *n* complemento; (*esp ship's crew*) dotación *f* ▷ *vt* ['kɔmplɪmɛnt] (*enhance*) complementar
complementary [kɔmplɪ'mɛntərɪ] *adj* complementario
complete [kəm'pli:t] *adj* (*full*) completo; (*finished*) acabado ▷ *vt* (*fulfil*) completar; (*finish*) acabar; (*a form*) rellenar; **it's a ~ disaster** es un desastre total
completely [kəm'pli:tlɪ] *adv* completamente
completion [kəm'pli:ʃən] *n* (*gen*) conclusión *f*, terminación *f*; **to be nearing ~** estar a punto de terminarse; **on ~ of contract** cuando se realice el contrato
complex ['kɔmplɛks] *adj* complejo ▷ *n* (*gen*) complejo
complexion [kəm'plɛkʃən] *n* (*of face*) tez *f*, cutis *m*; (*fig*) aspecto
complexity [kəm'plɛksɪtɪ] *n* complejidad *f*
compliance [kəm'plaɪəns] *n* (*submission*) sumisión *f*; (*agreement*) conformidad *f*; **in ~ with** de acuerdo con
complicate ['kɔmplɪkeɪt] *vt* complicar
complicated ['kɔmplɪkeɪtɪd] *adj* complicado
complication [kɔmplɪ'keɪʃən] *n* complicación *f*
compliment ['kɔmplɪmənt] *n* (*formal*) cumplido; (*flirtation*) piropo ▷ *vt* felicitar;
compliments *npl* saludos *mpl*; **to pay sb a ~** (*formal*) hacer cumplidos a algn; (*flirt*) piropear, echar piropos a algn; **to ~ sb (on sth/on doing sth)** felicitar a algn (por algo/ por haber hecho algo)
complimentary [kɔmplɪ'mɛntərɪ] *adj* elogioso; (*copy*) de regalo; **~ ticket** invitación *f*
comply [kəm'plaɪ] *vi*: **to ~ with** acatar
component [kəm'pəunənt] *adj* componente ▷ *n* (*Tech*) pieza, componente *m*
compose [kəm'pəuz] *vt* componer; **to be ~d of** componerse de, constar de; **to ~ o.s.** tranquilizarse
composed [kəm'pəuzd] *adj* sosegado
composer [kəm'pəuzəʳ] *n* (*Mus*) compositor(a) *m(f)*
composition [kɔmpə'zɪʃən] *n* composición *f*
compost ['kɔmpɔst] *n* abono
composure [kəm'pəuʒəʳ] *n* serenidad *f*, calma
compound ['kɔmpaund] *n* (*Chem*) compuesto; (*Ling*) término compuesto; (*enclosure*) recinto ▷ *adj* (*gen*) compuesto; (*fracture*) complicado ▷ *vt* [kəm'paund] (*fig*: *problem, difficulty*) agravar
comprehend [kɔmprɪ'hɛnd] *vt* comprender
comprehension [kɔmprɪ'hɛnʃən] *n* comprensión *f*
comprehensive [kɔmprɪ'hɛnsɪv] *adj* (*broad*) exhaustivo; (*general*) de conjunto; **~ (school)** *n* *centro estatal de enseñanza secundaria*, ≈ Instituto Nacional de Bachillerato (*Sp*); *ver nota*

COMPREHENSIVE SCHOOL

En los años 60 se creó un nuevo tipo de centro educativo de enseñanza secundaria (aproximadamente de los once años en adelante) denominado *comprehensive school*, abierto a todos los alumnos independientemente de sus capacidades, con el que se intentó poner fin a la división tradicional entre centros de enseñanzas teóricas para acceder a la educación superior ("grammar schools") y otros de enseñanzas básicamente profesionales ("secondary modern schools").

comprehensive insurance policy *n* seguro a todo riesgo
compress [kəm'prɛs] *vt* comprimir; (*Comput*) comprimir ▷ *n* ['kɔmprɛs] (*Med*) compresa
comprise [kəm'praɪz] *vt* (*also*: **be ~d of**) comprender, constar de
compromise ['kɔmprəmaɪz] *n* solución *f* intermedia; (*agreement*) arreglo ▷ *vt* comprometer ▷ *vi* transigir, transar (*LAm*) ▷ *cpd* (*decision, solution*) de término medio
compulsion [kəm'pʌlʃən] *n* obligación *f*; **under ~** a la fuerza, por obligación

compulsive [kəm'pʌlsɪv] *adj* compulsivo; (*viewing, reading*) obligado
compulsory [kəm'pʌlsərɪ] *adj* obligatorio
computer [kəm'pju:tə^r] *n* ordenador *m*, computador *m*, computadora
computer game *n* juego de ordenador
computerize [kəm'pju:təraɪz] *vt* (*data*) computerizar; (*system*) informatizar
computer literate *adj*: **to be ~** tener conocimientos de informática a nivel de usuario
computer programmer *n* programador(a) *m(f)*
computer programming *n* programación *f*
computer science *n* informática
computer studies *npl* informática *fsg*, computación *fsg* (*LAm*)
computing [kəm'pju:tɪŋ] *n* (*activity*) informática
comrade ['kɔmrɪd] *n* compañero(-a)
con [kɔn] *vt* timar, estafar ▷ *n* timo, estafa; **to ~ sb into doing sth** (*inf*) engañar a algn para que haga algo
conceal [kən'si:l] *vt* ocultar; (*thoughts etc*) disimular
concede [kən'si:d] *vt* (*point, argument*) reconocer; (*game*) darse por vencido en; (*territory*) ceder; **to ~ (defeat)** darse por vencido; **to ~ that** admitir que
conceit [kən'si:t] *n* orgullo, presunción *f*
conceited [kən'si:tɪd] *adj* orgulloso
conceivable [kən'si:vəbl] *adj* concebible; **it is ~ that ...** es posible que ...
conceive [kən'si:v] *vt, vi* concebir; **to ~ of sth/of doing sth** imaginar algo/imaginarse haciendo algo
concentrate ['kɔnsəntreɪt] *vi* concentrarse ▷ *vt* concentrar
concentration [kɔnsən'treɪʃən] *n* concentración *f*
concentration camp *n* campo de concentración
concept ['kɔnsɛpt] *n* concepto
conception [kən'sɛpʃən] *n* (*idea*) concepto, idea; (*Biol*) concepción *f*
concern [kən'sə:n] *n* (*matter*) asunto; (*Comm*) empresa; (*anxiety*) preocupación *f* ▷ *vt* (*worry*) preocupar; (*involve*) afectar; (*relate to*) tener que ver con; **to be ~ed (about)** interesarse (por), preocuparse (por)
concerning [kən'sə:nɪŋ] *prep* sobre, acerca de
concert ['kɔnsət] *n* concierto
concerted [kən'sə:təd] *adj* (*efforts etc*) concertado
concert hall *n* sala de conciertos
concerto [kən'tʃə:təu] *n* concierto
concession [kən'sɛʃən] *n* concesión *f*; (*price concession*) descuento; **tax ~** privilegio fiscal
conciliation [kənsɪlɪ'eɪʃən] *n* conciliación *f*
concise [kən'saɪs] *adj* conciso
conclude [kən'klu:d] *vt* (*finish*) concluir; (*treaty etc*) firmar; (*agreement*) llegar a; (*decide*): **to ~ that ...** llegar a la conclusión de que ... ▷ *vi* (*events*) concluir, terminar
concluding [kən'klu:dɪŋ] *adj* (*remarks etc*) final
conclusion [kən'klu:ʒən] *n* conclusión *f*; **to come to the ~ that** llegar a la conclusión de que
conclusive [kən'klu:sɪv] *adj* decisivo, concluyente
concoct [kən'kɔkt] *vt* (*food, drink*) preparar; (*story*) inventar; (*plot*) tramar
concoction [kən'kɔkʃən] *n* (*food*) mezcla; (*drink*) brebaje *m*
concourse ['kɔŋkɔ:s] *n* (*hall*) vestíbulo
concrete ['kɔnkri:t] *n* hormigón *m* ▷ *adj* de hormigón; (*fig*) concreto
concur [kən'kə:^r] *vi* estar de acuerdo
concurrently [kən'kʌrntlɪ] *adv* al mismo tiempo
concussion [kən'kʌʃən] *n* conmoción *f* cerebral
condemn [kən'dɛm] *vt* condenar; (*building*) declarar en ruina
condensation [kɔndɛn'seɪʃən] *n* condensación *f*
condense [kən'dɛns] *vi* condensarse ▷ *vt* condensar; (*text*) abreviar
condensed milk *n* leche *f* condensada
condescending [kɔndɪ'sɛndɪŋ] *adj* superior
condition [kən'dɪʃən] *n* condición *f*; (*of health*) estado; (*disease*) enfermedad *f* ▷ *vt* condicionar; **on ~ that** a condición (de) que; **weather ~s** condiciones atmosféricas; **in good/poor ~** en buenas/malas condiciones, en buen/mal estado; **~s of sale** condiciones de venta
conditional [kən'dɪʃənl] *adj* condicional
conditioner [kən'dɪʃənə^r] *n* (*for hair*) suavizante *m*, acondicionador *m*
condo ['kɔndəu] *n abbr* (*US inf*) = **condominium**
condolences [kən'dəulənsɪz] *npl* pésame *msg*
condom ['kɔndəm] *n* condón *m*
condominium [kɔndə'mɪnɪəm] *n* (*US: building*) bloque *m* de pisos *or* apartamentos (*propiedad de quienes lo habitan*), condominio (*LAm*); (*: apartment*) piso *or* apartamento (en propiedad), condominio (*LAm*)
condone [kən'dəun] *vt* condonar
conducive [kən'dju:sɪv] *adj*: **~ to** conducente a
conduct ['kɔndʌkt] *n* conducta, comportamiento ▷ *vt* [kən'dʌkt] (*lead*) conducir; (*manage*) llevar, dirigir; (*Mus*) dirigir ▷ *vi* (*Mus*) llevar la batuta; **to ~ o.s.** comportarse
conducted tour *n* (*Brit*) visita con guía
conductor [kən'dʌktə^r] *n* (*of orchestra*) director(a) *m(f)*; (*US: on train*) revisor(a) *m(f)*; (*on bus*) cobrador *m*; (*Elec*) conductor *m*
cone [kəun] *n* cono; (*pine cone*) piña; (*for ice cream*) cucurucho

confectioner [kən'fɛkʃənəʳ] *n* (*of cakes*) pastelero(-a); (*of sweets*) confitero(-a); **~'s (shop)** *n* pastelería; confitería
confectionery [kən'fɛkʃənrɪ] *n* pasteles *mpl*; dulces *mpl*
confer [kən'fəːʳ] *vt*: **to ~ (on)** otorgar (a) ▷ *vi* conferenciar; **to ~ (with sb about sth)** consultar (con algn sobre algo)
conference ['kɔnfərns] *n* (*meeting*) reunión *f*; (*convention*) congreso; **to be in ~** estar en una reunión
confess [kən'fɛs] *vt* confesar ▷ *vi* confesar; (*Rel*) confesarse
confession [kən'fɛʃən] *n* confesión *f*
confessional [kən'fɛʃənl] *n* confesionario
confessor [kən'fɛsəʳ] *n* confesor *m*
confetti [kən'fɛtɪ] *n* confeti *m*
confide [kən'faɪd] *vi*: **to ~ in** confiar en
confidence ['kɔnfɪdns] *n* (*gen*: *also*: **self-~**) confianza; (*secret*) confidencia; **in ~** (*speak, write*) en confianza; **to have (every) ~ that** estar seguro *or* confiado de que; **motion of no ~** moción *f* de censura; **to tell sb sth in strict ~** decir algo a algn de manera confidencial
confidence trick *n* timo
confident ['kɔnfɪdənt] *adj* seguro de sí mismo
confidential [kɔnfɪ'dɛnʃəl] *adj* confidencial; (*secretary*) de confianza
confidentiality [kɔnfɪdɛnʃɪ'ælɪtɪ] *n* confidencialidad *f*
confine [kən'faɪn] *vt* (*limit*) limitar; (*shut up*) encerrar; **to ~ o.s. to doing sth** limitarse a hacer algo
confined [kən'faɪnd] *adj* (*space*) reducido
confinement [kən'faɪnmənt] *n* (*prison*) reclusión *f*; (*Med*) parto; **in solitary ~** incomunicado
confines ['kɔnfaɪnz] *npl* confines *mpl*
confirm [kən'fəːm] *vt* confirmar
confirmation [kɔnfə'meɪʃən] *n* confirmación *f*
confirmed [kən'fəːmd] *adj* empedernido
confiscate ['kɔnfɪskeɪt] *vt* confiscar
conflict ['kɔnflɪkt] *n* conflicto ▷ *vi* [kən'flɪkt] (*opinions*) estar reñido; (*reports, evidence*) contradecirse
conflicting [kən'flɪktɪŋ] *adj* (*reports, evidence, opinions*) contradictorio
conform [kən'fɔːm] *vi*: **to ~ to** (*laws*) someterse a; (*usages, mores*) amoldarse a; (*standards*) ajustarse a
confound [kən'faund] *vt* confundir; (*amaze*) pasmar
confront [kən'frʌnt] *vt* (*problems*) hacer frente a; (*enemy, danger*) enfrentarse con
confrontation [kɔnfrən'teɪʃən] *n* enfrentamiento, confrontación *f*
confuse [kən'fjuːz] *vt* (*perplex*) desconcertar; (*mix up*) confundir; (*complicate*) complicar
confused [kən'fjuːzd] *adj* confuso; (*person*) desconcertado; **to get ~** desconcertarse; (*muddled up*) hacerse un lío
confusing [kən'fjuːzɪŋ] *adj* confuso
confusion [kən'fjuːʒən] *n* confusión *f*
congeal [kən'dʒiːl] *vi* coagularse
congenial [kən'dʒiːnɪəl] *adj* agradable
congested [kən'dʒɛstɪd] *adj* (*gen*) atestado; (*telephone lines*) saturado
congestion [kən'dʒɛstʃən] *n* congestión *f*
conglomerate [kən'glɔmərət] *n* (*Comm, Geo*) conglomerado
congratulate [kən'grætjuleɪt] *vt* felicitar
congratulations [kəngrætju'leɪʃənz] *npl*: **~ (on)** felicitaciones *fpl* (por); **~!** ¡enhorabuena!, ¡felicidades!
congregate ['kɔŋgrɪgeɪt] *vi* congregarse
congregation [kɔŋgrɪ'geɪʃən] *n* (*in church*) fieles *mpl*
congress ['kɔŋgrɛs] *n* congreso; (*US Pol*): **C~** el Congreso (de los Estados Unidos); *ver nota*

CONGRESS

En el Congreso de los Estados Unidos (*Congress*) se elaboran y aprueban las leyes federales. Consta de dos cámaras: la Cámara de Representantes ("House of Representatives"), cuyos 435 miembros son elegidos cada dos años por voto popular directo y en número proporcional a los habitantes de cada estado, y el Senado ("Senate"), con 100 senadores ("senators"), 2 por estado, de los que un tercio se elige cada dos años y el resto cada seis.

congressman ['kɔŋgrɛsmən] *n* (*US*) diputado, miembro del Congreso
congresswoman ['kɔŋgrɛswumən] *n* (*US*) diputada, miembro *f* del Congreso
conifer ['kɔnɪfəʳ] *n* conífera
conjecture [kən'dʒɛktʃəʳ] *n* conjetura
conjugate ['kɔndʒugeɪt] *vt* conjugar
conjugation [kɔndʒə'geɪʃən] *n* conjugación *f*
conjunction [kən'dʒʌŋkʃən] *n* conjunción *f*; **in ~ with** junto con
conjunctivitis [kəndʒʌŋktɪ'vaɪtɪs] *n* conjuntivitis *f*
conjure ['kʌndʒəʳ] *vi* hacer juegos de manos; **conjure up** *vt* (*ghost, spirit*) hacer aparecer; (*memories*) evocar
conjurer ['kʌndʒərəʳ] *n* ilusionista *m/f*
conk out [kɔŋk-] *vi* (*inf*) estropearse, fastidiarse, descomponerse (*LAm*)
con man *n* timador *m*
connect [kə'nɛkt] *vt* juntar, unir; (*Elec*) conectar; (*pipes*) empalmar; (*fig*) relacionar, asociar ▷ *vi*: **to ~ with** (*train*) enlazar con; **to be ~ed with** (*associated*) estar relacionado con; (*related*) estar emparentado con; **I am**

trying to ~ you (*Tel*) estoy intentando ponerle al habla
connecting flight *n* vuelo *m* de enlace
connection [kəˈnɛkʃən] *n* juntura, unión *f*; (*Elec*) conexión *f*; (*Tech*) empalme *m*; (*Rail*) enlace *m*; (*Tel*) comunicación *f*; (*fig*) relación *f*; **what is the ~ between them?** ¿qué relación hay entre ellos?; **in ~ with** con respecto a, en relación a; **she has many business ~s** tiene muchos contactos profesionales; **to miss/make a ~** perder/coger el enlace
connive [kəˈnaɪv] *vi*: **to ~ at** hacer la vista gorda a
connotation [kɔnəˈteɪʃən] *n* connotación *f*
conquer [ˈkɔŋkə^r] *vt* (*territory*) conquistar; (*enemy, feelings*) vencer
conquest [ˈkɔŋkwɛst] *n* conquista
cons [kɔnz] *npl see* **convenience, pro**
conscience [ˈkɔnʃəns] *n* conciencia; **in all ~** en conciencia
conscientious [kɔnʃɪˈɛnʃəs] *adj* concienzudo; (*objection*) de conciencia
conscious [ˈkɔnʃəs] *adj* consciente; (*deliberate: insult, error*) premeditado, intencionado; **to become ~ of sth/that** darse cuenta de algo/de que
consciousness [ˈkɔnʃəsnɪs] *n* conciencia; (*Med*) conocimiento
conscript [ˈkɔnskrɪpt] *n* recluta *m/f*
conscription [kənˈskrɪpʃən] *n* servicio militar (obligatorio)
consecrate [ˈkɔnsɪkreɪt] *vt* consagrar
consecutive [kənˈsɛkjutɪv] *adj* consecutivo; **on 3 ~ occasions** en 3 ocasiones consecutivas
consensus [kənˈsɛnsəs] *n* consenso; **the ~ of opinion** el consenso general
consent [kənˈsɛnt] *n* consentimiento ▷ *vi*: **to ~ to** consentir en; **by common ~** de común acuerdo
consequence [ˈkɔnsɪkwəns] *n* consecuencia; **in ~** por consiguiente
consequently [ˈkɔnsɪkwəntlɪ] *adv* por consiguiente
conservation [kɔnsəˈveɪʃən] *n* conservación *f*; (*of nature*) conservación, protección *f*
conservationist [kɔnsəˈveɪʃnɪst] *n* conservacionista *m/f*
conservative [kənˈsəːvətɪv] *adj* conservador(a); (*cautious*) moderado; **C~** *adj, n* (*Brit Pol*) conservador(a) *m(f)*; **the C~ Party** el partido conservador (británico)
conservatory [kənˈsəːvətrɪ] *n* (*greenhouse*) invernadero
conserve [kənˈsəːv] *vt* conservar ▷ *n* conserva
consider [kənˈsɪdə^r] *vt* considerar; (*take into account*) tener en cuenta; (*study*) estudiar, examinar; **to ~ doing sth** pensar en (la posibilidad de) hacer algo; **all things ~ed** pensándolo bien; **~ yourself lucky** ¡date por satisfecho!
considerable [kənˈsɪdərəbl] *adj* considerable
considerably [kənˈsɪdərəblɪ] *adv* bastante, considerablemente
considerate [kənˈsɪdərɪt] *adj* considerado
consideration [kənsɪdəˈreɪʃən] *n* consideración *f*; (*reward*) retribución *f*; **to be under ~** estar estudiándose; **my first ~ is my family** mi primera consideración es mi familia
considered [kənˈsɪdəd] *adj*: **it's my ~ opinion that ...** después de haber reflexionado mucho, pienso que ...
considering [kənˈsɪdərɪŋ] *prep*: **~ (that)** teniendo en cuenta (que)
consign [kənˈsaɪn] *vt* consignar
consignment [kənˈsaɪnmənt] *n* envío
consist [kənˈsɪst] *vi*: **to ~ of** consistir en
consistency [kənˈsɪstənsɪ] *n* (*of person etc*) consecuencia, coherencia; (*thickness*) consistencia
consistent [kənˈsɪstənt] *adj* (*person, argument*) consecuente, coherente; (*results*) constante
consolation [kɔnsəˈleɪʃən] *n* consuelo
console [kənˈsəul] *vt* consolar ▷ *n* [ˈkɔnsəul] (*control panel*) consola
consolidate [kənˈsɔlɪdeɪt] *vt* consolidar
consonant [ˈkɔnsənənt] *n* consonante *f*
consortium [kənˈsɔːtɪəm] *n* consorcio
conspicuous [kənˈspɪkjuəs] *adj* (*visible*) visible; (*garish etc*) llamativo; (*outstanding*) notable; **to make o.s. ~** llamar la atención
conspiracy [kənˈspɪrəsɪ] *n* conjura, complot *m*
constable [ˈkʌnstəbl] *n* (*Brit*) agente *m/f* (de policía); **chief ~** ≈ jefe *m/f* de policía
constabulary [kənˈstæbjulərɪ] *n* ≈ policía
constant [ˈkɔnstənt] *adj* (*gen*) constante; (*loyal*) leal, fiel
constantly [ˈkɔnstəntlɪ] *adv* constantemente
constellation [kɔnstəˈleɪʃən] *n* constelación *f*
consternation [kɔnstəˈneɪʃən] *n* consternación *f*
constipated [ˈkɔnstɪpeɪtəd] *adj* estreñido
constipation [kɔnstɪˈpeɪʃən] *n* estreñimiento
constituency [kənˈstɪtjuənsɪ] *n* (*Pol*) distrito electoral; (*people*) electorado
constituent [kənˈstɪtjuənt] *n* (*Pol*) elector(a) *m(f)*; (*part*) componente *m*
constitute [ˈkɔnstɪtjuːt] *vt* constituir
constitution [kɔnstɪˈtjuːʃən] *n* constitución *f*
constitutional [kɔnstɪˈtjuːʃənl] *adj* constitucional; **~ monarchy** monarquía constitucional
constraint [kənˈstreɪnt] *n* (*force*) fuerza; (*limit*) restricción *f*; (*restraint*) reserva; (*embarrassment*) cohibición *f*
construct [kənˈstrʌkt] *vt* construir

C

construction [kən'strʌkʃən] *n* construcción *f*; (*fig*: *interpretation*) interpretación *f*; **under ~** en construcción
constructive [kən'strʌktɪv] *adj* constructivo
construe [kən'struː] *vt* interpretar
consul ['kɔnsl] *n* cónsul *m/f*
consulate ['kɔnsjulɪt] *n* consulado
consult [kən'sʌlt] *vt, vi* consultar; **to ~ sb (about sth)** consultar a algn (sobre algo)
consultancy [kən'sʌltənsɪ] *n* (*Comm*) consultoría; (*Med*) puesto de especialista
consultant [kən'sʌltənt] *n* (*Brit Med*) especialista *m/f*; (*other specialist*) asesor(a) *m(f)*, consultor(a) *m(f)*
consultation [kɔnsəl'teɪʃən] *n* consulta; **in ~ with** en consulta con
consulting room *n* (*Brit*) consulta, consultorio
consume [kən'sjuːm] *vt* (*eat*) comerse; (*drink*) beberse; (*fire etc*) consumir; (*Comm*) consumir
consumer [kən'sjuːməʳ] *n* (*of electricity, gas etc*) consumidor(a) *m(f)*
consumer goods *npl* bienes *mpl* de consumo
consumer society *n* sociedad *f* de consumo
consumer watchdog *n* organización *f* protectora del consumidor
consummate ['kɔnsʌmeɪt] *vt* consumar
consumption [kən'sʌmpʃən] *n* consumo; (*Med*) tisis *f*; **not fit for human ~** no apto para el consumo humano
cont. *abbr* (= *continued*) sigue
contact ['kɔntækt] *n* contacto; (*person*: *pej*) enchufe *m* ▹ *vt* ponerse en contacto con; **~ lenses** *npl* lentes *fpl* de contacto; **to be in ~ with sb/sth** estar en contacto con algn/algo; **business ~s** relaciones *fpl* comerciales
contagious [kən'teɪdʒəs] *adj* contagioso
contain [kən'teɪn] *vt* contener; **to ~ o.s.** contenerse
container [kən'teɪnəʳ] *n* recipiente *m*; (*for shipping etc*) contenedor *m*
container ship *n* buque *m* contenedor, portacontenedores *m inv*
contaminate [kən'tæmɪneɪt] *vt* contaminar
contamination [kəntæmɪ'neɪʃən] *n* contaminación *f*
cont'd *abbr* (= *continued*) sigue
contemplate ['kɔntəmpleɪt] *vt* (*gen*) contemplar; (*reflect upon*) considerar; (*intend*) pensar
contemplation [kɔntəm'pleɪʃən] *n* contemplación *f*
contemporary [kən'tɛmpərərɪ] *adj, n* (*of the same age*) contemporáneo(-a) *m(f)*
contempt [kən'tɛmpt] *n* desprecio; **~ of court** (*Law*) desacato (a los tribunales *or* a la justicia)
contemptuous [kən'tɛmptjuəs] *adj* desdeñoso
contend [kən'tɛnd] *vt* (*argue*) afirmar ▹ *vi*: **to ~ with/for** luchar contra/por; **he has a lot to ~ with** tiene que hacer frente a muchos problemas
contender [kən'tɛndəʳ] *n* (*Sport*) contendiente *m/f*
content [kən'tɛnt] *adj* (*happy*) contento; (*satisfied*) satisfecho ▹ *vt* contentar; satisfacer ▹ *n* ['kɔntɛnt] contenido; **contents** *npl* contenido *msg*; **(table of) ~s** índice *m* de materias; (*in magazine*) sumario; **to be ~ with** conformarse con; **to ~ o.s. with sth/with doing sth** conformarse con algo/con hacer algo
contented [kən'tɛntɪd] *adj* contento; satisfecho
contention [kən'tɛnʃən] *n* discusión *f*; (*belief*) argumento; **bone of ~** manzana de la discordia
contentious [kən'tɛnʃəs] *adj* discutible
contentment [kən'tɛntmənt] *n* satisfacción *f*
contest ['kɔntɛst] *n* contienda; (*competition*) concurso ▹ *vt* [kən'tɛst] (*dispute*) impugnar; (*Law*) disputar, litigar; (*Pol*: *election, seat*) presentarse como candidato(-a) a
contestant [kən'tɛstənt] *n* concursante *m/f*; (*in fight*) contendiente *m/f*
context ['kɔntɛkst] *n* contexto; **in/out of ~** en/fuera de contexto
continent ['kɔntɪnənt] *n* continente *m*; **the C~** (*Brit*) el continente europeo, Europa; **on the C~** en el continente europeo, en Europa
continental [kɔntɪ'nɛntl] *adj* continental; (*Brit*: *European*) europeo
continental breakfast *n* desayuno estilo europeo
continental quilt *n* (*Brit*) edredón *m*
contingency [kən'tɪndʒənsɪ] *n* contingencia
contingent [kən'tɪndʒənt] *n* (*group*) representación *f*
continual [kən'tɪnjuəl] *adj* continuo
continually [kən'tɪnjuəlɪ] *adv* continuamente
continuation [kəntɪnju'eɪʃən] *n* prolongación *f*; (*after interruption*) reanudación *f*; (*of story, episode*) continuación *f*
continue [kən'tɪnjuː] *vi, vt* seguir, continuar; **~d on page 10** sigue en la página 10
continuing education [kən'tɪnjuɪŋ-] *n* educación *f* continua de adultos
continuity [kɔntɪ'njuɪtɪ] *n* (*also Cine*) continuidad *f*
continuous [kən'tɪnjuəs] *adj* continuo; **~ performance** (*Cine*) sesión *f* continua
continuous assessment *n* (*Brit*) evaluación *f* continua
continuously [kən'tɪnjuəslɪ] *adv* continuamente
contort [kən'tɔːt] *vt* retorcer
contour ['kɔntuəʳ] *n* contorno; (*also*: **~ line**) curva de nivel
contraband ['kɔntrəbænd] *n* contrabando ▹ *adj* de contrabando

contraception [kɔntrəˈsɛpʃən] *n* contracepción *f*
contraceptive [kɔntrəˈsɛptɪv] *adj, n* anticonceptivo
contract [*n* ˈkɔntrækt, *vb* kɔnˈtrækt] *n* contrato ▷ *cpd* [ˈkɔntrækt] (*price, date*) contratado, de contrato; (*work*) bajo contrato ▷ *vi* (*Comm*): **to ~ to do sth** comprometerse por contrato a hacer algo; (*become smaller*) contraerse, encogerse ▷ *vt* contraer; **to be under ~ to do sth** estar bajo contrato para hacer algo; **~ of employment** *or* **of service** contrato de trabajo; **contract in** *vi* tomar parte; **contract out** *vi*: **to ~ out (of)** optar por no tomar parte (en); **to ~ out of a pension scheme** dejar de cotizar en un plan de jubilación
contraction [kənˈtrækʃən] *n* contracción *f*
contractor [kənˈtræktəʳ] *n* contratista *m/f*
contractual [kənˈtræktjuəl] *adj* contractual
contradict [kɔntrəˈdɪkt] *vt* (*declare to be wrong*) desmentir; (*be contrary to*) contradecir
contradiction [kɔntrəˈdɪkʃən] *n* contradicción *f*; **to be in ~ with** contradecir
contradictory [kɔntrəˈdɪktərɪ] *adj* (*statements*) contradictorio; **to be ~ to** contradecir
contralto [kənˈtræltəu] *n* contralto *f*
contraption [kənˈtræpʃən] *n* (*pej*) artilugio *m*
contrary[1] [ˈkɔntrərɪ] *adj* contrario ▷ *n* lo contrario; **on the ~** al contrario; **~ to what we thought** al contrario de lo que pensábamos; **unless you hear to the ~** a no ser que le digan lo contrario
contrary[2] [kənˈtrɛərɪ] *adj* (*perverse*) terco
contrast [ˈkɔntrɑːst] *n* contraste *m* ▷ *vt* [kənˈtrɑːst] contrastar; **in ~ to** *or* **with** a diferencia de
contravene [kɔntrəˈviːn] *vt* contravenir
contravention [kɔntrəˈvɛnʃən] *n*: **~ (of)** contravención *f* (de)
contribute [kənˈtrɪbjuːt] *vi* contribuir ▷ *vt*: **to ~ to** (*gen*) contribuir a; (*newspaper*) colaborar en; (*discussion*) intervenir en
contribution [kɔntrɪˈbjuːʃən] *n* (*money*) contribución *f*; (*to debate*) intervención *f*; (*to journal*) colaboración *f*
contributor [kənˈtrɪbjutəʳ] *n* (*to newspaper*) colaborador(a) *m(f)*
contrive [kənˈtraɪv] *vt* (*invent*) idear ▷ *vi*: **to ~ to do** lograr hacer; (*try*) procurar hacer
control [kənˈtrəul] *vt* controlar; (*traffic etc*) dirigir; (*machinery*) manejar; (*temper*) dominar; (*disease, fire*) dominar, controlar ▷ *n* (*command*) control *m*; (*of car*) conducción *f*; (*check*) freno; **controls** *npl* (*of vehicle*) instrumentos *mpl* de mando; (*of radio*) controles *mpl*; (*governmental*) medidas *fpl* de control; **to ~ o.s.** controlarse, dominarse; **everything is under ~** todo está bajo control; **to be in ~ of** estar al mando de; **the car went out of ~** perdió el control del coche
control panel *n* (*on aircraft, ship, TV etc*) tablero de instrumentos
control room *n* (*Naut, Mil*) sala de mandos; (*Radio, TV*) sala de control
control tower *n* (*Aviat*) torre *f* de control
controversial [kɔntrəˈvəːʃl] *adj* polémico
controversy [ˈkɔntrəvəːsɪ] *n* polémica
convalesce [kɔnvəˈlɛs] *vi* convalecer
convector [kənˈvɛktəʳ] *n* calentador *m* de convección
convene [kənˈviːn] *vt* (*meeting*) convocar ▷ *vi* reunirse
convenience [kənˈviːnɪəns] *n* (*comfort*) comodidad *f*; (*advantage*) ventaja; **at your earliest ~** (*Comm*) tan pronto como le sea posible; **all modern ~s** (*Brit*) todo confort
convenient [kənˈviːnɪənt] *adj* (*useful*) útil; (*place*) conveniente; (*time*) oportuno; **if it is ~ for you** si le viene bien
convent [ˈkɔnvənt] *n* convento
convention [kənˈvɛnʃən] *n* convención *f*; (*meeting*) asamblea
conventional [kənˈvɛnʃənl] *adj* convencional
conversant [kənˈvəːsnt] *adj*: **to be ~ with** estar familiarizado con
conversation [kɔnvəˈseɪʃən] *n* conversación *f*
converse [ˈkɔnvəːs] *n* inversa ▷ *vi* [kənˈvəːs] conversar; **to ~ (with sb about sth)** conversar *or* platicar (*LAm*) (con algn de algo)
conversely [kɔnˈvəːslɪ] *adv* a la inversa
conversion [kənˈvəːʃən] *n* conversión *f*; (*house conversion*) reforma, remodelación *f*
convert [kənˈvəːt] *vt* (*Rel, Comm*) convertir; (*alter*) transformar ▷ *n* [ˈkɔnvəːt] converso(-a)
convertible [kənˈvəːtəbl] *adj* convertible ▷ *n* descapotable *m*; **~ loan stock** obligaciones *fpl* convertibles
convey [kənˈveɪ] *vt* transportar; (*thanks*) comunicar; (*idea*) expresar
conveyancing [kənˈveɪənsɪŋ] *n* (*Law*) preparación *f* de escrituras de traspaso
conveyor belt [kənˈveɪəʳ-] *n* cinta transportadora
convict [kənˈvɪkt] *vt* (*gen*) condenar; (*find guilty*) declarar culpable a ▷ *n* [ˈkɔnvɪkt] presidiario(-a)
conviction [kənˈvɪkʃən] *n* condena; (*belief*) creencia, convicción *f*
convince [kənˈvɪns] *vt* convencer; **to ~ sb (of sth/that)** convencer a algn (de algo/de que)
convinced [kənˈvɪnst] *adj*: **~ of/that** convencido de/de que
convincing [kənˈvɪnsɪŋ] *adj* convincente
convoluted [ˈkɔnvəluːtɪd] *adj* (*argument etc*) enrevesado; (*shape*) enrollado, enroscado
convoy [ˈkɔnvɔɪ] *n* convoy *m*
convulse [kənˈvʌls] *vt* convulsionar; **to be ~d with laughter** dislocarse de risa
convulsion [kənˈvʌlʃən] *n* convulsión *f*
coo [kuː] *vi* arrullar

C

cook [kuk] *vt* cocinar; (*stew etc*) guisar; (*meal*) preparar ▷ *vi* hacerse; (*person*) cocinar ▷ *n* cocinero(-a); **cook up** *vt* (*inf*: *excuse, story*) inventar
cookbook ['kukbuk] *n* libro de cocina
cooker ['kukəʳ] *n* cocina
cookery ['kukərɪ] *n* cocina
cookery book *n* (*Brit*) = **cookbook**
cookie ['kukɪ] *n* (*US*) galleta; (*Comput*) cookie *f*
cooking ['kukɪŋ] *n* cocina ▷ *cpd* (*apples*) para cocinar; (*utensils, salt, foil*) de cocina
cool [ku:l] *adj* fresco; (*not hot*) tibio; (*not afraid*) tranquilo; (*unfriendly*) frío ▷ *vt* enfriar ▷ *vi* enfriarse; **it is ~** (*weather*) hace fresco; **to keep sth ~** *or* **in a ~ place** conservar algo fresco *or* en un sitio fresco; **cool down** *vi* enfriarse; (*fig*: *person, situation*) calmarse; **cool off** *vi* (*become calmer*) calmarse, apaciguarse; (*lose enthusiasm*) perder (el) interés, enfriarse
coolant ['ku:lənt] *n* refrigerante *m*
coop [ku:p] *n* gallinero ▷ *vt*: **to ~ up** (*fig*) encerrar
co-op ['kəuɔp] *n abbr* (= *cooperative (society)*) cooperativa
cooperate [kəu'ɔpəreɪt] *vi* cooperar, colaborar; **will he ~?** ¿querrá cooperar?
cooperation [kəuɔpə'reɪʃən] *n* cooperación *f*, colaboración *f*
cooperative [kəu'ɔpərətɪv] *adj* cooperativo; (*person*) dispuesto a colaborar ▷ *n* cooperativa
coordinate [kəu'ɔ:dɪneɪt] *vt* coordinar ▷ *n* [kəu'ɔ:dɪnət] (*Math*) coordenada; **coordinates** *npl* (*clothes*) coordinados *mpl*
coordination [kəuɔ:dɪ'neɪʃən] *n* coordinación *f*
co-ownership [kəu'əunəʃɪp] *n* copropiedad *f*
cop [kɔp] *n* (*inf*) poli *m*
cope [kəup] *vi*: **to ~ with** poder con; (*problem*) hacer frente a
copier ['kɔpɪəʳ] *n* (*photocopier*) (foto)copiadora
copper ['kɔpəʳ] *n* (*metal*) cobre *m*; (*inf*: *policeman*) poli *m*; **coppers** *npl* perras *fpl*; (*small change*) calderilla
copy ['kɔpɪ] *n* copia; (*of book*) ejemplar *m*; (*of magazine*) número; (*material*: *for printing*) original *m* ▷ *vt* (*also Comput*) copiar; (*imitate*) copiar, imitar; **to make good ~** (*fig*) ser una noticia de interés; **rough ~** borrador *m*; **fair ~** copia en limpio; **copy out** *vt* copiar
copycat ['kɔpɪkæt] *n* (*pej*) imitador(a) *m(f)*
copyright ['kɔpɪraɪt] *n* derechos *mpl* de autor
coral ['kɔrəl] *n* coral *m*
coral reef *n* arrecife *m* (de coral)
cord [kɔ:d] *n* cuerda; (*Elec*) cable *m*; (*fabric*) pana; **cords** *npl* (*trousers*) pantalones *mpl* de pana
cordial ['kɔ:dɪəl] *adj* cordial ▷ *n* cordial *m*
cordless ['kɔ:dlɪs] *adj* sin hilos; **~ telephone** teléfono inalámbrico
cordon ['kɔ:dn] *n* cordón *m*; **cordon off** *vt* acordonar
corduroy ['kɔ:dərɔɪ] *n* pana
core [kɔ:ʳ] *n* (*of earth, nuclear reactor*) centro, núcleo; (*of fruit*) corazón *m*; (*of problem etc*) esencia, meollo ▷ *vt* quitar el corazón de
coriander [kɔrɪ'ændəʳ] *n* culantro, cilantro
cork [kɔ:k] *n* corcho; (*tree*) alcornoque *m*
corkscrew ['kɔ:kskru:] *n* sacacorchos *m inv*
corn [kɔ:n] *n* (*Brit*: *wheat*) trigo; (*US*: *maize*) maíz *m*, choclo (*LAm*); (*on foot*) callo; **~ on the cob** (*Culin*) maíz en la mazorca
corned beef ['kɔ:nd-] *n* carne *f* de vaca acecinada
corner ['kɔ:nəʳ] *n* (*outside*) esquina; (*inside*) rincón *m*; (*in road*) curva; (*Football*) córner *m*, saque *m* de esquina ▷ *vt* (*trap*) arrinconar; (*Comm*) acaparar ▷ *vi* (*in car*) tomar las curvas; **to cut ~s** atajar
corner shop *n* (*Brit*) tienda de la esquina
cornerstone ['kɔ:nəstəun] *n* piedra angular
cornet ['kɔ:nɪt] *n* (*Mus*) corneta; (*Brit*: *of ice cream*) cucurucho
cornflakes ['kɔ:nfleɪks] *npl* copos *mpl* de maíz, cornflakes *mpl*
cornflour ['kɔ:nflauəʳ] *n* (*Brit*) harina de maíz
cornstarch ['kɔ:nstɑ:tʃ] *n* (*US*) = **cornflour**
Cornwall ['kɔ:nwəl] *n* Cornualles *m*
corny ['kɔ:nɪ] *adj* (*inf*) gastado
coronary ['kɔrənərɪ] *n*: **~ (thrombosis)** infarto
coronation [kɔrə'neɪʃən] *n* coronación *f*
coroner ['kɔrənəʳ] *n* juez *m/f* de instrucción
corporal ['kɔ:pərl] *n* cabo ▷ *adj*: **~ punishment** castigo corporal
corporate ['kɔ:pərɪt] *adj* (*action, ownership*) colectivo; (*finance, image*) corporativo
corporation [kɔ:pə'reɪʃən] *n* (*of town*) ayuntamiento; (*Comm*) corporación *f*
corps [kɔ:ʳ] (*pl* **corps** [kɔ:z]) *n* cuerpo; **press ~** gabinete *m* de prensa
corpse [kɔ:ps] *n* cadáver *m*
correct [kə'rɛkt] *adj* correcto; (*accurate*) exacto ▷ *vt* corregir; **you are ~** tiene razón
correction [kə'rɛkʃən] *n* (*act*) corrección *f*; (*instance*) rectificación *f*; (*erasure*) tachadura
correlation [kɔrɪ'leɪʃən] *n* correlación *f*
correspond [kɔrɪs'pɔnd] *vi*: **to ~ (with)** (*write*) escribirse (con); (*be in accordance*) corresponder (con); (*be equivalent to*): **to ~ (to)** corresponder (a)
correspondence [kɔrɪs'pɔndəns] *n* correspondencia
correspondence course *n* curso por correspondencia
correspondent [kɔrɪs'pɔndənt] *n* corresponsal *m/f*
corresponding [kɔrɪs'pɔndɪŋ] *adj* correspondiente
corridor ['kɔrɪdɔ:ʳ] *n* pasillo
corroborate [kə'rɔbəreɪt] *vt* corroborar
corrode [kə'rəud] *vt* corroer ▷ *vi* corroerse
corrosion [kə'rəuʒən] *n* corrosión *f*
corrugated ['kɔrəgeɪtɪd] *adj* ondulado
corrugated iron *n* chapa ondulada

C

corrupt [kə'rʌpt] *adj* corrompido; (*person*) corrupto ▷ *vt* corromper; (*bribe*) sobornar; (*Comput: data*) degradar; **~ practices** (*dishonesty, bribery*) corrupción *f*
corruption [kə'rʌpʃən] *n* corrupción *f*; (*Comput: of data*) alteración *f*
corset ['kɔːsɪt] *n* faja; (*old-style*) corsé *m*
Corsica ['kɔːsɪkə] *n* Córcega
cortège [kɔː'teɪʒ] *n* cortejo, comitiva
cortisone ['kɔːtɪzəun] *n* cortisona
cosh [kɔʃ] *n* (*Brit*) cachiporra
cosmetic [kɔz'mɛtɪk] *n* cosmético ▷ *adj* (*also fig*) cosmético
cosmetic surgery *n* cirugía *f* estética
cosmic ['kɔzmɪk] *adj* cósmico
cosmopolitan [kɔzmə'pɔlɪtn] *adj* cosmopolita
cosmos ['kɔzmɔs] *n* cosmos *m*
cosset ['kɔsɪt] *vt* mimar
cost [kɔst] (*pt, pp* **cost**) *n* (*gen*) coste *m*, costo; (*price*) precio; **costs** *npl* (*Law*) costas *fpl* ▷ *vi* costar, valer ▷ *vt* preparar el presupuesto de; **how much does it ~?** ¿cuánto cuesta?, ¿cuánto vale?; **what will it ~ to have it repaired?** ¿cuánto costará repararlo?; **the ~ of living** el coste *or* costo de la vida; **to ~ sb time/effort** costarle a algn tiempo/esfuerzo; **it ~ him his life** le costó la vida; **at all ~s** cueste lo que cueste
co-star ['kəustɑːʳ] *n* coprotagonista *m/f*
Costa Rica ['kɔstə'riːkə] *n* Costa Rica
Costa Rican ['kɔstə'riːkən] *adj, n* costarriqueño(-a) *m(f)*, costarricense *m/f*
cost-effective [kɔstɪ'fɛktɪv] *adj* (*Comm*) rentable
costly ['kɔstlɪ] *adj* (*expensive*) costoso
cost-of-living [kɔstəv'lɪvɪŋ] *adj*: **~ allowance** *n* plus *m* de carestía de vida; **~ index** *n* índice *m* del coste de vida
cost price *n* (*Brit*) precio de coste
costume ['kɔstjuːm] *n* traje *m*; (*Brit: also:* **swimming ~**) traje de baño
costume jewellery *n* bisutería
cosy, cozy (*US*) ['kəuzɪ] *adj* cómodo, a gusto; (*room, atmosphere*) acogedor(a)
cot [kɔt] *n* (*Brit: child's*) cuna; (*US: folding bed*) cama plegable
cot death *n* muerte *f* en la cuna
Cotswolds ['kɔtswəuldz] *npl región de colinas del suroeste inglés*
cottage ['kɔtɪdʒ] *n* casita de campo
cottage cheese *n* requesón *m*
cottage industry *n* industria artesanal
cotton ['kɔtn] *n* algodón *m*; (*thread*) hilo; **cotton on** *vi* (*inf*): **to ~ on (to sth)** caer en la cuenta (de algo)
cotton bud *n* (*Brit*) bastoncillo *m* de algodón
cotton candy *n* (*US*) algodón *m* (azucarado)
cotton wool *n* (*Brit*) algodón *m* (hidrófilo)
couch [kautʃ] *n* sofá *m*; (*in doctor's surgery*) camilla; (*psychiatrist's*) diván *m*
couchette [kuː'ʃɛt] *n* litera
couch potato *n* (*inf*) *persona comodona que no se mueve en todo el día*
cough [kɔf] *vi* toser ▷ *n* tos *f*; **cough up** *vt* escupir
cough drop *n* pastilla para la tos
cough mixture *n* jarabe *m* para la tos
could [kud] *pt of* **can**
couldn't ['kudnt] = **could not**
council ['kaunsl] *n* consejo; **city** *or* **town ~** ayuntamiento, consejo municipal; **C~ of Europe** Consejo de Europa
council estate *n* (*Brit*) barriada de viviendas sociales de alquiler
council house *n* (*Brit*) vivienda social de alquiler
councillor ['kaunsləʳ] *n* concejal *m/f*
council tax *n* (*Brit*) contribución *f* municipal (*dependiente del valor de la vivienda*)
counsel ['kaunsl] *n* (*advice*) consejo; (*lawyer*) abogado(-a) ▷ *vt* aconsejar; **~ for the defence/the prosecution** abogado(-a) defensor(a)/fiscal; **to ~ sth/sb to do sth** aconsejar algo/a algn que haga algo
counselling, (*US*) **counseling** *n* (*Psych*) asistencia *f* psicológica
counsellor, counselor (*US*) ['kaunsləʳ] *n* consejero(-a); (*US Law*) abogado(-a)
count [kaunt] *vt* (*gen*) contar; (*include*) incluir ▷ *vi* contar ▷ *n* cuenta; (*of votes*) escrutinio; (*nobleman*) conde *m*; (*sum*) total *m*, suma; **to ~ the cost of** calcular el coste de; **not ~ing the children** niños aparte; **10 ~ing him** diez incluyéndolo a él, diez con él; **~ yourself lucky** date por satisfecho; **that doesn't ~!** ¡eso no vale!; **to ~ (up) to 10** contar hasta diez; **it ~s for very little** cuenta poco; **to keep ~ of sth** llevar la cuenta de algo; **count in** (*inf*) *vt*: **to ~ sb in on sth** contar con algn para algo; **count on** *vt fus* contar con; **to ~ on doing sth** contar con hacer algo; **count up** *vt* contar
countdown ['kauntdaun] *n* cuenta atrás
countenance ['kauntɪnəns] *n* semblante *m*, rostro ▷ *vt* (*tolerate*) aprobar, consentir
counter ['kauntəʳ] *n* (*in shop*) mostrador *m*; (*position: in post office, bank*) ventanilla; (*in games*) ficha; (*Tech*) contador *m* ▷ *vt* contrarrestar; (*blow*) parar; (*attack*) contestar a ▷ *adv*: **~ to** contrario a; **to buy under the ~** (*fig*) comprar de estraperlo *or* bajo mano; **to ~ sth with sth/by doing sth** contestar algo con algo/haciendo algo
counteract ['kauntər'ækt] *vt* contrarrestar
counterattack ['kauntərə'tæk] *n* contraataque *m* ▷ *vi* contraatacar
counter-clockwise ['kauntə'klɔkwaɪz] *adv* en sentido contrario al de las agujas del reloj
counterfeit ['kauntəfɪt] *n* falsificación *f* ▷ *vt* falsificar ▷ *adj* falso, falsificado
counterfoil ['kauntəfɔɪl] *n* (*Brit*) matriz *f*, talón *m*
countermand ['kauntəmɑːnd] *vt* revocar

counterpart ['kauntəpɑːt] *n* (*of person*) homólogo(-a)
countersign ['kauntəsaɪn] *vt* ratificar, refrendar
counterterrorism [kauntə'tɛrərɪzəm] *n* antiterrorismo
countess ['kauntɪs] *n* condesa
countless ['kauntlɪs] *adj* innumerable
country ['kʌntrɪ] *n* país *m*; (*native land*) patria; (*as opposed to town*) campo; (*region*) región *f*, tierra; **in the ~** en el campo; **mountainous ~** región *f* montañosa
country and western, country and western music *n* música country
country dancing *n* (*Brit*) baile *m* regional
country house *n* casa de campo
countryman ['kʌntrɪmən] *n* (*national*) compatriota *m*; (*rural*) hombre *m* del campo
countryside ['kʌntrɪsaɪd] *n* campo
countrywide ['kʌntrɪ'waɪd] *adj* nacional ▷ *adv* por todo el país
county ['kauntɪ] *n* condado; *see also* **district council**
county council *n* (*Brit*) ≈ diputación *f* provincial
coup [kuː] (*pl* **coups** [kuːz]) *n* golpe *m*; (*triumph*) éxito; (*also*: **~ d'état**) golpe de estado
couple ['kʌpl] *n* (*of things*) par *m*; (*of people*) pareja; (*married couple*) matrimonio ▷ *vt* (*ideas, names*) unir, juntar; (*machinery*) acoplar; **a ~ of** un par de
coupon ['kuːpɔn] *n* cupón *m*; (*voucher*) valé *m*; (*pools coupon*) boleto (de quiniela)
courage ['kʌrɪdʒ] *n* valor *m*, valentía
courageous [kə'reɪdʒəs] *adj* valiente
courgette [kuə'ʒɛt] *n* (*Brit*) calabacín *m*
courier ['kurɪəʳ] *n* mensajero(-a); (*diplomatic*) correo; (*for tourists*) guía *m/f* (de turismo)
course [kɔːs] *n* (*direction*) dirección *f*; (*of river*) curso; (*Scol*) curso; (*of ship*) rumbo; (*fig*) proceder *m*; (*Golf*) campo; (*part of meal*) plato; **of ~** *adv* desde luego, naturalmente; **of ~!** ¡claro!, ¡cómo no! (*LAm*); **(no) of ~ not!** ¡claro que no!, ¡por supuesto que no!; **in due ~** a su debido tiempo; **in the ~ of the next few days** durante los próximos días; **we have no other ~ but to ...** no tenemos más remedio que ...; **there are 2 ~s open to us** se nos ofrecen dos posibilidades; **the best ~ would be to ...** lo mejor sería ...; **~ of treatment** (*Med*) tratamiento
court [kɔːt] *n* (*royal*) corte *f*; (*Law*) tribunal *m*, juzgado; (*Tennis*) pista, cancha (*LAm*) ▷ *vt* (*woman*) cortejar; (*fig: favour, popularity*) solicitar, buscar; (*: death, disaster, danger etc*) buscar; **to take to ~** demandar; **~ of appeal** tribunal *m* de apelación
courteous ['kəːtɪəs] *adj* cortés
courtesy ['kəːtəsɪ] *n* cortesía; **by ~ of** (por) cortesía de
courtesy bus, courtesy coach *n* autobús *m* gratuito
courthouse ['kɔːthaus] *n* (*US*) palacio de justicia
courtier ['kɔːtɪəʳ] *n* cortesano
court martial (*pl* **courts martial**) ['kɔːt'mɑːʃəl] *n* consejo de guerra ▷ *vt* someter a consejo de guerra
courtroom ['kɔːtrum] *n* sala de justicia
courtyard ['kɔːtjɑːd] *n* patio
cousin ['kʌzn] *n* primo(-a); **first ~** primo(-a) carnal
cove [kəuv] *n* cala, ensenada
covenant ['kʌvənənt] *n* convenio ▷ *vt*: **to ~ £20 per year to a charity** concertar el pago de veinte libras anuales a una sociedad benéfica
cover ['kʌvəʳ] *vt* cubrir; (*with lid*) tapar; (*chairs etc*) revestir; (*distance*) cubrir, recorrer; (*include*) abarcar; (*protect*) abrigar; (*journalist*) investigar; (*issues*) tratar ▷ *n* cubierta; (*lid*) tapa; (*for chair etc*) funda; (*for bed*) manta/sábana; (*envelope*) sobre *m*; (*of magazine*) portada; (*shelter*) abrigo; (*insurance*) cobertura; **to take ~** (*shelter*) protegerse, resguardarse; **under ~** (*indoors*) bajo techo; **under ~ of darkness** al amparo de la oscuridad; **under separate ~** (*Comm*) por separado; **£10 will ~ everything** con diez libras cubriremos todos los gastos; **cover up** *vt* (*child, object*) cubrir completamente, tapar; (*fig: hide: truth, facts*) ocultar ▷ *vi*: **to ~ up for sb** (*fig*) encubrir a algn
coverage ['kʌvərɪdʒ] *n* alcance *m*; (*in media*) cobertura informativa; (*Insurance*) cobertura
cover charge *n* precio del cubierto
covering ['kʌvərɪŋ] *n* cubierta, envoltura
covering letter, cover letter (*US*) *n* carta de explicación
cover note *n* (*Insurance*) póliza provisional
covert ['kəuvət] *adj* (*secret*) secreto, encubierto; (*dissembled*) furtivo
cover-up ['kʌvərʌp] *n* encubrimiento
covet ['kʌvɪt] *vt* codiciar
cow [kau] *n* vaca ▷ *vt* intimidar
coward ['kauəd] *n* cobarde *m/f*
cowardice ['kauədɪs] *n* cobardía
cowardly ['kauədlɪ] *adj* cobarde
cowboy ['kaubɔɪ] *n* vaquero
cower ['kauəʳ] *vi* encogerse (de miedo)
coy [kɔɪ] *adj* tímido
cozy ['kəuzɪ] *adj* (*US*) = **cosy**
CPA *n abbr* (*US*) = **certified public accountant**
CPI *n abbr* (= *Consumer Price Index*) IPC *m*
CPU *n abbr* = **central processing unit**
crab [kræb] *n* cangrejo
crab apple *n* manzana silvestre
crack [kræk] *n* grieta; (*noise*) crujido; (*: of whip*) chasquido; (*joke*) chiste *m*; (*inf: drug*) crack *m*; (*attempt*): **to have a ~ at sth** intentar algo ▷ *vt* agrietar, romper; (*nut*) cascar; (*safe*) forzar; (*whip etc*) chasquear; (*knuckles*) crujir; (*joke*) contar; (*case: solve*) resolver; (*code*) descifrar ▷ *adj* (*athlete*) de primera clase;

to ~ jokes (*inf*) bromear; **crack down on** *vt fus* reprimir fuertemente, adoptar medidas severas contra; **crack up** *vi* sufrir una crisis nerviosa
cracked [krækt] *adj* (*cup, window*) rajado; (*wall*) resquebrajado
cracker ['krækəʳ] *n* (*biscuit*) galleta salada, cráckerm; (*Christmas cracker*) petardo sorpresa
crackle ['krækl] *vi* crepitar
crackpot ['krækpɔt] (*inf*) *n* pirado(-a) ▷ *adj* de pirado
cradle ['kreɪdl] *n* cuna ▷ *vt* (*child*) mecer, acunar; (*object*) abrazar
craft [krɑːft] *n* (*skill*) arte *m*; (*trade*) oficio; (*cunning*) astucia; (*boat*) embarcación *f*
craftsman ['krɑːftsmən] *n* artesano
craftsmanship ['krɑːftsmənʃɪp] *n* destreza
crafty ['krɑːftɪ] *adj* astuto
crag [kræg] *n* peñasco
cram [kræm] *vt* (*fill*): **to ~ sth with** llenar algo (a reventar) de; (*put*): **to ~ sth into** meter algo a la fuerza en ▷ *vi* (*for exams*) empollar
cramp [kræmp] *n* (*Med*) calambre *m*; (*Tech*) grapa ▷ *vt* (*limit*) poner trabas a
cramped [kræmpt] *adj* apretado; (*room*) minúsculo
cranberry ['krænbərɪ] *n* arándano agrio
crane [kreɪn] *n* (*Tech*) grúa; (*bird*) grulla ▷ *vt*, *vi*: **to ~ forward, to ~ one's neck** estirar el cuello
crank [kræŋk] *n* manivela; (*person*) chiflado(-a)
crankshaft ['kræŋkʃɑːft] *n* cigüeñal *m*
cranky ['kræŋkɪ] *adj* (*eccentric*) maniático; (*bad-tempered*) de mal genio
cranny ['krænɪ] *n see* **nook**
crap [kræp] *n* (*inf!*) mierda (*!*)
crash [kræʃ] *n* (*noise*) estrépito; (*of cars, plane*) accidente *m*; (*of business*) quiebra; (*Stock Exchange*) crac *m* ▷ *vt* (*plane*) estrellar ▷ *vi* (*plane*) estrellarse; (*two cars*) chocar; (*fall noisily*) caer con estrépito; **he ~ed the car into a wall** estrelló el coche contra una pared *or* tapia; **crash out** *vi* (*inf: sleep*) quedarse frito; (*from competition*) quedar eliminado
crash barrier *n* (*Aut*) barrera de protección
crash course *n* curso acelerado
crash helmet *n* casco (protector)
crash landing *n* aterrizaje *m* forzoso
crass [kræs] *adj* grosero, maleducado
crate [kreɪt] *n* cajón *m* de embalaje; (*for bottles*) caja; (*inf*) armatoste *m*
crater ['kreɪtəʳ] *n* cráter *m*
crave [kreɪv] *vt*, *vi*: **to ~ (for)** ansiar, anhelar
crawl [krɔːl] *vi* (*drag o.s.*) arrastrarse; (*child*) andar a gatas, gatear; (*vehicle*) avanzar (lentamente); (*inf*): **to ~ to sb** dar coba a algn, hacerle la pelota a algn ▷ *n* (*Swimming*) crol *m*
crawler lane [krɔːlə-] *n* (*Brit Aut*) carril *m* para tráfico lento
crayfish ['kreɪfɪʃ] *n pl inv* (*freshwater*) cangrejo (de río); (*saltwater*) cigala
crayon ['kreɪən] *n* lápiz *m* de color
craze [kreɪz] *n* manía; (*fashion*) moda
crazy ['kreɪzɪ] *adj* (*person*) loco; (*idea*) disparatado; **to go ~** volverse loco; **to be ~ about sb/sth** (*inf*) estar loco por algn/algo
creak [kriːk] *vi* crujir; (*hinge etc*) chirriar, rechinar
cream [kriːm] *n* (*of milk*) nata, crema; (*lotion*) crema; (*fig*) flor *f* y nata ▷ *adj* (*colour*) color *m* crema; **whipped ~** nata batida; **cream off** *vt* (*fig: best talents, part of profits*) separar lo mejor de
cream cake *n* pastel *m* de nata
cream cheese *n* queso blanco cremoso
creamy ['kriːmɪ] *adj* cremoso
crease [kriːs] *n* (*fold*) pliegue *m*; (*in trousers*) raya; (*wrinkle*) arruga ▷ *vt* (*fold*) doblar, plegar; (*wrinkle*) arrugar ▷ *vi* (*wrinkle up*) arrugarse
create [kriː'eɪt] *vt* (*also Comput*) crear; (*impression*) dar; (*fuss, noise*) hacer
creation [kriː'eɪʃən] *n* creación *f*
creative [kriː'eɪtɪv] *adj* creativo
creativity [kriːeɪ'tɪvɪtɪ] *n* creatividad *f*
creator [kriː'eɪtəʳ] *n* creador(a) *m(f)*
creature ['kriːtʃəʳ] *n* (*living thing*) criatura; (*animal*) animal *m*; (*insect*) bicho; (*person*) criatura
creature comforts *npl* comodidades *fpl* materiales
crèche, creche [krɛʃ] *n* (*Brit*) guardería (infantil)
credence ['kriːdəns] *n*: **to lend** *or* **give ~ to** creer en, dar crédito a
credentials [krɪ'dɛnʃlz] *npl* credenciales *fpl*; (*letters of reference*) referencias *fpl*
credibility [krɛdɪ'bɪlɪtɪ] *n* credibilidad *f*
credible ['krɛdɪbl] *adj* creíble; (*witness, source*) fidedigno
credit ['krɛdɪt] *n* (*gen*) crédito; (*merit*) honor *m*, mérito ▷ *vt* (*Comm*) abonar; (*believe*) creer, dar crédito a ▷ *adj* crediticio; **to be in ~** (*person, bank account*) tener saldo a favor; **on ~** a crédito; (*inf*) al fiado; **he's a ~ to his family** hace honor a su familia; **to ~ sb with** (*fig*) reconocer a algn el mérito de; *see also* **credits**
credit card *n* tarjeta de crédito
credit crunch *n* crisis *f* crediticia
credit note *n* nota de crédito
creditor ['krɛdɪtəʳ] *n* acreedor(a) *m(f)*
credits ['krɛdɪts] *npl* (*Cine*) títulos *mpl or* rótulos *mpl* de crédito, ficha técnica
creed [kriːd] *n* credo
creek [kriːk] *n* cala, ensenada; (*US*) riachuelo
creep [kriːp] (*pt, pp* **crept** [krɛpt]) *vi* (*animal*) deslizarse; (*plant*) trepar; **to ~ up on sb** acercarse sigilosamente a algn; (*fig: old age etc*) acercarse ▷ *n* (*inf*): **he's a ~** ¡qué lameculos es!; **it gives me the ~s** me da escalofríos

creeper ['kri:pə^r] *n* enredadera
creepy ['kri:pɪ] *adj* (*frightening*) horripilante
cremate [krɪ'meɪt] *vt* incinerar
cremation [krɪ'meɪʃən] *n* incineración *f*, cremación *f*
crematorium [krɛmə'tɔ:rɪəm] (*pl* **crematoria**) [krɛmə'tɔ:rɪə] *n* crematorio
creosote ['krɪəsəut] *n* creosota
crêpe [kreɪp] *n* (*fabric*) crespón *m*; (*also*: **~ rubber**) crep(é) *m*
crêpe bandage *n* (*Brit*) venda elástica
crêpe paper *n* papel *m* crep(é)
crept [krɛpt] *pt, pp of* **creep**
crescent ['krɛsnt] *n* media luna; (*street*) calle *f* (*en forma de semicírculo*)
cress [krɛs] *n* berro
crest [krɛst] *n* (*of bird*) cresta; (*of hill*) cima, cumbre *f*; (*of helmet*) cimera; (*of coat of arms*) blasón *m*
crestfallen ['krɛstfɔ:lən] *adj* alicaído
crevice ['krɛvɪs] *n* grieta, hendedura
crew [kru:] *n* (*of ship etc*) tripulación *f*; (*Cine etc*) equipo; (*gang*) pandilla, banda; (*Mil*) dotación *f*
crew-cut ['kru:kʌt] *n* corte *m* al rape
crew-neck ['kru:nɛk] *n* cuello a la caja
crib [krɪb] *n* cuna ▷ *vt* (*inf*) plagiar; (*Scol*) copiar
crick [krɪk] *n*: **~ in the neck** tortícolis *f inv*
cricket ['krɪkɪt] *n* (*insect*) grillo; (*game*) críquet *m*
cricketer ['krɪkɪtə^r] *n* jugador(a) *m(f)* de críquet
crime [kraɪm] *n* crimen *m*; (*less serious*) delito
criminal ['krɪmɪnl] *n* criminal *m/f*, delincuente *m/f* ▷ *adj* criminal; (*law*) penal
Criminal Investigation Department *n* ≈ Brigada de Investigación Criminal *f* (*Sp*)
crimson ['krɪmzn] *adj* carmesí
cringe [krɪndʒ] *vi* encogerse
crinkle ['krɪŋkl] *vt* arrugar
cripple ['krɪpl] *n* (*inf!*) lisiado(-a), cojo(-a) ▷ *vt* lisiar, mutilar; (*ship, plane*) inutilizar; (*production, exports*) paralizar; **~d with arthritis** paralizado por la artritis
crisis ['kraɪsɪs] (*pl* **crises** ['kraɪsi:z]) *n* crisis *f*
crisp [krɪsp] *adj* fresco; (*toast, snow*) crujiente; (*manner*) seco
crisps [krɪsps] *npl* (*Brit*) patatas *fpl* fritas (chips)
crispy *adj* crujiente
crisscross ['krɪskrɔs] *adj* entrelazado, entrecruzado ▷ *vt* entrecruzar(se)
criterion [kraɪ'tɪərɪən] (*pl* **criteria** [kraɪ'tɪərɪə]) *n* criterio
critic ['krɪtɪk] *n* crítico(-a)
critical ['krɪtɪkl] *adj* (*gen*) crítico; (*illness*) grave; **to be ~ of sb/sth** criticar a algn/algo
critically ['krɪtɪklɪ] *adv* (*speak etc*) en tono crítico; (*ill*) gravemente
criticism ['krɪtɪsɪzm] *n* crítica
criticize ['krɪtɪsaɪz] *vt* criticar
croak [krəuk] *vi* (*frog*) croar; (*raven*) graznar ▷ *n* (*of raven*) graznido
Croat ['krəuæt] *adj, n* = **Croatian**
Croatia [krəu'eɪʃə] *n* Croacia
Croatian [krəu'eɪʃən] *adj, n* croata *m/f* ▷ *n* (*Ling*) croata *m*
crochet ['krəuʃeɪ] *n* ganchillo
crockery ['krɔkərɪ] *n* (*plates, cups etc*) loza, vajilla
crocodile ['krɔkədaɪl] *n* cocodrilo
crocus ['krəukəs] *n* crocus *m*, croco
croft [krɔft] *n* granja pequeña
croissant ['krwasã] *n* croissant *m*, medialuna (*esp LAm*)
crony ['krəunɪ] *n* compinche *m/f*
crook [kruk] *n* (*inf*) ladrón(-ona) *m(f)*; (*of shepherd*) cayado; (*of arm*) pliegue *m*
crooked ['krukɪd] *adj* torcido; (*path*) tortuoso; (*inf*) corrupto
crop [krɔp] *n* (*produce*) cultivo; (*amount produced*) cosecha; (*riding crop*) látigo de montar; (*of bird*) buche *m* ▷ *vt* cortar, recortar; (*animals*: *grass*) pacer; **crop up** *vi* surgir, presentarse
croquet ['krəukeɪ] *n* croquet *m*
cross [krɔs] *n* cruz *f* ▷ *vt* (*street etc*) cruzar, atravesar; (*thwart*: *person*) contrariar, ir contra ▷ *vi*: **the boat ~es from Santander to Plymouth** el barco hace la travesía de Santander a Plymouth ▷ *adj* de mal humor, enojado; **it's a ~ between geography and sociology** es una mezcla de geografía y sociología; **to ~ o.s.** santiguarse; **they've got their lines ~ed** (*fig*) hay un malentendido entre ellos; **to be/get ~ with sb (about sth)** estar enfadado/enfadarse con algn (por algo); **cross off** *vt* tachar; **cross out** *vt* tachar; **cross over** *vi* cruzar
crossbar ['krɔsbɑ:^r] *n* travesaño; (*of bicycle*) barra
crossbow ['krɔsbəu] *n* ballesta
cross-Channel ferry ['krɔs'tʃænl-] *n* transbordador *m* que cruza el Canal de la Mancha
cross-country ['krɔs'kʌntrɪ], **cross-country race** *n* carrera a campo traviesa, cross *m*
cross-dressing [krɔs'drɛsɪŋ] *n* travestismo
cross-examination ['krɔsɪgzæmɪ'neɪʃən] *n* interrogatorio
cross-examine ['krɔsɪg'zæmɪn] *vt* interrogar
cross-eyed ['krɔsaɪd] *adj* bizco
crossfire ['krɔsfaɪə^r] *n* fuego cruzado
crossing ['krɔsɪŋ] *n* (*on road*) cruce *m*; (*Rail*) paso a nivel; (*sea passage*) travesía; (*also*: **pedestrian ~**) paso de peatones
crossing guard *n* (*US*) *persona encargada de ayudar a los niños a cruzar la calle*
crossing point *n* paso; (*at border*) paso fronterizo

cross purposes *npl*: **to be at ~ with sb** tener un malentendido con algn
cross-question ['krɔs'kwɛstʃən] *vt* interrogar
cross-reference ['krɔs'rɛfrəns] *n* remisión *f*
crossroads ['krɔsrəudz] *nsg* cruce *m*; (*fig*) encrucijada
cross section *n* corte *m* transversal; (*of population*) muestra (representativa)
crosswalk ['krɔswɔ:k] *n* (*US*) paso de peatones
crosswind ['krɔswɪnd] *n* viento de costado
crossword ['krɔswə:d] *n* crucigrama *m*
crotch [krɔtʃ] *n* (*of garment*) entrepierna
crotchet ['krɔtʃɪt] *n* (*Brit Mus*) negra
crouch [krautʃ] *vi* agacharse, acurrucarse
crouton ['kru:tɔn] *n* cubito de pan frito
crow [krəu] *n* (*bird*) cuervo; (*of cock*) canto, cacareo ▷ *vi* (*cock*) cantar; (*fig*) jactarse
crowbar ['krəubɑ:ʳ] *n* palanca
crowd [kraud] *n* muchedumbre *f*; (*Sport*) público; (*common herd*) vulgo ▷ *vt* (*gather*) amontonar; (*fill*) llenar ▷ *vi* (*gather*) reunirse; (*pile up*) amontonarse; **~s of people** gran cantidad de gente
crowded ['kraudɪd] *adj* (*full*) atestado; (*well-attended*) concurrido; (*densely populated*) superpoblado
crown [kraun] *n* corona; (*of head*) coronilla; (*of hat*) copa; (*of hill*) cumbre *f*; (*for tooth*) funda ▷ *vt* (*also tooth*) coronar; **and to ~ it all ...** (*fig*) y para colmo *or* remate ...
crown court *n* (*Law*) tribunal *m* superior
crown jewels *npl* joyas *fpl* reales
crown prince *n* príncipe *m* heredero
crow's feet ['krəuzfi:t] *npl* patas *fpl* de gallo
crucial ['kru:ʃl] *adj* crucial, decisivo; **his approval is ~ to the success of the project** su aprobación es crucial para el éxito del proyecto
crucifix ['kru:sɪfɪks] *n* crucifijo
crucifixion [kru:sɪ'fɪkʃən] *n* crucifixión *f*
crucify ['kru:sɪfaɪ] *vt* crucificar; (*fig*) martirizar
crude [kru:d] *adj* (*materials*) bruto; (*fig: basic*) tosco; (*: vulgar*) ordinario ▷ *n* (*also*: **~ oil**) (petróleo) crudo
cruel ['kruəl] *adj* cruel
cruelty ['kruəltɪ] *n* crueldad *f*
cruise [kru:z] *n* crucero ▷ *vi* (*ship*) navegar; (*holidaymakers*) hacer un crucero; (*car*) ir a velocidad constante
cruiser ['kru:zəʳ] *n* crucero
crumb [krʌm] *n* miga, migaja
crumble ['krʌmbl] *vt* desmenuzar ▷ *vi* (*gen*) desmenuzarse; (*building*) desmoronarse
crumbly ['krʌmblɪ] *adj* desmenuzable
crumpet ['krʌmpɪt] *n* ≈ bollo para tostar
crumple ['krʌmpl] *vt* (*paper*) estrujar; (*material*) arrugar
crunch [krʌntʃ] *vt* (*with teeth*) mascar; (*underfoot*) hacer crujir ▷ *n* (*fig*) hora de la verdad
crunchy ['krʌntʃɪ] *adj* crujiente
crusade [kru:'seɪd] *n* cruzada ▷ *vi*: **to ~ for/against** (*fig*) hacer una campaña en pro de/en contra de
crush [krʌʃ] *n* (*crowd*) aglomeración *f* ▷ *vt* (*gen*) aplastar; (*paper*) estrujar; (*cloth*) arrugar; (*grind, break up: garlic, ice*) picar; (*fruit*) exprimir; (*grapes*) exprimir, prensar; (*opposition*) aplastar; (*hopes*) destruir; **to have a ~ on sb** estar enamorado de algn
crushing ['krʌʃɪŋ] *adj* aplastante; (*burden*) agobiante
crust [krʌst] *n* corteza
crusty ['krʌstɪ] *adj* (*bread*) crujiente; (*person*) de mal carácter; (*remark*) brusco
crutch [krʌtʃ] *n* (*Med*) muleta; (*support*) apoyo
crux [krʌks] *n*: **the ~** lo esencial, el quid
cry [kraɪ] *vi* llorar; (*shout: also*: **~ out**) gritar ▷ *n* grito; (*of animal*) aullido; (*weep*): **she had a good ~** lloró a lágrima viva; **what are you ~ing about?** ¿por qué lloras?; **to ~ for help** pedir socorro a voces; **it's a far ~ from ...** (*fig*) dista mucho de ...; **cry off** *vi* retirarse; **cry out** *vi* (*call out, shout*) lanzar un grito, echar un grito ▷ *vt* gritar
cryptic ['krɪptɪk] *adj* enigmático
crystal ['krɪstl] *n* cristal *m*
crystal-clear ['krɪstl'klɪəʳ] *adj* claro como el agua; (*fig*) cristalino
CS gas *n* (*Brit*) gas *m* lacrimógeno
cub [kʌb] *n* cachorro; (*also*: **~ scout**) niño explorador
Cuba ['kju:bə] *n* Cuba
Cuban ['kju:bən] *adj, n* cubano(-a) *m(f)*
cubbyhole ['kʌbɪhəul] *n* cuchitril *m*
cube [kju:b] *n* cubo; (*of sugar*) terrón *m* ▷ *vt* (*Math*) elevar al cubo
cubic ['kju:bɪk] *adj* cúbico; **~ capacity** (*Aut*) capacidad *f* cúbica
cubicle ['kju:bɪkl] *n* (*at pool*) caseta; (*for bed*) cubículo
cuckoo ['kuku:] *n* cuco
cuckoo clock *n* reloj *m* de cuco
cucumber ['kju:kʌmbəʳ] *n* pepino
cuddle ['kʌdl] *vt* abrazar ▷ *vi* abrazarse
cue [kju:] *n* (*snooker cue*) taco; (*Theat etc*) entrada
cuff [kʌf] *n* (*Brit: of shirt, coat etc*) puño; (*US: of trousers*) vuelta; (*blow*) bofetada ▷ *vt* bofetear; **off the ~** *adv* improvisado
cufflinks ['kʌflɪŋks] *npl* gemelos *mpl*
cuisine [kwɪ'zi:n] *n* cocina
cul-de-sac ['kʌldəsæk] *n* callejón *m* sin salida
cull [kʌl] *vt* (*select*) entresacar; (*kill selectively: animals*) matar selectivamente ▷ *n* matanza selectiva; **seal ~** matanza selectiva de focas
culminate ['kʌlmɪneɪt] *vi*: **to ~ in** culminar en
culmination [kʌlmɪ'neɪʃən] *n* culminación *f*, colmo
culottes [ku:'lɔts] *npl* falda *f* pantalón
culprit ['kʌlprɪt] *n* culpable *m/f*

cult [kʌlt] *n* culto; **a ~ figure** un ídolo
cultivate ['kʌltɪveɪt] *vt* (*also fig*) cultivar
cultivation [kʌltɪ'veɪʃən] *n* cultivo; (*fig*) cultura
cultural ['kʌltʃərəl] *adj* cultural
culture ['kʌltʃəʳ] *n* (*also fig*) cultura; (*Biol*) cultivo
cultured ['kʌltʃəd] *adj* culto
cumbersome ['kʌmbəsəm] *adj* voluminoso
cumin ['kʌmɪn] *n* (*spice*) comino
cunning ['kʌnɪŋ] *n* astucia ▷ *adj* astuto; (*clever*: *device, idea*) ingenioso
cup [kʌp] *n* taza; (*prize, event*) copa; **a ~ of tea** una taza de té
cupboard ['kʌbəd] *n* armario, placar(d) *m* (*LAm*); (*in kitchen*) alacena
cup final *n* (*Football*) final *f* de copa
cuppa ['kʌpa] *n* (*Brit inf*) (taza de) té *m*
cup-tie ['kʌptaɪ] *n* (*Brit*) partido de copa
curate ['kjuərɪt] *n* coadjutor *m*
curator [kjuə'reɪtəʳ] *n* director(a) *m(f)*
curb [kə:b] *vt* refrenar; (*powers, spending*) limitar ▷ *n* freno; (*US*: *kerb*) bordillo
curdle ['kə:dl] *vi* cuajarse
cure [kjuəʳ] *vt* curar ▷ *n* cura, curación *f*; (*fig*: *solution*) remedio; **to be ~d of sth** curarse de algo; **to take a ~** tomar un remedio
curfew ['kə:fju:] *n* toque *m* de queda
curio ['kjuərɪəu] *n* curiosidad *f*
curiosity [kjuərɪ'ɔsɪtɪ] *n* curiosidad *f*
curious ['kjuərɪəs] *adj* curioso; **I'm ~ about him** me intriga
curl [kə:l] *n* rizo; (*of smoke etc*) espiral *f*, voluta ▷ *vt* (*hair*) rizar; (*paper*) arrollar; (*lip*) fruncir ▷ *vi* rizarse; arrollarse; **curl up** *vi* arrollarse; (*person*) hacerse un ovillo; (*inf*) morirse de risa
curler ['kə:ləʳ] *n* bigudí *m*, rulo
curly ['kə:lɪ] *adj* rizado
currant ['kʌrnt] *n* pasa; (*black, red*) grosella
currency ['kʌrnsɪ] *n* moneda; **to gain ~** (*fig*) difundirse
current ['kʌrnt] *n* corriente *f* ▷ *adj* actual; **direct/alternating ~** corriente directa/alterna; **the ~ issue of a magazine** el último número de una revista; **in ~ use** de uso corriente
current account *n* (*Brit*) cuenta corriente
current affairs *npl* (noticias *fpl* de) actualidad *f*
currently ['kʌrntlɪ] *adv* actualmente
curriculum (*pl* **curriculums** *or* **curricula**) [kə'rɪkjuləm, -lə] *n* plan *m* de estudios
curriculum vitae [-'vi:taɪ] *n* currículum *m* (vitae)
curry ['kʌrɪ] *n* curry *m* ▷ *vt*: **to ~ favour with** buscar el favor de
curry powder *n* curry *m* en polvo
curse [kə:s] *vi* echar pestes, soltar palabrotas ▷ *vt* maldecir ▷ *n* maldición *f*; (*swearword*) palabrota, taco
cursor ['kə:səʳ] *n* (*Comput*) cursor *m*
cursory ['kə:sərɪ] *adj* rápido, superficial
curt [kə:t] *adj* seco
curtail [kə:'teɪl] *vt* (*cut short*) acortar; (*restrict*) restringir
curtain ['kə:tn] *n* cortina; (*Theat*) telón *m*; **to draw the ~s** (*together*) cerrar las cortinas; (*apart*) abrir las cortinas
curve [kə:v] *n* curva ▷ *vi* (*road*) hacer una curva; (*line etc*) curvarse
curved [kə:vd] *adj* curvo
cushion ['kuʃən] *n* cojín *m*; (*Snooker*) banda ▷ *vt* (*seat*) acolchar; (*shock*) amortiguar
cushy ['kuʃɪ] *adj* (*inf*): **a ~ job** un chollo; **to have a ~ time** tener la vida arreglada
custard ['kʌstəd] *n* (*for pouring*) natillas *fpl*
custodial sentence [kʌs'təudɪəl-] *n* pena de prisión
custody ['kʌstədɪ] *n* custodia; **to take sb into ~** detener a algn; **in the ~ of** al cuidado *or* cargo de
custom ['kʌstəm] *n* costumbre *f*; (*Comm*) clientela; *see also* **customs**
customary ['kʌstəmərɪ] *adj* acostumbrado; **it is ~ to do ...** es la costumbre hacer ...
customer ['kʌstəməʳ] *n* cliente *m/f*; **he's an awkward ~** (*inf*) es un tipo difícil
customized ['kʌstəmaɪzd] *adj* (*car etc*) hecho a encargo
custom-made ['kʌstəm'meɪd] *adj* hecho a la medida
customs ['kʌstəmz] *npl* aduana *sg*; **to go through (the) ~** pasar la aduana
customs officer *n* aduanero(-a), funcionario(-a) de aduanas
cut [kʌt] (*pt, pp* **cut**) *vt* cortar; (*price*) rebajar; (*record*) grabar; (*reduce*) reducir; (*inf*: *avoid*: *class, lecture*) fumarse, faltar a ▷ *vi* cortar; (*intersect*) cruzarse ▷ *n* corte *m*; (*in skin*) corte, cortadura; (*with sword*) tajo; (*of knife*) cuchillada; (*in salary etc*) rebaja; (*in spending*) reducción *f*, recorte *m*; (*slice of meat*) tajada; **to ~ one's finger** cortarse un dedo; **to get one's hair ~** cortarse el pelo; **to ~ and paste** (*Comput*) cortar y pegar; **to ~ sb dead** negarle el saludo *or* cortarle (*LAm*) a algn; **it ~s both ways** (*fig*) tiene doble filo; **to ~ a tooth** echar un diente; **power ~** (*Brit*) apagón *m*; **cut back** *vt* (*plants*) podar; (*production, expenditure*) reducir; **cut down** *vt* (*tree*) cortar, derribar; (*consumption, expenses*) reducir; **to ~ sb down to size** (*fig*) bajarle los humos a algn; **cut in** *vi*: **to ~ in (on)** (*interrupt*: *conversation*) interrumpir, intervenir (en); (*Aut*) cerrar el paso (a); **cut off** *vt* cortar; (*fig*) aislar; (*troops*) cercar; **we've been ~ off** (*Tel*) nos han cortado la comunicación; **cut out** *vt* (*shape*) recortar; (*delete*) suprimir; **cut up** *vt* cortar (en pedazos); (*chop*: *food*) trinchar, cortar
cutback ['kʌtbæk] *n* reducción *f*
cute [kju:t] *adj* lindo, mono; (*shrewd*) listo
cuticle ['kju:tɪkl] *n* cutícula
cutlery ['kʌtlərɪ] *n* cubiertos *mpl*
cutlet ['kʌtlɪt] *n* chuleta

cutout ['kʌtaut] *n* (*cardboard cutout*) recortable *m*
cut-price ['kʌt'praɪs], **cut-rate** (*US*) ['kʌt'reɪt] *adj* a precio reducido
cutting ['kʌtɪŋ] *adj* (*gen*) cortante; (*remark*) mordaz ▷ *n* (Brit: *from newspaper*) recorte *m*; (*from plant*) esqueje *m*; (*Rail*) desmonte *m*; (*Cine*) montaje *m*
cutting edge *n* (*of knife*) filo; (*fig*) vanguardia; **a country on** *or* **at the ~ of space technology** un país puntero en tecnología del espacio
CV *n abbr* = **curriculum vitae**
cwt. *abbr* = **hundredweight**
cyanide ['saɪənaɪd] *n* cianuro
cybercafé ['saɪbəˌkæfeɪ] *n* cibercafé *m*
cyberspace ['saɪbəspeɪs] *n* ciberespacio
cyberterrorism ['saɪbətɛrərɪzəm] *n* ciberterrorismo *m*
cycle ['saɪkl] *n* ciclo; (*bicycle*) bicicleta ▷ *vi* ir en bicicleta
cycle hire *n* alquiler *m* de bicicletas
cycle lane *n* carril *m* de bicicleta, carril *m* bici
cycle path *n* carril-bici *m*
cycling ['saɪklɪŋ] *n* ciclismo
cyclist ['saɪklɪst] *n* ciclista *m/f*
cyclone ['saɪkləun] *n* ciclón *m*
cygnet ['sɪgnɪt] *n* pollo de cisne
cylinder ['sɪlɪndəʳ] *n* cilindro
cylinder-head gasket *n* junta de culata
cymbals ['sɪmblz] *npl* platillos *mpl*, címbalos *mpl*
cynic ['sɪnɪk] *n* cínico(-a)
cynical ['sɪnɪkl] *adj* cínico
cynicism ['sɪnɪsɪzəm] *n* cinismo
Cypriot ['sɪprɪət] *adj, n* chipriota *m/f*
Cyprus ['saɪprəs] *n* Chipre *f*
cyst [sɪst] *n* quiste *m*
cystitis [sɪs'taɪtɪs] *n* cistitis *f*
czar [zɑːʳ] *n* zar *m*
Czech [tʃɛk] *adj* checo ▷ *n* checo(-a); (*Ling*) checo; **the ~ Republic** la República Checa

d

D, d [diː] *n* (*letter*) D, d; (*Mus*): **D** re *m*; **D for David**, (*US*) **D for Dog** D de Dolores
D *abbr* (*US Pol*) = **democrat**; **democratic**
DA *n abbr* (*US*) = **district attorney**
dab [dæb] *vt*: **to ~ ointment onto a wound** aplicar pomada sobre una herida; **to ~ with paint** dar unos toques de pintura ▷ *n* (*light stroke*) toque *m*; (*small amount*) pizca
dabble ['dæbl] *vi*: **to ~ in** hacer por afición
dad [dæd], **daddy** ['dædɪ] *n* papá *m*
daddy-long-legs [dædɪ'lɔŋlɛgz] *n* típula
daffodil ['dæfədɪl] *n* narciso
daft [dɑːft] *adj* tonto
dagger ['dægəʳ] *n* puñal *m*, daga; **to look ~s at sb** fulminar a algn con la mirada
daily ['deɪlɪ] *adj* diario, cotidiano ▷ *n* (*paper*) diario; (*domestic help*) asistenta ▷ *adv* todos los días, cada día; **twice ~** dos veces al día
dainty ['deɪntɪ] *adj* delicado; (*tasteful*) elegante
dairy ['dɛərɪ] *n* (*shop*) lechería; (*on farm*) vaquería; (*products*) lácteos *pl* ▷ *adj* (*cow etc*) lechero
dairy produce *n* productos *mpl* lácteos
dais ['deɪɪs] *n* estrado
daisy ['deɪzɪ] *n* margarita
dale [deɪl] *n* valle *m*
dally ['dælɪ] *vi* entretenerse
dam [dæm] *n* presa; (*reservoir*) embalse ▷ *vt* embalsar
damage ['dæmɪdʒ] *n* daño; (*fig*) perjuicio; (*to machine*) avería ▷ *vt* dañar; perjudicar;

averiar; **~ to property** daños materiales; **damages** *npl* (*Law*) daños y perjuicios; **to pay £5000 in ~s** pagar £5000 por daños y perjuicios

damaging ['dæmɪdʒɪŋ] *adj*: **~ (to)** perjudicial (a)

dame [deɪm] *n* (*title*) dama; (*US inf*) tía; (*Theat*) vieja; *see also* **pantomime**

damn [dæm] *vt* condenar; (*curse*) maldecir ▷ *n* (*inf*): **I don't give a ~** me importa un pito ▷ *adj* (*inf*: *also*: **~ed**) maldito, fregado (*LAm*); **~ (it)!** ¡maldito sea!

damnation [dæm'neɪʃən] *n* (*Rel*) condenación *f* ▷ *excl* (*inf*) ¡maldición!, ¡maldito sea!

damning ['dæmɪŋ] *adj* (*evidence*) irrecusable

damp [dæmp] *adj* húmedo, mojado ▷ *n* humedad *f* ▷ *vt* (*also*: **~en**: *cloth, rag*) mojar; (*enthusiasm*) enfriar

damper ['dæmpəʳ] *n* (*Mus*) sordina; (*of fire*) regulador *m* de tiro; **to put a ~ on things** ser un jarro de agua fría

dampness ['dæmpnɪs] *n* humedad *f*

damson ['dæmzən] *n* ciruela damascena

dance [dɑːns] *n* baile *m* ▷ *vi* bailar; **to ~ about** saltar

dance floor *n* pista *f* de baile

dance hall *n* salón *m* de baile

dancer ['dɑːnsəʳ] *n* bailador(a) *m(f)*; (*professional*) bailarín(-ina) *m(f)*

dancing ['dɑːnsɪŋ] *n* baile *m*

dandelion ['dændɪlaɪən] *n* diente *m* de león

dandruff ['dændrəf] *n* caspa

D & T (*Brit*: *Scol*) *n abbr* (= *design and technology*) diseño y pretecnología

Dane [deɪn] *n* danés(-esa) *m(f)*

danger ['deɪndʒəʳ] *n* peligro; (*risk*) riesgo; **~!** (*on sign*) ¡peligro!; **to be in ~ of** correr riesgo de; **out of ~** fuera de peligro

danger list *n* (*Med*): **to be on the ~** estar grave

dangerous ['deɪndʒərəs] *adj* peligroso

dangle ['dæŋgl] *vt* colgar ▷ *vi* pender, estar colgado

Danish ['deɪnɪʃ] *adj* danés(-esa) ▷ *n* (*Ling*) danés *m*

dapper ['dæpəʳ] *adj* pulcro, apuesto

dare [dɛəʳ] *vt*: **to ~ sb to do** desafiar a algn a hacer ▷ *vi*: **to ~ (to) do sth** atreverse a hacer algo; **I ~ say** (*I suppose*) puede ser, a lo mejor; **I ~ say he'll turn up** puede ser que *or* quizás venga; **I ~n't tell him** no me atrevo a decírselo

daredevil ['dɛədɛvl] *n* temerario(-a), atrevido(-a)

daring ['dɛərɪŋ] *adj* (*person*) osado; (*plan, escape*) atrevido ▷ *n* atrevimiento, osadía

dark [dɑːk] *adj* oscuro; (*hair, complexion*) moreno; (*fig*: *cheerless*) triste, sombrío ▷ *n* (*gen*) oscuridad *f*; (*night*) tinieblas *fpl*; **~ chocolate** chocolate *m* amargo; **in the ~** a oscuras; **it is/is getting ~** es de noche/está oscureciendo; **in the ~ about** (*fig*) ignorante de; **after ~** después del anochecer

darken ['dɑːkn] *vt* oscurecer; (*colour*) hacer más oscuro ▷ *vi* oscurecerse; (*cloud over*) nublarse

dark glasses *npl* gafas *fpl* oscuras

dark horse *n* (*fig*) incógnita

darkness ['dɑːknɪs] *n* (*in room*) oscuridad *f*; (*night*) tinieblas *fpl*

darkroom ['dɑːkrum] *n* cuarto oscuro

darling ['dɑːlɪŋ] *adj, n* querido(-a) *m(f)*

darn [dɑːn] *vt* zurcir

dart [dɑːt] *n* dardo; (*in sewing*) pinza ▷ *vi* precipitarse; **to ~ away/along** salir/marchar disparado

dartboard ['dɑːtbɔːd] *n* diana

darts [dɑːts] *n* dardos *mpl*

dash [dæʃ] *n* (*small quantity*: *of liquid*) gota, chorrito; (: *of solid*) pizca; (*sign*) guión *m*; (: *long*) raya ▷ *vt* (*break*) romper, estrellar; (*hopes*) defraudar ▷ *vi* precipitarse, ir de prisa; **a ~ of soda** un poco *or* chorrito de sifón *or* soda; **dash away, dash off** *vi* marcharse apresuradamente

dashboard ['dæʃbɔːd] *n* (*Aut*) salpicadero

dashing ['dæʃɪŋ] *adj* gallardo

data ['deɪtə] *npl* datos *mpl*

database ['deɪtəbeɪs] *n* base *f* de datos

data processing *n* proceso *or* procesamiento de datos

date [deɪt] *n* (*day*) fecha; (*with friend*) cita; (*fruit*) dátil *m* ▷ *vt* fechar; (*inf*: *girl etc*) salir con; **what's the ~ today?** ¿qué fecha es hoy?; **~ of birth** fecha de nacimiento; **closing ~** fecha tope; **to ~** *adv* hasta la fecha; **out of ~** pasado de moda; **up to ~** moderno; puesto al día; **to bring up to ~** (*correspondence, information*) poner al día; (*method*) actualizar; **to bring sb up to ~** poner a algn al corriente; **letter ~d 5th July** *or* (*US*) **July 5th** carta fechada el 5 de julio

dated ['deɪtɪd] *adj* anticuado

daub [dɔːb] *vt* embadurnar

daughter ['dɔːtəʳ] *n* hija

daughter-in-law ['dɔːtərɪnlɔː] *n* nuera, hija política

daunting ['dɔːntɪŋ] *adj* desalentador(-a)

dawdle ['dɔːdl] *vi* (*waste time*) perder el tiempo; (*go slowly*) andar muy despacio; **to ~ over one's work** trabajar muy despacio

dawn [dɔːn] *n* alba, amanecer *m*; (*fig*) nacimiento ▷ *vi* amanecer; (*fig*): **it ~ed on him that ...** cayó en la cuenta de que ...; **at ~** al amanecer; **from ~ to dusk** de sol a sol

day [deɪ] *n* día *m*; (*working day*) jornada; **the ~ before** el día anterior; **the ~ after tomorrow** pasado mañana; **the ~ before yesterday** anteayer, antes de ayer; **the ~ after, the following ~** el día siguiente; **by ~** de día; **~ by ~** día a día; **(on) the ~ that ...** el día que ...; **to work an eight-hour ~** trabajar ocho horas diarias *or* al día; **he**

works eight hours a ~ trabaja ocho horas al día; **paid by the ~** pagado por día; **these ~s, in the present ~** hoy en día

daybreak ['deɪbreɪk] *n* amanecer *m*

day-care centre ['deɪkɛə-] *n* centro de día; (*for children*) guardería infantil

daydream ['deɪdri:m] *n* ensueño ▷ *vi* soñar despierto

daylight ['deɪlaɪt] *n* luz *f* (del día)

daylight robbery *n*: **it's ~!** (*fig, inf*) ¡es un robo descarado!

Daylight Saving Time *n* (*US*) hora de verano

day return, day return ticket *n* (*Brit*) billete *m* de ida y vuelta (en un día)

daytime ['deɪtaɪm] *n* día *m*

day-to-day ['deɪtə'deɪ] *adj* cotidiano, diario; (*expenses*) diario; **on a ~ basis** día por día

day trip *n* excursión *f* (de un día)

day tripper *n* excursionista *m/f*

daze [deɪz] *vt* (*stun*) aturdir ▷ *n*: **in a ~** aturdido

dazed [deɪzd] *adj* aturdido

dazzle ['dæzl] *vt* deslumbrar

dazzling ['dæzlɪŋ] *adj* (*light, smile*) deslumbrante; (*colour*) fuerte

DC *abbr* (*Elec*) = **direct current**

D-day ['di:deɪ] *n* (*fig*) día *m* clave

DEA *n abbr* (*US*: = *Drug Enforcement Administration*) *brigada especial dedicada a la lucha contra el tráfico de estupefacientes*

dead [dɛd] *adj* muerto; (*limb*) dormido; (*battery*) agotado ▷ *adv* (*completely*) totalmente; (*exactly*) justo; **he was ~ on arrival** ingresó cadáver; **to shoot sb ~** matar a algn a tiros; **~ tired** muerto (de cansancio); **to stop ~** parar en seco; **the line has gone ~** (*Tel*) se ha cortado la línea; **the ~** *npl* los muertos

deaden ['dɛdn] *vt* (*blow, sound*) amortiguar; (*pain*) calmar, aliviar

dead end *n* callejón *m* sin salida

dead-end ['dɛdɛnd] *adj*: **a ~ job** un trabajo sin porvenir

dead heat *n* (*Sport*) empate *m*

deadline ['dɛdlaɪn] *n* fecha tope; **to work to a ~** trabajar con una fecha tope

deadlock ['dɛdlɔk] *n* punto muerto

dead loss *n* (*inf*): **to be a ~** (*person*) ser un inútil; (*thing*) ser una birria

deadly ['dɛdlɪ] *adj* mortal, fatal; **~ dull** aburridísimo

deadpan ['dɛdpæn] *adj* sin expresión

Dead Sea *n*: **the ~** el Mar Muerto

deaf [dɛf] *adj* sordo; **to turn a ~ ear to sth** hacer oídos sordos a algo

deaf-and-dumb ['dɛfən'dʌm] (*inf!*) *adj* (*person*) sordomudo; (*alphabet*) para sordomudos

deafen ['dɛfn] *vt* ensordecer

deafening ['dɛfnɪŋ] *adj* ensordecedor(-a)

deaf-mute ['dɛfmju:t] *n* (*inf!*) sordomudo(-a)

deafness ['dɛfnɪs] *n* sordera

deal [di:l] *n* (*agreement*) pacto, convenio; (*business*) negocio, transacción *f*; (*Cards*) reparto ▷ *vt* (*pt, pp* **dealt**) (*gen*) dar; (*card*) repartir; **a great ~ (of)** bastante, mucho; **it's a ~!** (*inf*) ¡trato hecho!, ¡de acuerdo!; **to do a ~ with sb** hacer un trato con algn; **he got a bad/fair ~ from them** le trataron mal/bien; **deal in** *vt fus* tratar en, comerciar en; **deal with** *vt fus* (*people*) tratar con; (*problem*) ocuparse de; (*subject*) tratar de

dealer ['di:ləʳ] *n* comerciante *m/f*; (*Cards*) mano *f*

dealership ['di:ləʃɪp] *n* concesionario

dealings ['di:lɪŋz] *npl* (*Comm*) transacciones *fpl*; (*relations*) relaciones *fpl*

dealt [dɛlt] *pt, pp of* **deal**

dean [di:n] *n* (*Rel*) deán *m*; (*Scol*) decano(-a)

dear [dɪəʳ] *adj* querido; (*expensive*) caro ▷ *n*: **my ~** querido(-a); **~ me!** ¡Dios mío!; **D~ Sir/Madam** (*in letter*) Muy señor mío, Estimado señor/Estimada señora, De mi/nuestra (mayor) consideración (*esp LAm*); **D~ Mr/Mrs X** Estimado(-a) señor(a) X

dearly ['dɪəlɪ] *adv* (*love*) mucho; (*pay*) caro

dearth [də:θ] *n* (*of food, resources, money*) escasez *f*

death [dɛθ] *n* muerte *f*

deathbed ['dɛθbɛd] *n* lecho de muerte

death certificate *n* partida de defunción

deathly ['dɛθlɪ] *adj* mortal; (*silence*) profundo

death penalty *n* pena de muerte

death rate *n* tasa de mortalidad

death row *n*: **to be on ~** (*US*) estar condenado a muerte

death sentence *n* condena a muerte

death squad *n* escuadrón *m* de la muerte

death trap ['dɛθtræp] *n* lugar *m* (*or* vehículo *etc*) muy peligroso

debacle [deɪ'bɑ:kl] *n* desastre *m*, catástrofe *f*

debase [dɪ'beɪs] *vt* degradar

debatable [dɪ'beɪtəbl] *adj* discutible; **it is ~ whether ...** es discutible si ...

debate [dɪ'beɪt] *n* debate *m* ▷ *vt* discutir

debauchery [dɪ'bɔ:tʃərɪ] *n* libertinaje *m*

debenture [dɪ'bɛntʃəʳ] *n* (*Comm*) bono, obligación *f*

debilitating [dɪ'bɪlɪteɪtɪŋ] *adj* (*illness etc*) debilitante

debit ['dɛbɪt] *n* debe *m* ▷ *vt*: **to ~ a sum to sb** *or* **to sb's account** cargar una suma en cuenta a algn

debit card *n* tarjeta *f* de débito

debrief [di:'bri:f] *vt* hacer dar parte

debriefing [di:'bri:fɪŋ] *n* relación *f* (de un informe)

debris ['dɛbri:] *n* escombros *mpl*

debt [dɛt] *n* deuda; **to be in ~** tener deudas; **~s of £5000** deudas de cinco mil libras; **bad ~** deuda incobrable

debt collector *n* cobrador(a) *m(f)* de deudas

debtor ['dɛtəʳ] *n* deudor(a) *m(f)*

debug [di:'bʌg] *vt* (*Comput*) depurar, limpiar

d

debunk [di:ˈbʌŋk] *vt* (*inf: theory*) desprestigiar, desacreditar; (*claim*) desacreditar; (*person, institution*) desenmascarar
début [ˈdeɪbju:] *n* presentación *f*
Dec. *abbr* (= *December*) dic
decade [ˈdɛkeɪd] *n* década, decenio
decadence [ˈdɛkədəns] *n* decadencia
decadent [ˈdɛkədənt] *adj* decadente
de-caff [ˈdi:kæf] *n* (*inf*) descafeinado
decaffeinated [dɪˈkæfɪneɪtɪd] *adj* descafeinado
decanter [dɪˈkæntəʳ] *n* jarra, decantador *m*
decathlon [dɪˈkæθlən] *n* decatlón *m*
decay [dɪˈkeɪ] *n* (*fig*) decadencia; (*of building*) desmoronamiento; (*of tooth*) caries *f inv* ▷ *vi* (*rot*) pudrirse; (*fig*) decaer
deceased [dɪˈsi:st] *n*: **the ~** el/la difunto(-a) ▷ *adj* difunto
deceit [dɪˈsi:t] *n* engaño
deceitful [dɪˈsi:tful] *adj* engañoso
deceive [dɪˈsi:v] *vt* engañar
December [dɪˈsɛmbəʳ] *n* diciembre *m*; *see also* **July**
decency [ˈdi:sənsɪ] *n* decencia
decent [ˈdi:sənt] *adj* (*proper*) decente; (*person*) amable, bueno
deception [dɪˈsɛpʃən] *n* engaño
deceptive [dɪˈsɛptɪv] *adj* engañoso
decibel [ˈdɛsɪbɛl] *n* decibel(io) *m*
decide [dɪˈsaɪd] *vt* (*person*) decidir; (*question, argument*) resolver ▷ *vi* decidir; **to ~ to do/that** decidir hacer/que; **to ~ on sth** tomar una decisión sobre algo; **to ~ against doing sth** decidir en contra de hacer algo
decided [dɪˈsaɪdɪd] *adj* (*resolute*) decidido; (*clear, definite*) indudable
decidedly [dɪˈsaɪdɪdlɪ] *adv* decididamente
deciduous [dɪˈsɪdjuəs] *adj* de hoja caduca
decimal [ˈdɛsɪməl] *adj* decimal ▷ *n* decimal *f*; **to three ~ places** con tres cifras decimales
decimal point *n* coma decimal
decipher [dɪˈsaɪfəʳ] *vt* descifrar
decision [dɪˈsɪʒən] *n* decisión *f*; **to make a ~** tomar una decisión
decisive [dɪˈsaɪsɪv] *adj* (*influence*) decisivo; (*manner, person*) decidido; (*reply*) tajante
deck [dɛk] *n* (*Naut*) cubierta; (*of bus*) piso; (*of cards*) baraja; **record ~** platina; **to go up on ~** subir a (la) cubierta; **below ~** en la bodega
deckchair [ˈdɛktʃɛəʳ] *n* tumbona
declaration [dɛkləˈreɪʃən] *n* declaración *f*
declare [dɪˈklɛəʳ] *vt* (*gen*) declarar
decline [dɪˈklaɪn] *n* decaimiento, decadencia; (*lessening*) disminución *f* ▷ *vt* rehusar ▷ *vi* (*person, business*) decaer; (*strength*) disminuir; **~ in living standards** disminución *f* del nivel de vida; **to ~ to do sth** rehusar hacer algo
decoder [di:ˈkəudəʳ] *n* (*Comput, TV*) de(s)codificador *m*
decompose [di:kəmˈpəuz] *vi* descomponerse
decomposition [di:kɔmpəˈzɪʃən] *n* descomposición *f*
decompression [di:kəmˈprɛʃən] *n* descompresión *f*
decongestant [di:kənˈdʒɛstənt] *n* descongestionante *m*
decontaminate [di:kənˈtæmɪneɪt] *vt* descontaminar
décor [ˈdeɪkɔ:ʳ] *n* decoración *f*; (*Theat*) decorado
decorate [ˈdɛkəreɪt] *vt* (*paint*) pintar; (*paper*) empapelar; (*adorn*): **to ~ (with)** adornar (de), decorar (de)
decoration [dɛkəˈreɪʃən] *n* adorno; (*act*) decoración *f*; (*medal*) condecoración *f*
decorator [ˈdɛkəreɪtəʳ] *n* (*workman*) pintor *m* decorador
decoy [ˈdi:kɔɪ] *n* señuelo; **police ~** trampa *or* señuelo policial
decrease [*n* ˈdi:kri:s] *n* disminución *f* ▷ *vt* [dɪˈkri:s] disminuir, reducir ▷ *vi* reducirse; **to be on the ~** ir disminuyendo
decree [dɪˈkri:] *n* decreto ▷ *vt*: **to ~ (that)** decretar (que); **~ absolute/nisi** sentencia absoluta/provisional de divorcio
decrepit [dɪˈkrɛpɪt] *adj* (*person*) decrépito; (*building*) ruinoso
dedicate [ˈdɛdɪkeɪt] *vt* dedicar
dedicated [ˈdɛdɪkeɪtɪd] *adj* dedicado; (*Comput*) especializado; **~ word processor** procesador *m* de textos especializado *or* dedicado
dedication [dɛdɪˈkeɪʃən] *n* (*devotion*) dedicación *f*; (*in book*) dedicatoria
deduce [dɪˈdju:s] *vt* deducir
deduct [dɪˈdʌkt] *vt* restar; (*from wage etc*) descontar, deducir
deduction [dɪˈdʌkʃən] *n* (*amount deducted*) descuento; (*conclusion*) deducción *f*, conclusión *f*
deed [di:d] *n* hecho, acto; (*feat*) hazaña; (*Law*) escritura; **~ of covenant** escritura de contrato
deem [di:m] *vt* (*formal*) juzgar, considerar; **to ~ it wise to do** considerar prudente hacer
deep [di:p] *adj* profundo; (*voice*) bajo; (*breath*) profundo, a pleno pulmón ▷ *adv*: **the spectators stood 20 ~** los espectadores se formaron de 20 en fondo; **to be four metres ~** tener cuatro metros de profundidad
deepen [ˈdi:pn] *vt* ahondar, profundizar ▷ *vi* (*darkness*) intensificarse
deep-freeze [ˈdi:pˈfri:z] *n* arcón *m* congelador
deep-fry [ˈdi:pˈfraɪ] *vt* freír en aceite abundante
deeply [ˈdi:plɪ] *adv* (*breathe*) profundamente, a pleno pulmón; (*interested, moved, grateful*) profundamente, hondamente; **to regret sth ~** sentir algo profundamente
deep-rooted [ˈdi:pˈru:tɪd] *adj* (*prejudice, habit*) profundamente arraigado; (*affection*) profundo

deep-sea ['di:p'si:] *adj*: **~ diver** buzo; **~ diving** buceo de altura
deep-seated ['di:p'si:tɪd] *adj* (*beliefs*) (profundamente) arraigado
deer (*pl* **deer**) [dɪəʳ] *n* ciervo
deface [dɪ'feɪs] *vt* desfigurar, mutilar
defamation [dɛfə'meɪʃən] *n* difamación *f*
default [dɪ'fɔ:lt] *vi* faltar al pago; (*Sport*) no presentarse, no comparecer ▷ *n* (*Comput*) defecto; **by ~** (*Law*) en rebeldía; (*Sport*) por incomparecencia; **to ~ on a debt** dejar de pagar una deuda
defeat [dɪ'fi:t] *n* derrota ▷ *vt* derrotar, vencer; (*fig*: *efforts*) frustrar
defecate ['dɛfəkeɪt] *vi* defecar
defect ['di:fɛkt] *n* defecto ▷ *vi* [dɪ'fɛkt]: **to ~ to the enemy** pasarse al enemigo; **physical ~** defecto físico; **mental ~** (*pej*) deficiencia mental
defective [dɪ'fɛktɪv] *adj* (*gen*) defectuoso; (*pej*: *person*) anormal
defector [dɪ'fɛktə] *n* tránsfuga *m/f*
defence, defense (US) [dɪ'fɛns] *n* defensa; **the Ministry of D~** el Ministerio de Defensa; **witness for the ~** testigo de descargo
defenceless [dɪ'fɛnslɪs] *adj* indefenso
defend [dɪ'fɛnd] *vt* defender; (*decision, action*) defender; (*opinion*) mantener
defendant [dɪ'fɛndənt] *n* acusado(-a); (*in civil case*) demandado(-a)
defender [dɪ'fɛndəʳ] *n* defensor(a) *m(f)*; (*Sport*) defensa *m/f*
defense [dɪ'fɛns] *n* (US) = **defence**
defensive [dɪ'fɛnsɪv] *adj* defensivo ▷ *n* defensiva; **on the ~** a la defensiva
defer [dɪ'fə:ʳ] *vt* (*postpone*) aplazar; **to ~ to** diferir a; (*submit*): **to ~ to sb/sb's opinion** someterse a algn/a la opinión de algn
deference ['dɛfərəns] *n* deferencia, respeto; **out of** *or* **in ~ to** por respeto a
defiance [dɪ'faɪəns] *n* desafío; **in ~ of** en contra de
defiant [dɪ'faɪənt] *adj* (*insolent*) insolente; (*challenging*) retador(a), desafiante
deficiency [dɪ'fɪʃənsɪ] *n* (*lack*) falta; (*Comm*) déficit *m*; (*defect*) defecto
deficient [dɪ'fɪʃənt] *adj* (*lacking*) insuficiente; (*incomplete*) incompleto; (*defective*) defectuoso; **~ in** deficiente en
deficit ['dɛfɪsɪt] *n* déficit *m*
defile [dɪ'faɪl] *vt* manchar; (*violate*) violar
define [dɪ'faɪn] *vt* (*Comput*) definir; (*limits etc*) determinar
definite ['dɛfɪnɪt] *adj* (*fixed*) determinado; (*clear, obvious*) claro; **he was ~ about it** no dejó lugar a dudas (sobre ello)
definitely ['dɛfɪnɪtlɪ] *adv*: **he's ~ mad** no cabe duda de que está loco
definition [dɛfɪ'nɪʃən] *n* definición *f*
deflate [di:'fleɪt] *vt* (*gen*) desinflar; (*pompous person*) quitar *or* rebajar los humos a; (*Econ*) deflacionar
deflect [dɪ'flɛkt] *vt* desviar
deform [dɪ'fɔ:m] *vt* deformar
deformed [dɪ'fɔ:md] *adj* deformado
deformity [dɪ'fɔ:mɪtɪ] *n* deformación *f*
defraud [dɪ'frɔ:d] *vt* estafar; **to ~ sb of sth** estafar algo a algn
defrost [di:'frɔst] *vt* (*frozen food, fridge*) descongelar
defroster [di:'frɔstəʳ] *n* (US) eliminador *m* de vaho
deft [dɛft] *adj* diestro, hábil
defunct [dɪ'fʌŋkt] *adj* difunto; (*organization etc*) ya desaparecido
defuse [di:'fju:z] *vt* desarmar; (*situation*) calmar, apaciguar
defy [dɪ'faɪ] *vt* (*resist*) oponerse a; (*challenge*) desafiar; (*order*) contravenir; **it defies description** resulta imposible describirlo
degenerate [dɪ'dʒɛnəreɪt] *vi* degenerar ▷ *adj* [dɪ'dʒɛnərɪt] degenerado
degradation [dɛgrə'deɪʃən] *n* degradación *f*
degree [dɪ'gri:] *n* grado; (*Scol*) título; **10 ~s below freezing** 10 grados bajo cero; **to have a ~ in maths** ser licenciado(-a) en matemáticas; **by ~s** (*gradually*) poco a poco, por etapas; **to some ~, to a certain ~** hasta cierto punto; **a considerable ~ of risk** un gran índice de riesgo
dehydrated [di:haɪ'dreɪtɪd] *adj* deshidratado; (*milk*) en polvo
dehydration [di:haɪ'dreɪʃən] *n* deshidratación *f*
de-ice [di:'aɪs] *vt* (*windscreen*) deshelar
de-icer [di:'aɪsəʳ] *n* descongelador *m*
deign [deɪn] *vi*: **to ~ to do** dignarse hacer
deity ['di:ɪtɪ] *n* deidad *f*, divinidad *f*
déjà vu [deɪʒɑ:'vu:] *n*: **I had a sense of ~** sentía como si ya lo hubiera vivido
dejected [dɪ'dʒɛktɪd] *adj* abatido, desanimado
dejection [dɪ'dʒɛkʃən] *n* abatimiento
delay [dɪ'leɪ] *vt* demorar, aplazar; (*person*) entretener; (*train*) retrasar; (*payment*) aplazar ▷ *vi* tardar ▷ *n* demora, retraso; **without ~** en seguida, sin tardar
delectable [dɪ'lɛktəbl] *adj* (*person*) encantador(-a); (*food*) delicioso
delegate ['dɛlɪgɪt] *n* delegado(-a) ▷ *vt* ['dɛlɪgeɪt] (*person*) delegar en; (*task*) delegar; **to ~ sth to sb/sb to do sth** delegar algo en algn/en algn para hacer algo
delegation [dɛlɪ'geɪʃən] *n* (*of work etc*) delegación *f*
delete [dɪ'li:t] *vt* suprimir, tachar; (*Comput*) suprimir, borrar
deli ['dɛlɪ] *n* = **delicatessen**
deliberate [dɪ'lɪbərɪt] *adj* (*intentional*) intencionado; (*slow*) pausado, lento ▷ *vi* [dɪ'lɪbəreɪt] deliberar
deliberately [dɪ'lɪbərɪtlɪ] *adv* (*on purpose*) a propósito; (*slowly*) pausadamente

deliberation [dɪlɪbə'reɪʃən] *n* (*consideration*) reflexión *f*; (*discussion*) deliberación *f*, discusión *f*
delicacy ['dɛlɪkəsɪ] *n* delicadeza; (*choice food*) manjar *m*
delicate ['dɛlɪkɪt] *adj* (*gen*) delicado; (*fragile*) frágil
delicatessen [dɛlɪkə'tɛsn] *n tienda especializada en alimentos de calidad*
delicious [dɪ'lɪʃəs] *adj* delicioso, rico
delight [dɪ'laɪt] *n* (*feeling*) placer *m*, deleite *m*; (*object*) encanto, delicia ▷ *vt* encantar, deleitar; **to take ~ in** deleitarse en
delighted [dɪ'laɪtɪd] *adj*: **~ (at** *or* **with/to do)** encantado (con/de hacer); **to be ~ that** estar encantado de que; **I'd be ~** con mucho *or* todo gusto
delightful [dɪ'laɪtful] *adj* encantador(a), delicioso
delinquent [dɪ'lɪŋkwənt] *adj, n* delincuente *m/f*
delirious [dɪ'lɪrɪəs] *adj* (*Med: fig*) delirante; **to be ~** delirar, desvariar
deliver [dɪ'lɪvəʳ] *vt* (*distribute*) repartir; (*hand over*) entregar; (*message*) comunicar; (*speech*) pronunciar; (*blow*) lanzar, dar; (*Med*) asistir al parto de
delivery [dɪ'lɪvərɪ] *n* reparto; entrega; (*of speaker*) modo de expresarse; (*Med*) parto, alumbramiento; **to take ~ of** recibir
delude [dɪ'lu:d] *vt* engañar
deluge ['dɛlju:dʒ] *n* diluvio ▷ *vt* (*fig*): **to ~ (with)** inundar (de)
delusion [dɪ'lu:ʒən] *n* ilusión *f*, engaño
de luxe [də'lʌks] *adj* de lujo
delve [dɛlv] *vi*: **to ~ into** hurgar en
Dem. *abbr* (*US Pol*) = **Democrat**; **Democratic**
demand [dɪ'mɑ:nd] *vt* (*gen*) exigir; (*rights*) reclamar; (*need*) requerir ▷ *n* (*gen*) exigencia; (*claim*) reclamación *f*; (*Econ*) demanda; **to ~ sth (from** *or* **of sb)** exigir algo (a algn); **to be in ~** ser muy solicitado; **on ~** a solicitud
demanding [dɪ'mɑ:ndɪŋ] *adj* (*boss*) exigente; (*work*) absorbente
demean [dɪ'mi:n] *vt*: **to ~ o.s.** rebajarse
demeanour, demeanor (*US*) [dɪ'mi:nəʳ] *n* porte *m*, conducta, comportamiento
demented [dɪ'mɛntɪd] *adj* demente
demilitarize [di:'mɪlɪtəraɪz] *vt* desmilitarizar; **~d zone** zona desmilitarizada
demise [dɪ'maɪz] *n* (*death*) fallecimiento
demister [di:'mɪstəʳ] *n* (*Aut*) eliminador *m* de vaho
demo ['dɛməu] *n abbr* (*inf*: = *demonstration*) manifestación *f*
democracy [dɪ'mɔkrəsɪ] *n* democracia
democrat ['dɛməkræt] *n* demócrata *m/f*
democratic [dɛmə'krætɪk] *adj* democrático; **the D~ Party** el partido demócrata (estadounidense)
demography [dɪ'mɔgrəfɪ] *n* demografía
demolish [dɪ'mɔlɪʃ] *vt* derribar, demoler; (*fig: argument*) destruir
demolition [dɛmə'lɪʃən] *n* derribo, demolición *f*
demon ['di:mən] *n* (*evil spirit*) demonio ▷ *cpd* temible
demonstrate ['dɛmənstreɪt] *vt* demostrar ▷ *vi* manifestarse; **to ~ (for/against)** manifestarse (a favor de/en contra de)
demonstration [dɛmən'streɪʃən] *n* (*Pol*) manifestación *f*; (*proof*) prueba, demostración *f*; **to hold a ~** (*Pol*) hacer una manifestación
demonstrator ['dɛmənstreɪtəʳ] *n* (*Pol*) manifestante *m/f*
demote [dɪ'məut] *vt* degradar
demotion [dɪ'məuʃən] *n* degradación *f*; (*Comm*) descenso
demure [dɪ'mjuəʳ] *adj* recatado
den [dɛn] *n* (*of animal*) guarida; (*study*) estudio
denial [dɪ'naɪəl] *n* (*refusal*) denegación *f*; (*of report etc*) desmentido
denim ['dɛnɪm] *n* tela vaquera; *see also* **denims**
denims ['dɛnɪms] *npl* vaqueros *mpl*
Denmark ['dɛnmɑ:k] *n* Dinamarca
denomination [dɪnɔmɪ'neɪʃən] *n* valor *m*; (*Rel*) confesión *f*
denominator [dɪ'nɔmɪneɪtəʳ] *n* denominador *m*
denote [dɪ'nəut] *vt* indicar, significar
denounce [dɪ'nauns] *vt* denunciar
dense [dɛns] *adj* (*thick*) espeso; (*foliage etc*) tupido; (*stupid*) torpe
densely [dɛnslɪ] *adv*: **~ populated** con una alta densidad de población
density ['dɛnsɪtɪ] *n* densidad *f*; **single/double-~ disk** *n* (*Comput*) disco de densidad sencilla/de doble densidad
dent [dɛnt] *n* abolladura ▷ *vt* (*also*: **make a ~ in**) abollar
dental ['dɛntl] *adj* dental
dental floss [-flɔs] *n* seda dental
dental surgeon *n* odontólogo(-a)
dental surgery *n* clínica *f* dental, consultorio *m* dental
dentist ['dɛntɪst] *n* dentista *m/f*; **~'s surgery** (*Brit*) consultorio dental
dentistry ['dɛntɪstrɪ] *n* odontología
dentures ['dɛntʃəz] *npl* dentadura *sg* (postiza)
denunciation [dɪnʌnsɪ'eɪʃən] *n* denuncia, denunciación *f*
deny [dɪ'naɪ] *vt* negar; (*charge*) rechazar; (*report*) desmentir; **to ~ o.s.** privarse (de); **he denies having said it** niega haberlo dicho
deodorant [di:'əudərənt] *n* desodorante *m*
depart [dɪ'pɑ:t] *vi* irse, marcharse; (*train*) salir; **to ~ from** (*fig: differ from*) apartarse de
departed [dɪ'pɑ:tɪd] *adj* (*bygone: days, glory*) pasado; (*dead*) difunto ▷ *n*: **the (dear) ~** el/la/los/las difunto/a/os/as

department [dɪ'pɑːtmənt] *n* (*Comm*) sección *f*; (*Scol*) departamento; (*Pol*) ministerio; **that's not my ~** (*fig*) no tiene que ver conmigo; **D~ of State** (*US*) Ministerio de Asuntos Exteriores
department store *n* grandes almacenes *mpl*
departure [dɪ'pɑːtʃəʳ] *n* partida, ida; (*of train*) salida; **a new ~** un nuevo rumbo
departure lounge *n* (*at airport*) sala de embarque
depend [dɪ'pɛnd] *vi*: **to ~ (up)on** (*be dependent upon*) depender de; (*rely on*) contar con; **it ~s** depende, según; **~ing on the result** según el resultado
dependable [dɪ'pɛndəbl] *adj* (*person*) formal, serio
dependant [dɪ'pɛndənt] *n* dependiente *m/f*
dependence [dɪ'pɛndəns] *n* dependencia
dependent [dɪ'pɛndənt] *adj*: **to be ~ (on)** depender (de) ▷ *n* = **dependant**
depict [dɪ'pɪkt] *vt* (*in picture*) pintar; (*describe*) representar
depleted [dɪ'pliːtɪd] *adj* reducido
deplorable [dɪ'plɔːrəbl] *adj* deplorable
deploy [dɪ'plɔɪ] *vt* desplegar
deport [dɪ'pɔːt] *vt* deportar
deportation [diːpɔː'teɪʃən] *n* deportación *f*
deportee [diːpɔː'tiː] *n* deportado(-a)
deposit [dɪ'pɔzɪt] *n* depósito; (*Chem*) sedimento; (*of ore, oil*) yacimiento ▷ *vt* (*gen*) depositar; **to put down a ~ of £50** dejar un depósito de 50 libras
deposit account *n* (*Brit*) cuenta de ahorros
depot ['dɛpəu] *n* (*storehouse*) depósito; (*for vehicles*) parque *m*
depraved [dɪ'preɪvd] *adj* depravado, vicioso
depravity [dɪ'prævɪtɪ] *n* depravación *f*, vicio
depreciate [dɪ'priːʃɪeɪt] *vi* depreciarse, perder valor
depreciation [dɪpriːʃɪ'eɪʃən] *n* depreciación *f*
depress [dɪ'prɛs] *vt* deprimir; (*press down*) apretar
depressant [dɪ'prɛsnt] *n* (*Med*) calmante *m*, sedante *m*
depressed [dɪ'prɛst] *adj* deprimido; (*Comm: market, economy*) deprimido; (*area*) deprimido (económicamente); **to get ~** deprimirse
depressing [dɪ'prɛsɪŋ] *adj* deprimente
depression [dɪ'prɛʃən] *n* depresión *f*; **the economy is in a state of ~** la economía está deprimida
deprivation [dɛprɪ'veɪʃən] *n* privación *f*; (*loss*) pérdida
deprive [dɪ'praɪv] *vt*: **to ~ sb of** privar a algn de
deprived [dɪ'praɪvd] *adj* necesitado
dept. *abbr* (= *department*) dto
depth [dɛpθ] *n* profundidad *f*; **at a ~ of three metres** a tres metros de profundidad; **to be out of one's ~** (*swimmer*) perder pie; (*fig*) sentirse perdido; **to study sth in ~** estudiar algo a fondo; **in the ~s of** en lo más hondo de
deputize ['dɛpjutaɪz] *vi*: **to ~ for sb** sustituir a algn
deputy ['dɛpjutɪ] *adj*: **~ head** subdirector(a) *m(f)* ▷ *n* sustituto(-a), suplente *m/f*; (*Pol*) diputado(-a); (*agent*) representante *m/f*
derail [dɪ'reɪl] *vt*: **to be ~ed** descarrilarse
deranged [dɪ'reɪndʒd] *adj* trastornado
derby ['dəːbɪ] *n* (*US*) hongo
deregulation [diːrɛgju'leɪʃən] *n* desreglamentación *f*
derelict ['dɛrɪlɪkt] *adj* abandonado
derision [dɪ'rɪʒən] *n* irrisión *f*, mofas *fpl*
derisory [dɪ'raɪzərɪ] *adj* (*sum*) irrisorio; (*laughter, person*) burlón(-ona), irónico
derivative [dɪ'rɪvətɪv] *n* derivado ▷ *adj* (*work*) poco original
derive [dɪ'raɪv] *vt* derivar; (*benefit etc*) obtener ▷ *vi*: **to ~ from** derivarse de
dermatitis [dəːmə'taɪtɪs] *n* dermatitis *f*
derogatory [dɪ'rɔgətərɪ] *adj* despectivo
derv [dəːv] *n* (*Brit*) gasoil *m*
descend [dɪ'sɛnd] *vt, vi* descender, bajar; **to ~ from** descender de; **in ~ing order of importance** de mayor a menor importancia;
descend on *vt fus* (*enemy, angry person*) caer sobre; (*misfortune*) sobrevenir; (*gloom, silence*) invadir; **visitors ~ed on us** las visitas nos invadieron
descendant [dɪ'sɛndənt] *n* descendiente *m/f*
descent [dɪ'sɛnt] *n* descenso; (*Geo*) pendiente *f*, declive *m*; (*origin*) descendencia
describe [dɪs'kraɪb] *vt* describir
description [dɪs'krɪpʃən] *n* descripción *f*; (*sort*) clase *f*, género; **of every ~** de toda clase
descriptive [dɪs'krɪptɪv] *adj* descriptivo
desecrate ['dɛsɪkreɪt] *vt* profanar
desert [*n* 'dɛzət, *vb* dɪ'zəːt] *n* desierto ▷ *vt* abandonar, desamparar ▷ *vi* (*Mil*) desertar; *see also* **deserts**
deserted [dɪ'zəːtɪd] *adj* desierto
deserter [dɪ'zəːtəʳ] *n* desertor(-a) *m(f)*
desertion [dɪ'zəːʃən] *n* deserción *f*
desert island *n* isla desierta
deserts [dɪ'zəːts] *npl*: **to get one's just ~** llevarse su merecido
deserve [dɪ'zəːv] *vt* merecer, ser digno de, ameritar (*LAm*)
deserving [dɪ'zəːvɪŋ] *adj* (*person*) digno; (*action, cause*) meritorio
design [dɪ'zaɪn] *n* (*sketch*) bosquejo; (*of dress, car*) diseño; (*pattern*) dibujo ▷ *vt* (*gen*) diseñar; **industrial ~** diseño industrial; **to have ~s on sb** tener la(s) mira(s) puesta(s) en algn; **to be ~ed for sb/sth** estar hecho para algn/algo
design and technology *n* (*Brit Scol*) diseño y tecnología
designate ['dɛzɪgneɪt] *vt* (*appoint*) nombrar; (*destine*) designar ▷ *adj* ['dɛzɪgnɪt] designado
designer [dɪ'zaɪnəʳ] *n* diseñador(-a) *m(f)*

d

desirable [dɪ'zaɪərəbl] *adj* (*proper*) deseable; (*attractive*) atractivo; **it is ~ that** es conveniente que
desire [dɪ'zaɪəʳ] *n* deseo ▷ *vt* desear; **to ~ sth/ to do sth/that** desear algo/hacer algo/que
desk [dɛsk] *n* (*in office*) escritorio; (*for pupil*) pupitre *m*; (*in hotel, at airport*) recepción *f*; (*Brit: in shop, restaurant*) caja
desktop ['dɛsktɔp] *n* (*Comput*) escritorio
desktop computer *n* ordenador *m* de sobremesa
desktop publishing *n* autoedición *f*
desolate ['dɛsəlɪt] *adj* (*place*) desierto; (*person*) afligido
desolation [dɛsə'leɪʃən] *n* (*of place*) desolación *f*; (*of person*) aflicción *f*
despair [dɪs'pɛəʳ] *n* desesperación *f* ▷ *vi*: **to ~ of** desesperar de; **in ~** desesperado
despatch [dɪs'pætʃ] *n, vt* = **dispatch**
desperate ['dɛspərɪt] *adj* desesperado; (*fugitive*) peligroso; (*measures*) extremo; **we are getting ~** estamos al borde de desesperación; **to be ~ for sth/to do** necesitar urgentemente algo/hacer
desperately ['dɛspərɪtlɪ] *adv* desesperadamente; (*very*) terriblemente, gravemente; **~ ill** gravemente enfermo
desperation [dɛspə'reɪʃən] *n* desesperación *f*; **in ~** desesperado
despicable [dɪs'pɪkəbl] *adj* vil, despreciable
despise [dɪs'paɪz] *vt* despreciar
despite [dɪs'paɪt] *prep* a pesar de, pese a
despondent [dɪs'pɔndənt] *adj* deprimido, abatido
dessert [dɪ'zə:t] *n* postre *m*
dessertspoon [dɪ'zə:tspu:n] *n* cuchara (de postre)
destination [dɛstɪ'neɪʃən] *n* destino
destine ['dɛstɪn] *vt* destinar
destined ['dɛstɪnd] *adj*: **~ for London** con destino a Londres
destiny ['dɛstɪnɪ] *n* destino
destitute ['dɛstɪtju:t] *adj* desamparado, indigente
destitution [dɛstɪ'tju:ʃən] *n* indigencia, miseria
destroy [dɪs'trɔɪ] *vt* destruir; (*finish*) acabar con
destroyer [dɪs'trɔɪəʳ] *n* (*Naut*) destructor *m*
destruction [dɪs'trʌkʃən] *n* destrucción *f*; (*fig*) ruina
destructive [dɪs'trʌktɪv] *adj* destructivo, destructor(a)
detach [dɪ'tætʃ] *vt* separar; (*unstick*) despegar
detached [dɪ'tætʃt] *adj* (*attitude*) objetivo, imparcial
detached house *n* chalé *m*, chalet *m*
detachment [dɪ'tætʃmənt] *n* separación *f*; (*Mil*) destacamento; (*fig*) objetividad *f*, imparcialidad *f*
detail ['di:teɪl] *n* detalle *m*; (*Mil*) destacamento ▷ *vt* detallar; (*Mil*) destacar; **in ~** detalladamente; **to go into ~(s)** entrar en detalles
detailed ['di:teɪld] *adj* detallado
detain [dɪ'teɪn] *vt* retener; (*in captivity*) detener
detainee [di:teɪ'ni:] *n* detenido(-a)
detect [dɪ'tɛkt] *vt* (*discover*) descubrir; (*Med, Police*) identificar; (*Mil, Radar, Tech*) detectar; (*notice*) percibir
detection [dɪ'tɛkʃən] *n* descubrimiento; identificación *f*; **crime ~** investigación *f*; **to escape ~** (*criminal*) escaparse sin ser descubierto; (*mistake*) pasar inadvertido
detective [dɪ'tɛktɪv] *n* detective *m*
detective story *n* novela policíaca
detector [dɪ'tɛktəʳ] *n* detector *m*
detention [dɪ'tɛnʃən] *n* detención *f*, arresto; (*Scol*) castigo
deter [dɪ'tə:ʳ] *vt* (*dissuade*) disuadir; (*prevent*) impedir; **to ~ sb from doing sth** disuadir a algn de que haga algo
detergent [dɪ'tə:dʒənt] *n* detergente *m*
deteriorate [dɪ'tɪərɪəreɪt] *vi* deteriorarse
determination [dɪtə:mɪ'neɪʃən] *n* resolución *f*
determine [dɪ'tə:mɪn] *vt* determinar; **to ~ to do sth** decidir hacer algo
determined [dɪ'tə:mɪnd] *adj*: **to be ~ to do sth** estar decidido *or* resuelto a hacer algo; **a ~ effort** un esfuerzo enérgico
deterrent [dɪ'tɛrənt] *n* fuerza de disuasión; **to act as a ~** servir para prevenir
detest [dɪ'tɛst] *vt* aborrecer
detonate ['dɛtəneɪt] *vi* estallar ▷ *vt* hacer detonar
detonator ['dɛtəneɪtəʳ] *n* detonador *m*, fulminante *m*
detour ['di:tuəʳ] *n* (*gen, US Aut: diversion*) desvío ▷ *vt* (*US: traffic*) desviar; **to make a ~** dar un rodeo
detox ['di:tɔks] *vi* desintoxicarse ▷ *n* desintoxicación *f*
detract [dɪ'trækt] *vt*: **to ~ from** quitar mérito a, restar valor a
detractor [dɪ'træktəʳ] *n* detractor(-a) *m(f)*
detriment ['dɛtrɪmənt] *n*: **to the ~ of** en perjuicio de; **without ~ to** sin detrimento de, sin perjuicio para
detrimental [dɛtrɪ'mɛntl] *adj*: **~ (to)** perjudicial (a)
deuce [dju:s] *n* (*Tennis*) cuarenta iguales
devaluation [dɪvælju'eɪʃən] *n* devaluación *f*
devalue [dɪ'vælju:] *vt* devaluar
devastate ['dɛvəsteɪt] *vt* devastar; **he was ~d by the news** las noticias le dejaron desolado
devastating ['dɛvəsteɪtɪŋ] *adj* devastador(-a); (*fig*) arrollador(-a)
devastation [dɛvəs'teɪʃən] *n* devastación *f*, ruina
develop [dɪ'vɛləp] *vt* desarrollar; (*Phot*) revelar; (*disease*) contraer; (*habit*) adquirir ▷ *vi* desarrollarse; (*advance*) progresar; **this land is to be ~ed** se va a construir en este terreno;

to ~ a taste for sth tomar gusto a algo; **to ~ into** transformarse *or* convertirse en
developer [dɪ'vɛləpəʳ] *n* (*property developer*) promotor(-a) *m(f)*
developing country *n* país *m* en (vías de) desarrollo
development [dɪ'vɛləpmənt] *n* desarrollo; (*advance*) progreso; (*of affair, case*) desenvolvimiento; (*of land*) urbanización *f*
deviant ['di:vɪənt] *adj* anómalo, pervertido
deviate ['di:vɪeɪt] *vi*: **to ~ (from)** desviarse (de)
device [dɪ'vaɪs] *n* (*scheme*) estratagema, recurso; (*apparatus*) aparato, mecanismo; (*explosive device*) artefacto explosivo
devil ['dɛvl] *n* diablo, demonio
devil's advocate *n*: **to play (the) ~** hacer de abogado del diablo
devious ['di:vɪəs] *adj* intricado, enrevesado; (*person*) taimado
devise [dɪ'vaɪz] *vt* idear, inventar
devoid [dɪ'vɔɪd] *adj*: **~ of** desprovisto de
devolution [di:və'lu:ʃən] *n* (*Pol*) descentralización *f*
devote [dɪ'vəut] *vt*: **to ~ sth to** dedicar algo a
devoted [dɪ'vəutɪd] *adj* (*loyal*) leal, fiel; **to be ~ to sb** querer con devoción a algn; **the book is ~ to politics** el libro trata de política
devotee [dɛvəu'ti:] *n* devoto(-a)
devotion [dɪ'vəuʃən] *n* dedicación *f*; (*Rel*) devoción *f*
devour [dɪ'vauəʳ] *vt* devorar
devout [dɪ'vaut] *adj* devoto
dew [dju:] *n* rocío
dexterity [dɛks'tɛrɪtɪ] *n* destreza
diabetes [daɪə'bi:ti:z] *n* diabetes *f*
diabetic [daɪə'bɛtɪk] *n* diabético(-a) ▷ *adj* diabético; (*chocolate, jam*) para diabéticos
diabolical [daɪə'bɔlɪkəl] *adj* diabólico; (*inf: dreadful*) horrendo, horroroso
diagnose ['daɪəgnəuz] *vt* diagnosticar
diagnosis (*pl* **diagnoses**) [daɪəg'nəusɪs, -si:z] *n* diagnóstico
diagonal [daɪ'ægənl] *adj* diagonal ▷ *n* diagonal *f*
diagram ['daɪəgræm] *n* diagrama *m*, esquema *m*
dial ['daɪəl] *n* esfera; (*of radio*) dial *m*; (*tuner*) sintonizador *m*; (*of phone*) disco ▷ *vt* (*number*) marcar, discar (*LAm*); **to ~ a wrong number** equivocarse de número; **can I ~ London direct?** ¿puedo marcar un número de Londres directamente?
dial code *n* (*US*) prefijo
dialect ['daɪəlɛkt] *n* dialecto
dialling code ['daɪəlɪŋ-] *n* (*Brit*) prefijo
dialling tone *n* (*Brit*) señal *f or* tono de marcar
dialogue, dialog (*US*) ['daɪəlɔg] *n* diálogo
dial tone *n* (*US*) señal *f or* tono de marcar
dialysis [daɪ'ælɪsɪs] *n* diálisis *f*
diameter [daɪ'æmɪtəʳ] *n* diámetro
diamond ['daɪəmənd] *n* diamante *m*; **diamonds** *npl* (*Cards*) diamantes *mpl*
diaper ['daɪəpəʳ] *n* (*US*) pañal *m*
diaphragm ['daɪəfræm] *n* diafragma *m*
diarrhoea, diarrhea (*US*) [daɪə'ri:ə] *n* diarrea
diary ['daɪərɪ] *n* (*daily account*) diario; (*book*) agenda; **to keep a ~** escribir un diario
dice [daɪs] *n pl inv* dados *mpl* ▷ *vt* (*Culin*) cortar en cuadritos
Dictaphone® ['dɪktəfəun] *n* dictáfono®
dictate [dɪk'teɪt] *vt* dictar ▷ *n* ['dɪkteɪt] dictado; **dictate to** *vt fus* (*person*) dar órdenes a; **I won't be ~d to** no recibo órdenes de nadie
dictation [dɪk'teɪʃən] *n* (*to secretary etc*) dictado; **at ~ speed** para tomar al dictado
dictator [dɪk'teɪtəʳ] *n* dictador *m*
dictatorship [dɪk'teɪtəʃɪp] *n* dictadura
diction ['dɪkʃən] *n* dicción *f*
dictionary ['dɪkʃənrɪ] *n* diccionario
did [dɪd] *pt of* **do**
didactic [daɪ'dæktɪk] *adj* didáctico
diddle ['dɪdl] *vt* estafar, timar
didn't ['dɪdənt] = **did not**
die [daɪ] *vi* morir; **to ~ (of** *or* **from)** morirse (de); **to be dying** morirse, estar muriéndose; **to be dying for sth/to do sth** morirse por algo/de ganas de hacer algo; **die away** *vi* (*sound, light*) desvanecerse; **die down** *vi* (*gen*) apagarse; (*wind*) amainar; **die out** *vi* desaparecer, extinguirse
diehard ['daɪha:d] *n* intransigente *m/f*
diesel ['di:zl] *n* diesel *m*
diesel engine *n* motor *m* diesel
diesel fuel, diesel oil *n* gas-oil *m*
diet ['daɪət] *n* dieta; (*restricted food*) régimen *m* ▷ *vi* (*also*: **be on a ~**) estar a dieta, hacer régimen; **to live on a ~ of** alimentarse de
dietician [daɪə'tɪʃən] *n* dietista *m/f*
differ ['dɪfəʳ] *vi* (*be different*) ser distinto, diferenciarse; (*disagree*) discrepar
difference ['dɪfrəns] *n* diferencia; (*quarrel*) desacuerdo; **it makes no ~ to me** me da igual *or* lo mismo; **to settle one's ~s** arreglarse
different ['dɪfrənt] *adj* diferente, distinto
differentiate [dɪfə'rɛnʃɪeɪt] *vt* distinguir ▷ *vi* diferenciarse; **to ~ between** distinguir entre
differently ['dɪfrəntlɪ] *adv* de otro modo, en forma distinta
difficult ['dɪfɪkəlt] *adj* difícil; **~ to understand** difícil de entender
difficulty ['dɪfɪkəltɪ] *n* dificultad *f*; **to have difficulties with** (*police, landlord etc*) tener problemas con; **to be in ~** estar en apuros
diffident ['dɪfɪdənt] *adj* tímido
dig [dɪg] *vt* (*pt, pp* **dug** [dʌg]) (*hole*) cavar; (*ground*) remover; (*coal*) extraer; (*nails etc*) clavar ▷ *n* (*prod*) empujón *m*; (*archaeological*) excavación *f*; (*remark*) indirecta; **to ~ into** (*savings*) consumir; **to ~ into one's pockets**

d

for sth hurgar en el bolsillo buscando algo; **to ~ one's nails into** clavar las uñas en; *see also* **digs**; **dig in** *vi* (*also*: **~ o.s. in**: *Mil*) atrincherarse; (*inf*: *eat*) hincar los dientes ▷ *vt* (*compost*) añadir al suelo; (*knife, claw*) clavar; **to ~ in one's heels** (*fig*) mantenerse en sus trece; **dig out** *vt* (*hole*) excavar; (*survivors, car from snow*) sacar; **dig up** *vt* desenterrar; (*plant*) desarraigar

digest [daɪ'dʒɛst] *vt* (*food*) digerir; (*facts*) asimilar ▷ *n* ['daɪdʒɛst] resumen *m*

digestion [dɪ'dʒɛstʃən] *n* digestión *f*

digit ['dɪdʒɪt] *n* (*number*) dígito; (*finger*) dedo

digital ['dɪdʒɪtl] *adj* digital

digital camera *n* cámara digital

digital TV *n* televisión *f* digital

dignified ['dɪgnɪfaɪd] *adj* grave, solemne; (*action*) decoroso

dignitary ['dɪgnɪtərɪ] *n* dignatario(-a)

dignity ['dɪgnɪtɪ] *n* dignidad *f*

digress [daɪ'grɛs] *vi*: **to ~ from** apartarse de

digression [daɪ'grɛʃən] *n* digresión *f*

digs [dɪgz] *npl* (*Brit*: *inf*) pensión *f*, alojamiento

dilapidated [dɪ'læpɪdeɪtɪd] *adj* desmoronado, ruinoso

dilate [daɪ'leɪt] *vt* dilatar ▷ *vi* dilatarse

dilemma [daɪ'lɛmə] *n* dilema *m*; **to be in a ~** estar en un dilema

diligence ['dɪlɪdʒəns] *n* diligencia

diligent ['dɪlɪdʒənt] *adj* diligente

dill [dɪl] *n* eneldo

dilute [daɪ'lu:t] *vt* diluir

dim [dɪm] *adj* (*light*) débil; (*sight*) turbio; (*outline*) borroso; (*stupid*) lerdo; (*room*) oscuro ▷ *vt* (*light*) bajar; **to take a ~ view of sth** tener una pobre opinión de algo

dime [daɪm] *n* (*US*) *moneda de diez centavos*

dimension [dɪ'mɛnʃən] *n* dimensión *f*

dimensions [dɪ'mɛnʃənz] *npl* dimensiones *fpl*

diminish [dɪ'mɪnɪʃ] *vt, vi* disminuir

diminished [dɪ'mɪnɪʃt] *adj*: **~ responsibility** (*Law*) responsabilidad *f* disminuida

diminutive [dɪ'mɪnjutɪv] *adj* diminuto ▷ *n* (*Ling*) diminutivo

dimmer ['dɪmə^r] *n* (*also*: **~ switch**) regulador *m* (de intensidad); (*US Aut*) interruptor *m*

dimple ['dɪmpl] *n* hoyuelo

din [dɪn] *n* estruendo, estrépito ▷ *vt*: **to ~ sth into sb** (*inf*) meter algo en la cabeza a algn

dine [daɪn] *vi* cenar

diner ['daɪnə^r] *n* (*person*: *in restaurant*) comensal *m/f*; (*US*) restaurante económico; (*Brit Rail*) = **dining car**

dinghy ['dɪŋgɪ] *n* bote *m*; (*also*: **rubber ~**) lancha (neumática)

dingy ['dɪndʒɪ] *adj* (*room*) sombrío; (*dirty*) sucio; (*dull*) deslucido

dining car ['daɪnɪŋ-] *n* (*Brit*) coche-restaurante *m*

dining room ['daɪnɪŋ-] *n* comedor *m*

dining table *n* mesa *f* de comedor

dinner ['dɪnə^r] *n* (*evening meal*) cena, comida (*LAm*); (*lunch*) comida; (*public*) cena, banquete *m*; **~'s ready!** ¡la cena está servida!

dinner jacket *n* smoking *m*

dinner party *n* cena

dinner time *n* (*evening*) hora de cenar; (*midday*) hora de comer

dinosaur ['daɪnəsɔ:^r] *n* dinosaurio

dint [dɪnt] *n*: **by ~ of (doing) sth** a fuerza de (hacer) algo

diocese ['daɪəsɪs] *n* diócesis *f*

dioxide [daɪ'ɔksaɪd] *n* bióxido; **carbon ~** bióxido de carbono

Dip. *abbr* (*Brit*) = **diploma**

dip [dɪp] *n* (*slope*) pendiente *f*; (*in sea*) chapuzón *m* ▷ *vt* (*in water*) mojar; (*ladle etc*) meter; (*Brit Aut*): **to ~ one's lights** poner la luz de cruce ▷ *vi* descender, bajar

diphtheria [dɪf'θɪərɪə] *n* difteria

diphthong ['dɪfθɔŋ] *n* diptongo

diploma [dɪ'pləumə] *n* diploma *m*

diplomacy [dɪ'pləuməsɪ] *n* diplomacia

diplomat ['dɪpləmæt] *n* diplomático(-a) *m(f)*

diplomatic [dɪplə'mætɪk] *adj* diplomático; **to break off ~ relations** romper las relaciones diplomáticas

diplomatic immunity *n* inmunidad *f* diplomática

dipstick ['dɪpstɪk] *n* (*Aut*) varilla de nivel (del aceite)

dipswitch ['dɪpswɪtʃ] *n* (*Brit Aut*) interruptor *m*

dire [daɪə^r] *adj* calamitoso

direct [daɪ'rɛkt] *adj* (*gen*) directo; (*manner, person*) franco ▷ *vt* dirigir; **can you ~ me to ...?** ¿puede indicarme dónde está ...?; **to ~ sb to do sth** mandar a algn hacer algo

direct current *n* corriente *f* continua

direct debit *n* domiciliación *f* bancaria de recibos; **to pay by ~** domiciliar el pago

direct dialling *n* servicio automático de llamadas

direction [dɪ'rɛkʃən] *n* dirección *f*; **sense of ~** sentido de la orientación; **directions** *npl* (*advice*) órdenes *fpl*, instrucciones *fpl*; (*to a place*) señas *fpl*; **in the ~ of** hacia, en dirección a; **~s for use** modo de empleo; **to ask for ~s** preguntar el camino

directive [daɪ'rɛktɪv] *n* orden *f*, instrucción *f*; **a government ~** una orden del gobierno

directly [dɪ'rɛktlɪ] *adv* (*in straight line*) directamente; (*at once*) en seguida

directness [dɪ'rɛktnɪs] *n* (*of person, speech*) franqueza

director [dɪ'rɛktə^r] *n* director(a) *m(f)*; **managing ~** director(a) *m(f)* gerente

Director of Public Prosecutions *n* ≈ fiscal *m/f* general del Estado

directory [dɪ'rɛktərɪ] *n* (*Tel*) guía (telefónica); (*street directory*) callejero; (*trade directory*) directorio de comercio; (*Comput*) directorio

directory enquiries, directory assistance (*US*) *n* (*service*) (servicio *m* de) información
dirt [dəːt] *n* suciedad *f*
dirt-cheap ['dəːt'tʃiːp] *adj* baratísimo
dirty ['dəːtɪ] *adj* sucio; (*joke*) verde, colorado (*LAm*) ▷ *vt* ensuciar; (*stain*) manchar
disability [dɪsə'bɪlɪtɪ] *n* incapacidad *f*
disabled [dɪs'eɪbld] *adj* (*physically*) minusválido(-a); (*mentally*) deficiente mental
disadvantage [dɪsəd'vɑːntɪdʒ] *n* desventaja, inconveniente *m*
disagree [dɪsə'griː] *vi* (*differ*) discrepar; **to ~ (with)** no estar de acuerdo (con); **I ~ with you** no estoy de acuerdo contigo
disagreeable [dɪsə'grɪəbl] *adj* desagradable
disagreement [dɪsə'griːmənt] *n* (*gen*) desacuerdo; (*quarrel*) riña; **to have a ~ with sb** estar en desacuerdo con algn
disallow ['dɪsə'lau] *vt* (*goal*) anular; (*claim*) rechazar
disappear [dɪsə'pɪəʳ] *vi* desaparecer
disappearance [dɪsə'pɪərəns] *n* desaparición *f*
disappoint [dɪsə'pɔɪnt] *vt* decepcionar; (*hopes*) defraudar
disappointed [dɪsə'pɔɪntɪd] *adj* decepcionado
disappointing [dɪsə'pɔɪntɪŋ] *adj* decepcionante
disappointment [dɪsə'pɔɪntmənt] *n* decepción *f*
disapproval [dɪsə'pruːvəl] *n* desaprobación *f*
disapprove [dɪsə'pruːv] *vi*: **to ~ of** desaprobar
disarm [dɪs'ɑːm] *vt* desarmar
disarmament [dɪs'ɑːməmənt] *n* desarme *m*
disarray [dɪsə'reɪ] *n*: **in ~** (*troops*) desorganizado; (*thoughts*) confuso; (*hair, clothes*) desarreglado; **to throw into ~** provocar el caos
disaster [dɪ'zɑːstəʳ] *n* desastre *m*
disastrous [dɪ'zɑːstrəs] *adj* desastroso
disband [dɪs'bænd] *vt* disolver ▷ *vi* desbandarse
disbelief [dɪsbə'liːf] *n* incredulidad *f*; **in ~** con incredulidad
disc [dɪsk] *n* disco; (*Comput*) = **disk**
discard [dɪs'kɑːd] *vt* tirar; (*fig*) descartar
discern [dɪ'səːn] *vt* percibir, discernir; (*understand*) comprender
discerning [dɪ'səːnɪŋ] *adj* perspicaz
discharge [dɪs'tʃɑːdʒ] *vt* (*task, duty*) cumplir; (*ship etc*) descargar; (*patient*) dar de alta; (*employee*) despedir; (*soldier*) licenciar; (*defendant*) poner en libertad; (*settle: debt*) saldar ▷ *n* ['dɪstʃɑːdʒ] (*Elec*) descarga; (*dismissal*) despedida; (*of duty*) desempeño; (*of debt*) pago, descargo; (*of gas, chemicals*) escape *m*; **~d bankrupt** quebrado/a rehabilitado/a
disciple [dɪ'saɪpl] *n* discípulo(-a)
discipline ['dɪsɪplɪn] *n* disciplina ▷ *vt* disciplinar; **to ~ o.s. to do sth** obligarse a hacer algo
disc jockey, DJ *n* pinchadiscos *m/f inv*
disclaim [dɪs'kleɪm] *vt* negar tener
disclaimer [dɪs'kleɪməʳ] *n* rectificación *f*; **to issue a ~** hacer una rectificación
disclose [dɪs'kləuz] *vt* revelar
disclosure [dɪs'kləuʒəʳ] *n* revelación *f*
disco ['dɪskəu] *n abbr* = **discothèque**
discoloured, discolored (*US*) [dɪs'kʌləd] *adj* descolorido
discomfort [dɪs'kʌmfət] *n* incomodidad *f*; (*unease*) inquietud *f*; (*physical*) malestar *m*
disconcert [dɪskən'səːt] *vt* desconcertar
disconnect [dɪskə'nɛkt] *vt* (*gen*) separar; (*Elec etc*) desconectar; (*supply*) cortar (el suministro) a
disconsolate [dɪs'kɔnsəlɪt] *adj* desconsolado
discontent [dɪskən'tɛnt] *n* descontento
discontented [dɪskən'tɛntɪd] *adj* descontento
discontinue [dɪskən'tɪnjuː] *vt* interrumpir; (*payments*) suspender
discord ['dɪskɔːd] *n* discordia; (*Mus*) disonancia
discordant [dɪs'kɔːdənt] *adj* disonante
discothèque ['dɪskəutɛk] *n* discoteca
discount ['dɪskaunt] *n* descuento ▷ *vt* [dɪs'kaunt] descontar; (*report etc*) descartar; **at a ~** con descuento; **~ for cash** descuento por pago en efectivo; **to give sb a ~ on sth** hacer un descuento a algn en algo
discourage [dɪs'kʌrɪdʒ] *vt* desalentar; (*oppose*) oponerse a; (*dissuade, deter*) desanimar, disuadir; **to ~ sb from doing** disuadir a algn de hacer
discouraging [dɪs'kʌrɪdʒɪŋ] *adj* desalentador(a)
discourteous [dɪs'kəːtɪəs] *adj* descortés
discover [dɪs'kʌvəʳ] *vt* descubrir
discovery [dɪs'kʌvərɪ] *n* descubrimiento
discredit [dɪs'krɛdɪt] *vt* desacreditar
discreet [dɪ'skriːt] *adj* (*tactful*) discreto; (*careful*) circunspecto, prudente
discrepancy [dɪ'skrɛpənsɪ] *n* (*difference*) diferencia; (*disagreement*) discrepancia
discretion [dɪ'skrɛʃən] *n* (*tact*) discreción *f*; (*care*) prudencia, circunspección *f*; **use your own ~** haz lo que creas oportuno; **at the ~ of** a criterio de
discriminate [dɪ'skrɪmɪneɪt] *vi*: **to ~ between** distinguir entre; **to ~ against** discriminar contra
discriminating [dɪ'skrɪmɪneɪtɪŋ] *adj* entendido
discrimination [dɪskrɪmɪ'neɪʃən] *n* (*discernment*) perspicacia; (*bias*) discriminación *f*; **racial/sexual ~** discriminación racial/sexual

discus ['dɪskəs] *n* disco
discuss [dɪ'skʌs] *vt* (*gen*) discutir; (*a theme*) tratar
discussion [dɪ'skʌʃən] *n* discusión *f*; **under ~** en discusión
disdain [dɪs'deɪn] *n* desdén *m* ▷ *vt* desdeñar
disease [dɪ'zi:z] *n* enfermedad *f*
diseased [dɪ'zi:zd] *adj* enfermo
disembark [dɪsɪm'bɑ:k] *vt, vi* desembarcar
disengage [dɪsɪn'geɪdʒ] *vt* soltar; **to ~ the clutch** (*Aut*) desembragar
disentangle [dɪsɪn'tæŋgl] *vt* desenredar
disfigure [dɪs'fɪgə^r] *vt* desfigurar
disgrace [dɪs'greɪs] *n* ignominia; (*downfall*) caída; (*shame*) vergüenza, escándalo ▷ *vt* deshonrar
disgraceful [dɪs'greɪsful] *adj* vergonzoso; (*behaviour*) escandaloso
disgruntled [dɪs'grʌntld] *adj* disgustado, descontento
disguise [dɪs'gaɪz] *n* disfraz *m* ▷ *vt* disfrazar; (*voice*) disimular; (*feelings etc*) ocultar; **in ~** disfrazado; **to ~ o.s. as** disfrazarse de; **there's no disguising the fact that ...** no puede ocultarse el hecho de que ...
disgust [dɪs'gʌst] *n* repugnancia ▷ *vt* repugnar, dar asco a
disgusted [dɪs'gʌstɪd] *adj* indignado
disgusting [dɪs'gʌstɪŋ] *adj* repugnante, asqueroso
dish [dɪʃ] *n* (*gen*) plato; **to do** *or* **wash the ~es** fregar los platos; **dish out** *vt* (*money, exam papers*) repartir; (*food*) servir; (*advice*) dar; **dish up** *vt* servir
dishcloth ['dɪʃklɔθ] *n* (*for washing*) bayeta; (*for drying*) paño de cocina
dishearten [dɪs'hɑ:tn] *vt* desalentar
dishevelled, disheveled (*US*) [dɪ'ʃɛvəld] *adj* (*hair*) despeinado; (*clothes, appearance*) desarreglado
dishonest [dɪs'ɔnɪst] *adj* (*person*) poco honrado, tramposo; (*means*) fraudulento
dishonesty [dɪs'ɔnɪstɪ] *n* falta de honradez
dishonour, dishonor (*US*) [dɪs'ɔnə^r] *n* deshonra
dishtowel ['dɪʃtauəl] *n* (*US*) bayeta
dishwasher ['dɪʃwɔʃə^r] *n* lavaplatos *m inv*; (*person*) friegaplatos *m/f inv*
dishy ['dɪʃɪ] *adj* (*Brit inf*) buenón(-ona)
disillusion [dɪsɪ'lu:ʒən] *vt* desilusionar; **to become ~ed (with)** quedar desilusionado (con)
disincentive [dɪsɪn'sɛntɪv] *n* freno; **to act as a ~ (to)** actuar de freno (a); **to be a ~ to** ser un freno a
disinfect [dɪsɪn'fɛkt] *vt* desinfectar
disinfectant [dɪsɪn'fɛktənt] *n* desinfectante *m*
disinformation [dɪsɪnfə'meɪʃən] *n* desinformación *f*
disintegrate [dɪs'ɪntɪgreɪt] *vi* disgregarse, desintegrarse
disinterested [dɪs'ɪntrəstɪd] *adj* desinteresado
disjointed [dɪs'dʒɔɪntɪd] *adj* inconexo
disk [dɪsk] *n* (*Comput*) disco, disquete *m*; **single-/double-sided ~** disco de una cara/dos caras
disk drive *n* unidad *f* (de disco)
diskette [dɪs'kɛt] *n* diskette *m*, disquete *m*, disco flexible
disk operating system *n* sistema *m* operativo de discos
dislike [dɪs'laɪk] *n* antipatía, aversión *f* ▷ *vt* tener antipatía a; **to take a ~ to sb/sth** cogerle *or* (*LAm*) agarrarle antipatía a algn/algo; **I ~ the idea** no me gusta la idea
dislocate ['dɪsləkeɪt] *vt* dislocar; **he ~d his shoulder** se dislocó el hombro
dislodge [dɪs'lɔdʒ] *vt* sacar; (*enemy*) desalojar
disloyal [dɪs'lɔɪəl] *adj* desleal
dismal ['dɪzml] *adj* (*dark*) sombrío; (*depressing*) triste; (*very bad*) fatal
dismantle [dɪs'mæntl] *vt* desmontar, desarmar
dismay [dɪs'meɪ] *n* consternación *f* ▷ *vt* consternar; **much to my ~** para gran consternación mía
dismiss [dɪs'mɪs] *vt* (*worker*) despedir; (*official*) destituir; (*idea*) rechazar; (*Law*) rechazar; (*possibility*) descartar ▷ *vi* (*Mil*) romper filas
dismissal [dɪs'mɪsl] *n* despido; destitución *f*
dismount [dɪs'maunt] *vi* apearse; (*rider*) desmontar
disobedience [dɪsə'bi:dɪəns] *n* desobediencia
disobedient [dɪsə'bi:dɪənt] *adj* desobediente
disobey [dɪsə'beɪ] *vt* desobedecer; (*rule*) infringir
disorder [dɪs'ɔ:də^r] *n* desorden *m*; (*rioting*) disturbio; (*Med*) trastorno; (*disease*) enfermedad *f*; **civil ~** desorden *m* civil
disorderly [dɪs'ɔ:dəlɪ] *adj* (*untidy*) desordenado; (*meeting*) alborotado; **~ conduct** (*Law*) conducta escandalosa
disorganized [dɪs'ɔ:gənaɪzd] *adj* desorganizado
disorientated [dɪs'ɔ:rɪɛnteɪtəd] *adj* desorientado
disown [dɪs'əun] *vt* renegar de
disparaging [dɪs'pærɪdʒɪŋ] *adj* despreciativo; **to be ~ about sth/sb** menospreciar algo/a algn
dispassionate [dɪs'pæʃənɪt] *adj* (*unbiased*) imparcial; (*unemotional*) desapasionado
dispatch [dɪs'pætʃ] *vt* enviar; (*kill*) despachar; (*deal with: business*) despachar ▷ *n* (*sending*) envío; (*speed*) prontitud *f*; (*Press*) informe *m*; (*Mil*) parte *m*
dispel [dɪs'pɛl] *vt* disipar, dispersar
dispense [dɪs'pɛns] *vt* dispensar, repartir; (*medicine*) preparar; **dispense with** *vt fus* (*make unnecessary*) prescindir de

dispenser [dɪs'pɛnsəʳ] *n (container)* distribuidor *m* automático
dispensing chemist [dɪs'pɛnsɪŋ-] *n (Brit)* farmacia
disperse [dɪs'pəːs] *vt* dispersar ▷ *vi* dispersarse
dispirited [dɪ'spɪrɪtɪd] *adj* desanimado, desalentado
displace [dɪs'pleɪs] *vt (person)* desplazar; *(replace)* reemplazar
display [dɪs'pleɪ] *n (in shop window)* escaparate *m*; *(exhibition)* exposición *f*; *(Comput)* visualización *f*; *(Mil)* desfile *m*; *(of feeling)* manifestación *f*; *(pej)* aparato, pompa ▷ *vt* exponer; manifestar; *(ostentatiously)* lucir; **on ~** *(exhibits)* expuesto, exhibido; *(goods)* en el escaparate
displease [dɪs'pliːz] *vt (offend)* ofender; *(annoy)* fastidiar; **~d with** disgustado con
displeasure [dɪs'plɛʒəʳ] *n* disgusto
disposable [dɪs'pəuzəbl] *adj (not reusable)* desechable; **~ personal income** ingresos *mpl* personales disponibles
disposable nappy *n* pañal *m* desechable
disposal [dɪs'pəuzl] *n (sale)* venta; *(of house)* traspaso; *(by giving away)* donación *f*; *(arrangement)* colocación *f*; *(of rubbish)* destrucción *f*; **at one's ~** a la disposición de algn; **to put sth at sb's ~** poner algo a disposición de algn
dispose [dɪs'pəuz] *vi*: **~ of** *(time, money)* disponer de; *(unwanted goods)* deshacerse de; *(Comm: sell)* traspasar, vender; *(throw away)* tirar
disposed [dɪs'pəuzd] *adj*: **~ to do** dispuesto a hacer
disposition [dɪspə'zɪʃən] *n* disposición *f*; *(temperament)* carácter *m*
disproportionate [dɪsprə'pɔːʃənət] *adj* desproporcionado
disprove [dɪs'pruːv] *vt* refutar
dispute [dɪs'pjuːt] *n* disputa; *(verbal)* discusión *f*; *(also:* **industrial ~***)* conflicto (laboral) ▷ *vt (argue)* disputar; *(question)* cuestionar; **to be in** *or* **under ~** *(matter)* discutirse; *(territory)* estar en disputa; *(Law)* estar en litigio
disqualification [dɪskwɔlɪfɪ'keɪʃən] *n* inhabilitación *f*; *(Sport)* descalificación *f*; *(from driving)* descalificación *f*
disqualify [dɪs'kwɔlɪfaɪ] *vt (Sport)* desclasificar; **to ~ sb for sth/from doing sth** incapacitar a algn para algo/para hacer algo
disquiet [dɪs'kwaɪət] *n* preocupación *f*, inquietud *f*
disregard [dɪsrɪ'gɑːd] *vt* desatender; *(ignore)* no hacer caso de ▷ *n (indifference: to feelings, danger, money)*: **~ (for)** indiferencia (a); **~ (of)** *(non-observance: of law, rules)* violación *f* (de)
disrepair [dɪsrɪ'pɛəʳ] *n*: **to fall into ~** *(building)* desmoronarse; *(street)* deteriorarse
disreputable [dɪs'rɛpjutəbl] *adj (person, area)* de mala fama; *(behaviour)* vergonzoso
disrespectful [dɪsrɪ'spɛktful] *adj* irrespetuoso
disrupt [dɪs'rʌpt] *vt (plans)* desbaratar, alternar, trastornar; *(meeting, public transport, conversation)* interrumpir
disruption [dɪs'rʌpʃən] *n* desbaratamiento; trastorno; interrupción *f*
disruptive [dɪs'rʌptɪv] *adj (influence)* disruptivo; *(strike action)* perjudicial
dissatisfaction [dɪssætɪs'fækʃən] *n* disgusto, descontento
dissatisfied [dɪs'sætɪsfaɪd] *adj* insatisfecho
dissect [dɪ'sɛkt] *vt (also fig)* disecar
disseminate [dɪ'sɛmɪneɪt] *vt* divulgar, difundir
dissent [dɪ'sɛnt] *n* disensión *f*
dissertation [dɪsə'teɪʃən] *n (Univ)* tesina; *see also* **master's degree**
disservice [dɪs'səːvɪs] *n*: **to do sb a ~** perjudicar a algn
dissimilar [dɪ'sɪmɪləʳ] *adj* distinto
dissipate ['dɪsɪpeɪt] *vt* disipar; *(waste)* desperdiciar
dissolute ['dɪsəluːt] *adj* disoluto
dissolve [dɪ'zɔlv] *vt* disolver ▷ *vi* disolverse
dissuade [dɪ'sweɪd] *vt*: **to ~ sb (from)** disuadir a algn (de)
distance ['dɪstns] *n* distancia; **in the ~** a lo lejos; **what ~ is it to London?** ¿qué distancia hay de aquí a Londres?; **it's within walking ~** se puede ir andando
distant ['dɪstnt] *adj* lejano; *(manner)* reservado, frío
distaste [dɪs'teɪst] *n* repugnancia
distasteful [dɪs'teɪstful] *adj* repugnante, desagradable
distemper [dɪs'tɛmpəʳ] *n (of dogs)* moquillo
distended [dɪ'stɛndɪd] *adj (stomach)* hinchado
distil, distill (*US*) [dɪs'tɪl] *vt* destilar
distillery [dɪs'tɪlərɪ] *n* destilería
distinct [dɪs'tɪŋkt] *adj (different)* distinto; *(clear)* claro; *(unmistakeable)* inequívoco; **as ~ from** a diferencia de
distinction [dɪs'tɪŋkʃən] *n* distinción *f*; *(in exam)* sobresaliente *m*; **a writer of ~** un escritor destacado; **to draw a ~ between** hacer una distinción entre
distinctive [dɪs'tɪŋktɪv] *adj* distintivo
distinctly [dɪs'tɪŋktlɪ] *adv* claramente
distinguish [dɪs'tɪŋgwɪʃ] *vt* distinguir ▷ *vi*: **to ~ (between)** distinguir (entre)
distinguished [dɪs'tɪŋgwɪʃt] *adj (eminent)* distinguido; *(career)* eminente; *(refined)* distinguido, de categoría
distinguishing [dɪs'tɪŋgwɪʃɪŋ] *adj (feature)* distintivo
distort [dɪs'tɔːt] *vt* deformar; *(sound)* distorsionar; *(account, news)* tergiversar

d

distortion [dɪs'tɔːʃən] *n* deformación *f*; (*of sound*) distorsión *f*; (*of truth etc*) tergiversación *f*; (*of facts*) falseamiento
distract [dɪs'trækt] *vt* distraer
distracted [dɪs'træktɪd] *adj* distraído
distraction [dɪs'trækʃən] *n* distracción *f*; (*confusion*) aturdimiento; (*amusement*) diversión *f*; **to drive sb to ~** (*distress, anxiety*) volver loco a algn
distraught [dɪs'trɔːt] *adj* turbado, enloquecido
distress [dɪs'trɛs] *n* (*anguish*) angustia; (*want*) miseria; (*pain*) dolor *m*; (*danger*) peligro ▷ *vt* afligir; (*pain*) doler; **in ~** (*ship etc*) en peligro
distressing [dɪs'trɛsɪŋ] *adj* angustioso; doloroso
distribute [dɪs'trɪbjuːt] *vt* (*gen*) distribuir; (*share out*) repartir
distribution [dɪstrɪ'bjuːʃən] *n* distribución *f*
distributor [dɪs'trɪbjutəʳ] *n* (*Aut*) distribuidor *m*; (*Comm*) distribuidora
district ['dɪstrɪkt] *n* (*of country*) zona, región *f*; (*of town*) barrio; (*Admin*) distrito
district attorney *n* (*US*) fiscal *m/f*
district council *n* ≈ municipio; *ver nota*
district nurse *n* (*Brit*) *enfermera que atiende a pacientes a domicilio*
distrust [dɪs'trʌst] *n* desconfianza ▷ *vt* desconfiar de
disturb [dɪs'təːb] *vt* (*person: bother, interrupt*) molestar; (*meeting*) interrumpir; (*disorganize*) desordenar; **sorry to ~ you** perdone la molestia
disturbance [dɪs'təːbəns] *n* (*political etc*) disturbio; (*violence*) alboroto; (*of mind*) trastorno; **to cause a ~** causar alboroto; **~ of the peace** alteración *f* del orden público
disturbed [dɪs'təːbd] *adj* (*worried, upset*) preocupado, angustiado; **to be emotionally/mentally ~** tener problemas emocionales/ser un trastornado mental
disturbing [dɪs'təːbɪŋ] *adj* inquietante, perturbador(a)
disuse [dɪs'juːs] *n*: **to fall into ~** caer en desuso
disused [dɪs'juːzd] *adj* abandonado
ditch [dɪtʃ] *n* zanja; (*irrigation ditch*) acequia ▷ *vt* (*inf: partner*) deshacerse de; (*: plan, car etc*) abandonar
dither ['dɪðəʳ] *vi* vacilar
ditto ['dɪtəu] *adv* ídem, lo mismo
dive [daɪv] *n* (*from board*) salto; (*underwater*) buceo; (*of submarine*) inmersión *f*; (*Aviat*) picada ▷ *vi* (*swimmer: into water*) saltar; (*: under water*) zambullirse, bucear; (*fish, submarine*) sumergirse; (*bird*) lanzarse en picado; **to ~ into** (*bag etc*) meter la mano en; (*place*) meterse de prisa en
diver ['daɪvəʳ] *n* (*Sport*) saltador(a) *m(f)*; (*underwater*) buzo
diverse [daɪ'vəːs] *adj* diversos(-as), varios(-as)
diversification [daɪvəːsɪfɪ'keɪʃən] *n* diversificación *f*
diversion [daɪ'vəːʃən] *n* (*Brit Aut*) desviación *f*; (*distraction*) diversión *f*; (*Mil*) diversión *f*
diversity [daɪ'vəːsɪtɪ] *n* diversidad *f*
divert [daɪ'vəːt] *vt* (*Brit: train, plane, traffic*) desviar; (*amuse*) divertir
divide [dɪ'vaɪd] *vt* dividir; (*separate*) separar ▷ *vi* dividirse; (*road*) bifurcarse; **to ~ (between, among)** repartir *or* dividir (entre); **40 ~d by 5** 40 dividido por 5; **divide out** *vt*: **to ~ out (between, among)** (*sweets, tasks etc*) repartir (entre)
divided [dɪ'vaɪdɪd] *adj* (*country, couple*) dividido, separado; (*opinions*) en desacuerdo
divided highway *n* (*US*) carretera de doble calzada
dividend ['dɪvɪdɛnd] *n* dividendo; (*fig*) beneficio
divine [dɪ'vaɪn] *adj* divino ▷ *vt* (*future*) vaticinar; (*truth*) alumbrar; (*water, metal*) descubrir, detectar
diving ['daɪvɪŋ] *n* (*Sport*) salto; (*underwater*) buceo
diving board *n* trampolín *m*
divinity [dɪ'vɪnɪtɪ] *n* divinidad *f*; (*Scol*) teología
division [dɪ'vɪʒən] *n* (*also Brit Football*) división *f*; (*sharing out*) reparto; (*disagreement*) diferencias *fpl*; (*Comm*) sección *f*; (*Brit Pol*) votación *f*; **~ of labour** división *f* del trabajo
divisive [dɪ'vaɪsɪv] *adj* divisivo
divorce [dɪ'vɔːs] *n* divorcio ▷ *vt* divorciarse de
divorced [dɪ'vɔːst] *adj* divorciado
divorcee [dɪvɔː'siː] *n* divorciado(-a)
divot ['dɪvət] *n* (*Golf*) chuleta
divulge [daɪ'vʌldʒ] *vt* divulgar, revelar
DIY *adj, n abbr* (*Brit*) = **do-it-yourself**
dizziness ['dɪzɪnɪs] *n* vértigo
dizzy ['dɪzɪ] *adj* (*person*) mareado; (*height*) vertiginoso; **to feel ~** marearse; **I feel ~** estoy mareado
DJ *n abbr see* **disc jockey**
DNA *n abbr* (*= deoxyribonucleic acid*) ADN *m*

KEYWORD

do [duː] (*pt* **did**, *pp* **done**) *n* **1** (*inf: party etc*): **we're having a little do on Saturday** damos una fiestecita el sábado; **it was rather a grand do** fue un acontecimiento a lo grande
2: **the dos and don'ts** lo que se debe y no se debe hacer
▷ *aux vb* **1** (*in negative constructions: not translated*): **I don't understand** no entiendo
2 (*to form questions: not translated*): **do you speak English?** ¿habla (usted) inglés?; **didn't you know?** ¿no lo sabías?; **what do you think?** ¿qué opinas?

3 (*for emphasis, in polite expressions*): **people do make mistakes sometimes** a veces sí se cometen errores; **she does seem rather late** a mí también me parece que se ha retrasado; **do sit down/help yourself** siéntate/sírvete por favor; **do take care!** ¡ten cuidado! ¿eh?; **I DO wish I could ...** ojalá (que) pudiera ...; **but I DO like it** pero, sí (que) me gusta
4 (*used to avoid repeating vb*): **she sings better than I do** canta mejor que yo; **do you agree? — yes, I do/no, I don't** ¿estás de acuerdo? — sí (lo estoy)/no (lo estoy); **she lives in Glasgow — so do I** vive en Glasgow — yo también; **he didn't like it and neither did we** no le gustó y a nosotros tampoco; **who made this mess? — I did** ¿quién hizo esta chapuza? — yo; **he asked me to help him and I did** me pidió que le ayudara y lo hice
5 (*in question tags*): **you like him, don't you?** te gusta, ¿verdad? *or* ¿no?; **I don't know him, do I?** creo que no le conozco; **he laughed, didn't he?** se rió ¿no?
▷ *vt* **1** (*gen*): **what are you doing tonight?** ¿qué haces esta noche?; **what can I do for you?** (*in shop*) ¿en qué puedo servirle?; **what does he do for a living?** ¿a qué se dedica?; **I'll do all I can** haré todo lo que pueda; **what have you done with my slippers?** ¿qué has hecho con mis zapatillas?; **to do the washing-up/cooking** fregar los platos/ cocinar; **to do one's teeth/hair/nails** lavarse los dientes/arreglarse el pelo/ arreglarse las uñas
2 (*Aut etc*): **the car was doing 100** el coche iba a 100; **we've done 200 km already** ya hemos hecho 200 km; **he can do 100 in that car** puede ir a 100 en ese coche
3 (*visit*: *city, museum*) visitar, recorrer
4 (*cook*): **a steak – well done please** un filete bien hecho, por favor
▷ *vi* **1** (*act, behave*) hacer; **do as I do** haz como yo
2 (*get on, fare*): **he's doing well/badly at school** va bien/mal en la escuela; **the firm is doing well** la empresa anda *or* va bien; **how do you do?** mucho gusto; (*less formal*) ¿qué tal?
3 (*suit*): **will it do?** ¿sirve?, ¿está *or* va bien?; **it doesn't do to upset her** cuidado en ofenderla
4 (*be sufficient*) bastar; **will £10 do?** ¿será bastante con £10?; **that'll do** así está bien; **that'll do!** (*in annoyance*) ¡ya está bien!, ¡basta ya!; **to make do (with)** arreglárselas (con)
do away with *vt fus* (*kill*) eliminar; (*eradicate*: *disease*) eliminar; (*abolish*: *law etc*) abolir; (*withdraw*) retirar
do out of *vt fus*: **to do sb out of sth** pisar algo a algn
do up *vt* (*laces*) atar; (*zip, dress, shirt*) abrochar; (*renovate*: *room, house*) renovar
do with *vt fus* (*need*): **I could do with a drink/some help** no me vendría mal un trago/un poco de ayuda; (*be connected with*) tener que ver con; **what has it got to do with you?** ¿qué tiene que ver contigo?
do without *vi*: **if you're late for dinner then you'll do without** si llegas tarde tendrás que quedarte sin cenar ▷ *vt fus* pasar sin; **I can do without a car** puedo pasar sin coche

DOA *abbr* = **dead on arrival**
doc [dɔk] *n* (*inf*) médico(-a)
dock [dɔk] *n* (*Naut*: *wharf*) dársena, muelle *m*; (*Law*) banquillo (de los acusados); **docks** *npl* muelles *mpl*, puerto *sg* ▷ *vi* (*enter dock*) atracar (en el muelle) ▷ *vt* (*pay etc*) descontar
docker ['dɔkəʳ] *n* trabajador *m* portuario, estibador *m*
dockyard ['dɔkjɑːd] *n* astillero
doctor ['dɔktəʳ] *n* médico; (*Ph.D. etc*) doctor(a) *m(f)* ▷ *vt* (*fig*) arreglar, falsificar; (*drink etc*) adulterar
doctorate ['dɔktərɪt] *n* doctorado
Doctor of Philosophy *n* Doctor *m* (en Filosofía y Letras)
doctrine ['dɔktrɪn] *n* doctrina
docudrama [dɔkju'drɑːmə] *n* (TV) docudrama *m*
document ['dɔkjumənt] *n* documento ▷ *vt* documentar
documentary [dɔkju'mɛntərɪ] *adj* documental ▷ *n* documental *m*
documentation [dɔkjumɛn'teɪʃən] *n* documentación *f*
doddering ['dɔdərɪŋ], **doddery** ['dɔdərɪ] *adj* vacilante
doddle ['dɔdl] *n*: **it's a ~** (*Brit*: (*inf*)) es pan comido
dodge [dɔdʒ] *n* (*of body*) regate *m*; (*fig*) truco ▷ *vt* (*gen*) evadir; (*blow*) esquivar ▷ *vi* escabullirse; (*Sport*) hacer una finta; **to ~ out of the way** echarse a un lado; **to ~ through the traffic** esquivar el tráfico
dodgems ['dɔdʒəmz] *npl* (*Brit*) autos *or* coches *mpl* de choque
dodgy ['dɔdʒɪ] *adj* (*inf*: *uncertain*) dudoso; (*shady*) sospechoso; (*risky*) arriesgado
doe [dəu] *n* (*deer*) cierva, gama; (*rabbit*) coneja
does [dʌz] *vb see* **do**
doesn't ['dʌznt] = **does not**
dog [dɔg] *n* perro ▷ *vt* seguir (de cerca); (*fig*: *memory etc*) perseguir; **to go to the ~s** (*person*) echarse a perder; (*nation etc*) ir a la ruina
dog collar *n* collar *m* de perro; (*fig*) alzacuello(s) *msg*
dog-eared ['dɔgɪəd] *adj* sobado; (*page*) con la esquina doblada
dogged ['dɔgɪd] *adj* tenaz, obstinado
doggy ['dɔgɪ] *n* (*inf*) perrito
doggy bag *n* *bolsa para llevarse las sobras de la comida*

d

dogma ['dɔgmə] *n* dogma *m*
dogmatic [dɔg'mætɪk] *adj* dogmático
dogsbody ['dɔgzbɔdɪ] *n* (*Brit*) burro de carga
doily ['dɔɪlɪ] *n* pañito de adorno
doings ['duɪŋz] *npl* (*events*) sucesos *mpl*; (*acts*) hechos *mpl*
do-it-yourself [du:ɪtjɔ:'sɛlf] *n* bricolaje *m*
doldrums ['dɔldrəmz] *npl*: **to be in the ~** (*person*) estar abatido; (*business*) estar estancado
dole [dəul] *n* (*Brit*: *payment*) subsidio de paro; **on the ~** parado; **dole out** *vt* repartir
doleful ['dəulful] *adj* triste, lúgubre
doll [dɔl] *n* muñeca; **doll up** *vt*: **to ~ o.s. up** ataviarse
dollar ['dɔlə^r^] *n* dólar *m*
dollop ['dɔləp] *n* buena cucharada
dolphin ['dɔlfɪn] *n* delfín *m*
domain [də'meɪn] *n* (*fig*) campo, competencia; (*land*) dominios *mpl*
dome [dəum] *n* (*Arch*) cúpula; (*shape*) bóveda
domestic [də'mɛstɪk] *adj* (*animal, duty*) doméstico; (*flight, news, policy*) nacional
domestic appliance *n* aparato *m* doméstico, aparato *m* de uso doméstico
domesticated [də'mɛstɪkeɪtɪd] *adj* domesticado; (*person*: *home-loving*) casero, hogareño
dominant ['dɔmɪnənt] *adj* dominante
dominate ['dɔmɪneɪt] *vt* dominar
domination [dɔmɪ'neɪʃən] *n* dominación *f*
domineering [dɔmɪ'nɪərɪŋ] *adj* dominante
Dominican Republic [də'mɪnɪkən-] *n* República Dominicana
dominion [də'mɪnɪən] *n* dominio
domino (*pl* **dominoes**) ['dɔmɪnəu] *n* ficha de dominó
dominoes ['dɔmɪnəuz] *n* (*game*) dominó
don [dɔn] *n* (*Brit*) profesor(a) *m(f)* de universidad
donate [də'neɪt] *vt* donar
donation [də'neɪʃən] *n* donativo
done [dʌn] *pp of* **do**
donkey ['dɔŋkɪ] *n* burro
donor ['dəunə^r^] *n* donante *m/f*
donor card *n* carnet *m* de donante de órganos
don't [dəunt] = **do not**
donut ['dəunʌt] *n* (*US*) = **doughnut**
doodle ['du:dl] *n* garabato ▷ *vi* pintar dibujitos *or* garabatos
doom [du:m] *n* (*fate*) suerte *f*; (*death*) muerte *f* ▷ *vt*: **to be ~ed to failure** estar condenado al fracaso
doomsday ['du:mzdeɪ] *n* día *m* del juicio final
door [dɔ:^r^] *n* puerta; (*of car*) portezuela; (*entry*) entrada; **from ~ to ~** de puerta en puerta
doorbell ['dɔ:bɛl] *n* timbre *m*
door handle *n* tirador *m*; (*of car*) manija
doorknob *n* pomo *m* de la puerta, manilla *f* (*LAm*)
doorman ['dɔ:mən] *n* (*in hotel*) portero
doormat ['dɔ:mæt] *n* felpudo, estera
doorstep ['dɔ:stɛp] *n* peldaño; **on your ~** en la puerta de casa; (*fig*) al lado de casa
doorway ['dɔ:weɪ] *n* entrada, puerta; **in the ~** en la puerta
dope [dəup] *n* (*inf*: *illegal drug*) droga; (: *person*) imbécil *m/f*; (: *information*) información *f*, informes *mpl* ▷ *vt* (*horse etc*) drogar
dopey ['dəupɪ] *adj* atontado
dormant ['dɔ:mənt] *adj* inactivo; (*latent*) latente
dormitory ['dɔ:mɪtrɪ] *n* (*Brit*) dormitorio; (*US*: *hall of residence*) residencia, colegio mayor
dormouse (*pl* **dormice**) ['dɔ:maus, -maɪs] *n* lirón *m*
DOS [dɔs] *n abbr* = **disk operating system**
dosage ['dəusɪdʒ] *n* (*on medicine bottle*) dosis *f inv*, dosificación *f*
dose [dəus] *n* (*of medicine*) dosis *f inv*; **a ~ of flu** un ataque de gripe ▷ *vt*: **to ~ o.s. with** automedicarse con
dosser ['dɔsə^r^] *n* (*Brit inf*) mendigo(-a); (*lazy person*) vago(-a)
doss house ['dɔs-] *n* (*Brit*) pensión *f* de mala muerte
dossier ['dɔsɪeɪ] *n*: **~ (on)** expediente *m* (sobre)
dot [dɔt] *n* punto ▷ *vi*: **~ted with** salpicado de; **on the ~** en punto
dotcom ['dɔtkɔm] *n* puntocom *f*
dote [dəut]: **to ~ on** *vt fus* adorar, idolatrar
dot-matrix printer [dɔt'meɪtrɪks-] *n* impresora matricial *or* de matriz
dotted line ['dɔtɪd-] *n* línea de puntos; **to sign on the ~** firmar
double ['dʌbl] *adj* doble ▷ *adv* (*twice*): **to cost ~** costar el doble ▷ *n* (*gen*) doble *m* ▷ *vt* doblar; (*efforts*) redoblar ▷ *vi* doblarse; (*have two uses etc*): **to ~ as** hacer las veces de; **~ five two six (5526)** (*Telec*) cinco cinco dos seis; **spelt with a ~ "s"** escrito con dos "eses"; **on the ~** (*Brit*), **at the ~** corriendo; **double back** *vi* (*person*) volver sobre sus pasos; **double up** *vi* (*bend over*) doblarse; (*share bedroom*) compartir
double bass *n* contrabajo
double bed *n* cama de matrimonio
double-breasted ['dʌbl'brɛstɪd] *adj* cruzado
double-check ['dʌbltʃɛk] *vt* volver a revisar ▷ *vi*: **I'll ~** voy a revisarlo otra vez
double-click ['dʌbl,klɪk] (*Comput*) *vi* hacer doble clic
double-cross ['dʌbl'krɔs] *vt* (*trick*) engañar; (*betray*) traicionar
doubledecker ['dʌbl'dɛkə^r^] *n* autobús *m* de dos pisos
double glazing *n* (*Brit*) doble acristalamiento
double room *n* habitación *f* doble
doubles ['dʌblz] *n* (*Tennis*) juego de dobles
double whammy [-'wæmɪ] *n* (*inf*) palo doble

double yellow lines *npl* (*Brit*: *Aut*) *línea doble amarilla de prohibido aparcar*, ≈ línea *fsg* amarilla continua
doubly ['dʌblɪ] *adv* doblemente
doubt [daut] *n* duda ▷ *vt* dudar; (*suspect*) dudar de; **to ~ that** dudar que; **there is no ~ that** no cabe duda de que; **without (a) ~** sin duda (alguna); **beyond ~** fuera de duda; **I ~ it very much** lo dudo mucho
doubtful ['dautful] *adj* dudoso; (*arousing suspicion*: *person*) sospechoso; **to be ~ about sth** tener dudas sobre algo; **I'm a bit ~** no estoy convencido
doubtless ['dautlɪs] *adv* sin duda
dough [dəu] *n* masa, pasta; (*inf*: *money*) pasta, lana (*LAm*)
doughnut ['dəunʌt] *n* dónut *m*
douse [daus] *vt* (*drench*: *with water*) mojar; (*extinguish*: *flames*) apagar
dove [dʌv] *n* paloma
Dover ['dəuvəʳ] *n* Dover
dovetail ['dʌvteɪl] *vi* (*fig*) encajar
dowdy ['daudɪ] *adj* desaliñado; (*inelegant*) poco elegante
down [daun] *n* (*fluff*) pelusa; (*feathers*) plumón *m*, flojel *m*; (*hill*) loma ▷ *adv* (*also*: **~wards**) abajo, hacia abajo; (*on the ground*) por/en tierra ▷ *prep* abajo ▷ *vt* (*inf*: *drink*) beberse, tragar(se); **~ with X!** ¡abajo X!; **~ there** allí abajo; **~ here** aquí abajo; **I'll be ~ in a minute** ahora bajo; **England is two goals ~** Inglaterra está perdiendo por dos tantos; **I've been ~ with flu** he estado con gripe; **the price of meat is ~** ha bajado el precio de la carne; **I've got it ~ in my diary** lo he apuntado en mi agenda; **to pay £2 ~** dejar £2 de depósito; **he went ~ the hill** fue cuesta abajo; **~ under** (*in Australia etc*) en Australia/Nueva Zelanda; **to ~ tools** (*fig*) declararse en huelga
down-and-out ['daunəndaut] *n* (*tramp*) vagabundo(-a)
down-at-heel ['daunət'hiːl] *adj* venido a menos; (*appearance*) desaliñado
downcast ['daunkɑːst] *adj* abatido
downfall ['daunfɔːl] *n* caída, ruina
downhearted [daun'hɑːtɪd] *adj* desanimado
downhill [daun'hɪl] *adv*: **to go ~** ir cuesta abajo; (*business*) estar en declive
Downing Street ['daunɪŋ-] *n* (*Brit*) Downing Street *f*; *ver nota*

DOWNING STREET

Downing Street es la calle de Londres en la que tienen su residencia oficial tanto el Primer Ministro ("Prime Minister") como el Ministro de Economía ("Chancellor of the Exchequer"). El primero vive en el nº10 y el segundo en el nº11. Es una calle cerrada al público que se encuentra en el barrio de Westminster, en el centro de Londres. *Downing Street* se usa también en lenguaje periodístico para referirse al jefe del gobierno británico.

download ['daunləud] *vt* (*Comput*) transferir, telecargar
downloadable [daun'ləudəbl] *adj* (*Comput*) descargable
down payment *n* entrada, pago al contado
downpour ['daunpɔːʳ] *n* aguacero
downright ['daunraɪt] *adj* (*nonsense, lie*) manifiesto; (*refusal*) terminante
downsize [daun'saɪz] *vt* reducir la plantilla de
Down's syndrome [daunz-] *n* síndrome *m* de Down
downstairs [daun'stɛəz] *adv* (*below*) (en el piso de) abajo; (*motion*) escaleras abajo; **to come (*or* go) ~** bajar la escalera
downstream [daun'striːm] *adv* aguas *or* río abajo
down-to-earth [dauntu'əːθ] *adj* práctico
downtown [daun'taun] *adv* en el centro de la ciudad
down under *adv* en Australia (*or* Nueva Zelanda)
downward ['daunwəd] *adv* hacia abajo; **face ~** (*person*) boca abajo; (*object*) cara abajo ▷ *adj*: **a ~ trend** una tendencia descendente
downwards ['daunwədz] *adv* hacia abajo; **face ~** (*person*) boca abajo; (*object*) cara abajo
dowry ['daurɪ] *n* dote *f*
doz. *abbr* = **dozen**
doze [dəuz] *vi* dormitar; **doze off** *vi* echar una cabezada
dozen ['dʌzn] *n* docena; **a ~ books** una docena de libros; **~s of** cantidad de; **~s of times** cantidad de veces; **80p a ~** 80 peniques la docena
DPP *n abbr* (*Brit*) = **Director of Public Prosecutions**
Dr, Dr. *abbr* (= *doctor*) Dr
Dr. *abbr* (= *in street names*) = **Drive**
drab [dræb] *adj* gris, monótono
draft [drɑːft] *n* (*first copy*: *of document, report*) borrador *m*; (*Comm*) giro; (*US*: *call-up*) quinta ▷ *vt* (*write roughly*) hacer un borrador de; *see also* **draught**
drag [dræg] *vt* arrastrar; (*river*) dragar, rastrear ▷ *vi* arrastrarse por el suelo ▷ *n* (*Aviat*: *resistance*) resistencia aerodinámica; (*inf*) lata; (*women's clothing*): **in ~** vestido de mujer; **to ~ and drop** (*Comput*) arrastrar y soltar; **drag away** *vt*: **to ~ away (from)** separar a rastras (de); **drag on** *vi* ser interminable
dragon ['drægən] *n* dragón *m*
dragonfly ['drægənflaɪ] *n* libélula
drain [dreɪn] *n* desaguadero; (*in street*) sumidero; (*drain cover*) rejilla del sumidero

▷ *vt* (*land, marshes*) desecar; (*Med*) drenar; (*reservoir*) desecar; (*fig*) agotar ▷ *vi* escurrirse; **to be a ~ on** consumir, agotar; **to feel ~ed (of energy)** (*fig*) sentirse agotado
drainage ['dreɪnɪdʒ] *n* (*act*) desagüe *m*; (*Med, Agr*) drenaje *m*; (*sewage*) alcantarillado
draining board ['dreɪnɪŋ-], **drainboard** (*US*) ['dreɪnbɔːd] *n* escurridero, escurridor *m*
drainpipe ['dreɪnpaɪp] *n* tubo de desagüe
dram [dræm] *n* (*drink*) traguito, copita
drama ['drɑːmə] *n* (*art*) teatro; (*play*) drama *m*
dramatic [drə'mætɪk] *adj* dramático; (*sudden, marked*) espectacular
dramatist ['dræmətɪst] *n* dramaturgo(-a)
dramatize ['dræmətaɪz] *vt* (*events etc*) dramatizar; (*adapt*: *novel*: *for TV, cinema*) adaptar
drank [dræŋk] *pt of* **drink**
drape [dreɪp] *vt* (*cloth*) colocar; (*flag*) colgar
drapes [dreɪps] *npl* (*US*) cortinas *fpl*
drastic ['dræstɪk] *adj* (*measure, reduction*) severo; (*change*) radical
draught, draft (*US*) [drɑːft] *n* (*of air*) corriente *f* de aire; (*drink*) trago; (*Naut*) calado; **on ~** (*beer*) de barril
draught beer *n* cerveza de barril
draughtboard ['drɑːftbɔːd] (*Brit*) *n* tablero de damas
draughts [drɑːfts] *n* (*Brit*) juego de damas
draughtsman, draftsman (*US*) ['drɑːftsmən] *n* proyectista *m*, delineante *m*
draw [drɔː] (*pt* **drew**, *pp* **drawn**) ▷ *vt* (*pull*) tirar; (*take out*) sacar; (*attract*) atraer; (*picture*) dibujar; (*money*) retirar; (*formulate*: *conclusion*): **to ~ (from)** sacar (de); (*comparison, distinction*): **to ~ (between)** hacer (entre) ▷ *vi* (*Sport*) empatar ▷ *n* (*Sport*) empate *m*; (*lottery*) sorteo; (*attraction*) atracción *f*; **to ~ near** *vi* acercarse; **draw back** *vi*: **to ~ back (from)** echarse atrás (de); **draw in** *vi* (*car*) aparcar; (*train*) entrar en la estación; **draw on** *vt* (*resources*) utilizar, servirse de; (*imagination, person*) recurrir a; **draw out** *vi* (*lengthen*) alargarse; **draw up** *vi* (*stop*) pararse ▷ *vt* (*document*) redactar; (*plan*) trazar
drawback ['drɔːbæk] *n* inconveniente *m*, desventaja
drawbridge ['drɔːbrɪdʒ] *n* puente *m* levadizo
drawer [drɔːʳ] *n* cajón *m*; (*of cheque*) librador(a) *m(f)*
drawing ['drɔːɪŋ] *n* dibujo
drawing board *n* tablero (de dibujante)
drawing pin *n* (*Brit*) chincheta *m*
drawing room *n* salón *m*
drawl [drɔːl] *n* habla lenta y cansina
drawn [drɔːn] *pp of* **draw** ▷ *adj* (*haggard*: *with tiredness*) ojeroso; (*: with pain*) macilento
dread [drɛd] *n* pavor *m*, terror *m* ▷ *vt* temer, tener miedo *or* pavor a
dreadful ['drɛdful] *adj* espantoso; **I feel ~!** (*ill*) ¡me siento fatal *or* malísimo!; (*ashamed*) ¡qué vergüenza!
dream [driːm] *n* sueño ▷ *vt, vi* (*pt, pp* **dreamed** *or* **dreamt** [drɛmt]) soñar; **to have a ~ about sb/sth** soñar con algn/algo; **sweet ~s!** ¡que sueñes con los angelitos!; **dream up** *vt* (*reason, excuse*) inventar; (*plan, idea*) idear
dreamer ['driːməʳ] *n* soñador(a) *m(f)*
dreamt [drɛmt] *pt, pp of* **dream**
dreamy ['driːmɪ] *adj* (*person*) soñador(a), distraído; (*music*) de sueño
dreary ['drɪərɪ] *adj* monótono, aburrido
dredge [drɛdʒ] *vt* dragar; **dredge up** *vt* sacar con draga; (*fig*: *unpleasant facts*) pescar, sacar a luz
dregs [drɛgz] *npl* heces *fpl*
drench [drɛntʃ] *vt* empapar; **~ed to the skin** calado hasta los huesos
dress [drɛs] *n* vestido; (*clothing*) ropa ▷ *vt* vestir; (*wound*) vendar; (*Culin*) aliñar; (*shop window*) decorar, arreglar ▷ *vi* vestirse; **to ~ o.s., get ~ed** vestirse; **she ~es very well** se viste muy bien; **dress up** *vi* vestirse de etiqueta; (*in fancy dress*) disfrazarse
dress circle *n* (*Brit*) principal *m*
dresser ['drɛsəʳ] *n* (*furniture*) aparador *m*; (*: US*) tocador *m*; (*Theat*) camarero(-a)
dressing ['drɛsɪŋ] *n* (*Med*) vendaje *m*; (*Culin*) aliño
dressing gown *n* (*Brit*) bata
dressing room *n* (*Theat*) camarín *m*; (*Sport*) vestuario
dressing table *n* tocador *m*
dressmaker ['drɛsmeɪkəʳ] *n* modista, costurera
dress rehearsal *n* ensayo general
drew [druː] *pt of* **draw**
dribble ['drɪbl] *vi* gotear, caer gota a gota; (*baby*) babear ▷ *vt* (*ball*) driblar, regatear
dried [draɪd] *adj* (*gen*) seco; (*fruit*) paso; (*milk*) en polvo
drier ['draɪəʳ] *n* = **dryer**
drift [drɪft] *n* (*of current etc*) flujo; (*of sand*) montón *m*; (*of snow*) ventisquero; (*meaning*) significado ▷ *vi* (*boat*) ir a la deriva; (*sand, snow*) amontonarse; **to catch sb's ~** cogerle el hilo a algn; **to let things ~** dejar las cosas como están; **to ~ apart** (*friends*) seguir su camino; (*lovers*) disgustarse, romper
driftwood ['drɪftwud] *n* madera flotante
drill [drɪl] *n* taladro; (*bit*) broca; (*of dentist*) fresa; (*for mining etc*) perforadora, barrena; (*Mil*) instrucción *f* ▷ *vt* perforar, taladrar; (*soldiers*) ejercitar; (*pupils*: *in grammar*) hacer ejercicios con ▷ *vi* (*for oil*) perforar
drink [drɪŋk] *n* bebida ▷ *vt, vi* (*pt* **drank**, *pp* **drunk**) beber, tomar (*LAm*); **to have a ~** tomar algo; tomar una copa *or* un trago; **a ~ of water** un trago de agua; **to invite sb for ~s** invitar a algn a tomar unas copas; **there's food and ~ in the kitchen** hay de comer y de beber en la cocina; **would you like something to ~?** ¿quieres beber or

tomar algo?; **drink in** *vt* (*person: fresh air*) respirar; (*: story, sight*) beberse
drink-driving [drɪŋk'draɪvɪŋ] *n*: **to be charged with ~** ser acusado de conducir borracho *or* en estado de embriaguez
drinker ['drɪŋkəʳ] *n* bebedor(a) *m(f)*
drinking water *n* agua potable
drip [drɪp] *n* (*act*) goteo; (*one drip*) gota; (*Med*) gota a gota *m*; (*sound: of water etc*) goteo; (*inf: spineless person*) soso(-a) ▷ *vi* gotear, caer gota a gota
drip-dry ['drɪp'draɪ] *adj* (*shirt*) de lava y pon
dripping ['drɪpɪŋ] *n* (*animal fat*) pringue *m* ▷ *adj*: **~ wet** calado
drive [draɪv] (*pt* **drove**, *pp* **driven**) *n* paseo (en coche); (*journey*) viaje *m* (en coche); (*also*: **~way**) entrada; (*street*) calle; (*energy*) energía, vigor *m*; (*Psych*) impulso; (*Sport*) ataque *m*; (*Comput*: *also*: **disk ~**) unidad *f* (de disco) ▷ *vt* (*car*) conducir, manejar (*LAm*); (*nail*) clavar; (*push*) empujar; (*Tech: motor*) impulsar ▷ *vi* (*Aut: at controls*) conducir, manejar (*LAm*); (*: travel*) pasearse en coche; **to go for a ~** dar una vuelta en coche; **it's three hours' ~ from London** es un viaje de tres horas en coche desde Londres; **left-/right-hand ~** conducción *f* a la izquierda/derecha; **front-/rear-wheel ~** tracción *f* delantera/trasera; **sales ~** promoción *f* de ventas; **to ~ sb mad** volverle loco a algn; **to ~ sb to (do) sth** empujar a algn a (hacer) algo; **he ~s a taxi** es taxista; **he ~s a Mercedes** tiene un Mercedes; **can you ~?** ¿sabes conducir *or* (*LAm*) manejar?; **to ~ at 50 km an hour** ir a 50km por hora; **drive at** *vt fus* (*fig: intend, mean*) querer decir, insinuar; **drive on** *vi* no parar, seguir adelante ▷ *vt* (*incite, encourage*) empujar; **drive out** *vt* (*force out*) expulsar, echar
drive-by ['draɪvbaɪ] *n*: **~ shooting** tiroteo desde el coche
drive-in ['draɪvɪn] *adj* (*esp US*): **~ cinema** autocine *m*
drivel ['drɪvl] *n* (*inf*) tonterías *fpl*
driven ['drɪvn] *pp of* **drive**
driver ['draɪvəʳ] *n* conductor(a) *m(f)*, chofer *m* (*LAm*); (*of taxi*) taxista *m/f*
driver's license *n* (*US*) carnet *m or* permiso de conducir
driveway ['draɪvweɪ] *n* camino de entrada
driving ['draɪvɪŋ] *n* conducir *m*, manejar *m* (*LAm*) ▷ *adj* (*force*) impulsor(a)
driving instructor *n* instructor(a) *m(f)* de autoescuela
driving lesson *n* clase *f* de conducir
driving licence *n* (*Brit*) carnet *m or* permiso de conducir
driving school *n* autoescuela
driving test *n* examen *m* de conducir
drizzle ['drɪzl] *n* llovizna, garúa (*LAm*) ▷ *vi* lloviznar
drone [drəun] *vi* (*bee, aircraft, engine*) zumbar; (*also*: **~ on**) murmurar sin interrupción ▷ *n* zumbido; (*male bee*) zángano
drool [dru:l] *vi* babear; **to ~ over sb/sth** caérsele la baba por algn/algo
droop [dru:p] *vi* (*flower*) marchitarse; (*shoulders*) encorvarse; (*head*) inclinarse
drop [drɔp] *n* (*of water*) gota; (*fall: in price*) bajada; (*: in salary*) disminución *f* ▷ *vt* (*allow to fall*) dejar caer; (*voice, eyes, price*) bajar; (*set down from car*) dejar ▷ *vi* (*object*) caer; (*price, temperature*) bajar; (*wind*) calmarse, amainar; (*numbers, attendance*) disminuir; **drops** *npl* (*Med*) gotas *fpl*; **cough ~s** pastillas *fpl* para la tos; **a ~ of 10%** una bajada del 10 por ciento; **to ~ anchor** echar el ancla; **to ~ sb a line** mandar unas líneas a algn; **drop in** *vi* (*inf: visit*): **to ~ in (on)** pasar por casa (de); **drop off** *vi* (*sleep*) dormirse ▷ *vt* (*passenger*) bajar, dejar; **drop out** *vi* (*withdraw*) retirarse
dropout ['drɔpaut] *n* (*from society*) marginado(-a); (*from university*) estudiante *m/f* que ha abandonado los estudios
dropper ['drɔpəʳ] *n* (*Med*) cuentagotas *m inv*
droppings ['drɔpɪŋz] *npl* excremento *sg*
dross [drɔs] *n* (*fig*) escoria
drought [draut] *n* sequía
drove [drəuv] *pt of* **drive**
drown [draun] *vt* (*also*: **~ out**: *sound*) ahogar ▷ *vi* ahogarse
drowsy ['drauzɪ] *adj* soñoliento; **to be ~** tener sueño
drudgery ['drʌdʒərɪ] *n* trabajo pesado *or* monótono
drug [drʌg] *n* (*Med*) medicamento, droga; (*narcotic*) droga ▷ *vt* drogar; **to be on ~s** drogarse; **he's on ~s** se droga
drug addict *n* drogadicto(-a)
drug dealer *n* traficante *m/f* de drogas
druggist ['drʌgɪst] *n* (*US*) farmacéutico(-a)
drugstore ['drʌgstɔ:ʳ] *n* (*US*) tienda (*de comestibles, periódicos y medicamentos*)
drug trafficker *n* narcotraficante *m/f*
drum [drʌm] *n* tambor *m*; (*large*) bombo; (*for oil, petrol*) bidón *m* ▷ *vi* tocar el tambor; (*with fingers*) tamborilear ▷ *vt*: **to ~ one's fingers on the table** tamborilear con los dedos sobre la mesa; **drums** *npl* batería *sg*
drummer ['drʌməʳ] *n* (*in military band*) tambor *m/f*; (*in jazz/pop group*) batería *m/f*
drumstick ['drʌmstɪk] *n* (*Mus*) palillo, baqueta; (*chicken leg*) muslo (de pollo)
drunk [drʌŋk] *pp of* **drink** ▷ *adj* borracho ▷ *n* (*also*: **~ard**) borracho(-a); **to get ~** emborracharse
drunken ['drʌŋkən] *adj* borracho
dry [draɪ] *adj* seco; (*day*) sin lluvia; (*climate*) árido, seco; (*humour*) agudo; (*uninteresting: lecture*) aburrido, pesado ▷ *vt* secar; (*tears*) enjugarse ▷ *vi* secarse; **on ~ land** en tierra firme; **to ~ one's hands/hair/eyes** secarse las manos/el pelo/las lágrimas; **dry up** *vi*

(*river*) secarse; (*supply, imagination etc*) agotarse; (*in speech*) atascarse
dry-clean ['draɪ'kliːn] *vt* limpiar *or* lavar en seco; **"~ only"** (*on label*) "limpieza *or* lavado en seco"
dry-cleaner's ['draɪ'kliːnəz] *n* tintorería
dry-cleaning ['draɪ'kliːnɪŋ] *n* lavado en seco
dryer ['draɪə^r] *n* (*for hair*) secador *m*; (*for clothes*) secadora
dryness ['draɪnɪs] *n* sequedad *f*
dry rot *n* putrefacción *f*
DSS *n abbr* (*Brit*) = **Department of Social Security**; *see* **social security**
DTP *n abbr* = **desktop publishing**; (*Med: vaccination*) = **diphtheria, tetanus, pertussis**
dual ['djuəl] *adj* doble
dual carriageway *n* (*Brit*) ≈ autovía
dual nationality *n* doble nacionalidad *f*
dual-purpose ['djuəl'pəːpəs] *adj* de doble uso
dubbed [dʌbd] *adj* (*Cine*) doblado
dubious ['djuːbɪəs] *adj* indeciso; (*reputation, company*) dudoso; (*character*) sospechoso; **I'm very ~ about it** tengo mis dudas sobre ello
Dublin ['dʌblɪn] *n* Dublín
duchess ['dʌtʃɪs] *n* duquesa
duck [dʌk] *n* pato ▷ *vi* agacharse ▷ *vt* (*plunge in water*) zambullir
duckling ['dʌklɪŋ] *n* patito
duct [dʌkt] *n* conducto, canal *m*
dud [dʌd] *n* (*shell*) obús *m* que no estalla; (*object, tool*): **it's a ~** es una filfa ▷ *adj*: **~ cheque** (*Brit*) cheque *m* sin fondos
due [djuː] *adj* (*proper*) debido; (*fitting*) conveniente, oportuno ▷ *adv*: **~ north** derecho al norte; **dues** *npl* (*for club, union*) cuota *sg*; (*in harbour*) derechos *mpl*; **in ~ course** a su debido tiempo; **~ to** debido a; **to be ~ to** deberse a; **the train is ~ to arrive at 8.00** el tren tiene (prevista) la llegada a las ocho; **the rent's ~ on the 30th** hay que pagar el alquiler el día 30; **I am ~ six days' leave** me deben seis días de vacaciones; **she is ~ back tomorrow** ella debe volver mañana
duel ['djuəl] *n* duelo
duet [djuː'ɛt] *n* dúo
duffel bag ['dʌfl-] *n* macuto
duffel coat ['dʌfl-] *n* trenca
dug [dʌg] *pt, pp of* **dig**
dugout ['dʌgaut] *n* (*canoe*) piragua (*hecha de un solo tronco*); (*Sport*) banquillo; (*Mil*) refugio subterráneo
duke [djuːk] *n* duque *m*
dull [dʌl] *adj* (*light*) apagado; (*stupid*) torpe; (*boring*) pesado; (*sound, pain*) sordo; (*weather, day*) gris ▷ *vt* (*pain, grief*) aliviar; (*mind, senses*) entorpecer
duly ['djuːlɪ] *adv* debidamente; (*on time*) a su debido tiempo
dumb [dʌm] *adj* (*inf!*) mudo; (*stupid*) estúpido; **to be struck ~** (*fig*) quedar boquiabierto
dumbfounded [dʌm'faundɪd] *adj* pasmado
dummy ['dʌmɪ] *n* (*tailor's model*) maniquí *m*; (*Brit: for baby*) chupete *m* ▷ *adj* falso, postizo; **~ run** ensayo
dump [dʌmp] *n* (*heap*) montón *m* de basura; (*place*) basurero, vertedero; (*inf*) tugurio; (*Mil*) depósito; (*Comput*) copia vaciada ▷ *vt* (*put down*) dejar; (*get rid of*) deshacerse de; (*Comput*) tirar (a la papelera); (*Comm: goods*) inundar el mercado de; **to be (down) in the ~s** (*inf*) tener murria, estar deprimido
dumpling ['dʌmplɪŋ] *n bola de masa hervida*
dumpy ['dʌmpɪ] *adj* regordete(-a)
dunce [dʌns] *n* zopenco
dune [djuːn] *n* duna
dung [dʌŋ] *n* estiércol *m*
dungarees [dʌŋgə'riːz] *npl* mono *sg*, overol *msg* (*LAm*)
dungeon ['dʌndʒən] *n* calabozo
duplex ['djuːplɛks] *n* (*US: also:* **~ apartment**) dúplex *m*
duplicate ['djuːplɪkət] *n* duplicado; (*copy of letter etc*) copia ▷ *adj* (*copy*) duplicado ▷ *vt* ['djuːplɪkeɪt] duplicar; (*photocopy*) fotocopiar; (*repeat*) repetir; **in ~** por duplicado
durable ['djuərəbl] *adj* duradero
duration [djuə'reɪʃən] *n* duración *f*
duress [djuə'rɛs] *n*: **under ~** por coacción
during ['djuərɪŋ] *prep* durante
dusk [dʌsk] *n* crepúsculo, anochecer *m*
dust [dʌst] *n* polvo ▷ *vt* (*furniture*) desempolvar; (*cake etc*): **to ~ with** espolvorear de; **dust off** *vt* (*also fig*) desempolvar, quitar el polvo de
dustbin ['dʌstbɪn] *n* (*Brit*) cubo de la basura, balde *m* (*LAm*)
duster ['dʌstə^r] *n* paño, trapo; (*feather duster*) plumero
dust jacket *n* sobrecubierta
dustman ['dʌstmən] *n* (*Brit*) basurero
dustpan ['dʌstpæn] *n* cogedor *m*
dusty ['dʌstɪ] *adj* polvoriento
Dutch [dʌtʃ] *adj* holandés(-esa) ▷ *n* (*Ling*) holandés *m* ▷ *adv*: **to go ~** pagar a escote; **the Dutch** *npl* los holandeses
Dutchman ['dʌtʃmən], **Dutchwoman** ['dʌtʃwumən] *n* holandés(-esa) *m(f)*
dutiful ['djuːtɪful] *adj* (*child*) obediente; (*husband*) sumiso; (*employee*) cumplido
duty ['djuːtɪ] *n* deber *m*; (*tax*) derechos *mpl* de aduana; (*Med: in hospital*) servicio, guardia; **on ~** de servicio; (*at night etc*) de guardia; **off ~** libre (de servicio); **to make it one's ~ to do sth** encargarse de hacer algo sin falta; **to pay ~ on sth** pagar los derechos sobre algo
duty-free [djuːtɪ'friː] *adj* libre de impuestos; **~ shop** tienda libre de impuestos
duvet ['duːveɪ] *n* (*Brit*) edredón *m* (nórdico)
DVD *n abbr* (= *digital versatile or video disc*) DVD *m*
DVD player *n* lector *m* de DVD
DVD writer *n* grabadora de DVD

DVLA *n abbr* (*Brit*: = *Driver and Vehicle Licensing Agency*) *organismo encargado de la expedición de permisos de conducir y matriculación de vehículos*
dwarf [dwɔ:f] (*pl* **dwarves** [dwɔ:vz]) *n* (*inf!*) enano(-a) *m(f)* ▷ *vt* empequeñecer
dwell [dwɛl] (*pt, pp* **dwelt** [dwɛlt]) *vi* morar; **dwell on** *vt fus* explayarse en
dwelling ['dwɛlɪŋ] *n* vivienda
dwelt [dwɛlt] *pt, pp of* **dwell**
dwindle ['dwɪndl] *vi* menguar, disminuir
dwindling ['dwɪndlɪŋ] *adj* (*strength, interest*) menguante; (*resources, supplies*) en disminución
dye [daɪ] *n* tinte *m* ▷ *vt* teñir; **hair ~** tinte *m* para el pelo
dying ['daɪɪŋ] *adj* moribundo, agonizante; (*moments*) final; (*words*) último
dyke [daɪk] *n* (*Brit*) dique *m*; (*channel*) arroyo, acequia; (*causeway*) calzada
dynamic [daɪ'næmɪk] *adj* dinámico
dynamite ['daɪnəmaɪt] *n* dinamita ▷ *vt* dinamitar
dynamo ['daɪnəməu] *n* dinamo *f*, dínamo *m* (*LAm*)
dynasty ['dɪnəstɪ] *n* dinastía
dysentery ['dɪsɪntrɪ] *n* disentería
dyslexia [dɪs'lɛksɪə] *n* dislexia
dyslexic [dɪs'lɛksɪk] *adj, n* disléxico(-a) *m(f)*

e

E, e [i:] *n* (*letter*) E, e *f*; (*Mus*) mi *m*; **E for Edward**, (*US*) **E for Easy** E de Enrique
E *abbr* (= *east*) E ▷ *n abbr* (= *Ecstasy*) éxtasis *m*
each [i:tʃ] *adj* cada *inv* ▷ *pron* cada uno; (*also*: **~ other**) el uno al otro; **they hate ~ other** se odian (entre ellos *or* mutuamente); **~ day** cada día; **they have two books ~** tienen dos libros cada uno; **they cost £5 ~** cuestan cinco libras cada uno; **~ of us** cada uno de nosotros
eager ['i:gəʳ] *adj* (*gen*) impaciente; (*hopeful*) ilusionado; (*keen*) entusiasmado; (*pupil*) apasionado; **to be ~ to do sth** estar deseoso de hacer algo; **to be ~ for** tener muchas ganas de, ansiar
eagle ['i:gl] *n* águila
ear [ɪəʳ] *n* oreja; (*sense of hearing*) oído; (*of corn*) espiga; **up to the ~s in debt** abrumado de deudas
earache ['ɪəreɪk] *n* dolor *m* de oídos
eardrum ['ɪədrʌm] *n* tímpano
earful ['ɪəful] *n*: **to give sb an ~** (*inf*) echar una bronca a algn
earl [ə:l] *n* conde *m*
earlier ['ə:lɪəʳ] *adj* anterior ▷ *adv* antes
early ['ə:lɪ] *adv* (*gen*) temprano; (*ahead of time*) con tiempo, con anticipación ▷ *adj* (*gen*) temprano; (*reply*) pronto; (*man*) primitivo; (*first: Christians, settlers*) primero; **to have an ~ night** acostarse temprano; **in the ~** *or* **~ in the spring/19th century** a principios de primavera/del siglo diecinueve; **you're ~!**

¡has llegado temprano *or* pronto!; **~ in the morning/afternoon** a primeras horas de la mañana/tarde; **she's in her ~ forties** tiene poco más de cuarenta años; **at your earliest convenience** (*Comm*) con la mayor brevedad posible; **I can't come any earlier** no puedo llegar antes

early retirement *n* jubilación *f* anticipada

earmark ['ɪəmɑːk] *vt*: **to ~ for** reservar para, destinar a

earn [əːn] *vt* (*gen*) ganar; (*salary*) percibir; (*interest*) devengar; (*praise*) ganarse; **to ~ one's living** ganarse la vida

earnest ['əːnɪst] *adj* (*wish*) fervoroso; (*person*) serio, formal ▷ *n* (*also*: **~ money**) anticipo, señal *f*; **in ~** *adv* en serio

earnings ['əːnɪŋz] *npl* (*personal*) ingresos *mpl*; (*of company etc*) ganancias *fpl*

earphones ['ɪəfəunz] *npl* auriculares *mpl*

earplugs ['ɪəplʌgz] *npl* tapones *mpl* para los oídos

earring ['ɪərɪŋ] *n* pendiente *m*, arete *m* (*LAm*)

earshot ['ɪəʃɔt] *n*: **out of/within ~** fuera del/al alcance del oído

earth [əːθ] *n* (*gen*) tierra; (*Brit Elec*) toma de tierra ▷ *vt* (*Brit Elec*) conectar a tierra

earthenware ['əːθnwɛəʳ] *n* loza (de barro)

earthly ['əːθlɪ] *adj* terrenal, mundano; **~ paradise** paraíso terrenal; **there is no ~ reason to think ...** no existe razón para pensar ...

earthquake ['əːθkweɪk] *n* terremoto

earth-shattering ['əːθʃætərɪŋ] *adj* trascendental

earthy ['əːθɪ] *adj* (*fig*: *uncomplicated*) sencillo; (*coarse*) grosero

ease [iːz] *n* facilidad *f*; (*comfort*) comodidad *f* ▷ *vt* (*task*) facilitar; (*problem*) mitigar; (*pain*) aliviar; (*loosen*) soltar; (*relieve*: *pressure, tension*) aflojar; (*weight*) aligerar; (*help pass*): **to ~ sth in/out** meter/sacar algo con cuidado ▷ *vi* (*situation*) relajarse; **with ~** con facilidad; **to feel at ~/ill at ~** sentirse a gusto/a disgusto; **at ~!** (*Mil*) ¡descansen!; **ease off, ease up** *vi* (*work, business*) aflojar; (*person*) relajarse

easel ['iːzl] *n* caballete *m*

easily ['iːzɪlɪ] *adv* fácilmente

east [iːst] *n* este *m*, oriente *m* ▷ *adj* del este, oriental ▷ *adv* al este, hacia el este; **the E~** el Oriente; (*Pol*) el Este

eastbound *adj* en dirección este

Easter ['iːstəʳ] *n* Pascua (de Resurrección)

Easter egg *n* huevo de Pascua

easterly ['iːstəlɪ] *adj* (*to the east*) al este; (*from the east*) del este

Easter Monday *n* lunes *m* de Pascua

eastern ['iːstən] *adj* del este, oriental; **E~ Europe** Europa del Este; **the E~ bloc** (*Pol*) los países del Este

Easter Sunday *n* Domingo de Resurrección

East Germany *n* (*formerly*) Alemania Oriental *or* del Este

easy ['iːzɪ] *adj* fácil; (*life*) holgado, cómodo; (*relaxed*) natural ▷ *adv*: **to take it** *or* **things ~** (*not worry*) no preocuparse; (*go slowly*) tomarlo con calma; (*rest*) descansar; **payment on ~ terms** (*Comm*) facilidades de pago; **I'm ~** (*inf*) me da igual, no me importa; **easier said than done** del dicho al hecho hay buen trecho

easy chair *n* butaca

easy-going ['iːzɪ'gəuɪŋ] *adj* acomodadizo

eat (*pt* **ate**, *pp* **eaten**) [iːt, eɪt, 'iːtn] *vt* comer; **eat away** *vt* (*sea*) desgastar; (*acid*) corroer; **eat away at, eat into** *vt fus* corroer; **eat out** *vi* comer fuera; **eat up** *vt* (*meal etc*) comerse; **it ~s up electricity** devora la electricidad

eau de Cologne [əudəkə'ləun] *n* (agua de) colonia

eaves [iːvz] *npl* alero *sg*

eavesdrop ['iːvzdrɔp] *vi*: **to ~ (on sb)** escuchar a escondidas *or* con disimulo (a algn)

ebb [ɛb] *n* reflujo ▷ *vi* bajar; (*fig*: *also*: **~ away**) decaer; **~ and flow** el flujo y reflujo; **to be at a low ~** (*fig*: *person*) estar de capa caída

ebony ['ɛbənɪ] *n* ébano

e-book ['iːbuk] *n* libro electrónico, e-book *m*

e-business [iːbɪznɪs] *n* (*commerce*) comercio electrónico; (*company*) negocio electrónico

EC *n abbr* (= *European Community*) CE *f*

e-card ['iːkɑːd] *n* tarjeta de felicitación electrónica, e-card *f*

ECB *n abbr* (= *European Central Bank*) BCE *m*

eccentric [ɪk'sɛntrɪk] *adj, n* excéntrico(-a)

ECG *n abbr* (= *electrocardiogram*) E.C.G. *m*

echo (*pl* **echoes**) ['ɛkəu] *n* eco *m* ▷ *vt* (*sound*) repetir ▷ *vi* resonar, hacer eco

e-cigarette ['iːsɪgərɛt] *n* cigarrillo electrónico

eclipse [ɪ'klɪps] *n* eclipse *m* ▷ *vt* eclipsar

eco-friendly ['iːkəufrɛndlɪ] *adj* ecológico

ecological [iːkə'lɔdʒɪkl] *adj* ecológico

ecologist [ɪ'kɔlədʒɪst] *n* ecologista *m/f*; (*scientist*) ecólogo(-a) *m(f)*

ecology [ɪ'kɔlədʒɪ] *n* ecología

e-commerce ['iːkɔməːs] *n* comercio electrónico

economic [iːkə'nɔmɪk] *adj* (*profitable*: *price*) económico; (*business etc*) rentable

economical [iːkə'nɔmɪkl] *adj* económico

economics [iːkə'nɔmɪks] *n* (*Scol*) economía ▷ *npl* (*financial aspects*) finanzas *fpl*

economist [ɪ'kɔnəmɪst] *n* economista *m/f*

economize [ɪ'kɔnəmaɪz] *vi* economizar, ahorrar

economy [ɪ'kɔnəmɪ] *n* economía; **economies of scale** economías *fpl* de escala

economy class *n* (*Aviat etc*) clase *f* turista

economy class syndrome *n* síndrome *m* de la clase turista

economy size *n* tamaño familiar

ecosystem ['iːkəusɪstəm] *n* ecosistema *m*

eco-tourism [iːkəu'tuərɪzm] *n* turismo verde *or* ecológico

ecstasy [ˈɛkstəsɪ] *n* éxtasis *m inv*; (*drug*) éxtasis *m inv*
ecstatic [ɛksˈtætɪk] *adj* extático, extasiado
ECT *n abbr* (= *electroconvulsive therapy*) = **shock therapy**
Ecuador [ˈɛkwədɔːʳ] *n* Ecuador *m*
ecumenical [iːkjuˈmɛnɪkl] *adj* ecuménico
eczema [ˈɛksɪmə] *n* eczema *m*
edge [ɛdʒ] *n* (*of knife etc*) filo; (*of object*) borde *m*; (*of lake etc*) orilla ▷ *vt* (*Sewing*) ribetear ▷ *vi*: **to ~ past** pasar con dificultad; **on ~** (*fig*) = **edgy**; **to ~ away from** alejarse poco a poco de; **to ~ forward** avanzar poco a poco; **to ~ up** subir lentamente
edgeways [ˈɛdʒweɪz] *adv*: **he couldn't get a word in ~** no pudo meter baza
edgy [ˈɛdʒɪ] *adj* nervioso, inquieto
edible [ˈɛdɪbl] *adj* comestible
edict [ˈiːdɪkt] *n* edicto
Edinburgh [ˈɛdɪnbərə] *n* Edimburgo
edit [ˈɛdɪt] *vt* (*be editor of*) dirigir; (*re-write*) redactar; (*cut*) cortar; (*Comput*) editar
edition [ɪˈdɪʃən] *n* (*gen*) edición *f*; (*number printed*) tirada
editor [ˈɛdɪtəʳ] *n* (*of newspaper*) director(a) *m(f)*; (*of book*) redactor(a) *m(f)*; (*also*: **film ~**) montador(a) *m(f)*
editorial [ɛdɪˈtɔːrɪəl] *adj* editorial ▷ *n* editorial *m*; **~ staff** redacción *f*
EDT *n abbr* (*US*: = *Eastern Daylight Time*) *hora de verano de Nueva York*
educate [ˈɛdjukeɪt] *vt* (*gen*) educar; (*instruct*) instruir
educated [ˈɛdjukeɪtɪd] *adj* culto
education [ɛdjuˈkeɪʃən] *n* educación *f*; (*schooling*) enseñanza; (*Scol*: *subject etc*) pedagogía; **primary/secondary ~** enseñanza primaria/secundaria
educational [ɛdjuˈkeɪʃənl] *adj* (*policy etc*) de educación, educativo; (*teaching*) docente; (*instructive*) educativo; **~ technology** tecnología educacional
eel [iːl] *n* anguila
eerie [ˈɪərɪ] *adj* (*sound, experience*) espeluznante
effect [ɪˈfɛkt] *n* efecto ▷ *vt* efectuar, llevar a cabo; **effects** *npl* (*property*) efectos *mpl*; **to take ~** (*law*) entrar en vigor *or* vigencia; (*drug*) surtir efecto; **in ~** en realidad; **to have an ~ on sb/sth** hacerle efecto a algn/afectar algo; **to put into ~** (*plan*) llevar a la práctica; **his letter is to the ~ that ...** su carta viene a decir que ...
effective [ɪˈfɛktɪv] *adj* (*gen*) eficaz; (*striking: display, outfit*) impresionante; (*real*) efectivo; **to become ~** (*law*) entrar en vigor; **~ date** fecha de vigencia
effectively [ɪˈfɛktɪvlɪ] *adv* (*efficiently*) eficazmente; (*strikingly*) de manera impresionante; (*in reality*) de hecho
effectiveness [ɪˈfɛktɪvnɪs] *n* eficacia
effeminate [ɪˈfɛmɪnɪt] *adj* afeminado
effervescent [ɛfəˈvɛsnt] *adj* efervescente
efficiency [ɪˈfɪʃənsɪ] *n* (*gen*) eficiencia; (*of machine*) rendimiento
efficient [ɪˈfɪʃənt] *adj* eficiente; (*remedy, product, system*) eficaz; (*machine, car*) de buen rendimiento
efficiently [ɪˈfɪʃəntlɪ] *adv* eficientemente, de manera eficiente
effort [ˈɛfət] *n* esfuerzo; **to make an ~ to do sth** hacer un esfuerzo *or* esforzarse para hacer algo
effortless [ˈɛfətlɪs] *adj* sin ningún esfuerzo
effusive [ɪˈfjuːsɪv] *adj* efusivo
EFL *n abbr* (*Scol*) = **English as a foreign language**
e.g. *adv abbr* (= *exempli gratia*) p.ej.
egg [ɛg] *n* huevo; **hard-boiled/soft-boiled/ poached ~** huevo duro *or* (*LAm*) a la copa *or* (*LAm*) tibio/pasado por agua/escalfado; **scrambled ~s** huevos revueltos; **egg on** *vt* incitar
eggcup [ˈɛgkʌp] *n* huevera
eggplant [ˈɛgplɑːnt] *n* (*esp US*) berenjena
eggshell [ˈɛgʃɛl] *n* cáscara de huevo
egg white *n* clara de huevo
egg yolk *n* yema de huevo
ego [ˈiːgəu] *n* ego
egotism [ˈɛgəutɪzəm] *n* egoísmo
egotist [ˈɛgəutɪst] *n* egoísta *m/f*
Egypt [ˈiːdʒɪpt] *n* Egipto
Egyptian [ɪˈdʒɪpʃən] *adj, n* egipcio(-a) *m(f)*
eiderdown [ˈaɪdədaun] *n* edredón *m*
eight [eɪt] *num* ocho
eighteen [eɪˈtiːn] *num* dieciocho
eighteenth [eɪˈtːinθ] *adj* decimoctavo; **the ~ floor** la planta dieciocho; **the ~ of August** el dieciocho de agosto
eighth [eɪtθ] *adj* octavo
eightieth [ˈeɪtɪɪθ] *adj* octogésimo
eighty [ˈeɪtɪ] *num* ochenta
Eire [ˈɛərə] *n* Eire *m*
either [ˈaɪðəʳ] *adj* cualquiera de los dos ...; (*both, each*) cada ▷ *pron*: **~ (of them)** cualquiera (de los dos) ▷ *adv* tampoco ▷ *conj*: **~ yes or no** o sí o no; **on ~ side** en ambos lados; **I don't like ~** no me gusta ninguno de los dos; **no, I don't ~** no, yo tampoco
eject [ɪˈdʒɛkt] *vt* echar; (*tenant*) desahuciar ▷ *vi* eyectarse
eke out [iːk-] *vt fus* (*money*) hacer que llegue
EKG *n abbr* (*US*) *see* **electrocardiogram**
elaborate [*adj* ɪˈlæbərɪt, *vb* ɪˈlæbəreɪt] *adj* (*design, pattern*) complejo ▷ *vt* elaborar; (*expand*) ampliar; (*refine*) refinar ▷ *vi* explicarse con muchos detalles
elapse [ɪˈlæps] *vi* transcurrir
elastic [ɪˈlæstɪk] *adj, n* elástico
elastic band *n* (*Brit*) gomita
elated [ɪˈleɪtɪd] *adj*: **to be ~** estar eufórico
elation [ɪˈleɪʃən] *n* euforia
elbow [ˈɛlbəu] *n* codo ▷ *vt*: **to ~ one's way through the crowd** abrirse paso a codazos por la muchedumbre

elbow grease *n* (*inf*): **to use some** *or* **a bit of ~** menearse
elder ['ɛldəʳ] *adj* mayor ▷ *n* (*tree*) saúco; (*person*) mayor; (*of tribe*) anciano
elderly ['ɛldəlɪ] *adj* de edad, mayor ▷ *npl*: **the ~** los mayores, los ancianos
eldest ['ɛldɪst] *adj, n* el/la mayor
elect [ɪ'lɛkt] *vt* elegir; (*choose*): **to ~ to do** optar por hacer ▷ *adj*: **the president ~** el presidente electo
election [ɪ'lɛkʃən] *n* elección *f*; **to hold an ~** convocar elecciones
election campaign *n* campaña electoral
electioneering [ɪlɛkʃə'nɪərɪŋ] *n* campaña electoral
elector [ɪ'lɛktəʳ] *n* elector(a) *m(f)*
electoral [ɪ'lɛktərəl] *adj* electoral
electoral college *n* colegio electoral
electoral roll *n* censo electoral
electorate [ɪ'lɛktərɪt] *n* electorado
electric [ɪ'lɛktrɪk] *adj* eléctrico
electrical [ɪ'lɛktrɪkl] *adj* eléctrico
electric blanket *n* manta eléctrica
electric chair *n* silla eléctrica
electric cooker *n* cocina eléctrica
electric current *n* corriente *f* eléctrica
electric fire *n* estufa eléctrica
electrician [ɪlɛk'trɪʃən] *n* electricista *m/f*
electricity [ɪlɛk'trɪsɪtɪ] *n* electricidad *f*; **to switch on/off the ~** conectar/desconectar la electricidad
electricity board *n* (*Brit*) compañía eléctrica (estatal)
electric light *n* luz *f* eléctrica
electric shock *n* electrochoque *m*
electrify [ɪ'lɛktrɪfaɪ] *vt* (*Rail*) electrificar; (*fig*: *audience*) electrizar
electrocardiogram [ɪ'lɛktrə'kɑːdɪəgræm] *n* electrocardiograma *m*
electrocute [ɪ'lɛktrəukjuːt] *vt* electrocutar
electrode [ɪ'lɛktrəud] *n* electrodo
electron [ɪ'lɛktrɔn] *n* electrón *m*
electronic [ɪlɛk'trɔnɪk] *adj* electrónico
electronic mail *n* correo electrónico
electronics [ɪlɛk'trɔnɪks] *n* electrónica
elegance ['ɛlɪgəns] *n* elegancia
elegant ['ɛlɪgənt] *adj* elegante
elegy ['ɛlɪdʒɪ] *n* elegía
element ['ɛlɪmənt] *n* (*gen*) elemento; (*of heater, kettle etc*) resistencia
elementary [ɛlɪ'mɛntərɪ] *adj* elemental; (*primitive*) rudimentario; (*school, education*) primario
elementary school *n* (*US*) escuela de enseñanza primaria
elephant ['ɛlɪfənt] *n* elefante *m*
elevate ['ɛlɪveɪt] *vt* (*gen*) elevar; (*in rank*) ascender
elevation [ɛlɪ'veɪʃən] *n* elevación *f*; (*rank*) ascenso; (*height*) altitud *f*
elevator ['ɛlɪveɪtəʳ] *n* (*US*) ascensor *m*, elevador *m* (*LAm*)
eleven [ɪ'lɛvn] *num* once
elevenses [ɪ'lɛvnzɪz] *npl* (*Brit*) ≈ café *m* de media mañana
eleventh [ɪ'lɛvnθ] *adj* undécimo; **at the ~ hour** (*fig*) a última hora
elf (*pl* **elves**) [ɛlf, ɛlvz] *n* duende *m*
elicit [ɪ'lɪsɪt] *vt*: **to ~ sth (from sb)** obtener algo (de algn)
eligible ['ɛlɪdʒəbl] *adj*: **an ~ young man/woman** un buen partido; **to be ~ for sth** llenar los requisitos para algo; **to be ~ for a pension** tener derecho a una pensión
eliminate [ɪ'lɪmɪneɪt] *vt* eliminar; (*score out*) suprimir; (*a suspect, possibility*) descartar
elite [eɪ'liːt] *n* élite *f*
elm [ɛlm] *n* olmo
elocution [ɛlə'kjuːʃən] *n* elocución *f*
elongated ['iːlɔŋgeɪtɪd] *adj* alargado
elope [ɪ'ləup] *vi* fugarse
elopement [ɪ'ləupmənt] *n* fuga
eloquent ['ɛləkwənt] *adj* elocuente
else [ɛls] *adv*: **or ~** si no; **something ~** otra cosa *or* algo más; **somewhere ~** en otra parte; **everywhere ~** en todas partes menos aquí; **everyone ~** todos los demás; **nothing ~** nada más; **is there anything ~ I can do?** ¿puedo hacer algo más?; **where ~?** ¿dónde más?, ¿en qué otra parte?; **there was little ~ to do** apenas quedaba otra cosa que hacer; **nobody ~** nadie más
elsewhere [ɛls'wɛəʳ] *adv* (*be*) en otra parte; (*go*) a otra parte
ELT *n abbr* (*Scol*) = **English Language Teaching**
elude [ɪ'luːd] *vt* eludir; (*blow, pursuer*) esquivar
elusive [ɪ'luːsɪv] *adj* esquivo; (*answer*) difícil de encontrar; **he is very ~** no es fácil encontrarlo
elves [ɛlvz] *npl of* **elf**
emaciated [ɪ'meɪsɪeɪtɪd] *adj* escuálido
email ['iːmeɪl] *n abbr* (= *electronic mail*) email *m*, correo electrónico ▷ *vt*: **to ~ sb** mandar un email *or* un correo electrónico a algn; **to ~ sb sth** mandar algo a algn por Internet, mandar algo a algn en un email *or* un correo electrónico
email address *n* dirección *f* electrónica, email *m*
emancipate [ɪ'mænsɪpeɪt] *vt* emancipar
embankment [ɪm'bæŋkmənt] *n* (*of railway*) terraplén *m*; (*riverside*) dique *m*
embargo (*pl* **embargoes**) [ɪm'bɑːgəu] *n* prohibición *f*; (*Comm, Naut*) embargo; **to put an ~ on sth** poner un embargo en algo
embark [ɪm'bɑːk] *vi* embarcarse ▷ *vt* embarcar; **to ~ on** (*journey*) emprender, iniciar; (*fig*) emprender
embarkation [ɛmbɑː'keɪʃən] *n* (*of people*) embarco; (*of goods*) embarque *m*
embarrass [ɪm'bærəs] *vt* avergonzar, dar vergüenza a; (*financially etc*) poner en un aprieto

embarrassed [ɪm'baerəst] *adj* azorado, violento; **to be ~** sentirse azorado *or* violento
embarrassing [ɪm'bærəsɪŋ] *adj* (*situation*) violento; (*question*) embarazoso
embarrassment [ɪm'bærəsmənt] *n* vergüenza, azoramiento; (*financial*) apuros *mpl*
embassy ['ɛmbəsɪ] *n* embajada
embed [ɪm'bɛd] *vt* (*jewel*) empotrar; (*teeth etc*) clavar
embellish [ɪm'bɛlɪʃ] *vt* embellecer; (*fig: story, truth*) adornar
embezzle [ɪm'bɛzl] *vt* desfalcar, malversar
embezzlement [ɪm'bɛzlmənt] *n* desfalco, malversación *f*
embitter [ɪm'bɪtə^r] *vt* (*person*) amargar; (*relationship*) envenenar
emblem ['ɛmbləm] *n* emblema *m*
embody [ɪm'bɔdɪ] *vt* (*spirit*) encarnar; (*ideas*) expresar
embossed [ɪm'bɔst] *adj* realzado; **~ with ...** con ... en relieve
embrace [ɪm'breɪs] *vt* abrazar, dar un abrazo a; (*include*) abarcar; (*adopt: idea*) adherirse a ▹ *vi* abrazarse ▹ *n* abrazo
embroider [ɪm'brɔɪdə^r] *vt* bordar; (*fig: story*) adornar, embellecer
embroidery [ɪm'brɔɪdərɪ] *n* bordado
embryo ['ɛmbrɪəu] *n* (*also fig*) embrión *m*
emcee [ɛm'siː] *n abbr* (*US: = master of ceremonies*) presentador(a) *m(f)*
emend [ɪ'mɛnd] *vt* (*text*) enmendar
emerald ['ɛmərəld] *n* esmeralda
emerge [ɪ'məːdʒ] *vi* (*gen*) salir; (*arise*) surgir; **it ~s that** resulta que
emergency [ɪ'məːdʒənsɪ] *n* (*event*) emergencia; (*crisis*) crisis *f inv*; **in an ~** en caso de urgencia; **(to declare a) state of ~** (declarar) estado de emergencia *or* de excepción
emergency brake *n* (*US*) freno de mano
emergency cord *n* (*US*) timbre *m* de alarma
emergency exit *n* salida de emergencia
emergency landing *n* aterrizaje *m* forzoso
emergency room (*US: Med*) *n* sala *f* de urgencias
emergency service *n* servicio de urgencia
emergent [ɪ'məːdʒənt] *adj* (*nation*) recientemente independizado
emery board ['ɛmərɪ-] *n* lima de uñas
emigrant ['ɛmɪgrənt] *n* emigrante *m/f*
emigrate ['ɛmɪgreɪt] *vi* emigrar
emigration [ɛmɪ'greɪʃən] *n* emigración *f*
émigré ['ɛmɪgreɪ] *n* emigrado(-a)
eminence ['ɛmɪnəns] *n* eminencia; **to gain** *or* **win ~** ganarse fama
eminent ['ɛmɪnənt] *adj* eminente
emission [ɪ'mɪʃən] *n* emisión *f*
emit [ɪ'mɪt] *vt* emitir; (*smell, smoke*) despedir
emoticon [ɪ'məutɪkɔn] *n* emoticón *m*
emotion [ɪ'məuʃən] *n* emoción *f*
emotional [ɪ'məuʃənl] *adj* (*person*) sentimental; (*scene*) conmovedor(a), emocionante
emotive [ɪ'məutɪv] *adj* emotivo
empathy ['ɛmpəθɪ] *n* empatía; **to feel ~ with sb** sentirse identificado con algn
emperor ['ɛmpərə^r] *n* emperador *m*
emphasis (*pl* **emphases**) ['ɛmfəsɪs, -siːz] *n* énfasis *m inv*; **to lay** *or* **place ~ on sth** (*fig*) hacer hincapié en algo; **the ~ is on sport** se da mayor importancia al deporte
emphasize ['ɛmfəsaɪz] *vt* (*word, point*) subrayar, recalcar; (*feature*) hacer resaltar
emphatic [ɛm'fætɪk] *adj* (*condemnation*) enérgico; (*denial*) rotundo
emphatically [ɛm'fætɪklɪ] *adv* con énfasis
empire ['ɛmpaɪə^r] *n* imperio
employ [ɪm'plɔɪ] *vt* (*give job to*) emplear; (*make use of: thing, method*) emplear, usar; **he's ~ed in a bank** está empleado en un banco
employee [ɪmplɔɪ'iː] *n* empleado(-a)
employer [ɪm'plɔɪə^r] *n* patrón(-ona) *m(f)*; (*businessman*) empresario(-a)
employment [ɪm'plɔɪmənt] *n* empleo; **full ~** pleno empleo; **without ~** sin empleo; **to find ~** encontrar trabajo; **place of ~** lugar *m* de trabajo
employment agency *n* agencia de colocaciones *or* empleo
empower [ɪm'pauə^r] *vt*: **to ~ sb to do sth** autorizar a algn para hacer algo
empress ['ɛmprɪs] *n* emperatriz *f*
emptiness ['ɛmptɪnɪs] *n* vacío
empty ['ɛmptɪ] *adj* vacío; (*street, area*) desierto; (*threat*) vano ▹ *n* (*bottle*) envase *m* ▹ *vt* vaciar; (*place*) dejar vacío ▹ *vi* vaciarse; (*house*) quedar(se) vacío *or* desocupado; (*place*) quedar(se) desierto; **to ~ into** (*river*) desembocar en
empty-handed ['ɛmptɪ'hændɪd] *adj* con las manos vacías
EMS *n abbr* (= *European Monetary System*) SME *m*
EMU *n abbr* (= *European Monetary Union, Economic and Monetary Union*) UME *f*
emulate ['ɛmjuleɪt] *vt* emular
emulsion [ɪ'mʌlʃən] *n* emulsión *f*
enable [ɪ'neɪbl] *vt*: **to ~ sb to do sth** (*allow*) permitir a algn hacer algo; (*prepare*) capacitar a algn para hacer algo
enact [ɪn'ækt] *vt* (*law*) promulgar; (*play, scene, role*) representar
enamel [ɪ'næməl] *n* esmalte *m*
enamoured [ɪ'næməd] *adj*: **to be ~ of** (*person*) estar enamorado de; (*activity etc*) tener gran afición a; (*idea*) aferrarse a
encased [ɪn'keɪst] *adj*: **~ in** (*covered*) revestido de
enchant [ɪn'tʃɑːnt] *vt* encantar
enchanting [ɪn'tʃɑːntɪŋ] *adj* encantador(a)
encl. *abbr* (= *enclosed*) adj
enclose [ɪn'kləuz] *vt* (*land*) cercar; (*with letter etc*) adjuntar; (*in receptacle*): **to ~ (with)**

encerrar (con); **please find ~d** le mandamos adjunto
enclosure [ɪn'kləuʒəʳ] *n* cercado, recinto; (*Comm*) carta adjunta
encompass [ɪn'kʌmpəs] *vt* abarcar
encore [ɔŋ'kɔːʳ] *excl* ¡otra!, ¡bis! ▷ *n* bis *m*
encounter [ɪn'kauntəʳ] *n* encuentro ▷ *vt* encontrar, encontrarse con; (*difficulty*) tropezar con
encourage [ɪn'kʌrɪdʒ] *vt* alentar, animar; (*growth*) estimular; **to ~ sb (to do sth)** animar a algn (a hacer algo)
encouragement [ɪn'kʌrɪdʒmənt] *n* estímulo; (*of industry*) fomento
encouraging [ɪn'kʌrɪdʒɪŋ] *adj* alentador(a)
encroach [ɪn'krəutʃ] *vi*: **to ~ (up)on** (*gen*) invadir; (*time*) adueñarse de
encyclopaedia, encyclopedia [ɛnsaɪkləu'piːdɪə] *n* enciclopedia
end [ɛnd] *n* fin *m*; (*of table*) extremo; (*of line, rope etc*) cabo; (*of pointed object*) punta; (*of town*) barrio; (*of street*) final *m*; (*Sport*) lado ▷ *vt* terminar, acabar; (*also*: **bring to an ~, put an ~ to**) acabar con ▷ *vi* terminar, cabar; **to ~ (with)** terminar (con); **in the ~** al final; **to be at an ~** llegar a su fin; **at the ~ of the day** (*fig*) al fin y al cabo, a fin de cuentas; **to this ~, with this ~ in view** con este propósito; **from ~ to ~** de punta a punta; **on ~** (*object*) de punta, de cabeza; **to stand on ~** (*hair*) erizarse, ponerse de punta; **for hours on ~** hora tras hora; **end up** *vi*: **to ~ up in** terminar en; (*place*) ir a parar a
endanger [ɪn'deɪndʒəʳ] *vt* poner en peligro; **an ~ed species** (*of animal*) una especie en peligro de extinción
endearing [ɪn'dɪərɪŋ] *adj* entrañable
endeavour, endeavor (*US*) [ɪn'dɛvəʳ] *n* esfuerzo; (*attempt*) tentativa ▷ *vi*: **to ~ to do** esforzarse por hacer; (*try*) procurar hacer
ending ['ɛndɪŋ] *n* fin *m*, final *m*; (*of book*) desenlace *m*; (*Ling*) terminación *f*
endive ['ɛndaɪv] *n* (*curly*) escarola; (*smooth, flat*) endibia
endless ['ɛndlɪs] *adj* interminable, inacabable; (*possibilities*) infinito
endorse [ɪn'dɔːs] *vt* (*cheque*) endosar; (*approve*) aprobar
endorsement [ɪn'dɔːsmənt] *n* (*approval*) aprobación *f*; (*signature*) endoso; (*Brit*: *on driving licence*) nota de sanción
endow [ɪn'dau] *vt* (*provide with money*) dotar; (*found*) fundar; **to be ~ed with** (*fig*) estar dotado de
endowment mortgage *n* hipoteca dotal
endowment policy *n* póliza dotal
endurance [ɪn'djuərəns] *n* resistencia
endure [ɪn'djuəʳ] *vt* (*bear*) aguantar, soportar; (*resist*) resistir ▷ *vi* (*last*) perdurar; (*resist*) resistir
enema ['ɛnɪmə] *n* (*Med*) enema *m*
enemy ['ɛnəmɪ] *adj, n* enemigo(-a) *m(f)*; **to make an ~ of sb** enemistarse con algn
energetic [ɛnə'dʒɛtɪk] *adj* enérgico
energy ['ɛnədʒɪ] *n* energía
enforce [ɪn'fɔːs] *vt* (*law*) hacer cumplir
engage [ɪn'geɪdʒ] *vt* (*attention*) captar; (*in conversation*) abordar; (*worker, lawyer*) contratar ▷ *vi* (*Tech*) engranar; **to ~ in** dedicarse a, ocuparse en; **to ~ sb in conversation** entablar conversación con algn; **to ~ the clutch** embragar
engaged [ɪn'geɪdʒd] *adj* (*Brit*: *busy, in use*) ocupado; (*betrothed*) prometido; **to get ~** prometerse; **he is ~ in research** se dedica a la investigación
engaged tone *n* (*Brit Tel*) señal *f* de comunicando
engagement [ɪn'geɪdʒmənt] *n* (*appointment*) compromiso, cita; (*battle*) combate *m*; (*to marry*) compromiso; (*period*) noviazgo; **I have a previous ~** ya tengo un compromiso
engagement ring *n* anillo de pedida
engaging [ɪn'geɪdʒɪŋ] *adj* atractivo, simpático
engender [ɪn'dʒɛndəʳ] *vt* engendrar
engine ['ɛndʒɪn] *n* (*Aut*) motor *m*; (*Rail*) locomotora
engine driver *n* (*Brit*: *of train*) maquinista *m/f*
engineer [ɛndʒɪ'nɪəʳ] *n* ingeniero(-a); (*Brit*: *for repairs*) técnico(-a); (*US Rail*) maquinista *m/f*; **civil/mechanical ~** ingeniero(-a) de caminos, canales y puertos/industrial
engineering [ɛndʒɪ'nɪərɪŋ] *n* ingeniería ▷ *cpd* (*works, factory*) de componentes mecánicos
England ['ɪŋglənd] *n* Inglaterra
English ['ɪŋglɪʃ] *adj* inglés(-esa) ▷ *n* (*Ling*) el inglés; **the English** *npl* los ingleses
English Channel *n*: **the ~** el Canal de la Mancha
Englishman ['ɪŋglɪʃmən], **Englishwoman** ['ɪŋglɪʃwumən] *n* inglés(-esa) *m(f)*
English-speaker ['ɪŋglɪʃspiːkəʳ] *n* persona de habla inglesa
English-speaking ['ɪŋglɪʃspiːkɪŋ] *adj* de habla inglesa
engrave [ɪn'greɪv] *vt* grabar
engraving [ɪn'greɪvɪŋ] *n* grabado
engrossed [ɪn'grəust] *adj*: **~ in** absorto en
engulf [ɪn'gʌlf] *vt* sumergir, hundir; (*fire*) devorar
enhance [ɪn'hɑːns] *vt* (*gen*) aumentar; (*beauty*) realzar; (*position, reputation*) mejorar
enigma [ɪ'nɪgmə] *n* enigma *m*
enjoy [ɪn'dʒɔɪ] *vt* (*have*: *health, fortune*) disfrutar de, gozar de; (*food*) comer con gusto; **I ~ doing ...** me gusta hacer ...; **to ~ o.s.** divertirse, pasarlo bien
enjoyable [ɪn'dʒɔɪəbl] *adj* (*pleasant*) agradable; (*amusing*) divertido
enjoyment [ɪn'dʒɔɪmənt] *n* (*use*) disfrute *m*; (*joy*) placer *m*

enlarge [ɪn'lɑːdʒ] *vt* aumentar; (*broaden*) extender; (*Phot*) ampliar ▷ *vi*: **to ~ on** (*subject*) tratar con más detalles
enlargement [ɪn'lɑːdʒmənt] *n* (*Phot*) ampliación *f*
enlighten [ɪn'laɪtn] *vt* informar, instruir
enlightened [ɪn'laɪtnd] *adj* iluminado; (*tolerant*) comprensivo
Enlightenment [ɪn'laɪtnmənt] *n* (*History*): **the ~** la Ilustración, el Siglo de las Luces
enlist [ɪn'lɪst] *vt* alistar; (*support*) conseguir ▷ *vi* alistarse; **~ed man** (*US Mil*) soldado raso
enmity ['ɛnmɪtɪ] *n* enemistad *f*
enormity [ɪ'nɔːmɪtɪ] *n* enormidad *f*
enormous [ɪ'nɔːməs] *adj* enorme
enough [ɪ'nʌf] *adj*: **~ time/books** bastante tiempo/bastantes libros ▷ *n*: **have you got ~?** ¿tiene usted bastante? ▷ *adv*: **big ~** bastante grande; **he has not worked ~** no ha trabajado bastante; **(that's) ~!** ¡basta ya!, ¡ya está bien!; **that's ~, thanks** con eso basta, gracias; **will five be ~?** ¿bastará con cinco?; **I've had ~** estoy harto; **he was kind ~ to lend me the money** tuvo la bondad *or* amabilidad de prestarme el dinero; **... which, funnily ~ ...** ... lo que, por extraño que parezca ...
enquire [ɪn'kwaɪə^r] *vt, vi* = **inquire**
enrage [ɪn'reɪdʒ] *vt* enfurecer
enrich [ɪn'rɪtʃ] *vt* enriquecer
enrol, enroll (*US*) [ɪn'rəul] *vt* (*member*) inscribir; (*Scol*) matricular ▷ *vi* inscribirse; (*Scol*) matricularse
enrolment, enrollment (*US*) [ɪn'rəulmənt] *n* inscripción *f*; matriculación *f*
en route [ɔn'ruːt] *adv* durante el viaje; **~ for/from/to** camino de/de/a
ensconce [ɪn'skɔns] *vt*: **to ~ o.s.** instalarse cómodamente, acomodarse
ensue [ɪn'sjuː] *vi* seguirse; (*result*) resultar
en suite [ɔn'swiːt] *adj*: **with ~ bathroom** con baño
ensure [ɪn'ʃuə^r] *vt* asegurar
entail [ɪn'teɪl] *vt* (*imply*) suponer; (*result in*) acarrear
entangle [ɪn'tæŋgl] *vt* (*thread etc*) enredar, enmarañar; **to become ~d in sth** (*fig*) enredarse en algo
enter ['ɛntə^r] *vt* (*room, profession*) entrar en; (*club*) hacerse socio de; (*army*) alistarse en; (*sb for a competition*) inscribir; (*write down*) anotar, apuntar; (*Comput*) introducir ▷ *vi* entrar; **enter for** *vt fus* presentarse a; **enter into** *vt fus* (*relations*) establecer; (*plans*) formar parte de; (*debate*) tomar parte en; (*negotiations*) entablar; (*agreement*) llegar a, firmar; **enter (up)on** *vt fus* (*career*) emprender
enterprise ['ɛntəpraɪz] *n* empresa; (*spirit*) iniciativa; **free ~** la libre empresa; **private ~** la iniciativa privada
enterprising ['ɛntəpraɪzɪŋ] *adj* emprendedor(a)
entertain [ɛntə'teɪn] *vt* (*amuse*) divertir; (*receive: guest*) recibir (en casa); (*idea*) abrigar
entertainer [ɛntə'teɪnə^r] *n* artista *m/f*
entertaining [ɛntə'teɪnɪŋ] *adj* divertido, entretenido ▷ *n*: **to do a lot of ~** dar muchas fiestas, tener muchos invitados
entertainment [ɛntə'teɪnmənt] *n* (*amusement*) diversión *f*; (*show*) espectáculo; (*party*) fiesta
enthralled [ɪn'θrɔːld] *adj* cautivado
enthralling [ɪn'θrɔːlɪŋ] *adj* cautivador(a)
enthusiasm [ɪn'θuːzɪæzəm] *n* entusiasmo
enthusiast [ɪn'θuːzɪæst] *n* entusiasta *m/f*
enthusiastic [ɪnθuːzɪ'æstɪk] *adj* entusiasta; **to be ~ about sb/sth** estar entusiasmado con algn/algo
entice [ɪn'taɪs] *vt* tentar; (*seduce*) seducir
entire [ɪn'taɪə^r] *adj* entero, todo
entirely [ɪn'taɪəlɪ] *adv* totalmente
entirety [ɪn'taɪərətɪ] *n*: **in its ~** en su totalidad
entitle [ɪn'taɪtl] *vt*: **to ~ sb to sth** dar a algn derecho a algo
entitled [ɪn'taɪtld] *adj* (*book*) titulado; **to be ~ to sth/to do sth** tener derecho a algo/a hacer algo
entity ['ɛntɪtɪ] *n* entidad *f*
entourage [ɔntu'rɑːʒ] *n* séquito
entrance ['ɛntrəns] *n* entrada ▷ *vt* [ɪn'trɑːns] encantar, hechizar; **to gain ~ to** (*university etc*) ingresar en
entrance examination *n* (*to school*) examen *m* de ingreso
entrance fee *n* (*to a show*) entrada; (*to a club*) cuota
entrance ramp *n* (*US Aut*) rampa de acceso
entrant ['ɛntrənt] *n* (*in race, competition*) participante *m/f*; (*in exam*) candidato(-a)
entrenched [ɛn'trɛntʃd] *adj*: **~ interests** intereses *mpl* creados
entrepreneur [ɔntrəprə'nəː^r] *n* empresario(-a), capitalista *m/f*
entrust [ɪn'trʌst] *vt*: **to ~ sth to sb** confiar algo a algn
entry ['ɛntrɪ] *n* entrada; (*permission to enter*) acceso; (*in register, diary, ship's log*) apunte *m*; (*in account book, ledger, list*) partida; **no ~** prohibido el paso; (*Aut*) dirección prohibida; **single/double ~ book-keeping** contabilidad *f* simple/por partida doble
entry form *n* boletín *m* de inscripción
entry phone *n* (*Brit*) portero automático
E-number ['iːnʌmbə^r] *n* número E
enunciate [ɪ'nʌnsɪeɪt] *vt* pronunciar; (*principle etc*) enunciar
envelop [ɪn'vɛləp] *vt* envolver
envelope ['ɛnvələup] *n* sobre *m*
enviable ['ɛnvɪəbl] *adj* envidiable
envious ['ɛnvɪəs] *adj* envidioso; (*look*) de envidia
environment [ɪn'vaɪərnmənt] *n* medio ambiente; (*surroundings*) entorno;

Department of the E~ ministerio del medio ambiente
environmental [ɪnvaɪərn'mɛntl] *adj* (medio) ambiental; **~ studies** (*in school etc*) ecología *sg*
environmentalist [ɪnvaɪərn'mɛntlɪst] *n* ecologista *m/f*
environmentally [ɪnvaɪərn'mɛntlɪ] *adv*: **~ sound/friendly** ecológico
envisage [ɪn'vɪzɪdʒ] *vt* (*foresee*) prever; (*imagine*) concebir
envoy ['ɛnvɔɪ] *n* enviado(-a)
envy ['ɛnvɪ] *n* envidia ▷ *vt* tener envidia a; **to ~ sb sth** envidiar algo a algn
EPA *n abbr* (*US*: = *Environmental Protection Agency*) *Agencia del Medio Ambiente*
epic ['ɛpɪk] *n* épica ▷ *adj* épico
epicentre, epicenter (US) ['ɛpɪsɛntəʳ] *n* epicentro
epidemic [ɛpɪ'dɛmɪk] *n* epidemia
epilepsy ['ɛpɪlɛpsɪ] *n* epilepsia
epileptic [ɛpɪ'lɛptɪk] *adj, n* epiléptico(-a) *m(f)*
epileptic fit [ɛpɪ'lɛptɪk-] *n* ataque *m* de epilepsia, acceso *m* epiléptico
epilogue ['ɛpɪlɔg] *n* epílogo
episode ['ɛpɪsəud] *n* episodio
epitome [ɪ'pɪtəmɪ] *n* arquetipo
epitomize [ɪ'pɪtəmaɪz] *vt* representar
epoch ['i:pɔk] *n* época
equable ['ɛkwəbl] *adj* (*climate*) estable; (*character*) ecuánime
equal ['i:kwl] *adj* (*gen*) igual; (*treatment*) equitativo ▷ *n* igual *m/f* ▷ *vt* ser igual a; (*fig*) igualar; **to be ~ to** (*task*) estar a la altura de; **the E~ Opportunities Commission** (*Brit*) *comisión para la igualdad de la mujer en el trabajo*
equality [i:'kwɔlɪtɪ] *n* igualdad *f*
equalize ['i:kwəlaɪz] *vt, vi* igualar; (*Sport*) empatar
equally ['i:kwəlɪ] *adv* igualmente; (*share etc*) a partes iguales; **they are ~ clever** son tan listos uno como otro
equanimity [ɛkwə'nɪmɪtɪ] *n* ecuanimidad *f*
equate [ɪ'kweɪt] *vt*: **to ~ sth with** equiparar algo con
equation [ɪ'kweɪʒən] *n* (*Math*) ecuación *f*
equator [ɪ'kweɪtəʳ] *n* ecuador *m*
equilibrium [i:kwɪ'lɪbrɪəm] *n* equilibrio
equip [ɪ'kwɪp] *vt* (*gen*) equipar; (*person*) proveer; **~ped with** (*machinery etc*) provisto de; **to be well ~ped** estar bien equipado; **he is well ~ped for the job** está bien preparado para este puesto
equipment [ɪ'kwɪpmənt] *n* equipo
equities ['ɛkwɪtɪz] *npl* (*Brit Comm*) acciones *fpl* ordinarias
equivalent [ɪ'kwɪvəlnt] *adj, n* equivalente *m*; **to be ~ to** equivaler a
equivocal [ɪ'kwɪvəkl] *adj* equívoco
ER *abbr* (*Brit*: = *Elizabeth Regina*) *la reina Isabel*; (*US*: *Med*) = **emergency room**
era ['ɪərə] *n* era, época
eradicate [ɪ'rædɪkeɪt] *vt* erradicar, extirpar
erase [ɪ'reɪz] *vt* (*Comput*) borrar
eraser [ɪ'reɪzəʳ] *n* goma de borrar
e-reader ['i:'ri:dəʳ] *n* lector *m* de libros electrónicos, e-reader *m*
erect [ɪ'rɛkt] *adj* erguido ▷ *vt* erigir, levantar; (*assemble*) montar
erection [ɪ'rɛkʃən] *n* (*of building*) construcción *f*; (*of machinery*) montaje *m*; (*structure*) edificio; (*Med*) erección *f*
Eritrea [ɛrɪ'treɪə] *n* Eritrea
ERM *n abbr* (= *Exchange Rate Mechanism*) (mecanismo de cambios del) SME *m*
erode [ɪ'rəud] *vt* (*Geo*) erosionar; (*metal*) corroer, desgastar
erosion [ɪ'rəuʒən] *n* erosión *f*; desgaste *m*
erotic [ɪ'rɔtɪk] *adj* erótico
err [ə:ʳ] *vi* errar; (*Rel*) pecar
errand ['ɛrnd] *n* recado, mandado (*LAm*); **to run ~s** hacer recados; **~ of mercy** misión *f* de caridad
erratic [ɪ'rætɪk] *adj* variable; (*results etc*) desigual, poco uniforme
error ['ɛrəʳ] *n* error *m*, equivocación *f*; **typing/spelling ~** error de mecanografía/ortografía; **in ~** por equivocación; **~s and omissions excepted** salvo error u omisión
erupt [ɪ'rʌpt] *vi* entrar en erupción; (*Med*) hacer erupción; (*fig*) estallar
eruption [ɪ'rʌpʃən] *n* erupción *f*; (*fig*: *of anger, violence*) explosión *f*, estallido
escalate ['ɛskəleɪt] *vi* extenderse, intensificarse; (*costs*) aumentar vertiginosamente
escalator ['ɛskəleɪtəʳ] *n* escalera mecánica
escapade [ɛskə'peɪd] *n* aventura
escape [ɪ'skeɪp] *n* (*gen*) fuga; (*Tech*) escape *m*; (*from duties*) escapatoria; (*from chase*) evasión *f* ▷ *vi* (*gen*) escaparse; (*flee*) huir, evadirse ▷ *vt* evitar, eludir; (*consequences*) escapar a; **his name ~s me** no me sale su nombre; **to ~ from** (*place*) escaparse de; (*person*) huir de; (*clutches*) librarse de; **to ~ to** (*another place, freedom, safety*) huir a; **to ~ notice** pasar desapercibido
escapism [ɪ'skeɪpɪzəm] *n* escapismo, evasión *f*
eschew [ɪs'tʃu:] *vt* evitar, abstenerse de
escort ['ɛskɔ:t] *n* acompañante *m/f*; (*Mil*) escolta; (*Naut*) convoy *m* ▷ *vt* [ɪ'skɔ:t] acompañar; (*Mil, Naut*) escoltar
Eskimo ['ɛskɪməu] *adj* esquimal ▷ *n* esquimal *m/f*; (*Ling*) esquimal *m*
ESL *n abbr* (*Scol*) = **English as a Second Language**
esophagus [i:'sɔfəgəs] *n* (*US*) = **oesophagus**
ESP *n abbr* = **extrasensory perception**; (*Scol*: = *English for Specific (or Special) Purposes*) *inglés especializado*
esp. *abbr* = **especially**
especially [ɪ'spɛʃlɪ] *adv* (*gen*) especialmente; (*above all*) sobre todo; (*particularly*) en especial

espionage ['ɛspɪənɑːʒ] *n* espionaje *m*
Esq. *abbr* (= *Esquire*) D.
Esquire [ɪ'skwaɪə^r] *n*: **J. Brown, ~** Sr. D. J. Brown
essay ['ɛseɪ] *n* (*Scol*) redacción *f*; (*: longer*) trabajo
essence ['ɛsns] *n* esencia; **in ~** esencialmente; **speed is of the ~** es esencial hacerlo con la mayor prontitud
essential [ɪ'sɛnʃl] *adj* (*necessary*) imprescindible; (*basic*) esencial ▷ *n often pl* lo esencial; **it is ~ that** es imprescindible que
essentially [ɪ'sɛnʃlɪ] *adv* esencialmente
EST *n abbr* (*US*: = *Eastern Standard Time*) *hora de invierno de Nueva York*
establish [ɪ'stæblɪʃ] *vt* establecer; (*prove: fact*) comprobar, demostrar; (*identity*) verificar; (*relations*) entablar
established [ɪ'stæblɪʃt] *adj* (*business*) de buena reputación; (*staff*) de plantilla
establishment [ɪ'stæblɪʃmənt] *n* establecimiento; (*also*: **the E~**) la clase dirigente; **a teaching ~** un centro de enseñanza
estate [ɪ'steɪt] *n* (*land*) finca, hacienda; (*property*) propiedad *f*; (*inheritance*) herencia; (*Pol*) estado; **housing ~** (*Brit*) urbanización *f*; **industrial ~** polígono industrial
estate agent *n* (*Brit*) agente *m/f* inmobiliario(-a)
estate car *n* (*Brit*) ranchera, coche *m* familiar
esteem [ɪ'stiːm] *n*: **to hold sb in high ~** estimar en mucho a algn ▷ *vt* estimar
esthetic [iːs'θɛtɪk] *adj* (*US*) = **aesthetic**
estimate ['ɛstɪmət] *n* estimación *f*; (*assessment*) tasa, cálculo; (*Comm*) presupuesto ▷ *vt* ['ɛstɪmeɪt] estimar; tasar, calcular; **to give sb an ~ of** presentar a algn un presupuesto de; **at a rough ~** haciendo un cálculo aproximado; **to ~ for** (*Comm*) hacer un presupuesto de, presupuestar
estimation [ɛstɪ'meɪʃən] *n* opinión *f*, juicio; (*esteem*) aprecio; **in my ~** a mi juicio
Estonia [ɛ'stəunɪə] *n* Estonia
estranged [ɪ'streɪndʒd] *adj* separado
e-tailing ['iːteɪlɪŋ] *n* venta en línea, venta vía *or* por Internet
et al. *abbr* (= *et alii: and others*) et al.
etc *abbr* (= *et cetera*) etc
etching ['ɛtʃɪŋ] *n* aguafuerte *m or f*
eternal [ɪ'təːnl] *adj* eterno
eternity [ɪ'təːnɪtɪ] *n* eternidad *f*
ethical ['ɛθɪkl] *adj* ético; (*honest*) honrado
ethics ['ɛθɪks] *n* ética ▷ *npl* moralidad *f*
Ethiopia [iːθɪ'əupɪə] *n* Etiopía
ethnic ['ɛθnɪk] *adj* étnico
ethnic cleansing [-klɛnzɪŋ] *n* limpieza étnica
ethnic minority *n* minoría étnica
ethos ['iːθɔs] *n* (*of culture, group*) sistema *m* de valores
e-ticket ['iːtɪkɪt] *n* billete electrónico, boleto electrónico (*LAm*)
etiquette ['ɛtɪkɛt] *n* etiqueta
EU *n abbr* (= *European Union*) UE *f*
Eucharist ['juːkərɪst] *n* Eucaristía
euphemism ['juːfəmɪzm] *n* eufemismo
euphoria [juː'fɔːrɪə] *n* euforia
Eurasia [juə'reɪʃə] *n* Eurasia
Eurasian [juə'reɪʃən] *adj, n* eurasiático(-a) *m(f)*
euro ['jʊərəʊ] *n* (*currency*) euro
Eurocheque ['juərəutʃɛk] *n* Eurocheque *m*
Euroland ['jʊərəʊlænd] *n* Eurolandia
Europe ['juərəp] *n* Europa
European [juərə'piːən] *adj, n* europeo(-a) *m(f)*
European Community *n* Comunidad *f* Europea
European Court of Justice *n* Tribunal *m* de Justicia de las Comunidades Europeas
European Union *n* Unión *f* Europea
Euro-sceptic [juərəu'skɛptɪk] *n* euroescéptico(-a)
Eurostar® ['juərəustɑː^r] *n* Eurostar(r) *m*
Eurozone ['juərəuzəun] *n* eurozona, zona euro
euthanasia [juːθə'neɪzɪə] *n* eutanasia
evacuate [ɪ'vækjueɪt] *vt* evacuar; (*place*) desocupar
evacuation [ɪvækju'eɪʃən] *n* evacuación *f*
evacuee [ɪvækju'iː] *n* evacuado(-a)
evade [ɪ'veɪd] *vt* evadir, eludir
evaluate [ɪ'væljueɪt] *vt* evaluar; (*value*) tasar; (*evidence*) interpretar
evangelist [ɪ'vændʒəlɪst] *n* evangelista *m*; (*preacher*) evangelizador(a) *m(f)*
evaporate [ɪ'væpəreɪt] *vi* evaporarse; (*fig*) desvanecerse ▷ *vt* evaporar
evaporation [ɪvæpə'reɪʃən] *n* evaporación *f*
evasion [ɪ'veɪʒən] *n* evasión *f*
evasive [ɪ'veɪsɪv] *adj* evasivo
eve [iːv] *n*: **on the ~ of** en vísperas de
even ['iːvn] *adj* (*level*) llano; (*smooth*) liso; (*speed, temperature*) uniforme; (*number*) par; (*Sport*) igual(es) ▷ *adv* hasta, incluso; **~ if, ~ though** aunque + *subjun*, así + *subjun* (*LAm*); **~ more** aun más; **~ so** aun así; **not ~** ni siquiera; **~ he was there** hasta él estaba allí; **~ on Sundays** incluso los domingos; **~ faster** aún más rápido; **to break ~** cubrir los gastos; **to get ~ with sb** ajustar cuentas con algn; **to ~ out** *vi* nivelarse
evening ['iːvnɪŋ] *n* tarde *f*; (*dusk*) atardecer *m*; (*night*) noche *f*; **in the ~** por la tarde; **this ~** esta tarde *or* noche; **tomorrow/yesterday ~** mañana/ayer por la tarde *or* noche
evening class *n* clase *f* nocturna
evening dress *n* (*man's*) traje *m* de etiqueta; (*woman's*) traje *m* de noche
event [ɪ'vɛnt] *n* suceso, acontecimiento; (*Sport*) prueba; **in the ~ of** en caso de; **in the ~** en realidad; **in the course of ~s** en el curso de los acontecimientos; **at all ~s, in any ~** en cualquier caso

eventful [ɪ'vɛntful] *adj* (*life*) azaroso; (*day*) ajetreado; (*game*) lleno de emoción; (*journey*) lleno de incidentes
eventual [ɪ'vɛntʃuəl] *adj* final
eventuality [ɪvɛntʃu'ælɪtɪ] *n* eventualidad *f*
eventually [ɪ'vɛntʃuəlɪ] *adv* (*finally*) por fin; (*in time*) con el tiempo
ever ['ɛvə^r] *adv* nunca, jamás; (*at all times*) siempre; **for ~** (para) siempre; **the best ~** lo nunca visto; **did you ~ meet him?** ¿llegaste a conocerle?; **have you ~ been there?** ¿has estado allí alguna vez?; **have you ~ seen it?** ¿lo has visto alguna vez?; **better than ~** mejor que nunca; **thank you ~ so much** muchísimas gracias; **yours ~** (*in letters*) un abrazo de; **~ since** *adv* desde entonces ▷ *conj* después de que
evergreen ['ɛvəgri:n] *n* árbol *m* de hoja perenne
everlasting [ɛvə'lɑ:stɪŋ] *adj* eterno, perpetuo

KEYWORD

every ['ɛvrɪ] *adj* **1** (*each*) cada; **every one of them** (*persons*) todos ellos(-as); (*objects*) cada uno de ellos(-as); **every shop in the town was closed** todas las tiendas de la ciudad estaban cerradas
2 (*all possible*) todo(-a); **I gave you every assistance** te di toda la ayuda posible; **I have every confidence in him** tiene toda mi confianza; **we wish you every success** te deseamos toda suerte de éxitos
3 (*showing recurrence*) todo(-a); **every day/week** todos los días/todas las semanas; **every other car had been broken into** habían forzado uno de cada dos coches; **she visits me every other/third day** me visita cada dos/tres días; **every now and then** de vez en cuando

everybody ['ɛvrɪbɔdɪ] *pron* todos *pron pl*, todo el mundo; **~ knows about it** todo el mundo lo sabe; **~ else** todos los demás
everyday ['ɛvrɪdeɪ] *adj* (*daily*: *use, occurrence, experience*) diario, cotidiano; (*usual*: *expression*) corriente; (*common*) vulgar; (*routine*) rutinario
everyone ['ɛvrɪwʌn] *pron* = **everybody**
everything ['ɛvrɪθɪŋ] *pron* todo; **~ is ready** todo está dispuesto; **he did ~ possible** hizo todo lo posible
everywhere ['ɛvrɪwɛə^r] *adv* (*be*) en todas partes; (*go*) a *or* por todas partes; **~ you go you meet ...** en todas partes encuentras ...
evict [ɪ'vɪkt] *vt* desahuciar
eviction [ɪ'vɪkʃən] *n* desahucio
evidence ['ɛvɪdəns] *n* (*proof*) prueba; (*of witness*) testimonio; (*facts*) datos *mpl*, hechos *mpl*; **to give ~** prestar declaración, dar testimonio
evident ['ɛvɪdənt] *adj* evidente, manifiesto
evidently ['ɛvɪdəntlɪ] *adv* (*obviously*) obviamente, evidentemente; (*apparently*) por lo visto
evil ['i:vl] *adj* malo; (*influence*) funesto; (*smell*) horrible ▷ *n* mal *m*
evoke [ɪ'vəuk] *vt* evocar; (*admiration*) provocar
evolution [i:və'lu:ʃən] *n* evolución *f*, desarrollo
evolve [ɪ'vɔlv] *vt* desarrollar ▷ *vi* evolucionar, desarrollarse
ewe [ju:] *n* oveja
ex [eks] (*inf*) *n*: **my ex** mi ex
ex- [ɛks] *pref* (*former*: *husband, president etc*) ex-; (*out of*): **the price ~works** precio de fábrica
exact [ɪg'zækt] *adj* exacto ▷ *vt*: **to ~ sth (from)** exigir algo (de)
exacting [ɪg'zæktɪŋ] *adj* exigente; (*conditions*) arduo
exactly [ɪg'zæktlɪ] *adv* exactamente; (*time*) en punto; **~!** ¡exacto!
exaggerate [ɪg'zædʒəreɪt] *vt, vi* exagerar
exaggeration [ɪgzædʒə'reɪʃən] *n* exageración *f*
exalted [ɪg'zɔ:ltɪd] *adj* (*position*) elevado; (*elated*) enardecido
exam [ɪg'zæm] *n abbr* (*Scol*) = **examination**
examination [ɪgzæmɪ'neɪʃən] *n* (*gen*) examen *m*; (*Law*) interrogación *f*; (*Med*) reconocimiento; (*inquiry*) investigación *f*; **to take** *or* **sit an ~** hacer un examen; **the matter is under ~** se está examinando el asunto
examine [ɪg'zæmɪn] *vt* (*gen*) examinar; (*inspect*: *machine, premises*) inspeccionar; (*Scol, Law*: *person*) interrogar; (*at customs*: *luggage, passport*) registrar; (*Med*) reconocer, examinar
examiner [ɪg'zæmɪnə^r] *n* examinador(a) *m(f)*
example [ɪg'zɑ:mpl] *n* ejemplo; **for ~** por ejemplo; **to set a good/bad ~** dar buen/mal ejemplo
exasperate [ɪg'zɑ:spəreɪt] *vt* exasperar, irritar; **~d by** *or* **at** *or* **with** exasperado por *or* con
exasperation [ɪgzɑ:spə'reɪʃən] *n* exasperación *f*, irritación *f*
excavate ['ɛkskəveɪt] *vt* excavar
excavation [ɛkskə'veɪʃən] *n* excavación *f*
exceed [ɪk'si:d] *vt* exceder; (*number*) pasar de; (*speed limit*) sobrepasar; (*limits*) rebasar; (*powers*) excederse en; (*hopes*) superar
exceedingly [ɪk'si:dɪŋlɪ] *adv* sumamente, sobremanera
excel [ɪk'sɛl] *vi* sobresalir; **to ~ o.s.** lucirse
excellence ['ɛksələns] *n* excelencia
Excellency ['ɛksələnsɪ] *n*: **His ~** Su Excelencia
excellent ['ɛksələnt] *adj* excelente
except [ɪk'sɛpt] *prep* (*also*: **~ for, ~ing**) excepto, salvo ▷ *vt* exceptuar, excluir; **~ if/when** excepto si/cuando; **~ that** salvo que

exception [ɪk'sɛpʃən] *n* excepción *f*; **to take ~ to** ofenderse por; **with the ~ of** a excepción de; **to make an ~** hacer una excepción
exceptional [ɪk'sɛpʃənl] *adj* excepcional
exceptionally [ɪk'sɛpʃənəlɪ] *adv* excepcionalmente, extraordinariamente
excerpt ['ɛksə:pt] *n* extracto
excess [ɪk'sɛs] *n* exceso; **in ~ of** superior a
excess baggage *n* exceso de equipaje
excess fare *n* suplemento
excessive [ɪk'sɛsɪv] *adj* excesivo
exchange [ɪks'tʃeɪndʒ] *n* cambio; (*of prisoners*) canje *m*; (*of ideas*) intercambio; (*also:* **telephone ~**) central *f* (telefónica) ▷ *vt* intercambiar; **to ~ (for)** cambiar (por); **in ~ for** a cambio de; **foreign ~** (*Comm*) divisas *fpl*
exchange rate *n* tipo de cambio
exchequer [ɪks'tʃɛkəʳ] *n*; **the ~** (*Brit*) Hacienda
excise ['ɛksaɪz] *n* impuestos sobre el consumo interior
excite [ɪk'saɪt] *vt* (*stimulate*) estimular; (*anger*) suscitar, provocar; (*move*) emocionar; **to get ~d** emocionarse
excitement [ɪk'saɪtmənt] *n* emoción *f*
exciting [ɪk'saɪtɪŋ] *adj* emocionante
excl. *abbr* = **excluding; exclusive (of)**
exclaim [ɪk'skleɪm] *vi* exclamar
exclamation [ɛksklə'meɪʃən] *n* exclamación *f*
exclamation mark, exclamation point (*US*) *n* signo de admiración
exclude [ɪk'sklu:d] *vt* excluir; (*except*) exceptuar
excluding [ɪks'klu:dɪŋ] *prep*: **~ VAT** IVA no incluido
exclusion [ɪk'sklu:ʒən] *n* exclusión *f*; **to the ~ of** con exclusión de
exclusion zone *n* zona de exclusión
exclusive [ɪk'sklu:sɪv] *adj* exclusivo; (*club, district*) selecto; **~ of tax** excluyendo impuestos; **~ of postage/service** franqueo/servicio no incluido; **from 1st to 13th March ~** del 1 al 13 de marzo exclusive
exclusively [ɪk'sklu:sɪvlɪ] *adv* únicamente
excommunicate [ɛkskə'mju:nɪkeɪt] *vt* excomulgar
excrement ['ɛkskrəmənt] *n* excremento
excruciating [ɪk'skru:ʃɪeɪtɪŋ] *adj* (*pain*) agudísimo, atroz
excursion [ɪk'skə:ʃən] *n* excursión *f*
excuse *n* [ɪk'skju:s] disculpa, excusa; (*evasion*) pretexto ▷ *vt* [ɪk'skju:z] disculpar, perdonar; (*justify*) justificar; **to make ~s for sb** presentar disculpas por algn; **to ~ sb from doing sth** dispensar a algn de hacer algo; **to ~ o.s. (for (doing) sth)** pedir disculpas a algn (por (hacer) algo); **~ me!** ¡perdone!; (*attracting attention*) ¡oiga (, por favor)!; **if you will ~ me** con su permiso
ex-directory ['ɛksdɪ'rɛktərɪ] *adj* (*Brit*): **~ (phone) number** número que no figura en la guía (telefónica)
execute ['ɛksɪkju:t] *vt* (*plan*) realizar; (*order*) cumplir; (*person*) ajusticiar, ejecutar
execution [ɛksɪ'kju:ʃən] *n* realización *f*; cumplimiento; ejecución *f*
executioner [ɛksɪ'kju:ʃənəʳ] *n* verdugo
executive [ɪg'zɛkjutɪv] *n* (*Comm*) ejecutivo(-a); (*Pol*) poder *m* ejecutivo ▷ *adj* ejecutivo; (*car, plane, position*) de ejecutivo; (*offices, suite*) de la dirección; (*secretary*) de dirección
executor [ɪg'zɛkjutəʳ] *n* albacea *m*, testamentario
exemplary [ɪg'zɛmplərɪ] *adj* ejemplar
exemplify [ɪg'zɛmplɪfaɪ] *vt* ejemplificar
exempt [ɪg'zɛmpt] *adj*: **~ from** exento de ▷ *vt*: **to ~ sb from** eximir a algn de
exemption [ɪg'zɛmpʃən] *n* exención *f*; (*immunity*) inmunidad *f*
exercise ['ɛksəsaɪz] *n* ejercicio ▷ *vt* ejercer; (*patience etc*) proceder con; (*dog*) sacar de paseo ▷ *vi* hacer ejercicio
exercise bike *n* bicicleta estática
exercise book *n* cuaderno de ejercicios
exert [ɪg'zə:t] *vt* ejercer; (*strength, force*) emplear; **to ~ o.s.** esforzarse
exertion [ɪg'zə:ʃən] *n* esfuerzo
exhale [ɛks'heɪl] *vt* despedir, exhalar ▷ *vi* espirar, exhalar
exhaust [ɪg'zɔ:st] *n* (*pipe*) (tubo de) escape *m*; (*fumes*) gases *mpl* de escape ▷ *vt* agotar; **to ~ o.s.** agotarse
exhausted [ɪg'zɔ:stɪd] *adj* agotado
exhausting [ɪg'zɔ:stɪŋ] *adj*: **an ~ journey/day** un viaje/día agotador
exhaustion [ɪg'zɔ:stʃən] *n* agotamiento; **nervous ~** agotamiento nervioso
exhaustive [ɪg'zɔ:stɪv] *adj* exhaustivo
exhibit [ɪg'zɪbɪt] *n* (*Art*) obra expuesta; (*Law*) objeto expuesto ▷ *vt* (*show: emotions*) manifestar; demostrar; (*paintings*) exponer
exhibition [ɛksɪ'bɪʃən] *n* exposición *f*
exhilarating [ɪg'zɪləreɪtɪŋ] *adj* estimulante, tónico
exile ['ɛksaɪl] *n* exilio; (*person*) exiliado(-a) ▷ *vt* desterrar, exiliar
exist [ɪg'zɪst] *vi* existir
existence [ɪg'zɪstəns] *n* existencia
existing [ɪg'zɪstɪŋ] *adj* existente, actual
exit ['ɛksɪt] *n* salida ▷ *vi* (*Theat*) hacer mutis; (*Comput*) salir (del sistema)
exit poll *n encuesta a la salida de los colegios electorales*
exit ramp *n* (*US Aut*) vía de acceso
exodus ['ɛksədəs] *n* éxodo
exonerate [ɪg'zɔnəreɪt] *vt*: **to ~ from** exculpar de
exotic [ɪg'zɔtɪk] *adj* exótico
expand [ɪk'spænd] *vt* ampliar, extender; (*number*) aumentar ▷ *vi* (*trade etc*) ampliarse, expandirse; (*gas, metal*) dilatarse; **to ~ on** (*notes, story etc*) ampliar

expanse [ɪk'spæns] *n* extensión *f*
expansion [ɪk'spænʃən] *n* ampliación *f*; aumento; (*of trade*) expansión *f*
expect [ɪk'spɛkt] *vt* (*gen*) esperar; (*count on*) contar con; (*suppose*) suponer ▷ *vi*: **to be ~ing** estar encinta; **to ~ to do sth** esperar hacer algo; **as ~ed** como era de esperar; **I ~ so** supongo que sí
expectancy [ɪk'spɛktənsɪ] *n* (*anticipation*) expectación *f*; **life ~** esperanza de vida
expectant mother [ɪk'spɛktənt-] *n* futura madre *f*
expectation [ɛkspɛk'teɪʃən] *n* (*hope*) esperanza; (*belief*) expectativa; **in ~ of** esperando; **against** *or* **contrary to all ~(s)** en contra de todas las previsiones; **to come** *or* **live up to sb's ~s** resultar tan bueno como se esperaba; **to fall short of sb's ~s** no cumplir las esperanzas de algn, decepcionar a algn
expedient [ɪk'spi:dɪənt] *adj* conveniente, oportuno ▷ *n* recurso, expediente *m*
expedition [ɛkspə'dɪʃən] *n* expedición *f*
expel [ɪk'spɛl] *vt* expulsar
expend [ɪk'spɛnd] *vt* gastar; (*use up*) consumir
expendable [ɪk'spɛndəbl] *adj* prescindible
expenditure [ɪk'spɛndɪtʃə^r] *n* gastos *mpl*, desembolso; (*of time, effort*) gasto
expense [ɪk'spɛns] *n* gasto, gastos *mpl*; (*high cost*) coste *m*; **expenses** *npl* (*Comm*) gastos *mpl*; **at the ~ of** a costa de; **to meet the ~ of** hacer frente a los gastos de
expense account *n* cuenta de gastos (de representación)
expensive [ɪk'spɛnsɪv] *adj* caro, costoso
experience [ɪk'spɪərɪəns] *n* experiencia ▷ *vt* experimentar; (*suffer*) sufrir; **to learn by ~** aprender con la experiencia
experienced [ɪk'spɪərɪənst] *adj* experimentado
experiment [ɪk'spɛrɪmənt] *n* experimento ▷ *vi* hacer experimentos, experimentar; **to perform** *or* **carry out an ~** realizar un experimento; **as an ~** como experimento; **to ~ with a new vaccine** experimentar con una vacuna nueva
experimental [ɪkspɛrɪ'mɛntl] *adj* experimental; **the process is still at the ~ stage** el proceso está todavía en prueba
expert ['ɛkspə:t] *adj* experto, perito ▷ *n* experto(-a), perito(-a); (*specialist*) especialista *m/f*; **~ witness** (*Law*) testigo pericial; **~ in** *or* **at doing sth** experto *or* perito en hacer algo; **an ~ on sth** un experto en algo
expertise [ɛkspə:'ti:z] *n* pericia
expire [ɪk'spaɪə^r] *vi* (*gen*) caducar, vencerse
expiry [ɪk'spaɪərɪ] *n* caducidad *f*, vencimiento
expiry date *n* (*of medicine, food item*) fecha de caducidad
explain [ɪk'spleɪn] *vt* explicar; (*mystery*) aclarar; **explain away** *vt* justificar
explanation [ɛksplə'neɪʃən] *n* explicación *f*; aclaración *f*; **to find an ~ for sth** encontrarle una explicación a algo
explanatory [ɪk'splænətrɪ] *adj* explicativo; aclaratorio
explicit [ɪk'splɪsɪt] *adj* explícito
explode [ɪk'spləud] *vi* estallar, explotar; (*with anger*) reventar ▷ *vt* hacer explotar; (*fig: theory, myth*) demoler
exploit ['ɛksplɔɪt] *n* hazaña ▷ *vt* [ɪk'splɔɪt] explotar
exploitation [ɛksplɔɪ'teɪʃən] *n* explotación *f*
exploratory [ɪk'splɔrətrɪ] *adj* (*fig: talks*) exploratorio, preliminar
explore [ɪk'splɔ:^{r}] *vt* explorar; (*fig*) examinar, sondear
explorer [ɪk'splɔ:rə^r] *n* explorador(a) *m(f)*
explosion [ɪk'spləuʒən] *n* explosión *f*
explosive [ɪk'spləusɪv] *adj, n* explosivo
exponent [ɪk'spəunənt] *n* partidario(-a); (*of skill, activity*) exponente *m/f*
export *vt* [ɛk'spɔ:t] exportar ▷ *n* ['ɛkspɔ:t] exportación *f* ▷ *cpd* de exportación
exporter [ɛk'spɔ:tə^r] *n* exportador(a) *m(f)*
expose [ɪk'spəuz] *vt* exponer; (*unmask*) desenmascarar
exposed [ɪk'spəuzd] *adj* expuesto; (*land, house*) desprotegido; (*Elec: wire*) al aire; (*pipe, beam*) al descubierto
exposure [ɪk'spəuʒə^r] *n* exposición *f*; (*Phot: speed*) (tiempo *m* de) exposición *f*; (*: shot*) fotografía; **to die from ~** (*Med*) morir de frío
exposure meter *n* fotómetro
express [ɪk'sprɛs] *adj* (*definite*) expreso, explícito; (*Brit: letter etc*) urgente ▷ *n* (*train*) rápido ▷ *adv* (*send*) por correo extraordinario ▷ *vt* expresar; (*squeeze*) exprimir; **to send sth ~** enviar algo por correo urgente; **to ~ o.s.** expresarse
expression [ɪk'sprɛʃən] *n* expresión *f*
expressive [ɪk'sprɛsɪv] *adj* expresivo
expressly [ɪk'sprɛslɪ] *adv* expresamente
expressway [ɪk'sprɛsweɪ] *n* (*US: urban motorway*) autopista
expulsion [ɪk'spʌlʃən] *n* expulsión *f*
exquisite [ɛk'skwɪzɪt] *adj* exquisito
ext. *abbr* (*Tel*) = **extension**
extend [ɪk'stɛnd] *vt* (*visit, street*) prolongar; (*building*) ampliar; (*thanks, friendship etc*) extender; (*Comm: credit*) conceder; (*deadline*) prorrogar; (*invitation*) ofrecer ▷ *vi* (*land*) extenderse; **the contract ~s to/for ...** el contrato se prolonga hasta/por ...
extension [ɪk'stɛnʃən] *n* extensión *f*; (*building*) ampliación *f*; (*Tel: line*) extensión *f*; (*: telephone*) supletorio *m*; (*of deadline*) prórroga; **~ 3718** extensión 3718
extensive [ɪk'stɛnsɪv] *adj* (*gen*) extenso; (*damage*) importante; (*knowledge*) amplio
extensively [ɪk'stɛnsɪvlɪ] *adv* (*altered, damaged etc*) extensamente; **he's travelled ~** ha viajado por muchos países

extent [ɪk'stɛnt] *n* (*breadth*) extensión *f*; (*scope: of knowledge, activities*) alcance *m*; (*degree: of damage, loss*) grado; **to some ~** hasta cierto punto; **to a certain ~** hasta cierto punto; **to a large ~** en gran parte; **to the ~ of ...** hasta el punto de ...; **to such an ~ that ...** hasta tal punto que ...; **to what ~?** ¿hasta qué punto?; **debts to the ~ of £5000** deudas por la cantidad de £5000
extenuating [ɪk'stɛnjueɪtɪŋ] *adj*: **~ circumstances** circunstancias *fpl* atenuantes
exterior [ɛk'stɪərɪə^r] *adj* exterior, externo ▷ *n* exterior *m*
exterminate [ɪk'stə:mɪneɪt] *vt* exterminar
external [ɛk'stə:nl] *adj* externo, exterior ▷ *n*: **the ~s** la apariencia exterior; **~ affairs** asuntos *mpl* exteriores; **for ~ use only** (*Med*) para uso tópico
extinct [ɪk'stɪŋkt] *adj* (*volcano*) extinguido, apagado; (*race*) extinguido
extinction [ɪk'stɪŋkʃən] *n* extinción *f*
extinguish [ɪk'stɪŋgwɪʃ] *vt* extinguir, apagar
extinguisher [ɪk'stɪŋgwɪʃə^r] *n* extintor *m*
extol, extoll (*US*) [ɪk'stəul] *vt* (*merits, virtues*) ensalzar, alabar; (*person*) alabar, elogiar
extort [ɪk'stɔ:t] *vt* sacar a la fuerza; (*confession*) arrancar
extortion [ɪk'stɔ:ʃən] *n* extorsión *f*
extortionate [ɪk'stɔ:ʃnət] *adj* excesivo, exorbitante
extra ['ɛkstrə] *adj* adicional ▷ *adv* (*in addition*) más ▷ *n* (*addition*) extra *m*, suplemento; (*Theat*) extra *m/f*, comparsa *m/f*; (*newspaper*) edición *f* extraordinaria; **wine will cost ~** el vino se paga aparte; **~ large sizes** tallas extragrandes
extract *vt* [ɪk'strækt] sacar; (*tooth*) extraer; (*confession*) arrancar ▷ *n* ['ɛkstrækt] fragmento; (*Culin*) extracto
extraction [ɪk'strækʃən] *n* extracción *f*; (*origin*) origen *m*
extracurricular [ɛkstrəkə'rɪkjulə^r] *adj* (*Scol*) extraescolar
extradite ['ɛkstrədaɪt] *vt* extraditar
extradition [ɛkstrə'dɪʃən] *n* extradición *f*
extramarital [ɛkstrə'mærɪtl] *adj* extramatrimonial
extramural [ɛkstrə'mjuərl] *adj* extra-académico
extraneous [ɪk'streɪnɪəs] *adj* extraño, ajeno
extraordinary [ɪk'strɔ:dnrɪ] *adj* extraordinario; (*odd*) raro; **the ~ thing is that ...** lo más extraordinario es que ...
extraordinary general meeting *n* junta general extraordinaria
extrasensory perception ['ɛkstrə'sɛnsərɪ-] *n* percepción *f* extrasensorial
extra time *n* (*Football*) prórroga
extravagance [ɪk'strævəgəns] *n* (*excessive spending*) derroche *m*; (*thing bought*) extravagancia
extravagant [ɪk'strævəgənt] *adj* (*wasteful*) derrochador(a); (*taste, gift*) excesivamente caro; (*price*) exorbitante; (*praise*) excesivo
extreme [ɪk'stri:m] *adj* extremo; (*poverty etc*) extremado; (*case*) excepcional ▷ *n* extremo; **the ~ left/right** (*Pol*) la extrema izquierda/derecha; **~s of temperature** temperaturas extremas
extremely [ɪk'stri:mlɪ] *adv* sumamente, extremadamente
extremist [ɪk'stri:mɪst] *adj, n* extremista *m/f*
extremity [ɪk'strɛmətɪ] *n* extremidad *f*, punta; (*need*) apuro, necesidad *f*; **extremities** *npl* (*hands and feet*) extremidades *fpl*
extricate ['ɛkstrɪkeɪt] *vt*: **to ~ o.s. from** librarse de
extrovert ['ɛkstrəvə:t] *n* extrovertido(-a)
exuberance [ɪg'zju:bərns] *n* exuberancia
exuberant [ɪg'zju:bərnt] *adj* (*person*) eufórico; (*style*) exuberante
exude [ɪg'zju:d] *vt* rezumar
eye [aɪ] *n* ojo ▷ *vt* mirar; **to keep an ~ on** vigilar; **as far as the ~ can see** hasta donde alcanza la vista; **with an ~ to doing sth** con vistas *or* miras a hacer algo; **to have an ~ for sth** tener mucha vista *or* buen ojo para algo; **there's more to this than meets the ~** esto tiene su miga
eyeball ['aɪbɔ:l] *n* globo ocular
eyebath ['aɪbɑ:θ] *n* baño ocular, lavaojos *m inv*
eyebrow ['aɪbrau] *n* ceja
eyebrow pencil *n* lápiz *m* de cejas
eyedrops ['aɪdrɔps] *npl* gotas *fpl* para los ojos
eyeful ['aɪful] *n* (*inf*): **to get an ~ of sth** ver bien algo
eyelash ['aɪlæʃ] *n* pestaña
eyelid ['aɪlɪd] *n* párpado
eyeliner ['aɪlaɪnə^r] *n* lápiz *m* de ojos
eye-opener ['aɪəupnə^r] *n* revelación *f*, gran sorpresa
eyeshadow ['aɪʃædəu] *n* sombra de ojos
eyesight ['aɪsaɪt] *n* vista
eyesore ['aɪsɔ:^r] *n* monstruosidad *f*
eye witness *n* testigo *m/f* ocular
eyrie ['ɪərɪ] *n* aguilera

f

F, f [ɛf] *n* (*letter*) F, f *f*; (*Mus*) fa *m*; **F for Frederick**, (*US*) **F for Fox** F de Francia

FA *n abbr* (*Brit*: = *Football Association*) ≈ AFE *f* (*Sp*)

fable ['feɪbl] *n* fábula

fabric ['fæbrɪk] *n* tejido, tela

fabricate ['fæbrɪkeɪt] *vt* fabricar; (*fig*) inventar

fabrication [fæbrɪ'keɪʃən] *n* fabricación *f*; (*fig*) invención *f*

fabulous ['fæbjuləs] *adj* fabuloso

façade [fə'sɑːd] *n* fachada

face [feɪs] *n* (*Anat*) cara, rostro; (*of clock*) esfera; (*side*) cara; (*surface*) superficie *f* ▷ *vt* (*direction*) estar de cara a; (*situation*) hacer frente a; (*facts*) aceptar; **~ down** (*person, card*) boca abajo; **to lose ~** desprestigiarse; **to save ~** salvar las apariencias; **to make** *or* **pull a ~** hacer muecas; **in the ~ of** (*difficulties etc*) en vista de, ante; **on the ~ of it** a primera vista; **~ to ~** cara a cara; **to ~ the fact that ...** reconocer que ...; **face up to** *vt fus* hacer frente a, enfrentarse a

face cloth *n* (*Brit*) toallita

face cream *n* crema (de belleza)

face lift *n* lifting *m*, estirado facial

face pack *n* (*Brit*) mascarilla

face powder *n* polvos *mpl* para la cara

facet ['fæsɪt] *n* faceta

facetious [fə'siːʃəs] *adj* chistoso

face value *n* (*of stamp*) valor *m* nominal; **to take sth at ~** (*fig*) tomar algo en sentido literal, aceptar las apariencias de algo

facial ['feɪʃəl] *adj* de la cara ▷ *n* (*also*: **beauty ~**) tratamiento facial, limpieza

facile ['fæsaɪl] *adj* superficial

facilitate [fə'sɪlɪteɪt] *vt* facilitar

facility [fə'sɪlɪtɪ] *n* facilidad *f*; **facilities** *npl* instalaciones *fpl*; **credit ~** facilidades de crédito

facing ['feɪsɪŋ] *prep* frente a ▷ *adj* de enfrente

facsimile [fæk'sɪmɪlɪ] *n* facsímil(e) *m*

fact [fækt] *n* hecho; **in ~** en realidad; **to know for a ~ that ...** saber a ciencia cierta que ...

faction ['fækʃən] *n* facción *f*

factional ['fækʃənl] *adj* (*fighting*) entre distintas facciones

factor ['fæktəʳ] *n* factor *m*; (*Comm*: *person*) agente *m/f* comisionado(-a) ▷ *vi* (*Comm*) comprar deudas; **safety ~** factor de seguridad

factory ['fæktərɪ] *n* fábrica

factory floor *n* (*workers*) trabajadores *mpl*, mano *f* de obra directa; (*area*) talleres *mpl*

factual ['fæktjuəl] *adj* basado en los hechos

faculty ['fækəltɪ] *n* facultad *f*; (*US*: *teaching staff*) personal *m* docente

fad [fæd] *n* novedad *f*, moda

fade [feɪd] *vi* descolorarse, desteñirse; (*sound, hope*) desvanecerse; (*light*) apagarse; (*flower*) marchitarse; **fade away** *vi* (*sound*) apagarse; **fade in** *vt* (*TV, Cine*) fundir; (*Radio*: *sound*) mezclar ▷ *vi* (*TV, Cine*) fundirse; (*Radio*) oírse por encima; **fade out** *vt* (*TV, Cine*) fundir; (*Radio*) apagar, disminuir el volumen de ▷ *vi* (*TV, Cine*) desvanecerse; (*Radio*) apagarse, dejarse de oír

faeces, feces (*US*) ['fiːsiːz] *npl* excremento *sg*, heces *fpl*

fag [fæg] *n* (*Brit inf*: *cigarette*) pitillo (*Sp*), cigarro; (*US inf*: *homosexual*) maricón *m*

Fahrenheit ['fɑːrənhaɪt] *n* Fahrenheit *m*

fail [feɪl] *vt* suspender; (*memory etc*) fallar a ▷ *vi* suspender; (*be unsuccessful*) fracasar; (*strength, brakes, engine*) fallar; **to ~ to do sth** (*neglect*) dejar de hacer algo; (*be unable*) no poder hacer algo; **without ~** sin falta; **words ~ me!** ¡no sé qué decir!

failing ['feɪlɪŋ] *n* falta, defecto ▷ *prep* a falta de; **~ that** de no ser posible eso

failure ['feɪljəʳ] *n* fracaso; (*person*) fracasado(-a); (*mechanical etc*) fallo; (*in exam*) suspenso; (*of crops*) pérdida, destrucción *f*; **it was a complete ~** fue un fracaso total

faint [feɪnt] *adj* débil; (*smell, breeze, trace*) leve; (*recollection*) vago; (*mark*) apenas visible ▷ *n* desmayo ▷ *vi* desmayarse; **to feel ~** estar mareado, marearse

faintest ['feɪntɪst] *adj*: **I haven't the ~ idea** no tengo la más remota idea

faintly ['feɪntlɪ] *adv* débilmente; (*vaguely*) vagamente

fair [fɛəʳ] *adj* justo; (*hair, person*) rubio; (*weather*) bueno; (*good enough*) suficiente; (*sizeable*) considerable ▷ *adv*: **to play ~** jugar limpio ▷ *n* feria; (*Brit: funfair*) parque *m* de atracciones; **it's not ~!** ¡no es justo!, ¡no hay derecho!; **~ copy** copia en limpio; **~ play** juego limpio; **a ~ amount of** bastante; **~ wear and tear** desgaste *m* natural; **trade ~** feria de muestras

fairground ['fɛəgraund] *n* recinto ferial

fair-haired [fɛə'hɛəd] *adj* (*person*) rubio

fairly ['fɛəlɪ] *adv* (*justly*) con justicia; (*equally*) equitativamente; (*quite*) bastante; **I'm ~ sure** estoy bastante seguro

fairness ['fɛənɪs] *n* justicia; (*impartiality*) imparcialidad *f*; **in all ~** a decir verdad

fair trade *n* comercio justo

fairway ['fɛəweɪ] *n* (*Golf*) calle *f*

fairy ['fɛərɪ] *n* hada

fairy tale *n* cuento de hadas

faith [feɪθ] *n* fe *f*; (*trust*) confianza; (*sect*) religión *f*; **to have ~ in sb/sth** confiar en algn/algo

faithful ['feɪθful] *adj*, *adj* (*loyal: troops etc*) leal; (*spouse*) fiel; (*account*) exacto

faithfully ['feɪθfulɪ] *adv* fielmente; **yours ~** (*Brit: in letters*) le saluda atentamente

fake [feɪk] *n* (*painting etc*) falsificación *f*; (*person*) impostor(a) *m(f)* ▷ *adj* falso ▷ *vt* fingir; (*painting etc*) falsificar

falcon ['fɔːlkən] *n* halcón *m*

Falkland Islands ['fɔːlklənd-] *npl* Islas *fpl* Malvinas

fall [fɔːl] *n* caída; (*US*) otoño; (*decrease*) disminución *f* ▷ *vi* (*pt* **fell**, *pp* **fallen** ['fɔːlən]) caer; (*accidentally*) caerse; (*price*) bajar; **falls** *npl* (*waterfall*) cataratas *fpl*, salto *sg* de agua; **a ~ of earth** un desprendimiento de tierra; **a ~ of snow** una nevada; **to ~ flat** *vi* (*on one's face*) caerse de bruces; (*joke, story*) no hacer gracia; **to ~ short of sb's expectations** decepcionar a algn; **to ~ in love (with sb/sth)** enamorarse (de algn/algo); **fall apart** *vi* deshacerse; **fall back** *vi* retroceder; **fall back on** *vt fus* (*remedy etc*) recurrir a; **to have sth to ~ back on** tener algo a que recurrir; **fall behind** *vi* quedarse atrás; (*fig: with payments*) retrasarse; **fall down** *vi* (*person*) caerse; (*building*) derrumbarse; **fall for** *vt fus* (*trick*) tragar; (*person*) enamorarse de; **fall in** *vi* (*roof*) hundirse; (*Mil*) alinearse; **fall in with** *vt fus*: **to ~ in with sb's plans** acomodarse con los planes de algn; **fall off** *vi* caerse; (*diminish*) disminuir; **fall out** *vi* (*friends etc*) reñir; (*hair, teeth*) caerse; (*Mil*) romper filas; **fall over** *vi* caer(se); **fall through** *vi* (*plan, project*) fracasar

fallacy ['fæləsɪ] *n* error *m*

fallen ['fɔːlən] *pp of* **fall**

fallible ['fæləbl] *adj* falible

fallout ['fɔːlaut] *n* lluvia radioactiva

fallout shelter *n* refugio antinuclear

fallow ['fæləu] *adj* (*land, field*) en barbecho

false [fɔːls] *adj* (*gen*) falso; (*teeth etc*) postizo; (*disloyal*) desleal, traidor(a); **under ~ pretences** con engaños

false alarm *n* falsa alarma

falsehood ['fɔːlshud] *n* falsedad *f*

falsely ['fɔːlslɪ] *adv* falsamente

false teeth *npl* (*Brit*) dentadura *sg* postiza

falsify ['fɔːlsɪfaɪ] *vt* falsificar

falter ['fɔːltəʳ] *vi* vacilar

fame [feɪm] *n* fama

familiar [fə'mɪlɪəʳ] *adj* familiar; (*well-known*) conocido; (*tone*) de confianza; **to be ~ with** (*subject*) conocer (bien); **to make o.s. ~ with** familiarizarse con; **to be on ~ terms with sb** tener confianza con algn

familiarity [fəmɪlɪ'ærɪtɪ] *n* familiaridad *f*

familiarize [fə'mɪlɪəraɪz] *vt*: **to ~ o.s. with** familiarizarse con

family ['fæmɪlɪ] *n* familia

family credit *n* (*Brit*) ≈ ayuda familiar

family doctor *n* médico(-a) de cabecera

family man *n* (*home-loving*) hombre *m* casero; (*having family*) padre *m* de familia

family planning *n* planificación *f* familiar

family tree *n* árbol *m* genealógico

famine ['fæmɪn] *n* hambre *f*, hambruna

famished ['fæmɪʃt] *adj* hambriento; **I'm ~!** (*inf*) ¡estoy muerto de hambre!, ¡tengo un hambre canina!

famous ['feɪməs] *adj* famoso, célebre

famously ['feɪməslɪ] *adv* (*get on*) estupendamente

fan [fæn] *n* abanico; (*Elec*) ventilador *m*; (*person*) aficionado(-a); (*Sport*) hincha *m/f*; (*of pop star*) fan *m/f* ▷ *vt* abanicar; (*fire, quarrel*) atizar; **fan out** *vi* desplegarse

fanatic [fə'nætɪk] *n* fanático(-a)

fanatical [fə'nætɪkəl] *adj* fanático

fan belt *n* correa del ventilador

fanciful ['fænsɪful] *adj* (*gen*) fantástico; (*imaginary*) fantasioso; (*design*) rebuscado

fan club *n* club *m* de fans

fancy ['fænsɪ] *n* (*whim*) capricho, antojo; (*imagination*) imaginación *f* ▷ *adj* (*luxury*) de lujo; (*price*) exorbitado ▷ *vt* (*feel like, want*) tener ganas de; (*imagine*) imaginarse, figurarse; **to take a ~ to sb** tomar cariño a algn; **when the ~ takes him** cuando se le antoja; **it took** *or* **caught my ~** me cayó en gracia; **to ~ that ...** imaginarse que ...; **he fancies her** le gusta (ella) mucho

fancy dress *n* disfraz *m*

fancy-dress ball ['fænsɪdrɛs-] *n* baile *m* de disfraces

fang [fæŋ] *n* colmillo

fan heater *n* calefactor *m* de aire

fantasize ['fæntəsaɪz] *vi* fantasear, hacerse ilusiones

fantastic [fæn'tæstɪk] *adj* fantástico

fantasy ['fæntəzɪ] *n* fantasía

fanzine ['fænziːn] *n* fanzine *m*

FAQs *npl abbr* (= *frequently asked questions*) preguntas *fpl* frecuentes

far [fɑːʳ] *adj* (*distant*) lejano ▷ *adv* lejos; **the ~ left/right** (*Pol*) la extrema izquierda/

derecha; **~ away**, **~ off** (a lo) lejos; **~ better** mucho mejor; **~ from** lejos de; **by ~** con mucho; **it's by ~ the best** es con mucho el mejor; **go as ~ as the farm** vaya hasta la granja; **is it ~ to London?** ¿estamos lejos de Londres?, ¿Londres queda lejos?; **it's not ~ (from here)** no está lejos (de aquí); **as ~ as I know** que yo sepa; **how ~?** ¿hasta dónde?; (*fig*) ¿hasta qué punto?; **how ~ have you got with your work?** ¿hasta dónde has llegado en tu trabajo?

faraway ['fɑ:rəweɪ] *adj* remoto; (*look*) ausente, perdido

farce [fɑ:s] *n* farsa

farcical ['fɑ:sɪkəl] *adj* absurdo

fare [fɛəʳ] *n* (*on trains, buses*) precio (del billete); (*in taxi: cost*) tarifa; (*: passenger*) pasajero; (*food*) comida; **half/full ~** medio billete *m*/billete *m* completo

Far East *n*: **the ~** el Extremo *or* Lejano Oriente

farewell [fɛə'wɛl] *excl, n* adiós *m*

farm [fɑ:m] *n* granja, finca, estancia (*LAm*), chacra (*LAm*) ▷ *vt* cultivar; **farm out** *vt* (*work*): **to ~ out (to sb)** mandar hacer fuera (a algn)

farmer ['fɑ:məʳ] *n* granjero(-a), estanciero(-a) (*LAm*)

farmhand ['fɑ:mhænd] *n* peón *m*

farmhouse ['fɑ:mhaus] *n* granja, casa de hacienda (*LAm*)

farming ['fɑ:mɪŋ] *n* (*gen*) agricultura; (*tilling*) cultivo; **sheep ~** cría de ovejas

farmland ['fɑ:mlænd] *n* tierra de cultivo

farm worker *n* = **farmhand**

farmyard ['fɑ:mjɑ:d] *n* corral *m*

far-reaching [fɑ:'ri:tʃɪŋ] *adj* (*reform, effect*) de gran alcance

fart [fɑ:t] (*inf!*) *n* pedo (*!*) ▷ *vi* tirarse un pedo (*!*)

farther ['fɑ:ðəʳ] *adv* más lejos, más allá ▷ *adj* más lejano

farthest ['fɑ:ðɪst] *superlative of* **far**

fascinate ['fæsɪneɪt] *vt* fascinar

fascinated ['fæsɪneɪtəd] *adj* fascinado

fascinating ['fæsɪneɪtɪŋ] *adj* fascinante

fascination [fæsɪ'neɪʃən] *n* fascinación *f*

fascism ['fæʃɪzəm] *n* fascismo

fascist ['fæʃɪst] *adj, n* fascista *m/f*

fashion ['fæʃən] *n* moda; (*fashion industry*) industria de la moda; (*manner*) manera ▷ *vt* formar; **in ~** a la moda; **out of ~** pasado de moda; **in the Greek ~** a la griega, al estilo griego; **after a ~** (*finish, manage etc*) en cierto modo

fashionable ['fæʃnəbl] *adj* de moda; (*writer*) de moda, popular; **it is ~ to do ...** está de moda hacer ...

fashion show *n* desfile *m* de modelos

fast [fɑ:st] *adj* (*also Phot: film*) rápido; (*dye, colour*) sólido; (*clock*): **to be ~** estar adelantado ▷ *adv* rápidamente, de prisa; (*stuck, held*) firmemente ▷ *n* ayuno ▷ *vi* ayunar; **~ asleep** profundamente dormido; **in the ~ lane** (*Aut*) en el carril de adelantamiento; **my watch is five minutes ~** mi reloj está adelantado cinco minutos; **as ~ as I** *etc* **can** lo más rápido posible; **to make a boat ~** amarrar una barca

fasten ['fɑ:sn] *vt* asegurar, sujetar; (*coat, belt*) abrochar ▷ *vi* cerrarse; **fasten (up)on** *vt fus* (*idea*) aferrarse a

fastener ['fɑ:snəʳ] *n* cierre *m*; (*of door etc*) cerrojo; (*Brit: also*: **zip ~**) cremallera

fastening ['fɑ:snɪŋ] *n* = **fastener**

fast food *n* comida rápida, platos *mpl* preparados

fastidious [fæs'tɪdɪəs] *adj* (*fussy*) delicado; (*demanding*) exigente

fat [fæt] *adj* gordo; (*meat*) con mucha grasa; (*greasy*) grasiento; (*book*) grueso; (*profit*) grande, pingüe ▷ *n* grasa; (*on person*) carnes *fpl*; (*lard*) manteca; **to live off the ~ of the land** vivir a cuerpo de rey

fatal ['feɪtl] *adj* (*mistake*) fatal; (*injury*) mortal; (*consequence*) funesto

fatality [fə'tælɪtɪ] *n* (*road death etc*) víctima *f* mortal

fatally ['feɪtəlɪ] *adv*: **~ injured** herido de muerte

fate [feɪt] *n* destino, sino

fateful ['feɪtful] *adj* fatídico

fat-free ['fætfri:] *adj* sin grasa

father ['fɑ:ðəʳ] *n* padre *m*

Father Christmas *n* Papá *m* Noel

fatherhood ['fɑ:ðəhud] *n* paternidad *f*

father-in-law ['fɑ:ðərɪnlɔ:] *n* suegro

fatherly ['fɑ:ðəlɪ] *adj* paternal

fathom ['fæðəm] *n* braza ▷ *vt* (*unravel*) desentrañar; (*understand*) explicarse

fatigue [fə'ti:g] *n* fatiga, cansancio; **metal ~** fatiga del metal

fatten ['fætn] *vt, vi* engordar; **chocolate is ~ing** el chocolate engorda

fatty ['fætɪ] *adj* (*food*) graso ▷ *n* (*inf*) gordito(-a), gordinflón(-ona) *m(f)*

fatuous ['fætjuəs] *adj* fatuo, necio

faucet ['fɔ:sɪt] *n* (*US*) grifo, llave *f*, canilla (*LAm*)

fault [fɔ:lt] *n* (*blame*) culpa; (*defect: in character*) defecto; (*in manufacture*) desperfecto; (*Geo*) falla ▷ *vt* criticar; **it's my ~** es culpa mía; **to find ~ with** criticar, poner peros a; **at ~** culpable

faulty ['fɔ:ltɪ] *adj* defectuoso

fauna ['fɔ:nə] *n* fauna

faux pas ['fəu'pɑ:] *n* desacierto

favour, favor (*US*) ['feɪvəʳ] *n* favor *m*; (*approval*) aprobación *f* ▷ *vt* (*proposition*) estar a favor de, aprobar; (*person etc*) preferir; (*assist*) favorecer; **to ask a ~ of** pedir un favor a; **to do sb a ~** hacer un favor a algn; **to find ~ with sb** (*person*) caer en gracia a algn; (*: suggestion*) tener buena acogida por parte de algn; **in ~ of** a favor de; **to be in ~ of sth/of doing sth** ser partidario *or* estar a favor de algo/de hacer algo

favourable, favorable (US) ['feɪvərəbl] *adj* favorable

favourably, favorably (US) ['feɪvərəblɪ] *adv* favorablemente

favourite, favorite (US) ['feɪvərɪt] *adj, n* favorito(-a) *m(f)*, preferido(-a) *m(f)*

favouritism, favoritism (US) ['feɪvərɪtɪzəm] *n* favoritismo

fawn [fɔ:n] *n* cervato ▷ *adj* (*also*: **~-coloured**) de color cervato, leonado ▷ *vi*: **to ~ (up)on** adular

fax [fæks] *n* fax *m* ▷ *vt* mandar *or* enviar por fax

FBI *n abbr* (*US*: = *Federal Bureau of Investigation*) FBI *m*

FE *n abbr* = **further education**

fear [fɪəʳ] *n* miedo, temor *m* ▷ *vt* temer; **for ~ of** por temor a; **~ of heights** vértigo; **to ~ for/that** temer por/que

fearful ['fɪəful] *adj* temeroso; (*awful*) espantoso; **to be ~ of** (*frightened*) tener miedo de

fearless ['fɪəlɪs] *adj* (*gen*) sin miedo *or* temor; (*bold*) audaz

feasibility [fi:zə'bɪlɪtɪ] *n* factibilidad *f*, viabilidad *f*

feasible ['fi:zəbl] *adj* factible, viable

feast [fi:st] *n* banquete *m*; (*Rel*: *also*: **~ day**) fiesta ▷ *vi* festejar

feat [fi:t] *n* hazaña

feather ['fɛðəʳ] *n* pluma ▷ *vt*: **to ~ one's nest** (*fig*) hacer su agosto, sacar tajada ▷ *cpd* (*mattress, bed, pillow*) de plumas

feature ['fi:tʃəʳ] *n* (*gen*) característica; (*Anat*) rasgo; (*article*) reportaje *m* ▷ *vt* (*film*) presentar ▷ *vi* figurar; **features** *npl* (*of face*) facciones *fpl*; **a (special) ~ on sth/sb** un reportaje (especial) sobre algo/algn; **it ~d prominently in ...** tuvo un papel destacado en ...

feature film *n* largometraje *m*

Feb. *abbr* (= *February*) feb

February ['fɛbruərɪ] *n* febrero; *see also* **July**

feces ['fi:si:z] *npl* (*US*) = **faeces**

fed [fɛd] *pt, pp of* **feed**

federal ['fɛdərəl] *adj* federal

Federal Republic of Germany *n* República Federal de Alemania

federation [fɛdə'reɪʃən] *n* federación *f*

fed up [fɛd'ʌp] *adj*: **to be ~ (with)** estar harto (de)

fee [fi:] *n* (*professional*) honorarios *mpl*; (*for examination*) derechos *mpl*; (*of school*) matrícula; (*also*: **membership ~**) cuota; (*also*: **entrance ~**) entrada; **for a small ~** por poco dinero

feeble ['fi:bl] *adj* débil

feed [fi:d] *n* (*gen*) comida; (*of animal*) pienso; (*on printer*) dispositivo de alimentación ▷ *vt* (*pp, pt* **fed**) (*gen*) alimentar; (*Brit*: *breastfeed*) dar el pecho a; (*animal, baby*) dar de comer a ▷ *vi* (*baby, animal*) comer; **feed back** *vt* (*results*) pasar; **feed in** *vt* (*Comput*) introducir; **feed into** *vt* (*data, information*) suministrar a; **to ~ sth into a machine** introducir algo en una máquina; **feed on** *vt fus* alimentarse de

feedback ['fi:dbæk] *n* (*from person*) reacción *f*; (*Tech*) realimentación *f*, feedback *m*

feeding bottle ['fi:dɪŋ-] *n* (*Brit*) biberón *m*

feel [fi:l] *n* (*sensation*) sensación *f*; (*sense of touch*) tacto ▷ *vt* (*pt, pp* **felt**) tocar; (*cold, pain etc*) sentir; (*think, believe*) creer; **to get the ~ of sth** (*fig*) acostumbrarse a algo; **to ~ hungry/cold** tener hambre/frío; **to ~ lonely/better** sentirse solo/mejor; **I don't ~ well** no me siento bien; **it ~s soft** es suave al tacto; **it ~s colder out here** se siente más frío aquí fuera; **to ~ like** (*want*) tener ganas de; **I'm still ~ing my way** (*fig*) todavía me estoy orientando; **I ~ that you ought to do it** creo que debes hacerlo; **feel about** *or* **around** *vi* tantear

feeler ['fi:ləʳ] *n* (*of insect*) antena; **to put out ~s** (*fig*) tantear el terreno

feeling ['fi:lɪŋ] *n* (*physical*) sensación *f*; (*foreboding*) presentimiento; (*impression*) impresión *f*; (*emotion*) sentimiento; **what are your ~s about the matter?** ¿qué opinas tú del asunto?; **to hurt sb's ~s** herir los sentimientos de algn; **~s ran high about it** causó mucha controversia; **I got the ~ that ...** me dio la impresión de que ...; **there was a general ~ that ...** la opinión general fue que ...

fee-paying school ['fi:peɪɪŋ-] *n* colegio de pago

feet [fi:t] *npl of* **foot**

feign [feɪn] *vt* fingir

fell [fɛl] *pt of* **fall** ▷ *vt* (*tree*) talar ▷ *adj*: **with one ~ blow** con un golpe feroz; **at one ~ swoop** de un solo golpe ▷ *n* (*Brit*: *mountain*) montaña; (*moorland*): **the ~s** los páramos

fellow ['fɛləu] *n* tipo, tío (*Sp*), (*of learned society*) socio(-a); (*Univ*) *miembro de la junta de gobierno de un colegio* ▷ *cpd*: **~ students** compañeros(-as) *m(f)pl* de curso

fellow citizen *n* conciudadano(-a)

fellow countryman *n* compatriota *m*

fellow men *npl* semejantes *mpl*

fellowship ['fɛləuʃɪp] *n* compañerismo; (*grant*) beca

felony ['fɛlənɪ] *n* crimen *m*, delito mayor

felt [fɛlt] *pt, pp of* **feel** ▷ *n* fieltro

felt-tip pen ['fɛlttɪp-] *n* rotulador *m*

female ['fi:meɪl] *n* (*woman*) mujer *f*; (*Zool*) hembra ▷ *adj* femenino

feminine ['fɛmɪnɪn] *adj* femenino

feminism ['fɛmɪnɪzəm] *n* feminismo

feminist ['fɛmɪnɪst] *n* feminista *m/f*

fence [fɛns] *n* valla, cerca; (*Racing*) valla ▷ *vt* (*also*: **~ in**) cercar ▷ *vi* hacer esgrima; **to sit on the ~** (*fig*) nadar entre dos aguas; **fence in** *vt* cercar; **fence off** *vt* separar con cerca

fencing ['fɛnsɪŋ] *n* esgrima

fend [fɛnd] *vi*: **to ~ for o.s.** valerse por sí mismo; **fend off** *vt* (*attack, attacker*) rechazar, repeler; (*blow*) desviar; (*awkward question*) esquivar
fender ['fɛndəʳ] *n* pantalla; (*US Aut*) parachoques *m inv*; (*Rail*) trompa
fennel ['fɛnl] *n* hinojo
ferment *vi* [fə'mɛnt] fermentar ▷ *n* ['fə:mɛnt] (*fig*) agitación *f*
fern [fə:n] *n* helecho
ferocious [fə'rəuʃəs] *adj* feroz
ferocity [fə'rɔsɪtɪ] *n* ferocidad *f*
ferret ['fɛrɪt] *n* hurón *m*; **ferret about, ferret around** *vi* rebuscar; **ferret out** *vt* (*secret, truth*) desentrañar
ferry ['fɛrɪ] *n* (*small*) barca de pasaje, balsa; (*large*: *also*: **~boat**) transbordador *m*, ferry *m* ▷ *vt* transportar; **to ~ sth/sb across** *or* **over** transportar algo/a algn a la otra orilla; **to ~ sb to and fro** llevar a algn de un lado para otro
fertile ['fə:taɪl] *adj* fértil; (*Biol*) fecundo
fertility [fə'tɪlɪtɪ] *n* fertilidad *f*; fecundidad *f*
fertilize ['fə:tɪlaɪz] *vt* fertilizar; (*Biol*) fecundar; (*Agr*) abonar
fertilizer ['fə:tɪlaɪzəʳ] *n* abono, fertilizante *m*
fervent ['fə:vənt] *adj* ferviente
fester ['fɛstəʳ] *vi* supurar
festival ['fɛstɪvəl] *n* (*Rel*) fiesta; (*Art, Mus*) festival *m*
festive ['fɛstɪv] *adj* festivo; **the ~ season** (*Brit*: *Christmas*) las Navidades
festivities [fɛs'tɪvɪtɪz] *npl* festejos *mpl*
festoon [fɛs'tu:n] *vt*: **to ~ with** festonear *or* engalanar de
fetch [fɛtʃ] *vt* ir a buscar; (*Brit*: *sell for*) venderse por; **how much did it ~?** ¿por cuánto se vendió?; **fetch up** *vi* ir a parar
fetching ['fɛtʃɪŋ] *adj* atractivo
fête [feɪt] *n* fiesta
fetish ['fɛtɪʃ] *n* fetiche *m*
fetus ['fi:təs] *n* (*US*) = **foetus**
feud [fju:d] *n* (*hostility*) enemistad *f*; (*quarrel*) disputa; **a family ~** una pelea familiar
feudal ['fju:dl] *adj* feudal
fever ['fi:vəʳ] *n* fiebre *f*; **he has a ~** tiene fiebre
feverish ['fi:vərɪʃ] *adj* febril
few [fju:] *adj* (*not many*) pocos; (*some*) algunos, unos ▷ *pron* algunos; **a ~** *adj* unos pocos; **~ people** poca gente; **a good ~, quite a ~** bastantes; **in** *or* **over the next ~ days** en los próximos días; **every ~ weeks** cada dos o tres semanas; **a ~ more days** unos días más
fewer ['fju:əʳ] *adj* menos
fewest ['fju:ɪst] *adj* los/las menos
fiancé [fɪ'ã:ŋseɪ] *n* novio, prometido
fiancée [fɪ'ã:ŋseɪ] *n* novia, prometida
fiasco [fɪ'æskəu] *n* fiasco
fib [fɪb] *n* mentirijilla ▷ *vi* decir mentirijillas
fibre, fiber (*US*) ['faɪbəʳ] *n* fibra
fibreglass, fiberglass (*US*) ['faɪbəglɑ:s] *n* fibra de vidrio
fickle ['fɪkl] *adj* inconstante
fiction ['fɪkʃən] *n* (*gen*) ficción *f*
fictional ['fɪkʃənl] *adj* novelesco
fictitious [fɪk'tɪʃəs] *adj* ficticio
fiddle ['fɪdl] *n* (*Mus*) violín *m*; (*cheating*) trampa ▷ *vt* (*Brit*: *accounts*) falsificar; **tax ~** evasión *f* fiscal; **to work a ~** hacer trampa; **fiddle with** *vt fus* juguetear con
fiddler ['fɪdləʳ] *n* violinista *m/f*
fiddly ['fɪdlɪ] *adj* (*task*) delicado, mañoso; (*object*) enrevesado
fidelity [fɪ'dɛlɪtɪ] *n* fidelidad *f*
fidget ['fɪdʒɪt] *vi* moverse (nerviosamente)
fidgety ['fɪdʒɪtɪ] *adj* nervioso
field [fi:ld] *n* (*gen*) campo; (*Comput*) campo; (*fig*) campo, esfera; (*Sport*) campo, cancha (*LAm*); (*competitors*) competidores *mpl* ▷ *cpd*: **to have a ~ day** (*fig*) ponerse las botas; **to lead the ~** (*Sport, Comm*) llevar la delantera; **to give sth a year's trial in the ~** (*fig*) sacar algo al mercado a prueba por un año; **my particular ~** mi especialidad
field hospital *n* hospital *m* de campaña
field marshal *n* mariscal *m*
fieldwork ['fi:ldwə:k] *n* (*Archaeology, Geo*) trabajo de campo
fiend [fi:nd] *n* demonio
fiendish ['fi:ndɪʃ] *adj* diabólico
fierce [fɪəs] *adj* feroz; (*wind, attack*) violento; (*heat*) intenso; (*fighting, enemy*) encarnizado
fiery ['faɪərɪ] *adj* (*burning*) ardiente; (*temperament*) apasionado
FIFA ['fi:fə] *n abbr* (= *Fédération Internationale de Football Association*) FIFA *f*
fifteen [fɪf'ti:n] *num* quince
fifteenth [fɪf'ti:nθ] *adj* decimoquinto; **the ~ floor** la planta quince; **the ~ of August** el quince de agosto
fifth [fɪfθ] *adj* quinto
fiftieth ['fɪftɪɪθ] *adj* quincuagésimo
fifty ['fɪftɪ] *num* cincuenta; **the fifties** los años cincuenta; **to be in one's fifties** andar por los cincuenta
fifty-fifty ['fɪftɪ'fɪftɪ] *adj* (*deal, split*) a medias ▷ *adv*: **to go ~ with sb** ir a medias con algn; **we have a ~ chance of success** tenemos un cincuenta por ciento de posibilidades de tener éxito
fig [fɪg] *n* higo
fight [faɪt] (*pt, pp* **fought**) *n* (*gen*) pelea; (*Mil*) combate *m*; (*struggle*) lucha ▷ *vt* luchar contra; (*cancer, alcoholism*) combatir; (*Law*): **to ~ a case** defenderse ▷ *vi* pelear, luchar; (*quarrel*): **to ~ (with sb)** pelear (con algn); (*fig*): **to ~ (for/against)** luchar (por/contra); **fight back** *vi* defenderse; (*after illness*) recuperarse ▷ *vt* (*tears*) contener; **fight down** *vt* (*anger, anxiety, urge*) reprimir; **fight off** *vt* (*attack, attacker*) rechazar; (*disease, sleep, urge*) luchar contra; **fight out** *vt*: **to ~ it out** decidirlo en una pelea

fighter ['faɪtə^r] *n* combatiente *m/f*; (*fig*) luchador(a) *m(f)*; (*plane*) caza *m*

fighting ['faɪtɪŋ] *n* (*gen*) luchas *fpl*; (*battle*) combate *m*, pelea; (*in streets*) disturbios *mpl*

figment ['fɪgmənt] *n*: **a ~ of the imagination** un producto de la imaginación

figurative ['fɪgjurətɪv] *adj* (*meaning*) figurado; (*Art*) figurativo

figure ['fɪgə^r] *n* (*Drawing, Geom*) figura, dibujo; (*number, cipher*) cifra; (*person, outline*) figura; (*body shape*) línea; (*: attractive*) tipo ▷ *vt* (*esp US: think, calculate*) calcular, imaginarse ▷ *vi* (*appear*) figurar; (*esp US: make sense*) ser lógico; **~ of speech** (*Ling*) figura retórica; **public ~** personaje *m*; **figure on** *vt fus* (*US*) contar con; **figure out** *vt* (*work out*) resolver; (*understand*) comprender

figurehead ['fɪgəhɛd] *n* (*fig*) figura decorativa

file [faɪl] *n* (*tool*) lima; (*for nails*) lima de uñas; (*dossier*) expediente *m*; (*folder*) carpeta; (*in cabinet*) archivo; (*Comput*) fichero; (*row*) fila ▷ *vt* limar; (*papers*) clasificar; (*Law: claim*) presentar; (*store*) archivar; **to open/close a ~** (*Comput*) abrir/cerrar un fichero; **to ~ in/out** *vi* entrar/salir en fila; **to ~ a suit against sb** entablar pleito contra algn; **to ~ past** desfilar ante

filing ['faɪlɪŋ] *n*: **to do the ~** llevar los archivos

filing cabinet *n* archivo

Filipino [fɪlɪ'pi:nəu] *adj* filipino ▷ *n* (*person*) filipino(-a) *m/f*; (*Ling*) tagalo

fill [fɪl] *vt* llenar; (*tooth*) empastar; (*vacancy*) cubrir ▷ *n*: **to eat one's ~** comer hasta hartarse; **we've already ~ed that vacancy** ya hemos cubierto esa vacante; **~ed with admiration (for)** lleno de admiración (por); **fill in** *vt* rellenar; (*details, report*) completar; **to ~ sb in on sth** (*inf*) poner a algn al corriente *or* al día sobre algo; **fill out** *vt* (*form, receipt*) rellenar; **fill up** *vt* llenar (hasta el borde) ▷ *vi* (*Aut*) echar gasolina

fillet ['fɪlɪt] *n* filete *m*

fillet steak *n* filete *m* de ternera

filling ['fɪlɪŋ] *n* (*Culin*) relleno; (*for tooth*) empaste *m*

filling station *n* estación *f* de servicio

fillip ['fɪlɪp] *n* estímulo

film [fɪlm] *n* película ▷ *vt* (*scene*) filmar ▷ *vi* rodar

film star *n* estrella de cine

Filofax® ['faɪləufæks] *n* agenda (profesional)

filter ['fɪltə^r] *n* filtro ▷ *vt* filtrar; **filter in, filter through** *vi* filtrarse

filter lane *n* (*Brit*) carril *m* de selección

filter-tipped ['fɪltətɪpt] *adj* con filtro

filth [fɪlθ] *n* suciedad *f*

filthy ['fɪlθɪ] *adj* sucio; (*language*) obsceno

fin [fɪn] *n* (*gen*) aleta

final ['faɪnl] *adj* (*last*) final, último; (*definitive*) definitivo ▷ *n* (*Sport*) final *f*; **finals** *npl* (*Scol*) exámenes *mpl* finales

finale [fɪ'nɑ:lɪ] *n* final *m*

finalist ['faɪnəlɪst] *n* (*Sport*) finalista *m/f*

finalize ['faɪnəlaɪz] *vt* ultimar

finally ['faɪnəlɪ] *adv* (*lastly*) por último, finalmente; (*eventually*) por fin; (*irrevocably*) de modo definitivo; (*once and for all*) definitivamente

finance [faɪ'næns] *n* (*money, funds*) fondos *mpl*; **finances** *npl* finanzas *fpl* ▷ *cpd* (*page, section, company*) financiero ▷ *vt* financiar

financial [faɪ'nænʃəl] *adj* financiero

financial year *n* ejercicio (financiero)

find [faɪnd] *vt* (*pt, pp* **found** [faund]) (*gen*) encontrar, hallar; (*come upon*) descubrir ▷ *n* hallazgo; descubrimiento; **to ~ sb guilty** (*Law*) declarar culpable a algn; **I ~ it easy** me resulta fácil; **find out** ▷ *vt* averiguar; (*truth, secret*) descubrir ▷ *vi*: **to ~ out about** enterarse de

findings ['faɪndɪŋz] *npl* (*Law*) veredicto *sg*, fallo *sg*; (*of report*) recomendaciones *fpl*

fine [faɪn] *adj* (*delicate*) fino; (*beautiful*) hermoso ▷ *adv* (*well*) bien ▷ *n* (*Law*) multa ▷ *vt* (*Law*) multar; **the weather is ~** hace buen tiempo; **he's ~** está muy bien; **you're doing ~** lo estás haciendo muy bien; **to cut it ~** (*of time, money*) calcular muy justo; **to get a ~ for (doing) sth** recibir una multa por (hacer) algo

fine arts *npl* bellas artes *fpl*

fine print *n*: **the ~** la letra pequeña *or* menuda

finery ['faɪnərɪ] *n* galas *fpl*

finger ['fɪŋgə^r] *n* dedo ▷ *vt* (*touch*) manosear; (*Mus*) puntear; **little/index ~** (dedo) meñique *m*/índice *m*

fingernail ['fɪŋgəneɪl] *n* uña

fingerprint ['fɪŋgəprɪnt] *n* huella dactilar

fingertip ['fɪŋgətɪp] *n* yema del dedo; **to have sth at one's ~s** saberse algo al dedillo

finicky ['fɪnɪkɪ] *adj* (*fussy*) delicado

finish ['fɪnɪʃ] *n* (*end*) fin *m*; (*Sport*) meta; (*polish etc*) acabado ▷ *vt, vi* acabar, terminar; **to ~ doing sth** acabar de hacer algo; **to ~ first/second/third** (*Sport*) llegar el primero/segundo/tercero; **I've ~ed with the paper** he terminado con el periódico; **she's ~ed with him** ha roto *or* acabado con él; **finish off** *vt* acabar, terminar; (*kill*) rematar; **finish up** *vt* acabar, terminar ▷ *vi* ir a parar, terminar

finishing line *n* línea de llegada *or* meta

finishing school *n* *colegio para la educación social de señoritas*

finite ['faɪnaɪt] *adj* finito

Finland ['fɪnlənd] *n* Finlandia

Finn [fɪn] *n* finlandés(-esa) *m(f)*

Finnish ['fɪnɪʃ] *adj* finlandés(-esa) ▷ *n* (*Ling*) finlandés *m*

fir [fə:^r] *n* abeto

fire ['faɪə^r] *n* fuego; (*accidental, damaging*) incendio; (*heater*) estufa ▷ *vt* (*gun*) disparar;

(*set fire to*) incendiar; (*excite*) exaltar; (*interest*) despertar; (*dismiss*) despedir ▷ *vi* encenderse; (*Aut: engine*) encender; **electric/gas ~** estufa eléctrica/de gas; **on ~** ardiendo, en llamas; **to be on ~** estar ardiendo; **to catch ~** prenderse fuego; **to set ~ to sth, set sth on ~** prender fuego a algo; **insured against ~** asegurado contra incendios; **to be/come under ~** estar/caer bajo el fuego enemigo
fire alarm *n* alarma de incendios
firearm ['faɪərɑːm] *n* arma de fuego
fire brigade, fire department (*US*) *n* (cuerpo de) bomberos *mpl*
fire door *n* puerta contra incendios
fire engine *n* coche *m* de bomberos
fire escape *n* escalera de incendios
fire exit *n* salida de incendios
fire extinguisher *n* extintor *m*
fireman ['faɪəmən] *n* bombero
fireplace ['faɪəpleɪs] *n* chimenea
fireplug ['faɪəplʌg] *n* (*US*) boca de incendios
fireproof ['faɪəpruːf] *adj* a prueba de fuego; (*material*) incombustible
fireside ['faɪəsaɪd] *n*: **by the ~** al lado de la chimenea
fire station *n* parque *m* de bomberos
firetruck *n* (*US*) = **fire engine**
firewall ['faɪəwɔːl] *n* (*Internet*) firewall *m*
firewood ['faɪəwud] *n* leña
fireworks ['faɪəwəːks] *npl* fuegos *mpl* artificiales
firing squad *n* pelotón *m* de ejecución
firm [fəːm] *adj* firme; (*offer, decision*) en firme ▷ *n* empresa; **to be a ~ believer in sth** ser un partidario convencido de algo; **to stand ~** *or* **take a ~ stand on sth** (*fig*) mantenerse firme ante algo
firmly ['fəːmlɪ] *adv* firmemente
first [fəːst] *adj* primero ▷ *adv* (*before others*) primero; (*when listing reasons etc*) en primer lugar, primeramente ▷ *n* (*person: in race*) primero(-a); (*Aut: also:* **~ gear**) primera; **at ~** al principio; **~ of all** ante todo; **the ~ of January** el uno *or* primero de enero; **in the ~ instance** en primer lugar; **I'll do it ~ thing tomorrow** lo haré mañana a primera hora; **for the ~ time** por primera vez; **head ~** de cabeza; **from the (very) ~** desde el principio
first aid *n* primeros auxilios *mpl*
first aid kit *n* botiquín *m*
first-class ['fəːstklɑːs] *adj* de primera clase; **~ ticket** (*Rail etc*) billete *m or* (*LAm*) boleto de primera clase; **~ mail** correo de primera clase
first-hand [fəːst'hænd] *adj* de primera mano
first lady *n* (*esp US*) primera dama
firstly ['fəːstlɪ] *adv* en primer lugar
first name *n* nombre *m* de pila
first-rate [fəːst'reɪt] *adj* de primera (clase)
first-time buyer [fəːsttaɪm-] *n* *persona que compra su primera vivienda*
fiscal ['fɪskəl] *adj* fiscal; **~ year** año fiscal, ejercicio
fish [fɪʃ] *n pl inv* pez *m*; (*food*) pescado ▷ *vt* pescar en ▷ *vi* pescar; **to go ~ing** ir de pesca; **fish out** *vt* (*from water, box etc*) sacar; **~ and chips** pescado frito con patatas fritas
fish-and-chip shop *n* = **chip shop**
fisherman ['fɪʃəmən] *n* pescador *m*
fish farm *n* piscifactoría
fish fingers *npl* (*Brit*) palitos *mpl* de pescado (empanado)
fishing boat ['fɪʃɪŋ-] *n* barca de pesca
fishing industry ['fɪʃɪŋ-] *n* industria pesquera
fishing line ['fɪʃɪŋ-] *n* sedal *m*
fishing net ['fɪʃɪŋ-] *n* red *f* de pesca
fishing rod ['fɪʃɪŋ-] *n* caña (de pescar)
fishmonger ['fɪʃmʌŋgə^r] *n* (*Brit*) pescadero(-a)
fishmonger's, fishmonger's shop *n* (*Brit*) pescadería
fish sticks *npl* (*US*) = **fish fingers**
fishy ['fɪʃɪ] *adj* (*fig*) sospechoso
fist [fɪst] *n* puño
fit [fɪt] *adj* (*Med, Sport*) en (buena) forma; (*proper*) adecuado, apropiado ▷ *vt* (*clothes*) quedar bien a; (*try on: clothes*) probar; (*instal*) poner; (*equip*) proveer; (*match: facts*) cuadrar *or* corresponder *or* coincidir con; (*: description*) estar de acuerdo con; (*accommodate*) ajustar, adaptar ▷ *vi* (*clothes*) quedar bien; (*in space, gap*) caber; (*facts*) coincidir ▷ *n* (*Med*) ataque *m*; (*outburst*) arranque *m*; **~ to** apto para; **~ for** apropiado para; **do as you think** *or* **see ~** haz lo que te parezca mejor; **to keep ~** mantenerse en forma; **to be ~ for work** (*after illness*) estar en condiciones para trabajar; **~ of coughing** acceso de tos; **~ of anger/enthusiasm** arranque de cólera/entusiasmo; **to have** *or* **suffer a ~** tener un ataque *or* acceso; **this dress is a good ~** este vestido me queda bien; **by ~s and starts** a rachas; **fit in** *vi* encajar ▷ *vt* (*object*) acomodar; (*fig: appointment, visitor*) encontrar un hueco para; **to ~ in with sb's plans** acomodarse a los planes de algn; **fit out** (*Brit*), **fit up** *vt* equipar
fitful ['fɪtful] *adj* espasmódico, intermitente
fitment ['fɪtmənt] *n* mueble *m*
fitness ['fɪtnɪs] *n* (*Med*) forma física; (*of remark*) conveniencia
fitted ['fɪtɪd] *adj* (*jacket, shirt*) entallado; (*sheet*) de cuatro picos
fitted carpet ['fɪtɪd-] *n* moqueta
fitted kitchen ['fɪtɪd-] *n* cocina amueblada
fitter ['fɪtə^r] *n* ajustador(a) *m(f)*
fitting ['fɪtɪŋ] *adj* apropiado ▷ *n* (*of dress*) prueba; *see also* **fittings**
fitting room *n* (*in shop*) probador *m*
fittings ['fɪtɪŋz] *npl* instalaciones *fpl*
five [faɪv] *num* cinco; **she is ~ (years old)** tiene cinco años (de edad); **it costs ~ pounds** cuesta cinco libras; **it's ~ (o'clock)** son las cinco

fiver ['faɪvəʳ] *n* (*inf*: *Brit*) billete *m* de cinco libras; (: *US*) billete *m* de cinco dólares
fix [fɪks] *vt* (*secure*) fijar, asegurar; (*mend*) arreglar; (*make ready*: *meal, drink*) preparar ▷ *n*: **to be in a ~** estar en un aprieto; **to ~ sth in one's mind** fijar algo en la memoria; **the fight was a ~** (*inf*) la pelea estaba amañada; **fix on** *vt* (*decide on*) fijar; **fix up** *vt* (*arrange*: *date, meeting*) arreglar; **to ~ sb up with sth** conseguirle algo a algn
fixation [fɪk'seɪʃən] *n* (*Psych*) fijación *f*
fixed [fɪkst] *adj* (*prices etc*) fijo; **how are you ~ for money?** (*inf*) ¿qué tal andas de dinero?
fixture ['fɪkstʃəʳ] *n* (*Sport*) encuentro; **fixtures** *npl* instalaciones *fpl* fijas
fizzle out ['fɪzl-] *vi* apagarse; (*enthusiasm, interest*) decaer; (*plan*) quedar en agua de borrajas
fizzy ['fɪzɪ] *adj* (*drink*) gaseoso
flabbergasted ['flæbəgɑːstɪd] *adj* pasmado
flabby ['flæbɪ] *adj* flojo (de carnes); (*skin*) fofo
flag [flæg] *n* bandera; (*stone*) losa ▷ *vi* decaer; **~ of convenience** pabellón *m* de conveniencia; **flag down** *vt*: **to ~ sb down** hacer señas a algn para que se pare; **flag up** *vt* recalcar
flagpole ['flægpəul] *n* asta de bandera
flagrant ['fleɪgrənt] *adj* flagrante
flagship ['flægʃɪp] *n* buque *m* insignia *or* almirante
flair [flɛəʳ] *n* aptitud *f* especial
flak [flæk] *n* (*Mil*) fuego antiaéreo; (*inf*: *criticism*) lluvia de críticas
flake [fleɪk] *n* (*of rust, paint*) desconchón *m*; (*of snow*) copo; (*of soap powder*) escama ▷ *vi* (*also*: **~ off**: *paint*) desconcharse; (*skin*) descamarse
flamboyant [flæm'bɔɪənt] *adj* (*dress*) vistoso; (*person*) extravagante
flame [fleɪm] *n* llama; **to burst into ~s** incendiarse; **old ~** (*inf*) antiguo amor *m/f*
flamingo [flə'mɪŋgəu] *n* flamenco
flammable ['flæməbl] *adj* inflamable
flan [flæn] *n* (*Brit*) tarta
flank [flæŋk] *n* flanco; (*of person*) costado ▷ *vt* flanquear
flannel ['flænl] *n* (*Brit*: *also*: **face ~**) toallita; (*fabric*) franela; **flannels** *npl* pantalones *mpl* de franela
flap [flæp] *n* (*of pocket, envelope*) solapa; (*of table*) hoja (plegadiza); (*wing movement*) aletazo; (*Aviat*) flap *m* ▷ *vt* (*wings*) batir ▷ *vi* (*sail, flag*) ondear
flare [flɛəʳ] *n* llamarada; (*Mil*) bengala; (*in skirt etc*) vuelo; **flares** *npl* (*trousers*) pantalones *mpl* de campana; **flare up** *vi* encenderse; (*fig*: *person*) encolerizarse; (: *revolt*) estallar
flash [flæʃ] *n* relámpago; (*also*: **news ~**) noticias *fpl* de última hora; (*Phot*) flash *m*; (*US*: *torch*) linterna ▷ *vt* (*light, headlights*) lanzar destellos con; (*torch*) encender ▷ *vi* brillar; (*hazard light etc*) lanzar destellos; **in a ~** en un instante; **~ of inspiration** ráfaga de inspiración; **to ~ sth about** (*fig, col*: *flaunt*) ostentar algo, presumir con algo; **he ~ed by** *or* **past** pasó como un rayo
flashback ['flæʃbæk] *n* flashback *m*, escena retrospectiva
flashbulb ['flæʃbʌlb] *n* bombilla de flash
flash drive *n* (*Comput*) memoria flash, flash drive *m*
flashlight ['flæʃlaɪt] *n* (*US*: *torch*) linterna
flashy ['flæʃɪ] *adj* (*pej*) ostentoso
flask [flɑːsk] *n* petaca; (*also*: **vacuum ~**) termo
flat [flæt] *adj* llano; (*smooth*) liso; (*tyre*) desinflado; (*battery*) descargado; (*beer*) sin gas; (*Mus*: *instrument*) desafinado ▷ *n* (*Brit*: *apartment*) piso (*Sp*), departamento (*LAm*), apartamento; (*Aut*) pinchazo; (*Mus*) bemol *m*; **(to work) ~ out** (trabajar) a tope; **~ rate of pay** sueldo fijo
flatly ['flætlɪ] *adv* rotundamente, de plano
flatmate ['flætmeɪt] *n* compañero(-a) de piso
flat pack *n*: **it comes in a ~** viene en un paquete plano para su automontaje
flatscreen ['flætskriːn] *adj* pantalla plana
flatten ['flætn] *vt* (*also*: **~ out**) allanar; (*smooth out*) alisar; (*house, city*) arrasar
flatter ['flætəʳ] *vt* adular, halagar; (*show to advantage*) favorecer
flattering ['flætərɪŋ] *adj* halagador(a); (*clothes etc*) que favorece, favorecedor(a)
flattery ['flætərɪ] *n* adulación *f*
flaunt [flɔːnt] *vt* ostentar, lucir
flavour, flavor (*US*) ['fleɪvəʳ] *n* sabor *m*, gusto ▷ *vt* sazonar, condimentar; **strawberry ~ed** con sabor a fresa
flavouring, flavoring (*US*) ['fleɪvərɪŋ] *n* (*in product*) aromatizante *m*
flaw [flɔː] *n* defecto
flawless ['flɔːlɪs] *adj* impecable
flax [flæks] *n* lino
flaxen ['flæksən] *adj* muy rubio
flea [fliː] *n* pulga
flea market *n* rastro, mercadillo
fleck [flɛk] *n* mota ▷ *vt* (*with blood, mud etc*) salpicar; **brown ~ed with white** marrón con motas blancas
flee [fliː] (*pt, pp* **fled** [flɛd]) *vt* huir de, abandonar ▷ *vi* huir
fleece [fliːs] *n* (*of sheep*) vellón *m*; (*wool*) lana; (*top*) forro polar ▷ *vt* (*inf*) desplumar
fleet [fliːt] *n* flota; (*of cars, lorries etc*) parque *m*
fleeting ['fliːtɪŋ] *adj* fugaz
Flemish ['flɛmɪʃ] *adj* flamenco ▷ *n* (*Ling*) flamenco; **the ~** los flamencos
flesh [flɛʃ] *n* carne *f*; (*skin*) piel *f*; (*of fruit*) pulpa; **of ~ and blood** de carne y hueso
flesh wound *n* herida superficial
flew [fluː] *pt of* **fly**
flex [flɛks] *n* cable *m* ▷ *vt* (*muscles*) tensar
flexibility [flɛksɪ'bɪlɪtɪ] *n* flexibilidad *f*
flexible ['flɛksəbl] *adj* flexible; **~ working hours** horario *sg* flexible

f

flexitime ['flɛksɪtaɪm] *n* horario flexible
flick [flɪk] *n* golpecito; (*with finger*) capirotazo; (*Brit: inf: film*) película ▷ *vt* dar un golpecito a; **flick off** *vt* quitar con el dedo; **flick through** *vt fus* hojear
flicker ['flɪkəʳ] *vi* (*light*) parpadear; (*flame*) vacilar ▷ *n* parpadeo
flier ['flaɪəʳ] *n* aviador(a) *m(f)*
flies [flaɪz] *npl of* **fly**
flight [flaɪt] *n* vuelo; (*escape*) huida, fuga; (*also*: **~ of steps**) tramo (de escaleras); **to take ~** huir, darse a la fuga; **to put to ~** ahuyentar; **how long does the ~ take?** ¿cuánto dura el vuelo?
flight attendant *n* (*US*) auxiliar *m/f* de vuelo
flight deck *n* (*Aviat*) cabina de mandos
flight path *n* trayectoria de vuelo
flight recorder *n* registrador *m* de vuelo
flimsy ['flɪmzɪ] *adj* (*thin*) muy ligero; (*excuse*) flojo
flinch [flɪntʃ] *vi* encogerse; **to ~ from** retroceder ante
fling [flɪŋ] *vt* (*pt, pp* **flung** [flʌŋ]) arrojar ▷ *n* (*love affair*) aventura amorosa
flint [flɪnt] *n* pedernal *m*; (*in lighter*) piedra
flip [flɪp] *vt*: **to ~ a coin** echar a cara o cruz; **flip over** *vt* dar la vuelta a; **flip through** *vt fus* (*book*) hojear; (*records*) ver de pasada
flip-flops ['flɪpflɔps] *npl* (*esp Brit*) chancletas *fpl*
flippant ['flɪpənt] *adj* poco serio
flipper ['flɪpəʳ] *n* aleta
flirt [flə:t] *vi* coquetear, flirtear ▷ *n* coqueta *f*
flit [flɪt] *vi* revolotear
float [fləut] *n* flotador *m*; (*in procession*) carroza; (*sum of money*) reserva ▷ *vi* (*Comm: currency*) flotar; (*swimmer*) hacer la plancha ▷ *vt* (*gen*) hacer flotar; (*company*) lanzar; **to ~ an idea** plantear una idea
flock [flɔk] *n* (*of sheep*) rebaño; (*of birds*) bandada; (*of people*) multitud *f* ▷ *vi*: **to ~ to** acudir en tropel a
flog [flɔg] *vt* azotar; (*inf*) vender
flood [flʌd] *n* inundación *f*; (*of words, tears etc*) torrente *m*; (*of letters, imports etc*) avalancha ▷ *vt* (*Aut: carburettor*) inundar ▷ *vi* (*place*) inundarse; (*people*): **to ~ into** inundar; **to ~ the market** (*Comm*) inundar el mercado
flooding ['flʌdɪŋ] *n* inundaciones *fpl*
floodlight ['flʌdlaɪt] *n* foco ▷ *vt* (*irreg: like* **light**) iluminar con focos
floodwater ['flʌdwɔ:təʳ] *n* aguas *fpl* (*de la inundación*)
floor [flɔ:ʳ] *n* suelo, piso (*LAm*); (*storey*) piso; (*of sea, valley*) fondo; (*dance floor*) pista ▷ *vt* (*with blow*) derribar; (*fig: baffle*) dejar anonadado; **ground ~** (*US*), **first ~** planta baja; **first ~** (*US*), **second ~** primer piso; **top ~** último piso; **to have the ~** (*speaker*) tener la palabra
floorboard ['flɔ:bɔ:d] *n* tabla
flooring ['flɔ:rɪŋ] *n* suelo; (*material*) solería
floor show *n* cabaret *m*
flop [flɔp] *n* fracaso ▷ *vi* (*fail*) fracasar
floppy ['flɔpɪ] *adj* flojo ▷ *n* (*Comput: also*: **~ disk**) floppy *m*
flora ['flɔ:rə] *n* flora
floral ['flɔ:rl] *adj* floral; (*pattern*) floreado; (*dress, wallpaper*) de flores
florid ['flɔrɪd] *adj* (*style*) florido
florist ['flɔrɪst] *n* florista *m/f*; **~'s (shop)** *n* floristería
flotation [fləu'teɪʃən] *n* (*of shares*) emisión *f*; (*of company*) lanzamiento
flounce [flauns] *n* volante *m*; **flounce in** *vi* entrar con gesto exagerado; **flounce out** *vi* salir con gesto airado
flounder ['flaundəʳ] *vi* tropezar ▷ *n* (*Zool*) platija
flour ['flauəʳ] *n* harina
flourish ['flʌrɪʃ] *vi* florecer ▷ *n* ademán *m*, movimiento (ostentoso)
flout [flaut] *vt* burlarse de; (*order*) no hacer caso de, hacer caso omiso de
flow [fləu] *n* (*movement*) flujo; (*of traffic*) circulación *f*; (*direction*) curso; (*Elec*) corriente *f* ▷ *vi* (*river, blood*) fluir; (*traffic*) circular
flow chart *n* organigrama *m*
flower ['flauəʳ] *n* flor *f* ▷ *vi* florecer; **in ~** en flor
flower bed *n* macizo
flowerpot ['flauəpɔt] *n* tiesto
flowery ['flauərɪ] *adj* florido; (*perfume, pattern*) de flores
flown [fləun] *pp of* **fly**
fl. oz. *abbr* = **fluid ounce**
flu [flu:] *n* gripe *f*; **to have ~** tener la gripe
fluctuate ['flʌktjueɪt] *vi* fluctuar
fluency ['flu:ənsɪ] *n* fluidez *f*, soltura
fluent ['flu:ənt] *adj* (*speech*) elocuente; **he speaks ~ French, he's ~ in French** domina el francés
fluently ['flu:əntlɪ] *adv* con soltura
fluff [flʌf] *n* pelusa
fluffy ['flʌfɪ] *adj* de pelo suave
fluid ['flu:ɪd] *adj* (*movement*) fluido, líquido; (*situation*) inestable ▷ *n* fluido, líquido; (*in diet*) líquido
fluid ounce *n* onza *f* líquida
fluke [flu:k] *n* (*inf*) chiripa
flung [flʌŋ] *pt, pp of* **fling**
fluorescent [fluə'rɛsnt] *adj* fluorescente
fluoride ['fluəraɪd] *n* fluoruro
fluoride toothpaste *n* pasta de dientes con flúor
flurry ['flʌrɪ] *n* (*of snow*) ventisca; (*haste*) agitación *f*; **~ of activity** frenesí *m* de actividad
flush [flʌʃ] *n* (*on face*) rubor *m*; (*fig: of youth, beauty*) resplandor *m* ▷ *vt* limpiar con agua; (*also*: **~ out**: *game, birds*) levantar; (*fig: criminal*) poner al descubierto ▷ *vi* ruborizarse ▷ *adj*: **~ with** a ras de; **to ~ the toilet** tirar de la cadena (del wáter); **hot ~es** (*Med*) sofocos *mpl*
flushed [flʌʃt] *adj* ruborizado

flustered ['flʌstəd] *adj* aturdido
flute [flu:t] *n* flauta travesera
flutter ['flʌtəʳ] *n* (*of wings*) revoloteo, aleteo; (*inf*: *bet*) apuesta ▷ *vi* revolotear; **to be in a ~** estar nervioso
flux [flʌks] *n* flujo; **in a state of ~** cambiando continuamente
fly [flaɪ] (*pt* **flew**, *pp* **flown**) *n* (*insect*) mosca; (*on trousers*: *also*: **flies**) bragueta ▷ *vt* (*plane*) pilotar; (*cargo*) transportar (en avión); (*distance*) recorrer (en avión) ▷ *vi* volar; (*passenger*) ir en avión; (*escape*) evadirse; (*flag*) ondear; **fly away** *vi* (*bird, insect*) irse volando; **fly in** *vi* (*person*) llegar en avión; (*plane*) aterrizar; **he flew in from Bilbao** llegó en avión desde Bilbao; **fly off** *vi* irse volando; **fly out** *vi* irse en avión
fly-drive *n*: **~ holiday** *vacaciones que incluyen vuelo y alquiler de coche*
flying ['flaɪɪŋ] *n* (*activity*) (el) volar ▷ *adj*: **~ visit** visita relámpago; **with ~ colours** con lucimiento
flying picket *n* piquete *m* volante
flying saucer *n* platillo volante
flying squad *n* (*Police*) brigada móvil
flying start *n*: **to get off to a ~** empezar con buen pie
flyover ['flaɪəuvəʳ] *n* (*Brit*: *bridge*) paso elevado *or* (*LAm*) a desnivel
flysheet ['flaɪʃi:t] *n* (*for tent*) doble techo
flyweight ['flaɪweɪt] *adj* de peso mosca ▷ *n* peso mosca
FM *abbr* (*Radio*: = *frequency modulation*) FM; (*Brit Mil*) = **field marshal**
FO *n abbr* (*Brit*: = *Foreign Office*) ≈ Min. de AA. EE. (= *Ministerio de Asuntos Exteriores*)
foal [fəul] *n* potro
foam [fəum] *n* espuma ▷ *vi* hacer espuma
fob [fɔb] *n* (*also*: **watch ~**) leontina ▷ *vt*: **to ~ sb off with sth** deshacerse de algn con algo
focal ['fəukəl] *adj* focal; **~ point** punto focal; (*fig*) centro de atención
focus ['fəukəs] (*pl* **focuses**) *n* foco; (*centre*) centro ▷ *vt* (*field glasses etc*) enfocar ▷ *vi*: **to ~ (on)** enfocar (a); (*issue etc*) centrarse en; **in/out of ~** enfocado/desenfocado
fodder ['fɔdəʳ] *n* pienso
foe [fəu] *n* enemigo
foetus, fetus (US) ['fi:təs] *n* feto
fog [fɔg] *n* niebla
foggy ['fɔgɪ] *adj*: **it's ~** hay niebla
fog lamp, fog light (US) *n* (*Aut*) faro antiniebla
foil [fɔɪl] *vt* frustrar ▷ *n* hoja; (*also*: **kitchen ~**) papel *m* (de) aluminio; (*Fencing*) florete *m*
fold [fəuld] *n* (*bend, crease*) pliegue *m*; (*Agr*) redil *m* ▷ *vt* doblar; **to ~ one's arms** cruzarse de brazos; **fold up** *vi* plegarse, doblarse; (*business*) quebrar ▷ *vt* (*map etc*) plegar
folder ['fəuldəʳ] *n* (*for papers*) carpeta; (*binder*) carpeta de anillas; (*brochure*) folleto; (*Comput*) directorio
folding ['fəuldɪŋ] *adj* (*chair, bed*) plegable
foliage ['fəulɪɪdʒ] *n* follaje *m*
folk [fəuk] *npl* gente *f* ▷ *adj* popular, folklórico; **folks** *npl* familia, parientes *mpl*
folklore ['fəuklɔ:ʳ] *n* folklore *m*
folk music *n* música folk
folk singer *n* cantante *m/f* de música folk
folk song *n* canción *f* popular *or* folk
follow ['fɔləu] *vt* (*also on Twitter*) seguir ▷ *vi* seguir; (*result*) resultar; **he ~ed suit** hizo lo mismo; **to ~ sb's advice** seguir el consejo de algn; **I don't quite ~ you** no te comprendo muy bien; **to ~ in sb's footsteps** seguir los pasos de algn; **it doesn't ~ that ...** no se deduce que ....; **follow on** *vi* seguir; (*continue*): **to ~ on from** ser la consecuencia lógica de; **follow out** *vt* (*implement*: *idea, plan*) realizar, llevar a cabo; **follow through** *vt* llevar hasta el fin ▷ *vi* (*Sport*) dar el remate; **follow up** *vt* (*letter, offer*) responder a; (*case*) investigar
follower ['fɔləuəʳ] *n* seguidor(a) *m(f)*; (*Pol*) partidario(-a)
following ['fɔləuɪŋ] *adj* siguiente ▷ *n* seguidores *mpl*, afición *f*
follow-up ['fɔləuʌp] *n* continuación *f*
folly ['fɔlɪ] *n* locura
fond [fɔnd] *adj* (*loving*) cariñoso; **to be ~ of sb** tener cariño a algn; **she's ~ of swimming** tiene afición a la natación, le gusta nadar
fondle ['fɔndl] *vt* acariciar
font [fɔnt] *n* pila bautismal
food [fu:d] *n* comida
food chain *n* cadena alimenticia
food mixer *n* batidora
food poisoning *n* intoxicación *f* alimentaria
food processor *n* robot *m* de cocina
food stamp *n* (US) vale *m* para comida
foodstuffs ['fu:dstʌfs] *npl* comestibles *mpl*
fool [fu:l] *n* tonto(-a); (*Culin*) puré *m* de frutas con nata ▷ *vt* engañar; **to make a ~ of o.s.** ponerse en ridículo; **you can't ~ me** a mí no me engañas; *see also* **April Fools' Day**; **fool about, fool around** *vi* hacer el tonto
foolhardy ['fu:lhɑ:dɪ] *adj* temerario
foolish ['fu:lɪʃ] *adj* tonto; (*careless*) imprudente
foolproof ['fu:lpru:f] *adj* (*plan etc*) infalible
foot [fut] (*pl* **feet**) *n* (*Anat*) pie *m*; (*of page, stairs, mountain*) pie *m*; (*measure*) pie (= *304 mm*); (*of animal, table*) pata ▷ *vt* (*bill*) pagar; **on ~** a pie; **to find one's feet** acostumbrarse; **to put one's ~ down** (*say no*) plantarse; (*Aut*) pisar el acelerador
footage ['futɪdʒ] *n* (*Cine*) imágenes *fpl*
foot-and-mouth [futənd'mauθ], **foot-and-mouth disease** *n* fiebre *f* aftosa
football ['futbɔ:l] *n* balón *m*; (*game*: *Brit*) fútbol *m*; (US) fútbol *m* americano
footballer ['futbɔ:ləʳ] *n* (*Brit*) = **football player**
football match *n* partido de fútbol

football player *n* futbolista *m/f*, jugador(a) *m(f)* de fútbol
footbrake ['futbreɪk] *n* freno de pie
footbridge ['futbrɪdʒ] *n* pasarela, puente *m* para peatones
foothills ['futhɪlz] *npl* estribaciones *fpl*
foothold ['futhəuld] *n* pie *m* firme
footing ['futɪŋ] *n* (*fig*) nivel *m*; **to lose one's ~** perder pie; **on an equal ~** en pie de igualdad
footlights ['futlaɪts] *npl* candilejas *fpl*
footman ['futmən] *n* lacayo
footnote ['futnəut] *n* nota (de pie de página)
footpath ['futpɑ:θ] *n* sendero
footprint ['futprɪnt] *n* huella, pisada
footsie ['futsɪ] *n*: **to play ~ with sb** (*inf*) juguetear con los pies de algn
footstep ['futstɛp] *n* paso
footwear ['futwɛəʳ] *n* calzado

KEYWORD

for [fɔ:] *prep* **1** (*indicating destination, intention*) para; **the train for London** el tren para Londres; (*in announcements*) el tren con destino a Londres; **he left for Rome** marchó para Roma; **he went for the paper** fue por el periódico; **is this for me?** ¿es esto para mí?; **it's time for lunch** es la hora de comer
2 (*indicating purpose*) para; **what('s it) for?** ¿para qué (es)?; **what's this button for?** ¿para qué sirve este botón?; **to pray for peace** rezar por la paz
3 (*on behalf of, representing*): **the MP for Hove** el diputado por Hove; **he works for the government/a local firm** trabaja para el gobierno/en una empresa local; **I'll ask him for you** se lo pediré por ti; **G for George** G de Gerona
4 (*because of*) por esta razón; **for fear of being criticized** por temor a ser criticado
5 (*with regard to*) para; **it's cold for July** hace frío para julio; **he has a gift for languages** tiene don de lenguas
6 (*in exchange for*) por; **I sold it for £5** lo vendí por £5; **to pay 50 pence for a ticket** pagar 50 peniques por un billete
7 (*in favour of*): **are you for or against us?** ¿estás con nosotros o contra nosotros?; **I'm all for it** estoy totalmente a favor; **vote for X** vote (a) X
8 (*referring to distance*): **there are roadworks for 5 km** hay obras en 5 km; **we walked for miles** caminamos kilómetros y kilómetros
9 (*referring to time*): **he was away for two years** estuvo fuera (durante) dos años; **it hasn't rained for three weeks** no ha llovido durante *or* en tres semanas; **I have known her for years** la conozco desde hace años; **can you do it for tomorrow?** ¿lo podrás hacer para mañana?
10 (*with infinitive clauses*): **it is not for me to decide** la decisión no es cosa mía; **it would be best for you to leave** sería mejor que te fueras; **there is still time for you to do it** todavía te queda tiempo para hacerlo; **for this to be possible ...** para que esto sea posible ...
11 (*in spite of*) a pesar de; **for all his complaints** a pesar de sus quejas
▷ *conj* (*since, as: rather formal*) puesto que

forage ['fɔrɪdʒ] *n* forraje *m*
foray ['fɔreɪ] *n* incursión *f*
forbid (*pt* **forbad(e)**, *pp* **forbidden**) [fə'bɪd, -'bæd, -'bɪdn] *vt* prohibir; **to ~ sb to do sth** prohibir a algn hacer algo
forbidden [fə'bɪdn] *pt of* **forbid** ▷ *adj* (*food, area*) prohibido; (*word, subject*) tabú
forbidding [fə'bɪdɪŋ] *adj* (*landscape*) inhóspito; (*severe*) severo
force [fɔ:s] *n* fuerza ▷ *vt* obligar, forzar; **to ~ o.s. to do** hacer un esfuerzo por hacer; **the F~s** *npl* (*Brit*) las Fuerzas Armadas; **sales ~** (*Comm*) personal *m* de ventas; **a ~ 5 wind** un viento fuerza 5; **to join ~s** unir fuerzas; **in ~** (*law etc*) en vigor; **to ~ sb to do sth** obligar a algn a hacer algo; **force back** *vt* (*crowd, enemy*) hacer retroceder; (*tears*) reprimir; **force down** *vt* (*food*) tragar con esfuerzo
forced [fɔ:st] *adj* (*smile*) forzado; (*landing*) forzoso
force-feed ['fɔ:sfi:d] *vt* (*animal, prisoner*) alimentar a la fuerza
forceful ['fɔ:sful] *adj* enérgico
forceps ['fɔ:sɛps] *npl* fórceps *m inv*
forcibly ['fɔ:səblɪ] *adv* a la fuerza
ford [fɔ:d] *n* vado ▷ *vt* vadear
fore [fɔ:ʳ] *n*: **to bring to the ~** sacar a la luz pública; **to come to the ~** empezar a destacar
forearm ['fɔ:rɑ:m] *n* antebrazo
foreboding [fɔ:'bəudɪŋ] *n* presentimiento
forecast ['fɔ:kɑ:st] *n* pronóstico ▷ *vt* (*irreg: like* **cast**) pronosticar; **weather ~** previsión *f* meteorológica
forecourt ['fɔ:kɔ:t] *n* patio; (*of garage*) área de entrada
forefathers ['fɔ:fɑ:ðəz] *npl* antepasados *mpl*
forefinger ['fɔ:fɪŋgəʳ] *n* (dedo) índice *m*
forefront ['fɔ:frʌnt] *n*: **in the ~ of** en la vanguardia de
forego (*pt* **forewent**, *pp* **foregone**) [fɔ:'gəu, -'wɛnt, -'gɔn] *vt* = **forgo**
foregone ['fɔ:gɔn] *pp of* **forego** ▷ *adj*: **it's a ~ conclusion** es una conclusión inevitable
foreground ['fɔ:graund] *n* (*also Comput*) primer plano *m*
forehand ['fɔ:hænd] *n* (*Tennis*) derechazo directo
forehead ['fɔrɪd] *n* frente *f*
foreign ['fɔrɪn] *adj* extranjero; (*trade*) exterior
foreign currency *n* divisas *fpl*
foreigner ['fɔrɪnəʳ] *n* extranjero(-a)

foreign exchange *n* (*system*) cambio de divisas; (*money*) divisas *fpl*, moneda extranjera
Foreign Minister *n* Ministro(-a) de Asuntos Exteriores, Canciller *m* (*LAm*)
Foreign Office *n* (*Brit*) Ministerio de Asuntos Exteriores
Foreign Secretary *n* (*Brit*) Ministro(-a) de Asuntos Exteriores, Canciller *m* (*LAm*)
foreleg ['fɔːlɛg] *n* pata delantera
foreman ['fɔːmən] *n* capataz *m*; (*Law*: *of jury*) presidente *m/f*
foremost ['fɔːməust] *adj* principal ▷ *adv*: **first and ~** ante todo, antes que nada
forename ['fɔːneɪm] *n* nombre *m* (de pila)
forensic [fə'rɛnsɪk] *adj* forense; **~ scientist** forense *m/f*
foreplay ['fɔːpleɪ] *n* preámbulos *mpl* (*de estimulación sexual*)
forerunner ['fɔːrʌnər] *n* precursor(a) *m(f)*
foresee (*pt* **foresaw**, *pp* **foreseen**) [fɔː'siː, -'sɔː, -'siːn] *vt* prever
foreseeable [fɔː'siːəbl] *adj* previsible
foreshadow [fɔː'ʃædəu] *vt* prefigurar, anunciar
foresight ['fɔːsaɪt] *n* previsión *f*
foreskin ['fɔːskɪn] *n* (*Anat*) prepucio
forest ['fɔrɪst] *n* bosque *m*
forestall [fɔː'stɔːl] *vt* anticiparse a
forestry ['fɔrɪstrɪ] *n* silvicultura
foretaste ['fɔːteɪst] *n* anticipo
foretell (*pt, pp* **foretold**) [fɔː'tɛl, -'təuld] *vt* predecir, pronosticar
forever [fə'rɛvər] *adv* siempre; (*for good*) para siempre; (*endlessly*) constantemente
forewent [fɔː'wɛnt] *pt of* **forego**
foreword ['fɔːwəːd] *n* prefacio
forfeit ['fɔːfɪt] *n* (*in game*) prenda ▷ *vt* perder (derecho a)
forgave [fə'geɪv] *pt of* **forgive**
forge [fɔːdʒ] *n* fragua; (*smithy*) herrería ▷ *vt* (*signature*: *Brit*: *money*) falsificar; (*metal*) forjar; **forge ahead** *vi* avanzar mucho
forger ['fɔːdʒər] *n* falsificador(a) *m(f)*
forgery ['fɔːdʒərɪ] *n* falsificación *f*
forget (*pt* **forgot**, *pp* **forgotten**) [fə'gɛt, -'gɔt, -'gɔtn] *vt* olvidar, olvidarse de ▷ *vi* olvidarse
forgetful [fə'gɛtful] *adj* olvidadizo, despistado
forget-me-not [fə'gɛtmɪnɔt] *n* nomeolvides *f inv*
forgive (*pt* **forgave**, *pp* **forgiven**) [fə'gɪv, -'geɪv, -'gɪvn] *vt* perdonar; **to ~ sb for sth/ for doing sth** perdonar algo a algn/a algn por haber hecho algo
forgiveness [fə'gɪvnɪs] *n* perdón *m*
forgo (*pt* **forwent**, *pp* **forgone**) [fɔː'gəu, -'wɛnt, -'gɔn] *vt* (*give up*) renunciar a; (*go without*) privarse de
forgot [fə'gɔt] *pt of* **forget**
forgotten [fə'gɔtn] *pp of* **forget**
fork [fɔːk] *n* (*for eating*) tenedor *m*; (*for gardening*) horca; (*of roads*) bifurcación *f*; (*in tree*) horcadura ▷ *vi* (*road*) bifurcarse; **fork out** *vt* (*inf*: *pay*) soltar
fork-lift truck ['fɔːklɪft-] *n* máquina elevadora
forlorn [fə'lɔːn] *adj* (*person*) triste, melancólico; (*deserted*: *cottage*) abandonado; (*desperate*: *attempt*) desesperado
form [fɔːm] *n* forma; (*Brit Scol*) curso; (*document*) formulario, planilla (*LAm*) ▷ *vt* formar; **in the ~ of** en forma de; **in top ~** en plena forma; **to be in good ~** (*Sport*: *fig*) estar en plena forma; **to ~ part of sth** formar parte de algo; **to ~ a circle/a queue** hacer una curva/una cola
formal ['fɔːməl] *adj* (*offer, receipt*) por escrito; (*person etc*) correcto; (*occasion, dinner*) ceremonioso; **~ dress** traje *m* de vestir; (*evening dress*) traje *m* de etiqueta
formalities [fɔː'mælɪtɪz] *npl* formalidades *fpl*
formality [fɔː'mælɪtɪ] *n* ceremonia
formally ['fɔːməlɪ] *adv* oficialmente
format ['fɔːmæt] *n* formato ▷ *vt* (*Comput*) formatear
formation [fɔː'meɪʃən] *n* formación *f*
formative ['fɔːmətɪv] *adj* (*years*) de formación
former ['fɔːmər] *adj* anterior; (*earlier*) antiguo; (*ex*) ex; **the ~ ... the latter ...** aquél ... éste ...; **the ~ president** el antiguo *or* ex presidente; **the ~ Yugoslavia/Soviet Union** la antigua *or* ex Yugoslavia/Unión Soviética
formerly ['fɔːməlɪ] *adv* antes
formidable ['fɔːmɪdəbl] *adj* formidable
formula ['fɔːmjulə] *n* fórmula; **F~ One** (*Aut*) Fórmula Uno
forsake (*pt* **forsook**, *pp* **forsaken**) [fə'seɪk, -'suk, -'seɪkən] *vt* (*gen*) abandonar; (*plan*) renunciar a
fort [fɔːt] *n* fuerte *m*; **to hold the ~** (*fig*) quedarse a cargo
forte ['fɔːtɪ] *n* fuerte *m*
forth [fɔːθ] *adv*: **back and ~** de acá para allá; **and so ~** y así sucesivamente
forthcoming [fɔːθ'kʌmɪŋ] *adj* próximo, venidero; (*character*) comunicativo
forthright ['fɔːθraɪt] *adj* franco
forthwith ['fɔːθ'wɪθ] *adv* en el acto, acto seguido
fortieth ['fɔːtɪɪθ] *adj* cuadragésimo
fortify ['fɔːtɪfaɪ] *vt* fortalecer
fortitude ['fɔːtɪtjuːd] *n* (*city*) fortificar; (*person*) fortalecer
fortnight ['fɔːtnaɪt] *n* (*Brit*) quincena; **it's a ~ since ...** hace quince días que ...
fortnightly ['fɔːtnaɪtlɪ] *adj* quincenal ▷ *adv* quincenalmente
fortress ['fɔːtrɪs] *n* fortaleza
fortunate ['fɔːtʃənɪt] *adj*: **it is ~ that ...** (es una) suerte que ...
fortunately ['fɔːtʃənɪtlɪ] *adv* afortunadamente

f

fortune ['fɔːtʃən] *n* suerte *f*; (*wealth*) fortuna; **to make a ~** hacer un dineral
fortune-teller ['fɔːtʃəntɛləʳ] *n* adivino(-a)
forty ['fɔːtɪ] *num* cuarenta
forum ['fɔːrəm] *n* (*also fig*) foro
forward ['fɔːwəd] *adj* (*position*) avanzado; (*movement*) hacia delante; (*front*) delantero; (*not shy*) atrevido ▷ *n* (*Sport*) delantero ▷ *vt* (*letter*) remitir; (*career*) promocionar; **to move ~** avanzar; **"please ~"** "remítase al destinatario"
forwarding address *n* destinatario
forward planning *n* planificación *f* por anticipado
forward slash *n* barra diagonal
forwent [fɔː'wɛnt] *pt of* **forgo**
fossil ['fɔsl] *n* fósil *m*
foster ['fɔstəʳ] *vt* (*child*) acoger en familia; (*idea*) fomentar
foster child *n* hijo(-a) adoptivo(-a)
foster mother *n* madre *f* adoptiva
fought [fɔːt] *pt, pp of* **fight**
foul [faul] *adj* (*gen*) sucio, puerco; (*weather, smell etc*) asqueroso; (*language*) grosero; (*temper*) malísimo ▷ *n* (*Football*) falta ▷ *vt* (*dirty*) ensuciar; (*block*) atascar; (*entangle: anchor, propeller*) atascar, enredarse en; (*football player*) cometer una falta contra
foul play *n* (*Sport*) mala jugada; (*Law*) muerte *f* violenta
found [faund] *pt, pp of* **find** ▷ *vt* (*establish*) fundar
foundation [faun'deɪʃən] *n* (*act*) fundación *f*; (*basis*) base *f*; (*also*: **~ cream**) crema de base; **foundations** *npl* (*of building*) cimientos *mpl*
foundations [faun'deɪʃənz] *npl* (*of building*) cimientos *mpl*; **to lay the ~** poner los cimientos
founder ['faundəʳ] *n* fundador(a) *m(f)* ▷ *vi* irse a pique
foundry ['faundrɪ] *n* fundición *f*
fountain ['fauntɪn] *n* fuente *f*
fountain pen *n* (pluma) estilográfica, plumafuente *f* (*LAm*)
four [fɔːʳ] *num* cuatro; **on all ~s** a gatas
four-by-four ['fɔbaɪ'fɔʳ] *n* todoterreno, 4x4 *m* (*cuatro por cuatro*)
four-letter word ['fɔːlɛtə-] *n* taco
four-poster ['fɔː'pəustəʳ] *n* (*also*: **~ bed**) cama de columnas
foursome ['fɔːsəm] *n* grupo de cuatro personas
fourteen ['fɔː'tiːn] *num* catorce
fourteenth [fɔː'tiːnθ] *adj* decimocuarto
fourth [fɔːθ] *adj* cuarto ▷ *n* (*Aut*: *also*: **~ gear**) cuarta (velocidad)
four-wheel drive ['fɔːwiːl-] *n* tracción *f* a las cuatro ruedas
fowl [faul] *n* ave *f* (de corral)
fox [fɔks] *n* zorro ▷ *vt* confundir
foyer ['fɔɪeɪ] *n* vestíbulo
Fr. *abbr* (*Rel*: *= father*) P.; (*= friar*) Fr.
fracas ['frækɑː] *n* gresca, refriega
fracking ['frækɪŋ] *n* fracturación *f* or fractura hidráulica
fraction ['frækʃən] *n* fracción *f*
fracture ['fræktʃəʳ] *n* fractura ▷ *vt* fracturar
fragile ['frædʒaɪl] *adj* frágil
fragment ['frægmənt] *n* fragmento
fragrance ['freɪgrəns] *n* fragancia
fragrant ['freɪgrənt] *adj* fragante, oloroso
frail [freɪl] *adj* (*fragile*) frágil, quebradizo; (*weak*) delicado
frame [freɪm] *n* (*Tech*) armazón *f*; (*of picture, door etc*) marco; (*of spectacles*: *also*: **~s**) montura ▷ *vt* encuadrar; (*picture*) enmarcar; (*reply*) formular; **to ~ sb** (*inf*) inculpar por engaños a algn
frame of mind *n* estado de ánimo
framework ['freɪmwəːk] *n* marco
France [frɑːns] *n* Francia
franchise ['fræntʃaɪz] *n* (*Pol*) derecho al voto, sufragio; (*Comm*) licencia, concesión *f*
frank [fræŋk] *adj* franco ▷ *vt* (*Brit*: *letter*) franquear
frankly ['fræŋklɪ] *adv* francamente
frankness ['fræŋknɪs] *n* franqueza
frantic ['fræntɪk] *adj* (*desperate*: *need, desire*) desesperado; (*: search*) frenético; (*: person*) desquiciado
fraternity [frə'təːnɪtɪ] *n* (*club*) fraternidad *f*; (*US*) club *m* de estudiantes; (*guild*) gremio
fraud [frɔːd] *n* fraude *m*; (*person*) impostor(a) *m(f)*
fraught [frɔːt] *adj* (*tense*) tenso; **~ with** cargado de
fray [freɪ] *n* combate *m*, lucha, refriega ▷ *vi* deshilacharse; **tempers were ~ed** el ambiente se ponía tenso
freak [friːk] *n* (*person*) fenómeno; (*event*) suceso anormal; (*inf*: *enthusiast*) adicto(-a) ▷ *adj* (*storm, conditions*) anormal; **health ~** (*inf*) maniático(-a) en cuestión de salud; **freak out** *vi* (*inf*: *on drugs*) flipar
freckle ['frɛkl] *n* peca
free [friː] *adj* (*person*: *at liberty*) libre; (*not fixed*) suelto; (*gratis*) gratuito; (*unoccupied*) desocupado; (*liberal*) generoso ▷ *vt* (*prisoner etc*) poner en libertad; (*jammed object*) soltar; **to give sb a ~ hand** dar carta blanca a algn; **~ and easy** despreocupado; **is this seat ~?** ¿está libre este asiento?; **~ of tax** libre de impuestos; **admission ~** entrada libre; **~ (of charge)**, **for ~** *adv* gratis
freedom ['friːdəm] *n* libertad *f*; **~ of association** libertad de asociación
Freefone® ['friːfəun] *n* (*Brit*) número gratuito
free-for-all ['friːfərɔːl] *n* riña general
free gift *n* regalo
freehold ['friːhəuld] *n* propiedad *f* absoluta
free kick *n* tiro libre
freelance ['friːlɑːns] *adj* independiente ▷ *adv* por cuenta propia; **to do ~ work** trabajar por su cuenta

freely ['fri:lɪ] *adv* libremente; (*liberally*) generosamente

free-market economy ['fri:'mɑ:kɪt-] *n* economía de libre mercado

freemason ['fri:meɪsn] *n* francmasón *m*

Freepost® ['fri:pəust] *n* porte *m* pagado

free-range ['fri:'reɪndʒ] *adj* (*hen, egg*) de granja

free speech *n* libertad *f* de expresión

free trade *n* libre comercio

freeway ['fri:weɪ] *n* (*US*) autopista

free will *n* libre albedrío; **of one's own ~** por su propia voluntad

freeze [fri:z] (*pt* **froze**, *pp* **frozen**) *vi* helarse, congelarse ▷ *vt* helar; (*prices, food, salaries*) congelar ▷ *n* helada; (*on arms, wages*) congelación *f*; **freeze over** *vi* (*lake, river*) helarse, congelarse; (*window, windscreen*) cubrirse de escarcha; **freeze up** *vi* helarse, congelarse

freeze-dried ['fri:zdraɪd] *adj* liofilizado

freezer ['fri:zəʳ] *n* congelador *m*, congeladora

freezing ['fri:zɪŋ] *adj* helado

freezing point *n* punto de congelación; **3 degrees below ~** tres grados bajo cero

freight [freɪt] *n* (*goods*) carga; (*money charged*) flete *m*

freight train *n* (*US*) tren *m* de mercancías

French [frɛntʃ] *adj* francés(-esa) ▷ *n* (*Ling*) francés *m*; **the French** *npl* los franceses

French bean *n* judía verde

French bread *n* pan *m* francés

French dressing *n* (*Culin*) vinagreta

French fried potatoes, French fries (*US*) *npl* patatas *fpl* or (*LAm*) papas *fpl* fritas

French loaf *n* barra de pan

Frenchman ['frɛntʃmən] *n* francés *m*

French stick *n* barra de pan

French window *n* puerta ventana

Frenchwoman ['frɛntʃwumən] *n* francesa

frenzy ['frɛnzɪ] *n* frenesí *m*

frequency ['fri:kwənsɪ] *n* frecuencia

frequent *adj* ['fri:kwənt] frecuente ▷ *vt* [frɪ'kwɛnt] frecuentar

frequently ['fri:kwəntlɪ] *adv* frecuentemente, a menudo

fresco ['frɛskəu] *n* fresco

fresh [frɛʃ] *adj* (*gen*) fresco; (*bread*) tierno; (*new*) nuevo; (*water*) dulce; **to make a ~ start** empezar de nuevo

freshen ['frɛʃən] *vi* (*wind*) arreciar; (*air*) refrescar; **freshen up** *vi* (*person*) arreglarse

fresher ['frɛʃəʳ] *n* (*Brit Scol: inf*) estudiante *m/f* de primer año

freshly ['frɛʃlɪ] *adv*: **~ painted/arrived** recién pintado/llegado

freshman ['frɛʃmən] *n* (*US Scol*) = **fresher**

freshness ['frɛʃnɪs] *n* frescura

freshwater ['frɛʃwɔ:təʳ] *adj* (*fish*) de agua dulce

fret [frɛt] *vi* inquietarse

FRG *n abbr* (= *Federal Republic of Germany*) RFA *f*

Fri. *abbr* (= *Friday*) vier

friar ['fraɪəʳ] *n* fraile *m*; (*before name*) fray

friction ['frɪkʃən] *n* fricción *f*

Friday ['fraɪdɪ] *n* viernes *m inv*; *see also* **Tuesday**

fridge [frɪdʒ] *n* (*Brit*) nevera, frigo, refrigeradora (*LAm*), heladera (*LAm*)

fridge-freezer ['frɪdʒ'fri:zəʳ] *n* frigorífico-congelador *m*, combi *m*

fried [fraɪd] *pt, pp of* **fry** ▷ *adj*: **~ egg** huevo frito, huevo estrellado

friend [frɛnd] *n* amigo(-a) ▷ *vt* (*Internet*) agregar como amigo

friendly ['frɛndlɪ] *adj* simpático; (*government*) amigo; (*place*) acogedor(a); (*match*) amistoso

friendly fire *n* fuego amigo, disparos *mpl* del propio bando

friendship ['frɛndʃɪp] *n* amistad *f*

fries [fraɪz] *npl* (*esp US*) = **French fried potatoes**

frieze [fri:z] *n* friso

frigate ['frɪgɪt] *n* fragata

fright [fraɪt] *n* susto; **to take ~** asustarse

frighten ['fraɪtn] *vt* asustar; **frighten away, frighten off** *vt* (*birds, children etc*) espantar, ahuyentar

frightened ['fraɪtnd] *adj* asustado

frightening ['fraɪtnɪŋ] *adj*: **it's ~** da miedo

frightful ['fraɪtful] *adj* espantoso, horrible

frigid ['frɪdʒɪd] *adj* (*Med*) frígido

frill [frɪl] *n* volante *m*; **without ~s** (*fig*) sin adornos

frilly ['frɪlɪ] *adj* con volantes

fringe [frɪndʒ] *n* (*Brit: of hair*) flequillo; (*edge: of forest etc*) borde *m*, margen *m*

fringe benefits *npl* ventajas *fpl* complementarias

Frisbee® ['frɪzbɪ] *n* frisbee® *m*

frisk [frɪsk] *vt* cachear, registrar

frisky ['frɪskɪ] *adj* juguetón(-ona)

fritter ['frɪtəʳ] *n* buñuelo; **fritter away** *vt* desperdiciar

frivolous ['frɪvələs] *adj* frívolo

frizzy ['frɪzɪ] *adj* crespo

fro [frəu] *see* **to**

frock [frɔk] *n* vestido

frog [frɔg] *n* rana; **to have a ~ in one's throat** tener carraspera

frogman ['frɔgmən] *n* hombre-rana *m*

frolic ['frɔlɪk] *vi* juguetear

KEYWORD

from [frɔm] *prep* **1** (*indicating starting place*) de, desde; **where do you come from?, where are you from?** ¿de dónde eres?; **where has he come from?** ¿de dónde ha venido?; **from London to Glasgow** de Londres a Glasgow; **to escape from sth/sb** escaparse de algo/algn

2 (*indicating origin etc*) de; **a letter/telephone call from my sister** una carta/llamada de

mi hermana; **tell him from me that ...** dígale de mi parte que ...
3 (*indicating time*): **from one o'clock to** *or* **until** *or* **till nine** de la una a las nueve, desde la una hasta las nueve; **from January (on)** a partir de enero; **(as) from Friday** a partir del viernes
4 (*indicating distance*) de; **the hotel is 1 km from the beach** el hotel está a 1 km de la playa
5 (*indicating price, number etc*) de; **prices range from £10 to £50** los precios van desde £10 a *or* hasta £50; **the interest rate was increased from 9% to 10%** el tipo de interés fue incrementado de un 9% a un 10%
6 (*indicating difference*) de; **he can't tell red from green** no sabe distinguir el rojo del verde; **to be different from sb/sth** ser diferente a algn/algo
7 (*because of, on the basis of*): **from what he says** por lo que dice; **weak from hunger** debilitado por el hambre

front [frʌnt] *n* (*foremost part*) parte *f* delantera; (*of house*) fachada; (*promenade: also:* **sea ~**) paseo marítimo; (*Mil, Pol, Meteorology*) frente *m*; (*fig: appearances*) apariencia ▷ *adj* (*wheel, leg*) delantero; (*row, line*) primero ▷ *vi*: **to ~ onto sth** dar a algo; **in ~ (of)** delante (de)
frontage ['frʌntɪdʒ] *n* (*of building*) fachada
front bench *n* (*Brit: Pol*) *ver nota*
frontbencher ['frʌnt'bɛntʃəʳ] *n* (*Brit*) *see* **front bench**
front door *n* puerta principal
frontier ['frʌntɪəʳ] *n* frontera
front page *n* primera plana
front room *n* (*Brit*) salón *m*, sala
front-wheel drive ['frʌntwi:l-] *n* tracción *f* delantera
frost [frɔst] *n* (*gen*) helada; (*also:* **hoar~**) escarcha ▷ *vt* (*US Culin*) escarchar
frostbite ['frɔstbaɪt] *n* congelación *f*
frosted ['frɔstɪd] *adj* (*glass*) esmerilado; (*esp US: cake*) glaseado
frosting ['frɔstɪŋ] *n* (*esp US: icing*) glaseado
frosty ['frɔstɪ] *adj* (*weather*) de helada; (*surface*) cubierto de escarcha; (*welcome etc*) glacial
froth [frɔθ] *n* espuma
frothy ['frɔθɪ] *adj* espumoso
frown [fraun] *vi* fruncir el ceño ▷ *n*: **with a ~** frunciendo el entrecejo; **frown on** *vt fus* desaprobar
froze [frəuz] *pt of* **freeze**
frozen ['frəuzn] *pp of* **freeze** ▷ *adj* (*food*) congelado; (*Comm*): **~ assets** activos *mpl* congelados *or* bloqueados
frugal ['fru:gəl] *adj* (*person*) frugal
fruit [fru:t] *n pl inv* fruta
fruiterer ['fru:tərəʳ] *n* frutero(-a); **~'s (shop)** frutería
fruit fly *n* mosca de la fruta
fruitful ['fru:tful] *adj* provechoso
fruition [fru:'ɪʃən] *n*: **to come to ~** realizarse
fruit juice *n* jugo *or* (*Sp*) zumo de fruta
fruitless ['fru:tlɪs] *adj* (*fig*) infructuoso, inútil
fruit machine *n* (*Brit*) máquina tragaperras
fruit salad *n* macedonia *or* (*LAm*) ensalada de frutas
frustrate [frʌs'treɪt] *vt* frustrar
frustrated [frʌs'treɪtɪd] *adj* frustrado
frustrating [frʌs'treɪtɪŋ] *adj* (*job, day*) frustrante
frustration [frʌs'treɪʃən] *n* frustración *f*
fry (*pt, pp* **fried**) [fraɪ, -d] *vt* freír ▷ *n*: **small ~** gente *f* menuda
frying pan ['fraɪɪŋ-] *n* sartén *f*, sartén *m* (*LAm*)
FT *n abbr* (*Brit: = Financial Times*) *periódico financiero*; (*= the FT index*) *el índice de valores del Financial Times*
ft. *abbr* = **foot**; **feet**
fuddy-duddy ['fʌdɪdʌdɪ] (*pej*) *n* carcamal *m*, carroza *m/f* ▷ *adj* chapado a la antigua
fudge [fʌdʒ] *n* (*Culin*) *caramelo blando* ▷ *vt* (*issue, problem*) rehuir, esquivar
fuel [fjuəl] *n* (*for heating*) combustible *m*; (*coal*) carbón *m*; (*wood*) leña; (*for engine*) carburante *m* ▷ *vt* (*furnace etc*) alimentar; (*aircraft, ship etc*) aprovisionar de combustible
fuel oil *n* fuel oil *m*
fuel tank *n* depósito de combustible
fugitive ['fju:dʒɪtɪv] *n* (*from prison*) fugitivo(-a)
fulfil, fulfill (*US*) [ful'fɪl] *vt* (*function*) desempeñar; (*condition*) cumplir; (*wish, desire*) realizar
full [ful] *adj* lleno; (*fig*) pleno; (*complete*) completo; (*maximum*) máximo; (*information*) detallado; (*price*) íntegro, sin descuento ▷ *adv*: **~ well** perfectamente; **we're ~ up for July** estamos completos para julio; **I'm ~ (up)** estoy lleno; **~ employment** pleno empleo; **~ name** nombre *m* completo; **a ~ two hours** dos horas enteras; **at ~ speed** a toda velocidad; **in ~** (*reproduce, quote*) íntegramente; **to write sth in ~** escribir algo por extenso; **to pay in ~** pagar la deuda entera
full-length ['ful'lɛŋθ] *adj* (*portrait*) de cuerpo entero; (*film*) de largometraje
full moon *n* luna llena, plenilunio
full-scale ['fulskeɪl] *adj* (*attack, war, search, retreat*) en gran escala; (*plan, model*) de tamaño natural
full stop *n* punto
full-time ['fultaɪm] *adj* (*work*) de tiempo completo ▷ *adv*: **to work ~** trabajar a tiempo completo
fully ['fulɪ] *adv* completamente; (*at least*) al menos
fully-fledged ['fulɪ'flɛdʒd], **full-fledged** (*US*) *adj* (*teacher, barrister*) diplomado; (*bird*) con todas sus plumas, capaz de volar; (*fig*) de pleno derecho

fumble ['fʌmbl] *vi*: **to ~ with** manejar torpemente, manosear
fume [fjuːm] *vi* estar furioso, echar humo
fumes [fjuːmz] *npl* humo *sg*, gases *mpl*
fun [fʌn] *n* (*amusement*) diversión *f*; (*joy*) alegría; **to have ~** divertirse; **for ~** por gusto; **to make ~ of** reírse de
function ['fʌŋkʃən] *n* función *f* ▷ *vi* funcionar; **to ~ as** hacer (las veces) de, fungir de (*LAm*)
functional ['fʌŋkʃənl] *adj* funcional
fund [fʌnd] *n* fondo; (*reserve*) reserva; **funds** *npl* (*money*) fondos *mpl*
fundamental [fʌndə'mɛntl] *adj* fundamental; **fundamentals** *npl* fundamentos *mpl*
fundamentalism [fʌndə'mɛntəlɪzəm] *n* fundamentalismo, integrismo
fundamentalist [fʌndə'mɛntəlɪst] *n* fundamentalista *m/f* integrista *m/f*
funding ['fʌndɪŋ] *n* financiación *f*
fund-raising ['fʌndreɪzɪŋ] *n* recaudación *f* de fondos
funeral ['fjuːnərəl] *n* (*burial*) entierro; (*ceremony*) funerales *mpl*
funeral director *n* director(a) *m(f)* de pompas fúnebres
funeral parlour *n* (*Brit*) funeraria
funeral service *n* misa de cuerpo presente
funfair ['fʌnfɛəʳ] *n* (*Brit*) parque *m* de atracciones; (*travelling*) feria
fungus (*pl* **fungi**) ['fʌŋgəs, -gaɪ] *n* hongo; (*mould*) moho
funky ['fʌŋkɪ] *adj* (*music*) funky; (*inf: good*) guay
funnel ['fʌnl] *n* embudo; (*of ship*) chimenea
funny ['fʌnɪ] *adj* gracioso, divertido; (*strange*) curioso, raro
fun run *n* maratón *m* popular
fur [fəːʳ] *n* piel *f*; (*Brit: on tongue etc*) sarro
fur coat *n* abrigo de pieles
furious ['fjuərɪəs] *adj* furioso; (*effort, argument*) violento; **to be ~ with sb** estar furioso con algn
furlong ['fəːlɔŋ] *n* *octava parte de una milla*
furlough ['fəːləu] *n* (*US Mil*) permiso
furnace ['fəːnɪs] *n* horno
furnish ['fəːnɪʃ] *vt* amueblar; (*supply*) proporcionar; (*information*) facilitar
furnished ['fəːnɪʃt] *adj*: **~ flat** *or* (*US*) **apartment** piso amueblado
furnishings ['fəːnɪʃɪŋz] *npl* mobiliario *sg*
furniture ['fəːnɪtʃəʳ] *n* muebles *mpl*; **piece of ~** mueble *m*
furore [fjuə'rɔːrɪ] *n* (*protests*) escándalo
furrow ['fʌrəu] *n* surco ▷ *vt* (*forehead*) arrugar
furry ['fəːrɪ] *adj* peludo; (*toy*) de peluche
further ['fəːðəʳ] *adj* (*new*) nuevo; (*place*) más lejano ▷ *adv* más lejos; (*more*) más; (*moreover*) además ▷ *vt* hacer avanzar; **how much ~ is it?** ¿a qué distancia queda?; **~ to your letter of ...** (*Comm*) con referencia a su carta de ...; **to ~ one's interests** fomentar sus intereses
further education *n* educación *f* postescolar
furthermore [fəːðə'mɔːʳ] *adv* además
furthest ['fəːðɪst] *superlative of* **far**
furtive ['fəːtɪv] *adj* furtivo
fury ['fjuərɪ] *n* furia
fuse, fuze (*US*) [fjuːz] *n* fusible *m*; (*for bomb etc*) mecha ▷ *vt* (*metal*) fundir; (*fig*) fusionar ▷ *vi* fundirse; fusionarse; (*Brit Elec*): **to ~ the lights** fundir los plomos; **a ~ has blown** se ha fundido un fusible
fuse box *n* caja de fusibles
fuse wire *n* hilo fusible
fusion ['fjuːʒən] *n* fusión *f*
fuss [fʌs] *n* (*excitement*) conmoción *f*; (*complaint*) alboroto, protesta ▷ *vi* preocuparse (por pequeñeces) ▷ *vt* (*person*) molestar; **to make a ~** armar jaleo; **fuss over** *vt fus* (*person*) contemplar, mimar
fusspot ['fʌspɔt] *n* (*inf*) quisquilloso(-a)
fussy ['fʌsɪ] *adj* (*person*) quisquilloso; **I'm not ~** (*inf*) me da igual
fusty ['fʌstɪ] *adj* (*pej*) rancio; **to smell ~** oler a cerrado
futile ['fjuːtaɪl] *adj* vano
futon ['fuːtɔn] *n* futón *m*
future ['fjuːtʃəʳ] *adj* (*gen*) futuro; (*coming*) venidero ▷ *n* futuro, porvenir; **in ~** de ahora en adelante
futures ['fjuːtʃəz] *npl* (*Comm*) operaciones *fpl* a término, futuros *mpl*
fuze [fjuːz] *n, vb* (*US*) = **fuse**
fuzzy ['fʌzɪ] *adj* (*Phot*) borroso; (*hair*) muy rizado
fwd. *abbr* = **forward**
FYI *abbr* = **for your information**

f

g

G, g [dʒiː] *n* (*letter*) G, g *f*; **G** (*Mus*) sol *m*; **G for George** G de Gerona
G *n abbr* (*Brit Scol: mark: = good*) N; (*US Cine: = general audience*) todos los públicos
g. *abbr* (*= gram(s), gravity*) g
gab [gæb] *n*: **to have the gift of the ~** (*inf*) tener mucha labia
gabble ['gæbl] *vi* hablar atropelladamente; (*gossip*) cotorrear
gable ['geɪbl] *n* aguilón *m*
gadget ['gædʒɪt] *n* aparato
Gaelic ['geɪlɪk] *adj, n* (*Ling*) gaélico
gag [gæg] *n* (*on mouth*) mordaza; (*joke*) chiste *m* ▷ *vt* (*prisoner etc*) amordazar ▷ *vi* (*choke*) tener arcadas
gaiety ['geɪɪtɪ] *n* alegría
gain [geɪn] *n* ganancia ▷ *vt* ganar ▷ *vi* (*watch*) adelantarse; **to ~ by sth** ganar con algo; **to ~ ground** ganar terreno; **to ~ 3 lbs (in weight)** engordar 3 libras; **gain (up)on** *vt fus* alcanzar
gainfully ['geɪnfulɪ] *adv*: **to be ~ employed** tener un trabajo remunerado
gait [geɪt] *n* forma de andar, andares *mpl*
gal., gall. *abbr* = **gallon(s)**
gala ['gɑːlə] *n* gala; **swimming ~** certamen *m* de natación
galaxy ['gæləksɪ] *n* galaxia
gale [geɪl] *n* (*wind*) vendaval *m*; **~ force 10** vendaval de fuerza 10
gallant ['gælənt] *adj* valeroso; (*towards ladies*) galante
gall bladder *n* vesícula biliar
gallery ['gælərɪ] *n* (*Theat*) galería; (*for spectators*) tribuna; (*also*: **art ~**: *state-owned*) pinacoteca *or* museo de arte; (: *private*) galería de arte
galley ['gælɪ] *n* (*ship's kitchen*) cocina; (*ship*) galera
gallon ['gæln] *n* galón *m* (*= 8 pintas; Brit = 4,546 litros; US = 3,785 litros*)
gallop ['gæləp] *n* galope *m* ▷ *vi* galopar; **~ing inflation** inflación *f* galopante
gallows ['gæləuz] *n* horca
gallstone ['gɔːlstəun] *n* cálculo biliar
Gallup poll ['gæləp-] *n* sondeo de opinión
galore [gə'lɔːʳ] *adv* en cantidad, en abundancia
galvanize ['gælvənaɪz] *vt* (*metal*) galvanizar; (*fig*): **to ~ sb into action** mover *or* impulsar a algn a actuar
Gambia ['gæmbɪə] *n* Gambia
gambit ['gæmbɪt] *n* (*fig*): **opening ~** táctica inicial
gamble ['gæmbl] *n* (*risk*) jugada arriesgada; (*bet*) apuesta ▷ *vt*: **to ~ on** apostar a; (*fig*) contar con, confiar en que ▷ *vi* jugar; (*take a risk*) jugárselas; (*Comm*) especular; **to ~ on the Stock Exchange** jugar a la bolsa
gambler ['gæmbləʳ] *n* jugador(a) *m(f)*
gambling ['gæmblɪŋ] *n* juego
game [geɪm] *n* (*gen*) juego; (*match*) partido; (*of cards*) partida; (*Hunting*) caza ▷ *adj* valiente; (*ready*): **to be ~ for anything** estar dispuesto a todo; **~s** (*Scol*) deportes *mpl*; **big ~** caza mayor
gamekeeper ['geɪmkiːpəʳ] *n* guardabosque *m/f*
game plan *n* (*for game*) plan *m* de juego; (*gen*) táctica
games console [geɪmz-] *n* consola de juegos
game show *n* programa *m* concurso *inv*, concurso
gammon ['gæmən] *n* (*bacon*) tocino ahumado; (*ham*) jamón *m* ahumado
gamut ['gæmət] *n* (*Mus*) gama; **to run the (whole) ~ of emotions** (*fig*) recorrer toda la gama de emociones
gang [gæŋ] *n* (*of criminals etc*) banda; (*of kids*) pandilla; (*of colleagues*) peña; (*of workmen*) brigada ▷ *vi*: **to ~ up on sb** conchabarse contra algn
gangly ['gæŋglɪ] *adj* desgarbado
gangrene ['gæŋgriːn] *n* gangrena
gangster ['gæŋstəʳ] *n* gángster *m*
gang warfare *n* guerra entre bandas
gangway ['gæŋweɪ] *n* (*Brit: in theatre, bus etc*) pasillo; (*on ship*) pasarela
gantry ['gæntrɪ] *n* (*for crane, railway signal*) pórtico; (*for rocket*) torre *f* de lanzamiento
gaol [dʒeɪl] *n, vt* (*Brit*) = **jail**
gap [gæp] *n* hueco; (*in trees, traffic*) claro; (*in market, records*) laguna; (*in time*) intervalo
gape [geɪp] *vi* mirar boquiabierto
gaping ['geɪpɪŋ] *adj* (*hole*) muy abierto

gap year *n* año sabático (*antes de empezar a estudiar en la universidad*)
garage ['gærɑ:ʒ] *n* garaje *m*; (*for repairs*) taller *m*
garage sale *n* venta de objetos usados (*en el jardín de una casa particular*)
garbage ['gɑ:bɪdʒ] *n* (US) basura; (*nonsense*) bobadas *fpl*; (*fig: film, book etc*) basura
garbage can *n* (US) cubo *or* balde *m* (*LAm*) *or* bote *m* (*LAm*) de la basura
garbage collector *n* (US) basurero(-a)
garbage truck *n* (US) camión *m* de la basura
garbled ['gɑ:bld] *adj* (*account, explanation*) confuso
garden ['gɑ:dn] *n* jardín *m*; **gardens** *npl* (*public*) parque *m*, jardines *mpl*; (*private*) huertos *mpl*
garden centre *n* (*Brit*) centro de jardinería
garden city *n* (*Brit*) ciudad *f* jardín
gardener ['gɑ:dnəʳ] *n* jardinero(-a)
gardening ['gɑ:dnɪŋ] *n* jardinería
gargle ['gɑ:gl] *vi* hacer gárgaras, gargarear (*LAm*)
garish ['gɛərɪʃ] *adj* chillón(-ona)
garland ['gɑ:lənd] *n* guirnalda
garlic ['gɑ:lɪk] *n* ajo
garment ['gɑ:mənt] *n* prenda (de vestir)
garnish ['gɑ:nɪʃ] *vt* adornar; (*Culin*) aderezar
garrison ['gærɪsn] *n* guarnición *f* ▷ *vt* guarnecer
garrulous ['gærjuləs] *adj* charlatán(-ana)
garter ['gɑ:təʳ] *n* (US) liga
gas [gæs] *n* gas *m*; (*US: gasoline*) gasolina ▷ *vt* asfixiar con gas; **Calor ~**® (gas *m*) butano
gas cooker *n* (*Brit*) cocina de gas
gas cylinder *n* bombona de gas
gas fire *n* estufa de gas
gas-fired ['gæsfaɪəd] *adj* de gas
gash [gæʃ] *n* brecha, raja; (*from knife*) cuchillada ▷ *vt* rajar; (*with knife*) acuchillar
gasket ['gæskɪt] *n* (*Aut*) junta
gas mask *n* careta antigás
gas meter *n* contador *m* de gas
gasoline ['gæsəli:n] *n* (US) gasolina
gasp [gɑ:sp] *n* grito sofocado ▷ *vi* (*pant*) jadear; **gasp out** *vt* (*say*) decir jadeando
gas pedal *n* (*esp US*) acelerador *m*
gas station *n* (US) gasolinera
gassy ['gæsɪ] *adj* con mucho gas
gas tank *n* (*US Aut*) depósito (de gasolina)
gas tap *n* llave *f* del gas
gastric ['gæstrɪk] *adj* gástrico
gate [geɪt] *n* (*also at airport*) puerta; (*Rail: at level crossing*) barrera; (*metal*) verja
gâteau (*pl* **gâteaux**) ['gætəu, z] *n* tarta
gatecrash ['geɪtkræʃ] *vt* colarse en
gateway ['geɪtweɪ] *n* puerta
gather ['gæðəʳ] *vt* (*flowers, fruit*) coger (*Sp*), recoger (*LAm*); (*assemble*) reunir; (*pick up*) recoger; (*Sewing*) fruncir; (*understand*) sacar en consecuencia ▷ *vi* (*assemble*) reunirse; (*dust*) acumularse; (*clouds*) cerrarse; **to ~ speed** ganar velocidad; **to ~ (from/that)** deducir (por/que); **as far as I can ~** por lo que tengo entendido
gathering ['gæðərɪŋ] *n* reunión *f*, asamblea
gaudy ['gɔ:dɪ] *adj* chillón(-ona)
gauge, gage (US) [geɪdʒ] *n* calibre *m*; (*Rail*) ancho de vía, entrevía; (*instrument*) indicador *m* ▷ *vt* medir; (*fig: sb's capabilities, character*) juzgar, calibrar; **petrol ~** indicador *m* (del nivel) de gasolina; **to ~ the right moment** elegir el momento (oportuno)
gaunt [gɔ:nt] *adj* descarnado; (*fig*) adusto
gauntlet ['gɔ:ntlɪt] *n* (*fig*): **to run the ~ of sth** exponerse a algo; **to throw down the ~** arrojar el guante
gauze [gɔ:z] *n* gasa
gave [geɪv] *pt of* **give**
gawk [gɔ:k] *vi* mirar pasmado
gay [geɪ] *adj* (*homosexual*) gay; (*colour, person*) alegre
gaze [geɪz] *n* mirada fija ▷ *vi*: **to ~ at sth** mirar algo fijamente
gazump [gə'zʌmp] *vt, vi* (*Brit*) *echarse atrás en la venta ya acordada de una casa por haber una oferta más alta*
GB *abbr* (= *Great Britain*) GB
GBH *n abbr* (*Brit Law: inf*) = **grievous bodily harm**
GCE *n abbr* (*Brit: = General Certificate of Education*) ≈ certificado de bachillerato
GCSE *n abbr* (*Brit: = General Certificate of Secondary Education*) *certificado del último ciclo de la enseñanza secundaria obligatoria*
Gdns. *abbr* (= *gardens*) jdns
GDP *n abbr* (= *gross domestic product*) PIB *m*
GDR *n abbr* (= *German Democratic Republic*) RDA *f*
gear [gɪəʳ] *n* equipo; (*Tech*) engranaje *m*; (*Aut*) velocidad *f*, marcha ▷ *vt* (*fig: adapt*): **to ~ sth to** adaptar *or* ajustar algo a; **top** *or* (US) **high/low ~** cuarta/primera; **in ~** con la marcha metida; **our service is ~ed to meet the needs of disabled people** nuestro servicio va enfocado a responder a las necesidades de los minusválidos; **gear up** *vi* prepararse
gear box *n* caja de cambios
gear lever, gear shift (US) *n* palanca de cambio
gear stick *n* (*Brit*) = **gear lever**
geese [gi:s] *npl of* **goose**
gel [dʒɛl] *n* gel *m*
gelignite ['dʒɛlɪgnaɪt] *n* gelignita
gem [dʒɛm] *n* gema, piedra preciosa; (*fig*) joya
Gemini ['dʒɛmɪnaɪ] *n* Géminis *m*
gen [dʒɛn] *n* (*Brit inf*): **to give sb the ~ on sth** poner a algn al tanto de algo
Gen. *abbr* (*Mil: = General*) Gen., Gral
gen. *abbr* (= *general*) grl.; = **generally**
gender ['dʒɛndəʳ] *n* género
gene [dʒi:n] *n* gen(e) *m*
general ['dʒɛnərl] *n* general *m* ▷ *adj* general; **in ~** en general; **~ audit** auditoría general; **the ~ public** el gran público

general anaesthetic, general anesthetic (*US*) *n* anestesia general
general delivery *n* (*US*) lista de correos
general election *n* elecciones *fpl* generales
generalization [dʒɛnrəlaɪ'zeɪʃən] *n* generalización *f*
generalize ['dʒɛnrəlaɪz] *vi* generalizar
generally ['dʒɛnrəlɪ] *adv* generalmente, en general
general practitioner *n* médico(-a) de medicina general
general store *n* tienda (*que vende de todo*) (*LAm, Sp*), almacén *m* (*SC, Sp*)
general strike *n* huelga general
generate ['dʒɛnəreɪt] *vt* generar
generation [dʒɛnə'reɪʃən] *n* (*of electricity etc*) generación *f*
generator ['dʒɛnəreɪtə^r] *n* generador *m*
generosity [dʒɛnə'rɔsɪtɪ] *n* generosidad *f*
generous ['dʒɛnərəs] *adj* generoso; (*copious*) abundante
genetic [dʒɪ'nɛtɪk] *adj* genético; **~ engineering** ingeniería genética; **~ fingerprinting** identificación *f* genética
genetically modified organism [dʒɪ'nɛtɪkəlɪ-] *n* organismo genéticamente modificado, organismo transgénico
genetic engineering *n* ingeniería genética
genetic fingerprinting [-'fɪŋgəprɪntɪŋ] *n* identificación *f* genética
genetics [dʒɪ'nɛtɪks] *n* genética
Geneva [dʒɪ'ni:və] *n* Ginebra
genial ['dʒi:nɪəl] *adj* afable
genitals ['dʒɛnɪtlz] *npl* (órganos *mpl*) genitales *mpl*
genitive ['dʒɛnɪtɪv] *n* genitivo
genius ['dʒi:nɪəs] *n* genio
genocide ['dʒɛnəusaɪd] *n* genocidio
genome ['gi:nəum] *n* genoma *m*
gent [dʒɛnt] *n abbr* (*Brit inf*) = **gentleman**
genteel [dʒɛn'ti:l] *adj* fino, distinguido
gentle ['dʒɛntl] *adj* (*sweet*) dulce; (*touch etc*) ligero, suave
gentleman ['dʒɛntlmən] *n* señor *m*; (*well-bred man*) caballero; **~'s agreement** acuerdo entre caballeros
gently ['dʒɛntlɪ] *adv* suavemente
gentry ['dʒɛntrɪ] *npl* pequeña nobleza *sg*
gents [dʒɛnts] *n* servicios *mpl* (de caballeros)
genuine ['dʒɛnjuɪn] *adj* auténtico; (*person*) sincero
genuinely ['dʒɛnjuɪnlɪ] *adv* sinceramente
geographic [dʒɪə'græfɪk], **geographical** [dʒɪə'græfɪkl] *adj* geográfico
geography [dʒɪ'ɔgrəfɪ] *n* geografía
geological [dʒɪə'lɔdʒɪkl] *adj* geológico
geologist [dʒɪ'ɔlədʒɪst] *n* geólogo(-a)
geology [dʒɪ'ɔlədʒɪ] *n* geología
geometry [dʒɪ'ɔmətrɪ] *n* geometría
Geordie ['dʒɔ:dɪ] *n* habitante *m/f* de Tyneside
Georgia ['dʒɔ:dʒə] *n* Georgia
geranium [dʒɪ'reɪnjəm] *n* geranio
gerbil ['dʒerbl] *n* gerbo
geriatric [dʒɛrɪ'ætrɪk] *adj, n* geriátrico(-a) *m(f)*
germ [dʒə:m] *n* (*microbe*) microbio, bacteria; (*seed*) germen *m*
German ['dʒə:mən] *adj* alemán(-ana) ▷ *n* alemán(-ana) *m(f)*; (*Ling*) alemán *m*
German Democratic Republic *n* República Democrática Alemana
germane [dʒə:'meɪn] *adj*: **~ (to)** pertinente (a)
German measles *n* rubeola, rubéola
Germany ['dʒə:mənɪ] *n* Alemania; **East/ West ~** (*History*) Alemania Oriental *or* Democrática/Occidental *or* Federal
gesticulate [dʒɛs'tɪkjuleɪt] *vi* gesticular
gesture ['dʒɛstjə^r] *n* gesto; **as a ~ of friendship** en señal de amistad

KEYWORD

get [gɛt] (*pt, pp* **got**, (*US*) *pp* **gotten**) *vi* **1** (*become, be*) ponerse, volverse; **to get old/ tired** envejecer/cansarse; **to get drunk** emborracharse; **to get dirty** ensuciarse; **to get ready/washed** prepararse/lavarse; **to get married** casarse; **when do I get paid?** ¿cuándo me pagan *or* se me paga?; **it's getting late** se está haciendo tarde
2 (*go*): **to get to/from** llegar a/de; **to get home** llegar a casa; **he got under the fence** pasó por debajo de la barrera
3 (*begin*) empezar a; **to get to know sb** (llegar a) conocer a algn; **I'm getting to like him** me está empezando a gustar; **let's get going** *or* **started** ¡vamos (a empezar)!
4 (*modal aux vb*): **you've got to do it** tienes que hacerlo
▷ *vt* **1**: **to get sth done** (*finish*) hacer algo; (*have done*) mandar hacer algo; **to get one's hair cut** cortarse el pelo; **to get the car going** *or* **to go** arrancar el coche; **to get sb to do sth** conseguir *or* hacer que algn haga algo; **to get sth/sb ready** preparar algo/a algn
2 (*obtain: money, permission, results*) conseguir; (*find: job, flat*) encontrar; (*fetch: person, doctor*) buscar; (*object*) ir a buscar, traer; **to get sth for sb** conseguir algo para algn; **get me Mr Jones, please** (*Tel*) póngame *or* (*LAm*) comuníqueme con el Sr. Jones, por favor; **can I get you a drink?** ¿quieres algo de beber?
3 (*receive: present, letter*) recibir; (*acquire: reputation*) alcanzar; (*: prize*) ganar; **what did you get for your birthday?** ¿qué te regalaron por tu cumpleaños?; **how much did you get for the painting?** ¿cuánto sacaste por el cuadro?
4 (*catch*) coger (*Sp*), agarrar (*LAm*); (*hit: target etc*) dar en; **to get sb by the arm/throat** coger *or* agarrar a algn por el brazo/cuello; **get him!** ¡cógelo! (*Sp*), ¡atrápalo! (*LAm*); **the bullet got him in the leg** la bala le dio en la pierna

5 (*take, move*) llevar; **to get sth to sb** hacer llegar algo a algn; **do you think we'll get it through the door?** ¿crees que lo podremos meter por la puerta?
6 (*catch, take*: *plane, bus etc*) coger (*Sp*), tomar (*LAm*); **where do I get the train for Birmingham?** ¿dónde se coge *or* se toma el tren para Birmingham?
7 (*understand*) entender; (*hear*) oír; **I've got it!** ¡ya lo tengo!, ¡eureka!; **I don't get your meaning** no te entiendo; **I'm sorry, I didn't get your name** lo siento, no me he enterado de tu nombre
8 (*have, possess*): **to have got** tener
9 (*inf*: *annoy*) molestar; (: *thrill*) chiflar
get about *vi* salir mucho; (*news*) divulgarse
get across *vt* (*message, meaning*) lograr comunicar ▷ *vi*: **to get across to sb** hacer que algn comprenda
get along *vi* (*agree*) llevarse bien; (*depart*) marcharse; (*manage*) = **get by**
get at *vt fus* (*attack*) meterse con; (*reach*) alcanzar; (*the truth*) descubrir; **what are you getting at?** ¿qué insinúas?
get away *vi* marcharse; (*escape*) escaparse
get away with *vt fus* hacer impunemente
get back *vi* (*return*) volver ▷ *vt* recobrar
get back at *vt fus* (*inf*): **to get back at sb (for sth)** vengarse de algn (por algo)
get by *vi* (*pass*) (lograr) pasar; (*manage*) arreglárselas; **I can get by in Dutch** me defiendo en holandés
get down *vi* bajar(se) ▷ *vt fus* bajar ▷ *vt* bajar; (*depress*) deprimir
get down to *vt fus* (*work*) ponerse a
get in *vi* entrar; (*train*) llegar; (*arrive home*) volver a casa, regresar; (*political party*) salir ▷ *vt* (*bring in*: *harvest*) recoger; (: *coal, shopping, supplies*) comprar, traer; (*insert*) meter
get into *vt fus* entrar en; (*vehicle*) subir a; **to get into a rage** enfadarse
get off *vi* (*from train etc*) bajar(se); (*depart*: *person, car*) marcharse ▷ *vt* (*remove*) quitar; (*send off*) mandar; (*have as leave*: *day, time*) tener libre ▷ *vt fus* (*train, bus*) bajar(se) de; **to get off to a good start** (*fig*) empezar muy bien *or* con buen pie
get on ▷ *vi* (*at exam etc*): **how are you getting on?** ¿cómo te va?; (*agree*): **to get on (with)** llevarse bien (con) ▷ *vt fus* subir(se) a
get on to *vt fus* (*deal with*) ocuparse de; (*inf*: *contact on phone etc*) hablar con
get out *vi* salir; (*of vehicle*) bajar(se); (*news*) saberse ▷ *vt* sacar
get out of *vt fus* salir de; (*duty etc*) escaparse de; (*gain from*: *pleasure, benefit*) sacar de
get over *vt fus* (*illness*) recobrarse de
get round *vt fus* rodear; (*fig*: *person*) engatusar a ▷ *vi*: **to get round to doing sth** encontrar tiempo para hacer algo
get through *vt fus* (*finish*) acabar ▷ *vi* (*Tel*) (lograr) comunicar
get through to *vt fus* (*Tel*) comunicar con
get together *vi* reunirse ▷ *vt* reunir, juntar
get up *vi* (*rise*) levantarse ▷ *vt fus* subir; **to get up enthusiasm for sth** cobrar entusiasmo por algo
get up to *vt fus* (*reach*) llegar a; (*prank*) hacer

getaway ['gɛtəweɪ] *n* fuga
get-together ['gɛttəgɛðəʳ] *n* reunión *f*; (*party*) fiesta
get-up ['gɛtʌp] *n* (*Brit inf*: *outfit*) atavío, atuendo
get-well card [gɛt'wɛl-] *n* *tarjeta en la que se desea a un enfermo que se mejore*
geyser ['gi:zəʳ] *n* (*water heater*) calentador *m* de agua; (*Geo*) géiser *m*
Ghana ['gɑ:nə] *n* Ghana
ghastly ['gɑ:stlɪ] *adj* horrible; (*pale*) pálido
gherkin ['gə:kɪn] *n* pepinillo
ghetto ['gɛtəu] *n* gueto
ghetto blaster [-'blɑ:stəʳ] *n* radiocas(s)et(t)e *m* portátil (*de gran tamaño*)
ghost [gəust] *n* fantasma *m* ▷ *vt* (*book*) escribir por otro
ghost story *n* cuento de fantasmas
GI *n abbr* (*US inf*: = *government issue*) *soldado del ejército norteamericano*
giant ['dʒaɪənt] *n* gigante *m/f* ▷ *adj* gigantesco, gigante; **~ (size) packet** paquete *m* (de tamaño) gigante *or* familiar
giant killer *n* (*Sport*) matagigantes *m inv*
gibberish ['dʒɪbərɪʃ] *n* galimatías *m*
giblets ['dʒɪblɪts] *npl* menudillos *mpl*
Gibraltar [dʒɪ'brɔ:ltəʳ] *n* Gibraltar *m*
giddy ['gɪdɪ] *adj* (*dizzy*) mareado; (*height, speed*) vertiginoso; **it makes me ~** me marea; **I feel ~** me siento mareado
gift [gɪft] *n* (*gen*) regalo; (*Comm*: *also*: **free ~**) obsequio; (*ability*) don *m*; **to have a ~ for sth** tener dotes para algo
gifted ['gɪftɪd] *adj* dotado
gift shop, gift store (*US*) *n* tienda de regalos
gift token, gift voucher *n* vale-regalo *m*
gig¹ [gɪg] *n* (*inf*: *concert*) actuación *f*
gig² [gɪg] *n abbr* (*inf*: = *gigabyte*) giga *m*
gigabyte ['gɪgəbaɪt] *n* gigabyte *m*
gigantic [dʒaɪ'gæntɪk] *adj* gigantesco
giggle ['gɪgl] *vi* reírse tontamente ▷ *n* risilla
gill [dʒɪl] *n* (*measure*) *0.25 pintas* (*Brit = 0,148 litros; US = 0,118 litros.*)
gills [gɪlz] *npl* (*of fish*) branquias *fpl*, agallas *fpl*
gilt [gɪlt] *adj, n* dorado
gilt-edged ['gɪltɛdʒd] *adj* (*Comm*: *stocks, securities*) de máxima garantía
gimmick ['gɪmɪk] *n* reclamo; **sales ~** reclamo promocional
gin [dʒɪn] *n* (*liquor*) ginebra
ginger ['dʒɪndʒəʳ] *n* jengibre *m*
ginger ale *n* ginger ale *m*
ginger beer *n* refresco *m* de jengibre
gingerbread ['dʒɪndʒəbrɛd] *n* pan *m* de jengibre

gingerly ['dʒɪndʒəlɪ] *adv* con pies de plomo
ginseng ['dʒɪnsɛŋ] *n* ginseng *m*
gipsy ['dʒɪpsɪ] *n* gitano(-a)
giraffe [dʒɪ'rɑːf] *n* jirafa
girder ['gəːdəʳ] *n* viga
girdle ['gəːdl] *n* (*corset*) faja ▷ *vt* ceñir
girl [gəːl] *n* (*small*) niña; (*young woman*) chica, joven *f*, muchacha; **an English ~** una (chica) inglesa
girl band *n* girl band *m* (*grupo musical de chicas*)
girlfriend ['gəːlfrɛnd] *n* (*of girl*) amiga; (*of boy*) novia
girlish ['gəːlɪʃ] *adj* de niña
giro ['dʒaɪrəu] *n* (*Brit: bank giro*) giro bancario; (*post office giro*) giro postal
girth [gəːθ] *n* circunferencia; (*of saddle*) cincha
gist [dʒɪst] *n* lo esencial
give [gɪv] (*pt* **gave**, *pp* **given** [geɪv, 'gɪvn]) *vt* dar; (*deliver*) entregar; (*as gift*) regalar ▷ *vi* (*break*) romperse; (*stretch: fabric*) dar de sí; **to ~ sb sth, ~ sth to sb** dar algo a algn; **how much did you ~ for it?** ¿cuánto pagaste por él?; **12 o'clock, ~ or take a few minutes** más o menos las doce; **~ them my regards** dales recuerdos de mi parte; **I can ~ you 10 minutes** le puedo conceder 10 minutos; **to ~ way** (*Brit Aut*) ceder el paso; **to ~ way to despair** ceder a la desesperación; **give away** *vt* (*give free*) regalar; (*betray*) traicionar; (*disclose*) revelar; **give back** *vt* devolver; **give in** *vi* ceder ▷ *vt* entregar; **give off** *vt* despedir; **give out** *vt* distribuir ▷ *vi* (*be exhausted: supplies*) agotarse; (*fail: engine*) averiarse; (*strength*) fallar; **give up** *vi* rendirse, darse por vencido ▷ *vt* renunciar a; **to ~ up smoking** dejar de fumar; **to ~ o.s. up** entregarse
giveaway ['gɪvəweɪ] *n* (*inf*): **her expression was a ~** su expresión la delataba; **the exam was a ~!** ¡el examen estaba tirado! ▷ *cpd*: **~ prices** precios *mpl* de regalo
given ['gɪvn] *pp of* **give** ▷ *adj* (*fixed: time, amount*) determinado ▷ *conj*: **~ (that) ...** dado (que) ...; **~ the circumstances ...** dadas las circunstancias ...
glacier ['glæsɪəʳ] *n* glaciar *m*
glad [glæd] *adj* contento; **to be ~ about sth/that** alegrarse de algo/de que; **I was ~ of his help** agradecí su ayuda
gladly ['glædlɪ] *adv* con mucho gusto
glamorous ['glæmərəs] *adj* con glamour, glam(o)uroso
glamour, glamor (US) ['glæməʳ] *n* encanto, atractivo
glance [glɑːns] *n* ojeada, mirada ▷ *vi*: **to ~ at** echar una ojeada a; **glance off** *vt fus* (*bullet*) rebotar en
glancing ['glɑːnsɪŋ] *adj* (*blow*) oblicuo
gland [glænd] *n* glándula
glare [glɛəʳ] *n* deslumbramiento, brillo ▷ *vi* deslumbrar; **to ~ at** mirar con odio
glaring ['glɛərɪŋ] *adj* (*mistake*) manifiesto
glass [glɑːs] *n* vidrio, cristal *m*; (*for drinking*) vaso; (*with stem*) copa; (*also*: **looking ~**) espejo
glass ceiling *n* (*fig*) techo *or* barrera invisible (*que impide ascender profesionalmente a las mujeres o miembros de minorías étnicas*)
glasses ['glɑːsəs] *npl* gafas *fpl*, anteojos *mpl* (*LAm*)
glasshouse ['glɑːshaus] *n* invernadero
glassware ['glɑːswɛəʳ] *n* cristalería
Glaswegian [glæs'wiːdʒən] *adj* de Glasgow ▷ *n* nativo(-a) *or* habitante *m(f)* de Glasgow
glaze [gleɪz] *vt* (*window*) acristalar; (*pottery*) vidriar; (*Culin*) glasear ▷ *n* barniz *m*; (*Culin*) glaseado
glazed [gleɪzd] *adj* (*eye*) vidrioso; (*pottery*) vidriado
glazier ['gleɪzɪəʳ] *n* vidriero(-a)
gleam [gliːm] *n* destello ▷ *vi* relucir; **a ~ of hope** un rayo de esperanza
glean [gliːn] *vt* (*gather: information*) recoger
glee [gliː] *n* alegría, regocijo
glen [glɛn] *n* cañada
glib [glɪb] *adj* (*person*) de mucha labia; (*comment*) fácil
glide [glaɪd] *vi* deslizarse; (*Aviat: bird*) planear
glider ['glaɪdəʳ] *n* (*Aviat*) planeador *m*
gliding ['glaɪdɪŋ] *n* (*Aviat*) vuelo sin motor
glimmer ['glɪməʳ] *n* luz *f* tenue; (*of hope*) rayo
glimpse [glɪmps] *n* vislumbre *m* ▷ *vt* vislumbrar, entrever; **to catch a ~ of** vislumbrar
glint [glɪnt] *n* destello; (*in the eye*) chispa ▷ *vi* centellear
glisten ['glɪsn] *vi* relucir, brillar
glitter ['glɪtəʳ] *vi* relucir, brillar ▷ *n* brillo
gloat [gləut] *vi*: **to ~ over** regodearse con
global ['gləubl] *adj* (*world-wide*) mundial; (*comprehensive*) global
globalization ['gləubəlaɪzeɪʃən] *n* globalización *f*, mundialización *f*
global warming [-'wɔːmɪŋ] *n* (re)calentamiento global *or* de la tierra
globe [gləub] *n* globo, esfera; (*model*) bola del mundo; globo terráqueo
gloom [gluːm] *n* penumbra; (*sadness*) desaliento, melancolía
gloomy ['gluːmɪ] *adj* (*dark*) oscuro; (*sad*) triste; (*pessimistic*) pesimista; **to feel ~** sentirse pesimista
glorify ['glɔːrɪfaɪ] *vt* glorificar
glorious ['glɔːrɪəs] *adj* glorioso; (*weather, sunshine*) espléndido
glory ['glɔːrɪ] *n* gloria
gloss [glɔs] *n* (*shine*) brillo; (*also*: **~ paint**) (pintura) esmalte *m*; **gloss over** *vt fus* restar importancia a; (*omit*) pasar por alto
glossary ['glɔsərɪ] *n* glosario
glossy ['glɔsɪ] *adj* lustroso; (*hair*) brillante; (*photograph*) con brillo; (*magazine*) de papel satinado *or* cuché
glove [glʌv] *n* guante *m*

glove compartment *n* (*Aut*) guantera

glow [gləu] *vi* (*shine*) brillar ▷ *n* brillo

glower ['glauə^r] *vi*: **to ~ at** mirar con ceño

glucose ['glu:kəus] *n* glucosa

glue [glu:] *n* pegamento, cemento (*LAm*) ▷ *vt* pegar

glum [glʌm] *adj* (*mood*) abatido; (*person, tone*) melancólico

glut [glʌt] *n* superabundancia

glutton ['glʌtn] *n* glotón(-ona) *m(f)*; **~ for punishment** masoquista *m/f*

gluttony ['glʌtənɪ] *n* gula, glotonería

GM *adj abbr* (= *genetically-modified*) transgénico

gm *abbr* (= *gram*) g

GM crop *n* cultivo transgénico

GMT *abbr* (= *Greenwich Mean Time*) GMT

gnarled [nɑ:ld] *adj* nudoso

gnat [næt] *n* mosquito

gnaw [nɔ:] *vt* roer

gnome [nəum] *n* gnomo

GNP *n abbr* (= *gross national product*) PNB *m*

go [gəu] (*pt* **went**, *pp* **gone**) *vi* ir; (*travel*) viajar; (*depart*) irse, marcharse; (*work*) funcionar, marchar; (*be sold*) venderse; (*time*) pasar; (*become*) ponerse; (*break etc*) estropearse, romperse ▷ *n* (*pl* **goes**) **to have a go (at)** probar suerte (con); **to be on the go** no parar; **whose go is it?** ¿a quién le toca?; **to go by car/on foot** ir en coche/a pie; **he's going to do it** va a hacerlo; **to go for a walk** ir a dar un paseo; **to go dancing** ir a bailar; **to go looking for sth/sb** ir a buscar algo/a algn; **to make sth go, get sth going** poner algo en marcha; **my voice has gone** he perdido la voz; **the cake is all gone** se acabó la tarta; **the money will go towards our holiday** el dinero es para (ayuda de) nuestras vacaciones; **how did it go?** ¿qué tal salió *or* resultó?, ¿cómo ha ido?; **the meeting went well** la reunión salió bien; **to go and see sb** ir a ver a algn; **to go to sleep** dormirse; **I'll take whatever is going** acepto lo que haya; **... to go** (*US*: *food*) ... para llevar; **go about** *vi* (*rumour*) propagarse; (*also*: **go round**: *wander about*) andar (de un sitio para otro) ▷ *vt fus*: **how do I go about this?** ¿cómo me las arreglo para hacer esto?; **to go about one's business** ocuparse de sus asuntos; **go after** *vt fus* (*pursue*) perseguir; (*job, record etc*) andar tras; **go against** *vt fus* (*be unfavourable to*: *results*) ir en contra de; (*be contrary to*: *principles*) ser contrario a; **go ahead** *vi* seguir adelante; **go along** *vi* ir; **as you go along** sobre la marcha ▷ *vt fus* bordear; **go along with** *vt fus* (*accompany*) acompañar; (*agree with*: *idea*) estar de acuerdo con; **go around** *vi* = **go round**; **go away** *vi* irse, marcharse; **go back** *vi* volver; **go back on** *vt fus* (*promise*) faltar a; **go by** *vi* (*years, time*) pasar ▷ *vt fus* guiarse por; **go down** *vi* bajar; (*ship*) hundirse; (*sun*) ponerse ▷ *vt fus* bajar por; **that should go down well with him** eso le va a gustar; **he's gone down with flu** ha cogido la gripe; **go for** *vt fus* (*fetch*) ir por; (*like*) gustar; (*attack*) atacar; **go in** *vi* entrar; **go in for** *vt fus* (*competition*) presentarse a; **go into** *vt fus* entrar en; (*investigate*) investigar; (*embark on*) dedicarse a; **go off** *vi* irse, marcharse; (*food*) pasarse; (*lights etc*) apagarse; (*explode*) estallar; (*event*) realizarse ▷ *vt fus* perder el interés por; **I'm going off him/the idea** ya no me gusta tanto él/la idea; **the party went off well** la fiesta salió bien; **go on** *vi* (*continue*) seguir, continuar; (*lights*) encenderse; (*happen*) pasar, ocurrir; (*be guided by*: *evidence etc*) partir de; **to go on doing sth** seguir haciendo algo; **what's going on here?** ¿qué pasa aquí?; **go on at** *vt fus* (*nag*) soltarle el rollo a; **go out** *vi* salir; (*fire, light*) apagarse; (*ebb*: *tide*) bajar, menguar; **to go out with sb** salir con algn; **go over** *vi* (*ship*) zozobrar ▷ *vt fus* (*check*) revisar; **to go over sth in one's mind** repasar algo mentalmente; **go past** *vi, vt fus* pasar; **go round** *vi* (*circulate*: *news, rumour*) correr; (*suffice*) alcanzar, bastar; (*revolve*) girar, dar vueltas; (*visit*): **to go round (to sb's)** pasar a ver (a algn); **to go round (by)** (*make a detour*) dar la vuelta (por) ▷ *vt fus* **to go round the back** pasar por detrás; **go through** *vt fus* (*town etc*) atravesar; (*search through*) revisar; (*perform*: *ceremony*) realizar; (*examine*: *list, book*) repasar; **go through with** *vt fus* (*plan, crime*) llevar a cabo; **I couldn't go through with it** no pude llevarlo a cabo; **go together** *vi* entenderse; **go under** *vi* (*sink*: *ship, person*) hundirse; (*fig*: *business, firm*) quebrar; **go up** *vi* subir; **to go up in flames** estallar en llamas; **go with** *vt fus* (*accompany*) ir con, acompañar a; (*fit, suit*) hacer juego con; **go without** *vt fus* pasarse sin

goad [gəud] *vt* aguijonear

go-ahead ['gəuəhɛd] *adj* emprendedor(a) ▷ *n* luz *f* verde; **to give sth/sb the ~** dar luz verde a algo/algn

goal [gəul] *n* meta, arco (*LAm*); (*score*) gol *m*

goalkeeper ['gəulki:pə^r] *n* portero, guardameta *m/f*, arquero (*LAm*)

goal post *n* poste *m* (de la portería)

goat [gəut] *n* cabra *f*

gobble ['gɔbl] *vt* (*also*: **~ down, ~ up**) engullir

go-between ['gəubɪtwi:n] *n* intermediario(-a)

goblin ['gɔblɪn] *n* duende *m*

go-cart ['gəukɑ:t] *n* = **go-kart**

god [gɔd] *n* dios *m*; **G~** Dios *m*

godchild ['gɔdtʃaɪld] *n* ahijado(-a)

goddamn ['gɔddæm] *adj* (*inf*: *also*: **~ed**) maldito, puñetero ▷ *excl*: **~!** ¡cagüen diez!

goddaughter ['gɔddɔ:tə^r] *n* ahijada

goddess ['gɔdɪs] *n* diosa

godfather ['gɔdfɑ:ðə^r] *n* padrino

god-forsaken ['gɔdfəseɪkən] *adj* dejado de la mano de Dios

godmother ['gɔdmʌðə^r] *n* madrina

godparents ['gɔdpɛərənts] *npl*: **the ~** los padrinos
godsend ['gɔdsɛnd] *n*: **to be a ~** venir como llovido del cielo
godson ['gɔdsʌn] *n* ahijado
goes [gəuz] *vb see* **go**
gofer ['gəufə^r] *n* (*inf*) chico(-a) para todo
goggles ['gɔglz] *npl* (*Aut*) gafas *fpl*, anteojos *mpl* (*LAm*); (*diver's*) gafas *fpl* submarinas
going ['gəuɪŋ] *n* (*conditions*) cosas *fpl* ▷ *adj*: **the ~ rate** la tarifa corriente *or* en vigor; **it was slow ~** las cosas iban lentas
goings-on ['gəuɪŋz'ɔn] *npl* (*inf*) tejemanejes *mpl*
go-kart ['gəukɑːt] *n* kart *m*
gold [gəuld] *n* oro ▷ *adj* (*reserves*) de oro
golden ['gəuldn] *adj* (*made of gold*) de oro; (*colour*) dorado
golden rule *n* regla de oro
goldfish ['gəuldfɪʃ] *n* pez *m* de colores
goldmine ['gəuldmaɪn] *n* mina de oro
gold-plated ['gəuld'pleɪtɪd] *adj* chapado en oro
goldsmith ['gəuldsmɪθ] *n* orfebre *m/f*
golf [gɔlf] *n* golf *m*
golf ball *n* (*for game*) pelota de golf; (*on typewriter*) esfera impresora
golf club *n* club *m* de golf; (*stick*) palo (de golf)
golf course *n* campo de golf
golfer ['gɔlfə^r] *n* jugador(a) *m(f)* de golf, golfista *m/f*
golfing ['gɔlfɪŋ] *n*: **to go ~** jugar al golf
gone [gɔn] *pp of* **go**
goner ['gɔnə^r] *n* (*inf*): **to be a ~** estar en las últimas
gong [gɔŋ] *n* gong *m*
good [gud] *adj* bueno; (*before m sing n*) buen; (*well-behaved*) educado ▷ *n* bien *m*; **~!** ¡qué bien!; **he's ~ at it** se le da bien; **to be ~ for** servir para; **it's ~ for you** te hace bien; **would you be ~ enough to ...?** ¿podría hacerme el favor de ...?, ¿sería tan amable de ...?; **that's very ~ of you** es usted muy amable; **to feel ~** sentirse bien; **it's ~ to see you** me alegro de verte; **a ~ deal (of)** mucho; **a ~ many** muchos; **to make ~** reparar; **it's no ~ complaining** no sirve de nada quejarse; **is this any ~?** (*will it do?*) ¿sirve esto?; (*what's it like?*) ¿qué tal es esto?; **it's a ~ thing you were there** menos mal que estabas allí; **for ~** (*for ever*) para siempre, definitivamente; **~ morning/afternoon** ¡buenos días/buenas tardes!; **~ evening!** ¡buenas noches!; **~ night!** ¡buenas noches!; **he's up to no ~** está tramando algo; **for the common ~** para el bien común; *see also* **goods**
goodbye [gud'baɪ] *excl* ¡adiós!; **to say ~ (to)** (*person*) despedirse (de)
Good Friday *n* Viernes *m* Santo
good-looking ['gud'lukɪŋ] *adj* guapo
good-natured ['gud'neɪtʃəd] *adj* (*person*) de buen carácter; (*discussion*) cordial
goodness ['gudnɪs] *n* (*of person*) bondad *f*; **for ~ sake!** ¡por Dios!; **~ gracious!** ¡madre mía!
goods [gudz] *npl* bienes *mpl*; (*Comm etc*) géneros *mpl*, mercancías *fpl*, artículos *mpl*; **all his ~ and chattels** todos sus bienes
goods train *n* (*Brit*) tren *m* de mercancías
goodwill [gud'wɪl] *n* buena voluntad *f*; (*Comm*) fondo de comercio; (*customer connections*) clientela
Google® ['guːgəl] *n* Google® *m* ▷ *vi* hacer búsquedas en Internet ▷ *vt* buscar información en Internet sobre
goose (*pl* **geese**) [guːs, giːs] *n* ganso, oca
gooseberry ['guzbərɪ] *n* grosella espinosa *or* silvestre; **to play ~** hacer de carabina
gooseflesh ['guːsflɛʃ] *n*, **goosepimples** ['guːspɪmplz] *npl* carne *f* de gallina
gopher ['gəufə^r] *n* = **gofer**
gore [gɔː^r] *vt* dar una cornada a, cornear ▷ *n* sangre *f*
gorge [gɔːdʒ] *n* garganta ▷ *vr*: **to ~ o.s. (on)** atracarse (de)
gorgeous ['gɔːdʒəs] *adj* precioso; (*weather*) estupendo; (*person*) guapísimo
gorilla [gə'rɪlə] *n* gorila *m*
gorse [gɔːs] *n* tojo
gory ['gɔːrɪ] *adj* sangriento
gosh [gɔʃ] (*inf*) *excl* ¡cielos!
go-slow ['gəu'sləu] *n* (*Brit*) huelga de celo
gospel ['gɔspl] *n* evangelio
gossip ['gɔsɪp] *n* cotilleo; (*person*) cotilla *m/f* ▷ *vi* cotillear, comadrear (*LAm*); **a piece of ~** un cotilleo
gossip column *n* ecos *mpl* de sociedad
got [gɔt] *pt, pp of* **get**
Gothic ['gɔθɪk] *adj* gótico
gotten ['gɔtn] (*US*) *pp of* **get**
gourmet ['guəmeɪ] *n* gastrónomo(-a) *m(f)*
gout [gaut] *n* gota
govern ['gʌvən] *vt* (*gen*) gobernar; (*event, conduct*) regir
governess ['gʌvənɪs] *n* institutriz *f*
government ['gʌvnmənt] *n* gobierno; **local ~** administración *f* municipal
governor ['gʌvənə^r] *n* gobernador(a) *m(f)*; (*of school etc*) miembro del consejo; (*of jail*) director(a) *m(f)*
gown [gaun] *n* vestido; (*of teacher*: *Brit*: *of judge*) toga
GP *n abbr* (*Med*) = **general practitioner**
GPO *n abbr* (*Brit*: *old*) = **General Post Office**; (*US*) = **Government Printing Office**
gr. *abbr* (*Comm*: = *gross*) bto
grab [græb] *vt* coger (*Sp*) *or* agarrar; **to ~ at** intentar agarrar
grace [greɪs] *n* (*Rel*) gracia; (*gracefulness*) elegancia, gracia; (*graciousness*) cortesía, gracia ▷ *vt* (*favour*) honrar; (*adorn*) adornar; **5 days' ~** un plazo de 5 días; **to say ~** bendecir la mesa; **his sense of humour is his saving ~** lo que le salva es su sentido del humor

graceful ['greɪsful] *adj* grácil, ágil; (*style, shape*) elegante, gracioso
gracious ['greɪʃəs] *adj* amable ▷ *excl*: **good ~!** ¡Dios mío!
grade [greɪd] *n* (*quality*) clase *f*, calidad *f*; (*in hierarchy*) grado; (*Scol: mark*) nota; (*US Scol*) curso; (*: gradient*) pendiente *f*, cuesta ▷ *vt* clasificar; **to make the ~** (*fig*) dar el nivel
grade crossing *n* (*US*) paso a nivel
grade school *n* (*US*) escuela primaria
gradient ['greɪdɪənt] *n* pendiente *f*
gradual ['grædjuəl] *adj* gradual
gradually ['grædjuəlɪ] *adv* gradualmente
graduate *n* ['grædjuɪt] licenciado(-a), graduado(-a), egresado(-a) (*LAm*); (*US Scol*) bachiller *m/f* ▷ *vi* ['grædjueɪt] licenciarse, graduarse, recibirse (*LAm*); (*US*) obtener el título de bachillerato
graduation [grædju'eɪʃən] *n* graduación *f*; (*US Scol*) entrega de los títulos de bachillerato
graffiti [grə'fi:tɪ] *npl* pintadas *fpl*
graft [grɑ:ft] *n* (*Agr, Med*) injerto; (*bribery*) corrupción *f* ▷ *vt* injertar; **hard ~** (*inf*) trabajo duro
grain [greɪn] *n* (*single particle*) grano *no pl* (*cereals*) cereales *mpl*; (*US: corn*) trigo; (*in wood*) veta
gram [græm] *n* (*US*) gramo
grammar ['græmə^r] *n* gramática
grammar school *n* (*Brit*) ≈ instituto (de segunda enseñanza); (*US*) escuela primaria; *see also* **comprehensive school**
grammatical [grə'mætɪkl] *adj* gramatical
gramme [græm] *n* = **gram**
gran [græn] *n* (*Brit: inf*) abuelita
grand [grænd] *adj* magnífico, imponente; (*wonderful*) estupendo; (*gesture etc*) grandioso ▷ *n* (*US: inf*) mil dólares *mpl*
grandad (*inf*) ['grændæd] *n* = **granddad**
grandchild ['grændtʃaɪld] (*pl* **grandchildren**) *n* nieto(-a) *m/f*
granddad ['grændæd] *n* yayo, abuelito
granddaughter ['grændɔ:tə^r] *n* nieta
grandfather ['grænfɑ:ðə^r] *n* abuelo
grand jury *n* (*US*) jurado de acusación
grandma ['grænmɑ:] *n* yaya, abuelita
grandmother ['grænmʌðə^r] *n* abuela
grandpa ['grænpɑ:] *n* = **granddad**
grandparents ['grændpɛərənts] *npl* abuelos *mpl*
grand piano *n* piano de cola
Grand Prix ['grɑ̃:'pri:] *n* (*Aut*) gran premio, Grand Prix *m*
grandson ['grænsʌn] *n* nieto
grandstand ['grændstænd] *n* (*Sport*) tribuna
grand total *n* suma total, total *m*
granite ['grænɪt] *n* granito
granny ['grænɪ] *n* abuelita, yaya
grant [grɑ:nt] *vt* (*concede*) conceder; (*admit*): **to ~ (that)** reconocer (que) ▷ *n* (*Scol*) beca; **to take sth for ~ed** dar algo por sentado
granulated sugar ['grænjuleɪtɪd-] *n* (*Brit*) azúcar *m* granulado
granule ['grænju:l] *n* gránulo
grape [greɪp] *n* uva; **sour ~s** (*fig*) envidia *sg*; **a bunch of ~s** un racimo de uvas
grapefruit ['greɪpfru:t] *n* pomelo (*SC, Sp*), toronja (*LAm*)
grapevine ['greɪpvaɪn] *n* vid *f*, parra; **I heard it on the ~** (*fig*) me enteré, me lo contaron
graph [grɑ:f] *n* gráfica
graphic ['græfɪk] *adj* gráfico
graphic equalizer *n* ecualizador *m* gráfico
graphics ['græfɪks] *n* (*art, process*) artes *fpl* gráficas ▷ *npl* (*drawings: Comput*) gráficos *mpl*
grapple ['græpl] *vi* (*also*: **to ~ with a problem**) enfrentarse a un problema
grasp [grɑ:sp] *vt* agarrar, asir; (*understand*) comprender ▷ *n* (*grip*) asimiento; (*reach*) alcance *m*; (*understanding*) comprensión *f*; **to have a good ~ of** (*subject*) dominar; **grasp at** *vt fus* (*rope etc*) tratar de agarrar; (*fig: opportunity*) aprovechar
grasping ['grɑ:spɪŋ] *adj* avaro
grass [grɑ:s] *n* hierba; (*lawn*) césped *m*; (*pasture*) pasto; (*inf: informer*) soplón(-ona) *m(f)*
grasshopper ['grɑ:shɔpə^r] *n* saltamontes *m inv*
grass roots *adj* de base ▷ *npl* (*Pol*) bases *fpl*
grate [greɪt] *n* parrilla ▷ *vi* chirriar, rechinar ▷ *vt* (*Culin*) rallar
grateful ['greɪtful] *adj* agradecido
grater ['greɪtə^r] *n* rallador *m*
gratifying ['grætɪfaɪɪŋ] *adj* gratificante
grating ['greɪtɪŋ] *n* (*iron bars*) rejilla ▷ *adj* (*noise*) chirriante
gratitude ['grætɪtju:d] *n* agradecimiento
gratuitous [grə'tju:ɪtəs] *adj* gratuito
gratuity [grə'tju:ɪtɪ] *n* gratificación *f*
grave [greɪv] *n* tumba ▷ *adj* serio, grave
gravel ['grævl] *n* grava
gravestone ['greɪvstəun] *n* lápida
graveyard ['greɪvjɑ:d] *n* cementerio, camposanto
gravity ['grævɪtɪ] *n* gravedad *f*; (*seriousness*) seriedad *f*
gravy ['greɪvɪ] *n* salsa de carne
gray [greɪ] *adj* (*US*) = **grey**
graze [greɪz] *vi* pacer ▷ *vt* (*touch lightly, scrape*) rozar ▷ *n* (*Med*) rozadura
grease [gri:s] *n* (*fat*) grasa; (*lubricant*) lubricante *m* ▷ *vt* engrasar; **to ~ the skids** (*US: fig*) engrasar el mecanismo
greaseproof ['gri:spru:f] *adj* a prueba de grasa; (*Brit: paper*) de grasa
greasy ['gri:sɪ] *adj* (*hands, clothes*) grasiento; (*road, surface*) resbaladizo
great [greɪt] *adj* grande; (*before n sing*) gran; (*inf*) estupendo, macanudo (*LAm*), regio (*LAm*); (*pain, heat*) intenso; **we had a ~ time** nos lo pasamos muy bien; **they're ~ friends** son íntimos *or* muy amigos; **the ~ thing is that ...** lo bueno es que ...; **it was ~!** ¡fue estupendo!
Great Barrier Reef *n* Gran Barrera de Coral
Great Britain *n* Gran Bretaña

greater ['greɪtəʳ] *adj* mayor; **G~ London** el área metropolitana de Londres
greatest ['greɪtɪst] *adj* (el/la) mayor
great-grandchild (*pl* **-children**) [greɪt'grændtʃaɪld, 'tʃɪldrən] *n* bisnieto(-a)
great-grandfather [greɪt'grændfɑːðəʳ] *n* bisabuelo
great-grandmother [greɪt'grændmʌðəʳ] *n* bisabuela
Great Lakes *npl*: **the ~** los Grandes Lagos
greatly ['greɪtlɪ] *adv* muy; (*with verb*) mucho
greatness ['greɪtnɪs] *n* grandeza
Greece [griːs] *n* Grecia
greed [griːd] *n* (*also*: **~iness**) codicia; (*for food*) gula; (*for power etc*) avidez *f*
greedy ['griːdɪ] *adj* codicioso; (*for food*) glotón(-ona)
Greek [griːk] *adj* griego ▷ *n* griego(-a); (*Ling*) griego; **ancient/modern ~** griego antiguo/moderno
green [griːn] *adj* verde; (*inexperienced*) novato ▷ *n* verde *m*; (*stretch of grass*) césped *m*; (*of golf course*) campo, green *m*; **the G~ party** (*Pol*) el partido verde; **greens** *npl* verduras *fpl*; **to have ~ fingers** (*fig*) tener buena mano para las plantas
green belt *n* cinturón *m* verde
green card *n* (*Aut*) carta verde; (*US*: *work permit*) *permiso de trabajo para los extranjeros en* EE. UU.
greenery ['griːnərɪ] *n* vegetación *f*
greengage ['griːngeɪdʒ] *n* (ciruela) claudia
greengrocer ['griːngrəusəʳ] *n* (*Brit*) frutero(-a), verdulero(-a)
greenhouse ['griːnhaus] *n* invernadero
greenhouse effect *n* efecto invernadero
greenhouse gas *n* gas *m* que produce el efecto invernadero
greenish ['griːnɪʃ] *adj* verdoso
Greenland ['griːnlənd] *n* Groenlandia
green light *n* luz *f* verde
green pepper *n* pimiento verde
green salad *n* ensalada *f* (*de lechuga, pepino, pimiento verde, etc*)
green tax *n* impuesto ambiental
greet [griːt] *vt* saludar; (*news*) recibir
greeting ['griːtɪŋ] *n* (*gen*) saludo; (*welcome*) bienvenida; **~s** saludos *mpl*; **season's ~s** Felices Pascuas
greeting card, greetings card *n* tarjeta de felicitación
gregarious [grə'gɛərɪəs] *adj* gregario
grenade [grə'neɪd] *n* (*also*: **hand ~**) granada
grew [gruː] *pt of* **grow**
grey [greɪ] *adj* gris; **to go ~** salirle canas
grey-haired [greɪ'hɛəd] *adj* canoso
greyhound ['greɪhaund] *n* galgo
grid [grɪd] *n* rejilla; (*Elec*) red *f*
gridlock ['grɪdlɔk] *n* (*esp US*) retención *f*
grief [griːf] *n* dolor *m*, pena; **to come to ~** (*plan*) fracasar, ir al traste; (*person*) acabar mal, desgraciarse
grievance ['griːvəns] *n* (*cause for complaint*) motivo de queja, agravio
grieve [griːv] *vi* afligirse, acongojarse ▷ *vt* afligir, apenar; **to ~ for** llorar por; **to ~ for sb** (*dead person*) llorar la pérdida de algn
grievous ['griːvəs] *adj* grave; (*loss*) cruel; **~ bodily harm** (*Law*) daños *mpl* corporales graves
grill [grɪl] *n* (*on cooker*) parrilla ▷ *vt* (*Brit*) asar a la parrilla; (*question*) interrogar; **~ed meat** carne *f* (asada) a la parrilla *or* plancha
grille [grɪl] *n* rejilla
grim [grɪm] *adj* (*place*) lúgubre; (*person*) adusto
grimace [grɪ'meɪs] *n* mueca ▷ *vi* hacer muecas
grime [graɪm] *n* mugre *f*
grin [grɪn] *n* sonrisa abierta ▷ *vi*: **to ~ (at)** sonreír abiertamente (a)
grind [graɪnd] (*pt, pp* **ground**) *vt* (*coffee, pepper etc*) moler; (*US*: *meat*) picar; (*make sharp*) afilar; (*polish*: *gem, lens*) esmerilar ▷ *vi* (*car gears*) rechinar ▷ *n*: **the daily ~** (*inf*) la rutina diaria; **to ~ one's teeth** hacer rechinar los dientes; **to ~ to a halt** (*vehicle*) pararse con gran estruendo de frenos; (*fig*: *talks, scheme*) interrumpirse; (*work, production*) paralizarse
grip [grɪp] *n* (*hold*) asimiento; (*of hands*) apretón *m*; (*handle*) asidero; (*of racquet etc*) mango; (*understanding*) comprensión *f* ▷ *vt* agarrar; **to get to ~s with** enfrentarse con; **to lose one's ~** (*fig*) perder el control; **he lost his ~ of the situation** la situación se le fue de las manos
gripping ['grɪpɪŋ] *adj* absorbente
grisly ['grɪzlɪ] *adj* horripilante, horrible
gristle ['grɪsl] *n* cartílago
grit [grɪt] *n* gravilla; (*courage*) valor *m* ▷ *vt* (*road*) poner gravilla en; **I've got a piece of ~ in my eye** tengo una arenilla en el ojo; **to ~ one's teeth** apretar los dientes
grits [grɪts] *npl* (*US*) maíz *msg* a medio moler
groan [grəun] *n* gemido, quejido ▷ *vi* gemir, quejarse
grocer ['grəusəʳ] *n* tendero (de ultramarinos); **~'s (shop)** *n* tienda de ultramarinos *or* (*LAm*) de abarrotes
groceries ['grəusərɪz] *npl* comestibles *mpl*
grocery ['grəusərɪ] *n* (*shop*) tienda de ultramarinos
groin [grɔɪn] *n* ingle *f*
groom [gruːm] *n* mozo(-a) de cuadra; (*also*: **bride~**) novio ▷ *vt* (*horse*) almohazar; (*fig*): **to ~ sb for** preparar a algn para; **well-~ed** acicalado
groove [gruːv] *n* ranura; (*of record*) surco
grope [grəup] *vi* ir a tientas; **to ~ for** buscar a tientas
gross [grəus] *adj* (*neglect, injustice*) grave; (*vulgar*: *behaviour*) grosero; (*: appearance*) de mal gusto; (*Comm*) bruto ▷ *vt* (*Comm*) recaudar en bruto

gross domestic product *n* producto interior bruto

grossly ['grəuslı] *adv* (*greatly*) enormemente

gross national product *n* producto nacional bruto

grotesque [grə'tɛsk] *adj* grotesco

grotto ['grɔtəu] *n* gruta

grotty ['grɔtı] *adj* asqueroso

ground [graund] *pt, pp of* **grind** ▷ *n* suelo, tierra; (*Sport*) campo, terreno; (*reason*) *gen pl* motivo, razón *f*; (*US*: *also*: **~ wire**) tierra ▷ *vt* (*plane*) mantener en tierra; (*US Elec*) conectar con tierra ▷ *vi* (*ship*) varar, encallar ▷ *adj* (*coffee etc*) molido; **grounds** *npl* (*of coffee etc*) poso *sg*; (*gardens etc*) jardines *mpl*, parque *m*; **on the ~** en el suelo; **common ~** terreno común; **to gain/lose ~** ganar/perder terreno; **to the ~** al suelo; **below ~** bajo tierra; **he covered a lot of ~ in his lecture** abarcó mucho en la clase

ground cloth *n* (*US*) = **groundsheet**

ground floor *n* (*Brit*) planta baja

grounding ['graundıŋ] *n* (*in education*) conocimientos *mpl* básicos

groundless ['graundlıs] *adj* infundado, sin fundamento

ground rules *npl* normas básicas

groundsheet ['graundʃi:t] (*Brit*) *n* tela impermeable

ground staff *n* personal *m* de tierra

ground swell *n* mar *m or f* de fondo; (*fig*) ola

ground-to-air ['grauntə'ɛə] *adj* tierra-aire

ground-to-ground ['grauntə'graund] *adj* tierra-tierra

groundwork ['graundwə:k] *n* trabajo preliminar

group [gru:p] *n* grupo; (*Mus*: *pop group*) conjunto, grupo ▷ *vt* (*also*: **~ together**) agrupar ▷ *vi* agruparse

grouse [graus] *n pl inv* (*bird*) urogallo ▷ *vi* (*complain*) quejarse

grove [grəuv] *n* arboleda

grovel ['grɔvl] *vi* (*fig*) arrastrarse

grow (*pt* **grew**, *pp* **grown**) [grəu, gru:, grəun] *vi* crecer; (*increase*) aumentar; (*expand*) desarrollarse; (*become*) volverse ▷ *vt* cultivar; (*hair, beard*) dejar crecer; **to ~ rich/weak** enriquecerse/debilitarse; **to ~ tired of waiting** cansarse de esperar; **grow apart** *vi* (*fig*) alejarse uno del otro; **grow away from** *vt fus* (*fig*) alejarse de; **grow on** *vt fus*: **that painting is ~ing on me** ese cuadro me gusta cada vez más; **grow out of** *vt fus* (*habit*) perder; (*clothes*): **I've ~n out of this shirt** esta camisa se me ha quedado pequeña; **grow up** *vi* crecer, hacerse hombre/mujer

grower ['grəuə^r] *n* (*Agr*) cultivador(a) *m(f)*, productor(a) *m(f)*

growing ['grəuıŋ] *adj* creciente; **~ pains** (*also fig*) problemas *mpl* de crecimiento

growl [graul] *vi* gruñir

grown [grəun] *pp of* **grow**

grown-up [grəun'ʌp] *n* adulto(-a), mayor *m/f*

growth [grəuθ] *n* crecimiento, desarrollo; (*what has grown*) brote *m*; (*Med*) tumor *m*

grub [grʌb] *n* gusano; (*inf*: *food*) comida

grubby ['grʌbı] *adj* sucio, mugriento, mugroso (*LAm*)

grudge [grʌdʒ] *n* rencor ▷ *vt*: **to ~ sb sth** dar algo a algn de mala gana; **to bear sb a ~** guardar rencor a algn; **he ~s (giving) the money** da el dinero de mala gana

gruelling, grueling (*US*) ['gruəlıŋ] *adj* agotador

gruesome ['gru:səm] *adj* horrible

gruff [grʌf] *adj* (*voice*) ronco; (*manner*) brusco

grumble ['grʌmbl] *vi* refunfuñar, quejarse

grumpy ['grʌmpı] *adj* gruñón(-ona)

grunt [grʌnt] *vi* gruñir ▷ *n* gruñido

G-string ['dʒi:strıŋ] *n* tanga *m*

guarantee [gærən'ti:] *n* garantía ▷ *vt* garantizar; **he can't ~ (that) he'll come** no está seguro de poder venir

guard [gɑ:d] *n* guardia; (*person*) guarda *m/f*; (*Brit Rail*) jefe *m* de tren; (*safety device*: *on machine*) cubierta de protección; (*protection*) protección *f*; (*fireguard*) pantalla; (*mudguard*) guardabarros *m inv* ▷ *vt* guardar; **to ~ (against** *or* **from)** proteger (de); **to be on one's ~** (*fig*) estar en guardia; **guard against** *vi*: **to ~ against doing sth** guardarse de hacer algo

guarded ['gɑ:dıd] *adj* (*fig*) cauteloso

guardian ['gɑ:dıən] *n* guardián(-ana) *m(f)*; (*of minor*) tutor(a) *m(f)*

guard's van *n* (*Brit Rail*) furgón *m* del jefe de tren

Guatemala [gwɑ:tə'mɑ:lə] *n* Guatemala

Guatemalan [gwɑ:tə'mɑ:lən] *adj, n* guatemalteco(-a) *m(f)*

guerrilla [gə'rılə] *n* guerrillero(-a)

guess [gɛs] *vi, vt* (*gen*) adivinar; (*suppose*) suponer ▷ *n* suposición *f*, conjetura; **I ~ you're right** (*esp US*) supongo que tienes razón; **to keep sb ~ing** mantener a algn a la expectativa; **to take** *or* **have a ~** tratar de adivinar; **my ~ is that ...** yo creo que ...

guesswork ['gɛswə:k] *n* conjeturas *fpl*; **I got the answer by ~** acerté a ojo de buen cubero

guest [gɛst] *n* invitado(-a); (*in hotel*) huésped(a) *m(f)*; **be my ~** (*inf*) estás en tu casa

guest-house ['gɛsthaus] *n* casa de huéspedes, pensión *f*

guest room *n* cuarto de huéspedes

guff [gʌf] *n* (*inf*) bobadas *fpl*

guffaw [gʌ'fɔ:] *n* carcajada ▷ *vi* reírse a carcajadas

guidance ['gaıdəns] *n* (*gen*) dirección *f*; (*advice*) consejos *mpl*; **marriage/vocational ~** orientación *f* matrimonial/profesional

guide [gaıd] *n* (*person*) guía *m/f*; (*book*) guía *f*; (*fig*) guía *f*; (*also*: **girl ~**) exploradora ▷ *vt*

guiar; **to be ~d by sb/sth** dejarse guiar por algn/algo
guidebook ['gaɪdbuk] *n* guía
guide dog *n* perro guía
guided tour *n* visita *f* con guía
guidelines ['gaɪdlaɪnz] *npl* (*fig*) directrices *fpl*
guild [gɪld] *n* gremio
guildhall ['gɪldhɔ:l] *n* (*Brit: town hall*) ayuntamiento
guile [gaɪl] *n* astucia
guillotine ['gɪlətiːn] *n* guillotina
guilt [gɪlt] *n* culpabilidad *f*
guilty ['gɪltɪ] *adj* culpable; **to feel ~ (about)** sentirse culpable (de); **to plead ~/not ~** declararse culpable/inocente
guinea pig *n* cobaya; (*fig*) conejillo de Indias
guise [gaɪz] *n*: **in** *or* **under the ~ of** bajo la apariencia de
guitar [gɪ'tɑːʳ] *n* guitarra
guitarist [gɪ'tɑːrɪst] *n* guitarrista *m/f*
gulf [gʌlf] *n* golfo; (*abyss*) abismo; **the G~** el Golfo (Pérsico)
Gulf States *npl*: **the ~** los países del Golfo
gull [gʌl] *n* gaviota
gullet ['gʌlɪt] *n* esófago
gullible ['gʌlɪbl] *adj* crédulo
gully ['gʌlɪ] *n* barranco
gulp [gʌlp] *vi* tragar saliva ▷ *vt* (*also*: **~ down**) tragarse ▷ *n* (*of liquid*) trago; (*of food*) bocado; **in** *or* **at one ~** de un trago
gum [gʌm] *n* (*Anat*) encía; (*glue*) goma, cemento (*LAm*); (*sweet*) gominola; (*also*: **chewing-~**) chicle *m* ▷ *vt* pegar con goma; **gum up** *vt*: **to ~ up the works** (*inf*) entorpecerlo todo
gumboots ['gʌmbuːts] *npl* (*Brit*) botas *fpl* de goma
gun [gʌn] *n* (*small*) pistola; (*shotgun*) escopeta; (*rifle*) fusil *m*; (*cannon*) cañón *m* ▷ *vt* (*also*: **~ down**) abatir a tiros; **to stick to one's ~s** (*fig*) mantenerse firme *or* en sus trece
gunboat ['gʌnbəut] *n* cañonero
gunfire ['gʌnfaɪəʳ] *n* disparos *mpl*
gunman ['gʌnmən] *n* pistolero
gunpoint ['gʌnpɔɪnt] *n*: **at ~** a mano armada
gunpowder ['gʌnpaudəʳ] *n* pólvora
gunshot ['gʌnʃɔt] *n* disparo
gurgle ['gəːgl] *vi* gorgotear
gush [gʌʃ] *vi* chorrear, salir a raudales; (*fig*) deshacerse en efusiones
gust [gʌst] *n* (*of wind*) ráfaga
gusto ['gʌstəu] *n* entusiasmo
gut [gʌt] *n* intestino; (*Mus etc*) cuerda de tripa ▷ *vt* (*poultry, fish*) destripar; (*building*): **the blaze ~ted the entire building** el fuego destruyó el edificio entero
guts [gʌts] *npl* (*courage*) agallas *fpl*, valor *m*; (*inf: innards: of people, animals*) tripas *fpl*; **to hate sb's ~** odiar a algn (a muerte)
gutted ['gʌtɪd] *adj* (*inf: disappointed*): **I was ~** me quedé hecho polvo
gutter ['gʌtəʳ] *n* (*of roof*) canalón *m*; (*in street*) cuneta; **the ~** (*fig*) el arroyo
gutter press *n* (*inf*): **the ~** la prensa sensacionalista *or* amarilla; *see also* **tabloid press**
guy [gaɪ] *n* (*also*: **~rope**) viento, cuerda; (*inf: man*) tío (*Sp*), tipo
Guy Fawkes' Night [gaɪ'fɔːks-] *n ver nota*

GUY FAWKES' NIGHT

La noche del cinco de noviembre, *Guy Fawkes' Night*, se celebra el fracaso de la conspiración de la pólvora ("Gunpowder Plot"), el intento fallido de volar el parlamento de Jaime 1 en 1605. Esa noche se lanzan fuegos artificiales y se queman en muchas hogueras muñecos de trapo que representan a "Guy Fawkes", uno de los cabecillas. Días antes los niños tienen por costumbre pedir a los viandantes "a penny for the guy", dinero para comprar los cohetes.

guzzle ['gʌzl] *vi* tragar ▷ *vt* engullir
gym [dʒɪm] *n* (*also*: **~nasium**) gimnasio; (*also*: **~nastics**) gimnasia
gymnasium [dʒɪm'neɪzɪəm] *n* gimnasio
gymnast ['dʒɪmnæst] *n* gimnasta *m/f*
gymnastics [dʒɪm'næstɪks] *n* gimnasia
gym shoes *npl* zapatillas *fpl* de gimnasia
gym slip *n* (*Brit*) pichi *m*
gynaecologist, gynecologist (*US*) [gaɪnɪ'kɔlədʒɪst] *n* ginecólogo(-a)
gynaecology, gynecology (*US*) [gaɪnə-'kɔlədʒɪ] *n* ginecología
gypsy ['dʒɪpsɪ] *n* = **gipsy**

h

H, h [eɪtʃ] *n* (*letter*) H, h *f*; **H for Harry**, (*US*) **H for How** H de Historia
haberdashery ['hæbə'dæʃərɪ] *n* (*Brit*) mercería; (*US*: *men's clothing*) prendas *fpl* de caballero
habit ['hæbɪt] *n* hábito, costumbre *f*; (*drug habit*) adicción *f*; **to get out of/into the ~ of doing sth** perder la costumbre de/acostumbrarse a hacer algo
habitat ['hæbɪtæt] *n* hábitat *m*
habitual [hə'bɪtjuəl] *adj* acostumbrado, habitual; (*drinker, liar*) empedernido
hack [hæk] *vt* (*cut*) cortar; (*slice*) tajar ▷ *n* corte *m*; (*axe blow*) hachazo; (*pej*: *writer*) escritor(a) *m(f)* a sueldo; (*old horse*) jamelgo
hacker ['hækəʳ] *n* (*Comput*) pirata *m* informático
hackneyed ['hæknɪd] *adj* trillado, gastado
hacksaw ['hæksɔː] *n* sierra para metales
had [hæd] *pt, pp of* **have**
haddock (*pl* **haddock** *or* **haddocks**) ['hædək] *n especie de merluza*
hadn't ['hædnt] = **had not**
haematology, hematology (*US*) ['hiːmə'tɔlədʒɪ] *n* hematología
haemophilia, hemophilia (*US*) ['hiːmə'fɪlɪə] *n* hemofilia
haemorrhage, hemorrhage (*US*) ['hɛmərɪdʒ] *n* hemorragia
haemorrhoids, hemorrhoids (*US*) ['hɛmərɔɪdz] *npl* hemorroides *fpl*, almorranas *fpl*
hag [hæg] *n* (*ugly*) vieja fea, tarasca; (*nasty*) bruja; (*witch*) hechicera
haggard ['hægəd] *adj* ojeroso
haggis ['hægɪs] *n* (*Scottish*) *asadura de cordero cocida*; *see also* **Burns' Night**
haggle ['hægl] *vi* (*argue*) discutir; (*bargain*) regatear
haggling ['hæglɪŋ] *n* regateo
Hague [heɪg] *n*: **The ~** La Haya
hail [heɪl] *n* (*weather*) granizo ▷ *vt* saludar; (*call*) llamar a ▷ *vi* granizar; **to ~ (as)** aclamar (como), celebrar (como); **he ~s from Scotland** es natural de Escocia
hailstone ['heɪlstəun] *n* (piedra de) granizo
hailstorm ['heɪlstɔːm] *n* granizada
hair [hɛəʳ] *n* (*gen*) pelo, cabellos *mpl*; (*one hair*) pelo, cabello; (*head of hair*) pelo, cabellera; (*on legs etc*) vello; **to do one's ~** arreglarse el pelo; **grey ~** canas *fpl*
hairband ['hɛəbænd] *n* cinta
hairbrush ['hɛəbrʌʃ] *n* cepillo (para el pelo)
haircut ['hɛəkʌt] *n* corte *m* de pelo
hairdo ['hɛəduː] *n* peinado
hairdresser ['hɛədrɛsəʳ] *n* peluquero(-a); **~'s** peluquería
hairdryer ['hɛədraɪəʳ] *n* secador *m* (de pelo)
hair gel *n* fijador
hairgrip ['hɛəgrɪp] *n* horquilla
hairnet ['hɛənɛt] *n* redecilla
hairpiece ['hɛəpiːs] *n* trenza postiza
hairpin ['hɛəpɪn] *n* horquilla
hairpin bend, hairpin curve (*US*) *n* curva muy cerrada
hair-raising ['hɛəreɪzɪŋ] *adj* espeluznante
hair spray *n* laca
hairstyle ['hɛəstaɪl] *n* peinado
hairy ['hɛərɪ] *adj* peludo, velludo; (*inf*: *frightening*) espeluznante
hake [heɪk] *n* merluza
half [hɑːf] *n* (*pl* **halves** [hɑːvz]) mitad *f*; (*Sport*: *of match*) tiempo, parte *f*; (: *of ground*) campo; (*of beer*) ≈ caña (*Sp*), media pinta; (*Rail, Bus*) billete *m* de niño ▷ *adj* medio ▷ *adv* medio, a medias; **~-an-hour** media hora; **two and a ~** dos y media; **~ a dozen** media docena; **~ a pound** media libra, ≈ 250 gr.; **to cut sth in ~** cortar algo por la mitad; **to go halves (with sb)** ir a medias (con algn); **~ empty/closed** medio vacío/entreabierto; **~ asleep** medio dormido; **~ past 3** las 3 y media
half-baked ['hɑːf'beɪkt] *adj* (*inf*: *idea, scheme*) mal concebido *or* pensado
half board *n* (*Brit*: *in hotel*) media pensión
half-brother ['hɑːfbrʌðəʳ] *n* hermanastro
half-caste ['hɑːfkɑːst] *n* mestizo(-a)
half day *n* medio día *m*, media jornada
half fare *n* medio pasaje *m*
half-hearted ['hɑːf'hɑːtɪd] *adj* indiferente, poco entusiasta
half-hour [hɑːf'auəʳ] *n* media hora
half-mast ['hɑːf'mɑːst] *n*: **at ~** (*flag*) a media asta

halfpenny ['heɪpnɪ] *n* medio penique *m*
half-price ['hɑ:f'praɪs] *adj* a mitad de precio
half term *n* (*Brit Scol*) *vacaciones de mediados del trimestre*
half-time [hɑ:f'taɪm] *n* descanso
halfway ['hɑ:f'weɪ] *adv* a medio camino; **to meet sb ~** (*fig*) llegar a un acuerdo con algn
halfway house *n centro de readaptación de antiguos presos*; (*fig*) solución *f* intermedia
half-wit ['hɑ:fwɪt] *n* (*inf*) zoquete *m*
hall [hɔ:l] *n* (*for concerts*) sala; (*entrance way*) entrada, vestíbulo
hallmark ['hɔ:lmɑ:k] *n* (*mark*) rasgo distintivo; (*seal*) sello
hallo [hə'ləu] *excl* = **hello**
hall of residence *n* (*Brit*) colegio mayor, residencia universitaria
Hallowe'en [hæləu'i:n] *n* víspera de Todos los Santos; *ver nota*

HALLOWE'EN

La tradición anglosajona dice que en la noche del 31 de octubre, *Hallowe'en*, víspera de Todos los Santos, es fácil ver a brujas y fantasmas. Es una ocasión festiva en la que los niños se disfrazan y van de puerta en puerta llevando un farol hecho con una calabaza en forma de cabeza humana. Cuando se les abre la puerta gritan "trick or treat" para indicar que gastarán una broma a quien no les dé un pequeño regalo (como golosinas o dinero).

hallucination [həlu:sɪ'neɪʃən] *n* alucinación *f*
hallway ['hɔ:lweɪ] *n* vestíbulo
halo ['heɪləu] *n* (*of saint*) aureola, halo
halt [hɔ:lt] *n* (*stop*) alto, parada; (*Rail*) apeadero ▷ *vt* parar ▷ *vi* pararse; (*process*) interrumpirse; **to call a ~ (to sth)** (*fig*) poner fin (a algo)
halve [hɑ:v] *vt* partir por la mitad
halves [hɑ:vz] *pl of* **half**
ham [hæm] *n* jamón *m* (cocido); (*inf*: *also*: **radio ~**) radioaficionado(-a) *m*(*f*); (: *also*: **~ actor**) comicastro
hamburger ['hæmbə:gə^r] *n* hamburguesa
hamlet ['hæmlɪt] *n* aldea
hammer ['hæmə^r] *n* martillo ▷ *vt* (*nail*) clavar; **to ~ a point home to sb** remacharle un punto a algn; **hammer out** *vt* (*metal*) forjar a martillo; (*fig*: *solution, agreement*) elaborar (trabajosamente)
hammock ['hæmək] *n* hamaca
hamper ['hæmpə^r] *vt* estorbar ▷ *n* cesto
hamster ['hæmstə^r] *n* hámster *m*
hamstring ['hæmstrɪŋ] *n* (*Anat*) tendón *m* de la corva
hand [hænd] *n* mano *f*; (*of clock*) aguja, manecilla; (*writing*) letra; (*worker*) obrero; (*measurement*: *of horse*) palmo ▷ *vt* (*give*) dar, pasar; (*deliver*) entregar; **to give sb a ~** echar una mano a algn, ayudar a algn; **to force sb's ~** forzarle la mano a algn; **at ~** a mano; **in ~** entre manos; **we have the matter in ~** tenemos el asunto entre manos; **to have in one's ~** (*knife, victory*) tener en la mano; **to have a free ~** tener carta blanca; **on ~** (*person, services*) a mano, al alcance; **to ~** (*information etc*) a mano; **on the one ~ ..., on the other ~ ...** por una parte ... por otra (parte) ...; **hand down** *vt* pasar, bajar; (*tradition*) transmitir; (*heirloom*) dejar en herencia; (*US*: *sentence, verdict*) imponer; **hand in** *vt* entregar; **hand out** *vt* (*leaflets, advice*) repartir, distribuir; **hand over** *vt* (*deliver*) entregar; (*surrender*) ceder; **hand round** *vt* (*Brit*: *information, papers*) pasar (de mano en mano); (: *chocolates etc*) ofrecer
handbag ['hændbæg] *n* bolso, cartera (*LAm*)
hand baggage *n* = **hand luggage**
handbasin ['hændbeɪsn] *n* lavabo
handbook ['hændbuk] *n* manual *m*
handbrake ['hændbreɪk] *n* freno de mano
hand cream *n* crema para las manos
handcuffs ['hændkʌfs] *npl* esposas *fpl*
handful ['hændful] *n* puñado
hand-held ['hænd'hɛld] *adj* de mano
handicap ['hændɪkæp] *n* desventaja; (*Sport*) hándicap *m* ▷ *vt* estorbar
handicapped ['hændɪkæpt] *adj*: **to be mentally ~** (*pej*) ser mentalmente *m/f* discapacitado; **to be physically ~** (*pej*) ser minusválido(-a)
handicraft ['hændɪkrɑ:ft] *n* artesanía
handiwork ['hændɪwə:k] *n* manualidad(es) *f*(*pl*); (*fig*) obra; **this looks like his ~** (*pej*) es obra de él, parece
handkerchief ['hæŋkətʃɪf] *n* pañuelo
handle ['hændl] *n* (*of door etc*) pomo, tirador *m*; (*of cup etc*) asa; (*of knife etc*) mango; (*for winding*) manivela ▷ *vt* (*touch*) tocar; (*deal with*) encargarse de; (*treat*: *people*) manejar; **"~ with care"** "(manéjese) con cuidado"; **to fly off the ~** perder los estribos
handlebar ['hændlbɑ:^r] *n*, **handlebars** ['hændlbɑ:z] *npl* manillar *msg*
hand luggage *n* equipaje *m* de mano
handmade ['hændmeɪd] *adj* hecho a mano
handout ['hændaut] *n* (*distribution*) repartición *f*; (*charity*) limosna; (*leaflet*) folleto, octavilla; (*press handout*) nota
handrail ['hændreɪl] *n* (*on staircase etc*) pasamanos *m inv*, barandilla
handset ['hændsɛt] *n* (*Tel*) auricular *m*
hands-free ['hændzfri:] *adj* (*Tel*: *telephone*) manos libres; **~ kit** manos libres *m inv*
handshake ['hændʃeɪk] *n* apretón *m* de manos; (*Comput*) coloquio
handsome ['hænsəm] *adj* guapo
hands-on ['hændz'ɔn] *adj* práctico; **she has a very ~ approach** le gusta tomar parte

activa; ~ **experience** (*Comput*) experiencia práctica

handstand ['hændstænd] *n* voltereta, salto mortal

handwriting ['hændraɪtɪŋ] *n* letra

handwritten ['hændrɪtn] *adj* escrito a mano, manuscrito

handy ['hændɪ] *adj* (*close at hand*) a mano; (*useful*: *machine, tool etc*) práctico; (*skilful*) hábil, diestro; **to come in ~** venir bien

handyman ['hændɪmæn] *n* manitas *m inv*

hang (*pt, pp* **hung**) [hæŋ, hʌŋ] *vt* colgar; (*head*) bajar; (*criminal*: *pt, pp* **hanged**) ahorcar; **to get the ~ of sth** (*inf*) coger el tranquillo a algo; **hang about** *or* **around** *vi* haraganear; **hang back** *vi* (*hesitate*): **to ~ back (from doing)** vacilar (en hacer); **hang down** *vi* colgar, pender; **hang on** *vi* (*wait*) esperar ▷ *vt fus* (*depend on*: *decision etc*) depender de; **to ~ on to** (*keep*) guardar, quedarse con; **hang out** *vt* (*washing*) tender, colgar ▷ *vi* (*inf*: *live*) vivir; (: *often be found*) moverse; **to ~ out of sth** colgar fuera de algo; **hang round** *vi* = **hang around**; **hang together** *vi* (*cohere*: *argument etc*) sostenerse; **hang up** *vt* (*coat*) colgar ▷ *vi* (*Tel*) colgar; **to ~ up on sb** colgarle a algn

hangar ['hæŋəʳ] *n* hangar *m*

hanger ['hæŋəʳ] *n* percha

hanger-on [hæŋər'ɔn] *n* parásito

hang-gliding ['hæŋglaɪdɪŋ] *n* vuelo con ala delta

hanging ['hæŋɪŋ] *n* (*execution*) ejecución *f* (en la horca)

hangover ['hæŋəuvəʳ] *n* (*after drinking*) resaca

hang-up ['hæŋʌp] *n* complejo

hanker ['hæŋkəʳ] *vi*: **to ~ after** (*miss*) echar de menos; (*long for*) añorar

hankie, hanky ['hæŋkɪ] *n abbr* = **handkerchief**

Hansard ['hænsɑ:d] *n actas oficiales de las sesiones del parlamento británico*

haphazard [hæp'hæzəd] *adj* fortuito

happen ['hæpən] *vi* suceder, ocurrir; (*take place*) tener lugar, realizarse; (*chance*): **he ~ed to hear/see** dió la casualidad de que oyó/vió; **as it ~s** da la casualidad de que; **what's ~ing?** ¿qué pasa?; **happen (up)on** *vt fus* tropezar *or* dar con

happening ['hæpnɪŋ] *n* suceso, acontecimiento

happily ['hæpɪlɪ] *adv* (*luckily*) afortunadamente; (*cheerfully*) alegremente

happiness ['hæpɪnɪs] *n* (*contentment*) felicidad *f*; (*joy*) alegría

happy ['hæpɪ] *adj* feliz; (*cheerful*) alegre; **to be ~ (with)** estar contento (con); **yes, I'd be ~ to** sí, con mucho gusto; **H~ Christmas!** ¡Feliz Navidad!; **H~ New Year!** ¡Feliz Año Nuevo!; **~ birthday!** ¡feliz cumpleaños!

happy-go-lucky ['hæpɪgəu'lʌkɪ] *adj* despreocupado

happy hour *n horas en las que la bebida es más barata en un bar*

harass ['hærəs] *vt* acosar, hostigar

harassed ['hærəst] *adj* agobiado, presionado

harassment ['hærəsmənt] *n* persecución *f*, acoso; (*worry*) preocupación *f*

harbour, harbor (*US*) ['hɑ:bəʳ] *n* puerto ▷ *vt* (*fugitive*) dar abrigo a; (*hope etc*) abrigar; (*hide*) dar abrigo a; (*retain*: *grudge etc*) guardar

hard [hɑ:d] *adj* duro; (*difficult*) difícil; (*work*) arduo; (*person*) severo ▷ *adv* (*work*) mucho, duro; (*think*) profundamente; **to look ~ at sb/sth** clavar los ojos en algn/algo; **to try ~** esforzarse; **no ~ feelings!** ¡sin rencor(es)!; **to be ~ of hearing** ser duro de oído; **to be ~ done by** ser tratado injustamente; **to be ~ on sb** ser muy duro con algn; **I find it ~ to believe that ...** me cuesta trabajo creer que ...

hardback ['hɑ:dbæk] *n* libro de tapa dura

hardboard ['hɑ:dbɔ:d] *n* aglomerado *m* (*de madera*)

hard cash *n* dinero en efectivo

hard copy *n* (*Comput*) copia impresa

hard-core ['hɑ:d'kɔ:ʳ] *adj* (*pornography*) duro; (*supporters*) incondicional

hard disk *n* (*Comput*) disco duro

harden ['hɑ:dn] *vt* endurecer; (*steel*) templar; (*fig*) curtir; (: *determination*) fortalecer ▷ *vi* (*substance*) endurecerse; (*fig*) curtirse

hard-headed ['hɑ:d'hɛdɪd] *adj* poco sentimental, realista

hard-hitting ['hɑ:d'hɪtɪŋ] *adj* (*speech, article*) contundente

hard labour *n* trabajos *mpl* forzados

hardly ['hɑ:dlɪ] *adv* (*scarcely*) apenas; **that can ~ be true** eso difícilmente puede ser cierto; **~ ever** casi nunca; **I can ~ believe it** apenas me lo puedo creer

hard sell *n* publicidad *f* agresiva; **~ techniques** técnicas *fpl* agresivas de venta

hardship ['hɑ:dʃɪp] *n* (*troubles*) penas *fpl*; (*financial*) apuro

hard shoulder *n* (*Aut*) arcén *m*

hard-up [hɑ:d'ʌp] *adj* (*inf*) sin un duro (*Sp*), sin plata (*LAm*)

hardware ['hɑ:dwɛəʳ] *n* ferretería; (*Comput*) hardware *m*

hardware shop, hardware store (*US*) *n* ferretería

hard-wearing [hɑ:d'wɛərɪŋ] *adj* resistente, duradero; (*shoes*) resistente

hard-won ['hɑ:d'wʌn] *adj* ganado con esfuerzo

hard-working [hɑ:d'wə:kɪŋ] *adj* trabajador(a)

hardy ['hɑ:dɪ] *adj* fuerte; (*plant*) resistente

hare [hɛəʳ] *n* liebre *f*

hare-brained ['hɛəbreɪnd] *adj* atolondrado

harem [hɑ:'ri:m] *n* harén *m*

hark back [hɑ:k-] *vi*: **to ~ to** (*former days, earlier occasion*) recordar

harm [hɑːm] *n* daño, mal *m* ▷ *vt* (*person*) hacer daño a; (*health, interests*) perjudicar; (*thing*) dañar; **out of ~'s way** a salvo; **there's no ~ in trying** no se pierde nada con intentar
harmful [ˈhɑːmful] *adj* (*gen*) dañino; (*reputation*) perjudicial
harmless [ˈhɑːmlɪs] *adj* (*person*) inofensivo; (*drug*) inocuo; (*joke etc*) inocente
harmonica [hɑːˈmɔnɪkə] *n* armónica
harmonize [ˈhɑːmənaɪz] *vt, vi* armonizar
harmony [ˈhɑːmənɪ] *n* armonía
harness [ˈhɑːnɪs] *n* arreos *mpl* ▷ *vt* (*horse*) enjaezar; (*resources*) aprovechar
harp [hɑːp] *n* arpa ▷ *vi*: **to ~ on (about)** machacar (con)
harpoon [hɑːˈpuːn] *n* arpón *m*
harrowing [ˈhærəuɪŋ] *adj* angustioso
harsh [hɑːʃ] *adj* (*cruel*) duro, cruel; (*severe*) severo; (*words*) hosco; (*colour*) chillón(-ona); (*contrast*) violento
harvest [ˈhɑːvɪst] *n* (*harvest time*) siega; (*of cereals etc*) cosecha; (*of grapes*) vendimia ▷ *vt, vi* cosechar
has [hæz] *vb see* **have**
has-been [ˈhæzbiːn] *n* (*inf*: *person*) persona acabada; (: *thing*) vieja gloria
hash [hæʃ] *n* (*Culin*) picadillo; (*fig: mess*) lío
hashish [ˈhæʃɪʃ] *n* hachís *m*
hashtag [ˈhæʃtæg] *n* (*on Twitter*) hashtag m, etiqueta
hasn't [ˈhæznt] = **has not**
hassle [ˈhæsl] *n* (*inf*) lío, rollo ▷ *vt* incordiar
haste [heɪst] *n* prisa
hasten [ˈheɪsn] *vt* acelerar ▷ *vi* darse prisa; **I ~ to add that ...** me apresuro a añadir que ...
hastily [ˈheɪstɪlɪ] *adv* de prisa
hasty [ˈheɪstɪ] *adj* apresurado
hat [hæt] *n* sombrero
hatch [hætʃ] *n* (*Naut*: *also*: **~way**) escotilla ▷ *vi* salir del cascarón ▷ *vt* incubar; (*fig: scheme, plot*) idear, tramar; **5 eggs have ~ed** han salido 5 pollos
hatchback [ˈhætʃbæk] *n* (*Aut*) tres *or* cinco puertas *m*
hatchet [ˈhætʃɪt] *n* hacha
hate [heɪt] *vt* odiar, aborrecer ▷ *n* odio; **I ~ to trouble you, but ...** siento *or* lamento molestarle, pero ...
hateful [ˈheɪtful] *adj* odioso
hatred [ˈheɪtrɪd] *n* odio
hat trick *n*: **to score a ~** (*Brit Sport*) marcar tres tantos (*or* triunfos) seguidos
haughty [ˈhɔːtɪ] *adj* altanero, arrogante
haul [hɔːl] *vt* tirar, jalar (*LAm*); (*by lorry*) transportar ▷ *n* (*of fish*) redada; (*of stolen goods etc*) botín *m*
haulage [ˈhɔːlɪdʒ] *n* (*Brit*) transporte *m*; (*costs*) gastos *mpl* de transporte
haulier [ˈhɔːlɪə^r], **hauler** (*US*) [ˈhɔːlə^r] *n* transportista *m/f*
haunch [hɔːntʃ] *n* anca; (*of meat*) pierna
haunt [hɔːnt] *vt* (*ghost*) aparecer en; (*frequent*) frecuentar; (*obsess*) obsesionar ▷ *n* guarida
haunted [ˈhɔːntɪd] *adj* (*castle etc*) embrujado; (*look*) de angustia
Havana [həˈvɑːnə] *n* La Habana

KEYWORD

have [haev] (*pt, pp* **had**) *aux vb* **1** (*gen*) haber; **to have arrived/eaten** haber llegado/comido; **having finished** *or* **when he had finished, he left** cuando hubo acabado, se fue
2 (*in tag questions*): **you've done it, haven't you?** lo has hecho, ¿verdad? *or* ¿no?
3 (*in short answers and questions*): **I haven't** no; **so I have** pues, es verdad; **we haven't paid — yes we have!** no hemos pagado — ¡sí que hemos pagado!; **I've been there before, have you?** he estado allí antes, ¿y tú?
▷ *modal aux vb* (*be obliged*): **to have (got) to do sth** tener que hacer algo; **you haven't to tell her** no hay que *or* no debes decírselo
▷ *vt* **1** (*possess*) tener; **he has (got) blue eyes/dark hair** tiene los ojos azules/el pelo negro
2 (*referring to meals etc*): **to have breakfast/lunch/dinner** desayunar/comer/cenar; **to have a drink/a cigarette** tomar algo/fumar un cigarrillo
3 (*receive*) recibir; (*obtain*) obtener; **may I have your address?** ¿puedes darme tu dirección?; **you can have it for £5** te lo puedes quedar por £5; **I must have it by tomorrow** lo necesito para mañana; **to have a baby** tener un niño *or* bebé
4 (*maintain, allow*): **I won't have it!** ¡no lo permitiré!; **I won't have this nonsense!** ¡no permitiré estas tonterías!; **we can't have that** no podemos permitir eso
5: **to have sth done** hacer *or* mandar hacer algo; **to have one's hair cut** cortarse el pelo; **to have sb do sth** hacer que algn haga algo
6 (*experience, suffer*): **to have a cold/flu** tener un resfriado/la gripe; **she had her bag stolen/her arm broken** le robaron el bolso/se rompió un brazo; **to have an operation** operarse
7 (*+ noun*): **to have a swim/walk/bath/rest** nadar/dar un paseo/darse un baño/descansar; **let's have a look** vamos a ver; **to have a meeting/party** celebrar una reunión/una fiesta; **let me have a try** déjame intentarlo
have in *vt*: **to have it in for sb** (*inf*) tenerla tomada con algn
have on *vt*: **have you anything on tomorrow?** ¿vas a hacer algo mañana?; **I don't have any money on me** no llevo dinero (encima); **to have sb on** (*Brit*: (*inf*)) tomarle el pelo a algn
have out *vt*: **to have it out with sb** (*settle a problem etc*) dejar las cosas en claro con algn

haven [ˈheɪvn] *n* puerto; (*fig*) refugio

haven't ['hævnt] = **have not**
havoc ['hævək] *n* estragos *mpl*; **to play ~ with sth** hacer estragos en algo
Hawaii [hə'waii:] *n* (Islas *fpl*) Hawai *m*
hawk [hɔ:k] *n* halcón *m* ▷ *vt* (*goods for sale*) pregonar
hawthorn ['hɔ:θɔ:n] *n* espino
hay [heɪ] *n* heno
hay fever *n* fiebre *f* del heno
haystack ['heɪstæk] *n* almiar *m*
haywire ['heɪwaɪə^r] *adj* (*inf*): **to go ~** (*person*) volverse loco; (*plan*) irse al garete
hazard ['hæzəd] *n* riesgo; (*danger*) peligro ▷ *vt* (*remark*) aventurar; (*one's life*) arriesgar; **to be a health ~** ser un peligro para la salud; **to ~ a guess** aventurar una respuesta *or* hipótesis
hazardous ['hæzədəs] *adj* (*dangerous*) peligroso; (*risky*) arriesgado
hazard warning lights *npl* (*Aut*) señales *fpl* de emergencia
haze [heɪz] *n* neblina
hazel ['heɪzl] *n* (*tree*) avellano ▷ *adj* (*eyes*) color *m* de avellano
hazelnut ['heɪzlnʌt] *n* avellana
hazy ['heɪzɪ] *adj* brumoso; (*idea*) vago
h & c *abbr* (*Brit*) = **hot and cold (water)**
he [hi:] *pron* él; **he who ...** aquél que ..., quien ...
head [hɛd] *n* cabeza; (*leader*) jefe(-a) *m(f)* ▷ *vt* (*list*) encabezar; (*group*) capitanear; **~s (or tails)** cara (o cruz); **~ first** de cabeza; **~ over heels** patas arriba; **~ over heels in love** perdidamente enamorado; **on your ~ be it!** ¡allá tú!; **they went over my ~ to the manager** fueron directamente al gerente sin hacerme caso; **it was above** *or* **over their ~s** no alcanzaron a entenderlo; **to come to a ~** (*fig: situation etc*) llegar a un punto crítico; **to have a ~ for business** tener talento para los negocios; **to have no ~ for heights** no resistir las alturas; **to lose/keep one's ~** perder la cabeza/mantener la calma; **to sit at the ~ of the table** sentarse a la cabecera de la mesa; **to ~ the ball** cabecear (el balón); **head for** *vt fus* dirigirse a; (*disaster*) ir camino de; **head off** *vt* (*threat, danger*) evitar
headache ['hɛdeɪk] *n* dolor *m* de cabeza; **to have a ~** tener dolor de cabeza
headband ['hɛdbænd] *n* cinta (para la cabeza), vincha (*LAm*)
headdress ['hɛddrɛs] *n* (*of bride, Indian*) tocado
header ['hɛdə^r] *n* (*Brit inf: Football*) cabezazo; (*: fall*) caída de cabeza
headhunt ['hɛdhʌnt] *vt*: **to be ~ed** ser seleccionado por un cazatalentos
heading ['hɛdɪŋ] *n* título
headlamp ['hɛdlæmp] *n* (*Brit*) = **headlight**
headland ['hɛdlənd] *n* promontorio
headlight ['hɛdlaɪt] *n* faro
headline ['hɛdlaɪn] *n* titular *m*
headlong ['hɛdlɔŋ] *adv* (*fall*) de cabeza; (*rush*) precipitadamente
head office *n* oficina central, central *f*
head-on [hɛd'ɔn] *adj* (*collision*) de frente
headphones ['hɛdfəunz] *npl* auriculares *mpl*
headquarters ['hɛdkwɔ:təz] *npl* sede *f* central; (*Mil*) cuartel *m* general
head-rest ['hɛdrɛst] *n* reposa-cabezas *m inv*
headroom ['hɛdrum] *n* (*in car*) altura interior; (*under bridge*) (límite *m* de) altura
headscarf ['hɛdskɑ:f] *n* pañuelo
headset ['hɛdsɛt] *n* cascos *mpl*
headstrong ['hɛdstrɔŋ] *adj* testarudo
head teacher *n* director(a)
head waiter *n* maître *m*
headway ['hɛdweɪ] *n*: **to make ~** (*fig*) hacer progresos
headwind ['hɛdwɪnd] *n* viento contrario
heady ['hɛdɪ] *adj* (*experience, period*) apasionante; (*wine*) fuerte
heal [hi:l] *vt* curar ▷ *vi* cicatrizar
health [hɛlθ] *n* salud *f*
health care *n* asistencia sanitaria
health centre *n* ambulatorio, centro médico
health food *n*, **health foods** *npl* alimentos *mpl* orgánicos
health hazard *n* riesgo para la salud
Health Service *n* (*Brit*) servicio de salud pública, ≈ Insalud *m* (*Sp*)
healthy ['hɛlθɪ] *adj* (*gen*) sano; (*economy, bank balance*) saludable
heap [hi:p] *n* montón *m* ▷ *vt* amontonar; (*plate*) colmar; **~s of** (*inf: lots*) montones de; **to ~ favours/praise/gifts** *etc* **on sb** colmar a algn de favores/elogios/regalos *etc*
hear (*pt, pp* **heard**) [hɪə^r, hə:d] *vt* oír; (*perceive*) sentir; (*listen to*) escuchar; (*lecture*) asistir a; (*Law: case*) ver ▷ *vi* oír; **to ~ about** oír hablar de; **to ~ from sb** tener noticias de algn; **I've never ~d of that book** nunca he oído hablar de ese libro; **hear out** *vt*: **to ~ sb out** dejar que algn termine de hablar
heard [hə:d] *pt, pp of* **hear**
hearing ['hɪərɪŋ] *n* (*sense*) oído; (*Law*) vista; **to give sb a ~** dar a algn la oportunidad de hablar, escuchar a algn
hearing aid *n* audífono
hearsay ['hɪəseɪ] *n* rumores *mpl*, habladurías *fpl*
hearse [hə:s] *n* coche *m* fúnebre
heart [hɑ:t] *n* corazón *m*; (*fig*) valor *m*; (*of lettuce*) cogollo; **hearts** *npl* (*Cards*) corazones *mpl*; **at ~** en el fondo; **by ~** (*learn, know*) de memoria; **to have a weak ~** tener el corazón débil; **to set one's ~ on sth/on doing sth** anhelar algo/hacer algo; **I did not have the ~ to tell her** no tuve valor para decírselo; **to take ~** cobrar ánimos; **the ~ of the matter** lo esencial *or* el meollo del asunto
heartache ['hɑ:teɪk] *n* angustia
heart attack *n* infarto (de miocardio)
heartbeat ['hɑ:tbi:t] *n* latido (del corazón)
heartbreak ['hɑ:tbreɪk] *n* angustia, congoja

heartbreaking ['hɑ:tbreɪkɪŋ] *adj* desgarrador(a)
heartbroken ['hɑ:tbrəukən] *adj*: **she was ~ about it** eso le partió el corazón
heartburn ['hɑ:tbə:n] *n* acedía
heart disease *n* enfermedad *f* cardíaca
heartfelt ['hɑ:tfɛlt] *adj* (*cordial*) cordial; (*deeply felt*) sincero
hearth [hɑ:θ] *n* (*gen*) hogar *m*; (*fireplace*) chimenea
heartily ['hɑ:tɪlɪ] *adv* sinceramente, cordialmente; (*laugh*) a carcajadas; (*eat*) con buen apetito; **to be ~ sick of** estar completamente harto de
heartland ['hɑ:tlænd] *n* zona interior *or* central; (*fig*) corazón *m*
heartless ['hɑ:tlɪs] *adj* despiadado
heart-to-heart ['hɑ:ttə'hɑ:t] *n* (*also*: **~ talk**) conversación *f* íntima
heart transplant *n* transplante *m* de corazón
hearty ['hɑ:tɪ] *adj* (*person*) campechano; (*laugh*) sano; (*dislike, support*) absoluto
heat [hi:t] *n* (*gen*) calor *m*; (*Sport*: *also*: **qualifying ~**) prueba eliminatoria; (*Zool*): **in** *or* **on ~** en celo ▷ *vt* calentar; **heat up** *vi* (*gen*) calentarse ▷ *vt* calentar
heated ['hi:tɪd] *adj* caliente; (*fig*) acalorado
heater ['hi:təʳ] *n* calentador *m*, estufa
heath [hi:θ] *n* (*Brit*) brezal *m*
heather ['hɛðəʳ] *n* brezo
heating ['hi:tɪŋ] *n* calefacción *f*
heatstroke ['hi:tstrəuk] *n* insolación *f*
heatwave ['hi:tweɪv] *n* ola de calor
heave [hi:v] *vt* (*pull*) tirar; (*push*) empujar con esfuerzo; (*lift*) levantar (con esfuerzo) ▷ *vi* (*water*) subir y bajar ▷ *n* tirón *m*; empujón *m*; (*effort*) esfuerzo; (*throw*) echada; **to ~ a sigh** dar *or* echar un suspiro, suspirar; **heave to** *vi* (*Naut*) ponerse al pairo
heaven ['hɛvn] *n* cielo; (*Rel*) paraíso; **thank ~!** ¡gracias a Dios!; **for ~'s sake!** (*pleading*) ¡por el amor de Dios!, ¡por lo que más quiera!; (*protesting*) ¡por Dios!
heavenly ['hɛvnlɪ] *adj* celestial; (*Rel*) divino
heavily ['hɛvɪlɪ] *adv* pesadamente; (*drink, smoke*) en exceso; (*sleep, sigh*) profundamente
heavy ['hɛvɪ] *adj* pesado; (*work*) duro; (*sea, rain, meal*) fuerte; (*drinker, smoker*) empedernido; (*eater*) comilón(-ona); (*responsibility*) grave; (*schedule*) ocupado; (*weather*) bochornoso
heavy goods vehicle *n* (*Brit*) vehículo pesado
heavyweight ['hɛvɪweɪt] *n* (*Sport*) peso pesado
Hebrew ['hi:bru:] *adj, n* (*Ling*) hebreo
Hebrides ['hɛbrɪdi:z] *npl*: **the ~** las Hébridas
heck [hɛk] *n* (*inf*): **why the ~ ...?** ¿por qué porras ...?; **a ~ of a lot of** cantidad de
heckle ['hɛkl] *vt* interrumpir
heckler ['hɛkləʳ] *n* *el/la que interrumpe a un orador*
hectare ['hɛktɑ:ʳ] *n* (*Brit*) hectárea
hectic ['hɛktɪk] *adj* agitado; (*busy*) ocupado
he'd [hi:d] = **he would**; **he had**
hedge [hɛdʒ] *n* seto ▷ *vt* cercar (con un seto) ▷ *vi* contestar con evasivas; **as a ~ against inflation** como protección contra la inflación; **to ~ one's bets** (*fig*) cubrirse
hedgehog ['hɛdʒhɔg] *n* erizo
heed [hi:d] *vt* (*also*: **take ~ of**: *pay attention*) hacer caso de; (*bear in mind*) tener en cuenta; **to pay (no) ~ to, take (no) ~ of** (no) hacer caso a, (no) tener en cuenta
heedless ['hi:dlɪs] *adj* desatento
heel [hi:l] *n* talón *m*; (*of shoe*) tacón *m* ▷ *vt* (*shoe*) poner tacón a; **to take to one's ~s** (*inf*) poner pies en polvorosa; **to bring to ~** meter en cintura; *see also* **dig**
hefty ['hɛftɪ] *adj* (*person*) fornido; (*piece*) grande; (*price*) alto
heifer ['hɛfəʳ] *n* novilla, ternera
height [haɪt] *n* (*of person*) talla, estatura; (*of building*) altura; (*high ground*) cerro; (*altitude*) altitud *f*; **what ~ are you?** ¿cuánto mides?; **of average ~** de estatura mediana; **to be afraid of ~s** tener miedo a las alturas; **at the ~ of summer** en los días más calurosos del verano; **it's the ~ of fashion** es el último grito en moda
heighten ['haɪtn] *vt* elevar; (*fig*) aumentar
heir [ɛəʳ] *n* heredero
heiress ['ɛərɛs] *n* heredera
heirloom ['ɛəlu:m] *n* reliquia de familia
held [hɛld] *pt, pp of* **hold**
helicopter ['hɛlɪkɔptəʳ] *n* helicóptero
helium ['hi:lɪəm] *n* helio
hell [hɛl] *n* infierno; **oh ~!** (*inf*) ¡demonios!, ¡caramba!
he'll [hi:l] = **he will**; **he shall**
hellish ['hɛlɪʃ] *adj* infernal; (*inf*) horrible
hello [hə'ləu] *excl* ¡hola!; (*to attract attention*) ¡oiga!; (*surprise*) ¡caramba!; (*Tel*) ¡dígame! (*esp Sp*), ¡aló! (*LAm*)
helm [hɛlm] *n* (*Naut*) timón *m*
helmet ['hɛlmɪt] *n* casco
help [hɛlp] *n* ayuda; (*cleaner etc*) criada, asistenta ▷ *vt* ayudar; **~!** ¡socorro!; **with the ~ of** con la ayuda de; **can I ~ you?** (*in shop*) ¿qué desea?; **to be of ~ to sb** servir a algn; **to ~ sb (to) do sth** echarle una mano *or* ayudar a algn a hacer algo; **~ yourself** sírvete; **he can't ~ it** no lo puede evitar; **help out** *vi* ayudar, echar una mano ▷ *vt*: **to ~ sb out** ayudar a algn, echar una mano a algn
helper ['hɛlpəʳ] *n* ayudante *m/f*
helpful ['hɛlpful] *adj* útil; (*person*) servicial
helping ['hɛlpɪŋ] *n* ración *f*
helping hand *n*: **to give sb a ~** echar una mano a algn
helpless ['hɛlplɪs] *adj* (*incapable*) incapaz; (*defenceless*) indefenso
helpline ['hɛlplaɪn] *n* teléfono de asistencia al público

hem [hɛm] *n* dobladillo ▷ *vt* poner *or* coser el dobladillo a; **hem in** *vt* cercar; **to feel ~med in** (*fig*) sentirse acosado
hematology [hi:mə'tɔlədʒɪ] *n* (*US*) = **haematology**
hemisphere ['hɛmɪsfɪə^r] *n* hemisferio
hemophilia [hi:mə'fɪlɪə] *n* (*US*) = **haemophilia**
hemorrhage ['hɛmərɪdʒ] *n* (*US*) = **haemorrhage**
hemorrhoids ['hɛmərɔɪdz] *npl* (*US*) = **haemorrhoids**
hen [hɛn] *n* gallina; (*female bird*) hembra
hence [hɛns] *adv* (*therefore*) por lo tanto; **two years ~** de aquí a dos años
henceforth [hɛns'fɔ:θ] *adv* de hoy en adelante
henchman ['hɛntʃmən] *n* (*pej*) secuaz *m*
hen night *n* (*inf*) despedida de soltera
hepatitis [hɛpə'taɪtɪs] *n* hepatitis *f inv*
her [hə:^r] *pron* (*direct*) la; (*indirect*) le; (*stressed, after prep*) ella ▷ *adj* su; *see also* **me, my**
herald ['hɛrəld] *n* (*forerunner*) precursor(a) *m(f)* ▷ *vt* anunciar
heraldry ['hɛrəldrɪ] *n* heráldica
herb [hə:b] *n* hierba
herbal ['hə:bl] *adj* de hierbas
herbal tea *n* infusión *f* de hierbas
herbicide ['hə:bɪsaɪd] *n* herbicida *m*
herd [hə:d] *n* rebaño; (*of wild animals, swine*) piara ▷ *vt* (*drive, gather: animals*) llevar en manada; (*: people*) reunir; **herd together** *vt* agrupar, reunir ▷ *vi* apiñarse, agruparse
here [hɪə^r] *adv* aquí; **~!** (*present*) ¡presente!; **~ is/are** aquí está/están; **~ she is** aquí está; **come ~!** ¡ven aquí *or* acá!; **~ and there** aquí y allá
hereafter [hɪər'ɑ:ftə^r] *adv* en el futuro ▷ *n*: **the ~** el más allá
hereby [hɪə'baɪ] *adv* (*in letter*) por la presente
hereditary [hɪ'rɛdɪtrɪ] *adj* hereditario
heresy ['hɛrəsɪ] *n* herejía
heretic ['hɛrətɪk] *n* hereje *m/f*
heritage ['hɛrɪtɪdʒ] *n* (*gen*) herencia; (*fig*) patrimonio; **our national ~** nuestro patrimonio nacional
hermit ['hə:mɪt] *n* ermitaño(-a)
hernia ['hə:nɪə] *n* hernia
hero (*pl* **heroes**) ['hɪərəu] *n* héroe *m*; (*in book, film*) protagonista *m*
heroic [hɪ'rəuɪk] *adj* heroico
heroin ['hɛrəuɪn] *n* heroína
heroine ['hɛrəuɪn] *n* heroína; (*in book, film*) protagonista
heron ['hɛrən] *n* garza
herring ['hɛrɪŋ] *n* arenque *m*
hers [hə:z] *pron* (el) suyo/(la) suya *etc*; **a friend of ~** un amigo suyo; **this is ~** esto es suyo *or* de ella; *see also* **mine**
herself [hə:'sɛlf] *pron* (*reflexive*) se; (*emphatic*) ella misma; (*after prep*) sí (misma); *see also* **oneself**
he's [hi:z] = **he is**; **he has**
hesitant ['hɛzɪtənt] *adj* indeciso; **to be ~ about doing sth** no decidirse a hacer algo
hesitate ['hɛzɪteɪt] *vi* dudar, vacilar; (*in speech*) titubear; (*be unwilling*) resistirse a; **don't ~ to ask (me)** no dudes en pedírmelo
hesitation [hɛzɪ'teɪʃən] *n* indecisión *f*; **I have no ~ in saying (that) ...** no tengo el menor reparo en afirmar que ...
heterosexual [hɛtərəu'sɛksjuəl] *adj, n* heterosexual *m/f*
het up [hɛt'ʌp] *adj* (*inf*) agitado, nervioso
hew [hju:] *vt* cortar
hexagon ['hɛksəgən] *n* hexágono
hey [heɪ] *excl* ¡oye!, ¡oiga!
heyday ['heɪdeɪ] *n*: **the ~ of** el apogeo de
HGV *n abbr* = **heavy goods vehicle**
hi [haɪ] *excl* ¡hola!
hiatus [haɪ'eɪtəs] *n* vacío, interrupción *f*; (*Ling*) hiato
hibernate ['haɪbəneɪt] *vi* invernar
hibernation [haɪbə'neɪʃən] *n* hibernación *f*
hiccough, hiccup ['hɪkʌp] *vi* hipar; **hiccoughs** *npl* hipo *sg*
hid [hɪd] *pt of* **hide**
hidden ['hɪdn] *pp of* **hide** ▷ *adj*: **there are no ~ extras** no hay suplementos ocultos; **~ agenda** plan *m* encubierto
hide [haɪd] (*pt* **hid**, *pp* **hidden**) *n* (*skin*) piel *f* ▷ *vt* esconder, ocultar; (*feelings, truth*) encubrir, ocultar ▷ *vi*: **to ~ (from sb)** esconderse *or* ocultarse (de algn)
hide-and-seek ['haɪdən'si:k] *n* escondite *m*
hideaway ['haɪdəweɪ] *n* escondite *m*
hideous ['hɪdɪəs] *adj* horrible
hiding ['haɪdɪŋ] *n* (*beating*) paliza; **to be in ~** (*concealed*) estar escondido
hierarchy ['haɪərɑ:kɪ] *n* jerarquía
hi-fi ['haɪfaɪ] *abbr* = **high fidelity** ▷ *n* estéreo, hifi *m* ▷ *adj* de alta fidelidad
high [haɪ] *adj* alto; (*speed, number*) grande, alto; (*price*) elevado; (*wind*) fuerte; (*voice*) agudo; (*inf: on drugs*) colocado; (*: on drink*) borracho; (*Culin: meat, game*) pasado; (*: spoilt*) estropeado ▷ *adv* alto, a gran altura ▷ *n*: **exports have reached a new ~** las exportaciones han alcanzado niveles inusitados; **it is 20 m ~** tiene 20 m de altura; **~ in the air** en las alturas; **to pay a ~ price for sth** pagar algo muy caro
highbrow ['haɪbrau] *adj* culto
highchair ['haɪtʃɛə^r] *n* silla alta (para niños)
high-class ['haɪ'klɑ:s] *adj* (*neighbourhood*) de alta sociedad; (*hotel*) de lujo; (*person*) distinguido, de categoría; (*food*) de alta categoría
High Court *n* (*Law*) tribunal *m* supremo; *ver nota*
higher ['haɪə^r] *adj* (*form of life, study etc*) superior ▷ *adv* más alto ▷ *n* (*Scottish Scol*): ***H~** cada una de las asignaturas que se estudian entre los 16 y los 17 años generalmente, así como el certificado de haberlas probado*

h

higher education *n* educación *f or* enseñanza superior
high-flier, high-flyer [haɪˈflaɪəʳ] *n* ambicioso(-a)
high-handed [haɪˈhændɪd] *adj* despótico
high heels *npl* (*heels*) tacones *mpl* altos; (*shoes*) zapatos *mpl* de tacón
highjack [ˈhaɪdʒæk] *vb, n* = **hijack**
high jump *n* (*Sport*) salto de altura
highlands [ˈhaɪləndz] *npl* tierras *fpl* altas; **the H~** (*in Scotland*) las Tierras Altas de Escocia
highlight [ˈhaɪlaɪt] *n* (*fig*: *of event*) punto culminante ▷ *vt* subrayar; **highlights** *npl* (*in hair*) reflejos *mpl*
highlighter *n* rotulador
highly [ˈhaɪlɪ] *adv* sumamente; **~ paid** muy bien pagado; **to speak ~ of** hablar muy bien de; **~ strung** muy excitable
highness [ˈhaɪnɪs] *n* altura; **Her** *or* **His H~** Su Alteza
high-pitched [haɪˈpɪtʃt] *adj* agudo
high-rise [ˈhaɪraɪz] *n* (*also*: **~ block, ~ building**) torre *f* de pisos
high school *n* centro de enseñanza secundaria, ≈ Instituto Nacional de Bachillerato (*Sp*), liceo (*LAm*)
high season *n* (*Brit*) temporada alta
high street *n* (*Brit*) calle *f* mayor
high-tech (*inf*) *adj* al-tec (*fam*), de alta tecnología
high tide *n* marea alta
highway [ˈhaɪweɪ] *n* carretera; (*US*) autopista
Highway Code *n* (*Brit*) código de la circulación
hijack [ˈhaɪdʒæk] *vt* secuestrar ▷ *n* (*also*: **~ing**) secuestro
hijacker [ˈhaɪdʒækəʳ] *n* secuestrador(a) *m(f)*
hike [haɪk] *vi* (*go walking*) ir de excursión (a pie); (*tramp*) caminar ▷ *n* caminata; (*inf*: *in prices etc*) aumento; **hike up** *vt* (*raise*) aumentar
hiker [ˈhaɪkəʳ] *n* excursionista *m/f*
hiking [ˈhaɪkɪŋ] *n* senderismo
hilarious [hɪˈlɛərɪəs] *adj* divertidísimo
hill [hɪl] *n* colina; (*high*) montaña; (*slope*) cuesta
hillside [ˈhɪlsaɪd] *n* ladera
hilltop [ˈhɪltɔp] *n* cumbre *f*
hill walking *n* senderismo (de montaña)
hilly [ˈhɪlɪ] *adj* montañoso; (*uneven*) accidentado
hilt [hɪlt] *n* (*of sword*) empuñadura; **to the ~** (*fig*: *support*) incondicionalmente; **to be in debt up to the ~** estar hasta el cuello de deudas
him [hɪm] *pron* (*direct*) le, lo; (*indirect*) le; (*stressed, after prep*) él; *see also* **me**
Himalayas [hɪməˈleɪəz] *npl*: **the ~** el Himalaya
himself [hɪmˈsɛlf] *pron* (*reflexive*) se; (*emphatic*) él mismo; (*after prep*) sí (mismo); *see also* **oneself**
hind [haɪnd] *adj* posterior ▷ *n* cierva
hinder [ˈhɪndəʳ] *vt* estorbar, impedir
hindrance [ˈhɪndrəns] *n* estorbo, obstáculo
hindsight [ˈhaɪndsaɪt] *n* percepción *f* tardía *or* retrospectiva; **with ~** en retrospectiva; **with the benefit of ~** con la perspectiva del tiempo transcurrido
Hindu [ˈhɪndu:] *n* hindú *m/f*
Hinduism [ˈhɪndu:ɪzm] *n* (*Rel*) hinduismo
hinge [hɪndʒ] *n* bisagra, gozne *m* ▷ *vi* (*fig*): **to ~ on** depender de
hint [hɪnt] *n* indirecta; (*advice*) consejo ▷ *vt*: **to ~ that** insinuar que ▷ *vi*: **to ~ at** aludir a; **to drop a ~** soltar *or* tirar una indirecta; **give me a ~** dame una pista
hip [hɪp] *n* cadera; (*Bot*) escaramujo
hippie [ˈhɪpɪ] *n* hippie *m/f*, jipi *m/f*
hippo [ˈhɪpəu] (*pl* **hippos**) *n* hipopótamo
hippopotamus (*pl* **hippopotamuses** *or* **hippopotami**) [hɪpəˈpɔtəməs, -ˈpɔtəmaɪ] *n* hipopótamo
hippy [ˈhɪpɪ] *n* = **hippie**
hire [ˈhaɪəʳ] *vt* (*Brit*: *car, equipment*) alquilar; (*worker*) contratar ▷ *n* alquiler *m*; **for ~** se alquila; (*taxi*) libre; **on ~** de alquiler; **hire out** *vt* alquilar, arrendar
hire car, hired car *n* (*Brit*) coche *m* de alquiler
hire purchase *n* (*Brit*) compra a plazos; **to buy sth on ~** comprar algo a plazos
his [hɪz] *pron* (el) suyo/(la) suya *etc* ▷ *adj* su; **this is ~** esto es suyo *or* de él; *see also* **my**; **mine**
Hispanic [hɪsˈpænɪk] *adj* hispánico
hiss [hɪs] *vi* sisear; (*in protest*) silbar ▷ *n* siseo; silbido
historian [hɪˈstɔ:rɪən] *n* historiador(a) *m(f)*
historic [hɪˈstɔrɪk], **historical** [hɪˈstɔrɪkl] *adj* histórico
history [ˈhɪstərɪ] *n* historia; **there's a long ~ of that illness in his family** esa enfermedad corre en su familia
hit [hɪt] *vt* (*pt, pp* **hit**) (*strike*) golpear, pegar; (*reach*: *target*) alcanzar; (*collide with*: *car*) chocar contra; (*fig*: *affect*) afectar ▷ *n* golpe *m*; (*success*) éxito; (*on website*) visita; (*in web search*) correspondencia; **to ~ the headlines** salir en primera plana; **to ~ the road** (*inf*) largarse; **to ~ it off with sb** llevarse bien con algn; **hit back** *vi* defenderse; (*fig*) devolver golpe por golpe; **hit out at** *vt fus* asestar un golpe a; (*fig*) atacar; **hit (up)on** *vt fus* (*answer*) dar con; (*solution*) hallar, encontrar
hit-and-run driver [ˈhɪtənˈrʌn-] *n conductor que tras atropellar a algn se da a la fuga*
hitch [hɪtʃ] *vt* (*fasten*) atar, amarrar; (*also*: **~ up**) arremangarse ▷ *n* (*difficulty*) problema, pega; **to ~ a lift** hacer autostop; **technical ~** problema *m* técnico; **hitch up** *vt* (*horse, cart*) enganchar, uncir
hitch-hike [ˈhɪtʃhaɪk] *vi* hacer autostop
hitch-hiker [ˈhɪtʃhaɪkəʳ] *n* autostopista *m/f*
hitch-hiking [ˈhɪtʃhaɪkɪŋ] *n* autostop *m*
hi-tech [haɪˈtɛk] *adj* de alta tecnología

hitherto [hɪðə'tu:] *adv* hasta ahora, hasta aquí

hit list *n* lista negra

hitman ['hɪtmæn] *n* asesino a sueldo

HIV *n abbr* (= *human immunodeficiency virus*) VIH *m*; **~-negative** VIH negativo; **~-positive** VIH positivo, seropositivo

hive [haɪv] *n* colmena; **the shop was a ~ of activity** (*fig*) la tienda era una colmena humana; **hive off** *vt* (*inf: separate*) separar; (*: privatize*) privatizar

HM *abbr* (= *His* (or *Her*) *Majesty*) S.M.

HMS *abbr* = **His** (*or* **Her**) **Majesty's Ship**

HMSO *n abbr* (*Brit:* = *His* (or *Her*) *Majesty's Stationery Office*) *distribuidor oficial de las publicaciones del gobierno del Reino Unido*

HNC *n abbr* (*Brit:* = *Higher National Certificate*) *título académico*

HND *n abbr* (*Brit:* = *Higher National Diploma*) *título académico*

hoard [hɔ:d] *n* (*treasure*) tesoro; (*stockpile*) provisión *f* ▷ *vt* acumular

hoarding ['hɔ:dɪŋ] *n* (*for posters*) valla publicitaria

hoarse [hɔ:s] *adj* ronco

hoax [həuks] *n* engaño

hob [hɔb] *n* quemador *m*

hobble ['hɔbl] *vi* cojear

hobby ['hɔbɪ] *n* pasatiempo, afición *f*

hobby-horse ['hɔbɪhɔ:s] *n* (*fig*) tema preferido

hobo ['həubəu] *n* (*US*) vagabundo

hockey ['hɔkɪ] *n* hockey *m*

hockey stick *n* palo *m* de hockey

hodge-podge ['hɔdʒpɔdʒ] *n* (*US*) = **hotchpotch**

hog [hɔg] *n* cerdo, puerco ▷ *vt* (*fig*) acaparar; **to go the whole ~** echar el todo por el todo

Hogmanay [hɔgmə'neɪ] *n* (*Scottish*) Nochevieja; *ver nota*

> **HOGMANAY**
>
> La Nochevieja o "New Year's Eve" se conoce como "Hogmanay" en Escocia, donde se festeje de forma especial. La familia y los amigos se suelen juntar para oír las campanadas del reloj y luego se hace el "first-footing", costumbre que consiste en visitar a los amigos y vecinos llevando algo de beber (generalmente whisky) y un trozo de carbón que se supone que traerá buena suerte para el año entrante.

hoist [hɔɪst] *n* (*crane*) grúa ▷ *vt* levantar, alzar

hold [həuld] (*pt, pp* **held**) *vt* sostener; (*contain*) contener; (*have: power, qualification*) tener; (*keep back*) retener; (*believe*) sostener; (*take hold of*) coger (*Sp*), agarrar (*LAm*); (*bear: weight*) soportar; (*meeting*) celebrar ▷ *vi* (*withstand: pressure*) resistir; (*be valid*) ser válido; (*stick*) pegarse ▷ *n* (*grasp*) asimiento; (*fig*) dominio; (*Wrestling*) presa; (*Naut*) bodega; **~ the line!** (*Tel*) ¡no cuelgue!; **to ~ one's own** (*fig*) defenderse; **to ~ office** (*Pol*) ocupar un cargo; **to ~ firm** *or* **fast** mantenerse firme; **he ~s the view that ...** opina *or* es su opinión que ...; **to ~ sb responsible for sth** culpar *or* echarle la culpa a algn de algo; **where can I get ~ of ...?** ¿dónde puedo encontrar (a) ...?; **to catch** *or* **get (a) ~ of** agarrarse *or* asirse de; **hold back** *vt* retener; (*secret*) ocultar; **to ~ sb back from doing sth** impedir a algn hacer algo, impedir que algn haga algo; **hold down** *vt* (*person*) sujetar; (*job*) mantener; **hold forth** *vi* perorar; **hold off** *vt* (*enemy*) rechazar ▷ *vi*: **if the rain ~s off** si no llueve; **hold on** *vi* agarrarse bien; (*wait*) esperar; **~ on!** (*Tel*) ¡(espere) un momento!; **hold on to** *vt fus* agarrarse a; (*keep*) guardar; **hold out** *vt* ofrecer ▷ *vi* (*resist*) resistir; **to ~ out (against)** resistir (a), sobrevivir; **hold over** *vt* (*meeting etc*) aplazar; **hold up** *vt* (*raise*) levantar; (*support*) apoyar; (*delay*) retrasar; (*: traffic*) demorar; (*rob: bank*) asaltar, atracar

holdall ['həuldɔ:l] *n* (*Brit*) bolsa

holder ['həuldə^r] *n* (*of ticket, record*) poseedor(a) *m(f)*; (*of passport, post, office, title etc*) titular *m/f*

holding ['həuldɪŋ] *n* (*share*) participación *f*

holdup ['həuldʌp] *n* (*robbery*) atraco; (*delay*) retraso; (*Brit: in traffic*) embotellamiento

hole [həul] *n* agujero ▷ *vt* agujerear; **~ in the heart** (*Med*) boquete *m* en el corazón; **to pick ~s in** (*fig*) encontrar defectos en; **the ship was ~d** se abrió una vía de agua en el barco; **hole up** *vi* esconderse

holiday ['hɔlədɪ] *n* vacaciones *fpl*; (*day off*) (día *m* de) fiesta, día *m* festivo *or* feriado (*LAm*); **on ~** de vacaciones; **to be on ~** estar de vacaciones

holiday camp *n* colonia *or* centro vacacional; (*for children*) colonia veraniega infantil

holiday job *n* (*Brit*) trabajo para las vacaciones

holidaymaker ['hɔlədɪmeɪkə^r] *n* (*Brit*) turista *m/f*

holiday pay *n* paga de las vacaciones

holiday resort *n* centro turístico

Holland ['hɔlənd] *n* Holanda

holler ['hɔlə^r] *vi* (*inf*) gritar, vocear

hollow ['hɔləu] *adj* hueco; (*fig*) vacío; (*eyes*) hundido; (*sound*) sordo ▷ *n* (*gen*) hueco; (*in ground*) hoyo ▷ *vt*: **to ~ out** ahuecar

holly ['hɔlɪ] *n* acebo

Hollywood ['hɔlɪwud] *n* Hollywood *m*

holocaust ['hɔləkɔ:st] *n* holocausto

hologram ['hɔləgræm] *n* holograma *m*

holster ['həulstə^r] *n* pistolera

holy ['həulɪ] *adj* (*gen*) santo, sagrado; (*water*) bendito; **the H~ Father** el Santo Padre

Holy Communion *n* Sagrada Comunión *f*

Holy Ghost, Holy Spirit *n* Espíritu *m* Santo

homage ['hɔmɪdʒ] *n* homenaje *m*; **to pay ~ to** rendir homenaje a
home [həum] *n* casa; (*country*) patria; (*institution*) asilo; (*Comput*) punto inicial *or* de partida ▹ *adj* (*domestic*) casero, de casa; (*Econ, Pol*) nacional; (*Sport: team*) de casa; (*: match, win*) en casa ▹ *adv* (*direction*) a casa; **at ~** en casa; **to go/come ~** ir/volver a casa; **make yourself at ~** ¡estás en tu casa!; **it's near my ~** está cerca de mi casa; **home in on** *vt fus* (*missile*) dirigirse hacia
home address *n* domicilio
home-brew [həum'bru] *n* cerveza *etc* casera
Home Counties *npl condados que rodean Londres*
home economics *n* economía doméstica
home help *n* (*Brit*) trabajador(a) *m(f)* del servicio de atención domiciliaria
homeland ['həumlænd] *n* tierra natal
homeless ['həumlɪs] *adj* sin hogar, sin casa ▹ *npl*: **the ~** las personas sin hogar
homely ['həumlɪ] *adj* (*domestic*) casero; (*simple*) sencillo
home-made [həum'meɪd] *adj* casero
home match *n* partido en casa
Home Office *n* (*Brit*) Ministerio del Interior
homeopathy *etc* [həumɪ'ɔpəθɪ] (*US*) = **homoeopathy** *etc*
home owner *n* propietario(-a) *m/f* de una casa
home page *n* (*Comput*) página de inicio
home rule *n* autonomía
Home Secretary *n* (*Brit*) Ministro del Interior
homesick ['həumsɪk] *adj*: **to be ~** tener morriña *or* nostalgia
home town *n* ciudad *f* natal
home truth *n*: **to tell sb a few ~s** decir cuatro verdades a algn
homeward ['həumwəd] *adj* (*journey*) de vuelta ▹ *adv* hacia casa
homework ['həumwə:k] *n* deberes *mpl*
homicidal [hɔmɪ'saɪdl] *adj* homicida
homicide ['hɔmɪsaɪd] *n* (*US*) homicidio
homoeopath, homeopath (*US*) ['həumɪəupæθ] *n* homeópata *m/f*
homoeopathic, homeopathic (*US*) [həumɪəu'pæθɪk] *adj* homeopático
homoeopathy, homeopathy (*US*) [həumɪ'ɔpəθɪ] *n* homeopatía
homogeneous [hɔmə'dʒi:nɪəs] *adj* homogéneo
homosexual [hɔməu'sɛksjuəl] *adj, n* homosexual *m/f*
Hon *abbr* (*= honourable, honorary*) *en títulos*
Honduras [hɔn'djuərəs] *n* Honduras *fpl*
honest ['ɔnɪst] *adj* honrado; (*sincere*) franco, sincero; **to be quite ~ with you ...** para serte franco ...
honestly ['ɔnɪstlɪ] *adv* honradamente; francamente, de verdad
honesty ['ɔnɪstɪ] *n* honradez *f*
honey ['hʌnɪ] *n* miel *f*; (*US inf*) cariño; (*: to strangers*) guapo, linda
honeycomb ['hʌnɪkəum] *n* panal *m*; (*fig*) laberinto
honeymoon ['hʌnɪmu:n] *n* luna de miel
honeysuckle ['hʌnɪsʌkl] *n* madreselva
Hong Kong ['hɔŋ'kɔŋ] *n* Hong-Kong *m*
honk [hɔŋk] *vi* (*Aut*) tocar la bocina
honorary ['ɔnərərɪ] *adj* no remunerado; (*duty, title*) honorífico; **~ degree** doctorado honoris causa
honour, honor (*US*) ['ɔnə^r] *vt* honrar; (*commitment, promise*) cumplir con ▹ *n* honor *m*, honra; **in ~ of** en honor de; **it's a great ~** es un gran honor
honourable, honorable (*US*) ['ɔnərəbl] *adj* honrado, honorable
honours degree *n* (*Univ*) *licenciatura superior*
honours list *n* (*Brit*) *lista de distinciones honoríficas que entrega la reina*; *ver nota*
Hons. [ɔnz] *abbr* (*Univ*) = **hono(u)rs degree**
hood [hud] *n* capucha; (*Brit Aut*) capota; (*US Aut*) capó *m*; (*US inf*) matón *m*; (*of cooker*) campana de humos
hoodie ['hudɪ] *n* (*pullover*) sudadera *f* con capucha; (*young person*) capuchero(-a) *m(f)*
hoof (*pl* **hoofs** *or* **hooves**) [hu:f, hu:vz] *n* pezuña
hook [huk] *n* gancho; (*on dress*) corchete *m*, broche *m*; (*for fishing*) anzuelo ▹ *vt* enganchar; **~s and eyes** corchetes *mpl*, macho y hembra *m*; **by ~ or by crook** por las buenas o por las malas, cueste lo que cueste; **to be ~ed on** (*inf*) estar enganchado a; **hook up** *vt* (*Radio, TV*) transmitir en cadena
hooligan ['hu:lɪgən] *n* gamberro
hooliganism ['hu:lɪgənɪzəm] *n* gamberrismo
hoop [hu:p] *n* aro
hooray [hu:'reɪ] *excl* = **hurrah**
hoot [hu:t] *vi* (*Brit Aut*) tocar la bocina; (*siren*) sonar; (*owl*) ulular ▹ *n* bocinazo, toque *m* de sirena; **to ~ with laughter** morirse de risa
hooter ['hu:tə^r] *n* (*Brit Aut*) bocina; (*of ship, factory*) sirena
hoover® ['hu:və^r] (*Brit*) *n* aspiradora ▹ *vt* pasar la aspiradora por
hooves [hu:vz] *pl of* **hoof**
hop [hɔp] *vi* saltar, brincar; (*on one foot*) saltar con un pie ▹ *n* salto, brinco; *see also* **hops**
hope [həup] *vt, vi* esperar ▹ *n* esperanza; **I ~ so/not** espero que sí/no
hopeful ['həupful] *adj* (*person*) optimista; (*situation*) prometedor(a); **I'm ~ that she'll manage to come** confío en que podrá venir
hopefully ['həupfulɪ] *adv* con optimismo, con esperanza; **~ he will recover** esperamos que se recupere
hopeless ['həuplɪs] *adj* desesperado
hops [hɔps] *npl* lúpulo *sg*
horizon [hə'raɪzn] *n* horizonte *m*
horizontal [hɔrɪ'zɔntl] *adj* horizontal

hormone ['hɔːməun] *n* hormona
horn [hɔːn] *n* cuerno, cacho (*LAm*); (*Mus*: *also*: **French ~**) trompa; (*Aut*) bocina, claxon *m*
hornet ['hɔːnɪt] *n* avispón *m*
horny ['hɔːnɪ] *adj* (*material*) córneo; (*hands*) calloso; (*US inf*) cachondo
horoscope ['hɔrəskəup] *n* horóscopo
horrendous [hɔ'rɛndəs] *adj* horrendo
horrible ['hɔrɪbl] *adj* horrible
horrid ['hɔrɪd] *adj* horrible, horroroso
horrific [hɔ'rɪfɪk] *adj* (*accident*) horroroso; (*film*) horripilante
horrify ['hɔrɪfaɪ] *vt* horrorizar
horrifying ['hɔrɪfaɪɪŋ] *adj* horroroso
horror ['hɔrəʳ] *n* horror *m*
horror film *n* película de terror *or* miedo
hors d'œuvre [ɔː'dəːvrə] *n* entremeses *mpl*
horse [hɔːs] *n* caballo
horseback ['hɔːsbæk] *n*: **on ~** a caballo
horse chestnut *n* (*tree*) castaño de Indias; (*nut*) castaña de Indias
horseman ['hɔːsmən] *n* jinete *m*
horsepower ['hɔːspauəʳ] *n* caballo (de fuerza), potencia en caballos
horse-racing ['hɔːsreɪsɪŋ] *n* carreras *fpl* de caballos
horseradish ['hɔːsrædɪʃ] *n* rábano picante
horse riding *n* (*Brit*) equitación *f*
horseshoe ['hɔːsʃuː] *n* herradura
hose [həuz] *n* (*also*: **~pipe**) manguera; **hose down** *vt* limpiar con manguera
hospice ['hɔspɪs] *n* hospicio
hospitable ['hɔspɪtəbl] *adj* hospitalario
hospital ['hɔspɪtl] *n* hospital *m*
hospitality [hɔspɪ'tælɪtɪ] *n* hospitalidad *f*
host [həust] *n* anfitrión *m*; (*TV, Radio*) presentador(a) *m(f)*; (*of inn etc*) mesonero; (*Rel*) hostia; (*large number*): **a ~ of** multitud de
hostage ['hɔstɪdʒ] *n* rehén *m*
hostel ['hɔstl] *n* hostal *m*; (*for students, nurses etc*) residencia; (*also*: **youth ~**) albergue *m* juvenil; (*for homeless people*) hospicio
hostess ['həustɪs] *n* anfitriona; (*Brit*: *air hostess*) azafata; (*TV, Radio*) presentadora; (*in night-club*) señorita de compañía
hostile ['hɔstaɪl] *adj* hostil
hostility [hɔ'stɪlɪtɪ] *n* hostilidad *f*
hot [hɔt] *adj* caliente; (*weather*) caluroso, de calor; (*as opposed to only warm*) muy caliente; (*spicy*) picante; (*fig*) ardiente, acalorado; **to be ~** (*person*) tener calor; (*object*) estar caliente; (*weather*) hacer calor; **hot up** *vi* (*inf*: *situation*) ponerse difícil *or* apurado; (: *party*) animarse ▷ *vt* (*inf*: *pace*) apretar; (: *engine*) aumentar la potencia de
hotbed ['hɔtbɛd] *n* (*fig*) semillero
hotchpotch ['hɔtʃpɔtʃ] *n* mezcolanza, baturrillo
hot dog *n* perrito caliente
hotel [həu'tɛl] *n* hotel *m*
hotelier [həu'tɛlɪəʳ] *n* hotelero
hot-headed [hɔt'hɛdɪd] *adj* exaltado
hothouse ['hɔthaus] *n* invernadero
hot line *n* (*Pol*) teléfono rojo, línea directa
hotly ['hɔtlɪ] *adv* con pasión, apasionadamente
hotplate ['hɔtpleɪt] *n* (*on cooker*) hornillo
hot potato *n* (*Brit inf*) asunto espinoso; **to drop sth/sb like a ~** no querer saber ya nada de algo/algn
hot seat *n* primera fila
hotspot ['hɔt'spɔt] *n* (*Comput*: *also*: **wireless ~**) punto de acceso inalámbrico
hot spot *n* (*trouble spot*) punto caliente; (*night club etc*) lugar *m* popular
hot-water bottle [hɔt'wɔːtə-] *n* bolsa de agua caliente
hot-wire ['hɔtwaɪəʳ] *vt* (*inf*: *car*) hacer el puente en
hound [haund] *vt* acosar ▷ *n* perro de caza
hour ['auəʳ] *n* hora; **at 30 miles an ~** a 30 millas por hora; **lunch ~** la hora del almuerzo *or* de comer; **to pay sb by the ~** pagar a algn por horas
hourly ['auəlɪ] *adj* (de) cada hora; (*rate*) por hora ▷ *adv* cada hora
house *n* [haus] (*pl* **houses** ['hauzɪz]) casa; (*Pol*) cámara; (*Theat*) sala ▷ *vt* [hauz] (*person*) alojar; **at/to my ~** en/a mi casa; **the H~ of Commons/Lords** (*Brit*) la Cámara de los Comunes/Lores; **the H~ of Representatives** (*US*) la Cámara de Representantes; **it's on the ~** (*fig*) la casa invita
house arrest *n* arresto domiciliario
houseboat ['hausbəut] *n* casa flotante
housebound ['hausbaund] *adj* confinado en casa
housebreaking ['hausbreɪkɪŋ] *n* allanamiento de morada
housecoat ['hauskəut] *n* bata
household ['haushəuld] *n* familia
householder ['haushəuldəʳ] *n* propietario(-a); (*head of house*) cabeza de familia
housekeeper ['hauskiːpəʳ] *n* ama de llaves
housekeeping ['hauskiːpɪŋ] *n* (*work*) trabajos *mpl* domésticos; (*Comput*) gestión *f* interna; (*also*: **~ money**) dinero para gastos domésticos
house plant *n* planta de interior
house-proud ['hauspraud] *adj* preocupado por el embellecimiento de la casa
house-warming ['hauswɔːmɪŋ] *n* (*also*: **~ party**) fiesta de estreno de una casa
housewife ['hauswaɪf] *n* ama de casa
house wine *n* vino *m* de la casa
housework ['hauswəːk] *n* faenas *fpl* (de la casa)
housing ['hauzɪŋ] *n* (*act*) alojamiento; (*houses*) viviendas *fpl* ▷ *cpd* (*problem, shortage*) de (la) vivienda
housing association *n* asociación *f* de la vivienda

h

housing benefit *n* (*Brit*) subsidio por alojamiento
housing development, housing estate (*Brit*) *n* urbanización *f*
hovel ['hɔvl] *n* casucha
hover ['hɔvəʳ] *vi* flotar (en el aire); (*helicopter*) cernerse; **to ~ on the brink of disaster** estar al borde mismo del desastre
hovercraft ['hɔvəkrɑːft] *n* aerodeslizador *m*, hovercraft *m*
how [hau] *adv* cómo; **~ are you?** ¿cómo estás?; (*formal*) ¿cómo está usted?; **~ do you do?** encantado, mucho gusto; **~ far is it to ...?** ¿qué distancia hay de aquí a ...?; **~ long have you been here?** ¿cuánto (tiempo) hace que estás aquí?, ¿cuánto (tiempo) llevas aquí?; **~ lovely!** ¡qué bonito!; **~ many/much?** ¿cuántos/cuánto?; **~ much does it cost?** ¿cuánto cuesta?; **~ old are you?** ¿cuántos años tienes?; **~ is school?** ¿qué tal la escuela?; **~ was the film?** ¿qué tal la película?; **~ about a drink?** ¿te gustaría algo de beber?, ¿qué te parece una copa?
however [hau'ɛvəʳ] *adv* de cualquier manera; (*+ adjective*) por muy ... que; (*in questions*) cómo ▷ *conj* sin embargo, no obstante; **~ I do it** lo haga como lo haga; **~ cold it is** por mucho frío que haga; **~ did you do it?** ¿cómo lo hiciste?
howl [haul] *n* aullido ▷ *vi* aullar; (*person*) dar alaridos; (*wind*) ulular
HP *n abbr* (*Brit*) = **hire purchase**
hp *abbr* (*Aut*) = **horsepower**
HQ *n abbr* = **headquarters**
HR *n abbr* (*US*) = **House of Representatives**; **human resources**
hr, hrs *abbr* (= *hour(s)*) h
HRH *abbr* (= *His* (or *Her*) *Royal Highness*) S.A.R.
HTML *n abbr* (*Comput*: = *hypertext markup language*) HTML *m*
hub [hʌb] *n* (*of wheel*) cubo; (*fig*) centro
hubbub ['hʌbʌb] *n* barahúnda, barullo
hubcap ['hʌbkæp] *n* tapacubos *m inv*
huddle ['hʌdl] *vi*: **to ~ together** amontonarse
hue [hjuː] *n* color *m*, matiz *m*; **~ and cry** *n* protesta
huff [hʌf] *n*: **in a ~** enojado
hug [hʌg] *vt* abrazar ▷ *n* abrazo
huge [hjuːdʒ] *adj* enorme
hulk [hʌlk] *n* (*ship*) barco viejo; (*person, building etc*) mole *f*
hull [hʌl] *n* (*of ship*) casco
hullo [hə'ləu] *excl* = **hello**
hum [hʌm] *vt* tararear, canturrear ▷ *vi* tararear, canturrear; (*insect*) zumbar ▷ *n* (*Elec*) zumbido; (*of traffic, machines*) zumbido, ronroneo; (*of voices etc*) murmullo
human ['hjuːmən] *adj* humano ▷ *n* (*also*: **~ being**) ser *m* humano
humane [hjuː'meɪn] *adj* humano, humanitario
humanitarian [hjuːmænɪ'tɛərɪən] *adj* humanitario
humanity [hjuː'mænɪtɪ] *n* humanidad *f*
human rights *npl* derechos *mpl* humanos
humble ['hʌmbl] *adj* humilde ▷ *vt* humillar
humbug ['hʌmbʌg] *n* patrañas *fpl*; (*Brit: sweet*) caramelo de menta
humdrum ['hʌmdrʌm] *adj* (*boring*) monótono, aburrido; (*routine*) rutinario
humid ['hjuːmɪd] *adj* húmedo
humidity [hju'mɪdɪtɪ] *n* humedad *f*
humiliate [hjuː'mɪlɪeɪt] *vt* humillar
humiliating [hjuː'mɪlɪeɪtɪŋ] *adj* humillante, vergonzoso
humiliation [hjuːmɪlɪ'eɪʃən] *n* humillación *f*
humility [hjuː'mɪlɪtɪ] *n* humildad *f*
hummus ['huməs] *n* humus *m*
humorous ['hjuːmərəs] *adj* gracioso, divertido
humour, humor (*US*) ['hjuːməʳ] *n* humorismo, sentido del humor; (*mood*) humor *m* ▷ *vt* (*person*) complacer; **sense of ~** sentido del humor; **to be in a good/bad ~** estar de buen/mal humor
hump [hʌmp] *n* (*in ground*) montículo; (*camel's*) giba
hunch [hʌntʃ] *n* (*premonition*) presentimiento; **I have a ~ that** tengo la corazonada *or* el presentimiento de que
hunchback ['hʌntʃbæk] *n* jorobado(-a)
hunched [hʌntʃt] *adj* jorobado
hundred ['hʌndrəd] *num* ciento; (*before n*) cien; **about a ~ people** unas cien personas, alrededor de cien personas; **~s of** centenares de; **~s of people** centenares de personas; **I'm a ~ per cent sure** estoy completamente seguro
hundredth ['hʌndrɪdθ] *adj* centésimo
hundredweight ['hʌndrədweɪt] *n* (*Brit*) = *50.8 kg; 112 lb;* (*US*) = *45.3 kg; 100 lb*
hung [hʌŋ] *pt, pp of* **hang**
Hungarian [hʌŋ'gɛərɪən] *adj* húngaro ▷ *n* húngaro(-a) *m(f)*; (*Ling*) húngaro
Hungary ['hʌŋgərɪ] *n* Hungría
hunger ['hʌŋgəʳ] *n* hambre *f* ▷ *vi*: **to ~ for** (*fig*) tener hambre de, anhelar
hungover [hʌŋ'əuvəʳ] *adj* (*inf*): **to be ~** tener resaca
hungry ['hʌŋgrɪ] *adj* hambriento; **to be ~** tener hambre; **~ for** (*fig*) sediento de
hunk [hʌŋk] *n* (*of bread etc*) trozo, pedazo
hunt [hʌnt] *vt* (*seek*) buscar; (*Sport*) cazar ▷ *vi* (*search*): **to ~ (for)** buscar; (*Sport*) cazar ▷ *n* caza, cacería; **hunt down** *vt* acorralar, seguir la pista a
hunter ['hʌntəʳ] *n* cazador(a) *m(f)*; (*horse*) caballo de caza
hunting ['hʌntɪŋ] *n* caza
hurdle ['həːdl] *n* (*Sport*) valla; (*fig*) obstáculo
hurl [həːl] *vt* lanzar, arrojar
hurling ['həːlɪŋ] *n* (*Sport*) *juego irlandés semejante al hockey*

hurrah [hu'rɑː], **hurray** [hu'reɪ] *n* ¡viva!, ¡hurra!
hurricane ['hʌrɪkən] *n* huracán *m*
hurried ['hʌrɪd] *adj* (*fast*) apresurado; (*rushed*) hecho de prisa
hurriedly ['hʌrɪdlɪ] *adv* con prisa, apresuradamente
hurry ['hʌrɪ] *n* prisa ▷ *vb* (*also*: **~ up**) ▷ *vi* apresurarse, darse prisa, apurarse (*LAm*) ▷ *vt* (*person*) dar prisa a; (*work*) apresurar, hacer de prisa; **to be in a ~** tener prisa, tener apuro (*LAm*), estar apurado (*LAm*); **to ~ back/home** darse prisa en volver/volver a casa; **hurry along** *vi* pasar de prisa; **hurry away, hurry off** *vi* irse corriendo; **hurry on** *vi*: **to ~ on to say** apresurarse a decir; **hurry up** *vi* darse prisa, apurarse (*LAm*)
hurt [həːt] (*pt, pp* **hurt**) *vt* hacer daño a; (*business, interests etc*) perjudicar ▷ *vi* doler ▷ *adj* lastimado; **I ~ my arm** me lastimé el brazo; **where does it ~?** ¿dónde te duele?
hurtful ['həːtful] *adj* (*remark etc*) hiriente, dañino
hurtle ['həːtl] *vi*: **to ~ past** pasar como un rayo
husband ['hʌzbənd] *n* marido
hush [hʌʃ] *n* silencio ▷ *vt* hacer callar; (*cover up*) encubrir; **~!** ¡chitón!, ¡cállate!; **hush up** *vt* (*fact*) encubrir, callar
husk [hʌsk] *n* (*of wheat*) cáscara
husky ['hʌskɪ] *adj* ronco; (*burly*) fornido ▷ *n* perro esquimal
hustle ['hʌsl] *vt* (*push*) empujar; (*hurry*) dar prisa a ▷ *n* bullicio, actividad *f* febril; **~ and bustle** ajetreo
hut [hʌt] *n* cabaña; (*shed*) cobertizo
hutch [hʌtʃ] *n* conejera
hyacinth ['haɪəsɪnθ] *n* jacinto
hybrid ['haɪbrɪd] *adj, n* híbrido; **~ car** coche híbrido; **~ engine** motor híbrido
hydrangea [haɪ'dreɪnʒə] *n* hortensia
hydrant ['haɪdrənt] *n* (*also*: **fire ~**) boca de incendios
hydraulic [haɪ'drɔːlɪk] *adj* hidráulico
hydroelectric [haɪdrəuɪ'lɛktrɪk] *adj* hidroeléctrico
hydrofoil ['haɪdrəfɔɪl] *n* aerodeslizador *m*
hydrogen ['haɪdrədʒən] *n* hidrógeno
hyena [haɪ'iːnə] *n* hiena
hygiene ['haɪdʒiːn] *n* higiene *f*
hygienic [haɪ'dʒiːnɪk] *adj* higiénico
hymn [hɪm] *n* himno
hype [haɪp] *n* (*inf*) bombo
hyperactive [haɪpər'æktɪv] *adj* hiperactivo
hyperlink ['haɪpəlɪŋk] *n* hiperenlace *m*
hypermarket ['haɪpəmɑːkɪt] *n* hipermercado
hyphen ['haɪfn] *n* guión *m*
hypnosis [hɪp'nəusɪs] *n* hipnosis *f*
hypnotic [hɪp'nɔtɪk] *adj* hipnótico
hypnotism ['hɪpnətɪzəm] *n* hipnotismo
hypnotist ['hɪpnətɪst] *n* hipnotista *m/f*
hypnotize ['hɪpnətaɪz] *vt* hipnotizar
hypochondriac [haɪpəu'kɔndrɪæk] *n* hipocondríaco(-a)
hypocrisy [hɪ'pɔkrɪsɪ] *n* hipocresía
hypocrite ['hɪpəkrɪt] *n* hipócrita *m/f*
hypocritical [hɪpə'krɪtɪkl] *adj* hipócrita
hypodermic [haɪpə'dəːmɪk] *adj* hipodérmico ▷ *n* (*syringe*) aguja hipodérmica
hypotenuse [haɪ'pɔtɪnjuːz] *n* hipotenusa
hypothermia [haɪpəu'θəːmɪə] *n* hipotermia
hypothesis, hypotheses [haɪ'pɔθɪsɪs, -siːz] *n* hipótesis *f inv*
hypothetical [haɪpə'θɛtɪkl] *adj* hipotético
hysterectomy [hɪstə'rɛktəmɪ] *n* histerectomía
hysteria [hɪ'stɪərɪə] *n* histeria
hysterical [hɪ'stɛrɪkl] *adj* histérico
hysterics [hɪ'stɛrɪks] *npl* histeria *sg*, histerismo *sg*; **to have ~** ponerse histérico; **to be in ~** (*fig*) morirse de risa

i

I, i [aɪ] *n* (*letter*) I, i *f*; **I for Isaac**, (*US*) **I for Item** I de Inés, I de Israel
I [aɪ] *pron* yo ▷ *abbr* = **island; isle**
IBA *n abbr* (*Brit*: = *Independent Broadcasting Authority*) *see* **ITV**
Iberian [aɪ'bɪərɪən] *adj* ibero, ibérico
Iberian Peninsula *n*: **the ~** la Península Ibérica
ice [aɪs] *n* hielo ▷ *vt* (*cake*) alcorzar ▷ *vi* (*also*: **~ over, ~ up**) helarse; **to keep sth on ~** (*fig*: *plan, project*) tener algo en reserva
iceberg ['aɪsbəːg] *n* iceberg *m*; **the tip of the ~** la punta del iceberg
icebox ['aɪsbɔks] *n* (*Brit*) congelador *m*; (*US*) nevera, refrigeradora (*LAm*)
ice bucket *n* cubo para el hielo
ice cream *n* helado
ice cube *n* cubito de hielo
iced [aɪst] *adj* (*drink*) con hielo; (*cake*) escarchado
ice hockey *n* hockey *m* sobre hielo
Iceland ['aɪslənd] *n* Islandia
Icelander ['aɪsləndəʳ] *n* islandés(-esa) *m(f)*
Icelandic [aɪs'lændɪk] *adj* islandés(-esa) ▷ *n* (*Ling*) islandés *m*
ice lolly *n* (*Brit*) polo
ice rink *n* pista de hielo
ice-skating ['aɪsskeɪtɪŋ] *n* patinaje *m* sobre hielo
icicle ['aɪsɪkl] *n* carámbano
icing ['aɪsɪŋ] *n* (*Culin*) alcorza; (*Aviat etc*) formación *f* de hielo
icing sugar *n* (*Brit*) azúcar *m* glas(eado)
icon ['aɪkɔn] *n* (*gen*) icono; (*Comput*) icono
ICT *n abbr* (= *Information and Communication(s) Technology*) TIC *f*, tecnología de la información; (*Brit Scol*) informática
ICU *n abbr* (= *intensive care unit*) UVI *f*
icy ['aɪsɪ] *adj* (*road*) helado; (*fig*) glacial
I'd [aɪd] = **I would; I had**
ID card *n* (*identity card*) DNI *m*
idea [aɪ'dɪə] *n* idea; **good ~!** ¡buena idea!; **to have an ~ that ...** tener la impresión de que ...; **I haven't the least ~** no tengo ni (la más remota) idea
ideal [aɪ'dɪəl] *n* ideal *m* ▷ *adj* ideal
idealism [aɪ'dɪəlɪzəm] *n* idealismo
idealist [aɪ'dɪəlɪst] *n* idealista *m/f*
ideally [aɪ'dɪəlɪ] *adv*: **~, the book should have ...** lo ideal sería que el libro tuviera ...
identical [aɪ'dɛntɪkl] *adj* idéntico
identification [aɪdɛntɪfɪ'keɪʃən] *n* identificación *f*; **means of ~** documentos *mpl* personales
identify [aɪ'dɛntɪfaɪ] *vt* identificar ▷ *vi*: **to ~ with** identificarse con
Identikit® [aɪ'dɛntɪkɪt] *n*: **~ (picture)** retrato-robot *m*
identity [aɪ'dɛntɪtɪ] *n* identidad *f*
identity card *n* carnet *m* de identidad, cédula (de identidad) (*LAm*)
identity parade *n* identificación *f* de acusados
identity theft *n* robo de identidad
ideological [aɪdɪə'lɔdʒɪkəl] *adj* ideológico
ideology [aɪdɪ'ɔlədʒɪ] *n* ideología
idiom ['ɪdɪəm] *n* modismo; (*style of speaking*) lenguaje *m*
idiomatic [ɪdɪə'mætɪk] *adj* idiomático
idiosyncrasy [ɪdɪəu'sɪŋkrəsɪ] *n* idiosincrasia
idiot ['ɪdɪət] *n* (*gen*) idiota *m/f*; (*fool*) tonto(-a)
idiotic [ɪdɪ'ɔtɪk] *adj* idiota; tonto
idle ['aɪdl] *adj* (*inactive*) ocioso; (*lazy*) holgazán(-ana); (*unemployed*) parado, desocupado; (*talk*) frívolo ▷ *vi* (*machine*) funcionar *or* marchar en vacío; **~ capacity** (*Comm*) capacidad *f* sin utilizar; **~ money** (*Comm*) capital *m* improductivo; **~ time** (*Comm*) tiempo de paro; **idle away** *vt*: **to ~ away one's time** malgastar *or* desperdiciar el tiempo
idol ['aɪdl] *n* ídolo
idolize ['aɪdəlaɪz] *vt* idolatrar
idyllic [ɪ'dɪlɪk] *adj* idílico
i.e. *abbr* (= *id est*: *that is*) es decir
if [ɪf] *conj* si ▷ *n*: **there are a lot of ifs and buts** hay muchas dudas sin resolver; **(even) if** aunque, si bien; **I'd be pleased if you could do it** yo estaría contento si pudieras hacerlo; **if necessary** si resultase necesario; **if I were you** yo en tu lugar; **if only** si solamente; **as if** como si
iffy ['ɪfɪ] *adj* (*inf*) dudoso
igloo ['ɪgluː] *n* iglú *m*

ignite [ɪg'naɪt] *vt* (*set fire to*) encender ▷ *vi* encenderse
ignition [ɪg'nɪʃən] *n* (*Aut: process*) ignición *f*; (*: mechanism*) encendido; **to switch on/off the ~** arrancar/apagar el motor
ignition key *n* (*Aut*) llave *f* de contacto
ignorance ['ɪgnərəns] *n* ignorancia; **to keep sb in ~ of sth** ocultarle algo a algn
ignorant ['ɪgnərənt] *adj* ignorante; **to be ~ of** (*subject*) desconocer; (*events*) ignorar
ignore [ɪg'nɔːʳ] *vt* (*person*) no hacer caso de; (*fact*) pasar por alto
ill [ɪl] *adj* enfermo, malo ▷ *n* mal *m*; (*fig*) infortunio ▷ *adv* mal; **to take** *or* **be taken ~** caer *or* ponerse enfermo; **to feel ~ (with)** encontrarse mal (de); **to speak/think ~ of sb** hablar/pensar mal de algn
I'll [aɪl] = **I will; I shall**
ill-advised [ɪləd'vaɪzd] *adj* poco recomendable; **he was ~ to go** se equivocaba al ir
ill-at-ease [ɪlət'iːz] *adj* incómodo
illegal [ɪ'liːgl] *adj* ilegal
illegible [ɪ'lɛdʒɪbl] *adj* ilegible
illegitimate [ɪlɪ'dʒɪtɪmət] *adj* ilegítimo
ill-fated [ɪl'feɪtɪd] *adj* malogrado
ill feeling *n* rencor *m*
ill health *n* mala salud *f*; **to be in ~** estar mal de salud
illicit [ɪ'lɪsɪt] *adj* ilícito
illiterate [ɪ'lɪtərət] *adj* analfabeto
ill-mannered [ɪl'mænəd] *adj* mal educado
illness ['ɪlnɪs] *n* enfermedad *f*
ill-treat [ɪl'triːt] *vt* maltratar
illuminate [ɪ'luːmɪneɪt] *vt* (*room, street*) iluminar, alumbrar; (*subject*) aclarar; **~d sign** letrero luminoso
illumination [ɪluːmɪ'neɪʃən] *n* alumbrado; **illuminations** *npl* luminarias *fpl*, luces *fpl*
illusion [ɪ'luːʒən] *n* ilusión *f*; **to be under the ~ that ...** estar convencido de que ...
illustrate ['ɪləstreɪt] *vt* ilustrar
illustration [ɪlə'streɪʃən] *n* (*example*) ejemplo, ilustración *f*; (*in book*) lámina, ilustración *f*
illustrious [ɪ'lʌstrɪəs] *adj* ilustre
ill will *n* rencor *m*
I'm [aɪm] = **I am**
image ['ɪmɪdʒ] *n* imagen *f*
imagery ['ɪmɪdʒərɪ] *n* imágenes *fpl*
imaginary [ɪ'mædʒɪnərɪ] *adj* imaginario
imagination [ɪmædʒɪ'neɪʃən] *n* imaginación *f*; (*inventiveness*) inventiva; (*illusion*) fantasía
imaginative [ɪ'mædʒɪnətɪv] *adj* imaginativo
imagine [ɪ'mædʒɪn] *vt* imaginarse; (*suppose*) suponer
imam [ɪ'mɑːm] *n* imán *m*
imbalance [ɪm'bæləns] *n* desequilibrio
imbue [ɪm'bjuː] *vt*: **to ~ sth with** imbuir algo de
IMF *n abbr* (= *International Monetary Fund*) FMI *m*
imitate ['ɪmɪteɪt] *vt* imitar
imitation [ɪmɪ'teɪʃən] *n* imitación *f*; (*copy*) copia; (*pej*) remedo
immaculate [ɪ'mækjulət] *adj* limpísimo, inmaculado; (*Rel*) inmaculado
immaterial [ɪmə'tɪərɪəl] *adj* incorpóreo; **it is ~ whether ...** no importa si ...
immature [ɪmə'tjuəʳ] *adj* (*person*) inmaduro; (*of one's youth*) joven
immaturity [ɪmə'tjuərɪtɪ] *n* inmadurez *f*
immediate [ɪ'miːdɪət] *adj* inmediato; (*pressing*) urgente, apremiante; (*nearest: family*) próximo; (*: neighbourhood*) inmediato; **in the ~ future** en un futuro próximo
immediately [ɪ'miːdɪətlɪ] *adv* (*at once*) en seguida; (*directly*) inmediatamente; **~ next to** justo al lado de
immense [ɪ'mɛns] *adj* inmenso, enorme
immensely [ɪ'mɛnslɪ] *adv* enormemente
immerse [ɪ'məːs] *vt* (*submerge*) sumergir; **to be ~d in** (*fig*) estar absorto en
immersion heater [ɪ'məːʃən-] *n* (*Brit*) calentador *m* de inmersión
immigrant ['ɪmɪgrənt] *n* inmigrante *m/f*
immigrate ['ɪmɪgreɪt] *vi* inmigrar
immigration [ɪmɪ'greɪʃən] *n* inmigración *f*
imminent ['ɪmɪnənt] *adj* inminente
immobilize [ɪ'məubɪlaɪz] *vt* inmovilizar
immoral [ɪ'mɔrl] *adj* inmoral
immorality [ɪmɔ'rælɪtɪ] *n* inmoralidad *f*
immortal [ɪ'mɔːtl] *adj* inmortal
immortality [ɪmɔː'tælɪtɪ] *n* inmortalidad *f*
immortalize [ɪ'mɔːtlaɪz] *vt* inmortalizar
immune [ɪ'mjuːn] *adj*: **~ (to)** inmune (a)
immune system *n* sistema *m* inmunitario
immunity [ɪ'mjuːnɪtɪ] *n* (*Med: of diplomat*) inmunidad *f*; (*Comm*) exención *f*
immunization [ɪmjunaɪ'zeɪʃən] *n* inmunización *f*
immunize ['ɪmjunaɪz] *vt* inmunizar
imp [ɪmp] *n* (*small devil, child*) diablillo
impact ['ɪmpækt] *n* (*gen*) impacto
impair [ɪm'pɛəʳ] *vt* perjudicar
impart [ɪm'pɑːt] *vt* comunicar; (*make known*) participar; (*bestow*) otorgar
impartial [ɪm'pɑːʃl] *adj* imparcial
impassable [ɪm'pɑːsəbl] *adj* (*barrier*) infranqueable; (*road*) intransitable
impassive [ɪm'pæsɪv] *adj* impasible
impatience [ɪm'peɪʃəns] *n* impaciencia
impatient [ɪm'peɪʃənt] *adj* impaciente; **to get** *or* **grow ~** impacientarse
impeccable [ɪm'pɛkəbl] *adj* impecable
impede [ɪm'piːd] *vt* estorbar, dificultar
impediment [ɪm'pɛdɪmənt] *n* obstáculo, estorbo; (*also*: **speech ~**) defecto (del habla)
impending [ɪm'pɛndɪŋ] *adj* inminente
imperative [ɪm'pɛrətɪv] *adj* (*tone*) imperioso; (*necessary*) imprescindible ▷ *n* (*Ling*) imperativo
imperfect [ɪm'pəːfɪkt] *adj* imperfecto; (*goods etc*) defectuoso ▷ *n* (*Ling: also*: **~ tense**) imperfecto
imperfection [ɪmpəː'fɛkʃən] *n* (*blemish*) desperfecto; (*fault, flaw*) defecto

imperial [ɪmˈpɪərɪəl] *adj* imperial
imperialism [ɪmˈpɪərɪəlɪzəm] *n* imperialismo
impersonal [ɪmˈpəːsənl] *adj* impersonal
impersonate [ɪmˈpəːsəneɪt] *vt* hacerse pasar por
impersonation [ɪmpəːsəˈneɪʃən] *n* imitación *f*
impertinence [ɪmˈpəːtɪnəns] *n* impertinencia, insolencia
impertinent [ɪmˈpəːtɪnənt] *adj* impertinente, insolente
impervious [ɪmˈpəːvɪəs] *adj* impermeable; (*fig*): **~ to** insensible a
impetuous [ɪmˈpɛtjuəs] *adj* impetuoso
impetus [ˈɪmpətəs] *n* ímpetu *m*; (*fig*) impulso
impinge [ɪmˈpɪndʒ]: **to ~ on** *vt fus* (*affect*) afectar a
implant [ɪmˈplɑːnt] *vt* (*Med*) injertar, implantar; (*fig: idea, principle*) inculcar
implausible [ɪmˈplɔːzɪbl] *adj* implausible
implement *n* [ˈɪmplɪmənt] instrumento, herramienta ▷ *vt* [ˈɪmplɪmɛnt] hacer efectivo; (*carry out*) realizar
implicate [ˈɪmplɪkeɪt] *vt* (*compromise*) comprometer; (*involve*) enredar; **to ~ sb in sth** comprometer a algn en algo
implication [ɪmplɪˈkeɪʃən] *n* consecuencia; **by ~** indirectamente
implicit [ɪmˈplɪsɪt] *adj* (*gen*) implícito; (*complete*) absoluto
implicitly [ɪmˈplɪsɪtlɪ] *adv* implícitamente
imply [ɪmˈplaɪ] *vt* (*involve*) implicar, suponer; (*hint*) insinuar
impolite [ɪmpəˈlaɪt] *adj* mal educado
import *vt* [ɪmˈpɔːt] importar ▷ *n* [ˈɪmpɔːt] (*Comm*) importación *f*; (*: article*) producto importado; (*meaning*) significado, sentido ▷ *cpd* (*duty, licence etc*) de importación
importance [ɪmˈpɔːtəns] *n* importancia; **to be of great/little ~** tener mucha/poca importancia
important [ɪmˈpɔːtənt] *adj* importante; **it's not ~** no importa, no tiene importancia; **it is ~ that** es importante que
importer [ɪmˈpɔːtəʳ] *n* importador(a) *m(f)*
impose [ɪmˈpəuz] *vt* imponer ▷ *vi*: **to ~ on sb** abusar de algn
imposing [ɪmˈpəuzɪŋ] *adj* imponente, impresionante
imposition [ɪmpəˈzɪʃn] *n* (*of tax etc*) imposición *f*; **to be an ~** (*on person*) molestar
impossible [ɪmˈpɔsɪbl] *adj* imposible; (*person*) insoportable; **it is ~ for me to leave now** me es imposible salir ahora
impostor [ɪmˈpɔstəʳ] *n* impostor(a) *m(f)*
impotence [ˈɪmpətəns] *n* impotencia
impotent [ˈɪmpətənt] *adj* impotente
impound [ɪmˈpaund] *vt* embargar
impoverished [ɪmˈpɔvərɪʃt] *adj* necesitado; (*land*) agotado
impractical [ɪmˈpræktɪkl] *adj* (*person*) poco práctico
imprecise [ɪmprɪˈsaɪs] *adj* impreciso
impregnable [ɪmˈprɛgnəbl] *adj* invulnerable; (*castle*) inexpugnable
impress [ɪmˈprɛs] *vt* impresionar; (*mark*) estampar ▷ *vi* causar buena impresión; **to ~ sth on sb** convencer a algn de la importancia de algo
impression [ɪmˈprɛʃən] *n* impresión *f*; (*footprint etc*) huella; (*print run*) edición *f*; **to be under the ~ that** tener la impresión de que; **to make a good/bad ~ on sb** causar buena/mala impresión a algn
impressionist [ɪmˈprɛʃənɪst] *n* impresionista *m/f*
impressive [ɪmˈprɛsɪv] *adj* impresionante
imprint [ˈɪmprɪnt] *n* (*Publishing*) pie *m* de imprenta; (*fig*) sello
imprison [ɪmˈprɪzn] *vt* encarcelar
imprisonment [ɪmˈprɪznmənt] *n* encarcelamiento; (*term of imprisonment*) cárcel *f*; **life ~** cadena perpetua
improbable [ɪmˈprɔbəbl] *adj* improbable, inverosímil
impromptu [ɪmˈprɔmptjuː] *adj* improvisado ▷ *adv* de improviso
improper [ɪmˈprɔpəʳ] *adj* (*incorrect*) impropio; (*unseemly*) indecoroso; (*indecent*) indecente; (*dishonest: activities*) deshonesto
improve [ɪmˈpruːv] *vt* mejorar; (*foreign language*) perfeccionar ▷ *vi* mejorar; **improve (up)on** *vt fus* (*offer*) mejorar
improvement [ɪmˈpruːvmənt] *n* mejora; perfeccionamiento; **to make ~s to** mejorar
improvise [ˈɪmprəvaɪz] *vt, vi* improvisar
imprudent [ɪmˈpruːdnt] *adj* imprudente
impudent [ˈɪmpjudnt] *adj* descarado, insolente
impulse [ˈɪmpʌls] *n* impulso; **to act on ~** actuar sin reflexionar, dejarse llevar por el impulso
impulsive [ɪmˈpʌlsɪv] *adj* irreflexivo, impulsivo
impure [ɪmˈpjuəʳ] *adj* (*adulterated*) adulterado; (*morally*) impuro
impurity [ɪmˈpjuərɪtɪ] *n* impureza

KEYWORD

in [ɪn] *prep* **1** (*indicating place, position, with place names*) en; **in the house/garden** en (la) casa/el jardín; **in here/there** aquí/ahí *or* allí dentro; **in London/England** en Londres/Inglaterra; **in town** en el centro (de la ciudad)
2 (*indicating time*) en; **in spring** en (la) primavera; **in 1988/May** en 1988/mayo; **in the afternoon** por la tarde; **at four o'clock in the afternoon** a las cuarto de la tarde; **I did it in three hours/days** lo hice en tres horas/días; **I'll see you in two weeks**

or **in two weeks' time** te veré dentro de dos semanas; **once in a hundred years** una vez cada cien años
3 (*indicating manner etc*) en; **in a loud/soft voice** en voz alta/baja; **in pencil/ink** a lápiz/bolígrafo; **the boy in the blue shirt** el chico de la camisa azul; **in writing** por escrito; **to pay in dollars** pagar en dólares
4 (*indicating circumstances*): **in the sun/shade** al sol/a la sombra; **in the rain** bajo la lluvia; **a change in policy** un cambio de política; **a rise in prices** un aumento de precios
5 (*indicating mood, state*): **in tears** llorando; **in anger/despair** enfadado/desesperado; **to live in luxury** vivir lujosamente
6 (*with ratios, numbers*): **1 in 10 households, 1 household in 10** una de cada 10 familias; **20 pence in the pound** 20 peniques por libra; **they lined up in twos** se alinearon de dos en dos; **in hundreds** a *or* por centenares
7 (*referring to people, works*) en; entre; **the disease is common in children** la enfermedad es común entre los niños; **in (the works of) Dickens** en (las obras de) Dickens
8 (*indicating profession etc*): **to be in teaching** dedicarse a la enseñanza
9 (*after superlative*) de; **the best pupil in the class** el/la mejor alumno(-a) de la clase
10 (*with present participle*): **in saying this** al decir esto
▷ *adv*: **to be in** (*person*: *at home*) estar en casa; (*: at work*) estar; (*train, ship, plane*) haber llegado; (*in fashion*) estar de moda; **she'll be in later today** llegará más tarde hoy; **to ask sb in** hacer pasar a algn; **to run/limp** *etc* **in** entrar corriendo/cojeando *etc*; **in that** *conj* ya que
▷ *npl*: **the ins and outs** (*of proposal, situation etc*) los detalles

in., ins *abbr* = **inch(es)**
inability [ɪnəˈbɪlɪtɪ] *n*: **~ (to do)** incapacidad *f* (de hacer)
inaccuracy [ɪnˈækjurəsɪ] *n* inexactitud *f*
inaccurate [ɪnˈækjurət] *adj* inexacto, incorrecto
inadequate [ɪnˈædɪkwət] *adj* (*insufficient*) insuficiente; (*unsuitable*) inadecuado; (*person*) incapaz
inadmissible [ɪnədˈmɪsəbl] *adj* improcedente, inadmisible
inadvertent [ɪnədˈvəːtənt] *adj* descuidado, involuntario
inadvertently [ɪnədˈvəːtntlɪ] *adv* por descuido
inadvisable [ɪnədˈvaɪzəbl] *adj* poco aconsejable
inane [ɪˈneɪn] *adj* necio, fatuo
inanimate [ɪnˈænɪmət] *adj* inanimado
inapplicable [ɪnˈæplɪkəbl] *adj* inaplicable
inappropriate [ɪnəˈprəuprɪət] *adj* inadecuado
inarticulate [ɪnɑːˈtɪkjulət] *adj* (*person*) incapaz de expresarse; (*speech*) mal pronunciado
inasmuch as [ɪnəzˈmʌtʃ-] *adv* en la medida en que
inaugural [ɪˈnɔːgjurəl] *adj* inaugural; (*speech*) de apertura
inaugurate [ɪˈnɔːgjureɪt] *vt* inaugurar; (*president, official*) investir
inauguration [ɪnɔːgjuˈreɪʃən] *n* inauguración *f*; (*of official*) investidura; (*of event*) ceremonia de apertura
in-between [ɪnbɪˈtwiːn] *adj* intermedio
inborn [ɪnˈbɔːn] *adj* (*feeling*) innato
inbred [ɪnˈbrɛd] *adj* innato; (*family*) consanguíneo
Inc. *abbr* = **incorporated**
Inca [ˈɪŋkə] *adj* (*also*: **~n**) inca, de los incas ▷ *n* inca *m/f*
incapable [ɪnˈkeɪpəbl] *adj*: **~ (of doing sth)** incapaz (de hacer algo)
incapacitate [ɪnkəˈpæsɪteɪt] *vt*: **to ~ sb** incapacitar a algn
incapacity [ɪnkəˈpæsɪtɪ] *n* (*inability*) incapacidad *f*
incarcerate [ɪnˈkɑːsəreɪt] *vt* encarcelar
incarnate *adj* [ɪnˈkɑːnɪt] en persona ▷ *vt* [ˈɪnkɑːneɪt] encarnar
incarnation [ɪnkɑːˈneɪʃən] *n* encarnación *f*
incendiary [ɪnˈsɛndɪərɪ] *adj* incendiario ▷ *n* (*bomb*) bomba incendiaria
incense *n* [ˈɪnsɛns] incienso ▷ *vt* [ɪnˈsɛns] (*anger*) indignar, encolerizar
incentive [ɪnˈsɛntɪv] *n* incentivo, estímulo
incessant [ɪnˈsɛsnt] *adj* incesante, continuo
incessantly [ɪnˈsɛsəntlɪ] *adv* constantemente
incest [ˈɪnsɛst] *n* incesto
inch [ɪntʃ] *n* pulgada; **to be within an ~ of** estar a dos dedos de; **he didn't give an ~** no hizo la más mínima concesión; **a few ~es** unas pulgadas; **inch forward** *vi* avanzar palmo a palmo
incidence [ˈɪnsɪdns] *n* (*of crime, disease*) incidencia
incident [ˈɪnsɪdnt] *n* incidente *m*; (*in book*) episodio
incidental [ɪnsɪˈdɛntl] *adj* circunstancial, accesorio; (*unplanned*) fortuito; **~ to** relacionado con; **~ expenses** (gastos *mpl*) imprevistos *mpl*
incidentally [ɪnsɪˈdɛntəlɪ] *adv* (*by the way*) por cierto
incident room *n* (*Police*) centro de coordinación
incinerate [ɪnˈsɪnəreɪt] *vt* incinerar, quemar
incinerator [ɪnˈsɪnəreɪtəʳ] *n* incinerador *m*, incineradora
incision [ɪnˈsɪʒən] *n* incisión *f*
incisive [ɪnˈsaɪsɪv] *adj* (*mind*) penetrante; (*remark etc*) incisivo
incite [ɪnˈsaɪt] *vt* provocar, incitar

i

incl. *abbr* = **including; inclusive (of)**
inclination [ɪnklɪ'neɪʃən] *n* (*tendency*) tendencia, inclinación *f*
incline [*n* 'ɪnklaɪn, *vb* ɪn'klaɪn] *n* pendiente *f*, cuesta ▷ *vt* (*slope*) inclinar; (*head*) poner de lado ▷ *vi* inclinarse; **to be ~d to** (*tend*) ser propenso a; (*be willing*) estar dispuesto a
include [ɪn'klu:d] *vt* incluir, comprender; (*in letter*) adjuntar; **the tip is/is not ~d** la propina está/no está incluida
including [ɪn'klu:dɪŋ] *prep* incluso, inclusive; **~ tip** propina incluida
inclusion [ɪn'klu:ʒən] *n* inclusión *f*
inclusive [ɪn'klu:sɪv] *adj* inclusivo ▷ *adv* inclusive; **~ of tax** incluidos los impuestos; **$50, ~ of all surcharges** 50 dólares, incluidos todos los recargos
incognito [ɪnkɔg'ni:təu] *adv* de incógnito
incoherent [ɪnkəu'hɪərənt] *adj* incoherente
income ['ɪnkʌm] *n* (*personal*) ingresos *mpl*; (*from property etc*) renta; (*profit*) rédito; **gross/net ~** ingresos *mpl* brutos/netos; **~ and expenditure account** cuenta de gastos e ingresos
income support *n* (*Brit*) ≈ ayuda familiar
income tax *n* impuesto sobre la renta
incoming ['ɪnkʌmɪŋ] *adj* (*passengers, flight*) de llegada; (*government*) entrante; (*tenant*) nuevo
incompatible [ɪnkəm'pætɪbl] *adj* incompatible
incompetence [ɪn'kɔmpɪtəns] *n* incompetencia
incompetent [ɪn'kɔmpɪtənt] *adj* incompetente
incomplete [ɪnkəm'pli:t] *adj* incompleto; (*unfinished*) sin terminar
incomprehensible [ɪnkɔmprɪ'hɛnsɪbl] *adj* incomprensible
inconceivable [ɪnkən'si:vəbl] *adj* inconcebible
inconclusive [ɪnkən'klu:sɪv] *adj* sin resultado (definitivo); (*argument*) poco convincente
incongruous [ɪn'kɔŋgruəs] *adj* discordante
inconsiderate [ɪnkən'sɪdərət] *adj* desconsiderado; **how ~ of him!** ¡qué falta de consideración (de su parte)!
inconsistency [ɪnkən'sɪstənsɪ] *n* inconsecuencia; (*of actions etc*) falta de lógica; (*of work*) carácter *m* desigual, inconsistencia; (*of statement etc*) contradicción *f*
inconsistent [ɪnkən'sɪstnt] *adj* inconsecuente; (*contradictory*) incongruente; **~ with** que no concuerda con
inconspicuous [ɪnkən'spɪkjuəs] *adj* (*discreet*) discreto; (*person*) que llama poco la atención
incontinent [ɪn'kɔntɪnənt] *adj* incontinente
inconvenience [ɪnkən'vi:njəns] *n* (*gen*) inconvenientes *mpl*; (*trouble*) molestia ▷ *vt* incomodar; **to put sb to great ~** causar mucha molestia a algn; **don't ~ yourself** no se moleste
inconvenient [ɪnkən'vi:njənt] *adj* incómodo, poco práctico; (*time, place*) inoportuno; **that time is very ~ for me** esa hora me es muy inconveniente
incorporate [ɪn'kɔ:pəreɪt] *vt* incorporar; (*contain*) comprender; (*add*) agregar
incorporated [ɪn'kɔ:pəreɪtɪd] *adj*: **~ company** (*US*) ≈ Sociedad *f* Anónima (S.A.)
incorrect [ɪnkə'rɛkt] *adj* incorrecto
increase [*n* 'ɪnkri:s, *vb* ɪn'kri:s] *n* aumento ▷ *vi* aumentar; (*grow*) crecer; (*price*) subir ▷ *vt* aumentar; (*price*) subir; **an ~ of 5%** un aumento de 5%; **to be on the ~** ir en aumento
increasing [ɪn'kri:sɪŋ] *adj* (*number*) creciente, que va en aumento
increasingly [ɪn'kri:sɪŋlɪ] *adv* cada vez más
incredible [ɪn'krɛdɪbl] *adj* increíble
incredibly [ɪn'krɛdɪblɪ] *adv* increíblemente
incredulous [ɪn'krɛdjuləs] *adj* incrédulo
increment ['ɪnkrɪmənt] *n* aumento, incremento
incriminate [ɪn'krɪmɪneɪt] *vt* incriminar
incubate ['ɪnkjubeɪt] *vt* (*egg*) incubar, empollar ▷ *vi* (*egg, disease*) incubar
incubation [ɪnkju'beɪʃən] *n* incubación *f*
incubator ['ɪnkjubeɪtə^r] *n* incubadora
incumbent [ɪn'kʌmbənt] *n* ocupante *m/f* ▷ *adj*: **it is ~ on him to ...** le incumbe ...
incur [ɪn'kə:^r] *vt* (*expenses*) incurrir en; (*loss*) sufrir; (*anger, disapproval*) provocar
incurable [ɪn'kjuərəbl] *adj* incurable
indebted [ɪn'dɛtɪd] *adj*: **to be ~ to sb** estar agradecido a algn
indecency [ɪn'di:snsɪ] *n* indecencia
indecent [ɪn'di:snt] *adj* indecente
indecent assault *n* (*Brit*) atentado contra el pudor
indecent exposure *n* exhibicionismo
indecision [ɪndɪ'sɪʒən] *n* indecisión *f*
indecisive [ɪndɪ'saɪsɪv] *adj* indeciso; (*discussion*) no resuelto, inconcluyente
indeed [ɪn'di:d] *adv* efectivamente, en realidad; (*in fact*) en efecto; (*furthermore*) es más; **yes ~!** ¡claro que sí!
indefinite [ɪn'dɛfɪnɪt] *adj* indefinido; (*uncertain*) incierto
indefinitely [ɪn'dɛfɪnɪtlɪ] *adv* (*wait*) indefinidamente
indemnity [ɪn'dɛmnɪtɪ] *n* (*insurance*) indemnidad *f*; (*compensation*) indemnización *f*
indent [ɪn'dɛnt] *vt* (*text*) sangrar
independence [ɪndɪ'pɛndns] *n* independencia
Independence Day *n* Día *m* de la Independencia

INDEPENDENCE DAY

El cuatro de julio es la fiesta nacional de los Estados Unidos, *Independence Day*, en conmemoración de la Declaración de

Independencia escrita por Thomas Jefferson y adoptada en 1776. En ella se proclamaba la ruptura total con Gran Bretaña de las trece colonias americanas que fueron el origen de los Estados Unidos de América.

independent [ɪndɪ'pɛndənt] *adj* independiente; **to become ~** independizarse
independent school *n* (*Brit*) escuela *f* privada, colegio *m* privado
in-depth ['ɪndɛpθ] *adj* en profundidad, a fondo
index ['ɪndɛks] *n* (*pl* **indexes**: *in book*) índice *m*; (*: in library etc*) catálogo; (*pl* **indices** ['ɪndɪsi:z] *: ratio, sign*) exponente *m*
index card *n* ficha
index finger *n* índice *m*
index-linked ['ɪndɛks'lɪŋkt], **indexed** (*US*) ['ɪndɛkst] *adj* indexado
India ['ɪndɪə] *n* la India
Indian ['ɪndɪən] *adj, n* indio(-a) *m(f)*; (*also*: **American ~**) indio(-a) *m(f)* de América, amerindio(-a) *m(f)*; (*pej*): **Red ~** piel roja *m/f*
Indian Ocean *n*: **the ~** el Océano Índico, el Mar de las Indias
Indian summer *n* (*fig*) veranillo de San Martín
indicate ['ɪndɪkeɪt] *vt* indicar ▷ *vi* (*Brit Aut*): **to ~ left/right** indicar a la izquierda/a la derecha
indication [ɪndɪ'keɪʃən] *n* indicio, señal *f*
indicative [ɪn'dɪkətɪv] *adj*: **to be ~ of sth** indicar algo ▷ *n* (*Ling*) indicativo
indicator ['ɪndɪkeɪtə^r] *n* (*gen*) indicador *m*; (*Aut*) intermitente *m*, direccional *m* (*LAm*)
indices ['ɪndɪsi:z] *npl of* **index**
indict [ɪn'daɪt] *vt* acusar
indictment [ɪn'daɪtmənt] *n* acusación *f*
indifference [ɪn'dɪfrəns] *n* indiferencia
indifferent [ɪn'dɪfrənt] *adj* indiferente; (*poor*) regular
indigenous [ɪn'dɪdʒɪnəs] *adj* indígena
indigestion [ɪndɪ'dʒɛstʃən] *n* indigestión *f*
indignant [ɪn'dɪgnənt] *adj*: **to be ~ about sth** indignarse por algo
indignation [ɪndɪg'neɪʃən] *n* indignación *f*
indignity [ɪn'dɪgnɪtɪ] *n* indignidad *f*
indigo ['ɪndɪgəu] *adj* (*colour*) (de color) añil ▷ *n* añil *m*
indirect [ɪndɪ'rɛkt] *adj* indirecto
indiscreet [ɪndɪ'skri:t] *adj* indiscreto, imprudente
indiscriminate [ɪndɪ'skrɪmɪnət] *adj* indiscriminado
indispensable [ɪndɪ'spɛnsəbl] *adj* indispensable, imprescindible
indisputable [ɪndɪ'spju:təbl] *adj* incontestable
indistinct [ɪndɪ'stɪŋkt] *adj* indistinto
indistinguishable [ɪndɪ'stɪŋgwɪʃəbl] *adj* indistinguible
individual [ɪndɪ'vɪdjuəl] *n* individuo ▷ *adj* individual; (*personal*) personal; (*particular*) particular
individuality [ɪndɪvɪdju'ælɪtɪ] *n* individualidad *f*
individually [ɪndɪ'vɪdjuəlɪ] *adv* individualmente; particularmente
indoctrination [ɪndɔktrɪ'neɪʃən] *n* adoctrinamiento
Indonesia [ɪndə'ni:zɪə] *n* Indonesia
indoor ['ɪndɔ:^r] *adj* (*swimming pool*) cubierto; (*plant*) de interior; (*sport*) bajo cubierta
indoors [ɪn'dɔ:z] *adv* dentro; (*at home*) en casa
induce [ɪn'dju:s] *vt* inducir, persuadir; (*bring about*) producir; **to ~ sb to do sth** persuadir a algn a que haga algo
inducement [ɪn'dju:smənt] *n* (*incentive*) incentivo, aliciente *m*
induction [ɪn'dʌkʃən] *n* (*Med: of birth*) inducción *f*
indulge [ɪn'dʌldʒ] *vt* (*whim*) satisfacer; (*person*) complacer; (*child*) mimar ▷ *vi*: **to ~ in** darse el gusto de
indulgence [ɪn'dʌldʒəns] *n* vicio
indulgent [ɪn'dʌldʒənt] *adj* indulgente
industrial [ɪn'dʌstrɪəl] *adj* industrial
industrial action *n* huelga
industrial estate *n* (*Brit*) polígono *or* (*LAm*) zona industrial
industrialist [ɪn'dʌstrɪəlɪst] *n* industrial *m/f*
industrialize [ɪn'dʌstrɪəlaɪz] *vt* industrializar
industrial park *n* (*US*) = **industrial estate**
industrial relations *npl* relaciones *fpl* empresariales
industrious [ɪn'dʌstrɪəs] *adj* (*gen*) trabajador(a); (*student*) aplicado
industry ['ɪndəstrɪ] *n* industria; (*diligence*) aplicación *f*
inebriated [ɪ'ni:brɪeɪtɪd] *adj* borracho
inedible [ɪn'ɛdɪbl] *adj* incomible; (*plant etc*) no comestible
ineffective [ɪnɪ'fɛktɪv], **ineffectual** [ɪnɪ'fɛktʃuəl] *adj* ineficaz, inútil
inefficiency [ɪnɪ'fɪʃənsɪ] *n* ineficacia
inefficient [ɪnɪ'fɪʃənt] *adj* ineficaz, ineficiente
ineligible [ɪn'ɛlɪdʒɪbl] *adj* inelegible
inept [ɪ'nɛpt] *adj* incompetente, incapaz
inequality [ɪnɪ'kwɔlɪtɪ] *n* desigualdad *f*
inertia [ɪ'nə:ʃə] *n* inercia; (*laziness*) pereza
inescapable [ɪnɪ'skeɪpəbl] *adj* ineludible, inevitable
inevitable [ɪn'ɛvɪtəbl] *adj* inevitable; (*necessary*) forzoso
inevitably [ɪn'ɛvɪtəblɪ] *adv* inevitablemente; **as ~ happens ...** como siempre pasa ...
inexact [ɪnɪg'zaekt] *adj* inexacto
inexcusable [ɪnɪks'kju:zəbl] *adj* imperdonable
inexhaustible [ɪnɪg'zɔ:stɪbl] *adj* inagotable
inexpensive [ɪnɪk'spɛnsɪv] *adj* económico

inexperience [ɪnɪk'spɪərɪəns] *n* falta de experiencia
inexperienced [ɪnɪk'spɪərɪənst] *adj* inexperto; **to be ~ in sth** no tener experiencia en algo
inexplicable [ɪnɪk'splɪkəbl] *adj* inexplicable
infallible [ɪn'fælɪbl] *adj* infalible
infamous ['ɪnfəməs] *adj* infame
infancy ['ɪnfənsɪ] *n* infancia
infant ['ɪnfənt] *n* niño(-a); (*baby*) niño(-a) pequeño(-a), bebé *m/f*
infantry ['ɪnfəntrɪ] *n* infantería
infant school *n* (*Brit*) escuela infantil
infatuated [ɪn'fætjueɪtɪd] *adj*: **~ with** (*in love*) loco por; **to become ~ (with sb)** enamoriscarse (de algn), encapricharse (con algn)
infatuation [ɪnfætju'eɪʃən] *n* enamoramiento
infect [ɪn'fɛkt] *vt* (*wound*) infectar; (*food*) contaminar; (*person, animal*) contagiar; (*fig: pej*) corromper; **~ed with** (*illness*) contagiado de; **to become ~ed** (*wound*) infectarse
infection [ɪn'fɛkʃən] *n* infección *f*; (*fig*) contagio
infectious [ɪn'fɛkʃəs] *adj* contagioso; (*fig*) infeccioso
infer [ɪn'fəːʳ] *vt* deducir, inferir; **to ~ (from)** inferir (de), deducir (de)
inference ['ɪnfərəns] *n* deducción *f*, inferencia
inferior [ɪn'fɪərɪəʳ] *adj, n* inferior *m/f*; **to feel ~** sentirse inferior
inferiority [ɪnfɪərɪ'ɔrətɪ] *n* inferioridad *f*
inferiority complex *n* complejo de inferioridad
inferno [ɪn'fəːnəu] *n* infierno; (*fig*) hoguera
infertile [ɪn'fəːtaɪl] *adj* estéril; (*person*) infecundo
infertility [ɪnfəː'tɪlɪtɪ] *n* esterilidad *f*; infecundidad *f*
infested [ɪn'fɛstɪd] *adj*: **~ (with)** plagado (de)
infidelity [ɪnfɪ'dɛlɪtɪ] *n* infidelidad *f*
in-fighting ['ɪnfaɪtɪŋ] *n* (*fig*) lucha(s) *f(pl)* interna(s)
infinite ['ɪnfɪnɪt] *adj* infinito; **an ~ amount of money/time** un sinfín de dinero/tiempo
infinitely ['ɪnfɪnɪtlɪ] *adv* infinitamente
infinitive [ɪn'fɪnɪtɪv] *n* infinitivo
infinity [ɪn'fɪnɪtɪ] *n* (*Math*) infinito; **an ~** infinidad *f*
infirm [ɪn'fəːm] *adj* enfermizo, débil
infirmary [ɪn'fəːmərɪ] *n* hospital *m*
inflamed [ɪn'fleɪmd] *adj*: **to become ~** inflamarse
inflammable [ɪn'flæməbl] *adj* (*Brit*) inflamable; (*situation etc*) explosivo
inflammation [ɪnflə'meɪʃən] *n* inflamación *f*
inflatable [ɪn'fleɪtəbl] *adj* inflable
inflate [ɪn'fleɪt] *vt* (*tyre*) inflar; (*fig*) hinchar
inflation [ɪn'fleɪʃən] *n* (*Econ*) inflación *f*
inflationary [ɪn'fleɪʃnərɪ] *adj* inflacionario
inflexible [ɪn'flɛksɪbl] *adj* inflexible
inflict [ɪn'flɪkt] *vt*: **to ~ on** infligir en; (*tax etc*) imponer a
influence ['ɪnfluəns] *n* influencia ▷ *vt* influir en, influenciar; **under the ~ of alcohol** en estado de embriaguez
influential [ɪnflu'ɛnʃl] *adj* influyente
influenza [ɪnflu'ɛnzə] *n* gripe *f*
influx ['ɪnflʌks] *n* afluencia
info (*inf*) ['ɪnfəu] *n* = **information**
inform [ɪn'fɔːm] *vt*: **to ~ sb of sth** informar a algn sobre *or* de algo; (*warn*) avisar a algn de algo; (*communicate*) comunicar algo a algn ▷ *vi*: **to ~ on sb** delatar a algn
informal [ɪn'fɔːml] *adj* (*manner, tone*) desenfadado; (*dress, occasion*) informal; (*visit, meeting*) extraoficial
informality [ɪnfɔː'mælɪtɪ] *n* falta de ceremonia; (*intimacy*) intimidad *f*; (*familiarity*) familiaridad *f*; (*ease*) afabilidad *f*
informant [ɪn'fɔːmənt] *n* informante *m/f*
information [ɪnfə'meɪʃən] *n* información *f*; (*news*) noticias *fpl*; (*knowledge*) conocimientos *mpl*; (*Law*) delación *f*; **a piece of ~** un dato; **for your ~** para su información
information office *n* información *f*
information science *n* gestión *f* de la información
information technology *n* informática
informative [ɪn'fɔːmətɪv] *adj* informativo
informer [ɪn'fɔːməʳ] *n* delator(a) *m(f)*; (*also*: **police ~**) soplón(-ona) *m(f)*
infra-red [ɪnfrə'rɛd] *adj* infrarrojo
infrastructure ['ɪnfrəstrʌktʃəʳ] *n* infraestructura
infrequent [ɪn'friːkwənt] *adj* infrecuente
infringe [ɪn'frɪndʒ] *vt* infringir, violar ▷ *vi*: **to ~ on** invadir
infringement [ɪn'frɪndʒmənt] *n* infracción *f*; (*of rights*) usurpación *f*; (*Sport*) falta
infuriate [ɪn'fjuərɪeɪt] *vt*: **to become ~d** ponerse furioso
infuriating [ɪn'fjuərɪeɪtɪŋ] *adj* (*habit, noise*) enloquecedor(a); **I find it ~** me saca de quicio
ingenious [ɪn'dʒiːnjəs] *adj* ingenioso
ingenuity [ɪndʒɪ'njuːɪtɪ] *n* ingeniosidad *f*
ingenuous [ɪn'dʒɛnjuəs] *adj* ingenuo
ingot ['ɪŋgət] *n* lingote *m*, barra
ingrained [ɪn'greɪnd] *adj* arraigado
ingratiate [ɪn'greɪʃɪeɪt] *vt*: **to ~ o.s. with** congraciarse con
ingratitude [ɪn'grætɪtjuːd] *n* ingratitud *f*
ingredient [ɪn'griːdɪənt] *n* ingrediente *m*
ingrowing ['ɪngrəuɪŋ] *adj*: **~ (toe)nail** uña encarnada
inhabit [ɪn'hæbɪt] *vt* vivir en; (*occupy*) ocupar
inhabitant [ɪn'hæbɪtənt] *n* habitante *m/f*
inhale [ɪn'heɪl] *vt* inhalar ▷ *vi* (*breathe in*) aspirar; (*in smoking*) tragar
inhaler [ɪn'heɪləʳ] *n* inhalador *m*
inherent [ɪn'hɪərənt] *adj*: **~ in** *or* **to** inherente a

inherit [ɪnˈhɛrɪt] *vt* heredar
inheritance [ɪnˈhɛrɪtəns] *n* herencia; (*fig*) patrimonio
inhibit [ɪnˈhɪbɪt] *vt* inhibir, impedir; **to ~ sb from doing sth** impedir a algn hacer algo
inhibited [ɪnˈhɪbɪtɪd] *adj* (*person*) cohibido
inhibition [ɪnhɪˈbɪʃən] *n* cohibición *f*
in-house [ˈɪnhaus] *adj* dentro de la empresa
inhuman [ɪnˈhjuːmən] *adj* inhumano
inhumane [ɪnhjuːˈmeɪn] *adj* inhumano
inimitable [ɪˈnɪmɪtəbl] *adj* inimitable
initial [ɪˈnɪʃl] *adj* inicial; (*first*) primero ▷ *n* inicial *f* ▷ *vt* firmar con las iniciales; **initials** *npl* iniciales *fpl*; (*abbreviation*) siglas *fpl*
initially [ɪˈnɪʃəlɪ] *adv* en un principio
initiate [ɪˈnɪʃɪeɪt] *vt* (*start*) iniciar; **to ~ sb into a secret** iniciar a algn en un secreto; **to ~ proceedings against sb** (*Law*) poner una demanda contra algn
initiation [ɪnɪʃɪˈeɪʃən] *n* (*into secret etc*) iniciación *f*; (*beginning*) comienzo
initiative [ɪˈnɪʃətɪv] *n* iniciativa; **to take the ~** tomar la iniciativa
inject [ɪnˈdʒɛkt] *vt* inyectar; (*money, enthusiasm*) aportar
injection [ɪnˈdʒɛkʃən] *n* inyección *f*; **to have an ~** ponerse una inyección
injure [ˈɪndʒəʳ] *vt* herir; (*hurt*) lastimar; (*fig: reputation etc*) perjudicar; (*feelings*) herir; **to ~ o.s.** hacerse daño, lastimarse
injured [ˈɪndʒəd] *adj* (*also fig*) herido; **~ party** (*Law*) parte *f* perjudicada
injury [ˈɪndʒərɪ] *n* herida, lesión *f*; (*wrong*) perjuicio, daño; **to escape without ~** salir ileso
injury time *n* (*Sport*) descuento
injustice [ɪnˈdʒʌstɪs] *n* injusticia; **you do me an ~** usted es injusto conmigo
ink [ɪŋk] *n* tinta
ink-jet printer [ˈɪŋkdʒɛt-] *n* impresora de chorro de tinta
inkling [ˈɪŋklɪŋ] *n* sospecha; (*idea*) idea
inlaid [ˈɪnleɪd] *adj* (*wood*) taraceado; (*tiles*) entarimado
inland *adj* [ˈɪnlənd] interior; (*town*) del interior ▷ *adv* [ɪnˈlænd] tierra adentro
Inland Revenue *n* (*Brit*) ≈ Hacienda, ≈ Agencia Tributaria
in-laws [ˈɪnlɔːz] *npl* suegros *mpl*
inlet [ˈɪnlɛt] *n* (*Geo*) ensenada, cala; (*Tech*) admisión *f*, entrada
inmate [ˈɪnmeɪt] *n* (*in prison*) preso(-a), presidiario(-a); (*in asylum*) internado(-a)
inmost [ˈɪnməust] *adj* más íntimo, más secreto
inn [ɪn] *n* posada, mesón *m*
innate [ɪˈneɪt] *adj* innato
inner [ˈɪnəʳ] *adj* interior, interno; (*feelings*) íntimo
inner-city *adj* (*schools, problems*) de las zonas céntricas pobres, de los barrios céntricos pobres
inner city *n barrios deprimidos del centro de una ciudad*
innermost [ˈɪnəməust] *adj* más íntimo, más secreto
inner tube *n* (*of tyre*) cámara, llanta (*LAm*)
inning [ˈɪnɪŋ] *n* (*US: Baseball*) inning *m*, entrada; **~s** (*Cricket*) entrada, turno
innocence [ˈɪnəsns] *n* inocencia
innocent [ˈɪnəsnt] *adj* inocente
innocuous [ɪˈnɔkjuəs] *adj* inocuo
innovation [ɪnəuˈveɪʃən] *n* novedad *f*
innovative [ˈɪnəuˈveɪtɪv] *adj* innovador
innuendo (*pl* **innuendoes**) [ɪnjuˈɛndəu, -əuz] *n* indirecta
innumerable [ɪˈnjuːmrəbl] *adj* innumerable
inoculate [ɪˈnɔkjuleɪt] *vt*: **to ~ sb with sth/against sth** inocular *or* vacunar a algn con algo/contra algo
inoculation [ɪnɔkjuˈleɪʃən] *n* inoculación *f*
inoffensive [ɪnəˈfɛnsɪv] *adj* inofensivo
inordinate [ɪˈnɔːdɪnət] *adj* excesivo, desmesurado
inordinately [ɪˈnɔːdɪnətlɪ] *adv* excesivamente, desmesuradamente
in-patient [ˈɪnpeɪʃənt] *n* (paciente *m/f*) interno(-a)
input [ˈɪnput] *n* (*Elec*) entrada; (*of resources*) inversión *f*; (*Comput*) entrada de datos ▷ *vt* (*Comput*) introducir, entrar
inquest [ˈɪnkwɛst] *n* (*coroner's*) investigación *f* post-mortem
inquire [ɪnˈkwaɪəʳ] *vi* preguntar ▷ *vt*: **to ~ when/where/whether** preguntar cuándo/dónde/si; **to ~ about** (*person*) preguntar por; (*fact*) informarse de; **inquire into** *vt fus*: **to ~ into sth** investigar *or* indagar algo
inquiry [ɪnˈkwaɪərɪ] *n* pregunta; (*Law*) investigación *f*, pesquisa; (*commission*) comisión *f* investigadora; **to hold an ~ into sth** emprender una investigación sobre algo; **"Inquiries"** "Información"
inquiry office *n* (*Brit*) oficina de información
inquisition [ɪnkwɪˈzɪʃən] *n* inquisición *f*
inquisitive [ɪnˈkwɪzɪtɪv] *adj* (*mind*) inquisitivo; (*person*) fisgón(-ona)
inroad [ˈɪnrəud] *n* incursión *f*; (*fig*) invasión *f*; **to make ~s into** (*time*) ocupar parte de; (*savings, supplies*) agotar parte de
insane [ɪnˈseɪn] *adj* loco; (*Med*) demente
insanity [ɪnˈsænɪtɪ] *n* demencia, locura
inscribe [ɪnˈskraɪb] *vt* inscribir; (*book etc*): **to ~ (to sb)** dedicar (a algn)
inscription [ɪnˈskrɪpʃən] *n* (*gen*) inscripción *f*; (*in book*) dedicatoria
inscrutable [ɪnˈskruːtəbl] *adj* inescrutable, insondable
insect [ˈɪnsɛkt] *n* insecto
insecticide [ɪnˈsɛktɪsaɪd] *n* insecticida *m*
insect repellent *n* loción *f* contra los insectos
insecure [ɪnsɪˈkjuəʳ] *adj* inseguro
insecurity [ɪnsɪˈkjuərɪtɪ] *n* inseguridad *f*

insemination [ɪnsɛmɪ'neɪʃn] *n*: **artificial ~** inseminación *f* artificial
insensitive [ɪn'sɛnsɪtɪv] *adj* insensible
inseparable [ɪn'sɛprəbl] *adj* inseparable; **they were ~ friends** los unía una estrecha amistad
insert *vt* [ɪn'səːt] (*into sth*) introducir; (*Comput*) insertar ▷ *n* ['ɪnsəːt] encarte *m*
insertion [ɪn'səːʃən] *n* inserción *f*
in-service [ɪn'səːvɪs] *adj* (*training, course*) en el trabajo, a cargo de la empresa
inshore [ɪn'ʃɔːʳ] *adj*: **~ fishing** pesca *f* costera ▷ *adv* (*fish*) a lo largo de la costa; (*move*) hacia la orilla
inside ['ɪn'saɪd] *n* interior *m*; (*lining*) forro; (*of road: Brit*) izquierdo; (*: in US, Europe etc*) derecho ▷ *adj* interior, interno ▷ *adv* (*within*) (por) dentro, adentro (*esp LAm*); (*with movement*) hacia dentro; (*inf: in prison*) en chirona ▷ *prep* dentro de; (*of time*): **~ 10 minutes** en menos de 10 minutos; **insides** *npl* (*inf*) tripas *fpl*; **~ out** *adv* (*turn*) al revés; (*know*) a fondo
inside lane *n* (*Aut: Brit*) carril *m* izquierdo; (*: in US, Europe etc*) carril *m* derecho
insider [ɪn'saɪdəʳ] *n* enterado(-a)
insider dealing, insider trading *n* (*Stock Exchange*) abuso de información privilegiada
insight ['ɪnsaɪt] *n* perspicacia, percepción *f*; **to gain** *or* **get an ~ into sth** comprender algo mejor
insignificant [ɪnsɪg'nɪfɪknt] *adj* insignificante
insincere [ɪnsɪn'sɪəʳ] *adj* poco sincero
insinuate [ɪn'sɪnjueɪt] *vt* insinuar
insinuation [ɪnsɪnju'eɪʃən] *n* insinuación *f*
insist [ɪn'sɪst] *vi* insistir; **to ~ on doing** empeñarse en hacer; **to ~ that** insistir en que; (*claim*) exigir que
insistence [ɪn'sɪstəns] *n* insistencia; (*stubbornness*) empeño
insistent [ɪn'sɪstənt] *adj* insistente; (*noise, action*) persistente
insofar as [ɪnsəu'fɑː-] *conj* en la medida en que, en tanto que
insole ['ɪnsəul] *n* plantilla
insolence ['ɪnsələns] *n* insolencia, descaro
insolent ['ɪnsələnt] *adj* insolente, descarado
insolvent [ɪn'sɔlvənt] *adj* insolvente
insomnia [ɪn'sɔmnɪə] *n* insomnio
insomniac [ɪn'sɔmnɪæk] *n* insomne *m/f*
inspect [ɪn'spɛkt] *vt* inspeccionar, examinar; (*troops*) pasar revista a
inspection [ɪn'spɛkʃən] *n* inspección *f*, examen *m*; (*of troops*) revista
inspector [ɪn'spɛktəʳ] *n* inspector(a) *m(f)*; (*Brit: on buses, trains*) revisor(a) *m(f)*
inspiration [ɪnspə'reɪʃən] *n* inspiración *f*
inspire [ɪn'spaɪəʳ] *vt* inspirar; **to ~ sb (to do sth)** alentar a algn (a hacer algo)
inspiring [ɪn'spaɪərɪŋ] *adj* inspirador(a)
instability [ɪnstə'bɪlɪtɪ] *n* inestabilidad *f*
install, instal (*US*) [ɪn'stɔːl] *vt* instalar
installation [ɪnstə'leɪʃən] *n* instalación *f*
instalment, installment (*US*) [ɪn'stɔːl-mənt] *n* plazo; (*of story*) entrega; (*of TV serial etc*) capítulo; **in ~s** (*pay, receive*) a plazos; **to pay in ~s** pagar a plazos *or* por abonos
instance ['ɪnstəns] *n* ejemplo, caso; **for ~** por ejemplo; **in the first ~** en primer lugar; **in that ~** en ese caso
instant ['ɪnstənt] *n* instante *m*, momento ▷ *adj* inmediato; (*coffee*) instantáneo
instantly ['ɪnstəntlɪ] *adv* en seguida, al instante
instant message *n* mensaje *m* instantáneo
instant messaging [-'mɛsədʒɪŋ] *n* mensajería instantánea
instead [ɪn'stɛd] *adv* en cambio; **~ of** en lugar de, en vez de
instep ['ɪnstɛp] *n* empeine *m*
instigate ['ɪnstɪgeɪt] *vt* (*rebellion, strike, crime*) instigar; (*new ideas etc*) fomentar
instigation [ɪnstɪ'geɪʃən] *n* instigación *f*; **at sb's ~** a instigación de algn
instil [ɪn'stɪl] *vt*: **to ~ into** inculcar a
instinct ['ɪnstɪŋkt] *n* instinto
instinctive [ɪn'stɪŋktɪv] *adj* instintivo
institute ['ɪnstɪtjuːt] *n* instituto; (*professional body*) colegio ▷ *vt* (*begin*) iniciar, empezar; (*proceedings*) entablar
institution [ɪnstɪ'tjuːʃən] *n* institución *f*; (*beginning*) iniciación *f*; (*Med: home*) asilo; (*asylum*) manicomio; (*custom*) costumbre *f* arraigada
instruct [ɪn'strʌkt] *vt*: **to ~ sb in sth** instruir a algn en *or* sobre algo; **to ~ sb to do sth** dar instrucciones a algn de *or* mandar a algn hacer algo
instruction [ɪn'strʌkʃən] *n* (*teaching*) instrucción *f*; **instructions** *npl* órdenes *fpl*; **~s (for use)** modo *sg* de empleo
instructor [ɪn'strʌktəʳ] *n* instructor(a) *m(f)*
instrument ['ɪnstrəmənt] *n* instrumento
instrumental [ɪnstrə'mɛntl] *adj* (*Mus*) instrumental; **to be ~ in** ser el artífice de; **to be ~ in sth/in doing sth** ser responsable de algo/de hacer algo
instrument panel *n* tablero (de instrumentos)
insufficient [ɪnsə'fɪʃənt] *adj* insuficiente
insular ['ɪnsjuləʳ] *adj* insular; (*outlook*) estrecho de miras
insulate ['ɪnsjuleɪt] *vt* aislar
insulating tape ['ɪnsjuleɪtɪŋ-] *n* cinta aislante
insulation [ɪnsju'leɪʃən] *n* aislamiento
insulin ['ɪnsjulɪn] *n* insulina
insult *n* ['ɪnsʌlt] insulto; (*offence*) ofensa ▷ *vt* [ɪn'sʌlt] insultar; ofender
insulting [ɪn'sʌltɪŋ] *adj* insultante; ofensivo
insurance [ɪn'ʃuərəns] *n* seguro; **fire/life ~** seguro contra incendios/de vida; **to take out ~ (against)** hacerse un seguro (contra)

insurance company *n* compañía *f* de seguros
insurance policy *n* póliza (de seguros)
insure [ɪn'ʃuəʳ] *vt* asegurar; **to ~ sb** *or* **sb's life** hacer un seguro de vida a algn; **to ~ (against)** asegurar (contra); **to be ~d for £5000** tener un seguro de 5000 libras
insured [ɪn'ʃuəd] *n*: **the ~** el/la asegurado(-a)
insurer [ɪn'ʃuərəʳ] *n* asegurador(a)
intact [ɪn'tækt] *adj* íntegro; (*untouched*) intacto
intake ['ɪnteɪk] *n* (*Tech*) entrada, toma; (*: pipe*) tubo de admisión; (*of food*) ingestión *f*; (*Brit Scol*): **an ~ of 200 a year** 200 matriculados al año
integer ['ɪntɪdʒəʳ] *n* (número) entero
integral ['ɪntɪgrəl] *adj* (*whole*) íntegro; (*part*) integrante
integrate ['ɪntɪgreɪt] *vt* integrar ▷ *vi* integrarse
integrity [ɪn'tɛgrɪtɪ] *n* honradez *f*, rectitud *f*; (*Comput*) integridad *f*
intellect ['ɪntəlɛkt] *n* intelecto
intellectual [ɪntə'lɛktjuəl] *adj, n* intelectual *m/f*
intelligence [ɪn'tɛlɪdʒəns] *n* inteligencia
Intelligence Service *n* Servicio de Inteligencia
intelligence test *n* prueba de inteligencia
intelligent [ɪn'tɛlɪdʒənt] *adj* inteligente
intend [ɪn'tɛnd] *vt* (*gift etc*): **to ~ sth for** destinar algo a; **to ~ to do sth** tener intención de *or* pensar hacer algo
intended [ɪn'tɛndɪd] *adj* (*effect*) deseado
intense [ɪn'tɛns] *adj* intenso; **to be ~** (*person*) tomárselo todo muy en serio
intensely [ɪn'tɛnslɪ] *adv* intensamente; (*very*) sumamente
intensify [ɪn'tɛnsɪfaɪ] *vt* intensificar; (*increase*) aumentar
intensity [ɪn'tɛnsɪtɪ] *n* (*gen*) intensidad *f*
intensive [ɪn'tɛnsɪv] *adj* intensivo
intensive care *n*: **to be in ~** estar bajo cuidados intensivos; **~ unit** *n* unidad *f* de vigilancia intensiva
intent [ɪn'tɛnt] *n* propósito; (*Law*) premeditación *f* ▷ *adj* (*absorbed*) absorto; (*attentive*) atento; **to all ~s and purposes** a efectos prácticos; **to be ~ on doing sth** estar resuelto *or* decidido a hacer algo
intention [ɪn'tɛnʃən] *n* intención *f*, propósito
intentional [ɪn'tɛnʃənl] *adj* deliberado
intently [ɪn'tɛntlɪ] *adv* atentamente, fijamente
interact [ɪntər'ækt] *vi* (*substances*) influirse mutuamente; (*people*) relacionarse
interaction [ɪntər'ækʃən] *n* interacción *f*, acción *f* recíproca
interactive [ɪntər'æktɪv] *adj* (*Comput*) interactivo
intercept [ɪntə'sɛpt] *vt* interceptar; (*stop*) detener
interception [ɪntə'sɛpʃən] *n* interceptación *f*; detención *f*
interchange *n* ['ɪntətʃeɪndʒ] intercambio; (*on motorway*) intersección *f* ▷ *vt* [ɪntə'tʃeɪndʒ] intercambiar
interchangeable [ɪntə'tʃeɪndʒəbl] *adj* intercambiable
intercity [ɪntə'sɪtɪ] *adj*: **~ (train)** (tren *m*) intercity *m*
intercom ['ɪntəkɔm] *n* interfono
intercourse ['ɪntəkɔ:s] *n* (*also*: **sexual ~**) relaciones *fpl* sexuales, contacto sexual; (*social*) trato
interest ['ɪntrɪst] *n* (*Comm*) interés *m* ▷ *vt* interesar; **compound/simple ~** interés compuesto/simple; **business ~s** negocios *mpl*; **British ~s in the Middle East** los intereses británicos en el Medio Oriente
interested ['ɪntrɪstɪd] *adj* interesado; **to be ~ in** interesarse por
interesting ['ɪntrɪstɪŋ] *adj* interesante
interest rate *n* tipo de interés
interface ['ɪntəfeɪs] *n* (*Comput*) junción *f*, interface *m*
interfere [ɪntə'fɪəʳ] *vi*: **to ~ in** (*quarrel, other people's business*) entrometerse en; **to ~ with** (*hinder*) estorbar; (*damage*) estropear; (*Radio*) interferir con
interference [ɪntə'fɪərəns] *n* (*gen*) intromisión *f*; (*Radio, TV*) interferencia
interim ['ɪntərɪm] *adj* provisional ▷ *n*: **in the ~** en el ínterin; **~ dividend** dividendo parcial
interior [ɪn'tɪərɪəʳ] *n* interior *m* ▷ *adj* interior
interior decorator, interior designer *n* interiorista *m/f*, diseñador(a) *m(f)* de interiores
interior design *n* interiorismo, decoración *f* de interiores
interjection [ɪntə'dʒɛkʃən] *n* interrupción *f*
interlock [ɪntə'lɔk] *vi* entrelazarse; (*wheels etc*) endentarse
interlude ['ɪntəlu:d] *n* intervalo; (*rest*) descanso; (*Theat*) intermedio
intermediary [ɪntə'mi:dɪərɪ] *n* intermediario(-a)
intermediate [ɪntə'mi:dɪət] *adj* intermedio
intermission [ɪntə'mɪʃən] *n* (*Theat*) descanso
intermittent [ɪntə'mɪtnt] *adj* intermitente
intern *vt* [ɪn'tə:n] internar; (*enclose*) encerrar ▷ *n* ['ɪntə:n] (*US*) médico(-a) *m(f)* interno(-a)
internal [ɪn'tə:nl] *adj* interno, interior; (*injury, structure, memo*) internal; **~ injuries** heridas *fpl or* lesiones *fpl* internas
internally [ɪn'tə:nəlɪ] *adv* interiormente; **"not to be taken ~"** "uso externo"
Internal Revenue Service *n* (*US*) ≈ Hacienda, ≈ Agencia Tributaria
international [ɪntə'næʃənl] *adj* internacional; **~ (game)** partido internacional; **~ (player)** jugador(a) *m(f)* internacional
internee [ɪntə:'ni:] *n* interno(-a), recluso(-a)

i

internet, Internet ['ɪntənɛt] *n*: **the ~** (el *or* la) Internet
internet café *n* cibercafé *m*
Internet Service Provider *n* proveedor *m* de (acceso a) Internet
internet user *n* internauta *m/f*
internment [ɪn'tə:nmənt] *n* internamiento
interplay ['ɪntəpleɪ] *n* interacción *f*
interpret [ɪn'tə:prɪt] *vt* interpretar; (*translate*) traducir; (*understand*) entender ▷ *vi* hacer de intérprete
interpretation [ɪntə:prɪ'teɪʃən] *n* interpretación *f*; traducción *f*
interpreter [ɪn'tə:prɪtəʳ] *n* intérprete *m/f*
interrelated [ɪntərɪ'leɪtɪd] *adj* interrelacionado
interrogate [ɪn'tɛrəugeɪt] *vt* interrogar
interrogation [ɪntɛrəu'geɪʃən] *n* interrogatorio
interrogative [ɪntə'rɔgətɪv] *adj* interrogativo
interrupt [ɪntə'rʌpt] *vt, vi* interrumpir
interruption [ɪntə'rʌpʃən] *n* interrupción *f*
intersect [ɪntə'sɛkt] *vt* cruzar ▷ *vi* (*roads*) cruzarse
intersection [ɪntə'sɛkʃən] *n* intersección *f*; (*of roads*) cruce *m*
intersperse [ɪntə'spə:s] *vt*: **to ~ with** salpicar de
interstate ['ɪntərsteɪt] *n* (*US*) carretera interestatal
intertwine [ɪntə'twaɪn] *vt* entrelazar ▷ *vi* entrelazarse
interval ['ɪntəvl] *n* intervalo; (*Brit Theat, Sport*) descanso; (*Scol*) recreo; **at ~s** a ratos, de vez en cuando; **sunny ~s** (*Meteorology*) claros *mpl*
intervene [ɪntə'vi:n] *vi* intervenir; (*take part*) participar; (*occur*) sobrevenir
intervention [ɪntə'vɛnʃən] *n* intervención *f*
interview ['ɪntəvju:] *n* (*Radio, TV etc*) entrevista ▷ *vt* entrevistar a
interviewee [ɪntəvju:'i:] *n* entrevistado(-a)
interviewer ['ɪntəvju:əʳ] *n* entrevistador(a) *m(f)*
intestate [ɪn'tɛstɛɪt] *adj* intestado
intestine [ɪn'tɛstɪn] *n*: **large/small ~** intestino grueso/delgado
intimacy ['ɪntɪməsɪ] *n* intimidad *f*; (*relations*) relaciones *fpl* íntimas
intimate *adj* ['ɪntɪmət] íntimo; (*friendship*) estrecho; (*knowledge*) profundo ▷ *vt* ['ɪntɪmeɪt] (*announce*) dar a entender
intimidate [ɪn'tɪmɪdeɪt] *vt* intimidar, amedrentar
intimidating [ɪn'tɪmɪdeɪtɪŋ] *adj* amedrentador, intimidante
intimidation [ɪntɪmɪ'deɪʃən] *n* intimidación *f*
into ['ɪntu:] *prep* (*gen*) en; (*towards*) a; (*inside*) hacia el interior de; **~ three pieces/French** en tres pedazos/al francés; **to change pounds ~ euros** cambiar libras por euros
intolerable [ɪn'tɔlərəbl] *adj* intolerable, insoportable
intolerant [ɪn'tɔlərənt] *adj*: **~ (of)** intolerante (con)
intoxicated [ɪn'tɔksɪkeɪtɪd] *adj* embriagado
intoxication [ɪntɔksɪ'keɪʃən] *n* embriaguez *f*
intractable [ɪn'træktəbl] *adj* (*person*) intratable; (*problem*) irresoluble; (*illness*) incurable
intranet ['ɪntrənet] *n* intranet *f*
intransitive [ɪn'trænsɪtɪv] *adj* intransitivo
intravenous [ɪntrə'vi:nəs] *adj* intravenoso
in-tray ['ɪntreɪ] *n* bandeja de entrada
intrepid [ɪn'trɛpɪd] *adj* intrépido
intricate ['ɪntrɪkət] *adj* (*design, pattern*) intrincado; (*plot, problem*) complejo
intrigue [ɪn'tri:g] *n* intriga ▷ *vt* fascinar ▷ *vi* andar en intrigas
intriguing [ɪn'tri:gɪŋ] *adj* fascinante
intrinsic [ɪn'trɪnsɪk] *adj* intrínseco
introduce [ɪntrə'dju:s] *vt* introducir, meter; (*speaker, TV show etc*) presentar; **to ~ sb (to sb)** presentar algn (a algn); **to ~ sb to** (*pastime, technique*) introducir a algn a; **may I ~ ...?** permítame presentarle a ...
introduction [ɪntrə'dʌkʃən] *n* introducción *f*; (*of person*) presentación *f*; **a letter of ~** una carta de recomendación
introductory [ɪntrə'dʌktərɪ] *adj* introductorio; **an ~ offer** una oferta introductoria; **~ remarks** comentarios *mpl* preliminares
introvert ['ɪntrəuvə:t] *adj, n* introvertido(-a) *m(f)*
intrude [ɪn'tru:d] *vi* (*person*) entrometerse; **to ~ on** estorbar
intruder [ɪn'tru:dəʳ] *n* intruso(-a)
intrusion [ɪn'tru:ʒən] *n* invasión *f*
intuition [ɪntju:'ɪʃən] *n* intuición *f*
intuitive [ɪn'tju:ɪtɪv] *adj* intuitivo
inundate ['ɪnʌndeɪt] *vt*: **to ~ with** inundar de
invade [ɪn'veɪd] *vt* invadir
invalid *n* ['ɪnvəlɪd] minusválido(-a) ▷ *adj* [ɪn'vælɪd] (*not valid*) inválido, nulo
invaluable [ɪn'væljuəbl] *adj* inestimable
invariably [ɪn'vɛərɪəblɪ] *adv* sin excepción, siempre; **she is ~ late** siempre llega tarde
invasion [ɪn'veɪʒən] *n* invasión *f*
invent [ɪn'vɛnt] *vt* inventar
invention [ɪn'vɛnʃən] *n* invento; (*inventiveness*) inventiva; (*lie*) invención *f*
inventive [ɪn'vɛntɪv] *adj* inventivo
inventor [ɪn'vɛntəʳ] *n* inventor(a) *m(f)*
inventory ['ɪnvəntrɪ] *n* inventario
invert [ɪn'və:t] *vt* invertir
inverted commas [ɪn'və:tɪd-] *npl* (*Brit*) comillas *fpl*
invest [ɪn'vɛst] *vt* invertir; (*fig: time, effort*) dedicar ▷ *vi*: **to ~ in** (*company etc*) invertir dinero en; (*fig: sth useful*) comprar; **to ~ sb with sth** conferir algo a algn

investigate [ɪnˈvɛstɪgeɪt] *vt* investigar; (*study*) estudiar, examinar
investigation [ɪnvɛstɪˈgeɪʃən] *n* investigación *f*, pesquisa; examen *m*
investigator [ɪnˈvɛstɪgeɪtəʳ] *n* investigador(a) *m(f)*; **private ~** investigador(a) *m(f)* privado(-a)
investment [ɪnˈvɛstmənt] *n* inversión *f*
investor [ɪnˈvɛstəʳ] *n* inversor(a) *m(f)*
invigilator [ɪnˈvɪdʒɪleɪtəʳ] *n* celador(a) *m(f)*
invigorating [ɪnˈvɪgəreɪtɪŋ] *adj* vigorizante
invisible [ɪnˈvɪzɪbl] *adj* invisible
invitation [ɪnvɪˈteɪʃən] *n* invitación *f*; **at sb's ~** a invitación de algn; **by ~ only** solamente por invitación
invite [ɪnˈvaɪt] *vt* invitar; (*opinions etc*) solicitar, pedir; (*trouble*) buscarse; **to ~ sb (to do)** invitar a algn (a hacer); **to ~ sb to dinner** invitar a algn a cenar; **invite out** *vt* invitar a salir; **invite over** *vt* invitar a casa
inviting [ɪnˈvaɪtɪŋ] *adj* atractivo; (*look*) provocativo; (*food*) apetitoso
invoice [ˈɪnvɔɪs] *n* factura ▷ *vt* facturar; **to ~ sb for goods** facturar a algn las mercancías
involuntary [ɪnˈvɔləntrɪ] *adj* involuntario
involve [ɪnˈvɔlv] *vt* (*entail*) suponer, implicar, tener que ver con; (*concern, affect*) corresponder a; **to ~ sb (in sth)** involucrar a algn (en algo), comprometer a algn (con algo)
involved [ɪnˈvɔlvd] *adj* complicado; **to be ~ in sth** (*take part*) estar involucrado en algo; (*engrossed in*) estar muy metido
involvement [ɪnˈvɔlvmənt] *n* participación *f*, dedicación *f*; (*obligation*) compromiso; (*difficulty*) apuro
inward [ˈɪnwəd] *adj* (*movement*) interior, interno; (*thought, feeling*) íntimo ▷ *adv* hacia dentro
inwards [ˈɪnwədz] *adv* hacia dentro
I/O *abbr* (*Comput*; = *input/output*) E/S; **~ error** error *m* de E/S
iodine [ˈaɪəudiːn] *n* yodo
ioniser [ˈaɪənaɪzəʳ] *n* ionizador *m*
iota [aɪˈəutə] *n* (*fig*) jota, ápice *m*
IOU *n abbr* (= *I owe you*) pagaré *m*
IPA *n abbr* (= *International Phonetic Alphabet*) AFI *m*
iPod® [ˈaɪpɔd] *n* iPod® *m*
IQ *n abbr* (= *intelligence quotient*) C.I. *m*
IRA *n abbr* (= *Irish Republican Army*) IRA *m*; (*US*) = **individual retirement account**
Iran [ɪˈrɑːn] *n* Irán *m*
Iranian [ɪˈreɪnɪən] *adj* iraní ▷ *n* iraní *m/f*; (*Ling*) iraní *m*
Iraq [ɪˈrɑːk] *n* Irak *m*
Iraqi [ɪˈrɑːkɪ] *adj, n* irakí *m/f*
irate [aɪˈreɪt] *adj* enojado, airado
Ireland [ˈaɪələnd] *n* Irlanda; **Republic of ~** República de Irlanda
iris (*pl* **irises**) [ˈaɪrɪs, -ɪz] *n* (*Anat*) iris *m*; (*Bot*) lirio
Irish [ˈaɪrɪʃ] *adj* irlandés(-esa) ▷ *n* (*Ling*) irlandés *m*; **the ~** *npl* los irlandeses
Irishman [ˈaɪrɪʃmən] *n* irlandés *m*
Irish Sea *n*: **the ~** el Mar de Irlanda
Irishwoman [ˈaɪrɪʃwumən] *n* irlandesa
irk [əːk] *vt* fastidiar
irksome [ˈəːksəm] *adj* fastidioso
IRN *n abbr* (= *Independent Radio News*) *servicio de noticias en las cadenas de radio privadas*
iron [ˈaɪən] *n* hierro; (*for clothes*) plancha ▷ *adj* de hierro ▷ *vt* (*clothes*) planchar; **irons** *npl* (*chains*) grilletes *mpl*; **iron out** *vt* (*crease*) quitar; (*fig*) allanar, resolver
Iron Curtain *n*: **the ~** el Telón de Acero
ironic [aɪˈrɔnɪk], **ironical** [aɪˈrɔnɪkl] *adj* irónico
ironically [aɪˈrɔnɪklɪ] *adv* irónicamente
ironing [ˈaɪənɪŋ] *n* (*act*) planchado; (*ironed clothes*) ropa planchada; (*clothes to be ironed*) ropa por planchar
ironing board *n* tabla de planchar
ironmonger [ˈaɪənmʌŋgəʳ] *n* (*Brit*) ferretero(-a); **~'s (shop)** ferretería
irony [ˈaɪrənɪ] *n* ironía; **the ~ of it is that ...** lo irónico del caso es que ...
irrational [ɪˈræʃənl] *adj* irracional
irregular [ɪˈrɛgjuləʳ] *adj* irregular; (*surface*) desigual; (*action, event*) anómalo; (*behaviour*) poco ortodoxo
irrelevant [ɪˈrɛləvənt] *adj* irrelevante; **to be ~** estar fuera de lugar, no venir al caso
irresistible [ɪrɪˈzɪstɪbl] *adj* irresistible
irrespective [ɪrɪˈspɛktɪv]: **~ of** *prep* sin tener en cuenta, no importa
irresponsible [ɪrɪˈspɔnsɪbl] *adj* (*act*) irresponsable; (*person*) poco serio
irreverent [ɪˈrɛvərnt] *adj* irreverente, irrespetuoso
irrevocable [ɪˈrɛvəkəbl] *adj* irrevocable
irrigate [ˈɪrɪgeɪt] *vt* regar
irrigation [ɪrɪˈgeɪʃən] *n* riego
irritable [ˈɪrɪtəbl] *adj* (*person: temperament*) irritable; (*: mood*) de mal humor
irritate [ˈɪrɪteɪt] *vt* fastidiar; (*Med*) picar
irritating [ˈɪrɪteɪtɪŋ] *adj* fastidioso
irritation [ɪrɪˈteɪʃən] *n* fastidio; picazón *f*, picor *m*
IRS *n abbr* (*US*) = **Internal Revenue Service**
is [ɪz] *vb see* **be**
ISA [ˈaɪsə] *n abbr* (*Brit*: = *individual savings account*) *plan de ahorro personal para pequeños inversores con fiscalidad cero*
ISBN *n abbr* (= *International Standard Book Number*) ISBN *m*
ISDN *n abbr* (= *Integrated Services Digital Network*) RDSI *f*
Islam [ˈɪzlɑːm] *n* Islam *m*
Islamic [ɪzˈlæmɪk] *adj* islámico
island [ˈaɪlənd] *n* isla; (*also*: **traffic ~**) isleta
islander [ˈaɪləndəʳ] *n* isleño(-a)
isle [aɪl] *n* isla
isn't [ˈɪznt] = **is not**
isobar [ˈaɪsəubɑːʳ] *n* isobara
isolate [ˈaɪsəleɪt] *vt* aislar

isolated ['aɪsəleɪtɪd] *adj* aislado
isolation [aɪsə'leɪʃən] *n* aislamiento
isotope ['aɪsəutəup] *n* isótopo
ISP *n abbr* = **Internet Service Provider**
Israel ['ɪzreɪl] *n* Israel *m*
Israeli [ɪz'reɪlɪ] *adj, n* israelí *m/f*
issue ['ɪsju:] *n* cuestión *f*, asunto; (*outcome*) resultado; (*of banknotes etc*) emisión *f*; (*of newspaper etc*) número; (*offspring*) sucesión *f*, descendencia ▷ *vt* (*rations, equipment*) distribuir, repartir; (*orders*) dar; (*certificate, passport*) expedir; (*decree*) promulgar; (*magazine*) publicar; (*cheque*) extender; (*banknotes, stamp*) emitir ▷ *vi*: **to ~ (from)** derivar (de), brotar (de); **at ~** en cuestión; **to take ~ with sb (over)** disentir con algn (en); **to avoid the ~** andarse con rodeos; **to confuse** *or* **obscure the ~** confundir las cosas; **to make an ~ of sth** dar a algo más importancia de lo necesario; **to ~ sth to sb, ~ sb with sth** entregar algo a algn
isthmus ['ɪsməs] *n* istmo
IT *n abbr* = **information technology**

KEYWORD

it [ɪt] *pron* **1** (*specific subject: not generally translated*) él/ella; (*: direct object*) lo/la; (*: indirect object*) le; (*after prep*) él/ella; (*abstract concept*) ello; **it's on the table** está en la mesa; **I can't find it** no lo (*or* la) encuentro; **give it to me** dámelo (*or* dámela); **I spoke to him about it** le hablé del asunto; **what did you learn from it?** ¿qué aprendiste de él (*or* ella)?; **did you go to it?** (*party, concert etc*) ¿fuiste?
2 (*impersonal*): **it's raining** llueve, está lloviendo; **it's 6 o'clock/the 10th of August** son las 6/es el 10 de agosto; **how far is it? — it's 10 miles/2 hours on the train** ¿a qué distancia está? — a 10 millas/2 horas en tren; **who is it? — it's me** ¿quién es? — soy yo

Italian [ɪ'tæljən] *adj* italiano ▷ *n* italiano(-a); (*Ling*) italiano
italic [ɪ'tælɪk] *adj* cursivo; **italics** *npl* cursiva *sg*
Italy ['ɪtəlɪ] *n* Italia
itch [ɪtʃ] *n* picazón *f*; (*fig*) prurito ▷ *vi* (*person*) sentir *or* tener comezón; (*part of body*) picar; **to be ~ing to do sth** rabiar por *or* morirse de ganas de hacer algo
itchy ['ɪtʃɪ] *adj*: **to be ~** picar; **my hand is ~** me pica la mano
it'd ['ɪtd] = **it would; it had**
item ['aɪtəm] *n* artículo; (*on agenda*) asunto (a tratar); (*in programme*) número; (*also*: **news ~**) noticia; **~s of clothing** prendas *fpl* de vestir
itemize ['aɪtəmaɪz] *vt* detallar
itinerary [aɪ'tɪnərərɪ] *n* itinerario
it'll ['ɪtl] = **it will; it shall**
ITN *n abbr* (*Brit*) = **Independent Television News**
its [ɪts] *adj* su
it's [ɪts] = **it is; it has**
itself [ɪt'sɛlf] *pron* (*reflexive*) sí mismo(-a); (*emphatic*) él/ella mismo(-a)
ITV *n abbr* (*Brit*: = *Independent Television*)
IUD *n abbr* (= *intra-uterine device*) DIU *m*
I've [aɪv] = **I have**
ivory ['aɪvərɪ] *n* marfil *m*
ivy ['aɪvɪ] *n* hiedra
Ivy League *n* (*US*) *ver nota*

J

J, j [dʒeɪ] *n* (*letter*) J, j *f*; **J for Jack**, (*US*) **J for Jig** J de José
jab [dʒæb] *vt* (*elbow*) dar un codazo a; (*punch*) dar un golpe rápido a ▷ *vi*: **to ~ at** intentar golpear a; **to ~ sth into sth** clavar algo en algo ▷ *n* codazo; golpe *m* (rápido); (*Med*: *inf*) pinchazo
jack [dʒæk] *n* (*Aut*) gato; (*Bowls*) boliche *m*; (*Cards*) sota; **jack in** *vt* (*inf*) dejar; **jack up** *vt* (*Aut*) levantar con el gato
jackal [ˈdʒækl] *n* (*Zool*) chacal *m*
jackdaw [ˈdʒækdɔː] *n* grajo(-a), chova
jacket [ˈdʒækɪt] *n* chaqueta, americana, saco (*LAm*); (*of boiler etc*) camisa; (*of book*) sobrecubierta
jacket potato *n* patata asada (con piel)
jack-in-the-box [ˈdʒækɪnðəbɔks] *n* caja sorpresa, caja de resorte
jack-knife [ˈdʒæknaɪf] *vi* colear
jack plug *n* (*Elec*) enchufe *m* de clavija
jackpot [ˈdʒækpɔt] *n* premio gordo
Jacuzzi® [dʒəˈkuːzɪ] *n* jacuzzi® *m*
jaded [ˈdʒeɪdɪd] *adj* (*tired*) cansado; (*fed up*) hastiado
jagged [ˈdʒægɪd] *adj* dentado
jail [dʒeɪl] *n* cárcel *f* ▷ *vt* encarcelar
jail sentence *n* pena *f* de cárcel
jam [dʒæm] *n* mermelada; (*also*: **traffic ~**) atasco, embotellamiento; (*difficulty*) apuro ▷ *vt* (*passage etc*) obstruir; (*mechanism, drawer etc*) atascar; (*Radio*) interferir ▷ *vi* atascarse, trabarse; **to get sb out of a ~** sacar a algn del paso *or* de un apuro; **to ~ sth into sth** meter algo a la fuerza en algo; **the telephone lines are ~med** las líneas están saturadas
Jamaica [dʒəˈmeɪkə] *n* Jamaica
jamb [dʒæm] *n* jamba
jammed [dʒæmd] *adj* atascado
Jan *abbr* (= *January*) ene
jangle [ˈdʒæŋgl] *vi* sonar (de manera) discordante
janitor [ˈdʒænɪtəʳ] *n* (*caretaker*) portero, conserje *m*
January [ˈdʒænjuərɪ] *n* enero; *see also* **July**
Japan [dʒəˈpæn] *n* (el) Japón
Japanese [dʒæpəˈniːz] *adj* japonés(-esa) ▷ *n pl inv* japonés(-esa) *m(f)*; (*Ling*) japonés *m*
jar [dʒɑːʳ] *n* (*glass*: *large*) jarra; (*small*) tarro ▷ *vi* (*sound*) chirriar; (*colours*) desentonar
jargon [ˈdʒɑːgən] *n* jerga
jaundice [ˈdʒɔːndɪs] *n* ictericia
jaundiced [ˈdʒɔːndɪst] *adj* (*fig*: *embittered*) amargado; (: *disillusioned*) desilusionado
javelin [ˈdʒævlɪn] *n* jabalina
jaw [dʒɔː] *n* mandíbula; **jaws** *npl* (*Tech*: *of vice etc*) mordaza *sg*
jay [dʒeɪ] *n* (*Zool*) arrendajo
jaywalker [ˈdʒeɪwɔːkəʳ] *n* peatón(-ona) *m(f)* imprudente
jazz [dʒæz] *n* jazz *m*; **jazz up** *vt* (*liven up*) animar
JCB® *n abbr* excavadora
jealous [ˈdʒɛləs] *adj* (*gen*) celoso; (*envious*) envidioso; **to be ~** tener celos
jealousy [ˈdʒɛləsɪ] *n* celos *mpl*; envidia
jeans [dʒiːnz] *npl* (pantalones *mpl*) vaqueros *mpl or* tejanos *mpl*, bluejean *m inv* (*LAm*)
Jeep® [dʒiːp] *n* jeep *m*
jeer [dʒɪəʳ] *vi*: **to ~ (at)** (*boo*) abuchear; (*mock*) mofarse (de)
Jello® [ˈdʒɛləu] *n* (*US*) gelatina
jelly [ˈdʒɛlɪ] *n* (*jam*) jalea; (*dessert etc*) gelatina
jellyfish [ˈdʒɛlɪfɪʃ] *n* medusa
jeopardize [ˈdʒɛpədaɪz] *vt* arriesgar, poner en peligro
jeopardy [ˈdʒɛpədɪ] *n*: **to be in ~** estar en peligro
jerk [dʒəːk] *n* (*jolt*) sacudida; (*wrench*) tirón *m*; (*US inf*) imbécil *m/f*, pendejo(-a) (*LAm*) ▷ *vt* dar una sacudida a; tirar bruscamente de ▷ *vi* (*vehicle*) dar una sacudida
Jersey [ˈdʒəːzɪ] *n* Jersey *m*
jersey [ˈdʒəːzɪ] *n* jersey *m*; (*fabric*) tejido de punto
Jesus [ˈdʒiːzəs] *n* Jesús *m*; **~ Christ** Jesucristo
jet [dʒɛt] *n* (*of gas, liquid*) chorro; (*Aviat*) avión *m* a reacción
jet-black [ˈdʒɛtˈblæk] *adj* negro como el azabache
jet engine *n* motor *m* a reacción
jet lag *n* desorientación *f* por desfase horario
jet-setter [ˈdʒɛtsɛtəʳ] *n* personaje *m* de la jet
jet-ski [ˈdʒɛtskiː] *vi* practicar el motociclismo acuático

jettison ['dʒɛtɪsn] *vt* desechar
jetty ['dʒɛtɪ] *n* muelle *m*, embarcadero
Jew [dʒu:] *n* judío(-a)
jewel ['dʒu:əl] *n* joya; (*in watch*) rubí *m*
jeweller, jeweler (*US*) ['dʒu:ələʳ] *n* joyero(-a); **~'s (shop)** joyería
jewellery, jewelry (*US*) ['dʒu:əlrɪ] *n* joyas *fpl*, alhajas *fpl*
Jewess ['dʒu:ɪs] *n* judía
Jewish ['dʒu:ɪʃ] *adj* judío
jibe [dʒaɪb] *n* mofa
jiffy ['dʒɪfɪ] *n* (*inf*): **in a ~** en un santiamén
jigsaw ['dʒɪgsɔ:] *n* (*also*: **~ puzzle**) rompecabezas *m inv*, puzle *m*; (*tool*) sierra de vaivén
jilt [dʒɪlt] *vt* dejar plantado a
jingle ['dʒɪŋgl] *n* (*advert*) musiquilla ▷ *vi* tintinear
jinx [dʒɪŋks] *n*: **there's a ~ on it** está gafado
jitters ['dʒɪtəz] *npl* (*inf*): **to get the ~** ponerse nervioso
jittery ['dʒɪtərɪ] *adj* (*inf*) agitado
job [dʒɔb] *n* trabajo; (*task*) tarea; (*duty*) deber *m*; (*post*) empleo; (*inf*: *difficulty*) dificultad *f*; **it's a good ~ that ...** menos mal que ...; **just the ~!** ¡justo lo que necesito!; **a part-time/full-time ~** un trabajo a tiempo parcial/tiempo completo; **that's not my ~** eso no me incumbe *or* toca a mí; **he's only doing his ~** está cumpliendo nada más
job centre *n* (*Brit*) oficina de empleo
jobless ['dʒɔblɪs] *adj* sin trabajo ▷ *n*: **the ~** los parados
job satisfaction *n* satisfacción *f* en el trabajo
job security *n* garantía de trabajo
jockey ['dʒɔkɪ] *n* jockey *m/f* ▷ *vi*: **to ~ for position** maniobrar para sacar delantera
jockstrap ['dʒɔkstræp] *n* suspensorio
jocular ['dʒɔkjuləʳ] *adj* (*humorous*) gracioso; (*merry*) alegre
jog [dʒɔg] *vt* empujar (ligeramente) ▷ *vi* (*run*) hacer footing; **to ~ along** (*fig*) ir tirando; **to ~ sb's memory** refrescar la memoria a algn
jogger ['dʒɔgəʳ] *n* corredor(a) *m(f)*
jogging ['dʒɔgɪŋ] *n* footing *m*
join [dʒɔɪn] *vt* (*things*) unir, juntar; (*become member of*: *club*) hacerse socio de; (*Pol*: *party*) afiliarse a; (*meet*: *people*) reunirse con; (*fig*) unirse a ▷ *vi* (*roads*) empalmar; (*rivers*) confluir ▷ *n* juntura; **will you ~ us for dinner?** ¿quieres cenar con nosotros?; **I'll ~ you later** me reuniré contigo luego; **to ~ forces (with)** aliarse (con); **join in** *vi* tomar parte, participar ▷ *vt fus* tomar parte *or* participar en; **join up** *vi* unirse; (*Mil*) alistarse
joiner ['dʒɔɪnəʳ] *n* carpintero(-a)
joint [dʒɔɪnt] *n* (*Tech*) juntura, unión *f*; (*Anat*) articulación *f*; (*Brit Culin*) pieza de carne (para asar); (*inf*: *place*) garito; (*of cannabis*) porro ▷ *adj* (*common*) común; (*combined*) conjunto; (*responsibility*) compartido; (*committee*) mixto
joint account *n* (*with bank etc*) cuenta común
jointly ['dʒɔɪntlɪ] *adv* (*gen*) en común; (*together*) conjuntamente
joist [dʒɔɪst] *n* viga
joke [dʒəuk] *n* chiste *m*; (*also*: **practical ~**) broma ▷ *vi* bromear; **to play a ~ on** gastar una broma a
joker ['dʒəukəʳ] *n* chistoso(-a), bromista *m/f*; (*Cards*) comodín *m*
jolly ['dʒɔlɪ] *adj* (*merry*) alegre; (*enjoyable*) divertido ▷ *adv* (*inf*) muy, la mar de ▷ *vt*: **to ~ sb along** animar *or* darle ánimos a algn; **~ good!** ¡estupendo!
jolt [dʒəult] *n* (*shake*) sacudida; (*blow*) golpe *m*; (*shock*) susto ▷ *vt* (*physically*) sacudir; (*emotionally*) asustar
Jordan ['dʒɔ:dən] *n* (*country*) Jordania; (*river*) Jordán *m*
jostle ['dʒɔsl] *vt* dar empujones *or* empellones a
jot [dʒɔt] *n*: **not one ~** ni pizca, ni un ápice; **jot down** *vt* apuntar
jotter ['dʒɔtəʳ] *n* (*Brit*) bloc *m*
journal ['dʒə:nl] *n* (*paper*) periódico; (*magazine*) revista; (*diary*) diario
journalism ['dʒə:nəlɪzəm] *n* periodismo
journalist ['dʒə:nəlɪst] *n* periodista *m/f*
journey ['dʒə:nɪ] *n* viaje *m*; (*distance covered*) trayecto ▷ *vi* viajar; **return ~** viaje de regreso; **a five-hour ~** un viaje de cinco horas
joy [dʒɔɪ] *n* alegría
joyful ['dʒɔɪful] *adj* alegre
joyrider ['dʒɔɪraɪdəʳ] *n* *persona que se da una vuelta en un coche robado*
joystick ['dʒɔɪstɪk] *n* (*Aviat*) palanca de mando; (*Comput*) palanca de control
JP *n abbr see* **Justice of the Peace**
Jr *abbr* = **junior**
jubilant ['dʒu:bɪlnt] *adj* jubiloso
judge [dʒʌdʒ] *n* juez *m/f* ▷ *vt* juzgar; (*competition*) actuar de *or* ser juez en; (*estimate*) considerar; (: *weight, size etc*) calcular ▷ *vi*: **judging** *or* **to ~ by his expression** a juzgar por su expresión; **as far as I can ~** por lo que puedo entender, a mi entender; **I ~d it necessary to inform him** consideré necesario informarle
judicial [dʒu:'dɪʃl] *adj* judicial
judiciary [dʒu:'dɪʃɪərɪ] *n* poder *m* judicial, magistratura
judo ['dʒu:dəu] *n* judo
jug [dʒʌg] *n* jarra
juggernaut ['dʒʌgənɔ:t] *n* (*Brit*: *huge truck*) camión *m* de carga pesada
juggle ['dʒʌgl] *vi* hacer juegos malabares
juggler ['dʒʌgləʳ] *n* malabarista *m/f*
juice [dʒu:s] *n* jugo, zumo (*Sp*); (*of meat*) jugo; (*inf*: *petrol*): **we've run out of ~** se nos acabó la gasolina

juicy ['dʒu:sɪ] *adj* jugoso
jukebox ['dʒu:kbɔks] *n* máquina de discos
Jul. *abbr* (= *July*) jul
July [dʒu:'laɪ] *n* julio; **the first of ~** el uno *or* primero de julio; **during ~** en el mes de julio; **in ~ of next year** en julio del año que viene
jumble ['dʒʌmbl] *n* revoltijo ▷ *vt* (*also*: **~ together, ~ up**: *mix up*) revolver; (: *disarrange*) mezclar
jumble sale *n* (*Brit*) mercadillo; *ver nota*

JUMBLE SALE

En cada *jumble sale* pueden comprarse todo tipo de objetos baratos de segunda mano, especialmente ropa, juguetes, libros, vajillas y muebles. Suelen organizarse en los locales de un colegio, iglesia, ayuntamiento o similar, con fines benéficos, bien en ayuda de una organización benéfica conocida o para solucionar problemas más concretos de la comunidad.

jumbo ['dʒʌmbəu], **jumbo jet** *n* jumbo
jump [dʒʌmp] *vi* saltar, dar saltos; (*start*) sobresaltarse; (*increase*) aumentar ▷ *vt* saltar ▷ *n* salto; (*fence*) obstáculo; (*increase*) aumento; **to ~ the queue** (*Brit*) colarse; **jump about** *vi* dar saltos, brincar; **jump at** *vt fus* (*fig*) apresurarse a aprovechar; **he ~ed at the offer** se apresuró a aceptar la oferta; **jump down** *vi* bajar de un salto, saltar a tierra; **jump up** *vi* levantarse de un salto
jumper ['dʒʌmpə^r] *n* (*Brit*: *pullover*) jersey *m*, suéter *m*; (*US*: *pinafore dress*) pichi *m*; (*Sport*) saltador(a) *m(f)*
jump leads, jumper cables (*US*) *npl* cables *mpl* puente de batería
jump-start ['djʌmpstɑ:t] *vt* (*car*) arrancar con ayuda de otra batería *or* empujando; (*fig*: *economy*) reactivar
jumpy ['dʒʌmpɪ] *adj* nervioso
Jun. *abbr* = **junior**; (= *June*) jun
junction ['dʒʌŋkʃən] *n* (*Brit*: *of roads*) cruce *m*; (*Rail*) empalme *m*
juncture ['dʒʌŋktʃə^r] *n*: **at this ~** en este momento, en esta coyuntura
June [dʒu:n] *n* junio; *see also* **July**
jungle ['dʒʌŋgl] *n* selva, jungla
junior ['dʒu:nɪə^r] *adj* (*in age*) menor, más joven; (*competition*) juvenil; (*position*) subalterno ▷ *n* menor *m/f*, joven *m/f*; **he's ~ to me** es menor que yo
junior high school *n* (*US*) *centro de educación secundaria*
junior school *n* (*Brit*) escuela primaria
junk [dʒʌŋk] *n* (*cheap goods*) baratijas *fpl*; (*lumber*) trastos *mpl* viejos; (*rubbish*) basura; (*ship*) junco ▷ *vt* (*esp US*) deshacerse de
junk bond *n* (*Comm*) obligación *f* basura *inv*
junket ['dʒʌŋkɪt] *n* (*Culin*) *dulce de leche cuajada*; (*Brit inf*): **to go on a ~, go ~ing** viajar a costa ajena *or* del erario público
junk food *n* comida basura *or* de plástico
junkie ['dʒʌŋkɪ] *n* (*inf*) yonqui *m/f*, heroinómano(-a)
junk mail *n* propaganda (buzoneada), correo *m* basura *inv*
junk shop *n* tienda de objetos usados
Jupiter ['dʒu:pɪtə^r] *n* (*Mythology, Astro*) Júpiter *m*
jurisdiction [dʒuərɪs'dɪkʃən] *n* jurisdicción *f*; **it falls** *or* **comes within/outside our ~** es/no es de nuestra competencia
jurisprudence [dʒuərɪs'pru:dəns] *n* jurisprudencia
juror ['dʒuərə^r] *n* jurado
jury ['dʒuərɪ] *n* jurado
just [dʒʌst] *adj* justo ▷ *adv* (*exactly*) exactamente; (*only*) sólo, solamente, no más (*LAm*); **he's ~ done it/left** acaba de hacerlo/irse; **I've ~ seen him** acabo de verle; **~ right** perfecto; **~ two o'clock** las dos en punto; **she's ~ as clever as you** es tan lista como tú; **~ as well that ...** menos mal que ...; **it's ~ as well you didn't go** menos mal que no fuiste; **it's ~ as good (as)** es igual (que), es tan bueno (como); **~ as he was leaving** en el momento en que se marchaba; **we were ~ going** ya nos íbamos; **I was ~ about to phone** estaba a punto de llamar; **~ before/enough** justo antes/lo suficiente; **~ here** aquí mismo; **he ~ missed** falló por poco; **~ listen to this** escucha esto un momento; **~ ask someone the way** simplemente pregúntale a alguien por dónde se va; **not ~ now** ahora no
justice ['dʒʌstɪs] *n* justicia; (*US*: *judge*) juez *m/f*; **to do ~ to** (*fig*) hacer justicia a; **this photo doesn't do you ~** esta foto no te favorece
Justice of the Peace *n* juez *m/f* de paz; *see also* **Crown Court**
justification [dʒʌstɪfɪ'keɪʃən] *n* justificación *f*
justify ['dʒʌstɪfaɪ] *vt* justificar; (*text*) alinear, justificar; **to be justified in doing sth** tener motivo para *or* razón al hacer algo
jut [dʒʌt] *vi* (*also*: **~ out**) sobresalir
juvenile ['dʒu:vənaɪl] *adj* juvenil; (*humour, mentality*) infantil; (*court*) de menores ▷ *n* joven *m/f*, menor *m/f* de edad

K

K, k [keɪ] *n (letter)* K, k *f*; **K for King** K de Kilo

K *n abbr (= one thousand)* mil ▷ *abbr (Brit: = Knight) título*; *(= kilobyte)* K

kamikaze [kæmɪˈkɑːzɪ] *adj* kamikaze

kangaroo [kæŋgəˈruː] *n* canguro

karaoke [kɑːrəˈəukɪ] *n* karaoke

karate [kəˈrɑːtɪ] *n* karate *m*

Kazakhstan [kɑːzɑːkˈstæn] *n* Kazajstán *m*

kebab [kəˈbæb] *n* pincho moruno, brocheta

keel [kiːl] *n* quilla; **on an even ~** *(fig)* en equilibrio; **keel over** *vi (Naut)* zozobrar, volcarse; *(person)* desplomarse

keen [kiːn] *adj (interest, desire)* grande, vivo; *(eye, intelligence)* agudo; *(competition)* reñido; *(edge)* afilado; *(Brit: eager)* entusiasta; **to be ~ to do** *or* **on doing sth** tener muchas ganas de hacer algo; **to be ~ on sth/sb** interesarse por algo/algn; **I'm not ~ on going** no tengo ganas de ir

keep [kiːp] *(pt, pp* **kept***) vt (retain, preserve)* guardar; *(hold back)* quedarse con; *(shop)* ser propietario de; *(feed: family etc)* mantener; *(promise)* cumplir; *(chickens, bees etc)* criar ▷ *vi (food)* conservarse; *(remain)* seguir, continuar ▷ *n (of castle)* torreón *m*; *(food etc)* comida, sustento; **to ~ doing sth** seguir haciendo algo; **to ~ sb from doing sth** impedir a algn hacer algo; **to ~ sth from happening** impedir que algo ocurra; **to ~ sb happy** tener a algn contento; **to ~ sb waiting** hacer esperar a algn; **to ~ a place tidy** mantener un lugar limpio; **to ~ sth to o.s.** no decirle algo a nadie; **to ~ time** *(clock)* mantener la hora exacta; **~ the change** quédese con la vuelta; **to ~ an appointment** acudir a una cita; **to ~ a record** *or* **note of sth** tomar nota de *or* apuntar algo; *see also* **keeps**; **keep away** *vt*: **to ~ sth/sb away from sb** mantener algo/a algn apartado de algn ▷ *vi*: **to ~ away (from)** mantenerse apartado (de); **keep back** *vt (crowd, tears)* contener; *(money)* quedarse con; *(conceal: information)*: **to ~ sth back from sb** ocultar algo a algn ▷ *vi* hacerse a un lado; **keep down** *vt (control: prices, spending)* controlar; *(retain: food)* retener ▷ *vi* seguir agachado, no levantar la cabeza; **keep in** ▷ *vt (invalid, child)* impedir que salga, no dejar salir; *(Scol)* castigar (a quedarse en el colegio) ▷ *vi (inf)*: **to ~ in with sb** mantener la relación con algn; **keep off** ▷ *vt (dog, person)* mantener a distancia ▷ *vi* evitar; **~ your hands off!** ¡no toques!; **"~ off the grass"** "prohibido pisar el césped"; **keep on** *vi* seguir, continuar; **to ~ on doing** seguir *or* continuar haciendo; **to ~ on (about sth)** no parar de hablar (de algo); **keep out** *vi (stay out)* permanecer fuera; **"~ out"** "prohibida la entrada"; **keep up** *vt* mantener, conservar ▷ *vi* no rezagarse; *(fig: in comprehension)* seguir (el hilo); **to ~ up with** *(pace)* ir al paso de; *(level)* mantenerse a la altura de; **to ~ up with sb** seguir el ritmo a algn; *(fig)* seguir a algn

keeper [ˈkiːpəʳ] *n* guarda *m/f*

keep-fit [kiːpˈfɪt] *n* gimnasia (de mantenimiento)

keeping [ˈkiːpɪŋ] *n (care)* cuidado; **in ~ with** de acuerdo con

keeps [kiːps] *n*: **for ~** *(inf)* para siempre

keepsake [ˈkiːpseɪk] *n* recuerdo

keg [kɛg] *n* barrilete *m*, barril *m*

kennel [ˈkɛnl] *n* perrera; **kennels** *npl* residencia canina

Kenya [ˈkɛnjə] *n* Kenia

kept [kɛpt] *pt, pp of* **keep**

kerb [kəːb] *n (Brit)* bordillo

kerb crawler [-krɔːləʳ] *n conductor en busca de prostitutas desde su coche*

kernel [ˈkəːnl] *n (nut)* fruta; *(fig)* meollo

kerosene [ˈkɛrəsiːn] *n* keroseno

ketchup [ˈkɛtʃəp] *n* salsa de tomate, ketchup *m*

kettle [ˈkɛtl] *n* hervidor *m*

kettle drum *n (Mus)* timbal *m*

key [kiː] *n (gen)* llave *f*; *(Mus)* tono; *(of piano, typewriter)* tecla; *(on map)* clave *f* ▷ *cpd (vital: position, issue, industry etc)* clave ▷ *vt (also:* **~ in***)* teclear

keyboard [ˈkiːbɔːd] *n* teclado ▷ *vt (text)* teclear

keyboarder [ˈkiːbɔːdəʳ] *n* teclista *m/f*

keyed up [kiːd-] *adj (person)* nervioso; **to be (all) ~** estar nervioso *or* emocionado

keyhole [ˈkiːhəul] *n* ojo (de la cerradura)

keyhole surgery *n* cirugía cerrada *or* no invasiva
keynote ['ki:nəut] *n* (*Mus*) tónica; (*fig*) idea fundamental
keypad ['ki:pæd] *n* teclado numérico
keyring ['ki:rɪŋ] *n* llavero
kg *abbr* (= *kilogram*) kg
khaki ['kɑ:kɪ] *n* caqui
kick [kɪk] *vt* (*person*) dar una patada a; (*ball*) dar un puntapié a; (*habit*) quitarse de ▷ *vi* (*horse*) dar coces ▷ *n* patada; puntapié *m*, tiro; (*of rifle*) culetazo; (*inf*: *thrill*): **he does it for ~s** lo hace por pura diversión; **kick around** *vt* (*idea*) dar vueltas a; (*person*) tratar a patadas a; **kick off** *vi* (*Sport*) hacer el saque inicial
kick-off ['kɪkɔf] *n* saque inicial; **the ~ is at 10 o'clock** el partido empieza a las diez
kid [kɪd] *n* (*inf*: *child*) niño(-a), chiquillo(-a); (*animal*) cabrito; (*leather*) cabritilla ▷ *vi* (*inf*) bromear
kid gloves *npl*: **to treat sb with ~** andarse con pies de plomo con algn
kidnap ['kɪdnæp] *vt* secuestrar
kidnapper ['kɪdnæpə^r] *n* secuestrador(a) *m(f)*
kidnapping ['kɪdnæpɪŋ] *n* secuestro
kidney ['kɪdnɪ] *n* riñón *m*
kidney bean *n* judía, alubia
kill [kɪl] *vt* matar; (*murder*) asesinar; (*fig*: *rumour, conversation*) acabar con ▷ *n* matanza; **to ~ time** matar el tiempo; **kill off** *vt* exterminar, terminar con; (*fig*) echar por tierra
killer ['kɪlə^r] *n* asesino(-a)
killer instinct *n*: **to have the ~** ir a por todas
killing ['kɪlɪŋ] *n* (*one*) asesinato; (*several*) matanza; **to make a ~** (*Comm*) hacer su agosto
killjoy ['kɪldʒɔɪ] *n* (*Brit*) aguafiestas *m/f inv*
kiln [kɪln] *n* horno
kilo ['ki:ləu] *n abbr* (= *kilogram(me)*) kilo
kilobyte ['kɪləubaɪt] *n* (*Comput*) kilobyte *m*
kilogram, kilogramme ['kɪləugræm] *n* kilogramo
kilometre, kilometer (*US*) ['kɪləmi:tə^r] *n* kilómetro
kilowatt ['kɪləuwɔt] *n* kilovatio
kilt [kɪlt] *n* falda escocesa
kin [kɪn] *n* parientes *mpl*
kind [kaɪnd] *adj* (*treatment*) bueno, cariñoso; (*person, act, word*) amable, atento ▷ *n* clase *f*, especie *f*; (*species*) género; **in ~** (*Comm*) en especie; **a ~ of** una especie de; **to be two of a ~** ser tal para cual; **would you be ~ enough to ...?, would you be so ~ as to ...?** ¿me hace el favor de ...?; **it's very ~ of you (to do)** le agradezco mucho (el que haya hecho)
kindergarten ['kɪndəgɑ:tn] *n* jardín *m* de infancia
kind-hearted [kaɪnd'hɑ:tɪd] *adj* bondadoso, de buen corazón
kindle ['kɪndl] *vt* encender
kindly ['kaɪndlɪ] *adj* bondadoso; (*gentle*) cariñoso ▷ *adv* bondadosamente, amablemente; **will you ~ ...** sería usted tan amable de ...
kindness ['kaɪndnɪs] *n* bondad *f*, amabilidad *f*; (*act*) favor *m*
kindred ['kɪndrɪd] *n* familia, parientes *mpl* ▷ *adj*: **~ spirits** almas *fpl* gemelas
kinetic [kɪ'nɛtɪk] *adj* cinético
king [kɪŋ] *n* rey *m*
kingdom ['kɪŋdəm] *n* reino
kingfisher ['kɪŋfɪʃə^r] *n* martín *m* pescador
king-size ['kɪŋsaɪz], **king-sized** ['kɪŋsaɪzd] *adj* de tamaño gigante; (*cigarette*) extra largo; **~ bed** cama de matrimonio extragrande
kinky ['kɪŋkɪ] *adj* (*pej*) perverso
kiosk ['ki:ɔsk] *n* quiosco; (*Brit Tel*) cabina; **newspaper ~** quiosco, kiosco
kipper ['kɪpə^r] *n* arenque *m* ahumado
Kirghizia [kə:'gɪzɪə] *n* Kirguizistán *m*
kiss [kɪs] *n* beso ▷ *vt* besar; **~ of life** (*artificial respiration*) respiración *f* boca a boca; **to ~ sb goodbye** dar un beso de despedida a algn; **to ~ (each other)** besarse
kissagram ['kɪsəgræm] *n servicio de felicitaciones mediante el que se envía a una persona vestida de manera sugerente para besar a algn*
kit [kɪt] *n* equipo; (*set of tools etc*) (caja de) herramientas *fpl*; (*assembly kit*) juego de armar; **tool ~** juego *or* estuche *m* de herramientas; **kit out** *vt* equipar
kitchen ['kɪtʃɪn] *n* cocina
kitchen sink *n* fregadero
kite [kaɪt] *n* (*toy*) cometa
kith [kɪθ] *n*: **~ and kin** parientes *mpl* y allegados
kitten ['kɪtn] *n* gatito(-a)
kitty ['kɪtɪ] *n* (*pool of money*) fondo común; (*Cards*) bote *m*
kiwi ['ki:wi:] *n* (*inf*: *New Zealander*) neozelandés(-esa) *m(f)*; (*also*: **~ fruit**) kiwi *m*
km *abbr* (= *kilometre*) km
km/h *abbr* (= *kilometres per hour*) km/h
knack [næk] *n*: **to have the ~ of doing sth** tener facilidad para hacer algo
knackered ['nækəd] *adj* (*inf*) hecho polvo
knapsack ['næpsæk] *n* mochila
knead [ni:d] *vt* amasar
knee [ni:] *n* rodilla
kneecap ['ni:kæp] *vt* destrozar a tiros la rótula de ▷ *n* rótula
kneel [ni:l] (*pt, pp* **knelt**) [nɛlt] *vi* (*also*: **~ down**) arrodillarse
knelt [nɛlt] *pt, pp of* **kneel**
knew [nju:] *pt of* **know**
knickers ['nɪkəz] *npl* (*Brit*) bragas *fpl*, calzones *mpl* (*LAm*)
knife [naɪf] (*pl* **knives**) *n* cuchillo ▷ *vt* acuchillar; **~, fork and spoon** cubiertos *mpl*
knife edge *n*: **to be on a ~** estar en la cuerda floja
knight [naɪt] *n* caballero; (*Chess*) caballo

knighthood ['naɪthud] *n* (*title*): **to get a ~** recibir el título de *Sir*
knit [nɪt] *vt* tejer, tricotar; (*brows*) fruncir; (*fig*): **to ~ together** unir, juntar ▷ *vi* hacer punto, tejer, tricotar; (*bones*) soldarse
knitting ['nɪtɪŋ] *n* labor *f* de punto
knitting needle, knit pin (*US*) *n* aguja de hacer punto *or* tejer
knitwear ['nɪtwɛəʳ] *n* prendas *fpl* de punto
knives [naɪvz] *pl of* **knife**
knob [nɔb] *n* (*of door*) pomo; (*of stick*) puño; (*on radio, TV*) botón *m*; (*lump*) bulto; (*fig*): **a ~ of butter** (*Brit*) un pedazo de mantequilla
knock [nɔk] *vt* (*strike*) golpear; (*bump into*) chocar contra; (*fig: inf*) criticar ▷ *vi* (*at door etc*): **to ~ at/on** llamar a ▷ *n* golpe *m*; (*on door*) llamada; **he ~ed at the door** llamó a la puerta; **knock down** *vt* (*pedestrian*) atropellar; (*price*) rebajar; **knock off** *vi* (*inf: finish*) salir del trabajo ▷ *vt* (*inf: steal*) birlar; (*strike off*) quitar; (*fig: from price, record*): **to ~ off £10** rebajar en £10; **knock out** *vt* dejar sin sentido; (*Boxing*) poner fuera de combate, dejar K.O.; (*in competition*) eliminar; (*stop*) estropear, dejar fuera de servicio; **knock over** *vt* (*object*) derribar, tirar; (*pedestrian*) atropellar
knockdown ['nɔkdaun] *adj* (*price*) de saldo
knocker ['nɔkəʳ] *n* (*on door*) aldaba
knockout ['nɔkaut] *n* (*Boxing*) K.O. *m*, knockout *m*
knot [nɔt] *n* (*gen*) nudo ▷ *vt* anudar; **to tie a ~** hacer un nudo
knotty ['nɔtɪ] *adj* (*fig*) complicado
know [nəu] (*pt* **knew**, *pp* **known** [nju:, nəun]) *vt* (*gen*) saber; (*person, author, place*) conocer; (*recognize*) reconocer ▷ *vi*: **as far as I ~ ...** que yo sepa ...; **yes, I ~** sí, ya lo sé; **I don't ~** no lo sé; **to ~ how to do** saber hacer; **to ~ how to swim** saber nadar; **to ~ about** *or* **of sb/sth** saber de algn/algo; **to get to ~ sth** enterarse de algo; **I ~ nothing about it** no sé nada de eso; **I don't ~ him** no lo *or* le conozco; **to ~ right from wrong** saber distinguir el bien del mal
know-all ['nəuɔ:l] *n* (*Brit pej*) sabelotodo *m/f inv*, sabihondo(-a)
know-how ['nəuhau] *n* conocimientos *mpl*
knowing ['nəuɪŋ] *adj* (*look etc*) de complicidad
knowingly ['nəuɪŋlɪ] *adv* (*purposely*) a sabiendas; (*smile, look*) con complicidad
know-it-all ['nəuɪtɔ:l] *n* (*US*) = **know-all**
knowledge ['nɔlɪdʒ] *n* (*gen*) conocimiento; (*learning*) saber *m*, conocimientos *mpl*; **to have no ~ of** no saber nada de; **with my ~** con mis conocimientos, sabiéndolo; **to (the best of) my ~** a mi entender, que yo sepa; **not to my ~** que yo sepa, no; **it is common ~ that ...** es del dominio público que ...; **it has come to my ~ that ...** me he enterado de que ...; **to have a working ~ of Spanish** defenderse con el español
knowledgeable ['nɔlɪdʒəbl] *adj* entendido, erudito
known [nəun] *pp of* **know** ▷ *adj* (*thief, facts*) conocido; (*expert*) reconocido
knuckle ['nʌkl] *n* nudillo; **knuckle down** *vi* (*inf*) ponerse a trabajar en serio; **knuckle under** *vi* someterse
KO *abbr* (= *knock out*) K.O. *m* ▷ *vt* (*knock out*) dejar K.O.
koala [kəu'ɑ:lə] *n* (*also*: **~ bear**) koala *m*
Koran [kɔ'rɑ:n] *n* Corán *m*
Korea [kə'rɪə] *n* Corea; **North/South ~** Corea del Norte/Sur
Korean [kə'rɪən] *adj, n* coreano(-a) *m(f)*
kosher ['kəuʃəʳ] *adj* autorizado por la ley judía
Kosovar ['kɔsəvɑ:ʳ], **Kosovan** ['kɔsəvən] *adj* kosovar
Kosovo ['kɒsəvəu] *n* Kosovo *m*
Kremlin ['kremlɪn] *n*: **the ~** el Kremlin
kudos ['kju:dɔs] *n* gloria, prestigio
Kuwait [ku'weɪt] *n* Kuwait *m*
kW *abbr* (= *kilowatt*) Kv

l

L, l [ɛl] *n* (*letter*) L, l *f*; **L for Lucy**, (*US*) **L for Love** L de Lorenzo
L *abbr* (*on maps etc*) = **lake**; (*size*) = **large**; (= *left*) izq.; (*Brit Aut*: = *learner*) L
LA *n abbr* (*US*) = **Los Angeles**
lab [læb] *n abbr* = **laboratory**
label ['leɪbl] *n* etiqueta; (*brand*: *of record*) sello (discográfico) ▷ *vt* poner una etiqueta a, etiquetar
labor ['leɪbəʳ] *n*, *vb* (*US*) = **labour**
laboratory [lə'bɔrətərɪ] *n* laboratorio
Labor Day *n* (*US*) día *m* de los trabajadores (*primer lunes de septiembre*)
laborious [lə'bɔːrɪəs] *adj* penoso
labor union *n* (*US*) sindicato
Labour ['leɪbəʳ] *n* (*Brit Pol*: *also*: **the ~ Party**) el partido laborista, los laboristas
labour, labor (*US*) ['leɪbəʳ] *n* (*task*) trabajo; (*also*: **~ force**) mano *f* de obra; (*workers*) trabajadores *mpl*; (*Med*) (dolores *mpl* de) parto ▷ *vi*: **to ~ (at)** trabajar (en) ▷ *vt*: **to ~ a point** insistir en un punto; **hard ~** trabajos *mpl* forzados; **to be in ~** estar de parto; **the L~ party** (*Brit*) el partido laborista, los laboristas *mpl*
labourer, laborer (*US*) ['leɪbərəʳ] *n* peón *m*; (*on farm*) peón *m*, obrero; (*day labourer*) jornalero
labyrinth ['læbɪrɪnθ] *n* laberinto
lace [leɪs] *n* encaje *m*; (*of shoe etc*) cordón *m* ▷ *vt* (*shoes*: *also*: **~ up**) atarse; (*drink*: *fortify with spirits*) echar licor a
laceration [læsə'reɪʃən] *n* laceración *f*
lack [læk] *n* (*absence*) falta, carencia; (*scarcity*) escasez *f* ▷ *vt* faltarle a algn, carecer de; **through** *or* **for ~ of** por falta de; **to be ~ing** faltar, no haber; **to be ~ing in sth** faltarle a algn algo
lacquer ['lækəʳ] *n* laca; **hair ~** laca para el pelo
lacy ['leɪsɪ] *adj* (*like lace*) como de encaje
lad [læd] *n* muchacho, chico; (*in stable etc*) mozo
ladder ['lædəʳ] *n* escalera (de mano); (*Brit*: *in tights*) carrera ▷ *vt* (*Brit*: *tights*) hacer una carrera en
laden ['leɪdn] *adj*: **~ (with)** cargado (de); **fully ~** (*truck, ship*) cargado hasta el tope
ladle ['leɪdl] *n* cucharón *m*
lady ['leɪdɪ] *n* señora; (*distinguished, noble*) dama; **young ~** señorita; **the ladies' (room)** los servicios de señoras; **"ladies and gentlemen ..."** "señoras y caballeros ..."
ladybird ['leɪdɪbəːd], **ladybug** (*US*) ['leɪdɪbʌg] *n* mariquita
ladylike ['leɪdɪlaɪk] *adj* fino
Ladyship ['leɪdɪʃɪp] *n*: **your ~** su Señoría
LAFTA *n abbr* (= *Latin American Free Trade Association*) ALALC *f*
lag [læg] *vi* (*also*: **~ behind**) retrasarse, quedarse atrás ▷ *vt* (*pipes*) revestir
lager ['lɑːgəʳ] *n* cerveza (rubia)
lager lout *n* (*Brit inf*) gamberro borracho
lagoon [lə'guːn] *n* laguna
laid [leɪd] *pt*, *pp of* **lay**
laid-back [leɪd'bæk] *adj* (*inf*) tranquilo, relajado
laid up *adj*: **to be ~** (*person*) tener que guardar cama
lain [leɪn] *pp of* **lie**
lair [lɛəʳ] *n* guarida
laity ['leɪtɪ] *n* laicado
lake [leɪk] *n* lago
Lake District *n* (*Brit*): **the ~** la Región de los Lagos
lamb [læm] *n* cordero; (*meat*) carne *f* de cordero
lamb chop *n* chuleta de cordero
lame [leɪm] *adj* cojo, rengo (*LAm*); (*weak*) débil; (*excuse*) poco convincente; **~ duck** (*fig*: *person*) inútil *m/f*; (: *firm*) empresa en quiebra
lament [lə'mɛnt] *n* lamento ▷ *vt* lamentarse de
laminated ['læmɪneɪtɪd] *adj* laminado
lamp [læmp] *n* lámpara
lamppost ['læmppəust] *n* (*Brit*) farola
lampshade ['læmpʃeɪd] *n* pantalla
lance [lɑːns] *n* lanza ▷ *vt* (*Med*) abrir con lanceta
land [lænd] *n* tierra; (*country*) país *m*; (*piece of land*) terreno; (*estate*) tierras *fpl*, finca; (*Agr*) campo ▷ *vi* (*from ship*) desembarcar; (*Aviat*) aterrizar; (*fig*: *fall*) caer ▷ *vt* (*obtain*) conseguir; (*passengers, goods*) desembarcar; **to go/travel by ~** ir/viajar por tierra;

to own ~ ser dueño de tierras; **to ~ on one's feet** caer de pie; (*fig: to be lucky*) salir bien parado; **to ~ sb with sth** (*inf*) hacer cargar a algn con algo; **land up** *vi*: **to ~ up in/at** ir a parar a/en
landfill site ['lændfɪl-] *n* vertedero
landing ['lændɪŋ] *n* desembarco; aterrizaje *m*; (*of staircase*) rellano
landing card *n* tarjeta de desembarque
landing gear *n* (*Aviat*) tren *m* de aterrizaje
landing strip *n* pista de aterrizaje
landlady ['lændleɪdɪ] *n* (*of boarding house*) patrona; (*owner*) dueña
landline ['lændlaɪn] *n* (teléfono) fijo
landlocked ['lændlɔkt] *adj* cercado de tierra
landlord ['lændlɔːd] *n* propietario; (*of pub etc*) patrón *m*
landmark ['lændmɑːk] *n* lugar *m* conocido; **to be a ~** (*fig*) hacer época
landowner ['lændəunə^r] *n* terrateniente *m/f*
landscape ['lænskeɪp] *n* paisaje *m*
landscape gardener *n* diseñador(-a) *m(f)* de paisajes
landslide ['lændslaɪd] *n* (*Geo*) corrimiento de tierras; (*fig: Pol*) victoria arrolladora
lane [leɪn] *n* (*in country*) camino; (*in town*) callejón *m*; (*Aut*) carril *m*; (*in race*) calle *f*; (*for air or sea traffic*) ruta; **shipping ~** ruta marina
language ['læŋgwɪdʒ] *n* lenguaje *m*; (*national tongue*) idioma *m*, lengua; **bad ~** palabrotas *fpl*
language laboratory *n* laboratorio de idiomas
language school *n* academia de idiomas
language studies *npl* estudios *mpl* filológicos
languid ['læŋgwɪd] *adj* lánguido
languish ['læŋgwɪʃ] *vi* languidecer
lank [læŋk] *adj* (*hair*) lacio
lanky ['læŋkɪ] *adj* larguirucho
lantern ['læntn] *n* linterna, farol *m*
lap [læp] *n* (*of track*) vuelta; (*of body*) regazo ▷ *vi* (*waves*) chapotear; **to sit on sb's ~** sentarse en las rodillas de algn; **lap up** *vt* beber a lengüetadas *or* con la lengua; (*fig: compliments, attention*) disfrutar; (*: lies etc*) tragarse
lapdog ['læpdɔg] *n* perro faldero
lapel [lə'pɛl] *n* solapa
Lapland ['læplænd] *n* Laponia
lapse [læps] *n* (*fault*) error *m*, fallo; (*moral*) desliz *m* ▷ *vi* (*expire*) caducar; (*morally*) cometer un desliz; (*time*) pasar, transcurrir; **to ~ into bad habits** volver a las andadas; **~ of time** lapso, intervalo; **a ~ of memory** un lapsus de memoria
laptop ['læptɔp] *n* (*also:* **~ computer**) (ordenador *m*) portátil *m*
larceny ['lɑːsənɪ] *n* latrocinio
lard [lɑːd] *n* manteca (de cerdo)
larder ['lɑːdə^r] *n* despensa
large [lɑːdʒ] *adj* grande ▷ *adv*: **by and ~** en general, en términos generales; **at ~** (*free*) en libertad; (*generally*) en general; **to make ~(r)** hacer mayor *or* más extenso; **a ~ number of people** una gran cantidad de personas; **on a ~ scale** a gran escala
largely ['lɑːdʒlɪ] *adv* (*mostly*) en su mayor parte; (*introducing reason*) en gran parte
large-scale ['lɑːdʒ'skeɪl] *adj* (*map, drawing*) a gran escala; (*reforms, business activities*) importante
lark [lɑːk] *n* (*bird*) alondra; (*joke*) broma; **lark about** *vi* bromear, hacer el tonto
larva (*pl* **larvae**) ['lɑːvə, -iː] *n* larva
laryngitis [lærɪn'dʒaɪtɪs] *n* laringitis *f*
larynx ['lærɪŋks] *n* laringe *f*
lasagne [lə'zænjə] *n* lasaña
laser ['leɪzə^r] *n* láser *m*
laser beam *n* rayo láser
laser printer *n* impresora láser
lash [læʃ] *n* latigazo; (*punishment*) azote *m*; (*also:* **eye~**) pestaña ▷ *vt* azotar; (*tie*) atar; **lash down** *vt* sujetar con cuerdas ▷ *vi* (*rain*) caer a trombas; **lash out** *vi* (*inf: spend*) gastar a la loca; **to ~ out (at sb)** (*hit*) arremeter (contra algn); **to ~ out against sb** lanzar invectivas contra algn
lass [læs] *n* chica
lasso [læ'suː] *n* lazo ▷ *vt* coger con lazo
last [lɑːst] *adj* (*gen*) último; (*final*) último, final ▷ *adv* (*finally*) por último ▷ *vi* (*endure*) durar; (*continue*) continuar, seguir; **~ night** anoche; **~ week** la semana pasada; **at ~** por fin; **~ but one** penúltimo; **~ time** la última vez; **it ~s (for) two hours** dura dos horas
last-ditch ['lɑːst'dɪtʃ] *adj* (*attempt*) de último recurso, último, desesperado
lasting ['lɑːstɪŋ] *adj* duradero
lastly ['lɑːstlɪ] *adv* por último, finalmente
last-minute ['lɑːstmɪnɪt] *adj* de última hora
latch [lætʃ] *n* picaporte *m*, pestillo; **latch on to** *vt fus* (*cling to: person*) pegarse a; (*: idea*) aferrarse a
late [leɪt] *adj* (*not on time*) tarde, atrasado; (*towards end of period, life*) tardío; (*hour*) avanzado; (*deceased*) fallecido ▷ *adv* tarde; (*behind time, schedule*) con retraso; **to be (10 minutes) ~** llegar con (10 minutos de) retraso; **to be ~ with** estar atrasado con; **~ delivery** entrega tardía; **~ in life** a una edad avanzada; **of ~** últimamente; **~ at night** a última hora de la noche; **in ~ May** hacia fines de mayo; **the ~ Mr X** el difunto Sr. X; **to work ~** trabajar hasta tarde
latecomer ['leɪtkʌmə^r] *n* recién llegado(-a)
lately ['leɪtlɪ] *adv* últimamente
latent ['leɪtnt] *adj* latente; **~ defect** defecto latente
later ['leɪtə^r] *adj* (*date etc*) posterior; (*version etc*) más reciente ▷ *adv* más tarde, después; **~ on today** hoy más tarde
latest ['leɪtɪst] *adj* último; **at the ~** a más tardar
latex ['leɪtɛks] *n* látex *m*
lathe [leɪð] *n* torno

lather ['lɑːðəʳ] *n* espuma (de jabón) ▷ *vt* enjabonar
Latin ['lætɪn] *n* latín *m* ▷ *adj* latino
Latin America *n* América Latina, Latinoamérica
Latin American *adj, n* latinoamericano(-a) *m(f)*
Latino [læ'tiːnəu] *adj, n* latino(-a) *m(f)*
latitude ['lætɪtjuːd] *n* latitud *f*; (*fig: freedom*) libertad *f*
latter ['lætəʳ] *adj* último; (*of two*) segundo ▷ *n*: **the ~** el último, éste
latterly ['lætəlɪ] *adv* últimamente
Latvia ['lætvɪə] *n* Letonia
laudable ['lɔːdəbl] *adj* loable
laugh [lɑːf] *n* risa; (*loud*) carcajada ▷ *vi* reírse, reír; reírse a carcajadas; **(to do sth) for a ~** (hacer algo) en broma; **laugh at** *vt fus* reírse de; **laugh off** *vt* tomar a risa
laughable ['lɑːfəbl] *adj* ridículo
laughing ['lɑːfɪŋ] *adj* risueño ▷ *n*: **it's no ~ matter** no es cosa de risa
laughing stock *n*: **to be the ~ of the town** ser el hazmerreír de la ciudad
laughter ['lɑːftəʳ] *n* risa
launch [lɔːntʃ] *n* (*boat*) lancha; *see also* **launching** ▷ *vt* (*ship*) botar; (*rocket, plan*) lanzar; (*fig*) comenzar; **launch forth** *vi*: **to ~ forth (into)** lanzarse a *or* en, emprender; **launch into** *vt fus* lanzarse a; **launch out** *vi* = **launch forth**
launching ['lɔːntʃɪŋ] *n* (*of rocket etc*) lanzamiento; (*inauguration*) estreno
launder ['lɔːndəʳ] *vt* lavar
Launderette® [lɔːn'drɛt], **Laundromat®** (*US*) ['lɔːndrəmæt] *n* lavandería (automática)
laundry ['lɔːndrɪ] *n* lavandería; (*clothes: dirty*) ropa sucia; (*clean*) colada; **to do the ~** hacer la colada
laureate ['lɔːrɪət] *adj see* **poet laureate**
laurel ['lɔrl] *n* laurel *m*; **to rest on one's ~s** dormirse en *or* sobre los laureles
lava ['lɑːvə] *n* lava
lavatory ['lævətərɪ] *n* wáter *m*; **lavatories** *npl* servicios *mpl*, aseos *mpl*, sanitarios *mpl* (*LAm*)
lavender ['lævəndəʳ] *n* lavanda
lavish ['lævɪʃ] *adj* abundante; (*giving freely*): **~ with** pródigo en ▷ *vt*: **to ~ sth on sb** colmar a algn de algo
law [lɔː] *n* ley *f*; (*study*) derecho; (*of game*) regla; **against the ~** contra la ley; **to study ~** estudiar derecho; **to go to ~** recurrir a la justicia
law-abiding ['lɔːəbaɪdɪŋ] *adj* respetuoso con la ley
law and order *n* orden *m* público
law court *n* tribunal *m* (de justicia)
lawful ['lɔːful] *adj* legítimo, lícito
lawless ['lɔːlɪs] *adj* (*act*) ilegal; (*person*) rebelde; (*country*) ingobernable
Law Lord *n* (*Brit*) *miembro de la Cámara de los Lores y del más alto tribunal de apelación*
lawn [lɔːn] *n* césped *m*
lawnmower ['lɔːnməuəʳ] *n* cortacésped *m*
lawn tennis *n* tenis *m* sobre hierba
law school *n* (*US*) facultad *f* de derecho
lawsuit ['lɔːsuːt] *n* pleito; **to bring a ~ against** entablar un pleito contra
lawyer ['lɔːjəʳ] *n* abogado(-a); (*for sales, wills etc*) notario(-a)
lax [læks] *adj* (*discipline*) relajado; (*person*) negligente
laxative ['læksətɪv] *n* laxante *m*
lay [leɪ] *pt of* **lie** ▷ *adj* laico; (*not expert*) lego ▷ *vt* (*pt, pp* **laid** [leɪd]) (*place*) colocar; (*eggs, table*) poner; (*trap*) tender; (*carpet*) extender; **to ~ the facts/one's proposals before sb** presentar los hechos/sus propuestas a algn; **lay aside, lay by** *vt* dejar a un lado; **lay down** *vt* (*pen etc*) dejar; (*arms*) rendir; (*policy*) trazar; (*rules etc*) establecer; **to ~ down the law** imponer las normas; **lay in** *vt* abastecerse de; **lay into** *vt fus* (*inf: attack, scold*) arremeter contra; **lay off** *vt* (*workers*) despedir; **lay on** *vt* (*water, gas*) instalar; (*meal, facilities*) proveer; **lay out** *vt* (*plan*) trazar; (*display*) exponer; (*spend*) gastar; **lay up** *vt* (*store*) guardar; (*ship*) desarmar; (*illness*) obligar a guardar cama
layabout ['leɪəbaut] *n* vago(-a)
lay-by ['leɪbaɪ] *n* (*Brit Aut*) área de descanso
layer ['leɪəʳ] *n* capa
layman ['leɪmən] *n* lego
layout ['leɪaut] *n* (*design*) plan *m*, trazado; (*disposition*) disposición *f*; (*Press*) composición *f*
laze [leɪz] *vi* no hacer nada; (*pej*) holgazanear
lazy ['leɪzɪ] *adj* perezoso, vago, flojo (*LAm*)
lb. *abbr* = **pound** (*weight*)
lead¹ [liːd] (*pt, pp* **led** [lɛd]) *n* (*front position*) delantera; (*distance, time ahead*) ventaja; (*clue*) pista; (*Elec*) cable *m*; (*for dog*) correa; (*Theat*) papel *m* principal ▷ *vt* conducir; (*life*) llevar; (*be leader of*) dirigir; (*Sport*) ir en cabeza de; (*orchestra: Brit*) ser el primer violín en; (*: US*) dirigir ▷ *vi* ir primero; **to be in the ~** (*Sport*) llevar la delantera; (*fig*) ir a la cabeza; **to take the ~** (*Sport*) tomar la delantera; (*fig*) tomar la iniciativa; **to ~ sb to believe that ...** hacer creer a algn que ...; **to ~ sb to do sth** llevar a algn a hacer algo; **lead astray** *vt* llevar por mal camino; **lead away** *vt* llevar; **lead back** *vt* hacer volver; **lead off** *vt* llevar ▷ *vi* (*in game*) abrir; **lead on** *vt* (*tease*) engañar; **to ~ sb on to** (*induce*) incitar a algn a; **lead to** *vt fus* producir, provocar; **lead up to** *vt fus* (*events*) conducir a; (*in conversation*) preparar el terreno para
lead² [lɛd] *n* (*metal*) plomo; (*in pencil*) mina
leaded ['lɛdɪd] *adj*: **~ windows** ventanas *fpl* emplomadas
leaden ['lɛdn] *adj* (*sky, sea*) plomizo; (*heavy: footsteps*) pesado
leader ['liːdəʳ] *n* jefe(-a) *m(f)*, líder *m*; (*of union etc*) dirigente *m/f*; (*guide*) guía *m/f*; (*of newspaper*) editorial *m*; **they are ~s in their**

L

field (*fig*) llevan la delantera en su especialidad

leadership ['li:dəʃɪp] *n* dirección *f*; **qualities of ~** iniciativa *sg*; **under the ~ of ...** bajo la dirección de ..., al mando de ...

lead-free ['lɛdfri:] *adj* sin plomo

leading ['li:dɪŋ] *adj* (*main*) principal; (*outstanding*) destacado; (*first*) primero; (*front*) delantero; **a ~ question** una pregunta tendenciosa

leading lady *n* (*Theat*) primera actriz *f*

leading light *n* (*fig*: *person*) figura principal

leading man *n* (*Theat*) primer actor *m*

lead singer [li:d-] *n* cantante *m/f*

lead-up ['li:dʌp] *n*: **in the ~ to the election** cuando falta *etc* poco para las elecciones

leaf (*pl* **leaves**) [li:f, li:vz] *n* hoja; **to turn over a new ~** (*fig*) hacer borrón y cuenta nueva; **to take a ~ out of sb's book** (*fig*) seguir el ejemplo de algn; **leaf through** *vt fus* (*book*) hojear

leaflet ['li:flɪt] *n* folleto

league [li:g] *n* sociedad *f*; (*Football*) liga; **to be in ~ with** estar confabulado con

league table *n* clasificación *f*

leak [li:k] *n* (*of liquid, gas*) escape *m*, fuga; (*in pipe*) agujero; (*in roof*) gotera; (*fig*: *of information, in security*) filtración *f* ▷ *vi* (*ship*) hacer agua; (*shoes*) tener un agujero; (*pipe*) tener un escape; (*roof*) tener goteras; (*also*: **~ out**: *liquid, gas*) escaparse, salirse; (*fig*: *news*) trascender, divulgarse ▷ *vt* (*gen*) dejar escapar; (*fig*: *information*) filtrar

leakage ['li:kɪdʒ] *n* (*of water, gas etc*) escape *m*, fuga

lean [li:n] (*pt, pp* **leaned** *or* **leant**) *adj* (*thin*) flaco; (*meat*) magro ▷ *vt*: **to ~ sth on sth** apoyar algo en algo ▷ *vi* (*slope*) inclinarse; (*rest*): **to ~ against** apoyarse contra; **to ~ on** apoyarse en; **lean back** *vi* inclinarse hacia atrás; **lean forward** *vi* inclinarse hacia adelante; **lean out** *vi*: **to ~ out (of)** asomarse (a); **lean over** *vi* inclinarse

leaning ['li:nɪŋ] *adj* inclinado ▷ *n*: **~ (towards)** inclinación *f* (hacia); **the L~ Tower of Pisa** la Torre Inclinada de Pisa

leant [lɛnt] *pt, pp of* **lean**

leap [li:p] *n* salto ▷ *vi* (*pt, pp* **leaped** *or* **leapt** [lɛpt]) saltar; **to ~ at an offer** apresurarse a aceptar una oferta; **leap up** *vi* (*person*) saltar

leapfrog ['li:pfrɔg] *n* pídola ▷ *vi*: **to ~ over sb/sth** saltar por encima de algn/algo

leapt [lɛpt] *pt, pp of* **leap**

leap year *n* año bisiesto

learn (*pt, pp* **learned** *or* **learnt**) [lə:n, -t] *vt* (*gen*) aprender; (*come to know of*) enterarse de ▷ *vi* aprender; **to ~ how to do sth** aprender a hacer algo; **to ~ that ...** enterarse *or* informarse de que ...; **to ~ about sth** (*Scol*) aprender algo; (*hear*) enterarse *or* informarse de algo; **we were sorry to ~ that ...** nos dio tristeza saber que ...

learned ['lə:nɪd] *adj* erudito

learner ['lə:nə[r]] *n* principiante *m/f*; (*Brit*: *also*: **~ driver**) conductor(a) *m(f)* en prácticas; *see also* **L-plates**

learning ['lə:nɪŋ] *n* saber *m*, conocimientos *mpl*

learnt [lə:nt] *pp of* **learn**

lease [li:s] *n* arriendo ▷ *vt* arrendar; **on ~** en arriendo; **lease back** *vt* subarrendar

leash [li:ʃ] *n* correa

least [li:st] *adj* (*slightest*) menor, más pequeño; (*smallest amount of*) mínimo ▷ *adv* menos ▷ *n*: **the ~** lo menos; **the ~ expensive car** el coche menos caro; **at ~** por lo menos, al menos; **not in the ~** en absoluto

leather ['lɛðə[r]] *n* cuero ▷ *cpd*: **~ goods** artículos *mpl* de cuero *or* piel

leave [li:v] (*pt, pp* **left**) *vt* dejar; (*go away from*) abandonar ▷ *vi* irse; (*train*) salir ▷ *n* permiso; **to ~ school** dejar la escuela *or* el colegio; **~ it to me!** ¡yo me encargo!; **he's already left for the airport** ya se ha marchado al aeropuerto; **to be left** quedar, sobrar; **there's some milk left over** sobra *or* queda algo de leche; **on ~** de permiso; **to take one's ~ of** despedirse de; **leave behind** *vt* (*on purpose*) dejar (atrás); (*accidentally*) olvidar; **leave off** *vt* (*lid*) no poner; (*switch*) no encender; (*inf*: *stop*): **to ~ off doing sth** dejar de hacer algo; **leave on** *vt* (*lid*) dejar puesto; (*light, fire, cooker*) dejar encendido; **leave out** *vt* omitir; **leave over** *vt* (*postpone*) dejar, aplazar

leave of absence *n* excedencia

leaves [li:vz] *pl of* **leaf**

Lebanon ['lɛbənən] *n*: **the ~** el Líbano

lecherous ['lɛtʃərəs] *adj* lascivo

lectern ['lɛktə:n] *n* atril *m*

lecture ['lɛktʃə[r]] *n* conferencia; (*Scol*) clase *f* ▷ *vi* dar clase(s) ▷ *vt* (*scold*) sermonear; (*reprove*) echar una reprimenda a; **to give a ~ on** dar una conferencia sobre

lecture hall *n* sala de conferencias; (*Univ*) aula

lecturer ['lɛktʃərə[r]] *n* conferenciante *m/f*; (*Brit*: *at university*) profesor(a) *m(f)*

lecture theatre *n* = **lecture hall**

LED *n abbr* (*Elec*: = *light-emitting diode*) LED *m*

led [lɛd] *pt, pp of* **lead**

ledge [lɛdʒ] *n* (*on wall*) repisa; (*of window*) alféizar *m*; (*of mountain*) saliente *m*

ledger ['lɛdʒə[r]] *n* libro mayor

lee [li:] *n* sotavento; **in the ~ of** al abrigo de

leech [li:tʃ] *n* sanguijuela

leek [li:k] *n* puerro

leer [lɪə[r]] *vi*: **to ~ at sb** mirar de manera lasciva a algn

leeway ['li:weɪ] *n* (*fig*): **to have some ~** tener cierta libertad de acción

left [lɛft] *pt, pp of* **leave** ▷ *adj* izquierdo; (*remaining*): **there are two ~** quedan dos ▷ *n* izquierda ▷ *adv* a la izquierda; **on** *or* **to the ~** a la izquierda; **the L~** (*Pol*) la izquierda

left-hand *adj*: **the ~ side** la izquierda
left-hand drive ['lɛfthænd-] *n* conducción *f* por la izquierda
left-handed [lɛft'hændɪd] *adj* zurdo; **~ scissors** tijeras *fpl* zurdas *or* para zurdos
left-hand side ['lɛfthænd-] *n* izquierda
left-luggage [lɛft'lʌgɪdʒ], **left-luggage office** *n* (*Brit*) consigna
left-luggage locker *n* (*Brit*) consigna *f* automática
left-overs ['lɛftəuvəz] *npl* sobras *fpl*
left-wing [lɛft'wɪŋ] *adj* (*Pol*) de izquierda(s), izquierdista
lefty ['lɛftɪ] *n* (*inf*: *Pol*) rojillo(-a)
leg [lɛg] *n* pierna; (*of animal, chair*) pata; (*Culin*: *of meat*) pierna; (*of journey*) etapa; **1st/2nd ~** (*Sport*) partido de ida/de vuelta; **to pull sb's ~** tomar el pelo a algn; **to stretch one's ~s** dar una vuelta
legacy ['lɛgəsɪ] *n* herencia; (*fig*) herencia, legado
legal ['li:gl] *adj* (*permitted by law*) lícito; (*of law*) legal; (*inquiry etc*) jurídico; **to take ~ action** *or* **proceedings against sb** entablar *or* levantar un pleito contra algn
legal holiday *n* (*US*) fiesta oficial
legality [lɪ'gælɪtɪ] *n* legalidad *f*
legalize ['li:gəlaɪz] *vt* legalizar
legally ['li:gəlɪ] *adv* legalmente; **~ binding** con fuerza legal
legal tender *n* moneda de curso legal
legend ['lɛdʒənd] *n* leyenda
legendary ['lɛdʒəndərɪ] *adj* legendario
leggings ['legɪŋz] *npl* mallas *fpl*, leggins *mpl*
legible ['lɛdʒəbl] *adj* legible
legion ['li:dʒən] *n* legión *f*
legionnaire [li:dʒə'nɛəʳ] *n* legionario
legislation [lɛdʒɪs'leɪʃən] *n* legislación *f*; **a piece of ~** (*bill*) un proyecto de ley; (*act*) una ley
legislative ['lɛdʒɪslətɪv] *adj* legislativo
legislator ['lɛdʒɪsleɪtəʳ] *n* legislador(a) *m(f)*
legislature ['lɛdʒɪslətʃəʳ] *n* cuerpo legislativo
legitimacy [lɪ'dʒɪtɪməsɪ] *n* legitimidad *f*
legitimate [lɪ'dʒɪtɪmət] *adj* legítimo
legitimize [lɪ'dʒɪtɪmaɪz] *vt* legitimar
legless ['lɛglɪs] *adj* (*Brit inf*) mamado
leg-room ['lɛgru:m] *n* espacio para las piernas
leisure ['lɛʒəʳ] *n* ocio, tiempo libre; **at ~** con tranquilidad
leisure centre *n* polideportivo
leisurely ['lɛʒəlɪ] *adj* sin prisa; lento
lemon ['lɛmən] *n* limón *m*
lemonade [lɛmə'neɪd] *n* (*fruit juice*) limonada; (*fizzy*) gaseosa
lemon tea *n* té *m* con limón
lend [lɛnd] (*pt, pp* **lent** [lɛnt]) *vt*: **to ~ sth to sb** prestar algo a algn
lender ['lɛndəʳ] *n* prestamista *m/f*
length [lɛŋθ] *n* (*size*) largo, longitud *f*; (*section*: *of road, pipe*) tramo; (: *of rope etc*) largo; (*of wood, string*) trozo; (*amount of time*) duración *f*; **at ~** (*at last*) por fin, finalmente; (*lengthily*) largamente; **it is two metres in ~** tiene dos metros de largo; **what ~ is it?** ¿cuánto tiene de largo?; **to fall full ~** caer de bruces; **to go to any ~(s) to do sth** ser capaz de hacer cualquier cosa para hacer algo
lengthen ['lɛŋθn] *vt* alargar ▷ *vi* alargarse
lengthways ['lɛŋθweɪz] *adv* a lo largo
lengthy ['lɛŋθɪ] *adj* largo, extenso; (*meeting*) prolongado
lenient ['li:nɪənt] *adj* indulgente
lens [lɛnz] *n* (*of spectacles*) lente *f*; (*of camera*) objetivo
Lent [lɛnt] *n* Cuaresma
lent [lɛnt] *pt, pp of* **lend**
lentil ['lɛntl] *n* lenteja
Leo ['li:əu] *n* Leo
leopard ['lɛpəd] *n* leopardo
leotard ['li:ətɑ:d] *n* malla
leper ['lɛpəʳ] *n* leproso(-a)
leprosy ['lɛprəsɪ] *n* lepra
lesbian ['lɛzbɪən] *adj* lesbiano ▷ *n* lesbiana
lesion ['li:ʒən] *n* (*Med*) lesión *f*
less [lɛs] *adj* (*in size, degree etc*) menor; (*in quantity*) menos ▷ *pron, adv* menos; **~ than half** menos de la mitad; **~ than £1/a kilo/3 metres** menos de una libra/un kilo/3 metros; **~ than ever** menos que nunca; **~ 5%** menos el cinco por ciento; **~ and ~** cada vez menos; **the ~ he works ...** cuanto menos trabaja ...
lessen ['lɛsn] *vi* disminuir, reducirse ▷ *vt* disminuir, reducir
lesser ['lɛsəʳ] *adj* menor; **to a ~ extent** *or* **degree** en menor grado
lesson ['lɛsn] *n* clase *f*; **a maths ~** una clase de matemáticas; **to give ~s in** dar clases de; **it taught him a ~** (*fig*) le sirvió de lección
lest [lɛst] *conj*: **~ it happen** para que no pase
let (*pt, pp* **let**) [lɛt] *vt* (*allow*) dejar, permitir; (*Brit*: *lease*) alquilar; **to ~ sb do sth** dejar que algn haga algo; **to ~ sb have sth** dar algo a algn; **to ~ sb know sth** comunicar algo a algn; **~'s go** ¡vamos!; **~ him come** que venga; **"to ~"** "se alquila"; **let down** *vt* (*lower*) bajar; (*dress*) alargar; (*tyre*) desinflar; (*hair*) soltar; (*disappoint*) defraudar; **let go** *vi* soltar; (*fig*) dejarse ir ▷ *vt* soltar; **let in** *vt* dejar entrar; (*visitor etc*) hacer pasar; **what have you ~ yourself in for?** ¿en qué te has metido?; **let off** *vt* dejar escapar; (*firework etc*) disparar; (*bomb*) accionar; (*passenger*) dejar, bajar; **to ~ off steam** (*fig, inf*) desahogarse, desfogarse; **let on** *vi*: **to ~ on that ...** revelar que ...; **let out** *vt* dejar salir; (*dress*) ensanchar; (*rent out*) alquilar; **let up** *vi* disminuir; (*rain etc*) amainar
lethal ['li:θl] *adj* (*weapon*) mortífero; (*poison, wound*) mortal
lethargic [lɛ'θɑ:dʒɪk] *adj* aletargado
letter ['lɛtəʳ] *n* (*of alphabet*) letra; (*correspondence*) carta; **letters** *npl* (*literature,*

l

learning) letras *fpl*; **small/capital ~** minúscula/mayúscula; **covering ~** carta adjunta
letter bomb *n* carta-bomba
letterbox ['lɛtəbɔks] *n* (*Brit*) buzón *m*
lettering ['lɛtərɪŋ] *n* letras *fpl*
letter-opener ['lɛtərəupnə^r] *n* abrecartas *m inv*
lettuce ['lɛtɪs] *n* lechuga
let-up ['lɛtʌp] *n* descanso, tregua
leukaemia, leukemia (*US*) [luː'kiːmɪə] *n* leucemia
level ['lɛvl] *adj* (*flat*) llano; (*flattened*) nivelado; (*uniform*) igual ▷ *adv* a nivel ▷ *n* nivel *m*; (*height*) altura ▷ *vt* nivelar, allanar; (*destroy: building*) derribar; (*gun*) apuntar; (*accusation*): **to ~ (against)** levantar (contra) ▷ *vi* (*inf*): **to ~ with sb** ser franco con algn; **to be ~ with** estar a nivel de; **a ~ spoonful** (*Culin*) una cucharada rasa; **to draw ~ with** (*team*) igualar; (*runner, car*) alcanzar a; **A ~s** (*Brit*) ≈ exámenes *mpl* de bachillerato superior, B.U.P.; **O ~s** *npl* (*Brit: formerly*) ≈ bachillerato *sg* elemental, octavo *sg* de Básica; **on the ~** (*fig: honest*) en serio; **talks at ministerial ~** charlas *fpl* a nivel ministerial; **level off** *or* **out** *vi* (*prices etc*) estabilizarse; (*ground*) nivelarse; (*aircraft*) ponerse en una trayectoria horizontal
level crossing *n* (*Brit*) paso a nivel
level-headed [lɛvl'hɛdɪd] *adj* sensato
level playing field *n* situación *f* de igualdad; **to compete on a ~** competir en igualdad de condiciones
lever ['liːvə^r] *n* palanca ▷ *vt*: **to ~ up** levantar con palanca
leverage ['liːvərɪdʒ] *n* (*fig: influence*) influencia
levity ['lɛvɪtɪ] *n* frivolidad *f*, informalidad *f*
levy ['lɛvɪ] *n* impuesto ▷ *vt* exigir, recaudar
lewd [luːd] *adj* lascivo, obsceno, colorado (*LAm*)
lexicographer [lɛksɪ'kɔgrəfə^r] *n* lexicógrafo(-a) *m(f)*
lexicography [lɛksɪ'kɔgrəfɪ] *n* lexicografía
LGV *n abbr* (= *Large Goods Vehicle*) vehículo pesado
liability [laɪə'bɪlətɪ] *n* (*pej: person, thing*) estorbo, lastre *m*; (*Law: responsibility*) responsabilidad *f*; (*handicap*) desventaja
liable ['laɪəbl] *adj* (*subject*): **~ to** sujeto a; (*responsible*): **~ for** responsable de; (*likely*): **~ to do** propenso a hacer; **to be ~ to a fine** exponerse a una multa
liaise [liː'eɪz] *vi*: **to ~ (with)** colaborar (con); **to ~ with sb** mantener informado a algn
liaison [liː'eɪzɔn] *n* (*coordination*) enlace *m*; (*affair*) relación *f*
liar ['laɪə^r] *n* mentiroso(-a)
libel ['laɪbl] *n* calumnia ▷ *vt* calumniar
libellous ['ləɪbləs] *adj* difamatorio, calumnioso
liberal ['lɪbərl] *adj* (*gen*) liberal; (*generous*): **~ with** generoso con ▷ *n*: **L~** (*Pol*) liberal *m/f*
Liberal Democrat *n* (*Brit*) demócrata *m/f* liberal
liberalize ['lɪbərəlaɪz] *vt* liberalizar
liberate ['lɪbəreɪt] *vt* (*people: from poverty etc*) librar; (*prisoner*) libertar; (*country*) liberar
liberation [lɪbə'reɪʃən] *n* liberación *f*
liberation theology *n* teología de la liberación
liberty ['lɪbətɪ] *n* libertad *f*; **to be at ~** (*criminal*) estar en libertad; **to be at ~ to do** estar libre para hacer; **to take the ~ of doing sth** tomarse la libertad de hacer algo
Libra ['liːbrə] *n* Libra
librarian [laɪ'brɛərɪən] *n* bibliotecario(-a)
library ['laɪbrərɪ] *n* biblioteca
libretto [lɪ'brɛtəu] *n* libreto
Libya ['lɪbɪə] *n* Libia
lice [laɪs] *pl of* **louse**
licence, license (*US*) ['laɪsns] *n* licencia; (*permit*) permiso; (*also*: **driving ~**, (*US*): **driver's license**) carnet *m* de conducir, permiso de manejar (*LAm*); (*excessive freedom*) libertad *f*; **import ~** licencia *or* permiso de importación; **produced under ~** elaborado bajo licencia
licence number *n* (número de) matrícula
licence plate *n* (placa de) matrícula
license ['laɪsns] *n* (*US*) = **licence** ▷ *vt* autorizar, dar permiso a; (*car*) sacar la matrícula de *or* (*LAm*) la patente de
licensed ['laɪsnst] *adj* (*for alcohol*) autorizado para vender bebidas alcohólicas
licensee [laɪsən'siː] *n* (*in a pub*) concesionario(-a), dueño(-a) de un bar
license plate *n* (*US*) placa (de matrícula)
licensing hours *npl* (*Brit*) *horas durante las cuales se permite la venta y consumo de alcohol* (*en un bar etc*)
lick [lɪk] *vt* lamer; (*inf: defeat*) dar una paliza a ▷ *n* lamedura; **a ~ of paint** una mano de pintura; **to ~ one's lips** relamerse
licorice ['lɪkərɪs] *n* = **liquorice**
lid [lɪd] *n* (*of box, case, pan*) tapa, tapadera; **to take the ~ off sth** (*fig*) exponer algo a la luz pública
lie [laɪ] *n* mentira ▷ *vi* mentir (*pt* **lay**, *pp* **lain** [leɪ, leɪn]) (*rest*) estar echado, estar acostado; (*of object: be situated*) estar, encontrarse; **to tell ~s** mentir; **to ~ low** (*fig*) mantenerse a escondidas; **lie about, lie around** *vi* (*things*) estar tirado; (*Brit: people*) estar acostado *or* tumbado; **lie back** *vi* recostarse; **lie down** *vi* echarse, tumbarse; **lie up** *vi* (*hide*) esconderse
Liechtenstein ['lɪktənstaɪn] *n* Liechtenstein *m*
lie detector *n* detector *m* de mentiras
lie-down ['laɪdaun] *n* (*Brit*): **to have a ~** echarse (una siesta)
lie-in ['laɪɪn] *n* (*Brit*): **to have a ~** quedarse en la cama
lieu [luː]: **in ~ of** *prep* en lugar de

lieutenant [lɛf'tɛnənt, (*US*) lu:'tɛnənt] *n* (*Mil*) teniente *m*
life (*pl* **lives**) [laɪf, laɪvz] *n* vida; (*of licence etc*) vigencia; **to be sent to prison for ~** ser condenado a cadena perpetua; **country/city ~** la vida en el campo/en la ciudad; **true to ~** fiel a la realidad; **to paint from ~** pintar del natural; **to put** *or* **breathe new ~ into** (*person*) reanimar; (*project, area etc*) infundir nueva vida a
life assurance *n* (*Brit*) seguro de vida
lifebelt ['laɪfbɛlt] *n* (*Brit*) cinturón *m* salvavidas
lifeboat ['laɪfbəut] *n* lancha de socorro
life-buoy ['laɪfbɔɪ] *n* boya *or* guindola salvavidas
life expectancy *n* esperanza de vida
lifeguard ['laɪfgɑ:d] *n* vigilante *m/f*, socorrista *m/f*
life insurance *n* = **life assurance**
life jacket *n* chaleco salvavidas
lifeless ['laɪflɪs] *adj* sin vida; (*dull*) soso
lifelike ['laɪflaɪk] *adj* natural
lifeline ['laɪflaɪn] *n* (*fig*) cordón *m* umbilical
lifelong ['laɪflɔŋ] *adj* de toda la vida
life preserver *n* (*US*) = **lifebelt**
lifer ['laɪfəʳ] *n* (*inf*) condenado(-a) *m*(*f*) a cadena perpetua
life sentence *n* cadena perpetua
life-sized ['laɪfsaɪzd] *adj* de tamaño natural
life span *n* vida
lifestyle ['laɪfstaɪl] *n* estilo de vida
life support system *n* (*Med*) sistema *m* de respiración asistida
lifetime ['laɪftaɪm] *n*: **in his ~** durante su vida; **once in a ~** una vez en la vida; **the chance of a ~** una oportunidad única
lift [lɪft] *vt* levantar; (*copy*) plagiar ▷ *vi* (*fog*) disiparse ▷ *n* (*Brit: elevator*) ascensor *m*, elevador *m* (*LAm*); **to give sb a ~** (*Brit*) llevar a algn en coche; **lift off** *vt* levantar, quitar ▷ *vi* (*rocket, helicopter*) despegar; **lift out** *vt* sacar; (*troops, evacuees etc*) evacuar; **lift up** *vt* levantar
lift-off ['lɪftɔf] *n* despegue *m*
ligament ['lɪgəmənt] *n* ligamento
light [laɪt] *n* luz *f*; (*flame*) lumbre *f*; (*lamp*) luz *f*, lámpara; (*daylight*) luz *f* del día; (*headlight*) faro; (*rear light*) luz *f* trasera; (*for cigarette etc*): **have you got a ~?** ¿tienes fuego? ▷ *vt* (*pt, pp* **lighted** *or* **lit** [lɪt]) (*candle, cigarette, fire*) encender; (*room*) alumbrar ▷ *adj* (*colour*) claro; (*room*) con mucha luz ▷ *adv* (*travel*) con poco equipaje; **lights** *npl* (*traffic lights*) semáforos *mpl*; **to turn the ~ on/off** encender/apagar la luz; **in the ~ of** a la luz de; **to come to ~** salir a la luz; **to cast** *or* **shed** *or* **throw ~ on** arrojar luz sobre; **to make ~ of sth** (*fig*) no dar importancia a algo; **light up** *vi* (*smoke*) encender un cigarrillo; (*face*) iluminarse ▷ *vt* (*illuminate*) iluminar, alumbrar; (*set fire to*) encender
light bulb *n* bombilla, bombillo (*LAm*), foco (*LAm*)
lighten ['laɪtn] *vi* (*grow light*) clarear ▷ *vt* (*give light to*) iluminar; (*make lighter*) aclarar; (*make less heavy*) aligerar
lighter ['laɪtəʳ] *n* (*also*: **cigarette ~**) encendedor *m* (*LAm*), mechero
light-headed [laɪt'hɛdɪd] *adj* (*dizzy*) mareado; (*excited*) exaltado; (*by nature*) atolondrado
light-hearted [laɪt'hɑ:tɪd] *adj* (*person*) alegre; (*remark etc*) divertido
lighthouse ['laɪthaus] *n* faro
lighting ['laɪtɪŋ] *n* (*act*) iluminación *f*; (*system*) alumbrado
lightly ['laɪtlɪ] *adv* ligeramente; (*not seriously*) con poca seriedad; **to get off ~** ser castigado con poca severidad
lightness ['laɪtnɪs] *n* claridad *f*; (*in weight*) ligereza
lightning ['laɪtnɪŋ] *n* relámpago, rayo
lightning conductor, lightning rod (*US*) *n* pararrayos *m inv*
lightweight ['laɪtweɪt] *adj* (*suit*) ligero ▷ *n* (*Boxing*) peso ligero
light year *n* año luz
like [laɪk] *vt* (*person*) querer a; (*thing*): **I ~ swimming/apples** me gusta nadar/me gustan las manzanas ▷ *prep* como ▷ *adj* parecido, semejante ▷ *n*: **did you ever see the ~ (of it)?** ¿has visto cosa igual?; **his ~s and dislikes** sus gustos y aversiones; **the ~s of him** personas como él; **I would ~, I'd ~** me gustaría; (*for purchase*) quisiera; **would you ~ a coffee?** ¿te apetece un café?; **I ~ swimming** me gusta nadar; **to be** *or* **look ~ sb/sth** parecerse a algn/algo; **that's just ~ him** es muy de él, es típico de él; **do it ~ this** hazlo así; **it is nothing ~ ...** no tiene parecido alguno con ...; **what's he ~?** ¿cómo es (él)?; **what's the weather ~?** ¿qué tiempo hace?; **something ~ that** algo así *or* por el estilo; **I feel ~ a drink** me apetece algo de beber; **if you ~** si quieres
likeable ['laɪkəbl] *adj* simpático, agradable
likelihood ['laɪklɪhud] *n* probabilidad *f*; **in all ~** según todas las probabilidades
likely ['laɪklɪ] *adj* probable, capaz (*LAm*); **he's ~ to leave** es probable *or* (*LAm*) capaz que se vaya; **not ~!** ¡ni hablar!
liken ['laɪkən] *vt*: **to ~ to** comparar con
likeness ['laɪknɪs] *n* (*similarity*) semejanza, parecido
likewise ['laɪkwaɪz] *adv* igualmente; **to do ~** hacer lo mismo
liking ['laɪkɪŋ] *n*: **~ (for)** (*person*) cariño (a); (*thing*) afición (a); **to take a ~ to sb** tomar cariño a algn; **to be to sb's ~** ser del gusto de algn
lilac ['laɪlək] *n* (*tree*) lilo; (*flower*) lila ▷ *adj* (*colour*) de color lila
Lilo® ['laɪləu] *n* colchoneta inflable
lily ['lɪlɪ] *n* lirio, azucena; **~ of the valley** *n* lirio de los valles
lily of the valley *n* lirio de los valles

limb [lɪm] *n* miembro; (*of tree*) rama; **to be out on a ~** (*fig*) estar aislado
limber up ['lɪmbəʳ-] *vi* (*fig*) entrenarse; (*Sport*) hacer (ejercicios de) precalentamiento
limbo ['lɪmbəu] *n*: **to be in ~** (*fig*) quedar a la expectativa
lime [laɪm] *n* (*tree*) limero; (*fruit*) lima; (*Geo*) cal *f*
limelight ['laɪmlaɪt] *n*: **to be in the ~** (*fig*) ser el centro de atención
limerick ['lɪmərɪk] *n* quintilla humorística
limestone ['laɪmstəun] *n* piedra caliza
limit ['lɪmɪt] *n* límite *m* ▷ *vt* limitar; **weight/speed ~** peso máximo/velocidad *f* máxima; **within ~s** entre límites
limitation [lɪmɪ'teɪʃən] *n* limitación *f*
limited ['lɪmɪtɪd] *adj* limitado; **to be ~ to** limitarse a; **~ edition** edición limitada
limousine ['lɪməzi:n] *n* limusina
limp [lɪmp] *n*: **to have a ~** tener cojera ▷ *vi* cojear, renguear (*LAm*) ▷ *adj* flojo
limpet ['lɪmpɪt] *n* lapa
line [laɪn] *n* (*Comm*) línea; (*straight line*) raya; (*rope*) cuerda; (*for fishing*) sedal *m*; (*wire*) hilo; (*row, series*) fila, hilera; (*of writing*) renglón *m*; (*on face*) arruga; (*Rail*) vía; (*speciality*) rama ▷ *vt* (*Sewing*): **to ~ (with)** forrar (de); **to ~ the streets** ocupar las aceras; **in ~ with** de acuerdo con; **she's in ~ for promotion** (*fig*) tiene muchas posibilidades de que la asciendan; **to bring sth into ~ with sth** poner algo de acuerdo con algo; **~ of research/business** campo de investigación/comercio; **to take the ~ that ...** ser de la opinión que ...; **hold the ~ please** (*Tel*) no cuelgue usted, por favor; **to draw the ~ at doing sth** negarse a hacer algo; no permitir que se haga algo; **on the right ~s** por buen camino; **a new ~ in cosmetics** una nueva línea en cosméticos; **line up** *vi* hacer cola ▷ *vt* alinear, poner en fila; **to have sth ~d up** tener algo arreglado
linear ['lɪnɪəʳ] *adj* lineal
lined [laɪnd] *adj* (*face*) arrugado; (*paper*) rayado; (*clothes*) forrado
lineman ['laɪnmən] *n* (*US*) técnico de las líneas; (*Football*) delantero
linen ['lɪnɪn] *n* ropa blanca; (*cloth*) lino
liner ['laɪnəʳ] *n* vapor *m* de línea transatlántico; **dustbin ~** bolsa de la basura
linesman ['laɪnzmən] *n* (*Sport*) juez *m* de línea
line-up ['laɪnʌp] *n* (*US: queue*) cola; (*Sport*) alineación *f*
linger ['lɪŋgəʳ] *vi* retrasarse, tardar en marcharse; (*smell, tradition*) persistir
lingerie ['lænʒəri:] *n* ropa interior (de mujer), lencería
lingo (*pl* **lingoes**) ['lɪŋgəu, -gəuz] *n* (*pej*) jerga
linguist ['lɪŋgwɪst] *n* lingüista *m/f*
linguistic [lɪŋ'gwɪstɪk] *adj* lingüístico
linguistics [lɪŋ'gwɪstɪks] *n* lingüística
lining ['laɪnɪŋ] *n* forro; (*Tech*) revestimiento; (*of brake*) guarnición *f*
link [lɪŋk] *n* (*of chain*) eslabón *m*; (*connection*) conexión *f*; (*relationship*) relación *f*; (*bond*) vínculo, lazo; (*Internet*) enlace *m* ▷ *vt* vincular, unir; (*associate*): **to ~ with** *or* **to** relacionar con; **rail ~** línea de ferrocarril, servicio de trenes; **links** *npl* (*Golf*) campo de golf; **link up** *vt* acoplar ▷ *vi* unirse
lino ['laɪnəu], **linoleum** (*Brit*) [lɪ'nəulɪəm] *n* linóleo
lion ['laɪən] *n* león *m*
lioness ['laɪənɪs] *n* leona
lip [lɪp] *n* labio; (*of jug*) pico; (*of cup etc*) borde *m*
liposuction ['lɪpəusʌkʃən] *n* liposucción *f*
lip-read ['lɪpri:d] *vi* leer los labios
lip salve *n* crema protectora para labios
lip service *n*: **to pay ~ to sth** alabar algo pero sin hacer nada
lipstick ['lɪpstɪk] *n* lápiz *m or* barra de labios, carmín *m*
liqueur [lɪ'kjuəʳ] *n* licor *m*
liquid ['lɪkwɪd] *adj, n* líquido
liquidation [lɪkwɪ'deɪʃən] *n* liquidación *f*; **o go into ~** entrar en liquidación
liquidize ['lɪkwɪdaɪz] *vt* (*Culin*) licuar
liquidizer ['lɪkwɪdaɪzəʳ] *n* (*Culin*) licuadora
liquor ['lɪkəʳ] *n* licor *m*, bebidas *fpl* alcohólicas
liquorice ['lɪkərɪs] *n* regaliz *m*
liquor store *n* (*US*) bodega, *tienda de vinos y bebidas alcohólicas*
Lisbon ['lɪzbən] *n* Lisboa
lisp [lɪsp] *n* ceceo ▷ *vi* cecear
list [lɪst] *n* lista; (*of ship*) inclinación *f* ▷ *vt* (*write down*) hacer una lista de; (*mention*) enumerar; (*Comput*) hacer un listado de ▷ *vi* (*ship*) inclinarse; **shopping ~** lista de las compras; *see also* **lists**
listed building ['lɪstɪd-] *n* (*Arch*) edificio de interés histórico-artístico
listen ['lɪsn] *vi* escuchar, oír; (*pay attention*) atender
listener ['lɪsnəʳ] *n* oyente *m/f*
listeria [lɪs'tɪərɪə] *n* listeria
listing ['lɪstɪŋ] *n* (*Comput*) listado
listless ['lɪstlɪs] *adj* apático, indiferente
lists [lɪsts] *npl* (*History*) liza *sg*; **to enter the ~ (against sb/sth)** salir a la palestra (contra algn/algo)
lit [lɪt] *pt, pp of* **light**
litany ['lɪtənɪ] *n* letanía
liter ['li:təʳ] *n* (*US*) = **litre**
literacy ['lɪtərəsɪ] *n* capacidad *f* de leer y escribir
literal ['lɪtərl] *adj* literal
literally ['lɪtrəlɪ] *adv* literalmente
literary ['lɪtərərɪ] *adj* literario
literate ['lɪtərət] *adj* que sabe leer y escribir; (*educated*) culto
literature ['lɪtərɪtʃəʳ] *n* literatura; (*brochures etc*) folletos *mpl*
lithe [laɪð] *adj* ágil
Lithuania [lɪθju'eɪnɪə] *n* Lituania

litigate ['lɪtɪgeɪt] *vi* litigar
litigation [lɪtɪ'geɪʃən] *n* litigio
litmus paper ['lɪtməs-] *n* papel *m* de tornasol
litre, liter (*US*) ['li:təʳ] *n* litro
litter ['lɪtəʳ] *n* (*rubbish*) basura; (*paper*) papeles *mpl* (tirados); (*young animals*) camada, cría
litter bin *n* (*Brit*) papelera
littered ['lɪtəd] *adj*: **~ with** lleno de
little ['lɪtl] *adj* (*small*) pequeño, chico (*LAm*); (*not much*) poco; (*often translated by suffix, eg*): **~ house** casita ▷ *adv* poco; **a ~** un poco (de); **a ~ bit** un poquito; **~ by ~** poco a poco; **~ finger** (dedo) meñique *m*; **for a ~ while** (durante) un rato; **with ~ difficulty** sin problema *or* dificultad; **as ~ as possible** lo menos posible
little finger *n* dedo meñique
little-known ['lɪtl'nəun] *adj* poco conocido
liturgy ['lɪtədʒɪ] *n* liturgia
live[1] [laɪv] *adj* (*animal*) vivo; (*wire*) conectado; (*broadcast*) en directo; (*issue*) de actualidad; (*unexploded*) sin explotar
live[2] [lɪv] *vi* vivir ▷ *vt* (*a life*) llevar; (*experience*) vivir; **to ~ in London** vivir en Londres; **to ~ together** vivir juntos; **live down** *vt* hacer olvidar; **live off** *vt fus* (*land, fish etc*) vivir de; (*pej: parents etc*) vivir a costa de; **live on** *vt fus* (*food*) vivir de, alimentarse de; **to ~ on £50 a week** vivir con 50 libras semanales *or* a la semana; **live out** *vi* (*student*) ser externo ▷ *vt*: **to ~ out one's days** *or* **life** pasar el resto de la vida; **live up** *vt*: **to ~ it up** (*inf*) tirarse la gran vida; **live up to** *vt fus* (*fulfil*) cumplir con; (*justify*) justificar
livelihood ['laɪvlɪhud] *n* sustento
lively ['laɪvlɪ] *adj* (*gen*) vivo; (*interesting: place, book etc*) animado; (*pace*) rápido; (*party, tune*) alegre
liven up ['laɪvn-] *vt* (*discussion, evening*) animar ▷ *vi* animarse
liver ['lɪvəʳ] *n* hígado
lives [laɪvz] *npl of* **life**
livestock ['laɪvstɔk] *n* ganado
livid ['lɪvɪd] *adj* lívido; (*furious*) furioso
living ['lɪvɪŋ] *adj* (*alive*) vivo ▷ *n*: **to earn** *or* **make a ~** ganarse la vida; **cost of ~** coste *m* de la vida; **in ~ memory** que se recuerde *or* recuerda
living conditions *npl* condiciones *fpl* de vida
living room *n* sala (de estar), living *m* (*LAm*)
living standards *npl* nivel *msg* de vida
living wage *n* sueldo suficiente para vivir
lizard ['lɪzəd] *n* lagartija
llama ['lɑ:mə] *n* llama
load [ləud] *n* (*gen*) carga; (*weight*) peso ▷ *vt* (*Comput*) cargar; (*also*: **~ up**): **to ~ (with)** cargar (con *or* de); **a ~ of, ~s of** (*fig*) (gran) cantidad de, montones de
loaded ['ləudɪd] *adj* (*dice*) cargado; (*question*) intencionado; (*inf: rich*) forrado (de dinero)
loaf (*pl* **loaves**) [ləuf, ləuvz] *n* (barra de) pan *m* ▷ *vi* (*also*: **~ about, ~ around**) holgazanear
loan [ləun] *n* préstamo; (*Comm*) empréstito ▷ *vt* prestar; **on ~** (*book, painting*) prestado; **to raise a ~** (*money*) procurar un empréstito
loath [ləuθ] *adj*: **to be ~ to do sth** ser reacio a hacer algo
loathe [ləuð] *vt* aborrecer; (*person*) odiar
loaves [ləuvz] *pl of* **loaf**
lob [lɔb] *vt* (*ball*) volear por alto
lobby ['lɔbɪ] *n* vestíbulo, sala de espera; (*Pol: pressure group*) grupo de presión ▷ *vt* presionar
lobbyist ['lɔbɪɪst] *n* cabildero(-a)
lobe [ləub] *n* lóbulo
lobster ['lɔbstəʳ] *n* langosta
local ['ləukl] *adj* local ▷ *n* (*pub*) bar *m*; **the locals** *npl* los vecinos, los del lugar
local anaesthetic, local anesthetic (*US*) *n* (*Med*) anestesia local
local authority *n* municipio, ayuntamiento (*Sp*)
local call *n* (*Tel*) llamada local
local government *n* gobierno municipal
locality [ləu'kælɪtɪ] *n* localidad *f*
locally ['ləukəlɪ] *adv* en la vecindad
locate [ləu'keɪt] *vt* (*find*) localizar; (*situate*): **to be ~d in** estar situado en
location [ləu'keɪʃən] *n* situación *f*; **on ~** (*Cine*) en exteriores, fuera del estudio
loch [lɔx] *n* lago
lock [lɔk] *n* (*of door, box*) cerradura, chapa (*LAm*); (*of canal*) esclusa; (*of hair*) mechón *m* ▷ *vt* (*with key*) cerrar con llave; (*immobilize*) inmovilizar ▷ *vi* (*door etc*) cerrarse con llave; (*wheels*) trabarse; **~ stock and barrel** (*fig*) por completo *or* entero; **on full ~** (*Aut*) con el volante girado al máximo; **lock away** *vt* (*valuables*) guardar bajo llave; (*criminal*) encerrar; **lock in** *vt* encerrar; **lock out** *vt* (*person*) cerrar la puerta a; **the workers were ~ed out** los trabajadores tuvieron que enfrentarse con un cierre patronal; **lock up** *vt* (*criminal*) meter en la cárcel; (*psychiatric patient*) encerrar; (*house*) cerrar (con llave) ▷ *vi* echar la llave
locker ['lɔkəʳ] *n* casillero
locker-room ['lɔkərum] *n* (*US Sport*) vestuario
locket ['lɔkɪt] *n* medallón *m*
locksmith ['lɔksmɪθ] *n* cerrajero(-a)
lock-up ['lɔkʌp] *n* (*prison*) cárcel *f*; (*cell*) jaula; (*also*: **~ garage**) jaula, cochera
locomotive [ləukə'məutɪv] *n* locomotora
locum ['ləukəm] *n* (*Med*) (médico(-a)) suplente *m(f)*
locust ['ləukəst] *n* langosta
lodge [lɔdʒ] *n* casa del guarda; (*porter's*) portería; (*Freemasonry*) logia ▷ *vi* (*person*): **to ~ (with)** alojarse (en casa de) ▷ *vt* (*complaint*) presentar
lodger ['lɔdʒəʳ] *n* huésped *m/f*
lodging ['lɔdʒɪŋ] *n* alojamiento, hospedaje *m*
lodgings ['lɔdʒɪŋz] *npl* alojamiento *sg*; (*house*) casa *sg* de huéspedes

loft [lɔft] *n* desván *m*
lofty ['lɔftɪ] *adj* alto; (*haughty*) altivo, arrogante; (*sentiments, aims*) elevado, noble
log [lɔg] *n* (*of wood*) leño, tronco; (*written account*) diario; (*book*) = **logbook** ▷ *n abbr* (= *logarithm*) log ▷ *vt* anotar, registrar; **log in, log on** *vi* (*Comput*) iniciar la sesión; **log off, log out** *vi* (*Comput*) finalizar la sesión
logarithm ['lɔgərɪðəm] *n* logaritmo
logbook ['lɔgbuk] *n* (*Naut*) diario de a bordo; (*Aviat*) libro de vuelo; (*of car*) documentación *f* (del coche)
logger ['lɔgə^r] *n* leñador(a) *m(f)*
loggerheads ['lɔgəhɛdz] *npl*: **at ~ (with)** de pique (con)
logic ['lɔdʒɪk] *n* lógica
logical ['lɔdʒɪkl] *adj* lógico
login ['lɔgɪn] *n* (*Comput*) login *m*
logo ['ləugəu] *n* logotipo
loin [lɔɪn] *n* (*Culin*) lomo, solomillo; **loins** *npl* lomos *mpl*
loiter ['lɔɪtə^r] *vi* vagar; (*pej*) merodear
loll [lɔl] *vi* (*also*: **~ about**) repantigarse
lollipop ['lɔlɪpɔp] *n* pirulí *m*; (*iced*) polo
lollipop lady *n* (*Brit*) *ver nota*
lollipop man, lollipop lady *n* (*Brit*) *persona encargada de ayudar a los niños a cruzar la calle*
lolly ['lɔlɪ] *n* (*inf*: *ice cream*) polo; (: *lollipop*) piruleta; (: *money*) guita
London ['lʌndən] *n* Londres *m*
Londoner ['lʌndənə^r] *n* londinense *m/f*
lone [ləun] *adj* solitario
loneliness ['ləunlɪnɪs] *n* soledad *f*, aislamiento
lonely ['ləunlɪ] *adj* (*situation*) solitario; (*person*) solo; (*place*) aislado
loner ['ləunə^r] *n* solitario(-a)
long [lɔŋ] *adj* largo ▷ *adv* mucho tiempo, largamente ▷ *vi*: **to ~ for sth** anhelar algo ▷ *n*: **the ~ and the short of it is that ...** (*fig*) en resumidas cuentas ...; **in the ~ run** a la larga; **so** *or* **as ~ as** mientras, con tal de que; **don't be ~!** ¡no tardes!, ¡vuelve pronto!; **how ~ is the street?** ¿cuánto tiene la calle de largo?; **how ~ is the lesson?** ¿cuánto dura la clase?; **six metres ~** que mide seis metros, de seis metros de largo; **six months ~** que dura seis meses, de seis meses de duración; **all night ~** toda la noche; **~ ago** hace mucho (tiempo); **he no ~er comes** ya no viene; **~ before** mucho antes; **before ~** (+ *future*) dentro de poco; (+ *past*) poco tiempo después; **at ~ last** al fin, por fin; **I shan't be ~** termino pronto
long-distance [lɔŋ'dɪstəns] *adj* (*race*) de larga distancia; (*call*) interurbano
longhand ['lɔŋhænd] *n* escritura (corriente)
long-haul ['lɔŋhɔ:l] *adj* (*flight*) de larga distancia
longing ['lɔŋɪŋ] *n* anhelo, ansia; (*nostalgia*) nostalgia ▷ *adj* anhelante
longitude ['lɔŋgɪtju:d] *n* longitud *f*
long jump *n* salto de longitud
long-life ['lɔŋlaɪf] *adj* (*batteries*) de larga duración; (*milk*) uperizado
long-lost ['lɔŋlɔst] *adj* desaparecido hace mucho tiempo
long-playing record ['lɔŋpleɪɪŋ-] *n* elepé *m*, disco de larga duración
long-range ['lɔŋ'reɪndʒ] *adj* de gran alcance; (*weather forecast*) a largo plazo
long-sighted ['lɔŋ'saɪtɪd] *adj* (*Brit*) présbita
long-standing ['lɔŋ'stændɪŋ] *adj* de mucho tiempo
long-suffering [lɔŋ'sʌfərɪŋ] *adj* sufrido
long-term ['lɔŋtə:m] *adj* a largo plazo
long wave *n* onda larga
long-winded [lɔŋ'wɪndɪd] *adj* prolijo
loo [lu:] *n* (*Brit*: *inf*) wáter *m*
look [luk] *vi* mirar; (*seem*) parecer; (*building etc*): **to ~ south/on to the sea** dar al sur/al mar ▷ *n* mirada; (*glance*) vistazo; (*appearance*) aire *m*, aspecto; **looks** *npl* físico *sg*, belleza *sg*; **to ~ ahead** mirar hacia delante; **it ~s about four metres long** yo calculo que tiene unos cuarto metros de largo; **it ~s all right to me** a mí me parece que está bien; **to have a ~ at sth** echar un vistazo a algo; **to have a ~ for sth** buscar algo; **~ (here)!** (*expressing annoyance etc*) ¡oye!; **~!** (*expressing surprise*) ¡mira!; **look after** *vt fus* (*care for*) cuidar a; (*deal with*) encargarse de; **look around** *vi* echar una mirada alrededor; **look at** *vt fus* mirar; (*consider*) considerar; **look back** *vi* mirar hacia atrás; **to ~ back at sb/sth** mirar hacia atrás algo/a algn; **to ~ back on** (*event, period*) recordar; **look down on** *vt fus* (*fig*) despreciar, mirar con desprecio; **look for** *vt fus* buscar; **look forward to** *vt fus* esperar con ilusión; (*in letters*): **we ~ forward to hearing from you** quedamos a la espera de su respuesta *or* contestación; **I'm not ~ing forward to it** no tengo ganas de eso, no me hace ilusión; **look in** *vi*: **to ~ in on sb** (*visit*) pasar por casa de algn; **look into** *vt fus* investigar; **look on** *vi* mirar (como espectador); **look out** *vi* (*beware*): **to ~ out (for)** tener cuidado (de); **look out for** *vt fus* (*seek*) buscar; (*await*) esperar; **look over** *vt* (*essay*) revisar; (*town, building*) inspeccionar, registrar; (*person*) examinar; **look round** *vi* (*turn*) volver la cabeza; **to ~ round for sth** buscar algo; **look through** *vt fus* (*papers, book*) hojear; (*briefly*) echar un vistazo a; (*telescope*) mirar por; **look to** *vt fus* ocuparse de; (*rely on*) contar con; **look up** *vi* mirar hacia arriba; (*improve*) mejorar ▷ *vt* (*word*) buscar; (*friend*) visitar; **look up to** *vt fus* admirar
look-out ['lukaut] *n* (*tower etc*) puesto de observación; (*person*) vigía *m/f*; **to be on the ~ for sth** estar al acecho de algo
loom [lu:m] *n* telar *m* ▷ *vi*: **~ (up)** (*threaten*) surgir, amenazar; (*event: approach*) aproximarse

loony ['lu:nɪ] *adj, n (inf!)* loco(-a) *m(f)*
loop [lu:p] *n* lazo; (*bend*) vuelta, recodo; (*Comput*) bucle *m*
loophole ['lu:phəul] *n* laguna
loose [lu:s] *adj* (*gen*) suelto; (*not tight*) flojo; (*wobbly etc*) movedizo; (*clothes*) ancho; (*morals, discipline*) relajado ▷ *vt* (*free*) soltar; (*slacken*) aflojar; (*also*: **~ off**: *arrow*) disparar, soltar; **~ connection** (*Elec*) hilo desempalmado; **to be at a ~ end** *or* (*US*) **at ~ ends** no saber qué hacer; **to tie up ~ ends** (*fig*) no dejar ningún cabo suelto, atar cabos
loose change *n* cambio
loose chippings [-'tʃɪpɪŋz] *npl* (*on road*) gravilla *sg* suelta
loosely ['lu:slɪ] *adv* libremente, aproximadamente
loosely-knit [-nɪt] *adj* de estructura abierta
loosen ['lu:sn] *vt* (*free*) soltar; (*untie*) desatar; (*slacken*) aflojar; **loosen up** *vi* (*before game*) hacer (ejercicios de) precalentamiento; (*inf: relax*) soltarse, relajarse
loot [lu:t] *n* botín *m* ▷ *vt* saquear
looting ['lu:tɪŋ] *n* pillaje *m*
lop-sided ['lɔp'saɪdɪd] *adj* torcido; (*fig*) desequilibrado
lord [lɔ:d] *n* señor *m*; **L~ Smith** Lord Smith; **the L~** el Señor; **the (House of) L~s** (*Brit*) la Cámara de los Lores
Lordship ['lɔ:dʃɪp] *n*: **your ~** su Señoría
lore [lɔ:ʳ] *n* saber *m* popular, tradiciones *fpl*
lorry ['lɔrɪ] *n* (*Brit*) camión *m*
lorry driver *n* camionero(-a)
lose (*pt, pp* **lost**) [lu:z, lɔst] *vt* perder ▷ *vi* perder, ser vencido; **to ~ (time)** (*clock*) atrasarse; **to ~ no time (in doing sth)** no tardar (en hacer algo); **to get lost** (*object*) extraviarse; (*person*) perderse; **lose out** *vi* salir perdiendo
loser ['lu:zəʳ] *n* perdedor(a) *m(f)*; **to be a bad ~** no saber perder
loss [lɔs] *n* pérdida; **heavy ~es** (*Mil*) grandes pérdidas *fpl*; **to be at a ~** no saber qué hacer; **to be a dead ~** ser completamente inútil; **to make a ~** sufrir pérdidas; **to cut one's ~es** reducir las pérdidas; **to sell sth at a ~** vender algo perdiendo dinero
lost [lɔst] *pt, pp of* **lose** ▷ *adj* perdido; **~ in thought** absorto, ensimismado
lost and found *n* (*US*) = **lost property**; **lost property office** *or* **department**
lost cause *n* causa perdida
lost property *n* (*Brit*) objetos *mpl* perdidos
lost property office *or* **department** *n* (*Brit*) departamento de objetos perdidos
lot [lɔt] *n* (*at auction*) lote *m*; (*destiny*) suerte *f*; **the ~** el todo, todos *mpl*, todas *fpl*; **a ~** mucho, bastante; **a ~ of, ~s of** muchos(-as), mucho(-a) *adj sg*; **I read a ~** leo bastante; **to draw ~s (for sth)** echar suertes (para decidir algo)
lotion ['ləuʃən] *n* loción *f*
lottery ['lɔtərɪ] *n* lotería
loud [laud] *adj* (*voice, sound*) fuerte; (*laugh, shout*) estrepitoso; (*gaudy*) chillón(-ona) ▷ *adv* (*speak etc*) fuerte; **out ~** en voz alta
loudhailer [laud'heɪləʳ] *n* (*Brit*) megáfono
loudly ['laudlɪ] *adv* (*noisily*) fuerte; (*aloud*) en alta voz
loudspeaker [laud'spi:kəʳ] *n* altavoz *m*
lounge [laundʒ] *n* salón *m*, sala de estar; (*of hotel*) salón *m*; (*of airport*) sala de embarque ▷ *vi* (*also*: **~ about, ~ around**) holgazanear, no hacer nada
lounge bar *n* salón *m*
lounge suit *n* (*Brit*) traje *m* de calle
louse (*pl* **lice**) [laus, laɪs] *n* piojo; **louse up** *vt* (*inf*) echar a perder
lousy ['lauzɪ] *adj* (*fig*) vil, asqueroso; (*ill*) fatal
lout [laut] *n* gamberro(-a)
lovable ['lʌvəbl] *adj* amable, simpático
love [lʌv] *n* (*romantic, sexual*) amor *m*; (*kind, caring*) cariño ▷ *vt* amar, querer; **to send one's ~ to sb** dar sus recuerdos a algn; **~ from Anne** (*in letter*) con cariño de Anne; **I ~ to read** me encanta leer; **to be in ~ with** estar enamorado de; **to make ~** hacer el amor; **I ~ you** te quiero; **for the ~ of** por amor a; **"15 ~"** (*Tennis*) "15 a cero"; **I ~ paella** me encanta la paella; **I'd ~ to come** me gustaría muchísimo venir
love affair *n* aventura sentimental *or* amorosa
loved ones ['lʌvdwʌnz] *npl* seres *mpl* queridos
love-hate relationship ['lʌvheɪt-] *n* relación *f* de amor y odio
love life *n* vida sentimental
lovely ['lʌvlɪ] *adj* (*delightful*) precioso, encantador(a), lindo (*esp LAm*); (*beautiful*) precioso, lindo (*esp LAm*); **we had a ~ time** lo pasamos estupendo
lover ['lʌvəʳ] *n* amante *m/f*; (*amateur*): **a ~ of** un(a) aficionado(-a) *or* un(a) amante de
lovesick ['lʌvsɪk] *adj* enfermo de amor, amartelado
loving ['lʌvɪŋ] *adj* amoroso, cariñoso
low [ləu] *adj, adv* bajo ▷ *n* (*Meteorology*) área de baja presión ▷ *vi* (*cow*) mugir; **to feel ~** sentirse deprimido; **to turn (down) ~** bajar; **to reach a new** *or* **an all-time ~** llegar a su punto más bajo
low-alcohol [ləu'ælkəhɔl] *adj* bajo en alcohol
low-calorie ['ləu'kælərɪ] *adj* bajo en calorías
low-cut ['ləukʌt] *adj* (*dress*) escotado
lower ['ləuəʳ] *adj* más bajo; (*less important*) menos importante ▷ *vt* bajar; (*reduce: price*) reducir, rebajar; (*: resistance*) debilitar; **to ~ o.s. to** (*fig*) rebajarse a ▷ *vi* ['lauəʳ]: **to ~ (at sb)** fulminar (a algn) con la mirada
Lower House *n* (*Pol*): **the ~** la Cámara baja
low-fat ['ləu'fæt] *adj* (*milk, yoghurt*) desnatado; (*diet*) bajo en calorías

lowland [ˈləulənd] *n* tierra baja
lowly [ˈləulɪ] *adj* humilde
low-tech [ˈləutɛk] *adj* de baja tecnología, tradicional
loyal [ˈlɔɪəl] *adj* leal
loyalist [ˈlɔɪəlɪst] *n* legitimista *m/f*
loyalty [ˈlɔɪəltɪ] *n* lealtad *f*
loyalty card *n* (*Brit*) tarjeta cliente
lozenge [ˈlɔzɪndʒ] *n* (*Med*) pastilla
LP *n abbr* (= *long-playing record*) elepé *m*
L-plates [ˈɛlpleɪts] *npl* (*Brit*) (placas *fpl* de) la L; *ver nota*

L-PLATES

En el Reino Unido las personas que están aprendiendo a conducir han de llevar indicativos blancos con una L en rojo llamados normalmente *L-plates* (de "learner") en la parte delantera y trasera de los automóviles que conducen. No tienen que ir a clases teóricas, sino que desde el principio se les entrega un carnet de conducir provisional ("provisional driving licence") para que realicen sus prácticas, que han de estar supervisadas por un conductor con carnet definitivo ("full driving licence"). Tampoco se les permite hacer prácticas en autopistas aunque vayan acompañados.

Lt. *abbr* (= *lieutenant*) Tte.
Ltd *abbr* (*Comm*: = *limited company*) S.A.
lubricant [ˈluːbrɪkənt] *n* lubricante *m*
lubricate [ˈluːbrɪkeɪt] *vt* lubricar, engrasar
lucid [ˈluːsɪd] *adj* lúcido
luck [lʌk] *n* suerte *f*; **good/bad ~** buena/mala suerte; **good ~!** ¡(que tengas) suerte!; **to be in ~** estar de suerte; **to be out of ~** tener mala suerte; **bad** *or* **hard** *or* **tough ~!** ¡qué pena!
luckily [ˈlʌkɪlɪ] *adv* afortunadamente
lucky [ˈlʌkɪ] *adj* afortunado; (*at cards etc*) con suerte; (*object*) que trae suerte
lucrative [ˈluːkrətɪv] *adj* lucrativo
ludicrous [ˈluːdɪkrəs] *adj* absurdo
lug [lʌg] *vt* (*drag*) arrastrar
luggage [ˈlʌgɪdʒ] *n* equipaje *m*
luggage rack *n* (*in train*) rejilla, redecilla; (*on car*) baca, portaequipajes *m inv*
lukewarm [ˈluːkwɔːm] *adj* tibio, templado
lull [lʌl] *n* tregua ▷ *vt* (*child*) acunar; (*person, fear*) calmar; **to ~ sb to sleep** arrullar a algn; **to ~ sb into a false sense of security** dar a algn una falsa sensación de seguridad
lullaby [ˈlʌləbaɪ] *n* nana
lumbago [lʌmˈbeɪgəu] *n* lumbago
lumber [ˈlʌmbəʳ] *n* (*junk*) trastos *mpl* viejos; (*wood*) maderos *mpl* ▷ *vt* (*Brit inf*): **to ~ sb with sth/sb** hacer que algn cargue con algo/algn ▷ *vi* (*also*: **~ about, ~ along**) moverse pesadamente
lumberjack [ˈlʌmbədʒæk] *n* maderero
luminous [ˈluːmɪnəs] *adj* luminoso
lump [lʌmp] *n* terrón *m*; (*fragment*) trozo; (*in sauce*) grumo; (*in throat*) nudo; (*swelling*) bulto ▷ *vt* (*also*: **~ together**) juntar; (*persons*) poner juntos
lump sum *n* suma global
lumpy [ˈlʌmpɪ] *adj* (*sauce*) lleno de grumos
lunacy [ˈluːnəsɪ] *n* locura
lunar [ˈluːnəʳ] *adj* lunar
lunatic [ˈluːnətɪk] *adj, n* (*inf!*) loco(-a) *m(f)*
lunch [lʌntʃ] *n* almuerzo, comida ▷ *vi* almorzar; **to invite sb to** *or* **for ~** invitar a algn a almorzar
lunch break, lunch hour *n* hora del almuerzo
luncheon [ˈlʌntʃən] *n* almuerzo
luncheon meat *n tipo de fiambre*
luncheon voucher *n* vale *m* de comida
lunchtime [ˈlʌntʃtaɪm] *n* hora del almuerzo *or* de comer
lung [lʌŋ] *n* pulmón *m*
lunge [lʌndʒ] *vi* (*also*: **~ forward**) abalanzarse; **to ~ at** arremeter contra
lurch [ləːtʃ] *vi* dar sacudidas ▷ *n* sacudida; **to leave sb in the ~** dejar a algn plantado
lure [luəʳ] *n* (*bait*) cebo; (*decoy*) señuelo; (*attraction*) atracción *f* ▷ *vt* convencer con engaños
lurid [ˈluərɪd] *adj* (*colour*) chillón(-ona); (*account*) sensacional; (*detail*) horripilante
lurk [ləːk] *vi* (*hide*) esconderse; (*wait*) estar al acecho; (*fig*) acechar
luscious [ˈlʌʃəs] *adj* delicioso
lush [lʌʃ] *adj* exuberante
lust [lʌst] *n* lujuria; (*greed*) codicia; **lust after** *vt fus* codiciar
lusty [ˈlʌstɪ] *adj* robusto, fuerte
lute [luːt] *n* laúd *m*
Luxembourg [ˈlʌksəmbəːg] *n* Luxemburgo
luxurious [lʌgˈzjuərɪəs] *adj* lujoso
luxury [ˈlʌkʃərɪ] *n* lujo ▷ *cpd* de lujo
LV *n abbr* (*Brit*) = **luncheon voucher**
LW *abbr* (*Radio*) = **long wave**
Lycra® [ˈlaɪkrə] *n* licra®
lying [ˈlaɪɪŋ] *n* mentiras *fpl* ▷ *adj* (*statement, story*) falso; (*person*) mentiroso
lyric [ˈlɪrɪk] *adj* lírico; **lyrics** *npl* (*of song*) letra *sg*
lyrical [ˈlɪrɪkl] *adj* lírico

m

M, m [ɛm] *n* (*letter*) M, m *f*; **M for Mary**, (*US*) **M for Mike** M de Madrid
M *n abbr* (*Brit*: = *motorway*): **the M8** ≈ la A8 ▷ *abbr* (= *medium*) M
m *abbr* (= *metre*) m.; = **metre**; **mile**; **million**
ma [mɑː] (*inf*) *n* mamá
MA *n abbr* (*Scol*) = **Master of Arts**; (*US*) = **Military Academy**
mac [mæk] *n* (*Brit*) impermeable *m*
macaroni [mækə'rəunɪ] *n* macarrones *mpl*
Macedonia [mæsɪ'dəunɪə] *n* Macedonia
Macedonian [mæsɪ'dəunɪən] *adj* macedonio ▷ *n* macedonio(-a); (*Ling*) macedonio
machine [mə'ʃiːn] *n* máquina ▷ *vt* (*dress etc*) coser a máquina; (*Tech*) trabajar a máquina
machine gun *n* ametralladora
machine language *n* (*Comput*) lenguaje *m* máquina
machinery [mə'ʃiːnərɪ] *n* maquinaria; (*fig*) mecanismo
machine translation *n* traducción *f* automática
machine washable *adj* lavable a máquina
macho ['mætʃəu] *adj* macho
mackerel ['mækrl] *n pl inv* caballa
mackintosh ['mækɪntɔʃ] *n* (*Brit*) impermeable *m*
mad [mæd] *adj* loco; (*idea*) disparatado; (*angry*) furioso, enojado (*LAm*); **~ (at** *or* **with sb)** furioso (con algn); **to be ~ (keen) about** *or* **on sth** estar loco por algo; **to go ~** volverse loco, enloquecer(se)
madam ['mædəm] *n* señora; **can I help you, ~?** ¿le puedo ayudar, señora?; **M~ Chairman** señora presidenta
mad cow disease *n* encefalopatía espongiforme bovina
madden ['mædn] *vt* volver loco
made [meɪd] *pt, pp of* **make**
Madeira [mə'dɪərə] *n* (*Geo*) Madeira; (*wine*) madeira *m*
made-to-measure ['meɪdtəmɛʒəʳ] *adj* (*Brit*) hecho a la medida
made-up ['meɪdʌp] *adj* (*story*) ficticio
madhouse ['mædhaus] *n* (*also fig*) manicomio
madly ['mædlɪ] *adv* locamente
madman ['mædmən] *n* loco
madness ['mædnɪs] *n* locura
Madrid [mə'drɪd] *n* Madrid *m*
Mafia ['mæfɪə] *n* Mafia
mag [mæg] *n abbr* (*Brit inf*) = **magazine**
magazine [mægə'ziːn] *n* revista; (*Mil*: *store*) almacén *m*; (*of firearm*) recámara
maggot ['mægət] *n* gusano
magic ['mædʒɪk] *n* magia ▷ *adj* mágico
magical ['mædʒɪkəl] *adj* mágico
magician [mə'dʒɪʃən] *n* mago(-a)
magistrate ['mædʒɪstreɪt] *n* juez *m/f* (municipal)
magnesium [mæg'niːzɪəm] *n* magnesio
magnet ['mægnɪt] *n* imán *m*
magnetic [mæg'nɛtɪk] *adj* magnético
magnetic tape *n* cinta magnética
magnificent [mæg'nɪfɪsnt] *adj* magnífico
magnify ['mægnɪfaɪ] *vt* (*object*) ampliar; (*sound*) aumentar; (*fig*) exagerar
magnifying glass ['mægnɪfaɪɪŋ-] *n* lupa
magnitude ['mægnɪtjuːd] *n* magnitud *f*
magpie ['mægpaɪ] *n* urraca
mahogany [mə'hɔgənɪ] *n* caoba ▷ *cpd* de caoba
maid [meɪd] *n* criada; **old ~** (*pej*) solterona
maiden ['meɪdn] *n* doncella ▷ *adj* (*aunt etc*) solterona; (*speech, voyage*) inaugural
maiden name *n* apellido de soltera
mail [meɪl] *n* correo; (*letters*) cartas *fpl* ▷ *vt* (*post*) echar al correo; (*send*) mandar por correo; **by ~** por correo
mailbox ['meɪlbɔks] *n* (*US*: *for letters etc*: *Comput*) buzón *m*
mailing list ['meɪlɪŋ-] *n* lista de direcciones
mailman ['meɪlmæn] *n* (*US*) cartero
mail-order ['meɪlɔːdəʳ] *n* pedido postal; (*business*) venta por correo ▷ *adj*: **~ firm** *or* **house** casa de venta por correo
maim [meɪm] *vt* mutilar, lisiar
main [meɪn] *adj* principal, mayor ▷ *n* (*pipe*) cañería principal *or* maestra; (*US*) red *f* eléctrica; **the ~s** (*Brit Elec*) la red eléctrica; **in the ~** en general
main course *n* (*Culin*) plato principal
mainframe ['meɪnfreɪm] *n* (*also*: **~ computer**) ordenador *m or* computadora central

mainland ['meɪnlənd] *n* continente *m*
mainly ['meɪnlɪ] *adv* principalmente, en su mayoría
main road *n* carretera principal
mainstay ['meɪnsteɪ] *n* (*fig*) pilar *m*
mainstream ['meɪnstri:m] *n* (*fig*) corriente *f* principal
main street *n* calle *f* mayor
maintain [meɪn'teɪn] *vt* mantener; (*affirm*) sostener; **to ~ that ...** mantener *or* sostener que ...
maintenance ['meɪntənəns] *n* mantenimiento; (*alimony*) pensión *f* alimenticia
maisonette [meɪzə'nɛt] *n* dúplex *m*
maize [meɪz] *n* (*Brit*) maíz *m*, choclo (*LAm*)
majestic [mə'dʒɛstɪk] *adj* majestuoso
majesty ['mædʒɪstɪ] *n* majestad *f*; **Your M~** Su Majestad
major ['meɪdʒə^r] *n* (*Mil*) comandante *m* ▷ *adj* principal; (*Mus*) mayor ▷ *vi* (*US Univ*): **to ~ in** especializarse en; **a ~ operation** una operación *or* intervención de gran importancia
Majorca [mə'jɔ:kə] *n* Mallorca
majority [mə'dʒɔrɪtɪ] *n* mayoría ▷ *cpd* (*verdict*) mayoritario
make [meɪk] *vt* (*pt, pp* **made** [meɪd]) hacer; (*manufacture*) hacer, fabricar; (*mistake*) cometer; (*speech*) pronunciar; (*cause to be*): **to ~ sb sad** poner triste *or* entristecer a algn; (*force*): **to ~ sb do sth** obligar a algn a hacer algo; (*equal*): **2 and 2 ~ 4** 2 y 2 son 4 ▷ *n* marca; **to ~ a fool of sb** poner a algn en ridículo; **to ~ a profit/loss** obtener ganancias/sufrir pérdidas; **to ~ a profit of £500** sacar una ganancia de 500 libras; **to ~ it** (*arrive*) llegar; (*achieve sth*) tener éxito; **what time do you ~ it?** ¿qué hora tienes?; **to ~ do with** contentarse con; **make for** *vt fus* (*place*) dirigirse a; **make off** *vi* largarse; **make out** *vt* (*decipher*) descifrar; (*understand*) entender; (*see*) distinguir; (*write*: *cheque*) extender; **to ~ out (that)** (*claim, imply*) dar a entender (que); **to ~ out a case for sth** dar buenas razones en favor de algo; **make over** *vt* (*assign*): **to ~ over (to)** ceder *or* traspasar (a); **make up** *vt* (*invent*) inventar; (*parcel*) hacer ▷ *vi* reconciliarse; (*with cosmetics*) maquillarse; **to be made up of** estar compuesto de; **make up for** *vt fus* compensar
make-believe ['meɪkbɪli:v] *n* ficción *f*, fantasía
makeover ['meɪkəuvə^r] *n* cambio de imagen; **to give sb a ~** hacerle a algn un cambio de imagen
maker ['meɪkə^r] *n* fabricante *m/f*; (*of film, programme*) autor(a) *m(f)*
makeshift ['meɪkʃɪft] *adj* improvisado
make-up ['meɪkʌp] *n* maquillaje *m*
make-up remover *n* desmaquillador *m*
making ['meɪkɪŋ] *n* (*fig*): **in the ~** en vías de formación; **to have the ~s of** (*person*) tener madera de
malaria [mə'lɛərɪə] *n* malaria
Malaysia [mə'leɪzɪə] *n* Malaisia, Malaysia
male [meɪl] *n* (*Biol, Elec*) macho ▷ *adj* (*sex, attitude*) masculino; (*child etc*) varón
malevolent [mə'lɛvələnt] *adj* malévolo
malfunction [mæl'fʌŋkʃən] *n* mal funcionamiento
malice ['mælɪs] *n* (*ill will*) malicia; (*rancour*) rencor *m*
malicious [mə'lɪʃəs] *adj* malicioso; rencoroso
malign [mə'laɪn] *vt* difamar, calumniar ▷ *adj* maligno
malignant [mə'lɪgnənt] *adj* (*Med*) maligno
mall [mɔ:l] *n* (*US*: *also*: **shopping ~**) centro comercial
mallet ['mælɪt] *n* mazo
malnutrition [mælnju:'trɪʃən] *n* desnutrición *f*
malpractice [mæl'præktɪs] *n* negligencia profesional
malt [mɔ:lt] *n* malta; (*whisky*) whisky *m* de malta
Malta ['mɔ:ltə] *n* Malta
Maltese [mɔ:l'ti:z] *adj* maltés(-esa) ▷ *n* (*pl inv*) maltés(-esa) *m(f)*; (*Ling*) maltés *m*
malware ['mælwɛə^r] *n* (*Comput*) malware *m*, software *m* malicioso
mammal ['mæml] *n* mamífero
mammoth ['mæməθ] *n* mamut *m* ▷ *adj* gigantesco
man (*pl* **men**) [mæn, mɛn] *n* hombre *m*; (*mankind*) el hombre; (*Chess*) pieza ▷ *vt* (*Naut*) tripular; (*Mil*) defender; (*operate*: *machine*) manejar; **an old ~** un viejo; **~ and wife** marido y mujer
manage ['mænɪdʒ] *vi* arreglárselas ▷ *vt* (*be in charge of*) dirigir; (*person etc*) manejar; **to ~ to do sth** conseguir hacer algo; **to ~ without sth/sb** poder prescindir de algo/algn
manageable ['mænɪdʒəbl] *adj* manejable
management ['mænɪdʒmənt] *n* dirección *f*, administración *f*; **"under new ~"** "bajo nueva dirección"
manager ['mænɪdʒə^r] *n* director(a) *m(f)*; (*of pop star*) mánager *m/f*; (*Sport*) entrenador(a) *m(f)*; **sales ~** jefe(-a) *m(f)* de ventas
manageress ['mænɪdʒərɛs] *n* directora; (*Sport*) entrenadora
managerial [mænə'dʒɪerɪəl] *adj* directivo
managing director ['mænɪdʒɪŋ-] *n* director(a) *m(f)* general
Mancunian [mæŋ'kju:nɪən] *adj* de Manchester ▷ *n* nativo(-a) *or* habitante *m(f)* de Manchester
mandarin ['mændərɪn] *n* (*also*: **~ orange**) mandarina; (*person*) mandarín *m*
mandate ['mændeɪt] *n* mandato
mandatory ['mændətərɪ] *adj* obligatorio

mane [meɪn] *n* *(of horse)* crin *f*; *(of lion)* melena
maneuver [mə'nuːvə^{r}] *vb, n (US)* = **manoeuvre**
manfully ['mænfəlɪ] *adv* resueltamente
mangetout [mɔnʒ'tuː] *n* tirabeque *m*
mangle ['mæŋgl] *vt* mutilar, destrozar ▷ *n* escurridor *m*
mango *(pl* **mangoes***)* ['mæŋgəu] *n* mango
mangy ['meɪndʒɪ] *adj* roñoso; *(Med)* sarnoso
manhandle ['mænhændl] *vt* maltratar; *(move by hand: goods)* manipular
manhole ['mænhəul] *n* boca de alcantarilla
manhood ['mænhud] *n* edad *f* viril; *(manliness)* virilidad *f*
man-hour ['mæn'auə^{r}] *n* hora-hombre *f*
manhunt ['mænhʌnt] *n* caza de hombre
mania ['meɪnɪə] *n* manía
maniac ['meɪnɪæk] *n* maníaco(-a); *(fig)* maniático
manic ['mænɪk] *adj* *(behaviour, activity)* frenético
manicure ['mænɪkjuə^{r}] *n* manicura
manicure set *n* estuche *m* de manicura
manifest ['mænɪfɛst] *vt* manifestar, mostrar ▷ *adj* manifiesto ▷ *n* manifiesto
manifesto [mænɪ'fɛstəu] *n* manifiesto
manipulate [mə'nɪpjuleɪt] *vt* manipular
mankind [mæn'kaɪnd] *n* humanidad *f*, género humano
manly ['mænlɪ] *adj* varonil
man-made ['mæn'meɪd] *adj* artificial
manner ['mænə^{r}] *n* manera, modo; *(behaviour)* conducta, manera de ser; *(type)* clase *f*; **manners** *npl* modales *mpl*, educación *fsg*; **(good) ~s** (buena) educación *fsg*, (buenos) modales *mpl*; **bad ~s** falta *sg* de educación, malos modales *mpl*; **all ~ of** toda clase *or* suerte de
mannerism ['mænərɪzəm] *n* gesto típico
manoeuvre, maneuver *(US)* [mə'nuːvə^{r}] *vt, vi* maniobrar ▷ *n* maniobra; **to ~ sb into doing sth** manipular a algn para que haga algo
manor ['mænə^{r}] *n* *(also:* **~ house***)* casa solariega
manpower ['mænpauə^{r}] *n* mano *f* de obra
mansion ['mænʃən] *n* mansión *f*
manslaughter ['mænslɔːtə^{r}] *n* homicidio involuntario
mantelpiece ['mæntlpiːs] *n* repisa de la chimenea
manual ['mænjuəl] *adj* manual ▷ *n* manual *m*; **~ worker** obrero(-a), trabajador(a) *m(f)* manual
manufacture [mænju'fæktʃə^{r}] *vt* fabricar ▷ *n* fabricación *f*
manufacturer [mænju'fæktʃərə^{r}] *n* fabricante *m/f*
manure [mə'njuə^{r}] *n* estiércol *m*, abono
manuscript ['mænjuskrɪpt] *n* manuscrito
Manx [mæŋks] *adj* de la Isla de Man
many ['mɛnɪ] *adj* muchos(-as) ▷ *pron* muchos(-as); **a great ~** muchísimos, un buen número de; **~ a time** muchas veces; **too ~ difficulties** demasiadas dificultades; **twice as ~** el doble; **how ~?** ¿cuántos?
map [mæp] *n* mapa *m* ▷ *vt* trazar el mapa de; **map out** *vt* *(fig: career, holiday, essay)* proyectar, planear
maple ['meɪpl] *n* arce *m*, maple *m* *(LAm)*
mar [mɑː^{r}] *vt* estropear
Mar *abbr (= March)* mar
marathon ['mærəθən] *n* maratón *m* ▷ *adj*: **a ~ session** una sesión maratoniana
marble ['mɑːbl] *n* mármol *m*; *(toy)* canica
March [mɑːtʃ] *n* marzo; *see also* **July**
march [mɑːtʃ] *vi* *(Mil)* marchar; *(demonstrators)* manifestarse; *(fig)* caminar con resolución ▷ *n* marcha; *(demonstration)* manifestación *f*
mare [mɛə^{r}] *n* yegua
margarine [mɑːdʒə'riːn] *n* margarina
marg(e) [mɑːdʒ] *n abbr (inf)* = **margarine**
margin ['mɑːdʒɪn] *n* margen *m*; *(Comm: profit margin)* margen *m* de beneficios
marginal ['mɑːdʒɪnl] *adj* marginal
marginally ['mɑːdʒɪnəlɪ] *adv* ligeramente
marginal seat *n (Pol)* circunscripción *f* políticamente no definida
marigold ['mærɪgəuld] *n* caléndula
marijuana [mærɪ'wɑːnə] *n* marihuana
marina [mə'riːnə] *n* puerto deportivo
marinade [mærɪ'neɪd] *n* adobo
marinate ['mærɪneɪt] *vt* adobar
marine [mə'riːn] *adj* marino ▷ *n* soldado de infantería de marina
marital ['mærɪtl] *adj* matrimonial; **~ status** estado civil
maritime ['mærɪtaɪm] *adj* marítimo
marjoram ['mɑːdʒərəm] *n* mejorana
mark [mɑːk] *n* marca, señal *f*; *(in snow, mud etc)* huella; *(stain)* mancha; *(Brit Scol)* nota; *(currency)* marco ▷ *vt* *(Sport: player)* marcar; *(stain)* manchar; *(Brit Scol)* calificar, corregir; **punctuation ~s** signos *mpl* de puntuación; **to be quick off the ~** *(fig)* ser listo; **up to the ~** *(in efficiency)* a la altura de las circunstancias; **to ~ time** marcar el paso; *(fig)* marcar(se) un ritmo; **mark down** *vt* *(reduce: prices, goods)* rebajar; **mark off** *vt* *(tick)* indicar, señalar; **mark out** *vt* trazar; **mark up** *vt* *(price)* aumentar
marked [mɑːkt] *adj* marcado, acusado
marker ['mɑːkə^{r}] *n* *(sign)* marcador *m*; *(bookmark)* registro
market ['mɑːkɪt] *n* mercado ▷ *vt* *(Comm)* comercializar; *(promote)* publicitar; **open ~** mercado libre; **to be on the ~** estar en venta; **to play the ~** jugar a la bolsa
market economy *n* economía de mercado
market garden *n (Brit)* huerto
marketing ['mɑːkɪtɪŋ] *n* marketing *m*, mercadotecnia

m

marketplace ['mɑːkɪtpleɪs] *n* mercado
market research *n* (*Comm*) estudios *mpl* de mercado
marksman ['mɑːksmən] *n* tirador *m*
marmalade ['mɑːməleɪd] *n* mermelada de naranja
maroon [mə'ruːn] *vt*: **to be ~ed** (*shipwrecked*) quedar aislado; (*fig*) quedar abandonado ▷ *n* (*colour*) granate *m*
marquee [mɑː'kiː] *n* carpa, entoldado
marriage ['mærɪdʒ] *n* (*state*) matrimonio; (*wedding*) boda; (*act*) casamiento
marriage bureau *n* agencia matrimonial
marriage certificate *n* partida de casamiento
marriage of convenience *n* matrimonio de conveniencia
married ['mærɪd] *adj* casado; (*life, love*) conyugal
marrow ['mærəu] *n* médula; (*vegetable*) calabacín *m*
marry ['mærɪ] *vt* casarse con; (*father, priest etc*) casar ▷ *vi* (*also*: **get married**) casarse
Mars [mɑːz] *n* Marte *m*
marsh [mɑːʃ] *n* pantano; (*salt marsh*) marisma
marshal ['mɑːʃl] *n* (*Mil*) mariscal *m*; (*at sports meeting, demonstration etc*) oficial *m*; (*US*: *of police, fire department*) jefe(-a) *m(f)* ▷ *vt* (*facts*) ordenar; (*soldiers*) formar
marshy ['mɑːʃɪ] *adj* pantanoso
martial arts *npl* artes *fpl* marciales
martial law *n* ley *f* marcial
martyr ['mɑːtə^r] *n* mártir *m/f* ▷ *vt* martirizar
martyrdom ['mɑːtədəm] *n* martirio
marvel ['mɑːvl] *n* maravilla, prodigio ▷ *vi*: **to ~ (at)** maravillarse (de)
marvellous, marvelous (*US*) ['mɑːvləs] *adj* maravilloso
Marxism ['mɑːksɪzəm] *n* marxismo
Marxist ['mɑːksɪst] *adj, n* marxista *m/f*
marzipan ['mɑːzɪpæn] *n* mazapán *m*
mascara [mæs'kɑːrə] *n* rimel *m*
mascot ['mæskət] *n* mascota
masculine ['mæskjulɪn] *adj* masculino
mash [mæʃ] *vt* machacar ▷ *n* (*mix*) mezcla; (*Culin*) puré *m*; (*pulp*) amasijo
mashed potatoes [mæʃt-] *npl* puré *m* de patatas *or* (*LAm*) papas
mask [mɑːsk] *n* máscara ▷ *vt* (*cover*): **to ~ one's face** ocultarse la cara; (*hide*: *feelings*) esconder
masochist ['mæsəukɪst] *n* masoquista *m/f*
mason ['meɪsn] *n* (*also*: **stone~**) albañil *m*; (*also*: **free~**) masón *m*
masonic [mə'sɔnɪk] *adj* masónico
masonry ['meɪsnrɪ] *n* masonería; (*in building*) mampostería
masquerade [mæskə'reɪd] *n* baile *m* de máscaras; (*fig*) mascarada ▷ *vi*: **to ~ as** disfrazarse de, hacerse pasar por
mass [mæs] *n* (*people*) muchedumbre *f*; (*Physics*) masa; (*Rel*) misa; (*great quantity*) montón *m* ▷ *vi* reunirse; (*Mil*) concentrarse; **the ~es** las masas; **to go to ~** ir a *or* oír misa
massacre ['mæsəkə^r] *n* masacre *f* ▷ *vt* masacrar
massage ['mæsɑːʒ] *n* masaje *m* ▷ *vt* dar masajes *or* un masaje a
massive ['mæsɪv] *adj* enorme; (*support, intervention*) masivo
mass media *npl* medios *mpl* de comunicación de masas
mass-produce ['mæsprə'djuːs] *vt* fabricar en serie
mast [mɑːst] *n* (*Naut*) mástil *m*; (*Radio etc*) torre *f*, antena
mastectomy [mæs'tɛktəmɪ] *n* mastectomía
master ['mɑːstə^r] *n* (*of servant, animal*) amo; (*fig*: *of situation*) dueño; (*Art, Mus*) maestro; (*in secondary school*) profesor *m*; (*title for boys*): **M~ X** Señorito X ▷ *vt* dominar
masterly ['mɑːstəlɪ] *adj* magistral
mastermind ['mɑːstəmaɪnd] *n* inteligencia superior ▷ *vt* dirigir, planear
Master of Arts *n* licenciatura superior en Letras; *see also* **master's degree**
Master of Science *n* licenciatura superior en Ciencias; *see also* **master's degree**
masterpiece ['mɑːstəpiːs] *n* obra maestra
master plan *n* plan *m* rector
master's degree *n* máster *m*

MASTER'S DEGREE

Los estudios de postgrado británicos que llevan a la obtención de un *master's degree* consisten generalmente en una combinación de curso(s) académico(s) y tesina ("dissertation") sobre un tema original, o bien únicamente la redacción de una tesina. El primer caso es el más frecuente para los títulos de "MA" ("Master of Arts") y "MSc" ("Master of Science"), mientras que los de "MLitt" ("Master of Letters") o "MPhil" ("Master of Philosophy") se obtienen normalmente mediante tesina. En algunas universidades, como las escocesas, el título de *master's degree* no es de postgrado, sino que corresponde a la licenciatura.

mastery ['mɑːstərɪ] *n* maestría
masturbate ['mæstəbeɪt] *vi* masturbarse
masturbation [mæstə'beɪʃən] *n* masturbación *f*
mat [mæt] *n* alfombrilla; (*also*: **door~**) felpudo ▷ *adj* = **matt**
match [mætʃ] *n* cerilla, fósforo; (*game*) partido; (*fig*) igual *m/f* ▷ *vt* emparejar; (*go well with*) hacer juego con; (*equal*) igualar; (*correspond to*) corresponderse con; (*pair*: *also*:

~ up) casar con ▷ *vi* hacer juego; **to be a good ~** hacer buena pareja
matchbox ['mætʃbɔks] *n* caja de cerillas
matching ['mætʃɪŋ] *adj* que hace juego
mate [meɪt] *n* (*workmate*) compañero(-a), colega *m/f*; (*inf: friend*) amigo(-a), compadre *m/f* (*LAm*); (*animal*) macho/hembra; (*in merchant navy*) primer oficial *m*, segundo de a bordo ▷ *vi* acoplarse, aparearse ▷ *vt* acoplar, aparear
material [mə'tɪərɪəl] *n* (*substance*) materia; (*equipment*) material *m*; (*cloth*) tela, tejido ▷ *adj* material; (*important*) esencial; **materials** *npl* materiales *mpl*; (*equipment etc*) artículos *mpl*
materialize [mə'tɪərɪəlaɪz] *vi* materializarse
maternal [mə'tə:nl] *adj* maternal; **~ grandmother** abuela materna
maternity [mə'tə:nɪtɪ] *n* maternidad *f*
maternity dress *n* vestido premamá
maternity hospital *n* hospital *m* de maternidad
maternity leave *n* baja por maternidad
math [mæθ] *n abbr* (*US: = mathematics*) matemáticas *fpl*
mathematical [mæθə'mætɪkl] *adj* matemático
mathematician [mæθəmə'tɪʃən] *n* matemático(-a) *m(f)*
mathematics [mæθə'mætɪks] *n* matemáticas *fpl*
maths [mæθs] *n abbr* (*Brit: = mathematics*) matemáticas *fpl*
matinée ['mætɪneɪ] *n* sesión *f* de tarde, vermú(t) *m* (*LAm*)
mating call *n* llamada del macho
matrices ['meɪtrɪsi:z] *pl of* **matrix**
matriculation [mətrɪkju'leɪʃən] *n* matriculación *f*, matrícula
matrimonial [mætrɪ'məunɪəl] *adj* matrimonial
matrimony ['mætrɪmənɪ] *n* matrimonio
matrix (*pl* **matrices**) ['meɪtrɪks, 'meɪtrɪsi:z] *n* matriz *f*
matron ['meɪtrən] *n* (*in hospital*) enfermera jefe; (*in school*) ama de llaves
matt [mæt] *adj* mate
matted ['mætɪd] *adj* enmarañado
matter ['mætə^r] *n* cuestión *f*, asunto; (*Physics*) sustancia, materia; (*content*) contenido; (*Med: pus*) pus *m* ▷ *vi* importar; **it doesn't ~** no importa; **what's the ~?** ¿qué pasa?; **no ~ what** pase lo que pase; **as a ~ of course** por rutina; **as a ~ of fact** en realidad; **printed ~** impresos *mpl*; **reading ~** material *m* de lectura, lecturas *fpl*
matter-of-fact ['mætərəv'fækt] *adj* (*style*) prosaico; (*person*) práctico; (*voice*) neutro
mattress ['mætrɪs] *n* colchón *m*
mature [mə'tjuə^r] *adj* maduro ▷ *vi* madurar
mature student *n estudiante de más de 21 años*
maturity [mə'tjuərɪtɪ] *n* madurez *f*
maul [mɔ:l] *vt* magullar
mausoleum [mɔ:sə'lɪəm] *n* mausoleo
mauve [məuv] *adj* de color malva
maverick ['mævrɪk] *n* (*fig*) inconformista *m/f*, persona independiente
max *abbr* = **maximum**
maximize ['mæksɪmaɪz] *vt* (*profits etc*) llevar al máximo; (*chances*) maximizar
maximum ['mæksɪməm] *adj* máximo ▷ *n* (*pl* **maxima** ['mæksɪmə]) máximo
May [meɪ] *n* mayo; *see also* **July**
may [meɪ] *vi* (*conditional* **might**) (*indicating possibility*): **he ~ come** puede que venga; (*be allowed to*): **~ I smoke?** ¿puedo fumar?; (*wishes*): **~ God bless you!** ¡que Dios le bendiga!; **~ I sit here?** ¿me puedo sentar aquí?
maybe ['meɪbi:] *adv* quizá(s); **~ not** quizá(s) no
May Day *n* el primero de Mayo
mayday ['meɪdeɪ] *n* señal *f* de socorro
mayhem ['meɪhɛm] *n* caos *m* total
mayonnaise [meɪə'neɪz] *n* mayonesa
mayor [mɛə^r] *n* alcalde *m*
mayoress ['mɛərɛs] *n* alcaldesa
maze [meɪz] *n* laberinto
MBE *n abbr* (*Brit: = Member of the Order of the British Empire*) *título ceremonial*
MC *n abbr* (*= master of ceremonies*) e.p.; (*US: = Member of Congress*) *diputado del Congreso de los Estados Unidos*
MD *n abbr* (*= Doctor of Medicine*) *título universitario*; (*Comm*) = **managing director**; (*= MiniDisc*) MiniDisc® *m*, minidisc *m*
MD player *n* MiniDisc *m*, minidisc *m*
me [mi:] *pron* (*direct*) me; (*stressed, after pronoun*) mí; **can you hear me?** ¿me oyes?; **he heard ME!** me oyó a mí; **it's me** soy yo; **give them to me** dámelos; **with/without me** conmigo/sin mí; **it's for me** es para mí
meadow ['mɛdəu] *n* prado, pradera
meagre, meager (*US*) ['mi:gə^r] *adj* escaso, pobre
meal [mi:l] *n* comida; (*flour*) harina; **to go out for a ~** salir a comer
meals on wheels *nsg* (*Brit*) *servicio de alimentación a domicilio para necesitados y tercera edad*
mealtime ['mi:ltaɪm] *n* hora de comer
mean [mi:n] *adj* (*with money*) tacaño; (*unkind*) mezquino, malo; (*average*) medio; (*US: vicious: animal*) resabiado; (*: person*) malicioso ▷ *vt* (*pt, pp* **meant** [mɛnt]) (*signify*) querer decir, significar; (*intend*): **to ~ to do sth** tener la intención de *or* pensar hacer algo ▷ *n* medio, término medio; **do you ~ it?** ¿lo dices en serio?; **what do you ~?** ¿qué quiere decir?; **to be meant for sb/sth** ser para algn/algo; *see also* **means**
meander [mɪ'ændə^r] *vi* (*river*) serpentear; (*person*) vagar
meaning ['mi:nɪŋ] *n* significado, sentido
meaningful ['mi:nɪŋful] *adj* significativo

meaningless ['mi:nɪŋlɪs] *adj* sin sentido
meanness ['mi:nnɪs] *n* (*with money*) tacañería; (*unkindness*) maldad *f*, mezquindad *f*
means [mi:nz] *npl* medio *sg*, manera *sg*; (*resource*) recursos *mpl*, medios *mpl*; **by ~ of** mediante, por medio de; **by all ~!** ¡naturalmente!, ¡claro que sí!
meant [mɛnt] *pt, pp of* **mean**
meantime ['mi:ntaɪm], **meanwhile** ['mi:nwaɪl] *adv* (*also*: **in the ~**) mientras tanto
measles ['mi:zlz] *n* sarampión *m*
measly ['mi:zlɪ] *adj* (*inf*) miserable
measure ['mɛʒəʳ] *vt* medir; (*for clothes etc*) tomar las medidas a ▷ *vi* medir ▷ *n* medida; (*ruler*) cinta métrica, metro; **a litre ~** una medida de un litro; **some ~ of success** cierto éxito; **to take ~s to do sth** tomar medidas para hacer algo; **measure up** *vi*: **to ~ up (to)** estar a la altura (de)
measurement ['mɛʒəmənt] *n* (*measure*) medida; (*act*) medición *f*; **to take sb's ~s** tomar las medidas a algn
meat [mi:t] *n* carne *f*; **cold ~s** fiambres *mpl*; **crab ~** carne *f* de cangrejo
meatball ['mi:tbɔ:l] *n* albóndiga
Mecca ['mɛkə] *n* (*city*) la Meca; (*fig*) meca
mechanic [mɪ'kænɪk] *n* mecánico(-a)
mechanical [mɪ'kænɪkl] *adj* mecánico
mechanics [mə'kænɪks] *n* mecánica ▷ *npl* mecanismo *sg*
mechanism ['mɛkənɪzəm] *n* mecanismo
medal ['mɛdl] *n* medalla
medallion [mɪ'dælɪən] *n* medallón *m*
medallist, medalist (US) ['mɛdlɪst] *n* (*Sport*) medallista *m/f*
meddle ['mɛdl] *vi*: **to ~ in** entrometerse en; **to ~ with sth** manosear algo
media ['mi:dɪə] *npl* medios *mpl* de comunicación
media circus *n excesivo despliegue informativo*
mediaeval [mɛdɪ'i:vl] *adj* = **medieval**
median ['mi:dɪən] *n* (*US*: *also*: **~ strip**) mediana
mediate ['mi:dɪeɪt] *vi* mediar
mediator ['mi:dɪeɪtəʳ] *n* mediador(a) *m(f)*
Medicaid ['mɛdɪkeɪd] *n* (*US*) *programa de ayuda médica*
medical ['mɛdɪkl] *adj* médico ▷ *n* (*also*: **~ examination**) reconocimiento médico
medical certificate *n* certificado *m* médico
Medicare ['mɛdɪkɛəʳ] *n* (*US*) *seguro médico del Estado*
medicated ['mɛdɪkeɪtɪd] *adj* medicinal
medication [mɛdɪ'keɪʃən] *n* (*drugs etc*) medicación *f*
medicine ['mɛdsɪn] *n* medicina; (*drug*) medicamento
medieval, mediaeval [mɛdɪ'i:vl] *adj* medieval
mediocre [mi:dɪ'əukəʳ] *adj* mediocre
mediocrity [mi:dɪ'ɔkrɪtɪ] *n* mediocridad *f*
meditate ['mɛdɪteɪt] *vi* meditar
meditation [mɛdɪ'teɪʃən] *n* meditación *f*
Mediterranean [mɛdɪtə'reɪnɪən] *adj* mediterráneo; **the ~ (Sea)** el (Mar *m*) Mediterráneo
medium ['mi:dɪəm] *adj* mediano; (*level, height*) medio ▷ *n* (*pl* **media**: *means*) medio; (*pl* **mediums**: *person*) médium *m/f*; **happy ~** punto justo
medium-dry ['mi:dɪəm'draɪ] *adj* semiseco
medium-sized ['mi:dɪəm'saɪzd] *adj* de tamaño mediano; (*clothes*) de (la) talla mediana
medium wave *n* onda media
medley ['mɛdlɪ] *n* mezcla; (*Mus*) popurrí *m*
meek [mi:k] *adj* manso, sumiso
meet [mi:t] (*pt, pp* **met**) *vt* encontrar; (*accidentally*) encontrarse con; (*by arrangement*) reunirse con; (*for the first time*) conocer; (*go and fetch*) ir a buscar; (*opponent*) enfrentarse con; (*obligations*) cumplir; (*bill, expenses*) pagar, costear ▷ *vi* encontrarse; (*in session*) reunirse; (*join*: *objects*) unirse; (*get to know*) conocerse ▷ *n* (*Brit Hunting*) cacería; (*US Sport*) encuentro; **pleased to ~ you!** ¡encantado (de conocerle)!, ¡mucho gusto!; **meet up** *vi*: **to ~ up with sb** reunirse con algn; **meet with** *vt fus* reunirse con; (*difficulty*) tropezar con
meeting ['mi:tɪŋ] *n* (*also Sport*: *rally*) encuentro; (*arranged*) cita, compromiso (*LAm*); (*formal session, business meeting*) reunión *f*; (*Pol*) mítin *m*; **to call a ~** convocar una reunión
meeting place *n* lugar *m* de reunión *or* encuentro
meg [mɛg] *n abbr* (*inf*: = *megabyte*) megabyte
megabyte ['mɛgə'baɪt] *n* (*Comput*) megabyte *m*, megaocteto
megaphone ['mɛgəfəun] *n* megáfono
megapixel ['mɛgəpɪksl] *n* megapíxel *m*
megawatt ['mɛgəwɔt] *n* megavatio
melancholy ['mɛlənkəlɪ] *n* melancolía ▷ *adj* melancólico
mellow ['mɛləu] *adj* (*wine*) añejo; (*sound, colour*) suave; (*fruit*) maduro ▷ *vi* (*person*) madurar
melody ['mɛlədɪ] *n* melodía
melon ['mɛlən] *n* melón *m*
melt [mɛlt] *vi* (*metal*) fundirse; (*snow*) derretirse; (*fig*) ablandarse ▷ *vt* (*also*: **~ down**) fundir; **~ed butter** mantequilla derretida; **melt away** *vi* desvanecerse
meltdown ['mɛltdaun] *n* (*in nuclear reactor*) fusión *f* (de un reactor nuclear)
melting pot ['mɛltɪŋ-] *n* (*fig*) crisol *m*; **to be in the ~** estar sobre el tapete
member ['mɛmbəʳ] *n* (*of political party*) miembro; (*of club*) socio(-a); **M~ of Parliament (MP)** (*Brit*) diputado(-a); **M~ of the European Parliament (MEP)** (*Brit*) eurodiputado(-a); **M~ of Congress** (US)

miembro del Congreso; **M~ of the House of Representatives (MHR)** (*US*) miembro *m/f* de la Cámara de Representantes; **M~ of the Scottish Parliament (MSP)** (*Brit*) diputado(-a) *m(f)* del Parlamento escocés
membership ['mɛmbəʃɪp] *n* (*members*) miembros *mpl*; socios *mpl*; (*numbers*) número de miembros *or* socios; **to seek ~ of** pedir el ingreso a
membership card *n* carnet *m* de socio
memento [mə'mɛntəu] *n* recuerdo
memo ['mɛməu] *n* apunte *m*, nota
memoirs ['mɛmwɑ:z] *npl* memorias *fpl*
memorable ['mɛmərəbl] *adj* memorable
memorandum (*pl* **memoranda**) [mɛmə'rændəm, -də] *n* nota (de servicio); (*Pol*) memorándum *m*
memorial [mɪ'mɔ:rɪəl] *n* monumento conmemorativo ▷ *adj* conmemorativo
Memorial Day *n* (*US*) *día de conmemoración de los caídos en la guerra*
memorize ['mɛməraɪz] *vt* aprender de memoria
memory ['mɛmərɪ] *n* memoria; (*recollection*) recuerdo; (*Comput*) memoria; **to have a good/bad ~** tener buena/mala memoria; **loss of ~** pérdida de memoria
memory card *n* tarjeta de memoria
memory stick *n* (*Comput*) barra de memoria
men [mɛn] *pl of* **man**
menace ['mɛnəs] *n* amenaza; (*inf: nuisance*) lata ▷ *vt* amenazar; **a public ~** un peligro público
menacing ['mɛnɪsɪŋ] *adj* amenazador(-a)
mend [mɛnd] *vt* reparar, arreglar; (*darn*) zurcir ▷ *vi* reponerse ▷ *n* (*gen*) remiendo; (*darn*) zurcido; **to be on the ~** ir mejorando; **to ~ one's ways** enmendarse
mending ['mɛndɪŋ] *n* arreglo, reparación *f*; (*clothes*) ropa por remendar
menial ['mi:nɪəl] *adj* (*pej*) bajo, servil
meningitis [mɛnɪn'dʒaɪtɪs] *n* meningitis *f*
menopause ['mɛnəupɔ:z] *n* menopausia
men's room *n* (*US*): **the ~** el servicio de caballeros
menstruate ['mɛnstrueɪt] *vi* menstruar
menstruation [mɛnstru'eɪʃən] *n* menstruación *f*
menswear ['mɛnzwɛə^r] *n* confección *f* de caballero
mental ['mɛntl] *adj* mental; **~ illness** enfermedad *f* mental
mentality [mɛn'tælɪtɪ] *n* mentalidad *f*
mentally ['mɛntlɪ] *adv*: **to be ~ ill** tener una enfermedad mental
menthol ['mɛnθɔl] *n* mentol *m*
mention ['mɛnʃən] *n* mención *f* ▷ *vt* mencionar; (*speak of*) hablar de; **don't ~ it!** ¡de nada!; **I need hardly ~ that ...** huelga decir que ...; **not to ~, without ~ing** sin contar
menu ['mɛnju:] *n* (*set menu*) menú *m*; (*printed*) carta; (*Comput*) menú *m*
MEP *n abbr* = **Member of the European Parliament**
mercenary ['mə:sɪnərɪ] *adj, n* mercenario(-a)
merchandise ['mə:tʃəndaɪz] *n* mercancías *fpl*
merchant ['mə:tʃənt] *n* comerciante *m/f*
merchant bank *n* (*Brit*) banco comercial
merchant navy, merchant marine (*US*) *n* marina mercante
merciful ['mə:sɪful] *adj* compasivo
merciless ['mə:sɪlɪs] *adj* despiadado
mercury ['mə:kjurɪ] *n* mercurio
mercy ['mə:sɪ] *n* compasión *f*; (*Rel*) misericordia; **at the ~ of** a la merced de
mere [mɪə^r] *adj* simple, mero
merely ['mɪəlɪ] *adv* simplemente, sólo
merge [mə:dʒ] *vt* (*join*) unir; (*mix*) mezclar; (*fuse*) fundir; (*Comput: files, text*) intercalar ▷ *vi* unirse; (*Comm*) fusionarse
merger ['mə:dʒə^r] *n* (*Comm*) fusión *f*
meringue [mə'ræŋ] *n* merengue *m*
merit ['mɛrɪt] *n* mérito ▷ *vt* merecer
mermaid ['mə:meɪd] *n* sirena
merry ['mɛrɪ] *adj* alegre; **M~ Christmas!** ¡Felices Pascuas!
merry-go-round ['mɛrɪgəuraund] *n* tiovivo
mesh [mɛʃ] *n* malla; (*Tech*) engranaje *m* ▷ *vi* (*gears*) engranar; **wire ~** tela metálica
mesmerize ['mɛzməraɪz] *vt* hipnotizar
mess [mɛs] *n* confusión *f*; (*of objects*) revoltijo; (*dirt*) porquería; (*tangle*) lío; (*Mil*) comedor *m*; **to be (in) a ~** (*room*) estar revuelto; **to be/get o.s. in a ~** estar/meterse en un lío; **mess about, mess around** *vi* (*inf*) perder el tiempo; (*pass the time*) pasar el rato; **mess about** *or* **around with** *vt fus* (*inf: play with*) divertirse con; (*: handle*) manosear; **mess up** *vt* (*disarrange*) desordenar; (*spoil*) estropear; (*dirty*) ensuciar; **mess with** (*inf*) *vt fus* (*challenge, confront*) meterse con (*fam*); (*interfere with*) interferir con
message ['mɛsɪdʒ] *n* recado, mensaje *m*; **to get the ~** (*fig, inf*) enterarse
message board *n* (*Internet*) foro de debate
messenger ['mɛsɪndʒə^r] *n* mensajero(-a)
Messiah [mɪ'saɪə] *n* Mesías *m*
Messrs, Messrs. *abbr* (*on letters:* = *Messieurs*) Sres
messy ['mɛsɪ] *adj* (*dirty*) sucio; (*untidy*) desordenado; (*confused: situation etc*) confuso
met [mɛt] *pt, pp of* **meet** ▷ *adj abbr* = **meteorological**
metabolism [mɛ'tæbəlɪzəm] *n* metabolismo
metal ['mɛtl] *n* metal *m*
metallic [mɛ'tælɪk] *adj* metálico
metaphor ['mɛtəfə^r] *n* metáfora
mete [mi:t]: **to ~ out** *vt fus* (*punishment*) imponer
meteor ['mi:tɪə^r] *n* meteoro
meteorite ['mi:tɪəraɪt] *n* meteorito

m

meteorological [mi:tɪərə'lɔdʒɪkl] *adj* meteorológico
meteorology [mi:tɪə'rɔlədʒɪ] *n* meteorología
meter ['mi:tə^r] *n* (*instrument*) contador *m*; (*US: unit*) = **metre** ▷ *vt* (*US Post*) franquear; **parking ~** parquímetro
methane ['mi:θeɪn] *n* metano
method ['mɛθəd] *n* método; **~ of payment** método de pago
methodical [mɪ'θɔdɪkl] *adj* metódico
Methodist ['mɛθədɪst] *adj, n* metodista *m/f*
methodology [mɛθə'dɔlədʒɪ] *n* metodología
meths [mɛθs] *n* (*Brit*) = **methylated spirit**
methylated spirit ['mɛθɪleɪtɪd-] *n* (*Brit*) alcohol *m* metilado *or* desnaturalizado
meticulous [mɛ'tɪkjuləs] *adj* meticuloso
metre, meter (*US*) ['mi:tə^r] *n* metro
metric ['mɛtrɪk] *adj* métrico; **to go ~** pasar al sistema métrico
metropolitan [mɛtrə'pɔlɪtən] *adj* metropolitano
Metropolitan Police *n* (*Brit*): **the ~** la policía londinense
mettle ['mɛtl] *n* valor *m*, ánimo
mew [mju:] *vi* (*cat*) maullar
mews [mju:z] (*Brit*) *n*: **~ cottage** *casa acondicionada en antiguos establos o cocheras*; **~ flat** *piso en antiguos establos o cocheras*
Mexican ['mɛksɪkən] *adj, n* mejicano(-a) *m(f)*, mexicano(-a) *m(f)* (*LAm*)
Mexico ['mɛksɪkəu] *n* Méjico, México (*LAm*)
Mexico City *n* Ciudad *f* de Méjico *or* (*LAm*) México
mezzanine ['mɛtsəni:n] *n* entresuelo
mg *abbr* (= *milligram*) mg
Mgr *abbr* (= *Monseigneur, Monsignor*) Mons; (*Comm*) = **manager**
MHz *abbr* (= *megahertz*) MHz
MI5 *n abbr* (*Brit*: = *Military Intelligence, section five*) *servicio de contraespionaje del gobierno británico*
MI6 *n abbr* (*Brit*: = *Military Intelligence, section six*) *servicio de inteligencia del gobierno británico*
MIA *abbr* (*Mil*: = *missing in action*) desaparecido
miaow [mi:'au] *vi* maullar
mice [maɪs] *pl of* **mouse**
mickey ['mɪkɪ] *n*: **to take the ~ out of sb** tomar el pelo a algn
micro... [maɪkrəu] *pref* micro...
microbe ['maɪkrəub] *n* microbio
microbiology [maɪkrəubaɪ'ɔlədʒɪ] *n* microbiología
microchip ['maɪkrəutʃɪp] *n* microchip *m*, microplaqueta
microcosm ['maɪkrəukɔzəm] *n* microcosmo
microfiche ['maɪkrəufi:ʃ] *n* microficha
microfilm ['maɪkrəufɪlm] *n* microfilm *m*
microlight ['maɪkrəulaɪt] *n* ultraligero
microphone ['maɪkrəfəun] *n* micrófono
microprocessor ['maɪkrəu'prəusɛsə^r] *n* microprocesador *m*
microscope ['maɪkrəskəup] *n* microscopio; **under the ~** al microscopio
microwave ['maɪkrəuweɪv] *n* (*also*: **~ oven**) horno microondas
mid [mɪd] *adj*: **in ~ May** a mediados de mayo; **in ~ afternoon** a media tarde; **in ~ air** en el aire; **he's in his ~ thirties** tiene unos treinta y cinco años
midday [mɪd'deɪ] *n* mediodía *m*
middle ['mɪdl] *n* centro; (*half-way point*) medio; (*waist*) cintura ▷ *adj* de en medio; **in the ~ of the night** en plena noche; **I'm in the ~ of reading it** lo estoy leyendo ahora mismo
middle-aged [mɪdl'eɪdʒd] *adj* de mediana edad
Middle Ages *npl*: **the ~** la Edad *sg* Media
middle class *n*: **the ~(es)** la clase media ▷ *adj*: **middle-class** de clase media
Middle East *n* Oriente *m* Medio
middleman ['mɪdlmæn] *n* intermediario
middle name *n* segundo nombre *m*
middle-of-the-road ['mɪdləvðə'rəud] *adj* moderado
middle school *n* (*US*) *colegio para niños de doce a catorce años*; (*Brit*) *colegio para niños de ocho o nueve a doce o trece años*
middleweight ['mɪdlweɪt] *n* (*Boxing*) peso medio
middling ['mɪdlɪŋ] *adj* mediano
midge [mɪdʒ] *n* mosquito
midget ['mɪdʒɪt] *n* (*inf!*) enano(-a)
midi system *n* cadena midi
Midlands ['mɪdləndz] *npl* *región central de Inglaterra*
midnight ['mɪdnaɪt] *n* medianoche *f*; **at ~** a medianoche
midriff ['mɪdrɪf] *n* diafragma *m*
midst [mɪdst] *n*: **in the ~ of** entre, en medio de; (*situation, action*) en mitad de
midsummer [mɪd'sʌmə^r] *n*: **a ~ day** un día de pleno verano
midway [mɪd'weɪ] *adj, adv*: **~ (between)** a medio camino (entre); **~ through** a la mitad (de)
midweek [mɪd'wi:k] *adv* entre semana
midwife (*pl* **midwives**) ['mɪdwaɪf, -waɪvz] *n* matrona, comadrona
midwinter [mɪd'wɪntə^r] *n*: **in ~** en pleno invierno
might [maɪt] *vb see* **may** ▷ *n* fuerza, poder *m*; **he ~ be there** puede que esté allí, a lo mejor está allí; **I ~ as well go** más vale que vaya; **you ~ like to try** podría intentar
mightn't ['maɪtnt] = **might not**
mighty ['maɪtɪ] *adj* fuerte, poderoso
migraine ['mi:greɪn] *n* jaqueca
migrant ['maɪgrənt] *adj* migratorio; (*worker*) emigrante ▷ *n* (*bird*) ave *f* migratoria; (*worker*) emigrante *m/f*
migrate [maɪ'greɪt] *vi* emigrar
migration [maɪ'greɪʃən] *n* emigración *f*

mike [maɪk] *n abbr* (= *microphone*) micro
mild [maɪld] *adj* (*person*) apacible; (*climate*) templado; (*slight*) ligero; (*taste*) suave; (*illness*) leve
mildly ['maɪldlɪ] *adv* ligeramente; suavemente; **to put it ~** por no decir algo peor
mile [maɪl] *n* milla; **to do 20 ~s per gallon** hacer 20 millas por galón
mileage ['maɪlɪdʒ] *n* número de millas; (*Aut*) kilometraje *m*
mileometer [maɪ'lɔmɪtəʳ] *n* (*Brit*) = **milometer**
milestone ['maɪlstəun] *n* mojón *m*; (*fig*) hito
militant ['mɪlɪtnt] *adj, n* militante *m/f*
military ['mɪlɪtərɪ] *adj* militar
military service *n* servicio militar
militate ['mɪlɪteɪt] *vi*: **to ~ against** militar en contra de
militia [mɪ'lɪʃə] *n* milicia
milk [mɪlk] *n* leche *f* ▷ *vt* (*cow*) ordeñar; (*fig*) chupar
milk chocolate *n* chocolate *m* con leche
milkman ['mɪlkmən] *n* lechero, repartidor *m* de la leche
milk shake *n* batido, malteada (*LAm*)
milky ['mɪlkɪ] *adj* lechoso
Milky Way *n* Vía Láctea
mill [mɪl] *n* (*windmill etc*) molino; (*coffee mill*) molinillo; (*factory*) fábrica; (*spinning mill*) hilandería ▷ *vt* moler ▷ *vi* (*also*: **~ about**) arremolinarse
millennium (*pl* **millenniums** *or* **millennia**) [mɪ'lɛnɪəm, -'lɛnɪə] *n* milenio, milenario
miller ['mɪləʳ] *n* molinero
milli... ['mɪlɪ] *pref* mili...
milligram, milligramme ['mɪlɪgraem] *n* miligramo
millilitre, milliliter (*US*) ['mɪlɪli:təʳ] *n* mililitro
millimetre, millimeter (*US*) ['mɪlɪmi:təʳ] *n* milímetro
millinery ['mɪlɪnərɪ] *n* sombrerería
million ['mɪljən] *n* millón *m*; **a ~ times** un millón de veces
millionaire [mɪljə'nɛəʳ] *n* millonario(-a)
millionth ['mɪljənθ] *adj* millonésimo
milometer [maɪ'lɔmɪtəʳ] *n* (*Brit*) cuentakilómetros *m inv*
mime [maɪm] *n* mímica; (*actor*) mimo(-a) ▷ *vt* remedar ▷ *vi* actuar de mimo
mimic ['mɪmɪk] *n* imitador(a) *m(f)* ▷ *adj* mímico ▷ *vt* remedar, imitar
min. *abbr* (= *minute(s)*) m.; = **minimum**
mince [mɪns] *vt* picar ▷ *vi* (*in walking*) andar con pasos menudos ▷ *n* (*Brit Culin*) carne *f* picada, picadillo
mincemeat ['mɪnsmi:t] *n conserva de fruta picada*; (*US*: *meat*) carne *f* picada
mince pie *n pastelillo relleno de fruta picada*
mincer ['mɪnsəʳ] *n* picadora de carne
mind [maɪnd] *n* (*gen*) mente *f*; (*contrasted with matter*) espíritu *m* ▷ *vt* (*attend to, look after*) ocuparse de, cuidar; (*be careful of*) tener cuidado con; (*object to*): **I don't ~ the noise** no me molesta el ruido; **it is on my ~** me preocupa; **to my ~** a mi parecer *or* juicio; **to change one's ~** cambiar de idea *or* de parecer; **to bring** *or* **call sth to ~** recordar algo; **to have sth/sb in ~** tener algo/a algn en mente; **to be out of one's ~** haber perdido el juicio; **to bear sth in ~** tomar *or* tener algo en cuenta; **to make up one's ~** decidirse; **it went right out of my ~** se me fue por completo (de la cabeza); **to be in two ~s about sth** estar indeciso *or* dudar ante algo; **I don't ~** me es igual; **~ you, ...** te advierto que ...; **never ~!** ¡es igual!, ¡no importa!; (*don't worry*) ¡no te preocupes!; **"~ the step"** "cuidado con el escalón"
minder ['maɪndəʳ] *n* guardaespaldas *m inv*
mindful ['maɪndful] *adj*: **~ of** consciente de
mindless ['maɪndlɪs] *adj* (*violence, crime*) sin sentido; (*work*) de autómata
mine [maɪn] *pron* (el) mío/(la) mía *etc*; **a friend of ~** un(a) amigo(-a) mío/mía ▷ *adj*: **this book is ~** este libro es mío ▷ *n* mina ▷ *vt* (*coal*) extraer; (*ship, beach*) minar
minefield ['maɪnfi:ld] *n* campo de minas
miner ['maɪnəʳ] *n* minero(-a)
mineral ['mɪnərəl] *adj* mineral ▷ *n* mineral *m*; **minerals** *npl* (*Brit*: *soft drinks*) refrescos *mpl* con gas
mineral water *n* agua mineral
mingle ['mɪŋgl] *vi*: **to ~ with** mezclarse con
miniature ['mɪnətʃəʳ] *adj* (en) miniatura ▷ *n* miniatura
minibar ['mɪnɪbɑ:ʳ] *n* minibar *m*
minibus ['mɪnɪbʌs] *n* microbús *m*
minicab ['mɪnɪkæb] *n* taxi *m* (*que sólo puede pedirse por teléfono*)
MiniDisc® ['mɪnɪdɪsk] *n* MiniDisc® *m*
minim ['mɪnɪm] *n* (*Brit Mus*) blanca
minimal ['mɪnɪml] *adj* mínimo
minimalist ['mɪnɪməlɪst] *adj, n* minimalista *m/f*
minimize ['mɪnɪmaɪz] *vt* minimizar; (*play down*) empequeñecer
minimum ['mɪnɪməm] *n* (*pl* **minima** ['mɪnɪmə]) mínimo ▷ *adj* mínimo; **to reduce to a ~** reducir algo al mínimo; **~ wage** salario mínimo
mining ['maɪnɪŋ] *n* minería ▷ *adj* minero
mini-series ['mɪnɪsɪəri:z] *n* serie *f* de pocos capítulos, miniserie *f*
miniskirt ['mɪnɪskə:t] *n* minifalda
minister ['mɪnɪstəʳ] *n* (*Brit Pol*) ministro(-a); (*junior*) secretario(-a) de Estado; (*Rel*) pastor *m* ▷ *vi*: **to ~ to** atender a
ministerial [mɪnɪs'tɪərɪəl] *adj* (*Brit Pol*) ministerial
ministry ['mɪnɪstrɪ] *n* (*Brit Pol*) ministerio; (*Rel*) sacerdocio; **M~ of Defence** Ministerio de Defensa

mink [mɪŋk] *n* visón *m*
minor ['maɪnə^r^] *adj* (*repairs, injuries*) leve; (*poet, planet*) menor; (*unimportant*) secundario; (*Mus*) menor ▷ *n* (*Law*) menor *m/f* de edad
Minorca [mɪ'nɔ:kə] *n* Menorca
minority [maɪ'nɔrɪtɪ] *n* minoría; **to be in a ~** estar en *or* ser minoría
mint [mɪnt] *n* (*plant*) menta, hierbabuena; (*sweet*) caramelo de menta ▷ *vt* (*coins*) acuñar; **the (Royal) M~**, (*US*) **the (US) M~** la Casa de la Moneda; **in ~ condition** en perfecto estado
minus ['maɪnəs] *n* (*also*: **~ sign**) signo menos ▷ *prep* menos; **12 ~ 6 equals 6** 12 menos 6 son 6; **~ 24°C** menos 24 grados
minuscule ['mɪnəskju:l] *adj* minúsculo
minute¹ ['mɪnɪt] *n* minuto; (*fig*) momento; **minutes** *npl* (*of meeting*) actas *fpl*; **it is 5 ~s past 3** son las 3 y 5 (minutos); **at the last ~** a última hora; **wait a ~!** ¡espera un momento!; **up to the ~** de última hora
minute² [maɪ'nju:t] *adj* diminuto; (*search*) minucioso; **in ~ detail** con todo detalle
minutiae [mɪ'nju:ʃɪi:] *npl* minucias *fpl*
miracle ['mɪrəkl] *n* milagro
miraculous [mɪ'rækjuləs] *adj* milagroso
mirage ['mɪrɑ:ʒ] *n* espejismo
mirror ['mɪrə^r^] *n* espejo; (*in car*) retrovisor *m* ▷ *vt* reflejar
mirth [mə:θ] *n* alegría; (*laughter*) risa, risas *fpl*
misadventure [mɪsəd'vɛntʃə^r^] *n* desventura; **death by ~** muerte *f* accidental
misapprehension ['mɪsæprɪ'hɛnʃən] *n* equivocación *f*
misappropriate [mɪsə'prəuprɪeɪt] *vt* (*funds*) malversar
misbehave [mɪsbɪ'heɪv] *vi* portarse mal
misbehaviour, misbehavior (*US*) [mɪsbɪ'heɪvjə^r^] *n* mala conducta
misc. *abbr* = **miscellaneous**
miscalculate [mɪs'kælkjuleɪt] *vt* calcular mal
miscalculation [mɪskælkju'leɪʃən] *n* error *m* (de cálculo)
miscarriage ['mɪskærɪdʒ] *n* (*Med*) aborto (no provocado); **~ of justice** error *m* judicial
miscarry [mɪs'kærɪ] *vi* (*Med*) abortar (de forma natural); (*fail*: *plans*) fracasar, malograrse
miscellaneous [mɪsɪ'leɪnɪəs] *adj* varios(-as), diversos(-as); **~ expenses** gastos diversos
mischief ['mɪstʃɪf] *n* (*naughtiness*) travesura; (*harm*) mal *m*, daño; (*maliciousness*) malicia
mischievous ['mɪstʃɪvəs] *adj* travieso; dañino; (*playful*) malicioso
misconception ['mɪskən'sɛpʃən] *n* idea equivocada; equivocación *f*
misconduct [mɪs'kɔndʌkt] *n* mala conducta; **professional ~** falta profesional
misconstrue [mɪskən'stru:] *vt* interpretar mal
misdemeanour, misdemeanor (*US*) [mɪsdɪ'mi:nə^r^] *n* delito, ofensa
misdirect [mɪsdɪ'rɛkt] *vt* (*person*) informar mal; (*letter*) poner señas incorrectas en
miser ['maɪzə^r^] *n* avaro(-a)
miserable ['mɪzərəbl] *adj* (*unhappy*) triste, desgraciado; (*wretched*) miserable; **to feel ~** sentirse triste
miserly ['maɪzəlɪ] *adj* avariento, tacaño
misery ['mɪzərɪ] *n* (*unhappiness*) tristeza; (*wretchedness*) miseria, desdicha
misfire [mɪs'faɪə^r^] *vi* fallar
misfit ['mɪsfɪt] *n* (*person*) inadaptado(-a)
misfortune [mɪs'fɔ:tʃən] *n* desgracia
misgiving [mɪs'gɪvɪŋ] *n*, **misgivings** [mɪs'gɪvɪŋz] *npl* (*mistrust*) recelo; (*apprehension*) presentimiento; **to have ~s about sth** tener dudas sobre algo
misguided [mɪs'gaɪdɪd] *adj* equivocado
mishandle [mɪs'hændl] *vt* (*treat roughly*) maltratar; (*mismanage*) manejar mal
mishap ['mɪshæp] *n* desgracia, contratiempo
misinform [mɪsɪn'fɔ:m] *vt* informar mal
misinterpret [mɪsɪn'tə:prɪt] *vt* interpretar mal
misjudge [mɪs'dʒʌdʒ] *vt* juzgar mal
mislay [mɪs'leɪ] *vt* (*irreg*: *like* **lay**) extraviar, perder
mislead [mɪs'li:d] *vt* (*irreg*: *like* **lead**) llevar a conclusiones erróneas; (*deliberately*) engañar
misleading [mɪs'li:dɪŋ] *adj* engañoso
mismanage [mɪs'mænɪdʒ] *vt* administrar mal
mismanagement [mɪs'mænɪdʒmənt] *n* mala administración *f*
misnomer [mɪs'nəumə^r^] *n* término inapropiado *or* equivocado
misogynist [mɪ'sɔdʒɪnɪst] *n* misógino
misplace [mɪs'pleɪs] *vt* (*lose*) extraviar; **~d** (*trust etc*) inmerecido
misprint ['mɪsprɪnt] *n* errata, error *m* de imprenta
mispronounce [mɪsprə'nauns] *vt* pronunciar mal
misquote ['mɪs'kwəut] *vt* citar incorrectamente
misread [mɪs'ri:d] *vt* (*irreg*: *like* **read**) leer mal
misrepresent [mɪsrɛprɪ'zɛnt] *vt* falsificar
Miss [mɪs] *n* Señorita; **Dear ~ Smith** Estimada Señorita Smith
miss [mɪs] *vt* (*train etc*) perder; (*target*) errar; (*appointment, class*) faltar a; (*escape, avoid*) evitar; (*notice loss of*: *money etc*) notar la falta de, echar en falta; (*regret the absence of*): **I ~ him** le echo de menos ▷ *vi* fallar ▷ *n* (*shot*) tiro fallido; **the bus just ~ed the wall** faltó poco para que el autobús se estrella contra el muro; **you're ~ing the point** no has entendido la idea; **miss out** *vt* (*Brit*) omitir; **miss out on** *vt fus* (*fun, party, opportunity*) perderse
misshapen [mɪs'ʃeɪpən] *adj* deforme

missile ['mɪsaɪl] *n* (*Aviat*) misil *m*; (*object thrown*) proyectil *m*
missing ['mɪsɪŋ] *adj* (*pupil*) ausente, que falta; (*thing*) perdido; **to be ~** faltar; **~ person** desaparecido(-a); **~ in action** desaparecido en combate
mission ['mɪʃən] *n* misión *f*; **on a ~ for sb** en una misión para algn
missionary ['mɪʃənrɪ] *n* misionero(-a)
misspell [mɪs'spɛl] *vt* (*irreg: like* **spell**) escribir mal
misspent ['mɪs'spɛnt] *adj*: **his ~ youth** su juventud disipada
mist [mɪst] *n* (*light*) neblina; (*heavy*) niebla; (*at sea*) bruma ▷ *vi* (*also:* **~ over, ~ up**: *weather*) nublarse; (*Brit: windows*) empañarse
mistake [mɪs'teɪk] *n* error *m* ▷ *vt* (*irreg: like* **take**) entender mal; **by ~** por equivocación; **to make a ~** (*about sb/sth*) equivocarse; (*in writing, calculating etc*) cometer un error; **to ~ A for B** confundir A con B
mistaken [mɪs'teɪkən] *pp of* **mistake** ▷ *adj* (*idea etc*) equivocado; **to be ~** equivocarse, engañarse; **~ identity** identificación *f* errónea
mister ['mɪstə^r] *n* (*inf*) señor *m*; *see* **Mr**
mistletoe ['mɪsltəu] *n* muérdago
mistook [mɪs'tuk] *pt of* **mistake**
mistreat [mɪs'tri:t] *vt* maltratar, tratar mal
mistress ['mɪstrɪs] *n* (*lover*) amante *f*; (*of house*) señora (de la casa); (*Brit: in primary school*) maestra; (*in secondary school*) profesora; *see also* **Mrs**
mistrust [mɪs'trʌst] *vt* desconfiar de ▷ *n*: **~ (of)** desconfianza (de)
misty ['mɪstɪ] *adj* nebuloso, brumoso; (*day*) de niebla; (*glasses*) empañado
misunderstand [mɪsʌndə'stænd] *vt, vi* (*irreg: like* **understand**) entender mal
misunderstanding [mɪsʌndə'stændɪŋ] *n* malentendido
misunderstood [mɪsʌndə'stud] *pt, pp of* **misunderstand** ▷ *adj* (*person*) incomprendido
misuse *n* [mɪs'ju:s] mal uso; (*of power*) abuso; (*of funds*) malversación *f* ▷ *vt* [mɪs'ju:z] abusar de; (*funds*) malversar
mitigate ['mɪtɪgeɪt] *vt* mitigar; **mitigating circumstances** circunstancias *fpl* atenuantes
mitigation [mɪtɪ'geɪʃən] *n* mitigación *f*, alivio
mix [mɪks] *vt* (*gen*) mezclar; (*combine*) unir ▷ *vi* mezclarse; (*people*) llevarse bien ▷ *n* mezcla; **to ~ sth with sth** mezclar algo con algo; **to ~ business with pleasure** combinar los negocios con el placer; **cake ~** preparado para pastel; **mix in** *vt* (*eggs etc*) añadir; **mix up** *vt* mezclar; (*confuse*) confundir; **to be ~ed up in sth** estar metido en algo
mixed [mɪkst] *adj* (*assorted*) variado, surtido; (*school, marriage etc*) mixto; (*feelings etc*) encontrado
mixed grill *n* (*Brit*) parrillada mixta
mixed salad *n* ensalada mixta
mixed-up [mɪkst'ʌp] *adj* (*confused*) confuso, revuelto
mixer ['mɪksə^r] *n* (*for food*) batidora; (*person*): **he's a good ~** tiene don de gentes
mixer tap *n* (grifo) monomando
mixture ['mɪkstʃə^r] *n* mezcla
mix-up ['mɪksʌp] *n* confusión *f*
ml *abbr* (= *millilitre(s)*) ml
mm *abbr* (= *millimetre*) mm
MMS *n abbr* (= *multimedia messaging service*) MMS *m*
moan [məun] *n* gemido ▷ *vi* gemir; (*inf: complain*): **to ~ (about)** quejarse (de)
moat [məut] *n* foso
mob [mɔb] *n* multitud *f*; (*pej*): **the ~** el populacho ▷ *vt* acosar
mobile ['məubaɪl] *adj* móvil ▷ *n* móvil *m*
mobile home *n* caravana
mobile phone *n* teléfono móvil
mobility [məu'bɪlɪtɪ] *n* movilidad *f*; **~ of labour** *or* (*US*) **labor** movilidad *f* de la mano de obra
mobilize ['məubɪlaɪz] *vt* movilizar
mock [mɔk] *vt* (*make ridiculous*) ridiculizar; (*laugh at*) burlarse de ▷ *adj* fingido; **~ exams** (*Brit: Scol*) exámenes *mpl* de prueba
mockery ['mɔkərɪ] *n* burla; **to make a ~ of** desprestigiar
mock-up ['mɔkʌp] *n* maqueta
mod cons ['mɔd'kɔnz] *npl abbr* (= *modern conveniences*) *see* **convenience**
mode [məud] *n* modo; (*of transport*) medio; (*Comput*) modo, modalidad *f*
model ['mɔdl] *n* (*gen*) modelo; (*Arch*) maqueta; (*person: for fashion, art*) modelo *m/f* ▷ *adj* modelo *inv* ▷ *vt* modelar; **to ~ o.s. on** tomar como modelo a ▷ *vi* ser modelo; **~ railway** ferrocarril *m* de juguete; **to ~ clothes** pasar modelos, ser modelo; **to ~ on** crear a imitación de
modem ['məudəm] *n* módem *m*
moderate [*adj, n* 'mɔdərət, *vb* 'mɔdəreɪt] *adj, n* moderado(-a) *m(f)* ▷ *vi* moderarse, calmarse ▷ *vt* moderar
moderation [mɔdə'reɪʃən] *n* moderación *f*; **in ~** con moderación
moderator ['mɔdəreɪtə^r] *n* (*mediator*) moderador(a) *m(f)*
modern ['mɔdən] *adj* moderno; **~ languages** lenguas *fpl* modernas
modernize ['mɔdənaɪz] *vt* modernizar
modest ['mɔdɪst] *adj* modesto; (*small*) módico
modesty ['mɔdɪstɪ] *n* modestia
modicum ['mɔdɪkəm] *n*: **a ~ of** un mínimo de
modification [mɔdɪfɪ'keɪʃən] *n* modificación *f*; **to make ~s** hacer cambios *or* modificaciones
modify ['mɔdɪfaɪ] *vt* modificar

module ['mɔdju:l] *n* módulo
mogul ['məugəl] *n* (*fig*) magnate *m*
mohair ['məuhɛəʳ] *n* mohair *m*
Mohammed [mə'hæmɛd] *n* Mahoma *m*
moist [mɔɪst] *adj* húmedo
moisten ['mɔɪsn] *vt* humedecer
moisture ['mɔɪstʃəʳ] *n* humedad *f*
moisturize ['mɔɪstʃəraɪz] *vt* (*skin*) hidratar
moisturizer ['mɔɪstʃəraɪzəʳ] *n* crema hidratante
molar ['məuləʳ] *n* muela
molasses [məu'læsɪz] *n* melaza
mold [məuld] *n, vt* (*US*) = **mould**
Moldavia [mɔl'deɪvɪə], **Moldova** [mɔl'dəuvə] *n* Moldavia, Moldova
mole [məul] *n* (*animal*) topo; (*spot*) lunar *m*
molecule ['mɔlɪkju:l] *n* molécula
molest [məu'lɛst] *vt* importunar; (*sexually*) abusar sexualmente de
mollycoddle ['mɔlɪkɔdl] *vt* mimar
Molotov cocktail ['mɔlətɔf-] *n* cóctel *m* Molotov
molt [məult] *vi* (*US*) = **moult**
molten ['məultən] *adj* fundido; (*lava*) líquido
mom [mɔm] *n* (*US*) = **mum**
moment ['məumənt] *n* momento; **at** *or* **for the ~** de momento, por el momento, por ahora; **in a ~** dentro de un momento
momentarily ['məuməntrɪlɪ] *adv* momentáneamente; (*US: very soon*) de un momento a otro
momentary ['məuməntərɪ] *adj* momentáneo
momentous [məu'mɛntəs] *adj* trascendental, importante
momentum [məu'mɛntəm] *n* momento; (*fig*) ímpetu *m*; **to gather ~** cobrar velocidad; (*fig*) cobrar fuerza
mommy ['mɔmɪ] *n* (*US*) = **mummy**
Mon *abbr* (= *Monday*) lun
Monaco ['mɔnəkəu] *n* Mónaco
monarch ['mɔnək] *n* monarca *m/f*
monarchy ['mɔnəkɪ] *n* monarquía
monastery ['mɔnəstərɪ] *n* monasterio
Monday ['mʌndɪ] *n* lunes *m inv*; *see also* **Tuesday**
monetary ['mʌnɪtərɪ] *adj* monetario
money ['mʌnɪ] *n* dinero, plata (*LAm*); **to make ~** ganar dinero; **I've got no ~ left** no me queda dinero
money belt *n* riñonera
money order *n* giro
money-spinner ['mʌnɪspɪnəʳ] *n* (*inf: person, idea, business*) filón *m*
mongrel ['mʌŋgrəl] *n* (*dog*) perro cruzado
monitor ['mɔnɪtəʳ] *n* (*Scol*) monitor *m*; (*also:* **television ~**) receptor *m* de control; (*of computer*) monitor *m* ▷ *vt* controlar; (*foreign station*) escuchar
monk [mʌŋk] *n* monje *m*
monkey ['mʌŋkɪ] *n* mono
monkey nut *n* (*Brit*) cacahuete *m*, maní *m* (*LAm*)
monkey wrench *n* llave *f* inglesa
monogamous [mə'nɔgəməs] *adj* monógamo
monologue ['mɔnəlɔg] *n* monólogo
monopolize [mə'nɔpəlaɪz] *vt* monopolizar
monopoly [mə'nɔpəlɪ] *n* monopolio; **Monopolies and Mergers Commission** (*Brit*) *comisión reguladora de monopolios y fusiones*
monosyllable ['mɔnəsɪləbl] *n* monosílabo
monotone ['mɔnətəun] *n* voz *f* (*or* tono) monocorde
monotonous [mə'nɔtənəs] *adj* monótono
monotony [mə'nɔtənɪ] *n* monotonía
monoxide [mə'nɔksaɪd] *n*: **carbon ~** monóxido de carbono
monseigneur [mɔnsɛn'jə:ʳ], **monsignor** [mɔn'si:njəʳ] *n* monseñor *m*
monsoon [mɔn'su:n] *n* monzón *m*
monster ['mɔnstəʳ] *n* monstruo
monstrosity [mɔns'trɔsɪtɪ] *n* monstruosidad *f*
monstrous ['mɔnstrəs] *adj* (*huge*) enorme; (*atrocious*) monstruoso
month [mʌnθ] *n* mes *m*; **300 dollars a ~** 300 dólares al mes; **every ~** cada mes
monthly ['mʌnθlɪ] *adj* mensual ▷ *adv* mensualmente ▷ *n* (*magazine*) revista, mensual; **twice ~** dos veces al mes; **~ instalment** mensualidad *f*
monument ['mɔnjumənt] *n* monumento
moo [mu:] *vi* mugir
mood [mu:d] *n* humor *m*; **to be in a good/bad ~** estar de buen/mal humor
moody ['mu:dɪ] *adj* (*changeable*) de humor variable; (*sullen*) malhumorado
moon [mu:n] *n* luna
moonlight ['mu:nlaɪt] *n* luz *f* de la luna ▷ *vi* hacer pluriempleo
moonlighting ['mu:nlaɪtɪŋ] *n* pluriempleo
moonlit ['mu:nlɪt] *adj*: **a ~ night** una noche de luna
Moor [muəʳ] *n* moro(-a)
moor [muəʳ] *n* páramo ▷ *vt* (*ship*) amarrar ▷ *vi* echar las amarras
moorings ['muərɪŋz] *npl* (*chains*) amarras *fpl*; (*place*) amarradero *sg*
Moorish ['muərɪʃ] *adj* moro; (*architecture*) árabe
moorland ['muələnd] *n* páramo, brezal *m*
moose [mu:s] *n pl inv* alce *m*
mop [mɔp] *n* fregona; (*of hair*) melena ▷ *vt* fregar; **mop up** *vt* limpiar
mope [məup] *vi* estar deprimido; **mope about, mope around** *vi* andar abatido
moped ['məupɛd] *n* ciclomotor *m*
moral ['mɔrl] *adj* moral ▷ *n* moraleja; **morals** *npl* moralidad *f*, moral *f*
morale [mɔ'rɑ:l] *n* moral *f*
morality [mə'rælɪtɪ] *n* moralidad *f*

moralize ['mɔrəlaɪz] *vi*: **to ~ (about)** moralizar (sobre)
morally ['mɔrəlɪ] *adv* moralmente
moral victory *n* victoria moral
morass [mə'ræs] *n* pantano
morbid ['mɔ:bɪd] *adj* (*interest*) morboso; (*Med*) mórbido

KEYWORD

more [mɔ:ʳ] *adj* **1** (*greater in number etc*) más; **more people/work than before** más gente/trabajo que antes
2 (*additional*) más; **do you want (some) more tea?** ¿quieres más té?; **is there any more wine?** ¿queda vino?; **it'll take a few more weeks** tardará unas semanas más; **it's 2 kms more to the house** faltan 2 kms para la casa; **more time/letters than we expected** más tiempo del que/más cartas de las que esperábamos; **I have no more money, I don't have any more money** (ya) no tengo más dinero
▷ *pron* (*greater amount, additional amount*) más; **more than 10** más de 10; **it cost more than the other one/than we expected** costó más que el otro/más de lo que esperábamos; **is there any more?** ¿hay más?; **I want more** quiero más; **and what's more ...** y además ...; **many/much more** muchos(-as)/mucho(-a) más
▷ *adv* más; **more dangerous/easily (than)** más peligroso/fácilmente (que); **more and more expensive** cada vez más caro; **more or less** más o menos; **more than ever** más que nunca; **she doesn't live here any more** ya no vive aquí

moreover [mɔ:'rəuvəʳ] *adv* además, por otra parte
morgue [mɔ:g] *n* depósito de cadáveres
Mormon ['mɔ:mən] *n* mormón(-ona) *m(f)*
morning ['mɔ:nɪŋ] *n* (*gen*) mañana; (*early morning*) madrugada; **in the ~** por la mañana; **7 o'clock in the ~** las 7 de la mañana; **this ~** esta mañana
morning-after pill ['mɔ:nɪŋ'ɑ:ftə-] *n* píldora del día después
morning sickness *n* (*Med*) náuseas *fpl* del embarazo
Moroccan [mə'rɔkən] *adj, n* marroquí *m/f*
Morocco [mə'rɔkəu] *n* Marruecos *m*
moron ['mɔ:rɔn] *n* (*inf!*) imbécil *m/f*
morphine ['mɔ:fi:n] *n* morfina
Morse [mɔ:s] *n* (*also*: **~ code**) (código) morse *m*
morsel ['mɔ:sl] *n* (*of food*) bocado
mortal ['mɔ:tl] *adj, n* mortal *m*
mortality [mɔ:'tælɪtɪ] *n* mortalidad *f*
mortar ['mɔ:təʳ] *n* argamasa; (*implement*) mortero
mortgage ['mɔ:gɪdʒ] *n* hipoteca ▷ *vt* hipotecar; **to take out a ~** sacar una hipoteca
mortgage company *n* (*US*) ≈ banco hipotecario
mortician [mɔ:'tɪʃən] *n* (*US*) director(a) *m(f)* de pompas fúnebres
mortified ['mɔ:tɪfaɪd] *adj*: **I was ~** me dio muchísima vergüenza
mortuary ['mɔ:tjuərɪ] *n* depósito de cadáveres
mosaic [məu'zeɪɪk] *n* mosaico
Moscow ['mɔskəu] *n* Moscú *m*
Moslem ['mɔzləm] *adj, n* = **Muslim**
mosque [mɔsk] *n* mezquita
mosquito (*pl* **mosquitoes**) [mɔs'ki:təu] *n* mosquito, zancudo (*LAm*)
moss [mɔs] *n* musgo
most [məust] *adj* la mayor parte de, la mayoría de ▷ *pron* la mayor parte, la mayoría ▷ *adv* el más; (*very*) muy; **the ~** (*also*: + *adjective*) el más; **~ of them** la mayor parte de ellos; **I saw the ~** yo fui el que más vi; **at the (very) ~** a lo sumo, todo lo más; **to make the ~ of** aprovechar (al máximo); **a ~ interesting book** un libro interesantísimo
mostly ['məustlɪ] *adv* en su mayor parte, principalmente
MOT *n abbr* (*Brit*: = *Ministry of Transport*): **the ~ (test)** ≈ la ITV
motel [məu'tɛl] *n* motel *m*
moth [mɔθ] *n* mariposa nocturna; (*clothes moth*) polilla
mothball ['mɔθbɔ:l] *n* bola de naftalina
mother ['mʌðəʳ] *n* madre *f* ▷ *adj* materno ▷ *vt* (*care for*) cuidar (como una madre)
motherhood ['mʌðəhud] *n* maternidad *f*
mother-in-law ['mʌðərɪnlɔ:] *n* suegra
motherly ['mʌðəlɪ] *adj* maternal
mother-of-pearl ['mʌðərəv'pə:l] *n* nácar *m*
Mother's Day *n* Día *m* de la Madre
mother-to-be ['mʌðətə'bi:] *n* futura madre
mother tongue *n* lengua materna
motif [məu'ti:f] *n* motivo; (*theme*) tema *m*
motion ['məuʃən] *n* movimiento; (*gesture*) ademán *m*, señal *f*; (*at meeting*) moción *f*; (*Brit*: *also*: **bowel ~**) evacuación *f* intestinal ▷ *vt, vi*: **to ~ (to) sb to do sth** hacer señas a algn para que haga algo; **to be in ~** (*vehicle*) estar en movimiento; **to set in ~** poner en marcha; **to go through the ~s of doing sth** (*fig*) hacer algo mecánicamente *or* sin convicción
motionless ['məuʃənlɪs] *adj* inmóvil
motion picture *n* película
motivate ['məutɪveɪt] *vt* motivar
motivated ['məutɪveɪtɪd] *adj* motivado
motivation [məutɪ'veɪʃən] *n* motivación *f*
motive ['məutɪv] *n* motivo; **from the best ~s** con las mejores intenciones
motley ['mɔtlɪ] *adj* variopinto
motor ['məutəʳ] *n* motor *m*; (*Brit*: *inf*: *vehicle*) coche *m*, carro (*LAm*), automóvil *m*, auto *m* (*LAm*) ▷ *adj* motor/motora, motriz
motorbike ['məutəbaɪk] *n* moto *f*
motorboat ['məutəbəut] *n* lancha motora

motorcar ['məutəkɑːʳ] *n* (*Brit*) coche *m*, carro (*LAm*), automóvil *m*, auto *m* (*LAm*)
motorcycle ['məutəsaɪkl] *n* motocicleta
motorcycle racing *n* motociclismo
motorcyclist ['məutəsaɪklɪst] *n* motociclista *m/f*
motoring ['məutərɪŋ] *n* (*Brit*) automovilismo ▷ *adj* (*accident, offence*) de tráfico *or* tránsito
motorist ['məutərɪst] *n* conductor(a) *m(f)*, automovilista *m/f*
motor racing *n* (*Brit*) carreras *fpl* de coches, automovilismo
motorway ['məutəweɪ] *n* (*Brit*) autopista
mottled ['mɔtld] *adj* moteado
motto (*pl* **mottoes**) ['mɔtəu] *n* lema *m*; (*watchword*) consigna
mould, mold (*US*) [məuld] *n* molde *m*; (*mildew*) moho ▷ *vt* moldear; (*fig*) formar
mouldy, moldy (*US*) ['məuldɪ] *adj* enmohecido
moult, molt (*US*) [məult] *vi* mudar la piel; (*bird*) mudar las plumas
mound [maund] *n* montón *m*, montículo
mount [maunt] *n* monte *m*; (*horse*) montura; (*for jewel etc*) engarce *m*; (*for picture*) marco ▷ *vt* montar en, subir a; (*stairs*) subir; (*exhibition*) montar; (*attack*) lanzar; (*stamp*) pegar, fijar; (*picture*) enmarcar ▷ *vi* (*increase*) aumentar; (*also*: **~ up**: *on horse*) montar
mountain ['mauntɪn] *n* montaña ▷ *cpd* de montaña; **to make a ~ out of a molehill** hacer una montaña de un grano de arena
mountain bike *n* bicicleta de montaña
mountaineer [mauntɪ'nɪəʳ] *n* montañero(-a), alpinista *m/f*, andinista *m/f* (*LAm*)
mountaineering [mauntɪ'nɪərɪŋ] *n* montañismo, alpinismo, andinismo (*LAm*)
mountainous ['mauntɪnəs] *adj* montañoso
mountain range *n* sierra
mountain rescue team *n* equipo de rescate de montaña
mountainside ['mauntɪnsaɪd] *n* ladera de la montaña
mourn [mɔːn] *vt* llorar, lamentar ▷ *vi*: **to ~ for** llorar la muerte de, lamentarse por
mourner ['mɔːnəʳ] *n* doliente *m/f*
mournful ['mɔːnful] *adj* triste, lúgubre
mourning ['mɔːnɪŋ] *n* luto ▷ *cpd* (*dress*) de luto; **in ~** de luto
mouse (*pl* **mice**) [maus, maɪs] *n* (*also Comput*) ratón *m*
mouse mat, mouse pad *n* (*Comput*) alfombrilla, almohadilla
mousetrap ['maustræp] *n* ratonera
mousse [muːs] *n* (*Culin*) mousse *f*; (*for hair*) espuma (moldeadora)
moustache [məs'tɑːʃ], **mustache** (*US*) ['mʌstæʃ] *n* bigote *m*
mousy ['mausɪ] *adj* (*person*) tímido; (*hair*) pardusco
mouth (*pl* **mouths**) [mauθ, -ðz] *n* boca; (*of river*) desembocadura
mouthful ['mauθful] *n* bocado
mouth organ *n* armónica
mouthpiece ['mauθpiːs] *n* (*of musical instrument*) boquilla; (*Tel*) micrófono; (*spokesman*) portavoz *m/f*
mouthwash ['mauθwɔʃ] *n* enjuague *m* bucal
mouth-watering ['mauθwɔːtərɪŋ] *adj* apetitoso
movable ['muːvəbl] *adj* movible
move [muːv] *n* (*movement*) movimiento; (*in game*) jugada; (*: turn to play*) turno; (*change of house*) mudanza ▷ *vt* mover; (*emotionally*) conmover; (*Pol*: *resolution etc*) proponer ▷ *vi* (*gen*) moverse; (*traffic*) circular; (*Brit*: *also*: **~ house**) trasladarse, mudarse; **to ~ sb to do sth** mover a algn a hacer algo; **to be ~d** estar conmovido; **to get a ~ on** darse prisa; **move about** *or* **around** *vi* moverse; (*travel*) viajar; **move along** *vi* (*stop loitering*) circular; (*along seat etc*) correrse; **move away** *vi* (*leave*) marcharse; **move back** *vi* (*return*) volver; **move down** *vt* (*demote*) degradar; **move forward** *vi* avanzar ▷ *vt* adelantar; **move in** *vi* (*to a house*) instalarse; **move off** *vi* ponerse en camino; **move on** *vi* seguir viaje ▷ *vt* (*onlookers*) hacer circular; **move out** *vi* (*of house*) mudarse; **move over** *vi* hacerse a un lado, correrse; **move up** *vi* subir; (*employee*) ascender
movement ['muːvmənt] *n* movimiento; (*Tech*) mecanismo; **~ (of the bowels)** (*Med*) evacuación *f*
movie ['muːvɪ] *n* película; **to go to the ~s** ir al cine
movie camera *n* cámara cinematográfica
movie theater *n* (*US*) cine *m*
moving ['muːvɪŋ] *adj* (*emotional*) conmovedor(a); (*that moves*) móvil; (*instigating*) motor(a)
mow (*pt* **mowed**, *pp* **mowed** *or* **mown**) [məu, -n] *vt* (*grass*) cortar; (*corn*) segar; (*also*: **~ down**: *shoot*) acribillar
mower ['məuəʳ] *n* (*also*: **lawn~**) cortacésped *m*
Mozambique [məuzæm'biːk] *n* Mozambique *m*
MP *n abbr* (= *Military Police*) PM; (*Brit*) = **Member of Parliament**
mpg *n abbr* (= *miles per gallon*) *30 mpg = 9.4 l. per 100 km*
mph *abbr* (= *miles per hour*) *60 mph = 96 km/h*
MP3 ['ɛmpiː'θriː] *n* MP3 *m*
MP3 player *n* reproductor *m* MP3
Mr, Mr. ['mɪstəʳ] *n*: **Mr Smith** (el) Sr. Smith
Mrs, Mrs. ['mɪsɪz] *n*: **~ Smith** (la) Sra. de Smith
Ms, Ms. [mɪz] *n* (*Miss or Mrs*) *abreviatura con la que se evita hacer expreso el estado civil de una mujer*; **Ms Smith** (la) Sr(t)a. Smith
MSc *abbr see* **Master of Science**
MSP *n abbr* (*Brit*) = **Member of the Scottish Parliament**

Mt *abbr* (*Geo*: = *mount*) m
much [mʌtʃ] *adj* mucho ▷ *adv, n, pron* mucho; (*before pp*) muy; **how ~ is it?** ¿cuánto es?, ¿cuánto cuesta?; **too ~** demasiado; **so ~** tanto; **it's not ~** no es mucho; **as ~ as** tanto como; **however ~ he tries** por mucho que se esfuerce; **I like it very/so ~** me gusta mucho/tanto; **thank you very ~** muchas gracias, muy agradecido
muck [mʌk] *n* (*dirt*) suciedad *f*; (*fig*) porquería; **muck about** *or* **around** *vi* (*inf*) perder el tiempo; (*enjoy o.s.*) entretenerse; (*tinker*) manosear; **muck in** *vi* (*inf*) arrimar el hombro; **muck out** *vt* (*stable*) limpiar; **muck up** *vt* (*inf*: *dirty*) ensuciar; (: *spoil*) echar a perder; (: *ruin*) estropear
mucky ['mʌkɪ] *adj* (*dirty*) sucio
mucus ['mju:kəs] *n* mucosidad *f*, moco
mud [mʌd] *n* barro, lodo
muddle ['mʌdl] *n* desorden *m*, confusión *f*; (*mix up*) embrollo, lío ▷ *vt* (*also*: **~ up**) embrollar, confundir; **muddle along, muddle on** *vi* arreglárselas de alguna manera; **muddle through** *vi* salir del paso
muddy ['mʌdɪ] *adj* fangoso, cubierto de lodo
mudguard ['mʌdgɑ:d] *n* guardabarros *m inv*
mudslide ['mʌdslaid] *n* desprendimiento de tierra
muesli ['mju:zlɪ] *n* muesli *m*
muffin ['mʌfɪn] *n* bollo, ≈ magdalena
muffle ['mʌfl] *vt* (*sound*) amortiguar; (*against cold*) abrigar
muffled ['mʌfld] *adj* sordo, apagado; (*noise etc*) amortiguado
muffler ['mʌflə^r] *n* (*scarf*) bufanda; (*US Aut*) silenciador *m*; (*on motorbike*) silenciador *m*, mofle *m*
mug [mʌg] *n* (*cup*) taza alta; (*for beer*) jarra; (*inf*: *face*) jeta; (: *fool*) bobo ▷ *vt* (*assault*) atracar; **it's a ~'s game** es cosa de bobos; **mug up** *vt* (*inf*: *also*: **~ up on**) empollar
mugger ['mʌgə^r] *n* atracador(a) *m(f)*
mugging ['mʌgɪŋ] *n* atraco callejero
muggins ['mʌgɪnz] *nsg* (*inf*) tonto(-a) el bote
muggy ['mʌgɪ] *adj* bochornoso
mule [mju:l] *n* mula
mull [mʌl]: **to ~ over** *vt* meditar sobre
multicoloured, multicolored (*US*) ['mʌltɪkʌləd] *adj* multicolor
multi-level [mʌltɪ'lɛvl] *adj* (*US*) = **multistorey**
multimedia ['mʌltɪ'mi:dɪə] *adj* multimedia
multinational [mʌltɪ'næʃənl] *n* multinacional *f* ▷ *adj* multinacional
multiple ['mʌltɪpl] *adj* múltiple ▷ *n* múltiplo; (*Brit*: *also*: **~ store**) (cadena de) grandes almacenes *mpl*
multiple choice *n* (*also*: **~ test**) examen *m* de tipo test
multiple sclerosis [-sklɪ'rəusɪs] *n* esclerosis *f* múltiple
multiplex ['mʌltɪplɛks] *n* (*also*: **~ cinema**) multicines *m inv*
multiplication [mʌltɪplɪ'keɪʃən] *n* multiplicación *f*
multiply ['mʌltɪplaɪ] *vt* multiplicar ▷ *vi* multiplicarse
multistorey [mʌltɪ'stɔ:rɪ] *adj* (*Brit*: *building, car park*) de muchos pisos
multitude ['mʌltɪtju:d] *n* multitud *f*
mum [mʌm] *n* (*Brit*) mamá ▷ *adj*: **to keep ~ (about sth)** no decir ni mu (de algo)
mumble ['mʌmbl] *vt* decir entre dientes ▷ *vi* hablar entre dientes, musitar
mummy ['mʌmɪ] *n* (*Brit*: *mother*) mamá; (*embalmed*) momia
mumps [mʌmps] *n* paperas *fpl*
munch [mʌntʃ] *vt, vi* mascar
mundane [mʌn'deɪn] *adj* mundano
municipal [mju:'nɪsɪpl] *adj* municipal
munitions [mju:'nɪʃənz] *npl* municiones *fpl*
mural ['mjuərl] *n* (pintura) mural *m*
murder ['mə:də^r] *n* asesinato; (*in law*) homicidio ▷ *vt* asesinar, matar; **to commit ~** cometer un asesinato *or* homicidio
murderer ['mə:dərə^r] *n* asesino
murderous ['mə:dərəs] *adj* homicida
murky ['mə:kɪ] *adj* (*water, past*) turbio; (*room*) sombrío
murmur ['mə:mə^r] *n* murmullo ▷ *vt, vi* murmurar; **heart ~** soplo cardíaco
muscle ['mʌsl] *n* músculo; (*fig*: *strength*) garra, fuerza; **muscle in** *vi* entrometerse
muscular ['mʌskjulə^r] *adj* muscular; (*person*) musculoso
muscular dystrophy *n* distrofia muscular
muse [mju:z] *vi* meditar ▷ *n* musa
museum [mju:'zɪəm] *n* museo
mushroom ['mʌʃrum] *n* (*gen*) seta, hongo; (*small*) champiñón *m* ▷ *vi* (*fig*) crecer de la noche a la mañana
music ['mju:zɪk] *n* música
musical ['mju:zɪkl] *adj* musical; (*sound*) melodioso; (*person*) con talento musical ▷ *n* (*show*) (comedia) musical *m*
musical instrument *n* instrumento musical
music centre *n* equipo de música
musician [mju:'zɪʃən] *n* músico(-a)
Muslim ['mʌzlɪm] *adj, n* musulmán(-ana) *m(f)*
muslin ['mʌzlɪn] *n* muselina
mussel ['mʌsl] *n* mejillón *m*
must [mʌst] *aux vb* (*obligation*): **I ~ do it** debo hacerlo, tengo que hacerlo; (*probability*): **he ~ be there by now** ya debe (de) estar allí ▷ *n*: **it's a ~** es imprescindible
mustache ['mʌstæʃ] *n* (*US*) = **moustache**
mustard ['mʌstəd] *n* mostaza
muster ['mʌstə^r] *vt* juntar, reunir; (*also*: **~ up**) reunir; (: *courage*) armarse de
mustn't ['mʌsnt] = **must not**
mutant ['mju:tənt] *adj, n* mutante *m*

m

mutate [mju:'teɪt] *vi* sufrir mutación, transformarse
mute [mju:t] *adj* mudo(-a)
muted ['mju:tɪd] *adj* (*noise*) sordo; (*criticism*) callado
mutilate ['mju:tɪleɪt] *vt* mutilar
mutiny ['mju:tɪnɪ] *n* motín *m* ▷ *vi* amotinarse
mutter ['mʌtəʳ] *vt, vi* murmurar
mutton ['mʌtn] *n* (carne *f* de) cordero
mutual ['mju:tʃuəl] *adj* mutuo; (*friend*) común
mutually ['mju:tʃuəlɪ] *adv* mutuamente
Muzak® ['mju:zæk] *n* hilo musical
muzzle ['mʌzl] *n* hocico; (*protective device*) bozal *m*; (*of gun*) boca ▷ *vt* amordazar; (*dog*) poner un bozal a
MW *abbr* (*Radio: = medium wave*) onda media
my [maɪ] *adj* mi(s); **my house/brother/sisters** mi casa/hermano/mis hermanas; **I've washed my hair/cut my finger** me he lavado el pelo/cortado un dedo; **is this my pen or yours?** ¿este bolígrafo es mío o tuyo?
Myanmar ['maɪænmɑ:ʳ] *n* Myanmar
myself [maɪ'sɛlf] *pron* (*reflexive*) me; (*emphatic*) yo mismo; (*after prep*) mí (mismo); *see also* **oneself**
mysterious [mɪs'tɪərɪəs] *adj* misterioso
mystery ['mɪstərɪ] *n* misterio
mystical ['mɪstɪkl] *adj* místico
mystify ['mɪstɪfaɪ] *vt* (*perplex*) dejar perplejo; (*disconcert*) desconcertar
myth [mɪθ] *n* mito
mythical ['mɪθɪkl] *adj* mítico
mythology [mɪ'θɔlədʒɪ] *n* mitología

n

N, n [ɛn] *n* (*letter*) N, n *f*; **N for Nellie**, (*US*) **N for Nan** N de Navarra
N *abbr* (= *North*) N
n/a *abbr* (= *not applicable*) no interesa; (*Comm etc*) = **no account**
naan [nɑ:n] *n* = **nan bread**
nab [næb] *vt* (*inf: grab*) coger (*Sp*), agarrar (*LAm*); (*: catch out*) pillar
NAFTA ['næftə] *n abbr* (= *North Atlantic Free Trade Agreement*) TLC *m*
nag [næg] *n* (*pej: horse*) rocín *m* ▷ *vt* (*scold*) regañar; (*annoy*) fastidiar
nagging ['nægɪŋ] *adj* (*doubt*) persistente; (*pain*) continuo ▷ *n* quejas *fpl*
nail [neɪl] *n* (*human*) uña; (*metal*) clavo ▷ *vt* clavar; (*fig: catch*) coger (*Sp*), pillar; **to pay cash on the ~** pagar a tocateja; **to ~ sb down to a date/price** hacer que algn se comprometa a una fecha/un precio
nailbrush ['neɪlbrʌʃ] *n* cepillo para las uñas
nailfile ['neɪlfaɪl] *n* lima para las uñas
nail polish *n* esmalte *m or* laca para las uñas
nail polish remover *n* quitaesmalte *m*
nail scissors *npl* tijeras *fpl* para las uñas
nail varnish *n* (*Brit*) = **nail polish**
naïve [naɪ'i:v] *adj* ingenuo
naked ['neɪkɪd] *adj* (*nude*) desnudo; (*flame*) expuesto al aire; **with the ~ eye** a simple vista
name [neɪm] *n* (*gen*) nombre *m*; (*surname*) apellido; (*reputation*) fama, renombre *m* ▷ *vt* (*child*) poner nombre a; (*criminal*) identificar;

(*price, date etc*) fijar; (*appoint*) nombrar; **by ~** de nombre; **in the ~ of** en nombre de; **what's your ~?** ¿cómo se llama usted?; **my ~ is Peter** me llamo Pedro; **to give one's ~ and address** dar sus señas; **to take sb's ~ and address** apuntar las señas de algn; **to make a ~ for o.s.** hacerse famoso; **to get (o.s.) a bad ~** forjarse una mala reputación
nameless ['neɪmlɪs] *adj* anónimo, sin nombre
namely ['neɪmlɪ] *adv* a saber
namesake ['neɪmseɪk] *n* tocayo(-a)
nan bread [nɑːn-] *n pan indio sin apenas levadura*
nanny ['nænɪ] *n* niñera
nap [næp] *n* (*sleep*) sueñecito, siesta; **they were caught ~ping** les pilló desprevenidos
nape [neɪp] *n*: **~ of the neck** nuca, cogote *m*
napkin ['næpkɪn] *n* (*also*: **table ~**) servilleta
nappy ['næpɪ] *n* (*Brit*) pañal *m*
nappy rash *n* prurito
narcissus (*pl* **narcissi**) [nɑː'sɪsəs, -saɪ] *n* narciso
narcotic [nɑː'kɔtɪk] *adj, n* narcótico; **narcotics** *npl* estupefacientes *mpl*, narcóticos *mpl*
narrate [nə'reɪt] *vt* narrar, contar
narrative ['nærətɪv] *n* narrativa ▷ *adj* narrativo
narrator [nə'reɪtə^r] *n* narrador(a) *m(f)*
narrow ['nærəu] *adj* estrecho; (*resources, means*) escaso ▷ *vi* estrecharse; (*diminish*) reducirse; **to have a ~ escape** escaparse por los pelos; **narrow down** *vt* (*search, investigation, possibilities*) restringir, limitar; (*list*) reducir
narrowly ['nærəlɪ] *adv* (*miss*) por poco
narrow-minded [nærəu'maɪndɪd] *adj* de miras estrechas
NASA *n abbr* (*US*: = *National Aeronautics and Space Administration*) NASA *f*
nasal ['neɪzl] *adj* nasal
nasty ['nɑːstɪ] *adj* (*remark*) feo; (*person*) antipático; (*revolting*: *taste, smell*) asqueroso; (*wound, disease etc*) peligroso, grave; **to turn ~** (*situation*) ponerse feo; (*weather*) empeorar; (*person*) ponerse negro
nation ['neɪʃən] *n* nación *f*
national ['næʃənl] *adj* nacional ▷ *n* súbdito(-a)
national anthem *n* himno nacional
National Curriculum *n* (*Brit*) plan *m* general de estudios (*en Inglaterra y Gales*)
national debt *n* deuda pública
national dress *n* traje *m* típico del país
National Guard *n* (*US*) Guardia Nacional
National Health Service *n* (*Brit*) servicio nacional de salud, ≈ INSALUD *m* (*Sp*)
National Insurance *n* (*Brit*) seguro social nacional, ≈ Seguridad *f* Social
nationalism ['næʃnəlɪzəm] *n* nacionalismo
nationalist ['næʃnəlɪst] *adj, n* nacionalista *m/f*
nationality [næʃə'nælɪtɪ] *n* nacionalidad *f*
nationalization [næʃnəlaɪ'zeɪʃən] *n* nacionalización *f*
nationalize ['næʃnəlaɪz] *vt* nacionalizar; **~d industry** industria nacionalizada
nationally ['næʃnəlɪ] *adv* (*nationwide*) a escala nacional; (*as a nation*) como nación
national service *n* (*Mil*) servicio militar
National Trust *n* (*Brit*) *organización encargada de preservar el patrimonio histórico británico*
nationwide ['neɪʃənwaɪd] *adj* a escala nacional
native ['neɪtɪv] *n* (*local inhabitant*) natural *m/f*; (*in colonies*) indígena *m/f*, nativo(-a) ▷ *adj* (*indigenous*) indígena; (*country*) natal; (*innate*) natural, innato; **a ~ of Russia** un(a) natural de Rusia; **~ language** lengua materna; **a ~ speaker of French** un hablante nativo de francés
Native American *adj, n* americano(-a) indígena *m(f)*, amerindio(-a) *m(f)*
native speaker *n* hablante *m/f* nativo(-a)
Nativity [nə'tɪvɪtɪ] *n*: **the ~** Navidad *f*
nativity play *n* auto del nacimiento
NATO ['neɪtəu] *n abbr* (= *North Atlantic Treaty Organization*) OTAN *f*
natural ['nætʃrəl] *adj* natural; **death from ~ causes** (*Law*) muerte *f* por causas naturales
natural gas *n* gas *m* natural
natural history *n* historia natural
naturalize ['nætʃrəlaɪz] *vt*: **to become ~d** (*person*) naturalizarse; (*plant*) aclimatarse
naturally ['nætʃrəlɪ] *adv* (*speak etc*) naturalmente; (*of course*) desde luego, por supuesto, ¡cómo no! (*LAm*); (*instinctively*) por naturaleza
natural resources *npl* recursos *mpl* naturales
natural selection *n* selección *f* natural
nature ['neɪtʃə^r] *n* naturaleza; (*group, sort*) género, clase *f*; (*character*) modo de ser, carácter *m*; **by ~** por naturaleza; **documents of a confidential ~** documentos *mpl* de tipo confidencial
nature reserve *n* reserva natural
naught [nɔːt] *n* = **nought**
naughty ['nɔːtɪ] *adj* (*child*) travieso; (*story, film*) picante, escabroso, colorado (*LAm*)
nausea ['nɔːsɪə] *n* náusea
nauseate ['nɔːsɪeɪt] *vt* dar náuseas a; (*fig*) dar asco a
naval ['neɪvl] *adj* naval, de marina
naval officer *n* oficial *m/f* de marina
nave [neɪv] *n* nave *f*
navel ['neɪvl] *n* ombligo
navigate ['nævɪgeɪt] *vt* (*ship*) gobernar; (*river etc*) navegar por ▷ *vi* navegar; (*Aut*) ir de copiloto
navigation [nævɪ'geɪʃən] *n* (*action*) navegación *f*; (*science*) náutica
navvy ['nævɪ] *n* (*Brit*) peón *m* caminero

n

navy ['neɪvɪ] *n* marina de guerra; (*ships*) armada, flota ▷ *adj* azul marino
Nazi ['nɑ:tsɪ] *adj, n* nazi *m/f*
NB *abbr* (= *nota bene*) nótese
NBA *n abbr* (*US*) = **National Basketball Association**; **National Boxing Association**
NBC *n abbr* (*US*: = *National Broadcasting Company*) *cadena de televisión*
near [nɪə^r] *adj* (*place, relation*) cercano; (*time*) próximo ▷ *adv* cerca ▷ *prep* (*also*: **~ to**: *space*) cerca de, junto a; (: *time*) cerca de ▷ *vt* acercarse a, aproximarse a; **~ here/there** cerca de aquí/de allí; **£25,000 or ~est offer** 25,000 libras o precio a discutir; **in the ~ future** en fecha próxima; **the building is ~ing completion** el edificio está casi terminado
nearby [nɪə'baɪ] *adj* cercano, próximo ▷ *adv* cerca
nearly ['nɪəlɪ] *adv* casi, por poco; **I ~ fell** por poco me caigo; **not ~** ni mucho menos, ni con mucho
near miss *n* (*shot*) tiro casi en el blanco; (*Aviat*) *accidente evitado por muy poco*
nearside ['nɪəsaɪd] *n* (*Aut*: *right-hand drive*) lado izquierdo; (: *left-hand drive*) lado derecho
near-sighted [nɪə'saɪtɪd] *adj* miope, corto de vista
neat [ni:t] *adj* (*place*) ordenado, bien cuidado; (*person*) pulcro; (*plan*) ingenioso; (*spirits*) solo
neatly ['ni:tlɪ] *adv* (*tidily*) con esmero; (*skilfully*) ingeniosamente
neatness ['ni:tnɪs] *n* (*tidiness*) orden *m*; (*skilfulness*) destreza, habilidad *f*
necessarily ['nɛsɪsrɪlɪ] *adv* necesariamente; **not ~** no necesariamente
necessary ['nɛsɪsrɪ] *adj* necesario, preciso; **he did all that was ~** hizo todo lo necesario; **if ~** si es necesario
necessity [nɪ'sɛsɪtɪ] *n* necesidad *f*; **necessities** *npl* artículos *mpl* de primera necesidad; **in case of ~** en caso de urgencia
neck [nɛk] *n* (*Anat*) cuello; (*of animal*) pescuezo ▷ *vi* besuquearse; **~ and ~** parejos; **to stick one's ~ out** (*inf*) arriesgarse
necklace ['nɛklɪs] *n* collar *m*
neckline ['nɛklaɪn] *n* escote *m*
necktie ['nɛktaɪ] *n* (*US*) corbata
nectarine ['nɛktərɪn] *n* nectarina
née [neɪ] *adj*: **~ Scott** de soltera Scott
need [ni:d] *n* (*lack*) escasez *f*, falta; (*necessity*) necesidad *f* ▷ *vt* (*require*) necesitar; **in case of ~** en caso de necesidad; **there's no ~ for ...** no hace(n) falta ...; **to be in ~ of, have ~ of** necesitar; **10 will meet my immediate ~s** 10 satisfacerán mis necesidades más apremiantes; **the ~s of industry** las necesidades de la industria; **I ~ it** lo necesito; **a signature is ~ed** se requiere una firma; **I ~ to do it** tengo que hacerlo; **you don't ~ to go** no hace falta que vayas
needle ['ni:dl] *n* aguja ▷ *vt* (*fig*: *inf*) picar, fastidiar
needless ['ni:dlɪs] *adj* innecesario, inútil; **~ to say** huelga decir que
needlework ['ni:dlwə:k] *n* (*activity*) costura, labor *f* de aguja
needn't ['ni:dnt] = **need not**
needy ['ni:dɪ] *adj* necesitado
negative ['nɛgətɪv] *n* (*Phot*) negativo; (*answer*) negativa; (*Ling*) negación *f* ▷ *adj* negativo
negative equity *n situación en la que el valor de la vivienda es menor que el de la hipoteca que pesa sobre ella*
neglect [nɪ'glɛkt] *vt* (*one's duty*) faltar a, no cumplir con; (*child*) descuidar, desatender ▷ *n* (*state*) abandono; (*personal*) dejadez *f*; (*of child*) desatención *f*; (*of duty*) incumplimiento; **to ~ to do sth** olvidarse de hacer algo
negligee ['nɛglɪʒeɪ] *n* (*nightdress*) salto de cama
negligence ['nɛglɪdʒəns] *n* negligencia
negligent ['nɛglɪdʒənt] *adj* negligente; (*casual*) descuidado
negligible ['nɛglɪdʒɪbl] *adj* insignificante, despreciable
negotiable [nɪ'gəuʃɪəbl] *adj*: **not ~** (*cheque*) no trasferible
negotiate [nɪ'gəuʃɪeɪt] *vt* (*treaty, loan*) negociar; (*obstacle*) franquear; (*bend in road*) tomar ▷ *vi*: **to ~ (with)** negociar (con); **to ~ with sb for sth** tratar *or* negociar con algn por algo
negotiating table [nɪ'gəuʃɪeɪtɪŋ-] *n* mesa de negociaciones
negotiation [nɪgəuʃɪ'eɪʃən] *n* negociación *f*, gestión *f*; **negotiations** *npl* negociaciones; **to enter into ~s with sb** entrar en negociaciones con algn
negotiator [nɪ'gəuʃɪeɪtə^r] *n* negociador(a) *m(f)*
neigh [neɪ] *n* relincho ▷ *vi* relinchar
neighbour, neighbor (*US*) ['neɪbə^r] *n* vecino(-a)
neighbourhood, neighborhood (*US*) ['neɪbəhud] *n* (*place*) vecindad *f*, barrio; (*people*) vecindario
neighbourhood watch *n* (*Brit*: *also*: **~ scheme**) *vigilancia del barrio por los propios vecinos*
neighbouring, neighboring (*US*) ['neɪbərɪŋ] *adj* vecino
neither ['naɪðə^r] *adj* ni ▷ *conj*: **I didn't move and ~ did John** no me he movido, ni Juan tampoco ▷ *pron* ninguno; **~ is true** ninguno(-a) de los/las dos es cierto(-a) ▷ *adv*: **~ good nor bad** ni bueno ni malo
neologism [nɪ'ɔlədʒɪzəm] *n* neologismo
neon ['ni:ɔn] *n* neón *m*
neon light *n* lámpara de neón
Nepal [nɪ'pɔ:l] *n* Nepal *m*
nephew ['nɛvju:] *n* sobrino
nerd [nə:d] *n* (*inf*) primo(-a)

nerve [nə:v] *n* (*Anat*) nervio; (*courage*) valor *m*; (*impudence*) descaro, frescura; **nerves** (*nervousness*) nerviosismo *msg*, nervios *mpl*; **a fit of ~s** un ataque de nervios; **to lose one's ~** (*self-confidence*) perder el valor

nerve centre *n* (*Anat*) centro nervioso; (*fig*) punto neurálgico

nerve-racking ['nə:vrækɪŋ] *adj* angustioso

nervous ['nə:vəs] *adj* (*anxious*) nervioso; (*Anat*) nervioso; (*timid*) tímido, miedoso

nervous breakdown *n* crisis *f* nerviosa

nervous wreck *n* (*inf*): **to be a ~** estar de los nervios

nervy ['nə:vɪ] *adj*: **to be ~** estar nervioso

nest [nɛst] *n* (*of bird*) nido ▷ *vi* anidar

nest egg *n* (*fig*) ahorros *mpl*

nestle ['nɛsl] *vi*: **to ~ down** acurrucarse

Net ['nɛt] *n* (*Comput*) Internet *m or f*

net [nɛt] *n* (*gen*) red *f*; (*fabric*) tul *m* ▷ *adj* (*Comm*) neto, líquido; (*weight, price, salary*) neto ▷ *vt* coger (*Sp*) *or* agarrar (*LAm*) con red; (*money: person*) cobrar; (*: deal, sale*) conseguir; (*Sport*) marcar; **~ of tax** neto; **he earns £10,000 ~ per year** gana 10,000 libras netas por año; **the N~** (*Internet*) la Red

netball ['nɛtbɔ:l] *n* balonred *m*

net curtain *n* visillo

Netherlands ['nɛðələndz] *npl*: **the ~** los Países Bajos

net profit *n* beneficio neto

nett [nɛt] *adj* = **net**

netting ['nɛtɪŋ] *n* red *f*, redes *fpl*

nettle ['nɛtl] *n* ortiga

network ['nɛtwə:k] *n* red *f* ▷ *vt* (*Radio, TV*) difundir por la red de emisores; **local area ~** red local; **there's no ~ coverage here** (*Tel*) aquí no hay cobertura

neurological [njuərə'lɔdʒɪkl] *adj* neurológico

neurosis (*pl* **neuroses**) [njuə'rəusɪs, -si:z] *n* neurosis *f inv*

neurotic [njuə'rɔtɪk] *adj, n* neurótico(-a) *m(f)*

neuter ['nju:tə^r] *adj* (*Ling*) neutro ▷ *vt* castrar, capar

neutral ['nju:trəl] *adj* (*person*) neutral; (*colour etc*) neutro; (*Elec*) neutro ▷ *n* (*Aut*) punto muerto

neutralize ['nju:trəlaɪz] *vt* neutralizar

neutron ['nju:trɔn] *n* neutrón *m*

never ['nɛvə^r] *adv* nunca, jamás; **I ~ went** no fui nunca; **~ in my life** jamás en la vida; *see also* **mind**

never-ending [nɛvər'ɛndɪŋ] *adj* interminable, sin fin

nevertheless [nɛvəðə'lɛs] *adv* sin embargo, no obstante

new [nju:] *adj* nuevo; (*recent*) reciente; **as good as ~** como nuevo

New Age *n* Nueva era

newborn ['nju:bɔ:n] *adj* recién nacido

newcomer ['nju:kʌmə^r] *n* recién venido *or* llegado

new-fangled ['nju:fæŋgld] *adj* (*pej*) modernísimo

new-found ['nju:faund] *adj* (*friend*) nuevo; (*enthusiasm*) recién adquirido

newly ['nju:lɪ] *adv* recién

newly-weds ['nju:lɪwɛdz] *npl* recién casados

new moon *n* luna nueva

news [nju:z] *n* noticias *fpl*; **a piece of ~** una noticia; **the ~** (*Radio, TV*) las noticias *fpl*, el telediario; **good/bad ~** buenas/malas noticias *fpl*; **financial ~** noticias *fpl* financieras

news agency *n* agencia de noticias

newsagent ['nju:zeɪdʒənt] *n* (*Brit*) vendedor(a) *m(f)* de periódicos

newscaster ['nju:zkɑ:stə^r] *n* presentador(a) *m(f)*, locutor(a) *m(f)*

news dealer *n* (*US*) = **newsagent**

news flash *n* noticia de última hora

newsletter ['nju:zlɛtə^r] *n* hoja informativa, boletín *m*

newspaper ['nju:zpeɪpə^r] *n* periódico, diario; **daily ~** diario; **weekly ~** periódico semanal

newsprint ['nju:zprɪnt] *n* papel *m* de periódico

newsreader ['nju:zri:də^r] *n* = **newscaster**

newsreel ['nju:zri:l] *n* noticiario

newsroom ['nju:zru:m] *n* (*Press, Radio, TV*) sala de redacción

news stand *n* quiosco *or* puesto de periódicos

newsworthy ['nju:zwə:ðɪ] *adj*: **to be ~** ser de interés periodístico

newt [nju:t] *n* tritón *m*

new town *n* (*Brit*) ciudad *f* nueva (*construida con subsidios estatales*)

New Year *n* Año Nuevo; **Happy ~!** ¡Feliz Año Nuevo!; **to wish sb a happy ~** desear a algn un feliz año nuevo

New Year's Day *n* Día *m* de Año Nuevo

New Year's Eve *n* Nochevieja

New York [-'jɔ:k] *n* Nueva York

New Zealand [-'zi:lənd] *n* Nueva Zelanda (*Sp*), Nueva Zelandia (*LAm*) ▷ *adj* neozelandés(-esa)

New Zealander [-'zi:ləndə^r] *n* neozelandés(-esa) *m(f)*

next [nɛkst] *adj* (*house, room*) vecino, de al lado; (*meeting*) próximo; (*page*) siguiente ▷ *adv* después; **the ~ day** el día siguiente; **~ time** la próxima vez; **~ year** el año próximo *or* que viene; **~ month** el mes que viene *or* entrante; **the week after ~** no la semana que viene sino la otra; **"turn to the ~ page"** "vuelva a la página siguiente"; **you're ~** le toca; **~ to** *prep* junto a, al lado de; **~ to nothing** casi nada

next door *adv* en la casa de al lado ▷ *adj* vecino, de al lado

next-of-kin ['nɛkstəv'kɪn] *n* pariente(s) *m(pl)* más cercano(s)

NHS *n abbr* (*Brit*) = **National Health Service**

NI *abbr* = **Northern Ireland**; (*Brit*) = **National Insurance**
nib [nɪb] *n* plumilla
nibble [ˈnɪbl] *vt* mordisquear
Nicaragua [nɪkəˈrægjuə] *n* Nicaragua
Nicaraguan [nɪkəˈrægjuən] *adj, n* nicaragüense *m/f*, nicaragüeño(-a) *m(f)*
nice [naɪs] *adj* (*likeable*) simpático, majo; (*kind*) amable; (*pleasant*) agradable; (*attractive*) bonito, mono; (*distinction*) fino; (*taste, smell, meal*) rico
nicely [ˈnaɪslɪ] *adv* amablemente; (*of health etc*) bien; **that will do ~** perfecto
niceties [ˈnaɪsɪtɪz] *npl* detalles *mpl*
niche [niːʃ] *n* (*Arch*) nicho, hornacina
nick [nɪk] *n* (*wound*) rasguño; (*cut, indentation*) mella, muesca ▷ *vt* (*cut*) cortar; (*inf*) birlar, mangar; (*: arrest*) pillar; **in the ~ of time** justo a tiempo; **in good ~** en buen estado; **to ~ o.s.** cortarse
nickel [ˈnɪkl] *n* níquel *m*; (*US*) *moneda de 5 centavos*
nickname [ˈnɪkneɪm] *n* apodo, mote *m* ▷ *vt* apodar
nicotine [ˈnɪkətiːn] *n* nicotina
nicotine patch *n* parche *m* de nicotina
niece [niːs] *n* sobrina
Nigeria [naɪˈdʒɪərɪə] *n* Nigeria
Nigerian [naɪˈdʒɪərɪən] *adj, n* nigeriano(-a) *m(f)*
niggling [ˈnɪglɪŋ] *adj* (*detail: trifling*) nimio, insignificante; (*annoying*) molesto; (*doubt, pain*) constante
night [naɪt] *n* (*gen*) noche *f*; (*evening*) tarde *f*; **last ~** anoche; **the ~ before last** anteanoche, antes de ayer por la noche; **at ~, by ~** de noche, por la noche; **in the ~, during the ~** durante la noche, por la noche
nightcap [ˈnaɪtkæp] *n* (*drink*) *bebida que se toma antes de acostarse*
night club *n* club nocturno, discoteca
nightdress [ˈnaɪtdrɛs] *n* (*Brit*) camisón *m*
nightfall [ˈnaɪtfɔːl] *n* anochecer *m*
nightgown [ˈnaɪtgaun], **nightie** [ˈnaɪtɪ] (*Brit*) *n* = **nightdress**
nightingale [ˈnaɪtɪŋgeɪl] *n* ruiseñor *m*
night life *n* vida nocturna
nightly [ˈnaɪtlɪ] *adj* de todas las noches ▷ *adv* todas las noches, cada noche
nightmare [ˈnaɪtmɛəʳ] *n* pesadilla
night porter *n* guardián *m* nocturno
night school *n* clase(s) *f(pl)* nocturna(s)
night shift *n* turno nocturno *or* de noche
night-time [ˈnaɪttaɪm] *n* noche *f*
night watchman *n* vigilante *m* nocturno, sereno
nil [nɪl] *n* (*Brit Sport*) cero, nada
Nile [naɪl] *n*: **the ~** el Nilo
nimble [ˈnɪmbl] *adj* (*agile*) ágil, ligero; (*skilful*) diestro
nine [naɪn] *num* nueve
nineteen [ˈnaɪnˈtiːn] *num* diecinueve
nineteenth [naɪnˈtiːnθ] *adj* decimonoveno, decimonono
ninetieth [ˈnaɪntɪɪθ] *adj* nonagésimo
ninety [ˈnaɪntɪ] *num* noventa
ninth [naɪnθ] *adj* noveno
nip [nɪp] *vt* (*pinch*) pellizcar; (*bite*) morder ▷ *vi* (*Brit inf*): **to ~ out/down/up** salir/bajar/subir un momento ▷ *n* (*drink*) trago
nipple [ˈnɪpl] *n* (*Anat*) pezón *m*; (*of bottle*) tetilla; (*Tech*) boquilla, manguito
nippy [ˈnɪpɪ] *adj* (*Brit: person*) rápido; (*taste*) picante; **it's a very ~ car** es un coche muy potente para el tamaño que tiene
nit [nɪt] *n* (*of louse*) liendre *f*; (*inf: idiot*) imbécil *m/f*
nitrogen [ˈnaɪtrədʒən] *n* nitrógeno
NM, N. Mex. *abbr* (*US*) = **New Mexico**

KEYWORD

no [nəu] (*pl* **noes**) *adv* (*opposite of "yes"*) no; **are you coming? — no (I'm not)** ¿vienes? — no; **would you like some more? — no thank you** ¿quieres más? — no gracias
▷ *adj* **1** (*not any*): **I have no money/time/books** no tengo dinero/tiempo/libros; **no other man would have done it** ningún otro lo hubiera hecho;
2: **"no entry"** "prohibido el paso"; **"no smoking"** "prohibido fumar"
▷ *n* no *m*

no. *abbr* (= *number*) nº, núm
Nobel prize [nəuˈbɛl-] *n* premio Nobel
nobility [nəuˈbɪlɪtɪ] *n* nobleza
noble [ˈnəubl] *adj* (*person*) noble; (*title*) de nobleza
nobody [ˈnəubədɪ] *pron* nadie
no-claims bonus [ˈnəukleɪmz-] *n* bonificación *f* por carencia de reclamaciones
nod [nɔd] *vi* saludar con la cabeza; (*in agreement*) asentir con la cabeza ▷ *vt*: **to ~ one's head** inclinar la cabeza ▷ *n* inclinación *f* de cabeza; **they ~ded their agreement** asintieron con la cabeza; **nod off** *vi* cabecear
no-fly zone [nəuˈflaɪ-] *n* zona de exclusión aérea
noise [nɔɪz] *n* ruido; (*din*) escándalo, estrépito
noisy [ˈnɔɪzɪ] *adj* (*gen*) ruidoso; (*child*) escandaloso
nominal [ˈnɔmɪnl] *adj* nominal
nominate [ˈnɔmɪneɪt] *vt* (*propose*) proponer; (*appoint*) nombrar
nomination [nɔmɪˈneɪʃən] *n* propuesta; nombramiento
nominee [nɔmɪˈniː] *n* candidato(-a)
nonalcoholic [nɔnælkəˈhɔlɪk] *adj* sin alcohol
noncommittal [ˈnɔnkəˈmɪtl] *adj* (*reserved*) reservado; (*uncommitted*) evasivo

nondescript ['nɔndɪskrɪpt] *adj* anodino, soso
none [nʌn] *pron* ninguno(-a) ▷ *adv* de ninguna manera; ~ **of you** ninguno de vosotros; **I've ~ left** no me queda ninguno(-a); **he's ~ the worse for it** no le ha perjudicado; **I have ~** no tengo ninguno; ~ **at all** (*not one*) ni uno
nonentity [nɔ'nɛntɪtɪ] *n* cero a la izquierda, nulidad *f*
nonetheless [nʌnðə'lɛs] *adv* sin embargo, no obstante, aún así
non-event [nɔnɪ'vɛnt] *n* acontecimiento sin importancia; **it was a ~** no pasó absolutamente nada
nonexistent [nɔnɪg'zɪstənt] *adj* inexistente
non-fiction [nɔn'fɪkʃən] *n* no ficción *f*
no-no ['nəunəu] *n* (*inf*): **it's a ~** de eso ni hablar
no-nonsense [nəu'nɔnsəns] *adj* sensato
nonplussed [nɔn'plʌst] *adj* perplejo
nonsense ['nɔnsəns] *n* tonterías *fpl*, disparates *fpl*; **~!** ¡qué tonterías!; **it is ~ to say that ...** es absurdo decir que ...
nonsensical [nɔn'sɛnsɪkl] *adj* disparatado, absurdo
non-smoker ['nɔn'sməukə^r] *n* no fumador(a) *m(f)*
non-smoking ['nɔn'sməukɪŋ] *adj* (de) no fumador
nonstarter [nɔn'stɑːtə^r] *n*: **it's a ~** no tiene futuro
non-stick ['nɔn'stɪk] *adj* (*pan, surface*) antiadherente
nonstop ['nɔn'stɔp] *adj* continuo; (*Rail*) directo ▷ *adv* sin parar
noodles ['nuːdlz] *npl* tallarines *mpl*
nook [nuk] *n* rincón *m*; **~s and crannies** escondrijos *mpl*
noon [nuːn] *n* mediodía *m*
no-one ['nəuwʌn] *pron* = **nobody**
noose [nuːs] *n* lazo corredizo
nor [nɔː^r] *conj* = **neither** ▷ *adv see* **neither**
norm [nɔːm] *n* norma
normal ['nɔːml] *adj* normal; **to return to ~** volver a la normalidad
normality [nɔː'mælɪtɪ] *n* normalidad *f*
normally ['nɔːməlɪ] *adv* normalmente
Normandy ['nɔːməndɪ] *n* Normandía
north [nɔːθ] *n* norte *m* ▷ *adj* (del) norte ▷ *adv* al *or* hacia el norte
North Africa *n* África del Norte
North America *n* América del Norte
North American *adj, n* norteamericano(-a) *m(f)*
northbound ['nɔːθbaund] *adj* (*traffic*) que se dirige al norte; (*carriageway*) de dirección norte
north-east [nɔːθ'iːst] *n* nor(d)este *m*
northeastern [nɔːθ'iːstən] *adj* nor(d)este, del nor(d)este
northerly ['nɔːðəlɪ] *adj* (*point, direction*) hacia el norte, septentrional; (*wind*) del norte
northern ['nɔːðən] *adj* norteño, del norte
Northern Ireland *n* Irlanda del Norte
North Korea *n* Corea del Norte
North Pole *n*: **the ~** el Polo Norte
North Sea *n*: **the ~** el Mar del Norte
North Sea oil *n* petróleo del Mar del Norte
north-west [nɔːθ'wɛst] *n* noroeste *m*
northwestern ['nɔːθ'wɛstən] *adj* noroeste, del noroeste
Norway ['nɔːweɪ] *n* Noruega
Norwegian [nɔː'wiːdʒən] *adj* noruego(-a) ▷ *n* noruego(-a); (*Ling*) noruego
nos. *abbr* (= *numbers*) núms.
nose [nəuz] *n* (*Anat*) nariz *f*; (*Zool*) hocico; (*sense of smell*) olfato ▷ *vi* (*also*: **~ one's way**) avanzar con cautela; **to pay through the ~ (for sth)** (*inf*) pagar un dineral (por algo);
nose about, nose around *vi* curiosear
nosebleed ['nəuzbliːd] *n* hemorragia nasal
nose-dive ['nəuzdaɪv] *n* picado vertical
nosey ['nəuzɪ] *adj* curioso, fisgón(-ona)
nostalgia [nɔs'tældʒɪə] *n* nostalgia
nostalgic [nɔs'tældʒɪk] *adj* nostálgico
nostril ['nɔstrɪl] *n* ventana *or* orificio de la nariz
nosy ['nəuzɪ] *adj* = **nosey**
not [nɔt] *adv* no; **~ at all** no ... en absoluto; **~ that ...** no es que ...; **it's too late, isn't it?** es demasiado tarde, ¿verdad?; **~ yet** todavía no; **~ now** ahora no; **why ~?** ¿por qué no?; **I hope ~** espero que no; **~ at all** no ... nada; (*after thanks*) de nada
notable ['nəutəbl] *adj* notable
notably ['nəutəblɪ] *adv* especialmente; (*in particular*) sobre todo
notary ['nəutərɪ] *n* (*also*: **~ public**) notario(-a)
notation [nəu'teɪʃən] *n* notación *f*
notch [nɔtʃ] *n* muesca, corte *m*; **notch up** *vt* (*score, victory*) apuntarse
note [nəut] *n* (*Mus*: *record, letter*) nota; (*banknote*) billete *m*; (*tone*) tono ▷ *vt* (*observe*) notar, observar; (*write down*) apuntar, anotar; **delivery ~** nota de entrega; **to compare ~s** (*fig*) cambiar impresiones; **of ~** conocido, destacado; **to take ~** prestar atención a; **just a quick ~ to let you know that ...** sólo unas líneas para informarte que ...
notebook ['nəutbuk] *n* libreta, cuaderno; (*for shorthand*) libreta
noted ['nəutɪd] *adj* célebre, conocido
notepad ['nəutpæd] *n* bloc *m*
notepaper ['nəutpeɪpə] *n* papel *m* para cartas
noteworthy ['nəutwəːðɪ] *adj* notable, digno de atención
nothing ['nʌθɪŋ] *n* nada; (*zero*) cero; **he does ~** no hace nada; **~ new** nada nuevo; **~ much** no mucho; **for ~** (*free*) gratis; (*in vain*) en balde; **~ at all** nada en absoluto
notice ['nəutɪs] *n* (*announcement*) anuncio; (*warning*) aviso; (*dismissal*) despido; (*resignation*) dimisión *f*; (*review*: *of play etc*)

reseña ▷ *vt* (*observe*) notar, observar; **to bring sth to sb's ~** (*attention*) llamar la atención de algn sobre algo; **to take ~ of** hacer caso de, prestar atención a; **at short ~** con poca antelación; **without ~** sin previo aviso; **advance ~** previo aviso; **until further ~** hasta nuevo aviso; **to give sb ~ of sth** avisar a algn de algo; **to give ~, hand in one's ~** dimitir, renunciar; **it has come to my ~ that ...** he llegado a saber que ...; **to escape** *or* **avoid ~** pasar inadvertido

noticeable ['nəutɪsəbl] *adj* evidente, obvio

notice board *n* (*Brit*) tablón *m* de anuncios

notification [nəutɪfɪ'keɪʃən] *n* aviso; (*announcement*) anuncio

notify ['nəutɪfaɪ] *vt*: **to ~ sb (of sth)** comunicar (algo) a algn

notion ['nəuʃən] *n* noción *f*, idea; (*opinion*) opinión *f*

notions ['nəuʃənz] *npl* (*US*) mercería

notoriety [nəutə'raɪətɪ] *n* notoriedad *f*, mala fama

notorious [nəu'tɔːrɪəs] *adj* notorio, tristemente célebre

notwithstanding [nɔtwɪθ'stændɪŋ] *adv* no obstante, sin embargo; **~ this** a pesar de esto

nougat ['nuːgɑː] *n* turrón *m*

nought [nɔːt] *n* cero

noun [naun] *n* nombre *m*, sustantivo

nourish ['nʌrɪʃ] *vt* nutrir; (*fig*) alimentar

nourishing ['nʌrɪʃɪŋ] *adj* nutritivo, rico

nourishment ['nʌrɪʃmənt] *n* alimento, sustento

Nov. *abbr* (= *November*) nov

novel ['nɔvl] *n* novela ▷ *adj* (*new*) nuevo, original; (*unexpected*) insólito

novelist ['nɔvəlɪst] *n* novelista *m/f*

novelty ['nɔvəltɪ] *n* novedad *f*

November [nəu'vɛmbə^r] *n* noviembre *m*; *see also* **July**

novice ['nɔvɪs] *n* principiante *m/f*, novato(-a); (*Rel*) novicio(-a)

now [nau] *adv* (*at the present time*) ahora; (*these days*) actualmente, hoy día ▷ *conj*: **~ (that)** ya que, ahora que; **right ~** ahora mismo; **by ~** ya; **I'll do it just ~** ahora mismo lo hago; **~ and then, ~ and again** de vez en cuando; **from ~ on** de ahora en adelante; **between ~ and Monday** entre hoy y el lunes; **in 3 days from ~** de hoy en 3 días; **that's all for ~** eso es todo por ahora

nowadays ['nauədeɪz] *adv* hoy (en) día, actualmente

nowhere ['nəuwɛə^r] *adv* (*direction*) a ninguna parte; (*location*) en ninguna parte; **~ else** en *or* a ninguna otra parte

no-win situation [nəu'wɪn-] *n*: **I'm in a ~** haga lo que haga, llevo las de perder

nozzle ['nɔzl] *n* boquilla

NP *n abbr* = **notary public**

nr *abbr* (*Brit*) = **near**

nth [ɛnθ] *adj*: **for the ~ time** (*inf*) por enésima vez

nuclear ['njuːklɪə^r] *adj* nuclear

nuclear family *n* familia nuclear

nuclear-free zone ['njuːklɪə'friː-] *n* zona desnuclearizada

nucleus (*pl* **nuclei**) ['njuːklɪəs, 'njuːklɪaɪ] *n* núcleo

nude [njuːd] *adj, n* desnudo(-a) *m(f)*; **in the ~** desnudo

nudge [nʌdʒ] *vt* dar un codazo a

nudist ['njuːdɪst] *n* nudista *m/f*

nudity ['njuːdɪtɪ] *n* desnudez *f*

nuisance ['njuːsns] *n* molestia, fastidio; (*person*) pesado, latoso; **what a ~!** ¡qué lata!

null [nʌl] *adj*: **~ and void** nulo y sin efecto

numb [nʌm] *adj* entumecido; (*fig*) insensible ▷ *vt* quitar la sensación a, entumecer, entorpecer; **to be ~ with cold** estar entumecido de frío; **~ with fear/grief** paralizado de miedo/dolor

number ['nʌmbə^r] *n* número; (*numeral*) número, cifra; (*quantity*) cantidad *f* ▷ *vt* (*pages etc*) numerar, poner número a; (*amount to*) sumar, ascender a; **reference ~** número de referencia; **telephone ~** número de teléfono; **wrong ~** (*Tel*) número equivocado; **opposite ~** (*person*) homólogo(-a); **to be ~ed among** figurar entre; **a ~ of** varios, algunos; **they were ten in ~** eran diez

number plate *n* (*Brit*) matrícula, placa

Number Ten *n* (*Brit*: *10 Downing Street*) *residencia del primer ministro*

numbskull ['nʌmskʌl] *n* (*inf*) papanatas *m/f inv*

numeral ['njuːmərəl] *n* número, cifra

numerate ['njuːmərɪt] *adj* competente en aritmética

numerical [njuː'mɛrɪkl] *adj* numérico

numerous ['njuːmərəs] *adj* numeroso, muchos

nun [nʌn] *n* monja, religiosa

nunnery ['nʌnərɪ] *n* convento de monjas

nurse [nəːs] *n* enfermero(-a); (*nanny*) niñera ▷ *vt* (*patient*) cuidar, atender; (*baby*: *Brit*) mecer; (: *US*) criar, amamantar; **male ~** enfermero

nursery ['nəːsərɪ] *n* (*institution*) guardería infantil; (*room*) cuarto de los niños; (*for plants*) criadero, semillero

nursery rhyme *n* canción *f* infantil

nursery school *n* escuela infantil

nursery slope *n* (*Brit Ski*) cuesta para principiantes

nursing ['nəːsɪŋ] *n* (*profession*) profesión *f* de enfermera; (*care*) asistencia, cuidado ▷ *adj* (*mother*) lactante

nursing home *n* clínica de reposo

nurture ['nəːtʃə^r] *vt* (*child, plant*) alimentar, nutrir

nut [nʌt] *n* (*Tech*) tuerca; (*Bot*) nuez *f* ▷ *adj* (*chocolate etc*) con nueces; **~s** (*Culin*) frutos secos

nutcrackers ['nʌtkrækəz] *npl* cascanueces *m inv*
nutmeg ['nʌtmɛg] *n* nuez *f* moscada
nutrient ['nju:triənt] *adj* nutritivo ▷ *n* elemento nutritivo
nutrition [nju:'trɪʃən] *n* nutrición *f*, alimentación *f*
nutritionist [nju:'trɪʃənɪst] *n* dietista *m/f*
nutritious [nju:'trɪʃəs] *adj* nutritivo
nuts [nʌts] *adj* (*inf*) chiflado
nutshell ['nʌtʃɛl] *n* cáscara de nuez; **in a ~** en resumidas cuentas
nutty ['nʌtɪ] *adj* (*flavour*) a frutos secos; (*inf: foolish*) chalado
NVQ *n abbr* (*Brit: = national vocational qualification*) *título de formación profesional*
NY *abbr* (*US*) = **New York**
nylon ['naɪlɔn] *n* nylon *m*, nilón *m* ▷ *adj* de nylon *or* nilón

O

O, o [əu] *n* (*letter*) O, o *f*; **O for Oliver**, (*US*) **O for Oboe** O de Oviedo
oak [əuk] *n* roble *m* ▷ *adj* de roble
OAP *n abbr* (*Brit*) = **old-age pensioner**
oar [ɔ:ʳ] *n* remo; **to put** *or* **shove one's ~ in** (*fig, inf*) entrometerse
oasis (*pl* **oases**) [əu'eɪsɪs, əu'eɪsi:z] *n* oasis *m inv*
oath [əuθ] *n* juramento; (*swear word*) palabrota; **on** (*Brit*) *or* **under ~** bajo juramento
oatmeal ['əutmi:l] *n* harina de avena
oats [əuts] *npl* avena
OBE *n abbr* (*Brit: = Order of the British Empire*) *título ceremonial*
obedience [ə'bi:dɪəns] *n* obediencia; **in ~ to** de acuerdo con
obedient [ə'bi:dɪənt] *adj* obediente
obese [əu'bi:s] *adj* obeso
obesity [əu'bi:sɪtɪ] *n* obesidad *f*
obey [ə'beɪ] *vt* obedecer; (*instructions*) cumplir
obituary [ə'bɪtjuərɪ] *n* necrología
object ['ɔbdʒɪkt] *n* (*gen*) objeto; (*purpose*) objeto, propósito; (*Ling*) objeto, complemento ▷ *vi* [əb'dʒɛkt]: **to ~ to** (*attitude*) estar en contra de; (*proposal*) oponerse a; **to ~ that** objetar que; **expense is no ~** no importa lo que cueste; **I ~!** ¡protesto!; **to ~ that** objetar que
objection [əb'dʒɛkʃən] *n* objeción *f*; **I have no ~ to …** no tengo inconveniente en que …

O

objectionable [əb'dʒɛkʃənəbl] *adj* (*gen*) desagradable; (*conduct*) censurable
objective [əb'dʒɛktɪv] *adj, n* objetivo
obligation [ɔblɪ'geɪʃən] *n* obligación *f*; (*debt*) deber *m*; **"without ~"** "sin compromiso"; **to be under an ~ to sb/to do sth** estar comprometido con algn/ a hacer algo
obligatory [ə'blɪgətərɪ] *adj* obligatorio
oblige [ə'blaɪdʒ] *vt* (*do a favour for*) complacer, hacer un favor a; **to ~ sb to do sth** obligar a algn a hacer algo; **to be ~d to sb for sth** estarle agradecido a algn por algo; **anything to ~!** todo sea por complacerte
obliging [ə'blaɪdʒɪŋ] *adj* servicial, atento
oblique [ə'bli:k] *adj* oblicuo; (*allusion*) indirecto ▷ *n* (*Typ*) barra
obliterate [ə'blɪtəreɪt] *vt* arrasar; (*memory*) borrar
oblivion [ə'blɪvɪən] *n* olvido
oblivious [ə'blɪvɪəs] *adj*: **~ of** inconsciente de
oblong ['ɔblɔŋ] *adj* rectangular ▷ *n* rectángulo
obnoxious [əb'nɔkʃəs] *adj* odioso, detestable; (*smell*) nauseabundo
oboe ['əubəu] *n* oboe *m*
obscene [əb'si:n] *adj* obsceno
obscenity [əb'sɛnɪtɪ] *n* obscenidad *f*
obscure [əb'skjuə[r]] *adj* oscuro ▷ *vt* oscurecer; (*hide: sun*) ocultar
obscurity [əb'skjuərɪtɪ] *n* oscuridad *f*; (*obscure point*) punto oscuro; **to rise from ~** salir de la nada
observant [əb'zə:vnt] *adj* observador(a)
observation [ɔbzə'veɪʃən] *n* (*Med*) observación *f*; (*by police etc*) vigilancia
observatory [əb'zə:vətrɪ] *n* observatorio
observe [əb'zə:v] *vt* (*gen*) observar; (*rule*) cumplir
observer [əb'zə:və[r]] *n* observador(a) *m(f)*
obsess [əb'sɛs] *vt* obsesionar; **to be ~ed by** *or* **with sb/sth** estar obsesionado con algn/ algo
obsession [əb'sɛʃən] *n* obsesión *f*
obsessive [əb'sɛsɪv] *adj* obsesivo
obsolescence [ɔbsə'lɛsns] *n* obsolescencia
obsolete ['ɔbsəli:t] *adj* obsoleto
obstacle ['ɔbstəkl] *n* obstáculo; (*nuisance*) estorbo
obstacle race *n* carrera de obstáculos
obstetrician [ɔbstə'trɪʃən] *n* obstetra *m/f*
obstinate ['ɔbstɪnɪt] *adj* terco, obstinado; (*determined*) tenaz
obstruct [əb'strʌkt] *vt* (*block*) obstruir; (*hinder*) estorbar, obstaculizar
obstruction [əb'strʌkʃən] *n* obstrucción *f*; (*object*) estorbo, obstáculo
obtain [əb'teɪn] *vt* (*get*) obtener; (*achieve*) conseguir; **to ~ sth (for o.s.)** conseguir *or* adquirir algo
obtainable [əb'teɪnəbl] *adj* asequible
obtuse [əb'tju:s] *adj* obtuso
obvious ['ɔbvɪəs] *adj* (*clear*) obvio, evidente; (*unsubtle*) poco sutil; **it's ~ that ...** está claro que ..., es evidente que ...
obviously ['ɔbvɪəslɪ] *adv* obviamente, evidentemente; **~ not!** ¡por supuesto que no!; **he was ~ not drunk** era evidente que no estaba borracho; **he was not ~ drunk** no se le notaba que estaba borracho
occasion [ə'keɪʒən] *n* oportunidad *f*, ocasión *f*; (*event*) acontecimiento ▷ *vt* ocasionar, causar; **on that ~** esa vez, en aquella ocasión; **to rise to the ~** ponerse a la altura de las circunstancias
occasional [ə'keɪʒənl] *adj* poco frecuente, ocasional
occasionally [ə'keɪʒənlɪ] *adv* de vez en cuando; **very ~** muy de tarde en tarde, en muy contadas ocasiones
occult [ɔ'kʌlt] *adj* (*gen*) oculto
occupant ['ɔkjupənt] *n* (*of house*) inquilino(-a); (*of boat, car*) ocupante *m/f*
occupation [ɔkju'peɪʃən] *n* (*of house*) tenencia; (*job*) trabajo; (*pastime*) ocupaciones *fpl*; (*calling*) oficio
occupational hazard *n* gajes *mpl* del oficio
occupier ['ɔkjupaɪə[r]] *n* inquilino(-a)
occupy ['ɔkjupaɪ] *vt* (*seat, post, time*) ocupar; (*house*) habitar; **to ~ o.s. with** *or* **by doing** (*as job*) dedicarse a hacer; (*to pass time*) entretenerse haciendo; **to be occupied with sth/in doing sth** estar ocupado con algo/haciendo algo
occur [ə'kə:[r]] *vi* ocurrir, suceder; **to ~ to sb** ocurrírsele a algn
occurrence [ə'kʌrəns] *n* suceso
ocean ['əuʃən] *n* océano; **~s of** (*inf*) la mar de
ocean-going ['əuʃəngəuɪŋ] *adj* de alta mar
o'clock [ə'klɔk] *adv*: **it is five ~** son las cinco
OCR *n abbr* = **optical character recognition/ reader**
Oct. *abbr* (= *October*) oct
octane ['ɔkteɪn] *n* octano; **high ~ petrol** *or* (*US*) **gas** gasolina de alto octanaje
octave ['ɔktɪv] *n* octava
October [ɔk'təubə[r]] *n* octubre *m*; *see also* **July**
octopus ['ɔktəpəs] *n* pulpo
odd [ɔd] *adj* (*strange*) extraño, raro; (*number*) impar; (*sock, shoe etc*) suelto; **60-~** 60 y pico; **at ~ times** de vez en cuando; **to be the ~ one out** estar de más; **if you have the ~ minute** si tienes unos minutos libres; *see also* **odds**
oddity ['ɔdɪtɪ] *n* rareza; (*person*) excéntrico(-a)
odd-job man [ɔd'dʒɔb-] *n* hombre *m* que hace chapuzas
odd jobs *npl* chapuzas *fpl*
oddly ['ɔdlɪ] *adv* extrañamente
oddments ['ɔdmənts] *npl* (*Brit Comm*) restos *mpl*
odds [ɔdz] *npl* (*in betting*) puntos *mpl* de ventaja; **it makes no ~** da lo mismo; **at ~** reñidos(-as); **to succeed against all the ~**

tener éxito contra todo pronóstico; **~ and ends** cachivaches *mpl*
odds-on [ɔdz'ɔn] *adj* (*inf*): **the ~ favourite** el máximo favorito; **it's ~ he'll come** seguro que viene
odometer [ɔ'dɔmɪtəʳ] *n* (*US*) cuentakilómetros *m inv*
odour, odor (*US*) ['əudəʳ] *n* olor *m*; (*unpleasant*) hedor *m*; (*perfume*) perfume *m*
oesophagus, esophagus (*US*) [iː'sɔfəgəs] *n* esófago
oestrogen, estrogen (*US*) ['iːstrədʒən] *n* estrógeno

KEYWORD

of [ɔv, əv] *prep* **1** (*gen*) de; **a friend of ours** un amigo nuestro; **a boy of 10** un chico de 10 años; **that was kind of you** eso fue muy amable de tu parte
2 (*expressing quantity, amount, dates etc*) de; **a kilo of flour** un kilo de harina; **there were three of them** había tres; **three of us went** tres de nosotros fuimos; **the 5th of July** el 5 de julio; **a quarter of four** (*US*) las cuarto menos cuarto
3 (*from, out of*) de; **made of wood** (hecho) de madera

off [ɔf] *adj, adv* (*engine, light*) apagado; (*tap*) cerrado; (*Brit*: *food*: *bad*) pasado, malo; (: *milk*) cortado; (*cancelled*) suspendido; (*removed*): **the lid was ~** no estaba puesta la tapadera ▷ *prep* de; **to be ~** (*leave*) irse, marcharse; **to be ~ sick** estar enfermo *or* de baja; **a day ~** un día libre; **to have an ~ day** tener un mal día; **he had his coat ~** se había quitado el abrigo; **10% ~** (*Comm*) (con el) 10% de descuento; **it's a long way ~** está muy lejos; **5 km ~ (the road)** a 5 km (de la carretera); **~ the coast** frente a la costa; **I'm ~ meat** (*no longer eat/like it*) paso de la carne; **on the ~ chance** por si acaso; **~ and on, on and ~** de vez en cuando; **I must be ~** tengo que irme; **to be well/badly ~** andar bien/mal de dinero; **I'm afraid the chicken is ~** desgraciadamente ya no queda pollo; **that's a bit ~, isn't it?** (*fig, inf*) ¡eso no se hace!
offal ['ɔfl] *n* (*Brit Culin*) menudillos *mpl*, asaduras *fpl*
off-colour ['ɔf'kʌləʳ] *adj* (*Brit*: *ill*) indispuesto; **to feel ~** sentirse *or* estar mal
offence, offense (*US*) [ə'fɛns] *n* (*crime*) delito; (*insult*) ofensa; **to take ~ at** ofenderse por; **to commit an ~** cometer un delito
offend [ə'fɛnd] *vt* (*person*) ofender ▷ *vi*: **to ~ against** (*law, rule*) infringir
offender [ə'fɛndəʳ] *n* delincuente *m/f*; (*against regulations*) infractor(a) *m(f)*
offense [ə'fɛns] *n* (*US*) = **offence**
offensive [ə'fɛnsɪv] *adj* ofensivo; (*smell etc*) repugnante ▷ *n* (*Mil*) ofensiva
offer ['ɔfəʳ] *n* (*gen*) oferta, ofrecimiento; (*proposal*) propuesta ▷ *vt* ofrecer; **"on ~"** (*Comm*) "en oferta"; **to make an ~ for sth** hacer una oferta por algo; **to ~ sth to sb, ~ sb sth** ofrecer algo a algn; **to ~ to do sth** ofrecerse a hacer algo
offering ['ɔfərɪŋ] *n* (*Rel*) ofrenda
offertory ['ɔfətrɪ] *n* (*Rel*) ofertorio
offhand [ɔf'hænd] *adj* informal; (*brusque*) desconsiderado ▷ *adv* de improviso, sin pensarlo; **I can't tell you ~** no te lo puedo decir así de improviso *or* (*LAm*) así nomás
office ['ɔfɪs] *n* (*place*) oficina; (*room*) despacho; (*position*) cargo, oficio; **doctor's ~** (*US*) consultorio; **to take ~** entrar en funciones; **through his good ~s** gracias a sus buenos oficios; **O~ of Fair Trading** (*Brit*) *oficina que regula normas comerciales*
office automation *n* ofimática, buromática
office block, office building (*US*) *n* bloque *m* de oficinas
office hours *npl* horas *fpl* de oficina; (*US Med*) horas *fpl* de consulta
officer ['ɔfɪsəʳ] *n* (*Mil etc*) oficial *m/f*, (*of organization*) director(a) *m(f)*; (*also*: **police ~**) agente *m/f* de policía
office work *n* trabajo de oficina
office worker *n* oficinista *m/f*
official [ə'fɪʃl] *adj* (*authorized*) oficial, autorizado; (*strike*) oficial ▷ *n* funcionario(-a)
officialdom [ə'fɪʃldəm] *n* burocracia
officiate [ə'fɪʃɪeɪt] *vi* (*Rel*) oficiar; **to ~ as Mayor** ejercer las funciones de alcalde; **to ~ at a marriage** celebrar una boda
officious [ə'fɪʃəs] *adj* oficioso
offing ['ɔfɪŋ] *n*: **in the ~** (*fig*) en perspectiva
off-licence ['ɔflaɪsns] *n* (*Brit*: *shop*) *tienda de bebidas alcohólicas*; *ver nota*

OFF-LICENCE

En el Reino Unido una *off-licence* es una tienda especializada en la venta de bebidas alcohólicas para el consumo fuera del establecimiento. De ahí su nombre, pues se necesita un permiso especial para tal venta, que está estrictamente regulada. Suelen vender además bebidas sin alcohol, tabaco, chocolate, patatas fritas etc y a menudo son parte de grandes cadenas nacionales.

off-load ['ɔfləud] *vt* descargar, desembarcar
off-peak ['ɔf'piːk] *adj* (*holiday*) de temporada baja; (*electricity*) de banda económica; (*ticket*) *billete de precio reducido por viajar fuera de las horas punta*
off-putting ['ɔfputɪŋ] *adj* (*Brit*: *person*) poco amable, difícil; (*behaviour*) chocante; (*remark*) desalentador(a)

O

off-season ['ɔf'si:zn] *adj, adv* fuera de temporada
offset ['ɔfsɛt] *vt* (*irreg: like* **set**) (*counteract*) contrarrestar, compensar ▷ *n* (*also:* **~ printing**) offset *m*
offshoot ['ɔfʃu:t] *n* (*Bot*) vástago; (*fig*) ramificación *f*
offshore [ɔf'ʃɔ:ʳ] *adj* (*breeze, island*) costero; (*fishing*) de bajura; **~ oilfield** campo petrolífero submarino
offside ['ɔf'saɪd] *n* (*Aut: with right-hand drive*) lado derecho; (*: with left-hand drive*) lado izquierdo ▷ *adj* (*Sport*) fuera de juego; (*Aut: in UK*) del lado derecho; (*: in US, Europe etc*) del lado izquierdo
offspring ['ɔfsprɪŋ] *n* descendencia
offstage [ɔf'steɪdʒ] *adv* entre bastidores
off-the-cuff [ɔfðə'kʌf] *adj* espontáneo
off-the-peg [ɔfðə'pɛg], **off-the-rack** (*US*) [ɔfðə'ræk] *adv* confeccionado
off-the-record ['ɔfðə'rɛkɔ:d] *adj* extraoficial, confidencial ▷ *adv* extraoficialmente, confidencialmente
off-white ['ɔfwaɪt] *adj* blanco grisáceo
often ['ɔfn] *adv* a menudo, con frecuencia, seguido (*LAm*); **how ~ do you go?** ¿cada cuánto vas?
ogle ['əugl] *vt* comerse con los ojos a
oh [əu] *excl* ¡ah!
oil [ɔɪl] *n* aceite *m*; (*petroleum*) petróleo ▷ *vt* (*machine*) engrasar; **fried in ~** frito en aceite
oilcan ['ɔɪlkæn] *n* lata de aceite
oilfield ['ɔɪlfi:ld] *n* campo petrolífero
oil filter *n* (*Aut*) filtro de aceite
oil painting *n* pintura al óleo
oil refinery *n* refinería de petróleo
oil rig *n* torre *f* de perforación
oilskins ['ɔɪlskɪnz] *npl* impermeable *msg*, chubasquero *sg*
oil slick *n* marea negra
oil tanker *n* petrolero; (*truck*) camión *m* cisterna
oil well *n* pozo (de petróleo)
oily ['ɔɪlɪ] *adj* aceitoso; (*food*) grasiento
ointment ['ɔɪntmənt] *n* ungüento
O.K., okay ['əu'keɪ] *excl* O.K., ¡está bien!, ¡vale! ▷ *adj* bien ▷ *n*: **to give sth one's ~** dar el visto bueno a *or* aprobar algo ▷ *vt* dar el visto bueno a; **it's ~ with** *or* **by me** estoy de acuerdo, me parece bien; **are you ~ for money?** ¿andas *or* vas bien de dinero?
old [əuld] *adj* viejo; (*former*) antiguo; **how ~ are you?** ¿cuántos años tienes?, ¿qué edad tienes?; **he's 10 years ~** tiene 10 años; **~er brother** hermano mayor; **any ~ thing will do** sirve cualquier cosa
old age *n* vejez *f*
old-age pension ['əuldeɪdʒ-] *n* (*Brit*) jubilación *f*, pensión *f*
old-age pensioner ['əuldeɪdʒ-] *n* (*Brit*) jubilado(-a)
old-fashioned ['əuld'fæʃənd] *adj* anticuado, pasado de moda
old people's home *n* (*esp Brit*) residencia *f* de ancianos
olive ['ɔlɪv] *n* (*fruit*) aceituna; (*tree*) olivo ▷ *adj* (*also:* **~-green**) verde oliva *inv*
olive oil *n* aceite *m* de oliva
Olympic [əu'lɪmpɪk] *adj* olímpico; **the ~ Games, the ~s** *npl* las Olimpíadas
omelette, omelet ['ɔmlɪt] *n* tortilla, tortilla de huevo (*LAm*)
omen ['əumən] *n* presagio
ominous ['ɔmɪnəs] *adj* de mal agüero, amenazador(a)
omission [əu'mɪʃən] *n* omisión *f*; (*error*) descuido
omit [əu'mɪt] *vt* omitir; (*by mistake*) olvidar, descuidar; **to ~ to do sth** olvidarse *or* dejar de hacer algo

KEYWORD

on [ɔn] *prep* **1** (*indicating position*) en; sobre; **on the wall** en la pared; **it's on the table** está sobre *or* en la mesa; **on the left** a la izquierda; **I haven't got any money on me** no llevo dinero encima
2 (*indicating means, method, condition etc*): **on foot** a pie; **on the train/plane** (*go*) en tren/avión; (*be*) en el tren/el avión; **on the radio/television** por *or* en la radio/televisión; **on the telephone** al teléfono; **to be on drugs** drogarse; (*Med*) estar a tratamiento; **to be on holiday/business** estar de vacaciones/en viaje de negocios; **we're on irregular verbs** estamos con los verbos irregulares
3 (*referring to time*): **on Friday** el viernes; **on Fridays** los viernes; **on June 20th** el 20 de junio; **a week on Friday** del viernes en una semana; **on arrival** al llegar; **on seeing this** al ver esto
4 (*about, concerning*) sobre, acerca de; **a book on physics** un libro de *or* sobre física
5 (*at the expense of*): **this round's on me** esta ronda la pago yo, invito yo a esta ronda; (*earning*): **he's on sixteen thousand pounds a year** gana dieciséis mil libras al año
▷ *adv* **1** (*referring to dress*): **to have one's coat on** tener *or* llevar el abrigo puesto; **she put her gloves on** se puso los guantes
2 (*referring to covering*): **"screw the lid on tightly"** "cerrar bien la tapa"
3 (*further, continuously*): **to walk/run** *etc* **on** seguir caminando/corriendo *etc*; **from that day on** desde aquel día; **it was well on in the evening** estaba ya entrada la tarde
4 (*in phrases*): **I'm on to sth** creo haber encontrado algo; **my father's always on at me to get a job** (*inf*) mi padre siempre me está dando la lata para que me ponga a trabajar

▷ *adj* **1** (*functioning, in operation: machine, radio, TV, light*) encendido(-a) (*Sp*), prendido(-a) (*LAm*); (*: tap*) abierto(-a); (*: brakes*) echado(-a), puesto(-a); **is the meeting still on?** (*in progress*) ¿todavía continúa la reunión?; (*not cancelled*) ¿va a haber reunión al fin?; **there's a good film on at the cinema** ponen una buena película en el cine
2: **that's not on!** (*inf: not possible*) ¡eso ni hablar!; (*: not acceptable*) ¡eso no se hace!

once [wʌns] *adv* una vez; (*formerly*) antiguamente ▷ *conj* una vez que; **~ he had left/it was done** una vez que se había marchado/se hizo; **at ~** en seguida, inmediatamente; (*simultaneously*) a la vez; **~ a week** una vez a la semana; **~ more** otra vez; **~ and for all** de una vez por todas; **~ upon a time** érase una vez; **I knew him ~** le conocía hace tiempo
oncoming ['ɔnkʌmɪŋ] *adj* (*traffic*) que viene de frente

KEYWORD

one [wʌn] *num* un/una; **one hundred and fifty** ciento cincuenta; **one by one** uno a uno; **it's one (o'clock)** es la una
▷ *adj* **1** (*sole*) único; **the one book which** el único libro que; **the one man who** el único que
2 (*same*) mismo(-a); **they came in the one car** vinieron en un solo coche
▷ *pron* **1**: **this one** éste/ésta; **that one** ése/ésa; (*more remote*) aquél/aquélla; **I've already got (a red) one** ya tengo uno(-a) (rojo(-a)); **one by one** uno(-a) por uno(-a); **to be one up on sb** llevar ventaja a algn; **to be at one (with sb)** estar completamente de acuerdo (con algn)
2: **one another** (*us*) nos; (*you*) os (*Sp*); (*you: polite: them*) se; **do you two ever see one another?** ¿os veis alguna vez? (*Sp*), ¿se ven alguna vez?; **the two boys didn't dare look at one another** los dos chicos no se atrevieron a mirarse (el uno al otro); **they all kissed one another** se besaron unos a otros
3 *impers*; **one never knows** nunca se sabe; **to cut one's finger** cortarse el dedo; **one needs to eat** hay que comer

one-day excursion ['wʌndeɪ-] *n* (*US*) billete *m* de ida y vuelta en un día
one-man ['wʌn'mæn] *adj* (*business*) individual
one-man band *n* hombre-orquesta *m*
one-off [wʌn'ɔf] *n* (*Brit inf: object*) artículo único; (*: event*) caso especial
one-parent family ['wʌnpɛərənt-] *n* familia monoparental
oneself [wʌn'sɛlf] *pron* (*reflexive*) se; (*after prep*) sí; (*emphatic*) uno(-a) mismo(-a); **to hurt ~** hacerse daño; **to keep sth for ~** guardarse algo; **to talk to ~** hablar solo
one-shot [wʌn'ʃɔt] *n* (*US*) = **one-off**
one-sided [wʌn'saɪdɪd] *adj* (*argument*) parcial; (*decision, view*) unilateral; (*game, contest*) desigual
one-to-one ['wʌntəwʌn] *adj* (*relationship*) individualizado
one-upmanship [wʌn'ʌpmənʃɪp] *n*: **the art of ~** el arte de quedar siempre por encima
one-way ['wʌnweɪ] *adj* (*street, traffic*) de dirección única; (*ticket*) sencillo
ongoing ['ɔngəuɪŋ] *adj* continuo
onion ['ʌnjən] *n* cebolla
online [ɔn'laɪn] *adj, adv* (*Comput*) en línea; (*switched on*) conectado
onlooker ['ɔnlukə^{r}] *n* espectador(a) *m(f)*
only ['əunlɪ] *adv* solo, sólo, solamente, nomás (*LAm*) ▷ *adj* único, solo ▷ *conj* solamente que, pero; **an ~ child** un hijo único; **not ~ ... but also ...** no solo ... sino también ...; **I'd be ~ too pleased to help** encantado de ayudarles; **I saw her ~ yesterday** le vi ayer mismo; **I would come, ~ I'm very busy** iría, solo que estoy muy atareado
on-screen [ɔn'skri:n] *adj* (*Comput etc*) en pantalla; (*romance, kiss*) cinematográfico
onset ['ɔnsɛt] *n* comienzo
onshore ['ɔnʃɔ:^{r}] *adj* (*wind*) que sopla del mar hacia la tierra
onslaught ['ɔnslɔ:t] *n* ataque *m*, embestida
onto ['ɔntu] *prep* = **on to**
onus ['əunəs] *n* responsabilidad *f*; **the ~ is upon him to prove it** le incumbe a él demostrarlo
onward ['ɔnwəd], **onwards** ['ɔnwədz] *adv* (*move*) (hacia) adelante; **from that time ~** desde entonces en adelante
oops [ups] *excl* (*also*: **~-a-daisy!**) ¡huy!
ooze [u:z] *vi* rezumar
opaque [əu'peɪk] *adj* opaco
OPEC ['əupɛk] *n abbr* (= *Organization of Petroleum-Exporting Countries*) OPEP *f*
open ['əupn] *adj* abierto; (*car*) descubierto; (*road, view*) despejado; (*meeting*) público; (*admiration*) manifiesto ▷ *vt* abrir ▷ *vi* (*flower, eyes, door, debate*) abrirse; (*book etc: commence*) comenzar; **in the ~ (air)** al aire libre; **~ verdict** veredicto inconcluso; **~ ticket** billete *m* sin fecha; **~ ground** (*among trees*) claro; (*waste ground*) solar *m*; **to have an ~ mind (on sth)** estar sin decidirse aún (sobre algo); **to ~ a bank account** abrir una cuenta en el banco; **open on to** *vt fus* (*room, door*) dar a; **open out** *vt* abrir ▷ *vi* (*person*) abrirse; **open up** *vt* abrir; (*blocked road*) despejar ▷ *vi* abrirse
open day *n* (*Brit*) jornada de puertas abiertas *or* acceso público
opening ['əupnɪŋ] *n* abertura; (*beginning*) comienzo; (*opportunity*) oportunidad *f*; (*job*) puesto vacante, vacante *f*

opening hours *npl* horario de apertura
open learning *n enseñanza flexible a tiempo parcial*
openly ['əupnlɪ] *adv* abiertamente
open-minded [əupn'maɪndɪd] *adj* de amplias miras, sin prejuicios
open-necked ['əupnnɛkt] *adj* sin corbata
open-plan ['əupn'plæn] *adj* diáfano, sin tabiques
open prison *n* centro penitenciario de régimen abierto
Open University *n* (*Brit*) ≈ Universidad *f* Nacional de Enseñanza a Distancia, UNED *f*; *ver nota*

OPEN UNIVERSITY

La *Open University*, fundada en 1969, está especializada en impartir cursos a distancia y a tiempo parcial con sus propios materiales de apoyo diseñados para tal fin, entre ellos programas de radio y televisión emitidos por la "BBC". Los trabajos se envían por correo y se complementan con la asistencia obligatoria a cursos de verano. Para obtener la licenciatura es necesario estudiar un mínimo de módulos y alcanzar un determinado número de créditos.

opera ['ɔpərə] *n* ópera
opera house *n* teatro de la ópera
opera singer *n* cantante *m/f* de ópera
operate ['ɔpəreɪt] *vt* (*machine*) hacer funcionar; (*company*) dirigir ▷ *vi* funcionar; (*drug*) hacer efecto; **to ~ on sb** (*Med*) operar a algn
operatic [ɔpə'rætɪk] *adj* de ópera
operating room *n* (*US*) quirófano, sala de operaciones
operating table *n* mesa de operaciones
operating theatre *n* quirófano, sala de operaciones
operation [ɔpə'reɪʃən] *n* (*gen*) operación *f*; (*of machine*) funcionamiento; **to be in ~** estar funcionando *or* en funcionamiento; **to have an ~** (*Med*) ser operado; **to have an ~ for** operarse de; **the company's ~s during the year** las actividades de la compañía durante el año
operational [ɔpə'reɪʃənl] *adj* operacional, en buen estado; (*Comm*) en condiciones de servicio; (*ready for use or action*) en condiciones de funcionar; **when the service is fully ~** cuando el servicio esté en pleno funcionamiento
operative ['ɔpərətɪv] *adj* (*measure*) en vigor; **the ~ word** la palabra clave
operator ['ɔpəreɪtə^r] *n* (*of machine*) operario(-a), maquinista *m/f*; (*Tel*) operador(a) *m(f)*, telefonista *m/f*
opinion [ə'pɪnjən] *n* (*gen*) opinión *f*; **in my ~** en mi opinión, a mi juicio; **to seek a second ~** pedir una segunda opinión
opinionated [ə'pɪnjəneɪtɪd] *adj* testarudo
opinion poll *n* encuesta, sondeo
opponent [ə'pəunənt] *n* adversario(-a), contrincante *m/f*
opportune ['ɔpətju:n] *adj* oportuno
opportunity [ɔpə'tju:nɪtɪ] *n* oportunidad *f*, chance *m or f* (*LAm*); **to take the ~ to do** *or* **of doing** aprovechar la ocasión para hacer
oppose [ə'pəuz] *vt* oponerse a; **to be ~d to sth** oponerse a algo; **as ~d to** en vez de; (*unlike*) a diferencia de
opposing [ə'pəuzɪŋ] *adj* (*side*) opuesto, contrario
opposite ['ɔpəzɪt] *adj* opuesto, contrario; (*house etc*) de enfrente ▷ *adv* en frente ▷ *prep* en frente de, frente a ▷ *n* lo contrario; **the ~ sex** el otro sexo, el sexo opuesto
opposite number *n* (*Brit*) homólogo(-a)
opposition [ɔpə'zɪʃən] *n* oposición *f*
oppress [ə'prɛs] *vt* oprimir
oppression [ə'prɛʃən] *n* opresión *f*
oppressive [ə'prɛsɪv] *adj* opresivo
opt [ɔpt] *vi*: **to ~ for** optar por; **to ~ to do** optar por hacer; **opt out** *vi*: **to ~ out of** optar por no hacer
optical ['ɔptɪkl] *adj* óptico
optical character reader *n* lector *m* óptico de caracteres
optical character recognition *n* reconocimiento *m* óptico de caracteres
optician [ɔp'tɪʃən] *n* óptico *m/f*
optimism ['ɔptɪmɪzəm] *n* optimismo
optimist ['ɔptɪmɪst] *n* optimista *m/f*
optimistic [ɔptɪ'mɪstɪk] *adj* optimista
optimum ['ɔptɪməm] *adj* óptimo
option ['ɔpʃən] *n* opción *f*; **to keep one's ~s open** (*fig*) mantener las opciones abiertas; **I have no ~** no tengo más *or* otro remedio
optional ['ɔpʃənl] *adj* opcional; (*course*) optativo; **~ extras** opciones *fpl* extras
or [ɔ:^r] *conj* o; (*before o, ho*) u; (*with negative*): **he hasn't seen or heard anything** no ha visto ni oído nada; **or else** si no; **let me go or I'll scream!** ¡suéltame, o me pongo a gritar!
oral ['ɔ:rəl] *adj* oral ▷ *n* examen *m* oral
orange ['ɔrɪndʒ] *n* (*fruit*) naranja ▷ *adj* (de color) naranja
orange juice *n* jugo *m* de naranja, zumo *m* de naranja (*Sp*)
orange squash *n* bebida de naranja
orator ['ɔrətə^r] *n* orador(a) *m(f)*
orbit ['ɔ:bɪt] *n* órbita ▷ *vt, vi* orbitar; **to be in/go into ~ (round)** estar en/entrar en órbita (alrededor de)
orbital ['ɔ:bɪtl] *n* (*also*: **~ motorway**) autopista de circunvalación
orchard ['ɔ:tʃəd] *n* huerto; **apple ~** manzanar *m*, manzanal *m*

orchestra ['ɔ:kɪstrə] *n* orquesta; (*US: seating*) platea
orchid ['ɔ:kɪd] *n* orquídea
ordain [ɔ:'deɪn] *vt* (*Rel*) ordenar
ordeal [ɔ:'di:l] *n* experiencia terrible
order ['ɔ:dər] *n* orden *m*; (*command*) orden *f*; (*type, kind*) clase *f*; (*state*) estado; (*Comm*) pedido, encargo ▷ *vt* (*also*: **put in ~**) ordenar, poner en orden; (*Comm*) encargar, pedir; (*command*) mandar, ordenar; **in ~** (*gen*) en orden; (*of document*) en regla; **in (working) ~** en funcionamiento; **a machine in working ~** una máquina en funcionamiento; **to be out of ~** estar desordenado; (*not working*) no funcionar; **in ~ to do** para hacer; **in ~ that** para que + *subjun*; **on ~** (*Comm*) pedido; **to be on ~** estar pedido; **we are under ~s to do it** tenemos orden de hacerlo; **a point of ~** una cuestión de procedimiento; **to place an ~ for sth with sb** hacer un pedido de algo a algn; **made to ~** hecho a la medida; **his income is of the ~ of £24,000 per year** sus ingresos son del orden de 24 mil libras al año; **to the ~ of** (*Banking*) a la orden de; **to ~ sb to do sth** mandar a algn hacer algo
order form *n* hoja de pedido
orderly ['ɔ:dəlɪ] *n* (*Mil*) ordenanza *m*; (*Med*) auxiliar *m/f* (de hospital) ▷ *adj* ordenado
ordinary ['ɔ:dnrɪ] *adj* corriente, normal; (*pej*) común y corriente; **out of the ~** fuera de lo común, extraordinario
ordinary degree *n* (*Brit*) diploma *m*; *ver nota*
ordination [ɔ:dɪ'neɪʃən] *n* ordenación *f*
Ordnance Survey *n* (*Brit*) *servicio oficial de topografía y cartografía*
ore [ɔ:r] *n* mineral *m*
oregano [ɔrɪ'gɑ:nəu] *n* orégano
organ ['ɔ:gən] *n* órgano
organic [ɔ:'gænɪk] *adj* orgánico; (*vegetables, produce*) biológico
organism ['ɔ:gənɪzəm] *n* organismo
organist ['ɔ:gənɪst] *n* organista *m/f*
organization [ɔ:gənaɪ'zeɪʃən] *n* organización *f*
organize ['ɔ:gənaɪz] *vt* organizar
organized ['ɔ:gənaizd] *adj* organizado; **to get ~** organizarse
organized crime *n* crimen organizado
organizer ['ɔ:gənaɪzər] *n* organizador(-a) *m(f)*
orgasm ['ɔ:gæzəm] *n* orgasmo
orgy ['ɔ:dʒɪ] *n* orgía
Orient ['ɔ:rɪənt] *n* Oriente *m*
oriental [ɔ:rɪ'ɛntl] *adj* oriental
orientation [ɔ:rɪen'teɪʃən] *n* orientación *f*
origin ['ɔrɪdʒɪn] *n* origen *m*; (*point of departure*) procedencia
original [ə'rɪdʒɪnl] *adj* original; (*first*) primero; (*earlier*) primitivo ▷ *n* original *m*
originality [ərɪdʒɪ'nælɪtɪ] *n* originalidad *f*
originally [ə'rɪdʒɪnəlɪ] *adv* (*at first*) al principio; (*with originality*) con originalidad
originate [ə'rɪdʒɪneɪt] *vi*: **to ~ from, to ~ in** surgir de, tener su origen en
Orkneys ['ɔ:knɪz] *npl*: **the ~** (*also*: **the Orkney Islands**) las Orcadas
ornament ['ɔ:nəmənt] *n* adorno; (*trinket*) chuchería
ornamental [ɔ:nə'mɛntl] *adj* decorativo, de adorno
ornate [ɔ:'neɪt] *adj* recargado
ornithology [ɔ:nɪ'θɔlədʒɪ] *n* ornitología
orphan ['ɔ:fn] *n* huérfano(-a) ▷ *vt*: **to be ~ed** quedar huérfano(-a)
orphanage ['ɔ:fənɪdʒ] *n* orfanato
orthodox ['ɔ:θədɔks] *adj* ortodoxo
orthopaedic, orthopedic (*US*) [ɔ:θə'pi:dɪk] *adj* ortopédico
Oscar ['ɔskər] *n* óscar *m*
ostensible [ɔs'tɛnsɪbl] *adj* aparente
ostensibly [ɔs'tɛnsɪblɪ] *adv* aparentemente
ostentatious [ɔstɛn'teɪʃəs] *adj* pretencioso, aparatoso; (*person*) ostentativo
osteopath ['ɔstɪəpæθ] *n* osteópata *m/f*
ostracize ['ɔstrəsaɪz] *vt* hacer el vacío a
ostrich ['ɔstrɪtʃ] *n* avestruz *m*
other ['ʌðər] *adj* otro ▷ *pron*: **the ~ one** el/la otro(-a); **~s** (*other people*) otros; **~ than** (*apart from*) aparte de; **the ~ day** el otro día; **some ~ people have still to arrive** quedan por llegar otros; **some actor or ~** un actor cualquiera; **somebody or ~** alguien, alguno; **it was no ~ than the bishop** no era otro que el obispo
otherwise ['ʌðəwaɪz] *adv, conj* de otra manera; (*if not*) si no; **an ~ good piece of work** un trabajo que, quitando eso, es bueno
OTT *abbr* (*inf*) = **over the top**; *see* **top**
otter ['ɔtər] *n* nutria
ouch [autʃ] *excl* ¡ay!
ought (*pt* **ought**) [ɔ:t] *aux vb*: **I ~ to do it** debería hacerlo; **this ~ to have been corrected** esto debiera de haberse corregido; **he ~ to win** (*probability*) debiera ganar; **you ~ to go and see it** vale la pena ir a verlo
ounce [auns] *n* onza (*=28.35g: 16oz = 1lb*)
our ['auər] *adj* nuestro; *see also* **my**
ours ['auəz] *pron* (el) nuestro/(la) nuestra *etc*; *see also* **mine**
ourselves [auə'sɛlvz] *pron pl* (*reflexive, after prep*) nosotros; (*emphatic*) nosotros mismos; **we did it (all) by ~** lo hicimos nosotros solos; *see also* **oneself**
oust [aust] *vt* desalojar
out [aut] *adv* fuera, afuera; (*not at home*) fuera (de casa); (*light, fire*) apagado; (*on strike*) en huelga ▷ *vt*: **to ~ sb** revelar públicamente la homosexualidad de algn; **~ there** allí (fuera); **he's ~** (*absent*) no está, ha salido; **to be ~ in one's calculations** equivocarse (en sus cálculos); **to run ~** salir corriendo; **~ loud** en alta voz; **~ of** *prep* (*outside*) fuera de; (*because of: anger etc*) por; **to look ~ of the window** mirar por la ventana; **to drink ~**

O

of a cup beber de una taza; **made ~ of wood** de madera; **~ of petrol** sin gasolina; **"~ of order"** "no funciona"; **it's ~ of stock** (*Comm*) está agotado; **to be ~ and about again** estar repuesto y levantado; **the journey ~** el viaje de ida; **the boat was 10 km ~** el barco estaba a 10 kilómetros de la costa; **before the week was ~** antes del fin de la semana; **he's ~ for all he can get** busca sus propios fines, anda detrás de lo suyo
out-and-out ['autəndaut] *adj* (*liar, thief etc*) redomado, empedernido
outback ['autbæk] *n* interior *m*
outboard ['autbɔ:d] *adj*: **~ motor** (motor *m*) fuera borda *m*
outbound ['autbaund] *adj* (*flight*) de salida; (*flight: not return*) de ida; **~ from/for** con salida de/hacia
outbreak ['autbreɪk] *n* (*of war*) comienzo; (*of disease*) epidemia; (*of violence etc*) ola
outburst ['autbə:st] *n* explosión *f*, arranque *m*
outcast ['autkɑ:st] *n* paria *m/f*
outcome ['autkʌm] *n* resultado
outcrop ['autkrɔp] *n* (*of rock*) afloramiento
outcry ['autkraɪ] *n* protestas *fpl*
outdated [aut'deɪtɪd] *adj* anticuado
outdo [aut'du:] *vt* (*irreg: like* **do**) superar
outdoor [aut'dɔ:ʳ] *adj* al aire libre; (*clothes*) de calle
outdoors [aut'dɔ:z] *adv* al aire libre
outer ['autəʳ] *adj* exterior, externo
outer space *n* espacio exterior
outfit ['autfɪt] *n* equipo; (*clothes*) traje *m*; (*inf: organization*) grupo, organización *f*
outgoing ['autgəuɪŋ] *adj* (*president, tenant*) saliente; (*means of transport*) que sale; (*character*) extrovertido
outgoings ['autgəuɪŋz] *npl* (*Brit*) gastos *mpl*
outgrow [aut'grəu] *vt* (*irreg: like* **grow**): **he has ~n his clothes** su ropa le queda pequeña ya
outhouse ['authaus] *n* dependencia
outing ['autɪŋ] *n* excursión *f*, paseo
outlandish [aut'lændɪʃ] *adj* estrafalario
outlaw ['autlɔ:] *n* proscrito(-a) ▷ *vt* (*person*) declarar fuera de la ley; (*practice*) declarar ilegal
outlay ['autleɪ] *n* inversión *f*
outlet ['autlɛt] *n* salida; (*of pipe*) desagüe *m*; (*US Elec*) toma de corriente; (*for emotion*) desahogo; (*also:* **retail ~**) punto de venta
outline ['autlaɪn] *n* (*shape*) contorno, perfil *m*; (*sketch, plan*) esbozo ▷ *vt* (*plan etc*) esbozar; **in ~** (*fig*) a grandes rasgos
outlive [aut'lɪv] *vt* sobrevivir a
outlook ['autluk] *n* (*fig: prospects*) perspectivas *fpl*; (*: for weather*) pronóstico; (*opinion*) punto de vista
outlying ['autlaɪɪŋ] *adj* remoto, aislado
outmoded [aut'məudɪd] *adj* anticuado, pasado de moda
outnumber [aut'nʌmbəʳ] *vt* exceder *or* superar en número
out-of-date [autəv'deɪt] *adj* (*passport*) caducado, vencido; (*theory, idea*) anticuado; (*clothes, customs*) pasado de moda
out-of-doors [autəv'dɔ:z] *adv* al aire libre
out-of-the-way [autəvðə'weɪ] *adj* (*remote*) apartado; (*unusual*) poco común *or* corriente
out-of-town [autəv'taun] *adj* (*shopping centre etc*) en las afueras
outpatient ['autpeɪʃənt] *n* paciente *m/f* externo(-a)
outpost ['autpəust] *n* puesto avanzado
output ['autput] *n* (volumen *m* de) producción *f*, rendimiento; (*Comput*) salida ▷ *vt* (*Comput: to power*) imprimir
outrage ['autreɪdʒ] *n* (*scandal*) escándalo; (*atrocity*) atrocidad *f* ▷ *vt* ultrajar
outrageous [aut'reɪdʒəs] *adj* (*clothes*) extravagante; (*behaviour*) escandaloso
outright [aut'raɪt] *adv* (*ask, deny*) francamente; (*refuse*) rotundamente; (*win*) de manera absoluta; (*be killed*) en el acto; (*completely*) completamente ▷ *adj* ['autraɪt] completo; (*winner*) absoluto; (*refusal*) rotundo
outset ['autsɛt] *n* principio
outside [aut'saɪd] *n* exterior *m* ▷ *adj* exterior, externo ▷ *adv* fuera, afuera (*LAm*) ▷ *prep* fuera de; (*beyond*) más allá de; **at the ~** (*fig*) a lo sumo; **an ~ chance** una posibilidad remota; **~ left/right** (*esp Football*) extremo izquierdo/derecho
outside lane *n* (*Aut: in Britain*) carril *m* de la derecha; (*: in US, Europe etc*) carril *m* de la izquierda
outside line *n* (*Tel*) línea (exterior)
outsider [aut'saɪdəʳ] *n* (*stranger*) forastero(-a)
outsize ['autsaɪz] *adj* (*clothes*) de talla grande
outskirts ['autskə:ts] *npl* alrededores *mpl*, afueras *fpl*
outspoken [aut'spəukən] *adj* muy franco
outstanding [aut'stændɪŋ] *adj* excepcional, destacado; (*unfinished*) pendiente
outstay [aut'steɪ] *vt*: **to ~ one's welcome** quedarse más de la cuenta
outstretched [aut'strɛtʃt] *adj* (*arm*) extendido
outstrip [aut'strɪp] *vt* (*competitors, demand: also fig*) dejar atrás, aventajar
out-tray ['auttreɪ] *n* bandeja de salida
outward ['autwəd] *adj* (*sign, appearances*) externo; (*journey*) de ida
outwardly ['autwədlɪ] *adv* por fuera
outwards [autwədz] *adj* (*esp Brit*) = **outward**
outweigh [aut'weɪ] *vt* pesar más que
outwit [aut'wɪt] *vt* ser más listo que
oval ['əuvl] *adj* ovalado ▷ *n* óvalo
ovary ['əuvərɪ] *n* ovario
ovation [əu'veɪʃən] *n* ovación *f*
oven ['ʌvn] *n* horno
oven glove *n* guante *m* para el horno, manopla para el horno

ovenproof ['ʌvnpru:f] *adj* refractario, resistente al horno
oven-ready ['ʌvnrɛdɪ] *adj* listo para el horno
over ['əuvəʳ] *adv* encima, por encima ▷ *adj* (*finished*) terminado; (*surplus*) de sobra; (*excessively*) demasiado ▷ *prep* (por) encima de; (*above*) sobre; (*on the other side of*) al otro lado de; (*more than*) más de; (*during*) durante; (*about, concerning*): **they fell out ~ money** riñeron por una cuestión de dinero; **~ here** (por) aquí; **~ there** (por) allí *or* allá; **all ~** (*everywhere*) por todas partes; **~ and ~ (again)** una y otra vez; **~ and above** además de; **to ask sb ~** invitar a algn a casa; **to bend ~** inclinarse; **now ~ to our Paris correspondent** damos la palabra a nuestro corresponsal de París; **the world ~** en todo el mundo, en el mundo entero; **she's not ~ intelligent** no es muy lista que digamos
overall ['əuvərɔ:l] *adj* (*length*) total; (*study*) de conjunto ▷ *adv* [əuvər'ɔ:l] en conjunto ▷ *n* (*Brit*) guardapolvo; **overalls** *npl* mono *sg*, overol *msg* (*LAm*)
overall majority *n* mayoría absoluta
overanxious [əuvər'æŋkʃəs] *adj* demasiado preocupado *or* ansioso
overawe [əuvər'ɔ:] *vt* intimidar
overbalance [əuvə'bæləns] *vi* perder el equilibrio
overbearing [əuvə'bɛərɪŋ] *adj* autoritario, imperioso
overboard ['əuvəbɔ:d] *adv* (*Naut*) por la borda; **to go ~ for sth** (*fig*) enloquecer por algo
overbook [əuvə'buk] *vt* sobrereservar, reservar con exceso
overcame [əuvə'keɪm] *pt of* **overcome**
overcast ['əuvəkɑ:st] *adj* encapotado
overcharge [əuvə'tʃɑ:dʒ] *vt*: **to ~ sb** cobrar un precio excesivo a algn
overcoat ['əuvəkəut] *n* abrigo
overcome [əuvə'kʌm] *vt* (*irreg: like* **come**) (*gen*) vencer; (*difficulty*) superar; **she was quite ~ by the occasion** la ocasión le conmovió mucho
overconfident [əuvə'kɔnfɪdənt] *adj* demasiado confiado
overcrowded [əuvə'kraudɪd] *adj* atestado de gente; (*city, country*) superpoblado
overdo [əuvə'du:] *vt* (*irreg: like* **do**) exagerar; (*overcook*) cocer demasiado; **to ~ it** (*work etc*) pasarse
overdone [əuvə'dʌn] *adj* (*vegetables*) recocido; (*steak*) demasiado hecho
overdose ['əuvədəus] *n* sobredosis *f inv*
overdraft ['əuvədrɑ:ft] *n* saldo deudor
overdrawn [əuvə'drɔ:n] *adj* (*account*) en descubierto
overdrive ['əuvədraɪv] *n* (*Aut*) sobremarcha, superdirecta
overdue [əuvə'dju:] *adj* retrasado; (*recognition*) tardío; (*bill*) vencido y no pagado; **that change was long ~** ese cambio tenía que haberse hecho hace tiempo
overemphasis [əuvər'ɛmfəsɪs] *n*: **to put an ~ on** poner énfasis excesivo en
overestimate [əuvər'ɛstɪmeɪt] *vt* sobreestimar
overexcited [əuvərɪk'saɪtɪd] *adj* sobreexcitado
overflow [əuvə'fləu] *vi* desbordarse ▷ *n* ['əuvəfləu] (*excess*) exceso; (*of river*) desbordamiento; (*also*: **~ pipe**) (cañería de) desagüe *m*
overgrown [əuvə'grəun] *adj* (*garden*) cubierto de hierba; **he's just an ~ schoolboy** es un niño en grande
overhaul *vt* [əuvə'hɔ:l] revisar, repasar ▷ *n* ['əuvəhɔ:l] revisión *f*
overhead *adv* [əuvə'hɛd] por arriba *or* encima ▷ *adj* ['əuvəhɛd] (*cable*) aéreo; (*railway*) elevado, aéreo ▷ *n* ['əuvəhɛd] (*US*) = **overheads**
overhead projector *n* retroproyector
overheads ['əuvəhɛdz] *npl* (*Brit*) gastos *mpl* generales
overhear [əuvə'hɪəʳ] *vt* (*irreg: like* **hear**) oír por casualidad
overheat [əuvə'hi:t] *vi* (*engine*) recalentarse
overjoyed [əuvə'dʒɔɪd] *adj* encantado, lleno de alegría
overkill ['əuvəkɪl] *n* (*Mil*) capacidad *f* excesiva de destrucción; (*fig*) exceso
overland ['əuvəlænd] *adj, adv* por tierra
overlap *vi* [əuvə'læp] superponerse ▷ *n* ['əuvəlæp] superposición *f*
overleaf [əuvə'li:f] *adv* al dorso
overload [əuvə'ləud] *vt* sobrecargar
overlook [əuvə'luk] *vt* (*have view of*) dar a, tener vistas a; (*miss*) pasar por alto; (*excuse*) perdonar
overnight [əuvə'naɪt] *adv* durante la noche; (*fig*) de la noche a la mañana ▷ *adj* de noche; **to stay ~** pasar la noche
overnight bag *n* fin *m* de semana, neceser *m* de viaje
overpass ['əuvəpɑ:s] *n* (*US*) paso elevado *or* a desnivel
overpay [əuvə'peɪ] *vt*: **to ~ sb by £50** pagar 50 libras de más a algn
overplay [əuvə'pleɪ] *vt* exagerar; **to ~ one's hand** desmedirse
overpower [əuvə'pauəʳ] *vt* dominar; (*fig*) embargar
overpowering [əuvə'pauərɪŋ] *adj* (*heat*) agobiante; (*smell*) penetrante
overrate [əuvə'reɪt] *vt* sobrevalorar
overreact [əuvərɪ'ækt] *vi* reaccionar de manera exagerada
override [əuvə'raɪd] *vt* (*irreg: like* **ride**) (*order, objection*) no hacer caso de
overriding [əuvə'raɪdɪŋ] *adj* predominante
overrule [əuvə'ru:l] *vt* (*decision*) anular; (*claim*) denegar

overrun [əuvə'rʌn] *vt (irreg: like* **run***)* (*Mil: country*) invadir; (*time limit*) rebasar, exceder ▷ *vi* rebasar el límite previsto; **the town is ~ with tourists** el pueblo está inundado de turistas

overseas [əuvə'si:z] *adv* en ultramar; (*abroad*) en el extranjero ▷ *adj* (*trade*) exterior; (*visitor*) extranjero

oversee [əuvə'si:] (*irreg: like* **see**) *vt* supervisar

overshadow [əuvə'ʃædəu] *vt* (*fig*) eclipsar; **to be ~ed by** estar a la sombra de

oversight ['əuvəsaɪt] *n* descuido; **due to an ~** a causa de un descuido *or* una equivocación

oversleep [əuvə'sli:p] *vi (irreg: like* **sleep***)* dormir más de la cuenta, no despertarse a tiempo

overspend [əuvə'spɛnd] *vi (irreg: like* **spend***)* gastar más de la cuenta; **we have overspent by five dollars** hemos excedido el presupuesto en cinco dólares

overstate [əuvə'steɪt] *vt* exagerar

overstay [əuvə'steɪ] *vt*: **to ~ one's time** *or* **welcome** quedarse más de lo conveniente

overstep [əuvə'stɛp] *vt*: **to ~ the mark** *or* **the limits** pasarse de la raya

overt [əu'və:t] *adj* abierto

overtake [əuvə'teɪk] *vt (irreg: like* **take***)* sobrepasar; (*Brit Aut*) adelantar

overthrow [əuvə'θrəu] *vt (irreg: like* **throw***)* (*government*) derrocar

overtime ['əuvətaɪm] *n* horas *fpl* extraordinarias; **to do** *or* **work ~** hacer *or* trabajar horas extraordinarias *or* extras

overtone ['əuvətəun] *n* (*fig*) tono

overtook [əuvə'tuk] *pt of* **overtake**

overture ['əuvətʃuə^r] *n* (*Mus*) obertura; (*fig*) propuesta

overturn [əuvə'tə:n] *vt* volcar; (*fig: plan*) desbaratar; (*: government*) derrocar ▷ *vi* volcar

overview ['əuvəvju:] *n* visión *f* de conjunto

overweight [əuvə'weɪt] *adj* demasiado gordo *or* pesado

overwhelm [əuvə'wɛlm] *vt* aplastar

overwhelming [əuvə'wɛlmɪŋ] *adj* (*victory, defeat*) arrollador(a); (*desire*) irresistible; **one's ~ impression is of heat** lo que más impresiona es el calor

overwork [əuvə'wə:k] *n* trabajo excesivo ▷ *vt* hacer trabajar demasiado ▷ *vi* trabajar demasiado

overwrite [əuvə'raɪt] *vt (irreg: like* **write***)* (*Comput: file, disk*) sobre(e)scribir

overwrought [əuvə'rɔ:t] *adj* sobreexcitado

owe [əu] *vt* deber; **to ~ sb sth, to ~ sth to sb** deber algo a algn

owing to ['əuɪŋtu:] *prep* debido a, por causa de

owl [aul] *n* (*also:* **long-eared ~**) búho; (*also:* **barn ~**) lechuza

own [əun] *vt* tener, poseer ▷ *vi*: **to ~ to sth/to having done sth** confesar *or* reconocer algo/haber hecho algo ▷ *adj* propio; **a room of my ~** mi propia habitación; **to get one's ~ back** tomarse la revancha; **on one's ~** solo, a solas; **can I have it for my (very) ~?** ¿puedo quedarme con él?; **to come into one's ~** llegar a realizarse; **own up** *vi* confesar

owner ['əunə^r] *n* dueño(-a)

ownership ['əunəʃɪp] *n* posesión *f*; **it's under new ~** está bajo nueva dirección

own goal *n* (*Sport*) autogol *m*; **to score an ~** marcar un gol en propia puerta, marcar un autogol

ox (*pl* **oxen**) [ɔks, 'ɔksn] *n* buey *m*

Oxbridge ['ɔksbrɪdʒ] *n universidades de Oxford y Cambridge; ver nota*

OXBRIDGE

El término *Oxbridge* es una fusión de Ox(ford) y (Cam)bridge, las dos universidades británicas más antiguas y con mayor prestigio académico y social. Muchos miembros destacados de la clase dirigente del país son antiguos alumnos de una de las dos. El mismo término suele aplicarse a todo lo que ambas representan en cuestión de prestigio y privilegios sociales.

oxen ['ɔksən] *npl of* **ox**

oxide ['ɔksaɪd] *n* óxido

oxtail ['ɔksteɪl] *n*: **~ soup** sopa de rabo de buey

oxygen ['ɔksɪdʒən] *n* oxígeno

oxygen mask *n* máscara de oxígeno

oyster ['ɔɪstə^r] *n* ostra

oz. *abbr* = **ounce(s)**

ozone ['əuzəun] *n* ozono

ozone friendly *adj* que no daña la capa de ozono

ozone layer *n* capa de ozono

P

P, p [piː] *n* (*letter*) P, p *f*; **P for Peter** P de París
P *abbr* = **president**; **prince**
p *abbr* (= *page*) pág.; (*Brit*) = **penny**; **pence**
PA *n abbr* = **personal assistant**; **public address system**
pa [pɑː] *n* (*inf*) papá *m*
p.a. *abbr* = **per annum**
pace [peɪs] *n* paso; (*rhythm*) ritmo ▷ *vi*: **to ~ up and down** pasearse de un lado a otro; **to keep ~ with** llevar el mismo paso que; (*events*) mantenerse a la altura de *or* al corriente de; **to set the ~** (*running*) marcar el paso; (*fig*) marcar la pauta; **to put sb through his ~s** (*fig*) poner a algn a prueba
pacemaker ['peɪsmeɪkəʳ] *n* (*Med*) marcapasos *m inv*; (*Sport*: *also*: **pacesetter**) liebre *f*
pacific [pə'sɪfɪk] *adj* pacífico ▷ *n*: **the P~ (Ocean)** el (Océano) Pacífico
pacifier ['pæsɪfaɪəʳ] *n* (*US*: *dummy*) chupete *m*
pacifist ['pæsɪfɪst] *n* pacifista *m/f*
pack [pæk] *n* (*packet*) paquete *m*; (*Comm*) embalaje *m*; (*of hounds*) jauría; (*of people*) manada; (*of thieves etc*) banda; (*of cards*) baraja; (*bundle*) fardo; (*US*: *of cigarettes*) paquete *m*, cajetilla ▷ *vt* (*wrap*) empaquetar; (*fill*) llenar; (*in suitcase etc*) meter, poner; (*cram*) llenar, atestar; (*fig*: *meeting etc*) llenar de partidarios; (*Comput*) comprimir; **to ~ (one's bags)** hacer las maletas; **to ~ sb off** despachar a algn; **the place was ~ed** el local estaba (lleno) hasta los topes; **to send sb ~ing** (*inf*) echar a algn con cajas destempladas; **pack in** *vi* (*break down*: *watch, car*) estropearse ▷ *vt* (*inf*) dejar; **~ it in!** ¡para!, ¡basta ya!; **pack up** *vi* (*inf*: *machine*) estropearse; (*person*) irse ▷ *vt* (*belongings, clothes*) recoger; (*goods, presents*) empaquetar, envolver
package ['pækɪdʒ] *n* paquete *m*; (*bulky*) bulto; (*Comput*) paquete *m* (*de software*); (*also*: **~ deal**) acuerdo global ▷ *vt* (*Comm*: *goods*) envasar, embalar
package holiday *n* viaje *m* organizado (con todo incluido)
package tour *n* viaje *m* organizado
packaging ['pækɪdʒɪŋ] *n* envase *m*
packed [pækt] *adj* abarrotado
packed lunch [pækt-] *n* almuerzo frío
packet ['pækɪt] *n* paquete *m*
packing ['pækɪŋ] *n* embalaje *m*
packing case *n* cajón *m* de embalaje
pact [pækt] *n* pacto
pad [pæd] *n* (*of paper*) bloc *m*; (*cushion*) cojinete *m*; (*launching pad*) plataforma (de lanzamiento); (*inf*: *flat*) casa ▷ *vt* rellenar
padded [pædɪd] *adj* (*jacket*) acolchado; (*bra*) reforzado
padded cell *n* celda acolchada
padding ['pædɪŋ] *n* relleno; (*fig*) paja
paddle ['pædl] *n* (*oar*) canalete *m*, pala; (*US*: *for table tennis*) pala ▷ *vt* remar ▷ *vi* (*with feet*) chapotear
paddle steamer *n* vapor *m* de ruedas
paddling pool ['pædlɪŋ-] *n* (*Brit*) piscina para niños
paddock ['pædək] *n* (*field*) potrero
paddy field ['pædɪ-] *n* arrozal *m*
padlock ['pædlɔk] *n* candado ▷ *vt* cerrar con candado
paediatrician, pediatrician (*US*) [piːdɪə'trɪʃən] *n* pediatra *m/f*
paediatrics, pediatrics (*US*) [piːdɪ'ætrɪks] *n* pediatría
paedophile, pedophile (*US*) ['piːdəufaɪl] *adj* de pedófilos ▷ *n* pedófilo(-a)
pagan ['peɪgən] *adj, n* pagano(-a) *m(f)*
page [peɪdʒ] *n* página; (*of newspaper*) plana; (*also*: **~ boy**) paje *m* ▷ *vt* (*in hotel etc*) llamar por altavoz a
pageant ['pædʒənt] *n* (*procession*) desfile *m*; (*show*) espectáculo
pageantry ['pædʒəntrɪ] *n* pompa
pager ['peɪdʒəʳ] *n* busca *m*
pagination [pædʒɪ'neɪʃən] *n* paginación *f*
paid [peɪd] *pt, pp of* **pay** ▷ *adj* (*work*) remunerado; (*holiday*) pagado; (*official*) a sueldo; **to put ~ to** (*Brit*) acabar con
paid-up ['peɪdʌp], **paid-in** (*US*) ['peɪdɪn] *adj* (*member*) con sus cuotas pagadas *or* al día; (*share*) liberado; **~ capital** capital *m* desembolsado
pail [peɪl] *n* cubo, balde *m*
pain [peɪn] *n* dolor *m*; **to be in ~** sufrir; **on ~ of death** so *or* bajo pena de muerte; *see also* **pains**

pained [peɪnd] *adj* (*expression*) afligido
painful ['peɪnful] *adj* doloroso; (*difficult*) penoso; (*disagreeable*) desagradable
painfully ['peɪnfəlɪ] *adv* (*fig: very*) terriblemente
painkiller ['peɪnkɪləʳ] *n* analgésico
painless ['peɪnlɪs] *adj* sin dolor; (*method*) fácil
pains [peɪnz] *npl* (*efforts*) esfuerzos *mpl*; **to take ~ to do sth** tomarse el trabajo de hacer algo
painstaking ['peɪnzteɪkɪŋ] *adj* (*person*) concienzudo, esmerado
paint [peɪnt] *n* pintura ▷ *vt* pintar; **a tin of ~** un bote de pintura; **to ~ the door blue** pintar la puerta de azul
paintbrush ['peɪntbrʌʃ] *n* (*artist's*) pincel *m*; (*decorator's*) brocha
painter ['peɪntəʳ] *n* pintor(a) *m(f)*
painting ['peɪntɪŋ] *n* pintura
paintwork ['peɪntwəːk] *n* pintura
pair [pɛəʳ] *n* (*of shoes, gloves etc*) par *m*; (*of people*) pareja; **a ~ of scissors** unas tijeras; **a ~ of trousers** unos pantalones, un pantalón;
pair off *vi*: **to ~ off (with sb)** hacer pareja (con algn)
pajamas [pɪ'dʒɑːməz] *npl* (US) pijama *msg*, piyama *msg* (*LAm*)
Pakistan [pɑːkɪ'stɑːn] *n* Paquistán *m*
Pakistani [pɑːkɪ'stɑːnɪ] *adj, n* paquistaní *m/f*
pal [pæl] *n* (*inf*) amiguete(-a) *m(f)*, colega *m/f*
palace ['pæləs] *n* palacio
palatable ['pælɪtəbl] *adj* sabroso; (*acceptable*) aceptable
palate ['pælɪt] *n* paladar *m*
pale [peɪl] *adj* (*gen*) pálido; (*colour*) claro ▷ *n*: **to be beyond the ~** pasarse de la raya ▷ *vi* palidecer; **to grow** *or* **turn ~** palidecer; **to ~ into insignificance (beside)** no poderse comparar (con)
Palestine ['pælɪstaɪn] *n* Palestina
Palestinian [pælɪs'tɪnɪən] *adj, n* palestino(-a) *m(f)*
palette ['pælɪt] *n* paleta
pall [pɔːl] *n* (*of smoke*) cortina ▷ *vi* cansar
pallet ['pælɪt] *n* (*for goods*) pallet *m*
pallid ['pælɪd] *adj* pálido
palm [pɑːm] *n* (*Anat*) palma; (*also*: **~ tree**) palmera, palma ▷ *vt*: **to ~ sth off on sb** (*Brit: (inf)*) endosarle algo a algn
Palm Sunday *n* Domingo de Ramos
palpable ['pælpəbl] *adj* palpable
paltry ['pɔːltrɪ] *adj* (*amount etc*) miserable; (*insignificant: person*) insignificante
pamper ['pæmpəʳ] *vt* mimar
pamphlet ['pæmflət] *n* folleto; (*political: handed out in street*) panfleto
pan [pæn] *n* (*also*: **sauce~**) cacerola, cazuela, olla; (*also*: **frying ~**) sartén *f*; (*of lavatory*) taza ▷ *vi* (*Cine*) tomar panorámicas; **to ~ for gold** cribar oro
pan- [pæn] *pref* pan-
Panama ['pænəmɑː] *n* Panamá *m*
Panama Canal *n* el Canal de Panamá
pancake ['pænkeɪk] *n* crepe *f*, panqueque *m* (*LAm*)
pancreas ['pæŋkrɪəs] *n* páncreas *m*
panda ['pændə] *n* panda *m*
panda car *n* (*Brit*) coche *m* de la policía
pandemonium [pændɪ'məunɪəm] *n* (*noise*): **there was ~** se armó un tremendo jaleo; (*mess*) caos *m*
pander ['pændəʳ] *vi*: **to ~ to** complacer a
p & p *abbr* (*Brit: = postage and packing*) gastos de envío
pane [peɪn] *n* cristal *m*
panel ['pænl] *n* (*of wood*) panel *m*; (*of cloth*) paño; (*Radio, TV*) panel *m* de invitados
panelling, paneling (US) ['pænəlɪŋ] *n* paneles *mpl*
pang [pæŋ] *n*: **~s of conscience** remordimientos *mpl*; **~s of hunger** dolores *mpl* del hambre
panhandler ['pænhændləʳ] *n* (*US inf*) mendigo(-a)
panic ['pænɪk] *n* pánico ▷ *vi* dejarse llevar por el pánico
panic buying [-baɪɪŋ] *n* *compras masivas por miedo a futura escasez*
panicky ['pænɪkɪ] *adj* (*person*) asustadizo
panic-stricken ['pænɪkstrɪkən] *adj* preso del pánico
panorama [pænə'rɑːmə] *n* panorama *m*
pansy ['pænzɪ] *n* (*Bot*) pensamiento; (*inf!*) maricón *m*
pant [pænt] *vi* jadear
panther ['pænθəʳ] *n* pantera
panties ['pæntɪz] *npl* bragas *fpl*
pantihose ['pæntɪhəuz] *n* (US) medias *fpl*, panties *mpl*
panto ['pæntəu] *n* (*Brit inf*) = **pantomime**
pantomime ['pæntəmaɪm] *n* (*Brit*) representación *f* musical navideña; *ver nota*

PANTOMIME

En época navideña los teatros británicos ponen en escena representaciones llamadas *pantomimes*, versiones libres de cuentos tradicionales como Aladino o El gato con botas. En ella nunca faltan personajes como la dama ("dame"), papel que siempre interpreta un actor; el protagonista joven ("principal boy"), normalmente interpretado por una actriz, y el malvado ("villain"). Es un espectáculo familiar dirigido a los niños pero con grandes dosis de humor para adultos en el que se alienta la participación del público.

pantry ['pæntrɪ] *n* despensa
pants [pænts] *npl* (*Brit: underwear: woman's*) bragas *fpl*; (*: man's*) calzoncillos *mpl*; (*US: trousers*) pantalones *mpl*

paparazzi [pæpə'rætsɪ] *npl* paparazzi *mpl*
paper ['peɪpə^r] *n* papel *m*; (*also*: **news~**) periódico, diario; (*study, article*) artículo; (*exam*) examen *m* ▷ *adj* de papel ▷ *vt* empapelar; **(identity) ~s** *npl* papeles *mpl*, documentos *mpl*; **a piece of ~** un papel; **to put sth down on ~** poner algo por escrito
paperback ['peɪpəbæk] *n* libro de bolsillo
paper bag *n* bolsa de papel
paper clip *n* clip *m*
paper hankie *n* pañuelo de papel
paper shop *n* (*Brit*) tienda de periódicos
paperweight ['peɪpəweɪt] *n* pisapapeles *m inv*
paperwork ['peɪpəwə:k] *n* trabajo administrativo; (*pej*) papeleo
paprika ['pæprɪkə] *n* pimentón *m*
par [pɑ:^r] *n* par *f*; (*Golf*) par *m* ▷ *adj* a la par; **to be on a ~ with** estar a la par con; **at ~** a la par; **to be above/below ~** estar sobre/bajo par; **to feel under ~** sentirse en baja forma
parable ['pærəbl] *n* parábola
paracetamol [pærə'si:təmɔl] *n* (*Brit*) paracetamol *m*
parachute ['pærəʃu:t] *n* paracaídas *m inv* ▷ *vi* lanzarse en paracaídas
parade [pə'reɪd] *n* desfile *m* ▷ *vt* (*gen*) recorrer, desfilar por; (*show off*) hacer alarde de ▷ *vi* desfilar; (*Mil*) pasar revista; **a fashion ~** un desfile de modelos
paradise ['pærədaɪs] *n* paraíso
paradox ['pærədɔks] *n* paradoja
paradoxically [pærə'dɔksɪklɪ] *adv* paradójicamente
paraffin ['pærəfɪn] *n* (*Brit*): **~ (oil)** parafina
paragon ['pærəgən] *n* modelo
paragraph ['pærəgrɑ:f] *n* párrafo, acápite *m* (*LAm*); **new ~** punto y aparte, punto acápite (*LAm*)
Paraguay ['pærəgwaɪ] *n* Paraguay *m*
Paraguayan [pærə'gwaɪən] *adj, n* paraguayo(-a) *m(f)*, paraguayano(-a) *m(f)*
parallel ['pærəlɛl] *adj*: **~ (with/to)** en paralelo (con/a); (*fig*) semejante (a) ▷ *n* (*line*) paralela; (*fig*) paralelo; (*Geo*) paralelo
paralysis [pə'rælɪsɪs] *n* parálisis *f inv*
paralytic [pærə'lɪtɪk] *adj* paralítico
paralyze ['pærəlaɪz] *vt* paralizar; **~d** paralizado
paramedic [pærə'mɛdɪk] *n* auxiliar *m/f* sanitario(-a)
parameter [pə'ræmɪtə^r] *n* parámetro
paramilitary [pærə'mɪlɪtərɪ] *adj* (*organization, operations*) paramilitar
paramount ['pærəmaunt] *adj*: **of ~ importance** de suma importancia
paranoia [pærə'nɔɪə] *n* paranoia
paranoid ['pærənɔɪd] *adj* (*person, feeling*) paranoico
paranormal [pærə'nɔ:ml] *adj* paranormal
paraphernalia [pærəfə'neɪlɪə] *n* parafernalia
paraphrase ['pærəfreɪz] *vt* parafrasear
parasite ['pærəsaɪt] *n* parásito(-a)
parasol ['pærəsɔl] *n* sombrilla, quitasol *m*
paratrooper ['pærətru:pə^r] *n* paracaidista *m/f*
parcel ['pɑ:sl] *n* paquete *m* ▷ *vt* (*also*: **~ up**) empaquetar, embalar; **to be part and ~ of** ser parte integrante de; **parcel out** *vt* parcelar, repartir
parcel bomb *n* paquete *m* bomba
parcel post *n* servicio de paquetes postales
parch [pɑ:tʃ] *vt* secar, resecar
parched [pɑ:tʃt] *adj* (*person*) muerto de sed
parchment ['pɑ:tʃmənt] *n* pergamino
pardon ['pɑ:dn] *n* perdón *m*; (*Law*) indulto ▷ *vt* perdonar; indultar; **~ me!, I beg your ~!** ¡perdone usted!; **(I beg your) ~?**, (*US*) **~ me?** ¿cómo (dice)?
parent ['pɛərənt] *n* (*mother*) madre *f*; (*father*) padre *m*; **parents** *npl* padres *mpl*
parentage ['pɛərəntɪdʒ] *n* familia, linaje *m*; **of unknown ~** de padres desconocidos
parental [pə'rɛntl] *adj* paternal/maternal
parenthesis (*pl* **parentheses**) [pə'rɛnθɪsɪs, -θɪsi:z] *n* paréntesis *m inv*; **in parentheses** entre paréntesis
Paris ['pærɪs] *n* París *m*
parish ['pærɪʃ] *n* parroquia
parishioner [pə'rɪʃənə^r] *n* feligrés(-esa) *m(f)*
Parisian [pə'rɪzɪən] *adj, n* parisino(-a) *m(f)*, parisiense *m/f*
parity ['pærɪtɪ] *n* paridad *f*, igualdad *f*
park [pɑ:k] *n* parque *m*, jardín *m* público ▷ *vt* aparcar, estacionar ▷ *vi* aparcar, estacionar
parking ['pɑ:kɪŋ] *n* aparcamiento, estacionamiento; **"no ~"** "prohibido aparcar *or* estacionarse"
parking lot *n* (*US*) parking *m*, aparcamiento, playa *f* de estacionamiento (*LAm*)
parking meter *n* parquímetro
parking place *n* sitio para aparcar, aparcamiento
parking ticket *n* multa de aparcamiento
Parkinson's *n* (*also*: **~ disease**) (enfermedad *f* de) Parkinson *m*
parkway ['pɑ:kweɪ] *n* (*US*) alameda
parlance ['pɑ:ləns] *n* lenguaje *m*; **in common/modern ~** en lenguaje corriente/moderno
parliament ['pɑ:ləmənt] *n* parlamento; (*Spanish*) las Cortes *fpl*; *ver nota*

PARLIAMENT

El Parlamento británico (*Parliament*) tiene como sede el palacio de Westminster, también llamado "Houses of Parliament". Consta de dos cámaras: la Cámara de los Comunes ("House of Commons") está formada por 650 diputados ("Members of Parliament") que acceden a ella tras ser elegidos por sufragio universal en su respectiva área o circunscripción electoral ("constituency"). Se reúne

P

175 días al año y sus sesiones son presididas y moderadas por el Presidente de la Cámara ("Speaker"). La cámara alta es la Cámara de los Lores ("House of Lords") y sus miembros son nombrados por el monarca o bien han heredado su escaño. Su poder es limitado, aunque actúa como tribunal supremo de apelación, excepto en Escocia.

parliamentary [pɑːləˈmɛntərɪ] *adj* parlamentario

parlour, parlor (*US*) [ˈpɑːləʳ] *n* salón *m*, living *m* (*LAm*)

Parmesan [pɑːmɪˈzæn] *n* (*also*: **~ cheese**) queso parmesano

parochial [pəˈrəukɪəl] *adj* parroquial; (*pej*) de miras estrechas

parody [ˈpærədɪ] *n* parodia ▷ *vt* parodiar

parole [pəˈrəul] *n*: **on ~** en libertad condicional

parrot [ˈpærət] *n* loro, papagayo

parry [ˈpærɪ] *vt* parar

parsley [ˈpɑːslɪ] *n* perejil *m*

parsnip [ˈpɑːsnɪp] *n* chirivía

parson [ˈpɑːsn] *n* cura *m*

part [pɑːt] *n* (*gen*) parte *f*; (*Mus*) parte *f*; (*bit*) trozo; (*of machine*) pieza; (*Theat etc*) papel *m*; (*of serial*) entrega; (*US*: *in hair*) raya ▷ *adv* = **partly** ▷ *vt* separar; (*break*) partir ▷ *vi* (*people*) separarse; (*roads*) bifurcarse; (*crowd*) apartarse; (*break*) romperse; **to take ~ in** participar *or* tomar parte en; **to take sb's ~** tomar partido por algn; **for my ~** por mi parte; **for the most ~** en su mayor parte; (*people*) en su mayoría; **for the better ~ of the day** durante la mayor parte del día; **~ of speech** (*Ling*) categoría gramatical, parte *f* de la oración; **to take sth in good/bad ~** aceptar algo bien/tomarse algo a mal; **part with** *vt fus* ceder, entregar; (*money*) pagar; (*get rid of*) deshacerse de

part exchange *n* (*Brit*): **in ~** como parte del pago

partial [ˈpɑːʃl] *adj* parcial; **to be ~ to** (*like*) ser aficionado a

participant [pɑːˈtɪsɪpənt] *n* (*in competition*) concursante *m/f*

participate [pɑːˈtɪsɪpeɪt] *vi*: **to ~ in** participar en

participation [pɑːtɪsɪˈpeɪʃən] *n* participación *f*

participle [ˈpɑːtɪsɪpl] *n* participio

particle [ˈpɑːtɪkl] *n* partícula; (*of dust*) mota; (*fig*) pizca

particular [pəˈtɪkjuləʳ] *adj* (*special*) particular; (*concrete*) concreto; (*given*) determinado; (*detailed*) detallado, minucioso; (*fussy*) quisquilloso; (*demanding*) exigente; **particulars** *npl* (*information*) datos *mpl*, detalles *mpl*; (*details*) pormenores *mpl*; **in ~** en particular; **to be very ~ about** ser muy exigente en cuanto a; **I'm not ~** me es *or* da igual

particularly [pəˈtɪkjuləlɪ] *adv* (*in particular*) sobre todo; (*difficult, good etc*) especialmente

parting [ˈpɑːtɪŋ] *n* (*act of*) separación *f*; (*farewell*) despedida; (*Brit*: *in hair*) raya ▷ *adj* de despedida; **~ shot** (*fig*) golpe *m* final

partisan [pɑːtɪˈzæn] *adj* partidista ▷ *n* partidario(-a); (*fighter*) partisano(-a)

partition [pɑːˈtɪʃən] *n* (*Pol*) división *f*; (*wall*) tabique *m* ▷ *vt* dividir; dividir con tabique

partly [ˈpɑːtlɪ] *adv* en parte

partner [ˈpɑːtnəʳ] *n* (*Comm*) socio(-a); (*Sport*) pareja; (*at dance*) pareja; (*spouse*) cónyuge *m/f*; (*friend etc*) compañero(-a) ▷ *vt* acompañar

partnership [ˈpɑːtnəʃɪp] *n* (*gen*) asociación *f*; (*Comm*) sociedad *f*; **to go into ~ (with), form a ~ (with)** asociarse (con)

partridge [ˈpɑːtrɪdʒ] *n* perdiz *f*

part-time [ˈpɑːtˈtaɪm] *adj, adv* a tiempo parcial

party [ˈpɑːtɪ] *n* (*Pol*) partido; (*celebration*) fiesta; (*group*) grupo; (*Law*) parte *f*, interesado ▷ *adj* (*Pol*) de partido; (*dress etc*) de fiesta, de gala; **to have** *or* **give** *or* **throw a ~** organizar una fiesta; **dinner ~** cena; **to be a ~ to a crime** ser cómplice *m/f* de un crimen

party line *n* (*Pol*) línea política del partido; (*Tel*) línea compartida

party political broadcast *n* ≈ espacio electoral

pass [pɑːs] *vt* (*time, object*) pasar; (*place*) pasar por; (*exam, law*) aprobar; (*overtake, surpass*) rebasar; (*approve*) aprobar ▷ *vi* pasar; (*Scol*) aprobar ▷ *n* (*permit*) permiso, pase *m*; (*membership card*) carnet *m*; (*in mountains*) puerto; (*Sport*) pase *m*; (*Scol*: *also*: **~ mark**) aprobado; **to ~ sth through sth** pasar algo por algo; **to ~ the time of day with sb** pasar el rato con algn; **things have come to a pretty ~!** ¡hasta dónde hemos llegado!; **to make a ~ at sb** (*inf*) insinuársele a algn; **pass away** *vi* fallecer; **pass by** *vi* pasar ▷ *vt* (*ignore*) pasar por alto; **pass down** *vt* (*customs, inheritance*) pasar, transmitir; **pass for** *vt fus* pasar por; **she could ~ for 25** se podría creer que sólo tiene 25 años; **pass on** *vi* (*die*) fallecer, morir ▷ *vt* (*hand on*): **to ~ on (to)** transmitir (a); (*cold, illness*) pegar (a); (*benefits*) dar (a); (*price rises*) pasar (a); **pass out** *vi* desmayarse; (*Mil*) graduarse; **pass over** *vi* (*die*) fallecer ▷ *vt* omitir, pasar por alto; **pass up** *vt* (*opportunity*) dejar pasar, no aprovechar

passable [ˈpɑːsəbl] *adj* (*road*) transitable; (*tolerable*) pasable

passage [ˈpæsɪdʒ] *n* pasillo; (*act of passing*) tránsito; (*fare, in book*) pasaje *m*; (*by boat*) travesía

passenger [ˈpæsɪndʒəʳ] *n* pasajero(-a), viajero(-a)

passer-by [pɑːsəˈbaɪ] *n* transeúnte *m/f*

passing ['pɑːsɪŋ] *adj* (*fleeting*) pasajero; **in ~** de paso
passing place *n* (*Aut*) apartadero
passion ['pæʃən] *n* pasión *f*
passionate ['pæʃənɪt] *adj* apasionado
passion fruit *n* fruta de la pasión, granadilla
passion play *n* drama *m* de la Pasión
passive ['pæsɪv] *adj* (*also Ling*) pasivo
passive smoking *n* *efectos del tabaco en fumadores pasivos*
Passover ['pɑːsəuvəʳ] *n* Pascua (de los judíos)
passport ['pɑːspɔːt] *n* pasaporte *m*
passport control *n* control *m* de pasaporte
passport office *n* oficina de pasaportes
password ['pɑːswəːd] *n* (*also Comput*) contraseña
past [pɑːst] *prep* (*further than*) más allá de; (*later than*) después de ▷ *adj* pasado; (*president etc*) antiguo ▷ *n* (*time*) pasado; (*of person*) antecedentes *mpl*; **quarter/half ~ four** las cuatro y cuarto/media; **he's ~ forty** tiene más de cuarenta años; **I'm ~ caring** ya no me importa; **to be ~ it** (*inf: person*) estar acabado; **for the ~ few/three days** durante los últimos días/últimos tres días; **to run ~** pasar corriendo por; **in the ~** en el pasado, antes
pasta ['pæstə] *n* pasta
paste [peɪst] *n* (*gen*) pasta; (*glue*) engrudo ▷ *vt* (*stick*) pegar; (*glue*) engomar; **tomato ~** tomate concentrado
pastel ['pæstl] *adj* pastel; (*painting*) al pastel
pasteurized ['pæstəraɪzd] *adj* pasteurizado
pastille ['pæstl] *n* pastilla
pastime ['pɑːstaɪm] *n* pasatiempo
pastor ['pɑːstəʳ] *n* pastor *m*
past participle [-'pɑːtɪsɪpl] *n* (*Ling*) participio *m* (de) pasado *or* (de) pretérito *or* pasivo
pastry ['peɪstrɪ] *n* (*dough*) pasta; (*cake*) pastel *m*
pasture ['pɑːstʃəʳ] *n* (*grass*) pasto
pasty *n* ['pæstɪ] empanada ▷ *adj* ['peɪstɪ] pastoso; (*complexion*) pálido
pat [pæt] *vt* dar una palmadita a; (*dog etc*) acariciar ▷ *n* (*of butter*) porción *f* ▷ *adj*: **he knows it (off) ~** se lo sabe de memoria *or* al dedillo; **to give sb/o.s. a ~ on the back** (*fig*) felicitar a algn/felicitarse
patch [pætʃ] *n* (*of material*) parche *m*; (*mended part*) remiendo; (*of land*) terreno; (*Comput*) ajuste *m* ▷ *vt* (*clothes*) remendar; **(to go through) a bad ~** (pasar por) una mala racha; **patch up** *vt* (*mend temporarily*) reparar; **to ~ up a quarrel** hacer las paces
patchy ['pætʃɪ] *adj* desigual
pâté ['pæteɪ] *n* paté *m*
patent ['peɪtnt] *n* patente *f* ▷ *vt* patentar ▷ *adj* patente, evidente
patent leather *n* charol *m*
paternal [pə'təːnl] *adj* paternal; (*relation*) paterno
paternity [pə'təːnɪtɪ] *n* paternidad *f*
paternity leave *n* permiso *m* por paternidad, licencia por paternidad
path [pɑːθ] *n* camino, sendero; (*trail, track*) pista; (*of missile*) trayectoria
pathetic [pə'θɛtɪk] *adj* (*pitiful*) penoso, patético; (*very bad*) malísimo; (*moving*) conmovedor(a)
pathname ['pɑθneɪm] *n* (*Comput*) nombre *m* del directorio
pathological [pæθə'lɔdʒɪkəl] *adj* patológico
pathologist [pə'θɔlədʒɪst] *n* patólogo(-a)
pathos ['peɪθɔs] *n* patetismo
pathway ['pɑːθweɪ] *n* sendero, vereda
patience ['peɪʃns] *n* paciencia; (*Brit Cards*) solitario; **to lose one's ~** perder la paciencia
patient ['peɪʃnt] *n* paciente *m/f* ▷ *adj* paciente, sufrido; **to be ~ with sb** tener paciencia con algn
patio ['pætɪəu] *n* patio
patriot ['peɪtrɪət] *n* patriota *m/f*
patriotic [pætrɪ'ɔtɪk] *adj* patriótico
patriotism ['pætrɪətɪzəm] *n* patriotismo
patrol [pə'trəul] *n* patrulla ▷ *vt* patrullar por; **to be on ~** patrullar, estar de patrulla
patrol car *n* coche *m* patrulla
patrolman [pə'trəulmən] *n* (*US*) policía *m*
patron ['peɪtrən] *n* (*in shop*) cliente *m/f*; (*of charity*) patrocinador(a) *m(f)*; **~ of the arts** mecenas *m*
patronize ['pætrənaɪz] *vt* (*shop*) ser cliente de; (*look down on*) tratar con condescendencia a
patronizing ['pætrənaɪzɪŋ] *adj* condescendiente
patron saint *n* santo(-a) patrón(-ona)
patter ['pætəʳ] *n* golpeteo; (*sales talk*) labia ▷ *vi* (*rain*) tamborilear
pattern ['pætən] *n* (*Sewing*) patrón *m*; (*design*) dibujo; (*behaviour, events*) esquema *m*; **~ of events** curso de los hechos; **behaviour ~s** modelos *mpl* de comportamiento
patterned ['pætənd] *adj* (*material*) estampado
paunch [pɔːntʃ] *n* panza, barriga
pauper ['pɔːpəʳ] *n* pobre *m/f*
pause [pɔːz] *n* pausa; (*interval*) intervalo ▷ *vi* hacer una pausa; **to ~ for breath** detenerse para tomar aliento
pave [peɪv] *vt* pavimentar; **to ~ the way for** preparar el terreno para
pavement ['peɪvmənt] *n* (*Brit*) acera, vereda (*LAm*), andén *m* (*LAm*), banqueta (*LAm*); (*US*) calzada, pavimento
pavilion [pə'vɪlɪən] *n* pabellón *m*; (*Sport*) vestuarios *mpl*
paving ['peɪvɪŋ] *n* pavimento, enlosado
paving stone *n* losa
paw [pɔː] *n* pata; (*claw*) garra ▷ *vt* (*animal*) tocar con la pata; (*pej: touch*) tocar, manosear
pawn [pɔːn] *n* (*Chess*) peón *m*; (*fig*) instrumento ▷ *vt* empeñar
pawnbroker ['pɔːnbrəukəʳ] *n* prestamista *m/f*
pawnshop ['pɔːnʃɔp] *n* casa de empeños

P

pay [peɪ] (*pt, pp* **paid**) *n* paga; (*wage etc*) sueldo, salario ▷ *vt* pagar; (*visit*) hacer; (*respect*) ofrecer ▷ *vi* pagar; (*be profitable*) rendir, compensar, ser rentable; **to be in sb's ~** estar al servicio de algn; **to ~ attention (to)** prestar atención (a); **I paid £5 for that record** pagué 5 libras por ese disco; **how much did you ~ for it?** ¿cuánto pagaste por él?; **to ~ one's way** (*contribute one's share*) pagar su parte; (*remain solvent: company*) ser solvente; **to ~ dividends** (*Comm*) pagar dividendos; (*fig*) compensar; **it won't ~ you to do that** no te merece la pena hacer eso; **to put paid to** (*plan, person*) acabar con; **pay back** *vt* (*money*) devolver, reembolsar; (*person*) pagar; **pay for** *vt fus* pagar; **pay in** *vt* ingresar; **pay off** *vt* liquidar; (*person*) pagar; (*debts*) liquidar, saldar; (*creditor*) cancelar, redimir; (*workers*) despedir; (*mortgage*) cancelar, redimir ▷ *vi* (*scheme, decision*) dar resultado; **to ~ sth off in instalments** pagar algo a plazos; **pay out** *vt* (*rope*) ir dando; (*money*) gastar, desembolsar; **pay up** *vt* pagar

payable ['peɪəbl] *adj* pagadero; **to make a cheque ~ to sb** extender un cheque a favor de algn

pay award *n* aumento de sueldo

pay day *n* día *m* de paga

PAYE *n abbr* (*Brit: = pay as you earn*) *sistema de retención fiscal en la fuente de ingresos*

payee [peɪ'iː] *n* portador(a) *m(f)*

pay envelope *n* (*US*) = **pay packet**

payment ['peɪmənt] *n* pago; **advance ~** (*part sum*) anticipo, adelanto; (*total sum*) saldo; **monthly ~** mensualidad *f*; **deferred ~, ~ by instalments** pago a plazos *or* diferido; **on ~ of £5** mediante pago de *or* pagando £5; **in ~ for** en pago de

payout ['peɪjaut] *n* pago; (*in competition*) premio en metálico

pay packet *n* (*Brit*) sobre *m* (de la paga)

pay-phone ['peɪfəun] *n* teléfono público

payroll ['peɪrəul] *n* plantilla, nómina; **to be on a firm's ~** estar en la plantilla *or* nómina de una empresa

pay slip *n* nómina, hoja del sueldo

pay television *n* televisión *f* de pago

PC *n abbr* (*= personal computer*) PC *m*, OP *m*; (*Brit*) = **police constable** ▷ *adj abbr* = **politically correct**

pc *abbr* = **per cent**; **postcard**

PDA *n abbr* (*= personal digital assistant*) agenda electrónica

PE *n abbr* (*= physical education*) ed. física

pea [piː] *n* guisante *m*, chícharo (*LAm*), arveja (*LAm*)

peace [piːs] *n* paz *f*; (*calm*) paz *f*, tranquilidad *f*; **to be at ~ with sb/sth** estar en paz con algn/algo; **to keep the ~** (*policeman*) mantener el orden; (*citizen*) guardar el orden

peaceful ['piːsful] *adj* (*gentle*) pacífico; (*calm*) tranquilo, sosegado

peacekeeping ['piːskiːpɪŋ] *adj* de pacificación ▷ *n* pacificación *f*

peacekeeping force *n* fuerza de pacificación

peach [piːtʃ] *n* melocotón *m*, durazno (*LAm*)

peacock ['piːkɔk] *n* pavo real

peak [piːk] *n* (*of mountain: top*) cumbre *f*, cima; (*: point*) pico; (*of cap*) visera; (*fig*) cumbre *f*

peak hours *npl*, **peak period** *n* horas *fpl* punta

peak rate *n* tarifa máxima

peal [piːl] *n* (*of bells*) repique *m*; **~ of laughter** carcajada

peanut ['piːnʌt] *n* cacahuete *m*, maní *m* (*LAm*)

peanut butter *n* mantequilla de cacahuete

pear [pɛəʳ] *n* pera

pearl [pəːl] *n* perla

peasant ['pɛznt] *n* campesino(-a)

peat [piːt] *n* turba

pebble ['pɛbl] *n* guijarro

peck [pɛk] *vt* (*also:* **~ at**) picotear; (*food*) comer sin ganas ▷ *n* picotazo; (*kiss*) besito

pecking order ['pɛkɪŋ-] *n* orden *m* de jerarquía

peckish ['pɛkɪʃ] *adj* (*Brit inf*): **I feel ~** tengo ganas de picar algo

peculiar [pɪ'kjuːlɪəʳ] *adj* (*odd*) extraño, raro; (*typical*) propio, característico; (*particular: importance, qualities*) particular; **~ to** propio de

pedal ['pɛdl] *n* pedal *m* ▷ *vi* pedalear

pedalo ['pɛdələu] *n* patín *m* a pedal

pedantic [pɪ'dæntɪk] *adj* pedante

peddle ['pɛdl] *vt* (*goods*) ir vendiendo *or* vender de puerta en puerta; (*drugs*) traficar con; (*gossip*) divulgar

peddler ['pɛdləʳ] *n* vendedor(a) *m(f)* ambulante

pedestal ['pɛdəstl] *n* pedestal *m*

pedestrian [pɪ'dɛstrɪən] *n* peatón *m* ▷ *adj* pedestre

pedestrian crossing *n* (*Brit*) paso de peatones

pedestrianized *adj*: **a ~ street** una calle peatonal

pedestrian precinct, pedestrian zone (*US*) *n* zona reservada para peatones

pediatrics [piːdɪ'ætrɪks] *n* (*US*) = **paediatrics**

pedigree ['pɛdɪgriː] *n* genealogía; (*of animal*) pedigrí *m* ▷ *cpd* (*animal*) de raza, de casta

pedophile ['piːdəufaɪl] *n* (*US*) = **paedophile**

pee [piː] *vi* (*inf*) mear

peek [piːk] *vi* mirar a hurtadillas; (*Comput*) inspeccionar

peel [piːl] *n* piel *f*; (*of orange, lemon*) cáscara; (*: removed*) peladuras *fpl* ▷ *vt* pelar ▷ *vi* (*paint etc*) desconcharse; (*wallpaper*) despegarse, desprenderse; (*skin*) pelar; **peel back** *vt* pelar

peep [piːp] *n* (*Brit: look*) mirada furtiva; (*sound*) pío ▷ *vi* (*Brit: look*) mirar furtivamente; **peep out** *vi* asomar la cabeza

peephole ['piːphəul] *n* mirilla

peer [pɪəʳ] *vi*: **to ~ at** escudriñar ▷ *n* (*noble*) par *m*; (*equal*) igual *m*; (*contemporary*) contemporáneo(-a)

peerage ['pɪərɪdʒ] *n* nobleza
peeved [pi:vd] *adj* enojado
peg [pɛg] *n* clavija; (*for coat etc*) gancho, colgador *m*; (*Brit*: *also*: **clothes ~**) pinza; (*also*: **tent ~**) estaca ▷ *vt* (*clothes*) tender; (*groundsheet*) fijar con estacas; (*fig*: *wages, prices*) fijar
pejorative [pɪ'dʒɔrətɪv] *adj* peyorativo
pekinese [pi:kɪ'ni:z] *n* pequinés(-esa) *m(f)*
pelican ['pɛlɪkən] *n* pelícano
pelican crossing *n* (*Brit Aut*) paso de peatones señalizado
pellet ['pɛlɪt] *n* bolita; (*bullet*) perdigón *m*
pelt [pɛlt] *vt*: **to ~ sb with sth** arrojarle algo a algn ▷ *vi* (*rain*: *also*: **~ down**) llover a cántaros; (*inf*: *run*) correr ▷ *n* pellejo
pelvis ['pɛlvɪs] *n* pelvis *f*
pen [pɛn] *n* (*also*: **ballpoint ~**) bolígrafo; (*also*: **fountain ~**) pluma; (*for sheep*) redil *m*; (*US inf*: *prison*) cárcel *f*, chirona; **to put ~ to paper** tomar la pluma
penal ['pi:nl] *adj* penal; **~ servitude** trabajos *mpl* forzados
penalize ['pi:nəlaɪz] *vt* (*punish*) castigar; (*Sport*) sancionar, penalizar
penalty ['pɛnltɪ] *n* (*gen*) pena; (*fine*) multa; (*Sport*) sanción *f*; (*also*: **~ kick**: *Football*) penalty *m*
penalty area *n* (*Brit Sport*) área de castigo
penalty shoot-out [-'ʃu:taut] *n* (*Football*) tanda de penaltis
penance ['pɛnəns] *n* penitencia
pence [pɛns] *pl of* **penny**
penchant ['pɑ̃:ʃɑ̃:ŋ] *n* predilección *f*, inclinación *f*
pencil ['pɛnsl] *n* lápiz *m*, lapicero (*LAm*) ▷ *vt* (*also*: **~ in**) escribir con lápiz; (*fig*) apuntar con carácter provisional
pencil case *n* estuche *m*
pencil sharpener *n* sacapuntas *m inv*
pendant ['pɛndnt] *n* pendiente *m*
pending ['pɛndɪŋ] *prep* antes de ▷ *adj* pendiente; **~ the arrival of ...** hasta que llegue ..., hasta llegar ...
pendulum ['pɛndjuləm] *n* péndulo
penetrate ['pɛnɪtreɪt] *vt* penetrar
penetration [pɛnɪ'treɪʃən] *n* penetración *f*
penfriend ['pɛnfrɛnd] *n* (*Brit*) amigo(-a) por correspondencia
penguin ['pɛŋgwɪn] *n* pingüino
penicillin [pɛnɪ'sɪlɪn] *n* penicilina
peninsula [pə'nɪnsjulə] *n* península
penis ['pi:nɪs] *n* pene *m*
penitence ['pɛnɪtns] *n* penitencia
penitentiary [pɛnɪ'tɛnʃərɪ] *n* (*US*) cárcel *f*, presidio
penknife ['pɛnnaɪf] *n* navaja
pen name *n* seudónimo
pennant ['pɛnənt] *n* banderola; banderín *m*
penniless ['pɛnɪlɪs] *adj* sin dinero
Pennines ['pɛnaɪnz] *npl* (Montes *mpl*) Peninos *mpl*
penny (*pl* **pennies** *or* (*Brit*) **pence**) ['pɛnɪ, 'pɛnɪz, pɛns] *n* (*Brit*) penique *m*; (*US*) centavo
penpal ['pɛnpæl] *n* amigo(-a) por correspondencia
penpusher ['pɛnpuʃə^r] *n* (*pej*) chupatintas *m/f inv*
pension ['pɛnʃən] *n* (*allowance, state payment*) pensión *f*; (*old-age*) jubilación *f*; **pension off** *vt* jubilar
pensioner ['pɛnʃənə^r] *n* (*Brit*) jubilado(-a)
pension fund *n* fondo de pensiones
pensive ['pɛnsɪv] *adj* pensativo; (*withdrawn*) preocupado
pentagon ['pɛntəgən] *n* pentágono; **the P~** (*US Pol*) el Pentágono

PENTAGON

Se conoce como el Pentágono (*the Pentagon*) al edificio de planta pentagonal que acoge las dependencias del Ministerio de Defensa estadounidense ("Department of Defense") en Arlington, Virginia. En lenguaje periodístico se aplica también a la dirección militar del país.

Pentecost ['pɛntɪkɔst] *n* Pentecostés *m*
penthouse ['pɛnthaus] *n* ático (de lujo)
pent-up ['pɛntʌp] *adj* (*feelings*) reprimido
penultimate [pɛ'nʌltɪmət] *adj* penúltimo
people ['pi:pl] *npl* gente *f*; (*citizens*) pueblo *sg*, ciudadanos *mpl*; (*Pol*): **the ~** el pueblo ▷ *n* (*nation, race*) pueblo, nación *f* ▷ *vt* poblar; **several ~ came** vinieron varias personas; **~ say that ...** dice la gente que ...; **old/young ~** los ancianos/jóvenes; **~ at large** la gente en general; **a man of the ~** un hombre del pueblo
pep [pɛp] *n* (*inf*) energía; **pep up** *vt* animar
pepper ['pɛpə^r] *n* (*spice*) pimienta; (*vegetable*) pimiento, ají *m* (*LAm*), chile *m* (*LAm*) ▷ *vt*: **to ~ with** (*fig*) salpicar de
peppermint ['pɛpəmɪnt] *n* menta; (*sweet*) pastilla de menta
pepperoni [pɛpə'rəunɪ] *n* ≈ salchichón *m* picante
per [pə:^r] *prep* por; **~ day/person** por día/persona; **~ annum** al año; **as ~ your instructions** de acuerdo con sus instrucciones
per capita *adj, adv* per cápita
perceive [pə'si:v] *vt* percibir; (*realize*) darse cuenta de
per cent, percent (US) [pə'sɛnt] *n* por ciento; **a 20 ~ discount** un descuento del 20 por ciento
percentage [pə'sɛntɪdʒ] *n* porcentaje *m*; **to get a ~ on all sales** percibir un tanto por ciento sobre todas las ventas; **on a ~ basis** a porcentaje
percentage point *n* punto (porcentual)

P

perception [pə'sɛpʃən] *n* percepción *f*; (*insight*) perspicacia
perceptive [pə'sɛptɪv] *adj* perspicaz
perch [pə:tʃ] *n* (*fish*) perca; (*for bird*) percha ▹ *vi*: **to ~ (on)** (*bird*) posarse (en); (*person*) encaramarse (en)
percolate ['pə:kəleɪt] *vt* (*coffee*) filtrar ▹ *vi* (*coffee*) filtrarse; (*fig*) filtrarse
percolator ['pə:kəleɪtəʳ] *n* cafetera de filtro
percussion [pə'kʌʃən] *n* percusión *f*
perennial [pə'rɛnɪəl] *adj* perenne
perfect *adj* ['pə:fɪkt] perfecto ▹ *n* (*also*: **~ tense**) perfecto ▹ *vt* [pə'fɛkt] perfeccionar; **he's a ~ stranger to me** no le conozco de nada, me es completamente desconocido
perfection [pə'fɛkʃən] *n* perfección *f*
perfectly ['pə:fɪktlɪ] *adv* perfectamente; **I'm ~ happy with the situation** estoy muy contento con la situación; **you know ~ well** lo sabes muy bien *or* perfectamente
perforate ['pə:fəreɪt] *vt* perforar
perforation [pə:fə'reɪʃən] *n* perforación *f*
perform [pə'fɔ:m] *vt* (*carry out*) realizar, llevar a cabo; (*Theat*) representar; (*piece of music*) interpretar ▹ *vi* (*Theat*) actuar; (*Tech*) funcionar
performance [pə'fɔ:məns] *n* (*of task*) realización *f*; (*of a play*) representación *f*; (*of player etc*) actuación *f*; (*of engine*) rendimiento; (*of car*) prestaciones *fpl*; (*of function*) desempeño; **the team put up a good ~** el equipo se defendió bien
performer [pə'fɔ:məʳ] *n* (*actor*) actor *m*, actriz *f*; (*Mus*) intérprete *m/f*
performing arts *npl*: **the ~** las artes teatrales
perfume ['pə:fju:m] *n* perfume *m*
perfunctory [pə'fʌŋktərɪ] *adj* superficial
perhaps [pə'hæps] *adv* quizá(s), tal vez; **~ so/not** puede que sí/no
peril ['pɛrɪl] *n* peligro, riesgo
perilous ['pɛrɪləs] *adj* peligroso
perimeter [pə'rɪmɪtəʳ] *n* perímetro
period ['pɪərɪəd] *n* período, periodo; (*History*) época; (*Scol*) clase *f*; (*full stop*) punto; (*Med*) regla, periodo; (*US Sport*) tiempo ▹ *adj* (*costume, furniture*) de época; **for a ~ of three weeks** durante (un período de) tres semanas; **the holiday ~** el período de vacaciones
periodical [pɪərɪ'ɔdɪkl] *adj* periódico ▹ *n* revista, publicación *f* periódica
periodically [pɪərɪ'ɔdɪklɪ] *adv* de vez en cuando, cada cierto tiempo
period pains *npl* dolores *mpl* de la regla *or* de la menstruación
peripheral [pə'rɪfərəl] *adj* periférico ▹ *n* (*Comput*) periférico, unidad *f* periférica
periphery [pə'rɪfərɪ] *n* periferia
perish ['pɛrɪʃ] *vi* perecer; (*decay*) echarse a perder
perishable ['pɛrɪʃəbl] *adj* perecedero
perjure ['pə:dʒəʳ] *vt*: **to ~ o.s.** perjurar
perjury ['pə:dʒərɪ] *n* (*Law*) perjurio
perk [pə:k] *n* beneficio, extra *m*; **perk up** *vi* (*cheer up*) animarse
perky ['pə:kɪ] *adj* alegre, animado
perm [pə:m] *n* permanente *f* ▹ *vt*: **to have one's hair ~ed** hacerse una permanente
permanent ['pə:mənənt] *adj* permanente; (*job, position*) fijo; (*dye, ink*) indeleble; **~ address** domicilio permanente; **I'm not ~ here** no estoy fijo aquí
permanently ['pə:mənəntlɪ] *adv* (*lastingly*) para siempre, de modo definitivo; (*all the time*) permanentemente
permeate ['pə:mɪeɪt] *vi* penetrar, trascender ▹ *vt* penetrar, trascender a
permissible [pə'mɪsɪbl] *adj* permisible, lícito
permission [pə'mɪʃən] *n* permiso; **to give sb ~ to do sth** autorizar a algn para que haga algo; **with your ~** con su permiso
permissive [pə'mɪsɪv] *adj* permisivo
permit *n* ['pə:mɪt] permiso, licencia; (*entrance pass*) pase *m* ▹ *vt* [pə'mɪt] permitir; (*accept*) tolerar ▹ *vi* [pə'mɪt]: **weather ~ting** si el tiempo lo permite; **fishing ~** permiso de pesca; **building/export ~** licencia *or* permiso de construcción/exportación
perpendicular [pə:pən'dɪkjuləʳ] *adj* perpendicular
perpetual [pə'pɛtjuəl] *adj* perpetuo
perplex [pə'plɛks] *vt* dejar perplejo
perplexed [pə'plɛkst] *adj* perplejo, confuso
persecute ['pə:sɪkju:t] *vt* (*pursue*) perseguir; (*harass*) acosar
persecution [pə:sɪ'kju:ʃən] *n* persecución *f*
perseverance [pə:sɪ'vɪərəns] *n* perseverancia
persevere [pə:sɪ'vɪəʳ] *vi* perseverar
Persia ['pə:ʃə] *n* Persia
Persian ['pə:ʃən] *adj, n* persa *m/f* ▹ *n* (*Ling*) persa *m*; **the ~ Gulf** el Golfo Pérsico
persist [pə'sɪst] *vi* persistir; **to ~ in doing sth** empeñarse en hacer algo
persistence [pə'sɪstəns] *n* empeño
persistent [pə'sɪstənt] *adj* (*lateness, rain*) persistente; (*determined*) porfiado; (*continuing*) constante; **~ offender** (*Law*) multirreincidente *m/f*
person ['pə:sn] *n* persona; **in ~** en persona; **on** *or* **about one's ~** encima; **a ~ to ~ call** una llamada (de) persona a persona
personal ['pə:snl] *adj* personal, individual; (*visit*) en persona; (*Brit Tel*) (de) persona a persona
personal assistant *n* ayudante *m/f* personal
personal column *n* anuncios *mpl* personales
personal computer *n* ordenador *m* personal
personal identification number *n* número personal de identificación
personality [pə:sə'nælɪtɪ] *n* personalidad *f*
personally ['pə:snəlɪ] *adv* personalmente; (*in person*) en persona; **to take sth ~** tomarse algo a mal
personal organizer *n* agenda; (*electronic*) agenda electrónica

personal property *n* bienes *mpl* muebles
personal stereo *n* walkman® *m*
personify [pəːˈsɔnɪfaɪ] *vt* encarnar, personificar
personnel [pəːsəˈnɛl] *n* personal *m*
personnel department *n* departamento de personal
personnel manager *n* jefe *m* de personal
perspective [pəˈspɛktɪv] *n* perspectiva; **to get sth into ~** ver algo en perspectiva *or* como es
Perspex® [ˈpəːspɛks] *n* (*Brit*) vidrio acrílico, plexiglás® *m*
perspiration [pəːspɪˈreɪʃən] *n* transpiración *f*, sudor *m*
perspire [pəˈspaɪəʳ] *vi* transpirar, sudar
persuade [pəˈsweɪd] *vt*: **to ~ sb to do sth** persuadir a algn para que haga algo; **to ~ sb of sth/that** persuadir *or* convencer a algn de algo/de que; **I am ~d that ...** estoy convencido de que ...
persuasion [pəˈsweɪʒən] *n* persuasión *f*; (*persuasiveness*) persuasiva; (*creed*) creencia
persuasive [pəˈsweɪsɪv] *adj* persuasivo
pertaining [pəːˈteɪnɪŋ]: **~ to** *prep* relacionado con
pertinent [ˈpəːtɪnənt] *adj* pertinente, a propósito
perturb [pəˈtəːb] *vt* perturbar
Peru [pəˈruː] *n* el Perú
peruse [pəˈruːz] *vt* (*examine*) leer con detención, examinar; (*glance at*) mirar por encima
Peruvian [pəˈruːvɪən] *adj, n* peruano(-a) *m(f)*
pervade [pəˈveɪd] *vt* impregnar; (*influence, ideas*) extenderse por
perverse [pəˈvəːs] *adj* perverso; (*stubborn*) terco; (*wayward*) travieso
perversion [pəˈvəːʃən] *n* perversión *f*
pervert *n* [ˈpəːvəːt] pervertido(-a) ▷ *vt* [pəˈvəːt] pervertir
pessimism [ˈpɛsɪmɪzəm] *n* pesimismo
pessimist [ˈpɛsɪmɪst] *n* pesimista *m/f*
pessimistic [pɛsɪˈmɪstɪk] *adj* pesimista
pest [pɛst] *n* (*insect*) insecto nocivo; (*fig*) lata, molestia; **pests** *npl* plaga
pester [ˈpɛstəʳ] *vt* molestar, acosar
pesticide [ˈpɛstɪsaɪd] *n* pesticida *m*
pet [pɛt] *n* animal *m* doméstico; (*favourite*) favorito(-a) ▷ *vt* acariciar ▷ *vi* (*inf*) besuquearse ▷ *cpd*: **teacher's ~** favorito(-a) (del profesor); **~ hate** manía
petal [ˈpɛtl] *n* pétalo
peter [ˈpiːtəʳ]: **to ~ out** *vi* agotarse, acabarse
petite [pəˈtiːt] *adj* menuda, chiquita
petition [pəˈtɪʃən] *n* petición *f* ▷ *vt* presentar una petición a ▷ *vi*: **to ~ for divorce** pedir el divorcio
petrified [ˈpɛtrɪfaɪd] *adj* (*fig*) pasmado, horrorizado
petrol [ˈpɛtrəl] (*Brit*) *n* gasolina; (*for lighter*) bencina; **two/four-star ~** gasolina normal/súper
petrol bomb *n* cóctel *m* Molotov
petrol can *n* bidón *m* de gasolina
petroleum [pəˈtrəulɪəm] *n* petróleo
petrol pump *n* (*Brit: in car*) bomba de gasolina; (*in garage*) surtidor *m* de gasolina
petrol station *n* (*Brit*) gasolinera
petrol tank *n* (*Brit*) depósito (de gasolina)
petticoat [ˈpɛtɪkəut] *n* combinación *f*, enagua(s) *f(pl)* (*LAm*)
petty [ˈpɛtɪ] *adj* (*mean*) mezquino; (*unimportant*) insignificante
petty cash *n* dinero para gastos menores
petty officer *n* contramaestre *m*
petulant [ˈpɛtjulənt] *adj* malhumorado
pew [pjuː] *n* banco
pewter [ˈpjuːtəʳ] *n* peltre *m*
PG *n abbr* (*Cine*) = **parental guidance**
pH *n abbr* (= *pH value*) pH
phantom [ˈfæntəm] *n* fantasma *m*
pharmacist [ˈfɑːməsɪst] *n* farmacéutico(-a)
pharmacy [ˈfɑːməsɪ] *n* (*US*) farmacia
phase [feɪz] *n* fase *f* ▷ *vt*: **~d withdrawal** retirada progresiva; **phase in** *vt* introducir progresivamente; **phase out** *vt* (*machinery, product*) retirar progresivamente; (*job, subsidy*) eliminar por etapas
PhD *abbr* = **Doctor of Philosophy**
pheasant [ˈfɛznt] *n* faisán *m*
phenomena [fəˈnɔmɪnə] *npl of* **phenomenon**
phenomenal [fɪˈnɔmɪnl] *adj* fenomenal, extraordinario
phenomenon (*pl* **phenomena**) [fəˈnɔmɪnən, -nə] *n* fenómeno
Philippines [ˈfɪlɪpiːnz] *npl*: **the ~** (las Islas) Filipinas
philosopher [fɪˈlɔsəfəʳ] *n* filósofo(-a)
philosophical [fɪləˈsɔfɪkl] *adj* filosófico
philosophy [fɪˈlɔsəfɪ] *n* filosofía
phlegm [flɛm] *n* flema
phobia [ˈfəubjə] *n* fobia
phone [fəun] *n* teléfono ▷ *vt* telefonear, llamar por teléfono; **to be on the ~** tener teléfono; (*be calling*) estar hablando por teléfono; **phone back** *vt*, ▷ *vi* volver a llamar; **phone up** *vt*, ▷ *vi* llamar por teléfono
phone book *n* guía telefónica
phone box, phone booth *n* cabina telefónica
phone call *n* llamada (telefónica)
phonecard [ˈfəunkɑːd] *n* tarjeta telefónica
phone-in [ˈfəunɪn] *n* (*Brit Radio, TV*) *programa de radio o televisión con las líneas abiertas al público*
phone number *n* número de teléfono
phone tapping [-tæpɪŋ] *n* escuchas telefónicas
phonetics [fəˈnɛtɪks] *n* fonética
phoney [ˈfəunɪ] *adj, n* = **phony**
phony [ˈfəunɪ] *adj* falso ▷ *n* (*person*) farsante *m/f*
photo [ˈfəutəu] *n* foto *f*
photo album *n* álbum *m* de fotos

photocall ['fəutəukɔ:l] *n* sesión *f* fotográfica para la prensa
photocopier ['fəutəukɔpɪəʳ] *n* fotocopiadora
photocopy ['fəutəukɔpɪ] *n* fotocopia ▷ *vt* fotocopiar
Photofit® ['fəutəufɪt] *n* (*also*: **~ picture**) retrato robot
photograph ['fəutəgræf] *n* fotografía ▷ *vt* fotografiar; **to take a ~ of sb** sacar una foto de algn
photographer [fə'tɔgrəfəʳ] *n* fotógrafo
photography [fə'tɔgrəfɪ] *n* fotografía
photo opportunity *n oportunidad de salir en la foto*
phrase [freɪz] *n* frase *f* ▷ *vt* (*letter*) expresar, redactar
phrase book *n* libro de frases
physical ['fɪzɪkl] *adj* físico; **~ examination** reconocimiento médico; **~ exercises** ejercicios *mpl* físicos
physical education *n* educación *f* física
physically ['fɪsɪklɪ] *adv* físicamente
physician [fɪ'zɪʃən] *n* médico(-a)
physicist ['fɪzɪsɪst] *n* físico(-a)
physics ['fɪzɪks] *n* física
physiotherapist [fɪzɪəu'θɛrəpɪst] *n* fisioterapeuta
physiotherapy [fɪzɪəu'θɛrəpɪ] *n* fisioterapia
physique [fɪ'zi:k] *n* físico
pianist ['pɪənɪst] *n* pianista *m/f*
piano [pɪ'ænəu] *n* piano
pick [pɪk] *n* (*tool*: *also*: **~axe**) pico, piqueta ▷ *vt* (*select*) elegir, escoger; (*gather*) coger (*Sp*), recoger (*LAm*); (*lock*) abrir con ganzúa; (*scab, spot*) rascar ▷ *vi*: **to ~ and choose** ser muy exigente; **take your ~** escoja lo que quiera; **the ~ of** lo mejor de; **to ~ one's nose/teeth** hurgarse la nariz/escarbarse los dientes; **to ~ pockets** ratear, ser carterista; **to ~ one's way through** andar a tientas, abrirse camino; **to ~ a fight/quarrel with sb** buscar pelea/camorra con algn; **to ~ sb's brains** aprovecharse de los conocimientos de algn; **pick at** *vt fus*: **to ~ at one's food** comer con poco apetito; **pick off** *vt* (*kill*) matar de un tiro; **pick on** *vt fus* (*person*) meterse con; **pick out** *vt* escoger; (*distinguish*) identificar; **pick up** *vi* (*improve*: *sales*) ir mejor; (: *patient*) reponerse; (: *Finance*) recobrarse ▷ *vt* (*from floor*) recoger; (*buy*) comprar; (*find*) encontrar; (*learn*) aprender; (*Police*: *arrest*) detener; (*Radio, TV, Tel*) captar; **to ~ up speed** acelerarse; **to ~ o.s. up** levantarse; **to ~ up where one left off** volver a empezar algo donde lo había dejado
pickaxe, pickax (*US*) ['pɪkæks] *n* pico, zapapico
picket ['pɪkɪt] *n* (*in strike*) piquete *m* ▷ *vt* hacer un piquete en, piquetear; **to be on ~ duty** estar de piquete
pickle ['pɪkl] *n* (*also*: **~s**: *as condiment*) escabeche *m*; (*fig*: *mess*) apuro ▷ *vt* conservar en escabeche; (*in vinegar*) conservar en vinagre; **in a ~** en un lío, en apuros
pickpocket ['pɪkpɔkɪt] *n* carterista *m/f*
pickup ['pɪkʌp] *n* (*also*: **~ truck, ~ van**) furgoneta, camioneta
picnic ['pɪknɪk] *n* picnic *m*, merienda ▷ *vi* hacer un picnic
picnic area *n* zona de picnic; (*Aut*) área de descanso
picture ['pɪktʃəʳ] *n* cuadro; (*painting*) pintura; (*photograph*) fotografía; (*film*) película; (*TV*) imagen *f*; (*fig*: *description*) descripción *f*; (: *situation*) situación *f* ▷ *vt* pintar; (*imagine*) imaginar; **the ~s** (*Brit*) el cine; **we get a good ~ here** captamos bien la imagen aquí; **to take a ~ of sb/sth** hacer *or* sacar una foto a algn/de algo; **the garden is a ~ in June** el jardín es una preciosidad en junio; **the overall ~** la impresión general; **to put sb in the ~** poner a algn al corriente *or* al tanto
picture book *n* libro de dibujos
picture frame *n* marco
picture messaging *n* (envío de) mensajes *mpl* con imágenes
picturesque [pɪktʃə'rɛsk] *adj* pintoresco
pie [paɪ] *n* (*of meat etc*: *large*) pastel *m*; (: *small*) empanada; (*sweet*) tarta
piece [pi:s] *n* pedazo, trozo; (*of cake*) trozo; (*Draughts etc*) ficha; (*Chess*) pieza; (*part of a set*) pieza; (*item*): **a ~ of furniture/advice** un mueble/un consejo ▷ *vt*: **to ~ together** juntar; (*Tech*) armar; **to take to ~s** desmontar; **a ~ of news** una noticia; **a 10p ~** una moneda de 10 peniques; **a six-~ band** un conjunto de seis (músicos); **in one ~** (*object*) de una sola pieza; **~ by ~** pieza por *or* a pieza; **to say one's ~** decir su parecer
piecemeal ['pi:smi:l] *adv* poco a poco
piecework ['pi:swə:k] *n* trabajo a destajo
pie chart *n* gráfico de sectores *or* de tarta
pier [pɪəʳ] *n* muelle *m*, embarcadero
pierce [pɪəs] *vt* penetrar en, perforar; **to have one's ears ~d** hacerse los agujeros de las orejas
pig [pɪg] *n* cerdo, puerco, chancho (*LAm*); (*person*: *greedy*) tragón(-ona) *m(f)*, comilón(-ona) *m(f)*; (*nasty*) cerdo(-a)
pigeon ['pɪdʒən] *n* paloma; (*as food*) pichón *m*
pigeonhole ['pɪdʒənhəul] *n* casilla
piggy bank ['pɪgɪbæŋk] *n* hucha (*en forma de cerdito*)
piglet ['pɪglɪt] *n* cerdito, cochinillo
pigmentation [pɪgmən'teɪʃən] *n* pigmentación *f*
pigmy ['pɪgmɪ] *n* = **pygmy**
pigskin ['pɪgskɪn] *n* piel *f* de cerdo
pigsty ['pɪgstaɪ] *n* pocilga
pigtail ['pɪgteɪl] *n* (*girl's*) trenza; (*Chinese*) coleta; (*Taur*) coleta
pike [paɪk] *n* (*spear*) pica; (*fish*) lucio
pilchard ['pɪltʃəd] *n* sardina

pile [paɪl] *n* (*heap*) montón *m*; (*of carpet*) pelo; **in a ~** en un montón; **to ~ into** (*car*) meterse en; **pile on** *vt*: **to ~ it on** (*inf*) exagerar; **pile up** *vi* (*accumulate*: *work*) amontonarse, acumularse ▷ *vt* (*put in a heap*: *books, clothes*) apilar, amontonar; (*accumulate*) acumular
piles [paɪlz] *npl* (*Med*) almorranas *fpl*, hemorroides *mpl*
pile-up ['paɪlʌp] *n* (*Aut*) accidente *m* múltiple
pilfering ['pɪlfərɪŋ] *n* ratería
pilgrim ['pɪlgrɪm] *n* peregrino(-a); **the P~ Fathers** *or* **P~s** *los primeros colonos norteamericanos*; *see also* **Thanksgiving**
pilgrimage ['pɪlgrɪmɪdʒ] *n* peregrinación *f*, romería
pill [pɪl] *n* píldora; **the ~** la píldora; **to be on the ~** tomar la píldora (anticonceptiva)
pillage ['pɪlɪdʒ] *vt* pillar, saquear
pillar ['pɪlə^r] *n* pilar *m*, columna
pillar box *n* (*Brit*) buzón *m*
pillion ['pɪljən] *n* (*of motorcycle*) asiento trasero; **to ride ~** ir en el asiento trasero
pillow ['pɪləu] *n* almohada
pillowcase ['pɪləukeɪs], **pillowslip** ['pɪləuslɪp] *n* funda (de almohada)
pilot ['paɪlət] *n* piloto *inv* ▷ *adj* (*scheme etc*) piloto ▷ *vt* pilotar; (*fig*) guiar, conducir
pilot light *n* piloto
pimp [pɪmp] *n* chulo, cafiche *m* (*LAm*)
pimple ['pɪmpl] *n* grano
PIN *n abbr* (= *personal identification number*) PIN *m*
pin [pɪn] *n* alfiler *m*; (*Elec*: *of plug*) clavija; (*Tech*) perno; (: *wooden*) clavija; (*drawing pin*) chincheta; (*in grenade*) percutor *m* ▷ *vt* prender con (alfiler); sujetar con perno; **~s and needles** hormigueo *sg*; **to ~ sth on sb** (*fig*) cargar a algn con la culpa de algo; **pin down** *vt* (*fig*): **there's something strange here, but I can't quite ~ it down** aquí hay algo raro pero no puedo precisar qué es; **to ~ sb down** hacer que algn concrete
pinafore ['pɪnəfɔː^r] *n* delantal *m*
pinball ['pɪnbɔːl] *n* (*also*: **~ machine**) millón *m*, fliper *m*
pincers ['pɪnsəz] *npl* pinzas *fpl*, tenazas *fpl*
pinch [pɪntʃ] *n* pellizco; (*of salt etc*) pizca ▷ *vt* pellizcar; (*inf*: *steal*) birlar ▷ *vi* (*shoe*) apretar; **at a ~** en caso de apuro; **to feel the ~** (*fig*) pasar apuros *or* estrecheces
pincushion ['pɪnkuʃən] *n* acerico
pine [paɪn] *n* (*also*: **~ tree**) pino ▷ *vi*: **to ~ for** suspirar por; **pine away** *vi* morirse de pena
pineapple ['paɪnæpl] *n* piña, ananá(s) *m* (*LAm*)
ping [pɪŋ] *n* (*noise*) sonido agudo
Ping-Pong® ['pɪŋpɔŋ] *n* pingpong *m*
pink [pɪŋk] *adj* (de color) rosa ▷ *n* (*colour*) rosa; (*Bot*) clavel *m*
pinpoint ['pɪnpɔɪnt] *vt* precisar
pint [paɪnt] *n* pinta (*Brit* = *0,57 l*, *US* = *0,47 l*); (*Brit inf*: *of beer*) pinta de cerveza, ≈ jarra (*Sp*)
pin-up ['pɪnʌp] *n* (*picture*) *fotografía de mujer u hombre medio desnudos*; **~ (girl)** ≈ chica de calendario
pioneer [paɪə'nɪə^r] *n* pionero(-a) ▷ *vt* promover
pious ['paɪəs] *adj* piadoso, devoto
pip [pɪp] *n* (*seed*) pepita; **the ~s** (*Brit Tel*) la señal
pipe [paɪp] *n* tubería, cañería; (*for smoking*) pipa, cachimba (*LAm*), cachimbo (*LAm*) ▷ *vt* conducir en cañerías; **(bag)~s** *npl* gaita *sg*; **pipe down** *vi* (*inf*) callarse
pipe cleaner *n* limpiapipas *m inv*
pipe dream *n* sueño imposible
pipeline ['paɪplaɪn] *n* tubería, cañería; (*for oil*) oleoducto; (*for natural gas*) gasoducto; **it is in the ~** (*fig*) está en trámite
piper ['paɪpə^r] *n* (*gen*) flautista *m/f*; (*with bagpipes*) gaitero(-a)
piping ['paɪpɪŋ] *adv*: **to be ~ hot** estar calentito
pique [piːk] *n* pique *m*, resentimiento
pirate ['paɪərət] *n* pirata *m/f* ▷ *vt* (*record, video, book*) hacer una copia pirata de, piratear
Pisces ['paɪsiːz] *n* Piscis *m*
piss [pɪs] *vi* (*inf*) mear
pissed [pɪst] *adj* (*inf*: *drunk*) mamado, pedo
pistol ['pɪstl] *n* pistola
piston ['pɪstən] *n* pistón *m*, émbolo
pit [pɪt] *n* hoyo; (*also*: **coal ~**) mina; (*in garage*) foso de inspección; (*also*: **orchestra ~**) foso de la orquesta; (*quarry*) cantera ▷ *vt* (*chickenpox*) picar; (*rust*) comer; **to ~ A against B** oponer A a B; **pits** *npl* (*Aut*) box *msg*; **~ted with** (*chickenpox*) picado de; **to ~ one's wits against sb** medir fuerzas con algn
pitch [pɪtʃ] *n* (*throw*) lanzamiento; (*Mus*) tono; (*Brit Sport*) campo, terreno; (*tar*) brea; (*in market etc*) puesto; (*fig*: *degree*) nivel *m*, grado ▷ *vt* (*throw*) arrojar, lanzar ▷ *vi* (*fall*) caer(se); (*Naut*) cabecear; **I can't keep working at this ~** no puedo seguir trabajando a este ritmo; **at its (highest) ~** en su punto máximo; **his anger reached such a ~ that ...** su ira *or* cólera llegó a tal extremo que ...; **to ~ a tent** montar una tienda (de campaña); **to ~ one's aspirations too high** tener ambiciones desmesuradas
pitch-black ['pɪtʃ'blæk] *adj* negro como boca de lobo
pitched battle [pɪtʃt-] *n* batalla campal
piteous ['pɪtɪəs] *adj* lastimoso
pitfall ['pɪtfɔːl] *n* riesgo
pith [pɪθ] *n* (*of orange*) piel *f* blanca; (*fig*) meollo
pithy ['pɪθɪ] *adj* jugoso
pitiful ['pɪtɪful] *adj* (*touching*) lastimoso, conmovedor(a); (*contemptible*) lamentable
pitiless ['pɪtɪlɪs] *adj* despiadado, implacable
pittance ['pɪtns] *n* miseria
pity ['pɪtɪ] *n* (*compassion*) compasión *f*, piedad *f*; (*shame*) lástima ▷ *vt* compadecer(se de);

P

to have *or* **take ~ on sb** compadecerse de algn; **what a ~!** ¡qué pena!; **it is a ~ that you can't come** ¡qué pena que no puedas venir!
pivot ['pɪvət] *n* eje *m* ▷ *vi*: **to ~ on** girar sobre; (*fig*) depender de
pixel ['pɪksl] *n* (*Comput*) pixel *m*, punto
pizza ['pi:tsə] *n* pizza
placard ['plækɑ:d] *n* (*in march etc*) pancarta
placate [plə'keɪt] *vt* apaciguar
place [pleɪs] *n* lugar *m*, sitio; (*rank*) rango; (*seat*) plaza, asiento; (*post*) puesto; (*in street names*) plaza; (*home*): **at/to his ~** en/a su casa ▷ *vt* (*object*) poner, colocar; (*identify*) reconocer; (*find a post for*) dar un puesto a, colocar; (*goods*) vender; **to take ~** tener lugar; **to be ~d** (*in race, exam*) colocarse; **out of ~** (*not suitable*) fuera de lugar; **in the first ~** (*first of all*) en primer lugar; **to change ~s with sb** cambiarse de sitio con algn; **~ of birth** lugar *m* de nacimiento; **from ~ to ~** de un sitio a *or* para otro; **all over the ~** por todas partes; **he's going ~s** (*fig, inf*) llegará lejos; **I feel rather out of ~ here** me encuentro algo desplazado; **to put sb in his ~** (*fig*) poner a algn en su lugar; **it is not my ~ to do it** no me incumbe a mí hacerlo; **to ~ an order with sb (for)** hacer un pedido a algn (de); **we are better ~d than a month ago** estamos en mejor posición que hace un mes
place mat *n* (*wooden etc*) salvamanteles *m inv*; (*in linen etc*) mantel *m* individual
placement ['pleɪsmənt] *n* colocación *f*; (*at work*) emplazamiento
placid ['plæsɪd] *adj* apacible, plácido
plagiarism ['pleɪdʒjərɪzm] *n* plagio
plague [pleɪg] *n* plaga; (*Med*) peste *f* ▷ *vt* (*fig*) acosar, atormentar; **to ~ sb with questions** acribillar a algn a preguntas
plaice [pleɪs] *n pl inv* platija
plaid [plæd] *n* (*material*) tela de cuadros
plain [pleɪn] *adj* (*clear*) claro, evidente; (*simple*) sencillo; (*frank*) franco, abierto; (*not handsome*) poco atractivo; (*pure*) natural, puro ▷ *adv* claramente ▷ *n* llano, llanura; **in ~ clothes** (*police*) vestido de paisano; **to make sth ~ to sb** dejar algo en claro a algn
plain chocolate *n* chocolate *m* oscuro *or* amargo
plainly ['pleɪnlɪ] *adv* claramente, evidentemente; (*frankly*) francamente
plaintiff ['pleɪntɪf] *n* demandante *m/f*
plaintive ['pleɪntɪv] *adj* (*cry, voice*) lastimero, quejumbroso; (*look*) que da lástima
plait [plæt] *n* trenza ▷ *vt* trenzar
plan [plæn] *n* (*drawing*) plano; (*scheme*) plan *m*, proyecto ▷ *vt* (*think*) pensar; (*prepare*) proyectar, planear; (*intend*) pensar, tener la intención de ▷ *vi* hacer proyectos; **have you any ~s for today?** ¿piensas hacer algo hoy?; **to ~ to do** pensar hacer; **how long do you ~ to stay?** ¿cuánto tiempo piensas quedarte?; **to ~ (for)** planear, proyectar; **plan out** *vt* planear detalladamente
plane [pleɪn] *n* (*Aviat*) avión *m*; (*tree*) plátano; (*tool*) cepillo; (*Math*) plano
planet ['plænɪt] *n* planeta *m*
plank [plæŋk] *n* tabla
planner ['plænə^r] *n* planificador(-a) *m(f)*; (*chart*) diagrama *m* de planificación; **town ~** urbanista *m/f*
planning ['plænɪŋ] *n* (*Pol, Econ*) planificación *f*; **family ~** planificación familiar
planning permission *n* licencia de obras
plant [plɑ:nt] *n* planta; (*machinery*) maquinaria; (*factory*) fábrica ▷ *vt* plantar; (*field*) sembrar; (*bomb*) colocar
plantation [plæn'teɪʃən] *n* plantación *f*; (*estate*) hacienda
plant pot *n* maceta, tiesto
plaque [plæk] *n* placa
plasma ['plæzmə] *n* plasma *m*
plasma screen *n* pantalla de plasma
plaster ['plɑ:stə^r] *n* (*for walls*) yeso; (*also*: **~ of Paris**) yeso mate; (*Med*: *for broken leg etc*) escayola; (*Brit*: *also*: **sticking ~**) tirita, esparadrapo ▷ *vt* enyesar; (*cover*): **to ~ with** llenar *or* cubrir de; **to be ~ed with mud** estar cubierto de barro
plaster cast *n* (*Med*) escayola; (*model, statue*) vaciado de yeso
plastered ['plɑ:stəd] *adj* (*inf*) borracho
plastic ['plæstɪk] *n* plástico ▷ *adj* de plástico
plastic bag *n* bolsa de plástico
plastic bullet *n* bala de goma
plastic explosive *n* goma 2®
plasticine® ['plæstɪsi:n] *n* (*Brit*) plastilina®
plastic surgery *n* cirugía plástica
plate [pleɪt] *n* (*dish*) plato; (*metal, in book*) lámina; (*Phot*) placa; (*on door*) placa; (*Aut*: *also*: **number ~**) matrícula; (*dental plate*) placa de dentadura postiza
plateau (*pl* **plateaus** *or* **plateaux**) ['plætəu, -z] *n* meseta, altiplanicie *f*
plate glass *n* vidrio *or* cristal *m* cilindrado
platform ['plætfɔ:m] *n* (*Rail*) andén *m*; (*stage*) plataforma; (*at meeting*) tribuna; (*Pol*) programa *m* (electoral); **the train leaves from ~ seven** el tren sale del andén número siete
platinum ['plætɪnəm] *n* platino
platoon [plə'tu:n] *n* pelotón *m*
platter ['plætə^r] *n* fuente *f*
plausible ['plɔ:zɪbl] *adj* verosímil; (*person*) convincente
play [pleɪ] *n* (*gen*) juego; (*Theat*) obra ▷ *vt* (*game*) jugar; (*compete against*) jugar contra; (*instrument*) tocar; (*Theat*) representar; (*: part*) hacer el papel de; (*fig*) desempeñar ▷ *vi* jugar; (*band*) tocar; (*tape, record*) sonar; (*frolic*) juguetear; **to ~ safe** ir a lo seguro; **to bring** *or* **call into ~** poner en juego; **to ~ a trick on sb** gastar una broma a algn; **they're ~ing at soldiers** están jugando a (los) soldados; **to ~ for time** (*fig*) tratar de ganar tiempo; **to ~ into sb's hands** (*fig*) hacerle el juego a algn;

a smile ~ed on his lips una sonrisa le bailaba en los labios; **play about, play around** *vi* (*person*) hacer el tonto; **to ~ about** *or* **around with** (*fiddle with*) juguetear con; (*idea*) darle vueltas a; **play along** *vi*: **to ~ along with** seguirle el juego a ▷ *vt*: **to ~ sb along** (*fig*) jugar con algn; **play back** *vt* (*tape*) poner; **play down** *vt* quitar importancia a; **play on** *vt fus* (*sb's feelings, credulity*) aprovecharse de; **to ~ on sb's nerves** atacarle los nervios a algn; **play up** *vi* (*cause trouble*) dar guerra

playact ['pleɪækt] *vi* (*fig*) hacer comedia *or* teatro

playboy ['pleɪbɔɪ] *n* playboy *m*

player ['pleɪəʳ] *n* jugador(a) *m(f)*; (*Theat*) actor *m*, actriz *f*; (*Mus*) músico(-a) *m(f)*

playful ['pleɪful] *adj* juguetón(-ona)

playground ['pleɪgraund] *n* (*in school*) patio de recreo; (*in park*) parque *m* infantil

playgroup ['pleɪgru:p] *n* jardín *m* de infancia

playing card ['pleɪɪŋ-] *n* naipe *m*, carta

playing field *n* campo de deportes

playmaker ['pleɪmeɪkəʳ] *n* (*Sport*) *jugador encargado de facilitar buenas jugadas a sus compañeros*

playmate ['pleɪmeɪt] *n* compañero(-a) de juego

play-off ['pleɪɔf] *n* (*Sport*) (partido de) desempate *m*

playpen ['pleɪpɛn] *n* corral *m*

playschool ['pleɪsku:l] *n* = **playgroup**

plaything ['pleɪθɪŋ] *n* juguete *m*

playtime ['pleɪtaɪm] *n* (*Scol*) (hora de) recreo

playwright ['pleɪraɪt] *n* dramaturgo(-a)

plc *abbr* (*Brit*: = *public limited company*) S.A.

plea [pli:] *n* (*request*) súplica, petición *f*; (*excuse*) pretexto, disculpa; (*Law*) alegato, defensa

plea bargaining *n* (*Law*) *acuerdo entre fiscal y defensor para agilizar los trámites judiciales*

plead [pli:d] *vt* (*Law*): **to ~ sb's case** defender a algn; (*give as excuse*) poner como pretexto ▷ *vi* (*Law*) declararse; (*beg*): **to ~ with sb** suplicar *or* rogar a algn; **to ~ guilty/not guilty** (*defendant*) declararse culpable/inocente; **to ~ for sth** (*beg for*) suplicar algo

pleasant ['plɛznt] *adj* agradable

pleasantries ['plɛzntrɪz] *npl* (*polite remarks*) cortesías *fpl*; **to exchange ~** conversar amablemente

please [pli:z] *excl* ¡por favor! ▷ *vt* (*give pleasure to*) dar gusto a, agradar ▷ *vi* (*think fit*): **do as you ~** haz lo que quieras *or* lo que te dé la gana; **to ~ o.s.** hacer lo que le parezca; **~!** ¡por favor!; **~ yourself!** ¡haz lo que quieras!, ¡como quieras!; **~ don't cry!** ¡no llores! te lo ruego

pleased [pli:zd] *adj* (*happy*) alegre, contento; (*satisfied*): **~ (with)** satisfecho (de); **~ to meet you** ¡encantado!, ¡tanto *or* mucho gusto!; **to be ~ (about sth)** alegrarse (de algo); **we are ~ to inform you that ...** tenemos el gusto de comunicarle que ...

pleasing ['pli:zɪŋ] *adj* agradable, grato

pleasure ['plɛʒəʳ] *n* placer *m*, gusto; (*will*) voluntad *f* ▷ *cpd* de recreo; **"it's a ~"** "el gusto es mío"; **it's a ~ to see him** da gusto verle; **I have much ~ in informing you that ...** tengo el gran placer de comunicarles que ...; **with ~** con mucho *or* todo gusto; **is this trip for business or ~?** ¿este viaje es de negocios o de placer?

pleasure cruise *n* crucero de placer

pleat [pli:t] *n* pliegue *m*

pleb [plɛb] *n*: **the ~s** la gente baja, la plebe

plebiscite ['plɛbɪsɪt] *n* plebiscito

plectrum ['plɛktrəm] *n* plectro

pledge [plɛdʒ] *n* (*object*) prenda; (*promise*) promesa, voto ▷ *vt* (*pawn*) empeñar; (*promise*) prometer; **to ~ support for sb** prometer su apoyo a algn; **to ~ sb to secrecy** hacer jurar a algn que guardará el secreto

plentiful ['plɛntɪful] *adj* copioso, abundante

plenty ['plɛntɪ] *n* abundancia; **~ of** mucho(s) (-a(s)); **we've got ~ of time to get there** tenemos tiempo de sobra para llegar

pleurisy ['pluərɪsɪ] *n* pleuresía

pliable ['plaɪəbl] *adj* flexible

pliers ['plaɪəz] *npl* alicates *mpl*, tenazas *fpl*

plight [plaɪt] *n* condición *f or* situación *f* difícil

plimsolls ['plɪmsəlz] *npl* (*Brit*) zapatillas *fpl* de tenis

plinth [plɪnθ] *n* plinto

plod [plɔd] *vi* caminar con paso pesado; (*fig*) trabajar laboriosamente

plonk [plɔŋk] (*inf*) *n* (*Brit*: *wine*) vino peleón ▷ *vt*: **to ~ sth down** dejar caer algo

plot [plɔt] *n* (*scheme*) complot *m*, conjura; (*of story, play*) argumento; (*of land*) terreno, parcela ▷ *vt* (*mark out*) trazar; (*conspire*) tramar, urdir ▷ *vi* conspirar; **a vegetable ~** un cuadro de hortalizas

plough, plow (*US*) [plau] *n* arado ▷ *vt* (*earth*) arar; **plough back** *vt* (*Comm*) reinvertir; **plough through** *vt fus* (*crowd*) abrirse paso a la fuerza por

ploughman ['plaumən] *n*: **~'s lunch** pan *m* con queso y cebolla

plow [plau] *n, vb* (*US*) = **plough**

ploy [plɔɪ] *n* truco, estratagema

pluck [plʌk] *vt* (*fruit*) coger (*Sp*), recoger (*LAm*); (*musical instrument*) puntear; (*bird*) desplumar ▷ *n* valor *m*, ánimo; **to ~ up courage** hacer de tripas corazón; **to ~ one's eyebrows** depilarse las cejas

plucky ['plʌkɪ] *adj* valiente

plug [plʌg] *n* tapón *m*; (*Elec*) enchufe *m*, clavija; (*Aut*: *also*: **spark(ing) ~**) bujía ▷ *vt* (*hole*) tapar; (*inf*: *advertise*) dar publicidad a; **to give sb/sth a ~** dar publicidad a algn/algo; **to ~ a lead into a socket** enchufar un hilo en una toma; **plug in** *vt*, ▷ *vi* (*Elec*) enchufar

plughole ['plʌghəul] *n* desagüe *m*

plum [plʌm] *n* (*fruit*) ciruela; (*also*: **~ job**) chollo
plumb [plʌm] *adj* vertical ▷ *n* plomo ▷ *adv* (*exactly*) exactamente, en punto ▷ *vt* sondar; (*fig*) sondear; **plumb in** *vt* (*washing machine*) conectar
plumber ['plʌməʳ] *n* fontanero(-a), plomero(-a) (*LAm*)
plumbing ['plʌmɪŋ] *n* (*trade*) fontanería, plomería (*LAm*); (*piping*) cañerías
plummet ['plʌmɪt] *vi*: **to ~ (down)** caer a plomo
plump [plʌmp] *adj* rechoncho, rollizo ▷ *vt*: **to ~ sth (down) on** dejar caer algo en; **plump for** *vt fus* (*inf*: *choose*) optar por; **plump up** *vt* ahuecar
plunder ['plʌndəʳ] *n* pillaje *m*; (*loot*) botín *m* ▷ *vt* saquear, pillar
plunge [plʌndʒ] *n* zambullida ▷ *vt* sumergir, hundir ▷ *vi* (*fall*) caer; (*dive*) saltar; (*person*) arrojarse; (*sink*) hundirse; **to take the ~** lanzarse; **to ~ a room into darkness** sumir una habitación en la oscuridad
plunger ['plʌndʒəʳ] *n* émbolo; (*for drain*) desatascador *m*
plunging ['plʌndʒɪŋ] *adj* (*neckline*) escotado
pluperfect [plu:'pə:fɪkt] *n* pluscuamperfecto
plural ['pluərl] *adj* plural ▷ *n* plural *m*
plus [plʌs] *n* (*also*: **~ sign**) signo más; (*fig*) punto a favor ▷ *adj*: **a ~ factor** (*fig*) un factor *m* a favor ▷ *prep* más, y, además de; **ten/twenty ~** más de diez/veinte
plush [plʌʃ] *adj* de felpa
plus-one ['plʌs'wʌn] *n* (*inf*) acompañante *mf*
ply [plaɪ] *vt* (*a trade*) ejercer ▷ *vi* (*ship*) ir y venir; (*for hire*) ofrecerse (para alquilar); **three ~** (*wool*) de tres cabos; **to ~ sb with drink** no dejar de ofrecer copas a algn
plywood ['plaɪwud] *n* madera contrachapada
PM *n abbr* (*Brit*) = **Prime Minister**
p.m. *adv abbr* (= *post meridiem*) de la tarde *or* noche
PMS *n abbr* (= *premenstrual syndrome*) SPM *m*
PMT *n abbr* (= *premenstrual tension*) SPM *m*
pneumatic [nju:'mætɪk] *adj* neumático
pneumatic drill *n* taladradora neumática
pneumonia [nju:'məunɪə] *n* pulmonía, neumonía
PO *n abbr* (= *Post Office*) Correos *mpl*; (*Naut*) = **petty officer**
po *abbr* = **postal order**
poach [pəutʃ] *vt* (*cook*) escalfar; (*steal*) cazar/pescar en vedado ▷ *vi* cazar/pescar en vedado
poached [pəutʃt] *adj* (*egg*) escalfado
poacher ['pəutʃəʳ] *n* cazador(a) *m(f)* furtivo(-a)
PO Box *n abbr* (= *Post Office Box*) apdo., aptdo.
pocket ['pɔkɪt] *n* bolsillo; (*of air*, *Geo*, *fig*) bolsa; (*Billiards*) tronera ▷ *vt* meter en el bolsillo; (*steal*) embolsarse; (*Billiards*) entronerar; **breast ~** bolsillo de pecho; **~ of resistance** foco de resistencia; **~ of warm air** bolsa de aire caliente; **to be out of ~** salir perdiendo; **to be £5 in/out of ~** salir ganando/perdiendo 5 libras
pocketbook ['pɔkɪtbuk] *n* (*US*: *wallet*) cartera; (: *handbag*) bolso
pocket knife *n* navaja
pocket money *n* asignación *f*
pod [pɔd] *n* vaina
podcast ['pɔdkɑ:st] *n* podcast *m* ▷ *vi* podcastear
podgy ['pɔdʒɪ] *adj* gordinflón(-ona)
podiatrist [pɔ'di:ətrɪst] *n* (*US*) podólogo(-a)
podium ['pəudɪəm] *n* podio
poem ['pəuɪm] *n* poema *m*
poet ['pəuɪt] *n* poeta *m/f*
poetic [pəu'ɛtɪk] *adj* poético
poet laureate [-'lɔ:rɪɪt] *n* poeta *m* laureado
poetry ['pəuɪtrɪ] *n* poesía
poignant ['pɔɪnjənt] *adj* conmovedor(a)
point [pɔɪnt] *n* punto; (*tip*) punta; (*purpose*) fin *m*, propósito; (*Brit Elec*: *also*: **power ~**) toma de corriente, enchufe *m*; (*use*) utilidad *f*; (*significant part*) lo esencial; (*place*) punto, lugar *m*; (*also*: **decimal ~**): **2 ~ 3 (2.3)** dos coma tres (2,3) ▷ *vt* (*gun etc*): **to ~ sth at sb** apuntar con algo a algn ▷ *vi*: **to ~ at** señalar; **points** *npl* (*Aut*) contactos *mpl*; (*Rail*) agujas *fpl*; **to be on the ~ of doing sth** estar a punto de hacer algo; **to make a ~ of doing sth** poner empeño en hacer algo; **to get the ~** comprender; **to come to the ~** ir al meollo; **there's no ~ (in doing)** no tiene sentido (hacer); **~ of departure** (*also fig*) punto de partida; **~ of order** cuestión *f* de procedimiento; **~ of sale** (*Comm*) punto de venta; **~-of-sale advertising** publicidad *f* en el punto de venta; **the train stops at Carlisle and all ~s south** el tren para en Carlisle, y en todas las estaciones al sur; **when it comes to the ~** a la hora de la verdad; **in ~ of fact** en realidad; **that's the whole ~!** ¡de eso se trata!; **to be beside the ~** no venir al caso; **you've got a ~ there!** ¡tienes razón!; **point out** *vt* señalar; **point to** *vt fus* indicar con el dedo; (*fig*) indicar, señalar
point-blank ['pɔɪnt'blæŋk] *adv* (*say*, *refuse*) sin más hablar; (*also*: **at ~ range**) a quemarropa
pointed ['pɔɪntɪd] *adj* (*shape*) puntiagudo, afilado; (*remark*) intencionado
pointer ['pɔɪntəʳ] *n* (*stick*) puntero; (*needle*) aguja, indicador *m*; (*clue*) indicación *f*, pista; (*advice*) consejo
pointless ['pɔɪntlɪs] *adj* sin sentido
point of view *n* punto de vista
poise [pɔɪz] *n* (*of head*, *body*) porte *m*; (*calmness*) aplomo
poison ['pɔɪzn] *n* veneno ▷ *vt* envenenar
poisonous ['pɔɪznəs] *adj* venenoso; (*fumes etc*) tóxico; (*fig*: *ideas*, *literature*) pernicioso; (: *rumours*, *individual*) nefasto

poke [pəuk] *vt* (*fire*) hurgar, atizar; (*jab with finger, stick etc*) dar; (*Comput*) almacenar; (*put*): **to ~ sth in(to)** introducir algo en ▷ *n* (*jab*) empujoncito; (*with elbow*) codazo; **to ~ one's head out of the window** asomar la cabeza por la ventana; **to ~ fun at sb** ridiculizar a algn; **to give the fire a ~** atizar el fuego; **poke about** *vi* fisgonear; **poke out** *vi* (*stick out*) salir

poker ['pəukəʳ] *n* atizador *m*; (*Cards*) póker *m*

poky ['pəukɪ] *adj* estrecho

Poland ['pəulənd] *n* Polonia

polar ['pəuləʳ] *adj* polar

polar bear *n* oso polar

polarize ['pəuləraɪz] *vt* polarizar

Pole [pəul] *n* polaco(-a)

pole [pəul] *n* palo; (*Geo*) polo; (*Tel*) poste *m*; (*flagpole*) asta; (*tent pole*) mástil *m*

poleaxe ['pəulæks] *vt* (*fig*) desnucar

pole bean *n* (*US*) judía trepadora

pole star *n* estrella polar

pole vault *n* salto con pértiga

police [pə'li:s] *n* policía ▷ *vt* (*streets, city, frontier*) vigilar

police car *n* coche-patrulla *m*

police constable *n* (*Brit*) guardia *m*, policía *m*

police department *n* (*US*) policía

police force *n* cuerpo de policía

policeman [pə'li:smən] *n* guardia *m*, policía *m*, agente *m* (*LAm*)

police officer *n* guardia *m*, policía *m*

police station *n* comisaría

policewoman [pə'li:swumən] *n* mujer *f* policía

policy ['pɔlɪsɪ] *n* política; (*also*: **insurance ~**) póliza; (*of newspaper, company*) política; **it is our ~ to do that** tenemos por norma hacer eso; **to take out a ~** sacar una póliza, hacerse un seguro

polio ['pəulɪəu] *n* polio *f*

Polish ['pəulɪʃ] *adj* polaco ▷ *n* (*Ling*) polaco

polish ['pɔlɪʃ] *n* (*for shoes*) betún *m*; (*for floor*) cera (de lustrar); (*for nails*) esmalte *m*; (*shine*) brillo, lustre *m*; (*fig*: *refinement*) refinamiento ▷ *vt* (*shoes*) limpiar; (*make shiny*) pulir, sacar brillo a; (*fig*: *improve*) perfeccionar, refinar; **polish off** *vt* (*work*) terminar; (*food*) despachar; **polish up** *vt* (*shoes, furniture etc*) limpiar, sacar brillo a; (*fig*: *language*) perfeccionar

polished ['pɔlɪʃt] *adj* (*fig*: *person*) refinado

polite [pə'laɪt] *adj* cortés, atento; (*formal*) correcto; **it's not ~ to do that** es de mala educación hacer eso

politeness [pə'laɪtnɪs] *n* cortesía

political [pə'lɪtɪkl] *adj* político

politically [pə'lɪtɪkəlɪ] *adv* políticamente

politically correct *adj* políticamente correcto

politician [pɔlɪ'tɪʃən] *n* político(-a)

politics ['pɔlɪtɪks] *n* política

poll [pəul] *n* (*votes*) votación *f*, votos *mpl*; (*also*: **opinion ~**) sondeo, encuesta ▷ *vt* (*votes*) obtener; (*in opinion poll*) encuestar; **to go to the ~s** (*voters*) votar; (*government*) acudir a las urnas

pollen ['pɔlən] *n* polen *m*

pollen count *n* índice *m* de polen

polling booth *n* cabina de votar

polling day *n* día *m* de elecciones

polling station *n* centro electoral

pollster ['pəulstəʳ] *n* (*person*) encuestador(a) *m(f)*; (*organization*) empresa de encuestas *or* sondeos

poll tax *n* (*Brit*) contribución *f* municipal (*no progresiva*)

pollutant [pə'lu:tənt] *n* (agente *m*) contaminante *m*

pollute [pə'lu:t] *vt* contaminar

pollution [pə'lu:ʃən] *n* contaminación *f*

polo ['pəuləu] *n* (*sport*) polo

polo-neck ['pəuləunɛk] *adj* de cuello vuelto ▷ *n* (*sweater*) suéter *m* de cuello vuelto

polo shirt *n* polo, niqui *m*

poly bag *n* (*Brit inf*) bolsa de plástico

polyester [pɔlɪ'ɛstəʳ] *n* poliéster *m*

polygraph ['pɔlɪgrɑ:f] *n* polígrafo

polystyrene [pɔlɪ'staɪri:n] *n* poliestireno

polytechnic [pɔlɪ'tɛknɪk] *n* escuela politécnica

polythene ['pɔlɪθi:n] *n* (*Brit*) polietileno

polythene bag *n* bolsa de plástico

polyurethane [pɔlɪ'juərɪθeɪn] *n* poliuretano

pomegranate ['pɔmɪgrænɪt] *n* granada

pomp [pɔmp] *n* pompa

pompous ['pɔmpəs] *adj* pomposo; (*person*) presumido

pond [pɔnd] *n* (*natural*) charca; (*artificial*) estanque *m*

ponder ['pɔndəʳ] *vt* meditar

ponderous ['pɔndərəs] *adj* pesado

pong [pɔŋ] *n* (*Brit inf*) peste *f* ▷ *vi* (*Brit inf*) apestar

pontiff ['pɔntɪf] *n* pontífice *m*

pony ['pəunɪ] *n* poney *m*, potro

ponytail ['pəunɪteɪl] *n* coleta, cola de caballo

pony trekking *n* (*Brit*) excursión *f* a caballo

poodle ['pu:dl] *n* caniche *m*

pool [pu:l] *n* (*natural*) charca; (*pond*) estanque *m*; (*also*: **swimming ~**) piscina, alberca (*LAm*); (*billiards*) billar *m* americano; (*Comm*: *consortium*) consorcio; (: *US*: *monopoly trust*) trust *m* ▷ *vt* juntar; **typing ~** servicio de mecanografía; **(football) ~s** *npl* quinielas *fpl*

poor [puəʳ] *adj* pobre; (*bad*) malo ▷ *npl*: **the ~** los pobres

poorly ['puəlɪ] *adj* mal, enfermo ▷ *adv* mal

pop [pɔp] *n* ¡pum!; (*sound*) ruido seco; (*Mus*) (música) pop *m*; (*US inf*: *father*) papá *m*; (*inf*: *drink*) gaseosa ▷ *vt* (*burst*) hacer reventar ▷ *vi* reventar; (*cork*) saltar; **she ~ped her head out (of the window)** sacó de repente la cabeza (por la ventana); **pop in** *vi* entrar un momento; **pop out** *vi* salir un momento; **pop up** *vi* aparecer inesperadamente

P

pop concert *n* concierto pop
popcorn ['pɔpkɔ:n] *n* palomitas *fpl* (de maíz)
pope [pəup] *n* papa *m*
poplar ['pɔplə^r] *n* álamo
popper ['pɔpə^r] *n* corchete *m*, automático
poppy ['pɔpɪ] *n* amapola; *see also* **Remembrance Day**
Popsicle® ['pɔpsɪkl] *n* (*US*) polo
pop star *n* estrella del pop
popular ['pɔpjulə^r] *adj* popular; **a ~ song** una canción popular; **to be ~ (with)** (*person*) caer bien (a); (*decision*) ser popular (entre)
popularity [pɔpju'lærɪtɪ] *n* popularidad *f*
population [pɔpju'leɪʃən] *n* población *f*
pop-up ['pɔpʌp] *adj* desplegable, pop-up *inv* ▷ *n* desplegable *m*
pop-up book *n* libro desplegable
pop-up menu *n* (*Comput*) menú *m* desplegable
porcelain ['pɔ:slɪn] *n* porcelana
porch [pɔ:tʃ] *n* pórtico, entrada; (*US*) veranda
porcupine ['pɔ:kjupaɪn] *n* puerco *m* espín
pore [pɔ:^r] *n* poro ▷ *vi*: **to ~ over** enfrascarse en
pork [pɔ:k] *n* (carne *f* de) cerdo *or* chancho (*LAm*)
pork chop *n* chuleta de cerdo
pork pie *n* (*Brit*: *Culin*) empanada de carne de cerdo
porn [pɔ:n] *adj* (*inf*) porno *inv* ▷ *n* porno
pornographic [pɔ:nə'græfɪk] *adj* pornográfico
pornography [pɔ:'nɔgrəfɪ] *n* pornografía
porpoise ['pɔ:pəs] *n* marsopa
porridge ['pɔrɪdʒ] *n* gachas *fpl* de avena
port [pɔ:t] *n* (*harbour*) puerto; (*Naut*: *left side*) babor *m*; (*wine*) oporto; (*Comput*) puerta, puerto, port *m*; **~ of call** puerto de escala
portable ['pɔ:təbl] *adj* portátil
porter ['pɔ:tə^r] *n* (*for luggage*) maletero; (*doorkeeper*) portero(-a), conserje *m/f*; (*US Rail*) mozo de los coches-cama
portfolio [pɔ:t'fəulɪəu] *n* (*case, of artist*) cartera, carpeta; (*Pol, Finance*) cartera
porthole ['pɔ:thəul] *n* portilla
portion ['pɔ:ʃən] *n* porción *f*; (*helping*) ración *f*
portly ['pɔ:tlɪ] *adj* corpulento
portrait ['pɔ:treɪt] *n* retrato
portray [pɔ:'treɪ] *vt* retratar; (*in writing*) representar
portrayal [pɔ:'treɪəl] *n* representación *f*
Portugal ['pɔ:tjugl] *n* Portugal *m*
Portuguese [pɔ:tju'gi:z] *adj* portugués(-esa) ▷ *n pl inv* portugués(-esa) *m(f)*; (*Ling*) portugués *m*
pose [pəuz] *n* postura, actitud *f*; (*pej*) afectación *f*, pose *f* ▷ *vi* posar; (*pretend*): **to ~ as** hacerse pasar por ▷ *vt* (*question*) plantear; **to ~ for** posar para; **to strike a ~** tomar *or* adoptar una pose *or* actitud
poser ['pəuzə^r] *n* problema *m*/pregunta difícil; (*person*) = **poseur**
poseur [pəu'zə:^r] *n* presumido(-a), persona afectada
posh [pɔʃ] *adj* (*inf*) elegante, de lujo ▷ *adv* (*inf*): **to talk ~** hablar con acento afectado
position [pə'zɪʃən] *n* posición *f*; (*job*) puesto ▷ *vt* colocar; **to be in a ~ to do sth** estar en condiciones de hacer algo
positive ['pɔzɪtɪv] *adj* positivo; (*certain*) seguro; (*definite*) definitivo; **we look forward to a ~ reply** (*Comm*) esperamos que pueda darnos una respuesta en firme; **he's a ~ nuisance** es un auténtico pelmazo; **~ cash flow** (*Comm*) flujo positivo de efectivo
positively ['pɔzɪtɪvlɪ] *adv* (*affirmatively, enthusiastically*) de forma positiva; (*inf*: *really*) absolutamente
posse ['pɔsɪ] *n* (*US*) pelotón *m*
possess [pə'zɛs] *vt* poseer; **like one ~ed** como un poseído; **whatever can have ~ed you?** ¿cómo se te ocurrió?
possessed [pə'zɛst] *adj* poseso, poseído
possession [pə'zɛʃən] *n* posesión *f*; **possessions** *npl* (*belongings*) pertenencias *fpl*; **to take ~ of sth** tomar posesión de algo
possessive [pə'zɛsɪv] *adj* posesivo
possessiveness [pə'zɛsɪvnɪs] *n* posesividad *f*
possibility [pɔsɪ'bɪlɪtɪ] *n* posibilidad *f*; **he's a ~ for the part** es uno de los posibles para el papel
possible ['pɔsɪbl] *adj* posible; **as big as ~** lo más grande posible; **it is ~ to do it** es posible hacerlo; **as far as ~** en la medida de lo posible; **a ~ candidate** un(a) posible candidato(-a)
possibly ['pɔsɪblɪ] *adv* (*perhaps*) posiblemente, tal vez; **I cannot ~ come** me es imposible venir; **could you ~ ...?** ¿podrías ...?
post [pəust] *n* (*Brit*: *system*) correos *mpl*; (*letters, delivery*) correo; (*job, situation*) puesto; (*trading post*) factoría; (*pole*) poste *m*; (*on internet forum*) anuncio, post *m* ▷ *vt* (*Brit*: *send by post*) mandar por correo; (: *put in mailbox*) echar al correo; (*Mil*) apostar; (*bills*) fijar, pegar; (*to internet*) colgar; (*Brit*: *appoint*): **to ~ to** destinar a; **by ~** por correo; **by return of ~** a vuelta de correo; **to keep sb ~ed** tener a algn al corriente
postage ['pəustɪdʒ] *n* porte *m*, franqueo
postage stamp *n* sello (de correo)
postal ['pəustl] *adj* postal, de correos
postal order *n* giro postal
postbox ['pəustbɔks] *n* (*Brit*) buzón *m*
postcard ['pəustkɑ:d] *n* (tarjeta) postal *f*
postcode ['pəustkəud] *n* (*Brit*) código postal
poster ['pəustə^r] *n* cartel *m*, afiche *m* (*LAm*)
poste restante [pəust'rɛstɔ̃nt] *n* (*Brit*) lista de correos
posterior [pɔs'tɪərɪə^r] *n* (*inf*) trasero
posterity [pɔs'tɛrɪtɪ] *n* posteridad *f*
postgraduate ['pəust'grædjuɪt] *n* posgraduado(-a)
posthumous ['pɔstjuməs] *adj* póstumo

postman ['pəustmən] (*Brit*) (*irreg: like* **man**) *n* cartero
postmark ['pəustmɑ:k] *n* matasellos *m inv*
post-mortem [pəust'mɔ:təm] *n* autopsia
post office *n* (*building*) (oficina de) correos *m*; (*organization*): **the Post Office** Dirección *f* General de Correos
postpone [pəs'pəun] *vt* aplazar, postergar (*LAm*)
postponement [pəs'pəunmənt] *n* aplazamiento
posture ['pɔstʃəʳ] *n* postura, actitud *f*
post-war [pəust'wɔ:ʳ] *adj* de la posguerra
postwoman ['pəustwumən] (*irreg: like* **woman**) *n* (*Brit*) cartera
posy ['pəuzɪ] *n* ramillete *m* (de flores)
pot [pɔt] *n* (*for cooking*) olla; (*teapot*) tetera; (*coffeepot*) cafetera; (*for flowers*) maceta; (*for jam*) tarro, pote *m* (*LAm*); (*piece of pottery*) cacharro; (*inf: marijuana*) costo, chocolate *m* ▷ *vt* (*plant*) poner en tiesto; (*conserve*) conservar (en tarros); **~s of** (*inf*) montones de; **to go to ~** (*inf: work, performance*) irse al traste
potato (*pl* **potatoes**) [pə'teɪtəu] *n* patata, papa (*LAm*)
potato crisps, potato chips (*US*) *npl* patatas *fpl or* papas *fpl* (*LAm*)
potato peeler *n* pelapatatas *m inv*
potent ['pəutnt] *adj* potente, poderoso; (*drink*) fuerte
potential [pə'tɛnʃl] *adj* potencial, posible ▷ *n* potencial *m*; **to have ~** prometer
pothole ['pɔthəul] *n* (*in road*) bache *m*; (*Brit: underground*) gruta
potholing ['pɔthəulɪŋ] *n* (*Brit*): **to go ~** dedicarse a la espeleología
potion ['pəuʃən] *n* poción *f*, pócima
potluck [pɔt'lʌk] *n*: **to take ~** conformarse con lo que haya
pot plant *n* planta de interior
potted ['pɔtɪd] *adj* (*food*) en conserva; (*plant*) en tiesto *or* maceta; (*fig: shortened*) resumido
potter ['pɔtəʳ] *n* alfarero(-a) ▷ *vi*: **to ~ around, ~ about** entretenerse haciendo cosillas; **to ~ round the house** estar en casa haciendo cosillas; **~'s wheel** torno de alfarero
pottery ['pɔtərɪ] *n* cerámica; (*factory*) alfarería; **a piece of ~** un objeto de cerámica
potty ['pɔtɪ] *adj* (*inf: mad*) chiflado ▷ *n* orinal *m* de niño
pouch [pautʃ] *n* (*Zool*) bolsa; (*for tobacco*) petaca
poultry ['pəultrɪ] *n* aves *fpl* de corral; (*meat*) pollo
pounce [pauns] *vi*: **to ~ on** precipitarse sobre ▷ *n* salto, ataque *m*
pound [paund] *n* libra; (*for dogs*) perrera; (*for cars*) depósito ▷ *vt* (*beat*) golpear; (*crush*) machacar ▷ *vi* (*beat*) dar golpes; **half a ~** media libra; **a one ~ note** un billete de una libra
pound sterling *n* libra esterlina
pour [pɔ:ʳ] *vt* echar; (*tea*) servir ▷ *vi* correr, fluir; (*rain*) llover a cántaros; **pour away, pour off** *vt* vaciar, verter; **to ~ sb a drink** servirle a algn una copa; **pour in** *vi* (*people*) entrar en tropel; **to come ~ing in** (*water*) entrar a raudales; (*letters*) llegar a montones; (*cars, people*) llegar en tropel; **pour out** *vi* (*people*) salir en tropel ▷ *vt* (*drink*) echar, servir; (*fig*): **to ~ out one's feelings** desahogarse
pouring ['pɔ:rɪŋ] *adj*: **~ rain** lluvia torrencial
pout [paut] *vi* hacer pucheros
poverty ['pɔvətɪ] *n* pobreza, miseria; (*fig*) falta, escasez *f*
poverty line *n*: **below the ~** por debajo del umbral de pobreza
poverty-stricken ['pɔvətɪstrɪkn] *adj* necesitado
POW *n abbr* = **prisoner of war**
powder ['paudəʳ] *n* polvo; (*also*: **face ~**) polvos *mpl*; (*also*: **gun ~**) pólvora ▷ *vt* empolvar; **to ~ one's face** empolvarse la cara; **to ~ one's nose** empolvarse la nariz, ponerse polvos; (*euphemism*) ir al baño
powder compact *n* polvera
powdered milk ['paudəd-] *n* leche *f* en polvo
powder keg *n* (*fig*) polvorín *m*
powder puff *n* borla (para empolvarse)
powder room *n* aseos *mpl*
power ['pauəʳ] *n* poder *m*; (*strength*) fuerza; (*nation*) potencia; (*drive*) empuje *m*; (*Tech*) potencia; (*Elec*) energía ▷ *vt* impulsar; **to be in ~** (*Pol*) estar en el poder; **to do all in one's ~ to help sb** hacer todo lo posible por ayudar a algn; **the world ~s** las potencias mundiales
power cut *n* (*Brit*) apagón *m*
powered ['pauəd] *adj*: **~ by** impulsado por; **nuclear-~ submarine** submarino nuclear
power failure *n* = **power cut**
powerful ['pauəful] *adj* poderoso; (*engine*) potente; (*strong*) fuerte; (*play, speech*) convincente
powerless ['pauəlɪs] *adj* impotente
power of attorney *n* poder *m*, procuración *f*
power point *n* (*Brit*) enchufe *m*
power station *n* central *f* eléctrica
pp *abbr* (= *per procurationem: by proxy*) p.p.; = **pages**
PPS *n abbr* (= *post postscriptum*) *posdata adicional*; (*Brit*: = *Parliamentary Private Secretary*) *ayudante de un ministro*
PR *n abbr see* **proportional representation**; (= *public relations*) relaciones *fpl* públicas
practical ['præktɪkl] *adj* práctico
practicality [præktɪ'kælɪtɪ] *n* (*of situation etc*) aspecto práctico
practical joke *n* broma pesada
practically ['præktɪklɪ] *adv* (*almost*) casi, prácticamente

P

practice ['præktɪs] *n* (*habit*) costumbre *f*; (*exercise*) práctica; (*training*) adiestramiento; (*Med*: *of profession*) práctica, ejercicio; (*Med, Law*: *business*) consulta ▷ *vt, vi* (*US*) = **practise**; **in ~** (*in reality*) en la práctica; **out of ~** desentrenado; **to put sth into ~** poner algo en práctica; **it's common ~** es bastante corriente; **target ~** práctica de tiro; **he has a small ~** (*doctor*) tiene pocos pacientes; **to set up in ~ as** establecerse como

practise, practice (*US*) ['præktɪs] *vt* (*carry out*) practicar; (*profession*) ejercer; (*train at*) practicar ▷ *vi* ejercer; (*train*) practicar

practising, practicing (*US*) ['præktɪsɪŋ] *adj* (*Christian etc*) practicante; (*lawyer*) en ejercicio; (*homosexual*) activo

practitioner [præk'tɪʃənəʳ] *n* practicante *m/f*; (*Med*) médico(-a)

pragmatic [præg'mætɪk] *adj* pragmático

prairie ['prɛərɪ] *n* (*US*) pampa

praise [preɪz] *n* alabanza(s) *f(pl)*, elogio(s) *m(pl)* ▷ *vt* alabar, elogiar

praiseworthy ['preɪswəːðɪ] *adj* loable

pram [præm] *n* (*Brit*) cochecito de niño

prance [prɑːns] *vi* (*horse*) hacer cabriolas

prank [præŋk] *n* travesura

prat [præt] *n* (*Brit inf*) imbécil *m/f*

prawn [prɔːn] *n* gamba

prawn cocktail *n* cóctel *m* de gambas

pray [preɪ] *vi* rezar; **to ~ for forgiveness** pedir perdón

prayer [prɛəʳ] *n* oración *f*, rezo; (*entreaty*) ruego, súplica

preach [priːtʃ] *vi* predicar

preacher ['priːtʃəʳ] *n* predicador(a) *m(f)*; (*US*: *minister*) pastor(a) *m(f)*

prearrange [priːə'reɪndʒ] *vt* organizar *or* acordar de antemano

precarious [prɪ'kɛərɪəs] *adj* precario

precaution [prɪ'kɔːʃən] *n* precaución *f*

precede [prɪ'siːd] *vt, vi* preceder

precedent ['prɛsɪdənt] *n* precedente *m*; **to establish** *or* **set a ~** sentar un precedente

preceding [prɪ'siːdɪŋ] *adj* precedente

precinct ['priːsɪŋkt] *n* recinto; (*US*: *district*) distrito, barrio; **precincts** *npl* recinto; **pedestrian ~** (*Brit*) zona peatonal; **shopping ~** (*Brit*) centro comercial

precious ['prɛʃəs] *adj* precioso; (*treasured*) querido; (*stylized*) afectado ▷ *adv* (*inf*): **~ little/few** muy poco/pocos; **your ~ dog** (*ironic*) tu querido perro

precipitate *adj* [prɪ'sɪpɪtɪt] (*hasty*) precipitado ▷ *vt* [prɪ'sɪpɪteɪt] precipitar

precise [prɪ'saɪs] *adj* preciso, exacto; (*person*) escrupuloso

precisely [prɪ'saɪslɪ] *adv* exactamente, precisamente

precision [prɪ'sɪʒən] *n* precisión *f*

preclude [prɪ'kluːd] *vt* excluir

precocious [prɪ'kəuʃəs] *adj* precoz

precondition [priːkən'dɪʃən] *n* condición *f* previa

predator ['prɛdətəʳ] *n* depredador *m*

predecessor ['priːdɪsɛsəʳ] *n* antecesor(a) *m(f)*

predestination [priːdɛstɪ'neɪʃən] *n* predestinación *f*

predicament [prɪ'dɪkəmənt] *n* apuro

predict [prɪ'dɪkt] *vt* predecir, pronosticar

predictable [prɪ'dɪktəbl] *adj* previsible

prediction [prɪ'dɪkʃən] *n* pronóstico, predicción *f*

predominant [prɪ'dɔmɪnənt] *adj* predominante

predominantly [prɪ'dɔmɪnəntlɪ] *adv* en su mayoría

pre-eminent [priː'ɛmɪnənt] *adj* preeminente

pre-empt [priː'ɛmt] *vt* (*Brit*) adelantarse a

preen [priːn] *vt*: **to ~ itself** (*bird*) limpiarse las plumas; **to ~ o.s.** pavonearse

prefab ['priːfæb] *n* casa prefabricada

preface ['prɛfəs] *n* prefacio

prefect ['priːfɛkt] *n* (*Brit*: *in school*) monitor(a) *m(f)*

prefer [prɪ'fəːʳ] *vt* preferir; (*Law*: *charges, complaint*) presentar; (*: action*) entablar; **to ~ coffee to tea** preferir el café al té

preferable ['prɛfrəbl] *adj* preferible

preferably ['prɛfrəblɪ] *adv* preferentemente, más bien

preference ['prɛfrəns] *n* preferencia; (*priority*) prioridad *f*; **in ~ to sth** antes que algo

preferential [prɛfə'rɛnʃəl] *adj* preferente

prefix ['priːfɪks] *n* prefijo

pregnancy ['prɛgnənsɪ] *n* (*of woman*) embarazo; (*of animal*) preñez *f*

pregnancy test *n* prueba del embarazo

pregnant ['prɛgnənt] *adj* (*woman*) embarazada; (*animal*) preñada; **3 months ~** embarazada de tres meses; **~ with meaning** cargado de significado

prehistoric ['priːhɪs'tɔrɪk] *adj* prehistórico

prejudge [priː'dʒʌdʒ] *vt* prejuzgar

prejudice ['prɛdʒudɪs] *n* (*bias*) prejuicio; (*harm*) perjuicio ▷ *vt* (*bias*) predisponer; (*harm*) perjudicar; **to ~ sb in favour of/against** (*bias*) predisponer a algn a favor de/en contra de

prejudiced ['prɛdʒudɪst] *adj* (*person*) predispuesto; (*view*) parcial, interesado; **to be ~ against sb/sth** estar predispuesto en contra de algn/algo

preliminary [prɪ'lɪmɪnərɪ] *adj* preliminar

prelude ['prɛljuːd] *n* preludio

premarital ['priː'mærɪtl] *adj* prematrimonial, premarital

premature ['prɛmətʃuəʳ] *adj* (*arrival etc*) prematuro; **you are being a little ~** te has adelantado

premeditation [priːmɛdɪ'teɪʃən] *n* premeditación *f*

premier ['prɛmɪəʳ] *adj* primero, principal ▷ *n* (*Pol*) primer(a) ministro(-a)
première ['prɛmɪɛəʳ] *n* estreno
Premier League [prɛmɪə'li:g] *n* primera división
premise ['prɛmɪs] *n* premisa
premises ['prɛmɪsɪs] *npl* local *msg*; **on the ~** en el lugar mismo; **business ~** locales *mpl* comerciales
premium ['pri:mɪəm] *n* premio; (*insurance*) prima; **to be at a ~** estar muy solicitado; **to sell at a ~** (*shares*) vender caro
premium bond *n* (*Brit*) *bono del estado que participa en una lotería nacional*; *ver nota*
premonition [prɛmə'nɪʃən] *n* presentimiento
preoccupied [pri:'ɔkjupaɪd] *adj* (*worried*) preocupado; (*absorbed*) ensimismado
prep [prɛp] *adj abbr*: **~ school** = **preparatory school** ▷ *n abbr* (*Scol*: = *preparation*) deberes *mpl*
prepaid [pri:'peɪd] *adj* porte pagado; **~ envelope** sobre *m* de porte pagado
preparation [prɛpə'reɪʃən] *n* preparación *f*; **preparations** *npl* preparativos *mpl*; **in ~ for sth** en preparación para algo
preparatory [prɪ'pærətərɪ] *adj* preparatorio, preliminar; **~ to sth/to doing sth** como preparación para algo/para hacer algo
preparatory school *n* (*Brit*) *colegio privado de enseñanza primaria*; (*US*) *colegio privado de enseñanza secundaria*
prepare [prɪ'pɛəʳ] *vt* preparar, disponer; (*Culin*) preparar ▷ *vi*: **to ~ for** (*action*) prepararse *or* disponerse para; (*event*) hacer preparativos para
prepared [prɪ'pɛəd] *adj* (*willing*): **to be ~ to help sb** estar dispuesto a ayudar a algn; **~ for** listo para
preposition [prɛpə'zɪʃən] *n* preposición *f*
preposterous [prɪ'pɔstərəs] *adj* absurdo, ridículo
prep school [prɛp-] *n* = **preparatory school**
prerequisite [pri:'rɛkwɪzɪt] *n* requisito previo
preschool ['pri:'sku:l] *adj* (*child, age*) preescolar
prescribe [prɪ'skraɪb] *vt* prescribir; (*Med*) recetar; **~d books** (*Brit Scol*) libros *mpl* del curso
prescription [prɪ'skrɪpʃən] *n* (*Med*) receta; **to make up a ~** (*US*), **fill a ~** preparar una receta; **only available on ~** se vende solamente con receta (médica)
presence ['prɛzns] *n* presencia; (*attendance*) asistencia; **in sb's ~** en presencia de algn; **~ of mind** aplomo
presence of mind *n* aplomo
present *adj* ['prɛznt] (*in attendance*) presente; (*current*) actual ▷ *n* ['prɛznt] (*gift*) regalo; (*actuality*): **the ~** la actualidad, el presente ▷ *vt* [prɪ'zɛnt] (*introduce*) presentar; (*expound*) exponer; (*give*) presentar, dar, ofrecer; (*Theat*) representar; **to be ~ at** asistir a, estar presente en; **those ~** los presentes; **to give sb a ~, make sb a ~ of sth** regalar algo a algn; **at ~** actualmente; **to ~ o.s. for an interview** presentarse a una entrevista; **may I ~ Miss Clark** permítame presentarle *or* le presento a la Srta Clark
presentable [prɪ'zɛntəbl] *adj*: **to make o.s. ~** arreglarse
presentation [prɛzn'teɪʃən] *n* presentación *f*; (*gift*) obsequio; (*of case*) exposición *f*; (*Theat*) representación *f*; **on ~ of the voucher** al presentar el vale
present-day ['prɛzntdeɪ] *adj* actual
presenter [prɪ'zɛntəʳ] *n* (*Radio, TV*) locutor(a) *m(f)*
presently ['prɛzntlɪ] *adv* (*soon*) dentro de poco; (*US*: *now*) ahora
present participle *n* participio (de) presente
preservation [prɛzə'veɪʃən] *n* conservación *f*
preservative [prɪ'zə:vətɪv] *n* conservante *m*
preserve [prɪ'zə:v] *vt* (*keep safe*) preservar, proteger; (*maintain*) mantener; (*food*) conservar; (*in salt*) salar ▷ *n* (*for game*) coto, vedado *often pl* (*jam*) confitura
preside [prɪ'zaɪd] *vi* presidir
presidency ['prɛzɪdənsɪ] *n* presidencia
president ['prɛzɪdənt] *n* presidente *m/f*; (*US*: *of company*) director(a) *m(f)*
presidential [prɛzɪ'dɛnʃl] *adj* presidencial
press [prɛs] *n* (*tool, machine, newspapers*) prensa; (*printer's*) imprenta; (*of hand*) apretón *m* ▷ *vt* (*push*) empujar; (*squeeze*) apretar; (*grapes*) pisar; (*clothes*: *iron*) planchar; (*pressure*) presionar; (*doorbell*) apretar, pulsar, tocar; (*insist*): **to ~ sth on sb** insistir en que algn acepte algo ▷ *vi* (*squeeze*) apretar; (*pressurize*) ejercer presión; **to go to ~** (*newspaper*) entrar en prensa; **to be in the ~** (*being printed*) estar en prensa; (*in the newspapers*) aparecer en la prensa; **we are ~ed for time** tenemos poco tiempo; **to ~ sb to do** *or* **into doing sth** (*urge, entreat*) presionar a algn para que haga algo; **to ~ sb for an answer** insistir a algn para que conteste; **to ~ charges against sb** (*Law*) demandar a algn; **press ahead** *vi* seguir adelante; **press on** *vi* avanzar; (*hurry*) apretar el paso
press agency *n* agencia de prensa
press conference *n* rueda de prensa
pressing ['prɛsɪŋ] *adj* apremiante
press officer *n* jefe(-a) *m(f)* de prensa
press release *n* comunicado de prensa
press stud *n* (*Brit*) botón *m* de presión
press-up ['prɛsʌp] *n* (*Brit*) flexión *f*
pressure ['prɛʃəʳ] *n* presión *f*; (*urgency*) apremio, urgencia; (*influence*) influencia; **high/low ~** alta/baja presión; **to put ~ on sb** presionar a algn, hacer presión sobre algn
pressure cooker *n* olla a presión
pressure gauge *n* manómetro

P

pressure group *n* grupo de presión
pressurized ['prɛʃəraɪzd] *adj* (*container*) a presión
prestige [prɛs'ti:ʒ] *n* prestigio
prestigious [prɛs'tɪdʒəs] *adj* prestigioso
presumably [prɪ'zju:məblɪ] *adv* es de suponer que, cabe presumir que; **~ he did it** es de suponer que lo hizo él
presume [prɪ'zju:m] *vt*: **to ~ (that)** presumir (que), suponer (que); **to ~ to do** (*dare*) atreverse a hacer
presumption [prɪ'zʌmpʃən] *n* suposición *f*; (*pretension*) presunción *f*
presuppose [pri:sə'pəuz] *vt* presuponer
pretence, pretense (*US*) [prɪ'tɛns] *n* (*claim*) pretensión *f*; (*pretext*) pretexto; (*make-believe*) fingimiento; **on** *or* **under the ~ of doing sth** bajo *or* con el pretexto de hacer algo; **she is devoid of all ~** no es pretenciosa; **under false ~s** con engaños
pretend [prɪ'tɛnd] *vt* (*feign*) fingir ▷ *vi* (*feign*) fingir; (*claim*): **to ~ to sth** pretender a algo
pretense [prɪ'tɛns] *n* (*US*) = **pretence**
pretension [pri'tɛnʃən] *n* (*claim*) pretensión *f*; **to have no ~s to sth/to being sth** no engañarse en cuanto a algo/a ser algo
pretentious [prɪ'tɛnʃəs] *adj* pretencioso; (*ostentatious*) ostentoso, aparatoso
pretext ['pri:tɛkst] *n* pretexto; **on** *or* **under the ~ of doing sth** con el pretexto de hacer algo
pretty ['prɪtɪ] *adj* (*gen*) bonito, lindo (*LAm*) ▷ *adv* bastante
prevail [prɪ'veɪl] *vi* (*gain mastery*) prevalecer; (*be current*) predominar; (*persuade*): **to ~ (up)on sb to do sth** persuadir a algn para que haga algo
prevailing [prɪ'veɪlɪŋ] *adj* (*dominant*) predominante
prevalent ['prɛvələnt] *adj* (*dominant*) dominante; (*widespread*) extendido; (*fashionable*) de moda
prevent [prɪ'vɛnt] *vt*: **to ~ (sb) from doing sth** impedir (a algn) hacer algo; **to ~ sth from happening** evitar que ocurra algo
preventative [prɪ'vɛntətɪv] *adj* preventivo
prevention [prɪ'vɛnʃən] *n* prevención *f*
preventive [prɪ'vɛntɪv] *adj* preventivo
preview ['pri:vju:] *n* (*of film*) preestreno
previous ['pri:vɪəs] *adj* previo, anterior; **he has no ~ experience in that field** no tiene experiencia previa en ese campo; **I have a ~ engagement** tengo un compromiso anterior
previously ['pri:vɪəslɪ] *adv* antes
prewar [pri:'wɔ:ʳ] *adj* antes de la guerra
prey [preɪ] *n* presa ▷ *vi*: **to ~ on** vivir a costa de; (*feed on*) alimentarse de; **it was ~ing on his mind** le obsesionaba
price [praɪs] *n* precio; (*Betting: odds*) puntos *mpl* de ventaja ▷ *vt* (*goods*) fijar el precio de; **to go up** *or* **rise in ~** subir de precio; **what is the ~ of ...?** ¿qué precio tiene ...?; **to put a ~ on sth** poner precio a algo; **what ~ his promises now?** ¿para qué sirven ahora sus promesas?; **he regained his freedom, but at a ~** recobró su libertad, pero le había costado caro; **to be ~d out of the market** (*article*) no encontrar comprador por ese precio; (*nation*) no ser competitivo
priceless ['praɪslɪs] *adj* que no tiene precio; (*inf: amusing*) divertidísimo
price list *n* tarifa
pricey ['praɪsɪ] *adj* (*Brit inf*) caro
prick [prɪk] *n* pinchazo; (*with pin*) alfilerazo; (*sting*) picadura ▷ *vt* pinchar; (*hurt*) picar; **to ~ up one's ears** aguzar el oído
prickle ['prɪkl] *n* (*sensation*) picor *m*; (*Bot*) espina; (*Zool*) púa
prickly ['prɪklɪ] *adj* espinoso; (*fig: person*) enojadizo
prickly heat *n* sarpullido causado por exceso de calor
pride [praɪd] *n* orgullo; (*pej*) soberbia ▷ *vt*: **to ~ o.s. on** enorgullecerse de; **to take (a) ~ in** enorgullecerse de; **her ~ and joy** su orgullo; **to have ~ of place** tener prioridad
priest [pri:st] *n* sacerdote *m*
priesthood ['pri:sthud] *n* (*practice*) sacerdocio; (*priests*) clero
prim [prɪm] *adj* (*demure*) remilgado; (*prudish*) gazmoño
primal ['praɪməl] *adj* original; (*important*) principal
primarily ['praɪmərɪlɪ] *adv* (*above all*) ante todo, primordialmente
primary ['praɪmərɪ] *adj* primario; (*first in importance*) principal ▷ *n* (*US: also*: **~ election**) (elección *f*) primaria; *ver nota*

PRIMARY

Las elecciones primarias (*primaries*) sirven para preseleccionar a los candidatos de los partidos Demócrata ("Democratic") y Republicano ("Republican") durante la campaña que precede a las elecciones a presidente de los Estados Unidos. Se inician en New Hampshire y tienen lugar en 35 estados de febrero a junio. El número de votos obtenidos por cada candidato determina el número de delegados que votarán en el congreso general ("National Convention") de julio y agosto, cuando se decide el candidato definitivo de cada partido.

primary school *n* (*Brit*) escuela primaria
primate *n* ['praɪmɪt] (*Rel*) primado ▷ *n* ['praɪmeɪt] (*Zool*) primate *m*
prime [praɪm] *adj* primero, principal; (*basic*) fundamental; (*excellent*) selecto, de primera clase ▷ *n*: **in the ~ of life** en la flor de la vida ▷ *vt* (*gun, pump*) cebar; (*wood: fig*) preparar; **~ example** ejemplo típico

Prime Minister *n* primer(a) ministro(-a); *see also* **Downing Street**
primer ['praɪməʳ] *n* (*book*) texto elemental; (*paint*) capa preparatoria
primeval [praɪ'mi:vəl] *adj* primitivo
primitive ['prɪmɪtɪv] *adj* primitivo; (*crude*) rudimentario; (*uncivilized*) inculto
primrose ['prɪmrəuz] *n* primavera, prímula
prince [prɪns] *n* príncipe *m*
princess [prɪn'sɛs] *n* princesa
principal ['prɪnsɪpl] *adj* principal ▷ *n* director(a) *m(f)*; (*in play*) protagonista principal *m/f*; (*Comm*) capital *m*, principal *m*; *see also* **pantomime**
principally ['prɪnsɪplɪ] *adv* principalmente
principle ['prɪnsɪpl] *n* principio; **in ~** en principio; **on ~** por principio
print [prɪnt] *n* (*impression*) marca, impresión *f*; (*footprint*) huella; (*fingerprint*) huella dactilar; (*letters*) letra de molde; (*fabric*) estampado; (*Art*) grabado; (*Phot*) impresión *f* ▷ *vt* (*gen*) imprimir; (*on mind*) grabar; (*write in capitals*) escribir en letras de molde; **out of ~** agotado; **print out** *vt* (*Comput*) imprimir
printed matter *n* impresos *mpl*
printer ['prɪntəʳ] *n* (*person*) impresor(a) *m(f)*; (*machine*) impresora
printing ['prɪntɪŋ] *n* (*art*) imprenta; (*act*) impresión *f*; (*quantity*) tirada
printout ['prɪntaut] *n* (*Comput*) copia impresa
prior ['praɪəʳ] *adj* anterior, previo; (*more important*) más importante ▷ *n* prior *m*; **~ to doing** antes de *or* hasta hacer; **without ~ notice** sin previo aviso; **to have a ~ claim to sth** tener prioridad en algo
priority [praɪ'ɔrɪtɪ] *n* prioridad *f*; **to have** *or* **take ~ over sth** tener prioridad sobre algo
prise, prize (*US*) [praɪz] *vt*: **to ~ open** abrir con palanca
prism ['prɪzəm] *n* prisma *m*
prison ['prɪzn] *n* cárcel *f*, prisión *f* ▷ *cpd* carcelario
prisoner ['prɪznəʳ] *n* (*in prison*) preso(-a); (*captured person*) prisionero; (*under arrest*) detenido(-a); (*in dock*) acusado(-a); **the ~ at the bar** el/la acusado(-a); **to take sb ~** hacer *or* tomar prisionero a algn
prisoner of war *n* prisionero(-a) *or* preso(-a) de guerra
pristine ['prɪsti:n] *adj* pristino
privacy ['prɪvəsɪ] *n* (*seclusion*) soledad *f*; (*intimacy*) intimidad *f*; **in the strictest ~** con el mayor secreto
private ['praɪvɪt] *adj* (*personal*) particular; (*confidential*) secreto, confidencial; (*property, industry, discussion etc*) privado; (*person*) reservado; (*place*) tranquilo; (*sitting etc*) a puerta cerrada ▷ *n* soldado raso; **"~"** (*on envelope*) "confidencial"; (*on door*) "privado"; **in ~** en privado; **in (his) ~ life** en su vida privada; **to be in ~ practice** tener consulta particular
private enterprise *n* la empresa privada
private eye *n* detective *m/f* privado(-a)
private limited company *n* (*Brit*) sociedad *f* de responsabilidad limitada
privately ['praɪvɪtlɪ] *adv* en privado; (*in o.s.*) en secreto
private property *n* propiedad *f* privada
private school *n* colegio privado
privatize ['praɪvɪtaɪz] *vt* privatizar
privet ['prɪvɪt] *n* alheña
privilege ['prɪvɪlɪdʒ] *n* privilegio; (*prerogative*) prerrogativa
privy ['prɪvɪ] *adj*: **to be ~ to** estar enterado de
Privy Council *n* consejo privado (de la Corona)
prize [praɪz] *n* premio ▷ *adj* (*first class*) de primera clase ▷ *vt* apreciar, estimar; (*US*) = **prise**
prize-giving ['praɪzgɪvɪŋ] *n* distribución *f* de premios
prizewinner ['praɪzwɪnəʳ] *n* premiado(-a)
pro [prəu] *n* (*Sport*) profesional *m/f*; **the ~s and cons** los pros y los contras
pro- [prəu] *pref* (*in favour of*) pro, en pro de; **~Soviet** pro soviético
proactive [prəu'æktɪv] *adj*: **to be ~** impulsar la actividad
probability [prɔbə'bɪlɪtɪ] *n* probabilidad *f*; **in all ~** lo más probable
probable ['prɔbəbl] *adj* probable; **it is ~/hardly ~ that** es probable/poco probable que
probably ['prɔbəblɪ] *adv* probablemente
probation [prə'beɪʃən] *n*: **on ~** (*employee*) a prueba; (*Law*) en libertad condicional
probation officer *n persona a cargo de los presos en libertad condicional*
probe [prəub] *n* (*Med, Space*) sonda; (*enquiry*) investigación *f* ▷ *vt* sondar; (*investigate*) investigar
problem ['prɔbləm] *n* problema *m*; **what's the ~?** ¿cuál es el problema?, ¿qué pasa?; **no ~!** ¡por supuesto!; **to have ~s with the car** tener problemas con el coche
procedure [prə'si:dʒəʳ] *n* procedimiento; (*bureaucratic*) trámites *mpl*; **cashing a cheque is a simple ~** cobrar un cheque es un trámite sencillo
proceed [prə'si:d] *vi* proceder; (*continue*): **to ~ (with)** continuar (con); **to ~ against sb** (*Law*) proceder contra algn; **I am not sure how to ~** no sé cómo proceder; *see also* **proceeds**
proceedings [prə'si:dɪŋz] *npl* acto *sg*, actos *mpl*; (*Law*) proceso *sg*; (*meeting*) función *fsg*; (*records*) actas *fpl*
proceeds ['prəusi:dz] *npl* ganancias *fpl*, ingresos *mpl*
process ['prəusɛs] *n* proceso; (*method*) método, sistema *m*; (*proceeding*) procedimiento ▷ *vt* tratar, elaborar ▷ *vi* [prə'sɛs] (*Brit*: *formal*: *go in procession*) desfilar; **in ~** en curso; **we are in the ~ of moving to ...** estamos en vías de mudarnos a ...

P

processing ['prəusɛsɪŋ] *n* elaboración *f*
procession [prə'sɛʃən] *n* desfile *m*; **funeral ~** cortejo fúnebre
proclaim [prə'kleɪm] *vt* proclamar; (*announce*) anunciar
procrastinate [prəu'kræstɪneɪt] *vi* demorarse
procreation [prəukrɪ'eɪʃən] *n* procreación *f*
Procurator Fiscal ['prɔkjureɪtə-] *n* (*Scottish*) fiscal *m/f*
procure [prə'kjuə^r] *vt* conseguir, obtener
prod [prɔd] *vt* (*push*) empujar; (*with elbow*) dar un codazo a ▹ *n* empujoncito; codazo
prodigal ['prɔdɪgl] *adj* pródigo
prodigious [prə'dɪdʒəs] *adj* prodigioso
prodigy ['prɔdɪdʒɪ] *n* prodigio
produce *n* ['prɔdju:s] (*Agr*) productos *mpl* agrícolas ▹ *vt* [prə'dju:s] producir; (*yield*) rendir; (*bring*) sacar; (*show*) presentar, mostrar; (*proof of identity*) enseñar, presentar; (*Theat*) presentar, poner en escena; (*offspring*) dar a luz
producer [prə'dju:sə^r] *n* (*Theat*) director(a) *m(f)*; (*Agr, Cine*) productor(a) *m(f)*
product ['prɔdʌkt] *n* producto
production [prə'dʌkʃən] *n* (*act*) producción *f*; (*Theat*) representación *f*, montaje *m*; **to put into ~** lanzar a la producción
production line *n* línea de producción
productive [prə'dʌktɪv] *adj* productivo
productivity [prɔdʌk'tɪvɪtɪ] *n* productividad *f*
Prof. [prɔf] *abbr* (= *professor*) Prof
profane [prə'feɪn] *adj* profano
profess [prə'fɛs] *vt* profesar; **I do not ~ to be an expert** no pretendo ser experto
profession [prə'fɛʃən] *n* profesión *f*
professional [prə'fɛʃnl] *n* profesional *m/f*; (*skilled person*) perito ▹ *adj* profesional; (*by profession*) de profesión; **to take ~ advice** buscar un consejo profesional
professor [prə'fɛsə^r] *n* (*Brit*) catedrático(-a) *m(f)*; (*US: teacher*) profesor(a) *m(f)*
proficiency [prə'fɪʃənsɪ] *n* capacidad *f*, habilidad *f*
proficient [prə'fɪʃənt] *adj* experto, hábil
profile ['prəufaɪl] *n* perfil *m*; **to keep a high/low ~** tratar de llamar la atención/pasar inadvertido
profit ['prɔfɪt] *n* (*Comm*) ganancia; (*fig*) provecho ▹ *vi*: **to ~ by** *or* **from** aprovechar *or* sacar provecho de; **~ and loss account** cuenta de ganancias y pérdidas; **with ~s endowment assurance** seguro dotal con beneficios; **to sell sth at a ~** vender algo con ganancia
profitability [prɔfɪtə'bɪlɪtɪ] *n* rentabilidad *f*
profitable ['prɔfɪtəbl] *adj* (*Econ*) rentable; (*beneficial*) provechoso, útil
profound [prə'faund] *adj* profundo
profusely [prə'fju:slɪ] *adv* profusamente
programme, program (*US*) ['prəugræm] *n* programa *m* ▹ *vt* programar
programmer, programer (*US*) ['prəugræmə^r] *n* programador(a) *m(f)*
programming, programing (*US*) ['prəugræmɪŋ] *n* programación *f*
progress *n* ['prəugrɛs] progreso; (*development*) desarrollo ▹ *vi* [prə'grɛs] progresar, avanzar; desarrollarse; **in ~** (*meeting, work etc*) en curso; **as the match ~ed** a medida que avanzaba el partido
progression [prə'grɛʃən] *n* progresión *f*
progressive [prə'grɛsɪv] *adj* progresivo; (*person*) progresista
prohibit [prə'hɪbɪt] *vt* prohibir; **to ~ sb from doing sth** prohibir a algn hacer algo; **"smoking ~ed"** "prohibido fumar"
prohibition [prəuɪ'bɪʃən] *n* (*US*) prohibicionismo
project [*n* 'prɔdʒɛkt, *vb* prə'dʒɛkt] *n* proyecto; (*Scol, Univ: research*) trabajo, proyecto ▹ *vt* proyectar ▹ *vi* (*stick out*) salir, sobresalir
projection [prə'dʒɛkʃən] *n* proyección *f*; (*overhang*) saliente *m*
projector [prə'dʒɛktə^r] *n* proyector *m*
proletariat [prəulɪ'tɛərɪət] *n* proletariado
prolific [prə'lɪfɪk] *adj* prolífico
prologue, prolog (*US*) ['prəulɔg] *n* prólogo
prolong [prə'lɔŋ] *vt* prolongar, extender
prom [prɔm] *n abbr* (*Brit*) = **promenade**; **promenade concert**; (*US: ball*) baile *m* de gala; *ver nota*

PROM

Los conciertos de música clásica más conocidos en Inglaterra son los llamados *Proms* (o *promenade concerts*), que tienen lugar en el "Royal Albert Hall" de Londres, aunque también se llama así a cualquier concierto de esas características. Su nombre se debe al hecho de que en un principio el público paseaba durante las actuaciones; en la actualidad parte de la gente que acude a ellos permanece de pie. En Estados Unidos se llama *prom* a un baile de gala en un colegio o universidad.

promenade [prɔmə'nɑ:d] *n* (*by sea*) paseo marítimo ▹ *vi* (*stroll*) pasearse
promenade concert *n* concierto (*en que parte del público permanece de pie*)
prominence ['prɔmɪnəns] *n* (*fig*) importancia
prominent ['prɔmɪnənt] *adj* (*standing out*) saliente; (*important*) eminente, importante; **he is ~ in the field of ...** destaca en el campo de ...
promiscuity [prɔmɪs'kju:ɪtɪ] *n* promiscuidad *f*
promiscuous [prə'mɪskjuəs] *adj* (*sexually*) promiscuo
promise ['prɔmɪs] *n* promesa ▹ *vt, vi* prometer; **to make sb a ~** prometer algo

a algn; **a young man of ~** un joven con futuro; **to ~ (sb) to do sth** prometer (a algn) hacer algo; **to ~ well** ser muy prometedor
promising ['prɔmɪsɪŋ] *adj* prometedor(a)
promote [prə'məut] *vt* promover; (*new product*) dar publicidad a, lanzar; (*Mil*) ascender; (*employee*) ascender; (*ideas*) fomentar; **the team was ~d to the second division** (*Brit Football*) el equipo ascendió a la segunda división
promoter [prə'məutəʳ] *n* (*of sporting event*) promotor(a) *m(f)*; (*of company, business*) patrocinador(a) *m(f)*
promotion [prə'məuʃən] *n* (*gen*) promoción *f*; (*Mil*) ascenso
prompt [prɔmpt] *adj* pronto ▹ *adv*: **at six o'clock ~** a las seis en punto ▹ *n* (*Comput*) aviso, guía ▹ *vt* (*urge*) mover, incitar; (*when talking*) instar; (*Theat*) apuntar; **to ~ sb to do sth** instar a algn a hacer algo; **to be ~ to do sth** no tardar en hacer algo; **they're very ~** (*punctual*) son muy puntuales
promptly ['prɔmptlɪ] *adv* (*punctually*) puntualmente; (*rapidly*) rápidamente
prone [prəun] *adj* (*lying*) postrado; **~ to** propenso a
prong [prɔŋ] *n* diente *m*, punta
pronoun ['prəunaun] *n* pronombre *m*
pronounce [prə'nauns] *vt* pronunciar; (*declare*) declarar ▹ *vi*: **to ~ (up)on** pronunciarse sobre; **they ~d him unfit to plead** le declararon incapaz de defenderse
pronunciation [prənʌnsɪ'eɪʃən] *n* pronunciación *f*
proof [pru:f] *n* prueba; **70° ~** graduación *f* del 70 por 100 ▹ *adj*: **~ against** a prueba de ▹ *vt* (*tent, anorak*) impermeabilizar
proofreader ['pru:fri:dəʳ] *n* corrector(a) *m(f)* de pruebas
prop [prɔp] *n* apoyo; (*fig*) sostén *m*; **props** accesorios *mpl*, at(t)rezzo *msg* ▹ *vt* (*lean*): **to ~ sth against** apoyar algo contra; **prop up** *vt* (*roof, structure*) apuntalar; (*economy*) respaldar
propaganda [prɔpə'gændə] *n* propaganda
propel [prə'pɛl] *vt* impulsar, propulsar
propeller [prə'pɛləʳ] *n* hélice *f*
propensity [prə'pɛnsɪtɪ] *n* propensión *f*
proper ['prɔpəʳ] *adj* (*suited, right*) propio; (*exact*) justo; (*apt*) apropiado, conveniente; (*timely*) oportuno; (*seemly*) correcto, decente; (*authentic*) verdadero; (*inf: real*) auténtico; **to go through the ~ channels** (*Admin*) ir por la vía oficial
properly ['prɔpəlɪ] *adv* (*adequately*) correctamente; (*decently*) decentemente
proper noun *n* nombre *m* propio
property ['prɔpətɪ] *n* propiedad *f*; (*estate*) finca; **lost ~** objetos *mpl* perdidos; **personal ~** bienes *mpl* muebles
prophecy ['prɔfɪsɪ] *n* profecía
prophesy ['prɔfɪsaɪ] *vt* profetizar; (*fig*) predecir
prophet ['prɔfɪt] *n* profeta *m/f*
proportion [prə'pɔ:ʃən] *n* proporción *f*; (*share*) parte *f*; **proportions** *npl* (*size*) dimensiones *fpl*; **to be in/out of ~ to** *or* **with sth** estar en/no guardar proporción con algo; **to see sth in ~** (*fig*) ver algo en su justa medida
proportional [prə'pɔ:ʃənl] *adj* proporcional; **~ (to)** en proporción (con)
proportional representation *n* (*Pol*) representación *f* proporcional
proposal [prə'pəuzl] *n* propuesta; (*offer of marriage*) oferta de matrimonio; (*plan*) proyecto; (*suggestion*) sugerencia
propose [prə'pəuz] *vt* proponer; (*have in mind*): **to ~ sth/to do** *or* **doing sth** proponer algo/ proponerse hacer algo ▹ *vi* declararse; **to ~ to do** tener intención de hacer
proposer [prə'pəuzəʳ] *n* (*of motion*) proponente *m/f*
proposition [prɔpə'zɪʃən] *n* propuesta, proposición *f*; **to make sb a ~** proponer algo a algn
proprietor [prə'praɪətəʳ] *n* propietario(-a), dueño(-a)
propriety [prə'praɪətɪ] *n* decoro
pro rata [prəu'rɑ:tə] *adv* a prorrata
prose [prəuz] *n* prosa; (*Scol*) traducción *f* inversa
prosecute ['prɔsɪkju:t] *vt* (*Law*) procesar; **"trespassers will be ~d"** (*Law*) "se procesará a los intrusos"
prosecution [prɔsɪ'kju:ʃən] *n* proceso, causa; (*accusing side*) acusación *f*
prosecutor ['prɔsɪkju:təʳ] *n* acusador(a) *m(f)*; (*also*: **public ~**) fiscal *m/f*
prospect [*n* 'prɔspɛkt, *vb* prə'spɛkt] *n* (*chance*) posibilidad *f*; (*outlook*) perspectiva; (*hope*) esperanza ▹ *vt* explorar ▹ *vi* buscar; **prospects** *npl* (*for work etc*) perspectivas *fpl*; **to be faced with the ~ of** tener que enfrentarse a la posibilidad de que ...; **we were faced with the ~ of leaving early** se nos planteó la posibilidad de marcharnos pronto; **there is every ~ of an early victory** hay buenas perspectivas de una pronta victoria
prospecting [prə'spɛktɪŋ] *n* prospección *f*
prospective [prə'spɛktɪv] *adj* (*possible*) probable, eventual; (*certain*) futuro; (*buyer*) presunto; (*legislation, son-in-law*) futuro
prospectus [prə'spɛktəs] *n* prospecto
prosper ['prɔspəʳ] *vi* prosperar
prosperity [prɔ'spɛrɪtɪ] *n* prosperidad *f*
prosperous ['prɔspərəs] *adj* próspero
prostate ['prɔsteɪt] *n* (*also*: **~ gland**) próstata
prostitute ['prɔstɪtju:t] *n* prostituta; **male ~** prostituto
prostitution [prɔstɪ'tju:ʃən] *n* prostitución *f*
prostrate ['prɔstreɪt] *adj* postrado; (*fig*) abatido ▹ *vt*: **to ~ o.s.** postrarse
protagonist [prə'tægənɪst] *n* protagonista *m/f*

P

protect [prə'tɛkt] *vt* proteger
protection [prə'tɛkʃən] *n* protección *f*; **to be under sb's ~** estar amparado por algn
protective [prə'tɛktɪv] *adj* protector(a); **~ custody** (*Law*) detención *f* preventiva
protégé ['prəutɛʒeɪ] *n* protegido(-a)
protein ['prəuti:n] *n* proteína
protest [*n* 'prəutɛst, *vb* prə'tɛst] *n* protesta ▷ *vi*: **to ~ about** *or* **at/against** protestar de/contra ▷ *vt* (*affirm*) afirmar, declarar; (*insist*): **to ~ (that)** insistir en (que); **to do sth under ~** hacer algo bajo protesta; **to ~ against/about** protestar en contra de/por
Protestant ['prɔtɪstənt] *adj, n* protestante *m/f*
protester, protestor [prə'tɛstə^r] *n* (*in demonstration*) manifestante *m/f*
protocol ['prəutəkɔl] *n* protocolo
prototype ['prəutətaɪp] *n* prototipo
protracted [prə'træktɪd] *adj* prolongado
protractor [prə'træktə^r] *n* (*Geom*) transportador *m*
protrude [prə'tru:d] *vi* salir, sobresalir
proud [praud] *adj* orgulloso; (*pej*) soberbio, altanero ▷ *adv*: **to do sb ~** tratar a algn a cuerpo de rey; **to do o.s. ~** no privarse de nada; **to be ~ to do sth** estar orgulloso de hacer algo
prove [pru:v] *vt* probar; (*verify*) comprobar; (*show*) demostrar ▷ *vi*: **to ~ correct** resultar correcto; **to ~ o.s.** ponerse a prueba; **he was ~d right in the end** al final se vio que tenía razón
proverb ['prɔvə:b] *n* refrán *m*
provide [prə'vaɪd] *vt* proporcionar, dar; **to ~ sb with sth** proveer a algn de algo; **to be ~d with** ser provisto de; **provide for** *vt fus* (*person*) mantener a; (*problem etc*) tener en cuenta
provided [prə'vaɪdɪd] *conj*: **~ (that)** con tal de que, a condición de que
providing [prə'vaɪdɪŋ] *conj*: **~ (that)** a condición de que, con tal de que
province ['prɔvɪns] *n* provincia; (*fig*) esfera
provincial [prə'vɪnʃəl] *adj* provincial; (*pej*) provinciano
provision [prə'vɪʒən] *n* provisión *f*; (*supply*) suministro, abastecimiento; **provisions** *npl* provisiones *fpl*, víveres *mpl*; **to make ~ for** (*one's family, future*) atender las necesidades de
provisional [prə'vɪʒənl] *adj* provisional, provisorio (*LAm*); (*temporary*) interino ▷ *n*: **P~** (*Ireland Pol*) Provisional *m* (*miembro de la tendencia activista del IRA*)
provisional driving licence *n* (*Brit Aut*) carnet *m* de conducir provisional; *see also* **L-plates**
proviso [prə'vaɪzəu] *n* condición *f*, estipulación *f*; **with the ~ that** a condición de que
provocation [prɔvə'keɪʃən] *n* provocación *f*
provocative [prə'vɔkətɪv] *adj* provocativo
provoke [prə'vəuk] *vt* (*arouse*) provocar, incitar; (*cause*) causar, producir; (*anger*) enojar; **to ~ sb to sth/to do** *or* **into doing sth** provocar a algn a algo/a hacer algo
provost ['prɔvəst] *n* (*Brit: of university*) rector(a) *m(f)*; (*Scottish*) alcalde(-esa) *m(f)*
prow [prau] *n* proa
prowess ['prauɪs] *n* (*skill*) destreza, habilidad *f*; (*courage*) valor *m*; **his ~ as a footballer** (*skill*) su habilidad como futbolista
prowl [praul] *vi* (*also*: **~ about, ~ around**) merodear ▷ *n*: **on the ~** de merodeo, merodeando
prowler ['praulə^r] *n* merodeador(a) *m(f)*
proximity [prɔk'sɪmɪtɪ] *n* proximidad *f*
proxy ['prɔksɪ] *n* poder *m*; (*person*) apoderado(-a); **by ~** por poderes
prudent ['pru:dnt] *adj* prudente
prune [pru:n] *n* ciruela pasa ▷ *vt* podar
pry [praɪ] *vi*: **to ~ into** entrometerse en
PS *abbr* (= *postscript*) P.D.
psalm [sɑ:m] *n* salmo
PSBR *n abbr* (*Brit: = public sector borrowing requirement*) *necesidades de endeudamiento del sector público*
pseudonym ['sju:dənɪm] *n* seudónimo
PSHE *n abbr* (*Brit Scol: = personal, social, and health education*) *formación social y sanitaria para la vida adulta*
psyche ['saɪkɪ] *n* psique *f*
psychiatric [saɪkɪ'ætrɪk] *adj* psiquiátrico
psychiatrist [saɪ'kaɪətrɪst] *n* psiquiatra *m/f*
psychiatry [saɪ'kaɪətrɪ] *n* psiquiatría
psychic ['saɪkɪk] *adj* (*also*: **~al**) psíquico
psychoanalysis (*pl* **psychoanalyses**) [saɪkəuə'nælɪsɪs, -si:z] *n* psicoanálisis *m inv*
psychoanalyst [saɪkəu'ænəlɪst] *n* psicoanalista *m/f*
psychological [saɪkə'lɔdʒɪkl] *adj* psicológico
psychologist [saɪ'kɔlədʒɪst] *n* psicólogo(-a)
psychology [saɪ'kɔlədʒɪ] *n* psicología
psychopath ['saɪkəupæθ] *n* psicópata *m/f*
psychosis (*pl* **psychoses**) [saɪ'kəusɪs, -si:z] *n* psicosis *f inv*
psychotherapy [saɪkəu'θɛrəpɪ] *n* psicoterapia
PT *n abbr* (*Brit: = physical training*) Ed. Fís.
pt *abbr* = **pint(s); point(s)**
PTA *n abbr* (*Brit: = Parent-Teacher Association*) ≈ Asociación *f* de Padres de Alumnos
PTO *abbr* (= *please turn over*) sigue
pub [pʌb] *n abbr* (= *public house*) pub *m*, bar *m*
pub crawl *n* (*inf*): **to go on a ~** ir a recorrer bares
puberty ['pju:bətɪ] *n* pubertad *f*
public ['pʌblɪk] *adj* público ▷ *n*: **the ~** el público; **in ~** en público; **to make sth ~** revelar *or* hacer público algo; **to be ~ knowledge** ser del dominio público; **to go ~** (*Comm*) proceder a la venta pública de acciones
public address system *n* megafonía, sistema *m* de altavoces

publican ['pʌblɪkən] *n* dueño(-a) *or* encargado(-a) de un bar
publication [pʌblɪ'keɪʃən] *n* publicación *f*
public company *n* sociedad *f* anónima
public convenience *n* (*Brit*) aseos *mpl* públicos, sanitarios *mpl* (*LAm*)
public holiday *n* día *m* de fiesta, (día) feriado (*LAm*)
public house *n* (*Brit*) bar *m*, pub *m*
publicity [pʌb'lɪsɪtɪ] *n* publicidad *f*
publicize ['pʌblɪsaɪz] *vt* publicitar; (*advertise*) hacer propaganda para
public limited company *n* sociedad *f* anónima (S.A.)
publicly ['pʌblɪklɪ] *adv* públicamente, en público
public opinion *n* opinión *f* pública
public relations *n* relaciones *fpl* públicas
public relations officer *n* encargado(-a) de relaciones públicas
public school *n* (*Brit*) colegio privado; (*US*) instituto
public sector *n* sector *m* público
public-spirited [pʌblɪk'spɪrɪtɪd] *adj* cívico
public transport, public transportation (*US*) *n* transporte *m* público
public utility *n* servicio público
publish ['pʌblɪʃ] *vt* publicar
publisher ['pʌblɪʃə^r] *n* (*person*) editor(a) *m(f)*; (*firm*) editorial *f*
publishing ['pʌblɪʃɪŋ] *n* (*industry*) industria del libro
pub lunch *n* *almuerzo que se sirve en un pub*; **to go for a ~** almorzar *o* comer en un pub
puck [pʌk] *n* (*Ice Hockey*) puck *m*
pucker ['pʌkə^r] *vt* (*pleat*) arrugar; (*brow etc*) fruncir
pudding ['pudɪŋ] *n* pudín *m*; (*Brit*: *sweet*) postre *m*; **black ~** morcilla; **rice ~** arroz *m* con leche
puddle ['pʌdl] *n* charco
puerile ['pjuəraɪl] *adj* pueril
Puerto Rican ['pwə:təu'ri:kən] *adj, n* puertorriqueño(-a) *m(f)*
Puerto Rico [-'ri:kəu] *n* Puerto Rico
puff [pʌf] *n* soplo; (*of smoke*) bocanada; (*of breathing, engine*) resoplido; (*also*: **powder ~**) borla ▷ *vt*: **to ~ one's pipe** dar chupadas a la pipa; (*also*: **~ out**: *sails, cheeks*) hinchar, inflar ▷ *vi* (*gen*) soplar; (*pant*) jadear; **to ~ out smoke** echar humo
puffed [pʌft] *adj* (*inf*: *out of breath*) sin aliento
puffin ['pʌfɪn] *n* frailecillo
puff pastry, puff paste (*US*) *n* hojaldre *m*
puffy ['pʌfɪ] *adj* hinchado
pull [pul] *n* (*tug*): **to give sth a ~** dar un tirón a algo; (*fig*: *advantage*) ventaja; (: *influence*) influencia ▷ *vt* tirar de, jalar (*LAm*); (*haul*) tirar, jalar (*LAm*), arrastrar; (*strain*): **to ~ a muscle** sufrir un tirón ▷ *vi* tirar, jalar (*LAm*); **to ~ to pieces** hacer pedazos; **to ~ one's punches** andarse con bromas; **to ~ one's weight** hacer su parte; **to ~ o.s. together** tranquilizarse, sobreponerse; **to ~ sb's leg** tomar el pelo a algn; **to ~ strings (for sb)** enchufar (a algn); **pull about** *vt* (*handle roughly*: *object*) manosear; (: *person*) maltratar; **pull apart** *vt* (*take apart*) desmontar; (*break*) romper; **pull away** *vi* (*vehicle*: *move off*) salir, arrancar; (*draw back*) apartarse bruscamente; **pull back** *vt* (*lever etc*) tirar hacia sí; (*curtains*) descorrer ▷ *vi* (*refrain*) contenerse; (*Mil*: *withdraw*) retirarse; **pull down** *vt* (*house*) derribar; **pull in** *vi* (*Aut*: *at the kerb*) parar (junto a la acera); (*Rail*) llegar; **pull off** *vt* (*deal etc*) cerrar; **pull out** *vi* irse, marcharse; (*car, train etc*) salir ▷ *vt* sacar, arrancar; **pull over** *vi* (*Aut*) hacerse a un lado; **pull round, pull through** *vi* salvarse; (*Med*) recobrar la salud; **pull up** *vi* (*stop*) parar ▷ *vt* (*uproot*) arrancar, desarraigar; (*stop*) parar
pulley ['pulɪ] *n* polea
pull-out ['pulaut] *n* suplemento ▷ *cpd* (*pages, magazine*) separable
pullover ['puləuvə^r] *n* jersey *m*, suéter *m*
pulp [pʌlp] *n* (*of fruit*) pulpa; (*for paper*) pasta; (*pej*: *also*: **~ magazines** *etc*) prensa amarilla; **to reduce sth to ~** hacer algo papilla
pulpit ['pulpɪt] *n* púlpito
pulsate [pʌl'seɪt] *vi* pulsar, latir
pulse [pʌls] *n* (*Anat*) pulso; (*of music, engine*) pulsación *f*; (*Bot*) legumbre *f*; **pulses** *npl* legumbres; **to feel** *or* **take sb's ~** tomar el pulso a algn
pulverize ['pʌlvəraɪz] *vt* pulverizar; (*fig*) hacer polvo
puma ['pju:mə] *n* puma *m*
pump [pʌmp] *n* bomba; (*shoe*) zapatilla de tenis ▷ *vt* sacar con una bomba; (*fig*: *inf*) (son)sacar; **to ~ sb for information** (son) sacarle información a algn; **pump up** *vt* inflar
pumpkin ['pʌmpkɪn] *n* calabaza
pun [pʌn] *n* juego de palabras
punch [pʌntʃ] *n* (*blow*) golpe *m*, puñetazo; (*tool*) punzón *m*; (*for paper*) perforadora; (*for tickets*) taladro; (*drink*) ponche *m* ▷ *vt* (*hit*): **to ~ sb/sth** dar un puñetazo *or* golpear a algn/algo; (*make a hole in*) punzar; perforar
punch line *n* (*of joke*) remate *m*
punch-up ['pʌntʃʌp] *n* (*Brit inf*) riña
punctual ['pʌŋktjuəl] *adj* puntual
punctuality [pʌŋktju'ælɪtɪ] *n* puntualidad *f*
punctuate ['pʌŋktjueɪt] *vt* puntuar; (*fig*) interrumpir
punctuation [pʌŋktju'eɪʃən] *n* puntuación *f*
punctuation mark *n* signo de puntuación
puncture ['pʌŋktʃə^r] (*Brit*) *n* pinchazo ▷ *vt* pinchar; **to have a ~** tener un pinchazo
pundit ['pʌndɪt] *n* experto(-a)
pungent ['pʌndʒənt] *adj* acre
punish ['pʌnɪʃ] *vt* castigar; **to ~ sb for sth/for doing sth** castigar a algn por algo/por haber hecho algo

P

punishment ['pʌnɪʃmənt] *n* castigo; (*fig, inf*): **to take a lot of ~** (*boxer*) recibir una paliza; (*car*) ser maltratado
punk [pʌŋk] *n* (*also*: **~ rocker**) punki *m/f*; (*also*: **~ rock**) música punk; (*US inf*: *hoodlum*) matón *m*
punt [pʌnt] *n* (*boat*) batea; (*Ireland*) libra irlandesa ▷ *vi* (*bet*) apostar
punter ['pʌntəʳ] *n* (*gambler*) jugador(a) *m(f)*
puny ['pju:nɪ] *adj* enclenque
pup [pʌp] *n* cachorro
pupil ['pju:pl] *n* alumno(-a); (*of eye*) pupila
puppet ['pʌpɪt] *n* títere *m*
puppy ['pʌpɪ] *n* cachorro, perrito
purchase ['pə:tʃɪs] *n* compra; (*grip*) agarre *m*, asidero ▷ *vt* comprar
purchaser ['pə:tʃɪsəʳ] *n* comprador(a) *m(f)*
pure [pjuəʳ] *adj* puro; **a ~ wool jumper** un jersey de pura lana; **it's laziness, ~ and simple** es pura vagancia
purée ['pjuəreɪ] *n* puré *m*
purely ['pjuəlɪ] *adv* puramente
purgatory ['pə:gətərɪ] *n* purgatorio
purge [pə:dʒ] *n* (*Med, Pol*) purga ▷ *vt* purgar
purify ['pjuərɪfaɪ] *vt* purificar, depurar
purist ['pjuərɪst] *n* purista *m/f*
puritan ['pjuərɪtən] *n* puritano(-a)
purity ['pjuərɪtɪ] *n* pureza
purple ['pə:pl] *adj* morado
purport [pə:'pɔ:t] *vi*: **to ~ to be/do** dar a entender que es/hace
purpose ['pə:pəs] *n* propósito; **on ~** a propósito, adrede; **to no ~** para nada, en vano; **for teaching ~s** con fines pedagógicos; **for the ~s of this meeting** para los fines de esta reunión
purposeful ['pə:pəsful] *adj* resuelto, determinado
purr [pə:ʳ] *n* ronroneo ▷ *vi* ronronear
purse [pə:s] *n* monedero; (*US*: *handbag*) bolso, cartera (*LAm*) ▷ *vt* fruncir
purser ['pə:səʳ] *n* (*Naut*) comisario(-a)
pursue [pə'sju:] *vt* seguir; (*harass*) perseguir; (*profession*) ejercer; (*pleasures*) buscar; (*inquiry, matter*) seguir
pursuit [pə'sju:t] *n* (*chase*) caza; (*of pleasure etc*) busca; (*occupation*) actividad *f*; **in (the) ~ of sth** en busca de algo
pus [pʌs] *n* pus *m*
push [puʃ] *n* empujón *m*; (*Mil*) ataque *m*; (*drive*) empuje *m* ▷ *vt* empujar; (*button*) apretar; (*promote*) promover; (*fig*: *press, advance*: *views*) fomentar; (*thrust*): **to ~ sth (into)** meter algo a la fuerza (en) ▷ *vi* empujar; (*fig*) hacer esfuerzos; **at a ~** (*inf*) a duras penas; **she is ~ing 50** (*inf*) raya en los 50; **to be ~ed for time/money** andar justo de tiempo/escaso de dinero; **to ~ a door open/shut** abrir/cerrar una puerta empujándola; **to ~ for** (*better pay, conditions*) reivindicar; **"~"** (*on door*) "empujar"; (*on bell*) "pulse"; **push aside** *vt* apartar con la mano; **push in** *vi* colarse; **push off** *vi* (*inf*) largarse; **push on** *vi* (*continue*) seguir adelante; **push over** *vt* (*cause to fall*) hacer caer, derribar; (*knock over*) volcar; **push through** *vi* (*crowd*) abrirse paso a empujones ▷ *vt* (*measure*) despachar; **push up** *vt* (*total, prices*) hacer subir
pushchair ['puʃtʃɛəʳ] *n* (*Brit*) silla de niño
pusher ['puʃəʳ] *n* (*also*: **drug ~**) traficante *m/f* de drogas
pushover ['puʃəuvəʳ] *n* (*inf*): **it's a ~** está tirado
push-up ['puʃʌp] *n* (*US*) flexión *f*
pushy ['puʃɪ] *adj* (*pej*) agresivo
puss [pus], **pussy** ['pusɪ], **pussy-cat** ['pusɪkæt] *n* minino
put [put] (*pt, pp* **put**) *vt* (*place*) poner, colocar; (*put into*) meter; (*express, say*) expresar; (*a question*) hacer; (*estimate*) calcular; (*cause to be*): **to ~ sb in a good/bad mood** poner a algn de buen/mal humor; **to ~ a lot of time into sth** dedicar mucho tiempo a algo; **to ~ money on a horse** apostar dinero en un caballo; **to ~ money into a company** invertir dinero en una compañía; **to ~ sb to a lot of trouble** causar mucha molestia a algn; **we ~ the children to bed** acostamos a los niños; **how shall I ~ it?** ¿cómo puedo explicarlo *or* decirlo?; **I ~ it to you that ...** le sugiero que ...; **to stay ~** no moverse; **put about** *vi* (*Naut*) virar ▷ *vt* (*rumour*) hacer correr; **put across** *vt* (*ideas etc*) comunicar; **put aside** *vt* (*lay down*: *book etc*) dejar *or* poner a un lado; (*save*) ahorrar; (*in shop*) guardar; **put away** *vt* (*store*) guardar; **put back** *vt* (*replace*) devolver a su lugar; (*postpone*) aplazar; (*set back*: *watch, clock*) retrasar; **this will ~ us back 10 years** esto nos retrasará 10 años; **put by** *vt* (*money*) guardar; **put down** *vt* (*on ground*) poner en el suelo; (*animal*) sacrificar; (*in writing*) apuntar; (*suppress*: *revolt etc*) sofocar; (*attribute*) atribuir; **~ me down for £15** apúntame por 15 libras; **~ it down on my account** (*Comm*) póngalo en mi cuenta; **put forward** *vt* (*ideas*) presentar, proponer; (*date*) adelantar; **put in** *vt* (*application, complaint*) presentar; (*time*) dedicar; **put in for** *vt fus* (*job*) solicitar; (*promotion*) pedir; **put off** *vt* (*postpone*) aplazar; (*discourage*) desanimar, quitar las ganas a; **put on** *vt* (*clothes, lipstick etc*) ponerse; (*light etc*) encender; (*play etc*) presentar; (*gain*): **to ~ on weight** engordar; (*brake*) echar; (*record, kettle etc*) poner; (*assume*: *accent, manner*) afectar, fingir; (*airs*) adoptar, darse; (*concert, exhibition etc*) montar; (*extra bus, train etc*) poner; (*inf*: *kid, have on*: *esp US*) tomar el pelo a; (*inform, indicate*): **to ~ sb on to sb/sth** informar a algn de algn/algo; **to ~ on weight** engordar; **put out** *vt* (*fire, light*) apagar; (*rubbish etc*) sacar; (*cat etc*) echar; (*one's hand*) alargar; (*news, rumour*) hacer circular; (*tongue etc*) sacar; (*person*: *inconvenience*) molestar, fastidiar; (*dislocate*:

shoulder, vertebra, knee) dislocar(se) ▷ *vi* (*Naut*): **to ~ out to sea** hacerse a la mar; **to ~ out from Plymouth** salir de Plymouth; **put through** *vt* (*call*) poner; (*plan etc*) hacer aprobar; **~ me through to Mr Low** póngame *or* comuníqueme (*LAm*) con el Señor Low; **put together** *vt* unir, reunir; (*assemble*: *furniture*) armar, montar; (*meal*) preparar; **put up** *vt* (*raise*) levantar, alzar; (*hang*) colgar; (*build*) construir; (*increase*) aumentar; (*accommodate*) alojar; (*incite*): **to ~ sb up to doing sth** instar *or* incitar a algn a hacer algo; **to ~ sth up for sale** poner algo a la venta; **put upon** *vt fus*: **to be ~ upon** (*imposed upon*) dejarse explotar; **put up with** *vt fus* aguantar

putt [pʌt] *vt* hacer un putt ▷ *n* putt *m*

putter ['pʌtəʳ] *n* putter *m*

putting green ['pʌtɪŋ-] *n* green *m*, minigolf *m*

putty ['pʌtɪ] *n* masilla

put-up ['putʌp] *adj*: **~ job** (*Brit*) estafa

puzzle ['pʌzl] *n* (*riddle*) acertijo; (*jigsaw*) rompecabezas *m inv*; (*also*: **crossword ~**) crucigrama *m*; (*mystery*) misterio ▷ *vt* dejar perplejo, confundir ▷ *vi*: **to ~ about** quebrar la cabeza por; **to ~ over** (*sb's actions*) quebrarse la cabeza por; (*mystery, problem*) devanarse los sesos sobre; **to be ~d about sth** no llegar a entender algo

puzzling ['pʌzlɪŋ] *adj* (*question*) misterioso, extraño; (*attitude, instructions*) extraño

PVC *n abbr* (= *polyvinyl chloride*) P.V.C. *m*

pygmy ['pɪgmɪ] *n* pigmeo(-a)

pyjamas, pajamas (US) [pɪ'dʒɑ:məz] *npl* pijama *m*, piyama *m* (*LAm*); **a pair of ~** un pijama

pylon ['paɪlən] *n* torre *f* de conducción eléctrica

pyramid ['pɪrəmɪd] *n* pirámide *f*

Pyrenean [pɪrə'ni:ən] *adj* pirenaico

Pyrenees [pɪrə'ni:z] *npl*: **the ~** los Pirineos

Pyrex® ['paɪreks] *n* pírex *m* ▷ *cpd*: **~ casserole** cazuela de pírex

python ['paɪθən] *n* pitón *m*

q

Q, q [kju:] *n* (*letter*) Q, q *f*; **Q for Queen** Q de Quebec

QC *n abbr* (*Brit*: = *Queen's Counsel*) *título concedido a determinados abogados*

QED *abbr* (= *quod erat demonstrandum*) Q.E.D.

qty *abbr* (= *quantity*) cantidad

quack [kwæk] *n* (*of duck*) graznido; (*pej*: *doctor*) curandero(-a), matasanos *m inv* ▷ *vi* graznar

quad [kwɔd] *abbr* = **quadrangle**; **quadruple**; **quadruplet**

quadrangle ['kwɔdræŋgl] *n* (*Brit*: *courtyard*) patio

quadruple [kwɔ'dru:pl] *vt, vi* cuadruplicar

quadruplet [kwɔ'dru:plɪt] *n* cuatrillizo

quagmire ['kwægmaɪəʳ] *n* lodazal *m*, cenegal *m*

quail [kweɪl] *n* (*bird*) codorniz *f* ▷ *vi* amedrentarse

quaint [kweɪnt] *adj* extraño; (*picturesque*) pintoresco

quake [kweɪk] *vi* temblar ▷ *n abbr* = **earthquake**

qualification [kwɔlɪfɪ'keɪʃən] *n* (*ability*) capacidad *f*; (*often pl*: *diploma etc*) título; (*reservation*) salvedad *f*; (*modification*) modificación *f*; (*act*) calificación *f*; **what are your ~s?** ¿qué títulos tienes?

qualified ['kwɔlɪfaɪd] *adj* (*trained*) cualificado; (*fit*) capacitado; (*limited*) limitado; (*professionally*) titulado; **~ for/to do sth** capacitado para/para hacer algo; **he's not ~ for the job** no está capacitado para ese trabajo; **it was a ~ success** fue un éxito relativo

qualify ['kwɔlɪfaɪ] *vt* (*Ling*) calificar a; (*capacitate*) capacitar; (*modify*) matizar; (*limit*) moderar ▷ *vi* (*in competition*): **to ~ (for)** calificarse (para); (*pass examination(s)*): **to ~ (as)** calificarse (de), graduarse (en), recibirse (de) (*LAm*); (*be eligible*): **to ~ (for)** reunir los requisitos (para); **to ~ as an engineer** sacar el título de ingeniero

quality ['kwɔlɪtɪ] *n* calidad *f*; (*moral*) cualidad *f*; **of good/poor ~** de buena *or* alta/poca calidad

quality press *n* prensa seria

qualm [kwɑːm] *n* escrúpulo; **to have ~s about sth** sentir escrúpulos por algo

quandary ['kwɔndrɪ] *n*: **to be in a ~** verse en un dilema

quango ['kwæŋgəu] *n abbr* (*Brit*: = *quasi-autonomous non-governmental organization*) *organismo semiautónomo de subvención estatal*

quantifiable [kwɔntɪ'faɪəbl] *adj* cuantificable

quantify ['kwɔntɪfaɪ] *vt* cuantificar

quantity ['kwɔntɪtɪ] *n* cantidad *f*; **in ~** en grandes cantidades

quantity surveyor *n* aparejador(a) *m(f)*

quantum leap ['kwɔntəm-] *n* (*fig*) avance *m* espectacular

quarantine ['kwɔrntiːn] *n* cuarentena

quarrel ['kwɔrl] *n* riña, pelea ▷ *vi* reñir, pelearse; **to have a ~ with sb** reñir *or* pelearse con algn; **I can't ~ with that** no le veo pegas

quarrelsome ['kwɔrəlsəm] *adj* pendenciero

quarry ['kwɔrɪ] *n* (*for stone*) cantera; (*animal*) presa

quart [kwɔːt] *n cuarto de galón* = *1.136 l*

quarter ['kwɔːtəʳ] *n* cuarto, cuarta parte *f*; (*US*: *coin*) *moneda de 25 centavos*; (*of year*) trimestre *m*; (*district*) barrio ▷ *vt* dividir en cuartos; (*Mil*: *lodge*) alojar; **quarters** *npl* (*barracks*) cuartel *m*; (*living quarters*) alojamiento *sg*; **a ~ of an hour** un cuarto de hora; **to pay by the ~** pagar trimestralmente *or* cada tres meses; **it's a ~ to** *or* (*US*) **of three** son las tres menos cuarto; **it's a ~ past** *or* (*US*) **after three** son las tres y cuarto; **from all ~s** de todas partes; **at close ~s** de cerca

quarterback ['kwɔːtəbæk] *n* (*US*: *football*) mariscal *m* de campo

quarter final *n* cuarto de final

quarterly ['kwɔːtəlɪ] *adj* trimestral ▷ *adv* cada 3 meses, trimestralmente

quartet, quartette [kwɔː'tɛt] *n* cuarteto

quartz [kwɔːts] *n* cuarzo

quash [kwɔʃ] *vt* (*verdict*) anular, invalidar

quaver ['kweɪvəʳ] *n* (*Brit Mus*) corchea ▷ *vi* temblar

quay [kiː] *n* (*also*: **~side**) muelle *m*

queasy ['kwiːzɪ] *adj*: **to feel ~** tener náuseas

queen [kwiːn] *n* reina; (*Cards etc*) dama

queen mother *n* reina madre

Queen's Speech [kwiːnz-] *n ver nota*

QUEEN'S SPEECH

Se llama *Queen's Speech* (o "King's Speech") al discurso que pronuncia el monarca durante la sesión de apertura del Parlamento británico, en el que se expresan las líneas generales de la política del gobierno para la nueva legislatura. El Primer Ministro se encarga de redactarlo con la ayuda del Consejo de Ministros y es leído en la Cámara de los Lores ("House of Lords") ante los miembros de ambas cámaras.

queer [kwɪəʳ] *adj* (*odd*) raro, extraño ▷ *n* (*pej*: *inf!*) marica *m* (*!*)

quell [kwɛl] *vt* calmar; (*put down*) sofocar

quench [kwɛntʃ] *vt* (*flames*) apagar; **to ~ one's thirst** apagar la sed

querulous ['kwɛruləs] *adj* (*person, voice*) quejumbroso

query ['kwɪərɪ] *n* (*question*) pregunta; (*doubt*) duda ▷ *vt* preguntar; (*disagree with, dispute*) no estar conforme con, dudar de

quest [kwɛst] *n* busca, búsqueda

question ['kwɛstʃən] *n* pregunta; (*matter*) asunto, cuestión *f* ▷ *vt* (*doubt*) dudar de; (*interrogate*) interrogar, hacer preguntas a; **to ask sb a ~, put a ~ to sb** hacerle una pregunta a algn; **the ~ is ...** el asunto es ...; **to bring** *or* **call sth into ~** poner algo en (tela de) duda; **beyond ~** fuera de toda duda; **out of the ~** imposible, ni hablar

questionable ['kwɛstʃənəbl] *adj* discutible; (*doubtful*) dudoso

question mark *n* punto de interrogación

questionnaire [kwɛstʃə'nɛəʳ] *n* cuestionario

queue [kjuː] (*Brit*) *n* cola ▷ *vi* hacer cola; **to jump the ~** colarse

quibble ['kwɪbl] *vi* andarse con sutilezas

quiche [kiːʃ] *n* quiche *m*

quick [kwɪk] *adj* rápido; (*temper*) vivo; (*agile*) ágil; (*mind*) listo; (*eye*) agudo; (*ear*) fino ▷ *n*: **cut to the ~** (*fig*) herido en lo más vivo; **be ~!** ¡date prisa!; **to be ~ to act** obrar con prontitud; **she was ~ to see that** se dio cuenta de eso en seguida

quicken ['kwɪkən] *vt* apresurar ▷ *vi* apresurarse, darse prisa

quick fix *n* (*pej*) parche *m*

quickly ['kwɪklɪ] *adv* rápidamente, de prisa; **we must act ~** tenemos que actuar cuanto antes

quicksand ['kwɪksænd] *n* arenas *fpl* movedizas

quick-witted [kwɪk'wɪtɪd] *adj* listo, despabilado

quid [kwɪd] *n pl inv* (*Brit*: *inf*) libra

quiet ['kwaɪət] *adj* (*voice, music etc*) bajo; (*person, place*) tranquilo; (*silent*) callado;

(*reserved*) reservado; (*discreet*) discreto; (*not noisy: engine*) silencioso ▷ *n* silencio; (*calm*) tranquilidad *f* ▷ *vt, vi* (*US*) = **quieten**; **keep ~!** ¡cállate!, ¡silencio!; **business is ~ at this time of year** hay poco movimiento en esta época

quieten ['kwaɪətn] (*also*: **~ down**) *vi* (*grow calm*) calmarse; (*grow silent*) callarse ▷ *vt* calmar; hacer callar

quietly ['kwaɪətlɪ] *adv* tranquilamente; (*silently*) silenciosamente

quietness ['kwaɪətnɪs] *n* (*silence*) silencio; (*calm*) tranquilidad *f*

quilt [kwɪlt] *n* (*Brit*) edredón *m*

quin [kwɪn] *n abbr* = **quintuplet**

quintuplet [kwɪn'tju:plɪt] *n* quintillizo

quip [kwɪp] *n* ocurrencia ▷ *vi* decir con ironía

quirk [kwə:k] *n* peculiaridad *f*; **by some ~ of fate** por algún capricho del destino

quirky ['kw3:kɪ] *adj* raro, estrafalario

quit (*pt, pp* **quit** *or* **quitted**) [kwɪt] *vt* dejar, abandonar; (*premises*) desocupar; (*Comput*) abandonar ▷ *vi* (*give up*) renunciar; (*go away*) irse; (*resign*) dimitir; **~ stalling!** (*US*: (*inf*)) ¡déjate de evasivas!

quite [kwaɪt] *adv* (*rather*) bastante; (*entirely*) completamente; **~ a few of them** un buen número de ellos; **~ (so)!** ¡así es!, ¡exactamente!; **~ new** bastante nuevo; **that's not ~ right** eso no está del todo bien; **not ~ as many as last time** no tantos como la última vez; **she's ~ pretty** es bastante guapa

quits [kwɪts] *adj*: **~ (with)** en paz (con); **let's call it ~** quedamos en paz

quiver ['kwɪvə^r] *vi* estremecerse ▷ *n* (*for arrows*) carcaj *m*

quiz [kwɪz] *n* (*game*) concurso; (*: TV, Radio*) programa-concurso; (*questioning*) interrogatorio ▷ *vt* interrogar

quizzical ['kwɪzɪkl] *adj* burlón(-ona)

quorum ['kwɔ:rəm] *n* quórum *m*

quota ['kwəutə] *n* cuota

quotation [kwəu'teɪʃən] *n* cita; (*estimate*) presupuesto

quotation marks *npl* comillas *fpl*

quote [kwəut] *n* cita ▷ *vt* (*sentence*) citar; (*Comm: sum, figure*) cotizar ▷ *vi*: **to ~ from** citar de; **quotes** *npl* (*inverted commas*) comillas *fpl*; **in ~s** entre comillas; **the figure ~d for the repairs** el presupuesto dado para las reparaciones; **~ ... unquote** (*in dictation*) comillas iniciales ... finales

quotient ['kwəuʃənt] *n* cociente *m*

qv *n abbr* (= *quod vide: which see*) q.v.

r

R, r [ɑ:^r] *n* (*letter*) R, r *f*; **R for Robert**, (*US*) **R for Roger** R de Ramón

R *abbr* (= *right*) dcha.; (= *river*) R.; (= *Réaumur (scale)*) R; (*US Cine*: = *restricted*) *sólo mayores*; (*US Pol*) = **republican**; (*Brit*: = *Rex, Regina*) R

rabbi ['ræbaɪ] *n* rabino

rabbit ['ræbɪt] *n* conejo ▷ *vi*: **to ~ (on)** (*Brit*: (*inf*)) hablar sin ton ni son

rabbit hutch *n* conejera

rabble ['ræbl] *n* (*pej*) chusma, populacho

rabies ['reɪbi:z] *n* rabia

RAC *n abbr* (*Brit*: = *Royal Automobile Club*) ≈ RACE *m* (*Sp*)

raccoon [rə'ku:n] *n* mapache *m*

race [reɪs] *n* carrera; (*species*) raza ▷ *vt* (*horse*) hacer correr; (*person*) competir contra; (*engine*) acelerar ▷ *vi* (*compete*) competir; (*run*) correr; (*pulse*) latir a ritmo acelerado; **the arms ~** la carrera armamentista; **the human ~** el género humano; **he ~d across the road** cruzó corriendo la carretera; **to ~ in/out** entrar/salir corriendo

race car *n* (*US*) = **racing car**

race car driver *n* (*US*) = **racing driver**

racecourse ['reɪskɔ:s] *n* hipódromo

racehorse ['reɪshɔ:s] *n* caballo de carreras

racetrack ['reɪstræk] *n* hipódromo; (*for cars*) circuito de carreras

racial ['reɪʃl] *adj* racial

racing ['reɪsɪŋ] *n* carreras *fpl*

racing car *n* (*Brit*) coche *m* de carreras

racing driver *n* (*Brit*) piloto *m/f* de carreras

racism ['reɪsɪzəm] *n* racismo
racist ['reɪsɪst] *adj, n* racista *m/f*
rack [ræk] *n* (*also*: **luggage ~**) rejilla (portaequipajes); (*shelf*) estante *m*; (*also*: **roof ~**) baca; (*also*: **clothes ~**) perchero ▷ *vt* (*cause pain to*) atormentar; **to go to ~ and ruin** venirse abajo; **to ~ one's brains** devanarse los sesos; **rack up** *vt* conseguir, ganar
racket ['rækɪt] *n* (*for tennis*) raqueta; (*noise*) ruido, estrépito; (*swindle*) estafa, timo
racquet ['rækɪt] *n* raqueta
racy ['reɪsɪ] *adj* picante, subido
radar ['reɪdɑːʳ] *n* radar *m*
radial ['reɪdɪəl] *adj* (*tyre*: *also*: **~-ply**) radial
radiant ['reɪdɪənt] *adj* brillante, resplandeciente
radiate ['reɪdɪeɪt] *vt* (*heat*) radiar, irradiar ▷ *vi* (*lines*) extenderse
radiation [reɪdɪ'eɪʃən] *n* radiación *f*
radiator ['reɪdɪeɪtəʳ] *n* (*Aut*) radiador *m*
radical ['rædɪkl] *adj* radical
radii ['reɪdɪaɪ] *npl of* **radius**
radio ['reɪdɪəu] *n* radio *f* ▷ *vi*: **to ~ to sb** mandar un mensaje por radio a algn ▷ *vt* (*information*) radiar, transmitir por radio; (*one's position*) indicar por radio; (*person*) llamar por radio; **on the ~** en *or* por la radio
radioactive [reɪdɪəu'æktɪv] *adj* radi(o)activo
radioactivity [reɪdɪəuæk'tɪvɪtɪ] *n* radi(o) actividad *f*
radio station *n* emisora
radio taxi *n* radio taxi *m*
radiotherapy ['reɪdɪəuθɛrəpɪ] *n* radioterapia
radish ['rædɪʃ] *n* rábano
radium ['reɪdɪəm] *n* radio
radius (*pl* **radii**) ['reɪdɪəs, -ɪaɪ] *n* radio; **within a ~ of 50 miles** en un radio de 50 millas
RAF *n abbr* (*Brit*) *see* **Royal Air Force**
raffle ['ræfl] *n* rifa, sorteo ▷ *vt* (*object*) rifar
raft [rɑːft] *n* (*craft*) balsa; (*also*: **life ~**) balsa salvavidas
rafter ['rɑːftəʳ] *n* viga
rag [ræg] *n* (*piece of cloth*) trapo; (*torn cloth*) harapo; (*pej*: *newspaper*) periodicucho; (*for charity*) *actividades estudiantiles benéficas* ▷ *vt* (*Brit*) tomar el pelo a; **rags** *npl* harapos *mpl*; **in ~s** en harapos, hecho jirones
rag doll *n* muñeca de trapo
rage [reɪdʒ] *n* (*fury*) rabia, furor *m* ▷ *vi* (*person*) rabiar, estar furioso; (*storm*) bramar; **to fly into a ~** montar en cólera; **it's all the ~** es lo último; (*very fashionable*) está muy de moda
ragged ['rægɪd] *adj* (*edge*) desigual, mellado; (*cuff*) roto; (*appearance*) andrajoso, harapiento; **~ left/right** (*text*) margen *m* izquierdo/derecho irregular
rag week *n ver nota*
raid [reɪd] *n* (*Mil*) incursión *f*; (*criminal*) asalto; (*by police*) redada, allanamiento (*LAm*) ▷ *vt* invadir, atacar; asaltar
rail [reɪl] *n* (*on stair*) barandilla, pasamanos *m inv*; (*on bridge*) pretil *m*; (*of balcony, ship*) barandilla; (*for train*) riel *m*, carril *m*; **rails** *npl* vía *sg*; **by ~** por ferrocarril, en tren
railcard ['reɪlkɑːd] *n* (*Brit*) *tarjeta para obtener descuentos en el tren*; **Young Person's R~** ≈ Tarjeta joven (*Sp*)
railing ['reɪlɪŋ] *n*, **railings** ['reɪlɪŋz] *npl* verja *sg*
railway ['reɪlweɪ], **railroad** (*US*) ['reɪlrəud] *n* ferrocarril *m*, vía férrea
railway line *n* (*Brit*) línea (de ferrocarril)
railwayman ['reɪlweɪmən] *n* (*Brit*) ferroviario
railway station *n* (*Brit*) estación *f* de ferrocarril
rain [reɪn] *n* lluvia ▷ *vi* llover; **in the ~** bajo la lluvia; **it's ~ing** llueve, está lloviendo; **it's ~ing cats and dogs** está lloviendo a cántaros *or* a mares
rainbow ['reɪnbəu] *n* arco iris
raincoat ['reɪnkəut] *n* impermeable *m*
raindrop ['reɪndrɔp] *n* gota de lluvia
rainfall ['reɪnfɔːl] *n* lluvia
rainforest ['reɪnfɔrɪst] *n* selva tropical
rainstorm ['reɪnstɔːm] *n* temporal *m* (de lluvia)
rainwater ['reɪnwɔːtəʳ] *n* agua de lluvia
rainy ['reɪnɪ] *adj* lluvioso
raise [reɪz] *n* aumento ▷ *vt* (*lift*) levantar; (*build*) erigir, edificar; (*increase*) aumentar; (*improve*: *morale*) subir; (: *standards*) mejorar; (*doubts*) suscitar; (*a question*) plantear; (*cattle, family*) criar; (*crop*) cultivar; (*army*) reclutar; (*funds*) reunir; (*loan*) obtener; (*end*: *embargo*) levantar; **to ~ one's voice** alzar la voz; **to ~ one's glass to sb/sth** brindar por algn/algo; **to ~ a laugh/a smile** provocar risa/una sonrisa; **to ~ sb's hopes** dar esperanzas a algn
raisin ['reɪzn] *n* pasa de Corinto
rake [reɪk] *n* (*tool*) rastrillo; (*person*) libertino ▷ *vt* (*garden*) rastrillar; (*fire*) hurgar; (*with machine gun*) barrer; **rake in, rake together** *vt* sacar
rally ['rælɪ] *n* reunión *f*; (*Pol*) mitin *m*; (*Aut*) rallye *m*; (*Tennis*) peloteo ▷ *vt* reunir ▷ *vi* reunirse; (*sick person*) recuperarse; (*Stock Exchange*) recuperarse; **rally round** *vt fus* (*fig*) dar apoyo a
RAM [ræm] *n abbr* (*Comput*: = *random access memory*) RAM *f*
ram [ræm] *n* carnero; (*Tech*) pisón *m*; (*also*: **battering ~**) ariete *m* ▷ *vt* (*crash into*) dar contra, chocar con; (*push*: *fist etc*) empujar con fuerza; (*tread down*) apisonar
Ramadan ['ræmədæn] *n* Ramadán *m*
ramble ['ræmbl] *n* caminata, excursión *f* en el campo ▷ *vi* (*pej*: *also*: **~ on**) divagar
rambler ['ræmbləʳ] *n* excursionista *m/f*; (*Bot*) trepadora
rambling ['ræmblɪŋ] *adj* (*speech*) inconexo; (*Bot*) trepador(a); (*house*) laberíntico

ramp [ræmp] *n* rampa; **on/off ~** *n* (*US Aut*) vía de acceso/salida; **"~"** (*Aut*) "rampa"

rampage [ræm'peɪdʒ] *n*: **to be on the ~** desmandarse ▷ *vi*: **they went rampaging through the town** recorrieron la ciudad armando alboroto

rampant ['ræmpənt] *adj* (*disease etc*): **to be ~** estar muy extendido

rampart ['ræmpɑ:t] *n* terraplén *m*; (*wall*) muralla

ram raid *vt* atracar (*rompiendo el escaparate con un coche*)

ramshackle ['ræmʃækl] *adj* destartalado

ran [ræn] *pt of* **run**

ranch [rɑ:ntʃ] *n* (*US*) hacienda, estancia

rancher ['rɑ:ntʃə^r] *n* ganadero

rancid ['rænsɪd] *adj* rancio

rancour, rancor (*US*) ['ræŋkə^r] *n* rencor *m*

random ['rændəm] *adj* fortuito, sin orden; (*Comput, Math*) aleatorio ▷ *n*: **at ~** al azar

random access *n* (*Comput*) acceso aleatorio

randy ['rændɪ] *adj* (*Brit inf*) cachondo, caliente

rang [ræŋ] *pt of* **ring**

range [reɪndʒ] *n* (*of mountains*) cadena de montañas, cordillera; (*of missile*) alcance *m*; (*of voice*) registro; (*series*) serie *f*; (*of products*) surtido; (*Mil: also*: **shooting ~**) campo de tiro; (*also*: **kitchen ~**) fogón *m* ▷ *vt* (*place*) colocar; (*arrange*) arreglar ▷ *vi*: **to ~ over** (*wander*) recorrer; (*extend*) extenderse por; **within (firing) ~** a tiro; **do you have anything else in this price ~?** ¿tiene algo más de esta gama de precios?; **intermediate-/short-~ missile** proyectil *m* de medio/corto alcance; **to ~ from ... to ...** oscilar entre ... y ...; **~d left/right** (*text*) alineado a la izquierda/derecha

ranger [reɪndʒə^r] *n* guardabosques *m inv*

rank [ræŋk] *n* (*row*) fila; (*Mil*) rango; (*status*) categoría; (*Brit: also*: **taxi ~**) parada ▷ *vi*: **to ~ among** figurar entre ▷ *adj* (*stinking*) fétido, rancio; (*hypocrisy, injustice etc*) manifiesto; **the ~ and file** (*fig*) las bases; **to close ~s** (*Mil*) cerrar filas; (*fig*) hacer un frente común; **~ outsider** participante *m/f* sin probabilidades de vencer; **I ~ him sixth** yo le pongo en sexto lugar

rankle ['ræŋkl] *vi* (*insult*) doler

ransack ['rænsæk] *vt* (*search*) registrar; (*plunder*) saquear

ransom ['rænsəm] *n* rescate *m*; **to hold sb to ~** (*fig*) poner a algn entre la espada y la pared

rant [rænt] *vi* despotricar

rap [ræp] *vt* golpear, dar un golpecito en ▷ *n* (*music*) rap *m*

rape [reɪp] *n* violación *f*; (*Bot*) colza ▷ *vt* violar

rapid ['ræpɪd] *adj* rápido

rapidly ['ræpɪdlɪ] *adv* rápidamente

rapids ['ræpɪdz] *npl* (*Geo*) rápidos *mpl*

rapist ['reɪpɪst] *n* violador *m*

rapport [ræ'pɔ:^r] *n* entendimiento

rapture ['ræptʃə^r] *n* éxtasis *m*

rapturous ['ræptʃərəs] *adj* extático; (*applause*) entusiasta; **a ~ (party)** *macrofiesta con música máquina*; **~ music** música máquina

rare [rɛə^r] *adj* raro, poco común; (*Culin: steak*) poco hecho; **it is ~ to find that ...** es raro descubrir que ...

rarely ['rɛəlɪ] *adv* rara vez, pocas veces

raring ['rɛərɪŋ] *adj*: **to be ~ to go** (*inf*) tener muchas ganas de empezar

rascal ['rɑ:skl] *n* pillo(-a), pícaro(-a)

rash [ræʃ] *adj* imprudente, precipitado ▷ *n* (*Med*) sarpullido, erupción *f* (cutánea); **to come out in a ~** salir salpullidos

rasher ['ræʃə^r] *n* loncha

raspberry ['rɑ:zbərɪ] *n* frambuesa

rasping ['rɑ:spɪŋ] *adj*: **a ~ noise** un ruido áspero

rat [ræt] *n* rata

ratchet ['rætʃɪt] *n* (*Tech*) trinquete *m*

rate [reɪt] *n* (*ratio*) razón *f*; (*percentage*) tanto por ciento; (*price*) precio; (*: of hotel*) tarifa; (*of interest*) tipo; (*speed*) velocidad *f* ▷ *vt* (*value*) tasar; (*estimate*) estimar; **to ~ as** ser considerado como; **rates** *npl* (*Brit*) impuesto *sg* municipal; (*fees*) tarifa *sg*; **failure ~** porcentaje *m* de fallos; **pulse ~** pulsaciones *fpl* por minuto; **~ of pay** tipos *mpl* de sueldo; **at a ~ of 60 kph** a una velocidad de 60 kph; **~ of growth** ritmo de crecimiento; **~ of return** (*Comm*) tasa de rendimiento; **bank ~** tipo *or* tasa de interés bancario; **at any ~** en todo caso; **to ~ sb/sth highly** tener a algn/algo en alta estima; **the house is ~d at £84 per annum** (*Brit*) la casa está tasada en 84 libras al año

rateable value ['reɪtəbl-] *n* (*Brit*) valor *m* impuesto

ratepayer ['reɪtpeɪə^r] *n* (*Brit*) contribuyente *m/f*

rather ['rɑ:ðə^r] *adv* antes, más bien; (*somewhat*) algo, un poco; (*quite*) bastante; **it's ~ expensive** es algo caro; (*too much*) es demasiado caro; **there's ~ a lot** hay bastante; **I would** *or* **I'd ~ go** preferiría ir; **I'd ~ not** prefiero que no; **I ~ think he won't come** me inclino a creer que no vendrá; **or ~** (*more accurately*) o mejor dicho

ratify ['rætɪfaɪ] *vt* ratificar

rating ['reɪtɪŋ] *n* (*valuation*) tasación *f*; (*standing*) posición *f*; (*Brit Naut: sailor*) marinero; **ratings** *npl* (*Radio, TV*) niveles *mpl* de audiencia

ratio ['reɪʃɪəu] *n* razón *f*; **in the ~ of 100 to 1** a razón de *or* en la proporción de 100 a 1

ration ['ræʃən] *n* ración *f*; **rations** *npl* víveres *mpl* ▷ *vt* racionar

rational ['ræʃənl] *adj* racional; (*solution, reasoning*) lógico, razonable; (*person*) cuerdo, sensato

rationale [ræʃə'nɑ:l] *n* razón *f* fundamental

rationalize ['ræʃnəlaɪz] *vt* (*reorganize: industry*) racionalizar

r

rationally [ˈræʃnəlɪ] *adv* racionalmente; (*logically*) lógicamente
ratpack [ˈrætpæk] *n* (*Brit inf*) *periodistas que persiguen a los famosos*
rat race *n lucha incesante por la supervivencia*
rattle [ˈrætl] *n* golpeteo; (*of train etc*) traqueteo; (*object: of baby*) sonaja, sonajero; (*: of sports fan*) matraca ▷ *vi* (*small objects*) castañetear; (*car, bus*): **to ~ along** traquetear ▷ *vt* hacer sonar agitando; (*inf: disconcert*) poner nervioso a
rattlesnake [ˈrætlsneɪk] *n* serpiente *f* de cascabel
ratty [ˈrætɪ] *adj* (*inf*) furioso; **to get ~** mosquearse
raucous [ˈrɔːkəs] *adj* estridente, ronco
raunchy [ˈrɔːntʃɪ] *adj* (*inf*) lascivo
ravage [ˈrævɪdʒ] *vt* hacer estragos en, destrozar; **ravages** *npl* estragos *mpl*
rave [reɪv] *vi* (*in anger*) encolerizarse; (*with enthusiasm*) entusiasmarse; (*Med*) delirar, desvariar ▷ *cpd*: **~ review** reseña entusiasta; **a ~ (party)** *macrofiesta con música máquina*; **~ music** música máquina ▷ *n* (*inf: party*) rave *m*
raven [ˈreɪvən] *n* cuervo
ravenous [ˈrævənəs] *adj*: **to be ~** tener un hambre canina
ravine [rəˈviːn] *n* barranco
raving [ˈreɪvɪŋ] *adj*: **~ lunatic** loco de atar
ravioli [rævɪˈəulɪ] *n* ravioles *mpl*, ravioli *mpl*
ravish [ˈrævɪʃ] *vt* (*charm*) encantar, embelesar; (*rape*) violar
ravishing [ˈrævɪʃɪŋ] *adj* encantador(a)
raw [rɔː] *adj* (*uncooked*) crudo; (*not processed*) bruto; (*sore*) vivo; (*inexperienced*) novato, inexperto; **~ materials** materias primas
raw material *n* materia prima
ray [reɪ] *n* rayo; **~ of hope** (rayo de) esperanza
raze [reɪz] *vt* (*also*: **~ to the ground**) arrasar, asolar
razor [ˈreɪzəʳ] *n* (*open*) navaja; (*safety razor*) máquina de afeitar; (*electric razor*) máquina (eléctrica) de afeitar
razor blade *n* hoja de afeitar
RC *abbr* = **Roman Catholic**
Rd *abbr* = **road**
RE *n abbr* (*Brit*: = *religious education*)
re [riː] *prep* con referencia a
reach [riːtʃ] *n* alcance *m*; (*Boxing*) envergadura; (*of river etc*) extensión *f* entre dos recodos ▷ *vt* alcanzar, llegar a; (*achieve*) lograr ▷ *vi* extenderse; (*stretch out hand*: *also*: **~ down, ~ over, ~ across** *etc*) tender la mano; **within ~** al alcance (de la mano); **out of ~** fuera del alcance; **can I ~ you at your hotel?** ¿puedo localizarte en tu hotel?; **to ~ sb by phone** comunicarse con algn por teléfono; **reach out** *vt* (*hand*) tender ▷ *vi*: **to ~ out for sth** alargar *or* tender la mano para tomar algo
react [riːˈækt] *vi* reaccionar
reaction [riːˈækʃən] *n* reacción *f*
reactionary [riːˈækʃənrɪ] *adj, n* reaccionario(-a) *m(f)*
reactor [riːˈæktəʳ] *n* (*also*: **nuclear ~**) reactor *m* (nuclear)
read (*pt, pp* **read**) [riːd, rɛd] *vi* leer ▷ *vt* leer; (*understand*) entender; (*study*) estudiar; **to take sth as ~** (*fig*) dar algo por sentado; **do you ~ me?** (*Tel*) ¿me escucha?; **to ~ between the lines** leer entre líneas; **read out** *vt* leer en alta voz; **read over** *vt* repasar; **read through** *vt* (*quickly*) leer rápidamente, echar un vistazo a; (*thoroughly*) leer con cuidado *or* detenidamente; **read up, read up on** *vt fus* documentarse sobre
readable [ˈriːdəbl] *adj* (*writing*) legible; (*book*) que merece la pena leer
reader [ˈriːdəʳ] *n* lector(a) *m(f)*; (*book*) libro de lecturas; (*Brit: at university*) profesor(a) *m(f)*
readership [ˈriːdəʃɪp] *n* (*of paper etc*) número de lectores
readily [ˈrɛdɪlɪ] *adv* (*willingly*) de buena gana; (*easily*) fácilmente; (*quickly*) en seguida
readiness [ˈrɛdɪnɪs] *n* buena voluntad; (*preparedness*) preparación *f*; **in ~** (*prepared*) listo, preparado
reading [ˈriːdɪŋ] *n* lectura; (*understanding*) comprensión *f*; (*on instrument*) indicación *f*
readjustment [riːəˈdʒʌstmənt] *n* reajuste *m*
ready [ˈrɛdɪ] *adj* listo, preparado; (*willing*) dispuesto; (*available*) disponible ▷ *adv*: **~-cooked** listo para comer ▷ *n*: **at the ~** (*Mil*) listo para tirar; **~ for use** listo para usar; **to be ~ to do sth** estar listo para hacer algo; **to get ~** *vi* prepararse ▷ *vt* preparar
ready-made [ˈrɛdɪˈmeɪd] *adj* confeccionado
ready money *n* dinero contante
ready-to-wear [ˈrɛdɪtəˈwɛəʳ] *adj* confeccionado
reaffirm [riːəˈfəːm] *vt* reafirmar
real [rɪəl] *adj* verdadero, auténtico; **in ~ terms** en términos reales; **in ~ life** en la vida real, en la realidad
real ale *n* cerveza elaborada tradicionalmente
real estate *n* bienes *mpl* raíces
realism [ˈrɪəlɪzəm] *n* (*also Art*) realismo
realist [ˈrɪəlɪst] *n* realista *m/f*
realistic [rɪəˈlɪstɪk] *adj* realista
realistically [rɪəˈlɪstɪklɪ] *adv* de modo realista
reality [riːˈælɪtɪ] *n* realidad *f*; **in ~** en realidad
reality TV *n* telerrealidad *f*
realization [rɪəlaɪˈzeɪʃən] *n* comprensión *f*; (*of a project*) realización *f*; (*Comm: of assets*) realización *f*
realize [ˈrɪəlaɪz] *vt* (*understand*) darse cuenta de; (*a project*) realizar; (*Comm: asset*) realizar; **I ~ that ...** comprendo *or* entiendo que ...
really [ˈrɪəlɪ] *adv* realmente; (*for emphasis*) verdaderamente; (*actually*): **what ~ happened** lo que pasó en realidad; **~?** ¿de veras?; **~!** (*annoyance*) ¡vamos!, ¡por favor!

realm [rɛlm] *n* reino; (*fig*) esfera
realtor ['rɪəltɔːʳ] *n* (*US*) corredor(a) *m(f)* de bienes raíces
reap [riːp] *vt* segar; (*fig*) cosechar, recoger
reappear [riːə'pɪəʳ] *vi* reaparecer
reappraisal [riːə'preɪzl] *n* revaluación *f*
rear [rɪəʳ] *adj* trasero ▷ *n* parte *f* trasera ▷ *vt* (*cattle, family*) criar ▷ *vi* (*also*: **~ up**: *animal*) encabritarse
rearguard ['rɪəgɑːd] *n* retaguardia
rearrange [riːə'reɪndʒ] *vt* ordenar *or* arreglar de nuevo
rear-view ['rɪəvjuː]: **~ mirror** *n* (*Aut*) espejo retrovisor
rear-wheel drive *n* tracción *f* trasera
reason ['riːzn] *n* razón *f* ▷ *vi*: **to ~ with sb** tratar de que algn entre en razón; **it stands to ~ that ...** es lógico que ...; **the ~ for/why** la causa de/la razón por la cual; **she claims with good ~ that she's underpaid** dice con razón que está mal pagada; **all the more ~ why you should not sell it** razón de más para que no lo vendas
reasonable ['riːznəbl] *adj* razonable; (*sensible*) sensato
reasonably ['riːznəblɪ] *adv* razonablemente; **a ~ accurate report** un informe bastante exacto
reasoning ['riːznɪŋ] *n* razonamiento, argumentos *mpl*
reassurance [riːə'ʃuərəns] *n* consuelo
reassure [riːə'ʃuəʳ] *vt* tranquilizar; **to ~ sb that** tranquilizar a algn asegurándole que
rebate ['riːbeɪt] *n* (*on product*) rebaja; (*on tax etc*) desgravación *f*; (*repayment*) reembolso
rebel ['rɛbl] *n* rebelde *m/f* ▷ *vi* [rɪ'bɛl] rebelarse, sublevarse
rebellion [rɪ'bɛljən] *n* rebelión *f*, sublevación *f*
rebellious [rɪ'bɛljəs] *adj* rebelde; (*child*) revoltoso
rebirth [riː'bəːθ] *n* renacimiento
rebound [rɪ'baund] *vi* (*ball*) rebotar ▷ *n* ['riːbaund] rebote *m*
rebuff [rɪ'bʌf] *n* desaire *m*, rechazo ▷ *vt* rechazar
rebuild [riː'bɪld] *vt* (*irreg: like* **build**) reconstruir
rebuke [rɪ'bjuːk] *n* reprimenda ▷ *vt* reprender
rebut [rɪ'bʌt] *vt* rebatir
recall [rɪ'kɔːl] *vt* (*remember*) recordar; (*ambassador etc*) retirar; (*Comput*) volver a llamar ▷ *n* recuerdo
recant [rɪ'kænt] *vi* retractarse
recap ['riːkæp] *vt, vi* recapitular
recd., rec'd *abbr* (= *received*) recibido
recede [rɪ'siːd] *vi* retroceder
receding [rɪ'siːdɪŋ] *adj* (*forehead, chin*) hundido; **~ hairline** entradas *fpl*
receipt [rɪ'siːt] *n* (*document*) recibo; (*act of receiving*) recepción *f*; **receipts** *npl* (*Comm*) ingresos *mpl*; **to acknowledge ~ of** acusar recibo de; **we are in ~ of ...** obra en nuestro poder ...
receive [rɪ'siːv] *vt* recibir; (*guest*) acoger; (*wound*) sufrir; **"~d with thanks"** "recibí"
receiver [rɪ'siːvəʳ] *n* (*Tel*) auricular *m*; (*Radio*) receptor *m*; (*of stolen goods*) perista *m/f*; (*Law*) administrador *m* jurídico
receivership [rɪ'siːvəʃɪp] *n*: **to go into ~** entrar en liquidación
recent ['riːsnt] *adj* reciente; **in ~ years** en los últimos años
recently ['riːsntlɪ] *adv* recientemente, recién (*LAm*); **~ arrived** recién llegado; **until ~** hasta hace poco
receptacle [rɪ'sɛptɪkl] *n* receptáculo
reception [rɪ'sɛpʃən] *n* (*in building, office etc*) recepción *f*; (*welcome*) acogida
reception desk *n* recepción *f*
receptionist [rɪ'sɛpʃənɪst] *n* recepcionista *m/f*
recess [rɪ'sɛs] *n* (*in room*) hueco; (*for bed*) nicho; (*secret place*) escondrijo; (*Pol etc: holiday*) período vacacional; (*US Law: short break*) descanso; (*Scol: esp US*) recreo
recession [rɪ'sɛʃən] *n* recesión *f*, depresión *f*
recharge [riː'tʃɑːdʒ] *vt* (*battery*) recargar
recipe ['rɛsɪpɪ] *n* receta; (*for disaster, success*) fórmula
recipient [rɪ'sɪpɪənt] *n* recibidor(a) *m(f)*; (*of letter*) destinatario(-a)
reciprocate [rɪ'sɪprəkeɪt] *vt* devolver, corresponder a ▷ *vi* corresponder
recital [rɪ'saɪtl] *n* (*Mus*) recital *m*
recitation [rɛsɪ'teɪʃən] *n* (*of poetry*) recitado; (*of complaints etc*) enumeración *f*, relación *f*
recite [rɪ'saɪt] *vt* (*poem*) recitar; (*complaints etc*) enumerar
reckless ['rɛkləs] *adj* temerario, imprudente; (*speed*) peligroso
reckon ['rɛkən] *vt* (*calculate*) calcular; (*consider*) considerar ▷ *vi*: **to ~ without sb/sth** dejar de contar con algn/algo; **he is somebody to be ~ed with** no se le puede descartar; **I ~ that ...** me parece que ..., creo que ...; **reckon on** *vt fus* contar con
reckoning ['rɛkənɪŋ] *n* (*calculation*) cálculo
reclaim [rɪ'kleɪm] *vt* (*land*) recuperar; (*: from sea*) rescatar; (*demand back*) reclamar
recline [rɪ'klaɪn] *vi* reclinarse
reclining [rɪ'klaɪnɪŋ] *adj* (*seat*) reclinable
recluse [rɪ'kluːs] *n* recluso(-a)
recognition [rɛkəg'nɪʃən] *n* reconocimiento; **transformed beyond ~** irreconocible; **in ~ of** en reconocimiento de
recognize ['rɛkəgnaɪz] *vt* reconocer, conocer; **to ~ (by/as)** reconocer (por/como)
recoil [rɪ'kɔɪl] *vi* (*person*): **to ~ from doing sth** retraerse de hacer algo ▷ *n* (*of gun*) retroceso
recollect [rɛkə'lɛkt] *vt* recordar, acordarse de
recollection [rɛkə'lɛkʃən] *n* recuerdo; **to the best of my ~** que yo recuerde

r

recommend [rɛkə'mɛnd] *vt* recomendar; **she has a lot to ~ her** tiene mucho a su favor
recommendation [rɛkəmɛn'deɪʃən] *n* recomendación *f*
reconcile ['rɛkənsaɪl] *vt* (*two people*) reconciliar; (*two facts*) conciliar; **to ~ o.s. to sth** resignarse *or* conformarse a algo
reconciliation [rɛkənsɪlɪ'eɪʃən] *n* reconciliación *f*
recondition [ri:kən'dɪʃən] *vt* (*machine*) reparar, reponer
reconditioned [ri:kən'dɪʃənd] *adj* renovado, reparado
reconnoitre, reconnoiter (*US*) [rɛkə'nɔɪtə^r] *vt, vi* (*Mil*) reconocer
reconsider [ri:kən'sɪdə^r] *vt* repensar
reconstruct [ri:kən'strʌkt] *vt* reconstruir
reconvene [ri:kən'vi:n] *vt* volver a convocar ▷ *vi* volver a reunirse
record *n* ['rɛkɔ:d] (*Mus*) disco; (*of meeting etc*) acta; (*register*) registro, partida; (*file*) archivo; (*also*: **police** *or* **criminal ~**) antecedentes *mpl* penales; (*written*) expediente *m*; (*Sport*) récord *m*; (*Comput*) registro ▷ *vt* [rɪ'kɔ:d] (*set down*) registrar; (*Comput*) registrar; (*relate*) hacer constar; (*Mus*: *song etc*) grabar; **in ~ time** en un tiempo récord; **public ~s** archivos *mpl* nacionales; **he is on ~ as saying that ...** hay pruebas de que ha dicho públicamente que ...; **Spain's excellent ~** el excelente historial de España; **off the ~** *adj* no oficial ▷ *adv* confidencialmente
record card *n* (*in file*) ficha
recorded delivery [rɪ'kɔ:dɪd-] *n* (*Brit Post*) entrega con acuse de recibo
recorder [rɪ'kɔ:də^r] *n* (*Mus*) flauta de pico; (*Tech*) contador *m*
record holder *n* (*Sport*) actual poseedor(a) *m(f)* del récord
recording [rɪ'kɔ:dɪŋ] *n* (*Mus*) grabación *f*
recording studio *n* estudio de grabación
record library *n* discoteca
record player *n* tocadiscos *m inv*
recount *vt* [rɪ'kaunt] contar
re-count ['ri:kaunt] *n* (*Pol*: *of votes*) segundo escrutinio, recuento ▷ *vt* [ri:'kaunt] volver a contar
recoup [rɪ'ku:p] *vt*: **to ~ one's losses** recuperar las pérdidas
recourse [rɪ'kɔ:s] *n* recurso; **to have ~ to** recurrir a
recover [rɪ'kʌvə^r] *vt* recuperar; (*rescue*) rescatar ▷ *vi* recuperarse
recovery [rɪ'kʌvərɪ] *n* recuperación *f*; rescate *m*; (*Med*): **to make a ~** restablecerse
recreate [ri:krɪ'eɪt] *vt* recrear
recreation [rɛkrɪ'eɪʃən] *n* recreación *f*; (*amusement*) recreo
recreational [rɛkrɪ'eɪʃənl] *adj* de, recreo; **~ drug** droga recreativa
recreational vehicle *n* (*US*) caravana *or* roulotte *f* pequeña
recrimination [rɪkrɪmɪ'neɪʃən] *n* recriminación *f*
recruit [rɪ'kru:t] *n* recluta *m/f* ▷ *vt* reclutar; (*staff*) contratar
recruitment [rɪ'kru:tmənt] *n* reclutamiento
rectangle ['rɛktæŋgl] *n* rectángulo
rectangular [rɛk'tæŋgjulə^r] *adj* rectangular
rectify ['rɛktɪfaɪ] *vt* rectificar
rector ['rɛktə^r] *n* (*Rel*) párroco; (*Scol*) rector(a) *m(f)*
rectum ['rɛktəm] *n* (*Anat*) recto
recuperate [rɪ'ku:pəreɪt] *vi* reponerse, restablecerse
recur [rɪ'kə:^r] *vi* repetirse; (*pain, illness*) producirse de nuevo
recurrence [rɪ'kə:rns] *n* repetición *f*
recurrent [rɪ'kə:rnt] *adj* repetido
recurring [rɪ'kə:rɪŋ] *adj* (*problem*) repetido, constante
recyclable [ri:'saɪkləbl] *adj* reciclable
recycle [ri:'saɪkl] *vt* reciclar
recycling [ri:'saɪklɪŋ] *n* reciclaje *m*
red [rɛd] *n* rojo ▷ *adj* rojo; (*hair*) pelirrojo; (*wine*) tinto; **to be in the ~** (*account*) estar en números rojos; (*business*) tener un saldo negativo; **to give sb the ~ carpet treatment** recibir a algn con todos los honores
red alert *n* alerta roja
red-blooded ['rɛd'blʌdɪd] *adj* (*inf*) viril
Red Cross *n* Cruz *f* Roja
redcurrant ['rɛdkʌrənt] *n* grosella roja
redden ['rɛdn] *vt* enrojecer ▷ *vi* enrojecerse
reddish ['rɛdɪʃ] *adj* (*hair*) rojizo
redecorate [ri:'dɛkəreɪt] *vt* pintar de nuevo; volver a decorar
redeem [rɪ'di:m] *vt* redimir; (*promises*) cumplir; (*sth in pawn*) desempeñar; (*Rel*) rescatar; (*fig*) rescatar
redeeming [rɪ'di:mɪŋ] *adj*: **~ feature** punto bueno *or* favorable
redefine [ri:dɪ'faɪn] *vt* redefinir
redemption [rɪ'dɛmpʃən] *n* (*Rel*) redención *f*; **to be past** *or* **beyond ~** no tener remedio
redeploy [ri:dɪ'plɔɪ] *vt* disponer de nuevo
redeployment [ri:dɪ'plɔɪmənt] *n* redistribución *f*
red-handed [rɛd'hændɪd] *adj*: **he was caught ~** le pillaron con las manos en la masa
redhead ['rɛdhɛd] *n* pelirrojo(-a)
red herring *n* (*fig*) pista falsa
red-hot [rɛd'hɔt] *adj* candente
redirect [ri:daɪ'rɛkt] *vt* (*mail*) reexpedir
rediscover [ri:dɪs'kʌvə^r] *vt* redescubrir
redistribute [ri:dɪs'trɪbju:t] *vt* redistribuir, hacer una nueva distribución de
red light *n*: **to go through** *or* **jump a ~** (*Aut*) saltarse un semáforo
red-light district *n* barrio chino, zona de tolerancia
red meat *n* carne *f* roja

redo [riː'duː] *vt* (*irreg: like* **do**) rehacer
redolent ['rɛdələnt] *adj*: **~ of** (*smell*) con fragancia a; **to be ~ of** (*fig*) evocar
redouble [riː'dʌbl] *vt*: **to ~ one's efforts** redoblar los esfuerzos
redraft [riː'drɑːft] *vt* volver a redactar
redress [rɪ'drɛs] *n* reparación *f* ▷ *vt* reparar, corregir; **to ~ the balance** restablecer el equilibrio
Red Sea *n*: **the ~** el mar Rojo
redskin ['rɛdskɪn] *n* piel roja *m/f*
red tape *n* (*fig*) trámites *mpl*, papeleo (*fam*)
reduce [rɪ'djuːs] *vt* reducir; (*lower*) rebajar; **to ~ sth by/to** reducir algo en/a; **to ~ sb to silence/despair/tears** hacer callar/desesperarse/llorar a algn; **"~ speed now"** (*Aut*) "reduzca la velocidad"
reduced [rɪ'djuːst] *adj* (*decreased*) reducido, rebajado; **at a ~ price** con rebaja *or* descuento; **"greatly ~ prices"** "grandes rebajas"
reduction [rɪ'dʌkʃən] *n* reducción *f*; (*of price*) rebaja; (*discount*) descuento
redundancy [rɪ'dʌndənsɪ] *n* despido; (*unemployment*) desempleo; **voluntary ~** baja voluntaria
redundant [rɪ'dʌndənt] *adj* (*Brit: worker*) parado, sin trabajo; (*detail, object*) superfluo; **to be made ~** quedar(se) sin trabajo, perder el empleo
reed [riːd] *n* (*Bot*) junco, caña; (*Mus: of clarinet etc*) lengüeta
re-educate [riː'ɛdjukeɪt] *vt* reeducar
reef [riːf] *n* (*at sea*) arrecife *m*
reek [riːk] *vi*: **to ~ (of)** oler *or* apestar (a)
reel [riːl] *n* carrete *m*, bobina; (*of film*) rollo ▷ *vt* (*Tech*) devanar; (*also*: **~ in**) sacar ▷ *vi* (*sway*) tambalear(se); **my head is ~ing** me da vueltas la cabeza; **reel off** *vt* recitar de memoria
ref [rɛf] *n abbr* (*inf*) = **referee**
ref. *abbr* (*Comm*: = *with reference to*) Ref
refectory [rɪ'fɛktərɪ] *n* comedor *m*
refer [rɪ'fəː^{r}] *vt* (*send: patient*) referir; (*: matter*) remitir; (*ascribe*) referir a, relacionar con ▷ *vi*: **to ~ to** (*allude to*) referirse a, aludir a; (*apply to*) relacionarse con; (*consult*) remitirse a; **he ~red me to the manager** me envió al gerente
referee [rɛfə'riː] *n* árbitro; (*Brit: for job application*): **to be a ~ for sb** proporcionar referencias a algn ▷ *vt* (*match*) arbitrar en
reference ['rɛfrəns] *n* (*mention: in book*) referencia; (*sending*) remisión *f*; (*relevance*) relación *f*; (*for job application: letter*) carta de recomendación; **with ~ to** con referencia a; (*Comm: in letter*) me remito a
reference book *n* libro de consulta
reference library *n* biblioteca de consulta
reference number *n* número de referencia
referendum (*pl* **referenda**) [rɛfə'rɛndəm, -də] *n* referéndum *m*
referral [rɪ'fəːrəl] *n* remisión *f*
refill *vt* [riː'fɪl] rellenar ▷ *n* ['riːfɪl] repuesto, recambio
refine [rɪ'faɪn] *vt* (*sugar, oil*) refinar
refined [rɪ'faɪnd] *adj* (*person, taste*) refinado, fino
refinement [rɪ'faɪnmənt] *n* (*of person*) cultura, educación *f*
refinery [rɪ'faɪnərɪ] *n* refinería
refit (*also Naut*) *n* ['riːfɪt] reparación *f* ▷ *vt* [riː'fɪt] reparar
reflect [rɪ'flɛkt] *vt* (*light, image*) reflejar ▷ *vi* (*think*) reflexionar, pensar; **it ~s badly/well on him** le perjudica/le hace honor
reflection [rɪ'flɛkʃən] *n* (*act*) reflexión *f*; (*image*) reflejo; (*discredit*) crítica; **on ~** pensándolo bien
reflector [rɪ'flɛktə^{r}] *n* (*Aut*) catafaros *m inv*; (*telescope*) reflector *m*
reflex ['riːflɛks] *adj, n* reflejo
reflexive [rɪ'flɛksɪv] *adj* (*Ling*) reflexivo
reform [rɪ'fɔːm] *n* reforma ▷ *vt* reformar
reformat [riː'fɔːmæt] *vt* (*Comput*) recomponer
Reformation [rɛfə'meɪʃən] *n*: **the ~** la Reforma
reformatory [rɪ'fɔːmətərɪ] *n* (*US*) reformatorio
refrain [rɪ'freɪn] *vi*: **to ~ from doing** abstenerse de hacer ▷ *n* (*Mus etc*) estribillo
refresh [rɪ'frɛʃ] *vt* refrescar
refresher course [rɪ'frɛʃə-] *n* (*Brit*) curso de repaso
refreshing [rɪ'frɛʃɪŋ] *adj* (*drink*) refrescante; (*sleep*) reparador; (*change etc*) estimulante; (*idea, point of view*) estimulante, interesante
refreshments [rɪ'frɛʃmənts] *npl* (*drinks*) refrescos *mpl*
refrigeration [rɪfrɪdʒə'reɪʃən] *n* refrigeración *f*
refrigerator [rɪ'frɪdʒəreɪtə^{r}] *n* frigorífico, refrigeradora (*LAm*), heladera (*LAm*)
refuel [riː'fjuəl] *vi* repostar (combustible)
refuge ['rɛfjuːdʒ] *n* refugio, asilo; **to take ~ in** refugiarse en
refugee [rɛfju'dʒiː] *n* refugiado(-a)
refugee camp *n* campamento para refugiados
refund *n* ['riːfʌnd] reembolso ▷ *vt* [rɪ'fʌnd] devolver, reembolsar
refurbish [riː'fəːbɪʃ] *vt* restaurar, renovar
refusal [rɪ'fjuːzəl] *n* negativa; **first ~** primera opción; **to have first ~ on sth** tener la primera opción a algo
refuse[1] ['rɛfjuːs] *n* basura
refuse[2] [rɪ'fjuːz] *vt* (*reject*) rechazar; (*invitation*) declinar; (*permission*) denegar; (*say no to*) negarse a ▷ *vi* negarse; (*horse*) rehusar; **to ~ to do sth** negarse a *or* rehusar hacer algo
refuse collection *n* recogida de basuras
regain [rɪ'geɪn] *vt* recobrar, recuperar
regal ['riːgl] *adj* regio, real
regard [rɪ'gɑːd] *n* (*gaze*) mirada; (*aspect*) respecto; (*esteem*) respeto; (*attention*)

r

consideración *f* ▷ *vt* (*consider*) considerar; (*look at*) mirar; **to give one's ~s to** saludar de su parte a; **"(kind) ~s"** "muy atentamente"; **"with kindest ~s"** "con muchos recuerdos"; **~s to María, please give my ~s to María** recuerdos a María, dele recuerdos a María de mi parte; **as ~s, with ~ to** con respecto a, en cuanto a
regarding [rɪ'gɑ:dɪŋ] *prep* con respecto a, en cuanto a
regardless [rɪ'gɑ:dlɪs] *adv* a pesar de todo; **~ of** sin reparar en
regatta [rɪ'gætə] *n* regata
regenerate [rɪ'dʒɛnəreɪt] *vt* regenerar
reggae ['rɛgeɪ] *n* reggae *m*
régime [reɪ'ʒi:m] *n* régimen *m*
regiment *n* ['rɛdʒɪmənt] regimiento ▷ *vt* ['rɛdʒɪmɛnt] reglamentar
regimental [rɛdʒɪ'mɛntl] *adj* militar
region ['ri:dʒən] *n* región *f*; **in the ~ of** (*fig*) alrededor de
regional ['ri:dʒənl] *adj* regional
register ['rɛdʒɪstə^r] *n* registro ▷ *vt* registrar; (*birth*) declarar; (*car*) matricular; (*letter*) certificar; (*instrument*) marcar, indicar ▷ *vi* (*at hotel*) registrarse; (*as student*) matricularse; (*sign on*) inscribirse; (*make impression*) producir impresión; **to ~ a protest** presentar una queja; **to ~ for a course** matricularse *or* inscribirse en un curso
registered ['rɛdʒɪstəd] *adj* (*design*) registrado; (*Brit: letter*) certificado; (*student*) matriculado; (*voter*) registrado
registered trademark *n* marca registrada
registrar ['rɛdʒɪstrɑ:^r] *n* secretario(-a) (del registro civil)
registration [rɛdʒɪs'treɪʃən] *n* (*act*) declaración *f*; (*Aut: also:* **~ number**) matrícula
registry ['rɛdʒɪstrɪ] *n* registro
registry office *n* (*Brit*) registro civil; **to get married in a ~** casarse por lo civil
regret [rɪ'grɛt] *n* sentimiento, pesar *m*; (*remorse*) remordimiento ▷ *vt* sentir, lamentar; (*repent of*) arrepentirse de; **we ~ to inform you that ...** sentimos informarle que ...
regretfully [rɪ'grɛtfəlɪ] *adv* con pesar, sentidamente
regrettable [rɪ'grɛtəbl] *adj* lamentable; (*loss*) sensible
regular ['rɛgjulə^r] *adj* regular; (*soldier*) profesional; (*inf: intensive*) verdadero; (*listener, reader*) asiduo; (*usual*) habitual ▷ *n* (*client etc*) cliente(-a) *m(f)* habitual
regularity [rɛgju'lærɪtɪ] *n* regularidad *f*
regularly ['rɛgjuləlɪ] *adv* con regularidad
regulate ['rɛgjuleɪt] *vt* (*gen*) controlar; (*Tech*) regular, ajustar
regulation [rɛgju'leɪʃən] *n* (*rule*) regla, reglamento; (*adjustment*) regulación *f*
rehabilitate [ri:ə'bɪlɪteɪt] *vt* rehabilitar
rehabilitation ['ri:əbɪlɪ'teɪʃən] *n* rehabilitación *f*
rehash [ri:'hæʃ] *vt* (*inf*) hacer un refrito de
rehearsal [rɪ'hə:səl] *n* ensayo; **dress ~** ensayo general *or* final
rehearse [rɪ'hə:s] *vt* ensayar
rehouse [ri:'hauz] *vt* dar nueva vivienda a
reign [reɪn] *n* reinado; (*fig*) predominio ▷ *vi* reinar; (*fig*) imperar
reigning ['reɪnɪŋ] *adj* (*monarch*) reinante, actual; (*predominant*) imperante
reimburse [ri:ɪm'bə:s] *vt* reembolsar
rein [reɪn] *n* (*for horse*) rienda; **to give sb free ~** dar rienda suelta a algn
reincarnation [ri:ɪnkɑ:'neɪʃən] *n* reencarnación *f*
reindeer ['reɪndɪə^r] *n pl inv* reno
reinforce [ri:ɪn'fɔ:s] *vt* reforzar
reinforced concrete [ri:ɪn'fɔ:st-] *n* hormigón *m* armado
reinforcement [ri:ɪn'fɔ:smənt] *n* (*action*) refuerzo; **reinforcements** *npl* (*Mil*) refuerzos *mpl*
reinstate [ri:ɪn'steɪt] *vt* (*worker*) reintegrar (a su puesto); (*tax, law*) reinstaurar
reiterate [ri:'ɪtəreɪt] *vt* reiterar, repetir
reject *n* ['ri:dʒɛkt] (*thing*) desecho ▷ *vt* [rɪ'dʒɛkt] rechazar; (*proposition, offer etc*) descartar
rejection [rɪ'dʒɛkʃən] *n* rechazo
rejoice [rɪ'dʒɔɪs] *vi*: **to ~ at** *or* **over** regocijarse *or* alegrarse de
rejuvenate [rɪ'dʒu:vəneɪt] *vt* rejuvenecer
relapse [rɪ'læps] *n* (*Med*) recaída; (*into crime*) reincidencia
relate [rɪ'leɪt] *vt* (*tell*) contar, relatar; (*connect*) relacionar ▷ *vi* relacionarse; **to ~ to** (*connect*) relacionarse *or* tener que ver con
related [rɪ'leɪtɪd] *adj* afín; (*person*) emparentado; **to be ~ to** (*connected*) guardar relación con; (*by family*) ser pariente de
relating [rɪ'leɪtɪŋ]: **~ to** *prep* referente a
relation [rɪ'leɪʃən] *n* (*person*) pariente *m/f*; (*link*) relación *f*; **in ~ to** en relación con, en lo que se refiere a; **to bear a ~ to** guardar relación con; **diplomatic ~s** relaciones *fpl* diplomáticas; **relations** *npl* (*relatives*) familiares *mpl*
relationship [rɪ'leɪʃənʃɪp] *n* relación *f*; (*personal*) relaciones *fpl*; (*also:* **family ~**) parentesco
relative ['rɛlətɪv] *n* pariente *m/f*, familiar *m/f* ▷ *adj* relativo
relatively ['rɛlətɪvlɪ] *adv* (*fairly, rather*) relativamente
relax [rɪ'læks] *vi* descansar; (*quieten down*) relajarse ▷ *vt* relajar; (*grip*) aflojar; **~!** (*calm down*) ¡tranquilo!
relaxation [ri:læk'seɪʃən] *n* (*rest*) descanso; (*easing*) relajación *f*, relajamiento *m*; (*amusement*) recreo; (*entertainment*) diversión *f*
relaxed [rɪ'lækst] *adj* relajado; (*tranquil*) tranquilo
relaxing [rɪ'læksɪŋ] *adj* relajante

relay *n* ['ri:leɪ] (*race*) carrera de relevos ▷ *vt* [rɪ'leɪ] (*Radio, TV*) retransmitir; (*pass on*) retransmitir
release [rɪ'li:s] *n* (*liberation*) liberación *f*; (*discharge*) puesta en libertad *f*; (*of gas etc*) escape *m*; (*of film etc*) estreno; (*of record*) lanzamiento ▷ *vt* (*prisoner*) poner en libertad; (*film*) estrenar; (*book*) publicar; (*piece of news*) difundir; (*gas etc*) despedir, arrojar; (*free: from wreckage etc*) liberar; (*Tech: catch, spring etc*) desenganchar; (*let go*) soltar, aflojar
relegate ['rɛləgeɪt] *vt* relegar; (*Sport*): **to be ~d to** bajar a
relent [rɪ'lɛnt] *vi* ceder, ablandarse; (*let up*) descansar
relentless [rɪ'lɛntlɪs] *adj* implacable
relevance ['rɛləvəns] *n* relación *f*
relevant ['rɛləvənt] *adj* (*fact*) pertinente; **~ to** relacionado con
reliability [rɪlaɪə'bɪlɪtɪ] *n* fiabilidad *f*; seguridad *f*; veracidad *f*
reliable [rɪ'laɪəbl] *adj* (*person, firm*) de confianza, de fiar; (*method, machine*) seguro; (*source*) fidedigno
reliably [rɪ'laɪəblɪ] *adv*: **to be ~ informed that ...** saber de fuente fidedigna que ...
reliance [rɪ'laɪəns] *n*: **~ (on)** dependencia (de)
relic ['rɛlɪk] *n* (*Rel*) reliquia; (*of the past*) vestigio
relief [rɪ'li:f] *n* (*from pain, anxiety*) alivio, desahogo; (*help, supplies*) socorro, ayuda; (*Art, Geo*) relieve *m*; **by way of light ~** a modo de diversión
relieve [rɪ'li:v] *vt* (*pain, patient*) aliviar; (*bring help to*) ayudar, socorrer; (*burden*) aligerar; (*take over from: gen*) sustituir a; (*: guard*) relevar; **to ~ sb of sth** quitar algo a algn; **to ~ sb of his command** (*Mil*) relevar a algn de su mando; **to ~ o.s.** hacer sus necesidades
relieved [rɪ'li:vd] *adj*: **to be ~** sentir un gran alivio
religion [rɪ'lɪdʒən] *n* religión *f*
religious [rɪ'lɪdʒəs] *adj* religioso
religious education *n* educación *f* religiosa
relinquish [rɪ'lɪŋkwɪʃ] *vt* abandonar; (*plan, habit*) renunciar a
relish ['rɛlɪʃ] *n* (*Culin*) salsa; (*enjoyment*) entusiasmo; (*flavour*) sabor *m*, gusto ▷ *vt* (*food, challenge etc*) saborear; **to ~ doing** gozar haciendo
relive [ri:'lɪv] *vt* vivir de nuevo, volver a vivir
relocate [ri:ləu'keɪt] *vt* trasladar ▷ *vi* trasladarse
reluctance [rɪ'lʌktəns] *n* desgana, renuencia
reluctant [rɪ'lʌktənt] *adj* reacio; **to be ~ to do sth** resistirse a hacer algo
reluctantly [rɪ'lʌktəntlɪ] *adv* de mala gana
rely [rɪ'laɪ]: **to ~ on** *vt fus* confiar en, fiarse de; (*be dependent on*) depender de; **you can ~ on my discretion** puedes contar con mi discreción
remain [rɪ'meɪn] *vi* (*survive*) quedar; (*be left*) sobrar; (*continue*) quedar(se), permanecer; **to ~ silent** permanecer callado; **I ~, yours faithfully** (*in letters*) le saluda atentamente
remainder [rɪ'meɪndə^r] *n* resto
remaining [rɪ'meɪnɪŋ] *adj* restante, que queda(n)
remains [rɪ'meɪnz] *npl* restos *mpl*
remand [rɪ'mɑ:nd] *n*: **on ~** detenido (bajo custodia) ▷ *vt*: **to ~ in custody** mantener bajo custodia
remand home *n* (*Brit*) reformatorio
remark [rɪ'mɑ:k] *n* comentario ▷ *vt* comentar; **to ~ on sth** hacer observaciones sobre algo
remarkable [rɪ'mɑ:kəbl] *adj* notable; (*outstanding*) extraordinario
remarry [ri:'mærɪ] *vi* casarse por segunda vez, volver a casarse
remedial [rɪ'mi:dɪəl] *adj*: **~ education** educación *f* de los niños atrasados
remedy ['rɛmədɪ] *n* remedio ▷ *vt* remediar, curar
remember [rɪ'mɛmbə^r] *vt* recordar, acordarse de; (*bear in mind*) tener presente; **I ~ seeing it, I ~ having seen it** recuerdo haberlo visto; **she ~ed doing it** se acordó de hacerlo; **~ me to your wife and children!** ¡déle recuerdos a su familia!
remembrance [rɪ'mɛmbrəns] *n* (*memory, souvenir*) recuerdo; **in ~ of** en conmemoración de
Remembrance Day, Remembrance Sunday *n* (*Brit*) *ver nota*

REMEMBRANCE DAY

En el Reino Unido el domingo más cercano al 11 de noviembre es *Remembrance Day* o *Remembrance Sunday*, aniversario de la firma del armisticio de 1918 que puso fin a la Primera Guerra Mundial. Tal día se recuerda a todos aquellos que murieron en las dos guerras mundiales con dos minutos de silencio a las once de la mañana hora en que se firmó el armisticio durante los actos de conmemoración celebrados en los monumentos a los caídos. Allí se colocan coronas de amapolas, flor que también se suele llevar prendida en el pecho tras pagar un donativo para los inválidos de guerra.

remind [rɪ'maɪnd] *vt*: **to ~ sb to do sth** recordar a algn que haga algo; **to ~ sb of sth** recordar algo a algn; **she ~s me of her mother** me recuerda a su madre; **that ~s me!** ¡a propósito!
reminder [rɪ'maɪndə^r] *n* notificación *f*; (*memento*) recuerdo

reminisce [rɛmɪ'nɪs] *vi* recordar (viejas historias)
reminiscent [rɛmɪ'nɪsnt] *adj*: **to be ~ of sth** recordar algo
remiss [rɪ'mɪs] *adj* descuidado; **it was ~ of me** fue un descuido de mi parte
remission [rɪ'mɪʃən] *n* remisión *f*; (*of sentence*) reducción *f* de la pena
remit [rɪ'mɪt] *vt* (*send: money*) remitir, enviar
remittance [rɪ'mɪtns] *n* remesa, envío
remnant ['rɛmnənt] *n* resto; (*of cloth*) retal *m*, retazo; **remnants** *npl* (*Comm*) restos de serie
remorse [rɪ'mɔːs] *n* remordimientos *mpl*
remorseful [rɪ'mɔːsful] *adj* arrepentido
remorseless [rɪ'mɔːslɪs] *adj* (*fig*) implacable, inexorable
remote [rɪ'məut] *adj* remoto; (*distant*) lejano; (*person*) distante; **there is a ~ possibility that ...** hay una posibilidad remota de que ...
remote control *n* mando a distancia
remotely [rɪ'məutlɪ] *adv* remotamente; (*slightly*) levemente
remould ['riːməuld] *n* (*Brit: tyre*) neumático *or* llanta (*LAm*) recauchutado(-a)
removable [rɪ'muːvəbl] *adj* (*detachable*) separable
removal [rɪ'muːvəl] *n* (*taking away*) (el) quitar; (*Brit: from house*) mudanza; (*from office: dismissal*) destitución *f*; (*Med*) extirpación *f*
removal man *n* (*Brit*) mozo de mudanzas
removal van *n* (*Brit*) camión *m* de mudanzas
remove [rɪ'muːv] *vt* quitar; (*employee*) destituir; (*name: from list*) tachar, borrar; (*doubt*) disipar; (*Tech*) retirar, separar; (*Med*) extirpar; **first cousin once ~d** (*parent's cousin*) tío(-a) segundo(-a); (*cousin's child*) sobrino(-a) segundo(-a)
remuneration [rɪmjuːnə'reɪʃən] *n* remuneración *f*
Renaissance [rɪ'neɪsɔ̃ns] *n*: **the ~** el Renacimiento
rename [riː'neɪm] *vt* poner nuevo nombre a
render ['rɛndə^r] *vt* (*thanks*) dar; (*aid*) proporcionar; (*honour*) dar, conceder; (*assistance*) dar, prestar; **to ~ sth** + *adj* volver algo + *adj*; **to ~ sth useless** hacer algo inútil
rendering ['rɛndərɪŋ] *n* (*Mus etc*) interpretación *f*
rendez-vous ['rɔndɪvuː] *n* cita ▷ *vi* reunirse, encontrarse; (*spaceship*) efectuar una reunión espacial
rendition [rɛn'dɪʃən] *n* (*Mus*) interpretación *f*
renew [rɪ'njuː] *vt* renovar; (*resume*) reanudar; (*extend date*) prorrogar; (*negotiations*) volver a
renewable [rɪ'njuːəbl] *adj* renovable; **~ energy, ~s** energías renovables
renewal [rɪ'njuːəl] *n* renovación *f*; reanudación *f*; prórroga
renounce [rɪ'nauns] *vt* renunciar a; (*right, inheritance*) renunciar
renovate ['rɛnəveɪt] *vt* renovar
renovation [rɛnə'veɪʃən] *n* renovación *f*
renown [rɪ'naun] *n* renombre *m*
renowned [rɪ'naund] *adj* renombrado
rent [rɛnt] *n* alquiler *m*; (*for house*) arriendo, renta ▷ *vt* (*also:* **~ out**) alquilar
rental ['rɛntl] *n* (*for television, car*) alquiler *m*
rent boy *n* (*Brit inf*) chapero
reopen [riː'əupən] *vt* volver a abrir, reabrir
reorder [riː'ɔːdə^r] *vt* volver a pedir, repetir el pedido de; (*rearrange*) volver a ordenar *or* arreglar
reorganization [riːɔːgənaɪ'zeɪʃən] *n* reorganización *f*
reorganize [riː'ɔːgənaɪz] *vt* reorganizar
rep [rɛp] *n abbr* (*Comm*) = **representative**; (*Theat*) = **repertory**
repair [rɪ'pɛə^r] *n* reparación *f*, arreglo; (*patch*) remiendo ▷ *vt* reparar, arreglar; **in good/bad ~** en buen/mal estado; **under ~** en obras
repair kit *n* caja de herramientas
repatriate [riː'pætrɪeɪt] *vt* repatriar
repay [riː'peɪ] *vt* (*irreg: like* **pay**) (*money*) devolver, reembolsar; (*person*) pagar; (*debt*) liquidar; (*sb's efforts*) devolver, corresponder a
repayment [riː'peɪmənt] *n* reembolso, devolución *f*; (*sum of money*) recompensa
repeal [rɪ'piːl] *n* revocación *f* ▷ *vt* revocar
repeat [rɪ'piːt] *n* (*Radio, TV*) reposición *f* ▷ *vt* repetir ▷ *vi* repetirse
repeatedly [rɪ'piːtɪdlɪ] *adv* repetidas veces
repeat prescription *n* (*Brit*) receta renovada
repel [rɪ'pɛl] *vt* repugnar
repellent [rɪ'pɛlənt] *adj* repugnante ▷ *n*: **insect ~** crema/loción *f* antiinsectos
repent [rɪ'pɛnt] *vi*: **to ~ (of)** arrepentirse (de)
repentance [rɪ'pɛntəns] *n* arrepentimiento
repercussion [riːpə'kʌʃən] *n* (*consequence*) repercusión *f*; **to have ~s** repercutir
repertoire ['rɛpətwɑː^r] *n* repertorio
repertory ['rɛpətərɪ] *n* (*also:* **~ theatre**) teatro de repertorio
repertory company *n* compañía de repertorio
repetition [rɛpɪ'tɪʃən] *n* repetición *f*
repetitive [rɪ'pɛtɪtɪv] *adj* (*movement, work*) repetitivo, reiterativo; (*speech*) lleno de repeticiones
rephrase [riː'freɪz] *vt* decir *or* formular de otro modo
replace [rɪ'pleɪs] *vt* (*put back*) devolver a su sitio; (*take the place of*) reemplazar, sustituir
replacement [rɪ'pleɪsmənt] *n* reemplazo; (*act*) reposición *f*; (*thing*) recambio; (*person*) suplente *m/f*
replay ['riːpleɪ] *n* (*Sport*) partido de desempate; (*TV: playback*) repetición *f*
replenish [rɪ'plɛnɪʃ] *vt* (*tank etc*) rellenar; (*stock etc*) reponer; (*with fuel*) repostar
replica ['rɛplɪkə] *n* réplica, reproducción *f*
reply [rɪ'plaɪ] *n* respuesta, contestación *f* ▷ *vi* contestar, responder; **in ~** en respuesta; **there's no ~** (*Tel*) no contestan
reply coupon *n* cupón-respuesta *m*

report [rɪ'pɔ:t] *n* informe *m*; (*Press etc*) reportaje *m*; (*Brit*: *also*: **school ~**) informe *m* escolar; (*of gun*) detonación *f* ▷ *vt* informar sobre; (*Press etc*) hacer un reportaje sobre; (*notify*: *accident, culprit*) denunciar ▷ *vi* (*make a report*) presentar un informe; (*present o.s.*): **to ~ (to sb)** presentarse (ante algn); **annual ~** (*Comm*) informe *m* anual; **to ~ (on)** hacer un informe (sobre); **it is ~ed from Berlin that ...** se informa desde Berlín que ...
report card *n* (*US, Scottish*) cartilla escolar
reportedly [rɪ'pɔ:tɪdlɪ] *adv* según se dice, según se informa
reporter [rɪ'pɔ:tər] *n* (*Press*) periodista *m/f*, reportero(-a); (*Radio, TV*) locutor(a) *m(f)*
repose [rɪ'pəuz] *n*: **in ~** (*face, mouth*) en reposo
repossession order [ri:pə'zɛʃən-] *n orden de devolución de la vivienda por el impago de la hipoteca*
represent [rɛprɪ'zɛnt] *vt* representar; (*Comm*) ser agente de
representation [rɛprɪzɛn'teɪʃən] *n* representación *f*; (*petition*) petición *f*; **representations** *npl* (*protest*) quejas *fpl*
representative [rɛprɪ'zɛntətɪv] *n* (*US Pol*) representante *m/f*, diputado(-a); (*Comm*) representante *m/f* ▷ *adj*: **~ (of)** representativo (de)
repress [rɪ'prɛs] *vt* reprimir
repression [rɪ'prɛʃən] *n* represión *f*
reprieve [rɪ'pri:v] *n* (*Law*) indulto; (*fig*) alivio ▷ *vt* indultar; (*fig*) salvar
reprimand ['rɛprɪmɑ:nd] *n* reprimenda ▷ *vt* reprender
reprint ['ri:prɪnt] *n* reimpresión *f* ▷ *vt* [ri:'prɪnt] reimprimir
reprisal [rɪ'praɪzl] *n* represalia; **to take ~s** tomar represalias
reproach [rɪ'prəutʃ] *n* reproche *m* ▷ *vt*: **to ~ sb with sth** reprochar algo a algn; **beyond ~** intachable
reproachful [rɪ'prəutʃful] *adj* de reproche, de acusación
reproduce [ri:prə'dju:s] *vt* reproducir ▷ *vi* reproducirse
reproduction [ri:prə'dʌkʃən] *n* reproducción *f*
reproof [rɪ'pru:f] *n* reproche *m*
reptile ['rɛptaɪl] *n* reptil *m*
republic [rɪ'pʌblɪk] *n* república
republican [rɪ'pʌblɪkən] *adj, n* republicano(-a) *m(f)*
repudiate [rɪ'pju:dɪeɪt] *vt* (*accusation*) rechazar; (*obligation*) negarse a reconocer
repugnant [rɪ'pʌgnənt] *adj* repugnante
repulsive [rɪ'pʌlsɪv] *adj* repulsivo
reputable ['rɛpjutəbl] *adj* (*make etc*) de renombre
reputation [rɛpju'teɪʃən] *n* reputación *f*; **he has a ~ for being awkward** tiene fama de difícil
repute [rɪ'pju:t] *n* reputación *f*, fama
reputed [rɪ'pju:tɪd] *adj* supuesto; **to be ~ to be rich/intelligent** *etc* tener fama de rico/inteligente *etc*
reputedly [rɪ'pju:tɪdlɪ] *adv* según dicen *or* se dice
request [rɪ'kwɛst] *n* solicitud *f*, petición *f* ▷ *vt*: **to ~ sth of** *or* **from sb** solicitar algo a algn; **at the ~ of** a petición de; **"you are ~ed not to smoke"** "se ruega no fumar"
request stop *n* (*Brit*) parada discrecional
requiem ['rɛkwɪəm] *n* réquiem *m*
require [rɪ'kwaɪər] *vt* (*need*: *person*) necesitar, tener necesidad de; (*: thing, situation*) exigir, requerir; (*want*) pedir; (*demand*) insistir en que; **to ~ sb to do sth/sth of sb** exigir que algn haga algo; **what qualifications are ~d?** ¿qué títulos se requieren?; **~d by law** requerido por la ley
requirement [rɪ'kwaɪəmənt] *n* requisito; (*need*) necesidad *f*
requisite ['rɛkwɪzɪt] *n* requisito ▷ *adj* necesario, requerido
requisition [rɛkwɪ'zɪʃən] *n* solicitud *f*; (*Mil*) requisa ▷ *vt* (*Mil*) requisar
reroute [ri:'ru:t] *vt* desviar
resat [ri:'sæt] *pt, pp of* **resit**
rescue ['rɛskju:] *n* rescate *m* ▷ *vt* rescatar; **to come/go to sb's ~** ir en auxilio de uno, socorrer a algn; **to ~ from** librar de
rescuer ['rɛskjuər] *n* salvador(a) *m(f)*
research [rɪ'sə:tʃ] *n* investigaciones *fpl* ▷ *vt* investigar; **a piece of ~** un trabajo de investigación; **to ~ (into sth)** investigar (algo)
researcher [rɪ'sə:tʃər] *n* investigador(a) *m(f)*
resemblance [rɪ'zɛmbləns] *n* parecido; **to bear a strong ~ to** parecerse mucho a
resemble [rɪ'zɛmbl] *vt* parecerse a
resent [rɪ'zɛnt] *vt* resentirse por, ofenderse por; **he ~s my being here** le molesta que esté aquí
resentful [rɪ'zɛntful] *adj* resentido
resentment [rɪ'zɛntmənt] *n* resentimiento
reservation [rɛzə'veɪʃən] *n* reserva; (*Brit*: *also*: **central ~**) mediana; **with ~s** con reservas
reservation desk *n* (*US*: *in hotel*) recepción *f*
reserve [rɪ'zə:v] *n* reserva; (*Sport*) suplente *m/f* ▷ *vt* (*seats etc*) reservar; **reserves** *npl* (*Mil*) reserva *sg*; **in ~** en reserva
reserved [rɪ'zə:vd] *adj* reservado
reservoir ['rɛzəvwɑ:r] *n* (*artificial lake*) embalse *m*, represa; (*tank*) depósito
reset [ri:'sɛt] *vt* (*Comput*) reinicializar
reshape [ri:'ʃeɪp] *vt* (*policy*) reformar, rehacer
reshuffle [ri:'ʃʌfl] *n*: **Cabinet ~** (*Pol*) remodelación *f* del gabinete
reside [rɪ'zaɪd] *vi* residir
residence ['rɛzɪdəns] *n* residencia; (*formal*: *home*) domicilio; (*length of stay*) permanencia; **in ~** (*doctor*) residente; **to take up ~** instalarse

r

residence permit *n* (*Brit*) permiso de residencia
resident ['rɛzɪdənt] *n* vecino(-a); (*in hotel*) huésped(a) *m(f)* ▷ *adj* residente; (*population*) permanente
residential [rɛzɪ'dɛnʃəl] *adj* residencial
residue ['rɛzɪdju:] *n* resto, residuo
resign [rɪ'zaɪn] *vt* (*gen*) renunciar a ▷ *vi*: **to ~ (from)** dimitir (de), renunciar (a); **to ~ o.s. to** (*endure*) resignarse a
resignation [rɛzɪg'neɪʃən] *n* dimisión *f*; (*state of mind*) resignación *f*; **to tender one's ~** presentar la dimisión
resigned [rɪ'zaɪnd] *adj* resignado
resilience [rɪ'zɪlɪəns] *n* (*of material*) elasticidad *f*; (*of person*) resistencia
resilient [rɪ'zɪlɪənt] *adj* (*person*) resistente
resin ['rɛzɪn] *n* resina
resist [rɪ'zɪst] *vt* resistirse a; (*temptation, damage*) resistir
resistance [rɪ'zɪstəns] *n* resistencia
resistant [rɪ'zɪstənt] *adj*: **~ (to)** resistente (a)
resit ['ri:sɪt] (*pt, pp* **resat**) *vt* (*Brit*: *exam*) volver a presentarse a; (: *subject*) recuperar, volver a examinarse de (*Sp*)
resolute ['rɛzəlu:t] *adj* resuelto
resolution [rɛzə'lu:ʃən] *n* (*gen*) resolución *f*; (*purpose*) propósito; (*Comput*) definición *f*; **to make a ~** tomar una resolución
resolve [rɪ'zɔlv] *n* (*determination*) resolución *f*; (*purpose*) propósito ▷ *vt* resolver ▷ *vi* resolverse; **to ~ to do** resolver hacer
resolved [rɪ'zɔlvd] *adj* resuelto
resort [rɪ'zɔ:t] *n* (*town*) centro turístico; (*recourse*) recurso ▷ *vi*: **to ~ to** recurrir a; **in the last ~** como último recurso; **seaside/ winter sports ~** playa, estación *f* balnearia/ centro de deportes de invierno
resound [rɪ'zaund] *vi*: **to ~ (with)** resonar (con)
resounding [rɪ'zaundɪŋ] *adj* sonoro; (*fig*) clamoroso
resource [rɪ'sɔ:s] *n* recurso; **resources** *npl* recursos *mpl*; **natural ~s** recursos *mpl* naturales; **to leave sb to his/her own ~s** (*fig*) abandonar a algn/a sus propios recursos
resourceful [rɪ'sɔ:sful] *adj* ingenioso
respect [rɪs'pɛkt] *n* (*consideration*) respeto; (*relation*) respecto; **respects** *npl* recuerdos *mpl*, saludos *mpl* ▷ *vt* respetar; **with ~ to** con respecto a; **in this ~** en cuanto a eso; **to have** *or* **show ~ for** tener *or* mostrar respeto a; **out of ~ for** por respeto a; **in some ~s** en algunos aspectos; **with due ~ I still think you're wrong** con el respeto debido, sigo creyendo que está equivocado
respectable [rɪs'pɛktəbl] *adj* respetable; (*quite big*: *amount etc*) apreciable; (*passable*) tolerable; (*quite good*: *player, result etc*) bastante bueno
respected [rɪs'pɛktɪd] *adj* respetado, estimado
respectful [rɪs'pɛktful] *adj* respetuoso
respective [rɪs'pɛktɪv] *adj* respectivo
respectively [rɪs'pɛktɪvlɪ] *adv* respectivamente
respiration [rɛspɪ'reɪʃən] *n* respiración *f*
respite ['rɛspaɪt] *n* respiro; (*Law*) prórroga
resplendent [rɪs'plɛndənt] *adj* resplandeciente
respond [rɪs'pɔnd] *vi* responder; (*react*) reaccionar
response [rɪs'pɔns] *n* respuesta; (*reaction*) reacción *f*; **in ~ to** como respuesta a
responsibility [rɪspɔnsɪ'bɪlɪtɪ] *n* responsabilidad *f*; **to take ~ for sth/sb** admitir responsabilidad por algo/uno
responsible [rɪs'pɔnsɪbl] *adj* (*liable*): **~ (for)** responsable (de); (*character*) serio, formal; (*job*) de responsabilidad; **to be ~ to sb (for sth)** ser responsable ante algn (de algo)
responsibly [rɪs'pɔnsɪblɪ] *adv* con seriedad
responsive [rɪs'pɔnsɪv] *adj* sensible
rest [rɛst] *n* descanso, reposo; (*Mus*) pausa, silencio; (*support*) apoyo; (*remainder*) resto ▷ *vi* descansar; (*be supported*): **to ~ on** apoyarse en ▷ *vt* (*lean*): **to ~ sth on/against** apoyar algo en *or* sobre/contra; **the ~ of them** (*people, objects*) los demás; **to set sb's mind at ~** tranquilizar a algn; **to ~ one's eyes** *or* **gaze on** fijar la mirada en; **it ~s with him** depende de él; **~ assured that ...** tenga por seguro que ...
restaurant ['rɛstərɔŋ] *n* restaurante *m*
restaurant car *n* (*Brit*) coche-comedor *m*
restful ['rɛstful] *adj* descansado, tranquilo
restitution [rɛstɪ'tju:ʃən] *n*: **to make ~ to sb for sth** restituir algo a algn; (*paying*) indemnizar a algn por algo
restive ['rɛstɪv] *adj* inquieto; (*horse*) rebelón(-ona)
restless ['rɛstlɪs] *adj* inquieto; **to get ~** impacientarse
restoration [rɛstə'reɪʃən] *n* restauración *f*; (*giving back*) devolución *f*, restitución *f*
restore [rɪ'stɔ:ʳ] *vt* (*building*) restaurar; (*sth stolen*) devolver, restituir; (*health*) restablecer
restrain [rɪs'treɪn] *vt* (*feeling*) contener, refrenar; (*person*): **to ~ (from doing)** disuadir (de hacer)
restrained [rɪs'treɪnd] *adj* (*style*) reservado
restraint [rɪs'treɪnt] *n* (*restriction*) freno, control *m*; (*of style*) reserva; **wage ~** control *m* de los salarios
restrict [rɪs'trɪkt] *vt* restringir, limitar
restriction [rɪs'trɪkʃən] *n* restricción *f*, limitación *f*
rest room *n* (*US*) aseos *mpl*
restructure [ri:'strʌktʃəʳ] *vt* reestructurar
result [rɪ'zʌlt] *n* resultado ▷ *vi*: **to ~ in** terminar en, tener por resultado; **as a ~ of** a *or* como consecuencia de; **to ~ (from)** resultar (de)

resume [rɪ'zju:m] *vt* (*work, journey*) reanudar; (*sum up*) resumir ▷ *vi* (*meeting*) continuar
résumé ['reɪzju:meɪ] *n* resumen *m*
resumption [rɪ'zʌmpʃən] *n* reanudación *f*
resurgence [rɪ'sə:dʒəns] *n* resurgimiento
resurrection [rɛzə'rɛkʃən] *n* resurrección *f*
resuscitate [rɪ'sʌsɪteɪt] *vt* (*Med*) resucitar
retail ['ri:teɪl] *n* venta al por menor ▷ *cpd* al por menor ▷ *vt* vender al por menor *or* al detalle ▷ *vi*: **to ~ at** (*Comm*) tener precio de venta al público de
retailer ['ri:teɪlə^r] *n* minorista *m/f*, detallista *m/f*
retail price *n* precio de venta al público, precio al detalle *or* al por menor
retain [rɪ'teɪn] *vt* (*keep*) retener, conservar; (*employ*) contratar
retainer [rɪ'teɪnə^r] *n* (*servant*) criado; (*fee*) anticipo
retaliate [rɪ'tælɪeɪt] *vi*: **to ~ (against)** tomar represalias (contra)
retaliation [rɪtælɪ'eɪʃən] *n* represalias *fpl*; **in ~ for** como represalia por
retarded [rɪ'tɑ:dɪd] *adj* (*inf!*) retrasado (*mentalmente*) (*!*)
retch [rɛtʃ] *vi* darle a algn arcadas
retentive [rɪ'tɛntɪv] *adj* (*memory*) retentivo
reticence ['rɛtɪsns] *n* reticencia, reserva
retina ['rɛtɪnə] *n* retina
retire [rɪ'taɪə^r] *vi* (*give up work*) jubilarse; (*withdraw*) retirarse; (*go to bed*) acostarse
retired [rɪ'taɪəd] *adj* (*person*) jubilado
retirement [rɪ'taɪəmənt] *n* jubilación *f*; **early ~** jubilación *f* anticipada
retiring [rɪ'taɪərɪŋ] *adj* (*departing: chairman*) saliente; (*shy*) retraído
retort [rɪ'tɔ:t] *n* (*reply*) réplica ▷ *vi* replicar
retrace [ri:'treɪs] *vt*: **to ~ one's steps** volver sobre sus pasos, desandar lo andado
retract [rɪ'trækt] *vt* (*statement*) retirar; (*claws*) retraer; (*undercarriage, aerial*) replegar ▷ *vi* retractarse
retrain [ri:'treɪn] *vt* reciclar
retread ['ri:trɛd] *n* neumático *or* llanta (*LAm*) recauchutado(-a)
retreat [rɪ'tri:t] *n* (*place*) retiro; (*Mil*) retirada ▷ *vi* retirarse; (*flood*) bajar; **to beat a hasty ~** (*fig*) retirarse en desbandada
retrial ['ri:traɪəl] *n* nuevo proceso
retribution [rɛtrɪ'bju:ʃən] *n* desquite *m*
retrieval [rɪ'tri:vəl] *n* recuperación *f*; **information ~** recuperación *f* de datos
retrieve [rɪ'tri:v] *vt* recobrar; (*situation, honour*) salvar; (*Comput*) recuperar; (*error*) reparar
retriever [rɪ'tri:və^r] *n* perro cobrador
retrospect ['rɛtrəspɛkt] *n*: **in ~** retrospectivamente
retrospective [rɛtrə'spɛktɪv] *adj* retrospectivo; (*law*) retroactivo ▷ *n* exposición *f* retrospectiva
return [rɪ'tə:n] *n* (*going or coming back*) vuelta, regreso; (*of sth stolen etc*) devolución *f*; (*recompense*) recompensa; (*Finance: from land, shares*) ganancia, ingresos *mpl*; (*Comm: of merchandise*) devolución *f* ▷ *cpd* (*journey*) de regreso; (*Brit: ticket*) de ida y vuelta; (*match*) de vuelta ▷ *vi* (*person etc: come or go back*) volver, regresar; (*symptoms etc*) reaparecer ▷ *vt* devolver; (*favour, love etc*) corresponder a; (*verdict*) pronunciar; (*Pol: candidate*) elegir; **returns** *npl* (*Comm*) ingresos *mpl*; **tax ~** declaración *f* de la renta; **in ~ (for)** a cambio (de); **by ~ of post** a vuelta de correo; **many happy ~s (of the day)!** ¡feliz cumpleaños!
returning officer [rɪ'tə:nɪŋ-] *n* (*Brit Pol*) escrutador(a) *m(f)*
return ticket *n* (*esp Brit*) billete *m* (*Sp*) *or* boleto *m* (*LAm*) de ida y vuelta, billete *m* redondo (*Mex*)
retweet [ri:'twi:t] (*on Twitter*) *vt* retuitear ▷ *n* retuit *m*
reunion [ri:'ju:nɪən] *n* (*of family*) reunión *f*; (*of two people, school*) reencuentro
reunite [ri:ju:'naɪt] *vt* reunir; (*reconcile*) reconciliar
rev [rɛv] *n abbr* (*Aut: = revolution*) revolución *f* ▷ *vt* (*also*: **~ up**) acelerar
revaluation [ri:vælju:'eɪʃən] *n* revalorización *f*
revamp [ri:'væmp] *vt* renovar
reveal [rɪ'vi:l] *vt* (*make known*) revelar
revealing [rɪ'vi:lɪŋ] *adj* revelador(a)
reveille [rɪ'vælɪ] *n* (*Mil*) diana
revel ['rɛvl] *vi*: **to ~ in sth/in doing sth** gozar de algo/haciendo algo
revelation [rɛvə'leɪʃən] *n* revelación *f*
revelry ['rɛvlrɪ] *n* jarana, juerga
revenge [rɪ'vɛndʒ] *n* venganza; (*in sport*) revancha; **to take ~ on** vengarse de; **to get one's ~ (for sth)** vengarse (de algo)
revenue ['rɛvənju:] *n* ingresos *mpl*, rentas *fpl*
reverberate [rɪ'və:bəreɪt] *vi* (*sound*) resonar, retumbar
reverence ['rɛvərəns] *n* reverencia
Reverend ['rɛvərənd] *adj* (*in titles*): **the ~ John Smith** (*Anglican*) el Reverendo John Smith; (*Catholic*) el Padre John Smith; (*Protestant*) el Pastor John Smith
reverent ['rɛvərənt] *adj* reverente
reverie ['rɛvərɪ] *n* ensueño
reversal [rɪ'və:sl] *n* (*of order*) inversión *f*; (*of policy*) cambio de rumbo; (*of decision*) revocación *f*
reverse [rɪ'və:s] *n* (*opposite*) contrario; (*back: of cloth*) revés *m*; (*: of coin*) reverso; (*: of paper*) dorso; (*Aut: also*: **~ gear**) marcha atrás ▷ *adj* (*order*) inverso; (*direction*) contrario ▷ *vt* (*decision*) dar marcha atrás a; (*Aut*) dar marcha atrás a; (*position, function*) invertir ▷ *vi* (*Brit Aut*) poner en marcha atrás; **in ~ order** en orden inverso; **the ~** lo contrario; **to go into ~** dar marcha atrás
reverse-charge call [rɪ'və:stʃɑ:dʒ-] *n* (*Brit*) llamada a cobro revertido
reversing lights [rɪ'və:sɪŋ-] *npl* (*Brit Aut*) luces *fpl* de marcha atrás

r

revert [rɪ'vəːt] *vi*: **to ~ to** volver *or* revertir a
review [rɪ'vjuː] *n* (*magazine*) revista; (*Mil*) revista; (*of book, film*) reseña; (*US: examination*) repaso, examen *m* ▷ *vt* repasar, examinar; (*Mil*) pasar revista a; (*book, film*) reseñar; **to come under ~** ser examinado
reviewer [rɪ'vjuːəʳ] *n* crítico(-a)
revile [rɪ'vaɪl] *vt* injuriar, vilipendiar
revise [rɪ'vaɪz] *vt* (*manuscript*) corregir; (*opinion*) modificar; (*price, procedure*) revisar; (*Brit: study: subject*) repasar; (*look over*) revisar; **~d edition** edición *f* corregida
revision [rɪ'vɪʒən] *n* corrección *f*; modificación *f*; (*of subject*) repaso; (*revised version*) revisión *f*
revitalize [riː'vaɪtəlaɪz] *vt* revivificar
revival [rɪ'vaɪvəl] *n* (*recovery*) reanimación *f*; (*Pol*) resurgimiento; (*of interest*) renacimiento; (*Theat*) reestreno; (*of faith*) despertar *m*
revive [rɪ'vaɪv] *vt* resucitar; (*custom*) restablecer; (*hope, courage*) reanimar; (*play*) reestrenar ▷ *vi* (*person*) volver en sí; (*from tiredness*) reponerse; (*business*) reactivarse
revoke [rɪ'vəuk] *vt* revocar
revolt [rɪ'vəult] *n* rebelión *f* ▷ *vi* rebelarse, sublevarse ▷ *vt* dar asco a, repugnar; **to ~ (against sb/sth)** rebelarse (contra algn/algo)
revolting [rɪ'vəultɪŋ] *adj* asqueroso, repugnante
revolution [rɛvə'luːʃən] *n* revolución *f*
revolutionary [rɛvə'luːʃənrɪ] *adj, n* revolucionario(-a) *m(f)*
revolutionize [rɛvə'luːʃənaɪz] *vt* revolucionar
revolve [rɪ'vɔlv] *vi* dar vueltas, girar; **to ~ (a) round** girar en torno a
revolver [rɪ'vɔlvəʳ] *n* revólver *m*
revolving [rɪ'vɔlvɪŋ] *adj* (*chair, door etc*) giratorio
revue [rɪ'vjuː] *n* (*Theat*) revista
revulsion [rɪ'vʌlʃən] *n* asco, repugnancia
reward [rɪ'wɔːd] *n* premio, recompensa ▷ *vt*: **to ~ (for)** recompensar *or* premiar (por)
rewarding [rɪ'wɔːdɪŋ] *adj* (*fig*) gratificante; **financially ~** económicamente provechoso
rewind [riː'waɪnd] *vt* (*tape*) rebobinar; (*watch*) dar cuerda a; (*wool etc*) devanar
rewire [riː'waɪəʳ] *vt* (*house*) renovar la instalación eléctrica de
reword [riː'wəːd] *vt* expresar en otras palabras
rewritable [riː'raɪtəbl] *adj* reescribible
rewrite [riː'raɪt] *vt* (*irreg: like* **write**) reescribir
Rh *abbr* (= *rhesus*) Rh *m*
rheumatism ['ruːmətɪzəm] *n* reumatismo, reúma
rheumatoid arthritis ['ruːmətɔɪd-] *n* reúma *m* articular
Rhine [raɪn] *n*: **the ~** el (río) Rin
rhinoceros [raɪ'nɔsərəs] *n* rinoceronte *m*
Rhone [rəun] *n*: **the ~** el (río) Ródano
rhubarb ['ruːbɑːb] *n* ruibarbo
rhyme [raɪm] *n* rima; (*verse*) poesía ▷ *vi*: **to ~ (with)** rimar (con); **without ~ or reason** sin ton ni son
rhythm ['rɪðm] *n* ritmo
rhythm method *n* método (de) Ogino
RI *n abbr* (*Brit*: = *religious instruction*) ed. religiosa ▷ *abbr*
rib [rɪb] *n* (*Anat*) costilla ▷ *vt* (*mock*) tomar el pelo a
ribbon ['rɪbən] *n* cinta; **in ~s** (*torn*) hecho trizas
rice [raɪs] *n* arroz *m*
rice pudding *n* arroz *m* con leche
rich [rɪtʃ] *adj* rico; (*soil*) fértil; (*food*) pesado; (*: sweet*) empalagoso; **the rich** *npl* los ricos; **riches** *npl* riqueza *sg*; **to be ~ in sth** abundar en algo
rickets ['rɪkɪts] *n* raquitismo
rickety ['rɪkɪtɪ] *adj* (*old*) desvencijado; (*shaky*) tambaleante
rickshaw ['rɪkʃɔː] *n* carro de culí
rid (*pt, pp* **rid**) [rɪd] *vt*: **to ~ sb of sth** librar a algn de algo; **to get ~ of** deshacerse *or* desembarazarse de
riddance ['rɪdns] *n*: **good ~!** ¡y adiós muy buenas!
riddle ['rɪdl] *n* (*conundrum*) acertijo; (*mystery*) enigma *m*, misterio ▷ *vt*: **to be ~d with** ser lleno *or* plagado de
ride [raɪd] (*pt* **rode**, *pp* **ridden**) *n* paseo; (*distance covered*) viaje *m*, recorrido ▷ *vi* (*on horse: as sport*) montar; (*go somewhere: on horse, bicycle*) dar un paseo, pasearse; (*journey: on bicycle, motor cycle, bus*) viajar ▷ *vt* (*a horse*) montar a; (*distance*) recorrer; **to ~ a bicycle** andar en bicicleta; **to ~ at anchor** (*Naut*) estar fondeado; **can you ~ a bike?** ¿sabes montar en bici(cleta)?; **to go for a ~** dar un paseo; **to take sb for a ~** (*fig*) tomar el pelo a algn; **ride out** *vt*: **to ~ out the storm** (*fig*) capear el temporal
rider ['raɪdəʳ] *n* (*on horse*) jinete *m*; (*on bicycle*) ciclista *m/f*; (*on motorcycle*) motociclista *m/f*
ridge [rɪdʒ] *n* (*of hill*) cresta; (*of roof*) caballete *m*; (*wrinkle*) arruga
ridicule ['rɪdɪkjuːl] *n* irrisión *f*, burla ▷ *vt* poner en ridículo a, burlarse de; **to hold sth/sb up to ~** poner algo/a algn en ridículo
ridiculous [rɪ'dɪkjuləs] *adj* ridículo
riding ['raɪdɪŋ] *n* equitación *f*; **I like ~** me gusta montar a caballo
riding school *n* escuela de equitación
rife [raɪf] *adj*: **to be ~** ser muy común; **to be ~ with** abundar en
riffraff ['rɪfræf] *n* chusma, gentuza
rifle ['raɪfl] *n* rifle *m*, fusil *m* ▷ *vt* saquear; **rifle through** *vt fus* saquear
rifle range *n* campo de tiro; (*at fair*) tiro al blanco
rift [rɪft] *n* (*fig: between friends*) desavenencia; (*: in party*) escisión *f*

rig [rɪg] *n* (*also*: **oil ~**: *on land*) torre *f* de perforación; (: *at sea*) plataforma petrolera ▷ *vt* (*election etc*) amañar los resultados de; **rig out** *vt* (*Brit*) ataviar; **rig up** *vt* improvisar

rigging ['rɪgɪŋ] *n* (*Naut*) aparejo

right [raɪt] *adj* (*true, correct*) correcto, exacto; (*suitable*) indicado, debido; (*proper*) apropiado, propio; (*just*) justo; (*morally good*) bueno; (*not left*) derecho ▷ *n* (*title, claim*) derecho; (*not left*) derecha ▷ *adv* (*correctly*) bien, correctamente; (*straight*) derecho, directamente; (*not on the left*) a la derecha; (*to the right*) hacia la derecha ▷ *vt* (*put straight*) enderezar; (*correct*) corregir ▷ *excl* ¡bueno!, ¡está bien!; **to be ~** (*person*) tener razón; (*answer*) ser correcto; **to get sth ~** acertar en algo; **you did the ~ thing** hiciste bien; **let's get it ~ this time!** ¡a ver si esta vez nos sale bien!; **to put a mistake ~** corregir un error; **the ~ time** la hora exacta; (*fig*) el momento oportuno; **by ~s** en justicia; **~ and wrong** el bien y el mal; **film ~s** derechos *mpl* de la película; **on the ~** a la derecha; **to be in the ~** tener razón; **~ now** ahora mismo; **~ before/after** inmediatamente antes/después; **~ in the middle** exactamente en el centro; **~ away** en seguida; **to go ~ to the end of sth** llegar hasta el final de algo; **~, who's next?** bueno, ¿quién sigue?; **all ~!** ¡vale!; **I'm/I feel all ~ now** ya estoy bien

right angle *n* ángulo recto

righteous ['raɪtʃəs] *adj* justo, honrado; (*anger*) justificado

rightful ['raɪtful] *adj* (*heir*) legítimo

right-hand ['raɪthænd] *adj*: **~ drive** conducción *f* por la derecha; **the ~ side** derecha

right-handed [raɪt'hændɪd] *adj* (*person*) que usa la mano derecha, diestro

right-hand man *n* brazo derecho

right-hand side *n* derecha

rightly ['raɪtlɪ] *adv* correctamente, debidamente; (*with reason*) con razón; **if I remember ~** si recuerdo bien

right of way *n* (*on path etc*) derecho de paso; (*Aut*) prioridad *f* de paso

right-wing [raɪt'wɪŋ] *adj* (*Pol*) de derechas, derechista

rigid ['rɪdʒɪd] *adj* rígido; (*person, ideas*) inflexible

rigidly ['rɪdʒɪdlɪ] *adv* rígidamente; (*inflexibly*) inflexiblemente

rigmarole ['rɪgmərəul] *n* galimatías *m inv*

rigor mortis ['rɪgə'mɔ:tɪs] *n* rigidez *f* cadavérica

rigorous ['rɪgərəs] *adj* riguroso

rile [raɪl] *vt* irritar

rim [rɪm] *n* borde *m*; (*of spectacles*) montura, aro; (*of wheel*) llanta

rind [raɪnd] *n* (*of bacon, cheese*) corteza; (*of lemon etc*) cáscara

ring [rɪŋ] (*pt* **rang**, *pp* **rung**) *n* (*of metal*) aro; (*on finger*) anillo; (*of people*) corro; (*of objects*) círculo; (*gang*) banda; (*for boxing*) cuadrilátero; (*of circus*) pista; (*bull ring*) ruedo, plaza; (*sound of bell*) toque *m*; (*telephone call*) llamada ▷ *vi* (*on telephone*) llamar por teléfono; (*large bell*) repicar; (*doorbell, phone*) sonar; (*also*: **~ out**: *voice, words*) sonar; (*ears*) zumbar ▷ *vt* (*Brit Tel*: *also*: **~ up**) llamar; (*bell etc*) hacer sonar; (*doorbell*) tocar; **that has the ~ of truth about it** eso suena a verdad; **to give sb a ~** (*Brit Tel*) llamar a algn, dar un telefonazo a algn; **the name doesn't ~ a bell (with me)** el nombre no me suena; **to ~ sb (up)** llamar a algn; **ring back** *vt*, ▷ *vi* (*Tel*) devolver la llamada; **ring off** *vi* (*Brit Tel*) colgar, cortar la comunicación; **ring up** *vt* (*Brit*: *Tel*) llamar, telefonear

ring binder *n* carpeta de anillas

ringing ['rɪŋɪŋ] *n* (*of bell*) toque *m*, tañido, (*of large bell*) repique *m*; (*in ears*) zumbido

ringing tone *n* (*Tel*) tono de llamada

ringleader ['rɪŋli:dər] *n* cabecilla *m/f*

ringlets ['rɪŋlɪts] *npl* tirabuzones *mpl*, bucles *mpl*

ring road *n* (*Brit*) carretera periférica *or* de circunvalación

ringtone ['rɪŋtəun] *n* tono de llamada

rink [rɪŋk] *n* (*also*: **ice ~**) pista de hielo; (*for roller-skating*) pista de patinaje

rinse [rɪns] *n* (*of dishes*) enjuague *m*; (*of clothes*) aclarado; (*hair colouring*) reflejo ▷ *vt* enjuagar, aclarar; (*hair*) dar reflejos a

riot ['raɪət] *n* motín *m*, disturbio ▷ *vi* amotinarse; **to run ~** desmandarse

riot gear *n* uniforme *m* antidisturbios *inv*

riotous ['raɪətəs] *adj* alborotado; (*party*) bullicioso; (*uncontrolled*) desenfrenado

riot police *n* policía antidisturbios

RIP *abbr* (= *requiescat or requiescant in pace*: *rest in peace*) q.e.p.d.

rip [rɪp] *n* rasgón *m*, desgarrón *m* ▷ *vt* rasgar, desgarrar ▷ *vi* rasgarse; **rip off** *vt* (*inf*: *cheat*) estafar; **rip up** *vt* hacer pedazos

ripcord ['rɪpkɔ:d] *n* cabo de desgarre

ripe [raɪp] *adj* (*fruit*) maduro

ripen ['raɪpən] *vt*, *vi* madurar

rip-off ['rɪpɔf] *n* (*inf*): **it's a ~!** ¡es una estafa!, ¡es un timo!

ripple ['rɪpl] *n* onda, rizo; (*sound*) murmullo ▷ *vi* rizarse ▷ *vt* rizar

rise [raɪz] (*pt* **rose**, *pp* **risen** [rəuz, 'rɪzn]) *n* (*slope*) cuesta, pendiente *f*; (*hill*) altura; (*increase*: *in wages*: *Brit*) aumento; (: *in prices, temperature*) subida, alza; (*fig*: *to power etc*) ascenso; (: *ascendancy*) auge *m* ▷ *vi* (*gen*) elevarse; (*prices*) subir; (*waters*) crecer; (*river*) nacer; (*sun*) salir; (*person*: *from bed etc*) levantarse; (*also*: **~ up**: *rebel*) sublevarse; (*in rank*) ascender; **~ to power** ascenso al poder; **to give ~ to** dar lugar *or* origen a; **to ~ to the occasion** ponerse a la altura de las circunstancias

risen ['rɪzn] *pp of* **rise**
rising ['raɪzɪŋ] *adj (increasing: number)* creciente; *(: prices)* en aumento *or* alza; *(tide)* creciente; *(sun, moon)* naciente ▷ *n (uprising)* sublevación *f*
rising star *n (fig)* figura en alza
risk [rɪsk] *n* riesgo, peligro ▷ *vt (gen)* arriesgar; *(dare)* atreverse a; **to take** *or* **run the ~ of doing** correr el riesgo de hacer; **at ~** en peligro; **at one's own ~** bajo su propia responsabilidad; **fire/health/security ~** peligro de incendio/ para la salud/para la seguridad
risky ['rɪskɪ] *adj* arriesgado, peligroso
risqué ['riːskeɪ] *adj (joke)* subido de color
rissole ['rɪsəul] *n* croqueta
rite [raɪt] *n* rito; **last ~s** últimos sacramentos *mpl*
ritual ['rɪtjuəl] *adj* ritual ▷ *n* ritual *m*, rito
rival ['raɪvl] *n* rival *m/f*; *(in business)* competidor(a) *m(f)* ▷ *adj* rival, opuesto ▷ *vt* competir con
rivalry ['raɪvlrɪ] *n* rivalidad *f*, competencia
river ['rɪvə^r] *n* río ▷ *cpd (port, traffic)* de río, del río; **up/down ~** río arriba/abajo
riverbank ['rɪvəbæŋk] *n* orilla (del río)
rivet ['rɪvɪt] *n* roblón *m*, remache *m* ▷ *vt* remachar; *(fig)* fascinar
riveting ['rɪvɪtɪŋ] *adj (fig)* fascinante
Riviera [rɪvɪ'ɛərə] *n*: **the (French) ~** la Costa Azul, la Riviera (francesa); **the Italian ~** la Riviera italiana
road [rəud] *n (gen)* camino; *(motorway etc)* carretera; *(in town)* calle *f*; **major/minor ~** carretera general/secundaria; **main ~** carretera; **it takes four hours by ~** se tarda cuarto horas por carretera; **on the ~ to success** camino del éxito
roadblock ['rəudblɔk] *n* barricada, control *m*, retén *m (LAm)*
road hog ['rəudhɔg] *n* loco(-a) del volante
road map *n* mapa *m* de carreteras
road rage *n conducta agresiva de los conductores*
road safety *n* seguridad *f* vial
roadside ['rəudsaɪd] *n* borde *m* (del camino) ▷ *cpd* al lado de la carretera; **by the ~** al borde del camino
roadsign ['rəudsaɪn] *n* señal *f* de tráfico
road tax *n (Brit)* impuesto de rodaje
roadway ['rəudweɪ] *n* calzada
roadworks ['rəudwəːks] *npl* obras *fpl*
roadworthy ['rəudwəːðɪ] *adj (car)* en buen estado para circular
roam [rəum] *vi* vagar ▷ *vt* vagar por
roar [rɔː^r] *n (of animal)* rugido, bramido; *(of crowd)* clamor *m*, rugido; *(of vehicle, storm)* estruendo; *(of laughter)* carcajada ▷ *vi* rugir, bramar; hacer estruendo; **to ~ with laughter** reírse a carcajadas
roaring ['rɔːrɪŋ] *adj*: **a ~ success** un tremendo éxito; **to do a ~ trade** hacer buen negocio
roast [rəust] *n* carne *f* asada, asado ▷ *vt (meat)* asar; *(coffee)* tostar
roast beef *n* rosbif *m*
roasting ['rəustɪŋ] *n*: **to give sb a ~** *(inf)* echar una buena bronca a algn
rob [rɔb] *vt* robar; **to ~ sb of sth** robar algo a algn; *(fig: deprive)* quitar algo a algn
robber ['rɔbə^r] *n* ladrón(-ona) *m(f)*
robbery ['rɔbərɪ] *n* robo
robe [rəub] *n (for ceremony etc)* toga; *(also:* **bath ~**) bata, albornoz *m*
robin ['rɔbɪn] *n* petirrojo
robot ['rəubɔt] *n* robot *m*
robust [rəu'bʌst] *adj* robusto, fuerte
rock [rɔk] *n (gen)* roca; *(boulder)* peña, peñasco; *(Brit: sweet)* ≈ pirulí *m* ▷ *vt (swing gently)* mecer; *(shake)* sacudir ▷ *vi* mecerse, balancearse; sacudirse; **on the ~s** *(drink)* con hielo; **their marriage is on the ~s** su matrimonio se está yendo a pique; **to ~ the boat** *(fig)* crear problemas
rock and roll *n* rock and roll *m*, rocanrol *m*
rock-bottom ['rɔk'bɔtəm] *adj (fig)* por los suelos; **to reach** *or* **touch ~** *(price)* estar por los suelos; *(person)* tocar fondo
rock climbing *n (Sport)* escalada
rockery ['rɔkərɪ] *n* cuadro alpino
rocket ['rɔkɪt] *n* cohete *m* ▷ *vi (prices)* dispararse, ponerse por las nubes
rocking chair ['rɔkɪŋ-] *n* mecedora
rocking horse *n* caballo de balancín
rocky ['rɔkɪ] *adj (gen)* rocoso; *(unsteady: table)* inestable
rod [rɔd] *n* vara, varilla; *(Tech)* barra; *(also:* **fishing ~**) caña
rode [rəud] *pt of* **ride**
rodent ['rəudnt] *n* roedor *m*
rodeo ['rəudɪəu] *n* rodeo
roe [rəu] *n (species: also:* **~ deer**) corzo; *(of fish)*: **hard/soft ~** hueva/lecha
rogue [rəug] *n* pícaro, pillo
role [rəul] *n* papel *m*, rol *m*
role-model ['rəulmɔdl] *n* modelo a imitar
role play *n (also:* **~ing**) juego de papeles *or* roles
roll [rəul] *n* rollo; *(of bank notes)* fajo; *(also:* **bread ~**) panecillo; *(register)* lista, nómina; *(sound: of drums etc)* redoble *m*; *(movement: of ship)* balanceo ▷ *vt* hacer rodar; *(also:* **~ up**: *string)* enrollar; *(: sleeves)* arremangar; *(cigarettes)* liar; *(also:* **~ out**: *pastry)* aplanar ▷ *vi (gen)* rodar; *(drum)* redoblar; *(in walking)* bambolearse; *(ship)* balancearse; **cheese ~** panecillo de queso; **roll about, roll around** *vi (person)* revolcarse; **roll by** *vi (time)* pasar; **roll in** *vi (mail, cash)* entrar a raudales; **roll over** *vi* dar una vuelta; **roll up** *vi (inf: arrive)* presentarse, aparecer ▷ *vt (carpet, cloth, map)* arrollar; *(sleeves)* arremangar; **to ~ o.s. up into a ball** acurrucarse, hacerse un ovillo
roll call *n*: **to take a ~** pasar lista
roller ['rəulə^r] *n* rodillo; *(wheel)* rueda; *(for road)* apisonadora; *(for hair)* rulo
Rollerblades® ['rəuləbleɪdz] *npl* patines *mpl* en línea

roller coaster *n* montaña rusa
roller skates *npl* patines *mpl* de rueda
roller-skating ['rəuləskeɪtɪŋ] *n* patinaje sobre ruedas; **to go ~** ir a patinar (*sobre ruedas*)
rolling ['rəulɪŋ] *adj* (*landscape*) ondulado
rolling pin *n* rodillo (de cocina)
rolling stock *n* (*Rail*) material *m* rodante
ROM [rɔm] *n abbr* (*Comput*: = *read-only memory*) (memoria) ROM *f*
Roman ['rəumən] *adj, n* romano(-a) *m(f)*
Roman Catholic *adj, n* católico(-a) *m(f)* (romano(-a))
romance [rə'mæns] *n* (*love affair*) amor *m*, idilio; (*charm*) lo romántico; (*novel*) novela de amor
Romania [ru:'meɪnɪə] *n* = **Rumania**
Romanian [ru:'meɪnɪən] *adj, n* = **Rumanian**
Roman numeral *n* número romano
romantic [rə'mæntɪk] *adj* romántico
Rome [rəum] *n* Roma
romp [rɔmp] *n* retozo, jugueteo ▷ *vi* (*also*: **~ about**) juguetear; **to ~ home** (*horse*) ganar fácilmente
rompers ['rɔmpəz] *npl* pelele *m*
roof [ru:f] *n* (*gen*) techo; (*of house*) tejado ▷ *vt* techar, poner techo a; **~ of the mouth** paladar *m*
roofing ['ru:fɪŋ] *n* techumbre *f*
roof rack *n* (*Aut*) baca, portaequipajes *msg*
rook [ruk] *n* (*bird*) graja; (*Chess*) torre *f*
rookie ['rukɪ] *n* (*inf*) novato(-a); (*Mil*) chivo
room [ru:m] *n* (*in house*) cuarto, habitación *f*, pieza (*esp LAm*); (*also*: **bed~**) dormitorio; (*in school etc*) sala; (*space*) sitio; **rooms** *npl* (*lodging*) alojamiento *sg*; **"~s to let"**, (*US*) **"~s for rent"** "se alquilan pisos *or* cuartos"; **single/double ~** habitación individual/ doble *or* para dos personas; **is there ~ for this?** ¿cabe esto?; **to make ~ for sb** hacer sitio para algn; **there is ~ for improvement** podría mejorarse
rooming house ['ru:mɪŋ-] *n* (*US*) pensión *f*
roommate ['ru:mmeɪt] *n* compañero(-a) de cuarto
room service *n* servicio de habitaciones
roomy ['ru:mɪ] *adj* espacioso
roost [ru:st] *n* percha ▷ *vi* pasar la noche
rooster ['ru:stə^r] *n* gallo
root [ru:t] *n* (*Bot, Math*) raíz *f* ▷ *vi* (*plant, belief*) arraigar(se); **to take ~** (*plant*) echar raíces; (*idea*) arraigar(se); **the ~ of the problem is that ...** la raíz del problema es que ...; **root about** *vi* (*fig*) rebuscar; **root for** *vt fus* apoyar a; **root out** *vt* desarraigar
root beer *n* (*US*) *refresco sin alcohol de extractos de hierbas*
rope [rəup] *n* cuerda; (*Naut*) cable *m* ▷ *vt* (*box*) atar *or* amarrar con (una) cuerda; (*climbers*: *also*: **~ together**) encordarse; (*an area*: *also*: **~ off**) acordonar; **to ~ sb in** (*fig*) persuadir a algn a tomar parte; **to know the ~s** (*fig*) conocer los trucos (del oficio)
ropey ['rəupɪ] *adj* (*inf*) chungo
rosary ['rəuzərɪ] *n* rosario
rose [rəuz] *pt of* **rise** ▷ *n* rosa; (*also*: **~bush**) rosal *m*; (*on watering can*) roseta ▷ *adj* color de rosa
rosé ['rəuzeɪ] *n* vino rosado, clarete *m*
rosebud ['rəuzbʌd] *n* capullo de rosa
rosebush ['rəuzbuʃ] *n* rosal *m*
rosemary ['rəuzmərɪ] *n* romero
rosette [rəu'zɛt] *n* rosetón *m*
roster ['rɔstə^r] *n*: **duty ~** lista de tareas
rostrum ['rɔstrəm] *n* tribuna
rosy ['rəuzɪ] *adj* rosado, sonrosado; **the future looks ~** el futuro parece prometedor
rot [rɔt] *n* (*decay*) putrefacción *f*, podredumbre *f*; (*fig*: *pej*) tonterías *fpl* ▷ *vt* pudrir, corromper ▷ *vi* pudrirse, corromperse; **it has ~ted** está podrido; **to stop the ~** (*fig*) poner fin a las pérdidas
rota ['rəutə] *n* lista (de tareas)
rotary ['rəutərɪ] *adj* rotativo
rotate [rəu'teɪt] *vt* (*revolve*) hacer girar, dar vueltas a; (*change round*: *crops*) cultivar en rotación; (*: jobs*) alternar ▷ *vi* (*revolve*) girar, dar vueltas
rotating [rəu'teɪtɪŋ] *adj* (*movement*) rotativo
rote [rəut] *n*: **by ~** de memoria
rotor ['rəutə^r] *n* rotor *m*
rotten ['rɔtn] *adj* (*decayed*) podrido; (*: wood*) carcomido; (*fig*) corrompido; (*inf*: *bad*) pésimo; **to feel ~** (*ill*) sentirse fatal; **~ to the core** completamente podrido
rotund [rəu'tʌnd] *adj* rotundo
rough [rʌf] *adj* (*skin, surface*) áspero; (*terrain*) accidentado; (*road*) desigual; (*voice*) bronco; (*person, manner*: *coarse*) tosco, grosero; (*weather*) borrascoso; (*treatment*) brutal; (*sea*) embravecido; (*town, area*) peligroso; (*cloth*) basto; (*plan*) preliminar; (*guess*) aproximado; (*violent*) violento ▷ *n* (*Golf*): **in the ~** en las hierbas altas; **to ~ it** vivir sin comodidades; **to sleep ~** (*Brit*) pasar la noche al raso; **the sea is ~ today** el mar está agitado hoy; **to have a ~ time (of it)** pasar una mala racha; **~ estimate** cálculo aproximado
roughage ['rʌfɪdʒ] *n* fibra(s) *f(pl)*, forraje *m*
rough-and-ready ['rʌfən'rɛdɪ] *adj* improvisado, tosco
rough copy, rough draft *n* borrador *m*
roughly ['rʌflɪ] *adv* (*handle*) torpemente; (*make*) toscamente; (*approximately*) aproximadamente; **~ speaking** más o menos
roughness ['rʌfnɪs] *n* aspereza; tosquedad *f*; brutalidad *f*
roulette [ru:'lɛt] *n* ruleta
Roumania [ru:'meɪnɪə] *n* = **Rumania**
round [raund] *adj* redondo ▷ *n* círculo; (*of policeman*) ronda; (*of milkman*) recorrido; (*of doctor*) visitas *fpl*; (*game*: *in competition, cards*) partida; (*of ammunition*) cartucho; (*Boxing*) asalto; (*of talks*) ronda ▷ *vt* (*corner*) doblar ▷ *prep* alrededor de; (*surrounding*): **~ his neck/**

r

the table en su cuello/alrededor de la mesa; (*in a circular movement*): **to move ~ the room/ sail ~ the world** dar una vuelta a la habitación/circumnavigar el mundo; (*in various directions*): **to move ~ a room/house** moverse por toda la habitación/casa ▷ *adv*: **all ~** por todos lados; **the long way ~** por el camino menos directo; **all the year ~** durante todo el año; **it's just ~ the corner** (*fig*) está a la vuelta de la esquina; **to ask sb ~** invitar a algn a casa; **I'll be ~ at six o'clock** llegaré a eso de las seis; **she arrived ~ (about) noon** llegó alrededor del mediodía; **~ the clock** *adv* las 24 horas; **to go ~ to sb's (house)** ir a casa de algn; **to go ~ the back** pasar por atrás; **enough to go ~** bastante (para todos); **in ~ figures** en números redondos; **to go the ~s** (*story*) divulgarse; **a ~ of applause** una salva de aplausos; **a ~ of drinks/sandwiches** una ronda de bebidas/ bocadillos; **a ~ of toast** (*Brit*) una tostada; **the daily ~** la rutina cotidiana; **round off** *vt* (*speech etc*) acabar, poner término a; **round up** *vt* (*cattle*) acorralar; (*people*) reunir; (*prices*) redondear

roundabout ['raundəbaut] *n* (*Brit: Aut*) glorieta, rotonda; (: *at fair*) tiovivo ▷ *adj* (*route, means*) indirecto

rounders ['raundəz] *n* (*Brit: game*) *juego similar al béisbol*

roundly ['raundlı] *adv* (*fig*) rotundamente

round-shouldered ['raund'ʃəuldəd] *adj* cargado de espaldas

round trip *n* viaje *m* de ida y vuelta

roundup ['raundʌp] *n* rodeo; (*of criminals*) redada; **a ~ of the latest news** un resumen de las últimas noticias

rouse [rauz] *vt* (*wake up*) despertar; (*stir up*) suscitar

rousing ['rauzıŋ] *adj* (*applause*) caluroso; (*speech*) conmovedor(a)

rout [raut] *n* (*Mil*) derrota; (*flight*) desbandada ▷ *vt* derrotar

route [ru:t] *n* ruta, camino; (*of bus*) recorrido; (*of shipping*) rumbo, derrota; **the best ~ to London** el mejor camino *or* la mejor ruta para ir a Londres; **en ~ from ... to** en el viaje de ... a; **en ~ for** rumbo a, con destino en

route map *n* (*Brit: for journey*) mapa *m* de carreteras

router ['ru:tə^r, (*US*) 'rautə^r] *n* (*Comput*) router *m*

routine [ru:'ti:n] *adj* (*work*) rutinario ▷ *n* rutina; (*Theat*) número; (*Comput*) rutina; **~ procedure** trámite *m* rutinario

row¹ [rəu] *n* (*line*) fila, hilera; (*Knitting*) vuelta ▷ *vi* (*in boat*) remar ▷ *vt* (*boat*) conducir remando; **four days in a ~** cuarto días seguidos

row² [rau] *n* (*noise*) escándalo; (*dispute*) bronca, pelea; (*fuss*) jaleo; (*scolding*) reprimenda ▷ *vi* reñir(se); **to make a ~** armar un lío; **to have a ~** pelearse, reñir

rowboat ['rəubəut] *n* (*US*) bote *m* de remos

rowdy ['raudı] *adj* (*person: noisy*) ruidoso; (: *quarrelsome*) pendenciero; (*occasion*) alborotado ▷ *n* pendenciero

rowing ['rəuıŋ] *n* remo

rowing boat *n* (*Brit*) bote *m or* barco de remos

royal ['rɔıəl] *adj* real

Royal Air Force *n* Fuerzas Aéreas Británicas *fpl*

royalist ['rɔıəlıst] *adj, n* monárquico(-a) *m(f)*

royalty ['rɔıəltı] *n* (*royal persons*) (miembros *mpl* de la) familia real; (*payment to author*) derechos *mpl* de autor

rpm *abbr* (= *revolutions per minute*) r.p.m.

RSPB *n abbr* (*Brit*) = **Royal Society for the Protection of Birds**

RSPCA *n abbr* (*Brit*) = **Royal Society for the Prevention of Cruelty to Animals**

RSVP *abbr* (= *répondez s'il vous plaît*) SRC

RTA *n abbr* (= *road traffic accident*) accidente *m* de carretera

Rt. Hon. *abbr* (*Brit*: = *Right Honourable*) *tratamiento honorífico de diputado*

Rt. Rev. *abbr* (= *Right Reverend*) Rvdo.

rub [rʌb] *vt* (*gen*) frotar; (*hard*) restregar ▷ *n* (*gen*) frotamiento; (*touch*) roce *m*; **to give sth a ~** frotar algo; **to ~ sb up** *or* (*US*) **~ sb the wrong way** sacar de quicio a algn; **rub down** *vt* (*body*) secar frotando; (*horse*) almohazar; **rub in** *vt* (*ointment*) frotar; **rub off** *vt* borrarse ▷ *vi* quitarse (frotando); **to ~ off on sb** influir en algn, pegársele a algn; **rub out** *vt* borrar ▷ *vi* borrarse

rubber ['rʌbə^r] *n* caucho, goma; (*Brit: eraser*) goma de borrar

rubber band *n* goma, gomita

rubber bullet *n* bala de goma

rubber gloves *npl* guantes *mpl* de goma

rubber plant *n* ficus *m*

rubber ring *n* (*for swimming*) flotador *m*

rubbish ['rʌbıʃ] (*Brit*) *n* (*from household*) basura; (*waste*) desperdicios *mpl*; (*fig: pej*) tonterías *fpl*; (*trash*) basura, porquería ▷ *vt* (*inf*) poner por los suelos; **what you've just said is ~** lo que acabas de decir es una tontería

rubbish bin *n* cubo *or* bote *m* (*LAm*) de la basura

rubbish dump *n* (*in town*) vertedero, basurero

rubble ['rʌbl] *n* escombros *mpl*

ruby ['ru:bı] *n* rubí *m*

RUC *n abbr* (= *Royal Ulster Constabulary*) *fuerza de policía en Irlanda del Norte*

rucksack ['rʌksæk] *n* mochila

rudder ['rʌdə^r] *n* timón *m*

ruddy ['rʌdı] *adj* (*face*) rubicundo; (*inf: damned*) condenado

rude [ru:d] *adj* (*impolite: person*) grosero, maleducado; (: *word, manners*) rudo, grosero; (*indecent*) indecente; **to be ~ to sb** ser grosero con algn

rudimentary [ru:dı'mɛntərı] *adj* rudimentario

rue [ru:] *vt* arrepentirse de

rueful ['ru:ful] *adj* arrepentido
ruffian ['rʌfɪən] *n* matón *m*, criminal *m*
ruffle ['rʌfl] *vt* (*hair*) despeinar; (*clothes*) arrugar; (*fig: person*) agitar
rug [rʌg] *n* alfombra; (*Brit: for knees*) manta
rugby ['rʌgbɪ] *n* (*also:* **~ football**) rugby *m*
rugged ['rʌgɪd] *adj* (*landscape*) accidentado; (*features*) robusto
rugger ['rʌgə^r] *n* (*Brit inf*) rugby *m*
ruin ['ru:ɪn] *n* ruina ▷ *vt* arruinar; (*spoil*) estropear; **ruins** *npl* ruinas *fpl*, restos *mpl*; **in ~s** en ruinas
rule [ru:l] *n* (*norm*) norma, costumbre *f*; (*regulation, ruler*) regla; (*government*) dominio; (*dominion etc*): **under British ~** bajo el dominio británico ▷ *vt* (*country, person*) gobernar; (*decide*) disponer; (*draw lines*) trazar ▷ *vi* gobernar; (*Law*) fallar; **to ~ against/in favour of/on** fallar en contra de/a favor de/sobre; **to ~ that ...** (*umpire, judge*) fallar que ...; **it's against the ~s** está prohibido; **as a ~** por regla general, generalmente; **by ~ of thumb** por experiencia; **majority ~** (*Pol*) gobierno mayoritario; **rule out** *vt* excluir
ruled [ru:ld] *adj* (*paper*) rayado
ruler ['ru:lə^r] *n* (*sovereign*) soberano; (*for measuring*) regla
ruling ['ru:lɪŋ] *adj* (*party*) gobernante; (*class*) dirigente ▷ *n* (*Law*) fallo, decisión *f*
rum [rʌm] *n* ron *m*
Rumania [ru:'meɪnɪə] *n* Rumanía
Rumanian [ru:'meɪnɪən] *adj, n* rumano(-a) *m(f)*
rumble ['rʌmbl] *n* ruido sordo; (*of thunder*) redoble *m* ▷ *vi* retumbar, hacer un ruido sordo; (*stomach, pipe*) sonar
rummage ['rʌmɪdʒ] *vi* revolverlo todo
rumour, rumor (*US*) ['ru:mə^r] *n* rumor *m* ▷ *vt*: **it is ~ed that ...** se rumorea que ...; **~ has it that ...** corre la voz de que ...
rump [rʌmp] *n* (*of animal*) ancas *fpl*, grupa
rump steak *n* filete *m* de lomo
rumpus ['rʌmpəs] *n* (*inf*) lío, jaleo; (*quarrel*) pelea, riña; **to kick up a ~** armar un follón *or* armar bronca
run [rʌn] (*pt* **ran**, *pp* **run**) *n* (*Sport*) carrera; (*outing*) paseo, excursión *f*; (*distance travelled*) trayecto; (*series*) serie *f*; (*Theat*) temporada; (*Ski*) pista; (*in tights, stockings*) carrera ▷ *vt* (*operate: business*) dirigir; (*: competition, course*) organizar; (*: hotel, house*) administrar, llevar; (*Comput: program*) ejecutar; (*to pass: hand*) pasar; (*Press: feature*) publicar ▷ *vi* (*gen*) correr; (*work: machine*) funcionar, marchar; (*bus, train: operate*) circular, ir; (*: travel*) ir; (*continue: play*) seguir en cartel; (*: contract*) ser válido; (*flow: river, bath*) fluir; (*colours, washing*) desteñirse; (*in election*) ser candidato; **to go for a ~** ir a correr; **to make a ~ for it** echar(se) a correr, escapar(se), huir; **to have the ~ of sb's house** tener el libre uso de la casa de algn; **a ~ of luck** una racha de suerte; **there was a ~ on** (*meat, tickets*) hubo mucha demanda de; **in the long ~** a la larga; **on the ~** en fuga; **I'll ~ you to the station** te llevaré a la estación en coche; **to ~ a risk** correr un riesgo; **to ~ a bath** llenar la bañera; **to ~ errands** hacer recados; **it's very cheap to ~** es muy económico; **to be ~ off one's feet** estar ocupadísimo; **to ~ for the bus** correr tras el autobús; **we shall have to ~ for it** tendremos que escapar; **the train ~s between Gatwick and Victoria** el tren circula entre Gatwick y Victoria; **the bus ~s every 20 minutes** el autobús pasa cada 20 minutos; **to ~ on petrol/on diesel/off batteries** funcionar con gasolina/gasoil/baterías; **my salary won't ~ to a car** mi sueldo no me da para comprarme un coche; **the car ran into the lamppost** el coche chocó contra el farol; **run about, run around** *vi* (*children*) correr por todos lados; **run across** *vt fus* (*find*) dar *or* topar con; **run after** *vt fus* (*to catch up*) correr tras; (*chase*) perseguir; **run away** *vi* huir; **run down** *vi* (*clock*) pararse ▷ *vt* (*reduce: production*) ir reduciendo; (*factory*) restringir la producción de; (*Aut*) atropellar; (*criticize*) criticar; **to be ~ down** (*person: tired*) encontrarse agotado; **run in** *vt* (*Brit: car*) rodar; **run into** *vt fus* (*meet: person, trouble*) tropezar con; (*collide with*) chocar con; **to ~ into debt** contraer deudas, endeudarse; **run off** *vt* (*water*) dejar correr ▷ *vi* huir corriendo; **run out** *vi* (*person*) salir corriendo; (*liquid*) irse; (*lease*) caducar, vencer; (*money*) acabarse; **run out of** *vt fus* quedar sin; **I've ~ out of petrol** se me acabó la gasolina; **run over** *vt* (*Aut*) atropellar ▷ *vt fus* (*revise*) repasar; **run through** *vt fus* (*instructions*) repasar; **run up** *vt* (*debt*) incurrir en; **to ~ up against** (*difficulties*) tropezar con
run-around ['rʌnəraund] *n*: **to give sb the ~** traer a algn al retortero
runaway ['rʌnəweɪ] *adj* (*horse*) desbocado; (*truck*) sin frenos; (*person*) fugitivo
rung [rʌŋ] *pp of* **ring** ▷ *n* (*of ladder*) escalón *m*, peldaño
run-in ['rʌnɪn] *n* (*inf*) altercado
runner ['rʌnə^r] *n* (*in race: person*) corredor(a) *m(f)*; (*: horse*) caballo; (*on sledge*) patín *m*; (*wheel*) ruedecilla
runner bean *n* (*Brit*) judía verde
runner-up [rʌnər'ʌp] *n* subcampeón(-ona) *m(f)*
running ['rʌnɪŋ] *n* (*sport*) atletismo; (*race*) carrera ▷ *adj* (*costs, water*) corriente; (*commentary*) en directo; **to be in/out of the ~ for sth** tener/no tener posibilidades de ganar algo; **6 days ~** 6 días seguidos
running costs *npl* (*of business*) gastos *mpl* corrientes; (*of car*) gastos *mpl* de mantenimiento
runny ['rʌnɪ] *adj* líquido; (*eyes*) lloroso; **to have a ~ nose** tener mocos

run-of-the-mill ['rʌnəvðə'mɪl] *adj* común y corriente
runt [rʌnt] *n* (*also pej*) enano
run-up ['rʌnʌp] *n*: **~ to** (*election etc*) período previo a
runway ['rʌnweɪ] *n* (*Aviat*) pista (de aterrizaje)
rupee [ru:'pi:] *n* rupia
rupture ['rʌptʃəʳ] *n* (*Med*) hernia ▷ *vt*: **to ~ o.s.** causarse una hernia
rural ['ruərl] *adj* rural
rush [rʌʃ] *n* ímpetu *m*; (*hurry*) prisa, apuro (*LAm*); (*Comm*) demanda repentina; (*Bot*) junco; (*current*) corriente *f* fuerte, ráfaga; (*of feeling*) torrente *m* ▷ *vt* apresurar; (*work*) hacer de prisa; (*attack*: *town etc*) asaltar ▷ *vi* correr, precipitarse; **gold ~** fiebre *f* del oro; **we've had a ~ of orders** ha habido una gran demanda; **I'm in a ~ (to do)** tengo prisa *or* apuro (*LAm*) (por hacer); **is there any ~ for this?** ¿te corre prisa esto?; **to ~ sth off** hacer algo de prisa y corriendo; **rush through** *vt fus* (*meal*) comer de prisa; (*book*) leer de prisa; (*work*) hacer de prisa; (*town*) atravesar a toda velocidad ▷ *vt sep* (*Comm*: *order*) despachar rápidamente
rush hour *n* horas *fpl* punta
rusk [rʌsk] *n* bizcocho tostado
Russia ['rʌʃə] *n* Rusia
Russian ['rʌʃən] *adj* ruso ▷ *n* ruso(-a); (*Ling*) ruso
rust [rʌst] *n* herrumbre *f*, moho ▷ *vi* oxidarse
rustic ['rʌstɪk] *adj* rústico
rustle ['rʌsl] *vi* susurrar ▷ *vt* (*paper*) hacer crujir; (*US*: *cattle*) hurtar, robar
rustproof ['rʌstpru:f] *adj* inoxidable
rusty ['rʌstɪ] *adj* oxidado
rut [rʌt] *n* surco; (*Zool*) celo; **to be in a ~** ser esclavo de la rutina
ruthless ['ru:θlɪs] *adj* despiadado
RV *abbr* (*= revised version*) *traducción inglesa de la Biblia de 1855* ▷ *n abbr* (*US*) = **recreational vehicle**
rye [raɪ] *n* centeno
rye bread *n* pan de centeno

S

S, s [ɛs] *n* (*letter*) S, s *f*; **S for Sugar** S de sábado
S *abbr* (*= Saint*) Sto.(-a.); (*US Scol*: *mark*: *= satisfactory*) suficiente; (*= south*) S; (*on clothes*) = **small**
SA *n abbr* = **South Africa**; **South America**
Sabbath ['sæbəθ] *n* domingo; (*Jewish*) sábado
sabotage ['sæbətɑ:ʒ] *n* sabotaje *m* ▷ *vt* sabotear
saccharin, saccharine ['sækərɪn] *n* sacarina
sachet ['sæʃeɪ] *n* sobrecito
sack [sæk] *n* (*bag*) saco, costal *m* ▷ *vt* (*dismiss*) despedir, echar; (*plunder*) saquear; **to get the ~** ser despedido; **to give sb the ~** despedir *or* echar a algn
sacking ['sækɪŋ] *n* (*material*) arpillera
sacrament ['sækrəmənt] *n* sacramento
sacred ['seɪkrɪd] *adj* sagrado, santo
sacrifice ['sækrɪfaɪs] *n* sacrificio ▷ *vt* sacrificar; **to make ~s (for sb)** sacrificarse (por algn)
sacrilege ['sækrɪlɪdʒ] *n* sacrilegio
sad [sæd] *adj* (*unhappy*) triste; (*deplorable*) lamentable
saddle ['sædl] *n* silla (de montar); (*of cycle*) sillín *m* ▷ *vt* (*horse*) ensillar; **to ~ sb with sth** (*inf*: *task, bill, name*) cargar a algn con algo; (*responsibility*) gravar a algn con algo; **to be ~d with sth** (*inf*) quedar cargado con algo
saddlebag ['sædlbæg] *n* alforja
sadist ['seɪdɪst] *n* sádico(-a)
sadistic [sə'dɪstɪk] *adj* sádico

sadly ['sædlɪ] *adv* tristemente; (*regrettably*) desgraciadamente; **~ lacking (in)** muy deficiente (en)
sadness ['sædnɪs] *n* tristeza
sae *abbr* (*Brit: = stamped addressed envelope*) *sobre con las propias señas de uno y con sello*
safari [sə'fɑːrɪ] *n* safari *m*
safe [seɪf] *adj* (*out of danger*) fuera de peligro; (*not dangerous, sure*) seguro; (*unharmed*) ileso; (*trustworthy*) digno de confianza ▷ *n* caja de caudales, caja fuerte; **~ and sound** sano y salvo; **(just) to be on the ~ side** para mayor seguridad; **~ journey!** ¡buen viaje!; **it is ~ to say that ...** se puede decir con confianza que ...
safe-conduct [seɪf'kɔndʌkt] *n* salvoconducto
safe-deposit ['seɪfdɪpɔzɪt] *n* (*vault*) cámara acorazada; (*box*) caja de seguridad *or* de caudales
safeguard ['seɪfgɑːd] *n* protección *f*, garantía ▷ *vt* proteger, defender
safe haven *n* refugio
safekeeping ['seɪf'kiːpɪŋ] *n* custodia
safely ['seɪflɪ] *adv* seguramente, con seguridad; (*without mishap*) sin peligro; **I can ~ say** puedo decir *or* afirmar con toda seguridad; **to arrive ~** llegar bien
safe sex *n* sexo seguro *or* sin riesgo
safety ['seɪftɪ] *n* seguridad *f* ▷ *cpd* de seguridad; **road ~** seguridad *f* en carretera; **~ first!** ¡precaución!
safety belt *n* cinturón *m* (de seguridad)
safety catch *n* seguro
safety pin *n* imperdible *m*, seguro (*LAm*)
safety valve *n* válvula de seguridad *or* de escape
saffron ['sæfrən] *n* azafrán *m*
sag [sæg] *vi* aflojarse
saga ['sɑːgə] *n* (*History*) saga; (*fig*) epopeya
sage [seɪdʒ] *n* (*herb*) salvia; (*man*) sabio
Sagittarius [sædʒɪ'tɛərɪəs] *n* Sagitario
Sahara [sə'hɑːrə] *n*: **the ~ (Desert)** el Sáhara
said [sɛd] *pt, pp of* **say**
sail [seɪl] *n* (*on boat*) vela ▷ *vt* (*boat*) gobernar ▷ *vi* (*travel: ship*) navegar; (*passenger*) pasear en barco; (*Sport*) hacer vela; (*set off: also:* **to set ~**) zarpar; **to go for a ~** dar un paseo en barco; **they ~ed into Copenhagen** arribaron a Copenhague; **sail through** *vt fus* (*exam*) aprobar fácilmente
sailboat ['seɪlbəut] *n* (*US*) velero, barco de vela
sailing ['seɪlɪŋ] *n* (*Sport*) vela; **to go ~** hacer vela
sailing boat *n* barco de vela
sailing ship *n* barco de vela
sailor ['seɪlə^r] *n* marinero, marino
saint [seɪnt] *n* santo; **S~ John** San Juan
sake [seɪk] *n*: **for the ~ of** por; **for the ~ of argument** digamos, es un decir; **art for art's ~** el arte por el arte
salad ['sæləd] *n* ensalada; **tomato ~** ensalada de tomate
salad bowl *n* ensaladera
salad cream *n* (*Brit*) mayonesa
salad dressing *n* aliño
salami [sə'lɑːmɪ] *n* salami *m*, salchichón *m*
salary ['sælərɪ] *n* sueldo
sale [seɪl] *n* venta; (*at reduced prices*) liquidación *f*, saldo; (*auction*) subasta; **sales** *npl* (*total amount sold*) ventas *fpl*, facturación *f*; **"for ~"** "se vende"; **on ~** en venta; **on ~ or return** (*goods*) venta por reposición; **closing-down** *or* (*US*) **liquidation ~** liquidación *f*; **~ and lease back** venta y arrendamiento al vendedor
saleroom ['seɪlruːm] *n* sala de subastas
sales assistant *n* (*Brit*) dependiente(-a) *m(f)*
sales clerk *n* (*US*) dependiente(-a) *m(f)*
sales conference *n* conferencia de ventas
sales figures *npl* cifras *fpl* de ventas
sales force *n* personal *m* de ventas
salesman ['seɪlzmən] *n* vendedor *m*; (*in shop*) dependiente *m*; (*representative*) viajante *m*
salesperson ['seɪlzpəːsən] *irreg n* vendedor(a) *m(f)*, dependiente(-a) *m/f*
sales rep *n* representante *mf*, agente *m/f* comercial
saleswoman ['seɪlzwumən] *n* vendedora; (*in shop*) dependienta; (*representative*) viajante *f*
saline ['seɪlaɪn] *adj* salino
saliva [sə'laɪvə] *n* saliva
sallow ['sæləu] *adj* cetrino
sally forth, sally out ['sælɪ-] *vi* salir, ponerse en marcha
salmon ['sæmən] *n pl inv* salmón *m*
salon ['sælɔn] *n* (*hairdressing salon, beauty salon*) salón *m*
saloon [sə'luːn] *n* (*US*) bar *m*, taberna; (*Brit Aut*) (coche *m* de) turismo; (*ship's lounge*) cámara, salón *m*
salt [sɔːlt] *n* sal *f* ▷ *vt* salar; (*put salt on*) poner sal en; **an old ~** un lobo de mar; **salt away** *vt* (*inf: money*) ahorrar
salt cellar *n* salero
saltwater ['sɔːlt'wɔːtə^r] *adj* (*fish etc*) de agua salada, de mar
salty ['sɔːltɪ] *adj* salado
salute [sə'luːt] *n* saludo; (*of guns*) salva ▷ *vt* saludar
salvage ['sælvɪdʒ] *n* (*saving*) salvamento, recuperación *f*; (*things saved*) objetos *mpl* salvados ▷ *vt* salvar
salvation [sæl'veɪʃən] *n* salvación *f*
Salvation Army *n* Ejército de Salvación
Samaritan [sə'mærɪtən] *n*: **to call the ~s** llamar al teléfono de la esperanza
same [seɪm] *adj* mismo ▷ *pron*: **the ~** el mismo/la misma; **the ~ book as** el mismo libro que; **on the ~ day** el mismo día; **at the ~ time** (*at the same moment*) al mismo tiempo; (*yet*) sin embargo; **all** *or* **just the ~** sin

S

embargo, aun así; **they're one and the ~** (*person*) son la misma persona; (*thing*) son iguales; **to do the ~ (as sb)** hacer lo mismo (que otro); **and the ~ to you!** ¡igualmente!; **~ here!** ¡yo también!; **the ~ again** (*in bar etc*) otro igual
sample ['sɑːmpl] *n* muestra ▷ *vt* (*food, wine*) probar; **to take a ~** tomar una muestra; **free ~** muestra gratuita
sanatorium (*pl* **sanatoria**) [sænə'tɔːrɪəm, -rɪə] *n* (*Brit*) sanatorio
sanctimonious [sæŋktɪ'məunɪəs] *adj* santurrón(-ona)
sanction ['sæŋkʃən] *n* sanción *f* ▷ *vt* sancionar; **sanctions** *npl* (*Pol*) sanciones *fpl*; **to impose economic ~s on** *or* **against** imponer sanciones económicas a *or* contra
sanctity ['sæŋktɪtɪ] *n* (*gen*) santidad *f*; (*inviolability*) inviolabilidad *f*
sanctuary ['sæŋktjuərɪ] *n* (*gen*) santuario; (*refuge*) asilo, refugio; (*for wildlife*) reserva
sand [sænd] *n* arena; (*beach*) playa ▷ *vt* (*also*: **~ down**: *wood etc*) lijar
sandal ['sændl] *n* sandalia
sandbag ['sændbæg] *n* saco de arena
sandbox ['sændbɔks] *n* (*US*) = **sandpit**
sandcastle ['sændkɑːsl] *n* castillo de arena
sand dune *n* duna
sandpaper ['sændpeɪpə^r] *n* papel *m* de lija
sandpit ['sændpɪt] *n* (*for children*) cajón *m* de arena
sands [sændz] *npl* playa *sg* de arena
sandstone ['sændstəun] *n* piedra arenisca
sandstorm ['sændstɔːm] *n* tormenta de arena
sandwich ['sændwɪtʃ] *n* bocadillo (*Sp*), sandwich *m* (*LAm*) ▷ *vt* (*also*: **~ in**) intercalar; **to be ~ed between** estar apretujado entre; **cheese/ham ~** sandwich de queso/jamón
sandy ['sændɪ] *adj* arenoso; (*colour*) rojizo
sane [seɪn] *adj* cuerdo, sensato
sang [sæŋ] *pt of* **sing**
sanitary ['sænɪtərɪ] *adj* (*system, arrangements*) sanitario; (*clean*) higiénico
sanitary towel, sanitary napkin (*US*) *n* paño higiénico, compresa
sanitation [sænɪ'teɪʃən] *n* (*in house*) servicios *mpl* higiénicos; (*in town*) servicio de desinfección
sanitation department *n* (*US*) departamento de limpieza y recogida de basuras
sanity ['sænɪtɪ] *n* cordura; (*of judgment*) sensatez *f*
sank [sæŋk] *pt of* **sink**
Santa Claus [sæntə'klɔːz] *n* San Nicolás *m*, Papá Noel *m*
sap [sæp] *n* (*of plants*) savia ▷ *vt* (*strength*) minar, agotar
sapling ['sæplɪŋ] *n* árbol nuevo *or* joven
sapphire ['sæfaɪə^r] *n* zafiro
sarcasm ['sɑːkæzm] *n* sarcasmo
sarcastic [sɑː'kæstɪk] *adj* sarcástico; **to be ~** ser sarcástico
sardine [sɑː'diːn] *n* sardina
Sardinia [sɑː'dɪnɪə] *n* Cerdeña
SARS ['sɑːz] *n abbr* (= *severe acute respiratory syndrome*) neumonía asiática, SARS *m*
SAS *n abbr* (*Brit Mil*: = *Special Air Service*) *cuerpo del ejército británico encargado de misiones clandestinas*
SASE *n abbr* (*US*: = *self-addressed stamped envelope*) *sobre con las propias señas de uno y con sello*
sash [sæʃ] *n* faja
Sat. *abbr* (= *Saturday*) sáb
sat [sæt] *pt, pp of* **sit**
Satan ['seɪtn] *n* Satanás *m*
satchel ['sætʃl] *n* bolsa; (*child's*) cartera, mochila (*LAm*)
satellite ['sætəlaɪt] *n* satélite *m*
satellite dish *n* (antena) parabólica
satellite television *n* televisión *f* por satélite
satin ['sætɪn] *n* raso ▷ *adj* de raso; **with a ~ finish** satinado
satire ['sætaɪə^r] *n* sátira
satisfaction [sætɪs'fækʃən] *n* satisfacción *f*; **it gives me great ~** es para mí una gran satisfacción; **has it been done to your ~?** ¿se ha hecho a su satisfacción?
satisfactory [sætɪs'fæktərɪ] *adj* satisfactorio
satisfied ['sætɪsfaɪd] *adj* satisfecho; **to be ~ (with sth)** estar satisfecho (de algo)
satisfy ['sætɪsfaɪ] *vt* satisfacer; (*pay*) liquidar; (*convince*) convencer; **to ~ the requirements** llenar los requisitos; **to ~ sb that** convencer a algn de que; **to ~ o.s. of sth** convencerse de algo
satisfying ['sætɪsfaɪɪŋ] *adj* satisfactorio
satsuma [sæt'suːmə] *n* satsuma
saturated fat [sætʃəreɪtɪd-] *n* grasa saturada
saturation [sætʃə'reɪʃən] *n* saturación *f*
Saturday ['sætədɪ] *n* sábado; *see also* **Tuesday**
sauce [sɔːs] *n* salsa; (*sweet*) crema; (*fig: cheek*) frescura
saucepan ['sɔːspən] *n* cacerola, olla
saucer ['sɔːsə^r] *n* platillo
saucy ['sɔːsɪ] *adj* fresco, descarado
Saudi Arabia *n* Arabia Saudí *or* Saudita
sauna ['sɔːnə] *n* sauna
saunter ['sɔːntə^r] *vi* deambular
sausage ['sɔsɪdʒ] *n* salchicha; (*salami etc*) salchichón *m*
sausage roll *n* empanadilla de salchicha
sautéed ['səuteɪd] *adj* salteado
savage ['sævɪdʒ] *adj* (*cruel, fierce*) feroz, furioso; (*primitive*) salvaje ▷ *n* salvaje *m/f* ▷ *vt* (*attack*) embestir
save [seɪv] *vt* (*rescue*) salvar, rescatar; (*money, time*) ahorrar; (*put by*) guardar; (*Comput*) salvar (y guardar); (*avoid: trouble*) evitar; (*Sport*) parar ▷ *vi* (*also*: **~ up**) ahorrar ▷ *n* (*Sport*) parada ▷ *prep* salvo, excepto; **to ~ face** salvar las apariencias; **God ~ the Queen!**

¡Dios guarde a la Reina!, ¡Viva la Reina!; **I ~d you a piece of cake** te he guardado un trozo de tarta; **it will ~ me an hour** con ello ganaré una hora
saving ['seɪvɪŋ] *n* (*on price etc*) economía ▷ *adj*: **the ~ grace of** el único mérito de; **savings** *npl* ahorros *mpl*; **to make ~s** economizar
savings account *n* cuenta de ahorros
savings and loan association *n* (*US*) sociedad *f* de ahorro y préstamo
savings bank *n* caja de ahorros
saviour, savior (*US*) ['seɪvjə^r] *n* salvador(a) *m(f)*
savour, savor (*US*) ['seɪvə^r] *n* sabor *m*, gusto ▷ *vt* saborear
savoury, savory (*US*) ['seɪvərɪ] *adj* sabroso; (*dish: not sweet*) salado
saw [sɔː] *pt of* **see** ▷ *n* (*tool*) sierra ▷ *vt* (*pt* **sawed**, *pp* **sawed** *or* **sawn** [sɔːn]) serrar; **to ~ sth up** (a)serrar algo
sawdust ['sɔːdʌst] *n* (a)serrín *m*
sawmill ['sɔːmɪl] *n* aserradero
sawn [sɔːn] *pp of* **saw**
sawn-off ['sɔːnɔf], **sawed-off** (*US*) ['sɔːdɔf] *adj*: **~ shotgun** escopeta de cañones recortados
saxophone ['sæksəfəun] *n* saxófono
say [seɪ] (*pt, pp* **said** [sɛd]) *n*: **to have one's ~** expresar su opinión ▷ *vt, vi* decir; **to have a** *or* **some ~ in sth** tener voz y voto en algo; **to ~ yes/no** decir que sí/no; **my watch ~s 3 o'clock** mi reloj marca las tres; **that is to ~** es decir; **that goes without ~ing** ni que decir tiene; **she said (that) I was to give you this** me pidió que te diera esto; **I should ~ it's worth about £100** yo diría que vale unas 100 libras; **~ after me** repite lo que yo diga; **shall we ~ Tuesday?** ¿quedamos, por ejemplo, el martes?; **that doesn't ~ much for him** eso no dice nada a su favor; **when all is said and done** al fin y al cabo, a fin de cuentas; **there is something** *or* **a lot to be said for it** hay algo *or* mucho que decir a su favor
saying ['seɪɪŋ] *n* dicho, refrán *m*
say-so ['seɪsəu] *n* (*inf*) autorización *f*
scab [skæb] *n* costra; (*pej*) esquirol(a) *m(f)*
scaffold ['skæfəld] *n* (*for execution*) cadalso
scaffolding ['skæfəldɪŋ] *n* andamio, andamiaje *m*
scald [skɔːld] *n* escaldadura ▷ *vt* escaldar
scale [skeɪl] *n* (*gen*) escala; (*Mus*) escala; (*of fish*) escama; (*of salaries, fees etc*) escalafón *m* ▷ *vt* (*mountain*) escalar; (*tree*) trepar; **scales** *npl* (*small*) balanza *sg*; (*large*) báscula *sg*; **on a large ~** a gran escala; **~ of charges** tarifa, lista de precios; **pay ~** escala salarial; **to draw sth to ~** dibujar algo a escala; **scale down** *vt* reducir
scallion ['skæljən] *n* (*US*) cebolleta
scallop ['skɔləp] *n* (*Zool*) venera; (*Sewing*) festón *m*
scalp [skælp] *n* cabellera ▷ *vt* escalpar
scalpel ['skælpl] *n* bisturí *m*
scam [skæm] *n* (*inf*) estafa, timo
scamper ['skæmpə^r] *vi*: **to ~ away, ~ off** escabullirse
scampi ['skæmpɪ] *npl* gambas *fpl*
scan [skæn] *vt* (*examine*) escudriñar; (*glance at quickly*) dar un vistazo a; (*TV, Radar*) explorar, registrar; (*Comput*) escanear ▷ *n* (*Med*) examen *m* ultrasónico; **to have a ~** pasar por el escáner
scandal ['skændl] *n* escándalo; (*gossip*) chismes *mpl*
scandalize ['skændəlaɪz] *vt* escandalizar
scandalous ['skændələs] *adj* escandaloso
Scandinavia [skændɪ'neɪvɪə] *n* Escandinavia
Scandinavian [skændɪ'neɪvɪən] *adj, n* escandinavo(-a) *m(f)*
scanner ['skænə^r] *n* (*Radar, Med, Comput*) escáner *m*
scant [skænt] *adj* escaso
scanty ['skæntɪ] *adj* (*meal*) insuficiente; (*clothes*) ligero
scapegoat ['skeɪpgəut] *n* cabeza de turco, chivo expiatorio
scar [skɑː] *n* cicatriz *f* ▷ *vt* marcar con una cicatriz ▷ *vi* cicatrizarse
scarce [skɛəs] *adj* escaso; **to make o.s. ~** (*inf*) esfumarse
scarcely ['skɛəslɪ] *adv* apenas; **~ anybody** casi nadie; **I can ~ believe it** casi no puedo creerlo
scare [skɛə^r] *n* susto, sobresalto; (*panic*) pánico ▷ *vt* asustar, espantar; **to ~ sb stiff** dar a algn un susto de muerte; **bomb ~** amenaza de bomba; **scare away, scare off** *vt* espantar, ahuyentar
scarecrow ['skɛəkrəu] *n* espantapájaros *m inv*
scared [skɛəd] *adj*: **to be ~** asustarse, estar asustado
scarf (*pl* **scarves**) [skɑːf, skɑːvz] *n* (*long*) bufanda; (*square*) pañuelo
scarlet ['skɑːlɪt] *adj* escarlata
scarlet fever *n* escarlatina
scarper ['skɑːpə^r] *vi* (*Brit inf*) largarse
scarves [skɑːvz] *npl of* **scarf**
scary ['skɛərɪ] *adj* (*inf*) de miedo; **it's ~** da miedo
scathing ['skeɪðɪŋ] *adj* mordaz; **to be ~ about sth** criticar algo duramente
scatter ['skætə^r] *vt* (*spread*) esparcir, desparramar; (*put to flight*) dispersar ▷ *vi* desparramarse; dispersarse
scatterbrained ['skætəbreɪnd] *adj* ligero de cascos
scavenge ['skævɪndʒ] *vi*: **to ~ (for)** (*person*) revolver entre la basura (para encontrar); **to ~ for food** (*hyenas etc*) nutrirse de carroña
scavenger ['skævɪndʒə^r] *n* (*person*) *mendigo/a que rebusca en la basura*; (*Zool: animal*) animal *m* de carroña; (*: bird*) ave *f* de carroña

S

scenario [sɪ'nɑːrɪəu] *n* (*Theat*) argumento; (*Cine*) guión *m*; (*fig*) escenario
scene [siːn] *n* (*Theat*) escena; (*of crime, accident*) escenario; (*sight, view*) vista, panorama; (*fuss*) escándalo; **the political ~ in Spain** el panorama político español; **behind the ~s** (*also fig*) entre bastidores; **to appear** *or* **come on the ~** (*also fig*) aparecer, presentarse; **to make a ~** (*inf: fuss*) armar un escándalo
scenery ['siːnərɪ] *n* (*Theat*) decorado; (*landscape*) paisaje *m*
scenic ['siːnɪk] *adj* (*picturesque*) pintoresco
scent [sɛnt] *n* perfume *m*, olor *m*; (*fig: track*) rastro, pista; (*sense of smell*) olfato ▷ *vt* perfumar; (*suspect*) presentir; **to put** *or* **throw sb off the ~** (*fig*) despistar a algn
sceptic, skeptic (US) ['skɛptɪk] *n* escéptico(-a)
sceptical, skeptical (US) ['skɛptɪkl] *adj* escéptico
schedule ['ʃɛdjuːl, (US) 'skɛdjuːl] *n* (*of trains*) horario; (*of events*) programa *m*; (*list*) lista ▷ *vt* (*timetable*) establecer el horario de; (*list*) catalogar; (*visit*) fijar la hora de; **on ~** a la hora, sin retraso; **to be ahead of/behind ~** ir adelantado/retrasado; **we are working to a very tight ~** tenemos un programa de trabajo muy apretado; **everything went according to ~** todo salió según lo previsto; **the meeting is ~d for seven** *or* **to begin at seven** la reunión está fijada para las siete
scheduled ['ʃɛdjuːld, (US) 'skɛdjuːld] *adj* (*date, time*) fijado; (*visit, event, bus, train*) programado; (*stop*) previsto; **~ flight** vuelo regular
scheme [skiːm] *n* (*plan*) plan *m*, proyecto; (*method*) esquema *m*; (*plot*) intriga; (*trick*) ardid *m*; (*arrangement*) disposición *f*; (*pension scheme etc*) sistema *m* ▷ *vt* proyectar ▷ *vi* (*plan*) hacer proyectos; (*intrigue*) intrigar; **colour ~** combinación *f* de colores
scheming ['skiːmɪŋ] *adj* intrigante
schism ['skɪzəm] *n* cisma *m*
schizophrenia [skɪtsə'friːnɪə] *n* esquizofrenia
schizophrenic [skɪtsə'frɛnɪk] *adj* esquizofrénico
scholar ['skɔləʳ] *n* (*pupil*) alumno(-a), estudiante *m/f*; (*learned person*) sabio(-a), erudito(-a)
scholarly ['skɔləlɪ] *adj* erudito
scholarship ['skɔləʃɪp] *n* erudición *f*; (*grant*) beca
school [skuːl] *n* (*gen*) escuela, colegio; (*in university*) facultad *f*; (*of fish*) banco ▷ *vt* (*animal*) amaestrar; **to be at** *or* **go to ~** ir al colegio *or* a la escuela
school age *n* edad *f* escolar
schoolbook ['skuːlbuk] *n* libro de texto
schoolboy ['skuːlbɔɪ] *n* alumno
schoolchild (*pl* **schoolchildren**) ['skuːltʃaɪld, -tʃɪldrən] *n* alumno(-a)
schoolgirl ['skuːlgəːl] *n* alumna
schooling ['skuːlɪŋ] *n* enseñanza
school-leaver ['skuːlliːvəʳ] *n* (*Brit*) *joven que ha terminado la educación secundaria*
schoolmaster ['skuːlmɑːstəʳ] *n* (*primary*) maestro; (*secondary*) profesor *m*
schoolmistress ['skuːlmɪstrɪs] *n* (*primary*) maestra; (*secondary*) profesora
schoolteacher ['skuːltiːtʃəʳ] *n* (*primary*) maestro(-a); (*secondary*) profesor(a) *m(f)*
schoolyard ['skuːljɑːd] *n* (US) patio del colegio
sciatica [saɪ'ætɪkə] *n* ciática
science ['saɪəns] *n* ciencia; **the ~s** las ciencias
science fiction *n* ciencia-ficción *f*
scientific [saɪən'tɪfɪk] *adj* científico
scientist ['saɪəntɪst] *n* científico(-a)
sci-fi ['saɪfaɪ] *n abbr* (*inf*) = **science fiction**
Scilly Isles ['sɪlɪ-], **Scillies** ['sɪlɪz] *npl*: **the ~** las Islas Sorlingas
scissors ['sɪzəz] *npl* tijeras *fpl*; **a pair of ~** unas tijeras
scoff [skɔf] *vt* (*Brit inf: eat*) engullir ▷ *vi*: **to ~ (at)** (*mock*) mofarse (de)
scold [skəuld] *vt* regañar
scone [skɔn] *n pastel de pan*
scoop [skuːp] *n* cucharón *m*; (*for flour etc*) pala; (*Press*) exclusiva ▷ *vt* (*Comm: market*) adelantarse a; (*: profit*) sacar; (*Comm, Press: competitors*) adelantarse a; **scoop out** *vt* excavar; **scoop up** *vt* recoger
scooter ['skuːtəʳ] *n* (*motor cycle*) Vespa®; (*toy*) patinete *m*
scope [skəup] *n* (*of plan, undertaking*) ámbito; (*reach*) alcance *m*; (*of person*) competencia; (*opportunity*) libertad *f* (de acción); **there is plenty of ~ for improvement** hay bastante campo para efectuar mejoras
scorch [skɔːtʃ] *vt* (*clothes*) chamuscar; (*earth, grass*) quemar, secar
scorching ['skɔːtʃɪŋ] *adj* abrasador(a)
score [skɔːʳ] *n* (*points etc*) puntuación *f*; (*Mus*) partitura; (*reckoning*) cuenta; (*twenty*) veintena ▷ *vt* (*goal, point*) ganar; (*mark, cut*) rayar ▷ *vi* marcar un tanto; (*Football*) marcar un gol; (*keep score*) llevar el tanteo; **to keep (the) ~** llevar la cuenta; **to have an old ~ to settle with sb** (*fig*) tener cuentas pendientes con algn; **on that ~** en lo que se refiere a eso; **~s of people** (*fig*) muchísima gente, cantidad de gente; **to ~ 6 out of 10** obtener una puntuación de 6 sobre 10; **score out** *vt* tachar
scoreboard ['skɔːbɔːd] *n* marcador *m*
scoreline ['skɔːlaɪn] *n* (*Sport*) resultado final
scorer ['skɔːrəʳ] *n* marcador *m*; (*keeping score*) encargado(-a) del marcador
scorn [skɔːn] *n* desprecio ▷ *vt* despreciar
Scorpio ['skɔːpɪəu] *n* Escorpión *m*
scorpion ['skɔːpɪən] *n* alacrán *m*, escorpión *m*
Scot [skɔt] *n* escocés(-esa) *m(f)*

Scotch [skɔtʃ] *n* whisky *m* escocés

scotch [skɔtʃ] *vt* (*rumour*) desmentir; (*plan*) frustrar

Scotch tape® *n* (*US*) cinta adhesiva, celo, scotch® *m*

scot-free [skɔt'fri:] *adv*: **to get off ~** (*unpunished*) salir impune; (*unhurt*) salir ileso

Scotland ['skɔtlənd] *n* Escocia

Scots [skɔts] *adj* escocés(-esa)

Scotsman ['skɔtsmən] *n* escocés *m*

Scotswoman ['skɔtswumən] *n* escocesa

Scottish ['skɔtɪʃ] *adj* escocés(-esa); **the ~ National Party** *partido político independista escocés*; **the ~ Parliament** el Parlamento escocés

scoundrel ['skaundrəl] *n* canalla *m/f*, sinvergüenza *m/f*

scour ['skauə^{r}] *vt* (*clean*) fregar, estregar; (*search*) recorrer, registrar

scourge [skə:dʒ] *n* azote *m*

scout [skaut] *n* explorador *m*; **girl ~** (*US*) niña exploradora; **scout around** *vi* reconocer el terreno

scowl [skaul] *vi* fruncir el ceño; **to ~ at sb** mirar con ceño a algn

scrabble ['skræbl] *vi* (*claw*): **to ~ (at)** arañar ▷ *n*: **S~®** Scrabble® *m*, Intelect® *m*; **to ~ around for sth** revolver todo buscando algo

scram [skræm] *vi* (*inf*) largarse

scramble ['skræmbl] *n* (*climb*) subida (difícil); (*struggle*) pelea ▷ *vi*: **to ~ out/through** salir/abrirse paso con dificultad; **to ~ for** pelear por; **to go scrambling** (*Sport*) hacer motocrós

scrambled eggs ['skræmbld-] *npl* huevos *mpl* revueltos

scrap [skræp] *n* (*bit*) pedacito; (*fig*) pizca; (*fight*) riña, bronca; (*also*: **~ iron**) chatarra, hierro viejo ▷ *vt* (*discard*) desechar, descartar ▷ *vi* reñir, armar (una) bronca; **scraps** *npl* (*waste*) sobras *fpl*, desperdicios *mpl*; **to sell sth for ~** vender algo como chatarra

scrapbook ['skræpbuk] *n* álbum *m* de recortes

scrap dealer *n* chatarrero(-a)

scrape [skreɪp] *n* (*fig*) lío, apuro ▷ *vt* raspar; (*skin etc*) rasguñar; (*also*: **~ against**) rozar; **to get into a ~** meterse en un lío; **scrape through** *vi* (*succeed*) salvarse por los pelos; (*exam*) aprobar por los pelos

scrap heap *n* (*fig*): **on the ~** desperdiciado; **to throw sth on the ~** desechar *or* descartar algo

scrap merchant *n* (*Brit*) chatarrero(-a)

scrap paper *n* pedazos *mpl* de papel

scrap yard *n* depósito de chatarra; (*for cars*) cementerio de coches

scratch [skrætʃ] *n* rasguño; (*from claw*) arañazo ▷ *adj*: **~ team** equipo improvisado ▷ *vt* (*paint, car*) rayar; (*with claw, nail*) rasguñar, arañar; (*Comput*) borrar ▷ *vi* rascarse; **to start from ~** partir de cero; **to be up to ~** cumplir con los requisitos

scratch card *n* (*Brit*) tarjeta *f* de "rasque y gane"

scrawl [skrɔ:l] *n* garabatos *mpl* ▷ *vi* hacer garabatos

scrawny ['skrɔ:nɪ] *adj* (*person, neck*) flaco

scream [skri:m] *n* chillido ▷ *vi* chillar; **it was a ~** (*fig, inf*) fue para morirse de risa *or* muy divertido; **he's a ~** (*fig, inf*) es muy divertido *or* de lo más gracioso; **to ~ at sb (to do sth)** gritarle a algn (para que haga algo)

screech [skri:tʃ] *vi* chirriar

screen [skri:n] *n* (*Cine, TV*) pantalla; (*movable*) biombo; (*wall*) tabique *m*; (*also*: **wind~**) parabrisas *m inv* ▷ *vt* (*conceal*) tapar; (*from the wind etc*) proteger; (*film*) proyectar; (*fig: person: for security*) investigar; (*: for illness*) hacer una exploración a

screenful ['skri:nful] *n* pantalla

screening ['skri:nɪŋ] *n* (*of film*) proyección *f*; (*for security*) investigación *f*; (*Med*) exploración *f*

screenplay ['skri:npleɪ] *n* guión *m*

screen saver [-seɪvə^{r}] *n* (*Comput*) salvapantallas *m inv*

screenshot ['skri:nʃɔt] *n* (*Comput*) screenshot *m*, captura de pantalla

screw [skru:] *n* tornillo; (*propeller*) hélice *f* ▷ *vt* atornillar; **to ~ sth to the wall** fijar algo a la pared con tornillos; **screw up** *vt* (*paper, material etc*) arrugar; (*inf: ruin*) fastidiar; **to ~ up one's eyes** arrugar el entrecejo; **to ~ up one's face** torcer *or* arrugar la cara

screwdriver ['skru:draɪvə^{r}] *n* destornillador *m*

screwed-up ['skru:d'ʌp] *adj* (*inf*): **she's totally ~** está trastornada

scribble ['skrɪbl] *n* garabatos *mpl* ▷ *vi* garabatear ▷ *vt* escribir con prisa; **to ~ sth down** garabatear algo

script [skrɪpt] *n* (*Cine etc*) guión *m*; (*writing*) escritura, letra

Scripture ['skrɪptʃə^{r}] *n* Sagrada Escritura

scroll [skrəul] *n* rollo ▷ *vt* (*Comput*) desplazar

scrotum ['skrəutəm] *n* escroto

scrounge [skraundʒ] (*inf*) *vt*: **to ~ sth off** *or* **from sb** gorronear algo a algn ▷ *vi*: **to ~ on sb** vivir a costa de algn

scrounger ['skraundʒə^{r}] *n* gorrón(-ona) *m(f)*

scrub [skrʌb] *n* (*clean*) fregado; (*land*) maleza ▷ *vt* fregar, restregar; (*reject*) cancelar, anular

scruff [skrʌf] *n*: **by the ~ of the neck** por el pescuezo

scruffy ['skrʌfɪ] *adj* desaliñado, desaseado

scrum ['skrʌm], **scrummage** ['skrʌmɪdʒ] *n* (*Rugby*) melée *f*

scruple ['skru:pl] *n* escrúpulo; **to have no ~s about doing sth** no tener reparos en *or* escrúpulos para hacer algo

scrupulous ['skru:pjuləs] *adj* escrupuloso

scrutinize ['skru:tɪnaɪz] *vt* escudriñar; (*votes*) escrutar

S

scrutiny ['skru:tɪnɪ] *n* escrutinio, examen *m*; **under the ~ of sb** bajo la mirada *or* el escrutinio de algn
scuba diving ['sku:bə'daɪvɪŋ] *n* submarinismo
scuff [skʌf] *vt* (*shoes, floor*) rayar
scuffle ['skʌfl] *n* refriega
scullery ['skʌlərɪ] *n* trascocina
sculptor ['skʌlptə^r] *n* escultor(a) *m(f)*
sculpture ['skʌlptʃə^r] *n* escultura
scum [skʌm] *n* (*on liquid*) espuma; (*pej: people*) escoria
scupper ['skʌpə^r] *vt* (*Brit: boat*) hundir; (*: fig: plans etc*) acabar con
scurrilous ['skʌrɪləs] *adj* difamatorio, calumnioso
scurry ['skʌrɪ] *vi*: **to ~ off** escabullirse
scuttle ['skʌtl] *n* (*also*: **coal ~**) cubo, carbonera ▷ *vt* (*ship*) barrenar ▷ *vi* (*scamper*): **to ~ away, ~ off** escabullirse
scythe [saɪð] *n* guadaña
sea [si:] *n* mar *m/f*; **by ~** (*travel*) en barco; **on the ~** (*boat*) en el mar; (*town*) junto al mar; **to be all at ~** (*fig*) estar despistado; **out to** *or* **at ~** en alta mar; **to go by ~** ir en barco; **heavy** *or* **rough ~s** marejada; **by** *or* **beside the ~** (*holiday*) en la playa; (*village*) a orillas del mar; **a ~ of faces** una multitud de caras
sea bed *n* fondo del mar
seaboard ['si:bɔ:d] *n* litoral *m*
seafood ['si:fu:d] *n* mariscos *mpl*
sea front *n* (*beach*) playa; (*prom*) paseo marítimo
seagoing ['si:gəuɪŋ] *adj* (*ship*) de alta mar
seagull ['si:gʌl] *n* gaviota
seal [si:l] *n* (*animal*) foca; (*stamp*) sello ▷ *vt* (*close*) cerrar; (*: with seal*) sellar; (*decide: sb's fate*) decidir; (*: bargain*) cerrar; **~ of approval** sello de aprobación; **seal off** *vt* obturar
sea level *n* nivel *m* del mar
sea lion *n* león *m* marino
seam [si:m] *n* costura; (*of metal*) juntura; (*of coal*) veta, filón *m*; **the hall was bursting at the ~s** la sala rebosaba de gente
seaman ['si:mən] *n* marinero
seance ['seɪɔns] *n* sesión *f* de espiritismo
seaplane ['si:pleɪn] *n* hidroavión *m*
search [sə:tʃ] *n* (*for person, thing*) busca, búsqueda; (*of drawer, pockets*) registro; (*inspection*) reconocimiento ▷ *vt* (*look in*) buscar en; (*examine*) examinar; (*person, place*) registrar; (*Comput*) buscar ▷ *vi*: **to ~ for** buscar; **in ~ of** en busca de; **"~ and replace"** (*Comput*) "buscar y reemplazar"; **search through** *vt fus* registrar
search engine *n* (*Comput, Internet*) buscador *m*
searching ['sə:tʃɪŋ] *adj* (*question*) penetrante
searchlight ['sə:tʃlaɪt] *n* reflector *m*
search party *n* equipo de salvamento
search warrant *n* mandamiento judicial
seashore ['si:ʃɔ^r] *n* playa, orilla del mar; **on the ~** a la orilla del mar
seasick ['si:sɪk] *adj* mareado; **to be ~** marearse
seaside ['si:saɪd] *n* playa, orilla del mar; **to go to the ~** ir a la playa
seaside resort *n* centro turístico costero
season ['si:zn] *n* (*of year*) estación *f*; (*sporting etc*) temporada; (*gen*) época, período ▷ *vt* (*food*) sazonar; **to be in/out of ~** estar en sazón/fuera de temporada; **the busy ~** (*for shops, hotels etc*) la temporada alta; **the open ~** (*Hunting*) la temporada de caza *or* de pesca
seasonal ['si:znl] *adj* estacional
seasoned ['si:znd] *adj* (*wood*) curado; (*fig: worker, actor*) experimentado; (*troops*) curtido; **~ campaigner** veterano(-a)
seasoning ['si:znɪŋ] *n* condimento
season ticket *n* abono
seat [si:t] *n* (*in bus, train: place*) asiento; (*chair*) silla; (*Parliament*) escaño; (*buttocks*) trasero; (*centre: of government etc*) sede *f* ▷ *vt* sentar; (*have room for*) tener cabida para; **are there any ~s left?** ¿quedan plazas?; **to take one's ~** sentarse, tomar asiento; **to be ~ed** estar sentado, sentarse
seat belt *n* cinturón *m* de seguridad
seating ['si:tɪŋ] *n* asientos *mpl*
sea water *n* agua *m* del mar
seaweed ['si:wi:d] *n* alga marina
seaworthy ['si:wə:ðɪ] *adj* en condiciones de navegar
sec. *abbr* = **second(s)**
secluded [sɪ'klu:dɪd] *adj* retirado
seclusion [sɪ'klu:ʒən] *n* retiro
second ['sɛkənd] *adj* segundo ▷ *adv* (*in race etc*) en segundo lugar ▷ *n* (*gen*) segundo; (*Aut: also*: **~ gear**) segunda; (*Comm*) artículo con algún desperfecto; (*Brit Scol: degree*) título universitario de segunda clase ▷ *vt* (*motion*) apoyar; [sɪ'kɔnd] (*employee*) trasladar temporalmente; **~ floor** (*Brit*) segundo piso; (*US*) primer piso; **Charles the S~** Carlos Segundo; **to ask for a ~ opinion** (*Med*) pedir una segunda opinión; **just a ~!** ¡un momento!; **to have ~ thoughts** cambiar de opinión; **on ~ thoughts** *or* (*US*) **thought** pensándolo bien; **~ mortgage** segunda hipoteca
secondary ['sɛkəndərɪ] *adj* secundario
secondary education *n* enseñanza secundaria
secondary school *n* escuela secundaria
second-class ['sɛkənd'klɑ:s] *adj* de segunda clase ▷ *adv*: **to send sth ~** enviar algo por correo de segunda clase; **to travel ~** viajar en segunda; **~ citizen** ciudadano(-a) de segunda (clase)
second cousin *n* primo(-a) segundo(-a)
second-guess ['sɛkənd'gɛs] *vt* (*evaluate*) juzgar (a posteriori); (*anticipate*): **to ~ sth/sb** (intentar) adivinar algo/lo que va a hacer algn

secondhand ['sɛkənd'hænd] *adj* de segunda mano, usado ▷ *adv*: **to buy sth ~** comprar algo de segunda mano; **to hear sth ~** oír algo indirectamente
second hand *n* (*on clock*) segundero
secondly ['sɛkəndlɪ] *adv* en segundo lugar
secondment [sɪ'kɔndmənt] *n* (*Brit*) traslado temporal
second-rate ['sɛkənd'reɪt] *adj* de segunda categoría
secrecy ['si:krəsɪ] *n* secreto
secret ['si:krɪt] *adj, n* secreto; **in ~** *adv* en secreto; **to keep sth ~ (from sb)** ocultarle algo (a algn); **to make no ~ of sth** no ocultar algo
secret agent *n* agente *m/f* secreto(-a), espía *m/f*
secretary ['sɛkrətərɪ] *n* secretario(-a); **S~ of State** (*Brit Pol*) Ministro (con cartera)
secretary-general ['sɛkrətərɪ'dʒɛnərl] *n* secretario(-a) general
secrete [sɪ'kri:t] *vt* (*Med, Anat, Bio*) secretar; (*hide*) ocultar, esconder
secretive ['si:krətɪv] *adj* reservado, sigiloso
secretly ['si:krɪtlɪ] *adv* en secreto
secret police *n* policía secreta
secret service *n* servicio secreto
sect [sɛkt] *n* secta
sectarian [sɛk'tɛərɪən] *adj* sectario
section ['sɛkʃən] *n* sección *f*; (*part*) parte *f*; (*of document*) artículo; (*of opinion*) sector *m*; **business ~** (*Press*) sección *f* de economía
sector ['sɛktə^r] *n* sector *m*
secular ['sɛkjulə^r] *adj* secular, seglar
secure [sɪ'kjuə^r] *adj* (*free from anxiety*) seguro; (*firmly fixed*) firme, fijo ▷ *vt* (*fix*) asegurar, afianzar; (*get*) conseguir; (*Comm: loan*) garantizar; **to make sth ~** afianzar algo; **to ~ sth for sb** conseguir algo para algn
security [sɪ'kjuərɪtɪ] *n* seguridad *f*; (*for loan*) fianza; (*: object*) prenda; **securities** *npl* (*Comm*) valores *mpl*, títulos *mpl*; **~ of tenure** tenencia asegurada; **to increase/tighten ~** aumentar/estrechar las medidas de seguridad; **job ~** seguridad *f* en el empleo
Security Council *n*: **the ~** el Consejo de Seguridad
security forces *npl* fuerzas *fpl* de seguridad
security guard *n* guardia *m/f* de seguridad
sedan [sɪ'dæn] *n* (*US Aut*) sedán *m*
sedate [sɪ'deɪt] *adj* tranquilo ▷ *vt* administrar sedantes a, sedar
sedation [sɪ'deɪʃən] *n* (*Med*) sedación *f*; **to be under ~** estar bajo sedación
sedative ['sɛdɪtɪv] *n* sedante *m*, calmante *m*
sediment ['sɛdɪmənt] *n* sedimento
seduce [sɪ'dju:s] *vt* (*gen*) seducir
seduction [sɪ'dʌkʃən] *n* seducción *f*
seductive [sɪ'dʌktɪv] *adj* seductor(-a)
see [si:] (*pt* **saw**, *pp* **seen**) *vt* (*gen*) ver; (*understand*) ver, comprender; (*look at*) mirar ▷ *vi* ver ▷ *n* sede *f*; **to ~ sb to the door** acompañar a algn a la puerta; **to ~ that** (*ensure*) asegurarse de que; **~ you soon/later/tomorrow!** ¡hasta pronto/luego/mañana!; **as far as I can ~** por lo visto *or* por lo que veo; **there was nobody to be ~n** no se veía a nadie; **let me ~** (*show me*) a ver; (*let me think*) vamos a ver; **to go and ~ sb** ir a ver a algn; **~ for yourself** compruébalo tú mismo; **I don't know what she ~s in him** no sé qué le encuentra; **see about** *vt fus* atender a, encargarse de; **see off** *vt* despedir; **see out** *vt* (*take to the door*) acompañar hasta la puerta; **see through** *vt fus* calar ▷ *vt* llevar a cabo; **see to** *vt fus* atender a, encargarse de
seed [si:d] *n* semilla; (*in fruit*) pepita; (*fig*) germen *m*; (*Tennis*) preseleccionado(-a); **to go to ~** (*plant*) granar; (*fig*) descuidarse
seedling ['si:dlɪŋ] *n* planta de semillero
seedy ['si:dɪ] *adj* (*person*) desaseado; (*place*) sórdido
seeing ['si:ɪŋ] *conj*: **~ (that)** visto que, en vista de que
seek (*pt, pp* **sought**) [si:k, sɔ:t] *vt* (*gen*) buscar; (*post*) solicitar; **to ~ advice/help from sb** pedir consejos/solicitar ayuda a algn; **seek out** *vt* (*person*) buscar
seem [si:m] *vi* parecer; **there ~s to be ...** parece que hay ...; **it ~s (that) ...** parece que ...; **what ~s to be the trouble?** ¿qué pasa?; **I did what ~ed best** hice lo que parecía mejor
seemingly ['si:mɪŋlɪ] *adv* aparentemente, según parece
seen [si:n] *pp of* **see**
seep [si:p] *vi* filtrarse
seesaw ['si:sɔ:] *n* balancín *m*, subibaja *m*
seethe [si:ð] *vi* hervir; **to ~ with anger** enfurecerse
see-through ['si:θru:] *adj* transparente
segment ['sɛgmənt] *n* segmento; (*of citrus fruit*) gajo
segregate ['sɛgrɪgeɪt] *vt* segregar
seize [si:z] *vt* (*grasp*) agarrar, asir; (*take possession of*) secuestrar; (*: territory*) apoderarse de; (*opportunity*) aprovecharse de; **seize up** *vi* (*Tech*) agarrotarse; **seize (up)on** *vt fus* valerse de
seizure ['si:ʒə^r] *n* (*Med*) ataque *m*; (*Law*) incautación *f*
seldom ['sɛldəm] *adv* rara vez
select [sɪ'lɛkt] *adj* selecto, escogido; (*hotel, restaurant, clubs*) exclusivo ▷ *vt* escoger, elegir; (*Sport*) seleccionar; **a ~ few** una minoría selecta
selection [sɪ'lɛkʃən] *n* selección *f*, elección *f*; (*Comm*) surtido
selective [sɪ'lɛktɪv] *adj* selectivo
self [sɛlf] *n* (*pl* **selves** [sɛlvz]) uno mismo ▷ *pref* auto...; **the ~** el yo
self-appointed [sɛlfə'pɔɪntɪd] *adj* autonombrado
self-assurance [sɛlfə'ʃuərəns] *n* confianza en sí mismo

self-assured [sɛlfə'ʃuəd] *adj* seguro de sí mismo
self-catering [sɛlf'keɪtərɪŋ] *adj* (*Brit*) sin pensión *or* servicio de comida; **~ apartment** apartamento con cocina propia
self-centred, self-centered (*US*) [sɛlf'sɛntəd] *adj* egocéntrico
self-confessed [sɛlfkən'fɛst] *adj* (*alcoholic etc*) confeso
self-confidence [sɛlf'kɔnfɪdns] *n* confianza en sí mismo
self-confident [sɛlf'kɔnfɪdnt] *adj* seguro de sí (mismo), lleno de confianza en sí mismo
self-conscious [sɛlf'kɔnʃəs] *adj* cohibido
self-contained [sɛlfkən'teɪnd] *adj* (*gen*) independiente; (*Brit: flat*) con entrada particular
self-control [sɛlfkən'trəul] *n* autodominio
self-defence, self-defense (*US*) [sɛlfdɪ'fɛns] *n* defensa propia
self-discipline [sɛlf'dɪsɪplɪn] *n* autodisciplina
self-employed [sɛlfɪm'plɔɪd] *adj* que trabaja por cuenta propia, autónomo
self-esteem [sɛlfɪ'sti:m] *n* amor *m* propio
self-evident [sɛlf'ɛvɪdnt] *adj* patente
self-explanatory [sɛlfɪks'plænətərɪ] *adj* que no necesita explicación
self-governing [sɛlf'gʌvənɪŋ] *adj* autónomo
self-harm [sɛlf'hɑ:m] *vi* autolesionarse
self-help ['sɛlf'hɛlp] *n* autosuficiencia, ayuda propia
self-indulgent [sɛlfɪn'dʌldʒənt] *adj* indulgente consigo mismo
self-inflicted [sɛlfɪn'flɪktɪd] *adj* infligido a sí mismo
self-interest [sɛlf'ɪntrɪst] *n* egoísmo
selfish ['sɛlfɪʃ] *adj* egoísta
selfishness ['sɛlfɪʃnɪs] *n* egoísmo
selfless ['sɛlflɪs] *adj* desinteresado
self-pity [sɛlf'pɪtɪ] *n* lástima de sí mismo
self-portrait [sɛlf'pɔ:treɪt] *n* autorretrato
self-possessed [sɛlfpə'zɛst] *adj* sereno, dueño de sí mismo
self-preservation ['sɛlfprɛzə'veɪʃən] *n* propia conservación *f*
self-raising [sɛlf'reɪzɪŋ], **self-rising** (*US*) [sɛlf'raɪzɪŋ] *adj*: **~ flour** harina con levadura
self-respect [sɛlfrɪ'spɛkt] *n* amor *m* propio
self-righteous [sɛlf'raɪtʃəs] *adj* santurrón(-ona)
self-sacrifice [sɛlf'sækrɪfaɪs] *n* abnegación *f*
self-same [sɛlfseɪm] *adj* mismo, mismísimo
self-satisfied [sɛlf'sætɪsfaɪd] *adj* satisfecho de sí mismo
self-service [sɛlf'sə:vɪs] *adj* de autoservicio
self-sufficient [sɛlfsə'fɪʃənt] *adj* autosuficiente
self-tanning [sɛlf'tænɪŋ] *adj* autobronceador
self-taught [sɛlf'tɔ:t] *adj* autodidacta
sell (*pt, pp* **sold**) [sɛl, səuld] *vt* vender ▷ *vi* venderse; **to ~ at** *or* **for £10** venderse a 10 libras; **to ~ sb an idea** (*fig*) convencer a algn de una idea; **sell off** *vt* liquidar; **sell out** *vi* transigir, transar (*LAm*); **to ~ out (to sb/sth)** (*Comm*) vender su negocio (a algn/algo) ▷ *vt* agotar las existencias de, venderlo todo; **the tickets are all sold out** las entradas están agotadas; **sell up** *vi* (*Comm*) liquidarse
sell-by date ['sɛlbaɪ-] *n* fecha de caducidad
seller ['sɛlə^r] *n* vendedor(a) *m(f)*; **~'s market** mercado de demanda
selling price ['sɛlɪŋ-] *n* precio de venta
Sellotape® ['sɛləuteɪp] *n* (*Brit*) cinta adhesiva, celo, scotch® *m*
sellout ['sɛlaut] *n* traición *f*; **it was a ~** (*Theat etc*) fue un éxito de taquilla
selves [sɛlvz] *npl of* **self**
semblance ['sɛmbləns] *n* apariencia
semen ['si:mən] *n* semen *m*
semester [sɪ'mɛstə^r] *n* (*US*) semestre *m*
semi ['sɛmɪ] *n* = **semidetached house**
semi... [sɛmɪ] *pref* semi..., medio...
semicircle ['sɛmɪsə:kl] *n* semicírculo
semicolon [sɛmɪ'kəulən] *n* punto y coma
semiconductor [sɛmɪkən'dʌktə^r] *n* semiconductor *m*
semidetached [sɛmɪdɪ'tætʃt], **semidetached house** *n* casa adosada
semi-final [sɛmɪ'faɪnl] *n* semifinal *f*
seminar ['sɛmɪnɑ:^r] *n* seminario
seminary ['sɛmɪnərɪ] *n* (*Rel*) seminario
semiskilled ['sɛmɪskɪld] *adj* (*work, worker*) semicualificado
semi-skimmed ['sɛmi'skɪmd] *adj* semidesnatado
semi-skimmed (milk) *n* leche semidesnatada
Sen., sen. *abbr* = **senator**; **senior**
senate ['sɛnɪt] *n* senado; *see also* **Congress**
senator ['sɛnɪtə^r] *n* senador(a) *m(f)*
send (*pt, pp* **sent**) [sɛnd, sɛnt] *vt* mandar, enviar; **to ~ by post** mandar por correo; **to ~ sb for sth** mandar a algn a buscar algo; **to ~ word that ...** avisar *or* mandar aviso de que ...; **she ~s (you) her love** te manda *or* envía cariñosos recuerdos; **to ~ sb to sleep/into fits of laughter** dormir/hacer reír a algn; **to ~ sb flying** echar a algn; **to ~ sth flying** tirar algo; **send away** *vt* (*letter, goods*) despachar; **send away for** *vt fus* pedir; **send back** *vt* devolver; **send for** *vt fus* mandar traer; (*by post*) escribir pidiendo algo; **send in** *vt* (*report, application, resignation*) mandar; **send off** *vt* (*goods*) despachar; (*Brit Sport: player*) expulsar; **send on** *vt* (*letter*) mandar, expedir; (*luggage etc: in advance*) facturar; **send out** *vt* (*invitation*) mandar; (*emit: light, heat*) emitir, difundir; (*signal*) emitir; **send round** *vt* (*letter, document etc*) hacer circular; **send up** *vt* (*person, price*) hacer subir; (*Brit: parody*) parodiar
sender ['sɛndə^r] *n* remitente *m/f*
send-off ['sɛndɔf] *n*: **a good ~** una buena despedida

send-up ['sɛndʌp] *n* (*inf*) parodia, sátira
senile ['si:naɪl] *adj* senil
senior ['si:nɪə^r] *adj* (*older*) mayor, más viejo; (*: on staff*) de más antigüedad; (*of higher rank*) superior ▷ *n* mayor *m*; **P. Jones ~** P. Jones padre
senior citizen *n* persona de la tercera edad
senior high school *n* (*US*) ≈ instituto de enseñanza media
seniority [si:nɪ'ɔrɪtɪ] *n* antigüedad *f*; (*in rank*) rango superior
sensation [sɛn'seɪʃən] *n* (*physical feeling, impression*) sensación *f*
sensational [sɛn'seɪʃənl] *adj* sensacional
sense [sɛns] *n* (*faculty, meaning*) sentido; (*feeling*) sensación *f*; (*good sense*) sentido común, juicio ▷ *vt* sentir, percibir; **~ of humour** sentido del humor; **it makes ~** tiene sentido; **there is no ~ in (doing) that** no tiene sentido (hacer) eso; **to come to one's ~s** (*regain consciousness*) volver en sí, recobrar el sentido; **to take leave of one's ~s** perder el juicio
senseless ['sɛnslɪs] *adj* estúpido, insensato; (*unconscious*) sin conocimiento
sense of humour *n* (*Brit*) sentido del humor
sensibility [sɛnsɪ'bɪlɪtɪ] *n* sensibilidad *f*; **sensibilities** *npl* delicadeza *sg*
sensible ['sɛnsɪbl] *adj* sensato; (*reasonable*) razonable, lógico
sensibly ['sɛnsɪblɪ] *adv* sensatamente; razonablemente, de modo lógico
sensitive ['sɛnsɪtɪv] *adj* sensible; (*touchy*) susceptible; **he is very ~ about it** es muy susceptible acerca de eso
sensitivity [sɛnsɪ'tɪvɪtɪ] *n* sensibilidad *f*; susceptibilidad *f*
sensual ['sɛnsjuəl] *adj* sensual
sensuous ['sɛnsjuəs] *adj* sensual
sent [sɛnt] *pt, pp of* **send**
sentence ['sɛntəns] *n* (*Ling*) frase *f*, oración *f*; (*Law*) sentencia, fallo ▷ *vt*: **to ~ sb to death/ to five years** condenar a algn a muerte/a cinco años de cárcel; **to pass ~ on sb** (*also fig*) sentenciar *or* condenar a algn
sentiment ['sɛntɪmənt] *n* sentimiento; (*opinion*) opinión *f*
sentimental [sɛntɪ'mɛntl] *adj* sentimental
sentry ['sɛntrɪ] *n* centinela *m*
Sep. *abbr* (= *September*) sep., set.
separate [*adj* 'sɛprɪt, *vb* 'sɛpəreɪt] *adj* separado; (*distinct*) distinto ▷ *vt* separar; (*part*) dividir ▷ *vi* separarse; **~ from** separado *or* distinto de; **under ~ cover** (*Comm*) por separado; **to ~ into** dividir *or* separar en; **he is ~d from his wife, but not divorced** está separado de su mujer, pero no (está) divorciado
separately ['sɛprɪtlɪ] *adv* por separado
separates ['sɛprɪts] *npl* (*clothes*) coordinados *mpl*
separation [sɛpə'reɪʃən] *n* separación *f*
September [sɛp'tɛmbə^r] *n* se(p)tiembre *m*; *see also* **July**
septic ['sɛptɪk] *adj* séptico; **to go ~** ponerse séptico
septic tank *n* fosa séptica
sequel ['si:kwl] *n* consecuencia, resultado; (*of story*) continuación *f*
sequence ['si:kwəns] *n* sucesión *f*, serie *f*; (*Cine*) secuencia; **in ~** en orden *or* serie
sequin ['si:kwɪn] *n* lentejuela
Serb [sə:b] *adj, n* = **Serbian**
Serbia ['sə:bɪə] *n* Serbia
Serbian ['sə:bɪən] *adj* serbio ▷ *n* serbio(-a); (*Ling*) serbio
serenade [sɛrə'neɪd] *n* serenata ▷ *vt* dar serenata a
serene [sɪ'ri:n] *adj* sereno, tranquilo
sergeant ['sɑ:dʒənt] *n* sargento
serial ['sɪərɪəl] *n* novela por entregas; (*TV*) serie *f*
serial killer *n* asesino(-a) múltiple
serial number *n* número de serie
series ['sɪəri:z] *n pl inv* serie *f*
serious ['sɪərɪəs] *adj* serio; (*grave*) grave; **are you ~ (about it)?** ¿lo dices en serio?
seriously ['sɪərɪəslɪ] *adv* en serio; (*ill, wounded etc*) gravemente; (*inf: extremely*) de verdad; **to take sth/sb ~** tomar algo/a algn en serio; **he's ~ rich** es una pasada de rico
sermon ['sə:mən] *n* sermón *m*
serpent ['sə:pənt] *n* serpiente *f*
serrated [sɪ'reɪtɪd] *adj* serrado, dentellado
serum ['sɪərəm] *n* suero
servant ['sə:vənt] *n* (*gen*) servidor(a) *m(f)*; (*also*: **house ~**) criado(-a) *m(f)*
serve [sə:v] *vt* servir; (*customer*) atender; (*train*) tener parada en; (*apprenticeship*) hacer; (*prison term*) cumplir ▷ *vi* (*servant, soldier etc*) servir; (*Tennis*) sacar ▷ *n* (*Tennis*) saque *m*; **it ~s him right** se lo merece, se lo tiene merecido; **to ~ a summons on sb** entregar una citación a algn; **it ~s my purpose** me sirve para lo que quiero; **are you being ~d?** ¿le atienden?; **the power station ~s the entire region** la central eléctrica abastece a toda la región; **to ~ as/for/to do** servir de/para/para hacer; **to ~ on a committee/ a jury** ser miembro de una comisión/un jurado; **serve out, serve up** *vt* (*food*) servir
server *n* (*Comput*) servidor *m*
service ['sə:vɪs] *n* (*gen*) servicio; (*Rel: Catholic*) misa; (*: other*) oficio (religioso); (*Aut*) mantenimiento; (*of dishes*) juego ▷ *vt* (*car, washing machine*) revisar; (*: repair*) reparar; **the S~s** las fuerzas armadas; **funeral ~** exequias *fpl*; **to hold a ~** celebrar un oficio religioso; **the essential ~s** los servicios esenciales; **medical/social ~s** servicios *mpl* médicos/ sociales; **the train ~ to London** los trenes a Londres; **to be of ~ to sb** ser útil a algn; **~ included/not included** servicio incluido/ no incluido; **services** (*Econ: tertiary sector*)

sector *m* terciario *or* (de) servicios; (*Brit*: *on motorway*) área de servicio
serviceable ['sə:vɪsəbl] *adj* servible, utilizable
service area *n* (*on motorway*) área de servicios
service charge *n* (*Brit*) servicio
serviceman ['sə:vɪsmən] *n* militar *m*
service station *n* estación *f* de servicio
serviette [sə:vɪ'ɛt] *n* (*Brit*) servilleta
session ['sɛʃən] *n* (*sitting*) sesión *f*; **to be in ~** estar en sesión
set [sɛt] (*pt*, *pp* **set**) *n* juego; (*Radio*) aparato; (*TV*) televisor *m*; (*of utensils*) batería; (*of cutlery*) cubierto; (*of books*) colección *f*; (*Tennis*) set *m*; (*group of people*) grupo; (*Cine*) plató *m*; (*Theat*) decorado; (*Hairdressing*) marcado ▷ *adj* (*fixed*) fijo; (*ready*) listo; (*resolved*) resuelto, decidido ▷ *vt* (*place*) poner, colocar; (*fix*) fijar; (*adjust*) ajustar, arreglar; (*decide*: *rules etc*) establecer, decidir; (*assign*: *task*) asignar; (: *homework*) poner ▷ *vi* (*sun*) ponerse; (*jam, jelly*) cuajarse; (*concrete*) fraguar; **a ~ of false teeth** una dentadura postiza; **a ~ of dining-room furniture** muebles *mpl* de comedor; **~ in one's ways** con costumbres arraigadas; **a ~ phrase** una frase hecha; **to be all ~ to do sth** estar listo para hacer algo; **to be ~ on doing sth** estar empeñado en hacer algo; **a novel ~ in Valencia** una novela ambientada en Valencia; **to ~ to music** poner música a; **to ~ on fire** incendiar, prender fuego a; **to ~ free** poner en libertad; **to ~ sth going** poner algo en marcha; **to ~ sail** zarpar, hacerse a la mar; **set about** *vt fus*: **to ~ about doing sth** ponerse a hacer algo; **set aside** *vt* poner aparte, dejar de lado; **set back** *vt* (*progress*): **to ~ back (by)** retrasar (por); **a house ~ back from the road** una casa apartada de la carretera; **set down** *vt* (*bus, train*) dejar; (*record*) poner por escrito; **set in** *vi* (*infection*) declararse; (*complications*) comenzar; **the rain has ~ in for the day** parece que va a llover todo el día; **set off** *vi* partir ▷ *vt* (*bomb*) hacer estallar; (*cause to start*) poner en marcha; (*show up well*) hacer resaltar; **set out** *vi* partir ▷ *vt* (*arrange*) disponer; (*state*) exponer; **to ~ out to do sth** proponerse hacer algo; **to ~ out (from)** salir (de); **set up** *vt* (*organization*) establecer
setback ['sɛtbæk] *n* (*hitch*) revés *m*, contratiempo; (*in health*) recaída
set menu *n* menú *m*
set phrase *n* frase *f* hecha
settee [sɛ'ti:] *n* sofá *m*
setting ['sɛtɪŋ] *n* (*scenery*) marco; (*of jewel*) engaste *m*, montadura
settle ['sɛtl] *vt* (*argument, matter*) resolver; (*pay*: *bill, accounts*) pagar, liquidar; (*colonize*: *land*) colonizar; (*Med*: *calm*) calmar, sosegar ▷ *vi* (*dust etc*) depositarse; (*weather*) estabilizarse; **to ~ for sth** convenir en aceptar algo; **to ~ on sth** decidirse por algo; **that's ~d then** bueno, está arreglado; **to ~ one's stomach** asentar el estómago; **settle down** *vi* (*get comfortable*) ponerse cómodo, acomodarse; (*calm down*) calmarse, tranquilizarse; (*live quietly*) echar raíces; **settle in** *vi* instalarse; **settle up** *vi*: **to ~ up with sb** ajustar cuentas con algn
settlement ['sɛtlmənt] *n* (*payment*) liquidación *f*; (*agreement*) acuerdo, convenio; (*village etc*) poblado; **in ~ of our account** (*Comm*) en pago *or* liquidación de nuestra cuenta
settler ['sɛtlə^r] *n* colono(-a), colonizador(a) *m(f)*
setup ['sɛtʌp] *n* sistema *m*
seven ['sɛvn] *num* siete
seventeen [sɛvn'ti:n] *num* diez y siete, diecisiete
seventeenth [sevn'ti:nθ] *adj* decimoséptimo
seventh ['sɛvnθ] *adj* séptimo
seventieth ['sevntɪɪθ] *adj* septuagésimo
seventy ['sɛvntɪ] *num* setenta
sever ['sɛvə^r] *vt* cortar; (*relations*) romper
several ['sɛvərl] *adj, pron* varios(-as) *m(f)pl*, algunos(-as) *m(f)pl*; **~ of us** varios de nosotros; **~ times** varias veces
severance ['sɛvərəns] *n* (*of relations*) ruptura
severance pay *n* indemnización *f* por despido
severe [sɪ'vɪə^r] *adj* severo; (*serious*) grave; (*hard*) duro; (*pain*) intenso
severity [sɪ'vɛrɪtɪ] *n* severidad *f*; gravedad *f*; intensidad *f*
Seville [sə'vɪl] *n* Sevilla
sew (*pt* **sewed**, *pp* **sewn**) [səu, səud, səun] *vt, vi* coser; **sew up** *vt* coser
sewage ['su:ɪdʒ] *n* (*effluence*) aguas *fpl* residuales; (*system*) alcantarillado
sewer ['su:ə^r] *n* alcantarilla, cloaca
sewing ['səuɪŋ] *n* costura
sewing machine *n* máquina de coser
sewn [səun] *pp of* **sew**
sex [sɛks] *n* sexo; **the opposite ~** el sexo opuesto; **to have ~** hacer el amor
sex appeal *n* sex-appeal *m*, gancho
sex education *n* educación *f* sexual
sexism ['sɛksɪzəm] *n* sexismo
sexist ['sɛksɪst] *adj, n* sexista *m/f*
sex life *n* vida sexual
sex object *n* objeto sexual
sexual ['sɛksjuəl] *adj* sexual; **~ assault** atentado contra el pudor; **~ harassment** acoso sexual; **~ intercourse** relaciones *fpl* sexuales
sexuality [seksju'ælɪtɪ] *n* sexualidad *f*
sexy ['sɛksɪ] *adj* sexy
shabby ['ʃæbɪ] *adj* (*person*) desharrapado; (*clothes*) raído, gastado
shack [ʃæk] *n* choza, chabola
shackles ['ʃæklz] *npl* grillos *mpl*, grilletes *mpl*

shade [ʃeɪd] *n* sombra; (*for lamp*) pantalla; (*for eyes*) visera; (*of colour*) tono *m*, tonalidad *f*; (*US: window shade*) persiana ▷ *vt* dar sombra a; **shades** *npl* (*US: sunglasses*) gafas *fpl* de sol; **in the ~** a la sombra; (*small quantity*): **a ~ of** un poquito de; **a ~ smaller** un poquito más pequeño
shadow [ˈʃædəu] *n* sombra ▷ *vt* (*follow*) seguir y vigilar; **without** *or* **beyond a ~ of doubt** sin lugar a dudas
shadow cabinet *n* (*Brit Pol*) gobierno en la oposición
shadowy [ˈʃædəuɪ] *adj* oscuro; (*dim*) indistinto
shady [ˈʃeɪdɪ] *adj* sombreado; (*fig: dishonest*) sospechoso; (*deal*) turbio
shaft [ʃɑːft] *n* (*of arrow, spear*) astil *m*; (*Aut, Tech*) eje *m*, árbol *m*; (*of mine*) pozo; (*of lift*) hueco, caja; (*of light*) rayo; **ventilator ~** chimenea de ventilación
shaggy [ˈʃægɪ] *adj* peludo
shake [ʃeɪk] (*pt* **shook**, *pp* **shaken** [ˈʃeɪkn]) *vt* sacudir; (*building*) hacer temblar; (*perturb*) inquietar, perturbar; (*weaken*) debilitar; (*alarm*) trastornar ▷ *vi* estremecerse; (*tremble*) temblar ▷ *n* (*movement*) sacudida; **to ~ one's head** (*in refusal*) negar con la cabeza; (*in dismay*) mover *or* menear la cabeza, incrédulo; **to ~ hands with sb** estrechar la mano a algn; **to ~ in one's shoes** (*fig*) temblar de miedo; **shake off** *vt* sacudirse; (*fig*) deshacerse de; **shake up** *vt* agitar
shake-up [ˈʃeɪkʌp] *n* reorganización *f*
shaky [ˈʃeɪkɪ] *adj* (*unstable*) inestable, poco firme; (*trembling*) tembloroso; (*health*) delicado; (*memory*) defectuoso; (*person: from illness*) temblando; (*premise etc*) incierto
shall [ʃæl] *aux vb*: **I ~ go** iré; **~ I help you?** ¿quieres que te ayude?; **I'll buy three, ~ I?** compro tres, ¿no te parece?
shallot [ʃəˈlɔt] *n* (*Brit*) cebollita, chalote *m*
shallow [ˈʃæləu] *adj* poco profundo; (*fig*) superficial
sham [ʃæm] *n* fraude *m*, engaño ▷ *adj* falso, fingido ▷ *vt* fingir, simular
shambles [ˈʃæmblz] *n* desorden *m*, confusión *f*; **the economy is (in) a complete ~** la economía está en un estado desastroso
shame [ʃeɪm] *n* vergüenza; (*pity*) lástima, pena ▷ *vt* avergonzar; **it is a ~ that/to do** es una lástima *or* pena que/hacer; **what a ~!** ¡qué lástima *or* pena!; **to put sth/sb to ~** (*fig*) ridiculizar algo/a algn
shamefaced [ˈʃeɪmfeɪst] *adj* avergonzado
shameful [ˈʃeɪmful] *adj* vergonzoso
shameless [ˈʃeɪmlɪs] *adj* descarado
shampoo [ʃæmˈpuː] *n* champú *m* ▷ *vt* lavar con champú
shamrock [ˈʃæmrɔk] *n* trébol *m*
shandy [ˈʃændɪ], **shandygaff** (*US*) [ˈʃændɪgæf] *n* clara, cerveza con gaseosa
shan't [ʃɑːnt] = **shall not**
shanty town [ˈʃæntɪ-] *n* barrio de chabolas
shape [ʃeɪp] *n* forma ▷ *vt* formar, dar forma a; (*clay*) modelar; (*stone*) labrar; (*sb's ideas*) formar; (*sb's life*) determinar ▷ *vi* (*also*: **~ up**: *events*) desarrollarse; (*person*) formarse; **to take ~** tomar forma; **to get o.s. into ~** ponerse en forma *or* en condiciones; **in the ~ of a heart** en forma de corazón; **I can't bear gardening in any ~ or form** no aguanto la jardinería de ningún modo
shapeless [ˈʃeɪplɪs] *adj* informe, sin forma definida
shapely [ˈʃeɪplɪ] *adj* bien formado *or* proporcionado
share [ʃɛəʳ] *n* (*part*) parte *f*, porción *f*; (*contribution*) cuota; (*Comm*) acción *f* ▷ *vt* dividir; (*fig: have in common*) compartir; **to have a ~ in the profits** tener una proporción de las ganancias; **he has a 50% ~ in a new business venture** tiene una participación del 50% en un nuevo negocio; **to ~ in** participar en; **to ~ out (among** *or* **between)** repartir (entre)
share certificate *n* certificado *or* título de una acción
shareholder [ˈʃɛəhəuldəʳ] *n* (*Brit*) accionista *m/f*
share issue *n* emisión *f* de acciones
shark [ʃɑːk] *n* tiburón *m*
sharp [ʃɑːp] *adj* (*razor, knife*) afilado; (*point*) puntiagudo; (*outline*) definido; (*pain*) intenso; (*Mus*) desafinado; (*contrast*) marcado; (*voice*) agudo; (*curve, bend*) cerrado; (*person: quick-witted*) avispado; (*: dishonest*) poco escrupuloso ▷ *n* (*Mus*) sostenido ▷ *adv*: **at two o'clock ~** a las dos en punto; **to be ~ with sb** hablar a algn de forma brusca y tajante; **turn ~ left** tuerce del todo a la izquierda
sharpen [ˈʃɑːpn] *vt* afilar; (*pencil*) sacar punta a; (*fig*) agudizar
sharpener [ˈʃɑːpnəʳ] *n* (*gen*) afilador *m*; (*also*: **pencil ~**) sacapuntas *m inv*
sharp-eyed [ʃɑːpˈaɪd] *adj* de vista aguda
sharply [ˈʃɑːplɪ] *adv* (*abruptly*) bruscamente; (*clearly*) claramente; (*harshly*) severamente
shatter [ˈʃætəʳ] *vt* hacer añicos *or* pedazos; (*fig: ruin*) destruir, acabar con ▷ *vi* hacerse añicos
shattered [ˈʃætəd] *adj* (*grief-stricken*) destrozado, deshecho; (*exhausted*) agotado, hecho polvo
shave [ʃeɪv] *vt* afeitar, rasurar ▷ *vi* afeitarse ▷ *n*: **to have a ~** afeitarse
shaver [ˈʃeɪvəʳ] *n* (*also*: **electric ~**) máquina de afeitar (eléctrica)
shaving [ˈʃeɪvɪŋ] *n* (*action*) afeitado; **shavings** *npl* (*of wood etc*) virutas *fpl*
shaving brush *n* brocha (de afeitar)
shaving cream *n* crema (de afeitar)
shaving foam *n* espuma de afeitar
shawl [ʃɔːl] *n* chal *m*

she [ʃiː] *pron* ella; **there ~ is** allí está; **~-cat** gata
sheaf (*pl* **sheaves**) [ʃiːf, ʃiːvz] *n* (*of corn*) gavilla; (*of arrows*) haz *m*; (*of papers*) fajo
shear [ʃɪəʳ] *vt* (*pt, pp* **sheared** *or* **shorn** [ʃɔːn]) (*sheep*) esquilar, trasquilar; **shear off** *vi* romperse
shears ['ʃɪəz] *npl* (*for hedge*) tijeras *fpl* de jardín
sheath [ʃiːθ] *n* vaina; (*contraceptive*) preservativo
shed [ʃɛd] (*pt, pp* **shed**) *n* cobertizo; (*Industry, Rail*) nave *f* ▷ *vt* (*skin*) mudar; (*tears*) derramar; (*workers*) despedir; **to ~ light on** (*problem, mystery*) aclarar, arrojar luz sobre
she'd [ʃiːd] = **she had**; **she would**
sheen [ʃiːn] *n* brillo, lustre *m*
sheep [ʃiːp] *n pl inv* oveja
sheepdog ['ʃiːpdɔg] *n* perro pastor
sheepish ['ʃiːpɪʃ] *adj* tímido, vergonzoso
sheepskin ['ʃiːpskɪn] *n* piel *f* de carnero
sheer [ʃɪəʳ] *adj* (*utter*) puro, completo; (*steep*) escarpado; (*material*) diáfano ▷ *adv* verticalmente; **by ~ chance** de pura casualidad
sheet [ʃiːt] *n* (*on bed*) sábana; (*of paper*) hoja; (*of glass, metal*) lámina
sheik, sheikh [ʃeɪk] *n* jeque *m*
shelf (*pl* **shelves**) [ʃɛlf, ʃɛlvz] *n* estante *m*
shelf life *n* (*Comm*) periodo de conservación antes de la venta
shell [ʃɛl] *n* (*on beach*) concha, caracol (*LAm*); (*of egg, nut etc*) cáscara; (*explosive*) proyectil *m*, obús *m*; (*of building*) armazón *m* ▷ *vt* (*peas*) desenvainar; (*Mil*) bombardear; **shell out** *vi* (*inf*): **to ~ out (for)** soltar el dinero (para), desembolsar (para)
she'll [ʃiːl] = **she will**; **she shall**
shellfish ['ʃɛlfɪʃ] *n pl inv* crustáceo *pl* (*as food*) mariscos *mpl*
shellsuit ['ʃɛlsuːt] *n* chándal *m* (de tactel®)
shelter ['ʃɛltəʳ] *n* abrigo, refugio ▷ *vt* (*aid*) amparar, proteger; (*give lodging to*) abrigar; (*hide*) esconder ▷ *vi* abrigarse, refugiarse; **to take ~ (from)** refugiarse *or* asilarse (de); **bus ~** parada de autobús cubierta
sheltered ['ʃɛltəd] *adj* (*life*) protegido; (*spot*) abrigado
shelve [ʃɛlv] *vt* (*fig*) dar carpetazo a
shelves [ʃɛlvz] *npl of* **shelf**
shelving ['ʃɛlvɪŋ] *n* estantería
shepherd ['ʃɛpəd] *n* pastor *m* ▷ *vt* (*guide*) guiar, conducir
shepherd's pie *n* *pastel de carne y puré de patatas*
sheriff ['ʃɛrɪf] *n* (*US*) sheriff *m*
sherry ['ʃɛrɪ] *n* jerez *m*
she's [ʃiːz] = **she is**; **she has**
Shetland ['ʃɛtlənd] *n* (*also*: **the ~s, the ~ Isles**) las Islas *fpl* Shetland
Shetland pony *n* pony *m* de Shetland
shield [ʃiːld] *n* escudo; (*Tech*) blindaje *m* ▷ *vt*: **to ~ (from)** proteger (de)
shift [ʃɪft] *n* (*change*) cambio; (*at work*) turno ▷ *vt* trasladar; (*remove*) quitar ▷ *vi* moverse; (*change place*) cambiar de sitio; **the wind has ~ed to the south** el viento ha virado al sur; **a ~ in demand** (*Comm*) un desplazamiento de la demanda
shift work *n* (*Brit*) trabajo por turnos; **to do ~** trabajar por turnos
shifty ['ʃɪftɪ] *adj* tramposo; (*eyes*) furtivo
Shiite ['ʃiːaɪt] *adj, n* shiíta *m/f*
shilling ['ʃɪlɪŋ] *n* (*Brit*: *formerly*) chelín *m* (= *12 peniques antiguos; una libra tenía 20 chelines*)
shilly-shally ['ʃɪlɪʃælɪ] *vi* titubear, vacilar
shimmer ['ʃɪməʳ] *n* reflejo trémulo ▷ *vi* relucir
shin [ʃɪn] *n* espinilla ▷ *vi*: **to ~ down/up a tree** bajar de/trepar un árbol
shine [ʃaɪn] (*pt, pp* **shone**) *n* brillo, lustre *m* ▷ *vi* brillar, relucir ▷ *vt* (*shoes*) lustrar, sacar brillo a; **to ~ a torch on sth** dirigir una linterna hacia algo
shingle ['ʃɪŋgl] *n* (*on beach*) guijarras *fpl*
shingles ['ʃɪŋglz] *n* (*Med*) herpes *msg*
shiny ['ʃaɪnɪ] *adj* brillante, lustroso
ship [ʃɪp] *n* buque *m*, barco ▷ *vt* (*goods*) embarcar; (*oars*) desarmar; (*send*) transportar *or* enviar por vía marítima; **~'s manifest** manifiesto del buque; **on board ~** a bordo
shipbuilding ['ʃɪpbɪldɪŋ] *n* construcción *f* naval
shipment ['ʃɪpmənt] *n* (*act*) embarque *m*; (*goods*) envío
shipper ['ʃɪpəʳ] *n* compañía naviera
shipping ['ʃɪpɪŋ] *n* (*act*) embarque *m*; (*traffic*) buques *mpl*
shipwreck ['ʃɪprɛk] *n* naufragio ▷ *vt*: **to be ~ed** naufragar
shipyard ['ʃɪpjɑːd] *n* astillero
shire ['ʃaɪəʳ] *n* (*Brit*) condado
shirk [ʃəːk] *vt* eludir, esquivar; (*obligations*) faltar a
shirt [ʃəːt] *n* camisa; **in ~ sleeves** en mangas de camisa
shirty ['ʃəːtɪ] *adj* (*Brit inf*): **to be ~** estar de malas pulgas
shit [ʃɪt] (*inf!*) *n* mierda (*!*); (*nonsense*) chorradas *fpl*; **to be a ~** ser un cabrón (*!*) ▷ *excl* ¡mierda! (*!*); **tough ~!** ¡te jodes! (*!*)
shiver ['ʃɪvəʳ] *n* escalofrío ▷ *vi* temblar, estremecerse; (*with cold*) tiritar
shoal [ʃəul] *n* (*of fish*) banco
shock [ʃɔk] *n* (*impact*) choque *m*; (*Elec*) descarga (eléctrica); (*emotional*) conmoción *f*; (*start*) sobresalto, susto; (*Med*) postración *f* nerviosa ▷ *vt* dar un susto a; (*offend*) escandalizar; **to get a ~** (*Elec*) sentir una sacudida eléctrica; **to give sb a ~** dar un susto a algn; **to be suffering from ~** padecer una postración nerviosa; **it came as a ~ to hear that ...** me *etc* asombró descubrir que ...
shock absorber [-əbsɔːbəʳ] *n* amortiguador *m*

shocking ['ʃɔkɪŋ] *adj* (*awful*: *weather, handwriting*) espantoso, horrible; (*improper*) escandaloso; (*result*) inesperado
shock wave *n* onda expansiva *or* de choque
shod [ʃɔd] *pt, pp of* **shoe** ▷ *adj* calzado
shoddy ['ʃɔdɪ] *adj* de pacotilla
shoe [ʃuː] (*pt, pp* **shod** [ʃɔd]) *n* zapato; (*for horse*) herradura; (*brake shoe*) zapata ▷ *vt* (*horse*) herrar
shoelace ['ʃuːleɪs] *n* cordón *m*
shoe polish *n* betún *m*
shoeshop ['ʃuːʃɔp] *n* zapatería
shoestring ['ʃuːstrɪŋ] *n* (*shoelace*) cordón *m*; (*fig*): **on a ~** con muy poco dinero, a lo barato
shone [ʃɔn] *pt, pp of* **shine**
shoo [ʃuː] *excl* ¡fuera!; (*to animals*) ¡zape! ▷ *vt* (*also*: **~ away, ~ off**) ahuyentar
shook [ʃuk] *pt of* **shake**
shoot [ʃuːt] (*pt, pp* **shot**) *n* (*on branch, seedling*) retoño, vástago; (*shooting party*) cacería; (*competition*) concurso de tiro; (*preserve*) coto de caza ▷ *vt* disparar; (*kill*) matar a tiros; (*execute*) fusilar; (*Cine*: *film, scene*) rodar, filmar ▷ *vi* (*Football*) chutar; **to ~ (at)** tirar (a); **to ~ past** pasar como un rayo; **to ~ in/out** *vi* entrar corriendo/salir disparado; **shoot down** *vt* (*plane*) derribar; **shoot up** *vi* (*prices*) dispararse
shooting ['ʃuːtɪŋ] *n* (*shots*) tiros *mpl*, tiroteo; (*Hunting*) caza con escopeta; (*act*: *murder*) asesinato (a tiros); (*Cine*) rodaje *m*
shooting star *n* estrella fugaz
shop [ʃɔp] *n* tienda; (*workshop*) taller *m* ▷ *vi* (*also*: **go ~ping**) ir de compras; **to talk ~** (*fig*) hablar del trabajo; **repair ~** taller *m* de reparaciones; **shop around** *vi* comparar precios
shopaholic [ʃɔpə'hɔlɪk] *n* (*inf*) adicto(-a) a las compras
shop assistant *n* (*Brit*) dependiente(-a) *m(f)*
shop floor *n* (*Brit fig*) taller *m*, fábrica
shopkeeper ['ʃɔpkiːpəʳ] *n* (*Brit*) tendero(-a)
shoplift ['ʃɔplɪft] *vi* robar en las tiendas
shoplifter ['ʃɔplɪftəʳ] *n* ratero(-a)
shoplifting ['ʃɔplɪftɪŋ] *n* ratería, robo (en las tiendas)
shopper ['ʃɔpəʳ] *n* comprador(a) *m(f)*
shopping ['ʃɔpɪŋ] *n* (*goods*) compras *fpl*
shopping bag *n* bolsa (de compras)
shopping centre, shopping center (*US*) *n* centro comercial
shopping mall *n* centro comercial
shopping trolley *n* (*Brit*) carrito de la compra
shop steward *n* (*Brit Industry*) enlace *m/f* sindical
shop window *n* escaparate *m*, vidriera (*LAm*)
shore [ʃɔːʳ] *n* (*of sea, lake*) orilla ▷ *vt*: **to ~ (up)** reforzar; **on ~** en tierra
shorn [ʃɔːn] *pp of* **shear**
short [ʃɔːt] *adj* (*not long*) corto; (*in time*) breve, de corta duración; (*person*) bajo; (*curt*) brusco, seco ▷ *vi* (*Elec*) ponerse en cortocircuito ▷ *n* (*also*: **~ film**) cortometraje *m*; **(a pair of) ~s** (unos) pantalones *mpl* cortos; **to be ~ of sth** estar falto de algo; **in ~** en pocas palabras; **a ~ time ago** hace poco (tiempo); **in the ~ term** a corto plazo; **to be in ~ supply** escasear, haber escasez de; **I'm ~ of time** me falta tiempo; **~ of doing ...** a menos que hagamos *etc* ...; **everything ~ of ...** todo menos ...; **it is ~ for** es la forma abreviada de; **to cut ~** (*speech, visit*) interrumpir, terminar inesperadamente; **to fall ~ of** no alcanzar; **to run ~ of sth** acabársele algo; **to stop ~** parar en seco; **to stop ~ of** detenerse antes de
shortage ['ʃɔːtɪdʒ] *n* escasez *f*, falta
shortbread ['ʃɔːtbred] *n galleta de mantequilla, especie de mantecada*
short-change [ʃɔːt'tʃeɪndʒ] *vt*: **to ~ sb** no dar el cambio completo a algn
short-circuit [ʃɔːt'səːkɪt] *n* cortocircuito ▷ *vt* poner en cortocircuito ▷ *vi* ponerse en cortocircuito
shortcoming ['ʃɔːtkʌmɪŋ] *n* defecto, deficiencia
shortcrust pastry ['ʃɔːtkrʌst-], **short pastry** *n* (*Brit*) pasta quebradiza
shortcut ['ʃɔːtkʌt] *n* atajo
shorten ['ʃɔːtn] *vt* acortar; (*visit*) interrumpir
shortfall ['ʃɔːtfɔːl] *n* déficit *m*, deficiencia
shorthand ['ʃɔːthænd] *n* (*Brit*) taquigrafía; **to take sth down in ~** taquigrafiar algo
shorthand typist *n* (*Brit*) taquimecanógrafo(-a)
short list *n* (*Brit*: *for job*) lista de candidatos pre-seleccionados
short-lived ['ʃɔːt'lɪvd] *adj* efímero
shortly ['ʃɔːtlɪ] *adv* en breve, dentro de poco
short-sighted [ʃɔːt'saɪtɪd] *adj* (*Brit*) miope, corto de vista; (*fig*) imprudente
short-sleeved *adj* de manga corta
short-staffed [ʃɔːt'stɑːft] *adj* falto de personal
short story *n* cuento
short-tempered [ʃɔːt'tɛmpəd] *adj* enojadizo
short-term ['ʃɔːttəːm] *adj* (*effect*) a corto plazo
short wave *n* (*Radio*) onda corta
shot [ʃɔt] *pt, pp of* **shoot** ▷ *n* (*sound*) tiro, disparo; (*person*) tirador(a) *m(f)*; (*try*) tentativa; (*injection*) inyección *f*; (*Phot*) toma, fotografía; (*shotgun pellets*) perdigones *mpl*; **to fire a ~ at sb/sth** tirar *or* disparar contra algn/algo; **to have a ~ at (doing) sth** probar suerte con algo; **like a ~** (*without any delay*) como un rayo; **a big ~** (*inf*) un pez gordo; **to get ~ of sth/sb** (*inf*) deshacerse de algo/algn, quitarse algo/a algn de encima
shotgun ['ʃɔtgʌn] *n* escopeta
should [ʃud] *aux vb*: **I ~ go now** debo irme ahora; **he ~ be there now** debe de haber llegado (ya); **I ~ go if I were you** yo en tu lugar me iría; **I ~ like to** me gustaría; **~ he**

S

phone ... si llamara ..., en caso de que llamase ...
shoulder ['ʃəuldəʳ] *n* hombro; (*Brit*: *of road*): **hard ~** arcén *m* ▷ *vt* (*fig*) cargar con; **to look over one's ~** mirar hacia atrás; **to rub ~s with sb** (*fig*) codearse con algn; **to give sb the cold ~** (*fig*) dar de lado a algn
shoulder bag *n* bolso de bandolera
shoulder blade *n* omóplato
shoulder strap *n* tirante *m*
shouldn't ['ʃudnt] = **should not**
shout [ʃaut] *n* grito ▷ *vt* gritar ▷ *vi* gritar, dar voces; **shout down** *vt* hundir a gritos
shouting ['ʃautɪŋ] *n* griterío
shouting match *n* (*inf*) discusión *f* a voz en grito
shove [ʃʌv] *n* empujón *m* ▷ *vt* empujar; (*inf*: *put*): **to ~ sth in** meter algo a empellones; **he ~d me out of the way** me quitó de en medio de un empujón; **shove off** *vi* (*Naut*) alejarse del muelle; (*fig*: *inf*) largarse
shovel ['ʃʌvl] *n* pala; (*mechanical*) excavadora ▷ *vt* mover con pala
show [ʃəu] (*pt* **showed**, *pp* **shown**) *n* (*of emotion*) demostración *f*; (*semblance*) apariencia; (*Comm, Tech*: *exhibition*) exhibición *f*, exposición *f*; (*Theat*) función *f*, espectáculo; (*organization*) negocio, empresa ▷ *vt* mostrar, enseñar; (*courage etc*) mostrar, manifestar; (*exhibit*) exponer; (*film*) proyectar ▷ *vi* mostrarse; (*appear*) aparecer; **on ~** (*exhibits etc*) expuesto; **to be on ~** estar expuesto; **it's just for ~** es sólo para impresionar; **to ask for a ~ of hands** pedir una votación a mano alzada; **who's running the ~ here?** ¿quién manda aquí?; **to ~ a profit/loss** (*Comm*) arrojar un saldo positivo/negativo; **I have nothing to ~ for it** no saqué ningún provecho (de ello); **to ~ sb to his seat/to the door** acompañar a algn a su asiento/a la puerta; **as ~n in the illustration** como se ve en el grabado; **it just goes to ~ that ...** queda demostrado que ...; **it doesn't ~** no se ve *or* nota; **show in** *vt* (*person*) hacer pasar; **show off** *vi* (*pej*) presumir ▷ *vt* (*display*) lucir; (*pej*) hacer alarde de; **show out** *vt*: **to ~ sb out** acompañar a algn a la puerta; **show up** *vi* (*stand out*) destacar; (*inf*: *turn up*) presentarse ▷ *vt* descubrir; (*unmask*) desenmascarar
showbiz ['ʃəubɪz] *n* (*inf*) = **show business**
show business *n* el mundo del espectáculo
showdown ['ʃəudaun] *n* crisis *f*, momento decisivo
shower ['ʃauəʳ] *n* (*rain*) chaparrón *m*, chubasco; (*of stones etc*) lluvia; (*also*: **~ bath**) ducha ▷ *vi* llover ▷ *vt*: **to ~ sb with sth** colmar a algn de algo; **to have** *or* **take a ~** ducharse
shower cap *n* gorro de baño
shower gel *n* gel de ducha
showery ['ʃauərɪ] *adj* (*weather*) lluvioso
showing ['ʃəuɪŋ] *n* (*of film*) proyección *f*
show jumping *n* hípica
shown [ʃəun] *pp of* **show**
show-off ['ʃəuɔf] *n* (*inf*: *person*) fanfarrón(-ona) *m(f)*
showpiece ['ʃəupi:s] *n* (*of exhibition etc*) objeto más valioso, joya; **that hospital is a ~** ese hospital es un modelo del género
showroom ['ʃəuru:m] *n* sala de muestras
show trial *n* juicio propagandístico
shrank [ʃræŋk] *pt of* **shrink**
shrapnel ['ʃræpnl] *n* metralla
shred [ʃrɛd] *n gen pl* triza, jirón *m*; (*fig*: *of truth, evidence*) pizca, chispa ▷ *vt* hacer trizas; (*documents*) triturar; (*Culin*) desmenuzar
shredder ['ʃrɛdəʳ] *n* (*vegetable shredder*) picadora; (*document shredder*) trituradora (de papel)
shrewd [ʃru:d] *adj* astuto
shriek [ʃri:k] *n* chillido ▷ *vt, vi* chillar
shrill [ʃrɪl] *adj* agudo, estridente
shrimp [ʃrɪmp] *n* camarón *m*
shrine [ʃraɪn] *n* santuario, sepulcro
shrink (*pt* **shrank**, *pp* **shrunk**) [ʃrɪŋk, ʃræŋk, ʃrʌŋk] *vi* encogerse; (*be reduced*) reducirse ▷ *vt* encoger ▷ *n* (*inf, pej*) loquero(-a); **to ~ from (doing) sth** no atreverse a hacer algo; **shrink away** *vi* retroceder, retirarse
shrinkage ['ʃrɪŋkɪdʒ] *n* encogimiento; reducción *f*; (*Comm*: *in shops*) pérdidas *fpl*
shrink-wrap ['ʃrɪŋkræp] *vt* empaquetar en envase termorretráctil
shrivel ['ʃrɪvl] (*also*: **~ up**) *vt* (*dry*) secar; (*crease*) arrugar ▷ *vi* secarse; arrugarse
shroud [ʃraud] *n* sudario ▷ *vt*: **~ed in mystery** envuelto en el misterio
Shrove Tuesday ['ʃrəuv-] *n* martes *m* de carnaval
shrub [ʃrʌb] *n* arbusto
shrubbery ['ʃrʌbərɪ] *n* arbustos *mpl*
shrug [ʃrʌg] *n* encogimiento de hombros ▷ *vt, vi*: **to ~ (one's shoulders)** encogerse de hombros; **shrug off** *vt* negar importancia a; (*cold, illness*) deshacerse de
shrunk [ʃrʌŋk] *pp of* **shrink**
shrunken ['ʃrʌŋkn] *adj* encogido
shudder ['ʃʌdəʳ] *n* estremecimiento, escalofrío ▷ *vi* estremecerse
shuffle ['ʃʌfl] *vt* (*cards*) barajar; **to ~ (one's feet)** arrastrar los pies
shun [ʃʌn] *vt* rehuir, esquivar
shunt [ʃʌnt] *vt* (*Rail*) maniobrar
shut (*pt, pp* **shut**) [ʃʌt] *vt* cerrar ▷ *vi* cerrarse; **shut down** *vt*, ▷ *vi* cerrar; (*machine*) parar; **shut off** *vt* (*stop*: *power, water supply etc*) interrumpir, cortar; (*engine*) parar; **shut out** *vt* (*person*) excluir, dejar fuera; (*noise, cold*) no dejar entrar; (*block*: *view*) tapar; (*memory*) tratar de olvidar; **shut up** *vi* (*inf*: *keep quiet*) callarse ▷ *vt* (*close*) cerrar; (*silence*) callar
shutter ['ʃʌtəʳ] *n* contraventana; (*Phot*) obturador *m*

shuttle ['ʃʌtl] *n* lanzadera; (*also*: **~ service**: *Aviat*) puente *m* aéreo ▷ *vi* (*vehicle, person*) ir y venir ▷ *vt* (*passengers*) transportar, trasladar
shuttlecock ['ʃʌtlkɔk] *n* volante *m*
shy [ʃaɪ] *adj* tímido ▷ *vi*: **to ~ away from doing sth** (*fig*) rehusar hacer algo; **to be ~ of doing sth** esquivar hacer algo
Siberia [saɪ'bɪərɪə] *n* Siberia
sibling ['sɪblɪŋ] *n* (*formal*) hermano(-a)
Sicily ['sɪsɪlɪ] *n* Sicilia
sick [sɪk] *adj* (*ill*) enfermo; (*nauseated*) mareado; (*humour*) morboso; **to be ~** (*Brit*) vomitar; **to feel ~** tener náuseas; **to be ~ of** (*fig*) estar harto de; **a ~ person** un(a) enfermo(-a); **to be (off) ~** estar ausente por enfermedad; **to fall** *or* **take ~** ponerse enfermo
sickbag ['sɪkbæg] *n* bolsa para el mareo
sick bay *n* enfermería
sick building syndrome *n enfermedad causada por falta de ventilación y luz natural en un edificio*
sicken ['sɪkn] *vt* dar asco a ▷ *vi* enfermar; **to be ~ing for** (*cold, flu etc*) mostrar síntomas de
sickening ['sɪknɪŋ] *adj* (*fig*) asqueroso
sickle ['sɪkl] *n* hoz *f*
sick leave *n* baja por enfermedad
sickly ['sɪklɪ] *adj* enfermizo; (*taste*) empalagoso
sickness ['sɪknɪs] *n* enfermedad *f*, mal *m*; (*vomiting*) náuseas *fpl*
sick pay *n prestación por enfermedad pagada por la empresa*
side [saɪd] *n* (*gen*) lado; (*face, surface*) cara; (*of paper*) cara; (*slice of bread*) rebanada; (*of body*) costado; (*of animal*) ijar *m*, ijada; (*of lake*) orilla; (*part*) lado; (*aspect*) aspecto; (*team*: *Sport*) equipo; (: *Pol etc*) partido; (*of hill*) ladera ▷ *adj* (*door, entrance*) lateral ▷ *vi*: **to ~ with sb** tomar partido por algn; **by the ~ of** al lado de; **~ by ~** juntos(-as); **from all ~s** de todos lados; **to take ~s (with)** tomar partido (por); **~ of beef** flanco de vaca; **the right/wrong ~** el derecho/revés; **from ~ to ~** de un lado a otro
sideboard ['saɪdbɔːd] *n* aparador *m*
sideboards ['saɪdbɔːdz], **sideburns** (*Brit*) ['saɪdbəːnz] *npl* patillas *fpl*
side effect *n* efecto secundario
sidelight ['saɪdlaɪt] *n* (*Aut*) luz *f* lateral
sideline ['saɪdlaɪn] *n* (*Sport*) línea de banda; (*fig*) empleo suplementario
sidelong ['saɪdlɔŋ] *adj* de soslayo; **to give a ~ glance at sth** mirar algo de reojo
side road *n* (*Brit*) calle *f* lateral
side-saddle ['saɪdsædl] *adv* a la amazona
side show *n* (*stall*) caseta; (*fig*) atracción *f* secundaria
sidestep ['saɪdstɛp] *vt* (*question*) eludir; (*problem*) esquivar ▷ *vi* (*Boxing etc*) dar un quiebro
side street *n* calle *f* lateral
sidetrack ['saɪdtræk] *vt* (*fig*) desviar (de su propósito)
sidewalk ['saɪdwɔːk] *n* (*US*) acera, vereda (*LAm*), andén *m* (*LAm*), banqueta (*LAm*)
sideways ['saɪdweɪz] *adv* de lado
siding ['saɪdɪŋ] *n* (*Rail*) apartadero, vía muerta
sidle ['saɪdl] *vi*: **to ~ up (to)** acercarse furtivamente (a)
siege [siːdʒ] *n* cerco, sitio; **to lay ~ to** cercar, sitiar
sieve [sɪv] *n* colador *m* ▷ *vt* cribar
sift [sɪft] *vt* cribar ▷ *vi*: **to ~ through** (*information*) examinar cuidadosamente
sigh [saɪ] *n* suspiro ▷ *vi* suspirar
sight [saɪt] *n* (*faculty*) vista; (*spectacle*) espectáculo; (*on gun*) mira, alza ▷ *vt* ver, divisar; **in ~** a la vista; **out of ~** fuera de (la) vista; **at ~** a la vista; **at first ~** a primera vista; **to lose ~ of sth/sb** perder algo/a algn de vista; **to catch ~ of sth/sb** divisar algo/a algn; **I know her by ~** la conozco de vista; **to set one's ~s on (doing) sth** aspirar a *or* ambicionar (hacer) algo
sightseeing ['saɪtsiːɪŋ] *n* turismo; **to go ~** hacer turismo
sign [saɪn] *n* (*with hand*) señal *f*, seña; (*trace*) huella, rastro; (*notice*) letrero; (*written*) signo; (*also*: **road ~**) indicador *m*; (: *with instructions*) señal *f* de tráfico ▷ *vt* firmar; (*Sport*) fichar; **as a ~ of** en señal de; **it's a good/bad ~** es buena/mala señal; **plus/minus ~** signo de más/de menos; **to ~ one's name** firmar; **sign away** *vt* (*rights etc*) ceder; **sign in** *vi* firmar el registro (al entrar); **sign off** *vi* (*Radio, TV*) cerrar el programa; **sign on** *vi* (*Mil*) alistarse; (*as unemployed*) apuntarse al paro; (*employee*) firmar un contrato ▷ *vt* (*Mil*) alistar; (*employee*) contratar; **to ~ on for a course** matricularse en un curso; **sign out** *vi* firmar el registro (al salir); **sign over** *vt*: **to ~ sth over to sb** traspasar algo a algn; **sign up** *vi* (*Mil*) alistarse; (*for course*) inscribirse ▷ *vt* (*player*) fichar; (*contract*) contratar
signal ['sɪgnl] *n* señal *f* ▷ *vi* (*Aut*) señalizar ▷ *vt* (*person*) hacer señas a; (*message*) transmitir; **the engaged ~** (*Tel*) la señal de comunicando; **the ~ is very weak** (*TV*) no captamos bien el canal; **to ~ a left/right turn** (*Aut*) indicar que se va a doblar a la izquierda/derecha; **to ~ to sb (to do sth)** hacer señas a algn (para que haga algo)
signalman ['sɪgnlmən] *n* (*Rail*) guardavía *m*
signature ['sɪgnətʃəʳ] *n* firma
signature tune *n* sintonía
signet ring ['sɪgnət-] *n* (anillo de) sello
significance [sɪg'nɪfɪkəns] *n* significado; (*importance*) trascendencia; **that is of no ~** eso no tiene importancia
significant [sɪg'nɪfɪkənt] *adj* significativo; (*important*) trascendente; **it is ~ that ...** es significativo que ...

S

signify ['sɪgnɪfaɪ] *vt* significar
sign language *n* mímica, lenguaje *m* por *or* de señas
signpost ['saɪnpəust] *n* indicador *m*
Sikh [si:k] *adj, n* sij *m/f*
silence ['saɪlns] *n* silencio ▷ *vt* hacer callar, acallar; (*guns*) reducir al silencio
silencer ['saɪlnsə^r] *n* silenciador *m*
silent ['saɪlnt] *adj* (*gen*) silencioso; (*not speaking*) callado; (*film*) mudo; **to keep** *or* **remain ~** guardar silencio
silent partner *n* (*Comm*) socio(-a) comanditario(-a)
silhouette [sɪlu:'ɛt] *n* silueta; **~d against** destacado sobre *or* contra
silicon ['sɪlɪkən] *n* silicio
silicon chip *n* chip *m*, plaqueta de silicio
silicone ['sɪlɪkəun] *n* silicona
silk [sɪlk] *n* seda ▷ *cpd* de seda
silky ['sɪlkɪ] *adj* sedoso
silly ['sɪlɪ] *adj* (*person*) tonto; (*idea*) absurdo; **to do sth ~** hacer una tontería
silt [sɪlt] *n* sedimento
silver ['sɪlvə^r] *n* plata; (*money*) moneda suelta ▷ *adj* de plata
silver foil, silver paper (*Brit*) *n* papel *m* de plata
silver-plated [sɪlvə'pleɪtɪd] *adj* plateado
silversmith ['sɪlvəsmɪθ] *n* platero(-a)
silvery ['sɪlvrɪ] *adj* plateado
SIM card ['sɪm-] *n* (*Tel*) SIM card *m o f*, tarjeta SIM
similar ['sɪmɪlə^r] *adj*: **~ to** parecido *or* semejante a
similarity [sɪmɪ'lærɪtɪ] *n* parecido, semejanza
similarly ['sɪmɪləlɪ] *adv* del mismo modo; (*in a similar way*) de manera parecida; (*equally*) igualmente
simile ['sɪmɪlɪ] *n* símil *m*
simmer ['sɪmə^r] *vi* hervir a fuego lento; **simmer down** *vi* (*fig, inf*) calmarse, tranquilizarse
simple ['sɪmpl] *adj* (*easy*) sencillo; (*foolish*) simple; (*Comm*) simple; **the ~ truth** la pura verdad
simplicity [sɪm'plɪsɪtɪ] *n* sencillez *f*; (*foolishness*) ingenuidad *f*
simplify ['sɪmplɪfaɪ] *vt* simplificar
simply ['sɪmplɪ] *adv* (*in a simple way: live, talk*) sencillamente; (*just, merely*) sólo
simulate ['sɪmjuleɪt] *vt* simular
simultaneous [sɪməl'teɪnɪəs] *adj* simultáneo
simultaneously [sɪməl'teɪnɪəslɪ] *adv* simultáneamente, a la vez
sin [sɪn] *n* pecado ▷ *vi* pecar
since [sɪns] *adv* desde entonces ▷ *prep* desde ▷ *conj* (*time*) desde que; (*because*) ya que, puesto que; **~ then, ever ~** desde entonces; **~ Monday** desde el lunes; **(ever) ~ I arrived** desde que llegué
sincere [sɪn'sɪə^r] *adj* sincero
sincerely [sɪn'sɪəlɪ] *adv* sinceramente; **yours ~** (*in letters*) le saluda (afectuosamente); **~ yours** (*US: in letters*) le saluda atentamente
sincerity [sɪn'sɛrɪtɪ] *n* sinceridad *f*
sinew ['sɪnju:] *n* tendón *m*
sinful ['sɪnful] *adj* (*thought*) pecaminoso; (*person*) pecador(a)
sing (*pt* **sang**, *pp* **sung**) [sɪŋ, sæŋ, sʌŋ] *vt* cantar ▷ *vi* (*gen*) cantar; (*bird*) trinar; (*ears*) zumbar
Singapore [sɪŋə'pɔ:^r] *n* Singapur *m*
singe [sɪndʒ] *vt* chamuscar
singer ['sɪŋə^r] *n* cantante *m/f*
singing ['sɪŋɪŋ] *n* (*of person, bird*) canto; (*songs*) canciones *fpl*; (*in the ears*) zumbido; (*of kettle*) silbido
single ['sɪŋgl] *adj* único, solo; (*unmarried*) soltero; (*not double*) individual, sencillo ▷ *n* (*Brit: also:* **~ ticket**) billete *m* sencillo; (*record*) sencillo, single *m*; **singles** *npl* (*Tennis*) individual *msg*; **not a ~ one was left** no quedaba ni uno; **every ~ day** todos los días (sin excepción); **single out** *vt* (*choose*) escoger; (*point out*) singularizar
single bed *n* cama individual
single-breasted [sɪŋgl'brɛstɪd] *adj* (*jacket, suit*) recto, sin cruzar
single file *n*: **in ~** en fila de uno
single-handed [sɪŋgl'hændɪd] *adv* sin ayuda
single-minded [sɪŋgl'maɪndɪd] *adj* resuelto, firme
single parent *n* (*mother*) madre *f* soltera; (*father*) padre *m* soltero; **~ family** familia monoparental
single room *n* habitación *f* individual
singly ['sɪŋglɪ] *adv* uno por uno
singular ['sɪŋgjulə^r] *adj* singular, extraordinario, raro, extraño; (*outstanding*) excepcional; (*Ling*) singular ▷ *n* (*Ling*) singular *m*; **in the feminine ~** en femenino singular
sinister ['sɪnɪstə^r] *adj* siniestro
sink [sɪŋk] (*pt* **sank**, *pp* **sunk**) *n* fregadero ▷ *vt* (*ship*) hundir, echar a pique; (*foundations*) excavar; (*piles etc*): **to ~ sth into** hundir algo en ▷ *vi* (*gen*) hundirse; **he sank into a chair/the mud** se dejó caer en una silla/se hundió en el barro; **the shares** *or* **share prices have sunk to three dollars** las acciones han bajado a tres dólares; **sink in** *vi* (*fig*) penetrar, calar; **the news took a long time to ~ in** la noticia tardó mucho en hacer mella en él (*or mí etc*)
sinner ['sɪnə^r] *n* pecador(a) *m(f)*
sinus ['saɪnəs] *n* (*Anat*) seno
sip [sɪp] *n* sorbo ▷ *vt* sorber, beber a sorbitos
siphon ['saɪfən] *n* sifón *m* ▷ *vt* (*also:* **~ off**: *funds*) desviar
sir [sə:^r] *n* señor *m*; **S~ John Smith** el Señor John Smith; **yes ~** sí, señor; **Dear S~** (*in letter*)

Muy señor mío, Estimado Señor; **Dear S~s** Muy señores nuestros, Estimados Señores
siren ['saɪərn] *n* sirena
sirloin ['sə:lɔɪn] *n* solomillo
sirloin steak *n* filete *m* de solomillo
sissy ['sɪsɪ] *n* (*inf*) marica *m*
sister ['sɪstə^r] *n* hermana; (*Brit: nurse*) enfermera jefe
sister-in-law ['sɪstərɪnlɔ:] *n* cuñada
sit (*pt, pp* **sat**) [sɪt, sæt] *vi* sentarse; (*be sitting*) estar sentado; (*assembly*) reunirse; (*dress etc*) caer, sentar; (*for painter*) posar ▷ *vt* (*exam*) presentarse a; **that jacket ~s well** esa chaqueta sienta bien; **to ~ on a committee** ser miembro de una comisión *or* un comité; **sit about, sit around** *vi* holgazanear; **sit back** *vi* (*in seat*) recostarse; **sit down** *vi* sentarse; **to be ~ting down** estar sentado; **sit in on** *vt fus*: **to ~ in on a discussion** asistir a una discusión; **sit on** *vt fus* (*jury, committee*) ser miembro de, formar parte de; **sit up** *vi* incorporarse; (*not go to bed*) no acostarse
sitcom ['sɪtkɔm] *n abbr* (*TV*: = *situation comedy*) telecomedia
site [saɪt] *n* sitio; (*also*: **building ~**) solar *m* ▷ *vt* situar
sit-in ['sɪtɪn] *n* (*demonstration*) sentada *f*
sitting ['sɪtɪŋ] *n* (*of assembly etc*) sesión *f*; (*in canteen*) turno
sitting room *n* sala de estar
situated ['sɪtjueɪtɪd] *adj* situado, ubicado (*LAm*)
situation [sɪtju'eɪʃən] *n* situación *f*; **"~s vacant"** (*Brit*) "ofertas de trabajo"
situation comedy *n* (*TV, Radio*) serie *f* cómica, comedia de situación
six [sɪks] *num* seis
sixteen [sɪks'ti:n] *num* dieciséis
sixteenth [sɪks'ti:nθ] *adj* decimosexto
sixth [sɪksθ] *adj* sexto; **the upper/lower ~** (*Scol*) el séptimo/sexto año
sixth form *n* (*Brit*) clase *f* de alumnos del sexto año (*de 16 a 18 años de edad*)
sixth-form college *n* instituto *m* para alumnos de 16 a 18 años
sixtieth ['sɪkstɪɪθ] *adj* sexagésimo
sixty ['sɪkstɪ] *num* sesenta
size [saɪz] *n* (*gen*) tamaño; (*extent*) extensión *f*; (*of clothing*) talla; (*of shoes*) número; **I take ~ 5 shoes** calzo el número cinco; **I take ~ 14** mi talla es la 42; **I'd like the small/large ~** (*of soap powder etc*) quisiera el tamaño pequeño/grande; **size up** *vt* formarse una idea de
sizeable ['saɪzəbl] *adj* importante, considerable
sizzle ['sɪzl] *vi* crepitar
skate [skeɪt] *n* patín *m*; (*fish*) *pl inv* raya ▷ *vi* patinar; **skate over, skate round** *vt fus* (*problem, issue*) pasar por alto
skateboard ['skeɪtbɔ:d] *n* monopatín *m*
skateboarding *n* monopatín *m*
skater ['skeɪtə^r] *n* patinador(a) *m(f)*
skating ['skeɪtɪŋ] *n* patinaje *m*; **figure ~** patinaje *m* artístico
skating rink *n* pista de patinaje
skeleton ['skɛlɪtn] *n* esqueleto; (*Tech*) armazón *m*; (*outline*) esquema *m*
skeleton staff *n* personal *m* reducido
skeptic *etc* ['skɛptɪk] (*US*) = **sceptic** *etc*
sketch [skɛtʃ] *n* (*drawing*) dibujo; (*outline*) esbozo, bosquejo; (*Theat*) pieza corta, sketch *m* ▷ *vt* dibujar; (*plan etc*: *also*: **~ out**) esbozar
sketch book *n* bloc *m* de dibujo
sketchy ['skɛtʃɪ] *adj* incompleto
skewer ['skju:ə^r] *n* broqueta
ski [ski:] *n* esquí *m* ▷ *vi* esquiar
ski boot *n* bota de esquí
skid [skɪd] *n* patinazo ▷ *vi* patinar; **to go into a ~** comenzar a patinar
skier ['ski:ə^r] *n* esquiador(a) *m(f)*
skiing ['ski:ɪŋ] *n* esquí *m*; **to go ~** practicar el esquí, (ir a) esquiar
ski jump *n* pista para salto de esquí
skilful, skillful (*US*) ['skɪlful] *adj* diestro, experto
ski lift *n* telesilla *m*, telesquí *m*
skill [skɪl] *n* destreza, pericia; (*technique*) arte *m*, técnica; **there's a certain ~ to doing it** se necesita cierta habilidad para hacerlo
skilled [skɪld] *adj* hábil, diestro; (*worker*) cualificado
skillful ['skɪlful] (*US*) = **skilful**
skim [skɪm] *vt* (*milk*) desnatar; (*glide over*) rozar, rasar ▷ *vi*: **to ~ through** (*book*) hojear
skimmed milk [skɪmd] *n* leche *f* desnatada *or* descremada
skimp [skɪmp] *vt* (*work*) chapucear; (*cloth etc*) escatimar; **to ~ on** (*material etc*) economizar; (*work*) escatimar
skimpy ['skɪmpɪ] *adj* (*meagre*) escaso; (*skirt*) muy corto
skin [skɪn] *n* (*gen*) piel *f*; (*complexion*) cutis *m*; (*of fruit, vegetable*) piel *f*, cáscara; (*crust*: *on pudding, paint*) nata ▷ *vt* (*fruit etc*) pelar; (*animal*) despellejar; **wet** *or* **soaked to the ~** calado hasta los huesos
skin cancer *n* cáncer *m* de piel
skin-deep ['skɪn'di:p] *adj* superficial
skin diving *n* buceo
skinhead ['skɪnhɛd] *n* cabeza *m/f* rapada, skin(head) *m/f*
skinny ['skɪnɪ] *adj* flaco, magro
skintight ['skɪntaɪt] *adj* (*dress etc*) muy ajustado
skip [skɪp] *n* brinco, salto; (*container*) contenedor *m* ▷ *vi* brincar; (*with rope*) saltar a la comba ▷ *vt* (*pass over*) omitir, saltarse
ski pants *npl* pantalones *mpl* de esquí
ski pass *n* forfait *m* (de esquí)
ski pole *n* bastón *m* de esquiar
skipper ['skɪpə^r] *n* (*Naut, Sport*) capitán *m*
skipping rope ['skɪpɪŋ-] *n* (*Brit*) comba, cuerda (de saltar)

skirmish ['skə:mɪʃ] *n* escaramuza
skirt [skə:t] *n* falda, pollera (*LAm*) ▷ *vt* (*surround*) ceñir, rodear; (*go round*) ladear
skirting board ['skə:tɪŋ-] *n* (*Brit*) rodapié *m*
ski slope *n* pista de esquí
ski suit *n* traje *m* de esquiar
skittle ['skɪtl] *n* bolo; **~s** (*game*) boliche *m*
skive [skaɪv] *vi* (*Brit*: *inf*) gandulear
skulk [skʌlk] *vi* esconderse
skull [skʌl] *n* calavera; (*Anat*) cráneo
skunk [skʌŋk] *n* mofeta
sky [skaɪ] *n* cielo; **to praise sb to the skies** poner a algn por las nubes
skydiving ['skaɪdaɪvɪŋ] *n* paracaidismo acrobático
sky-high ['skaɪ'haɪ] *adj* (*inf*) por las nubes ▷ *adv* (*throw*) muy alto; **prices have gone ~** (*inf*) los precios están por las nubes
skylight ['skaɪlaɪt] *n* tragaluz *m*, claraboya
skyline ['skaɪlaɪn] *n* (*horizon*) horizonte *m*; (*of city*) perfil *m*
skyscraper ['skaɪskreɪpə^r] *n* rascacielos *m inv*
slab [slæb] *n* (*stone*) bloque *m*; (*of wood*) tabla, plancha; (*flat*) losa; (*of cake*) trozo; (*of meat, cheese*) tajada, trozo
slack [slæk] *adj* (*loose*) flojo; (*slow*) de poca actividad; (*careless*) descuidado; (*Comm*: *market*) poco activo; (: *demand*) débil; (*period*) bajo; **business is ~** hay poco movimiento en el negocio
slacken ['slækn] (*also*: **~ off**) *vi* aflojarse ▷ *vt* aflojar; (*speed*) disminuir
slacks [slæks] *npl* pantalones *mpl*
slag [slæg] *n* escoria, escombros *mpl*
slag heap *n* escorial *m*, escombrera
slain [sleɪn] *pp of* **slay**
slam [slæm] *vt* (*door*) cerrar de golpe; (*throw*) arrojar (violentamente); (*criticize*) vapulear, vituperar ▷ *vi* cerrarse de golpe; **to ~ the door** dar un portazo
slander ['slɑ:ndə^r] *n* calumnia, difamación *f* ▷ *vt* calumniar, difamar
slang [slæŋ] *n* argot *m*; (*jargon*) jerga
slanging match ['slæŋɪŋ-] *n* (*Brit inf*) bronca gorda
slant [slɑ:nt] *n* sesgo, inclinación *f*; (*fig*) punto de vista, interpretación *f*; **to get a new ~ on sth** obtener un nuevo punto de vista sobre algo
slanted ['slɑ:ntɪd], **slanting** ['slɑ:ntɪŋ] *adj* inclinado
slap [slæp] *n* palmada; (*in face*) bofetada ▷ *vt* dar una palmada/bofetada a; (*paint etc*): **to ~ sth on sth** embadurnar algo con algo ▷ *adv* (*directly*) de lleno
slapdash ['slæpdæʃ] *adj* chapucero
slapstick ['slæpstɪk] *n*: **~ comedy** comedia de payasadas
slap-up ['slæpʌp] *adj*: **a ~ meal** (*Brit*) un banquetazo, una comilona
slash [slæʃ] *vt* acuchillar; (*fig*: *prices*) fulminar
slat [slæt] *n* (*of wood, plastic*) tablilla, listón *m*
slate [sleɪt] *n* pizarra ▷ *vt* (*Brit*: *fig*: *criticize*) vapulear
slaughter ['slɔ:tə^r] *n* (*of animals*) matanza; (*of people*) carnicería ▷ *vt* matar
slaughterhouse ['slɔ:təhaus] *n* matadero
Slav [slɑ:v] *adj* eslavo
slave [sleɪv] *n* esclavo(-a) ▷ *vi* (*also*: **~ away**) trabajar como un negro; **to ~ (away) at sth** trabajar como un negro en algo
slave driver *n* (*inf, pej*) tirano(-a)
slavery ['sleɪvərɪ] *n* esclavitud *f*
slavish ['sleɪvɪʃ] *adj* (*devotion*) de esclavo; (*imitation*) servil
slay (*pt* **slew**, *pp* **slain**) [sleɪ, slu:, sleɪn] *vt* (*literary*) matar
sleazy ['sli:zɪ] *adj* (*fig*: *place*) sórdido
sledge [slɛdʒ], **sled** (*US*) [slɛd] *n* trineo
sledgehammer ['slɛdʒhæmə^r] *n* mazo
sleek [sli:k] *adj* (*shiny*) lustroso
sleep [sli:p] (*pt, pp* **slept**) *n* sueño ▷ *vi* dormir ▷ *vt*: **we can ~ 4** podemos alojar a 4, tenemos cabida para 4; **to go to ~** dormirse; **to have a good night's ~** dormir toda la noche; **to put to ~** (*patient*) dormir; (*animal*: *euphemism*: *kill*) sacrificar; **to ~ lightly** tener el sueño ligero; **to ~ with sb** (*euphemism*) acostarse con algn; **sleep in** *vi* (*oversleep*) quedarse dormido
sleeper ['sli:pə^r] *n* (*person*) durmiente *m/f*; (*Brit Rail*: *on track*) traviesa; (: *train*) coche-cama *m*
sleeping bag ['sli:pɪŋ-] *n* saco de dormir
sleeping car *n* coche-cama *m*
sleeping partner *n* (*Comm*) socio(-a) comanditario(-a)
sleeping pill *n* somnífero
sleepless ['sli:plɪs] *adj*: **a ~ night** una noche en blanco
sleepover ['sli:pəuvə^r] *n*: **we're having a ~ at Fiona's** nos quedamos a dormir en casa de Fiona
sleepwalk ['sli:pwɔ:k] *vi* caminar dormido; (*habitually*) ser sonámbulo
sleepwalker ['sli:pwɔ:kə^r] *n* sonámbulo(-a)
sleepy ['sli:pɪ] *adj* soñoliento; (*place*) soporífero; **to be** *or* **feel ~** tener sueño
sleet [sli:t] *n* aguanieve *f*
sleeve [sli:v] *n* manga; (*Tech*) manguito; (*of record*) funda
sleeveless ['sli:vlɪs] *adj* (*garment*) sin mangas
sleigh [sleɪ] *n* trineo
sleight [slaɪt] *n*: **~ of hand** prestidigitación *f*
slender ['slɛndə^r] *adj* delgado; (*means*) escaso
slept [slɛpt] *pt, pp of* **sleep**
slew [slu:] *vi* (*veer*) torcerse ▷ *pt of* **slay**
slice [slaɪs] *n* (*of meat*) tajada; (*of bread*) rebanada; (*of lemon*) rodaja; (*utensil*) paleta ▷ *vt* cortar, tajar; rebanar; **~d bread** pan *m* de molde
slick [slɪk] *adj* (*skilful*) hábil, diestro; (*clever*) astuto ▷ *n* (*also*: **oil ~**) marea negra
slid [slɪd] *pt, pp of* **slide**

slide [slaɪd] (*pt, pp* **slid**) *n* (*in playground*) tobogán *m*; (*Phot*) diapositiva; (*microscope slide*) portaobjetos *m inv*, plaquilla de vidrio; (*Brit: also:* **hair ~**) pasador *m* ▷ *vt* correr, deslizar ▷ *vi* (*slip*) resbalarse; (*glide*) deslizarse; **to let things ~** (*fig*) dejar que ruede la bola
sliding ['slaɪdɪŋ] *adj* (*door*) corredizo; **~ roof** (*Aut*) techo de corredera
sliding scale *n* escala móvil
slight [slaɪt] *adj* (*slim*) delgado; (*frail*) delicado; (*pain etc*) leve; (*trifling*) insignificante; (*small*) pequeño ▷ *n* desaire *m* ▷ *vt* (*offend*) ofender, desairar; **a ~ improvement** una ligera mejora; **not in the ~est** en absoluto; **there's not the ~est possibility** no hay la menor *or* más mínima posibilidad
slightly ['slaɪtlɪ] *adv* ligeramente, un poco; **~ built** delgado
slim [slɪm] *adj* delgado, esbelto ▷ *vi* adelgazar
slime [slaɪm] *n* limo, cieno
slimming ['slɪmɪŋ] *n* adelgazamiento ▷ *adj* (*diet, pills*) adelgazante
slimy ['slaɪmɪ] *adj* cenagoso; (*covered with mud*) fangoso; (*also fig: person*) adulón, zalamero
sling [slɪŋ] (*pt, pp* **slung** [slʌŋ]) *n* (*Med*) cabestrillo; (*weapon*) honda ▷ *vt* tirar, arrojar; **to have one's arm in a ~** llevar el brazo en cabestrillo
slip [slɪp] *n* (*slide*) resbalón *m*; (*mistake*) descuido; (*underskirt*) combinación *f*; (*of paper*) papelito ▷ *vt* (*slide*) deslizar ▷ *vi* (*slide*) deslizarse; (*stumble*) resbalar(se); (*decline*) decaer; (*move smoothly*): **to ~ into/out of** (*room etc*) colarse en/salirse de; **to let a chance ~ by** dejar escapar la oportunidad; **to ~ sth on/off** ponerse/quitarse algo; **to ~ on a jumper** ponerse un jersey *or* un suéter; **it ~ped from her hand** se la cayó de la mano; **to give sb the ~** dar esquinazo a algn; **wages ~** (*Brit*) hoja del sueldo; **a ~ of the tongue** un lapsus; **slip away** *vi* escabullirse; **slip in** *vt* meter ▷ *vi* meterse, colarse; **slip out** *vi* (*go out*) salir (un momento); **slip up** *vi* (*make mistake*) equivocarse; meter la pata
slipped disc [slɪpt-] *n* vértebra dislocada
slipper ['slɪpə^r] *n* zapatilla, pantufla
slippery ['slɪpərɪ] *adj* resbaladizo
slip road *n* (*Brit*) carretera de acceso
slipshod ['slɪpʃɔd] *adj* descuidado, chapucero
slip-up ['slɪpʌp] *n* (*error*) desliz *m*
slipway ['slɪpweɪ] *n* grada, gradas *fpl*
slit [slɪt] (*pt, pp* **slit**) *n* raja; (*cut*) corte *m* ▷ *vt* rajar, cortar; **to ~ sb's throat** cortarle el pescuezo a algn
slither ['slɪðə^r] *vi* deslizarse
sliver ['slɪvə^r] *n* (*of glass, wood*) astilla; (*of cheese, sausage*) lonja, loncha
slob [slɔb] *n* (*inf*) patán(-ana) *m(f)*, palurdo(-a) *m(f)*
slog [slɔg] (*Brit*) *vi* sudar tinta ▷ *n*: **it was a ~** costó trabajo (hacerlo)
slogan ['sləugən] *n* eslogan *m*, lema *m*
slop [slɔp] *vi* (*also:* **~ over**) derramarse, desbordarse ▷ *vt* derramar, verter
slope [sləup] *n* (*up*) cuesta, pendiente *f*; (*down*) declive *m*; (*side of mountain*) falda, vertiente *f* ▷ *vi*: **to ~ down** estar en declive; **to ~ up** subir (en pendiente)
sloping ['sləupɪŋ] *adj* en pendiente; en declive
sloppy ['slɔpɪ] *adj* (*work*) descuidado; (*appearance*) desaliñado
slot [slɔt] *n* ranura; (*fig: in timetable*) hueco; (*Radio, TV*) espacio ▷ *vt*: **to ~ into** encajar en
sloth [sləuθ] *n* (*vice*) pereza; (*Zool*) oso perezoso
slot machine *n* (*Brit: vending machine*) máquina expendedora; (*for gambling*) máquina tragaperras
slouch [slautʃ] *vi*: **to ~ about, ~ around** (*laze*) gandulear
Slovak ['sləuvæk] *adj* eslovaco ▷ *n* eslovaco(-a); (*Ling*) eslovaco; **the ~ Republic** Eslovaquia
Slovakia [sləu'vækɪə] *n* Eslovaquia
Slovakian [sləu'vækɪən] *adj, n* = **Slovak**
Slovene [sləu'vi:n] *adj* esloveno ▷ *n* esloveno(-a); (*Ling*) esloveno
Slovenia [sləu'vi:nɪə] *n* Eslovenia
Slovenian [sləu'vi:nɪən] *adj, n* = **Slovene**
slovenly ['slʌvənlɪ] *adj* (*dirty*) desaliñado, desaseado; (*careless*) descuidado
slow [sləu] *adj* lento; (*watch*): **to be ~** ir atrasado ▷ *adv* lentamente, despacio ▷ *vt* (*also:* **~ down, ~ up**) retardar; (*engine, machine*) reducir la marcha de ▷ *vi* (*also:* **~ down, ~ up**) ir más despacio; **"~"** (*road sign*) "disminuir la velocidad"; **at a ~ speed** a una velocidad lenta; **the ~ lane** el carril derecho; **business is ~** (*Comm*) hay poca actividad; **my watch is 20 minutes ~** mi reloj lleva 20 minutos de retraso; **bake for two hours in a ~ oven** cocer *or* asar dos horas en el horno a fuego lento; **to be ~ to act/decide** tardar en obrar/decidir; **to go ~** (*driver*) conducir despacio; (*in industrial dispute*) trabajar a ritmo lento
slowly ['sləulɪ] *adv* lentamente, despacio; **to drive ~** conducir despacio; **~ but surely** lento pero seguro
slow motion *n*: **in ~** a cámara lenta
sludge [slʌdʒ] *n* lodo, fango
slug [slʌg] *n* babosa; (*bullet*) posta
sluggish ['slʌgɪʃ] *adj* (*slow*) lento; (*lazy*) perezoso; (*business, market, sales*) inactivo
sluice [slu:s] *n* (*gate*) esclusa; (*channel*) canal *m* ▷ *vt*: **to ~ down** *or* **out** regar
slum [slʌm] *n* (*area*) barrios *mpl* bajos; (*house*) casucha
slump [slʌmp] *n* (*economic*) depresión *f* ▷ *vi* hundirse; (*prices*) caer en picado; **the ~ in the price of copper** la baja repentina del precio del cobre; **he was ~ed over the wheel** se había desplomado encima del volante

S

slung [slʌŋ] *pt, pp of* **sling**
slur [slə:ʳ] *n* calumnia ▷ *vt* calumniar, difamar; (*word*) pronunciar mal; **to cast a ~ on sb** manchar la reputación de algn, difamar a algn
slurp [slə:p] *vt, vi* sorber ruidosamente
slurred [slə:d] *adj* (*pronunciation*) poco claro
slush [slʌʃ] *n* nieve *f* a medio derretir
slush fund *n* fondos *mpl* para sobornar
slut [slʌt] *n* marrana
sly [slaɪ] *adj* (*clever*) astuto; (*nasty*) malicioso
smack [smæk] *n* (*slap*) bofetada; (*blow*) golpe *m* ▷ *vt* dar una manotada a; golpear con la mano ▷ *vi*: **to ~ of** saber a, oler a ▷ *adv*: **it fell ~ in the middle** (*inf*) cayó justo en medio
small [smɔ:l] *adj* pequeño, chico (*LAm*); (*in height*) bajo, chaparro (*LAm*); (*letter*) en minúscula ▷ *n*: **~ of the back** región *f* lumbar; **~ shopkeeper** pequeño(-a) comerciante *m(f)*; **to get** *or* **grow ~er** (*stain, town*) empequeñecer; (*debt, organization, numbers*) reducir, disminuir; **to make ~er** (*amount, income*) reducir; (*garden, object, garment*) achicar
small ads *npl* (*Brit*) anuncios *mpl* por palabras
small business *n* pequeño negocio; **~es** la pequeña empresa
small change *n* suelto, cambio
smallholder ['smɔ:lhəuldəʳ] *n* (*Brit*) granjero(-a), parcelero(-a)
small hours *npl*: **in the ~** a altas horas de la noche
smallpox ['smɔ:lpɔks] *n* viruela
small talk *n* cháchara
smarmy ['smɑ:mɪ] *adj* (*Brit pej*) pelotillero (*fam*)
smart [smɑ:t] *adj* elegante; (*clever*) listo, inteligente; (*quick*) rápido, vivo; (*weapon*) inteligente ▷ *vi* escocer, picar; **the ~ set** la gente de buen tono; **to look ~** estar elegante; **my eyes are ~ing** me pican los ojos
smartcard ['smɑ:tkɑ:d] *n* tarjeta inteligente
smart phone *n* smartphone *m*
smash [smæʃ] *n* (*also*: **~-up**) choque *m*; (*sound*) estrépito ▷ *vt* (*break*) hacer pedazos; (*car etc*) estrellar; (*Sport*: *record*) batir ▷ *vi* hacerse pedazos; (*against wall etc*) estrellarse; **smash up** *vt* (*car*) hacer pedazos; (*room*) destrozar
smashing ['smæʃɪŋ] *adj* (*inf*) estupendo
smattering ['smætərɪŋ] *n*: **a ~ of Spanish** algo de español
smear [smɪəʳ] *n* mancha; (*Med*) frotis *m inv* (cervical); (*insult*) calumnia ▷ *vt* untar; (*fig*) calumniar, difamar; **his hands were ~ed with oil/ink** tenía las manos manchadas de aceite/tinta
smear campaign *n* campaña de calumnias
smear test *n* (*Med*) citología, frotis *m inv* (cervical)
smell [smɛl] (*pt, pp* **smelt** *or* **smelled**) *n* olor *m*; (*sense*) olfato ▷ *vt, vi* oler; **it ~s good/of garlic** huele bien/a ajo
smelly ['smɛlɪ] *adj* maloliente
smelt [smɛlt] *vt* (*ore*) fundir ▷ *pt, pp of* **smell**
smile [smaɪl] *n* sonrisa ▷ *vi* sonreír
smirk [smə:k] *n* sonrisa falsa *or* afectada
smock [smɔk] *n* blusón; (*children's*) babi *m*; (*US*: *overall*) guardapolvo, bata
smog [smɔg] *n* smog *m*
smoke [sməuk] *n* humo ▷ *vi* fumar; (*chimney*) echar humo ▷ *vt* (*cigarettes*) fumar; **to go up in ~** quemarse; (*fig*) quedar en agua de borrajas
smoke alarm *n* detector *m* de humo, alarma contra incendios
smoked [sməukt] *adj* (*bacon, glass*) ahumado
smokeless fuel ['sməuklɪs-] *n* combustible *m* sin humo
smoker ['sməukəʳ] *n* fumador(a) *m(f)*
smoke screen *n* cortina de humo
smoking ['sməukɪŋ] *n*: **"no ~"** "prohibido fumar"; **he's given up ~** ha dejado de fumar
smoky ['sməukɪ] *adj* (*room*) lleno de humo
smolder ['sməuldəʳ] *vi* (*US*) = **smoulder**
smooth [smu:ð] *adj* liso; (*sea*) tranquilo; (*flavour, movement*) suave; (*person*: *pej*) meloso ▷ *vt* alisar; (*also*: **~ out**: *creases*) alisar; (*difficulties*) allanar; **smooth over** *vt*: **to ~ things over** (*fig*) limar las asperezas
smother ['smʌðəʳ] *vt* sofocar; (*repress*) contener
smoulder, smolder (*US*) ['sməuldəʳ] *vi* arder sin llama
SMS *n abbr* (= *short message service*) SMS *m*
SMS message *n* (mensaje *m*) SMS *m*
smudge [smʌdʒ] *n* mancha ▷ *vt* manchar
smug [smʌg] *adj* engreído
smuggle ['smʌgl] *vt* pasar de contrabando; **to ~ in/out** (*goods etc*) meter/sacar de contrabando
smuggler ['smʌgləʳ] *n* contrabandista *m/f*
smuggling ['smʌglɪŋ] *n* contrabando
smutty ['smʌtɪ] *adj* (*fig*) verde, obsceno
snack [snæk] *n* bocado, tentempié *m*; **to have a ~** tomar un bocado
snack bar *n* cafetería
snag [snæg] *n* problema *m*; **to run into** *or* **hit a ~** encontrar inconvenientes, dar con un obstáculo
snail [sneɪl] *n* caracol *m*
snake [sneɪk] *n* (*gen*) serpiente *f*; (*harmless*) culebra; (*poisonous*) víbora
snap [snæp] *n* (*sound*) chasquido; golpe *m* seco; (*photograph*) foto *f* ▷ *adj* (*decision*) instantáneo ▷ *vt* (*fingers etc*) castañetear; (*break*) partir, quebrar; (*photograph*) tomar una foto de ▷ *vi* (*break*) partirse, quebrarse; (*fig*: *person*) contestar bruscamente; **to ~ shut** cerrarse de golpe; **a cold ~** (*of weather*) una ola de frío; **snap at** *vt fus*: **to ~ (at sb)** (*person*) hablar con brusquedad (a algn); (*dog*) intentar morder (a algn); **to ~ one's fingers at sth/sb** (*fig*) burlarse de algo/uno; **snap off** *vi* (*break*) partirse; **snap up** *vt* agarrar

galletas; **have some tea** tómese un té; **there's some milk in the fridge** hay leche en el frigo; **there were some people outside** había algunas personas fuera; **I've got some money, but not much** tengo algo de dinero, pero no mucho
2 (*certain*: *in contrasts*) algunos(-as); **some people say that ...** hay quien dice que ...; **some films were excellent, but most were mediocre** hubo películas excelentes, pero la mayoría fueron mediocres
3 (*unspecified*): **some woman was asking for you** una mujer estuvo preguntando por ti; **some day** algún día; **some day next week** un día de la semana que viene; **he was asking for some book (or other)** pedía no sé qué libro; **in some way or other** de alguna que otra manera
4 (*considerable amount of*) bastante; **some days ago** hace unos cuantos días; **after some time** pasado algún tiempo; **at some length** con mucho detalle
5 (*inf*: *intensive*): **that was some party!** ¡menuda fiesta!
▷ *pron* 1 (*a certain number*): **I've got some** (*books etc*) tengo algunos(-as)
2 (*a certain amount*) algo; **I've got some** (*money, milk*) tengo algo; **would you like some?** (*coffee etc*) ¿quiere un poco?; (*books etc*) ¿quiere alguno?; **could I have some of that cheese?** ¿me puede dar un poco de ese queso?; **I've read some of the book** he leído parte del libro
▷ *adv*: **some 10 people** unas 10 personas, una decena de personas

somebody ['sʌmbədɪ] *pron* alguien; **~ or other** alguien
somehow ['sʌmhau] *adv* de alguna manera; (*for some reason*) por una u otra razón
someone ['sʌmwʌn] *pron* = **somebody**
someplace ['sʌmpleɪs] *adv* (*US*) = **somewhere**
somersault ['sʌməsɔ:lt] *n* (*deliberate*) salto mortal; (*accidental*) vuelco ▷ *vi* dar un salto mortal; dar vuelcos
something ['sʌmθɪŋ] *pron* algo ▷ *adv*: **he's ~ like me** es un poco como yo; **~ to do** algo que hacer; **it's ~ of a problem** es bastante problemático; **would you like ~ to eat/drink?** ¿te gustaría cenar/tomar algo?
sometime ['sʌmtaɪm] *adv* (*in future*) algún día, en algún momento; **~ last month** durante el mes pasado; **I'll finish it ~** lo terminaré un día de éstos
sometimes ['sʌmtaɪmz] *adv* a veces
somewhat ['sʌmwɔt] *adv* algo
somewhere ['sʌmwɛə^r] *adv* (*be*) en alguna parte; (*go*) a alguna parte; **~ else** (*be*) en otra parte; (*go*) a otra parte
son [sʌn] *n* hijo
sonar ['səunɑ:^r] *n* sonar *m*
song [sɔŋ] *n* canción *f*
songwriter ['sɔŋraɪtə^r] *n* compositor(a) *m(f)* de canciones
sonic ['sɔnɪk] *adj* (*boom*) sónico
son-in-law ['sʌnɪnlɔ:] *n* yerno
sonnet ['sɔnɪt] *n* soneto
sonny ['sʌnɪ] *n* (*inf*) hijo
soon [su:n] *adv* pronto, dentro de poco; **~ afterwards** poco después; **very/quite ~** muy/bastante pronto; **how ~ can you be ready?** ¿cuánto tardas en prepararte?; **it's too ~ to tell** es demasiado pronto para saber; **see you ~!** ¡hasta pronto!; *see also* **as**
sooner ['su:nə^r] *adv* (*time*) antes, más temprano; **I would ~ do that** preferiría hacer eso; **~ or later** tarde o temprano; **no ~ said than done** dicho y hecho; **the ~ the better** cuanto antes mejor; **no ~ had we left than ...** apenas nos habíamos marchado cuando ...
soot [sut] *n* hollín *m*
soothe [su:ð] *vt* tranquilizar; (*pain*) aliviar
sophisticated [sə'fɪstɪkeɪtɪd] *adj* sofisticado
sophomore ['sɔfəmɔ:^r] *n* (*US*) estudiante *m/f* de segundo año
sopping ['sɔpɪŋ] *adj*: **~ (wet)** empapado
soppy ['sɔpɪ] *adj* (*pej*) bobo, tonto
soprano [sə'prɑ:nəu] *n* soprano *f*
sorbet ['sɔ:beɪ] *n* sorbete *m*
sorcerer ['sɔ:sərə^r] *n* hechicero
sordid ['sɔ:dɪd] *adj* (*place etc*) sórdido; (*motive etc*) mezquino
sore [sɔ:^r] *adj* (*painful*) doloroso, que duele; (*offended*) resentido ▷ *n* llaga; **~ throat** dolor *m* de garganta; **my eyes are ~, I have ~ eyes** me duelen los ojos; **it's a ~ point** es un asunto delicado *or* espinoso
sorely *adv*: **I am ~ tempted to (do it)** estoy muy tentado a (hacerlo)
sorrow ['sɔrəu] *n* pena, dolor *m*
sorry ['sɔrɪ] *adj* (*regretful*) arrepentido; (*condition, excuse*) lastimoso; (*sight, failure*) triste; **~!** ¡perdón!, ¡perdone!; **~?** ¿cómo?; **I am ~** lo siento; **I feel ~ for him** me da lástima *or* pena; **I'm ~ to hear that ...** siento saber que ...; **to be ~ about sth** lamentar algo
sort [sɔ:t] *n* clase *f*, género, tipo; (*make*: *of coffee, car etc*) marca ▷ *vt* (*also*: **~ out**) (*papers*) clasificar; (*organize*) ordenar, organizar; (*resolve*: *problem, situation etc*) arreglar, solucionar; (*Comput*) clasificar; **what ~ do you want?** (*make*) ¿qué marca quieres?; **what ~ of car?** ¿qué tipo de coche?; **I shall do nothing of the ~** no pienso hacer nada parecido; **it's ~ of awkward** (*inf*) es bastante difícil
sorting office ['sɔ:tɪŋ-] *n* oficina de clasificación del correo
SOS *n* SOS *m*
so-so ['səusəu] *adv* regular, así así
soufflé ['su:fleɪ] *n* suflé *m*

sought [sɔːt] *pt, pp of* **seek**
soul [səul] *n* alma *f*; **God rest his ~** Dios le reciba en su seno *or* en su gloria; **I didn't see a ~** no vi a nadie; **the poor ~ had nowhere to sleep** el pobre no tenía dónde dormir
soulful [ˈsəulful] *adj* lleno de sentimiento
sound [saund] *adj* (*healthy*) sano; (*safe, not damaged*) en buen estado; (*valid: argument, policy, claim*) válido; (*: move*) acertado; (*dependable: person*) de fiar; (*sensible*) sensato, razonable ▷ *adv*: **~ asleep** profundamente dormido ▷ *n* (*noise*) sonido, ruido; (*volume: on TV etc*) volumen *m*; (*Geo*) estrecho ▷ *vt* (*alarm*) sonar; (*also*: **~ out**: *opinions*) consultar, sondear ▷ *vi* sonar, resonar; (*fig: seem*) parecer; **to ~ like** sonar a; **to be of ~ mind** estar en su sano juicio; **I don't like the ~ of it** no me gusta nada; **it ~s as if ...** parece que ...; **sound off** *vi* (*inf*): **to ~ off (about)** (*give one's opinions*) despotricar (contra)
sound barrier *n* barrera del sonido
sound bite *n* cita jugosa
sound effects *npl* efectos *mpl* sonoros
soundly [ˈsaundlɪ] *adv* (*sleep*) profundamente; (*beat*) completamente
soundproof [ˈsaundpruːf] *adj* insonorizado
sound system *n* equipo de sonido
soundtrack [ˈsaundtræk] *n* (*of film*) banda sonora
soup [suːp] *n* (*thick*) sopa; (*thin*) caldo; **in the ~** (*fig*) en apuros
soup plate *n* plato sopero
soupspoon [ˈsuːpspuːn] *n* cuchara sopera
sour [ˈsauəʳ] *adj* agrio; (*milk*) cortado; **it's just ~ grapes!** (*fig*) ¡pura envidia!, ¡están verdes!; **to go** *or* **turn ~** (*milk*) cortarse; (*wine*) agriarse; (*fig: relationship*) agriarse; (*: plans*) irse a pique
source [sɔːs] *n* fuente *f*; **I have it from a reliable ~ that ...** sé de fuente fidedigna que ...
south [sauθ] *n* sur *m* ▷ *adj* del sur ▷ *adv* al sur, hacia el sur; **(to the) ~ of** al sur de; **the S~ of France** el Sur de Francia; **to travel ~** viajar hacia el sur
South Africa *n* Sudáfrica
South African *adj, n* sudafricano(-a) *m(f)*
South America *n* América del Sur, Sudamérica
South American *adj, n* sudamericano(-a) *m(f)*
southbound [ˈsauθbaund] *adj* (con) rumbo al sur
south-east [sauθˈiːst] *n* sudeste *m* ▷ *adj* (*counties etc*) (del) sudeste
southeastern [sauθˈiːstən] *adj* sureste, del sureste
southerly [ˈsʌðəlɪ] *adj* sur; (*from the south*) del sur
southern [ˈsʌðən] *adj* del sur, meridional; **the ~ hemisphere** el hemisferio sur
South Korea *n* Corea del Sur
South Pole *n* Polo Sur
southward [ˈsauθwəd], **southwards** [ˈsauθwədz] *adv* hacia el sur
south-west [sauθˈwɛst] *n* suroeste *m*
southwestern [sauθˈwɛstən] *adj* suroeste
souvenir [suːvəˈnɪəʳ] *n* recuerdo
sovereign [ˈsɔvrɪn] *adj, n* soberano(-a) *m(f)*
soviet [ˈsəuvɪət] *adj* soviético
sow [sau] *n* cerda, puerca
sow [səu] (*pt* **sowed**, *pp* **sown** [səun]) *vt* sembrar
soya [ˈsɔɪə], **soy** (*US*) [sɔɪ] *n* soja
sozzled [ˈsɔzld] *adj* (*Brit inf*) mamado
spa [spɑː] *n* balneario
space [speɪs] *n* espacio; (*room*) sitio ▷ *vt* (*also*: **~ out**) espaciar; **to clear a ~ for sth** hacer sitio para algo; **in a confined ~** en un espacio restringido; **in a short ~ of time** en poco *or* un corto espacio de tiempo; **(with)in the ~ of an hour/three generations** en el espacio de una hora/ tres generaciones
spacecraft [ˈspeɪskrɑːft] *n* nave *f* espacial, astronave *f*
spaceman [ˈspeɪsmæn] *n* astronauta *m*, cosmonauta *m*
spaceship [ˈspeɪsʃɪp] *n* = **spacecraft**
spacesuit [ˈspeɪssuːt] *n* traje *m* espacial
spacewoman [ˈspeɪswumən] *n* astronauta, cosmonauta
spacing [ˈspeɪsɪŋ] *n* espacio
spacious [ˈspeɪʃəs] *adj* amplio
spade [speɪd] *n* (*tool*) pala; **spades** *npl* (*Cards: British*) picas *fpl*; (*Spanish*) espadas *fpl*
spaghetti [spəˈgɛtɪ] *n* espaguetis *mpl*
Spain [speɪn] *n* España
spam [spæm] *n* (*junk email*) correo basura
span [spæn] *n* (*of bird, plane*) envergadura; (*of hand*) palmo; (*of arch*) luz *f*; (*in time*) lapso ▷ *vt* extenderse sobre, cruzar; (*fig*) abarcar
Spaniard [ˈspænjəd] *n* español(a) *m(f)*
spaniel [ˈspænjəl] *n* perro de aguas
Spanish [ˈspænɪʃ] *adj* español(a) ▷ *n* (*Ling*) español *m*, castellano; **the Spanish** *npl* (*people*) los españoles; **~ omelette** tortilla española *or* de patata
spank [spæŋk] *vt* zurrar, dar unos azotes a
spanner [ˈspænəʳ] *n* (*Brit*) llave *f* inglesa
spar [spɑːʳ] *n* palo, verga ▷ *vi* (*Boxing*) entrenarse (en el boxeo)
spare [spɛəʳ] *adj* de reserva; (*surplus*) sobrante, de más ▷ *n* (*part*) pieza de repuesto ▷ *vt* (*do without*) pasarse sin; (*afford to give*) tener de sobra; (*refrain from hurting*) perdonar; (*details etc*) ahorrar; **to ~** (*surplus*) sobrante, de sobra; **there are two going ~** sobran *or* quedan dos; **to ~ no expense** no escatimar gastos; **can you ~ (me) £10?** ¿puedes prestarme *or* darme 10 libras?; **can you ~ the time?** ¿tienes tiempo?; **I've a few minutes to ~** tengo unos minutos libres; **there is no time to ~** no hay tiempo que perder
spare part *n* pieza de repuesto

spare room *n* cuarto de los invitados
spare time *n* ratos *mpl* de ocio, tiempo libre
spare tyre, spare tire (*US*) *n* (*Aut*) neumático *or* llanta (*LAm*) de recambio
spare wheel *n* (*Aut*) rueda de recambio
sparing ['spɛərɪŋ] *adj*: **to be ~ with** ser parco en
sparingly ['spɛərɪŋlɪ] *adv* escasamente
spark [spɑːk] *n* chispa; (*fig*) chispazo
sparking plug ['spɑːk(ɪŋ)-] *n* = **spark plug**
sparkle ['spɑːkl] *n* centelleo, destello ▷ *vi* centellear; (*shine*) relucir, brillar
sparkler ['spɑːkləʳ] *n* bengala
sparkling ['spɑːklɪŋ] *adj* centelleante; (*wine*) espumoso
spark plug *n* bujía
sparring partner ['spɑːrɪŋ-] *n* sparring *m*; (*fig*) contrincante *m/f*
sparrow ['spærəu] *n* gorrión *m*
sparse [spɑːs] *adj* esparcido, escaso
spartan ['spɑːtən] *adj* (*fig*) espartano
spasm ['spæzəm] *n* (*Med*) espasmo; (*fig*) arranque *m*, ataque *m*
spasmodic [spæz'mɔdɪk] *adj* espasmódico
spastic ['spæstɪk] *n* espástico(-a)
spat [spæt] *pt, pp of* **spit** ▷ *n* (*US*) riña
spate [speɪt] *n* (*fig*): **~ of** torrente *m* de; **in ~** (*river*) crecido
spatter ['spætəʳ] *vt*: **to ~ with** salpicar de
spatula ['spætjulə] *n* espátula
spawn [spɔːn] *vt* (*pej*) engendrar ▷ *vi* desovar, frezar ▷ *n* huevas *fpl*
speak (*pt* **spoke**, *pp* **spoken**) [spiːk, spəuk, 'spəukn] *vt* (*language*) hablar; (*truth*) decir ▷ *vi* hablar; (*make a speech*) intervenir; **to ~ one's mind** hablar claro *or* con franqueza; **to ~ to sb/of** *or* **about sth** hablar con algn/de *or* sobre algo; **to ~ at a conference/in a debate** hablar en un congreso/un debate; **he has no money to ~ of** no tiene mucho dinero que digamos; **~ing!** ¡al habla!; **~ up!** ¡habla más alto!; **speak for** *vt fus*: **to ~ for sb** hablar por *or* en nombre de algn; **that picture is already spoken for** (*in shop*) ese cuadro está reservado
speaker ['spiːkəʳ] *n* (*in public*) orador(a) *m(f)*; (*also*: **loud~**) altavoz *m*; (*for stereo etc*) bafle *m*; (*Pol*): **the S~** (*Brit*) *el Presidente de la Cámara de los Comunes*; (*US*) *el Presidente del Congreso*; **are you a Welsh ~?** ¿habla Vd galés?
spear [spɪəʳ] *n* lanza; (*for fishing*) arpón *m* ▷ *vt* alancear; arponear
spearhead ['spɪəhɛd] *vt* (*attack etc*) encabezar ▷ *n* punta de lanza, vanguardia
spec [spɛk] *n* (*inf*): **on ~** por si acaso; **to buy on ~** arriesgarse a comprar
special ['spɛʃl] *adj* especial; (*edition etc*) extraordinario; (*delivery*) urgente ▷ *n* (*train*) tren *m* especial; **nothing ~** nada de particular, nada extraordinario
special delivery *n* (*Post*): **by ~** por entrega urgente
special effects *npl* (*Cine*) efectos *mpl* especiales
specialist ['spɛʃəlɪst] *n* especialista *m/f*; **a heart ~** (*Med*) un(-a) especialista del corazón
speciality [spɛʃɪ'ælɪtɪ], **specialty** (*US*) ['spɛʃəltɪ] *n* especialidad *f*
specialize ['spɛʃəlaɪz] *vi*: **to ~ (in)** especializarse (en)
specially ['spɛʃlɪ] *adv* especialmente
special offer *n* (*Comm*) oferta especial
special school *n* (*Brit*) colegio *m* de educación especial
specialty ['spɛʃəltɪ] *n* (*US*) = **speciality**
species ['spiːʃiːz] *n* especie *f*
specific [spə'sɪfɪk] *adj* específico
specifically [spə'sɪfɪklɪ] *adv* (*explicitly*: *state, warn*) específicamente, expresamente; (*especially*: *design, intend*) especialmente
specification [spɛsɪfɪ'keɪʃən] *n* especificación *f*; **specifications** *npl* (*plan*) presupuesto *sg*; (*of car, machine*) descripción *f* técnica; (*for building*) plan *msg* detallado
specify ['spɛsɪfaɪ] *vt, vi* especificar, precisar; **unless otherwise specified** salvo indicaciones contrarias
specimen ['spɛsɪmən] *n* ejemplar *m*; (*Med*: *of urine*) espécimen *m*; (: *of blood*) muestra
speck [spɛk] *n* grano, mota
speckled ['spɛkld] *adj* moteado
specs [spɛks] *npl* (*inf*) gafas *fpl* (*Sp*), anteojos *mpl*
spectacle ['spɛktəkl] *n* espectáculo; **spectacles** *npl* (*Brit*: *glasses*) gafas *fpl* (*Sp*), anteojos *mpl*
spectacular [spɛk'tækjuləʳ] *adj* espectacular; (*success*) impresionante
spectator [spɛk'teɪtəʳ] *n* espectador(a) *m(f)*
spectator sport *n* deporte *m* espectáculo
spectrum (*pl* **spectra**) ['spɛktrəm, -trə] *n* espectro
speculate ['spɛkjuleɪt] *vi* especular; (*try to guess*): **to ~ about** especular sobre
speculation [spɛkju'leɪʃən] *n* especulación *f*
sped [spɛd] *pt, pp of* **speed**
speech [spiːtʃ] *n* (*faculty*) habla; (*formal talk*) discurso; (*words*) palabras *fpl*; (*manner of speaking*) forma de hablar; (*language*) idioma *m*, lenguaje *m*
speechless ['spiːtʃlɪs] *adj* mudo, estupefacto
speed [spiːd] (*pt, pp* **sped** [spɛd]) *n* (*also Aut, Tech*: *gear*) velocidad *f*; (*haste*) prisa; (*promptness*) rapidez *f* ▷ *vi* (*Aut*: *exceed speed limit*) conducir con exceso de velocidad; **at full** *or* **top ~** a máxima velocidad; **at a ~ of 70 km/h** a una velocidad de 70 km por hora; **at ~** a gran velocidad; **a five-~ gearbox** una caja de cambios de cinco velocidades; **shorthand/typing ~** rapidez *f* en taquigrafía/mecanografía; **the years sped by** los años pasaron volando; **speed up** ▷ *vi* acelerarse ▷ *vt* acelerar
speedboat ['spiːdbəut] *n* lancha motora

S

speed camera *n* cámara de control de velocidad
speedily ['spi:dɪlɪ] *adv* rápido, rápidamente
speeding ['spi:dɪŋ] *n* (*Aut*) exceso de velocidad
speed limit *n* límite *m* de velocidad, velocidad *f* máxima
speedometer [spɪ'dɔmɪtə^r] *n* velocímetro
speed trap *n* (*Aut*) control *m* de velocidades
speedway ['spi:dweɪ] *n* (*Sport*) pista de carrera
speedy ['spi:dɪ] *adj* (*fast*) veloz, rápido; (*prompt*) pronto
spell [spɛl] (*pt, pp* **spelt** *or* **spelled** [spɛlt, spɛld]) *n* (*also*: **magic ~**) encanto, hechizo; (*period of time*) rato, período; (*turn*) turno ▷ *vt* deletrear; (*fig*) anunciar, presagiar; **to cast a ~ on sb** hechizar a algn; **he can't ~** no sabe escribir bien, comete faltas de ortografía; **can you ~ it for me?** ¿cómo se deletrea *or* se escribe?; **how do you ~ your name?** ¿cómo se escribe tu nombre?; **spell out** *vt* (*explain*): **to ~ sth out for sb** explicar algo a algn en detalle
spellbound ['spɛlbaund] *adj* embelesado, hechizado
spellchecker *n* (*Comput*) corrector *m* (ortográfico)
spelling ['spɛlɪŋ] *n* ortografía
spelling mistake *n* falta de ortografía
spelt [spɛlt] *pt, pp of* **spell**
spend (*pt, pp* **spent**) [spɛnd, spɛnt] *vt* (*money*) gastar; (*time*) pasar; (*life*) dedicar; **to ~ time/money/effort on sth** gastar tiempo/dinero/energías en algo
spending ['spɛndɪŋ] *n*: **government ~** gastos *mpl* del gobierno
spending money *n* dinero para gastos
spendthrift ['spɛndθrɪft] *n* derrochador(a) *m(f)* manirroto(-a)
spent [spɛnt] *pt, pp of* **spend** ▷ *adj* (*cartridge, bullets, match*) usado
sperm [spə:m] *n* esperma
sperm bank *n* banco de esperma
spew [spju:] *vt* vomitar, arrojar
sphere [sfɪə^r] *n* esfera
spice [spaɪs] *n* especia ▷ *vt* especiar
spick-and-span ['spɪkən'spæn] *adj* impecable
spicy ['spaɪsɪ] *adj* picante
spider ['spaɪdə^r] *n* araña
spider's web *n* telaraña
spiel [ʃpi:l] *n* (*inf*) rollo
spike [spaɪk] *n* (*point*) punta; (*Zool*) pincho, púa; (*Bot*) espiga; (*Elec*) pico parásito ▷ *vt*: **to ~ a quote** cancelar una cita; **spikes** *npl* (*Sport*) zapatillas *fpl* con clavos
spill (*pt, pp* **spilt** *or* **spilled**) [spɪl, spɪlt, spɪld] *vt* derramar, verter; (*blood*) derramar ▷ *vi* derramarse; **to ~ the beans** (*inf*) descubrir el pastel; **spill out** *vi* derramarse, desparramarse; **spill over** *vi* desbordarse
spillage ['spɪlɪdʒ] *n* (*event*) derrame *m*; (*substance*) vertidos
spin [spɪn] (*pt, pp* **spun**) *n* (*revolution of wheel*) vuelta, revolución *f*; (*Aviat*) barrena; (*trip in car*) paseo (en coche) ▷ *vt* (*wool etc*) hilar; (*wheel*) girar ▷ *vi* girar, dar vueltas; **the car spun out of control** el coche se descontroló y empezó a dar vueltas; **spin out** *vt* alargar, prolongar
spina bifida ['spaɪnə'bɪfɪdə] *n* espina *f* bífida
spinach ['spɪnɪtʃ] *n* espinacas *fpl*
spinal ['spaɪnl] *adj* espinal
spinal cord *n* médula espinal
spindly ['spɪndlɪ] *adj* (*leg*) zanquivano
spin doctor *n* (*inf*) *informador(a) parcial al servicio de un partido político*
spin-dryer [spɪn'draɪə^r] *n* (*Brit*) secadora centrífuga
spine [spaɪn] *n* espinazo, columna vertebral; (*thorn*) espina
spineless ['spaɪnlɪs] *adj* (*fig*) débil, flojo
spinning ['spɪnɪŋ] *n* (*of thread*) hilado; (*art*) hilandería; (*Sport*) spinning *m*
spinning top *n* peonza
spinning wheel *n* rueca, torno de hilar
spin-off ['spɪnɔf] *n* derivado, producto secundario
spinster ['spɪnstə^r] *n* soltera; (*pej*) solterona
spiral ['spaɪərl] *n* espiral *f* ▷ *adj* en espiral ▷ *vi* (*prices*) dispararse; **the inflationary ~** la espiral inflacionista
spiral staircase *n* escalera de caracol
spire ['spaɪə^r] *n* aguja, chapitel *m*
spirit ['spɪrɪt] *n* (*soul*) alma *f*; (*ghost*) fantasma *m*; (*attitude*) espíritu *m*; (*courage*) valor *m*, ánimo; **spirits** *npl* (*drink*) alcohol *msg*, bebidas *fpl* alcohólicas; **in good ~s** alegre, de buen ánimo; **Holy S~** Espíritu *m* Santo; **community ~**, **public ~** civismo
spirited ['spɪrɪtɪd] *adj* enérgico, vigoroso
spirit level *n* nivel *m* de aire
spiritual ['spɪrɪtjuəl] *adj* espiritual ▷ *n* (*also*: **Negro ~**) canción *f* religiosa, espiritual *m*
spiritualism ['spɪrɪtjuəlɪzəm] *n* espiritualismo
spit [spɪt] (*pt, pp* **spat** [spæt]) *n* (*for roasting*) asador *m*, espetón *m*; (*spittle*) esputo, escupitajo; (*saliva*) saliva ▷ *vi* escupir; (*sound*) chisporrotear
spite [spaɪt] *n* rencor *m*, ojeriza ▷ *vt* fastidiar; **in ~ of** a pesar de, pese a
spiteful ['spaɪtful] *adj* rencoroso, malévolo
spittle ['spɪtl] *n* saliva, baba
splash [splæʃ] *n* (*sound*) chapoteo; (*of colour*) mancha ▷ *vt* salpicar de ▷ *vi* (*also*: **~ about**) chapotear; **to ~ paint on the floor** manchar el suelo de pintura; **splash out** (*inf*) *vi* (*Brit*) derrochar dinero
spleen [spli:n] *n* (*Anat*) bazo
splendid ['splɛndɪd] *adj* espléndido
splint [splɪnt] *n* tablilla
splinter ['splɪntə^r] *n* astilla; (*in finger*) espigón *m* ▷ *vi* astillarse, hacer astillas

split [splɪt] (*pt, pp* **split**) *n* hendedura, raja; (*fig*) división *f*; (*Pol*) escisión *f* ▷ *vt* partir, rajar; (*party*) dividir; (*work, profits*) repartir ▷ *vi* (*divide*) dividirse, escindirse; **to ~ the difference** partir la diferencia; **to do the ~s** hacer el spagat; **to ~ sth down the middle** (*also fig*) dividir algo en dos; **split up** *vi* (*couple*) separarse, romper; (*meeting*) acabarse
split personality *n* doble personalidad *f*
split second *n* fracción *f* de segundo
splutter ['splʌtəʳ] *vi* chisporrotear; (*person*) balbucear
spoil (*pt, pp* **spoilt** *or* **spoiled**) [spɔɪl, spɔɪlt, spɔɪld] *vt* (*damage*) dañar; (*ruin*) estropear, echar a perder; (*child*) mimar, consentir; (*ballot paper*) invalidar ▷ *vi*: **to be ~ing for a fight** estar con ganas de lucha, andar con ganas de pelea
spoiled [spɔɪld] *adj* (*US: food: bad*) pasado, malo; (*milk*) cortado
spoils [spɔɪlz] *npl* despojo *sg*, botín *msg*
spoilsport ['spɔɪlspɔ:t] *n* aguafiestas *m inv*
spoilt [spɔɪlt] *pt, pp of* **spoil** ▷ *adj* (*child*) mimado, consentido; (*ballot paper*) invalidado
spoke [spəuk] *pt of* **speak** ▷ *n* rayo, radio
spoken ['spəukn] *pp of* **speak**
spokesman ['spəuksmən] *n* portavoz *m*, vocero (*LAm*)
spokesperson ['spəukspə:sn] *n* portavoz *m/f*, vocero(-a) (*LAm*)
spokeswoman ['spəukswumən] *n* portavoz *f*, vocera (*LAm*)
sponge [spʌndʒ] *n* esponja; (*Culin: also:* **~ cake**) bizcocho ▷ *vt* (*wash*) lavar con esponja ▷ *vi*: **to ~ on** *or* (*US*) **off sb** vivir a costa de algn
sponge bag *n* (*Brit*) neceser *m*
sponsor ['spɔnsəʳ] *n* (*Radio, TV*) patrocinador(a) *m(f)*; (*for membership*) padrino/madrina; (*Comm*) fiador(a) *m(f)*, avalador(a) *m(f)* ▷ *vt* patrocinar; apadrinar; (*parliamentary bill*) apoyar, respaldar; (*idea etc*) presentar, promover; **I ~ed him at 3p a mile** (*in fund-raising race*) me apunté para darle 3 peniques la milla
sponsorship ['spɔnsəʃɪp] *n* patrocinio
spontaneous [spɔn'teɪnɪəs] *adj* espontáneo
spooky ['spu:kɪ] *adj* (*inf: place, atmosphere*) espeluznante, horripilante
spool [spu:l] *n* carrete *m*; (*of sewing machine*) canilla
spoon [spu:n] *n* cuchara
spoon-feed ['spu:nfi:d] *vt* dar de comer con cuchara a; (*fig*) dárselo todo mascado a
spoonful ['spu:nful] *n* cucharada
sporadic [spə'rædɪk] *adj* esporádico
sport [spɔ:t] *n* deporte *m*; (*person*): **to be a good ~** ser muy majo; (*amusement*) juego, diversión *f*; **indoor/outdoor ~s** deportes *mpl* en sala cubierta/al aire libre; **to say sth in ~** decir algo en broma
sporting ['spɔ:tɪŋ] *adj* deportivo; **to give sb a ~ chance** darle a algn su oportunidad
sport jacket *n* (*US*) = **sports jacket**
sports car *n* coche *m* sport
sports centre *n* (*Brit*) polideportivo
sports ground *n* campo de deportes, centro deportivo
sports jacket, sport jacket (*US*) *n* chaqueta deportiva
sportsman ['spɔ:tsmən] *n* deportista *m*
sportsmanship ['spɔ:tsmənʃɪp] *n* deportividad *f*
sports utility vehicle *n* todoterreno *m inv*
sportswear ['spɔ:tswɛəʳ] *n* ropa de deporte
sportswoman ['spɔ:tswumən] *n* deportista
sporty ['spɔ:tɪ] *adj* deportivo
spot [spɔt] *n* sitio, lugar *m*; (*dot: on pattern*) punto, mancha; (*pimple*) grano; (*also:* **advertising ~**) spot *m*; (*small amount*): **a ~ of** un poquito de ▷ *vt* (*notice*) notar, observar ▷ *adj* (*Comm*) inmediatamente efectivo; **on the ~** en el acto; (*in difficulty*) en un aprieto; **to do sth on the ~** hacer algo en el acto; **to put sb on the ~** poner a algn en un apuro
spot check *n* reconocimiento rápido
spotless ['spɔtlɪs] *adj* (*clean*) inmaculado; (*reputation*) intachable
spotlight ['spɔtlaɪt] *n* foco, reflector *m*; (*Aut*) faro auxiliar
spot-on [spɔt'ɔn] *adj* (*Brit inf*) exacto
spotted ['spɔtɪd] *adj* (*pattern*) de puntos
spotty ['spɔtɪ] *adj* (*face*) con granos
spouse [spauz] *n* cónyuge *m/f*
spout [spaut] *n* (*of jug*) pico; (*pipe*) caño ▷ *vi* chorrear
sprain [spreɪn] *n* torcedura, esguince *m* ▷ *vt*: **to ~ one's ankle** torcerse el tobillo
sprang [spræŋ] *pt of* **spring**
sprawl [sprɔ:l] *vi* tumbarse ▷ *n*: **urban ~** crecimiento urbano descontrolado; **to send sb ~ing** tirar a algn al suelo
spray [spreɪ] *n* rociada; (*of sea*) espuma; (*container*) atomizador *m*; (*of paint*) pistola rociadora; (*of flowers*) ramita ▷ *vt* rociar; (*crops*) regar ▷ *cpd* (*deodorant*) en atomizador
spread [sprɛd] (*pt, pp* **spread**) *n* extensión *f*; (*of idea*) diseminación *f*; (*inf: food*) comilona; (*Press, Typ: two pages*) plana ▷ *vt* extender; diseminar; (*butter*) untar; (*wings, sails*) desplegar; (*scatter*) esparcir ▷ *vi* (*also:* **~ out**: *stain*) extenderse; (*news*) diseminarse; **middle-age ~** gordura de la mediana edad; **repayments will be ~ over 18 months** los pagos se harán a lo largo de 18 meses; **spread out** *vi* (*move apart*) separarse
spread-eagled ['sprɛdi:gld] *adj*: **to be ~** estar despatarrado
spreadsheet ['sprɛdʃi:t] *n* (*Comput*) hoja de cálculo
spree [spri:] *n*: **to go on a ~** ir de juerga *or* farra (*LAm*)
sprightly ['spraɪtlɪ] *adj* vivo, enérgico

spring [sprɪŋ] (*pt* **sprang**, *pp* **sprung**) *n* (*season*) primavera; (*leap*) salto, brinco; (*coiled metal*) resorte *m*; (*of water*) fuente *f*, manantial *m*; (*bounciness*) elasticidad *f* ▷ *vi* (*arise*) brotar, nacer; (*leap*) saltar, brincar ▷ *vt*: **to ~ a leak** (*pipe etc*) empezar a hacer agua; **he sprang the news on me** de repente me soltó la noticia; **in (the) ~** en (la) primavera; **to walk with a ~ in one's step** andar dando saltos *or* brincos; **to ~ into action** lanzarse a la acción; **spring up** *vi* (*thing: appear*) aparecer; (*problem*) surgir

springboard ['sprɪŋbɔːd] *n* trampolín *m*

spring-clean [sprɪŋ'kliːn] *n* (*also*: **~ing**) limpieza general

spring onion *n* cebolleta

spring roll *n* rollito de primavera

springtime ['sprɪŋtaɪm] *n* primavera

sprinkle ['sprɪŋkl] *vt* (*pour: liquid*) rociar; (*: salt, sugar*) espolvorear; **to ~ water** *etc* **on**, **~ with water** *etc* rociar *or* salpicar de agua *etc*

sprinkler ['sprɪŋkləʳ] *n* (*for lawn*) aspersor *m*; (*to put out fire*) aparato de rociadura automática

sprint [sprɪnt] *n* (e)sprint *m* ▷ *vi* (*gen*) correr a toda velocidad; (*Sport*) esprintar; **the 200 metres ~** el (e)sprint de 200 metros

sprinter ['sprɪntəʳ] *n* velocista *m/f*

spritzer ['sprɪtsəʳ] *n* vino blanco con soda

sprout [spraut] *vi* brotar, retoñar ▷ *n*: **(Brussels) ~s** *npl* coles *fpl* de Bruselas

spruce [spruːs] *n* (*Bot*) pícea ▷ *adj* aseado, pulcro; **spruce up** *vt* (*tidy*) arreglar, acicalar; (*smarten up: room etc*) ordenar; **to ~ o.s. up** arreglarse

sprung [sprʌŋ] *pp of* **spring**

spry [spraɪ] *adj* ágil, activo

spun [spʌn] *pt, pp of* **spin**

spur [spəːʳ] *n* espuela; (*fig*) estímulo, aguijón *m* ▷ *vt* (*also*: **~ on**) estimular, incitar; **on the ~ of the moment** de improviso

spurious ['spjuərɪəs] *adj* falso

spurn [spəːn] *vt* desdeñar, rechazar

spurt [spəːt] *n* chorro; (*of energy*) arrebato ▷ *vi* chorrear; **to put in** *or* **on a ~** (*runner*) acelerar; (*fig: in work etc*) hacer un gran esfuerzo

spy [spaɪ] *n* espía *m/f* ▷ *vi*: **to ~ on** espiar a ▷ *vt* (*see*) divisar, lograr ver ▷ *cpd* (*film, story*) de espionaje

spying ['spaɪɪŋ] *n* espionaje *m*

spyware ['spaɪwɛəʳ] *n* (*Comput*) spyware *m*

sq. *abbr* (*Math etc*) = **square**

squabble ['skwɔbl] *n* riña, pelea ▷ *vi* reñir, pelear

squad [skwɔd] *n* (*Mil*) pelotón *m*; (*Police*) brigada; (*Sport*) equipo; **flying ~** (*Police*) brigada móvil

squaddie ['skwɔdɪ] *n* (*Mil: inf*) chivo

squadron ['skwɔdrn] *n* (*Mil*) escuadrón *m*; (*Aviat, Naut*) escuadra

squalid ['skwɔlɪd] *adj* miserable

squall [skwɔːl] *n* (*storm*) chubasco; (*wind*) ráfaga

squalor ['skwɔləʳ] *n* miseria

squander ['skwɔndəʳ] *vt* (*money*) derrochar, despilfarrar; (*chances*) desperdiciar

square [skwɛəʳ] *n* cuadro; (*in town*) plaza; (*US: block of houses*) manzana, cuadra (*LAm*); (*inf: person*) carca *m/f* ▷ *adj* cuadrado; (*inf: ideas, tastes*) trasnochado ▷ *vt* (*arrange*) arreglar; (*Math*) cuadrar; (*reconcile*) compaginar ▷ *vi* cuadrar, conformarse; **all ~** igual(es); **a ~ meal** una comida decente; **two metres ~** dos metros por dos; **one ~ metre** un metro cuadrado; **to get one's accounts ~** dejar las cuentas claras; **I'll ~ it with him** (*inf*) yo lo arreglo con él; **can you ~ it with your conscience?** ¿cómo se justifica ante sí mismo?; **we're back to ~ one** (*fig*) hemos vuelto al punto de partida; **square up** *vi* (*settle*): **to ~ up (with sb)** ajustar cuentas (con algn)

squarely ['skwɛəlɪ] *adv* (*fully*) de lleno; (*honestly, fairly*) honradamente, justamente

square root *n* raíz *f* cuadrada

squash [skwɔʃ] *n* (*vegetable*) calabaza; (*Sport*) squash *m*; (*Brit: drink*): **lemon/orange ~** zumo (*Sp*) *or* jugo (*LAm*) de limón/naranja ▷ *vt* aplastar

squat [skwɔt] *adj* achaparrado ▷ *vi* agacharse, sentarse en cuclillas; (*on property*) ocupar ilegalmente

squatter ['skwɔtəʳ] *n* ocupante *m/f* ilegal, okupa *m/f*

squawk [skwɔːk] *vi* graznar

squeak [skwiːk] *vi* (*hinge, wheel*) chirriar, rechinar; (*shoe, wood*) crujir; (*mouse*) chillar ▷ *n* (*of hinge, wheel etc*) chirrido, rechinamiento; (*of shoes*) crujir *m*; (*of mouse etc*) chillido

squeaky ['skwiːkɪ] *adj* que cruje; **to be ~ clean** (*fig*) ser superhonrado

squeal [skwiːl] *vi* chillar, dar gritos agudos

squeamish ['skwiːmɪʃ] *adj* delicado, remilgado

squeeze [skwiːz] *n* presión *f*; (*of hand*) apretón *m*; (*Comm: credit squeeze*) restricción *f* ▷ *vt* (*lemon etc*) exprimir; (*hand, arm*) apretar; **a ~ of lemon** unas gotas de limón; **to ~ past/under sth** colarse al lado de/por debajo de algo; **squeeze out** *vt* exprimir; (*fig*) excluir; **squeeze through** *vi* abrirse paso con esfuerzos

squelch [skwɛltʃ] *vi* chapotear

squid [skwɪd] *n* calamar *m*

squiggle ['skwɪgl] *n* garabato

squint [skwɪnt] *vi* bizquear, ser bizco ▷ *n* (*Med*) estrabismo; **to ~ at sth** mirar algo entornando los ojos

squirm [skwəːm] *vi* retorcerse, revolverse

squirrel ['skwɪrəl] *n* ardilla

squirt [skwəːt] *vi* salir a chorros ▷ *vt* chiscar

Sr *abbr* = **senior**; (*Rel*) = **sister**

Sri Lanka [srɪ'læŋkə] *n* Sri Lanka *m*
SS *abbr* (= *steamship*) M.V.
St *abbr* (= *saint*) Sto.(-a); (= *street*) c/
stab [stæb] *n* (*with knife etc*) puñalada; (*of pain*) pinchazo; **to have a ~ at (doing) sth** (*inf*) probar (a hacer) algo ▹ *vt* apuñalar; **to ~ sb to death** matar a algn a puñaladas
stability [stə'bɪlɪtɪ] *n* estabilidad *f*
stable ['steɪbl] *adj* estable ▹ *n* cuadra, caballeriza; **riding ~s** escuela hípica
stack [stæk] *n* montón *m*, pila; (*inf*) mar *f* ▹ *vt* amontonar, apilar; **there's ~s of time to finish it** hay cantidad de tiempo para acabarlo
stadium ['steɪdɪəm] *n* estadio
staff [stɑːf] *n* (*work force*) personal *m*, plantilla; (*Brit Scol*: *also*: **teaching ~**) cuerpo docente; (*stick*) bastón *m* ▹ *vt* proveer de personal; **to be ~ed by Asians/women** tener una plantilla asiática/femenina
stag [stæg] *n* ciervo, venado; (*Brit Stock Exchange*) especulador *m* con nuevas emisiones
stage [steɪdʒ] *n* escena; (*point*) etapa; (*platform*) plataforma; **the ~** el escenario, el teatro ▹ *vt* (*play*) poner en escena, representar; (*organize*) montar, organizar; (*fig*: *perform*: *recovery etc*) efectuar; **in ~s** por etapas; **in the early/final ~s** en las primeras/últimas etapas; **to go through a difficult ~** pasar una fase *or* etapa mala
stagecoach ['steɪdʒkəutʃ] *n* diligencia
stage manager *n* director(a) *m(f)* de escena
stagger ['stægə^r^] *vi* tambalear ▹ *vt* (*amaze*) asombrar; (*hours, holidays*) escalonar
staggering ['stægərɪŋ] *adj* (*amazing*) asombroso, pasmoso
stagnant ['stægnənt] *adj* estancado
stagnate [stæg'neɪt] *vi* estancarse; (*fig*: *economy, mind*) quedarse estancado
stag night, stag party *n* despedida de soltero
staid [steɪd] *adj* (*clothes*) serio, formal
stain [steɪn] *n* mancha; (*colouring*) tintura ▹ *vt* manchar; (*wood*) teñir
stained glass *n* vidrio *m* de color
stained glass window [steɪnd-] *n* vidriera de colores
stainless ['steɪnlɪs] *adj* (*steel*) inoxidable
stainless steel *n* acero inoxidable
stain remover *n* quitamanchas *m inv*
stair [stɛə^r^] *n* (*step*) peldaño, escalón *m*; **stairs** *npl* escaleras *fpl*
staircase ['stɛəkeɪs], **stairway** ['stɛəweɪ] *n* escalera
stake [steɪk] *n* estaca, poste *m*; (*Comm*) interés *m*; (*Betting*) apuesta ▹ *vt* (*bet*) apostar; (*also*: **~ out**: *area*) cercar con estacas; **to be at ~** estar en juego; **to have a ~ in sth** tener interés en algo; **to ~ a claim to (sth)** presentar reclamación por *or* reclamar (algo)
stalactite ['stæləktaɪt] *n* estalactita
stalagmite ['stæləgmaɪt] *n* estalagmita
stale [steɪl] *adj* (*bread*) duro; (*food*) pasado; (*smell*) rancio; (*beer*) agrio
stalemate ['steɪlmeɪt] *n* tablas *fpl*; **to reach ~** (*fig*) estancarse, alcanzar un punto muerto
stalk [stɔːk] *n* tallo, caña ▹ *vt* acechar, cazar al acecho; **to ~ off** irse airado
stall [stɔːl] *n* (*in market*) puesto; (*in stable*) casilla (de establo) ▹ *vt* (*Aut*) parar, calar; (*fig*) dar largas a ▹ *vi* (*Aut*) pararse, calarse; (*fig*) buscar evasivas; **stalls** *npl* (*Brit*: *in cinema, theatre*) butacas *fpl*; **a newspaper ~** un quiosco (de periódicos); **a flower ~** un puesto de flores
stallion ['stælɪən] *n* semental *m*, garañón *m*
stalwart ['stɔːlwət] *n* partidario(-a) incondicional
stamina ['stæmɪnə] *n* resistencia
stammer ['stæmə^r^] *n* tartamudeo, balbuceo ▹ *vi* tartamudear, balbucir
stamp [stæmp] *n* sello, estampilla (*LAm*); (*mark*) marca, huella; (*on document*) timbre *m* ▹ *vi* (*also*: **~ one's foot**) patear ▹ *vt* patear, golpear con el pie; (*letter*) poner sellos en, franquear; (*with rubber stamp*) marcar con sello; **~ed addressed envelope (sae)** sobre *m* franqueado con la dirección propia; **stamp out** *vt* (*fire*) apagar con el pie; (*crime, opposition*) acabar con
stamp album *n* álbum *m* para sellos
stamp collecting *n* filatelia
stampede [stæm'piːd] *n* (*of cattle*) estampida
stance [stæns] *n* postura
stand [stænd] (*pt, pp* **stood**) *n* (*attitude*) posición *f*, postura; (*for taxis*) parada; (*also*: **music ~**) atril *m*; (*Sport*) tribuna; (*at exhibition*) stand *m* ▹ *vi* (*be*) estar, encontrarse; (*be on foot*) estar de pie; (*rise*) levantarse; (*remain*) quedar en pie ▹ *vt* (*place*) poner, colocar; (*tolerate, withstand*) aguantar, soportar; **to make a ~** (*fig*) resistir, mantener una postura firme; **to take a ~ on an issue** adoptar una actitud hacia una cuestión; **to ~ for parliament** (*Brit*) presentarse (como candidato) a las elecciones; **nothing ~s in our way** nada nos lo impide; **to ~ still** quedarse inmóvil; **to let sth ~ as it is** dejar algo como está; **as things ~** tal como están las cosas; **to ~ sb a drink/meal** invitar a algn a una copa/a comer; **the company will have to ~ the loss** la empresa tendrá que hacer frente a las pérdidas; **I can't ~ him** no le aguanto, no le puedo ver; **to ~ guard** *or* **watch** (*Mil*) hacer guardia; **stand aside** *vi* apartarse, mantenerse aparte; **stand back** *vi* retirarse; **stand by** ▹ *vi* (*be ready*) estar listo ▹ *vt fus* (*opinion*) mantener; **stand down** *vi* (*withdraw*) ceder el puesto; (*Mil, Law*) retirarse; **stand for** *vt fus* (*signify*) significar; (*tolerate*) aguantar, permitir; **stand in for** *vt fus* suplir a; **stand out** *vi* (*be prominent*) destacarse; **stand up** *vi* (*rise*)

levantarse, ponerse de pie; **stand up for** *vt fus* defender; **stand up to** *vt fus* hacer frente a
standard ['stændəd] *n* patrón *m*, norma; (*flag*) estandarte *m* ▷ *adj* (*size etc*) normal, corriente, estándar; **standards** *npl* (*morals*) valores *mpl* morales; **the gold ~** (*Comm*) el patrón oro; **high/low ~** de alto/bajo nivel; **below** *or* **not up to ~** (*work*) de calidad inferior; **to be** *or* **come up to ~** satisfacer los requisitos; **to apply a double ~** aplicar un doble criterio
standardize ['stændədaɪz] *vt* estandarizar
standard lamp *n* (*Brit*) lámpara de pie
standard of living *n* nivel *m* de vida
stand-by ['stændbaɪ] *n* (*alert*) alerta, aviso; (*also*: **~ ticket**: *Theat*) *entrada reducida de última hora*; (: *Aviat*) billete *m* standby; **to be on ~** estar preparado; (*doctor*) estar listo para acudir; (*Aviat*) estar en la lista de espera
stand-in ['stændɪn] *n* suplente *m/f*; (*Cine*) doble *m/f*
standing ['stændɪŋ] *adj* (*upright*) derecho; (*on foot*) de pie, en pie; (*permanent*: *committee*) permanente; (: *rule*) fijo; (: *army*) permanente, regular; (*grievance*) constante, viejo ▷ *n* reputación *f*; (*duration*): **of six months' ~** que lleva seis meses; **of many years' ~** que lleva muchos años; **he was given a ~ ovation** le dieron una calurosa ovación de pie; **~ joke** motivo constante de broma; **a man of some ~** un hombre de cierta posición *or* categoría
standing order *n* (*Brit*: *at bank*) giro bancario; **~s** *npl* (*Mil*) reglamento *sg* general
standing room *n* sitio para estar de pie
stand-off ['stændɔf] *n* punto muerto
stand-offish [stænd'ɔfɪʃ] *adj* distante
standpoint ['stændpɔɪnt] *n* punto de vista
standstill ['stændstɪl] *n*: **at a ~** (*industry, traffic*) paralizado, en un punto muerto; **to come to a ~** pararse, quedar paralizado
stank [stæŋk] *pt of* **stink**
staple ['steɪpl] *n* (*for papers*) grapa; (*product*) producto *or* artículo de primeva necesidad ▷ *adj* (*crop, industry, food etc*) básico ▷ *vt* grapar
stapler ['steɪpləʳ] *n* grapadora
star [stɑːʳ] *n* estrella; (*celebrity*) estrella, astro ▷ *vi*: **to ~ in** ser la estrella de; **four-~ hotel** hotel *m* de cuatro estrellas; **4-~ petrol** gasolina extra ▷ *vt* (*Theat, Cine*) ser el/la protagonista de; **the stars** *npl* (*Astrology*) el horóscopo
starboard ['stɑːbəd] *n* estribor *m*
starch [stɑːtʃ] *n* almidón *m*
stardom ['stɑːdəm] *n* estrellato
stare [stɛəʳ] *n* mirada fija ▷ *vi*: **to ~ at** mirar fijo
starfish ['stɑːfɪʃ] *n* estrella de mar
stark [stɑːk] *adj* (*bleak*) severo, escueto; (*simplicity, colour*) austero; (*reality, truth*) puro; (*poverty*) absoluto ▷ *adv*: **~ naked** en cueros
starkers ['stɑːkəz] *adj* (*Brit inf*): **to be ~** estar en cueros
starling ['stɑːlɪŋ] *n* estornino
starry ['stɑːrɪ] *adj* estrellado
starry-eyed [stɑːrɪ'aɪd] *adj* (*gullible, innocent*) inocentón(-ona), ingenuo; (*idealistic*) idealista; (*from wonder*) asombrado; (*from love*) enamoradísimo
Stars and Stripes *npl*: **the ~** las barras y las estrellas, la bandera de EEUU
star sign *n* signo del zodíaco
start [stɑːt] *n* (*beginning*) principio, comienzo; (*departure*) salida; (*sudden movement*) sobresalto; (*advantage*) ventaja ▷ *vt* empezar, comenzar; (*cause*) causar; (*found*: *business, newspaper*) establecer, fundar; (*engine*) poner en marcha ▷ *vi* (*begin*) comenzar, empezar; (*with fright*) asustarse, sobresaltarse; (*train etc*) salir; **to give sb a ~** dar un susto a algn; **at the ~** al principio; **for a ~** en primer lugar; **to make an early ~** ponerse en camino temprano; **the thieves had three hours' ~** los ladrones llevaban tres horas de ventaja; **to ~ a fire** provocar un incendio; **to ~ doing** *or* **to do sth** empezar a hacer algo; **to ~ (off) with ...** (*firstly*) para empezar; (*at the beginning*) al principio; **start off** *vi* empezar, comenzar; (*leave*) salir, ponerse en camino; **start out** *vi* (*begin*) empezar; (*set out*) partir, salir; **start over** *vi* (*US*) volver a empezar; **start up** *vi* comenzar; (*car*) ponerse en marcha ▷ *vt* comenzar; (*car*) poner en marcha
starter ['stɑːtəʳ] *n* (*Aut*) botón *m* de arranque; (*Sport*: *official*) juez *m/f* de salida; (: *runner*) corredor(a) *m(f)*; (*Brit Culin*) entrada, entrante *m*
starting point ['stɑːtɪŋ-] *n* punto de partida
startle ['stɑːtl] *vt* sobresaltar
startling ['stɑːtlɪŋ] *adj* alarmante
starvation [stɑː'veɪʃən] *n* hambre *f*, hambruna (*LAm*); (*Med*) inanición *f*
starve [stɑːv] *vi* pasar hambre; (*to death*) morir de hambre ▷ *vt* hacer pasar hambre; (*fig*) privar; **I'm starving** estoy muerto de hambre
stash [stæʃ] *vt*: **to ~ sth away** (*inf*) poner algo a buen recaudo
state [steɪt] *n* estado; (*pomp*): **in ~** con mucha ceremonia ▷ *vt* (*say, declare*) afirmar; (*a case*) presentar, exponer; **~ of emergency** estado de excepción *or* emergencia; **~ of mind** estado de ánimo; **to lie in ~** (*corpse*) estar de cuerpo presente; **to be in a ~** estar agitado; **the S~s** los Estados Unidos
State Department *n* (*US*) Ministerio de Asuntos Exteriores
stately ['steɪtlɪ] *adj* majestuoso, imponente
statement ['steɪtmənt] *n* afirmación *f*; (*Law*) declaración *f*; (*Comm*) estado; **official ~** informe *m* oficial; **~ of account, bank ~** estado de cuenta
States [steɪts] *npl*: **the ~** los Estados Unidos

state school *n* escuela *or* colegio estatal
statesman ['steɪtsmən] *n* estadista *m*
static ['stætɪk] *n* (*Radio*) parásitos *mpl* ▷ *adj* estático
station ['steɪʃən] *n* (*gen*) estación *f*; (*place*) puesto, sitio; (*Radio*) emisora; (*rank*) posición *f* social ▷ *vt* colocar, situar; (*Mil*) apostar; **action ~s!** ¡a los puestos de combate!; **to be ~ed in** (*Mil*) estar estacionado en
stationary ['steɪʃnərɪ] *adj* estacionario, fijo
stationer ['steɪʃənəʳ] *n* papelero(-a)
stationer's, stationer's shop *n* (*Brit*) papelería
stationery ['steɪʃənərɪ] *n* (*writing paper*) papel *m* de escribir; (*writing materials*) artículos *mpl* de escritorio
station master *n* (*Rail*) jefe *m* de estación
station wagon *n* (*US*) coche *m* familiar con ranchera
statistic [stə'tɪstɪk] *n* estadística
statistics [stə'tɪstɪks] *n* (*science*) estadística
statue ['stætju:] *n* estatua
stature ['stætʃəʳ] *n* estatura; (*fig*) talla
status ['steɪtəs] *n* condición *f*, estado; (*reputation*) reputación *f*, estatus *m*
status quo *n* (e)statu quo *m*
status symbol *n* símbolo de prestigio
statute ['stætju:t] *n* estatuto, ley *f*
statutory ['stætjutrɪ] *adj* estatutario; **~ meeting** junta ordinaria
staunch [stɔ:ntʃ] *adj* leal, incondicional ▷ *vt* (*flow, blood*) restañar
stave [steɪv] *vt*: **to ~ off** (*attack*) rechazar; (*threat*) evitar
stay [steɪ] *n* (*period of time*) estancia; (*Law*): **~ of execution** aplazamiento de una sentencia ▷ *vi* (*remain*) quedar(se); (*as guest*) hospedarse; **to ~ put** seguir en el mismo sitio; **to ~ the night/5 days** pasar la noche/estar *or* quedarse 5 días; **stay away** *vi* (*from person, building*) no acercarse; (*from event*) no acudir; **stay behind** *vi* quedar atrás; **stay in** *vi* (*at home*) quedarse en casa; **stay on** *vi* quedarse; **stay out** *vi* (*of house*) no volver a casa; (*strikers*) no volver al trabajo; **stay up** *vi* (*at night*) velar, no acostarse
staycation [steɪ'keɪʃən] *n* (*inf*) vacaciones *fpl* en casa
staying power ['steɪɪŋ-] *n* resistencia, aguante *m*
STD *n abbr* (= *sexually transmitted disease*) ETS *f*
stead [stɛd] *n*: **in sb's ~** en lugar de algn; **to stand sb in good ~** ser muy útil a algn
steadfast ['stɛdfɑ:st] *adj* firme, resuelto
steadily ['stɛdɪlɪ] *adv* (*firmly*) firmemente; (*unceasingly*) sin parar; (*fixedly*) fijamente; (*drive*) a velocidad constante
steady ['stɛdɪ] *adj* (*fixed*) firme, fijo; (*regular*) regular; (*boyfriend etc*) formal, fijo; (*person, character*) sensato, juicioso ▷ *vt* (*hold*) mantener firme; (*stabilize*) estabilizar; (*nerves*) calmar; **to ~ o.s. on** *or* **against sth** afirmarse en algo
steak [steɪk] *n* (*gen*) filete *m*; (*beef*) bistec *m*
steal (*pt* **stole**, *pp* **stolen**) [sti:l, stəul, 'stəuln] *vt, vi* robar; **steal away, steal off** *vi* marcharse furtivamente, escabullirse
stealth [stɛlθ] *n*: **by ~** a escondidas, sigilosamente
stealthy ['stɛlθɪ] *adj* cauteloso, sigiloso
steam [sti:m] *n* vapor *m*; (*mist*) vaho, humo ▷ *vt* (*Culin*) cocer al vapor ▷ *vi* echar vapor; (*ship*): **to ~ along** avanzar, ir avanzando; **under one's own ~** (*fig*) por sus propios medios *or* propias fuerzas; **to run out of ~** (*fig: person*) quedar(se) agotado, quemarse; **to let off ~** (*fig*) desahogarse; **steam up** *vi* (*window*) empañarse; **to get ~ed up about sth** (*fig*) ponerse negro por algo
steam engine *n* máquina de vapor
steamer ['sti:məʳ] *n* (buque *m* de) vapor *m*; (*Culin*) *recipiente para cocinar al vapor*
steamroller ['sti:mrəuləʳ] *n* apisonadora
steamship ['sti:mʃɪp] *n* = **steamer**
steamy ['sti:mɪ] *adj* (*room*) lleno de vapor; (*window*) empañado; (*heat, atmosphere*) bochornoso
steel [sti:l] *n* acero ▷ *adj* de acero
steelworks ['sti:lwə:ks] *n* acería, fundición *f* de acero
steep [sti:p] *adj* escarpado, abrupto; (*stair*) empinado; (*price*) exorbitante, excesivo ▷ *vt* empapar, remojar
steeple ['sti:pl] *n* aguja, campanario
steeplejack ['sti:pldʒæk] *n* reparador(a) *m(f)* de chimeneas *or* de campanarios
steer [stɪəʳ] *vt* (*car*) conducir (*Sp*), manejar (*LAm*); (*person*) dirigir, guiar ▷ *vi* conducir (*Sp*), manejar (*LAm*); **to ~ clear of sb/sth** (*fig*) esquivar a algn/evadir algo
steering ['stɪərɪŋ] *n* (*Aut*) dirección *f*
steering wheel *n* volante *m*
stem [stɛm] *n* (*of plant*) tallo; (*of glass*) pie *m*; (*of pipe*) cañón *m* ▷ *vt* detener; (*blood*) restañar; **stem from** *vt fus* ser consecuencia de
stench [stɛntʃ] *n* hedor *m*
stencil ['stɛnsl] *n* (*typed*) cliché *m*, clisé *m*; (*lettering*) plantilla ▷ *vt* hacer un cliché de
stenographer [stɛ'nɔgrəfəʳ] *n* (*US*) taquígrafo(-a)
step [stɛp] *n* paso; (*sound*) paso, pisada; (*stair*) peldaño, escalón *m* ▷ *vi*: **to ~ forward** dar un paso adelante; **steps** *npl* (*Brit*) = **stepladder**; **~ by ~** paso a paso; (*fig*) poco a poco; **to keep in ~ (with)** llevar el paso de; (*fig*) llevar el paso de, estar de acuerdo con; **to be in/out of ~ with** estar acorde con/estar en disonancia con; **to take ~s to solve a problem** tomar medidas para resolver un problema; **step down** *vi* (*fig*) retirarse; **step in** *vi* entrar; (*fig*) intervenir; **step off** *vt fus* bajar de; **step on** *vt fus* pisar; **step over** *vt fus*

S

pasar por encima de; **step up** *vt* (*increase*) aumentar
step aerobics *npl* step *m*
stepbrother ['stɛpbrʌðəʳ] *n* hermanastro
stepchild ['stɛptʃaɪld] (*pl* **stepchildren**) *n* hijastro(-a) *m/f*
stepdaughter ['stɛpdɔːtəʳ] *n* hijastra
stepfather ['stɛpfɑːðəʳ] *n* padrastro
stepladder ['stɛplædəʳ] *n* escalera doble *or* de tijera
stepmother ['stɛpmʌðəʳ] *n* madrastra
stepping stone ['stɛpɪŋ-] *n* pasadera
stepsister ['stɛpsɪstəʳ] *n* hermanastra
stepson ['stɛpsʌn] *n* hijastro
stereo ['stɛrɪəu] *n* estéreo ▷ *adj* (*also*: **~phonic**) estéreo, estereofónico; **in ~** en estéreo
stereotype ['stɪərɪətaɪp] *n* estereotipo ▷ *vt* estereotipar
sterile ['stɛraɪl] *adj* estéril
sterilization [stɛrɪlaɪ'zeɪʃən] *n* esterilización *f*
sterilize ['stɛrɪlaɪz] *vt* esterilizar
sterling ['stəːlɪŋ] *adj* (*silver*) de ley ▷ *n* (*Econ*) libras *fpl* esterlinas; **a pound ~** una libra esterlina; **he is of ~ character** tiene un carácter excelente
stern [stəːn] *adj* severo, austero ▷ *n* (*Naut*) popa
steroid ['stɪərɔɪd] *n* esteroide *m*
stethoscope ['stɛθəskəup] *n* estetoscopio
stew [stjuː] *n* cocido, estofado, guisado (*LAm*) ▷ *vt, vi* estofar, guisar; (*fruit*) cocer; **~ed fruit** compota de fruta
steward ['stjuːəd] *n* (*Brit*: *gen*) camarero; (*shop steward*) enlace *m/f* sindical
stewardess ['stjuədəs] *n* azafata
stewardship ['stjuədʃɪp] *n* tutela
St. Ex. *abbr* = **stock exchange**
stg *abbr* (= *sterling*) ester
stick [stɪk] (*pt, pp* **stuck**) *n* palo; (*as weapon*) porra; (*also*: **walking ~**) bastón *m* ▷ *vt* (*glue*) pegar; (*inf*: *put*) meter; (*: tolerate*) aguantar, soportar ▷ *vi* pegarse; (*come to a stop*) quedarse parado; (*get jammed*: *door, lift*) atascarse; **to get hold of the wrong end of the ~** entender al revés; **to ~ to** (*word, principles*) atenerse a, ser fiel a; (*promise*) cumplir; **it stuck in my mind** se me quedó grabado; **to ~ sth into** clavar *or* hincar algo en; **stick around** *vi* (*inf*) quedarse; **stick out** *vi* sobresalir ▷ *vt*: **to ~ it out** (*inf*) aguantar; **stick up** *vi* sobresalir; **stick up for** *vt fus* defender
sticker ['stɪkəʳ] *n* (*label*) etiqueta adhesiva; (*with slogan*) pegatina
sticking plaster ['stɪkɪŋ-] *n* (*Brit*) esparadrapo
sticking point *n* (*fig*) punto de fricción
stick insect *n* insecto palo
stickler ['stɪkləʳ] *n*: **to be a ~ for** insistir mucho en
stick shift *n* (*US Aut*) palanca de cambios
stick-up ['stɪkʌp] *n* asalto, atraco
sticky ['stɪkɪ] *adj* pegajoso; (*label*) adhesivo; (*fig*) difícil
stiff [stɪf] *adj* rígido, tieso; (*hard*) duro; (*difficult*) difícil; (*person*) inflexible; (*price*) exorbitante; **to have a ~ neck/back** tener tortícolis/dolor de espalda; **the door's ~** la puerta está atrancada ▷ *adv*: **scared/bored ~** muerto de miedo/aburrimiento
stiffen ['stɪfn] *vt* hacer más rígido; (*limb*) entumecer ▷ *vi* endurecerse; (*grow stronger*) fortalecerse
stifle ['staɪfl] *vt* ahogar, sofocar
stifling ['staɪflɪŋ] *adj* (*heat*) sofocante, bochornoso
stigma ['stɪgmə] *n* (*Bot, Med, Rel, pl* **stigmata** [stɪg'mɑːtə], *fig*: *pl* **stigmas**) estigma *m*
stile [staɪl] *n* escalera (*para pasar una cerca*)
stiletto [stɪ'lɛtəu] *n* (*Brit*: *also*: **~ heel**) tacón *m* de aguja
still [stɪl] *adj* inmóvil, quieto; (*orange juice etc*) sin gas ▷ *adv* (*up to this time*) todavía; (*even*) aún; (*nonetheless*) sin embargo, aun así ▷ *n* (*Cine*) foto *f* fija; **keep ~!** ¡estate quieto!, ¡no te muevas!; **he ~ hasn't arrived** todavía no ha llegado
stillborn ['stɪlbɔːn] *adj* nacido muerto
still life *n* naturaleza muerta
stilt [stɪlt] *n* zanco; (*pile*) pilar *m*, soporte *m*
stilted ['stɪltɪd] *adj* afectado, artificial
stimulant ['stɪmjulənt] *n* estimulante *m*
stimulate ['stɪmjuleɪt] *vt* estimular
stimulating ['stɪmjuleɪtɪŋ] *adj* estimulante
stimulation [stɪmju'leɪʃən] *n* estímulo
stimulus (*pl* **stimuli**) ['stɪmjuləs, -laɪ] *n* estímulo, incentivo
sting [stɪŋ] (*pt, pp* **stung**) *n* (*wound*) picadura; (*pain*) escozor *m*, picazón *m*; (*organ*) aguijón *m*; (*inf*: *confidence trick*) timo ▷ *vt* picar ▷ *vi* picar, escocer; **my eyes are ~ing** me pican *or* escuecen los ojos
stingy ['stɪndʒɪ] *adj* tacaño
stink [stɪŋk] (*pt* **stank**, *pp* **stunk** [stæŋk, stʌŋk]) *n* hedor *m*, tufo ▷ *vi* heder, apestar
stinking ['stɪŋkɪŋ] *adj* hediondo, fétido; (*fig*: *inf*) horrible
stint [stɪnt] *n* tarea, destajo; **to do one's ~ (at sth)** hacer su parte (de algo), hacer lo que corresponde (de algo) ▷ *vi*: **to ~ on** escatimar
stir [stəːʳ] *n* (*fig*: *agitation*) conmoción *f* ▷ *vt* (*tea etc*) remover; (*fire*) atizar; (*move*) agitar; (*fig*: *emotions*) provocar ▷ *vi* moverse; **to give sth a ~** remover algo; **to cause a ~** causar conmoción *or* sensación; **stir up** *vt* excitar; (*trouble*) fomentar
stir-fry ['stəːfraɪ] *vt* sofreír removiendo ▷ *n* *plato preparado sofriendo y removiendo los ingredientes*
stirrup ['stɪrəp] *n* estribo

stitch [stɪtʃ] *n* (*Sewing*) puntada; (*Knitting*) punto; (*Med*) punto (de sutura); (*pain*) punzada ▹ *vt* coser; (*Med*) suturar

stoat [stəut] *n* armiño

stock [stɔk] *n* (*Comm*: *reserves*) existencias *fpl*, stock *m*; (: *selection*) surtido; (*Agr*) ganado, ganadería; (*Culin*) caldo; (*fig*: *lineage*) estirpe *f*, cepa; (*Finance*) capital *m*; (: *shares*) acciones *fpl*; (*Rail*: *rolling stock*) material *m* rodante ▹ *adj* (*Comm*: *goods, size*) normal, de serie; (*fig*: *reply etc*) clásico, trillado; (: *greeting*) acostumbrado ▹ *vt* (*have in stock*) tener existencias de; (*supply*) proveer, abastecer; **in ~** en existencia *or* almacén; **to have sth in ~** tener existencias de algo; **out of ~** agotado; **to take ~ of** (*fig*) considerar, examinar; **stocks** *npl* (*History*: *punishment*) cepo *sg*; **~s and shares** acciones y valores; **government ~** papel *m* del Estado; **stock up with** *vt fus* abastecerse de

stockbroker ['stɔkbrəukəʳ] *n* agente *m/f or* corredor(a) *m(f)* de bolsa

stock cube *n* pastilla *or* cubito de caldo

stock exchange *n* bolsa

stockholder ['stɔkhəuldəʳ] *n* (*US*) accionista *m/f*

stocking ['stɔkɪŋ] *n* media

stock market *n* bolsa (de valores)

stock phrase *n* vieja frase *f*

stockpile ['stɔkpaɪl] *n* reserva ▹ *vt* acumular, almacenar

stockroom ['stɔkruːm] *n* almacén *m*, depósito

stocktaking ['stɔkteɪkɪŋ] *n* (*Brit Comm*) inventario, balance *m*

stocky ['stɔkɪ] *adj* (*strong*) robusto; (*short*) achaparrado

stodgy ['stɔdʒɪ] *adj* indigesto, pesado

stoke [stəuk] *vt* atizar

stole [stəul] *pt of* **steal** ▹ *n* estola

stolen ['stəuln] *pp of* **steal**

stolid ['stɔlɪd] *adj* (*person*) imperturbable, impasible

stomach ['stʌmək] *n* (*Anat*) estómago; (*belly*) vientre *m* ▹ *vt* tragar, aguantar

stomach ache *n* dolor *m* de estómago

stone [stəun] *n* piedra; (*in fruit*) hueso; (*Brit*: *weight*) = *6.348 kg; 14lb* ▹ *adj* de piedra ▹ *vt* apedrear; (*fruit*) deshuesar; **within a ~'s throw of the station** a tiro de piedra *or* a dos pasos de la estación

stone-cold ['stəun'kəuld] *adj* helado

stone-deaf ['stəun'dɛf] *adj* sordo como una tapia

stonewall [stəun'wɔːl] *vi* alargar la cosa innecesariamente ▹ *vt* dar largas a

stonework ['stəunwəːk] *n* (*art*) cantería

stood [stud] *pt, pp of* **stand**

stooge [stuːdʒ] *n* (*inf*) hombre *m* de paja

stool [stuːl] *n* taburete *m*

stoop [stuːp] *vi* (*also*: **~ down**) doblarse, agacharse; (*also*: **have a ~**) ser cargado de espaldas; (*bend*) inclinarse, encorvarse; **to ~ to (doing) sth** rebajarse a (hacer) algo

stop [stɔp] *n* parada, alto; (*in punctuation*) punto ▹ *vt* parar, detener; (*break off*) suspender; (*block*: *pay*) suspender; (: *cheque*) invalidar; (*prevent*) impedir; (*also*: **put a ~ to**) poner término a ▹ *vi* pararse, detenerse; (*end*) acabarse; **to ~ doing sth** dejar de hacer algo; **to ~ sb (from) doing sth** impedir a algn hacer algo; **to ~ dead** pararse en seco; **~ it!** ¡basta ya!, ¡párate!; **stop by** *vi* pasar por; **stop off** *vi* interrumpir el viaje; **stop up** *vt* (*hole*) tapar

stopgap ['stɔpgæp] *n* interino; (*person*) sustituto(-a); (*measure*) medida provisional ▹ *cpd* (*situation*) provisional

stopover ['stɔpəuvəʳ] *n* parada intermedia; (*Aviat*) escala

stoppage ['stɔpɪdʒ] *n* (*strike*) paro; (*temporary stop*) interrupción *f*; (*of pay*) suspensión *f*; (*blockage*) obstrucción *f*

stopper ['stɔpəʳ] *n* tapón *m*

stop press *n* noticias *fpl* de última hora

stopwatch ['stɔpwɔtʃ] *n* cronómetro

storage ['stɔːrɪdʒ] *n* almacenaje *m*; (*Comput*) almacenamiento

storage heater *n* acumulador *m* de calor

store [stɔːʳ] *n* (*stock*) provisión *f*; (*depot*) almacén *m*; (*Brit*: *large shop*) almacén *m*; (*US*) tienda; (*reserve*) reserva, repuesto ▹ *vt* (*gen*) almacenar; (*Comput*) almacenar; (*keep*) guardar; (*in filing system*) archivar; **stores** *npl* víveres *mpl*; **who knows what is in ~ for us** quién sabe lo que nos espera; **to set great/little ~ by sth** dar mucha/poca importancia a algo, valorar mucho/poco algo; **store up** *vt* acumular

storekeeper ['stɔːkiːpəʳ] *n* (*US*) tendero(-a)

storeroom ['stɔːruːm] *n* despensa

storey, story (*US*) ['stɔːrɪ] *n* piso

stork [stɔːk] *n* cigüeña

storm [stɔːm] *n* tormenta; (*wind*) vendaval *m*; (*fig*: *of applause*) salva; (: *of criticism*) nube *f* ▹ *vi* (*fig*) rabiar ▹ *vt* tomar por asalto, asaltar; **to take a town by ~** (*Mil*) tomar una ciudad por asalto

stormy ['stɔːmɪ] *adj* tempestuoso

story ['stɔːrɪ] *n* historia; (*Press*) artículo; (*joke*) cuento, chiste *m*; (*plot*) argumento; (*lie*) cuento; (*US*) = **storey**

storybook ['stɔːrɪbuk] *n* libro de cuentos

stout [staut] *adj* (*strong*) sólido; (*fat*) gordo, corpulento ▹ *n* cerveza negra

stove [stəuv] *n* (*for cooking*) cocina; (*for heating*) estufa; **gas/electric ~** cocina de gas/eléctrica

stow [stəu] *vt* meter, poner; (*Naut*) estibar

stowaway ['stəuəweɪ] *n* polizón(-ona) *m(f)*

straddle ['strædl] *vt* montar a horcajadas

straggle ['strægl] *vi* (*wander*) vagar en desorden; (*lag behind*) rezagarse

straight [streɪt] *adj* (*direct*) recto, derecho; (*plain, uncomplicated*) sencillo; (*frank*) franco, directo; (*in order*) en orden; (*continuous*) continuo; (*Theat*: *part, play*) serio; (*person*: *conventional*) recto, convencional; (: *heterosexual*) heterosexual ▷ *adv* derecho, directamente; (*drink*) solo; **to put** *or* **get sth ~** dejar algo en claro; **10 ~ wins** 10 victorias seguidas; **to be (all) ~** (*tidy*) estar en orden; (*clarified*) estar claro; **I went ~ home** (me) fui directamente a casa; **~ away, ~ off** (*at once*) en seguida

straighten ['streɪtn] *vt* (*also*: **~ out**) enderezar, poner derecho ▷ *vi* (*also*: **~ up**) enderezarse, ponerse derecho; **to ~ things out** poner las cosas en orden

straight-faced [streɪt'feɪst] *adj* serio ▷ *adv* sin mostrar emoción, impávido

straightforward [streɪt'fɔːwəd] *adj* (*simple*) sencillo; (*honest*) sincero

strain [streɪn] *n* (*gen*) tensión *f*; (*Tech*) presión *f*; (*Med*) distensión *f*, torcedura; (*breed*) raza; (*lineage*) linaje *m*; (*of virus*) variedad *f* ▷ *vt* (*back etc*) distender, torcerse; (*resources*) agotar; (*tire*) cansar; (*stretch*) estirar; (*filter*) filtrar; (*meaning*) tergiversar ▷ *vi* esforzarse; **strains** *npl* (*Mus*) son *m*; **she's under a lot of ~** está bajo mucha tensión

strained [streɪnd] *adj* (*muscle*) torcido; (*laugh*) forzado; (*relations*) tenso

strainer ['streɪnəʳ] *n* colador *m*

strait [streɪt] *n* (*Geo*) estrecho; **to be in dire ~s** (*fig*) estar en un gran aprieto

straitjacket ['streɪtdʒækɪt] *n* camisa de fuerza

strait-laced [streɪt'leɪst] *adj* mojigato, gazmoño

strand [strænd] *n* (*of thread*) hebra; (*of rope*) ramal *m*; **a ~ of hair** un pelo

stranded ['strændɪd] *adj* (*person*: *without money*) desamparado; (: *without transport*) colgado

strange [streɪndʒ] *adj* (*not known*) desconocido; (*odd*) extraño, raro

strangely *adv* de un modo raro; *see also* **enough**

stranger ['streɪndʒəʳ] *n* desconocido(-a); (*from another area*) forastero(-a); **I'm a ~ here** no soy de aquí

strangle ['stræŋgl] *vt* estrangular

stranglehold ['stræŋglhəuld] *n* (*fig*) dominio completo

strap [stræp] *n* correa; (*of slip, dress*) tirante *m* ▷ *vt* atar con correa

strapped [stræpt] *adj*: **to be ~ for cash** (*inf*) andar mal de dinero

strapping ['stræpɪŋ] *adj* robusto, fornido

strategic [strə'tiːdʒɪk] *adj* estratégico

strategy ['strætɪdʒɪ] *n* estrategia

straw [strɔː] *n* paja; (*also*: **drinking ~**) caña, pajita; **that's the last ~!** ¡eso es el colmo!

strawberry ['strɔːbərɪ] *n* fresa, frutilla (*LAm*)

stray [streɪ] *adj* (*animal*) extraviado; (*bullet*) perdido; (*scattered*) disperso ▷ *vi* extraviarse, perderse; (*wander*: *walker*) vagar, ir sin rumbo fijo; (: *speaker*) desvariar

streak [striːk] *n* raya; (*fig*: *of madness etc*) vena ▷ *vt* rayar ▷ *vi*: **to ~ past** pasar como un rayo; **to have ~s in one's hair** tener vetas en el pelo; **a winning/losing ~** una racha de buena/mala suerte

streaker ['striːkəʳ] *n* corredor(a) *m(f)* desnudo(-a)

stream [striːm] *n* riachuelo, arroyo; (*jet*) chorro; (*flow*) corriente *f*; (*of people*) oleada ▷ *vt* (*Scol*) dividir en grupos por habilidad ▷ *vi* correr, fluir; **to ~ in/out** (*people*) entrar/salir en tropel; **against the ~** a contracorriente; **on ~** (*new power plant etc*) en funcionamiento

streamer ['striːməʳ] *n* serpentina

streamline ['striːmlaɪn] *vt* aerodinamizar; (*fig*) racionalizar

streamlined ['striːmlaɪnd] *adj* aerodinámico

street [striːt] *n* calle *f* ▷ *adj* callejero; **the back ~s** las callejuelas; **to be on the ~s** (*homeless*) estar sin vivienda; (*as prostitute*) hacer la calle

streetcar ['striːtkɑː] *n* (*US*) tranvía *m*

street lamp *n* farol *m*

street light *n* farol *m* (*LAm*), farola (*Sp*)

street map *n* plano (de la ciudad)

street plan *n* plano callejero

streetwise ['striːtwaɪz] *adj* (*inf*) pícaro

strength [strɛŋθ] *n* fuerza; (*of girder, knot etc*) resistencia; (*of chemical solution*) potencia; (*of wine*) graduación *f* de alcohol; (*fig*: *power*) poder *m*; **on the ~ of** a base de, en base a; **to be at full/below ~** tener/no tener completo el cupo

strengthen ['strɛŋθn] *vt* fortalecer, reforzar

strenuous ['strɛnjuəs] *adj* (*tough*) arduo; (*energetic*) enérgico; (*opposition*) firme, tenaz; (*efforts*) intensivo

stress [strɛs] *n* (*force, pressure*) presión *f*; (*mental strain*) estrés *m*, tensión *f*; (*accent, emphasis*) énfasis *m*, acento; (*Ling, Poetry*) acento; (*Tech*) tensión *f*, carga ▷ *vt* subrayar, recalcar; **to be under ~** estar estresado; **to lay great ~ on sth** hacer hincapié en algo

stressed [strɛst] *adj* (*tense*) estresado, agobiado; (*syllable*) acentuado

stressful ['strɛsful] *adj* (*job*) estresante

stretch [strɛtʃ] *n* (*of sand etc*) trecho; (*of road*) tramo; (*of time*) período, tiempo ▷ *vi* estirarse; (*extend*): **to ~ to** *or* **as far as** extenderse hasta; (*be enough*: *money, food*): **to ~ to** alcanzar para, dar de sí para ▷ *vt* extender, estirar; (*make demands of*) exigir el máximo esfuerzo a; **to ~ one's legs** estirar las piernas; **stretch out** *vi* tenderse ▷ *vt* (*arm etc*) extender; (*spread*) estirar

stretcher ['strɛtʃəʳ] *n* camilla

strewn [struːn] *adj*: **~ with** cubierto *or* sembrado de

stricken ['strɪkən] *adj* (*person*) herido; (*city, industry etc*) condenado; **~ with** (*arthritis,* *disease*) afligido por; **grief-~** destrozado por el dolor

strict [strɪkt] *adj* (*order, rule etc*) estricto; (*discipline, ban*) severo; **in ~ confidence** en la más absoluta confianza

strictly ['strɪktlɪ] *adv* estrictamente; (*totally*) terminantemente; **~ confidential** estrictamente confidencial; **~ speaking** en (el) sentido estricto (de la palabra); **~ between ourselves ...** entre nosotros ...

stride [straɪd] (*pt* **strode**, *pp* **stridden** [strəud, 'strɪdn]) *n* zancada, tranco ▷ *vi* dar zancadas, andar a trancos; **to take in one's ~** (*fig*: *changes etc*) tomar con calma

strife [straɪf] *n* lucha

strike [straɪk] (*pt, pp* **struck**) *n* huelga; (*of oil etc*) descubrimiento; (*attack*) ataque *m*; (*Sport*) golpe *m* ▷ *vt* golpear, pegar; (*oil etc*) descubrir; (*obstacle*) topar con; (*produce*: *coin, medal*) acuñar; (: *agreement, deal*) alcanzar ▷ *vi* declarar la huelga; (*attack*: *Mil etc*) atacar; (*clock*) dar la hora; **on ~** (*workers*) en huelga; **to call a ~** declarar una huelga; **to go on** *or* **come out on ~** ponerse *or* declararse en huelga; **to ~ a match** encender una cerilla; **to ~ a balance** (*fig*) encontrar un equilibrio; **to ~ a bargain** cerrar un trato; **the clock struck nine o'clock** el reloj dio las nueve; **strike back** *vi* (*Mil*) contraatacar; (*fig*) devolver el golpe; **strike down** *vt* derribar; **strike off** *vt* (*from list*) tachar; (*doctor etc*) suspender; **strike out** *vt* borrar, tachar; **strike up** *vt* (*Mus*) empezar a tocar; (*conversation*) entablar; (*friendship*) trabar

striker ['straɪkəʳ] *n* huelguista *m/f*; (*Sport*) delantero

striking ['straɪkɪŋ] *adj* (*colour*) llamativo; (*obvious*) notorio

Strimmer® ['strɪməʳ] *n* cortacéspedes *m inv* (*especial para los bordes*)

string [strɪŋ] (*pt, pp* **strung** [strʌŋ]) *n* (*gen*) cuerda; (*row*) hilera; (*Comput*) cadena ▷ *vt*: **to ~ together** ensartar; **to ~ out** extenderse; **the strings** *npl* (*Mus*) los instrumentos de cuerda; **to pull ~s** (*fig*) mover palancas; **to get a job by pulling ~s** conseguir un trabajo por enchufe; **with no ~s attached** (*fig*) sin compromiso

string bean *n* judía verde, habichuela

stringent ['strɪndʒənt] *adj* riguroso, severo

strip [strɪp] *n* tira; (*of land*) franja; (*of metal*) cinta, lámina ▷ *vt* desnudar; (*also*: **~ down**: *machine*) desmontar ▷ *vi* desnudarse; **strip off** *vt* (*paint etc*) quitar ▷ *vi* (*person*) desnudarse

strip cartoon *n* tira cómica, historieta (*LAm*)

stripe [straɪp] *n* raya; (*Mil*) galón *m*; **white with green ~s** blanco con rayas verdes

striped [straɪpt] *adj* a rayas, rayado

strip lighting *n* alumbrado fluorescente

stripper ['strɪpəʳ] *n* artista *m/f* de striptease

strip-search ['strɪpsəːtʃ] *vt*: **to ~ sb** desnudar y registrar a algn

strive (*pt* **strove**, *pp* **striven**) [straɪv, strəuv, 'strɪvn] *vi*: **to ~ to do sth** esforzarse *or* luchar por hacer algo

strode [strəud] *pt of* **stride**

stroke [strəuk] *n* (*blow*) golpe *m*; (*Swimming*) brazada; (*Med*) apoplejía; (*caress*) caricia; (*of pen*) trazo; (*Swimming*: *style*) estilo; (*of piston*) carrera ▷ *vt* acariciar; **at a ~** de golpe; **a ~ of luck** un golpe de suerte; **two-~ engine** motor *m* de dos tiempos

stroll [strəul] *n* paseo, vuelta ▷ *vi* dar un paseo *or* una vuelta; **to go for a ~, have** *or* **take a ~** dar un paseo

stroller ['strəuləʳ] *n* (*US*: *pushchair*) cochecito

strong [strɔŋ] *adj* fuerte; (*bleach, acid*) concentrado ▷ *adv*: **to be going ~** (*company*) marchar bien; (*person*) conservarse bien; **they are 50 ~** son 50

stronghold ['strɔŋhəuld] *n* fortaleza; (*fig*) baluarte *m*

strongly ['strɔŋlɪ] *adv* fuertemente, con fuerza; (*believe*) firmemente; **to feel ~ about sth** tener una opinión firme sobre algo

strongroom ['strɔŋruːm] *n* cámara acorazada

stroppy ['strɔpɪ] *adj* (*Brit inf*) borde; **to get ~** ponerse borde

strove [strəuv] *pt of* **strive**

struck [strʌk] *pt, pp of* **strike**

structural ['strʌktʃərəl] *adj* estructural

structure ['strʌktʃəʳ] *n* estructura; (*building*) construcción *f*

struggle ['strʌgl] *n* lucha ▷ *vi* luchar; **to have a ~ to do sth** esforzarse por hacer algo

strum [strʌm] *vt* (*guitar*) rasguear

strung [strʌŋ] *pt, pp of* **string**

strut [strʌt] *n* puntal *m* ▷ *vi* pavonearse

stub [stʌb] *n* (*of ticket etc*) matriz *f*; (*of cigarette*) colilla ▷ *vt*: **to ~ one's toe on sth** dar con el dedo del pie contra algo; **stub out** *vt* (*cigarette*) apagar

stubble ['stʌbl] *n* rastrojo; (*on chin*) barba (incipiente)

stubborn ['stʌbən] *adj* terco, testarudo

stuck [stʌk] *pt, pp of* **stick** ▷ *adj* (*jammed*) atascado

stuck-up [stʌk'ʌp] *adj* engreído, presumido

stud [stʌd] *n* (*shirt stud*) corchete *m*; (*of boot*) taco; (*earring*) pendiente *m* (de bolita); (*also*: **~ farm**) caballeriza; (*also*: **~ horse**) caballo semental ▷ *vt* (*fig*): **~ded with** salpicado de

student ['stjuːdənt] *n* estudiante *m/f* ▷ *adj* estudiantil; **a law/medical ~** un(a) estudiante de derecho/medicina

student driver *n* (*US Aut*) aprendiz(a) *m(f)* de conductor

students' union *n* (*Brit*: *association*) sindicato de estudiantes; (: *building*) centro de estudiantes

studio ['stjuːdɪəu] *n* estudio; (*artist's*) taller *m*

studio flat, studio apartment (*US*) *n* estudio
studious ['stju:dɪəs] *adj* estudioso; (*studied*) calculado
studiously ['stju:dɪəslɪ] *adv* (*carefully*) con esmero
study ['stʌdɪ] *n* estudio ▷ *vt* estudiar; (*examine*) examinar, investigar ▷ *vi* estudiar; **to make a ~ of sth** realizar una investigación de algo; **to ~ for an exam** preparar un examen
stuff [stʌf] *n* materia; (*cloth*) tela; (*substance*) material *m*, sustancia; (*things, belongings*) cosas *fpl* ▷ *vt* llenar; (*Culin*) rellenar; (*animal: for exhibition*) disecar; **my nose is ~ed up** tengo la nariz tapada; **~ed toy** juguete *m or* muñeco de trapo
stuffing ['stʌfɪŋ] *n* relleno
stuffy ['stʌfɪ] *adj* (*room*) mal ventilado; (*person*) de miras estrechas
stumble ['stʌmbl] *vi* tropezar, dar un traspié;
stumble across *vt fus* (*fig*) tropezar con
stumbling block ['stʌmblɪŋ-] *n* tropiezo, obstáculo
stump [stʌmp] *n* (*of tree*) tocón *m*; (*of limb*) muñón *m* ▷ *vt*: **to be ~ed** quedarse perplejo; **to be ~ed for an answer** quedarse sin saber qué contestar
stun [stʌn] *vt* aturdir
stung [stʌŋ] *pt, pp of* **sting**
stunk [stʌŋk] *pp of* **stink**
stunned [stʌnd] *adj* (*dazed*) aturdido, atontado; (*amazed*) pasmado; (*shocked*) anonadado
stunning ['stʌnɪŋ] *adj* (*fig: news*) pasmoso; (*: outfit etc*) sensacional
stunt [stʌnt] *n* (*Aviat*) vuelo acrobático; (*in film*) escena peligrosa; (*also:* **publicity ~**) truco publicitario
stunted ['stʌntɪd] *adj* enano, achaparrado
stuntman ['stʌntmæn] *n* especialista *m*
stupendous [stju:'pɛndəs] *adj* estupendo, asombroso
stupid ['stju:pɪd] *adj* estúpido, tonto
stupidity [stju:'pɪdɪtɪ] *n* estupidez *f*
sturdy ['stə:dɪ] *adj* robusto, fuerte
stutter ['stʌtəʳ] *n* tartamudeo ▷ *vi* tartamudear
sty [staɪ] *n* (*for pigs*) pocilga
stye [staɪ] *n* (*Med*) orzuelo
style [staɪl] *n* estilo; (*fashion*) moda; (*of dress etc*) hechura; (*hair style*) corte *m*; **in the latest ~** en el último modelo
stylish ['staɪlɪʃ] *adj* elegante, a la moda
stylist ['staɪlɪst] *n* (*hair stylist*) peluquero(-a)
stylus (*pl* **styli** *or* **styluses**) ['staɪləs, -laɪ] *n* (*of record player*) aguja
suave [swɑ:v] *adj* cortés, fino
sub [sʌb] *n abbr* = **submarine**; **subscription**
sub... [sʌb] *pref* sub...
subconscious [sʌb'kɔnʃəs] *adj* subconsciente ▷ *n* subconsciente *m*
subcontinent [sʌb'kɔntɪnənt] *n*: **the Indian ~** el subcontinente (de la India)
subcontract *n* ['sʌb'kɔntrækt] subcontrato ▷ *vt* ['sʌbkən'trækt] subcontratar
subcontractor ['sʌbkən'træktəʳ] *n* subcontratista *m/f*
subdue [səb'dju:] *vt* sojuzgar; (*passions*) dominar
subdued [səb'dju:d] *adj* (*light*) tenue; (*person*) sumiso, manso
subject *n* ['sʌbdʒɪkt] súbdito; (*Scol*) tema *m*, materia; (*Grammar*) sujeto ▷ *vt* [səb'dʒɛkt]: **to ~ sb to sth** someter a algn a algo ▷ *adj* ['sʌbdʒɪkt]: **to be ~ to** (*law*) estar sujeto a; (*person*) ser propenso a; **to change the ~** cambiar de tema; **~ to confirmation in writing** sujeto a confirmación por escrito
subjective [səb'dʒɛktɪv] *adj* subjetivo
subject matter *n* materia; (*content*) contenido
subjunctive [səb'dʒʌŋktɪv] *adj, n* subjuntivo
sublet [sʌb'lɛt] *vt, vi* subarrendar, realquilar
submarine [sʌbmə'ri:n] *n* submarino
submerge [səb'mə:dʒ] *vt* sumergir; (*flood*) inundar ▷ *vi* sumergirse
submission [səb'mɪʃən] *n* sumisión *f*; (*to committee etc*) ponencia
submissive [səb'mɪsɪv] *adj* sumiso
submit [səb'mɪt] *vt* someter; (*proposal, claim*) presentar ▷ *vi* someterse; **I ~ that ...** me permito sugerir que ...
subnormal [sʌb'nɔ:məl] *adj* subnormal
subordinate [sə'bɔ:dɪnət] *adj, n* subordinado(-a) *m(f)*
subpoena [səb'pi:nə] (*Law*) *n* citación *f* ▷ *vt* citar
subscribe [səb'skraɪb] *vi* suscribir; **to ~ to** (*fund*) suscribir, aprobar; (*opinion*) estar de acuerdo con; (*newspaper*) suscribirse a
subscriber [səb'skraɪbəʳ] *n* (*to periodical*) suscriptor(a) *m(f)*; (*to telephone*) abonado(-a)
subscription [səb'skrɪpʃən] *n* (*to club*) abono; (*to magazine*) suscripción *f*; **to take out a ~ to** suscribirse a
subsequent ['sʌbsɪkwənt] *adj* subsiguiente, posterior; **~ to** posterior a
subsequently ['sʌbsɪkwəntlɪ] *adv* posteriormente, más tarde
subside [səb'saɪd] *vi* hundirse; (*flood*) bajar; (*wind*) amainar
subsidence [səb'saɪdns] *n* hundimiento; (*in road*) socavón *m*
subsidiarity [səbsɪdɪ'ærɪtɪ] *n* (*Pol*) subsidiariedad *f*
subsidiary [səb'sɪdɪərɪ] *n* sucursal *f*, filial *f* ▷ *adj* (*Univ: subject*) secundario
subsidize ['sʌbsɪdaɪz] *vt* subvencionar
subsidy ['sʌbsɪdɪ] *n* subvención *f*
subsistence [səb'sɪstəns] *n* subsistencia
substance ['sʌbstəns] *n* sustancia; (*fig*) esencia; **to lack ~** (*argument*) ser poco convincente; (*accusation*) no tener

fundamento; (*film, book*) tener poca profundidad
substance abuse *n* uso indebido de sustancias tóxicas
substantial [səb'stænʃl] *adj* sustancial, sustancioso; (*fig*) importante
substantially [səb'stænʃəlɪ] *adv* sustancialmente; **~ bigger** bastante más grande
substantiate [səb'stænʃɪeɪt] *vt* comprobar
substitute ['sʌbstɪtju:t] *n* (*person*) suplente *m/f*; (*thing*) sustituto ▷ *vt*: **to ~ A for B** sustituir B por A, reemplazar A por B
substitution [sʌbstɪ'tju:ʃən] *n* sustitución *f*
subterranean [sʌbtə'reɪnɪən] *adj* subterráneo
subtitle ['sʌbtaɪtl] *n* subtítulo
subtle ['sʌtl] *adj* sutil
subtlety ['sʌtltɪ] *n* sutileza
subtotal [sʌb'təutl] *n* subtotal *m*
subtract [səb'trækt] *vt* restar; sustraer
subtraction [səb'trækʃən] *n* resta; sustracción *f*
suburb ['sʌbə:b] *n* barrio residencial; **the ~s** las afueras (de la ciudad)
suburban [sə'bə:bən] *adj* suburbano; (*train etc*) de cercanías
suburbia [sə'bə:bɪə] *n* barrios *mpl* residenciales
subversive [səb'və:sɪv] *adj* subversivo
subway ['sʌbweɪ] *n* (*Brit*) paso subterráneo *or* inferior; (*US*) metro
succeed [sək'si:d] *vi* (*person*) tener éxito; (*plan*) salir bien ▷ *vt* suceder a; **to ~ in doing** lograr hacer
succeeding [sək'si:dɪŋ] *adj* (*following*) sucesivo; **~ generations** generaciones *fpl* futuras
success [sək'sɛs] *n* éxito; (*gain*) triunfo
successful [sək'sɛsful] *adj* (*venture*) de éxito, exitoso (*esp LAm*); **to be ~ (in doing)** lograr (hacer)
successfully [sək'sɛsfulɪ] *adv* con éxito
succession [sək'sɛʃən] *n* (*series*) sucesión *f*, serie *f*; (*descendants*) descendencia; **in ~** sucesivamente
successive [sək'sɛsɪv] *adj* sucesivo, consecutivo; **on three ~ days** tres días seguidos
successor [sək'sɛsəʳ] *n* sucesor(a) *m(f)*
succinct [sək'sɪŋkt] *adj* sucinto
succulent ['sʌkjulənt] *adj* suculento; **succulents** *npl* (*Bot*) plantas *fpl* carnosas
succumb [sə'kʌm] *vi* sucumbir
such [sʌtʃ] *adj* tal, semejante; (*of that kind*): **~ a book** tal libro; **~ books** tales libros; (*so much*): **~ courage** tanto valor ▷ *adv* tan; **~ a long trip** un viaje tan largo; **~ a lot of** tanto; **~ as** (*like*) tal como; **a noise ~ as to** un ruido tal que; **~ books as I have** cuantos libros tengo; **I said no ~ thing** no dije tal cosa; **it's ~ a long time since we saw each other** hace tanto tiempo que no nos vemos; **~ a long time ago** hace tantísimo tiempo; **as ~** *adv* como tal
such-and-such ['sʌtʃənsʌtʃ] *adj* tal o cual
suchlike ['sʌtʃlaɪk] *pron* (*inf*): **and ~** y cosas por el estilo
suck [sʌk] *vt* chupar; (*bottle*) sorber; (*breast*) mamar; (*pump, machine*) aspirar
sucker ['sʌkəʳ] *n* (*Bot*) serpollo; (*Zool*) ventosa; (*inf*) bobo, primo
suction ['sʌkʃən] *n* succión *f*
Sudan [su'dæn] *n* Sudán *m*
sudden ['sʌdn] *adj* (*rapid*) repentino, súbito; (*unexpected*) imprevisto; **all of a ~** de repente
sudden-death [sʌdn'dɛθ] *n* (*also*: **~ play off**) desempate *m* instantáneo, muerte *f* súbita
suddenly ['sʌdnlɪ] *adv* de repente
sudoku [su'dəuku:] *n* sudoku *m*
suds [sʌdz] *npl* espuma *sg* de jabón
sue [su:] *vt* demandar; **to ~ (for)** demandar (por); **to ~ for divorce** solicitar *or* pedir el divorcio; **to ~ for damages** demandar por daños y perjuicios
suede [sweɪd] *n* ante *m*, gamuza (*LAm*)
suet ['suɪt] *n* sebo
suffer ['sʌfəʳ] *vt* sufrir, padecer; (*tolerate*) aguantar, soportar; (*undergo: loss, setback*) experimentar ▷ *vi* sufrir, padecer; **to ~ from** padecer, sufrir; **to ~ from the effects of alcohol/a fall** sufrir los efectos del alcohol/ resentirse de una caída
sufferer ['sʌfərəʳ] *n* víctima *f*; (*Med*): **~ from** enfermo(-a) de
suffering ['sʌfərɪŋ] *n* (*hardship, deprivation*) sufrimiento; (*pain*) dolor *m*
suffice [sə'faɪs] *vi* bastar, ser suficiente
sufficient [sə'fɪʃənt] *adj* suficiente, bastante
sufficiently [sə'fɪʃəntlɪ] *adv* suficientemente, bastante
suffix ['sʌfɪks] *n* sufijo
suffocate ['sʌfəkeɪt] *vi* ahogarse, asfixiarse
sugar ['ʃugəʳ] *n* azúcar *m* ▷ *vt* echar azúcar a, azucarar
sugar beet *n* remolacha
sugar cane *n* caña de azúcar
suggest [sə'dʒɛst] *vt* sugerir; (*recommend*) aconsejar; **what do you ~ I do?** ¿qué sugieres que haga?; **this ~s that ...** esto hace pensar que ...
suggestion [sə'dʒɛstʃən] *n* sugerencia; **there's no ~ of ...** no hay indicación *or* evidencia de ...
suicide ['suɪsaɪd] *n* suicidio; (*person*) suicida *m/f*; **to commit ~** suicidarse
suicide attack *n* atentado suicida
suicide bomber *n* terrorista *m/f* suicida
suicide bombing *n* atentado *m* suicida
suit [su:t] *n* traje *m*; (*Law*) pleito; (*Cards*) palo ▷ *vt* convenir; (*clothes*) sentar bien a, ir bien a; (*adapt*): **to ~ sth to** adaptar *or* ajustar algo a; **to be ~ed to sth** (*suitable for*) ser apto para algo; **well ~ed** (*couple*) hechos el uno para

el otro; **to bring a ~ against sb** entablar demanda contra algn; **to follow ~** (*Cards*) seguir el palo; (*fig*) seguir el ejemplo (de algn); **that ~s me** me va bien

suitable ['su:təbl] *adj* conveniente; (*apt*) indicado

suitably ['su:təblɪ] *adv* convenientemente; (*appropriately*) en forma debida

suitcase ['su:tkeɪs] *n* maleta, valija (*LAm*)

suite [swi:t] *n* (*of rooms*) suite *f*; (*Mus*) suite *f*; (*furniture*): **bedroom/dining room ~** (juego de) dormitorio/comedor *m*; **a three-piece ~** un tresillo

suitor ['su:tə^r] *n* pretendiente *m*

sulfur ['sʌlfə^r] *n* (*US*) = **sulphur**

sulk [sʌlk] *vi* estar de mal humor

sulky ['sʌlkɪ] *adj* malhumorado

sullen ['sʌlən] *adj* hosco, malhumorado

sulphur, sulfur (*US*) ['sʌlfə^r] *n* azufre *m*

sultana [sʌl'tɑ:nə] *n* (*fruit*) pasa de Esmirna

sultry ['sʌltrɪ] *adj* (*weather*) bochornoso; (*seductive*) seductor(a)

sum [sʌm] *n* suma; (*total*) total *m*; **sum up** *vt* resumir; (*evaluate rapidly*) evaluar ▷ *vi* hacer un resumen

summarize ['sʌməraɪz] *vt* resumir

summary ['sʌmərɪ] *n* resumen *m* ▷ *adj* (*justice*) sumario

summer ['sʌmə^r] *n* verano ▷ *adj* de verano; **in (the) ~** en (el) verano

summer holidays *npl* vacaciones *fpl* de verano

summerhouse ['sʌməhaus] *n* (*in garden*) cenador *m*, glorieta

summertime ['sʌmətaɪm] *n* (*season*) verano

summer time *n* (*by clock*) hora de verano

summit ['sʌmɪt] *n* cima, cumbre *f*; (*also*: **~ conference**) (conferencia) cumbre *f*

summon ['sʌmən] *vt* (*person*) llamar; (*meeting*) convocar; **to ~ a witness** citar a un testigo; **summon up** *vt* (*courage*) armarse de

summons ['sʌmənz] *n* llamamiento, llamada ▷ *vt* citar, emplazar; **to serve a ~ on sb** citar a algn ante el juicio

sumo ['su:məu] *n* (*also*: **~ wrestling**) sumo

sump [sʌmp] *n* (*Brit Aut*) cárter *m*

Sun *abbr* (= *Sunday*) dom

sun [sʌn] *n* sol *m*; **they have everything under the ~** no les falta nada, tienen de todo

sunbathe ['sʌnbeɪð] *vi* tomar el sol

sunbed ['sʌnbɛd] *n* cama solar

sunblock ['sʌnblɔk] *n* filtro solar

sunburn ['sʌnbə:n] *n* (*painful*) quemadura del sol; (*tan*) bronceado

sunburnt ['sʌnbə:nt], **sunburned** ['sʌnbə:nd] *adj* (*tanned*) bronceado; (*painfully*) quemado por el sol

Sunday ['sʌndɪ] *n* domingo; *see also* **Tuesday**

Sunday paper *n* (periódico) dominical *m*

Sunday school *n* catequesis *f*

sundial ['sʌndaɪəl] *n* reloj *m* de sol

sundown ['sʌndaun] *n* anochecer *m*, puesta de sol

sundries ['sʌndrɪz] *npl* géneros *mpl* diversos

sundry ['sʌndrɪ] *adj* varios, diversos; **all and ~** todos sin excepción

sunflower ['sʌnflauə^r] *n* girasol *m*

sung [sʌŋ] *pp of* **sing**

sunglasses ['sʌnglɑ:sɪz] *npl* gafas *fpl* de sol

sunk [sʌŋk] *pp of* **sink**

sunlight ['sʌnlaɪt] *n* luz *f* del sol

sunlit ['sʌnlɪt] *adj* iluminado por el sol

sun lounger *n* tumbona, perezosa (*LAm*)

sunny ['sʌnɪ] *adj* soleado; (*day*) de sol; (*fig*) alegre; **it is ~** hace sol

sunrise ['sʌnraɪz] *n* salida del sol

sun roof *n* (*Aut*) techo corredizo *or* solar; (*on building*) azotea, terraza

sunscreen ['sʌnskri:n] *n* protector *m* solar

sunset ['sʌnsɛt] *n* puesta del sol

sunshade ['sʌnʃeɪd] *n* (*over table*) sombrilla

sunshine ['sʌnʃaɪn] *n* sol *m*

sunstroke ['sʌnstrəuk] *n* insolación *f*

suntan ['sʌntæn] *n* bronceado

suntan lotion *n* bronceador *m*

suntanned ['sʌntænd] *adj* bronceado

suntan oil *n* aceite *m* bronceador

super ['su:pə^r] *adj* (*inf*) genial

superannuation [su:pərænju'eɪʃən] *n* jubilación *f*, pensión *f*

superb [su:'pə:b] *adj* magnífico, espléndido

Super Bowl *n* (*US Sport*) *super copa de fútbol americano*

supercilious [su:pə'sɪlɪəs] *adj* (*disdainful*) desdeñoso; (*haughty*) altanero

superconductor [su:pəkən'dʌktə^r] *n* superconductor *m*

superficial [su:pə'fɪʃəl] *adj* superficial

superfluous [su'pə:fluəs] *adj* superfluo, de sobra

superglue ['su:pəglu:] *n* cola de contacto, supercola

superhighway ['su:pəhaɪweɪ] *n* (*US*) superautopista; **the information ~** la superautopista de la información

superimpose ['su:pərɪm'pəuz] *vt* sobreponer

superintendent [su:pərɪn'tɛndənt] *n* director(a) *m(f)*; (*also*: **police ~**) subjefe(-a) *m(f)*

superior [su'pɪərɪə^r] *adj* superior; (*smug*: *person*) altivo, desdeñoso; (*: smile, air*) de suficiencia; (*: remark*) desdeñoso ▷ *n* superior *m*; **Mother S~** (*Rel*) madre *f* superiora

superiority [supɪərɪ'ɔrɪtɪ] *n* superioridad *f*; desdén *m*

superlative [su'pə:lətɪv] *adj, n* superlativo

superman ['su:pəmæn] *n* superhombre *m*

supermarket ['su:pəmɑ:kɪt] *n* supermercado

supermodel ['su:pəmɔdl] *n* top model *f*, supermodelo *f*

supernatural [su:pə'nætʃərəl] *adj* sobrenatural ▷ *n*: **the ~** lo sobrenatural

supernova [su:pə'nəuvə] *n* supernova
superpower ['su:pəpauə^r] *n* (*Pol*) superpotencia
supersede [su:pə'si:d] *vt* suplantar
supersonic ['su:pə'sɔnɪk] *adj* supersónico
superstar ['su:pəstɑ:^r] *n* superestrella ▷ *adj* de superestrella
superstition [su:pə'stɪʃən] *n* superstición *f*
superstitious [su:pə'stɪʃəs] *adj* supersticioso
superstore ['su:pəstɔ:^r] *n* (*Brit*) hipermercado
supervise ['su:pəvaɪz] *vt* supervisar
supervision [su:pə'vɪʒən] *n* supervisión *f*
supervisor ['su:pəvaɪzə^r] *n* supervisor(a) *m(f)*
supper ['sʌpə^r] *n* cena; **to have ~** cenar
supple ['sʌpl] *adj* flexible
supplement *n* ['sʌplɪmənt] suplemento ▷ *vt* [sʌplɪ'mɛnt] suplir
supplementary [sʌplɪ'mɛntərɪ] *adj* suplementario
supplier [sə'plaɪə^r] *n* suministrador(a) *m(f)*; (*Comm*) distribuidor(a) *m(f)*
supply [sə'plaɪ] *vt* (*provide*) suministrar; (*information*) facilitar; (*fill: need, want*) suplir, satisfacer; (*equip*): **to ~ (with)** proveer (de) ▷ *n* provisión *f*; (*of gas, water etc*) suministro ▷ *adj* (*Brit: teacher etc*) suplente; **supplies** *npl* (*food*) víveres *mpl*; (*Mil*) pertrechos *mpl*; **office supplies** materiales *mpl* para oficina; **to be in short ~** escasear, haber escasez de; **the electricity/water/gas ~** el suministro de electricidad/agua/gas; **~ and demand** la oferta y la demanda
support [sə'pɔ:t] *n* (*moral, financial etc*) apoyo; (*Tech*) soporte *m* ▷ *vt* apoyar; (*financially*) mantener; (*uphold*) sostener; (*Sport: team*) seguir, ser hincha de; **they stopped work in ~ (of)** pararon de trabajar en apoyo (de); **to ~ o.s.** (*financially*) ganarse la vida
supporter [sə'pɔ:tə^r] *n* (*Pol etc*) partidario(-a); (*Sport*) aficionado(-a); (*Football*) hincha *m/f*
supporting [sə'pɔ:tɪŋ] *adj* (*wall*) de apoyo; **~ role** papel *m* secundario; **~ actor/actress** actor/actriz *m/f* secundario(-a)
supportive [sə'pɔ:tɪv] *adj* de apoyo; **I have a ~ family/wife** mi familia/mujer me apoya
suppose [sə'pəuz] *vt, vi* suponer; (*imagine*) imaginarse; **to be ~d to do sth** deber hacer algo; **I don't ~ she'll come** no creo que venga; **he's ~d to be an expert** se le supone un experto
supposedly [sə'pəuzɪdlɪ] *adv* según cabe suponer
supposing [sə'pəuzɪŋ] *conj* en caso de que; **always ~ (that) he comes** suponiendo que venga
suppress [sə'prɛs] *vt* suprimir; (*yawn*) ahogar
supreme [su'pri:m] *adj* supremo
Supreme Court *n* (*US*) Tribunal *m* Supremo, Corte *f* Suprema
supremo [su'pri:məu] *n* autoridad *f* máxima
surcharge ['sə:tʃɑ:dʒ] *n* sobretasa, recargo
sure [ʃuə^r] *adj* seguro; (*definite, convinced*) cierto; (*aim*) certero ▷ *adv*: **that ~ is pretty, that's ~ pretty** (*US*) ¡qué bonito es!; **to be ~ of sth** estar seguro de algo; **to be ~ of o.s.** estar seguro de sí mismo; **to make ~ of sth/that** asegurarse de algo/asegurar que; **I'm not ~ how/why/when** no estoy seguro de cómo/por qué/cuándo; **~!** (*of course*) ¡claro!, ¡por supuesto!; **~ enough** efectivamente
sure-fire ['ʃuəfaɪə^r] *adj* (*inf*) infalible
surely ['ʃuəlɪ] *adv* (*certainly*) seguramente; **~ you don't mean that!** ¡no lo dices en serio!
surety ['ʃuərətɪ] *n* fianza; (*person*) fiador(a) *m(f)*; **to go** *or* **stand ~ for sb** ser fiador de algn, salir garante por algn
surf [sə:f] *n* olas *fpl* ▷ *vi* hacer surf ▷ *vt* (*Internet*): **to ~ the Net** navegar por Internet
surface ['sə:fɪs] *n* superficie *f* ▷ *vt* (*road*) revestir ▷ *vi* salir a la superficie ▷ *cpd* (*Mil, Naut*) de (la) superficie; **on the ~ it seems that ...** (*fig*) a primera vista parece que ...
surface mail *n* vía terrestre
surfboard ['sə:fbɔ:d] *n* tabla (de surf)
surfeit ['sə:fɪt] *n*: **a ~ of** un exceso de
surfer ['sə:fə^r] *n* surfista *m/f*; **web** *or* **net ~** internauta *m/f*
surfing ['sə:fɪŋ] *n* surf *m*
surge [sə:dʒ] *n* oleada, oleaje *m*; (*Elec*) sobretensión *f* transitoria ▷ *vi* (*wave*) romper; (*people*) avanzar a tropel; **to ~ forward** avanzar rápidamente
surgeon ['sə:dʒən] *n* cirujano(-a)
surgery ['sə:dʒərɪ] *n* cirugía; (*Brit: room*) consultorio; (*: Pol*) *horas en las que los electores pueden reunirse personalmente con su diputado*; **to undergo ~** operarse
surgical ['sə:dʒɪkl] *adj* quirúrgico
surgical spirit *n* (*Brit*) alcohol *m*
surly ['sə:lɪ] *adj* hosco, malhumorado
surname ['sə:neɪm] *n* apellido
surpass [sə:'pɑ:s] *vt* superar, exceder
surplus ['sə:pləs] *n* excedente *m*; (*Comm*) superávit *m* ▷ *adj* (*Comm*) excedente, sobrante; **to have a ~ of sth** tener un excedente de algo; **it is ~ to our requirements** nos sobra; **~ stock** saldos *mpl*
surprise [sə'praɪz] *n* sorpresa ▷ *vt* sorprender; **to take by ~** (*person*) coger desprevenido *or* por sorpresa a, sorprender a; (*Mil: town, fort*) atacar por sorpresa
surprised [sə'praɪzd] *adj* (*look, smile*) de sorpresa; **to be ~** sorprenderse
surprising [sə'praɪzɪŋ] *adj* sorprendente
surprisingly [sə'praɪzɪŋlɪ] *adv* (*easy, helpful*) de modo sorprendente; **(somewhat) ~, he agreed** para sorpresa de todos, aceptó
surrealism [sə'rɪəlɪzəm] *n* surrealismo
surrender [sə'rɛndə^r] *n* rendición *f*, entrega ▷ *vi* rendirse, entregarse ▷ *vt* renunciar
surreptitious [sʌrəp'tɪʃəs] *adj* subrepticio
surrogate ['sʌrəgɪt] *n* (*Brit*) sustituto(-a)
surrogate mother *n* madre *f* de alquiler

S

surround [sə'raund] *vt* rodear, circundar; (*Mil etc*) cercar
surrounding [sə'raundɪŋ] *adj* circundante
surroundings [sə'raundɪŋz] *npl* alrededores *mpl*, cercanías *fpl*
surveillance [səː'veɪləns] *n* vigilancia
survey *n* ['səːveɪ] inspección *f* reconocimiento; (*inquiry*) encuesta; (*comprehensive view: of situation etc*) vista de conjunto ▷ *vt* [səː'veɪ] examinar, inspeccionar; (*Surveying: building*) inspeccionar; (*: land*) hacer un reconocimiento de, reconocer; (*look at*) mirar, contemplar; (*make inquiries about*) hacer una encuesta de; **to carry out a ~ of** inspeccionar, examinar
surveyor [sə'veɪə^r] *n* (*Brit: of building*) perito *m/f*; (*of land*) agrimensor(a) *m(f)*
survival [sə'vaɪvl] *n* supervivencia
survive [sə'vaɪv] *vi* sobrevivir; (*custom etc*) perdurar ▷ *vt* sobrevivir a
survivor [sə'vaɪvə^r] *n* superviviente *m/f*
susceptible [sə'sɛptəbl] *adj* (*easily influenced*) influenciable; (*to disease, illness*): **~ to** propenso a
suspect *adj, n* ['sʌspɛkt] sospechoso(-a) *m(f)* ▷ *vt* [səs'pɛkt] sospechar
suspected [səs'pɛktɪd] *adj* presunto; **to have a ~ fracture** tener una posible fractura
suspend [səs'pɛnd] *vt* suspender
suspended animation [səs'pɛndəd-] *n*: **in a state of ~** en (estado de) hibernación
suspended sentence *n* (*Law*) libertad *f* condicional
suspender belt [səs'pɛndə^r-] *n* (*Brit*) liguero, portaligas *m inv* (*LAm*)
suspenders [səs'pɛndəz] *npl* (*Brit*) ligas *fpl*; (*US*) tirantes *mpl*
suspense [səs'pɛns] *n* incertidumbre *f*, duda; (*in film etc*) suspense *m*; **to keep sb in ~** mantener a algn en suspense
suspension [səs'pɛnʃən] *n* (*gen*) suspensión *f*; (*of driving licence*) privación *f*
suspension bridge *n* puente *m* colgante
suspicion [səs'pɪʃən] *n* sospecha; (*distrust*) recelo; (*trace*) traza; **to be under ~** estar bajo sospecha; **arrested on ~ of murder** detenido bajo sospecha de asesinato
suspicious [səs'pɪʃəs] *adj* (*suspecting*) receloso; (*causing suspicion*) sospechoso; **to be ~ of** *or* **about sb/sth** tener sospechas de algn/algo
sustain [səs'teɪn] *vt* sostener, apoyar; (*suffer*) sufrir, padecer
sustainable [səs'teɪnəbl] *adj* sostenible; **~ development** desarrollo sostenible
sustained [səs'teɪnd] *adj* (*effort*) sostenido
sustenance ['sʌstɪnəns] *n* sustento
SUV ['ɛs'juː'viː] *n abbr* (= *sports utility vehicle*) todoterreno *m inv*, cuatro por cuatro
swab [swɔb] *n* (*Med*) algodón *m*, frotis *m inv* ▷ *vt* (*Naut: also:* **~ down**) limpiar, fregar
swagger ['swægə^r] *vi* pavonearse
swallow ['swɔləu] *n* (*bird*) golondrina; (*of food*) bocado; (*of drink*) trago ▷ *vt* tragar; **swallow up** *vt* (*savings etc*) consumir
swam [swæm] *pt of* **swim**
swamp [swɔmp] *n* pantano, ciénaga ▷ *vt* abrumar, agobiar
swan [swɔn] *n* cisne *m*
swap [swɔp] *n* canje *m*, trueque *m* ▷ *vt*: **to ~ (for)** canjear (por), cambiar (por)
swarm [swɔːm] *n* (*of bees*) enjambre *m*; (*fig*) multitud *f* ▷ *vi* (*bees*) formar un enjambre; (*fig*) hormiguear, pulular
swarthy ['swɔːðɪ] *adj* moreno
swastika ['swɔstɪkə] *n* esvástika, cruz *f* gamada
swat [swɔt] *vt* aplastar ▷ *n* (*also:* **fly ~**) matamoscas *m inv*
sway [sweɪ] *vi* mecerse, balancearse ▷ *vt* (*influence*) mover, influir en ▷ *n* (*rule, power*): **~ (over)** dominio (sobre); **to hold ~ over sb** dominar a algn, mantener el dominio sobre algn
swear (*pt* **swore**, *pp* **sworn**) [swɛə^r, swɔː^r, swɔːn] *vi* jurar; (*with swearwords*) decir tacos ▷ *vt*: **to ~ an oath** prestar juramento, jurar; **to ~ to sth** declarar algo bajo juramento; **swear in** *vt* tomar juramento (a); **to be sworn in** prestar juramento
swearword ['swɛəwəːd] *n* taco, palabrota
sweat [swɛt] *n* sudor *m* ▷ *vi* sudar
sweatband ['swɛtbænd] *n* (*Sport: on head*) banda; (*: on wrist*) muñequera
sweater ['swɛtə^r] *n* suéter *m*
sweatshirt ['swɛtʃəːt] *n* sudadera
sweaty ['swɛtɪ] *adj* sudoroso
Swede [swiːd] *n* sueco(-a)
swede [swiːd] *n* (*Brit*) nabo
Sweden ['swiːdn] *n* Suecia
Swedish ['swiːdɪʃ] *adj, n* (*Ling*) sueco
sweep [swiːp] (*pt, pp* **swept**) *n* (*act*) barrida; (*of arm*) manotazo *m*; (*curve*) curva, alcance *m*; (*also:* **chimney ~**) deshollinador(a) *m(f)* ▷ *vt* barrer; (*with arm*) empujar; (*current*) arrastrar; (*disease, fashion*) recorrer ▷ *vi* barrer; **sweep away** *vt* barrer; (*rub out*) borrar; **sweep past** *vi* pasar rápidamente; (*brush by*) rozar; **sweep up** *vi* barrer
sweeper ['swiːpə^r] *n* (*person*) barrendero(-a); (*machine*) barredora; (*Football*) líbero, libre *m*
sweeping ['swiːpɪŋ] *adj* (*gesture*) dramático; (*generalized*) generalizado; (*changes, reforms*) radical
sweet [swiːt] *n* (*candy*) dulce *m*, caramelo; (*Brit: pudding*) postre *m* ▷ *adj* dulce; (*sugary*) azucarado; (*charming: person*) encantador(a); (*: smile, character*) dulce, amable, agradable ▷ *adv*: **to smell/taste ~** oler/saber dulce
sweet and sour *adj* agridulce
sweetcorn ['swiːtkɔːn] *n* maíz *m* (dulce)
sweeten ['swiːtn] *vt* (*person*) endulzar; (*add sugar to*) poner azúcar a
sweetener ['swiːtnə^r] *n* (*Culin*) edulcorante *m*

sweetheart ['swi:thɑ:t] *n* amor *m*, novio(-a); (*in speech*) amor, cariño
sweetness ['swi:tnɪs] *n* (*gen*) dulzura
sweet pea *n* guisante *m* de olor
sweetshop ['swi:tʃɔp] *n* (*Brit*) confitería, bombonería
swell [swɛl] (*pt* **swelled**, *pp* **swollen** *or* **swelled**) *n* (*of sea*) marejada, oleaje *m* ▷ *adj* (*US*: *inf*: *excellent*) estupendo, fenomenal ▷ *vt* hinchar, inflar ▷ *vi* (*also*: **~ up**) hincharse; (*numbers*) aumentar; (*sound, feeling*) ir aumentando
swelling ['swɛlɪŋ] *n* (*Med*) hinchazón *f*
sweltering ['swɛltərɪŋ] *adj* sofocante, de mucho calor
swept [swɛpt] *pt, pp of* **sweep**
swerve [swə:v] *n* regate *m*; (*in car*) desvío brusco ▷ *vi* desviarse bruscamente
swift [swɪft] *n* (*bird*) vencejo ▷ *adj* rápido, veloz
swig [swɪg] *n* (*inf*: *drink*) trago
swill [swɪl] *n* bazofia ▷ *vt* (*also*: **~ out, ~ down**) lavar, limpiar con agua
swim [swɪm] (*pt* **swam**, *pp* **swum**) *n*: **to go for a ~** ir a nadar *or* a bañarse ▷ *vi* nadar; (*head, room*) dar vueltas ▷ *vt* pasar a nado; **to go ~ming** ir a nadar; **to ~ a length** nadar *or* hacer un largo
swimmer ['swɪmə^r] *n* nadador(a) *m(f)*
swimming ['swɪmɪŋ] *n* natación *f*
swimming cap *n* gorro de baño
swimming costume *n* bañador *m*, traje *m* de baño
swimmingly ['swɪmɪŋlɪ] *adv*: **to go ~** (*wonderfully*) ir como una seda *or* sobre ruedas
swimming pool *n* piscina, alberca (*LAm*)
swimming trunks *npl* bañador *msg*
swimsuit ['swɪmsu:t] *n* = **swimming costume**
swindle ['swɪndl] *n* estafa ▷ *vt* estafar
swine [swaɪn] *n pl inv* cerdo, puerco; (*inf!*) canalla *m* (*!*)
swing [swɪŋ] (*pt, pp* **swung**) *n* (*in playground*) columpio; (*movement*) balanceo, vaivén *m*; (*change of direction*) viraje *m*; (*rhythm*) ritmo; (*Pol*: *in votes etc*): **there has been a ~ towards/away from Labour** ha habido un viraje en favor/en contra del Partido Laborista ▷ *vt* balancear; (*on a swing*) columpiar; (*also*: **~ round**) voltear, girar ▷ *vi* balancearse, columpiarse; (*also*: **~ round**) dar media vuelta; **a ~ to the left** un movimiento hacia la izquierda; **to be in full ~** estar en plena marcha; **to get into the ~ of things** meterse en situación; **the road ~s south** la carretera gira hacia el sur
swing bridge *n* puente *m* giratorio
swing door, swinging door (*US*) ['swɪŋɪŋ-] *n* puerta giratoria
swingeing ['swɪndʒɪŋ] *adj* (*Brit*) abrumador(a)
swipe [swaɪp] *n* golpe *m* fuerte ▷ *vt* (*hit*) golpear fuerte; (*inf*: *steal*) guindar; (*credit card etc*) pasar
swipe card [swaɪp-] *n* tarjeta magnética deslizante, tarjeta swipe
swirl [swə:l] *vi* arremolinarse
swish [swɪʃ] *n* (*sound*: *of whip*) chasquido; (*: of skirts*) frufrú *m*; (*: of grass*) crujido ▷ *adj* (*inf*: *smart*) elegante ▷ *vi* chasquear
Swiss [swɪs] *adj, n pl inv* suizo(-a) *m(f)*
switch [swɪtʃ] *n* (*for light, radio etc*) interruptor *m*; (*change*) cambio ▷ *vt* (*change*) cambiar de; (*invert*: *also*: **~ round, ~ over**) intercambiar; **switch off** *vt* apagar; (*engine*) parar; **switch on** *vt* (*Aut*: *ignition*) encender, prender (*LAm*); (*engine, machine*) arrancar; (*water supply*) conectar
switchboard ['swɪtʃbɔ:d] *n* (*Tel*) centralita (de teléfonos), conmutador *m* (*LAm*)
Switzerland ['swɪtsələnd] *n* Suiza
swivel ['swɪvl] *vi* (*also*: **~ round**) girar
swollen ['swəulən] *pp of* **swell**
swoon [swu:n] *vi* desmayarse
swoop [swu:p] *n* (*by police etc*) redada; (*of bird etc*) descenso en picado, calada ▷ *vi* (*also*: **~ down**) caer en picado
swop [swɔp] *n, vb* = **swap**
sword [sɔ:d] *n* espada
swordfish ['sɔ:dfɪʃ] *n* pez *m* espada
swore [swɔ:^{r}] *pt of* **swear**
sworn [swɔ:n] *pp of* **swear** ▷ *adj* (*statement*) bajo juramento; (*enemy*) implacable
swot [swɔt] (*Brit*) *vt, vi* empollar ▷ *n* empollón(-ona) *m(f)*
swum [swʌm] *pp of* **swim**
swung [swʌŋ] *pt, pp of* **swing**
syllable ['sɪləbl] *n* sílaba
syllabus ['sɪləbəs] *n* programa *m* de estudios; **on the ~** en el programa de estudios
symbol ['sɪmbl] *n* símbolo
symbolic [sɪm'bɔlɪk], **symbolical** [sɪm'bɔlɪkl] *adj* simbólico; **to be ~ of sth** simbolizar algo
symbolism ['sɪmbəlɪzəm] *n* simbolismo
symbolize ['sɪmbəlaɪz] *vt* simbolizar
symmetrical [sɪ'mɛtrɪkl] *adj* simétrico
symmetry ['sɪmɪtrɪ] *n* simetría
sympathetic [sɪmpə'θɛtɪk] *adj* compasivo; (*understanding*) comprensivo; **to be ~ to a cause** (*well disposed*) apoyar una causa; **to be ~ towards** (*person*) ser comprensivo con
sympathize ['sɪmpəθaɪz] *vi*: **to ~ with** (*person*) compadecerse de; (*feelings*) comprender; (*cause*) apoyar
sympathizer ['sɪmpəθaɪzə^r] *n* (*Pol*) simpatizante *m/f*
sympathy ['sɪmpəθɪ] *n* (*pity*) compasión *f*; (*understanding*) comprensión *f*; **a letter of ~** un pésame; **with our deepest ~** nuestro más sentido pésame
symphony ['sɪmfənɪ] *n* sinfonía
symposium [sɪm'pəuzɪəm] *n* simposio
symptom ['sɪmptəm] *n* síntoma *m*, indicio
synagogue ['sɪnəgɔg] *n* sinagoga

S

sync [sɪŋk] *n* (*inf*): **to be in/out of ~ (with)** ir/no ir al mismo ritmo (que); (*fig*: *people*) conectar/no conectar con
synchronized swimming ['sɪŋkrənaɪzd-] *n* natación *f* sincronizada
syndicate ['sɪndɪkɪt] *n* (*gen*) sindicato; (*Press*) agencia (de noticias)
syndrome ['sɪndrəum] *n* síndrome *m*
synonym ['sɪnənɪm] *n* sinónimo
synopsis, synopses [sɪ'nɔpsɪs, -si:z] *n* sinopsis *f inv*
syntax ['sɪntæks] *n* sintaxis *f*
synthetic [sɪn'θɛtɪk] *adj* sintético ▷ *n* sintético
syphilis ['sɪfɪlɪs] *n* sífilis *f*
syphon ['saɪfən] *n, vb* = **siphon**
Syria ['sɪrɪə] *n* Siria
syringe [sɪ'rɪndʒ] *n* jeringa
syrup ['sɪrəp] *n* jarabe *m*, almíbar *m*
system ['sɪstəm] *n* sistema *m*; (*Anat*) organismo; **it was quite a shock to his ~** fue un golpe para él
systematic [sɪstə'mætɪk] *adj* sistemático; metódico
system disk *n* (*Comput*) disco del sistema
systems analyst *n* analista *m/f* de sistemas

t

T, t [ti:] *n* (*letter*) T, t *f*; **T for Tommy** T de Tarragona
TA *n abbr* (*Brit*) = **Territorial Army**
ta [tɑ:] *excl* (*Brit*: *inf*) ¡gracias!
tab [tæb] *n abbr* = **tabulator** ▷ *n* lengüeta; (*label*) etiqueta; **to keep ~s on** (*fig*) vigilar
tabby ['tæbɪ] *n* (*also*: **~ cat**) gato atigrado
tabernacle ['tæbənækl] *n* tabernáculo
table ['teɪbl] *n* mesa; (*chart*: *of statistics etc*) cuadro, tabla ▷ *vt* (*Brit*: *motion etc*) presentar; **to lay** *or* **set the ~** poner la mesa; **to clear the ~** quitar *or* levantar la mesa; **league ~** (*Football, Rugby*) clasificación *f* del campeonato; **~ of contents** índice *m* de materias
tablecloth ['teɪblklɔθ] *n* mantel *m*
table d'hôte [tɑ:bl'dəut] *n* menú *m*
table lamp *n* lámpara de mesa
tablemat ['teɪblmæt] *n* (*for plate*) posaplatos *m inv*; (*for hot dish*) salvamantel *m*
tablespoon ['teɪblspu:n] *n* cuchara grande; (*also*: **~ful**: *as measurement*) cucharada grande
tablet ['tæblɪt] *n* (*Med*) pastilla, comprimido; (*for writing*) bloc *m*; (*of stone*) lápida; (*Comput*) tableta, tablet *f*; **~ of soap** pastilla de jabón
table tennis *n* ping-pong *m*, tenis *m* de mesa
table wine *n* vino de mesa
tabloid ['tæblɔɪd] *n* (*newspaper*) periódico popular sensacionalista
tabloid press *n ver nota*

TABLOID PRESS

El término genérico *tabloid press* o "tabloids" se usa para referirse a los periódicos populares británicos, por su tamaño reducido. A diferencia de la llamada quality press, estos periódicos se caracterizan por su lenguaje sencillo, presentación llamativa y contenido a menudo sensacionalista, con gran énfasis en noticias sobre escándalos financieros y sexuales de los famosos, por lo que también reciben el nombre peyorativo de "gutter press".

taboo [tə'buː] *adj, n* tabú *m*
tabulate ['tæbjuleɪt] *vt* disponer en tablas
tabulator ['tæbjuleɪtə^r] *n* tabulador *m*
tachograph ['tækəgrɑːf] *n* tacógrafo
tacit ['tæsɪt] *adj* tácito
tack [tæk] *n (nail)* tachuela; *(stitch)* hilván *m*; *(Naut)* bordada ▷ *vt (nail)* clavar con tachuelas; *(stitch)* hilvanar ▷ *vi* virar; **to ~ sth on to (the end of) sth** *(of letter, book)* añadir algo a(l final de) algo
tackle ['tækl] *n (gear)* equipo; *(fishing tackle, for lifting)* aparejo; *(Football)* entrada, tackle *m*; *(Rugby)* placaje *m* ▷ *vt (difficulty)* enfrentarse a, abordar; *(challenge: person)* hacer frente a; *(grapple with)* agarrar; *(Football)* entrar a; *(Rugby)* placar
tacky ['tækɪ] *adj* pegajoso; *(inf)* hortera *inv*, de mal gusto
tact [tækt] *n* tacto, discreción *f*
tactful ['tæktful] *adj* discreto, diplomático; **to be ~** tener tacto, actuar discretamente
tactical ['tæktɪkl] *adj* táctico
tactical voting *n* voto útil
tactician [tæk'tɪʃən] *n* táctico(-a)
tactics ['tæktɪks] *n, npl* táctica *sg*
tactless ['tæktlɪs] *adj* indiscreto
tadpole ['tædpəul] *n* renacuajo
taffy ['tæfɪ] *n (US)* melcocha
tag [tæg] *n (label)* etiqueta; **price/name ~** etiqueta del precio/con el nombre; **tag along** *vi*: **to ~ along with sb** engancharse a algn
tail [teɪl] *n* cola; *(Zool)* rabo; *(of shirt, coat)* faldón *m* ▷ *vt (follow)* vigilar a; **heads or ~s** cara o cruz; **to turn ~** volver la espalda; **tails** *npl (formal suit)* levita; **tail away, tail off** *vi (in size, quality etc)* ir disminuyendo
tailback ['teɪlbæk] *n (Brit Aut)* cola
tail end *n* cola, parte *f* final
tailgate ['teɪlgeɪt] *n (Aut)* puerta trasera
tailor ['teɪlə^r] *n* sastre *m* ▷ *vt*: **to ~ sth (to)** confeccionar algo a medida (para); **~'s (shop)** sastrería
tailoring ['teɪlərɪŋ] *n (cut)* corte *m*; *(craft)* sastrería
tailor-made ['teɪlə'meɪd] *adj (also fig)* hecho a (la) medida
tailwind ['teɪlwɪnd] *n* viento de cola
tainted ['teɪntɪd] *adj (water, air)* contaminado; *(fig)* manchado
Taiwan [taɪ'wɑːn] *n* Taiwán *m*
Taiwanese [taɪwə'niːz] *adj, n* taiwanés(-esa) *m/f*
Tajikistan [tɑːdʒɪkɪ'stɑːn] *n* Tayikistán *m*
take [teɪk] *(pt* **took**, *pp* **taken**) *vt* tomar; *(grab)* coger *(Sp)*, agarrar *(LAm)*; *(gain: prize)* ganar; *(require: effort, courage)* exigir; *(support weight of)* aguantar; *(hold: passengers etc)* tener cabida para; *(accompany, bring, carry)* llevar; *(exam)* presentarse a; *(conduct: meeting)* presidir ▷ *vi (fire)* prender; *(dye)* coger *(Sp)*, agarrar, tomar ▷ *n (Cine)* toma; **to ~ sth from** *(drawer etc)* sacar algo de; *(person)* quitar algo a, coger algo a *(Sp)*; **to ~ sb's hand** tomar de la mano a algn; **to ~ notes** tomar apuntes; **to be ~n ill** ponerse enfermo; **~ the first on the left** toma la primera a la izquierda; **I only took Russian for one year** sólo estudié ruso un año; **I took him for a doctor** le tenía por médico; **it won't ~ long** durará poco; **it will ~ at least five litres** tiene cabida por lo menos para cinco litros; **to be ~n with sb/sth** *(attracted)* tomarle cariño a algn/tomarle gusto a algo; **I ~ it that ...** supongo que ...; **take after** *vt fus* parecerse a; **take apart** *vt* desmontar; **take away** *vt (remove)* quitar; *(carry off)* llevar ▷ *vi*: **to ~ away from** quitar mérito a; **take back** *vt (return)* devolver; *(one's words)* retractar; **take down** *vt (building)* derribar; *(dismantle: scaffolding)* desmantelar; *(message etc)* apuntar, tomar nota de; **take in** *vt (Brit: deceive)* engañar; *(understand)* entender; *(include)* abarcar; *(lodger)* acoger, recibir; *(orphan, stray dog)* recoger; *(Sewing)* achicar; **take off** *vi (Aviat)* despegar, decolar *(LAm)* ▷ *vt (remove)* quitar; *(imitate)* imitar, remedar; **take on** *vt (work)* emprender; *(employee)* contratar; *(opponent)* desafiar; **take out** *vt* sacar; *(remove)* quitar; **don't ~ it out on me!** ¡no te desquites conmigo!; **take over** *vt (business)* tomar posesión de ▷ *vi*: **to ~ over from sb** reemplazar a algn; **take to** *vt fus (person)* coger cariño a *(Sp)*, encariñarse con *(LAm)*; *(activity)* aficionarse a; **to ~ to doing sth** aficionarse a (hacer) algo; **take up** *vt (a dress)* acortar; *(occupy: time, space)* ocupar; *(engage in: hobby etc)* dedicarse a; *(absorb: liquids)* absorber; *(accept: offer, challenge)* aceptar ▷ *vi*: **to ~ up with sb** hacerse amigo de algn; **to ~ sb up on** aceptar algo de algn; **take upon** *vt*: **to ~ it upon o.s. to do sth** encargarse de hacer algo
takeaway ['teɪkəweɪ] *adj (Brit: food)* para llevar ▷ *n* tienda *or* restaurante *m* de comida para llevar
taken ['teɪkən] *pp of* **take**
takeoff ['teɪkɔf] *n (Aviat)* despegue *m*, decolaje *m (LAm)*
takeover ['teɪkəuvə^r] *n (Comm)* absorción *f*

t

takeover bid *n* oferta pública de adquisición
takings ['teɪkɪŋz] *npl* (*Comm*) ingresos *mpl*
talc [tælk] *n* (*also*: **~um powder**) talco
tale [teɪl] *n* (*story*) cuento; (*account*) relación *f*; **to tell ~s** (*fig*) contar chismes
talent ['tælnt] *n* talento
talented ['tæləntɪd] *adj* talentoso, de talento
talisman ['tælɪzmən] *n* talismán *m*
talk [tɔːk] *n* charla; (*gossip*) habladurías *fpl*, chismes *mpl*; (*conversation*) conversación *f* ▷ *vi* (*speak*) hablar; (*chatter*) charlar; **talks** *npl* (*Pol etc*) conversaciones *fpl*; **to give a ~** dar una charla *or* conferencia; **to ~ about** hablar de; **to ~ sb into doing sth** convencer a algn para que haga algo; **to ~ sb out of doing sth** disuadir a algn de que haga algo; **to ~ shop** hablar del trabajo; **~ing of films, have you seen ...?** hablando de películas, ¿has visto ...?; **talk over** *vt* discutir
talkative ['tɔːkətɪv] *adj* hablador(a)
talking point ['tɔːkɪŋ-] *n* tema *m* de conversación
talking-to ['tɔːkɪŋtuː] *n*: **to give sb a good ~** echar una buena bronca a algn
talk show *n* programa *m* magazine
tall [tɔːl] *adj* alto; (*tree*) grande; **to be 6 feet ~** ≈ medir 1 metro 80, tener 1 metro 80 de alto; **how ~ are you?** ¿cuánto mides?
tall story *n* cuento chino
tally ['tælɪ] *n* cuenta ▷ *vi*: **to ~ (with)** concordar (con), cuadrar (con); **to keep a ~ of sth** llevar la cuenta de algo
talon ['tælən] *n* garra
tambourine [tæmbə'riːn] *n* pandereta
tame [teɪm] *adj* (*mild*) manso; (*tamed*) domesticado; (*fig*: *story, style, person*) soso, anodino
tamper ['tæmpə^r] *vi*: **to ~ with** (*lock etc*) intentar forzar; (*papers*) falsificar
tampon ['tæmpən] *n* tampón *m*
tan [tæn] *n* (*also*: **sun~**) bronceado ▷ *vt* broncear ▷ *vi* ponerse moreno ▷ *adj* (*colour*) marrón; **to get a ~** broncearse, ponerse moreno
tandem ['tændəm] *n* tándem *m*
tang [tæŋ] *n* sabor *m* fuerte
tangent ['tændʒənt] *n* (*Math*) tangente *f*; **to go off at a ~** (*fig*) salirse por la tangente
tangerine [tændʒə'riːn] *n* mandarina
tangible ['tændʒəbl] *adj* tangible; **~ assets** bienes *mpl* tangibles
tangle ['tæŋgl] *n* enredo; **to get in(to) a ~** enredarse
tank [tæŋk] *n* (*also*: **water ~**) depósito, tanque *m*; (*for fish*) acuario; (*Mil*) tanque *m*
tanker ['tæŋkə^r] *n* (*ship*) petrolero; (*truck*) camión *m* cisterna
tankini [taŋ'kiːnɪ] *n* tankini *m*
tanned [tænd] *adj* (*skin*) moreno, bronceado
tannoy® ['tænɔɪ] *n*: **over the ~** por el altavoz
tantalizing ['tæntəlaɪzɪŋ] *adj* tentador(a)
tantamount ['tæntəmaunt] *adj*: **~ to** equivalente a
tantrum ['tæntrəm] *n* rabieta; **to throw a ~** coger una rabieta
Tanzania [tænzə'nɪə] *n* Tanzania
tap [tæp] *n* (*Brit*: *on sink etc*) grifo, canilla (*LAm*); (*gentle blow*) golpecito; (*gas tap*) llave *f* ▷ *vt* (*table etc*) tamborilear; (*shoulder etc*) dar palmaditas en; (*resources*) utilizar, explotar; (*telephone conversation*) intervenir, pinchar; **on ~** (*fig*: *resources*) a mano; **beer on ~** cerveza de barril
tap dancing ['tæpdɑːnsɪŋ] *n* claqué *m*
tape [teɪp] *n* cinta; (*also*: **magnetic ~**) cinta magnética; (*sticky tape*) cinta adhesiva ▷ *vt* (*record*) grabar (en cinta); **on ~** (*song etc*) grabado (en cinta)
tape deck *n* pletina
tape measure *n* cinta métrica, metro
taper ['teɪpə^r] *n* cirio ▷ *vi* afilarse
tape recorder *n* grabadora
tapestry ['tæpɪstrɪ] *n* (*object*) tapiz *m*; (*art*) tapicería
tar [tɑː^r] *n* alquitrán *m*, brea; **low/middle ~ cigarettes** cigarrillos con contenido bajo/medio de alquitrán
target ['tɑːgɪt] *n* (*gen*) blanco; **to be on ~** (*project*) seguir el curso previsto
tariff ['tærɪf] *n* (*on goods*) arancel *m*; (*Brit*: *in hotels etc*) tarifa
tarmac ['tɑːmæk] *n* (*Brit*: *on road*) asfalto; (*Aviat*) pista (de aterrizaje)
tarnish ['tɑːnɪʃ] *vt* deslustrar
tarot ['tærəu] *n* tarot *m*
tarpaulin [tɑː'pɔːlɪn] *n* lona (impermeabilizada)
tarragon ['tærəgən] *n* estragón *m*
tart [tɑːt] *n* (*Culin*) tarta; (*Brit inf*: *pej*: *woman*) fulana ▷ *adj* (*flavour*) agrio, ácido; **tart up** *vt* (*room, building*) dar tono a
tartan ['tɑːtn] *n* tartán *m*, tela escocesa ▷ *adj* de tartán
tartar ['tɑːtə^r] *n* (*on teeth*) sarro
tartar sauce *n* salsa tártara
task [tɑːsk] *n* tarea; **to take to ~** reprender
task force *n* (*Mil, Police*) grupo de operaciones
tassel ['tæsl] *n* borla
taste [teɪst] *n* sabor *m*, gusto; (*also*: **after~**) dejo; (*sip*) sorbo; (*fig*: *glimpse, idea*) muestra, idea ▷ *vt* probar ▷ *vi*: **to ~ of** *or* **like** (*fish etc*) saber a; **you can ~ the garlic (in it)** se nota el sabor a ajo; **can I have a ~ of this wine?** ¿puedo probar este vino?; **to have a ~ for sth** ser aficionado a algo; **in good/bad ~** de buen/mal gusto; **to be in bad** *or* **poor ~** ser de mal gusto
tasteful ['teɪstful] *adj* de buen gusto
tasteless ['teɪstlɪs] *adj* (*food*) soso; (*remark*) de mal gusto
tasty ['teɪstɪ] *adj* sabroso, rico
ta-ta ['tæ'tɑː] *interj* (*Brit inf*) hasta luego, adiós
tatters ['tætəz] *npl*: **in ~** (*also*: **tattered**) hecho jirones
tattoo [tə'tuː] *n* tatuaje *m*; (*spectacle*) espectáculo militar ▷ *vt* tatuar

tatty ['tætɪ] *adj* (*Brit inf*) cochambroso
taught [tɔ:t] *pt, pp of* **teach**
taunt [tɔ:nt] *n* pulla ▷ *vt* lanzar pullas a
Taurus ['tɔ:rəs] *n* Tauro
taut [tɔ:t] *adj* tirante, tenso
tax [tæks] *n* impuesto ▷ *vt* gravar (con un impuesto); (*fig: test*) poner a prueba; (*: patience*) agotar; **before/after ~** impuestos excluidos/incluidos; **free of ~** libre de impuestos
taxable ['tæksəbl] *adj* (*income*) imponible, sujeto a impuestos
taxation [tæk'seɪʃən] *n* impuestos *mpl*; **system of ~** sistema *m* tributario
tax avoidance *n* evasión *f* de impuestos
tax disc *n* (*Brit Aut*) pegatina del impuesto de circulación
tax evasion *n* evasión *f* fiscal
tax-free ['tæksfri:] *adj* libre de impuestos
taxi ['tæksɪ] *n* taxi *m* ▷ *vi* (*Aviat*) rodar por la pista
taxi driver *n* taxista *m/f*
taxi rank, taxi stand (*Brit*) *n* parada de taxis
tax payer *n* contribuyente *m/f*
tax rebate *n* devolución *f* de impuestos, reembolso fiscal
tax relief *n* desgravación *f* fiscal
tax return *n* declaración *f* de la renta
TB *n abbr* = **tuberculosis**
tbc *abbr* (= *to be confirmed*) por confirmar
TD *n abbr* (*US*) = **Treasury Department**; (*: Football*) = **touchdown**
tea [ti:] *n* té *m*; (*Brit: snack*) ≈ merienda; **high ~** (*Brit*) ≈ merienda-cena
tea bag *n* bolsita de té
tea break *n* (*Brit*) descanso para el té
teach (*pt, pp* **taught**) [ti:tʃ, tɔ:t] *vt*: **to ~ sb sth, ~ sth to sb** enseñar algo a algn ▷ *vi* enseñar; (*be a teacher*) ser profesor(a); **it taught him a lesson** (eso) le sirvió de escarmiento
teacher ['ti:tʃə^r] *n* (*in secondary school*) profesor(a) *m(f)*; (*in primary school*) maestro(-a); **Spanish ~** profesor(a) *m(f)* de español
teaching ['ti:tʃɪŋ] *n* enseñanza
tea cloth *n* (*Brit*) paño de cocina, trapo de cocina (*LAm*)
tea cosy *n* cubretetera *m*
teacup ['ti:kʌp] *n* taza de té
teak [ti:k] *n* (madera de) teca
tea leaves *npl* hojas *fpl* de té
team [ti:m] *n* equipo; (*of animals*) pareja;
team up *vi* asociarse
teamwork ['ti:mwə:k] *n* trabajo en equipo
teapot ['ti:pɔt] *n* tetera
tear[1] [tɪə^r] *n* lágrima; **in ~s** llorando; **to burst into ~s** deshacerse en lágrimas
tear[2] [tɛə^r] (*pt* **tore**, *pp* **torn**) *n* rasgón *m*, desgarrón *m* ▷ *vt* romper, rasgar ▷ *vi* rasgarse; **to ~ to pieces** *or* **to bits** *or* **to shreds** (*also fig*) hacer pedazos, destrozar;
tear along *vi* (*rush*) precipitarse; **tear apart** *vt* (*also fig*) hacer pedazos; **tear away** *vt*: **to ~ o.s. away (from sth)** alejarse (de algo); **tear down** *vt* (*building, statue*) derribar; (*poster, flag*) arrancar; **tear off** *vt* (*sheet of paper etc*) arrancar; (*one's clothes*) quitarse a tirones;
tear out *vt* (*sheet of paper, cheque*) arrancar;
tear up *vt* (*sheet of paper etc*) romper
tearful ['tɪəful] *adj* lloroso
tear gas *n* gas *m* lacrimógeno
tearoom ['ti:ru:m] *n* salón *m* de té
tease [ti:z] *n* bromista *m/f* ▷ *vt* tomar el pelo a
tea set *n* servicio de té
teaspoon ['ti:spu:n] *n* cucharita; (*also*: **~ful**: *as measurement*) cucharadita
teat [ti:t] *n* (*of bottle*) boquilla, tetilla
teatime ['ti:taɪm] *n* hora del té
tea towel *n* (*Brit*) paño de cocina
technical ['tɛknɪkl] *adj* técnico
technical college *n* centro de formación profesional
technicality [tɛknɪ'kælɪtɪ] *n* detalle *m* técnico; **on a legal ~** por una cuestión formal
technically ['tɛknɪklɪ] *adv* técnicamente
technician [tɛk'nɪʃn] *n* técnico(-a)
technique [tɛk'ni:k] *n* técnica
technological [tɛknə'lɔdʒɪkl] *adj* tecnológico
technology [tɛk'nɔlədʒɪ] *n* tecnología
teddy ['tɛdɪ], **teddy bear** *n* osito de peluche
tedious ['ti:dɪəs] *adj* pesado, aburrido
tee [ti:] *n* (*Golf*) tee *m*
teem [ti:m] *vi*: **to ~ with** rebosar de; **it is ~ing (with rain)** llueve a mares
teen [ti:n] *adj* = **teenage** ▷ *n* (*US*) = **teenager**
teenage ['ti:neɪdʒ] *adj* (*fashions etc*) juvenil
teenager ['ti:neɪdʒə^r] *n* adolescente *m/f*, quinceañero(-a)
teens [ti:nz] *npl*: **to be in one's ~** ser adolescente
tee-shirt ['ti:ʃə:t] *n* = **T-shirt**
teeter ['ti:tə^r] *vi* balancearse
teeth [ti:θ] *npl of* **tooth**
teethe [ti:ð] *vi* echar los dientes
teething ring ['ti:ðɪŋ-] *n* mordedor *m*
teething troubles ['ti:ðɪŋ] *npl* (*fig*) dificultades *fpl* iniciales
teetotal ['ti:'təutl] *adj* (*person*) abstemio
TEFL ['tɛfl] *n abbr* (= *Teaching of English as a Foreign Language*); **~ qualification** *título para la enseñanza del inglés como lengua extranjera*
tel. *abbr* (= *telephone*) tel
telecommunications ['tɛlɪkəmju:nɪ] *n* telecomunicaciones *fpl*
teleconferencing ['telɪkɒnfərənsɪŋ] *n* teleconferencias *fpl*
telegram ['tɛlɪgræm] *n* telegrama *m*
telegraph ['tɛlɪgrɑ:f] *n* telégrafo
telegraph pole *n* poste *m* telegráfico
telepathic [tɛlɪ'pæθɪk] *adj* telepático
telephone ['tɛlɪfəun] *n* teléfono ▷ *vt* llamar por teléfono, telefonear; **to be on the ~**

t

(*subscriber*) tener teléfono; (*be speaking*) estar hablando por teléfono
telephone book *n* guía *f* telefónica
telephone booth, telephone box (*Brit*) *n* cabina telefónica
telephone call *n* llamada telefónica
telephone directory *n* guía telefónica
telephone number *n* número de teléfono
telephonist [tə'lɛfənɪst] *n* (*Brit*) telefonista *m/f*
telesales ['tɛlɪseɪlz] *npl* televentas *fpl*
telescope ['tɛlɪskəup] *n* telescopio
Teletext® ['tɛlɪtɛkst] *n* teletexto *m*
telethon ['tɛlɪθɔn] *n* telemaratón *m*, maratón *m* televisivo (*con fines benéficos*)
televise ['tɛlɪvaɪz] *vt* televisar
television ['tɛlɪvɪʒən] *n* televisión *f*; **to watch ~** mirar *or* ver la televisión
television licence *n* impuesto por uso de televisor
television programme *n* programa *m* de televisión
television set *n* televisor *m*
teleworking ['telɪwɜːkɪŋ] *n* teletrabajo
telex ['tɛlɛks] *n* télex *m* ▷ *vt* (*message*) enviar por télex; (*person*) enviar un télex a ▷ *vi* enviar un télex
tell (*pt, pp* **told**) [tɛl, təuld] *vt* decir; (*relate: story*) contar; (*distinguish*): **to ~ sth from** distinguir algo de ▷ *vi* (*talk*): **to ~ (of)** contar; (*have effect*) tener efecto; **to ~ sb to do sth** decir a algn que haga algo; **to ~ sb about sth** contar algo a algn; **to ~ the time** dar *or* decir la hora; **can you ~ me the time?** ¿me puedes decir la hora?; **(I) ~ you what ...** fíjate ...; **I couldn't ~ them apart** no podía distinguirlos; **tell off** *vt*: **to ~ sb off** regañar a algn; **tell on** *vt fus*: **to ~ on sb** chivarse de algn
teller ['tɛlə^r] *n* (*in bank*) cajero(-a)
telling ['tɛlɪŋ] *adj* (*remark, detail*) revelador(a)
telltale ['tɛlteɪl] *adj* (*sign*) indicador(a)
telly ['tɛlɪ] *n* (*Brit inf*) tele *f*
temp [tɛmp] *n abbr* (*Brit: = temporary office worker*) empleado(-a) eventual ▷ *vi* trabajar como empleado(-a) eventual
temper ['tɛmpə^r] *n* (*mood*) humor *m*; (*bad temper*) (mal) genio; (*fit of anger*) ira; (*of child*) rabieta ▷ *vt* (*moderate*) moderar; **to be in a ~** estar furioso; **to lose one's ~** enfadarse, enojarse (*LAm*); **to keep one's ~** contenerse, no alterarse
temperament ['tɛmprəmənt] *n* (*nature*) temperamento
temperamental [tɛmprə'mɛntl] *adj* temperamental
temperate ['tɛmprət] *adj* moderado; (*climate*) templado
temperature ['tɛmprətʃə^r] *n* temperatura; **to have** *or* **run a ~** tener fiebre
template ['tɛmplɪt] *n* plantilla
temple ['tɛmpl] *n* (*building*) templo; (*Anat*) sien *f*
temporary ['tɛmpərərɪ] *adj* provisional, temporal; (*passing*) transitorio; (*worker*) eventual; (*job*) temporal; **~ teacher** maestro(-a) interino(-a)
tempt [tɛmpt] *vt* tentar; **to ~ sb into doing sth** tentar *or* inducir a algn a hacer algo; **to be ~ed to do sth** (*person*) sentirse tentado de hacer algo
temptation [tɛmp'teɪʃən] *n* tentación *f*
tempting ['tɛmptɪŋ] *adj* tentador(a); (*food*) apetitoso(-a)
ten [tɛn] *num* diez; **~s of thousands** decenas *fpl* de miles
tenacity [tə'næsɪtɪ] *n* tenacidad *f*
tenancy ['tɛnənsɪ] *n* alquiler *m*
tenant ['tɛnənt] *n* (*rent-payer*) inquilino(-a); (*occupant*) habitante *m/f*
tend [tɛnd] *vt* (*sick etc*) cuidar, atender; (*cattle, machine*) vigilar, cuidar ▷ *vi*: **to ~ to do sth** tener tendencia a hacer algo
tendency ['tɛndənsɪ] *n* tendencia
tender ['tɛndə^r] *adj* tierno, blando; (*delicate*) delicado; (*meat*) tierno; (*sore*) sensible; (*affectionate*) tierno, cariñoso ▷ *n* (*Comm: offer*) oferta; (*money*): **legal ~** moneda de curso legal ▷ *vt* ofrecer; **to put in a ~ (for)** hacer una oferta (para); **to put work out to ~** ofrecer un trabajo a contrata; **to ~ one's resignation** presentar la dimisión
tendon ['tɛndən] *n* tendón *m*
tenement ['tɛnəmənt] *n* casa *or* bloque *m* de pisos *or* vecinos (*LAm*)
tenet ['tɛnət] *n* principio
tenner ['tɛnə^r] *n* (billete *m* de) diez libras *fpl*
tennis ['tɛnɪs] *n* tenis *m*
tennis ball *n* pelota de tenis
tennis court *n* cancha de tenis
tennis match *n* partido de tenis
tennis player *n* tenista *m/f*
tennis racket *n* raqueta de tenis
tennis shoes *npl* zapatillas *fpl* de tenis
tenor ['tɛnə^r] *n* (*Mus*) tenor *m*
tenpin bowling ['tɛnpɪn-] *n* bolos *mpl*
tense [tɛns] *adj* tenso; (*stretched*) tirante; (*stiff*) rígido, tieso; (*person*) nervioso ▷ *n* (*Ling*) tiempo ▷ *vt* (*tighten: muscles*) tensar
tension ['tɛnʃən] *n* tensión *f*
tent [tɛnt] *n* tienda (de campaña), carpa (*LAm*)
tentative ['tɛntətɪv] *adj* (*person*) indeciso; (*provisional*) provisional
tenterhooks ['tɛntəhuks] *npl*: **on ~** sobre ascuas
tenth [tɛnθ] *adj* décimo
tent peg *n* clavija, estaca
tent pole *n* mástil *m*
tenuous ['tɛnjuəs] *adj* tenue
tenure ['tɛnjuə^r] *n* posesión *f*, tenencia; **to have ~** tener posesión *or* título de propiedad
tepid ['tɛpɪd] *adj* tibio
term [təːm] *n* (*limit*) límite *m*; (*Comm*) plazo; (*word*) término; (*period*) período; (*Scol*) trimestre *m* ▷ *vt* llamar, calificar de; **terms**

npl (*conditions*) condiciones *fpl*; (*Comm*) precio, tarifa; **in the short/long ~** a corto/largo plazo; **during his ~ of office** bajo su mandato; **to be on good ~s with sb** llevarse bien con algn; **to come to ~s with** (*problem*) aceptar; **in ~s of ...** en cuanto a ..., en términos de ...
terminal ['tə:mɪnl] *adj* (*disease*) mortal; (*patient*) terminal ▷ *n* (*Elec*) borne *m*; (*Comput*) terminal *m*; (*also*: **air ~**) terminal *f*; (*Brit*: *also*: **coach ~**) (estación *f*) terminal *f*
terminate ['tə:mɪneɪt] *vt* poner término a; (*pregnancy*) interrumpir ▷ *vi*: **to ~ in** acabar en
termini ['tə:mɪnaɪ] *npl of* **terminus**
terminology [tə:mɪ'nɔlədʒɪ] *n* terminología
terminus (*pl* **termini**) ['tə:mɪnəs, 'tə:mɪnaɪ] *n* término, (estación *f*) terminal *f*
termite ['tə:maɪt] *n* termita, comején *m*
term paper *n* (*US Univ*) trabajo escrito trimestral *or* semestral
terrace ['tɛrəs] *n* terraza; (*Brit*: *row of houses*) hilera de casas adosadas; **the ~s** (*Brit Sport*) las gradas *fpl*
terraced ['tɛrəst] *adj* (*garden*) escalonado; (*house*) adosado
terracotta ['tɛrə'kɔtə] *n* terracota
terrain [tɛ'reɪn] *n* terreno
terrestrial [tɪ'restrɪəl] *adj* (*life*) terrestre; (*Brit*: *channel*) de transmisión (por) vía terrestre
terrible ['tɛrɪbl] *adj* terrible, horrible; (*inf*) malísimo
terribly ['tɛrɪblɪ] *adv* terriblemente; (*very badly*) malísimamente
terrier ['tɛrɪə^r] *n* terrier *m*
terrific [tə'rɪfɪk] *adj* fantástico, fenomenal, macanudo (*LAm*); (*wonderful*) maravilloso
terrify ['tɛrɪfaɪ] *vt* aterrorizar; **to be terrified** estar aterrado *or* aterrorizado
terrifying ['tɛrɪfaɪɪŋ] *adj* aterrador(a)
territorial [tɛrɪ'tɔ:rɪəl] *adj* territorial
territory ['tɛrɪtərɪ] *n* territorio
terror ['tɛrə^r] *n* terror *m*
terror attack *n* atentado (terrorista)
terrorism ['tɛrərɪzəm] *n* terrorismo
terrorist ['tɛrərɪst] *n* terrorista *m/f*
terrorist attack *n* atentado (terrorista)
terrorize ['tɛrəraɪz] *vt* aterrorizar
terse [tə:s] *adj* (*style*) conciso; (*reply*) brusco
TESL [tɛsl] *n abbr* = **Teaching of English as a Second Language**
test [tɛst] *n* (*trial, check*) prueba, ensayo; (*: of goods in factory*) control *m*; (*of courage etc*) prueba; (*Chem, Med*) prueba; (*of blood, urine*) análisis *m inv*; (*exam*) examen *m*, test *m*; (*also*: **driving ~**) examen *m* de conducir ▷ *vt* probar, poner a prueba; (*Med*) examinar; (*: blood*) analizar; **to put sth to the ~** someter algo a prueba; **to ~ sth for sth** analizar algo en busca de algo
testament ['tɛstəmənt] *n* testamento; **the Old/New T~** el Antiguo/Nuevo Testamento
testicle ['tɛstɪkl] *n* testículo
testify ['tɛstɪfaɪ] *vi* (*Law*) prestar declaración; **to ~ to sth** atestiguar algo
testimony ['tɛstɪmənɪ] *n* (*Law*) testimonio, declaración *f*
test match *n* partido internacional
testosterone [tɛs'tɔstərəun] *n* testosterona
test pilot *n* piloto *m/f* de pruebas
test tube *n* probeta
tetanus ['tɛtənəs] *n* tétano
tether ['tɛðə^r] *vt* atar ▷ *n*: **to be at the end of one's ~** no aguantar más
text [tɛkst] *n* texto; (*on mobile*) mensaje *m* de texto ▷ *vt*: **to ~ sb** enviar un mensaje (de texto) a algn
textbook ['tɛkstbuk] *n* libro de texto
textiles ['tɛkstaɪlz] *npl* tejidos *mpl*
text message *n* mensaje *m* de texto
text messaging [-'mɛsɪdʒɪŋ] *n* (envío de) mensajes *mpl* de texto
textual ['tɛkstjuəl] *adj* del texto, textual
texture ['tɛkstʃə^r] *n* textura
Thai [taɪ] *adj, n* tailandés(-esa) *m(f)*
Thailand ['taɪlænd] *n* Tailandia
Thames [tɛmz] *n*: **the ~** el (río) Támesis
than [ðæn, ðən] *conj* que; (*with numerals*): **more ~ 10/once** más de 10/una vez; **I have more/less ~ you** tengo más/menos que tú; **it is better to phone ~ to write** es mejor llamar por teléfono que escribir; **no sooner did he leave ~ the phone rang** en cuanto se marchó, sonó el teléfono
thank [θæŋk] *vt* dar las gracias a, agradecer; **~ you (very much)** (muchas) gracias; **~ heavens, ~ God!** ¡gracias a Dios!, ¡menos mal!; *see also* **thanks**
thankful ['θæŋkful] *adj*: **~ for** agradecido (por)
thankfully ['θæŋkfəlɪ] *adv* (*gratefully*) con agradecimiento; (*with relief*) por suerte; **~ there were few victims** afortunadamente hubo pocas víctimas
thankless ['θæŋklɪs] *adj* ingrato
thanks [θæŋks] *npl* gracias *fpl* ▷ *excl* ¡gracias!; **many ~, ~ a lot** ¡muchas gracias!; **~ to** *prep* gracias a
Thanksgiving ['θæŋksgɪvɪŋ], **Thanksgiving Day** *n* día *m* de Acción de Gracias; *ver nota*

THANKSGIVING DAY

En Estados Unidos el cuarto jueves de noviembre es *Thanksgiving Day*, fiesta oficial en la que se conmemora la celebración que tuvieron los primeros colonos norteamericanos ("Pilgrims" o "Pilgrim Fathers") tras la estupenda cosecha de 1621, por la que se dan gracias a Dios. En Canadá se celebra una fiesta semejante el segundo lunes de octubre, aunque no está relacionada con dicha fecha histórica.

KEYWORD

that [ðæt] (*pl* **those**) *adj* (*demonstrative*) ese(-a), esos(-as) *pl*; (*more remote*) aquel/aquella *m/f*, aquellos(-as) *m(f)pl*; **leave those books on the table** deja esos libros sobre la mesa; **that one** ése/ésa; (*more remote*) aquél/aquélla; **that one over there** ése/ésa de ahí; aquél/aquélla de allí
▷ *pron* **1** (*demonstrative*) ese(-a); ése(-a), esos(-as) *pl*; ésos(-as) *pl*; (*neuter*) eso; (*more remote*) aquel/aquella *m/f*; aquél/aquélla *m/f*, aquellos(-as) *m(f)pl*; aquéllos(-as) *m(f)pl*, aquello *neuter*; **what's that?** ¿qué es eso (*or* aquello)?; **who's that?** ¿quién es?; (*pointing etc*) ¿quién es ése/a?; **is that you?** ¿eres tú?; **will you eat all that?** ¿vas a comer todo eso?; **that's my house** ésa es mi casa; **that's what he said** eso es lo que dijo; **that is (to say)** es decir; **at** *or* **with that she ...** en eso, ella ...; **do it like that** hazlo así
2 (*relative*: *subject, object*) que; (*with preposition*) (el/la) que, el/la cual; **the book (that) I read** el libro que leí; **the books that are in the library** los libros que están en la biblioteca; **all (that) I have** todo lo que tengo; **the box (that) I put it in** la caja en la que *or* donde lo puse; **the people (that) I spoke to** la gente con la que hablé; **not that I know of** que yo sepa, no
3 (*relative*: *of time*) que; **the day (that) he came** el día (en) que vino
▷ *conj* que; **he thought that I was ill** creyó que yo estaba enfermo
▷ *adv* (*demonstrative*): **I can't work that much** no puedo trabajar tanto; **I didn't realize it was that bad** no creí que fuera tan malo; **that high** así de alto

thatched [θætʃt] *adj* (*roof*) de paja; **~ cottage** casita con tejado de paja
thaw [θɔː] *n* deshielo ▷ *vi* (*ice*) derretirse; (*food*) descongelarse ▷ *vt* descongelar

KEYWORD

the [ðiː, ðə] *def art* **1** (*gen*) el, la *f*, los *pl*, las *fpl*; (*NB = el immediately before feminine noun beginning with stressed (h)a; a+el = al; de + el = del*): **the boy/girl** el chico/la chica; **the books/flowers** los libros/las flores; **to the postman/from the drawer** al cartero/del cajón; **I haven't the time/money** no tengo tiempo/dinero; **1.10 euros to the dollar** 1,10 euros por dólar; **paid by the hour** pagado por hora
2 (*+adj to form noun*) los; lo; **the rich and the poor** los ricos y los pobres; **to attempt the impossible** intentar lo imposible
3 (*in titles, surnames*): **Elizabeth the First** Isabel Primera; **Peter the Great** Pedro el Grande; **do you know the Smiths?** ¿conoce a los Smith?
4 (*in comparisons*): **the more he works the more he earns** cuanto más trabaja más gana

theatre, theater (*US*) [ˈθɪətəʳ] *n* teatro; (*also*: **lecture ~**) aula; (*Med*: *also*: **operating ~**) quirófano
theatre-goer, theater-goer (*US*) [ˈθɪətəgəuəʳ] *n* aficionado(-a) al teatro
theatrical [θɪˈætrɪkl] *adj* teatral
theft [θɛft] *n* robo
their [ðɛəʳ] *adj* su
theirs [ðɛəz] *pron* (el) suyo/(la) suya *etc*; *see also* **my**; **mine**
them [ðɛm, ðəm] *pron* (*direct*) los/las; (*indirect*) les; (*stressed, after prep*) ellos/ellas; **I see ~** los veo; **both of ~** ambos(-as), los/las dos; **give me a few of ~** dame algunos(-as); *see also* **me**
theme [θiːm] *n* tema *m*
theme park *n* parque *m* temático
theme song *n* tema *m* (musical)
themselves [ðəmˈsɛlvz] *pron pl* (*subject*) ellos mismos/ellas mismas; (*complement*) se; (*after prep*) sí (mismos(-as)); *see also* **oneself**
then [ðɛn] *adv* (*at that time*) entonces; (*next*) pues; (*later*) luego, después; (*and also*) además ▷ *conj* (*therefore*) en ese caso, entonces ▷ *adj*: **the ~ president** el entonces presidente; **from ~ on** desde entonces; **until ~** hasta entonces; **and ~ what?** y luego, ¿qué?; **what do you want me to do, ~?** ¿entonces, qué quiere que haga?
theologian [θɪəˈləudʒən] *n* teólogo(-a)
theology [θɪˈɔlədʒɪ] *n* teología
theoretical [θɪəˈrɛtɪkl] *adj* teórico
theorize [ˈθɪəraɪz] *vi* teorizar
theory [ˈθɪərɪ] *n* teoría
therapist [ˈθɛrəpɪst] *n* terapeuta *m/f*
therapy [ˈθɛrəpɪ] *n* terapia

KEYWORD

there [ˈðɛəʳ] *adv* **1**: **there is, there are** hay; **there is no-one here** no hay nadie aquí; **there is no bread left** no queda pan; **there has been an accident** ha habido un accidente
2 (*referring to place*) ahí; (*distant*) allí; **it's there** está ahí; **put it in/on/up/down there** ponlo ahí dentro/encima/arriba/abajo; **I want that book there** quiero ese libro de ahí; **there he is!** ¡ahí está!; **there's the bus** ahí *or* ya viene el autobús; **back/down there** allí atrás/abajo; **over there, through there** por allí
3: **there, there** (*esp to child*) venga, venga, bueno

thereabouts [ˈðɛərəˈbauts] *adv* por ahí
thereafter [ðɛərˈɑːftəʳ] *adv* después
thereby [ˈðɛəbaɪ] *adv* así, de ese modo
therefore [ˈðɛəfɔːʳ] *adv* por lo tanto
there's [ðɛəz] = **there is**; **there has**

thereupon [ðɛərə'pɔn] *adv* (*at that point*) en eso, en seguida
thermal ['θə:ml] *adj* termal; (*paper*) térmico
thermometer [θə'mɔmɪtə^r] *n* termómetro
Thermos® ['θə:məs] *n* (*also*: **~ flask**) termo
thermostat ['θə:məustæt] *n* termostato
thesaurus [θɪ'sɔ:rəs] *n* tesoro, diccionario de sinónimos
these [ði:z] *adj pl* estos(-as) ▷ *pron pl* éstos(-as)
thesis (*pl* **theses**) ['θi:sɪs, -si:z] *n* tesis *f inv*
they [ðeɪ] *pron pl* ellos/ellas; **~ say that …** (*it is said that*) se dice que …
they'd [ðeɪd] = **they had; they would**
they'll [ðeɪl] = **they shall; they will**
they're [ðɛə^r] = **they are**
they've [ðeɪv] = **they have**
thick [θɪk] *adj* (*wall, slice*) grueso; (*dense: liquid, smoke etc*) espeso; (*vegetation, beard*) tupido; (*stupid*) torpe ▷ *n*: **in the ~ of the battle** en lo más reñido de la batalla; **it's 20 cm ~** tiene 20 cm de espesor
thicken ['θɪkn] *vi* espesarse ▷ *vt* (*sauce etc*) espesar
thicket ['θɪkɪt] *n* espesura
thickness ['θɪknɪs] *n* espesor *m*, grueso
thickset [θɪk'sɛt] *adj* fornido
thick-skinned [θɪk'skɪnd] *adj* (*fig*) insensible
thief (*pl* **thieves**) [θi:f, θi:vz] *n* ladrón(-ona) *m(f)*
thigh [θaɪ] *n* muslo
thimble ['θɪmbl] *n* dedal *m*
thin [θɪn] *adj* delgado; (*wall, layer*) fino; (*watery*) aguado; (*light*) tenue; (*hair*) escaso; (*fog*) ligero; (*crowd*) disperso ▷ *vt*: **to ~ (down)** (*sauce, paint*) diluir ▷ *vi* (*fog*) aclararse; (*also*: **~ out**: *crowd*) dispersarse; **his hair is ~ning** se está quedando calvo
thing [θɪŋ] *n* cosa; (*object*) objeto, artículo; (*contraption*) chisme *m*; (*mania*) manía; **things** *npl* (*belongings*) cosas *fpl*; **the best ~ would be to …** lo mejor sería …; **the main ~ is …** lo principal es …; **first ~ (in the morning)** a primera hora (de la mañana); **last ~ (at night)** a última hora (de la noche); **the ~ is …** lo que pasa es que …; **how are ~s?** ¿qué tal van las cosas?; **she's got a ~ about mice** le dan no sé qué los ratones; **poor ~!** ¡pobre! *m/f*, ¡pobrecito(-a)!
think (*pl* **thought**) [θɪŋk, θɔ:t] *vi* pensar ▷ *vt* pensar, creer; (*imagine*) imaginar; **what did you ~ of it?** ¿qué te parece?; **what did you ~ of them?** ¿qué te parecieron?; **to ~ about sth/sb** pensar en algo/uno; **I'll ~ about it** lo pensaré; **to ~ of doing sth** pensar en hacer algo; **I ~ so/not** creo que sí/no; **~ again!** ¡piénsalo bien!; **to ~ aloud** pensar en voz alta; **to ~ well of sb** tener buen concepto de algn; **think out** *vt* (*plan*) elaborar, tramar; (*solution*) encontrar; **think over** *vt* reflexionar sobre, meditar; **I'd like to ~ things over** me gustaría pensármelo; **think through** *vt* pensar bien; **think up** *vt* imaginar
think tank *n* grupo de expertos
thinly ['θɪnlɪ] *adv* (*cut*) en lonchas finas; (*spread*) en una capa fina
third [θə:d] *adj* (*before n*) tercer(a); (*following n*) tercero(-a) ▷ *n* tercero(-a); (*fraction*) tercio; (*Brit Scol: degree*) *título universitario de tercera clase*
thirdly ['θə:dlɪ] *adv* en tercer lugar
third party insurance *n* (*Brit*) seguro a terceros
third-rate ['θə:d'reɪt] *adj* de poca calidad
Third World *n*: **the ~** el Tercer Mundo ▷ *cpd* tercermundista
thirst [θə:st] *n* sed *f*
thirsty ['θə:stɪ] *adj* (*person*) sediento; **to be ~** tener sed
thirteen [θə:'ti:n] *num* trece
thirteenth [θə:'ti:nθ] *adj* decimotercero ▷ *n* (*in series*) decimotercero(-a); (*fraction*) decimotercio
thirtieth ['θə:tɪəθ] *adj* trigésimo ▷ *n* (*in series*) trigésimo(-a); (*fraction*) treintavo
thirty ['θə:tɪ] *num* treinta

KEYWORD

this [ðɪs] (*pl* **these**) *adj* (*demonstrative*) este(-a), estos(-as) *pl*, esto *neuter*; **this man/woman** este hombre/esta mujer; **these children/flowers** estos chicos/estas flores; **this way** por aquí; **this time last year** hoy hace un año; **this one (here)** éste(-a), esto (de aquí) ▷ *pron* (*demonstrative*) este(-a); éste(-a), estos(-as) *pl*; éstos(-as) *pl*, esto *neuter*; **who is this?** ¿quién es éste/ésta?; **what is this?** ¿qué es esto?; **this is where I live** aquí vivo; **this is what he said** esto es lo que dijo; **this is Mr Brown** (*in introductions*) le presento al Sr. Brown; (*photo*) éste es el Sr. Brown; (*on telephone*) habla el Sr. Brown; **they were talking of this and that** hablaban de esto y lo otro ▷ *adv* (*demonstrative*): **this high/long** así de alto/largo; **this far** hasta aquí

thistle ['θɪsl] *n* cardo
thorn [θɔ:n] *n* espina
thorough ['θʌrə] *adj* (*search*) minucioso; (*knowledge*) profundo; (*research*) a fondo
thoroughbred ['θʌrəbrɛd] *adj* (*horse*) de pura sangre
thoroughfare ['θʌrəfɛə^r] *n* calle *f*; **"no ~"** "prohibido el paso"
thoroughly ['θʌrəlɪ] *adv* (*search*) minuciosamente; (*study*) profundamente; (*wash*) a fondo; (*utterly: bad, wet etc*) completamente, totalmente
those [ðəuz] *pron pl* ésos/ésas; (*more remote*) aquéllos(-as) ▷ *adj pl* esos/esas; aquellos(-as)
though [ðəu] *conj* aunque ▷ *adv* sin embargo, aún así; **even ~** aunque; **it's not so easy, ~** sin embargo no es tan fácil
thought [θɔ:t] *pt, pp of* **think** ▷ *n* pensamiento; (*opinion*) opinión *f*; (*intention*)

t

intención *f*; **to give sth some ~** pensar algo detenidamente; **after much ~** después de pensarlo bien; **I've just had a ~** se me acaba de ocurrir una idea
thoughtful ['θɔ:tful] *adj* pensativo; (*considerate*) atento
thoughtless ['θɔ:tlɪs] *adj* desconsiderado
thousand ['θauzənd] *num* mil; **two ~** dos mil; **~s of** miles de
thousandth ['θauzəntθ] *num* milésimo
thrash [θræʃ] *vt* dar una paliza a; **thrash about** *vi* revolverse; **thrash out** *vt* discutir a fondo
thread [θrɛd] *n* hilo; (*of screw*) rosca ▷ *vt* (*needle*) enhebrar
threadbare ['θrɛdbɛəʳ] *adj* raído
threat [θrɛt] *n* amenaza; **to be under ~ of** estar amenazado de
threaten ['θrɛtn] *vi* amenazar ▷ *vt*: **to ~ sb with sth/to do** amenazar a algn con algo/con hacer
threatening ['θrɛtnɪŋ] *adj* amenazador(a), amenazante
three [θri:] *num* tres
three-dimensional [θri:dɪ'mɛnʃənl] *adj* tridimensional
threefold ['θri:fəuld] *adv*: **to increase ~** triplicar
three-piece ['θri:pi:s]: **~ suit** traje *m* de tres piezas; **~ suite** tresillo
three-ply [θri:'plaɪ] *adj* (*wood*) de tres capas; (*wool*) triple
three-quarter [θri:'kwɔ:təʳ] *adj*: **~ length sleeves** mangas *fpl* tres cuartos
three-quarters [θri:'kwɔ:təz] *npl* tres cuartas partes; **~ full** tres cuartas partes lleno
thresh [θrɛʃ] *vt* (*Agr*) trillar
threshold ['θrɛʃhəuld] *n* umbral *m*; **to be on the ~ of** (*fig*) estar al borde de
threw [θru:] *pt of* **throw**
thrift [θrɪft] *n* economía
thrifty ['θrɪftɪ] *adj* económico
thrill [θrɪl] *n* (*excitement*) emoción *f* ▷ *vt* emocionar; **to be ~ed** (*with gift etc*) estar encantado
thriller ['θrɪləʳ] *n* película/novela de suspense
thrilling ['θrɪlɪŋ] *adj* emocionante
thrive (*pt* **thrived, throve**, *pp* **thrived, thriven**) [θraɪv, θrəuv, 'θrɪvn] *vi* (*grow*) crecer; (*do well*) prosperar
thriving ['θraɪvɪŋ] *adj* próspero
throat [θrəut] *n* garganta; **I have a sore ~** me duele la garganta
throb [θrɔb] *n* (*of heart*) latido; (*of engine*) vibración *f* ▷ *vi* latir; vibrar; (*with pain*) dar punzadas; **my head is ~bing** la cabeza me da punzadas
throes [θrəuz] *npl*: **in the ~ of** en medio de
thrombosis [θrɔm'bəusɪs] *n* trombosis *f*
throne [θrəun] *n* trono
throng [θrɔŋ] *n* multitud *f*, muchedumbre *f* ▷ *vt, vi* apiñarse, agolparse
throttle ['θrɔtl] *n* (*Aut*) acelerador *m* ▷ *vt* estrangular
through [θru:] *prep* por, a través de; (*time*) durante; (*by means of*) por medio de, mediante; (*owing to*) gracias a ▷ *adj* (*ticket, train*) directo ▷ *adv* completamente, de parte a parte; de principio a fin; **(from) Monday ~ Friday** (*US*) de lunes a viernes; **to go ~ sb's papers** mirar entre los papeles de algn; **I am halfway ~ the book** voy por la mitad del libro; **the soldiers didn't let us ~** los soldados no nos dejaron pasar; **to put sb ~ to sb** (*Tel*) poner *or* pasar a algn con algn; **to be ~** (*Tel*) tener comunicación; (*have finished*) haber terminado; **"no ~ road"** (*Brit*) "calle sin salida"
throughout [θru:'aut] *prep* (*place*) por todas partes de, por todo; (*time*) durante todo ▷ *adv* por *or* en todas partes
throve [θrəuv] *pt of* **thrive**
throw [θrəu] (*pt* **threw**, *pp* **thrown** [θru:, θrəun]) *n* tiro; (*Sport*) lanzamiento ▷ *vt* tirar, echar, botar (*LAm*); (*Sport*) lanzar; (*rider*) derribar; (*fig*) desconcertar; **to ~ a party** dar una fiesta; **throw about, throw around** *vt* (*litter etc*) tirar, esparcir; **throw away** *vt* tirar; **throw in** *vt* (*Sport: ball*) sacar; (*include*) incluir; **throw off** *vt* deshacerse de; **throw open** *vt* (*doors, windows*) abrir de par en par; (*house, gardens etc*) abrir al público; (*competition, race*) abrir a todos; **throw out** *vt* tirar, botar (*LAm*); **throw together** *vt* (*clothes*) amontonar; (*meal*) preparar a la carrera; (*essay*) hacer sin cuidado; **throw up** *vi* vomitar, devolver
throwaway ['θrəuəweɪ] *adj* para tirar, desechable
throw-in ['θrəuɪn] *n* (*Sport*) saque *m* de banda
thrown [θrəun] *pp of* **throw**
thru [θru:] *prep, adj, adv* (*US*) = **through**
thrush [θrʌʃ] *n* zorzal *m*, tordo; (*Med*) candiasis *f*
thrust [θrʌst] (*pt, pp* **thrust**) *n* (*Tech*) empuje *m* ▷ *vt* empujar; (*push in*) introducir
thud [θʌd] *n* golpe *m* sordo
thug [θʌg] *n* gamberro(-a)
thumb [θʌm] *n* (*Anat*) pulgar *m* ▷ *vt*: **to ~ a lift** hacer dedo; **to give sth/sb the ~s up/down** aprobar/desaprobar algo/a algn; **thumb through** *vt fus* (*book*) hojear
thumbtack ['θʌmtæk] *n* (*US*) chincheta, chinche *f*
thump [θʌmp] *n* golpe *m*; (*sound*) ruido seco *or* sordo ▷ *vt, vi* golpear
thunder ['θʌndəʳ] *n* trueno; (*of applause etc*) estruendo ▷ *vi* tronar; (*train etc*): **to ~ past** pasar como un trueno
thunderbolt ['θʌndəbəult] *n* rayo
thunderclap ['θʌndəklæp] *n* trueno
thunderstorm ['θʌndəstɔ:m] *n* tormenta
thundery ['θʌndərɪ] *adj* tormentoso
Thur., Thurs. *abbr* (= *Thursday*) juev
Thursday ['θə:zdɪ] *n* jueves *m inv*; *see also* **Tuesday**

thus [ðʌs] *adv* así, de este modo
thwart [θwɔ:t] *vt* frustrar
thyme [taɪm] *n* tomillo
tiara [tɪ'ɑ:rə] *n* tiara, diadema
Tibet [tɪ'bɛt] *n* el Tibet
tick [tɪk] *n* (*sound: of clock*) tictac *m*; (*mark*) señal *f* (de visto bueno), palomita (*LAm*); (*Zool*) garrapata; (*Brit inf*): **in a ~** en un instante; (*Brit*: (*inf*): *credit*): **to buy sth on ~** comprar algo a crédito ▷ *vi* hacer tictac ▷ *vt* marcar, señalar; **to put a ~ against sth** poner una señal en algo; **tick off** *vt* marcar; (*person*) reñir; **tick over** *vi* (*Brit*: *engine*) girar en marcha lenta; (: *fig*) ir tirando
ticket ['tɪkɪt] *n* billete *m*, tíquet *m*, boleto (*LAm*); (*for cinema etc*) entrada, boleto (*LAm*); (*in shop: on goods*) etiqueta; (*for library*) tarjeta; (*US Pol*) lista (de candidatos); **to get a parking ~** (*Aut*) ser multado por estacionamiento ilegal
ticket barrier *n* (*Brit: Rail*) *barrera más allá de la cual se necesita billete/boleto*
ticket collector *n* revisor(a) *m(f)*
ticket inspector *n* revisor(a) *m(f)*, inspector(a) *m(f)* de boletos (*LAm*)
ticket machine *n* máquina de billetes (*Sp*) *or* boletos (*LAm*)
ticket office *n* (*Theat*) taquilla, boletería (*LAm*); (*Rail*) despacho de billetes *or* boletos (*LAm*)
tickle ['tɪkl] *n*: **to give sb a ~** hacer cosquillas a algn ▷ *vt* hacer cosquillas a ▷ *vi* hacer cosquillas
ticklish ['tɪklɪʃ] *adj* (*which tickles: blanket*) que pica; (: *cough*) irritante; (*fig: problem*) delicado; **to be ~** tener cosquillas
tidal ['taɪdl] *adj* de marea
tidal wave *n* maremoto
tidbit ['tɪdbɪt] *n* (*US*) = **titbit**
tiddlywinks ['tɪdlɪwɪŋks] *n* juego de la pulga
tide [taɪd] *n* marea; (*fig: of events*) curso, marcha ▷ *vt*: **to ~ sb over** *or* **through (until)** sacar a algn del apuro (hasta); **high/low ~** marea alta/baja; **the ~ of public opinion** la tendencia de la opinión pública
tidy ['taɪdɪ] *adj* (*room*) ordenado; (*drawing, work*) limpio; (*person*) (bien) arreglado; (: *in character*) metódico; (*mind*) claro, metódico ▷ *vt* (*also*: **~ up**) ordenar, poner en orden
tie [taɪ] *n* (*string etc*) atadura; (*Brit: necktie*) corbata; (*fig: link*) vínculo, lazo; (*Sport: draw*) empate *m* ▷ *vt* atar ▷ *vi* (*Sport*) empatar; **family ~s** obligaciones *fpl* familiares; **cup ~** (*Sport: match*) partido de copa; **to ~ in a bow** hacer un lazo; **to ~ a knot in sth** hacer un nudo en algo; **tie down** *vt* atar; (*fig*): **to ~ sb down to** obligar a algn a; **tie in** *vi*: **to ~ in (with)** (*correspond*) concordar (con); **tie on** *vt* (*Brit: label etc*) atar; **tie up** *vt* (*parcel*) envolver; (*dog*) atar; (*boat*) amarrar; (*arrangements*) concluir; **to be ~d up** (*busy*) estar ocupado
tier [tɪə^r] *n* grada; (*of cake*) piso
tiger ['taɪgə^r] *n* tigre *m*
tight [taɪt] *adj* (*rope*) tirante; (*money*) escaso; (*clothes, budget*) ajustado; (*programme*) apretado; (*budget*) ajustado; (*security*) estricto; (*inf: drunk*) borracho ▷ *adv* (*squeeze*) muy fuerte; (*shut*) herméticamente; **to be packed ~** (*suitcase*) estar completamente lleno; (*people*) estar apretados; **everybody hold ~!** ¡agárense bien!
tighten ['taɪtn] *vt* (*rope*) tensar, estirar; (*screw*) apretar ▷ *vi* estirarse; apretarse
tight-fisted [taɪt'fɪstɪd] *adj* tacaño
tight-lipped ['taɪt'lɪpt] *adj*: **to be ~** (*silent*) rehusar hablar; (*angry*) apretar los labios
tightly ['taɪtlɪ] *adv* (*grasp*) muy fuerte
tightrope ['taɪtrəup] *n* cuerda floja
tights [taɪts] *npl* (*Brit*) medias *fpl*, panties *mpl*
tile [taɪl] *n* (*on roof*) teja; (*on floor*) baldosa; (*on wall*) azulejo ▷ *vt* (*floor*) poner baldosas en; (*wall*) alicatar
tiled [taɪld] *adj* (*floor*) embaldosado; (*wall, bathroom*) alicatado; (*roof*) con tejas
till [tɪl] *n* caja (registradora) ▷ *vt* (*land*) cultivar ▷ *prep, conj* = **until**
tiller ['tɪlə^r] *n* (*Naut*) caña del timón
tilt [tɪlt] *vt* inclinar ▷ *vi* inclinarse ▷ *n* (*slope*) inclinación *f*; **to wear one's hat at a ~** llevar el sombrero echado a un lado *or* terciado; **(at) full ~** a toda velocidad *or* carrera
timber [tɪmbə^r] *n* (*material*) madera; (*trees*) árboles *mpl*
time [taɪm] *n* tiempo; (*epoch*) *often pl* época; (*by clock*) hora; (*moment*) momento; (*occasion*) vez *f*; (*Mus*) compás *m* ▷ *vt* calcular *or* medir el tiempo de; (*race*) cronometrar; (*remark etc*) elegir el momento para; **a long ~** mucho tiempo; **four at a ~** cuarto a la vez; **for the ~ being** de momento, por ahora; **at ~s** a veces, a ratos; **~ after ~, ~ and again** repetidas veces, una y otra vez; **from ~ to ~** de vez en cuando; **in ~** (*soon enough*) a tiempo; (*after some time*) con el tiempo; (*Mus*) al compás; **in a week's ~** dentro de una semana; **in no ~** en un abrir y cerrar de ojos; **any ~** cuando sea; **on ~** a la hora; **to be 30 minutes behind/ahead of ~** llevar media hora de retraso/adelanto; **to take one's ~** tomárselo con calma; **he'll do it in his own ~** (*without being hurried*) lo hará sin prisa; (*out of working hours*) lo hará en su tiempo libre; **by the ~ he arrived** cuando llegó; **5 ~s 5** 5 por 5; **what ~ is it?** ¿qué hora es?; **what ~ do you make it?** ¿qué hora es *or* tiene?; **to be behind the ~s** estar atrasado; **to carry three boxes at a ~** llevar tres cajas a la vez; **to keep ~** llevar el ritmo *or* el compás; **to have a good ~** pasarlo bien, divertirse; **to ~ sth well/badly** elegir un buen/mal momento para algo; **the bomb was ~d to explode five minutes later** la bomba estaba programada para explotar cinco minutos más tarde
time bomb *n* bomba de relojería

time frame *n* plazo
time lag *n* desfase *m*
timeless ['taɪmlɪs] *adj* eterno
time limit *n* (*gen*) límite *m* de tiempo; (*Comm*) plazo
timeline ['taimlain] *n* línea de tiempo
timely ['taɪmlɪ] *adj* oportuno
time off *n* tiempo libre
timer ['taɪməʳ] *n* (*also*: **~ switch**) interruptor *m*; (*in kitchen*) temporizador *m*; (*Tech*) temporizador *m*
time scale *n* escala de tiempo
time switch *n* (*Brit*) interruptor *m* (horario)
timetable ['taɪmteɪbl] *n* horario; (*programme of events etc*) programa *m*
time zone *n* huso horario
timid ['tɪmɪd] *adj* tímido
timing ['taɪmɪŋ] *n* (*Sport*) cronometraje *m*; **the ~ of his resignation** el momento que eligió para dimitir
timpani ['tɪmpənɪ] *npl* tímpanos *mpl*
tin [tɪn] *n* estaño; (*also*: **~ plate**) hojalata; (*Brit*: *can*) lata
tinfoil ['tɪnfɔɪl] *n* papel *m* de estaño
tinge [tɪndʒ] *n* matiz *m* ▷ *vt*: **~d with** teñido de
tingle ['tɪŋgl] *n* hormigueo ▷ *vi* (*cheeks, skin*: *from cold*) sentir comezón; (: *from bad circulation*) sentir hormigueo; **to ~ with** estremecerse de
tinker ['tɪŋkəʳ] *n* calderero(-a); (*gipsy*) gitano(-a); **tinker with** *vt fus* jugar con, tocar
tinkle ['tɪŋkl] *vi* tintinear
tinned [tɪnd] *adj* (*Brit*: *food*) en lata, en conserva
tinnitus ['tɪnɪtəs] *n* (*Med*) acufeno
tin opener [-əupnəʳ] *n* (*Brit*) abrelatas *m inv*
tinsel ['tɪnsl] *n* oropel *m*
tint [tɪnt] *n* matiz *m*; (*for hair*) tinte *m* ▷ *vt* (*hair*) teñir
tinted ['tɪntɪd] *adj* (*hair*) teñido; (*glass, spectacles*) ahumado
tiny ['taɪnɪ] *adj* minúsculo, pequeñito
tip [tɪp] *n* (*end*) punta; (*gratuity*) propina; (*Brit*: *for rubbish*) vertedero; (*advice*) consejo ▷ *vt* (*waiter*) dar una propina a; (*tilt*) inclinar; (*empty*: *also*: **~ out**) vaciar, echar; (*predict*: *winner*) pronosticar; (: *horse*) recomendar; **he ~ped out the contents of the box** volcó el contenido de la caja; **tip off** *vt* avisar, poner sobre aviso a; **tip over** *vt* volcar ▷ *vi* volcarse
tip-off ['tɪpɔf] *n* (*hint*) advertencia
tipped [tɪpt] *adj* (*Brit*: *cigarette*) con filtro
Tipp-Ex® ['tɪpɛks] *n* Tipp-Ex® *m*
tipster ['tɪpstəʳ] *n* (*Racing*) pronosticador(a) *m(f)*
tipsy ['tɪpsɪ] *adj* alegre, achispado
tiptoe ['tɪptəu] *n* (*Brit*): **on ~** de puntillas
tiptop ['tɪptɔp] *adj*: **in ~ condition** en perfectas condiciones
tirade [taɪ'reɪd] *n* diatriba
tire ['taɪəʳ] *n* (*US*) = **tyre** ▷ *vt* cansar ▷ *vi* (*gen*) cansarse; (*become bored*) aburrirse; **tire out** *vt* agotar, rendir
tired ['taɪəd] *adj* cansado; **to be ~ of sth** estar harto de algo; **to be/feel/look ~** estar/sentirse/parecer cansado
tireless ['taɪəlɪs] *adj* incansable
tire pressure *n* (*US*) = **tyre pressure**
tiresome ['taɪəsəm] *adj* aburrido
tiring ['taɪrɪŋ] *adj* cansado
tissue ['tɪʃu:] *n* tejido; (*paper handkerchief*) pañuelo de papel, kleenex® *m*
tissue paper *n* papel *m* de seda
tit [tɪt] *n* (*bird*) herrerillo común; **to give ~ for tat** dar ojo por ojo
titbit ['tɪtbɪt], **tidbit** (*US*) ['tɪdbɪt] *n* (*food*) golosina; (*news*) pedazo
title ['taɪtl] *n* título; (*Law*: *right*): **~ (to)** derecho (a)
title deed *n* (*Law*) título de propiedad
title role *n* papel *m* principal
titter ['tɪtəʳ] *vi* reírse entre dientes
T-junction ['ti:dʒʌŋkʃən] *n* cruce *m* en T
TM *abbr* (= *trademark*) marca de fábrica; = **transcendental meditation**

KEYWORD

to [tu:, tə] *prep* **1** (*direction*) a; **to go to France/London/school/the station** ir a Francia/Londres/al colegio/a la estación; **to go to Claude's/the doctor's** ir a casa de Claude/al médico; **the road to Edinburgh** la carretera de Edimburgo; **to the left/right** a la izquierda/derecha
2 (*as far as*) hasta, a; **from here to London** de aquí a *or* hasta Londres; **to count to 10** contar hasta 10; **from 40 to 50 people** entre 40 y 50 personas
3 (*with expressions of time*): **a quarter/twenty to five** las cuarto menos cuarto/veinte
4 (*for, of*): **the key to the front door** la llave de la puerta principal; **she is secretary to the director** es la secretaria del director; **a letter to his wife** una carta a *or* para su mujer
5 (*expressing indirect object*) a; **to give sth to sb** darle algo a algn; **give it to me** dámelo; **to talk to sb** hablar con algn; **to be a danger to sb** ser un peligro para algn; **to carry out repairs to sth** hacer reparaciones en algo
6 (*in relation to*): **3 goals to 2** 3 goles a 2; **30 miles to the gallon** ≈ 9,4 litros a los cien (kilómetros); **8 apples to the kilo** 8 manzanas por kilo
7 (*purpose, result*): **to come to sb's aid** venir en auxilio *or* ayuda de algn; **to sentence sb to death** condenar a algn a muerte; **to my great surprise** con gran sorpresa mía
▷ *infin particle* **1** (*simple infin*): **to go/eat** ir/comer
2 (*following another vb; see also relevant vb*): **to want/try/start to do** querer/intentar/empezar a hacer
3 (*with vb omitted*): **I don't want to** no quiero

4 (*purpose, result*) para; **I did it to help you** lo hice para ayudarte; **he came to see you** vino a verte
5 (*equivalent to relative clause*): **I have things to do** tengo cosas que hacer; **the main thing is to try** lo principal es intentarlo
6 (*after adj etc*): **ready to go** listo para irse; **too old to ...** demasiado viejo (como) para ...
▷ *adv*: **pull/push the door to** tirar de/empujar la puerta; **to go to and fro** ir y venir

toad ['təud] *n* sapo
toadstool ['təudstu:l] *n* seta venenosa
toast [təust] *n* (*Culin*: *also*: **piece of ~**) tostada; (*drink, speech*) brindis *m inv* ▷ *vt* (*Culin*) tostar; (*drink to*) brindar por
toaster ['təustə^r] *n* tostador *m*
tobacco [tə'bækəu] *n* tabaco; **pipe ~** tabaco de pipa
tobacconist [tə'bækənɪst] *n* estanquero(-a), tabaquero(-a) (*LAm*); **~'s (shop)** (*Brit*) estanco, tabaquería (*LAm*)
toboggan [tə'bɔgən] *n* tobogán *m*
today [tə'deɪ] *adv, n* (*also fig*) hoy *m*; **what day is it ~?** ¿qué día es hoy?; **what date is it ~?** ¿a qué fecha estamos hoy?; **~ is the 4th of March** hoy es el 4 de marzo; **~'s paper** el periódico de hoy; **a fortnight ~** de hoy en 15 días, dentro de 15 días
toddler ['tɔdlə^r] *n* niño(-a) (que empieza a andar)
toe [təu] *n* dedo (del pie); (*of shoe*) punta ▷ *vt*: **to ~ the line** (*fig*) acatar las normas; **big/little ~** dedo gordo/pequeño del pie
TOEFL ['təufl] *n abbr* = **Test(ing) of English as a Foreign Language**
toenail ['təuneɪl] *n* uña del pie
toffee ['tɔfɪ] *n* caramelo
toffee apple *n* (*Brit*) manzana de caramelo
tofu ['təufu:] *n* tofu *m*
toga ['təugə] *n* toga
together [tə'gɛðə^r] *adv* juntos; (*at same time*) al mismo tiempo, a la vez; **~ with** junto con
toil [tɔɪl] *n* trabajo duro, labor *f* ▷ *vi* esforzarse
toilet ['tɔɪlət] *n* (*Brit*: *lavatory*) servicios *mpl*, baño ▷ *cpd* (*bag, soap etc*) de aseo; **to go to the ~** ir al baño; *see also* **toilets**
toilet bag *n* neceser *m*, bolsa de aseo
toilet paper *n* papel *m* higiénico
toiletries ['tɔɪlətrɪz] *npl* artículos *mpl* de aseo; (*make-up etc*) artículos *mpl* de tocador
toilet roll *n* rollo de papel higiénico
toilets ['tɔɪləts] *npl* (*Brit*) servicios *mpl*
toilet water *n* (agua de) colonia
token ['təukən] *n* (*sign*) señal *f*, muestra; (*souvenir*) recuerdo; (*voucher*) vale *m*; (*disc*) ficha ▷ *cpd* (*fee, strike*) nominal, simbólico; **book/record ~** (*Brit*) vale *m* para comprar libros/discos; **by the same ~** (*fig*) por la misma razón
tokenism ['təukənɪzəm] *n* (*Pol*) política simbólica *or* de fachada
Tokyo ['təukjəu] *n* Tokio, Tokío
told [təuld] *pt, pp of* **tell**
tolerable ['tɔlərəbl] *adj* (*bearable*) soportable; (*fairly good*) pasable
tolerance ['tɔlərns] *n* (*also Tech*) tolerancia
tolerant ['tɔlərnt] *adj*: **~ of** tolerante con
tolerate ['tɔləreɪt] *vt* tolerar
toll [təul] *n* (*of casualties*) número de víctimas; (*tax, charge*) peaje *m* ▷ *vi* (*bell*) doblar
toll bridge *n* puente *m* de peaje
toll call *n* (*US Telec*) conferencia, llamada interurbana
toll-free ['tɔl'fri:] *adj, adv* (*US*) gratis
tomato (*pl* **tomatoes**) [tə'mɑ:təu] *n* tomate *m*
tomato sauce *n* salsa de tomate
tomb [tu:m] *n* tumba
tomboy ['tɔmbɔɪ] *n* marimacho
tombstone ['tu:mstəun] *n* lápida
tomcat ['tɔmkæt] *n* gato
tomorrow [tə'mɔrəu] *adv, n* (*also fig*) mañana; **the day after ~** pasado mañana; **~ morning** mañana por la mañana; **a week ~** de mañana en ocho (días)
ton [tʌn] *n* tonelada; **~s of** (*inf*) montones de
tone [təun] *n* tono ▷ *vi* armonizar; **dialling ~** (*Tel*) señal *f* para marcar; **tone down** *vt* (*criticism*) suavizar; (*colour*) atenuar; **tone up** *vt* (*muscles*) tonificar
tone-deaf [təun'dɛf] *adj* sin oído musical
tongs [tɔŋz] *npl* (*for coal*) tenazas *fpl*; (*for hair*) tenacillas *fpl*
tongue [tʌŋ] *n* lengua; **~ in cheek** en broma
tongue-tied ['tʌŋtaɪd] *adj* (*fig*) mudo
tongue-twister ['tʌŋtwɪstə^r] *n* trabalenguas *m inv*
tonic ['tɔnɪk] *n* (*Med*) tónico; (*Mus*) tónica; (*also*: **~ water**) (agua) tónica
tonight [tə'naɪt] *adv, n* esta noche; **I'll see you ~** nos vemos esta noche
tonsil ['tɔnsl] *n* amígdala; **to have one's ~s out** sacarse las amígdalas *or* anginas
tonsillitis [tɔnsɪ'laɪtɪs] *n* amigdalitis *f*
too [tu:] *adv* (*excessively*) demasiado; (*very*) muy; (*also*) también; **it's ~ sweet** está demasiado dulce; **I'm not ~ sure about that** no estoy muy seguro de eso; **I went ~** yo también fui; **~ much** *adv, adj* demasiado; **~ many** *adj* demasiados(-as); **~ bad!** ¡mala suerte!
took [tuk] *pt of* **take**
tool [tu:l] *n* herramienta; (*fig*: *person*) instrumento
tool box *n* caja de herramientas
tool kit *n* juego de herramientas
toot [tu:t] *n* (*of horn*) bocinazo; (*of whistle*) silbido ▷ *vi* (*with car horn*) tocar la bocina
tooth (*pl* **teeth**) [tu:θ, ti:θ] *n* (*Anat, Tech*) diente *m*; (*molar*) muela; **to clean one's teeth** lavarse los dientes; **to have a ~ out** sacarse una muela; **by the skin of one's teeth** por un pelo

toothache ['tu:θeɪk] *n* dolor *m* de muelas
toothbrush ['tu:θbrʌʃ] *n* cepillo de dientes
toothpaste ['tu:θpeɪst] *n* pasta de dientes
toothpick ['tu:θpɪk] *n* palillo
top [tɔp] *n* (*of mountain*) cumbre *f*, cima; (*of head*) coronilla; (*of ladder*) (lo) alto; (*of cupboard, table*) superficie *f*; (*lid: of box, jar*) tapa; (*: of bottle*) tapón *m*; (*of list, table, queue, page*) cabeza; (*toy*) peonza; (*Dress: blouse*) blusa; (*: T-shirt*) camiseta; (*: of pyjamas*) chaqueta ▷ *adj* de arriba; (*in rank*) principal, primero; (*best*) mejor ▷ *vt* (*exceed*) exceder; (*be first in*) encabezar; **on ~ of** sobre, encima de; **from ~ to bottom** de pies a cabeza; **the ~ of the milk** la nata; **at the ~ of the stairs** en lo alto de la escalera; **at the ~ of the street** al final de la calle; **at the ~ of one's voice** (*fig*) a voz en grito; **at ~ speed** a máxima velocidad; **a ~ surgeon** un cirujano eminente; **over the ~** (*inf*) excesivo, desmesurado; **to go over the ~** pasarse; **top off** (*US*) *vt* volver a llenar; **top up** *vt* volver a llenar; (*mobile phone*) recargar el saldo de
top-class ['tɔp'klɑ:s] *adj* de primera clase
top floor *n* último piso
top hat *n* sombrero de copa
top-heavy [tɔp'hɛvɪ] *adj* (*object*) con más peso en la parte superior
topic ['tɔpɪk] *n* tema *m*
topical ['tɔpɪkl] *adj* actual
topless ['tɔplɪs] *adj* (*bather etc*) topless
top-level ['tɔplɛvl] *adj* (*talks*) al más alto nivel
topmost ['tɔpməust] *adj* más alto
top-notch ['tɔp'nɔtʃ] *adj* (*inf*) de primerísima categoría
topping ['tɔpɪŋ] *n* (*Culin*): **with a ~ of cream** con nata por encima
topple ['tɔpl] *vt* volcar, derribar ▷ *vi* caerse
top-secret [tɔp'si:krɪt] *adj* de alto secreto
topsy-turvy ['tɔpsɪ'tə:vɪ] *adj, adv* patas arriba
top-up card *n* (*for mobile phone*) tarjeta prepago
top-up loan *n* (*Brit*) préstamo complementario
torch [tɔ:tʃ] *n* antorcha; (*Brit: electric*) linterna
tore [tɔ:ʳ] *pt of* **tear**
torment *n* ['tɔ:mɛnt] tormento ▷ *vt* [tɔ:'mɛnt] atormentar; (*fig: annoy*) fastidiar
torn [tɔ:n] *pp of* **tear**
tornado (*pl* **tornadoes**) [tɔ:'neɪdəu] *n* tornado
torpedo (*pl* **torpedoes**) [tɔ:'pi:dəu] *n* torpedo
torrent ['tɔrnt] *n* torrente *m*
torrential [tɔ'rɛnʃl] *adj* torrencial
torrid ['tɔrɪd] *adj* tórrido; (*fig*) apasionado
torso ['tɔ:səu] *n* torso
tortoise ['tɔ:təs] *n* tortuga
torture ['tɔ:tʃəʳ] *n* tortura ▷ *vt* torturar; (*fig*) atormentar
Tory ['tɔ:rɪ] *adj, n* (*Brit Pol*) conservador(a) *m(f)*
toss [tɔs] *vt* tirar, echar; (*head*) sacudir ▷ *n* (*movement: of head etc*) sacudida; (*of coin*) tirada, echada (*LAm*); **to ~ a coin** echar a cara o cruz; **to ~ up for sth** jugar algo a cara o cruz; **to ~ and turn** (*in bed*) dar vueltas (en la cama); **to win/lose the ~** (*also Sport*) ganar/perder (a cara o cruz)
tot [tɔt] *n* (*Brit: drink*) copita; (*child*) nene(-a) *m(f)*; **tot up** *vt* sumar
total ['təutl] *adj* total, entero; (*emphatic: failure etc*) completo, total ▷ *n* total *m*, suma ▷ *vt* (*add up*) sumar; (*amount to*) ascender a; **grand ~** cantidad *f* total; (*cost*) importe *m* total; **in ~** en total, en suma
totalitarian [təutælɪ'tɛərɪən] *adj* totalitario
totality [təu'tælɪtɪ] *n* totalidad *f*
totally ['təutəlɪ] *adv* totalmente
totter ['tɔtəʳ] *vi* tambalearse
touch [tʌtʃ] *n* (*sense*) tacto; (*contact*) contacto; (*Football*) fuera de juego ▷ *vt* tocar; (*emotionally*) conmover; **a ~ of** (*fig*) una pizca *or* un poquito de; **to get in ~ with sb** ponerse en contacto con algn; **I'll be in ~** le llamaré/escribiré; **to lose ~** (*friends*) perder contacto; **to be out of ~ with events** no estar al corriente (de los acontecimientos); **the personal ~** el toque personal; **to put the finishing ~es to sth** dar el último toque a algo; **no artist in the country can ~ him** no hay artista en todo el país que le iguale; **touch down** *vi* (*on land*) aterrizar; **touch on** *vt fus* (*topic*) aludir (brevemente) a; **touch up** *vt* (*paint*) retocar
touch-and-go ['tʌtʃən'gəu] *adj* arriesgado
touchdown ['tʌtʃdaun] *n* aterrizaje *m*; (*US Football*) ensayo
touched [tʌtʃt] *adj* conmovido; (*inf*) chiflado
touching ['tʌtʃɪŋ] *adj* conmovedor(a)
touchline ['tʌtʃlaɪn] *n* (*Sport*) línea de banda
touch-sensitive ['tʌtʃsɛnsɪtɪv] *adj* sensible al tacto
touchy ['tʌtʃɪ] *adj* (*person*) quisquilloso
tough [tʌf] *adj* (*meat*) duro; (*journey*) penoso; (*task, problem, situation*) difícil; (*resistant*) resistente; (*person*) fuerte; (*: pej*) bruto ▷ *n* (*gangster etc*) gorila *m*; **they got ~ with the workers** se pusieron muy duros con los trabajadores
toughen ['tʌfn] *vt* endurecer
toupée ['tu:peɪ] *n* peluquín *m*
tour ['tuəʳ] *n* viaje *m*; (*also*: **package ~**) viaje *m* con todo incluido; (*of town, museum*) visita ▷ *vt* viajar por; **to go on a ~ of** (*region, country*) ir de viaje por; (*museum, castle*) visitar; **to go on ~** partir *or* ir de gira
tour guide *n* guía *m/f* turístico(-a)
tourism ['tuərɪzm] *n* turismo
tourist ['tuərɪst] *n* turista *m/f* ▷ *cpd* turístico; **the ~ trade** el turismo
tourist class *n* (*Aviat*) clase *f* turista
tourist office *n* oficina de turismo
tournament ['tuənəmənt] *n* torneo
tour operator *n* touroperador(a) *m(f)*, operador(a) *m(f)* turístico(-a)

tousled ['tauzld] *adj* (*hair*) despeinado
tout [taut] *vi*: **to ~ for business** solicitar clientes ▷ *n*: **ticket ~** revendedor(a) *m(f)*
tow [təu] *n*: **to give sb a ~** (*Aut*) remolcar a algn ▷ *vt* remolcar; **"on** *or* (*US*) **in ~"** (*Aut*) "a remolque"; **tow away** *vt* llevarse a remolque
toward [tə'wɔːd], **towards** [tə'wɔːdz] *prep* hacia; (*of attitude*) respecto a, con; (*of purpose*) para; **~noon** alrededor de mediodía; **~the end of the year** hacia finales de año; **to feel friendly ~sb** sentir amistad hacia algn
towel ['tauəl] *n* toalla; **to throw in the ~** (*fig*) darse por vencido, renunciar
towelling ['tauəlɪŋ] *n* (*fabric*) felpa
towel rail, towel rack (*US*) *n* toallero
tower ['tauə^r] *n* torre *f* ▷ *vi* (*building, mountain*) elevarse; **to ~ above** *or* **over sth/sb** dominar algo/destacarse sobre algn
tower block *n* (*Brit*) bloque *m* de pisos
towering ['tauərɪŋ] *adj* muy alto, imponente
town [taun] *n* ciudad *f*; **to go to ~** ir a la ciudad; (*fig*) tirar la casa por la ventana; **in the ~** en la ciudad; **to be out of ~** estar fuera de la ciudad
town centre *n* centro de la ciudad
town council *n* Ayuntamiento, consejo municipal
town hall *n* ayuntamiento
townie ['taunɪ] *n* (*Brit inf*) persona de la ciudad
town plan *n* plano de la ciudad
town planning *n* urbanismo
township ['taunʃɪp] *n* *municipio habitado sólo por negros en Sudáfrica*
towrope ['təurəup] *n* cable *m* de remolque
tow truck *n* (*US*) camión *m* grúa
toxic ['tɔksɪk] *adj* tóxico
toxin ['tɔksɪn] *n* toxina
toy [tɔɪ] *n* juguete *m*; **toy with** *vt fus* jugar con; (*idea*) acariciar
toyshop ['tɔɪʃɔp] *n* juguetería
trace [treɪs] *n* rastro ▷ *vt* (*draw*) trazar, delinear; (*locate*) encontrar; **there was no ~ of it** no había ningún indicio de ello
tracing paper ['treɪsɪŋ-] *n* papel *m* de calco
track [træk] *n* (*mark*) huella, pista; (*path*: *gen*) camino, senda; (: *of bullet etc*) trayectoria; (: *of suspect, animal*) pista, rastro; (*Rail*) vía; (*Comput, Sport*) pista; (*on album*) canción *f* ▷ *vt* seguir la pista de; **to keep ~ of** mantenerse al tanto de, seguir; **a four-~ tape** una cinta de cuarto pistas; **the first ~ on the record/tape** la primera canción en el disco/la cinta; **to be on the right ~** (*fig*) ir por buen camino; **track down** *vt* (*person*) localizar; (*sth lost*) encontrar
track meet *n* (*US*) concurso de carreras y saltos
track record *n*: **to have a good ~** (*fig*) tener un buen historial
tracksuit ['træksuːt] *n* chandal *m*
tract [trækt] *n* (*Geo*) región *f*; (*pamphlet*) folleto
traction ['trækʃən] *n* (*Aut*: *power*) tracción *f*; **in ~** (*Med*) en tracción
tractor ['træktə^r] *n* tractor *m*
trade [treɪd] *n* comercio, negocio; (*skill, job*) oficio, empleo; (*industry*) industria ▷ *vi* negociar, comerciar; **foreign ~** comercio exterior ▷ *vt* (*exchange*): **to ~ sth (for sth)** cambiar algo (por algo); **trade in** *vt* (*old car etc*) ofrecer como parte del pago
Trade Descriptions Act *n* (*Brit*) *ley sobre descripciones comerciales*
trade fair *n* feria de muestras
trade-in ['treɪdɪn] *adj*: **~ price/value** *precio/valor de un artículo usado que se descuenta del precio de otro nuevo*
trademark ['treɪdmɑːk] *n* marca de fábrica
trade name *n* marca registrada
trade-off ['treɪdɔf] *n*: **a ~ (between)** un equilibrio (entre)
trader ['treɪdə^r] *n* comerciante *m/f*
trade secret *n* secreto profesional
tradesman ['treɪdzmən] *n* (*shopkeeper*) comerciante *m/f*
trade union *n* sindicato
trade unionist [-'juːnjənɪst] *n* sindicalista *m/f*
trading ['treɪdɪŋ] *n* comercio
tradition [trə'dɪʃən] *n* tradición *f*
traditional [trə'dɪʃənl] *adj* tradicional
traffic ['træfɪk] *n* tráfico, circulación *f*, tránsito ▷ *vi*: **to ~ in** (*pej*: *liquor, drugs*) traficar en; **air ~** tráfico aéreo
traffic calming [-'kɑːmɪŋ] *n* reducción *f* de la velocidad de la circulación
traffic circle *n* (*US*) rotonda, glorieta
traffic island *n* refugio, isleta
traffic jam *n* embotellamiento, atasco
traffic lights *npl* semáforo *sg*
traffic warden *n* guardia *m/f* de tráfico
tragedy ['trædʒədɪ] *n* tragedia
tragic ['trædʒɪk] *adj* trágico
trail [treɪl] *n* (*tracks*) rastro, pista; (*path*) camino, sendero; (*dust, smoke*) estela ▷ *vt* (*drag*) arrastrar; (*follow*) seguir la pista de; (*follow closely*) vigilar ▷ *vi* arrastrarse; (*in contest etc*) ir perdiendo; **to be on sb's ~** seguir la pista de algn; **trail away, trail off** *vi* (*sound*) desvanecerse; (*interest, voice*) desaparecer; **trail behind** *vi* quedar a la zaga
trailer ['treɪlə^r] *n* (*Aut*) remolque *m*; (*caravan*) caravana; (*Cine*) trailer *m*, avance *m*
train [treɪn] *n* tren *m*; (*of dress*) cola; (*series*): **~ of events** curso de los acontecimientos ▷ *vt* (*educate*) formar; (*teach skills to*) adiestrar; (*sportsman*) entrenar; (*dog*) adiestrar, amaestrar; (*point*: *gun etc*): **to ~ on** apuntar a ▷ *vi* (*Sport*) entrenarse; (*be educated, learn a skill*) formarse; **to go by ~** ir en tren; **to ~ as a teacher** *etc* estudiar para profesor *etc*; **one's ~ of thought** el razonamiento de algn; **to ~ sb to do sth** enseñar a algn a hacer algo
trained [treɪnd] *adj* (*worker*) cualificado; (*animal*) amaestrado

t

trainee [treɪ'niː] *n* trabajador(a) *m(f)* en prácticas ▷ *cpd*: **he's a ~ teacher** (*primary*) es estudiante de magisterio; (*secondary*) está haciendo las prácticas del I.C.E.
trainer ['treɪnə^r] *n* (*Sport*) entrenador(a) *m(f)*; (*of animals*) domador(a) *m(f)*; **trainers** *npl* (*shoes*) zapatillas *fpl* (de deporte)
training ['treɪnɪŋ] *n* formación *f*; entrenamiento; **to be in ~** (*Sport*) estar entrenando; (*: fit*) estar en forma
training college *n* (*gen*) colegio de formación profesional; (*for teachers*) escuela normal
training course *n* curso de formación
training shoes *npl* zapatillas *fpl* (de deporte)
traipse [treɪps] *vi* andar penosamente
trait [treɪt] *n* rasgo
traitor ['treɪtə^r] *n* traidor(a) *m(f)*
tram [træm] *n* (*Brit*: *also*: **~car**) tranvía *m*
tramp [træmp] *n* (*person*) vagabundo(-a); (*inf, pej*: *woman*) puta ▷ *vi* andar con pasos pesados
trample ['træmpl] *vt*: **to ~ (underfoot)** pisotear
trampoline ['træmpəliːn] *n* trampolín *m*
trance [trɑːns] *n* trance *m*; **to go into a ~** entrar en trance
tranquil ['træŋkwɪl] *adj* tranquilo
tranquillizer, tranquilizer (US) ['træŋkwɪlaɪzə^r] *n* (*Med*) tranquilizante *m*
transact [træn'zækt] *vt* (*business*) tramitar
transaction [træn'zækʃən] *n* transacción *f*, operación *f*; **cash ~s** transacciones al contado
transatlantic ['trænzət'læntɪk] *adj* transatlántico
transcend [træn'sɛnd] *vt* rebasar
transcendental [trænsɛn'dɛntl] *adj*: **~ meditation** meditación *f* transcendental
transcribe [træn'skraɪb] *vt* transcribir, copiar
transcript ['trænskrɪpt] *n* copia
transcription [træn'skrɪpʃən] *n* transcripción *f*
transfer *n* ['trænsfə^r] transferencia; (*Sport*) traspaso; (*picture, design*) calcomanía ▷ *vt* [træns'fəː^r] trasladar, pasar; **to ~ the charges** (*Brit Tel*) llamar a cobro revertido; **by bank ~** por transferencia bancaria *or* giro bancario; **to ~ money from one account to another** transferir dinero de una cuenta a otra; **to ~ sth to sb's name** transferir algo al nombre de algn
transform [træns'fɔːm] *vt* transformar
transformation [trænsfə'meɪʃən] *n* transformación *f*
transfusion [træns'fjuːʒən] *n* transfusión *f*
transient ['trænzɪənt] *adj* transitorio
transistor [træn'zɪstə^r] *n* (*Elec*) transistor *m*
transit ['trænzɪt] *n*: **in ~** en tránsito
transition [træn'zɪʃən] *n* transición *f*
transition period *n* período de transición
transitive ['trænzɪtɪv] *adj* (*Ling*) transitivo
translate [trænz'leɪt] *vt*: **to ~ (from/into)** traducir (de/a)
translation [trænz'leɪʃən] *n* traducción *f*
translator [trænz'leɪtə^r] *n* traductor(a) *m(f)*
transmission [trænz'mɪʃən] *n* transmisión *f*
transmit [trænz'mɪt] *vt* transmitir
transmitter [trænz'mɪtə^r] *n* transmisor *m*; (*station*) emisora
transparency [træns'pɛərnsɪ] *n* (*Brit Phot*) diapositiva
transparent [træns'pærnt] *adj* transparente
transpire [træns'paɪə^r] *vi* (*turn out*) resultar (ser); (*happen*) ocurrir, suceder; (*become known*): **it finally ~d that ...** por fin se supo que ...
transplant *vt* [træns'plɑːnt] transplantar ▷ *n* ['trænsplɑːnt] (*Med*) transplante *m*; **to have a heart ~** hacerse un transplante de corazón
transport *n* ['trænspɔːt] transporte *m* ▷ *vt* [træns'pɔːt] transportar; **public ~** transporte *m* público
transportation [trænspɔː'teɪʃən] *n* transporte *m*; (*of prisoners*) deportación *f*
transport café *n* (*Brit*) bar-restaurante *m* de carretera
transsexual [trænz'sɛksjuəl] *adj, n* transexual *m/f*
transvestite [trænz'vɛstaɪt] *n* travesti *m/f*
trap [træp] *n* (*snare, trick*) trampa ▷ *vt* coger (*Sp*) *or* agarrar (*LAm*) en una trampa; (*trick*) engañar; (*confine*) atrapar; (*immobilize*) bloquear; (*jam*) atascar; **to set** *or* **lay a ~ (for sb)** poner(le) una trampa (a algn); **to ~ one's finger in the door** pillarse el dedo en la puerta
trap door *n* escotilla
trapeze [trə'piːz] *n* trapecio
trappings ['træpɪŋz] *npl* adornos *mpl*
trash [træʃ] *n* basura; (*nonsense*) tonterías *fpl*; **the book/film is ~** el libro/la película no vale nada
trash can *n* (*US*) cubo, balde *m* (*LAm*) *or* bote *m* (*LAm*) de la basura
trashy ['træʃɪ] *adj* (*inf*) chungo
trauma ['trɔːmə] *n* trauma *m*
traumatic [trɔː'mætɪk] *adj* traumático
travel ['trævl] *n* viaje *m* ▷ *vi* viajar ▷ *vt* (*distance*) recorrer; **this wine doesn't ~ well** este vino pierde con los viajes
travel agency *n* agencia de viajes
travel agent *n* agente *m/f* de viajes
travel insurance *n* seguro de viaje
traveller, traveler (US) ['trævlə^r] *n* viajero(-a); (*Comm*) viajante *m/f*
traveller's cheque, traveler's check (US) *n* cheque *m* de viaje
travelling, traveling (US) ['trævlɪŋ] *n* los viajes, el viajar ▷ *adj* (*circus, exhibition*) ambulante ▷ *cpd* (*bag, clock*) de viaje
travel-sick ['trævəlsɪk] *adj*: **to get ~** marearse al viajar

travel sickness *n* mareo
travesty ['trævəstɪ] *n* parodia
trawler ['trɔːləʳ] *n* pesquero de arrastre
tray [treɪ] *n* (*for carrying*) bandeja; (*on desk*) cajón *m*
treacherous ['trɛtʃərəs] *adj* traidor(a); **road conditions are ~** el estado de las carreteras es peligroso
treachery ['trɛtʃərɪ] *n* traición *f*
treacle ['triːkl] *n* (*Brit*) melaza
tread [trɛd] (*pt* **trod**, *pp* **trodden** [trɔd, 'trɔdn]) *n* paso, pisada; (*of tyre*) banda de rodadura ▷ *vi* pisar; **tread on** *vt fus* pisar
treason ['triːzn] *n* traición *f*
treasure ['trɛʒəʳ] *n* tesoro ▷ *vt* (*value*) apreciar, valorar
treasurer ['trɛʒərəʳ] *n* tesorero(-a)
treasury ['trɛʒərɪ] *n*: **the T~** (*US*), **the T~ Department** ≈ el Ministerio de Economía y de Hacienda
treat [triːt] *n* (*present*) regalo; (*pleasure*) placer *m* ▷ *vt* tratar; (*consider*) considerar; **to give sb a ~** hacer un regalo a algn; **to ~ sb to sth** invitar a algn a algo; **to ~ sth as a joke** tomar algo a broma
treatise ['triːtɪz] *n* tratado
treatment ['triːtmənt] *n* tratamiento; **to have ~ for sth** recibir tratamiento por algo
treaty ['triːtɪ] *n* tratado
treble ['trɛbl] *adj* triple ▷ *vt* triplicar ▷ *vi* triplicarse
treble clef *n* (*Mus*) clave *f* de sol
tree [triː] *n* árbol *m*
tree trunk *n* tronco de árbol
trek [trɛk] *n* (*long journey*) expedición *f*; (*tiring walk*) caminata
trellis ['trɛlɪs] *n* enrejado
tremble ['trɛmbl] *vi* temblar
tremendous [trɪ'mɛndəs] *adj* tremendo; (*enormous*) enorme; (*excellent*) estupendo
tremor ['trɛməʳ] *n* temblor *m*; (*also*: **earth ~**) temblor *m* de tierra
trench [trɛntʃ] *n* zanja; (*Mil*) trinchera
trend [trɛnd] *n* (*tendency*) tendencia; (*of events*) curso; (*fashion*) moda; **~ towards/away from sth** tendencia hacia/en contra de algo; **to set the ~** marcar la pauta
trendy ['trɛndɪ] *adj* de moda
trepidation [trɛpɪ'deɪʃən] *n* inquietud *f*
trespass ['trɛspəs] *vi*: **to ~ on** entrar sin permiso en; **"no ~ing"** "prohibido el paso"
trestle ['trɛsl] *n* caballete *m*
trial ['traɪəl] *n* (*Law*) juicio, proceso; (*test: of machine etc*) prueba; (*hardship*) desgracia; **trials** *npl* (*Athletics*) pruebas *fpl*; (*of horses*) pruebas *fpl*; **to bring sb to ~ (for a crime)** llevar a algn a juicio (por un delito); **~ by jury** juicio ante jurado; **to be sent for ~** ser remitido al tribunal; **by ~ and error** a fuerza de probar
trial period *n* periodo de prueba
triangle ['traɪæŋgl] *n* (*Math, Mus*) triángulo
triangular [traɪ'æŋgjuləʳ] *adj* triangular
triathlon [traɪ'æθlən] *n* triatlón *m*
tribe [traɪb] *n* tribu *f*
tribesman ['traɪbzmən] *n* miembro de una tribu
tribunal [traɪ'bjuːnl] *n* tribunal *m*
tributary ['trɪbjuːtərɪ] *n* (*river*) afluente *m*
tribute ['trɪbjuːt] *n* homenaje *m*, tributo; **to pay ~ to** rendir homenaje a
trice [traɪs] *n*: **in a ~** en un santiamén
trick [trɪk] *n* trampa; (*conjuring trick, deceit*) truco; (*joke*) broma; (*Cards*) baza ▷ *vt* engañar; **it's a ~ of the light** es una ilusión óptica; **to play a ~ on sb** gastar una broma a algn; **that should do the ~** eso servirá; **to ~ sb out of sth** quitarle algo a algn con engaños; **to ~ sb into doing sth** hacer que algn haga algo con engaños
trickery ['trɪkərɪ] *n* engaño
trickle ['trɪkl] *n* (*of water etc*) hilo ▷ *vi* gotear
tricky ['trɪkɪ] *adj* difícil; (*problem*) delicado
tricycle ['traɪsɪkl] *n* triciclo
tried [traɪd] *adj* probado
trifle ['traɪfl] *n* bagatela; (*Culin*) *dulce de bizcocho, gelatina, fruta y natillas* ▷ *adv*: **a ~ long** un pelín largo ▷ *vi*: **to ~ with** jugar con
trifling ['traɪflɪŋ] *adj* insignificante
trigger ['trɪgəʳ] *n* (*of gun*) gatillo; **trigger off** *vt* desencadenar
trilogy ['trɪlədʒɪ] *n* trilogía
trim [trɪm] *adj* (*elegant*) aseado; (*house, garden*) en buen estado; (*figure*): **to be ~** tener buen talle ▷ *n* (*haircut etc*) recorte *m* ▷ *vt* (*neaten*) arreglar; (*cut*) recortar; (*decorate*) adornar; (*Naut: a sail*) orientar; **to keep in (good) ~** mantener en buen estado
trimmings ['trɪmɪŋz] *npl* (*extras*) accesorios *mpl*; (*cuttings*) recortes *mpl*
Trinity ['trɪnɪtɪ] *n*: **the ~** la Trinidad
trinket ['trɪŋkɪt] *n* chuchería, baratija
trio ['triːəu] *n* trío
trip [trɪp] *n* viaje *m*; (*excursion*) excursión *f*; (*stumble*) traspié *m* ▷ *vi* (*stumble*) tropezar; (*go lightly*) andar a paso ligero; **on a ~** de viaje; **trip over** *vt fus* tropezar con; **trip up** *vi* tropezar, caerse ▷ *vt* hacer tropezar *or* caer
tripe [traɪp] *n* (*Culin*) callos *mpl*; (*pej: rubbish*) bobadas *fpl*
triple ['trɪpl] *adj* triple ▷ *adv*: **~ the distance/the speed** 3 veces la distancia/la velocidad
triple jump *n* triple salto
triplets ['trɪplɪts] *npl* trillizos(-as) *m(f)pl*
triplicate ['trɪplɪkət] *n*: **in ~** por triplicado
tripod ['traɪpɔd] *n* trípode *m*
tripwire ['trɪpwaɪəʳ] *n* cable *m* de trampa
trite [traɪt] *adj* trillado
triumph ['traɪʌmf] *n* triunfo ▷ *vi*: **to ~ (over)** vencer
triumphant [traɪ'ʌmfənt] *adj* triunfante
trivia ['trɪvɪə] *npl* trivialidades *fpl*
trivial ['trɪvɪəl] *adj* insignificante, trivial
trod [trɔd] *pt of* **tread**

t

trodden ['trɔdn] *pp of* **tread**
trolley ['trɔlɪ] *n* carrito; (*in hospital*) camilla
trolley bus *n* trolebús *m*
trombone [trɔm'bəun] *n* trombón *m*
troop [tru:p] *n* grupo, banda; **troops** *npl* (*Mil*) tropas *fpl*; **troop in** *vi* entrar en tropel; **troop out** *vi* salir en tropel
trophy ['trəufɪ] *n* trofeo
tropic ['trɔpɪk] *n* trópico; **the ~s** los trópicos, la zona tropical; **T~ of Cancer/Capricorn** trópico de Cáncer/Capricornio
tropical ['trɔpɪkl] *adj* tropical
trot [trɔt] *n* trote *m* ▷ *vi* trotar; **on the ~** (*Brit fig*) seguidos(-as); **trot out** *vt* (*excuse, reason*) volver a usar; (*names, facts*) sacar a relucir
trouble ['trʌbl] *n* problema *m*, dificultad *f*; (*worry*) preocupación *f*; (*bother, effort*) molestia, esfuerzo; (*unrest*) inquietud *f*; (*with machine etc*) fallo, avería; (*Med*): **stomach ~** problemas *mpl* gástricos ▷ *vt* molestar; (*worry*) preocupar, inquietar ▷ *vi*: **to ~ to do sth** molestarse en hacer algo; **troubles** *npl* (*Pol etc*) conflictos *mpl*; **to be in ~** estar en un apuro; (*for doing wrong*) tener problemas; **to have ~ doing sth** tener dificultad en *or* para hacer algo; **to go to the ~ of doing sth** tomarse la molestia de hacer algo; **it's no ~!** ¡no es molestia (ninguna)!; **what's the ~?** ¿qué pasa?; **the ~ is ...** el problema es ..., lo que pasa es ...; **please don't ~ yourself** por favor no se moleste
troubled ['trʌbld] *adj* (*person*) preocupado; (*epoch, life*) agitado
troublemaker ['trʌblmeɪkə^r] *n* agitador(a) *m(f)*
troubleshooter ['trʌblʃu:tə^r] *n* (*in conflict*) mediador(a) *m(f)*
troublesome ['trʌblsəm] *adj* molesto, inoportuno
troubling ['trʌblɪŋ] *adj* (*thought*) preocupante; **these are ~ times** son malos tiempos
trough [trɔf] *n* (*also*: **drinking ~**) abrevadero; (*also*: **feeding ~**) comedero; (*channel*) canal *m*
trounce [trauns] *vt* dar una paliza a
troupe [tru:p] *n* grupo
trousers ['trauzəz] *npl* pantalones *mpl*; **short ~** pantalones *mpl* cortos
trouser suit *n* traje *m* de chaqueta y pantalón
trout [traut] *n pl inv* trucha
trowel ['trauəl] *n* paleta
truant ['truənt] *n*: **to play ~** (*Brit*) hacer novillos
truce [tru:s] *n* tregua
truck [trʌk] *n* (*US*) camión *m*; (*Rail*) vagón *m*
truck driver *n* camionero(-a)
trucker ['trʌkə^r] *n* (*esp US*) camionero(-a)
truck farm *n* (*US*) huerto de hortalizas
trudge [trʌdʒ] *vi* caminar penosamente
true [tru:] *adj* verdadero; (*accurate*) exacto; (*genuine*) auténtico; (*faithful*) fiel; (*wheel*) centrado; (*wall*) a plomo; (*beam*) alineado; **~ to life** verídico; **to come ~** realizarse, cumplirse
truffle ['trʌfl] *n* trufa
truly ['tru:lɪ] *adv* realmente; (*faithfully*) fielmente; **yours ~** (*in letter-writing*) atentamente
trump [trʌmp] *n* (*Cards*) triunfo; **to turn up ~s** (*fig*) salir *or* resultar bien
trumped-up ['trʌmptʌp] *adj* inventado
trumpet ['trʌmpɪt] *n* trompeta
truncheon ['trʌntʃən] *n* (*Brit*) porra
trundle ['trʌndl] *vt, vi*: **to ~ along** rodar haciendo ruido
trunk [trʌŋk] *n* (*of tree, person*) tronco; (*of elephant*) trompa; (*case*) baúl *m*; (*US Aut*) maletero, baúl *m* (*LAm*)
trunks [trʌŋks] *npl* (*also*: **swimming ~**) bañador *m*
truss [trʌs] *n* (*Med*) braguero ▷ *vt*: **to ~ (up)** atar
trust [trʌst] *n* confianza; (*Comm*) trust *m*; (*Law*) fideicomiso ▷ *vt* (*rely on*) tener confianza en; (*entrust*): **to ~ sth to sb** confiar algo a algn; (*hope*): **to ~ (that)** esperar (que); **in ~** en fideicomiso; **you'll have to take it on ~** tienes que aceptarlo a ojos cerrados
trusted ['trʌstɪd] *adj* de confianza, fiable, de fiar
trustee [trʌs'ti:] *n* (*Law*) fideicomisario
trustful ['trʌstful] *adj* confiado
trustworthy ['trʌstwə:ðɪ] *adj* digno de confianza, fiable, de fiar
truth, truths [tru:θ, tru:ðz] *n* verdad *f*
truthful ['tru:θfəl] *adj* (*person*) sincero; (*account*) fidedigno
try [traɪ] *n* tentativa, intento; (*Rugby*) ensayo ▷ *vt* (*Law*) juzgar, procesar; (*test: sth new*) probar, someter a prueba; (*attempt*) intentar; (*strain: patience*) hacer perder ▷ *vi* probar; **to give sth a ~** intentar hacer algo; **to ~ one's (very) best** *or* **hardest** poner todo su empeño, esmerarse; **to ~ to do sth** intentar hacer algo; **~ again!** ¡vuelve a probar!; **~ harder!** ¡esfuérzate más!; **well, I tried** al menos lo intenté; **try on** *vt* (*clothes*) probarse; **try out** *vt* probar, poner a prueba
trying ['traɪɪŋ] *adj* cansado; (*person*) pesado
T-shirt ['ti:ʃə:t] *n* camiseta
T-square ['ti:skwɛə^r] *n* regla en T
tub [tʌb] *n* cubo (*Sp*), balde *m* (*LAm*); (*bath*) bañera, tina (*LAm*)
tubby ['tʌbɪ] *adj* regordete
tube [tju:b] *n* tubo; (*Brit: underground*) metro; (*US inf: television*) tele *f*
tuberculosis [tjubə:kju'ləusɪs] *n* tuberculosis *f inv*
tube station *n* (*Brit*) estación *f* de metro
TUC *n abbr* (*Brit: = Trades Union Congress*) *federación nacional de sindicatos*
tuck [tʌk] *n* (*Sewing*) pliegue *m* ▷ *vt* (*put*) poner; **tuck away** *vt* esconder; **tuck in** *vt* meter; (*child*) arropar ▷ *vi* (*eat*) comer con apetito; **tuck up** *vt* (*child*) arropar

tuck shop *n* (*Scol*) tienda de golosinas
Tue., Tues. *abbr* (= *Tuesday*) mart
Tuesday ['tju:zdɪ] *n* martes *m inv*; **on ~** el martes; **on ~s** los martes; **every ~** todos los martes; **every other ~** cada dos martes, un martes sí y otro no; **last/next ~** el martes pasado/próximo; **a week/fortnight on ~, ~ week/fortnight** del martes en 8/15 días, del martes en una semana/dos semanas
tuft [tʌft] *n* mechón *m*; (*of grass etc*) manojo
tug [tʌg] *n* (*ship*) remolcador *m* ▷ *vt* remolcar
tug-of-love [tʌgəv'lʌv] *n*: **~ children** *hijos envueltos en el litigio de los padres por su custodia*
tug-of-war [tʌgəv'wɔ:ʳ] *n* juego de la cuerda
tuition [tju:'ɪʃən] *n* (*Brit*) enseñanza; (*: private tuition*) clases *fpl* particulares; (*US: school fees*) matrícula
tulip ['tju:lɪp] *n* tulipán *m*
tumble ['tʌmbl] *n* (*fall*) caída ▷ *vi* caerse, tropezar; **to ~ to sth** (*inf*) caer en la cuenta de algo
tumbledown ['tʌmbldaun] *adj* ruinoso
tumble dryer *n* (*Brit*) secadora
tumbler ['tʌmbləʳ] *n* vaso
tummy ['tʌmɪ] *n* (*inf*) barriga, vientre *m*
tumour, tumor (*US*) ['tju:məʳ] *n* tumor *m*
tuna ['tju:nə] *n pl inv* (*also*: **~ fish**) atún *m*
tune [tju:n] *n* (*melody*) melodía ▷ *vt* (*Mus*) afinar; (*Radio, TV, Aut*) sintonizar; **to be in/out of ~** (*instrument*) estar afinado/desafinado; (*singer*) afinar/desafinar; **to be in/out of ~ with** (*fig*) armonizar/desentonar con; **to the ~ of** (*fig: amount*) por (la) cantidad de; **tune in** *vi* (*Radio, TV*): **to ~ in (to)** sintonizar (con); **tune up** *vi* (*musician*) afinar (su instrumento)
tuneful ['tju:nful] *adj* melodioso
tuner ['tju:nəʳ] *n* (*radio set*) sintonizador *m*; **piano ~** afinador(a) *m(f)* de pianos
tunic ['tju:nɪk] *n* túnica
Tunisia [tju:'nɪzɪə] *n* Túnez *m*
tunnel ['tʌnl] *n* túnel *m*; (*in mine*) galería ▷ *vi* construir un túnel/una galería
tunnel vision *n* (*Med*) visión *f* periférica restringida; (*fig*) estrechez *f* de miras
turbo ['tə:bəu] *n* turbo
turbulence ['tə:bjuləns] *n* (*Aviat*) turbulencia
tureen [tə'ri:n] *n* sopera
turf [tə:f] *n* césped *m*; (*clod*) tepe *m* ▷ *vt* cubrir con césped; **turf out** *vt* (*inf*) echar a la calle
turgid ['tə:dʒɪd] *adj* (*prose*) pesado
Turk [tə:k] *n* turco(-a)
Turkey ['tə:kɪ] *n* Turquía
turkey ['tə:kɪ] *n* pavo
Turkish ['tə:kɪʃ] *adj* turco ▷ *n* (*Ling*) turco
turmoil ['tə:mɔɪl] *n* desorden *m*, alboroto; **in ~** revuelto
turn [tə:n] *n* turno; (*in road*) curva; (*Theat*) número; (*Med*) ataque *m* ▷ *vt* girar, volver, voltear (*LAm*); (*collar, steak*) dar la vuelta a; (*shape: wood, metal*) tornear; (*change*): **to ~ sth into** convertir algo en ▷ *vi* volver, voltearse (*LAm*); (*person: look back*) volverse; (*reverse direction*) dar la vuelta, voltear (*LAm*); (*milk*) cortarse; (*change*) cambiar; (*become*): **to ~ into sth** convertirse *or* transformarse en algo; **a good ~** un favor; **it gave me quite a ~** me dio un susto; **"no left ~"** (*Aut*) "prohibido girar a la izquierda"; **it's your ~** te toca a ti; **in ~** por turnos; **to take ~s** turnarse; **at the ~ of the year/century** a fin de año/a finales de siglo; **to take a ~ for the worse** (*situation, patient*) empeorar; **they ~ed him against us** le pusieron en contra nuestra; **the car ~ed the corner** el coche dobló la esquina; **to ~ left** (*Aut*) torcer *or* girar a la izquierda; **she has no-one to ~ to** no tiene a quién recurrir; **turn around** *vi* (*person*) volverse, darse la vuelta ▷ *vt* (*object*) dar la vuelta a, voltear (*LAm*); **turn away** *vi* apartar la vista ▷ *vt* (*reject: person, business*) rechazar; **turn back** *vi* volverse atrá ▷ *vt* hacer retroceder; (*clock*) retrasar; **turn down** *vt* (*refuse*) rechazar; (*reduce*) bajar; (*fold*) doblar; **turn in** *vi* (*inf: go to bed*) acostarse ▷ *vt* (*fold*) doblar hacia dentro; **turn off** *vi* (*from road*) desviarse ▷ *vt* (*light, radio etc*) apagar; (*engine*) parar; **turn on** *vt* (*light, radio etc*) encender, prender (*LAm*); (*engine*) poner en marcha; **turn out** *vt* (*light, gas*) apagar; (*produce: goods, novel etc*) producir ▷ *vi* (*attend: troops*) presentarse; (*: doctor*) atender; **to ~ out to be ...** resultar ser ...; **turn over** *vi* (*person*) volverse ▷ *vt* (*mattress, card*) dar la vuelta a; (*page*) volver; **turn round** *vi* volverse; (*rotate*) girar; **turn to** *vt fus*: **to ~ to sb** acudir a algn; **turn up** *vi* (*person*) llegar, presentarse; (*lost object*) aparecer ▷ *vt* (*radio*) subir, poner más alto; (*heat, gas*) poner más fuerte
turning ['tə:nɪŋ] *n* (*side road*) bocacalle *f*; (*bend*) curva; **the first ~ on the right** la primera bocacalle a la derecha
turning point *n* (*fig*) momento decisivo
turnip ['tə:nɪp] *n* nabo
turnout ['tə:naut] *n* (*attendance*) asistencia; (*number of people attending*) número de asistentes; (*spectators*) público
turnover ['tə:nəuvəʳ] *n* (*Comm: amount of money*) facturación *f*; (*of goods*) movimiento; **there is a rapid ~ in staff** hay mucho movimiento de personal
turnpike ['tə:npaɪk] *n* (*US*) autopista de peaje
turnstile ['tə:nstaɪl] *n* torniquete *m*
turntable ['tə:nteɪbl] *n* plato
turn-up ['tə:nʌp] *n* (*Brit: on trousers*) vuelta
turpentine ['tə:pəntaɪn] *n* (*also*: **turps**) trementina
turquoise ['tə:kwɔɪz] *n* (*stone*) turquesa ▷ *adj* color turquesa
turret ['tʌrɪt] *n* torreón *m*
turtle ['tə:tl] *n* tortuga (marina)
turtleneck ['tə:tlnɛk], **turtleneck sweater** *n* (jersey *m* de) cuello cisne
tusk [tʌsk] *n* colmillo

tussle ['tʌsl] *n* lucha, pelea
tutor ['tju:tə^r] *n* profesor(a) *m(f)*
tutorial [tju:'tɔ:rɪəl] *n* (*Scol*) seminario
tuxedo [tʌk'si:dəu] *n* (*US*) smóking *m*, esmoquin *m*
TV [ti:'vi:] *n abbr* (= *television*) televisión *f*
TV dinner *n* cena precocinada
TV licence *n licencia que se paga por el uso del televisor, destinada a financiar la BBC*
twang [twæŋ] *n* (*of instrument*) tañido; (*of voice*) timbre *m* nasal
tweed [twi:d] *n* tweed *m*
tweet [twi:t] (*on Twitter*) *n* tuit *m* ▷ *vt* tuitear
tweezers ['twi:zəz] *npl* pinzas *fpl* (de depilar)
twelfth [twɛlfθ] *num* duodécimo
twelve [twɛlv] *num* doce; **at ~ o'clock** (*midday*) a mediodía; (*midnight*) a medianoche
twentieth ['twɛntɪɪθ] *num* vigésimo
twenty ['twɛntɪ] *num* veinte
twerp [twə:p] *n* (*inf*) idiota *m/f*
twice [twaɪs] *adv* dos veces; **~ as much** dos veces más, el doble; **she is ~ your age** ella te dobla edad; **~ a week** dos veces a la *or* por semana
twiddle ['twɪdl] *vt, vi*: **to ~ (with) sth** dar vueltas a algo; **to ~ one's thumbs** (*fig*) estar de brazos cruzados
twig [twɪg] *n* ramita ▷ *vi* (*inf*) caer en la cuenta
twilight ['twaɪlaɪt] *n* crepúsculo; (*morning*) madrugada; **in the ~** en la media luz
twin [twɪn] *adj, n* gemelo(-a) *m(f)* ▷ *vt* hermanar
twin-bedded room ['twɪn'bɛdɪd-] *n* = **twin room**
twin beds *npl* camas *fpl* gemelas
twine [twaɪn] *n* bramante *m* ▷ *vi* (*plant*) enroscarse
twinge [twɪndʒ] *n* (*of pain*) punzada; (*of conscience*) remordimiento
twinkle ['twɪŋkl] *n* centelleo ▷ *vi* centellear; (*eyes*) parpadear
twin room *n* habitación *f* con dos camas
twin town *n* ciudad *f* hermanada *or* gemela
twirl [twə:l] *n* giro ▷ *vt* dar vueltas a ▷ *vi* piruetear
twist [twɪst] *n* (*action*) torsión *f*; (*in road, coil*) vuelta; (*in wire, flex*) doblez *f*; (*in story*) giro ▷ *vt* torcer, retorcer; (*roll around*) enrollar; (*fig*) deformar ▷ *vi* serpentear; **to ~ one's ankle/wrist** (*Med*) torcerse el tobillo/la muñeca
twisted ['twɪstɪd] *adj* (*wire, rope*) trenzado, enroscado; (*ankle, wrist*) torcido; (*fig: logic, mind*) retorcido
twit [twɪt] *n* (*inf*) tonto
twitch [twɪtʃ] *n* sacudida; (*nervous*) tic *m* nervioso ▷ *vi* moverse nerviosamente
two [tu:] *num* dos; **~ by ~, in ~s** de dos en dos; **to put ~ and ~ together** (*fig*) atar cabos
two-bit [tu:'bɪt] *adj* (*esp US: inf, pej*) de poca monta, de tres al cuarto
two-door [tu:'dɔ:^r] *adj* (*Aut*) de dos puertas
two-faced [tu:'feɪst] *adj* (*pej: person*) falso, hipócrita
twofold ['tu:fəuld] *adv*: **to increase ~** duplicarse ▷ *adj* (*increase*) doble; (*reply*) en dos partes
two-piece [tu:'pi:s] *n* (*also*: **~ suit**) traje *m* de dos piezas; (*also*: **~ swimsuit**) dos piezas *m inv*, bikini *m*
twosome ['tu:səm] *n* (*people*) pareja
two-way ['tu:weɪ] *adj*: **~ traffic** circulación *f* de dos sentidos; **~ radio** radio *f* emisora y receptora
tycoon [taɪ'ku:n] *n*: **(business) ~** magnate *m/f*
type [taɪp] *n* (*category*) tipo, género; (*model*) modelo; (*Typ*) tipo, letra ▷ *vt* (*letter etc*) escribir a máquina; **what ~ do you want?** ¿qué tipo quieres?; **in bold/italic ~** en negrita/cursiva
type-cast ['taɪpkɑ:st] *adj* (*actor*) encasillado
typeface ['taɪpfeɪs] *n* tipo de letra
typescript ['taɪpskrɪpt] *n* texto mecanografiado
typesetter ['taɪpsɛtə^r] *n* cajista *m/f*
typewriter ['taɪpraɪtə^r] *n* máquina de escribir
typewritten ['taɪprɪtn] *adj* mecanografiado
typhoid ['taɪfɔɪd] *n* (fiebre *f*) tifoidea
typhoon [taɪ'fu:n] *n* tifón *m*
typhus ['taɪfəs] *n* tifus *m*
typical ['tɪpɪkl] *adj* típico
typically ['tɪpɪklɪ] *adv* típicamente
typing ['taɪpɪŋ] *n* mecanografía
typist ['taɪpɪst] *n* mecanógrafo(-a)
tyrant ['taɪərənt] *n* tirano(-a)
tyre, tire (*US*) ['taɪə^r] *n* neumático, llanta (*LAm*)
tyre pressure *n* presión *f* de los neumáticos

U

U, u [ju:] *n* (*letter*) U, u *f*; **U for Uncle** U de Uruguay
U *n abbr* (*Brit Cine*: = *universal*) todos los públicos
U-bend ['ju:bɛnd] *n* recodo
ubiquitous [ju:'bɪkwɪtəs] *adj* omnipresente, ubicuo
udder ['ʌdəʳ] *n* ubre *f*
UEFA [ju:'eɪfə] *n abbr* (= *Union of European Football Associations*) U.E.F.A. *f*
UFO ['ju:fəu] *n abbr* (= *unidentified flying object*) OVNI *m*
Uganda [ju:'gændə] *n* Uganda
ugh [ə:h] *excl* ¡uf!
ugly ['ʌglɪ] *adj* feo; (*dangerous*) peligroso
UHF *abbr* (= *ultra-high frequency*) UHF *f*
UHT *adj abbr* (= *ultra heat treated*); **~ milk** leche *f* uperizada
UK *n abbr* (= *United Kingdom*) Reino Unido, R.U.
Ukraine [ju:'kreɪn] *n* Ucrania
ulcer ['ʌlsəʳ] *n* úlcera; **mouth ~** llaga bucal
Ulster ['ʌlstəʳ] *n* Ulster *m*
ulterior [ʌl'tɪərɪəʳ] *adj* ulterior; **~ motive** segundas intenciones *fpl*
ultimate ['ʌltɪmət] *adj* último, final; (*greatest*) mayor ▷ *n*: **the ~ in luxury** el colmo del lujo
ultimately ['ʌltɪmətlɪ] *adv* (*in the end*) por último, al final; (*fundamentally*) a fin de cuentas
ultimatum (*pl* **ultimatums** *or* **ultimata**) [ʌltɪ'meɪtəm, -tə] *n* ultimátum *m*
ultrasound ['ʌltrəsaund] *n* (*Med*) ultrasonido
ultraviolet ['ʌltrə'vaɪəlɪt] *adj* ultravioleta
umbilical cord [ʌmbɪ'laɪkl-] *n* cordón *m* umbilical
umbrella [ʌm'brɛlə] *n* paraguas *m inv*; **under the ~ of** (*fig*) bajo la protección de
umlaut ['umlaut] *n* diéresis *f inv*
umpire ['ʌmpaɪəʳ] *n* árbitro ▷ *vt* arbitrar
umpteen [ʌmp'ti:n] *num* enésimos(-as); **for the ~th time** por enésima vez
UN *n abbr* (= *United Nations*) ONU *f*
unable [ʌn'eɪbl] *adj*: **to be ~ to do sth** no poder hacer algo; (*not know how to*) ser incapaz de hacer algo, no saber hacer algo
unacceptable [ʌnək'sɛptəbl] *adj* (*proposal, behaviour, price*) inaceptable; **it's ~ that** no se puede aceptar que
unaccompanied [ʌnə'kʌmpənɪd] *adj* no acompañado; (*singing, song*) sin acompañamiento
unaccountably [ʌnə'kauntəblɪ] *adv* inexplicablemente
unaccustomed [ʌnə'kʌstəmd] *adj*: **to be ~ to** no estar acostumbrado a
unanimous [ju:'nænɪməs] *adj* unánime
unanimously [ju:'nænɪməslɪ] *adv* unánimemente
unarmed [ʌn'ɑ:md] *adj* (*person*) desarmado; (*combat*) sin armas
unashamed [ʌnə'ʃeɪmd] *adj* desvergonzado
unassuming [ʌnə'sju:mɪŋ] *adj* modesto, sin pretensiones
unattached [ʌnə'tætʃt] *adj* (*person*) soltero; (*part etc*) suelto
unattended [ʌnə'tɛndɪd] *adj* (*car, luggage*) desatendido
unattractive [ʌnə'træktɪv] *adj* poco atractivo
unauthorized [ʌn'ɔ:θəraɪzd] *adj* no autorizado
unavailable [ʌnə'veɪləbl] *adj* (*article, room, book*) no disponible; (*person*) ocupado
unavoidable [ʌnə'vɔɪdəbl] *adj* inevitable
unaware [ʌnə'wɛəʳ] *adj*: **to be ~ of** ignorar
unawares [ʌnə'wɛəz] *adv*: **to catch sb ~** pillar a algn desprevenido
unbalanced [ʌn'bælənst] *adj* desequilibrado; (*mentally*) trastornado
unbearable [ʌn'bɛərəbl] *adj* insoportable
unbeatable [ʌn'bi:təbl] *adj* (*gen*) invencible; (*price*) inmejorable
unbeaten [ʌn'bi:tn] *adj* (*team*) imbatido; (*army*) invicto; (*record*) no batido
unbelievable [ʌnbɪ'li:vəbl] *adj* increíble
unbend [ʌn'bɛnd] *vi* (*irreg*: *like* **bend**) (*fig*: *person*) relajarse ▷ *vt* (*wire*) enderezar
unborn [ʌn'bɔ:n] *adj* que va a nacer
unbreakable [ʌn'breɪkəbl] *adj* irrompible
unbroken [ʌn'brəukən] *adj* (*seal*) intacto; (*series*) continuo, ininterrumpido; (*record*) no batido; (*spirit*) indómito
unbutton [ʌn'bʌtn] *vt* desabrochar
uncalled-for [ʌn'kɔ:ldfɔ:ʳ] *adj* gratuito, inmerecido

uncanny [ʌn'kænɪ] *adj* extraño, extraordinario
unceasing [ʌn'siːsɪŋ] *adj* incesante
unceremonious ['ʌnsɛrɪ'məunɪəs] *adj* (*abrupt, rude*) brusco, hosco
uncertain [ʌn'səːtn] *adj* incierto; (*indecisive*) indeciso; **it's ~ whether** no se sabe si; **in no ~ terms** sin dejar lugar a dudas
uncertainty [ʌn'səːtntɪ] *n* incertidumbre *f*
unchanged [ʌn'tʃeɪndʒd] *adj* sin cambiar *or* alterar
unchecked [ʌn'tʃɛkt] *adj* desenfrenado
uncivilized [ʌn'sɪvɪlaɪzd] *adj* (*gen*) inculto, poco civilizado; (*fig: behaviour etc*) bárbaro
uncle ['ʌŋkl] *n* tío
unclear [ʌn'klɪəʳ] *adj* poco claro; **I'm still ~ about what I'm supposed to do** todavía no tengo muy claro lo que tengo que hacer
uncomfortable [ʌn'kʌmfətəbl] *adj* incómodo; (*uneasy*) inquieto
uncommon [ʌn'kɔmən] *adj* poco común, raro
uncompromising [ʌn'kɔmprəmaɪzɪŋ] *adj* intransigente
unconcerned [ʌnkən'səːnd] *adj* indiferente; **to be ~ about** ser indiferente a, no preocuparse de
unconditional [ʌnkən'dɪʃənl] *adj* incondicional
unconnected [ʌnkə'nɛktɪd] *adj* (*unrelated*): **to be ~ with** no estar relacionado con
unconscious [ʌn'kɔnʃəs] *adj* sin sentido; (*unaware*) inconsciente ▷ *n*: **the ~** el inconsciente; **to knock sb ~** dejar a algn sin sentido
unconsciously [ʌn'kɔnʃəslɪ] *adv* inconscientemente
unconstitutional [ʌnkɔnstɪ'tjuːʃənl] *adj* anticonstitucional
uncontrollable [ʌnkən'trəuləbl] *adj* (*temper*) indomable; (*laughter*) incontenible
unconventional [ʌnkən'vɛnʃənl] *adj* poco convencional
unconvinced [ʌnkən'vɪnst] *adj*: **to be** *or* **remain ~** seguir sin convencerse
uncouth [ʌn'kuːθ] *adj* grosero, inculto
uncover [ʌn'kʌvəʳ] *vt* (*gen*) descubrir; (*take lid off*) destapar
undecided [ʌndɪ'saɪdɪd] *adj* (*person*) indeciso; (*question*) no resuelto, pendiente
undeniable [ʌndɪ'naɪəbl] *adj* innegable
under ['ʌndəʳ] *prep* debajo de; (*less than*) menos de; (*according to*) según, de acuerdo con ▷ *adv* debajo, abajo; **~ there** ahí debajo; **~ construction** en construcción; en obras; **~ the circumstances** dadas las circunstancias; **in ~ 2 hours** en menos de dos horas; **~ anaesthetic** bajo los efectos de la anestesia; **~ discussion** en discusión, sobre el tapete
under-age [ʌndər'eɪdʒ] *adj* menor de edad
undercarriage ['ʌndəkærɪdʒ] *n* (*Brit Aviat*) tren *m* de aterrizaje
undercharge [ʌndə'tʃɑːdʒ] *vt* cobrar de menos
underclass ['ʌndəklɑːs] *n* clase *f* marginada
undercoat ['ʌndəkəut] *n* (*paint*) primera mano
undercover [ʌndə'kʌvəʳ] *adj* clandestino
undercurrent ['ʌndəkʌrnt] *n* corriente *f* submarina; (*fig*) tendencia oculta
undercut ['ʌndəkʌt] *vt* (*irreg: like* **cut**) vender más barato que; fijar un precio más barato que
underdog ['ʌndədɔg] *n* desvalido(-a)
underdone [ʌndə'dʌn] *adj* (*Culin*) poco hecho
underestimate [ʌndər'ɛstɪmeɪt] *vt* subestimar
underfed [ʌndə'fɛd] *adj* subalimentado
underfoot [ʌndə'fut] *adv*: **it's wet ~** el suelo está mojado
undergo [ʌndə'gəu] *vt* (*irreg: like* **go**) sufrir; (*treatment*) recibir, someterse a; **the car is ~ing repairs** están reparando el coche
undergraduate ['ʌndə'grædjuət] *n* estudiante *m/f* ▷ *cpd*: **~ courses** cursos *mpl* de licenciatura
underground ['ʌndəgraund] *n* (*Brit: railway*) metro; (*Pol*) movimiento clandestino ▷ *adj* subterráneo ▷ *adv* (*work*) en la clandestinidad
undergrowth ['ʌndəgrəuθ] *n* maleza
underlie [ʌndə'laɪ] *vt* (*irreg: like* **lie**) (*fig*) ser la razón fundamental de; **the underlying cause** la causa fundamental
underline [ʌndə'laɪn] *vt* subrayar
underling ['ʌndəlɪŋ] *n* (*pej*) subalterno(-a)
undermine [ʌndə'maɪn] *vt* socavar, minar
underneath [ʌndə'niːθ] *adv* debajo ▷ *prep* debajo de, bajo
underpaid [ʌndə'peɪd] *adj* mal pagado
underpants ['ʌndəpænts] *npl* calzoncillos *mpl*
underpass ['ʌndəpɑːs] *n* (*Brit*) paso subterráneo
underprivileged [ʌndə'prɪvɪlɪdʒd] *adj* desposeído
underrate [ʌndə'reɪt] *vt* infravalorar, subestimar
underscore ['ʌndəskɔːʳ] *vt* subrayar, sostener
undershirt ['ʌndəʃəːt] *n* (*US*) camiseta
undershorts ['ʌndəʃɔːts] *npl* (*US*) calzoncillos *mpl*
underside ['ʌndəsaɪd] *n* parte *f* inferior, revés *m*
undersigned ['ʌndəsaɪnd] *adj, n*: **the ~** el/la *etc* abajo firmante
underskirt ['ʌndəskəːt] *n* (*Brit*) enaguas *fpl*
understand [ʌndə'stænd] *vt, vi* (*irreg: like* **stand**) entender, comprender; (*assume*) tener entendido; **to make o.s. understood** hacerse entender; **I ~ you have been absent** tengo entendido que (usted) ha estado ausente

understandable [ʌndə'stændəbl] *adj* comprensible
understanding [ʌndə'stændɪŋ] *adj* comprensivo ▷ *n* comprensión *f*, entendimiento; (*agreement*) acuerdo; **to come to an ~ with sb** llegar a un acuerdo con algn; **on the ~ that** a condición de que + *subjun*
understate [ʌndə'steɪt] *vt* minimizar
understatement [ʌndə'steɪtmənt] *n* subestimación *f*; (*modesty*) modestia (excesiva); **to say it was good is quite an ~** decir que estuvo bien es quedarse corto
understood [ʌndə'stud] *pt, pp of* **understand** ▷ *adj* entendido; (*implied*): **it is ~ that** se sobreentiende que
understudy ['ʌndəstʌdɪ] *n* suplente *m/f*
undertake [ʌndə'teɪk] *vt* (*irreg*: *like* **take**) emprender; **to ~ to do sth** comprometerse a hacer algo
undertaker ['ʌndəteɪkə^r] *n* director(a) *m(f)* de pompas fúnebres
undertaking ['ʌndəteɪkɪŋ] *n* empresa; (*promise*) promesa
undertone ['ʌndətəun] *n* (*of criticism*) connotación *f*; (*low voice*): **in an ~** en voz baja
underwater [ʌndə'wɔːtə^r] *adv* bajo el agua ▷ *adj* submarino
underway [ʌndə'weɪ] *adj*: **to be ~** (*meeting*) estar en marcha; (*investigation*) estar llevándose a cabo
underwear ['ʌndəwɛə^r] *n* ropa interior *or* íntima (*LAm*)
underwent [ʌndə'wɛnt] *vb see* **undergo**
underworld ['ʌndəwəːld] *n* (*of crime*) hampa, inframundo
underwrite [ʌndə'raɪt] *vt* (*irreg*: *like* **write**) (*Comm*) suscribir; (*Insurance*) asegurar (*contra riesgos*)
underwriter ['ʌndəraɪtə^r] *n* (*Insurance*) asegurador(a) *m(f)*
undesirable [ʌndɪ'zaɪərəbl] *adj* indeseable
undies ['ʌndɪz] *npl* (*inf*) paños *mpl* menores
undiluted [ʌndaɪ'luːtɪd] *adj* (*concentrate*) concentrado
undiplomatic [ʌndɪplə'mætɪk] *adj* poco diplomático
undisciplined [ʌn'dɪsɪplɪnd] *adj* indisciplinado
undisputed [ʌndɪ'spjuːtɪd] *adj* incontestable
undivided [ʌndɪ'vaɪdɪd] *adj*: **I want your ~ attention** quiero su completa atención
undo [ʌn'duː] *vt* (*irreg*: *like* **do**) (*laces*) desatar; (*button etc*) desabrochar; (*spoil*) deshacer
undoing [ʌn'duːɪŋ] *n* ruina, perdición *f*
undone [ʌn'dʌn] *pp of* **undo** ▷ *adj*: **to come ~** (*clothes*) desabrocharse; (*parcel*) desatarse
undoubted [ʌn'dautɪd] *adj* indudable
undoubtedly [ʌn'dautɪdlɪ] *adv* indudablemente, sin duda
undress [ʌn'drɛs] *vi* desnudarse, desvestirse (*esp LAm*)
undue [ʌn'djuː] *adj* indebido, excesivo
undulating ['ʌndjuleɪtɪŋ] *adj* ondulante
unduly [ʌn'djuːlɪ] *adv* excesivamente, demasiado
undying [ʌn'daɪɪŋ] *adj* eterno
unearth [ʌn'əːθ] *vt* desenterrar
unearthly [ʌn'əːθlɪ] *adj*: **~ hour** (*inf*) hora intempestiva
unease [ʌn'iːz] *n* malestar *m*
uneasy [ʌn'iːzɪ] *adj* intranquilo; (*worried*) preocupado; **to feel ~ about doing sth** sentirse incómodo con la idea de hacer algo
uneducated [ʌn'ɛdjukeɪtɪd] *adj* ignorante, inculto
unemployed [ʌnɪm'plɔɪd] *adj* parado, sin trabajo ▷ *n*: **the ~** los parados
unemployment [ʌnɪm'plɔɪmənt] *n* paro, desempleo, cesantía (*LAm*)
unemployment benefit *n* (*Brit*) subsidio de desempleo *or* paro
unending [ʌn'ɛndɪŋ] *adj* interminable
unenviable [ʌn'ɛnvɪəbl] *adj* poco envidiable
unequal [ʌn'iːkwəl] *adj* (*length, objects etc*) desigual; (*amounts*) distinto; (*division of labour*) poco justo
unerring [ʌn'əːrɪŋ] *adj* infalible
uneven [ʌn'iːvn] *adj* desigual; (*road etc*) con baches
uneventful [ʌnɪ'vɛntful] *adj* sin incidentes
unexpected [ʌnɪk'spɛktɪd] *adj* inesperado
unexpectedly [ʌnɪk'spɛktɪdlɪ] *adv* inesperadamente
unexplained [ʌnɪks'pleɪnd] *adj* inexplicado
unfailing [ʌn'feɪlɪŋ] *adj* (*support*) indefectible; (*energy*) inagotable
unfair [ʌn'fɛə^r] *adj*: **~ (to sb)** injusto (con algn); **it's ~ that ...** es injusto que ..., no es justo que ...
unfaithful [ʌn'feɪθful] *adj* infiel
unfamiliar [ʌnfə'mɪlɪə^r] *adj* extraño, desconocido; **to be ~ with sth** desconocer *or* ignorar algo
unfashionable [ʌn'fæʃnəbl] *adj* (*clothes*) pasado *or* fuera de moda; (*district*) poco elegante
unfasten [ʌn'fɑːsn] *vt* desatar
unfavourable, unfavorable (*US*) [ʌn'feɪvərəbl] *adj* desfavorable
unfeeling [ʌn'fiːlɪŋ] *adj* insensible
unfinished [ʌn'fɪnɪʃt] *adj* inacabado, sin terminar
unfit [ʌn'fɪt] *adj* en baja forma; (*incompetent*) incapaz; **~ for work** no apto para trabajar
unfold [ʌn'fəuld] *vt* desdoblar; (*fig*) revelar ▷ *vi* abrirse; revelarse
unforeseen ['ʌnfɔː'siːn] *adj* imprevisto
unforgettable [ʌnfə'gɛtəbl] *adj* inolvidable
unforgivable [ʌnfə'gɪvəbl] *adj* imperdonable
unfortunate [ʌn'fɔːtʃnət] *adj* desgraciado; (*event, remark*) inoportuno
unfortunately [ʌn'fɔːtʃnətlɪ] *adv* desgraciadamente, por desgracia

unfounded [ʌn'faundɪd] *adj* infundado
unfriendly [ʌn'frɛndlɪ] *adj* antipático; (*behaviour, remark*) hostil, poco amigable
unfurl [ʌn'fə:l] *vt* desplegar
unfurnished [ʌn'fə:nɪʃt] *adj* sin amueblar
ungainly [ʌn'geɪnlɪ] *adj* (*walk*) desgarbado
ungodly [ʌn'gɔdlɪ] *adj*: **at an ~ hour** a una hora intempestiva
ungrateful [ʌn'greɪtful] *adj* ingrato
unhappiness [ʌn'hæpɪnɪs] *n* tristeza
unhappy [ʌn'haepɪ] *adj* (*sad*) triste; (*unfortunate*) desgraciado; (*childhood*) infeliz; **~ with** (*arrangements etc*) poco contento con, descontento de
unharmed [ʌn'hɑ:md] *adj* (*person*) ileso
UNHCR *n abbr* (= *United Nations High Commission for Refugees*) ACNUR *m*
unhealthy [ʌn'hɛlθɪ] *adj* (*gen*) malsano, insalubre; (*person*) enfermizo; (*interest*) morboso
unheard-of [ʌn'hə:dɔv] *adj* inaudito, sin precedente
unhelpful [ʌn'hɛlpful] *adj* (*person*) poco servicial; (*advice*) inútil
unholy [ʌn'həulɪ] *adj*: **an ~ alliance** una alianza nefasta; **he returned at an ~ hour** volvió a una hora intempestiva
unhurt [ʌn'hə:t] *adj* ileso
unhygienic [ʌnhaɪ'dʒi:nɪk] *adj* antihigiénico
UNICEF ['ju:nɪsɛf] *n abbr* (= *United Nations International Children's Emergency Fund*) UNICEF *f*
unidentified [ʌnaɪ'dɛntɪfaɪd] *adj* no identificado; **~ flying object (UFO)** objeto volante no identificado
uniform ['ju:nɪfɔ:m] *n* uniforme *m* ▷ *adj* uniforme
uniformity [ju:nɪ'fɔ:mɪtɪ] *n* uniformidad *f*
unify ['ju:nɪfaɪ] *vt* unificar, unir
unimportant [ʌnɪm'pɔ:tənt] *adj* sin importancia
uninhabited [ʌnɪn'hæbɪtɪd] *adj* desierto; (*country*) despoblado; (*house*) deshabitado, desocupado
uninspiring [ʌnɪn'spaɪərɪŋ] *adj* anodino
unintentional [ʌnɪn'tɛnʃənəl] *adj* involuntario
union ['ju:njən] *n* unión *f*; (*also*: **trade ~**) sindicato ▷ *cpd* sindical; **the U~** (*US*) la Unión
Union Jack *n* bandera del Reino Unido
unique [ju:'ni:k] *adj* único
unisex ['ju:nɪsɛks] *adj* unisex
unison ['ju:nɪsn] *n*: **in ~** en armonía
unit ['ju:nɪt] *n* unidad *f*; (*team, squad*) grupo; **kitchen ~** módulo de cocina; **production ~** taller *m* de fabricación; **sink ~** fregadero
unite [ju:'naɪt] *vt* unir ▷ *vi* unirse
united [ju:'naɪtɪd] *adj* unido
United Kingdom *n* Reino Unido
United Nations, United Nations Organization *n* Naciones Unidas *fpl*
United States, United States of America *n* Estados Unidos *mpl* (de América)
unit trust *n* (*Brit*) bono fiduciario
unity ['ju:nɪtɪ] *n* unidad *f*
Univ. *abbr* = **university**
universal [ju:nɪ'və:sl] *adj* universal
universe ['ju:nɪvə:s] *n* universo
university [ju:nɪ'və:sɪtɪ] *n* universidad *f* ▷ *cpd* (*student, professor, education, degree*) universitario; (*year*) académico; **to be at/go to ~** estudiar en/ir a la universidad
unjust [ʌn'dʒʌst] *adj* injusto
unkempt [ʌn'kɛmpt] *adj* descuidado; (*hair*) despeinado
unkind [ʌn'kaɪnd] *adj* poco amable; (*comment etc*) cruel
unknown [ʌn'nəun] *adj* desconocido ▷ *adv*: **~ to me** sin saberlo yo; **~ quantity** incógnita
unlawful [ʌn'lɔ:ful] *adj* ilegal, ilícito
unleaded [ʌn'lɛdɪd] *n* (*also*: **~ petrol**) gasolina sin plomo
unleash [ʌn'li:ʃ] *vt* desatar
unless [ʌn'lɛs] *conj* a menos que; **~ he comes** a menos que venga; **~ otherwise stated** salvo indicación contraria; **~ I am mistaken** si no mi equivoco
unlike [ʌn'laɪk] *adj* distinto ▷ *prep* a diferencia de
unlikely [ʌn'laɪklɪ] *adj* improbable
unlimited [ʌn'lɪmɪtɪd] *adj* ilimitado; **~ liability** responsabilidad *f* ilimitada
unlisted [ʌn'lɪstɪd] *adj* (*US Tel*) que no figura en la guía; **~ company** empresa sin cotización en bolsa
unload [ʌn'ləud] *vt* descargar
unlock [ʌn'lɔk] *vt* abrir (con llave)
unlucky [ʌn'lʌkɪ] *adj* desgraciado; (*object, number*) que da mala suerte; **to be ~** (*person*) tener mala suerte
unmarked [ʌn'mɑ:kt] *adj* (*unstained*) sin mancha; **~ police car** vehículo policial camuflado
unmarried [ʌn'mærɪd] *adj* soltero
unmistakable [ʌnmɪs'teɪkəbl] *adj* inconfundible
unmitigated [ʌn'mɪtɪgeɪtɪd] *adj* rematado, absoluto
unnamed [ʌn'neɪmd] *adj* (*nameless*) sin nombre; (*anonymous*) anónimo
unnatural [ʌn'nætʃrəl] *adj* (*gen*) antinatural; (*manner*) afectado; (*habit*) perverso
unnecessary [ʌn'nɛsəsərɪ] *adj* innecesario, inútil
unnerve [ʌn'nə:v] *vt* (*accident*) poner nervioso; (*hostile attitude*) acobardar; (*long wait, interview*) intimidar
unnoticed [ʌn'nəutɪst] *adj*: **to go** *or* **pass ~** pasar desapercibido
UNO ['ju:nəu] *n abbr* (= *United Nations Organization*) ONU *f*
unobtainable [ʌnəb'teɪnəbl] *adj* inasequible; (*Tel*) inexistente
unobtrusive [ʌnəb'tru:sɪv] *adj* discreto
unofficial [ʌnə'fɪʃl] *adj* no oficial; **~ strike** huelga no oficial

unorthodox [ʌn'ɔ:θədɔks] *adj* poco ortodoxo
unpack [ʌn'pæk] *vi* deshacer las maletas, desempacar (*LAm*) ▷ *vt* deshacer
unpaid [ʌn'peɪd] *adj* (*bill, debt*) sin pagar, impagado; (*Comm*) pendiente; (*holiday*) sin sueldo; (*work*) sin pago, voluntario
unpalatable [ʌn'pælətəbl] *adj* (*truth*) desagradable
unparalleled [ʌn'pærəlɛld] *adj* (*unequalled*) sin par; (*unique*) sin precedentes
unpleasant [ʌn'plɛznt] *adj* (*disagreeable*) desagradable; (*person, manner*) antipático
unplug [ʌn'plʌg] *vt* desenchufar, desconectar
unpopular [ʌn'pɔpjulə^r] *adj* poco popular; **to be ~ with sb** (*person, law*) no ser popular con algn; **to make o.s. ~ (with)** hacerse impopular (con)
unprecedented [ʌn'prɛsɪdəntɪd] *adj* sin precedentes
unpredictable [ʌnprɪ'dɪktəbl] *adj* imprevisible
unprofessional [ʌnprə'fɛʃənl] *adj* poco profesional; **~ conduct** negligencia
UNPROFOR *n abbr* (= *United Nations Protection Force*) FORPRONU *f*, Unprofor *f*
unprotected ['ʌnprə'tɛktɪd] *adj* (*sex*) sin protección
unpunished [ʌn'pʌnɪʃt] *adj*: **to go ~** quedar sin castigo, salir impune
unqualified [ʌn'kwɔlɪfaɪd] *adj* sin título, no cualificado; (*success*) total, incondicional
unquestionably [ʌn'kwɛstʃənəblɪ] *adv* indiscutiblemente
unravel [ʌn'rævl] *vt* desenmarañar
unreal [ʌn'rɪəl] *adj* irreal
unrealistic [ʌnrɪə'lɪstɪk] *adj* poco realista
unreasonable [ʌn'ri:znəbl] *adj* irrazonable; **to make ~ demands on sb** hacer demandas excesivas a algn
unrecognizable [ʌn'rɛkəgnaɪzəbl] *adj* irreconocible
unrelated [ʌnrɪ'leɪtɪd] *adj* sin relación; (*family*) no emparentado
unrelenting [ʌnrɪ'lɛntɪŋ] *adj* implacable
unreliable [ʌnrɪ'laɪəbl] *adj* (*person*) informal; (*machine*) poco fiable
unremitting [ʌnrɪ'mɪtɪŋ] *adj* incesante
unrepeatable [ʌnrɪ'pi:təbl] *adj* irrepetible
unrepentant [ʌnrɪ'pɛntənt] *adj* (*smoker, sinner*) impenitente; **to be ~ about sth** no arrepentirse de algo
unreservedly [ʌnrɪ'zə:vɪdlɪ] *adv* sin reserva
unrest [ʌn'rɛst] *n* inquietud *f*, malestar *m*; (*Pol*) disturbios *mpl*
unripe [ʌn'raɪp] *adj* verde, inmaduro
unrivalled, unrivaled (*US*) [ʌn'raɪvəld] *adj* incomparable, sin par
unroll [ʌn'rəul] *vt* desenrollar
unruly [ʌn'ru:lɪ] *adj* indisciplinado
unsafe [ʌn'seɪf] *adj* (*journey*) peligroso; (*car etc*) inseguro; (*method*) arriesgado; **~ to drink/ eat** no apto para el consumo humano
unsaid [ʌn'sɛd] *adj*: **to leave sth ~** dejar algo sin decir
unsatisfactory ['ʌnsætɪs'fæktərɪ] *adj* poco satisfactorio
unsavoury, unsavory (*US*) [ʌn'seɪvərɪ] *adj* (*fig*) repugnante
unscathed [ʌn'skeɪðd] *adj* ileso
unscrew [ʌn'skru:] *vt* destornillar
unscrupulous [ʌn'skru:pjuləs] *adj* sin escrúpulos
unseat [ʌn'si:t] *vt* (*rider*) hacer caerse de la silla a; (*fig: official*) hacer perder su escaño a
unseeded [ʌn'si:dɪd] *adj* (*Sport*) no preseleccionado
unseen [ʌn'si:n] *adj* (*person, danger*) oculto
unselfish [ʌn'sɛlfɪʃ] *adj* generoso, poco egoísta; (*act*) desinteresado
unsettled [ʌn'sɛtld] *adj* inquieto; (*situation*) inestable; (*weather*) variable
unsettling [ʌn'sɛtlɪŋ] *adj* perturbador(a), inquietante
unshaven [ʌn'ʃeɪvn] *adj* sin afeitar
unsightly [ʌn'saɪtlɪ] *adj* desagradable
unskilled [ʌn'skɪld] *adj*: **~ workers** mano *f* de obra no cualificada
unspeakable [ʌn'spi:kəbl] *adj* indecible; (*awful*) incalificable
unspoiled ['ʌn'spɔɪld], **unspoilt** ['ʌn'spɔɪlt] *adj* (*place*) que no ha perdido su belleza natural
unstable [ʌn'steɪbl] *adj* inestable
unsteady [ʌn'stɛdɪ] *adj* inestable
unstuck [ʌn'stʌk] *adj*: **to come ~** despegarse; (*fig*) fracasar
unsubscribe [ʌnsəb'skraɪb] *vt* (*Internet*) borrarse
unsuccessful [ʌnsək'sɛsful] *adj* (*attempt*) infructuoso; (*writer, proposal*) sin éxito; **to be ~** (*in attempting sth*) no tener éxito, fracasar
unsuitable [ʌn'su:təbl] *adj* inconveniente, inapropiado; (*time*) inoportuno
unsung ['ʌnsʌŋ] *adj*: **an ~ hero** un héroe desconocido
unsure [ʌn'ʃuə^r] *adj* inseguro, poco seguro; **to be ~ of o.s.** estar poco seguro de sí mismo
unsuspecting [ʌnsə'spɛktɪŋ] *adj* confiado
unsympathetic [ʌnsɪmpə'θɛtɪk] *adj* (*attitude*) poco comprensivo; (*person*) sin compasión; **~ (to)** indiferente (a)
untapped [ʌn'tæpt] *adj* (*resources*) sin explotar
unthinkable [ʌn'θɪŋkəbl] *adj* inconcebible, impensable
untidy [ʌn'taɪdɪ] *adj* (*room*) desordenado, en desorden; (*appearance*) desaliñado
untie [ʌn'taɪ] *vt* desatar
until [ən'tɪl] *prep* hasta ▷ *conj* hasta que; **~ he comes** hasta que venga; **~ now** hasta ahora; **~ then** hasta entonces; **from morning ~ night** de la mañana a la noche
untimely [ʌn'taɪmlɪ] *adj* inoportuno; (*death*) prematuro

U

untold [ʌn'təuld] *adj (story)* nunca contado; *(suffering)* indecible; *(wealth)* incalculable
untoward [ʌntə'wɔ:d] *adj (behaviour)* impropio; *(event)* adverso
untrue [ʌn'tru:] *adj (statement)* falso
unused [ʌn'ju:zd] *adj* sin usar, nuevo; **to be ~ to (doing) sth** no estar acostumbrado a (hacer) algo
unusual [ʌn'ju:ʒuəl] *adj* insólito, poco común
unusually [ʌn'ju:ʒuəlɪ] *adv*: **he arrived ~ early** llegó más temprano que de costumbre
unveil [ʌn'veɪl] *vt (statue)* descubrir
unwanted [ʌn'wɔntɪd] *adj (person, effect)* no deseado
unwelcome [ʌn'wɛlkəm] *adj (at a bad time)* inoportuno, molesto; **to feel ~** sentirse incómodo
unwell [ʌn'wɛl] *adj*: **to feel ~** estar indispuesto, sentirse mal
unwieldy [ʌn'wi:ldɪ] *adj* difícil de manejar
unwilling [ʌn'wɪlɪŋ] *adj*: **to be ~ to do sth** estar poco dispuesto a hacer algo
unwillingly [ʌn'wɪlɪŋlɪ] *adv* de mala gana
unwind [ʌn'waɪnd] *(irreg: like* **wind***) vt* desenvolver ▷ *vi (relax)* relajarse
unwise [ʌn'waɪz] *adj* imprudente
unwitting [ʌn'wɪtɪŋ] *adj* inconsciente
unwittingly [ʌn'wɪtɪŋlɪ] *adv* inconscientemente, sin darse cuenta
unworkable [ʌn'wə:kəbl] *adj (plan)* impracticable
unworthy [ʌn'wə:ðɪ] *adj* indigno; **to be ~ of sth/to do sth** ser indigno de algo/de hacer algo
unwrap [ʌn'ræp] *vt* desenvolver
unwritten [ʌn'rɪtn] *adj (agreement)* tácito; *(rules, law)* no escrito
unzip [ʌn'zɪp] *vt* abrir la cremallera de; *(Comput)* descomprimir

KEYWORD

up [ʌp] *prep*: **to go/be up sth** subir/estar subido en algo; **he went up the stairs/the hill** subió las escaleras/la colina; **we walked/climbed up the hill** subimos la colina; **they live further up the street** viven más arriba en la calle; **go up that road and turn left** sigue por esa calle y gira a la izquierda
▷ *adv* **1** *(upwards, higher)* más arriba; **up in the mountains** en lo alto (de la montaña); **put it a bit higher up** ponlo un poco más arriba *or* alto; **to stop halfway up** pararse a la mitad del camino *or* de la subida; **up there** ahí *or* allí arriba; **up above** en lo alto, por encima, arriba; **"this side up"** "este lado hacia arriba"; **to live/go up North** vivir en el norte/ir al norte
2: **to be up** *(out of bed)* estar levantado; *(prices, level)* haber subido; *(building)* estar construido; *(tent)* estar montado; *(curtains, paper etc)* estar puesto; **time's up** se acabó el tiempo; **when the year was up** al terminarse el año; **he's well up in** *or* **on politics** *(Brit: knowledgeable)* está muy al día en política; **what's up?** *(wrong)* ¿qué pasa?; **what's up with him?** ¿qué le pasa?; **prices are up on last year** los precios han subido desde el año pasado
3: **up to** *(as far as)* hasta; **up to now** hasta ahora *or* la fecha
4: **to be up to** *(depending on)*: **it's up to you** depende de ti; **he's not up to it** *(job, task etc)* no es capaz de hacerlo; **I don't feel up to it** no me encuentro con ánimos para ello; **his work is not up to the required standard** su trabajo no da la talla; *(inf: be doing)*: **what is he up to?** ¿qué estará tramando?
▷ *vi (inf)*: **she upped and left** se levantó y se marchó
▷ *vt (inf: price)* subir
▷ *n*: **ups and downs** altibajos *mpl*

up-and-coming [ʌpənd'kʌmɪŋ] *adj* prometedor(a)
upbringing ['ʌpbrɪŋɪŋ] *n* educación *f*
upcoming ['ʌpkʌmɪŋ] *adj* próximo
update [ʌp'deɪt] *vt* poner al día
upfront [ʌp'frʌnt] *adj* claro, directo ▷ *adv* a las claras; *(pay)* por adelantado; **to be ~ about sth** admitir algo claramente
upgrade [ʌp'greɪd] *vt* ascender; *(Comput)* modernizar
upheaval [ʌp'hi:vl] *n* trastornos *mpl*; *(Pol)* agitación *f*
uphill [ʌp'hɪl] *adj* cuesta arriba; *(fig: task)* penoso, difícil ▷ *adv*: **to go ~** ir cuesta arriba
uphold [ʌp'həuld] *vt (irreg: like* **hold***)* sostener
upholstery [ʌp'həulstərɪ] *n* tapicería
upkeep ['ʌpki:p] *n* mantenimiento
upmarket [ʌp'mɑ:kɪt] *adj (product)* de categoría
upon [ə'pɔn] *prep* sobre
upper ['ʌpə[r]] *adj* superior, de arriba ▷ *n (of shoe: also:* **~s***)* pala
upper-class [ʌpə'klɑ:s] *adj (district, people, accent)* de clase alta; *(attitude)* altivo
uppercut ['ʌpəkʌt] *n* uppercut *m*, gancho a la cara
uppermost ['ʌpəməust] *adj* el más alto; **what was ~ in my mind** lo que me preocupaba más
upright ['ʌpraɪt] *adj* vertical; *(fig)* honrado
uprising ['ʌpraɪzɪŋ] *n* sublevación *f*
uproar ['ʌprɔ:[r]] *n* tumulto, escándalo
uproarious [ʌp'rɔ:rɪəs] *adj* escandaloso; *(hilarious)* graciosísimo
uproot [ʌp'ru:t] *vt* desarraigar
upset *n* ['ʌpsɛt] *(to plan etc)* revés *m*, contratiempo; *(Med)* trastorno ▷ *vt* [ʌp'sɛt] *(irreg: like* **set***) (glass etc)* volcar; *(spill)* derramar; *(plan)* alterar; *(person)* molestar, perturbar ▷ *adj* [ʌp'sɛt] preocupado, perturbado;

(*stomach*) revuelto; **to have a stomach ~** (*Brit*) tener el estómago revuelto; **to get ~** molestarse, llevarse un disgusto

upsetting [ʌp'sɛtɪŋ] *adj* (*worrying*) inquietante; (*offending*) ofensivo; (*annoying*) molesto

upshot ['ʌpʃɔt] *n* resultado

upside-down ['ʌpsaɪd'daun] *adv* al revés; **to turn a place ~** (*fig*) revolverlo todo

upstage ['ʌp'steɪdʒ] *vt* robar protagonismo a

upstairs [ʌp'stɛəz] *adv* arriba ▷ *adj* (*room*) de arriba ▷ *n* el piso superior

upstart ['ʌpstɑːt] *n* advenedizo

upstream [ʌp'striːm] *adv* río arriba

uptake ['ʌpteɪk] *n*: **he is quick/slow on the ~** es muy listo/torpe

uptight [ʌp'taɪt] *adj* tenso, nervioso

up-to-date ['ʌptə'deɪt] *adj* actual, moderno; **to bring sb ~ (on sth)** poner a algn al corriente/tanto (de algo)

uptown ['ʌptaun] *adv* (*US*) hacia las afueras ▷ *adj* exterior, de las afueras

upturn ['ʌptəːn] *n* (*in luck*) mejora; (*Comm: in market*) resurgimiento económico; (*: in value of currency*) aumento

upward, upwards ['ʌpwəd(z)] *adv* hacia arriba; (*more than*): **~(s) of** más de

upwardly-mobile ['ʌpwədlɪ'məubaɪl] *adj*: **to be ~** mejorar socialmente

upwards ['ʌpwədz] *adv* = **upward**

uranium [juə'reɪnɪəm] *n* uranio

Uranus [juə'reɪnəs] *n* (*Astro*) Urano

urban ['əːbən] *adj* urbano

urbane [əː'beɪn] *adj* cortés, urbano

urchin ['əːtʃɪn] *n* pilluelo, golfillo

Urdu ['uəduː] *n* urdu *m*

urge [əːdʒ] *n* (*force*) impulso; (*desire*) deseo ▷ *vt*: **to ~ sb to do sth** animar a algn a hacer algo; **urge on** *vt* animar

urgency ['əːdʒənsɪ] *n* urgencia

urgent ['əːdʒənt] *adj* (*earnest, persistent: plea*) insistente; (*: tone*) urgente

urinal ['juərɪnl] *n* (*building*) urinario; (*vessel*) orinal *m*

urinate ['juərɪneɪt] *vi* orinar

urine ['juərɪn] *n* orina

urn [əːn] *n* urna; (*also*: **tea ~**) tetera (grande)

Uruguay ['juərəgwaɪ] *n* el Uruguay

Uruguayan [juərə'gwaɪən] *adj, n* uruguayo(-a) *m(f)*

US *n abbr* (= *United States*) EE.UU. (= *Estados Unidos*)

us [ʌs] *pron* nos; (*after prep*) nosotros(-as); (*inf: me*): **give us a kiss** dame un beso; *see also* **me**

USA *n abbr* = **United States of America**; (*Mil*) = **United States Army**

usable ['juːzəbl] *adj* utilizable

usage ['juːzɪdʒ] *n* (*Ling*) uso; (*utilization*) utilización *f*

USB stick *n* memoria USB, llave *f* de memoria

use *n* [juːs] uso, empleo; (*usefulness*) utilidad *f* ▷ *vt* [juːz] usar, emplear; **in ~** en uso; **out of ~** en desuso; **to be of ~** servir; **ready for ~** listo (para usar); **to make ~ of sth** aprovecharse *or* servirse de algo; **it's no ~** (*pointless*) es inútil; (*not useful*) no sirve; **what's this ~d for?** ¿para qué sirve esto?; **to be ~d to** estar acostumbrado a (*Sp*), acostumbrar; **to get ~d to** acostumbrarse a; **she ~d to do it** (ella) solía *or* acostumbraba hacerlo; **use up** *vt* (*food*) consumir; (*money*) gastar

used [juːzd] *adj* (*car*) usado

useful ['juːsful] *adj* útil; **to come in ~** ser útil

usefulness ['juːsfəlnɪs] *n* utilidad *f*

useless ['juːslɪs] *adj* inútil; (*unusable: object*) inservible

user ['juːzə^r] *n* usuario(-a); (*of petrol, gas etc*) consumidor(a) *m(f)*

user-friendly ['juːzə'frɛndlɪ] *adj* (*Comput*) fácil de utilizar

username ['juːzəneɪm] *n* (*Comput*) nombre *m* de usuario

usher ['ʌʃə^r] *n* (*at wedding*) ujier *m*; (*in cinema etc*) acomodador *m* ▷ *vt*: **to ~ sb in** (*into room*) hacer pasar a algn; **it ~ed in a new era** (*fig*) inició una nueva era

usherette [ʌʃə'rɛt] *n* (*in cinema*) acomodadora

USSR *n abbr* (*History*: = *Union of Soviet Socialist Republics*): **the (former) ~** la (antigua) U.R.S.S. (= *Unión de Repúblicas Socialistas Soviéticas*)

usu. *abbr* = **usually**

usual ['juːʒuəl] *adj* normal, corriente; **as ~** como de costumbre, como siempre

usually ['juːʒuəlɪ] *adv* normalmente

utensil [juː'tɛnsl] *n* utensilio; **kitchen ~s** batería de cocina

uterus ['juːtərəs] *n* útero

utility [juː'tɪlɪtɪ] *n* utilidad *f*; (*public utility*) (empresa de) servicio público

utility room *n* trascocina

utilize ['juːtɪlaɪz] *vt* utilizar

utmost ['ʌtməust] *adj* mayor ▷ *n*: **to do one's ~** hacer todo lo posible; **it is of the ~ importance that ...** es de la mayor importancia que ...

utter ['ʌtə^r] *adj* total, completo ▷ *vt* pronunciar, proferir

utterance ['ʌtərns] *n* palabras *fpl*, declaración *f*

utterly ['ʌtəlɪ] *adv* completamente, totalmente

U-turn ['juː'təːn] *n* cambio de sentido; (*fig*) giro de 180 grados

Uzbekistan [ʌzbɛkɪ'stɑːn] *n* Uzbekistán *m*

V

V, v [vi:] *n* (*letter*) V, v *f*; **V for Victor** V de Valencia
v. *abbr* (= *verse*) vers.º; (= *vide*: *see*) V, vid., vide; (= *versus*) vs.; = **volt**
vac [væk] *n abbr* (*Brit inf*) = **vacation**
vacancy ['veɪkənsɪ] *n* (*Brit*: *job*) vacante *f*; (*room*) cuarto libro; **have you any vacancies?** ¿tiene *or* hay alguna habitación *or* algún cuarto libre?; **"no vacancies"** "completo"
vacant ['veɪkənt] *adj* desocupado, libre; (*expression*) distraído
vacate [və'keɪt] *vt* (*house*) desocupar; (*job*) dejar (vacante)
vacation [və'keɪʃən] *n* vacaciones *fpl*; **on ~** de vacaciones; **to take a ~** (*esp US*) tomarse unas vacaciones
vacationer [və'keɪʃənə^r], **vacationist** [və'keɪʃənɪst] *n* (*US*) turista *m/f*
vaccinate ['væksɪneɪt] *vt* vacunar
vaccination [væksɪ'neɪʃən] *n* vacunación *f*
vaccine ['væksi:n] *n* vacuna
vacuum ['vækjum] *n* vacío
vacuum cleaner *n* aspiradora
vacuum-packed ['vækjum'pækt] *adj* envasado al vacío
vagina [və'dʒaɪnə] *n* vagina
vagrant ['veɪgrənt] *n* vagabundo(-a)
vague [veɪg] *adj* vago; (*blurred*: *memory*) borroso; (*uncertain*) incierto; (*ambiguous*) impreciso; (*person*: *absent-minded*) distraído; (: *evasive*): **to be ~** no decir las cosas claramente; **I haven't the ~st idea** no tengo la más remota idea
vaguely ['veɪglɪ] *adv* vagamente
vain [veɪn] *adj* (*conceited*) presumido; (*useless*) vano, inútil; **in ~** en vano
vainly ['veɪnlɪ] *adv* (*to no effect*) en vano; (*conceitedly*) vanidosamente
valentine ['væləntaɪn] *n* (*also*: **~ card**) tarjeta del Día de los Enamorados
Valentine's Day *n* día de los enamorados (*el 14 de febrero, día de San Valentín*)
valiant ['væljənt] *adj* valiente
valid ['vælɪd] *adj* válido; (*ticket*) valedero; (*law*) vigente
valley ['vælɪ] *n* valle *m*
valour, valor (*US*) ['vælə^r] *n* valor *m*, valentía
valuable ['væljuəbl] *adj* (*jewel*) de valor; (*time*) valioso; **valuables** *npl* objetos *mpl* de valor
valuation [vælju'eɪʃən] *n* tasación *f*, valuación *f*
value ['vælju:] *n* valor *m*; (*importance*) importancia ▷ *vt* (*fix price of*) tasar, valorar; (*esteem*) apreciar; **values** *npl* (*moral*) valores *mpl* morales; **to lose (in) ~** (*currency*) bajar; (*property*) desvalorizarse; **to gain (in) ~** (*currency*) subir; (*property*) revalorizarse; **you get good ~ (for money) in that shop** la relación calidad-precio es muy buena en esa tienda; **to be of great ~ to sb** ser de gran valor para algn; **it is ~d at £8** está valorado en ocho libras
valued ['vælju:d] *adj* (*appreciated*) apreciado
valve [vælv] *n* (*Anat, Tech*) válvula
vampire ['væmpaɪə^r] *n* vampiro
van [væn] *n* (*Aut*) furgoneta, camioneta (*LAm*); (*Brit Rail*) furgón *m* (de equipajes)
vandal ['vændl] *n* vándalo(-a)
vandalism ['vændəlɪzəm] *n* vandalismo
vandalize ['vændəlaɪz] *vt* dañar, destruir, destrozar
vanguard ['vængɑ:d] *n* vanguardia
vanilla [və'nɪlə] *n* vainilla
vanish ['vænɪʃ] *vi* desaparecer, esfumarse
vanity ['vænɪtɪ] *n* vanidad *f*
vantage point ['vɑ:ntɪdʒ-] *n* posición *f* ventajosa
vapour, vapor (*US*) ['veɪpə^r] *n* vapor *m*; (*on breath, window*) vaho
variable ['vɛərɪəbl] *adj* variable ▷ *n* variable *f*
variance ['vɛərɪəns] *n*: **to be at ~ (with)** estar en desacuerdo (con), no cuadrar (con)
variant ['vɛərɪənt] *n* variante *f*
variation [vɛərɪ'eɪʃən] *n* variación *f*
varicose ['værɪkəus] *adj*: **~ veins** varices *fpl*
varied ['vɛərɪd] *adj* variado
variety [və'raɪətɪ] *n* variedad *f*, diversidad *f*; (*quantity*) surtido; **for a ~ of reasons** por varias *or* diversas razones
variety show *n* espectáculo de variedades
various ['vɛərɪəs] *adj* varios(-as), diversos(-as); **at ~ times** (*different*) en distintos momentos; (*several*) varias veces

varnish ['vɑːnɪʃ] *n* (*gen*) barniz *m*; (*also*: **nail ~**) esmalte *m* ▷ *vt* (*gen*) barnizar; (*nails*) pintar (con esmalte)
vary ['vɛərɪ] *vt* variar; (*change*) cambiar ▷ *vi* variar; (*disagree*) discrepar; **to ~ with** *or* **according to** variar según *or* de acuerdo con
vase [vɑːz] *n* florero, jarrón *m*
vasectomy [və'sɛktəmɪ] *n* vasectomía
Vaseline® ['væsɪliːn] *n* vaselina®
vast [vɑːst] *adj* enorme; (*success*) abrumador(a), arrollador(a)
vastly ['vɑːstlɪ] *adv* enormemente
VAT [væt] *n abbr* (*Brit*: = *value added tax*) IVA *m*
vat [væt] *n* tina, tinaja
Vatican ['vætɪkən] *n*: **the ~** el Vaticano
vault [vɔːlt] *n* (*of roof*) bóveda; (*tomb*) panteón *m*; (*in bank*) cámara acorazada ▷ *vt* (*also*: **~ over**) saltar (por encima de)
vaunted ['vɔːntɪd] *adj*: **much ~** cacareado
VCR *n abbr* = **video cassette recorder**
VD *n abbr* = **venereal disease**
VDU *n abbr* (= *visual display unit*) UPV *f*
veal [viːl] *n* ternera
veer [vɪəʳ] *vi* (*vehicle*) virar; (*wind*) girar
veg. [vɛdʒ] *n abbr* (*Brit inf*) = **vegetable(s)**
vegan ['viːgən] *n* vegetariano(-a) estricto(-a)
vegeburger, veggieburger ['vɛdʒɪbəːgəʳ] *n* hamburguesa vegetal
vegetable ['vɛdʒtəbl] *n* (*Bot*) vegetal *m*; (*edible plant*) legumbre *f*, hortaliza ▷ *adj* vegetal; **vegetables** *npl* (*cooked*) verduras *fpl*
vegetarian [vɛdʒɪ'tɛərɪən] *adj, n* vegetariano(-a) *m(f)*
vegetation [vɛdʒɪ'teɪʃən] *n* vegetación *f*
vegetative ['vɛdʒɪtətɪv] *adj* vegetativo; (*Bot*) vegetal
vehement ['viːɪmənt] *adj* vehemente, apasionado; (*dislike, hatred*) violento
vehicle ['viːɪkl] *n* vehículo; (*fig*) vehículo, medio
veil [veɪl] *n* velo ▷ *vt* velar; **under a ~ of secrecy** (*fig*) en el mayor secreto
veiled [veɪld] *adj* (*also fig*) disimulado, velado
vein [veɪn] *n* vena; (*of ore etc*) veta
Velcro® ['vɛlkrəu] *n* velcro® *m*
velour [və'luəʳ] *n* terciopelo
velvet ['vɛlvɪt] *n* terciopelo ▷ *adj* aterciopelado
vending machine ['vɛndɪŋ-] *n* máquina expendedora, expendedor *m*
vendor ['vɛndəʳ] *n* vendedor(a) *m(f)*; **street ~** vendedor(a) *m(f)* callejero(-a)
veneer [və'nɪəʳ] *n* chapa, enchapado; (*fig*) barniz *m*
venereal [vɪ'nɪərɪəl] *adj*: **~ disease (VD)** enfermedad *f* venérea
Venetian blind [vɪ'niːʃən-] *n* persiana
Venezuela [vɛnɛ'zweɪlə] *n* Venezuela
Venezuelan [vɛnɛ'zweɪlən] *adj, n* venezolano(-a) *m(f)*
vengeance ['vɛndʒəns] *n* venganza; **with a ~** (*fig*) con creces
venison ['vɛnɪsn] *n* carne *f* de venado
venom ['vɛnəm] *n* veneno
venomous ['vɛnəməs] *adj* venenoso
vent [vɛnt] *n* (*opening*) abertura; (*air-hole*) respiradero; (*in wall*) rejilla (de ventilación) ▷ *vt* (*fig*: *feelings*) desahogar
ventilation [vɛntɪ'leɪʃən] *n* ventilación *f*
ventilator ['vɛntɪleɪtəʳ] *n* ventilador *m*
ventriloquist [vɛn'trɪləkwɪst] *n* ventrílocuo(-a)
venture ['vɛntʃəʳ] *n* empresa ▷ *vt* arriesgar; (*opinion*) ofrecer ▷ *vi* arriesgarse, lanzarse; **a business ~** una empresa comercial; **to ~ to do sth** aventurarse a hacer algo
venue ['vɛnjuː] *n* (*meeting place*) lugar *m* de reunión; (*for concert*) local *m*
Venus ['viːnəs] *n* (*Astro*) Venus *m*
verb [vəːb] *n* verbo
verbal ['vəːbl] *adj* verbal
verbatim [vəː'beɪtɪm] *adj, adv* al pie de la letra, palabra por palabra
verdict ['vəːdɪkt] *n* veredicto, fallo; (*fig*: *opinion*) opinión *f*, juicio; **~ of guilty/not guilty** veredicto de culpabilidad/inocencia
verge [vəːdʒ] *n* (*Brit*) borde *m*; **to be on the ~ of doing sth** estar a punto de hacer algo; **verge on** *vt fus* rayar en
verify ['vɛrɪfaɪ] *vt* comprobar, verificar; (*prove the truth of*) confirmar
vermin ['vəːmɪn] *npl* (*animals*) bichos *mpl*; (*insects*) sabandijas *fpl*; (*fig*) sabandijas *fpl*
vermouth ['vəːməθ] *n* vermut *m*
versatile ['vəːsətaɪl] *adj* (*person*) polifacético; (*machine, tool etc*) versátil
verse [vəːs] *n* versos *mpl*, poesía; (*stanza*) estrofa; (*in bible*) versículo; **in ~** en verso
version ['vəːʃən] *n* versión *f*
versus ['vəːsəs] *prep* contra
vertical ['vəːtɪkl] *adj* vertical
vertigo ['vəːtɪgəu] *n* vértigo; **to suffer from ~** tener vértigo
verve [vəːv] *n* brío
very ['vɛrɪ] *adv* muy ▷ *adj*: **the ~ book which** el mismo libro que; **the ~ last** el último (de todos); **at the ~ least** al menos; **~ much** muchísimo; **~ well/little** muy bien/poco; **~ high frequency** (*Radio*) frecuencia muy alta; **it's ~ cold** hace mucho frío; **the ~ thought (of it) alarms me** con sólo pensarlo me entra miedo
vessel ['vɛsl] *n* (*Anat*) vaso; (*ship*) barco; (*container*) vasija
vest [vɛst] *n* (*Brit*) camiseta; (*US*: *waistcoat*) chaleco
vested interests ['vɛstɪd-] *npl* (*Comm*) intereses *mpl* creados
vet [vɛt] *n abbr* = **veterinary surgeon**; (*US*: *inf*) = **veteran** ▷ *vt* revisar; **to ~ sb for a job** someter a investigación a algn para un trabajo

veteran ['vɛtərn] *n* veterano(-a) ▷ *adj*: **she is a ~ campaigner for ...** es una veterana de la campaña de ...
veterinarian [vɛtrɪ'nɛərɪən] *n* (*US*) = **veterinary surgeon**
veterinary surgeon *n* (*Brit*) veterinario(-a)
veto ['vi:təu] *n* (*pl* **vetoes**) veto ▷ *vt* prohibir, vedar; **to put a ~ on** vetar
vetting ['vɛtɪŋ] *n*: **positive ~** *investigación gubernamental de los futuros altos cargos de la Administración*
vex [vɛks] *vt* (*irritate*) fastidiar; (*make impatient*) impacientar
vexed [vɛkst] *adj* (*question*) controvertido
VG *n abbr* (*Brit Scol etc*: = *very good*) S (= *sobresaliente*)
VHF *abbr* (= *very high frequency*) VHF *f*
via ['vaɪə] *prep* por, por vía de
viable ['vaɪəbl] *adj* viable
vial ['vaɪəl] *n* frasco pequeño
vibes [vaɪbz] *npl* (*inf*): **I got good/bad ~** me dio buen/mal rollo
vibrate [vaɪ'breɪt] *vi* vibrar
vibration [vaɪ'breɪʃən] *n* vibración *f*
vicar ['vɪkə^r] *n* párroco
vicarage ['vɪkərɪdʒ] *n* parroquia
vicarious [vɪ'kɛərɪəs] *adj* indirecto; (*responsibility*) delegado
vice [vaɪs] *n* (*evil*) vicio; (*Tech*) torno de banco
vice- [vaɪs] *pref* vice...
vice-chairman ['vaɪs'tʃɛəmən] *n* vicepresidente *m*
vice versa ['vaɪsɪ'və:sə] *adv* viceversa
vicinity [vɪ'sɪnɪtɪ] *n* (*area*) vecindad *f*; (*nearness*) proximidad *f*; **in the ~ (of)** cercano (a)
vicious ['vɪʃəs] *adj* (*remark*) malicioso; (*blow*) brutal; (*dog, horse*) resabido; **a ~ circle** un círculo vicioso
victim ['vɪktɪm] *n* víctima; **to be the ~ of** ser víctima de
victimize ['vɪktɪmaɪz] *vt* (*strikers etc*) tomar represalias contra
victor ['vɪktə^r] *n* vencedor(a) *m(f)*
Victorian [vɪk'tɔ:rɪən] *adj* victoriano
victorious [vɪk'tɔ:rɪəs] *adj* vencedor(a)
victory ['vɪktərɪ] *n* victoria; **to win a ~ over sb** obtener una victoria sobre algn
video ['vɪdɪəu] *cpd* de vídeo ▷ *n* vídeo ▷ *vt* grabar (en vídeo)
video call *n* videollamada
video camera *n* videocámara, cámara de vídeo
video cassette *n* videocassette *f*
video cassette recorder *n* = **video recorder**
video game *n* videojuego
videophone ['vɪdɪəufəun] *n* videoteléfono, videófono
video recorder *n* vídeo, videocassette *f*
video tape *n* cinta de vídeo
vie [vaɪ] *vi*: **to ~ with** competir con
Vienna [vɪ'ɛnə] *n* Viena
Vietnam, Viet Nam [vjɛt'næm] *n* Vietnam *m*
Vietnamese [vjɛtnə'mi:z] *adj* vietnamita ▷ *n pl inv* vietnamita *m/f*; (*Ling*) vietnamita *m*
view [vju:] *n* vista; (*landscape*) paisaje *m*; (*opinion*) opinión *f*, criterio ▷ *vt* (*look at*) mirar; (*examine*) examinar; **on ~** (*in museum etc*) expuesto; **in full ~ of sb** a la vista de algn; **to be within ~ (of sth)** estar a la vista (de algo); **an overall ~ of the situation** una visión de conjunto de la situación; **in ~ of the fact that** en vista de que; **to take** *or* **hold the ~ that ...** opinar *or* pensar que ...; **with a ~ to doing sth** con miras *or* vistas a hacer algo
viewer ['vju:ə^r] *n* (*small projector*) visionadora; (*TV*) televidente *m/f*, telespectador(a) *m(f)*
viewfinder ['vju:faɪndə^r] *n* visor *m* de imagen
viewpoint ['vju:pɔɪnt] *n* punto de vista
vigil ['vɪdʒɪl] *n* vigilia; **to keep ~** velar
vigilant ['vɪdʒɪlənt] *adj* vigilante
vigilante [vɪdʒɪ'læntɪ] *n vecino/a que se toma la justicia por su mano*
vigorous ['vɪgərəs] *adj* enérgico, vigoroso
vile [vaɪl] *adj* (*action*) vil, infame; (*smell*) repugnante; (*temper*) endemoniado
villa ['vɪlə] *n* (*country house*) casa de campo; (*suburban house*) chalet *m*
village ['vɪlɪdʒ] *n* aldea
villager ['vɪlɪdʒə^r] *n* aldeano(-a)
villain ['vɪlən] *n* (*scoundrel*) malvado(-a); (*criminal*) maleante *m/f*; *see also* **pantomime**
vinaigrette [vɪneɪ'grɛt] *n* vinagreta
vindicate ['vɪndɪkeɪt] *vt* vindicar, justificar
vindictive [vɪn'dɪktɪv] *adj* vengativo
vine [vaɪn] *n* vid *f*
vinegar ['vɪnɪgə^r] *n* vinagre *m*
vineyard ['vɪnjɑ:d] *n* viña, viñedo
vintage ['vɪntɪdʒ] *n* (*year*) vendimia, cosecha; **the 1970 ~** la cosecha de 1970
vintage car *n* coche *m* antiguo *or* de época
vintage wine *n* vino añejo
vinyl ['vaɪnl] *n* vinilo
viola [vɪ'əulə] *n* (*Mus*) viola
violate ['vaɪəleɪt] *vt* violar
violation [vaɪə'leɪʃən] *n* violación *f*; **in ~ of sth** en violación de algo
violence ['vaɪələns] *n* violencia; **acts of ~** actos *mpl* de violencia
violent ['vaɪələnt] *adj* (*gen*) violento; (*pain*) intenso; **a ~ dislike of sb/sth** una profunda antipatía *or* manía a algn/algo
violet ['vaɪələt] *adj* violado, violeta ▷ *n* (*plant*) violeta
violin [vaɪə'lɪn] *n* violín *m*
violinist [vaɪə'lɪnɪst] *n* violinista *m/f*
VIP *n abbr* (= *very important person*) VIP *m*
viral ['vaɪərəl] *adj* (*Med*) vírico; (*Comput*) viral
virgin ['və:dʒɪn] *n* virgen *m/f* ▷ *adj* virgen; **the Blessed V~** la Santísima Virgen
virginity [və:'dʒɪnɪtɪ] *n* virginidad *f*
Virgo ['və:gəu] *n* Virgo

virile ['vɪraɪl] *adj* viril
virtual ['vəːtjuəl] *adj* (*also Comput, Physics*) virtual
virtually ['vəːtjuəlɪ] *adv* (*almost*) prácticamente, virtualmente; **it is ~ impossible** es prácticamente imposible
virtual reality *n* (*Comput*) realidad *f* virtual
virtue ['vəːtjuː] *n* virtud *f*; **by ~ of** en virtud de
virtuosity [vəːtju'ɔsɪtɪ] *n* virtuosismo
virtuous ['vəːtjuəs] *adj* virtuoso
virus ['vaɪərəs] *n* virus *m inv*
visa ['viːzə] *n* visado, visa (*LAm*)
vise [vaɪs] *n* (*US Tech*) = **vice**
visibility [vɪzɪ'bɪlɪtɪ] *n* visibilidad *f*
visible ['vɪzəbl] *adj* visible; **~ exports/imports** exportaciones *fpl*/importaciones *fpl* visibles
vision ['vɪʒən] *n* (*sight*) vista; (*foresight, in dream*) visión *f*
visit ['vɪzɪt] *n* visita ▷ *vt* (*person*) visitar, hacer una visita a; (*place*) ir a, (ir a) conocer; **to pay a ~ to** (*person*) visitar a; **on a private/official ~** en visita privada/oficial
visiting hours *npl* (*in hospital etc*) horas *fpl* de visita
visitor ['vɪzɪtə^r] *n* (*gen*) visitante *m/f*; (*to one's house*) visita; (*tourist*) turista *m/f*; (*tripper*) excursionista *m/f*; **to have ~s** (*at home*) tener visita
visitor centre, visitor center (*US*) *n* centro *m* de información
visitors' book *n* libro de visitas
visor ['vaɪzə^r] *n* visera
vista ['vɪstə] *n* vista, panorama
visual ['vɪzjuəl] *adj* visual
visual aid *n* medio visual
visual arts *npl* artes *fpl* plásticas
visualize ['vɪzjuəlaɪz] *vt* imaginarse; (*foresee*) prever
vital ['vaɪtl] *adj* (*essential*) esencial, imprescindible; (*crucial*) crítico; (*person*) enérgico, vivo; (*organ*) vital; **of ~ importance (to sb/sth)** de suma importancia (para algn/algo)
vitality [vaɪ'tælɪtɪ] *n* energía, vitalidad *f*
vitally ['vaɪtəlɪ] *adv*: **~ important** de suma importancia
vital statistics *npl* (*of population*) estadísticas *fpl* demográficas; (*inf: of woman*) medidas *fpl* (corporales)
vitamin ['vɪtəmɪn] *n* vitamina
vitamin pill *n* pastilla de vitaminas
viva ['vaɪvə] *n* (*also:* **~ voce**) examen *m* oral
vivacious [vɪ'veɪʃəs] *adj* vivaz, alegre
vivid ['vɪvɪd] *adj* (*account*) gráfico; (*light*) intenso; (*imagination*) vivo
vividly ['vɪvɪdlɪ] *adv* (*describe*) gráficamente; (*remember*) como si fuera hoy
viz *abbr* (= *vide licet: namely*) v.gr.
V-neck ['viːnɛk] *n* cuello de pico
vocabulary [vəu'kæbjulərɪ] *n* vocabulario
vocal ['vəukl] *adj* vocal; (*articulate*) elocuente
vocal cords *npl* cuerdas *fpl* vocales
vocalist ['vəukəlɪst] *n* cantante *m/f*
vocation [vəu'keɪʃən] *n* vocación *f*
vocational [vəu'keɪʃənl] *adj* profesional; **~ guidance** orientación *f* profesional; **~ training** formación *f* profesional
vociferous [və'sɪfərəs] *adj* vociferante
vodka ['vɔdkə] *n* vodka *m*
vogue [vəug] *n* boga, moda; **to be in ~, be the ~** estar de moda *or* en boga
voice [vɔɪs] *n* voz *f* ▷ *vt* (*opinion*) expresar; **in a loud/soft ~** en voz alta/baja; **to give ~ to** expresar
voice mail *n* (*Tel*) fonobuzón *m*
voice-over ['vɔɪsəuvə^r] *n* voz *f* en off
void [vɔɪd] *n* vacío; (*hole*) hueco ▷ *adj* (*invalid*) nulo, inválido; (*empty*): **~ of** carente *or* desprovisto de
vol. *abbr* (= *volume*) t
volatile ['vɔlətaɪl] *adj* (*situation*) inestable; (*person*) voluble; (*liquid*) volátil; (*Comput: memory*) no permanente
volcano (*pl* **volcanoes**) [vɔl'keɪnəu] *n* volcán *m*
volition [və'lɪʃən] *n*: **of one's own ~** por su propia voluntad
volley ['vɔlɪ] *n* (*of gunfire*) descarga; (*of stones etc*) lluvia; (*Tennis etc*) volea
volleyball ['vɔlɪbɔːl] *n* voleibol *m*, balonvolea *m*
volt [vəult] *n* voltio
voltage ['vəultɪdʒ] *n* voltaje *m*; **high/low ~** alto/bajo voltaje, alta/baja tensión
volume ['vɔljuːm] *n* (*of tank*) volumen *m*; (*book*) tomo; **~ one/two** (*of book*) tomo primero/segundo; **volumes** *npl* (*great quantities*) cantidad *fsg*; **his expression spoke ~s** su expresión (lo) decía todo
voluntarily ['vɔləntrɪlɪ] *adv* libremente, voluntariamente
voluntary ['vɔləntərɪ] *adj* voluntario, espontáneo
volunteer [vɔlən'tɪə^r] *n* voluntario(-a) ▷ *vt* (*information*) ofrecer ▷ *vi* ofrecerse (de voluntario); **to ~ to do** ofrecerse a hacer
vomit ['vɔmɪt] *n* vómito ▷ *vt, vi* vomitar
voracious [və'reɪʃəs] *adj* voraz; (*reader*) ávido
vote [vəut] *n* voto; (*votes cast*) votación *f*; (*right to vote*) derecho a votar; (*franchise*) sufragio ▷ *vt* (*chairman*) elegir ▷ *vi* votar, ir a votar; **~ of thanks** voto de gracias; **to put sth to the ~, to take a ~ on sth** someter algo a votación; **~ for** *or* **in favour of/against** voto a favor de/en contra de; **to ~ to do sth** votar por hacer algo; **he was ~d secretary** fue elegido secretario por votación; **to pass a ~ of confidence/no confidence** aprobar un voto de confianza/de censura
voter ['vəutə^r] *n* votante *m/f*
voting ['vəutɪŋ] *n* votación *f*

V

vouch [vautʃ]: **to ~ for** *vt fus* garantizar, responder de
voucher ['vautʃəʳ] *n* (*for meal, petrol*) vale *m*; **luncheon/travel ~** vale *m* de comida/de viaje
vow [vau] *n* voto ▷ *vi* hacer voto ▷ *vt*: **to ~ to do/that** jurar hacer/que; **to take** *or* **make a ~ to do sth** jurar hacer algo, comprometerse a hacer algo
vowel ['vauəl] *n* vocal *f*
voyage ['vɔɪɪdʒ] *n* (*journey*) viaje *m*; (*crossing*) travesía
voyeur [vwɑː'jəːʳ] *n* voyeur *m/f*, mirón(-ona) *m(f)*
vs *abbr* (= *versus*) vs
VSO *n abbr* (Brit: = *Voluntary Service Overseas*) *organización que envía jóvenes voluntarios a trabajar y enseñar en los países del Tercer Mundo*
vulgar ['vʌlgəʳ] *adj* (*rude*) ordinario, grosero; (*in bad taste*) de mal gusto
vulnerable ['vʌlnərəbl] *adj* vulnerable
vulture ['vʌltʃəʳ] *n* buitre *m*, gallinazo (*LAm*)

W

W, w ['dʌbljuː] *n* (*letter*) W, w *f*; **W for William** W de Washington
W *abbr* (= *west*) O; (*Elec*: = *watt*) v
wad [wɔd] *n* (*of cotton wool, paper*) bolita; (*of banknotes etc*) fajo
waddle ['wɔdl] *vi* andar como un pato
wade [weɪd] *vi*: **to ~ through** caminar por el agua; (*fig*: *a book*) leer con dificultad
wafer ['weɪfəʳ] *n* (*biscuit*) barquillo; (*Rel*) oblea; (: *consecrated*) hostia; (*Comput*) oblea, microplaqueta
waffle ['wɔfl] *n* (*Culin*) gofre *m* ▷ *vi* meter el rollo
waft [wɔft] *vt* llevar por el aire ▷ *vi* flotar
wag [wæg] *vt* menear, agitar ▷ *vi* moverse, menearse; **the dog ~ged its tail** el perro meneó la cola
wage [weɪdʒ] *n* (*also*: **~s**) sueldo, salario ▷ *vt*: **to ~ war** hacer la guerra; **a day's ~** el sueldo de un día
wage earner *n* asalariado(-a)
wage packet *n* sobre *m* de la paga
wager ['weɪdʒəʳ] *n* apuesta ▷ *vt* apostar
waggle ['wægl] *vt* menear, mover
wagon, waggon ['wægən] *n* (*horse-drawn*) carro; (*Brit Rail*) vagón *m*
wail [weɪl] *n* gemido ▷ *vi* gemir
waist [weɪst] *n* cintura, talle *m*
waistcoat ['weɪstkəut] *n* (*Brit*) chaleco
waistline ['weɪstlaɪn] *n* talle *m*
wait [weɪt] *n* espera; (*interval*) pausa ▷ *vi* esperar; **to lie in ~ for** acechar a; **I can't ~ to**

(*fig*) estoy deseando; **to ~ for** esperar (a); **to keep sb ~ing** hacer esperar a algn; **~ a moment!** ¡un momento!, ¡un momentito!; **"repairs while you ~"** "reparaciones en el acto"; **wait behind** *vi* quedarse; **wait on** *vt fus* servir a; **wait up** *vi* esperar levantado

waiter ['weɪtəʳ] *n* camarero

waiting list *n* lista de espera

waiting room *n* sala de espera

waitress ['weɪtrɪs] *n* camarera

waive [weɪv] *vt* suspender

wake [weɪk] (*pt* **woke** *or* **waked**, *pp* **woken** *or* **waked**) *vt* (*also*: **~ up**) despertar ▷ *vi* (*also*: **~ up**) despertarse ▷ *n* (*for dead person*) velatorio; (*Naut*) estela; **to ~ up to sth** (*fig*) darse cuenta de algo; **in the ~ of** tras, después de; **to follow in sb's ~** (*fig*) seguir las huellas de algn

waken ['weɪkn] *vt, vi* = **wake**

Wales [weɪlz] *n* País *m* de Gales

walk [wɔːk] *n* (*stroll*) paseo; (*hike*) excursión *f* a pie, caminata; (*gait*) paso, andar *m*; (*in park etc*) paseo ▷ *vi* andar, caminar; (*for pleasure, exercise*) pasearse ▷ *vt* (*distance*) recorrer a pie, andar; (*dog*) (sacar a) pasear; **to go for a ~** ir a dar un paseo; **10 minutes' ~ from here** a 10 minutos de aquí andando; **people from all ~s of life** gente de todas las esferas; **to ~ in one's sleep** ser sonámbulo(-a); **I'll ~ you home** te acompañaré a casa; **walk out** *vi* (*go out*) salir; (*as protest*) marcharse, salirse; (*strike*) declararse en huelga; **to ~ out on sb** abandonar a algn

walkabout ['wɔːkəbaut] *n*: **to go (on a) ~** darse un baño de multitudes

walker ['wɔːkəʳ] *n* (*person*) paseante *m/f*, caminante *m/f*

walkie-talkie ['wɔːkɪ'tɔːkɪ] *n* walkie-talkie *m*

walking ['wɔːkɪŋ] *n* (el) andar; **it's within ~ distance** se puede ir andando *or* a pie

walking shoes *npl* zapatos *mpl* para andar

walking stick *n* bastón *m*

Walkman® ['wɔːkmən] *n* walkman® *m*

walkout ['wɔːkaut] *n* (*of workers*) huelga

walkover ['wɔːkəuvəʳ] *n* (*inf*) pan *m* comido

walkway ['wɔːkweɪ] *n* paseo

wall [wɔːl] *n* pared *f*; (*exterior*) muro; (*city wall etc*) muralla; **to go to the ~** (*fig*: *firm etc*) quebrar, ir a la bancarrota; **wall in** *vt* (*garden etc*) cercar con una tapia

walled [wɔːld] *adj* (*city*) amurallado; (*garden*) con tapia

wallet ['wɔlɪt] *n* cartera, billetera (*esp LAm*)

wallflower ['wɔːlflauəʳ] *n* alhelí *m*; **to be a ~** (*fig*) comer pavo

wallop ['wɔləp] *vt* (*inf*) zurrar

wallow ['wɔləu] *vi* revolcarse; **to ~ in one's grief** sumirse en su pena

wallpaper ['wɔːlpeɪpəʳ] *n* (*for walls*) papel *m* pintado; (*Comput*) fondo de escritorio ▷ *vt* empapelar

wally ['wɔlɪ] *n* (*inf*) majadero(-a)

walnut ['wɔːlnʌt] *n* nuez *f*; (*tree*) nogal *m*

walrus (*pl* **walrus** *or* **walruses**) ['wɔːlrəs] *n* morsa

waltz [wɔːlts] *n* vals *m* ▷ *vi* bailar el vals

wan [wɔn] *adj* pálido

wand [wɔnd] *n* (*also*: **magic ~**) varita (mágica)

wander ['wɔndəʳ] *vi* (*person*) vagar; deambular; (*thoughts*) divagar; (*get lost*) extraviarse ▷ *vt* recorrer, vagar por

wane [weɪn] *vi* menguar

wangle ['wæŋgl] (*Brit inf*) *vt*: **to ~ sth** agenciarse *or* conseguir algo ▷ *n* chanchullo

want [wɔnt] *vt* (*wish for*) querer, desear; (*need*) necesitar; (*lack*) carecer de ▷ *n* (*poverty*) pobreza; **for ~ of** por falta de; **wants** *npl* (*needs*) necesidades *fpl*; **to ~ to do** querer hacer; **to ~ sb to do sth** querer que algn haga algo; **you're ~ed on the phone** te llaman al teléfono; **to be in ~** estar necesitado

wanted [wɔntɪd] *adj* (*criminal*) buscado; **"~"** (*in advertisements*) "se busca"

wanting ['wɔntɪŋ] *adj*: **to be ~ (in)** estar falto (de); **to be found ~** no estar a la altura de las circunstancias

wanton ['wɔntn] *adj* (*licentious*) lascivo

war [wɔːʳ] *n* guerra; **to make ~** hacer la guerra; **the First/Second World W~** la primera/segunda guerra mundial

ward [wɔːd] *n* (*in hospital*) sala; (*Pol*) distrito electoral; (*Law*: *child*: *also*: **~ of court**) pupilo(-a); **ward off** *vt* desviar, parar; (*attack*) rechazar

warden ['wɔːdn] *n* (*Brit*: *of institution*) director(a) *m(f)*; (*of park, game reserve*) guardián(-ana) *m(f)*; (*Brit*: *also*: **traffic ~**) guardia *m/f*

warder ['wɔːdəʳ] *n* (*Brit*) guardián(-ana) *m(f)*, carcelero(-a) *m(f)*

wardrobe ['wɔːdrəub] *n* armario, guardarropa, ropero, clóset/closet *m* (*LAm*)

warehouse ['wɛəhaus] *n* almacén *m*, depósito

wares [wɛəz] *npl* mercancías *fpl*

warfare ['wɔːfɛəʳ] *n* guerra

warhead ['wɔːhɛd] *n* cabeza armada; **nuclear ~s** cabezas *fpl* nucleares

warily ['wɛərɪlɪ] *adv* con cautela, cautelosamente

warm [wɔːm] *adj* caliente; (*person, greeting, heart*) afectuoso, cariñoso; (*supporter*) entusiasta; (*thanks, congratulations, apologies*) efusivo; (*clothes etc*) que abriga; (*welcome, day*) caluroso; **it's ~** hace calor; **I'm ~** tengo calor; **to keep sth ~** mantener algo caliente; **warm up** *vi* (*room*) calentarse; (*person*) entrar en calor; (*athlete*) hacer ejercicios de calentamiento; (*discussion*) acalorarse ▷ *vt* calentar

war memorial *n* monumento a los caídos

warm-hearted [wɔːm'hɑːtɪd] *adj* afectuoso

warmly ['wɔːmlɪ] *adv* afectuosamente

warmth [wɔːmθ] *n* calor *m*
warm-up [ˈwɔːmʌp] *n* (*Sport*) ejercicios *mpl* de calentamiento
warn [wɔːn] *vt* avisar, advertir; **to ~ sb not to do sth** *or* **against doing sth** aconsejar a algn que no haga algo
warning [ˈwɔːnɪŋ] *n* aviso, advertencia; **gale ~** (*Meteorology*) aviso de vendaval; **without (any) ~** sin aviso *or* avisar
warning light *n* luz *f* de advertencia
warning triangle *n* (*Aut*) triángulo señalizador
warp [wɔːp] *vi* (*wood*) combarse
warrant [ˈwɔrnt] *n* (*Law: to arrest*) orden *f* de detención; (*: to search*) mandamiento de registro ▷ *vt* (*justify, merit*) merecer
warranty [ˈwɔrəntɪ] *n* garantía; **under ~** (*Comm*) bajo garantía
warren [ˈwɔrən] *n* (*of rabbits*) madriguera; (*fig*) laberinto
warrior [ˈwɔrɪəʳ] *n* guerrero(-a)
Warsaw [ˈwɔːsɔː] *n* Varsovia
warship [ˈwɔːʃɪp] *n* buque *m or* barco de guerra
wart [wɔːt] *n* verruga
wartime [ˈwɔːtaɪm] *n*: **in ~** en tiempos de guerra, en la guerra
wary [ˈwɛərɪ] *adj* cauteloso; **to be ~ about** *or* **of doing sth** tener cuidado con hacer algo
was [wɔz] *pt of* **be**
wash [wɔʃ] *vt* lavar; (*sweep, carry: sea etc*) llevar ▷ *vi* lavarse ▷ *n* (*clothes etc*) lavado; (*bath*) baño; (*of ship*) estela; **he was ~ed overboard** fue arrastrado del barco por las olas; **to have a ~** lavarse; **wash away** *vt* (*stain*) quitar lavando; (*river etc*) llevarse; (*fig*) limpiar; **wash down** *vt* lavar; **wash off** *vt* quitar lavando; **wash up** *vi* (*Brit*) fregar los platos; (*US: have a wash*) lavarse
washable [ˈwɔʃəbl] *adj* lavable
washbasin [ˈwɔʃbeɪsn], **washbowl** (*US*) [ˈwɔʃbəul] *n* lavabo
washcloth [ˈwɔʃklɔθ] *n* (*US*) manopla
washer [ˈwɔʃəʳ] *n* (*Tech*) arandela
washing [ˈwɔʃɪŋ] *n* (*dirty*) ropa sucia; (*clean*) colada
washing line *n* cuerda de (colgar) la ropa
washing machine *n* lavadora
washing powder *n* (*Brit*) detergente *m* (en polvo)
Washington [ˈwɔʃɪŋtən] *n* (*city, state*) Washington *m*
washing-up [wɔʃɪŋˈʌp] *n* fregado; (*dishes*) platos *mpl* (para fregar); **to do the ~** fregar los platos
washing-up liquid *n* lavavajillas *m inv*
wash-out [ˈwɔʃaut] *n* (*inf*) fracaso
washroom [ˈwɔʃrum] *n* servicios *mpl*
wasn't [ˈwɔznt] = **was not**
wasp [wɔsp] *n* avispa
wastage [ˈweɪstɪdʒ] *n* desgaste *m*; (*loss*) pérdida; **natural ~** desgaste natural
waste [weɪst] *n* derroche *m*, despilfarro; (*misuse*) desgaste *m*; (*of time*) pérdida; (*food*) sobras *fpl*; (*rubbish*) basura, desperdicios *mpl* ▷ *adj* (*material*) de desecho; (*left over*) sobrante; (*energy, heat*) desperdiciado; (*land, ground: in city*) sin construir; (*: in country*) baldío ▷ *vt* (*squander*) malgastar, derrochar; (*time*) perder; (*opportunity*) desperdiciar; **wastes** *npl* (*area of land*) tierras *fpl* baldías; **to lay ~** devastar, arrasar; **it's a ~ of money** es tirar el dinero; **to go to ~** desperdiciarse; **waste away** *vi* consumirse
wastebasket [ˈweɪstbɑːskɪt] *n* (*esp US*) = **wastepaper basket**
wasteful [ˈweɪstful] *adj* derrochador(a); (*process*) antieconómico
waste ground *n* (*Brit*) terreno baldío
wastepaper basket [ˈweɪstpeɪpə-] *n* papelera; (*Comput*) papelera de reciclaje
waste pipe *n* tubo de desagüe
waster [ˈweɪstəʳ] *n* (*inf*) gandul *m/f*
watch [wɔtʃ] *n* reloj *m*; (*vigil*) vigilia; (*vigilance*) vigilancia; (*Mil: guard*) centinela *m*; (*Naut: spell of duty*) guardia ▷ *vt* (*look at*) mirar, observar; (*: match, programme*) ver; (*spy on, guard*) vigilar; (*be careful of*) cuidar, tener cuidado de ▷ *vi* ver, mirar; (*keep guard*) montar guardia; **to keep a close ~ on sth/sb** vigilar algo/a algn de cerca; **~ how you drive/what you're doing** ten cuidado al conducir/con lo que haces; **watch out** *vi* cuidarse, tener cuidado
watchdog [ˈwɔtʃdɔg] *n* perro guardián; (*fig*) organismo de control
watchful [ˈwɔtʃful] *adj* vigilante, sobre aviso
watchmaker [ˈwɔtʃmeɪkəʳ] *n* relojero(-a)
watchman [ˈwɔtʃmən] (*irreg: like* **man**) *n* guardián *m*; (*also:* **night ~**) sereno, vigilante *m*; (*in factory*) vigilante *m* nocturno
watch strap *n* pulsera (de reloj)
watchword [ˈwɔtʃwəːd] *n* consigna, contraseña
water [ˈwɔːtəʳ] *n* agua ▷ *vt* (*plant*) regar ▷ *vi* (*eyes*) llorar; **I'd like a drink of ~** quisiera un vaso de agua; **in British ~s** en aguas británicas; **to pass ~** orinar; **his mouth ~ed** se le hizo la boca agua; **water down** *vt* (*milk etc*) aguar; (*fig: story*) dulcificar, diluir
watercolour, watercolor (*US*) [ˈwɔːtəkʌləʳ] *n* acuarela
watercress [ˈwɔːtəkrɛs] *n* berro
waterfall [ˈwɔːtəfɔːl] *n* cascada, salto de agua
water heater *n* calentador *m* de agua
watering can [ˈwɔːtərɪŋ-] *n* regadera
water lily *n* nenúfar *m*
waterline [ˈwɔːtəlaɪn] *n* (*Naut*) línea de flotación
waterlogged [ˈwɔːtəlɔgd] *adj* (*boat*) anegado; (*ground*) inundado
water main *n* cañería del agua
watermark [ˈwɔːtəmɑːk] *n* (*on paper*) filigrana

watermelon ['wɔːtəmɛlən] *n* sandía
waterproof ['wɔːtəpruːf] *adj* impermeable
watershed ['wɔːtəʃɛd] *n* (*Geo*) cuenca; (*fig*) momento crítico
water-skiing ['wɔːtəskiːɪŋ] *n* esquí *m* acuático
water tank *n* depósito de agua
watertight ['wɔːtətaɪt] *adj* hermético
waterway ['wɔːtəweɪ] *n* vía fluvial *or* navegable
waterworks ['wɔːtəwəːks] *npl* central *fsg* depuradora
watery ['wɔːtərɪ] *adj* (*colour*) desvaído; (*coffee*) aguado; (*eyes*) lloroso
watt [wɔt] *n* vatio
wave [weɪv] *n* ola; (*of hand*) señal *f* con la mano; (*Radio*) onda; (*in hair*) onda; (*fig*: *of enthusiasm, strikes*) oleada ▷ *vi* agitar la mano; (*flag*) ondear ▷ *vt* (*handkerchief, gun*) agitar; **short/medium/long ~** (*Radio*) onda corta/media/larga; **the new ~** (*Cine, Mus*) la nueva ola; **to ~ goodbye to sb** decir adiós a algn con la mano; **he ~d us over to his table** nos hizo señas (con la mano) para que nos acercásemos a su mesa; **wave aside, wave away** *vt* (*person*): **to ~ sb aside** apartar a algn con la mano; (*fig*: *suggestion, objection*) rechazar; (*doubts*) desechar
wavelength ['weɪvlɛŋθ] *n* longitud *f* de onda
waver ['weɪvəʳ] *vi* oscilar; (*confidence*) disminuir; (*faith*) flaquear
wavy ['weɪvɪ] *adj* ondulado
wax [wæks] *n* cera ▷ *vt* encerar ▷ *vi* (*moon*) crecer
waxworks ['wækswəːks] *npl* museo *sg* de cera
way [weɪ] *n* camino; (*distance*) trayecto, recorrido; (*direction*) dirección *f*, sentido; (*manner*) modo, manera; (*habit*) costumbre *f*; **which ~? — this ~** ¿por dónde? *or* ¿en qué dirección? — por aquí; **on the ~** (*en route*) en (el) camino; (*expected*) en camino; **to be on one's ~** estar en camino; **you pass it on your ~ home** está de camino a tu casa; **to be in the ~** bloquear el camino; (*fig*) estorbar; **to keep out of sb's ~** esquivar a algn; **to make ~ (for sb/sth)** dejar paso (a algn/algo); (*fig*) abrir camino (a algn/algo); **to go out of one's ~ to do sth** desvivirse por hacer algo; **to lose one's ~** perderse, extraviarse; **to be the wrong ~ round** estar del *or* al revés; **in a ~** en cierto modo *or* sentido; **by the ~** a propósito; **by ~ of** (*via*) pasando por; (*as a sort of*) como, a modo de; **"~ in"** (*Brit*) "entrada"; **"~ out"** (*Brit*) "salida"; **the ~ back** el camino de vuelta; **the village is rather out of the ~** el pueblo está un poco apartado *or* retirado; **it's a long ~ away** está muy lejos; **to get one's own ~** salirse con la suya; **"give ~"** (*Brit Aut*) "ceda el paso"; **no ~!** (*inf*) ¡ni pensarlo!; **put it the right ~ up** ponlo boca arriba; **he's in a bad ~** está grave; **to be under ~** (*work, project*) estar en marcha
waylay [weɪ'leɪ] *vt* (*irreg: like* **lay**) atacar
wayward ['weɪwəd] *adj* díscolo, caprichoso
WC ['dʌbljuˈsiː] *n abbr* (*Brit*: = *water closet*) wáter *m*
we [wiː] *pron pl* nosotros(-as); **we understand** (nosotros) entendemos; **here we are** aquí estamos
weak [wiːk] *adj* débil, flojo; (*tea, coffee*) flojo, aguado; **to grow ~(er)** debilitarse
weaken ['wiːkən] *vi* debilitarse; (*give way*) ceder ▷ *vt* debilitar
weakling ['wiːklɪŋ] *n* debilucho(-a)
weakness ['wiːknɪs] *n* debilidad *f*; (*fault*) punto débil; **to have a ~ for** tener debilidad por
wealth [wɛlθ] *n* (*money, resources*) riqueza; (*of details*) abundancia
wealthy ['wɛlθɪ] *adj* rico
wean [wiːn] *vt* destetar
weapon ['wɛpən] *n* arma; **~s of mass destruction** armas de destrucción masiva
wear [wɛəʳ] (*pt* **wore**, *pp* **worn**) *n* (*use*) uso; (*deterioration through use*) desgaste *m*; (*clothing*): **sports/baby ~** ropa de deportes/de niños ▷ *vt* (*clothes, beard*) llevar; (*shoes*) calzar; (*look, smile*) tener; (*damage*: *through use*) gastar, usar ▷ *vi* (*last*) durar; (*rub through etc*) desgastarse; **evening ~** (*man's*) traje *m* de etiqueta; (*woman's*) traje *m* de noche; **to ~ a hole in sth** hacer un agujero en algo; **wear away** *vt* gastar ▷ *vi* desgastarse; **wear down** *vt* gastar; (*strength*) agotar; **wear off** *vi* (*pain, excitement etc*) pasar, desaparecer; **wear out** *vt* desgastar; (*person, strength*) agotar
wear and tear *n* desgaste *m*
weary ['wɪərɪ] *adj* (*tired*) cansado; (*dispirited*) abatido ▷ *vt* cansar ▷ *vi*: **to ~ of** cansarse de, aburrirse de
weasel ['wiːzl] *n* (*Zool*) comadreja
weather ['wɛðəʳ] *n* tiempo ▷ *vt* (*storm, crisis*) hacer frente a; **under the ~** (*fig*: *ill*) mal, pachucho; **what's the ~ like?** ¿qué tiempo hace?, ¿cómo hace?
weather-beaten ['wɛðəbiːtn] *adj* curtido
weathercock ['wɛðəkɔk] *n* veleta
weather forecast *n* boletín *m* meteorológico
weatherman ['wɛðəmæn] *n* hombre *m* del tiempo
weather vane *n* = **weathercock**
weave (*pt* **wove**, *pp* **woven**) [wiːv, wəuv, 'wəuvn] *vt* (*cloth*) tejer; (*fig*) entretejer ▷ *vi* (*pt, pp* **weaved**) (*fig*: *move in and out*) zigzaguear
weaver ['wiːvəʳ] *n* tejedor(a) *m(f)*
web [wɛb] *n* (*of spider*) telaraña; (*on foot*) membrana; (*Comput*: *network*) red *f*; **the W~** la Red
web address *n* dirección *f* de página web
webcam ['wɛbkæm] *n* webcam *f*
web page *n* página web

website ['wɛbsaɪt] *n* sitio web
wed [wɛd] (*pt, pp* **wedded**) *vt* casar ▷ *vi* casarse ▷ *n*: **the newly--s** los recién casados
Wed. *abbr* (= *Wednesday*) miérc
we'd [wi:d] = **we had**; **we would**
wedding ['wɛdɪŋ] *n* boda, casamiento
wedding anniversary *n* aniversario de boda; **silver/golden ~** bodas *fpl* de plata/ de oro
wedding day *n* día *m* de la boda
wedding dress *n* traje *m* de novia
wedding present *n* regalo de boda
wedding ring *n* alianza
wedge [wɛdʒ] *n* (*of wood etc*) cuña; (*of cake*) trozo ▷ *vt* acuñar; (*push*) apretar
Wednesday ['wɛdnzdɪ] *n* miércoles *m inv*; *see also* **Tuesday**
wee [wi:] *adj* (*Scottish*) pequeñito
weed [wi:d] *n* mala hierba, maleza ▷ *vt* escardar, desherbar; **weed out** *vt* eliminar
weedkiller ['wi:dkɪlə^r] *n* herbicida *m*
weedy ['wi:dɪ] *adj* (*person*) debilucho
week [wi:k] *n* semana; **a ~ today** de hoy en ocho días; **Tuesday ~, a ~ on Tuesday** del martes en una semana; **once/twice a ~** una vez/dos veces a la semana; **this ~** esta semana; **in two ~s' time** dentro de dos semanas; **every other ~** cada dos semanas
weekday ['wi:kdeɪ] *n* día *m* laborable; **on ~s** entre semana, en días laborables
weekend [wi:k'ɛnd] *n* fin *m* de semana
weekly ['wi:klɪ] *adv* semanalmente, cada semana ▷ *adj* semanal ▷ *n* semanario; **~ newspaper** semanario
weep (*pt, pp* **wept**) [wi:p, wɛpt] *vi, vt* llorar; (*Med: wound etc*) supurar
weeping willow ['wi:pɪŋ-] *n* sauce *m* llorón
weepy ['wi:pɪ] *n* (*inf: film*) película lacrimógena; (*: story*) historia lacrimógena
weigh [weɪ] *vt, vi* pesar; **to ~ anchor** levar anclas; **to ~ the pros and cons** pesar los pros y los contras; **weigh down** *vt* sobrecargar; (*fig: with worry*) agobiar; **weigh out** *vt* (*goods*) pesar; **weigh up** *vt* sopesar
weight [weɪt] *n* peso; (*on scale*) pesa; **to lose/ put on ~** adelgazar/engordar; **~s and measures** pesas y medidas
weighting ['weɪtɪŋ] *n* (*allowance*): **(London) ~** *dietas (por residir en Londres)*
weight lifter *n* levantador(a) *m(f)* de pesas
weightlifting ['weɪtlɪftɪŋ] *n* levantamiento de pesas
weight training *n* musculación *f* (con pesas)
weighty ['weɪtɪ] *adj* pesado
weir [wɪə^r] *n* presa
weird [wɪəd] *adj* raro, extraño
weirdo ['wɪədəu] *n* (*inf*) tío(-a) raro(-a)
welcome ['wɛlkəm] *adj* bienvenido ▷ *n* bienvenida ▷ *vt* dar la bienvenida a; (*be glad of*) alegrarse de; **to make sb ~** recibir *or* acoger bien a algn; **thank you — you're ~** gracias — de nada; **you're ~ to try** puede intentar cuando quiera; **we ~ this step** celebramos esta medida
weld [wɛld] *n* soldadura ▷ *vt* soldar
welfare ['wɛlfɛə^r] *n* bienestar *m*; (*social aid*) asistencia social; **W~** (*US*) subsidio de paro; **to look after sb's ~** cuidar del bienestar de algn
welfare state *n* estado del bienestar
welfare work *n* asistencia social
well [wɛl] *n* pozo ▷ *adv* bien ▷ *adj*: **to be ~** estar bien (de salud) ▷ *excl* ¡vaya!, ¡bueno!; **as ~** (*in addition*) además, también; **as ~ as** además de; **you might as ~ tell me** más vale que me lo digas; **it would be as ~ to ask** más valdría preguntar; **~ done!** ¡bien hecho!; **get ~ soon!** ¡que te mejores pronto!; **to do ~** (*business*) ir bien; **I did ~ in my exams** me han salido bien los exámenes; **they are doing ~ now** les va bien ahora; **to think ~ of sb** pensar bien de algn; **I don't feel ~** no me encuentro *or* siento bien; **~, as I was saying ...** bueno, como decía ...; **well up** *vi* brotar
we'll [wi:l] = **we will**; **we shall**
well-behaved ['wɛlbɪ'heɪvd] *adj*: **to be ~** portarse bien
well-being ['wɛl'bi:ɪŋ] *n* bienestar *m*
well-built ['wɛl'bɪlt] *adj* (*person*) fornido
well-deserved ['wɛldɪ'zə:vd] *adj* merecido
well-dressed ['wɛl'drɛst] *adj* bien vestido
well-heeled ['wɛl'hi:ld] *adj* (*inf: wealthy*) rico
wellies ['welɪz] (*inf*) *npl* (*Brit*) botas de goma
wellingtons ['wɛlɪŋtənz] *npl* (*also*: **Wellington boots**) botas *fpl* de goma
well-known ['wɛl'nəun] *adj* (*person*) conocido
well-mannered ['wɛl'mænəd] *adj* educado
well-meaning ['wɛl'mi:nɪŋ] *adj* bienintencionado
well-off ['wɛl'ɔf] *adj* acomodado
well-paid [wel'peɪd] *adj* bien pagado, bien retribuido
well-read ['wɛl'rɛd] *adj* culto
well-to-do ['wɛltə'du:] *adj* acomodado
well-wisher ['wɛlwɪʃə^r] *n* admirador(a) *m(f)*
Welsh [wɛlʃ] *adj* galés(-esa) ▷ *n* (*Ling*) galés *m*; **the Welsh** *npl* los galeses; **the ~ Assembly** el Parlamento galés
Welshman ['wɛlʃmən] *n* galés *m*
Welsh rarebit [-'rɛəbɪt] *n* pan *m* con queso tostado
Welshwoman ['wɛlʃwumən] *n* galesa
went [wɛnt] *pt of* **go**
wept [wɛpt] *pt, pp of* **weep**
were [wə:^{r}] *pt of* **be**
we're [wɪə^r] = **we are**
weren't [wə:nt] = **were not**
west [wɛst] *n* oeste *m* ▷ *adj* occidental, del oeste ▷ *adv* al *or* hacia el oeste; **the W~** Occidente *m*
westbound ['wɛstbaund] *adj* (*traffic, carriageway*) con rumbo al oeste

West Country *n*: **the ~** el suroeste de Inglaterra
westerly ['wɛstəlɪ] *adj* (*wind*) del oeste
western ['wɛstən] *adj* occidental ▷ *n* (*Cine*) película del oeste
westerner ['wɛstənəʳ] *n* (*Pol*) occidental *m/f*
West German (*formerly*) *adj* de Alemania Occidental ▷ *n* alemán(-ana) *m(f)* (de Alemania Occidental)
West Germany *n* (*formerly*) Alemania Occidental
West Indian *adj, n* antillano(-a) *m(f)*
West Indies [-'ɪndɪz] *npl*: **the ~** las Antillas
Westminster ['wɛstmɪnstəʳ] *n el parlamento británico*, Westminster *m*
wet [wɛt] *adj* (*damp*) húmedo; (*wet through*) mojado; (*rainy*) lluvioso ▷ *vt*: **to ~ one's pants** *or* **o.s.** mearse; **to get ~** mojarse; **"~ paint"** "recién pintado"
wet blanket *n*: **to be a ~** (*fig*) ser un/una aguafiestas
wetsuit ['wɛtsu:t] *n* traje *m* de buzo
we've [wi:v] = **we have**
whack [wæk] *vt* dar un buen golpe a
whale [weɪl] *n* (*Zool*) ballena
whaling ['weɪlɪŋ] *n* pesca de ballenas
wharf (*pl* **wharves**) [wɔ:f, wɔ:vz] *n* muelle *m*

KEYWORD

what [wɔt] *adj* **1** (*in direct/indirect questions*) qué; **what size is he?** ¿qué talla usa?; **what colour/shape is it?** ¿de qué color/forma es?; **what books do you need?** ¿qué libros necesitas?
2 (*in exclamations*): **what a mess!** ¡qué desastre!; **what a fool I am!** ¡qué tonto soy!
▷ *pron* **1** (*interrogative*) qué; **what are you doing?** ¿qué haces *or* estás haciendo?; **what is happening?** ¿qué pasa *or* está pasando?; **what is it called?** ¿cómo se llama?; **what about me?** ¿y yo qué?; **what about doing ...?** ¿qué tal si hacemos ...?; **what is his address?** ¿cuáles son sus señas?; **what will it cost?** ¿cuánto costará?
2 (*relative*) lo que; **I saw what you did/was on the table** vi lo que hiciste/había en la mesa; **what I want is a cup of tea** lo que quiero es una taza de té; **I don't know what to do** no sé qué hacer; **tell me what you're thinking about** dime en qué estás pensando
3 (*reported questions*): **she asked me what I wanted** me preguntó qué quería
▷ *excl* (*disbelieving*) ¡cómo!; **what, no coffee!** ¡que no hay café!

whatever [wɔt'ɛvəʳ] *adj*: **~ book you choose** cualquier libro que elijas ▷ *pron*: **do ~ is necessary** haga lo que sea necesario; **no reason ~** ninguna razón en absoluto; **nothing ~** nada en absoluto; **~ it costs** cueste lo que cueste
whatsoever [wɔtsəu'ɛvəʳ] *adj see* **whatever**
wheat [wi:t] *n* trigo
wheedle ['wi:dl] *vt*: **to ~ sb into doing sth** engatusar a algn para que haga algo; **to ~ sth out of sb** sonsacar algo a algn
wheel [wi:l] *n* rueda; (*Aut*: *also*: **steering ~**) volante *m*; (*Naut*) timón *m* ▷ *vt* (*pram etc*) empujar ▷ *vi* (*also*: **~ round**) dar la vuelta, girar; **four-~ drive** tracción *f* en las cuatro ruedas; **front-/rear-~ drive** tracción *f* delantera/trasera
wheelbarrow ['wi:lbærəu] *n* carretilla
wheelchair ['wi:ltʃɛəʳ] *n* silla de ruedas
wheel clamp *n* (*Aut*) cepo
wheelie-bin ['wi:lɪbɪn] *n* (*Brit*) contenedor *m* de basura
wheeze [wi:z] *vi* resollar
wheezy ['wi:zɪ] *adj* silbante

KEYWORD

when [wɛn] *adv* cuando; **when did it happen?** ¿cuándo ocurrió?; **I know when it happened** sé cuándo ocurrió
▷ *conj* **1** (*at, during, after the time that*) cuando; **be careful when you cross the road** ten cuidado al cruzar la calle; **that was when I needed you** entonces era cuando te necesitaba; **I'll buy you a car when you're 18** te compraré un coche cuando cumplas 18 años
2 (*on, at which*): **on the day when I met him** el día en qué le conocí
3 (*whereas*) cuando; **you said I was wrong when in fact I was right** dijiste que no tenía razón, cuando en realidad sí la tenía

whenever [wɛn'ɛvəʳ] *conj* cuando; (*every time*) cada vez que; **I go ~ I can** voy siempre *or* todas las veces que puedo
where [wɛəʳ] *adv* dónde ▷ *conj* donde; **this is ~** aquí es donde; **~ possible** donde sea posible; **~ are you from?** ¿de dónde es usted?
whereabouts ['wɛərəbauts] *adv* dónde ▷ *n*: **nobody knows his ~** nadie conoce su paradero
whereas [wɛər'æz] *conj* mientras
whereby [wɛə'baɪ] *adv* mediante el/la cual *etc*, por lo/la cual *etc*
whereupon [wɛərə'pɔn] *conj* con lo cual, después de lo cual
wherever [wɛər'ɛvəʳ] *adv* dondequiera que; (*interrogative*) dónde; **sit ~ you like** siéntese donde quiera
wherewithal ['wɛəwɪðɔ:l] *n* recursos *mpl*; **the ~ (to do sth)** los medios económicos (para hacer algo)
whet [wɛt] *vt* estimular; (*appetite*) abrir

whether ['wɛðəʳ] *conj* si; **I don't know ~ to accept or not** no sé si aceptar o no; **~ you go or not** vayas o no vayas

KEYWORD

which [wɪtʃ] *adj* **1** (*interrogative: direct, indirect*) qué; **which picture(s) do you want?** ¿qué cuadro(s) quieres?; **which one?** ¿cuál?; **which one of you?** ¿cuál de vosotros?; **tell me which one you want** dime cuál (es el que) quieres
2: **in which case** en cuyo caso; **we got there at eight pm, by which time the cinema was full** llegamos allí a las ocho, cuando el cine estaba lleno
▷ *pron* (*interrogative*) cual; **I don't mind which** el(-la) que sea; **which do you want?** ¿cuál quieres?
3 (*relative: replacing noun*) que; (*: replacing clause*) lo que; (*: after preposition*) (el(-la)) que, el(-la) cual; **the apple which you ate/which is on the table** la manzana que comiste/que está en la mesa; **the chair on which you are sitting** la silla en la que estás sentado; **he didn't believe it, which upset me** no se lo creyó, lo cual *or* lo que me disgustó; **after which** después de lo cual

whichever [wɪtʃ'ɛvəʳ] *adj*: **take ~ book you prefer** coja el libro que prefiera; **~ book you take** cualquier libro que coja
whiff [wɪf] *n* bocanada; **to catch a ~ of sth** oler algo
while [waɪl] *n* rato, momento ▷ *conj* durante; (*whereas*) mientras; (*although*) aunque ▷ *vt*: **to ~ away the time** pasar el rato; **for a ~** durante algún tiempo; **in a ~** dentro de poco; **all the ~** todo el tiempo; **we'll make it worth your ~** te compensaremos generosamente
whilst [waɪlst] *conj* = **while**
whim [wɪm] *n* capricho
whimper ['wɪmpəʳ] *n* (*weeping*) lloriqueo; (*moan*) quejido ▷ *vi* lloriquear; quejarse
whimsical ['wɪmzɪkl] *adj* (*person*) caprichoso
whine [waɪn] *n* (*of pain*) gemido; (*of engine*) zumbido ▷ *vi* gemir; zumbar; (*fig: complain*) gimotear
whip [wɪp] *n* látigo; (*Brit: Pol*) *diputado encargado de la disciplina del partido en el parlamento* ▷ *vt* azotar; (*snatch*) arrebatar; (*US Culin*) batir; **whip up** *vt* (*cream etc*) batir (rápidamente); (*inf: meal*) preparar rápidamente; (*: stir up: support, feeling*) avivar; *ver nota*
whipped cream [wɪpt-] *n* nata montada
whip-round ['wɪpraund] *n* (*Brit*) colecta
whirl [wəːl] *n* remolino ▷ *vt* hacer girar, dar vueltas a ▷ *vi* (*dancers*) girar, dar vueltas; (*leaves, dust, water etc*) arremolinarse
whirlpool ['wəːlpuːl] *n* remolino
whirlwind ['wəːlwɪnd] *n* torbellino
whirr [wəːʳ] *vi* zumbar
whisk [wɪsk] *n* (*Brit Culin*) batidor *m* ▷ *vt* (*Brit Culin*) batir; **to ~ sb away** *or* **off** llevarse volando a algn
whiskers [wɪskəz] *npl* (*of animal*) bigotes *mpl*; (*of man*) patillas *fpl*
whisky, whiskey (*US, Ireland*) ['wɪskɪ] *n* whisky *m*
whisper ['wɪspəʳ] *n* cuchicheo; (*rumour*) rumor *m*; (*fig*) susurro, murmullo ▷ *vi* cuchichear, hablar bajo; (*fig*) susurrar ▷ *vt* susurrar; **to ~ sth to sb** decirle algo al oído a algn
whistle ['wɪsl] *n* (*sound*) silbido; (*object*) silbato ▷ *vi* silbar; **to ~ a tune** silbar una melodía
white [waɪt] *adj* blanco; (*pale*) pálido ▷ *n* blanco; (*of egg*) clara; **to turn** *or* **go ~** (*person*) palidecer, ponerse blanco; (*hair*) encanecer; **the ~s** (*washing*) la ropa blanca; **tennis ~s** ropa *f* de tenis
whiteboard ['waɪtbɔːd] *n* pizarra blanca; **interactive ~** pizarra interactiva
white coffee *n* (*Brit*) café *m* con leche
white-collar worker ['waɪtkɔlə-] *n* oficinista *m/f*
white elephant *n* (*fig*) maula
White House *n* (*US*) Casa Blanca
white lie *n* mentirijilla
white paper *n* (*Pol*) libro blanco
whitewash ['waɪtwɔʃ] *n* (*paint*) cal *f*, jalbegue *m* ▷ *vt* encalar, blanquear; (*fig*) encubrir
whiting ['waɪtɪŋ] *n pl inv* (*fish*) pescadilla
Whitsun ['wɪtsn] *n* (*Brit*) Pentecostés *m*
whittle ['wɪtl] *vt*: **to ~ away**: **whittle down** ir reduciendo
whizz [wɪz] *vi*: **to ~ past** *or* **by** pasar a toda velocidad
whizz kid *n* (*inf*) prodigio(-a)
WHO *n abbr* (= *World Health Organization*) OMS *f*

KEYWORD

who [huː] *pron* **1** (*interrogative*) quién; **who is it?, who's there?** ¿quién es?; **who are you looking for?** ¿a quién buscas?; **I told her who I was** le dije quién era yo
2 (*relative*) que; **the man/woman who spoke to me** el hombre/la mujer que habló conmigo; **those who can swim** los que saben *or* sepan nadar

whoever [huː'ɛvəʳ] *pron*: **~ finds it** cualquiera *or* quienquiera que lo encuentre; **ask ~ you like** pregunta a quien quieras; **~ he marries** se case con quien se case
whole [həul] *adj* (*complete*) todo, entero; (*not broken*) intacto ▷ *n* (*total*) total *m*; (*sum*) conjunto; **~ villages were destroyed** pueblos enteros fueron destruídos; **the ~ of**

the town toda la ciudad, la ciudad entera; **on the ~, as a ~** en general

wholefood(s) [həulfu:d(z)] *n(pl)* alimento(s) *m(pl)* integral(es)

wholehearted [həul'hɑ:tɪd] *adj* (*support, approval*) total; (*sympathy*) todo

wholeheartedly [həul'hɑ:tɪdlɪ] *adv* con entusiasmo

wholemeal ['həulmi:l] *adj* (*Brit*: *flour, bread*) integral

wholesale ['həulseɪl] *n* venta al por mayor ▷ *adj* al por mayor; (*destruction*) sistemático

wholesaler ['həulseɪlə^r] *n* mayorista *m/f*

wholesome ['həulsəm] *adj* sano

wholewheat ['həulwi:t] *adj* = **wholemeal**

wholly ['həulɪ] *adv* totalmente, enteramente

KEYWORD

whom [hu:m] *pron* **1** (*interrogative*): **whom did you see?** ¿a quién viste?; **to whom did you give it?** ¿a quién se lo diste?; **tell me from whom you received it** dígame de quién lo recibiste
2 (*relative*) que; **to whom** a quien(es); **of whom** de quien(es), del/de la que; **the man whom I saw** el hombre qui vi; **the man to whom I wrote** el hombre a quien escribí, **the lady about whom I was talking** la señora de (la) que hablaba; **the lady with whom I was talking** la señora con quien *or* (la) que hablaba

whooping cough ['hu:pɪŋ-] *n* tos *f* ferina

whoops [wu:ps] *excl* (*also*: **~-a-daisy!**) ¡huy!

whore [hɔ:^r] *n* (*inf*: *pej*) puta

KEYWORD

whose [hu:z] *adj* **1** (*possessive*: *interrogative*) de quién; **whose book is this?, whose is this book?** ¿de quién es este libro?; **whose pencil have you taken?** ¿de quién es el lápiz que has cogido?; **whose daughter are you?** ¿de quién eres hija?
2 (*possessive*: *relative*) cuyo(-a) *m(f)*, cuyos(-as) *m(f)pl*; **the man whose son they rescued** el hombre cuyo hijo rescataron; **the girl whose sister he was speaking to** la chica con cuya hermana estaba hablando; **those whose passports I have** aquellas personas cuyos pasaportes tengo; **the woman whose car was stolen** la mujer a quien le robaron el coche
▷ *pron* de quién; **whose is this?** ¿de quién es esto?; **I know whose it is** sé de quién es

KEYWORD

why [waɪ] *adv* por qué; **why not?** ¿por qué no?; **why not do it now?** ¿por qué no lo haces (*or* hacemos ahora?
▷ *conj*: **I wonder why he said that** me pregunto por qué dijo eso; **that's not why I'm here** no es por eso (por lo) que estoy aquí; **the reason why** la razón por la que
▷ *excl* (*expressing surprise, shock, annoyance*) ¡hombre!, ¡vaya!; (*explaining*): **why, it's you!** ¡hombre, eres tú!; **why, that's impossible** ¡pero si eso es imposible!

whyever [waɪ'ɛvə^r] *adv* por qué

wicked ['wɪkɪd] *adj* malvado, cruel

wicket ['wɪkɪt] *n* (*Cricket*) palos *mpl*

wide [waɪd] *adj* ancho; (*area, knowledge*) vasto, grande; (*choice*) amplio ▷ *adv*: **to open ~** abrir de par en par; **to shoot ~** errar el tiro; **it is three metres ~** tiene tres metros de ancho

wide-angle lens ['waɪdæŋgl-] *n* (objetivo) gran angular *m*

widely ['waɪdlɪ] *adv* (*differing*) muy; **it is ~ believed that ...** existe la creencia generalizada de que ...; **to be ~ read** (*author*) ser muy leído; (*reader*) haber leído mucho

widen ['waɪdn] *vt* ensanchar; (*experience*) ampliar ▷ *vi* ensancharse

wide open *adj* abierto de par en par

widespread ['waɪdsprɛd] *adj* (*belief etc*) extendido, general

widow ['wɪdəu] *n* viuda

widowed ['wɪdəud] *adj* viudo

widower ['wɪdəuə^r] *n* viudo

width [wɪdθ] *n* anchura; (*of cloth*) ancho; **it's seven metres in ~** tiene siete metros de ancho

wield [wi:ld] *vt* (*sword*) blandir; (*power*) ejercer

wife (*pl* **wives**) [waɪf, waɪvz] *n* mujer *f*, esposa

Wi-Fi ['waɪfaɪ] *n abbr* (= *wireless fidelity*) wi-fi *m* ▷ *adj* (*hot spot, network etc*) wi-fi

wig [wɪg] *n* peluca

wiggle ['wɪgl] *vt* menear ▷ *vi* menearse

wiki ['wɪki:] *n* (*Comput*) wiki *f*

wild [waɪld] *adj* (*animal*) salvaje; (*plant*) silvestre; (*rough*) furioso, violento; (*idea*) descabellado; (*rough*: *sea*) bravo; (: *land*) agreste; (: *weather*) muy revuelto; (*inf*: *angry*) furioso ▷ *n*: **the ~** la naturaleza; **wilds** *npl* regiones *fpl* salvajes, tierras *fpl* vírgenes; **to be ~ about** (*enthusiastic*) estar *or* andar loco por; **in its ~ state** en estado salvaje

wild card *n* (*Comput*) comodín *m*

wildcat ['waɪldkæt] *n* gato montés

wilderness ['wɪldənɪs] *n* desierto; (*jungle*) jungla

wildfire ['waɪldfaɪə^r] *n*: **to spread like ~** correr como un reguero de pólvora

wild-goose chase [waɪld'gu:s-] *n* (*fig*) búsqueda inútil

wildlife ['waɪldlaɪf] *n* fauna

wildly ['waɪldlɪ] *adv* (*roughly*) violentamente; (*foolishly*) locamente; (*rashly*) descabelladamente; (*lash out*) a diestro y siniestro; (*guess*) a lo loco; (*happy*) a más no poder

wilful, willful (*US*) ['wɪlful] *adj* (*action*) deliberado; (*obstinate*) testarudo

KEYWORD

will [wɪl] *aux vb* **1** (*forming future tense*): **I will finish it tomorrow** lo terminaré *or* voy a terminar mañana; **I will have finished it by tomorrow** lo habré terminado para mañana; **will you do it? — yes I will/no I won't** ¿lo harás? — sí/no; **you won't lose it, will you?** no lo vayas a perder *or* no lo perderás ¿verdad?
2 (*in conjectures, predictions*): **he will** *or* **he'll be there by now** ya habrá llegado, ya debe (de) haber llegado; **that will be the postman** será el cartero, debe ser el cartero
3 (*in commands, requests, offers*): **will you be quiet!** ¿quieres callarte?; **will you help me?** ¿quieres ayudarme?; **will you have a cup of tea?** ¿te apetece un té?; **I won't put up with it!** ¡no lo soporto!
4 (*habits, persistence*): **the car won't start** el coche no arranca; **accidents will happen** son cosas que pasan
▷ *vt* (*pt, pp* **willed**): **to will sb to do sth** desear que algn haga algo; **he willed himself to go on** con gran fuerza de voluntad, continuó
▷ *n* **1** (*desire*) voluntad *f*; **against sb's will** contra la voluntad de algn; **he did it of his own free will** lo hizo por su propia voluntad
2 (*Law*) testamento; **to make a** *or* **one's will** hacer su testamento

willing ['wɪlɪŋ] *adj* (*with goodwill*) de buena voluntad; (*enthusiastic*) entusiasta; **he's ~ to do it** está dispuesto a hacerlo; **to show ~** mostrarse dispuesto

willingly ['wɪlɪŋlɪ] *adv* con mucho gusto

willingness ['wɪlɪŋnɪs] *n* buena voluntad

willow ['wɪləu] *n* sauce *m*

willpower ['wɪlpauə^r] *n* fuerza de voluntad

willy-nilly [wɪlɪ'nɪlɪ] *adv* quiérase o no

wilt [wɪlt] *vi* marchitarse

wily ['waɪlɪ] *adj* astuto

wimp [wɪmp] *n* (*inf*) enclenque *m/f*; (*character*) calzonazos *m inv*

win [wɪn] (*pt, pp* **won**) *n* (*in sports etc*) victoria, triunfo ▷ *vt* ganar; (*obtain*: *contract etc*) conseguir, lograr ▷ *vi* ganar; **win over, win round** (*Brit*) *vt* convencer a

wince [wɪns] *vi* encogerse

winch [wɪntʃ] *n* torno

wind[1] [wɪnd, *n* viento; (*Med*) gases *mpl*; (*breath*) aliento *vt* (*take breath away from*) dejar sin aliento a; **into** *or* **against the ~** contra el viento; **to get ~ of sth** enterarse de algo; **to break ~** ventosear

wind[2] [waɪnd] (*pt, pp* **wound**) *vt* enrollar; (*wrap*) envolver; (*clock, toy*) dar cuerda a ▷ *vi* (*road, river*) serpentear; **wind down** *vt* (*car window*) bajar; (*fig*: *production, business*) disminuir; **wind up** *vt* (*clock*) dar cuerda a; (*debate*) concluir, terminar

windfall ['wɪndfɔːl] *n* golpe *m* de suerte

wind farm *n* parque *m* eólico

winding ['waɪndɪŋ] *adj* (*road*) tortuoso

wind instrument *n* (*Mus*) instrumento de viento

windmill ['wɪndmɪl] *n* molino de viento

window ['wɪndəu] *n* ventana; (*in car, train*) ventana; (*in shop etc*) escaparate *m*, vitrina (*LAm*), vidriera (*LAm*); (*Comput*) ventana

window box *n* jardinera (de ventana)

window cleaner *n* (*person*) limpiacristales *m inv*

window ledge *n* alféizar *m*, repisa

window pane *n* cristal *m*

window seat *n* asiento junto a la ventana

window-shopping [wɪndəu'ʃɔpɪŋ] *n*: **to go ~** ir a ver *or* mirar escaparates

windowsill ['wɪndəusɪl] *n* alféizar *m*, repisa

windpipe ['wɪndpaɪp] *n* tráquea

wind power *n* energía eólica

windscreen ['wɪndskriːn], **windshield** (*US*) ['wɪndʃiːld] *n* parabrisas *m inv*

windscreen washer, windshield washer (*US*) *n* lavaparabrisas *m inv*

windscreen wiper, windshield wiper (*US*) *n* limpiaparabrisas *m inv*

windsurfing ['wɪndsəːfɪŋ] *n* windsurf *m*

windswept ['wɪndswɛpt] *adj* azotado por el viento

windy ['wɪndɪ] *adj* de mucho viento; **it's ~** hace viento

wine [waɪn] *n* vino ▷ *vt*: **to ~ and dine sb** agasajar *or* festejar a algn

wine bar *n* *bar especializado en vinos*

wine cellar *n* bodega

wine glass *n* copa (de *or* para vino)

wine list *n* lista de vinos

wine tasting *n* degustación *f* de vinos

wine waiter *n* escanciador *m*

wing [wɪŋ] *n* ala; (*Brit Aut*) aleta; **wings** *npl* (*Theat*) bastidores *mpl*

winger ['wɪŋə^r] *n* (*Sport*) extremo

wing mirror *n* (espejo) retrovisor *m*

wink [wɪŋk] *n* guiño; (*blink*) pestañeo ▷ *vi* guiñar; (*blink*) pestañear; (*light etc*) parpadear

winner ['wɪnə^r] *n* ganador(a) *m(f)*

winning ['wɪnɪŋ] *adj* (*team*) ganador(a); (*goal*) decisivo; (*charming*) encantador(a)

winnings ['wɪnɪŋz] *npl* ganancias *fpl*

winter ['wɪntə^r] *n* invierno ▷ *vi* invernar

winter sports *npl* deportes *mpl* de invierno

wintertime ['wɪntətaɪm] *n* invierno

wintry ['wɪntrɪ] *adj* invernal

wipe [waɪp] *n*: **to give sth a ~** pasar un trapo sobre algo ▷ *vt* limpiar; (*tape*) borrar; **to ~ one's nose** limpiarse la nariz; **wipe off** *vt*

limpiar con un trapo; **wipe out** *vt* (*debt*) liquidar; (*memory*) borrar; (*destroy*) destruir; **wipe up** *vt* limpiar
wire ['waɪəʳ] *n* alambre *m*; (*Elec*) cable *m* (eléctrico); (*Tel*) telegrama *m* ▷ *vt* (*house*) poner la instalación eléctrica en; (*also*: **~ up**) conectar
wireless ['waɪəlɪs] *n* (*Brit*) radio *f* ▷ *adj* inalámbrico
wire service *n* (*US*) agencia de noticias
wiring ['waɪərɪŋ] *n* instalación *f* eléctrica
wiry ['waɪərɪ] *adj* enjuto y fuerte
wisdom ['wɪzdəm] *n* sabiduría, saber *m*; (*good sense*) cordura
wisdom tooth *n* muela del juicio
wise [waɪz] *adj* sabio; (*sensible*) juicioso; **I'm none the ~r** sigo sin entender; **wise up** *vi* (*inf*): **to ~ up (to sth)** enterarse (de algo)
wisecrack ['waɪzkræk] *n* broma
wish [wɪʃ] *n* (*desire*) deseo ▷ *vt* desear; (*want*) querer; **best ~es** (*on birthday etc*) felicidades *fpl*; **with best ~es** (*in letter*) saludos *mpl*, recuerdos *mpl*; **he ~ed me well** me deseó mucha suerte; **to ~ sth on sb** imponer algo a algn; **to ~ to do/sb to do sth** querer hacer/que algn haga algo; **to ~ for** desear
wishbone ['wɪʃbəun] *n* espoleta (*de la que tiran dos personas quien se quede con el hueso más largo pide un deseo*)
wishful ['wɪʃful] *adj*: **it's ~ thinking** eso es hacerse ilusiones
wistful ['wɪstful] *adj* pensativo; (*nostalgic*) nostálgico
wit [wɪt] *n* (*wittiness*) ingenio, gracia; (*intelligence*: *also*: **~s**) inteligencia; (*person*) chistoso(-a); **to have** *or* **keep one's ~s about one** no perder la cabeza
witch [wɪtʃ] *n* bruja
witchcraft ['wɪtʃkrɑːft] *n* brujería

KEYWORD

with [wɪð, wɪθ] *prep* **1** (*accompanying, in the company of*) con (*con +mí, ti, sí = conmigo, contigo, consigo*); **I was with him** estaba con él; **we stayed with friends** nos quedamos en casa de unos amigos
2 (*descriptive, indicating manner etc*) con; de; **a room with a view** una habitación con vistas; **the man with the grey hat/blue eyes** el hombre del sombrero gris/de los ojos azules; **red with anger** rojo de ira; **to shake with fear** temblar de miedo; **to fill sth with water** llenar algo de agua
3: **I'm with you/I'm not with you** (*understand*) ya te entiendo/no te entiendo; **to be with it** (*inf*: *person*: *up-to-date*) estar al tanto; (: *alert*) ser despabilado; **I'm not really with it today** no doy pie con bola hoy

withdraw [wɪθ'drɔː] *vt* (*irreg*: *like* **draw**) retirar ▷ *vi* retirarse; (*go back on promise*) retractarse; **to ~ money (from the bank)** retirar fondos (del banco); **to ~ into o.s.** ensimismarse
withdrawal [wɪθ'drɔːəl] *n* retirada; (*of money*) reintegro
withdrawal symptoms *npl* síndrome *m* de abstinencia
withdrawn [wɪθ'drɔːn] *adj* (*person*) reservado, introvertido ▷ *pp of* **withdraw**
withdrew [wɪθ'druː] *pt of* **withdraw**
wither ['wɪðəʳ] *vi* marchitarse
withhold [wɪθ'həuld] *vt* (*irreg*: *like* **hold**) (*money*) retener; (*decision*) aplazar; (*permission*) negar; (*information*) ocultar
within [wɪð'ɪn] *prep* dentro de ▷ *adv* dentro; **~ reach** al alcance de la mano; **~ sight of** a la vista de; **~ the week** antes de que acabe la semana; **to be ~ the law** atenerse a la legalidad; **~ an hour from now** dentro de una hora; **~ a mile (of)** a menos de una milla (de)
without [wɪð'aut] *prep* sin; **to go** *or* **do ~ sth** prescindir de algo; **~ anybody knowing** sin saberlo nadie
withstand [wɪθ'stænd] *vt* (*irreg*: *like* **stand**) resistir a
witness ['wɪtnɪs] *n* (*person*) testigo *m/f*; (*evidence*) testimonio ▷ *vt* (*event*) presenciar, ser testigo de; (*document*) atestiguar la veracidad de; **~ for the prosecution/defence** testigo de cargo/descargo; **to ~ to (having seen) sth** dar testimonio de (haber visto) algo; **to bear ~ to** (*fig*) ser testimonio de
witness box, witness stand (*US*) *n* tribuna de los testigos
witticism ['wɪtɪsɪzm] *n* dicho ingenioso
witty ['wɪtɪ] *adj* ingenioso
wives [waɪvz] *npl of* **wife**
wizard ['wɪzəd] *n* hechicero
wk *abbr* = **week**
wobble ['wɔbl] *vi* tambalearse
woe [wəu] *n* desgracia
woeful ['wəuful] *adj* (*bad*) lamentable; (*sad*) apesadumbrado
wok [wɔk] *n* wok *m*
woke [wəuk] *pt of* **wake**
woken ['wəukn] *pp of* **wake**
wolf (*pl* **wolves**) [wulf, wulvz] *n* lobo
woman (*pl* **women**) ['wumən, 'wɪmɪn] *n* mujer *f*; **young ~** (mujer *f*) joven *f*; **women's page** (*Press*) sección *f* de la mujer
womanly ['wumənlɪ] *adj* femenino
womb [wuːm] *n* (*Anat*) matriz *f*, útero
women ['wɪmɪn] *npl of* **woman**
won [wʌn] *pt, pp of* **win**
wonder ['wʌndəʳ] *n* maravilla, prodigio; (*feeling*) asombro ▷ *vi*: **to ~ whether** preguntarse si; **to ~ at** asombrarse de; **to ~ about** pensar sobre *or* en; **it's no ~ that** no es de extrañar que
wonderful ['wʌndəful] *adj* maravilloso

wonky ['wɔŋkɪ] *adj* (*Brit inf: unsteady*) poco seguro, cojo; (*: broken down*) estropeado
wont [wɔnt] *n*: **as is his/her ~** como tiene por costumbre
won't [wəunt] = **will not**
woo [wu:] *vt* (*woman*) cortejar
wood [wud] *n* (*timber*) madera; (*forest*) bosque *m* ▷ *cpd* de madera
wood carving *n* tallado en madera
wooded ['wudɪd] *adj* arbolado
wooden ['wudn] *adj* de madera; (*fig*) inexpresivo
woodpecker ['wudpɛkə^r^] *n* pájaro carpintero
woodwind ['wudwɪnd] *n* (*Mus*) instrumentos *mpl* de viento de madera
woodwork ['wudwə:k] *n* carpintería
woodworm ['wudwə:m] *n* carcoma
wool [wul] *n* lana; **knitting ~** lana (de hacer punto); **to pull the ~ over sb's eyes** (*fig*) dar a algn gato por liebre
woollen, woolen (US) ['wulən] *adj* de lana ▷ *n*: **~s** géneros *mpl* de lana
woolly, wooly (US) ['wulɪ] *adj* de lana; (*fig: ideas*) confuso
woozy ['wu:zɪ] *adj* (*inf*) mareado
word [wə:d] *n* palabra; (*news*) noticia; (*promise*) palabra (de honor) ▷ *vt* redactar; **~ for ~** palabra por palabra; **what's the ~ for "pen" in Spanish?** ¿cómo se dice "pen" en español?; **to put sth into ~s** expresar algo en palabras; **to have a ~ with sb** hablar (dos palabras) con algn; **in other ~s** en otras palabras; **to break/keep one's ~** faltar a la palabra/cumplir la promesa; **to leave ~ (with/for sb) that ...** dejar recado (con/para algn) de que ...; **to have ~s with sb** (*quarrel with*) discutir *or* reñir con algn
wording ['wə:dɪŋ] *n* redacción *f*
word-of-mouth [wə:dəv'mauθ] *n*: **by** *or* **through ~** de palabra, por el boca a boca
word processing *n* procesamiento *or* tratamiento de textos
word processor [-'prəusɛsə^r^] *n* procesador *m* de textos
wore [wɔ:^r^] *pt of* **wear**
work [wə:k] *n* trabajo; (*job*) empleo, trabajo; (*Art, Lit*) obra ▷ *vi* trabajar; (*mechanism*) funcionar, marchar; (*medicine*) ser eficaz, surtir efecto ▷ *vt* (*shape*) trabajar; (*stone etc*) tallar; (*mine etc*) explotar; (*machine*) manejar, hacer funcionar; (*cause*) producir; **to go to ~** ir a trabajar *or* al trabajo; **to be at ~ (on sth)** estar trabajando (en algo); **to set to ~, start ~** ponerse a trabajar; **to be out of ~** estar parado, no tener trabajo; **his life's ~** el trabajo de su vida; **to ~ hard** trabajar mucho *or* duro; **to ~ to rule** (*Industry*) hacer una huelga de celo; **to ~ loose** (*part*) desprenderse; (*knot*) aflojarse; *see also* **works**; **work off** *vt*: **to ~ off one's feelings** desahogarse; **work on** *vt fus* trabajar en, dedicarse a; (*principle*) basarse en; **he's ~ing on the car** está reparando el coche; **work out** *vi* (*plans etc*) salir bien, funcionar; (*Sport*) hacer ejercicios ▷ *vt* (*problem*) resolver; (*plan*) elaborar; **it ~s out at £100** asciende a 100 libras; **work up** *vt*: **he ~ed his way up in the company** ascendió en la compañía mediante sus propios esfuerzos
workable ['wə:kəbl] *adj* (*solution*) práctico, factible
workaholic [wə:kə'hɔlɪk] *n* adicto(-a) al trabajo
worked up [wə:kt-] *adj*: **to get ~** excitarse
worker ['wə:kə^r^] *n* trabajador(a) *m(f)*, obrero(-a) *m(f)*; **office ~** oficinista *m/f*
work experience *n*: **I'm going to do my ~ in a factory** voy a hacer las prácticas en una fábrica
work force *n* mano *f* de obra
working class *n* clase *f* obrera ▷ *adj*: **working-class** obrero
working order *n*: **in ~** en funcionamiento
working week *n* semana laboral
workload ['wə:kləud] *n* cantidad *f* de trabajo
workman ['wə:kmən] *n* obrero
workmanship ['wə:kmənʃɪp] *n* (*art*) hechura; (*skill*) habilidad *f*
workmate ['wə:kmeɪt] *n* compañero(-a) de trabajo
work of art *n* obra de arte
workout ['wə:kaut] *n* (*Sport*) sesión *f* de ejercicios
work permit *n* permiso de trabajo
workplace ['wəkpleɪs] *n* lugar *m* de trabajo
works [wə:ks] *nsg* (*Brit: factory*) fábrica ▷ *npl* (*of clock, machine*) mecanismo; **road ~** obras *fpl*
worksheet ['wə:kʃi:t] *n* (*Comput*) hoja de trabajo; (*Scol*) hoja de ejercicios
workshop ['wə:kʃɔp] *n* taller *m*
work station *n* estación *f* de trabajo
work surface *n* encimera
worktop ['wə:ktɔp] *n* encimera
work-to-rule ['wə:ktə'ru:l] *n* (*Brit*) huelga de celo
world [wə:ld] *n* mundo ▷ *cpd* (*champion*) del mundo; (*power, war*) mundial; **all over the ~** por todo el mundo, en el mundo entero; **the business ~** el mundo de los negocios; **what in the ~ is he doing?** ¿qué diablos está haciendo?; **to think the ~ of sb** (*fig*) tener un concepto muy alto de algn; **to do sb a ~ of good** sentar muy bien a algn; **W~ War One/Two** la primera/segunda Guerra Mundial
World Cup *n* (*Football*): **the ~** el Mundial, los Mundiales
worldly ['wə:ldlɪ] *adj* mundano
World Series *n*: **the ~** (*US Baseball*) el campeonato nacional de béisbol de EEUU
World Service *n see* **BBC**
world-wide ['wə:ldwaɪd] *adj* mundial, universal
World-Wide Web *n*: **the ~** el World Wide Web

worm [wəːm] *n* gusano; (*earthworm*) lombriz *f*
worn [wɔːn] *pp of* **wear** ▷ *adj* usado
worn-out ['wɔːnaut] *adj* (*object*) gastado; (*person*) rendido, agotado
worried ['wʌrɪd] *adj* preocupado; **to be ~ about sth** estar preocupado por algo
worry ['wʌrɪ] *n* preocupación *f* ▷ *vt* preocupar, inquietar ▷ *vi* preocuparse; **to ~ about** *or* **over sth/sb** preocuparse por algo/algn
worrying ['wʌrɪɪŋ] *adj* inquietante
worse [wəːs] *adj, adv* peor ▷ *n* el peor, lo peor; **a change for the ~** un empeoramiento; **so much the ~ for you** tanto peor para ti; **he is none the ~ for it** se ha quedado tan fresco *or* tan tranquilo; **to get ~, to grow ~** empeorar
worsen ['wəːsn] *vt, vi* empeorar
worse off *adj* (*financially*): **to be ~** tener menos dinero; (*fig*): **you'll be ~ this way** de esta forma estarás peor que antes
worship ['wəːʃɪp] *n* (*organized worship*) culto; (*act*) adoración *f* ▷ *vt* adorar; **Your W~** (*Brit: to mayor*) su Ilustrísima; (*: to judge*) su señoría
worst [wəːst] *adj* (el/la) peor ▷ *adv* peor ▷ *n* lo peor; **at ~** en el peor de los casos; **to come off ~** llevar la peor parte; **if the ~ comes to the ~** en el peor de los casos
worth [wəːθ] *n* valor *m* ▷ *adj*: **to be ~** valer; **how much is it ~?** ¿cuánto vale?; **it's ~ it** vale *or* merece la pena; **to be ~ one's while (to do)** merecer la pena (hacer); **it's not ~ the trouble** no vale *or* merece la pena
worthless ['wəːθlɪs] *adj* sin valor; (*useless*) inútil
worthwhile ['wəːθwaɪl] *adj* (*activity*) que merece la pena; (*cause*) loable
worthy ['wəːðɪ] *adj* (*person*) respetable; (*motive*) honesto; **~ of** digno de

KEYWORD

would [wud] *aux vb* **1** (*conditional tense*): **if you asked him he would do it** si se lo pidieras, lo haría; **if you had asked him he would have done it** si se lo hubieras pedido, lo habría *or* hubiera hecho
2 (*in offers, invitations, requests*): **would you like a biscuit?** ¿quieres una galleta?; (*formal*) ¿querría una galleta?; **would you ask him to come in?** ¿quiere hacerle pasar?; **would you open the window please?** ¿quiere *or* podría abrir la ventana, por favor?
3 (*in indirect speech*): **I said I would do it** dije que lo haría
4 (*emphatic*): **it WOULD have to snow today!** ¡tenía que nevar precisamente hoy!
5 (*insistence*): **she wouldn't behave** no quiso comportarse bien
6 (*conjecture*): **it would have been midnight** sería medianoche; **it would seem so** parece ser que sí
7 (*indicating habit*): **he would go there on Mondays** iba allí los lunes

would-be ['wudbiː] *adj* (*pej*) presunto
wouldn't ['wudnt] = **would not**
wound[1] [wuːnd] *n* herida ▷ *vt* herir
wound[2] [waund] *pt, pp of* **wind[2]**
wove [wəuv] *pt of* **weave**
woven ['wəuvən] *pp of* **weave**
WP *n abbr* = **word processing; word processor** ▷ *abbr* (*Brit inf: = weather permitting*) si lo permite el tiempo
WPC *n abbr* (*Brit*) = **woman police constable**
wpm *abbr* (*= words per minute*) p.p.m.
wrap [ræp] *n* (*stole*) chal *m* ▷ *vt* (*also:* **~ up**) envolver; (*gift*) envolver, abrigar ▷ *vi* (*dress warmly*) abrigarse; **under ~s** (*fig: plan, scheme*) oculto, tapado
wrapper ['ræpəʳ] *n* (*Brit: of book*) sobrecubierta; (*on chocolate etc*) envoltura
wrapping paper ['ræpɪŋ-] *n* papel *m* de envolver
wrath [rɔθ] *n* cólera
wreak [riːk] *vt* (*destruction*) causar; **to ~ havoc (on)** hacer *or* causar estragos (en); **to ~ vengeance (on)** vengarse (en)
wreath (*pl* **wreaths**) [riːθ, riːðz] *n* (*also:* **funeral ~**) corona; (*of flowers*) guirnalda
wreck [rɛk] *n* (*ship: destruction*) naufragio; (*: remains*) restos *mpl* del barco; (*pej: person*) ruina ▷ *vt* destrozar; (*chances*) arruinar; **to be ~ed** (*Naut*) naufragar
wreckage ['rɛkɪdʒ] *n* (*remains*) restos *mpl*; (*of building*) escombros *mpl*
wren [rɛn] *n* (*Zool*) reyezuelo
wrench [rɛntʃ] *n* (*Tech*) llave *f* inglesa; (*tug*) tirón *m* ▷ *vt* arrancar; **to ~ sth from sb** arrebatar algo violentamente a algn
wrestle ['rɛsl] *vi*: **to ~ (with sb)** luchar (con *or* contra algn)
wrestler ['rɛsləʳ] *n* luchador(a) *m(f)* (de lucha libre)
wrestling ['rɛslɪŋ] *n* lucha libre
wretched ['rɛtʃɪd] *adj* miserable
wriggle ['rɪgl] *vi* serpentear; (*also:* **~ about**) menearse, retorcerse
wring (*pt, pp* **wrung**) [rɪŋ, rʌŋ] *vt* torcer, retorcer; (*wet clothes*) escurrir; (*fig*): **to ~ sth out of sb** sacar algo por la fuerza a algn
wrinkle ['rɪŋkl] *n* arruga ▷ *vt* arrugar ▷ *vi* arrugarse
wrist [rɪst] *n* muñeca
wrist watch *n* reloj *m* de pulsera
writ [rɪt] *n* mandato judicial; **to serve a ~ on sb** notificar un mandato judicial a algn
writable ['raɪtəbl] *adj* (*CD, DVD*) escribible
write (*pt* **wrote**, *pp* **written**) [raɪt, rəut, 'rɪtn] *vt* escribir; (*cheque*) extender ▷ *vi* escribir; **to ~ sb a letter** escribir una carta a algn; **write away** *vi*: **to ~ away for** (*information, goods*) pedir por escrito *or* carta; **write down** *vt* escribir; (*note*) apuntar; **write off** *vt* (*debt*) borrar (como incobrable); (*fig*) desechar por inútil; (*smash up: car*) destrozar; **write out** *vt* escribir; **write up** *vt* redactar

write-off ['raɪtɔf] *n* siniestro total; **the car is a ~** el coche es pura chatarra
writer ['raɪtə^r] *n* escritor(a) *m(f)*
writhe [raɪð] *vi* retorcerse
writing ['raɪtɪŋ] *n* escritura; (*handwriting*) letra; (*of author*) obras *fpl*; **in ~** por escrito; **to put sth in ~** poner algo por escrito; **in my own ~** escrito por mí
writing paper *n* papel *m* de escribir
written ['rɪtn] *pp of* **write**
wrong [rɔŋ] *adj* (*wicked*) malo; (*unfair*) injusto; (*incorrect*) equivocado, incorrecto; (*not suitable*) inoportuno, inconveniente ▷ *adv* mal ▷ *n* mal *m*; (*injustice*) injusticia ▷ *vt* ser injusto con; (*hurt*) agraviar; **to be ~** (*answer*) estar equivocado; (*in doing, saying*) equivocarse; **it's ~ to steal, stealing is ~** es mal robar; **you are ~ to do it** haces mal en hacerlo; **you are ~ about that, you've got it ~** en eso estás equivocado; **to be in the ~** no tener razón; (*guilty*) tener la culpa; **what's ~?** ¿qué pasa?; **what's ~ with the car?** ¿qué le pasa al coche?; **there's nothing ~** no pasa nada; **you have the ~ number** (*Tel*) se ha equivocado de número; **to go ~** (*person*) equivocarse; (*plan*) salir mal; (*machine*) estropearse
wrongdoer ['rɔŋduə^r] *n* malhechor(a) *m(f)*
wrong-foot [rɔŋ'fut] *vt* (*Sport*) hacer perder el equilibrio a; (*fig*) poner en un aprieto a
wrongful ['rɔŋful] *adj* injusto; **~ dismissal** (*Industry*) despido improcedente
wrongly ['rɔŋlɪ] *adv* (*answer, do, count*) incorrectamente; (*treat*) injustamente
wrong number *n* (*Tel*): **you've got the ~** se ha equivocado de número
wrote [rəut] *pt of* **write**
wrought [rɔːt] *adj*: **~ iron** hierro forjado
wrung [rʌŋ] *pt, pp of* **wring**
WRVS *n abbr* (*Brit: = Women's Royal Voluntary Service*) *cuerpo de voluntarias al servicio de la comunidad*
wry [raɪ] *adj* irónico
wt. *abbr* = **weight**
WWW *n abbr* (= *World Wide Web*) WWW *m or f*

X

X, x [eks] *n* (*letter*) X, x *f*; (*Brit Cine: formerly*) no apto para menores de 18 años; **X for Xmas** X de Xiquena; **if you earn X dollars a year** si ganas X dólares al año
X-certificate ['ɛkssə'tɪfɪkɪt] *adj* (*Brit: film: formerly*) no apto para menores de 18 años
Xerox® ['zɪərɔks] *n* (*also:* **~ machine**) fotocopiadora; (*photocopy*) fotocopia ▷ *vt* fotocopiar
XL *abbr* = **extra large**
Xmas ['ɛksməs] *n abbr* = **Christmas**
X-rated ['eks'reɪtɪd] *adj* (*US: film*) no apto para menores de 18 años
X-ray [ɛks'reɪ] *n* radiografía; **X-rays** *npl* rayos *mpl* X ▷ *vt* radiografiar
xylophone ['zaɪləfəun] *n* xilófono

y

Y, y [waɪ] *n* (*letter*) Y, y *f*; **Y for Yellow**, (*US*) **Y for Yoke** Y de Yegua
yacht [jɔt] *n* yate *m*
yachting ['jɔtɪŋ] *n* (*sport*) balandrismo
yachtsman ['jɔtsmən] *n* balandrista *m*
Yank [jæŋk], **Yankee** ['jæŋkɪ] *n* (*pej*) yanqui *m/f*
yank [jæŋk] *vt* tirar de, jalar de (*LAm*) ▷ *n* tirón *m*
yap [jæp] *vi* (*dog*) aullar
yard [jɑːd] *n* patio; (*US*: *garden*) jardín *m*; (*measure*) yarda; **builder's ~** almacén *m*
yard sale *n* (*US*) venta de objetos usados (*en el jardín de una casa particular*)
yardstick ['jɑːdstɪk] *n* (*fig*) criterio, norma
yarn [jɑːn] *n* hilo; (*tale*) cuento (chino), historia
yawn [jɔːn] *n* bostezo ▷ *vi* bostezar
yawning ['jɔːnɪŋ] *adj* (*gap*) muy abierto
yd. *abbr* (= *yard*) yda
yeah [jɛə] *adv* (*inf*) sí
year [jɪə^r] *n* año; (*Scol*, *Univ*) curso; **this ~** este año; **~ in, ~ out** año tras año; **a** *or* **per ~** al año; **to be eight ~s old** tener ocho años; **she's three ~s old** tiene tres años; **an eight-~-old child** un niño de ocho años (de edad)
yearly ['jɪəlɪ] *adj* anual ▷ *adv* anualmente, cada año; **twice ~** dos veces al año
yearn [jəːn] *vi*: **to ~ for sth** añorar algo, suspirar por algo
yeast [jiːst] *n* levadura
yell [jɛl] *n* grito, alarido ▷ *vi* gritar
yellow ['jɛləu] *adj*, *n* amarillo
Yellow Pages® *npl* páginas *fpl* amarillas
yelp [jɛlp] *n* aullido ▷ *vi* aullar
yeoman ['jəumən] *n*: **Y~ of the Guard** *alabardero de la Casa Real*
yes [jɛs] *adv*, *n* sí *m*; **to say/answer ~** decir/contestar que sí; **to say ~ (to)** decir que sí (a), conformarse (con)
yesterday ['jɛstədɪ] *adv*, *n* ayer *m*; **~ morning/evening** ayer por la mañana/tarde; **all day ~** todo el día de ayer; **the day before ~** antes de ayer, anteayer
yet [jɛt] *adv* todavía ▷ *conj* sin embargo, a pesar de todo; **~ again** de nuevo; **it is not finished ~** todavía no está acabado; **the best ~** el/la mejor hasta ahora; **as ~** hasta ahora, todavía
yew [juː] *n* tejo
Y-fronts® ['waɪfrʌnts] *npl* (*Brit*) calzoncillos *mpl*, eslip *msg* tradicional
Yiddish ['jɪdɪʃ] *n* yiddish *m*
yield [jiːld] *n* producción *f*; (*Agr*) cosecha; (*Comm*) rendimiento ▷ *vt* producir, dar; (*profit*) rendir ▷ *vi* rendirse, ceder; (*US Aut*) ceder el paso; **a ~ of 5%** un rédito del 5 por ciento
YMCA *n abbr* (= *Young Men's Christian Association*) Asociación *f* de Jóvenes Cristianos
yob ['jɔb], **yobbo** ['jɔbbəu] *n* (*Brit inf*) gamberro
yoga ['jəugə] *n* yoga *m*
yoghurt, yogurt ['jəugət] *n* yogur *m*
yoke [jəuk] *n* (*of oxen*) yunta; (*on shoulders*) balancín *m*; (*fig*) yugo ▷ *vt* (*also*: **~ together**: *oxen*) uncir
yolk [jəuk] *n* yema (de huevo)
yonder ['jɔndə^r] *adv* allá (a lo lejos)
yonks [jɔŋks] *npl* (*inf*): **I haven't seen him for ~** hace siglos que no lo veo

KEYWORD

you [juː] *pron* **1** (*subject*: *familiar*: *singular*) tú; (: *plural*) vosotros(-as) (*Sp*), ustedes (*LAm*); (*polite*) usted, ustedes *pl*; **you are very kind** eres/es *etc* muy amable; **you French enjoy your food** a vosotros (*or* ustedes) los franceses os (*or* les) gusta la comida; **you and I will go** iremos tú y yo
2 (*object*: *direct*: *familiar*: *singular*) te; (: *plural*) os (*Sp*), les (*LAm*); (*polite*: *singular masc*) lo *or* le; (: *plural masc*) los *or* les; (*singular fem*) la; (*plural fem*) las; **I know you** te/le *etc* conozco
3 (*object*: *indirect*: *familiar*: *singular*) te; (: *plural*) os (*Sp*), les (*LAm*); (*polite*) le, les *pl*; **I gave the letter to you yesterday** te/os *etc* di la carta ayer
4 (*stressed*): **I told YOU to do it** te dije a ti que lo hicieras, es a ti a quien dije que lo hicieras; *see also* **3, 5**
5 (*after prep*: *NB*: *con +ti = contigo*: *familiar*: *singular*) ti; (: *plural*) vosotros(-as) (*Sp*), ustedes (*LAm*); (*polite*) usted, ustedes *pl*; **it's for you** es para ti/vosotros *etc*

6 (*comparisons*: *familiar*: *singular*) tú; (: *plural*) vosotros(-as) (*Sp*), ustedes (*LAm*); (*polite*) usted, ustedes *pl*; **she's younger than you** es más joven que tú/vosotros *etc*
7 (*impersonal*: *one*): **fresh air does you good** el aire puro (te) hace bien; **you never know** nunca se sabe; **you can't do that!** ¡eso no se hace!

you'd [ju:d] = **you had**; **you would**
you'll [ju:l] = **you will**; **you shall**
young [jʌŋ] *adj* joven ▷ *npl* (*of animal*) cría; (*people*): **the ~** los jóvenes, la juventud; **a ~ man/lady** un(a) joven; **my ~er brother** mi hermano menor *or* pequeño; **the ~er generation** la nueva generación
youngster ['jʌŋstəʳ] *n* joven *m/f*
your [jɔːʳ] *adj* tu, vuestro *pl*; (*formal*) su; **~ house** tu *etc* casa; *see also* **my**
you're [juəʳ] = **you are**
yours [jɔːz] *pron* tuyo, vuestro *pl*; (*formal*) suyo; **a friend of ~** un amigo tuyo *etc*; *see also* **faithfully**; **mine**; **sincerely**
yourself [jɔː'sɛlf] *pron* (*reflexive*) tú mismo; (*complement*) te; (*after prep*) ti (mismo); (*formal*) usted mismo; (: *complement*) se; (: *after prep*) sí (mismo); **you ~ told me** me lo dijiste tú mismo; **(all) by ~** sin ayuda de nadie, solo; *see also* **oneself**
yourselves [jɔː'sɛlvz] *pron pl* vosotros mismos; (*after prep*) vosotros (mismos); (*formal*) ustedes (mismos); (: *complement*) se; (: *after prep*) sí mismos
youth [ju:θ] *n* juventud *f*; (*young man*) (*pl* **youths**) [ju:ðz] joven *m*; **in my ~** en mi juventud
youth club *n* club *m* juvenil
youthful ['ju:θful] *adj* juvenil
youth hostel *n* albergue *m* juvenil
you've [ju:v] = **you have**
yr *abbr* (= *year*) a
Yugoslav ['ju:gəuslɑ:v] *adj*, *n* yugoslavo(-a) *m(f)*
Yugoslavia [ju:gəu'slɑ:vɪə] *n* Yugoslavia
yuppie ['jʌpɪ] (*inf*) *adj*, *n* yuppie *m/f*
YWCA *n abbr* (= *Young Women's Christian Association*) Asociación *f* de Jóvenes Cristianas

Z

Z, z [zɛd, (*US*) zi:] *n* (*letter*) Z, z *f*; **Z for Zebra** Z de Zaragoza
zany ['zeɪnɪ] *adj* estrafalario
zap [zæp] *vt* (*Comput*) borrar
zeal [zi:l] *n* celo, entusiasmo
zebra ['zi:brə] *n* cebra
zebra crossing *n* (*Brit*) paso de peatones
zero ['zɪərəu] *n* cero; **5 degrees below ~** 5 grados bajo cero
zest [zɛst] *n* ánimo, vivacidad *f*; (*of orange*) piel *f*; **~ for living** brío
zigzag ['zɪgzæg] *n* zigzag *m* ▷ *vi* zigzaguear
Zimbabwe [zɪm'bɑ:bwɪ] *n* Zimbabwe *m*
Zimmer® ['zɪməʳ] *n* (*also*: **~ frame**) andador *m*, andaderas *fpl*
zinc [zɪŋk] *n* cinc *m*, zinc *m*
zip [zɪp] *n* (*also*: **~ fastener**, *US*: *also*: **~per**) cremallera, cierre *m* relámpago (*LAm*); (*energy*) energía, vigor *m* ▷ *vt* (*Comput*) comprimir; (*also*: **~ up**) cerrar la cremallera de ▷ *vi*: **to ~ along to the shops** ir de compras volando
zip code *n* (*US*) código postal
zip file *n* (*Comput*) archivo *m* comprimido
zipper [zɪpəʳ] *n* (*US*) cremallera
zit [zɪt] *n* grano
zodiac ['zəudɪæk] *n* zodíaco
zombie ['zɔmbɪ] *n* zombi *m*
zone [zəun] *n* zona
zonked [zɔŋkt] *adj* (*inf*) hecho polvo
zoo [zu:] *n* zoo, (parque *m*) zoológico
zoologist [zu'ɔlədʒɪst] *n* zoólogo(-a)

zoology [zuːˈɔlədʒɪ] *n* zoología
zoom [zuːm] *vi*: **to ~ past** pasar zumbando; **to ~ in (on sth/sb)** (*Phot*, *Cine*) enfocar (algo/ a algn) con el zoom
zoom lens *n* zoom *m*
zucchini [zuːˈkiːnɪ] *n(pl)* (*US*) calabacín(-ines) *m(pl)*

Grammar
Gramática

Using the grammar

The Grammar section deals systematically and comprehensively with all the information you will need in order to communicate accurately in Spanish. The numbers, → ❶ etc, direct you to the relevant example in every case.

Abbreviations

cond.	*conditional*
fem.	*feminine*
masc.	*masculine*
plur.	*plural*
sing.	*singular*
subj.	*subjunctive*
sb	somebody
sth	something

Contents

Glossary

VERBS

VERB a 'doing' word which describes what someone or something does, is, or what happens to them, for example, *be, sing, live*.

ACTIVE a form of the verb that is used when the subject of the verb is the person or thing doing the action.

AGREE (to) in the case of adjectives and pronouns, to have the correct word ending or form according to whether what is referred to is masculine, feminine, singular or plural; in the case of verbs, to have the form which goes with the person or thing carrying out the action.

AUXILIARY VERB a verb such as *be, have* or *do* used with a main verb to form tenses and questions.

BASE FORM the form of the verb without any endings added to it.

CONDITIONAL a verb form used to talk about things that would happen or would be true under certain conditions, for example, *I would help you if I could*. It is also used to say what you would like or need, for example, *Could you give me the bill?*

CONJUGATE (to) to give a verb different endings according to whether you are referring to *I, you, they* and so on, and according to whether you are referring to the present, past or future.

CONJUGATION a group of verbs which have the same endings as each other or change according to the same pattern.

CONTINUOUS TENSE a verb tense formed using *to be* and the *-ing* form of the main verb.

DIRECT OBJECT a noun or pronoun used with verbs to show who or what is acted on by the verb. For example, in *He wrote a letter*, *letter* is the direct object.

ENDING a form added to a verb, for example, *go* → *goes*, and to adjectives, nouns and pronouns depending on whether they refer to masculine, feminine, singular or plural things or persons.

FUTURE a verb tense used to talk about something that will happen or will be true.

GERUND a verb form in English ending in *-ing*, for example, *eating, sleeping*.

IMPERATIVE the form of a verb used when giving orders and instructions, for example, *Shut the door!*

IMPERFECT one of the verb tenses used to talk about the past, especially in descriptions, and to say what was happening or used to happen, for example, *It was sunny at the weekend*.

IMPERSONAL VERB a verb whose subject is *it*, but where the *it* does not refer to any specific thing, for example, *It's raining; It's 10 o'clock*.

INDICATIVE ordinary verb forms that aren't subjunctive, such as the present.

INDIRECT OBJECT a noun or pronoun used with verbs to show who benefits or is harmed by an action. For example, in *I gave the carrot to the rabbit*, *the rabbit* is the indirect object and *the carrot* is the direct object.

INFINITIVE a form of the verb that hasn't any endings added to it and doesn't relate to any particular tense. In English the infinitive is usually shown with *to*, as in *to speak, to eat*.

INTRANSITIVE VERB a type of verb that does not take a direct object, for example, *to sleep, to rise, to swim*.

IRREGULAR VERB a verb whose forms do not follow a general pattern.

OBJECT a noun or pronoun which refers to a person or thing that is affected by the action described by the verb.

PASSIVE a form of the verb that is used when the subject of the verb is the person or thing that is affected by the action, for example, *we were told*.

PAST PARTICIPLE a verb form which is used to form perfect and pluperfect tenses and passives, for example, *watched, swum*.

PAST PERFECT see **pluperfect**.

PERFECT a verb form used to talk about what has or hasn't happened, for example, *I've broken my glasses*.

PERSON one of the three classes: the first person (*I, we*), the second person (*you* singular and *you* plural), and the third person (*he, she, it* and *they*).

PLUPERFECT one of the verb tenses used to describe something that had happened or had been true at a point in the past.

PRESENT a verb form used to talk about what is true at the moment, what happens regularly, and what is happening now, for example, *I'm a student; I'm studying languages*.

PRESENT PARTICIPLE a verb form in English ending in *-ing*, for example, *eating, sleeping*.

REFLEXIVE VERB a verb where the subject and object are the same, and where the action 'reflects back' on the subject. A reflexive verb is used with a reflexive pronoun such as *myself*, for example, *I washed myself*.

REGULAR VERB a verb whose forms follow a general pattern or the normal rules.

SIMPLE TENSE a verb tense in which the verb form is made up of one word, rather than being formed from *to have* and a past participle or *to be* and an *–ing* form; for example, *She wrote a book*.

STEM the main part of a verb to which endings are added.

SUBJECT a noun or pronoun that refers to the person or thing doing the action or being in the state described by the verb, for example, *My cat doesn't drink milk*.

SUBJUNCTIVE a verb form used in certain circumstances to indicate some sort of feeling, or to show doubt about whether something will happen or whether something is true. It is only used occasionally in modern English, for example, *If I were you*.

TENSE the form of a verb which shows whether you are referring to the past, present or future.

TRANSITIVE VERB a type of verb that takes a direct object, for example, *to spend*.

NOUNS

NOUN a 'naming' word for a living being, thing or idea, for example, *woman, desk, happiness, Andrew*.

FEMININE a form of noun, pronoun or adjective that is used to refer to a living being, thing or idea that is not classed as masculine.

GENDER whether a noun, pronoun or adjective is feminine or masculine.

MASCULINE a form of noun, pronoun or adjective that is used to refer to a living being, thing or idea that is not classed as feminine.

NOUN GROUP, NOUN PHRASE a word or group of words that acts as the subject or object of a verb, or as the object of a preposition, for example, *my older sister; the man next door*.

PLURAL the form of a word which is used to refer to more than one person or thing.

SINGULAR the form of a word which is used to refer to one person or thing.

ARTICLES

ARTICLE a word like *the, a* and *an*, which is used in front of a noun.

DEFINITE ARTICLE the word *the*.

INDEFINITE ARTICLE the words *a* and *an*.

ADJECTIVES

ADJECTIVE a 'describing' word that tells you more about a person or thing, such as their appearance, colour, size or other qualities.

COMPARATIVE an adjective or adverb with *-er* on the end of it or *more* or *less* in front of it that is used to compare people, things or actions.

INVARIABLE used to describe a form which does not change.

SUPERLATIVE an adjective or adverb with *-est* on the end of it or *most* or *least* in front of it that is used to compare people, things or actions.

PRONOUNS

PRONOUN a word which you use instead of a noun, when you do not need or want to name someone or something directly, for example, *it, you, none*.

REFLEXIVE PRONOUN a word ending in *-self* or *-selves*, such as *myself* or *themselves*, which refers back to the subject, for example, *He hurt himself*.

ADVERBS

ADVERB a word usually used with verbs, adjectives or other adverbs that gives more information about when, where, how or in what circumstances something happens or to what degree something is true.

COMPARATIVE an adjective or adverb with *-er* on the end of it or *more* or *less* in front of it that is used to compare people, things or actions.

SUPERLATIVE an adjective or adverb with *-est* on the end of it or *most* or *least* in front of it that is used to compare people, things or actions.

PREPOSITIONS

PREPOSITION a word such as *at, for, with, into* or *from*, which is usually followed by a noun, pronoun or, in English, a word ending in *-ing*. Prepositions show how people and things relate to the rest of the sentence, for example, *She's at home*.

CONJUNCTIONS

CONJUNCTION a word such as *and, because* or *but* that links two words or phrases of a similar type or two parts of a sentence.

NEGATIVES

NEGATIVE a question or statement which contains a word such as *not, never* or *nothing*, and is used to say that something is not happening, is not true or is absent, for example, *I never eat meat*.

QUESTIONS

QUESTION a sentence which is used to ask someone about something and which normally has a verb in front of the subject, for example, *Where are you going?*

Verbs

Simple Tenses: Formation of Regular Verbs

Simple tenses are one-word tenses formed by adding endings to a stem. The different endings identify the subject of the verb. The stem and endings of regular verbs are totally predictable. For irregular verbs see page 42 onwards.

First Conjugation

First conjugation verbs end in **-ar** e.g. **hablar** *to speak*. For the present, imperfect, preterite, present subjunctive and imperfect subjunctive, the stem is the infinitive minus **-ar** (e.g. **habl-**). For the future and conditional the stem is the infinitive (e.g. **hablar**-).

To the appropriate stem add the following endings:

		❶ PRESENT	❷ IMPERFECT	❸ PRETERITE
	1st person	**-o**	**-aba**	**-é**
sing.	2nd person	**-as**	**-abas**	**-aste**
	3rd person	**-a**	**-aba**	**-ó**
	1st person	**-amos**	**-ábamos**	**-amos**
plur.	2nd person	**-áis**	**-abais**	**-asteis**
	3rd person	**-an**	**-aban**	**-aron**

		❹ PRESENT SUBJUNCTIVE	❺ IMPERFECT SUBJUNCTIVE
	1st person	**-e**	**-ara** *or* **-ase**
sing.	2nd person	**-es**	**-aras** *or* **-ases**
	3rd person	**-e**	**-ara** *or* **-ase**
	1st person	**-emos**	**-áramos** *or* **-ásemos**
plur.	2nd person	**-éis**	**-arais** *or* **-aseis**
	3rd person	**-en**	**-aran** *or* **-asen**

		❻ FUTURE	❼ CONDITIONAL
	1st person	**-é**	**-ía**
sing.	2nd person	**-ás**	**-ías**
	3rd person	**-á**	**-ía**
	1st person	**-emos**	**-íamos**
plur.	2nd person	**-éis**	**-íais**
	3rd person	**-án**	**-ían**

Examples

	❶ PRESENT	❷ IMPERFECT	❸ PRETERITE
(yo)	habl**o**	habl**aba**	habl**é**
(tú)	habl**as**	habl**abas**	habl**aste**
(él/ella/Vd)	habl**a**	habl**aba**	habl**ó**
(nosotros/as)	habl**amos**	habl**ábamos**	habl**amos**
(vosotros/as)	habl**áis**	habl**abais**	habl**asteis**
(ellos/as/Vds)	habl**an**	habl**aban**	habl**aron**

	❹ PRESENT SUBJUNCTIVE	❺ IMPERFECT SUBJUNCTIVE
(yo)	habl**e**	habl**ara** *or* habl**ase**
(tú)	habl**es**	habl**aras** *or* habl**ases**
(él/ella/Vd)	habl**e**	habl**ara** *or* habl**ase**
(nosotros/as)	habl**emos**	habl**áramos** *or* habl**ásemos**
(vosotros/as)	habl**éis**	habl**arais** *or* habl**aseis**
(ellos/as/Vds)	habl**en**	habl**aran** *or* habl**asen**

	❻ FUTURE	❼ CONDITIONAL
(yo)	hablar**é**	hablar**ía**
(tú)	hablar**ás**	hablar**ías**
(él/ella/Vd)	hablar**á**	hablar**ía**
(nosotros/as)	hablar**emos**	hablar**íamos**
(vosotros/as)	hablar**éis**	hablar**íais**
(ellos/as/Vds)	hablar**án**	hablar**ían**

Note that the subject pronouns appear in brackets because they are not normally necessary in Spanish (see page 96).

Verbs

Simple Tenses: Second Conjugation

Second conjugation verbs end in **-er** e.g. **comer** to eat. For the present, imperfect, preterite, present subjunctive and imperfect subjunctive, the stem is the infinitive minus **-er** (e.g. **com-**). For irregular verbs see 42. For the future and conditional the stem is the infinitive (e.g. **comer-**).

To the appropriate stem add the following endings:

		❶ PRESENT	❷ IMPERFECT	❸ PRETERITE
sing.	1st person	**-o**	**-ía**	**-í**
	2nd person	**-es**	**-ías**	**-iste**
	3rd person	**-e**	**-ía**	**-ió**
plur.	1st person	**-emos**	**-íamos**	**-imos**
	2nd person	**-éis**	**-íais**	**-isteis**
	3rd person	**-en**	**-ían**	**-ieron**

		❹ PRESENT SUBJUNCTIVE	❺ IMPERFECT SUBJUNCTIVE
sing.	1st person	**-a**	**-iera** *or* **-iese**
	2nd person	**-as**	**-ieras** *or* **-ieses**
	3rd person	**-a**	**-iera** *or* **-iese**
plur.	1st person	**-amos**	**-iéramos** *or* **-iésemos**
	2nd person	**-áis**	**-ierais** *or* **-ieseis**
	3rd person	**-an**	**-ieran** *or* **-iesen**

		❻ FUTURE	❼ CONDITIONAL
sing.	1st person	**-é**	**-ía**
	2nd person	**-ás**	**-ías**
	3rd person	**-á**	**-ía**
plur.	1st person	**-emos**	**-íamos**
	2nd person	**-éis**	**-íais**
	3rd person	**-án**	**-ían**

Examples

	❶ PRESENT	❷ IMPERFECT	❸ PRETERITE
(yo)	com**o**	com**ía**	com**í**
(tú)	com**es**	com**ías**	com**iste**
(él/ella/Vd)	com**e**	com**ía**	com**ió**
(nosotros/as)	com**emos**	com**íamos**	com**imos**
(vosotros/as)	com**éis**	com**íais**	com**isteis**
(ellos/as/Vds)	com**en**	com**ían**	com**ieron**

	❹ PRESENT SUBJUNCTIVE	❺ IMPERFECT SUBJUNCTIVE
(yo)	com**a**	com**iera** *or* com**iese**
(tú)	com**as**	com**ieras** *or* com**ieses**
(él/ella/Vd)	com**a**	com**iera** *or* com**iese**
(nosotros/as)	com**amos**	com**iéramos** *or* com**iésemos**
(vosotros/as)	com**áis**	com**ierais** *or* com**ieseis**
(ellos/as/Vds)	com**an**	com**ieran** *or* com**iesen**

	❻ FUTURE	❼ CONDITIONAL
(yo)	comer**é**	comer**ía**
(tú)	comer**ás**	comer**ías**
(él/ella/Vd)	comer**á**	comer**ía**
(nosotros/as)	comer**emos**	comer**íamos**
(vosotros/as)	comer**éis**	comer**íais**
(ellos/as/Vds)	comer**án**	comer**ían**

Note that the subject pronouns appear in brackets because they are not normally necessary in Spanish (see page 96).

Verbs

Simple Tenses: Third Conjugation

Third conjugation verbs end in **-ir** e.g. **vivir** to live. For the present, imperfect, preterite, present subjunctive and imperfect subjunctive the stem is the infinitive minus **-ir** (e.g. **viv-**). For irregular verbs see 42. For the future and conditional the stem is the infinitive (e.g. **vivir-**).

To the appropriate stem add the following endings:

		❶ PRESENT	❷ IMPERFECT	❸ PRETERITE
	1st person	**-o**	**-ía**	**-í**
sing.	2nd person	**-es**	**-ías**	**-iste**
	3rd person	**-e**	**-ía**	**-ió**
	1st person	**-imos**	**-íamos**	**-imos**
plur.	2nd person	**-ís**	**-íais**	**-isteis**
	3rd person	**-en**	**-ían**	**-ieron**

		❹ PRESENT SUBJUNCTIVE	❺ IMPERFECT SUBJUNCTIVE
	1st person	**-a**	**-iera** *or* **-iese**
sing.	2nd person	**-as**	**-ieras** *or* **-ieses**
	3rd person	**-a**	**-iera** *or* **-iese**
	1st person	**-amos**	**-iéramos** *or* **-iésemos**
plur.	2nd person	**-áis**	**-ierais** *or* **-ieseis**
	3rd person	**-an**	**-ieran** *or* **-iesen**

		❻ FUTURE	❼ CONDITIONAL
	1st person	**-é**	**-ía**
sing.	2nd person	**-ás**	**-ías**
	3rd person	**-á**	**-ía**
	1st person	**-emos**	**-íamos**
plur.	2nd person	**-éis**	**-íais**
	3rd person	**-án**	**-ían**

Examples

	❶ PRESENT	❷ IMPERFECT	❸ PRETERITE
(yo)	viv**o**	viv**ía**	viv**í**
(tú)	viv**es**	viv**ías**	viv**iste**
(él/ella/Vd)	viv**e**	viv**ía**	viv**ió**
(nosotros/as)	viv**imos**	viv**íamos**	viv**imos**
(vosotros/as)	viv**ís**	viv**íais**	viv**isteis**
(ellos/as/Vds)	viv**en**	viv**ían**	viv**ieron**

	❹ PRESENT SUBJUNCTIVE	❺ IMPERFECT SUBJUNCTIVE
(yo)	viv**a**	viv**iera** *or* viv**iese**
(tú)	viv**as**	viv**ieras** *or* viv**ieses**
(él/ella/Vd)	viv**a**	viv**iera** *or* viv**iese**
(nosotros/as)	viv**amos**	viv**iéramos** *or* viv**iésemos**
(vosotros/as)	viv**áis**	viv**ierais** *or* viv**ieseis**
(ellos/as/Vds)	viv**an**	viv**ieran** *or* viv**iesen**

	❻ FUTURE	❼ CONDITIONAL
(yo)	vivir**é**	vivir**ía**
(tú)	vivir**ás**	vivir**ías**
(él/ella/Vd)	vivir**á**	vivir**ía**
(nosotros/as)	vivir**emos**	vivir**íamos**
(vosotros/as)	vivir**éis**	vivir**íais**
(ellos/as/Vds)	vivir**án**	vivir**ían**

Note that the subject pronouns appear in brackets because they are not normally necessary in Spanish (see page 96).

Verbs

The Imperative

The imperative is the form of the verb used to give commands or orders. It can be used politely, as in English 'Shut the door, please'.

In *positive* commands, the imperative forms for **Vd**, **Vds** and **nosotros** are the same as the subjunctive. The other forms are as follows:

tú (same as 3rd person singular present indicative in regular verbs)
vosotros (final **-r** of infinitive changes to **-d** in regular verbs) → ❶

(tú)	**habla** speak	**come** eat	**vive** live
(Vd)	**hable** speak	**coma** eat	**viva** live
(nosotros)	**hablemos** let's speak	**comamos** let's eat	**vivamos** let's live
(vosotros)	**hablad** speak	**comed** eat	**vivid** live
(Vds)	**hablen** speak	**coman** eat	**vivan** live

In *negative* commands, all the imperative forms are exactly the same as the present subjunctive.

Position of object pronouns with the imperative:

- in *positive* commands: they follow the verb and are attached to it. An accent may be needed to show the stress (see page 127 . The **nosotros** form drops the final **-s** before the pronoun **se** → ❷
- in *negative* commands: they precede the verb → ❸

For reflexive verbs – e.g. **levantarse** to get up – the object pronoun is the reflexive pronoun. An accent may be needed to show the stress (see page 127). The **nosotros** and **vosotros** forms also drop the final **-s** and **-d** respectively before the pronouns **nos** and **os** → ❹

BUT: **idos (vosotros)** go

ⓘ Note: For general instructions, the infinitive is used instead of the imperative → ❺

Examples

1	cantar	to sing
	cantad	sing
2	Perdóneme	Excuse me
	Enviémoselos	Let's send them to him/her/them
	Elíjanos	Choose us
	Explíquemelo	Explain it to me
	Esperémosla	Let's wait for her/it
	Devuélvaselo	Give it back to him/her/them
3	No me molestes	Don't disturb me
	No se la devolvamos	Let's not give it back to him/her/them
	No les castiguemos	Let's not punish them
	No me lo mandes	Don't send it to me
	No las conteste	Don't answer them
	No nos lo hagan	Don't do it to us
4	Levántate Get up	No te levantes Don't get up
	Levántese (Vd) Get up	No se levante (Vd) Don't get up
	Levantémonos Let's get up	No nos levantemos Let's not get up
	Levantaos Get up	No os levantéis Don't get up
	Levántense (Vds) Get up	No se levanten (Vds) Don't get up
5	Ver pág ...	See page ...
	No pasar	Do not pass

For the order of object pronouns, see page 100.

Compound Tenses: Formation of Regular Verbs

In Spanish the compound tenses of both regular and irregular verbs are formed using the past participle of the main verb together with the auxiliary verb **haber**. See opposite for the compound tenses of **hablar** as an example.

The Past Participle

For all compound tenses you need to know how to form the past participle of the verb. For regular verbs this is as follows:

First conjugation: replace the **-ar** of the infinitive by **-ado**
(e.g. **cantar** *to sing* → **cantado** *sung*)

Second conjugation: replace the **-er** of the infinitive by **-ido**
(e.g. **comer** *to eat* → **comido** *eaten*)

Third conjugation: replace the **-ir** of the infinitive by **-ido**
(e.g. **vivir** *to live* → **vivido** *lived*)

The past participle of irregular verbs is given for each verb in the verb tables, pages 42 to 76.

Examples

	PERFECT (have/has spoken)	PLUPERFECT (had spoken)
(yo)	**he** habl**ado**	**había** habl**ado**
(tú)	**has** habl**ado**	**habías** habl**ado**
(él/ella/Vd)	**ha** habl**ado**	**había** habl**ado**
(nosotros/as)	**hemos** habl**ado**	**habíamos** habl**ado**
(vosotros/as)	**habéis** habl**ado**	**habíais** habl**ado**
(ellos/as/Vds)	**han** habl**ado**	**habían** habl**ado**

	FUTURE PERFECT (shall/will have spoken)	CONDITIONAL PERFECT (would have spoken)
(yo)	**habré** habl**ado**	**habría** habl**ado**
(tú)	**habrás** habl**ado**	**habrías** habl**ado**
(él/ella/Vd)	**habrá** habl**ado**	**habría** habl**ado**
(nosotros/as)	**habremos** habl**ado**	**habríamos** habl**ado**
(vosotros/as)	**habréis** habl**ado**	**habríais** habl**ado**
(ellos/as/Vds)	**habrán** habl**ado**	**habrían** habl**ado**

	PAST ANTERIOR (had spoken)	PERFECT SUBJUNCTIVE (have spoken/spoke)
(yo)	**hube** habl**ado**	**haya** habl**ado**
(tú)	**hubiste** habl**ado**	**hayas** habl**ado**
(él/ella/Vd)	**hubo** habl**ado**	**haya** habl**ado**
(nosotros/as)	**hubimos** habl**ado**	**hayamos** habl**ado**
(vosotros/as)	**hubisteis** habl**ado**	**hayáis** habl**ado**
(ellos/as/Vds)	**hubieron** habl**ado**	**hayan** habl**ado**

	PLUPERFECT SUBJUNCTIVE (had spoken)
(yo)	**hubiera** *or* **hubiese** habl**ado**
(tú)	**hubieras** *or* **hubieses** habl**ado**
(él/ella/Vd)	**hubiera** *or* **hubiese** habl**ado**
(nosotros/as)	**hubiéramos** *or* **hubiésemos** habl**ado**
(vosotros/as)	**hubierais** *or* **hubieseis** habl**ado**
(ellos/as/Vds)	**hubieran** *or* **hubiesen** habl**ado**

Verbs

Reflexive Verbs

A reflexive verb is one accompanied by a reflexive pronoun. The infinitive of a reflexive verb ends with the pronoun **se**, which is added to the verb form e.g. **lavarse** to wash (oneself).
The pronouns are:

	SINGULAR	PLURAL
1st person	**me**	**nos**
2nd person	**te**	**os**
3rd person	**se**	**se**

The reflexive pronoun is not always translated in English → ❶

The plural pronouns are sometimes translated as 'one another', 'each other' (the *reciprocal* meaning). The reciprocal meaning may be emphasized by **el uno al otro/la una a la otra** etc. → ❷

Reflexive verbs are conjugated in the same way as non-reflexive verbs, but see page 12 for an ending change needed in the imperative.

Position of reflexive pronouns

The pronoun comes before the verb, except with the infinitive, gerund and positive commands, when it is attached to the end of the verb (but see also page 98). → ❸

Use of reflexive verbs

Verbs can often be used both reflexively and non-reflexively but with a different but closely related meaning. → ❹

Often a reflexive verb can be used to avoid the passive (see page 20) or in impersonal expressions (see page 22) → ❺

Examples

1	Me visto	I'm dressing (myself)
	Nos lavamos	We're washing (ourselves)
	Se levanta	He gets up
2	Nos queremos	We love each other
	Se parecen	They resemble one another
	Se miraban el uno al otro	They were looking at each other
3	¿Cómo se llama Vd?	What is your name?
	No se ha despertado	He hasn't woken up
	No te levantes	Don't get up
	Quiero irme	I want to go away
	Estoy levantándome	I am getting up
	Siéntense	Sit down
	Vámonos	Let's go
4	NON-REFLEXIVE	REFLEXIVE
	caer to fall	caerse to fall down (by accident)
	dormir to sleep	dormirse to go to sleep
	enfadar to annoy	enfadarse to get annoyed
	hacer to make	hacerse to become
	ir to go	irse to leave, go away
	lavar to wash	lavarse to get washed
	levantar to raise	levantarse to get up
	llamar to call	llamarse to be called
	morir to die, be killed (by accident or on purpose)	morirse to die (from natural causes)
	vestir to dress (someone)	vestirse to get dressed
	volver to return	volverse to turn round
5	Se perdió la batalla	The battle was lost
	No se veían las casas	The houses could not be seen
	Se dice que ...	(It is said that) People say that ...
	No se puede entrar	You/One can't go in
	No se permite	It is not allowed

Reflexive Verbs *continued*

Conjugation of: **lavarse** to wash (oneself)

1 SIMPLE TENSES

	PRESENT	IMPERFECT
(yo)	**me** lav**o**	**me** lav**aba**
(tú)	**te** lav**as**	**te** lav**abas**
(él/ella/Vd)	**se** lav**a**	**se** lav**aba**
(nosotros/as)	**nos** lav**amos**	**nos** lav**ábamos**
(vosotros/as)	**os** lav**áis**	**os** lav**abais**
(ellos/as/Vds)	**se** lav**an**	**se** lav**aban**

	FUTURE	CONDITIONAL
(yo)	**me** lavar**é**	**me** lavar**ía**
(tú)	**te** lavar**ás**	**te** lavar**ías**
(él/ella/Vd)	**se** lavar**á**	**se** lavar**ía**
(nosotros/as)	**nos** lavar**emos**	**nos** lavar**íamos**
(vosotros/as)	**os** lavar**éis**	**os** lavar**íais**
(ellos/as/Vds)	**se** lavar**án**	**se** lavar**ían**

	PRETERITE	PRESENT SUBJUNCTIVE
(yo)	**me** lav**é**	**me** lav**e**
(tú)	**te** lav**aste**	**te** lav**es**
(él/ella/Vd)	**se** lav**ó**	**se** lav**e**
(nosotros/as)	**nos** lav**amos**	**nos** lav**emos**
(vosotros/as)	**os** lav**asteis**	**os** lav**éis**
(ellos/as/Vds)	**se** lav**aron**	**se** lav**en**

	IMPERFECT SUBJUNCTIVE
(yo)	**me** lav**ara** *or* lav**ase**
(tú)	**te** lav**aras** *or* lav**ases**
(él/ella/Vd)	**se** lav**ara** *or* lav**ase**
(nosotros/as)	**nos** lav**áramos** *or* lav**ásemos**
(vosotros/as)	**os** lav**arais** *or* lav**aseis**
(ellos/as/Vds)	**se** lav**aran** *or* lav**asen**

Examples

Reflexive Verbs *continued*

Conjugation of: **lavarse** to wash (oneself)

2 COMPOUND TENSES

	PERFECT	PLUPERFECT
(yo)	**me he** lav**ado**	**me había** lav**ado**
(tú)	**te has** lav**ado**	**te habías** lav**ado**
(él/ella/Vd)	**se ha** lav**ado**	**se había** lav**ado**
(nosotros/as)	**nos hemos** lav**ado**	**nos habíamos** lav**ado**
(vosotros/as)	**os habéis** lav**ado**	**os habíais** lav**ado**
(ellos/as/Vds)	**se han** lav**ado**	**se habían** lav**ado**

	FUTURE PERFECT	PAST ANTERIOR
(yo)	**me habré** lav**ado**	**me hube** lav**ado**
(tú)	**te habrás** lav**ado**	**te hubiste** lav**ado**
(él/ella/Vd)	**se habrá** lav**ado**	**se hubo** lav**ado**
(nosotros/as)	**nos habremos** lav**ado**	**nos hubimos** lav**ado**
(vosotros/as)	**os habréis** lav**ado**	**os hubisteis** lav**ado**
(ellos/as/Vds)	**se habrán** lav**ado**	**se hubieron** lav**ado**

	PERFECT SUBJUNCTIVE
(yo)	**me haya** lav**ado**
(tú)	**te hayas** lav**ado**
(él/ella/Vd)	**se haya** lav**ado**
(nosotros/as)	**nos hayamos** lav**ado**
(vosotros/as)	**os hayáis** lav**ado**
(ellos/as/Vds)	**se hayan** lav**ado**

	PLUPERFECT SUBJUNCTIVE
(yo)	**me hubiera** *or* **hubiese** lav**ado**
(tú)	**te hubieras** *or* **hubieses** lav**ado**
(él/ella/Vd)	**se hubiera** *or* **hubiese** lav**ado**
(nosotros/as)	**nos hubiéramos** *or* **hubiésemos** lav**ado**
(vosotros/as)	**os hubierais** *or* **hubieseis** lav**ado**
(ellos/as/Vds)	**se hubieran** *or* **hubiesen** lav**ado**

Verbs

The Passive

In the passive, the subject of the verb receives the action (e.g. *I was hit*) instead of performing it (e.g. *I hit the ball*).

In the same way that English uses 'to be' with the past participle to form the passive, Spanish uses a tense of **ser** with the past participle, which agrees in number and gender with the subject → ❶

The word that corresponds to 'by' in Spanish passive sentences is **por** → ❷

Whereas in English an active sentence with an indirect object can be made into two passive sentences (e.g. active = *His mother gave him the book*; passive: *The book was given to him by his mother* or *He was given the book by his mother*), in Spanish only the direct object of an active verb can become the subject of a passive one → ❸

Less common in Spanish than English, the passive is used where the identity of the agent is unknown or unimportant → ❹

Otherwise, active constructions are generally preferred, such as specifying the subject or using the 3rd person plural (equivalent to 'they') → ❺

When the action of the sentence is performed on a person, the reflexive form of the verb can be used in the 3rd person singular, and the person becomes the object → ❻

When the action is performed on a thing, this becomes the subject of the sentence and the verb is made reflexive, agreeing in number with the subject → ❼

Examples

❶	Pablo ha sido despedido	Paul has been sacked
	Su madre era muy admirada	His mother was greatly admired
	El palacio será vendido	The palace will be sold
	Las puertas habían sido cerradas	The doors had been closed
❷	La casa fue diseñada por mi hermano	The house was designed by my brother
❸	Su madre le regaló el libro	His mother gave him the book
	BECOMES:	
	El libro le fue regalado por su madre	The book was given to him by his mother
❹	La ciudad fue conquistada tras un largo asedio	The city was conquered after a long siege
	Ha sido declarado el estado de excepción	A state of emergency has been declared
❺	La policía interrogó al sospechoso	The suspect was questioned by the police
	RATHER THAN:	
	El sospechoso fue interrogado por la policía	
	Usan demasiada publicidad en la televisión	Too much advertising is used on television
❻	Últimamente no se lo/los ha visto mucho en público	He has/They have not been seen much in public recently
❼	Esta palabra ya no se usa	This word is no longer used
	Todos los libros se han vendido	All the books have been sold

Verbs

Verbal Idioms

Although we think of **gustar** as meaning *to like*, the way it is used is more like *to be pleasing to*, as the subject of the verb is the thing that pleases and it is used with an indirect object → ❶

Other Spanish verbs and expressions behave similarly → ❷

Impersonal Verbs

Spanish impersonal verbs are used only in the infinitive, the gerund, and in the 3rd person without a subject pronoun, e.g.

llueve it's raining
es fácil decir que ... it's easy to say that ...

The most common impersonal verbs are ones to do with the weather, such as **amanecer**, **anochecer**, **granizar**, **llover**, **lloviznar**, **nevar**, **tronar** → ❸

Some reflexive verbs are also used impersonally:

INFINITIVE	CONSTRUCTION
creerse	**se cree que*** + *indicative* → ❹
decirse	**se dice que*** + *indicative* → ❺
poderse	**se puede** + *infinitive* → ❻
tratarse de	**se trata de** + *noun* → ❼
	se trata de + *infinitive* → ❽
venderse	**se vende*** + *noun* → ❾

*This impersonal construction conveys the same meaning as the 3rd person plural of these verbs; **creen que**, **dicen que**, **venden**.

Examples

❶	Me gusta este vestido	I like this dress (This dress pleases me)
	Me gustan los animales	I like animals
❷	Me gustan más estas	I prefer these
	Nos encanta hacer deporte	We love doing sport
	Me duele la cabeza	I have a headache
	Le faltaban tres dientes	He had three teeth missing
❸	Amanece/Está amaneciendo	It's daybreak
	Anochece/Está anocheciendo	It's getting dark
	Graniza/Está granizando	It's hailing
	Llueve/Está lloviendo	It's raining
	Llovizna/Está lloviznando	It's drizzling
	Nieva/Está nevando	It's snowing
	Truena/Está tronando	It's thundering
❹	Se cree que llegarán mañana	It is thought they will arrive tomorrow
❺	Se dice que ha sido el peor invierno en 50 años	People say it's been the worst winter in 50 years
❻	Aquí se puede aparcar	You can park here
❼	No se trata de dinero	It isn't a question/matter of money
❽	Se trata de poner fin al asunto	We must put an end to the matter
❾	Se vende coche	Car for sale

Verbs

The Infinitive

The infinitive is the form of the verb found in dictionary entries meaning 'to ...', e.g. **hablar** to speak, **vivir** to live. It is used in the following ways:

- After a preposition → ❶
- As a verbal noun → ❷

In this use the article may precede the infinitive, especially when the infinitive is the subject and begins the sentence → ❸

- After another verb or a verb followed by a preposition → ❹

The following construction should also be noted:

indefinite pronoun + **que** + *infinitive* → ❺

Object pronouns generally follow the infinitive and are attached to it. For exceptions see page 98.

Verbs followed by an infinitive with no linking preposition

deber, **poder**, **saber**, **querer** and **tener que** (**hay que** in impersonal constructions) → ❻

verbs of seeing or hearing, e.g. **ver** *to see*, **oír** *to hear* → ❼

dejar, hacer → ❽

The following common verbs:

aconsejar to advise → ❾
conseguir to manage to → ❿
decidir to decide
desear to wish, want → ⓫
esperar to hope → ⓬
evitar to avoid → ⓭
impedir to prevent → ⓮
intentar to try → ⓯
lograr to manage to → ❿
necesitar to need → ⓰
odiar to hate
olvidar to forget → ⓱
pensar to think → ⓲
preferir to prefer → ⓳
procurar to try → ⓯
prohibir to forbid → ⓴
prometer to promise → ㉑
proponer to propose → ㉒

Examples

1	Me hizo daño sin saberlo	She hurt me without realizing
2	Su deporte preferido es montar a caballo	Her favourite sport is horse riding
	Ver es creer	Seeing is believing
3	El viajar tanto me resulta cansado	I find so much travelling tiring
4	¿Quiere Vd esperar?	Would you like to wait?
	Aprenderán pronto a nadar	They will soon learn to swim
	Pronto dejará de llover	It'll stop raining soon
5	Tengo algo que decirte	I have something to tell you
6	No puede venir	She can't come
7	Nos ha visto llegar	She saw us arriving
8	No me hagas reír	Don't make me laugh
9	Le aconsejamos olvidarlo	We'd advise you to forget it
10	Aún no he conseguido/logrado entenderlo	I still haven't managed to work it out
11	No desea tener más hijos	She doesn't want to have any more children
12	Esperamos casarnos	We are hoping to get married
13	Evite beber cuando conduzca	Avoid drinking and driving
14	No pudo impedirle hablar	He couldn't prevent him from speaking
15	Intentamos/Procuramos pasar desapercibidos	We tried not to be noticed
16	Necesitaba salir a la calle	I needed to go out
17	Olvidó dejar su dirección	He forgot to leave his address
18	¿Piensan venir?	Are you thinking of coming?
19	Preferiría elegirlo yo mismo	I'd rather choose it myself
20	Prohibió fumar a los alumnos	He forbade the pupils to smoke
21	Prometieron volver pronto	They promised to come back soon
22	Propongo salir cuanto antes	I propose to leave ASAP

Verbs

The Gerund

Formation

First conjugation:

- replace the **-ar** of the infinitive by **-ando** → ❶

Second conjugation:

- replace the **-er** of the infinitive by **-iendo** → ❷

Third conjugation:

- replace the **-ir** of the infinitive by **-iendo** → ❸

For irregular gerunds, see irregular verbs, page 42 onwards.

Uses

After the verb **estar**, to form the continuous tenses → ❹

After the verbs **seguir** and **continuar** *to continue*, and **ir** when meaning to *happen gradually* → ❺

In time constructions, after **llevar** → ❻

When the action in the main clause needs to be complemented by another action → ❼

The position of object pronouns is the same as for the infinitive (see pages 24 and 98).

The gerund is invariable and strictly verbal in sense.

Examples

1. cantar to sing → cantando singing

2. temer to fear → temiendo fearing

3. partir to leave → partiendo leaving

4	Estoy escribiendo una carta	I am writing a letter
	Estaban esperándonos	They were waiting for us
5	Sigue viniendo todos los días	He/She is still coming every day
	Continuarán subiendo los precios	Prices will continue to go up
	El ejército iba avanzando poco a poco	The army was advancing little by little
6	Lleva dos años estudiando inglés	He/She has been studying English for two years
7	Pasamos el día tomando el sol en la playa	We spent the day sunbathing on the beach
	Iba cojeando	He/She/I was limping
	Salieron corriendo	They ran out

Verbs

Use of Tenses

The Present

Unlike English, Spanish can use both the simple present and the continuous present to talk about what is happening now → ❶

Normally, however, the continuous present is used to describe actions that are going on at this very moment → ❷

Spanish uses the present tense where English uses the perfect in the following cases:

- with certain expressions of time – notably **desde** *for/since* – when an action begun in the past is continued in the present → ❸

ⓘ Note: The perfect can be used as in English when the verb is negative → ❹

- in the construction **acabar de hacer** *to have just done* → ❺

Like English, Spanish often uses the present where a future action is implied → ❻

The Future

The future is generally used as in English → ❼, but note the following:

Immediate future time is often expressed by means of the present tense of **ir** + **a** + infinitive → ❽

When 'will' or 'shall' mean 'wish to', 'are willing to', **querer** is used → ❾

The Future Perfect

Used as in English shall/will have done → ❿

It can also express conjecture, usually about things in the recent past → ⓫

Examples

❶	Fumo	I smoke *or* I am smoking
	Lee	He reads *or* He is reading
	Vivimos	We live *or* We are living
❷	Está fumando	He is smoking
❸	Linda estudia español desde hace seis meses	Linda's been learning Spanish for six months (and still is)
	Estoy de pie desde las siete	I've been up since seven
	¿Hace mucho que esperan?	Have you been waiting long?
	Ya hace dos semanas que estamos aquí	We've been here for two weeks now
❹	No se han visto desde hace meses	They haven't seen each other for months
❺	Isabel acaba de salir	Isabel has just left
❻	Mañana voy a Madrid	I am going to Madrid tomorrow
❼	Lo haré mañana	I'll do it tomorrow
❽	Te vas a caer si no tienes cuidado	You'll fall if you're not careful
	Va a perder el tren	He's going to miss the train
	Va a llevar una media hora	It'll take about half an hour
❾	¿Me quieres esperar un momento, por favor?	Will you wait for me a second, please?
❿	Lo habré acabado para mañana	I will have finished it for tomorrow
⓫	Ya habrán llegado a casa	They must have arrived home by now

Use of Tenses *continued*

The Imperfect

The imperfect describes:

- an action or state in the past without definite limits in time → ❶
- habitual action(s) in the past (often expressed in English by means of *would* or *used to*) → ❷

Spanish uses the imperfect tense where English uses the pluperfect in the following cases:

- with certain expressions of time – notably **desde** *for/since* – when an action begun in the remoter past was continued in the more recent past → ❸

ⓘ Note: The pluperfect is used as in English when the verb is negative or the action has been completed → ❹

- in the construction **acabar de hacer** *to have just done* → ❺

Both the continuous and simple forms in English can be translated by the Spanish simple imperfect, but the continuous imperfect is used when the emphasis is on the fact that an action was going on at a precise moment in the past → ❻

The Perfect

The perfect is generally used much as it is in English → ❼

The Preterite

The preterite generally corresponds to the English simple past in both written and spoken Spanish → ❽

However, while English can use the simple past to describe habitual actions or settings, Spanish uses the imperfect (see above) → ❾

The Past Anterior

This tense is only ever used in written, literary Spanish, to replace the pluperfect in time clauses where the verb in the main clause is in the preterite → ❿

Examples

1	Todos mirábamos en silencio	We were all watching in silence
	Nuestras habitaciones daban a la playa	Our rooms overlooked the beach
2	En su juventud se levantaba de madrugada	In his youth he used to get up really early
	Hablábamos sin parar durante horas	We would talk non-stop for hours on end
	Mi hermano siempre me tomaba el pelo	My brother was always teasing me
3	Hacía dos años que vivíamos en Irlanda	We had been living in Ireland for two years
	Estaba enfermo desde 2005	He had been ill since 2005
	Hacía mucho tiempo que salían juntos	They had been going out together for a long time
4	Hacía un año que no le había visto	I hadn't seen him for a year
	Hacía una hora que había llegado	She had arrived an hour before
5	Acababa de encontrármelos	I had just found them
6	Cuando llegué, todos estaban fumando	When I arrived, they were all smoking
7	Todavía no han salido	They haven't come out yet
8	Me desperté y salté de la cama	I woke up and jumped out of bed
9	Siempre iban en coche al trabajo	They always travelled to work by car
10	Apenas hubo acabado, se oyeron unos golpes en la puerta	She had scarcely finished when there was a knock at the door

Verbs

The Subjunctive: when to use it

After verbs of:

- 'wishing'

querer que **desear que**	to wish that, want → ❶

- 'emotion' (e.g. regret, surprise, shame, pleasure, etc)

sentir que	to be sorry that → ❷
sorprender que	to be surprised that → ❸
alegrarse de que	to be pleased that → ❹

- 'asking' and 'advising'

pedir que	to ask that → ❺
aconsejar que	to advise that → ❻

In all the above constructions, when the subject of the verbs in the main and subordinate clause is the same, the infinitive is used, and the conjunction **que** omitted → ❼

- 'ordering', 'forbidding', 'allowing'

mandar que* **ordenar que**	to order that → ❽
permitir que* **dejar que***	to allow that → ❾
prohibir que*	to forbid that → ❿
impedir que*	to prevent that → ⓫

* With these verbs either the subjunctive or the infinitive is used when the object of the main verb is the subject of the subordinate verb → ⓬

Always after verbs expressing doubt or uncertainty, and verbs of opinion used negatively.

dudar que	to doubt that → ⓭
no creer que **no pensar que**	not to think that → ⓮

Examples

1	Queremos que esté contenta	We want her to be happy (*literally*: We want that she is happy)
	¿Desea Vd que lo haga yo?	Do you want me to do it?
2	Sentí mucho que no vinieran	I was very sorry that they didn't come
3	Nos sorprendió que no les vieran Vds	We were surprised you didn't see them
4	Me alegro de que te gusten	I'm pleased that you like them
5	Solo les pedimos que tengan cuidado	We're only asking you to take care
6	Le aconsejé que no llegara tarde	I advised him not to be late
7	Quiero que lo termines pronto	I want you to finish it soon
	BUT:	
	Quiero terminarlo pronto	I want to finish it soon
8	Ha mandado que vuelvan	He has ordered them to come back
	Ordenó que fueran castigados	He ordered them to be punished
9	No permitas que te tomen el pelo	Don't let them pull your leg
	No me dejó que la llevara a casa	She wouldn't let me take her home
10	Te prohíbo que digas eso	I forbid you to say that
11	No les impido que vengan	I am not preventing them from coming
12	Les ordenó que salieran *or* Les ordenó salir	She ordered them to go out
13	Dudo que lo sepan hacer	I doubt they can do it
14	No creo que sean tan listos	I don't think they are as clever as that

The Subjunctive: when to use it *continued*

In impersonal constructions which express necessity, possibility, etc:

hace falta que **es necesario que**	it is necessary that → ❶
es posible que	it is possible that → ❷
más vale que	it is better that → ❸
es una lástima que	it is a pity that → ❹

ⓘ Note: In impersonal constructions which state a fact or express certainty the indicative is used when the impersonal verb is affirmative. When it is negative, the subjunctive is used → ❺

After certain conjunctions:

para que **a fin de que***	so that → ❻
como si	as if → ❼
sin que*	without → ❽
a condición de que* **con tal (de) que*** **siempre que**	provided that, on condition that → ❾
a menos que **a no ser que**	unless → ❿
antes (de) que*	before → ⓫
no sea que	lest/in case → ⓬
mientras (que) **siempre que**	as long as → ⓭
(el) que	the fact that → ⓮

* When the subject of both verbs is the same, the infinitive is used, and the final **que** is omitted → ❽

Examples

❶ ¿Hace falta que vaya Jaime?	Does Jaime have to go?
❷ Es posible que tengan razón	It's possible that they are right
❸ Más vale que se quede Vd en su casa	You'd be better to stay at home
❹ Es una lástima que haya perdido su perrito	It's a shame/pity that she has lost her puppy
❺ Es verdad que va a venir	It's true that he's coming
BUT:	
No es verdad que vayan a hacerlo	It's not true that they are going to do it
❻ Átalas bien para que no se caigan	Tie them on securely so that they won't fall off
❼ Hablaba como si no creyera en sus propias palabras	He talked as if he didn't believe in his own words
❽ Salimos sin que nos vieran	We left without them seeing us
BUT:	
Me fui sin esperarla	I left without waiting for her
❾ Lo haré con tal de que me cuentes todo lo que pasó	I'll do it provided you tell me exactly what happened
❿ Saldremos de paseo a menos que esté lloviendo	We'll go for a walk unless it's raining
⓫ Avísale antes de que sea demasiado tarde	Tell him before it's too late
⓬ Habla en voz baja, no sea que alguien nos oiga	Speak quietly in case anyone hears us
⓭ Eso no pasará mientras yo sea el jefe aquí	That won't happen as long as I am the boss here
⓮ El que no me escribiera no me importaba demasiado	The fact that he didn't write didn't bother me too much

The Subjunctive: when to use it *continued*

After the conjunctions:

de modo que **de forma que** **de manera que**	so that (*indicating a purpose*) → ❶

ⓘ Note: When these conjunctions introduce a result rather than a purpose the indicative is used → ❷

In relative clauses with an antecedent which is:

- negative → ❸
- indefinite → ❹
- non-specific → ❺

In main clauses, to express a wish or exhortation. The verb may be preceded by expressions like **ojalá** or **que** → ❻

In the **si** clause of conditions where the English sentence contains a conditional tense → ❼

In set expressions → ❽

In the following constructions which translate *however*:

- **por** + *adjective* + **que** + *subjunctive* → ❾
- **por** + *adverb* + **que** + *subjunctive* → ❿
- **por** + **mucho** + **que** + *subjunctive* → ⓫

Examples

1	Vuélvanse de manera que los vea bien	Turn round so that I can see you properly
2	No quieren hacerlo, de manera que tendré que hacerlo yo	They won't do it, so I'll have to do it myself
3	No he encontrado a nadie que la conociera	I haven't met anyone who knows her
	No dijo nada que no supiéramos ya	He/She didn't say anything we didn't already know
4	Necesito alguien que sepa conducir	I need someone who can drive
	Busco algo que me distraiga	I'm looking for something to take my mind off it
5	Busca una casa que tenga calefacción central	He/She's looking for a house which has central heating (*subjunctive used since such a house may or may not exist*)
	El que lo haya visto tiene que decírmelo	Anyone who has seen it must tell me (*subjunctive used since it is not known who has seen it*)
6	¡Ojalá haga buen tiempo!	Let's hope the weather will be good!
	¡Que te diviertas!	Have a good time!
7	Si fuéramos en coche llegaríamos a tiempo	If we went by car we'd be there in time
8	Diga lo que diga ...	Whatever he may say ...
	Sea lo que sea ...	Be that as it may ...
	Pase lo que pase ...	Come what may ...
	Sea como sea ...	One way or another ...
9	Por cansado que esté, seguirá trabajando	No matter how/However tired he may be, he'll go on working
10	Por lejos que viva, iremos a buscarlo	No matter how/However far away he lives, we'll go and find him
11	Por mucho que lo intente, nunca lo conseguirá	No matter how/However hard he tries, he'll never succeed

The Subjunctive: when to use it *continued*

Clauses taking either a subjunctive or an indicative

In certain constructions, a subjunctive is needed when the action refers to future events or hypothetical situations, whereas an indicative is used when stating a fact or experience → ❶

The commonest of these are:

The conjunctions:

cuando	when → ❶
en cuanto / **tan pronto como**	as soon as → ❷
después (de) que*	after → ❸
hasta que	until → ❹
mientras	while → ❺
siempre que	whenever → ❻
aunque	even if/though → ❼

All conjunctions and pronouns ending in **-quiera** (*-ever*) → ❽

* ⓘ Note: If the subject of both verbs is the same, the subjunctive introduced by **después (de) que** may be replaced by **después de** + *infinitive* → ❾

Sequence of tenses in Subordinate Clauses

If the verb in the main clause is in the present, future or imperative, the verb in the dependent clause will be in the present or perfect subjunctive → ❿

If the verb in the main clause is in the conditional or any past tense, the verb in the dependent clause will be in the imperfect or pluperfect subjunctive → ⓫

Examples

❶ Le aconsejé que oyera música cuando estuviera nervioso	I advised him to listen to music when he felt nervous
Me gusta nadar cuando hace calor	I like to swim when it is warm
❷ Te devolveré el libro tan pronto como lo haya leído	I'll give you back the book as soon as I have read it
❸ Te lo diré después de que te hayas sentado	I'll tell you after you've sat down
❹ Quédate aquí hasta que volvamos	Stay here until we come back
❺ No hablen en voz alta mientras estén ellos aquí	Don't speak loudly while they are here
❻ Vuelvan por aquí siempre que quieran	Come back whenever you want
❼ No le creeré aunque diga la verdad	I won't believe him even if he's telling the truth
❽ La encontraré dondequiera que esté	I will find her wherever she may be
❾ Después de cenar nos fuimos al cine	After dinner we went to the cinema
❿ Quiero que lo hagas (*pres + pres subj*)	I want you to do it
Temo que no haya venido (*pres + perf subj*)	I fear he hasn't come (may not have come)
Iremos por aquí para que no nos vean (*future + pres subj*)	We'll go this way so that they won't see us
⓫ Me gustaría que llegaras temprano (*cond + imperf subj*)	I'd like you to arrive early
Les pedí que me esperaran (*preterite + imperf subj*)	I asked them to wait for me
Sentiría mucho que hubiese muerto (*cond + pluperf subj*)	I would be very sorry if he were dead

Verbs

Ser and Estar

Spanish has two verbs – **ser** and **estar** – for 'to be'.

They are not interchangeable and each one is used in defined contexts.

ser is used:
- with an adjective, to express a permanent or inherent quality → ❶
- to express occupation or nationality → ❷
- to express possession → ❸
- to express origin or the material something is made from → ❹
- with a noun, pronoun or infinitive following the verb → ❺
- to express the time and date → ❻
- to form the passive, with the past participle (see page 20).

ⓘ Note: This use emphasizes the action of the verb. If, however, the resultant state or condition needs to be emphasized, **estar** is used. The past participle then functions as an adjective → ❼

estar is used:
- to indicate place or location of a person, animal or thing* → ❽
- with an adjective or adjectival phrase, to express a quality or state seen by the speaker as subject to change or different from expected → ❾
- when speaking of a person's state of health → ❿
- to form the continuous tenses → ⓫
- with **de** + *noun*, to indicate a temporary occupation → ⓬

With certain adjectives both **ser** and **estar** can be used, but with a different meaning:
- **ser** will express a permanent or inherent quality → ⓭
- **estar** will express a temporary state or quality → ⓮

*To talk about where an event is taking place, use **ser** → ⓯

Examples

1	Mi hermano es alto	My brother is tall
	María es inteligente	María is intelligent
2	Javier es aviador	Javier is a pilot
	Sus padres son italianos	His parents are Italian
3	La casa es de Miguel	The house belongs to Miguel
4	Mi mujer es de Granada	My wife is from Granada
	Las paredes son de ladrillo	The walls are made of brick
5	Andrés es un niño travieso	Andrés is a naughty boy
	Soy yo, Enrique	It's me, Enrique
	Todo es proponérselo	It's all a question of putting your mind to it
6	Son las tres y media	It's half past three
	Mañana es sábado	Tomorrow is Saturday
7	Las puertas eran cerradas sigilosamente	The doors were being silently closed
	Las puertas estaban cerradas	The doors were closed (resultant action)
8	La comida está en la mesa	The meal is on the table
9	El lavabo está ocupado	The toilet is engaged
	Hoy estoy de mal humor	I'm in a bad mood today
	El café estaba frío	The coffee was cold
10	¿Cómo están Vds?	How are you?
	Estamos todos bien	We are all well
	Su amigo está enfermo	Her friend is ill
11	Estamos aprendiendo mucho	We are learning a great deal
12	Mi primo está de camarero en un bar	My cousin is working as a waiter in a bar
13	Su hermana es muy joven/vieja	His sister is very young/old
	Mi hijo es bueno/malo	My son is good/naughty
	Viajar es cansado	Travelling is tiring
14	Está muy joven/vieja con ese vestido	She looks very young/old in that dress
	El café está bueno/malo	The coffee tastes good/bad
	Hoy estoy cansada	I am tired today
15	La boda será en Madrid	The wedding will be in Madrid

Irregular Verbs

Irregular Verbs

The verbs on the following pages provide the main patterns for irregular verbs and verbs that change their stems (radical-changing verbs). They are given in their most common simple tenses, together with the imperative and the gerund. The past participle is also shown, to enable you to form all the compound tenses (see pages 14 to 15.)

Note that **escribir** and **romper** are not shown in the tables as only their past participles are irregular (**escrito** and **roto**).

Also not shown are verbs that make predictable spelling changes such as **c** to **qu** and **g** to **gu** before **e** (e.g. **sacar** and **pagar**). See page 128.

The pronouns **ella** and **Vd** take the same verb endings as **él**, while **ellas** and **Vds** take the same endings as **ellos**.

> All the verbs included in the tables differ from the three conjugations set out on pages 6 to 11. Many – e.g. **contar** – serve as models for groups of verbs, while others – e.g. **ir** – are unique.

Imperfect Subjunctive of Irregular Verbs

For verbs with an irregular stem in the preterite tense – e.g. **andar** → **anduvieron** – the imperfect subjunctive is formed by using the root form of the 3rd person plural of the preterite tense, and adding the imperfect subjunctive endings **-iera/-iese** etc where the verb has an '**i**' in the preterite ending – e.g. anduv**ieron** → anduv**iera/iese**. Where the verb has no '**i**' in the preterite ending, add **-era/-ese** etc – e.g. produj**eron** → produj**era/ese**.

abrir (to open)

	PAST PARTICIPLE	GERUND	IMPERATIVE
	abierto	abr**iendo**	abr**e**
			abri**d**
	PRESENT	**FUTURE**	**IMPERFECT**
(yo)	abr**o**	abrir**é**	abr**ía**
(tú)	abr**es**	abrir**ás**	abr**ías**
(él)	abr**e**	abrir**á**	abr**ía**
(nosotros)	abr**imos**	abrir**emos**	abr**íamos**
(vosotros)	abr**ís**	abrir**éis**	abr**íais**
(ellos)	abr**en**	abrir**án**	abr**ían**
	PRESENT SUBJUNCTIVE	**CONDITIONAL**	**PRETERITE**
(yo)	abr**a**	abrir**ía**	abr**í**
(tú)	abr**as**	abrir**ías**	abr**iste**
(él)	abr**a**	abrir**ía**	abr**ió**
(nosotros)	abr**amos**	abrir**íamos**	abr**imos**
(vosotros)	abr**áis**	abrir**íais**	abr**isteis**
(ellos)	abr**an**	abrir**ían**	abr**ieron**

actuar (to act)

	PAST PARTICIPLE	GERUND	IMPERATIVE
	actu**ado**	actu**ando**	**actúa**
			actua**d**
	PRESENT	**FUTURE**	**IMPERFECT**
(yo)	**actúo**	actuar**é**	actu**aba**
(tú)	**actúas**	actuar**ás**	actu**abas**
(él)	**actúa**	actuar**á**	actu**aba**
(nosotros)	actu**amos**	actuar**emos**	actu**ábamos**
(vosotros)	actu**áis**	actuar**éis**	actu**abais**
(ellos)	**actúan**	actuar**án**	actu**aban**
	PRESENT SUBJUNCTIVE	**CONDITIONAL**	**PRETERITE**
(yo)	**actúe**	actuar**ía**	actu**é**
(tú)	**actúes**	actuar**ías**	actu**aste**
(él)	**actúe**	actuar**ía**	actu**ó**
(nosotros)	actu**emos**	actuar**íamos**	actu**amos**
(vosotros)	actu**éis**	actuar**íais**	actu**asteis**
(ellos)	**actúen**	actuar**ían**	actu**aron**

adquirir (to acquire)

	PAST PARTICIPLE	GERUND	IMPERATIVE
	adquir**ido**	adquir**iendo**	**adquiere**
			adquiri**d**

	PRESENT	FUTURE	IMPERFECT
(yo)	**adquiero**	adquirir**é**	adquir**ía**
(tú)	**adquieres**	adquirir**ás**	adquir**ías**
(él)	**adquiere**	adquirir**á**	adquir**ía**
(nosotros)	adquir**imos**	adquirir**emos**	adquir**íamos**
(vosotros)	adquir**ís**	adquirir**éis**	adquir**íais**
(ellos)	**adquieren**	adquirir**án**	adquir**ían**

	PRESENT SUBJUNCTIVE	CONDITIONAL	PRETERITE
(yo)	**adquiera**	adquirir**ía**	adquir**í**
(tú)	**adquieras**	adquirir**ías**	adquir**iste**
(él)	**adquiera**	adquirir**ía**	adquir**ió**
(nosotros)	adquir**amos**	adquirir**íamos**	adquir**imos**
(vosotros)	adquir**áis**	adquirir**íais**	adquir**isteis**
(ellos)	**adquieran**	adquirir**ían**	adquir**ieron**

almorzar (to have lunch)

	PAST PARTICIPLE	GERUND	IMPERATIVE
	almorz**ado**	almorz**ando**	**almuerza**
			almorza**d**

	PRESENT	FUTURE	IMPERFECT
(yo)	**almuerzo**	almorzar**é**	almorz**aba**
(tú)	**almuerzas**	almorzar**ás**	almorz**abas**
(él)	**almuerza**	almorzar**á**	almorz**aba**
(nosotros)	almorz**amos**	almorzar**emos**	almorz**ábamos**
(vosotros)	almorz**áis**	almorzar**éis**	almorz**abais**
(ellos)	**almuerzan**	almorzar**án**	almorz**aban**

	PRESENT SUBJUNCTIVE	CONDITIONAL	PRETERITE
(yo)	**almuerce**	almorzar**ía**	**almorcé**
(tú)	**almuerces**	almorzar**ías**	almorz**aste**
(él)	**almuerce**	almorzar**ía**	almorz**ó**
(nosotros)	**almorcemos**	almorzar**íamos**	almorz**amos**
(vosotros)	**almorcéis**	almorzar**íais**	almorz**asteis**
(ellos)	**almuercen**	almorzar**ían**	almorz**aron**

andar (to walk)

	PAST PARTICIPLE	GERUND	IMPERATIVE
	and**ado**	and**ando**	and**a** anda**d**
	PRESENT	FUTURE	IMPERFECT
(yo)	and**o**	andar**é**	and**aba**
(tú)	and**as**	andar**ás**	and**abas**
(él)	and**a**	andar**á**	and**aba**
(nosotros)	and**amos**	andar**emos**	and**ábamos**
(vosotros)	and**áis**	andar**éis**	and**abais**
(ellos)	and**an**	andar**án**	and**aban**
	PRESENT SUBJUNCTIVE	CONDITIONAL	PRETERITE
(yo)	and**e**	andar**ía**	**anduve**
(tú)	and**es**	andar**ías**	**anduviste**
(él)	and**e**	andar**ía**	**anduvo**
(nosotros)	and**emos**	andar**íamos**	**anduvimos**
(vosotros)	and**éis**	andar**íais**	**anduvisteis**
(ellos)	and**en**	andar**ían**	**anduvieron**

avergonzar (to shame)

	PAST PARTICIPLE	GERUND	IMPERATIVE
	avergonz**ado**	avergonz**ando**	**avergüenza** avergonza**d**
	PRESENT	FUTURE	IMPERFECT
(yo)	**avergüenzo**	avergonzar**é**	avergonz**aba**
(tú)	**avergüenzas**	avergonzar**ás**	avergonz**abas**
(él)	**avergüenza**	avergonzar**á**	avergonz**aba**
(nosotros)	avergonz**amos**	avergonzar**emos**	avergonz**ábamos**
(vosotros)	avergonz**áis**	avergonzar**éis**	avergonz**abais**
(ellos)	**avergüenzan**	avergonzar**án**	avergonz**aban**
	PRESENT SUBJUNCTIVE	CONDITIONAL	PRETERITE
(yo)	**avergüence**	avergonzar**ía**	**avergoncé**
(tú)	**avergüences**	avergonzar**ías**	avergonz**aste**
(él)	**avergüence**	avergonzar**ía**	avergonz**ó**
(nosotros)	**avergoncemos**	avergonzar**íamos**	avergonz**amos**
(vosotros)	**avergoncéis**	avergonzar**íais**	avergonz**asteis**
(ellos)	**avergüencen**	avergonzar**ían**	avergonz**aron**

Irregular Verbs

caber (to fit)

	PAST PARTICIPLE	GERUND	IMPERATIVE
	cab**ido**	cab**iendo**	cab**e** cab**ed**

	PRESENT	FUTURE	IMPERFECT
(yo)	**quepo**	**cabré**	cab**ía**
(tú)	cab**es**	**cabrás**	cab**ías**
(él)	cab**e**	**cabrá**	cab**ía**
(nosotros)	cab**emos**	**cabremos**	cab**íamos**
(vosotros)	cab**éis**	**cabréis**	cab**íais**
(ellos)	cab**en**	**cabrán**	cab**ían**

	PRESENT SUBJUNCTIVE	CONDITIONAL	PRETERITE
(yo)	**quepa**	**cabría**	**cupe**
(tú)	**quepas**	**cabrías**	**cupiste**
(él)	**quepa**	**cabría**	**cupo**
(nosotros)	**quepamos**	**cabríamos**	**cupimos**
(vosotros)	**quepáis**	**cabríais**	**cupisteis**
(ellos)	**quepan**	**cabrían**	**cupieron**

caer (to fall)

	PAST PARTICIPLE	GERUND	IMPERATIVE
	caído	**cayendo**	ca**e** ca**ed**

	PRESENT	FUTURE	IMPERFECT
(yo)	**caigo**	caer**é**	**caía**
(tú)	ca**es**	caer**ás**	**caías**
(él)	ca**e**	caer**á**	**caía**
(nosotros)	ca**emos**	caer**emos**	**caíamos**
(vosotros)	ca**éis**	caer**éis**	**caíais**
(ellos)	ca**en**	caer**án**	**caían**

	PRESENT SUBJUNCTIVE	CONDITIONAL	PRETERITE
(yo)	**caiga**	caer**ía**	**caí**
(tú)	**caigas**	caer**ías**	**caíste**
(él)	**caiga**	caer**ía**	**cayó**
(nosotros)	**caigamos**	caer**íamos**	**caímos**
(vosotros)	**caigáis**	caer**íais**	**caísteis**
(ellos)	**caigan**	caer**ían**	**cayeron**

cocer (to boil)

	PAST PARTICIPLE	GERUND	IMPERATIVE
	coc**ido**	coc**iendo**	**cuece**
			coce**d**

	PRESENT	FUTURE	IMPERFECT
(yo)	**cuezo**	cocer**é**	coc**ía**
(tú)	**cueces**	cocer**ás**	coc**ías**
(él)	**cuece**	cocer**á**	coc**ía**
(nosotros)	coc**emos**	cocer**emos**	coc**íamos**
(vosotros)	coc**éis**	cocer**éis**	coc**íais**
(ellos)	**cuecen**	cocer**án**	coc**ían**

	PRESENT SUBJUNCTIVE	CONDITIONAL	PRETERITE
(yo)	**cueza**	cocer**ía**	coc**í**
(tú)	**cuezas**	cocer**ías**	coc**iste**
(él)	**cueza**	cocer**ía**	coc**ió**
(nosotros)	**cozamos**	cocer**íamos**	coc**imos**
(vosotros)	**cozáis**	cocer**íais**	coc**isteis**
(ellos)	**cuezan**	cocer**ían**	coc**ieron**

coger (to take)

	PAST PARTICIPLE	GERUND	IMPERATIVE
	cog**ido**	cog**iendo**	cog**e**
			coge**d**

	PRESENT	FUTURE	IMPERFECT
(yo)	**cojo**	coger**é**	cog**ía**
(tú)	cog**es**	coger**ás**	cog**ías**
(él)	cog**e**	coger**á**	cog**ía**
(nosotros)	cog**emos**	coger**emos**	cog**íamos**
(vosotros)	cog**éis**	coger**éis**	cog**íais**
(ellos)	cog**en**	coger**án**	cog**ían**

	PRESENT SUBJUNCTIVE	CONDITIONAL	PRETERITE
(yo)	**coja**	coger**ía**	cog**í**
(tú)	**cojas**	coger**ías**	cog**iste**
(él)	**coja**	coger**ía**	cog**ió**
(nosotros)	**cojamos**	coger**íamos**	cog**imos**
(vosotros)	**cojáis**	coger**íais**	cog**isteis**
(ellos)	**cojan**	coger**ían**	cog**ieron**

conducir (to drive, to lead)

	PAST PARTICIPLE	GERUND	IMPERATIVE
	conduc**ido**	conduc**iendo**	conduc**e**
			conduc**id**

	PRESENT	FUTURE	IMPERFECT
(yo)	**conduzco**	conducir**é**	conduc**ía**
(tú)	conduc**es**	conducir**ás**	conduc**ías**
(él)	conduc**e**	conducir**á**	conduc**ía**
(nosotros)	conduc**imos**	conducir**emos**	conduc**íamos**
(vosotros)	conduc**ís**	conducir**éis**	conduc**íais**
(ellos)	conduc**en**	conducir**án**	conduc**ían**

	PRESENT SUBJUNCTIVE	CONDITIONAL	PRETERITE
(yo)	**conduzca**	conducir**ía**	**conduje**
(tú)	**conduzcas**	conducir**ías**	**condujiste**
(él)	**conduzca**	conducir**ía**	**condujo**
(nosotros)	**conduzcamos**	conducir**íamos**	**condujimos**
(vosotros)	**conduzcáis**	conducir**íais**	**condujisteis**
(ellos)	**conduzcan**	conducir**ían**	**condujeron**

construir (to build)

	PAST PARTICIPLE	GERUND	IMPERATIVE
	constru**ido**	**construyendo**	**construye**
			constru**id**

	PRESENT	FUTURE	IMPERFECT
(yo)	**construyo**	construir**é**	constru**ía**
(tú)	**construyes**	construir**ás**	constru**ías**
(él)	**construye**	construir**á**	constru**ía**
(nosotros)	constru**imos**	construir**emos**	constru**íamos**
(vosotros)	constru**ís**	construir**éis**	constru**íais**
(ellos)	**construyen**	construir**án**	constru**ían**

	PRESENT SUBJUNCTIVE	CONDITIONAL	PRETERITE
(yo)	**construya**	construir**ía**	constru**í**
(tú)	**construyas**	construir**ías**	constru**iste**
(él)	**construya**	construir**ía**	**construyó**
(nosotros)	**construyamos**	construir**íamos**	constru**imos**
(vosotros)	**construyáis**	construir**íais**	constru**isteis**
(ellos)	**construyan**	construir**ían**	**construyeron**

contar (to tell, to count)

	PAST PARTICIPLE	GERUND	IMPERATIVE
	cont**ado**	cont**ando**	**cuenta**
			conta**d**
	PRESENT	**FUTURE**	**IMPERFECT**
(yo)	**cuento**	contar**é**	cont**aba**
(tú)	**cuentas**	contar**ás**	cont**abas**
(él)	**cuenta**	contar**á**	cont**aba**
(nosotros)	cont**amos**	contar**emos**	cont**ábamos**
(vosotros)	cont**áis**	contar**éis**	cont**abais**
(ellos)	**cuentan**	contar**án**	cont**aban**
	PRESENT SUBJUNCTIVE	**CONDITIONAL**	**PRETERITE**
(yo)	**cuente**	contar**ía**	cont**é**
(tú)	**cuentes**	contar**ías**	cont**aste**
(él)	**cuente**	contar**ía**	cont**ó**
(nosotros)	cont**emos**	contar**íamos**	cont**amos**
(vosotros)	cont**éis**	contar**íais**	cont**asteis**
(ellos)	**cuenten**	contar**ían**	cont**aron**

crecer (to grow)

	PAST PARTICIPLE	GERUND	IMPERATIVE
	crec**ido**	crec**iendo**	crec**e**
			crece**d**
	PRESENT	**FUTURE**	**IMPERFECT**
(yo)	**crezco**	crecer**é**	crec**ía**
(tú)	crec**es**	crecer**ás**	crec**ías**
(él)	crec**e**	crecer**á**	crec**ía**
(nosotros)	crec**emos**	crecer**emos**	crec**íamos**
(vosotros)	crec**éis**	crecer**éis**	crec**íais**
(ellos)	crec**en**	crecer**án**	crec**ían**
	PRESENT SUBJUNCTIVE	**CONDITIONAL**	**PRETERITE**
(yo)	**crezca**	crecer**ía**	crec**í**
(tú)	**crezcas**	crecer**ías**	crec**iste**
(él)	**crezca**	crecer**ía**	crec**ió**
(nosotros)	**crezcamos**	crecer**íamos**	crec**imos**
(vosotros)	**crezcáis**	crecer**íais**	crec**isteis**
(ellos)	**crezcan**	crecer**ían**	crec**ieron**

cruzar (to cross)

	PAST PARTICIPLE	GERUND	IMPERATIVE
	cruz**ado**	cruz**ando**	cruz**a**
			cruza**d**
	PRESENT	**FUTURE**	**IMPERFECT**
(yo)	cruz**o**	cruzar**é**	cruz**aba**
(tú)	cruz**as**	cruzar**ás**	cruz**abas**
(él)	cruz**a**	cruzar**á**	cruz**aba**
(nosotros)	cruz**amos**	cruzar**emos**	cruz**ábamos**
(vosotros)	cruz**áis**	cruzar**éis**	cruz**abais**
(ellos)	cruz**an**	cruzar**án**	cruz**aban**
	PRESENT SUBJUNCTIVE	**CONDITIONAL**	**PRETERITE**
(yo)	**cruce**	cruzar**ía**	**crucé**
(tú)	**cruces**	cruzar**ías**	cruz**aste**
(él)	**cruce**	cruzar**ía**	cruz**ó**
(nosotros)	**crucemos**	cruzar**íamos**	cruz**amos**
(vosotros)	**crucéis**	cruzar**íais**	cruz**asteis**
(ellos)	**crucen**	cruzar**ían**	cruz**aron**

dar (to give)

	PAST PARTICIPLE	GERUND	IMPERATIVE
	d**ado**	d**ando**	d**a**
			da**d**
	PRESENT	**FUTURE**	**IMPERFECT**
(yo)	**doy**	dar**é**	d**aba**
(tú)	d**as**	dar**ás**	d**abas**
(él)	d**a**	dar**á**	d**aba**
(nosotros)	d**amos**	dar**emos**	d**ábamos**
(vosotros)	d**ais**	dar**éis**	d**abais**
(ellos)	d**an**	dar**án**	d**aban**
	PRESENT SUBJUNCTIVE	**CONDITIONAL**	**PRETERITE**
(yo)	**dé**	dar**ía**	**di**
(tú)	d**es**	dar**ías**	**diste**
(él)	**dé**	dar**ía**	**dio**
(nosotros)	d**emos**	dar**íamos**	**dimos**
(vosotros)	d**eis**	dar**íais**	**disteis**
(ellos)	d**en**	dar**ían**	**dieron**

decir (to say)

	PAST PARTICIPLE	GERUND	IMPERATIVE
	dicho	**diciendo**	**di**
			deci**d**

	PRESENT	FUTURE	IMPERFECT
(yo)	**digo**	**diré**	dec**ía**
(tú)	**dices**	**dirás**	dec**ías**
(él)	**dice**	**dirá**	dec**ía**
(nosotros)	dec**imos**	**diremos**	dec**íamos**
(vosotros)	dec**ís**	**diréis**	dec**íais**
(ellos)	**dicen**	**dirán**	dec**ían**

	PRESENT SUBJUNCTIVE	CONDITIONAL	PRETERITE
(yo)	**diga**	**diría**	**dije**
(tú)	**digas**	**dirías**	**dijiste**
(él)	**diga**	**diría**	**dijo**
(nosotros)	**digamos**	**diríamos**	**dijimos**
(vosotros)	**digáis**	**diríais**	**dijisteis**
(ellos)	**digan**	**dirían**	**dijeron**

dirigir (to direct)

	PAST PARTICIPLE	GERUND	IMPERATIVE
	dirig**ido**	dirig**iendo**	dirig**e**
			dirigi**d**

	PRESENT	FUTURE	IMPERFECT
(yo)	**dirijo**	dirigir**é**	dirig**ía**
(tú)	dirig**es**	dirigir**ás**	dirig**ías**
(él)	dirig**e**	dirigir**á**	dirig**ía**
(nosotros)	dirig**imos**	dirigir**emos**	dirig**íamos**
(vosotros)	dirig**ís**	dirigir**éis**	dirig**íais**
(ellos)	dirig**en**	dirigir**án**	dirig**ían**

	PRESENT SUBJUNCTIVE	CONDITIONAL	PRETERITE
(yo)	**dirija**	dirigir**ía**	dirig**í**
(tú)	**dirijas**	dirigir**ías**	dirig**iste**
(él)	**dirija**	dirigir**ía**	dirig**ió**
(nosotros)	**dirijamos**	dirigir**íamos**	dirig**imos**
(vosotros)	**dirijáis**	dirigir**íais**	dirig**isteis**
(ellos)	**dirijan**	dirigir**ían**	dirig**ieron**

dormir (to sleep)

	PAST PARTICIPLE	GERUND	IMPERATIVE
	dorm**ido**	**durmiendo**	**duerme** dormi**d**

	PRESENT	FUTURE	IMPERFECT
(yo)	**duermo**	dormir**é**	dorm**ía**
(tú)	**duermes**	dormir**ás**	dorm**ías**
(él)	**duerme**	dormir**á**	dorm**ía**
(nosotros)	dorm**imos**	dormir**emos**	dorm**íamos**
(vosotros)	dorm**ís**	dormir**éis**	dorm**íais**
(ellos)	**duermen**	dormir**án**	dorm**ían**

	PRESENT SUBJUNCTIVE	CONDITIONAL	PRETERITE
(yo)	**duerma**	dormir**ía**	dorm**í**
(tú)	**duermas**	dormir**ías**	dorm**iste**
(él)	**duerma**	dormir**ía**	**durmió**
(nosotros)	**durmamos**	dormir**íamos**	dorm**imos**
(vosotros)	**durmáis**	dormir**íais**	dorm**isteis**
(ellos)	**duerman**	dormir**ían**	**durmieron**

elegir (to choose)

	PAST PARTICIPLE	GERUND	IMPERATIVE
	eleg**ido**	**eligiendo**	**elige** elegi**d**

	PRESENT	FUTURE	IMPERFECT
(yo)	**elijo**	elegir**é**	eleg**ía**
(tú)	**eliges**	elegir**ás**	eleg**ías**
(él)	**elige**	elegir**á**	eleg**ía**
(nosotros)	eleg**imos**	elegir**emos**	eleg**íamos**
(vosotros)	eleg**ís**	elegir**éis**	eleg**íais**
(ellos)	**eligen**	elegir**án**	eleg**ían**

	PRESENT SUBJUNCTIVE	CONDITIONAL	PRETERITE
(yo)	**elija**	elegir**ía**	eleg**í**
(tú)	**elijas**	elegir**ías**	eleg**iste**
(él)	**elija**	elegir**ía**	**eligió**
(nosotros)	**elijamos**	elegir**íamos**	eleg**imos**
(vosotros)	**elijáis**	elegir**íais**	eleg**isteis**
(ellos)	**elijan**	elegir**ían**	**eligieron**

empezar (to begin)

	PAST PARTICIPLE	GERUND	IMPERATIVE
	empez**ado**	empez**ando**	**empieza** empeza**d**

	PRESENT	FUTURE	IMPERFECT
(yo)	**empiezo**	empezar**é**	empez**aba**
(tú)	**empiezas**	empezar**ás**	empez**abas**
(él)	**empieza**	empezar**á**	empez**aba**
(nosotros)	empez**amos**	empezar**emos**	empez**ábamos**
(vosotros)	empez**áis**	empezar**éis**	empez**abais**
(ellos)	**empiezan**	empezar**án**	empez**aban**

	PRESENT SUBJUNCTIVE	CONDITIONAL	PRETERITE
(yo)	**empiece**	empezar**ía**	**empecé**
(tú)	**empieces**	empezar**ías**	empez**aste**
(él)	**empiece**	empezar**ía**	empez**ó**
(nosotros)	**empecemos**	empezar**íamos**	empez**amos**
(vosotros)	**empecéis**	empezar**íais**	empez**asteis**
(ellos)	**empiecen**	empezar**ían**	empez**aron**

entender (to understand)

	PAST PARTICIPLE	GERUND	IMPERATIVE
	entend**ido**	entend**iendo**	**entiende** entende**d**

	PRESENT	FUTURE	IMPERFECT
(yo)	**entiendo**	entender**é**	entend**ía**
(tú)	**entiendes**	entender**ás**	entend**ías**
(él)	**entiende**	entender**á**	entend**ía**
(nosotros)	entend**emos**	entender**emos**	entend**íamos**
(vosotros)	entend**éis**	entender**éis**	entend**íais**
(ellos)	**entienden**	entender**án**	entend**ían**

	PRESENT SUBJUNCTIVE	CONDITIONAL	PRETERITE
(yo)	**entienda**	entender**ía**	entend**í**
(tú)	**entiendas**	entender**ías**	entend**iste**
(él)	**entienda**	entender**ía**	entend**ió**
(nosotros)	entend**amos**	entender**íamos**	entend**imos**
(vosotros)	entend**áis**	entender**íais**	entend**isteis**
(ellos)	**entiendan**	entender**ían**	entend**ieron**

enviar (to send)

	PAST PARTICIPLE	GERUND	IMPERATIVE
	envi**ado**	envi**ando**	**envía** envia**d**

	PRESENT	FUTURE	IMPERFECT
(yo)	**envío**	enviar**é**	envi**aba**
(tú)	**envías**	enviar**ás**	envi**abas**
(él)	**envía**	enviar**á**	envi**aba**
(nosotros)	envi**amos**	enviar**emos**	envi**ábamos**
(vosotros)	envi**áis**	enviar**éis**	envi**abais**
(ellos)	**envían**	enviar**án**	envi**aban**

	PRESENT SUBJUNCTIVE	CONDITIONAL	PRETERITE
(yo)	**envíe**	enviar**ía**	envi**é**
(tú)	**envíes**	enviar**ías**	envi**aste**
(él)	**envíe**	enviar**ía**	envi**ó**
(nosotros)	envi**emos**	enviar**íamos**	envi**amos**
(vosotros)	envi**éis**	enviar**íais**	envi**asteis**
(ellos)	**envíen**	enviar**ían**	envi**aron**

erguir (to erect)

	PAST PARTICIPLE	GERUND	IMPERATIVE
	ergu**ido**	**irguiendo**	**yergue** ergui**d**

	PRESENT	FUTURE	IMPERFECT
(yo)	**yergo**	erguir**é**	ergu**ía**
(tú)	**yergues**	erguir**ás**	ergu**ías**
(él)	**yergue**	erguir**á**	ergu**ía**
(nosotros)	ergu**imos**	erguir**emos**	ergu**íamos**
(vosotros)	ergu**ís**	erguir**éis**	ergu**íais**
(ellos)	**yerguen**	erguir**án**	ergu**ían**

	PRESENT SUBJUNCTIVE	CONDITIONAL	PRETERITE
(yo)	**yerga**	erguir**ía**	ergu**í**
(tú)	**yergas**	erguir**ías**	ergu**iste**
(él)	**yerga**	erguir**ía**	**irguió**
(nosotros)	**irgamos**	erguir**íamos**	ergu**imos**
(vosotros)	**irgáis**	erguir**íais**	ergu**isteis**
(ellos)	**yergan**	erguir**ían**	**irguieron**

Irregular Verbs

errar (to err)

	PAST PARTICIPLE	GERUND	IMPERATIVE
	err**ado**	err**ando**	**yerra**
			erra**d**

	PRESENT	FUTURE	IMPERFECT
(yo)	**yerro**	errar**é**	err**aba**
(tú)	**yerras**	errar**ás**	err**abas**
(él)	**yerra**	errar**á**	err**aba**
(nosotros)	err**amos**	errar**emos**	err**ábamos**
(vosotros)	err**áis**	errar**éis**	err**abais**
(ellos)	**yerran**	errar**án**	err**aban**

	PRESENT SUBJUNCTIVE	CONDITIONAL	PRETERITE
(yo)	**yerre**	errar**ía**	err**é**
(tú)	**yerres**	errar**ías**	err**aste**
(él)	**yerre**	errar**ía**	err**ó**
(nosotros)	err**emos**	errar**íamos**	err**amos**
(vosotros)	err**éis**	errar**íais**	err**asteis**
(ellos)	**yerren**	errar**ían**	err**aron**

estar (to be)

	PAST PARTICIPLE	GERUND	IMPERATIVE
	est**ado**	est**ando**	**está**
			esta**d**

	PRESENT	FUTURE	IMPERFECT
(yo)	**estoy**	estar**é**	est**aba**
(tú)	**estás**	estar**ás**	est**abas**
(él)	**está**	estar**á**	est**aba**
(nosotros)	est**amos**	estar**emos**	est**ábamos**
(vosotros)	est**áis**	estar**éis**	est**abais**
(ellos)	**están**	estar**án**	est**aban**

	PRESENT SUBJUNCTIVE	CONDITIONAL	PRETERITE
(yo)	**esté**	estar**ía**	**estuve**
(tú)	**estés**	estar**ías**	**estuviste**
(él)	**esté**	estar**ía**	**estuvo**
(nosotros)	est**emos**	estar**íamos**	**estuvimos**
(vosotros)	est**éis**	estar**íais**	**estuvisteis**
(ellos)	**estén**	estar**ían**	**estuvieron**

freír (to fry)

	PAST PARTICIPLE	GERUND	IMPERATIVE
	frito	**friendo**	**fríe**
			freí**d**

	PRESENT	FUTURE	IMPERFECT
(yo)	**frío**	freir**é**	fre**ía**
(tú)	**fríes**	freir**ás**	fre**ías**
(él)	**fríe**	freir**á**	fre**ía**
(nosotros)	fre**ímos**	freir**emos**	fre**íamos**
(vosotros)	fre**ís**	freir**éis**	fre**íais**
(ellos)	**fríen**	freir**án**	fre**ían**

	PRESENT SUBJUNCTIVE	CONDITIONAL	PRETERITE
(yo)	**fría**	freir**ía**	fre**í**
(tú)	**frías**	freir**ías**	fre**íste**
(él)	**fría**	freir**ía**	**frio**
(nosotros)	**friamos**	freir**íamos**	fre**ímos**
(vosotros)	**friais**	freir**íais**	fre**ísteis**
(ellos)	**frían**	freir**ían**	**frieron**

haber (to have, *auxiliary*)

	PAST PARTICIPLE	GERUND	IMPERATIVE
	hab**ido**	hab**iendo**	**he**
			habe**d**

	PRESENT	FUTURE	IMPERFECT
(yo)	**he**	**habré**	hab**ía**
(tú)	**has**	**habrás**	hab**ías**
(él)	**ha**	**habrá**	hab**ía**
(nosotros)	**hemos**	**habremos**	hab**íamos**
(vosotros)	hab**éis**	**habréis**	hab**íais**
(ellos)	**han**	**habrán**	hab**ían**

	PRESENT SUBJUNCTIVE	CONDITIONAL	PRETERITE
(yo)	**haya**	**habría**	**hube**
(tú)	**hayas**	**habrías**	**hubiste**
(él)	**haya**	**habría**	**hubo**
(nosotros)	**hayamos**	**habríamos**	**hubimos**
(vosotros)	**hayáis**	**habríais**	**hubisteis**
(ellos)	**hayan**	**habrían**	**hubieron**

Irregular Verbs

hacer (to do, to make)

	PAST PARTICIPLE	GERUND	IMPERATIVE
	hecho	hac**iendo**	**haz**
			hace**d**
	PRESENT	FUTURE	IMPERFECT
(yo)	**hago**	**haré**	hac**ía**
(tú)	hac**es**	**harás**	hac**ías**
(él)	hac**e**	**hará**	hac**ía**
(nosotros)	hac**emos**	**haremos**	hac**íamos**
(vosotros)	hac**éis**	**haréis**	hac**íais**
(ellos)	hac**en**	**harán**	hac**ían**
	PRESENT SUBJUNCTIVE	CONDITIONAL	PRETERITE
(yo)	**haga**	**haría**	**hice**
(tú)	**hagas**	**harías**	**hiciste**
(él)	**haga**	**haría**	**hizo**
(nosotros)	**hagamos**	**haríamos**	**hicimos**
(vosotros)	**hagáis**	**haríais**	**hicisteis**
(ellos)	**hagan**	**harían**	**hicieron**

ir (to go)

	PAST PARTICIPLE	GERUND	IMPERATIVE
	ido	**yendo**	**ve**
			id
	PRESENT	FUTURE	IMPERFECT
(yo)	**voy**	ir**é**	**iba**
(tú)	**vas**	ir**ás**	**ibas**
(él)	**va**	ir**á**	**iba**
(nosotros)	**vamos**	ir**emos**	**íbamos**
(vosotros)	**vais**	ir**éis**	**ibais**
(ellos)	**van**	ir**án**	**iban**
	PRESENT SUBJUNCTIVE	CONDITIONAL	PRETERITE
(yo)	**vaya**	ir**ía**	**fui**
(tú)	**vayas**	ir**ías**	**fuiste**
(él)	**vaya**	ir**ía**	**fue**
(nosotros)	**vayamos**	ir**íamos**	**fuimos**
(vosotros)	**vayáis**	ir**íais**	**fuisteis**
(ellos)	**vayan**	ir**ían**	**fueron**

jugar (to play)

	PAST PARTICIPLE	GERUND	IMPERATIVE
	jug**ado**	jug**ando**	**juega**
			jug**ad**

	PRESENT	FUTURE	IMPERFECT
(yo)	**juego**	jugar**é**	jug**aba**
(tú)	**juegas**	jugar**ás**	jug**abas**
(él)	**juega**	jugar**á**	jug**aba**
(nosotros)	jug**amos**	jugar**emos**	jug**ábamos**
(vosotros)	jug**áis**	jugar**éis**	jug**abais**
(ellos)	**juegan**	jugar**án**	jug**aban**

	PRESENT SUBJUNCTIVE	CONDITIONAL	PRETERITE
(yo)	**juegue**	jugar**ía**	**jugué**
(tú)	**juegues**	jugar**ías**	jug**aste**
(él)	**juegue**	jugar**ía**	jug**ó**
(nosotros)	**juguemos**	jugar**íamos**	jug**amos**
(vosotros)	**juguéis**	jugar**íais**	jug**asteis**
(ellos)	**jueguen**	jugar**ían**	jug**aron**

leer (to read)

	PAST PARTICIPLE	GERUND	IMPERATIVE
	le**ído**	**leyendo**	le**e**
			lee**d**

	PRESENT	FUTURE	IMPERFECT
(yo)	le**o**	leer**é**	le**ía**
(tú)	le**es**	leer**ás**	le**ías**
(él)	le**e**	leer**á**	le**ía**
(nosotros)	le**emos**	leer**emos**	le**íamos**
(vosotros)	le**éis**	leer**éis**	le**íais**
(ellos)	le**en**	leer**án**	le**ían**

	PRESENT SUBJUNCTIVE	CONDITIONAL	PRETERITE
(yo)	le**a**	leer**ía**	**leí**
(tú)	le**as**	leer**ías**	**leíste**
(él)	le**a**	leer**ía**	**leyó**
(nosotros)	le**amos**	leer**íamos**	**leímos**
(vosotros)	le**áis**	leer**íais**	**leísteis**
(ellos)	le**an**	leer**ían**	**leyeron**

lucir (to shine)

	PAST PARTICIPLE	GERUND	IMPERATIVE
	luc**ido**	luc**iendo**	luc**e**
			luc**id**

	PRESENT	FUTURE	IMPERFECT
(yo)	**luzco**	lucir**é**	luc**ía**
(tú)	luc**es**	lucir**ás**	luc**ías**
(él)	luc**e**	lucir**á**	luc**ía**
(nosotros)	luc**imos**	lucir**emos**	luc**íamos**
(vosotros)	luc**ís**	lucir**éis**	luc**íais**
(ellos)	luc**en**	lucir**án**	luc**ían**

	PRESENT SUBJUNCTIVE	CONDITIONAL	PRETERITE
(yo)	**luzca**	lucir**ía**	luc**í**
(tú)	**luzcas**	lucir**ías**	luc**iste**
(él)	**luzca**	lucir**ía**	luc**ió**
(nosotros)	**luzcamos**	lucir**íamos**	luc**imos**
(vosotros)	**luzcáis**	lucir**íais**	luc**isteis**
(ellos)	**luzcan**	lucir**ían**	luc**ieron**

llover (to rain)

PAST PARTICIPLE	GERUND	IMPERATIVE
llov**ido**	llov**iendo**	*not used*

PRESENT	FUTURE	IMPERFECT
llueve	llover**á**	llov**ía**

PRESENT SUBJUNCTIVE	CONDITIONAL	PRETERITE
llueva	llover**ía**	llov**ió**

morir (to die)

	PAST PARTICIPLE	GERUND	IMPERATIVE
	muerto	**muriendo**	**muere**
			mori**d**

	PRESENT	FUTURE	IMPERFECT
(yo)	**muero**	morir**é**	mor**ía**
(tú)	**mueres**	morir**ás**	mor**ías**
(él)	**muere**	morir**á**	mor**ía**
(nosotros)	mor**imos**	morir**emos**	mor**íamos**
(vosotros)	mor**ís**	morir**éis**	mor**íais**
(ellos)	**mueren**	morir**án**	mor**ían**

	PRESENT SUBJUNCTIVE	CONDITIONAL	PRETERITE
(yo)	**muera**	morir**ía**	mor**í**
(tú)	**mueras**	morir**ías**	mor**iste**
(él)	**muera**	morir**ía**	**murió**
(nosotros)	**muramos**	morir**íamos**	mor**imos**
(vosotros)	**muráis**	morir**íais**	mor**isteis**
(ellos)	**mueran**	morir**ían**	**murieron**

mover (to move)

	PAST PARTICIPLE	GERUND	IMPERATIVE
	mov**ido**	mov**iendo**	**mueve**
			move**d**

	PRESENT	FUTURE	IMPERFECT
(yo)	**muevo**	mover**é**	mov**ía**
(tú)	**mueves**	mover**ás**	mov**ías**
(él)	**mueve**	mover**á**	mov**ía**
(nosotros)	mov**emos**	mover**emos**	mov**íamos**
(vosotros)	mov**éis**	mover**éis**	mov**íais**
(ellos)	**mueven**	mover**án**	mov**ían**

	PRESENT SUBJUNCTIVE	CONDITIONAL	PRETERITE
(yo)	**mueva**	mover**ía**	mov**í**
(tú)	**muevas**	mover**ías**	mov**iste**
(él)	**mueva**	mover**ía**	mov**ió**
(nosotros)	mov**amos**	mover**íamos**	mov**imos**
(vosotros)	mov**áis**	mover**íais**	mov**isteis**
(ellos)	**muevan**	mover**ían**	mov**ieron**

nacer (to be born)

	PAST PARTICIPLE	GERUND	IMPERATIVE
	nac**ido**	nac**iendo**	nac**e** nac**ed**

	PRESENT	FUTURE	IMPERFECT
(yo)	**nazco**	nacer**é**	nac**ía**
(tú)	nac**es**	nacer**ás**	nac**ías**
(él)	nac**e**	nacer**á**	nac**ía**
(nosotros)	nac**emos**	nacer**emos**	nac**íamos**
(vosotros)	nac**éis**	nacer**éis**	nac**íais**
(ellos)	nac**en**	nacer**án**	nac**ían**

	PRESENT SUBJUNCTIVE	CONDITIONAL	PRETERITE
(yo)	**nazca**	nacer**ía**	nac**í**
(tú)	**nazcas**	nacer**ías**	nac**iste**
(él)	**nazca**	nacer**ía**	nac**ió**
(nosotros)	**nazcamos**	nacer**íamos**	nac**imos**
(vosotros)	**nazcáis**	nacer**íais**	nac**isteis**
(ellos)	**nazcan**	nacer**ían**	nac**ieron**

negar (to deny)

	PAST PARTICIPLE	GERUND	IMPERATIVE
	neg**ado**	neg**ando**	**niega** nega**d**

	PRESENT	FUTURE	IMPERFECT
(yo)	**niego**	negar**é**	neg**aba**
(tú)	**niegas**	negar**ás**	neg**abas**
(él)	**niega**	negar**á**	neg**aba**
(nosotros)	neg**amos**	negar**emos**	neg**ábamos**
(vosotros)	neg**áis**	negar**éis**	neg**abais**
(ellos)	**niegan**	negar**án**	neg**aban**

	PRESENT SUBJUNCTIVE	CONDITIONAL	PRETERITE
(yo)	**niegue**	negar**ía**	**negué**
(tú)	**niegues**	negar**ías**	neg**aste**
(él)	**niegue**	negar**ía**	neg**ó**
(nosotros)	**neguemos**	negar**íamos**	neg**amos**
(vosotros)	**neguéis**	negar**íais**	neg**asteis**
(ellos)	**nieguen**	negar**ían**	neg**aron**

oír (to hear)

	PAST PARTICIPLE	GERUND	IMPERATIVE
	oído	oyendo	oye
			oíd
	PRESENT	FUTURE	IMPERFECT
(yo)	oigo	oiré	oía
(tú)	oyes	oirás	oías
(él)	oye	oirá	oía
(nosotros)	oímos	oiremos	oíamos
(vosotros)	oís	oiréis	oíais
(ellos)	oyen	oirán	oían
	PRESENT SUBJUNCTIVE	CONDITIONAL	PRETERITE
(yo)	oiga	oiría	oí
(tú)	oigas	oirías	oíste
(él)	oiga	oiría	oyó
(nosotros)	oigamos	oiríamos	oímos
(vosotros)	oigáis	oiríais	oísteis
(ellos)	oigan	oirían	oyeron

oler (to smell)

	PAST PARTICIPLE	GERUND	IMPERATIVE
	olido	oliendo	huele
			oled
	PRESENT	FUTURE	IMPERFECT
(yo)	huelo	oleré	olía
(tú)	hueles	olerás	olías
(él)	huele	olerá	olía
(nosotros)	olemos	oleremos	olíamos
(vosotros)	oléis	oleréis	olíais
(ellos)	huelen	olerán	olían
	PRESENT SUBJUNCTIVE	CONDITIONAL	PRETERITE
(yo)	huela	olería	olí
(tú)	huelas	olerías	oliste
(él)	huela	olería	olió
(nosotros)	olamos	oleríamos	olimos
(vosotros)	oláis	oleríais	olisteis
(ellos)	huelan	olerían	olieron

pedir (to ask for)

	PAST PARTICIPLE	GERUND	IMPERATIVE
	ped**ido**	**pidiendo**	**pide**
			ped**id**

	PRESENT	FUTURE	IMPERFECT
(yo)	**pido**	pedir**é**	ped**ía**
(tú)	**pides**	pedir**ás**	ped**ías**
(él)	**pide**	pedir**á**	ped**ía**
(nosotros)	ped**imos**	pedir**emos**	ped**íamos**
(vosotros)	ped**ís**	pedir**éis**	ped**íais**
(ellos)	**piden**	pedir**án**	ped**ían**

	PRESENT SUBJUNCTIVE	CONDITIONAL	PRETERITE
(yo)	**pida**	pedir**ía**	ped**í**
(tú)	**pidas**	pedir**ías**	ped**iste**
(él)	**pida**	pedir**ía**	**pidió**
(nosotros)	**pidamos**	pedir**íamos**	ped**imos**
(vosotros)	**pidáis**	pedir**íais**	ped**isteis**
(ellos)	**pidan**	pedir**ían**	**pidieron**

pensar (to think)

	PAST PARTICIPLE	GERUND	IMPERATIVE
	pens**ado**	pens**ando**	**piensa**
			pensa**d**

	PRESENT	FUTURE	IMPERFECT
(yo)	**pienso**	pensar**é**	pens**aba**
(tú)	**piensas**	pensar**ás**	pens**abas**
(él)	**piensa**	pensar**á**	pens**aba**
(nosotros)	pens**amos**	pensar**emos**	pens**ábamos**
(vosotros)	pens**áis**	pensar**éis**	pens**abais**
(ellos)	**piensan**	pensar**án**	pens**aban**

	PRESENT SUBJUNCTIVE	CONDITIONAL	PRETERITE
(yo)	**piense**	pensar**ía**	pens**é**
(tú)	**pienses**	pensar**ías**	pens**aste**
(él)	**piense**	pensar**ía**	pens**ó**
(nosotros)	pens**emos**	pensar**íamos**	pens**amos**
(vosotros)	pens**éis**	pensar**íais**	pens**asteis**
(ellos)	**piensen**	pensar**ían**	pens**aron**

poder (to be able)

	PAST PARTICIPLE	GERUND	IMPERATIVE
	pod**ido**	**pudiendo**	**puede**
			pode**d**
	PRESENT	FUTURE	IMPERFECT
(yo)	**puedo**	**podré**	pod**ía**
(tú)	**puedes**	**podrás**	pod**ías**
(él)	**puede**	**podrá**	pod**ía**
(nosotros)	pod**emos**	**podremos**	pod**íamos**
(vosotros)	pod**éis**	**podréis**	pod**íais**
(ellos)	**pueden**	**podrán**	pod**ían**
	PRESENT SUBJUNCTIVE	CONDITIONAL	PRETERITE
(yo)	**pueda**	**podría**	**pude**
(tú)	**puedas**	**podrías**	**pudiste**
(él)	**pueda**	**podría**	**pudo**
(nosotros)	pod**amos**	**podríamos**	**pudimos**
(vosotros)	pod**áis**	**podríais**	**pudisteis**
(ellos)	**puedan**	**podrían**	**pudieron**

poner (to put)

	PAST PARTICIPLE	GERUND	IMPERATIVE
	puesto	pon**iendo**	**pon**
			pone**d**
	PRESENT	FUTURE	IMPERFECT
(yo)	**pongo**	**pondré**	pon**ía**
(tú)	pon**es**	**pondrás**	pon**ías**
(él)	pon**e**	**pondrá**	pon**ía**
(nosotros)	pon**emos**	**pondremos**	pon**íamos**
(vosotros)	pon**éis**	**pondréis**	pon**íais**
(ellos)	pon**en**	**pondrán**	pon**ían**
	PRESENT SUBJUNCTIVE	CONDITIONAL	PRETERITE
(yo)	**ponga**	**pondría**	**puse**
(tú)	**pongas**	**pondrías**	**pusiste**
(él)	**ponga**	**pondría**	**puso**
(nosotros)	**pongamos**	**pondríamos**	**pusimos**
(vosotros)	**pongáis**	**pondríais**	**pusisteis**
(ellos)	**pongan**	**pondrían**	**pusieron**

prohibir (to forbid)

	PAST PARTICIPLE	GERUND	IMPERATIVE
	prohib**ido**	prohib**iendo**	**prohíbe**
			prohibi**d**
	PRESENT	FUTURE	IMPERFECT
(yo)	**prohíbo**	prohibir**é**	prohib**ía**
(tú)	**prohíbes**	prohibir**ás**	prohib**ías**
(él)	**prohíbe**	prohibir**á**	prohib**ía**
(nosotros)	prohib**imos**	prohibir**emos**	prohib**íamos**
(vosotros)	prohib**ís**	prohibir**éis**	prohib**íais**
(ellos)	**prohíben**	prohibir**án**	prohib**ían**
	PRESENT SUBJUNCTIVE	CONDITIONAL	PRETERITE
(yo)	**prohíba**	prohibir**ía**	prohib**í**
(tú)	**prohíbas**	prohibir**ías**	prohib**iste**
(él)	**prohíba**	prohibir**ía**	prohib**ió**
(nosotros)	prohib**amos**	prohibir**íamos**	prohib**imos**
(vosotros)	prohib**áis**	prohibir**íais**	prohib**isteis**
(ellos)	**prohíban**	prohibir**ían**	prohib**ieron**

querer (to want)

	PAST PARTICIPLE	GERUND	IMPERATIVE
	quer**ido**	quer**iendo**	**quiere**
			quere**d**
	PRESENT	FUTURE	IMPERFECT
(yo)	**quiero**	**querré**	quer**ía**
(tú)	**quieres**	**querrás**	quer**ías**
(él)	**quiere**	**querrá**	quer**ía**
(nosotros)	quer**emos**	**querremos**	quer**íamos**
(vosotros)	quer**éis**	**querréis**	quer**íais**
(ellos)	**quieren**	**querrán**	quer**ían**
	PRESENT SUBJUNCTIVE	CONDITIONAL	PRETERITE
(yo)	**quiera**	**querría**	**quise**
(tú)	**quieras**	**querrías**	**quisiste**
(él)	**quiera**	**querría**	**quiso**
(nosotros)	quer**amos**	**querríamos**	**quisimos**
(vosotros)	quer**áis**	**querríais**	**quisisteis**
(ellos)	**quieran**	**querrían**	**quisieron**

rehusar (to refuse)

	PAST PARTICIPLE	GERUND	IMPERATIVE
	rehus**ado**	rehus**ando**	**rehúsa**
			rehusa**d**

	PRESENT	FUTURE	IMPERFECT
(yo)	**rehúso**	rehusar**é**	rehus**aba**
(tú)	**rehúsas**	rehusar**ás**	rehus**abas**
(él)	**rehúsa**	rehusar**á**	rehus**aba**
(nosotros)	rehus**amos**	rehusar**emos**	rehus**ábamos**
(vosotros)	rehus**áis**	rehusar**éis**	rehus**abais**
(ellos)	**rehúsan**	rehusar**án**	rehus**aban**

	PRESENT SUBJUNCTIVE	CONDITIONAL	PRETERITE
(yo)	**rehúse**	rehusar**ía**	rehus**é**
(tú)	**rehúses**	rehusar**ías**	rehus**aste**
(él)	**rehúse**	rehusar**ía**	rehus**ó**
(nosotros)	rehus**emos**	rehusar**íamos**	rehus**amos**
(vosotros)	rehus**éis**	rehusar**íais**	rehus**asteis**
(ellos)	**rehúsen**	rehusar**ían**	rehus**aron**

reír (to laugh)

	PAST PARTICIPLE	GERUND	IMPERATIVE
	re**ído**	**riendo**	**ríe**
			reí**d**

	PRESENT	FUTURE	IMPERFECT
(yo)	**río**	**reiré**	re**ía**
(tú)	**ríes**	**reirás**	re**ías**
(él)	**ríe**	**reirá**	re**ía**
(nosotros)	**reímos**	**reiremos**	re**íamos**
(vosotros)	**reís**	**reiréis**	re**íais**
(ellos)	**ríen**	**reirán**	re**ían**

	PRESENT SUBJUNCTIVE	CONDITIONAL	PRETERITE
(yo)	**ría**	**reiría**	**reí**
(tú)	**rías**	**reirías**	**reíste**
(él)	**ría**	**reiría**	**rio**
(nosotros)	**riamos**	**reiríamos**	**reímos**
(vosotros)	**riais**	**reiríais**	**reísteis**
(ellos)	**rían**	**reirían**	**rieron**

reñir (to scold)

	PAST PARTICIPLE	GERUND	IMPERATIVE
	reñ**ido**	**riñendo**	**riñe**
			reñi**d**
	PRESENT	FUTURE	IMPERFECT
(yo)	**riño**	reñir**é**	reñ**ía**
(tú)	**riñes**	reñir**ás**	reñ**ías**
(él)	**riñe**	reñir**á**	reñ**ía**
(nosotros)	reñ**imos**	reñir**emos**	reñ**íamos**
(vosotros)	reñ**ís**	reñir**éis**	reñ**íais**
(ellos)	**riñen**	reñir**án**	reñ**ían**
	PRESENT SUBJUNCTIVE	CONDITIONAL	PRETERITE
(yo)	**riña**	reñir**ía**	reñ**í**
(tú)	**riñas**	reñir**ías**	reñ**iste**
(él)	**riña**	reñir**ía**	**riñó**
(nosotros)	**riñamos**	reñir**íamos**	reñ**imos**
(vosotros)	**riñáis**	reñir**íais**	reñ**isteis**
(ellos)	**riñan**	reñir**ían**	**riñeron**

resolver (to solve)

	PAST PARTICIPLE	GERUND	IMPERATIVE
	resuelto	resolv**iendo**	**resuelve**
			resolve**d**
	PRESENT	FUTURE	IMPERFECT
(yo)	**resuelvo**	resolver**é**	resolv**ía**
(tú)	**resuelves**	resolver**ás**	resolv**ías**
(él)	**resuelve**	resolver**á**	resolv**ía**
(nosotros)	resolv**emos**	resolver**emos**	resolv**íamos**
(vosotros)	resolv**éis**	resolver**éis**	resolv**íais**
(ellos)	**resuelven**	resolver**án**	resolv**ían**
	PRESENT SUBJUNCTIVE	CONDITIONAL	PRETERITE
(yo)	**resuelva**	resolver**ía**	resolv**í**
(tú)	**resuelvas**	resolver**ías**	resolv**iste**
(él)	**resuelva**	resolver**ía**	resolv**ió**
(nosotros)	resolv**amos**	resolver**íamos**	resolv**imos**
(vosotros)	resolv**áis**	resolver**íais**	resolv**isteis**
(ellos)	**resuelvan**	resolver**ían**	resolv**ieron**

reunir (to put together, to gather)

	PAST PARTICIPLE	GERUND	IMPERATIVE
	reun**ido**	reun**iendo**	**reúne**
			reuni**d**
	PRESENT	FUTURE	IMPERFECT
(yo)	**reúno**	reunir**é**	reun**ía**
(tú)	**reúnes**	reunir**ás**	reun**ías**
(él)	**reúne**	reunir**á**	reun**ía**
(nosotros)	reun**imos**	reunir**emos**	reun**íamos**
(vosotros)	reun**ís**	reunir**éis**	reun**íais**
(ellos)	**reúnen**	reunir**án**	reun**ían**
	PRESENT SUBJUNCTIVE	CONDITIONAL	PRETERITE
(yo)	**reúna**	reunir**ía**	reun**í**
(tú)	**reúnas**	reunir**ías**	reun**iste**
(él)	**reúna**	reunir**ía**	reun**ió**
(nosotros)	reun**amos**	reunir**íamos**	reun**imos**
(vosotros)	reun**áis**	reunir**íais**	reun**isteis**
(ellos)	**reúnan**	reunir**ían**	reun**ieron**

rogar (to beg)

	PAST PARTICIPLE	GERUND	IMPERATIVE
	rog**ado**	rog**ando**	**ruega**
			roga**d**
	PRESENT	FUTURE	IMPERFECT
(yo)	**ruego**	rogar**é**	rog**aba**
(tú)	**ruegas**	rogar**ás**	rog**abas**
(él)	**ruega**	rogar**á**	rog**aba**
(nosotros)	rog**amos**	rogar**emos**	rog**ábamos**
(vosotros)	rog**áis**	rogar**éis**	rog**abais**
(ellos)	**ruegan**	rogar**án**	rog**aban**
	PRESENT SUBJUNCTIVE	CONDITIONAL	PRETERITE
(yo)	**ruegue**	rogar**ía**	**rogué**
(tú)	**ruegues**	rogar**ías**	rog**aste**
(él)	**ruegue**	rogar**ía**	rog**ó**
(nosotros)	**roguemos**	rogar**íamos**	rog**amos**
(vosotros)	**roguéis**	rogar**íais**	rog**asteis**
(ellos)	**rueguen**	rogar**ían**	rog**aron**

saber (to know)

	PAST PARTICIPLE	GERUND	IMPERATIVE
	sab**ido**	sab**iendo**	sab**e**
			sab**ed**

	PRESENT	FUTURE	IMPERFECT
(yo)	**sé**	**sabré**	sab**ía**
(tú)	sab**es**	**sabrás**	sab**ías**
(él)	sab**e**	**sabrá**	sab**ía**
(nosotros)	sab**emos**	**sabremos**	sab**íamos**
(vosotros)	sab**éis**	**sabréis**	sab**íais**
(ellos)	sab**en**	**sabrán**	sab**ían**

	PRESENT SUBJUNCTIVE	CONDITIONAL	PRETERITE
(yo)	**sepa**	**sabría**	**supe**
(tú)	**sepas**	**sabrías**	**supiste**
(él)	**sepa**	**sabría**	**supo**
(nosotros)	**sepamos**	**sabríamos**	**supimos**
(vosotros)	**sepáis**	**sabríais**	**supisteis**
(ellos)	**sepan**	**sabrían**	**supieron**

salir (to go out)

	PAST PARTICIPLE	GERUND	IMPERATIVE
	sal**ido**	sal**iendo**	**sal**
			sali**d**

	PRESENT	FUTURE	IMPERFECT
(yo)	**salgo**	**saldré**	sal**ía**
(tú)	sal**es**	**saldrás**	sal**ías**
(él)	sal**e**	**saldrá**	sal**ía**
(nosotros)	sal**imos**	**saldremos**	sal**íamos**
(vosotros)	sal**ís**	**saldréis**	sal**íais**
(ellos)	sal**en**	**saldrán**	sal**ían**

	PRESENT SUBJUNCTIVE	CONDITIONAL	PRETERITE
(yo)	**salga**	**saldría**	sal**í**
(tú)	**salgas**	**saldrías**	sal**iste**
(él)	**salga**	**saldría**	sal**ió**
(nosotros)	**salgamos**	**saldríamos**	sal**imos**
(vosotros)	**salgáis**	**saldríais**	sal**isteis**
(ellos)	**salgan**	**saldrían**	sal**ieron**

satisfacer (to satisfy)

	PAST PARTICIPLE	GERUND	IMPERATIVE
	satisfecho	satisfac**iendo**	**satisfaz**/satisfac**e** satisfac**ed**

	PRESENT	FUTURE	IMPERFECT
(yo)	**satisfago**	**satisfaré**	satisfac**ía**
(tú)	satisfac**es**	**satisfarás**	satisfac**ías**
(él)	satisfac**e**	**satisfará**	satisfac**ía**
(nosotros)	satisfac**emos**	**satisfaremos**	satisfac**íamos**
(vosotros)	satisfac**éis**	**satisfaréis**	satisfac**íais**
(ellos)	satisfac**en**	**satisfarán**	satisfac**ían**

	PRESENT SUBJUNCTIVE	CONDITIONAL	PRETERITE
(yo)	**satisfaga**	**satisfaría**	**satisfice**
(tú)	**satisfagas**	**satisfarías**	**satisficiste**
(él)	**satisfaga**	**satisfaría**	**satisfizo**
(nosotros)	**satisfagamos**	**satisfaríamos**	**satisficimos**
(vosotros)	**satisfagáis**	**satisfaríais**	**satisficisteis**
(ellos)	**satisfagan**	**satisfarían**	**satisficieron**

seguir (to follow)

	PAST PARTICIPLE	GERUND	IMPERATIVE
	segu**ido**	**siguiendo**	**sigue** segui**d**

	PRESENT	FUTURE	IMPERFECT
(yo)	**sigo**	seguir**é**	segu**ía**
(tú)	**sigues**	seguir**ás**	segu**ías**
(él)	**sigue**	seguir**á**	segu**ía**
(nosotros)	segu**imos**	seguir**emos**	segu**íamos**
(vosotros)	segu**ís**	seguir**éis**	segu**íais**
(ellos)	**siguen**	seguir**án**	segu**ían**

	PRESENT SUBJUNCTIVE	CONDITIONAL	PRETERITE
(yo)	**siga**	seguir**ía**	segu**í**
(tú)	**sigas**	seguir**ías**	segu**iste**
(él)	**siga**	seguir**ía**	**siguió**
(nosotros)	**sigamos**	seguir**íamos**	segu**imos**
(vosotros)	**sigáis**	seguir**íais**	segu**isteis**
(ellos)	**sigan**	seguir**ían**	**siguieron**

sentir (to feel)

	PAST PARTICIPLE	GERUND	IMPERATIVE
	sent**ido**	**sintiendo**	**siente** senti**d**
	PRESENT	**FUTURE**	**IMPERFECT**
(yo)	**siento**	sentir**é**	sent**ía**
(tú)	**sientes**	sentir**ás**	sent**ías**
(él)	**siente**	sentir**á**	sent**ía**
(nosotros)	sent**imos**	sentir**emos**	sent**íamos**
(vosotros)	sent**ís**	sentir**éis**	sent**íais**
(ellos)	**sienten**	sentir**án**	sent**ían**
	PRESENT SUBJUNCTIVE	**CONDITIONAL**	**PRETERITE**
(yo)	**sienta**	sentir**ía**	sent**í**
(tú)	**sientas**	sentir**ías**	sent**iste**
(él)	**sienta**	sentir**ía**	**sintió**
(nosotros)	**sintamos**	sentir**íamos**	sent**imos**
(vosotros)	**sintáis**	sentir**íais**	sent**isteis**
(ellos)	**sientan**	sentir**ían**	**sintieron**

ser (to be)

	PAST PARTICIPLE	GERUND	IMPERATIVE
	sido	**siendo**	**sé** se**d**
	PRESENT	**FUTURE**	**IMPERFECT**
(yo)	**soy**	ser**é**	**era**
(tú)	**eres**	ser**ás**	**eras**
(él)	**es**	ser**á**	**era**
(nosotros)	**somos**	ser**emos**	**éramos**
(vosotros)	**sois**	ser**éis**	**erais**
(ellos)	**son**	ser**án**	**eran**
	PRESENT SUBJUNCTIVE	**CONDITIONAL**	**PRETERITE**
(yo)	**sea**	ser**ía**	**fui**
(tú)	**seas**	ser**ías**	**fuiste**
(él)	**sea**	ser**ía**	**fue**
(nosotros)	**seamos**	ser**íamos**	**fuimos**
(vosotros)	**seáis**	ser**íais**	**fuisteis**
(ellos)	**sean**	ser**ían**	**fueron**

tener (to have)

	PAST PARTICIPLE	GERUND	IMPERATIVE
	ten**ido**	ten**iendo**	**ten**
			tene**d**

	PRESENT	FUTURE	IMPERFECT
(yo)	**tengo**	**tendré**	ten**ía**
(tú)	**tienes**	**tendrás**	ten**ías**
(él)	**tiene**	**tendrá**	ten**ía**
(nosotros)	ten**emos**	**tendremos**	ten**íamos**
(vosotros)	ten**éis**	**tendréis**	ten**íais**
(ellos)	**tienen**	**tendrán**	ten**ían**

	PRESENT SUBJUNCTIVE	CONDITIONAL	PRETERITE
(yo)	**tenga**	**tendría**	**tuve**
(tú)	**tengas**	**tendrías**	**tuviste**
(él)	**tenga**	**tendría**	**tuvo**
(nosotros)	**tengamos**	**tendríamos**	**tuvimos**
(vosotros)	**tengáis**	**tendríais**	**tuvisteis**
(ellos)	**tengan**	**tendrían**	**tuvieron**

torcer (to twist)

	PAST PARTICIPLE	GERUND	IMPERATIVE
	torc**ido**	torc**iendo**	**tuerce**
			torce**d**

	PRESENT	FUTURE	IMPERFECT
(yo)	**tuerzo**	torcer**é**	torc**ía**
(tú)	**tuerces**	torcer**ás**	torc**ías**
(él)	**tuerce**	torcer**á**	torc**ía**
(nosotros)	torc**emos**	torcer**emos**	torc**íamos**
(vosotros)	torc**éis**	torcer**éis**	torc**íais**
(ellos)	**tuercen**	torcer**án**	torc**ían**

	PRESENT SUBJUNCTIVE	CONDITIONAL	PRETERITE
(yo)	**tuerza**	torcer**ía**	torc**í**
(tú)	**tuerzas**	torcer**ías**	torc**iste**
(él)	**tuerza**	torcer**ía**	torc**ió**
(nosotros)	**torzamos**	torcer**íamos**	torc**imos**
(vosotros)	**torzáis**	torcer**íais**	torc**isteis**
(ellos)	**tuerzan**	torcer**ían**	torc**ieron**

traer (to bring)

	PAST PARTICIPLE	GERUND	IMPERATIVE
	traído	**trayendo**	tra**e**
			trae**d**

	PRESENT	FUTURE	IMPERFECT
(yo)	**traigo**	traer**é**	tra**ía**
(tú)	tra**es**	traer**ás**	tra**ías**
(él)	tra**e**	traer**á**	tra**ía**
(nosotros)	tra**emos**	traer**emos**	tra**íamos**
(vosotros)	tra**éis**	traer**éis**	tra**íais**
(ellos)	tra**en**	traer**án**	tra**ían**

	PRESENT SUBJUNCTIVE	CONDITIONAL	PRETERITE
(yo)	**traiga**	traer**ía**	**traje**
(tú)	**traigas**	traer**ías**	**trajiste**
(él)	**traiga**	traer**ía**	**trajo**
(nosotros)	**traigamos**	traer**íamos**	**trajimos**
(vosotros)	**traigáis**	traer**íais**	**trajisteis**
(ellos)	**traigan**	traer**ían**	**trajeron**

valer (to be worth)

	PAST PARTICIPLE	GERUND	IMPERATIVE
	val**ido**	val**iendo**	vale
			vale**d**

	PRESENT	FUTURE	IMPERFECT
(yo)	**valgo**	**valdré**	val**ía**
(tú)	val**es**	**valdrás**	val**ías**
(él)	val**e**	**valdrá**	val**ía**
(nosotros)	val**emos**	**valdremos**	val**íamos**
(vosotros)	val**éis**	**valdréis**	val**íais**
(ellos)	val**en**	**valdrán**	val**ían**

	PRESENT SUBJUNCTIVE	CONDITIONAL	PRETERITE
(yo)	**valga**	**valdría**	val**í**
(tú)	**valgas**	**valdrías**	val**iste**
(él)	**valga**	**valdría**	val**ió**
(nosotros)	**valgamos**	**valdríamos**	val**imos**
(vosotros)	**valgáis**	**valdríais**	val**isteis**
(ellos)	**valgan**	**valdrían**	val**ieron**

venir (to come)

	PAST PARTICIPLE	GERUND	IMPERATIVE
	ven**ido**	**viniendo**	**ven**
			veni**d**

	PRESENT	FUTURE	IMPERFECT
(yo)	**vengo**	**vendré**	ven**ía**
(tú)	**vienes**	**vendrás**	ven**ías**
(él)	**viene**	**vendrá**	ven**ía**
(nosotros)	ven**imos**	**vendremos**	ven**íamos**
(vosotros)	ven**ís**	**vendréis**	ven**íais**
(ellos)	**vienen**	**vendrán**	ven**ían**

	PRESENT SUBJUNCTIVE	CONDITIONAL	PRETERITE
(yo)	**venga**	**vendría**	**vine**
(tú)	**vengas**	**vendrías**	**viniste**
(él)	**venga**	**vendría**	**vino**
(nosotros)	**vengamos**	**vendríamos**	**vinimos**
(vosotros)	**vengáis**	**vendríais**	**vinisteis**
(ellos)	**vengan**	**vendrían**	**vinieron**

ver (to see)

	PAST PARTICIPLE	GERUND	IMPERATIVE
	visto	viendo	ve
			ve**d**

	PRESENT	FUTURE	IMPERFECT
(yo)	**veo**	ver**é**	**veía**
(tú)	**ves**	ver**ás**	**veías**
(él)	ve	ver**á**	**veía**
(nosotros)	v**emos**	ver**emos**	**veíamos**
(vosotros)	v**eis**	ver**éis**	**veíais**
(ellos)	v**en**	ver**án**	**veían**

	PRESENT SUBJUNCTIVE	CONDITIONAL	PRETERITE
(yo)	**vea**	ver**ía**	vi
(tú)	**veas**	ver**ías**	v**iste**
(él)	**vea**	ver**ía**	v**io**
(nosotros)	**veamos**	ver**íamos**	v**imos**
(vosotros)	**veáis**	ver**íais**	v**isteis**
(ellos)	**vean**	ver**ían**	v**ieron**

volcar (to overturn)

	PAST PARTICIPLE	GERUND	IMPERATIVE
	volc**ado**	volc**ando**	**vuelca**
			volca**d**
	PRESENT	**FUTURE**	**IMPERFECT**
(yo)	**vuelco**	volcar**é**	volc**aba**
(tú)	**vuelcas**	volcar**ás**	volc**abas**
(él)	**vuelca**	volcar**á**	volc**aba**
(nosotros)	volc**amos**	volcar**emos**	volc**ábamos**
(vosotros)	volc**áis**	volcar**éis**	volc**abais**
(ellos)	**vuelcan**	volcar**án**	volc**aban**
	PRESENT SUBJUNCTIVE	**CONDITIONAL**	**PRETERITE**
(yo)	**vuelque**	volcar**ía**	**volqué**
(tú)	**vuelques**	volcar**ías**	volc**aste**
(él)	**vuelque**	volcar**ía**	volc**ó**
(nosotros)	**volquemos**	volcar**íamos**	volc**amos**
(vosotros)	**volquéis**	volcar**íais**	volc**asteis**
(ellos)	**vuelquen**	volcar**ían**	volc**aron**

volver (to return)

	PAST PARTICIPLE	GERUND	IMPERATIVE
	vuelto	volv**iendo**	**vuelve**
			volve**d**
	PRESENT	**FUTURE**	**IMPERFECT**
(yo)	**vuelvo**	volver**é**	volv**ía**
(tú)	**vuelves**	volver**ás**	volv**ías**
(él)	**vuelve**	volver**á**	volv**ía**
(nosotros)	volv**emos**	volver**emos**	volv**íamos**
(vosotros)	volv**éis**	volver**éis**	volv**íais**
(ellos)	**vuelven**	volver**án**	volv**ían**
	PRESENT SUBJUNCTIVE	**CONDITIONAL**	**PRETERITE**
(yo)	**vuelva**	volver**ía**	volv**í**
(tú)	**vuelvas**	volver**ías**	volv**iste**
(él)	**vuelva**	volver**ía**	volv**ió**
(nosotros)	volv**amos**	volver**íamos**	volv**imos**
(vosotros)	volv**áis**	volver**íais**	volv**isteis**
(ellos)	**vuelvan**	volver**ían**	volv**ieron**

Nouns

The Gender of Nouns

In Spanish, all nouns are either masculine or feminine, whether denoting people, animals or things. Gender is largely unpredictable and has to be learnt for each noun. However, the following guidelines will help you determine the gender for certain types of nouns:

Nouns denoting male people and animals are usually – but not always – masculine, e.g.

un hombre a man	**un enfermero** a (*male*) nurse
un toro a bull	**un semental** a stallion

Nouns denoting female people and animals are usually – but not always – feminine, e.g.

una niña a girl	**una enfermera** a nurse
una vaca a cow	**una yegua** a mare

Some nouns are masculine *or* feminine depending on the sex of the person to whom they refer, e.g.

un camarada a (*male*) comrade	**una camarada** a (*female*) comrade
un belga a Belgian (*man*)	**una belga** a Belgian (*woman*)

Other nouns referring to either men *or* women have only one gender which applies to both, e.g.

una persona a person	**una víctima** a victim
una visita a visitor	**una estrella** a star

Often the ending of a noun indicates its gender. Shown below and opposite are some of the most important to guide you.

Masculine endings

-o	**un clavo** a nail, **un plátano** a banana EXCEPTIONS: **mano** hand, **foto** photograph, **moto(cicleta)** motorbike
-r	**un tractor** a tractor, **el altar** the altar EXCEPTIONS: **coliflor** cauliflower, **flor** flower, **labor** task

Examples

Feminine endings

-a	**una casa** a house, **la cara** the face EXCEPTIONS: **día** day, **mapa** map, **planeta** planet, **tranvía** tram, and most words ending in **-ma** (**tema** subject, **problema** problem, etc)
-ión	**una canción** a song, **una procesión** a procession EXCEPTIONS: most nouns not ending in **-ción** or **-sión**, e.g. **avión** aeroplane, **camión** lorry, **gorrión** sparrow
-dad, -tad,	**una ciudad** a town, **la libertad** freedom
-itis	**una faringitis** pharyngitis, **la celulitis** cellulitis
-sis	**una tesis** a thesis, **una dosis** a dose EXCEPTIONS: **análisis** analysis, **énfasis** emphasis, **paréntesis** parenthesis

Some nouns change meaning according to gender:

	MASCULINE	FEMININE
capital	capital (*money*)	capital (*city*)
cometa	comet	kite
corte	cut	court (*royal*)
coma	coma	comma
cura	priest	cure
frente	front (*in war*)	forehead
guía	guide (*man*)	guide(book), guide (*woman*)
orden	order (*arrangement*)	order (*command*)
papa	Pope	potato
pendiente	earring	slope
policía	policeman	police, policewoman
radio	radius, radium	radio

Nouns

Gender: the Formation of Feminines

As in English, males and females are sometimes differentiated by the use of two quite separate words, e.g.

mi marido my husband — **mi mujer** my wife
un toro a bull — **una vaca** a cow

There are, however, some words in Spanish which show this distinction by the form of their ending:

Nouns ending in **-o** change to **-a** to form the feminine (e.g. **un amigo** a (*male*) friend → **una amiga** a (*female*) friend; **un gato** a cat → **una gata** a (*female*) cat).

If the masculine singular form already ends in **-a**, no further **-a** is added to the feminine (e.g. **un deportista** a sportsman → **una deportista** a sportswoman).

If the last letter of the masculine singular form is a consonant, an **-a** is normally added in the feminine (e.g. **un vendedor** a salesman → **una vendedora** a saleswoman).

* If the last syllable has an accent, it disappears in the feminine (e.g. **un león** a lion → **una leona** a lioness; see page 127)

Feminine forms to note

MASCULINE	FEMININE	
el abad	**la abadesa**	abbot/abbess
un actor	**una actriz**	actor/actress
el alcalde	**la alcaldesa**	mayor/mayoress
el conde	**la condesa**	count/countess
el duque	**la duquesa**	duke/duchess
el emperador	**la emperatriz**	emperor/empress
un poeta	**una poetisa**	poet/poetess
el príncipe	**la princesa**	prince/princess
el rey	**la reina**	king/queen
un sacerdote	**una sacerdotisa**	priest/priestess
un tigre	**una tigresa**	tiger/tigress
el zar	**la zarina**	tzar/tzarina

Nouns

The Formation of Plurals

Nouns ending in an unstressed vowel add **-s** to the singular form (e.g. **la casa** the house → **las casas** the houses; **el libro** the book → **los libros** the books).

Nouns ending in a consonant or a stressed vowel add **-es** to the singular form (e.g. **un rumor** a rumour → **unos rumores** (some) rumours; **un jabalí** a boar → **unos jabalíes** (some) boars).

ⓘ BUT: **café** coffee shop (*plural*: **cafés**)
mamá mummy (*plural*: **mamás**)
papá daddy (*plural*: **papás**)
pie foot (*plural*: **pies**)
sofá sofa (*plural*: **sofás**)
té tea (*plural*: **tes**)

and words of foreign origin ending in a consonant, e.g.:

coñac brandy (*plural*: **coñacs**)
ballet ballet (*plural*: **ballets**)

ⓘ Note:

- nouns ending in **-n** or **-s** with an accent on the last syllable drop this accent in the plural (e.g. **la canción** the song → **las canciones** the songs; **el autobús** the bus → **los autobuses** the buses); see page 127.
- nouns ending in **-n** with the stress on the last syllable but one in the singular add an accent to that syllable in the plural in order to show the correct position for stress (e.g. **un examen** an exam → **unos exámenes** (some) exams; **un crimen** a crime → **unos crímenes** (some) crimes; see page 127)
- nouns ending in **-z** change this to **c** in the plural (e.g. **la luz** the light → **las luces** the lights).

Nouns with an unstressed final syllable ending in **-s** do not change in the plural (e.g. **un paraguas** an umbrella → **unos paraguas** (some) umbrellas; **el lunes** Monday → **los lunes** Mondays).

Articles

The Definite Article

	WITH MASC. NOUN	WITH FEM. NOUN	
SING.	**el**	**la**	the
PLUR.	**los**	**las**	the

The article used depends on both the gender of the noun and whether it is singular or plural → ❶

ⓘ Note: use **el** not **la** immediately before a feminine singular noun starting with a stressed **a-** or **ha-** → ❷

a + **el** becomes **al** and **de** + **el** becomes **del** → ❸

Uses of the Definite Article

While the Spanish definite article ususally translates as 'the', it is often used where English has no article or uses another construction:

- with abstract nouns, except when following certain prepositions → ❹
- in generalizations, especially with plural or uncountable nouns → ❺
- with parts of the body → ❻
  Note that 'ownership' is often indicated by an indirect object pronoun or a reflexive pronoun → ❼
- with titles/ranks/professions followed by a proper name → ❽
  EXCEPTIONS: with **Don/Doña**, **San/Santo(a)** → ❾
- before nouns of official, academic and religious buildings, and names of meals and games → ❿

The definite article is *not* used with nouns in apposition unless those nouns are individualized → ⓫

Examples

1	el tren the train el actor the actor (*male*) los hoteles the hotels	la estación the station la actriz the actress las mujeres the women
2	el agua pura the pure water el hacha the axe	la misma agua the same water la mejor hacha the best axe
3	al cine al hospital del departamento del presidente	to the cinema to the hospital from/of the department from/of the president
4	El tiempo es oro BUT: con pasión sin esperanza	Time is money with passion without hope
5	No me gusta el café Los niños necesitan ser queridos Los precios suben	I don't like coffee Children need to be loved Prices are rising
6	No puedo mover las piernas	I can't move my legs
7	Lávate las manos	Wash your hands
8	el doctor Ochoa el señor Ramírez	Doctor Ochoa Mr Ramírez
9	Don Arturo Ruiz Santa Teresa	Mr Arturo Ruiz Saint Teresa
10	en la cárcel en la universidad en la iglesia la cena el tenis	in prison at university at church dinner tennis
11	Madrid, capital de España, es la ciudad que ... BUT: Maria Callas, la famosa cantante de ópera ...	Madrid, the capital of Spain, is the city which ... Maria Callas, the famous opera singer ...

Articles

The Indefinite Article

	WITH MASC. NOUN	WITH FEM. NOUN	
SING.	**un**	**una**	a
PLUR.	**unos**	**unas**	some

The indefinite article is used in Spanish largely as it is in English. However, there is no article when a person's profession is being stated → ❶ unless the profession is qualified by an adjective → ❷

The article is not used with the following words: → ❸

otro	another	**cien**	a hundred
cierto	certain	**mil**	a thousand
semejante	such (a)	**sin**	without
tal	such (a)	**qué**	what a

There is no article with a noun in apposition → ❹. When an abstract noun is qualified by an adjective, the indefinite article is used, but is not translated in English → ❺

The Article lo

This is never used with a noun. Instead, it is used in the following ways:

- as an intensifier before an adjective or adverb in the construction **lo** + adjective/adverb + **que** → ❻
  Note: The adjective agrees with the noun it refers to → ❼
- With an adjective or participle to form an abstract noun → ❽
- In the phrase **lo de** to refer to a subject of which speaker and listener are already aware. → ❾
- In certain set expressions, the commonest of which are: → ❿
  a lo mejor maybe, perhaps
  a lo lejos in the distance
  a lo largo de along, through
  por lo menos at least
  por lo tanto therefore, so
  por lo visto apparently

Examples

1	Es profesor	He's a teacher
	Mi madre es enfermera	My mother is a nurse
2	Es un buen médico	He's a good doctor
	Se hizo una escritora célebre	She became a famous writer
3	otro libro	another book
	cierta calle	a certain street
	tal mentira	such a lie
	cien/mil años	a hundred/thousand years
	sin casa	without a house
	¡Qué sorpresa!	What a surprise!
4	Baroja, gran escritor de la Generación del 98	Baroja, a great writer of the 'Generación del 98'
5	con una gran sabiduría	with great wisdom
	Dieron pruebas de una sangre fría increíble	They showed incredible coolness
6	No sabíamos lo pequeña que era la casa	We didn't know how small the house was
	Sé lo mucho que te gusta la música	I know how much you like music
7	No te imaginas lo simpáticos que son	You can't imagine how nice they are
8	Lo bueno de eso es que ...	The good thing about it is that ...
9	Lo de tu hermano me preocupa mucho	That business with your brother worries me a lot
10	A lo mejor ha salido	Perhaps he's gone out
	A lo lejos se veían unas casas	Some houses could be seen in the distance
	a lo largo de su vida	throughout his life
	a lo largo de la carretera	along the road
	Hubo por lo menos cincuenta heridos	At least fifty people were injured
	Por lo visto, no viene	He's not coming, it seems

Adjectives

Adjectives

Most adjectives agree in number and gender with the noun or pronoun.

ⓘ Note that:

- if the adjective refers to two or more singular nouns of the same gender, a plural ending of that gender is required → ❶
- if the adjective refers to two or more singular nouns of different genders, a masculine plural ending is required → ❷

The Formation of Feminines

Adjectives ending in **-o** change to **-a** → ❸

Some groups of adjectives add **-a**:

- adjectives of nationality or geographical origin → ❹
- adjectives ending in **-or** (except irregular comparatives: see page 88), **-án**, **-ón**, **-ín** → ❺

ⓘ Note: When there is an accent on the last syllable, it disappears in the feminine (see page 127).

Other adjectives do not change → ❻

The Formation of Plurals

Adjectives ending in an unstressed vowel add **-s** → ❼

Adjectives ending in a stressed vowel or a consonant add **-es** → ❽

ⓘ Note:

- if there is an accent on the last syllable of a word ending in a consonant, it will disappear in the plural (see page 127) → ❾
- if the last letter is a **z**, it will become a **c** in the plural → ❿

Examples

1	la lengua y la literatura españolas	(the) Spanish language and literature
2	Nunca había visto árboles y flores tan raros	I had never seen such strange trees and flowers
3	mi hermano pequeño	my little brother
	mi hermana pequeña	my little sister
4	un chico español	a Spanish boy
	una chica española	a Spanish girl
	el equipo barcelonés	the team from Barcelona
	la vida barcelonesa	the Barcelona way of life
5	un niño encantador	a charming little boy
	una niña encantadora	a charming little girl
	un hombre holgazán	an idle man
	una mujer holgazana	an idle woman
	un gesto burlón	a mocking gesture
	una sonrisa burlona	a mocking smile
	un chico cantarín	a boy who's fond of singing
	una chica cantarina	a girl who's fond of singing
6	un final feliz	a happy ending
	una infancia feliz	a happy childhood
	mi amigo belga	my Belgian (*male*) friend
	mi amiga belga	my Belgian (*female*) friend
	el vestido verde	the green dress
	la blusa verde	the green blouse
7	el último tren	the last train
	los últimos trenes	the last trains
	una casa vieja	an old house
	unas casas viejas	(some) old houses
8	un médico iraní	an Iranian doctor
	unos médicos iraníes	(some) Iranian doctors
	un examen fácil	an easy exam
	unos exámenes fáciles	(some) easy exams
9	un río francés	a French river
	unos ríos franceses	(some) French rivers
10	un día feliz	a happy day
	unos días felices	(some) happy days

Adjectives

Invariable Adjectives

Some adjectives and other parts of speech used adjectivally do not change in the feminine or plural. The commonest of these are:

- nouns used to denote colour → ❶
- compound adjectives → ❷
- nouns used as adjectives → ❸

Shortening of Adjectives

The following drop the final **-o** before a masculine singular noun:

bueno good → ❹
malo bad
alguno* some → ❺
ninguno* none
uno one → ❻
primero first → ❼
tercero third
postrero last → ❽

* ⓘ Note: An accent is required to show the correct position for stress.

Grande *big*, *great* is usually shortened to **gran** before a masculine *or* feminine singular noun → ❾

Santo *Saint* changes to **San** except with saints' names beginning with **Do-** *or* **To-** → ❿

Ciento *a hundred* is shortened to **cien** before a masculine *or* feminine plural noun → ⓫

Cualquiera drops the final **-a** before a singular noun → ⓬

Examples

❶ los vestidos naranja	the orange dresses
❷ las chaquetas azul marino	the navy blue jackets
❸ bebés probeta mujeres soldado	test-tube babies women soldiers
❹ un buen libro	a good book
❺ algún libro	some book
❻ cuarenta y un años	forty-one years
❼ el primer hijo	the first child
❽ un postrer deseo	a last wish
❾ un gran actor una gran decepción	a great actor a great disappointment
❿ San Antonio Santo Tomás	Saint Anthony Saint Thomas
⓫ cien años cien millones	a hundred years a hundred million
⓬ cualquier día a cualquier hora	any day any time

Adjectives

Comparatives and Superlatives

Comparatives

más ... (que) more ... (than) → ❶
menos ... (que) less ... (than) → ❷
tanto ... como as ... as → ❸
tan ... como as ... as → ❹
tan ... que so ... that → ❺

demasiado ...		too ...	
bastante ...	**para**	... enough	to → ❻
suficiente ...		... enough	

'Than' followed by a clause is translated by **de lo que** → ❼

Superlatives

el/la/los/las más ... (que) the most ... (that) → ❽
el/la/los/las menos ... (que) the least ... (that) → ❾
After a superlative, **de** is often translated as 'in' → ❿

Adjectives with irregular comparatives/superlatives

ADJECTIVE	COMPARATIVE	SUPERLATIVE
bueno/a	**mejor**	**el/la mejor**
good	better	the best
malo/a	**peor**	**el/la peor**
bad	worse	the worst
grande	**mayor** *or* **más grande**	**el/la mayor** *or* **el/la más grande**
big	bigger; older	the biggest; the oldest
pequeño/a	**menor** *or* **más pequeño/a**	**el/la menor** *or* **el/la más pequeño/a**
small	smaller; younger; lesser	the smallest; the youngest; the least

While the regular comparative and superlative forms of **grande** and **pequeño** are used mainly to express physical size (→ ⓫), the irregular forms are used mainly to express age, in which case they come after the noun (→ ⓬), and abstract size and degrees of importance, in which case they come before the noun (→ ⓭)

Examples

1	una razón más seria	a more serious reason
	Es más alto que mi hermano	He's taller than my brother
2	una película menos conocida	a less well-known film
	Luis es menos tímido que tú	Luis is less shy than you
3	Pablo tenía tanto miedo como yo	Pablo was as frightened as I was
4	No es tan grande como creía	It isn't as big as I thought
5	El examen era tan difícil que nadie aprobó	The exam was so difficult that nobody passed
6	Eres (lo) bastante grande para hacerlo solo	You're old enough to do it by yourself
7	Está más cansada de lo que parece	She is more tired than she seems
8	el caballo más veloz	the fastest horse
	la casa más pequeña	the smallest house
	los días más lluviosos	the wettest days
	las manzanas más maduras	the ripest apples
9	el hombre menos simpático	the least likeable man
	la niña menos habladora	the least talkative girl
	los cuadros menos bonitos	the least attractive paintings
	las camisas menos viejas	the least old shirts
10	la estación más ruidosa de Londres	the noisiest station in London
11	Este plato es más grande que aquel	This plate is bigger than that one
	Mi casa es más pequeña que la tuya	My house is smaller than yours
12	mis hermanos mayores	my older brothers
	la hija menor	the youngest daughter
13	el menor ruido	the slightest sound
	las mayores dificultades	the biggest difficulties

Adjectives

Interrogative Adjectives

	MASCULINE	FEMININE	
SING.	**¿qué?**	**¿qué?**	what?, which?
	¿cuánto?	**¿cuánta?**	how much?
PLUR.	**¿qué?**	**¿qué?**	what?, which?
	¿cuántos?	**¿cuántas?**	how many?

Interrogative adjectives, when not invariable, agree in number and gender with the noun → ❶

The forms shown above are also used in indirect questions → ❷

Exclamatory Adjectives

	MASCULINE	FEMININE	
SING.	**¡qué!**	**¡qué!**	what (a)!
	¡cuánto!	**¡cuánta!**	what (a lot of)!
PLUR.	**¡qué!**	**¡qué!**	what!
	¡cuántos!	**¡cuántas!**	what (a lot of)!

Exclamatory adjectives, when not invariable, agree in number and gender with the noun → ❸

Examples

1	¿Qué libro te gustó más?	Which book did you like most?
	¿Qué clase de hombre es?	What type of man is he?
	¿Qué instrumentos toca Vd?	What instruments do you play?
	¿Qué ofertas ha recibido Vd?	What offers have you received?
	¿Cuánto dinero te queda?	How much money have you got left?
	¿Cuánta lluvia ha caído?	How much rain have we had?
	¿Cuántos vestidos quieres comprar?	How many dresses do you want to buy?
	¿Cuántas personas van a venir?	How many people are coming?
2	No sé a qué hora llegó	I don't know what time she arrived at
	Dígame cuántas postales quiere	Tell me how many postcards you'd like
3	¡Qué pena!	What a shame!
	¡Qué tiempo tan/más malo!	What lousy weather!
	¡Cuánto tiempo!	What a long time!
	¡Cuánta pobreza!	What poverty!
	¡Cuántos autobuses!	What a lot of buses!
	¡Cuántas mentiras!	What a lot of lies!

Adjectives

Possessive Adjectives

Weak forms

WITH SING. NOUN		WITH PLUR. NOUN		
MASC.	FEM.	MASC.	FEM.	
mi	**mi**	**mis**	**mis**	my
tu	**tu**	**tus**	**tus**	your
su	**su**	**sus**	**sus**	his; her; its; your (of **Vd**)
nuestro	**nuestra**	**nuestros**	**nuestras**	our
vuestro	**vuestra**	**vuestros**	**vuestras**	your
su	**su**	**sus**	**sus**	their; your (of **Vds**)

All possessive adjectives agree in number and (when applicable) in gender with the noun described, not with the owner → ❶
The weak forms always precede the noun → ❶
Since the form **su(s)** can mean his, her, your (of **Vd**, **Vds**) or their, clarification is often needed. This is done by adding **de él**, **de ella**, **de Vds** etc to the noun, and usually (but not always) changing the possessive to a definite article → ❷

Strong forms

WITH SING. NOUN		WITH PLUR. NOUN		
MASC.	FEM.	MASC.	FEM.	
mío	**mía**	**míos**	**mías**	my
tuyo	**tuya**	**tuyos**	**tuyas**	your
suyo	**suya**	**suyos**	**suyas**	his; her; its; your (of **Vd**)
nuestro	**nuestra**	**nuestros**	**nuestras**	our
vuestro	**vuestra**	**vuestros**	**vuestras**	your
suyo	**suya**	**suyos**	**suyas**	their; your (of **Vds**)

The strong forms follow the noun, or the verb **ser**, and are used to translate the English (*of*) *mine*, etc → ❸ and to address people → ❹

Examples

❶	Pilar no ha traído nuestros libros	Pilar hasn't brought our books
	Antonio irá a vuestra casa	Antonio will go to your house
	¿Han vendido su coche tus vecinos?	Have your neighbours sold their car?
	Mi hermano y tu primo no se llevan bien	My brother and your cousin don't get on
❷	su casa → la casa de él	his house
	sus amigos → los amigos de Vd	your friends
	sus coches → los coches de ellos	their cars
	su abrigo → el abrigo de ella	her coat
❸	Es un capricho suyo	It's a whim of hers
	un amigo nuestro	a friend of ours
	una revista tuya	a magazine of yours
	Este abrigo es mío.	This coat is mine.
❹	Muy señor mío (in letters)	Dear Sir
	hija mía	my daughter
	¡Dios mío!	My God!
	Amor mío	Darling/My love

Adjectives

Position of Adjectives

Spanish adjectives usually follow the noun → ❶, ❷

Note that when used figuratively or to express a quality already inherent in the noun, adjectives can precede the noun → ❸

As in English, demonstrative, possessive (weak forms), numerical, interrogative and exclamatory adjectives precede the noun → ❹

Indefinite adjectives such as **ambos** *both* and **cada** *each* usually precede the noun → ❺

ⓘ Note: **alguno** *some/any* follows the noun in negative expressions → ❻

Some adjectives can precede or follow the noun, but their meaning varies according to their position:

	BEFORE NOUN	AFTER NOUN
antiguo	former	old, ancient → ❼
diferente	various	different → ❽
grande	great	big → ❾
medio	half	average → ❿
mismo	same	-self, very/precisely → ⓫
nuevo	new, another, fresh	brand new → ⓬
pobre	poor (wretched)	poor (not rich) → ⓭
puro	sheer, mere	pure (clear) → ⓮
varios	several	assorted, different → ⓯
viejo	old (long known, etc)	old (aged) → ⓰

Adjectives following the noun are linked by **y** → ⓱

Examples

❶	la página siguiente la hora exacta	the following page the right time
❷	una corbata azul una palabra española	a blue tie a Spanish word
❸	un dulce sueño un terrible desastre	a sweet dream a terrible disaster (*all disasters are terrible*)
❹	este sombrero mi padre ¿qué hombre?	this hat my father what man?
❺	cada día otra vez poco dinero	every day another time little money
❻	sin duda alguna	without any doubt
❼	un antiguo colega la historia antigua	a former colleague ancient history
❽	diferentes capítulos personas diferentes	various chapters different people
❾	un gran pintor una casa grande	a great painter a big house
❿	medio melón velocidad media	half a melon average speed
⓫	la misma respuesta yo mismo eso mismo	the same answer myself precisely that
⓬	mi nuevo coche unos zapatos nuevos	my new car (some) brand new shoes
⓭	esa pobre mujer un país pobre	that poor woman a poor country
⓮	la pura verdad aire puro	the plain truth fresh air
⓯	varios caminos artículos varios	several ways/paths assorted items
⓰	un viejo amigo esas toallas viejas	an old friend those old towels
⓱	una acción cobarde y falsa	a cowardly, deceitful act

Pronouns

Personal Pronouns: subject

	SUBJECT PRONOUNS		
	SINGULAR	PLURAL	
1st person	**yo** I	**nosotros** we	(*masc./masc. + fem.*)
		nosotras we	(*all fem.*)
2nd person	**tú** you	**vosotros** you	(*masc./masc. + fem.*)
		vosotras you	(*all fem.*)
3rd person	**él** he; it	**ellos** they	(*masc./masc. + fem.*)
	ella she; it	**ellas** they	(*all fem.*)
	usted (Vd) you	**ustedes (Vds)** you	

Subject pronouns have a limited usage in Spanish. Normally they are only used with a verb:

- for emphasis → ❶
- for clarity → ❷

BUT: **Vd** and **Vds** should always be used for politeness, whether they are otherwise needed or not → ❸

It as subject and *they*, referring to things, are never translated into Spanish → ❹

tú/usted

As a general rule, you should use **tú** (or **vosotros**, if plural) when addressing a friend, a child, a relative, someone you know well, or when invited to do so. In all other cases, use **usted** (or **ustedes**).

nosotros/as; **vosotros/as**; **él/ella**; **ellos/ellas**

All these forms reflect the number and gender of the noun(s) they replace. **Nosotros**, **vosotros** and **ellos** also replace a combination of masculine and feminine nouns.

Examples

❶	Ellos sí que llegaron tarde	They really did arrive late
	Tú no tienes por qué venir	There is no reason for you to come
	Ella jamás creería eso	She would never believe that
❷	Yo estudio español pero él estudia francés	I study Spanish but he studies French
	Ella era muy deportista pero él prefería jugar a las cartas	She was a sporty type but he preferred to play cards
	Vosotros saldréis primero y nosotros os seguiremos	You leave first and we will follow you
❸	Pase Vd por aquí	Please come this way
	¿Habían estado Vds antes en esta ciudad?	Had you been to this town before?
❹	¿Qué es? — Es una sorpresa	What is it? — It's a surprise
	¿Qué son? — Son abrelatas	What are they? — They are tin-openers

Pronouns

Personal Pronouns: object

		SINGULAR	PLURAL
		DIRECT OBJECT PRONOUNS	
1st	person	**me** me	**nos** us
2nd	person	**te** you	**os** you
3rd	person (*masc.*)	**lo** him; it; you (of **Vd**)	**los** them; you (of **Vds**)
	(*fem.*)	**la** her; it; you (of **Vd**)	**las** them; you (of **Vds**)
		INDIRECT OBJECT PRONOUNS	
1st	person	**me**	**nos**
2nd	person	**te**	**os**
3rd	person	**le**	**les**

lo sometimes functions as a 'neuter' pronoun, referring to an idea or information contained in a previous statement or question. It is often not translated → ❶

Indirect object pronouns replace the preposition **a** + noun → ❷

Use direct object pronouns instead to replace personal **a** + noun.

Position of object pronouns

In constructions other than the affirmative imperative, infinitive or gerund, the pronoun always comes before the verb → ❸
In the affirmative imperative, infinitive and gerund, the pronoun follows the verb and is attached to it. An accent is needed in certain cases to show the correct position for stress (see also page 127) → ❹
Where an infinitive or gerund depends on a previous verb, object pronouns, and also reflexive pronouns, may be used either after the infinitive or gerund, or before the main verb → ❺

For information on reflexive pronouns see page 16.

Examples

1	¿Va a venir María? — No lo sé	Is María coming? — I don't know
	Hay que regar las plantas — Yo lo haré	The plants need watering — I'll do it
	Habían comido ya pero no nos lo dijeron	They had already eaten, but they didn't tell us
	Yo conduzco de prisa pero él lo hace despacio	I drive fast but he drives slowly
2	Estoy escribiendo a Teresa	I am writing to Teresa
	Le estoy escribiendo	I am writing to her
	Da de comer al gato	Give the cat some food
	Dale de comer	Give it some food
3	Te quiero	I love you
	¿Las ve Vd?	Can you see them?
	Tu hija no nos conoce	Your daughter doesn't know us
	No los toques	Don't touch them
	Sofía os ha escrito	Sofía has written to you
	¿Os ha escrito Sofía?	Has Sofía written to you?
	¿Qué te pedían?	What were they asking you for?
4	Ayúdame	Help me
	Acompáñenos	Come with us
	Quiero decirte algo	I want to tell you something
	Estaban persiguiéndonos	They were coming after us
	No quería darte la noticia todavía	I didn't want to tell you the news yet
	Llegaron diciéndome que ...	They came telling me that ...
5	Lo está comiendo *or* Está comiéndolo	She is eating it
	Estoy afeitándome *or* Me estoy afeitando	I'm shaving
	Les voy a hablar *or* Voy a hablarles	I'm going to talk to them

Pronouns

Personal Pronouns *continued*

Order of object pronouns

When two object pronouns are combined, the order is: indirect before direct, i.e.

me	before	**lo**	→ ❶
te		**la**	
nos		**los**	
os		**las**	

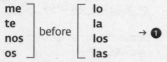

ⓘ Note: When two 3rd person object pronouns are combined, the first (i.e. the indirect object pronoun) becomes **se** → ❷

Points to note on object pronouns

As **le/les** can refer to either gender, and **se** to either gender, singular or plural, sometimes clarification is needed. This is done by adding **a él** *to him*, **a ella** *to her*, **a Vd** *to you* etc to the phrase, usually after the verb → ❸

When a noun object precedes the verb, the corresponding object pronoun must be used too → ❹

Indirect object pronouns are often used instead of possessive adjectives with parts of the body or clothing to indicate 'ownership', and also in certain common constructions involving reflexive verbs (see also Uses of the Definite Article, page 80) → ❺

Le and **les** are often used in Spanish instead of **lo** and **los** when referring to people. Equally **la** is sometimes used instead of **le** when referring to a feminine person or animal, although this usage is considered incorrect by some speakers of Spanish → ❻

Examples

❶	Paloma os lo mandará mañana	Paloma is sending it to you tomorrow
	¿Te los ha enseñado mi hermana?	Has my sister shown them to you?
	No me lo digas	Don't tell me (that)
	Todos estaban pidiéndotelo	They were all asking you for it
	No quiere prestárnosla	He won't lend it to us
❷	Se lo di ayer	I gave it to him/her/them yesterday
❸	Le escriben mucho a ella	They write to her often
	Se lo van a mandar pronto a ellos	They will be sending it to them soon
❹	A tu hermano lo conozco bien	I know your brother well
	A María la vemos algunas veces	We sometimes see María
❺	La chaqueta le estaba ancha	His jacket was too loose
	Me duele el tobillo	My ankle is aching
	Se me ha perdido el bolígrafo	I have lost my pen
❻	Le *or* Lo encontraron en el cine	They met him at the cinema
	Les *or* Los oímos llegar	We heard them coming

Personal Pronouns *continued*

Pronouns after prepositions

These are the same as the subject pronouns, except for the forms **mí** *me*, **ti** *you* (*singular*), and the reflexive **sí** *himself*, *herself*, *themselves*, *yourselves* → ❶

Con *with* combines with **mí**, **ti** and **sí** to form

conmigo	with me → ❷
contigo	with you
consigo	with him(self)/her(self) etc

The following prepositions always take a subject pronoun:

entre	between, among → ❸
hasta, **incluso**	even, including → ❹
salvo, **menos**	except → ❺
según	according to → ❻

ⓘ Note: Subject pronouns are also used in comparative constructions → ❼

These pronouns are used for emphasis, especially where contrast is involved → ❽

Ello *it*, *that* is used after a preposition when referring to an idea already mentioned, but never to a concrete noun → ❾

A él, **de él** never contract → ❿

Examples

1	Pienso en ti	I'm thinking about you
	¿Son para mí?	Are they for me?
	Es para ella	This is for her
	Iban hacia ellos	They were going towards them
	Volveréis sin nosotros	You'll come back without us
	Volaban sobre vosotros	They were flying above you
	Hablaba para sí	He was talking to himself
2	Venid conmigo	Come with me
	Lo trajeron consigo	They brought it/him with them
	BUT:	
	¿Hablaron con vosotros?	Did they talk to you?
3	entre tú y ella	between you and her
4	Hasta yo puedo hacerlo	Even I can do it
5	todos menos yo	everybody except me
6	según tú	according to you
7	Es más joven que yo	He is younger than me (*or* than I am)
8	¿A ti no te escriben?	Don't they write to you?
	Me lo manda a mí, no a ti	She is sending it to me, not to you
9	Nunca pensaba en ello	He never thought about it
	Por todo ello me parece que ...	For all those reasons it seems to me that ...
10	A él no lo conozco	I don't know him
	No he sabido nada de él	I haven't heard from him

Pronouns

Relative Pronouns

PEOPLE		
SINGULAR	PLURAL	
que	**que**	who, that (*subject*) → ❶
que	**que**	who(m), that (*direct object*) → ❷
a quien	**a quienes**	who(m), that (*direct object*) → ❷
a quien	**a quienes**	to whom, that → ❸
de que	**de que**	of whom, that → ❹
de quien	**de quienes**	of whom, that → ❹
cuyo/a	**cuyos/as**	whose → ❺

THINGS	
SINGULAR AND PLURAL	
que	which, that (*subject*) → ❻
que	which, that (*direct object*) → ❼
a que	to which, that → ❽
de que	of which, that → ❾
cuyo	whose → ❿

cuyo, which is in fact a relative adjective, agrees with the noun it accompanies → ❺/❿

You cannot omit the relative pronoun in Spanish as you can in English → ❷/❹/❼

el cual, **el que**, etc

These are used when the relative is separated from the word it refers to, or when it would otherwise be unclear which word it referred to. The pronouns always agree in number and gender with the noun → ⓫
El cual may also be used when the verb in the relative clause is separated from the relative pronoun → ⓬

lo que, **lo cual**

The neuter form **lo** is normally used when referring to an idea, statement or abstract noun. In certain expressions, the form **lo cual** may also be used as the subject of the relative clause → ⓭

Examples

❶	Mi hermano, que tiene veinte años, es el más joven	My brother, who is twenty, is the youngest
❷	Los amigos que más quiero son ...	The friends (that) I like best are ...
	María, a quien Daniel admira tanto, es ...	María, whom Daniel admires so much, is ...
❸	Mis abogados, a quienes he escrito hace poco, están ...	My lawyers, to whom I wrote recently, are ...
❹	la chica de que te hablé	the girl (that) I told you about
	los niños de quienes se ocupa Vd	the children (that) you look after
❺	Vendrá la mujer cuyo hijo está enfermo	The woman whose son is ill will be coming
❻	Hay una escalera que lleva a la buhardilla	There's a staircase which leads to the loft
❼	La casa que hemos comprado tiene ...	The house (which) we've bought has ...
	Este es el regalo que me ha mandado mi amiga	This is the present (that) my friend sent to me
❽	la tienda a que siempre va	the shop (which) she always goes to
❾	las injusticias de que se quejan	the injustices (that) they're complaining about
❿	la ventana cuyas cortinas están corridas	the window whose curtains are drawn
⓫	El padre de Elena, el cual tiene mucho dinero, es ...	Elena's father, who has a lot of money, is ...
	(el cual *is used here since* que *or* quien *might equally refer to Elena*)	
	Su hermana, a la cual/la que hacía mucho que no veía, estaba también allí	His sister, whom I hadn't seen for a long time, was also there
⓬	Vieron a su tío, el cual, después de levantarse, salió	They saw their uncle, who, after having got up, went out
⓭	Lo que dijiste fue una tontería	What you said was foolish
	Todo estaba en silencio, lo que (*or* lo cual) me pareció muy raro	All was silent, which I thought most odd

Relative Pronouns *continued*

Relative pronouns after prepositions

Que and **quienes** are generally used after the prepositions:

a	to	→ ❶
con	with	→ ❷
de	from, about, of	→ ❸
en	in, on, into	→ ❹

It should be noted that **en que** can sometimes be translated by:

- *where*. In this case it can also be replaced by **en donde** or **donde** → ❺
- *when*. Sometimes here it can be replaced by **cuando** → ❻

El que or **el cual** are used after other prepositions, and they always agree → ❼

el que, la que; los que, las que
These mean *the one(s) who/which, those who/that* → ❽

ⓘ Note: **quien(es)** can replace **el que** etc when used in a general sense referring to a person or people → ❾

todos los que, todas las que
These mean *all who, all those/the ones which* → ❿

todo lo que
This translates *all that, everything that* → ⓫

el de, la de; los de, las de
These can mean:

- *the one(s) of, that/those of* → ⓬
- *the one(s) with* → ⓭

Examples

1	las tiendas a (las) que íbamos	the shops we used to go to
2	la chica con quien (or la que) sale	the girl he's going out with
3	el libro de(l) que te hablé	the book I told you about
4	el lío en (el) que te has metido	the trouble you've got yourself into
5	el sitio en que (en donde/donde) se escondía	the place where he/she was hiding
6	el año en que naciste	the year (when) you were born
7	el puente debajo del que/cual pasa el río	the bridge under which the river flows
	las obras por las cuales/que es famosa	the plays for which she is famous
8	Esa película es la que quiero ver	That film is the one I want to see
	¿Te acuerdas de ese amigo? El que te presenté ayer	Do you remember that friend? The one I introduced you to yesterday
	Los que quieran entrar tendrán que pagar	Those who want to go in will have to pay
9	Quien (*or* El que) llegue antes ganará el premio	The person who arrives first will win the prize
10	Todos los que salían iban de negro	All those who were coming out were dressed in black
11	Quiero saber todo lo que ha pasado	I want to know all that has happened
12	Trae la foto de tu novio y la de tu hermano	Bring the photo of your boyfriend and the one of your brother
	Viajamos en mi coche y en el de María	We travelled in my car and María's
	Te doy estos libros y también los de mi hermana	I'll give you these books and my sister's too
13	Tu amigo, el de las gafas, me lo contó	Your friend, the one with glasses, told me

Pronouns

Interrogative Pronouns

¿qué? what?
¿cuál(es)? which?; what?
¿quién(es)? who?

qué

It translates *what* → ❶

ⓘ Note: **por** + **qué** is normally translated by *why* → ❷

cuál

It normally implies a choice, and translates *which* → ❸

ⓘ However, **cúal(es)** is also used in *what is/are* questions that require specific information rather than a definition as the answer → ❹

ⓘ Note: Whilst the pronoun **qué** can also work as an adjective meaning *what* or *which*, **cuál** only works as a pronoun → ❺

quién

SUBJECT *or* AFTER PREPOSITION	**quién(es)**	who → ❻
OBJECT	**a quién(es)**	whom → ❼
	de quién(es)	whose → ❽

All the forms shown above are also used in indirect questions → ❾

Examples

1	¿Qué están haciendo?	What are they doing?
	¿Qué dices?	What are you saying?
	¿Qué es un tractor, papá?	What's a tractor, Daddy?
	¿Qué son las alcaparras?	What are capers?
	¿Para qué lo quieres?	What do you want it for?
2	¿Por qué no llegaron Vds antes?	Why didn't you arrive earlier?
3	¿Cuál de estos vestidos te gusta más?	Which of these dresses do you like best?
	¿Cuáles viste?	Which ones did you see?
4	¿Cuál es la capital de España?	What is the capital of Spain?
	¿Cuál es tu consejo?	What is your advice?
	¿Cuál es su fecha de nacimiento?	What is your date of birth?
5	¿Qué libro es más interesante?	Which book is more interesting?
	¿Cuál (de estos libros) es más interesante?	Which (of these books) is more interesting?
6	¿Quién ganó la carrera?	Who won the race?
	¿Con quiénes los viste?	Who did you see them with?
	¿A quién se lo diste?	Who did you give it to?
7	¿A quiénes ayudaste?	Who(m) did you help?
8	¿De quién es este libro?	Whose book is this?
9	Le pregunté para qué lo quería	I asked him/her what he/she wanted it for
	No me dijeron cuáles preferían	They didn't tell me which ones they preferred
	No sabía a quién acudir	I didn't know who to turn to

Pronouns

Possessive Pronouns

These are the same as the strong forms of the possessive adjectives, but they are always accompanied by the definite article.

Singular:

MASCULINE	FEMININE	
el mío	**la mía**	mine
el tuyo	**la tuya**	yours (of **tú**)
el suyo	**la suya**	his; hers; its; yours (of **Vd**)
el nuestro	**la nuestra**	ours
el vuestro	**la vuestra**	yours (of **vosotros**)
el suyo	**la suya**	theirs; yours (of **Vds**)

Plural:

MASCULINE	FEMININE	
los míos	**las mías**	mine
los tuyos	**las tuyas**	yours (of **tú**)
los suyos	**las suyas**	his; hers; its; yours (of **Vd**)
los nuestros	**las nuestras**	ours
los vuestros	**las vuestras**	yours (of **vosotros**)
los suyos	**las suyas**	theirs; yours (of **Vds**)

The pronoun agrees in number and gender with the noun it replaces, not with the owner, and can also be translated as *my one(s)*, *your one(s)* etc → ❶

Alternative translations are 'my own', 'your own' etc → ❷

After the prepositions **a** and **de** the article **el** is contracted in the normal way (see page 80):

a + el mío → **al mío** → ❸
de + el mío → **del mío** → ❹

Examples

❶ Pregunta a Cristina si este bolígrafo es el suyo	Ask Cristina if this pen is hers *or* her one
¿Qué equipo ha ganado, el suyo o el nuestro?	Which team won – theirs or ours?
Mi perro es más joven que el tuyo	My dog is younger than yours
Daniel pensó que esos libros eran los suyos	Daniel thought those books were his
Si no tienes discos, te prestaré los míos	If you don't have any records, I'll lend you mine
Las habitaciones son menos amplias que las vuestras	The rooms are smaller than yours
❷ ¿Es su familia tan grande como la tuya?	Is his/her/their family as big as your own one?
Sus precios son más bajos que los nuestros	Their prices are lower than our own
❸ ¿Por qué prefieres este sombrero al mío?	Why do you prefer this hat to mine?
Su coche se parece al vuestro	His/her/their car looks like yours *or* your one
❹ Mi libro está encima del tuyo	My book is on top of yours *or* your one

Adverbs

Adverbs

Formation

Most adverbs are formed by adding **-mente** to the feminine form of the adjective. Accents on the adjective are not affected since the suffix **-mente** is stressed independently → ❶

ⓘ Note: **-mente** is omitted:
- in the first of two or more of these adverbs when joined by a conjunction → ❷
- **recientemente** *recently* is replaced by **recién** immediately before a past participle → ❸

The following adverbs are formed in an irregular way:

bueno →	**bien**	**malo** →	**mal**
good	well	bad	badly

Adjectives used as adverbs

Certain adjectives are used adverbially. These include:
alto, **bajo**, **barato**, **caro**, **claro**, **derecho**, **fuerte** and **rápido** → ❹

ⓘ Note: Other adjectives used where in English we would use an adverb agree with the subject, and can normally be replaced by the adverb ending in **-mente** or an adverbial phrase → ❺

Position of adverbs

When the adverb accompanies a verb, it may either immediately follow it or precede it for emphasis → ❻

ⓘ Note: The adverb can never be placed between **haber** and the past participle in compound tenses → ❼

When the adverb accompanies an adjective or another adverb, it generally precedes the adjective or adverb → ❽

Examples

❶	FEM ADJECTIVE	ADVERB
	lenta slow	lentamente slowly
	franca frank	francamente frankly
	feliz happy	felizmente happily
	fácil easy	fácilmente easily
❷	Lo hicieron lenta pero eficazmente	They did it slowly but efficiently
❸	El pan estaba recién hecho	The bread had just been baked
❹	hablar alto/bajo	to speak loudly/softly
	cortar derecho	to cut (in a) straight (line)
	costar barato/caro	to be cheap/expensive
	Habla muy fuerte	He talks very loudly
	ver claro	to see clearly
	correr rápido	to run fast
❺	Esperaban impacientes (*or* impacientemente/ con impaciencia)	They were waiting impatiently
	Vivieron muy felices (*or* muy felizmente)	They lived very happily
❻	No conocemos aún al nuevo médico	We still haven't met the new doctor
	Aún estoy esperando	I'm still waiting
	Han hablado muy bien	They spoke very well
	Siempre le regalaban flores	They always gave her flowers
❼	Lo he hecho ya	I've already done it
	No ha estado nunca en Italia	She's never been to Italy
❽	un sombrero muy bonito	a very nice hat
	hablar demasiado alto	to talk too loud
	mañana temprano	early tomorrow
	hoy mismo	today

Adverbs

Comparatives and Superlatives

Comparatives

These are formed using the following constructions:

más ... (que) more ... (than) → ❶
menos ... (que) less ... (than) → ❷
tanto como as much as → ❸
tan ... como as ... as → ❹
tan ... que so ... that → ❺
demasiado ... para too ... to → ❻
(lo) bastante ... / **(lo) suficientemente ...** **para** enough to → ❼
cada vez más/menos more and more/less and less → ❽

ⓘ To translate *more than/fewer than* with a number, use **más de/menos de** (e.g. **más de 10** more than 10; **menos de 100** fewer than 100).

Superlatives

These are formed by placing **más/menos** *the most/the least* before the adverb → ❾

lo is added before a superlative which is qualified → ❿

Adverbs with irregular comparatives/superlatives

ADVERB	COMPARATIVE	SUPERLATIVE
bien well	**mejor*** better	**(lo) mejor** (the) best
mal badly	**peor** worse	**(lo) peor** (the) worst
mucho a lot	**más** more	**(lo) más** (the) most
poco little	**menos** less	**(lo) menos** (the) least

* **más bien** also exists, meaning *rather* → ⓫

Examples

1	más de prisa	more quickly
	más abiertamente	more openly
	Mi hermana canta más fuerte que yo	My sister sings louder than me
2	menos fácilmente	less easily
	menos a menudo	less often
	Nos vemos menos frecuentemente que antes	We see each other less often than we used to
3	Daniel no lee tanto como Andrés	Daniel doesn't read as much as Andrés
4	Hágalo tan rápido como le sea posible	Do it as quickly as you can
	Ganan tan poco como nosotros	They earn as little as we do
5	Llegaron tan pronto que tuvieron que esperarnos	They arrived so early that they had to wait for us
6	Es demasiado tarde para ir al cine	It's too late to go to the cinema
7	Corrió lo suficientemente rápido para batir el récord	She ran fast enough to break the record
8	Me gusta el campo cada vez más	I like the countryside more and more
9	María es la que corre más rápido	María is the one who runs fastest
	El que llegó menos tarde fue Miguel	Miguel was the one who arrived the least late
10	Lo hice lo más de prisa que pude	I did it as quickly as I could
11	Era un hombre más bien bajito	He was a rather short man
	Estaba más bien inquieta que impaciente	I was restless rather than impatient

Prepositions

It is often difficult to give an English equivalent for Spanish prepositions, since usage varies so much between the two languages and the Spanish preposition may not always be the one that the English sentence leads you to expect, and vice versa. If in doubt you will find the examples in the dictionary will help you.

Note that English verbal constructions often contain a preposition (or adverb) where none exists in Spanish, and vice versa (e.g. to look *at* something **mirar algo**).

Below are some typical examples using **en**, **a**, **de**, **por** and **para**:

Trabaja **en** Madrid	He works in Madrid
Lo compramos **en** el supermercado	We bought it at the supermarket
Vivimos **en** la planta baja	We live on the ground floor
No entró **en** el bar	He didn't go into the bar
Vamos **en** tren	We're going by train
Nació **en** 2000	She was born in 2000
Voy **al** parque	I'm going to the park
¿Cuándo llegaste **a** Londres?	When did you arrive in London?
Fuimos **a** casa	We went home
Está **a** siete kilómetros de aquí	It's seven kilometres from here
Empieza **a** las dos	It starts at two o'clock
Estamos **a** tres de julio	It's the third of July
una taza **de** té	a cup of tea/a teacup
la casa **de** Julia	Julia's house
un médico **de** Vigo	a doctor from Vigo
la mujer **del** sombrero rojo	the woman in the red hat
del 15 al 30	from the 15th to the 30th
la cuidad más/menos bonita **del** mundo	the most/least beautiful city in the world
Había más/menos **de** cien personas	There were more/fewer than a hundred people

Examples

Fue pintado **por** Velázquez	It was painted by Velázquez
Fue **por** necesidad	It was out of necessity
Me castigaron **por** mentir	I was punished for lying
¿Cuánto me darás **por** este libro?	How much will you give me for this book?
Vaya **por** ese camino	Go along that path
por el túnel	through the tunnel
Tiene que estar **por** aquí	It's got to be around here somewhere
por correo áereo	by airmail
por la tarde	in the afternoon
90 km **por** hora	90 km per hour
Lo hago **por** ellos	I'm doing it for them
Es **para** ti	It's for you
Es **para** mañana	It's for tomorrow
una habitación **para** dos noches	a room for two nights
Para ser un niño, lo hace muy bien	For a child, he is very good at it
Salen **para** Cádiz	They are leaving for Cádiz
Es demasiado torpe **para** comprenderlo	He's too stupid to understand
hablar **para** sí	to talk to oneself
Todavía tengo **para** 1 hora	I'll be another hour (at it) yet

Personal a

When the direct object of a verb is a noun referring to a person or pet animal, **a** must be placed immediately before it:

Querían mucho **a** sus hijos	They loved their children dearly
El niño miraba **a** su perro con asombro	The boy kept looking at his dog in astonishment

EXCEPTION: **tener** to have

Tienen dos hijos	They have two children

Conjunctions

Some conjunctions introduce a main clause, e.g. **y** *and*, **pero** *but*, and some introduce a subordinate clause, e.g. **porque** *because* and **mientras que** *while*. They are used in much the same way as in English, but:

Some conjunctions in Spanish require a following subjunctive, see pages 34 to 36.

Some conjunctions are 'split' in Spanish like 'both ... and', 'either ... or' in English:

tanto ... como both ... and → ❶
ni ... ni neither ... nor → ❷
o (bien) ... o (bien) either ... or (else) → ❸
sea ... sea either ... or, whether ... or → ❹

y

- Before words beginning with **i-** or **hi-** + consonant it becomes **e** → ❺

o

- Before words beginning with **o-** or **ho-** it becomes **u** → ❻
- Between numerals it becomes **ó** → ❼

que

- meaning *that* → ❽
- in comparisons, meaning *than* → ❾
- followed by the subjunctive, see page 32.

porque (not to be confused with **por qué** *why*)

- **como** should be used instead at the beginning of a sentence → ❿

pero, sino

- **pero** normally translates *but* → ⓫
- **sino** is used when there is a direct contrast after a negative → ⓬

Examples

1	Estas flores crecen tanto en verano como en invierno	These flowers grow in both summer and winter
2	Ni él ni ella vinieron No tengo ni dinero ni comida	Neither he nor she came I have neither money nor food
3	Debe de ser o ingenua o tonta O bien me huyen o bien no me reconocen	She must be either naïve or stupid Either they're avoiding me or else they don't recognize me
4	Sea en verano, sea en invierno, siempre me gusta andar	I always like walking, whether in summer or in winter
5	Diana e Isabel madre e hija BUT: árboles y hierba	Diana and Isabel mother and daughter trees and grass
6	diez u once minutos u horas	ten or eleven minutes or hours
7	37 ó 38	37 or 38
8	Dicen que te han visto ¿Sabías que estábamos allí?	They say (that) they've seen you Did you know that we were there?
9	Le gustan más que nunca Miguel es menos guapo que su hermano	He likes them more than ever Miguel is less attractive than his brother
10	Como estaba lloviendo no pudimos salir (*Compare with:* No pudimos salir porque estaba lloviendo)	Because/As it was raining we couldn't go out
11	Me gustaría ir, pero estoy muy cansada	I'd like to go, but I am very tired
12	No es escocesa sino irlandesa	She isn't Scottish but Irish

Demonstratives

Demonstrative Adjectives

	MASCULINE	FEMININE	
SING.	**este**	**esta**	this
	ese	**esa**	that
	aquel	**aquella**	that
PLUR.	**estos**	**estas**	these
	esos	**esas**	those
	aquellos	**aquellas**	those

Demonstrative adjectives normally precede the noun and always agree in number and in gender with it → ❶

The forms **ese/a/os/as** are used:

- to indicate distance from the speaker but proximity to the person addressed → ❷
- to indicate a not too remote distance → ❸

The forms **aquel/la/los/las** are used to indicate distance, in space or time → ❹

Demonstrative Pronouns

Demonstrative pronouns → ❺ are identical to demonstrative adjectives with the following exceptions:

- neuter forms of the pronouns exist (**esto**, **eso** and **aquello**). These are used to refer to an idea or a statement or to an object when we want to identify it but don't have a specific noun in mind → ❻
- the masculine and feminine pronouns were always written with an accent in the past (**éste**, **ésta**, **éstos**, **éstas**; **ése**, **ésa**, **ésos**, **ésas**; **aquél**, **aquélla**, **aquéllos**, **aquéllas**) to distinguish them from demonstrative adjectives. Nowadays the accents are only considered essential where ambiguity is otherwise possible. The neuter forms are never written with an accent.

An additional meaning of **aquel** is *the former*, and of **este** *the latter* → ❼

Examples

1	Este bolígrafo no escribe	This pen is not working
	Esa revista es muy mala	That is a very bad magazine
	Aquella montaña es muy alta	That mountain (over there) is very high
	¿Conoces a esos señores?	Do you know those gentlemen?
	Siga Vd hasta aquellos edificios	Carry on until you come to those buildings
	¿Ves aquellas personas?	Can you see those people (over there)?
2	Ese papel en donde escribes ...	That paper you are writing on ...
3	No me gustan esos cuadros	I don't like those pictures
4	Aquella calle parece muy ancha	That street (over there) looks very wide
	Aquellos años sí que fueron felices	Those were really happy years
5	¿Qué abrigo te gusta más? — Este de aquí	Which coat do you like best? — This one here
	Aquella casa era más grande que esta	That house was bigger than this one
	estos libros y aquellos	these books and those (over there)
	Quiero estas sandalias y esas	I'd like these sandals and those ones
6	No puedo creer que esto me esté pasando a mí	I can't believe this is really happening to me
	Eso de madrugar es algo que no le gusta	(This business of) getting up early is something she doesn't like
	Aquello sí que me gustó	I really did like that
	Esto es una bicicleta	This is a bicycle
7	Hablaban Jaime y Andrés, este a voces y aquel casi en un susurro	Jaime and Andrés were talking, the latter in a loud voice and the former almost in a whisper

Sentence Stucture

Negatives

A sentence is made negative by adding **no** between the subject (if stated explicitly) and the verb (and any preceding object pronouns) → ❶

In phrases like *not her, not now* etc, the Spanish **no** usually comes after the word it qualifies → ❷
With verbs of saying, hoping, thinking etc, *not* is translated by **que no** → ❸

Double negatives

The following are the most common negative pairs:

no ... nada nothing (*not ... anything*)
no ... nadie nobody (*not ... anybody*)
no ... más no longer (*not ... any more*)
no ... nunca never (*not ... ever*)
no ... jamás never (stronger) (*not ... ever*)
no ... más que only (*not ... more than*)
no ... ningún/ninguno/a no (*not any*)
no ... tampoco not ... either
no ... ni ... ni neither ... nor
no ... ni siquiera not even

Word order

No precedes the verb (and any object pronouns) in both simple and compound tenses, and the second element follows the verb → ❹

Sometimes the above negatives are placed before the verb (with the exception of **más** and **más que**), and **no** is then dropped → ❺

Negatives in short replies

No is the usual negative response to a question → ❻

ⓘ Note: It is often translated as 'not' → ❼

Negative words like **nada**, **nunca** and **nadie** can also be used on their own in short replies → ❽

Examples

1	El coche no es suyo	The car is not his
	(Yo) no me lo pondré	I won't put it on
2	¿Quién lo ha hecho? — Ella no	Who did it? — Not her
	Ahora no	Not now
	Dame ese libro, el que está a tu lado no, el otro	Give me that book, not the one near you, the other one
3	Opino que no	I think not
	Dijeron que no	They said not
4	No dicen nada	They don't say anything
	No han visto a nadie	They haven't seen anybody
	No me veréis más	You won't see me any more
	No te olvidaré nunca/jamás	I'll never forget you
	No habían recorrido más que 40 kms cuando ...	They hadn't travelled more than 40 kms when ...
	No se me ha ocurrido ninguna idea	I haven't had any ideas
	No les estaban esperando ni mi hijo ni mi hija	Neither my son nor my daughter was waiting for them
	No ha venido ni siquiera Juan	Even Juan hasn't come
	No lo haré nunca más	I'll never do it again
	No se ve nunca a nadie por allí	You never see anybody around there
	No he hablado nunca más que con su mujer	I've only ever spoken to his wife
5	Nadie ha venido hoy	Nobody came today
	Nunca me han gustado	I've never liked them
	Ni mi hermano ni mi hermana fuman	Neither my brother nor my sister smokes
6	¿Quieres intentarlo? — No	Do you want to try? — No
7	¿Vienes o no?	Are you coming or not?
8	¿Ha venido alguien? — ¡Nadie!	Has anyone come? — Nobody!
	¿Has ido al Japón alguna vez? — Nunca	Have you ever been to Japan? — Never

Sentence Stucture

Question Forms

Direct

There are two ways of forming direct questions in Spanish:

by inverting the normal word order so that
subject + verb → *verb + subject* → ❶

by maintaining the word order *subject + verb*, but by using a rising intonation at the end of the sentence → ❷

ⓘ Note: In compound tenses the auxiliary may never be separated from the past participle, as happens in English → ❸

Indirect

An indirect question is one that is 'reported', e.g. he asked me 'what the time was', tell me 'which way to go'. Word order in indirect questions can adopt one of the two following patterns:

interrogative word + subject + verb → ❹

interrogative word + verb + subject → ❺

¿verdad?, ¿no?

These are used wherever English would use 'isn't it?', 'don't they?', 'weren't we?', 'is it?' etc tagged on to the end of a sentence → ❻

sí

Sí is the word for 'yes' in answer to a question put either in the affirmative or in the negative → ❼

Examples

1	¿Vendrá tu madre?	Will your mother come?
	¿Lo trajo Vd?	Did you bring it?
	¿Es posible eso?	Is it possible?
	¿Cuándo volverán Vds?	When will you come back?
2	El gato, ¿se bebió toda la leche?	Did the cat drink up all his milk?
	Andrés, ¿va a venir?	Is Andrés coming?
3	¿Lo ha terminado Vd?	Have you finished it?
	¿Había llegado tu amigo?	Had your friend arrived?
4	Dime qué autobuses pasan por aquí	Tell me which buses come this way
	No sé cuántas personas vendrán	I don't know how many people will turn up
5	Me preguntó dónde trabajaba mi hermano	He asked me where my brother worked
	No sabemos a qué hora empieza la película	We don't know what time the film starts
6	Hace calor, ¿verdad?	It's warm, isn't it?
	No se olvidará Vd, ¿verdad?	You won't forget, will you?
	Estaréis cansados, ¿no?	You must be tired, aren't you?
	Te lo dijo María, ¿no?	María told you, didn't she?
7	¿Lo has hecho? — Sí	Have you done it? — Yes (I have)
	¿No lo has hecho? — Sí	Haven't you done it? — Yes (I have)

Pronunciation

Normal Word Stress

There are simple rules to establish which syllable in a Spanish word is stressed. When an exception to these rules occurs an acute accent (stress-mark) is needed. These rules are as follows:

- words ending in a vowel or combination of vowels, or with the consonants **-s** or **-n** are stressed on the next to last syllable (**ca**sa; **ca**sas; **co**rre; **co**rren; pa**la**bra; pa**la**bras; **cri**sis)
- words ending in a consonant other than **-s** or **-n** bear the stress on the last syllable (re**loj**; ver**dad**; bati**dor**)
- a minority of words bear the stress on the second to last syllable, and these always need an accent (mur**cié**lago; **pá**jaro)
- some nouns change their stress from singular to plural (car**á**cter; caract**e**res; **ré**gimen; re**gí**menes)

Stress in Diphthongs

In the case of diphthongs there are rules to establish which of the vowels is stressed. These rules are as follows:

- diphthongs formed by the combination of a 'weak' vowel (**i**, **u**) and a 'strong' vowel (**a**, **e** or **o**) bear the stress on the strong vowel (**ba**ile; **bo**ina; **pe**ine; **ca**usa; **re**ina)
- diphthongs formed by the combination of two 'weak' vowels bear the stress on the second vowel (fu**i**; vi**u**do)

ⓘ Note: Two 'strong' vowels don't form a diphthong but are pronounced as two separate vowels. In these cases stress follows the normal rules (me ma**re**o; ca**er**; **ca**os; cor**re**a)

Spelling

The Acute Accent (´)

This is used in writing to show that a word is stressed contrary to the normal rules for stress (**autobús**; **revolución**; **relámpago**; **árboles**)

The following points should be noted:

The same syllable is stressed in the plural form of adjectives and nouns as in the singular. To show this, it is necessary to

- add an accent in the case of unaccented nouns and adjectives ending in **-n** (**orden**; **órdenes**; **examen**; **exámenes**; **joven**; **jóvenes**)
- drop the accent from nouns and adjectives ending in **-n** or **-s** which have an accent on the last syllable (**revolución**; **revoluciones**; **autobús**; **autobuses**; **parlanchín**; **parlanchines**)

The feminine form of accented nouns or adjectives does not have an accent (**marqués**; **marquesa**; **francés**; **francesa**)

When object pronouns are added to certain verb forms an accent is required to show that the syllable stressed in the verb form does not change. These verb forms are:

- the gerund (**comprando**; **comprándo(se)lo**)
- the infinitive, when followed by two pronouns (**vender**; **vendérselas**)
- imperative forms, except for the 2nd person plural (**compra**; **cómpralo**; **hagan**; **háganselo**)

Accents on adjectives are not affected by the addition of the adverbial suffix **-mente** (**fácil**; **fácilmente**)

Accents are also used to distinguish between the written forms of words which are pronounced the same but have a different meaning or function (e.g. **tú** *you* and **tu** *your*) interrogative and exclamatory forms of certain words (e.g. **¿dónde?** *where?*; **¡qué!** *what (a)!*).

Spelling

Regular Spelling Changes

The consonants **c**, **g** and **z** are modified by the addition of certain verb or plural endings and by some suffixes. Some of the cases where this occurs have already been dealt with under the appropriate part of speech, but are summarized here along with other instances not covered elsewhere.

Verbs

The changes set out below occur so that the consonant of the verb stem is always pronounced the same as in the infinitive.

INFINITIVE	CHANGE			TENSES AFFECTED
-car	**c + e**	→	**-que**	Present subj, pret
-cer, **-cir**	**c + a, o**	→	**-za**, **-zo**	Present, pres subj
-gar	**g + e, i**	→	**-gue**	Present subj, pret
-guar	**gu + e**	→	**-güe**	Present subj, pret
-ger, **-gir**	**g + a, o**	→	**-ja**, **-jo**	Present, pres subj
-guir	**gu + a, o**	→	**-ga**, **-go**	Present, pres subj
-zar	**z + e**	→	**-ce**	Present subj, pret

Noun and adjective plurals

SINGULAR		PLURAL
vowel + **z**	→	**-ces**

Nouns and adjectives + suffixes

ENDING	SUFFIX	NEW ENDING
vowel + **z** +	**-cito**	**-cecito**
-go, **-ga** +	**-ito**, **-illo**	**-guito/a**, **-guillo/a**
-co, **-ca** +	**-ito**, **-illo**	**-quito/a**, **-quillo/a**

-ísimo endings

ENDING	SUPERLATVE
-co	**-quísimo**
-go	**-guísimo**
vowel + **z**	**-císimo**